Encyclopedia of World History

Encyclopedia of World History

Compiled by
Market House Books Ltd

OXFORD UNIVERSITY PRESS
1998

Oxford University Press, Great Clarendon Street, Oxford OX2 6DP
Oxford New York
Athens Auckland Bangkok Bogota Buenos Aires Calcutta
Cape Town Chennai Dar es Salaam Delhi Florence Hong Kong Istanbul
Karachi Kuala Lumpur Madrid Melbourne Mexico City Mumbai
Nairobi Paris São Paulo Singapore Taipei Tokyo Toronto Warsaw
and associated companies in Berlin Ibadan

Oxford is a registered trade mark of Oxford University Press

Published in the United States
by Oxford University Press Inc., New York

British Library Cataloguing in Publication Data
Data available

Library of Congress Cataloging in Publication Data
Data available

ISBN 0-19-860223-5

10 9 8 7 6 5 4 3 2 1

Typeset by Market House Books Ltd
Printed in Great Britain
on acid-free paper
by The Bath Press

Preface

The *Encyclopedia of World History* is a new single-volume alphabetically arranged reference work that provides the reader with ready access to a wealth of historical information from a wide spectrum of global cultures. The core of the book has been derived from the two volumes devoted to world history in the *Oxford Illustrated Encyclopedia*.

Starting from this base, the editors of Market House Books Ltd. and their history advisers have adapted the text to create a coherent history encyclopedia by broadening many existing entries, updating information on contemporary subjects, and not least by adding articles to outline and illuminate many of the social, political, and economic ideologies that have motivated world cultures over the last 4,000 years.

The encyclopedia contains a wide variety of biographies, ranging from Moses to Tony Blair, as well as a detailed analysis of every country's history in the context of its physical location and economic development. Each country entry also includes statistical information as a ready reference source.

The encyclopedia is illustrated by 50 maps especially produced for this book as well as a selection of portraits and engravings depicting historical events. The detailed network of cross-references indicates where related entries may be found and is a feature of the book that is intended to provide the reader with quick access to a wide range of historical knowledge.

F. A.
1998

Acknowledgements

Market House Editors

Fran Alexander

Dr Alan Isaacs

Jonathan Law

Dr Peter Lewis

Picture Research

Linda Wells

Oxford Illustrated Encyclopedia Editors

Robert Blake

Harry Judge

The following copyrighted photographs appear in this Encyclopedia:

Archivi Alinari, Florence: 48
Associated Press: 143
By permission of the British Library: 6, 335, 654
Edinburgh University Library: 714
Germanisches Nationalmuseum, Nuremberg 400
Hulton Getty: 279, 367, 391, 480, 518
Musée du Château, Versailles/Giraudon: 459
Musée du Louvre/Réunion des Musées Nationaux: 17
The Board of Trinity College, Dublin: 152
The British Museum: 1, 109, 645
The Fotomas Index UK: 74, 82, 90, 215, 223, 272, 299, 334, 344, 423, 520, 531, 550, 719

Maps and Artwork:

The Map Studio, Romsey, Hants. [Maps on pages 8, 17, 21, 82, 84, 95, 127, 260, 304, 321, 324, 373, 484, 537, 567, 581, 625, 694, 707 prepared using MAPS IN MINUTES™ © RH PUBLICATIONS (1997).]

Vana Haggerty: 12, 34, 40, 41, 174, 416, 466, 467

Every endeavour has been made to obtain permission to use copyright material. The publishers would appreciate errors or omissions being brought to their attention.

Contents

A

Abbas I (the Great) (1571–1629) Shah of Persia (1588–1628). He ended an inherited war with the OTTOMANS by conceding territory (1590) in order to free himself to drive the UZBEKS from north-eastern Persia (1598). By 1618 he had strengthened his army by curbing the Turcoman chiefs who supplied his recruits, and by using foreign advisers, and had reconquered the lands ceded to the Ottomans, but he died before the end of a further war over MESOPOTAMIA (1623–29).

Abbas I *The arts flourished under Abbas I; this painting of a calligrapher is by his favourite painter, Reza Abbasi, and carries his personal seal.*

Abbasid A Muslim dynasty, ruling most of the central Middle East (750–1258) claiming descent from Abbas, uncle of the Prophet MUHAMMAD. The Abbasids utilized the Hashimiyya, an extremist group, to capitalize on tribal, sectarian, and ethnic rivalries and overthrow the UMAYYAD dynasty, starting in the frontier province of Khurasan. The CALIPH al-Mansur established a new capital at Baghdad, which, under HARUN AL-RASHID, became a celebrated centre of culture and prosperity. From *c.* 850 central power weakened in the face of local dynasties, as the Aghlabids took power in Ifriqiyya

(North Africa) and the Fatimids took over Egypt, while the dynasty itself fell in thrall to the SHIITE Buwayhids. SELJUKS took Baghdad and with it, effectively, the caliphate in 1055, though their rule was soon constrained by Crusader incursions from 1095 and decisively ended by the MONGOL destruction of Baghdad in 1258. A nominal line of Abbasid caliphs continued in Egypt until the OTTOMAN conquest of the MAMELUKES in 1517.

Abd-al Aziz ibn Saud SAUD.

Abd el-Krim (1881–1963) Moroccan Berber resistance leader. In 1921 he roused the Rif Berbers, and defeated a Spanish army of 20,000. He held out until 1925, when a joint Franco-Spanish force took him prisoner. He was exiled to Réunion until 1947, when he was given permission to go to France. On the way he escaped to Cairo, where he set up the Maghrib Bureau, or Liberation Committee of the Arab West. After Moroccan independence (1956), he refused to return as long as French troops remained on African soil.

Abdication crisis The renunciation of the British throne by EDWARD VIII in 1936. The king let it be known that he wished to marry Mrs Wallis Simpson, a twice-divorced American, which would have required legislative sanction from the British Parliament and from all the DOMINIONS. The British government under Stanley Baldwin, reflecting public opinion and strong opposition from the Church of England under the Archbishop of Canterbury (Cosmo Lang), opposed the king's wish, as did representatives of the dominions. Edward chose to abdicate, making a farewell broadcast to the nation, and commending his brother, the Duke of York, who succeeded him as GEORGE VI.

Abdul Hamid II (1842–1918) Ottoman sultan (1876–1909). He succeeded his brother Murad V and ruled until his deposition following the 1908 YOUNG TURK revolution. His war with Russia (1877–78) was resolved by the Treaty of San Stefano (1878), subsequently modified by the Congress of BERLIN (1878). An autocratic ruler, he suspended Parliament and the constitution, and ruled the empire until his deposition (1909). He was noted for his exploitation of the religious feelings of his Muslim subjects and, due to internal unrest within the empire, his suppression of his non-Muslim subjects, notably the ARMENIANS.

Abdullah, Sheikh Muhammad (1905–82) Kashmiri Muslim leader. He began his career as an activist in the Kashmir Muslim Conference in the 1930s, agitating against the arbitrary rule of the Hindu Dogra Maharaja of Kashmir. Later, as the leader of the Muslim National Conference, he established close links with the Indian National CONGRESS and Jawaharlal NEHRU. In 1947, when the Maharaja delayed his decision regarding accesion to India or Pakistan, and tribal groups from the North-West Frontier with Pakistani military support invaded KASHMIR, Abdullah approved of the decision to join India.

As Chief Minister of the now Indian state of Kashmir, he worked closely with Nehru until he was deposed from his office and imprisoned on suspicion that he was planning a separatist movement. He was later released by Indira GANDHI and in his last years again co-operated with the Indian government and Congress.

Abelard, Peter (or Pierre Abélard) (1079–1142) French theologian and logician, whose philosophical originality and emphasis on intention and personal conscience in moral theory and practice made him a controversial figure. His *Sic et Non (Yes and No)*, a collection of opposed texts from scripture, the Church fathers, and philosophers, whose resolution was left to the student, was, along with *Sentences* by Peter Lombard (*c.* 1100–60), influential in shaping the SCHOLASTIC method of disputation. His works also include *Ethics or Know Thyself*, an analysis of moral responsibility. His apparent stress upon reason rather than faith led to a clash between Abelard and St Bernard of Clairvaux at Sens in 1140 where Abelard was found guilty of heresy.

Abelard is most widely remembered for his relationship with Héloïse, niece of a canon of Paris, whom he secretly married. When her family discovered this, Abelard was punished with castration and retired to a monastery and Héloïse became a nun. Though the couple were never reunited, their correspondence reveals an undying devotion to each other.

Aberdeen, George Hamilton Gordon, 4th Earl of (1784–1860) British statesman. He was Foreign Secretary during 1828–30 and again from 1841 to 1846, when he concluded the WEBSTER–ASHBURTON and OREGON BOUNDARY treaties which settled boundary disputes between the USA and Canada. As a leader of those Conservatives who campaigned for FREE TRADE, he supported Sir Robert PEEL in repealing the CORN LAWS (1846). As Prime Minister (1852–55) of the 'Aberdeen Coalition', he reluctantly involved his country in the CRIMEAN WAR and was subsequently blamed for its mismanagement. He resigned in 1855.

abolitionists Militant opponents of slavery in the 19th-century USA. In the first two decades of the 19th century, there was only a handful of individual abolitionists, but thereafter, fired by religious revivalism, the abolition movement became a strong political force. Prominent as writers and orators were the Boston newspaper-owner William Lloyd Garrison, the author Harriet Beecher Stowe (whose anti-slavery novel *Uncle Tom's Cabin* sold 1.5 million copies within a year of its publication in 1852), and the ex-slave Frederick Douglass. The abolitionist cause at first found little support in Congress or the main political parties, except among a few individuals such as Charles SUMNER, but it played an increasing part in precipitating the political division which led to the AMERICAN CIVIL WAR.

abolition of slavery SLAVE TRADE, ABOLITION OF.

Aborigines The indigenous Australoid people of Australia and Tasmania, such as the Aranda. Prior to European settlement Australian Aborigines were semi-nomadic HUNTER-GATHERERS, with a complex series of myths and sacred rituals. Traditionally, the predominant form of social organization was the patrilineal descent group, based on a system of exogamous marriage (marriage outside an individual's group). This system served to link different kin groups, between which reciprocal exchanges of marriage partners would take place. Males were responsible for ritual observances, such as initiation and circumcision, and often these rites of passage would also involve food prohibitions, as in the female puberty rite. Some 300 different Australian Aboriginal languages were spoken; these were all based on an oral tradition, and no written language existed. The Aboriginal population in 1788 has been estimated at about 500,000. Within a hundred years it had declined to about 50,000, mainly as a result of loss of land, adoption of European habits, such as drinking alcohol, effects of European diseases, declining birthrates, and violence between Europeans and Aborigines. Aborigine reserves were created in central and northern Australia in the 1930s, but since World War II Aboriginal groups have emerged seeking to preserve their cultural heritage. On the northern reserves they have made demands for a share from the mining companies in the mineral exploitation, and in Western Australia they have formed trade unions on the sheep stations. Legally they have been Australian citizens since 1948, but there has been considerable variation in state and federal procedures requiring Aborigines to register and vote. Since 1948 there has been a marked cultural resurgence, together with demands for greater social and cultural equality. In 1992 a High Court ruling overturned the notion of *terra nullius* (the notion that Australia had been uninhabited when European colonization began), allowing Aborigines a measure of legal entitlement to their ancestral lands.

Aboukir Bay NILE, BATTLE OF THE.

Abraham First of the patriarchs of ISRAEL, from whom the Israelites traced their descent. He is revered by Jews, Christians, and Muslims. The biblical stories of Abraham are of varying date and origin, and it is uncertain how much historical fact they contain. According to the book of Genesis (the first book of the Old Testament) Abraham lived in the middle of the 2nd millennium BC at Haran in northern Mesopotamia. He was divinely called to leave his home and family and go to a new land, CANAAN. It is recorded that God made a covenant (or agreement) with him, promising him a multitude of descendants to whom he would give Canaan for ever, provided that he and all his male descendants were circumcised. Accordingly, Abraham's wife Sarah, although aged over 90, gave birth to a son, Isaac. God subsequently tested Abraham's faith by asking him to sacrifice Isaac to him. When Abraham showed his readiness to do this, a ram was substituted for the sacrifice and God confirmed his covenant. Through Ishmael, his son by Hagar, the maidservant of Sarah, he is considered by Muslims an ancestor of the Arabs, and is frequently mentioned (as Ibrahim) in the Koran.

Absaroke CROW AND HIDATSA.

absentee landlord A landowner not normally resident on the estate from which he derived income and which was generally managed through an agent. While some landlords cared for the welfare of their tenants, others engaged in such practices as the issue of very short leases, which gave unscrupulous agents opportunities to raise rents frequently and evict anyone unable to pay. Abuses were common in pre-revolutionary France and in Ireland, where successive confiscations had led to Irish estates falling into English hands.

Abu Bakr (*c.* 573–634) First CALIPH of Islam (632–34). He was one of the earliest converts to Islam and a close companion of the Prophet MUHAMMAD, who married his daughter Aisha. When he succeeded to Muhammad's position as temporal leader of the Muslim community, this pious and gentle man was chiefly concerned to reaffirm the allegiance of those Arabian tribes who had withdrawn it at the time of the Prophet's death. These 'wars of apostasy' initiated the ARAB CONQUESTS.

Abushiri Revolt (August 1888–89) Arab revolt against German traders on the East African coast north of ZANZIBAR. The Arab leader Abushiri (Abu Bashir ibn Salim al-Harthi) united local hostility to German colonization at Pangani when in August 1888 the Germans hauled down the Sultan of Zanzibar's flag and hoisted their own. British and German interference in the slave, ivory, and rubber trades, and their conduct in mosques, had already caused resentment. Abushiri's resistance spread inland to the Usambara mountains, and to Lake Victoria. The revolt was crushed by the German explorer and administrator Hermann von Wissmann in 1889.

Abydos Two ancient cities. Abydos on the south-eastern shore of the HELLESPONT stood where those waters are at their narrowest. It was from there that XERXES I crossed into Europe, via a bridge of boats, in 480 BC. It was also an important base for Antiochus the Great when he crossed into Europe in 197 BC. After his defeat at Magnesia, Abydos probably came under the control of PERGAMUM, and subsequently of Rome.

Abydos in Upper Egypt was specially venerated because of its association with the god Osiris. Its remains date from *c.* 3100–500 BC. The earliest pharaohs built funerary monuments there, and later kings such as Seti I and RAMESSES II built temples and sanctuaries there.

Abyssinia ETHIOPIA.

Abyssinian Campaigns (1935–41) Conflicts between Italy, Abyssinia (ETHIOPIA), and later Britain. War broke out from Italy's unfulfilled ambition of 1894–96 to link ERITREA with SOMALIA, and from MUSSOLINI's aim to provide colonies to absorb Italy's surplus unemployed population. In 1934 and 1935 incidents, possibly contrived, took place at Walwal and elsewhere. On 3 October 1935 an Italian army attacked the Ethiopian forces from the north and east. Eventually the Ethiopians mustered 40,000 men, but they were helpless against the highly trained troops and modern weapons of the Italians. During the Italian occupation (1936–41), fighting continued. In 1940 the Italians occupied British Somaliland, but in 1941 British troops evicted the Italians entirely from Eritrea, Ethiopia, and Somalia in a four-month campaign with support from Ethiopian nationalists.

academic freedom The right to pursue knowledge, to engage in research, or to teach independently of any political control. It is argued that academic freedom is desirable because knowledge is best discovered by the open investigation of facts and opinions. In 1632 the scientist Galileo was accused of heresy before the Inquisition for stating that the planets circled the Sun, not the Earth. With the secularization of education,

religious interference in academic enquiry has largely given way to political and commercial pressures. The majority of nations exercise some control over their academic and educational systems, but totalitarian regimes exploit this control for the purpose of indoctrination (see TOTALITARIANISM). In the 1930s, for example, thousands of Soviet scientists lost their jobs for teaching orthodox genetics, deemed to clash with Marxist principles. Thousands more (including 20 who were or became Nobel Prize winners) were dismissed by the Nazis because they were Jewish. In recent years, the introduction of 'value for money' criteria for government investment in research, and of 'user pays' sponsorship by businesses, has increasingly affected the direction of academic research.

Académie des Sciences French scientific society, one of the oldest and most prestigious in the world. Founded in 1666 by Jean-Baptiste COLBERT, four years after the ROYAL SOCIETY OF LONDON, it developed out of informal gatherings of scientists, including René Descartes, Christiaan Huygens, and PASCAL. The Académie was originally intended by Louis XIV (1638–1715) to embrace history and literature as well as science. The Académie was reorganized and given a formal constitution in 1699; in the 18th century it became the leading force in European science. Since its inception, the Académie has granted its members a state pension, plus financial assistance with their research.

Academy The school established at Athens by PLATO in the 380s BC, probably intended to prepare men to serve the city-state. It was as a philosophical centre that it became celebrated, its students including ARISTOTLE, EPICURUS, and ZENO OF CITIUM. Much of its history is obscure, but it survived until its closure by JUSTINIAN I in 529 AD.

Acadia NOVA SCOTIA.

Achaean League A confederacy of Achaean and other Peloponnesian states in ancient GREECE. Its name derived from the region of Achaea in north-east Greece. In the 4th century BC an alliance was forged which was dissolved in 338 BC. It was refounded in 280 BC, under the leadership of Aratus of Sicyon. It became involved in wars with Macedonia and Sparta, before allying itself with Rome in 198. However, war with Rome in 146 led to defeat and the dissolution of the League.

Achaemenid The dynasty established by CYRUS THE GREAT in the 6th century BC and named after his ancestor Achaemenes. Cyrus' predecessors ruled Parsumash, a vassal state of the Median empire, but he overthrew their king Astyages and incorporated the MEDES within his Persian empire, which by his death in 530 BC extended from Asia Minor to the River Indus. His successor Cambyses II (529–521 BC) added Egypt. DARIUS I instituted a major reorganization of the administration and finances of the empire, establishing 20 provinces ruled by SATRAPS. Both he and XERXES failed in their attempts to conquer Greece in the early 5th century. By the time ALEXANDER THE GREAT invaded with his Macedonian army (334 BC) the empire was much weakened. Darius III, defeated at Issus and Gaugamela, was killed by his own men in 330 BC. Achaemenid rule was tolerant of local customs, religions, and forms of government. The construction of a major road system, centred on Susa, facilitated trade and administration. The magnificent remains of PERSEPOLIS provide a glimpse of Achaemenid wealth and power.

Acheh A sultanate on the northern coast of Sumatra, claimed to be the first Muslim state in south-east Asia. After the fall of MALACCA to the Portuguese in 1511 many Muslim traders moved there. By the late 16th century it had reduced the power of JOHORE and controlled much of Sumatra and Malaya, deriving its wealth from pepper and tin. After the Dutch took Malacca in 1641, Acheh consolidated its rule in Sumatra.

Acheh War (1873–1903) A conflict in north Sumatra between the Dutch and the Achehnese. Trade rivalry and attempts by the sultan of Acheh to obtain foreign assistance against Dutch domination of north Sumatra caused the dispatch of an abortive Dutch expeditionary force in 1871. Although a larger force, sent later in the year, captured the sultan's capital, the Dutch met with fierce resistance in the interior, organized by the local religious leaders (*ulama*). The war was brought to an end between 1898 and January 1903 by military 'pacification' and concessions to the *ulama*, who were permitted to carry on their religious duties provided they kept out of politics. Anti-Dutch sentiments persisted, and the region was the first to rise against the colonial power when the Japanese invaded INDONESIA in 1942.

Acheson, Dean (Gooderham) (1893–1971) US politician. He served as Assistant Secretary of State, Under-Secretary, and Secretary of State (1949–53), urging international control of nuclear power in the Acheson-Lilienthal Report of 1946, formulating plans for NATO, implementing the MARSHALL PLAN, and the TRUMAN DOCTRINE of US support for nations threatened by communism.

Acheulian A prehistoric culture characterized by handaxes, named after St Acheul near Amiens, France, but widely distributed across Africa, Europe, the Middle East, and parts of Asia. The handaxes were general-purpose stone tools produced from a cobble or large flake by trimming it to an oval or pear-shaped form. They lacked a handle but were nonetheless efficient slicing tools. They first appear in Africa around 1.5 million years ago and continued to be made with little modification to the basic shape until 150,000 years ago. Sites with Acheulian tools have provided the earliest certain evidence of the control and use of fire by humans.

acropolis The CITADEL of an ancient Greek city, most notably of Athens. The Athenian citadel was destroyed by the invading Persians in 480 BC, but PERICLES instituted a rebuilding programme. The Parthenon, built 447–432 BC, was a Doric temple containing a gold and ivory statue of Athena. This was followed by the gateway or Propylaea, the temple of Athena Nike (commemorating victory over the Persians), and the Erectheum, which housed the shrines of various cults. Many of the sculptures on the Parthenon were removed by Lord Elgin in 1801–03 and purchased by the British government in 1816. The right to their possession is disputed between Britain and Greece.

Action Française An extreme right-wing group in France during the first half of the 20th century, and also the name of the newspaper published to promote its views. Founded by the poet and political journalist Charles Maurras, it aimed at overthrowing the parliamentary republic and restoring the monarchy. Strongly nationalist, its relationship with royalist pretenders and the papacy was not always good. It became discredited for its overt FASCISM and association with the VICHY government in 1940–44.

Actium A promontory on the south headland of the Ambracian gulf, north-west Greece. It was the base of MARK ANTONY and Cleopatra in their campaign (31 BC) against Octavian for supremacy in the Roman world. This was the last in the series of civil wars which had begun with Caesar's crossing of the RUBICON in 49 BC. After blockading Antony's larger fleet, Octavian and his admiral Agrippa scattered it at sea near Actium. Antony and Cleopatra escaped to Egypt and eventually committed suicide, leaving their land-forces to surrender. The victory gave Octavian undisputed supremacy in the Roman world and in 27 BC he gained official recognition as Caesar AUGUSTUS. The battle was widely used for some decades in the East as the starting date of a new era.

Act of Union (1800) An Act to abolish the Irish Parliament. Following rebellion in IRELAND (1798) the British Prime Minister William PITT resolved that Ireland should be united with the rest of Britain under a single Parliament. The Act had to be passed by the British Parliament in London and the Irish Parliament in Dublin, where it was deeply resented. Pitt promised that the reward would be CATHOLIC EMANCIPATION, although in the event he was to find this impossible to achieve.

Adams, Gerry (Gerard) (1948–) Northern Ireland politician, president of SINN FÉIN (1978–). He was interned for three years in the 1970s for suspected involvement in the terrorist activities of the IRISH REPUBLICAN ARMY (IRA), with which Sinn Féin is closely associated. Advocating a combination of violence with consitutional activity, he was twice elected to Parliament, in 1983 and 1997, but refused to take up his seat. In 1993 Adams agreed with the moderate nationalist Social Democratic and Labour Party (SDLP) on steps towards a possible settlement in Northern Ireland; this led to the DOWNING STREET DECLARATION and an IRA ceasefire in August 1994. The ceasefire broke down in February 1996 but was resumed in July 1997. In September of the same year, peace negotiations began between a Sinn Féin delegation led by Adams, representatives of the British and Irish governments, and most of the Unionist parties in the province. The outcome was the Good Friday agreement of April 1998, which proposed a comprehensive settlement for the province.

Adams, John (1735–1826) Second President of the USA (1797–1801). He was a lawyer from Quincy, Massachusetts, who was enlisted for the patriot cause by James OTIS and his cousin Samuel ADAMS. His *Dissertation on the Canon and Feudal Law* championed the rights of the individual. He helped to draft the DECLARATION OF INDEPENDENCE at the second CONTINENTAL CONGRESS and the conservative Massachusetts State Constitution (1780), which reflected his fear of popular licence. Service as American representative in France (1778–79), the Netherlands (1780–82), and Britain (1785–88), and as a peace commissioner (1782) led to his election as

WASHINGTON's Vice-President (1789–97) and successor as a moderate FEDERALIST. Rival sympathies in the European war heightened party conflict and precipitated the Alien and Sedition Acts, the Virginia and Kentucky Resolves, and the outrage over the XYZ AFFAIR. Adams's moral courage prevented HAMILTON's stampede into war against France in 1799. Due to JEFFERSON's opposition Adams failed to be re-elected and retired to Quincy.

Adams, John Quincy (1767–1848) Sixth President of the USA (1825–29). The eldest son of John Adams, second President of the USA, he was elected Federalist Senator for Massachusetts (1803–08). After five years as Minister to Russia (1809–14), Adams was one of the five commissioners sent to Ghent to negotiate the end of the WAR OF 1812. He was Minister in London (1815–17) and then became Secretary of State under Monroe, when he helped to shape the MONROE DOCTRINE. He succeeded as President in 1825, but little of note was achieved during his term, due in part to persistent opposition from supporters of Andrew JACKSON to his attempts to extend federal powers. After leaving office in 1829, Adams entered the House of Representatives (1831), where he served until his death, taking a prominent part in the anti-slavery campaign.

Adams, Samuel (1722–1803) American patriot, the leader of resistance to Britain in Massachusetts between 1763 and 1776. He founded the SONS OF LIBERTY in Boston and organized riots, propaganda, and boycotts against tax-raising. He attended the CONTINENTAL CONGRESS and signed the DECLARATION OF INDEPENDENCE. He later served as governor of Massachusetts and was drafter of its constitution (1780), but failed to achieve the 'Christian Sparta' of his evangelical dreams. He was only persuaded to support the CONSTITUTION OF THE USA by the promise of a BILL OF RIGHTS.

Addams, Jane (1860–1935) US social worker and reformer. With her friend Ellen Grates Starr, she opened Hull House in Chicago in 1889, a pioneer settlement house for workers and immigrants on the model of TOYNBEE HALL in London. A pioneer of the new discipline of sociology, she had considerable influence over the planning of neighbourhood welfare institutions throughout the country. She was a leader of the WOMEN'S SUFFRAGE movement and an active pacifist.

Addington, Henry, 1st Viscount Sidmouth (1757–1844) British statesman. He entered Parliament in 1783, and succeeded William PITT THE YOUNGER as Prime Minister in 1801. His peace treaty with France (Amiens, 1802) won him some popularity, but when the conflict was resumed in the following year it became clear that he lacked the qualities of a war leader. He resigned in 1804 and later, as Lord Sidmouth, held other cabinet posts. As Home Secretary (1812–21), he introduced repressive legislation in an attempt to suppress the LUDDITES and other protest groups.

Addled Parliament (5 April–7 June 1614) The nickname given to JAMES I of England's second Parliament. In the absence of effective guidance from crown or councillors, those opposed to the king's policies were able to divert the House of Commons to discussion of grievances, including Church reform, impositions (import duties), and court interference at the elections. The king dissolved the Parliament before it had passed any legislation – hence the nickname 'addled' meaning barren, empty, or muddled. He ruled without a Parliament until 1621.

Aden A port commanding the entrance to the Red Sea. In 1839 Aden was captured from the Abdali Sultan of Lahej by a British expedition and annexed to British India. It became a free port in 1850 and enjoyed commercial prosperity as an entrepôt for the East African trade and as a station on the route from Europe to the East, especially after the opening of the Suez Canal in 1869. In 1937 Aden became a crown colony and in 1963 part of the South Arabian Federation of Arab Emirates. In the civil war of 1965–67, British forces attempted to keep the peace, but when Britain withdrew its sponsorship of the Federation, Aden became part of the People's Republic of South Yemen. (See YEMEN.)

Adenauer, Konrad (1876–1967) German statesman. He became Mayor of Cologne in 1917, but because of his opposition to NAZISM he was removed from this post in 1933 and subsequently twice arrested. In 1945 he again became mayor, but was removed by the British authorities for alleged inefficiency. In the same year he helped to create the CHRISTIAN DEMOCRATIC PARTY. When the GERMAN FEDERAL REPUBLIC was created in 1949, he became the first Chancellor (1949–63). During his period in office a sound democratic system of government was established; friendship with the USA and France was secured; and the West German people started to enjoy the fruits of the so-called 'economic miracle' of the ERHARD years. However, his critics accused him of being too autocratic in manner and too little concerned about the possibility of German reunification.

Adowa, Battle of (1 March 1896) A decisive defeat of the Italians by the Ethiopian Emperor MENELIK II. Italy had established a protectorate in ETHIOPIA in 1889. In 1895 there was a rebellion, and at Adowa an Italian force of 10,000 was routed, losing 4,500 dead and 300 prisoners. In the resulting Treaty of Addis Ababa the Italians recognized the independence of Ethiopia and restricted themselves to the colony of Eritrea. The battle ensured Ethiopian survival as an independent kingdom in Africa after the era of imperial partition.

Adrian IV (Nicholas Breakspear) (c. 1100–59) The only Englishman to have held the office of pope (1154–59). He reorganized the Church in Norway, and in the bull *Laudabiliter* assisted HENRY II of England to gain control of Ireland. He opposed FREDERICK I BARBAROSSA's claims to power, using the interdict (EXCOMMUNICATION) against Frederick's supporters in Rome. The Diet of Besançon in 1157 did not resolve their differences and the dispute was still raging when he died.

Adrianople, Battle of (9 August 378 AD) The defeat of Roman forces by the VISIGOTHS at the Roman city of Adrianople 480 km (300 miles) west of Constantinople. Emperor Valens, who had hoped to prevent the Gothic invasion of the Roman empire, was killed.

Adrianople, Treaty of (1829) A peace treaty between Russia and the OTTOMAN EMPIRE. It terminated the war between them (1828–29) and gave Russia minor territorial gains in Europe, including access to the mouth of the Danube, and substantial gains in Asia Minor. The treaty also confirmed the autonomy of SERBIA, promised autonomy for Greece, and guaranteed free passage for merchant ships through the Dardanelles.

Aegean civilization MYCENAEAN CIVILIZATION.

Afghanistan   *This Mogul miniature depicts the construction of the Gardens of Fidelity in Kabul for the Mogul emperor Babur in 1504.*

Aegospotami The site of a naval battle (405 BC) fought in the HELLESPONT. It sealed the defeat of Athens in the PELOPONNESIAN WAR. For five days the Athenian fleet attempted to draw LYSANDER and the Spartan fleet into battle. As the Athenians were disembarking after the fifth attempt, Lysander launched a surprise attack and captured 160 out of 180 TRIREMES. He executed all the Athenians whom he took prisoner.

Aetolia A mountainous region in central Greece. In ancient times it was poor, its inhabitants dispersed in small isolated communities. In 426 BC its fierce, skilled troops defeated the invasion force led by the Athenian general DEMOSTHENES. In the 4th century BC the Aetolian League, a federation of its tribes, was formed. It enjoyed considerable success: in the 3rd century DELPHI fell under its influence, and it also became Rome's first effective ally in Greece. Later it turned against the Romans, but in 189 BC they forced it into submission, breaking its power though allowing it to continue in existence.

Afars and Issas DJIBOUTI.

Afghani, Jamal al-Din al- (1839–97) Muslim revivalist of Iranian origin. He advocated social and political reforms within Muslim countries and Pan-Islamism. Afghani was active as a teacher in Egypt during the 1870s, edited a newspaper (*al-Urwa al-Wuthqa*, 'the Unbreakable Link') in Paris during the 1880s, and played a part in the protest in Iran in 1891–92, which forced the government to cancel its concessions for the production of tobacco.

Afghanistan A mountainous, landlocked country in south-central Asia, bounded on the west by Iran, on the south and east by Pakistan, and on the north by Turkmenistan, Uzbekistan, and Tajikistan.

Physical. Afghanistan's eastern region is dominated by the vast mountain range of the Hindu Kush, and most of the country is high plateau. In winter much of it is under snow; but in spring grass appears, soon to be scorched dry and swept by the dust storms of summer.

Economy. Agriculture, mainly sheep-raising and subsistence farming, is the mainstay of the economy, which has been devastated by the civil war; there are widespread food shortages and illegal opium production is prevalent.

History. Afghanistan was conquered by ALEXANDER THE GREAT, and after his death became part of the BACTRIAN state. A succession of foreign overlords was followed by Arab conquest from the 7th century. The territory was converted to ISLAM, the most important Muslim ruler was MAHMUD OF GHAZNA. The country was overrun by MONGOLS in 1219 and remained under Mongol control until the fall of GENGHIS KHAN, when a number of principalities arose. Part of Afghanistan was then claimed by the Safavid Persians, while Kabul and the rest of the country became part of the MOGUL empire. The country was first united under an Afghan leader in 1747, when Ahmad Shah founded the Durrani dynasty at Kandahar.

In the 19th and early 20th centuries Afghanistan was the focal point of conflicting Russian and British interests. A British attempt to replace the Kabul ruler DOST MUHAMMAD was repulsed in the First ANGLO-AFGHAN WAR. Afghan foreign policy came under British control in 1879 by the Treaty of Gandamak, when Britain gained control of the Khyber Pass, an important route between India and Central Asia, thus alienating the PATHAN TRIBES. In 1880 Abdurrahman Khan became amir. Under him a strong central government was established, and his heirs achieved some modernization and social reform. In 1953 General Mohammad Daoud Khan seized power and was Prime Minister until 1963, during which time he obtained economic and military assistance from the Soviet Union. There were border disputes with Pakistan, but it was Daoud's policy to maintain 'non-alignment' between the two super-power blocs. In 1964 Afghanistan became a parliamentary democracy, but a military coup in 1973 overthrew the monarchy and Daoud reasserted control. In 1977 he issued a constitution for a one-party state. Within a year, however, he had been assassinated and the Democratic Republic of Afghanistan proclaimed, headed by a revolutionary council, whose first President was Nur Mohammad Taraki. The new regime embarked on reforms, but there was tension and rural unrest. In February 1979 the US ambassador was killed and one month later Taraki was assassinated by supporters of the deputy Prime Minister, Hafizullah Amin, who then sought US support. In December 1979 Soviet troops entered the country. Amin was killed and replaced by Babrak Karmal. Guerrilla Mujahidin forces, equipped with US arms, then waged a *jihad* or holy war against government troops armed and supported by Soviet forces. Some six million refugees fled to Iran and Pakistan. In 1987 the Soviet Union began to disengage, all troops being withdrawn by 1989. In 1992 Mujahidin guerrillas overthrew the Communist government of Mohammad Najibullah and proclaimed the Islamic State of Afghanistan. However, civil conflict between both rival Mujahidin factions and other militant groups continued. In 1996 the government was overthrown by the fundamentalist Islamic TALIBAN militia, who took control of Kabul and executed former President Najibullah. The north of the country remains under the control of anti-Taliban forces.

CAPITAL:	Kabul
AREA:	652,225 sq km (251,825 sq miles)
POPULATION:	22.264 million (1996)
CURRENCY:	1 afghani = 100 puls
RELIGIONS:	Sunni Muslim 93.0%; Shiite Muslim 7.0%
ETHNIC GROUPS:	Pathan (Pashto) 52.3%; Tajik 20.3%; Uzbek 8.7%; Hazara 8.7%; Chahar Aimak 2.9%; Turkmen 2.0%; Baluchi 1.0%
LANGUAGES:	Pashto, Dari (Persian) (both official); minority languages
INTERNATIONAL ORGANIZATIONS:	UN; Colombo Plan; Non-Aligned Movement

Afghan Wars ANGLO-AFGHAN WARS.

Africa The second largest continent, extending south from the Mediterranean Sea and bounded by the Atlantic and Indian oceans and the Red Sea.

Physical. The Equator passes through the middle of Africa, so that all but the very north and south are tropical, although regional differences in climate and landscape are vast. The cultivable north-west coastal plains rise up to the High Atlas Mountains, which, southward, fall more gently to the plateau of the Sahara. Most of northern Africa is desert, the only significant waterway being the Nile. The west, watered by the Niger and other rivers, is rich in tropical forests, though in many coastal regions there is only swamp. Inland the ground rises first to savannahs and then to hilly, wooded plateaux in the centre of the continent. Here are some of the largest copper deposits in the world, and also of gold, diamonds, uranium, cobalt, and other minerals. East Africa is a temperate region of great lakes, mountains, and high plateaux. It is split from north to south by the Great Rift Valley. South of the Zambezi River are more highlands, giving way in the south-west to the Kalahari Desert. Then the land rises again, to the temperate veld. This good farming country is very rich in minerals. The southernmost coastal plain is ideal for fruit and plantation crops.

History. Africa was the birthplace of the human race, as shown by finds at OLDUVAI GORGE and other sites. By the late Stone Age Proto-Berbers inhabited the north, Ethiopians the Nile valley, while NEGROID peoples moved southwards. Pygmies occupied the central forest, and San and Khoikhoi (called Bushmen and Hottentots by White colonists) roamed the south.

By the 4th millennium BC, one of the world's oldest civilizations had developed in EGYPT. In the north PHOENICIANS, and then CARTHAGINIANS, organized sea-borne empires which fell, with Egypt, to Rome in the last centuries BC. Indigenous kingdoms arose in NUBIA and AXUM. In the 7th century the Arabs seized the north, bringing to it the religion and culture of ISLAM.

In Cameroon *c.* 500 BC a population explosion sent the Bantu eastwards. They slowly occupied most of southern and central Africa, overwhelming the San people. There and in West Africa chieftainships developed, and some empires with sophisticated cultures, especially in Islamic states such as MALI and in Christian ETHIOPIA. Their intricate system of commerce reached from the Mediterranean to Indonesia and China. The Portuguese arrival in the 15th century heralded European intervention in Africa, stimulating trade in the west and centre, but interrupting it in the east. In the 16th century the north fell to the Ottomans, while south of the Sahara Europeans began the SLAVE TRADE to the Americas. From the 16th to the 18th century in the present Democratic Republic of the Congo (formerly Zaïre) and in central Africa Bantu states developed, some of them sizeable empires. During this period the Bantu were pushing their way southwards, but it was not until the 19th century that they began to form recognizable states in the present South Africa. While each tribe or state developed its individual pattern of constitution, some more sophisticated than others, power was generally concentrated in the hands of chieftains and regulated both by tribal conventions and by free public discussion in tribal assemblies.

During the 19th century the interior was gradually opened up to European explorers, traders, and MISSIONARIES in an extensive programme of colonization. Imperialist sentiments and the desire to exploit the continent's natural resources produced a series of military campaigns against the local states and tribes. After World War I Germany's former colonial empire was divided among the victorious Allies. After 1945 the rise of African nationalism accelerated the process of decolonization, most of the Black countries becoming independent between 1957 and 1980, sometimes as a result of peaceful negotiation and sometimes through armed rebellion (see illustration). In Namibia (until 1990) and South Africa (until 1994), small White élites held on to political power, but elsewhere the descendants of the original inhabitants assumed responsibility for their own government. The artificial boundaries imposed by colonialism, the rapidity of the transition to home rule, and the underdeveloped state of many of the local economies produced political, social, and economic problems of varying severity all over the continent. Many of the new nations remained unstable and politically impoverished, while drought in the 1980s and early 1990s, in both East and Southern Africa, caused terrible suffering. Multiparty democracies, which replaced single-party regimes in many African countries in the early 1990s, inherited vast burdens of World Bank and IMF debt.

African National Congress (ANC) A South African political party. It was established in Bloemfontein in 1912 as the South African Native National Congress by a Zulu Methodist minister, J. W. Dube. In 1914 he led a deputation to Britain protesting against the Native Land Act (1913), which restricted the purchase of land by

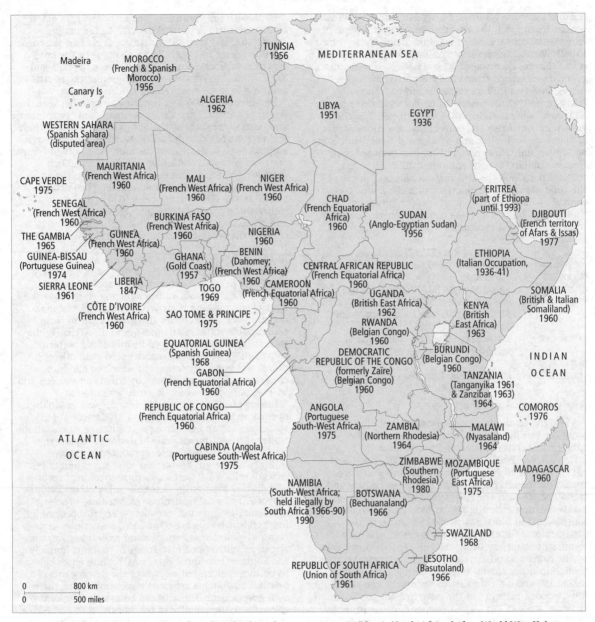

African decolonization *Agitation for political independence was strong in Islamic North Africa before World War II, but south of the Sahara the first Black African independent state to emerge was Ghana (1957). Within decades, White minority rule was confined to South Africa and Namibia.*

Black Africans. In 1926 the ANC established a united front with representatives of the Indian community, which aimed to create a racially integrated, democratic southern Africa. It sought to achieve racial equality by non-violent means, as practised by GANDHI in India, and from 1952 until 1967 was led by the Natal chieftain Albert LUTHULI. Together with the more militant break-away movement, the PAN-AFRICANIST CONGRESS (PAC), it was declared illegal by the South African government in 1960. Confronted by Afrikaner intransigence on racial issues, the ANC saw itself forced into a campaign of

violence. Maintaining that APARTHEID should be abolished, and every South African have the vote, it formed a liberation army, 'Umkhonto Wesizwe' (Spear of the Nation). In 1962 its vice-president, Nelson MANDELA, and some of his colleagues were convicted of sabotage and jailed for life. The exiled wing of the ANC maintained a campaign of violence during the 1980s, but following the election of President DE KLERK (1989) the party was legalized and Mandela was released from prison in 1990. The ANC subsequently entered into talks with the government and participated in the drafting of a new constitution, which gave the vote to all South African adults. The first multiracial elections, held in 1994, were won by the ANC and Mandela became President. Violence has been prevalent, both before and after the transition to majority rule, between ANC supporters and adherents of the mainly Zulu INKATHA FREEDOM PARTY, especially in Inkatha's power-base, the eastern region of KwaZulu/Natal. In December 1997 Thabo MBEKI succeeded Mandela as president of the ANC.

African traditional religions African traditional religions are closely linked to different ethnic groups, of which there are over 700 south of the Sahara. There is great diversity in both practice and belief, but there are certain common features on the basis of which generalizations may be made. Lacking extensive written scriptures, African traditional religions are based upon myths and rituals passed down by oral tradition and custom. African traditional religions may be described as systems of beliefs and rituals that make sense of daily experience, rather than metaphysical and moral systems which promise individual salvation in another (spiritual) world. Thus evil and misfortune, for example, are regarded as a disorder in the right harmony of things that may be set right by healing and propitiation rather than as the work of supernatural powers. In general, a supreme god or ultimate principle is acknowledged in a remote way, but far greater attention is paid to a range of minor deities and spirits. From about the 17th century, as colonization progressed, it seems that the concept of a supreme God became more significant, perhaps in response to the disintegration of political institutions. After contact with Islam and Christianity, many Africans recognized their supreme God to be the same as that in Christianity and Islam, allowing a ready synthesis of certain aspects of the different traditions. In most traditional African belief systems, ancestral spirits are particularly important. The spirits of leaders of the clan or family continue to concern themselves with the well-being of their descendants, and considerable efforts are made to propitiate these spirits through prayers and sacrifices. Other spirit beings may include evil spirits whose power can be harnessed by sorcerers and witches. Charms and amulets to ward off witchcraft are also widespread. In many parts of sub-Saharan Africa, the king or chief was traditionally regarded as semi-divine, and provided both religious and moral leadership. Others concerned with spiritual life include priests; mediums possessed by the spirit of a god or an ancestor; diviners, who foretell the future through magical acts such as throwing the bones; and herbalists. Communal rituals are held for specific purposes such as rain-making or involving a blessing on the harvest. Rites of passage mark the turning points in an individual's life and maintain the cohesion of the community. Holy places may be a grove or tree or a large temple-like building sacred to the god or spirit whose image may be stored there.

Afrikaner (or Boer) The White Afrikaans-speaking population of South Africa. It is used particularly to refer to the descendants of the families which emigrated from the Netherlands, Germany, and France before 1806, that is, before Britain seized the Cape Colony. Most Afrikaners follow the Christian Calvinist tradition, which, through the belief that salvation is only possible for a predetermined group of people and cannot be gained by any other individual, even by leading a religious life, contributed to the concept of APARTHEID.

Agade AKKAD.

Aga Khan (Turkish, *aga*, 'master', *khan*, 'ruler') Title borne by leaders of the Nizari or eastern branch of the Ismaili sect of Shiite Islam. The first Aga Khan, Hassan Ali Shah of Kirman (d. 1881), fled to Afghanistan and Sind after leading an unsuccessful revolt in Iran in 1838. Winning British favour he settled in Bombay, where in 1866 the Arnold judgment gave him control of the affairs of the Indian Khoja community. His grandson, Sultan Muhammad Shah (1877–1957), played an active part in Indian politics, attempting to secure Muslim support for British rule, particularly as President of the All-India MUSLIM LEAGUE (1913). He was leader of the Muslim delegation to the ROUND TABLE CONFERENCE in 1930–32. He was succeeded by his grandson, Prince Karim.

Agincourt, Battle of (25 October 1415) The defeat of a large French force by an English army led by HENRY V near the village of Agincourt in northern France. Henry's force invaded NORMANDY in 1415, captured Harfleur, but was intercepted by a large French army after a long march north towards Calais. The English troops, mainly archers and foot soldiers, dug in behind wooden stakes between thickly wooded ground. The next day the French cavalry advanced on a narrow front across muddy ground only to be killed by English archers and infantry. A dozen French notables, including the Constable of France, died, together with perhaps 1,500 knights and 4,500 men-at-arms, including prisoners massacred after French knights made a surprise attack on the English baggage train late in the day. English casualties were light but included the Duke of York and the Earl of Suffolk.

agnosticism (from Greek, *agnostos*, 'unknown') A term coined in 1869 by T. H. Huxley (1825–95), the British biologist and supporter of Charles Darwin's theories of evolution, to indicate his position with regard to orthodox religious belief. Influenced by modern scientific thought, the agnostic holds that phenomena (such as the existence of God), unprovable by material means, cannot be the subjects of belief or disbelief. Agnosticism is also popularly used to imply scepticism about, or indifference to, religious matters, but it should not be confused with ATHEISM, which is the denial of the existence of God or any supernatural being.

agora The market-place that stood at the centre of every Greek city, the equivalent of the Roman FORUM. In Athens, as well as being a trading centre, it included administrative buildings, temples, meeting places such as the Stoa Poikile where ZENO OF CITIUM taught, the mint, and, in Roman times, two libraries.

Agricola, Gnaeus Julius (40–93 AD) Governor of Roman Britain (78–84). He served with Paulinus against the Iceni queen BOUDICCA (61) and commanded the Twentieth Legion in the north-west (70–73). As governor he subjugated the Ordovices of north Wales and extended the frontier north to the rivers Forth and Clyde, defeating the Caledonians in the process. His successes irritated Emperor Domitian who recalled him to Rome in 84. His career, in particular the British governorship, is described in his *Life* by TACITUS, his son-in-law.

Agricultural Revolution The major changes in agriculture that took place in Britain during the 18th century. Some historians stress that agriculture was already undergoing evolutionary change, but that this was speeded up by ENCLOSURE, particularly the parliamentary enclosures of the 18th century. The medieval economy rested on the manorial system and open-field cultivation in STRIPS which hampered change. The Agricultural Revolution saw this replaced by large-scale farming in consolidated units, the extension of arable farming over heaths and commons, the adoption of intensive livestock husbandry, the conversion of a largely self-subsistent peasantry into a community of agricultural labourers, and considerable attention to the improvement of agricultural techniques like CROP ROTATION, new crops, for example turnips and potatoes, and improved grasses. Viscount Townshend (1674–1738) and Thomas Coke, Earl of Leicester (1752–1842) were notable for their adoption and promotion of crop rotation; Jethro Tull (1674–1741) for his seed drills; and Robert Bakewell (1725–95) was the most famous of the livestock improvers.

agriculture Cultivation of the soil, including the allied pursuits of gathering crops and rearing livestock. The 'Neolithic revolution', the change from an economy based on hunting and gathering to one based on settled agriculture, is thought to have begun in many independent centres around the world, at very roughly the same time (*c.* 9000 BC): changes in climate and population growth may have stimulated this process. Archaeological evidence suggests at least three independent centres of origin for agriculture based on grain crops (the Near East, the Far East, and meso-America), plus other sites (for example, Peru and Indonesia), where root vegetables formed the main crops. The most complete evidence has come from the Near East, where domesticated barley and emmer wheat strains have been found which date from about 8000 BC. Domesticated animals (e.g. sheep and goats) were reared in large numbers from at least 7000 BC, and there is evidence for the use of the ox-drawn wooden plough from 5000 BC. In the early civilizations of Babylonia, Egypt, the Indus Valley, and China (from *c.* 3000 BC), large-scale irrigation systems were developed.

Agricultural practices spread gradually from the different centres to other parts of the world, and were adapted to local conditions; many different field systems evolved. In Europe and the Mediterranean, practices, once established, remained basically unchanged for many years. Roman farmers used an ox-drawn, wheelless plough with iron shares or blades. They sowed seed by hand, harvested using a curved sickle, threshed grain with a hand flail, and winnowed it by throwing it into the air and letting the wind carry away the chaff. By the 4th century AD, high labour input, the transplanting of seedlings, and use of fertilizers were producing cereal yields in China not matched elsewhere until the 19th century. In the Americas, maize was the main crop in some areas, the potato in others. The llama was domesticated as a beast of burden, while the alpaca was kept for its wool, and the guinea-pig for meat. In medieval Europe, slow improvements were made in

agricultural practice, particularly in northern areas. From the 5th to the 12th centuries, agricultural land was created by forest clearance, or was reclaimed from marshland and the sea. From the late 13th to the early 15th centuries, much arable land fell into disuse due to the effects of floods, famine, plague, and wars. Recovery began slowly in the 15th century.

In the 17th and 18th centuries several different developments led to improvements in crop yields and in livestock production. In particular, the AGRICULTURAL REVOLUTION of 18th-century Britain introduced new, more efficient practices into farming. Principal among these was the Norfolk four-course system, in which grain and fodder or grazing crops were grown in a four-year rotation. The effects of this system were cumulative: grazing animals manured the land and increased its fertility, while the growing of winter fodder and summer grazing crops meant that animals were better fed, and more productive. In the 18th century selective breeding was introduced, and the Rotherham plough (the forerunner of the modern plough) was developed, along with a variety of simple machines for threshing, chopping animal feed, hoeing, and seed drilling. However, it was not until the mid-19th century that agricultural machinery, for example the reaper and the traction-engine, began to be adopted by farmers.

The 19th century also saw the development of agricultural science, with the introduction of the earliest chemical and synthetic fertilizers, and the opening of agricultural research stations in several countries. During this period large areas of the USA, Canada, South America, and Australia were settled: huge sheep and cattle ranches were established, and large areas were given over to wheat farming. In colonial countries, plantation farming of beverage crops, rubber, and sugar cane expanded tremendously, although these developments had little effect on indigenous agricultural practices. Much of the cheap food generated by the opening up of these new areas was exported to Europe.

The 20th century has seen far-reaching changes in farming practices. The internal-combustion engine has replaced steam-power for agricultural machinery, and improved transport has led to the development of a world market for some agricultural products. The green revolution saw increased crop production in developing countries. From 1965 to the early 1990s, world cereal production (the best indicator of agriculture and nutrition since cereals provide over half the calories in the human diet) increased by over 70%. Thus India, for example, which formerly suffered regularly from FAMINE and was forced to spend scarce foreign exchange on food imports is now self-sufficient in food, although its population has doubled since independence in 1947. Agrochemicals were being used in huge quantities by the 1960s, but since that time the hazards of indiscriminate pesticide use have led to the development of other strategies such as the breeding of disease-resistant plant strains and the use of biological methods of pest control favoured by organic farmers. Genetic development of plant strains and intensive animal breeding have greatly increased the productivity of croplands and livestock in developed countries. However, surpluses of some commodities in developed countries have not helped developing countries, in particular in Africa, where population growth has not been matched by increases in agricultural productivity. Western aid has too often failed to recognize the efficiency of local agricultural practices.

Economic thinking emphasizes the importance of agriculture in development: formerly industrialization was seen as the key to economic growth and the agricultural sector was taxed in order to finance investment in industry, but it is now recognized that it is essential to develop agriculture as well in order to alleviate poverty, provide employment, and to meet the basic needs for food of the population, and to boost the domestic market for industrial products. Agriculture is also an important source of export earnings for many developing countries, accounting for many primary-product exports. Typically, governments may encourage agricultural development by positive pricing and taxation policies, supporting transport, infrastructure, the use of marginal land, research, and education, providing subsidies, capital, and credit, and, in some cases, by implementing land reform. Agriculture forms a decreasing share of GNP and employment as development proceeds, and many industrialized countries import food, but most developed countries continue to subsidize agriculture, because it is regarded as a strategic industry, because they wish to preserve the rural environment, and, most importantly, because of the political power of farming lobbies.

Agrippa, Marcus Vipsanius (63–12 BC) Roman statesman. He accompanied the young AUGUSTUS to Rome after Julius CAESAR's murder, and later won decisive naval victories over Sextus Pompeius (Naulochus, 36 BC) and MARK ANTONY (Actium, 31 BC). Augustus consistently entrusted him with wide military and organizational responsibilities, and marked him out as his heir-apparent. His death in 12 BC was unexpected. A prolific builder, his best-known constructions are the Pantheon at Rome and the Pont du Gard and Maison Carré at Nîmes, southern France.

Aguinaldo, Emilio (1869–1964) Filipino nationalist leader. He became active in the nationalist movement in the early 1890s and led an armed uprising against Spanish rule (1895–96). He returned during the SPANISH-AMERICAN WAR (1898) and organized another guerrilla campaign, but, after the US victory, his nationalist aspirations resulted in war with US forces (1899–1901). Finally accepting US rule, he waged a peaceful campaign for independence for the next four decades before collaborating with the Japanese during World War II. Briefly imprisoned by the Americans in 1945, he retired from active politics after his release.

Ahab (9th century BC) Second king of the OMRI dynasty in northern Israel (c. 869–c. 850 BC). He campaigned in alliance with Syria against Assyria, but was defeated at the battle of Qarqar (853 BC). Three years later he allied with Jehoshaphat, King of Judah, to regain Transjordan from the Syrians. Although temporarily uniting the kingdoms, Ahab was defeated and killed. The stability of his kingdom was undermined by religious disputes. His wife Jezebel was a Phoenician from the city of Tyre. While the marriage brought political advantage, it introduced Phoenician traditions into Hebrew life and religion, and Ahab was publicly denounced by the prophet ELIJAH for attempting to unite the Canaanites and Israelites in the worship of Phoenician gods.

Aidan, St (d. 651) Irish missionary. While still a monk at the monastery of Iona (c. 635), he was made a bishop and chosen by King Oswald to act as a missionary in the English kingdom of Northumbria in northern England. With royal support, St Aidan established a monastery on the island of Lindisfarne where Celtic missionaries were trained; they played an instrumental role in promoting Christianity in northern England.

airforce The armed service concerned with attack and defence in the air. Aircraft were first used in World War I to locate targets for artillery on the WESTERN FRONT, but from 1916 onwards they were developed for bombing, while rival fighter aircraft engaged in aerial dogfights both in France and in the MESOPOTAMIA CAMPAIGN, where aircraft were also invaluable for reconnaissance. Airships were also constructed, especially by Germany, which used Zeppelin airships for bombing attacks against civilian targets. After disastrous crashes in the 1930s, however, airships lost popularity. Very rapid development in aircraft design between the wars meant that World War II began with both sides possessing formidable bomber and fighter capability. During the war dive-bombing techniques as well as heavily armed bombers for massed high altitude air raids (BOMBING OFFENSIVES) were developed, while the invention of radar assisted defenders in locating attacking aircraft. Large troop-carrying planes were also introduced, together with the helicopter, which became a key weapon in later wars in Korea, Vietnam, and Afghanistan. The Cold War, from the late 1940s to 1990, saw the deployment by the superpowers of strategic nuclear bombers and intercontinental ballistic missiles (ICBMs). With the advent of supersonic flight, the high costs of increasingly sophisticated aircraft since World War II have led to the design of aircraft that each fulfil several roles, often jointly developed by a consortium of nations. Air power was decisive in the GULF WAR of 1991. This saw the first large-scale use of several innovations, such as laser-guided bombs and computer-guided cruise missiles, that were able to pinpoint and destroy specific targets. A further development was the use of the Stealth bomber, which was designed to evade and destroy radar defences. (See illustration.)

air transport The movement of passengers and goods by air. Nineteenth-century air transport, on a very limited scale, was by hot-air balloon, glider, and airship, first using steam- and then petrol engines to drive a propeller. An integral part of the TRANSPORT REVOLUTION, airships continued to be developed, especially by Germany in World War I, and by Britain and the USA, until the loss of the *Hindenburg* (1937). Passenger and freight traffic, using land and sea-planes, increased during the 1920s and 1930s; many major national airlines (e.g. Air France, Swissair) were founded in this period. Commercial air transport has experienced massive growth since the late 1950s, with the advent of jet airliners. In 1970, the introduction of the wide-bodied Jumbo jet (Boeing 747), carrying 500 passengers, resulted in reduced fares, while in 1976 the Anglo-French *Concorde* cut the trans-Atlantic crossing to under four hours. For military transport, helicopters, developed during World War II, saw extensive service in the KOREAN WAR and the VIETNAM WAR; they also became increasingly used as taxis, in rescue operations, and for

(a)

Fokker Dr. I triplane fighter
(German)

DH4 bomber (British)

27 + E11

(b) Junker Ju 52/3m
(German)

(c) Hawker Hurricane fighter
(British)

2057

(d) MIG-15 fighter
(Soviet)

(e) Bell AH-1G Huey Cobra gunship
(US)

NATO OTAN

(f) Boeing G-3A Sentry AWACS
(USAF & NATO)

airforce   *Sketch (a) shows a German triplane fighter attacking a British bomber (460 lb bomb-load) in the last year of World War I. The Junker Ju 52/3m (b) was developed by Germany in the 1930s and adapted in the Spanish Civil War as a bomber. In World War II it served the Luftwaffe (German airforce) for troop-transport and bombing. Behind the Hurricane (c) are radar aerials, developed 1938–40, which were a vital British asset in the Battle of Britain. The Soviet MIG 15 (d) was first used in the Korean War. The US helicopter gunship (e), equipped with rockets, fought in the Vietnam War. Boeing AWACS (f) are used for surveillance and as flying communications centres.*

supplying isolated areas. Air-lifting of heavy military equipment and large numbers of troops is carried out by wide-bodied cargo aircraft.

Aix-la-Chapelle, Treaty of (1748) The treaty that concluded the War of the AUSTRIAN SUCCESSION. It restored conquered territory to its original owners, with a few exceptions. The terms were drawn up by the British and French and reluctantly accepted by Empress MARIA THERESA of Austria, who had to abandon Silesia to FREDERICK II of Prussia. In Italy Don Philip, the younger son of PHILIP V of Spain, received Parma. This treaty was a temporary truce in the Anglo-French conflict in India and North America. In North America colonists unwillingly ceded the French fortress of Louisburg, in order to secure the return of Madras to Britain. Prussia's rise to the rank of a great power was strongly resented by Austria. The treaty left many issues of conflict unresolved and war (the SEVEN YEARS WAR) broke out again eight years later.

Akbar (1542–1605) The third and greatest of the MOGULS, who ruled India from 1555 to 1605. At 13 he inherited a fragile empire, but military conquests brought Rajasthan, Gujarat, Bengal, Kashmir, and the north Deccan under his sway. He introduced a system of civil and military service which ensured loyalty and centralized control, and made modifications to the land revenue system which reduced pressure on peasant cultivators. Although he was illiterate, he had an enquiring mind and extended patronage to artists and scholars of all religions. Underlying his success was a statesmanlike attitude towards the majority Hindu population, symbolized by marriage with RAJPUT princesses, the suspension of discriminatory taxes, and the increased employment of Hindus in the imperial service. A man of contradictory and powerful impulses, Akbar created the basis for Mogul control over India until the early 18th century, and also left a distinctive mark on Muslim–Hindu relations in India.

Akhenaten (or Ikhnaton) (d. 1362 BC) Pharaoh of Egypt (1379–62) and husband of NEFERTITI. He was a very early monotheist who prohibited the worship of all gods except Aten, the sun disc. He replaced THEBES as the capital with his new foundation of Akhetaten, the focal point of which was a roofless temple dedicated to Aten. However, his religious reforms were unpopular, and the influence of the priests of Amon had them overturned at the beginning of TUTANKHAMUN's reign.

Akkad An area in central Mesopotamia, named after the city of Agade, which was founded by Sargon I *c.* 2350 BC. Sargon conquered the SUMERIANS in southern Mesopotamia after much hard fighting, and in later campaigns penetrated as far as Syria and eastern Asia Minor. He apparently ruled for 56 years, though revolts towards the end of his reign indicate the difficulties of holding together such a large empire. Even so, his successors maintained Akkadian supremacy for another hundred years. Thereafter Akkad was simply the name of an area, though Akkadian had become the major spoken language of Mesopotamia; examples of it have been preserved in CUNEIFORM texts.

Aksum AXUM.

Alamein, El, Battle of (October–November 1942) A critical battle in Egypt in World War II. In June 1942, the British took up a defensive position in Egypt. One

flank rested on the Mediterranean at El Alamein and the other on the salt marshes of the Qattara Depression. In August, General MONTGOMERY was appointed to command the defending 8th Army. He launched an offensive in which, after a heavy artillery preparation, about 1,200 tanks advanced, followed by infantry, against the German Afrika Korps commanded by General ROMMEL. Rommel was handicapped by a grave fuel shortage and had only about 500 tanks. The outnumbered Germans never regained the initiative. Rommel managed to withdraw most of his men back into Libya, but this battle marked the beginning of the end of the NORTH AFRICAN CAMPAIGN for Germany.

Alamo, the A mission fort in San Antonio, Texas, and scene of a siege during the TEXAS revolution against Mexico of 1836. A Mexican army of 3,000 led by SANTA ANNA besieged the fort held by fewer than 200 men, under the joint command of William B. Travis and James Bowie. The siege lasted from 24 February to 6 March, when the Mexicans finally breached the walls. Travis, Bowie, Davy CROCKETT, and all their men were killed. The defence of the Alamo became the symbol of Texan resistance.

Alanbrooke, Alan Francis Brooke, 1st Viscount (1883–1963) British field-marshal. He served with distinction during World War I, and in the 1930s was noted as an artillery expert. In World War II he was a corps commander during the withdrawal from DUNKIRK. Later, as Chief of the Imperial General Staff and Chairman of the Chiefs of Staff Committee (1941–46), he represented the service chiefs in discussions with Churchill. As Churchill's chief adviser on military strategy, he accompanied him to all his conferences with Roosevelt and Stalin.

Åland Islands A province of FINLAND, consisting of over 6,000 islands in the Gulf of Bothnia. The islands were Swedish until 1809, when, together with Finland, they became a Russian grand duchy. After the collapse of the Russian empire in 1917 Finland declared independence, and Swedish troops, who were occupying the archipelago, were ejected. The future of the islands was referred to the LEAGUE OF NATIONS (1921), which upheld the islands' autonomy as a part of Finland.

Alans A nomadic people from southern Russia who began to harass the Roman empire's eastern frontier in the 1st century AD. In the 4th century they were forced west by the conquering HUNS, finally reaching Gaul in 406 and Spain in 409. There they merged with the VANDALS and crossed into Africa in 429.

Alaric I (*c.* 370–410) King of the VISIGOTHS. He commanded THEODOSIUS' Gothic allies and helped put down the Western usurper emperor Eugenius. On Theodosius' death the Eastern and Western Roman empires were formally divided. Alaric revolted against the rule of CONSTANTINOPLE and moved with his people in search of homelands. He invaded Italy in 401. Twice defeated by Stilicho, the Roman general, he entered a treaty of alliance with him. After the execution of Stilicho by Emperor Honorius, Alaric repudiated the pact and ravaged Italy, laying siege to Rome three times. The city fell in 410. That same year he planned invasions of Sicily and Africa, but his fleet was destroyed by storms. He died at Cosenza and was buried with treasures looted, reputedly from Rome, in the bed of the River Busentus.

Alaska Purchase (1867) The purchase by the USA of Alaska from Russia for $7,200,000 (less than five cents a hectare) arranged by William H. SEWARD. It remained an unorganized territory until 1884. Despite extensive copper and gold discoveries there was little population growth. After World War II oil was discovered, and in the COLD WAR the area played an important strategic role.

Alba, Fernando Alvarez de Toledo, Duke of (*c.* 1507–82) Spanish statesman and general. He rose to prominence in the armies of Emperor CHARLES V. A stickler for discipline and a master of logistics, he contributed significantly to the defeat of the German Protestants at the battle of Mühlberg (1547). PHILIP II sent him as governor-general to deal with unrest in the Netherlands in 1567, but his notorious 'Council of Blood' executed or banished over a thousand men, and was responsible for sparking off the DUTCH REVOLTS. He was recalled to Spain at his own request in 1573, and in 1580 Philip gave him command of the forces which conquered Portugal.

Albania A small country in south-eastern Europe, on the Adriatic coast of the BALKANS, with Montenegro, Kosovo, and Macedonia to its north and east, and Greece to its south.

Physical. Its coastal plain is marshy in the north but mostly fertile. Inland are rugged mountains, forested hills, and fast-flowing rivers. It also has the shores of three large lakes within its frontiers. In winter the bora blows cold from the north and in summer the sirocco blows Saharan dust over the crops. Rainfall is generally moderate.

Economy. Formerly a centrally planned economy under communism, since 1992 Albania has undertaken economic reforms, which include the privatization of farmland, state enterprises, and housing, the abolition of price subsidies, and the liberalization of trade. The economy is primarily agricultural, but crude oil is exported, and petrol-refining is an important industry.

History. As part of the Ottoman empire from the 15th century, Albania was noted for the military dictatorship of Ali Pasha (*c.* 1744–1822), whose court was described by the English poet Byron in *Childe Harold*. Nationalist resistance was crushed in 1831, but discontent persisted and a national league was created during the RUSSO-TURKISH WAR of 1877–78. It became an independent state as a result of the BALKAN WARS in 1912, and after a brief period as a republic became a monarchy under King ZOG in 1928. Invaded by Italy in 1939, it became a communist state under Enver HOXHA after World War II. Under the strong influence of the Soviet Union until a rift in 1958, it became closely aligned with China until MAO ZEDONG's death in 1976. Albania was expelled from the WARSAW PACT in 1968, but remained Stalinist in policy and outlook until the death of Hoxha in 1985. From then on its isolationism began to ease, with cautious steps to restore democracy in 1990. The Communists held power in the first free elections in 1991, but were defeated in 1992 by the Democratic Party, led by Sali Berisha, who became President. A democratic parliamentary constitution was adopted in 1993. A collapse of the economy resulted in widespread poverty and

deprivation. During the early 1990s there were demonstrations by Albanians living in the province of Kosovo in Serbia who supported independence for the region. Elections in 1996 saw the return of Berisha's Democratic Party, but were widely suspected of being held under fraudulent conditions. In early 1997, the collapse of a number of pyramid investment schemes led to widespread rioting as many people lost their life-savings. Repressive measures by President Berisha were answered by armed resistance, especially in the south. Elections in June-July resulted in victory for the socialists under Fatos Nano, who became Prime Minister. Berisha resigned as head of state and Rexhep Medjani became President.

CAPITAL:	Tirana
AREA:	28,748 sq km (11,100 sq miles)
POPULATION:	3.249 million (1996)
CURRENCY:	1 lek = 100 qindars
RELIGIONS:	Non-religious 55.4%; Muslim 20.5%; atheist 18.7%; Eastern Orthodox 5.4%
ETHNIC GROUPS:	Albanian, with Greek and gypsy minorities
LANGUAGES:	Albanian (official); Greek; Macedonian; Romany
INTERNATIONAL ORGANIZATIONS:	UN; CSCE; North Atlantic Co-operation Council

Albany Congress (1754) A congress of seven colonies convened by the British Board of Trade at Albany, a town in New York State, to concert defence against the French and pacify the Iroquois. It was at Albany that Benjamin FRANKLIN presented his 'Plan of Union' for a Grand Council elected by the 13 colonies to control defence and Indian relations, but this first step towards American unity was rejected by the individual colonies.

Albemarle, George, 1st Duke of MONCK.

Alberoni, Giulio (1664–1752) Italian cardinal and statesman. In 1713 he arranged the marriage of the Duke of Parma's niece Elizabeth FARNESE with PHILIP V. He became effective ruler of Spain in 1715 and strengthened royal power in Spain at the expense of the nobles. His chief aims were to strengthen Spain, nullify the Peace of UTRECHT, and crush HABSBURG power in Italy. He was doubtful about the wisdom of declaring war on Austria in July 1717 and it proved to be a disastrous decision, mainly because of British and French intervention against Spain, and resulted in his dismissal by Philip in 1719. He retired to Rome.

Albert Francis Charles Augustus Emmanuel (1819–61) Prince-Consort of England, husband of Queen VICTORIA. The younger son of the Duke of Saxe-Coburg-Gotha, he married Victoria, his first cousin, in 1840. At first meeting with mistrust and prejudice, both because he was not British and because the queen would let him take no part in state affairs, he gradually exerted his influence and that of his own adviser, Baron Stockmar, over Victoria. Albert took a keen interest in industry, agriculture, and the arts, and presided over the Royal Commission that raised the money for the GREAT EXHIBITION of 1851. His diplomatic skills were shown in December 1861, when he moderated the government's hostile reaction to the USA over the TRENT AFFAIR. His death from typhoid was a great shock to Victoria, who withdrew from public life for several years.

Albigensians Followers of a form of the CATHAR heresy; they took their name from the town of Albi in Languedoc in southern France. There and in northern Italy the sect acquired immense popularity. The movement was condemned at the Council of Toulouse in 1119 and by the Third and Fourth LATERAN COUNCILS in 1179 and 1215, which opposed it not only as heretical but because it threatened the family and the state. St BERNARD and St DOMINIC were its vigorous opponents. Between 1209 and 1228 the wars known as the Albigensian Crusade were mounted, led principally by Simon de MONTFORT. By 1229 the heretics were largely crushed and the Treaty of Meaux delivered most of their territory to France.

Albion An ancient name, probably pre-Celtic, for the island now comprising England, Wales, and Scotland. Roman writers linked it with the Latin *albus* (white), in reference to the chalk cliffs and downlands of southern England. The Latin 'Britannia' soon replaced the term.

Albuquerque, Alfonso de (1453–1515) Governor of the Portuguese empire in Asia (1508–15). He captured key ports on the sea route to India and created a Portuguese monopoly of trade. After establishing a fortified factory at Cochin on the west coast of India (1505), he disrupted Arab trade with India by fortifications at key points on the East African coast and Persian Gulf. In 1510 he conquered GOA, which then expanded into a trading centre. By seizing MALACCA on the Malay peninsula (1511), he laid the basis for Portuguese monopoly of the spice trade of the southeast Asian archipelago, but died at sea, in disgrace, before the full results of his empire-building initiatives were appreciated.

Alcázar (Arabic *al-kasr*, 'the palace') A type of fortress in Spain, built by the Christians during their 14th- and 15th-century wars against the MOORS. It was usually rectangular with great corner towers, and contained an open space or patio, surrounded by chapels, hospitals, and salons. The most renowned is the Alcázar of Seville, built by King Pedro the Cruel (1334–69). The most splendid Muslim fortress-palace in Spain is the Alhambra (the red), built by the Moorish monarchs of Granada, chiefly between 1238 and 1358.

Alcazarquivir (locally called al-Kasr al-Kabir) A city in northern MOROCCO, famous for the battle of the Three Kings (1578). From the 15th century it suffered attacks from Portuguese coastal ports, and became an advanced post of the *mujahidin*, 'warriors for the faith', in retaliation. In 1578 Sebastian I of Portugal attacked with 20,000 men, but the Moroccans, mustering 50,000, defeated them utterly. Sebastian himself perished, with 8,000 men, and in 1580 Portugal fell into the hands of Spain.

alchemy A pseudo-science originating independently in China, Greece, and India in about the 3rd century BC, concerned with the possible transmutation of all matter, most famously the transmutation of base metals such as lead into gold. The transmutation was variously an end in itself, a means by which to make an elixir of life, and a route to the creation of a panacea, or universal medicine. Early alchemy degenerated into superstition and mysticism, but the art flourished once again in the 8th century AD in Arab countries.

Translations of Arabic alchemical texts led in the 12th century to a second revival of alchemy in Europe, notably in Prague. It attracted such medieval scholars as Roger Bacon and Albertus Magnus, and was patronized by princes and emperors. The influential Swiss writer Paracelsus (16th century) was primarily concerned with its medical application to his search for a chemical therapy for disease; his followers developed specialized chemical medicines and sought a universal elixir which they dreamed would prolong life and restore youth. During the Renaissance alchemy fell into disrepute, but the chemical experience accumulated by alchemists over many centuries became the basis upon which the modern science of chemistry was built. Many leading scientists, including Isaac Newton, retained an interest in transmutation. The rise of mechanical philosophy in the 17th century gradually undermined alchemy and other forms of the occult, and later alchemists chose to emphasize its mystical aspects in esoteric movements such as that of the Rosicrucians.

Alcibiades (*c.* 450–404 BC) An Athenian leader in the PELOPONNESIAN WAR. His plans to defeat Sparta on land faltered at the battle of Mantinea (418 BC). He advocated and was appointed one of the commanders of the ill-fated expedition to Sicily (415–413 BC), but was charged with the desecration of sacred statues and recalled to Athens. He fled to Sparta, where he gave advice that was seriously damaging to his own city. Nevertheless, after breaking with the Athenian oligarchs in 411 BC, he later won the confidence of the officers of the Athenian fleet based at Samos, leading it with conspicuous success. A defeat in his absence led to his downfall. He was murdered in Phrygia, Asia Minor.

Alcuin (*c.* 735–804) English scholar and theologian. He was educated in the cathedral school at York, later becoming its head. In 782 was employed by Emperor CHARLEMAGNE as head of his palace school at Aachen where his pupils included many of the outstanding figures in the 'Carolingian Renaissance'. Alcuin played a central role in fostering this cultural revival. In 796 he became abbot of St Martin at Tours where he continued his work until his death.

alderman (Old English, *ealdorman*, 'elderman') A title dating from the Anglo-Saxon period when ealdormen, nobles by birth, exercised considerable powers. They were initially appointed by the crown to administer the shire system (particularly the shire moot or assembly and FYRD). By the 10th century their influence extended beyond the shire, and in the early 11th century their title evolved into 'earl'. Under the Norman kings the senior shire official was the sheriff, and the title alderman later came to apply to those who held municipal office.

Alessandri, Arturo (1868–1950) Chilean statesman. In 1920 he was elected President on a liberal policy, but, finding his attempts at reform blocked, he went into voluntary exile in 1924. The following year he was brought back by the army when a new constitution was adopted. He extended the suffrage, separated Church and state while guaranteeing religious liberty, and made primary education compulsory. He resigned again in October 1925 and went to Italy. On his return he was re-elected President (1932–38). By now the economy was experiencing the Great DEPRESSION. He reorganized the nitrate industry, developed schools, and improved conditions in agriculture and industry.

Alexander I (*c.* 1078–1124) King of Scotland (1107–24). He succeeded his brother Edgar although the regions of Strathclyde, Lothian, and Cumbria were ruled with Anglo-Norman support by his younger brother (later DAVID I). Educated in England, Alexander encouraged the feudalization of his country while still retaining its independence of England. After crushing a Celtic revolt (*c.* 1115) he was styled 'the Fierce' although he was a pious man, founding Augustinian houses at Scone (1115) and Inchcolm. He refused the Bishop of St Andrews (1120, 1124) leave to acknowledge the ecclesiastical authority of York or Canterbury.

Alexander I (1777–1825) Emperor of Russia (1801–25). The son of Paul I (in whose murder he may indirectly have assisted), he set out to reform Russia and correct many of the injustices of the preceding reign. His private committee (Neglasny Komitet) introduced plans for public education, but his reliance on the nobility made it impossible for him to abolish serfdom. His adviser, M. Speransky, pressed for a more liberal constitution, but the nobles secured his fall in 1812. At first a supporter of the coalition against NAPOLEON, his defeats by the latter at AUSTERLITZ (1805) and Friedland (1807) resulted in the Treaties of TILSIT and in his support of the CONTINENTAL SYSTEM against the British. His wars with Persia (1804–13) and Turkey (1806–12) brought territorial gains, including the acquisition of Georgia. His armies helped to defeat Napoleon's *grande armée* at LEIPZIG, after its retreat from Moscow (1812). In an effort to uphold Christian morality in Europe he formed a HOLY ALLIANCE of European monarchs, and became increasingly conservative in his domestic policies. The constitution he gave to POLAND scarcely disguised the rule of the military there. He supported METTERNICH WINNEBURG in suppressing liberal and national movements, and gave no help to the Greeks in rebellion against the OTTOMAN Turks, although they were Orthodox Christians like himself. He was reported to have died while in the Crimea, but rumour persisted that he had escaped to Siberia and became a hermit.

Alexander I (1888–1934) King of Yugoslavia (1921–34). Of the Karageorgević dynasty of Serbia, he tried to overcome the ethnic, religious, and regional rivalries in his country by means of a personal dictatorship (1929), supported by the army. In the interest of greater unity, he changed the name of his kingdom, which consisted of Serbs, Croats, and Slovenes, to YUGOSLAVIA in 1929. In 1931 some civil rights were restored, but they proved insufficient to quell rising political and separatist dissent, aggravated by economic depression. He was planning to restore parliamentary government when he was assassinated by a Croatian terrorist.

Alexander II (1198–1249) King of Scotland (1214–49). He succeeded William the Lion. After supporting the English barons in the first BARONS' WAR against King John he had to suppress revolts in Moray (1221), Argyll (1222), Caithness (1222), and Galloway (1224). His campaigns against England and the Norse in the Western Isles (1249) were motivated by territorial ambitions.

Alexander II (1818–81) Emperor of Russia (1855–81). Known as the 'Tsar Liberator', he was the eldest son of NICHOLAS I and succeeded to the throne when the CRIMEAN WAR had revealed Russia's backwardness. His Emancipation Act of 1861 freed millions of serfs and led to an overhaul of Russia's archaic administrative institutions. Measures of reform, however, did not disguise his belief in the need to maintain autocratic rule and his commitment to military strength, as witnessed by the introduction of universal conscription in 1874. His reign saw great territorial gains in the Caucasus, Central Asia, and the Far East, to off-set the sale of ALASKA to the USA (1867). The growth of secret revolutionary societies such as the NIHILISTS and POPULISTS, culminating in an assassination attempt in 1862, completed his conversion to conservatism. After further assassination attempts, he was mortally wounded (1881) by a bomb, thrown by a member of the People's Will Movement.

Alexander III (1241–86) King of Scotland (1249–86). He defeated Haakon of Norway at the battle of Largs (1263) and received the Hebrides by the Treaty of Perth. Despite close ties with England (his father-in-law was HENRY III), Alexander resisted English claims to the Scottish kingdom. The early death of his children left the succession to his granddaughter, MARGARET, MAID OF NORWAY.

Alexander III (1845–94) Emperor of Russia (1881–94). Following the assassination of his father ALEXANDER II he rejected all plans of liberal reform, suppressing Russian NIHILISTS and POPULISTS, extending the powers of nominated landed proprietors over the peasantry, and strengthening the role of landowners in local government. A zealous Orthodox Christian, he was unsympathetic to non-Orthodox Christians and did nothing to prevent the anti-Semitic POGROMS of 1881 and later years. Autocratic in attitude, he was, however, genuinely interested in the principles of administration and his reign saw the abolition of the poll tax, the creation of a Peasant Land Bank, and tentative moves towards legalization of trade unions. Under his Minister of Finance Sergei WITTE the reign also saw large European investment in Russian railways and industry. Alexander's concept of *narodnost* (belief in the Russian people) led to the Russian language being imposed as the single language of education throughout the empire. Although he resented the loss of the Russian Balkans imposed by the Congress of BERLIN, he nevertheless continued to support Bismarck's League of the THREE EMPERORS, the Dreikaiserbund, until 1890, when the aggressive attitudes of the new German emperor WILLIAM II led to its replacement by an alliance with France.

Alexander Nevsky (*c.* 1220–63) Russian soldier, Grand Duke of Vladimir (1252–63). Born in Vladimir, son of the Grand Duke Jaroslav II of Novgorod, he acquired his second name after his defeat of the Swedish army on the banks of the River Neva in 1240. Wars against the Germans and Lithuanians culminated in a battle with the TEUTONIC KNIGHTS on the frozen Lake Peipus which he won decisively. After his death he was canonized as a saint of the Russian Orthodox Church.

Alexander of Tunis, Harold Rupert Leofric George Alexander, 1st Earl (1891–1969) British field-marshal. He served in the Irish Guards in World War I, and later in Latvia and India. In World War II he commanded the rearguard at DUNKIRK and the retreat in Burma. As commander-in-chief, Middle East, in 1942, he turned the tide against ROMMEL. In 1943 he was deputy to EISENHOWER, clearing Tunisia for the Allies. He then led the invasion of Sicily and commanded in Italy until the end of the war. He was governor-general of Canada (1946–52).

Alexander the Great (Alexander III; Arabic, Iskandar) (356–323 BC) King of Macedonia (336–323). Alexander succeeded his father PHILIP II in 336 BC and conquered the whole of the ACHAEMENID Persian empire in the course of his short reign. He inherited a highly professional army and commanded it with tactical brilliance: major victories were won at Granicus, Issus, Gaugamela, and Hydaspes, and his capture of the island-city of Tyre was a masterpiece of siege warfare. His conquest of Persia, however, was not merely the expedition of revenge that Greeks had talked about since the GREEK–PERSIAN wars. Rather than overthrow the Persian empire, he determined to rule it in co-operation with the Persian nobles, some of whom he appointed as his governors. He also drafted many non-Greeks into his army and adopted much of Persian court ceremonial. Such policies were resented by his fellow Macedonians who were reluctant to share power with the conquered barbarians.

His death at the age of 32, whether from fever or, less likely, poison, was untimely, but nevertheless his short

Alexander the Great   *A contemporary bust by Lysippus, Alexander's court sculptor.*

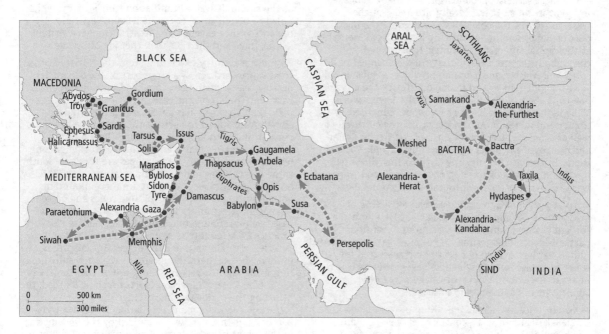

Alexander the Great   *Alexander's victorious progress through Asia Minor against the Persians culminated in the defeat of King Darius at Issus (333 BC). Advancing through Phoenicia, where he met resistance from Tyre and Gaza, he reached Egypt in 332 and was welcomed as a liberator. After founding Alexandria he turned eastwards and won a decisive battle at Gaugamela (331). Babylonia offered no serious resistance and he advanced through Bactria to the Jaxartes, founding Alexandria-the-Furthest as a defence against nomadic Scythians. His defeat of the Indian ruler Porus on the Hydaspes (326) took him into new territory, but his weary soldiers persuaded him to turn back. On the return journey he sailed down the Hydaspes to the Indus delta, as he was anxious both to conquer Sind and to see 'Ocean', which the Greeks believed encircled the world. After a gruelling desert march he reached Susa in 324. Alexander died at Babylon in 323, in his 33rd year.*

career changed the course of history. His conquests spread the Greek language and culture (see HELLENISTIC CIVILIZATION) over much of the known world. In areas as far east as Afghanistan and northern India the remains of Greek-type cities have been uncovered. After his death his empire was bitterly contested by his generals; the resultant 'successor' kingdoms — ANTIGONID Macedonia, SELEUCID Asia, and Ptolemaic EGYPT — were often at war with each other until each in turn was conquered by Rome.

Regarded as a god in his life-time and an important figure in Greek, Christian, Jewish, and Islamic legend, Alexander is a favourite figure in medieval legends and in European literature and art. As a prophet-like figure and considered a believer, he has assumed particular significance in Islam. As the *Dhu'l-Qarnayn* (he-of-the-two-horns/centuries) in the Koran he saved people from the depredations of Yajuj and Majuj. In Persian sources, his search for knowledge takes precedence over world conquest. In the *Iskandar-nāmah* (Book of Alexander) by the Persian poet Nizami, Alexander is depicted as the half-brother of the conquered King DARIUS I and therefore a legitimate successor to him.

Alexandria The name of six cities founded or refounded by ALEXANDER THE GREAT throughout the conquered Persian empire. In their architecture and their institutions they were very much Greek cities, and contributed greatly to the spread of HELLENISTIC CIVILIZATION.

The most successful foundation was that established in Egypt in 331 BC. It was ideally situated – at the western edge of the Nile delta – to become the main port of Egypt, and under Ptolemy I it replaced Memphis as the capital city of that country. It prospered throughout the PTOLEMAIC dynasty, and continued to do so after Egypt became a Roman province. A substantial Jewish population settled in one quarter of the city: at one time the city was the capital of the Jewish world. Violent anti-Jewish riots were frequent. Enhanced by its library and museum, Alexandria prospered culturally as well as economically. Arabs captured the city in 641 AD and destroyed the library, said to contain some 700,000 items. In the 14th century the canal to the Nile silted up, and at the end of the 15th the Cape of Good Hope was discovered as a new European route to the East.

Alfonso V (the Magnanimous) (1396–1458) King of ARAGON (1416–58) and of NAPLES (1443–58). He pursued a foreign policy committed to territorial expansion, particularly in Italy. Joanna II, Queen of NAPLES, adopted him as her heir and on her death he transferred his court to Naples in 1443, which he developed as a centre of RENAISSANCE culture. His patronage earned the admiration of contemporary HUMANISTS.

Alfonso X (the Wise) (1221–84) King of CASTILE and León (1252–84). His reign was a contrast between the failure of his political ambitions and his scholarly success as a law-giver. He spent fruitless years trying to become Holy Roman Emperor and failed to complete his father's Crusade against the MOORS in southern Spain. His indecision caused his son, Sancho IV, to rebel and isolate him in Seville. Of real importance was his *Siete Partidas* (1256), a collection of constitutional, civil, and criminal law, the first such work to be written in Spanish.

Alfred (the Great) (849–99) King of WESSEX (871–99). He became king in 871 at the time of Danish invasions. Earlier (865), the other English kingdoms of EAST ANGLIA, MERCIA, and NORTHUMBRIA had been overwhelmed by the Danes, who had even begun (871) to challenge the defences of Wessex. Three fierce Danish attacks (871–78) followed, the most serious being in 877 when, under Guthrum, they drove Alfred into hiding in the marshes of Athelney. Alfred's counter-offensive produced a decisive victory at Edington (878) and the Treaty of Wedmore (Chippenham) by which Guthrum agreed to withdraw to East Anglia and to become a Christian. In 886 Alfred, having captured London, defined with Guthrum the boundaries between Wessex and the DANELAW. Alfred improved the defences of England by reorganizing the FYRD, developing a navy, and improving the system of fortified towns.

Alfred also encouraged learning. He translated the Latin texts of BOETHIUS, BEDE, Orosius, and St GREGORY I (the Great), and may have suggested the writing of the ANGLO-SAXON CHRONICLE. He and other members of his family established fortified towns (burghs), many of which are still county towns. He was also renowned for the laws which he made. The probably apocryphal story of Alfred burning the cakes is told in the 12th century *Chronicle of St Neot's*.

Algeciras Conference (1906) An international meeting in Algeciras, Spain, held at Germany's request. Its treaty regulated French and Spanish intervention in Moroccan internal affairs and reaffirmed the authority of the sultan. It was a humiliation for Germany, which failed to obtain support for its hardline attitude towards France except from Austria-Hungary. Britain, Russia, Italy, and the USA took the side of France.

Algeria A country extending from the North African coast southward across a large part of the Sahara, its narrow coastal strip being bounded by Morocco on the west and Tunisia on the east.

Physical. The coast has an equable Mediterranean climate well suited to agriculture. Inland the ground rises until it is mountainous, though here also the valleys are fertile. Plains and plateaux provide grazing, while many of the mountain slopes are forested. South is the desert – dry and with temperatures over 35 °C (95 °F) – and further south-east are more mountains with desolate plateaux and volcanic cones and craters.

Economy. Algerian industry, mainly state-owned, is based on oil-refining, but cement and steel are also produced. The country's main exports are crude oil, petroleum products, and natural gas. Agriculture is limited: the northern mountainous region is suited only to grazing and timber, and the south of the country is the Sahara Desert. Algeria imports much of its food, the EU being the major trading partner.

History. The indigenous population of Algeria were Berbers, but the coast was colonized by the Phoenicians in the 9th century BC. In the 2nd century BC the Romans incorporated the whole region into the province of Africa. In the 7th century AD the Romanized Berbers resisted the Arab invasion fiercely. Once conquered they were converted to Islam, and became members of the extreme Kharijite sect. From the 11th century they were repeatedly ravaged by the Banu Hilal and other Arabs, and ruled by a series of dynasties until conquest by the

Ottoman empire in the 16th century. Throughout the 18th century, Algeria was notorious as a base for pirates raiding Mediterranean shipping.

Conquered by France in the 1830s (when its present boundaries were established) and formally annexed in 1842, Algeria was 'attached' to metropolitan France and heavily settled by European Christians. The refusal of the European settlers to grant equal rights to the native population led to increasing instability, and in 1954 a war of national independence broke out that was characterized by atrocities on both sides. In 1962, in spite of considerable resistance in both France and White Algeria, President DE GAULLE negotiated an end to hostilities in the ÉVIAN AGREEMENT, and Algeria was granted independence as the result of a referendum. In 1965 a coup established a left-wing government under Colonel Houari BOUMÉDIENNE and afterwards serious border disputes broke out with Tunisia, Morocco, and Mauritania. After Boumédienne's death in 1978, his successor Benjedid Chadli relaxed his repressive domestic policies and began to normalize Algeria's external relations. Algeria was a one-party state, ruled by the FLN (Front de Libération Nationale), from 1976 until 1989, when other political parties were legalized. The fundamentalist FIS (Front Islamique du Salut) party rapidly gained popular support. In 1992 the FIS seemed poised to win a general election but Chadli dissolved the government and resigned. A transitional military regime took over and cancelled the election. FIS supporters continued to wage a campaign of violence and terrorism; an estimated 75,000 people fell victim to political violence in the years 1992–97. Atrocities intensified during 1997 following the victory of pro-government parties in a general election.

CAPITAL: Algiers
AREA: 2,381,741 sq km (919,595 sq miles)
POPULATION: 28.566 million (1996)
CURRENCY: 1 Algerian dinar = 100 centimes
RELIGIONS: Sunni Muslim 99.1%; Roman Catholic 0.5%
ETHNIC GROUPS: Arab 82.6%; Berber 17.0%; French 0.1%
LANGUAGES: Arabic (official); Berber; French
INTERNATIONAL
ORGANIZATIONS: UN; Arab League; OAPEC; OPEC; Maghreb Union; Non-Aligned Movement; OAU

Algonquin An eastern Canadian group of Algonquian-speaking Native Americans inhabiting the Ottawa valley and adjacent regions in the 17th century, and southern Ontario in the 18th. They fought the IROQUOIS, especially the MOHAWK, from 1570 in alliance with the Montagnais, to the east, and from 1603 as allies of the French in a conflict over the European fur trade that lasted into the 18th century. They were essentially a hunting-fishing people, though some grew corn, beans, and squash in cleared areas of the bush. They lived in small groups in dwellings – pointed tipis or dome-shaped wigwams – made from birchbark laid over poles, and are associated with the light birchbark canoe, and with snowshoes, sleds, and toboggans, which they used for winter travel. A small number (c. 2000) survive today as hunters' guides and trappers.

Ali Pasha, Mehmed Emin (1815–71) Ottoman statesman and reformer. After service in the Foreign Ministry he became Grand Vizier in 1852. He became one of the leading statesmen of the TANZIMAT REFORM movement, and was responsible for the Hatt-i Humayun reform edict of 1856. This guaranteed Christians security of life and property, opened civil offices to all subjects, abolished torture, and allowed acquisition of property by foreigners. He believed in autocratic rule and opposed the granting of a parliamentary constitution.

Allen, Ethan (1738–89) American patriot. He migrated from Connecticut to the 'New Hampshire Grants', later VERMONT, in 1769. With his younger brothers, Ira and Levi, he organized the GREEN MOUNTAIN BOYS to combat New York's claims to the region. In 1775, together with Benedict ARNOLD, he helped overrun TICONDEROGA, but was captured while leading an expedition against Canada. Released in 1778, he continued to campaign for Vermont independence, even considering making it into a British province.

Allenby, Edmund Henry Hynman, 1st Viscount (1861–1936) British field-marshal. In World War I he defeated the Ottoman forces in Palestine and Syria, capturing Jerusalem, and ending Turkish resistance after the Battle of Megiddo (18–21 September 1918) and the fall of Damascus and Aleppo. He was appointed Special High Commissioner for Egypt and the Sudan (1919–25), and in 1922 persuaded the British government to end its protectorate over EGYPT.

Allende (Gossens), Salvador (1908–73) Chilean statesman. As President of Chile (1970–73), he was the first avowed Marxist to win a Latin American presidency in a free election. Having bid for the office unsuccessfully on two previous occasions (1958 and 1964), Allende's 1970 victory was brought about by a coalition of leftist parties. During his brief tenure he set the country on a socialist path, incurring the antipathy of the Chilean military establishment. Under General PINOCHET a military coup (which enjoyed some indirect support from the USA) overthrew him in 1973. Allende died in the fighting, and was given a state funeral in 1990.

Allied Intervention, War of RUSSIAN CIVIL WAR.

Almagro, Diego de PIZARRO, FRANCISCO.

Almohad (from the Arabic al-Muwahhiddun, unitarian) A Berber dynasty that originated in the Atlas Mountains of North Africa c. 1121. The founder, Ibn Tumart, claimed to be Mahdi (the divinely guided one), whose coming was foretold by MUHAMMAD, and he preached an extreme puritanical form of Islam. His successor, Abd al-Mumin, seized all North Africa and then southern Spain from the ALMORAVIDS in 1145. The Almohad empire was a great Islamic and Mediterranean power. A centrally directed administration with a professional civil service collected taxes and maintained a large fleet and army. Besides fine architecture the empire also produced influential international scholars, like the Spanish-Arabian philosopher AVERROËS. War in Spain proved disastrous, and the defeat at Las Navas de Tolosa (1212) ended the Almohad regime. The dynasty survived in Marrakesh until 1269.

Almoravid (from the Arabic al-Murabitun, 'member of a religious group') A Berber dynasty that originated in North Africa (1061–1145), and in Spain from 1086. It originated among the Lamtuna Tuareg, whose extreme

Islamic faith compelled even men to wear veils. The founder, Abu Bakr, built Marrakesh in 1070, and his cousin, Yusuf ibn Tashfin, conquered all of north-west Africa, and then Spain, to which he was invited in 1086 by al-Mutamid of Seville. His Berber army defeated Alfonso VI of León at Zallaqah, near Badajoz, in 1086. In 1088 he returned to Spain and began his new campaign by taking Granada. He took Seville and Córdoba in 1091, Badajoz in 1094, Valencia in 1102, and Saragossa in 1110, but he failed to overcome Alfonso VI, or to take Toledo. Yusuf and his followers were primarily fighting men and their time in Spain was one of confusion and cultural stagnation. It was a time of suffering and persecution for many Christians, Jews, and even liberal Muslims – divines as respected as al-Ghazzali had their works proscribed. The end of the dynasty came in 1145, with a further Berber invasion under the ALMOHADS, who succeeded to the conquests of the Almoravids.

almshouse A sanctuary for the reception and succour of the poor. Almshouses were originally those sections of medieval monasteries where alms (food and money) were distributed. Most medieval foundations were made by clergymen, like Bishop Henry of Blois, who set up the Hospital of St Cross in Winchester, England, *c*. 1135. The term was also used to describe privately financed dwellings, usually for the support of the old and infirm. Wealthy merchants, as individuals or in corporations, became especially active in endowing almshouses, as a way of showing their charitable intentions. From the 16th century the charitable relief supplied by almshouses was supplemented by a series of POOR LAWS.

Alsace-Lorraine A French region west of the Rhine. Alsace and the eastern part of Lorraine were ceded to Germany after the FRANCO-PRUSSIAN WAR (1871) and held in common by all the German states. Rich in both coal and iron-ore, Lorraine enabled Germany to expand its naval and military power. The subsequent policy of Germanization of the region was resented by French nationalists, and the province was restored to France by the Treaty of VERSAILLES after World War I. In 1940 Nazi troops occupied the region and it reverted to Germany. In 1945 French and US troops recovered Alsace-Lorraine for France.

Alva, Duke of ALBA.

Ambedkar, Bhimrao Ramji (1893–1956) Indian leader of the Untouchables (Hindus held to defile members of a caste on touch). He led the agitation for their constitutional rights in the 1930s and when GANDHI went on a fast against the provision of separate electorates for the Untouchables, agreed to the Poona Pact (1934) providing reserved seats for them in the legislatures. As the leader and founder of the Scheduled Castes Federation, he opposed the Indian National CONGRESS, but joined that party after independence. As a leading constitutional lawyer, he played a major role in formulating and drafting the Indian constitution.

Amboina (or Ambon) An island in the MOLUCCAS, a major centre for clove production. In 1521 the Portuguese established themselves there but were driven out by the Dutch in 1605. An English attempt to set up a trading station for spices ended in 1623 when all their men were tried and executed for conspiring against the Dutch in the so-called 'Amboina massacre'.

Dutch missions were active among the Ambonese, who became the most loyal of the Netherlands' overseas subjects

Ambrose, St (*c*. 340–97) Bishop of Milan. He was acclaimed bishop in 374 when he was Roman governor of the region and awaiting baptism. A renowned preacher and writer, he attacked ARIANISM, the pagan revival, and the Jews. Three Roman emperors came under his influence: THEODOSIUS was even compelled to perform penance for a massacre. He saw Church and state as complementary spiritual and temporal institutions facing shared threats from heretics and barbarians.

American Civil War (1861–65) A war between the Northern (Union) and Southern (CONFEDERACY) states of the USA. It was officially known as the War of the Rebellion and usually called the War between the States in the South. Economic divergence between the industrialized North and the agricultural, slave-based economy of the South was transformed into political rivalry by the ABOLITIONISTS, and by the dispute over the expansion of slavery into the western territories. By the late 1850s, all efforts at compromise had failed and violence had begun with John BROWN's armed descent on Harper's Ferry (1859). South Carolina seceded from the Union in December 1860 in the wake of Abraham LINCOLN's victory in the presidential election of that year. When the war began with the bombardment of FORT SUMTER (1861), the newly established Southern Confederacy increased to 11 states under the presidency of Jefferson DAVIS. The war itself is best considered as three simultaneous campaigns. At sea, the North held the upper hand, but the blockade imposed in 1861 took a long time to become effective. Virtually no cotton was exported. Massive naval expansion produced a blockade which helped to cripple the Confederate war effort. On land a series of engagements took place in the VIRGINIA CAMPAIGNS, where the close proximity of the Union and Confederacy capitals, Washington and Richmond, and the military genius of General LEE enabled the Confederacy to keep superior Union forces at bay for much of the war. In the more spacious western regions, after a series of abortive starts, the North managed to split the Confederacy in the VICKSBURG CAMPAIGN, by gaining control of the Mississippi. From here General GRANT moved through Tennessee in the CHATTANOOGA CAMPAIGN, opening the way for the drive by SHERMAN through Georgia to the sea. This ruthless strategy, together with Lee's surrender to Grant at APPOMATTOX, brought the war to an end in April 1865. Over 600,000 soldiers died in the Civil War. While the immediate results were the salvation of the union and the abolition of slavery, the challenges of revitalizing the South and promoting racial justice and equality persisted.

American Colonization Society Founded in the USA in 1817 in order to resettle in Africa free-born Africans and emancipated slaves. In 1821 the society bought the site of the future Monrovia, LIBERIA, which it controlled until Liberia declared its independence in 1847. After 1840 the society declined and was dissolved in 1912.

American Federation of Labor (AFL) Federation of North American labour unions, mainly of skilled workers, founded in 1886. From its formation until his retirement in 1924, it was decisively shaped by its president Samuel Gompers. After mass disorders culminating in the HAYMARKET SQUARE RIOT and the subsequent eclipse of the KNIGHTS OF LABOR, Gompers wanted a cohesive non-radical organization of skilled workers committed to collective bargaining for better wages and conditions. However, growing numbers of semi-skilled workers in mass-production industries found their champion in John L. Lewis, leader of the more militant United Mine Workers. When he failed to convince the AFL of the need to promote industry-wide unions in steel, automobiles, and chemicals, Lewis formed (1935) the Committee (later the Congress) of Industrial Organizations (CIO), its members seceding from the AFL. In 1955 the rival organizations were reconciled as the AFL–CIO under George Meany and Walter Reuther with a total of 15 million members. This body remained the recognized voice of organized labour in the USA and Canada.

American Party KNOW-NOTHINGS.

American Philosophical Society The first and still the most illustrious US scholarly association, founded in Philadelphia in 1743 by Benjamin FRANKLIN. The inventor and astronomer David Rittenhouse (1791) and Thomas JEFFERSON (1797) succeeded him as presidents. The Society has a major collection of scientific literature and sponsors academic research.

American Revolution INDEPENDENCE, AMERICAN WAR OF.

American System A programme of US economic reforms propounded in the 1820s by the politician Henry CLAY. He advocated a combination of a protective tariff, a national bank, and a system of internal improvements to expand the US domestic market and lessen dependence upon overseas sources. A nationalist policy, intended as a binding force in the face of demands for increased STATES' RIGHTS, the American System inspired much of the economic policy of the WHIG PARTY.

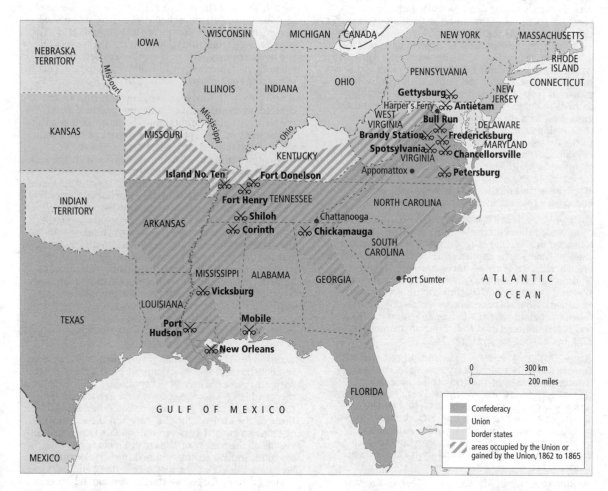

American Civil War (1861–65) *Often called the first really modern war, the American Civil War marked a milestone in military strategy. The deployment of the long-range rifle shattered the effectiveness of traditional attack, while the use of steam power lent speed of movement to both armies. The political objective of the North was to prevent the Southern states from seceding from the Union: the Confederate states, apprehensive of centralized government, sought to retain their independence, especially over their rights to buttress their economy with slave labour.*

Amerindians The indigenous peoples of North and South America. They are usually classified as a major branch of the MONGOLOID peoples but are sometimes described as a distinct racial group. With the Inuits and Aleuts (who are unquestionably Mongoloids), they were the inhabitants of the New World at the time of the first European exploration in the late 15th century. Their forebears came from north-eastern Asia, most probably taking advantage of low sea levels during the last Ice Age to cross the Bering Strait on land. The earliest certain evidence suggests that people were in America by 15,000 years ago but an earlier date seems increasingly likely. Recent controversial archaeological finds in Mexico, Chile, Brazil, and elsewhere suggest a human presence as early as 30,000 or more years ago. There could have been several separate colonizations; the Inuits (Eskimos) and Aleuts (inhabitants of the Aleutian Islands) are the descendants of the most recent one, within the past 10,000 years. The first colonizers brought little more than simple stone tools and perhaps domesticated dogs for hunting. As hunters and gatherers they spread quickly south; hunting the plentiful game using fine stone projectile points such as those of the CLOVIS tradition.

The cultural development of Amerindians provides an interesting comparison with the Old World. Agriculture, which started developing 7000 or more years ago, was based on maize, squash, and beans, with manioc being grown in tropical forest regions. With no suitable animals to domesticate, apart from the llama and the guinea-pig, and no draught animals to pull the plough, the development of more mixed farming was gradual. In the Andes, an advanced metallurgical technology developed from 1000 BC. Complex societies developed in many areas, which grew into sophisticated civilizations, for example, the AZTECS and INCAS, but most collapsed after the arrival of the CONQUISTADORES and other European explorers in the 16th century.

Amherst, Jeffrey, Baron (1717–97) British general. He commanded the combined operation which captured LOUISBURG in 1758. On his appointment as commander-in-chief in America, he applied widespread pressure on the French. His own army advanced northward up the Hudson Valley, taking TICONDEROGA and Crown Point in 1759 and Montreal in 1760, thus ending French control of Canada. He was then made governor of Virginia, but failed to contain PONTIAC's Indian Rebellion in 1763 and was recalled. He refused to fight against Americans in 1775, but advised on strategy.

Amin Dada, Idi (c. 1925–   ) Ugandan head of state. Possessed of only rudimentary education, Amin rose through the ranks of the army to become its commander. In 1971 he overthrew President OBOTE and seized power. His rule was characterized by the advancing of narrow tribal interests, the expulsion of non-Africans (most notably Ugandan Asians), and violence on a huge scale. He was overthrown with Tanzanian assistance in 1979 and went into exile in Saudi Arabia.

amphora A two-handled ancient Greek or Roman pottery jar with a pointed or knobbed bottom to facilitate its transport, used for the storage of wine and olive oil. The amphora was often stamped with a mark – a sign that it conformed to local regulations on size. This mark might include the potter's name, the name of the relevant annual magistrate, and the country of origin. Often located by marine archaeologists in wrecks, they provide valuable evidence of trade links.

Amritsar massacre (13 April 1919) A massacre of unarmed supporters of Indian self-government by British troops in the city of Amritsar, Punjab. Indian discontent against the British had been mounting as a result of the ROWLATT ACT. The massacre in Amritsar followed the killing, three days before, of five Englishmen and the beating of an Englishwoman. Gurkha troops under the command of Brigadier R. H. Dyer fired on a crowd gathered in the Jallianwala Bagh, an enclosed park, killing 379 and wounding over 1,200. Mounting agitation throughout India followed, and Dyer was given an official, if belated, censure.

In 1984 government troops stormed the Golden Temple of Amritsar and killed 400 members of a Sikh separatist group, in revenge for which Indira GANDHI was assassinated.

Amundsen, Roald (1872–1928) Norwegian explorer who in 1911 was the first to reach the South Pole, ahead of Robert SCOTT. In an earlier voyage (1903–06) he had also been the first to complete the long-sought north-west passage from the Atlantic to the Pacific, locating the northern magnetic pole on the way. He was lost when flying from Bergen to Spitsbergen to take part in the search for Umberto Nobile's airship *Italia* in 1928.

Anabaptism A Christian religious doctrine which centred on the baptism of believers, and held that people baptized as infants must be rebaptized as adults. Anabaptists or 'Re-baptists' formed part of the radical wing of the 16th-century REFORMATION. The sects originated mainly in Zürich in the 1520s, with the aim of restoring the spirit and institutions of the early Church. Their belief that the Church was not an earthly institution and that true earthly institutions were by their nature hopelessly corrupt, led them to a repudiation of the very basis of the authority of the civil power. Thus, though they were often law-abiding, they reserved the right in conscience to disobey the law, and for this they were feared and persecuted. They managed to establish centres in Saxony, Austria, Moravia, Poland, the Lower Rhine, and the Netherlands, but made almost no headway in the French-speaking world. In the 17th century the MENNONITES preserved some of the best of the Anabaptist traditions, which made a significant contribution to the religious history of modern Europe and America.

anarchism The belief that government and law should be abolished and society organized by voluntary means without resort to force or compulsion. The French social theorist Pierre Joseph PROUDHON first expounded the theory that equality and justice should be achieved through the abolition of the state and the substitution of free agreements between individuals. Other anarchist visions of the society of the future include the economic individualism, outlined in the US writer Benjamin Tucker's *Instead of a Book* (1893) and the communism envisaged by the Russian émigré Peter Kropotkin's work *The Conquest of Bread* (1906).

Groups of anarchists tried to find popular support in many European states in the 1860s and 1870s. They were hostile to MARXISM on the grounds that a seizure of state-power by the workers would only perpetuate oppression. The Russian anarchist Mikhail BAKUNIN founded a Social Democratic alliance (1868), which attempted to wrest control of the workers' INTERNATIONAL from MARX. Anarchists switched between strategies of spontaneous mutual association and violent acts against representatives of the state. The Presidents of France and Italy, the King of Italy, and the Empress of Austria were killed by anarchists between 1894 and 1901. Subsequently they tried to mobilize mass working-class support behind the Russian General Strike, which was a central feature of the RUSSIAN REVOLUTIONS of 1905 and 1917. Their influence in Europe declined after the rise of totalitarian states elsewhere. They were active in the SPANISH CIVIL WAR, and in the latter half of the 20th century anarchism attracted urban terrorists.

Anasazi A Native American culture centred in the 'four corners' region of modern Utah, Colorado, Arizona, and New Mexico, USA. It began *c.* 500 BC when a variant, called San Jose (*c.* 500–100 BC), of the hunter-gatherer DESERT CULTURES took the first steps towards agriculture and village life. Their abundant basketry has given the name BASKET MAKERS to their early stages. By 450 AD they were making pottery, and by 700–900 great kivas (round ceremonial chambers) were being built. In the 13th to 15th centuries droughts, crop failures, and the influx of Athapascan tribes (NAVAHO and APACHE) led to the abandonment of many of their settlements and the building of CLIFF-DWELLINGS, or pueblos, for defence. They were visited by Francisco Vasquez de Coronado's expedition of 1540–42, by which time they had begun to resettle some of their old territory. Initial relations were friendly, but a shortage of food led to resistance, ended by Coronado's mass execution of Indians. Spanish missions came in the 17th century, and attempts were made to expel the missionaries in the 1680s, followed by severe Spanish reprisals from 1692. They became known as the Pueblo Indians.

ancien régime The political and administrative systems in France in the 17th and 18th centuries under the Bourbon kings, before the FRENCH REVOLUTION; the term is also applied more widely to much of the rest of Europe. The monarch had (in theory) unlimited authority, including the right to imprison individuals without trial. There was no representative assembly. Privilege, above all, was the hallmark of the *ancien régime*: the nobility were privileged before the law, in matters of taxation, and in the holding of high offices. This was particularly resented by the increasingly prosperous middle class and in fact limited the power of the monarchy. The clergy were equally privileged and the Roman Catholic Church had extensive land-holdings in France. The peasants were over-taxed and though they were not SERFS, their landlords were able to exercise many rights over them.

The *ancien régime* was inefficient: reforms in law, taxation, and local government were long overdue, and it was government bankruptcy which was to be one of the causes of the Revolution. In spite of restraints on the freedom of the press by both Church and state, criticism was vigorous and widespread. The regime acted as a straitjacket on a society that was evolving rapidly and it was destroyed by the French Revolution.

Andalusia The southernmost region of Spain bordered by Portugal in the west and the Atlantic and Mediterranean to the south.

As the Roman province of Baetica, Andalusia was the birthplace of the emperors TRAJAN and HADRIAN. During the dissolution of the Roman empire it fell to the VANDALS. In 711 it was captured by the Muslims and it remained in their hands for many centuries. Internal strife between rival emirs allowed the recovery of much of the territory by Ferdinand II of Castile, but Granada continued to resist until 1492 when it too fell, to Ferdinand and Isabella of Spain. Following the Spanish conquest of South America it enjoyed a period of prosperity and many of the CONQUISTADORES were recruited from the region. In 1609 the Moriscos, Christian converts from the Muslim faith, were expelled, to the economic detriment of the area. In 1704 Gibraltar was lost to the British.

Andean Group A regional economic grouping comprising Colombia, Peru (suspended from 1992 to 1993), Bolivia, Chile (from 1969 to 1977), Venezuela, and Ecuador. Formally established by the Cartagena Agreement of 1969 – hence its official name, *Acuerdo de Cartagena* – it was an attempt to enhance the competitive edge of the member states in their economic relations with the more developed economies of the Latin American region. The two major goals – reduction of trade barriers and the stimulation of industrial development – encountered some measure of success. In 1987 members signed the Quito Protocol, which included a relaxation of the strict controls on foreign investors in the region (on such matters as share ownership and the repatriation of profits), which had acted as a deterrent to investment. The Andean Group committed itself in 1989 to both regional and political integration. Subsequent summit meetings attempted to accelerate the process of economic integration; the Andean Pact of 1991 (the Caracas Declaration) agreed to the abolition of internal trade tariffs by 1995. In 1994 it agreed to form a free trade area with MERCOSUR, another South American economic group.

Anderson, Elizabeth Garrett (1836–1917) British physician. Until her time medical schools would not admit women students, but she discovered that the Society of Apothecaries, by its constitution, could not prevent her taking its examinations. She qualified in 1865 and this entitled her to practise as a doctor. In 1866 she helped to found the Marylebone Dispensary for Women and Children (the present Elizabeth Garrett Hospital). She lectured on medicine (1875–97) at the London School of Medicine for Women and was the first woman elected to the British Medical Association (1873).

Andersonville Prison A prisoner-of-war camp used by the CONFEDERACY during the AMERICAN CIVIL WAR. Notorious for the high death rate among its inmates, it had been established in 1864 and suffered from shortage of food, clothing, and medical supplies in the war-stricken South. By the time of its capture by Union (Northern) forces, nearly half the prisoners had died from disease, and as a result of ensuing outcry the ex-commandant, Captain Henry Wirz, was tried and executed for murder. Subsequent investigation revealed the catastrophe to have been the product less of deliberate barbarity than of the collapse of the Confederate military machine.

Andorra A small co-principality in the Pyrenees, between France and Spain.

Physical. Andorra has a landscape of valleys at around 900 m (3,000 feet) which rise to peaks at 2,900 m (9,600 feet). Bisected by the Valira River, it contains three distinct natural regions: the valleys of the north and east Valira, and that of the Gran Valira. The attractive mountain scenery is snow-covered for several months of the year.

Economy. Tourism is the main industry, employing 37% of the labour-force, with commerce, forestry, and the construction industry also of importance.

History. According to tradition, Charlemagne granted independence to Andorra in 803 AD. Andorra came under the control of the Counts of Urgel and subsequently the Bishops of the diocese of Urgel. A dispute between the French and Spanish heirs of the Bishops and Counts in the late 13th century was resolved by making Andorra a co-principality, jointly ruled by a French and a Spanish prince. In 1993 Andorra adopted a democratic constitution which reduced the powers of the co-princes (who are now the President of France and the Spanish Bishop of Urgel), making them constitutional heads of state only, and which legalized political parties.

CAPITAL:	Andorra la Vella
AREA:	468 sq km (181 sq miles)
POPULATION:	64,100 (1996)
CURRENCY:	French francs, Spanish pesetas
RELIGIONS:	Roman Catholic 94.2%; Jewish 0.4%; Jehovah's Witnesses 0.3%; Protestant 0.2%
ETHNIC GROUPS:	Spanish 55.1%; Andorran 27.5%; French 7.4%; Portuguese 4.1%; British 1.5%
LANGUAGES:	Catalan (official); French; Spanish
INTERNATIONAL ORGANIZATIONS:	UN; Council of Europe

Andover scandal An event leading to improvement in workhouse conditions in Britain in the 1840s. The POOR LAW of 1834 had resulted in a worsening of conditions in workhouses to discourage all but the really needy from applying for admission. In 1845 able-bodied labourers at the workhouse at Andover, Hampshire, were found to be eating the gristle and marrow from bones they were crushing to make manure. A committee was set up to investigate and the result was the establishment of a new Poor Law Board, responsible to Parliament, and some improvement in workhouse conditions.

Andrada e Silva, José Bonifacio (1763–1838) Brazilian scientist and statesman. In 1821 he gave his support to the regent Pedro, who was left in charge when his father JOHN VI returned to Portugal. By mid-1822 leading Brazilians were determined that their country should become independent and in December PEDRO I was crowned Emperor of Brazil, with Andrada appointed as Prime Minister. With his two brothers he drew up a draft constitution, but antagonism developed with the emperor, and Andrada was exiled. In 1831 he was invited to return to Brazil by the emperor to become the tutor of his son. When Pedro I abdicated in April 1831 in favour of the boy, Pedro II, Andrada was confirmed as tutor by the council of regency. He was later arrested for 'political intrigue' and again left the country.

Andrassy, Julius, Count (1823–90) Hungarian statesman. One of the radical nationalist leaders of the unsuccessful Hungarian revolution of 1848, he rose to prominence with Francis DEÁK in the negotiations leading up to the AUSGLEICH (Compromise) of 1867. By now a moderate, he served as Hungary's first Prime Minister (1867–71). From 1871 to 1879 he was Foreign Minister of the Austro-Hungarian empire, during which time he limited Russian influence in the BALKAN states.

Andrewes, Lancelot (1555–1626) English prelate, successively Bishop of Chichester (1605), Ely (1609), and Winchester (1619). A celebrated scholar and famous preacher, he was prominent at the courts of ELIZABETH I and JAMES I. He was a key figure at the HAMPTON COURT CONFERENCE (1603–04), and was closely involved in producing the Authorized Version of the English Bible (1611). He played an important part in developing the theology of the ANGLICAN CHURCH.

Angevin The dynasty of the counts of Anjou in France which began with Fulk I (the 'Red'), under the Carolingian emperors of the 9th century. Their badge, a sprig of the broom plant *Genista*, gave rise later to the name of PLANTAGENET. Geoffrey of Anjou married MATILDA, the daughter of Henry I of England, in 1128, and their son, as HENRY II of England, was the first of an English royal dynasty. The power of the Angevins under Henry was formidable, overshadowing the CAPETIAN kings of France. Anjou remained in English hands until 1203 when Philip Augustus wrested it from John. Louis gave the Angevin title to his brother Charles who, as King of Naples and the Two Sicilies, established the second Angevin dynasty. In 1328 PHILIP IV inherited it together with Maine from his mother and thus it passed directly to the French crown.

Angkor In Cambodia, the site of several capitals of the KHMER empire. It is renowned for the temples which the Khmers built between the 9th and 12th centuries for their god-kings to live in after death. At Angkor Thom was the grandiose Bayon (temple) of Jayavarman VII (1181–*c*. 1220); on pinnacle after pinnacle the king's features live on in the faces of the Buddha. Under this Buddhist king, Angkor Thom reached its zenith. The city, with its 13 km (8 miles) of moated walls and position on the shores of the vast inland lake of Tonlé Sap, lay at the heart of an elaborate irrigation system which was partially laid out and controlled by the Khmer kings. For centuries the city and the great temples, with their bas-reliefs recording sacred myths and the daily lives and bloody battles of the Khmers, were lost to the jungle. After their rediscovery in the 19th century they were much restored.

Angles A Germanic tribe closely linked to the JUTES and SAXONS, thought to have originated in Schleswig-Holstein or Denmark. In the 5th century they settled in eastern Britain in EAST ANGLIA and NORTHUMBRIA. Because of their presence, the land of the ANGLO-SAXONS later became known as 'Englaland' and thereby England.

Anglican Church The established Church in England, recognized by the State and with the British monarch as titular head. The Church of England was established during the 16th-century Protestant REFORMATION. Although Henry VIII broke with the Roman Catholic Church and EDWARD VI made moves to establish Protestant doctrines and practices, the formulation of Anglican principles dates from the reign of ELIZABETH I. The second Book of Common Prayer of Edward VI's reign was revised with modifications (1559) and its use enforced by an Act of UNIFORMITY. In 1563 the THIRTY-NINE

ARTICLES were issued by Convocation (the highest assembly of the Church) and finally adopted by the Church of England (1571) as a statement of its beliefs and practices. The aim was to set up a comprehensive, national, episcopal Church with the monarch as supreme governor. Those who refused to attend church services were fined. The PURITANS were dissatisfied with the Elizabethan religious settlement but the queen opposed all their attempts to modify her Anglican Church.

The 'Catholicization' of the Church in the 1630s under Archbishop LAUD exacerbated Puritan antipathy to the bishops, and religion was a crucial factor in the outbreak of the ENGLISH CIVIL WAR. Although Anglicanism was banned during the Commonwealth and Protectorate, it returned with vigour at the Restoration (1660). The Clarendon Code and TEST ACTS created a breach between establishment Anglicanism and NONCONFORMISTS, and James II's pro-Catholic policies played a significant part in provoking the GLORIOUS REVOLUTION. The TOLERATION ACT (1689) secured limited toleration for Nonconformists, although clergymen refusing to swear the oath of allegiance to William III were deprived of their office. (Catholics were not emancipated until 1829.)

The 18th century witnessed disputes between High Anglicans, who maintained Laud's conservatism, and Low Anglicans, or Latitudinarians, who were less concerned with forms of worship. Opposition to the evangelism of John WESLEY led to the establishment of an independent METHODIST CHURCH in 1791. The 19th century saw growing divergence between the 'High' Church tradition, which was revived by the Oxford Movement of the 1830s, led by John Henry NEWMAN, and the burgeoning evangelical movement. The former claimed historical continuity with the pre-Reformation Roman Catholic Church, stressing the authority of the bishops and priesthood, the doctrinal centrality of the seven sacraments, and the importance of ceremony in worship. By contrast, the Evangelicals were more Protestant in outlook, setting less store by the sacraments and tradition, and emphasizing the importance of the Bible as the basis of faith. In the 19th century the Evangelicals were particularly active in MISSIONARY work and social reform.

Both traditions remain strongly represented in the modern Church of England. During the 20th century a third tradition, that of theological liberalism, has also been widely influential in its emphasis on the need for the Church to adapt to modern knowledge and conditions. The diversity of views in the modern Church emerged most clearly in the controversy over the ordination of women: the Church's General Synod voted to admit women to the priesthood in 1992.

Anglican Communion The body of Protestant Christian Churches around the world which claim descent from the Church in England as reformed in the 16th century. They all recognize the spiritual leadership of the Archbishop of Canterbury, though he does not have any jurisdiction over Anglicans outside England. There are 20 fully autonomous national member Churches, including the Church of England, the largest, with about 16 million full members; the Protestant Episcopal Church of America (the first diocese of which was formed in 1784); the Church of Wales; the Episcopal Church of Scotland; and Anglican and Episcopal Churches in former British colonies or areas of Anglican

Missionary activity, for example Japan. There is little formal structure linking the Anglican Churches, but since 1867 their bishops have gathered every 10 years at the Lambeth Conference in England, an occasion to affirm the unity of the Anglican Churches and to debate outstanding issues, though the resolutions of the conference have no binding authority. The Anglican Communion is distinguished by considerable diversity in both doctrine and liturgy, but the Churches unite in acknowledging the three-fold ministry of bishops, priests, and deacons, the authority of the BIBLE, and a tradition of liturgical practice or form of worship inherited from the 16th-century Book of Common Prayer. In recent times various issues have strained the unity of the various Churches, and on some, such as the ordination of women, there has been an agreement to differ. The Churches of the Anglican Communion each have individual membership of the WORLD COUNCIL OF CHURCHES, and have been active in the ecumenical movement. Many Anglicans see themselves as forming a 'bridge' between Roman Catholicism and the more strictly Protestant Churches.

Anglo-Afghan Wars A series of wars between Afghan rulers and British India. The first occurred (1838–42) when Britain, concerned about Russian influence in AFGHANISTAN, sent an army to replace DOST MUHAMMAD with a pro-British king, Shah Shuja al-Mulk. Resistance to Shuja's rule culminated in an uprising (1841) which led to the destruction of the British Indian forces in Kabul during their withdrawal to Jalalabad (1842). Kabul was reoccupied the same year, but British forces were withdrawn from Afghanistan. The second (1878–80) was also fought to exclude Russian influence. By the Treaty of Gandamak (1879) Britain acquired territory and the right to maintain a Resident in Kabul, but in September of the same year the Resident, Sir Louis Cavagnari, was killed in Kabul and further campaigns were fought before the British withdrawal was accomplished. The third war was fought in 1919, when the new amir of Afghanistan, Amanullah, attacked British India and, although repulsed, secured the independence of Afghanistan through the Treaty of Rawalpindi (1919).

Anglo-Burmese Wars (1824–26, 1852–53, 1885) Conflicts between British India and Burma (now called MYANMAR). In 1824 a threatened Burmese invasion of Bengal led to a British counter-invasion, which captured Rangoon and forced the cession to Britain of Arakan and Tenasserim, the payment of a large indemnity, and the renunciation of Burmese claims to Assam. After a period of relative harmony, hostile treatment of British traders led to a second invasion in 1852, as a result of which Rangoon and the Irrawaddy delta was annexed. In 1885, the alleged francophile tendencies of King Thibaw (1878–85) provoked a third invasion which captured the royal capital at Mandalay and led to Thibaw's exile. Upper Burma became a province of British India, although guerrilla resistance to British rule was not suppressed for another five years.

Anglo-Dutch Wars Three maritime wars, 1652–54, 1665–67, and 1672–74, fought between the United Provinces and Britain on grounds of commercial and naval rivalry. The Dutch navy was commanded by able admirals but the prevailing westerly winds gave the English sailors a significant advantage.

The first war began when the Dutch carrying-trade was undermined by the English NAVIGATION ACTS of 1651, and the Dutch refused to salute the English flag in the English Channel. TROMP defeated BLAKE off Dungeness in December 1652, but convoying Dutch merchant ships through the Channel proved difficult and de WITT settled for reasonable peace terms from Cromwell in 1654. The Dutch recognized English sovereignty in the English Channel, gave compensation for the massacre at AMBOINA, and promised not to assist the exiled CHARLES II. An encounter off the African coast began the second war, followed by the fall of New Amsterdam (renamed New York) to the English, who also defeated the Dutch off Lowestoft in June 1665. However in 1666 Charles II was in financial difficulties, Cornelius Tromp and RUYTER won the Four Days War, and Ruyter made his celebrated raid on the English dockyards at Chatham. Peace was made at Breda in 1667. The Navigation Acts were modified in favour of the Dutch and territories gained during the war were retained, the Dutch keeping Surinam and the British, Delaware and New England. In 1672 Charles II, dependent on French subsidies, supported LOUIS XIV against the Dutch. The Dutch admirals had the advantage and the Treaty of Westminster signed in 1674 renewed the terms of Breda.

Anglo-Japanese Alliance (1902) Diplomatic agreement between Britain and Japan. It improved Britain's international position and consolidated Japan's position in north-east Asia at a time of increasing rivalry with Russia. The two powers agreed to remain neutral in any war fought by the other to preserve the *status quo* and to join the other in any war fought against two powers. Britain and Japan began to drift apart after World War I, and when the WASHINGTON CONFERENCE was summoned in 1921, Britain decided not to renew the alliance, which ended in 1923.

Anglo-Maori Wars A complex series of conflicts following the colonization of New Zealand. In the mid-1840s there were rebellions under the Maori chiefs Hone Heke and Te Rauparaha. In 1860 the TARANAKI WARS began, but Wiremu Tamihana, a leader of the KINGITANGA unity movement, negotiated an uneasy truce in 1861. Governor Browne was replaced by Sir George GREY in an attempt to secure peace. Grey and his advisers were reluctant to see the Kingitanga consolidated, for fear that British authority could not be asserted throughout New Zealand, and that land purchases would be halted. Fighting resumed in Taranaki in May 1863 and in July the Waikato was invaded. Fighting with the Kingitanga stopped in 1865 but was sustained by resistance from the PAI MARIRE (1864–65) and from Titokowaru in Taranaki and TE KOOTI RIKIRANGI TE TURUKI on the east coast (1868). London recalled Grey and the British regiments that year, but the pursuit of Titokowaru and Te Kooti, masters of guerrilla warfare, was carried on by settler militia and Maori auxiliaries. The last engagement was in 1872, after which Maori resistance gradually subsided.

Anglo-Saxon Chronicle A collection of seven manuscripts written in Anglo-Saxon (Old English) that together provide a history of England from the beginning of the conversion to Christianity up to 1154. The major text (known as the *Parker Chronicle*) appears to have been written by one clerk until 891. Most of the copies end in the 11th century; after 1079 only the

Peterborough Chronicle continued, breaking off abruptly with an unfinished entry for 1154. The *Chronicle* probably originated as notes inserted in the tables used by the Christian Church when calculating the date of Easter.

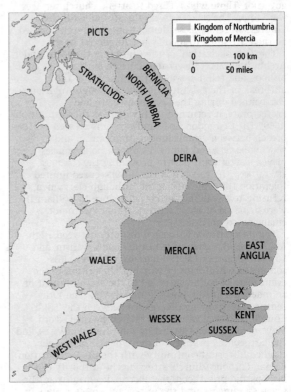

Anglo-Saxon England *Northumbria and Mercia were successively dominant in Anglo-Saxon England but the country's unification was not achieved until the early 10th century when the Wessex kings first resisted and then conquered the Vikings and Danes.*

Anglo-Saxons The ANGLES, SAXONS, and JUTES whose invasions of Britain (c. 450–c. 600) began with the departure of the Roman legions. They were probably joined by FRISIANS, SWABIANS, and settlers from southern Sweden.

The monk BEDE in his *Historia Ecclesiastica Gentis Anglorum* (Ecclesiastical History of the English People) explained the origins of the independent kingdoms that emerged. The East Angles (East Anglia), Middle Angles (East Midlands), Mercians (Midlands), and those who lived north of the Humber were descended from the Angles. The Saxons established the kingdoms of the East Saxons (Essex), the South Saxons (Sussex), and the West Saxons (Wessex). The Jutes settled in Kent, on the Isle of Wight, and in Hampshire. In the 7th century Northumbria under Edwin, OSWALD, and OSWY claimed authority (bretwaldaship) over all Anglo-Saxons. By the 8th century this hegemony had passed to Mercia under Ethelbald and OFFA and finally, by the 9th century, to Wessex, whose kings were able to resist the Viking invasions. Under ALFRED, EDWARD THE ELDER, ATHELSTAN, and

EDGAR, Wessex established an undisputed claim to the overlordship of England. The renewal of Scandinavian raids led to a Danish king, CANUTE (Cnut), becoming King of England in 1016. Although the West Saxon line was restored temporarily with EDWARD THE CONFESSOR in 1042, it finally ended with the Norman Conquest.

Until the conversion to Christianity of Ethelbert of Kent by St AUGUSTINE OF CANTERBURY (597) the Anglo-Saxons had been pagan. Thereafter their conversion proceeded rapidly. Church art and architecture contain some of the finest expressions of Anglo-Saxon culture and the monasteries, especially that at Winchester, produced beautiful illuminated manuscripts, noted particularly for their decorated initial letters.

Angola A country of south-central Africa bounded by the Atlantic on the west, the Democratic Republic of the Congo (Zaïre) and Zambia on the north and east, and Namibia on the south. While most of Angola lies south of the Congo River, the Cabinda province lies north of the Congo and is separated from the rest of Angola by a section of the Democratic Republic of the Congo (Zaïre).

Physical. Most of the country lies on a high plateau; but there is a coastal plain which, starting near the mouth of the Congo River, is broad and fertile until, southward, it becomes drier and narrower as it approaches the Namib desert. The vast plateau is a region of savannah, watered by rivers that flow outwards from highlands near the centre and usually have swamps along their valleys.

Economy. Potentially Africa's richest country, Angola has a wealth of mineral deposits, including the oil produced offshore from Cabinda, on which the economy is heavily dependent, diamonds, and iron ore. Exports include crude oil, petroleum products, coffee, diamonds, and mahogany hardwoods. Agricultural crops include sugar cane, bananas, palm oil, and tobacco. Industry is limited to food-processing and metal-refining. Electricity is generated mainly from hydroelectric dams. The economy has suffered major disruption from the civil war, which has caused widespread migration, famine, and destitution; it is badly in need of investment in infrastructure.

History. The coastal strip was colonized by the Portuguese in the 16th century, but it was not until the 19th century that, following wars with the Ovimbundu, Ambo, Humbo, and Kuvale, they began to exploit the mineral reserves of the hinterland. In 1951 Angola became an Overseas Province of Portugal. In 1954 a nationalist movement emerged, demanding independence. The Portuguese at first refused, but finally agreed in 1975 after a protracted guerrilla war, and 400,000 Portuguese were repatriated. Almost total economic collapse followed. Internal fighting continued between guerrilla factions. The ruling Marxist party, the Popular Movement for the Liberation of Angola (MPLA), was supported by Cuba, the Soviet Union, and East Germany, and its opponent, the National Union for the Total Independence of Angola (UNITA), by SOUTH AFRICA and the USA. Punitive South African raids took place from time to time, aimed at Namibian resistance forces operating from Angola. In 1988 there was a Geneva Accord between the various parties, intended to end violence. UNITA leader Jonas Savimbi at first refused to accept its terms, but more moderate MPLA policies, together with the withdrawal of South African aid, resulted in a peace treaty in 1991. Multiparty

elections were held in 1992. The MPLA won the elections but UNITA disputed the results and fighting broke out again. UNITA accepted the results in 1993 and peace talks were resumed, but sporadic violence continued. UN peacekeeping forces were sent to Angola in 1995. In April 1997, a new government of national unity was sworn in, boycotted by Savimbi.

CAPITAL:	Luanda
AREA:	1,246,700 sq km (481,354 sq miles)
POPULATION:	11.904 million (1996)
CURRENCY:	1 kwanza = 100 lwei
RELIGIONS:	Roman Catholic 68.7%; Protestant 19.8%; traditional beliefs 9.5%
ETHNIC GROUPS:	Ovimbundu 37.2%; Mbundu 21.6%; Kongo 13.2%; Portuguese and Mestizo 1%
LANGUAGES:	Portuguese (official); Umbundu; African Bantu languages
INTERNATIONAL ORGANIZATIONS:	UN; OAU; Non-Aligned Movement; SADC

Anguilla The most northerly of the Leeward Islands in the Caribbean. Flat and scrub-covered, its area is only 91 sq km (35 sq miles) of coral formation with fine, sandy beaches, but it is flanked by many islets. The climate is dry and warm, and fresh water is scarce. Salt deposits are the main natural resources, and fish and lobster are the island's chief export. A British colony since 1650, Anguilla formed part of the Federation of the West Indies (1958–62) and subsequently received associated state status with St Kitts and Nevis. Anguilla declared independence in 1967 and two years later was occupied by British troops, who reduced the island to colonial status once again. In 1980 it became a British dependency with full self-government.

animals, domestication of The process by which wild animals are bred and reared under human control and adapted for such purposes as meat, milk, or wool production, and hunting. Domestication has only been achieved with a small number of the wild species available. In most cases the time and place of domestication remain obscure, but cattle, goats, sheep, pigs, and camels were certainly domesticated at least 7,000 years ago. The initial reason for domestication was invariably the provision of meat. However, livestock were readily adapted to provide more than one resource. Cattle also supplied milk and hides, sheep gave wool, and domestic birds provided eggs. Domestication of multipurpose animals occurred worldwide. Llamas and reindeer provide region-specific examples. More recent domestications have been confined to specialized animals, like the silkworm.

Anjou Historically a province of western France, whose principal city was Angers. The Celtic inhabitants, the Andecavi, came under Roman domination during Julius CAESAR's conquest of Gaul but seceded from the Roman empire in the 5th century. In the 9th and 10th centuries it suffered depredations, first at the hands of the Vikings and then from the Normans.

In the 12th century the title of count passed to HENRY II of England and remained in English hands until 1203 when it reverted to France. In 1366 it became a duchy of the kingdom of Naples but in 1480 was restored to France under Louis XI. It ceased to exist as a province in 1790, as part of the French Revolutionary changes.

annals (Latin *annus*, 'year') The yearly records kept by the priests in Rome from the earliest times. They noted ceremonies, state enactments, and the holders of office. The high priest (Pontifex Maximus) was responsible for maintaining the records in his official residence. The accumulated material (mainly dating from after 300 BC) was published in eighty books known as the *Annales Maximi c.* 123 BC. CATO THE ELDER, LIVY, and TACITUS among other writers drew heavily on these records. The name came to be applied generally to the writing of history in strict chronological order.

Annam (Chinese, 'Pacified South') The central region of VIETNAM. It formerly covered Tonkin and northern Annam – those parts of Vietnam conquered by the Chinese in 111 BC. The original home of the Vietnamese was centred on the Red River and its delta in northern Vietnam. In 939 the Annamese drove out the Chinese and established an independent kingdom, though it continued to pay tribute to China until the 19th century. By 1471 it had conquered the CHAMPA. There followed a period of unrest and after a rebellion in 1558, the kingdom was divided in two. The Trinh ruled from Hanoi over an area that became known as Tonkin, and the Nguyen ruled southern Annam from Hué. The Nguyen expanded their rule over COCHIN CHINA in the 18th century and in 1802 Nguyen Anh, an Annamese general, reunited both parts of Annam with French assistance. Thereafter, he ruled as the Emperor Gia-Long. In 1807 a protectorate was enforced on Cambodia which led to frequent wars with Siam. Gia-Long's xenophobia and massacre of Catholics provoked French military intervention in 1858, and, by 1884, the seizure of the southern part of the country (also known as Cochin China) and the establishment of protectorates over the centre (Annam) and north (Tonkin). The imperial court at Hué remained, but had only nominal power except, briefly, under BAO DAI in the post-1945 period. Since the unification of North and South Vietnam, in 1976, Annam has been part of the Socialist Republic of Vietnam.

Annan, Kofi (1938–) Ghanaian diplomat, Secretary General of the United Nations (1997–). The son of a chief of the Fanti people, Annan studied in the USA and began work in the World Health Organization, a UN special agency, in 1962. He thereafter pursued a career in diplomacy before being appointed director of UN peacekeeping operations in 1993, in which role he was responsible for sending peacekeeping forces to Somalia (1993) and Bosnia-Herzegovina (1995). Annan became UN Secretary General after the USA had vetoed a second term of office for his predecessor, Boutros BOUTROS-GHALI. In February 1998 his intervention helped to prevent renewed war between the USA and Saddam HUSSEIN's Iraq.

Anne (1665–1714) Queen of England, Scotland, and Ireland (1702–07) and of Great Britain and Ireland (1707–14), the last STUART sovereign. She was the younger daughter of the Roman Catholic JAMES II and his first wife Anne Hyde, but was brought up as a Protestant and in 1683 married the Protestant Prince George of Denmark (d. 1708). During the GLORIOUS REVOLUTION she abandoned her father's cause and from 1689 gave support to her brother-in-law WILLIAM III. The death of her last surviving child in 1700 led to the Act of SETTLEMENT by which, after Anne's death, Parliament bestowed the succession to the throne on her Hanoverian (and Protestant) relations. Her reign was dominated on the one hand by the War of the SPANISH SUCCESSION (known in the American colonies as Queen Anne's War), and on the other hand by the struggle between the Whigs and Tories to control the queen's government. At first the Whigs dominated through the influence on the queen of Sarah Churchill, Duchess of MARLBOROUGH. From 1707 she was ousted by a new royal favourite, Abigail Masham, and in 1710 the Tories came to power, retaining it until Anne's sudden and fatal illness.

Anne was not a politically gifted woman and was easily influenced by the opinions of others and by her own prejudices. She was the last English monarch to veto an Act of Parliament and caused controversy when she created a dozen peers to give the Tories a working majority in the House of Lords in 1712. Her reign was notable for its many literary figures, including Alexander Pope and Jonathan Swift, which helped to justify its title of the 'Augustan Age', implying comparison with the greatest age of the ROMAN EMPIRE.

Anne of Austria (1601–66) Wife of Louis XIII of France whom she married in 1615. She was the daughter of Philip III of Spain. Her friend Madame de Chevreuse was involved in plots against RICHELIEU, and she was accused of encouraging the advances of the Duke of BUCKINGHAM. When her four-year-old son succeeded to the throne as LOUIS XIV in 1643 she was declared regent and gave her full support to MAZARIN during the FRONDE. She influenced her son until her death, though her regency ended in 1651.

Anne of Cleves (1515–57) German princess, Queen consort of HENRY VIII. She was chosen by Thomas CROMWELL to marry Henry VIII of England, and thereby seal a diplomatic alliance with the German Protestants. After a proxy courtship she became the king's fourth wife in January 1540. Six months later Henry had the marriage annulled, alleging that the marriage was unconsummated. She stayed in England, unmarried, on a generous pension for the rest of her life.

Anschluss (German, 'connection') HITLER's annexation of Austria in 1938. The GERMAN SECOND EMPIRE did not include Austrian Germans, who remained in Austria-Hungary. The Austrian Republic was proclaimed in 1918. In 1934 a coup by Austrian Nazis failed to achieve union with Germany. In February 1938 Hitler summoned Kurt von Schuschnigg, the Austrian Chancellor, to Berchtesgaden and demanded the admission of Nazis into his cabinet. Schuschnigg attempted to call a plebiscite on Austrian independence, failed, and was forced to resign. German troops entered Vienna and on 13 March 1938 the Anschluss was proclaimed. The majority of Austrians welcomed the union. The ban on such a union, laid down in the Treaties of VERSAILLES and St Germain (1919), was reiterated when the Allied Powers recognized the second Austrian republic in 1946.

Anselm, St (1033–1109) Philosopher, theologian, and Archbishop of Canterbury. He was a Benedictine monk at the monastery of Bec, in Normandy, where LANFRANC was prior, and he succeeded him as prior in 1063. Over the next thirty years Anselm established Bec as a major centre of scholarship and himself as 'the Father of Scholasticism'. He argued that faith was a necessary prerequisite for the understanding of the scriptures and was not itself dependent upon that understanding – although reason could be used constructively within the context of faith. Christian truths, he believed, were capable of rational exposition.

Anselm also succeeded Lanfranc as Archbishop of Canterbury, in 1093. His relationship with both WILLIAM II and HENRY I was uneasy, particularly over the election of bishops (INVESTITURE) without interference from the crown. Twice Anselm went into voluntary exile over this issue (1097–1100, 1103–06). Finally he accepted a compromise under which the king surrendered his claim to invest bishops but retained the right to their homage for lands held by virtue of their office.

Anson, George, Baron Anson (1697–1762) English admiral, remembered for his circumnavigation of the world, 1740–44. Due to shipwreck and scurvy among his crew he returned with only one of his original six ships though with almost £500,000 worth of Spanish treasure. In 1747, off Cape Finisterre, he captured six French enemy warships during the War of the AUSTRIAN SUCCESSION. Later, at the Board of Admiralty, he created the corps of marines, and by his reforms and effective planning, played a major part in securing Britain's naval successes in the SEVEN YEARS WAR.

Antarctica A continent surrounding the South Pole and lying almost wholly to the south of latitude 66° 33' S, the Antarctic Circle.

Physical. Within the Antarctic Circle the Sun neither rises at midwinter nor sets at midsummer. The average temperature at the South Pole is –50 °C (–58 °F), and an extremely thick ice-cap covers the continent, forming a vast plateau. Strong winds often blow from the centre of this ice-cap; it is usually too cold to snow, and such snow as does fall takes hundreds of years to turn to ice. The ice grows and moves so slowly that parts of the ice-cap are millions of years old. In several of the coastal regions there are mountain ranges through which glaciers flow. Where they emerge into the frozen sea the great ice-shelves make the continent on the map seem larger than it really is. In other places, where the rocky shore is exposed, little patches of summer moss and lichen can be seen. Recent scientific discoveries on Antarctica include the remains of a large number of meteorites, and a vast unfrozen lake deep under the ice-cap.

History. Fabian von Bellingshausen, a Russian, was probably the first person to sight the continent, in 1820. There were significant Russian, British, French, and US scientific and geographical expeditions to Antarctica during the 19th century. Many countries were involved in overland exploration during the first decades of the 20th century. Ernest Shackleton's British party sledged to within 156 km (97 miles) of the South Pole in 1909. Roald Amundsen's Norwegian party reached it in 1911. Soon after, Robert Falcon Scott's British party reached it (1912), but all members died on the return journey. Although Antarctica remains uninhabited, territorial claims have been made by several countries. Chief among these claims, not recognized by the USA or Russia, have been those made by Britain (British Antarctic Territory) in 1908, New Zealand (Ross Dependency) in 1923, Australia (Australian Antarctic Territory) in 1933, France (Adélie Land) in 1938, Norway (Queen Maud Land) in 1939, Chile (Antarctic Peninsula) in 1940, and Argentina (Antarctic Peninsula) in 1942. The Antarctic Treaty, signed in 1959, preserves Antarctica for peaceful purposes, pledges international scientific co-operation, and prohibits nuclear explosions and the disposal by any nation of radioactive waste. A 50-year ban on all exploitation of the continent's considerable coal and other mineral deposits was agreed in 1991.

Anthracite strike A strike by the United Mine Workers of America, called in 1902 in a bid for higher wages, shorter hours, and union recognition. The employers refused to arbitrate, and President Theodore ROOSEVELT appointed a commission to mediate, which led to the union to call off the strike. In 1903 the commission gave the miners a 10% wage increase but refused to recognize the union. The intransigent behaviour of the employers created public support for the federal government's intervention and the strike signalled an important extension of federal economic responsibilities.

anticlericalism An attitude of hostility toward the Christian clergy's involvement in political and secular affairs. It has existed since the earliest days of institutionalized Christianity. In medieval Europe it was unorganized and apolitical. Pluralism (the simultaneous holding of several church offices) and absenteeism (the non-residence of clergy) were prime targets of criticism, along with immoral conduct, the abuse of INDULGENCES, and the excessive powers of Church courts. Anticlerical sentiment helped to pave the way for the Reformation, as it coalesced with the calls for doctrinal reform from WYCLIF and LUTHER. Modern political anticlericalism dates from the ENLIGHTENMENT.

Anti-Comintern Pact (25 November 1936) An agreement between Germany and Japan ostensibly to collaborate against international communism (the COMINTERN). Italy signed the pact (1937), followed by other nations in 1941. It was in reality a union of aggressor states, first apparent in Japan's invasion of China in 1937.

Anti-Corn Law League A movement to bring about the repeal of the duties on imported grain in Britain known as the CORN LAWS. Founded in Manchester in 1839 under Richard COBDEN and John BRIGHT, the League conducted a remarkably successful campaign. It organized mass meetings, circulated pamphlets, and sought to influence Members of Parliament. A combination of bad harvests, trade depression, and the IRISH FAMINE strengthened the League's position and in 1846 the Prime Minister, Sir Robert PEEL, was persuaded to abolish the Corn Laws. The expected slump in agriculture did not take place.

Antietam (Sharpsburg), Battle of (17 September 1862) A battle in the AMERICAN CIVIL WAR, fought in Maryland. After his victory at the second Battle of Bull Run, General LEE invaded the North, but with only 30,000 men under his immediate command was attacked by a Union (Northern) army under General George MCCLELLAN at Sharpsburg on the Antietam Creek. Although the Confederates were badly mauled, they held their positions and were able to make an orderly retreat on the following day. The casualties of 23,000 (divided almost equally between the two sides) were the worst of any single day of the war. While the Confederate invasion was repulsed, McClellan missed his chance to destroy Lee's army and bring the war to an early end. The political advantages of the victory, however, were such as to deter Britain and France from diplomatic intervention and to provide LINCOLN with the opportunity to issue his Emancipation Proclamations (22 September 1862 and 1 January 1863), the executive order abolishing slavery in the areas under Confederate control.

Antigonus I (the 'One-eyed') (c. 382–301 BC) An officer in the army of ALEXANDER THE GREAT. After the latter's death (323), and that of the Macedonian regent, Antipater (319), he attempted, in the subsequent power struggle, to re-establish Alexander's empire under his own sole leadership, declaring himself king (306). His considerable success induced his rivals – Ptolemy, Seleucus, Cassander, and Lysimachus – to combine, defeat, and kill him at the 'battle of the kings' at Ipsus.

Antigua and Barbuda A country in the Leeward Island group of the Caribbean, comprising the islands of Antigua, Barbuda, and Redonda (uninhabited).

Physical. The main island, Antigua, comprises 280 sq km (108 sq miles) of fairly bare scrubland. Formed of volcanic rock in the south-west and coral in the north and east, it is moderately hilly, rising to 405 m (1,329 feet). The coastline is indented. The climate of the islands is dry and warm, although there are occasional hurricanes in summer. Water is scarce.

Economy. The mainstay of the economy is up-market tourism. Manufacturing industry includes clothing and the assembly of electrical components for re-export. Aside from some cultivation of sugar cane and cotton, agriculture has been neglected, resulting in dependence on food imports, which exacerbates the high foreign debt.

History. Antigua and Barbuda were colonized from the 17th century by the British, who brought slaves from Africa to work on the islands. From 1871 until 1956 the islands were part of the British colony of the Leeward Islands. Antigua and Barbuda joined the West Indian Federation (see WEST INDIAN INDEPENDENCE), and in 1967 became an Associated State of Britain, gaining internal autonomy. The country became fully independent in 1981. The Antiguan Labour Party (ALP) has held power since 1976.

CAPITAL:	Saint John's
AREA:	441.6 sq km (170.5 sq miles)
POPULATION:	64,400 (1996)
CURRENCY:	1 East Caribbean dollar = 100 cents
RELIGIONS:	Anglican 44.5%; other Protestant (mainly Moravian, Methodist, and Seventh-day Adventist) 41.6%; Roman Catholic 10.2%; Rastafarian 0.7%
ETHNIC GROUPS:	Black 94.4%; Mixed 3.5%; White 1.3%
LANGUAGES:	English (official); English creole
INTERNATIONAL ORGANIZATIONS:	UN; Commonwealth; CARICOM

Anti-Masonic Party A US political party of the 1820s and 1830s opposed to Freemasons. Formed in 1826 in the wake of the disappearance of William Morgan, a New York bricklayer alleged to have divulged lodge secrets, the Anti-Masonic Party was the product of hysteria, cleverly played upon by local politicians. It played an influential part in the politics of New York and surrounding states, and drew sufficient WHIG support away from Henry CLAY in the 1832 presidential election to help sweep President JACKSON back into office. The

Anti-Masonic Party was the first to hold a nominating convention, but otherwise made no lasting political contribution.

Antioch One of the most prosperous cities of antiquity, founded in 300 BC by Seleucus I. It stood strategically on the trade routes linking the East with the Mediterranean, and was the capital city of the SELEUCIDS. In 64 BC it was annexed by Pompey for Rome and remained a flourishing commercial and intellectual centre, though it had declined by the time of its capture by the Arabs in 637–38 AD. The Crusaders captured it in 1098 and it remained an important Christian city until it fell in 1268 to the MAMELUKES of Egypt. It came under OTTOMAN rule from 1516.

antipope A person who claims or exercises the office of pope (PAPACY) in opposition to the true pope of the time. There have been about 35 antipopes in the history of the Catholic Church, the last being Felix V (1439–49). There have been two main causes. First, a disputed election, in which there was disagreement among the electors or other interested parties as to which person was elected pope. Secondly, the desire of various HOLY ROMAN EMPERORS to have a more pliable person as pope, and their setting up of antipopes for this purpose. In some cases, especially during the GREAT SCHISM of 1378–1417, it is very difficult to say which person was the true pope and which was the antipope.

anti-Semitism Hostility towards and discrimination against JEWISH PEOPLE. The roots of anti-Semitism go back to the early history of the Jews in the Middle East. Jewish communities in the Middle East were scattered (see DIASPORA) from the 8th century BC. The Bible described the Jews as the betrayers of Jesus Christ and in medieval Europe Christian persecution of Jewish people was intense. The SPANISH INQUISITION forced Jewish people to flee Europe and many settled in North Africa. The ENLIGHTENMENT in the 18th century brought greater religious tolerance but the rise of NATIONALISM led to hostility towards minority peoples in many countries. In the late 19th and early 20th centuries anti-Semitism was strongly evident in France, Germany, Poland, Russia, and elsewhere, many Jewish emigrants fleeing from persecution or POGROMS in south-east Europe to Britain and the USA. After World War I early Nazi propaganda in Germany encouraged anti-Semitism, alleging Jewish responsibility for the nation's defeat. By 1933 Jewish persecution was active throughout the country. The 'final solution' which Hitler worked for was to be a HOLOCAUST or extermination of the entire Jewish race; some six million Jews were killed in CONCENTRATION CAMPS before the defeat of Nazism in 1945. Anti-Semitism was a strong feature of society within the former Soviet Union, especially after World War II. Anti-Semitism remains a problem in eastern Europe and in the former Soviet republics, although Jewish people are now allowed to emigrate from these countries. During the early 1990s in western Europe, especially in France and Germany, there was an increase in racist violence by neo-Nazi groups.

Anti-Trust laws US laws restricting business monopolies. After 25 years' agitation against monopolies, the CONGRESS passed the Sherman Anti-Trust Act (1890) that declared illegal 'every contract, combination, or conspiracy in restraint of trade'. The

Clayton Anti-Trust Act (1914), amended by the Robinson-Patman Act (1936), prohibited discrimination among customers and mergers of firms that would lessen competition. After World War II there was a further growth in giant multinational corporations and the Celler-Kefauver Antimerger Act (1950) was intended to prevent oligarchic tactics, such as elimination of price competition, as being against the public interest.

Antonescu, Ion (1882–1946) Romanian military leader and fascist dictator. In 1940 he assumed dictatorial powers. He forced the abdication of King CAROL II, and supported the Axis Powers. His participation in the Nazi invasion of the Soviet Union resulted, in 1944, in the fall of his regime as the Red Army entered Romania. In 1946 he was executed as a war criminal.

Antonines A Roman imperial dynasty beginning with Titus Aurelius Antoninus (86–161 AD). He succeeded HADRIAN in 137 and was entitled 'Pius' (Latin, 'the Devout') by the ROMAN SENATE. His reign was peaceful, by virtue of his respect for the traditional role of the Senate. The administration was streamlined and centralized and the weaker points of Rome's vast imperial frontiers were secured. The remains of a column and temple to his memory still exist in Rome. His nephew and son-in-law MARCUS AURELIUS was named his adopted son and heir. Aurelius' son, Commodus, was technically the last of the dynasty; but Lucius Septimius SEVERUS adopted himself into the line. Severus' son 'Caracalla' and great-nephew Elagabalus continued to use the name and the title 'Pius'.

Antonine Wall The Roman empire's northernmost fixed frontier in Britain, built c. 143 AD in what is now southern Scotland. Constructed by detachments of all three legions of the Roman army then stationed in Britain, it was a turf barricade standing some 3 m (10 feet) high. A ditch 12 m (40 feet) wide and over 3 m (10 feet) deep along its northern front was lined with sharp stakes. Nineteen forts marked its 60-km (37-mile) length, along with advanced outposts and signal towers. As a line of defence it was evacuated in about 155 AD, almost certainly for good, although there may have been a brief reoccupation some 20 years or so later.

Antony, Mark MARK ANTONY.

Anyang A city in Henan province, China. It is an important LONGSHAN site, and also the site of the most famous (c. 1300 BC) SHANG capital, which has been extensively excavated. Chinese characters scratched on to ORACLE bones found there, some stored in 'archive' pits, show that writing had already advanced well beyond the pictographic stage and that bamboo-slip books, writing brushes, and ink were in use. Excavated pit tombs provide evidence of the slaughter of human beings and of horses at royal funerals. Bronze vessels in these tombs are of sophisticated design and show great skill in the technique of bronze casting; distinctive shapes, in particular a tripod with udder-like hollow legs, link this mature Shang metallurgy with the shapes of earlier Longshan pottery.

ANZAC Acronym for the Australian and New Zealand Army Corps, which fought during World War I. Originally it was applied to those members of the Corps who took part in the GALLIPOLI CAMPAIGN. The name came to be applied to all Australian and New Zealand

servicemen. Anzac Day (25 April), commemorating the Gallipoli landing (and later contributions to other campaigns), has been observed since 1916.

ANZUS Acronym for the tripartite Pacific security treaty between Australia, New Zealand, and the USA, signed at San Francisco in 1951. Known also as the Pacific Security Treaty, it recognizes that an armed attack in the Pacific Area on any of the Parties would be dangerous to peace and safety, and declares that it would act to meet the common danger, in accordance with its constitutional processes. Following New Zealand's anti-nuclear policy, which included the banning of nuclear-armed ships from its ports, the USA suspended its security obligations to New Zealand in 1986. ANZUS continues to govern security relations between Australia and the USA, and between Australia and New Zealand.

Apache A group of PLAINS PEOPLES of the south-western USA. Traditionally, the Apache practised subsistence farming and hunting, and a system of matrilocal (at the home of the wife) residence. Their nomadic existence, using the dog-travois (sledge) in the central and southern Great Plains, gradually led them southwards into semi-desert regions during the 9th to the 15th centuries. They had a reputation as fierce fighters; they and the NAVAHO raided towns of the ANASAZI as early as c. 1275. Spanish explorers found them well established in Arizona, New Mexico, Texas, and northern Mexico in the late 16th century and regular contact with Spanish settlements was developed by the early 17th century. As they, and numerous other tribes on the eastern edges of the plains, acquired horses, competition for buffalo hunting became fierce and the COMANCHE eventually drove them off the Great Plains into the deserts by the mid-18th century. The Apache resisted domination by the Spanish and Mexicans until the mid-19th century, when their territory was incorporated into the USA. They were not finally subjugated, however, until the end of the 19th century, and many of their chiefs, such as Geronimo, entered into US folklore. They now live in the state of Arizona.

apartheid (Afrikaans, 'separateness') A racial policy in South Africa. It involved a strict segregation of Black, White, and 'Coloured' people, in land ownership, residence, marriage and other social intercourse, work, education, religion, and sport. As a word it was first used politically in 1943, but as a concept it goes back to the rigid segregation practised by the settlers since the 17th century. From 1948 onwards, it was expressed in statutes, in job reservation and trade union separation, and in the denial of the vote and parliamentary representation for Black people. In accordance with it BANTU HOMELANDS were created, depriving the Bantu-speaking peoples of South African citizenship for an illusory independence. From 1985 certain restrictions began to be mitigated by creating subordinate parliamentary chambers for Indians and Coloureds (people of mixed descent), by relaxation of rules for sport and leisure, by abolishing the Pass Laws, and by modifying the Group Areas Act. Increasing internal unrest along with international pressure for its abolition eventually swayed the government, and in July 1991 President DE KLERK repealed all remaining apartheid legislation, including the Population Registration Act. In December 1991 a Convention for a Democratic South

Africa (CODESA) was established, comprising the government and 18 political groups, including the AFRICAN NATIONAL CONGRESS and the INKATHA FREEDOM PARTY. In 1993 a new transitional constitution, drafted by CODESA, was ratified by the government. The constitution gave the vote to all South African adults and the first multiracial elections were held in 1994.

appeasement The efforts by the British Prime Minister, Neville CHAMBERLAIN, and his French counterpart, Édouard DALADIER, to satisfy the demands (1936–39) of the AXIS POWERS. Their policy of appeasement enabled Hitler to occupy the RHINELAND, to annex Austria, and to acquire the Sudetenland in Czechoslovakia after the MUNICH PACT of 1938. Appeasement ended when Hitler, in direct contravention of assurances given at Munich, invaded the rest of Czechoslovakia in March 1939. A policy of 'guarantees' was then instituted, by which Britain and France pledged themselves to protect Romania, Greece, and Poland should they be attacked by Germany or Italy. The German invasion of Poland five months later was the event that precipitated World War II.

Appian Way Ancient Rome's earliest major military road, named after Appius Claudius Caecus, who authorized its construction in 312 BC. It was described by the Roman poet Statius as the 'Queen of Roads'. The first stage, from Rome to Capua, was constructed during the SAMNITE WARS; it was later extended to Taranto and Brindisi. It was paved with cobblestones, and marked by milestones. TRAJAN added a spur-road to Bari, the Appia Traiana, in 109 AD. The first few miles from Rome still preserve many of the ancient tombs which lined the road and some of the original stone paving.

Apostles DISCIPLES.

apparitor SUMMONER.

Appomattox A village in Virginia, USA, scene of the surrender of the CONFEDERACY Army of Northern Virginia to the Union Army of the Potomac on 9 April 1865 at the end of the AMERICAN CIVIL WAR. Having been forced to evacuate Petersburg and Richmond a week before, General LEE found himself almost surrounded by greatly superior forces and decided that further resistance was pointless. He was granted generous surrender terms by his victorious opponent, General GRANT. The surrender terminated Confederate resistance in the east and marked the effective end of the war.

Aquinas, St Thomas (c. 1224–74) Dominican theologian and philosopher. Aquinas was born to a noble Italian family and despite opposition became a DOMINICAN friar, studying under Albertus Magnus of Cologne, one of the best teachers of the day. He then taught in Paris and was for a time attached to the papal court. He was the greatest theologian of the medieval Church and a powerful force in the movement known as SCHOLASTICISM. His main arguments are set out in his *Summa Theologica*, which covers the whole range of theology.

His metaphysics, a development of the teachings of Aristotle and of medieval Arab commentators on Aristotle's works, revolves around three contrasts, those of potentiality and actuality, form and matter (see ARISTOTLE), and essence and existence. Whether

something exists is not settled by an account of what it is; similarly, the existence of God is deduced from what could be observed about the nature of the world. The essence of a thing may involve materiality, but this is not implied by the notion of existence: to be is not to be material. In all material things Aquinas distinguishes their form, or organizing principle, from their matter, which is simply the potential to take on this or another form. Aquinas also followed Aristotle in identifying the mind or soul with the form of the body, and sought to reconcile this with the Christian belief in immortality. Thomism, a philosophy rooted in his doctrines, holds a central place in Roman Catholic education to this day.

Aquitaine A province in south-western France, originally the Roman Aquitania. Between the 3rd and 7th centuries it suffered from German and Gascon invasions. The attempts of the region to preserve some political independence were frustrated by the CAROLINGIANS, who made it part of their empire in the 8th century. It remained semi-independent, however, and, after the collapse of Carolingian power, emerged as a duchy in the 10th century under the counts of Poitiers. It passed briefly to France when Duchess ELEANOR married Louis VII, but they divorced in 1152 and when her new husband became HENRY II of England it came to the English crown. Nevertheless Henry had to do homage for it as a vassal of the King of France. Effective control of the territory fluctuated between France and England until the middle of the 15th century when all but the port of Calais had been recovered by France.

Arab conquests Wars which, in the century after the death of MUHAMMAD in 632, created an empire stretching from Spain to the Indus valley. Beginning as a JIHAD (holy war) against the apostasy of the Arabian tribes that had renounced ISLAM they acquired a momentum of their own as the Arabs, inspired by the prospect of vast booty and the belief that death in battle would gain them instant admission to paradise, confronted the waning power of BYZANTIUM and PERSIA.

In Syria and Egypt the conquerors allowed both Christians and Jews to keep their faiths as *dhimmi* (protected peoples) upon payment of a discriminatory tax. Local resistance in Persia and North Africa made the conquests there slower. After the first civil war (656–61) the Arab capital was moved from Medina to Damascus by the UMAYYADS, and under the ABBASIDS to the new city of Baghdad where, with the encouragement of the caliphs HARUN AL-RASHID and al-Mamun, Islamic culture flowered. The political unity of this empire was short-lived – rival CALIPHATES appeared in North Africa and Spain in the 9th and 10th centuries – but cultural coherence was maintained by the universality of the Arabic language and Islamic law (*shariah*), and by the traffic of traders, scholars, and pilgrims.

Arabi Pasha The English name of Ahmad Urabi Pasha al-Misri (1839–1911), Egyptian nationalist leader. A conscript in the Egyptian army, he rose to the rank of colonel in the Egyptian-Ethiopian War (1875–76). In 1879 he took part in an officers' revolt against the Turkish governor of Egypt, and led a further revolt in 1881. In 1882, when Britain and France intervened at the request of Khedive Tawfiq, bombarding the city of Alexandria, he organized a nationalist resistance movement. The British defeated him at TEL-EL-KEBIR, and exiled him to Sri Lanka. He returned to Egypt in 1901.

Arab League (League of Arab States) An organization of Arab states, founded in Cairo, Egypt in 1945. In 1991 its members were: Algeria, Bahrain, Comoros, Djibouti, Egypt, Iraq, Jordan, Kuwait, Lebanon, Libya, Mauritania, Morocco, Oman, Palestine, Qatar, Saudi Arabia, Somalia, Sudan, Syria, Tunisia, United Arab Emirates, and Yemen. An annexe to the League's Charter stipulates that Palestine is considered as an independent state and as a full member of the Arab League. The principal aims of the League are to protect the independence and sovereignty of its members, and to strengthen the ties between them by encouraging co-operation in different fields. Opposition to the state of Israel and the demand for the establishment of a PALESTINIAN state have been central to the policies of the League. The organization's headquarters were transferred to Tunis during the suspension of Egypt from the League because of President Sadat's peace agreement with Israel's Prime Minister Begin in 1978 (see CAMP DAVID ACCORD). Egypt was readmitted in 1989, and in 1990 Cairo once again became the League's headquarters. In 1989 a mediation committee consisting of three of the members of the Arab League helped to negotiate a ceasefire in Lebanon. In 1990 the League narrowly approved a proposal to dispatch Arab forces to support the US-led coalition against Saddam Hussein's invasion of Kuwait, but the conflict exposed serious divisions among members. The League supported the peace accord between Israel and the PLO (1993) but decided to uphold the boycott of Israel until it withdrew from all the occupied territories.

Arafat, Yasser (1929–   ) Palestinian politician. Born in Jerusalem, he helped to form the al-FATAH movement, emerging as its leader in 1968. The PALESTINE LIBERATION ORGANIZATION was founded in 1964; he became its chairman in 1969 and Commander-in-Chief of the Palestine Revolutionary Forces in 1971. As such he organized guerrilla raids on Israeli territory, assassinations, and anti-Israeli terrorist attacks. Although gaining support from Eastern bloc countries, he did not aspire to communism. He attended all-Arab summit conferences, and in 1974 was invited to address the UN General Assembly. In 1982 his organization was expelled by Israel from Lebanon. He was criticized by Marxist elements in the PLO as too conservative, failed to reach agreement with King HUSSEIN OF JORDAN, and quarrelled with President ASSAD of SYRIA. In 1983 he set up a new base in Tunisia and in 1988 he was again invited to address the General Assembly, when he rejected military violence, recognized the existence of the state of Israel, and called for a political solution to the Palestine problem. Although excluded from the 'peace-process' initiated by the USA in 1992, he remained a key figure behind the negotiations between Israel, Syria, and the Palestinians. In 1993 he signed a peace accord with Israel, in which Israel agreed to withdraw its troops from the West Bank and the Gaza Strip areas, and the PLO agreed to give up terrorism. Arafat, along with Yitzhak RABIN and Foreign Minister Shimon PERES of Israel, was awarded the Nobel Peace Prize in 1994. He was elected President of the newly formed Palestinian National Authority in 1996.

Aragon Formerly a kingdom, now a province in northern Spain. It became part of the Roman empire under Augustus, was taken by the Visigoths in the 5th century and by the Moors in the 8th century. In 1137 it was united with Catalonia by the marriage of the monarchs, and under James I acquired the Balearic Islands. During the 14th century Sardinia, Naples, and Sicily were added. In 1469 Ferdinand II married ISABELLA I of Castile, uniting the kingdoms of Aragon and Castile and becoming FERDINAND V of Castile.

Arakan The western coastal strip of MYANMAR (Burma), extending along the Bay of Bengal. It was formerly an independent kingdom, but in about 1600 its ruler, with help from Portuguese mercenaries, invaded the country and a Portuguese adventurer established himself as 'king' on the Irrawaddy delta. In 1784 Bodawpaya, King of Burma, conquered Arakan, bringing the Burmese frontier up to Chittagong. This threat to British India was followed by the First Anglo-Burmese War (1824–26) and Arakan's cession to the British.

Arapaho A Native American tribe who inhabited the hills bordering the northern Great Plains, along with the BLACKFOOT and Gros Ventre. In the late 17th century, they changed from being agriculturalists and seasonal buffalo hunters to nomads on horseback following the great herds. Alongside the Kiowa and COMANCHE they helped drive the APACHE off the Great Plains by the mid-18th century, and also fought the CROW, PAWNEE, and Cheyenne as they moved on to the plains.

Arbenz Guzmán, Jacobo (1913–71) Guatemalan statesman. A member of the Revolutionary Action Party, he served as President, 1951–54. Comprehensive agrarian reforms made possible the expropriation of large estates owned by Guatemalans and US conglomerates. When his administration was judged to be communist by the Roman Catholic Church and the US government, the EISENHOWER administration sent arms to Guatemala's neighbours enabling Carlos Castillo Armas to depose Arbenz in 1954.

Arcadia A mountainous region in the Peloponnese, Greece. It had no great political unity or strength in ancient times. Many of its communities were small and scattered, and its two leading cities, Tegea and Mantinea, were often at odds with each other. By the 480s BC it was a major supplier of mercenaries, but rose to political prominence only when Megalopolis was founded in 370–362 by the Theban general Epaminondas. This city led resistance to SPARTA, was well disposed towards MACEDONIA, and in 235 joined the ACHAEAN LEAGUE. Arcadia, which was regarded in Greek mythology as the home of the pastoral god Pan, was identified in classical times and during the Renaissance (for example, in Sir Philip Sidney's *Arcadia*) as an earthly paradise. The phrase *Et in Arcadia ego* refers to the presence of Death even in this idyllic region.

archaeology The study of the past of mankind, especially in the prehistoric period, and usually by excavation. Archaeological research includes four stages. The most obvious is recovery of material by excavation, chance find, surface survey, and observation from the air. Digging remains crucial because it alone can recover the precise context of finds, without which they lose much of their significance. It can take a wide variety of archaeology   *Archaeology is the study of the history and way of life of past cultures through the systematic and scientific excavation and analysis or remains in the ground. These remains may come from buildings, territorial boundaries, domestic, craft or industrial activities, or may merely be discarded debris. Location, excavation, interpretation, and restoration of archaeological remains involves many disciplines.*

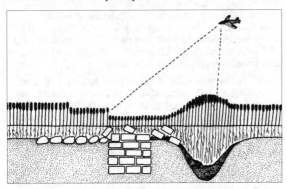

Archaeological artefacts in the ground may be caught by the plough and brought to the surface, or, if the ground is unploughed, features may survive as mounds or hollows, under a grass mantle. In this example, the crop will grow differently over the hidden cobbles, wall, and ditch. Under the right conditions, this pattern may be seen from the air, indicating the location of a site.

The process of excavating a site involves taking off the topsoil and cleaning, recording, drawing, and photographing the different sediments and features, together with any artefacts, such as pot sherds, bones, and metal objects that are found. Sediments may be sampled for microanalysis of their composition, and artefacts will be taken to laboratories for analysis and conservation.

The excavated data, including written records, plans, photographs, and artefacts are subsequently brought together to form an idea of what the site might have looked like in the past. In this example, the evidence of the excavations suggests that there was a wall and gateway, with cobbled roads, and ditches for rubbish.

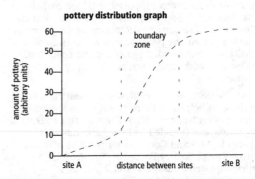

pottery distribution graph

The data gathered at one site may be analysed within a wider cultural context. Here, the amount of a particular type of pottery found at two neighbouring contemporary sites varies dramatically, and increases rapidly in the area between the sites. This intermediate area is a cultural or trading boundary zone separating the sites.

forms depending on the nature of the site – an isolated grave, a long-occupied cave, a wreck on the sea-bed, a standing building, a modern construction site, and many more. Then, finds have to be turned into evidence by analysis. Their form, composition, date, and associations all have information to impart. Typology (study of changes in forms) can link finds from different sites. A whole battery of scientific and mathematical aids can be brought to bear at this stage. Thirdly, the results have to be built into a coherent story to give an account of what happened when. Finally, and often the most difficult task, reasons must be sought for the processes of cultural change.

archer A soldier armed with bow and arrows. Archers have practised their deadly skill since prehistory in

most parts of the world, for example, the Romans employed SCYTHIAN archers on horseback. In the Middle Ages the cumbrous but powerful crossbow was widely used in continental Europe, despite being forbidden against all save infidels by the Lateran Council of 1139. In England the potential of the longbow was discovered in the time of Edward I, but it was in Edward III's reign that full use was first made of it; nearly 2 m (6 feet) long, and made of yew, oak, or maple, it enabled accurate firing of arrows at a range of up to about 320 m (350 yards), and it gave England such victories as CRÉCY in 1346 and POITIERS in 1356. Archery became the English national sport; Roger Ascham, tutor to the future ELIZABETH I, published *Toxophilus*, a treatise on archery (1545). The musketeer superseded the archer in Europe from the later 16th century, but in 19th-century North America the Native Americans proved how devastating the mounted archer could be, even against men armed with rifles.

Arctic exploration Exploration of the ice-covered ocean around the North Pole. The search for a north-west and a north-east passage from Europe to the Orient gave impetus to arctic explorations from the 16th century onwards. The British geographer Sir John Barrow promoted explorations in the early 19th century, while an attempt by Sir John Franklin (1845) to find the north-west passage led to his disappearance and ultimate confirmation of his death. The 40 or more search parties sent out after him brought back valuable information about the Arctic regions. In 1850 the British arctic explorer Robert McClure completed a west–east crossing, but the first continuous voyage remained unachieved. In 1878–79 the Swedish Baron Nordenskjöld undertook the first traverse of the north-east passage from Norway to the Bering Strait, but the north-west passage was not completed until the voyage of the Norwegian Roald AMUNDSEN in 1903–06. During the 20th century there have been many Arctic expeditions made by Soviet, US, and European scientists seeking ways to develop and exploit the region; a number of drifting observation stations have also been set up on ice floes. In 1968 oil was discovered in northern Alaska, and exploration for further Arctic oilfields has continued. The first vessel to cross the North Pole underwater was a US nuclear submarine, the *Nautilus*, in 1958 and in 1977 the Soviet icebreaker *Arktika* was the first surface ship to reach the Pole.

Arctic societies Two distinct cultural groups resident in the region around the North Pole; those of the western hemisphere, now known as the Inuit, and those of the eastern hemisphere, who include the Lapps. The societies of the eastern hemisphere are predominantly semi-nomadic pastoralists, while the Inuit are exclusively hunters. Arctic cultural boundaries are more difficult to define than geographical ones, especially in the eastern hemisphere where the social groupings are more diverse than those in the west. The pastoralists of the east often spend the winter in the coniferous forest, or taiga, of the region, and move their herds during the summer months to the pastures of the Arctic tundra. Shamanism and spirit worship or animism were common throughout this region, although such traditional beliefs are now in decline. The Inuit, by contrast, are mostly coastal dwellers, and hunt for fish and small aquatic mammals, such as seal and walrus. The basic unit of social organization is the family; during the winter, several families congregate in small settlements, and disperse throughout the brief months of summer, although many Inuit now live in permanent settlements.

Ardennes Campaign (also called Battle of the Bulge) (16–26 December 1944) The last serious German counter offensive against Allied armies advancing into Germany in World War II (NORMANDY CAMPAIGN). It resulted from a decision by Hitler to make an attack through hilly, wooded country and thereby take the US forces by surprise. Last-ditch resistance at several points, notably at Bastogne, held the Germans up long enough for the Allies to recover and prevent the Germans reaching their objective of Antwerp.

Areopagus A council which met on the hill of that name in ancient ATHENS. Drawn in the beginning from the richest class, the Eupatridae, it was originally an advisory body to the kings, but by the 7th century BC virtually ruled Athens. Its influence was still considerable in the early 5th century. Ephialtes' removal of its 'guardianship of the laws' in 462–61 marked the beginning of the radical ATHENIAN DEMOCRACY. It continued to judge some criminal and religious cases, but power thereafter lay with the popular assembly and the lawcourts.

Argentina The second largest country of South America, occupying nearly the whole of the south-east of the continent, from the Andes to the Atlantic Ocean and from tropical Bolivia to the Southern Ocean, the latter being a distance of nearly 3,700 km (2,300 miles).

Physical. In the west the cordillera, some of it volcanic, contains deposits of many minerals, copper, zinc, tungsten, and mica among them. The foothills are wooded, except in the south, and shelter valleys with vineyards and orchards. In the extreme north is the Gran Chaco, an area of subtropical forest and swamp, from which run tributaries of the Paraná. The Chaco yields hardwoods, and its southern part opens into land suitable for plantation crops. Southward, in the centre of the country, lie the pampas – a vast region of high plains which supports some of the best agricultural and livestock farming in the world. Further south is Patagonia, a series of cold, infertile plateaux which are suitable only for sheep grazing.

Economy. Argentina's principal exports are agricultural products such as cereals, soya beans, and meat, but there is also a broad range of manufacturing industry, of which petroleum products and chemicals are significant exports. A high percentage of agricultural land is taken up by large cattle-raising estates. Argentina has some oil and natural gas deposits (notably in Patagonia) whose exploitation is important to the development of industry. There is also a long-standing programme to develop nuclear technology. In recent years government policies, including extensive privatization, have successfully reduced very high rates of inflation.

History. Argentina was colonized by the Spanish from 1515 onwards, with settlers dedicating themselves to stock raising on the fertile pampas and agriculture in the areas of Salta, Jujuy, and Cordoba. In 1776 Argentina was incorporated into the viceroyalty of La Plata, with its capital in Buenos Aires; in addition to Argentina, the viceroyalty of La Plata comprised Uruguay, Paraguay, and Bolivia. The independence of the country, as the 'United Provinces of South America', was declared at the Congress of Tucuman in 1816. Divisional differences produced a series of conflicts between unitarios (centralists) and federales (federalists) which characterized much of the 19th century. The lack of political or constitutional legitimacy saw the emergence of the age of the CAUDILLOS until the promulgation of the National Constitution in 1853. The second half of the 19th century witnessed a demographic and agricultural revolution. The fertile plains (pampas) in the interior were transformed by means of foreign and domestic capital, while immigrant workers (principally from Spain and Italy), an extensive railway network, and the introduction of steamships and refrigeration vastly increased the export of cattle and grain. The influx of immigrants between 1870 and 1914 contributed to an increase in the national population from 1.2 million in 1852 to 8 million in 1914. Argentina's export-orientated economy proved vulnerable to the fluctuations of the international market, and the Great DEPRESSION saw a drop of 40% in the nation's exports. The military coup of 1930 saw the emergence of the armed forces as the arbiter of Argentinian politics. The failure of civilian democratic government and of achieving sustained economic growth has led to frequent military intervention. This was true even in the case of Peronism, the populist movement created with the support of trade unions by Juan Domingo PERON (1946–55). Perón was re-elected as President in 1973 after an 18-year exile. His death in 1974 was followed by another period of military dictatorship (1976–83) in a particularly bitter and tragic period of authoritarian rule, as a result of which an estimated 20,000 Argentinians lost their lives in the 'dirty war' waged by the junta against opposition groups. In 1982 the armed forces suffered a humiliating defeat in the war with Britain over the FALKLAND ISLANDS (Malvinas), and in 1983 a civilian administration was elected under President Raul Alfonsin of the Radical Party. The process of redemocratization in Argentina faced severe problems, most notably a virtually bankrupt economy and the political sensitivity of the armed forces to reform. The Perónist Justicialist Party came to power in 1989 with Carlos Menem as President. Diplomatic relations with Britain were restored and the economy deregulated. The constitution was amended in 1994, allowing the President to hold office for two terms. Menem triumphed again in presidential elections in 1995.

CAPITAL:	Buenos Aires
AREA:	2,780,092 sq km (1,073,399 sq miles)
POPULATION:	34.995 million (1996)
CURRENCY:	1 peso = 100 centavos
RELIGIONS:	Roman Catholic 92.0%; Protestant 3.0%; Jewish 2.0%
ETHNIC GROUPS:	White, mainly Spanish and Italian extraction 85.0%; Mestizo, Amerindian and other 15.0%
LANGUAGES:	Spanish (official); Italian; Amerindian languages
INTERNATIONAL ORGANIZATIONS:	UN; OAS; Non-Aligned Movement

Argos An important Peloponnesian city-state in ancient Greece. It reached a peak of power in the 7th century BC, possibly under King Pheidon. After his death it declined in influence, its position of supremacy in the Peloponnese being usurped by SPARTA. Argos remained neutral throughout the GREEK-PERSIAN WARS, and over the next century made unsuccessful attempts to reassert itself in the Peloponnese. It supported PHILIP II of Macedonia and finally joined the ACHAEAN LEAGUE.

Arianism The teaching of Arius (250–336 AD), a Libyan priest living in Alexandria, who preached a Christian heresy. He declared JESUS CHRIST was not divine, simply an exceptional human being. His teachings reached a wide audience, from the imperial household down to humble citizens. In 325 the Council of NICAEA excommunicated and banished him. After CONSTANTINE's death the Roman empire was divided on the issue, and another condemnation was issued at Constantinople in 381. Germanic invaders of the empire generally adopted Arianism as it was simpler than orthodox Christianity. It spread throughout western Europe and persisted in places until the 8th century.

Aristides (5th century BC) Athenian general and statesman. He fought at the Battle of MARATHON, was exiled in 482, but was recalled in time to fight at SALAMIS. He led the Athenian contingent at PLATAEA. He assessed the levels of tribute to be paid by members of the DELIAN LEAGUE and enjoyed a leading role in the early development of the ATHENIAN EMPIRE. He was famed for being scrupulously fair – hence his nickname 'the Just'.

Aristotle (384–322 BC) One of the most celebrated Greek philosophers. At the age of 17 he joined Plato's ACADEMY, where he stayed until shortly after Plato's death in 347. He was later (343–42) appointed tutor to ALEXANDER THE GREAT. In 335 he returned to Athens, where he established a school and a collection of manuscripts, which was the model for later libraries. He organized research projects, the fruit of one being a comparative study of 158 Greek constitutions. Following the death of Alexander in 323, he was charged with impiety and left Athens, dying soon afterwards in Chalcis.

His output was enormous and survives largely in the form of notes for lectures delivered at the Lyceum, successor to Plato's Academy. Aristotle's work encompasses dialogues which exist only in fragments; collections of historical information; the extant *Constitution of the Athenians* (though the authorship of this is now doubted); and scientific and philosophical works which are mostly extant, such as the *Nicomachaean Ethics*, the *Politics*, and the *Metaphysics*, some of which reveal the influence of Plato. These writings reveal the encyclopedic nature of Aristotle's interests and his logical, carefully organized work laid the foundations of many later philosophical enquiries. He introduced the systematic study of logic, developing a system for describing and assessing reasoning that remained the core of the discipline until the 19th century. Contemporary categorial grammar can be traced to Aristotle's interest in the functioning of words, giving him a special place in philosophical logic and in linguistics. The central questions of Aristotle's *Metaphysics* (What is substance?) and his *On Coming to be and Passing Away* (How do things come into existence and cease to exist?) are still hotly debated. In *De Anima* (On the Soul) Aristotle discussed the soul, or psyche; that which makes something alive and capable of the activities characteristic of life. In claiming that the psyche is dependent upon the body, Aristotle anticipated the mind/body debate current in philosophy of mind. Contemporary ETHICS also owes a debt to Aristotle's *Ethics*. His claim that all action aims at *eudaimonia*, or happiness, seemingly has much in common with modern-day UTILITARIANISM; however, Aristotle's stress on the several virtues is in tension with utilitarianism's promise of a single (if not simple) principle for deciding all moral questions.

Aristotle's work was rediscovered by Arab scholars, notably Avicenna and AVERROËS, and, translated into Latin, shaped the development of medieval thought in the arts and sciences. St Thomas AQUINAS reconciled the Aristotelian doctrines with those of Christian theology and they remained a key part of higher education in Europe from the 13th to the 17th centuries.

Armagnac A region in Gascony in south-west France. It was disputed by the English and French kings from the 12th century and gained independence from frequent changes of allegiance. Under English suzerainty by the Treaty of Calais in 1360 it continued to change hands in the HUNDRED YEARS WAR. The early 15th century saw a civil war fought between the Armagnacs against the Burgundians. The Armagnacs, led by their count, were supported by the nobility and the southern regions, while the Burgundians derived support in the north. In 1607 the whole region passed to the French crown.

Armenia A region south of the Caucasus in Asia Minor, comprising the Republic of Armenia (see ARMENIA, REPUBLIC OF) but also parts of eastern Turkey and northern Iran.
   Physical. The northern part of Armenia is very mountainous, containing high plateau-basins of which the largest is the vast Lake Sevan, while its Turkish part contains Mount Ararat and the sources of the Euphrates and Tigris Rivers.
   History. Armenian culture dates from the 6th century BC, when people who referred to themselves as the Hay and were descended from the ancient Phrygians founded a civilization on the ruins of the ancient kingdom of Urartu. After successive annexation over 500 years by the Persians, Macedonians (Alexander the Great), and Romans, the kingdom of Armenia reached its height under Tigranes II (95–55 BC). Further subjugation by Rome, the Byzantine Empire, Persia, and the Mongol Empire culminated in over two centuries of rule by the Turks, from the early 16th century onwards. In 1828 north-east Armenia was ceded by the OTTOMAN Turks to Russia. Agitation for independence developed in both Russian and Turkish Armenia, leading to a series of large-scale massacres that culminated in the deportation by the YOUNG TURK government of all Turkish Armenians to Syria and Palestine (1915), in which over one million died. A short-lived independent Transcaucasian Federal Republic, comprising Armenia, Azerbaijan, and Georgia, was created in 1917 but collapsed a year later. The separate republic of Armenia lasted from 1918 until 1920 when, following the Battle of Kars, Turkey captured some more Armenian territory. The remainder of Armenia proclaimed itself independent, but was again attacked by Turkey. It then became a Soviet Republic, and joined the Soviet Union. The Transcausian Republic was recreated as a Soviet Socialist Republic in 1922, but split in 1936. In Turkish Armenia, Turkish massacres and mass deportations continued until the Treaty of Lausanne (1923) confirmed incorporation of the region into the new republic of Turkey.

Armenia, Republic of A country in west Asia, formerly a constituent republic of the Soviet Union.
   Physical. The Republic of Armenia comprises the north-eastern part of the region of ARMENIA, the rest of the region forming part of Turkey.
   Economy. Mineral resources include copper, lead, and zinc, and there has been rapid industrial expansion, particularly in mechanical engineering, chemicals production, and mining. Agriculture, which includes cotton, rice, tobacco, fruit, and viticulture, remains important. There is considerable hydroelectric potential, but Armenia is dependent on imports for its other energy requirements.

   History. An independent Armenian republic was proclaimed in 1920, but in 1922 this was reunited with its former partners, Georgia and Azerbaijan, as the Transcaucasian Soviet Socialist Republic. This split in 1936 and the Soviet Socialist Republic of Armenia was proclaimed. In 1989 Armenian claims to Nagorno Karabagh, a predominantly Armenian and Christian region within Muslim AZERBAIJAN led to ethnic violence there. Armenia became independent in 1991, having declared itself no longer part of the Soviet Union. That same year the conflict in Nagorno-Karabagh escalated into full-scale fighting between Armenian and Azerbaijani troops. This continued until a ceasefire was agreed in 1994. In 1996 the region unilaterally declared independence. Attempts to broker a permanent peace settlement have continued.
   Armenia's first parliamentary elections since independence were held in 1995 and a new constitution was approved by a referendum. Further political crises ensued in the later 1990s, with allegations of fraud in the presidential elections and the resignation of the Prime Minister (1996) and the President (1998). In 1998 the hardline nationalist Robert Kocharyan was elected President by a landslide, giving rise to renewed fears for the stability of the region. Armenia is a member of the COMMONWEALTH OF INDEPENDENT STATES.

CAPITAL:	Yerevan
AREA:	29,766 sq km (11,490 sq miles)
POPULATION:	3.765 million (1996)
CURRENCY:	1 dram = 100 lumas
RELIGIONS:	Armenian Orthodox and Catholic Churches; minority faiths
ETHNIC GROUPS:	Armenian 93.0%; Azeri 2.0%; Russian and Kurdish minorities
LANGUAGES:	Armenian (official); Russian; minority languages
INTERNATIONAL ORGANIZATIONS:	UN; Commonwealth of Independent States; CSCE; North Atlantic Co-operation Council

Armenians A people of Indo-European origin who entered eastern Anatolia in the 8th and 7th centuries BC. They were incorporated within various empires, from that of the ACHAEMENIDS on, finally breaking free of the SELEUCIDS after the Battle of Magnesia in 189 BC. Tigranes the Great (c. 140–55 BC), who allied himself to MITHRIDATES VI, briefly carved out a sizeable empire, but in 66 BC he was defeated by POMPEY and became a client king of Rome. Armenia was subsequently a battle-ground for PARTHIA and Rome, and was divided between the SASSANIANS and BYZANTIUM in 387 AD. It had been converted to Christianity and its Church opposed the NESTORIANS, but following the Council of Chalcedon in 451 it broke with Western Christianity, and in c. 506 the Gregorian Church was established. The Arabs conquered the country c. 653, but in 885 an indigenous dynasty, the Bagatids, gained control. This lasted until the Seljuk Turks invaded, though many Armenians fled to CILICIA. Most of Armenia itself was ruled by the Ottomans from 1516.
   The latter-day history of the Armenian people has continued to be one of annexation and conquest. Subjected at the instigation of the Ottoman and Turkish republican governments to forced mass deportation or massacres in the late 19th and early 20th centuries, the Armenians are a tiny and inconspicuous minority

concentrated at present in Istanbul in Turkey; most Armenians are resident in Armenia, Azerbaijan, and Georgia, and in the USA, with minorities in Lebanon and Iran. Speaking Armenian, most Armenians are members of the Armenian Apostolic or the Armenian Catholic Churches. It is estimated that there are over 4 million worldwide. Since the 1970s Armenian terrorists (Armenian Secret Army for the Liberation of Armenia, ASALA) have conducted an efficient campaign, mostly against Turkish officials abroad, in an attempt to gain reparations for Turkey's atrocities against the Armenians, which have never been officially acknowledged by the Turkish government.

Arminius (*c.* 18 BC–19 AD) Leader of the Germanic resistance to Roman colonization. Son of a noble family, he served as an officer in the Roman auxiliary forces and became a Roman citizen. But he turned against Rome, and in 9 AD annihilated Quinctilius Varus and his three legions, thereby wrecking AUGUSTUS' German policy; and again in 16 he thwarted the attempt of TIBERIUS' nephew Germanicus to renew the conquest. However, he failed to unite the fragmented Germanic tribes; in 19 his own aspirations to kingship encountered popular opposition, and he was murdered. He was a superb tactician and a master of the surprise attack. TACITUS hailed him as 'the Liberator of Germany'.

Arminius, Jacobus (or Jakob Harmensen) (1560–1609) Dutch theologian, the founder of the theological movement known as Arminianism. He studied at Utrecht, Leiden, Basle, and Geneva before being ordained in 1588. The last six years of his life were spent as professor of theology at Leiden University, where he became involved in theological controversies with a colleague, Franciscus Gomarus. These centred on his rejection of the strict CALVINIST doctrine of absolute predestination or election and his arrival at a more liberal view of the relation between salvation and free will. Arminianism subsequently gave rise to the Dutch Remonstrant movement and in England it influenced Archbishop LAUD.

arms and armour Personal weapons and protective clothing used in combat or for ceremonial purposes, being regarded both as objects of beauty as well as of practical use. In Europe armourers have invariably been workers in metal, but in other parts of the world materials such as wickerwork, bone, and coconut fibre have been used. Outside Europe, the richest traditions of arms and armour have been in the Japanese and Indo-Persian cultures, in which metal (in the form of both mail and plate) is combined with leather and padded and studded textiles. European armour reached its highest peak of development in the 15th and 16th centuries, when plate armour, which had gradually replaced mail, encased the whole body in an ingeniously articulated suit. The finest armours were made in Germany and Milan, and the main English centre of production was Greenwich, where Henry VIII established workshops. Henry's own armours, however, were intended more for the tournament than the battlefield, because by the 16th century firearms were becoming so effective that armour could not be made proof against bullets without being excessively heavy. Cavalry continued to wear breast and back plates until the early 18th century, however. Among weapons, the sword occupies pride of place as the symbol of knighthood, justice, and power. Certain towns – notably Toledo in Spain in the 16th and 17th centuries – have been famous for their production, and in Japan the SAMURAI blades of the great swordsmiths are regarded with an almost religious veneration.

arms race A process in which two or more states, feeling themselves to be insecure or threatened, acquire armaments, each side responding to the acquisition of arms by the other with a further build-up of its own. This action-reaction mechanism may acquire a momentum of its own, fuelling perceptions of insecurity, threat, and the need for more armaments. This is particularly so during times of rapid technological innovation, as in the 'naval race' between Britain and Germany to build DREADNOUGHTS before World War I. A more recent example was the US-Soviet arms race, especially their competition for strategic nuclear weaponry, which started after World War II (see COLD WAR). Some believe arms races to be a cause of conflict; to others they are a reflection of underlying political distrust, not a cause of it. One theory on arms races is that, if controlled at a key stability point, they may contribute to some kind of strategic stability, akin to a BALANCE OF POWER.

army An organized force of men or women armed for fighting on land. Armies came into existence with the earliest states, and underpinned the great empires of antiquity: Egypt, Babylon, and Assyria. The essential components of armies in early history were infantry, with some chariots, and cavalry. In ancient Greece the tendency towards greater professionalism reached its climax with the Macedonian army of ALEXANDER THE GREAT. From this time on, the development of siege techniques was an important part of military practice. The generals of Carthage, especially HANNIBAL, hired mercenaries to great effect in their forces, but it was the armies of Rome, gradually evolving into fully professional standing forces, which dominated Europe from the 2nd century BC to the 5th century AD. Less organized but swiftly moving armies then came to the fore in the DARK AGES, from those of ATTILA the Hun to the MONGOLS. In Europe in the Middle Ages the limitations of the heavily armoured mounted knight were finally exposed by Swiss infantry armed with pikes or halberds and English infantry armed with longbows. The use of mercenaries (CONDOTTIERE) became commonplace.

The major advances of the 15th and 16th centuries were the invention of gunpowder and the development of cannon. Organization, discipline, and further advances in weaponry led to the creation of highly efficient armies, most notably those of FREDERICK II (the Great) of Prussia. In the late 18th century European armies were mainly of mercenaries recruited (often under pressure) and trained by a professional officer class. The first conscript armies were recruited in France to fight the REVOLUTIONARY and NAPOLEONIC WARS. During the 19th century most European countries adopted a system of conscription of young men to train and serve for about two years. (Britain only enforced conscription in 1916–18, and again between 1939 and 1959.) In 1800 military battles followed a strict and formal pattern. Infantry were lined into well-drilled rows, firing muskets and advancing with bayonets, backed up by field guns. Cavalry divisions, armed with sabres, provided mobility. European armies played an essential role in 19th- and early 20th-century IMPERIALISM, their superior fire-power enabling them to dominate the peoples of Africa and Asia. The AMERICAN CIVIL WAR 1861–65 saw large armies of the Union (the North) and the Confederacy (the South) engaged in a struggle in which railways were crucial for movement of troops, and new infantry weapons, such as the breech-loading rifle and the repeating carbine, were developed. By the time of the FRANCO-PRUSSIAN WAR in 1870–71 heavy artillery was developing, but infantry and cavalry tactics remained little changed until World War I, when motor transport and heavier artillery developed. Even then, armies were slow to adapt to armoured vehicles, and the massed infantry attacks of its battles still used rifle, bayonet, and hand-grenade as their basic weapons, now pitched against machine-guns. By World War II armies were fully motorized, and tanks played a major part in the NORTH AFRICAN CAMPAIGN and at the EASTERN FRONT. This mobility required large back-up fuel and maintenance services. Basic infantry tactics still remained essential (even though the rifle was being replaced by the semiautomatic or automatic submachine gun), especially in the jungle warfare of the BURMA CAMPAIGN. They remained so for later campaigns in Korea, Vietnam, and the Falklands. In the COLD WAR balance of power, large armies of NATO and the WARSAW PACT continued to face one another in Europe, armed with both conventional weapons and missiles. Allied victory in the GULF WAR was achieved through massive tank deployment. Since the end of the Cold War the armies of UN member nations have increasingly been combined to form multinational peacekeeping and 'rapid reaction' forces. (See illustration.)

Arnhem, Battle of (September 1944) Battle in Holland in World War II. Parachutists of the 1st Allied Airborne Division (British, US, Polish) were dropped in an attempt to capture key bridges over the Lower Rhine to enable the Allied armies to advance more rapidly into Germany. The attempt failed, and resulted in 7,000 Allied casualties. German units blocked the path of Allied divisions, which were attempting to reach and reinforce the airborne troops.

Arnold, Benedict (1741–1801) US soldier and traitor. He was a hero of the early stages of the War of INDEPENDENCE, serving with conspicuous valour at TICONDEROGA, the invasion of Canada, and SARATOGA. After 1778, possibly persuaded by his loyalist wife, he began plotting with George CLINTON to deliver West Point to the British. When his courier, Major André, was captured, he fled to the British, for whom he fought thereafter. He died, neglected, in England.

Artaxerxes II (c. 436–358 BC) King of Persia (404–358), the son of Darius II. He crushed the rebellion of his younger brother CYRUS II at Cunaxa in 401. By the peace of Antalcidas, made with the Spartans in 386, he recovered the Greek cities of Asia Minor, but he was unsuccessful in his attempts to repossess Egypt, and he put down the SATRAPS' revolt of 366–358 only with difficulty. His son, Artaxerxes III, killed his brothers and crushed two rebellious satraps in order to establish his power. In 343 he finally forced Egypt back into the empire, but his reign was one of terror and he was murdered by his minister Bagoas in 338.

art history The study of the history of the fine arts and of the applied arts. The term can embrace a variety of intellectual approaches, from the cataloguing of museum collections, where the primary object is to establish a body of factual information about each object, to philosophical musings on the relationship of art and society or the nature of beauty. It also includes the process of attribution: the assignment to an artist of a work of uncertain authorship, based on stylistic or written evidence (such as letters or dealers' records). As an academic discipline, art history developed in Germany in the 19th century, but its origins stretch back much further. Various Greek and Roman writers commented on the history of the arts, notably PLINY the Elder in his encyclopedic work *Natural History* (1st century), and the 15th-century Florentine sculptor Lorenzo Ghiberti wrote a manuscript called *Commentaries* that includes a survey of ancient art and the first artist's autobiography to have survived. The man who put art history on the map, however, was Giorgio Vasari, whose *Lives of the Artists* (1550) inspired many later collections of biographies. Vasari said that he aimed at 'investigating the causes and roots of styles and why the arts improved or declined', and this idea of art following an evolutionary pattern of decay and revival proved immensely influential. In the 18th century a new approach was initiated by Johann Joachim Winckelmann, who regarded art as the most noble manifestation of a nation's soul. Winckelmann played a major role in establishing Germany as the home of art-historical studies, and it was there, during the 19th century, that two contrasting approaches to the subject developed: on the one hand the analysis of the formal qualities of a work of art was seen as paramount; on the other, the work was studied in its historical context, with emphasis on subject-matter. In the 20th century art history has moved from being a somewhat elitist subject to one that is a popular part of the school curriculum.

Arthur A legendary figure, supposedly King of the Britons, for whom there is probably some historical basis. Son of Uther Pendragon and guided in childhood by the magician Merlin, Arthur won the crown by drawing the magic sword Excalibur from a stone. A hero of Celtic and medieval Christian mythology, Arthur is portrayed by writers as a powerful medieval king attracting to his court at Camelot an élite corps of knights (the 'Round Table') bound by the ideals of CHIVALRY and a semi-mystical form of Christianity. Knights of the Round Table include Launcelot, Gawain, Tristram, and Sir Galahad. Their highest quest was for the Holy Grail, the cup of the Last Supper and the symbol of perfection. Other legends give prominence to the love of Launcelot and Arthur's Queen, Guinevere, and the love of Tristram and Iseult. A rebellion led by Arthur's nephew (or son) Modred, who had seduced Guinevere, brought disaster to his kingdom and left Arthur mortally wounded.

Such legends have little connection with any historical Arthur. The writer NENNIUS (9th century) claimed that Arthur commanded a mixed Roman–British force against the Saxons, whose raids on Britain increased with the departure of the Roman legions (c. 450). According to Nennius, Arthur inflicted a major defeat on the SAXONS at Mount Badon (c. 518), but was mortally wounded in a later battle at Camlan (c. 537). GILDAS,

(a) Macedonian hoplite and phalanx
early 4th century BC

(b) Roman centurion
1st century AD

(c) Mongolian mounted archer
early 13th century

(d) mounted knight
mid 14th century

(e) Swiss halberdier
mid 15th century

(f) musketeer
early 16th century

(g) artilleryman and 6-pounder
mid 18th century

army   The basis of Alexander the Great's army was the hoplite (a), organized into phalanxes and supported by other lightly armed troops and cavalry. The Roman foot-soldiers (b) were also backed by cavalry. Mongol archers (c) used three types of arrow, suitable for different ranges. Chain mail (d) evolved to full plate armour by the 15th century, but the greater manoeuvrability of the Swiss pikemen and halberdiers (e) eventually led to the demise of the armoured knights. The invention of gunpowder contributed to the replacement of the archers and the foot-soldiers by musketeers (f) and during the reign of Frederick the Great quite sophisticated artillery (g) was being used.

(a) riflemen
*c.*1810 (British)

(b) cavalry
*c.*1855 (British)

(c) field-gun
*c.*1864 (US Gatling)

(d) field-gun
*c.*1917 (French long-range Filloux)

(e) tank
*c.*1941 (German PZkpfw III)

(f) mobile anti-aircraft missile launcher
*c.*1982 (British Rapier)

Sketch (a) is of British riflemen in the Peninsular War. They were armed with muzzle-loading flintlocks. Breach-loading rifles (Enfields) were first issued to British infantry in 1842. Mobility was provided by cavalry (sketch (b)), who were armed with such weapons as the sabre and sword, armies only slowly adapting to motorized fighting after World War I, with the development of the tank (e). Artillery field-guns (c) and (d) were developed rapidly in the second half of the 19th century as the armaments industry grew, while mobile launchers (f) were used from the 1960s onwards in Vietnam, the Falklands, Afghanistan, and the Gulf War.

writing before 547, mentioned Badon but did not connect Arthur with the victory, and neither Mount Badon nor Camlan has been identified. The great number of places in Britain associated with Arthur indicates that belief in his heroic deeds was widespread from the 6th century onwards.

Arthur, Chester A(lan) (1830–86) Twenty-first President (1881–85) of the USA. Born in Vermont, he campaigned for the abolition of slavery, while helping to organize his state's REPUBLICAN PARTY. In 1871 he became Collector of the Port of New York, one of the most lucrative sources of political patronage. Caught in the crossfire of the self-styled STALWARTS and 'Half Breeds' (Republican reformers) over the SPOILS SYSTEM during the presidency of HAYES, he was, nevertheless, nominated as James GARFIELD's running mate in the election of 1880. He became President when Garfield was assassinated in office. Arthur repudiated the spoils system, and supported the PENDLETON ACT, which reformed the civil services. He failed to secure re-nomination in 1884.

Artigas, José Gervasio (1764–1850) National hero of Uruguay. He led the Uruguyan movement for independence from Spain during the years 1811–13 and maintained this in the face of the territorial ambitions of Argentina in 1814. Uruguay also had to contend with Portuguese expansionists from Brazil, and Portuguese troops captured Montevideo in 1817. Artigas was unable to dislodge them. He conducted guerrilla warfare against them for three years but in 1820 was forced to retreat to Argentina, and never returned to Uruguay.

Artois, Charles, Comte d' CHARLES X.

Arusha Declaration (1967) A major policy statement by President Nyerere of TANZANIA. The text was agreed by the executive of the political party TANU (Tanganyika African National Union) and proposed that TANU implement a socialist programme by which the major means of production would be placed under the collective ownership of the farmers and workers of the country. No party member would be allowed more than one salary or to own more than one house, nor any capitalist stocks and shares. Banks were nationalized, followed by large industrial and insurance companies, as well as the larger trading firms. Nyerere was deeply committed to the concept of *ujamaa*, which saw all land and natural resources as belonging to the people within their village communities, and following the declaration there emerged many farm collectives. The policy was moderated after 1977 to allow some private investment, and largely abandoned after 1987.

Aryans Ancient settlers in the Indian subcontinent, speakers of an Indo-European language. The Aryans, a people of uncertain racial origin, invaded India from Persia, gradually conquering the resident Dravidian and Munda peoples in the period 2000–1200 BC. The following millennium witnessed gradual eastward expansion and progressive absorption of the indigenous population, as well as the evolution of the Vedic caste system, but the emerging hierarchical agrarian society remained split between warring petty states. In the late 4th century BC northern India was united for the first time by the MAURYAN dynasty, founded by Chandragupta, which ruled over an area stretching from Herat to the Ganges delta from its capital at Pataliputra, establishing an extensive administrative system and a regular army before being overthrown in the 2nd century BC by the Sunga dynasty. The upsurge of BUDDHISM led in the 3rd century BC to the establishment of the short-lived empire of ASOKA which at the pinnacle of its strength included most of the subcontinent, but the west remained the stronghold of the original Aryan culture, and served as the home for HINDUISM.

Arya Samaj A Hindu reform movement. Founded in 1875 by Swami Dayananda Saraswati (c. 1825–83), it appealed to the authority of the *Vedas* in support of programmes of social reform and education. Its supporters, such as Lala Rajpat Rai, were prominent in political movements opposed to British rule, and their activities aggravated Hindu relations with Sikhs and Muslims.

Asante (Ashanti) The largest and most prestigious of the chiefdoms of Ghana, in West Africa. It emerged, under the Asantehene Osei Tutu in the 1670s, as a powerful kingdom, the Asante Confederacy, ruled by the Asantehene from Kumasi (now in Ghana). The wealth of the confederacy was based on the control of trade, particularly of cola nuts, and of gold mines, and by selling slaves for European goods to the European trading stations established along the Gold Coast of West Africa. In 1807 the Asante occupied Fanti coastal territory. Following the British abolition of the slave trade they fought the British between 1824 and 1831, and again in 1874, when WOLSELEY took and burned Kumasi, the Asante capital. Further troubles (1895–96) ended in the establishment of a Protectorate and the exile of Asantehene PREMPEH I, and in 1901 Britain annexed the country. In 1924 Prempeh was allowed to return and an Asante Confederacy Council was set up in 1935 as an organ of local government, the Asantehene being head. In that year the Golden Stool, symbolizing the soul of the Asante people, was restored to Kumasi.

The people of the southern tropical forest of Ghana, who are also known as Asante, are a primarily agricultural people who farm crops for local consumption and produce cocoa as an important export crop. Asante society is organized on the principle of matrilineal descent (from men to men, via their mothers and sisters), but the Asante also recognize spiritual characteristics inherited from the father. The office of lineage head is symbolized by a lineage stool.

asceticism (from Greek, *askeo*, 'to exercise' or 'to train') A system of austere religious practices designed to combat the natural passions and inclinations in order to strengthen spiritual life. The word has its origins in strict regimes of training for athletes, but the idea has formed part of religions and philosophies throughout history. Ascetic practices range from abstinence, fasting, monastic codes, and a life of solitary contemplation and physical austerity as a hermit, to the extremes of flagellation and self-mutilation. Ascetic cults are found in CHRISTIANITY, HINDUISM, and ISLAM. In many cases, asceticism reflects a low estimation of the human body and physical life. Both Gnosticism and MANICHAEISM, heretical movements in the early Christian Church, subscribed to dualistic views of the universe, denigrating all that was physical, a belief which led to extreme asceticism among their followers. More orthodox Christians also viewed self-denial and sacrifice as a way of following Christ's example, and by the 4th century, monasticism, which stipulated celibacy, poverty, and obedience, had become established. Ascetic practices are still especially prominent in Eastern Orthodox communities. In Hinduism, the *sādhu* or holy man increases his spiritual strength through sexual abstinence and fasting, as well as through practices such as self-laceration. Within Islam, some SUFIS stress ascetic practices such as fasting and sleep deprivation. Although BUDDHISM, on the other hand, advocates the 'Middle Way', the avoidance of the extremes of both asceticism and hedonism, Buddhist monasticism includes many ascetic practices and exercises.

Ascham, Roger (1515–68) English scholar, an influential exponent of the NEW LEARNING. From 1540 he was reader in Greek at St John's College, Cambridge and in 1545 he published a popular treatise on archery, *Toxophilus*, which earned him a royal pension. He was tutor to the future ELIZABETH I for two years and subsequently engaged in diplomatic missions for MARY I and Elizabeth I. *The Scholemaster* (published in 1570) advocated an enlightened approach to education including the teaching of the English language as well as the classics.

Ashikaga (also called Muromachi, from the district in Kyoto where, after 1392, the shoguns lived) The SHOGUNATE in Japan from 1339 to 1573. In 1333 Ashikaga Takanju (1305–58) overthrew the HOJO, who had acted as regents for the KAMAKURA shoguns. Soon after he drove the emperor Go-Daigo from the capital of Kyoto. In the ensuing dynastic dispute he installed Koyo as emperor, and in return the emperor appointed him shogun in succession to the Kamakura shogunate, which had become ineffectual. He moved the shogunate from Kamakura to Kyoto. The Ashikaga shoguns never exercised great power as the shogunate witnessed much fighting between rival DAIMYO and their SAMURAI armies. The increasing disorder of the Ashikaga shogunate ended in 1573 when ODA NOBUNAGA and his army drove the shogun from Kyoto.

Ashley, William Henry (1778–1838) US fur-trader and politician. In 1822 he founded the Rocky Mountain Fur Company to develop the fur trade in the far west of North America. Between 1822 and 1826 he organized expeditions across the Rockies by the South Pass, penetrating to Great Salt Lake and the Green River valley, opening up rich fur areas and the route to be followed by later settlers travelling to Oregon. Instead of using the trading forts he introduced annual meetings of fur traders, the first being held in Green River, in 1825. The system revolutionized the fur trade and in two years made him a private fortune. He retired from trade in 1827 and devoted the rest of his life to politics, being elected to the House of Representatives in 1831.

Ashley Cooper, Anthony SHAFTESBURY.

Ashurbanipal Ruler of the ASSYRIAN empire (669–626 BC). His reign was the apogee of Assyrian power, although it collapsed soon after his death. Early in his reign, Egypt rebelled successfully and broke away, but when one of his half-brothers attempted the same thing in Babylon several years later, he crushed him. Although he campaigned vigorously in other parts of his empire

too, he was no mere warrior-king. A man of culture, and a patron of the arts, he assembled a large and wide-ranging library in Nineveh.

Asia The largest continent in the world, occupying a third of its land surface. Asia stretches from the Arctic to the Equator and from the Ural Mountains to the Pacific Ocean. Asia includes the Indian sub-continent, the peninsula of Asia Minor, and numerous islands, including JAPAN, the PHILIPPINES, and INDONESIA.

Physical. The extreme north is mainly tundra, which gives way to the vast expanse of Siberia. The land rises to the south and central Asia is mountainous, containing the Himalayas, the highest mountains in the world. Major rivers, including the Indus, the Ganges, the Mekong, and the Yangtze provide water and sediment for large areas of India and China. The volcanic and earthquake zone at the edge of the Eurasian plate runs from Japan, across the south of the continent to Turkey in the west.

History. The ancient civilizations of SUMERIA, BABYLON, ASSYRIA, Media, and Persia, as well as those of CHINA and INDIA, arose in Asia. The world's major religions originated in Asia, Judaism and Christianity expanding westwards. Population movements have been affected by the topography, many cultures surviving in isolation in the mountains while conquerers, such as the HUNS, MONGOLS, and COSSACKS, created vast empires. European trade with China was taking place via the SILK ROUTE as early as the 2nd centry BC. In the 15th century sea routes, discovered by such explorers as Vasco DA GAMA led to the creation of such companies as the EAST INDIA COMPANIES that were keen to exploit new resources. The European colonial powers acquired lands in Asia and it was not until the 20th century that European influence began to wane as former colonies gained independence. The creation of the SOVIET UNION saw the rise of communism. The USA became involved in the KOREAN WAR and its fears of a major communist alliance were only averted by the ideological divergence of the Soviet Union and China after 1960. The VIETNAM WAR proved disastrous for the USA. Meanwhile Japan led a regional economic boom, the 'tiger economies' of south-east Asian nations in particular growing rapidly in the 1980s and early 1990s. The Middle East has continued to be troubled by violent unrest, but advances have been made in relations between ISRAEL and the Palestinians (see PALESTINE LIBERATION ORGANIZATION).

asiento de negros A contract made between Britain and Spain in 1713 for the sale of slaves to the Spanish American colonies. In the Peace of UTRECHT (1713) Spain granted Britain a monopoly of the supply of slaves to the Spanish American colonies of 144,000 slaves at 4,800 a year for 30 years, with other privileges. They were the origin of the speculation which resulted in the SOUTH SEA BUBBLE. They led to endless disputes, and to the War of JENKINS'S EAR between England and Spain in 1739. The treaty was ended by agreement in 1750.

Askia Muhammad I (d. 1528) Emperor of SONGHAY (1493–1528) in West Africa. Originally named Muhammad Turé, he was SONNI ALI's best general. He usurped Songhay from Ali's son in 1493, thus founding a new dynasty, and took the title Askia. He was a convert to Islam, but tolerant towards pagans, and made the pilgrimage to MECCA, meeting many notable men, especially the great Muslim teacher al-Maghili. He had close political and commercial relationships with Morocco and Egypt, organized an efficient administration, and an army and a navy on the River Niger, and made TIMBUKTU the capital of the Songhay empire and an important intellectual and religious centre.

Asoka The last great MAURYAN Emperor of India (ruled c. 265–c. 238 BC). He is remembered chiefly for his patronage of Buddhism and his high ethical standards as a ruler. Adoption of the Buddhist *dharma* (teaching on religious truth) led him to an overriding concern for the spiritual and material welfare of his subjects, and to toleration of other religions.

He inherited an empire which already extended over the entire subcontinent except the extreme south. After one successful campaign he renounced warfare because of the suffering it generated. Although his empire disintegrated soon after his death, he is regarded as one of the greatest of the subcontinent's early rulers. Knowledge of his empire derives mainly from inscriptions carved on rocks and pillars in far-flung parts of the subcontinent and indicate that he was an efficient ruler who strengthened and humanized a remarkable administrative system, incorporating a standing army of 700,000, a widespread secret service, and a large bureaucracy. Asoka's lasting influence on India is embodied in the country's adoption of his Sarnath lion capital as one of its national emblems.

Asquith, Herbert Henry, 1st Earl of Oxford and Asquith (1852–1928) British statesman, Liberal Prime Minister (1908–16). He served as Home Secretary (1892–95) and in 1905 joined the government of CAMPBELL-BANNERMAN as Chancellor of the Exchequer. He introduced three skilful budgets, the third setting up Old Age Pensions, and he supported other important social legislation such as the abolition of sweatshops and the establishment of labour exchanges. When Campbell-Bannerman fell ill (April 1908) Asquith became Prime Minister, supporting LLOYD GEORGE in his fight for the People's Budget and the creation of the NATIONAL INSURANCE scheme of 1911. Other important legislation included the PARLIAMENT ACT (1911) and an Act to pay Members of Parliament. The later years of his ministry were beset with industrial unrest (TONYPANDY) and violence in parts of IRELAND over his HOME RULE BILL. The Bill to disestablish the Anglican Church in WALES provoked much hostility before being passed. In 1915 he formed a coalition government with the Conservatives, but in the conduct of World War I he was too detached to provide dynamic leadership. Discontent grew and in 1916 LLOYD GEORGE displaced him. The division in the Liberal Party between his supporters and those of Lloyd George lasted until 1926, when Asquith resigned the leadership of the party.

Assad, Hafez al (1928–) Syrian politician, secretary-general of the BA'ATHIST party and president of Syria from 1971. Assad is one of the longest-serving and most influential leaders of the Middle East; after positions as an air force general and defence minister, he became prime minister after a bloodless coup in 1970, and was elected president the following year. In the effectively one-party state that Assad created, he was re-elected president in 1978, 1985, and 1991. He lost the GOLAN HEIGHTS in the YOM KIPPUR WAR against Israel in 1973, but won increasing influence in Lebanon after committing some 50,000 troops to the civil war there (1975–90). Though initially allying Syria closely to the Soviet Union, and opposing the 1977 CAMP DAVID ACCORD between Egypt and Israel, Assad has adopted a more pro-Western stance since the late 1980s, opposing Iranian-sponsored terrorism in Lebanon, contributing forces to the UN coalition against Iraq in the GULF WAR of 1991, and entering into negotiations with Israel from 1995 as part of a US-brokered Middle East peace plan.

assassin (from the Arabic *hashishiyun*, 'smoker of hashish') A member of a secret sect of the ISMAILI branch of Shiite Islam. It was founded by Hasan ibn al-Sabbah in 1078 to support the claim of Nizar to the FATIMID caliphate, and established a headquarters at Alamut in north-west Persia. The assassins wielded influence through suicide squads of political murderers, confident of earning a place in paradise if they died while obeying orders. The MONGOL Hulagu took Alamut in 1256, executing the grand master of the order. Their last Syrian strongholds fell to the MAMELUKE Baybars in 1273. (The widely scattered Nizari branch of the Ismailis, who revere the Aga Khan, are their spiritual descendants.)

assizes A procedure introduced into English law in the later 12th century by HENRY II. The Assize of Clarendon (1166), which dealt with criminal trials and the Assize of Arms (1181), which reorganized local defence and police measures, were enactments made at sessions of the king's council. The assizes of novel disseisin and mort d'ancestor (both relating to tenancy), and the Grand Assize (to determine titles to disputed lands) were introduced by sessions of Henry II's council (1166, 1176, and the late 1170s); these procedures remained important throughout the Middle Ages.

Travelling justices were established in the 13th century; these justices came to be called justices of assize, and their sessions were called assizes. A system of such judicial sessions was regularized (1293–1328) and judicial circuits were established that remained in force until a new system of Crown Courts was set up in 1971.

Association of South-East Asian Nations (ASEAN) A regional organization formed by Indonesia, Malaysia, the Philippines, Singapore, and Thailand through the Bangkok Declaration of 1967. It has subsequently been joined by Brunei (1984), Vietnam (1995), Laos (1997), and Myanmar (Burma) (1997). ASEAN aims to accelerate and to promote regional stability. It has facilitated exchange of administrative and cultural resources and co-operation in transport and communication, with a permanent secretariat in Jakarta. In 1992 it agreed to create the ASEAN Free Trade Area (AFTA) as the first step towards the creation of an ASEAN common market. Since ASEAN members have historically given priority to external rather than intra-ASEAN trade, one of its principal roles has been to negotiate with other countries and with such organizations as the EUROPEAN UNION. From its inception ASEAN opposed communist regimes in other Asian countries such as North Vietnam and, subsequently, Laos and Cambodia (Kampuchea). From 1978 it gave political backing to the Khmer Rouge-dominated coalition in Kampuchea, which opposed the Vietnamese-backed regime, and sought diplomatic collaboration to end Vietnamese occupation.

Assyria An area of northern Mesopotamia centred on the city of Ashur (or Assur), which became a Semitic state. The first Assyrian empire was established early in the 2nd millennium BC, and many documents discovered in Anatolia attest to vigorous commercial intercourse with that part of the world. Shamshi-Adad I (ruled *c.* 1813–1781 BC) brought Mesopotamia under his control, but after his death his empire collapsed. It was attacked by HAMMURABI of BABYLON and then fell to the Mitanni, a people from the west. Assyria re-emerged as a political power under Ashur-uballit I (ruled *c.* 1362–1327 BC) and his successors. The Mitanni were conquered, northern Mesopotamia was secured, and under Tukulti-Ninurta I (ruled 1242–1206 BC) Babylon was captured. Following this king's death Assyrian fortunes declined until Tiglath-Pileser I (ruled *c.* 1114–1076 BC) revived them, although the pressure of Aramaean nomads migrating from the east posed a threat to the stability of the Assyrian civilization. The years 911 to 824 saw Assyrian expansion, with the empire extending to the Mediterranean coast. Iron was extensively traded and was the main source of wealth. The peak of Assyrian power and civilization began with the reign of Tiglath-Pileser III (ruled 744–727 BC), who reconquered Babylon but allowed it to retain limited autonomy. This policy did not ensure peace, and Babylon was destroyed in 689 by SENNACHERIB who made Nineveh his capital. His son Esarhaddon even conquered Egypt, which he ruled through native princes, but the Egyptians rebelled against his successor ASHURBANIPAL, who suffered other revolts which further weakened his empire. Finally Nabopolassar, a Chaldean, took control of Babylon in 625 BC, and under attack from him and the Medes Assyrian power collapsed. The Assyrians were famed as ruthless soldiers, armed with iron weapons, and were sophisticated not only in military technique, but also in administration, art, and architecture.

Astor, John Jacob (1763–1848) US fur trader and financier. Emigrating from Germany in 1779, he worked with his brother, a maker of musical instruments in London, until 1783, when he set sail for North America. He entered the US fur trade and by 1800 had established the beginnings of a commercial empire, with chartered ships plying both the Atlantic and the Pacific. His American Fur Company, formed in 1808, dominated the fur trade in the prairies and mountains within a decade. In 1834 he sold his interest in the fur trade and spent his remaining years managing his highly profitable property holdings.

Atahualpa (d. 1533) The last ruler of the INCA EMPIRE, son of Huayna Capac. Ruling from 1525 in QUITO, he defeated Huáscar, his half-brother and co-ruler in CUZCO, whom he killed after the battle of Huancavelica in 1530. In 1532 he marched against PIZARRO and remnants of the Huáscar faction, who had allied themselves to the Spaniards; at Cajamarca he was drawn into an ambush, captured, and held for ransom. He ordered a room to be filled with gold and silver objects while another army secretly marched to free him, but was murdered when Pizarro learned of it. Shortly thereafter Pizarro captured Cuzco and within a few years Spain ruled the lands of the Incas.

Atatürk, Mustafa Kemal (Turkish, 'Father of the Turks', 1881–1938) Founder of modern Turkey. An Ottoman officer, he distinguished himself during World War I. In May 1919 he was appointed inspector-general of the 9th Army in Samsun, Anatolia, and organized Turkish resistance to the proposed VERSAILLES PEACE SETTLEMENT for the OTTOMAN EMPIRE. The defeat of Greek forces in 1922 paved the way for the recognition of Turkey's independence at Lausanne (1923), the abolition of the sultanate, the establishment of the republic (1923), and the abolition (1924) of the caliphate (the temporal and spiritual leadership of the Muslim community). As first President of the republic (1923–38) Atatürk defined the principles of the state in the so-called six arrows of Kemalism: republicanism, nationalism, populism, statism, secularism, and revolution. His policies involved a rejection of the Islamic past and the creation of a secular Turkish state over which he ruled until his death.

Athanasius, St (*c.* 295–373) Bishop of Alexandria. He was a vehement opponent of ARIANISM and refused CONSTANTINE's request to restore the excommunicated Arius and was subsequently himself exiled five times by Constantine and later emperors. His theological position was confirmed at the first Council of Constantinople in 381 when Arianism was finally prohibited and the Nicene Creed, a statement of Christian belief, was approved.

atheism (from Greek, *a theos*, 'not god') The denial of the existence of any God or supernatural being. It should not be confused with the position of the AGNOSTIC, who holds that as the existence of God cannot be proved or disproved, it should not be subject to belief or disbelief. The atheist maintains, on the other hand, that the very notion of god is meaningless, a view also subscribed to by some Asian religious traditions, such as Theravada Buddhism. In the 19th century MARX based his atheism on materialism, and argued for the abolition of religion, which he saw as upholding an unjust socio-economic order. Communist theory, developed from Marxism, is strictly atheist. Friedrich Nietzsche proclaimed the 'death of God' and encouraged man to seek for the meaning of life in himself alone, a position also taken by 20th-century existentialists, such as Heidegger and Sartre. The modern philosophical school of logical positivism is also atheist, arguing that religious speculation is logically ill-founded, since knowledge can only be derived from observation and experience.

Athelstan (895–939) King of the English (926–39). As King of Wessex from 925 he established Wessex's supremacy throughout England, Wales, and southern Scotland, and defended it in an overwhelming defeat of a combined force of Scots and Danes at an unidentified place called Brunanburh (937) as recorded in the ANGLO-SAXON CHRONICLE. Athelstan's fame was not due solely to his military exploits. He provided sound government, reformed the coinage, granted charters to towns, and, in a century of legal reform, issued six series of laws.

Athenian democracy A form of popular government established in Athens by Cleisthenes in the last decade of the 6th century BC. At first, the AREOPAGUS retained considerable influence, during the GREEK-PERSIAN WARS, and it was only after Ephialtes stripped it of its powers in 462 that a more radical democracy came into being. Ephialtes died suddenly in mysterious circumstances but PERICLES pushed through further reforms, establishing in particular the important principle of pay for jury service.

The principal organ of democracy was the popular assembly (*ekklesia*), which was open to all Athenian male citizens aged over 18. All members had the right to speak, and it was the assembly which decided all legislative and policy matters. The council of 500 (*boule*), elected by lot for a year from Athenian male citizens over the age of 30, was an executive body which prepared business for the assembly and then saw that its decisions were carried out. Pericles dominated the democracy until his death in 429, but none of the 'demagogues' who followed him achieved the same level of influence. Radical democracy had its dangers, however: established laws were sometimes overridden by the assembly, and skilled orators could easily manipulate listeners' emotions.

Athenian empire The cities and islands mainly in the Aegean area that paid tribute to ATHENS in the 5th century BC. It developed out of the DELIAN LEAGUE as Athens, by virtue of its great naval superiority, imposed its will on its allies. A significant step was the transference of the League's treasury from Delos to Athens probably in 454 BC, since this ensured for Athens absolute control of the tribute. Inscriptions and literary sources reveal the means by which Athens controlled its subjects: the installation of garrisons; the establishment of clenruchies (colonies) of Athenian citizens in important or rebellious areas; the encouragement of local democracies; the referral of important judicial cases to Athens; the imposition of Athenian weights and measures throughout the empire, and officials to keep an eye on subject cities.

As long as it had a strong navy, Athens could crush revolts and enforce its will throughout the Aegean, but the empire died with Athens' final defeat in the PELOPONNESIAN WAR. Nevertheless it did establish the Second Athenian Confederacy in 377 BC, trying to avoid the mistakes of the 5th century.

Athens The capital of modern Greece, historically an ancient Greek city-state. It was formed as a result of the unification of a number of small villages of ATTICA. It was first under the rule of hereditary kings, and monarchy was followed by a long-lived aristocracy, first successfully challenged by SOLON in 594 BC. Tyranny was established by PISISTRATUS, temporarily in 561 and more permanently in 546, until his son Hippias was driven out in 510. Within a few years Cleisthenes had put the ATHENIAN DEMOCRACY on to a firm footing.

In 490 BC and 480–479 the city-state enjoyed success in the GREEK-PERSIAN wars. Subsequently its rulers transformed the DELIAN LEAGUE into the ATHENIAN EMPIRE. The city supported brilliant artistic activity, attracting artists from throughout the Mediterranean. However, it was defeated by Sparta in the PELOPONNESIAN WAR, losing by 404 the empire, almost all its fleet, and the city walls. It recovered remarkably in the 4th century BC and led the resistance to PHILIP II OF MACEDONIA. The city was a centre of philosophy, science, and the arts, centred on the ACADEMY.

Athens was prey to the successors of Alexander the Great, losing its independence in 262 BC, though regaining it in 228. After supporting MITHRIDATES VI, King of Pontus, (120–63 BC) against Rome, it was successfully besieged by his antagonist, SULLA, and sacked (87–86). From then on its importance was as a university town which attracted many young men, particularly Romans. This apart, the city underwent a prolonged period of historical obscurity and economic decline. It was captured by the Turks in 1456, and suffered during the Venetian siege of 1687.

Atkinson, Sir Harry Albert (1831–92) New Zealand statesman. A pioneer farmer, he served in the national Parliament and in various ministries for nearly 30 years. He was Premier, 1876–77, 1883, and 1887–90. Though generally representing the conservative rural interest in matters such as land tax and retrenchment of government spending, he was also noted for his advocacy of radical measures such as a national insurance scheme, leasehold tenure of crown land, proportional representation, and abolition of plural voting.

Atlantic, Battle of the The name given to a succession of sea-operations in World War II. They took place in the Atlantic, the Caribbean, and northern European waters and involved both submarine blockades and attacks on Allied shipping. German U-boats, sometimes assisted by Italian submarines, were the main weapon of attack, but aircraft and surface raiders also participated. About 2,800 Allied, mainly British, merchant ships were lost, placing the Allies in a critical situation. After summer 1943, with the introduction of better radar, the provision of long-distance aircraft and of escort carriers, and the breaking of German codes, the situation eased, although technical innovations subsequently increased the U-boats' effectiveness. It was only the capture of their bases by Allied land forces that finally put an end to the threat.

Atlantic Charter A joint declaration of principles to guide a post-World War II peace settlement. It resulted from a meeting at sea between CHURCHILL and F. D. ROOSEVELT on 14 August 1941. It stipulated freely chosen governments, free trade, freedom of the seas, and disarmament of current aggressor states, and it condemned territorial changes made against the wishes of local populations. A renunciation of territorial ambitions on the part of Britain and the USA was also prominent. In the following month other states fighting the AXIS POWERS, including the USSR, declared their support for these principles. The Atlantic Charter provided the ideological base for the UNITED NATIONS ORGANIZATION.

Atlantis According to a myth told by PLATO, a large island lying in the Atlantic Ocean, west of the mountains in north-west Africa, where Atlas supposedly supported the heavens. Supposedly a powerful kingdom, it was said to have disappeared beneath the sea, which has led some to equate it with the MINOAN CIVILIZATION of Crete, which they believe was destroyed by the eruption of the volcano of Thera (modern Santorini) *c.* 1500 BC. Classicists generally give no credence to the Platonic myth of Atlantis, though archaeologists continue to search for evidence to support the legend.

attainder The extinction of civil rights and powers when judgement of death or outlawry was recorded against a person convicted of treason or felony. It was the severest English common law penalty, for an attainted person lost all his goods and lands to the crown. Procedure by Act of Attainder became common in the Wars of the ROSES, when because it was reversible it could be used as a powerful threat. Of the 397 people condemned by process in Parliament between 1453 and 1509, over 250 ultimately had their attainders reversed. Acts of Attainder came to be disapproved of because an opportunity for defence was not necessarily given; they became rare in the 18th century and ceased after 1798.

Attica A region comprising the south-eastern portion of central Greece. In ancient times it contained a number of small villages and towns and these gradually were united politically into the city-state of ATHENS, the process being completed by the 7th century BC. Major land-owning families continued to live outside the city, though in the time of the PELOPONNESIAN WAR (431–404 BC) the countryside was abandoned temporarily to the depredations of the invading Spartans. Attica was rich in natural resources, notably clay for a thriving pottery industry, marble, lead, and the silver which financed the Athenian navy.

Attila (*c.* 406–53 AD) King of the HUNS. He became king in 434 jointly with his brother Bleda, whom he murdered in 445. He forcibly united the Hun tribes into a vast horde based in Hungary; they raided from the Rhine to the Caspian Sea, ravaging the divided ROMAN EMPIRE, and exacting tribute as the price of peace treaties. The historian Priscus has left a vivid description of the squat and wily Mongoloid conqueror and his court. Invading Gaul in 451, the 'Scourge of God' met his only defeat on the CATALAUNIAN FIELDS near Châlons at the hands of combined Roman, Frankish, and Visigothic forces. He then turned on Italy but spared Rome, perhaps in response to pleas or ransom from Pope Leo I. His sudden death was followed by the collapse of his dominion.

Attlee, Clement Richard, 1st Earl Attlee (1883–1967) British statesman. He was successively a lawyer, a social worker, and a university lecturer before entering politics, becoming a Labour Member of Parliament in 1922. He served in the government of Ramsay MACDONALD, and in 1935 succeeded George LANSBURY as leader of the Labour Party. During World War II he served in the government of Winston CHURCHILL and was Deputy Prime Minister (1942–45). After a landslide victory in 1945, the Labour Party came to power, with Attlee as Prime Minister. His two governments (1945–50; 1950–51) had to face many post-war problems but succeeded in establishing the WELFARE STATE. He was defeated in the 1951 election and accepted an earldom in 1955.

To the surprise of many, the Labour Party easily won the general election of 1945 against the Conservative Party led by Winston CHURCHILL. Despite a war debt of $20,000 million (about £5,000 million) and severe fiscal difficulties, the government embarked on an economic and social reform programme advocated by J. M. KEYNES. It implemented the BEVERIDGE Report of 1942 through the creation of a WELFARE STATE, supported by a policy of full employment. The National Insurance Act of 1946 introduced the National Health Service, a free medical service financed from general taxation, and the extension of NATIONAL INSURANCE to the entire adult population. Public ownership was extended, the Bank of England was nationalized, as were key industries and services, such as gas, coal, and railways. A full-employment policy was vigorously pursued through the relocation of industry, and the wartime policy of subsidizing agriculture was continued. The economic stability of the country was underpinned by the international agreements reached at the BRETTON WOODS CONFERENCE. The powers of the House of LORDS were further reduced by the Parliament Act of 1946. The process of decolonization began with the granting of independence to India and Pakistan (1947), as well as to Burma, while British withdrawal from Palestine allowed the creation of Israel (1948). In 1949, with the beginning of the COLD WAR, Britain helped to form NATO. The second ministry, following an election in February 1950, had a smaller majority. At home it faced fierce opposition in its attempts to nationalize the steel industry while entry into the KOREAN WAR necessitated increased rearmament. The Festival of Britain in the summer of 1951 encouraged a sense of optimism in the future of the nation, but it did not prevent Labour from losing the election to the Conservatives in October.

Auchinleck, Sir Claude John Eyre (1884–1981) British field-marshal. He served with distinction in World War I. He commanded the land forces at Narvik in the ineffectual Norwegian campaign in April–May 1940, was commander-in-chief in India (1940–41) and from mid-1941 he commanded in North Africa. He led the advance in Libya, but was driven back by stronger German forces in 1942. When TOBRUK surrendered, he took personal command of the troops, establishing the key defensive line at El ALAMEIN. Churchill then replaced him with MONTGOMERY and he returned to India as commander-in-chief.

Augsburg A city in Bavaria, from 1276 one of the great free imperial cities of Germany. It was an important member of the SWABIAN league and was famous in the 16th century for its merchant princes, the FUGGERS and Welsers. It was often chosen by CHARLES V as the venue for negotiations that might lead to religious unity. In 1530 the Confession of Augsburg was drawn up by MELANCHTHON; in moderate language it gave a statement of essential LUTHERAN doctrines, such as justification by faith. It was not accepted by the Roman Catholics but remains the chief standard of faith in the Lutheran churches. In 1548 the Interim of Augsburg, a Catholic statement with modest concessions to the Lutherans, was not accepted in Protestant areas. In 1555 the Peace of Augsburg was concluded by the new emperor Ferdinand and the ELECTORS: Catholicism and Lutheranism (but not CALVINISM) were recognized and each prince could impose the faith of his choice on his territories (the principle of *cuius regio, eius religio*, the ruler may dictate the religion); in free cities such as Augsburg both faiths could be practised; all ecclesiastical land already obtained by Protestants could be retained, but in future ecclesiastical princes who were converted had to give up the Church lands in their possession. This principle was often not observed by Protestant princes and was applied sporadically.

In 1686 the defensive League of Augsburg was formed by Emperor Leopold and some German princes to resist LOUIS XIV's advance into the Rhineland; it was joined by the Holy Roman Emperor, the Dutch, Spain, and Sweden. After the French invaded the PALATINATE

and WILLIAM III became King of England a new Grand
Alliance was formed; the ensuing NINE YEARS WAR is also
known as the War of the League of Augsburg or the
War of the Grand Alliance.

augur An official diviner or soothsayer in ancient
Rome. The augur's task was to watch for indications of
the attitude of the gods towards proposed activities of
the state or its officers. They played a key role
in choosing or 'inaugurating' successive non-
hereditary kings of early Rome. The name was
thought to be linked with birds (Latin, *aves*), since
they scrutinized the activities of birds, besides other
animals, as well as accidents, and dreams, particularly
on the eve of military expeditions and at the
moment of important births. All political assemblies of
the Roman people were preceded by the taking of
'auspices'.

Augustine of Canterbury, St (d. *c.* 605 AD) The first
Archbishop of Canterbury. He was chosen (596) by Pope
GREGORY I (the Great) to convert the English to
Christianity. With 40 monks Augustine came first to
Kent (597) and converted King Ethelbert, whose wife was
already a Christian. Consecrated archbishop (597),
Augustine organized the Church into 12 dioceses (598)
but failed at a meeting with the Celtic bishops in 603 to
resolve the differences between the Roman and Celtic
Churches, although these differences were resolved at
the Synod of WHITBY (664). Augustine's work was
instrumental in the re-establishment of Christianity in
England.

Augustine of Hippo, St (354–430 AD) Christian bishop,
one of the outstanding theologians of the early
Christian Church. Born in North Africa of a pagan
father and a Christian mother, he was early attracted to
MANICHAEISM, which he later rejected. He taught rhetoric
in Rome and Milan, where he was influenced by Bishop
AMBROSE. Augustine lived a monastic life for some time,
then becoming a priest and (after 395) Bishop of
Hippo in North Africa. His episcopate there was
marked by controversy with followers of heretical
Christian sects (Manichees, Donatists, and Pelagians) and
of pagan philosophies. He was an upholder of order in a
time of political strife caused by the disintegration of
the ROMAN EMPIRE and he died as the VANDALS reached
Hippo.

De Civitate Dei (*The City of God*), a vindication of the
Church against paganism, is perhaps his most important
work, apart from his *Confessions* which contains a
striking account of his early life and conversion. His
writings reached a wide audience after his death and
were known in Anglo-Saxon England in the reign of
King ALFRED. His theology influenced much subsequent
Christian theology; the 'rule of St Augustine' (see
AUGUSTINIAN) was based on his writings.

Augustinian A member of one of the religious orders
following the rule or code of conduct laid down by St
AUGUSTINE OF HIPPO. Augustine's rule proved practical and
adaptable to changing conditions over many centuries
and was used by both St Dominic and St Francis as a
model upon which to construct constitutions for the
DOMINICAN and FRANCISCAN orders. Essentially it required
men to live a communal life apart from the world but

allowed for involvement in missionary work and care of
the sick. The rule was endorsed and promoted by the
Fourth LATERAN COUNCIL of 1215.

Augustus   *A 1st-century bust of Emperor Augustus
in military dress, excavated at Prima Porta, near
Rome.*

Augustus (Gaius Julius Caesar Octavianus) (63 BC–14 AD)
The first Roman emperor (27 BC–14 AD). Born as Octavian
into the CAESAR family, he was Julius Caesar's nephew
and entered the power struggle after Caesar's death in
44 BC. Despite MARK ANTONY's opposition, he gained the
consulship and soon after joined Antony and Lepidus in
the 'Second Triumvirate', an alliance of three dictators.
Their republican opponents, BRUTUS and Cassius, were
defeated (see PHILIPPI, BATTLE OF) and Antony and Octavian
ruled the empire between them, Antony the eastern
part, and Octavian the western territories. The Battle of
ACTIUM in 31 BC gave Octavian victory, and, after
Antony's suicide, total supremacy. In 28 BC he took over
responsibility for Rome's military provinces and their
garrisons. His pre-eminence was reflected in the title of
'Augustus' bestowed upon him, which later became
synonymous with 'emperor'. His generals were
victorious in Asia, Spain, Pannonia, Dalmatia, and Gaul.
The only reversal was defeat by the Germans under
ARMINIUS. Augustus enjoyed formidable power, but
although an absolute ruler in all but name, he was
careful to preserve the institutions of republican
government. His achievement was the creation of the

Principate, a system of stable and effectively monarchic government, after half a century of strife. An efficient administration was formed out of the old governing class. The 'Augustan Age' brought security and prosperity to the Roman empire. His court circle provided patronage for writers such as Virgil, Horace, and Livy, and he adorned Rome and other cities with beautiful buildings.

Augustus II (the Strong) (1670–1733) King of Poland (1696–1733). He was Elector of Saxony from 1694 and succeeded John III (John SOBIESKI) as King of Poland in 1696. He joined Russia and Denmark against CHARLES XII OF SWEDEN without Polish support but was defeated. Charles had him banished and Stanislaus Leszczynski elected king in his place. Augustus recovered his position after Charles's defeat at POLTAVA (1709) and for the rest of his reign brought some economic prosperity to Saxony and Poland, although renewed war with Sweden lasted until 1718. A ruler of considerable extravagance, supposed to be the most dissolute monarch in Europe, he was a patron of the arts and gave special support to the Dresden and Meissen china factories.

Aung San (1914–47) Burmese nationalist leader. Head of the pre-war *Dobama Asiayone* (We Burmans' Association), whose members took the title of *Thakin* ('lord'), Aung San first achieved prominence as an organizer of the student strike in Rangoon in 1936. After a period of secret military training under the Japanese he returned to Burma in 1942 and became the leader of the Japanese-sponsored Burma National Army which defected to the Allies in the closing weeks of the Pacific War. As head of the Anti-Fascist People's Freedom League, he led the post-war Council of Ministers, and, in January 1947, negotiated a promise of full self-government from the British, but on 19 July 1947 he and six of his colleagues were assassinated at the behest of a political rival, U Saw.

Aung San Suu Kyi (1945–) Burmese politician and human-rights activist. The daughter of the nationalist leader AUNG SAN, Aung San Suu Kyi was educated in India and at Oxford University, England, before working for the United Nations. In 1988 she returned to Myanmar (Burma), where she was instrumental in founding the National League for Democracy (NLD) to campaign against the repressive military regime. She was placed under house arrest in 1989. Her party won overwhelming public support in the general elections of 1990, but was prevented from taking office by the military regime. In 1991 she was awarded the Nobel Peace Prize. On her release, her appointment to the presidency of the NLD was declared void by the country's leaders, who have disbarred her from holding political office. Aung San Suu Kyi's campaign has led to the imposition of sanctions on Myanmar by a number of countries; however, violent repression of her supporters has continued.

Aurangzeb (1618–1707) Known also as Alamgir ('world-holder'), Mogul Emperor of India (1659–1707). He was the last great ruler in his line, though the signs of subsequent decline first became apparent during his reign. After eliminating his brothers, he seized the throne from his father, and then pushed the boundaries of Mogul India to their fullest extent by defeating the Muslim rulers of Bijapur and Golconda. However, his obsession with expansion into the DECCAN severely overextended his resources. Desiring to reassert Muslim orthodoxy, he reversed the conciliatory gestures, notably in taxation, which had won Hindu support, particularly since AKBAR's reign. The result was intensified opposition to Mogul rule among newly assertive groups such as the MARATHAS and the SIKHS. His achievements and failures remain controversial.

Aurelian (Lucius Domitius Aurelianus) (215–75 AD) Roman emperor (270–75). After a career as a cavalry commander, he was adopted as co-emperor by Claudius II, who died that year. Under Aurelian's rule the rivers Rhine and Danube were temporarily regained as the empire's natural frontiers against the barbarian Alemanni and GOTHS. Internal threats from the Gallic usurper Tetricus (defeated at Châlons in 274) and the kingdom of Palmyra in Syria were suppressed. Aurelian was murdered while campaigning against the Persians.

Aurignacian UPPER PALAEOLITHIC.

Auriol, Vincent (1884–1966) French statesman. Elected as a Socialist Deputy in 1914, he served as Minister of Finance (1936) and Justice (1938). During World War II he spent two years in internment before escaping to join the FREE FRENCH in Britain. After the liberation he served in de Gaulle's government (1945–46) and played an active part in the formation of the Fourth Republic, being elected its first President (1947–53).

Ausgleich (1867; German, 'compromise') A constitutional compromise between Hungary and the AUSTRIAN EMPIRE following the defeat of Austria in Italy and Germany. It was drawn up by Francis DEÁK, and ratified by the Austrian emperor FRANCIS JOSEPH, granting Hungary its own parliament and constitution but retaining Francis Joseph as King of Hungary. A dual monarchy, the AUSTRO-HUNGARIAN EMPIRE, was created, in which the Magyars were permitted to dominate their subject peoples, and the Austrians the remaining 17 provinces of the empire.

Austerlitz, Battle of (2 December 1805) Fought by Austria and Russia against France, near the town of Austerlitz in Moravia. Alexander I of Russia persuaded FRANCIS I of Austria to attack before reinforcements arrived. Their complicated plan to encircle the French allowed NAPOLEON to split their army and defeat each half. It was a decisive battle; the Russian army had to withdraw from Austria, and Austria signed the Treaty of Pressburg (1805), in which it recognized Napoleon as King of Italy, and ceded territories in northern Italy, the Alpine regions, and on the Adriatic coast.

Australia An island country and continent in the Southern Hemisphere in the south-west Pacific Ocean. Surrounding it are numerous islands, the largest being Tasmania, and off its east coast lies the Great Barrier Reef.

Physical. Much of the continent has a hot, dry climate, and a large part of the central area is desert or semi-desert; the most fertile areas are on the eastern coastal plains and in the south-west corner of Western Australia. The south-western coastal areas are undulating, their hills supporting forests of hardwood trees. They rise to a low plateau of ancient rocks, and this gives way in turn to the Great Sandy and Gibson Deserts. In the centre of the continent are the Macdonnell Ranges, beyond which the land falls away to the Simpson Desert and Lake Eyre before gradually rising again to the Sturt Desert. The Murray–Darling basin is the country's largest water catchment area; its water supply for irrigation was greatly increased with the diversion of the Snowy River (1974) from its natural south-eastward course into the Murray River. Eastwards, the land rises to the Great Dividing Range and then falls sharply to the sea.

Economy. Australia's economy is based on mining, agriculture, and industry. Agricultural land, which is periodically devastated by drought, accounts for 64% of Australia's territory, almost all of this devoted to cattle and sheep. Australia is the world's leading wool producer and largest beef exporter, as well as being an important wheat producer. Paramount in mineral production, Australia is the world's leading exporter of iron ore and aluminium, and highly important in producing coal, nickel, zinc, and other metals. Australia's energy resources, which include high quality black coal, oil, natural gas, and uranium, constitute 18% of global reserves. Domestic crude oil meets most domestic needs and is also exported. Manufacturing industry is aimed principally at domestic markets, and is comparatively undeveloped and vulnerable to competition from Asian neighbours.

History. Australia was first inhabited by the ABORIGINES, who are thought to have migrated from south-east Asia *c.*50,000–40,000 years ago. Although the first known European discoveries of the continent were those made in the early 17th century, there may have been earlier Portuguese discoveries. It was visited by an Englishman, William Dampier, in 1688 and 1699. Captain James Cook claimed British possession of the eastern part of the continent in 1770, naming it New South Wales. The British penal colony of New South Wales was founded in 1788. Immigration of free settlers from 1820 onwards aided the colony's development, as did exploration, which opened pastures for the wool industry. SQUATTER settlement of much of eastern Australia led to conflict with the Aborigines, resulting in events such as the MYALL CREEK MASSACRE (1838). Van Diemen's Land (from 1855 Tasmania), settled in 1803, became a separate colony in 1825. Moreton Bay, founded as a PENAL SETTLEMENT in 1824, became the colony of Queensland in 1859. The colony of Western Australia was founded in 1829. The Port Phillip District, settled illegally in 1834, became the colony of Victoria in 1851. South Australia, founded as a province in 1834, became a crown colony in 1842. All of the colonies except Western Australia were granted responsible government during the 1850s. The GOLD RUSHES of the 1850s and 1860s brought many changes. The WHITE AUSTRALIA POLICY can be traced back to that period. Demands for land to be opened for SELECTORS increased. Western Australia, granted responsible government in 1890, developed more slowly than the other colonies.

In 1901 the six colonies were federated as self-governing states to form the Commonwealth of Australia. Powers were distributed between the Commonwealth and state governments, and with the crown through its representative, the governor-general, retaining (until 1931) overall responsibility for defence and foreign affairs. State legislators would have full responsibility for internal state affairs. BARTON, who had been prominent in the federation movement, was the first Prime Minister. The Northern Territory was transferred from South Australia to the Commonwealth in 1911. In the same year land was transferred to the Commonwealth from New South Wales, for the creation of the Australian Capital Territory, Canberra. (Jervis Bay was added to the Australian Capital Territory in 1915.) The Commonwealth Parliament met in Melbourne until 1927, when it was transferred to Canberra. In the 1930s reserves were established for the ABORIGINES, and in 1981 the Pitjantjara Aborigines were granted freehold titles to land in Southern Australia. Australia fought with the Allies in both WORLD WARS and with the USA in VIETNAM. After World War II ties with Britain diminished, and Australia joined the ANZUS and SEATO powers. The Labor governments of the 1970s and 1980s, led by Gough Whitlam (see WHITLAM CRISIS) and Bob HAWKE, strengthened trade ties with the non-communist Far East, but a deteriorating economy in the 1980s led to labour unrest and in 1991 to the replacement of Hawke (Prime Minister since 1983) by his deputy Paul KEATING. In 1996 Keating's Labor Party suffered a heavy electoral defeat by a Liberal-National Party coalition and John Howard was appointed Prime Minister. In response to increasing support for Australia becoming a republic, Queen Elizabeth II in 1993 announced that she would agree to such a constitutional change if the Australian people wanted it. Elections to a constitutional convention, which will decide whether to hold a referendum on the issue, were held in 1997.

CAPITAL:	Canberra
AREA:	7,682,300 sq km (2,966,200 sq miles)
POPULATION:	18.287 million (1996)
CURRENCY:	1 Australian dollar = 100 cents
RELIGIONS:	Anglican 26.1%; Roman Catholic 26.0%; other Protestant 20.8%; Eastern Orthodox, Muslim, Jewish, and Buddhist minorities
ETHNIC GROUPS:	native-born 78.2% (of which 1.5% Aboriginal); country of origin of foreign-born: UK 7.2%; Asia and Middle East 3.9%; New Zealand 1.9%; Italy 1.6%; Africa and Americas 1.5%; Yugoslavia 1.0%; Greece 1.0%
LANGUAGES:	English (official); minority and Aboriginal languages
INTERNATIONAL ORGANIZATIONS:	UN; OECD; Colombo Plan; ANZUS Pact; South Pacific Commission; Commonwealth

Australian federation movement (1890–1900) A movement to seek federation of the six Australian colonies and (initially) New Zealand. Two pressure groups for federation were the Australian Natives' Association and the Australasian Federation League. In 1889 the six Australian colonies and New Zealand agreed to send delegates to a federal conference in Melbourne in 1890. It was decided to hold a full convention the following year in Parliament House, Sydney, at which a draft constitution was drawn up. A second convention was held in 1893 in the small New South Wales town of Corowa convened by the Australian Natives' Association, at which it was proposed that a national referendum be held. By now indifference had increased in New Zealand as its trade shifted to Britain with the invention of refrigeration. In Australia too, opposition to New Zealand's participation was growing, and plans for the federation were dropped. In 1895 the Premiers of the six Australian colonies met to reconsider the draft constitution drawn up in 1891. New Zealand was now excluded. Ten delegates from each colony were chosen (elected by the people, except in the case of Western Australia) and the Australian Federation Convention first met in Adelaide (March 1897). It was agreed that a referendum should be held. It met again in January 1898, when after much compromise a proposed constitution was agreed. The first referendum failed. The second (held in 1899 after amendments were made) passed in all colonies and was given royal assent in 1900, the Commonwealth of AUSTRALIA coming into being on 1 January 1901.

Australoids ABORIGINES.

australopithecines Early members of the human line of evolution. The first australopithecine fossil was discovered at Taung in southern Africa in 1924 and named *Australopithecus africanus* (southern ape of Africa). Since then, australopithecine fossils have been found in southern and eastern Africa but the relationships between the different forms is still far from clear.

Current opinion divides them into two, or perhaps three main groups that date from over 5 million to nearly 1 million years ago. The oldest (5–3 million years ago) and most ape-like is *Australopithecus afarensis*, now known from eastern African sites including HADAR and LAETOLI. This species is often linked closely to *Australopithecus africanus* (3–2 million years ago), best represented at STERKFONTEIN and Makapansgat in southern Africa. Some authorities consider both these species are human ancestors; others rule out *A. africanus*, some even discount both from being human ancestors. These lightly built australopithecines are described as 'gracile' to distinguish them from the more heavily built, 'robust' forms – *Australopithecus robustus* (2–1.5 million years ago) from southern Africa (for example from Swartkrans), and the even heavier *Australopithecus boisei* (2.5–1.2 million years ago) from eastern Africa. These robust forms are widely regarded as off the direct human lineage. Australopithecines were clearly capable of walking upright but their brains were still ape-like. It is uncertain if they made tools.

Austria A country in central Europe, bounded by Italy, Slovenia, and Croatia to the south, Hungary and Slovakia to the east, the Czech Republic and Germany to the north, and Liechtenstein and Switzerland to the west.

Physical. Much of Austria is mountainous, with the River Danube flowing through the north-east of the country. Austria is the most densely forested nation in central Europe, with almost half of its land covered by trees. In the Alpine regions, south-facing mountain slopes have been cleared for pasture land and crops. In the Danube valley, arable land is characterized by very fertile soils. The warm, dry south wind, the Föhn, affects vegetation and land use. The country's steep topography provides potential for hydroelectric development.

Economy. Timber and paper products account for 10% of Austria's exports. Apart from this important silviculture, the economy is primarily industrial, with agriculture contributing only 3% of GDP. Foreign trade is the mainstay of the economy, with machinery accounting for over a quarter of exports. Austria is the world's largest source of high-grade graphite, and has other mineral deposits, including crude oil, natural gas, and uranium. Tourism is also important. Austria joined EU in 1995, and trade is largely with Western Europe, especially Germany. A large portion of the Austrian economy has been in public hands since World War II, but a privatization programme now aims to enhance productivity and reduce the large public debt.

History. The Celtic tribes which had settled in the area from about 500 to 200 BC were conquered by the Romans in 14 BC, and the region remained part of the ROMAN EMPIRE, with the Danube as its frontier. A succession of Germanic invaders (Vandals, Goths, Huns, Lombards, and Avars) in the 5th century AD ended with a short period of stability under CHARLEMAGNE. MAGYAR invaders then followed, but these were decisively defeated by OTTO I THE GREAT at the Battle of LECHFELD in 955. Otto invested Leopold of Babenberg with the title of Margrave of Austria, and the Babenberg dynasty lasted until 1246. In 1282 Rudolf I, Count of HABSBURG invested his two sons jointly as Dukes of Austria, the older son Albert (Duke of Austria 1282–1308) founding a dynasty which survived into the 20th century. The first Habsburg Holy Roman Emperor was FREDERICK III (1452–93) and perhaps the greatest CHARLES V (1530–56). From Vienna, the Habsburgs ruled the vast empire which, before its dissolution in 1918, included Hungary, Bohemia, Moravia, Burgundy, Tuscany, Piedmont, Croatia, Bosnia-Herzegovina, Bukovina, Slovenia, parts of Serbia, of Romania, and of Spanish America, Silesia, Spain, Luxembourg, The Netherlands, Venetia, and Naples. In 1575 the court moved from Vienna to Prague, where it remained until 1621. Vienna withstood a Muslim siege in 1529 and again in 1683, when the Polish army forced the OTTOMAN retreat. The War of the AUSTRIAN SUCCESSION brought the conflict over supremacy in the German orbit to a head, and the SEVEN YEARS WAR confirmed Prussia as a power of equal weight. The end of the 18th century saw almost continuous conflict, with Austrians fighting against the French revolutionary armies in The Netherlands, the Rhineland, and northern Italy.

The unification of Germany by Prussia (1866–71) excluded the AUSTRIAN EMPIRE from German affairs and destroyed hopes for the creation of a union of all the German-speaking peoples. Austria was forced to make concessions to the Hungarians by forming the AUSTRO-HUNGARIAN EMPIRE. Austrian diplomats, however, retained links with the new GERMAN SECOND EMPIRE, and tried to gain German support for their ambitions against Russia in the Balkans through an alliance system. During World War I the Austrian Imperial Army was virtually under German military control. Defeat and revolution destroyed the monarchy in 1918, and the first Austrian republic which followed it was only a rump of the former state. This was destabilized by the Nazis, who in 1934 murdered DOLLFUSS and staged an abortive coup. They were more successful in achieving ANSCHLUSS in 1938, when Hitler's army invaded the country without opposition. Defeated in World War II, Austria was invaded by Soviet troops, and divided into separate occupation zones, each controlled by an Allied Power. In 1955 a treaty between the Allies and Austria restored full sovereignty to the country. The treaty prohibited the possession of major offensive weapons and required Austria to pay heavy reparations to the USSR, as well as to give assurances that it would ally itself with neither East nor West Germany, nor restore the Habsburgs. It remained neutral, democratic, and increasingly prosperous under a series of socialist regimes. Extreme right-wing candidates won a number of seats in elections in 1994, but the socialists were re-elected in general elections in 1995, the year in which Austria also joined the EUROPEAN UNION.

CAPITAL:	Vienna
AREA:	83,857 sq km (32,377 sq miles)
POPULATION:	8.102 million (1996)
CURRENCY:	1 Schilling = 100 Groschen
RELIGIONS:	Roman Catholic 84.3%; non-religious and atheist 6.0%; Evangelical 5.6%; Muslim, Jewish, and other minorities
ETHNIC GROUPS:	Austrian 96.1%; Yugoslav 1.7%; Turkish 0.8%; German 0.5%
LANGUAGES:	German (official) and other minority languages
INTERNATIONAL ORGANIZATIONS:	UN; OECD; EU; Council of Europe; CSCE

Austria, House of HABSBURG.

Austrian empire (1806–67) Those territories and peoples from whom the Habsburg emperors in Vienna demanded allegiance. Following the dissolution of the Holy Roman Empire (1806) Emperor Francis II continued to rule as FRANCIS I (1804–35), Emperor of Austria and of the hereditary Habsburg lands of Bohemia, Hungary, Croatia and Transylvania, Galicia (once a province of Poland), and much of northern Italy (Venetia and Lombardy). He ruled by means of a large bureaucracy, a loyal army, the Roman Catholic Church, and an elaborate police force. His chief minister was Chancellor METTERNICH WINNEBURG. Nationalist feelings were emerging, and during the reign of his successor Ferdinand I (1835–48), liberal agitation for reform developed. Vienna was becoming rapidly industrialized and in March 1848, at a time of economic depression, riots in the capital led to Metternich's resignation. The emperor abolished censorship and promised a constitution. This, published in April, was not democratic enough for radical leaders, who organized a popular protest on 15 May 1848. The emperor fled to Innsbruck and later abdicated. His 18-year-old nephew FRANCIS JOSEPH succeeded. There were movements for independence among all the peoples of the empire, including the Hungarians led by KOSSUTH, the Czechs, Slovaks, Serbs, Croats, Romanians, and Italians. A PAN-SLAV conference met (1848) in Prague. But the opposition to the government in Vienna was divided and the Prime Minister, SCHWARZENBERG and Francis Joseph were able to regain control. The army crushed the reform movements in Prague and Vienna and with the help of Russia, subjugated Budapest. Alexander Bach, the new Minister of the Interior, greatly strengthened the centralized bureaucracy, and the empire regained some stability, until its defeat by France and Piedmont at MAGENTA and SOLFERINO, which ended Austrian rule in Italy. In an effort to appease nationalist feeling the emperor proposed a new federal constitution, but it came too late and after a further defeat at SADOWA he agreed to the AUSGLEICH (Compromise) of 1867 and the creation of the AUSTRO-HUNGARIAN EMPIRE.

Austrian Succession, War of the (1740–48) A complicated European conflict in which the key issue was the right of MARIA THERESA of Austria to succeed to the lands of her father, Emperor Charles VI, and that of her husband Francis of Lorraine to the imperial title. Francis's claims (in spite of the PRAGMATIC SANCTION) were disputed by Charles Albert, Elector of Bavaria, supported by Frederick II of Prussia and Louis XV of France. Additionally Philip V of Spain and Maria Theresa were in dispute over who should have control of Italy, and Britain was challenging France and Spain's domination of the Mediterranean (War of JENKINS'S EAR), and fighting for control of India and America (KING GEORGE'S WAR).

After the death of Charles VI in 1740 war was precipitated by Frederick II of Prussia, who seized Silesia. The war began badly for Austria: the French seized Prague, a Spanish army landed in north Italy, Charles Albert was elected Holy Roman Emperor, and Silesia was ceded by treaty to Frederick II in 1742. Britain now supported Austria by organizing the so-called Pragmatic Army (Britain, Austria, Hanover, and Hesse) and under the personal command of George II it defeated the French at DETTINGEN in 1743. Savoy joined Austria and Britain (Treaty of Worms, September 1743) and the tide of war began to turn in Austria's favour. In 1744–45 Frederick II re-entered the war, determined to retain Silesia. Meanwhile Charles Albert died and Francis was elected Holy Roman Emperor in exchange for the return of the lands of Bavaria to the Elector's heir. Frederick II won a series of victories against Austria, and the Treaty of Dresden (1745) confirmed his possession of Silesia.

The struggle between France and Britain intensified. The French supported the Jacobite invasion of Britain (the FORTY-FIVE) and in India the French captured the British town of Madras (1746). The British won major victories at sea: off Cape Finisterre, Spain and Belle-Ile, France in 1747.

By 1748 all participants were ready for peace, which was concluded at AIX-LA-CHAPELLE. The war had been a long and costly effort by Maria Theresa to keep her Habsburg inheritance intact and in this she largely succeeded. But Austria was weakened and Prussia, which held Silesia, consolidated its position as a significant European power.

Austro-Hungarian empire (Dual Monarchy) The Habsburg monarchy between 1867 and 1919. Following Austria's defeat by Prussia (1866) Francis Joseph, the Austrian emperor, realized that Austria's future lay along the Danube and into the Balkans. Before any such expansion could occur, the differences between the two dominating peoples in his empire, Germans and Hungarians, had to be overcome. By the AUSGLEICH (Compromise) of 1867 Austria and Hungary became autonomous states under a common sovereign. Each had its own parliament to control internal affairs: foreign policy, war, and finance were decided by common ministers. The dualist system came under increasing pressure from the other subject nations; in Hungary there was constant friction with the Croatians, Serbs, Slovaks, and Romanians (52% of the population). The

Czechs of BOHEMIA-Moravia resented the German-speaking government in Vienna, and found a potent advocate for Czech independence in Tomáš MASARYK. BOSNIA-HERZEGOVINA, formally annexed in 1908, developed a strong Serbian nationalist movement, and the failure to resolve nationalist aspirations within the empire was one of the main causes of World War I. After the death of Francis Joseph (1916) his successor Charles promised constitutional reforms, but the Allies gave their support to the emergent nations and the Austro-Hungarian empire was finally dissolved by the VERSAILLES PEACE SETTLEMENT.

Austro-Prussian War (June–August 1866) A war fought between Prussia, allied with Italy, and Austria, allied with Bavaria and other, smaller German states. War had become inevitable after BISMARCK challenged Austria's supremacy in the GERMAN CONFEDERATION. Hostilities finally broke out when Bismarck, having gained France's neutrality and the support of Italy, proposed that the German Confederation should be abolished. Prussian troops forced the Austrians out of Schleswig-Holstein, but the Austrians defeated the Italian army at Custozza. However, the Prussian army, better trained and equipped, crushed the main Austrian army at SADOWA. Seven weeks later the Austrians signed the Treaty of Prague, by which the German Confederation was dissolved. Austria ceded Venetia to Italy, while Prussia annexed the smaller states into the new North German Confederation. Austria, excluded from its territories in the south and from political influence to the north, turned towards the east, accepting the Hungarian AUSGLEICH and forming the AUSTRO-HUNGARIAN EMPIRE.

automation The use of automatic machinery and systems, particularly those manufacturing or data-processing systems which require little or no human intervention in their normal operation. Although the term was first used in 1946 to describe machinery being developed by the Ford Motor Company to move automobile components and workpieces automatically to and from other machines, the origins of the concept are much older. During the 19th century a number of machines such as looms and lathes became increasingly self-regulating. At the same time transfer-machines were developed, whereby a series of machine-tools, each doing one operation automatically, became linked in a continuous production line by pneumatic or hydraulic devices transferring components from one operation to the next. In addition to these technological advances in automation, the theory of 'scientific management', which was based on the early time-and-motion studies of Frederick Winslow Taylor in Philadelphia, USA, in the 1880s was designed by Taylor to enhance the efficiency and productivity of workers and machines. In the early 20th century, with the development of electrical devices and time-switches, more processes became automatically controlled, and a number of basic industries such as oil-refining, chemicals, and food-processing were increasingly automated. The development of computers after World War II enabled more sophisticated automation to be used in manufacturing industries, for example in iron and steel production. (See COMPUTER, HISTORY OF THE.)

Avars Central Asian nomads whose irruption into eastern Europe in 568 led to the creation of a large empire centred on the Danube valley. They drove the southern Slavs into the Balkans and the Germanic Lombards into northern Italy, thereby depriving BYZANTIUM of its Latin-speaking subjects and confirming its Greek character. Their empire was destroyed by Charlemagne in 791, and the resulting rebellions of their subject peoples led to their complete extermination.

Averroës (Ibn Rushd) (c. 1126–98) Islamic philosopher born in Cordoba, Spain. Averroës saw philosophy and religion as distinct ways of apprehending a single truth, and so was able to assert the authority of natural reason in his *Destruction* of al-Ghazāli's *Destruction of the Philosophers*. He considered ARISTOTLE's works the highest achievement of philosophy; his voluminous commentaries on these were important in introducing Aristotle's thought to Christian SCHOLASTICS. His confidence that philosophical truth, patiently expounded, would harmonize with religious doctrine was not accepted by later philosophers. Thus, his account of the unity of the intellect was held incompatible with personal immortality, and was criticized as such by AQUINAS.

Awami League A political party in East Pakistan. It was founded in 1952 as the Jinnah Awami Muslim League by H. S. Suhrawardy, although it existed informally before that date. It was renamed the Awami League under pressure from its East Bengal leader, Maulana Abdul Hamid Bhashani, who left the party in 1957 to form the National Awami Party. During the 1960s the Awami League grew rapidly under Sheikh Mujibur Rahman, who succeeded Suhrawardy as leader and in 1970 won a majority, completely dominating East Pakistan, which became BANGLADESH in December 1971. In August 1975 the Awami League was disbanded with other political parties. It was later reformed and became the largest opposition party in Bangladesh.

Axis Powers An alliance of fascist states fighting with Germany during WORLD WAR II. The term was used in an agreement (October 1936) between Hitler and Mussolini proclaiming the creation of a Rome–Berlin 'axis round which all European states can also assemble'. Japan joined the coalition on signing the ANTI-COMINTERN PACT (November 1936). A full military and political alliance between Germany and Italy (the Pact of Steel) followed in 1939. The Tripartite Pact between the three powers in 1940 cemented the alliance, and, by subsequently joining it, Hungary, Romania, and Bulgaria, as well as the Nazi-created states of Slovakia and Croatia, became members.

Axum (or Aksum) A town in northern Ethiopia. It was the capital of a trading kingdom between the 3rd and 1st centuries BC, selling ivory, gums, and spices at the port of Adulis, chiefly to Egyptian merchants. In the 4th century AD King Ezana minted its first gold coinage, and signed a treaty with Byzantium. The country was then slowly converted to Christianity. To this time belong the huge obelisk tombs for which Axum is famous. In the 6th century Axum controlled western Arabia for a short time, but lost it to the rising power of Persia. By 1000 the kingdom had collapsed.

Ayub Khan, Muhammad (1907–74) Military leader and President of Pakistan (1958–69). A Pathan from the Hazara district, he was a professional soldier who, when the state of Pakistan was created (1947), assumed command of military forces in East Pakistan (now Bangladesh). He was appointed commander-in-chief of the Pakistan Army in 1951, Minister of Defence (1954–56), and Chief Martial Law Administrator after the 1958 military coup. For the next ten years he ruled Pakistan as President, pursuing a policy of rapid economic growth, modest land reform, and restricted political life through 'basic democracies', introducing Pakistan's second constitution in 1962. In March 1968 he suffered a serious illness and thereafter lost political control, being replaced in March 1969 by General Yahya Khan.

Ayuthia SIAM.

Azerbaijan A country in western Asia, in the Caucasus. Situated on the west coast of the Caspian Sea, Azerbaijan is bordered by Armenia to the west, Georgia and Russia to the north, and Iraq to the south.

Physical. The Apsheron Peninsula in the north contains the long-established Baku oilfields. The hot and arid Kura valley runs towards the south-east below the Caucasian foothills, cotton and tobacco being cultivated along the river banks. The Caspian coastal plain with a subtropical climate is more naturally fertile; and round it lie well-wooded hills with deep valleys. The mountainous south-west contains the large and scenic Lake Gyoygyol and numerous deposits of copper, iron, and lead.

Economy. Azerbaijan was the world's leader in petroleum production at the beginning of the 20th century, and has rich mineral resources, including petroleum, gas, and metal ores. Industry concentrates on power, manufacturing, and chemicals production. Cotton and tobacco are the main crops; viticulture is also important.

History. The country comprises the part of the Azerbaijan area that was conquered by Russia in the 18th and 19th centuries (the remainder of the traditional Azerbaijan area is now incorporated in Iran). By 1914 it was the largest oil-producing area in the world, centred on Baku. After the Bolshevik Revolution in Russia of 1917, it declared its independence, but in 1920 was conquered by the Red Army. In 1922 Azerbaijan was combined with Armenia and Georgia as the Transcaucasian Soviet Federated Socialist Republic. This split in 1936 into three separate Soviet socialist republics. The autonomous region of Nakhichevan formed an exclave within Armenia, while a second area, that of Nagorno Karabagh, inhabited by Christian Armenians and claimed by Armenia, lay within Azerbaijan. Severe violence erupted over the latter, leading to military intervention by the Soviet Union in 1989. In 1991 Azerbaijan declared its independence, as a Shi'ite Muslim state. The autonomous region of Nakhichevan allegedly received aid from Iran during 1992 in a bid for its own independence. In 1991 the disputed status of Nagorno Karabagh led to fighting between Azerbaijani and Armenian troops, which continued until a ceasefire was agreed in 1994. Nagorno Karabagh declared itself to be independent in 1996, and attempts to negotiate a permanent agreement have continued.

In 1993 President Elchibey was ousted in a military coup; President Geidar Aliyev took over, his position being ratified in elections. The government agreed to several oil exploitation deals with foreign companies in 1994. Aliyev consolidated his hold on power in 1995, surviving a coup attempt and winning elections from which many opposition parties were excluded. Azerbaijan is a member of the COMMONWEALTH OF INDEPENDENT STATES.

CAPITAL:	Baku
AREA:	88,606 sq km (33,430 sq miles)
POPULATION:	7.570 million (1996)
CURRENCY:	1 manat = 100 gopik
RELIGIONS:	Shiite Muslim; minority religions
ETHNIC GROUPS:	Azeri 83.0%; Armenian 6.0%; Russian 6.0%
LANGUAGES:	Azeri Turkish (official); Armenian, Russian, and other minority languages
INTERNATIONAL ORGANIZATIONS:	UN; Commonwealth of Independent States; CSCE; North Atlantic Co-operation Council

Azikiwe, (Benjamin) Nnamdi (1904–96) Nigerian statesman, first President of NIGERIA (1963–66). An Ibo (Igbo), he founded the National Council of Nigeria and the Cameroons (NCNC) and exerted a strong influence throughout the 1940s on emerging Nigerian nationalism. He held a number of political posts before becoming the first governor-general of Nigeria (1960–63). He was deposed by a military coup (1966), which ousted the civilian government, but remained leader of the Nigerian People's Party (until political parties were banned in 1984) and was a member of the Nigerian Council of State (1979–83).

Azores A group of ten islands set out in three groups in the North Atlantic Ocean. Partially autonomous from Portugal, they are of volcanic origin and stand on the great mid-Atlantic ridge, the largest island being San Miguel some 66 km (41 miles) long and 15 km (9 miles) wide. Pico in the central group rises to 2,316 m (7,598 feet), and small volcanic eruptions still cause disturbances. Hot springs and fumaroles are a feature on some of the islands, which are steep and heavily dissected by valleys. The winters are mild and the soil fertile, yielding fruit, grain, tobacco, and rich pasture.

Uninhabited prior to their discovery by Portuguese explorers in the 14th century, the Azores were settled by colonists from Portugal and Flanders. The Portuguese crown took control after 1494. In 1581 the battle of Salga between the Spanish and Portuguese fleets took place off Terceira Island, and in 1591 British admiral Sir Richard GRENVILLE, in the *Revenge*, fought the entire Spanish fleet in a celebrated action off the Azores.

Aztec The Central American Indian people originally known as the *Méxica* (whence Mexico) or *Tenochea* (whence TENOCHTITLÁN, their capital). Like their TOLTEC predecessors, they originated somewhere in northern Mexico. During the early 13th century they migrated into the valley of Mexico and eventually settled on an island in Lake Texcoco (later mostly drained by the Spaniards), after the instructions of their gods to settle where they witnessed an eagle sitting on a cactus devouring a snake. From this base they formed an alliance with two other cities – Texcoco and Tlacopán – against Atzcapotzalco, defeated it, and proceeded through the 15th century to conquer the other cities of the valley, then to carve out an empire stretching from coast to coast, north to the deserts, and south to the MAYA kingdoms of YUCATÁN, by the early 16th century.

Three things characterized their culture: their religion which demanded large-scale human sacrifices particularly to their god of war, Huitzilopochtli; their efficient use of *chinampas* (artificial garden islands built in regular grids out into lakes and divided by canals) to feed their vast population; and their widespread trading network and system of tribute administration.

However, many of their subjects had only recently been subdued, and, eager to lose their tributary status, became allies of CORTÉS in 1519. The Aztec ruler MONTEZUMA considered that the Spaniards were descendants of the god-king QUETZALCÓATL, and did not appreciate the danger his kingdom faced. He received Cortés, who subsequently held him as a hostage. In 1520 there was an Aztec revolt and Montezuma was killed. His successor, Cuauhtémoc, the last Aztec ruler, resisted the invaders, but in 1521, Cortés captured Tenochtitlán and defeated the empire.

B

Baader-Meinhof gang Byname of the West German anarchist terrorist group, Red Army Faction. Its leaders were Andreas Baader (1943–77) and Ulrike Meinhof (1934–76). The group set itself to oppose the capitalist organization of German society and the presence of US armed forces by engaging in murders, bombings, and kidnappings. The leaders were arrested in 1972, and their trial and deaths (by suicide) received considerable publicity. The group continued its terrorist activities in the 1980s, forming a number of splinter cells.

Ba'athism An Arab political doctrine that combines elements of SOCIALIST thinking with pan-Arabism. This theory of Arab NATIONALISM conceives of the 'Arab nation' as a single entity stretching from Morocco to IRAQ, which has been artificially divided by IMPERIALISM. Ba'athism originated in SYRIA, where the first Ba'ath Party was founded in 1953. Ba'athists have held power in Syria since 1963 and Iraq since 1968, although the two branches of the movement are deeply divided. There have been further divisions between its civilian and military elements. While the Iraqi leader Saddam HUSSEIN employed the slogans of pan-Arabism to justify his invasion of Kuwait in 1990, the Ba'ath Party in Iraq has been reduced to an instrument of state power.

Babeuf, François Noël (1760–97) French Revolutionary who called himself 'Caius-GRACCHUS, tribune of the people'. A domestic servant before the French Revolution, he moved to Paris in 1794. There he started to publish the *Journal de la liberté de la presse*, in which he argued that the Revolution should go further than establishing political equality. He formed a small group (the Equals) of discontented artisans and soldiers and campaigned for the equal ownership of property by all. This idea thrived in the turmoil following ROBESPIERRE's execution but secret agents learnt of his plans for an armed rising on 11 May 1796. He was captured and was executed and his followers were executed or deported. His conspiracy influenced later revolutionary socialists, particularly in the 1830s.

Babington Plot (1586) A conspiracy to co-ordinate a Spanish invasion of England with a rising of English Catholics, to assassinate ELIZABETH I, and to replace her on the throne with MARY, Queen of Scots. Sir Anthony Babington (1561–86) was the go-between in the secret preparations. WALSINGHAM monitored Babington's correspondence with the captive Queen Mary until he had enough evidence of her treasonable intentions to have her tried and executed in 1587, Babington having been executed after torture at Tyburn.

Bábism The doctrines of a messianic Shiite Muslim sect founded in 1844 by the Persian Sayyid Ali Muhammad of Shiraz (1819–50). Known as the Báb ed-Din (the gate or intermediary between man and God), he declared himself to be the long-awaited Mahdi. For inciting insurrection the Báb was arrested in 1848 by the government and executed in 1850, his remains being

interred (1909) on Mt Carmel, Palestine. In 1863 Baha'ullah and his son Abdul Baha declared themselves the new leaders, and the religion they founded became known as BAHA'ISM.

Babur (1483–1530) The first MOGUL Emperor of India (1526–30). He was born in Ferghana, Central Asia, in a princely family of mixed Mongol and Turkish blood. Failure to recover his father's lands caused him to turn reluctantly south-east, for India seemed to present the last hope for his ambitions. Defeat of Ibrahim Lodi, the Afghan ruler of Delhi, at the battle of PANIPAT in 1526 initiated 200 years of strong Mogul rule in India. Having conquered much of northern India, Babur ruled by force, lacking any civil administration. In addition to his military genius, he possessed a love of learning and wrote his own memoirs.

Babylon An ancient city in Mesopotamia on the River Euphrates. Its ruins stand near the town of Al Hillah in Iraq, *c.* 90 km (55 miles) south of modern Baghdad. It was twice the centre of a major empire. The first was established by the Amorite Sumuabum in 1894 BC and augmented by his successors, above all HAMMURABI. Following a Hittite attack *c.* 1595, it fell under the rule of the Kassites (another Indo-European people) *c.* 1570 for over 400 years (although the ASSYRIANS captured it briefly in 1234), before being looted by the Elamites (also from western Persia) in 1158. They were in turn defeated by Nebuchadnezzar I (ruled 1124–1103) who established a dynasty that lasted into the early 10th century. Thereafter Babylon came much more under Assyrian influence, and SENNACHERIB, despairing of controlling the local tribesmen, destroyed the city in 689. His successor Esarhaddon had it rebuilt.

In 625 BC the Chaldeans, led by Nabopolassar, took control of Babylon, and under his son NEBUCHADNEZZAR II the second great Babylonian empire was extended as far as Palestine and Syria. Babylon itself was fortified with extensive new walls and was the scene of much building activity. The Chaldean dynasty continued until CYRUS II (the Great) captured the city in 539 BC. It flourished under the ACHAEMENIDS but never again became an independent power in its own right.

The city of Nebuchadnezzar II's time was the largest of the ancient world and included the Hanging Gardens (SEVEN WONDERS OF THE WORLD), and the temple of Marduk with its ziggurat, popularly identified with the Tower of Babel described in the Bible. It derived much wealth from its position on the north-south and east-west trade routes. Although considerable remains are still extant, there are fears that the recent attempts of Saddam Hussein's regime to rebuild Babylon may have done serious damage.

Bacon, Francis, 1st Baron Verulam, Viscount St Albans (1561–1626) English statesman and philosopher. He became a barrister in 1582 and entered Parliament two years later. In the 1590s he prospered as a member of the ESSEX faction at court, and published his first edition of witty, aphoristic *Essays* (1597). Under James I he had to compete with COKE for high legal office, but when Coke began to oppose the crown, Bacon was taken up by Villiers (Duke of BUCKINGHAM) and rose to be Lord Chancellor (1618). In 1621 he was impeached by Parliament for accepting bribes and his political career was ruined. In retirement he devoted himself to literary and philosophical work. His emphasis on the observation and classification of the natural world, in *The Advancement of Learning* (1605), *Novum Organum* (1620), and *New Atlantis* (1627), contributed significantly to the European SCIENTIFIC REVOLUTION and to the ENLIGHTENMENT. His *Essays* (1597–1625) and other writings mark him as a master of English prose.

Bacon's Rebellion (1676) An uprising in Virginia, North America, led by an English immigrant, Nathaniel Bacon. Dissident county leaders and landless ex-servants followed his opposition to Sir William BERKELEY. Though he was initially successful, Bacon died soon after the passage of reforms in the Virginian Assembly. Underlying the rebellion were problems caused by depressed tobacco prices and lack of colonial autonomy.

Bactria An area famed in antiquity for its fertility and approximating to northern Afghanistan and its environs. It was a SATRAPY (province) under the ACHAEMENIDS, and put up fierce resistance to ALEXANDER THE GREAT, who conquered it in 329 BC. In the mid-3rd century BC Diodotus I established a kingdom independent of the SELEUCIDS, and although his successor Euthydemus I (ruled 235–200 BC) was compelled to acknowledge Antiochus the Great as his overlord, Menander (ruled 155–130) brought under his control an area comprising all of modern Afghanistan and parts of Pakistan and southern Russia. In *c.* 130 BC the northern part was conquered by the Yueh-Chih (a nomadic tribe from western China) and *c.* 100 the southern part by the Sakas (a Scythian tribe). In the late 1st century BC part of the Chinese tribe, known as the Kushan dynasty, became dominant and made Bactria a centre of the growing faith of BUDDHISM. It subsequently came under the Sassanians, the White Huns, and in the late 7th century, Arabs.

Baden-Powell, Robert Stephenson Smyth Baden-Powell, 1st Baron (1857–1941) British soldier and founder of the Boy Scout movement (1907). As a soldier he had served in India and Afghanistan, and was the successful defender of Mafeking in the Second BOER WAR. His knowledge of the skill of gaining information about hostile territory was fundamental to the teachings of the Scout movement. Training in self-reliance and a code of moral conduct were to be the other hallmarks of the movement. By the end of World War I the movement was developing on an international scale. With his sister, Agnes, he founded the Girl Guide movement (1910).

Badoglio, Pietro (1871–1956) Italian general and Prime Minister. By 1925 he was chief of staff; MUSSOLINI appointed him governor of Libya (1929) and sent him (1935) to rescue the faltering Italian campaign in ETHIOPA. He captured Addis Ababa and became governor. When Mussolini was deposed in 1943, he was chosen to head the new non-fascist government. He made peace with the advancing Allies, declared war against Germany, but resigned soon afterwards.

Baganda A group of settled farmers in Uganda. The Baganda constituted a kingdom in the 19th century, in which the king was seen as the supreme ruler who exercised his power through a system of district chiefs. The Baganda consist of 50 exogamous (based on marriage outside the group) clans, each distinguished by totemic symbols. Originally practitioners of a form of ancestor worship, they are now predominantly Christian.

Bagehot, Walter (1826–77) British economist, journalist, and man of letters. He was joint editor of the *National Review* and later editor of *The Economist* (1860–77), which he made a journal of international importance. Bagehot is best known for his book *The English Constitution* (1867), in which he applied a rigorous analysis to his country's political system in order to distinguish between the realities of power which he saw as lying in the cabinet and the House of Commons, and its formal trappings, which he saw as the crown and the House of Lords.

Baha'ism A religion founded in Iran by Baha'ullah (Arabic, 'Glory of God') (1817–92) with about 5 million adherents throughout the world. Following the suppression of the MILLENARIAN movement BÁBISM in Iran and the execution of its leader, the Báb, in 1850, Baha'ullah declared himself in 1863 to be the new prophet heralded by the Báb. Baha'ullah acknowledged the revelations of earlier prophets such as Jesus and Muhammad, but held that the single identity of God must be retaught by new prophecy to each generation. Baha'is believe in the spiritual progression of the world to unity and their ideal is an international community with one language. Baha'i temples are open to the faithful of all creeds. A Universal House of Justice administers the religion, with its centres in Haifa and Akko (Acre) in Israel. There is no clergy or ritual; spiritual practice includes daily private prayer and an annual period of fasting, which ends with the festival of Nōw Rūz, the Persian New Year at the spring equinox. Baha'is stress the equality of women and the importance of monogamous family life. Although Baha'is regard the KORAN and Muhammad with reverence, to Muslims the Baha'is are heretics who have displaced the Koran from its position as the final and most important revelation; this has led to persecution in Iran since the religion's inception, with renewed force since the Islamic revolution of 1979. Furthermore, the location of the Baha'is world centre in Israel has led to an association of Baha'ism with that country and made the Baha'is a target of anti-Semitic sentiment.

Bahamas, The Commonwealth of The A country in the Caribbean, consisting of a group of islands in the western Atlantic Ocean, set between Florida and Hispaniola.

Physical. Of the 700 mainly coral islands some 30 are large enough to live on, the largest being the Grand Bahama and New Providence islands. The climate is very warm.

Economy. Tourism makes a large contribution to the economy, while exports are dominated by petroleum products, refined from imported crude oil. A favourable system of taxation has led to the Bahamas becoming an important financial centre. There is some industry, and shipping has expanded since free-flag status was established in 1976.

History. The earliest known inhabitants of the Bahamas were Arawak Indians. According to most historians, Guanahani was the site of Columbus's first landing in the Americas in 1492. The Spanish subsequently raided the islands, attacking and enslaving the Arawaks, but did not settle there. In 1629 the Bahamas were included in the British Carolina colonies, but actual settlement did not begin until 1648, with settlers from BERMUDA. By this time all the Arawaks had died out. Possession was disputed by Spain, but was acknowledged in 1670 under the Treaty of Madrid. The Bahamas became a British Crown Colony in 1717. Of major strategic importance, they were captured by the Spanish in 1782, but returned to Britain in 1783. There were also frequent raids by pirates. Many Africans were brought to the islands to work as slaves in the sugar plantations (SLAVE TRADE). A civil-rights movement led to the creation of the Progressive Liberal Party (PLP) in 1953. The PLP advocated parliamentary representation for the Black majority, and independence for the Bahamas. Internal self-government was achieved in 1964, the PLP were elected in 1967, and independence was gained in 1973. In 1992 the Free National Movement (FNM) won elections, ending 25 years of PLP government.

CAPITAL:	Nassau
AREA:	13,939 sq km (5,382 sq miles)
POPULATION:	280,000 (1996)
CURRENCY:	1 Bahamian dollar = 100 cents
RELIGIONS:	Non-Anglican Protestant 55.2%; Anglican 20.1%; Roman Catholic 18.8%
ETHNIC GROUPS:	Black 72.3%; Mixed 14.2%; White 12.9%
LANGUAGES:	English (official); English creole; French (Haitian) creole
INTERNATIONAL ORGANIZATIONS:	UN; OAS; Commonwealth; CARICOM

Bahmani A dynasty of sultans of the DECCAN plateau in central India (1347–1518). The dynasty was founded by Ala-ud-din Bahman Shah, who in 1347 rebelled against his Delhi suzerain. His successors expanded over the west-central Deccan, reaching a peak in the late 15th century under Mahmud Gawan, who successfully held encroaching Hindu and Muslim powers at bay. During the early 16th century the Hindu empire of VIJAYANAGAR to the south expanded at the Bahmanis' expense, and between 1490 and 1518 the sultanate gradually dissolved into five successor Muslim states, Bijapur, Ahmadnagar, Golconda, Berar, and Bidar.

Bahrain A sheikhdom consisting of a group of islands 32 km (20 miles) off the Arabian coast of the Gulf.

Physical. The largest island is some 16 km (10 miles) wide and three times as long. The climate is hot and humid, although rainfall is very light.

Economy. The country's exports are dominated by crude oil and petroleum products from a large oil refinery on Bahrain Island. An aluminium smelter constitutes the largest non-oil industry in the Gulf; there is also a growing banking and communications sector. Shipbuilding and repair in dry docks are also significant.

History. Iran, which ruled Bahrain from 1602 to 1783, was expelled by the al-Khalifas, who still reign. British political control dates from 1820. Oil was discovered in 1932, when the Bahrain National Oil Company was formed. After the withdrawal of Britain in 1971 and the abandonment by Iran of its claims, the country joined the Arab League. Tension between Shiite and Sunni communities increased, leading to the suspension of the National Assembly in 1975. Together with other members of the Gulf Co-operation Council (Saudi Arabia, Kuwait, Qatar, and Oman), Bahrain repeatedly called for an end to the IRAN–IRAQ WAR (1980–88), while retaining its neutrality then and in the GULF WAR (1991). Its economy became increasingly diversified as oil reserves dwindled. Increasing opposition to the government and demands for the restoration of the National Assembly led to rising civil unrest in the mid-1990s. The emir responded by instituting moves towards greater democratic representation in 1996.

CAPITAL:	Manama
AREA:	691 sq km (267 sq miles)
POPULATION:	598,000 (1996)
CURRENCY:	1 Bahrain dinar = 1,000 fils
RELIGIONS:	Shiite Muslim 60.0%; Sunni Muslim 40.0%; Christian minority
ETHNIC GROUPS:	Bahraini Arab 68.0%; Iranian, Indian, and Pakistani 24.7%; other Arab 4.1%; European 2.5%
LANGUAGES:	Arabic (official) and minority languages
INTERNATIONAL ORGANIZATIONS:	UN; Arab League; OAPEC; OPEC; GCC

bailiff The estate manager of the lord of the manor in England from the 11th century. In each medieval village there was usually one salaried bailiff (or else a serjeant or reeve, of lesser status). He would make sure that his village reached its annual production target for the lord, for he might be sued if it did not, while he gained the surplus if it was exceeded. The word 'bailiff' gradually shifted its meaning, and in the later Middle Ages, when lords more commonly let out their manors to farmers, the bailiff was one of the lesser officials of the sheriff. The bailiff had always had a legal role in the village, prosecuting on its behalf or acting as the legal representative of individual villagers, but from the 14th century he was primarily the sheriff's representative, authorized to make arrests, summon people to court, and seize property. Farmers and urban landlords also employed him as a rent-collector, knowing that his legal skills could be drawn on in cases of non-payment.

Baker, Sir Samuel White (1821–93) British explorer who traced the Nile tributaries in Ethiopia (1861–62). In 1864, despite the opposition of Arab slave traders, he located the Nile source in Lake Albert Nyanza. Khedive Ismail of Egypt sent him to put down the slave trade (1869–73), which he attempted by establishing Egyptian protectorates in the present UGANDA and opening the lake areas to commerce. Although he set up a skeletal administration, it was not strong enough to be effective.

Bakunin, Mikhail (1814–76) Russian revolutionary, leading exponent of ANARCHISM and founder member of the Russian POPULIST MOVEMENT. He served in the emperor's army until his dismissal in 1835. After taking part in the REVOLUTIONS OF 1848 he was exiled to Siberia. He escaped in 1861 and went to London, which was used as a headquarters for militant anarchists and communists. The first International Workingmen's Association, founded in 1864, was marred by the conflict between MARX and Bakunin, who called for violent means to destroy the existing political and social order, splitting the two factions for years to come.

Balaklava, Battle of (25 October 1854) An inconclusive battle during the CRIMEAN WAR. Following their defeat on the River Alma, the Russians retreated to Sevastopol, which was then besieged by British, French, and Turkish troops, supplied from the small port of Balaklava. Russian forces moved down into the Balaklava plain, where they were met by the British cavalry division under Lord Lucan. Lord Raglan, British commander-in-chief, sent orders to the Light Brigade under Lord Cardigan to 'prevent the enemy carrying away the guns'. It is assumed this order referred to guns on the Vorontsov Heights, but Cardigan understood it to require a direct frontal charge down the valley. Fired on by guns from both flanks and to the front, he and a few dragoons reached the Russian line before retreating. In this 'Charge of the Light Brigade' 247 men were killed out of a force of 673. The Russians failed to capture Balaklava, but they held on to the Vorontsov Heights and thus cut the paved supply-road from the port to the besieging allied forces above Sevastopol.

balance of power (in international relations) The maintenance of international order by means of an equilibrium of power among different states; the term can also refer to the deliberate policy of achieving this equilibrium. If one state or group of states seeks a preponderance of power, others may form alliances in order to counter its attempt at dominance. However, misperceptions of the relative powers of different states might result in war. The idea of the balance of power dominated the foreign policies of the GREAT POWERS during the 19th century; it succeeded in maintaining the independence of states, as well as providing some form of international order. After World War I there was a movement towards a system characterized by co-operation rather than the use of force to maintain equilibrium, but the underlying theory may be considered still to be a key concept in most strategic planning.

Balboa, Vasco Núñez de (c. 1475–1517) Spanish conquistador, the discoverer of the Pacific Ocean. He first arrived in the New World in 1501 and, after an unsuccessful period as a plantation owner in Hispaniola, he joined and soon became leader of an expedition that founded the town of Darien in the Gulf of Uraba in 1511. There he heard of an ocean beyond the mountains and of the gold of Peru, and in 1513 led an expedition of 190 Spaniards (including Francisco PIZARRO) and 1,000 Indians across the mountains to the ocean. He named it the 'Great South Sea' and took formal possession of it in the name of FERDINAND II (of Spain). The king made him admiral of the South Sea and governor of Panama and Coyba, and sent out a governor to take charge of Darien itself. This new governor, jealous of Balboa and encouraged by Pizarro, had him seized, charged with treason, and executed.

Baldwin, Robert (1804–58) Canadian statesman. Born in York (renamed Toronto in 1834), he was elected to the Assembly of Upper Canada (UPPER AND LOWER CANADA) in 1829, and became one of the leaders of the campaign for reformed government which would give more say to elected representatives. After the Act of Union (1840) he was elected for Canada West and in 1842–43 led a reformist ministry with LA FONTAINE. The DURHAM REPORT had recommended the development of 'responsible government' (responsible to an executive or cabinet dependent on the votes of a majority in the elected legislature), and in 1848 Lord ELGIN was appointed governor-general and instructed to implement this recommendation. Baldwin and LA FONTAINE formed a second coalition ministry (1848–51) which was to be based on such parliamentary procedures. It is sometimes called the 'Great Ministry' for its outstanding reformist accomplishments.

Baldwin, Stanley, 1st Earl Baldwin of Bewdley (1867–1947) British statesman. A Conservative Member of Parliament (1908–37), he was a member of LLOYD GEORGE's coalition (1918–22) but led the Conservative rebellion against him. He was Chancellor of the Exchequer under Bonar LAW and was chosen as Prime Minister in preference to Curzon when Law resigned in 1923. He lost the 1923 election in an attempt to introduce tariffs but returned to office in 1924. His premiership was marked by the return to the GOLD STANDARD, the GENERAL STRIKE, Neville CHAMBERLAIN's social legislation, and the Trades Dispute Act of 1927. He lost the 1929 election, but served under Ramsay MACDONALD in the coalition caused by the 1931 crisis, succeeding him as Prime Minister in 1935. His last ministry witnessed the ABDICATION CRISIS, which he handled skilfully. In 1935 he approved the Hoare-Laval pact which allowed fascist Italy to annex Ethiopia. Although international relations continued to deteriorate with the German occupation of the Rhineland and the outbreak of the SPANISH CIVIL WAR, Baldwin opposed demands for rearmament, believing that the public would not support it. He resigned the premiership in 1937.

Baldwin I (c. 1058–1118) King of Jerusalem (1100–18). On the death of his brother, GODFREY OF BOUILLON, he was crowned first King of Jerusalem. He foiled the ambitions of the Patriarch Daimbert and ensured that Jerusalem would become a secular kingdom with himself as its first monarch. His control of the Levantine ports secured vital sea communications with Europe, and by asserting his suzerainty over other Crusader principalities he consolidated the primacy of the Latin Kingdom of Jerusalem.

Balewa, Alhaji Sir Abubakar Tafawa (1912–66) Nigerian statesman. He entered politics in 1946, and became a member of the Central Legislative Council in 1947. The first Prime Minister of the Federation of Nigeria, he retained his office when the country became independent (1960) until he was killed in an army coup. He was a founder and deputy president general of the country's largest political party, the Northern People's Congress.

Balfour, Arthur James, 1st Earl (1848–1930) British statesman, nephew of Lord SALISBURY. As Chief Secretary of Ireland (1887–91) he was an opponent of HOME RULE and earned from the Irish the nickname 'Bloody Balfour'. His premiership of 1902–05 was undermined by his vacillation over tariff reform. His Education Act (1902) established a national system of secondary education. He created a Committee of Imperial Defence (1904), and helped to establish the *entente cordiale* (1904) with France, by which the supremacy of Britain in Egypt and of France in Morocco were recognized. The Conservatives were crushingly defeated in the 1906 general election. Balfour then used the House of Lords, described by Lloyd George as 'Mr Balfour's poodle', to attempt to block contentious Liberal legislation. He resigned the leadership of the Conservative Party in 1911. As Foreign Secretary in Lloyd George's war cabinet, he is associated with the BALFOUR DECLARATION (1917) promising the Jews a national home in Palestine. In the 1920s he supported the cause of DOMINION status. The Statute of WESTMINSTER owed much to his inspiration.

Balfour Declaration (2 November 1917) A declaration by Britain in favour of a Jewish national home in Palestine. It took the form of a letter from Lord BALFOUR (British Foreign Secretary) to Lord Rothschild, a prominent ZIONIST, announcing the support of the British government for the establishment of a national home for the Jewish people in Palestine without prejudice to the civil and religious rights of the non-Jewish peoples of Palestine or the rights and political status of Jews in other countries. The Declaration subsequently formed the basis of the mandate given to Britain for Palestine and of British policy in that country until 1947.

Bali An island in INDONESIA, lying immediately east of Java. Bali's palm-fringed beaches make the island a popular tourist destination.

History. Long controlled by Hindu states, Bali resisted ISLAM when it spread through Java in the 16th century. Refugee princes from MAJAPAHIT in the early 16th century and later from Belambangan in east Java, strengthened Hindu influence in the island, although the caste system was never fully adopted. (The Balinese religion is a unique form of HINDUISM, although it also incorporates some elements of animism, and is characterized by elaborate art forms such as wood carving, temple architecture, dance, and music.) The Balinese were divided into nine warring states and also engaged in piracy, slave trading, and shipwrecking, which brought them into conflict with the Dutch. Although three Dutch expeditions (1846, 1848, and 1849), established control in the north coast areas, the rulers in the south and east only submitted after the *prang puputan* (final battles) at Den Pasar, Pamĕcutan, and Klungkung in 1906 and 1908, when the white-clad Hindu *rajas* and their retainers allowed themselves to be ritually slaughtered by the Dutch forces. Occupied by the Japanese during World War II, Bali became a part of Indonesia after 1945.

Balkans A region of south-east Europe, consisting of a great peninsula bounded by the Adriatic, Aegean, and Black Seas. It now comprises ALBANIA, continental GREECE, BULGARIA, European TURKEY, south-east ROMANIA, CROATIA, BOSNIA-HERZEGOVINA, YUGOSLAVIA (Serbia and Montenegro), and the Former Yugoslav Republic of MACEDONIA.

Physical. The region is very mountainous, taking its name from the Balkan Mountains south of the Danube. The Dinaric Alps of Croatia, the Pindus Mountains of Greece, and the Rhodope Mountains of Bulgaria, the other main ranges, all act as barriers to the mild climate of the Mediterranean. The scenery varies greatly, from the barren Karst country of Croatia, to the wooded slopes of the Rila Mountains in Bulgaria, and to the flat Danubian plains.

History. The Balkans have been inhabited since *c.* 200,000 BC and there is archaeological evidence of the Aurignacian and Gravettian cultures (see UPPER PALAEOLITHIC). By 7,000 BC NEOLITHIC culture had developed, including a fine decorated pottery. The area was then settled by semi-nomadic farmers from the Russian steppes (*c.* 3,500 BC) and then by central European URNFIELD CULTURES. It was part of several empires, being dominated by the Persians, the Greeks, the Romans, and, in the early Middle Ages, by the Byzantines. Although Serbs, Bulgarians, and MAGYARS were able to carve brief empires in the area, by the late 14th century it yielded to the westward expansion of the OTTOMANS. They reached the Dardanelles in 1354, Macedonia by the 1370s, and, after the battle of KOSSOVO in 1389, marched on to SERBIA. The balance of power changed after the last siege of Vienna in 1683, and the Turks were gradually driven back by a revived HABSBURG empire, and by Russia.

Despite centuries of Turkish rule and periodic persecution, the subject nations largely retained their languages and religions. In the 19th century, the grip of Turkey weakened, and increasingly Russia and Austria quarrelled over the gains to be made there. Russia championed the Balkan peoples, many of whom were Slavs and Orthodox Christians, while Austria feared the rise of PAN-SLAVISM. Serbia, Bulgaria, and Montenegro all became independent states in the later 19th century. In 1912 these three countries and Greece formed the Balkan League to counter Turkish influence in the area, a development that led to the outbreak of the BALKAN WARS. After Serbia's success in the wars, Austria's hostility towards Pan-Slavism contributed to the outbreak of World War I. As a result of the VERSAILLES PEACE SETTLEMENT frontiers were re-drawn and attempts made to introduce democratic government. These failed and authoritarian regimes emerged in a majority of the states between the wars. The Balkan Pact of 1934 sought to unify the countries by a non-aggression treaty and guarantees of the Balkan frontiers. After 1945 the states varied in their allegiance between Soviet and Western politics. A second Balkan Pact between Yugoslavia, Greece, and Turkey was concluded in 1954, which provided for common military assistance in the face of aggression. It quickly collapsed over the issue of CYPRUS. The area was in turmoil from 1991 to 1995 as Yugoslavia disintegrated into its constituent republics and a savage ethnic conflict developed in Bosnia-Herzegovina.

Balkan Wars (1912–13) Two short wars, fought between Serbia, Montenegro, Greece, Romania, Turkey, and Bulgaria for the possession of remaining European territories of the OTTOMAN EMPIRE. In 1912 Greece, Serbia, Bulgaria, and Montenegro formed the Balkan League; officially to demand better treatment for Christians in Turkish Macedonia, in reality to seize the remaining Turkish territory in Europe while Turkey was embroiled in a war with Italy. In October 1912 the League armies captured all but Constantinople (now Istanbul). European ambassadors intervened to re-draw the Balkans map to the advantage of Bulgaria and detriment of Serbia in the Treaty of London (May 1913). A month later, Bulgaria launched a pre-emptive attack on the Serbs and Greeks, who coveted Bulgaria's gains, but was defeated. In the Treaty of Bucharest (August

1913) Greece and Serbia partitioned Macedonia, and Romania gained part of Bulgaria. Albania, which had been under Turkish suzerainty, was made an independent Muslim principality. A 'big Serbia' now presented a considerable threat to Austria-Hungary. Russia promised to support Serbia in its nationalist struggle, and Germany to give military aid to Austria-Hungary. The assassination of the Austrian heir apparent, Archduke Francis Ferdinand, at Sarajevo (1914) gave Austria-Hungary the pretext to invade Serbia, leading to the outbreak of World War I six weeks later.

Ball, John (d. 1381) English rebel. He was a priest who combined the religious teachings of John WYCLIF with an egalitarian social message. He was imprisoned for heresy, but released in June 1381 by the Kentish rebels in the PEASANTS' REVOLT. Outside London he preached to them and incited them to attack anyone opposed to his ideal of social equality. A month later he was captured, tried, and hanged as a traitor.

Ballance, John (1839–93) New Zealand statesman. In the 1890 elections the Liberals emerged as the first party in New Zealand politics, broadly united on a programme of radical reform, and Ballance became Premier (1891–93). His strong cabinet introduced land taxes to break up large estates, new leasehold tenures, and labour regulations. Ballance and his Liberal successors established the tradition of using the state to regulate the economy and protect poorer groups, laying the foundations of basic stability in New Zealand society.

Balliol, Edward (d. *c.* 1364) King of Scotland (1332–36), son of John Balliol. In 1332 he landed in Fife to reclaim the throne his father had given up. He defeated the Scots at Dupplin and was crowned at Scone. Within three months he was forced to flee but returned with the help of EDWARD III of England after his victory at Halidon Hill. In 1341 Balliol was again expelled from Scotland and in 1356 he resigned his claim to the Scottish throne.

Balliol, John (*c.* 1240–1314) King of Scotland (1292–96). He was descended through his maternal grandmother from DAVID I of Scotland, and in 1291–92 his claim to the crown was upheld in a trial between him and Robert Bruce, Lord of Annandale. The trial was arranged by EDWARD I of England, and less than a month after his coronation (30 November 1292) Balliol grudgingly did homage to Edward as his superior. In 1295 he attempted to ally with France, which resulted in an English invasion of Scotland. Balliol was forced to give up his kingdom to Edward and was taken as a captive to England, before retiring to his estates in France.

Balmaceda, José Manuel (1840–91) Chilean statesman and liberal reformer. He was first elected to the Chilean Congress as a Liberal in 1864. As leader of the anti-clerical group he was sent to Argentina in 1878 to persuade that country not to enter the War of the PACIFIC. He became a member of the cabinet of President Santa Maria (1881–86) and himself was then elected President (1886–91). Chile was experiencing rapid economic expansion with both the copper and nitrate industries booming. Balmaceda instituted wide reforms and a large public works programme. Despite national prosperity, however, tension arose between President and Congress, which Balmaceda increasingly ignored. In

January 1891 this resulted in civil war. Balmaceda took refuge in the Argentinian Embassy, where, rather than face trial, he shot himself.

Baltic Entente (1934) A mutual defence pact between Estonia, Latvia, and Lithuania. Soon after World War I there were negotiations for an alliance between all the countries which had recently broken away from the Russian empire, that is, Poland, Finland, Estonia, Latvia, and Lithuania, but these collapsed. Latvia and Estonia did however make an agreement in 1923, which Lithuania joined in 1934. The Pact helped to stimulate economic and cultural links, but in terms of defence proved unable to prevent the Nazi–Soviet Pact of 1939, whereby all three countries were to be absorbed into the Soviet Union.

Bancroft, Edward (1744–1821) American traitor. Born in Massachusetts, he studied medicine in London. He met Benjamin FRANKLIN, and during the War of Independence was a friend of Arthur Lee and Silas Dean when they were negotiating an alliance with the French and became secretary to the American peace delegation. Bancroft was actually an agent for England at an annual fee of £500 and a life pension and it was almost a century before his activities as a British agent were discovered.

Banda, Hastings Kamuzu (1906–97) Malawi statesman and President (1966–95). Son of a peasant in Nyasaland, he worked on the Rand goldfield and then went to the USA and Britain, where he trained and practised as a doctor, his home in London becoming a centre for African exiles. In 1953 he went to Ghana to work as a doctor, before returning to his homeland. Here he became politically active and was arrested for an alleged plot, and imprisoned for one year. On his release, he travelled to London for a constitutional conference on Nyasaland. When self-government was granted (1963) he became Prime Minister. In 1964 with independence, Nyasaland changed its name to Malawi and in 1966, when it became a republic, he was elected President, becoming President for Life in 1971. His cautious policies towards South Africa left him a somewhat isolated figure within the Commonwealth, and he was increasingly resented by younger Malawian politicians. For a long time known as 'the Little Messiah', his popularity began to wane in the early 1990s as calls for multiparty politics were ignored. After a year of civil unrest Banda agreed to hold a referendum in 1993 and the population voted in favour of introducing multiparty democracy. Parliament then approved a new constitution and Banda lost Malawi's first multiparty elections in 1994. In 1995 he was put on trial for allegedly ordering the murder in 1983 of four politicians, but was acquitted.

Bandaranaike, Sirimavo Ratwatte Dias (1916–   ) Sinhalese stateswoman, Prime Minister of Sri Lanka (1960–65, 1970–77, 1994–   ) The world's first woman Prime Minister, she succeeded her husband, S. W. R. BANDARANAIKE after his assassination. Opposition to her policies and continuing ethnic conflict resulted in an overwhelming defeat in the 1977 elections. She was charged with misuse of power in 1980, stripped of her civil rights for six years, and expelled from Parliament.

Her daughter, Chandrika Bandaranaike Kumaratunga, became Prime Minister and then President in 1994, being succeeded as Prime Minister by her mother.

Bandaranaike, S(olomon) W(est) R(idgeway) D(ias)

(1899–1959) Sinhalese statesman. He formed the Maha Sinhala Party in the 1920s. In 1931 he was elected to the new State Council and after independence he assumed ministerial power. In 1952 he founded the Sri Lanka Freedom Party (SLFP), which was the leading partner in the coalition which won the 1956 elections, attracting left-wing and Buddhist support. As Prime Minister (1956–59) Bandaranaike pursued a policy of promoting the Sinhalese language, Buddhism, socialism, and neutrality. His policy alienated the Tamils. After his assassination in September 1959 by a dissident Buddhist monk, his widow, Mrs Sirimavo BANDARANAIKE (1916–   ), succeeded him as Prime Minister.

bandkeramik A kind of pottery (decorated with incised ribbon-like ornament) that was characteristic of the first NEOLITHIC settlers in central Europe; it gives its name to their culture. These peoples spread up from the Balkans c. 5000 BC. They occupied small plots of land on fertile soil near rivers, where they built wooden longhouses for themselves and their livestock, and cultivated cereals, which they introduced to this area. They formed the basis of later Neolithic populations.

Bandung Conference (1955) A conference of Asian and African states at Bandung in Java, Indonesia. Organized on the initiative of President SUKARNO and other leaders of the Non-Aligned Movement, the Bandung Conference brought together 29 states in an attempt to form a non-aligned bloc opposed to colonialism and the 'imperialism' of the superpowers. The five principles of non-aggression, respect for sovereignty, non-interference in internal affairs, equality, and peaceful co-existence were adopted, but the subsequent emergence of the non-aligned movement was hamstrung by the deterioration of relations between India and China, and by the conflicting forces set loose by decolonization.

Bangladesh A tropical low-lying country of the Indian subcontinent.

Physical. Situated at the head of the Bay of Bengal, Bangladesh is mainly occupied by the deltas of the Ganges and the Brahmaputra. It is a land of rivers, which flood regularly in the monsoon season, leaving fertile soil on their banks. The south-west delta area, the Sundarbans, is mainly swamp and jungle; the region is subject to frequent cyclones, which cause immense damage.

Economy. The country grows 70% of the world's supply of jute, and jute products are an important export, despite falling world demand. Other exports include clothing, shrimp, and leather goods. Industry is limited; the economy is primarily agrarian, with rice the most important food crop. There are substantial undeveloped reserves of oil, coal, and natural gas. The country is one of the world's poorest and most densely populated, and relies heavily on foreign aid.

History. Bangladesh was established in 1971 from territories which had previously formed the eastern part of Pakistan. Evidence of discontent in East Pakistan first appeared in the 1952 Bengali-language agitation and became much stronger after the 1965 INDO-PAKISTAN WAR.

In 1966 the AWAMI LEAGUE put forward a demand for greater autonomy which it proposed to implement after its victory in the 1970 elections. In March 1971, when this demand was rejected by the military government of Pakistan, civil war began, leading to a massive exodus of refugees to India. India sent help to the East Pakistan guerrillas (the Mukti Bahini). In the war of December 1971, Indian troops defeated the Pakistan forces in East Pakistan. The independence of Bangladesh was proclaimed in 1971 and recognized by Pakistan in 1974. The first Prime Minister, Mujibur Rahman, was murdered in 1975 and a period of political chaos, ethnic riots, floods, and famine followed, Bangladesh being declared the world's poorest country in 1987. In 1990 the military leader President Ershad was forced to resign, was arrested, and imprisoned for corruption (he was released on bail in 1997). Elections in 1991 restored civilian rule under Prime Minister Begum Zia. The presidential form of government was replaced in 1991 when a parliamentary constitution was adopted. Abdur Rahman Biswas was elected to the Presidency, which had become primarily a ceremonial office. From 1995 Zia's government was troubled by strikes and mass protests against privatization and other policies. The political crisis deepened after elections held in February 1996 were boycotted by the opposition and much of the electorate. Following a second election in June 1996 Sheikha Hasina Wajed became the head of a coalition government.

CAPITAL:	Dhaka
AREA:	143,998 sq km (55,598 sq miles)
POPULATION:	123.063 million (1996)
CURRENCY:	1 Bangladesh taka = 100 paisa
RELIGIONS:	Muslim 86.6%; Hindu 12.1%; Buddhist 0.6%; Christian 0.3%
ETHNIC GROUPS:	Bengali 97.7%; Bihari 1.3%; minority tribes 1.0%
LANGUAGES:	Bengali (official) 99.0%; Urdu; Bihari; Hindi
INTERNATIONAL ORGANIZATIONS:	UN; Commonwealth; Colombo Plan

Bank of England The British central bank, popularly known as the 'Old Lady of Threadneedle Street', where its London office stands. It was founded in 1694 as an undertaking by 1268 shareholders to lend £1,200,000 to the government of William III to finance his wars against France. In return it received 8% interest and the right to issue notes against the security of the loan. These privileges were confirmed in 1708 when its capital was doubled, and it was given a monopoly of joint-stock banking, which lasted until 1826, thus preventing rival banks from having large numbers of shareholders. However, small family concerns multiplied and there were over 700 banks in London by 1800. The Bank played an important role in the SOUTH SEA BUBBLE crash of 1720, this time increasing its capital in order to take over some of the South Sea Company's obligations.

The foundation of the Bank of England, the institution of the National Debt, a debt secured against the national income (1694), and the setting up of the Stock Exchange (1773) were part of a financial revolution in England. The rewards from financial speculation led investors to look away from land, the traditional source of wealth, towards the City of London which became a centre of commercial activity and prosperity.

The bank is controlled by the Governor of the Bank of England and a court of 16 directors, appointed by the Crown. Its responsibilities include acting as banker to the government and as its agent in the issue of treasury bills; functioning as lender of last resort to the clearing banks, enabling it to control the amount of money in circulation; issuing the country's stock of money through its subsidiary, the Royal Mint; acting as registrar for government stocks; managing, on behalf of the Treasury, the money market and exchange equalization account; operational responsibility for setting interest rates was restored to the Bank by the Chancellor of the Exchequer in 1997.

Bannockburn, Battle of (24 June 1314). A major battle fought between EDWARD II of England and ROBERT I (the Bruce) at Bannockburn, about 4.5 km (2 miles) from Stirling in Scotland. Edward's large invading army, perhaps 20,000 strong, was outmanoevred and forced into the Bannock burn (or river) and adjacent marshes; it was a disastrous defeat for the English, and Edward was lucky to be able to flee to safety.

Bantam (or Bantĕn) A port in Java, commanding the Sunda Straits. It was a village when MALACCA fell to the Portuguese in 1511 and it attracted traders unfriendly to the Portuguese. After its conversion to ISLAM in the early 16th century, it became a centre for Islamic ideas. At its height, Bantam's control extended over the major pepper-growing areas of southern Sumatra. In 1604 the English built a trading post and the subsequent Dutch conquest of Malacca (1641) and MACASSAR (1667–68) increased the importance of Bantam. Its sultans stirred up anti-Dutch movements among Sumatran pepper-growers. The power of the Bantamese sultans was already waning, however, due to internal rivalries, which the Dutch exploited. In 1684 the Dutch expelled the British. After a rebellion in 1752 Bantam became a vassal of the DUTCH EAST INDIA COMPANY. Its sultanate was finally suppressed in 1832.

Bantu homelands The former 'homelands' reserved for Black Africans in the Republic of South Africa. Ten Bantu homelands were created by the Bantu Self-Government Act of 1959. The Bantu Homelands Constitution Act (1971) established them as Separate Development Self-Governing Areas and envisaged eventual 'independence'. This was in fact granted to four of the homelands, their largely non-resident populations automatically becoming citizens of the new states: Transkei, chiefly Xhosa people, in 1976; Bophuthatswana, chiefly Tswana, in 1977; Venda in 1979; and Ciskei in 1981. Most of these states were made up of separate tracts of poor-quality land and were not viable as independent countries; for this reason, and because many of their citizens were South African residents, they were not recognized in international law. Only South Africa recognized them. Each of the four began with a democratic constitution, but there were military coups and counter-coups in all four during the 1980s, while in 1992 Brigadier Gqozo's troops in Ciskei were involved in the Bisho massacre of ANC demonstrators. The KwaZulu homeland was the power-base of the INKATHA FREEDOM PARTY. The homelands were regarded by many as the clearest manifestation of the policy of APARTHEID. In Bophuthatswana in 1994, President Lucas Mangope unilaterally excluded the Bantu homeland from the forthcoming South African multiracial

elections, and received armed support from extreme right-wing Whites. The South African Defence forces restored order and Mangope was deposed; however, 60 people died in the violence. All the Bantu homelands were abolished following South Africa's adoption of a multiracial constitution in 1994 and South African nationality was restored to all their citizens.

Bao Dai (1913–97) Emperor of Vietnam (1926–45). His initial aim to reform Vietnam did not receive French colonial support. During World War II he collaborated with the Japanese and in 1945 he was forced to abdicate by the VIETMINH. In 1949 he renounced his title and returned to Saigon as head of the state of Vietnam within the French Union. In 1955, after the partition of Vietnam at the GENEVA CONFERENCE, he was once again deposed when power in the new republic of South Vietnam passed to NGO DINH DIEM. He spent the rest of his life in exile, mainly in France.

Baptist Church A Christian Protestant movement distinguished by its stress on baptism of adults by total immersion in water and the autonomy of local congregations. In the 16th century various religious groups in Europe (ANABAPTISM) established the ritual of adult baptism. The modern Baptist movement dates its beginnings from the English church established in Amsterdam in 1609 by John Smyth (1554–1612) and the church in London under Thomas Helwys (1612). They were 'General' or ARMINIAN BAPTISTS, as opposed to 'Particular' or Calvinist Baptists, who evolved between 1633 and 1638. After the RESTORATION they moved closer to the PRESBYTERIANS and Independents and were recognized as dissenters from the Anglican Church. America's first Baptist church was probably the one established at Providence, Rhode Island, with the help of Roger Williams (1639). From 1740, under the influence of the GREAT AWAKENING, the movement made considerable headway, especially in the southern states.

In both Britain and the USA Baptist Churches grew in the late 18th century. Baptist missionaries first went to India in 1792 and in the 19th century were active all over the world including in Russia. In 1813 the Baptist Union of Great Britain was organized and Baptist churches became very popular, especially in towns. In the USA in 1845, the Southern Baptist Convention was formed and split from the Northern (later National) Convention. Black Baptist Churches grew after 1865 and contributed significantly to Black culture. In 1905 the Baptist World Alliance was formed. By 1990 it included 144 churches with about 30 million full members in the USA, and a further 6 million in Africa, Asia, and elsewhere. Baptists constituted the largest Protestant group in the former Soviet Union, where many ministers were imprisoned. During the 1980s and 1990s, especially in the USA, there was a rise in the number of fundamentalist and militant Baptist groups. Many Baptist preachers have turned to such modern methods of communication as television and the Internet to spread their views to a wide audience.

Barbados An island country in the south-east Caribbean.

Physical. Barbados is the most easterly of the Windward Islands in the Caribbean Sea. Of coral formation, it is about 34 km (21 miles) long by 22 km (14 miles) wide and rises to some 336 m (1,100 feet). The climate is very warm and wet.

Economy. The principal economic activity is tourism, but agriculture, with sugar cane the main crop, remains important; a limited manufacturing industry includes food-processing, clothing, and assembly work. Offshore petroleum and natural gas reserves make an important contribution to the economy, and there is a developing services sector.

History. Barbados may have been visited by the conquistador Rodrigo de Bastidas in 1501; however the island that he called Isla Verde (because of its luxuriant vegetation) could have been Grenada rather than Barbados. The earliest inhabitants were thought to have been Arawak Indians, and later also some Carib Indians, but they had disappeared by the time British settlers began to colonize the island in 1627. Barbados became a British Crown colony in 1652. The British brought a large number of Africans to Barbados to work as slaves on sugar plantations SLAVE TRADE; when slavery was abolished in 1834 six-sevenths of the population was Black. Cane sugar remained the principal product of the island throughout the 17th, 18th, and 19th centuries. Barbados was also a strategic port for the British navy. In 1958 Barbados joined the West Indies Federation (see WEST INDIAN INDEPENDENCE) and in 1966 became fully independent within the Commonwealth. The Democratic Labour Party (DLP) was in power from 1961 until 1976 and from 1986 until 1994, when the Barbados Labour Party (BLP) won general elections.

CAPITAL:	Bridgetown
AREA:	430 sq km (166 sq miles)
POPULATION:	265,000 (1996)
CURRENCY:	1 Barbados dollar = 100 cents
RELIGIONS:	Anglican 39.7%; non-religious 17.5%; Pentecostal 7.6%; Methodist 7.1%; Roman Catholic 4.4%
ETHNIC GROUPS:	Black 80.0%; Mixed 16.0%; White 4.0%
LANGUAGES:	English (official)
INTERNATIONAL ORGANIZATIONS:	UN; OAS; CARICOM; Commonwealth

Barbarossa (Turkish, Khayr ad-Din Pasha) (*c.* 1483–1546) A famous CORSAIR, and later grand admiral of the OTTOMAN fleet. He and his brother Aruj first came to fame for their success against Christian vessels in the eastern Mediterranean. In 1516 Algiers appealed to Aruj to save it from Spain, and made him sultan. Aruj was killed fighting in 1518, and his brother Khayr ad-Din diplomatically ceded Algiers and its territory to the Ottoman sultan. He served as viceroy until 1533, when he was made grand admiral. In 1534 he took Tunis, but CHARLES V expelled him in 1535. After a number of minor engagements he retired in 1544.

Barbarossa, Frederick FREDERICK I.

Barbary Wars TRIPOLITAN WAR.

Bar Cochba (Simeon bar Kosiba, 'Simon son of the star') (d. 135) Leader of a Jewish rebellion against Roman rule in 132. He failed to gain general support and was killed with the fall of his stronghold, Betar. His life and military exploits have become legendary.

Barebones Parliament The assembly summoned by Oliver CROMWELL in July 1653, after he had dissolved the RUMP PARLIAMENT. It consisted of 140 members chosen partly by the army leaders and partly by congregations of 'godly men'. Known initially as the Parliament of Saints, it was later nicknamed after 'Praise-God' Barbon,

or Barebones (*c.* 1596–1679), one of its excessively pious leaders. Its attacks on the Court of Chancery and on the Church of England alarmed both Cromwell and its more moderate members. The dissolution of this Parliament was followed by the Instrument of Government and the proclamation of CROMWELL as Lord Protector.

Barents, Willem (*c.* 1550–97) Dutch explorer and leader of several expeditions in search of a north-east passage to Asia, south of the Arctic Ocean (see ARCTIC EXPLORATION). He discovered Spitsbergen and reached the Novaya Zemlya archipelago north of European Russia. His accurate charting and valuable meteorological data make him one of the most important of the early Arctic explorers. The Barents Sea is named after him.

Baring, Evelyn CROMER, EVELYN BARING, 1ST EARL OF.

Baring crisis (July 1890) A financial crisis in ARGENTINA. The London merchant bank of Baring Brothers was the country's financial agent in Europe, where a crisis of confidence occurred over the inflationary policy of President Juarez Celman (1886–90). The President gave way to his deputy Carlos Pellegrini, who had to stabilize the currency and adopt the GOLD STANDARD before London would give any more credit. One result was heavy urban unemployment, although the refrigerated beef and corn industries continued to expand. Approximately a century later (1995) Barings Bank collapsed as a result of unmonitored loss-making speculation in derivatives (especially financial futures) on the Singapore markets.

Barnardo, Thomas John (1845–1905) British doctor and social reformer who founded homes for destitute children. Born in Dublin of a Spanish Protestant family, he moved to London in 1862 and subsequently qualified as a doctor of medicine. He became concerned over the plight of children living in deprivation in the East End of London. In 1870 he established his first home for destitute boys and a similar institution for girls. By the time of his death nearly 60,000 children had been cared for in 'Dr Barnardo's Homes'. The homes were run by the Dr Barnardo's charity until the 1980s, when the charity was renamed Barnardo's and concentrated on providing help and support for children within families.

Barnet, Battle of (14 April 1471) A battle in the Wars of the ROSES fought between the Lancastrian forces, led by Richard Neville, Earl of WARWICK ('the Kingmaker') and the Yorkist troops of EDWARD IV. Both sides suffered heavy losses, but Warwick was slain and Edward's recovery of his throne was made almost certain.

baron A member of the lowest rank of the British peerage. Barons were originally the military tenants-in-chief of the crown. The title was introduced in England with the Norman Conquest and signified the vassal of a lord. Its limitation to those who held land directly from the king in return for military service occurred early. MAGNA CARTA (1215) made the distinction between the lesser baronage, summoned to the Great Council (Parliament) by general writ, and the greater baronage, called by personal writ, which was regarded as having conferred a hereditary peerage on the recipient. In 1387 Richard II made John de Beauchamp Baron of Kidderminster by letter patent (a letter from the sovereign) which gave this rank to Beauchamp and to his heirs. This new practice was regularly followed from

1446, establishing the principle that the peerage could be created either by writ of summons or by letters patent, the latter being more customary.

Barons' Wars (1215–17 and 1264–67) The civil wars fought in England between King JOHN and the barons. In June 1215 at Runnymede, King John, faced by the concerted opposition of the barons and Church, conceded MAGNA CARTA. He failed to honour his promise and thereby provoked the barons to offer the crown to Louis, Dauphin of France, who landed in Kent in May 1216. John's death (October 1216) and the reissue of Magna Carta by the regent of his son HENRY III prevented a major civil war. With his defeat at Lincoln and the capture of his supply ships off Sandwich, Louis accepted the Treaty of Kingston-upon-Thames in September 1217.

Baronial opposition to the incompetent Henry III led to his accepting a programme of reform, the Provisions of Oxford (1258). Henry's renunciation of those reforms led to civil war in 1264, the baronial forces being led by Simon de MONTFORT. The king's capture at the Battle of Lewes (May 1264) began a brief period of baronial control when de Montfort sought to broaden his support by extending parliamentary franchise to the shires and towns (1265). After his defeat and death at Evesham (August 1265), the struggle was continued unsuccessfully until 1267 by his supporters.

barrow (or tumulus) An earthen mound raised over a grave (if of stone, 'cairn' is the usual term). Grave-mounds of this type were characteristic throughout Europe and parts of central and southern Asia during the NEOLITHIC and BRONZE AGES, and in places much later. They occurred less frequently in other parts of the world.

Mounds could be raised over either inhumation or cremation burials, or sometimes over elaborate mortuary structures of stone or wood, houses of the dead. The best known examples include the Neolithic long barrows of Atlantic Europe, many enclosing spectacular chambers of MEGALITHS; the round barrows of the second millennium across most of the Continent; the ship burials of the VIKINGS and related peoples in the north; the richly furnished Scythic tombs on the Altai Mountains of central Asia; and the burial mounds of the Native Americans of the Mississippi valley in the USA.

Barth, Heinrich (1821–65) German explorer and geographer. The most influential of 19th-century European observers of West African life, Barth was a member of a British-sponsored expedition which left Tripoli in 1850 to explore the hinterland to the south. Having assumed command of the expedition in northern Nigeria, he explored the area around Lake Chad and Cameroon, stayed six months in Timbuktu, and recrossed the Sahara to complete a journey of some 16,090 km (10,000 miles). He returned to London in 1855. His five-volume account of his explorations, *Travels and Discoveries in North and Central Africa* (1857–58), contains much valuable anthropological, historical, and linguistic data. He also mapped the upper reaches of the River Benue and gave an accurate account of the River Niger.

Barton, Clara (1821–1912) US humanitarian, founder of the American Red Cross. She organized supplies and nursing in army camps and on the battlefields during the American Civil War (1861–65). In 1881 she established the American Red Cross, and successfully campaigned to extend Red Cross relief internationally to calamities not caused by war, such as famines and floods.

Barton, Sir Edmund (1849–1920) Australian statesman and jurist. He held high political offices in New South Wales for most of the 1880s and 1890s. Barton with Parkes and Deakin was an acknowledged leader of the AUSTRALIAN FEDERATION MOVEMENT. He was the Commonwealth of AUSTRALIA's first Prime Minister (1901–03), leading a ministry which sought to protect Australian industry.

Baruch, Bernard (Mannes) (1870–1965) US industrialist and financier. The respected adviser of presidents from Wilson to Eisenhower, he preferred to be an 'eminence grise' than to run for elective office. In World War I he served on the Council of National Defense and was the successful Chairman of the War Industries Board. Between the World Wars he was a member of various presidential conferences on capital, agriculture, transportation, and labour. In the 1940s he acted as special adviser on war mobilization and post-war planning. He was appointed to the UN Atomic Energy Commission, which proposed (1946) a World Atomic Authority with full control over the manufacture of atomic bombs throughout the world; this, however, was rejected by the Soviet Union.

basket-makers A group of Native Americans in Colorado and neighbouring areas who developed out of the DESERT CULTURES in the last centuries BC. They adopted farming from Mexico. The baskets they used instead of pottery have been preserved in the dry climatic conditions of their territory. In about 900 AD, improving agricultural techniques and increasing population led to the ANASAZI culture of the Pueblos.

Basques An ethnic group inhabiting the western Pyrenees on both sides of the French-Spanish border; this region in known as the Basque Country. They possess a distinctive culture and language, perhaps the result of their relative isolation from the rest of Europe until comparatively recently. Although the Basque country is divided between France and Spain, they have maintained an identity separate from both states. From the 14th century onwards the Basques were renowned for their fishing and whaling skills. Basque culture underwent a revival in the late 19th century, which ensured its continuance into the 20th century. During the SPANISH CIVIL WAR, the Basques supported the Republic; in reprisal, German aircraft acting on behalf of FRANCO's Nationalists destroyed the Basque town of Guernica in 1937. Under Franco's regime, concerted attempts were made to suppress the Basque culture and language. In response to what they consider continuing efforts to stifle their culture by the imposition of centralized authority, many Basques in Spain have campaigned for an independent Basque state, through the nationalist party *Herri Batasuna* or its violent military wing ETA (Basque Fatherland and Liberty).

Bastille A fortress in eastern Paris that was the French state prison in the 17th and 18th centuries, holding prisoners held under *lettre de cachet* or royal orders. In 1789 it held only seven prisoners but it was none the less regarded as a symbol of royal despotism and was believed to contain arms and ammunition. On 14 July it was attacked by crowds, including mutineers from the

Gardes Françaises. The governor, De Launay, surrendered, but he and his men were killed and the fortress demolished. The event is celebrated as the beginning of the French Revolution and Bastille Day (14 July) is a French national holiday.

Batavia DUTCH EAST INDIES.

Batistá y Zaldívar, Fulgencio (1901–73) Cuban statesman. He was President of Cuba (1933–44, 1952–58), having come to national prominence in 1933 when, as a sergeant in the army, he led a successful revolt against President Gerardo Machado y Morales. He established a strong, efficient government, but increasingly used terrorist methods to achieve his aims. He amassed fortunes for himself and his associates, and the dictatorial excesses of his second term abetted CASTRO's revolution, which drove Batistá from power in December 1958.

Batlle y Ordóñez, José (1856–1929) Uruguayan statesman. He was President of Uruguay (1903–07, 1911–15), and initiated legislation to increase public welfare. He believed that the Swiss Bundesrat or federal council was well suited to his own country's needs and during his second term he tried to have the office of president eliminated altogether. His political opponents compromised by agreeing to an executive branch in which power was shared between a president and a nine-man council. This decentralization of power placed Uruguay on a unique path in the 20th century.

Battenberg, Prince Louis (1854–1921) British admiral. Of Polish-German descent, he became a naturalized British subject in 1868 and joined the navy, becoming First Sea Lord in 1912 in the critical period before the outbreak of World War I. His decision, criticized by some, not to disperse the naval squadrons gathered for exercises at Portsmouth at the time of the assassination of the Archduke FRANCIS FERDINAND at Sarajevo in 1914, assisted Britain's readiness for war. Anti-German hysteria in the early months of the war forced his resignation in October 1914. He became a marquis in 1917, giving up his German titles, and adopting the equivalent English name of Mountbatten. He married Princess Alice, grand-daughter of Queen Victoria, in 1884. The younger of their two sons was Lord Louis Mountbatten, later Earl MOUNTBATTEN of Burma, and one grandson was Prince Philip, Duke of Edinburgh.

Bavaria (German, 'Bayern') The largest state of Germany, in the south of the country bordering Austria and the Czech Republic.
Physical. Bavaria is a plateau area with sandstone hills in the north-west and basalt hills in the north. Limestone hills along the River Danube separate North and South Bavaria and the Böhmerwald (Bohemian Forest) forms the eastern boundary.
Economy. Bavaria is mainly agricultural, with industry concentrated in the state capital of Munich. Tourism and forestry are important sources of revenue. Other economic activities include hop-growing and beer-making.
History. Bavaria became an independent duchy under the Wittelsbach dynasty in the late 12th century. Austria's attempts to dominate the region were thwarted in the War of the BAVARIAN SUCCESSION (1778–79). Subsequently Bavaria came under French influence, supporting Napoleon in the invasion of Austria (1800).

Although obliged (1801) by Napoleon to cede to France its territories on the Rhine (the Palatinate), it was enlarged and proclaimed a kingdom in 1805. In 1806 it was incorporated into Napoleon's CONFEDERATION OF THE RHINE. Shortly before the Battle of LEIPZIG it deserted Napoleon, joining the QUADRUPLE ALLIANCE and was rewarded with the restoration of the Rhineland Palatinate. The Wittelsbach king Maximilian I gave Bavaria a liberal constitution in 1818, and it became one of the three most powerful states in the GERMAN CONFEDERATION, holding the balance of power between Austria and Prussia. In 1866 it was defeated by the Prussians, but later joined Prussia in the FRANCO-PRUSSIAN WAR. Ludwig II secured sovereign rights for Bavaria within the new GERMAN SECOND EMPIRE, but withdrew from public life. Ludwig III came to the throne in 1913, to be deposed at the end of World War I, when his kingdom was declared a republic. A communist government was set up by the SPARTAKIST Kurt Eisner, and after the latter's assassination, a short-lived Communist Soviet Republic was proclaimed (1920–21). On its collapse, Bavaria became the centre of right-wing politics with the first attempted Nazi revolution in a Munich beer-hall (1923). In 1948 Bavaria became a state, minus the Rhenish Palatinate, in the Federal Republic of Germany. It was for long the political power base of the right-wing postwar politician Franz Josef Strauss (1915–88), leader of the Christian Social Union.

Bavarian Succession, War of the (1778–79) A war between Austria and Prussia resulting from JOSEPH II's ambition to add Bavaria to the HABSBURG dominions. The childless Maximilian Joseph of Bavaria (d. 1777) had designated Karl Theodore, Elector Palatine, as his heir. He was a weak man with illegitimate sons to provide for, and in January 1778 he agreed to sell a third of Bavaria to Joseph. FREDERICK II headed the opposition to this and the 'Potato War' (so called because the Prussian troops occupied their time by picking potatoes) took place in Bohemia: no battles were fought. Russia advanced into Poland, France offered mediation, and the Peace of Feschen was signed, under which Austria gained only the very small area of Innviertel.

Baxter, Richard (1615–91) English Puritan minister. He was ordained as an Anglican clergyman, but rejected belief in episcopacy and became a NONCONFORMIST. In 1645 he became chaplain to a ROUNDHEAD regiment. He published the first of some 150 pamphlets in 1649 and in 1650 *The Saints' Everlasting Rest*, an important devotional work. During the Commonwealth period, his appeals for tolerance did not succeed. At the Restoration he became a royal chaplain but refused a bishopric. The 1662 Act of UNIFORMITY forced his resignation, and in about 1673 he took out a licence as a Nonconformist minister. In 1685 he was imprisoned and fined by Judge JEFFREYS for 'libelling the Church'.

Bayard, Pierre Terrail, seigneur de (c. 1473–1524) French knight. He was celebrated by contemporary chroniclers as the outstanding knight of his generation '*sans peur et sans reproche*' ('without fear and without reproach'). He accompanied Charles VIII and Louis XII of France in their invasions of Italy. He was renowned for a heroic defence of Mézières against Emperor CHARLES V in 1521, which saved France from HABSBURG conquest. He died in battle.

Bayezid I (1347–1403) Ottoman sultan (1389–1402), known as Yildirim ('Thunderbolt'). He succeeded his father MURAD I and absorbed rival Turkish principalities in western Asia Minor, took Trnovo in Bulgaria (1393), and Thessaloniki in Greece (1394), blockaded Constantinople (1394–1401), and defeated a Christian army at Nicopolis in 1396. His thrust into eastern Asia Minor, however, brought him to disaster at Ankara in 1402, and he died a captive of his conqueror, TAMERLANE.

Bayezid II (c. 1447–1512) Ottoman sultan (1481–1512). He wrested the throne from his brother Jem on the death of their father MEHMED II, fought inconclusively with the MAMELUKES (1485–91), gained Greek and Adriatic territories from Venice, and was faced with the emerging power of ISMAIL I SAFAVI. He abdicated a month before his death in favour of his youngest son, Selim.

Bayle, Pierre (1647–1706) French philosopher and critic. He was professor of philosophy and history at Rotterdam University and an influential writer on scientific subjects who wished to encourage a sceptical attitude of mind. He argued that religion and morality were independent of one another, and championed the cause of universal religious toleration. His most famous work was a historical and analytical dictionary, the *Dictionnaire historique et critique* (1696).

Bay of Pigs An incident in Cuba in the area of that name. There in 1961 a small force of CIA-trained Cuban exiles from Miami was landed from US ships in an attempt to overthrow the Marxist regime of Fidel CASTRO. The invaders were swiftly crushed and rounded up by Castro's troops, and the incident was a grave blow to the prestige of the USA and of President KENNEDY. It strengthened the Castro regime and tightened Cuba's links with the former Soviet Union.

Bazaine, Achille François (1811–88) French general. During the FRANCO-PRUSSIAN WAR he was appointed commander-in-chief, but was reluctant to give battle. He withdrew to Metz with 176,000 French troops and capitulated to BISMARCK on 27 October 1870. Convicted of treason (1873), he was sentenced to death, but this was commuted to 20 years' imprisonment. After one year he escaped to Italy and then Spain, where he died.

Beaker cultures Peoples in many parts of western Europe at the end of the NEOLITHIC period (c. 2600–2200 BC) who made and used a particular type of decorated pottery drinking-vessel. It was shaped like an inverted bell, with or without handles, and ornamented with zones of stamped impressions. The style of 'Beaker' pottery seems to have developed in the Lower Rhine area, though it absorbed motifs from other areas with which it was in contact by sea and river routes. These pots were valuable to their owners, and are often found as grave-goods in male burials, along with weapons such as a copper dagger or the remains of archery equipment. Their wide distribution, from the western Mediterranean to northern Germany, led earlier investigators to postulate a 'Beaker Folk' spreading up from Portugal, or perhaps from central Europe. They are now seen more simply as part of a general trend to ostentatious display of personal wealth, introduced at that time from central Europe. These included copper metallurgy and horses for riding. Such personal wealth was buried with the individual in a new form of single grave under its own mound, a custom which superseded older funerary practices based on communal burial in MEGALITHIC monuments.

Beale, Dorothea (1831–1906) Pioneer, together with her friend Frances Mary Buss (1827–94), in higher education for women in Britain. In 1858 she was appointed principal of the recently established Cheltenham Ladies' College, a position she was to hold until her death. She founded (1885) St Hilda's College, Cheltenham, for women teachers and lent her support to the establishment of St Hilda's Hall (later College), Oxford, in 1893. She was also an enthusiastic advocate of women's suffrage.

Beaton, David (or Bethune) (1494–1546) Scottish churchman. He worked for the preservation of the Catholic religion, leading the anti-Protestant faction at court, and favouring the 'Auld Alliance' with France. Created cardinal in 1538, he succeeded his uncle as Archbishop of St Andrews in 1539 and was made Chancellor in 1543. His harsh persecution of Protestant preachers culminated in the execution of George WISHART, and Beaton was assassinated by Protestant nobles.

Beatty, David, 1st Earl (1871–1936) British admiral. He earned rapid promotion for his daring leadership in campaigns in Egypt and the Sudan, and in the BOXER RISING in China. Winston Churchill, First Lord of the Admiralty, secured for him in 1913 command of the battlecruiser squadrons. Beatty gained minor victories over German cruisers off Heligoland (1914) and the Dogger Bank (1915), and played a major role in the Battle of JUTLAND. He was commander-in-chief of the Grand Fleet (1916–19) and First Sea Lord (1919–27).

Beaufort An English family descending from three illegitimate sons of John of GAUNT (fourth son of Edward III) and Katherine Swynford. The children were legitimated in 1407 but with the exclusion of any claim to the crown. Their father and their half-brother HENRY IV made them powerful and wealthy: Thomas (d. 1427) became Duke of Exeter, John (c. 1371–1410) was made Lord High Admiral and Earl of Somerset, and Henry (d. 1447) was Bishop of Winchester and later a cardinal. As a court politician he led the so-called constitutional party against Humphrey, Duke of GLOUCESTER. The YORKISTS had no love for the Beauforts, and by 1471 all three of the Earl of Somerset's grandsons had been killed in battle or executed. The male line thus ended, but their niece Margaret Beaufort (1443–1509), daughter of John, Duke of Somerset, who married Edmund TUDOR, enjoyed a life of charity and patronage of learning after her son became king as HENRY VII.

Beauregard, Pierre Gustave Toutant (1818–93) US general. He served as an engineer during the MEXICAN-AMERICAN WAR and was appointed superintendent of West Point in 1860, but he resigned at the outbreak of the AMERICAN CIVIL WAR to join the CONFEDERACY. As commander at Charleston, he ordered the first shot of the war against the Union-held FORT SUMTER. Beauregard was the field commander in the Confederate victory at the first Battle of Bull Run (1861) before being promoted to full general and sent to the western theatre, where, after the battle of Shiloh (1862), he commanded the Army of Tennessee. Ill-health and bad relations with Jefferson DAVIS limited his influence for much of the remainder of the war, although he was back in the field when Confederate forces finally surrendered to General SHERMAN in 1865.

Beaverbrook, William Maxwell Aitken, Baron
(1879–1964) British financier, statesman, and newspaper owner. In 1910 he became a Conservative Member of Parliament and in 1916 took an important part in overthrowing ASQUITH and manoeuvring LLOYD GEORGE into the premiership. By 1918 he owned the *Evening Standard*, the *Sunday Express*, and *Daily Express*, with a record world circulation. Through these newspapers he supported the Hoare-LAVAL pact and Chamberlain's APPEASEMENT of Hitler by the MUNICH PACT (1938). In 1940 he became Minister of Aircraft Production and a member of Churchill's war cabinet, and it was in no small measure due to his efforts in producing fighter aircraft that the Battle of BRITAIN was won.

Bechuanaland BOTSWANA.

Becket, Thomas à, St
(1118–70) Archbishop of Canterbury (1162–70). Born in London, and educated in Paris and Bologna, Becket became archdeacon of Canterbury (1154) shortly before HENRY II made him Chancellor of England (1155) and he served the king as statesman and diplomat. However, when Becket became archbishop (1162) he became a determined defender of the rights of the Church. He came into conflict with the king in the councils of Westminster, Clarendon, and Northampton (1163–64), particularly over Henry's claim to try in the lay courts clergy who had already been convicted in an ecclesiastical court. Refusing to endorse the Constitutions of Clarendon (1164), Becket went into exile in France. On his return (1170), apparently reconciled to Henry, Becket suspended those bishops who had accepted these Constitutions. Henry's rage over this action was misinterpreted by four knights who assumed he would approve their murder of Becket in Canterbury Cathedral. Acclaimed a martyr, and canonized (1173), his shrine became a centre of Christian PILGRIMAGE.

Bede
(673–735) English scholar and historian, the author of the most famous work on Anglo-Saxon England, the *Historia Ecclesiastica Gentis Anglorum* ('Ecclesiastical History of the English People') (731). From the age of seven, he was educated at the Northumbrian monasteries of Wearmouth and Jarrow, where he remained as a monk for the rest of his life. He wrote (in Latin) lives of five abbots of his monastery and numerous biblical works, hymns, verse, books on astronomy, letters, and a martyrology of 114 saints. He popularized a new chronology using *anno domini* (AD) in dating. Although he probably did not travel further than York or Lindisfarne, Bede was the best-known Englishman of his time, and a synod at Aachen (836) awarded him the title 'Venerable'.

Bedford, John, Duke of
(1389–1435) Regent of France (1422–35). He was the third son of HENRY IV. While his brother HENRY V was in France, Bedford was appointed Guardian of England on several occasions between 1415 and 1421, and on Henry's death in 1422, he was made governor of Normandy and Regent of France. He succeeded in retaining England's French territories, despite the campaign of JOAN OF ARC and insufficient

funds; by his first marriage, to Anne of Burgundy, daughter of Duke John the Fearless, he cemented England's crucial Burgundian alliance.

Beecher, Lyman
(1775–1863) US temperance reformer and Presbyterian clergyman. In 1832 he was appointed first president of the Lane Theological Seminary in Cincinnati, where his daughter, Harriet Beecher Stowe, author of *Uncle Tom's Cabin* (1852), married Calvin Ellis Stowe, professor of biblical literature. Lane Seminary students were among the first ABOLITIONISTS. Beecher became a target for attack by conservative Presbyterians and had to face charges, of which he was finally acquitted, of slander, heresy, and hypocrisy.

Begin, Menachem (Wolfovitch)
(1913–92) Israeli statesman. Active in the ZIONIST movement throughout the 1930s, he was sent with the Polish army-in-exile to Palestine (1942), where he joined the militant IRGUN ZVAI LEUMI. On the creation of ISRAEL (1948) the Irgun regrouped as the Herut (Freedom) Party and elected Begin as its head. He was leader of the Opposition in the Knesset (Parliament) until 1967, when he joined the National Unity government. In 1970 he served as joint chairman of the Likud (Unity) coalition, and after its electoral victory in 1977 became Prime Minister (1977–83). His negotiations with President SADAT of Egypt resulted in the CAMP DAVID ACCORD, but remained opposed to the establishment of a Palestinian state.

Beit, Sir Alfred
(1853–1906) South African financier and philanthropist. Of German origin, he settled in Kimberley as a diamond merchant in 1875, and became a close friend of Cecil RHODES. His interest in gold greatly contributed to the development of the Rand and the British South African Company, and later of RHODESIA. He made benefactions to scholarship and the arts.

Belarus, Republic of
A landlocked country in eastern Europe, formerly a constituent republic of the Soviet Union. It is bounded on the west by Poland, on the north-west by Latvia and Lithuania, on the north and east by Russia, and on the south by Ukraine.

Physical. Gentle hills run through a series of low forested plains. The climate is predominantly wet, and many rivers drain the land into the vast area of the Pripet Marshes.

Economy. The rich plains of Belarus support agriculture and animal husbandry on a wide scale. Petroleum reserves in the south of the country are exploited, but other mineral resources are meagre. Belarus was the major Soviet supplier of engineering, transport, and agricultural equipment, electronic and consumer goods, chemicals, timber, and textiles. However, much industry was dependent on processing raw materials from other parts of the former Soviet Union and after independence the country's inability to pay market prices for supplies led to severe recession. In 1994 Belarus entered into monetary union with Russia, enabling it to obtain cheap Russian raw materials.

History. Belarus (once referred to as White Russia) had been part of Lithuania and later Poland until conquered by Russia under Catherine the Great. Heavy fighting took place during and after World War I, before the Treaty of Riga (1921) which divided the area between Poland and the newly declared Soviet Socialist Republic of Belorussia, which joined the Soviet Union. In 1939 the latter occupied all the area as far as the River Bug, and heavy fighting took place after the German invasion in 1941. In 1945 the Belorussian SS.R. was granted a seat in the UN National Assembly, and Poland abandoned its claim to western Belorussia, its Polish population being transferred to Poland. The rich steppe lands in the south of the republic suffered heavy pollution from the Chernobyl disaster of 1986. In April 1991 the Belorussian S.S.R. declared its independence from the Soviet Union, renaming itself the Republic of Belarus. Multiparty politics were adopted, but the communists have continued to dominate politics and the centrally planned economy has been maintained. A presidential constitution was adopted in 1994 and Aleksander Lukashenko (1954–) was elected President later that year. In four referendums in 1995 Belarussians voted in favour of establishing greater political, economic, and cultural links with Russia. Treaties establishing joint economic, foreign, and defence policies between the two countries, were signed in 1996 and 1997. Lukashenko's increasingly authoritarian style of leadership has provoked concern about the future of democracy in Belarus.

CAPITAL:	Minsk
AREA:	207,600 sq km (80,134 sq miles)
POPULATION:	10.442 million (1996)
CURRENCY:	1 rouble = 100 kopeks
RELIGIONS:	Eastern Orthodox Church
ETHNIC GROUPS:	Belorussian 78.0%; Russian 13.0%; Ukrainian, Polish, and Jewish minorities
LANGUAGES:	Belorussian (official); Russian (official); minority languages
INTERNATIONAL ORGANIZATIONS:	UN; Commonwealth of Independent States; CSCE; North Atlantic Co-operation Council

Belau PALAU.

Belaúnde, Terry Fernando (1912–) Peruvian statesman. He was elected to the Chamber of Deputies (1945–48). In 1956 he helped to found the moderate Popular Action Party and in 1963 was elected President with the support of both Popular Action and Christian Democrats in opposition to HAYA DE LA TORRE, the candidate for APRA (Alianja Popular Revolucionaria Americana). His first term of office (1963–68) is remembered for its social, educational, and land reforms, as well as for industrial development and the construction of a vast highway system across the Andes. He was a strong supporter of the US Alliance for Progress programme, but his economic policies resulted in high inflation. He was deposed by the army and fled to the USA. He returned briefly to Peru in 1970, but was deported. He returned again in 1976 and was again President (1980–85). During his second term inflation grew worse and he was unable to counter the terrorist activities of the Sendero Luminoso (the Shining Path organization).

Belgae German and Celtic tribes who inhabited the Rhine estuary, the Low Countries, and north-east France. Subdued by Julius CAESAR in the GALLIC WARS their name was given to 'Gallia Belgica', one of the three main administrative units of Gaul established by AUGUSTUS. During the last century BC a number of Belgae settled in southern Britain. They led resistance against the invasion of Britain in 43 AD, most notably the Catuvellauni under CARATACUS.

Belgium A country in north-west Europe on the North Sea. It is bounded inland by The Netherlands, Germany, Luxembourg, and France.

Physical. The coastal area comprises broad, sandy beaches backed by dunes. Inland, most of the rivers run across the flat, fertile Flanders Plain, north-eastward to The Netherlands. In the south-east the land rises to the highlands of the Ardennes. Here the soil is poor, and the land generally forested. The Campine coalfield is in the east.

Economy. Manufacturing industries such as steel, textiles, engineering, and chemicals dominate the economy, but service industries are of increasing importance due to the location of the EU's headquarters in Brussels. Other than coal, Belgium has no natural resources, and processes imported raw materials. Major exports include steel, chemicals, motor vehicles, and foodstuffs. Agriculture is limited to production for the domestic market.

History. Belgium takes its name from the BELGAE, one of the peoples of ancient Gaul, but by the 5th century immigrations from the north had resulted in a large settled German population. After several centuries under the Franks the region split into independent duchies and, especially in FLANDERS, free merchant cities. In the 15th century all of what is now Belgium became part of the duchy of BURGUNDY, but the Low Countries (which included Belgium) in 1477 passed by marriage to the Habsburg empire of MAXIMILIAN I. They were later absorbed into the Spanish empire, and in 1713 passed to AUSTRIA. Belgium was occupied by France in 1795 during the French Revolutionary wars.

Following the defeat of Napoleon, Belgium became one of the provinces of the kingdom of The NETHERLANDS in 1815. However, in 1830 it separated from The Netherlands following a national revolution, and Prince Leopold of Saxe-Coburg was elected king. After an unsuccessful Dutch invasion, an international treaty was drawn up guaranteeing Belgian neutrality in 1839. In the later 19th century Belgium's King Leopold II (1865–1909) headed an international Association of the Congo (1876), following the exploration of the River Congo by H. M. STANLEY. This association was recognized at the Berlin Conference (1884) as the Congo Free State, with Leopold as its unrestrained sovereign. As the Congo was opened for trade, appalling atrocities against Africans were committed, leading to its transfer from Leopold's personal control to the Belgian Parliament (1908). Independence was granted to the Congo in June 1960, but was immediately followed by violence and bloodshed (CONGO CRISIS).

In 1914 Germany's invasion of Belgium precipitated Britain's entry into World War I. The country was occupied by the Germans, against whom Albert I (1908–34) led the Belgian army on the WESTERN FRONT. When Germany invaded again in 1940 Leopold III (1901–83) at once surrendered. However, a government-in-exile in London continued the war, organizing a strong resistance movement. After the war Leopold was forced to abdicate (1951) in favour of his son Baudouin (1930–93). After World War II the main task for Belgium was to unite the Flemish-speaking northerners with the French-speaking Walloons of the south. In 1977 the Pact of Egmont, introduced by the Prime Minister, Leo Tindemans, recognized three semi-autonomous regions: that of the Flemings in the north, the Walloons in the south, and Brussels. The regions of Flanders, Wallonia, and Brussels were given greater autonomy by a constitution, adopted in 1993, that defines Belgium as a federal nation. Following his death in 1993, King Baudouin was succeeded by his younger brother, Albert II (1934–   ).

CAPITAL:	Brussels
AREA:	30,518 sq km (11,783 sq miles)
POPULATION:	10.185 million (1996)
CURRENCY:	1 Belgian franc = 100 centimes
RELIGIONS:	Roman Catholic 90.0%; Muslim 1.1%; Protestant 0.4%
ETHNIC GROUPS:	Belgian 91.1%; Italian 2.8%; Moroccan 1.1%; French 1.1%; Dutch, Turkish, and other minorities
LANGUAGES:	Flemish, French, German (all official); Italian
INTERNATIONAL ORGANIZATIONS:	UN; EU; NATO; OECD; Council of Europe; CSCE

Belisarius (505–65 AD) Roman general under JUSTINIAN. He was instrumental in halting the collapse of the Roman empire, if only temporarily. In 530 he defeated the Persians in the east, although they quickly reasserted themselves in Syria. Six years later he conquered VANDAL North Africa, capturing its king. In 535–40 he took back Italy from the OSTROGOTHS, advancing as far north as Ravenna, taking their king prisoner, and followed it with a second Italian campaign a few years later. He took Rome in 549 but was dismissed and even charged with conspiracy by a jealous Justinian, though reinstated in 564.

Belize A small tropical country lying at the south of the Yucatán Peninsula in Central America. It is bounded by Guatemala to the west and the Caribbean Sea to the east.

Physical. Belize is mainly low-lying and covered with rain forest; only in the south does it rise to pine forest and savannah. Sea breezes from the Caribbean temper the hot and humid climate.

Economy. Belize has a predominantly agricultural economy. Industry is limited mainly to food-processing, and the chief exports are processed sugar, clothing, and citrus products. Tourism is another important source of revenue.

History. The British settled Belize in the 17th century, proclaiming the area (as British Honduras) a crown colony in 1862. Subject to the jurisdiction of the governor of Jamaica, the colony sustained itself with little direct support from the British government. Grudging acceptance by its Latin American neighbours in the 19th century led to treaties recognizing its permanent boundaries. In 1964 the colony gained complete internal self-government. It adopted the name Belize in 1973, and in 1981 became an independent state within the COMMONWEALTH OF NATIONS. However, Guatemala continued its long-standing claim to the territory on the basis of old Spanish treaties. In 1991 Guatemala recognized Belize's independence, the two countries having reached a provisional agreement on mutual fishing rights. In 1993 Britain decided to withdraw almost all its troops from Belize as a Guatemalan invasion was no longer thought likely.

CAPITAL:	Belmopan
AREA:	22,965 sq km (8,867 sq miles)
POPULATION:	219,000 (1996)
CURRENCY:	1 Belize dollar = 100 cents
RELIGIONS:	Roman Catholic 62.0%; Anglican 12.0%; Methodist 6.0%
ETHNIC GROUPS:	Creole (predominantly Black) 40.0%; Mestizo (Mayo-Spanish) 33.0%; Garifuna 8.0%; Maya 7.0%; European 4.0%; Ketchi 3.0%; East Indian 2.0%
LANGUAGES:	English (official); English creole; Spanish; Mayan; Garifuna
INTERNATIONAL ORGANIZATIONS:	UN; Commonwealth; CARICOM

Bell, Alexander Graham (1847–1922) British-born US inventor of the telephone and pioneer of sound recording. Bell's father was an authority on speech correction and elocution, and from 1868 Bell worked with him, teaching deaf children to speak. In 1873, he was appointed Professor of Vocal Physiology at the University of Boston. Working in his spare time, he and a mechanic, Thomas Watson, developed his ideas for transmitting speech electrically, and in 1876 he was granted a patent for 'transmitting vocal or other sounds telegraphically'. He gave the first public demonstration of the telephone in Philadelphia later that year, and commercial development soon followed. The immensely successful Bell Telephone Company was founded in 1877. Bell continued to experiment in electrical communication. He developed a photophone, which transmitted sound on a light beam; he also made several improvements to Thomas Edison's gramophone, and developed a graphophone, a sound-recording device employing a stylus, wax cylinders, and discs. In his later years Bell extended his investigations into many other areas, including aeronautics and hydrofoil speedboats.

Bello, Alhaji Sir Ahmadu (1906–66) Nigerian statesman. He became leader of the Northern People's Congress, and, in 1952, the first elected minister in Northern Nigeria, and in 1954 Premier. When Nigeria became independent in 1960, his party combined with AZIKIWE's National Council of Nigeria and the Cameroons (NCNC) to control the federal Parliament. Bello's deputy in the NPC, Abubakar Tafawa BALEWA, became federal Prime Minister, while Bello himself remained to lead the party in the north. In 1966, when the army seized power, Bello was among the political leaders who were assassinated.

Belshazzar (6th century BC) Ruler of BABYLON. He was the son of Nabonidus, the last of the Chaldean kings of Babylon. When his father embarked on a prolonged campaign in Arabia *c.* 556 BC, he remained behind as ruler (probably with the title of king) in Babylon. The city was captured by CYRUS II (the Great) in 539 BC and he was killed.

In the biblical Book of Daniel (where he is wrongly called the son of Nebuchadnezzar), Belshazzar is described as giving a great feast at which a hand is seen writing the message, '*mene, mene, tekel*' and '*parsim*' on the wall of his palace, predicting the imminent downfall of his kingdom.

Benares VARANASI.

Ben Bella, Ahmed (1916–   ) Algerian revolutionary leader. He served in the French army in World War II, and in 1947 became a leader of the secret military wing of the Algerian nationalist movement. He organized revolutionary activities and was imprisoned by the French (1950–52). He then founded and directed the National Liberation Front (FLN), which began the Algerian war with France. In 1956, when he was on board a Moroccan airliner he was seized and interned in France. In 1962 he was freed under the ÉVIAN AGREEMENTS; he became Prime Minister of Algeria (1962–65) and was elected the first President of the Algerian Republic in 1963. In 1965 his government was overthrown in a military coup by Colonel Houari BOUMÉDIENNE. He was kept in prison until July 1979, and under house arrest until 1980, when he was freed unconditionally. He returned to Algeria from exile in 1990.

Benbow, John (1653–1702) English admiral. He was prominent in sea battles against the French for control of the English Channel during the early 1690s. He served in the West Indies for most of the period 1698–1702, where in his last engagement his daring plans for pursuing the retreating French were defied by his own captains. He died of his wounds in Jamaica, leaving a reputation for vigour, toughness, and bravery.

Benedictine A monk or nun of an order following the rule of St BENEDICT. From the original Benedictine foundations at Subiaco and Monte Cassino in Italy the number of monastic houses in Europe grew to many thousands. The order reached its peak of prestige and influence in the 10th and 11th centuries, with the abbey of CLUNY in Burgundy its most prestigious foundation. The basic concept of Benedictine monasticism was that it should encourage a way of life separated from the world, within which monks could achieve a life devoted to prayer.

Benedict of Nursia, St (*c.* 480–*c.* 550) Founder of the BENEDICTINE order of monks. He built his monastery at Monte Cassino in central Italy in *c.* 525. Monasticism then was lacking order and regulation, and he introduced his 'rule', which was a definition of the qualities and actions required of a monk. These were principally humility, prayer, obedience, silence, and solitude. St Benedict of Aniane (*c.* 750–821) systematized the Benedictine rule and his *capitulare monasticum* received official approval in 817 as the basis for the reform of French monastic houses.

benefit of clergy The privilege enabling a cleric, on being accused of a crime, to be exempted from trial by a secular court, and to be subject only to the Church courts, which usually dealt with him more leniently. It was a system open to abuse, especially when clerics were numerous and difficult to identify with certainty, as was the case in the Middle Ages. Indeed the mere ability to read was often accepted as proof of clerical status. In England it was a principal issue in the controversy between Archbishop Thomas à BECKET and HENRY II and the privilege was largely conceded by the crown in the aftermath of Becket's murder in 1170; later its application was limited by various Acts of Parliament and it was finally abolished in 1827.

Beneš, Edvard (1884–1948) Czechoslovak president (1935–38; 1946–48). He was, with Tomáš MASARYK, a founder of modern Czechoslovakia (1918). As leader of the Czech National Socialist Party, he was the country's foreign minister from 1918 until he succeeded Masaryk as President in 1935. In an attempt to keep the balance of power in Eastern Europe, he formed, in 1921, the LITTLE ENTENTE with Yugoslavia to enforce observance of the VERSAILLES PEACE SETTLEMENT by Hungary and prevent a restoration of the Habsburg King Charles. In 1924 he and the Greek jurist Nikolaos Politis drafted the abortive Geneva Protocol for the pacific settlement of international disputes. He strongly supported the LEAGUE OF NATIONS, helping to admit the Soviet Union in 1934. Exiled during WORLD WAR II, he returned as President in 1945. Refusing to sign Klement GOTTWALD's communist constitution, he resigned in 1948.

Bengal A region of the Indian subcontinent comprising BANGLADESH and the Indian state of West Bengal.

Physical. The region is dominated by the vast alluvial plains and deltas of the Ganges and Brahmaputra Rivers.

History. In early times the region was incorporated in some of the great BUDDHIST and HINDU empires of northern India, but a sense of separate identity was fostered by periods of independent rule. From the 13th century a series of Muslim invasions annexed Bengal to the Delhi sultanate. In succeeding centuries local governors maintained considerable autonomy until MOGUL conquest in 1576 brought subordination to Delhi. On Mogul decline in the 18th century the Bengali nawabs (governors) enjoyed a shortlived era of renewed autonomy. This was ended by the EAST INDIA COMPANY's ambitions. Its merchants had been trading in Calcutta since 1690, but in 1757 Robert CLIVE took advantage of the BLACK HOLE OF CALCUTTA incident to force a trial of strength. After his victory at PLASSEY the Company gradually ousted the local nawabs and their Mogul suzerains from the economic and judicial control of the province. By the 1790s the British controlled Bengal. The region was divided between India and Pakistan on independence in 1947. The Bengali part of Pakistan achieved independence as Bangladesh in 1972.

Ben-Gurion, David (1886–1973) Israeli statesman. Born in Russian Poland, he migrated to Palestine in 1906 and quickly entered politics. He was one of the organizers of the Israeli Workers' Party (Mapai) and of the Jewish Federation of Labour (Histadrut), which he served as General Secretary (1921–35). As Chairman of the Jewish Agency (1935–48) he was the leading figure in the Jewish community in Palestine. As Israel's first Prime Minister (1948–53, 1955–63), and Minister of Defence, he played the largest part in shaping Israel during its formative years. In 1965 he was expelled from the Labour Party and formed a new party known as Rafi.

Benin, kingdom of West African kingdom based on Benin City, now in southern Nigeria, probably founded in about the 13th century. Its iron work and bronze and ivory sculptures rank with the finest art of Africa. It developed by trading in ivory, pepper, cloth, metals, and, from the 15th century, slaves. The kingdom achieved its greatest power under Oba Equare, who ruled from about 1440 to 1481. With his powerful army he conquered Yoruba lands to the west and Lower Niger to the east. He initiated administrative reforms, established a sophisticated bureaucracy, and ensured that the Portuguese, who arrived on the coast in 1472, did not establish control over Benin. The kingdom expanded further in the 16th century but by the 18th century its power waned with the growing strength of OYO and other Yoruba states. Its extent declined further in the 19th century. Continuing slave-trading and the use of human sacrifice in religious rituals precipitated a British military expedition in 1897, which was massacred, whereupon a British force razed Benin city. The kingdom of Benin was incorporated into the new protectorate of southern NIGERIA in 1900. The republic of DAHOMEY subsequently took the name Benin.

Benin, Republic of A West African country lying between Togo and Nigeria on the Gulf of Guinea.

Physical. Benin has a southern coastline of only 125 km (78 miles) but extends inland for 700 km (460 miles) to Niger. The coast is sandy with large lagoons. Inland there is a fertile clay plain with thick tropical forest that rises to a sandy plateau with savannah vegetation.

Economy. Benin has an agricultural economy, with exports of cocoa, cotton, and palm products. There is some light industry, especially food-processing, brewing, and palm-oil processing. There are mineral deposits of off-shore oil, chromium, and phosphates; oil production began in 1982, but has disappointed expectations.

History. Formerly known as DAHOMEY, this region was ruled by kings of Yoruba origin until the French occupied it in 1892. It was constituted a territory of French West Africa in 1904. As Dahomey, it became an independent republic within the FRENCH COMMUNITY in 1960, after which periods of civilian government alternated with military rule. In 1972 it was declared a Marxist–Leninist state, and its name was altered (1975) to Benin. Under the leadership of Mathieu Kérékou (President 1972–91), Benin achieved greater domestic stability and international standing. In the country's first free elections, held in 1991, Kérékou was defeated by his Prime Minister Nicéphore Soglo, whose government moved towards a free-market economy with the support of the IMF. Legislative elections in 1995 led to the formation of a coalition government. However, presidential elections held in 1996 saw a surprise victory for the former dictator Kérékou.

CAPITAL:	Porto Novo
AREA:	112,600 sq km (43,450 sq miles)
POPULATION:	5.574 million (1996)
CURRENCY:	1 CFA franc = 100 centimes
RELIGIONS:	Traditional beliefs 61.4%; Roman Catholic 18.5%; Muslim 15.2%; Protestant 2.8%
ETHNIC GROUPS:	Fon-Ewe 55.5%; Bargu 22.5%; Yoruba 13.6%
LANGUAGES:	French (official); Fon-Ewe; Bargu; Yoruba
INTERNATIONAL ORGANIZATIONS:	UN; OAU; Non-Aligned Movement; ECOWAS; Franc Zone

Bennington, Battle of (16 August 1777) A battle of the American War of INDEPENDENCE in which 1,600 GREEN MOUNTAIN BOYS under General John Stark overwhelmed 1,200 German mercenaries of BURGOYNE's army. Encouraged by this success, the Americans forced Burgoyne to surrender after the defeat at SARATOGA.

Bentham, Jeremy (1748–1832) British philosopher, the founder of the UTILITARIAN school of ethics and political thought. He promoted the idea that the morality of an action could be measured by its effects on people: the greatest happiness of the greatest number should be the goal, and human institutions judged by the extent to which they contributed to that happiness. He supported much humanitarian reform and provided the inspiration for the founding of London University.

Bentinck, Lord William Cavendish (1774–1839) British statesman. After serving in Flanders and Italy, he was posted to India as governor of Madras (1803–07). He was recalled to Britain after a mutiny at Velore for which, by his prohibition of sepoy beards and turbans, he was held responsible. After serving in the PENINSULAR WAR he returned to India as governor-general of Bengal (1827–33). He was given considerable administrative responsibility and effectively was the first governor-general of all India (1833–35). A liberal reformer, his administration substituted English for Persian and Sanskrit in the courts, brought about many educational reforms, suppressed the practice of ritual strangling (see THUG), and abolished suttee, in which a widow was burned on her dead husband's pyre.

Bentinck, William Henry Cavendish, 3rd Duke of Portland (1738–1809) British statesman. As leader of the Whig Party he was briefly Prime Minister at the end of the American War of Independence in 1783. Later he supported the government of William PITT in its opposition to the French Revolution. He became Pitt's Home Secretary (1794–1801) and greatly assisted in the passing of the ACT OF UNION in 1801. After Pitt's death (January 1806) and the failure of the so-called 'Ministry of All the Talents' (1806–07), he was persuaded (1807) to take office again as Prime Minister. Then an old man, he failed to prevent internal dissension in his government, which led to the duel between CANNING and CASTLEREAGH, on news of which he resigned.

Berbers The indigenous peoples of northern and north-western Africa. Traditionally, they speak Berber languages, although most literate Berbers also speak Arabic. The Berbers are Sunni Muslims, and their local tribal groups are often led by a hereditary religious leader. The Berber peoples include several distinct groups: settled farmers living in the Atlas mountains; transhumance farmers (who move their livestock seasonally from region to region); and the nomadic Tuareg of the Sahara.

History. The Berbers have occupied the mountains and deserts of northern Africa since prehistoric times. HERODOTUS recorded that they were found in various tribes. They do not seem commonly to have formed kingdoms, although they co-operated on occasions, for example against Roman rule. Their extreme independence and austerity were exemplified by the DONATIST *circumcelliones* (violent bands of marauders) of the 4th and 5th centuries, by the Kharijite sect of early Islam, and by the cults of *marabouts*, Islamic holy men of ascetic devotion and organizers of fraternities. In this way they both resisted the ARAB conquest and transformed Islam to suit their own tastes. They supported the UMAYYADS in Spain, and the FATIMIDS in Morocco, and then set up several dynasties of their own, of whom the ALMOHADS and the ALMORAVIDS were the most important.

Beria, Lavrenti Pavlovich (1899–1953) Soviet politician who played a major role in organizing the large-scale purges of the Stalinist era, including the liquidation of police bureaucrats. Born in Georgia, he joined the Communist Party in 1917, and became head of the secret police (CHEKA) in that province (1921). In 1938 he took charge of the secret police as head of Internal Affairs and greatly expanded Soviet PRISON CAMPS. During World War II he intensified armaments production.

After Stalin's death he was defeated by a coalition led by Malenkov, Molotov, and Khrushchev. In July 1953 he was arrested on charges of conspiracy. He was tried in secret and executed.

Berkeley, George (1685–1753) Irish philosopher, Anglican Bishop of Cloyne. One of the British empiricists, he rejected the distinction, upheld by LOCKE, between primary qualities such as shape, which resemble our sensory ideas of them, and secondary ones such as colour which do not, claiming that the being of perceptible objects is simply to be perceived. He declared the notion of matter self-contradictory, as involving the causal operation of something inert: all that could exist were spirits (minds) and their contents. Since our perceptions are not of our making, they must be induced in us by another mind, that of God. His principal writings, which include *An Essay Towards a New Theory of Vision* (1709), and *Principles of Human Knowledge*, reveal him as one of the most elegant writers of philosophy. Berkeley also devoted much of his life to the encouragement and development of missionary work. He went to America in 1728 to found a missionary college, but had to return to Ireland because of shortage of funds.

Berkeley, Sir William (1606–77) Governor of Virginia (1642–52, 1660–76). A royalist aristocrat, he was removed from the governorship during the COMMONWEALTH. At the Restoration, Charles II renewed his commission and he won colonist popularity by his attempts to protect tobacco prices and gain a charter, but his regime grew corrupt and oligarchical, triggering BACON'S REBELLION in 1676. His cruelty against the rebels led to his recall.

Berlin, Congress of (1878) A conference of European powers. It revised the Treaty of San Stefano (1878) which had ended the war between the OTTOMAN EMPIRE and Russia (1877–78). Under the chairmanship of the German chancellor, Otto von BISMARCK, the congress limited Russian naval expansion; gave Montenegro, Serbia, and Romania independence; allowed Austro-Hungary to occupy Bosnia-Herzegovina; reduced BULGARIA to one-third of its size; and placed Cyprus under temporary occupation by the British. The congress left Russian nationalists and PAN-SLAVS dissatisfied, and the aspirations of Greece, Serbia, and Bulgaria unfulfilled. Bismarck's handling of the congress antagonized Russia, and the claim of DISRAELI, that it had achieved 'peace with honour', proved unfounded.

Berlin Airlift (1948–49) A measure undertaken by the US and British governments to counter the Soviet blockade of Berlin. In June 1948 the USA, Britain, and France announced a currency reform in their zones of occupied Germany. The Soviet Union, fearing this was a prelude to the unification of these zones, retaliated by closing all land and water communication routes from the western zones to Berlin. The western Allies in turn responded by supplying their sectors of Berlin with all necessities by cargo aircraft. The siege lasted until May 1949, when the Russians reopened the surface routes. The blockade confirmed the division of Berlin, and ultimately of Germany, into two administrative units.

Berlin Wall A barrier between East and West Berlin. It was built by the GERMAN DEMOCRATIC REPUBLIC in August 1961 in order to stem the flow of refugees from East Germany to the West: over three million had emigrated between 1945 and 1961. The Wall was heavily guarded and many people, especially in the 1960s, were killed or wounded while attempting to cross. It was demolished in 1989.

Bermuda A self-governing British colony consisting of some 150 tiny coral islands in the western Atlantic Ocean.

Physical. The islands are composed of a layer 60 m (200 feet) thick of limestone, coral, and other marine organisms, capping an extinct and submerged volcanic mountain range.

Economy. Tourism is the most important industry, while medical products account for over half of total exports. International finance and insurance flourish due to low levels of taxation. Over 10% of Bermuda's land is occupied by US military and naval bases.

History. The first European to visit the islands was the Spaniard, Juan de Bermundez (1515). First settled in 1609 by the Virginia Company, they have the oldest parliament in the New World, dating to 1620. A flourishing slave economy, based mainly on tobacco production, existed until 1834 when slavery was abolished. By the 20th century two-thirds of the population was of African or Indian descent. Strategically important to the British navy, Bermuda grew rich on trade and tourism, with close ties with the USA. US naval and air-bases were granted in 1940. Universal adult suffrage was introduced in 1944 and the present constitution in 1967, granting the colony considerable self-government. Political activity developed in the 1960s and there were sporadic and bitter race-riots in the 1970s. In a referendum in 1995 Bermudans rejected independence from Britain.

CAPITAL:	Hamilton
AREA:	54 sq km (21 sq miles)
POPULATION:	61,400 (1996)
CURRENCY:	1 Bermuda dollar = 100 cents
RELIGIONS:	Anglican 37.3%; Methodist 16.3%; Roman Catholic 13.8%; non-religious 7.8%
ETHNIC GROUPS:	Black 61.3%; White 37.3%
LANGUAGES:	English (official)
INTERNATIONAL ORGANIZATIONS:	Commonwealth

Bernadotte, Folke, Count (1895–1948) Swedish international mediator. The nephew of Gustav V, he entered the Swedish army as a young man. During World War II he worked for the Swedish Red Cross and in 1948 was appointed as UN mediator to supervise the implementation of the partition of PALESTINE and the creation of ISRAEL. He was murdered by Israeli terrorists.

Bernard of Clairvaux, St (1090–1153) Theologian and reformer, one of the most influential figures of the Middle Ages. He was born into a noble family in Burgundy but rejected this privileged existence to adopt a life of religious study and austerity. He became abbot of Clairvaux, a CISTERCIAN monastery which he founded and which became a model for reformed monastic houses. The Cistercian order grew rapidly under his influence. In the disputed papal election of 1130 he supported Pope Innocent II and throughout his life he attacked heresy. His preaching in support of Innocent II brought him a European-wide reputation, seen in the support he attracted for the Second CRUSADE

(1140). A fervent mystical religious thinker he clashed with the more intellectual approach of ABELARD, and helped to bring about his downfall.

Berwick, Treaty of Three treaties were named after Berwick, a town in Northumberland, sited on the border between England and Scotland. The first (3 October 1357) arranged for the release from captivity of David II of Scotland in return for a large ransom to be paid to Edward III of England, but this debt was never fully discharged. The second (27 February 1560) committed the English to send the Scottish Protestants military aid to help overthrow the Roman Catholic regent Mary of Guise. The third (18 June 1639) ended the first BISHOPS' WAR between Charles I and Scottish Covenanters, although it did not fully resolve the conflict and was regarded as unsatisfactory by both parties.

Besant, Annie (1847–1933) British social reformer and theosophist. She became a Fabian, a trade-union organizer (including the MATCH GIRLS' strike of 1888), and a propagandist for birth control. She campaigned tirelessly for intellectual freedom, social justice, and sexual equality. A campaigner for Indian independence, she founded the Hindu University in Benares, India, and helped to form, in 1916, the All India Home Rule League. She was President of the Indian National CONGRESS 1918–19, one of only three Britons to have held this office. She became a leading exponent of the religious movement known as theosophy and published numerous books on the subject.

Annie Besant   *According to the writer George Bernard Shaw, Besant was the greatest female orator of her era.*

Betancourt, Rómulo (1908–81) Venezuelan statesman. An avowed democrat, he served as President from 1959 to 1964, presiding over a period of redemocratization following a long period of military juntas. He initiated a modest programme of agrarian reform, increased the taxes paid by the foreign oil companies, and secured a series of benefits for organized labour. Attacked by the right-wing supporters of his predecessor and by the radical socialists, he turned the presidential office over to a freely elected successor in 1964.

Bethmann-Hollweg, Theobald von (1856–1921) German statesman. He was Prussian Minister of the Interior, then Secretary of State in the Imperial Ministry of the Interior. As Chancellor (1909–17) he instituted a number of electoral reforms and gave greater autonomy to ALSACE-LORRAINE. He greatly increased the German peacetime army, believing that Germany would be forced into a war by its neighbours. He hoped to retain British neutrality and, in 1912, worked successfully with Britain to keep peace in the BALKAN STATES. In July 1914 he and the Kaiser, WILLIAM II, convinced of the need for a short, preventive war, promised unconditional support to the AUSTRO-HUNGARIAN EMPIRE. In 1917 he opposed unrestricted submarine warfare, rightly foreseeing the entry of the USA into the war. He retired in July and Hindenburg and Ludendorff then set up a military dictatorship.

Bevan, Aneurin (1897–1960) British politician. He led the Welsh miners in the 1926 GENERAL STRIKE. He was elected Independent Labour Member of Parliament for Ebbw Vale in 1929, joining the more moderate Labour Party in 1931. His left-wing views and fiery personality made him a rebellious member of the Party. A founder and editor of *Tribune* magazine, he was one of Winston CHURCHILL's most constructive critics during World War II. As Minister of Health (1945–51), he was responsible for a considerable programme of house-building and for the creation, amid bitter controversy with the medical profession, of the National HEALTH SERVICE. In 1951 he became Minister of Labour, but resigned when charges were imposed for some medical services. The Bevanite group was then formed within the Party. As shadow minister for foreign affairs in opposition from 1957, he is remembered for his opposition to unilateral nuclear disarmament. Often in conflict with his own party, he was nevertheless elected deputy leader in 1959.

Beveridge, William Henry, 1st Baron Beveridge (1879–1963) British economist and social reformer. At the invitation of Winston CHURCHILL he entered (1908) the Board of Trade and published his notable report, *Unemployment*, in 1909. In it he argued that the regulation of society by an interventionist state would strengthen rather than weaken the free market economy. He was instrumental in drafting the Labour Exchanges Act (1909) and the National Insurance Act (1911). In 1941 he was commissioned by the government to chair an inquiry into the social services and produced the report *Social Insurance and Allied Services* (1942). This was to become the foundation of the British WELFARE STATE and the blueprint for much social legislation from 1944 to 1948.

Bevin, Ernest (1881–1951) British trade union leader and politician. He was General Secretary of the Transport and General Workers' Union (1922–40),

Minister of Labour and National Service (1940–45), and Foreign Secretary (1945–51). Bevin played a major role in the GENERAL STRIKE of 1926 and the crisis of 1931. His influence on Labour Party politics in the 1930s was considerable, but he did not enter Parliament until invited to join Winston CHURCHILL's war-time coalition government in 1940. His trade-union background was invaluable in mobilizing the labour force during World War II. As Foreign Secretary he took decisive action to extricate Britain from PALESTINE in 1948 and to involve the USA in post-war West European affairs through the MARSHALL PLAN and NATO.

Bhagavadgita (Sanskrit, 'Song of the Lord') A Hindu philosophical poem inserted into the sixth book of the Mahabharata. The poem, which is the most famous religious text of HINDUISM, consists of 700 Sanskrit verses and was probably written in the 1st or 2nd century AD. The Pandava prince Arjuna, revolted by the prospect of killing his kinsmen in battle, seeks guidance from Krishna, disguised as his charioteer. Krishna urges Arjuna to fulfil his caste duties as a warrior selflessly and, revealing his divinity, preaches absolute devotion (*bhakti*) to the all-loving Supreme Being incarnated from age to age to save mankind. This is the first clear presentation of this doctrine in Hindu texts, and represents a move away from the priestly sacrificial cult of the VEDAS to a devotional Hinduism open to all.

Bhave, Vinoba (1895–1982) Indian leader. A follower of GANDHI from 1916, he was active in attempts to re-vitalize Indian village life. Imprisoned by the British (1940–44) for defying wartime regulations, Bhave was, after Gandhi's assassination (1948), widely regarded as the leading exponent of Gandhism. He founded (1948) the Sarvodaya Samaj to work among refugees. In 1951 he began the BHOODAN or land-gift movement, and led the Shanti Sena movement for conflict resolution and economic and social reform.

Bhoodan A movement in India begun in 1951 by Vinoba BHAVE with the object of acquiring land for redistribution to landless villagers. At first the object was to acquire individual plots, but from the late 1950s an attempt was made to transfer ownership of entire villages to village councils. The movement had a measure of success in Bihar state.

Bhopal A city in Madhya Pradesh, India, the site of probably the largest industrial accident in history, when in 1984 large quantities of methyl isocyanate gas from a plant manufacturing insecticide were released over a densely populated area. In the mass panic as the inhabitants tried to escape, over 2,500 people were killed and 50,000 were injured. In the longer term, the gas caused chronic respiratory problems, eye irritation, and blindness in many thousands of people. Litigation for liability lasted for almost three years, with the owners of the US plant (Union Carbide) claiming that industrial sabotage was responsible for the disaster. The inquiry into the disaster found that poor operating and safety procedures plus inadequate staffing levels were the major causes.

Bhutan, Kingdom of A small country in south Asia, lying in the Himalayas between China in the north and India in the south.

Physical. Northern Bhutan is entirely mountainous with spectacular peaks rising to 7,300 m (nearly 24,000 feet). Deep valleys with fast-flowing rivers lead to warmer and lower land in the south, which is forested and offers soil for cultivation.

Economy. Tourism is significant in a largely agricultural economy with some light industry. Only about 9% of Bhutan's territory is cultivated; the chief crops are rice, maize, and fruit. Principal exports are electricity and wood products. India, the major export destination, provides an annual subsidy.

History. Bhutan existed as a political unit by the end of the 17th century. The country is referred to in earlier monastic texts, but its early history is not clear. The first rulers of Bhutan were religious and political leaders, but the functions were later divided between a spiritual leader, the Dharma Raja, and an administrator, the Deb Raja. The Deb Raja was in theory elected by the regional governors, but in practice the strongest governor claimed the position. During the 19th century there were frequent wars between rival governors. The Dharma Raja was succeeded by a person traditionally regarded as a reincarnation of him. The office ceased to exist in the early 20th century when no reincarnation of the last Dharma Raja could be agreed. In 1907 a powerful regional governor was elected as the first hereditary maharaja, or king, who is called the Druk Gyalpo. His great-grandson Jigme Singye Wangchuk became king in 1972.

In 1774 Bhutan and the EAST INDIA COMPANY signed a treaty of co-operation. This was replaced in 1865 by a treaty with Britain, which allowed Britain to supervise Bhutan's external affairs. This role was transferred to British India in 1910 and to the newly independent Indian government in 1949. During the 1950s and 1960s the king liberalized Bhutanese customs, abolishing slavery and the caste system and improving the status of women. He established a National Assembly in 1953. In 1969 a more democratic constitution was adopted, but political parties remain illegal. The country has received large numbers of Tibetan refugees and Nepalese immigrants. In 1990 ethnic conflict broke out in southern Bhutan, with many Nepalese demanding greater recognition and protesting against government measures aimed at preserving Bhutanese culture and language.

CAPITAL:	Thimphu
AREA:	47,000 sq km (18,150 sq miles)
POPULATION:	842,000 (1996)
CURRENCY:	1 ngultrum = 100 chetrum (Indian rupee also legal tender)
RELIGIONS:	Buddhist 69.6%; Hindu 24.6%; Muslim 5.0%
ETHNIC GROUPS:	Bhutia 62.5%; Gerung 15.5%; Assamese 13.2%
LANGUAGES:	Dzongkha (a Tibetan dialect) (official); Gurung; Assamese
INTERNATIONAL ORGANIZATIONS:	UN; Colombo Plan; Non-Aligned Movement

Bhutto, Benazir (1953–   ) Pakistani stateswoman, Prime Minister of Pakistan (1988–90, 1993–96). The daughter of Zulfikar Ali BHUTTO, she completed her studies at Harvard and Oxford Universities and went back to Pakistan only a few days before her father was deposed in a coup (1977). She was frequently held under house arrest from 1977 until 1984, when she went into exile. After her father's execution (1979) she led the

Pakistan People's Party (PPP) and campaigned for the restoration of democracy. Martial law was lifted in 1986 and Bhutto returned to Pakistan, leading opposition to General ZIA UL-HAQ's government. The PPP won elections in 1988 and Bhutto became Prime Minister until 1990, when her government was dismissed. She was charged with corruption and fraud, but was acquitted of most of the charges in 1994. In 1993 she was elected Prime Minister for the second time, as head of a PPP-led coalition. Her plans to implement social reforms and to liberalize Pakistani society were hampered by economic difficulties, violent social unrest, and rising Islamic fundamentalism. She was again accused of corruption and dismissed from office (1996) and was defeated in elections held in 1997.

Bhutto, Zulfikar Ali (1928–79) Pakistani statesman. In 1958 he joined AYUB KHAN's first military government as Minister of Fuel and Power and subsequently became Foreign Minister (1963). Dismissed from Ayub's cabinet in 1967 he formed the Pakistan People's Party with a policy of Islam, democracy, socialism, and populism. In the elections of 1970 the PPP secured the largest share of the vote in West Pakistan and, after the military government was discredited by the loss of Bangladesh, Bhutto became President (1971), but stepped down in 1973 to become Prime Minister. Bhutto concluded the Simla agreement with India in 1972; recognized Bangladesh in 1974, and cultivated China; and formulated a new constitution and an ambitious economic programme, whose failure contributed to his ejection in a military coup in 1977. Bhutto was subsequently hanged on the charge of complicity in a political murder. His widow, Begum Nusrat Bhutto (1934–), has also been active in politics and his daughter Benazir BHUTTO became Prime Minister.

Biafra An abortive NIGERIAN secessionist state (1967–70) in the south-east of the country, inhabited principally by Ibo people. It seceded after mounting antagonism between the eastern region and the western and northern regions led Colonel Ojukwu to declare the east independent. Civil war followed. Gabon, Ivory Coast, Tanzania, and Zambia recognized Biafra, while Britain and the Soviet Union supported the federal government. When Ojukwu fled to the Ivory Coast General Effiong capitulated in Lagos in 1970 and Biafra ceased to exist.

Bible The sacred book of Christianity. All Christian Churches accept two sections of the Bible: the Hebrew scriptures, known as the Old Testament, and specifically Christian writings, known as the New Testament. In addition, some Churches, including the Roman Catholic Church, accept a third section called the Apocrypha, found in the Greek version of the Old Testament (Septuagint). Each section consists of a number of separate books, written at different times by different authors. However, most Christians consider them to be endowed with unique divine authority.

The Old Testament contains 39 books. The first five books ('the Law', the TORAH, or Pentateuch) describe the origins of the Jewish people. 'The Prophets' give a history of the settlement in CANAAN, the period of the kingdom of ISRAEL, and prophetic commentaries. 'The Writings' consist of the remainder of the books including the Psalms, Job, and Daniel. The final content of the Hebrew Old Testament was probably agreed *c.* 100 AD. The New Testament consists of 27 books. The

four Gospels (meaning 'good news'), attributed to Matthew, Mark, Luke, and John, record the life, death, and resurrection of JESUS CHRIST. The Acts of the Apostles traces the development of the early Christian Church and the Epistles (or Letters), notably those of St PAUL, contain advice on worship, conduct, and organization for the first Christian communities. The Book of Revelation gives a prophetic description of the end of the world. Most of these books were acknowledged as canonical (accepted as sacred and genuine) by the middle of the 2nd century. The Apocrypha (Greek, 'hidden things') is the name given to a collection of 12 books written between 300 BC and 100 AD. They were included in the Septuagint, a Greek translation of the Old Testament of the 3rd and 2nd centuries BC that was used by the early Christian Church. These books do not appear in the Hebrew Old Testament and are not accepted by all Christian Churches.

The Bible was originally written in Hebrew, Aramaic, and Greek. The first translation of the whole book was the Latin Vulgate (405 AD) of St JEROME. The first translation into English was undertaken by John WYCLIF and his followers (1382–88). The development of PRINTING stimulated the production of vernacular editions. Martin LUTHER translated the New Testament into German in 1522 and William TYNDALE into English in 1525–26. William Coverdale's edition of the Bible, drawing heavily on Tyndale's work, was first published in 1535 and revised as the Great Bible in 1539. The Authorized or King James Version (1611), named after JAMES I who agreed to a new translation at the HAMPTON COURT CONFERENCE, was produced by about 50 scholars and remained for centuries the Bible of every English-speaking country. Modern English translations include the *New English Bible* (1961–70). There are now translations of all or part of the Bible in over 1760 languages.

Bidault, Georges (1899–1982) French statesman and journalist. After serving in World War I he became professor of history in Paris. During World War II he became a distinguished leader of the French RESISTANCE MOVEMENT. He was a founder-member and leader (1949) of the Mouvement Républicaine Populaire. Bidault was Foreign Minister in several administrations of the Fourth Republic (1944, 1947, 1953–54) and Prime Minister (1946, 1949–50, 1958). He subsequently became bitterly opposed to ALGERIAN independence: he became President of the National Resistance Council in 1962, was charged with plotting against the state, and went into exile in Brazil. He returned to France in 1968.

Bigge Inquiry (1819–21) A British government inquiry into New South Wales, Australia. It was conducted by John Bigge to inquire into the future potential of the penal colony as a free settlement. He visited New South Wales and Van Diemen's Land and produced three official reports in 1822 and 1823. He recommended limited constitutional government and the establishment of Van Diemen's Land as a separate colony. Other recommendations, many of which were implemented, included the encouragement of the pastoral industry. Bigge was critical of Governor MACQUARIE, especially in his treatment of convicts and EMANCIPISTS, which Bigge saw as being excessively lenient, and also of his expensive programme of public works.

Bihar A region in India comprising the middle Ganges plains and the Chota Nagpur plateau in north-eastern India. The region had its 'golden age' during the evolution of early Indian civilization. Among its ancient kingdoms was MAGADHA, where both Gautama BUDDHA and the JAIN seer, Mahavira, preached. Its capital, Pataliputra (now Patna), was adopted by several notable empire builders, including the MAURYAS and the GUPTAS. About 1200 it came under Muslim influence and remained subservient to the DELHI sultans until becoming a province of the MOGUL empire in the 16th century. In 1765 British victories resulted in its amalgamation with BENGAL and the introduction of indigo plantations.

Bijapur A city and former state on the Deccan plateau, south-western India. It was the capital of a Muslim kingdom, founded by the Yadava dynasty in the 12th century. It fell under the control of the BAHMANI Muslims in the 14th century. Its era of independent splendour was from 1489 to 1686 when the Adil Shahi sultans made it their capital and were responsible for Islamic architecture of outstanding quality. In 1686 the Mogul emperor AURANGZEB defeated Bijapur, but was unable to exert firm control and the region soon fell under MARATHA sway, from which it passed into East India Company hands in the early 19th century.

Bikini Atoll An atoll in the MARSHALL ISLANDS, west central Pacific. It was the site for 23 US nuclear bomb tests (1946–58). Despite expectations that it would be fit again for human habitation in 1968, the atoll remains too contaminated for the return of the Bikinians, who have been relocated on surrounding islands. In 1985 the USA agreed to decontaminate the atoll, a process that would take 10–15 years. During the 1990s Bikinians continued to pursue claims for compensation and the USA set up a fund for islanders who had suffered personal injury as a result of the nuclear tests.

Biko, Steve (1956–77) Student leader in South Africa. A medical student at the University of Natal, he was co-founder and president of the all-Black South African Students Association, whose aim was to raise Black consciousness. Active in the Black People's Convention, he was banned and then arrested on numerous occasions (1973–76). His death in custody, by falling from a window at police headquarters in Pretoria (officially suicide but widely regarded as murder), made him a symbol of heroism in Black South African townships and beyond. Following disclosures about his maltreatment in prison, the South African government prohibited numerous Black organizations and detained newspaper editors, thus provoking international anger. In post-apartheid South Africa, police officers giving evidence before the Truth and Reconciliation Commission in 1997 continued to maintain that Biko's death was not murder.

Bill of Rights (1689) A declaration of the conditions upon which WILLIAM III and Mary were to become joint sovereigns of England, Scotland, and Ireland which became an Act of Parliament. Its major important provisions were that the king could not levy taxes without the consent of Parliament, that he no longer had the power to suspend or dispense with the laws, and that there was to be no peacetime standing army without Parliament's consent. These terms dealt with

issues that had been raised by the actions of JAMES II and were seen as a guarantee of Englishmen's liberties, helping to justify the name GLORIOUS REVOLUTION for the events of 1688–89. American patriots often referred to the Bill of Rights when claiming, in the dispute with Britain in the late 18th century, that their liberties had been undermined.

Bill of Rights (1791) The first ten amendments to the CONSTITUTION OF THE USA. The constitutional arrangements of 1787 were assumed to guarantee human and civil rights, but omission of specific rights led to criticism. To prevent this issue jeopardizing ratification, a Bill of Rights was adopted in 1791. Based on features of the English BILL OF RIGHTS (1689) and common law principles, it guaranteed freedom of speech, press, worship, assembly, and petition (the first amendment). US citizens had the right to speedy and fair trial, reasonable bail, and to bear arms. They could not be forced to incriminate themselves (the fifth amendment) or suffer unwarranted search and seizure or cruel and unusual punishments.

Billy the Kid (William H. Bonney) (1859–81) US outlaw. He arrived in New Mexico in 1868. A frequenter of saloons, he moved effortlessly into robbery and murder. In 1878 he became prominent in a cattle war, killing the local sheriff, Jim Brady. The territorial governor, Lew Wallace, was unable to persuade Billy to cease his activities. Sheriff Pat Garrett captured him in 1880, but he escaped, only to be shot by Garrett at Fort Sumner, New Mexico.

Birch, John JOHN BIRCH SOCIETY.

Birla Indian commercial and industrial family of the Marwari or Hindu merchant caste. It is one of the two (with the Tatas) greatest Indian industrial families. The best known member of the family was Ghanshyam Das Birla, who became GANDHI's principal financial backer, paying most of the cost of the *ashram* (retreat), the Harijan organizations, the peasant uplift campaign, and the national language movement, as well as supporting many other Gandhian welfare projects. It was at Birla House, New Delhi, that Gandhi was killed. The Birla family has continued to manage a successful business empire.

Bishop, Maurice GRENADA.

Bishops' Wars (1639–40) Two brief conflicts over CHARLES I's attempt to impose Anglicanism on the Scots, and important as a factor leading to the outbreak of the ENGLISH CIVIL WAR. Since 1625 the king had been trying to take back former Church lands from Scottish noblemen, provoking great bitterness. In 1637, a modified version of the English Prayer Book was introduced in Scotland. This spurred the COVENANTERS into abolishing the episcopacy. The first war (May–June 1639) was a bloodless fiasco. Charles had refused to call a Parliament to vote funds and, acknowledging that his new recruits were no match for the Covenanters, he made peace at Berwick. For the second war (August–September 1640), refused supplies by the English 'Short Parliament', he obtained money from the Irish Parliament, but his army was routed by the Covenanters at Newburn, near Newcastle upon Tyne. With the Scots occupying Northumberland and Durham, Charles was forced to make peace at Ripon, and to call the LONG PARLIAMENT.

Bismarck, Otto von (1815–98) German statesman, known as the 'Iron Chancellor'. A Brandenburg nobleman, he entered the Prussian Parliament as an ultra-royalist and an opponent of democracy. During the REVOLUTIONS OF 1848 he opposed demands for constitutional reform and in 1851, as Prussian member of the Federal German Diet at Frankfurt, dominated by Austria, he demanded equal rights for Prussia. After a brief period as ambassador to St Petersburg (1859) and Paris (1862) he was made minister-president of Prussia (1862–90). He enlarged and reorganized the Prussian army. In 1864, in partnership with Austria, he led the German states in the defeat of Denmark, acquiring SCHLESWIG-HOLSTEIN, whose KIEL CANAL became of strategic importance to Germany. In 1866 he provoked a confrontation with Austria, known as the AUSTRO-PRUSSIAN WAR, or the Seven Weeks War, from which he emerged victorious. He then annexed Hanover and united most of the other German states in the North German Confederation, of which he became Chancellor. He instigated the FRANCO-PRUSSIAN WAR (1870–71), wresting ALSACE and Lorraine from France, capturing the French emperor, NAPOLEON III, and subjecting Paris to a long and terrible siege. He then proclaimed the King of Prussia, WILLIAM I, as emperor of a GERMAN SECOND EMPIRE in the French Palace of Versailles. At home, he introduced a common currency, a central bank, a single code of law, and various administrative reforms for the new empire. He unsuccessfully sought to weaken the power of the Catholic Church (the so-called KULTURKAMPF), but successfully introduced the Prussian school system, with its government inspectors, into the empire. He kept the German Parliament (Reichstag) weak and the executive strong. He dealt severely with socialist supporters. In an effort to keep the working class away from the socialists and to hold trade-unionists in check, he introduced the first industrial welfare scheme in history, a series of SOCIAL SECURITY laws (1883–87) to provide for sickness, accident, and old age benefits. In foreign affairs, as Chancellor, he initiated the THREE EMPERORS LEAGUE (Dreikaiserbund) and the later TRIPLE ALLIANCE. He presided with great success over the Congress of BERLIN (1878) and the Berlin Conference on Africa (1884). As a result of his economic nationalism and protective tariffs, German industry and commerce flourished and new colonies were acquired overseas. The death of William I showed the weakness of Bismarck's position, dependent as it was on the royal will and not on popular, democratic support. WILLIAM II saw Bismarck as a rival for power, and forced his resignation (1890). Bismarck spent the rest of his years in retirement.

Black-and-Tans An auxiliary force of the Royal Irish Constabulary. The demands of the Irish Republicans for a free IRELAND led in 1919 to violence against the Royal Irish Constabulary, an armed British police force. Many of the policemen resigned, so the British government in 1920 reinforced the RIC with British ex-soldiers. Their distinctive temporary uniforms gave them their nickname of Black-and-Tans. They adopted a policy of harsh reprisals against republicans, many people being killed in raids and property destroyed. Public opinion in Britain and the USA was shocked and the Black-and-Tans were withdrawn after the Anglo-Irish truce in 1921.

Black Churches Christian congregations of Afro-Americans. They may be of any PROTESTANT denomination, especially BAPTIST, METHODIST, or Pentecostal. Originating among Black slaves, Black Churches have a strong awareness of political and social injustice, and played an important part in the US Civil Rights Movement of the 1960s and 1970s. Black theology, like LIBERATION THEOLOGY, emphasizes the freedom of the oppressed and God's identification with the victims in society. Worship in Black Churches is often informal, with spontaneous singing, shouting, and dancing. Preaching is central, and the Black minister may also be active in community activities and politics.

Black Death (1347–50) The most virulent epidemic of bubonic and pneumonic plague ever recorded. It reached Europe from the TARTAR armies, fresh from campaigning in the Crimea, who besieged the port of Caffa (1347). Rats carrying infected fleas swarmed aboard trading vessels, thus transmitting the plague to southern Europe. By 1348 it reached France, Spain, and England; a year later Germany, Russia, and Scandinavia. Numbers of dead cannot be exact but up to 25,000,000 may have died in Europe; perhaps one-third of the population in England.

Effects were profound and lasting. Shortage of manpower put those peasants who survived in a strong position. The demand for labour led to the substitution of wages for labour services and peasants' agitation for further improvements led to agrarian revolts. The Church, too, was adversely affected, with inadequately trained clerics being ordained to replace dead parish priests. Mass hysteria caused by fear and helplessness was reflected in art and literature. Outbreaks of plague continued in Europe until the 17th century (GREAT PLAGUE).

Blackfoot A Native American people who inhabited southern Alberta and north-western Montana, originally a hunter-gatherer people similar to the CREE. The Shoshone of Idaho became nomadic once they acquired horses and firearms in the 18th century, and raided the horseless Blackfoot. The Blackfoot retaliated by stealing horses from the Shoshone and trading for firearms with the Cree. Thereafter they rapidly adopted nomadism on the northern Great Plains.

Black Hand Symbol and name for a number of secret societies that flourished in the 19th and early 20th centuries. It was the name adopted by a Serbian terrorist organization, founded in 1911 by Colonel Dimitrijevic largely from army officers, to liberate Serbs still under Habsburg or Turkish rule. It organized the assassination at Sarajevo of Archduke FRANCIS FERDINAND (1914), an event which contributed to the outbreak of World War I. The name and symbol were adopted by organizations controlled by the MAFIA in the USA and Italy, which used intimidation and murder to gain their ends.

Black Hawk War (1832) A Native American war. Between the LOUISIANA PURCHASE and the 1830s, there was steady pressure to remove the remaining Native Americans east of the Mississippi to the new territory, and their land rights were eaten away by a series of enforced treaties. In 1831, the Sauk and Fox people, led by Chief Black Hawk, were forced by the local militia to retreat across the Mississippi into Missouri. In the following year, threatened by famine and hostile Sioux, they recrossed the river to plant corn. When they

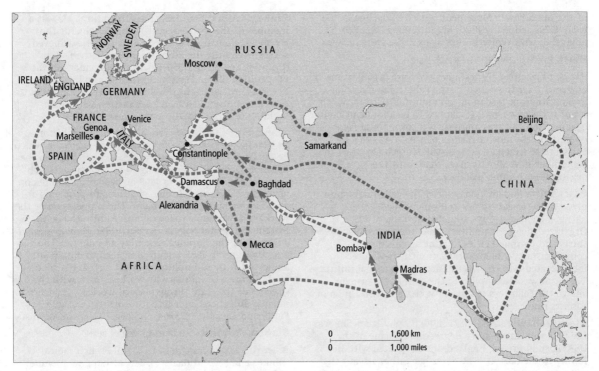

Black Death   *The Black Death was the most devastating of many outbreaks of plague. Although its origins are uncertain, it is believed to have come from the Far East and to have been carried westward to Europe by merchants, pilgrims, and other travellers. It spread especially fast along sea trade routes, transmitted by the fleas of rats on board ship. The particular virulence of this epidemic may have been due to the presence of the more deadly pneumonic variety of plague, the only form that can be directly transmitted from one human to another (by sneezing, for example). It is estimated that as much as one-third of the population of Europe and the Near East died as a result of this outbreak in less than 20 years.*

refused to comply with the local military commander's order to leave, a brief war broke out in which the starving Sauk and Fox were gradually driven back, before being trapped and massacred near the mouth of the Red Axe River in early August. Black Hawk's defeat and death allowed the final loss of Native American land rights east of the Mississippi in favour of the White settlers.

Black Hole of Calcutta A prison room at Fort William, Calcutta, India, so called after the alleged suffocation there in 1756 of some English prisoners. They had been incarcerated by the nawab, Siraj ud-Daula, in retaliation for extending the fort against previous agreements. The incident has an important place in British imperial mythology, for British accounts grossly exaggerated both the smallness of the room and the number of prisoners, thus suggesting an act of barbarism on the nawab's part.

Black Muslim Movement An Islamic organization in the USA. It was founded in 1930 and led by Elijah Muhammad from 1934 until his death in 1975. The Movement expanded greatly in the 1950s when MALCOLM X became one of its spokesmen; by the 1960s, at the height of the BLACK POWER MOVEMENT, it probably had over 100,000 members. With the suspension of Malcolm X from the Movement and his assassination in 1965, it lost some of its influence to the Black Panthers, but

continued to establish separate Black enterprises and to provide a source of inspiration for thousands of Black Americans. Elijah Muhammad was succeeded in 1975 by his son, Wallace D. Muhammad, who advocated a more moderate form of Islam and racial integration. This led to disagreements within the Movement and in 1976 it split into the American Muslim Mission and the radical Nation of Islam, led by Louis Farrakhan.

Black Power Movement A movement among Black people in the USA in the mid-1960s; it took a more militant approach towards securing CIVIL RIGHTS, and stressed the need for action by Black people alone, rather than in alliance with White liberals. Many Black people felt that the civil rights movement had done little to alter their lives, and under such leaders as Stokeley Carmichael they proposed that Black Americans should concentrate in their own communities to establish their own political and economic power. In 1966 a Student Non-Violent Co-ordinating Committee (SNCC) was formed by Carmichael to activate Black college students, and at the same time the BLACK MUSLIM MOVEMENT was advocating Islam as the Black salvation. Others, like the Black Panthers, emphasized violence and militancy, but all were concerned to stress the value of Black culture. The riots in the cities in the middle and late 1960s seemed to herald new waves of Black militancy, but the intensity of the Black Power Movement tended to decline in the early 1970s and many Black organizations began co-operating with White groups against the VIETNAM WAR.

Black Prince EDWARD THE BLACK PRINCE.

Black September Palestinian terrorist organization. It emerged after the defeat of the Palestinian guerrilla organizations in Jordan in September 1970, from which event it took its name. It claimed to be an independent organization, but was apparently a cover for al-Fatah operations, the most atrocious of which was the massacre of Israeli athletes at the Munich Olympics in September 1972. Shortly after that event the organization became inactive.

Blackshirts (Italian, *camicie nere*) The colloquial name given to the *Squadre d'Azione* (Action Squads), the national combat groups, founded in Italy in 1919. Organized along paramilitary lines, they wore black shirts and patrolled cities to fight socialism and communism by violent means. In 1921 they were incorporated into the FASCIST Party as a national militia. The term was also applied to the SS in Nazi Germany and to the followers of Oswald MOSLEY's British Union of Fascists in the 1930s.

Blackwell, Elizabeth (1821–1910) US physician. She was the first woman to gain a degree in medicine in the USA. Born in Bristol, England, she emigrated with her family to the USA in 1832. After her father's death she supported her family by teaching, and began studying medicine privately. Rejected by various medical schools, she was finally accepted by the Geneva Medical College, New York, graduating in 1849. She practised in New York but later lived in England, becoming professor of gynaecology at the London School of Medicine for Women (1875–1907).

Blaine, James Gillespie (1830–93) US politician. He was Secretary of State to President GARFIELD (1881), and to President William Henry HARRISON (1889–91). As leader of the so-called 'Half Breeds' Republicans (those committed to a conciliatory policy towards the South and to civil-service reform), he helped three lesser men (Hayes, Garfield, Harrison) attain the presidency but was denied the prize himself in the 1884 election against CLEVELAND. He aroused suspicion on account of his transactions with railway companies, to whom he owed his moderate wealth.

Blair, Tony (1953–) British politician and Prime Minister from 1997. A lawyer, Blair was elected as a Labour Member of Parliament in 1983, becoming a member of the shadow cabinet in 1984 and shadow spokesman for Home Affairs (1992–94). As leader of the Labour Party from 1994 he promoted dynamic reform within the Party, changing its constitution to end its traditional commitment to collective ownership of all industries and promising to support private enterprise. In 1997 he led the Labour Party to a landslide victory in the general election, ending 18 years of Conservative government. A popular and reforming Prime Minister, he has promoted major changes to the constitution of the UK, including devolved bodies in Scotland and Wales and a new political settlement in Northern Ireland (April 1998). His government has also promised major reforms of the Welfare State.

Blake, Robert (1599–1657) English admiral. He was a member of the LONG PARLIAMENT and fought for the ROUNDHEADS during the ENGLISH CIVIL WAR. He achieved successes against the Royalists (1649–51), the Dutch (1652–54), and Spain (1656–57). His involvement in the preparation of the *Fighting Instructions* and *Articles of War* was crucial to the developing professionalism of the English navy, as was his association with the building of large, heavily armed vessels.

Blanc, Louis (1811–82) French politician and historian. In 1839 he published *The Organization of Labour* in which he outlined his ideal of a new social order based on the principle 'from each according to his abilities, to each according to his needs'. In 1848 he headed a commission of workers' delegates to find solutions to problems of exploitation and unemployment. The suppression of the workers' revolt later that year forced him to flee to Britain and he did not return until 1871. He was elected a Deputy of the National Assembly and did not join the PARIS COMMUNE in 1871, but tried instead to obtain an amnesty for those implicated in the rising. His advocacy of the control of industry by working men with the support of the state through social workshops (*ateliers sociaux*) influenced later leftist reformers, notably Ferdinand Lassalle (1825–64) and other German socialists.

Blanco, Antonio Guzmán GUZMÁN BLANCO.

Blanqui, Louis Auguste (1805–81) French radical thinker and revolutionary leader. Although a member of the CARBONARI, he was decorated by LOUIS-PHILIPPE for his part in the 1830 July revolution which had deposed Charles X. Realizing that the only beneficiaries of the revolution had been bourgeois oligarchs, he took to conspiracy against them, launching an attack on the Paris Hotel de Ville in 1839. Sentenced to death, his sentence was later commuted to life imprisonment. A brief period of freedom allowed him to lead the republicans in the REVOLUTION OF 1848. He remained in prison until 1859, was re-arrested in 1861, and escaped to Belgium in 1865, where he organized the extremist republican opposition to NAPOLEON III in whose deposition he was instrumental. He was imprisoned in 1871, after attempting to overthrow the French provisional government. His influence over the PARIS COMMUNE was considerable, and his followers vainly offered their hostages in exchange for Blanqui. He died in 1881, two years after being finally released from prison.

Blenheim, Battle of (13 August 1704) A major battle of the War of the SPANISH SUCCESSION, fought at Blenheim, a Bavarian village on the north bank of the River Danube. In 1704 LOUIS XIV's armies were advancing towards Vienna and the French leader, Marshal Tallard, occupied the village while his ally, the Elector of Bavaria, held Lutzingen. John Churchill, Duke of MARLBOROUGH, captain-general of the allied armies, had made a brilliant march down the Rhine and joined forces with the Austrian commander, Prince EUGÈNE OF SAVOY. On 13 August Marlborough overwhelmed the French while Prince Eugène defeated the Elector. After heavy losses (12,000 Allies; *c.* 30,000 French) on both sides Tallard surrendered: Vienna was saved and Bavaria conquered.

Blenheim Palace was built at Woodstock in Oxfordshire as a gift to the Duke of Marlborough from the grateful British nation.

Bligh, William (1754–1817) British admiral. He accompanied Captain Cook on his second voyage (1772–75). On a further visit to the South Pacific islands in 1788, his irascible temper and overbearing conduct provoked the BOUNTY MUTINY. Returning to Britain, he served under Nelson at Copenhagen (1801) and in 1805 was appointed governor of New South Wales. Conflict with the New South Wales Corps culminated in the RUM REBELLION of 1808. Settling in England in 1810, he was promoted to the rank of vice-admiral.

Blitzkrieg (German, 'lightning war') A military tactic employed by the Germans in World War II that was especially successful in campaigns against Poland, France, Greece, and the Soviet Union. It employed fast-moving tanks and motorized infantry, supported by dive-bombers, to throw superior but slower enemy forces off balance and thereby win crushing victories rapidly and with small expenditure of men and materials. In Britain, where it was known as 'the Blitz' it consisted of an air assault on British cities in 1940–41. After 1941, Germany's enemies were better prepared and new battlefields in the Soviet Union and Africa were less suited to the technique.

Blood, Thomas (c. 1618–80) Irish colonel and adventurer. He lost his estates at the RESTORATION in 1660 and hoped to persuade the authorities to return them by his attack on Dublin castle in 1663. His most famous exploit was the theft of the English crown jewels from the Tower of London in 1671. CHARLES II, who examined Blood personally after his arrest, was so impressed with his audacity that he was pardoned and his estates restored.

Blood River, Battle of (16 December 1838) A battle fought between Voortrekkers and ZULUS, led by DINGAAN, near a tributary of the Buffalo River – subsequently called Blood River after its waters were reddened with the blood of some 3,000 Zulus, killed to avenge the slaughter of about 500 Boers (AFRIKANERS) earlier in the year. The Zulu defeat enabled the Boers to establish the Republic of NATAL.

Bloody Assizes A series of trials held in 1685 to punish those who took part in MONMOUTH'S REBELLION, conducted by Judge JEFFREYS, the Lord Chief Justice, in those centres of western England most affected by the rebellion. Of 1,400 prisoners brought before him, 300 were hanged and 800 more were sold as slaves in the colonies, some of the profits from this enslavement going to courtiers, and even to the queen and her ladies. The severity of the sentences helped to mobilize support for WILLIAM III (of Orange) in the West Country in 1688.

Blücher, Gebhard Leberecht von (1742–1819) Prussian field-marshal, whose victories were due more to dash and energy than to military tactics. Forced to surrender to the French in 1806, he helped to re-create his country's opposition to NAPOLEON, and was commander-in-chief of the armies in their victory at LEIPZIG in 1813. The following year he led the invasion of France, gaining a major victory at Laon, which led to the overthrow of Napoleon. He retired to Silesia, only to be recalled when Napoleon returned. His intervention at a late stage of the battle of WATERLOO was decisive.

Blum, Léon (1872–1950) French politician and writer. An established journalist and critic, he was first drawn to politics by the DREYFUS affair. He brought about the coalition of radical socialists, socialists, and communists which won power in 1936. As France's first Socialist Prime Minister, his government granted workers a 40-hour week, paid holidays, and collective bargaining, resulting in considerable hostility from industrialists. Radicals refused to support intervention in the SPANISH CIVIL WAR, while communists withdrew their support for his failure to intervene. His government fell. He was arrested in 1940, and charged with causing France's defeat, but his skilful defence obliged the authorities to call off his trial (1942). He was interned in a German concentration camp (1943–45), and returned briefly to power as the Prime Minister of a caretaker government in 1946–47.

Boadicea BOUDICCA.

Bodin, Jean (1530–96) French political philosopher and economist. In 1576 he published his great work on limited monarchy, *Les Six Livres de la République* ('Six Books of the Commonwealth'). Its argument that sovereignty arose from human needs rather than divine institution influenced the later English philosopher Thomas HOBBES. Unlike other contemporary Protestant writings, it held that citizens were never justified in rebelling against their ruler. Bodin was also a pioneer of the study of money and its effect on prices.

Boeotia A region in central Greece whose cities in classical times included THEBES and PLATAEA. It contained much good agricultural land, suitable for the growing of corn and rearing of horses. A Boeotian League was established c. 447 BC and lasted until 387, the city of Thebes controlling four of the 11 federal areas. In 424 Boeotian forces won an important victory over the invading Athenians at Delium, but Boeotia's strength ultimately depended on that of Thebes.

Boer AFRIKANER.

Boer Wars (1880–81, 1899–1902) (the South African, or Anglo-Boer, Wars; the First and Second Wars of Freedom) Two wars fought between Britain and Transvaal and between Britain and Transvaal and the Orange Free State. The first arose from the British annexation of the Transvaal in 1877 and the incompetent administration that followed. In 1880 it was thought that the GLADSTONE government would grant independence, or at least self-government; when hopes were dashed, KRUGER, Joubert, and PRETORIUS took power as a triumvirate. British disasters at the Battles of Laing's Nek, Ingogo, and Majuba Hill, forced peace upon Gladstone, who granted self-government. The second war was caused by multiple grievances. The Boers, under the leadership of Kruger, resented the imperialist policies of Joseph CHAMBERLAIN, which they feared would deprive the Transvaal of its independence. The refusal of political rights to UITLANDERS aggravated the situation, as did the aggressive attitude of Lord MILNER, British High Commissioner. For Britain, control of the Rand goldfield was all-important. In 1896 the Transvaal and the Orange Free State formed a military alliance. The Boers, equipped by Germany, never mustered more than 88,000 men, but defeated Britain in numerous initial engagements, for example, Spion Kop. British garrisons were besieged in Ladysmith, Kimberley, and Mafeking. In 1900 the British, under KITCHENER and Roberts, landed with reinforcements. The Boers were

Boer Wars *This contemporary drawing by R. Caton Woodville illustrates the capture of a Boer convoy led by Christian de Wet, commander of the Orange Free State forces at Reitz in 1901. The convoy had been attacked by British troops under Colonel de Lisle.*

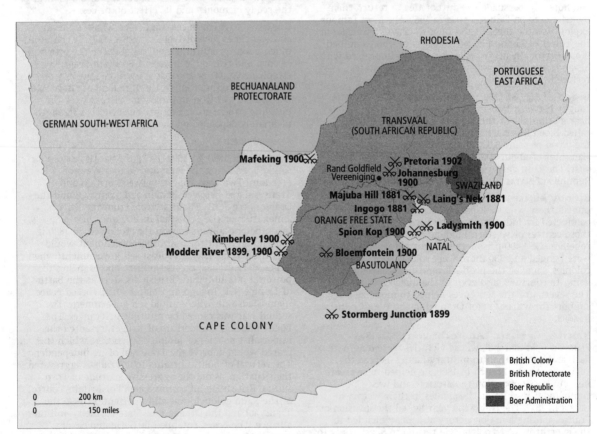

Boer Wars *The discovery of diamonds (1867) stimulated an influx of British settlers into the Boer Orange Free State and the Transvaal, where the First Boer War (1881) resulted in a British defeat. The Witwatersrand goldrush (1886) and British imperialist ambitions led to the Second War (1899–1902). The Act of Union (1909) was an uneasy compromise, preserving White domination over Black Africans and Asians.*

gradually defeated, despite the brilliant defence of the commandos. Kitchener adopted a scorched-earth policy, interning the civil population in CONCENTRATION CAMPS, and systematically destroying farms. Peace was offered in 1901, but terms that included the loss of Boer independence were not agreed until the Peace of VEREENIGING in 1902.

Boethius, Aricius Mantius Severinus (c. 475–525) One of the most influential authors of the Middle Ages. He was employed at the court of THEODORIC THE GREAT in Rome but was accused of treason, imprisoned, and executed. In prison he wrote the *De Consolatione Philosophiae* ('The Consolations of Philosophy') which owed much to Neoplatonic thought and discussed the value of philosophy to those Christians who suffer in a troubled world. The work was translated into English by ALFRED and later by Chaucer, who incorporated some of it in the *Canterbury Tales*. Boethius' chief significance is as a channel by which ancient learning passed into the monastic tradition. His translations of and commentaries on the logical works of ARISTOTLE provided almost all that was known to Christians of that philosopher until the 12th century, and helped to establish a rich Latin vocabulary of philosophical disputation. He also wrote at length on theology, mathematics, logic, art, and music.

Bohemia A region in central Europe, now the north-western part of the Czech Republic.
Physical. Bohemia is a dissected plateau rising to 1,602 m (5,256 feet) with subdued highland scenery. Bounded by the Ore Mountains (German, Erzgebirge) in the north-west and the Bohemian–Moravian heights in the south-east, it is drained by the Labe (Elbe) and its tributaries, notably the Vltava (Moldau).
History. Bohemia was established as a duchy by the Premyslid dynasty in the 9th century, but as a result of the rising power of the Ottonians was forced to accept the suzerainty of the German HOLY ROMAN EMPERORS in the following century. Having incorporated the neighbouring region of Moravia as a province, Bohemia remained under the Pre-myslids until 1306, becoming a kingdom in 1198. At the height of its power, under Ottakar II, it also controlled the duchies of Austria. In the later Middle Ages Bohemia was ruled by a number of families, most notably the German Luxemburgs and the Polish JAGIELLONS, and played a central role in the turbulent politics of the empire and papacy. In the early 15th century the martyrdom of the Prague religious reformer John HUSS (1415) solidified the identification of religious reform with an emerging popular nationalism; the Hussite wars of 1420–33 marked the departure of Bohemia from the German orbit and its assumption of a more overtly Slavic identity. In 1526 the kingdom was inherited by the imperial HABSBURG dynasty, but in the 17th century it was once again at the centre of politico-religious upheaval within the empire, Protestantism and resurgent nationalism helping precipitate a revolt against imperial power which led to the THIRTY YEARS WAR (1618–48).
In 1848, a Slav Congress demanding greater autonomy assembled in Prague under the leadership of PALACKÝ. Austrian domination was forcibly restored in 1849, and Moravia was made into a separate crown land. Concessions made to the Czechs by Vienna after 1867 served only to disconcert the Germans living in

Bohemia. Independence as part of the republic of CZECHOSLOVAKIA, incorporating Bohemia, Moravia, Slovakia, and Austrian Silesia, was achieved after the collapse of the AUSTRO-HUNGARIAN EMPIRE in 1918. In 1938, having earmarked Bohemia and Moravia for German colonization, Hitler invaded the SUDETENLAND and annexed the rest of the region in the following year. A lasting shift of population was effected by the expulsion by the Czechoslovak government of three million Germans, mainly from Bohemia and Moravia, after World War II. From 1948 until 1989 Czechoslovakia was under communist control. On the break-up of Czechoslovakia in 1993, Bohemia and Moravia together formed the Czech Republic.

Bohemond I (c. 1056–1111) Norman prince of Antioch, the eldest son of Robert GUISCARD. He fought for Guiscard against the Byzantine emperor, Alexius COMNENUS; after his father's death he joined the First CRUSADE and played a prominent part in the capture of the Syrian city of Antioch. He established himself as prince in Antioch but was captured by the TURKS and imprisoned for two years. In 1107 he led an expedition against the BYZANTINE EMPIRE and was defeated by Alexius, making peace at the Treaty of Devol (1108).

Bokassa, Jean-Bédel (1921–96) President of the Central African Republic (1966–76); emperor of the Central African Empire (1976–79). After a distinguished career in the French Army, Bokassa became commander-in-chief of the forces of his newly independent country in 1964 and seized power in a coup two years later. Bokassa's rule became increasingly arbitrary and authoritarian and he was implicated in the massacre of civilians. He proclaimed himself president for life in 1972 and was named emperor in a lavish investiture ceremony in 1976. In one of the poorest countries of Africa, he spent huge sums on maintaining a luxurious lifestyle modelled on that of Napoleon I. He was deposed, with French support, in 1979. After spending seven years in exile, Bokassa was condemned to death on his return, but this sentence was commuted to one of life imprisonment. He was given amnesty and freed in 1993.

Boleyn, Anne (1507–36) Second wife of HENRY VIII and mother of ELIZABETH I. By 1527 the king was conducting a secret affair with Anne and contemplating an annulment of his marriage to Catherine of Aragon, who had failed to provide him with a male heir. His liaison with Anne continued and in January 1533 they were secretly married. Archbishop CRANMER annulled Henry's first marriage in May 1533, and Anne was crowned in June, three months before the birth of Elizabeth. Anne and her family were supporters of the Protestant religion and she helped to promote REFORMATION doctrines at court. Anne, too, failed to produce a son, and in May 1536 she was tried on dubious charges of adultery. She was beheaded in the Tower of London.

Bolger, James Brendan (1935–   ) New Zealand politician; Prime Minister (1990–97). Originally a sheep-rancher, Bolger led the National Party to victory in the elections of 1990 and 1993. After elections in 1996 he lost his majority and formed a coalition government.

Bolingbroke, Henry of HENRY IV.

Bolingbroke, Henry St John, 1st Viscount (1678–1751) British politician. He entered Parliament as a

Tory in 1701, became Secretary of State following the Tory triumph of 1710, and was responsible for negotiating the Peace of UTRECHT in 1713, though he angered Britain's allies by abandoning the military effort before peace had been finally agreed. In the power struggle among the Tories shortly before the death of Queen ANNE he was victorious over HARLEY. Dismissed by George I in 1714, and impeached by the Whig Parliament of 1715, he fled to France, where he joined James Edward Stuart, but soon became disillusioned with the PRETENDER's cause. In 1723 he was pardoned by George I and allowed back into England. Though he was refused permission to return to Parliament, he remained politically active by contributing from 1725 to *The Craftsman*, a journal that attacked both WALPOLE and the system of political patronage. His *Idea of a Patriot King* was written in 1738 in order to flatter Prince FREDERICK LOUIS, but his political influence ceased after Walpole's fall in 1742.

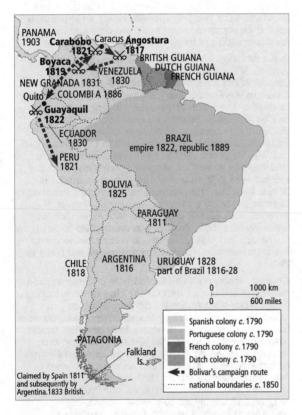

Bolívar and South American independence *Spanish control in South America was weakened when Napoleon forced Ferdinand VII to abdicate (1808). In Caracas Simón Bolívar and other young Venezuelan aristocrats, inspired by the French Revolution, established themselves at Angostura, from where, augmented by British mercenaries, they defeated Spanish troops in New Granada and Peru. Here, in 1824, Bolívar met up with José de San Martín, who had marched across the Andes, to liberate Chile. In 1826 Bolívar proclaimed the Republic of Gran Colombia, but this soon broke up. In 1825 Upper Peru was named Bolivia in his honour.*

Bolívar, Simón (1783–1830) South American soldier and statesman, and leader in the SPANISH-SOUTH AMERICAN WAR OF INDEPENDENCE. Inspired by European rationalists, he vowed to liberate Hispanic America. Participating in South American republican risings from 1812, Bolívar's crucial victory at Boyacá (1819) secured Colombia's independence from Spain, and two years later at the Battle of Carabobo (June 1821) his defeat of the Spanish royalists achieved the same for Venezuela. He then marched an army to Ecuador and drove the Spanish from Quito before meeting up with José de SAN MARTÍN at Guayaquil. The two independence leaders disagreed at the Guayaquil conference over the future of South America and ultimately San Martín resigned his command and allowed Bolívar to drive the Spanish army out of Peru, the last colonial stronghold on the continent. With the independence of South America assured, Bolívar accepted the presidency of the Confederation of Gran Colombia (Venezuela, Colombia, Ecuador, and Panama). Unable to prevent the break-up of the confederation into three independent nations, he resigned the presidency in April 1830.

Bolivia A landlocked country of central South America. It is bounded by Brazil and Paraguay to the north and east, Argentina to the south, and Peru and Chile to the west.

Physical. In the south-west is a great plateau, the Altiplano, some 800 km (500 miles) long and 3,660 m (12,000 feet) high, set between two ranges of the Andes. At its northern end is Lake Titicaca, while in the south there are vast salt pans. The north-east has low plains with hot, wet rain forest and several navigable rivers. Here and in the Gran Chaco to the east, the soil is fertile and suitable for sugar cane, rice, coffee, coca, and cotton. Southward the ground rises to plains which are covered with lighter woodland and grass.

Economy. The mountains of Bolivia offer large deposits of minerals: mining is the principal industry, and the country is developing its capacity to smelt mineral ore. Other industry includes chemicals, textiles, and food-processing. Natural gas accounts for 60% of exports, while tin, of which Bolivia is one of the world's largest producers, provides another 30%. Bolivia produces enough petroleum for internal consumption. Agriculture is the mainstay of the economy, with sugar cane, potatoes, and maize the principal crops. The coca plant, from the leaves of which the drug cocaine is produced, grows freely; it is smuggled to Colombia for processing. Bolivia's economy has suffered from protracted political instability, fluctuating commodity prices, a large external debt, high inflation, and lack of investment.

History. The area became an important Ayamará Indian state between 600 and 1000 AD but was conquered by the growing INCA state *c.* 1200. Some Ayamará continued to resist, however, and were not completely subdued until the late 15th century. Spanish conquest followed six years after PIZARRO's landing in Peru in 1532, and in 1539 the capital at Charcas (modern Sucre) was founded. The discovery of silver deposits in the Potosí mountains in 1545 led to the establishment of the Audiencia (a high court with a political role) of Charcas, under the viceroyalty of Peru. Revolutionary movements against Spain occurred here earlier than anywhere else in South America – at La Paz in 1661, Cochabamba in 1730, and Charcas, Cochabamba, La Paz, and Oruro in 1776–80 – but all failed.

Independence was finally won under José de Sucre, at the battle of Ayacucho (1824). A National Assembly declared Upper Peru independent, and named it Bolivia after Simón BOLÍVAR. A short-lived Peru-Bolivian Confederation was formed (1825–39). Control of the Atacama coast region, where rich guano nitrate deposits were found, was challenged by Chile in 1842 and finally lost in 1884 in the disastrous War of the PACIFIC. A series of military dictatorships (1839–80) was succeeded by more liberal regimes, with Liberal and Republican Parties alternating. In 1930 a popular revolution elected a reforming President, Daniel Salamanca. In 1936, following the disastrous CHACO WAR, military rule returned. In 1952 the Bolivian National Revolution overthrew the dictatorship of the junta, and PAZ ESTENSSORO, leader of the MNR (Movimento Nacionalista Revolucionario) Party returned from exile and was installed as President. Tin mines were nationalized, adult suffrage introduced, and a bold programme of social reforms begun. Paz was re-elected in 1960 but overthrown in 1964 by a military coup. In 1967 a communist revolutionary movement, led by Ché GUEVARA, was defeated. Military regimes followed each other quickly. Not all were right-wing, and that of General Juan José Torres (1970–71) sought to replace Congress by workers' soviets. Democratic elections were restored in 1978, when the first woman President, Lydia Guelier Tejada, briefly held office. There was another military coup in 1980 and a state of political tension continued until 1982, when civilian rule was restored. Paz Estenssoro resumed the presidency (1985–89) but faced extreme economic difficulties. His successor Jaime Paz Zamora, President from 1989 to 1993, initiated a campaign against the drug traffic. In 1993 Gonzalo Sánchez de Lozada was elected President. He continued the campaign against illegal drugs and pursued free-market reforms, despite widespread civil unrest. Disputes with Chile over the issue of access to the Pacific Coast have continued.

CAPITAL:	La Paz (administrative); Sucre (judicial)
AREA:	1,098,581 sq km (424,164 sq miles)
POPULATION:	7.593 million (1996)
CURRENCY:	1 boliviano = 100 centavos
RELIGIONS:	Roman Catholic 92.5%; Baha'i 2.6%
ETHNIC GROUPS:	Mestizo 31.0%; Quechua 25.0%; Aymara 17.0%; White (mainly Spanish extraction) 15.0%
LANGUAGES:	Spanish, Aymara, Quechua (all official)
INTERNATIONAL ORGANIZATIONS:	UN; OAS; Andean Group

Bolshevik (Russian, 'a member of the majority') The wing of the Social Democratic Party in Russia which, from 1903, and under the leadership of LENIN, favoured revolutionary tactics. It rejected co-operation with moderate reformers and favoured the instigation of a revolution by a small, dictatorial party prepared to control the working class. Their opponents, the Mensheviks ('members of the minority'), led by MARTOV and PLEKHANOV, favoured a loosely organized mass labour party, in which workers had more influence, and which was prepared to collaborate with the liberal bourgeoisie against the Tsarist autocracy. After the abortive RUSSIAN REVOLUTION of 1905 Bolshevik leaders fled abroad, having

made little appeal to the peasantry, and it was the Mensheviks led by KERENSKY who joined the Provisional Government, following the February RUSSIAN REVOLUTION in 1917. The infiltration by Bolsheviks into SOVIETS and factory committees contributed to the success of the October Revolution. During the RUSSIAN CIVIL WAR the Bolsheviks succeeded in seizing control of the country from other revolutionary groups. In 1918 they changed their name to the Russian Communist Party. The Mensheviks were formally suppressed in 1922.

bombing offensives (World War II) Attacks by bomber aircraft on military and civilian targets. As part of his BLITZKRIEG tactics, Hitler deployed dive-bombers in the offensives in Poland (1939) and western Europe (1940). In August 1940 the first major German offensive was launched against Britain, a series of daylight attacks by bombers, many of which were destroyed by fighter aircraft of the Royal Air Force in the Battle of BRITAIN. A German night-bombing offensive on civilian targets then began which lasted until May 1941, London being attacked on 57 consecutive nights and badly burned while large numbers of incendiary and high-explosive bombs were also dropped over other cities. The Allied air offensive against Germany and the occupied countries grew in intensity throughout the war. Increasing resources were made available to the British Bomber Command under Air Marshal Sir Arthur Harris, and daylight raids by the US Air Force, combined with British night-bombing, endeavoured to obliterate key German cities, one of the biggest such raids being against DRESDEN. Meanwhile the bulk of German bombing power was turned to the Eastern Front, where fighter-bombers supported the army, attacking besieged cities such as Leningrad and Stalingrad. Pilotless flying bombs (V1s) and rocket missiles (V2s), launched against southern England during 1944 and 1945, did relatively little damage. In the Far East a massive bomber offensive was launched by US forces against Japanese cities in October 1944. On 9 March 1945 much of Tokyo was destroyed by a fire-storm following raids. On 6 and 9 August 1945 respectively, US aircraft dropped the world's first atomic bombs on the Japanese cities of HIROSHIMA and NAGASAKI, bringing the war against Japan to a close.

Bonhoeffer, Dietrich (1906–45) German Lutheran theologian. An active opponent of Nazism, he signed (1934) the Barmen Declaration in protest against attempts by German Christians to synthesize Nazism with Christianity. He was forbidden by the government to teach, and in 1937 his seminary at Finkenwalde was closed. In 1942 he tried to form a link between the Germans opposed to Hitler and the British government. Arrested in 1943, he was executed in 1945.

Boniface VIII (1235–1303) Pope (1294–1303). A papal diplomat and lawyer who travelled widely, he succeeded Pope Celestine V. He quarrelled disastrously with PHILIP IV of France when he asserted papal authority to challenge Philip's right to tax the clergy. In response Philip had him siezed in 1303. The shock hastened the pope's death and contributed towards the transfer of the papacy from Italy to Avignon in France.

Bonner, Yelena SAKHAROV, ANDREY.

Bonnie Prince Charlie PRETENDER; STUART.

Bonus Army An assemblage of ex-servicemen in the USA. It was the popular name given to the so-called Bonus Expeditionary Force (BEF), a group of about 20,000 World War I veterans, roused by poverty in the Great DEPRESSION, who marched on Washington in the spring of 1932. Under their leader, Walter F. Waters, they demanded immediate payment of a war pension, or bonus, voted for them by Congress in 1924 but not to be paid until 1945. When the Senate rejected an enabling Bill, the Secretary of War, Patrick Hurley, had General Douglas MACARTHUR use federal troops to break up the various encampments and raze them, dispersing the BEF.

Boone, Daniel (c. 1735–1820) American pioneer. Born in Pennsylvania, he made trips into unexplored areas of Kentucky from 1767 onwards, organizing settlements and defending them against hostile Native Americans. In 1775 he opened the Wilderness Trail, which became the main route from Virginia to Kentucky. He later moved further west to Missouri, being granted land there by the Spanish in 1799. He remained there after Missouri became part of the USA in the Louisiana Purchase (1803). As a hunter, trail-blazer, and fighter against Native Americans he became a legend during his lifetime.

Booth, Charles (1840–1916) British social researcher. As the author of *Life and Labour of the People in London* (1891–1903) he presented an exhaustive study of poverty in London, showing its extent, causes, and location. Aided by Beatrice WEBB, his methods, based on observation and on searches into public records, pioneered an approach to social studies which has been influential ever since. His special interest in the problems of old age accelerated the Old Age Pensions Act (1908).

Booth, John Wilkes (1838–65) US assassin of President LINCOLN. Brother of the tragic actor Edwin Booth, and a sympathizer with the CONFEDERACY, he participated during the closing stages of the AMERICAN CIVIL WAR in a small conspiracy to overthrow the victorious Lincoln government. On 14 April 1865 he mortally wounded Lincoln in Ford's Theater in Washington and escaped to Virginia, but was discovered and killed on 26 April. Four of his fellow conspirators were hanged.

Booth, William (1829–1912) British religious leader and founder of the SALVATION ARMY (1878). Originally a Methodist preacher, Booth, assisted by his wife, Catherine, preached in the streets, and made singing, uniforms, and bands a part of his evangelical mission. He used his organizational gifts to inspire similar missions in other parts of the world. National concern over the poor and the aged was increased by his *In Darkest England and the Way Out* (1890), which showed that one tenth of the population of England and Wales was living in abject poverty.

Borden, Sir Robert Laird (1854–1937) Canadian statesman. He was chosen as leader of the Conservative Party in 1901. In the general election of 1911 he defeated the Liberals and succeeded LAURIER as Prime Minister of Canada. Knighted in 1914, he remained in office throughout World War I, leading a coalition government after 1917 and joining the imperial war cabinet. He retired from political life in 1920, but remained active in public affairs until his death.

Borgia, Cesare, Duke of Romagna (c. 1475–1507) The illegitimate son of Pope Alexander VI and his principal mistress, Vanozza dei Caltaneis. His career provides a classic example of how 15th-century popes used their families to recover power and prestige lost during the GREAT SCHISM (1378–1417). He was made archbishop and cardinal but his lack of religious vocation quickly became notorious. He went as papal legate to France where he married the daughter of the King of Navarre. His support of his father's ambitions was seen during the French invasions of Italy (after 1494) and in his attempted reconquest of papal lands in central Italy. His hopes of carving out his own kingdom there ended with the death of Alexander (1503). Imprisoned by Pope JULIUS II, he escaped to Navarre and was later killed fighting in Castile. Ruthless and unscrupulous, he served as a model for MACHIAVELLI's book *The Prince*.

Borgia, Lucrezia, Duchess of Ferrara (1480–1519) The beautiful illegitimate daughter of Pope Alexander VI; sister of Cesare Borgia. To further the ambitions of her father and brother she was married three times – to Giovanni Sforza of Pesaro (1493), a marriage annulled to enable that with Alfonso of Aragon (1500). Her third husband was Alfonso d'Este (1501) who became Duke of Ferrara (1505), ruling over a brilliant court. Henceforth she devoted herself to the patronage of art and literature, to works of charity, and the care of her children.

Boris Godunov (c. 1551–1605) Tsar of Russia (1598–1605). He began his career of court service under IVAN IV (the Terrible), became virtual ruler of Muscovy during the reign of his imbecile son Fyodor (1584–98), and engineered his own elevation to the Tsardom. He conducted a successful war against Sweden (1590–95), promoted foreign trade, and dealt ruthlessly with those BOYAR families which opposed him. In 1604 boyar animosity combined with popular dissatisfaction ushered in the 'Time of Troubles', a confused eight-year dynastic and political crisis, Boris having died suddenly in 1605.

Bormann, Martin (1900–c. 1945) German Nazi leader. He was briefly imprisoned for his part in a political murder in 1924, and then rewarded by appointment to HITLER's personal staff in 1928. After the departure of HESS in 1941 he headed the Party chancery. His intimacy with Hitler enabled him to wield great power unobtrusively. He was an extremist on racial questions, and was also behind the offensive against the churches in 1942. He was sentenced to death *in absentia* at the NUREMBERG TRIALS; in 1973, after identification of a skeleton exhumed in Berlin, the West German government declared that he had committed suicide after Hitler's death (1945).

Borneo An island east of the Malay peninsula in south-east Asia.

Physical. The world's third largest island, Borneo contains Brunei and two parts of Malaysia (Sarawak and Sabah) in the north, and a part of Indonesia (Kalimantan) in the south. Set in the path of the two monsoons, Borneo is one of the wettest places in the world. Much of the coast is swampy; there is luxuriant jungle inland; and evergreen forest covers even the central mountains, which rise to over 2,000 m (6,500 feet). The island is rich in mineral resources.

History. The name 'Borneo' is a European corruption of Brunei, a sultanate which reached the height of its influence in the 16th century just as Europeans were beginning to appear in south-east Asia. The name was extended to cover the whole island. Its original Negrito inhabitants were dispersed by Malays who began arriving *c.* 2000 BC. Living in river valleys separated by mountains and jungle, these early immigrants developed as isolated communities, some in longhouses, some in *kampongs* (villages) built over water, some nomadic. Apart from Indians and Chinese seeking kingfisher feathers, birds' nests for soup, and jungle produce, there was little outside contact until the 16th century when Portuguese and Spaniards began arriving. From the 16th century Chinese began establishing pepper plantations and mining communities. Brunei fended off Spanish attacks from the Philippines during this period. In the 17th and 18th centuries the Dutch and British gained footholds, and after the fall of JOHORE in the late 17th century many settlers came from the Malay peninsula. During the 19th century the Dutch and British effectively divided the island between them in order to protect the interests of their East India companies.

Bornu KANEM-BORNU.

Borodino, Battle of (7 September 1812) Fought between Russia and France, about 110 km (70 miles) west of Moscow. Here KUTUZOV chose to take his stand against NAPOLEON's army. The Russian position was centred upon a well-fortified hill. After 12 hours of fierce combat, a terrific artillery bombardment and a decisive cavalry charge split the Russian forces. They were forced to withdraw and Napoleon, claiming victory, marched on an undefended Moscow. Over 80,000 men were lost in the most bloody battle of the NAPOLEONIC WARS.

borough A town in England enjoying particular privileges. The boroughs evolved from the Anglo-Saxon *burhs* and from the 12th century benefited from royal and noble grants of CHARTERS. Their representatives attended Parliament regularly from the 14th century, having first been summoned in 1265 when Simon de MONTFORT called two representatives from each city and borough. The Scottish equivalent of the English borough was the burgh, of which there were three types. The Burgh of Barony was located within a barony and controlled by magistrates; the Burgh of Regality was similar, with exclusive legal jurisdiction over its land; the Royal Burgh had received its charter from the crown. Freeholders in a borough were known as burgesses.

Boscawen, Edward (1711–61) British admiral, known as 'Old Dreadnought'. He served in the West Indies during the War of JENKINS'S EAR and the War of the AUSTRIAN SUCCESSION, and was in charge of naval operations at the siege of LOUISBURG, Nova Scotia, in 1758, where his success opened the way for the conquest of Canada. His most famous exploit was the destruction of the French Mediterranean fleet off the Portuguese coast at Lagos in 1759, which helped to establish British naval supremacy in the SEVEN YEARS WAR.

Bosch, Juan (1909–   ) Dominican statesman. He founded the leftist Partido Revolucionario Dominicano (PRD) in 1939, and was exiled during the dictatorship of Rafael TRUJILLO. After the latter's assassination he returned (1961) to the Dominican Republic and was elected President (1962–63) in the first free elections for nearly 40 years. He introduced sweeping liberal and democratic reforms, but after nine months in office was overthrown by rightist military leaders with the backing of the Church, of landowners, and of industrialists. His supporters launched their revolt in 1965, a movement which prompted a military intervention by the USA. In 1966 he was defeated for the presidency by Joaquin Balaguer, who had heavy US backing. He remained active in politics and as a writer.

Bose, Subhas Chandra (1897–1945) Indian nationalist politician. With Jawaharlal NEHRU he founded the Indian Independence League in 1928. He became President of the Indian National CONGRESS Party (1938–39) but quarrelled with other leaders. He escaped from virtual house arrest (1941), went to Germany but failed to secure Nazi support and in 1943 went to Japan and Singapore. There he assumed command of the Indian National Army, recruited from Indian prisoners-of-war, and formed a provisional Indian government.

Bosnia-Herzegovina A country in south-east Europe, in the Balkan Peninsula. It is bordered by Croatia to the north and west, Serbia to the east, and Montenegro to the south-east.

Physical. The country is mostly mountainous and wooded. It has a short Adriatic coastline.

Economy. The poorest of the former Yugoslav republics, Bosnia-Herzegovina has suffered severe economic disruption from the civil war (1992–95). It has a variety of mineral resources, including coal, iron, copper, chrome, manganese, cinnabar, zinc, and mercury. Livestock and sheep are raised, and the principal crops are cereals, fruits, citrus, and tobacco. Industry comprises mining, steelworks, and oil refineries. Many Bosnians are migrant workers in Western Europe.

History. First inhabited by the ILLYRIANS, the region became part of the Roman province of Illyricum. SLAVS settled in the 7th century and, in 1137, it came under Hungarian rule. The Ottomans invaded in 1386 and after much resistance made it a province in 1463. They governed through Bosnian nobles, many of whom became Muslim, though much of the population became rebellious as Ottoman power declined. During the early 18th century Austrian forces began to push the Turks back. The rise of PAN-SLAVONIC nationalism provoked revolts in 1821, 1831, and 1837. A revolt in 1875 brought Austrian occupation, which was consolidated by formal annexation into the AUSTRO-HUNGARIAN EMPIRE in 1908. This provoked protest from Serbia and Russia. An international crisis only subsided when Germany threatened to intervene. Serbs continued to protest and to indulge in terrorist activity, culminating in the assassination of the Archduke FRANCIS FERDINAND and his wife in the capital Sarajevo in 1914. This sparked off World War I, after which Bosnia was integrated into the new Kingdom of Serbs, Croats, and Slovenes, later renamed YUGOSLAVIA. During World War II the two provinces were incorporated into the German puppet state of Croatia, and were the scene of much fighting by the Yugoslav partisans. After the war they were integrated into TITO's communist Yugoslavia.

Alija IZETBEGOVIĆ became President in 1990. In 1992, as Yugoslavia disintegrated, the mainly Muslim population of Bosnia-Herzegovina voted to become an independent country in a referendum. Although most Western countries recognized this decision, areas occupied mainly by the Serb and Croat minorities proclaimed themselves independent of the Muslim-dominated government and all three groups began fighting for territory. Attempts by the UN and the European Community to mediate in the ensuing ferocious civil war made little headway. The three main factions agreed in principle to Bosnia-Herzegovina being a federal nation with regions based on ethnic groupings but failed to agree on the borders of the proposed regions.

In April 1992 the Serbs besieged Sarajevo; by the end of that year, with backing from the Serb-led Yugoslav army, they had taken possession of over two-thirds of the country. Although a UN peace-keeping force intervened to defend Muslims and others fleeing from 'ethnic cleansing', it was unable to prevent thousands of civilians from being massacred. In 1994 NATO shot down Serb fighter planes that were flying in the UN-established 'no-fly zone' and bombed Serb ground targets. That same year Bosnian Muslims and Bosnian Croats formed an alliance, and by mid-1995, with support from the Croatian army, they had recaptured a large amount of territory from the Serbs. Further NATO air strikes led to the lifting of the siege of Sarajevo in September 1995. In December 1995 a US-brokered peace deal was signed. This stated that although Bosnia-Herzegovina would remain a single state with unchanged borders, it would henceforth be divided into a Bosnian–Croat Federation in the west and a Bosnian Serb Republic in the north and east. Although there has been no resumption of full-scale violence, a number of serious problems remain – notably the resettlement of many thousands of refugees and the capture and prosecution of war criminals on all sides. In 1996 Izetbegović was re-elected as the chairman of a new tripartite presidency, serving alongside a Serb and a Croat.

CAPITAL:	Sarajevo
AREA:	51,129 sq km (19,741 sq miles)
POPULATION:	3.524 million (1996)
CURRENCY:	dinar
RELIGIONS:	Muslim 44.0%; Eastern Orthodox 31.0%; Roman Catholic 17.0%
ETHNIC GROUPS:	Muslim Slav 44.0%; Serb 31.0%; Croat 17.0%
LANGUAGES:	Serbo-Croat (official)
INTERNATIONAL ORGANIZATIONS:	UN

Boston A city in the USA, in Massachusetts. It was founded on a peninsula at the mouth of the Charles River by Puritan emigrants in 1630. As the colony capital, it housed some 10,000 people by 1700 and was the leading trading centre of New England. Bostonians took the lead in resisting British attempts at taxation with the STAMP ACT Riots (1765). In 1770 troops threatened by a mob opened fire, killing five people in the Boston massacre. When tea ships from England in 1773 threatened other tea importers and clandestine revenue-raising under the TOWNSHEND ACTS, the SONS OF LIBERTY threw the cargo overboard in what was known as the Boston Tea Party. The city, having been evacuated by the British, was entered by WASHINGTON in 1776, and was a FEDERALIST stronghold in the early republic.

Bosworth Field, Battle of (22 August 1485) A battle fought close to the English town of Bosworth in Leicestershire; its outcome was to establish HENRY VII and the Tudor dynasty on the English throne. Just over a fortnight after Henry had landed on the Welsh coast, he and his army of Welsh followers were met in battle by RICHARD III's larger army. The issue was uncertain when Lord Stanley arrived and with his followers went over to Henry's side; Henry was victorious, Richard was killed, and at the end of the day Stanley placed Richard's crown on Henry's head.

Botany Bay An inlet on the eastern coast of Australia. Captain James Cook, the first White person to discover it, landed there in 1770 and named it Stingray Bay. The botanist Sir Joseph Banks observed many plants unknown to him, and its name was changed to Botany Bay. The British government instructed Captain Arthur Phillip to prepare a fleet for transportation to Botany Bay. The first fleet, consisting of convicts, marines, and some civilians, arrived at Botany Bay in 1788, but Phillip decided instead to establish a settlement further north in Port Jackson. During the era of CONVICT TRANSPORTATION, the name was sometimes used as a synonym for New South Wales.

Botha, Louis (1862–1919) Boer general and statesman. He was the first Prime Minister of the Union of SOUTH AFRICA. The son of a Voortrekker, he was elected to the Natal Volksraad (parliament) in 1897. In the BOER WAR he rose rapidly, and his successes at Spion Kop and elsewhere gained him promotion to general. After the Peace of VEREENIGING (1902), he worked for reconciliation with Britain. In 1910 he became Prime Minister, and in 1911 he established the South African Party. In 1915 some of his followers turned against him in an Afrikaner rebellion. He suppressed it, and then led a successful campaign against the Germans in South-West Africa (NAMIBIA).

Bothwell, James Hepburn, 4th Earl of (1536–78) Scottish Protestant nobleman, the third husband of MARY, QUEEN OF SCOTS. He was a supporter and adviser of Mary, while she was married to DARNLEY. In 1567 he was acquitted of Darnley's murder but then his swift divorce, promotion to the dukedom of Orkney and Shetland, and marriage to Mary caused the Scottish lords to rise against him. He fled from Scotland after the Battle of Carberry Hill (June 1567), when Mary's forces were defeated. He turned to piracy, but was captured in Norway, and died in a Danish prison.

Botswana A landlocked country in southern Africa. It is bordered by Namibia to the west and north, Zimbabwe to the east, and South Africa to the south.

Physical. Botswana lies in the hot, dry central region of southern Africa. The north-west drains into a swampy basin, the Okavango, the only surface water in the country. The centre and west is covered by the Kalahari Desert, while in the east is a large salt-pan, the Makgadikgadi.

Economy. Diamonds are the chief export, producing revenues that have made Botswana the world's fastest growing economy. In recent years a deterioration in the diamond market has caused severe economic difficulties. It is thought that further mineral wealth awaits discovery; other exports are copper-nickel matte and beef. Agriculture is mainly pastoral. A large proportion of the work-force is employed in South African mines. Landlocked, Botswana depends on South Africa for much of its trade and imports.

History. Botswana was formerly known as Bechuanaland. British missionaries visited the southern Tswana people in 1801, and in 1817 the London Missionary Society settled at Kuruman. David LIVINGSTONE and other missionaries operated from here during the second quarter of the 19th century. In 1885 the British protectorate of Bechuanaland was declared, to be administered from Mafeking. The success of the cattle industry led the Union of South Africa to seek to incorporate Botswana, along with Basutoland (Lesotho) and Swaziland, but this was rejected by the British government in 1935; no transfer would be tolerated until the inhabitants had been consulted and an agreement reached. The dominant tribe was the Ngwato, whose chief Seretse KHAMA was banned from the country from 1948 until 1956 for marrying an Englishwoman. By now a nationalist movement had begun, which culminated in a democratic constitution in 1965 followed by independence on 30 September 1966, as the republic of Botswana, with Seretse Khama as President. He was succeeded on his death in 1980 by the vice-president Quett Masire, who was re-elected in 1989 and again in 1994. On his retirement in 1998 Masire was succeeded by Festus Mogae.

CAPITAL:	Gaborone
AREA:	581,730 sq km (224,607 sq miles)
POPULATION:	1.478 million (1996)
CURRENCY:	1 pula = 100 thebe
RELIGIONS:	Traditional beliefs 49.2%; Protestant 29.0%; African Christian 11.8%; Roman Catholic 9.4%
ETHNIC GROUPS:	Tswana 97.0%; Shona, !Kung San (Bushmen), Khoikhoin (Hottentot), and Ndebele minorities
LANGUAGES:	Tswana, English (both official); Shona and local languages
INTERNATIONAL ORGANIZATIONS:	UN; OAU; SADC; Non-Aligned Movement; Commonwealth

Boudicca (or Boadicea) (d. 60 AD) Queen of the ICENI in East Anglia. She succeeded her husband Prasutagus, who had left his kingdom jointly to his daughters and the Roman emperor, on his death in 60 AD. The Romans displayed greed and brutality in taking over the kingdom, and her tribe was reduced to the status of an occupied people. She took advantage of the absence of the main Roman forces on a campaign in Wales and led the Iceni and Trinovantes in revolt. Roman settlements at Camulodunum (Colchester), Verulamium (St Albans), and Londinium (London) were burnt. Defeated by the governor Suetonius Paulinus, she committed suicide by taking poison.

Bougainville, Louis Antoine de (1729–1811) French explorer. Between 1766 and 1769 he led the first successful French circumnavigation of the globe, visiting many of the islands of the South Pacific and compiling a scientific record of his findings. The largest of the SOLOMON ISLANDS is named after him as is the tropical plant, bougainvillaea.

Boulanger, Georges Ernest (1837–91) French general and politician. He won increasing popular support for his campaign for revenge on Germany after the FRANCO-PRUSSIAN WAR (1870–71). In 1886 he became Minister of War but forfeited the support of moderate republicans who feared that he might provoke another war with Germany. Forced from his ministry in 1887, he became the focus of opposition to the government and won a series of by-elections. He failed to seize this opportunity to make himself President, and his popularity waned. The government prepared to have him tried for treason but he fled into exile.

Boumédienne, Houari (1925–78) Algerian statesman. In the early 1950s he joined a group of expatriate Algerian nationalists in Cairo which included BEN BELLA, and in 1955 he joined resistance forces in ALGERIA operating against the French. He became chief-of-staff of the exiled National Liberation Front in Tunisia (1960–62). In March 1962 his forces occupied Algiers for Ben Bella after which a peace treaty was signed with France. He displaced Ben Bella in a coup in 1965, ruling until his death in 1978. He had close ties with the Communist bloc, but also maintained friendly relations with Western countries.

Bounty mutiny (1789) A British mutiny that occurred near the Tongan Islands on HMS *Bounty*, under the command of Captain BLIGH. Some of the crew, resenting Bligh's harsh exercise of authority and insults, rebelled under the leadership of Fletcher Christian. Bligh and 18 others were cast off in a small, open boat with no chart. Thanks to Bligh's navigational skill and resource, they covered a distance of 5,822 km (3,618 miles), arriving in Timor about six weeks later. Bligh was exonerated at a court martial in Britain. Some of the mutineers surrendered and others were captured and court martialled. Fletcher Christian and some of the other mutineers, with a number of Tahitian men and women, settled on Pitcairn Island in 1790. Most of their descendants moved to Norfolk Island in 1856. (See illustration.)

Bourbon A great European ruling dynasty, founded when Robert of Clermont (1256–1317), the sixth son of Louis IX of France, married the heiress to the lordship of Bourbon. The first duke was their son, Louis I (1279–1341). In 1503 the title passed to the Montpensier branch of the family, but in 1527 headship of the house of Bourbon passed to the line of Marche-Vendôme. Antoine de Bourbon (1518–62), duc de Vendôme, became King Consort of Navarre, while his brother Louis (1530–69) was made Prince of CONDÉ. On the death of the last VALOIS king in 1589, Antoine's son became King of France as HENRY IV (ruled 1589–1610). His heirs ruled France without interruption until 1792: Louis XIII (ruled 1610–43), Louis XIV (ruled 1643–1715), LOUIS XV (ruled 1715–74) and LOUIS XVI (ruled 1774–92). The last was overthrown during the FRENCH REVOLUTION, and Louis XVII (titular king 1793–95) died without reigning; Louis XVI's brothers LOUIS XVIII (ruled 1814–24) and CHARLES X (ruled 1824–30) both ruled after the Bourbon restoration. LOUIS-PHILIPPE (ruled 1830–48), the last Bourbon King of France, was a member of the cadet ORLÉANS branch of the family.

In 1700 Louis XIV's second grandson became PHILIP V (ruled 1700–46) of Spain, thus setting in train the War of the SPANISH SUCCESSION. His successors have held the Spanish throne ever since (excepting the republican period, 1931–75).

Bounty Mutiny *This contemporary print from an engraving by Robert Dodd shows the mutineers casting the officers of the Bounty adrift. The story of the Bounty has continued to capture the public imagination and controversy over whether the mutiny was justified has persisted. There are descendants of Fletcher Christian still living on Pitcairn Island.*

Bourguiba, Habib Ali (1903–   ) Tunisian statesman. A staunch nationalist, he was imprisoned at different times by the French and during World War II by the Germans. He negotiated the agreement which led to Tunisian autonomy (1954) and when Tunisia became independent (1956), he was elected Prime Minister. In 1957 he deposed the Bey of Tunis, abolished the monarchy, and was himself chosen President of the Republic by the constituent Assembly, and President for life in 1975. A moderate, Bourguiba faced riots in 1978 and 1980. After 1981 he democratized the National Assembly of his one-party state, and recognized the right of opposition by forging a coalition alliance. He was deposed in 1987 and placed under house-arrest.

Boutros-Ghali, Boutros (1922–   ) Egyptian diplomat, Secretary-General of the United Nations (1992–96). A Coptic Christian from a distinguished family, he was educated in the USA and France, and lectured in law and political science in Cairo. Boutros-Ghali was a political ally of Anwar SADAT and was instrumental in bringing about the CAMP DAVID ACCORD with Israel in 1977. He served as Egypt's deputy Prime Minister (1991–92). In his first year of office as UN Secretary-General, he supported the ill-fated US-led UN military intervention in Somalia; however, growing antagonism between him and the USA, especially over UN funding and the ethnic conflicts in BOSNIA-HERZEGOVINA and RWANDA, led the USA to veto his reappointment for a second term.

bowl cultures WESTERN NEOLITHIC.

Bow Street Runners The first organized police force, based at Bow Street Magistrates' Court in London; they were recruited by the magistrate (and novelist) Henry Fielding from the 1740s to augment the forces at his disposal. With functions that included serving writs and acting as detectives, they gained a reputation for efficiency and were much feared by criminals. The formation of the London Metropolitan Police Force in 1829 brought their separate existence to an end.

Boxer Rising (1899–1900) A popular anti-Western movement in China. The secret society of Righteous and Harmonious Fists, which was opposed to foreign expansion and the Manchu court, claimed that by training (including ritual boxing) its members could become immune to bullets. The movement began in Shandong province and had its roots in rural poverty and unemployment, blamed partly on Western imports. Missionaries, Chinese Christians, and people handling foreign goods were among those attacked. The movement was backed by the empress dowager CIXI and some provincial governors. In 1900 the Boxers besieged the foreign legations in Beijing for two months until they were relieved by an international force which occupied and looted the capital; Cixi and the emperor fled in disguise. The foreign powers launched punitive raids in the Beijing region and negotiated heavy reparations in the Boxer Protocol (1901). The rising greatly increased foreign interference in China, and further reduced the authority of the QING dynasty.

boyar A member of the highest non-princely class of medieval Russian society. In the 10th to 12th century the boyars formed the senior levels of the princes' retinues. They received large grants of land, and exercised considerable independent power during the period of decentralization after the 13th-century Mongol conquest; but as the grand princes of Muscovy consolidated their own power, they managed to curb boyar independence.

From the 15th to the 17th century Muscovite boyars formed a closed aristocratic class drawn from about 200 families. They retained a stake in princely affairs through their membership of the boyar *duma* or council. IVAN IV (the Terrible) (ruled 1547–84) reduced their power significantly by relying on favourites and locally elected officials. Their social and political importance continued to decline throughout the 17th century, and PETER THE GREAT eventually abolished the rank and title.

Boycott, Charles Cunningham (1832–97) British land agent in Ireland. When, at the direction of the Land League, Irish tenants on the estate of Lord Erne in County Mayo asked for rent reductions and refused to pay their full rents, Boycott ordered their eviction (1880). PARNELL urged everyone to refuse all communication with Boycott and to ostracize his family. The policy was successful and Boycott was forced to leave. The practice of non-communication became known as 'boycotting'.

Boyne, Battle of the (1 July 1690) A major defeat for the Stuart cause which confirmed WILLIAM III's control over Ireland. It took place near Drogheda, where the recently deposed JAMES II and his Irish and French forces were greatly outnumbered by the Protestant army led by William III. When William attacked across the River Boyne James's troops broke and fled. He returned to exile in France, and William's position as King of England, Scotland, and Ireland was immeasurably strengthened. The victory is still commemorated annually by the Orange Order, a political society founded in 1795 to support Protestantism in Ireland.

Braddock, Edward (1695–1755) British general, who commanded forces in America against the French and Native Americans in 1755. In his advance on Fort Duquesne (Pittsburg) he allowed himself to be ambushed crossing the Monongahela River. He died in the Battle of the Wilderness and WASHINGTON took command of the retreat of the defeated army.

Bradford, William (1590–1657) English-born PILGRIM FATHER. He was born in Yorkshire and escaped to Holland with the Scrooby separatists. After the *Mayflower* reached Plymouth, he was elected governor and guided the colony until his death. He pacified the Native Americans, achieved financial independence from the London merchants, and wrote his *History of Plimmoth Plantation*.

Bradlaugh, Charles (1833–91) British social reformer. A republican and keen supporter of reform movements, he was tried, with Annie BESANT, in 1877–78 for printing a pamphlet on birth control. The charge failed and contraceptives could thereafter be openly advertised. When returned as Member of Parliament for Northampton in 1880 his refusal to take the Bible oath of allegiance to the crown was backed by his voters and led eventually in 1886 to British Members of Parliament having the right to affirm rather than to swear allegiance.

Bradley, Omar Nelson (1893–1981) US general. In World War II he commanded a corps in the NORTH AFRICAN and Sicilian campaigns. He commanded US land forces in the NORMANDY CAMPAIGN, and later, following the ARDENNES CAMPAIGN, went beyond Eisenhower's orders to link up with the Soviet forces on the Elbe in 1945. He was instrumental in building up NATO, formulating US global defence strategy in the post-war years, and in committing US troops to fight in the KOREAN WAR.

Braganza The ruling dynasty of Portugal (1640–1910). Alfonso, an illegitimate son of John I of Portugal, was made first Duke of Braganza (1442). His descendants became the wealthiest nobles in the kingdom, and, by marriage into the royal family, had a claim to the Portuguese throne before the Spaniards took control of the country in 1580. When the Portuguese threw off Spanish rule in 1640, the 8th Duke of Braganza ascended the throne as John IV. The title of Duke of Braganza was thenceforth borne by the heir to the throne.

Brahmo Samaj (Hindu, 'Society of God') Indian religious movement. It was a development of a Hindu social reform movement founded in Bengal in 1828 by Ram Mohan ROY and revived as a purely religious movement in 1842 by Maharshi Devendranath Tagore (1817–1905). Following the latter's repudiation of the vedic scriptures in 1850 the movement divided between a religious group, the Adi Brahmo Samaj, and the social reformers, Brahmo Samaj of India (under Keshab Chandra Sen (1838–84)). The latter sponsored a temperance movement and campaigned for women's education and social rights. Brahmo Samaj had a powerful influence on 20th-century Hindu society.

Brandenburg A German state, the nucleus of the kingdom of PRUSSIA. German conquest of its Slavic population began in the early 12th century. The margravate (established *c.* 1157) took its name from the town of Brandenburg, west of Berlin. In 1356 the MARGRAVE's status as an imperial ELECTOR was confirmed by the Golden Bull of CHARLES V.

Strong central government began with the advent of the HOHENZOLLERN dynasty in 1415. Brandenburg accepted the Lutheran REFORMATION after 1540, and in the early 17th century it acquired further territories in western Germany and also Prussia (1618). After an initial period of neutrality during the THIRTY YEARS WAR, FREDERICK WILLIAM (the 'Great Elector') (1620–88) entered the fighting and secured excellent terms at the Treaty of WESTPHALIA (1648). He subsequently achieved full sovereignty in Prussia (1660) and turned Brandenburg-Prussia into a centralized European power with a highly effective army and bureaucracy. He used the opportunity offered him by Louis XIV's persecution of the HUGUENOTS to develop his country's industry and trade. In 1701 Elector Frederick III (1657–1713) was granted the title of King in Prussia, and from that time Brandenburg was a province of the Prussian kingdom.

Brandreth, Jeremiah PENTRICH RISING.

Brandt, Willy (Herbert Ernst Karl Frahm) (1913–92) West German statesman. As a young Social Democrat he had to flee (1932) from the GESTAPO and assumed the name of Willy Brandt, living in Norway. As mayor of West Berlin (1957–66), he resisted Soviet demands that Berlin become a demilitarized free city (1958) and successfully survived the crisis arising out of the building of the BERLIN WALL in 1961. In 1964 he became Chairman of the Social Democratic Party, an office he held until 1987. He was elected Federal Chancellor in 1969. His main achievement was the policy of OSTPOLITIK or détente towards eastern Europe. In 1970 he negotiated an agreement with the Soviet Union accepting the *de facto* frontiers of Europe, making a second agreement on the status of Berlin in 1971. In 1971 he also signed a non-aggression agreement with the Soviet Union and Poland, accepting the Oder-Neisse boundary; in 1972 he negotiated the agreement with the

GERMAN DEMOCRATIC REPUBLIC which recognized the latter's existence and established diplomatic relations between the two nations. In 1974 he resigned as Chancellor over a spy scandal in his office, but accepted an invitation to chair the Independent Commission on International Development Issues which published its findings in 1980, known as the BRANDT REPORT.

Brandt Report (*North-South: A Programme for Survival*, 1980) Report by an international commission on the state of the world economy. Convened by the United Nations, it met from 1977 to 1979 under the chairmanship of Willy BRANDT. It recommended urgent improvement in the trade relations between the rich northern hemisphere and poor southern for the sake of both. Governments in the north were reluctant to accept the recommendations. Members of the commission therefore reconvened to produce a second report, *Common Crisis North-South: Co-operation for World Recovery* (1983), which perceived 'far greater dangers than three years ago', forecasting 'conflict and catastrophe' unless the imbalances in international finance could be solved.

Brandywine, Battle of (11 September 1777). An engagement in the American War of INDEPENDENCE when British forces were attacking Philadelphia. Washington was outmanoeuvred by Sir William Howe and was forced to retreat with heavy losses. The British occupied Philadelphia on 27 September, but this victory was offset by SARATOGA less than a month later.

Brauchitsch, Walter von (1881–1948) German field-marshal. As commander-in-chief of the German army (1938–41), he carried out the occupation of Austria (see ANSCHLUSS) and Czechoslovakia (see SUDETENLAND) and conducted the successful campaigns against Poland, the Netherlands, and France. He was relieved of his command by Hitler as a scapegoat for the German failure to capture Moscow.

Brazil The largest country in South America. Brazil borders ten countries, has a coastline 7,400 km (4,600 miles) long, and straddles the equator from latitude 4° N to past latitude 33° S.

Physical. The whole of the northern region lies in the vast Amazon basin with its tributary rivers. South of this are the Mato Grosso with its grassland plateau and the *campos*, mountain plateaux intersected by deep river valleys. In the region of great lakes the climate becomes suited to coffee-growing. Southward the land drops away to a vast plain suitable for livestock and plantation farming. The destruction in recent decades of up to 12% of the vast Amazonian rain forest is a cause for worldwide concern.

Economy. A huge newly industrialized country, Brazil has the eighth largest economy in the world. Industry is concentrated in the centre and south, while the drought-prone north and north-east remain undeveloped. Only about 7% of Brazil's land area is considered arable. While agriculture has been neglected in favour of industry, crops such as sugar and cocoa and exports such as coffee, soya beans, and orange concentrates remain important. Brazil is rich in minerals: it has the third largest reserves of bauxite in the world, the largest reserves of columbium (high-grade iron ore), and one of the largest reserves of beryllium. Tin, iron ore, machinery, and other industrial

products now account for more than half of all exports. At the same time high inflation, a massive foreign debt, and extreme inequalities in wealth have restricted economic growth and led to severe social problems.

History. Brazil is the only South American country originally established as a Portuguese colony, having been awarded to the Portuguese crown by the Treaty of TORDESILLAS (1494). Settlement began in 1532 with the foundation of São Vicente by Martim Afonso de SOUSA. During the first half of the 16th century 12 captaincies were established. No centralized government was established until 1549 when Thomé de Sousa was named governor-general and a capital was established at Salvador (Bahia). The north-eastern coast was lost to the Dutch briefly in the 17th century but was regained.

By 1800 the prosperity of the colony had outstripped that of Portugal. As a result of the NAPOLEONIC WARS, the Portuguese court was transferred to Rio de Janeiro, which was transformed into the centre of the Portuguese empire. When John VI returned to Lisbon in 1821, his son Pedro remained behind as regent. In 1822 he became Emperor Pedro I of Brazil in an almost bloodless coup, and established an independent empire which lasted until the abdication of his son Pedro II in 1889. Brazil's neo-colonial economy based upon agricultural exports such as coffee and wild rubber produced on the fazenda (estate), and dependent on slave labour, remained virtually intact until the downfall of the country's two predominant institutions – slavery (1888), and the monarchy (1889). In 1891 Brazil became a republic with a federal constitution. The fraudulent elections of 1930 and the effects of the Great DEPRESSION prompted the intervention of the military and the appointment of Getúlio VARGAS as provisional president. Vargas was to remain in power until he was deposed in 1945. He remained a powerful force in international politics until his suicide in 1954. Vargas' successor, Juscelino KUBITSCHEK (1956–61) embarked upon an ambitious expansion of the economy, including the construction of a futuristic capital city at Brazilia, intended to encourage development of the interior. President João Goulart (1961–64) had to face the consequent inflation and severe balance-of-payments deficit. In rural areas peasant leagues mobilized behind the cause of radical land reform. Faced with these threats, Brazil's landowners and industrialists backed the military coup of 1964 and the creation of a series of authoritarian regimes which sought to attract foreign investment. President Figueiredo (1978–84) re-established civilian rule and democracy, and under his successor José Sarne (1985–89) a new constitution was approved. Rapid industrialization, together with urbanization, had greatly increased inequalities of income. In the early 1990s very high inflation, together with an economic recession, challenged the government of President Collor de Mello, who himself was faced with allegations of corruption, and resigned in 1992. Itamar Franco then served as President until 1995, when Fernando Cardoso (elected in 1994) succeeded him. Cardoso pursued privatization policies but the economy has remained weak.

CAPITAL:	Brasília
AREA:	8,511,965 sq km (3,286,488 sq miles)
POPULATION:	157.872 million (1996)
CURRENCY:	1 real = 100 centavos
RELIGIONS:	Roman Catholic 87.8%; Protestant 6.1%

ETHNIC GROUPS: Mulatto 22.0%; Portuguese 15.0%;
                 Mestizo 12.0%; Italian 11.0%; Black 11.0%;
                 Spanish 10.0%; German 3.0%; Japanese
                 0.8%; Amerindian 0.1%
LANGUAGES: Portuguese (official); German; Japanese;
                 Italian; Amerindian languages
INTERNATIONAL
  ORGANIZATIONS: UN; OAS

Brazzaville Conference (1944) A meeting between
leaders from French West and Equatorial Africa and
General DE GAULLE as head of Free France. The African
leaders for the first time publicly called for reforms in
French colonial rule, and were given an assurance by de
Gaulle that these would be implemented. Independence
was still firmly ruled out.

Breakspear, Nicholas ADRIAN IV.

Breckinridge, John Cabell (1821–75) US politician and
general. He served as a Democrat member of the House
of Representatives (1851–55), before being elected as
BUCHANAN's Vice-President in 1856. He presided over the
Senate during the pre-war political crisis with noted
impartiality, despite his strong belief in slavery and
STATES' RIGHTS. When the Democratic Party split in 1860,
he ran for President against Abraham LINCOLN as the
candidate of the Southern Democrats. From November
1861, he saw extensive service as a major-general in the
army of the Confederacy Party before becoming
Secretary of State for War under Jefferson DAVIS in 1865.

Breda A Dutch city in North Brabant, historically an
important frontier town close to the Belgian border.
The Compromise of Breda in 1566 was a league
formed by Protestant and Catholic nobles and burghers
to fight against PHILIP II's policies in the Netherlands. The
most dramatic event in its history was its surrender to
the Spanish commander Spinola in 1625; it was retaken
by the Dutch in 1636 and finally became part of the
Netherlands in 1648. The Declaration of Breda was
made by CHARLES II in 1660 just before his Restoration,
promising an amnesty, religious toleration, and
payment of arrears to the army. The Treaty of Breda
(1667) ended the second ANGLO-DUTCH WAR.

Breitenfeld, Battles of Two battles during the THIRTY
YEARS WAR, which take their name from a village near
Leipzig (now in Germany). The first was fought on 17
September 1631, between Count Johannes TILLY's Catholic
forces and the Protestant army of GUSTAVUS ADOLPHUS (of
Sweden). Despite an early advantage, Tilly's traditional
infantry squares were overwhelmed by the Swedes'
flexible linear tactics. Gustavus's victory was the first
major Protestant success of the war, and it announced
the arrival of Sweden as a power on the European stage.
The second battle, on 2 November 1642, ended in
another Swedish victory.

Brendan, St (the Navigator) (c. 484–577) Founder and
abbot of the monastery of Clonfert in Galway, Ireland (c.
560). According to tradition he visited holy sites in
Ireland and western Scotland, including that of St
Columba on the island of Iona. His travels were
fictionalized in a remarkable 11th century work,
Brendan's Voyage, which makes use of tales from Irish
mythology. It relates some astonishing adventures when
St Brendan, with a group of monks, sailed in a leather

boat to a 'Land of Promise' in the Atlantic which has
been identified with a number of places, including the
Canary Islands, and even Newfoundland.

Brest-Litovsk, Treaty of (1918) An agreement
between Soviet Russia, Germany, and Austria-Hungary,
signed in the town of that name in Poland. The
conference opened in December 1917 in order to end
Soviet participation in World War I. TROTSKY skilfully
prolonged discussions in the hope of Allied help for the
RUSSIAN REVOLUTION or of a socialist uprising of German
and Austro-Hungarian workers. Neither happened. LENIN
capitulated and ordered his delegates to accept the
German terms. By the treaty, Russia surrendered nearly
half of its European territory: Finland, the Baltic
provinces, Belorussia (now Belarus), Poland, the Ukraine,
and parts of the Caucasus. The German armistice in the
west (November 1918) annulled the treaty, but at
VERSAILLES Russia only regained the Ukraine.

Brétigny, Treaty of (1360) A treaty concluded between
Edward III of England, and John II of France following
John's defeat and capture at POITIERS. It released John on
payment of a ransom of three million crowns, brought
the HUNDRED YEARS WAR temporarily to a halt, and saw
the English renounce claims to Anjou and Normandy
while retaining Gascony and Guyenne. It was never fully
implemented, and Anglo-French hostilities broke out
again in 1369.

Bretton Woods Conference (1944) A United Nations
monetary and financial conference. Representatives
from 44 nations met at Bretton Woods, New Hampshire,
USA, to consider the stabilization of world currencies
and the establishment of credit for international trade
in the post-war world. They drew up a project for an
International Bank for Reconstruction and Development
(see WORLD BANK), which would make long-term capital
available to states urgently needing such aid, and a plan
for an INTERNATIONAL MONETARY FUND (IMF) to finance
short-term imbalances in international trade and
payments. The Conference also hoped to see an
international financial system with stable exchange
rates, with exchange controls and discriminatory tariffs
being ended as soon as possible. The Bank and the Fund
continue as specialized agencies of the United Nations.

Brezhnev, Leonid Ilyich (1906–82) Soviet statesman.
He was President of the Praesidium of the Supreme
Soviet (i.e. titular head of state) (1960–64). As First
Secretary of the Communist Party, he replaced
KHRUSHCHEV (1964). Through these two offices he came to
exercise effective control over Soviet policy, though
initially he shared power with KOSYGIN. Brezhnev's period
in power was marked by the intensified persecution of
dissidents at home and attempted DÉTENTE, followed by
renewed COLD WAR, in foreign affairs. He was largely
responsible for the decision to invade CZECHOSLOVAKIA in
1968, maintaining the doctrine that one socialist state
may interfere in the affairs of another if the
continuance of socialism is at risk.

Brian Boru (c. 926–1014) The last High King of Ireland
(1011). He had previously made himself ruler of Munster
and Limerick in southern Ireland. In doing so Brian,
ruler of the Dal Cais dynasty of Munster, overcame the
influence of the powerful Uú Néill dynasty which had
dominated Ireland for three centuries. In 1012 the men
of Leinster, and supported by the Norse settlers of

Dublin, rose in revolt. The battle of Clontarf brought victory to Brian's forces, though he was killed in the fighting.

Briand, Aristide (1862–1932) French statesman. He was 11 times Premier, and Foreign Minister in 14 successive governments. He entered Parliament in 1903, a strong socialist and an impressive orator. In 1905 he took a leading part in the separation of Church from state and by 1909 had become Premier. In the 1920s he was a powerful advocate of peace and international co-operation, and supported the League of Nations. The cabinet he headed in 1921 fell because of his criticism of France's harsh treatment of Germany after the Treaty of VERSAILLES. Working closely with Austen CHAMBERLAIN and STRESEMANN, the British and German Foreign Ministers, his greatest achievements were the LOCARNO Pact (1925) and the KELLOGG–BRIAND PACT (1928).

Bridgewater, Francis Egerton, 3rd Duke of (1736–1803) British landowner and pioneer of canal construction. His estates included coal-mines and to move his coal cheaply, he financed the cutting of the Bridgewater canal from Worsley to Manchester. James Brindley (1716–72) was the gifted engineer he employed for this project, completed in 1772, which not only caused a dramatic reduction in the price of coal there, but introduced new methods of canal construction and inaugurated the great era of English canal-building in the 1770s and 1780s.

Brigantes ('mountain folk') The Celtic inhabitants of northern Britain between the Humber and the Tyne. After the Roman invasion in 43 AD, Emperor Claudius formed an alliance with their queen Cartimandua. Roman troops helped suppress at least three revolts against her; she also handed over the refugee CARATACUS. During the ROMAN CIVIL WARS 68–69 she was expelled by her anti-Roman husband. Petilius Cerealis was made governor (legatus) of Britain by Vespasian; he advanced north c. 71–74 AD, and established Eboracum (York) as a permanent legionary fortress for the Ninth Legion in this former tribal territory.

Bright, John (1811–89) British politician. An active supporter of radical causes in Victorian England, he became a founder-member of the ANTI-CORN LAW LEAGUE and was associated with its leader, COBDEN in the movement for FREE TRADE. Bright advocated the abolition of the East India Company, supported the Union (the North) in the AMERICAN CIVIL WAR, was prominent in the campaign which led to the REFORM ACT of 1867, and helped GLADSTONE to prepare his policy of Irish land reform. In old age he was a strong opponent of HOME RULE.

Brissot de Warville, Jacques Pierre (1754–93) French journalist, social reformer, and politician. He abandoned the legal profession in 1776 for a career in journalism. He was the founder of the French anti-slavery movement, and wrote pamphlets and newspapers in England, Switzerland, and America before founding an extremist newspaper, *Le Patriote Français* in 1789. He was a prominent member of the JACOBIN CLUB and was elected to the Legislative Assembly, where he pressed for war against the central European countries. His influence and that of his supporters (the Brissotins, later called GIRONDINS) declined after the military failures of 1792, and he died on the guillotine.

Britain UNITED KINGDOM.

Britain, Battle of (August–October 1940) A series of air battles between Britain and Germany fought over Britain. After the fall of France, German aircraft launched a BOMBING OFFENSIVE against British coastal shipping with the aim of attracting and then destroying British fighter aircraft, as a prelude to a general invasion of Britain. This action (July–August 1940) resulted in heavy German dive-bomber losses. Attacks were then made on southern England, but German losses were again heavy. In late August and early September mass bombing raids took place on British aircraft factories, radar installations, and fighter airfields; these caused heavy British losses, but Hitler ordered the offensive to be diverted to British cities just as RAF Fighter Command was exhausting its reserves of machines and pilots. Hitler's priority of the day bombing of London gave time for Fighter Command to recover. On 1 October day-bombing of major cities was replaced by night-bombing, but by this time it was clear that the major German objective, to destroy British air power, had failed. On 12 October Hitler postponed indefinitely his plan to invade Britain. Though heavily outnumbered by the Germans, the British lost 900 aircraft against 1,700 German losses. Radar, used by the British for the first time in battle, made a significant contribution.

British empire (formerly) Lands throughout the world linked by a common allegiance to the British crown. In 1800, although Britain had lost its 13 American colonies, it still retained Newfoundland, thinly populated parts of Canada, many West Indian islands, and other islands useful for trading purposes. It held Gibraltar from Spain and in 1788 had created a convict settlement in New South Wales, Australia. During the NAPOLEONIC WARS Britain acquired further islands, for example Malta, Mauritius, the Maldives, and also Ceylon and Cape Colony, which was particularly valuable for fresh food supplies for ships on the way to the East. Most of these belonged to the EAST INDIA COMPANY, which was steadily developing and exploiting its trade monopoly in India and beyond. All such acquisitions were seen as part of the development of British commerce, as was to be the seizure of HONG KONG in 1841. From the 1820s, a new colonial movement began, with British families taking passages abroad to develop British settlements. In 1857 the INDIAN MUTINY obliged the British government to take over from the East India Company the administration of that vast sub-continent; in January 1877 Queen Victoria was proclaimed Empress of India. New tropical colonies were competed for in the 'SCRAMBLE FOR AFRICA' and in the Pacific. In 1884 an Imperial Federation League was formed, seeking some form of political federation between Britain and its colonies. The scheme soon foundered, being rejected by the colonial Premiers when they gathered in London for the two Colonial Conferences of 1887 and 1897. Strategically, the key area was seen to be southern Africa, and it was the dream of Cecil RHODES and Alfred MILNER to create a single Cape-to-Cairo British dominion, linked by a railway, and acting as the pivot of the whole empire, a dream which faded with the Second BOER WAR. Another result of the Boer War was the creation of the permanent Committee of Imperial Defence (1902), whose function was to be the co-ordination of the defence of

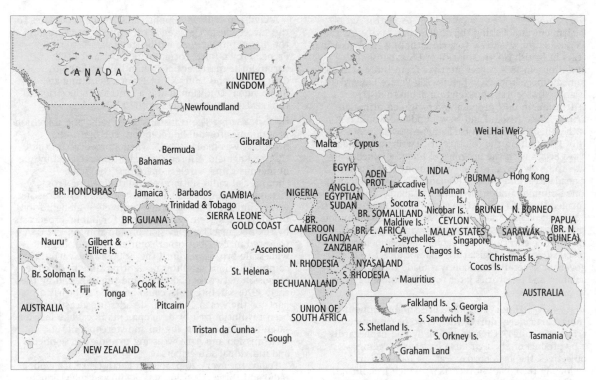

British empire *This map shows the extent of the British empire in 1923. The British empire, established over a period of three centuries, resulted primarily from commercial and political motives. At its height, during the late 19th and early 20th centuries, it comprised about one quarter of the world's area and population. It acquired pre-eminence over its Dutch, Portuguese, French, and Belgian rivals through its command of the seas and sustained its dominance through the flexibility of its rule, which encouraged the establishment of a regular civil service and relatively efficient colonial administrations. A pattern of devolution for its White colonies was inaugurated by the British North America Act of 1867, while the Crown Colonies, with their large indigenous populations, were ruled by a British governor and consultative councils, which delegated powers to local rulers. Nationalist agitation against economic disparities forced Britain to concede independence to most of its remaining colonies after World War II. Since then, most of the empire's former territories have elected to remain within the Commonwealth of Nations.*

the empire, and which was to continue until 1938. The empire reached its zenith after World War I, when German and Ottoman MANDATES were acquired, and over 600 million people were ruled from London. In the later 19th century movements for home-rule had begun in all the White colonies. Starting in Canada, but spreading to Australasia and South Africa, such moves resulted in 1931 in DOMINION status for these lands. Although the Indian National CONGRESS had been founded in 1885, attempts by the indigenous peoples of the empire to secure similar self-government proved more difficult. It was only after 1945 that the process of decolonization began, which by 1964 was largely complete. Most former colonies remained members of the COMMONWEALTH OF NATIONS after becoming independent. Fifteen Commonwealth members (other than Britain) recognize the British monarch as head of state; the others recognize the monarch as head of the Commonwealth. Queen ELIZABETH II consented to the ending of constitutional links between Britain and Canada in 1982 and between Britain and Australia in 1986. Republican movements in Australia and New Zealand gained support during the 1980s and 1990s. Britain has 13 remaining dependent territories including GIBRALTAR, the

FALKLAND ISLANDS, and BERMUDA, which rejected independence in a referendum in 1995: Hong Kong was handed back to China in 1997.

British Expeditionary Force (BEF) British army contingents sent to France at the outbreak of WORLD WAR I. Following the army reforms of Richard HALDANE a territorial reserve army had been created. This was immediately mobilized when war was declared on 4 August 1914 and, together with regular troops, sent to France under Sir John FRENCH. Here, as the Germans advanced into France, the BEF moved up the German western flank into Belgium before being halted and defeated at the Battle of Mons (23–24 August). From here they steadily retreated to Ypres, where they took part in the first Battle of Ypres (20 October–17 November). It is estimated that by the end of November, survivors from the original force averaged no more than one officer and 30 men per battalion of approximately 600 men. An expeditionary force was again mobilized and sent to France in September 1939 but, after failing to halt the German advance across the Low Countries and France, had to be rescued in the DUNKIRK EVACUATION.

British Honduras BELIZE.

British North America Act (1867) A British Act of Parliament establishing the DOMINION of CANADA. As the AMERICAN CIVIL WAR drew to a close there were increasing fears in British North America of US expansionist ambitions. In 1864 representatives from United Canada joined others from New Brunswick, Prince Edward Island, Nova Scotia, and Newfoundland to discuss federation. In 1867 proposals were agreed, although Prince Edward Island and Newfoundland would not ratify them. The British Parliament passed an Act in July 1867 uniting the colonies of New Brunswick and Nova Scotia with the province of Canada, which itself was to be divided into the two provinces of Quebec (Canada East) and Ontario (Canada West), thus creating 'one Dominion under the name of Canada'. The Act formed the basis of the Canadian Constitution until the Constitution of Canada Act of 1982. The new dominion retained the status of colony, but with a system of responsible government (a cabinet government responsible to the legislature and not direct to the governor general). Provision was made for other colonies and territories later to seek admission, as was to be the case.

British Raj (Hindi, 'rule') The British government in India, particularly during the period of Crown rule from 1858 to 1947. Created gradually and haphazardly as a by-product of the EAST INDIA COMPANY's trading objectives, the Raj's heyday was the half-century following the INDIAN MUTINY (1857), which had abruptly ended Company rule. It was an age of IMPERIALISM, symbolized by the proclamation of Queen Victoria as Empress of India (January 1877), and the viceroyalty of Lord CURZON (1899–1905) over an empire 'on which the sun never sets'. The Indian National CONGRESS, which initiated nationalist criticism of the Raj, and eventually succeeded it, was founded in 1885. Its influence extended over the subcontinent, although more than 500 PRINCELY STATES, bound by treaty to the crown, preserved control over their domestic affairs. Control over the directly ruled territories (about three-quarters of the total area) was exercised by a Secretary of State in the British cabinet, and a Viceroy-in-Council in India. The administration was staffed by the ICS (Indian Civil Service), which was open in later years to Indians. The Indian army, with British officers in controlling positions until the 1920s and recruited from British and Indian ranks, ensured the Raj's security in conjunction with a British army garrison. The Raj ended in 1947 when Britain transferred power to the new states of India and Pakistan. British personnel withdrew, but Western modes of thought, channelled through the army and the educational system, have made a continuing contribution to the character and administration of the subcontinent.

Brittany An isolated region in north-west France which has always enjoyed considerable autonomy, retaining a distinct local language and culture. After the Roman conquest in 56 BC it became part of the province of Armorica. Celtic missionaries brought Christianity by the 6th century and it developed a regional church distinguished by local saints and customs. It was able to withstand assault by MEROVINGIANS and CAROLINGIANS, achieved unity in the 9th century, and passed to the dukes of Brittany in the 10th century.

A civil war between English and French candidates for the succession to the French crown took place during the HUNDRED YEARS WAR, and Brittany passed to the French crown (1488; formally incorporated 1532) through the marriages of Breton heiress Anne to Charles VIII and Louis XII of France. Retaining an independent tradition, it was a centre of opposition to the FRENCH REVOLUTIONARIES in the 1790s.

broadcasting The transmission of radio and television programmes for public reception. The first radio broadcast was made in 1906, when a broadcast in the USA by Reginald Aubrey Fessenden was received by numerous ships' wireless operators. The first commercial radio station began broadcasting from Pittsburgh, USA, in 1920. By 1931 television broadcasting was technically feasible, and a complete high-definition broadcasting system was first used for public broadcasts by the BBC in 1935. Television broadcasting in the USA followed in 1939, but other countries did not begin wide-scale broadcasts until the 1950s. By the early 1960s communications satellites made it possible to link the television networks of Europe and the USA, and by the early 1970s satellite links could be made to nearly all parts of the world. In recent decades broadcasting has been revolutionized by developments in cable television, satellite transmission, digital and stereophonic transmission and narrowcasting to audience 'segments' and individual subscribers.

Today, for every 20 people on Earth there are eight radio and three television sets. Radio and television are key components of what are termed the mass media and broadcasting is a major source of news, entertainment, and education. In the USA it developed primarily as a local service financed by advertising, with only general supervision by the Federal Communications Commission. National networks provide programmes to affiliated stations and compete for advertising and audience share. In the UK, by contrast, a unified system of national public service broadcasting, was built around the non-commercial BBC. Independent radio and television services, funded by advertising and regulated by a national authority, came later. A similar 'mixed' approach operates in many continental countries. In countries under an authoritarian regime, where the state wishes to exert strong control over public opinion, ownership and control tend to be centralized. The PROPAGANDA potential of radio was demonstrated in World War II and during the Cold War, and since television became pre-eminent in the 1950s and 1960s, debates about the ownership, regulation, and underlying philosophy of broadcasting have intensified. Wider access to the airwaves has been demanded by sections of the public in both industrialized and developing countries. However, in the 1980s, commercial pressure for deregulation and privatization of broadcasting services increased everywhere. Concentration of media ownership continued, yet the number of radio and television stations proliferated.

Broken Hill A mine at Kabwe in central Zambia where a fossilized human skull and other bones representing three or four individuals were found in 1921. Bones of extinct animals and stone tools of late ACHEULIAN type were found with the remains. The skeletal material, once called Rhodesian Man, but now usually referred to as Kabwe or Broken Hill Man, is important because it represents a population in Africa 400,000–200,000 years ago that is transitional between late *homo erectus* and early or 'archaic' *homo sapiens*.

Bronze Age The prehistoric period during which bronze, an alloy of copper and tin, was the principal material used for tools and weapons. Appreciation of the advantages of alloying came slowly, and various mixes were tried before the optimum 10% tin was arrived at. The transition from the COPPER AGE is therefore difficult to fix, as is that to the IRON AGE which followed. It is now accepted that the technological advance to bronze was made on several separate occasions between 3500 and 3000 BC in the Near East, the Balkans, and south-east Asia, and not until the 15th century AD among the Aztecs of Mexico. Knowledge of the new alloy spread slowly, mainly because of the scarcity of tin, so the Bronze Age tends to have widely different dates in different parts of the world. Indeed sub-Saharan Africa and Australasia, nearly all of America, and much of Asia never experienced a Bronze Age at all.

Although much more metal came into circulation in Bronze Age cultures, the high cost of tin led to two significant results. International trade increased greatly in order to secure supplies, and greater emphasis on social stratification is noticeable practically everywhere following the introduction of bronze, as those able to produce or obtain it strengthened their power over those without it. In the Middle East the Bronze Age developed into the Iron Age from about 1200 BC, in southern Europe from about 1000 BC, and in northern Europe from about 500 BC.

Brooke, Sir James (1803–68) British adventurer and ruler of SARAWAK (1841–68). Arriving in Borneo in 1839 he helped one of the Brunei princes to put down a revolt and was rewarded with the governorship of Kuching in 1841. He established himself as an independent ruler (the 'White Raja') governing as a benevolent autocrat and extending his rule over much of Sarawak. Renowned for his legal reforms (which successfully adapted local custom) he resisted external attacks by Chinese opponents in 1857. Sarawak was effectively ruled by the Brooke family until the Japanese occupation of 1942–45.

Brougham, Henry Peter, 1st Baron Brougham and Vaux (1778–1868) British lawyer and statesman. A notable legal reformer, he, as Attorney-General, successfully defended Queen Caroline at her trial in 1820. An enthusiast for education, in 1828 he helped to found London University. As Lord Chancellor (1830–44) he was responsible for the setting up of the Central Criminal Court and the Judicial Committee of the Privy Council. He also helped to secure the passage of the 1832 REFORM ACT through the House of Lords and the Act of 1833 abolishing slavery in the British empire. However, his somewhat autocratic and eccentric behaviour made him enemies and, although he lived on until 1868, he never again held high office.

Brown, John (1800–59) US ABOLITIONIST. Fired by a mixture of religious fanaticism and a violent hatred of slavery, Brown was responsible for the Pottawatomie massacre, in which five pro-slavery men were murdered. He rapidly emerged as one of the leading figures in the violent local struggle which was making 'Bleeding

Kansas' into a national issue. His most dramatic gesture came in October 1859 when, at the head of a party of about 20, he seized the federal arsenal at Harper's Ferry, Virginia, in the belief that he could precipitate a slave uprising. The arsenal was recaptured by soldiers two days later, and Brown was hanged for treason and murder.

Browne, Robert (*c.* 1550–1633) English Protestant Nonconformist, founder of a religious sect, the 'Brownists'. His followers were the first to separate from the Anglican Church after the Reformation. His treatise *Reformation without Tarrying for Any* (1582) called for immediate separatism and doctrinal reform. Mental instability undermined his leadership, and by 1591 he was reconciled to the Anglican Church. He is seen by CONGREGATIONALISTS as the founder of their principles of Church government.

Brownshirts Members of an early Nazi paramilitary organization, the *Sturmabteilung* or SA ('assault division'). The Brownshirts, recruited from various rough elements of society, were founded by Adolf HITLER in Munich in 1921. Fitted out in brown uniforms reminiscent of Mussolini's BLACKSHIRTS, they figured prominently in organized marches and rallies. Their violent intimidation of political opponents and of Jews played a key role in Hitler's rise to power. From 1931 the SA was led by a radical anti-capitalist, Ernst Röhm. By 1933 it numbered some two million, double the size of the army, which was hostile to them. Röhm's ambition was that the SA should achieve parity with the army and the Nazi Party, and serve as the vehicle for a Nazi revolution in state and society. For Hitler the main consideration was to ensure the loyalty to his regime of the German establishment, and in particular of the German officer corps. Consequently, he had more than 70 members of the SA, including Röhm, summarily executed by the SS in the 'NIGHT OF THE LONG KNIVES', after which the revolutionary period of Nazism may be said to have ended.

Brown v. Board of Education of Topeka (1954) A US Supreme Court case. The Board of Education in Topeka (West Kansas) had established separate schools for White and Black children, in accordance with the Supreme Court decision of *Plessy* v. *Fergusson* of 1896. The Board's policy was challenged by the National Association for the Advancement of Colored People (NAACP) and the case brought before the US Supreme Court, where it was argued by a Black lawyer, Thurgood Marshall, who was himself to be the first Black justice to be appointed to the Court in 1967. The Court found unanimously that racial segregation in schools violated the FOURTEENTH AMENDMENT, thus reversing the decision of 1896 and opening the way for DESEGREGATION not only in schools but in other public facilities.

Bruce, Robert ROBERT I (THE BRUCE).

Bruce, Stanley Melbourne, Viscount Bruce of Melbourne (1883–1967) Australian statesman. A member of the House of Representatives, he represented the Nationalists and the United Australia Party. He became Prime Minister and Minister for External Affairs in the so-called Bruce–Page government. His government's policies were summed up in the slogan 'Men, Money, and Markets'. He served in the British War Cabinet and Pacific War Council

(1942–45). He chaired the World Food Council (1947–51) and the British Finance Corporation for Industry (1947–57).

Brunei A small country on the north-west coast of Borneo, comprising two enclaves surrounded by SARAWAK Malaysia.

Physical. A narrow coastal plain rises inland to rugged and infertile hill country, the highest point being Bukit Belalong at 913 m (2,997 feet) in the south-east. The coast is noted for its oil and natural gas, found both on shore and off-shore. The climate is tropical.

Economy. The economy is almost entirely dependent on oil and natural gas, with one of the world's largest gas liquefaction plants.

History. By 1800 the Brunei sultanate, which had once controlled all of Borneo, had been reduced to Sarawak and SABAH. Control of Sarawak was lost to Sir James BROOKE and his successors after 1841, and in 1888 further incursions drove the sultan to accept a British protectorate, which in 1906 was extended through the appointment of a British resident. The Brunei economy was revolutionized by the discovery of substantial onshore oil deposits in 1929 and offshore oil and gas fields in the early 1960s. The sultanate was put under pressure to join the newly formed Federation of MALAYSIA, provoking a brief rebellion in 1962 of Bruneians opposed to joining Malaysia. Brunei did not join, however, partly because of its natural resources. It achieved internal self-government in 1971 but did not become formally independent until 1984. A state of emergency has been in force since 1962, allowing the sultan to rule by decree. During the 1990s the level of unemployment and social unrest rose. In 1991 the sultan banned the import of alcohol and the celebration of Christmas, measures designed to encourage the population to adopt strict Islamic codes of behaviour.

CAPITAL:	Bandar Seri Begawan
AREA:	5,765 sq km (2,226 sq miles)
POPULATION:	300, 000 (1996)
CURRENCY:	1 Brunei dollar = 100 cents
RELIGIONS:	Muslim 63.4%; Buddhist 14.0%; Christian 9.7%
ETHNIC GROUPS:	Malay 68.8%; Chinese 18.3%; Indian and other 7.9%; other indigenous 5.0%
LANGUAGES:	Malay, English (both official); Chinese; minority languages
INTERNATIONAL ORGANIZATIONS:	UN; Commonwealth; ASEAN

Brunhilda (d.534–613) Visigothic queen of the MEROVINGIAN Kingdom of Austrasia. After her husband's assassination she tried to rule in the name of her son Childebert II but, faced with internal revolts and the opposition of the King of Neustria, she fled to Burgundy. In old age she claimed Burgundy and Austrasia in the name of her great-grandson, but Chlothar of Neustria defeated her. She is alleged to have been executed by being dragged to death by wild horses.

Brüning, Heinrich (1885–1970) German statesman. As leader of the Weimar Republic's Catholic Centre Party, he was Chancellor and Foreign Minister, 1930–32. He attempted to solve Germany's economic problems by unpopular deflationary measures such as higher taxation, cuts in government expenditure, and by trying to reduce REPARATION payments. But after the elections of 1930 he lost support in the Reichstag and ruled by

emergency decrees. He was forced to resign in 1932 by President Hindenburg, whose confidence he had lost. He escaped the 1934 purge and emigrated to the USA.

Bruno, Giordano (*c.* 1548–1600) Italian philosopher and astronomer. He entered the DOMINICAN order in 1562 and was ordained priest in 1572. Having been charged with heresy in 1576, he entered upon a peripatetic career of teaching and writing. He accepted the main astronomical teachings of Copernicus, and was the first to see the logical consequences of the removal of the Earth from its position at the centre of the universe. He held that the universe was infinite, with countless individual worlds similar to the Earth, rather than a fixed sphere of stars as in the Copernican system. He was arrested by the Inquisition of the Roman Catholic Church for his unorthodox beliefs and was burned to death. His philosophical ideas influenced later philosophers, notably Gottfried Wilhelm Leibniz (1646–1716) and Baruch Spinoza (1632–77).

Bruno of Cologne, St (*c.* 1032–1101) Founder of the CARTHUSIAN order of monks at La Grande Chartreuse in France, *c.* 1084, where he was the first prior. He advocated the separation of his monks from the secular world and adherence to a very strict regime of self-denial. Respect for the order grew rapidly and he was summoned to Rome around 1090 to advise Pope Urban II about the state of the Church. In England Carthusian houses were called charterhouses; they were forcibly closed during the dissolution of the monasteries in the 16th century.

Brusilov, Aleksky (1853–1926) Russian general. He won a brilliant campaign against Austro-Hungary (1916) in south-west Russia, which, although it cost Russia at least a million lives, forced Germany to divert troops from the SOMME and encouraged Romania to join the Allies. After the fall of the Russian emperor he sided with the BOLSHEVIKS and directed the war against Poland.

Brutus, Marcus Junius (*c.* 85–42 BC) Roman soldier, one of the assassins of Julius CAESAR. He was the nephew of CATO (the Younger) and a conservative republican Roman. He took POMPEY's side against Caesar in the ROMAN CIVIL WARS. Pardoned by Caesar after PHARSALUS, he became governor of Cisalpine GAUL, and then urban praetor in 44 through Caesar's favour. Together with Cassius he plotted Caesar's death. It was Brutus' idealism which confined the conspirators' action to the single act of killing Caesar: they thereby lost the political initiative to the consul Antony, whom they had spared, and were compelled to flee, afterwards forming a fleet and army in Greece against MARK ANTONY and Octavian (AUGUSTUS). Defeat at PHILIPPI in 42 was followed by his suicide.

Bryan, William Jennings (1860–1925) US politician. Elected to Congress as a Democrat, he delivered his celebrated Free-Silver speech, in which he attacked MCKINLEY's endorsement of the GOLD STANDARD ('You shall not crucify mankind upon a cross of gold'), at the Democratic Convention in 1896. The speech won him the presidential nomination, which he obtained again in 1900 and 1908. He supported Woodrow WILSON, who made him Secretary of State, but Bryan resigned over Wilson's note to Germany after the sinking of the LUSITANIA in

World War I. In 1925 he appeared for the prosecution in the celebrated SCOPES CASE. He won the case, but died five days after the trial was concluded.

buccaneer A pirate or privateer who preyed on Spanish shipping and settlements in the Caribbean and South America in the 17th century. Mainly of British, French, and Dutch stock, buccaneers made their headquarters first on Tortuga Island off Haiti and then on Jamaica. In wartime they formed a mercenary navy for Spain's enemies, fighting with reckless bravery. Their triumphs included the sackings of Porto Bello, Panama, Chagres, New Segovia, and Maracaibo. Henry MORGAN was their most famous commander. After 1680 they penetrated to the Pacific coast of South America. Their power and prosperity rapidly declined in the early 18th century.

Buchanan, James (1791–1868) Fifteenth President of the USA (1857–61). He served as a Democratic Senator (1835–45) and, as Secretary of State under Polk (1845–49), played a central role in the diplomatic events surrounding the MEXICAN–AMERICAN WAR, and the settlement of the OREGON BOUNDARY DISPUTE (1846). As minister to London (1853–56), he was one of the authors of the Ostend Manifesto, which backed the US claim to Cuba. As a Northerner acceptable to the South, Buchanan won the Democratic presidential nomination, and subsequently the presidency in 1856. Hard-working but limited in his vision, he consistently leaned towards the pro-slavery side in the developing dispute over slavery in the territories. He endorsed the candidacy of the Southern Democrat BRECKINRIDGE in 1860, but supported the Union (the North) in the AMERICAN CIVIL WAR.

Buckingham, George Villiers, 1st Duke of (1592–1628) English statesman, favourite of JAMES I and Charles I. In 1615 James appointed Villiers, a young man of no distinction but attractive to the king, to the office of Gentleman of the Bedchamber. Thereafter he amassed fortune and power for himself and his followers by distributing offices and favours. His personal extravagance, promotion of Archbishop LAUD, and political incompetence combined to tarnish the reputation of the court. He accompanied Charles, Prince of Wales, to Madrid in 1623 in the hopes of arranging a marriage for him with the Spanish Infanta, an expedition which served only to fuel hostile rumours of Charles's conversion to the Catholic faith. After Charles's accession in 1625 Buckingham remained the king's policy-maker, ignored Parliament's hostility towards war, and insisted on a costly campaign against Spain which ended with a disastrous expedition to Cadiz in 1625. Parliament attempted to impeach him, charging him with corruption and financial mismanagement, but the king dissolved Parliament and Buckingham pursued campaigns against both France and Spain, personally leading an unsuccessful expedition to the relief of the HUGUENOTS at La Rochelle. In 1628 he was murdered by a soldier aggrieved by the mismanagement of the war.

Buddha (Sanskrit, 'enlightened one') A title applied by Buddhists to anyone, earthly or transcendent, who has attained nirvana (complete liberation). However, the title is most commonly used to refer to Siddhartha Gautama (c. 480–400 BC), the historical founder of Buddhism. According to tradition, he left his life as the son of a prince and became a wandering ascetic in order to seek the meaning of existence. At the age of 35 he underwent an experience of enlightenment under a Bodhi tree. He realized that the root of all existence is suffering, but that by following a 'Middle Way' between self-indulgence and extreme asceticism, men and women may achieve enlightenment. Buddha travelled around northern India for about 45 years, preaching and gathering together a large number of followers. He attained nirvana at his enlightenment, and at his death, a final nirvana.

The Buddha's teaching is set in the context of the Indian belief in a cycle of rebirth, and the aim to find a complete liberation from it. Although he shared many ideas with other Indian religions, such as JAINISM and HINDUISM, his central teaching of the non-existence of any real soul or self set him apart from them. His first sermon outlines the 'Four Noble Truths': the omnipresence of suffering; its cause, desire; the elimination of suffering by the elimination of desire; and the Eightfold Path (comprising Right Understanding, Intention, Speech, Conduct, Livelihood, Effort, Mindfulness, and Meditation) that leads to this end.

Although the focus of Buddhism is on the teaching of the Buddha rather than on Gautama as a unique individual, he is nevertheless shown great reverence as a supreme teacher and exemplar. The Buddha is widely represented in art and sculpture, often in the seated, cross-legged posture of meditation.

Buddhism A major world religion numbering around 300 million followers (exact estimates are impossible since Buddhism does not preclude other religious beliefs). Early Buddhism developed from HINDUISM through the teaching of Siddhartha Gautama (the BUDDHA) and his disciples, around the 5th century BC in northern India. Under leaders such as the emperor ASOKA, who converted to Buddhism and encouraged its spread, the religion provided a stabilizing political structure throughout India. Offering a way to salvation that did not depend on caste or the ritualism of the Brahmin priesthood of Hinduism, and strengthened by a large, disciplined monastic order (the *sangha*), it made a very great impact; but by the end of the 1st millennium AD it had lost ground to a resurgent Hinduism, and the subsequent Muslim invasions virtually extinguished it in India. Meanwhile however, monks had taken the faith all over Asia, to central and northern areas now in Afghanistan, Mongolia, China, Japan, Korea and Vietnam; and in south and south-east Asia to Sri Lanka, Myanmar (Burma), Thailand, Cambodia, and Laos. The final phase of Buddhist expansion, after the 7th century, saw the emergence of Tantric and Tibetan Buddhism.

Owing to its linguistic diversity and geographical extent, Buddhist teaching, scriptures, and observance are complex and varied, but certain main doctrines are characteristic. Buddhism recognizes no creator God with a monopoly over knowledge and power; instead it asserts that all phenomena are linked together in an endless chain of dependency. Buddhism teaches that the suffering of the world is caused by desire conditioned by ignorance, but that by following the path of the Buddha, release from the cycle of rebirth can be achieved.

During the centuries following the Buddha's death, many different schools emerged, usually grouped into

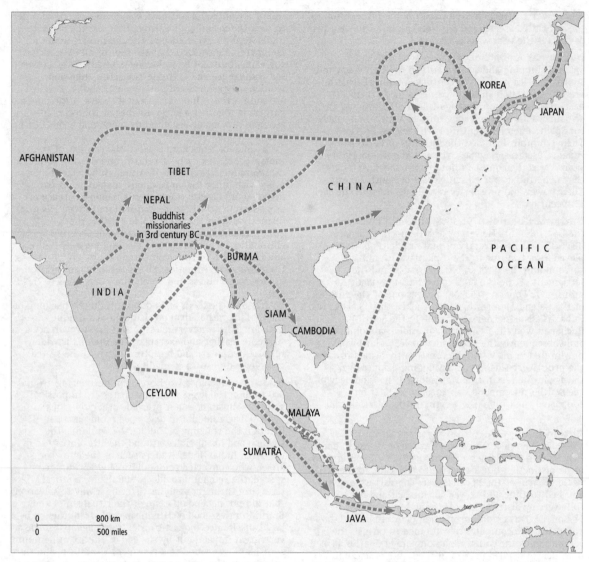

Buddhism   *This map shows the extent of Buddhism in about 1000 AD. The expansion of Buddhism beyond India can be traced to the reign of Asoka (273–232 BC), a convert to the religion. He sent out missions, notably to Anuradhapura, capital of Ceylon (Sri Lanka), where Buddhism was established by a relative, perhaps a son. The adoption of Buddhism in other countries was gradual. By the 1st century AD it was spreading throughout central Asia along the SILK ROUTE and was known in China, although it did not become widely popular therefor another four centuries. From China it reached Korea in the 4th century and Japan in the 6th century, challenging Shinto for a time. It was established in Sumatra and Java in the 5th century and had also spread to Siam (Thailand), Cambodia, and Tibet by the 7th century. Meanwhile Buddhism was in decline in India, where Hinduism was becoming the dominant religion.*

two 'vehicles': the MAHAYANA, 'the great vehicle', dominant in North Asia, and 'the lesser vehicle', Hinayana, of which the only form now remaining is the THERAVADA Buddhism of south and south-east Asia. This, the most conservative form of Buddhism, persists today in Sri Lanka, Thailand, Myanmar (Burma), and Laos; it is noted for its analytical and monastic approach. More widespread today is the teaching developed by the Mahayana school, which arose between 150 BC and 100 AD and became dominant in China, Japan, Vietnam, and Korea. There are many religious and philosophical

differences between the various schools of the Mahayana, which include the ZEN sect, but they all differ from the Theravada in giving a greater status to the Buddha, who is sometimes seen as an eternal being rather than a man, and in making it the aim of all Buddhists to become a Bodhisattva, a being who works for the salvation of all.

The last two centuries have demonstrated the resilience of Buddhism and its ability to communicate across cultural barriers. Despite communist revolutions, Western technology, and commercialism, its teaching and its ancient meditation techniques have maintained their appeal. Attempts to revive Buddhism in India are indebted to the impetus of the Theosophical Society, the spread of neo-Buddhism, particularly among the outcastes by AMBEDKAR and, in recent times, the presence of Tibetan Buddhist refugees. In Thailand, Buddhism continues to enjoy royal patronage, and the work of the *sangha* is seen as an important factor in social development in the region. Buddhism has survived even in communist China, while in Japan the Pure Land sects of Mahayana Buddhism remain popular. Like Zen, they are also represented in the USA and Europe. (See map.)

Buganda UGANDA.

Bugis Muslim mercenaries and traders of south-east Asia. They were enterprising seamen and traders living in villages in Sulawesi (Celebes). When MACASSAR fell to the Dutch (1667) they lost their livelihood. Thereafter they sought employment as mercenaries and engaged in piracy in Borneo, Java, Sumatra, and Malaya. They fought for and against the Dutch. They suffered a reverse when their leader Raja Haji was killed while assaulting MALACCA (1784), but went on to found states, like Selangor and Riao, on the Malay peninsula. Their prahus, boats with a triangular sail and a canoe-like outrigger, continued to trade throughout the archipelago.

building techniques Archaeological evidence suggests that building as a specialized activity probably began in Mesopotamia (*c.* 7000 BC), where there is little building stone. Mud buildings were generally roofed either with wooden beams supporting clay-daubed matting or with a vault (a three-dimensional arched structure). True arches were used for openings, and methods of building vaults without centring (using a wooden framework to support the vault while building) were also known. The Ur-Nammu ziggurat at UR, Mesopotamia (*c.* 2100 BC), had an adobe core that was faced with fired bricks bedded in bitumen and reinforced with reed mats.

Building with stone seems to have begun in the Nile valley, with the construction of important religious buildings. Although the arch was known to the Egyptians, they preferred massive columns supporting short lintels for their temples. The Great PYRAMID (*c.*2500 BC) was built with stones up to 200 tonnes each, faced with finely jointed limestone bedded in lime. Before stone-quarrying began, Egyptian buildings were made from reed bundles covered with reed matting, a technique still in use in southern Iraq. Buildings were often built from wood where it was plentiful. Early buildings used wooden posts, planking, or entire logs to form walls and roof; later, timber frame construction was introduced to save on wood. Roofs were covered with thatching (vegetable material such as reeds or brushwood laid over the rafters) or tiles. In Greece, this frame construction, translated into marble, is evident in such temples as the Parthenon, Athens (*c.* 450 BC). The Romans developed a strong, durable form of concrete by adding silica-rich crushed brick or pozzolana (volcanic ash) to lime. Large public buildings were roofed by concrete and masonry semicircular vaults or domes. The Pantheon dome in Rome (built in 27 BC) spans 43 m (141 feet) — a span unequalled until the 19th century.

Meanwhile, in China, there was a tradition of timber construction very different from that in the West. This type of design spread to Korea and Japan and lasted until modern times.

In Europe, the medieval mason extended Roman methods to develop slender Gothic churches with large tracery windows. Timber trussed roofs protected the masonry from the weather. Humbler buildings were still of timber, with the upper floors and roof supported by walls of closely spaced posts. During the Renaissance, masonry remained the material for large structures, with arches being used to span openings. The domes of St Peter's, Rome (1546–64), and of St Paul's, London (1685–1710), were not buttressed externally but were encircled by iron chains to contain the outward thrust on the supporting walls below. Increasingly, metal reinforcements were used to strengthen masonry. In France in the 1670s, Claude Perrault designed lintels for a colonnade at the Louvre, which were made from small stone blocks reinforced with an iron cage – a precursor of reinforced concrete.

By the late 1700s in Britain a number of disastrous fires in mill buildings prompted the replacement of wood with cast-iron columns and beams as the internal support for floors (external walls were still of masonry) and the development of iron windows and brick and iron vaulted floors. In a series of large botanical glasshouses, sheet glass (which could now be manufactured in large sizes) enclosed an iron framework; masonry walls were not used at all. This technique culminated in the Crystal Palace, London (1851), which was the first large building to be assembled from prefabricated components, and was also used to construct the roofs of many large train stations and sheds. The first fully framed building was probably the four-storey Menier chocolate factory built over the River Marne (to utilize water power) at Noisel, France (1871). In Chicago, development of a safe passenger lift led to the construction of skyscrapers. The Forth Bridge (1882–89) was the first major steel structure to be built in the UK.

Meanwhile, concrete had undergone significant development. In the 1760s, the British civil engineer John Smeaton (1724–92) discovered that mixtures of clay and limestone produced a hydraulic cement that hardened under water — essential for his work in rebuilding the Eddystone Lighthouse off Plymouth, UK. Subsequently, the compressive strength and reliability of these cements improved, but the concrete made with them lacked tensile strength, essential to resist the stresses in a floor or beam. In Britain and France reinforcement techniques were developed for concrete. In Britain in 1854, A. B. Wilkinson patented beams reinforced with wire ropes and iron bars and built a reinforced concrete house (1865). In France, Joseph Monier made reinforced concrete tubs for orange trees (1849), and in 1892 a reinforced concrete building frame was patented with many features still in use today.

Modern skyscrapers have hull-and-core structures, with a light-weight curtain wall enclosing the building. The central core is a reinforced concrete tower. While reinforced concrete is also often used as the skeleton frame for blocks of flats and similar buildings, a load-bearing wall structure is usually more appropriate. The main walls run across the building to support the floors and are buttressed by internal longitudinal walls (cross-wall construction) as in the Unités d'Habitation (1947–52) by the Swiss-born French architect Le Corbusier. For large-area single-storey buildings, both thin concrete shells and steel space frames are widely used, and by the 1980s the availability of durable polymer fabrics made possible the construction of tent-like tension structures typified by the Hajj terminal in Saudi Arabia. A major force for the development of building techniques has been the improvement in materials manufacture and in fabrication and jointing techniques. Another has been the better understanding of structural behaviour and the evolution of mathematical techniques of structural analysis since the 16th century.

Bukharin, Nikolai Ivanovich (1888–1938) Russian Bolshevik leader and theoretician. A member of the Social Democratic Party, he played an active part in the RUSSIAN REVOLUTION of 1917 and became editor of the Party newspaper, *Pravda* (Truth). He opposed LENIN's withdrawal from World War I (1918), arguing in favour of promoting a European revolution. After Lenin's death (1924) he was a member of the POLITBURO and of the COMINTERN. In the 1920s he supported the NEW ECONOMIC POLICY, arguing that industrialization required a healthy agricultural base, and opposed COLLECTIVIZATION. He lost favour with STALIN and was arrested as a 'Trotskyite' (1937). In 1938 he was put on trial, together with other prominent Bolsheviks, accused of wanting to restore bourgeois capitalism and of joining with TROTSKY in treasonable conspiracy. He was convicted and executed, but was rehabilitated in 1989.

Bulganin, Nikolai Alekandrovich (1895–1975) Soviet military leader and politician. He joined the Communist Party in 1917 and served in the secret police or CHEKA. He held various Party posts in Moscow during 1931–41 and helped organize the defence of the city during World War II. He became a Marshal of the Soviet Union in 1945, succeeding Stalin as Minister of Defence in 1946. He was Chairman of the Council of Ministers (1955–58), during which time he shared power with KHRUSHCHEV, who replaced him. He lost his membership of the Central Committee in 1958.

Bulgaria A country of the Balkan Peninsula in south-east Europe. It is bordered by Romania to the north, Serbia and Macedonia to the west, Greece and Turkey to the south, and the Black Sea.

Physical. The northern boundary of Bulgaria is formed by the River Danube, except in the north-east; about 80 km (50 miles) to the south the long Planina range of Balkan Mountains runs parallel to the river, dividing the country laterally. Further south the Rhodope ranges cut the country off from the mild climate of the Mediterranean Sea.

Economy. Until 1989 Bulgaria was a communist republic closely allied to the Soviet Union. An economic reform programme was introduced in 1991 with the support of the IMF; this involved the return of collectivized land to former owners and the privatization of small businesses. The removal of subsidies from food and other basic commodities caused considerable hardship and further reform stalled until 1994, when a mass privatization programme was launched. In 1996 the country was engulfed by an acute financial crisis when the national currency, the lev, collapsed. Bulgaria's mineral resources include coal, iron ore, copper, lead, zinc, and petroleum from the Black

Sea. Agricultural products include wheat, maize, barley, sugar beet, grapes, and tobacco, which are exported along with wine and spirits. Manufacturing industry specializes in electrical and transport equipment, steel, and chemicals. Tourism is a significant source of revenue.

History. Bulgaria was settled by central Asian tribesmen in the 5th century, colonized by the Romans, and then invaded by SLAV Bulgars. They killed Emperor Nicephorus in 811 AD, and captured ADRIANOPLE in 813. Christianity was introduced in the 9th century. Greek and MAGYAR threats were repulsed but rebellion, and incursions by Greeks, Russians, and SERBS resulted in the kingdom being divided into three in the 11th century. It was annexed by the OTTOMAN EMPIRE in 1396 and ruled by the Turks for nearly five centuries.

In the 19th century Bulgarian nationalism led to a series of insurrections against the Ottoman Turks culminating in 1876, when several thousand Bulgars were massacred. Russia gave its support to Bulgaria, and war between Russia and Turkey followed. This was ended by the Treaty of San Stefano (March 1878), which created a practically independent Bulgaria covering three-fifths of the Balkan Peninsula. Britain, however, now feared that the new state would become a puppet of Russia. The Treaty of BERLIN (1878) therefore split the country into Bulgaria and Eastern Roumelia, which remained nominally under Turkish rule. In 1879 a democratic constituent assembly elected the German Prince, Alexander of Battenburg, as ruling prince and in 1885 Alexander incorporated Eastern Roumelia into Bulgaria. For this he was kidnapped by Russian officers and forced to abdicate. His successor was another German prince, Ferdinand of Saxe-Coburg (1887–1918). Taking advantage of the YOUNG TURK movement Ferdinand formally proclaimed full independence from Turkish rule in 1908, and was crowned king. Participation in World War I on the side of Germany led to invasion by the Allies (1916), and the loss of territory through the VERSAILLES PEACE SETTLEMENT. Between 1919 and 1923 Bulgaria was virtually a peasant-dictatorship under Alexander Stamboliyski, the leader of the Agrarian Union. He was murdered and an attempt by communists under DIMITROV to seize power followed. Military and political instability persisted until 1935, when an authoritarian government was set up by Boris III (1918–43). World War II saw co-operation with Nazi Germany, followed by invasion by the Soviet Union. In 1946 the monarchy was abolished and a communist state proclaimed, Bulgaria becoming the most consistently pro-Soviet member of the WARSAW PACT countries. In 1989 the communist leader Todor Zhivkov, who had been in office since 1954, was ousted from power (in 1992 he was found guilty of embezzlement of state funds). Free elections followed, with a new constitution in 1990. The introduction of privatization and other economic reforms has proved particularly painful in Bulgaria. After elections in 1994 a coalition government was formed (1995), led by the former Communist Party under its new title, the Bulgarian Socialist Party. However, the country's economic and political crisis deepened in 1996–97; after a general strike and rapid inflation, the right-wing Union of Democratic Forces (UDF) won elections in April 1997. The new government aimed to stabilize the currency and sought full NATO membership.

CAPITAL:	Sofia
AREA:	110,994 sq km (42,855 sq miles)
POPULATION:	8.366 million (1996) ·
CURRENCY:	1 lev = 100 stotinki
RELIGIONS:	atheist 64.5%; Eastern Orthodox 26.7%; Muslim 7.5%; Protestant 0.7%; Roman Catholic 0.5%
ETHNIC GROUPS:	Bulgarian 85.3%; Turkish 8.5%; gypsy 2.6%; Macedonian 2.5%; Armenian 0.3%; Russian 0.2%
LANGUAGES:	Bulgarian (official); Turkish; Romany; Macedonian; minority languages
INTERNATIONAL ORGANIZATIONS:	UN; CSCE; North Atlantic Co-operation Council

Bulge, Battle of the ARDENNES.

Bülow, Bernard, Prince von (1849–1920) German statesman. He served in the FRANCO–PRUSSIAN WAR and the German Foreign Service before becoming German Foreign Minister (1897–1900) and then Chancellor (1900–09) under WILLIAM II. In domestic policies he was a cautious conservative, but in foreign affairs his policies were to support the emperor's wish for German imperial expansion. Following the BOER WAR, when William openly supported the Boers, von Bülow improved relations with Britain, who suggested in 1900 that Germany might assist to support the decaying regime of Abdul Aziz in Morocco. France was also interested and following the *entente* with Britain (1904) the latter supported its claim. At first von Bülow retaliated by sending the emperor on a provocative visit to Tangier (1905), when Franco–German tension developed. He then, however, helped to convene the ALGECIRAS CONFERENCE (1906) and in 1909 agreed that France be the protector of MOROCCO. He supported the Austrian annexation of BOSNIA-HERZEGOVINA, a move which was to help precipitate WORLD WAR I. Von Bülow retired when he lost the support of the Reichstag in 1909.

Bunche, Ralph (1904–71) US administrator and diplomat. He was professor of political science at Howard University when, during World War II, he served with the joint chiefs-of-staff and the State Department. In 1946 he joined the secretariat of the United Nations and served on the UN Palestine Commission in 1947. After Count BERNADOTTE was assassinated in 1948, he carried on negotiations between the warring Arabs and Jews with such skill that he was able to arrange an armistice between them. For this achievement he was awarded (1950) the Nobel Peace Prize, the first awarded to a Black American. He served as Director of the Trusteeship Division of the UN (1948–54).

Bunker Hill, Battle of (17 June 1775) A battle in the American War of INDEPENDENCE ending in a British victory. Thomas GAGE, the British commander besieged in Boston, sent 2,400 troops (redcoats) to take the heights occupied by 1,600 Americans under William Prescott. Only after three bloody uphill assaults, costing 1,000 British against 400 American casualties, were they successful. The impressive defence undermined the myth of redcoat invincibility and encouraged colonial unification.

Burger, Warren E. (1907–95) Chief Justice of the US Supreme Court (1969–86). In 1955 he was appointed judge in the Court of Appeal in the District of Columbia. A conservative republican, he was appointed by President Nixon as Chief Justice of the Supreme Court in May 1969, to succeed Chief Justice WARREN. He did not, however, seek to reverse all the liberal judgements of his predecessor, especially when civil rights were concerned. In 1971 the Court supported a policy of BUSING to lessen racial segregation in schools, but in 1974 its judgement on *Milliken* v. *Bradley* accepted the reality of racial segregation by housing. In the 1978 Bakke case it supported 'positive discrimination' in favour of disadvantaged candidates for university admission, i.e. Black or Hispanic students, even though it also ruled that in this particular case a rejected White candidate, Allan Bakke, be admitted. Burger also voted in favour of the right to have an abortion (*Roe* v. *Wade*; 1973). In 1974 Burger wrote a judgement for the case of *United States* v. *Richard M. Nixon*, in which he confirmed that the Supreme Court and not the President was the final arbiter of the US Constitution.

Burghley, Lord CECIL, WILLIAM.

Burgoyne, John (1722–92) British general, who fought against the colonial army in the American War of INDEPENDENCE. As commander-in-chief of the northern army, 'Gentleman Johnny' led the attack southward from Montreal towards the Hudson Valley in 1776 and 1777. He was unable to adapt to American conditions and was defeated at SARATOGA in 1777; this led to his recall and France's alliance with America.

Burgundy A former duchy in south-central France. The Burgundii, a Germanic tribe, settled there in the 5th century. It was under Merovingian control and then absorbed into the CAROLINGIAN EMPIRE. During the reign of strong Holy Roman Emperors most of it was under imperial control but in the late Middle Ages it was ruled by a series of strong dukes. PHILIP THE BOLD acquired Flanders and John the Fearless the Netherlands. Geographically the separation of territories made government difficult and CHARLES THE BOLD tried, but failed, to unite the northern and southern parts by annexing Lorraine. He was killed in 1477, leaving no son to succeed, and Louis XI of France claimed the duchy. The final subjection to France occurred when Louis XIV seized Franche-Comté.

During its history the duchy had achieved great power and influence, its court in the 15th century the most splendid in Europe. Certainly some of its dukes were more powerful than many kings of France and when they allied themselves with the English, as they did during the HUNDRED YEARS WAR, they posed a real threat to the security of the French monarch. The court of the dukes of Burgundy was renowned for its artistic patronage; the name Burgundian School is applied to a group of Flemish panel painters and miniaturists working for them between 1390 and 1420.

Burke, Edmund (1729–97) British statesman and political theorist. He was the son of an Irish lawyer, and went to London in 1750. In 1765 he became private secretary to the Prime Minister, the Marquis of ROCKINGHAM, soon afterwards entering Parliament, where he quickly gained a reputation as a skilful debater. On the American question he argued that Britain ought to abandon the abstract right to tax the Americans, on the ground of expediency. He became a friend of Charles James FOX in 1774, and in defence of liberty he attacked political corruption and injustice while demanding parliamentary reform. He took a leading role in the unsuccessful prosecution (1788–95) of Warren HASTINGS, former governor-general of India.

Burke split with Fox over the FRENCH REVOLUTION. While Fox could see little to criticize in the events in France, Burke saw liberty only in law and order. In his *Reflections on the Revolution in France* (1790) he denounced events in France as mob rule, and by supporting reform through evolution, not revolution, he laid down the basis of modern British conservatism. Burke's views on the French Revolution were more widely accepted than those of Fox's supporters, and at his retirement in 1794 he was granted a large pension by George III.

Burkina Faso A landlocked country in West Africa surrounded by Mali, Niger, Benin, Togo, Ghana, and Côte d'Ivoire.

Physical. Burkina Faso lies on a plateau, rising highest in the west and cut in the centre by the north–south route of the Volta River. The soils are mostly coarse and sandy, based on hard rock; the climate is hot and arid, and the natural vegetation except in the river valleys is thornscrub and thin savannah.

Economy. Burkina Faso is one of the poorest countries in the world, heavily dependent on Western aid. The economy is mainly agricultural and vulnerable to drought, with most of the population engaged in subsistence agriculture. The major exports are cotton and gold. There is some industry, mostly state-owned, with largely unexploited mineral deposits of gold, manganese, and zinc. Many Burkinabé seek employment abroad.

History. Before French colonization in the 19th century the region was ruled by a number of Mossi states. It was a French protectorate from 1898, originally as part of French Sudan (now Mali) and later as Haute Volta (Upper Volta). It became an autonomous republic within the FRENCH COMMUNITY in 1958 and independent in 1960. Following a military coup in 1970, a new constitution was adopted in 1977. A series of military governments followed, including those of Captain Thomas Sankara, who was assassinated in 1987, and of Blaise Compaore. The latter ended military rule in June 1991 and held multiparty elections, for which there were 44 eligible political parties. Compaore's Popular Front won these, and he became President. However, the opposition parties had withdrawn their candidates and there was a widespread boycott of the elections because of alleged corruption. Legislative elections, held in 1992, were won by supporters of Compaore.

CAPITAL:	Ouagadougou
AREA:	274,200 sq km (105,869 sq miles)
POPULATION:	10.615 million (1996)
CURRENCY:	1 CFA franc = 100 centimes
RELIGIONS:	Traditional beliefs 65.0%; Muslim 25.0%; Roman Catholic 9.8%; Protestant 2.4%
ETHNIC GROUPS:	Mossi 47.9%; Mande 8.8%; Fulani 8.3%; Lobi 6.9%; Bobo 6.8%; Senufo 6.0%; Grunshi 5.0%; Bunasi 5.0%; Gurma 4.5%
LANGUAGES:	French (official); Mossi; Dyula; Fulani; Lobi; local languages

INTERNATIONAL
ORGANIZATIONS: UN; OAU; Non-Aligned Movement; Franc Zone; ECOWAS

Burma MYANMAR.

Burma Campaigns (World War II) (January 1942–August 1945) In 1942 two Japanese divisions advanced into Burma (now MYANMAR), accompanied by the Burma National Army of AUNG SAN, capturing Rangoon, and forcing the British garrison to begin the long evacuation west. The Japanese reached Lashio at the southern end of the 'Burma Road', thus cutting off the supply link from India to Nationalist China. They captured Mandalay (May 1942) and the British forces under General ALEXANDER OF TUNIS withdrew to the Indian frontier. During 1943 there were attempts to reassert control over the Arakan, but these failed, although WINGATE with his Chindit units organized effective guerrilla activity behind Japanese lines, where an originally pro-Japanese population was becoming increasingly disillusioned. Early in the spring of 1944 heavy fighting took place in defence of Imphal, when an attempted Japanese invasion of Assam/Northern India was deflected in a series of bloody battles, of which Kohima was the most important. In October a three-pronged offensive was launched by British, Commonwealth, US, and Chinese Nationalist troops, and in January 1945 the 'Burma Road' was re-opened. By now a discontented Aung San had contacted MOUNTBATTEN and in March his troops joined the Allies. Rangoon was finally captured on 1 May 1945 by an Indian division.

Burnet, Gilbert (1643–1715) Scottish churchman and historian. He sought advancement in England from 1674, but moved to the Continent on the accession of James II. He became adviser to WILLIAM III (of Orange), accompanying him to England in 1688, and was rewarded with the bishopric of Salisbury in 1689. His greatest work was *The History of My Own Times*, published after his death, a valuable source of information on contemporary events, but coloured by Burnet's strong Whig bias.

Burns, John Elliott (1858–1943) British trade union leader and politician. He had been a factory worker as a child, and was largely self-educated, becoming a radical socialist. The 1889 LONDON DOCKERS' STRIKE owed much of its success to his leadership. Burns was one of the first Labour representatives to be elected to Parliament (1892), but he fell out with Keir HARDIE and turned his back on socialism. As a supporter of the Liberal Party he became president of the Local Government Board (1905–14) and introduced the first Town Planning Act (1909). He was president of the Board of Trade in 1914 but resigned from the cabinet in protest against Britain's entry into World War I.

Burr, Aaron (1756–1836) US Vice-President and political adventurer. He served with distinction in the War of Independence (1775–83) and then served in the Senate (1791–97). Allying himself with the Democratic-Republicans (DEMOCRATIC PARTY), Burr won the same number of electoral college votes as Thomas JEFFERSON in the presidential election of 1800, but was defeated in the House of Representatives and became Vice-President. His rivalry with Alexander Hamilton, who in 1804 thwarted Burr's ambition to become governor of New York, led to a duel in which Hamilton was killed and which effectively stopped Burr's public career. He became an adventurer, and was involved in a conspiracy allegedly intended to set up a separate confederacy in the west, allied to Spain, which in 1807 led to his trial (and acquittal) on a charge of treason.

Burton, Sir Richard Francis (1821–90) Anglo-Irish scholar and explorer. He joined the Indian Army in 1842 and while employed in military intelligence, he claimed to have learnt 35 languages. He travelled widely; in 1853, disguised as a Pathan, he went on a pilgrimage to Mecca. In 1857–59 he led an expedition into uncharted east central Africa to discover the source of the White NILE. It reached the great lakes of East Africa, but it was Burton's companion John SPEKE who made the final discovery. Later Burton explored West Africa and South America.

He drafted over 80 volumes on the sociology and anthropology of the countries he visited, most of which were published. He also published over 20 volumes of translations, including an unexpurgated translation of *The Arabian Nights*.

Burundi A small landlocked country on the east side of Lake Tanganyika in east central Africa. It is bounded to the north by Rwanda, to the east and south by Tanzania and to the west by the Democratic Republic of the Congo (Zaïre).

Physical. Burundi straddles the watershed of the Congo and the Nile Rivers, while the Ruzizi River in the west flows along the Great Rift Valley.

Economy. Burundi's economy depends heavily on coffee exports, with cotton and tea as subsidiary exports. The biggest sector of employment is subsistence agriculture. There are large unexploited nickel deposits, and uranium, vanadium, and gold. Industry is limited. Since the late 1980s the economy has been disrupted by endemic ethnic violence and an acute refugee problem.

History. Burundi was ruled as a monarchy in the 19th century by *Bami* (kings) of the Tutsi tribe, who dominated a population of Hutu. Germany annexed it as part of German East Africa in the 1890s and from 1914 it was administered by Belgium, which obtained a League of Nations MANDATE and ruled it as a part of Ruanda-Urundi. In 1962 it became independent and in 1964 its union with Ruanda (now Rwanda) was dissolved. Burundi became a republic after a coup in 1966, but tribal rivalries and violence obstructed the evolution of central government. There were military coups in 1976 and 1987, and renewed ethnic violence in 1988 that left 5,000 Hutu dead. In 1991 a referendum voted to restore the constitution with 'democracy within the single party'. President Pierre Buyoya (a Tutsi) increased the Hutu membership of his Council of Ministers, but violence continued with many seeking refuge in Zaïre and Rwanda. In 1992 a multiparty constitution was adopted. The first Hutu head of state, Melchior Ndadaye, was elected in 1993, along with a Hutu majority in the National Assembly, ending political dominance by the Tutsi. Tutsi army officers staged an unsuccessful coup six days after Ndadaye's election, but in a second coup a few months later killed Ndadaye and many other Hutu politicians. The coup triggered fierce ethnic violence and massacres throughout Burundi and over a million refugees fled their homes, many going to neighbouring countries. Ndadaye's successor, another Hutu, was killed in a plane crash in 1994. Violence and instability have continued, with ethnic killings reaching an average of 1,000 a month in 1996. In July of that year a Tutsi-led military coup ousted President Sylvestre Ntibantunganya and installed Pierre Buyoya in his place. In the ensuing months, Hutu rebels continued to wage war on the Tutsi regime.

CAPITAL:	Bujumbura
AREA:	27,834 sq km (10,747 sq miles)
POPULATION:	5.943 million (1995)
CURRENCY:	1 Burundi franc = 100 centimes
RELIGIONS:	Roman Catholic 62.0%; traditional beliefs 32.0%; Protestant 5.0%; Muslim 1.0%
ETHNIC GROUPS:	Rundi 96.4% (Hutu 81.9%; Tutsi 13.5%; Twa Pygmy 1.0%)
LANGUAGES:	Rundi, French (both official); Swahili
INTERNATIONAL ORGANIZATIONS:	UN; OAU

Bush, George (1924–) Forty-first President of the USA (1989–93). Son of a Connecticut banker and Senator, he served as a US navy pilot in World War II. In 1966 he was elected as a Republican to the House of Representatives, where he served until 1971, when President Nixon appointed him US ambassador to the UN. In 1974 he headed the Republican Party Committee which called on Nixon to resign. He headed the US Liaison Office in China (1974–75), and was then placed in charge of the CIA (1976–77). In 1980 he was elected Vice-President under Ronald Reagan, an office he held until his election as President in 1988. On taking office he was at once faced with the problem of the USA's vast balance-of-payments deficit. He gained considerable popularity in the USA for his intervention in Panama (1989–90), and won international backing for his decision to mount a campaign against Iraq, on the latter's invasion of Kuwait. The GULF WAR was followed by a 'Peace Process' for the Middle East, initiated by his Secretary of State, James Baker. During his presidency, private- and public-sector growth was more heavily based on borrowing than ever before; it was hoped that the NAFTA NORTH AMERICAN FREE TRADE AGREEMENT of 1992 might stimulate the economy. The country's economic problems contributed to his defeat by Bill CLINTON in the 1992 presidential elections.

bushido (Japanese, 'way of the warrior') The strict codes of behaviour, duties, and training of the SAMURAI, the traditional ruling warrior class of Japan. The *bushido* code was influenced by SHINTOISM, ZEN BUDDHISM, and CONFUCIANISM, but its predominant ideals were martial skills, including swordsmanship; duty to the emperor and feudal lords; and a strong emphasis on honour, which dominated everything from speech to ritual suicide or *seppuku* (less correctly termed hara-kiri). Bushido continues to provide inspirational models for modern Japanese capitalists.

bushrangers Law-breakers who lived in the Australian bush. The term came into use in the early 19th century and the first bushrangers were escaped convicts such as John DONAHOE. They often operated in well-organized gangs and attacked both White settlers and ABORIGINES. Bushranging was prevalent in Van Diemen's Land in the 1820s and 1830s. The main period of bushranging in the south-eastern colonies (where it was most common) was during the 1850s and 1860s.

busing (or **bussing**) An educational policy introduced in the USA in the 1960s. Children were taken by bus from Black, White, or Hispanic neighbourhoods, usually to suburban schools, in order to secure racially integrated schooling. The DESEGREGATION movement mainly affected the southern states, where busing was first introduced, against strong opposition from many White families. *De facto* segregation also existed in many northern cities, since the central areas were often inhabited entirely by Black people. In 1971 the Supreme Court approved the principle of busing but in 1972 Congress ordered that further schemes should be delayed. Busing remained a controversial issue and its use steadily declined as a means of racial integration.

Bustamante, Sir (William) Alexander (1884–1977) Jamaican statesman. He was a labour leader and founder of the Jamaican Labour Party, and became his country's first Prime Minister (1962–65) after independence from Britain in 1962. During this time he initiated an ambitious five-year plan which embraced major public works projects, agrarian reform, and social welfare.

Bustamante, Anastasio (1780–1853) Mexican statesman. As President of Mexico (1830–32, 1837–41) Bustamante posed as a champion of constitutionalism while violating Mexico's constitutions of 1824 and 1836. His regime was troubled by revolution and conflict with the French, who blockaded Vera Cruz (1838) as a means of obtaining compensation for damages suffered by French nationals.

Bute, John Stuart, 3rd Earl of (1713–92) Scottish courtier and statesman. He joined the household of Frederick, Prince of Wales, in 1747, and after Frederick's death exercised much influence over his widow Augusta and her son who became GEORGE III in 1760. The king appointed him Secretary of State in 1761, and in 1762 he succeeded the Elder PITT as Prime Minister. Bute was widely disliked and was lampooned by radicals such as WILKES. He resigned after forcing through the unpopular Treaty of PARIS and a contentious additional excise duty on cider. His influence with the king soon waned, and he retired from public life.

Buthelezi, Chief Mangosuthu Gatsha (1928–) South African politician and ethnic leader. A descendant of the 19th-century Zulu king CETSHWAYO, Buthelezi became chief of the Buthelezi tribe in 1953. In 1976 he was made chief minister of the KwaZulu BANTU HOMELAND; in the same year he founded the INKATHA FREEDOM PARTY. Buthelezi's policy of working within the apartheid system led to violent conflict between Inkatha and the AFRICAN NATIONAL CONGRESS (ANC). After initially boycotting South Africa's first multiracial elections in 1994, Inkatha eventually participated, winning 10% of the popular vote and control of the KwaZulu/Natal province. Buthelezi was appointed home affairs minister in the ANC-dominated government.

Butler, Joseph (1692–1752) British bishop and moral philosopher. He wrote *The Analogy of Religion* (1736), a defence of revealed religion against the deists and rationalists, whose attacks on Christianity were an important aspect of the ENLIGHTENMENT. Butler's own reasoning was rationalist in method, and he was much admired for coming as close to proving the existence of God by argument as would ever be possible. He is said to have declined the post of Archbishop of Canterbury in 1747, but became Bishop of Durham in 1750.

Butler, Josephine Elizabeth (Grey) (1828–1906) British social reformer. She is best known for her successful campaign against the Contagious Diseases Acts, whereby women operating as prostitutes were under regular police and medical inspection, which frequently exposed them to brutality and injustice. She was a keen supporter of higher education and social and political advancement for women. Settling with her husband in Liverpool in 1866, she devoted herself to the rescue and rehabilitation of prostitutes. She was also active in attempts to suppress the procuring of young girls for prostitution both in Britain and on the European mainland.

Butler of Saffron Walden, R(ichard) A(usten), Baron (1902–82) British statesman. He entered Parliament as a Conservative Member in 1929. During 1941–45 he was President of the Board of Education and was responsible for the Education Act of 1944, which laid down the framework for the post-war English free secondary education system and introduced the '11-plus' examination for the selection of grammar school children. He was an important influence in persuading the Conservative Party to accept the principles of the WELFARE STATE. Butler held several ministerial posts between 1951 and 1964, including Chancellor of the Exchequer (1951–55), but was defeated in the contest for the leadership of the Conservative Party by Harold MACMILLAN in 1957 and again by Sir Alec DOUGLAS-HOME in 1963. He became Master of Trinity College, Cambridge, and a life peer in 1965.

Buxar, Battle of (22 October 1764) A decisive battle fought at Buxar in north-east India, which confirmed the EAST INDIA COMPANY's control of Bengal and Bihar. Facing the Company were the combined forces of the MOGUL emperor (Shah Alam), the governor of Oudh (Shuja ad-Daula), and the dispossessed governor of Bengal (Mir Qasim). The Company's victory achieved recognition of its predominance in the region, demonstrated by the transfer of the *diwani* (revenue collecting powers) to the Company's agents in 1765.

Byng, George, Viscount Torrington (1663–1733) English admiral. He received promotion for his loyalty to William of Orange, and gained a great reputation for his successes in the War of the SPANISH SUCCESSION. His most famous battle was in 1718 at Cape Passaro, when he sank a Spanish fleet which was attempting to take Sicily.

His son **John Byng** (1704–57) owed his rapid and somewhat undeserved promotion to his father's influence. He was sent with an inadequate force in 1756 to save Minorca, then under siege by the French, and to protect Gibraltar, but returned to England having failed to do either. He was court-martialled for negligence and sentenced to death, providing a useful scapegoat for the government's mismanagement. His execution prompted Voltaire's famous remark that in England 'they like to shoot an admiral from time to time to encourage the others'.

Byzantine empire The eastern half of the Roman empire. Emperor CONSTANTINE (306–34) had reunited the two halves, divided by Diocletian (284–305), and had refounded the Greek city of Byzantium as his eastern capital, calling it CONSTANTINOPLE (330). At his death in 395 Emperor THEODOSIUS divided the empire between his sons. After the fall of Rome to the OSTROGOTHS (476) Constantinople was the capital of the empire and was famous for its art, architecture, and wealth. While barbarian invaders overran the Western empire, the Byzantine emperors always hoped to defeat them and reunite the empire. Emperor JUSTINIAN reconquered North Africa and part of Italy, making Ravenna the western capital, but his success was shortlived.

After MUHAMMAD's death (632) Muslim Arab forces swept through Persia and the Middle East, across North Africa, and into Spain. By 750 only the Balkans and Asia Minor remained unconquered. From the 9th century CHARLEMAGNE's Frankish empire dominated the West. In the 8th and 9th centuries religious disunity, notably the ICONCLASTIC CONTROVERSY, weakened the empire.

Theological and political differences between Rome and Constantinople led to the EAST-WEST SCHISM between Latin and Orthodox Christianity. (1054). The vigorous emperor Alexius COMNENUS (1081–1118) defeated barbarian attacks from the north and appealed to the Franks for help against the SELJUK Turks. In the 12th century, some reconquests were made in Asia Minor and the period was one of achievement in literature and art, only brought to an end by the Frankish sack of Constantinople in 1204. The failure to achieve any united Christian opposition to the Turks and the growing independence of the Balkan princedoms weakened the empire. Ottoman incursions in the 14th and 15th centuries culminated in the capture of Constantinople in 1453 and the end of the empire.

Byzantium CONSTANTINOPLE.

C

cabal A group or association of political intriguers. In England the term was generally pejoratively applied to the inner circle of the more important ministers, those who would be fully informed of all government secrets. Thus in the 17th century it was a precursor of the English CABINET, but in modern times the term is applied to any political group which pursues its aims by underhand methods. From 1667 to 1673 the word (though of older origin) was used somewhat misleadingly of Charles II's ministers, who did not really form a united group but the initials of whose names – Clifford, Ashley, Buckingham, Arlington, and Lauderdale – happened to spell CABAL.

Cabeza de Vaca, Alvar Núñez (c. 1490–c. 1557) Spanish soldier. He pursued a military career, serving in Europe before joining Pánfilo de NARVÁEZ in an expedition to Florida in 1527. When it failed, he and three other survivors spent ten years trekking 6,000 miles through the south of North America and back to New Spain. He hoped to command another expedition, but delays in returning to Spain lost him the opportunity. Instead he was made governor of Rio de La Plata, and led two 1,000-mile expeditions through the jungles and up the Rio Paraguay in 1541 and 1542. Arrested in 1543 by jealous colleagues, whom he had prohibited from looting and enslaving the local Indians, he was returned to Spain in chains. His sentence of eight years' exile in Africa was annulled, however, and a royal pension enabled him to write his *Commentarios* on his South American treks.

cabinet The group of ministers responsible for implementing government policy. The cabinet may make collective decisions, as it does in the UK and most European democracies, or it may have only an advisory status, as in the case of the President's cabinet in the USA. The size and membership of cabinets vary, but the holders of the major offices of state, such as the ministers responsible for finance, defence, and foreign affairs, are always included. In the USA, the cabinet consists of the heads of executive departments who are chosen by the President with the consent of the SENATE; they themselves are not members of CONGRESS. In countries which have coalition governments as a result of an electoral system of proportional representation, members of different parties may be represented in the cabinet. The UK cabinet has normally had around 20 members, chosen by the prime minister and appointed by the monarch, who are collectively responsible to Parliament for the policy and conduct of the government. The convention of collective responsibility means that all members of the cabinet must publicly support its policies or resign. Prime ministers in Australia and New Zealand have less discretion in cabinet selection. The kings of England always had advisers, but it was not until the RESTORATION in 1660 that a cabinet (or cabinet council) developed, consisting of the major office-bearers, and the king's most trusted members of the Privy Council, meeting as a committee in a private room (the cabinet, whence its name) and taking decisions without consulting the full Privy Council. In the time of Queen ANNE it became the main machinery of executive government and the Privy Council became formal. From about 1717 the monarch GEORGE I ceased to attend, and from that time the cabinet met independently. GEORGE III became obliged, through insanity and age, to leave more and more to his ministers, but it was not until after the Reform Act of 1832 that the royal power was dissolved and cabinets came to depend, for their existence and policies, upon the support of the majority in the House of Commons.

Cabot, John (or Giovanni Caboto) (c. 1450–98) Venetian navigator of Genoese origin, who at various times was in the service of Venice, England, and Spain. He was a successful merchant who settled in Bristol in 1484, hoping to find sponsors for a voyage in search of a route to the Orient across the Atlantic. Before he set out news came that COLUMBUS had already sailed and in 1496 HENRY VII granted him permission for a voyage of general exploration. In 1497 he set sail westwards in his small ship, *Matthew*, in search of a route to Cathay (China). On 24 June he reached the northern coast of North America, believing it to be north-east Asia, and took possession of the land for both the Venetian and the British kings. He set off on a second expedition to America in 1498, but his fleet was never heard of again. His son Sebastian Cabot (c. 1485–1557) led a Spanish expedition (1526) to La Plata in South America, but was turned back by hostile Indians on the Paraguay River. He was cartographer to King Henry VIII and in 1544 produced a notable map of the world as it was then known. He variously served in both the English and the Spanish armies and navies, and was expelled to Africa by the Spanish for disobeying orders. As Governor of the Merchant Adventurers in England, he organized an expedition to search for the North-East Passage from Europe to Asia. His efforts were ultimately to lead to the establishment of trade between Europe and Russia.

Cabral, Amilcar (1924–73) Guinean revolutionary. He founded a clandestine liberation organization against Portuguese rule. From 1963 to 1973 he led a successful guerrilla campaign which had gained control of much of the interior before he was assassinated, supposedly by a Portuguese agent. In the following year Portuguese Guinea became independent as GUINEA-BISSAU.

CACM CENTRAL AMERICAN COMMON MARKET.

Cadbury, George (1839–1922) British businessman and social reformer. A Quaker, he was part owner, with his brother Richard Cadbury (1835–99) of the cocoa and chocolate firm of Cadbury. They built the Bournville garden city estate near Birmingham, England, in 1885, for their employees. His concern for adult education and for the welfare of his workers set new standards in management. He and his wife, Elizabeth Cadbury

(1858–1935), herself a noted social worker and philanthropist, were influential in the improvement of housing and education, and in peace movements.

Cade, Jack (d. 1450) English rebel leader. In June 1450 he led a band of rebels from Kent in a protest against the financial oppression and general incompetence of HENRY VI's government. They occupied London for three days and put to death both the treasurer of England and the sheriff of Kent. Their rising differed from the PEASANTS' REVOLT of 1381 in having considerable support from the landed classes and clearer aims, but like Wat TYLER, Cade was captured and killed.

Cadwalader (or Cadwallon) (d. 633) King of Gwynedd, north Wales. His hatred of the Anglo-Saxon kingdom of NORTHUMBRIA intensified when his attempts at invasion (629) failed and he was forced to flee to Ireland. Although a Christian, he next allied with the heathen King PENDA of Mercia. Their victory at Hatfield Chase (632) over Edwin of Northumbria was followed by the devastation of Northumbria. Thereafter Northumbrian fortunes recovered and Cadwalader was killed in battle by Edwin's nephew Oswald at Heavenfield, near Hexham.

Caesar, Gaius Julius *This Roman coin, dating from c. 55 BC, bears the profile of Julius Caesar. The Latin inscription reads 'Ceasar, perpetual dictator.'*

Caesar, Gaius Julius (100–44 BC) Roman general and dictator. Born into a PATRICIAN FAMILY, he became Pontifex Maximus (High Priest) in 63 BC as part of a deal with POMPEY and CRASSUS, the so-called 'First Triumvirate'; as consul in 59 he obtained the provinces of Illyricum and Cisalpine and Transalpine GAUL. A superb general, able to inspire loyalty in his soldiers, he subjugated Gaul, crossed the River Rhine, and made two expeditions to Britain. He refused to surrender command until he had secured a second consulship for 48 BC, which would render him immune from prosecution by his enemies, by now including Pompey. When the Senate delivered

an ultimatum in January 49, he crossed the RUBICON, took Rome, and defeated Pompey at PHARSALUS in 48. He demonstrated clemency by permitting those who wished to do so to return to Italy. After campaigns in Asia Minor, Egypt, Africa, and Spain he returned to Rome in 45.

He governed Rome as dictator, finally as 'perpetual' dictator. His wide-ranging programme of reform, which included the institution of the Julian Calendar, reveals his breadth of vision, but he flaunted his ascendancy and ignored republican traditions. It was alleged that he wanted to be king, although this was anathema to the Romans. A conspiracy was formed, led by BRUTUS and Cassius, and he was assassinated on the Ides (15th) of March 44. He was later deified and a temple was dedicated to his worship in the Forum.

Caesars A branch of the aristocratic Roman Julia clan, the name of which passed from its most famous member Julius CAESAR to become an imperial title. Julius Caesar had no legitimate sons, and his young son Caesarion (by Cleopatra) was not recognized in Roman law. Octavian AUGUSTUS took the name as Caesar's adoptive son. It was used by the Julio-Claudian dynasty until the line died out with NERO in 68. All succeeding Roman emperors adopted it, conferring the title on their designated heirs so that it came to signify a 'prince'. The title was used in the Eastern empire as 'Kaisaros'. From this were later derived the imperial Russian and German titles Tsar and Kaiser.

Caetano, Marcello José das Neves Alves (1904–81) Portuguese statesman. As Minister for the Colonies in 1944 he drafted the law which integrated overseas territories with metropolitan Portugal. He was Prime Minister from 1968 to 1974. He was ousted from power by General Spinola in 1974 in a *putsch* which brought to an end half a century of dictatorship in Portugal, established by Caetano's predecessor, SALAZAR.

Cairo Conference (22–26 November 1943) A World War II meeting, attended by ROOSEVELT, CHURCHILL, and CHIANG KAI-SHEK, to decide on post-war policy for the Far East. Unconditional surrender by Japan was its prerequisite; Manchuria was to be returned to China, and Korea to its own people. At a second conference Roosevelt and Churchill met President INÖNÜ of Turkey, and confirmed that country's independence. The TEHERAN CONFERENCE was held immediately afterwards.

Caledonia The Roman name for Scotland north of the ANTONINE WALL, approximating to the Scottish Highlands. In 83 AD the governor of Britain, Agricola, invaded the territory of the Caledonii, ancestors of the later PICTS and defeated them, though they remained a constant threat to the Roman frontier in Britain, necessitating a further campaign by SEVERUS.

calendar Any system for fixing the beginning, length, order, and subdivisions of the year. Calendrical systems have been used by societies since the earliest times, nearly all of them based on one of two astronomical cycles: the cycle of the phases of the Moon (the synodic month or lunation), often of major ritual and religious significance, and the cycle of the seasons (the period of the Earth's orbit around the Sun), of importance in agriculture. The two cycles are incompatible in that the synodic month has a period of about 29.5 days, giving a lunar year (12 months) of just over 354 days, over 11 days shorter than the mean solar year of 365.2422 days. In most societies the lunar calendar, in which the month, not the year, is the basic interval, was the first to be used, and different systems were developed to reconcile this cycle with that of the seasons. The early Egyptians had two completely separate calendars running concurrently, one for religious purposes and one for agricultural use. A particular year was identified by reference to a king or official. For some early calendars the correspondence between the seasons and the phases of the Moon was secondary and an uninterrupted ritual cycle was of prime importance. For example, the Mayan civilization of Central America had two calendars: a ritual cycle of 260 days, formed by combining the numbers 1–13 with 20 days names, and a yearly cycle of 365 days consisting of 18 months of 20 days each and 5 additional days. The two cycles ran concurrently. The beginnings of the two cycles came into coincidence every 52 years, this being exactly 72 ritual cycles. By specifying a date in both systems it was possible to identify that date uniquely within this 52-year period. The Mayan civilization maintained this calendar over several millennia. For the Babylonians the first appearance of the new crescent moon in the western evening sky fixed the beginning of a new month, days being reckoned to begin at sunset. The average length of these months was therefore the synodic month, and the normal year had 12 months, that is, about 354 days. In order to maintain the correspondence of the calendar to the seasons an additional month was intercalated (added) as necessary. Usually the last month of the year (Adaru) was simply repeated. At first these intercalations were carried out empirically but by the early 4th century BC definite rules had been established based on the Metonic cycle, in which 19 years is equated to 235 months and to 6,940 days.

The earliest ancient Roman calendar had only ten lunar months, with March as its first month, although in 153 BC the calendar New Year was transferred to 1 January. The pontiffs inserted an extra month when necessary to keep the years in line with the solar year. Originally, therefore, September to December were months seven to ten as their names suggest. The two previous months were originally named Quintilis (fifth) and Sextilis (sixth) but were renamed July and August in honour of Julius Caesar and Augustus Caesar. The years were numbered from the foundation of the city (AUC, *ab urbe condita*), traditionally 753 BC, or, more usually, calculated by reference to the names of the consuls in office and emperors' reigns. Each month had three named days, the Kalends (1st), Nones (5th or 7th), and Ides (13th or 15th). The Julian calendar was introduced to the Roman Empire by Julius Caesar in 46 BC. It was developed from the traditional Roman lunar calendar, as is evident from its division into 12 months. However, the months no longer corresponded to lunations, as days were added to give a total year length of 365 days. Almost exact correspondence with the mean solar year was maintained by the intercalation of a leap year containing an extra day, on 29 February, every four years. The average length of the year was therefore 365.25 days which is only slightly longer than the length of the mean solar year. The discrepancy however amounted to one day in 128 years, and by the 16th century it was found that the vernal equinox was occurring about ten days early. The Gregorian

calendar, first introduced in 1582 by Pope Gregory XIII and in almost universal civil use today, superseded, with only slight modification, the Julian calendar. The Gregorian reform of 1582 omitted ten days from the calendar that year, the day after 4 October becoming 15 October. This restored the vernal equinox to 21 March and, to maintain this, three leap years are now suppressed every 400 years, centurial years ceasing to be leap years unless they are divisible by 400. For example, 1900 was not a leap year but 2000 is. The average length of the calendar year is now reduced to 365.2425 days, so close to the mean solar year that no adjustment will be required before 5000 AD. The Gregorian calendar was devised principally as a basis for fixing the date of Easter and therefore the whole ecclesiastical calendar. As such it was adopted at once in predominantly Roman Catholic countries but only gradually over the next two centuries in the Protestant countries of Western Europe. Britain came into line in 1752 by striking out 11 days. The Russians persisted with the old calendar until 1918. The Gregorian calendar only became established for international transactions early in the 20th century.

The system of numbering years from the beginning of the Christian era was introduced by a Roman monk, Dionysius Exiguus, in 525 AD. This system was soon generally adopted in Western Europe. In different countries, however, a variety of dates was adopted as the first day of the New Year, the most common choices, apart from 1 January, being 25 December, 1 March, and 25 March, and these differences persisted as late as the 18th century. The names of the months are of Roman origin.

Other calendrical systems continue to be used, particularly for religious purposes, alongside the Gregorian system. The present Jewish calendar uses the 19-year Metonic cycle made up of 12 common years and seven leap years. The common years have 12 months, each of 29 or 30 days, while the leap years have an additional month. The rules governing the detailed construction of the calendar are very complicated but the year begins on the first day of Tishri, an autumn month. Years are reckoned from the era of creation (*anno mundi*) for which the epoch adopted is 7 October 3761 BC. Thus the year beginning in autumn 1988 was AM 5749. The Islamic calendar is wholly lunar, the year always containing 12 months without intercalation. This means that the Muslim New Year occurs seasonally about 11 days earlier each year. The months have alternately 30 and 29 days and are fixed in length, except for the twelfth month (Dulheggia) which has one intercalatory day in 11 years out of a cycle of 30 calendar years. This period of 360 months amounts to 10,631 days which differs from 360 lunations by only 17.3 minutes. So, although the Islamic calendar bears no relation to the solar year, it is, within its own lunar terms of reference, of an accuracy comparable to the Gregorian calendar. The years in the Islamic calendar are reckoned from the Hegira, the flight of Mohammed, which was 16 July 622 (Julian calendar).

The week, unlike the day, month, or year, is an artificial device with no astronomical origin. First introduced by the Babylonians, it became established in the Christian era only when it was linked to the Julian calendar by Constantine in 321 AD. As a continuously uninterrupted cycle it can be useful in removing ambiguities. The ancient Chinese had a similar system of day naming but in cycles of 60 that were unaffected by any intercalation. As the day name is usually included with the date in Chinese records, it is possible to verify the exact epoch of early Chinese chronology.

Calhoun, John Caldwell (1782–1850) US statesman. He was elected to Congress in 1811. As a leader of the 'War Hawks', Calhoun committed the USA to the WAR OF 1812. He served as Secretary of War under President MONROE (1817–25), and as Vice-President to both John Quincy Adams (1825–29) and JACKSON (1829–32). The leading advocate of STATES' RIGHTS, he was the main architect of the theory of NULLIFICATION which led to the NULLIFICATION crisis of 1832–3. Calhoun was the spokesman of Southern interests who saw a North-South confrontation as inevitable. He served briefly as Secretary of State under TYLER (1844–45) before returning to the Senate.

Caligula (Gaius Julius Caesar Germanicus) (12–41 AD) Roman Emperor (37–41). His nickname derived from the miniature army-boots (*caligae*) which he wore as a child when his father Germanicus was commander-in-chief on the Rhine. He was the great-grandson of both AUGUSTUS and MARK ANTONY, and the great-nephew and successor of TIBERIUS. His reign was brief, bloody, and authoritarian, scarred by mental instability, personal excesses, and delusions of divinity. He was murdered in his palace together with his (fourth) wife and only child.

caliphate Formerly the central ruling office of Islam. The first caliph (Arabic, *khalifa*, 'deputy of God' or 'successor of his Prophet') after the Prophet Muhammad's death in 632 was his father-in-law ABU BAKR, and he was followed by UMAR, UTHMAN, and Ali: these four are called the Rashidun (rightly guided) caliphs. When Ali died in 661 SHIITE Muslims recognized his successors, the imams, as rightful possessors of the Prophet's authority, the rest of Islam accepting the UMAYYAD dynasty. They were overthrown in 750 by the ABBASIDS, but within two centuries they were virtually puppet rulers under Turkish control. Meanwhile an Umayyad refugee had established an independent emirate in Spain in 756 which survived for 250 years, and in North Africa a Shiite caliphate arose under the FATIMIDS, the imams of the Ismailis (909–1171). After the Mongols sacked Baghdad in 1258 the caliphate, now only a name, passed to the MAMELUKE rulers of Egypt, and from the OTTOMAN conquest of Egypt in 1517 the title was assumed by the Turkish sultans, until its abolition in 1924.

Callaghan, James (1912–   ) British Labour Prime Minister (1976–79). He was previously Chancellor of the Exchequer (1964–67), Home Secretary (1967–70), and Foreign Secretary (1974–76). During his ministry relations with the rest of the EUROPEAN ECONOMIC COMMUNITY remained cool: some members of the cabinet were opposed to Britain's continued membership. Domestically the government could not command a majority in the House of Commons. An agreement was therefore entered into with the Liberal Party – the 'Lib–Lab Pact' (1977–78). Partly to meet Liberal interests devolution bills were introduced for Scotland and Wales, though they were rejected in referenda (1979). The government's position became weakened by widespread strikes in the so-called 'winter of discontent' (1978–79) in protest at attempts to restrain wages and it was

defeated in the House of Commons on the devolution issue. The Conservatives won the election with a large majority, under Margaret THATCHER.

Calles, Plutarco Elías (1877–1945) Mexican statesman. He achieved prominence as a military leader during the MEXICAN REVOLUTION. As President of Mexico (1924–28), Calles implemented Mexico's constitution (1917) by supporting agrarian reform, organized labour, economic nationalism, and education. During 1928–34, although not in office himself, he continued to exert a powerful influence. This period, known as the *maximato* or chieftainship, was not as successful as the Calles administration itself and caused his reputation to suffer.

Calvin, John (1509–64) French theologian, the leading figure in the second generation of PROTESTANT reformers. He was the son of a clerk and was educated at Paris, Orleans, and Bourges. About 1533 he became a convert to the reformed faith. His *Institutes of the Christian Religion* (1536) was a lucid exposition of Reformed theology, minimizing the freedom of the human will. This was followed by his *Ecclesiastical Ordinances* (1541), in which he set forth a form of Church government which subsequently became a model for PRESBYTERIANS.

From 1536 to 1564, with a three-year interval in Strasburg from 1538, he devoted himself to imposing his version of liturgy, Church organization, doctrine, and moral behaviour upon the Swiss city of Geneva. It became a haven and inspiration for many European Protestants, and a base for worldwide missionary activity. Calvin's creed was particularly influential in France, the Netherlands, and Scotland. It also formed the bedrock of the PURITAN movement in England and North America. The Calvinist doctrines of predestination (God's foreordaining of what will come to pass) and legitimate resistance to 'ungodly authority' gave encouragement to Protestants who found themselves suffering at the hands of unsympathetic lay rulers.

Cambodia A tropical country in south-east Asia flanked by Thailand, Laos, and Vietnam.

Physical. Through it from the north flows the Mekong, while westward is a large lake, the Tonlé Sap. The climate is tropical monsoon, and most of the land marshy or forested, providing good crops of rice and timber. A short coastline faces south-west on the Gulf of Thailand.

Economy. Cambodia's economy is overwhelmingly agricultural, and rubber is a major export. There is limited light industry. The prolonged civil war and the KHMER ROUGE regime's policies of enforced resettlement decimated agriculture, and caused a sharp drop in productivity of rice, the staple crop. The economy is being rebuilt with the help of foreign aid donations.

History. Cambodia was occupied from the 1st to the 6th century AD by the Hindu kingdoms of Funan, and subsequently Chenla. The KHMER people overthrew the Hindu rulers of Chenla and established a Buddhist empire, centred around the region of ANGKOR. The classical, or Angkorean, period lasted from 802 to 1432, with the Kmer empire reaching its peak during the 12th century. After 1432 the empire went into decline and suffered frequent invasions from Vietnam and Thailand. Continuing foreign domination forced Cambodia to seek French protection in 1863, and from 1884 it was treated as part of FRENCH INDO-CHINA, although allowed to retain its royal dynasty. After Japanese occupation in World War II, King Norodom SIHANOUK achieved independence within the French Union (1949) and full independence in 1953. Sihanouk abdicated in 1955 to form a broad-based coalition government. Cambodia was drawn into the VIETNAM WAR in the 1960s, and US suspicions of Sihanouk's relations with communist forces led to his overthrow by the army under Lon Nol in 1970, following a US bombing offensive (1969–70) and invasion. The Lon Nol regime renamed Cambodia the Khmer Republic. The regime soon came under heavy pressure from the communist Khmer Rouge. Following the fall of Phnom Penh in 1975, the Khmer Rouge under POL POT renamed the country Democratic Kampuchea and launched a bloody reign of terror, which is estimated to have resulted in as many as two million deaths, or nearly a third of the population. Border tensions led to an invasion of the country by Vietnam in 1978, and the overthrow of the Pol Pot regime two weeks later. The Vietnamese installed a client regime under an ex-Khmer Rouge member, Heng Samrin, who proclaimed a new People's Republic of Kampuchea, but conflict with Khmer Rouge guerrillas continued. International relief organizations were active in Cambodia from 1980. A government in exile comprising anti-Vietnamese factions and led by Son Sann, the Coalition Government of Democratic Kampuchea (CGDK), was recognized by the United Nations in 1983. Civil war lasted until 1987, when inconclusive peace talks were held in Paris. These later moved to Jakarta, and in 1991 resulted in a peace agreement to end 13 years of civil strife. A UN Transitional Authority enforced a ceasefire and installed an interim Supreme Council, under Prince Norodom Sihanouk as head of state. The Council included representatives of the former pro-Vietnamese government, the Cambodian People's Party, now led by Hun Sen, and the three former guerrilla movements: the Party of Democratic Kampuchea (Khmer Rouge), whose former leader Pol Pot retained considerable influence; the Khmer People's National Liberation Front, led by Son Sann; and the National United Front, led by Norodom Ranariddh, son of Prince Sihanouk. Multiparty elections were held in 1993, and UN peace-keepers supervised the process and helped to repatriate and rehabilitate some half million refugees and released prisoners. No party won a clear majority of seats, but a democratic monarchist constitution was adopted, and Sihanouk became king (1993), with his son, Prince Norodom Ranariddh, as executive prime minister and Hun Sen as second prime minister. The Khmer Rouge refused to participate in the elections and continued to launch guerrilla attacks. In 1996 moves by some Khmer Rouge leaders to seek peace with the government led to a violent split in the movement, culminating in 1997 in the capture and imprisonment of Pol Pot, who died in 1998. Meanwhile rifts in the ruling coalition led to open fighting in July 1997, when supporters of Hun Sen ousted Prince Ranariddh, who fled the country.

CAPITAL: Phnom Penh
AREA: 181,035 sq km (69,898 sq miles)
POPULATION: 10.081 million (1996)
CURRENCY: 1 riel = 100 sen
RELIGIONS: Buddhist 88.4%; Muslim 2.4%
ETHNIC GROUPS: Khmer 88.1%; Chinese 4.6%; Vietnamese 4.6%
LANGUAGES: Khmer (official); Chinese; Vietnamese; French
INTERNATIONAL
ORGANIZATIONS: UN; Colombo Plan

Cambrai, League of (1508) An alliance of the PAPACY, the HOLY ROMAN EMPIRE, France, and Spain against VENICE. In 1529 the 'Ladies' Peace (the Peace of Cambrai) temporarily halted the Habsburg–Valois wars.

Camden, Battle of (16 August 1780) A battle of the American War of INDEPENDENCE in which some 2,000 American militiamen under Horatio GATES were defeated when attacked by CORNWALLIS's army 193 km (120 miles) north-north-west of Charleston, South Carolina. Gates was replaced by Nathanael GREENE as commander of the Southern Army, which revenged itself at the Battle of King's Mountain in October.

Cameroon A country in West Africa, with Nigeria and Chad to its west and north, the Central African Republic to its east, and Gabon and Congo to the south.

Physical. Most of the coastline is low, with creeks, lagoons, and swamps, although near Mount Cameroon, an active volcano, there are steep cliffs. The coastal plain is hot and very wet and covered with thick rain forest. Inland this becomes open woodland and then savannah as the ground rises to the plateau that makes up most of the country.

Economy. Crude oil is the largest export, followed by cocoa and coffee. Mineral deposits include oil and natural gas, gold, uranium, bauxite, nickel, and cobalt. Industries include aluminium smelting (from imported bauxite and alumina), food-processing, and brewing. Half the land is forested but poor transportation has restricted its development.

History. The Portuguese and other Europeans who explored Cameroon in the 15th and 16th centuries found that it was mainly uninhabited, but it was believed to be the original home of the Bantu. About 1810 King Mbwé-Mbwé walled his capital, Fomban, against the FULANI EMPIRE. Other peoples set up small kingdoms. Germans began trading c. 1860, and signed protectorate treaties in 1884. The German Protectorate of Kamerun was confirmed by the Franco-German Treaty of 1911, but in 1916 Anglo-French forces occupied it. From 1919 it was administered under LEAGUE OF NATIONS (later UN) trusteeship, having been divided into British and French MANDATES. In 1960 the French Cameroons became an independent republic, to be joined in 1961 by part of the British Cameroons, the remainder becoming part of Nigeria. The French and British territories in 1972 merged as the United Republic of Cameroon, later renamed the Republic of Cameroon. It was from 1972 a one-party republic ruled by the Cameroon People's Democratic Movement, from 1982 under President Paul Biya. Legislation providing for multiparty government was adopted in 1990 and, following strikes, demonstrations, and unrest through 1991, President Biya finally held elections in 1992. His party failed to win an overall majority and a coalition government was formed. Biya was re-elected in presidential elections (also held in 1992) but the result was rejected by opponents, who alleged that fraud had taken place. Political unrest continued. Cameroon applied to join the COMMONWEALTH OF NATIONS in 1993 and was accepted in 1995: the 25th member of the Commonwealth, Cameroon was the first never to have been fully under British rule.

CAPITAL:	Yaoundé
AREA:	475,458 sq km (179,714 sq miles)
POPULATION:	13.609 million (1995)
CURRENCY:	1 CFA franc = 100 centimes
RELIGIONS:	Roman Catholic 35.0%; traditional religions 25.0%; Muslim 22.0%; Protestant 18.0%
ETHNIC GROUPS:	Bamileke 27.0%; Beti-Pahonin 18.0%; Kirdi 15.0%; Fulani 9.5%; Bassa Bakoko 8.0%; Baya Mbum 6.0%
LANGUAGES:	French, English (both official); Bati-Pahonin, Bamileke, and almost one hundred other languages and dialects
INTERNATIONAL ORGANIZATIONS:	UN; Commonwealth; OAU; Non-Aligned Movement; Franc Zone

Camisards French Protestants, who in 1702 defied LOUIS XIV in the Cévennes, a mountainous region of southern France with a strong tradition of independence. The loss of their leaders in 1704 was followed by a period of savage persecution, but the rebels were bought off rather than defeated, and the authorities subsequently preferred to leave the area largely alone. Their name may come from the 'camise' or shirt they wore over their clothes.

Campaign for Nuclear Disarmament (CND) A British pressure group pledged to nuclear disarmament, including the unilateral abandonment of British nuclear weapons. CND was created in 1958 with the philosopher Bertrand Russell as President. Frustration at the lack of progress led to the creation of a splinter-group, the Committee of 100, led by Russell and pledged to civil disobedience. From 1963 to 1980 CND was in eclipse. It revived in 1980–84 mainly as a protest against the deployment of US cruise missiles at Greenham Common. In 1980 European Nuclear Disarmament (END) was formed, linking closely with dissident groups in Eastern Europe. Similar movements developed in France, Germany, Australasia, and the USA. Since the end of the COLD WAR, the main focus has been the prevention of nuclear proliferation.

Campbell-Bannerman, Sir Henry (1836–1908) British statesman. He was Prime Minister of a Liberal government (1906–08). As Secretary of State for War (1895) he secured the removal of the Duke of Cambridge as army commander-in-chief but failed to introduce any far-reaching army reforms. His brief premiership ended in 1908 with his resignation and death, but it included the grant of self-government for the TRANSVAAL and ORANGE FREE STATE in South Africa, support of the important 1906 Trade Disputes Act, the army reforms of HALDANE, and the Anglo-Russian *entente cordiale* in 1907.

Camp David Accord (1978) A Middle East peace agreement. It was named after the official country house of the US President in Maryland, where President CARTER met President SADAT of Egypt and Prime Minister BEGIN of Israel to negotiate a settlement of the disputes between the two countries. Peace was made between Egypt and Israel after some 30 years of conflict, and provisions were agreed for an Israeli withdrawal from Egyptian territory. This agreement did not bring about peace with the other Arab countries. Instead it led increasingly to Egypt being isolated from its Arab neighbours.

Camperdown, Battle of (11 October 1797) A naval battle fought off the coast of Holland in which the British fleet destroyed the Dutch fleet. The Dutch tried to lure the British commander on to the shoals, but he accepted the risk, chased them, and captured nine ships. This victory, and the defeat of the Spanish fleet in February at CAPE ST VINCENT, ended NAPOLEON's hopes of invading England and enabled PITT THE YOUNGER to negotiate the formation of another coalition.

Campion, Edmund, St (1540–81) English JESUIT scholar and Catholic martyr. He was ordained in the Church of England in 1568. In 1571 he left England for Douai in the Low Countries, where he joined the Roman Catholic Church; in Rome, two years later, he became a Jesuit. In 1580 he participated in the first secret Jesuit mission to England. Although he claimed that he came only to teach and minister to the Catholic community, he was arrested, tortured, tried, and executed for treason.

Canaan An ancient name for PALESTINE, the 'Promised Land' of the Israelites, promised by their God to ABRAHAM and his descendants. The Canaanites inhabited the area by about 2000 BC and from 1500 BC were periodically subject to the Egyptians and Hittites. The arrival of the Israelites in the 13th century BC following their EXODUS from Egypt and their gradual conquest of the area confined the Canaanites to the coastal strip of PHOENICIA. The region was to suffer further invasions, but under the leadership of King David (10th century BC) the Israelites secured control over all other groups. The religion of the Canaanites, including the worship of local deities called Baals, sacred prostitution, child sacrifice, and frenzied prophecy, all incurred the condemnation of the Hebrew prophets, particularly in the 9th century BC the period of ELIJAH and Elisha.

Canada The second largest country of the world, occupying the whole of the northern part of North America except for Alaska and bounded by three oceans: the Pacific on the west, the Arctic on the north, and the Atlantic on the east. Canada is a federation of ten North American provinces (Alberta, British Columbia, Manitoba, New Brunswick, Newfoundland, Nova Scotia, Ontario, Prince Edward Island, Quebec, Saskatchewan), the Yukon Territory, and the Northwest Territories.

Physical. Canada's southern boundary crosses the Rocky Mountains and continues eastward on latitude 49° N to the Great Lakes and the Saint Lawrence, and then crosses the northern Appalachian Mountains to join the sea along the Saint Croix River. While the Saint Lawrence is Canada's most important river, the Mackenzie in the north-west is the longest and the Fraser in the south-west the most beautiful. Northern Canada is a land of lakes, wide and winding rivers, low tundra vegetation, and dark coniferous forests. Snow lies for six to nine months in the year and there is much permafrost, making building and mining difficult and agriculture impossible. The west coast, with its mild climate and salmon rivers, is scored by fiords and over-hung by snow-capped mountains. Inland, the main Rocky Mountain chain yields rich mineral deposits, and its deep, sheltered valleys with hot, dry summers produce crops of vines and peaches. Through its eastern foothills, a major area of cattle-ranching and oil production, the land falls gently eastward to the prairies. This is the heart of the country and a vast grain-growing region, despite a harsh climate of very

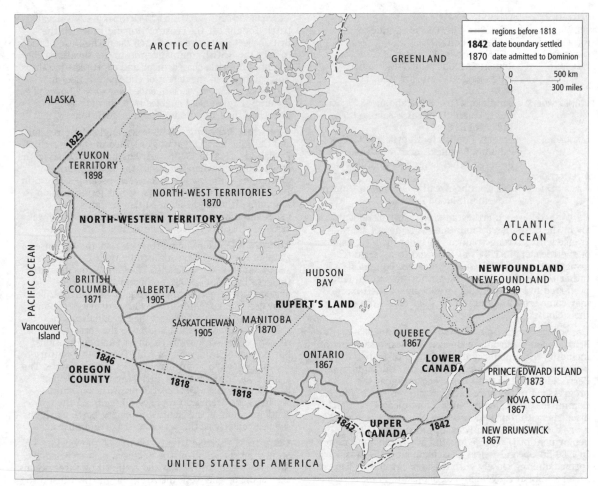

regions before 1818
1842 date boundary settled
1870 date admitted to Dominion

Canada *Following the American War of Independence (1775–83) many loyalists to the British crown moved north into the British colonies of Quebec and Nova Scotia. As the 19th century progressed, Canada evolved from colonial to dominion status (1867), establishing complete national sovereignty in 1982. The 20th century has seen an influx of immigrants from central and southern Europe to add to the earlier settlers of mainly French and British descent, the majority of residents of Quebec remaining Roman Catholic and French-speaking. Those descendants of the country's earlier inhabitants, the Indians and Inuits (Eskimos) who have not been attracted to the industrial south live in scattered settlements.*

cold winters and very warm but short summers. Huge mineral deposits exist here too. To the east lies the lowland of the Canadian Shield, also rich in minerals and covered by a mosaic of lakes and forest. Eastward again, between Lakes Huron, Erie, and Ontario, are rich farming lands. The land becomes more hilly in Quebec and the easternmost maritime provinces, and farmers concentrate on orchard crops. Fishing is an important activity as the waters of the North Atlantic Ocean are well stocked: this coast is less rugged than the west, but the cool, damp climate and poor, rocky ground limit agriculture. To the north are the plateaus of Labrador, and its huge deposits of iron ore and other minerals.

Economy. A leading industrial nation, Canada depends on the neighbouring USA, with whom it signed a free-trade agreement in 1989, for about 75% of its trade. Major exports include motor vehicles (assembled from imported components), machinery, crude oil, timber, natural gas, non-ferrous metals, chemicals, and

newsprint. Canada is the world's largest producer of zinc, nickel, and uranium and is rich in many other minerals. A little more than half the country's electricity comes from hydroelectric generation. Canadian agriculture is diverse, with extensive grain, dairy, and fruit-farming as well as ranching and fur-farming.

History. Originally inhabited by NATIVE AMERICANS and by Inuit in the far north, in the 10th century VIKINGS established a settlement at L'ANSE AUX MEADOWS. John CABOT landed in Labrador, Newfoundland, or Cape Breton Island, in 1497 and in 1534 Jacques CARTIER claimed the land for France. The first French settlement was begun by fur traders in Acadia (now NOVA SCOTIA) in 1604. In 1608 Samuel de CHAMPLAIN founded QUEBEC on the St Lawrence River. Governor FRONTENAC defended Quebec against Sir William Phips (1691) and led a successful campaign against the hostile IROQUOIS (1696). Explorers followed the routes of the Great Lakes and the

Mississippi Valley — LA SALLE reached the mouth of the Mississippi in 1682 — and the name Canada came to be used interchangeably with that of NEW FRANCE, which referred to all French possessions in North America. Conflict between Britain and France was mirrored in Canada in the FRENCH AND INDIAN WARS. By the Peace of UTRECHT (1713) France gave up most of Acadia, Newfoundland, and Hudson Bay. The remainder of New France was conquered by Britain and ceded in 1763. During or immediately after the American War of INDEPENDENCE some 40,000 UNITED EMPIRE LOYALISTS arrived in Nova Scotia (formerly Acadia) and present-day Ontario. St John's Island was renamed Prince Edward Island in 1799 and Cape Breton Island was joined to Nova Scotia in 1820. In 1791 Quebec was divided into UPPER AND LOWER CANADA, but following the Act of Union of 1840 the two were reunited to form the Province of Canada. Two frontier agreements were made with the USA: the WEBSTER–ASHBURTON TREATY (1842) and a treaty ending the OREGON BOUNDARY DISPUTE (1846). Fears of US expansion led to the British North America Act (1867), creating the Dominion of Canada. The new dominion acquired full responsibility for home affairs. In 1870 the Hudson's Bay Company's lands around the Red River were formed into the Province of Manitoba, while the Northwest Territories passed from control of the Company to the federal government. In 1873 Prince Edward Island joined the Confederation, British Columbia, including Vancouver Island, having done so in 1871. This had been on the promise of a CANADIAN PACIFIC RAILWAY, which was completed in 1885, enabling prairie wheat to flow east for export. Britain gave Canada title to the arctic islands in 1880. In 1896 the Yukon boomed briefly with the Klondike GOLD RUSH. In 1905 Alberta and Saskatchewan became federated provinces. Newfoundland joined the dominion in 1949. The Hudson's Bay Company gradually ceded all the lands for which it was responsible, but as a corporation it has retained a significant place in the Canadian economy. As the provinces developed, so did their strength *vis-à-vis* the central federal government, a strongly centralized political system being resisted. In 1982 the British Parliament accepted the 'patriation' of the British North America Act to Canada, establishing the complete national sovereignty of Canada, although it retained allegiance to the British crown as well as membership of the COMMONWEALTH OF NATIONS. Constitutional disputes continued through the 1980s and 1990s, with Newfoundland, Manitoba, and Quebec all rejecting proposed solutions, the latter insisting on 'distinct society' status, but rejecting independence in a provincial referendum in 1980. In 1992 Canada signed the NORTH AMERICAN FREE TRADE AGREEMENT. In the general election of 1993 the ruling Conservatives suffered a humiliating defeat by the Liberal Party under Jean CHRÉTIEN, retaining only two seats. The Bloc Québécois (Quebec separatists) became the official opposition. In a referendum in 1995 voters in Quebec only narrowly voted to reject secession from the Union. Chrétien and his party were returned to power in 1997 with a reduced majority.

CAPITAL: Ottawa
AREA: 9,970,610 sq km (3,849,675 sq miles)
POPULATION: 29.784 million (1995)
CURRENCY: 1 Canadian dollar = 100 cents
RELIGIONS: Roman Catholic 46.5%; Protestant 41.2%; non-religious 7.4%; Eastern Orthodox 1.5%; Jewish 1.2%; Muslim 0.4%; Hindu 0.3%; Sikh 0.3%
ETHNIC GROUPS: (by origin) British 34.4%; French 25.7%; German 3.6%; Italian 2.8%; Ukrainian 1.7%; Amerindian and Inuit (Eskimo) 1.5%; Chinese 1.4%; Dutch 1.4%
LANGUAGES: English, French (both official)
INTERNATIONAL
ORGANIZATIONS: UN; Commonwealth; OECD; NATO; OAS; CSCE; NAFTA

Canadian Pacific Railway The first transcontinental railway in Canada. Proposed in the 1840s, the idea was revived in 1871 on condition that British Columbia entered the new Confederation of Canada. Preparations for its undertaking led to the PACIFIC SCANDAL of 1873, when the Prime Minister, Sir John A. MACDONALD, was forced to resign. His return to office in 1878 brought the railway its charter: the line was completed in 1885.

canal An artificial waterway built for navigational purposes, for water supply, or for land drainage. Ship canals such as the PANAMA CANAL and the SUEZ CANAL are made for sea-going vessels. Canals built for inland navigation are much smaller and generally used by canal barges. In the late 18th and early 19th centuries hundreds of miles of canals were built by pick and shovel in Britain, the USA, and Europe to carry raw materials, and manufactured goods. Obstacles such as hills are negotiated by building the canal along the contours of the land wherever possible. However, it is occasionally necessary to tunnel beneath hills, or to climb over broad, high hills using locks. Where the slope is steep, a flight of locks is used, in which one lock's upper gate acts as the next lock's lower gate. This series of small rises reduces the water pressure on the gates. Very steep slopes require a canal lift: a wheeled container, large enough to carry a barge, that is winched up or down an incline. Water is fed into the summit of a canal either from reservoirs or by diverting river water. Narrow barges were at first towed along a footpath by horses, but later had their own steam or motor engine. Wider barges on rivers and broad canals used sail or were towed by a steam tug. By 1830 a canal network covered Britain, particularly the midlands. In the USA, the Erie Canal (1817–25) linked Buffalo on Lake Erie with Albany on the River Hudson and from there to New York, which then became the focal point of westward development.

Irrigation canals have been built since at least 3000 BC, and most of the ancient civilizations built extensive irrigation and canal networks. The most impressive of these early canals is the Nahrwan Canal between the Tigris and Euphrates rivers (c. 2400–2200 BC), which is 300 km (185 miles) long and 122 m (400 feet) wide. The Egyptian pharaohs built a canal linking the Mediterranean with the Red Sea, and this was used by Roman shipping, having been restored in 539 BC and again in 285 BC. In China, the first section of the GRAND CANAL was completed in 610 AD. Canals in Europe were not of importance until the late Middle Ages. The first developments were in the Netherlands, where in the 13th and 14th centuries drainage canals were adapted to carry boat traffic. In the 17th century several important canals were constructed in France, the greatest of which was the 240-km (150-mile) Languedoc Canal (Canal du Midi), built from 1661 by the engineer Riquet. In the UK, canal building started in about 1750, with Brindley's Bridgewater Canal in Lancashire. At its height, canal-building employed thousands of labourers known as navigators (navvies), but with the advent of the railways during the first half of the 19th century, canal-building virtually ceased.

Cannae, Battle of (216 BC) The village of Cannae in southern Italy was the site of one of the classic victories in military history. The Carthaginian general, HANNIBAL, his infantry considerably outnumbered, but stronger in cavalry, stationed his troops in a shallow crescent formation. The densely-packed Roman legionaries, under the consuls Aemilius Paullus and Terentius Varro, charged Hannibal's centre, forced it back, but failed to break it. As it slowly and deliberately gave ground, and the Romans pushed deeper, Hannibal effected his brilliant double-encirclement: his cavalry, having defeated the opposing right and left wings, closed the trap and assaulted the Romans from flanks and rear. Out of some 50,000 men the Romans lost 35,000 killed or captured, Hannibal only 5,700. Rome's hold on Italy was imperilled, and many of its allies in central and southern Italy defected to Hannibal.

Canning, Charles John, 1st Earl Canning (1812–62) British statesman. The son of George CANNING, he was governor-general of India at the time of the INDIAN MUTINY, and played a notable part in the work of reconciliation which followed it. He was subsequently first viceroy of India (1858–62), and was known as 'Clemency Canning' for his policy of no retribution.

Canning, George (1770–1827) British statesman. Entering Parliament in 1794, he became known as a firm opponent of revolutionary France. In 1807 he was appointed Foreign Secretary and was responsible for ordering the destruction of the Danish fleet at the second Battle of COPENHAGEN (1807) to prevent it falling into Napoleon's hands, and for the decision to wage the PENINSULAR WAR. After a quarrel with Lord CASTLEREAGH, which ended in a duel, he held no important office for some years. However, following Castlereagh's death in 1822 he again became Foreign Secretary. He openly supported the MONROE DOCTRINE and recognized the independence of Spain's South American colonies. He arranged the Anglo–French–Russian agreement that resulted in Greek independence from Turkey. He was Prime Minister for a few months before his death in August 1827, but had to rely on Whig support, since his policies, notably his advocacy of CATHOLIC EMANCIPATION, had antagonized his Tory colleagues.

canonist A compiler of or commentator on canon law, the law of the Western Christian Church. Church law evolved to deal with matters of discipline, organization, and administration, as well as of general morality and liturgy. Guidance was received from the scriptures, from the influence of Roman law, from Church councils and from the writings of St PAUL and of the Church Fathers. Important figures in the development of a body of law enforced by the PAPACY included Pope Gregory IX whose *Decretals* of 1234 represented the first official collection of papal law. Significant adjustments were

made within the Roman Catholic Church at the Council of TRENT, in response to the Protestant REFORMATION, and at the Vatican Council.

Canossa A castle in the Apennines, in Italy, where, in the winter of 1077, the German emperor Henry IV (1050–1106) waited for three days until Pope GREGORY VII granted absolution and removed a ban of EXCOMMUNICATION from him. Henry had been at odds with the papacy over ultimate control within the Holy Roman Empire. His penance greatly strengthened his hand against the German princes who threatened him, for they had been allies of the pope and when Henry was absolved the princes withdrew their support for Gregory.

Canton GUANGZHOU.

Canute (or Cnut) (*c*. 994–1035) King of England, Denmark, Norway, and Sweden, one of the most powerful rulers in Europe. He accompanied his father, SWEYN, in the invasion of England (1013) and was chosen King of Denmark on Sweyn's death in the following year. After a long struggle with ETHELRED II and his successor EDMUND II of Wessex which ended with Edmund's murder (1016), he became King of England (1017), marrying Emma, the widow of Ethelred. His reign was marked by legal and military reforms and by internal peace, Canute wisely using both Englishmen and Danes as advisers. A story is told by Henry of Huntingdon that he rebuked his flatterers by showing that even he, as king, could not stop the in-coming tide.

Cao Cao (or Ts'ao Ts'ao) (155–220) Chinese general. One of China's greatest soldiers, he unified much of northern China after the collapse of the HAN dynasty. His conquests enabled his son to found the Wei kingdom, one of the THREE KINGDOMS. His campaigns and adventures are recorded in one of the classics of Chinese literature, *The Romance of the Three Kingdoms*.

Cape Province A former province in South Africa, it was the largest and most southerly of the four provinces (the others were Natal, the Orange Free State, and Transvaal), which were abolished in 1994.
  History. The territory was inhabited by San (Bushmen), Khoikhoi (Hottentots), and Bantu-speaking Africans when the Dutch and French built up their trading settlements there from the 16th century onwards. In 1779 the first of the XHOSA WARS broke out. From 1795 to 1803 and from 1806 to 1815 the British held the Cape and this became permanent under the Treaty of Vienna (1815), when it became known as Cape Colony. Relations between the British settlers and the Boers (AFRIKANERS) over the anglicization of the courts and schools, the official use of English, control of farmland, and the emancipation of slaves quickly deteriorated. When the status of crown colony was granted in 1853, the franchise for the elected assembly was for males, whose property qualified them to vote, regardless of colour. In the 1890s the attempts by Cecil RHODES to unite the Cape with the three Dutch republics, under British rule, led to the Second BOER WAR (1899–1902). By the Act of Union (1910) Cape Colony joined the Union of South Africa as Cape Province, and the franchise was reduced, although partially extended again in 1956. In 1994 a new South African constitution enfranchised all adults, and the

province was replaced by the new regions of Northern Cape, Western Cape, Eastern Cape, and part of North West.

Cape St Vincent, Battle of (14 February 1797) A naval battle off the south-west coast of Portugal in which NELSON and JERVIS defeated a combined French and Spanish fleet of 27 ships. The British were outnumbered almost two to one, but the disorder of the Spanish fleet cancelled out its advantage in numbers. After this victory the British fleet was able to continue its blockade of Cadiz and to re-enter the Mediterranean in pursuit of Napoleon in Egypt.

Capetian (987–1328) The dynasty of French kings who succeeded the CAROLINGIANS. It was not until the reign of Louis VI (1108–1137) that the dynasty established firm control over its own territories around Paris and began the slow process of gaining real power in France. Philip Augustus (1180–1223) seized Normandy and recovered many other areas which had been occupied by, or were under the influence of, the English crown. This effectively doubled the size of the country. Paris became the true centre of government. By the end of the reign of Philip IV (1285–1314) France had achieved a great degree of stability and acquired many of the legal and governmental systems which were to survive up to the French Revolution. On the death of Charles IV in 1328 the throne passed to the House of VALOIS who, together with the later BOURBONS, could claim indirect descent from Hugh Capet (ruled 987–96), the first of the line.

Cape Verde A country comprising an archipelago of volcanic islands in the Atlantic Ocean, 563 km (350 miles) west of Cape Verde Peninsula, Senegal, the most westerly point of Africa.

Physical. The archipelago is in two groups, Windward and Leeward, and consists in all of ten islands and five islets. Sheer cliffs rise from the sea, and the inland slopes present a jagged landscape as a result of erosion by wind-blown sand. The prevailing winds are north-easterly trades, and the temperate maritime climate provides little temperature variation throughout the year. A dense haze containing Saharan sand often occurs.

Economy. Agriculture and fishing are the main productive sectors, with fish and salt dominating exports. The domestic economy relies heavily on remittances from Cape Verdeans working overseas.

History. The islands were uninhabited until they were colonized by the Portuguese from 1462, and were used as a base for the Portuguese slave trade. In 1951 Cape Verde became an overseas province of Portugal and its residents were given Portuguese citizenship in 1961. An independence movement for Cape Verde and GUINEA-BISSAU gained strength during the 1950s and 1960s, and later became the African Party for the Independence of Cape Verde and Guinea-Bissau (PAICVGB). Cape Verde gained full independence in 1975, but remained linked with Guinea-Bissau as the PAICVGB was the only legal political party in both countries. In 1980 the PAICVGB in Guinea-Bissau was ousted in a coup and the party in Cape Verde dropped the reference to Guinea-Bissau from its name. A multiparty constitution was adopted in 1991, and elections were won in the same year by the newly created Movement for Democracy Party.

CAPITAL: Praia
AREA: 4,033 sq km (1,557 sq miles)
POPULATION: 403,000 (1996)

CURRENCY: Escudo Caboverdiano = 100 centavos
RELIGIONS: Roman Catholic 80.0%; Protestant and
                 other 2.2%
ETHNIC GROUPS: Mixed 71.0%; Black 28.0%; White 1.0%
LANGUAGES: Portuguese (official); Portuguese creole
                 (crioulo)
INTERNATIONAL
ORGANIZATIONS: UN; OAU; ECOWAS; Non-Aligned
                 Movement

capitalism A system of economic organization, based on market competition, under which the means of production, distribution, and exchange are privately owned and directed by individuals or corporations. All human production requires both labour and capital. In a capitalist system, capital is supplied either by the single owner of a firm, or by shareholders in the case of a JOINT-STOCK COMPANY. Labour is supplied separately by employees who receive a wage or salary. The residual profit of the firm after wages and costs have been paid accrues to the owners of capital. Firms compete with one another to sell to customers in what is primarily a FREE MARKET. This system developed gradually in West European countries between the 16th and 19th centuries, replacing the older systems of production by merchant guilds and tied serfs. Capitalist methods were used in banking and commerce before being applied to industrial production at the time of the INDUSTRIAL REVOLUTION. In its most developed form capitalism, which is based on the principle that economic decisions should be taken by private individuals, restricts the role of the state in economic policy to the minimum. It thus stands for FREE TRADE. Capitalist industry has at times sought the protection of the state against foreign competition: this is known as protectionism. In the 20th century capitalist societies have been modified in various ways: often a capitalist economy is accompanied by the development of a WELFARE STATE, as in the 'welfare capitalism' of western Europe, or it is combined with a degree of government intervention, as for instance in F. D. ROOSEVELT's NEW DEAL or as advocated by J. M. KEYNES. Another development is the mixed economy, in which the production of certain goods or services is nationalized, while the rest of the economy remains in private ownership. A trend in 20th-century capitalism, particularly since World War II, has been the growth of multinational companies operating across national frontiers, often controlling greater economic resources than small- or medium-sized states.

Since the beginning of the 19th century capitalism's main competitor in the industrial societies has been SOCIALISM, which favours the social or public ownership of industry. Defenders of capitalism point to the high rates of economic growth which this system has achieved, and also to the personal freedom that private ownership of property bestows. Its critics such as MARX have claimed that capitalism necessarily involves the exploitation of workers by owners, and that it prevents people from controlling their own working lives. The force of the first charge has been diminished to some extent by state policies of income redistribution and welfare provision. With the collapse of the leading socialist economies in the 1980s, the main challenge now facing capitalism is to show that the pursuit of private profit can be reconciled with concern for the natural environment and the quality of life.

Capone, Al(fonso) (1899–1947) Italian-American gangster. Also known as 'Scarface', he was the most flamboyant and widely publicized criminal of the PROHIBITION ERA. In 1925 he took over Chicago's South Side gang from Johnny Torrio, and dominated the city's underworld, dealing in bootleg liquor, extortion, white slavery, and other rackets, and controlling the corrupt administration of Major Bill Thompson. His war on other syndicates, culminating in the St Valentine's Day Massacre of 1929 against the North Side gang, went unchecked until his indictment for federal income tax evasion in 1931 led to a prison sentence. Physically and mentally broken by syphilis, he was released in 1939.

Caporetto, Battle of (24 October 1917) A battle fought north of Trieste when Austro-Hungarian and German forces overwhelmed the Italian army. General Cadorna withdrew his demoralized troops north of Venice, where his new line held, eventually strengthened by British and French reinforcements. Some 300,000 Italian prisoners-of-war were taken and Italy was temporarily out of the war, and a German offensive for March 1918 on the WESTERN FRONT could now be planned.

Cappadocia The central area of ancient Asia Minor. Its SATRAP Ariarathes resisted ALEXANDER THE GREAT'S Macedonians until he was killed in 322 BC. After 301 his descendants re-established control and Ariarathes IV fought against the Romans at Magnesia in 190, though he and his successors thereafter aligned themselves with Rome. Cappadocia suffered badly at the hands of the neighbouring Armenians during the Mithridatic War, though the Roman general POMPEY aided recovery by granting loans for town building. The area was annexed to the Roman empire in 17 AD.

Caprivi, Leo, Graf von (1831–99) Prussian army officer and statesman. Chosen by WILLIAM II to succeed BISMARCK as Chancellor (1890–94) he had to face the consequences of the break-up of Bismarck's coalition in the Reichstag. He surrendered ZANZIBAR to Britain in exchange for Heligoland (1890). He favoured conciliation with the working classes, socialists, and Roman Catholics, and pleased industrialists with lower grain imports, thereby laying the foundation for German trade expansion. He resigned in 1894, having displeased the agrarians by encouraging industry above agriculture, and the militarists through the reduction of military service, and finding it increasingly difficult to work with the wilful and politically active, William II.

Caratacus (or Caractacus or Caradog) (d. 54 AD) King of the Catuvellauni, a tribe of southern Britain. He was the son of CUNOBELINUS. After his father's death *c.* 40 AD and the Roman capture of Camulodunum he resisted the Romans, but was defeated and fled to the BRIGANTES, who handed him to CLAUDIUS, in 51. He and his family were kept as respected hostages in Rome.

caravanserai (Persian, *karwansaray*, 'caravan place') An inn along Asia's caravan routes. The shelters, often under municipal supervision, provided a place for resting, making repairs, and preparing for the next stage of a journey. They were centres of news, information, and often espionage. At terminals like Damascus they were 'mansions', accommodating several hundred camels or mules, with storerooms at ground level and sleeping quarters above. On desert routes, at points where there was a little brackish water, they offered the barest facilities. Generally located outside the town walls, they were constructed round a courtyard, sometimes arcaded, usually with a well at the centre.

caravel A small Mediterranean trading ship, used in the 14th–17th centuries. It was lateen-rigged on two or sometimes three masts. Late in the 15th century, Spain and Portugal adapted the three-masted caravel for exploration and trade, square-rigged on the two forward masts and lateen-rigged on the mizen. The explorer Bartholomew DIAZ DE NOVAES rounded the Cape of Good Hope in 1488 in a caravel. The *Santa Maria*, in which Christopher COLUMBUS reached the West Indies in 1492, was a 29 m (95 feet) caravel. The ships used by the Portuguese navigators Vasco DA GAMA (who reached India in 1498) and Ferdinand MAGELLAN (whose ship in 1522 completed the first circumnavigation of the world) also included caravels.

Carbonari (Italian, 'charcoal burners') Secret revolutionary society formed in Italy, and active in France and the Iberian Peninsula. It was formed in the kingdom of Naples during the reign of Joachim Murat (1808–15) and its members plotted to free the country from foreign rule. The society was influential in the revolt in Naples in 1820 which resulted in the granting of a constitution to the kingdom of the Two Sicilies. Similar revolts took place in Spain and Portugal (1820), Piedmont (1821), Romagna and Parma (1831), all in turn being suppressed. It was supplanted in Italy by the more broadly based YOUNG ITALY movement. Meanwhile the French movement, after mutinies in 1821–22, also declined.

Cárdenas, Lázaro (1895–1970) Mexican statesman. As President of Mexico (1934–40), he carried the MEXICAN REVOLUTION to the left during his administration. He redistributed land, encouraged organized labour through support of the Confederación de Trabajadores de Mexico (CTM), and nationalized the property of the foreign-owned oil companies in 1938. Himself a mestizo (of mixed Native American and European descent), he won the support of the indigenous peoples and Mexican working classes.

Cardwell, Edward, Viscount (1813–86) British statesman. A supporter of Sir Robert PEEL, he served as Secretary to the Treasury (1845–46) and as Secretary for War in GLADSTONE's ministry of 1868–74. British incompetence in the CRIMEAN WAR (1853–56) and the efficiency of the German army in the European wars of the 1860s were the background to Cardwell's military reforms. These included subordination of the commander-in-chief to the Secretary of State for War, short service enlistment for six years in the army, and six years in the Reserves, and abolition of the purchase of commissions. This reorganized army, though much smaller than those of other large European powers, proved efficient in dealing with later 19th-century imperial crises, but inadequate in the Second BOER WAR, after which a more thoroughgoing reform was carried out by HALDANE.

Caribbean Community and Common Market (CARICOM) An organization formed in 1973 to promote unity among the many small nations of the Caribbean. The main purpose of the organization is to promote the economic integration of its 14 members by means of a Caribbean Common Market, replacing the former Caribbean Free Trade Association (CARIFTA). Member nations also co-operate on other projects in areas such as health, education, and agricultural development. A summit meeting in 1984 agreed to create a single market, but many issues were unresolved. At subsequent annual summit meetings disagreements were gradually settled and in 1995 the members decided to remove all internal trade tariffs by the end of the year. Its headquarters are in Georgetown, Guyana.

Caribs People of South American origin, who migrated to the islands of the Lesser Antilles from *c.* 1000 AD. There they replaced the agricultural Arawak culture, killing off most of the men and taking their women. Many Arawak men were eaten in ritual cannibalism. The Caribs were the first 'Indians' discovered by Columbus.

Carlist A conservative who supported the claims of Don Carlos (1788–1855) and his descendants to the throne of Spain. Don Carlos's religious orthodoxy and belief in the divine right of kings made him the natural leader of these traditionalists. In 1830, after Ferdinand VII had excluded his brother Don Carlos from the succession, preferring his daughter, Isabella, they formed the Carlist Party. Three years later, on the death of Ferdinand, they proclaimed Don Carlos as Charles V and a civil war followed. This lasted six years until Don Carlos fled to France. His two eldest sons continued the Carlist claims until they were forced to surrender them after an unsuccessful rising in 1860. The third son, John (1822–87), briefly advanced his claims before renouncing them in favour of his son, Charles, Don Carlos VII in 1868. In the same year a revolution overthrew ISABELLA II and the Carlists asserted his claim to the throne. Although routed by the new king Amadeus in 1872, the creation of a federal republic the following year gave the party renewed hope. But in 1874–75 Isabella's son was restored as Alfonso XII. After the abdication of his son Alfonso XIII (1886–1941) in 1931 and the establishment of a republic the Carlists emerged as a strong force with popular support. In the SPANISH CIVIL WAR the Carlists sided with the nationalists, and for many years obstructed Franco's aim to restore the Bourbon dynasty. In 1969 Franco overcame Carlist objections and named the grandson of Alfonso XIII, Juan Carlos, as his successor.

Carlyle, Thomas (1795–1881) Scottish historian, essayist, and political philosopher. He was for a time a teacher, contributed to the *Edinburgh Review*, and wrote a *Life of Schiller* (1824). In 1826 he married Jane Welsh, who was to become a noted letter writer and the constant support of her husband. His semi-autobiographical philosophical work, *Sartor Resartus* (1833–34), shows the influence of Richter and the German Romantic school. Carlyle moved in 1834 to London, where he wrote his celebrated *History of the French Revolution* (1837). In *On Heroes, Hero-Worship and the Heroic in History* (1841) he outlined his view that great men in the past shaped destiny through the genius of their spirit. He was a critic of 19th-century materialism and a sympathizer with the sufferings of the poor, whose plight he described in *Chartism* (1839), which attacked the consequences of the Industrial Revolution. In *Past and Present* (1843) he exalted the feudal past and paternalistic government. During his

lifetime his influence as a social prophet and critic was enormous; in the 20th century his reputation waned, partly because his ideas were interpreted as foreshadowings of fascism.

Carmelite A monk or nun who is a follower of the Order of Our Lady of Mount Carmel. Carmelites obey the strict monastic 'rule' of St Albert of Jerusalem. They originated in PALESTINE *c.* 1154 but came to western Europe when Palestine was conquered by the Muslims. Their order was approved by Pope Honorius III in 1226. The rule required strict isolation from the secular world but was later relaxed to allow a degree of involvement with the care of the laity. In 1452 the Carmelite Sisters was formed. In 1594 a reformed group of the order was established, the Discalced Carmelites, but it remained essentially similar in organization and objectives. The order has produced celebrated mystics including St JOHN OF THE CROSS and St TERESA OF ÁVILA.

Carnac A town in Brittany, France, near a major centre of ritual activity between the 5th and 3rd millennia BC. A peninsula is marked off by rows of MEGALITHS, presumably as some sort of sanctuary. There are numerous megalithic tombs in the area and nearby, at Locmariaquer, is the largest known MENHIR, originally standing 20 m (65 feet) high.

Carnegie, Andrew (1835–1919) Scottish-born US industrialist and philanthropist. The son of a weaver, he emigrated in 1848, and rose to become, at 18, personal assistant to Thomas A. Scott of the Pennsylvania Railroad. He invested in iron and steel production and launched his own steel company in 1872. He achieved control of steel production, ensuring greater and faster production than his rivals by technological improvement, and by demanding accountable management. In 1901 he sold out to the US Steel Corporation for the sum of $447 million, of which $250 million came to Carnegie himself. His belief that the rich should act as trustees of their wealth for the public good was set out in his essay *The Gospel of Wealth* (1889), and applied in the philanthropic distribution of over $350 million.

Carnot, Lazare Nicolas Marguerite (1753–1823) French general and military tactician. He entered the French army in 1784 and two years later published his influential *Essay on the Use of Machines in Warfare*. In 1791, after the FRENCH REVOLUTION, he was elected to the National Assembly and, as a republican, voted for the execution of Louis XVI. His reorganization of recruitment and administration of the army was mainly responsible for the successes of the revolutionary armies. He was a member of the COMMITTEE OF PUBLIC SAFETY, was in charge of the war department, and between 1795 and 1797 was a member of the DIRECTORY. He fled to Germany, falsely accused of treason in 1797, following the royalist victory in the elections. He returned to become Minister of War (1800) and continued with his administrative reforms for a year under NAPOLEON BONAPARTE, but resigned in 1801. He spent most of his retirement writing books on military fortifications. He served Napoleon during the HUNDRED DAYS of 1815, as Minister of the Interior. He brilliantly defended Antwerp, but went into exile in Germany after the second restoration. His heavy detached fortress wall (Carnot's Wall) and principle of active defence influenced modern fortifications.

Caro, Joseph (1488–1575) Jewish scholar and mystic, who wrote the last great codification of Jewish law. His family was among the Jews expelled from Spain in 1492. Caro finally settled in Safed in Palestine *c.* 1537, where he produced *House of Joseph* (1559); his popular condensation of this work, *Prepared Table* (1565), was initially opposed by some rabbinical authorities, but has since become the authoritative standard of JUDAISM. In 1646 his *Preacher of Righteousness*, a diary of his mystical experiences, was published.

Carol I (1839–1914) First King of Romania (1881–1914). A German-born prince and Prussian officer, he was elected in 1866 to succeed Alexander John Cuza as Prince of Romania. His pro-German sympathies made him unpopular during the FRANCO-PRUSSIAN WAR, but skill in manipulating politicians and elections saved him from abdication. As a result of his military leadership in the RUSSO–TURKISH WAR, he gained full independence for Romania at the Congress of BERLIN and declared a Romanian kingdom in 1881. In 1883 he concluded a secret alliance with Germany and Austro-Hungary. He reformed the Romanian constitution and the monetary system, army, and network of communication. Romanian oilfields first began to be exploited in his reign, but the problem of peasant land-hunger was not solved, and there was a Romanian peasant revolt in 1907.

Carol II (1893–1953) King of Romania. The great-nephew of CAROL I, he was exiled in 1925 for his scandalous domestic life. In 1930 he returned as king, and established a royal dictatorship inspired by intense admiration of MUSSOLINI. In 1940 he was forced to cede large parts of his kingdom to the AXIS POWERS, and to abdicate in favour of his son, Michael.

Caroline Islands A chain of 963 islands in the north-west Pacific, inhabited for over 2,000 years. Europeans maintained contact with the islands from the 16th century. From 1885 the Carolines were controlled by the Spanish, then, after 1899, the Germans, and, after 1914, the Japanese, who used the islands as a base for operations during World War II. In 1947 the Carolines, together with the Northern Mariana and Marshall Islands, became part of the UN Trust Territory of the Pacific, administered by the USA. The Marshall Islands left the Trust Territory in 1979 and the Northern Marianas left in 1986. The eastern part of the Caroline Islands became the Federated States of MICRONESIA, which gained independence in 1990. The western part became PALAU (also known as Belau), which gained independence in 1994. Micronesia and Palau signed Compacts of Free Association with the USA, which is responsible for their defence.

Caroline of Ansbach (1683–1737) German princess, Queen consort of GEORGE II, whom she married in 1705. She was a cultivated woman, possessed of much common sense and considerable political skill, and used her influence in support of WALPOLE. She was a popular queen, and during the king's absences in Hanover, she was four times appointed 'Guardian of the Realm'. She was responsible for enclosing 121 ha (300 acres) of London's Hyde Park to form Kensington Gardens.

Carolingian empire The collection of territories in Western Europe ruled by the family of CHARLEMAGNE (768–814 AD) from whom the dynasty took its name. Charlemagne's ancestors, Frankish aristocrats, fought their way to supreme power under the MEROVINGIAN kings, the last of whom was deposed by Charlemagne's father PEPIN III in 751. Under Charlemagne, the empire covered modern-day France, part of Spain, Germany to the River Elbe, and much of Italy. Charlemagne was crowned Emperor of the West by Pope Leo III in 800 and made his court a centre of learning (the 'Carolingian Renaissance'). After the division of the empire by the Treaty of VERDUN in 843, civil war among the Carolingians, VIKING raids, and the ambitions of rival families subjected the empire to intolerable strains. Nevertheless, Carolingians reigned in Germany till 911 and in France till 987 and they left behind a prestige which later kings of the Middle Ages sought to emulate.

carpetbaggers (USA) Northerners who moved into the post-Civil War American South. In the wake of the RECONSTRUCTION ACTS of 1867, large numbers of Northern entrepreneurs, educators, and missionaries arrived in the South to share in the rebuilding of the former states of the CONFEDERACY. Some carpetbaggers (so called because it was said that they could transport their entire assets in a carpetbag) hoped to help the Black ex-slave population, but others were interested only in making a quick profit. Some of the more politically active were influential in the Republican Party in the South, and were elected to various offices, including state governorships. Following the election of Rutherford HAYES to the Presidency (1876–80) and the restoration of home rule to the South in 1877, carpetbagger influence waned.

Carranza, Venustiano (1859–1920) Mexican statesman. As President of Mexico (1917–20), he played a minor role in the revolution against Porfirio DÍAZ but a major role in shaping the course of the MEXICAN REVOLUTION from 1913 to 1920. A voice for moderation during the violent decade of revolutionary politics, he defeated his rival 'Pancho' VILLA and reluctantly accepted the leftist constitution of 1917. During his administration he implemented the revolutionary provisions only when forced to do so. Driven from office before his presidential term expired, he was assassinated in the village of Tlaxcalantongo on his way into exile.

Carson, Edward Henry, Baron (1854–1935) Anglo-Irish statesman. Elected to the British Parliament in 1892, he became Solicitor General (1900–05) in the Conservative government. He was determined to preserve Ireland's constitutional relationship with Britain. He opposed the third HOME RULE Bill (1912) and organized a private army of ULSTER VOLUNTEERS, threatening that Ulster would set up a separate provisional government if the Bill proceeded. In 1914 he reluctantly agreed to Home Rule for southern Ireland but insisted that NORTHERN IRELAND, including the predominantly Catholic counties of Tyrone and Fermanagh, should remain under the British crown. He continued an inflammatory campaign against Home Rule after the war. Although he reluctantly accepted the Anglo-Irish Treaty (1921), he never ceased to speak for the interests of Ulster.

Carson, Kit (1809–68) US frontiersman and guide born in Kentucky, who established headquarters at Taos, New Mexico. He worked with FRÉMONT along the Oregon Trail in 1842–46, played an important role in the seizure of California from Mexico in 1847, and guided many groups of settlers west during the GOLD RUSH of 1849. He served as a US Indian agent and, during the AMERICAN CIVIL WAR, was responsible for Union (Northern) scouts in the western theatre. One of the most accomplished of the MOUNTAIN MEN, Carson was the subject of many of the legends of the early days of the American West.

Carter, James (Jimmy) Earl (1924–   ) The 39th President of the USA (1977–81). His Southern Baptist Christian background and his disassociation from the US political establishment, which had suffered from the revelations over the WATERGATE SCANDAL, helped him to win the Democratic nomination and election of 1976, with Walter Mondale for Vice-President. Initially regimes which failed to respect the basic human rights agreed on at the HELSINKI CONFERENCE were to be deprived of US aid, but this policy was soon abandoned. Carter's measures to pardon draft-dodgers (young men imprisoned for evading conscription in the VIETNAM WAR) and to introduce administrative and economic reforms were popular. Although Congress had a Democratic majority Carter was not always able to secure its support. He failed to obtain approval for his energy policy, which sought to reduce oil consumption, while the Senate in 1979 refused to ratify the agreement on STRATEGIC ARMS LIMITATION TALKS (SALT II). In foreign affairs the administration achieved the CAMP DAVID ACCORD between Israel and Egypt and the transference of the PANAMA CANAL to Panama. His reputation was harmed by the IRAN HOSTAGE CRISIS and, although renominated by the Democrats in the 1980 election he was defeated by the Republican Ronald REAGAN. After leaving office he led teams of international observers to troubled areas in Central America, went on peace missions in the Middle East, hosted peace negotiations between Ethiopia and Eritrean separatists (1989), helped to resolve the deadlock over North Korea's capacity to build nuclear weapons (1994), and brokered a deal to restore democracy in Haiti (1994).

Carthage A city on the coast of North Africa (in modern Tunisia). It was founded by colonists from TYRE (though later than the traditional date of 814 BC) and developed into one of the leading trading cities of the western Mediterranean, with footholds in Spain, Sardinia, and Sicily. Between the 5th and 3rd centuries BC it engaged in frequent hostilities with the Greeks of Sicily. It was on that island that Carthage first clashed with Rome, and the three PUNIC WARS ended with the razing Or the city, in 146 BC.

It was refounded as a Roman colony by CAESAR and AUGUSTUS, and again achieved great prosperity. As a centre of Christianity it opposed the DONATISTS. The Vandal GENSERIC occupied it in 439 and established it as his capital, but in 533–34 BELISARIUS overthrew the Vandals and from then until its capture and destruction by the Arabs in 697 it remained part of the Byzantine empire.

Carthusian A member of the monastic order founded by St BRUNO OF COLOGNE at Chartreuse in France in 1084. Their 'rule' is extremely severe, requiring solitude, abstinence from meat, regular fasting, and silence except for a few hours each week. Nuns affiliated to the order may eat together and, uniquely within the Roman Catholic Church, are allowed to become deaconesses. Lay brothers and sisters tend their needs and provide the minimum necessary contact with the outside world. They are governed by the general chapter, consisting of the priors of all houses together with the community of La Grande Chartreuse itself.

Cartier, Sir George-Etienne (1814–73) French-Canadian statesman. His involvement in 1837 in PAPINEAU'S REBELLION forced him into brief exile in the USA. In 1848 he was elected as a Conservative to the Canadian Legislative Assembly, holding a seat there, and later in the Canadian House of Commons, until his death. From 1857 to 1862 he was leader of the French-Canadian section of the government in the Macdonald–Cartier administration and after Confederation (1867) served as Minister of Militia in the first dominion government. One of the Fathers of Confederation and a promoter of improved relations between English and French Canada, Cartier was a central figure in the political campaign for unification, wielding immense influence as a result of his hold over the electors of French Canada.

Cartier, Jacques (1491–1557) French navigator, the discoverer of the St Lawrence River. Charged by François I to look for gold in the New World and for a North-West Passage to China, he set sail from Saint Malo in 1534 and landed off Newfoundland 20 days later. On his second expedition (1535–36) he discovered one of the world's great rivers, the Saint Lawrence, in a region which was to become the axis of French power in North America. He sailed up the river as far as the Île d'Orléans, and continued his journey in longboats. He is credited with the discovery (1535) of an area around Quebec, which he named Canada after the Huron-Iroquois *kanata*, meaning a village or settlement. Welcomed by the Iroquois of Hochelaga, he renamed their village Mont Royal, the present site of Montreal city. On his third voyage (1541–42) he wintered on the river but made no new geographical discoveries. Further exploration of Canada was undertaken by CHAMPLAIN.

Carver, John (c. 1576–1621) English-born PILGRIM FATHER. He had been deacon of the separatist church in Leiden and led the migration in the *Mayflower* in 1620. Elected first governor of Plymouth Plantation, he died shortly afterwards and was succeeded by William BRADFORD.

Casablanca Conference (14–24 January 1943) A meeting in Morocco between CHURCHILL and F. D. ROOSEVELT to determine Allied strategy for the continuation of World War II. Plans were made to increase bombing of Germany, invade Sicily, and transfer British forces to the Far East after the collapse of Germany. Both leaders expressed their determination to continue the war until Germany agreed to unconditional surrender.

Casanova de Seingalt, Giovanni Giacomo (1725–98) Venetian adventurer. He led a wandering existence as a gambler and spy. He had considerable personal charm and was notorious for the number of his seductions. He is celebrated for his escape (1756) from the state prison in Venice. His voluminous memoirs, written in French and published posthumously, give a lively account of his adventures and amours all over Europe as well as an entertaining picture of 18th-century society.

Casement, Roger David (1864–1916) Irish patriot. As a British consular official, he won respect for exposing cases of ill-treatment of native labour in Africa, particularly the Upper Congo, and in South America, and was awarded a knighthood by the British government. He retired from the consular service in 1913. An Ulster Protestant, he supported Irish independence and went to the USA and to Germany in 1914 to seek help for an Irish uprising. His attempt to recruit Irish prisoners-of-war in Germany to fight against the British in Ireland failed, nor would the Germans provide him with troops. Casement, however, was landed on the Irish coast in County Kerry from a German submarine in 1916, hoping to secure a postponement of the EASTER RISING. He was arrested, tried, and executed for treason. His request to be buried in Ireland, rejected at the time, was fulfilled in 1965.

Casey, Richard Gardiner, Baron (1890–1976) Australian diplomat and statesman. He was a United Australia Party Member of the House of Representatives (1931–40). He was Australia's first Minister to the USA (1940–42), joined the British war cabinet (1942–43), and was governor of Bengal (1944–46). On returning to the House of Representatives (1949–60), representing the Liberal Party, Casey held various portfolios including that of External Affairs (1951–60). He was governor-general of the Commonwealth of Australia (1965–69).

Casimir III (the Great) (1310–70) King of Poland (1333–70). He consolidated the achievements of his predecessor, Wladyslaw I, reorganizing the country's administration, codifying the law, and acquiring territory through diplomacy. Links with Lithuania, Hesse, Silesia, Brandenburg, and the Holy Roman Empire were forged through marriage. He successfully fought against RUSSIA, the TEUTONIC KNIGHTS, and the BOHEMIANS.

caste system A means of stratification, which groups people according to specific social rank. Variations of caste are found in all Indian religious communities, not only Hindu but Jain, Buddhist, Muslim, and Christian communities as well. All stem from the tripartite social division of the ARYANS, who invaded northern India c. 1500 BC. However, only Hindus developed theological and legal rationales for caste. The three divisions or *varnas* consisted of Brahmins (priests and professionals), Kshatriyas (rulers, warriors, and administrators), and Vaishyas (farmers and merchants). Later a fourth *varna* developed, the Shūdras (artisans and labourers). Each *varna* classifies many *jātis* or castes, traditionally determined by occupation, but often linked through geographical locality, marriage, or dietary customs. Religious justification for the *varna-jāti* system stems from the *Rigveda*, the earliest text of the VEDAS, which describes how Purusha, the original cosmic man, was divided by the gods into specific *varnas*, each of which has its own attributes and role in society. One of the preoccupations of the caste system is the notion of purity and pollution: varying degrees of defilement result from a *jāti's* occupation, dietary habits, or customs. Those who carried out the most polluting tasks became known as 'untouchables'. Untouchables are outside the *varna* system, although still part of the caste

system. Mahatma GANDHI, desiring to improve their status, renamed them *Harijans*, 'Children of God', a title subsequently rejected by them in favour of the name *dalit*, 'depressed'. They remain the most oppressed members of Indian society, despite legislation to reserve government jobs, education places, and parliamentary seats for them. In recent years proposals for similar positive discrimination for other castes have been a leading issue in Indian politics and caused widespread violence. Critics argue that in a democratic system such policies may amount to little more than electoral bribery and expect that urbanization and modernization will erode the caste system; others point to the entrenched nature of the caste system and the severe economic and social constraints it places on the lives of those in the lower *jātis*.

Castile A former kingdom in northern Spain, the name deriving from the castle-building activities there of Garcia of León in the early 10th century. The period which followed was a confused one in which alliances with the Spanish MOORS alternated with expansion at their expense, especially during the reigns of Alfonso VI and Alfonso VII. León was gained, lost, and finally reunited with the kingdom under Ferdinand III in the 13th century. Under ALFONSO X, the cultural life of the country developed but a long period of weak rule and internal turmoil followed. In 1469 ISABELLA I (of Castile), having married Ferdinand II of Aragon (FERDINAND V), inherited the crown and thus the two greatest kingdoms of Spain were united.

Castilla, Ramón (1797–1867) Peruvian statesman. He began his political career during the wars for independence against Spain. As President (1845–51, 1855–62), he encouraged railway development and telegraphic communication, and supported the commercial use of guano (the nitrogen-rich dropping of fish-eating seabirds) as a fertilizer. He developed the nitrate industries by establishing government monopolies and leasing them to private individuals. He abolished slavery, and freed the Peruvian Indian from tribute payments.

castle A fortified building for the defence of a town or district, doubling as the private residence of a BARON in the Middle Ages. Although also called 'castles', Celtic hill-forts, Roman camps, and Saxon burhs were designed to provide refuge for whole populations; archaeological evidence suggests that in England fortified private residences date from the 9th century. The 'motte and bailey' design of the 11th century comprised a palisaded 'motte' (a steep-sided earthen mound) and a 'bailey' (an enclosure or courtyard) separated from the motte by a ditch. Both were surrounded by a second ditch. Initially timber-built, and often prefabricated for rapid assembly, many were later rebuilt in stone. Design modifications in the 12th century included stone tower keeps (as at Rochester, c. 1130, and Castle Hedingham c. 1140) to replace the motte. The keep (the rounded form was called a shell keep) combined strong defence with domestic quarters. The need to extend these quarters meant that the courtyard had to be protected by a line of towers joined by 'curtain' walls. In the 12th century the concentric castle (one ring of defences enclosing another) was developed from the model of the castles built by the Crusaders, who themselves had copied the Saracens. Two of the greatest castles of the late 12th century were Château Gaillard in Normandy and the Krak des Chevaliers in Syria. At the end of the 13th century, EDWARD I of England, following a policy of subduing north Wales, built a series of castles at Caernarvon, Conway, Harlech, and Beaumaris. Design improvements saw the further development of rounded towers, which were more difficult to undermine, machicolations, which enabled objects to be dropped or poured on the besiegers, massive gatehouses, and refinements to the battlements, or crenellations, along the walls. Castles were built throughout Europe during the Middle Ages but although they continued to be built and improved in England in the 14th and 15th centuries, a more settled society encouraged the building of unfortified MANOR HOUSES. The invention of gunpowder had made castles obsolete for defensive purposes by the middle of the 16th century.

Castle Hill Uprising (1804) A convict rebellion at Castle Hill, a settlement in New South Wales, Australia. Several hundred convicts, many of them Irish nationalists, captured Castle Hill as part of a plan to gain control over other settlements. The rebellion was crushed by the New South Wales Corps, martial law was proclaimed, and the ringleaders hanged, flogged, or deported.

Castlereagh, Robert Stewart, Viscount (1769–1822) British statesman. He played a leading part in the coalition that defeated Napoleonic France and in the post-war settlement at the Congress of VIENNA. He entered the Irish House of Commons in 1790 and secured the passage of the ACT OF UNION which united Britain and Ireland. He resigned when George III rejected a plan for CATHOLIC EMANCIPATION. As Secretary for War (1807–09), he was not a success, and the attack upon his policies by George CANNING led to a duel between them. Appointed Foreign Secretary in 1812, he devoted his energies to the overthrow of Napoleon and the maintenance of the balance of power in Europe. At home, he was the focus of the hostility aroused by the British government's repressive measures. He committed suicide when overwork had disturbed the balance of his mind.

Castro (Ruz), Fidel (1927–) Cuban revolutionary and statesman. Son of an immigrant sugar planter, he joined the Cuban People's Party in 1947, and led a revolution in Santiago in 1953, for which he was imprisoned. His self-defence at this trial, known by its concluding words, *History Will Absolve Me*, was to become his major policy statement at the time. Exiled in 1955 he went to Mexico and in 1956 landed on the Cuban coast with 82 men, including Ché GUEVARA, but only 12 men survived the landing. He conducted successful guerrilla operations from the Sierra Maestra mountains, and in December 1958 led a march on Havana. The dictator, General BATISTA, fled, and on 1 January 1959 Castro proclaimed the Cuban Revolution, ordering the arrest and execution of many of Batista's supporters. Castro declared himself Prime Minister and, unable to establish diplomatic or commercial agreements with the USA, negotiated credit, arms, and food supplies with the former Soviet Union. He expropriated foreign industry, and collectivized agriculture. The USA cancelled all trade agreements (1960), and from 1961 Castro was openly aligned with the Soviet Union, emerging more and more strongly as a Marxist. The abortive US and Cuban invasion (April 1961)

of the 'BAY OF PIGS' boosted his popularity, as did his successful survival of the CUBAN MISSILE CRISIS (October 1962) and of several assassination plots. A keen promoter of revolution in other Latin American countries, and of liberation movements in Africa, he achieved considerable status in developing countries through his leadership of the NON-ALIGNED MOVEMENT. With the collapse of the Soviet Union and of COMECON in 1990, his government faced severe problems. He introduced economic austerity measures in 1991, and some degree of liberalization of Cuba's economy.

catacomb An underground burial gallery of early Christian Rome. Catacombs were named after the best known example, St Sebastian in the Hollow (*ad Catacumbas*). Forty such subterranean chambers are known in Rome, tunnelled through soft rock outside the ancient city boundaries. The anniversaries of MARTYRS were celebrated at the graves. Looted by barbarians and subject to collapse, they were virtually forgotten until their accidental rediscovery in the 16th century. Similar ones are also found as far apart as Salzburg and Malta.

Catalaunian Fields (or Plains) The site of a major battle in 451 AD, reputedly near Châlons-sur-Marne in France, but placed by some nearer Troyes. The Roman general Aetius with a combined force of Romans, Goths, and Burgundians defeated ATTILA the Hun, forcing his retreat from Gaul. He was expelled from Italy the following year.

Çatal Hüyük A large Neolithic settlement (about 13 ha, 32 acres), near Konya in south-central Turkey, which dates from *c.* 6500 BC. Its small houses, built of mud bricks, were so close together that all access had to be by way of the flat roofs. A high proportion of rooms are believed to have been shrines, on the basis of numerous bulls' horns mounted in benches. There were also wall decorations, votive offerings, and richly furnished burials beneath the floors. Only part of the site has been excavated.

Catalonia A semi-autonomous region in north-east Spain. Once a Roman colony, it was overrun by the VISIGOTHS in the 5th century and became independent under the counts of Barcelona from 874. Linked by marriage alliance to ARAGON in 1137, and to CASTILE in 1479, the Catalans rebelled in 1462–72 and 1640–52. In the second outbreak they appealed to the French for help. The French invaded from 1689 to 1697. In the War of the SPANISH SUCCESSION (1701–14) Catalonia supported the unsuccessful Austrian candidate, leading to a loss of privileges under the BOURBONS. During the Spanish Civil War (1936–39), in which Catalonia took a leading role on the Republican side, an autonomous government was once more established in the region. Catalonia remained a centre of opposition to the regime of General FRANCO. Limited self-government was restored in 1978. Catalan, a Romance language similar to Provençal, is the traditional language of Catalonia, Andorra, and the Balearic Islands.

Cathars (Greek *katharos*, 'pure') A medieval sect whose members sought to achieve a life of great purity. Cathars believed in a 'dualist' heresy. Their basic belief was that if God, being wholly good, had alone created the world it would have been impossible for evil to exist within it, and that another, diabolical, creative force must have taken part. They held that the material world and all within it were irredeemably evil. The human body and its appetites were despised. Marriage was rejected and suicide by starvation was admired. A pure life was impossible to all but a very few called the 'perfect', and the rest – known simply as 'believers' — could live as they wished. Salvation was assured if they took a form of confirmation known as the 'consolamentum' before death. This ceremony was to be delayed as long as possible to reduce the chance of the recipient's sinning further before he or she died. The heresy originated in Bulgaria and appeared in western Europe in the 1140s. In southern France this Christian heresy took the form of ALBIGENSIANISM.

Catherine I (c. 1684–1727) Empress of Russia (1725–27). She was a Lithuanian servant girl who was first the mistress and then the second wife of PETER I (the Great). On his death she was proclaimed ruler with the support of her husband's favourite, Menshikov, and the guards regiments. Menshikov became the effective head of government, working through the newly established Privy Council, but fell from power on Catherine's death. Her daughter Elizabeth became empress (1741–62).

Catherine II (the Great) (1729–96) Empress of Russia (1762–96). She was a German princess, Sophia of Anhalt-Zerbst, who in 1745 married the future emperor Peter III, a cruel and feeble-minded young man. In 1762, six months after his accession, he was murdered, and she was proclaimed empress with the support of the guards regiments of St Petersburg, and she ruled for 44 years. She was an intelligent and ambitious woman who corresponded with VOLTAIRE and considered herself a disciple of the ENLIGHTENMENT. However, her much-heralded Legislative Commission (1765–74) achieved nothing; and her charter of 1785 established the nobility as a privileged class and caused serfdom to be extended and made harsher. The revolt of PUGACHEV (1773–74) was difficult to suppress. Her claim to greatness rests mainly on her foreign policy: with the help of POTEMKIN and SUVAROV she obtained most of Poland in the partitions of 1772, 1793, and 1795, gained Azov in the first Turkish War, annexed the Crimea, and by 1792 the whole northern shore of the Black Sea.

Catherine of Aragon (1485–1536) Spanish princess, the first wife of HENRY VIII of England to whom she was married in 1509. She bore him a daughter, the future MARY I, but no male heir survived; the importance of the Spanish alliance diminished, and by 1527 Henry, infatuated with Anne BOLEYN, sought a papal annulment, claiming that Catherine's marriage in 1501 to his elder brother Arthur rendered his own marriage invalid. The pope was unco-operative, and CRANMER annulled the king's marriage in 1533. Thereafter Catherine lived in seclusion in England.

Catherine of Braganza (1638–1705) Portuguese princess and Queen consort of CHARLES II of England, whom she married in 1662, bringing Tangier and Bombay as part of her dowry. The marriage was childless and she had to tolerate the king's infidelities. As a Roman Catholic, she was unpopular and there were attempts to implicate her in the POPISH PLOT. In 1692, as a widow, she returned to Portugal, where she died.

Catholic emancipation The granting of full political and civil liberties to British and Irish Roman Catholics.

Partial religious toleration had been achieved in Britain by the late 17th century, but the TEST ACTS limited holders of public office to communicant Anglicans and placed additional disabilities on members of other Churches. Until 1745 the JACOBITE threat seemed to justify continued discrimination against Roman Catholics, and fears of Catholic emancipation led to the GORDON RIOTS in 1780. By the late 18th century many reformists were agitating for total religious freedom. In Ireland, where a majority were Catholics, concessions were made from 1778 onwards, culminating in the Relief Act of 1793, passed by the Irish Parliament and giving liberty of religious practice and the right to vote in elections, but not to sit in Parliament or hold public office. William PITT had become convinced of the need for full Catholic emancipation by 1798, and promises were made to the Irish Parliament when it agreed to the ACT OF UNION in 1800. Protestant landlords as well as George III resisted emancipation and Pitt resigned. Various attempts were made, for example in 1807, to ease restrictions, but all failed. Daniel O'CONNELL took up the cause for emancipation and founded the Catholic Association in 1823, dedicated to peaceful agitation. In 1828 O'Connell won a parliamentary election for County Clare, but as a Catholic could not take his seat. The Prime Minister, WELLINGTON, reluctantly introduced a Relief Bill to avoid civil war. The 1829 Act removed most civil restrictions; the only one to survive to the present is that no British monarch may be a Roman Catholic.

Catholic League HOLY LEAGUE.

Cato, Marcus Porcius (the Elder) (c. 234–149 BC) Roman statesman. As consul in 195 Cato suppressed revolt in former Carthaginian Spain with severity; as censor in 184 he was equally severe against private extravagance. *Delenda est Carthago* ('Carthage must be destroyed') became his slogan, although he did not live to see the event in 146. Cato prosecuted SCIPIO for corruption. His book on agriculture (*De agri cultura*) survives, but of his history of Rome, the *Origines*, there remain only a few fragments in existence.

Cato, Marcus Porcius (the Younger) (95–46 BC) Roman statesman, the great-grandson of CATO the Elder. He was known posthumously as 'Uticensis' after the place of his death. A conservative republican, he long opposed POMPEY, but finally sided with him against Julius CAESAR. He committed suicide at Utica in northern Africa after Caesar's victory at Thapsus rather than seek Caesar's pardon. Less noteworthy than his great-grandfather, he nevertheless became proverbial as an exemplar of republican and traditional Roman values.

Cato Street Conspiracy (1820) A plot to assassinate members of the British government. Under the leadership of Arthur Thistlewood, a revolutionary extremist, the conspirators planned to murder Lord CASTLEREAGH and other ministers while they were at dinner, as a prelude to a general uprising. However, government spies revealed the plot and possibly also provoked the conspirators to take action. They were arrested at a house in Cato Street, off the Edgware Road, in London. Convicted of high treason, Thistlewood and four others were executed, the rest being sentenced to transportation for life.

cattle trails Routes along which cattle in the USA were driven to the nearest railhead for despatch to market. When the AMERICAN CIVIL WAR ended many millions of wild cattle roamed the Texas range. Enterprising COWBOYS would round up herds, brand them, and then drive them along cattle trails to a railhead at such places as Abilene and, later, Dodge City. Two early trails from Texas were the Chisholm and the Shawnee trails. From the mid-1880s encroachments of homesteaders, the growth of large cattle ranches fenced by barbed wire, and the steady extension of railroads all contributed to the end of open-range ranching and made long-distance cattle drives uneconomical.

Caucasoids Fair-skinned 'European' people, named after the Caucasus Mountains between the Black and Caspian seas. They occupy Europe, Africa as far south as the Sahara, the Middle East, and the Indian subcontinent; in the past five centuries they have spread worldwide. In parts of Central Asia they were replaced in historic times by MONGOLOIDS. There was always admixture with, and incomplete differentiation from, neighbouring races, making a coherent story of the origin and dispersal of Caucasoids difficult. Modern-looking people (*homo sapiens sapiens*) had appeared in the Middle East by 50,000 years ago and in Europe by 35,000 years ago. It is now widely believed that these people came from Africa. They presumably replaced the NEANDERTHAL groups then occupying these regions although the Neanderthals are now considered a completely separate species. The CRO-MAGNON race of people, the forebears of modern Europeans, appeared around 35,000 years ago.

caudillo (Spanish, 'leader', 'hero') Military dictator in a Spanish-speaking country. In Latin American politics caudillos have tended to circumvent constitutions, and rule by military force. A product of the weakness of formal political structures and the prevalence of family and dynastic connections in politics they have nevertheless sometimes been able to bring about order, at least until they in turn have fallen.

Cavalier Parliament (or the Long Parliament of the Restoration) (1661–79) The first parliament in CHARLES II's reign to be elected by royal writ. Strongly Royalist and Anglican in composition, it contained 100 members from the LONG PARLIAMENT of Charles I. Its long duration enabled the Commons to claim a large part in affairs, despite being in session for only 60 months of the 18 years. Its early years were marked by harsh laws against Roman Catholics and Protestant Dissenters. As its membership changed it became increasingly critical of royal policy.

Cavaliers (French *chevalier*, 'horseman') The name of the Royalist party before, during, and after the ENGLISH CIVIL WAR. Opponents used the word from about 1641 as a term of abuse: later it acquired a romantic aura in contrast to the image of puritanical ROUNDHEADS. The party, made up of all social classes, but dominated by the country gentry and landowners, was defined by loyalty to the crown and the Anglican Church. The Restoration brought the Royalists back to power – the Parliament of 1661–79 is called the 'CAVALIER PARLIAMENT'.

cave-dwellers The name for the people who first used caves as shelters. This became widespread during the Middle and Upper PALAEOLITHIC periods, when humans penetrated for the first time into the northern tundra environments in front of the ice-sheets of the last glaciation. Since the remains of open-air campsites, such as wind-breaks or tents, are generally less well preserved and less likely to be discovered than bones and tools incorporated in cave sediments, early investigators imagined that STONE AGE people lived entirely in caves. This has now been refuted by the excavation of huts and tent-foundations preserved under wind-blown sediments in the Ukraine, central Europe, and France.

Cavell, Edith (1865–1915) English nurse. The daughter of a Norfolk vicar, in 1906 she helped establish a training school for nurses at the Berkendael Medical Institute in Brussels. Left in charge of the Institute after it had become a Red Cross hospital in World War I she nursed German and Allied soldiers alike. She believed it was her duty to help British, French, and Belgian soldiers to escape to neutral Holland. Unable to conceal these activities she was arrested, courtmartialled, and executed (1915). Her last words were, 'I realize that patriotism is not enough. I must have no hatred or bitterness towards anyone.'

Cavour, Camillo Benso, Count (1810–61) Piedmontese statesman. A leading agriculturalist, financier, and industrialist, he became a believer in the need for Italian unity and independence. In 1847 he founded the newspaper *Il* RISORGIMENTO (Italian, 'resurgence'), which advocated constitutional reforms. The REVOLUTIONS OF 1848 in Italy made it clear that unification would have to come through the action of the strongest Italian state, Piedmont. Elected to the first Parliament of PIEDMONT, he became Prime Minister in 1852, and quickly established Piedmont as a model of economic and military progress. A series of treaties with Britain, Belgium, and France encouraged free trade. The entry of Piedmont into the CRIMEAN WAR gave it an international voice and the chance of alliances essential to end Austrian control in Italy. His secret negotiations at Plombières in 1858 with NAPOLEON III resulted in the promise of Savoy and Nice to France as the price of French support which led to victory against the Austrians at MAGENTA and SOLFERINO the following year. The unexpected truce between the emperors of France and Austria at VILLAFRANCA, whereby Venetia was to remain an Austrian province precipitated Cavour's brief resignation. He returned to office at the beginning of 1860, when French support was again forthcoming, and master-minded the unification of all of northern Italy under Victor Emanuel II in 1859. He made use of GARIBALDI's expedition to Sicily and Naples the following year to bring those states also into a united Italy. Appointed Italy's first Premier in February 1861, Cavour died four months later, still negotiating to secure complete Italian unification with the inclusion of Venetia and the papal states.

Caxton, William (*c.* 1422–91) English printer. He spent most of his life as a mercer (cloth merchant), but in 1476 he set up the first printing press in England, in the precincts of Westminster Abbey. He was successful in producing a series of books in English, some from his own translations, which appealed to the taste of the court and gentry.

Ceausescu, Nicolae (1918–89) Romanian politician; secretary of the Communist Party and president of Romania (1967–89). After World War II, during which he was interned by the fascist government, Ceausescu rose to prominence in the ruling Communist Party. As president, he pursued a foreign policy that was markedly independent of the Soviet Union, especially in matters of Soviet military intervention in client states, which won him praise in the West. However, he presided over a regime that conducted massive internal repression (through the *Securitate* secret policy) and mismanaged the economy. His attempt to wipe out Romania's foreign debt through an austerity programme brought great hardship in the 1980s. With the collapse of communism in eastern Europe in late 1989, his grip on power loosened and he was toppled in the 'Christmas Revolution'. He and his wife Elena were executed by a firing squad on 25 December, 1989.

Cecil, Robert, 1st Earl of Salisbury and 1st Viscount Cranborne (1563–1612) English statesman. The son of William CECIL, Lord Burghley, he succeeded his father as ELIZABETH I's chief minister in 1598. He was responsible for ensuring the succession of JAMES I in 1603. He was created Viscount Cranborne (1604) and Earl of Salisbury (1605). He was made Lord Treasurer in 1608 and was faced with crown debts of nearly a million pounds. He increased the king's income by introducing additional customs duties (impositions) and attempted to improve the administrations of crown lands and revenues. In 1610 he proposed the 'Great Contract' by which Parliament would vote revenues annually to the king but it refused to ratify the scheme and he had to continue raising money by unpopular means, principally a forced loan (1611), and the sale of titles. After his death in 1612 expenditure not only continued to exceed income but increased under James I and his adviser BUCKINGHAM.

Cecil, William, 1st Baron Burghley (1520–98) English statesman. He trained as a lawyer and held office under HENRY VIII, EDWARD VI, and finally as ELIZABETH I's Secretary of State from 1558. Politically adept, he formulated the queen's policy at home and abroad and was rewarded by the offices of Master of the Courts of Wards and Liveries (1561) and Lord Treasurer (1572). He was created Lord Burghley in 1571.

For 40 years he ensured the stability of the Elizabethan regime. He promoted the ANGLICAN CHURCH by commissioning Bishop JEWEL to write his *Apologia Ecclesiae Anglicanae*. More Protestant in sympathy than the queen, he persuaded her to aid the French Huguenots (1567) and the Dutch Calvinists (1585). He exercised control of appointments to the universities of Oxford and Cambridge and was responsible for ordering the execution of MARY, QUEEN OF SCOTS, whose existence he perceived as a threat to the state. He encouraged new industries, particularly glass-making, and introduced financial reforms. He profited handsomely from his career and used his wealth to build the mansions of Burghley House, Lincolnshire, and Theobalds in Hertfordshire.

Celtic Church The Christian Church in Ireland and other Celtic parts of the British Isles from the 5th to the 8th centuries. It is probable that Ireland had early contacts with Christianity through Roman Britain, but the widespread conversion of the country to Christianity appears to have occurred in the 5th century, notably under St PATRICK (*c.* 390–460). For the next three centuries Ireland was the most important

centre of Christianity in north-western Europe. In the evangelization of Scotland, Irish missionaries played a prominent role, notably St COLUMBA (*c.* 521–97), who established many monasteries including one on the island of Iona. Celtic missionaries from Ireland also played a prominent role in the re-conversion of England in the 7th century. Others, such as St COLUMBANUS (*c.* 543–615), established monasteries in Gaul and north Italy. Celtic Christianity had its own strong characteristics. Its life-style was evangelical and ascetic, as shown by surviving Celtic 'Penitential Codes'; it was noted for its missionary zeal; and its organization was monastic rather than diocesan or parochial, with even bishops being subject to the abbots of monasteries. There flourished a rich visual and literary culture, most famously represented by the 'Book of Kells', on 8th-century illuminated manuscript of the gospels. Gradually the Celtic Church lost many of its distinctive features, as Ireland was absorbed into the mainstream of Western Christendom: the decisive moment in England was the Synod of WHITBY in 664, when the Roman date for Easter was preferred to the Irish; in Ireland and Scotland submission to Roman authority came about a century later.

Celts (often also called 'Gauls') A group of peoples identifiable by common cultural and linguistic features who occupied large areas of Iron Age Europe. Their earliest archaeological traces are found in the Upper Danube region (13th century BC), from where branches spread to Galatia in Asia Minor, Gaul (modern France), North Italy, Galicia and Celtiberia in Spain, and the British Isles. Their main expansion seems to have occurred after 800 BC. They sacked Rome in 390, and Delphi about a century later, when they also reached Asia Minor. Their artefacts are conventionally divided into URNFIELD CULTURES (earlier Danubian phase), HALLSTATT, and (after *c.* 500 BC) three successive LA TÈNE periods. They were gifted craftsmen and fierce fighters; but they lacked political cohesion, and by the end of the 1st millennium BC were increasingly 'squeezed' between the expanding power of Rome and migratory Germanic tribes, and settled in the remote areas of Europe (Brittany, Wales, and Ireland), where their dialects have survived.

CENTO CENTRAL TREATY ORGANIZATION.

Central African Federation (1953–63) A short-lived African federation, comprising the self-governing colony of Southern Rhodesia (ZIMBABWE) and the British protectorates of Northern Rhodesia (ZAMBIA) and Nyasaland (MALAWI). In the 1920s and 1930s Europeans in both Rhodesias had pressed for union, but Britain had rejected the proposal because of its responsibilities towards Africans in Northern Rhodesia and Nyasaland. In 1953 the Conservative government in Britain allowed economic arguments to prevail, and a federal constitution was devised by which the federal government handled external affairs, defence, currency, intercolonial relations, and federal taxes. Riots and demonstrations by African nationalists followed (1960–61), and in 1962 Britain accepted in principle Nyasaland's right to secede. A meeting of the four concerned governments at the Victoria Falls Conference agreed to dissolve the Federation, which came officially to an end in 1963. Nyasaland and Northern Rhodesia became independent. Southern RHODESIA refused to hand political control over to its African majority, and in 1965 the White government made a unilateral declaration of independence (UDI) from Britain. It was not until 1980 that the ensuing political impasse was ended, with the creation of the republic of Zimbabwe.

CARIBBEAN SEA

0   300 km
0   200 miles

United Provinces of Central America, 1823-38
Independent Mexican Empire, 1821-23
Gran Colombia, 1819-30
····· current national boundaries

CUBA
MEXICO 1821
BELIZE 1981 (British Honduras)
Bay Islands
GUATEMALA 1839
HONDURAS 1838
EL SALVADOR 1839
NICARAGUA 1838
Mosquito Coast
San Juan del Norte (Greytown)
COSTA RICA 1838
PANAMA 1903
COLUMBIA 1886
Panama Canal Zone (US protectorate 1903-39)

Central America *Central America formed part of the Spanish American empire as the captaincy-general of Guatemala and gained independence in 1821. When the United Provinces of Central America (1823–38) collapsed, the various provinces declared separate independence, except for British Honduras (Belize), which Britain had already seized from Spain in 1789. Early US attempts to build a canal (across Nicaragua) were thwarted by Britain (1855–57), but the successful Panama Canal was opened in 1914. US military intervention has taken place in Guatemala, El Salvador, Nicaragua, and Panama.*

Central African Republic A landlocked country in Africa stretching west-to-east from Cameroon to the Sudan and south-to-north from humid equatorial forests bordering the Democratic Republic of the Congo (Zaïre) to the savannah plains of the Chad basin.
Physical. The landscape mainly comprises low plateaux, with the highest point in the west. There is high ground also in the north, and from it streams flow south to the River Oubangi, which forms the southern boundary.
Economy. The Central African Republic is one of Africa's poorer countries, with a largely agricultural economy that is often adversely affected by drought. Diamonds, followed by coffee and cotton, constitute the largest export commodity.
History. Archaeological finds have shown that the area was inhabited from palaeolithic times (from about three million years ago) but there are no documentary records until the 19th century. The Central African Republic is thought to have been part of the empire of Gaoga, which flourished in the 16th century, and the region was raided for slaves during the 16th, 17th, and 18th centuries. The French began exploring the country in 1889 and by 1911 had taken full control of it. As the French colony of Ubangi Shari, it formed part of FRENCH EQUATORIAL AFRICA. In 1958 it became a republic within the FRENCH COMMUNITY, and fully independent in 1960. In 1976 its president, Jean Bedel BOKASSA, declared it an empire, and himself emperor. Following allegations of atrocities, he was deposed in 1979, and the country

reverted to a republic. Political instability persisted, and in 1981 General Kolingba seized power from the civilian government. This was restored in 1986 with Kolingba still President. There were demands for multiparty politics, and a new constitution was adopted in 1992. Elections were held in 1993: Ange-Félix Patasse became president and a coalition government was formed. In 1996 a military rebellion caused chaos for a week, but was suppressed with the help of French troops.

CAPITAL: Bangui
AREA: 622,436 sq km (240,324 sq miles)
POPULATION: 3.274 million (1996)
CURRENCY: 1 CFA franc = 100 centimes
RELIGIONS: Traditional beliefs 60.0%; Roman Catholic 25.0%; Muslim 9.0%; Protestant 6.0%
ETHNIC GROUPS: Banda 31.0%; Baya 29.0%; Mandjia 8.5%
LANGUAGES: French (official); Banda; Baya; Sango; local languages
INTERNATIONAL ORGANIZATIONS: UN; OAU; Non-Aligned Movement; Franc Zone

Central America The southernmost extension of the North American continent joining it to South America. In comprises Panama, Costa Rica, Nicaragua, El Salvador, Honduras, Guatemala, and Belize (British Honduras); Mexico, especially southern Mexico, is usually considered part of Central America.
Physical. Central America stretches between the isthmuses of Tehuantepec, Mexico, in the north-west and Panama in the south-east, and it separates the Pacific Ocean from the Caribbean Sea. Mountains run along its spine, those in the south being an extension of the Andes. Most are volcanic as the region is at a junction of crustal plates and an earthquake danger zone. The two great lakes of Nicaragua interrupt the chain. The climate is tropical, although above 760 m (2,500 feet) the temperature is mild. Dense jungle flourishes behind the mangrove swamps of the seashore.
Economy. Agriculture is important, the main crops being bananas, sugar cane, maize, and fruit. Cattle are bred, especially in Honduras. Manufacturing and tourism are increasingly important. The region contains large deposits of oil and gas, and of silver and gold.
History. Central America was populated by diverse aboriginal groups at the time of the first European contact in the early 16th century, and its colonization was the product of Spanish expansion from the Caribbean settlements of HISPANIOLA and CUBA. From 1535 to 1810, except for Panama, Central America was part of the viceroyalty of NEW SPAIN and subject to the jurisdiction of the viceroy in Mexico City. Independence from Spain came to Central America in 1821, most of the area being briefly annexed (1821–22) to the Mexican empire of Agustin de ITURBIDE. From 1823 to 1838 it experimented with political confederation within the United Provinces of Central America (Costa Rica, Guatemala, Honduras, Nicaragua, and El Salvador), but this soon fell victim to rivalries between liberals and conservatives, and to regional jealousies. By 1839 the political unity had ended. Military CAUDILLOS dominated the remainder of the 19th century. The US adventurer William Walker invaded Nicaragua (1855–57). The British occupied San Juan del Norte (Greytown) (1848) and the Bay Islands of Honduras to gain control of the Mosquito coast and to block US plans to build an inter-oceanic

canal, while the French applied diplomatic pressure to secure canal rights throughout the region. In 1951 the Organization of Central American States was formed to help solve common problems. The Economic Commission for Latin America, an organ of the United Nations, has encouraged co-operation concerning production, tariffs, and trade between member countries of the Latin American Free Trade Association (renamed LATIN AMERICAN INTEGRATION ASSOCIATION (LAIA) in 1980) and the CENTRAL AMERICAN COMMON MARKET.

Central American Common Market (ODECA or CACM) An economic organization comprising Guatemala, Honduras, El Salvador, Nicaragua, and Costa Rica. Beginning with a treaty signed by all five countries in 1960 the CACM sought to reduce trade barriers, stimulate exports, and encourage industrialization by means of regional co-operation. With a permanent secretariat at Guatemala City, its aim was co-operation with the member countries of the Latin American Free Trade Association (now called the Latin American Integration Association). During the 1970s, it somewhat lost impetus, owing to war, upheaval, international recession, and ideological differences among member states. A new tariff and customs agreement came into effect in 1986, when regional trade improved. In 1993 Panama agreed to implement full economic integration with the CACM nations.

Central Intelligence Agency (CIA) A US government agency. It was established by Congress in 1947 and is responsible to the President through the National Security Council. Its work consists of gathering and evaluating foreign intelligence, undertaking counter-intelligence operations overseas, and organizing secret political intervention and psychological warfare operations in foreign areas. The CIA has acquired immense power and influence, employing thousands of agents overseas, and it disposes of a large budget which is not subjected to Congressional scrutiny. During the 1980s it was actively involved in Nicaragua, Afghanistan, and Iran. In 1986 the CIA was criticized for its involvement in the Irangate scandal (see REAGAN). During the 1990s it sought to redefine its role following the end of the COLD WAR.

Central Pacific Railroad A US railway forming the western part of the first transcontinental route. The Central Pacific Railway was built eastward from Sacramento to meet the Union Pacific coming west. With a larger federal subsidy available for the company building the most track, the CPR was constructed rapidly over the most difficult territory, crossing the Sierras, passing along the Humboldt River through Nevada into Utah, where at Promontory Point on 10 May 1869 a golden spike was driven to mark the joining with the Union Pacific and the completion of the east–west rail link. Although the Union Pacific won the extra subsidy, the organizers of the CPR, Collis P. Huntington and Leland Stanford, were able to realize sufficient from the sale of millions of acres of land grants to cover the entire cost ($90 million) of construction.

Central Treaty Organization (CENTO) (1955–79) A mutual security organization composed of representatives of Britain, Turkey, Iran, Pakistan, and Iraq. In 1956 the USA became an associate member. Formed as a result of the Baghdad Pact (1955), it was designed in part as a defence against the Soviet Union and to consolidate the influence of Britain in the Arab world. Following the withdrawal of Iraq (1958), its headquarters were moved to Ankara. It became inactive after the withdrawal of Turkey, Pakistan, and Iran in 1979.

centurion A professional middle-ranking officer of the Roman army. The title means 'leader of a hundred'. A century was a military unit, based on early citizen lists drawn up for military service. In earlier days most centurions rose from the ranks; but in the later republic and under the emperors (Principate) some men enlisted directly as centurions. The rigorous discipline, leadership and experience of the centurions made them a vital factor in the success of the professional army.

ceorl A free peasant farmer of Anglo-Saxon England. In status ceorls were above the SERFS but below the THANES (noblemen), with a WERGILD of usually 200 shillings. They were liable to military service in the FYRD and to taxation. Although they could own land, they were often forced by economic pressures and by reasons of security to place themselves in the control of the richer landowners. After the Norman Conquest their status diminished rapidly and the term 'churl' came to mean an ill-bred serf.

Cetshwayo (often spelt Cetewayo) (1826–84) King of the ZULUS (1873–79). He first took part in raids against European settlers in 1838. When his father Mpande died in 1872 fighting broke out: six of his half-brothers were killed and two exiled to enable him to ascend the throne. His installation was performed by Sir Theophilus Shepstone. Cetshwayo was angered by Shepstone's support of Boer claims to his territory, and increased his army to defend it. This led to the ZULU WAR (1879), in which he defeated the British. The British captured his capital Ulundi eight months later. Cetshwayo was deposed and sent to London. In 1883 an attempt by the British to restore him failed; he was attacked by an old enemy and fled to a native reserve.

Ceylon SRI LANKA.

Chaco War (1932–35) A conflict between Paraguay and Bolivia. The Gran Chaco, an extensive lowland plain, had been an object of dispute between the two countries since the early 19th century, but Bolivia's final loss of its Pacific coast in 1929 (the TACNA–ARICA settlement) prompted it to push its claims to the Chaco. Border clashes in the late 1920s led to outright war in 1932. Bolivia had the larger army and superior military equipment, but the Aymará and Quechua Indian conscripts from the Andean highlands did not fare well in the low, humid Chaco. The Paraguayan colonel José Félix Estigarribia drove the Bolivians west across the Chaco and forced his enemies to sue for peace in 1935. Paraguay gained most of the disputed territory, but the price was immense for both countries. More than 50,000 Bolivians and 35,000 Paraguayans had lost their lives. Economic stagnation was to plague both combatants for years to come.

Chad A landlocked country in north-Central Africa surrounded by Libya to the north, Sudan to the east, the Central African Republic to the south, and Niger, Nigeria, and Cameroon to the west.

Physical. Out of the Sahara in its northern half rise the volcanic Tibesti Mountains, with reserves of tungsten, while in the east is the great depression surrounding Lake CHAD, with deposits of natron (hydrated sodium carbonate). The south has moderate summer rains which produce a savannah and the seasonal Chari and Logone Rivers and their tributaries.

Economy. Chad is one of the poorest countries in Africa, with a mainly agricultural economy which is vulnerable to drought. Major exports include cotton and livestock products. The industrial sector is small, mostly comprising textiles and food-processing.

History. Northern Chad has been inhabited for about 10,000 years and southern Chad since about 500 BC. During the 8th century BERBER peoples moved into the area and founded the empire of Kanem. This empire expanded and in the 13th century merged with the kingdom of Bornu. The neighbouring kingdoms of Baguirmi and Ouaddaï grew more powerful during the 16th century. The three kingdoms fought during the 17th century until in the early 1890s all fell under the control of the Sudanese conqueror, RABEH. French expeditions advanced into the region, and French sovereignty was recognized by the European powers. After FASHODA (1898) France declared a protectorate, and in 1908 Chad became part of French Equatorial Africa, though control was complete only in 1912. In 1920 Chad became a colony under French administration, its rich mineral deposits being rapidly exploited. In 1940 Chad was the first colony to declare for the FREE FRENCH. It became autonomous within the FRENCH COMMUNITY in 1958, and a fully independent republic in 1960, with François Tombalbaye as the first President. Since then the country has struggled to maintain unity between the Arabic-speaking Muslim peoples of the north and the more economically developed south and west. In 1980 Libya invaded, proposing union between the two countries. Civil war lasted until 1987, when French and US intervention led to Libya's withdrawal and the installation of Hissène Habré as President. Habré was deposed in 1990 by his one-time military commander Idriss Déby. A democratization process was agreed upon, and a transitional legislature was installed in 1993. In 1994 Libya agreed to hand back to Chad the Aouzou Strip, an area rich in minerals occupied by Libya since 1973.

Armed rebels, based in the south of the country, agreed to a ceasefire in 1996 and a constitutional referendum, which had been postponed several times, was held. A new constitution was approved, establishing Chad as a unitary state.

CAPITAL:	Ndjamena
AREA:	1,284,000 sq km (495,755 sq miles)
POPULATION:	6.543 million (1996)
CURRENCY:	1 CFA franc = 100 centimes
RELIGIONS:	Muslim 50.0%; traditional beliefs 45.0%; Christian 5.0%
ETHNIC GROUPS:	Arabic (Hassauna and Djoheina) 46.0%; Sudanic 28.0%; Nilotic 8.0%; Saharan 7.0%
LANGUAGES:	Arabic, French (both official); Sara; Nilotic; Saharan
INTERNATIONAL ORGANIZATIONS:	UN; OAU; Non-Aligned Movement; Franc Zone

Chadwick, Sir Edwin (1800–90) British public health reformer. A friend and disciple of Jeremy BENTHAM, he was the architect of the POOR LAW Amendment Act (1834). His report for the royal commission set up in 1833 to investigate the conditions of work of factory children resulted in the passing of the Ten Hours Act. In 1840, concerned at the number of people driven into pauperism by the death of the breadwinner during the numerous outbreaks of cholera, he conducted on behalf of the Poor Law Commissioners an *Inquiry into the Sanitary Condition of the Labouring Population*, published in 1842. As a result of this and subsequent agitation, an Act of 1848 gave municipalities powers to set up local boards of health, subject to Public Health Commissioners, among them Chadwick himself. During his term of office as Commissioner of the Board of Health (1848–54), he persuaded urban authorities to undertake major water, drainage, and slum clearance schemes to reduce DISEASE.

Chaeronea The northernmost city of BOEOTIA, ancient Greece, the scene of two important battles. In 338 BC PHILIP II of Macedonia crushed the Thebans, Athenians, and their allies there, and so brought mainland Greece under his control. An enormous stone lion, commemorating the site of the fighting, can still be seen.

In 86 BC two armies of MITHRIDATES VI, King of Pontus, combined there against the Roman forces of SULLA, but were defeated despite a considerable numerical superiority. A further Roman victory at Orchomenus ensured the ejection of the Pontic forces from Greece.

Chaka SHAKA.

Chalcedon, Council of (451) The fourth ecumenical council of the Christian Church, held at the city of Chalcedon in Greece. This rejected the view expressed by a meeting – convened without papal approval – at Ephesus in 449 which declared JESUS CHRIST to have a single nature, asserting instead that Christ's nature was both human and divine.

Chalcis In ancient times, the leading city of the island of Euboea, off the eastern coast of central Greece. It was a trading city, famous for its metal goods, and was important in transmitting Greek civilization to Sicily and southern Italy. In 506 BC it was forced to cede some of its territory to Athenian settlers. In 446 an attempt to secede from the Athenian empire was crushed. In 338 PHILIP II of Macedonia installed a garrison there – one of the 'fetters' of Greece – but the city thrived subsequently until it was partly destroyed by the Romans after having sided with the ACHAEAN LEAGUE against them in 146.

Chaldea An area at the head of the Persian Gulf. It was attacked by the Assyrian Shalmaneser II *c.* 850 BC. In 721–710 a Chaldean king managed to wrest Babylon from the Assyrians, but was later ejected. It was not until 626 that Nabopolassar established the great Chaldean dynasty of BABYLON, of which the most famous representative was NEBUCHADNEZZAR II. After it had been overthrown by Cyrus the Great in 539 BC the term 'Chaldean' became equivalent to 'Babylonian'.

Chamberlain, Arthur Neville (1869–1940) British statesman. Son of Joseph CHAMBERLAIN, he first entered Parliament in 1918. As Minister of Health (1923 and 1924–29), he was responsible for the reform of the POOR LAW, the promotion of council-house building, and the systematizing of local government. A skilful Chancellor of the Exchequer (1931–37), he steered the economy back towards prosperity with a policy of low interest rates and easy credit. As Prime Minister (1937–40) his hope for a large programme of social reform was ended by the necessity for rearmament, which began in 1937. His policy, largely popular at the time but later termed 'APPEASEMENT' by his critics, was to accommodate the European dictators in order to avoid war. At his three meetings with Hitler, at Berchtesgaden, at Godesberg, and at Munich, he made increasing concessions. He did not in fact save CZECHOSLOVAKIA from German invasion (March 1939). When Germany invaded Poland later in the year, Chamberlain had little choice but to declare war. In May 1940, following the routing of British forces in Norway, his own party rebelled against him and he was forced to resign the Premiership in favour of Winston CHURCHILL, whom he wholeheartedly supported.

Chamberlain, Sir Austen (1863–1937) British statesman. Son of Joseph CHAMBERLAIN, he entered Parliament in 1892 as a Liberal-Unionist. He was Chancellor of the Exchequer (1903–05) and Secretary of State for India (1915–17), resigning over alleged blunders in the MESOPOTAMIA CAMPAIGN. He became Chancellor of the Exchequer again in 1919 and leader of the Conservative Party in 1921, but loyalty to LLOYD GEORGE led to his resignation in 1922. He was Foreign Secretary (1924–29), playing a major part in securing the LOCARNO TREATIES.

Chamberlain, Joseph (1835–1914) British statesman. In local politics he won distinction as a Liberal mayor of Birmingham (1873–76), pioneering municipal reform. Elected to Parliament (1876), he organized national Liberal Associations throughout the country. These helped to win the election of 1880, when he joined the cabinet. Unable to support Gladstone's HOME RULE policy for Ireland, he left the Liberals to join the Conservatives as a Liberal-Unionist (1887). As Colonial Secretary (1895–1903) he distanced himself from the JAMESON RAID, but supported MILNER's policies in South Africa which precipitated the Second BOER WAR, and encouraged the formation of the Commonwealth of AUSTRALIA. A committed imperialist, he came increasingly to regard a trade policy of protection as essential to the British economy, resigning in 1903 to campaign for an end to FREE TRADE and the introduction of tariffs to encourage trade within the empire (imperial preference).

Champa The kingdom of the Chams, a Malay people, said to have been founded in the 2nd century AD in Vietnam. It was frequently at war with the KHMERS to its west, and succumbed in the 15th century to ANNAM to the north. Its people are commemorated in ANGKOR: in a bas-relief of a battle against the Khmers they are distinguished by their flat hats, each one decorated with a flower.

Champagne A province of north-eastern France adjoining Lorraine. International trade FAIRS were held there in the Middle Ages. In 1284 the marriage of Jeanne, daughter of Henry III, the last count, to PHILIP IV (the Fair) led to union with France. The discovery of the method of making its celebrated sparkling wine, champagne, is attributed to a Benedictine monk, Dom Perignon (1668–1715).

Champlain, Samuel de (1567–1635) French statesman and explorer of CANADA. After leading a Spanish expedition to the Caribbean in 1599, he made 11 voyages in French service to Canada, following CARTIER's discovery of the St Lawrence River and the site of Montreal, at the time an Iroquois village. He explored the New England coast and in 1608 founded a settlement at what is now Quebec, which he used as a base for exploring the Canadian interior, discovering lakes Champlain (named after him), Ontario, and Huron. He believed that the Great Lakes must lead to a way through to the Pacific, but was deflected from further exploration by his role as governor of the French colony, which he defended when it was attacked by hostile Native Americans. In 1629 Quebec was captured by the English and he remained for three years captive in England. On the return of Canada to France in 1633 he returned to Quebec and died there.

chancery (from the Latin *cancella*, 'screen', hence a screened-off place, or office) The writing-office attached to the court of a ruler – emperor, pope, or king. Since it supplied the writ necessary for a lawsuit to be heard by the king's judges, it came to be a law court itself, presided over by its head, the Chancellor. From the late 14th century in England its legal business grew rapidly; by the 16th century, it was notorious for delays and it was reformed in the 19th century.

Chandragupta Maurya MAURYAN EMPIRE.

Changamire (*fl. c.* 1500) East African ruler. The son of MWENE MATOPE, he added the Arabic title *amir* (commander) to his given name, Changa. On his father's death he killed Nyahuma, the lawful successor. His own son fought Chikuyo, Nyahuma's son, until 1502. He began the dismemberment of the ROZVI EMPIRE. His kingdom was known also as Butwa, and lasted until the early 19th century, when the Nguni destroyed it. His successors built a number of stone monuments and added to the Great ZIMBABWE.

Channel Tunnel A rail tunnel beneath the English Channel providing a fixed link between the UK and France. Several schemes were proposed from the early 19th century onwards. Work actually started twice, in 1882 and 1974, though it was soon abandoned. The present tunnel, which runs between Folkestone and Sangatte, was begun in 1986 and completed in 1994. It comprises two tunnels, each 7.6 m (25 feet) in diameter and 49.4 km (30.7 miles) long, 37.5 km (23.3 miles) of which is under water, and a service tunnel. The tunnels are, on average, 40 m (130 feet) below the sea-bed. A high-speed shuttle service carrying motor vehicles between the two terminals in about 35 minutes opened in 1994. A year later the Eurostar passenger service connecting London with Paris and Brussels began to operate: the centre of Paris can now be reached from the centre of London in about three hours. The Channel Tunnel was developed entirely as a private enterprise; as a result of spiralling construction costs and interest on loans, its developer Eurotunnel has incurred huge debts.

Chapultepec Conference (1945) An Inter-American conference, held in Mexico City. The Act of Chapultepec (1945), adopted by 20 republics, resolved to undertake joint action in repelling any aggression against an American state. This was formalized by the Inter-American Treaty of Reciprocal Assistance (the Rio Treaty, 1947), and constituted a significant step in the history of PAN-AMERICANISM.

chariot A fast, two-wheeled, horse-drawn vehicle. They were originally designed for use in war, and developed from the battle-wagons used by the SUMERIANS *c.* 2500 BC, which had four wheels, were drawn by onagers (wild asses), and served as mobile fighting platforms. The use of horses, and light two-wheeled vehicles adapted to them, was introduced to the Near East from the region between the Black Sea and the Caspian *c.* 2000 BC. (Horses, which were only the size of ponies, were rarely used for riding.) Their crews consisted of two or three people, who were generally armed with bows or javelins. In northern Europe, however, the chariot was used to carry into battle soldiers who fought on foot. A popular tactic was to equip chariot wheels with scythe blades to hack at the legs of enemy soldiers.

Chariots were the prized possessions of potentates, as much for prestige as for warfare, from Greece and Egypt as far as China throughout the 2nd millennium BC, but declined in importance in the 1st millennium when heavier horses made cavalry possible. By the time Julius CAESAR went to Britain in 55 BC, their use in war had ceased on the Continent, and he was interested to find them used by the Britons to give warriors mobility on the battlefield. In Rome, they continued to be used as sporting vehicles, in chariot races.

Charlemagne   *As Emperor of the West, Charlemagne fostered a major cultural revival. This 8th-century coin bearing his profile also illustrates the improved coin-making techniques developed during his reign.*

Charlemagne (*c.* 742–814) Frankish king and Emperor of the West (HOLY ROMAN EMPIRE) (800–14). He was the son of PEPIN III (the Short) and grandson of CHARLES MARTEL. As King of the Franks, reigning at first jointly with his brother Carloman, who died in 771, he set about the formidable task of imposing his rule. The Franks had long suffered from weak government and continuous invasions from the barbarian north and east and the Muslim south. His long campaign began in 772, directed initially at the pagan Saxons, then against the Avars to the east. Bavaria and Lombardy came under his control and he was then able to strengthen and support the

papacy by restoring papal lands in Italy. On Christmas Day 800 he was crowned as Emperor of the West by Pope Leo III.

The palace school at his capital city, Aachen, became the most important centre of learning in western Christendom, and there the emperor brought many great scholars and teachers including ALCUIN. He founded schools in cathedrals and monasteries throughout the Empire, initiating a revival in scholarship whose effects were profound and lasting, and a prime contribution to what is called the 'Carolingian Renaissance'. Charlemagne enjoyed a heroic posthumous reputation throughout the Middle Ages, witnessed in the poem the *Chanson de Roland.*

Charles I (1600–49) King of Great Britain and Ireland (1625–49). He was the second son of JAMES I and Anne of Denmark. He was neglected by his father in favour of his favourite, BUCKINGHAM, who also dominated Charles in the opening years of his reign. A disastrous foreign policy, Charles's illegal levying of TUNNAGE AND POUNDAGE, and the mildness of his policy towards Roman Catholics (RECUSANTS) culminated in the forcing through by a hostile Parliament of the PETITION OF RIGHT (1628). From 1629 he ruled without a Parliament.

Charles was a man of strong religious conviction: he was also stubborn and politically naïve. During the 'Eleven Year Tyranny' (1629–40) he relied increasingly on LAUD, STRAFFORD, and his French Catholic queen, HENRIETTA MARIA; their influence, and the king's use of unconstitutional measures, deepened the widespread antagonism to the court, especially after the SHIP MONEY crisis (1637). The fiasco of the BISHOPS' WARS drove him to recall Parliament in 1640. The LONG PARLIAMENT forced him to sacrifice Laud and Strafford, who were impeached and executed. He had to accept severe limitations of his powers, but an open breach came in January 1642, when he tried to arrest FIVE MEMBERS of the House of Commons, a blunder which united the Lords and Commons against the king and made the ENGLISH CIVIL WAR inevitable.

The royal standard was raised at Nottingham in August. Charles was soundly beaten at MARSTON MOOR (1644) and NASEBY (1645) and in 1646 surrendered to the Scots near Newark, was handed over to Parliament the following year, and subsequently captured by the Parliamentary army. After escaping to Carisbrooke Castle, Isle of Wight, he signed the 'Engagement' with the Scots (1647) that enabled him to renew the war with their help, but with little success. He was recaptured in 1648, tried, and publicly executed in London.

Charles I of Anjou (1226–85) King of Naples and Sicily (1266–85), son of Louis VIII of France. He acquired PROVENCE by marriage in 1246. Pope Urban IV was under severe threat from the HOHENSTAUFENS and gave him the kingdom of Sicily in order to curtail their power. He defeated and killed MANFRED at Benevento, effectively ending Hohenstaufen influence, but then went on to take Naples as well as most of northern Italy, himself becoming a real threat to papal interests. His ambitions were ended by the uprising known as the SICILIAN VESPERS in which he was assassinated and the French expelled.

Charles II (the Bald) (823–77) King of the West Franks (843–77) and Emperor of Germany (875–77). He was the son of Emperor Louis the Pious. After the death of their father he and his brother, Louis the German, made war on their eldest brother Lothair, who had inherited the title of King of the West Franks. By the Treaty of VERDUN in 843 Charles gained that kingdom. He and Louis divided Lothair's central kingdom between them in 870 by the Treaty of Mersen, and Charles gained the imperial title in 875. The internal conflicts of his reign were further complicated by VIKING incursions. He was a noted patron of scholarship and the arts.

Charles II (1630–85) King of England, Scotland, and Ireland (1660–85), the son of CHARLES I. In the first phase of the ENGLISH CIVIL WAR he was at the Battle of Edgehill (1642), and then took refuge in the west of England (1645–46) until he escaped to France. After his father's execution he was crowned in Scotland (1651), having signed the SOLEMN LEAGUE AND COVENANT, which he later repudiated. CROMWELL had already defeated the Scottish army at Dunbar, and Charles's advance into England was halted at the Battle of Worcester. He was on the run for six weeks, before escaping to the Continent. The efforts of General MONCK were largely responsible for his RESTORATION to the English throne in May 1660.

Charles shrewdly adopted conciliatory policies, offering indemnity to all but the regicides (those responsible for the death of his father) and attempting to wean England from religious prejudice. His marriage in 1662 to CATHERINE OF BRAGANZA increased anti-Catholic feeling, however; the union was childless, and the heir apparent, the king's brother James, Duke of York, was also a Roman Catholic. His foreign policy was originally directed against France in the Triple Alliance (1668) with Sweden and the United Provinces. He then signed the Treaty of Dover (1670) and agreed to support Louis XIV against the Dutch in return for financial and territorial gains; a secret clause committed him to announcing his conversion to Catholicism. He undermined the CLARENDON Code by Declarations of INDULGENCE, provoking the POPISH PLOT (1678) and the RYE HOUSE PLOT (1683), as well as the exclusion crisis of 1679–81 led by his chief opponent in Parliament, the Earl of SHAFTESBURY. After March 1684 he did not call Parliament though this was illegal under the terms of the Triennial Act. In the country he was a popular monarch and, although he is commonly remembered for his mistresses and his horse-racing, he was also a notable patron of the arts and sciences and a sponsor of the ROYAL SOCIETY.

Charles III (the Fat) (832–88) King of the Franks (884–87), Emperor of Germany (882–88). He was the youngest son of Louis the German. He inherited Swabia and acquired both east and west Frankish kingdoms by 884 after his older brothers died. He was unsuccessful in repelling SARACEN invaders and was obliged to buy a respite from attacks by the VIKINGS and so was deposed in 887. His death marked the end of the Carolingian monopoly of kingship over the Franks.

Charles III (1716–88) King of Spain (1759–88) and of Naples and Sicily (1734–59). His enlightened policies met with opposition in Spain. He tried to improve agriculture and industry, reformed the judicial system, and reduced the INQUISITION's powers. His foreign policy was dominated by alliance with France (the Family Compact, 1761). He lost Florida in 1763 but regained it with Minorca in 1783. In 1779 he began a three-year siege of Gibraltar but failed to retake it from Britain.

Charles IV (1316–78) King of Bohemia (1346–78), HOLY ROMAN EMPEROR (1347–78). He acquired authority over Austria and Hungary in 1364, and received the imperial crown from the pope, in Rome, in 1355. The Golden Bull (1356) issued in his reign formed the imperial constitution, regulating the duties of the seven ELECTORS. He was an intellectual, interested in the development of the German language, and founded the University of Prague in 1348.

Charles V (the Wise) (1337–80) King of France (1364–80). He earned his nickname from his intellectual pursuits which included book-collecting and artistic patronage, his religious piety, and his cautious adoption of delaying and 'scorched-earth' tactics in fighting the English during the HUNDRED YEARS WAR. Assuming responsibility as Regent of France in 1356 when his father, John II was captured at POITIERS, he quelled revolt in Paris and from the JACQUERIE and, aided by the Constable of France, Bertrand du GUESCLIN, was able to recover most of France from the invading English forces.

Charles V (1500–58) Holy Roman Emperor (1519–56) and (as Charles I) King of Spain (1516–56). The son of PHILIP I (the Handsome) and Joanna of Spain, and grandson of Emperor MAXIMILIAN I, Charles came to the throne of Spain in 1516 and united it with that of the empire when he inherited the latter in 1519. Tied down by such wide responsibilities, and hampered by the fact that his authority in his separate territories was established on different bases, Charles was never able to give proper attention to national and international problems. His achievements were none the less considerable. In Spain he survived an early revolt and laid the foundations of the strong government which underpinned Spanish greatness in the century after his death, while in Italy he overcame papal resistance to the establishment of Spanish hegemony. While his long war with FRANCIS I of France was not decisive, it did weaken France to the extent that it was unable to challenge Spain again before the outbreak of the THIRTY YEARS WAR. He blunted the OTTOMAN offensive against Christian Europe, and maintained his authority under difficult circumstances in the Netherlands. His greatest failure was in Germany, where he was unable either to check the spread of Protestantism or curb the independence of the local princes. Charles handed Naples (1554), the Netherlands (1555), and Spain (1556) over to his son PHILIP, and the imperial crown (1556) to his brother Ferdinand, and retired to a monastery in Spain.

Charles VII (1403–61) King of France (1422–61). During his youth France was badly ruled by his father Charles the Mad and much territory was lost. Internal quarrels and war with England dominated his reign. He was not crowned until 1429, and then only thanks to JOAN OF ARC. He established greater control over the Church in the Pragmatic Sanction of Bourges of 1438, which upheld the right of the French Church to administer its property and nominate clergy to benefices, independently of the papacy. He brought the HUNDRED YEARS WAR to an end, having recovered most of his land and established his authority.

Charles X (1757–1836) King of France (1824–30). As the Comte d'Artois, the dissolute and reactionary brother of Louis XVI, he was ordered by the king to leave France in 1789 and became the leader of the exiled royalists. He returned to France in 1814 and during the reign of his next brother, LOUIS XVIII, led the ultra-royalist party. His proclamation to rule by divine right and his choice of ministers who did not reflect liberal majorities in Parliament led to unrest. The defeat of an unpopular ministry in June 1830 prompted him to issue the July Ordinances, which established rigid control of the press, dissolved the newly elected chamber, and restricted suffrage. These measures enraged the populace and he was forced, in the JULY REVOLUTION, to abdicate. After the succession of LOUIS-PHILIPPE, he returned to Britain.

Charles XII (1682–1718) King of Sweden (1697–1718). The story of his reign is reflected in the progress of the NORTHERN WAR. He was attacked by a coalition of enemies and won a series of victories; then in 1707 he invaded Russia and was defeated at POLTAVA. He took refuge in Turkish territory was imprisoned and escaped and was finally killed while on another military campaign. His wars left Sweden financially drained and no longer one of the great powers of Europe.

Charles XIV (Jean Baptiste Jules Bernadotte) (1763–1844) King of Sweden and Norway (1818–44). A supporter of the French Revolution, he served brilliantly under NAPOLEON BONAPARTE in the Italian Campaign. At one time a rival to Napoleon, he nevertheless supported the latter when he proclaimed the empire in 1804. He fought at Austerlitz and Wagram and became governor of Hanover before being invited (1810) by the Swedish Riksdag (Parliament) to succeed the senile, childless Charles XIII. He accepted, becoming a member of the Lutheran Church. As crown prince he allied Sweden with Britain and Russia and played an important part in the defeat of Napoleon at the battle of Leipzig (1813). Having invaded Denmark, he obtained Danish agreement at the Treaty of Kiel (1814) for the transfer of NORWAY to Sweden. He succeeded Charles XIII in 1818. Autocratic in style and opposed to demands for a free press and more liberal government, he nevertheless maintained popular support throughout his reign. He was the founder of the present Swedish dynasty.

Charles Martel (c. 688–741) (French, *martel*, 'hammer') Frankish leader. He was the son of Pepin II, 'mayor of the palace' under MEROVINGIAN rule. He gained control of the Austrasian province and defeated the Neustrian mayor. Burgundy and Aquitaine were also acquired. His greatest achievement, and the one which made him a traditional French hero, was his defeat of the Muslim forces between Poitiers and Tours in 732, which signalled the end of their northward expansion.

Charles the Bold (1433–77) Duke of BURGUNDY (1467–77). He was the greatest of the dukes of Burgundy, and almost succeeded in creating a kingdom independent of France. He tried to persuade the HOLY ROMAN EMPEROR to grant him the title of king in 1473. He supported the League of the Public Weal against the French king, Louis XI, and, after 1467, concentrated with successful results on expansion into the Rhineland and Alsace. After 1475, war with the Swiss and defeat in battle culminated in his own death in battle. His realm was absorbed by the French and by MAXIMILIAN I.

Charlie, Bonnie Prince PRETENDER; STUART.

charter (Latin, *carta*, 'written document') A legal document from a ruler or government, conferring rights or laying down a constitution. Charters in England date from the 7th century, when they were used to confirm grants of land, usually recorded in Latin. Borough charters granting towns specific privileges, which could include self-government and freedom from certain fiscal burdens, were regularly awarded by English kings between 1066 and 1216 (over 300 were issued). MAGNA CARTA (1215) was a charter which sought to regularize the feudal contract between the crown and its BARONS.

The commercial and colonial expansion of England from the 16th century led to the use of charters to authorize the trading ventures of companies (CHARTERED COMPANY) and to form the first constitutions of the English colonies in America. Such colonial charters were in the form of a grant to a company (Virginia Company 1606), or gave recognition to the self-governing status of existing colonies (as with Connecticut in 1662). The importance of these charters was recognized by the Americans during the War of INDEPENDENCE.

chartered company A form of trading company which developed from the European medieval trading guilds, and which was prominent in the late 16th and 17th centuries. The discovery by explorers of India and America stimulated individual merchants into forming groups, safe-guarded by royal charter in order to monopolize trade. Governments awarded exclusive trading rights in a particular area to a few rich merchants. Such companies were easy to control and, with their specially granted diplomatic, legislative, and military authority, they acted as virtual representatives of the crown. Since the companies were so restrictive, they could arouse considerable domestic opposition.

The DUTCH EAST INDIA COMPANY (founded 1602) probably had the best record of profit of all the 'joint-stock' ventures. These were companies in which members held shares entitling them to a proportion of the profits. They differed significantly from the earlier 'regulated' companies, which were associations of individuals who traded alone with their own stock and employees, subject to the company's regulations.

Many European chartered companies were costly failures. In the 17th century the French monarchy set up some thirty – including its own FRENCH EAST INDIA COMPANY (1664) – most of which were unprofitable. Individual French traders were more successful in Haiti, Martinique, and Guadeloupe. The heyday of the chartered company was before 1800.

Charter 77 A Czechoslovak human rights movement. Named after a document delivered in 1977, initially signed by 242 academics, intellectuals, and churchmen, the charter appealed to the Czech government to adjust the country's laws in conformity with the Universal Declaration of Human Rights enshrined in the United Nations covenants, and to respect in practice the agreements of the HELSINKI CONFERENCE. It failed to win widespread support, but some of its members, among them Václav HAVEL, became leading figures in post-communist CZECHOSLOVAKIA.

Chartism A popular movement in Britain for electoral and social reform (1836–48). The REFORM ACT of 1832 had left the mass of the population without any voice in the country's affairs, and widespread discontent was fuelled by a slump in the economy. The Chartist movement began with the formation of the London Working Men's Association, led by William Lovett and Francis PLACE, who drew up a programme of reform for the common people. In 1838 *The People's Charter* was launched at a meeting in Birmingham: it called for universal male suffrage, annual parliaments, vote by ballot, abolition of the property qualification for Members of Parliament, payment of Members of Parliament, and equal electoral districts. In 1839, the Chartists, now strongly influenced by the Irish radical Feargus O'CONNOR, met in London to prepare a petition to the House of Commons. The meeting revealed deep differences of opinion and after Parliament had rejected the petition, there was uncertainty about the movement's future. During that year there were riots in Birmingham and throughout the north of England; the NEWPORT RISING took place in Monmouthshire, and several Chartist leaders were arrested and imprisoned. Reorganizing themselves, in 1842 the Chartists presented a second petition, signed by three million supporters, to Parliament, which again refused to listen to their claims. The plan for a final demonstration, to be held in London in 1848 for the purpose of presenting yet another petition, was called off after the government threatened military resistance, and the movement faded into insignificance, though many Chartists were later active in radical politics.

Chassey culture WESTERN NEOLITHIC.

Chatham, 1st Earl of PITT.

Chattanooga Campaign (1863) A campaign during the AMERICAN CIVIL WAR. On 9 September a Federal army under General W. Rosencrans occupied Chattanooga, a strategic communication centre for the CONFEDERACY and pushed on south-eastwards. Rosecrans's forces were attacked by a Confederate army under General Bragg, who successfully drove Rosecrans back to Chattanooga, where the Union army was besieged for several weeks. General Ulysses GRANT assumed direct command, broke the siege and counter-attacked, winning the Battle of Chattanooga and opening the way for the advance on Atlanta (1864) and later for the march of General William SHERMAN to the sea.

Chavín culture A civilization that flourished in Peru 1000–200 BC. The culture was based on the ceremonial centre of Chavín de Huantar, high in the Andes 280 km (175 miles) north of Lima. It united an area 800 km (500 miles) along the Peruvian coast in a common culture, and its influence spread almost as far again. The unifying force was probably religious rather than political, the most characteristic feature being figures, presumably gods, with jaguar fangs projecting from their lips. Notable advances included improved maize, the back-strap loom, and metallurgy. As its religious authority waned, regional groups appeared, that dominated Peru for the next thousand years.

Chechnya RUSSIA.

CHEKA Acronym for the All-Russian Extraordinary Commission for the Suppression of Counter-revolution and Sabotage, the earliest form of Soviet secret police. It was instituted by LENIN (1917) and run by Dzerzhinski, a Pole. Lenin envisaged the need for terror to protect his revolution and this was its purpose. Its headquarters, the Lubyanka prison in Moscow, contained offices and places for torture and execution. In 1922 the CHEKA became the GPU or secret police and later the OGPU (United State Political Administration). The OGPU was replaced in 1934 by the NKVD.

chemical and biological warfare (CBW) The use of synthetic poisonous substances, or organisms such as disease germs, to kill or injure the enemy. They include chlorine, phosgene, and mustard gas (first used in World War I), various nerve gases, defoliant agents, and viruses and bacteria (for example, anthrax). The use of chemical and biological weapons is prohibited by the GENEVA CONVENTION, but their production, possession, or transfer are not. Unlike their World War I counterparts, modern chemical weapons are sophisticated and may be delivered by long-range artillery or missiles, or sprayed from aircraft. The chemicals take effect when they are inhaled or come into contact with skin. The main defence against them is protective clothing – gas masks and special suits made of rubber or treated synthetic cloth – although some medical treatments have been used. The most notorious use of chemical weapons in recent years was Iraq's, against its Kurdish minority in 1988; similar weapons were deployed by Iraq, but not used, in the 1991 Gulf War. Biological weapons were banned under the Biological Weapons Convention of 1972, but research production was permitted for defensive purposes. Agreement regarding the limitation of chemical and biological weapons stands high on the agenda of the Conference on Disarmament, but many states, particularly in the developing world, are reluctant to give up possession of such weapons because they act as a deterrent. Verification of any total ban presents difficulties: declared stocks of chemical and biological weapons can be checked and destroyed, but detection of undeclared production and stockpiling is almost impossible. During 1997 Iraq refused to allow UN inspectors access to suspected weapons sites, fuelling fears that Iraq was secretly developing a chemical and biological arsenal.

Cheng Ho ZHENG HE.

Chernobyl A nuclear power-station near Kiev in Ukraine, the site in 1986 of the worst nuclear accident in the world to date. Thirty-one people died trying to fight subsequent fires, and many more received radiation burns or suffered from associated diseases. The reactor was one of a group of four at the site that used a light-water coolant and a graphite moderator. The accident was the result of unauthorized experiments by the operators, in which safety systems were deliberately circumvented in order to learn more about the plant's operation. As a result the reactor rapidly overheated, and the water coolant 'flashed' into steam. Hydrogen then formed by reaction of the steam with the graphite moderator, causing two major explosions and fire. Fall-out from the explosions, containing the radioactive isotope caesium-137, affected large areas of Europe. In particular, livestock in high-rainfall areas received unacceptable doses of radiation. In the mid-1990s large areas of land in Ukraine, Belarus, and south-west Russia were still contaminated and high levels of cancer (especially leukaemia in children) were reported.

Ukraine and a consortium of western companies intend to replace the nuclear reactor with a gas-fired power station by 2000.

Cherokee A Native American people (PLAINS PEOPLES) who traditionally inhabited a region stretching across western Virginia and the Carolinas, eastern Kentucky and Tennessee, and northern Georgia and Alabama.

Their pre-historic ancestors built ancient Etowah (Georgia), an important ceremonial centre of the eastern MISSISSIPPI CULTURES, visited by Hernando DE SOTO in his explorations of 1540–42. The Cherokee lived in towns composed of longhouses, and were at first easily assimilated into the expanding USA. Smallpox and other European-introduced diseases had greatly reduced their population by the 17th century, when French and English traders made contact. Conflict with White settlers moving westwards led to several wars, which reduced their lands. However, they adopted European methods of farming and government, including a bill of rights and a written constitution. The Cherokee also developed a distinct and original written language in the early 19th century, which gave rise to an indigenous literature and, later, a Cherokee-language newspaper.

The Cherokee had supported the British in 18th-century wars against the French and during the American War of INDEPENDENCE. American forces attacked them, and by the end of the war their population and territories had been greatly reduced and in 1827 they established the Cherokee Nation in north-west Georgia through a series of treaties with the US federal government. The discovery of gold on their land resulted in pressure from the White settlers to encroach further onto Cherokee territory. Although their treaty rights and tribal autonomy were upheld in the Supreme Court, they fell foul of both the state authorities and Jackson's policy of removal of Native American tribes to land west of the Mississippi. In 1838 President Van Buren ordered the deportation of the remaining Cherokee to the OKLAHOMA INDIAN TERRITORY (TRAIL OF TEARS). In 1906 the Cherokee finally gave up their tribal allegiance and in 1924 they gained the suffrage as US citizens.

Chesterfield, Earl of STANHOPE.

Chiang Kai-shek (or Jiang Jiehi) (1887–1975) Chinese general and statesman. He took control over the KUOMINTANG in 1926 and led the NORTHERN EXPEDITION (1926–28). He ruthlessly suppressed trade union and communist organizations and drove the communists out of the Kuomintang. His nationalist government, established in Nanjing in 1928, lasted until 1937 and succeeded in unifying most of CHINA. Major financial reforms were carried out, and communications and education were improved. Chiang promoted the New Life Movement (1934–37), which reasserted traditional Confucian values to combat communist ideas. His government was constantly at war with provincial warlords, with the communists in their rural bases, and with the invading Japanese. In 1936 he was kidnapped in the XI'AN INCIDENT and was released, having agreed to co-operate with the communists in resisting the Japanese. With US support, encouraged by the advocacy of his wife, Soong Mei-ling, he put nationalist forces against the Japanese from 1937 to the end of World War II, but he lost control of the coastal regions and most of the major cities to Japan early in the conflict. Talks with MAO ZEDONG failed to provide a basis for agreement in 1945 and in the ensuing CHINESE CIVIL WAR, Chiang's forces were gradually worn down until he was forced to resign as President and evacuate his remaining Kuomintang forces to TAIWAN in 1949. The administration he established there still continues as the Republic of China and Chiang was its President until his death.

Chicanos US citizens of Mexican descent. The descendants of Mexicans living in the south-west of the USA when the area was taken in the MEXICAN–AMERICAN WAR (1846–48), or of later immigrants from Mexico, they were long an underprivileged group. They were, however, encouraged by the CIVIL RIGHTS movement from the 1950s to launch Chicano organizations to secure improvements. In the 1960s Cesar Chavez wrung concessions for the California grape pickers by a series of strikes and boycotts, while in the 1970s advances were made in education, and some Mexican Americans secured high positions in government.

Chickasaw A Native American people that inhabited the region of modern northern Alabama and Mississippi, and southern Tennessee: they were descendants of the late prehistoric MISSISSIPPI CULTURES. In 1739 they were attacked by a French campaign from Montreal and Fort Michilimackinac (Michigan), aided by several Great Lakes tribes; and as allies of the British based in Charlestown they fought in the 18th century with pro-French tribes such as the Illinois in the north and the Choctaw in the south.

Chien-lung QIANLONG.

Chifley, Joseph Benedict (1885–1951) Australian statesman. An employee of the railways, he was active in union affairs and was dismissed during the Railway Strike of 1917. A Labor member of the federal Parliament, he held various offices, including that of Prime Minister (1945–49). He led the opposition from 1949 until his death. He successfully introduced the uniform tax scheme during the war. His attempt to nationalize the banks in the late 1940s was controversial and unsuccessful.

child labour Work performed by children, often under compulsion and in violation of national and international labour standards. Before the INDUSTRIAL REVOLUTION children had frequently been compelled to work from an early age, but by 1800 their employment under dirty and dangerous conditions in the new mines and factories had become a cause for public concern. In 1802 the British government enacted the first laws regulating child labour, but they proved ineffective. In 1833 a FACTORY ACT restricted working hours for children and provided for the appointment of inspectors. During the 19th century further factory acts and the introduction of compulsory education effectively limited child labour. In the USA some states passed laws to restrict the common use of child labour, but these were not always enforced. It was not until the enactment of a federal law, the Fair Labor Standards Act in 1938, that child labour could be brought to an end. Other western European countries, particularly Prussia after 1870, also began to make legislation regulating the employment of children.

In developing countries the employment of children in factories, mines, and agriculture has remained widespread. Most child labourers, some as young as four years old, are employed in agriculture, domestic service, or small, unregulated urban enterprises such as weavers' and mechanics' workshops or restaurants. In such societies, the child's contribution to the family's income may be vital to its survival. Child labour prevails where competition is strong, technologies are rudimentary, and production processes simple and routine. Children cannot cope as well as adults with complex work procedures, but they can work faster and are more agile and submissive. Employers use children to reduce labour and capital costs where there are fluctuations in demand and economic uncertainty. Children tend to be paid extremely low wages and some are bonded, working solely to pay off a debt. Many work long hours, frequently with no protection from toxic substances or dangerous machinery, no allowance being made for their physical vulnerability or developmental needs. They are likely to be powerless and unable to organize, and therefore experience severe employment instability. The United Nations Convention on the Rights of the Child contains articles requiring signatory states to take measures against child labour, and agencies such as UNICEF are committed to protecting child labourers. The UN estimates that by the end of the 20th century there will be 375 million child labourers worldwide; there are presently an estimated 175 million children working in India alone.

Children's Crusade (1212) A pathetic episode in the CRUSADES, growing out of simple faith and fanatical zeal for the recapture of PALESTINE from the Saracens. Some 50,000 children, mainly from France and Germany, are said to have taken part in the expedition, which probably included poor adults. It was doomed from the start. Those who did manage to embark from the ports of France and Italy were dispatched to Muslim slave markets. Very few ever returned to their homes. The legend of the Pied Piper of Hamelin telling of the loss of 130 children who followed a mysterious flautist 'to Calvary' may derive from this episode. Robert Browning based his poem (1842) on the legend.

Chile A long and narrow country on the west coast of South America, occupying some 4,600 km (2,860 miles) between Peru in the north and Cape Horn.

Physical. On average Chile is only 160 km (100 miles) in width from the Pacific to the high Andes, along which run the boundaries with Bolivia and Argentina. In the north is the arid Atacama Desert, while in the centre the climate is mild and conducive to most forms of agriculture. Here and in the south the lower slopes of the cordilleras are well forested and there are short, fertile river valleys. Tierra del Fuego, in the extreme south, on the other hand is cold, very wet, and relatively barren, suitable only for sheep grazing. Inland, along the whole length of the country, stretch mountains.

Economy. Chile's economy is based largely on exploitation of substantial mineral reserves, and agriculture. Copper accounts for almost half of exports, with other minerals and fruit, fishmeal, and timber products of secondary importance. About 80% of electricity is generated by hydroelectric power, and domestic oil production accounts for about half of total requirements. Manufacturing industry includes chemicals, brewing, wood-pulping, and tyre manufacture. The country has one of the best public education and social service systems in Latin America, although these suffered under military rule in the 1980s.

History. At the time of the first Spanish contact in 1536 the dominant Indian group, the Araucanians, were theoretically subject to the INCA empire, but in practice they retained considerable independence within the Inca realm. Though they resisted Spanish encroachments, the Araucanians were gradually pushed south of the Bío Bío River, where they were more or less kept under control. Spanish colonization began with the foundation of Santiago in 1541. The colony grew moderately but did not prosper for the next two centuries as it was overshadowed by wealthier Peru. Politically Chile became part of the Spanish viceroyalty of Peru. Chilean independence from Spain was proclaimed in 1810 by O'HIGGINS; it was achieved after the South American liberator José de SAN MARTIN crossed the Andes with an army of 3,200 men and defeated Spanish troops at the Battles of Chacabuco (1817), and Maipo (1818). The discovery of rich copper deposits in the northern Atacama desert had a dramatic impact on economic life, with a railway system developing from 1851. Following war with BOLIVIA and PERU (1879–83), rich natural nitrate deposits were annexed in the north, leading to a 50-year economic boom. By the 1920s synthetic nitrates were replacing saltpetre and dependence on copper exports placed Chile at the mercy of the world market. Political experiments after World War II failed to cope with a series of burgeoning social problems and prompted the election in 1970 of the Marxist democrat Salvador ALLENDE, the first avowed Marxist in world history to be elected President by popular vote. As the head of the Unidad Popular (a coalition of communists and socialists), Allende was faced with a majority opposition in Congress, and the hostility of the USA. He was increasingly frustrated in his attempts to implement his radical programme of nationalization and agrarian reform. Inflation, capital flight, and a balance-of-payments deficit contributed to an economic crisis in 1973. In September the army commander-in-chief PINOCHET led the military coup which cost Allende and 15,000 Chileans their lives, and prompted one-tenth of the population to emigrate. The military regime which replaced Chile's democracy brutally suppressed all labour unions and opposition groups, and pursued a free-market economy. Although inflation was dramatically reduced, so was demand, output, and employment. The economy continued on a downward spiral in the 1980s with the world's highest per-capita level of external debt. In 1988 Pinochet accepted a plebiscite decision for the 're-establishment' of 'workable democracy', and stepped down. In 1989 Patricio Aylwin was elected President and civilian rule was restored. Aylwin was succeeded in 1994 by Edúardo Frei Ruiz-Tagle, the son of the former president Edúardo FREI (MONTALVA). In 1994 Chile applied to join the NORTH AMERICAN FREE TRADE AGREEMENT.

CAPITAL:	Santiago
AREA:	756,626 sq km (292,135 sq miles)
POPULATION:	14.375 million (1996)
CURRENCY:	1 peso = 100 centavos
RELIGIONS:	Roman Catholic 80.7%; atheist and non-religious 12.8%; Protestant 6.1%; Jewish 0.2%
ETHNIC GROUPS:	Mestizo 91.6%; Amerindian (mostly Araucanian) 6.8%; others (mainly European) 1.6%
LANGUAGES:	Spanish (official); also Amerindian languages (mostly Araucanian)
INTERNATIONAL ORGANIZATIONS:	UN; OAS

Chilembwe, John (c. 1871–1915) MALAWI nationalist. A servant of the missionary Joseph Booth, who sent him to a Negro theological college in the USA, he became a church minister and in 1900 established the Providence Industrial Mission in Nyasaland (now Malawi). Chilembwe protested against the injustices of colonial rule. In 1915 he started a rebellion but it did not gain enough African support and he was shot by the police.

Chimú The most powerful state of the north coast of Peru between c. 1000 AD and 1476, when it was conquered by the INCAS. Its capital was Chan Chan (near modern Trujillo), a vast city with ten large rectangular enclosures measuring 400 by 200 m (1300 by 650 feet). These were built in sequence as the ruler died and was buried, and comprised a royal compound complete with residences, administrative rooms, gardens, kitchens, storerooms, and the royal tomb. Associated artefacts included a distinctive mould-made black pottery and some of the finest gold, silver, and bronze-work known from the New World.

China The third-largest country in the world, occupying most of eastern Asia and bounded by North Korea, Kazakhstan and Mongolia on the north, Russia on the west, Afghanistan, Pakistan, India, Nepal and Bhutan on the south-west and Myanmar (Burma), Laos, and Vietnam on the south-east.

Physical. China's coastline adjoins the South and East China Seas and the Yellow Sea. In the north-west lies Xinjiang (Sinkiang), an area of mountains and desert, and in the south-west is the mountainous region of Tibet. The remainder of China is divided laterally by the Yangtze (Chang) River. To the north-west is the high loess region, supporting millet and wheat. The wind carries the loess eastward to the flat northern plain, while the eastward-flowing rivers carry yellow silt. The plain, with a monsoon climate of warm, wet summers and very cold, arid winters, is highly cultivable. In the north-east lies Manchuria, on higher ground and with many rivers and lakes. In the west are the mountains and plateaux surrounding the red clay basin of Sichuan, which is well watered and supports a mass of paddy fields. Huge lakes occupy low-lying land to the south of the Yangtze, while southward the terrain rises to many ranges of high hills. Here the climate is subtropical. The plateaux support tea plantations, many of the slopes are terraced for rice, and the deep valleys are full of natural forests of bamboo. The province of Gansu in the north-west region is the principal centre of earthquakes in China, where major earthquakes take place on an average of once every 65 years.

Economy. Since the late 1970s China has adopted pragmatic policies of liberalizing the economy. Four Special Economic Zones were established to attract foreign investment, direct state control of factories has been loosened, stockmarkets have been set up, and responsibility for agriculture switched from collective farms to individual households. China's economy is predominantly agricultural, with rice, wheat, and pigs the main products. Agriculture prospers, although there is a need for investment in irrigation and fertilizers. Mineral extraction is important: crude oil is refined and exported, there are large coal, tin, and iron ore deposits, and China leads the world in tungsten ore production. Several nuclear energy plants are under construction. Industry is targeted for expansion, and major industrial products include textiles and clothing, cement, chemicals, steel, and consumer electrical goods. Japan is the main trading partner. Tourism is also of increasing economic importance.

History. China has a recorded history beginning nearly 4,000 years ago, with the SHANG who settled in the Huang He (Yellow River) valley. Under the Eastern ZHOU, from the 6th century BC, CONFUCIUS and MENCIUS formulated ideas that became the framework of Chinese society. TAOISM appeared during the 3rd century BC. Gradually Chinese culture spread out from the Huang He valley. A form of writing with characters representing meanings rather than sounds – and required by SHI HUANGDI, the first ruler of a unified China, to be written in a uniform style – bound together people divided by geography and different spoken dialects. From the QIN the concept of a unified empire prevailed, surviving periods of fragmentation and rule by non-Chinese dynasties such as the YUAN. Under strong dynasties such as the HAN and the TANG China's power extended far west into TURKISTAN and south into ANNAM. On its neighbours, particularly KOREA and Annam, it exercised a powerful influence. Barbarian invaders and dynasties usually adopted Chinese cultural traditions.

The ideas of BUDDHISM began to reach China from the 1st century AD and were gradually changed and assimilated into Chinese culture. The Chinese people, showing remarkable inventiveness, were ahead of the West in technology until about the end of the SONG dynasty. However, after the MONGOL conquest the country drew in on itself. Learning, in high esteem from early times, became rooted in the stereotyped study of the Confucian classics, for success in examinations based on the classics was for centuries the means to promotion in the civil service. In time, study of the classics had a deadening intellectual influence.

Throughout history, China, the 'Middle Kingdom', as it is called by the Chinese, regarded itself as superior to all others – a view shared by philosophers of the ENLIGHTENMENT. After the Manchu invasion of 1644, China was ruled by the QING dynasty, which was at its most powerful and prosperous in the 18th century. Western countries attempted to establish trading links with the Qing dynasty but with little success. As the power of the Qing dynasty weakened towards the end of the 18th century, Western pressure for change built up, leading to direct European involvement in China. Contact with the West precipitated crisis and decline. After the OPIUM WARS, TREATY PORTS became the focus for both Western expansion and demands for modernization. Nineteenth-century rebellions, such as the TAIPING devastated the country and undermined imperial rule in spite of the SELF-STRENGTHENING MOVEMENT and the abortive HUNDRED DAYS REFORM. Defeat in the SINO-JAPANESE WAR (1894–95) and the BOXER RISING stimulated reforms, but the dynasty ended in the CHINESE REVOLUTION OF 1911. The Republic that followed SUN YAT-SEN's brief presidency degenerated into WARLORD regimes after YUAN SHIKAI's attempt to restore the monarchy. CHIANG KAI-SHEK united much of China after the NORTHERN EXPEDITION and ruled from Nanjing with his nationalist KUOMINTANG, but his Republic of China collapsed in the face of the Japanese invasion of 1937 and the civil war with the communists, and continued only on the island of TAIWAN after his retreat there in 1949. The CHINESE COMMUNIST PARTY under MAO ZEDONG won the civil war, established the People's

Republic of China on the mainland, and set about revolutionizing and developing China's economy and society. In the 1950s, land reform led to the COMMUNES and the GREAT LEAP FORWARD, and urban industry was expanded and nationalized. Relations with the Soviet Union worsened and during 1966–76 the country was torn apart by the CULTURAL REVOLUTION, which ended only with Mao's death. During the 1980s DENG XIAOPING remained committed to economic reform through the FOUR MODERNIZATIONS, and to improving relations with the Soviet Union. Pressures for democratization grew, however, and a student demonstration in Beijing in June 1989 led to a massacre of unarmed protestors in Tiananmen Square. Gradual moves towards a controlled market economy have continued. Following the death of DENG XIAOPING in February 1997, JIANG ZEMIN emerged as the country's principal leader. In July of that year, Britain's 99-year lease of HONG KONG expired and the territory returned to mainland China. China continued to exert pressure on Taiwan to rejoin the 'motherland'.

CAPITAL:	Beijing
AREA:	9,572,900 sq km (3,696,100 sq miles)
POPULATION:	1,218.7 million (1996)
CURRENCY:	1 Renminbi (yuan) = 10 jiao = 100 fen
RELIGIONS:	Non-religious 59.2%; Chinese traditional religions 20.1%; atheist 12.0%; Buddhist 6.0%; Muslim 2.4%; Christian 0.2%
ETHNIC GROUPS:	Han (Chinese) 93.3%; Chuang 1.33%; Hui 0.72%; Uighur 0.59%; Yi 0.54%; Miao 0.5%; Manchu 0.43%; Tibetan 0.39%; Mongolian 0.34%; Tuchia 0.28%; Puyi 0.21%; Korean 0.18%; Tung 0.14%; Yao 0.14%; Pai 0.11%; Hani 0.11%; Kasakh 0.09%; Tai 0.08%; Li 0.08%
LANGUAGES:	Mandarin Chinese (official); six other dialects of Chinese; at least 41 other minority languages
INTERNATIONAL ORGANIZATIONS:	UN

China-Japan Peace and Friendship Treaty (1978) An agreement between China and Japan aimed at closer political and economic co-operation. Post-war Japanese foreign policy was characterized by a tension between dependence on the USA and popular pressure for closer relations with China. The growing western inclination of Chinese policy, the thaw in US–Chinese relations following the Nixon visit of 1972, and increasing Japanese dependence on Asia for its foreign trade improved Sino-Japanese contact, leading to the signing of the Treaty in 1978, one of the major aims of which was the establishment of closer trading links.

Chin dynasty JIN.

Ch'in dynasty QIN.

Chinese Civil War (1927–37; 1946–49) Conflicts between nationalist and communist Chinese forces. Hostilities broke out in 1927 during CHIANG KAI-SHEK'S NORTHERN EXPEDITION, with anti-leftist purges of the KUOMINTANG and a series of abortive communist urban uprisings. Communist strength was thereafter most successfully established in rural areas and its supporters were able to utilize guerrilla tactics to neutralize superior nationalist strength. After a three-year campaign, Chiang finally managed to destroy the JIANGXI SOVIET established by MAO ZEDONG, but after the LONG MARCH

(1934–35), the communists were able to re-establish themselves in Yan'an, in the north of the country. Hostilities between the two sides were reduced by the Japanese invasion of 1937, and, until the end of World War II in 1945, an uneasy truce was maintained as largely separate campaigns were fought against the common enemy. Violence broke out briefly immediately the war ended, resuming on a widespread basis in April 1946 after the US general George MARSHALL had failed to arrange a lasting compromise settlement. During the first year of the renewed conflict, numerically superior nationalist troops made large territorial gains, including the communist capital of Yan'an. Thereafter Kuomintang morale began to crumble in the face of successful military operations by the communists, decreasing confidence in their administration, and by the end of 1947 a successful communist counter-offensive was well under way. In November 1948 LIN BIAO completed his conquest of Manchuria, where the nationalists lost half a million men, many of whom defected to the communists. In Central China the nationalists lost Shandong, and in January 1949 were defeated at the battle of Huai-Hai (near Xuzhou). Beijing fell in January, and Nanjing and Shanghai in April. The People's Republic of China was proclaimed (1 October 1949), and the communist victory was complete when the nationalist government fled from Chongqing to TAIWAN in December.

Chinese Communist Party (CCP) Chinese political party. Interest in communism was stimulated by the RUSSIAN REVOLUTION (1917) and the MAY FOURTH MOVEMENT and promoted by Li Dazhao, librarian of Beijing University, and Chen Duxiu. They were co-founders of the Chinese Communist Party at its First Congress in Shanghai in July 1921. Under COMINTERN instructions, CCP members joined the KUOMINTANG and worked in it for national liberation. Early activities concentrated on trade union organization in Shanghai and other large cities, but a peasant movement was already being developed by PENG PAI. Purged by the Kuomintang in 1927 and forced out of the cities, the CCP had to rely on China's massive peasant population as its revolutionary base. It set up the JIANGXI SOVIET in southern China in 1931, and moved north under the leadership of MAO ZEDONG in the LONG MARCH (1934–35). Temporarily at peace with the Kuomintang after the XI'AN INCIDENT in 1936, the communists proved an effective resistance force when the Japanese invaded the country in 1937. After the end of World War II, the party's military strength and rural organization allowed it to triumph over the nationalists in the renewed civil war, and to proclaim a People's Republic in 1949. It has ruled China since 1949. Internal arguments over economic reform and political doctrine and organization led to the chaos of the CULTURAL REVOLUTION (1966–76), during which the CCP appeared to turn on itself. After the death of Mao Zedong and the purge of the GANG OF FOUR the CCP pursued a more stable political direction under the leadership of DENG XIAOPING. However, allegations of corruption and demands for more open government led to a prolonged crisis in 1987–89. In June 1989 thousands of unarmed protesters gathered throughout the country, with most in Tiananmen Square, in Beijing; the army was sent in to stop the demonstrations and western diplomats and journalists estimated several thousand people, mainly students, were massacred.

Chinese philosophy The essence of Chinese philosophy is humanism: people and society have captivated the Chinese mind since antiquity. Although there have been comparatively few metaphysical speculations, the Chinese generally see a unity between the individual and the universe. This harmonious relationship between the individual and the natural world characterizes the entire history of Chinese philosophy. During its 4,000 years of recorded history, Chinese philosophy has gone through four major periods. The first of these was the Classical Age, which culminated in the blossoming of the Hundred Schools during the Spring and Autumn (722–481 BC) and the Warring States (403–222 BC) Periods. It was followed by the Middle Period (206 BC–960 AD), when CONFUCIANISM first emerged supreme in the socio-political sphere, only to give way to Neo-TAOISM and BUDDHISM. The third period was the Neo-Confucian Stage (960–1850), during which Neo-Confucianism was the unchallenged state ideology. Last came the Modern Era, when MARXISM and MAOISM ousted the indigeneous Chinese schools of thought. Chinese philosophy in the 20th century is still in a formative stage, engaged in a sometimes confusing and chaotic attempt to bring together the whole of the Western philosophical tradition with its own native developments.

Chinese Revolution of 1911 The overthrow of the Manchu QING dynasty and the establishment of a Chinese republic. After half a century of anti-Manchu risings, the imperial government began a reform movement which gave limited authority to provincial assemblies, and these became power bases for constitutional reformers and republicans. Weakened by provincial opposition to the nationalization of some major railways, the government was unable to suppress the republican WUCHANG UPRISING (10 October 1911). By the end of November 15 provinces had seceded, and on 29 December 1911 provincial delegates proclaimed a republic, with SUN YAT-SEN as provisional President. In February 1912, the last Qing emperor PUYI was forced to abdicate and Sun stepped down to allow YUAN SHIKAI to become President. The Provisional Constitution of March 1912 allowed for the institution of a democratically elected parliament, but this was ignored and eventually dissolved by Yuan Shikai after the abortive Second Revolution of 1913 which challenged his authority. Yuan had himself proclaimed emperor in 1915, but by that time central government was ineffective, and China was controlled by provincial WARLORDS.

Chinese technology China has the longest unbroken history of progress in science and technology (over 4,000 years) of any nation in the world. Four inventions that had a major impact on Western culture were paper, printing from movable type, gunpowder, and the magnetic compass. Paper-making began in China around 50 BC and by the 7th century AD had spread to Korea, Japan, and the Arab world. Wood-block printing was well established in China by 1000 AD, while movable type came about a century later. Gunpowder was first used in China early in the 12th century. It reached Europe less than a century later, where it almost overnight transformed the art of warfare. A form of magnetic compass was probably used in China as early as the 5th century BC, but it was not used for navigation until the 12th century, almost the same time as in Europe. An enormous number of other inventions have their origins in China. Examples include the stern rudder and compartmentalized hulls for ships, horse-collar harness, paddle-wheel propulsion, and the seismograph. The GREAT WALL OF CHINA and the GRAND CANAL are outstanding Chinese civil engineering projects.

Ch'ing dynasty QING.

Chirac, Jacques (1932–) French statesman, President of France (1995–). Chirac served as an officer in Algeria (1956–57) and joined the civil service in 1959. A conservative, he entered politics in 1967 and was appointed Minister for Agriculture in 1972, under President POMPIDOU. He was given the nickname 'The Bulldozer', and served briefly as Minister for the Interior before being appointed Prime Minister by President Giscard d'Estaing in 1974. He resigned in 1976 following disagreements with Giscard and became Mayor of Paris in 1977.

In 1986 the right-wing coalition won legislative elections, and the socialist President MITTERRAND appointed Chirac Prime Minister, the first time since 1958 that the President and Prime Minister had come from opposing political camps. Chirac took responsibility for domestic matters, while Mitterrand dealt with foreign policy, an arrangement that was referred to as 'cohabitation'. Chirac, however, pursued a vigorous policy of privatization, reversing many of the nationalizations that Mitterrand had overseen.

Mitterrand defeated Chirac in presidential elections (1988) and Chirac resigned as Prime Minister. In 1995 Mitterrand retired and Chirac was subsequently elected President.

During the first months of his presidency Chirac incurred unpopularity abroad by resuming French nuclear testing in the Pacific. The imposition of a severe austerity programme led to a wave of strikes and protests in 1995–96. Since the general election of 1997 Chirac has been faced with a legislature controlled by the Socialist Party under Lionel Jospin.

chivalry The code of behaviour practised in the Middle Ages, especially in the 12th and 13th centuries, by the mounted soldier or KNIGHT. The chivalric ethic represented the fusion of Christian and military concepts of conduct. A knight was to be brave, loyal to his lord, and the protector of women. The songs of the TROUBADOURS celebrated these virtues.

It was a system of apprenticeship: as boys, knights' sons became pages in the castles of other knights; from the age of 14 they learnt horsemanship and military skills, and were themselves knighted at the age of 21. The CRUSADES saw the apogee of the chivalric ideal, as new Christian orders of knights (KNIGHTS TEMPLARS, KNIGHTS HOSPITALLERS), waged war in PALESTINE against the Muslims. During times of peace, the TOURNAMENT was the setting for displays of military and equestrian skill. The 15th century saw a decline in the real value of chivalry, and though new orders, such as the Order of the Golden Fleece (Burgundy) were created, tournaments survived merely as ritualized ceremonies.

Choctaw A Native American people who inhabited modern Mississippi south of the CHICKASAW, and whose ancestors formed the southern extent of the MISSISSIPPI CULTURES. Hernando DE SOTO explored their territory in

1540–42, and they competed with the NATCHEZ and CHICKASAW for trade with early Spanish settlers, and later with the French at New Orleans in the 17th and 18th centuries. Conflict with American colonists increased after the American War of INDEPENDENCE.

Choiseul, Étienne François, duc de (1719–85) French statesman, Secretary of State for Foreign Affairs (1758–70). He concluded the Family Compact of 1761 with CHARLES III of Spain and, considering the weakness of the French position, was a successful negotiator at the Treaty of PARIS in 1763. He then tried to reform the army and navy, but was dismissed in December 1770 when he tried to persuade LOUIS XV to support Spain against Britain over the FALKLAND ISLANDS. Lorraine and Corsica were both annexed during his period in office.

Chola A Tamil Hindu dynasty dominant in south India from the 9th to the 13th century. Their origins are uncertain, but they were influential from at least the 3rd century AD, becoming an imperial power on the overthrow of their PALLAVA neighbours in the late 9th century. Victory over the PANDYAS followed, and then expansion into the Deccan, Orissa, and Sri Lanka. Their peak was during the reigns of Rajaraja I (985–1014) and Rajendra I (1014–44), when Chola armies reached the Ganges and the Malay archipelago. The dynasty remained the paramount power in south India until the mid-13th century when HOYSALA and Pandya incursions and the rise of VIJAYANAGAR eventually destroyed its claims.

Chou dynasty ZHOU.

Chou En-lai ZHOU ENLAI.

Chrétien, (Joseph-Jacques) Jean (1934–   ) French-Canadian statesman and Prime Minister (1993–   ). A lawyer, he entered politics in 1963 and was appointed to nine successive cabinet posts, including Minister of Finance (1977–79). As Minister of Justice (1980–82) he handled negotiations with Britain over revising Canada's constitution to remove the few remaining traces of British colonial influence. Chrétien became Deputy Prime Minister in 1984 but resigned in 1986, returning to his law practice. In 1990 he resumed his political career and was elected leader of the Liberal Party. Chrétien became Prime Minister of Canada in 1993 when the Liberal Party won a landslide general election, ending nine years of Conservative rule. He was re-elected with a much smaller majority in 1997.

Christ JESUS CHRIST.

Christian I (1426–81) King of Denmark and Norway (1448–81) and Sweden (1457–64), who founded of the Oldenburg dynasty. Elected to power by the Danish Rigstad, and confirming his status by marriage to his predecessor's widow, he gained the Swedish throne after the war of 1451–57, but lost control to the Swedish nobility later. He also gained Schleswig and Holstein, and was at war with England (1469–74). Strongly Catholic, he founded the Catholic University of Copenhagen in 1479.

Christian Church The collective body of all Christian believers, or any particular denomination of Christians (CHRISTIANITY). The Christian Church is divided into three main groups, the ROMAN CATHOLIC CHURCH, the ORTHODOX CHURCHES, and the PROTESTANT Churches, the most prominent of which are the ANGLICAN COMMUNION, the

BAPTIST CHURCH, the Lutheran Church, and the METHODIST CHURCH. The variety of traditions within the present Christian Churches developed from the early Church as it spread around the world. Divisions between Christians were often occasioned by doctrinal disagreements, though social and political factors also played a part. The major traditions of Christianity are broadly divided along geographical lines. The Roman Catholic Church is dominant in many countries of southern Europe and their former colonies in Central and South America, and in Poland and Ireland. Protestant Churches, which broke away from Roman Catholicism in the 16th century, are concentrated in northern Europe and the USA. Emigration and missionary work have established both traditions in Australasia, Africa, and elsewhere. The Orthodox Church, which finally separated from the Roman Catholic Church in the EAST-WEST SCHISM of the 11th century, is primary in Belarus, Bulgaria, Georgia, Greece, Moldova, Russia, Serbia, and parts of the Ukraine, and is scattered throughout the Middle East. The Oriental tradition is one of the most ancient in Christianity, composed of two strands: Nestorian and Monophysite Christianity, which both originated from important differences in doctrine in the 5th century. The Nestorian Church held that Christ united two persons, one divine and one human, while the Monophysites taught that Christ has only one divine nature. The Monophysites broke with the mainstream Church in the 6th century, eventually forming four important Churches, which accept each other's ministries and sacraments: the Coptic, Ethiopian, Armenian, and Syrian Churches. These are sometimes known as the Oriental Orthodox Churches.

In the 19th century Christianity faced many challenges as a result of political, social, and scientific revolutions. There was a weakening of the close relationship between Church and state, and growing scientific knowledge questioned traditional biblical accounts, most notably the creation story, which was challenged by Darwin's theory of evolution (1859). The 19th century saw great MISSIONARY activity, particularly by the Protestant Churches. There was also an increasing awareness of social deprivation, and Christian belief was an important motivator behind campaigns for the abolition of slavery, the introduction of legislation to protect workers, and the establishment of education and welfare systems. Traditional Churches did not always serve growing urban areas, inspiring new Christian movements to grow, most notably the SALVATION ARMY. In the 20th century links between Church and state were further weakened, and after the communist revolutions in Russia and elsewhere, churches were forcibly suppressed. In 1948 the need for greater unity between the many Churches was recognized with the establishment of the WORLD COUNCIL OF CHURCHES. Since then church membership has been declining in Western Europe but continues to grow in many developing countries.

Christian Democracy The ideology of a number of Centre-Right parties in post-war Europe, attempting to apply Christian principles to the management of industrial society. Arising in reaction both to classical LIBERALISM and to MARXISM, it sought to create social harmony in place of class divisions, and to use the state as a means of humanizing the capitalist economy. Its religious inspiration was predominantly, though not exclusively, Roman Catholic in character. Much stress was laid on strengthening the family, work associations, and other forms of community. In economic policy, Christian Democrats have tended to embrace corporatism; in international relations they have advocated the protection of human rights, and been strong supporters of European integration. Christian Democratic parties have been powerful in Italy, Germany, and Belgium, often forming the main governing party; weaker, but still of some influence, in France and The Netherlands. The parties were especially strong during the first decade after World War II and counted some of the most distinguished West European politicians as members, among them ADENAUER, BIDAULT, DE GASPERI, and Schuman. Following the accession of President Kennedy in 1960, there was also an upsurge of Christian Democracy in Latin America, with particularly strong parties established in Chile and Venezuela; in the 1980s a similar tendency emerged in most of Central America.

Christian fundamentalism A Protestant religious movement that stresses traditional Christian doctrines, especially the literal truth of the Bible. Fundamentalism developed in the 1920s in opposition to modern techniques of biblical criticism; its adherents have been particularly powerful in the USA, especially among the various Baptist groups. Fundamentalists were and are particularly noted for their hostility to DARWIN's theory of evolution, as shown by the prosecution of the biology teacher John T. Scopes (see SCOPES CASE) in Tennessee. Fundamentalism is associated with aggressive evangelicalism and has re-emerged in recent years as an influential movement, particularly in the USA, where fundamentalist views reach a wide audience through religious broadcasting. Fundamentalists often have a clearly defined social agenda, which they see as traditionalist. They oppose abortion, support anti-pornography legislation, and promote the teaching of creationism (the biblical account of the creation as literally true) rather than evolutionary theories in schools. MILLENARIAN ideas rooted in biblical prophecies of the Second Coming have led to support for the state of Israel and for a strongly armed USA. US fundamentalists have been active missionaries and derivative or parallel movements are now found worldwide, among them being 'House Churches' in Britain. During the 1990s, especially in the USA, extreme fundamentalist groups became increasingly violent.

The term fundamentalist is loosely used of those in any religion who seek a return to literal interpretations of religious doctrines. (See also HINDU REVIVALISM, ISLAMIC FUNDAMENTALISM.)

Christianity The Christian religion, based on the belief that JESUS CHRIST is the incarnate Son of God and on his teachings. The world's largest religion, Christianity was originally a sect of JUDAISM, and shares the Jewish belief in one omnipotent God. Jesus, who was a Jew, was believed to be the Messiah and Son of God, the fulfilment in a new way of Jewish MILLENARIAN and eschatological prophecies of the Saviour. He proclaimed a new covenant between God and humanity. Central to Christianity is the belief that Jesus is the incarnate Son of God, from which developed the doctrine of the Trinity, whereby God is three persons, the Father, the Son, and the Holy Spirit, yet one God. Jesus is both God and man, one person in two natures. Jesus' death by crucifixion represents a sacrifice or atonement through which humanity may be redeemed from its sinful condition, and his resurrection from the dead symbolizes the hope of eternal life.

The Christian holy book is the BIBLE, the first part of which, the Old Testament, is the same as the Hebrew Scriptures. Christians acknowledge the moral force of the Ten Commandments, but add to these Jesus' teaching of divine love, found in the second part of the Bible, the New Testament, a compilation of writings on Jesus' life and the development of the early Church and Christian doctrines. The doctrine of divine love is considered to be at the heart of God's relationship with humanity, and Christians are called on to display equal love in human relationships. Christianity has from the earliest times been characterized by a strong tradition of communal worship and, in many cases, well-developed ritual, but the liturgy, or forms of worship, vary strikingly between the different CHRISTIAN CHURCHES. Christian Churches also vary in the importance attached to the sacraments, but the vast majority accept Baptism, in which the believer is initiated into membership of the Church, and the Eucharist, in which bread and wine are blessed and distributed between believers as a memorial or re-enactment of the Last Supper, the Passover meal celebrated by Jesus and his disciples on the eve of his death. Christians believe in life after death, but the Churches vary in their interpretation of the afterlife, heaven, and hell.

In the years after his death the teachings of Jesus began to spread, particularly through the missionary travels of the former pharisee, PAUL, who visited Asia Minor, Greece, and Rome. Paul's message that faith in Jesus was open to everyone brought Christianity to Gentiles (non-Jews) who were not willing to accept the ritual obligations of Judaism and enabled Christianity to spread rapidly. Initially Christians experienced intermittent harassment by the Roman authorities though there was no clear legal basis for this until the reign of Emperor Decius, who began systematic persecution of the Christians in 250 AD. By the 3rd century, Christianity was widespread throughout the Roman empire; in 313 CONSTANTINE ended persecution and in 380 Theodosius recognized it as the official religion of the empire. By this time Christianity had also reached Armenia, Egypt, Persia, and probably southern India.

Around 200, the Church leaders began to collect together the most authoritative Christian writings into the New Testament, the final selection being agreed by 382; and in 325 at the Council of NICAEA a statement of Christian belief was agreed. As the Church grew, however, there were disputes between Christians on matters of doctrine and later over church organization. A division, originally cultural and linguistic, grew between the Eastern Church based at Constantinople and the Western Church at Rome, culminating in the EAST-WEST SCHISM of 1054 and sealed by the sacking of Constantinople by the CRUSADERS in 1204. In the West the unity of the Church, focused on the PAPACY in Rome, was challenged by the Protestant REFORMATION in the 16th century and the emergence of autonomous reformed Churches. This period also saw renewed missionary activity, particularly by Catholic religious orders, as

European countries colonized other parts of the world. By 1800 the political influence of the Church was waning but its moral teachings continued to guide the behaviour of individuals.

Today Christianity is widespread throughout the world, with rapidly expanding congregations in Africa and South America, where movements such as LIBERATION THEOLOGY have attempted to apply the Church's teaching to the problems of poverty and social injustice. Organizations such as the WORLD COUNCIL OF CHURCHES promote greater unity within Christianity; Church leaders such as the pope, head of the ROMAN CATHOLIC CHURCH, have historically been based in the West or Near East, but it is expected that developing countries will play a larger part in the leadership of the churches in acknowledgement of their growing congregations.

Christian Science A religious movement founded in the USA by Mary Baker Eddy (1821–1910), a frail woman deeply interested in medicine and the Bible. Her commitment to religious healing was deepened by her recovery from a serious illness in 1866. In 1875 she published the first of many editions of the manual *Science and Health, with Key to the Scriptures*, and in 1879 she established the Church of Christ, Scientist. This teaches that God is divine mind. Only mind is real; matter, evil, sin, disease, and death are all unreal illusions.

Based in Boston, Massachusetts, it is found in all English-speaking countries. Membership has declined in North America and Europe since 1950, but there has been considerable growth in Africa and South America. No membership figures have been published since 1936, when there were 250,000 members in North America. Mrs Eddy founded the international daily newspaper the *Christian Science Monitor* in 1908.

Christian Socialism A form of SOCIALISM based on Protestant Christian ideals. The term was first used in Britain in the 1840s by clergy, including Charles Kingsley, who opposed the social consequences of competitive business and unrestricted individualism, their aim being to improve the status of workers. Late 19th-century urban and industrial conditions stimulated further opposition to unrestricted capitalism, with the establishment in 1889 of the British Christian Social Union and the US Society of Christian Socialists. A belief that the established Churches were more sympathetic to the interests of capital than to the conditions of labour gave rise to the more radical Social Gospel movement. Its leaders, mostly American, studied Christ's teaching for the purpose of tracing its implications in social and economic problems.

Christina (1626–89) Queen of Sweden (1632–54). She was the daughter and successor of GUSTAVUS II (Adolphus). During her minority, the kingdom was governed mainly by Chancellor Axel OXENSTIERNA. When she assumed power in 1644, she showed herself to be clever, restless, and headstrong. She attracted many foreign artists and scholars (including DESCARTES) to her court, but after a serious constitutional crisis in 1650, she made plans to abdicate in favour of her cousin, Charles X. This was partly because of the pressure of social unrest within Sweden, and partly because of her secret conversion to the proscribed Roman Catholic faith. In 1654 she

abdicated, and spent most of her remaining years in Rome. Her time was occupied in patronizing the arts and in intriguing for the crowns of Naples and Poland.

Chuang-tzu ZHUANGZI.

Chulalongkorn (1853–1910) King Rama V of Siam (Thailand) (1868–1910). Only 15 when his father Rama IV (MONGKUT) died, Chulalongkorn was represented by a regent until he reached his majority in 1873 and used the intervening years to travel and study administrative practices abroad. He then continued his father's reformist policies, undertaking a massive modernization of his country. This, together with his astute international diplomacy, in which rival British and French interests were played off against each other, helped to protect it from colonization, although he was forced to cede some territory to French Indo-China in 1907 and to British Malaya in 1909.

Church, Benjamin (1639–1718) American soldier, a Rhode Island militia captain in KING PHILIP'S WAR (1675–76). He cornered Philip in the Great Swamp near Kingston, destroying the remnant of his force. In 1705 he joined a New England expedition against the French in Nova Scotia. His *Entertaining Passages Relating to King Philip's War* appeared in 1716.

His grandson, Benjamin (1734–76) was a leading Boston doctor and patriot who in 1775 betrayed the American cause to the British. Paroled from life imprisonment, he died en route to the West Indies.

Churchill, Lord Randolph Henry Spencer (1849–94) British politician. Younger son of the Duke of Marlborough and father of Winston CHURCHILL, he was elected as Conservative Member of Parliament in 1874. He became prominent in the 1880–85 Parliament, when he and a group of young Tories became known in opposition to the Liberals as 'the Fourth Party'. Churchill emphasized the concept of Tory democracy to attract the middle and working classes, and looked on himself as the heir to DISRAELI. A gifted rhetorician, his comment in 1886 that 'Ulster will fight and Ulster will be right' became a slogan for those resisting HOME RULE for Ireland. Chancellor of the Exchequer in 1886, he resigned when the cabinet would not support him over foreign policy and cuts in military expenditure. Ill health ended his career and he died at the age of 46.

Churchill, Sir Winston Leonard Spencer (1874–1965) British statesman and war leader. The son of Lord Randolph CHURCHILL and of Jenny Jerome of New York, he fought at the Battle of Omdurman (1898). As a journalist he covered the BOER WAR, was captured, and escaped. Elected as Unionist Member of Parliament in 1900, he switched to the Liberals in 1904 as a supporter of FREE TRADE. He served as Under-Secretary of State for the Colonies (1906–08) and in ASQUITH's great reforming government from 1908. He introduced measures to improve working conditions, established Labour Exchanges, and supported LLOYD GEORGE's Insurance Bill against unemployment in Parliament (1911). At the Admiralty from 1911 until 1915, it was largely due to him that the navy was modernized in time to meet Germany in World War I. After resigning because of the evacuation of the Dardanelles, he served briefly on the Western Front. In 1917 he became Minister of Munitions, in 1918 Minister for War and Air. Back with the Conservatives, he was Chancellor of the Exchequer from 1924 to 1929, his return to the GOLD STANDARD bringing serious economic consequences including, indirectly, the GENERAL STRIKE, in which his bellicose attitude towards the trade unions was unhelpful. In the 1930s he was out of office, largely because of his extreme attitude to the India Bill, but his support for rearmament against Nazi Germany ensured his inclusion, as First Lord of the Admiralty, in CHAMBERLAIN's wartime government. In May 1940 he became Prime Minister (and Defence Minister) of a coalition government. As war leader, Churchill was

Churchill, Sir Winston Leonard Spencer *This photograph, taken two days after Churchill became Prime Minister in 1940, shows the new Premier on his way to the swearing-in of his cabinet ministers at Buckingham Palace.*

superb in maintaining popular morale and close relations with the USA and the Commonwealth. Together with Roosevelt he was instrumental in drawing up the ATLANTIC CHARTER as a buttress of the free world. Wary of Soviet expansionism, he was concerned that the USA should not concede too many of Stalin's demands as the war drew to its close. In the 1945 election he lost office, but returned as Prime Minister from 1951 to 1955. In failing health, he was preoccupied with the need for Western unity in the COLD WAR, and of a 'special relationship' between Britain and the USA. He suffered a stroke in 1953, and two years later resigned the Premiership. A master of the English language, he was a notable orator and a prolific writer.

Church of England ANGLICAN CHURCH; ANGLICAN COMMUNION.

churl CEORL.

Chu Teh ZHU DE.

Ciano, Count Galeazzo (1903–44) Italian politician. A leading fascist, he married MUSSOLINI's daughter and from 1936 to 1943 was Foreign Minister. He was among those leaders who voted for the deposition of Mussolini, and for this he was tried and shot in Verona by the puppet government established by Mussolini in northern Italy. Ciano's diaries confirm that although he arranged the pre-war agreements with Germany, he soon came to resent the German connection.

Cicero, Marcus Tullius (106–43 BC) Roman orator, statesman, and philosopher. He first made his name as a lawyer in civil and criminal trials. His brilliant prosecution of Verres, the corrupt Roman governor of Sicily, in 70, established his reputation and the nobility came to see in him a strong candidate for the consulship of 63. As consul he outmanoeuvred Catiline and his fellow conspirators, who were plotting to take over Rome. He spoke out against the First Triumvirate, and was exiled on the charge of executing the Cataline conspirators without trial. The exertions of his friends secured his recall in 57 amid popular acclaim. He returned to Rome just before the eruption of civil war, which he did his best to avert.

His allegiance lay with Pompey and the senatorial cause but he became disillusioned by Pompey's leadership and after his defeat at PHARSALUS, returned to Italy. Caesar admired him greatly and valued his political support but he rejected Caesar and immersed himself in his philosophical writings. After Caesar's assassination it fell to Cicero to rally the Senate. He denounced MARK ANTONY in the *Philippicae* ('Philippic Orations') and hoped that he could revive the republic. In 43 Antony, Octavian, and Lepidus ordered him to be put to death and he was captured and killed.

Although Cicero rated his political role most highly his lasting claim to greatness rests on his writings. Cicero was fascinated by the theory as well as the practice of oratory and its branches, such as rhetoric, and in a series of works expounded the principles of the art. No one, apart from himself, much admired Cicero's poetry; but his letters, especially those to his friend Atticus, which were not meant for publication, give an unrivalled view of contemporary Roman politics and social life, in a style of brilliant variety and vigour. No less remarkable is a series of philosophical works, written as a consolation during years of political inactivity. They are largely based on Greek sources, but, with their dialogue form (based on PLATO), they bring to life the basic philosophical quarrel between hedonistic Epicureans (see EPICURUS) and rigorous STOICS. Cicero found Latin a language ill-suited to abstract exposition, and it is an important part of his achievement that he greatly expanded its vocabulary and developed a fluent and adaptable style that enabled the Christian writers of the 4th century to expound and forward the doctrines of their faith. He has remained an influence on Western thought and literature to this day.

Cid Campeador EL CID.

Cilicia An ancient country, now part of south-eastern Turkey. Geographically, it fell into two distinct parts: the western area was mountainous, while the eastern consisted of a fertile plain with Tarsus as its main city. It came under the control of the HITTITES, the ASSYRIANS, the ACHAEMENIDS, and ALEXANDER THE GREAT and was fought over by the SELEUCIDS and PTOLEMIES. In the 2nd century BC it became a haven for pirates, who were finally crushed by the Roman general Pompey in 67 BC, and by the end of the century it was part of the ROMAN EMPIRE. It was occupied by migrating Armenians in 1080. In 1375 it was conquered by the Mamelukes of Egypt and in 1515 by the OTTOMAN Turks.

Çiller, Tansu (1946–) Turkish politician and economist; Prime Minister (1993–96). The leader of the centre-right True Path party, she became Turkey's first female premier following elections in 1993. Her administration was characterized by free-market policies, including privatization and reductions in public spending. Çiller adopted a hawkish policy on internal security issues, such as Kurdish militancy in support of a separate homeland (see KURDISTAN). Following the collapse of her coalition and an inconclusive election, she resigned the premiership in February 1996. Despite allegations of corruption, she returned as Deputy Prime Minister of a new coalition (with the Islamic Welfare Party) in June. She lost power altogether in July 1997.

Cincinnatus, Lucius Quinctius (c. 519–438 BC) Roman republican hero famous for his devotion to the republic in times of crisis. Appointed dictator in 458 when a Roman army was trapped in battle by the Aequi tribe, he won a crushing victory and rescued the beleaguered troops. After this success, he resigned his command and returned to farm his small estate. CATO (the Elder) and other later republicans regarded him as the ideal statesman, representing the old Roman values of rustic frugality, duty to fatherland, courage, and lack of personal ambition; consequently much of what was told about him by the historian LIVY was strongly infected by romantic invention, as in the famous picture of his being 'called from the plough' in 458 to take the supreme command. The 18th century also idealized him as the citizen-soldier *par excellence* and Cincinatti (USA) was so named to honour the contribution of volunteer officers in the War of INDEPENDENCE.

Cinque Ports A confederation of coastal towns in south-east England. They provided the crown with ships and men to patrol the Channel and to convey its armies to the Continent, from the 11th to 16th centuries. The original five (French, *cinque*) ports were Hastings, Romney, Hythe, Sandwich, and Dover – known collectively as the 'head' ports. They were joined by 32 other ports, known as 'limbs'. By the 14th century Winchelsea and Rye were also recognized as head ports. The ports of the confederation received privileges including exemption from taxes, the right to return members to Parliament (retained until the 19th century), and the honour of attending on the monarch at the coronation. Burgesses of the ports were in 1205 granted the title of 'barons'. A Warden of the Cinque Ports was created in 1268 as an extension of the powers of the Constable of Dover Castle. A royal CHARTER incorporating these privileges was granted in 1278. The Cinque Ports declined with the setting up of a permanent navy and the Warden's title became honorary.

circus A spectacle in which animal acts and human feats of daring are performed. In ancient Rome the circus, which took its name from the long racing 'circuit' of the arena, featured CHARIOT races as the chief attraction of the programme. Four rival teams represented the elements, wearing Green, Red, Blue, and White, and each drove four horses representing the seasons. A race lasted seven laps, and each day had 24 races. Ninety days a year came to be devoted to circuses. The Circus Maximus hippodrome held 350,000, one-third of Rome's population. Roman emperors staged elaborate shows featuring acrobats, jugglers, dancers, trained animals, mime artists, actors, and musicians and there were combats between GLADIATORS as well as chariot races. Such theatrical spectacles were thought to keep the Roman public content and docile. According to the satirist Juvenal all the Roman people cared about was 'bread and circuses'.

The modern circus dates from the late 18th century, when ex-sergeant-major Philip Astley gave horse-riding displays in London in 'Astley's Royal Amphitheatre of Arts,' an arena to which he had added a stage for singing, dancing, and pantomime. This form of entertainment proved so popular that similar shows were started elsewhere in Britain and in other countries of Europe, some permanent, others as 'tenting' circuses, with performers and equipment travelling in caravans and wagons. From the early 19th century they were often combined with the travelling menageries and wild animal performances that had become very popular, of which the most celebrated was the combined circus and menagerie owned by the Sangers. The USA was the home of the really big circus. Barnum and his partners opened their first show at Brooklyn in 1871, and combined in 1880 with his great rivals Cooper and Bailey. After losing its popularity in Britain in the early 20th century, the circus enjoyed a revival through the large and elaborate productions of C. B. Cochran (1912) and after World War I by new circuses such as that of Bertram Mills, but circuses are now rare in Britain and the USA. In the former Soviet Union the state-subsidized circus flourished. Concern for animal welfare has led to a decrease in the use of animals in circuses in favour of skilled human performers. Modern circuses use magicians or illusionists, or base their acts on highly choreographed and dramatic acrobatic routines; one such outstanding troupe is the French-Canadian Cirque du Soleil. Some attempt to reflect contemporary life; the French circus group Archaos perform with motor cars, motorcycles, and chainsaws.

CIS COMMONWEALTH OF INDEPENDENT STATES.

Cistercian A member of a monastic order founded by St Robert of Molesme in 1098 at Cîteaux in France. Cistercians followed a strict interpretation of the 'rule' of St BENEDICT; their constitution was laid down in the *Carta Caritatis* ('The Charter of Charity'). St BERNARD founded a daughter house at Clairvaux which rapidly gained a great reputation. The Cistercians followed a life of strict austerity and during the great spread of monastic houses in the 11th and 12th centuries they led the movement to bring formerly unproductive land (marsh and moor) into use for agriculture, pioneering many new techniques including the employment of water power, and became very wealthy as sheep farmers and wool traders. The monks are now divided into two observances, the strict observance (following the original rule), known as Trappists, and the common observance, which allows certain relaxations.

citadel A key feature of a Greek city, being the stronghold around which large communities originally developed. When a city expanded, and a protective encircling wall was built to protect the citizens' houses, the citadel lessened in importance, though it often became a religious centre and housed the public treasury. The ACROPOLIS of Athens is the most famous example.

Civil Rights Acts (1866, 1875, 1957, 1964) Legislation aimed at extending the legal and civil rights of the US Black population. The first Civil Rights Act of 1866 reversed the doctrine laid down by the DRED SCOTT decision of 1857 and bestowed citizenship on all persons born in the USA (except tribal Native Americans, not so treated until 1924). It also extended the principle of equal protection of the laws to all citizens. The provisions of the Act were reinforced by the FOURTEENTH AMENDMENT to the Constitution, but later decisions of the Supreme Court and lack of will on the part of administrators rendered them largely ineffective. For almost a century thereafter there were few effective federal attempts to protect the Black population against discrimination, and in the South in particular Black people remained persecuted second-class citizens. It was only a series of legislative acts commencing with the Civil Rights Act of 1957, and culminating in the Civil Rights Act of 1964 and the Voting Rights Act of 1965, which finally gave federal agencies effective power to enforce Black rights and thus opened the way to non-discrimination.

Civil War, English ENGLISH CIVIL WAR.

civil wars, French FRENCH WARS OF RELIGION.

civil wars, Roman ROMAN CIVIL WARS.

Cixi (or Tz'u-hsi) (*c.* 1834–1908) Empress dowager of China (1862–1908). A Manchu, she became a concubine of the emperor Xianfeng (ruled 1851–61), giving birth to a son in 1856 who came to the throne in 1862 as the emperor Tongzhi. Cixi acted as Regent for 12 years, and after Tongzhi's death, resumed her position after the elevation of the latter's four-year-old cousin to the throne as the emperor Guangxu. She maintained her power through a combination of ruthlessness and corruption, until the last decade of the century, when the emperor attempted to reverse her conservative policies (HUNDRED DAYS REFORM). She responded by imprisoning Guangxu, and encouraging the BOXER RISING.

Forced by foreign military forces to flee the capital, she returned in 1902, conceding some reforms, but still tried to delay the establishment of a constitutional monarchy.

clan A group of people within a wider society who claim descent from a common ancestor and are usually distinguished by a common clan name, as, for example, the Highland clans of Scotland. The term is rather a general one, and can refer to groups organized around different forms of lineage. In some societies, the ancestor from whom members claim descent may be a mythical figure or, as in forms of totemism, an animal or other non-human figure. Members of a clan have obligations towards each other, and their marriages are usually exogamous: that is, members must marry outside the clan.

Clans have always been politically significant in Scottish history and clan support was vital to the Scottish king, who often played upon clan rivalries to maintain his power. These rivalries, especially between the Highland and Lowland clans, intensified at the time of the Reformation. The Highland clans retained their Roman Catholic faith, they fought for the Royalists during the English Civil War, and their reluctance to accept WILLIAM III (of Orange) led to the GLENCOE MASSACRE in 1692. They also took the lead in the JACOBITE rebellions of 1715 and 1745, after which an attempt was made by the British government to break up the clans by banning the wearing of the kilt and by undermining the system of communal clan ownership of land.

In Ireland a clan-based social system prevailed until, after the 16th-century rebellions against English rule, their influence was progressively destroyed by military suppression and a policy of wholesale land confiscation.

Clare election (1828) An event in Ireland that led to the passing of the Roman Catholic Relief Act by the British government in 1829. In 1828 Daniel O'CONNELL, an Irish lawyer, stood for election to Parliament in the County Clare constituency, winning a resounding victory over his opponent. However, O'Connell, as a Roman Catholic, could not take his seat. The Prime Minister, the Duke of Wellington, felt that if O'Connell were excluded there would be violent disorders in Ireland. Accordingly, despite furious opposition, the government pushed through a CATHOLIC EMANCIPATION measure allowing Catholics to sit in Parliament and hold public office.

Clarence, George Plantagenet, Duke of (1449–78) One of EDWARD IV of England's younger brothers. He intrigued with the Burgundians and fell out with both Edward and his other brother, Richard, Duke of Gloucester (RICHARD III of England); he was found guilty of high treason and is supposed to have been drowned in a butt of malmsey wine.

Clarence, Lionel, 1st Duke of (1338–68) The second surviving son of EDWARD III of England and Philippa of Hainaut, known as Lionel of Antwerp from his birth in Antwerp. From about 1341 it was arranged that he would marry the Anglo-Irish heiress Elizabeth de Burgh (1332–63); he was created Earl of Ulster and in 1361 was sent to Ireland as governor, to reassert English rule there. In 1362 he was created Duke of Clarence, the title being derived from his wife's inheritance of the lordship of Clare in Suffolk. After her death another rich marriage was arranged for him, to Violante, the only daughter of Galeazzo Visconti, Lord of Pavia; he died only a few months after this wedding.

The title of Clarence was revived in 1412 for Thomas of Lancaster (1389–1421), second son of HENRY IV and Mary de Bohun; it lapsed again after his death.

Clarendon, Constitutions of A document presented by HENRY II of England to a council convened at Clarendon, near Salisbury, in 1166. The king sought to define certain relationships between the state and the Church according to established usage. Churchmen, in particular Thomas à BECKET, saw it as state interference. The most controversial issue, BENEFIT OF CLERGY, concerned Henry's claim to try in his law courts clerics who had already been convicted in the ecclesiastical courts. After Becket's murder in 1170 Henry conceded the benefit of clergy, but not other points at issue.

Clarendon, Edward Hyde, 1st Earl of (1609–74) English statesman and historian. He began his political career in the Short and Long Parliaments as an opponent of royal authority, but in 1641 he refused to support the Grand Remonstrance, changed sides, and became a trusted adviser of Charles I, and later of Charles II, with whom he shared exile. At the RESTORATION Charles II made him Lord Chancellor; he helped to carry out the king's conciliatory policies, and his influence reached its peak when his daughter Anne married the heir apparent, James, Duke of York. Clarendon had little sympathy with the so-called Clarendon Code (1661–65), a series of laws aimed at Roman Catholics and dissenters, but he enforced them against the king's wishes. He was popularly blamed for the naval disasters of the second ANGLO-DUTCH WAR. He fell from power in 1667 and fled to France to avoid impeachment. His *History of the Rebellion* (published 1702–04) is a masterly account of the English Civil War, written from a royalist standpoint but with a considerable degree of objectivity.

Clarkson, Thomas (1760–1846) British philanthropist. A strong opponent of slavery, he became a founder member of the Committee for the Suppression of the Slave Trade. He collected much information about the trade and conditions on slave ships, which was published in a pamphlet and used by William WILBERFORCE in his parliamentary campaign for abolition. In 1807 an Act was passed prohibiting British participation in the SLAVE TRADE. In 1823 Clarkson became a leading member of the Anti-Slavery Society, which saw its efforts rewarded with the 1833 Act abolishing slavery in the British empire.

classical economics The system of economic theory expounded in the writings of (mainly British) economists between Adam SMITH (whose *Wealth of Nations* was published in 1776) and John Stuart MILL (whose *Principles of Political Economy* appeared in 1848). The principal contributors to classical economic theory were Smith, Jean-Baptiste Say (1767–1832), David RICARDO, Robert Malthus (1766–1834), and Mill. The central idea in classical economics is that of competition. Although individuals behave solely to benefit themselves, competitive markets (Adam Smith's 'invisible hand') ensure that this is enough to lead to efficient allocation of resources and production, and no excess profits. Government has a desirable economic role (above that of

providing law and order) only in the context of market failure, that is, where competition does not exist. The supply of every good and every factor of production will be equal to demand. The equilibrating element in all markets is price, the price of labour being the wage. This was assumed by the classical economists to tend in the long run to subsistence level, any persistent wage above this level calling forth faster population growth. At the same time, Say's Law, that 'supply creates its own demand', was supposed to rule out persistent or involuntary unemployment of labour. The analysis of rent was another pre-occupation of classical economics because the need was felt to explain and justify the distribution of income among the owners of labour, capital, and land. Ricardo argued that rent was equal to the surplus producible on more fertile land in competition with less fertile land. Classical economics assumes both savings and investment to be predominantly determined by interest rates, one of the aspects disputed in the 20th century by John Maynard KEYNES. The classical view of growth theory and economic development was that a stationary state was expected to materialize at some stage in the future. Following the new marginal analysis pioneered in the second half of the 19th century by the British economist William Stanley Jevons (1835–82), and the Austrian economist Carl Menger (1840–1921), classical economics developed into the neo-classical economics of Marie-Esprit Walras, Vilfredo Pareto, Alfred Marshall, and others. Neo-classical theory remains the scientific core of economic, especially micro-economic, analysis today.

Claudius (Tiberius Claudius Drusus Nero Germanicus) (10 BC–54 AD) Roman emperor (41–54). He was the nephew of Tiberius and the uncle of Gaius CALIGULA. An intelligent man of poor physique, he devoted himself to scholarship before sharing consular office with Caligula. After his nephew's murder the PRAETORIANS proclaimed his accession. He set about repairing the damage of the previous reign, taking an interest in the army, the Senate, and the administration. He added Britain and Mauretania (in north Africa) to the empire. He took a formal personal part in the invasion of Britain and added 'Britannicus' to his son's names to indicate the Roman possession of Britain. In later years his court was dominated by freedmen. His third wife Messalina, the mother of his children Britannicus and Octavia, was notorious for her infidelities and was eventually put to death. His fourth wife Agrippina, mother of NERO, is said to have poisoned him with mushrooms to hasten her son's succession. He was declared a god although SENECA in his satire *Apocolocyntosis* mocked the deification ceremony.

Clausewitz, Karl von (1780–1831) Prussian general and military strategist. He served in the Rhine campaigns of 1793–94 before being admitted to the Berlin military academy (1801), where he came under the influence of the military reformer Gerhard von SCHARNHORST. Captured by the French after the Battle of Jena, he returned to Prussia in 1809 and assisted Scharnhorst in his reorganization of the Prussian army. He served briefly in the Russian army (1812–14) and helped negotiate the alliance between Prussia, Russia, and Britain against Napoleon. His most famous work, *On War*, was published after his death. It sees war as a continuation of politics, the ultimate arbiter when all else fails. He supported the conception of national war and insisted that war must be conducted swiftly and ruthlessly in order to reach a clear decision in the minimum time.

Clay, Henry (1777–1852) US statesman and orator. As Speaker of the House of Representatives (1811–14) he played a central role in the agitation leading to the WAR OF 1812, and was one of the commissioners responsible for the negotiation of the Treaty of GHENT which ended it. He was one of the architects of the MISSOURI COMPROMISE and won support for his AMERICAN SYSTEM, a policy to improve national unity through a programme of economic legislation. His final political achievement lay in helping the passage of the COMPROMISE OF 1850 between the opposing FREE-SOIL PARTY and pro-slavery interests. His role in arranging major sectional compromises between North and South (1820, 1833, and 1850) earned him the title of 'the Great Compromiser'.

Clemenceau, Georges (1849–1929) French statesman. He entered the National Assembly (1871) as an anti-clerical republican. He fought for justice for DREYFUS (1897) but as Minister of the Interior and Premier (1906–09) ruthlessly suppressed popular strikes and demonstrations. In 1917, with French defeatism at its peak, he formed his victory cabinet with himself as Minister of War, persuading the Allies to accept FOCH as allied commander-in-chief. Nicknamed 'The Tiger', he became chairman of the VERSAILLES Peace Conference of 1919, where in addition to the restoration of ALSACE-LORRAINE to France, he demanded the SAAR basin and the permanent separation of the Rhine left bank from Germany, which should also pay the total cost of the war. Failing to get all these demands he lost popularity and was defeated in the presidential election of 1920.

Cleopatra VII (69–30 BC) The last of the PTOLEMIES. She became co-ruler of Egypt with Ptolemy XIII in 51, but was driven out in 48. She was restored by Julius CAESAR, and in 47 bore a son whom she said was his. In 46 they both accompanied him to Rome. After his assassination in 44 she returned to Egypt, and in 41 met MARK ANTONY at Tarsus. He spent the following winter with her in Alexandria, and she in due course gave birth to twins. In 37 Antony acknowledged these children and restored the territories of Cyrene and elsewhere to her; she pledged Egypt's support to him. In 34 they formally announced the division of ALEXANDER THE GREAT's former empire between Cleopatra and her children. In 32 Octavian declared war on her, and in the following year the Battle of ACTIUM resulted in the collapse of her fortunes. In 30 she committed suicide and Egypt passed into Roman hands.

Cleveland, (Stephen) Grover (1837–1908) Twenty-second (1885–89) and twenty-fourth (1893–97) President of the USA. He became governor of New York (1883–84) and gained a reputation as a reform politician, independent of the corrupt machine politics of TAMMANY HALL. He won the Democratic nomination for President in 1884 and closely defeated his republican rival BLAINE by gaining the support of many reform Republicans – the mugwumps, who voted against their party. As President, he favoured low tariffs and civil service reforms, but he had no answer for the Depression of 1893–97. He refused arguments for FREE SILVER, relying on exorbitant loans from a bankers' consortium led by

J. P. MORGAN. In foreign affairs he opposed the rising tide of imperialist sentiment, resisting US intervention in Hawaii and Cuba, but he enlarged the scope of the MONROE DOCTRINE by his stand on the dispute between Britain and Venezuela over the Venezuelan-British Guiana boundary (1897), insisting that Britain should go to arbitration.

cliff-dwellers A generalized term for the ANASAZI peoples living at Mesa Verde, Colorado, and similar sites such as Montezuma Castle, Arizona, or sites in the Canyon de Chelly, Arizona, especially after c. 1150 AD. Such sites were partly defensive against internal Pueblo warfare and against APACHE and NAVAHO raids. Perhaps the most famous site is Cliff Palace, Mesa Verde, comprising several tiers of adobe brick structures under an overhanging cliff face – stout terrace walls, square and round apartment towers with over 200 rooms, and 23 large round *kiva* ceremonial chambers.

Clinton, Bill (1946–) Forty-second President of the USA, inaugurated in 1993. Born William Jefferson Blythe, in Arkansas, he was educated as a Rhodes Scholar at Oxford, and at Yale University. A Democrat, he defeated President BUSH on a programme of reducing the federal deficit by cutting military spending and reforming taxation, while increasing investment in education, training, and public infrastructure. He appointed his wife Hillary to head the administration's health-care taskforce; her plans to provide health insurance for all US citizens were rejected by Congress in 1994. Abroad, he pursued tighter controls against trading rivals while seeking to underpin Russia's reform economy. During 1994 Clinton agreed with Russian leader Boris YELTSIN not to keep nuclear weapons constantly aimed at each other's countries. He lifted the trade embargo on Vietnam, and pledged to work towards the creation of a trans-Pacific free-trade zone. He also decided to maintain trade links with China, despite its poor human rights record. Following mid-term elections in 1994, Clinton's position was weakened as the Republicans gained control of both the House of Representatives and the Senate. However, the next two years saw a major upturn in the economy as well as a number of foreign-policy successes, including important US-brokered peace deals in the Middle East (1994) and the former Yugoslavia (1995). Clinton also authorized the bombing of strategic targets in Iraq (1996) in response to Iraqi violations of a UN-imposed no-fly zone above Kurdish areas. He stood for re-election in 1996 against the Republican challenger Robert Dole and was returned with a comfortable majority. Despite persistent (if unproven) accusations of personal and financial impropriety Clinton has remained a popular figure.

Clinton, George (1739–1812) American patriot leader. He controlled the popular anti-British faction in New York City from 1768. After attending the second CONTINENTAL CONGRESS (1775–76) he helped draft the state's constitution and served as governor for 15 years. An opponent of Alexander HAMILTON, he joined Thomas JEFFERSON in founding the Democratic-Republican party, and was Vice-President (1805–12) to both Jefferson and James Madison.

Clinton, Sir Henry (c. 1738–95) British general. He was promoted to commander-in-chief in America after fighting at BUNKER HILL and the capture of New York.

Although victorious at Monmouth (1778) and Charleston (1780), he was hampered by problems of supply and by the jealousy of CORNWALLIS. His failure to prevent Franco-American concentration of troops at YORKTOWN or to reinforce Cornwallis contributed to Britain's defeat and his own resignation. In 1794 he was appointed governor of Gibraltar, where he died.

Clive of Plassey, Robert, Baron (1725–74) British general and first British governor of BENGAL (1757–60 and 1765–67). Sent to south India at 18 as an EAST INDIA COMPANY clerk, he demonstrated such military prowess against the French (notably in the Siege of Arcot, 1751), that he soon rose to the position of governor of Madras. He was responsible for securing south-east India as a sphere of British influence. In 1756 his decision to transfer Company forces to Bengal was the first step in securing control of the region. He defeated the Bengal nawab, Siraj ud-Daula, at PLASSEY in 1757, and assumed the governorship of Bengal. After consolidation of the Company's hold, during which he amassed a personal fortune, he returned home to a peerage.

He was recalled to Bengal in 1765 to extricate the Company from its growing economic difficulties. He attempted to reform the Company's exploitative government, but paid the price for his own earlier manipulations when Parliament censured him after his final return home. Not unusually dishonest for his day, he was the victim of changing, more critical attitudes to overseas ventures, and of jealousy of his NABOB life-style. Parliament reversed its verdict, but Clive, always melancholic, committed suicide in 1774.

clocks and time measurement Among the earliest time-measuring devices was the shadow clock, known from around 1500 BC. This was later developed into the sundial. Other early clocks were the clepsydra or water clock, and the sand glass (still familiar as the egg-timer). Mechanical clocks were first made in China, where the escapement, a system of gears basic to all mechanical clocks, was developed in the 8th century AD by Yi Xing and Liang Lingzan. By the 11th century, the Chinese astronomer Su Sung was building elaborate astronomical clocks. Early European mechanical clocks from the 14th century were driven by the controlled fall of a weight, but they were only accurate to within about an hour per day, so had no minute hand. Spring-driven mechanisms appeared in the mid-15th century, and were used to manufacture watches as well as clocks.

The evolution of the style and design of clocks can be traced back to the Gothic forms of medieval church architecture. Chamber clocks of the 15th and early 16th centuries were mostly made of iron, with arches, lancet 'windows', pinnacles, and figures in niches, which bore no relationship to their structural needs. The great schools of 16th-century clock-making were centred in southern Germany, of which a wide range of gilded or polished-bronze table clocks, iron and steel lantern clocks, ship clocks, and weight-driven wall-clocks survive.

It was not until the 17th century, when the Dutch scientist Christiaan Huygens adopted the pendulum and the balance spring, that more accurate timekeeping became possible. In the mid-18th century accurate chronometers, driven by balance springs, began to be used at sea for finding longitude. The application of a pendulum to control the motion of the clock altered its

appearance. Among the great clock-makers of the period was Thomas Tompion of London, who made the noted 'Mostyn' mantle clock, encased in veneered ebony with silver mounts. Baroque clock cases reflect the more classic architectural and sculptural forms, such as in the French 'tête de poupée' clock from a design by A.-C. Boulle, with marquetry and gilded bronze mounts, made by the Martinot family and now in the Wallace Collection in London. French clock cases of the 18th century were considered as works of art, and the names of their makers, such as Jacques Cafferi, were stamped on them. Neo-classicism was popularized by Robert Adam, Josiah Wedgwood, and Matthew Boulton, who characteristically made gilded bronze cases which were ornamented with Derby porcelain figures, marble bases, and jasperware medallions. A contemporary French long-case clock by Balthazar Lieutaud was veneered in tulipwood and kingwood, and had a dial in enamelled copper. Among notable clock-makers at the court of Louis XVI were Ferdinand Berthoud and Pierre Le Roy. In the USA, a distinctive family of Massachusetts clock-makers were the Williards, who introduced the 'banjo' wall-clock. Among the makers of US tall clocks which became popular in the early 1800s were Daniel Burnap of Connecticut and Eli Terry.

Electrically driven clocks appeared in the 19th century. As the 19th century progressed clock-makers began to mass produce both the movements and cases of clocks, and the factory took over from the craftsman. By the early 20th century pendulum clocks accurate to 0.01 s per day could be built, but in 1929 the quartz crystal clock was developed, capable of an accuracy of 0.0001 s per day. In a quartz clock, a crystal of quartz is stimulated by a small electric signal to vibrate at high frequency. The quartz crystal is piezo-electric, and so this vibration induces a very precise, constant, high-frequency electrical signal. This signal is fed to an integrated circuit, which reduces the signal frequency to one pulse per second. This pulse is then used to drive the clock mechanism. In 1955 the first atomic clock was installed at the National Physical Laboratory in the UK, regulated by the extremely rapid, fixed oscillation rate of a specified energy transition in the nucleus of a caesium atom. Such atomic clocks vary by as little as one second every 3 million years. They are now internationally used as time standards.

Clodius, Publius Claudius Pulcher (c. 92–52 BC) Roman statesman. Although Claudius was of PATRICIAN birth, in 59 CAESAR, POMPEY, and CRASSUS assisted his adoption into a plebeian family; thus he became eligible to stand for election as a tribune of the PLEBS, which office he held in 58. Active in Caesar's and Crassus' support, but also personally ambitious, he enacted several populist laws, including one for free corn distributions to the urban poor and another to exile CICERO. He was a brilliant organizer and director of para-military groups, and for several years Rome became a battleground of rival political gangs, until early in 52 he was killed in an ambush. The resultant chaos subsequently led to Pompey's appointment as sole consul to break the power of the gangs.

Clovis (c. 466–511) The founder of the Frankish kingdom. He ruled a tribe of Salian FRANKS at Tournai in what is now Belgium and defeated the last Roman governor of GAUL at Soissons in 486, bringing the area between the rivers Loire and Seine under his control. In 496 he acquired the upper Rhineland by defeating the tribe of the Alemanni. He conquered the VISIGOTHS near Poitiers, extending his lands south as far as the Pyrenees. Small independent kingdoms in northern France were absorbed into his domain. His conversion to Christianity gained him the support of the Catholic Church, and thus strengthened his dynasty, the MEROVINGIANS.

Clovis culture A prehistoric culture in North America, characterized by lance-shaped stone points, 7–12 cm (3–5 inches) long, fluted near the base. The tools are often found in association with bones of large mammals, such as bison and extinct mammoth, and are assumed to have been used as spear heads. Named after a town in western New Mexico, they are found at sites throughout the mid-west and south-west USA from a period between 12,000 and 10,000 years ago. At one time, Clovis hunters were regarded as typifying the first AMERINDIANS, but there is increasing evidence that people were in the Americas long before, perhaps by 30,000 years ago.

Cluny, Order of A reformed Benedictine monastic order, whose mother house was the abbey of Cluny in France, founded by Duke William of Aquitaine in 909. Under Abbot Odilo (994–1048) Cluny became the head of a system of dependent 'daughter houses' throughout western Europe. In the 11th and 12th centuries Cluny became a spiritual and cultural centre of vast influence; four of its members became popes and it inspired the zealous reforming innovations of Pope GREGORY VII from 1073. The monastery church at Cluny was a model for much ecclesiastical building in Europe. By the 13th century the period of greatest achievement was over, as the monastic ideal suffered from too close an involvement with the secular world and too great a share of its wealth and worldly power.

Cnut CANUTE.

Coates, Joseph Gordon (1878–1943) New Zealand statesman. He represented the interests of the rural poor, including the MAORI. Though he was of the conservative Reform Party he advanced the New Zealand tradition of state action for the public good, developing roads and railways, the state hydro-electricity programme, afforestation, and aiding Maori farming schemes. In coalition with FORBES during the DEPRESSION he broke the authority of the private banks, established the Reserve Bank, and laid the foundation for economic recovery.

Cobbett, William (1763–1835) British social reformer and journalist. In 1802 he began publishing a weekly journal, the *Political Register*. He began to denounce the British government's conduct of the war with France, calling for peace and parliamentary reform. His conversion to radical reform was completed by his observations of the sufferings of the rural poor. In 1810 he was imprisoned for denouncing flogging in the army. After a period in the USA, he spent much time travelling in the English countryside, recording his impressions in his *Rural Rides* (1830). He strongly supported the REFORM ACT of 1832 and was elected Member of Parliament the same year.

Cobden, Richard (1804–65) British political economist and statesman. A strong supporter of FREE TRADE, he believed that it would help to promote international peace. In 1839, together with John BRIGHT, he founded the ANTI-CORN LAW LEAGUE and was in part responsible for the repeal of the Corn Laws in 1846. He lost his seat in Parliament in 1857 but was re-elected two years later. In 1860 he helped to negotiate a commercial treaty with France, which was based on tariff reductions and expansion of trade between the two countries. During the AMERICAN CIVIL WAR he declared his support for the Union (the North) and helped to smooth the often difficult relationships between the US and British governments. Cobden's radicalism was tempered by doubts about the extension of the franchise, a belief in minimum state interference, and a dislike of trade unions, but he retained a hatred of any kind of injustice.

Cochin KERALA.

Cochin China The southern region of Vietnam, centred on the Mekong delta. It was so called to distinguish it from Cochin in India. The home of people akin to the KHMERS, it was not fully absorbed by the Vietnamese until the 18th century. It was the base from which Gia-Long, as emperor of ANNAM, unified Vietnam in 1802.

Cochise (*c*. 1815–74) Apache Native American chief. Noted for his courage and military prowess, he gave his word in 1860 that he would not molest US mail riders passing through his Arizona territory in spite of war. In 1872 he made a peace treaty with the US government. He maintained both agreements, despite hostile acts from Whites and Native Americans.

Cochrane, Thomas, 10th Earl of Dundonald (1775–1860) British naval officer. Elected to Parliament in 1806, he conducted a campaign against naval corruption, but was himself found guilty of fraud in 1814 and courtmartialled. After fruitless attempts to clear his name, in 1817 he took command of Chile's fleet during its struggle to win freedom from Spain. He subsequently commanded the navies of Brazil·(1823–25) and of Greece (1827–28) when those countries were fighting for their independence. He was reinstated in the Royal Navy in 1832 with the rank of rear-admiral. Cochrane was one of the first to advocate the use of steam power in warships.

Code Napoléon (or *Code Civil*) The first modern codification of French civil law, issued between 1804 and 1810, which sought, under the direction of J. J. Cambacérès, to reorganize the French legal system. Napoleon himself presided over the commission which drafted the laws, which drew on the philosophical heritage of the 18th-century Enlightenment, the articles of the laws representing a compromise between revolutionary principles and the ancient Roman (i.e. civil) law which prevailed generally throughout Europe. It may be considered a triumph of individual, bourgeois rights over those established by Church and customary law, and for a long time delayed the recognition of collective (e.g. trade-union) and workers' rights. The code enshrines the principles of equality, the separation of civil and ecclesiastical jurisdictions, and the freedom of the individual. With its compressed legislative style (the entire law of tort is set out in five articles), the *Code* represents perhaps the pinnacle of the codification achievement; versions of it were adopted in various

European countries, and later spread through colonization to Latin America and parts of Africa. It was revised in 1904, and has remained the basis of French private law. Today, certain parts of the *Code*, such as family law, have been amended to reflect changing public attitudes, removing, for example, the absolute power of the husband and father in the family. In addition to the *Code Civil*, Napoleon was responsible for the Code of Civil Procedure (1807), the Commercial Code (1808), the Code of Criminal Procedure (1811), and the Penal Code (1811).

Cod War (1972–76) A period of antagonism between Britain and Iceland over fishing rights. The cause was Iceland's unilateral extension of its fishing limits to protect against over-fishing. Icelandic warships harassed British trawlers fishing within this new limit (1975–76), prompting protective action by British warships. A compromise agreement was reached in 1976 which allowed 24 British trawlers within a 320-km (200-mile) limit. This hastened the decline of British fishing ports such as Hull and Grimsby.

Cody, William Frederick (Buffalo Bill) 'WILD WEST'.

Coercive Acts (1774) Legislation passed by the British Parliament as a punishment for the BOSTON Tea Party. They closed the port of Boston pending compensation, amended Massachusetts's charter, allowed trials to be transferred to other colonies, and troops to be quartered at Boston's expense. Though Lord NORTH's aim was to isolate Massachusetts, the 'Intolerable Acts', as they became known, stiffened American resistance and precipitated the CONTINENTAL CONGRESS.

coffee-house A public place of refreshment where the main beverage was coffee. Coffee had enjoyed varying popularity following its introduction into Europe in the 16th century, but with the opening of the first coffee-house in London in 1652 its future was assured. Most of the cities of Europe had coffee-houses by the late 17th century, and the institution spread into the American colonies in 1689. They became centres where business was transacted, newspapers were read, and literary and political opinions were exchanged. In London Lloyd's coffee-house was the centre for marine insurance, and in New York the Merchants coffee-house, opened in 1737, became of major political importance in the years leading up to the American War of INDEPENDENCE. The heyday of these establishments was over by the mid-18th century, especially in England, where their social role was taken over by gentlemen's clubs.

Coke, Sir Edward (1552–1634) English lawyer and politician. He rose to the position of Lord Chief Justice (1613), prosecuting such defendants as ESSEX (1601) and the GUNPOWDER PLOT conspirators (1606). In 1616 James I dismissed him, since, at first a supporter of the royal prerogative, Coke had become a defender of the common law against Church and crown: as a Member of Parliament he led opposition to James I and CHARLES I. He was largely responsible for drafting the PETITION OF RIGHT (1628) and wrote commentaries on medieval and contemporary English law.

Colbert, Jean Baptiste (1619–83) A leading minister of France from the mid-17th century. The son of a merchant who became an important financier in Paris, he rose to be one of the chief ministers of LOUIS XIV,

having shown his ability in building up MAZARIN's private fortune and in profiting from the fall of FOUQUET. He was loyal, dedicated, and hard-working, and when he became Controller-General of Finance in 1665 he halved the expense of tax collection and greatly increased the revenue. Putting MERCANTILIST theories into practice, he stimulated industry, improved communications, and established trading companies. He was constantly thwarted by the king's costly wars, but his aim was to make France great through the prosperity of the people. He did not remedy the basic weakness of the French fiscal system, however, and tended to burden industry with bureaucratic details, and his tariff policy was aggressive. He encouraged the construction of the Canal du Midi, linking Toulouse to the Mediterranean, and as Secretary of State he restored the French navy. In the artistic sphere Colbert supervised the reorganization of the Gobelins tapestry factory and the re-establishment of the Royal Academy of Painting and Sculpture. He was a collector himself and it was largely owing to his practical support for the king's ambitions that France replaced Italy as the artistic capital of Europe.

Cold War The struggle between the Soviet bloc countries and the Western countries from 1945 to 1990. The Soviet Union, the USA, and Britain had been wartime allies against Nazi Germany, but already before Germany was defeated they began to differ about the future of Germany and of Eastern Europe. Wartime summit meetings at YALTA (1945) and POTSDAM (1945) had laid down certain agreements, but as communist governments seized exclusive power in Eastern Europe, and Greece and Turkey were threatened with similar take-overs, the Western Powers became increasingly alarmed. From 1946 onwards popular usage spoke of a 'Cold War' (as opposed to an atomic 'hot war') between the two sides. The Western allies took steps to defend their position with the formation of the TRUMAN DOCTRINE (1947) and the MARSHALL PLAN (1947) to bolster the economies of Western Europe. In 1949 NATO was formed as a defence against possible attack. The communist bloc countered with the establishment of the Council for Mutual Aid and Assistance (COMECON, 1949), and the WARSAW PACT (1955). Over the following decades, the Cold War spread to every part of the world, and the USA sought CONTAINMENT of Soviet advances by forming alliances in the Pacific and south-east Asia. There were repeated crises (the KOREAN WAR, Indo-China, HUNGARY, the CUBAN MISSILE CRISIS, and the VIETNAM WAR), but there were also occasions when tension was reduced as both sides sought *détente*. The development of a nuclear arms race from the 1950s, only slightly modified by a NUCLEAR TEST-BAN TREATY in 1963 and STRATEGIC ARMS LIMITATION TALKS (1969–79), maintained tension at a high level. Tension intensified in the early 1980s with the installation of US Cruise missiles in Europe and the announcement of the US STRATEGIC DEFENSE INITIATIVE, and receded with an agreement in 1987 for limited arms control (see DISARMAMENT). It began to recede in 1985 with a resumption of START talks, followed by the INF Treaty (1987). Soviet forces withdrew from Afghanistan in 1989 and pacification in such troubled areas as Nicaragua and Angola followed. In December 1989 Presidents Bush and Gorbachev, at a summit meeting in Malta, declared the Cold War officially ended. By then the communist regimes of the Warsaw Pact countries were collapsing and the Soviet Union itself ceased to exist in late 1991. Aware of a need to rethink its role, NATO invited the former Warsaw Pact countries to join a 'partnership for peace' (inaugurated in 1994) as a first step towards granting them full NATO membership (if desired). In 1997 Russia was granted an official voice in NATO business in return for its acceptance of NATO's expansion into eastern Europe. Poland, Hungary, and the Czech Republic were then formally invited to join NATO. (See also EAST–WEST RELATIONS.)

Coligny, Gaspard de, seigneur de Châtillon (1519–72) French nobleman of the House of Montmorency, appointed Admiral of France in 1552. He was captured by the Spaniards in 1557, and during his incarceration in prison he became a committed Calvinist. His high personal standing subsequently conferred respectability on the HUGUENOT cause in the first phase of the FRENCH WARS OF RELIGION. On CONDÉ's death he was elected commander-in-chief (1569), and then helped to engineer the favourable Peace of St Germain (1570). But his ascendancy over the youthful Charles IX alienated him from Catherine de MEDICI, who almost certainly acquiesced in a plan to assassinate him. The ST BARTHOLOMEW'S DAY MASSACRE seems to have broken out spontaneously in the wake of his assassination.

collectivization The creation of collective or communal farms, to replace private ones. The policy was ruthlessly enforced in the Soviet Union by STALIN between 1929 and 1933 in an effort to overcome an acute grain shortage in the towns. The industrialization of the Soviet Union depended on cheap food and abundant labour. Bitter peasant resistance was overcome with brutality, but the liquidation of the KULAKS and slaughter by peasants of their own livestock resulted in famine (1932–33). Gradually more moderate methods were substituted with the development of state farms. An average collective farm in the former Soviet Union was about 6,000 hectares (15,000 acres) in extent, nine-tenths cultivated collectively, but each family owning a small plot for its own use. By the late 1980s these personal plots made up 3% of the nation's farmland, but accounted for over 25% of its agricultural output. Profits were shared in collective farms; in state farms workers received wages. In the early 1990s collective farms accounted for about 67% of the area of cultivated land, state farms about 30%, and privately owned farms about 1.6%. Private ownership of land was encouraged by GORBACHEV as part of his economic reforms. After 1945 a policy of collectivization was adopted in a number of socialist countries. The Soviet example was followed in China by MAO ZEDONG in his First Five Year Plan of 1953, but was only enforced by stages. China did not copy the ruthless subordination of agriculture to industry, preferring the peasant COMMUNE.

Collins, Michael (1890–1922) Irish patriot. A member of the IRISH REPUBLICAN BROTHERHOOD, he fought in the EASTER RISING (1916) in Dublin. Elected a Member of Parliament he was one of the members of SINN FEIN who set up the Dáil Éireann in 1919. He worked as Finance Minister in Arthur GRIFFITH's government and at the same time led the IRISH REPUBLICAN ARMY. In 1921 the British government offered a reward of £10,000 for him, dead or alive. He played a large part in the negotiations that led to the Anglo–Irish truce in 1921 and the Dáil approval of the treaty in 1922. He commanded the Irish

Free State Army at the start of the Irish civil war and was killed in an ambush at Beal-na-Blath, County Cork, in August 1922.

Colombia A country in the extreme north-west of the South American continent, the only South American country with coasts on both the Pacific and the Atlantic oceans, separated by the isthmus of Panama. To the east is Venezuela, and to the south Brazil, Peru, and Ecuador.

Physical. The northern end of the Andes occupies the north-western half of the country, here breaking into three great cordilleras which enclose high, cool plateaux. Running from them are several large rivers to water the hot northern coastal plains. South-east of the Andes, plains of rich pasture stretch away to the east and to the south, where the land falls in forested terraces towards the headstreams of the Amazon.

Economy. Colombia has a wide range of agricultural crops and is virtually self-sufficient in food production. About 5% of Colombia's total area is arable, while 30% is permanent pasture land. Colombia has large reserves of crude oil, coal, natural gas, gold, precious stones, platinum, bauxite, and copper. Coffee accounts for half of exports, and industrial products such as textiles, iron, chemicals, and petroleum products are also exported. Political instability has deterred much-needed foreign investment, and disrupted agriculture. Cannabis and coca are cultivated illicitly on a vast scale for the manufacture of illegal drugs. In July 1991 a major new oilfield was discovered.

History. Colombia was occupied by the Chibcha Indians before the Spanish conquest. The first permanent European settlements were made on the Caribbean coast, Santa Marta being founded in 1525 and Cartagena eight years later. Colonization of the interior was led by Gonzalo Jiménez de Quesada, who defeated the Chibchas and founded the city of Bogotá in 1538. The region was initially part of the viceroyalty of Peru, but a different political status came with the establishment of the viceroyalty of New Granada in the first half of the 18th century. The viceroy sitting in Bogotá was given jurisdiction over Colombia, but also over Venezuela, Ecuador, and Panama. Colombia remained a viceroyalty of Spain until the Battle of Boyacá (1819) during the SPANISH SOUTH-AMERICAN WARS OF INDEPENDENCE, when, joined with Venezuela, it was named by Simón BOLÍVAR the United States of Colombia. In 1822 under his leadership New Granada, Panama, Venezuela, and Ecuador were united as the Republic of Gran Colombia, which collapsed in 1830. In 1832 a constitution for New Granada was promulgated by Francisco Santander, which was amended in 1858 to allow a confederation of nine states within the central republic now known as the Granadine Confederation. In 1863 the country was renamed the United States of Colombia. The constitution of 1886 abolished the sovereignty of the states and the presidential system of the newly named Republic of Colombia was established. The War of the Thousand Days (1899–1902), encouraged by the USA, led to the separation of Panama from Colombia (1903). Violence broke out again in 1948 and moved from urban to rural areas, precipitating a military government between 1953 and 1958. A semi-representative democracy was restored that achieved a degree of political stability, and Colombia's economy has recovered from the setbacks of the early 1970s as diversification of production and foreign investment have increased.

Agriculture is the chief source of income in Colombia, but it is estimated that the country's illegal drugs trade supplies some 80% of the world's cocaine market. During the 1980s Colombia achieved sustained economic growth and a successful record of external debt management, but the drug trade increasingly dominated both internal affairs and its relations with the USA. At the same time numerous extremist guerrilla groups, of both Left and Right, resorted to violence, including assassinations. In 1990 the ruling Liberal Party convened a Constitutional Assembly, which produced a new constitution, this was followed by an agreement by some guerrillas (most notably the notorious M-19) to demobilize and take part in the political process. Nevertheless, violence and drug-related corruption have continued to be major problems. In 1995–96 a political crisis arose when President Ernesto Samper was charged with accepting funds from the drug cartels.

CAPITAL:	Bogotá
AREA:	1,141,748 sq km (440,831 sq miles)
POPULATION:	35.652 million (1996)
CURRENCY:	1 peso = 100 centavos
RELIGIONS:	Roman Catholic 95%
ETHNIC GROUPS:	Mestizo 58.0%; White 20.0%; Mulatto 14.0%; Black 4.0%; mixed Black-Indian 3.0%; Amerindian 1.0%
LANGUAGES:	Spanish (official); Amerindian languages
INTERNATIONAL ORGANIZATIONS:	UN; OAS; Andean Group

Colombian Independence War SPANISH SOUTH-AMERICAN WARS OF INDEPENDENCE.

Colombo Plan (for Co-operative Economic Development in South and South-East Asia) An international organization of 24 countries, established to assist the development of member countries in the Asian and Pacific regions. Based on an Australian initiative at the meeting of COMMONWEALTH ministers in Colombo in January 1950, it was originally intended to serve Commonwealth countries of the region. The scheme was later extended to cover 26 countries, with the USA and Japan as major donors; Britain and Canada left in 1991 and 1992 respectively. Assistance takes the form of educational aid, training programmes, food aid, loans, equipment, and technical co-operation. In 1977 its title was changed to the 'Colombo Plan for Co-operative Economic and Social Development in Asia and the Pacific' following the withdrawal of several south-east Asian nations that had adopted communism.

colonialism IMPERIALISM.

Colosseum (literally 'Colossal Building') The name dating from the 8th century, given to the Flavian Amphitheatre in Rome. It was built by the emperors VESPASIAN and Titus in front of NERO's 'Golden Palace'. Prisoners brought to Rome after the suppression of the JEWISH REVOLT laboured on it, completing it in 80 AD. With a seating capacity of 50,000 on three levels, it was shaded by adjustable awnings and flooded for mock sea-battles. A wooden floor covered in sand was the stage for GLADIATORS and wild beasts. In turn a fortress and a home for squatters, its preservation was ordered by the pope in the 11th century.

Columba, St (c. 521–97) Abbot and missionary. He was born in Donegal, Ireland, of the family of the Irish High

Kings. In 563 he and 12 monks founded the monastery of Iona, off the west coast of Scotland. For the next 30 years Columba continued the conversion of the heathen Picts. His consecration of King Aidan at the coronation (574) was the first royal consecration in Britain. Through the work of Columba and his successors Iona became the centre of Celtic Christianity (CELTIC CHURCH) in northern Britain.

Columba, St *A page from the* Book of Kells, *a superb example of an illuminated manuscript. It is thought to have been produced at the monastery founded by St Columba in the 6th century, at Kells, Co. Meath, in the Republic of Ireland.*

Columbanus, St (c. 543–615) Abbot and missionary, from his youth a monk at Bangor, Ireland. In about 590 he left for France and founded monasteries at Annegray and Luxeuil. His support for the CELTIC practice of Christianity, and especially for the Irish dating of Easter, upset Pope Gregory I and he was ordered back to Ireland (610). He promptly crossed the Alps to Lombardy in Italy and established an abbey at Bobbio (614). However, his austere monasticism lost its appeal before the more practical provisions of St BENEDICT.

Columbus, Christopher (c. 1451–1506) Genoese navigator and explorer, celebrated as the first European to discover America. His great interest was in what he called his 'Enterprise to the Indies', the search for a westward route to the Orient for trade in spices. For over a decade he tried to get financial support for his 'Enterprise', and at last in 1492 persuaded FERDINAND I and Isabella of Spain to sponsor an expedition. He set out in the *Santa Maria*, with two other small ships, expecting to reach Japan, and when he came on the islands of the Caribbean he named them the West Indies, and the native Arawak people Indians. On Cuba (which he thought was China) tobacco was discovered. His published record was the first real evidence in Europe of the existence of the New World. For his second voyage a year later he was provided with 17 ships and expected to trade for gold and establish colonies. He surveyed much of the Caribbean archipelago during the next three years, but then, with no gold forthcoming, he was recalled to Spain in disgrace. After months of lobbying, however, he was allowed again to search for Asia; and this time he took a more southerly route, discovering Trinidad and the mouth of the Orinoco River, but the colony he had left on HISPANIOLA was seething with rebellion. Ferdinand and Isabella sent a new governor to control it and paid off Columbus by allowing him to fit out a fourth voyage (1502–04) at their expense. He explored much of the coast of Central America vainly seeking at Panama a strait that would lead him to Japan, until his poorly equipped ships became worm-eaten and unfit for the voyage home. He chartered another vessel and reached Spain ill and discredited, and died forgotten.

Comanche A Native American people of the Great Plains. They used the dog-travois (sledge) to follow migrant game herds, but gained greater mobility after the introduction of horses in the 17th century from Spanish settlements in the south-west. Throughout the 18th century warfare was endemic against other tribes. The Comanche obtained firearms from the French, and continued raiding against the Utes and Spanish until 1786, when the Spanish began to give them guns, ammunition, and supplies to make them dependent and cause them to lose their skill as ARCHERS.

Combination Acts Laws passed by the British Parliament in 1799 and 1800 in order to prevent the meeting ('combining together') of two or more people to obtain improvements in their working conditions. Flouting the law resulted in trial before a magistrate, and TRADE UNIONS were thus effectively made illegal. The laws, which were largely inspired by the fear of radical ideas spreading from France to Britain, were nevertheless unsuccessful in preventing the formation of trade unions. The Combination Acts were repealed in 1824 as a result of the skilful campaign by Francis PLACE and Joseph HUME, and were followed by an outbreak of strikes. In 1825 another Act was passed which resulted in trade union activity but limited the right to strike.

COMECON (Council for Mutual Economic Assistance) An economic organization of Soviet-bloc countries that was established by Stalin among the communist countries of eastern Europe in 1949 to encourage interdependence in trade and production as the second pillar, with the WARSAW PACT, of Soviet influence in Europe. It achieved little until 1962, when agreements restricting the satellite countries to limited production and to economic dependency on the Soviet Union were enforced. Its members were: Bulgaria, Cuba, Czechoslovakia, German Democratic Republic, Hungary, Mongolian People's Republic, Poland, Romania, the Soviet Union, and Vietnam (Yugoslavia had associate status). Albania was expelled in 1961. In 1987 it began to discuss

co-operation with the EUROPEAN COMMUNITY, and it was dissolved in 1990, following the collapse of communist regimes in eastern Europe.

Cominform (Communist Information Bureau) An international communist organization to co-ordinate Party activities throughout Europe. Created in 1947, it assumed some of the functions of the INTERNATIONALS which had lapsed with the dissolution of the COMINTERN in 1943. After the quarrel of TITO and STALIN in 1948 Yugoslavia was expelled. The Cominform was abolished in 1956, partly as a gesture of renewed friendship with Yugoslavia and partly to improve relations with the West.

Comintern (Communist international) Organization of national communist parties for the propagation of communist doctrine with the aim of bringing about a world revolution. It was established by LENIN (1919) in Moscow at the Congress of the Third International (INTERNATIONALS) with ZINOVIEV as its chairman. At its second meeting in Moscow (1920), delegates from 37 countries attended, and Lenin established the Twenty-one Points, which required all parties to model their structure on disciplined lines in conformity with the Soviet pattern, and to expel moderate ideologies. In 1943 STALIN dissolved the Comintern, though in 1947 it was revived in a modified form as the COMINFORM, to co-ordinate the activities of European communism. This, in turn, was dissolved in 1956.

comitia Assemblies of Roman citizens meeting for elections or legislation. The oldest assembly, the 'Curiata', consisted of representatives of religious groups based on kinship: it survived later as a body which sanctioned adoptions and ratified wills. The creation of the 'Centuriata' as the assembly of the people in arms was attributed to King Servius Tullius. It originally elected magistrates and legislated. The citizens were organized in 'centuries' according to census rating and military equipment and function, and voting power was weighted in favour of wealth and age. It remained the electoral assembly for consuls and praetors.

The 'Tributa' was the meeting of the people in the 35 tribes, based on domicile, in which votes were equal, irrespective of property, but it was the tribal and not the individual vote which counted. Like the 'Centuriata' it was convened by consuls or praetors and became the main legislative body and elected most of the lower magistrates. It was perhaps modelled on the 'Concilium Plebis', under the presidency of the tribunes of the PLEBS. This was established early in the conflict between patricians and plebeians. It consisted of plebeians only and was convened by the tribunes. Bills carried here were 'plebiscita'; but after 287 BC 'plebiscita' were accorded the same form as laws of the whole Roman people, and were generally also called 'leges'.

Commines, Philippe de (or Commynes) (c. 1447–1511) French historian. Born in Flanders, the son of a noble BURGUNDIAN commander, he was raised at the Burgundian court, joined Louis XI of France in 1472, and was later disgraced for plotting against Charles VIII in 1486. Restored to favour, he joined Charles's invasion of Italy in 1494. He wrote his *Memoires*, six books on Louis and two on Charles during 1489–98.

Committee of Public Safety An emergency body set up in France in April 1793. It was the first effective executive government of the Revolutionary period and governed France during the most critical year of the Revolution. Its nine members (later 12) were chiefly drawn from the JACOBINS and it contained some of the ablest men in France, dominated at first by DANTON and then by ROBESPIERRE. It successfully defeated France's external enemies but was largely responsible for the Reign of TERROR, and its ruthless methods, at a time of growing economic distress, led to growing opposition. In March 1794 an attempt to overthrow it, led by HÉBERT, was quashed, but four months later the reaction which overthrew Robespierre marked the end of the Committee's power. It was restricted to foreign affairs until its influence was finally ended in October 1795.

common land (or common) Land that is subject to rights of common. These are rights to take the produce from land of which the right-holder is not the owner, for example a right of pasture. They are private rights, and need not be open to all. The right may be restricted, for example, to a portion of the year. The first commons were usually woodland or rough pasture for the villagers' animals in medieval England. By the Statute of Merton (1236) the lord of the manor or other owner of a village was allowed to enclose waste land for his own use only if he left adequate pasture for the villagers. ENCLOSURE of common land started in the 12th century, and increased dramatically in the second half of the 18th century, often arousing opposition and claims of theft.

In colonial America many village communities had large areas of common land, partly for defensive purposes as well as for pasturage. These areas sometimes survived to be used for recreation, the best known being Boston Common, today a public park but bought by the town for pasturage in 1634.

Commons, House of HOUSE OF COMMONS.

Commonwealth The republican government of England between the execution of Charles I in 1649 and the restoration of Charles II in 1660. The RUMP PARLIAMENT claimed to 'have the supreme power in this nation', and ruled through a nominated 40-man Council of State. In 1650 an 'Engagement' to be faithful to the Commonwealth was imposed on all adult males. While Oliver CROMWELL was eliminating Royalist resistance in Ireland and then Scotland (1649–51), the Rump disappointed expectations of radical reform. Unpopular taxes had to be raised to finance the army's expeditions. Furthermore, the Navigation Acts sparked off the much-resented ANGLO-DUTCH WAR of 1652–54.

Cromwell expelled the Rump in April 1653. He hoped to reach a political and religious settlement through the BAREBONES PARLIAMENT (July–December 1653), but in December he accepted the necessity of taking the headship of state himself. The period of Cromwellian rule is usually known as the PROTECTORATE.

Commonwealth of Independent States (CIS) (Russian, 'Sodruzhestvo Nezavisimykh Gosudarstv') A community of 12 independent countries, founded by the Alma Ata agreement on 8 December 1991 by Russia, Ukraine, and Belarus, as a successor to the Soviet Union.

Armenia, Kazakhstan, Kyrgyzstan, Moldova, Tajikistan, Turkmenistan, and Uzbekistan had joined by the end of 1991. Azerbaijan and Georgia joined in 1993.

The members of the CIS have agreed to co-operate in many areas, including politics, culture, public health, education, science, and trade, and to allow free movement of people and information from one member state to another. The CIS has unified military and armaments policies, although member states can choose to be neutral or non-nuclear. Nine CIS states are seeking to form a free-trade area with a single currency. The headquarters of the CIS are in Minsk.

Commonwealth of Nations An association of 54 nations, most of which were formerly members of the BRITISH EMPIRE. Although the nations of the Commonwealth are all independent in every aspect of domestic and external affairs, for historical reasons they accept the British monarch as the symbol of the free association of its members and as such the head of the Commonwealth. The term British Commonwealth began to be used after World War I when the military help given by the DOMINIONS to Britain had enhanced their status. Their independence, apart from the formal link of allegiance to the crown, was asserted at the Imperial Conference of 1926, and given legal authority by the Statute of WESTMINSTER (1931). The power of independent decision by Commonwealth countries was evident in 1936 over the abdication of EDWARD VIII, and in 1939 when they decided whether or not they wished to support Britain in World War II. In 1945 the British Commonwealth consisted of countries where the White population was dominant. Beginning with the granting of independence to India, Pakistan, and Burma (now Myanmar) in 1947, its composition changed and it adopted the title of Commonwealth of Nations. A minority of countries have withdrawn from the Commonwealth, notably Burma in 1947 and the Republic of Ireland in 1949. Pakistan left in 1972 but re-joined in 1989, SOUTH AFRICA withdrew in 1961 because of hostility to its apartheid policy but was formally re-admitted in 1995, and Fiji withdrew from 1987 to 1997.

In the 1950s pressure began to build up in Britain to end free immigration of Commonwealth citizens which was running at about 115,000 in 1959, mostly from the West Indies, India, and Pakistan. From 1962 onwards increasing immigration restrictions were reciprocally imposed by a series of legislative measures. Regular conferences and financial and cultural links help to maintain some degree of unity among Commonwealth members. In 1993 Cameroon applied to join the Commonwealth, and was accepted in 1995. It is the first country that has never been wholly ruled by Britain to seek Commonwealth membership. Mozambique, which also has no historical links with Britain, was admitted as a special case in 1995.

The Commonwealth Secretariat was set up in London in 1965. It operates as an international organization to foster financial and cultural links between all Commonwealth nations. The Commonwealth has no charter but all members subscribe to a set of declarations, among which NORTH–SOUTH RELATIONS and the eradication of racial prejudice have been prominent and often controversial themes. The 1979 Lusaka meeting of the Heads of Government paved the way for internationally recognized independence for Zimbabwe, and through the 1980s, the Heads of Government, with the exception of the UK, urged the imposition of economic sanctions against South Africa as a protest against apartheid. In 1995 the Heads of Government voted to suspend Nigeria's membership, following the execution of nine environmental and minority rights activists there.

communal conflict Conflict between different groups, often within one state, based upon different religion, race, language, culture, or history–factors which may all be described as their ethnicity. It may be expressed in a general tension, hostility, and competition for scarce resources, or in forms of oppression or prejudice by one group, often the majority, over another, such as racism, segregation, and discrimination. It may lead to unrest or protests which destabilize a state, separatist movements, or open armed conflict culminating in civil war, which undermines the integrity of the state and may lead to secession. Communal conflict may also be a major source of conflict between states. Conflict may be sparked by a particular issue, such as access to a mutually claimed religious place (the most famous example being Jerusalem, which is holy to Christians, Jews, and Muslims; while in Ayodhya, India, which is one of the seven most sacred Hindu sites, Hindus have attempted to demolish a mosque). Disputes often focus on language and education. Language conflicts in Canada and Belgium, for example, reinforced by religious differences, have been a focus of political tension for decades. In the UK, awareness of being Welsh, Scottish or Irish combines with resentment of English dominance to produce periodic nationalist upsurges. Ethnic conflict is particularly widespread in former colonies, as in Africa, where state borders were drawn with little regard for the cultural or linguistic boundaries of different peoples. It may also be the result of the lifting or loosening of central government authority, as in the former Soviet Union, where the upsurge of ethnic or communal conflicts, for example between Christian Armenians and Muslim Azeris, may be seen as a result of the weakening of central authority following the policies of reform introduced by Mikhail Gorbachev in the 1980s. The revival of religion as an increasingly important factor in world politics and the challenge to secularism (see RELIGION AND POLITICS) is also likely to increase communal conflict in the future. In Sri Lanka, religious and linguistic differences have been the basis of violent conflict between TAMILS and Sinhalese, a conflict with sufficiently destabilizing implications for the entire Indian subcontinent for the Indian army to intervene in an attempt to restore peace. India itself, with some 1,500 languages and dialects, seven religions, and varied ethnic groups and castes, is subject to incessant ethnic strife. In Lebanon, a complex web of ethnic conflict between Christians and Muslims on the one hand, and Sunni and Shiite Muslims on the other, caused a long and bloody civil war, exacerbated by external intervention, which led to the virtual disintegration of the state. Northern Ireland has seen a long-running conflict between the Catholic minority and the Protestant majority, also described as sectarianism because it is a conflict between sects of the same religion. Ostensibly political, ideological, or economic conflicts can often be shown to have a tribal, religious, or communal dimension. For example, in post-colonial Angola, the ideological conflict

between pro-Soviet and pro-Western groups paralleled the rivalries between different ethnic groups. It is estimated that half the independent states of the world have experienced some form of communal conflict in recent years; the Marxist prediction that distinctions of an ethnic nature would be replaced by a universal working class seems to have been disproved by the strength of ethnic allegiances, which some commentators take to be the strongest form of political awareness.

commune (in China) The basic unit of agricultural organization and rural local government in communist China from 1958 to about 1978. Co-operatives were formed when the mutual aid teams that emerged during the land reform of the early 1950s were merged as part of the 'high tide of socialism' of 1955–56. During the GREAT LEAP FORWARD these co-operatives were themselves combined to form large units known as communes which were responsible for planning local farming and for running public services. Commune power was gradually devolved to production brigades after the disastrous harvests of 1959–61. In the FOUR MODERNIZATIONS movement communes were virtually abolished.

commune (in Europe) A medieval western European town which had acquired specific privileges by purchase or force. The privileges might include a charter of liberties, freedom to elect councils, responsibility for regulating local order, justice, and trade, and powers to raise taxes and tolls. The burghers initially swore an oath binding themselves together. There were regional differences: in northern and central Italy where there was a strong tradition of municipal independence, a commercial boom in the Middle Ages enhanced the wealth of the towns and increased their power, some eventually becoming independent city-republics (VENICE, FLORENCE). The communes of Flanders, the German cities of the Holy Roman Empire, and of Spain all achieved a measure of independence as the high costs of warfare forced their rulers to surrender direct control in return for financial benefits. The communes often pursued their own diplomatic policies as political alliances shifted. They flourished where central government was weak and became bastions of local power, and after the Reformation, of religious loyalties. The growth of strong national monarchies reduced them in the 16th and 17th centuries.

Commune of Paris PARIS, COMMUNE OF.

communications revolution An unprecedented advance in the speed of message transmission. In 1794 the French army started to use semaphore to pass messages, and a hot-air balloon to observe the enemy. In 1837 Charles Wheatstone in Britain and Samuel Morse in the USA developed an electric telegraph, the latter sending electric signals by means of a 'Morse-code'. Telegraph lines were erected between Washington and Baltimore in 1844, then across Europe, and in 1866 across the Atlantic. One of the effects of the telegraph was that it linked international banking; another was that newspapers could print up-to-date international news; thirdly, governments could exert much closer control, for example in war or in their distant colonies. With the telephone (1876) direct speech communication replaced the telegram, while radio (1899) removed the need for communicants to be linked by electric cables. Television (1926) enabled visual images to be transmitted, while satellites (from the 1970s) enabled the whole world to watch events of supranational interest, with English becoming increasingly the language of the world. In the 1980s information technology emerged as a computer-based means of storing and transmitting information using networks of computers linked together, especially for academic or business use. The networks were subsequently connected into a global system using fibre-optic cables and existing telephone channels. During the 1990s, the use of this system, known as the Internet, expanded dramatically with an increase in the ownership of personal computers. The Internet came to be used for transmitting electronic mail, accessing and exchanging information, electronic on-line publishing, and, to some extent, entertainment.

communism A social and political ideology advocating that authority and property be vested in the community, each member working for the common benefit according to capacity and receiving according to needs.

The ideal of communism has been embraced by many thinkers, including PLATO, the early Christians and the 16th-century humanist Thomas More, who saw it as expressing man's social nature to the highest degree. It became the basis of a revolutionary movement through the work of Karl MARX, who saw communism as the final outcome of the proletarian REVOLUTION that would overthrow CAPITALISM. Specifically communist parties did not emerge until after 1918, when extreme Marxists broke away from the SOCIAL DEMOCRATS. Marx's theories were the moving force behind LENIN and the BOLSHEVIKS and the establishment of the political system in the UNION OF SOVIET SOCIALIST REPUBLICS.

In the hands of Vladimir Ilyich Lenin (1870–1924) and his successors in the Soviet Union, MARXISM was transformed into a doctrine justifying state control of all aspects of society. The doctrine had two main elements. The first was the leading role of the Communist Party, seen as representing the true interests of the working class. The party was to control the organs of the state: the membership of each body in the party hierarchy was formally chosen by the vote of the body below, but policy decisions were to be taken at the top and then imposed rigidly at all lower levels of the hierarchy. The second major element in communist doctrine was the social ownership of property and central planning of the economy. In principle, all private ownership of the means of production and all elements of the market economy were to be abolished, and economic life was to be controlled by planning ministries, which would set production targets for factories and collective farms, fix prices, direct labour, and so forth. Although this principle was never fully implemented, Soviet communism in its heyday stood alone as a society whose every aspect was controlled by a small political élite (during the Stalinist period, 1928–53, by a single individual), and was thus, for many, the leading example of TOTALITARIANISM. Its economic and military achievements nevertheless inspired revolutionary movements in many other countries, and in some developing countries, such as China, Vietnam, North Korea, and Cuba, communist parties came to power and established regimes based more or less closely on the Soviet model. In Eastern Europe,

communist governments were installed under Soviet influence at the end of World War II. But the communist model was increasingly criticized in the West, even by those sympathetic to Marxism, for its economic inefficiency, its lack of genuine democracy, and its denial of basic human freedoms. In the 1970s most Western communist parties adopted Eurocommunist ideas, which centrally involved the acceptance of democratic institutions and the abandonment of the Leninist theory of 'dictatorship of the proletariat'. During the next decade this questioning of orthodox communism spread to Eastern Europe and the Soviet Union, culminating in a remarkable series of largely peaceful revolutions which removed communist parties from power and opened the way to liberal democracy and the market economy.

Following the collapse of the Soviet Union in 1991, the communist countries of eastern Europe adopted pluralist, democratic systems. However, in several of these countries, for example Poland, Hungary, and Romania, the former communist parties have been re-elected. Communist parties have also been active within the multi-party systems of western European nations. Communism's historical significance will in future probably be seen as providing a possible path of transition from agrarian to industrial society based on an ideological alternative to western capitalism, not (as it portrays itself) as the final goal of human history.

Communist Manifesto The primary source of the social and economic doctrine of COMMUNISM. It was written as *Das Manifest der Kommunistischen Partei* in 1848 by Karl MARX and Friedrich ENGELS to provide a political programme that would establish a common tactic for the working-class movement. The manuscript was adopted by the German Socialist League of the Just as its manifesto. It proposed that all history had hitherto been a development of class struggles, and asserted that the industrialized proletariat would eventually establish a classless society safeguarded by social ownership. It linked SOCIALISM directly with COMMUNISM and set out measures by which the latter could be achieved. It had no immediate impact and Marx suggested it should be shelved when the REVOLUTIONS OF 1848 failed. Nevertheless, it continued to influence worldwide communist movements throughout the 20th century.

Communist Party of India A party that emerged in the 1920s. Originally functioning as a part of the Indian National CONGRESS, it was expelled for its co-operation with the war effort after the German invasion of Russia. After independence a programme of violent incursion and agrarian uprising was tried unsuccessfully in Telengana in Andhra Pradesh. The party returned to constitutional politics and formed the government in Kerala state, which was overthrown by an agitation organized by the Congress. After the Sino-Soviet rift, the party split into two and the CPI (Marxist) emerged as the more powerful wing. The latter has been the leading partner in a leftist coalition government in West Bengal, victorious in three successive elections.

Comnena, Anna (*c.* 1083–1148) Historian, daughter of the Byzantine emperor Alexius COMNENUS. She nurtured ambitions that her husband would usurp her brother as emperor but when she was widowed in 1137, she retired to a monastery. She wrote the *Alexiad*, a history in 15 books which was largely an account of the First CRUSADE and panegyric of her father's life.

Comnenus, Alexius (1048–1118) BYZANTINE EMPEROR

(1081–1118). In the mid-11th century Byzantine politics were dominated by a military aristocracy and court officials; Alexius Comnenus was an army general who forged an alliance between his military supporters and a number of court officials and so won the throne for himself. He succeeded in checking the challenge from the NORMANS under GUISCARD in the Mediterranean but was continually harassed by the threat of barbarian invasions. In 1095 he approached Pope Urban II for help in recruiting mercenaries, a call which led to the First CRUSADE which the pope hoped would save the empire from the Seljuk TURKS. The Crusade was to Alexius's advantage and he was able to leave his son John to inherit the Byzantine empire on his death.

Comoros, Federal Islamic Republic of the A

country made up of three main islands and several islets in the Indian Ocean.

Physical. The Comoro Islands are volcanic. They lie in the Mozambique Channel of the Indian Ocean, between the mainland of Africa and northern Madagascar. The chief islands are Great Comoro, Anjouan, and Mohéli. Great Comoro is well forested. Mayotte, geographically part of the archipelago, is a French dependency.

Economy. Exports are dominated by cloves, vanilla, and essential oils for perfume. Most foodstuffs are imported. France, the main trading partner, provides economic aid, while tourism is being developed by South African investors. There is high unemployment and the country suffers from lack of energy resources.

History. Arab peoples were living on the islands when the first Europeans encountered them in the 16th century. Since the 17th century the islands have been occupied by many different peoples, including Arab traders, Africans, Indonesians, and Madagascans. The islands became a French protectorate in 1886, a French overseas territory in 1947, and gained internal autonomy in 1961. In 1974 all the islanders voted for independence, except for those living on Mayotte, who voted to remain under French rule. The Comorian government declared the whole archipelago to be independent (1975) but France gave Mayotte the status of a 'special collectivity.' In 1978 European mercenaries, led by Bob Denard, overthrew the government and ruled until 1984 when democracy was restored. Denard returned from exile in 1995 to attempt another coup but French troops invaded and restored democracy. In 1997 secessionists on Anjouan and Mobeli declared independence from the Republic of the Comoros and demanded the resumption of French rule.

CAPITAL:	Moroni
AREA:	1,862 sq km (719 sq miles)
POPULATION:	562,000 (1996)
CURRENCY:	1 Comorian franc = 100 centimes
RELIGIONS:	Sunni Muslim 99.7%; Christian 0.2%; Baha'i 0.1%
ETHNIC GROUPS:	Comorian (a mixture of Bantu, Arab, and Malagasy peoples) 96.9%; Makua 1.6%; French 0.4%
LANGUAGES:	Arabic, French (both official); Comoran
INTERNATIONAL ORGANIZATIONS:	UN; Non-Aligned Movement; Franc Zone; OAU

Compromise of 1850 A political compromise between the North and South of the USA. Initiated by Henry CLAY, it became law in September 1850. In an attempt to resolve problems arising from slavery it provided for the admission of California as a free state; the organization of the Utah and New Mexico territories with no mention of slavery; the abolition of the slave trade in the District of Columbia (Washington); and a stricter fugitive slave law. Hopes that these measures would provide an enduring solution to North–South antagonism were dashed by the passage of the KANSAS-NEBRASKA ACT (1854) and other issues, including persistent popular interference with the return of fugitive slaves.

computer, history of the Although the development of the computer has been largely played out during the 20th century, there is a long history of automatic calculation. Hero wrote in the 1st century AD of representing numbers using a train of gears, but little real progress seems to have been made until the early 17th century, when the first calculators were built, and the German mathematician Gottfried Leibniz speculated (1679) on the possibility of building a calculator using moving balls to represent numbers in binary code. The notion of storing a sequence of instructions mechanically is also very old and was incorporated into self-playing musical instruments and other automata even in ancient times. In 1725 Basile Bouchon invented a method of producing intricate woven patterns on a draw loom from instructions on a perforated paper tape. By 1800 this method had been refined by Jacquard into a highly successful automatic loom controlled by punched cards. The idea of punched-card instructions was adapted by Hollerith to record and analyse the results of the 1890 US census in the earliest example of large-scale data processing.

In 1835 Babbage conceived of the basic idea of an analytical engine in which can be found most of the elements of a truly general-purpose computer. He drew together the ideas of mechanical calculation and a set of instructions recorded on perforated paper tape. The development costs of the machine were very high: the British government eventually withdrew funding, and this pioneering machine was never completed. Babbage's ideas were subsequently lost until the 1930s, when work on electromechanical computers was started independently in Germany and the USA. In 1941 Konrad Zuse in Germany built the world's first working stored-program computer. His Z_3 machine was based on electromechanical relays, and was used for military aircraft design. In the USA, the mathematician Howard Aiken, in association with IBM (International Business Machines), was working independently on a large electromechanical calculator that could be programmed using paper tape. The Automatic Sequence Controlled Calculator (ASCC), or Harvard Mark I, was completed in 1943; it was very similar in concept (although not in engineering realization), to Babbage's analytical machine.

Computers based on the electronic thermionic valve were a major development, since they were much faster and more reliable than electromechanical computers. Among the earliest electronic computers were the

Colossus series of special-purpose computers, developed secretly in the UK from 1943. They deciphered coded German messages produced on sophisticated mechanical systems called Enigma machines. An important member of the Colossus team was Turing, who in 1936 had published a paper that defined in abstract terms the generalized concept of a universal computer. The concept of the stored-program computer (an idea attributed to von Neumann), in which instructions for processing data are stored along with the data in the computer's own memory, proved to be very important, since it hugely enhanced the flexibility and potential of the computer. The earliest electronic stored-program computer was an experimental machine built under the leadership of Frederick Williams at Manchester University, UK, in 1948. This was followed by the Manchester Mark 1 computer in 1949 which, as the Ferranti Mark 1, was the first commercially available computer to be delivered. Other notable early computers in the UK were EDSAC at Cambridge, later marketed as LEO, and Turing's ACE at the National Physical Laboratory.

Mauchly and Eckert at the University of Pennsylvania (USA) developed the ENIAC and EDVAC computers based on the highly influential ideas of von Neumann; they later developed the successful UNIVAC computer, which became commercially available in 1951. The development of the transistor led to much cheaper, faster, and more reliable computers. The first transistorized computer was working at Manchester University in 1953, although the USA had a number of much larger computers operating within a few years. The first compiler was developed at Manchester in 1952, and in 1954 John Backus of IBM in the USA developed FORTRAN, the first internationally used computer language. A significant high point in this era was the joint development of the Atlas computer by Ferranti Ltd. and Manchester University. This was the world's first super-computer, and pioneered many aspects of computer architecture that are common today. After this, most major developments took place in the USA. Particularly crucial was the development of the integrated circuit (IC) in 1958 which allowed complete circuits to be manufactured on a tiny piece of silicon. In 1972 the Intel Corporation developed the world's first microprocessor, the Intel 4004, which was very limited but was an immediate commercial success and led directly to the development of today's cheap, fast, and reliable microcomputers as well as much more powerful mainframe computers. Modems linking individual computers to the global telephone network have enabled the almost instantaneous transfer of digital information around the world and, along with the Internet and related technologies, form the so-called 'information superhighway'.

concentration camp A prison camp in which large numbers of non-military prisoners are held without trial, usually in the most severe conditions. Concentration camps were first instituted by Lord KITCHENER during the Second Boer War (1899–1902). Non-combatant Boers, mainly women and children, were placed there for their own protection from Kitchener's 'scorched earth policy' in the Transvaal and Cape Colony, but mainly to prevent them from aiding the guerrillas. Some 20,000 detainees died, largely as a result of disease arising from unhygienic conditions. Boer indignation at

what they considered 'deliberate genocide' was intense, and in London Emily Hobhouse roused public opinion against such maladministration. A commission of investigation was appointed, headed by Elizabeth FAWCETT. It identified inadequate sanitary and medical facilities and recommended changes. Lord MILNER acted on the report, and before their closure the death rate was falling.

During the NAZI regime in Germany (1933–45) the term was applied to the place of internment of unwanted persons, specifically JEWISH PEOPLE, but also Protestant and Catholic dissidents, communists, gypsies, trade unionists, homosexuals, and the handicapped. Described by GOEBBELS in August 1934 as 'camps to turn anti-social members of society into useful members by the most humane means possible', they in fact came to witness some of the worst acts of torture, horror, and mass murder in the 20th century on a scale unprecedented in any century. Some 200,000 had been through the camps before World War II began, when they were increased in size and number. The camps (Konzentrazionslager, or KZ), administered by the SS, were categorized into *Arbeitslager*, where prisoners were organized into labour battalions, and *Vernichtungslager*, set up for the extermination and incineration of men, women, and children. In eastern Europe prisoners were used initially in labour battalions or in the tasks of genocide, until they too were exterminated. In camps such as Auschwitz, gas chambers could kill and incinerate 12,000 people daily. In the west, Belsen, Dachau, and Buchenwald (a forced labour camp where doctors conducted medical research on prisoners) were notorious. An estimated four to six million Jews died in the camps (the HOLOCAUST), as well as some half million gypsies; in addition, millions of Poles, Soviet prisoners-of-war, and other civilians perished. After the war many camp officials were tried and punished, but others escaped. Maidanek was the first camp to be liberated (by the Red Army, in July 1944). After 1953 West Germany paid $37 billion in reparations to Jewish victims of Nazism.

In the Soviet Union, Lenin greatly enlarged (1919) the Tzarist forced labour camps, which were renamed Gulags (Russian acronym for the Main Administration of Corrective Labour Camps) in 1930. An estimated 15 million prisoners were confined to the Gulags during Stalin's purges, of whom many succumbed to disease, famine, or the firing squad.

Conciliar Movement (1409–49) A Church movement centred on the three general (or ecumenical) councils of Pisa (1409), CONSTANCE (1414–18), and Basle (1431–49). Its original purpose was to heal the papal schism caused by there being two, and later three, popes at the same time (see ANTIPOPE). The movement was successful, deposing or accepting the resignation of the popes concerned. It declared the superiority of a general council of the Church over the papacy, formulated in the decree *Haec Sancta* (sometimes called *Sacrosancta*) of 1415, and tried to make general councils a regular feature of the Western Church. It also dealt with various heresies, the council of Constance burning John HUSS and condemning John WYCLIF in 1415, and it initiated some reforms. The movement, in so far as it challenged papal authority, was eventually defeated by the papacy, but its long-term influence upon Christian Churches was considerable.

Concord LEXINGTON AND CONCORD, BATTLE OF.

Concordat An agreement between the Roman Catholic Church and a secular power. One of the most important was the Concordat of 1801 between Pius VII and Napoleon I which re-established the Catholic Church in France. This provided that French archbishops and bishops should be appointed by the government, but confirmed by the pope. Church property confiscated during the Revolution was not to be restored, but the government was to provide adequate support for the clergy. This lasted until the separation of Church and State in France in 1905. Another concordat, in the form of the LATERAN TREATIES of 1929, regulated the status of the papacy in Italy, which had been a source of contention since unification in 1870 abolished the temporal power of the pope. It gave the pope sovereignty over VATICAN CITY and restored the influence of the Catholic Church in Italy.

Condé A junior branch of the French royal House of BOURBON. The name was first borne by Louis I de Bourbon (1530–69), prince de Condé, a military leader of the HUGUENOTS during the first phase of the FRENCH WARS OF RELIGION. A bitter enemy of the GUISE faction, he was killed at the Battle of Jarnac. Henry I de Bourbon (1552–88) took over his father's leadership of the Huguenots. He briefly renounced his faith at the time of the ST BARTHOLOMEW'S DAY MASSACRE (1572), but subsequently embarrassed his cousin, the future HENRY IV, with his Protestant fanaticism.

Henry II de Bourbon (1588–1646) was brought up as a Catholic; he plotted during the regency of Marie de Medici, and distinguished himself only by fathering Louis II de Bourbon, his successor, known as the Great Condé. The latter married a niece of Cardinal RICHELIEU, and excelled as a military commander in the last phase of the THIRTY YEARS WAR. During the first FRONDE he sided with the court party; disagreements with MAZARIN led to his arrest and imprisonment (1650), and on the failure of his insurrection against the government (1651–52), he fled and took service in the Spanish armies in the Netherlands. When he was allowed to return to France in 1660, he conquered Franche-Comté for LOUIS XIV (1668), and held high command in the war against the UNITED PROVINCES (1672); but Louis never really forgave him for his part in the Fronde, and his treasonable defection to the Spaniards.

Condorcet, Antoine Nicolas, marquis de (1743–94) French philosopher and politician. He was the only prominent French *philosophe* to play any real part in the events of the Revolution. As a GIRONDIN and a friend of SIEYÈS and BRISSOT he was elected to the National Convention. In October 1793 he was condemned by the Revolutionary Tribunal and eventually poisoned himself to avoid the guillotine. His best-known work *Esquisse d'un tableau historique des progrès de l'esprit humain* ('Sketch for a Historical Picture of the Progress of the Human Mind') was published in 1795.

Condor Legion A unit of the German airforce sent by HITLER to aid FRANCO in the SPANISH CIVIL WAR (1936) on condition that it remained under German command. It aided Franco in transporting troops from Morocco in the early days of the war, and played a major role in the bombing of rebel lines and civilian centres, notably the city of Guernica on 27 April 1937.

condottiere (Italian *condotta*, 'contract') A term for the leader of a medieval mercenary band of soldiers. Mercenaries flourished in the climate of economic prosperity and inter-municipal warfare of 14th- and 15th-century Italy. The earliest such mercenaries were recruited from the unemployed mercenary 'free companies' of the 1360s and included Catalans, the Germans and Hungarians of the so-called Grand Company, and the English Sir John Hawkwood, leader of the White Company in the 14th century. The system was refined in the 15th century by the SFORZAS, although the condottieri were always motivated by self-interest and changing of sides and loyalties was frequent. The system died out as a result of the Habsburg-Valois wars of the 16th century, which led to changes in the financing and organization of armies.

Confederacy The 11 southern US states that seceded from the Union of the United States in 1860–61. Seven states (Alabama, Florida, Georgia, Louisiana, Mississippi, South Carolina, and Texas) formed themselves into the Confederate States of America on 8 February 1861 at Montgomery, Alabama, with a constitution modelled on the US document but incorporating guarantees of STATES' RIGHTS and the institution of slavery. Jefferson DAVIS and Alexander H. Stephens were elected President and Vice-President. After the bombardment of FORT SUMTER, four further states joined the Confederacy (Arkansas, North Carolina, Tennessee, and Virginia). Although the Confederate flag contained 13 stars, two represented Kentucky and Missouri, border states which in fact remained largely under federal control. Despite the relative weakness of its central government based at Richmond, Virginia, the Confederacy managed to sustain the civil war until its collapse in April 1865 after four years of war with most of its territory occupied, its armies defeated, and its economy in ruins.

Confederation of the Rhine (1806–13) A grouping of middle and south German states. After Napoleon's victory at Austerlitz (1805) he announced the creation of a Confederation of the Rhine, whose members were obliged to abdicate from the old Holy Roman Empire, which was then declared dissolved. After the defeat of Prussia at Jena (1806) other princely states and cities joined. Napoleon had annexed for France all the left bank of the Rhine, but the new Confederation gradually extended from the Rhine to the Elbe. It was at first welcomed by the German people as a step towards unity, but it was really a barrier against Prussian and Austrian power, and as the CONTINENTAL SYSTEM began to result in economic hardship, it became less popular. It contributed a contingent to Napoleon's campaigns of 1813. After his defeat at Leipzig, however, the Confederation broke up; one by one the German states and cities made peace and supported the QUADRUPLE ALLIANCE of Prussia, Britain, Russia, and Austria. A new GERMAN CONFEDERATION was to emerge from the Congress of VIENNA.

Conference on Security and Co-operation in Europe HELSINKI CONFERENCE.

Confucianism (Chinese, *rujia* 'teaching of the scholars') The Chinese religious world-view and code of conduct loosely based on the teachings of Confucius (551–479 BC). The principal texts of Confucianism are the various works which are divided into groups known as the Five,

Six, Nine, Twelve, or Thirteen Classics, the last two of which include the *Analects* of Confucius. Most of these are not specifically Confucian; the *Sishu* (a collection of four independent books), was used as a basic Confucian educational text for many years. The philosophical and ethical code worked out by Confucius was adopted and developed into a state cult under the Han dynasty (206 BC–220 AD), with elaborate state ceremonies honouring the emperor and those who had served the empire well. The civil-service examination and educational system were based on the study of the Five Classics, and temples were built in veneration of Confucius throughout the empire. Traditional beliefs such as YIN AND YANG and the five elements of wood, fire, earth, metal, and water were also incorporated into Confucianism at about this period. Later, the scholar philosopher Zhu Xi (1130–1200) elaborated Confucian doctrines into a coherent spiritual and philosophical world-view known as Neo-Confucianism (*lixue* or *Daoxue*) developed partly as a response to the increased prominence of TAOISM and BUDDHISM in Chinese life. As well as developing a metaphysical system based on the twin but complementary concepts of *li*, principle, and *qi*, material force, Zhu Xi wrote authoritative commentaries on the Classics which were the official texts of the Chinese state examinations until 1905. The overwhelming influence of Confucianism on Chinese life has been much restricted in the 20th century since the abolition of the traditional educational system in 1905 and the establishment of the Republic in 1911. With the adoption of COMMUNISM as the state ideology under Mao Zedong (1893–1976), Confucian temples were destroyed and the classics banned, but none the less, Confucian elements prevail in various aspects of Chinese life and its teachings may be discerned in contemporary Chinese socio-political thinking and planning. Confucianism persists in Japan, Korea, Singapore, Taiwan, and Vietnam; today, it is strongest in South Korea and Taiwan, where Confucian shrines and education are maintained on traditional lines.

Congo A country in western Africa, formerly called Congo (Brazzaville) after the French explorer de Brazza, whose eastern boundary is the River Congo; it is bounded by Cameroon and the Central African Republic on the north and Gabon on the west.

Physical. On its short stretch of Atlantic Ocean coast there are lagoons, large deposits of potash and oil. A small plain rises inland to a forest-covered escarpment, while most of the country comprises savannah-covered plateaux. The climate is hot and generally very wet, the river valleys inland being marshy forest.

Economy. Crude oil is the principal export, and oil revenues have funded a growing manufacturing base which includes food-processing, textiles, chemicals, and metalwork. Lead, copper, zinc, and gold ore are mined. Cassava, sugar cane, and pineapples are the chief agricultural crops, and timber is an important export.

History. The Congo area is thought to have been uninhabited before the 15th century when Pygmies moved into the area from the north and Kongo (or Vili) people from the east. The two main kingdoms that flourished in pre-colonial times were the kingdoms of Loango and Teke, both of which prospered by supporting the slave trade. De Brazza began exploring the region in 1875 and he made the first of the series of treaties that brought it under French control in 1880. In 1888 it was united with Gabon, but was later separated from it as the Moyen Congo (Middle Congo). It was absorbed with Chad into French Equatorial Africa (1910–58). It became a member of the French Community as a constituent republic in 1958, and fully independent in 1960. In the 1960s and 1970s it suffered much from unstable governments, which alternated between civilian and military rule. Some measure of stability was achieved by the regime of Colonel Denis Sassou-Nguesso, who came to power in 1979 and was re-elected in 1989. Although a one-party Marxist state from 1970, Congo maintained links with Western nations, particularly France, from whom it gained economic assistance. In September 1990 a national conference agreed to adopt a multiparty political system. A new constitution was devised and accepted in a referendum in 1992. Elections held later that year produced no clear winner and a coalition was formed, which soon collapsed. Fresh elections were held in 1993 but the results were disputed and fraud was alleged. A campaign of protest was launched by one political faction, leading to fierce fighting between rival militias. Several ceasefire agreements were made and broken during 1994–95 and political instability continued. In September–October 1997, troops loyal to the former military leader General Dennis Sassou-Nguesso ousted President Pascal Lissouba, with Angolan help. Sassou-Nguesso was subsequently sworn in as president.

CAPITAL:	Brazzaville
AREA:	342,000 sq km (132,047 sq miles)
POPULATION:	2.665 million (1996)
CURRENCY:	1 CFA franc = 100 centimes
RELIGIONS:	Traditional religions 47.0%; Roman Catholic 33.0%; Protestant 17.0%; Muslim 2.0%
ETHNIC GROUPS:	Kongo 51.5%; Teke 17.3%; Mboshi 11.5%; Mbete 7.0%; Sanga 5.0%
LANGUAGES:	French (official); Kongo; Teke; local languages
INTERNATIONAL ORGANIZATIONS:	UN; OAU; Non-Aligned Movement; Franc Zone

Congo, Belgian CONGO, DEMOCRATIC REPUBLIC OF THE.

Congo, Democratic Republic of the (formerly Zaïre) The largest country in equatorial Africa; it is bounded by nine other countries and has an outlet to the Atlantic Ocean at the mouth of the River Congo.

Physical. The River Congo and its tributaries flow through the country. Thick forests cover the central districts and there is much swamp. In the south, however, are open highlands. The eastern boundary runs down the Great Rift Valley and includes the western shore of Lake Tanganyika.

Economy. The country has substantial agricultural, mineral, and energy resources, whose development is impeded by corruption, smuggling, lack of infrastructure and investment, and falling world commodity prices.

History. The pre-colonial 19th-century history of the Democratic Republic of the Congo was dominated by the Arab slave trade. LIVINGSTONE was the first European explorer of the country. In 1871 STANLEY undertook to sail down the River Congo. His reports prompted King LEOPOLD II of Belgium to found the International Association of the Congo (later termed the Congo Free

State). Stanley began to open up its resources. Maladministration by Leopold's agents obliged him to hand the state over to the Belgian Parliament (1908), but in the next 50 years little was done, except by Catholic mission schools, to prepare the country for self-government. The outbreak of unrest in 1959 led to the hasty granting of independence in the following year, but the regime of Patrice LUMUMBA was undermined by civil war, and disorder in the newly named Congo Republic remained endemic until the coup of General MOBUTU SESE SEKO in 1965. In 1967 the Union Minière, the largest copper-mining company, was nationalized and Mobutu achieved some measure of economic recovery. In 1971 the name of the country was changed to Zaïre. Falling copper prices and centralized policies undermined foreign business confidence, and two revolts followed in 1977 and 1978 in the province of Shaba (formerly Katanga), only put down with French military assistance. The 1980 constitution only recognized one political party, the Movement Populaire de la Révolution (MPR), and Mobutu was re-elected as sole candidate in 1977 and 1984. Multiparty elections were promised for 1991, during which the five main opposition parties all refused to support the president's nominated Prime Minister. Near economic collapse provoked riots, looting, and arson. In a confused situation, Mobutu cancelled elections for a renewal of his term of office in December 1991. During 1992 a national constitutional conference was convened by Mgr. Laurent Pasinya Monsengwo, Archbishop of Kisangani, which replaced the government with a High Council of the Republic. Political instability continued throughout 1993 and 1994, with the President and the High Council of the Republic appointing rival cabinets. An agreement was reached in 1994, when both cabinets were replaced by a new transitional legislature. Although its own population is subject to recurrent abuses of human rights, the Democratic Republic of the Congo has been host to large numbers of refugees, mainly from Angola and in 1994 over 1 million refugees entered the country, fleeing from the civil war in neighbouring Rwanda. In August 1995, government troops began the forcible repatriation of Rwandan refugees; however, after international condemnation, this policy was halted the following month. In April 1996 Tutsi rebels attacked Hutu militiamen who had fled from Rwanda. The Tutsi rebels overthrew the government in 1997 and Mobutu went into exile. The rebel leader, Laurent KABILA took over as head of state and renamed the country.

CAPITAL:	Kinshasa
AREA:	2,345,000 sq km (905,446 sq miles)
POPULATION:	45.259 million (1996)
CURRENCY:	1 Congolese franc = 100 centimes
RELIGIONS:	Roman Catholic 48.4%; Protestant 29.0%; indigenous Christian 17.1%; traditional beliefs 3.4%; Muslim 1.4%
ETHNIC GROUPS:	Luba 18.0%; Kongo 16.1%; Mongo 13.5%; Rwanda 10.3%; Azande 6.1%; Bangi and Ngale 5.8%; Rundi 3.8%; Teke 2.7%; Boa 2.3%; Chokwe 1.8%; Lugbara 1.6%; Banda 1.4%
LANGUAGES:	French (official); Lingala; Kongo; Swahili; local languages
INTERNATIONAL ORGANIZATIONS:	UN; OAU

Congo crisis (1960–65) Political disturbances in the Democratic Republic of the CONGO following its independence from Belgium. The sudden decision by Belgium to grant independence to its vast colony along the Congo was taken in January 1960. A single state was to be created, governed from Léopoldville (Kinshasa). Fighting began between tribes during parliamentary elections in May and further fighting occurred at independence (30 June). The Congolese troops of the Force Publique (armed police) mutinied against their Belgian officers. Europeans and their property were attacked, and Belgian refugees fled. In the rich mining province of Katanga, Moise TSHOMBÉ, supported by Belgian troops and white mercenaries, proclaimed an independent republic. The government appealed to the United Nations for troops to restore order, and the UN Secretary-General HAMMARSKJÖLD despatched a peace-keeping force to replace the Belgians. A military coup brought the army commander, Colonel MOBUTU, to power with a government which excluded the radical Prime Minister, Patrice LUMUMBA. In 1961 Lumumba was killed, allegedly by 'hostile tribesmen', and Hammarskjöld died in an air crash on a visit to the Congo. The fighting continued and independent regimes were established at different times in Katanga, Stanleyville, and Kasai. In November 1965 the Congolese army under Mobutu staged a second coup, and Mobutu declared himself President.

Congregationalism A a form of church organization in which each local church is independent. The system derives from the belief that JESUS CHRIST is the sole head of his Church, and it is held to represent the original form of the church's organization. Known at different times in England as Separatists or Independents, Congregationalists can be traced back to the 16th century followers of Robert BROWNE, who broke with the ANGLICAN CHURCH. Driven underground by persecution, they resurfaced in 17th-century Holland and America. They were among the PILGRIM FATHERS who sailed to the New World in 1620. Meanwhile in England, after figuring prominently in the NEW MODEL ARMY, they enjoyed freedom of worship under Oliver CROMWELL. This was abolished by the 1662 Act of Uniformity, then restored by the 1689 Toleration Act. In America they were allowed freedom of worship. Keen educationists, they played a major part in founding the universities of Harvard (1636) and Yale (1701).

Congress, Indian National A major Indian political party, historically the principal Indian party. It was founded in 1885 as an annual meeting of educated Indians desiring a greater share in government in co-operation with Britain. Later, divisions emerged between moderates and extremists, led by B. G. Tilak, and Congress split temporarily in 1907. Tilak died in 1920 and under the leadership of M. K. GANDHI Congress developed a powerful central organization, an elaborate branch organization in provinces and districts, and acquired a mass membership. It began to conduct major political campaigns for self-rule and independence. In 1937 it easily won the elections held under the Government of India Act (1935) in a majority of provinces. In 1939 it withdrew from government, and many of its leaders were imprisoned during the 1941 'Quit India' campaign. In 1945–47 Congress negotiated with Britain for Indian independence. Under Jawaharlal

NEHRU it continued to dominate independent INDIA. After his death a struggle ensued between the Congress Old Guard (the Syndicate) and younger, more radical elements of whom Mrs Indira GANDHI assumed the leadership. In 1969 it split between these two factions but was quickly rebuilt under Mrs Gandhi's leadership. In 1977 it was heavily defeated by the Janata (People's) Alliance Party, led by Morarji Desai (1896–1995), who became Prime Minister (1977–79). In 1978 Mrs Gandhi formed a new party, the 'real' Indian National Congress, or Congress (I) (for Indira). In 1979 she led this faction to victory in elections and again became Prime Minister in 1980. After her assassination in October 1984 the splits between factions largely healed and leadership of the Congress (I) Party passed to her son Rajiv Gandhi

(1944–91), who became Prime Minister (1984–89). He was assassinated in May 1991, during the run-up to a general election. The Congress (I) Party was re-elected under the leadership of P. V. Narasimha Rao (1921–   ), who served as Prime Minister until 1996, when the Party lost the general election in its worst ever defeat. Rao resigned as leader of the party later that year and was replaced by Sitaram Kesri. In 1998 Congress improved its position slightly in the general election and Kesri resigned to enable Sonia Gandhi, Rajiv Gandhi's Italian-born widow, to take over the leadership.

Congress of the USA The legislative branch of the US federal government. Provided for in Article I of the US Constitution, Congress is divided into two constituent houses: the lower, the House of REPRESENTATIVES, in which

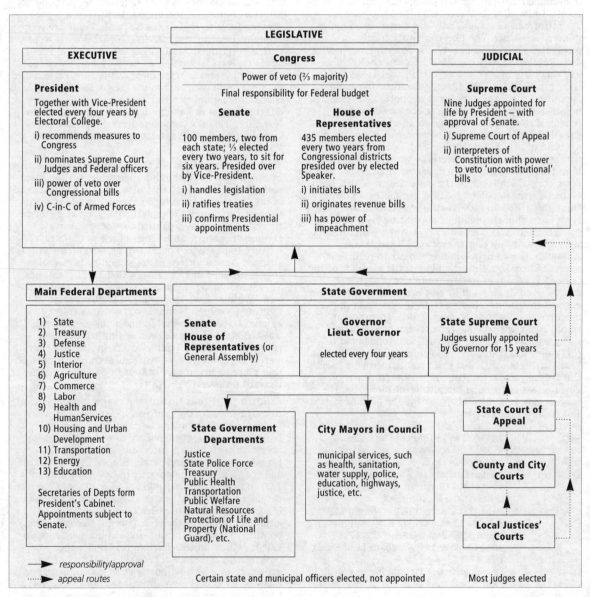

Congress of the USA   *The structure of the US government.*

membership is based on the population of each state; and the upper, the SENATE, in which each state has two members. Representatives serve a two-year term and Senators a six-year term. Congressional powers include the collection of taxes and duties, the provision for common defence, general welfare, the regulation of commerce, patents and copyrights, the declaration of war, raising of armies, and maintenance of a navy, and the establishment of the post offices and federal courts. Originally, Congress was expected to hold the initiative in the federal government, but the emergence of the President as a national party leader has resulted in the continuous fluctuation in the balance of power between legislature and executive. Much of the effective work of Congress is now done in powerful standing committees dealing with major areas of policy.

Conkling, Roscoe (1829–88) US politician. A prominent supporter of the WHIG PARTY, he joined the newly formed REPUBLICAN PARTY on its collapse and served in the House of Representatives from 1858 to 1864 as a strong supporter of President LINCOLN. After the AMERICAN CIVIL WAR he was distinguished for his support of radical measures against the former CONFEDERACY and for his insistence on retaining control of federal appointments within his state of New York. He remained a believer in the SPOILS SYSTEM and opponent of civil service reform, over which he resigned from the Senate.

Connaught (or Connacht) A province in the mid-west of Ireland. It was one of the five ancient Irish kingdoms, ruled from the 5th century AD by the O'Connors, kings of TARA. With the 12th-century Anglo-Norman conquest of Ireland the area passed through the hands of various Norman nobles, reverting to the English crown in 1461. In the Tudor period the province was divided into shires, and the Composition of Connaught (1585) confirmed the possession of the land to the local gentry, ensuring their loyalty to Elizabeth I during TYRONE's rising. Connaught suffered from the extortionary policies of CHARLES I.

Connecticut A state in the north-east USA, one of the original colonies of New England. Chartered in 1662, it combined the settlements round Hartford and New Haven. Its first governor was John WINTHROP junior. It was never subject to royal control. In the early national period, it was a leading stronghold of the FEDERALIST PARTY.

conquistadores Spanish soldiers and adventurers in the 16th century. The term stems in part from the *Reconquista* of Spain from Moorish rule, culminating in the capture of GRANADA by FERDINAND I and Isabella in 1492 after some 500 years of slow reconquest. The most famous conquistadores were Hérnan CORTÉS, the conqueror of Aztec Mexico, and Francisco PIZARRO, the conqueror of Inca Peru; but there were many others. Their discoveries and conquests included the Caribbean, Latin America, southern and south-western USA, and the Philippines. Many would-be conquistadores explored immense areas but conquered nothing and founded no permanent settlements. As proper colonial administrations were established their activity diminished, and they never again found such rich empires as those of the Aztecs or Incas. Not all were soldiers: some were Christian missionaries, often appalled by the heartless Spanish exploitation of the native races. Most notable was Bartolomé de LAS CASAS, who became an outspoken critic of the Spanish treatment of the Indians.

Conservative Party (Britain) A major political party in Britain. In 1830 it was suggested in the *Quarterly Review*, a TORY journal, that a better name for the old Tory Party might be Conservative since the Party stood for the preservation of existing institutions. The idea was favoured by Sir Robert PEEL, whose TAMWORTH MANIFESTO, which set out a programme of reforming Conservatism, brought him briefly to the premiership in 1834–35. Although Peel was re-elected in 1841, his conversion to FREE TRADE in 1846 split the Party. Peel's followers after a time joined the Liberals. The majority of the Party under Lord Derby and DISRAELI gradually adopted the title Conservative, though Tory continued to be used also. Between 1846 and 1874 the Conservatives were a minority party though they were in office in 1867 and passed a REFORM ACT. In 1867 they were the first party to create a national organization with the formation of the Central Office. Disraeli described the aims of the Party as: 'the preservation of our institutions, the maintenance of our Empire and the amelioration of the condition of the people'. In 1874, his government embarked on a programme of social reforms and increased the powers of central government. In 1886 those Liberals, led by Joseph CHAMBERLAIN, who rejected Gladstone's HOME RULE policy for Ireland, allied with the Party, whose full title then became the National Union of Conservative and Unionist Associations. The Party was strongly imperialist throughout the first half of the 20th century, although splitting in 1903 over the issue of free trade or empire preference. From 1915 until 1945 the Party either formed the government, except for 1924 and 1929–31, or governed in coalition with the Labour Party (1931–35, 1939–45). Since World War II it has again been in office for long periods (1951–64, 1970–74, 1979–97). With the growing crisis in NORTHERN IRELAND after 1968 the ULSTER UNIONISTS dissociated themselves from the Party. Until the later 1970s the Party's policies tended to be pragmatic, accepting the basic philosophy of the WELFARE STATE and being prepared to adjust in response to a consensus of public opinion. Under the leadership of Margaret THATCHER, however, it seemed to reassert the 19th-century liberal emphasis on individual free enterprise, challenging the need for state support and subsidy, while combining this with a strong assertion of state power against local authorities, a trend that continued under the leadership of John MAJOR. Many publicly owned companies, including British Airways, British Aerospace, British Gas, British Telecom, and British Rail were privatized by the Thatcher and Major governments. By the mid-1990s, however, the popularity of privatization was beginning to wane as criticism of the management of many of the newly privatized companies increased. In the General Election of May 1997, the Conservative Party suffered a devastating defeat, recording their lowest proportion of the vote (31%) since 1832 and winning their fewest seats (165) since 1906. John Major resigned as leader and was replaced by William Hague (1961–). In recent years the Party has tended to return to the use of the term Tory.

Conservative Party (Canada) Since 1942 the Progressive Conservative Party of Canada, a major

Canadian political party. Its origins go back to the early 19th century, when Tory supporters of the British were opposed to their critics, the 'Reformers', at the time of the MACKENZIE'S REBELLION in 1837. In 1864, under John A. MACDONALD, a coalition of Conservatives and Reformers was formed to work for Confederation (the union of the British colonies of British North America). When the Dominion of Canada was created in 1867, with Macdonald as the first Prime Minister, a LIBERAL PARTY (Canada) began to form and led the government from 1873 to 1878, when the Conservatives regained leadership. In 1896 they relinquished office to the Liberals under Wilfrid LAURIER, forming a coalition with the Liberals in 1917. They have since held power under Sir Robert BORDEN (1911–20), Arthur Meighen (1920–21, 1926), R. B. Bennett (1930–35). John DIEFENBAKER (1957–63), Joe Clark (1979–80), Brian Mulroney (1984–93), and Kim Campbell (1993). The party was humiliated in the General Election of 1993; Kim Campbell lost her seat and the Conservatives were left with only two parliamentary representatives. The Conservatives improved their position in the General Election of 1997.

conservatism A political outlook that values and supports established institutions and is critical of proposals for radical social change. Conservatism first took shape as an ideology at the time of the French Revolution, when thinkers such as Edmund BURKE (*Reflections on the Revolution in France*, 1790) and Joseph de Maistre (*Considerations on France*, 1796) denounced the revolutionary changes taking place in France as destructive of much that is valuable in society. Since then, conservatism has chiefly been opposed to LIBERALISM and SOCIALISM. Conservatives have a pessimistic view of human nature. They see people as standing in need of discipline and restraint, and are fearful of the consequences when authority is destroyed and individuals are left to their own devices. They respect tradition as embodying the accumulated wisdom of the ages, and are correspondingly sceptical about untested plans and policies put forward by would-be reformers. Conservatives typically favour: constitutional government as a way of preserving authority without concentrating it in the hands of a despot or dictator; an ordered or ranked society in which people know their proper place and defer to those placed above them in the hierarchy; established religion, in order to integrate people into the fabric of society; and the family, the primary source of moral values and the place where responsible citizens are formed. Conservative economic attitudes have varied with time. Originally conservatives tended to support protectionist policies in contrast to the LAISSEZ-FAIRE policies advocated by liberals, but in the 20th century they have increasingly turned to the FREE MARKET as the best means of organizing economic activity. This synthesis of conservative and classical liberal beliefs can be seen especially in the thinking of the NEW RIGHT. Political parties are rarely wholeheartedly conservative in outlook, but politicians of a conservative disposition can be found in the CHRISTIAN DEMOCRATIC parties of Europe, in the US Republican Party, and in the CONSERVATIVE (Tory) Party in the UK.

Constance, Council of (1414–18) An ecclesiastical council held at Constance in Germany that was called to deal with reform and heresy within the Christian Church. It resolved the GREAT SCHISM, decreed the regular calling of councils, and presided over the trial and burning of John HUSS. It failed, however, to produce effective reform of outstanding abuses in clerical finance and conduct, or to curb papal independence.

Constantine I (the Great) (Flavius Valerius Aurelius Constantinus) (*c.* 274–337) Roman emperor (324–37). On the death of his father Constantius I in 306 at Eboracum (York) the army proclaimed him emperor. After a period of political complications, with several emperors competing for power, Constantine and Licinius divided the empire between them, East and West. War was fought between the two rulers (314) and Constantine defeated and killed Licinius (323) and he became sole emperor, founding a new second capital at Byzantium which he named CONSTANTINOPLE.

He adopted Christian symbols for his battle standards in 312 prompted by a 'vision' of the sign of the cross in the rays of the sun. In the following year he proclaimed tolerance and recognition of Christianity in the 'Edict' of Milan. Although his own beliefs are uncertain he supported orthodox Christianity in an attempt to maintain the unity of the vast ROMAN EMPIRE. Sunday was declared a holiday in 326. He and his mother Helena took great interest in the Christian sites of ROME and PALESTINE. Basilicas were built on the site of the stable-cave in Bethlehem, where Jesus Christ was supposed to have been born, his alleged tomb in Jerusalem, and St PETER's grave on the Vatican hill in Rome, and at Constantinople (St Sophia). The Eastern Church lists him as a saint.

Constantinople A city in Turkey, formerly Byzantium, founded in 657 BC as a Greek colony. Early in the 4th century AD CONSTANTINE chose the site as the capital for the Eastern Empire in preference to DIOCLETIAN's nearby Nicomedia. It was designed as a new Rome, straddling seven hills and divided into 14 districts and was renamed Constantinople in 330. The second capital of a single Roman empire ruled by two emperors, in 395 it became the sole capital of the East as Italy and Rome came under barbarian threat.

A city of monuments, churches, but no pagan temples, it was decorated with material from 'old Rome'. The walls of this capital of the BYZANTINE EMPIRE withstood siege by Goths, Persians, and Arabs but was looted after a horrifying attack by Western Crusaders in 1204. It finally fell to the Ottoman Turks in 1453 and became the capital of the OTTOMAN EMPIRE until the 19th century. Today it is the Turkish city of Istanbul.

Constitution of the USA The fundamental written instrument of the US government. It replaced the Articles of Confederation (1781–87), a league of sovereign states, with an effective central, national, federal government. Three months' secret debate among the FOUNDING FATHERS at the Federal Constitutional Convention in Philadelphia in 1787 produced a series of modifications to MADISON's original Virginia Plan. The Great Compromise, between large and small states, gave equal representation in the Senate but by population in the House of Representatives. North and South finally agreed to slaves being counted as three-fifths of a person in representation and taxation, continuation of the slave trade until at least 1808, and no taxes on exports. Conflict between state and central power was reconciled by enumerating areas of federal concern. The principle of popular sovereignty with direct biennial election of congressmen was balanced by indirect election of senators and presidents for renewable six- and four-year terms. Within the federal system of executive (President, Vice-President, cabinet, and civil service), legislature (Senate and House of Representatives), and judiciary (Supreme and other federal courts), a series of checks and balances sought to share and divide power between these three components of government. Thus, for instance, the Supreme Court, appointed by the President with Senatorial approval, may declare actions of the executive or legislature unconstitutional, but may not initiate suits or legislation. The 1787 draft required ratification by nine state conventions. Major opposition in Virginia, Massachusetts, and New York came from the anti-Federalist, states' rights advocates like Patrick HENRY or George CLINTON. The constitution was defended in the *Federalist Papers* by MADISON, HAMILTON, and JAY and came into operation in 1789. Major shortcomings included failure to foresee political parties, initial absence of a BILL OF RIGHTS, complexity of electoral arrangements, and frustration of executive initiative. The loose definition of congressional powers and the persuasive influence of federal grants tipped the balance from state to central supremacy. This flexible guide for government has been amended 26 times, most notably to abolish slavery, to add a Bill of Rights, and to establish black and female enfranchisement.

containment A basic principle of US foreign policy after World War II. It aimed at the 'containment of Soviet expansionist tendencies' by the building of a circle of military pacts around the Soviet Union and its satellites. The policy was first adopted by President Truman with the creation of NATO in 1949. This was to be a major means of containment in Europe, armed with conventional forces and nuclear devices, and stretching from the Arctic Circle to Turkey. Similar pacts in the Far East were the ANZUS pact of 1951 and the SOUTH-EAST ASIA TREATY ORGANIZATION of 1954. In the 1960s the policy was extended to include the need to prevent Soviet participation in the affairs of states in Latin America and Africa, the most dramatic episode perhaps being the CUBAN MISSILE CRISIS of 1962.

Continental Congress (1774, 1775–89) The assembly that first met in Philadelphia to concert a colonial response to the 'Intolerable' COERCIVE ACTS. At its first session, the radicals, led by delegates from Massachusetts, Virginia, and South Carolina, outmanoeuvred the moderates from New York and Pennsylvania and adopted the Suffolk County (Massachusetts) Resolves, rejecting the Acts as 'the attempts of a wicked administration to enslave America'. The second Congress, convened in the wake of LEXINGTON AND CONCORD, created a Continental Army under WASHINGTON and, as a result of British intransigence and radical pressure, moved gradually towards the DECLARATION OF INDEPENDENCE (1776). The Congress undertook the central direction of the War of INDEPENDENCE, and, under the Articles of Confederation (1781), the government of the USA. Its delegates, however, were little more than ambassadors from the 13 sovereign states, lacking financial and disciplinary powers. It was superseded by the CONSTITUTION OF THE USA in 1789.

Continental System An economic strategy by which NAPOLEON aimed to cripple Britain's economy. It was based upon the Berlin (1806) and Milan (1807) decrees of Napoleon, which declared Britain to be in a state of blockade and forbade either neutral countries or French allies to trade with it or its colonies. At TILSIT (1807) Russia agreed to the system and in 1808 Spain was obliged to join it. Britain responded by issuing Orders in Council that blockaded the ports of France and its allies and allowed them to trade with each other and neutral countries only if they did so via Britain. The restrictions imposed by the system had serious effects on Britain and its allies, while Britain's countermeasures contributed to the WAR OF 1812 with the USA over the right of neutral ships to trade with Europe. The system gradually resulted in Napoleon losing support at home and being challenged abroad. His unsuccessful invasion of Russia in 1812 was provoked by Russian refusal to continue the system and it marked the beginning of his downfall.

Control Commissions Allied administrations established in Germany after both World Wars. After World War I the Commission supervised German demilitarization. During World War II it was agreed by the US, British, and Soviet leaders that, after its defeat, Germany should be divided. Four zones of occupation were created in 1945, administered until 1948 by these Allies and France, the four military commanders acting as a supreme Control Council. Their responsibility was to deal with matters relating to the whole of Germany. In practice the occupying powers administered their zones independently, while the British and US zones merged at the start of 1947. However, the Control Commission undertook significant work especially in the process of removing members of the Nazi Party from important positions. Tension between the Soviet and Western representatives led to the collapse of the system.

convict transportation The banishment of criminals to a penal settlement as a form of punishment. The system was used by France (to the West Indies) and in Russia (to Siberian PRISON CAMPS). It was used in Britain from the 17th century until 1868, with most of the convicts being sent to Britain's American and Australian colonies. The most common crime of Australian convicts was theft, although there were some socio-political prisoners, many of them Irish. At first, convicts were mostly used on public works. Later, the system of 'assignment', in which convicts were allotted as paid servants to colonists, came to be used extensively. Various forms of probation were used, especially in Van Diemen's Land (TASMANIA) during the 1840s and early 1850s and in New South Wales from MACQUARIE's time onwards. Secondary punishment included corporal punishment, solitary confinement, hard labour, confinement to segregated factories for women, and transportation to PENAL SETTLEMENTS.

convoy system During wartime, a system whereby merchant vessels sail in groups under armed naval escort. In 1917 Germany's policy of unrestricted submarine (U-boat) warfare nearly defeated Britain. One ship in four leaving British ports was sunk; new construction only replaced one-tenth of lost tonnage; loss of Norwegian pit props threatened the coal industry; only six weeks' supply of wheat remained. In the face of this crisis LLOYD GEORGE overruled the Admiralty's refusal to organize convoys, and by November 1918, 80% of shipping, including foreign vessels, came in convoy. In World War II transatlantic convoys were immediately instituted in spite of a shortage of destroyers, using long-range aircraft for protection. During 1942 they were extended to the USA as the Allies were losing an average of 96 ships a month.

Cook, James (1728–79) British naval captain, navigator, and explorer. Cook charted the coasts and seaways of Canada (1759, 1763–7), the St Lawrence Channel and the coasts of Nova Scotia and Newfoundland. He then commanded an expedition in HMS *Endeavour* (1768–71) to Tahiti and continued to chart the coasts of New Zealand and eastern Australia. On a second voyage (1772–5) he became the first navigator to cross the Antarctic Circle but was then driven back by ice. However, he explored vast areas of the Pacific. His third voyage (begun in 1776) was to find the North-West Passage. He sought it backwards, by entering the Pacific and sailing up the west coast of North America. He reached the Bering Strait before a wall of ice forced him to retreat. On the way he had discovered Hawaii, a perfect place for refitting his ships. Returning to Hawaii his crew became engaged in a fight with the islanders over the stealing of a cutter and he was stabbed to death.

Cook set new standards in the sea care of men exposed to lengthy voyages: in order to protect his crews from scurvy (a lethal disease caused by lack of ascorbic acid), he pioneered a diet that included cabbage, cress, and a kind of orange extract. His *Journals* give a detailed account of his three voyages to the Pacific.

Coolidge, (John) Calvin (1872–1933) Thirtieth President of the USA (1923–29). He won national fame by his firm action in face of the 1919 Boston police strike. This helped to win him the Republican nomination as Vice-President in 1920. When President HARDING died (1923) Coolidge succeeded him. Elected President in his own right (1924), he served only one full term of office, being seen as an embodiment of thrift, caution, and honesty in a decade when corruption in public life was common, even in his own administration. He showed no sympathy towards war-veterans, small farmers, miners, or textile workers, all of whom were seeking public support at that time. Foreign policy he left to his Secretaries of State, Hughes and Kellogg. Personally highly popular, he resisted pressures to stand for office again in 1928, preferring to retire into private life.

Cooper, Anthony Ashley SHAFTESBURY.

Co-operative Commonwealth Federation (CCF) A Canadian political party. It was founded in 1932, when about 12 Progressive Members of Parliament joined with supporters of the League for Social Reconstruction to form the Commonwealth Party. In 1933, at its convention, it put forward a programme for economic and social planning that would combat the depression affecting all Canada, but particularly the prairie provinces. The CCF returned members to all Canadian Parliaments after 1935, reaching a high point in 1945–49, before becoming the NEW DEMOCRATIC PARTY (NDP) with a closer relationship with organized labour in 1961.

Co-operative Movement An organization owned by and run for the benefit of its members. First developed in many of the new industrial towns in Britain at the end of the 18th century, the Co-operative Movement was largely an attempt to offer an alternative to competitive CAPITALISM. In the early 19th century the social reformer Robert OWEN made several attempts to set up his own co-operative communities, but it was with the founding of the Rochdale Pioneers in 1844 that the co-operative movement in Britain really got under way. In 1864 these came together in a federation known as the Co-operative Wholesale Society. In 1869 the Co-operative Union, an advisory and educational body, was formed. The Co-operative Wholesale Society developed as a manufacturer and wholesale trader, opening its first factories and developing its own farms. The Co-operative Party was established in 1917 to represent its members' interests in Parliament, and subsequently contested elections in alliance with the Labour Party. The movement spread rapidly to northern Europe. In the USA the first co-operatives were established at the end of the 18th and the beginning of the 19th centuries. In India and other developing countries, particularly in Africa after World War II, co-operatives have been an important factor in the growth of the economy.

Copenhagen, first Battle of (1801) A naval engagement between the British and Danish fleets. The northern powers (Russia, Prussia, Denmark, and Sweden) formed a league of armed neutrality to resist the British right of search at sea. Without declaring war, a British fleet, commanded by Admiral Sir Hyde Parker, was sent to destroy the Danish fleet, anchored in Copenhagen. The British divided their fleet, NELSON attacking the Danes from the more protected south whilst Parker attacked from the north. Despite bad weather and the loss of three ships Nelson, ignoring Parker's signal to discontinue action by fixing the telescope to his blind eye, was able to sink or take all but three of the Danish ships. The Danes agreed to an armistice and the league was disbanded.

Copenhagen, second Battle of (1807) A hostile incident between Denmark and Britain during the Napoleonic Wars. The news that Denmark was about to join Napoleon's CONTINENTAL SYSTEM and to declare war on Britain, led the British government to challenge Denmark. When the Danes refused to surrender, the British landed troops and shelled Copenhagen.

Copper Age The stage of technological development between the introduction of copper and the manufacture of bronze (an alloy of copper and tin) in the BRONZE AGE. As copper was initially very scarce, the impact of metallurgy was often slight, and it was used only for ornaments and rare daggers or flat axes.

Copper appeared at very different dates in various parts of the world. In some cases there was no separate stage before the adoption of true bronze or even iron: in others, Andean South America for example, it was in use for very much longer. It was often accompanied by gold and occasionally by silver. The beginning of the period is difficult to define, as the occasional trinket of copper is found sometimes many centuries before metal began to displace stone for tools or weapons. The use of cold-hammered native copper is held not to constitute a Copper Age; examples are found among the Inuit (Eskimos) of North America.

Copt A member of the Coptic Orthodox Church of Egypt and Ethiopia. The word comes from *Aiguptioi*,

(Greek, 'Egyptians'). According to tradition they were converted by St Mark. From the 2nd to the 5th century the Catechetical School of ALEXANDRIA was the most important intellectual institution in the Christian Church. Monasticism originated in the Coptic Church in the 3rd century and it spread along North Africa to Rome, and through Palestine to Syria and Asia Minor. The Copts suffered greatly in Diocletian's persecution: their Calendar dates from 284, the Year of the Martyrs. They broke away from the rest of the Church in 451, claiming that JESUS CHRIST has a single nature (part divine, part human) only. After the Muslim conquest of Egypt in 641 many Christians converted to Islam. The Coptic Church retained its position in ETHIOPIA.

Corday d'Armont, Charlotte (1768–93) French noblewoman, the murderess of MARAT. After a lonely childhood in Normandy she began to attend the meetings of the GIRONDINS, where she heard of Marat as a tyrant and conceived the idea of assassinating him. She arrived in Paris in 1793 and on 13 July murdered Marat in his bath. A plea of insanity was overruled and she was sentenced to death on the guillotine.

Corfu incident (31 August 1923) The naval bombardment and occupation of the Greek island of Corfu by Italian troops. An Italian general and four members of his staff, engaged under international authority in determining the boundary between Greece and ALBANIA, had been murdered three days before. Following the bombardment by Italy in which 16 people were killed, MUSSOLINI issued an ultimatum, demanding a heavy indemnity. Greece appealed to the LEAGUE OF NATIONS, which referred the dispute to the Council of Ambassadors. The Council ordered Greece to pay 50 million lire. Under pressure from Britain and France, Italian troops with drew. The outcome of the dispute raised serious doubts about the strength and efficiency of the League.

Corinth A port on the Isthmus of Corinth, southern Greece. Located at the crossroads of much land and sea trade (it was easier and safer for ships to cross or unload at the Isthmus than to risk the trip round the Peloponnese), it was strategically important. Its trade enabled it, by the mid-6th century BC, to become the most prosperous city in Greece, and a prolific exporter of high-quality pottery. Corinthians founded colonies in north-west Greece and in Sicily, thus transmitting Greek influence throughout the Mediterranean. In c. 657 BC Cypselus brought Corinth under a tyranny, which form of government lasted into the early 6th century. Its power was not checked until the rise of the ATHENIAN EMPIRE, which led Corinth to press Sparta to embark on the PELOPONNESIAN WAR against Athens. In the 4th century BC it fought against Sparta, but was neutral in the face of PHILIP II of Macedonia.

It joined the ACHAEAN LEAGUE in 243 BC and was sacked and destroyed by Rome in 146. Rebuilt in 44 BC as a Roman colony, an earthquake destroyed the ancient city in 521 AD.

Corn Laws Regulations applied in Britain to the import and export of grain (mainly wheat) in order to control its supply and price. In 1815, following the end of the Napoleonic Wars, Parliament passed a law permitting the import of foreign wheat free of duty only when the domestic price reached 80 shillings per quarter (8 bushels). A sliding scale of duties was introduced in 1828 in order to alleviate the distress being caused to poorer people by the rise in the price of bread. A slump in trade in the late 1830s and a succession of bad harvest made conditions worse and strengthened the hand of the ANTI-CORN LAW LEAGUE. In 1846 the Corn Laws were repealed save for a nominal shilling. This split the Conservative Party, but agriculture in Britain did not suffer as had been predicted. The repeal of the Corn Laws came to symbolize the success of FREE TRADE and liberal political economy.

Cornwallis, Charles, 1st Marquis (1738–1805) British general, who fought in the War of INDEPENDENCE at Long Island and BRANDYWINE. He took command of the southern campaign in 1780, defeating the Americans at CAMDEN and Guildford Court House, but by his relentless pursuit into the interior he lost contact with George CLINTON and exhausted his troops. His choice of YORKTOWN as a base proved disastrous, and he was forced to surrender (1781). Later reinstated, he served as governor-general of Bengal (1786–93, 1805) where he defeated TIPU SULTAN and his Cornwallis Code reformed land tenure. He was also viceroy of Ireland (1798–1801) and negotiator of the Treaty of Amiens (1802).

Coromandel A name used for the eastern coast of India between the Cauvery and Krishna deltas, where the English and French competed for supremacy in the 18th century. The name may have derived from the great medieval CHOLA dynasty which ruled this region ('cholamandala' means 'Chola kingdom').

corsair A privateer of the Barbary Coast of North Africa, and especially Algiers. Piracy existed here in Roman times, but, after the MOORS were expelled from Spain (1492), individuals (with government connivance) began attacks on Christian shipping. The early 17th century was the peak of their activity. In Algiers alone 80,000 Christian captives were held as slaves. Britain and France frequently attacked the corsairs and from 1800 to 1815 the USA made war on Tripoli and Algiers. Privateering ceased with the French occupation of Algiers in 1830.

Corsica A west Mediterranean island lying south of the Gulf of Genoa and just north of Sardinia, under French rule since 1768.

Physical. Corsica is the fourth largest island in the Mediterranean. It is about 100 km (60 miles) south-west of the Tuscan coast of Italy. Its north–south length is 183 km (114 miles) and its west–east width is 84 km (52 miles). A mountainous fragment of an old land mass, now submerged, it has high ridges separating secluded valleys, Mount Cinto rising to 2,710 m (8,891 feet). While the west coast is rocky and broken by deep bays, the east has an alluvial coastal plain which is very fertile.

History. Greeks, Etruscans, and Carthaginians all made settlements here before the Roman conquest of 259 BC. It became a Roman province, and was used as a place of political banishment. VANDAL conquest in c. 469 AD was followed by periods of Byzantine, Gothic, Lombard, Frankish, and Moorish domination. In 1077 the papacy assigned control of the island to the Bishop of Pisa. After a long period of conflict, Pisa's hegemony passed to Geneva in 1284. The Genoese subsequently withstood challenges from Aragon (1297–1453) and France (1553–59), and remained in control throughout the 17th century despite considerable popular discontent. There was an unsuccessful mass revolt in 1729, but in 1755 Pasquale de Paoli established an effectively independent Corsican state. In 1768 the French purchased all rights to the island from Genoa, and in 1769 defeated Paoli's troops. Corsica then became a French province, where on 15 August 1769 NAPOLEON was born.

Cortés, Hernan, Marqués del Valle de Oaxaca

(1485–1547) Spanish CONQUISTADOR and conqueror of MEXICO. He was born into a noble Spanish family and at 19 sailed for Hispaniola. In 1511 he joined Diego Velásquez's expedition to conquer Cuba, became a man of means as a result, and began to equip himself with help from Velásquez to lead an expedition to colonize the Mexican mainland. He sailed abruptly, after quarrelling with Velásquez, landing at Vera Cruz on 21 April 1519, and soon met envoys from the AZTECS.

His arrival coincided with the predicted return of the god-king of Aztec mythology, QUETZALCÓATL, and he was welcomed by the emperor MONTEZUMA in TENOCHTITLÁN, the Aztec capital. Suspicions grew among the Aztecs, however, and Cortés seized Montezuma as a hostage, forcing him to parley with his people. Meanwhile Velásquez sent a force under Pánfilo de NARVÁEZ to retrieve Cortés, but he won them over to his side at Vera Cruz in 1520. He then returned to Tenochtitlán, where fighting had broken out in his absence. Montezuma was mortally wounded and the new emperor, Cuauhtémoc, led the Aztecs in driving the Spanish from the city. Cortés returned the following year and the final siege lasted 93 days, the city falling on 13 August 1521. The rest of the empire was quickly subdued, but an expedition to Honduras in 1524 was unsuccessful. Cortés was forgiven for his 'rebellion' by Charles I of Spain, and was awarded estates, but spent most of the rest of his life fighting in Mexico and Spain.

Cosgrave, William Thomas

(1880–1965) Irish statesman. Determined to gain Irish independence from Britain, he took part in the EASTER RISING (1916). Elected to the British Parliament in 1918 as a SINN FEIN member, he became Minister for Local Government in the provisional government of the Dáil Éireann in 1919. He reluctantly accepted the Anglo-Irish Treaty creating the Irish Free State (see IRELAND, REPUBLIC OF). He was president of the Executive Council of the Free State from 1922 to 1932, during which time the international standing of the new state was greatly enhanced. He was Opposition Leader in the Dáil Eireann (1933–44). He was the father of Liam Cosgrave (1920–), who in turn became leader of the Fine Gael Party (1965–77) and later Taoiseach (Prime Minister) of the Republic of Ireland (1973–77).

Cossacks

(from the Turkish, adventurer or guerrilla) A people in south Russia. They were descended from refugees from religious persecution in POLAND and MUSCOVY, and from peasants fleeing the taxes and obligations of the feudal system. Settling in mainly autonomous tribal groups around the rivers Don and Dnieper, they played an important role in the history of the Ukraine. A frontier life-style encouraged military prowess and horsemanship, males aged 16–60 years being obliged to bear arms. They were democratic, directly electing their leaders or *hetmen*. Their relations with Russia included military service and military

alliance, especially against the Turks, but there were rebellions against Russia under the leaderships of Stenka Razin (1667–69), Iran Mazeppa (1709), and PUGACHEV (1773–74).

Costa Rica

A small country on the Central American isthmus, between Nicaragua and Panama.

Physical. It has a Caribbean coast on its north-east and a Pacific coast on its south-west. While the coastal lowlands have a tropical climate, a range of volcanic mountains occupies the centre of the country, providing plateaux which have a mild climate. There are several peaks over 3,350 m (11,000 feet).

Economy. The soil is very fertile and supports livestock farming and some of the finest coffee in the world. Bananas are grown and cattle-rearing is important. The chemical and textile industries also contribute to the economy.

History. Costa Rica was discovered by COLUMBUS during his fourth voyage to the New World in 1502. Permanent settlement did not occur until 1564 when Juan Vásquez de Coronado, with settlers from Nicaragua, founded Cartago on the Meseta Central. The small Indian population fell victim to disease, leaving the ethnic make-up of the area mostly European. Costa Rica formed part of the captaincy-general of Guatemala until 1821, when it joined the independent Mexican empire (1821–23) and then the United Provinces of Central America (1823–38). In 1838 it became an independent republic. A policy of isolation and stability, together with agricultural fertility, brought considerable British and US investment in the 19th century. Apart from the brief dictatorship of Federico Tinoco Granados (1917–19), Costa Rica was remarkable in the late 19th and early 20th centuries for its democratic tradition. After World War II left-wing parties emerged, including the communist party. The socialist presidents, Otilio Ulate (1948–53) and José Figueres (1953–58, 1970–74), tried to disband the army, nationalize banks, and curb US investment. A new constitution, granting universal suffrage and abolishing the armed forces, was introduced in 1949. Political tensions in the 1970s were aggravated by economic problems and by the arrival of many fugitives from neighbouring states. President Luis Alberto Monge (1982–86) had to impose severe economic restraint. In 1987 President Oscar Arias Sánchez (1986–90) put forward a peace-plan for Central America, to which President Reagan reacted by reducing US aid to the country. Severe economic difficulties continued under Presidents Rafael Calderón Fournier (1990–94) and José María Figueres (1994–98), with an IMF-imposed austerity programme and widespread industrial unrest in the early 1990s. The conservative economist Miguel Angel Rodriguez was elected President in 1998.

CAPITAL:	San José
AREA:	51,100 sq km (19,730 sq miles)
POPULATION:	3.400 million (1996)
CURRENCY:	1 Costa Rican colón = 100 céntimos
RELIGIONS:	Roman Catholic 88.6%; other (mostly Protestant) 11.4%
ETHNIC GROUPS:	European 87.0%; Mestizo 7.0%; Black/Mulatto 3.0%; East Asian (mostly Chinese) 2.0%; Amerindian 1.0%
LANGUAGES:	Spanish (official); other minority languages
INTERNATIONAL ORGANIZATIONS:	UN; OAS

Côte d'Ivoire (formerly Ivory Coast) A tropical West African country, bounded on the west by Liberia and Guinea, on the north by Mali and Burkina Faso, and on the east by Ghana.

Physical. Its south-facing coastline is rocky in the west but elsewhere has sand-bars and lagoons. Three rivers run through the hot, rain-forested lowlands. In the central belt coffee is grown. In winter the drying harmattan blows down from savannah-covered sandstone uplands. The Nimba Mountains in the west contain minerals, including iron.

Economy. The economy is primarily agricultural, with main exports including cocoa, coffee, cotton, tropical timber, and vegetable oils. Offshore oil reserves are being increasingly exploited. Industries, such as oil-refining, food-processing, textiles, and chemicals are well established, and there is a well-developed system of hydraulic electricity production from dams. Mineral deposits include iron, cobalt, bauxite, nickel, manganese, and diamonds.

History. There were scattered and isolated coastal settlements in the region when European slave traders arrived in the 15th century. The French had established trading posts in the area by the end of the 17th century and in the 19th century made treaties with local chiefs. France obtained rights on the coast in 1842, establishing a colony in 1893, which in 1904 became a territory of French West Africa. In 1933 most of the territory of Upper Volta was added to the Côte d'Ivoire, but in 1948 this area was returned to the reconstituted Upper Volta, today BURKINA FASO. The Côte d'Ivoire became an autonomous republic within the FRENCH COMMUNITY in 1958, and achieved full independence in 1960, becoming a one-party republic governed by the moderate Democratic Party of the Côte d'Ivoire and with Félix HOUPHOUËT-BOIGNY its president. The country has large petroleum deposits and a developing industrial sector, but falling cocoa and coffee prices adversely affected the economy during the late 1980s. The resulting policy of economic austerity caused unrest and demonstrations. In the first multiparty elections in November 1990, the President's Democratic Party won all but 10 seats in the National Assembly. Following Houphouët-Boigny's death in 1993, Henri Konan Bedie (1934–) became President. He and the Democratic Party were re-elected in 1995, though the main opposition parties were banned.

CAPITAL:	Abidjan (capital designate, Yamoussoukro)
AREA:	322,463 sq km (124,471 sq miles)
POPULATION:	14.733 million (1996)
CURRENCY:	1 CFA franc = 100 centimes
RELIGIONS:	Traditional beliefs 65.0%; Muslim 23.0%; Christian 12.0%
ETHNIC GROUPS:	Akan 27.0%; Mande 24.0%; Kru 18.0%; Senufo 12.0%; Lagoon 8.0%; Lobi 5.0%
LANGUAGES:	French (official); Akan; Kru; local languages
INTERNATIONAL ORGANIZATIONS:	ECOWAS; Non-Aligned Movement; OAU; UN; Franc Zone

Coughlin, Charles Edward (1891–1979) Canadian-born Roman Catholic priest. His radio broadcasts won him fame in the 1930s as the 'radio priest'. At first he spoke in support of the NEW DEAL and then, when F. D. Roosevelt refused Coughlin's plan for the coinage of silver to expand the currency, he made speeches against the President and his policies with ever-mounting vituperation. Isolationist, anti-Semitic, and pro-fascist, Coughlin used his magazine *Social Justice* to promote his causes. In 1942 it was barred from the mails (i.e. not allowed to be sent by post) for violating the Espionage Act, and with full US involvement in the war his influence quickly waned.

Council of Europe An association of West European states, independent of the EUROPEAN UNION. Founded in 1949, it is committed to the principles of freedom and the rule of law, to safeguarding the political and cultural heritage of Europe, and to promoting economic and social co-operation. With a membership of 39 European democracies (including Russia and the Ukraine, which joined in 1996), the Council is served by the Committee of Ministers, the European Court of Human Rights, the European Commission of Human Rights, and the Parliamentary Assembly at Strasbourg. The Council has limited powers but has made progress in furthering regional co-operation in a variety of fields, notably in working towards the harmonization of national laws within Europe or subjects such as the legal status of migrant workers and data protection. The Council is also a forum for discussion of political matters, such as UN activities, international relations, the prevention of TERRORISM, and the promotion of HUMAN RIGHTS. All members are party to the European Convention on Human Rights (1950).

Counter-Reformation A revival in the ROMAN CATHOLIC CHURCH between the mid-16th and mid-17th centuries. It had its origins in reform movements which were independent of the Protestant REFORMATION, but it increasingly became identified with, and took its name from, efforts to 'counter' the Protestant Reformation. There were three main ecclesiastical aspects. First a reformed papacy, with a succession of popes who had a notably more spiritual outlook than their immediate predecessors, and a number of reforms in the Church's central government initiated by them. Secondly, the foundation of new religious orders, notably the Oratorians and in 1540 the Society of Jesus (JESUITS), and the reform of older orders, notably the Capuchin reform of the FRANCISCANS. Thirdly, the Council of TRENT (1545–63), which defined and clarified Catholic doctrine on most points in dispute with Protestants and instituted important moral and disciplinary reforms within the Catholic Church, including the provision of a better education for the clergy through theological colleges called seminaries. Prominent Counter-Reformation figures were Ignatius LOYOLA (*c.* 1491–1556), founder of the Society of Jesus, Charles Borromeo, Archbishop of Milan 1560–84, Pope Pius V (1566–72), and the Spanish Carmelite mystics TERESA OF AVILA (1515–82) and JOHN OF THE CROSS (1542–91). All this led to a flowering of Catholic spirituality at the popular level, but also to an increasingly anti-Protestant mentality. The movement became political through its links with Catholic rulers, notably PHILIP II of Spain, who sought to re-establish Roman Catholicism by force. The stalemate between Catholics and Protestants was effectively recognized by the Treaty of WESTPHALIA in 1648, which brought to an end the Thirty Years War and in a sense concluded the Counter-Reformation period.

country house A large house standing in its own park or estate. Country houses in the grand manner were built in England by the wealthy from the 16th century onwards. The stability and prosperity of the TUDOR period meant that these great houses were built for comfort rather than for defence (unlike CASTLES), and to entertain Elizabeth I when she toured the country on a royal PROGRESS. Longleat House (Wiltshire) and Hardwick Hall (Derbyshire) date from the 16th century, and Hatfield House (Hertfordshire) is a fine Jacobean house of the early 17th century. The great age of country-house building was the 18th century: noble families recovered their estates after the RESTORATION, increased their income from agricultural land by ENCLOSURES, and the development of mineral resources, and built magnificent residences to display their collections of paintings, furniture, and silver (see also GRAND TOUR). Blenheim Palace, one of the most splendid, was a gift from the British nation to the Duke of Marlborough after his victory at the Battle of BLENHEIM. New wealth from trade, banking, or industry was invested in the purchase or construction of country-house estates during the 18th and 19th centuries, and the country-house 'weekend' became a characteristic of 19th- and early 20th-century social and political Britain. After World War I some houses continued to maintain their traditions, but increasing costs and a more fragmented society reduced their numbers considerably. Some houses fell into disrepair, others became conference centres, hotels, or institutions, or were given to the nation under the care of the National Trust, who open them to the public. Others continue to be lived in by their owners, helped by revenue from visitors who pay to be shown the house and grounds.

Courtrai, Battle of (11 July 1302) A battle between French and Flemish troops fought at the town of Courtrai in modern Belgium: it is sometimes known as the 'Battle of the Golden Spurs.' Philip IV of France had attempted to overrun FLANDERS but was halted at Courtrai, where Flemish burghers defeated the French nobility. In celebration of their victory, the burghers hung their spurs in the churches of Bruges. The Battle of Courtrai was one of the most significant defeats suffered by France in the 14th century. Charles VI of France avenged this insult by sacking Courtrai in 1382.

Covenanter Originally a Scot who opposed the ecclesiastical innovations of CHARLES I of England. Drawn from all parts of Scotland and all sections of society, Covenanters subscribed to the National Covenant of 1638. This was a revised version of a previous covenant (1581), which had been signed by James VI of Scotland. They swore to resist 'episcopal' (the Church governed by bishops) religious changes, and, in the event of such changes, they set up a full PRESBYTERIAN system and defended it in the BISHOPS' WARS. They hoped to impose their system on England in 1643, by drawing up the SOLEMN LEAGUE AND COVENANT with the LONG PARLIAMENT. Disappointed in this, they turned in 1650 to CHARLES II, who signed the Covenant, but then abjured it at his RESTORATION (1660), condemning it as an unlawful oath. In Scotland the episcopacy was re-established in 1661, and Covenanters were badly treated. In 1690 the Presbyterian Church of Scotland was established.

Coverdale, Miles (1488–1568) English scholar and translator of the BIBLE into English. A priest from 1514,

he came under the influence of William TYNDALE, and held increasingly Protestant views. His first translation of the Bible was printed in Zürich (1535), and he is claimed as the author of the 'Great Bible' (1539), commissioned by Thomas CROMWELL, which was placed by order in all parish churches. In 1551, he was made Bishop of Exeter, but fled abroad during the reign of Mary I. He possibly contributed to the Geneva Bible of 1560, and under Elizabeth I was one of the leaders of the PURITANS.

cowboy In the western USA, a man hired to herd cattle on horseback. The term was first applied to some pro-British marauders during the American War of Independence, who roamed the neutral ground of Westchester county in New York state (their Revolutionary counterparts were 'skinners'). By the 1870s the term was used to describe those who herded cattle on the Great Plains. Many of them were Black or Mexican; they rounded up cattle in an enclosure or rodeo, and, dividing them into herds of about 2,500 head, with a dozen cowboys for each herd, drove them along the CATTLE TRAILS to the nearest shipping points. The cattle industry spread across the Great Plains from Texas to Canada and westward to the Rocky Mountains. The introduction of barbed wire to fence in ranches rapidly encroached on the open ranges, and by 1895 railway expansion had made trail-driving uneconomical, and cowboys settled to work on the cattle ranches. By the end of the 19th century the cowboy had become a central figure in the mythology of the Wild West.

Cranmer, Thomas (1489–1556) English cleric, a founding father of the English Protestant Church. He served HENRY VIII on diplomatic missions before becoming Archbishop of Canterbury in 1532. He annulled Henry's marriages to Catherine of Aragon, Anne Boleyn, and Anne of Cleves. During EDWARD VI's reign, he was chiefly responsible for liturgical reform including the First and Second English Prayer Books (1549 and 1552) and the Forty-Two Articles (1553). He supported Lady Jane GREY's succession in 1553; after Queen Mary's accession he was tried for high treason, then for heresy, and finally burnt at the stake in Oxford.

Crassus, Marcus Licinius (c. 115–53 BC) Roman general and member of the 'First Triumvirate' with POMPEY and Julius CAESAR. He had fled from MARIUS as a young man and joined SULLA, whose troops he commanded at the Battle of the Colline Gate (November 82). Sulla rewarded him and he further increased his fortune by property speculation to become one of the richest men in Rome. After defeating SPARTACUS in 71 he and Pompey were elected consuls. Though hostile to each other during the sixties, in 59 they formed a junta or 'triumvirate' with Caesar to dominate Roman politics. Crassus was given command against the Parthians as governor of Syria for a five-year term in 55. Greed and ambition drove him to sack JERUSALEM and then to attack PARTHIA. Defeated at Carrhae, he was captured and executed by the PATRICIANS.

Crazy Horse (d. 1877) Native American chief. Of the Ogala Sioux tribe, he opposed White infiltration into the mineral-rich Black Hills. He was at the first military confrontation between the Sioux and White forces in 1854, and opposed Native American settlement on reservations. He was at the centre of the confederation that defeated Generals George Crook on the Rosebud River and CUSTER at LITTLE BIG HORN, both in 1876. He and his followers were starved into surrender (May 1877). Imprisoned because of a rumour that he was planning a revolt, he was reputedly stabbed to death while trying to escape.

Crécy, Battle of (26 August 1346) The defeat of the French under Philip VI by the ARCHERS of the English king, Edward III, at the village of Crécy in northern France. Edward's raiding army, anxious to avoid pitched battle, was trapped by a numerically superior French force. The English bowmen dug pits to impede advancing cavalry, while the knights dismounted and formed three supporting divisions, their right commanded by Edward's son and heir, EDWARD THE BLACK PRINCE. Genoese crossbowmen in French pay, handicapped by wet bowstrings and the slowness and short range of their weapons, were swiftly dispersed. The French knights charged forward only to have their horses shot from under them by longbow arrows. Wounded and trampled on, some were then killed by English pikes and knives and others held for ransom. Over 1,500 of the French died, including the cream of the nobility, as against 40 English dead. Edward was able to march north and besiege Calais. This was a decisive English victory at the outset of the HUNDRED YEARS WAR.

Crédit Mobilier of America A US finance company. It was acquired by Thomas Durant, vice-president of the Union Pacific Railroad, to raise money for its construction. The railway had cost at least $50 million, of which $23 million had been diverted into the pockets of the promoters, who had granted construction contracts to Crédit Mobilier at exorbitant rates. Thus the Union Pacific was forced to the verge of bankruptcy while Crédit Mobilier paid excessive dividends. It was a scandal that cut at the heart of US political corruption in the so-called Gilded Age. During the elections of 1872 15 leading politicians were damaged by their association with it.

Cree The largest and most widespread group of Algonquian-speaking Native Americans in Canada, originally from the Great Lakes area. Prehistorically they were hunters in the northern forest and tundra areas of central and mid-western Canada, living in small bands or hunting groups in conical or dome-shaped lodges, travelling by foot or canoe in summer and by snow shoes and toboggan in winter. The Cree split into two distinct groupings when they were displaced in the mid-19th century following contact with the HUDSON'S BAY COMPANY: one group became the Woodland Cree, practising sedentary farming, hunting, and gathering, while the other group moved into the Plains area to become the Plains Cree, practising nomadic buffalo hunting. With the introduction of firearms the Plains Cree became horse-mounted hunters of buffalo, virtually destroying these herds in the 1880s. Both groups are culturally and linguistically close to the OJIBWA.

Creek (or Muskogee) A Native American people who inhabited Alabama and Georgia, and were the prehistoric eastern extension of the MISSISSIPPI CULTURES. The Spanish explorer Hernando DE SOTO visited the region in 1540–42, and found them to have a powerful and highly organized political and social system. They lived in large fortified towns with central ceremonial mounds, linked in a loose confederacy, which bitterly fought European attempts at conquest but were defeated in the late 18th and early 19th centuries.

Crete The largest of the Greek islands, sited in the southern part of the Aegean Sea.

Physical. Crete is a long, narrow island, its west–east length being 257 km (160 miles) and its north–south breadth 56 km (35 miles) at its broadest point. High limestone mountains rise in long chains along its centre (Mount Ida reaching 2,456 m (8,058 feet)), and enclose a number of small, elevated plains, formerly the basins of lakes which dried up or drained away. These plains once were centres of ancient Greek civilization.

History. In the pre-historic period it was home to the MINOAN CIVILIZATION. Its continued importance was ensured by its position on the sea-routes to Egypt, the Levant, and Cyprus. It played a significant role in the development of archaic Greek art, and in early written law-codes, was well known as a home of mercenaries, and maintained an aristocratic society. It was neutral during the GREEK–PERSIAN WARS.

A league of Cretan cities was established in the 3rd century BC, and this accepted the protection of Philip V of Macedonia, who encouraged the pirates for which the island was then infamous. When Cretan pirates later threw their lot in with MITHRIDATES VI, an enemy of Rome, they provoked Roman retaliation and in 68–67 BC the island was subdued and KNOSSOS destroyed. The island subsequently became a Roman province. After Roman and Byzantine rule, it underwent a period of Arab control before being recaptured by the Byzantines in 960–61 AD. In 1210 it was taken over by the Venetians, who were not ejected until 1669 by the Turks who made Crete part of the Ottoman empire. The extant fortifications by the harbour of Heraklion are an impressive reminder of this period. The islanders rose unsuccessfully in revolt against their Turkish overlords in 1866, in a pursuit of *enosis*, or union with Greece. In 1897 a Greek force landed but the great powers supported Turkey. The island was declared independent, under Turkish suzerainty, but with Prince George of Greece as High Commissioner. Turkish troops were withdrawn in 1898 and after more unrest it was declared a part of Greece by the Treaty of London in 1913. In 1941 Germany attacked Crete and, despite resistance by Greek and Allied forces, made the first successful airborne invasion in military history, followed by a bloody 12-day battle and capturing some 18,000 Allied troops. Crete was liberated at the end of World War II.

Crimea A peninsula in southern Ukraine, bounded on the west and south by the Black Sea and on the east by the Sea of Azov.

Physical. Northward the 8-km (5-mile)-wide Perekop Isthmus joins it to the Ukraine mainland. The northern area comprises a low, flat plain of steppe grassland which has only 250–380 mm (10–15 inches) of precipitation a year. In the south mountain ridges rising to 1,545 m (4,769 feet) extend for 160 km (100 miles) in length and 48 km (30 miles) in width and protect the south coast from cold northerly winds, giving this coast a Mediterranean climate. The north-east shoreline is noted for its stagnant, shallow, but mineral-rich lagoons.

History. The area was colonized by the Greeks in the 6th century BC, and became a Roman protectorate in the 1st century AD. It was overrun by Ostrogoths, Huns, and others, and was partly under Byzantine control from the 6th to the 12th century. The 13th century saw it pillaged by Mongols, yet enjoying trade relations with Kievan Russia and Genoa. In the late 15th century a short-lived Tartar khanate was absorbed by the OTTOMANS, until Russia annexed it in 1783. Crimea remained Russian and became part of the Soviet Union. In 1921 the mainly TARTAR Crimean Autonomous Soviet Socialist Republic was formed but the Tartars were expelled in 1945 for alleged collaboration with the Nazis and Crimea reverted to the Russian Soviet Socialist Republic. It was transferred to Ukraine in 1954 and remained part of Ukraine (as an autonomous republic) following the collapse of the Soviet Union in 1991. In 1992 Crimea declared itself independent but this was rejected by Ukraine. A movement favouring unification with Russia developed, the majority of the population of Crimea are ethnic Russians, and the political crisis worsened. Direct rule was imposed by the Ukrainian government from March to August 1995 and support for the pro-Russian faction subsided.

Crimean War (1853–56) A war fought by Russia against Turkey, Britain, France, and Piedmont. The immediate cause was the dispute between France and Russia over the Palestinian holy places. War became inevitable after the Russians, having failed to obtain equal rights with the French, occupied territories of the OTTOMAN EMPIRE in July 1853. In a bid to prevent Russian expansion in the Black Sea area and to ensure existing trade routes, a conference was convened in Vienna. Turkey was pressed by the Powers to make some concessions to placate Russia, but it refused, and declared war. In November 1853 the Russians destroyed the Turkish fleet at Sinope, in the Black Sea. This forced the hand of Britain and France, who in March 1854 declared war, expecting, with their naval supremacy, a quick victory. Austria did not join the Allies but, by mobilizing its army, obliged the Russians to evacuate the provinces of Wallachia and Moldavia which they had occupied. The Allied forces were at first mustered at Varma, but in August 1854 they were transported to Eupatoria on the Crimea with Lord RAGLAN as Commander-in-Chief of an ill-prepared army which had been ravaged by cholera. They were able to defeat the Russian army, skilfully led by Menschikov, at the Battle of the Alma River (20 September 1854) and began bombarding the strongly armed fort of SEVASTOPOL. Following the Battle of BALAKLAVA, a long winter of siege warfare ensued, aggravated by lack of fuel, clothing, and supplies for the Allied armies. Public opinion in Britain became critical of the war after reading eyewitness reports in *The Times*, sent back by the Irishman W. H. Russell, the first journalist in history to write as a war correspondent using the telegraph. Florence NIGHTINGALE received permission to take nurses to the Crimea. Sevastopol fell on 8 September 1855; by that time the Russians, with a new emperor, ALEXANDER II, were already seeking peace. This was concluded at the Congress of PARIS in 1856.

Cripps, Sir (Richard) Stafford (1889–1952) British politician. He entered Parliament as a Labour Member in 1931, but was expelled from the Labour Party in 1939 because of his advocacy of a Popular Front. During World War II Cripps was Ambassador to Moscow (1940–42) and Minister for Aircraft Production (1942–45). During 1945–50 he served in ATTLEE's government successively as President of the Board of Trade and Chancellor of the Exchequer. In these posts he was responsible for the policy of austerity – a programme of rationing and controls introduced to adjust Britain to its reduced economy following the withdrawal of US LEND–LEASE. He also directed a notable expansion of exports, especially after devaluation of the pound in 1949.

Crispi, Francesco (1819–1901) Italian politician. He began as a Sicilian revolutionary republican supporting GARIBALDI's invasion (1860) and ended as a monarchist, a friend of BISMARCK, and twice a dictatorial Premier. During his first ministry (1887–91) a colonial administration was formally established (1889) in the Ethiopian province of Eritrea. Italy's economic distress was aggravated by his tariff war against France, and he brutally suppressed a socialist uprising in Sicily. His foreign policy was based on friendship with Germany and adherence to Bismarck's TRIPLE ALLIANCE. His second ministry (1893–96) witnessed the rout of the Italians by the Ethiopians at ADOWA (1896). Italy was obliged to sue for peace and Crispi was forced from office.

critical theory The radical social theory developed by members of the Institute for Social Research in Frankfurt, Germany (the FRANKFURT SCHOOL), during the 1930s and later. Following MARX, they criticized capitalist societies, believing that individuality and freedom were being destroyed, that social injustice was deepening, and that large corporations were eliminating competition and aggrandizing themselves. Through critical theory, they analysed these developments and sought to 'unmask' the discrepancies between the proclaimed goals of, for example, 'democratic' governments and 'FREE MARKET' economies and the principles by which they in truth operated. Critical theory has influenced scholars in diverse fields. Critical theorists look behind the apparent meaning of, for example, a literary work or the public justification of an institution in order to uncover what they believe to be a hidden, less palatable, reality.

Croatia A country in south-eastern Europe, formerly a constituent republic of Yugoslavia.
Physical. Croatia is bounded by Slovenia, Hungary, Bosnia-Herzegovina, Serbia, and the Adriatic Sea. In the south-west, the Dinaric Alps form a rugged chain, while the north-eastern part is mostly flat and fertile and well suited to agriculture.
Economy. Croatia has an industrialized economy in which mining, petroleum production, shipbuilding, and other heavy industry are important. Mineral resources include bauxite, petroleum, and natural gas. The civil war inflicted great damage on tourism, the principal earner of foreign exchange. The main agricultural products are grains, sugar beet, and potatoes. Grapes are grown mainly on the off-shore islands.
History. Once the Roman province of Illyricum, the area suffered successive barbarian invasions, with the Slavs becoming the majority population. Conquered by CHARLEMAGNE, the first Croatian state was formed with its own knezes or princes when the Carolingian empire collapsed. With papal support Kneze Tomislav became

the first king. Struggles between HUNGARY, VENICE, and the BYZANTINE EMPIRE resulted in rule by the Hungarian crown until 1301, when the House of Anjou took control. From 1381 there was a long period of civil war. The Battle of MOHÁCS in 1526 brought most of the country under OTTOMAN rule with the remainder governed by the HABSBURGS. From 1809 to 1813 Croatia was part of Napoleon's Illyrian province, during which time Croatian nationalism emerged, strongly resisting both Habsburg imperialism and Hungarian control. In 1848 a revolution reasserted Croatian independence, ending serfdom, and proclaiming all citizens equal. In the following year Austria countered by proclaiming the nation an Austrian crownland. In 1868, following the establishment of the AUSTRO-HUNGARIAN EMPIRE, it was pronounced to be the autonomous Hungarian crownland of Croatia-Slovenia, apart from the coastline of Dalmatia, which was to remain an Austrian province. The Hungarian authorities tried to crush all manifestations of Croatian nationalism, with little success, and in October 1918 an independent Croatia was again proclaimed. This then joined the Kingdom of the Serbs, Croats, and Slovenes (1921), later renamed Yugoslavia. In 1941 it was once again declared an independent state under the fascist leader Ante Pavelić, whose brutal government provoked a guerrilla war. Croatia joined the new Federal Republic of Yugoslavia in 1945. A movement for Croatian independence re-emerged in the late 1980s and a non-communist government was formed in May 1990 under Franjo TUDJMAN. In 1991 clashes between Croatian nationalists and ethnic Serbs led to an invasion by the Serbian-dominated Yugoslav army. A confused military situation developed with the ancient city of Dubrovnik being bombarded by Yugoslav artillery. Croatia was recognized as independent by the European Community in 1992. Fighting continued in the region of Krajina, which had declared itself to be a Serbian republic, and UN peacekeepers were sent in (1992). Croatian forces attacked Krajina in 1993, and in 1995 launched an offensive that enabled them to regain possession of much of the region; this military action earned the censure of the UN Security Council in 1996 for its human rights abuses. From 1992 Croatian forces were involved in the civil war in BOSNIA-HERZEGOVINA, fighting Bosnian Serbs and, in some areas, Bosnian Muslims. Some Bosnian Croat nationalists even proclaimed themselves to be a separate republic. In 1994 Croatia agreed to a plan of military co-operation with the Bosnian government. Fighting with the Bosnian Serbs continued until late 1995, when the governments of Croatia, Serbia, and Bosnia accepted a US-brokered peace plan for the region. The mid-1990s saw growing opposition to the authoritarian rule of Tudjman; he was re-elected President in 1996, in a poll that was regarded as free but unfair, owing to his control of the media.

CAPITAL:	Zagreb
AREA:	56,537 sq km (21,829 sq miles)
POPULATION:	4.775 million (1996)
CURRENCY:	1 kuna = 100 lipa
RELIGIONS:	Roman Catholic 75.0%; Eastern Orthodox 12.0%
ETHNIC GROUPS:	Croat 75.0%; Serb 12.0%
LANGUAGES:	Serbo-Croat (official)
INTERNATIONAL ORGANIZATIONS:	CSCE

Crockett, David (Davy) (1786–1836) US pioneer and adventurer. A hunter and frontier fighter, he fought against the Creek people in Andrew JACKSON's campaign of 1814, and went on to serve two terms in the state legislature and three terms in Congress as a Jacksonian Democrat, gaining considerable fame as a result of his backwoods manner and uninhibited sense of humour. Defection to the Whigs ended his political career, and Crockett returned to the frontier, where he took up the cause of Texan independence and died at the ALAMO.

Croesus King of LYDIA (c. 560–546 BC) He expanded his domains to include all the Greek cities on the coast of Asia Minor, and the stories of his wealth indicate the extent of his power. However, he was unable to withstand CYRUS II (the Great), and after his defeat Lydia entered the Persian empire of the Achaemenids.

Cro-Magnons Early modern people (*Homo sapiens sapiens*) found in Europe until about 10,000 years ago. They were generally more heavily built than humans today but otherwise had the same anatomical characteristics. They appeared around 35,000 years ago and are named after a rock shelter in the Dordogne, France, where four adult skeletons, an infant's skeleton, and other remains were found in 1868. With the skeletons were UPPER PALAEOLITHIC flint tools of Aurignacian type and signs of decorative art in the form of pierced sea shells. The ancestry of Cro-Magnons is unclear. It was once believed these people were the direct descendants of NEANDERTHALS, but it is now thought that they evolved elsewhere, probably in Africa, and replaced the Neanderthals within a few thousand years of reaching Europe.

Cromer, Evelyn Baring, 1st Earl of (1841–1917) British statesman, colonial administrator, and diplomatist. A professional soldier, he became secretary to the viceroy of India. In 1879 he became Commissioner of Debt in EGYPT, rescuing the country from near bankruptcy. He was in India again in 1880–83, and then became British Agent and Consul-General in Egypt at a critical time, following the Battle of TEL-EL-KEBIR and Britain's occupation of the country. His ability and imposing personality made him the real and absolute ruler of Egypt until he retired in 1907.

Cromwell, Oliver (1599–1658) English statesman and general, Lord Protector of the Commonwealth of England (1653–58). He was born of Huntingdon gentry stock, indirectly descended from Thomas CROMWELL. An opposition member of the Long Parliament, he rose to prominence during the ENGLISH CIVIL WAR. He helped to form the Eastern Association and secured East Anglia's support for the Roundheads. Until 1645, he displayed great skill in cavalry organization and tactics in the Army of the Eastern Association. After helping to engineer the SELF-DENYING ORDINANCE, he became Fairfax's second-in-command in the NEW MODEL ARMY in which he played a decisive role (1646–48). He supported the Army in its quarrel with the Parliamentary Presbyterians, and the Army Grandees against the LEVELLERS. During the war's second phase, he won the Battle of Preston, approved of PRIDE'S PURGE, and signed Charles I's death warrant.

Appointed a member of the COMMONWEALTH's Council of State, he repressed resistance to the regime in Ireland, Scotland, then England. In Ireland, Cromwell was responsible for widespread repression, culminating in massacres following the Siege of the Drogheda and Wexford garrisons (1649). He became the focus of general dissatisfaction with the policies of the Rump Parliament. In April 1653 he expelled it, becoming Lord Protector, and spent the rest of his life vainly trying to give constitutional permanence to his military regime. Although in effect dictator, he refused the crown urged on him by Parliament in 1657.

His Protectorate, based on the Instrument of Government, and upheld by the rule of major-generals in the counties, was unpopular. After his death his son Richard CROMWELL failed to keep the senior military commanders under control and factions emerged. Eighteen months after Cromwell's death one section of the army under General MONCK called for free elections and it was voted to recall CHARLES II from exile.

Cromwell, Richard (1626–1712) Son of Oliver CROMWELL, whom he succeeded as Lord Protector of the Commonwealth of England (1658–59). He was more interested in country life than in politics and, incapable of reconciling the military and civilian factions in Parliament, he retired after a few months. At the RESTORATION he fled to the Continent, returning c. 1689 to spend the rest of his life quietly in Hampshire.

Cromwell, Thomas, Earl of Essex (1485–1540) English statesman. His beginnings are obscure: in early life he appears to have travelled abroad, acquiring skills in commerce, law, languages, and mercenary warfare. After 1520, he obtained the patronage of Thomas WOLSEY, and by 1529, when his master was discredited, was attracting HENRY VIII's attention. By 1531 he belonged to the inner ring of the royal council, and his successive appointments included Chancellor of the Exchequer (1533), Principal Secretary of State (1534), Vicar-General (1535), and Lord Privy Seal (1536). From 1533 to 1540 he was the king's chief minister. His managerial genius accomplished the divorce from Catherine of Aragon, the break with the pope and the Roman Catholic Church, the Dissolution of the MONASTERIES, and what amounted to an administrative revolution. His Protestant sympathies led to the choice of ANNE OF CLEVES as the king's fourth wife, resulting in the loss of royal favour and arousing hostility both inside the court and out. The Catholic HOWARD faction contrived his execution for treason just after he had been made Earl of Essex.

crop rotation The practice of growing different crops in different years on the same land, in order to prevent the soil's nutrients from being exhausted and to reduce the risk of a build-up of diseases and pests specific to one crop. Crop rotation was widespread in Europe from

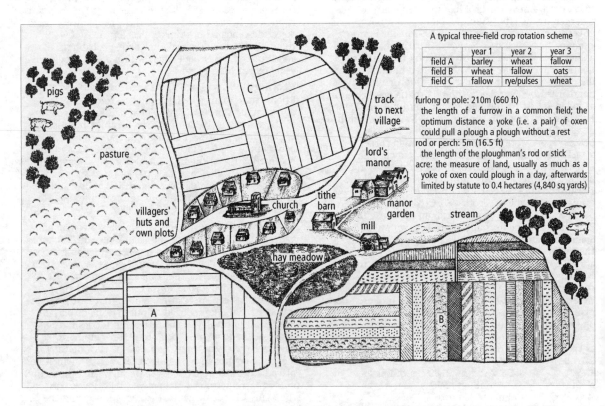

crop rotation *Villagers were tenants of the manor and were obliged to work a specified number of days a year on the manorial or 'demesne' land. One tenth, or a tithe, of everyone's produce was owed to the priest, who might also hold land. A typical village in England in the late Middle Ages might have been divided into three fields, each regulated into strips one furlong in length and one rod in width. The size of holdings varied according to the type of soil, but an average one might be 12 hectares (30 acres). The manor court, presided over by the bailiff in the absence of the lord, decided the allocation of strips and sequence of crops – barley, wheat, rye, oats, pulses – and the time of sowing.*

the time of the ROMAN EMPIRE. Two-field rotation was practised by the ancient Greeks: one half of a farmer's land was planted in the spring or autumn of each year, while the other half was left fallow (i.e. not planted with crops), to allow the soil to 'rest'. The Romans developed the three-course rotation, which was in use from the Middle Ages until the 18th century. A three-year cycle was followed on each of three fields, with an autumn-sown crop such as rye or winter wheat, a spring-sown crop such as oats or beans, and a year of lying fallow. Two out of three fields were thus in cultivation every year. The three-field system succeeded only in countries with mild climates, such as England. With the AGRICULTURAL REVOLUTION and the acceleration of ENCLOSURES in the 18th century, more scientific methods were applied to crop rotation. A four-course rotation was adopted based on turnips, clover, barley, and wheat. The introduction of root-crops (such as turnips) improved the soil and hence the quality of harvest and livestock; they also smother the weeds that have grown between plants of the previous crop. The replacement of the fallow with a leguminous crop, such as clover, peas, beans, or lentils, boosts the fertility of the soil since leguminous plants are able to 'fix' atmospheric nitrogen, which enriches the soil when they die. (See illustration.)

Crosland, (Charles) Anthony (Raven) (1918–77) British politician. He served as Labour Member of Parliament (1950–55, 1959–77). His book, *The Future of Socialism* (1956), gave an optimistic forecast of continuing economic growth which was to influence a whole generation. As Secretary of State for Education and Science (1964–67) his strongly held libertarian and egalitarian principles led to the closure of grammar schools, the establishment of a comprehensive state school system, and the growth of polytechnics. During 1965–70 and 1974–77 he held several cabinet posts, and was Foreign Secretary before his early death.

Crossman, Richard Howard Stafford (1907–74) British politician. He was assistant chief of the Psychological Warfare Division during World War II. He entered Parliament as a Labour Member in 1945. During the WILSON administrations he was successively Minister of Housing and Local Government, Leader of the House of Commons, and Secretary of State for Social Services. His posthumous *Diaries* (1975–77) provided revealing insights into the working of government.

Crow and Hidatsa (or Absaroke) Native Americans who inhabited Montana and northern Wyoming. In prehistoric times they lived in permanent villages and practised a well-balanced agricultural economy with seasonal buffalo hunts. When they acquired horses in the 18th century, the Crow abandoned their villages for a nomadic life of full-time buffalo-hunting, trading meat for some of the crops of the farmer Hidatsa.

crucifixion A form of capital punishment used by various ancient peoples including the Persians, Carthaginians, and Romans, who usually applied it only to slaves and other persons with no civil rights. The victim, nailed or roped to a crossbar, was hoisted on to an upright to form a 'T' or cross. Six thousand rebels with SPARTACUS were crucified in 71 BC, as was JESUS CHRIST

(in about 30 AD). Romans regarded the cross with horror. Only after Constantine abolished this form of penalty did Christians adopt the cross as a symbol.

Crusades A series of expeditions (11th–14th century) to secure Christian rule over the Muslim-controlled holy places of PALESTINE. (The term is by extension used to describe any religious war or even moral or political movement.) The wealthy powerful orders of KNIGHTS HOSPITALLERS and KNIGHTS TEMPLAR were created by the Crusades. The First Crusade was called by Pope Urban II, and was provoked by the rise to power of the SELJUK Turks, which interfered with traditional PILGRIMAGE to Palestine. The pope promised spiritual benefits to warriors willing to fight under Christian banners. The Crusaders captured JERUSALEM in 1099 and massacred its inhabitants, establishing a kingdom there under GODFREY OF BOUILLON. The Second Crusade (1147–49) succeeded only in souring relations between the Crusader kingdoms, the Byzantines, and friendly Muslim rulers. The Third Crusade (1189–92), prompted by SALADIN's capture of Jerusalem, recaptured Acre but achieved little more. The Fourth (1202–04) was diverted by Venetian interests to Constantinople, which was sacked, making the gulf between Eastern and Western Churches unbridgeable, though some Crusaders benefited from the division of Byzantine territories known as the Latin empire of the East (1204–61). This briefly replaced the Greek empire at Constantinople until MICHAEL VIII retook the city. Later expeditions concentrated on North Africa, but to little purpose. The fall of Acre in 1291 ended the Crusader presence in the Levant. All, except the peaceful Sixth Crusade (1228–29), were marred by greed and brutality: Jews and Christians in Europe were slaughtered by rabble armies on their way to the Holy Land. The papacy was incapable of controlling the immense forces at its disposal. However, the Crusades attracted such leaders as RICHARD I and LOUIS IX, greatly affected European CHIVALRY, and for centuries, its literature. While deepening the hostility between Christianity and Islam, they also stimulated economic and cultural contacts of lasting benefit to European civilization. (See also CHILDREN'S CRUSADE.)

CSCE HELSINKI CONFERENCE.

Ctesiphon An ancient city on the River Tigris, originally established as a military outpost of Parthia. The kings of the Arsacid dynasty of Parthia used it as their winter headquarters, and after nearby Seleucia was destroyed in 165 AD, it became the leading city of Babylonia. When Artaxerxes, son of Papek, established the SASSANIAN EMPIRE in 211–12, Ctesiphon became the capital. It was captured by the Arabs in 636.

Cuba An island country, the largest island in the Caribbean Islands.
Physical. Cuba is long and narrow – about 1,280 km (795 miles) from west to east yet rarely more than 160 km (100 miles) from north to south. Most of it is flat, with plains rising southward to heights seldom greater than 90 m (295 feet), except in the south-east, where the Sierra Maestra reaches 2,000 m (6,560 feet) and more. The climate is tropical, with heavy rain and easterly winds which often become hurricanes.
Economy. The world's second largest producer of sugar, Cuba has a centrally planned economy. Exports have been heavily dependent on sugar (75% in 1975, mainly to

the Soviet Union), though nickel and petroleum products (based on the resale of imported Soviet crude oil) have also been important. Agriculture is highly mechanized, and most farms are co-operatively run on state-owned land. Tobacco is another major crop. Iron, nickel, and manganese are Cuba's main mineral resources. Compared to its neighbours, Cuba has a sizeable industrial sector and high standards of social services. The loss of Soviet aid and trade since the Soviet Union's disintegration in 1991 has had serious consequences on the economy, and social services have suffered.

History. Cuba was first settled by migrating hunter-gatherer-fisher people, the Ciboney from South America, by *c.* 3000 BC. Migrations of agriculturist, pottery-making Arawak Indians from northern South America began to displace them in eastern Cuba after *c.* 1000 BC, but the Ciboney remained in the west. Cuba was discovered by Columbus in 1492 but it was not realized that it was an island until it was circumnavigated in 1508. Spanish settlement began in 1511 when Diego Velásquez founded Havana and several other towns. The Arawak became virtually extinct by the end of the century from exploitation and European-introduced diseases. Black slaves were imported for the plantations (especially sugar and tobacco) from 1526. Britain seized the island in 1762–63 but immediately exchanged it with the Spanish for Florida. Slave importation ended in 1865, but slavery was not abolished until 1886. Various attempts were made by US interests to acquire the island and many Americans fought in the unsuccessful first War of Independence (1868–78). Large US investments were maintained in the sugar industry, which by now was producing one-third of the world's sugar. The second War of Independence (1895–1901) was joined by the USA (1898) after a well-orchestrated press campaign, and Cuba was occupied by US troops (1899–1901). In 1902 the Republic of Cuba was proclaimed. A series of corrupt and socially insensitive governments followed, culminating in the brutal, authoritarian regime of Gerardo Machado (1925–33), which prompted the abortive revolution of 1933–34, the island remaining under US 'protection' until 1934. Fulengio BATISTA was President 1940–44 and 1952–59. Although supported by the USA, his second government was notoriously corrupt and ruthless. In 1956 Fidel CASTRO initiated a guerrilla war which led to the establishment of a socialist regime (1959) under his leadership. He repulsed the invasion by Cuban exiles at Cochinos Bay, the BAY OF PIGS (April 1961), and survived the CUBAN MISSILE CRISIS of October 1962. The accomplishments of his one-party regime in public health, education, and housing are considerable though his record on human rights remains poor. Castro maintained a high profile abroad and although the espousal of world revolution was tempered under pressure from Moscow, Cuban assistance to liberation movements in Latin America and Africa was consistent. At home, after the political turbulence of the 1960s, the revolution stabilized with the establishment of more broadly based representative assemblies at municipal, provincial, and national levels. In economic terms, the initial hopes of diversification and industrialization were not realized, and Cuba continued to rely on the export of sugar as well as on substantial financial subsidy from the Soviet Union. Agricultural production in the socialist state was generally poor, and shortages and rationing continued. Frustrations with the regime led to an exodus of 125,000 Cubans in 1980. Yet the regime survived when COMECON and the Soviet Union collapsed in 1990 and 1991 respectively, and the country found itself faced with a grave economic situation. In October 1991 the fourth Congress of the Communist Party endorsed the policy of centralized control, but an opposition group, the Cuban Democratic Convergence, did emerge. In June 1992 a successful international conference for capital investment was held in Havana, in spite of the continuing US embargo on trade. In 1994 an agreement on asylum seekers was signed between Cuba and the USA, in an attempt to regulate the continuing flow of economic migrants from the island to Florida.

CAPITAL:	Havana
AREA:	110,861 sq km (42,804 sq miles)
POPULATION:	11.117 million (1996)
CURRENCY:	1 Cuban peso = 100 centavos
RELIGIONS:	Non-religious 48.7%; Roman Catholic 39.6%; atheist 6.4%; Protestant 3.3%; Afro-Cuban syncretist 1.6%
ETHNIC GROUPS:	White 66.0%; Mixed 21.9%; Black 12.0%
LANGUAGES:	Spanish (official)
INTERNATIONAL ORGANIZATIONS:	UN; Non-Aligned Movement; suspended member of OAS

Cuban Missile Crisis (1962) An international crisis involving the USA and the Soviet Union. It was precipitated when US leaders learned that Soviet missiles with nuclear warheads capable of hitting the USA were being secretly installed in Cuba. President KENNEDY reinforced the US naval base at Guantanamo, ordered a naval blockade against Soviet military shipments to Cuba, and demanded that the Soviet Union remove its missiles and bases from the island. There seemed a real danger of nuclear war as the rival forces were placed on full alert, and the crisis sharpened as Soviet merchant vessels thought to be carrying missiles approached the island and the blockading US forces. However, the Soviet ships were ordered by KHRUSHCHEV to turn back, and the Soviet Union agreed to US demands to dismantle the rocket bases in return for a US pledge not to attack Cuba. An outcome of the crisis was the establishment of a direct, exclusive line of communication (the 'hot line') to be used in an emergency, between the President of the USA and the leader of the Soviet Union.

Culloden, Battle of (16 April 1746) A battle fought on a bleak moor in Scotland to the east of Inverness between the JACOBITE forces of Charles Edward Stuart and the English and German troops led by the Duke of CUMBERLAND. The Jacobite forces were routed during a sleet storm – a victory of trained professionals over enthusiastic amateurs. The battle was followed by ruthless slaughter of the Jacobite wounded and prisoners, with survivors hunted down and killed, earning Cumberland the nickname 'Butcher'. Culloden ended the FORTY-FIVE rebellion and virtually destroyed the Jacobite cause.

Culpeper's Rebellion (1677) A demonstration of local antagonism to the syndicate of proprietors who administered the new colony of North Carolina. It was brought to a head by attempts to enforce the NAVIGATION ACTS on tobacco and to collect land taxes, and by the example of BACON'S REBELLION in Virginia in 1676. A 'parliament' of 18 proclaimed one of the ringleaders, John Culpeper, governor and he ruled until replaced by a proprietorial nominee in 1679. The factionalism and insubordination of North Carolina continued until 1714, with further rebellions in 1689 and 1711.

Cultural Revolution (1966–76) A decade of chaos and political upheaval in China with its roots in a factional dispute over the future of Chinese socialism. Oblique criticisms of MAO ZEDONG in the early 1960s prompted him to retaliate against this threat to his ideology-led position from more pragmatic and bureaucratic modernizers with ideas closer to the Soviet Union. Unable to do so in the Communist Party, he utilized discontented students and young workers as his RED GUARDS to attack local and central party officials, who were then replaced by his own supporters and often had army backing. LIU SHAOQI, State Chairman of China since 1959 and Mao's heir-apparent, lost all his government and party posts and LIN BIAO became the designated successor. The most violent phase of the Cultural Revolution came to an end with the Ninth Party Congress in 1969, but its radical policies continued until Mao's death in 1976.

Cumberland, William Augustus, Duke of (1721–65) British army commander, second son of GEORGE II. He achieved military success at an early age, was made captain-general of the British army in 1745, and destroyed the Jacobites at CULLODEN in 1746. He was less successful against the French in the SEVEN YEARS WAR, losing the Battle of Hastenbeck in 1757 and agreeing by the Convention of Klosterseven to withdraw his troops from Hanover and Germany. His political influence with George II resulted in the collapse of the PITT-dominated Devonshire ministry in 1757, but his failures on the Continent, the death of his father, and the mistrust of GEORGE III's mother caused his influence to wane after 1760. He was an important focus for the Whig politicians who had been dismissed by George III, but he died soon after their leader, ROCKINGHAM, came into office.

Cunard, Sir Samuel (1787–1865) Canadian ship-owner. He became a successful merchant in Nova Scotia and in 1839, in partnership with George Burns and David MacIver, he successfully bid for a British government subsidy to run a steam mail-packet service between the USA and the UK. With others he established the British and North American Royal Mail Steam Packet Company, later known as the Cunard Line.

cuneiform A script, or rather a family of scripts, developed in the Middle East as a result of using split reeds for writing on soft clay. Incised free-hand signs were turned into groups of impressed triangles (cuneiform means wedge-shaped) by the Sumerians *c.* 2500 BC. Thereafter it was adapted for other languages, including Akkadian and Assyrian. All these were elaborate scripts with signs serving many different purposes; practice tablets and glossaries show that it required long training to write properly. The forms were rigidly maintained, even when inscriptions were carved on stone. About 1500 BC in Persia, alphabets of cuneiform signs were invented, eventually to be replaced by derivatives of the Phoenician alphabet.

Cunningham, Andrew Browne, Viscount Cunningham of Hyndhope (1883–1963) British admiral. At the beginning of World War II he was commander-in-chief in the Mediterranean. Here he was faced with an Italian fleet that was numerically superior to his own. However, he asserted British domination by his air attack on the Italian base of Taranto in 1940, and at Cape Matapan in 1941, where his victory effectually neutralized the Italian fleet for the rest of the war. As First Sea Lord from 1943 he was responsible for naval strategy and attended the meetings of Allied heads of government.

Cunobelinus King of the Belgic Catuvellauni in Britain (*c.* 5–40 AD). He advanced from his capital at Verulamium (St Albans) to take Camulodunum (Colchester) and control of much of south-east Britain. His growing power was seen by Rome as a threat and prompted CALIGULA to contemplate an invasion of Britain. His sons CARATACUS and Togodumnus pursued a policy which prompted Roman invasion in 43. Medieval tradition created the 'Cymbeline' of Shakespeare.

Curragh incident A mutiny at the British military centre on the Curragh plain near Dublin. In 1914 the British commander there, General Sir Arthur Paget, on the instructions of Colonel Seely, the Secretary of State for War, informed his officers that military action might be necessary against private armies in Ulster. Officers with Ulster connections were to be allowed to 'disappear' or resign. Such an action, threatening army discipline, brought about the resignation of many British army officers, as well as of Colonel Seely.

Cursus Honorum The name given to the ladder of (annual) offices which would-be Roman politicians had to climb. After a prescribed period of military service (though this requirement lapsed in the very late republic), or the tenure of certain minor magistracies, the first major rung was the quaestorship, which before SULLA effectively, and after Sulla statutorily, gave membership of the SENATE. Thereafter came praetorship and consulship (though not all achieved these offices), and finally the quinquennial office of censor, the crown of a republican politician's career. Other magistracies, the aedileship and the tribunate of the plebs, might be held between quaestorship and praetorship, but were not obligatory. In the middle and late republic, specific minimum ages and intervals between offices were established by statute. Quaestors, praetors, and consuls were often employed after their year of office at Rome as 'pro-magistrates' to administer the provinces of the Roman empire.

Curtin, John Joseph (1885–1945) Australian statesman. A Labor Member of the House of Representatives (1928–31, 1934–45), he led the Opposition from 1935 until 1941, and was Prime Minister from 1941 until his death. Curtin opposed conscription during World War I, but organized the defence of Australia in World War II, working closely with the USA. He introduced a limited form of conscription for overseas service and helped plan closer co-operation within the British COMMONWEALTH.

Curzon, George Nathaniel, 1st Marquis Curzon of Kedleston (1859–1925) British statesman. As viceroy of India (1899–1905) he achieved reforms in administration, education, and currency, and set up the

North-West Frontier province (1901). He was instrumental in the partitioning of Bengal in 1901, incurring thereby the ill-feeling of the Hindus. A strong supporter of imperialism, he resigned in 1905 in a dispute with KITCHENER. LLOYD GEORGE included him in his coalition war cabinet (1916–18). He became Foreign Secretary in 1919. Lloyd George's tendency to conduct foreign affairs himself irritated Curzon, who joined the Conservative rebellion in 1922 against the coalition government. Bonar LAW became Prime Minister and made Curzon his Foreign Secretary in 1922. As Foreign Secretary he gave his name to the frontier line proposed (1920) by Lloyd George, between Poland and Russia. The broad outline of the frontier became (1939) the boundary between the Soviet and German spheres of occupied Poland. It was imposed (1945) on Poland by the Allies as the definitive frontier between itself and the Soviet Union.

Cush NUBIANS.

Custer, George Armstrong (1839–76) US soldier. He served in most of the AMERICAN CIVIL WAR campaigns, gaining a reputation for personal courage. He personally received the Confederate white flag of truce from General Lee on 9 April 1865. In 1874 he led an expedition to look for gold in South Dakota in an area which had been agreed by treaty as a sacred hunting-ground for the Sioux and Cheyenne. A gold-rush followed and the Native Americans were ordered to move into a reservation by 1 January 1876 or be deemed hostile. In June Custer joined an expedition led by General Alfred Terry to round up such 'hostile' people. Custer went ahead of the main force towards Mount Little Big Horn in South Dakota and decided to attack. Possibly he underestimated the number of Native American warriors mustered – estimated at some 3,500. He occupied a hill position, only to be surrounded. He and his entire force of 266 men were killed.

customs and excise Duties charged on goods (both home-produced and imported) to raise revenue for governments. In England customs date from the reign of EDWARD I, when they were raised on wool and leather. TUNNAGE AND POUNDAGE was introduced under EDWARD II. Impositions, additional duties levied by the monarchy without Parliament's consent, became a source of controversy in the early 17th century. In 1606 Bate's case arose when John Bate, a merchant, challenged JAMES I's right to levy a duty on imported currants. The case was decided in the crown's favour, and CHARLES I continued to raise money from this source and from monopolies, despite opposition; monopolies were abolished by the LONG PARLIAMENT in 1643.

Excise was first introduced in 1643 to finance the parliamentary armies in the ENGLISH CIVIL WAR and was a tax on alcoholic beverages, mainly beer and ale. At the RESTORATION Charles II was granted excise duties for life by Parliament. However, the tax always remained unpopular, as WALPOLE discovered when he attempted to extend it in 1733. In 1799, William PITT (the Younger) introduced income tax to help finance the war effort, and gradually direct tax on income came to represent the main source of revenue for governments rather than indirect taxes on commodities. However, indirect taxes still persist. Customs duties are tariffs paid on goods entering (or occasionally leaving) a country. Excise duties are paid on the domestic sale of certain goods and activities, such as alcohol, tobacco, motor fuel, and betting.

Cuzco A city in Peru. It was established as the INCA capital c. 1200 but from 1438 was largely rebuilt by the emperor Pachacuti. There was an inner city, including the *Huacapata* or Holy Place, palaces, and administrative buildings, the *Sunturhuasi* tower in the square, and the *Coricancha* or Sun Temple. Around this were regularly planned city wards representing all the provinces of the empire. In 1535, after PIZARRO's defeat of the Incas, it was replaced by Lima as the viceregal capital of Peru. Its mountain location was impractical to the Spaniards, who needed a large port city to bring European trade to their colonial possessions. It remained an important provincial governorship, however, and was still sacred to the Incas, who set up a successor state at Vilcabamba in the hills to the north. They tried to recapture it in 1538 and were not finally defeated until 1572.

Cymbeline CUNOBELINUS.

Cynics A sect of ancient Greek philosophers popularly thought to have been established by DIOGENES, though his mentor, Antisthenes of Athens, should perhaps be accorded the title of founder. Since the Cynics were never a formal school, with no fully defined philosophy, considerable differences emerged amongst Diogenes' disciples, who adopted only those ideas which appealed to them. Crates of Thebes was his most faithful follower: he demonstrated how in troubled times happiness was possible for the man who gave up material possessions, kept his needs to an absolute minimum, and maintained his independence.

The Cynic philosophy flourished through the 3rd century BC, and the beggar-philosopher, knapsack on his back and stick in hand, became a familiar sight in Greece. A steady decline thereafter was reversed by a temporary revival in the 1st century AD, though the Cynics' readiness to criticize the conduct of the emperors led to many expulsions from Rome. The last recorded beggar-philosopher lived at the end of the 5th century.

Cyprus An island country in the north-east corner of the Mediterranean, with Turkey to the north and Syria to the east.
Physical. Cyprus is 225 km (140 miles) long and 97 km (60 miles) in breadth at its widest point. The Kyrenia coast on the north has a range of steep limestone mountains along most of its length. South of that is a treeless plain, hot and arid in summer, while further south still are igneous mountains rising to 1,950 m (6,400 feet). Here seasonally heavy rainfall has caused erosion, for winter torrents rush down unchecked. Lack of consistent rainfall is ameliorated by a high water-table which allows the use of wells.
Economy. In the south, exports of manufactured goods such as clothing, and agricultural products, together with the successful development of tourism, contribute to a thriving economy. Vineyards and orchards flourish, and sheep and goats graze the hills. Cyprus (Greek, 'copper') still has some copper, as well as iron pyrites and asbestos. The north, by contrast, is primarily agricultural and is dependent on Turkish aid.
History. A Mycenaean colony in the 14th century BC, it was ruled successively by the Assyrian, Persian, Roman,

and Byzantine empires. RICHARD I of England conquered it in 1191 and sold it to the French Crusader Guy de Lusignan under whom it became a feudal monarchy. An important base for the CRUSADES, it eventually came under the control of Italian trading states, until in 1571 it fell to the OTTOMAN EMPIRE. It remained part of the Ottoman empire until 1879, when it was placed under British administration. It was formally annexed by Britain in 1914 and in 1925 declared a crown colony. From the outset there was rivalry between Greek- and Turkish-speaking communities, the former, the majority, desiring union (ENOSIS) with Greece. After World War II there was much civil violence in which the Greek Cypriot terrorist organization EOKA played the leading role. In 1959 independence within the Commonwealth was granted under the presidency of Archbishop MAKARIOS, but by 1964 the government was in chaos and a United Nations peace-keeping force intervened. In 1974 a Greek Cypriot coup overthrew the president and Turkish forces invaded, gaining virtual control over most of the island. The Greek national government, which had backed the revolt, collapsed. Talks in Geneva between Britain, Turkey, Greece, and the two Cypriot communities failed, and, although Makarios was able to resume the presidency in 1975, the Turkish Federated State of Cyprus was formed in northern Cyprus, comprising some 35% of the island, with its own president. In 1983 it proclaimed itself the Turkish Republic of Northern Cyprus. Britain retained an important RAF base at Akrotiri in the Greek part of the island, which was also a key intelligence centre. In the early 1990s the presidents of the two communities held talks on uniting the island, but no agreement was reached. Tensions between the two communities rose again in 1997. Cyprus has been formally invited to join the European Union early in the new century.

CAPITAL:	Nicosia
AREA:	9,251 sq km (3,572 sq miles); south: 5,896 sq km (2,276 sq miles); north: 3,355 sq km (1,295 sq miles)
POPULATION:	767,000 (combined; 1996) 651,000 (south) 152,000 (north)
CURRENCY:	south: 1 Cyprus pound = 100 cents; north: 1 Turkish lira = 100 kurush
RELIGIONS:	south: predominantly Greek Orthodox; north: predominantly Muslim
ETHNIC GROUPS:	south: Greek 99.2%; north: Turkish 98.7%
LANGUAGES:	south: Greek; north: Turkish (both official)
INTERNATIONAL ORGANIZATIONS:	south: Council of Europe; UN; Commonwealth; Non-Aligned Movement; CSCE; the north is recognized only by Turkey

Cyril, St (c. 827–69) Greek missionary. Educated in the Byzantine court, he and his brother, St Methodius (c. 825–85), were sent to convert the Slavic tribes of Central Europe. Together they began, and Methodius completed, a translation of the liturgy and the Bible into Slavic, adopting what became known as the Cyrillic alphabet, still used in Russia. The introduction of the vernacular in the liturgy aroused opposition, especially from rival Latin missionaries in Bulgaria. This competitive conversion increased the tension between Rome and Constantinople.

Cyrus II (the Great) (d.530 BC) King of Persia (539–530 BC), who founded the ACHAEMENID Persian empire when he overthrew Astyages, King of Media, and took possession of his capital Ecbatana in c. 500. In 546 he defeated CROESUS to take control of Asia Minor and Nabonidus (the last of the Chaldean kings) to add Babylonia, Assyria, Syria, and Palestine to his domains. Further conquests to the north and east created a vast empire. His policies towards his subjects were enlightened and tolerant: the Medians had access to important administrative posts; the Jews were freed from their Babylonian EXILE and allowed to start rebuilding the Temple (their main religious centre) at Jerusalem; and generally he refrained from interfering with native customs and religions. He was probably killed in battle, and was buried at Pasargadae, where his tomb can still be seen.

Cyrus the Younger (d. 401 BC) A Persian prince, son of Darius II, who was given command of Asia Minor in 408 BC. He allied himself with LYSANDER, and supported the Spartans financially, enabling them to defeat the Athenians in the PELOPONNESIAN WAR. When his elder brother, ARTAXERXES II, ascended the throne, he narrowly avoided execution. He then raised an army which included many Greek mercenaries, among them XENOPHON, and marched east to depose his brother, but was defeated and killed at Cunaxa.

Czartoryski, Adam Jerzy, Prince (1770–1861) Polish statesman and nationalist leader. A cousin of the last independent king of POLAND, he worked unfailingly at the restoration of his country when Russia, Prussia, and Austria had partitioned it between them. He became the trusted adviser of the Russian Prince Alexander, who became emperor in 1801. The latter appointed him Russian Foreign Minister (1804–05). After the Battle of LEIPZIG (1813) he sought the re-creation of Poland from the Grand Duchy of Warsaw, formed by Napoleon. In this he was partially successful as the Polish representative at the Congress of VIENNA, which restored the kingdom of Poland, but with the Russian emperor as king. He was proclaimed President of the Provisional Government of Poland at the time of the Polish revolt of 1830–31, for which he was condemned to death but then escaped to Paris. He became known as the 'Polish king in exile' and helped to plan the two unsuccessful Polish rebellions of 1846–49 and 1863.

Czechoslovakia A former country in central Europe, created out of the northern part of the old AUSTRO-HUNGARIAN EMPIRE after its collapse at the end of World War I. It incorporated the Czechs of BOHEMIA-MORAVIA in the west with the Slovaks in the east. Tomáš MASARYK became the republic's first President and BENEŠ its Foreign Minister. Loyalty to the League of Nations, alliances with Yugoslavia and Romania (1921), France (1924), and the Soviet Union (1935) ensured a degree of stability, but danger lay in the national minorities, especially Germans and Hungarians, within its borders. In 1938, deserted by his allies, President Beneš accepted the terms dictated by Hitler in the MUNICH PACT, which deprived the country of the SUDETENLAND and of nearly five million inhabitants. In 1939 Hitler's troops occupied the country. During World War II a provisional government under Beneš was formed in London. After a brief period of restored independence (1945–48) under Beneš, the communists under Klement GOTTWALD and with the backing of the Soviet Union gained control of the government, making Czechoslovakia a satellite of the Soviet Union. In the 'Prague Spring' of 1968 an attempt by DUBČEK and other liberal communist reformers to gain a degree of independence failed as WARSAW PACT armies invaded the country. During the late 1970s and 1980s opposition to totalitarianism found expression in the CHARTER 77 movement. A series of demonstrations organized by students and the Civic Forum movement culminated in November 1989 when workers joined a national strike. President Husák (1913–91) resigned and the Communist Party lost power. Václav HAVEL was elected President of the new Federal Assembly. Both Czech and Slovak National Councils were formed, with equal legislative powers. Transition to a market economy was gradual, but in June 1992 the people of Slovakia, led by their Prime Minister Vladimir Mečiar, voted for national independence and a more centrally controlled economy. In January 1993 the CZECH REPUBLIC and SLOVAKIA formally came into being.

Czech Republic A landlocked country in central Europe, formerly part of CZECHOSLOVAKIA.

Physical. The Czech Republic comprises the historic regions of Bohemia and Moravia. It is bordered on the west by Germany, on the south by Austria, on the east by Slovakia, and on the north and east by Silesian Poland. The country lies in the headwater area of the main European watershed; the Labe–Vlatava (Moldau–Elba) river system flows in the Bohemian basin towards the North Sea, and the Odra (Oder) flows northwards towards the Baltic. Rich alluvial soils alongside river courses are characteristic. The country is rich in mineral springs. The Bohemian highlands form a large elevated basin encircled by mountain ranges that at Sněžka reach an altitude of 1,602 m (5,256 feet). South of the central Sudety (Sudeten) Mountains, which border on Germany, is found the spectacular Moravian karst. A moderate climate prevails.

Economy. The main mineral resources are brown coal, lignite, copper, and zinc, and large gold deposits have been found. Agriculturally, the country is to some extent reliant on imports, although wheat, barley, sugar beet, and hops are grown, and there is an extensive timber industry. Industry is in urgent need of modernization, and is hampered by the need to import energy, as the potential for hydroelectric power has not yet been exploited. Motor vehicles, glass, beer, ceramics, footwear, and textiles are the main exports. The programme of economic reform instituted after the collapse of communism began to bear fruit in the mid-1990s, with an annual growth rate of 5% and the implementation of popular privatization schemes.

History. The Czech Republic came into existence on 1 January 1993: it was, until then, part of Czechoslovakia, but an increasingly strong Slovakian independence movement led to plans to separate the two states. The separation process was set in motion in June 1992 and went so smoothly that it was referred to as the 'velvet divorce'. Václav Havel, formerly President of Czechoslovakia, was elected President of the Czech Republic (1993). The country was admitted into the United Nations in 1993 and in 1996 submitted an application for full membership of the European Union. In 1997 it was formally invited to join NATO.

CAPITAL:	Prague
AREA:	78,864 sq km (30,442 sq miles)
POPULATION:	10.316 million (1996)
CURRENCY:	1 koruna = 100 haléru
RELIGIONS:	Roman Catholic 39.3%; non-religious 39.7%; Protestant 4.1%; Orthodox 0.2%; other 0.5%
ETHNIC GROUPS:	Czech 94.0%; Slovak 4.1%; Hungarian 3.8%; other 1.7%
LANGUAGES:	Czech, Slovak (both official); Hungarian; Romany; other minority languages
INTERNATIONAL ORGANIZATIONS:	UN; CSCE; Council of Europe

D

Dacian wars Campaigns fought by successive Roman emperors over territory corresponding roughly to modern Romania and part of Hungary. The Dacians threatened the lands south of the River Danube which Rome regarded as a natural frontier. Under Emperor Domitian peace was agreed and considerable financial aid given to the Dacians. Then Emperor TRAJAN stopped payments, crossed the Lower Danube, and fought two campaigns 101 AD and 105–06 that were commemorated on Trajan's column in Rome, which is still standing today. Dacia became a Roman province, until Emperor Aurelian abandoned it to the Goths in 270.

da Gama, Vasco (c. 1469–1524) Portuguese navigator and conquistador, the first European to discover a sea route to India. In 1497 he was chosen by the King of Portugal to follow up the discovery made by Bartholomew DIAZ DE NOVAES of a great ocean east of the Cape of Good Hope. He rounded the Cape (1497) and sailed up the east coast of Africa and across the Indian Ocean to the Malabar coast; he returned home in 1499 with a rich cargo of spices. He was given command of a punitive expedition to India in 1502–03, Muslim traders having attacked a Portuguese settlement at Calicut; he bombarded the town before sailing on to Cochin for another cargo of spices. In 1524 he was recalled from retirement to restore Portuguese authority in the east, but fell ill shortly after his arrival at Goa and died at Cochin a few weeks later. Da Gama was instrumental in breaking the monopoly of trade with India and other eastern states which the Muslims had enjoyed, and he succeeded in establishing Portugal as a world power. His exploits were celebrated in the great epic poem, the *Lusiads* (1572), by Luis de Camoëns.

Dahomey A former kingdom in West Africa. In the 16th century the kingdom of Allada, with which the Portuguese had commercial relations, was founded. Two further kingdoms of Abomey and Adjatché (now Porto Novo), were founded c. 1625. These were united by conquest by Ouegbadja of Abomey between 1645 and 1685, and renamed Dahomey. The kingdom had a special notoriety with travellers from Europe for its 'customs': the 'grand customs' on the death of a king, and the biennial 'minor customs', at both of which captured slaves were sacrificed in numbers to provide the deceased king with attendants in the spirit world. Women soldiers were first trained by King Agadja (1708–32). French trading forts were established in the 18th and 19th centuries, but the rulers of Dahomey succeeded in limiting their influence and restricting the slave trade. Under French rule from 1892, it became independent in 1960, and changed its name in 1975 to the Republic of BENIN.

daimyo (Japanese, 'great names') Japan's feudal lords. They expanded their SAMURAI armies during the confusion of the ASHIKAGA period, and territorial disputes between daimyo threatened Japan's unity. A re-allocation of fiefs under HIDEYOSHI had reduced their

power by 1591. The TOKUGAWA controlled much of their activity, although during this SHOGUNATE (1600–1878) the daimyo continued to exercise local control over domains comprising two-thirds of Japan. The new national government at the time of the MEIJI RESTORATION persuaded the daimyo to surrender their titles, powers, and privileges as feudal landowners, compensating them by payment of a portion of their former revenues. This, along with the dismantling of the SAMURAI class of warriors who served the daimyo, helped transform Japan from a feudal to a centralized state.

Dakota The largest division of a Native American group of seven related peoples, commonly known as the Sioux, who inhabit areas of Nebraska, Montana, the woodlands of Minnesota, and the eastern Dakotas on the fringe of the northern Great Plains. During the mid-18th century they lost much of their lands to the OJIBWA. As French and English FUR TRADE increased, so did intertribal warfare, exterminating some tribes and driving others, including the Dakota, on to the plains. They raided the tribes of the Missouri River to the south-east, and also acted as middlemen, exchanging European goods, especially firearms, for corn, tobacco, and other produce. Traditional enemies and trade rivals were the CREE and Ojibwa to the north and east. In common with other PLAINS PEOPLES, the Dakota were nomadic buffalo hunters, who gathered in tribes during the summer, and dispersed into family groups during the winter. Before they acquired horses, buffalo hunting had been ecologically balanced; seasonal migrations were aided by the travois (sledge), pulled by dogs but later adapted for horses, and the tipi (Dakota for 'they dwell'). Over-hunting with horses began to deplete the herds, further exacerbated by White people moving on to tribal lands and systematically devastating the herds.

Daladier, Édouard (1884–1970) French statesman. With Neville CHAMBERLAIN he yielded to Hitler's demands to annex the SUDETENLAND of Czechoslovakia in the MUNICH PACT (1938). He had served as a Radical Socialist in various ministries, was briefly Premier in 1933 and 1934 and again in 1938–40. Arrested by the VICHY government in 1940, he was tried at Riom, together with other democratic leaders, accused of responsibility for France's military disasters. Although acquitted, he remained imprisoned in France and Germany. He was elected to the national assembly (1945–58) during the Fourth Republic.

Dalai Lama (Tibetan, 'Ocean of wisdom and compassion') Title bestowed upon the head of the Yellow Hat monks, the dominant sect in Tibetan BUDDHISM, by the Mongol ruler Altan Khan in 1578. The office was originally purely religious, but the fifth Dalai Lama (1617–82) also assumed authority in secular matters and unified Tibet. The concept of 'lama' (meaning 'none above') is central to the institutions of Tibetan Buddhism. Succession is by incarnation: that is, each monastic leader is regarded as a reincarnation of his predecessor. Years are spent seeking out and teaching each new incumbent. The present, 14th, Dalai Lama, Tenzin Gyatso (1935–), was sworn in in 1940, but was forced into exile in 1959 after the Chinese had annexed Tibet in 1950. His spiritual and political influence remains authoritative for Tibetans, and he was awarded the Nobel Peace Prize in 1989.

Dalhousie, James Ramsay, 1st Marquess of (1812–60) British statesman and colonial administrator. A Conservative Member of Parliament (1837), he became governor-general of India (1848–56), when he oversaw the extension of British rule through the annexation of the Punjab (1849), of Lower Burma (1852), of Oudh (1856), and of several smaller Indian states, through the use of the so-called Doctrine of Lapse. According to this Britain annexed those states where there was no heir who was recognized by Britain. Dalhousie initiated major developments in communications, including the railway (1853), the telegraph and postal system, the opening of the Ganges canal, and in public works and industry. He removed internal trade barriers, promoted social reform through legislation against female infanticide and the suppression of human sacrifice, and fostered the development of a popular educational system in India. He introduced improved training of the Indian civil service, which was opened to all British subjects of any race.

Dalriads SCOTS.

Dampier, William (1652–1715) English explorer and adventurer. After a career as a buccaneer, he returned to England in 1691. The success of his book *A New Voyage round the World* (1697) led to his being sent in command of HMS *Roebuck* on a voyage to Australia, where he made a survey of much of the west coast, which was then unknown. Although a good hydrographer, he proved incompetent in command; his harsh treatment of his men resulted in a mutiny and on his return to England he was court-martialled. In 1703 he joined a privateering expedition to the Pacific, and again his crew mutinied. The voyage is remembered as the occasion on which Alexander Selkirk, the master of one of his ships whose story inspired Daniel Defoe's *Robinson Crusoe*, was marooned at his own request on the uninhabited island of Juan Fernandez off the coast of Chile (in 1704). On a later privateering voyage to the Pacific, Selkirk was rescued after five years of solitary life.

Danby, Thomas Osborne, 1st Earl of (1631–1712) English statesman. He entered Parliament in 1665 as a supporter of the restored CHARLES II. He received rapid promotion, becoming Secretary of the Navy in 1671 and Lord Treasurer in 1673. His reluctant negotiations with LOUIS XIV of France to supply Charles II with money led in 1678 to accusations by Parliament of corruption and he was imprisoned until 1684. In 1688 he signed the invitation to WILLIAM OF ORANGE to come to England, regained royal favour, and became Duke of Leeds in 1694, but following further accusations of corruption he retired from public life after 1695.

Dandolo, Enrico (c. 1108–1205) Member of a Venetian family important in the Middle Ages, and DOGE of VENICE. He established military and naval power by personally directing the Fourth CRUSADE to attack Dalmatia and

sack CONSTANTINOPLE. Under him, Venice was victorious against Pisa, secured important treaties with Armenia and the HOLY ROMAN EMPIRE, and reformed its laws.

Danegeld The tribute paid in silver by ETHELRED II of England to buy peace from the invading Danes. It was raised by a tax levied on land. The first payment (991) was 10,000 pounds in weight of silver (1 pound equals 0.54 kg); later payments were greater — 16,000 pounds (994), 24,000 pounds (1002), 36,000 pounds (1007), and a massive 158,000 pounds (1012). Later (1012–51) it was levied to maintain a navy and the royal bodyguard (housecarls), when it was known as 'heregeld'; when raised by the NORMAN kings the levy was used for general as well as military purposes.

Danelaw The name given to the northern and eastern parts of Anglo-Saxon England settled by the Danes in the late 9th and 10th centuries and where Danish, rather than English, laws and customs applied. The earliest attempt to describe a boundary between these areas was made by King ALFRED and the Danish leader Guthrum (c. 886). The Danelaw was identified as being north and east of a line from the Thames estuary (but not including London), through Hertfordshire and Bedfordshire, then along the River Ouse and the Roman Watling Street to Chester. It was granted legal autonomy by King EDGAR.

D'Annunzio, Gabriele (1863–1938) Italian poet, dramatist, novelist, short-story writer, and military leader. His vast output of writing is of uneven quality; its tenor is generally pagan, evoking the Nietzschean superman-hero, and setting the tone for Mussolini's fascist regime. Among his best works are the autobiographical novel *The Child of Pleasure* (1898) and his collection of poetry *In Praise of Sky, Sea, Earth, and Heroes* (1899). He urged Italy to enter World War I and himself fought with spectacular daring in the air force (1915–18). In 1919 in defiance of the VERSAILLES PEACE SETTLEMENT, he seized the Adriatic port of Fiume (Rijeka), imposing an authoritarian and fascist government on it until, after 15 months, it was starved into surrender.

Danton, Georges Jacques (1759–94) French Revolutionary leader. In 1790 he founded the militant Cordelier Club and took part in JACOBIN debates, where he petitioned for the king's trial and the creation of a republic. Though he was a favourite of the SANSCULOTTES, he was forced to leave France briefly in 1791 but returned to become Minister of Justice. His calmness and authority during the crises of 1792, including his famous call for 'more daring', underlined his growing importance to the Revolution. Nevertheless, his criticism of the massacre of prisoners led to his resignation. He voted for the king's execution in January 1793, was appointed a member of the COMMITTEE OF PUBLIC SAFETY in April, and for three months effectively led the government. His attempts to negotiate and compromise with France's enemies failed and he was not re-elected. His disapproval of the repression of the TERROR and his growing moderation soon brought him into conflict with ROBESPIERRE and led to his execution in April 1794.

Dardanelles (Hellespont) A strait separating Europe from Asiatic Turkey and uniting the Sea of Marmara with the Aegean Sea. It is 76 km (47 miles) long and up to 5 km (3 to 4 miles) wide, with an average depth of 55 m (180 feet). A rapid surface current flows to the Aegean

Sea, more saline waters returning as an undercurrent. The waters contain many kinds of fish, which migrate between the Black and Aegean Seas.

By the 1841 London Convention the straits were closed to all warships in time of peace. The collapse of the Ottoman empire in 1918 permitted the establishment of a new system by the VERSAILLES PEACE SETTLEMENT (1919) under which the straits were placed under an international commission and opened to all vessels (including warships) at all times. This arrangement was modified at Lausanne (1923) to permit the passage of warships of less than 10,000 tonnes in peace-time only and reduce the powers of the Commission. By the Montreux Convention (1936) the International Commission was abolished and control of the straits fully restored to Turkey. The straits were to be closed to all warships in wartime if Turkey was neutral. The Convention remained effective despite attempts by the former Soviet Union to have it revised in its favour. The Dardanelles was the scene of an unsuccessful attack on the Ottoman empire by British and French troops in 1915, with Australian and New Zealand contingents playing a major part (GALLIPOLI CAMPAIGN).

Darius I (the Great) (d. 486 BC) Ruler of Achaemenid Persia from 521 to his death. The first years of his reign were overshadowed by uprisings in various parts of the empire, but after quelling them he embarked on a major task of reorganization. SATRAPS were established to rule the various provinces, though he allowed considerable local independence. He was tolerant towards the worship of local gods, overhauled the finances of the empire, and built a renowned road system and a palace at PERSEPOLIS.

He conducted various campaigns to secure his frontiers, but was unable to subdue the SCYTHIANS. The revolt of the Ionian Greeks (499–494) was suppressed but attempts to extract revenge on mainland Greece (GREEK–PERSIAN WARS) for assisting the rebels met with disaster: storms scattered the fleet in 492, and the army was defeated in battle at MARATHON in 490.

Dark Ages A term used to describe Europe in the 5th and 6th centuries. Following the collapse of the Roman empire, many Germanic tribes crossed through Italy, Germany, France, Spain, and North Africa, often attacking and destroying towns. Rome was sacked on three successive occasions. Many tribes formed their own kingdoms (for example, Vandals in North Africa; Visigoths in Spain; Ostrogoths and Lombards in northern Italy; FRANKS in France and western Germany; ANGLO-SAXONS in England). The Visigoths helped the Romans defeat the Huns of ATTILA at Châlons in 451. The Ostrogoth THEODORIC ruled in Italy (493–526) as the representative of the BYZANTINE EMPIRE, retaining Rome's administrative system.

The period of the Dark Ages saw cultural and economic decline though in the past this has been exaggerated. The period saw the foundation of Christian monasteries which kept scholarship alive. The 7th and 8th centuries saw relative stability and during the 9th century the encouragement of learning at the courts of CHARLEMAGNE and ALFRED THE GREAT.

Darlan, (Jean Louis Xavier) François (1881–1942) French admiral. He was the virtual creator of the French navy that entered World War II. After he became Minister of Marine in the VICHY GOVERNMENT in 1940 he was regarded by the British as pro-fascist. His secret order to his commanders to scuttle their vessels should the Germans attempt to take them over was not known to the British. When the Allies invaded North Africa in 1942 he was in Algiers, where he began negotiations with the USA. He ordered the Vichy French forces to cease fire and was proclaimed Head of State in French Africa. A month later he was assassinated.

Darling, Sir Ralph (1775–1858) British military commander and colonial administrator. He was the governor of New South Wales from 1825 until 1831. A rigid disciplinarian, he faced many difficulties, largely because of continuing conflict between EMANCIPISTS and EXCLUSIONISTS in the colony. In the controversial Sudds and Thompson affair (1826) Darling's harsh punishment of these two soldiers was by popular opinion held responsible for the death of Sudds. The continued agitation over instances of alleged misgovernment resulted in a British House of Commons select committee of inquiry (1835), which exonerated him.

Darnley, Henry Stuart, Lord (1545–67) Anglo-Scottish aristocrat, second husband of MARY, QUEEN OF SCOTS. After their union in 1565, Mary produced a son, the future James VI of Scotland and JAMES I of England. Mary's reliance on her secretary David RIZZIO (who may have been her lover) led Darnley to murder him. Darnley was subsequently murdered in a conspiracy involving the Earl of BOTHWELL.

Darrow, Clarence Seward (1857–1938) US lawyer. Known as the 'attorney for the damned', in 1894 he defended the railway leader Eugene DEBS for his part in the PULLMAN STRIKE; although he lost, he earned a reputation for taking on controversial cases. This flair for controversy brought him to the verge of bankruptcy (1911), when he was tried, but acquitted, of conspiring to bribe jurors. He defended over 50 people charged with murder, but only once did he lose a client to the executioner. In 1925 he defended the evolutionist biology teacher in the SCOPES TRIAL but lost the case.

dating systems Scientific evidence about the prehistory of the human race and of the Earth rests heavily on the accurate dating of recovered artefacts and rocks. Traditional methods of dating depend on stratigraphic succession – for instance, where a layer with one distinctive kind of artefact overlies another with different kinds – or it can be inferred from a sequence of gradual changes in the artefact. Stylistic comparisons with more securely dated objects can sometimes be made in order to establish a rough guide to age. These methods are now reinforced by several much more precise scientific techniques. Dendrochronology, developed in the 1930s, is based on measurement of growth rings in timber. Radio-carbon dating uses the decay of the radioisotope carbon-14 to date organic material up to 40,000 years old. A similar technique uses the decay of potassium-40 to argon-40 for dating volcanic rocks, and the decay of rubidium-87 to strontium-87 for dating other rocks. Both radio-carbon dating and dendrochronology are absolute dating systems; other methods must be calibrated first. Pottery and burnt flint are dated using thermoluminescence, which measures the light emitted when an object is heated. Electron spin resonance is used to date shells, corals, and tooth enamel. In optical dating, a laser is used to date silt and sediment samples.

Daughters of the American Revolution A US patriotic society. Founded in 1890, it is open to women directly descended from individuals who assisted in establishing American independence. Its stated aims are to perpetuate the spirit of the early patriots and to 'cherish, maintain, and extend the institutions of American freedom'. It encourages education and the study of American history, but it has tended to be conservative on such issues as foreign affairs and civil liberties.

Dauphiné A former province in south-east France. It was conquered by the Romans, Burgundians, and Franks. Once a fief of the HOLY ROMAN EMPIRE, it passed to the kingdom of Arles, and, in 1029 to the counts of D'Albon who, from 1133, took the title of Dauphin of Vienne. By 1282, it had acquired its regional name and it was sold to the future CHARLES V of France in 1346. Thereafter heirs to the French throne assumed the title of dauphin. It acquired a *parlement* in 1453, but was annexed to the crown in 1457 and lost its local privileges, especially during the FRENCH WARS OF RELIGION.

David (d. *c.* 961 BC) Second King of Israel (*c.* 1000–*c.* 961 BC). In the biblical account he appears initially as a harp player at SAUL's court and as the slayer of the Philistine Goliath. As a military commander David became a friend of Saul's son, Jonathan, and married his daughter, provoking the jealousy of Saul, who exiled him. After Saul's death, he ruled the tribe of Judah while Saul's son Ishbosheth ruled the rest of Israel. On Ishbosheth's death, David was chosen as the king of all Israel and his reign marks a change in the fortunes of the Jews from a confederation of tribes to a settled nation. He moved the capital from Hebron to JERUSALEM, which had no previous tribal loyalties and made it the religious centre of the Israelites by bringing the Ark of the Covenant (their most sacred object) with him. He expanded the territories over which he ruled and brought prosperity to Israel. His later years were troubled by rebellions led by his sons and family rivalries at court. He is traditionally regarded as the author of the Psalms, but only a fraction are now thought to be his work.

David I (*c.* 1084–1153) King of Scotland (1124–53) in succession to his brother ALEXANDER I. He had been brought up at the English court of WILLIAM II and HENRY I, whom his sister Matilda later married (1100). His own marriage (1113) gave him the earldom of Huntingdon and thus a right to intervene in English politics. David's English upbringing prompted him to introduce into Scotland Norman institutions of government and feudal tenure and to sponsor new monasteries and bishoprics – measures which led to Scottish resentment and rebellion. His claim to the northern counties of England, which was initially checked by a crushing English victory (Battle of the Standard, 1138), was eventually recognized by HENRY II.

David II (1324–71) King of Scotland (1329–71), the only son of ROBERT I (the Bruce). At the age of four he was married to Joan (1321–62), daughter of EDWARD II of England, and at the age of five he inherited the throne of Scotland. In 1334 he was forced off his throne by Edward BALLIOL, and fled to France; he returned to Scotland in 1341, invaded England, and was captured at the Battle of NEVILLE'S CROSS (1346). His subsequent years of captivity Anglicized him, so that when ultimately freed (1357) he found himself at odds with his people and disliked his heir-presumptive Robert the Steward.

David, St (d. *c.* 601) Patron saint of Wales. According to legend he was born in south-west Wales, the son of St Non and of Sant, a local prince. He is credited with founding 12 monasteries in Wales, the most important being at Mynyw (St David's), where he resided when he became Bishop of Wales. He took a prominent part in the synod of Llandewi-Brevi (*c.* 560) to suppress the PELAGIAN heresy, and supposedly persuaded the 'Synod of Victory' at Caerleon (*c.* 569) to adopt the teachings of St AUGUSTINE OF HIPPO instead.

Davis, Jefferson (1808–89) US statesman and president of the Southern CONFEDERACY (1861–65). He served in the BLACK HAWK WAR before leaving the army in 1835 to become a Mississippi planter. He commanded the Mississippi Rifles in the MEXICAN-AMERICAN WAR. Davis served two terms in the Senate (1847–51, 1857–61) and was Secretary of War in the administration of President PIERCE (1853–57). He left the Senate when Mississippi seceded from the Union, and in 1861 was named provisional President of the Confederacy. A year later he was elected to a six-year term. His aloofness and limited political skill, as well as his interference in military affairs, aroused considerable opposition, but it is doubtful whether any other Confederate leader could have been much more effective in the difficult wartime conditions of the South.

Davitt, Michael (1846–1906) Irish nationalist and land reformer. The son of an Irish farmer who had been evicted from his holding, he opposed the British-imposed land-holding system in Ireland. In 1865 he joined the IRISH REPUBLICAN BROTHERHOOD, a movement committed to the establishment of an independent republic of Ireland. He was sentenced to 15 years' penal servitude in 1870 for smuggling weapons for the FENIANS. Released in 1877, he helped found the Irish Land League in 1879, an organization formed to achieve land reform. With C. S. PARNELL, he sought to protect Irish peasants against evictions and high rents. He was elected a Member of Parliament in 1882 while in gaol, and again in 1892 and 1895. The agitation which he led influenced Gladstone to introduce the 1881 Irish Land Act, guaranteeing fair rents, fixety of tenure, and freedom to sell (the THREE FS) to tenants.

Davout, Louis Nicolas, Duke of Auerstädt (1770–1823) Marshal of France. He was made a general by Napoleon after the Battle of Marengo (1800) and marshal in 1804. One of Napoleon's ablest generals, his third corps played a major part at AUSTERLITZ, Auerstädt, Friedland (1807), and WAGRAM (1809). He was responsible for organizing the army that invaded Russia in 1812. During the HUNDRED DAYS, Davout was Minister of War. After the restoration of Louis XVIII he was deprived of his rank and title, but was reinstated two years later.

Dawes Plan (1924) An arrangement for collecting REPARATIONS from Germany after World War I. Following the collapse of the Deutschmark and the inability of the WEIMAR REPUBLIC to pay reparations, an Allied payments commission chaired by the US financier Charles G. Dawes put forward a plan whereby Germany would pay according to its abilities, on a sliding scale. To avoid a clash with France (which demanded heavy reparations and had occupied the RUHR to ensure collections) the experts evaded the question of determining the grand total of reparations, and scheduled annual payments instead. Germany's failure to meet these led to the Plan's collapse and its replacement by the YOUNG PLAN.

Dead Sea Scrolls A collection of Hebrew and Aramaic manuscripts, the first of which were found in 1947 by shepherds in a cave near the north-western shore of the Dead Sea. They belonged to the library of the Jewish (perhaps Essene) community at nearby Qumran, and were probably hidden shortly before the Roman destruction of 68 AD. The scrolls include fragments of nearly every book of the Hebrew BIBLE; those of special interest include the oldest known manuscript of the book of Isaiah; a commentary on the book of Habakkuk; a manual of teachings and rules of discipline for the community; the Temple Scroll, which lays down in detail how the ideal temple of Jerusalem should be built; and there are also many other biblical, sectarian, and apocryphal writings of varying importance and in varying states of preservation.

Until the discovery of the scrolls, the earliest surviving Hebrew biblical manuscripts dated from the 9th century AD. They are therefore immensely important for scholars of the Old Testament and confirm the care with which the biblical texts were preserved and copied by the Jews.

Deák, Francis (Ferenc) (1803–76) Hungarian statesman. He entered the Hungarian Diet in 1833, becoming the leader of the moderate faction for national emancipation from the AUSTRIAN EMPIRE. In 1848 as Minister of Justice he introduced the reforming Ten Points or 'March Law' which, together with further demands, would have made Hungary all but independent. He was briefly Minister of Justice (April–September 1848) in the independent Ministry of Count Bathyany, but retired as the counter-revolution developed. Five years later he returned to politics and was the architect of the AUSGLEICH of 1867, which gave Hungary internal autonomy within an AUSTRO-HUNGARIAN EMPIRE.

Deakin, Alfred (1856–1919) Australian statesman, lawyer, and journalist. He was a Member of the Victorian Legislative Assembly (1879, 1880–1900), where he held various portfolios, and was active in the AUSTRALIAN FEDERATION MOVEMENT. Deakin was a supporter of a WHITE AUSTRALIA POLICY. In the new federal parliament he was a Protectionist, and then Liberal, Member of the House of Representatives (1901–13). He was Prime Minister (1903–04, 1905–08, 1909–10), and attempted to implement the so-called New Protection based on the concept of a minimum 'fair wage'. New Protection was declared unconstitutional by the Federal High Court, after the defeat of his government by Labor in 1910. Deakin led the Opposition (by then called the Liberals) until his resignation in 1913.

de Almagro, Diego PIZARRO, FRANCISCO.

Debs, Eugene V(ictor) (1855–1926) US labour leader. In 1893 he founded the American Railway Union and led it in a secondary strike on behalf of the Pullman workers in 1894 (PULLMAN STRIKE). The strike was broken by the intervention of federal troops, and Debs was imprisoned in 1895 for conspiracy. Together with Victor Berger, Morris Hillquit, and others, he formed the Socialist Party of America (1901) and stood as its presidential candidate. A leading pacifist, he was briefly imprisoned for his sedition, that is, discouraging recruitment to the US armed services in World War I.

Decatur, Stephen (1779–1820) US naval commander. He was promoted captain following his daring recapture of the frigate *Philadelphia* in the TRIPOLITAN WAR (1801–05). After the WAR OF 1812 he became a national hero by forcing the Bey of Algiers to sign the treaty (1815) that ended US tribute to the Barbary pirates. He was killed in a duel with a suspended naval officer.

Deccan (Sanskrit *dakshin*, 'south') A triangular plateau covering most of peninsular India south of the Narbada River, bounded by the Satpura Range in the north and by the Western and Eastern Ghats on the other two sides. Tilting eastward, from about 900 m to 450 m (3,000 feet to 1,500 feet), it is drained by the Godavari, Krishna, and Cauvery rivers flowing into the Bay of Bengal. The lava beds in the north-west are characterized by water-retaining black soil, and cotton is grown.

Few empire-builders achieved full control over it, although some, notably ASOKA (c. 250 BC), AURANGZEB (late 17th century), and the British (19th century) claimed suzerainty. Between these eras of fragile, externally imposed unity, local dynasties struggled for hegemony, some like the CHOLAS (10th to 13th century AD) successfully dominating parts of the region. While Hindu power was maintained by the VIJAYANAGAR EMPIRE in the south (c. 1347–c. 1565), Muslim dynasties established the BAHMANI kingdom in the north (c. 1347). This later split into five sultanates which in turn fell to MOGUL expansion in the 17th century. Hindu strength was reasserted in the 18th century by various MARATHA clans, but after British victories in the early 19th century, most of the remaining kingdoms, Muslim and Hindu, were absorbed into the EAST INDIA COMPANY's Madras and Bombay presidencies. Survivors, such as Hyderabad, entered into treaty relationships with the British.

Decembrists Members of a Russian revolutionary society, the Northern Society. A group of Russian army officers, influenced by French liberal ideas, combined to lead a revolt against the accession of NICHOLAS I in 1825. Some of their supporters proclaimed their preference for a republic, others for Nicholas's eldest brother Constantine, in the hope that he would be in favour of constitutional reform and modernization. A few Guards regiments in St Petersburg refused to take an oath of allegiance to Nicholas and marched to the Senate House, where they were met by artillery fire. Betrayed by police spies, five of their leaders were executed, and 120 exiled to Siberia. The Decembrists' revolt profoundly affected Russia, leading to increased police terrorism and to the spread of revolutionary societies among the intellectuals.

Declaration of Independence The foundation document of the USA, which proclaimed American separation from Britain and was adopted by the CONTINENTAL CONGRESS on 4 July 1776. Its principal author was Thomas JEFFERSON, who based its arguments on John

LOCKE's ideas of contractual government. Its celebrated preamble declared that all men are created equal and have inalienable rights to life, liberty, and the pursuit of happiness. There followed a detailed list of acts of tyranny committed by George III, his ministers, and Parliament against the American people, similar in tone to those in the English BILL OF RIGHTS (1689). The original document had 56 signatories whose names were initially kept secret for fear of British reprisals in the event of American defeat.

Declarations of Indulgence Four proclamations issued by CHARLES II and JAMES II of England in an attempt to achieve religious toleration. Charles II issued Declarations in 1662 and 1672, stating that the penal laws against Roman Catholics and Protestant dissenters were to be suspended, but protests by Parliament caused both attempts to be abandoned. James II issued similar Declarations in 1687 and 1688, the latter leading to the trial of the Seven Bishops. James II insisted that the Declaration should be read in all churches; a Tory High Churchman, Archbishop Sancroft and six bishops who refused to do so were tried on a charge of seditious libel and were acquitted. The verdict was a popular one and widespread protest and defiance followed during the months leading up to the GLORIOUS REVOLUTION of 1688.

Defence of the Realm Acts (DORA) Legislation (1914, 1915, 1916) by the British Parliament during World War I. Under the Acts government took powers to commandeer factories and directly control all aspects of war production, making it unlawful for war-workers to move elsewhere. Left-wing agitators, especially on Clydeside, were 'deported' to other parts of the country. Strict press censorship was imposed. All Germans had already been interned but war hysteria led tribunals to harass anyone with a German name or connection (for example, the writer D. H. Lawrence) and to imprison or fine pacifists (for example, Bertrand Russell). The Act of May 1915 gave wide powers over the supply and sale of intoxicating liquor, powers which were widely resented but which nevertheless survived the war. An Emergency Powers Act of 1920 confirmed the government's power to issue regulations in times of emergency and in 1939 many such regulations were reintroduced.

de Gasperi, Alcide (1881–1954) Italian statesman. He was elected to the AUSTRO-HUNGARIAN Parliament in 1911, and became Secretary-General of the Italian People's Party (1919–25). From 1929 to 1943 he was given refuge from MUSSOLINI's regime by the Vatican. He played an important part in creating the Christian Democrat Party as a focus for moderate opinion after the fascist era. De Gasperi was Prime Minister from 1945 to 1953, during which time he adopted a strong stand against communism and in favour of European co-operation.

de Gaulle, Charles André Joseph Marie (1890–1970) French general and statesman. He first gained a reputation as a military theorist by arguing the case for the greater mechanization of the French army. When France surrendered in 1940 he fled to Britain, from where he led the FREE FRENCH forces. He was head of the provisional government (1944–46) and provisional President (1945–46), but then retired into private life following disagreement over the constitution adopted by the Fourth Republic. In 1947 he created the Rassemblement du Peuple Français, a party advocating

strong government. Its modest success disappointed de Gaulle, who dissolved it in 1953 and again retired. He re-entered public life in 1958 at the height of the crisis in ALGERIA. The Fourth Republic was dissolved and a new constitution was drawn up to strengthen the power of the President: the Fifth Republic thus came into being, with de Gaulle as President (1959–69). He conceded independence to Algeria and the African colonies. De Gaulle dominated the EUROPEAN ECONOMIC COMMUNITY, excluding Britain from membership. He developed an independent French nuclear deterrent and in 1966 withdrew French support from NATO. His position was shaken by a serious uprising in Paris (May–June 1968) by students discontented by the contrast between the high expenditure on defence and that on education and the social services. They were supported by industrial workers in what became the most sustained strike in France's history. De Gaulle was forced to liberalize the higher education system and make economic concessions to the workers. In 1969, following an adverse national referendum, he resigned from office.

de Klerk, Fredrik Willem (1936–   ) South African statesman. Son of a distinguished Afrikaner family, he was born in Johannesburg and practised law until entering politics in 1972. In 1982 he became Minister of Internal Affairs under President P. W. Botha. At that time he became leader of the National Party of Transvaal and pressed the concept of 'limited power-sharing' between the races. On becoming President in September 1989 he appeared to move steadily towards the position of accepting universal suffrage, while being threatened from the right by conservative and extremist groups, many of whom were clearly influencing his police force. In 1990 he opened discussion with Nelson MANDELA and the AFRICAN NATIONAL CONGRESS, and his government began to dismantle APARTHEID legislation. He established an all-party Convention for a Democratic South Africa (CODESA) and in March 1992 won a referendum to continue the reform process. In 1993 a new (transitional) constitution was adopted, which gave all South African adults the right to vote. De Klerk was awarded the Nobel Peace Prize, jointly with Mandela, in 1993. He served as Second Deputy President of South Africa from 1994, following the country's first multiracial elections, until 1996, when he withdrew his party from the governing coalition. De Klerk stood down as leader of the National Party in 1997.

Delaware A state of the USA situated on the east coast between New Jersey and Maryland. Though discovered by Henry Hudson, its name derives from Lord de la Warr, governor of Virginia in 1610. It was first settled as New Sweden in 1638, but came under English control in 1664. As the three 'Lower Counties' of Pennsylvania, it enjoyed virtual autonomy under the PENN family but in 1776 it achieved independent statehood. It was the first state to ratify the US constitution in 1787.

Delaware A Native American people who lived in the Delaware River valley of eastern Pennsylvania and New Jersey. Contacts with Spanish and Portuguese ships preceded Henry Hudson's arrival in 1609. Dutch settlements at Albany, New York (1614), Burlington, New Jersey (1624), and Fort Amsterdam (Manhattan, 1626) traded European goods for beaver pelts, but open warfare increased towards the middle of the century as more colonists arrived. Peace was officially concluded in

1645, but incidents continued to occur through the 18th century. The tribe was dispersed in the 18th and 19th centuries by the English and Americans.

Delcassé, Théophile (1852–1923) French statesman. As Foreign Minister in six successive governments between 1898 and 1905, he was the principal architect of the pre-1914 European alliances. He was the key figure in negotiations which resulted in the ENTENTE CORDIALE with Britain (1904) and he paved the way for the Triple Entente with Britain and Russia (1907). In 1911 as Minister of Marine he arranged for co-operation between British and French fleets in the event of war. In 1914 he was again Foreign Minister and helped to negotiate the secret Treaty of London (1915), which persuaded Italy to fight on the side of the Allies in World War I by guaranteeing the retention of the Dodecanese Islands.

Delhi The capital of India, situated on the banks of the River Jumna in the north Indian plains. According to legend the city has changed site seven times, and there is archaeological evidence for at least this number of previous strongholds. The earliest evidence belongs to the 6th century BC. In the 1st century BC a 'Raja Dhilu' gave his name to the site. Little is known until the 12th century when Muslim invaders wrested it from the Hindu king PRITHVIRAJ III, but the Tomar Rajputs occupied the site in the 8th century and made it their capital. During the Delhi sultanate era (12th–16th century) it was the capital of a succession of Muslim dynasties (MAMELUKE, KHALJI, TUGHLUQ, SAYYID, and LODI). The first Muslim capital is marked by the Qutb Minar, a carved tower, built by the founder of the Mameluke dynasty, Sultan Qutb ud-Din Aibak. Natural and strategic factors caused movements to new sites, but always within a few miles of the original settlement. In the Mogul era Emperor SHAH JAHAN built the Red Fort Palace and mosque which still dominate walled 'Old Delhi'. Mogul decline led to renewed invasions, notably the sack of Delhi by the Persian king, NADIR SHAH (1739). It was captured by the British in 1803.

Delian League A voluntary alliance formed by the Greek city-states in 478–447 BC to seek revenge for losses suffered during the GREEK–PERSIAN WARS. All members paid tribute in the form of ships or money, the latter being stored on the sacred island of Delos, the League's nominal base. At first, under the leadership of Athens, the League actively sought to drive Persian garrisons out of Europe and to liberate the Greek cities of Asia Minor. At Eurymedon in *c.* 466 a Persian fleet and army were crushed. However, Athens, which had by far the largest navy, had begun to dictate matters in a manner not foreseen by its allies. Thus in *c.* 472 Carystus had been compelled to join the League; and in 465–462 the revolt of Thasos was crushed, its mining and other commercial interests on the mainland taken over by Athens. PERICLES encouraged the conversion of the alliance into the beginnings of the ATHENIAN EMPIRE.

Delors, Jacques (Lucien Jean) (1925–) French socialist politician; president of the EUROPEAN COMMISSION (1984–94). Delors served as French minister of finance during the presidency of François MITTERRAND (1981–84), in which role he was responsible for introducing an austerity programme. During his presidency of the European Commission the MAASTRICHT TREATY (1992) was implemented and ratified by all member countries, and the Uruguay round of the GENERAL AGREEMENT ON TARIFFS AND TRADE negotiations was successfully concluded. His strong advocacy of European financial and political integration brought him into conflict with national leaders of a more sceptical disposition, notably Margaret THATCHER.

Delphi A site on Mount Parnassus in central Greece. It was the seat of the most respected ORACLE of ancient times. Individuals and city-states consulted Pythia, the priestess of Apollo, and her answers were interpreted by a prophet. Delphi endured largely unscathed, from attacks by Persians (480 BC) and Gauls (279), though the Roman emperor NERO removed 500 statues. The oracle survived until closed by THEODOSIUS in 390 AD. Remains of a number of buildings can be seen today, including a temple to Athena, national treasuries, and the *stadion* or running track used for the Pythian Games, a sprinting competition and festival.

demesne In the Middle Ages, the lands retained by a lord under his direct control. The medieval lord, whether a king or VASSAL, needed land to provide food and all other necessities for himself and his own household. Demesnes were the site of his residences which could be manors, palaces, or castles, and possibly all three. Lords with widespread territories would have demesne lands in several areas, especially where there was military threat. The day-to-day running of such estates was carried out by the lord's personal servants. Lords who failed to keep sufficient land in their own hands found themselves in great difficulty when times were troubled.

democracy A system of government in which sovereignty rests with the whole people, who rule either directly or through representatives. In the contemporary world, democracy is closely associated with the idea of choosing governments by periodic free multiparty elections, but in the past it was understood more literally to mean the people gathering together in an assembly to debate political issues and enact laws. As such, it was compared unfavourably to monarchy and aristocracy by most political thinkers, who saw it as unruly and inexpert, and also as impractical in societies bigger than the city-state. The representative system appeared to solve these problems (although it was fiercely criticized by ROUSSEAU, the greatest theorist of democracy). The chief elements of representative democracy are: freedom of speech and expression; periodic free elections to the legislature (the law-giving national assembly), in which all citizens are entitled to vote and to stand for office; the right to form competing parties to contest these elections; a government which is responsible to the legislature, and thereby to some degree responsive to public opinion. Where one or more of these elements is absent, as in the 'People's Democracies', the ONE-PARTY STATES of the communist bloc in the period following World War II, the system is unlikely to be genuinely democratic. Within the representative democracies, the major issue has been whether increased popular participation, through referenda and other such devices, might make these states more democratic in the original sense. There has also been pressure for more democracy at a lower level, particularly in the way that work is organized. The social conditions for stable democratic government have been extensively discussed, with level of economic development apparently the most important single factor: the advanced capitalist societies are nearly all representative democracies, whereas many developing societies (India being a striking exception) have authoritarian governments, despite often laying claim to a democratic structure.

Democratic Party A major political party in the USA. Known in its initial form as the Democratic-Republican Party, it emerged under Thomas JEFFERSON in the 1790s in opposition to the FEDERALIST PARTY, drawing its support from Southern planters and Northern yeoman farmers. In 1828, after a split with the National Republicans (soon called WHIGS) led by John Quincy ADAMS and Henry CLAY, a new Democratic Party was formed under the leadership of Andrew JACKSON and John C. CALHOUN. Its strong organization and popular appeal kept it in power for all but two presidential terms between then and 1860, when it divided over slavery. It only returned as a major national party in the last decades of the 19th century. By then, while retaining the loyalty of the deep South, it was gaining support from the ever expanding West and from the immigrant working classes of the industrialized north-east. In the early 20th century it adopted many of the policies of the PROGRESSIVE MOVEMENT and its candidate for President, Woodrow WILSON, was elected for two terms (1913–21). Although in eclipse in the 1920s, it re-emerged in the years of the Great DEPRESSION, capturing Congress and the presidency: its candidate, Franklin D. ROOSEVELT, is the only President to have been re-elected three times. Since then it has tended to dominate the House of Representatives, and has generally held the Senate as well. Following the CIVIL RIGHTS movement and DESEGREGATION in the 1950s and 1960s it lost much of its support from the DIXIECRAT Southern states, becoming less of a coalition party and more one which favours the working classes of the big cities and the small farmers, as against business and the middle classes. The Democratic presidencies of John F. KENNEDY and Lyndon B. JOHNSON saw fruitful partnership between Congress and President, although the VIETNAM WAR badly divided the Party in 1968. Under the Republican President NIXON it retained control of Congress and won the presidential elections for Jimmy CARTER in 1977. The Democrats lost control of the Senate in 1980, but regained it in 1986 and, despite losing the presidential election of 1988 to the Republican George BUSH, retained majorities within both Houses of Congress. The Democratic candidate Bill CLINTON won presidential elections in late 1992, but in mid-term elections in 1994 the Democrats suffered devastating losses, the Republicans gaining control of both Houses of Congress for the first time since 1954. Nevertheless, in 1996 Clinton became the first Democratic President since F. D. Roosevelt to be re-elected for a second term.

Demosthenes (384–322 BC) The greatest orator produced by ancient ATHENS. In his speeches on public policy he consistently urged the need to resist the encroachments of PHILIP II of Macedonia, and he twice served on embassies to that king. He fought at CHAERONEA in 338, and was a leading figure at Athens until the death of ALEXANDER THE GREAT. After Athens had been defeated by the Macedonians in 322 BC, he committed suicide to avoid execution.

Deng Xiaoping (Teng Hsiao-p'ing) (1904–97) Chinese statesman. He studied with ZHOU ENLAI in France in the early 1920s and spent some time in the Soviet Union before returning to China and working for the communists in Shanghai and Jiangxi. During the wars of 1937–49 he rose to prominence as a political commissar, and afterwards he held the senior party position in south-west China. He moved to Beijing in 1952 and became General Secretary of the Chinese Communist Party in 1956. Following the GREAT LEAP FORWARD, Deng was identified with the pragmatic wing of the CCP. He was discredited during the CULTURAL REVOLUTION and after one rehabilitation suffered again at the hands of the GANG OF FOUR. He re-emerged in 1977 as the real power behind the administration of HUA GUOFENG, and became the most prominent exponent of economic modernization and improved relations with the West. Although effective leader of China, he refrained from taking top party posts, but was for long in control of the armed forces as Chairman of the Central Military Commission. From 1981 his policies were to decentralize economic management and to purge corruption. Yet he was not prepared for the Communist Party of China to lose its monopoly of power, so that when pressures for democratization built up into a massed demonstration in Tiananmen Square in Beijing in June 1989, he ordered in 300,000 troops, and a massacre of an estimated 2600 demonstrators, mainly students, followed. During the early 1990s Deng encouraged rapid economic growth and continued to promote JIANG ZEMIN as his successor, making Jiang President in 1993.

Denikin, Anton Ivanovich (1872–1947) Russian general and counter-revolutionary. The son of a serf, he served the Provisional Government as commander of the WESTERN FRONT in 1917. After the OCTOBER REVOLUTION he assumed command of a 'white' army, the 'Armed Forces of the South', gaining control of a large part of southern Russia. In May 1919 Denikin launched an offensive against Moscow which the RED ARMY repulsed at Orel. He retreated to the Caucasus, where in 1920 his army disintegrated and he fled to France.

Denmark A Scandinavian country in northern Europe, situated between the North and Baltic Seas and comprising most of the peninsula of Jutland together with many islands, the largest of which are Sjaelland (Zealand), Fyn (Funen), Lolland, and Bornholm. Since the 14th century GREENLAND and the Faeroe Islands have been Danish sovereign territories. The northern end of the peninsula has coasts on the Skagerrak and Kattegat channels, while to the south there is a boundary with Schleswig-Holstein in Germany.

Physical. Denmark is a flat and low-lying country, the sea twisting into it at many points and outwash sand forming much of the subsoil. The climate is temperate with abundant rainfall.

Economy. Both industry and agriculture are important in the Danish economy: agricultural products account for about a quarter of exports, with machinery and chemicals taking another third. Engineering, shipbuilding, petroleum-refining, and furniture manufacture are important industries. In the Faeroe Islands and Greenland fishing is the primary economic activity.

History. There was active Danish participation in the VIKING explorations and conquests after *c.* 800. King CANUTE ruled over a great 11th-century empire comprising Denmark, England, Norway, southern Sweden, and parts of Finland. His reign was notable for the spread of Christianity, initially introduced in the 9th century.

After a period of internal disunity, Denmark re-emerged as the leading Scandinavian nation in the 13th century. Civil warfare and constitutional troubles continued, however, until Christopher II (1320–32) made major concessions to the nobles and clergy at the expense of royal authority. His son, Waldemar IV (1340–75), re-established royal power, and his daughter, Margaret I (1387–1412), succeeded in creating the Pan-Scandinavian Union of KALMAR (1397–1523). In 1448 the House of Oldenburg became the ruling dynasty. The 16th-century Protestant Reformation brought a national Lutheran Church, and Christian IV (1588–1648) intervened in the THIRTY YEARS WAR as a champion of Protestantism. A sequence of 17th-century wars with Sweden resulted in Denmark's eclipse as the leading Baltic power. ENLIGHTENMENT ideas reached Denmark in the late 18th century, leading to major land reforms in favour of the peasants.

Denmark supported France during the Napoleonic Wars, and in 1814 was forced to cede Norway to Sweden. In 1849 a new constitution ended absolute monarchy and introduced a more representative form of government under a constitutional monarch. In 1863 Denmark incorporated Schleswig (SCHLESWIG-HOLSTEIN), which its king ruled personally as a duke, but this was opposed by Prussia and Austria, whose troops invaded in 1864. Schleswig was then absorbed into the GERMAN SECOND EMPIRE. After World War I north Schleswig voted to return to Denmark, which had remained neutral during the war. Despite another declaration of neutrality at the start of World War II, the Germans occupied the country from 1940 to 1945 when all Schleswig-Holstein passed to the new German Federal Republic. After World War II Denmark joined NATO and in 1960 the newly formed EUROPEAN FREE TRADE ASSOCIATION. Like Britain, it later joined the European Community (1973), its farming community gaining considerably from membership. A close referendum decision in 1992 rejected the draft MAASTRICHT TREATY but in a subsequent referendum in 1993 the Danes voted to ratify the treaty.

CAPITAL:	Copenhagen
AREA:	43,092 sq km (16,638 sq miles)
POPULATION:	5.244 million (1996)
CURRENCY:	1 krone = 100 øre
RELIGIONS:	Evangelical Lutheran 90.6%; Roman Catholic 0.5%; Jewish 0.1%
ETHNIC GROUPS:	Danish 97.2%; Turkish 0.5%; other Scandinavian 0.4%; British 0.2%; Yugoslav 0.2%
LANGUAGES:	Danish (official); Turkish; other minority languages
INTERNATIONAL ORGANIZATIONS:	UN; NATO; OECD; EU; Council of Europe; CSCE

Depression, the Great (1929–33) The world economic crisis that began in October 1929, when the New York Stock Exchange collapsed in the so-called STOCK MARKET CRASH. As a result US banks began to call in international loans and were unwilling to continue loans to Germany for REPARATIONS and industrial development. In 1931 discussions took place between Germany and Austria for a customs union. In May, the French, who saw this as a first step towards a full union or ANSCHLUSS, withdrew funds from the large bank of Kredit-Anstalt, controlled by the Rothschilds. The bank announced its inability to fulfil its obligations and soon other Austrian and German banks were having to close. Although President HOOVER in the USA negotiated a one-year moratorium on reparations, it was too late. Because Germany had been the main recipient of loans from Britain and the USA, the German collapse was soon felt in other countries. Throughout the USA and Germany members of the public began a 'run on the banks', withdrawing their personal savings, and more and more banks had to close. Farmers could not sell crops, factories and industrial concerns could not borrow and had to close, workers were thrown out of work, retail shops went bankrupt, and governments could not afford to continue unemployment benefits, even where these had been available. In the colonies of the European powers and in Latin America demand for basic commodities collapsed, increasing unemployment, but also stimulating nationalist agitation. Unemployment in Germany rose to six million, in Britain to three million, and in the USA to 14 million, where by 1932 nearly every bank was closed. In Europe, where a process of democratization since World War I had reduced class tensions, the effect everywhere was to foster political extremism. Renewed fears of a BOLSHEVIK uprising produced extreme right-wing, militarist regimes, inspired by fascism, not only in Italy and Germany but throughout the Balkan countries. In 1932 Franklin D. ROOSEVELT was elected President of the USA, and gradually financial confidence there was restored, but not before the THIRD REICH in Germany had established itself as a means for the revitalization of the German economy.

Derby, Edward George Geoffrey Smith Stanley, 14th Earl of (1799–1869) British statesman. Entering Parliament in 1822 as a Whig, he served as Chief Secretary for Ireland (1830–33) and subsequently as Colonial Secretary (1833–34), when he introduced the successful proposals to abolish slavery in the British empire. In the later 1830s he left the Whigs and joined Sir Robert Peel's Conservative government of 1841, but resigned over the repeal of the CORN LAWS. Together with Benjamin DISRAELI he led the Conservative opposition to the succeeding Whig administration. He was Prime Minister in 1852, in 1858–59, and again from 1866 to 1868, when he carried the REFORM ACT of 1867 through Parliament. This act, which redistributed the parliamentary seats and more than doubled the electorate, gave the vote to many working men in the towns.

deregulation The reduction or elimination of specific government regulation of commercial enterprises and public bodies. In the 1970s the NEW RIGHT and others argued that excessive regulation was stifling initiative, preventing the emergence of new suppliers and patterns of service, and denying consumers the benefits of choice and competition. In several Western countries, transport, financial services, and telecommunications were among the many activities deregulated during the

1980s. By the early 1990s, deregulation was an important concomitant of privatization in formerly socialist countries, allowing existing enterprises more freedom, and permitting new enterprises to be set up. Experience in the USA of the deregulation of domestic airlines (1978) and of the savings-and-loans banks (1982) suggests that while diversity and choice may be evident at first, insufficient regulation may lead to savage price-wars and to fraud and, through the resulting collapse of some of the businesses, a 'reconcentration' of the activity in a few hands or even into a private monopoly. In consequence, most governments find it necessary to maintain some degree of regulation of important public services, and of businesses in key sectors of the economy: in Britain one measure to ensure public accountability has been the appointment of ombudsmen to oversee the activities of utilities.

Dermot McMurrough (Diarmuid MacMurragh) (*c.* 1110–71) King of Leinster (1126–71) in Ireland. In 1166, after feuding with his neighbours, he was defeated and banished by the Irish High King. He sought support from HENRY II of England and obtained the aid of Richard de Clare, Earl of Pembroke ('Strongbow'), offering him his daughter in marriage and the succession of Leinster. Dermot regained his kingdom in 1170 and after his death Leinster became an English fief and Henry II began to establish English dominance in Ireland.

Derry LONDONDERRY.

Desai, Morarji (Ranchhodji) (1896–1995) Indian statesman and nationalist leader. He made his reputation as Finance Minister (1946–52) and Chief Minister of Bombay (1952–56), and as Finance Minister in the Central Government (1958–63), overseeing a series of five-year plans for expanding industry, which led to a doubling of industrial output in ten years. After the death of Jawaharlal Nehru, he was a strong contender for the post of Prime Minister, but his austere and autocratic style made him too many enemies within the Congress Party. In 1977 he was the obvious candidate to lead the Janata opposition to Mrs Gandhi and led his party to victory in the election of that year. As Prime Minister (1977–79) his inflexible style handicapped him in dealing with the economic and factional problems which confronted him and he resigned in 1979.

Descartes, René (1596–1650) French mathematician, scientist, and philosopher. He received a Jesuit education before taking his degree in law (1616). From 1617 to 1619 he followed a military career in the armies of the Netherlands and Bavaria. After a period of travelling, he spent some time in Paris and finally settled in the Netherlands (1628), having begun his *Rules for the Direction of the Mind* (published in 1701). He then produced the works which bought him contemporary and posthumous fame: *Discours de la méthode* ('Discourse on Method', 1637), *Meditationes de Prima Philosophia* ('Meditations on First Philosophy', 1641), and *Principia Philosophiae* ('Principles of Philosophy', 1644). His views exposed him to persecution by the theologians, and he accepted Queen CHRISTINA's invitation to take refuge in Sweden, where he died.

According to Descartes' philosophy all the sciences, being interconnected, must be studied together, and by a single process designed to pursue certainty about the nature of knowledge – the Method of Doubt. This works by suspending judgement on any belief until it can be shown to be systematically derived from more certain beliefs. The aim of the Method is to reach a belief which cannot be doubted, and then to build up knowledge from that basis. In this way scepticism can be refuted. In *Discours de la méthode*, he claimed that the a priori belief in his own existence, *Cogito ergo sum* ('I think therefore I am'), was immune to doubt and could, therefore, serve as the basic belief. On this basis he came to hold a dualist philosophy of mind; believing the essence of the 'I' to be thinking, and of the physical body to be extension. He advanced mathematics by his development of analytical geometry through his invention of 'Cartesian co-ordinates' (which enabled geometrical properties to be represented numerically). In optics, he discovered the law of refraction. Descartes' influence has been profound and can be traced in the works of rationalists, empiricists, materialists, and even of philosophers who rejected his doctrines but benefited from his general intellectual rigour.

René Descartes *His philosophical rigour and courage in challenging accepted ways of thought, as well as his scientific and mathematical work, made Descartes one of the most influential thinkers of his age and a forefather of the Enlightenment in Europe.*

desegregation In the USA, the movement to end discrimination against its Black citizens. Many segregation laws were passed in the Southern states after the AMERICAN CIVIL WAR, and they were supported by a Supreme Court decision in 1896 which accepted as constitutional a Louisiana law requiring separate but equal facilities for White and Black people in trains. For the next 50 years, many Southern states continued to use the 'separate but equal' rule as an excuse for requiring segregated facilities. With the founding of the National Association for the Advancement of Colored People (NAACP) in 1909 Black and White Americans began making efforts to end segregation, but they met with fierce resistance from state authorities and White organizations, especially in the South. When World War II saw over one million Black people in active military service change was inevitable, and in 1948 President Truman issued a directive calling for an end to segregation in the forces. It was only with the CIVIL RIGHTS movement of the 1950s and 1960s that real social reforms were made. The Supreme Court decision in 1954 against segregation in state schools (BROWN V. BOARD OF EDUCATION OF TOPEKA) was a landmark. The efforts of Martin Luther KING, the FREEDOM RIDERS, and others ended segregation and led to the passing of the Civil Rights Act of 1964 and the Voting Rights Act of 1965, which effectively outlawed legal segregation and ended literacy tests. There were still Black ghettos in the northern cities, but the purely legal obstacles to the equality of the races were now essentially removed.

Desert cultures Early post-glacial groups of hunter-gatherers in the south-western USA and MEXICO from c. 8000 BC. They lived mostly on vegetables, and digging sticks and grinders are common among the archaeological finds. Spears were used for hunting. The spread of maize cultivation gave rise to the BASKET-MAKERS. Agriculture started in Mexico soon after 3500 BC, reaching some areas of the south-western USA around the beginning of the Christian era, but in others the Desert cultures continued into the 19th century.

Desmoulins, Camille (1760–94) French journalist and Revolutionary. He became an advocate in the Paris *parlement* in 1785, and four years later, after the dismissal of NECKER, he summoned the crowd outside the Palais Royal 'to arms'. On 14 July, the mob stormed the BASTILLE. Soon afterwards he began to publish his famous journal *Les Révolutions de France et de Brabant*, attacking the ANCIEN RÉGIME. He married Lucile Duplessis in 1790 and began a close association with DANTON. He voted for the execution of LOUIS XVI and campaigned against the GIRONDINS and BRISSOT. His support of Danton's policies of clemency angered ROBESPIERRE and led to his arrest and execution on 5 April 1794. A week later his wife followed him to the guillotine.

De Soto, Hernando (c. 1500–42) Spanish CONQUISTADOR and explorer. De Soto took part in the conquest of Central America, before joining Francisco Pizzaro's expedition in Peru; he returned to Spain when the Inca King Atahualpa, whom he had befriended, was executed by Pizarro. De Soto was then made governor of Cuba by Emperor CHARLES V, with the right to conquer the mainland of America. He landed on the Florida coast in 1539 and reached North Carolina before crossing the Appalachian Mountains and returning through Tennessee and Alabama. In 1541 he led another expedition, crossing the Mississippi (which he was probably the first White man to see) and going up the Arkansas River into Oklahoma. They were seeking gold, silver, and other treasure, but returned disappointed. De Soto died on reaching the banks of the Mississippi.

Despenser, Hugh le, Earl of Winchester (the Elder) (1262–1326) English aristocrat. He was loyal to EDWARD I and a favourite of EDWARD II. In 1321 he and his son, Hugh le Despenser (the Younger) were attacked in Parliament for their allegedly evil counselling of the king and were disinherited and exiled from the realm. These sentences were annulled in the following year, but when Edward was murdered in 1326 both the Despensers were captured and hanged.

Dessalines, Jean Jacques (1758–1806) Black emperor of Haiti. A former slave, he served under TOUSSAINT L'OUVERTURE in the wars that liberated Haiti from France. Although illiterate, he had a declaration of independence written in his name in 1804. With the defeat of the French in a war of extermination he became governor-general of Haiti, and in late 1804 had himself crowned Emperor Jacques I. The ferocity of his rule precipitated a revolt of mulattos in 1805. Dessalines was killed while trying to put down this rebellion in 1806.

Destroyer-Bases Deal (1940) A World War II agreement between F. D. Roosevelt and Churchill. Known as the Destroyer Transfer Agreement, it ensured the US transfer to Britain of 50 much-needed destroyers in exchange for leases of bases in British possessions in the West Indies, Newfoundland, and British Guiana. Being of World War I design, the destroyers became surplus to British requirements during the war, but in the early and critical stage of World War II they were an invaluable supplement to available escort vessels.

détente (French, 'relaxation') The easing of strained relations, especially between states. It was first employed in this sense in 1908. The word is particularly associated with the 'thaw' in the COLD WAR in the early 1970s and the policies of Richard NIXON as President and Henry KISSINGER as National Security Adviser (1969–75) and Secretary of State (1973–77). The more relaxed relations were marked by the holding of the Conference on Security and Co-operation in Europe in Helsinki (see HELSINKI CONFERENCE) in 1972–75; the signing of the Salt I Treaty (STRATEGIC ARMS LIMITATION TALKS) in 1973; and the improvement in West Germany's relations with the countries of Eastern Europe, particularly East Germany, following Chancellor Willy Brandt's OSTPOLITIK. Before the end of the Cold War, while points of conflict still remained, détente was a way of managing superpower relations at a time when the nuclear capabilities of both sides posed a threat to world peace.

Dettingen, Battle of (27 June 1743) An important victory for the British over the French in the War of the AUSTRIAN SUCCESSION. GEORGE II at the head of 40,000 British, Hanoverian, and Austrian troops marched from the Austrian Netherlands to the banks of the River Main. He was attacked by a larger French army under Noailles, but forced them back across the Main and finally across the River Rhine. George II was the last reigning British sovereign to take command on the battlefield.

de Valera, Eamon (1882–1975) Irish statesman. As a young man he devoted himself to securing independence for Ireland from Britain. He was imprisoned for his part in the EASTER RISING (1916) and would have been executed but for his US birth. After escaping from Lincoln gaol in 1919 he was active in the guerrilla fighting of 1919–21 as a member of the IRISH REPUBLICAN ARMY. Elected as a SINN FEIN Member of Parliament, he became president of the independent government (Dáil Éireann) set up by Sinn Fein in 1919. He did not attend the negotiations in London leading to the Anglo-Irish Treaty of 1921, and repudiated its concept of an IRISH FREE STATE from which six Ulster counties were to be excluded. The leading opponent of COSGRAVE between 1924 and 1932, he founded FÍANNA FÁIL in 1926, leading his party to victory in the 1932 election. He was president of the Executive Council of the Irish Free State from 1932 to 1937. He ended the oath of allegiance to the British crown and devised a new constitution in 1937, categorizing his country as 'a sovereign independent democratic state'. He stopped the payment of annuities to Britain and negotiated the return of naval bases held by Britain under the 1921 treaty. De Valera continued to have popular support and was twice elected President of the Republic of Ireland. His last presidency (until 1973) took him into his 90th year.

developing country (less developed country or underdeveloped country) An imprecise term used to describe the poorer countries of the world. One definition offered by the WORLD BANK includes all countries in the low or middle income group, that is with GNP per capita of less than $6,000 in 1988. Like the terms THIRD WORLD and South (see NORTH–SOUTH RELATIONS), it is applied to those countries whose economies are not fully modernized (nor centrally planned) and thus includes Latin America, Africa, and most of Asia, as well as a few countries in Europe. Despite diversities, most of these countries had many common economic, political, and social characteristics in the early years after World War II, while also sharing a colonial past. They have generally acted as a bloc in international politics, especially in the UN, to demand radical changes in the international economic order, in which they are seen to operate at a serious disadvantage. However, in the last 40 years there have been considerable differences in development experience, so it is less legitimate to classify these countries into a single group. The growing differences between economies in the developing country category, with some like the prosperous NEWLY INDUSTRIALIZING COUNTRIES (NICs) becoming richer and others, like Bangladesh or Somalia (sometimes termed the 'least developed countries'), having stagnant or even falling incomes, make it an inadequate term. Yet it remains a useful label to apply to those countries who lag behind the developed world in terms of economic development, technology, and social and political structures, and which, for the most part, face common problems while undergoing structural change and adjustment in the course of development.

Devolution, War of An attempt by LOUIS XIV of France to seize the Spanish Netherlands. In 1665, on the death of his father-in-law, Philip IV of Spain, he invoked dubious laws based on local customs by which a child of a first wife (as was his queen Maria Theresa) inherited titles and territory, rather than the son of a second wife. A campaign under TURENNE alarmed Europe, a defensive Triple Alliance was formed by the United Provinces, England, and Sweden to check the French

advance, and Louis made peace. He restored most of his conquests, hoping to obtain part of the Spanish empire peacefully on the death of Charles II.

Dewey, George (1837–1917) US admiral. He served in the Union (Northern) navy under Farragut during the AMERICAN CIVIL WAR. He was granted naval command of the Pacific (1897). His victory over the Spanish fleet at MANILA BAY on 1 May 1898 was not only decisive for the outcome of the SPANISH-AMERICAN WAR but also for the future of US imperialism in the Pacific. In 1899 he made a triumphal progress through New York and was created the first ever US admiral.

Diane de Poitiers, duchesse de Valentinois (1499–1566) Mistress of HENRY II of France. She came to court during the reign of Francis I (1515–47) and Prince Henry, 20 years her junior, fell passionately in love with her. On his accession she became queen in all but name displacing Henry's wife, Catherine de Medici. A beautiful and cultured woman, she was friend and patron of poets and artists. She played little part in politics, contenting herself with augmenting her income and providing for her family. On Henry's death (1559) Catherine forced her to surrender the crown jewels and banished her to Chaumont.

diaspora (from the Greek, 'dispersion') The collective term for Jewish communities outside Israel itself. The process began with Assyrian and Babylonian expulsions in 721 and 597 BC, was continued by voluntary migration, and accelerated by the Roman destruction of the Temple in Jerusalem in 70 AD. By the 1st century AD there were Jewish communities from the Levant to Italy, notably in Babylon and Egypt. The diaspora Jews of the Graeco-Roman world were mostly Greek-speaking but remained loyal to their faith, visited Jerusalem, and regarded Israel as their homeland. The existence of these diaspora communities was also an important factor in the spread of Christianity.

By the early Middle Ages Spain was the main centre of Jewish scholarship, which it remained until the INQUISITION expelled all Jews in 1492. Distinguished Jewish scholars were also found in France and Germany, but from the time of the Crusaders, ANTI-SEMITISM began to develop, many cities confining Jews to particular quarters or ghettos. At first Poland and Lithuania welcomed Jewish victims of persecution, and by the 17th century Eastern Europe had become the diaspora's centre of gravity until the pogroms of the 1880s drove many westwards, via Germany and Britain, to the USA. Some Jews interpret diaspora as exile, others as a positive aspect of Judaism's spiritual destiny.

Díaz, Porfirio (1830–1915) Mexican dictator of part-Indian descent. As President of Mexico he remained in control of his country for nearly 35 years (1877–80, 1884–1911). He began his military career by supporting JUÁREZ and the liberals during Mexico's War of Reform (1858–61) and during the fight against the French intervention in 1862. Responsible for the economic development and modernization of his country, he ruled in the interests of the privileged minority. The mineral resources of Mexico were largely exploited by foreigners, the PEONS, or indebted labourers, lost most of their communal land, and much of the rural population was bound to debt slavery. The harsh dictatorship which he initiated prompted the MEXICAN REVOLUTION of 1910 and led to civil war (1911–18).

Diaz de Novaes, Bartholomew (c. 1455–1500) Portuguese explorer who led the first European expedition (1488) to round the Cape of Good Hope, thus opening the sea route to Asia via the Atlantic and Indian Oceans. On a voyage surveying the West African coast he had sailed to latitude 26° S, off Namibia, when his ships were caught in a storm and swept further south for 13 days. His landfall (1488) was near the southernmost tip of Africa: coasting eastwards, he found that the land turned north. He is attributed with having named it variously as the Cape of Storms and the Cape of Good Hope; he perished just off the Cape in 1500, on a later voyage during which Brazil had been discovered.

Diderot, Denis (1713–84) French encyclopedist, novelist, critic, and dramatist. He worked initially as a teacher and writer, but his criticisms of the French ANCIEN RÉGIME political and administrative systems led to a short prison sentence (1749). In 1745 Diderot began work, in association with the scientist Jean Le Rond d'Alembert, on what was originally conceived of as a translation of Ephraim Chambers's *Cyclopaedia* (1728). The project grew, however, into the great *Encyclopédie, ou dictionnaire raisonné des sciences, des arts et des métiers* (1751–72), a lavishly illustrated review, in the broadest sense, of the science and technology of that period; its aim was the application of reason to all matters of human interest. Other works included his *Salons* (accounts of exhibitions of contemporary art), which inaugurated the genre of art criticism. He also wrote two plays, *Le Fils naturel* (1757) and *Le Père de famille* (1758), illustrating his concept of a new theatrical genre called *drame bourgeois* or serious comedy. These have little artistic merit, though his theories exercised some influence on other writers, including Beaumarchais. Diderot wrote two prose tales, *La Religieuse* and *Jacques le fataliste*, and an imaginary dialogue entitled *Le Neveu de Rameau*, which were published posthumously. He derived his ideas from natural science: he became an atheist, advocated a materialist philosophy, and attempted to found morality on reason. Like ROUSSEAU, he held that man, born good, was corrupted by society.

Diefenbaker, John George (1895–1979) Canadian statesman. He served as leader of the Progressive CONSERVATIVE PARTY (1956–67) and Prime Minister of Canada (1957–63). He introduced some important measures of social reform and sought to encourage economic development, but as Canada experienced increasing economic difficulties in the early 1960s he was forced to devalue the Canadian dollar. In foreign affairs he wished to reduce Canada's dependence on the USA, but his party lost the election of 1963 when he took issue with the USA over the arming with atomic warheads of missiles supplied to Canada.

Dienbienphu (1954) The decisive military engagement in the FRENCH INDO-CHINA WAR. In an attempt to defeat the VIETMINH guerrilla forces, French airborne troops seized and fortified the village of Dienbienphu overlooking the strategic route between Hanoi and the Laotian border in November 1953. Contrary to expectations, the Vietnamese commander General GIAP

was able to establish an effective siege with Chinese-supplied heavy artillery, denying the garrison of 16,500 men supply by air, and subjecting it to eight weeks of constant bombardment between March and May 1954, which finally forced its surrender. The ensuing armistice ended French rule in Indo-China within two months.

Dieppe raid (18–19 August 1942) An amphibious raid by the Allies on Dieppe, Normandy, in World War II. Its aim was to destroy the German port, airfield, and radar installations and to gain experience in amphibious operations. Some 1,000 British commando and 5,000 Canadian infantry troops were involved. There was considerable confusion as landing-craft approached the two landing beaches, where they met heavy fire. The assault was a failure and the order to withdraw was given. Not only were over two-thirds of the troops lost, but German shore guns sank one destroyer and 33 landing-craft, and shot down 106 aircraft. Although in itself a disaster, the raid taught many lessons for later landings in North Africa and Italy, and the NORMANDY LANDINGS of June 1944 – not least the need for careful planning.

Diet (from the medieval Latin, 'a meeting for a single day') A meeting of estates or representatives, or even a legislative assembly. The representatives of the German States in the Holy Roman Empire (and the Emperor) met at the Imperial Diet (Reichstag) until 1806. Important meetings took place at Augsburg (1500), Constance (1507), and Frankfurt (1518) between the princes and MAXIMILIAN I, attempting to reform the empire. The most famous was that of WORMS (1521), dealing with the confrontation of Martin LUTHER and CHARLES V. As the princes used Lutheranism to challenge Charles V's authority, further diets discussed religion. At Speier, a solution offering religious tolerance was submitted in 1526, and a strict Catholic alternative in 1529. The two sides further defined their terms at AUGSBURG in 1530, and a last attempt at conciliation was made at Regensberg in 1541. Further meetings at Augsburg in 1547–8 and 1555 brought religious settlement. Another important meeting, at Regensburg, in 1732, saw the princes accept the PRAGMATIC SANCTION. The GERMAN CONFEDERATION established a federal Diet in Frankfurt with Austria holding a casting vote. Other parliamentary bodies, including those of Hungary, Bohemia, Poland, and the Scandinavian countries, have also been called Diets, as is the current Japanese legislative assembly.

Digby, Sir Kenelm (1603–65) English diplomat and writer. He was the son of Sir Everard Digby, executed as a traitor for his involvement in the GUNPOWDER PLOT. He led a successful privateering expedition in the Mediterranean and Adriatic (1628). Thereafter he supported LAUD and from 1636 worked to achieve toleration for Catholics in England. He was imprisoned by Parliament, then banished, but in the 1650s undertook diplomatic missions in Europe for CROMWELL. An amateur scientist, he was one of the first members of the ROYAL SOCIETY.

Diggers A radical group that flourished briefly in 1649–50, when England's political future was uncertain. Led by Gerrard WINSTANLEY, the Diggers began seizing common land and sharing it out. They called themselves the True Levellers, but were opposed and denounced by the LEVELLERS, who disliked their communistic attitude towards property. Although they themselves rejected the use of force, their settlements in Surrey were dispersed by the authorities in March 1650.

Dimitrov, Georgi (1882–1949) Bulgarian communist leader. From 1929 he was head of the Bulgarian sector of the COMINTERN in Berlin. When the REICHSTAG was burned (1933) he was accused with other communists of complicity. His powerful defence at his trial forced the Nazis to release him and he settled in Moscow. In 1945 he was appointed head of the communist government in BULGARIA which led to the setting up of the Bulgarian People's Republic (1946) under his premiership, a period marked by ruthless Sovietization.

Dingaan (d. 1843) Zulu king (1828–40). He was half-brother to SHAKA, whom he murdered. At first friendly to European settlers, missionaries, and the VOORTREKKERS, he treacherously killed their leader Piet Retief and his followers. He attacked a White settlement near what is now Durban, but was defeated (1838) at the Battle of BLOOD RIVER. He then fled, and was succeeded in 1840 by his brother Mpande. Driven into SWAZILAND, he was assassinated there three years later.

Dingiswayo (d. 1817) Founder of the ZULU KINGDOM. In 1807 he became chief of the Mthethwa in the present northern NATAL. By conquering neighbouring NGUNI peoples he made himself paramount over all surrounding groups and established a rudimentary military state, developing trade with Mozambique. He had already designated SHAKA as his successor when he was assassinated by Zwide, chief of the Ndurande clan of the Zulu, in a rebellion against his rule.

Diocletian (Gaius Aurelius Valerius Diocletianus) (245–316 AD) Roman emperor (284–305). Born in humble circumstances in Dalmatia, he joined the Roman army, rose to become commander of the imperial household troops, and was acclaimed emperor by the army at Nicomedia in 284. His accession restored order after a long and chaotic period of short-lived emperors. He campaigned vigorously and successfully to protect the empire's collapsing frontiers and to repress internal rebellions, most notably in Britain and Egypt. He effected far-reaching and lasting military, financial, and administrative reforms. He established the so-called 'Tetrarchy': himself the 'Augustus', or emperor, in the East with Galerius as his 'Caesar', or deputy, he appointed Maximian as 'Augustus' of the Western Empire with Constantius Chlorus as his 'Caesar'. From 303 he ordered the systematic persecution of the Christians. He abdicated in 305, and apart from a brief re-emergence in 308 lived until his death in 316 in a splendid palace at Salonae (Split, now in Croatia), much of which survives. He provided the solid base from which Constantius and CONSTANTINE were to continue to restore the empire's fortunes and for most of the 4th century his system of appointing more than one emperor held firm.

Diogenes (c. 400–325 BC) Greek philosopher, popularly credited with being the founder of the CYNICS. He came to Athens, where he lived as a pauper and flouted conventional behaviour. He believed that an individual needed only to satisfy his natural needs in the simplest manner possible to be happy. His apparent

shamelessness led to his nickname 'the dog' (Greek *kuōn*, hence 'Cynic'). He is said to have lived in a barrel. His debt to Antisthenes of Athens, himself a devoted disciple of SOCRATES, was considerable, and many of the details of his particular philosophy are uncertain.

Diponegoro (or Dipanagara) (1785–1855) Javanese prince, leader of the JAVA WAR (1825–30) against the Dutch. This struggle gained the support of central Javanese society, many of whom saw the prince as a latter-day messiah, a Javanese 'Just King' (*Ratu Adil*), who would liberate Java from foreign influence. Fired by a mixture of Javanese mysticism and Islam, Diponegoro demanded recognition from the Dutch as protector of Islam in Java, but successful Dutch military tactics, in particular their use of mobile columns and fortified outposts (*bèntèng*), eventually forced him to the conference table, where he was treacherously arrested and exiled.

Directory, French (1795–99) The government of France in the difficult years between the JACOBIN dictatorship and the Consulate. It was composed of two legislative houses, a Council of Five Hundred and a Council of Ancients, and an executive (elected by the councils) of five Directors. It was dominated by moderates and sought to stabilize the country by overcoming the economic and financial problems at home and ending the war abroad. In 1796 it introduced measures to combat inflation and the monetary crisis, but popular distress increased and opposition grew as the Jacobins reassembled. A conspiracy, led by François BABEUF, was successfully crushed but it persuaded the Directory to seek support from the royalists. In the elections the next year, supported by NAPOLEON, it decided to resort to force.

This second Directory implemented an authoritarian domestic policy ('Directorial Terror'), which for a time established relative stability as financial and fiscal reforms met with some success. By 1798, however, economic difficulties in agriculture and industry led to renewed opposition which, after the defeats abroad in 1799, became a crisis. The Directors, fearing a foreign invasion and a Jacobin coup, turned to Napoleon who took this opportunity to seize power.

disarmament A policy aimed at the banning of armaments, or their reduction to the lowest level possible. It is different from arms control, which seeks to manage the ARMS RACE by maintaining a balance between the capabilities of both sides. Disarmament, on the other hand, envisages a dramatic reduction in arms in order to achieve peace. Attempts to achieve disarmament by international agreement began before World War I and in 1932 there was a World Disarmament Conference. In 1952 a permanent United Nations Disarmament Commission was established in Geneva. National disarmament pressure groups have tended to seek unilateral disarmament, for example the CAMPAIGN FOR NUCLEAR DISARMAMENT. Bilateral agreements are negotiated between two governments, while multilateral agreements are sought via international conferences or the UN Commission. Important arms limitation talks include the STRATEGIC ARMS LIMITATION TALKS and the STRATEGIC ARMS REDUCTION TALKS. Disarmament may also only apply to certain categories of weapons (as in the 1972 Convention on Biological Weapons) or geographical areas (as in the Antarctic

Treaty of 1959, banning the emplacement of nuclear weapons in Antarctica). Proponents of disarmament argue that the manufacture and maintenance of weapons consume vast resources, cause instabilities, and, given the sheer quantity of weaponry, create the risk of accidental war. On the other hand, it is argued that the build-up of weapons is a symptom of conflict and not a cause of it, and that stability is better achieved through a balance of arms. It tends to be in the interest of those who have power and resources to propose disarmament.

disciples The original followers of JESUS CHRIST. In the Jewish society of Jesus' time many religious teachers attracted disciples (pupils and learners) who came to be taught their master's interpretation of scriptures. Jesus' followers differed from such groups in several respects. For example, he actively sought out disciples and found many of them among people judged socially or morally as outcasts. The Apostles were the 12 chief disciples: PETER (the leader), Andrew, James, John, Philip, Bartholomew, Thomas, Matthew, James (the Less), Thaddeus, Simon, and Judas Iscariot. After the suicide of Judas, who betrayed Jesus, his place was taken by Matthias. PAUL and his original companion Barnabas are also considered as Apostles.

disease, communicable (contagious disease, infectious disease) An infection which can be transmitted from person to person.

At the beginning of the 19th century the belief that communicable diseases were caused by 'miasmata', poisonous vapours given off by sewage and rubbish, led to campaigns to improve public health by supplying clean water and drainage systems. In Britain this resulted in the Public Health Act (1848) drawn up by Edwin CHADWICK, in the same year that the London doctor, John Snow, showed that cholera was carried by dirty water. In the latter half of the 19th century, Louis Pasteur, Heinrich Koch, and others began to identify the micro-organisms that caused infectious diseases and this led to further research into their prevention and cure. Vaccination against smallpox, first described by Edward Jenner in 1798, resulted in its global eradication by 1979. In the 20th century drugs were developed that could cure many infectious diseases. In 1910 Paul Ehrlich introduced salvarsan, the first effective cure for syphilis and, following the development of sulphonamides in the 1930s and antibiotics in the 1940s (penicillin was first used in 1941), many life-threatening diseases caused by bacteria and fungi can now be treated, resulting in greater life expectancy. However, the indiscriminate use of antibiotics has resulted in the development of resistant strains of bacteria and a resurgence of the infections they cause. Treatment for some virus infections has proved difficult; antiviral drugs have had limited success. There is still no cure for influenza, an epidemic of which killed up to 15 million people in 1918–19, nor for HIV (human immunodeficiency virus) which can result in AIDS (acquired immune deficiency syndrome), whose symptoms were first recognized in 1979. Even where it seems that diseases have disappeared, they may reoccur, as was shown by the major cholera epidemic in Peru, which broke out in 1991, the first there for a century.

Disestablishment Acts Legislation in Britain to remove the financial and other privileges of the ANGLICAN CHURCH. The Anglican Church had been 'established' in the reign of Elizabeth I as the only Church allowed within the state, with large endowments and privileges. These came to be strongly resented by Non-Conformists in Victorian England; but proposals that all financial and other state support should be withdrawn failed. In Ireland, however, it came to be accepted as unjust that the Anglican Church should be the established Church in a predominantly Roman Catholic population. It lost its privileges by Gladstone's Irish Church Disestablishment Act (1869). The Welsh also pressed for the disestablishment of the Anglican Church in Wales. Heated arguments over the financial implications of Welsh disestablishment arose in the years just before World War I, the Welsh Church Disestablishment Bill eventually becoming law in 1920.

Disraeli, Benjamin, 1st Earl of Beaconsfield (1804–81) British statesman and novelist. He gave the modern CONSERVATIVE PARTY its identity and provided it with a policy of imperialism and social reform. Of Jewish descent, he was baptized a Christian. He entered Parliament in 1837. By the early 1840s he had become a member of the YOUNG ENGLAND movement of Tories who favoured an alliance between the old aristocracy and the mass of the people, in opposition to the increasingly powerful middle classes. These views provided the theme for his novels, in which he sees early Victorian England as deeply divided between the rich and the poor, many of whom were massed in the new northern cities; his books reveal a fascination and amused contempt for high society, together with a genuine sympathy for the poor and the oppressed. The first success of his literary career was the novel *Vivian Grey* (published anonymously, 1826), which together with *Alroy* (1833) and the autobiographical *Contarini Fleming* (1832) formed his first trilogy; the second was composed of *Coningsby; or The New Generation* (1844), *Sybil; or The Two Nations* (1845), and *Tancred* (1847).

In 1846 the Prime Minister, Sir Robert Peel, repealed the CORN LAWS. This provoked fierce opposition from Disraeli and a majority of the Tories, who supported a protectionist policy, and it split the Party. For the next 20 years Disraeli led the protectionist Conservatives in the House of Commons and was Chancellor of the Exchequer in 1852, 1858–59, and 1866–68. He introduced the REFORM ACT of 1867, which enfranchised much of the urban working class, and was briefly Prime Minister in the following year. In 1874 he became Prime Minister again. He bought the largest shareholding in the SUEZ CANAL Company (1875), procured the title of Empress of India for Queen Victoria (1876), and averted war with Russia through his skilful diplomacy at the Congress of BERLIN (1878). At home his government passed much useful social legislation (slum clearance, public health and trade union reform, and the improvement of working conditions in factories). Economic depression and unpopular colonial wars led to a Conservative defeat in the election of 1880 and Disraeli, though in poor health, continued to lead his party from the House of Lords, having been created 1st Earl of Beaconsfield in 1876.

Dissenter NONCONFORMIST.

Dissolution of the Monasteries MONASTERIES, DISSOLUTION OF THE.

Divine, Father (c. 1882–1965) Black US evangelist. Born George Baker in Georgia, he founded a Peace Mission movement in 1919. He opened a free employment bureau and fed the destitute in Sayville, New York. His house became known as 'Heaven' and he began styling himself first Major, then Father, Divine. By the 1940s his followers numbered thousands, both Black and White, and some 200 'Heavens' were established as centres for communal living. Many of his followers declared him to be the personification of God and endowed him with miraculous healing powers. His cult did not long outlast his death.

Divine Right of Kings A European doctrine that taught that monarchy was a divinely ordained institution, that hereditary right could not be abolished, that kings were answerable only to God, and that it was therefore sinful for their subjects to resist them actively. It evolved during the Middle Ages, in part as a reaction to papal intrusions into secular affairs. The extension of the principle, to justify absolute rule and illegal taxation, aroused controversy. JAMES I of England upheld the doctrine in his speeches and writings and his son CHARLES I was executed for refusing to accept parliamentary control of his policies. After the GLORIOUS REVOLUTION the doctrine was far less influential, yielding to anti-absolutist arguments like those of John LOCKE. In late 17th-century France LOUIS XIV's monarchy was based on the principle of Divine Right.

Dix, Dorothea Lynde (1802–87) US humanitarian and medical reformer. She campaigned for prison reform and improvement in the treatment of the mentally ill. During the AMERICAN CIVIL WAR Dix served as superintendent of nursing for the Union. Perhaps her greatest achievement was in persuading many states to assume direct responsibility for care of the mentally ill.

Dixiecrat Popular name for a US Democrat in a Southern state opposed to desegregation. In 1948 the STATES' RIGHTS Democratic Party was founded by diehard Southern Democrats ('Dixiecrats'), opposed to President Truman's renomination as Democratic candidate for President on account of his stand on civil rights (see CIVIL RIGHTS ACTS). Its members wished each state to be able to nominate its own presidential candidate without losing the label 'Democratic'. After Truman's victory they abandoned their presidential efforts but continued to resist the civil rights programme in Congress. Many Dixiecrats moved to support the Republican Party in the 1960s and 1970s.

Djibouti A small country of north-east Africa, formerly part of French Somaliland, on the south coast of the Gulf of Aden at the narrow entrance to the Red Sea, opposite Yemen.

Physical. It lies on the Great Rift Valley: Lake Assal lies at 155 m (509 feet) below sea-level. The climate is harsh and much of the country is semi-arid desert.

Economy. Trade is the mainstay of the economy; Djibouti City, the capital, is a free port and through its rail link to Addis Ababa handles trade for Ethiopia and other neighbouring African states. The main exports are livestock and foodstuffs. Agriculture is limited to livestock-rearing by the nomadic population, with market-gardening at the Ambouli oasis and near urban areas.

History. The small enclave of Djibouti was created as a port c. 1888 by the French and became the capital of French Somaliland (1892). Its importance results from its strategic position on the Gulf of Aden. In 1958 it was declared by France to be the Territory of the Afars and Issas, but in 1977 it was granted total independence as the Republic of Djibouti under President Hassan Gouled Aptidon (re-elected in 1981 and 1987), leading the Popular Rally for Progress (RPP) party. Famine and wars inland have produced many economic problems, with refugees arriving in large numbers from Ethiopia and Somalia. In November 1991 the Front pour la Restauration de la Unité et la Démocratie (FRUD) was formed, mostly of Afar opposition groups opposed to the one-party rule of Gouled Aptidon. There was fighting in the west and south until French mediation in February 1992. Later that year a multiparty constitution was adopted and elections were held. Only one opposition party was allowed to contest the elections; the others called for a boycott of the elections. Less than half the population voted and the RPP won all the seats. Fighting continued until late 1993, when a ceasefire was agreed.

CAPITAL:	Djibouti City
AREA:	23,200 sq km (8,950 sq miles)
POPULATION:	604,000 (1996)
CURRENCY:	1 Djibouti franc = 100 centimes
RELIGIONS:	Sunni Muslim 94%; Roman Catholic 4%; Protestant 1%; Orthodox 1%
ETHNIC GROUPS:	Somali (Issa 33.4%; Gadaboursi 15.0%; Issaq 13.3%;) 61.7%; Afar 20.0%; Arab (mostly Yemeni) 6.0%; European 4.0%; other (refugees) 8.3%
LANGUAGES:	Arabic, French (both official); Somali; minority languages
INTERNATIONAL ORGANIZATIONS:	UN; OAU; Arab League; Non-Aligned Movement

doge The title of the holder of the highest civil office in Venice, Genoa, and Amalfi from the 7th century until the 18th century. The office originated in Venice; in 1032 hereditary succession was formally banned and election was made increasingly complicated to prevent domination by particular factions, although the Participazio and Candiano families provided most candidates in the 9th and 10th centuries, and the Tiepolo and Dandolo in the 13th and 14th. The system ended with the Napoleonic conquest of 1797. The Genoese introduced a similar system after 1339. Democratic until 1515, it became an aristocratic office thereafter and also succumbed to NAPOLEON. The first doge's palace in Venice was built in 814 and destroyed in 976. Both in Venice and in Genoa, mercantile riches financed lavish residences for civic leaders; the 14th-century palace in Venice was decorated by the painters Tintoretto and Titian.

dole UNEMPLOYMENT ASSISTANCE.

dollar diplomacy A term used to describe foreign policies designed to subserve US business interests. It was first applied to the policy of President TAFT, whereby investments and loans, supported and secured by federal action, financed the building of railways in China after 1909. It spread to Haiti, Honduras, and Nicaragua, where US loans were underpinned by US forces and where a US collector of customs was installed in 1911. Although the policy was disavowed by President

Woodrow WILSON, comparable acts of intervention in support of US business interests, particularly in Latin America, remained a recurrent feature of US foreign policy.

Dollfuss, Engelbert (1892–1934) Austrian statesman. As Chancellor (1932–34), his term of office was troubled by his hostility to both socialists and nationalists. In an effort to relieve the economic depression and social unrest in the country, Dollfuss secured a generous loan from the LEAGUE OF NATIONS in 1932. Unrest and terrorism continued and in March 1933 he suspended parliamentary government. In February 1934 demonstrations by socialist workers led Dollfuss to order the bombardment of the socialist housing estate in Vienna. After fierce fighting the socialists were crushed and Dollfuss proclaimed an authoritarian constitution. By antagonizing the working classes he deprived himself of effective support against the NAZI threat. On 25 July 1934 he was assassinated in an abortive Nazi coup.

dolmen MEGALITH.

Domesday Book A survey of property in England conducted in 1086. Conceived by WILLIAM I, but probably to some extent based on pre-Conquest administrative records, it was the most comprehensive assessment of property and land ever undertaken in medieval Europe. The English shires were visited by royal commissioners and the survey yielded evidence relating to the identity of landholders, their status, the size of their holding, its use, its tax liability, and the number of animals maintained. The information for each shire was then condensed and reorganized into feudal groupings. The final version comprised two volumes – Little Domesday (Norfolk, Suffolk, and Essex) and Great Domesday (the rest of England except for the four northern shires, London, and Winchester). Its purpose was to maximize the revenues from the land tax and it caused resentment and even riots. It was given its name on account of its definitive nature; today its volumes are housed in the Public Record Office, London.

Dominic, St (1170–1221) Founder of the DOMINICAN order of friars. He was born in Spain, of noble family, but as a young man adopted an austere life, becoming a priest and canon of Osma Cathedral. In 1203 he was a missionary to the ALBIGENSIAN heretics of southern France, working also with the Crusaders who were trying to suppress them by force. In 1215 he attended the Fourth LATERAN COUNCIL. In that year he founded his own order known as the Dominicans or 'Black Friars'.

Dominica, Commonwealth of An island country, the second largest of the Windward group of the Caribbean Islands, some 750 sq km (290 sq miles) in area.
Physical. The loftiest island in the region, it has a mountainous ridge rising to Morne Diablotin, at 1,447 m (4,747 feet). Of volcanic origin, it offers beautiful scenery, with forests, waterfalls, craters, and springs. Only the coastline is cultivable on any scale.
Economy. Dominica's economy is primarily agricultural, with bananas the leading export crop. Other crops include root crops, coconuts, and citrus, but much land is still under forest. Tourism is being developed, while industry is limited to food-processing and soap-making.

History. When Europeans first arrived Dominica was inhabited by Carib Indians, who had driven out the earlier inhabitants, the Arawaks. During the 18th century the French and British fought with each other, and with the Caribs, for control of the island. Britain was in possession of the island in 1805, when the French made their last attempt to capture Dominica, but were driven out. In 1958 Dominica joined the West Indian Federation (see WEST INDIAN INDEPENDENCE), and became an autonomous British Associated State in 1967. It gained full independence in 1978.
Dominica was devastated by hurricanes in 1979 and 1980, and there were two attempted coups in 1981. The Dominican Freedom Party (DFP), under Dame Eugenia Charles (1919–   ), governed the country from 1980 until 1995, when the United Workers' Party (DUWP) won elections.

CAPITAL:	Roseau
AREA:	750 sq km (290 sq miles)
POPULATION:	73,800 (1996)
CURRENCY:	1 East Caribbean dollar = 100 cents
RELIGIONS:	Roman Catholic 76.9%; Methodist 5.0%; Seventh-day Adventist 3.2%; Pentecostal 2.9%
ETHNIC GROUPS:	Black 91.2%; mixed 6.0%; Amerindian 1.5%; White and other 1.3%
LANGUAGES:	English (official); French creole
INTERNATIONAL ORGANIZATIONS:	UN; OAS; CARICOM; Commonwealth

Dominican A member of the Order of Friars Preachers. They were founded by St DOMINIC and the order received papal approval in 1216. They are governed by their master-general and wear a white tunic with a black mantle which has given them the name of 'Black Friars'. They were a mendicant or begging order, devoted to teaching and preaching within the world and not confined within the walls of a monastery. Special emphasis on study was based on a teaching system involving houses of study, the 'Studia Generalia'. The philosopher and theologian St Thomas AQUINAS was a member of the order, as were four popes. The order gained great popularity during the 13th century; the popes used the Dominicans for preaching crusades and for the INQUISITION. With the rise of new orders during the COUNTER-REFORMATION their influence was reduced.

Dominican Republic A country in the Caribbean, comprising the eastern part of the island of HISPANIOLA.
Economy. Light industry, expansion of duty-free industrial zones, and tourism are being fostered in the Dominican Republic to diversify a primarily agricultural economy which exports sugar, cocoa, and coffee. Nickel is the chief export, and gold is also important.
History. The Dominican Republic declared its independence from Spain in 1821, although in the following year it was annexed by Haiti. In 1843 the Dominicans revolted from Haitian domination, winning their second independence in 1844. Between 1861 and 1865 the Dominican Republic was re-annexed to Spain and fought a third war for independence (1865) under Buenaventura Báez. Anarchy, revolutions, and dictatorships followed, and by 1905 the country was bankrupt. The USA assumed fiscal control, but disorder continued and the country was occupied (1916–24) by US marines. A constitutional government was established (1924), but this was overthrown by Rafael TRUJILLO, whose

military dictatorship lasted from 1930 to 1961. On his assassination, President Juan Bosch established (1962–63) a democratic government, until he was deposed by a military junta. Civil war and fear of a communist take-over brought renewed US intervention (1965), and a new constitution was introduced in 1966. Since then redemocratization has steadily advanced, the Partido Reformista being returned to power in the 1986 elections. The country occupies a strategic position on major sea routes leading from Europe and the USA to the Panama Canal. The Partido Reformista remained in power after the 1990 elections with Joaquín Balaguer as President. The latter resigned as party leader in 1991, but remained President. An IMF austerity programme in 1991 sharply reduced inflation and there were successful efforts to diversify the economy. In 1994 Balaguer was re-elected, but the result was contested with allegations of corruption and fraud being made. Fresh elections were promised to end the political crisis and these resulted in the election as President of Leonel Fernandez, leader of the centrist Liberation Party (in 1996).

CAPITAL:	Santo Domingo
AREA:	48,443 sq km (18,704 sq miles)
POPULATION:	7.502 million (1996)
CURRENCY:	1 Dominican peso = 100 centavos
RELIGIONS:	Roman Catholic 91.9%; other (mostly evangelical Protestant and followers of voodoo) 8.1%
ETHNIC GROUPS:	Mulatto 73.0%; Black 11.0%; White 10.0%
LANGUAGES:	Spanish (official); Haitian creole
INTERNATIONAL ORGANIZATIONS:	UN; OAS

dominions (between 1867 and 1947) Those countries from the BRITISH EMPIRE that had achieved a degree of autonomy while still owing allegiance to the British crown. The first country to call itself a dominion was Canada (1867), followed in 1907 by New Zealand. Australia called itself a Commonwealth (1901), South Africa a Union (1910). After World War I, in which all these countries had aided Britain, it was felt that there was a need to define their status. This came about at the Imperial Conference (1926), when they were given the general term dominion. Their power to legislate independently of the British government was confirmed and extended by the Statute of WESTMINSTER (1931). After World War II the concept became obsolete as the COMMONWEALTH OF NATIONS included countries that were republics and did not owe allegiance to the crown, though accepting the monarch as symbolic head of the Commonwealth.

domino theory A political theory based on an analogy with the way a row of dominoes falls until none remains standing. Popular in the COLD WAR, it holds that a political event in one country will lead to its repetition in another, usually neighbouring, country and so on. The term was coined by US President EISENHOWER in 1954 in reference to the communist threat to Indochina, although he also applied it to Central America. His fear was that the collapse of one state to communist forces would lead to the collapse of another, an argument that seemed to be confirmed when the fall of the non-communist government in South Vietnam in 1975 was soon followed by those of Laos and Cambodia. However, an alternative view holds that it is precisely

the intervention of the USA and its support for right-wing authoritarian regimes that fosters the spread of communism.

Donahoe, John (c. 1806–30) Australian BUSHRANGER. Born in Dublin, he was sentenced to transportation for life. He and two companions went bushranging in New South Wales from 1827 to 1830, when he was killed in a fight in the Bringelly scrub near Campbelltown. He, together with Ned Kelly (1855–80), inspired the glorification and cult of bushranging in Australian society.

Donatism The beliefs of a group that broke away from the Catholic Church in North Africa in the early 4th century AD. The Donatists were named after the Numidian Donatus, whom they set up as a rival bishop to the bishop of Carthage. Although Donatus was exiled by the Byzantine emperor Constans in 347, the Donatists continued to thrive, especially among the poor inhabitants of rural Numidia and Mauretania. In 411 a meeting of bishops declared against them, and they were persecuted until the VANDALS invaded in 429. Nevertheless, there was a revival of Donatism in the following century.

Don Pacifico affair An international incident provoked by the actions of a Greek mob, who in 1847 ransacked and burnt the house of Don Pacifico, a Portuguese moneylender who was also a Jew, injuring his wife and children. Pacifico, who had been born in Gibraltar and could therefore claim British nationality, demanded compensation from the Greek government. Insisting on Pacifico's rights as a British subject, the British Foreign Secretary, Lord PALMERSTON, took up the case in 1850 and decided to reinforce his entitlement to compensation by blockading Greece with the British fleet. He defended his action, which almost precipitated a war with France, with a masterly speech in Parliament.

Doria, Andrea (1466–1560) DOGE of GENOA (1528–60). An outstanding soldier and admiral, Doria at first fought for the French under FRANCIS I against the HOLY ROMAN EMPEROR CHARLES V, ousting Charles's troops from Genoa. He then made a pact with Charles and in return for Genoese independence, he expelled the French from Genoa in 1528 and took power himself, creating the aristocratic republic. His descendants contributed six doges and numerous officials to the state.

Dorians Invaders from the north who entered ancient Greece c. 1125–1025 BC. They settled first in the Peloponnese then also in the islands of Crete, Melos, and Thera, and the southern coast of Asia Minor. They spoke a dialect of the Greek language and seem to have come from EPIRUS and south-west MACEDONIA. They destroyed the MYCENAEAN CIVILIZATION, thereby ushering in the Greek 'Dark Age', an obscure period about which little is known. In Sparta and Crete they suppressed their subjects as HELOTS, but elsewhere a gradual fusion of conquerors and conquered took place.

Dost Muhammad (c. 1798–1863) Amir of Afghanistan. He was ruler of Kabul and Afghanistan (1826–39, 1843–63). Defeated in the first ANGLO-AFGHAN WAR, he regained power in 1843 and consolidated his rule in Afghanistan through control of Kandahar (1855), northern Afghanistan (1850–59), and Herat (1863), so establishing the territorial outlines of modern Afghanistan.

Douglas, Clifford (1879–1952) British engineer and economist. Before and during World War I he developed his theory of SOCIAL CREDIT, arguing that in every productive establishment the total cash issued in wages, salaries, and dividends was less than the collective price of the product. To remedy deficiencies of purchasing power, either subsidies should be paid to producers or additional moneys go to consumers. His ideas became fashionable in Britain (1921–22) and in the dominions, particularly in Canada and New Zealand.

Douglas-Home, Sir Alec (1903–95) British Conservative Prime Minister (1963–64). Important ministers in Douglas-Home's cabinet included Reginald Maudling (Chancellor of the Exchequer) and R. A. BUTLER (Foreign Secretary). The short ministry was notable for monetary expansion and the acceptance of the Robbins Report on higher education. The Conservatives were narrowly defeated in the general election in 1964 and Harold WILSON became Prime Minister.

Douglass, Frederick (c. 1817–95) US Black ABOLITIONIST. Born in slavery in Maryland, he made his escape to the free states in 1838. In 1841 he became an agent for the Massachusetts Anti-Slavery Society and a prominent advocate of abolition. An adviser of LINCOLN during the AMERICAN CIVIL WAR, he remained throughout his long life an advocate of full civil rights for all. From 1889 to 1891 he served as US minister to Haiti.

Dowding, Hugh Caswall Tremenheere, 1st Baron Dowding (1882–1970) British air chief marshal. On the outbreak of war in 1914 he was appointed commandant of the newly formed Royal Flying Corps and served as a pilot. In 1936 he was appointed commander-in-chief of Fighter Command. During the next three years he built up a force of Spitfire and Hurricane fighter aircraft, encouraged the key technological development of radar, and created an operations room which would be able to control his command. It was here that he fought the Battle of BRITAIN in September–October 1940. Mentally and physically exhausted, he was replaced in November 1940 when the German Luftwaffe had abandoned its daylight BOMBING OFFENSIVE.

Downing Street Declaration A document, signed on 15 December 1993 by the British Prime Minister, John MAJOR, and the Prime Minister of the Irish Republic, Albert Reynolds, declaring their principles and conditions for the conduct of negotiations to achieve peace in NORTHERN IRELAND. The declaration restated the existing positions of both governments, confirming that they would seek the agreement of the people of both Northern Ireland and the Irish Republic to any change to the status of Northern Ireland and would uphold all existing guarantees to Northern Ireland.

The British government confirmed that it would abide by any decision on Northern Ireland's future status made by a majority of its people, including the possibility that they would favour the formation of a united Ireland. The Irish government confirmed that any majority decisions about the status of Northern Ireland made by the Irish people as a whole would be subject to the separate consent of the majority of people in Northern Ireland. The government of the Republic would, in the event of a final settlement, support the alteration of Ireland's constitution to remove its territorial claim to Northern Ireland. The two governments also promised to set up a Forum for Peace and Reconciliation but asserted that they would only negotiate with parties that did not use or support violence. However, as an implicit invitation to SINN FEIN, they agreed to negotiate with any parties that decided to uphold peace and democracy.

On 31 August 1994 the IRA announced a ceasefire, which was followed a few weeks later by a similar announcement from Loyalist paramilitary groups. In 1995 the British government held its first meeting with Sinn Féin for over 20 years. However, progress towards full negotiations faltered over the IRA's unwillingness to decommission its armaments before the talks began. Owing to the breakdown of the IRA ceasefire in February 1996, Sinn Féin representatives were initially barred from the negotiating Forum that met for the first time in June 1996. Following the reinstatement of the ceasefire in July 1997 and a compromise on the decommissioning issue, Sinn Féin was admitted to full-scale talks in September. The talks led to the Good Friday agreement of 1998, to be approved by the Northern Irish and Irish electorates in referendums.

Draconian laws The first written code of laws drawn up at ATHENS, believed to have been introduced in 621 or 620 BC by a statesman named Draco. Although their details are obscure, they apparently covered a number of offences. The modern adjective 'Draconian' (excessively harsh) reflects the fact that penalties laid down in the code were extremely severe: pilfering received the same punishment as murder – death. A 4th-century BC politician quipped that Draco wrote his laws not in ink, but in blood.

Drago, Luis Maria (1859–1921) Argentine statesman, jurist, and writer on international law. The Drago Doctrine, enunciated in 1902 and intended as a corollary to the MONROE DOCTRINE, states that no country has the right to intervene militarily in a sovereign American state for the purpose of collecting debts. Drafted in response to a naval blockade (1902) of Venezuela by Britain, Italy, and Germany, the basic principles of the doctrine were accepted internationally by the Second Hague Conference in 1907.

dragoon A mounted infantry soldier, named in 16th-century France after the short musket called the 'dragon'. Originally trained to fight on foot, dragoons were organized in infantry companies, not cavalry squadrons, but were progressively trained to cavalry standard. Thus by the early 18th century they were known as medium cavalry in the Prussian army, and light cavalry in the British army. Their versatility on horse or foot made them ideal for the maintenance of public order or for dealing with guerrilla warfare. The 'dragonnades' against the French Huguenots in the 1680s were an example of their brutal effectiveness.

Drake, Sir Francis (c. 1540–96) English admiral and explorer, the first Englishman to circumnavigate the world. He sailed on a slave-trading voyage with his cousin, John HAWKINS, in 1567, and spent the next few years in privateering raids on the SPANISH MAIN. In 1577 he was engaged by a syndicate headed by ELIZABETH I to undertake a voyage of circumnavigation of which the chief object was undoubtedly plunder. Having passed through the Magellan Straits he plundered the Spanish South American settlements before sailing his ship, the *Golden Hind*, up the Californian coast, which he named New Albion. He was the first European to sight the west coast of Canada. From there he traversed the Pacific, sailed round the Cape of Good Hope, and arrived back in Plymouth in 1580 a rich man, being knighted in the following year.

In 1585 he commanded an expedition which was the first act of open war against Spain, sacking San Domingo, Cartagena, and St Augustine in Florida, and then rescuing RALEIGH's Virginia colonists. He returned to England to hear news of the preparations for the SPANISH ARMADA, some ships of which he proceeded to destroy at Cadiz in 1587, thus delaying the sailing of the Armada for a year, in the operation known as 'singeing the King of Spain's beard'. When the Armada sailed in 1588 Drake was appointed vice-admiral of the English fleet at Plymouth under Lord Howard of Effingham. The story of his finishing a game of bowls before going into battle is improbable. In command of the *Revenge*, he took a leading part in the defeat of the Armada and its pursuit into the North Sea. In 1595 he and Hawkins again sailed to the Caribbean, where they both died.

Dreadnoughts A class of battleship equipped with heavy guns. They were originally designed by Britain in response to a perceived threat from the German naval development of TIRPITZ (1898), with the first ship – HMS *Dreadnought* – being launched in 1906. Powered by steam turbine engines, they revolutionized naval warfare: their speed of 21 knots and heavy fire power enabled them to fight outside the range of enemy torpedoes.

Dred Scott decision (1857) A US Supreme Court decision regarding slave status. Dred Scott, a slave, had in 1834 been taken by his master into Illinois (a non-slave state) and later into territory in which slavery had been forbidden. Years later, his then owner sued for Scott's freedom in a Missouri (slave state) court, claiming that because of his earlier stay in free territory he should be free. In 1857 the case was decided by the US Supreme Court. The majority of the court held that Scott, as a slave and as a Black person, was not a citizen of the USA, nor was he entitled to use the Missouri courts. He was not free since his status was determined by the state in which he lived when the case was brought, i.e. Missouri. In the highly tense political atmosphere of the 1850s, the Dred Scott decision immediately deepened divisions over slavery, in particular because it declared unconstitutional the MISSOURI COMPROMISE of 1820 which had banned slavery from all territory north of the 36°30′ line of latitude.

Dreikaiserbund THREE EMPERORS' LEAGUE.

Dresden raid (February 1945) One of the heaviest air-raids on Germany in World War II. The main raid was on the night of 13–14 February 1945 by Britain's Bomber Command; 805 bombers attacked the city, which, because of its cultural significance and lack of strategic importance, had until then been safe. The main raid was followed by three more in daylight by the US 8th Air Force. The Allied commander-in-chief General EISENHOWER was anxious to link up with the advancing RED ARMY in south Germany, and Dresden came to be regarded as strategically important as a communications centre. The city was known to be overcrowded with some 200,000 refugees, but it was felt that the inevitably high casualties might in the end help to shorten the war. Over 30,000 buildings were flattened. The numbers of those who died in the bombing and the ensuing firestorm are still in dispute, estimates varying from 40,000 to 140,000.

Dreyfus, Alfred (1859–1935) French army officer, whose conviction for treason caused national controversy in France. Jewish by birth, he served in the French War Office, and in 1894 was accused and found guilty of selling military secrets to Germany. He was sentenced to life imprisonment in the penal colony on Devil's Island off the coast of French Guiana. Doubts quickly arose about the fairness of the trial. In 1896 Colonel Picquart, chief of the intelligence section, satisfied himself that Dreyfus was the innocent victim of a spy, Major Esterhazy. When Esterhazy was pronounced innocent by a military court the storm broke (1898). Encouraged by CLEMENÇEAU, Emile Zola published a newspaper article headed '*J'Accuse*', accusing the judges of having obeyed orders from the War Office in their verdict. The case was exploited by nationalist, militarist, and anti-semitic elements on the one hand, and republican, socialist, and anti-clerical supporters on the other. The case against Dreyfus collapsed as the forger, Major Henry, committed suicide (1898) and the real spy Esterhazy confessed. The Supreme Court ordered the military to re-try the case (1899). A military court found Dreyfus 'guilty with extenuating circumstances', and he was pardoned by the President of the republic. It was not until 1906 that he was fully exonerated and reinstated in the army. The French political left-wing was both strengthened and unified as a result of the affair, and army influence declined. Anticlericalism gained widespread support, and in 1905 the Roman Catholic Church was disestablished in France.

Drogheda, Siege of CROMWELL, Oliver.

Druids The ruling caste of the Gallic CELTS. Knowledge of the Druids is derived chiefly from the hostile accounts of them in the Roman authors Julius CAESAR and TACITUS. Caesar reports that they exercised judicial and priestly functions, worshipped in groves (clearings in forests), and cut mistletoe from the oak tree (sacred to them) with a golden sickle. The religion was stamped out by the Romans, lest it should become a force for resistance to Roman rule. Suetonius Paulinus destroyed the Druid centre at Mona (Anglesey, north Wales) in 61 AD, after which there is no further mention of them in England and Wales. The supposed association of the Druids with Stonehenge is rejected by scholars but the modern Druidical order seeks to make use of the site to conduct its annual solstice ceremonies.

Druze A closed, tightly knit, relatively small, religious and political sect of Islamic origin with SHIITE influences. The main communities are in Syria, Lebanon, and Israel. Founded by Ismail Darazi (d. 1019), from whom they take their name, the Druze maintain an ISMAILI notion that God manifests himself to mankind in different ages, the last manifestation being the Shiite Fatimid Caliph Hakim, who took the title *imam*. He is said not to have died, but to have hidden; he will reappear as a new Muslim messianic leader, or *mahdī* (see MILLENARIANISM). The Druze are led by a hereditary *rais* (chief). In the 18th and 19th centuries they expanded from southern Lebanon to south-western Syria, where they drove out the inhabitants of Jabal Hawran and became known as Jabal Druze. Throughout the 19th and 20th centuries the Druze have persistently been involved in clashes with MARONITE CHRISTIANS, but occasionally also with the Turks when under the OTTOMAN EMPIRE. After the French MANDATE was created in Syria (1920), Druze tribes rebelled (1925–27) against French social and administrative reforms. In retaliation the French bombarded Damascus city in 1925 and 1926. In 1944 the Druze of Syria became, theoretically, amalgamated under the country's central government; in reality, many fled. After 1945 in LEBANON, the Druze held high political office, and played a significant role in the civil war in Lebanon (1975–91).

Dual Monarchy AUSTRO-HUNGARIAN EMPIRE.

du Barry, Marie Jeanne, comtesse (1743–93) Favourite of LOUIS XV of France. She was a great beauty who in 1769 became the king's mistress and influenced him until his death in 1774. CHOISEUL criticized her and she may have helped to bring about his dismissal. During the FRENCH REVOLUTION she was arrested by the Revolutionary Tribunal and guillotined.

Dubček, Alexander (1921–92) Czechoslovak communist statesman. He fought with the Slovak Resistance in World War II and held several Communist Party posts between 1945 and 1968, when he became First Secretary and leader of his country. In what came to be known as the 'Prague Spring' he and other liberal members of the government set about freeing the country from rigid political and economic controls. He promised a gradual democratization of Czech political life and began to pursue a foreign policy independent of the Soviet Union. The latter organized an invasion by WARSAW PACT forces of Czechoslovakia. Dubček, together with other leaders, was called to Moscow and forced to consent to the rescinding of key reforms. He was removed from office in 1969 and expelled from the Party in 1970. He re-emerged in 1989 to be elected chairman of the new Federal Assembly in 1990. He remained a convinced federalist and was strongly opposed to the Slovak bid for independence in 1992.

Du Bois, William Edward Burghardt (1868–1963) US Black CIVIL RIGHTS leader and author. Seeking a self-sufficient Black society, he was a co-founder of the National Association for the Advancement of Colored People (NAACP, 1909). His enrolment in the Communist Party earned him the Lenin Peace Prize (1961); this followed federal indictment (and acquittal) during the years of the MCCARTHY witch-hunts.

Dudley, Robert LEICESTER, 1st Earl of.

Dulles, John Foster (1888–1959) US international lawyer and statesman. He served as adviser to the US delegation at the San Francisco Conference (1945) which set up the UNITED NATIONS, and as the chief author of the Japanese Peace Treaty (1951). As Secretary of State under EISENHOWER (1953–59) he became a protagonist of the COLD WAR and, advancing beyond the TRUMAN DOCTRINE of CONTAINMENT, he urged that the USA should prepare a nuclear arms build-up to deter Soviet aggression. He helped to prepare the EISENHOWER DOCTRINE of economic

and military aid to halt aggression in the Middle East, and gave clear assurances that the USA was prepared to defend West Berlin against any encroachment.

Duma An elective legislative assembly introduced in Russia by NICHOLAS II in 1906 in response to popular unrest. Boycotted by the socialist parties, its efforts to introduce taxation and agrarian reforms were nullified by the reactionary groups at court which persuaded the emperor to dissolve three successive Dumas. The fourth Duma (1912–17) refused an imperial decree in February 1917 ordering its dissolution and established a provisional government. Three days later it accepted the emperor's abdication, but soon began to disintegrate.

Dumbarton Oaks Conference (1944) An international conference at Dumbarton Oaks in Washington, DC, when representatives of the USA, Britain, the Soviet Union, and China drew up proposals that served as the basis for the charter of the UNITED NATIONS formulated at the San Francisco Conference the following year. Attention at Dumbarton Oaks was focused on measures to secure 'the maintenance of international peace and security', and one of its main achievements was the planning of the UNITED NATIONS SECURITY COUNCIL.

Dunant, Jean-Henri RED CROSS.

Dunbar, Battle of (3 September 1650) A battle fought between English and Scots armies near the port of Dunbar in Scotland. Oliver CROMWELL's force of 14,000 men won a victory over 27,000 Scots, and enormous numbers were taken prisoner together with all the Scottish guns. Cromwell's victory destroyed the STUART cause in Scotland for a decade.

Duncan I (c. 1010–40) King of Scotland (1034–40). He was ruler of Strathclyde which was added to the Scottish kingdom inherited from his grandfather Malcolm II. His accession was unpopular with the northern tribes and twice he was defeated by the Earl of Orkney before being killed in battle by the Earl of Moray, MACBETH.

Duncan II (c. 1060–94) King of Scotland (1094). He gained the throne through the support of William II of England, who provided the army with which Duncan defeated his uncle and rival Donald Bane. However, Duncan's English alliance was resented and he was murdered at his uncle's instigation.

Dunkirk evacuation A seaborne rescue of British and French troops in World War II (26 May–4 June 1940). German forces advancing into northern France cut off large numbers of British and French troops. General Gort, commanding the British Expeditionary Force, organized a withdrawal to the port and beaches of Dunkirk, where warships, aided by small private boats, carried off some 330,000 men – most, but not all, of the troops.

Duns Scotus, John (c. 1266–1308) Scholastic philosopher and theologian known as the Subtle Doctor. Born in Scotland (hence his name 'Scotus'), he became a Franciscan friar and then a priest and studied at Oxford and Paris. He later returned to both universities as a teacher before finally moving (1307) to Cologne University. In his writings and lectures he stressed the distinction between faith and reason, arguing the limitations of reason and that the will is superior to the intellect. His ideas were different from those of St

Thomas AQUINAS, who saw a possible harmony between faith and reason. His ideas were unpopular with 16th-century reformers who regarded his supporters as 'Dunsmen' or 'dunces'.

Dunstan, St (c. 909–88) Archbishop of Canterbury (959–88). He was a reformer of organized monasticism in England, and a counsellor to its kings. EDMUND I of Wessex made Dunstan abbot of the Benedictine house of Glastonbury, Somerset. Although exiled (956–57) by King Edwy, Dunstan was recalled by Edwy's successor EDGAR, and made successively Bishop of Worcester and London. With Edgar's support Dunstan founded or re-founded many abbeys and helped draw up a code of monastic observance, the *Regularis Concordis*, at the Synod of Winchester (c. 970). His formulation of the ceremony for Edgar's coronation became the basis of all subsequent coronations in England. Dunstan was also a skilful musician, draughtsman, and metalworker.

Dupleix, Joseph-François, Marquis de (1697–1763) Governor-general of the FRENCH EAST INDIA COMPANY in India (1742–54). He demonstrated able leadership of France's Indian interests, but was outmanoeuvred by Robert CLIVE during wars in south India. In 1754 he was recalled to Paris, where he died in ignominy, aware that Clive's subsequent victories in Bengal had finally destroyed his own dream of extending French influence in India. Historians differ in considering him gifted but unlucky, or rashly overambitious.

Durbar (Persian and Urdu, 'court') Term used by the Mogul emperors of India to describe their public audiences and appropriated under British rule to describe major ceremonial gatherings usually connected with some royal event. On 1 January 1877 the viceroy, Lord Lytton, held a Durbar at Delhi to proclaim the adoption by Queen Victoria of the title Empress of India, and thereafter such gatherings became features of the British Raj. The most magnificent was that attended by George V at Delhi in December 1911.

Durham Report (1838) A report on constitutional reform in British North America. In 1837 the liberal reformer John George Lambton, Earl of Durham (1792–1840), was appointed governor-general of British North America in the wake of the MACKENZIE and PAPINEAU'S REBELLION of 1837. Soon after his arrival he submitted the *Report on the Affairs of British North America*, recommending that UPPER AND LOWER CANADA be united under a single parliament and given freedom to govern itself. It also proposed a reform of the land laws, extensive railway building to unify the country, and an end to French nationalism in Canada. Its recommendations met with initial hostility in Britain, but it became the seminal document for British policy in the White dominions for the rest of the 19th century. It was partially implemented in 1841 following the Act of Union uniting Upper and Lower Canada.

Dutch East India Company A CHARTERED COMPANY established (1602) under the aegis of Prince Maurice of Nassau to co-ordinate the activities of companies competing for trade in the East Indies and to act as an arm of the Dutch state in its struggle against Spain. It was involved in attacks on the Portuguese (then part of the SPANISH EMPIRE), and warfare with native rulers, and created a virtual monopoly in trade in fine spices (for example cloves, nutmeg, and mace) grown under its supervision in the MOLUCCAS and the Banda Islands. In 1619 it made Batavia its headquarters. It ousted the Portuguese from Ceylon, set up trading posts in India, Persia, and Nagasaki, and made the Cape of Good Hope a base for Dutch ships en route to and from the East.

Its chief activities were in south-east Asia. One after another it brought to heel AMBOINA and the Moluccas, MALACCA, MACASSAR, and BANTAM. The subjection of the kingdom of Mataram in JAVA proved more difficult, bringing military, financial, and administrative problems.

Throughout the 18th century the Company operated at a loss. High mortality and inadequate salaries led to corruption among its officials. Nor did it succeed in making its monopoly in the Indies complete. In 1799 it was liquidated, its debts, possessions, and responsibilities being taken over by the Dutch state.

Dutch East Indies An area of south-east Asia formerly under the rule of the DUTCH EAST INDIA COMPANY, now mainly in INDONESIA. The archipelago has been subject to Indian and Chinese cultural influences over many centuries. Hinduism, Buddhism, and later Islam reached the islands and were grafted on to local cultures. Many Chinese settled in the islands as traders and planters, maintaining regular contact with China. Empires in the Indies based on sea-power were, except for SRIVIJAYA, relatively ephemeral, for example MACASSAR and Ternate in the MOLUCCAS. The land-based empires, in JAVA for example, were inclined to last longer. Islam spread throughout the Indies after 1300 (Hinduism survived only in BALI), and provided a weapon against the Portuguese and Dutch, who arrived in force in the 16th and 17th centuries. The Portuguese established footholds in the Moluccas but their presence proved to be short-lived. The Dutch, who were initially a sea-based trading power with many scattered bases, were drawn into land-based responsibilities, especially in Java. The Dutch East India Company became ever more deeply involved in the politics of the island of Java from the time of the establishment in Batavia (now Jakarta) in 1619.

Dutch empire The overseas territories of the UNITED PROVINCES OF THE NETHERLANDS. Dutch wealth rested on the fishing and shipping industries, assisted by Holland's position on the chief European trade routes. Amsterdam became the principal warehouse and trading centre for all Europe. Grain and naval stores from the Baltic, much of Spanish, Portuguese, and English trade, and the bulk of French exports were transported in efficiently designed vessels. Modern banking methods developed from Amsterdam's exchange bank (1609). Overseas trade with Asia, America, and Africa grew steadily even during war. Spain and Portugal's attempt to exclude the Dutch from the 'New World' prompted them to found the DUTCH EAST INDIA COMPANY (1602). From headquarters in Java they came to control the Indian Ocean and the spice trade and traded extensively in the China seas. The West India Company (1621) became primarily concerned with the African slave trade. In America a settlement, to become New York, was founded on the Hudson River (1609). Growing rivalry with Britain led to loss of maritime supremacy and of all Dutch colonies except in south-east Asia.

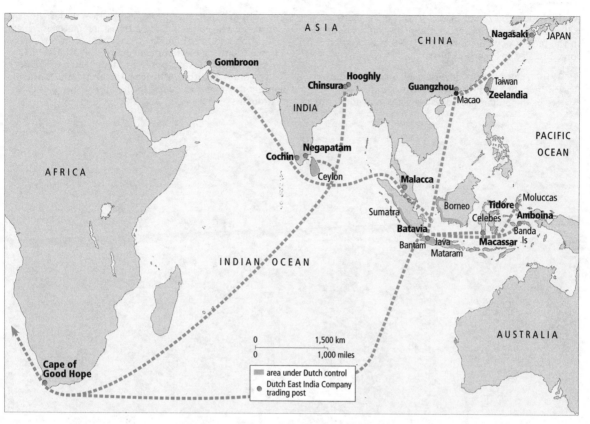

Dutch East India Company: 1602–1799   *The Dutch East India Company had two important strategic advantages in the cut-throat competition for trade and constant naval skirmishing among European powers in south-east Asia in the 17th century. Its base at Batavia was ideally placed to defend the company's interests in the Spice Islands, and the acquisition of the Cape of Good Hope in South Africa in 1652 provided a vital staging post for Dutch captains, who followed a direct route to Batavia, taking advantage of the prevailing westerlies. Dutch dominance in the area was largely secured at the expense of the Portuguese.*

Dutch Republic UNITED PROVINCES OF THE NETHERLANDS.

Dutch Revolts (1567–1648) The struggle by the NETHERLANDS for independence from Spain. The Low Countries formed part of the Spanish empire but the tactlessness of the Council of Regency for Philip II alienated the local nobles, who were excluded from government. High taxation, unemployment, and Calvinist fears of Catholic persecution aroused dangerous opposition which the Duke of ALBA came to crush (1567) with a reign of terror and punitive taxation. Open revolt led by WILLIAM I (the Silent) followed. He avoided pitched battles with the superior Spanish forces and exploited his local knowledge, saving besieged cities like Leiden (1573–74) by opening the dykes and flooding the countryside. The sack of Antwerp (1576) led to a temporary union of the whole Netherlands in the Pacification of Ghent. Calvinist excesses soon caused the southern provinces to form the Union of Arras (1579) and make peace with Spain. The northern provinces formed the Union of Utrecht and the war became a religious struggle for independence. William held out with foreign aid until assassinated (1584), when the leadership passed to Maurice of Nassau and the politician OLDENBARNEVELDT. The United Provinces were saved by Spain's commitment to wars against France, England, and Turkey. A truce (1609) was followed by recognition of full independence at the Peace of WESTPHALIA (1648).

Dutra, Eurico Gaspar (1885–1974) Brazilian statesman. He served as Minister of War before becoming President of Brazil (1946–51). Winning the presidency as the candidate of the Partido Social Democratico, Dutra had a new constitution adopted during his first year in office and promoted economic nationalism and industrialization. A political conservative, he did not repudiate the idea of state participation in the economy.

Duvalier, François (1907–71) Dictator of Haiti (1957–71). His 1957 election was the first held under the rule of universal adult suffrage, but within a year after coming to office he suspended all constitutional guarantees and established a reign of terror based on the Tontons Macoutes, a notorious police and spy organization. The economy of his country declined severely, and 90% of his subjects remained illiterate.

By the time of his death in 1971 'Papa Doc', as he was called, had assured the succession of his son, Jean-Claude. In the face of popular unrest the latter was deposed and forced to flee to France in 1986.

dyarchy The system of government introduced into British India by the 1919 Government of India Act. Powers in the Indian provinces were to be divided into a reserved area (finance, police, and justice) under the control of the governor, and a transferred area, such as education and health, under the control of ministers chosen from the elected members of a legislative council. The plan was devised by Lionel Curtis, founder of the Royal Institute of International Affairs. It was largely unsuccessful owing to the opposition of Indian nationalists.

E

earl British nobleman ranking third in the peerage, below a duke or a marquess but above a viscount. From Alfred's time ALDERMEN had charge of shires, but during the 10th century they became more important, with overall control of several shires. King CANUTE's dependence on his Scandinavian jarls (earls) gave them territorial power in England over the regions of Northumbria, East Anglia, and Wessex (where Godwin was earl). They presided over the shire court, commanded its FYRD, and retained one-third of the profits of justice (replaced later by King John with a fixed sum). Under the Norman kings in the 11th century shire administration passed to the sheriffs but the hereditary title of earl survived.

East African Community (1967–77) An economic association of East African countries. It began with a declaration of intent (June 1963) between Kenya, Tanzania, and Uganda to improve trade, communications, and economic development. This was the East African Common Services Organization and provided for common currency, common market, and customs. This was developed by the Treaty of Kampala (1967) into the East African Community with headquarters in Arusha, Tanzania. It made considerable economic headway before 1971 when Uganda came under AMIN's regime. The Community broke up in 1977.

East Anglia The region of eastern England occupied by the counties of Norfolk and Suffolk. The kingdom of the East Angles was formed from the end of the 5th century by Angles, Saxons, Frisians, and Swabians from the German Baltic coast. Initial settlements were made in Norfolk, but the settlements in Suffolk, especially around Ipswich, were to provide the nucleus of the kingdom, with the royal seat at Rendlesham on the River Deben. Protection against the Britons to the west was provided by the Middle Angles settled in the waterlands of the Fens and by the construction of earthworks (Devil's Dyke, Fleam Dyke, Heydon Dyke).

Little is known about its kings but Raedwald (d. *c.* 625), was briefly a Christian and was styled Bretwalda, or overlord, of the south, by BEDE. His is probably the rich barrow-burial at SUTTON HOO. Sigeberht, his son, founded the bishopric at Dunwich and a monastery at Burgh Castle. Although never again attaining overlordship, the kingdom continued until overrun by Danes in the later 9th century. It became part of the DANELAW and eventually (921) one of the four English earldoms.

Easter Island An island in the South Pacific some 3,800 km (2,400 miles) west of Chile. It was colonized by Polynesians from the nearest occupied islands 2,400 km (1,800 miles) to the west. At the time of its discovery by the Dutch navigator Jakob Roggeveen on Easter Day 1722, the Polynesians were no longer engaged on voyages of exploration, and had developed a complex system of chiefdoms. This involved the carving and erection of extraordinary stone heads, some of which were over 9 m (30 feet) high.

Eastern Front Campaigns (World War II, 1939–45) A series of military campaigns fought in eastern Europe. The first campaign (September 1939) followed the NAZI-SOVIET PACT (1939), when Germany invaded Poland. Soviet forces entered from the east, and Poland collapsed. Finland was defeated in the FINNISH-RUSSIAN WAR. In June 1941 Hitler launched a surprise offensive against his one-time ally, the Soviet Union. Italy, Romania, Hungary, Finland, and Slovakia joined in the invasion. By the end of 1941 Germany had overrun Belorussia and most of the Ukraine, had besieged Leningrad, and was converging on Moscow. The Russian winter halted the German offensive, and the attack on Moscow was foiled by a Soviet counter-offensive. Britain, now allied with the Soviet Union, launched a joint British-Soviet occupation of Iran (1941), thus providing a route for British and US supplies to the Red Army, as an alternative to ice-bound Murmansk. During 1942 LENINGRAD continued to be besieged, while a massive German offensive was launched towards STALINGRAD and the oil-fields of the Caucasus. KURSK, Kharkov, and Rostov all fell, as did the Crimea, and the oil centre of Maikop was reached. Here the Soviet line consolidated and forces were built up for a counter-offensive which began in December 1942, the relief of Stalingrad following in February 1943. The surrender of 330,000 German troops there marked a turning point in the war. A new German offensive recaptured Kharkov, but lost the massive Battle of Kursk in July. The Red Army now resumed its advance and by the winter of 1943–44 it was back on the River Dnieper. In November 1943 Hitler ordered forces to be recalled from the Eastern Front to defend the Atlantic. Soviet offensives from January to May 1944 relieved Leningrad, recaptured the Crimea and Odessa, and re-entered Poland. Through the rest of the year and into 1945 the Red Army continued its advance, finally entering Germany in January 1945. By April it was linking up with advance troops of the Allied armies from the west, and on 2 May Berlin surrendered to Soviet troops. Victory on the Eastern Front had been obtained at the cost of at least 20 million lives.

Eastern Orthodox Churches A group of CHRISTIAN CHURCHES, historically centred in Eastern Europe, Greece, Ukraine, Russia, Georgia, and the Middle East. Each Church is independent but they all acknowledge the primacy (not the supremacy) of the Patriarch of Constantinople. There are about 100 million full members worldwide; there is a sizeable Orthodox community in the USA, but most of the Orthodox population live in the countries of the former Soviet Union. The Orthodox Communion is made up of a number of independent autocephalous Churches with their own internal administration which share the same faith and doctrine. These are the four eastern Patriarchates of Constantinople, Alexandria, Antioch (Antakya), and Jerusalem; the Russian, Serbian, Romanian, Bulgarian, and Georgian Patriarchates; the Orthodox Churches of such countries as Greece,

Poland, and Albania, and certain other semi-independent Churches. Services have traditionally been held in the vernacular (now archaic in some cases, such as Old Slavonic), leading sometimes to an association with nationalism. The Orthodox Churches attach great importance to the role of Councils, in contrast to Roman Catholic emphasis on the pope's authority, and their central beliefs are based on the seven Church Councils held up to 787 AD. Doctrinally, the principal difference from Roman Catholicism is the role of the Holy Spirit in the Trinity. The Orthodox acknowledge seven sacraments, with some flexibility since, for example, burial or a monastic commitment may also be regarded as a sacrament. Communion is taken only four or five times a year, and parish priests are permitted to marry, although the higher clergy, who are usually from the monasteries, are not. Divorce is permitted under certain circumstances. Monasticism is important, but there are no centralized orders, each monastery being a self-governing unit. The veneration of icons, which are believed to have a mediatory role, is central in Orthodox worship. The Orthodox celebrate many of the principal festivals of the Christian year according to a different calendar from the Western Church. In recent years there has been some rapprochement between the Orthodox Churches and the Roman Catholic Church, following the lifting in 1965 of mutual excommunications imposed in 1054. Subject to much persecution during the era of communist ascendancy in Eastern Europe and the former Soviet Union, the Orthodox Churches have recently been permitted to operate freely again.

Easter Rising (April 1916) An insurrection in Dublin when some 2,000 members of the Irish Volunteers and the Irish Citizen Army took up arms against British rule in Ireland. The IRISH REPUBLICAN BROTHERHOOD had planned the uprising, supported by the SINN FEIN Party. A ship carrying a large consignment of arms from Germany was intercepted by the British navy. Roger CASEMENT of the IRB, acting as a link with Germany, was arrested soon after landing from a German U-boat. The military leaders, Pádraic Pearse and James Connolly, decided nevertheless to continue with the rebellion. The General Post Office in Dublin was seized along with other strategic buildings in the city. The Irish Republic was proclaimed on 24 April, Easter Monday, and a provisional government set up with Pearse as president. British forces forced their opponents to surrender by 29 April. The rising had little public support at first. Many Irishmen were serving in British forces during World War I. Sixteen leaders of the rebellion were executed and over 2,000 men and women imprisoned. The executions led to a change of feeling in Ireland and in the 1918 general election Sinn Féin won the majority vote.

East India Company, English A CHARTERED COMPANY of London merchants that gradually transformed trading privileges in Asia into a territorial empire centred on India. Chartered in 1600, the Company soon lost the Spice Islands (MOLUCCAS) to the Dutch, but by 1700 had secured important trading ports in India, notably Madras, Bombay, and Calcutta. In the mid-18th century Anglo-French hostility in Europe was reflected in a struggle for supremacy with the FRENCH EAST INDIA COMPANY. The English commander CLIVE outmanoeuvred

the French governor DUPLEIX in south India, then intervened in the rich north-eastern province of BENGAL. Victory over the Bengal ruler in 1757 initiated a century of expansion, the East India Company emerging as the greatest European trader in India, though with strong French competition. Increasingly the company acted as an instrument of colonial government; having lost its commercial monopolies by 1833, it served as Britain's administrative agent in India. Widespread risings in 1857 during the INDIAN MUTINY determined, through the INDIA ACTS, the transfer of India from company to British government control in 1858, and the company was finally dissolved in 1873.

East Timor The eastern part of the island of TIMOR, the largest and most easterly of the Lesser Sunda Islands of INDONESIA, lying between the Savu and Timor Seas and part of the Malay Archipelago.

Physical. The coastal plains often inundated with mangrove swamps gradually rise to a mountainous interior. The volcanic nature of the island is displayed by mud geysers but the volcanoes are not active.

History. A Portuguese colony for over 450 years, East Timor declared its independence in 1975, but was invaded by Indonesia; it was annexed as the province of Timor Timor in 1976. The UN does not recognize this annexation and separatists known as FRETILIN (the Revolutionary Front of Independent East Timor) have continued to wage a guerrilla war. There was a massive military strike by Indonesia in 1981 and in November 1991 some 200 demonstrators died in the capital, Dili, when fired on by the army. Human rights groups asserted that some 200,000 Timorese were killed or died in detention in the years 1976–91. Indonesia and Portugal have attended several rounds of UN-sponsored peace talks on the situation in East Timor since 1993. In 1996 the Nobel Peace Prize was jointly awarded to Jorge Ramos-Horta, a FRETILIN activist living in exile, and Bishop Carols Belo of East Timor, a champion of human rights on the island.

East–West relations The relationship existing from the end of World War II between the USA and its allies on one side (the West) and the former Soviet Union and its allies on the other (the East). After the war the USA and the Soviet Union emerged as superpowers based on opposing ideologies, with global interests. The USA had a stake in the security of Western Europe, while the Soviet Union extended its influence over the countries of the Eastern bloc, despite Eastern European discontent, leading to the Yugoslav break with Stalin in 1948 and Soviet repression of dissidents in Poland, Czechoslovakia, and elsewhere. Both sides possessed increasing nuclear capabilities. The bipolar split in world politics became evident in the alliance systems of NATO and the WARSAW PACT. The period of mutual distrust and rivalry that ensued, characterized by ideological differences, the dissemination of PROPAGANDA, the build-up of arms, military threat, and occasional misunderstandings and crises, became known as the COLD WAR. Each side built up its nuclear arsenals (see ARMS RACE) and attempted to extend its sphere of influence in the developing world. However, the rigid polarization of the first period of the Cold War was broken down in the early 1960s by an ideological split between the communist regimes of China and the Soviet Union, and the formation of the NON-ALIGNED

MOVEMENT, an attempt to remain independent from both East and West. During the 1970s there was a period of DÉTENTE when relations improved, only to deteriorate because of the Soviet invasion of Afghanistan (1979), which triggered what many called the second Cold War. However, the later 1980s saw the rise of GLASNOST AND PERESTROIKA in the Soviet Union, progress in arms agreements (see ARMS CONTROL), the withdrawal of the Soviet army from Afghanistan (1988), the demise of communism in the Eastern bloc, the reunification of Germany in 1990, and the disbanding of the Warsaw Pact in the same year. In 1991 the Soviet Union itself ceased to exist, as the constituent republics asserted their independence. With the demilitarization of East-West relations and prospects of greater co-operation between the two sides, the East-West balance of power may cease to be an overriding factor in shaping international relations.

East–West Schism The schism between the EASTERN ORTHODOX CHURCH and the Western (or Roman) Church, which became definitive in the year 1054. Tension between the two Churches dated back at least to the division of the ROMAN EMPIRE into an Eastern and a Western part, and the transferral of the capital city from Rome to CONSTANTINOPLE in the 4th century. An increasingly different mental outlook between the two Churches resulted from the occupation of the West by formerly barbarian invaders, while the East remained the heirs of the classical world. This was exacerbated when the popes turned for support to the HOLY ROMAN EMPIRE in the West rather than to the BYZANTINE EMPIRE in the East, especially from the time of CHARLEMAGNE onwards. There were also doctrinal disputes, and arguments over the nature of papal authority. Matters came to a head in 1054 when the two Churches, through their official representatives, excommunicated and anathematized (formally denounced) each other. The breach was deepened in 1204 when the Fourth CRUSADE was diverted to Constantinople and sacked the city, and a Latin (Western) Empire was established there for some time. There were various attempts to heal the schism, notably at the ecclesiastical councils of Lyons II (1274) and Florence (1439), but the reunions proved fleeting. These attempts were effectively brought to an end when the OTTOMAN Turks captured Constantinople in 1453 and occupied almost all of the former Byzantine empire for many centuries. It is only in recent years that the dialogue between the two Churches to heal the schism has been effectively re-opened.

Ebert, Friedrich (1871–1925) German statesman. When Germany collapsed at the end of World War I he was Chancellor for one day (9 November 1918). He steered a difficult course between revolution and counter-revolution in order to give Germany a liberal, parliamentary constitution and he became the first President (1920–25) of the unpopular WEIMAR REPUBLIC. He lost support from the Left for crushing the communists and from the Right for signing the Treaty of VERSAILLES.

Eboué, Félix (1884–1944) French colonial administrator. He was appointed governor of Martinique (1932), of Guadeloupe (1936), of Chad (1938), and then governor-general of French Equatorial Africa. In World War II he supported the FREE FRENCH army of DE GAULLE, sending men and materials from the French African colonies to support the Allies.

Ecgbert EGBERT.

Economic Community of West African States (ECOWAS) An economic grouping constituted largely on the initiative of General GOWON at Lagos in 1975 by 15 West African countries, and later (1977) joined by Cape Verde. Its object was to provide a programme of liberalization of trade and to bring about an eventual customs union. A common fund was established to promote development projects, with specialized commissions for trade, industry, transport, and social and cultural affairs. A new treaty was signed in 1993, designating the creation of a free-trade zone and a single currency as specific objectives and planning the establishment of a West African parliament and a new ECOWAS court of justice.

economics, schools of From the mid-16th century to the final quarter of the 20th century, economic thought can be split into five main historical schools: MERCANTILISM; the economics of the French physiocrats; CLASSICAL (and neoclassical) ECONOMICS; KEYNESIANISM; and MONETARISM. The schools overlap, and they represent broad categories of thought which do not necessarily encompass the views of all economists. The mercantilists, between the mid-16th and mid-18th centuries, argued that the wealth of nations depended on their balance of trade. With the simple monetary system that existed, proponents of the theory were concerned to maximize the amount of precious metals in the country. Protectionism was encouraged. Classical critics of mercantilism, beginning with the philosopher HUME, demonstrated that attempts to accumulate bullion were likely to prove self-defeating, because inflows of gold would raise domestic price levels to the point of making domestic producers uncompetitive, therefore causing gold to flow out again as more imports were bought. The French physiocrats of the 18th century, led by François Quesnay (1694–1774), accorded pre-eminence to the agricultural sector, which they saw as the only source of wealth, and also the source of tax revenue. They believed in the role of government being limited to preserving the natural order. They also believed in FREE TRADE. Thus their approach was LAISSEZ-FAIRE. The physiocrats' ideas of *laissez-faire* and free trade were adopted by the classical economists. Much of modern micro-economics stems from the theories of classical economics, centring on Adam SMITH's *Wealth of Nations* (1776). The marginal analysis of the 19th century led to the development of neo-classical economics as a refinement and progression from classical economics. It clarified the mode of interaction of supply and demand through the price mechanism, and resolved a number of problems that had troubled classical economic theory, for example the apparent paradox that diamonds (an inessential luxury) are usually more 'valuable' than water (a necessity of life). The principal contributors to classical and then neo-classical economics include, in chronological order: Smith, Robert Malthus (1766–1834), RICARDO, MILL, William Stanley Jevons (1835–82), Alfred Marshall (1842–1924), Arthur Cecil Pigou (1877–1959), Marie-Esprit Walras (1834–1910), Vilfredo Pareto (1848–1923), and Francis Ysidro Edgeworth (1845–1926). The central tenet in classical economics is competition. The law of supply and demand ensures that the price of a good balances supply and demand. Competitive markets ensure that the self-seeking behaviour of individuals results in efficient, socially optimal allocation of resources and production. This is Adam Smith's 'invisible hand'. The role of government is limited to intervention in cases where a market does not exist or works imperfectly. In the early part of the 20th century, economists argued over the role of government in controlling unemployment caused by fluctuations in demand. Those in the classical tradition argued that government should maintain a balanced budget; others argued for government expenditure financed by budget deficits. The issue was resolved by KEYNES in 1936 in *The General Theory of Employment, Interest and Money*. This work laid the foundation of what is now called macro-economics. Keynesianism favours demand management by government through the use of both fiscal and monetary policy. MONETARISM, prominent in the 1970s and 1980s, represented a resurgence and updating of pre-Keynesian thought on macro-economic issues. It stressed the importance of the money supply as the means of controlling aggregate money demand and inflation but rejected the notion that either monetary or fiscal policy could exercise any lasting influence on the level of output and employment: the money supply, it was argued, determined only the price level, not the volume of output and employment.

Ecuador A country on the north-west coast of South America.

Physical. Ecuador is bounded by Colombia on the north-east and Peru on the east and south. Palms flourish on the sandy, salty parts of the coast, and there are also mangrove swamps. Inland is a rich tropical plain, drained by several meandering rivers, and higher valleys where cocoa and coffee are grown; they extend into the foothills of the Andes, where there are cinchona and great mahogany trees. The Andes run north to south through the middle of the country. The peaks are lofty, COTOPAXI, at 5,897 m (19,347 feet), being the highest active volcano in the world, and between the peaks are high but fertile valleys where the climate is temperate.

Economy. The oil industry, nationalized since 1988, produces the country's chief export, but otherwise the economy is primarily agricultural with bananas (of which Ecuador is the world's leading exporter), coffee, and, increasingly, fish the other exports of importance. Oil revenues have been invested to develop some manufacturing industry. Ecuador was a member of OPEC until 1992. There are plentiful supplies of natural gas and hydroelectric power to meet domestic energy requirements, and also mineral deposits of lignite, gold, and silver.

History. By c. 500 AD independent kingdoms had developed with two cultural regions – a coastal one, adapted to the open sea, and one adapted to the interior environment. The Incas conquered the central valley in the 15th century, and their communications network included a road from CUZCO to QUITO, which they set up as their regional capital. The Spaniard Pizarro united the region to his Peruvian conquests in 1535 and installed his brother, Gonzalo, as governor. Internal dissensions led to a take-over by the Spanish crown and the establishment of Quito as an Audiencia (a high court with a political role) under the viceroy of Peru.

With the victory at Pichincha (1822) by Antonio SUCRE Ecuador gained independence, joining Gran COLOMBIA.

When this broke up (1830) it became a separate republic, whose politics reflected the tension between the conservative landowners of the interior and the more liberal, business community of the coastal plain. This led to an almost total breakdown in government (1845–60). Garcia Moreno ruthlessly re-established order as President (1860–75) and, on his assassination, there was a period of stable government under anti-clerical liberal governments. After World War I increasing poverty of the masses led to political turbulence. Although US military bases in World War II brought some economic gain, a disastrous war with Peru (1941) forced Ecuador to abandon claims on the Upper Amazon. Between 1944 and 1972 the CAUDILLO José Maria Velasco Ibarra alternated with the military as ruler, being elected President five times. The discovery of oil in the 1970s might have brought new prosperity, but in fact the mass of the population remained poor and illiterate, with the great HACIENDAS surviving intact. Democratic government was restored in 1979 with the election of the social democrat Jaimé Roldos Aquilera as President (1979–81). He had promised reform but died in a mysterious air-crash. His successor, Osvaldo Hurtado Larrea (1981–84), was accused of embezzlement, and President Febres Cordero (1984–88) faced military intervention, a major crisis of external indebtedness, trade union unrest, and a decline in the oil price. The Democratic Left Party under Rodrigo Borja Cevallos came to power in 1988. It took over management of the oil companies, but still faced grave economic problems, with over a third of its 1992 budget allocated to debt servicing. Following elections in 1992 a coalition government was formed under President Sixto Durán Ballén. He introduced free-market economic reforms and cut public spending, provoking popular unrest that led to the election in 1996 of the maverick populist Abdala Bucaram. In 1995 a recurrent border dispute with Peru flared up again, but was settled after several days of fighting. In February 1997 President Bucaram (known as 'El Loco' – the madman) was relieved of his office by the national congress, which appointed Fabian Alarçon in his place.

CAPITAL:	Quito
AREA:	269,178 sq km (103,930 sq miles)
POPULATION:	11.698 million (1996)
CURRENCY:	1 sucre = 100 centavos
RELIGIONS:	Roman Catholic 93.5%
ETHNIC GROUPS:	Quechua 49.9%; Mestizo 40.0%; White 8.5%; other Amerindian 1.6%
INTERNATIONAL ORGANIZATIONS:	UN; OAS; Andean Group; Non-Aligned Movement

Eden, (Robert) Anthony, 1st Earl of Avon (1897–1977) British statesman; Conservative Prime Minister (1955–57). As Foreign Secretary from 1935 to 1938, he was noted for his support for the LEAGUE OF NATIONS: he resigned over his opposition to APPEASEMENT but was again Foreign Secretary from 1940 to 1945 and from 1951 to 1955. He was also deputy leader of the Conservatives (1945–55) under CHURCHILL, whom he succeeded as Prime Minister. Eden's premiership was dominated by the SUEZ WAR. Owing to his experience of appeasement, he was determined to stand up to President NASSER of Egypt, whom he perceived as a potential aggressor. Widespread opposition to Britain's role in the Suez Crisis, together with his own failing health, led to his resignation.

Edgar (*c.* 944–75) King of Northumbria and Mercia (957–75) and of England (959–75). After the political failure of his brother Eadwig, he was chosen king of England north of the Thames (957). The southern part also became his on Edwy's death (959). Edgar's reign saw freedom from Danish raids (due in part to his building of an effective navy), hence his title of 'Edgar the Peaceful'. His authority was acknowledged (973) by the other kings in England, Scotland, and Wales. Edgar supported Saints Dunstan, Ethelwold, and Oswald in their reform of English monasteries. He was succeeded in turn by two of his sons, Edward the Martyr and Ethelred II.

Edgar the Aetheling (from Anglo-Saxon *aetheline*, 'prince') (*c.* 1050–1130) Anglo-Saxon prince, the grandson of EDMUND II. His father's death (1057) in exile left Edgar as the heir to EDWARD THE CONFESSOR in 1066, but because of his youth he was rejected in favour of HAROLD II. On Harold's death at the Battle of HASTINGS the Witan chose Edgar as king but, despite his involvement in a rebellion against WILLIAM I (1069), he was unable to organize any further resistance and became a member of William's court (1074). He was captured by HENRY I at Tinchebrai (1106) for supporting Henry's older brother Robert of Normandy (Curthose), but was later released.

Edgehill, Battle of (23 October 1642) The first battle of the ENGLISH CIVIL WAR. Charles I's Royalists, marching south from Shrewsbury, with the eventual aim of recapturing London, clashed with the Parliamentarians under the 3rd Earl of ESSEX, at Edgehill, near Warwick. Prince RUPERT and his Royalist cavalry gained an early advantage, but the brunt of the fighting was borne by both infantries. Darkness, and the exhaustion of the troops ended the struggle, with no clear victor and heavy losses on both sides.

Edmund I (921–46) King of England (939–46). He succeeded his brother Athelstan as king. In his brief reign he defended Athelstan's territorial gains and reconquered (944) Danish-occupied Mercia. He sought to stabilize his north-west border against Danish raids from Ireland by presenting (945) the region of Strathclyde to his ally the King of Scotland, Malcolm I. Edmund appointed DUNSTAN as abbot of Glastonbury and supported his reform of organized monasticism. He was murdered by a convicted robber in a banquet brawl.

Edmund II (Ironside) (*c.* 993–1016) King of Wessex. He was the son of ETHELRED II, who had temporarily (1013–14) lost his throne to Sweyn I of Denmark. Edmund's succession was challenged by Sweyn's son CANUTE. Over a period of eight months (1016) they fought six major battles. Defeated at Ashingdon in Essex (October 1016), Edmund agreed to rule southern England and Canute the remainder, either survivor succeeding to the whole country. Edmund died in the following month and Canute became overall ruler.

Edo, Treaty of (1858) Treaty between Japan and the USA. It extended the rights granted to the USA four years earlier by the Treaty of KANAGAWA, establishing diplomatic relations, accepting a conventional tariff, and granting US citizens extra-territorial rights in five treaty ports. Along with treaties signed with other foreign powers, this agreement opened the way to the westernization of Japan, but exposed the SHOGUNATE to nationalist hostility which was to play an important role in its downfall in 1868.

Edward I (1239–1307) King of England (1272–1307), in succession to his father HENRY III. He was married to Eleanor of Castile (1254), then to Margaret of France (1299). Edward's reputation as a successful ruler rests on his military and legal skills (for which he was called 'the English JUSTINIAN'). His military achievements, which were motivated by a determination to extend royal power, included the defeat of Simon de MONTFORT (1265), the conquest of Wales (1277–82), the suppression of rebellions in Wales (1294–95) and Scotland (1296–1305), and the defence of his lands in GASCONY against the French crown (1294–99). His legal reforms covered such matters as feudal administration (Statute of Westminster, 1275), crown lands (Quo Warranto, 1278), and law and order (Statute of Winchester, 1285), and he summoned the MODEL PARLIAMENT in 1295. He died during a vain expedition to subdue the Scots and was succeeded by EDWARD II.

Edward II (1284–1327) The first English Prince of Wales (1301–07) and King of England (1307–27). The fourth (but eldest surviving) son of EDWARD I and Eleanor of Castile, he was notorious in his own lifetime for his inordinate affection for Piers GAVESTON and for his unhappy marriage with ISABELLA, daughter of Philip IV of France. Gaveston dominated Edward by 1304 and helped alienate him from his barons; the barons, led by Edward's cousin, Thomas of Lancaster, hemmed Edward in by a set of Ordinances (1310) and had Gaveston killed in 1312. The king's prestige fell further when he was defeated by ROBERT I (the Bruce) at BANNOCKBURN in 1314, and although he attempted to reassert his royal authority and annulled the Ordinances (1322), his own wife and her lover, Roger MORTIMER, imprisoned him in 1326 and finally had him murdered.

Edward III (1312–77) King of England, Ireland, and France (1327–77). He succeeded his father, EDWARD II, though the throne was at first his in little more than name, power remaining in the hands of his mother, ISABELLA, and her lover Roger MORTIMER; but in 1330 Edward had Mortimer arrested and began his personal rule. He secured the Scottish frontier with relative ease by the victory of HALIDON HILL (1333); but his initial French strategy was less successful, for although he prudently bought up the allegiance of France's neighbours the cost proved excessive. By 1341 Edward was virtually bankrupt. In 1346 he sought to justify his claim to the French throne by the more direct means of leading a vast army to France, and victories at CRÉCY (1346) and in Brittany made him effectively king in France. The English by now were gaining a taste for foreign warfare and booty, and the truce of 1354 was ended by a fresh invasion of France two years later, crowned by the epic victory that Edward's son, EDWARD THE BLACK PRINCE, won at POITIERS.

The rest of Edward's long reign was less successful – there were failures in France between 1369 and 1375, and after the death of his wife, Philippa of Hainaut in 1369, his health and mind began to deteriorate; he fell under the influence of his mistress, Alice Perrers. Edward left his successor, RICHARD II, with a legacy of social discontent in England as well as the possession of vast tracts of France.

Edward IV (1442–83) King of England (1461–70, 1471–83). He was the eldest son of Richard, Duke of YORK and so had a clear hereditary right to the throne by descent from Edward III. He gained the throne at the age of 19 with the help of his cousin Richard Neville, Earl of WARWICK, while the Lancastrians hesitated after their victory of ST ALBANS, and he then defeated them at TOWTON. His marriage to Elizabeth Woodville and alliance with Burgundy alienated Warwick, who in October 1470 invaded England from France and secured HENRY VI's nominal restoration, but Edward won back the throne by victories at BARNET and TEWKESBURY (1471). Thereafter he was a strong ruler and promoter of English commerce, but his dissolute lifestyle probably caused his early death, which left England with a 12-year-old king, EDWARD V.

Edward V (1470–83) King of England (1483), the eldest son of EDWARD IV and Elizabeth Woodville. His short reign, which began on 9 April 1483, was little more than a power struggle between the Woodvilles and his paternal uncle Richard, Duke of Gloucester. In June, Richard assumed royal dignity as RICHARD III, and it was at some time between then and August of the same year that Edward and his brother were murdered in the Tower of London, probably at the instigation of Richard.

Edward VI (1537–53) King of England (1547–53). He was the son of HENRY VIII and Jane Seymour. During his minority effective power was exercised by Edward SEYMOUR, Duke of Somerset until 1549, and subsequently by John Dudley, Duke of NORTHUMBERLAND. He favoured the Protestant religion, endorsing Archbishop CRANMER's English Prayer Books (1549 and 1552). Contemporaries noted his studious, unemotional nature, and a callous streak reminiscent of his father. Always a sickly child, he died of tuberculosis aged 16.

Edward VII (1841–1910) King of Great Britain and Ireland and dependencies overseas, Emperor of India (1901–10). The eldest son of Queen VICTORIA and Prince Albert, he was 59 before he succeeded to the throne on the death of his mother. As Prince of Wales he served on the Royal Commission on working-class housing (1884–85), but in general the queen excluded him from public affairs, denying him access to reports of cabinet meetings until 1892. As monarch his state visit to Paris in 1903 improved relations between Britain and France, and promoted public acceptance of the ENTENTE CORDIALE. In domestic politics he was influential in 1910 through his insistence that his approval for the Parliament Bill to reform the House of LORDS must be preceded by a general election. He was succeeded in 1910 by his second son, GEORGE V.

Edward VIII (1894–1972) King of Great Britain and Northern Ireland and of dependencies overseas, Emperor of India (1936). The eldest son of King GEORGE V, he abandoned the crown owing to his desire to marry Wallis Simpson, a divorcee (see ABDICATION CRISIS). Created Duke of Windsor, he was governor of the Bahamas during World War II but took no subsequent public role. He settled in France, but was buried at Windsor, together with the duchess after her death in 1986.

Edwards, Jonathan (1703–58) American Puritan divine, the scion of two distinguished ministerial families in the Connecticut valley. He was the leading Puritan intellectual of his generation and one of the pioneers of the GREAT AWAKENING and of resistance to ARMINIANISM. His pastoral style and theological dogmatism led to his dismissal in 1750, and he died in 1758 shortly after becoming the president of Princeton University.

Edward the Black Prince (1330–76) Prince of Wales (1343–76), the eldest son of EDWARD III. He was an outstanding example of the chivalric ideal, a military leader who helped restore national pride to the English by a series of victories in the HUNDRED YEARS WAR. He commanded part of his father's army at CRÉCY (1346), and in 1356 won the Battle of POITIERS, capturing John II. In 1367 he restored King Pedro to the throne of Castile, but the campaign in Spain ruined his health. By his love match to Joan, the 'Fair Maid of Kent', he left one son, the future RICHARD II.

Edward the Confessor, St (c. 1003–66) King of England (1042–66). He succeeded King CANUTE's Danish heirs as king, temporarily re-establishing the West Saxon monarchy, although he favoured the Normans, among whom he had been brought up. In 1045 he married the daughter of Earl Godwin of Wessex and six years later put down a rebellion by the earl. It will never be known for certain whether, as the Normans claimed, he promised the crown to Duke William before his death; the succession after his death of Harold, Earl Godwin's son, caused the Normans to take England by conquest. Edward was the founder of Westminster Abbey (1045), and had a great reputation for piety. He was canonized in 1161.

Edward the Elder (d. 924) King of Wessex (899–924). He was the eldest son of King ALFRED, whom he succeeded in 899. He continued his father's policy of repossessing the DANELAW. A system of fortified towns was developed. A series of victories (909–18) secured the Midlands and the important towns of Derby, Leicester, Lincoln, Stamford, and Nottingham and convinced the Danes of the need to recognize English rule south of the Humber. Edward's authority was also acknowledged in southern Scotland.

Edward the Martyr, St (c. 963–79) King of England (975–78). He succeeded his father Edgar as king, but his accession was disputed by his stepbrother ETHELRED II, and while visiting him and his stepmother Alfrida at Corfe Castle in Dorset, Edward was murdered. Miracles were reported at his tomb at Shaftesbury and Ethelred had to pronounce the date of Edward's death (18 March) a solemn festival. He was canonized and became the focus of a considerable medieval cult.

Egbert (or Ecgbert) (d. 839) King of Wessex (802–39). He was elected king after living in exile (789–802) at the court of CHARLEMAGNE, having been expelled from England by OFFA. By 829 he had extended his authority over the other southern English kingdoms although Mercia regained its independence in 830. Egbert styled himself 'King of the English', but his authority was tested by the onset of the Danish raids towards the end of his reign. His victory at Hengist Down in Cornwall (837) provided only a brief respite from attack.

Egmont, Lamoral, Count of, Prince of Gavre (1522–68) Flemish statesman and soldier. He was made statholder (governor) of Flanders and Artois in 1559. Although he was a member of PHILIP II of Spain's regency council, he opposed his sovereign's policy of imposing Catholicism and Spanish government on the Netherlands, and helped to oust Cardinal Granvelle from his pre-eminent position in the government of the Netherlands (1564). In 1565 he withdrew from the council with HORN, but during the first phase of the DUTCH REVOLTS he vacillated, and refused to join WILLIAM I (the Silent) in armed resistance. He was seized by ALBA in 1567, and beheaded on a charge of treason.

Egypt A country in the north-east corner of Africa, bounded by its Mediterranean and Red Sea coasts, Israel in the north-east, Sudan in the south, and Libya in the west.

Physical. It is generally hot and arid and civilization depends on the waters of the Nile, which are regulated by the Aswan High Dam. To the west of the Nile valley is a desert of rock, sand, and gravel, with a few oases, and the great Qattara Depression. To the east is a range of hills with limestone and sandstone plateaux dissected by wadis, and on the east bank of the Gulf of Suez is the Sinai desert. The fan-shaped Nile delta in the north, where the climate is wetter, is very fertile.

Economy. Egypt's main exports are of crude oil, petroleum products, and cotton. Agriculture is the main economic activity, but Egypt is no longer self-sufficient in food, due partly to swift population growth and partly to the neglect of agriculture. Foreign-exchange earnings from the Suez Canal, from the estimated 3 million Egyptians working abroad, and from tourism, make an important contribution to the economy.

History. Egypt is the site of one of the first civilizations, together with Mesopotamia, of the Old World. Agriculture and metallurgy were both introduced from western Asia, and the great fertility of the Nile floodplain allowed the growth of a highly distinctive cultural tradition. Two kingdoms, one in the Delta (Lower Egypt) and one centred upstream around Thebes (Upper Egypt), were in existence during the 4th

Period	Dynasty	Dates	Pharaohs	Major Events
Archaic	1–2	c. 3000–2700	Menes	Unification of the Delta kingdom (Upper Egypt) and Thebes (Lower Egypt) by Menes, the first pharaoh. Memphis founded. Royal Monuments at Saqqara and Abydos.
Old Kingdom c. 2700–2200	3	c. 2700–2600	Zoser	Zoser's Step Pyramid, the first monumental building in stone, constructed by Imhotep.
	4	c. 2600–2500	Snofru, Cheops (Khufu), Chephren (Kha-f-Ra), Mycerinus (Menkaure)	The great age of pyramid building, including that of Khufu at Giza, the largest ever constructed at 147m (481 feet) high.
	5–6	c. 2500–2200	Teti, Pepi I, Pepi II	Growth of power of provincial governors (nomarchs).
First Intermediate Period	7–10	c. 2200–2050		Climatic deterioration leading to low inundations and famine. Collapse of central authority. Brief period of anarchy, followed by intermittent civil war between Heracleopolis (Dynasties 9 and 10) and Thebes (Dynasty 11). Thebes triumphant. Country reunited c. 2050 by Mentuhotep II.
Middle Kingdom	11	c. 2050–2000	Mentuhotep III	
	12	c. 2000–1750	Amenemhat I–III, Sesostris I–III	Golden age of art and craftsmanship. Curbing of nomarchs' power by Sesostris III. Conquest of Lower Nubia completed.
Second Intermediate Period	13–17	c. 1750–1550	Hyksos kings; Seqenenra, Kamose	Northern Egypt taken over by Asian kings, later called Hyksos (Dynasties 15 and 16). Thebans remain independent (Dynasty 17), eventually expel Hyksos and reunite the country.
New Kingdom c. 1550–1050	18	c. 1550–1300	Amenhotep I–III, Thutmose I–IV, Queen Hatshepsut, Akhenaten, Tutankhamun, Horemheb	Temples of Karnak and Luxor built. Great expansion of Egyptian power (Thutmose III). Akhenaten founds new religion. Egyptian civilization reaches its zenith under Amenhotep III.
	19	c. 1300–1200	Seti I, Ramesses II, Merenptah	Possible connection between the Exodus and Ramesses II. Ramesses fights the Hittites at Kadesh. Peace treaty later concluded between the two powers. Royal residence in the East Delta.
	20	c. 1200–1050	Ramesses III	Invasion by Sea Peoples thwarted by Ramesses III. Economic difficulties towards end of dynasty. First recorded strike in history. Tomb robbery trials.
Third Intermediate Period	21–25	c. 1050–650	Sheshonq I, Taharqa	High-priestly 'dynasty' at Thebes during Dynasty 21. Dynasty 22 kings of Libyan origin. Sheshonq I invades Palestine c. 925. Nubians invade and take over Egypt c. 750 (Dynasty 25). Assyrians invade c. 655 and sack Thebes.
Late Period	26–31	c. 650–332	Psammeticus I, Nectanebo II	Cultural renaissance during Dynasty 26. Two periods of Persian domination (Dynasties 27 and 31). Last native pharaoh, Nectanebo II. Alexander the Great reaches Egypt, 332, and defeats the Persians.

Egypt *Periods, dynasties, and pharaohs of ancient Egypt.*

millennium BC. These were unified by the conquest of Lower Egypt some time shortly before 3000 BC, initiating the Protodynastic period. The shift of the capital to Memphis, near the head of the Delta, in the Old Kingdom (2700–2200 BC) perhaps indicates the importance of sea-borne trade with the Levant. The major pyramids were constructed here on the desert edge overlooking the river. A period of fragmentation (the first of two 'intermediate' periods) separated the Old from the Middle Kingdom (c. 2050–1750), when some expansion into Palestine took place and the Nubian frontier was fortified. After a period of domination by foreign rulers (the 'HYKSOS'), the New Kingdom (1550–1050) was a period of imperial expansion when Egypt fought the Asiatic powers for control of Palestine. It was punctuated by the Amarna Period when AKHENATEN founded a new capital and religion. Egypt suffered from attacks of marauding SEA PEOPLES in the 12th century BC, but maintained continuity of tradition into the Late Period (c. 650–332). However, its independence came to an end with its successive incorporation into Assyrian, Persian, and Hellenistic empires. When the Romans took it, Egypt was virtually self-governing. It was a granary for Rome, and its capital, Alexandria, became the world's chief commercial centre, when, c. 106 AD, the sea route to India was opened.

Until 451 Alexandria was the intellectual centre of the Christian Church (see COPTS). When the Arab armies reached Egypt in 639, they had little difficulty in taking the country. Under Arab rule taxes were lighter, administration remained in local hands, and there was little pressure for conversion to Islam. The new capital of Misr, now Old Cairo, was the military base for the Arab conquest of North Africa. In the 9th century the CALIPHATE gradually weakened, and Ibn Tulun, a Turk, made it independent for a time. In 969 the FATIMIDS seized the country, and built a new capital named al-Qahira, Cairo. Local administration continued with little change, and the country's prosperity is reflected in Fatimid art and architecture. In 1171 there followed the Fatimid dynasty of Saladin, and then the MAMELUKES, foreign slave rulers under whom Egypt had the most prosperous period in her history (1250–1517). Then, with the rest of North Africa and the Middle East, Egypt fell to OTTOMAN Turkey, although Mamelukes still maintained much local power. In 1798 Napoleon invaded Egypt in an attempt to restrict British trade with the east, but was driven out by the Turkish and British armies in 1801.

Egypt was restored to the Ottoman empire in 1802 but enjoyed almost total independence under the rule of pashas (MEHEMET ALI) in Cairo. The construction of the Suez Canal in the 1860s made Egypt strategically important and in 1882 the British occupied the country in the wake of a nationalist revolt led by ARABI PASHA. They ruled the country in all but name through the Agent and Consul-General Lord CROMER. Egypt became a British protectorate in 1914 and received nominal independence in 1922 when Britain established a constitutional monarchy, with Sultan Ahmed as King Fuad I. Britain retained control of defence and imperial communications. In 1936 an Anglo-Egyptian treaty of alliance was signed, providing for a British garrison for 20 years, but for a gradual British withdrawal. This was interrupted by World War II. In 1948 Egyptian forces failed to defeat the emerging state of Israel, and in 1952 King FAROUK was overthrown by a group of army officers, one of whom, Colonel NASSER, emerged as the head of the new republic. Nasser's nationalization of the SUEZ CANAL in 1956 provoked abortive Anglo-French military intervention, and in the same year he embarked on another unsuccessful war against Israel. Helped by Soviet military and economic aid, Nasser dominated the Arab world, although he suffered another heavy defeat at Israeli hands in the SIX-DAY WAR of 1967. His successor, Anwar SADAT, continued his confrontationalist policies, but after defeat in the YOM KIPPUR WAR of 1973, he turned his back on the Soviet alliance, sought an accommodation with Israel, and strengthened his contacts with the West. This change of policy damaged Egypt's standing in the Arab world and in 1981 Sadat was assassinated by Islamic fundamentalists. His successor, President Hosni MUBARAK, has followed a policy of moderation and reconciliation. Egypt was formally re-admitted to the ARAB LEAGUE in 1989. In 1991 Egypt sent troops to support the US-led alliance in the GULF WAR and in return had its debts to the USA reduced. Although the Aswan Dam increased productivity of the land, poverty remains a major problem. During the 1990s militant Islamic fundamentalists grew increasingly violent, attacking and killing tourists as well as Egyptians.

CAPITAL:	Cairo
AREA:	997,739 sq km (385,229 sq miles)
POPULATION:	60.896 million (1996)
CURRENCY:	1 Egyptian pound = 100 piastres = 1,000 millièmes
RELIGIONS:	Sunni Muslim 90.0%; Christian (mostly Coptic) 10.0%
ETHNIC GROUPS:	Egyptian 99.8%
LANGUAGES:	Arabic (official)
INTERNATIONAL ORGANIZATIONS:	UN; OAU; Arab League; OAPEC; Non-Aligned Movement

Egyptian and Mesopotamian technology
Technology of the early civilizations in Egypt and in Mesopotamia, both of which arose in about 3000 BC. The early civilizations of Mesopotamia included the Sumerian, Assyrian, and Babylonian empires. These two areas provide the earliest known examples of many basic technologies – pottery and glass-making, the extraction and working of metals, textiles, woodworking, and building techniques – which were firmly established long before the Christian era. Both had highly developed agricultural systems in which strictly controlled irrigation played a critical role. They were skilled at astronomical observation and computation and devised intricate CALENDARS, important for observing the annual cycle of sowing, growth, and harvesting. Systems of pictographic writing were developed in both areas, and standardized weights and measures were introduced. Both civilizations had highly organized urban communities and established trading relationships with distant countries, facilitated by the development of shipbuilding and of road systems.

Eichmann, (Karl) Adolf (1906–62) Austrian Nazi
administrator. A salesman by trade, he joined the Austrian Nazi Party in 1932 and by 1935 was in charge of the GESTAPO's anti-Jewish section in Berlin. In 1942, at a conference in Wannsee on the 'final solution to the

Jewish problem', he was appointed to organize the logistic arrangements for the dispatch of Jews to CONCENTRATION CAMPS and promote the use of gas chambers for mass murder. Abducted (1960) by Israelis from Argentina, he was executed after trial in Israel.

Eighteen-Twelve, War of WAR OF 1812.

Einstein, Albert (1879–1955) German-born mathematical physicist whose relativity theory altered ideas about space, time, and the nature of the universe. Educated in Switzerland, he first took employment in a patent office in Berne. The work was undemanding, however, and he quickly turned his mind to problems in theoretical physics. In 1905, he successfully used the quantum theory to explain the photoelectric effect. He received the Nobel Prize for Physics in 1921 for this achievement. Also in 1905 he published a paper on molecular motion, as well as a paper in which he put forward the special theory of relativity, describing the effects of motion on observed values of length, mass, and time. One consequence of his theory is that mass, m, is equivalent to energy, E, a concept expressed by the equation $E = mc^2$, where c is the speed of light. This is the basis of all calculations of the energy released by nuclear reactions. He extended his ideas in the general theory of relativity, published in 1915, which is concerned with gravitation and the effects of accelerated motion. The first independent verification of general relativity was obtained in 1919 when the bending of light was observed during an eclipse. Einstein also made important contributions to quantum mechanics. However, he was unable to accept as final the probabilistic description of physics which quantum theory involved. In 1913 he returned to his native Germany to take up a professorship at the University of Berlin. As a Jew, however, he later experienced Nazi persecution, and in 1932 was forced to leave the country. After a brief stay in the UK he settled in the USA, and eventually became a US citizen. In a famous letter to President Roosevelt in 1939 he outlined the military potential of nuclear energy and the dangers of a Nazi lead in this field. His letter influenced the decision to build an atomic bomb, the use of which he greatly regretted. His last years were spent attempting to develop a grand unified theory – a single mathematical system incorporating the laws of gravitation and electromagnetism.

Eisenhower, Dwight D(avid) (1890–1969) US General and 34th President of the USA (1953–61). In World War II he was appointed to command the US forces in Europe. He was in overall command of the Allied landings in North Africa in 1942. In 1944–45 as Supreme Commander of the Allied expeditionary force he was responsible for the planning and execution of the NORMANDY landings and subsequent campaign in Europe. His success in rolling back German forces was limited by Soviet advances, and the pressure to bring US troops back home. The resultant vacuum of power in central Europe led to the COLD WAR and to the need to establish NATO.

At home his popularity led to nomination as Republican presidential candidate and a sweeping electoral victory with Richard NIXON as his Vice-President. Eisenhower's new 'modern Republicanism' sought reduced taxes, balanced budgets, and a decrease in federal control of the economy. The administration was embarrassed by the extreme right-wing 'witch-hunt' of Senator Joseph MCCARTHY, with its anti-communist hysteria. In spite of tough talk there was a move towards reconciliation with China and a decision not to become engaged in Indo-China following the defeat of France there in 1954. A truce to the KOREAN WAR was negotiated in July 1953. John DULLES, as Secretary of State, held to a firm policy of CONTAINMENT and deterrence by building up US nuclear power and conventional forces against possible Soviet aggression. Thus the NATO and ANZUS pacts of President Truman were extended by the SOUTH-EAST ASIA TREATY ORGANIZATION Pact of 1954. The EISENHOWER DOCTRINE (1957) committed the US to a policy of containment in the Middle East. After Dulles's death in 1959 Eisenhower took a more personal role in foreign policy, seeking to negotiate with the Soviet Union; however, his hopes of improving relations were destroyed in May 1960, when a US U-2 reconnaissance plane was shot down by the Russians over Soviet territory.

Eisenhower Doctrine A statement of US foreign policy issued by President EISENHOWER after the SUEZ WAR and approved by Congress in 1957. It proposed to offer economic aid and military advice to governments in the Middle East who felt their independence threatened and led to the USA sending 10,000 troops to Lebanon (1958) when its government, fearing a Muslim revolution, asked for assistance. Britain had also sent troops (1957) to protect Jordan, and despite Soviet protests US and British forces remained in the Middle East for some months. The Doctrine, whose assumption that Arab nationalism was Soviet-inspired came to be seen as fallacious, lapsed with the death (1959) of the US Secretary of State, John DULLES.

El Alamein ALAMEIN, El.

ELAS A communist-dominated guerrilla army in Greece. The initials stand for the Greek words meaning National People's Liberation Army. It was created during World War II by the communist-controlled National Liberation Front (EAM) to fight against German occupation forces. By the time of the German defeat and withdrawal (1944–45) EAM/ELAS controlled much of Greece and opposed the restoration of the monarchy, aiming to replace it with a communist regime. A bitter civil war broke out (1946–49), which prompted US promise of support in the TRUMAN DOCTRINE (1947). Stalin's unwillingness to support the Greek communists contributed to their defeat.

El Cid (Campeador) (c. 1040–99) (Arabic al-Said, 'the lord' and Spanish campeador, 'champion') Spanish hero. He was Rodrigo Díaz de Bivar, a Castilian nobleman, who was exiled after the war between the brothers Sancho II of Castile and Alfonso VI of León, becoming a mercenary captain fighting mainly for the MOORS. He captured Valencia on his own behalf but was expelled in 1099, dying shortly afterwards. Many of the legends concerning him bear little relation to historical facts.

El Dorado (Spanish, 'the gilded man') The name given by 16th-century Spanish CONQUISTADORES to a legendary gilded man, and to the land or city full of gold where he was reputed to live. When the Spanish defeated the Muisca Indians of central Colombia in the 1530s they heard tales of el indio dorado from captives. According to the tales, when a new ruler was appointed at Lake

Guatavita he was taken after a period of seclusion to the lake, stripped, covered with mud, then gold dust, and set on a raft laden with golden objects. Pushed out into the middle, he and companion chiefs offered the gifts to the waters. The name El Dorado has subsequently been given to any mythical place of riches and abundance.

Eleanor of Aquitaine (*c.* 1122–1204) A duchess in her own right, who by marriage became Queen of France and subsequently Queen of England. She married Louis VII of France and accompanied him on the Second CRUSADE (1147), but the marriage was annulled and in 1152 she married Henry, the Duke of Normandy and Count of Anjou. When he became the ANGEVIN king, HENRY II of England, the lands they claimed stretched from Scotland to the Mediterranean. Her ten children included Richard and John, future kings of England whose accession she acted zealously to ensure. She was imprisoned (1173–85) for plotting against her husband.

Eleanor of Castile (*c.* 1244–90) Queen of England (1272–90). She was the daughter of Ferdinand III of Castile in Spain and married EDWARD I of England in 1254. Eleanor bore 13 children and accompanied her husband on Crusade (1270–73). After her death at Hadby in Nottinghamshire, her body was embalmed and taken to Westminster Abbey. At each of the ten overnight stopping places Edward ordered a stone cross to be erected to her memory, the 'Eleanor crosses'.

Elector A prince of the HOLY ROMAN EMPIRE who had the right to elect the emperor. Although the monarchy was elective by the 12th century, it was not until the contested election of 1257 that the number of Electors was fixed at seven. They were: the Count Palatine of the Rhine (Imperial Steward), the Margrave of Brandenburg (Chamberlain), the Duke of Saxony (Marshal), the King of Bohemia (Imperial Cupbearer), and the Archbishops of Mainz, Trier, and Cologne (Chancellors). Additional Electorates were later created for Bavaria (1623–1778), Hanover (1708), and Hesse-Kassel (1803). The Electors exercised considerable power at disputed successions by reason of their independence, though the imperial crown gradually became, in practice, hereditary in the HABSBURG family. The office of Elector disappeared when Napoleon abolished the empire in 1806.

Electoral College A group of people chosen to elect a candidate to an office. Probably the oldest College is that which meets in Rome to elect a new pope, consisting of the cardinals of the Church. The idea was adapted by the framers of the American Constitution in 1787, each state appointing as many electors as it had members of Congress, these electors then meeting to choose the President of the USA. As states extended their franchise these electors came to be chosen by direct election. With the emergence of organized political parties, the holding of a national party convention to select presidential candidates developed. Candidates in each state are all now chosen beforehand by party associations and their vote is decided by their party's convention. Thus, for each state (except Maine since 1969), following a presidential election, the candidate who has won a majority of the popular vote in that state will gain all that state's electoral votes. In the event of a tied election the President is chosen by a vote in the House of Representatives.

Elgin, James Bruce, Earl (1811–63) British statesman and colonial administrator. As governor-general of British North America (1847–54) he was given the task of carrying out the recommendations made by the DURHAM REPORT. In 1848 he implemented 'responsible' government with the formation of the Baldwin-La Fontaine ministry to be responsible to the elected legislative assembly. He introduced measures to improve education in Canada and to stabilize the economy, which was depressed by the new British policy of FREE TRADE. After leaving Canada, he jointly led an Anglo-French force that marched into Beijing in 1860 to secure ratification of the Treaty of Tianjin. In 1862 he was appointed viceroy of India, dying in office a year later.

Elijah (9th century BC) Hebrew prophet at the time of King AHAB. His mission, as told in the Old Testament of the Bible, was to strengthen the worship of the God of the Israelites, to oppose the worship of all other gods, and to promote moral uprightness and social justice. He rebuked Ahab for his devotion to the fertility god Baal, worshipped by his wife Jezebel. He charged his successor, Elisha, with the destruction of the OMRI dynasty. Elisha became involved in court affairs, inspiring revolutions in Syria and Israel; by anointing Jehu as King of Israel, he instigated the downfall of the Omri.

According to tradition, Elijah was 'translated' into heaven (without dying) in a chariot of fire; there was a popular Jewish prophecy that he would return before the coming of the Messiah. Ilyas (Elijah) is one of the prophets mentioned in the Koran and a popular figure in Islamic legend, which closely follows the Bible account: Ilyas is said to have been given power over the rain after Ahab rejected his teaching, and to have caused a great drought during which he was miraculously provided with food while so many Israelites died that God eventually interceded on their behalf.

Elizabeth I (1533–1603) Queen of England and Ireland (1558–1603). She was the only child of HENRY VIII and Anne BOLEYN. After her mother's downfall she was temporarily illegitimized, then imprisoned under her half-sister MARY I for suspected implication in WYATT'S REBELLION. She was well educated in the humanities, and, succeeding to the throne on Mary's death, she proved an industrious and intelligent monarch. The regime she established with the indispensable aid of William CECIL enjoyed a considerable degree of popular support: the nation achieved stability and prosperity under her rule and enjoyed a 'golden age' of achievement in art, music, and literature.

She did not please everyone. Her ANGLICAN CHURCH settlement (1559–63) offended Catholics and Puritans alike by its very moderation. Her refusal to marry and ensure the succession irritated certain Members of Parliament, as did her financial demands and her lengthy procrastination over the execution of MARY, Queen of Scots. Abroad, meanwhile, her covert aid to the Dutch and French Protestants and her sponsorship of privateering against the Spanish helped to incite PHILIP II of Spain to open warfare against England. Yet there was no religious warfare under her rule; JAMES I succeeded peacefully when she died; and the navy not only resisted the attempted invasion by the SPANISH ARMADA (1588), but maintained England's advantage in the expensive Anglo-Spanish war which continued until 1604. The problems presented by Puritans, Catholics, and Parliamentary opposition remained to be faced by James I, but by force of character and clever temporizing Elizabeth dominated a remarkably talented array of Englishmen.

Elizabeth I   *The Elizabethan age was a golden era for English culture, commerce, and naval power.*

Elizabeth II (1926–   ) Queen of Great Britain and Northern Ireland and dependencies overseas, head of the COMMONWEALTH OF NATIONS (1952–   ). As elder daughter of GEORGE VI she became heir to the throne on the abdication in 1936 of her uncle EDWARD VIII. She was trained in motor transport driving and maintenance in the Auxiliary Territorial Service (ATS) late in World War II and in 1947 married her distant cousin Philip Mountbatten, formerly Prince Philip of Greece and Denmark. Their first child and heir to the throne, Prince Charles was born in 1948. Her coronation in 1953 was the first major royal occasion to be televised. Since then she has devoted much of her reign to ceremonial functions and to tours of the Commonwealth and other countries. While strictly adhering to the conventions of the British constitution, she has always held a weekly audience with her Prime Minister and shown a strong personal commitment to the Commonwealth. In the 1990s the Queen instituted changes to bring the Royal family more into line with contemporary public opinion; in 1993, she agreed to pay tax on her personal income, while in 1997, following the death of Diana, Princess of Wales, she indicated that the Royal Family is committed to greater openness and responsiveness.

Elizabeth Petrovna (1709–62) Empress of Russia (1741–62). She was the unmarried daughter of PETER THE GREAT, a beautiful and extravagant woman who seized the throne from the infant Ivan VI. She was more interested in social life and the arts than in affairs of state and government was conducted mainly by her ministers. The court became more westernized and the economy flourished. The nobility added to their privileges by increasing their power over the SERFS. Foreign affairs were managed by Count Bestuzhev until 1758. Russia increased its hold on Poland in the War of the POLISH SUCCESSION and the SEVEN YEARS WAR. On her death Peter III immediately changed sides, thus making possible the ultimate victory of FREDERICK II (the Great).

Ellis Island An island in New York Bay off Manhattan Island. Long used as an arsenal and a fort, from 1892 to 1943 it served as the centre for immigration control. From 1943 until 1954 it acted as a detention centre for aliens and deportees. In 1965 it became part of the Statue of Liberty National Monument, and open to sightseers.

El Salvador The smallest Central American country, situated on the Pacific coast. Only some 80 km (50 miles) wide, it is bounded on three sides by Guatemala, Honduras, and Nicaragua and has a 258-km (160-mile) southward-facing coastline.

Physical. It comprises a hot, very wet coastal plain with wooded inland slopes, above which rise volcanic mountains with cratered lakes; as the country is at a junction of two crustal plates, earthquakes occasionally occur.

Economy. The economy of El Salvador is primarily agricultural, with coffee and cotton important exports. There is some manufacturing industry, principally textiles, chemicals, food-processing, and paper.

History. After it was conquered by Pedro de Alvarado, a lieutenant of Hernan CORTÉS, El Salvador formed part of the viceroyalty of NEW SPAIN, but was subject to the jurisdiction of the captain-general sitting in Guatemala City.

The country gained independence from Spain in 1821, joined (1824) the United Provinces of CENTRAL AMERICA, and with the break-up of that entity in 1838, became an independent republic (1839). Internal struggles between liberals and conservatives and a series of border clashes with neighbours retarded development in the 19th century. By the early 20th century the conservatives had gained ascendancy and the presidency remained within a handful of élite families as if it were their personal patrimony. El Salvador's 20th-century history has been dominated by a series of military presidents. While some of them, such as Oscar Osorio (1950–56) and José M. Lemus (1956–60), appeared mildly sympathetic to badly needed social reform, they were held in check by their more conservative military colleagues in concert with the civilian oligarchy. Fidel CASTRO's Cuban revolution and leftist guerrilla activity in other Central American countries pushed the Salvadoran army steadily to the right. Repressive measures and violations of human rights by the army during the 1970s and 1980s were documented by a number of international agencies, and posed a large refugee problem. Under President Felix Cristiani (elected 1989) negotiations began with the extreme left-wing guerrilla group *Frente Farabundo Marti de Liberación* (FMLN). The UN Secretary-General

PÉREZ DE CUÉLLAR sponsored peace-talks throughout 1991 and a peace agreement was reached in 1992. The FMLN was recognized as a political party and took part in the 1994 elections, winning a few seats. The *Alianza Republicana Nacionalista* (ARENA), under President Armando Calderón Sol, won the majority of seats. In 1995 the government announced plans for economic reform.

CAPITAL:	San Salvador
AREA:	21,041 sq km (8,124 sq miles)
POPULATION:	5.897 million (1996)
CURRENCY:	1 colón = 100 centavos
RELIGIONS:	Roman Catholic 92.4%
ETHNIC GROUPS:	Mestizo 90.0%; Amerindian (mostly Pipil) 5.0%; White 5.0%
LANGUAGES:	Spanish (official)
INTERNATIONAL ORGANIZATIONS:	UN; OAS

emancipists Ex-convicts in early 19th-century Australia (see CONVICT TRANSPORTATION). In a narrow sense, the term referred only to those convicts who had been pardoned, conditionally or absolutely, by the governor. In a broader sense, it was applied to all ex-convicts who, having served their term of imprisonment or enforced servitude, had become free, and in some cases, wealthy. There was much conflict between emancipists and EXCLUSIONISTS in New South Wales, Australia, especially during MACQUARIE's governorship (1810–21). The term was also applied to members of a political group, consisting of emancipists and liberals, which campaigned for reforms during the 1820s, 1830s, and early 1840s. William Wentworth was the acknowledged leader of this group for many years. In 1835, it founded the Australian Patriotic Association.

Emin Pasha (Mehmed Eduard Schnitzer) (1840–92) German explorer and physician. He joined the Ottoman army in 1865, and in 1876 he served under General GORDON in Khartoum. Gordon used him for administrative duties and diplomatic missions and in 1878 appointed him governor of the Upper Nile area of Equatoria, where he surveyed the region and suppressed slavery. Isolated when the MAHDI controlled the Sudan, he was rescued in 1888 by H. M. STANLEY. In 1890 he was employed by the German government in East Africa. While engaged in exploration for Germany, Arab slave-raiders murdered him.

emirate A Muslim territory ruled by an emir (Arabic *amir*, 'lord' or 'prince'), who often united civil and military authority. Depending on the strength of the CALIPHATE, an emir might be either a diligent subordinate, subject to supervision and removal, as under the early ABBASIDS, or a virtually independent princeling, able to defy his nominal master. In the latter case recognition of overlordship was signified merely by symbolic acts, such as acceptance of caliphal confirmation of their office, acknowledgement of his title in Friday congregational prayers, and use of his name and title on coinage. Some dispensed with these formalities. The title *amir al-muminin* — 'commander of the faithful' — was taken by UMAR and borne by all subsequent caliphs, and some monarchs claiming independent authority, such as the kings of Morocco. The term *amir* could also be applied to a specific office such as commander-in-chief of the armies (*amir al-umara*) or leader of the pilgrimage (*amir al-hajj*).

It was also applied as a courtesy title to descendants of MUHAMMAD and is the origin, via medieval Italian, of the English title 'admiral'.

Emirates, Fulani FULANI EMPIRE OF SOKOTO.

Emmet, Robert (1778–1803) Irish nationalist. Involved in the United Irishmen movement, during 1800–02 he visited France in an attempt to win support for Irish independence. Returning to Ireland in 1803 with a small band of followers, he began an insurrection in Dublin against British rule, which ended in disaster. Emmet escaped but was subsequently captured and executed. Gallant and reckless, he was to become a potent symbol in the cause of Irish nationalism.

Ems telegram (13 July 1870) A dispatch from the Prussian king WILLIAM I to his chancellor, BISMARCK, that precipitated the outbreak of the FRANCO-PRUSSIAN WAR. A relative of the Prussian king, Prince Leopold of Hohenzollern-Sigmaringen, had accepted an offer to the Spanish throne. This alarmed the French, who feared Prussian influence south of the Pyrenees. Leopold withdrew his claim a few days later, but the French ambassador approached William at the German spa town of Ems, asking for an assurance that Leopold's candidacy would never be renewed. The king refused, politely but firmly, and he sent his chancellor a telegram to the effect that the crisis had passed. Bismarck, intent on provoking war with France, published a shortened version which turned the refusal into an insult. French public opinion was outraged and Napoleon III declared the Franco-Prussian War, whose consequences were to include the downfall of the French Second Empire and the creation of the GERMAN SECOND EMPIRE.

enclosure An area of land formed as the result of enclosing (with fences, ditches, and hedges) what had usually been COMMON LAND so as to make it private property. Enclosures gradually transformed English farming from the medieval system of communally controlled open fields farmed in strips by the villagers, into a system of individually owned fields whose cropping and stocking were their owner's choice. Enclosures were created for different reasons at different times, and the reaction to the process depended on whether it was affecting valuable arable land or common wastes. In Tudor times enclosure was popularly seen as the conversion of the peasants' tilled land to grass on which a landowner's sheep would graze: the sheep were eating men, it was said, because the villagers were losing both their employment and their tillage. Enclosures became a national issue, but although they were denounced by the Church (especially by Cardinal WOLSEY and Thomas MORE) and were penalized by statutes and royal proclamations, and even provoked Kett's Rebellion (1549), their financial advantages were so strong that they continued to be carried out.

In the second half of the 18th century enclosure by private Act of Parliament increased dramatically, and the General Enclosure Act of 1801 standardized the procedure. Enclosures were less unpopular in the 18th century, as they enabled farmers to introduce improvements in crops and breeding without reference to their neighbours'.

Encyclopédists The *philosophes* and others who contributed to and otherwise supported the *Encyclopédie*, published in France in 35 volumes between 1751 and 1780, one of the great literary achievements of the 18th century. It was a complete review of the arts and sciences of the day, explaining the new physics and cosmology and proclaiming a new philosophy of humanism. It was edited by DIDEROT and d'Alembert and articles were contributed by VOLTAIRE, MONTESQUIEU, ROUSSEAU, Buffon, and baron d'Holbach. The strict censorship laws in France prevented direct attacks on Church and state but these twin institutions were treated in the *Encyclopédie* with irony and disdain. A decree of 1752 suppressed the first volumes and in 1759 it was placed on the Index (of books forbidden to Roman Catholics), but it continued to circulate. The critical attitudes fostered by the *Encyclopédie* are believed to have contributed to the FRENCH REVOLUTION.

Engels, Friedrich (1820–95) German social philosopher and businessman. He was, with MARX, one of the founders of modern COMMUNISM. A partner in the Ermen and Engels cotton plant in Manchester, England, he was converted to communism by the radical, Moses Hess. Engels believed that England, with its advanced industry and rapidly growing proletariat, would lead the world in social upheaval. In 1844 his *The Condition of the Working Class in England in 1844*, based largely on official parliamentary reports, attracted wide attention. In the same year he met Karl Marx in Paris. Together they joined the socialist League of the Just in 1847, transforming it into the Communist League, and publishing its COMMUNIST MANIFESTO the following year. He participated in the revolutionary movement in Baden and later published a penetrating work on the failure of the REVOLUTIONS OF 1848 in Germany. Engels returned to England, working as a successful businessman whilst supporting Marx financially. After Marx's death he served as the foremost authority on MARXISM, continuing work on *Das Kapital* from Marx's drafts, publishing the second and third volumes in 1885 and 1894.

Enghien, Louis Antoine Henri de Bourbon-Condé, duc d' (1772–1804) French aristocrat and military leader. The only son of Henri, prince de Condé, he left France early in the Revolution. In 1792 he joined a force of exiled royalists (known as the *armée des émigrés* or *l'armée des princes*) and commanded them from 1796 until 1799. This was an army of princes who had left France after the Revolution, based at Worms, in Germany. Between 1793 and 1801 it was funded variously by Austria, Russia, and England, and fought against French Republican armies throughout Europe. This force was dissolved after the Peace of Lunéville in 1801 and he retired to Baden. Three years later he was wrongly accused by Napoleon of being involved in a plot to invade France, and he was kidnapped and shot. With his death, the House of Condé ended.

England The largest part of the island of Great Britain in north-west Europe, England is bounded by Scotland on the north and Wales on the west and forms the largest political division of the UK.

Physical. Roughly triangular in shape, it has a coastline of 3,200 km (2,000 miles); the land mass extends for some 560 km (or 350 miles) from the Cheviot Hills in the north to the South Downs, and from The Wash on its east coast to Land's End in the south-west. The highest point is Sca Fell at 978 m (3,209 feet), among the Cumbrian Mountains in the Lake District of the north-west, although there are peaks also in the central Pennine chain.

History. There were settlements in England from at least palaeolithic times, and considerable remains exist of neolithic and Bronze Age cultures. These were followed by the CELTS whose civilization spread over the whole country. The Romans under Julius CAESAR raided the south of Britain in 55 and 54 BC, but full-scale invasion did not take place until a century later; it was then ruled as a Roman province until the withdrawal of the last Roman garrison in the 5th century. In the 3rd to the 7th century ANGLES, SAXONS, and JUTES raided and settled, establishing independent kingdoms and when that of Wessex became dominant in the 9th century England emerged as a distinct political entity. From 1066 England under its Norman and PLANTAGENET kings was closely linked to France.

The neighbouring principality of WALES was conquered during the Middle Ages and politically incorporated in the 16th century. During the period of TUDOR rule England emerged as a Protestant state with a strong monarchy and as a naval power. In the 17th century the upheavals of the ENGLISH CIVIL WAR and the period of republican government under CROMWELL gave way to the RESTORATION of Charles II and the invitation to WILLIAM III. Scotland (ruled from England since 1603) was united with England in 1707 (Act of UNION), and it was then that Great BRITAIN was created.

English Civil War (1642–49) The armed struggle between the supporters of the king (CAVALIERS) and Parliamentarians (ROUNDHEADS), which erupted in 1642 and continued, with an interruption, until 1649. It arose from constitutional, religious, and economic differences between CHARLES I and the Members of the LONG PARLIAMENT. Of these the most decisive factor was religion since the attempts of LAUD to impose liturgical uniformity had alienated substantial numbers of clergy, gentry, and craftsmen. All sections of society were affected, though many in the localities desired peace not war, and sometimes families were divided by conflicting allegiances.

The king's primary objective in 1642 was the capture of London, a Parliamentary stronghold. After an indecisive engagement at EDGEHILL, he eventually had to take refuge in Oxford, which became his wartime capital. His plan in 1643 to bring together Cavalier armies from Oxford, Newcastle, and the south-west, followed by a march on London, was not realized. Meanwhile the balance was tipping toward the Roundheads, for by the SOLEMN LEAGUE AND COVENANT they secured Scottish assistance, of value in 1644 at MARSTON MOOR. Charles's attempt to march on London (1644) was frustrated at the Battle of Newbury. With the formation of the NEW MODEL ARMY, the Roundheads were able to inflict a crushing defeat on the Cavaliers at NASEBY (1645). Charles, having rejected terms previously offered him at the Uxbridge negotiations, eventually surrendered to the Scots near Newark (1646) after Oxford had fallen.

Charles's subsequent attempts to profit from divisions between the Parliamentary factions prevented a settlement from being reached in 1647. His escape to the Isle of Wight and 'Engagement' with the Scots sparked off the second phase of the war (1648). This consisted of unsuccessful Cavalier risings in Wales, Essex, and Kent, and a Scottish invasion which came to grief at PRESTON. PRIDE'S PURGE of Parliament then cleared the way for the trial and execution of the king and the establishment of the English COMMONWEALTH.

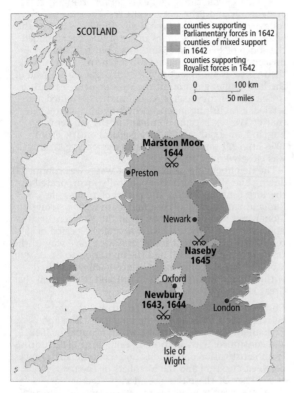

English Civil War (1642–49)   *London and south-east England were of particular strategic importance in the English Civil War. Charles I was forced to abandon the capital before the outbreak of fighting in 1642 and his failure to regain it made the Royalist defeat inevitable. The Royalists won a succession of minor victories in the south-east in 1642–43, but by the end of 1644 the Parliamentary forces were in the ascendant, having gained most of the Royalist strongholds in the north. By 1646 the military conflict was essentially at an end. An important factor in Parliament's success was its control of the navy, which denied the King the seaborne reinforcements and foreign subsidies made vital by Parliamentary control of most government revenue.*

Enlightenment (or 'Age of Reason') The philosophical, scientific, and rational attitudes, notably freedom from superstition and belief in religious tolerance, that characterized intellectual life in much of 18th-century Europe. In Germany the *Aufklärung* ('Enlightenment'), which extended from the middle of the 17th century to the beginning of the 19th century, was a literary and philosophical movement that included Goethe, Schiller, and Emanuel KANT. The Yiddish literature of Eastern Europe experienced a new dynamism, while a similarly invigorating freedom of ideas affected writers as far apart as Sweden, Russia, and Britain. In France the Enlightenment was associated with the *philosophes*, the literary men, scientists, and thinkers who were united

in their belief in the supremacy of reason and their desire to see practical change to combat inequality and injustice. The movement against established beliefs and institutions gained momentum throughout the 18th century under VOLTAIRE, ROUSSEAU, TURGOT, CONDORCET, and others. Through the publication of the *Encyclopédie* (1751–76) their attacks on the government, the Church, and the judiciary provided the intellectual basis for the French Revolution (see ENCYCLOPÉDISTS).

The English Enlightenment owed its origin both to the political theories of LOCKE, and to the French example. PAINE, an admirer of the French, advocated American independence, and many writers and poets transmitted Enlightenment ideas. In Scotland an intellectual movement flourished in Edinburgh between 1750 and 1800; its outstanding philosophers were Hume and Adam Smith and important scientific advances were made in chemistry, geology and medicine. The *Encyclopaedia Britannica*, began in 1768–71 as a dictionary of the arts and sciences, was issued by a 'Society of gentlemen in Scotland'. In literature, some have seen a connection between the philosophy of the Enlightenment, the growth of literary realism, and the rise of the novel. It influenced the Romantic movement in the arts by releasing the more individualist attitudes upon which this movement was based, and by inspiring the Romantics themselves to react against the coldly scientific intellectualism that the Enlightenment represented.

enosis (Greek, 'union') A Greek-Cypriot campaign for union of CYPRUS with Greece, launched by EOKA in the 1950s. Archbishop MAKARIOS's acceptance of independence from Britain without union (1960) led to renewed demands for *enosis* (1970), and its proclamation in 1974. In response Turkey invaded and partitioned the island to protect the Turkish minority.

entente cordiale (1904) (French, 'friendly understanding') An agreement between Britain and France. It aimed to settle territorial disputes and to encourage co-operation against perceived German pressure. Britain was to be given a free hand in Egyptian affairs and France in Morocco. Germany, concerned over this *entente*, tested its strength by provoking a crisis in Morocco in 1905, leading to the ALGECIRAS CONFERENCE (1906). The *entente* was extended in 1907 to include Russia and culminated in the formal alliance of Britain, France, and Russia in World War I against the Central Powers and the Ottoman empire.

Enver Pasha (1881–1922) Ottoman Turkish general and statesman. He played a prominent part in the 1908 YOUNG TURK revolution which restored the liberal constitution of 1876, and subsequently led a successful coup in 1913. As Minister of War (1913–18) he played the leading role in determining the entry of the Ottoman empire into World War I on the side of the Central Powers and in the conduct of Ottoman strategy during the war. In 1921 he fled to Turkistan, where he was killed leading opposition to Soviet rule.

EOKA (National Organization of Cypriot Fighters) The militant wing of the ENOSIS movement in Cyprus. Colonel Georgios Grivas (1898–1974), commander of the Greek Cypriot national guard, was its most famous leader. During 1954–59 guerrilla warfare and terrorist attacks were waged against the British forces. In 1956

MAKARIOS was exiled on the charge of being implicated with EOKA. After independence in 1960 the organization was revived as EOKA-B.

Ephesus An ancient city on the west coast of Asia Minor. It was founded by the Ionians, and maintained its independence against the kingdom of Lydia until CROESUS captured it in the middle of the 6th century BC. He assisted in the building of a famous temple there to Artemis, one of the SEVEN WONDERS OF THE WORLD, which was destroyed by fire in 356. The city was successively a member of the DELIAN LEAGUE and the ATHENIAN EMPIRE and fell under the overlordship of ALEXANDER THE GREAT, the Seleucids, and Pergamum, before becoming Roman territory in 133 BC. By this time it had outstripped its rival MILETUS to become one of the most prosperous cities of the eastern Mediterranean. Excavations have revealed much of the city, including shops, streets, temples, and a magnificent theatre. In 431 AD the Council of Ephesus, summoned by Theodosius II, confirmed the Nicean Creed and rejected the doctrine of Nestorius, who was excommunicated.

Epictetus (c. 50–135 AD) Phrygian STOIC philosopher. He was expelled from Rome c. 90 AD when Emperor Domitian proscribed all philosophers. Although he wrote nothing himself, the lecture notes taken by the historian Arrian, survived him. He was contemporary with the rise of Christianity and his Stoicism, combined with a strong belief in one God, has many similarities with the teaching of JESUS CHRIST. He insisted that trust in God was the only answer to the mysteries of pain, loss, and death. MARCUS AURELIUS admired him greatly.

Epicurus (341–270 BC) The founder of the philosophical school of Epicureans. He was educated at the ACADEMY in Athens and established his own school there (307–306). His followers (including women and slaves) lived very modestly, but his desire for privacy and his hedonistic doctrine led to many accusations of a selfish pursuit of pleasure from rival philosophers. Epicureans believed that pleasure was the only worthwhile aim in life, but not that life should be an endless search for new pleasures. Rather pleasure was a state of being, with natural and necessary desires being satisfied. Epicureans sought freedom from disturbances, and chose to avoid the stresses associated with involvement in politics and public life, and any deep emotional attachments.

Epidaurus An ancient Greek city-state in the north-east Peloponnese. It enjoyed close ties with nearby ARGOS and was famous for its oracular sanctuary to Asclepius, the god of healing (early 4th century BC). This comprised a large temple housing a gold and ivory statue of the god, and other religious and secular buildings. Its Greek theatre, marvellously well preserved and with excellent acoustics, is still used.

Epirus A coastal region in north-western Greece. It was famous in antiquity for its oracle at Dodona. The highpoint of its early history was the reign of the mercurial PYRRHUS, who considerably expanded and strengthened its territory. It fell foul of Rome after giving support to Macedonia, and in 167 BC 150,000 of its inhabitants were taken into slavery. Following the sacking of Constantinople by the knights of the Fourth Crusade in 1204, the despotate of Epirus was established by Byzantine Greeks, but in 1337 it returned to the re-established BYZANTINE EMPIRE. In 1430 it fell to the Ottoman Turks.

Equatorial Guinea A small country in equatorial West Africa on the Gulf of Guinea.

Physical. Equatorial Guinea includes the plateau of Río Muni bounded by Cameroon and Gabon, and the more mountainous and fertile, but smaller, island of Bioko (Fernando Póo).

Economy. Equatorial Guinea has a mainly agricultural economy, the main exports being timber and cocoa. Offshore oil and gold are exploited, and there are deposits of iron ore, copper, manganese, uranium, silica, and titanium. Equatorial Guinea is one of Africa's poorest countries; political upheaval has led to extensive emigration and agricultural neglect, with widespread food shortages. The economy is heavily dependent on foreign aid, largely from Spain.

History. Formerly a Spanish colony, it was a haunt of slave-traders and merchants. The mainland was not effectively occupied by Spain until 1926. Declared independent in 1968, a reign of terror followed until President Macias Nguema was overthrown and executed (1979) by his nephew, Obiang Nguema. The new regime pursued less repressive domestic policies with some degree of success. A referendum in November 1991 appeared to give overwhelming approval for multiparty politics, and in January 1992 an amnesty was granted by President Nguema to returning exiles; but in February a number of opposition leaders were arrested and some later died in prison. The Spanish government announced that promised economic aid was dependent upon implementation of democratization. Multiparty elections were planned, but opposition parties claimed they were not allowed to campaign freely, and called for a boycott of the elections. Few people voted in the elections, which were held in 1993 and were reported as being unfair by international observers. Nguema's ruling party were the official winners and retained power in February 1996, amid claims of electoral fraud. In 1995 the UN reiterated its concern about serious violations of human rights in the country.

CAPITAL:	Malabo
AREA:	28,051 sq km (10,831 sq miles)
POPULATION:	406,000 (1996)
CURRENCY:	1 CFA franc = 100 centimes
RELIGIONS:	Christian (mostly Roman Catholic) 88.8%; traditional beliefs 4.6%; atheist 1.4%; Muslim 0.5%
ETHNIC GROUPS:	Fang 72.0%; Bubi 14.7%; Duala 2.7%; Ibibio 1.3%; Maka 1.3%
LANGUAGES:	Spanish and French (official); Fang, Bubi, and local languages
INTERNATIONAL ORGANIZATIONS:	UN; OAU; Non-Aligned Movement; Franc Zone

Erasmus, Desiderius (c. 1467–1536) Dutch HUMANIST scholar. He was the first major European figure whose fame and influence were based on the printed word. He began life in poverty-stricken obscurity, the illegitimate son of a priest, entered the Augustinian order, but later left his monastery, and travelled extensively in Europe. In 1516 he published his own edition of the Greek New Testament, followed by a Latin translation. This was to have enormous significance to European disciples of the

NEW LEARNING. His many editions and translations of the Bible, early Christian authors, and the classics revolutionized European literary culture. His reputation was also enhanced by works like his *Adages* (1500) and *The Praise of Folly* (1511), a witty satire on monasticism and the Church, dedicated to his close friend, Thomas MORE. Until 1521 he moved throughout Europe, lecturing, debating, and writing letters to rulers and eminent men. He wished for peaceful, rational reform of the Church, and though he sympathized with Luther initially, he ultimately repudiated the Protestant Reformation. He retired to Basle, disillusioned by the sharpening religious conflict. In 1559 all his works were placed on the INQUISITION's Papal Index of prohibited books.

Erastus, Thomas (Thomas Lieber or Liebler) (1524–83) Swiss physician and Protestant theologian. He was appointed professor of medicine at Heidelberg University (1558), where he became closely associated with the introduction of reformed Protestantism into the Palatinate. He was a follower of ZWINGLI, and he tried unsuccessfully to prevent the imposition of a Calvinist system of Church government in Heidelberg in 1570. He was excommunicated for two years, and wrote his *Explication of the Gravest Question* at Basle (posthumously published in 1589). Later the term 'Erastian' was applied to those who wished to subordinate the interests and institutions of religion to the state, though Erastus himself never held such an extreme view.

Erhard, Ludwig (1897–1977) German economist and statesman, Chancellor of the German Federal Republic (1963–66). A Christian Democrat, he was Minister for Economic Affairs from 1949 to 1963, during which time he assisted in his country's 'economic miracle' (German, *Wirtschaftswunder*), which trebled the gross national product in theF post-war years.

Eric the Red (*fl.* 984) Norwegian explorer. Exiled from Iceland for manslaughter, Eric explored the land to the west, which had been skirted earlier in the 10th century by the Norwegian Gunnbjörn Ulfsson. He founded the first European settlement there, calling the region Greenland. He returned the following year with a party of colonists from Iceland to found the settlement of Brattahlid. His son Leif Ericsson sailed westward from Greenland *c.* 1001 and discovered land, which was probably Baffin Island, Labrador, and Newfoundland which he named VINLAND. He and his crew were the first Europeans known to have set foot on the American continent.

Eritrea A country in north-eastern Africa, on the Red Sea.

Physical. Eritrea consists of a narrow coastal low-lying area and rises towards the Ethiopian plateau in the south. It is very hot and arid.

Economy. The economy has been badly affected by the war of independence. Agricultural products include sorghum and livestock is raised. There are textile and footwear industries.

History. In 1869 Italy purchased the coastal town of Assab, and in 1885 began the occupation of the rest of Eritrea, which it declared a colony in 1889. It was from here that the Italians launched their disastrous campaign against ETHIOPIA in 1896, ending in their defeat at ADOWA. Under British military administration (1941–52), a plan to join the Muslim west with the Sudan and the Christian centre with Ethiopia failed. Instead, the United Nations voted to make Eritrea a federal area subject to Ethiopia. In 1962 Emperor HAILE SELASSIE declared it a province of Ethiopia and the Eritrean People's Liberation Front (EPLF) then emerged, seeking secession. Fierce fighting between the EPLF and the Ethiopian regime continued through the 1980s, in spite of drought and famine. In February 1990 the EPLF captured Massawa, and in 1991, in an alliance with the Ethiopian People's Revolutionary Democratic Front (EPRDF) and the Tigray People's Liberation Front, the EPLF defeated the Ethiopian government's forces. A transitional Eritrean government was set up by the EPLF and a referendum was held in 1993. Independence was approved by the referendum and was achieved later that year.

CAPITAL:	Asmara
AREA:	117,400 sq km (45,300 sq miles)
POPULATION:	3.627 million (1996)
CURRENCY:	nakfa
RELIGIONS:	Christian (Ethiopian Orthodox) 50.0%; Muslim 50.0%
LANGUAGES:	Arabic; Tigrinya; Tigré; minority languages
INTERNATIONAL ORGANIZATIONS:	UN; OAU

Ermine Street A Roman road in Britain that led northwards from Londinium (London) to Eboracum (York) by way of Lindum Colonia (Lincoln). Partly built *c.* 60–70 AD for the advance north of the FOSSE WAY, it followed some of the line of an earlier trackway. Its name came from the later Anglo-Saxons: a 'street' denoted a paved Roman road and it was linked with 'the people of Earna' (Earningas), a Germanic settlement leader.

escutage SCUTAGE.

esquire SQUIRE.

Essex, Robert Devereux, 2nd Earl of (1567–1601) English courtier, favourite of ELIZABETH I. He distinguished himself as a soldier during the DUTCH REVOLT (1586), but earned the queen's displeasure by participating in the disastrous Lisbon expedition (1589) and by marrying Sir Philip Sidney's widow (1590). The love-hate relationship between queen and courtier continued throughout the 1590s. He commanded an English contingent during the FRENCH WARS OF RELIGION (1591–92) and shared in the capture of Cadiz (1596). Gradually, his rivalry with the CECIL faction grew. In 1599 Elizabeth sent him as Lord Lieutenant of Ireland to put down TYRONE's rebellion. He failed ignominiously and was stripped of his offices. His subsequent attempt to raise the London people in an anti-Cecil coup (1601) led to his trial and execution for treason.

Essex, Robert Devereux, 3rd Earl of (1591–1646) English soldier, commander of the ROUNDHEADS. Although he served CHARLES I in 1625 he opposed him at the outbreak of the ENGLISH CIVIL WAR and in 1642 was appointed commander of the Roundhead forces, leading them at the Battle of EDGEHILL. After a number of Roundhead defeats, the NEW MODEL ARMY was organized in 1645 and Essex resigned his command.

Estates-General STATES-GENERAL.

Estonia A country of northern Europe, bounded on the north by the Gulf of Finland, on the east by Russia, on the south by Latvia, and on the west by the Baltic Sea.

Physical. Two large islands and numerous small ones lie off the coast, which is occasionally ice-bound in winter although the summers are warm. The mainland comprises a limestone plateau in the north, and a low-lying plain on which are situated forests and lakes of glacial origin.

Economy. The principal mineral resource is bituminous shale, together with peat; industries utilizing oil shale to produce artificial gas and electricity produce much of the power of north-west Russia and Belarus, but at serious environmental cost. Other industries include machinery, chemicals, timber, and textiles. Agriculture concentrates on animal husbandry.

History. Annexed by Russia in 1709, Estonia regained its independence in 1918, at the time of the Bolshevik revolution. Its history during the 1920s was of an agrarian revolution, whereby the great estates of the Baltic barons (mostly German) were broken up, creating a prosperous peasantry. An attempted communist uprising in 1924 was suppressed. The economy was adversely affected by the Great Depression and from 1934 until 1939 Estonia experienced a highly autocratic, neo-fascist regime led by Konstantin Paets. The latter admired Hitler, but his attempt to make a pact was invalidated by the NAZI-SOVIET PACT of August 1939. In September Soviet troops occupied key ports and in 1940 the whole country. Estonia welcomed German troops in 1941, but its anti-Bolshevik Resistance forces could not prevent the Red Army from reoccupying it in 1944 and it became a constituent republic of the Soviet Union. In February 1990 there were mass rallies in the capital Tallin demanding independence, and in May 1990 its Supreme Soviet reinstated the constitution of the Republic of Estonia of 1920. Talks began with the Soviet Union, which recognized the Republic's independence in September 1991, when it was admitted to the UN General Assembly. The collapse of its markets in Russia during 1991 resulted in an economic crisis, with food and fuel rationing in January 1992, eased by trade agreements with the European Community and by IMF support. In 1992 a new constitution was adopted and Lennart Meri (1929–   ) was elected President. Russian residents were disturbed by a proposed law that would have denied them Estonian citizenship. The law was amended (1993) before it was passed, making citizenship available to residents who passed Estonian language tests. Two mainly Russian cities voted for autonomy (1993) but the government declared their referendums illegal. In 1994 the last Russian troops withdrew from Estonia.

CAPITAL:	Tallin
AREA:	45,111 sq km (17,413 sq miles)
POPULATION:	1.475 million (1996)
CURRENCY:	1 kroon = 100 senti
RELIGIONS:	Lutheran Church
ETHNIC GROUPS:	Estonian 62.0%; Russian 30.0%
LANGUAGES:	Estonian (official); Russian
INTERNATIONAL ORGANIZATIONS:	UN; CSCE; North Atlantic Co-operation Council

Etaples, Treaty of (9 November 1492) A truce concluded between Charles VIII of France and Henry VII of England. The latter had revived claims from the HUNDRED YEARS WAR and raised an army, but little fighting took place following an invasion and Henry was bought off in return for a sum of 745,000 gold crowns paid in annual instalments. Charles was left free to proceed with his planned invasion of Italy.

Ethelred I (d. 871) King of Wessex (866–71). His rule coincided with unremitting Danish raids that assumed the scale of an invasion. Assisted by his younger brother, ALFRED, Ethelred had some success against those Danes advancing into neighbouring Mercia (868), and into Wessex itself (870). However, three major battles, including a defeat near the Danish base at Reading and a notable victory at Ashdown, and numerous skirmishes, failed to give any advantage to Ethelred who died of wounds received in the Battle at Merton.

Ethelred II (the Unready) (*c.* 968–1016) King of England (978–1016). He succeeded his stepbrother EDWARD THE MARTYR, who had been murdered on instructions from Ethelred's mother Alfrida. This inauspicious beginning to the reign was compounded by further blunders which earned Ethelred the title 'unready', meaning 'devoid of counsel'. Encouraged by his misfortunes the Danes renewed their invasions. Ethelred bought them off on five occasions (991, 994, 1002, 1007, 1012) with DANEGELD. His attempt (1002) to massacre all the Danes in his kingdom was answered (1013) by the invasion of the King of Denmark, SWEYN FORKBEARD, who ruled England until his death (1014) when Ethelred was restored.

ethics The philosophical study of the nature and grounds of moral thought and action. Ethical theories in this pure sense are sharply distinguished from moral systems, which are directed towards drawing up particular sets of rules by which to live (such as Christian morality), and from practical or applied ethics, the analysis of arguments advanced for particular moral conclusions (such as the rightness or wrongness of abortion). The most fundamental question in ethics is usually taken to be the justification of morality, that is whether or not it can be demonstrated that moral action is rational. Schools of ethics can be divided, very roughly, into three sorts. The first, which derives from ARISTOTLE's *Ethics*, gives pride of place to the virtues, such as justice, charity, and generosity, which are thought of as dispositions to act in ways that both tend to the fulfilment of the person who has them and to benefit the society of which he or she is a member. Aristotle's ethics are also often described as naturalistic, in that he seeks to exhibit a harmony between morality and human nature. The second, which is defended in most depth by KANT, is the school which makes the concept of duty central to morality (called 'deontology'). Kant argued that the only thing which is good in itself (as opposed to merely good as a means) is a 'good will', one which is freely in accordance with duty. Knowledge of one's duty, for Kant, follows from a realization that one is a rational being, and thus bound to obey what he called the 'categorical imperative', the requirement to respect all rational beings as autonomous 'ends in themselves'. Kant's views of morality are intimately connected with his view of free will. The third school of ethics is UTILITARIANISM whose goal is the 'greatest happiness of the greatest number'. Ethical theories may also be divided in another way, according to whether or not they allow that there is such a thing as objective moral truth; HUME, as a subjectivist, held that morality is profoundly rooted in our 'sentiments'. Ethics in the 20th century has been largely preoccupied with analysing the meaning of moral language, as in A. J. Ayer's theory of emotivism, whereby the meaning of a moral statement consists in its expressing an emotional attitude.

Ethiopia A country, formerly called Abyssinia, in north-eastern Africa. Sudan is on its eastern border, Eritrea on its northern border, and Kenya on its southern, while Somalia reaches round it on the east.

Physical. The low-lying Ogaden region in the east is very hot and arid; but the entire centre of the country is a group of volcanic mountain ranges with high plateaux where the air is mild and there is moderate summer rain. The Great Rift Valley runs through these, and the whole area is cut about with ravines and fertile valleys. In the north-west lies Lake Tana, the source of the Blue Nile, while in the south-west forests rise along the slopes of the mountain ranges.

Economy. The Ethiopian economy has been centrally planned and has been based on collectivized agriculture. Coffee, hides, and skins are the main exports. Ethiopia has an oil refinery, but derives most of its energy from firewood, charcoal, and dung. Industry is limited.

History. By the 2nd century AD the kingdom of AXUM had a brisk trade with Egypt, Syria, Arabia, and India in gold, ivory, and incense, and minted a gold currency. In the 4th century the court became Christian. Axum collapsed c. 1000, and, after a time of confusion, the ZAGWE dynasty emerged. In 1270 it was replaced by the Solomonic dynasty claiming lineal descent from SOLOMON and the Queen of Sheba, bringing the Amharas from the mountains of central Ethiopia to prominence. For Europe in the Middle Ages this was possibly the legendary kingdom of PRESTER JOHN. In the 16th century the Muslims of the lowlands attacked the Christian highlands, but were repulsed in 1542 with Portuguese artillery. When Jesuit missionaries came to Ethiopia Emperor Susenyos was converted to Roman Catholicism (1626). His son Fasilidas (1632–67), having forced him to abdicate, made Gondar the capital. Surrounded by Islam, and torn by warring factions, the empire foundered. The only unifying force was the Ethiopian COPTIC Church, and the empire was not reunited until 1855, when Emperor Tewodros II was crowned, and this was continued during the reign of MENELIK II.

Ethiopia successfully repelled Italian attempts at colonization by a decisive victory at ADOWA in 1896, but was conquered by MUSSOLINI in 1935–36. The Ethiopian emperor HAILE SELASSIE was restored in 1941 after the ABYSSINIAN CAMPAIGNS, and in the 1950s and 1960s Ethiopia emerged as a leading African neutralist state. Haile Selassie's failure to deal with severe social and economic problems led to his deposition by a group of radical army officers in 1974. A subsequent coup brought Colonel MENGISTU to power in 1977, but his centralized Marxist state was confronted by a Somali-backed guerrilla war in ERITREA. Famine broke out on a massive scale (1984–87), and despite Soviet and Cuban military assistance and an international relief effort to alleviate starvation, neither peace nor plenty returned. In May 1991 Mengistu was forced to flee the country by the Ethiopian People's Revolutionary Democratic Front (EPRDF) and their allies, who included the Eritrean People's Liberation Front (EPLF) and the Tigray People's Liberation Front. Peace talks in London resulted in the

recognition of an EPRDF government in Addis Ababa, which largely succeeded in restoring order. In 1991 the country was divided into nine regions, based on ethnic groupings. Eritrea voted to secede and became independent in 1993. A new constitution was adopted in 1994 for the so-called Federal Democratic Republic of Ethiopia, which gave the regions considerable autonomy. The first multiparty elections (1995) were won by the EPRDF, under Meles Zenawi, who became prime minister.

CAPITAL:	Addis Ababa
AREA:	1,223,500 sq km (472,400 sq miles)
POPULATION:	56.713 million (1996)
CURRENCY:	1 Ethiopian Birr = 100 cents
RELIGIONS:	Ethiopian Orthodox 40.0%; Muslim 40.0%; traditional beliefs 15.0%; other Christian 4.5%
ETHNIC GROUPS:	Galla 40.0%; Amhara-Tigre 32.0%; Kafa Sidano 9.0%; Somali 6.0%; Nilotic 6.0%; Afar 5.0%
LANGUAGES:	Amharic (official); Gallinya; local languages
INTERNATIONAL ORGANIZATIONS:	UN; OAU; Non-Aligned Movement

Etruscans The inhabitants of ancient Etruria, an Italian region west of the Apennines and the River Tiber approximating to modern Tuscany. Twelve independent cities including Vulci, Clusium, and Cortona were formed into a league and came to dominate central Italy in the 7th and 6th centuries BC. Tradition held that they came from Asia Minor in the 10th century BC, though it is now believed that they were native to Italy before that and only culturally influenced by the Greek colonies of south Italy. In the 6th century BC they were driven out of southern central Italy by the Greeks, Latins, and Samnites. In the following century their navy was defeated off Cumae. Traditionally, in 510 BC the last Etruscan king of Rome, TARQUIN, was expelled. In the 4th century they were driven out of Elba and Corsica, defeated by the Gauls in 390, and finally allied themselves with Rome after defeat in 283. From this time they came under Rome's control and began to lose their unique cultural identity.

Etruscan art reveals an aristocratic society in which women enjoyed an emancipated style of life. The Etruscan language has so far proved beyond translation; it was still spoken and written in the 1st century AD but no literature survives.

Eugène of Savoy (1663–1736) Prince of the House of Savoy. He was born in Paris; his mother, Olympe Mancini, was a niece of MAZARIN. When Vienna was besieged by the Turks in 1683 he entered the Austrian army and became one of the country's greatest generals. In 1697 he was given command of the Danube army and won a decisive victory over the Turks at Zente. In the War of the SPANISH SUCCESSION he was president of the Council of War, co-operated successfully with MARLBOROUGH at BLENHEIM and OUDENARDE, and won control of north Italy at the Battle of Turin in 1706. In 1716–17 he led another successful campaign against the Turks and recovered Belgrade.

eugenics The study and doctrine of improving a population by controlled breeding for desirable inherited characteristics. The concept was widely discussed in Britain, the USA, and Europe in the late

19th and early 20th centuries, the term having been coined by the British psychologist Sir Francis Galton in 1883. Advocates of eugenics seek either to encourage the procreation of supposedly superior human beings or to prevent the procreation of supposedly inferior ones. Any complete eugenic policy would involve decisions about which characteristics were desirable and which undesirable, assumptions that these characteristics were inherited rather than socially determined, and a degree of compulsion. Because eugenic ideas flourished under NAZISM, they became discredited and are not often voiced. However, implicitly eugenic practices continue in many parts of the world: for example, the denial to disabled people of the right to have children, selective sterilization, and amniocentesis followed by the offer of abortion if chromosomal abnormality emerges. Furthermore, advances in genetic engineering have raised serious concerns about the potential for cloning individual human beings and for genetic screening of individuals to determine if they or their offspring are at risk from hereditary diseases.

Eugénie, Marie de Montijo (1826–1920) Empress of the French and wife of NAPOLEON III. Throughout her husband's reign she contributed much to the brilliance of his court and acted as regent on three occasions. When the empire collapsed (September 1870), she fled to England. She retained a close interest in European affairs until her death in Spain in 1920.

eunuch A castrated human male. Eunuchs were used as guardians of harems in ancient China and in the Persian empire of the Achaemenids and also at the courts of the Byzantine emperors and the Ottoman sultans. They became the friends and advisers of the rulers of these powers, as they did of Roman emperors. Castration was also imposed as a form of punishment (ABELARD suffered in this way); was practised voluntarily by some Christian sects (the most notable Christian eunuch being the

theologian Origen); and was used to produce male adult sopranos — castrati — in Italy until Pope Leo XIII banned the practice in 1878.

Eureka Rebellion (1854) An armed conflict between diggers and authorities on the Ballarat gold fields of Australia. Gold had been found here in 1851; by 1853 over 20,000 diggers from around the world had crowded into Ballarat. Their grievances, which included the licence system and its administration, corruption among officials, lack of political representation, and limited access to land, culminated in an attack by soldiers and police on diggers who were in a stockade on the 'Eureka lead'. Thirteen diggers faced charges of high treason; one case was dropped and the others were acquitted. A royal commission led to reforms on the gold-fields.

Europe The smallest continent of the northern hemisphere, stretching westward from the Ural Mountains in Russia and surrounded on three sides by sea.

Physical. The structure of Europe is complex. In the north-west, mountains of old, hard rock occupy most of the Scandinavian Peninsula, the north-west of the British Isles, and Brittany in France; much of this area is covered by barren rocks and moorland. Most of it is separated by the shallow North and Baltic seas from the North European Plain, which spreads from England and France across the north of the continent to Finland and the Baltic states and down to the Black Sea. Southern Europe is hilly or mountainous, except for two plains: a triangular plain in northern Italy and the broad one of the middle Danube. From west to east is a curving chain of ranges – the Pyrenees, Alps, and Carpathians – while pointing southward are the Apennines and the parallel ranges of the Balkan Peninsula. They form barriers, yet are so cut by rivers and valleys that no part of Europe is completely isolated. The extreme south is volcanic, being close to the edge of the Eurasian plate.

Eureka Rebellion   *This sketch from a newspaper of 1853 shows gold-diggers in Australia. The gold-diggers were often accused of being no more than groups of lawless ex-convicts and vagabonds.*

History. Throughout its history Europe has exerted an influence disproportionate to its size. Its most important ancient civilizations developed in the Mediterranean region. Greek civilization reached its zenith between *c.* 500 and *c.* 300 BC, to be succeeded by that of ROME. CHRISTIANITY became the official religion of the Roman empire in the late 4th century, shortly before the empire's western section succumbed to Germanic invaders. The eastern section lived on as the BYZANTINE EMPIRE, centred on Constantinople, which eventually fell to the OTTOMAN Turks in 1453.

During the MIDDLE AGES a politically fragmented Europe underwent varying degrees of invasion and colonization from MOORS, VIKINGS, MAGYARS, and others. The attempt of the powerful FRANKS to re-establish the Western Roman empire soon failed, but the year 962 marked the foundation of what later became the HOLY ROMAN EMPIRE. The ROMAN CATHOLIC CHURCH became the unifying force throughout the continent; but in the wake of the RENAISSANCE, the 16th century bought about a religious schism (the REFORMATION) in western Christendom and ushered in an era of national and international politico-religious warfare.

Post-medieval Europe was characterized by the rise of strong individual nation-states such as Spain, France, England, the Netherlands, and eventually Russia. Their influence on the rest of the world was the result of their acquisition of vast empires outside Europe. Imperial expansion continued through the age of European revolutions, of which the FRENCH REVOLUTION was the most momentous. In the late 18th and early 19th centuries north-western Europe became the first region of the world to undergo industrialization (see INDUSTRIAL REVOLUTION).

The modern history of Europe is largely that of its constituent nations. In the 20th century European history has been dominated by WORLD WAR I and WORLD WAR II. Since the end of World War II the EUROPEAN COMMUNITY and its successor, the EUROPEAN UNION, have brought an altogether more hopeful era to the peoples of Europe.

European Commission (until 1993 the Commission of the European Communities) One of the principal institutions of the EUROPEAN UNION, and the one responsible for planning Union policies. Its loyalties are to the EU as a whole, rather than to the individual member states. The present-day European Commission dates from 1967, when a treaty merging the three executive bodies of the three different Communities (the EUROPEAN ECONOMIC COMMUNITY, the European Coal and Steel Community (ECSC), and the European Atomic Energy Community (EURATOM)) came into effect. The Commission heads a large Secretariat in Brussels, which submits proposals for consideration by the Council of Ministers. The Commission is also charged with the implementation of decisions, once they have been made by the Council. It also acts as a mediator between the different EU members. There are 17 commissioners, appointed by the governments of the member states: two from the UK, Germany, France, Italy, and Spain, and one from other EU member states. Each commissioner has responsibility for a different policy area. The President of the Commission is normally appointed for a four-year term. During the later 1980s, particularly in Britain under Margaret THATCHER, criticism developed against the growing bureaucracy of the Commission

under its President, Jacques DELORS, who held office from 1985 to 1994. He was succeeded as President by Jacques Santer.

European Community (EC) An organization of European states. It came into being (1967) through the merger of the EUROPEAN ECONOMIC COMMUNITY (EEC), the European Atomic Energy Community (EURATOM), and the European Coal and Steel Community (ECSC), and was committed to economic and political integration as envisaged by the Treaties of ROME. Its membership comprised the six original members of the EEC, together with Denmark, Ireland, and the UK (from 1973), Greece (1981), and Spain and Portugal (1986). Much controversy surrounded Britain's entry, which was delayed for 13 years from initial application, mainly by the use of the French veto under President DE GAULLE. It operated within a single institutional framework comprising the EUROPEAN COMMISSION, the European Council of Ministers, the European Court of Justice, and the EUROPEAN PARLIAMENT; these were assisted by the advisory Economic and Social Committee, and by the Court of Auditors. The Single European Act of 1986 had envisaged a single trading area by January 1993 but, to make this possible, members had to accept numerous compromises, many of which were not popular. In 1993 the European Community was succeeded by the EUROPEAN UNION, following the Treaty of MAASTRICHT in 1992.

European Economic Community (EEC, Common Market) An economic organization of European states set up by the Treaties of ROME in March 1957. Its member states agreed to co-ordinate their economic policies, and to establish common policies for agriculture, transport, the movement of capital and labour, the erection of common external tariffs, and the ultimate establishment of political unification. From its inception the EEC provided an extension of the functional co-operation inaugurated by the European Coal and Steel Community (made up of Belgium, France, Federal Republic of Germany, Italy, Luxembourg, and the Netherlands). It owed much to the campaigning initiative of Jean MONNET and to the detailed planning of Paul-Henri SPAAK. Preliminary meetings were held at Messina in 1955, which led to the Treaties of Rome in 1957 and the formal creation of the EEC in January 1958. Co-operation in the EEC was most organized in the area of agriculture, and the Common Agricultural Policy (CAP) was the largest item in the EC budget. The EEC merged with the European Atomic Energy Community (EURATOM) and the European Coal and Steel Community (ECSC) in 1967 to form the EUROPEAN COMMUNITY (EC).

European Free Trade Association (EFTA) An organization of western and northern European countries which created an industrial free-trade area among its members. Based in Geneva, the Association was set up in 1960 by eight countries who wished to reduce trade barriers and thereby create a larger market for their manufactured goods, but who were not ready to accept the broader political and economic obligations implied by membership of the EEC. By 1973 its membership was reduced to six (following the departure of the UK and Denmark, when they joined the EC), comprising: Austria, Finland, Iceland, Norway, Sweden, and Switzerland. A series of agreements linked

EC and EFTA members, with a trend towards growing collaboration. In 1984, an EFTA–EC tariff-free zone was established, and in the Luxembourg Declaration of the same year, guidelines were laid down for developing the EC–EFTA relationship and for the creation of a European Economic Area (EEA), comprising all EC–EFTA countries. The EEA came into existence in 1994, comprising member states of the European Union and EFTA (not including Switzerland). In 1995 Austria, Finland, and Sweden joined the EU, leaving EFTA much reduced in size and casting some doubt on its survival.

European Monetary System (EMS) A system devised by EUROPEAN COMMUNITY members with the aim of promoting monetary stability by limiting exchange-rate fluctuations. The system was set up in 1979 by the then nine members of the EC. The EMS comprised three principal elements: the European Currency Unit (ECU), the monetary unit used in EC transactions; the Exchange Rate Mechanism (ERM), whereby those member states taking part agreed to maintain currency fluctuations within certain agreed limits; and the European Monetary Co-operation Fund, which issues the ECU and oversees the ERM. The 1992 Maastricht Treaty set a timetable for the longer-term goal of Economic and Monetary Union (EMU) including the introduction of a single European currency and a European central bank. These goals suffered a major setback in autumn 1992, when the EMS effectively collapsed owing to the inability of the British, Italian, and Spanish governments to maintain their currencies above the floor levels set by the ERM. Several of the remaining currencies would also have been forced out if the limits of permitted fluctuation had not been relaxed in 1993. Despite this, moves to create a central bank and a single currency (to be known as the Euro) by 1999 gathered pace once more in the later 1990s.

European Parliament One of the constituent institutions of the EUROPEAN UNION (formerly the EUROPEAN COMMUNITY), meeting in Strasbourg or Luxembourg. Set up in 1952 under the terms of the treaty which established the European Steel and Coal Community (ECSC), the Parliament was replaced and extended in 1958 to serve two new communities, the EUROPEAN ECONOMIC COMMUNITY and the European Atomic Energy Community (EURATOM). From 1958 to 1979 it was composed of representatives drawn from the Assemblies of the member states. However, quinquennial direct elections have taken place since 1979, and it is now made up of 626 seats, distributed among member states, according to the size of their populations. Its powers have increased, and it is now consulted on all major EU issues, including the annual budget, and it advises on legislation. Although it has the theoretical power to dismiss the EUROPEAN COMMISSION by a vote of censure, its actual powers are restricted, and its role has been advisory rather than legislative. However, under the European Co-operation Procedure formalized under the Single European Act (1987), the Parliament was given a greater say over the proposals for the completion of a single European market in 1992, and under the Maastricht Treaty (1992) the powers of the Parliament were enhanced to include the right of veto on some bills, further budgetary control, and a say in the membership of the Commission.

European Union (EU) An organization of European countries that replaced the EUROPEAN COMMUNITY in 1993. The EU took over all the EC institutions, such as the EUROPEAN PARLIAMENT, but also extended the scope of the EC according to the terms of the Treaty of MAASTRICHT. The member countries agreed to add a shared foreign policy and a commitment to co-operation on security matters (including justice and policing) to their economic and political links under the EC. Consequently the EU is often said to have 'three pillars', one pillar being the former EC, another being the co-ordination of foreign and external security policies (with the WESTERN EUROPEAN UNION as the EU's defence wing), and the third being the co-ordination of internal matters and justice (particularly on immigration and political asylum). Despite the failure of the EUROPEAN MONETARY SYSTEM in 1992–93 and the uneasiness of some members, plans to create a single European currency by 1999 have gathered pace. There have also been disagreements over social policy and the sovereignty of member nations; the UK, which has opposed any suggestion of FEDERALISM, at first opted out of the common policy on social issues that was adopted by other members, but accepted it in 1997.

In 1995 Austria, Finland, and Sweden joined the EU, increasing the total number of members to 15. The EU has agreements of association with many countries. Turkey and Malta have been promised eventual admittance to the Union when they have fulfilled certain conditions. Morocco applied to join in 1987 but was rejected. Poland, Hungary, the Czech Republic, Estonia, and Cyprus have now been formally invited to join the Union early in the millenium, while the applications of Slovenia and Switzerland are also under consideration. The EU has agreed to co-operate with other former Eastern bloc countries, including Romania, Bulgaria, and Slovakia. More limited co-operation agreements were made in 1994 with Russia and the Ukraine. With the EUROPEAN FREE TRADE ASSOCIATION (EFTA), the EU established a frontier-free zone in 1994, known as the European Economic Area (EEA).

Evatt, Herbert Vere (1894–1965) Australian statesman. A federal politician (1925–30, 1940–60), he led the Labor Opposition (1951–60). Noted for his championship of the rights of the smaller nations, and for greater independence from Britain, Evatt presided over the UN General Assembly (1948–49).

Evesham, Battle of (4 August 1265). A crucial engagement in the second BARONS' WAR (1264–65) when Prince Edward defeated Simon de MONTFORT and rescued his father Henry III. Simon's headless corpse was buried in the abbey at Evesham which subsequently became a place of pilgrimage.

Évian Agreements (1962) A series of agreements negotiated at Évian-les-Bains in France. Secret negotiations between the government of General DE GAULLE and representatives of the provisional government of the Algerian Republic of BEN BELLA began in Switzerland in December 1961 and continued in March 1962 at Évian. A ceasefire commission was set up and the French government, subject to certain safeguards, agreed to the establishment of an independent Algeria following a referendum. The agreements were ratified by the French National Assembly but were violently attacked by the extremist Organization de l'Armée Secrète (OAS).

evolution, human The stages of development whereby humans diverged from ape-like ancestors and took on their present form. The process took at least five million years (HOMINIDS, AUSTRALOPITHECINES, HOMO HABILIS, HOMO ERECTUS, HOMO SAPIENS, and NEANDERTHALS). Many details remain uncertain, particularly of the relationship between the australopithecines and the *Homo* lineage, and the position of such remains as BROKEN HILL, and the later Neanderthals. However, the general outline is becoming clearer with every new discovery and as DATING SYSTEMS become more refined.

Exchequer A former English government department dealing with finance. The Normans created two departments dealing with finance. One was the Treasury, which received and paid out money on behalf of the monarch, the other was the Exchequer which was itself divided into two parts, lower and upper. The lower Exchequer was an office for receiving money and was connected to the Treasury; the upper Exchequer was a court of law dealing with cases related to revenue, and was merged with the High Court of Justice in 1880.

excise CUSTOMS AND EXCISE.

Exclusion crisis The attempt to exclude James, Duke of York, later JAMES II, from succeeding to the English throne because he was a Catholic. After the unmasking of the POPISH PLOT the Whigs tried in three successive parliamentary sessions to force through a bill to alter the succession but all three attempts (1679, 1680, 1681) failed. The Whig opposition eventually triumphed at the GLORIOUS REVOLUTION.

exclusionists (or exclusives) Australian settlers opposed to the emancipation of ex-convicts. The name was applied in New South Wales, during the period of CONVICT TRANSPORTATION, to those people who opposed the restoration of civil rights to ex-convicts or EMANCIPISTS. The exclusives were composed for the most part of civil and military officials and of gentleman squatters and settlers who were called in derision 'Pure Merinos'.

excommunication The exclusion of an individual from membership and especially the sacraments of the Christian Church. The process was first used against individuals holding unorthodox or heretical religious beliefs, but it was later employed as a disciplinary and political weapon against rulers who opposed the Church and especially the papacy; Pope Adrian IV was one of the first to use it in this way. It could include releasing subjects from their duty to obey their lord which could seriously threaten a weak king. King John of England was punished in this way, as was the Holy Roman Emperor Henry IV who finally submitted to Pope Gregory VII at CANOSSA. Its effectiveness as a weapon depended on the recipient's willingness to be frightened by it, which is why it was frequently employed in the medieval period when the majority of the populace was greatly concerned with its spiritual welfare. The interdict was a less severe punishment that was also used against the laity.

Exile The captivity of the Jews in BABYLON (the 'Babylonian Captivity'). In 597 BC the Babylonians captured JERUSALEM and took King Jehoiachin and many leaders of the Judaean community, including the prophet EZEKIEL, into exile in Babylon. Following further revolt, they again attacked Jerusalem and, after a three-year siege captured and destroyed it in 586 BC. Many of those taken to Babylon were settled in communities, with the result that distinctive Jewish teaching, religion, and life could continue. In 539 BC Babylon fell to Persia and one year later CYRUS II (the Great) gave permission for Jews who wished to do so to return home. The number returning was probably small and the return protracted over a long time.

Exodus The departure of the Israelites under MOSES from their captivity in Egypt in about 1300 BC; the story is recorded in the Old Testament book of Exodus. According to the biblical account, the Israelites were pursued by the pharaoh's army, but were saved by a tidal wave that swept across a region known as the Reed Sea (probably near one of the lakes now joined by the Suez Canal). The Israelites then spent over 40 years wandering in the wilderness of Sinai, during which time they received through MOSES the Ten Commandments which established their relationship with their God and between one another. After the death of Moses, Joshua became their leader, and his capture of Jericho led to the occupation of CANAAN. The variety of sources make it impossible to regard this narrative as a straightforward historical account, but it is central to Jewish history as evidence of God's favour to his chosen people and is commemorated annually in the Passover feast.

exploration The investigation of undiscovered territories. For the first explorers, travel was easier by sea than by land: PHOENICIAN traders frequently sailed to Galicia (in Spain) and Brittany, and perhaps even to Cornwall.

In the early Middle Ages the VIKINGS sailed as far west as Greenland and to North America (ERIC THE RED) and curiosity about the 'marvels of the east' led the Italian MARCO POLO overland to China (1271–95). The Chinese Ming emperors supported the seven voyages of discovery of ZHENG HE (1405–33). Under the patronage of Prince HENRY THE NAVIGATOR, the Portuguese in the 15th century sailed to the Indian Ocean, and in 1498 Vasco DA GAMA crossed the South Atlantic; in 1516 the Portuguese reached China. Probably with the aim of reaching the East, Christopher COLUMBUS crossed the North Atlantic (1492) and Ferdinand MAGELLAN found the strait which enabled him to reach the Chinese coast (1521). The North American landmass was such a deterrent that searches were long made for a navigable passage to the north of it: the search for a north-west passage led CABOT to what was probably Hudson Bay (1509) and CARTIER along the St Lawrence River (1534–41). North America's interior began to be explored in the 17th century, but it was not until *c.* 1730 that the Rocky Mountains were discovered, and the continent was not crossed until 1793, when Mackenzie traversed Canada. The United States was first crossed by Lewis and Clark, in 1803. His previous scientific research helped Captain James COOK secure backing from the ROYAL SOCIETY for his voyages to New Zealand and eastern Australia (1769–77).

The exploration and mapping of the interiors of continents continued throughout the 19th century and often accompanied colonialism. Only very remote areas of the world have remained uncharted.

Ezekiel (6th century BC) Hebrew prophet. He was a priest who was taken into EXILE by Nebuchadnezzar in

Babylon in 597 BC. He denounced religious apostasy and idolatry and prophesized the destruction of Jerusalem and the Jewish nation. As soon as Jerusalem fell, in 586 BC, he began to prophesy that God would restore the nation and that the Israelites would begin life back in their land in a new relationship with their God. Ezekiel's teaching paved the way for the religious nationalism of post-exilic Judaism. In Islam Ezekiel (Hizkil) is usually identified with Dhū-l-Kifl, a prophet mentioned in the Koran.

Ezra (5th or 4th century BC) Jewish priest who was instrumental in reforming Judaism after the EXILE in Babylon. Although the Biblical record is unclear, it is thought that Ezra arrived in Jerusalem in 397 BC with authority from the Persian king Artaxerxes II. He reformed the system of worship at the Jerusalem Temple and established a written code of laws. He also set up and organized the priestly leadership of Judaism. His work was facilitated by the political successes of NEHEMIAH.

F

Fabians A society of British socialists aiming at gradual social change through democratic means. They took their name from the Roman general Quintus FABIUS Maximus, who achieved his victories through a policy of attrition. The Fabian Society was founded in 1884 by a group of intellectuals who believed that new political pressures were needed to achieve social reforms. George Bernard Shaw, Beatrice and Sidney WEBB, Annie BESANT, and Hubert Bland were its leading members. The slogan of the early Fabians was 'the inevitability of gradualism'. Reforms would be secured by the patient, persistent use of argument, and propaganda through constitutional methods. It was one of the socialist societies that helped found the Labour Representation Committee, the origin of the LABOUR PARTY, in 1900. Trade Union militancy from 1910 to 1926, and the harshness of unemployment in the 1930s, weakened the appeal of Fabian gradualism but by 1939, with moderate leaders, such as Clement ATTLEE, coming to the forefront, their influence revived. The Fabian Society has continued to conduct research and publicize its ideas.

Fabius, Quintus, Maximus Verrucosus Cunctator ('the Delayer') (d. 203 BC) Roman general and consul five times between 233 and 209. He was appointed dictator in 221 and again for a second time in 217 after the Battle of Trasimene, during the Second PUNIC WAR. Appreciating that the Carthaginian forces were superior to his own, he declined to engage in pitched battles. His unspectacular tactics of slow harassment against Hannibal's army in Italy at first won little popular support, and the nickname Cunctator was intended as an insult. After the defeat at Cannae (216) the feeling against his strategy waned and the insult became a title of approval. He opposed SCIPIO's aggressive war against Carthage on the African mainland.

Factory Acts Laws to regulate conditions of employment of factory workers. Textile factories first developed in Britain and the USA in the late 18th century, employing many workers, especially women and children, and replacing the older 'domestic' textile industry. Conditions were sometimes dangerous and working hours were long. In Britain two early Acts of Parliament in 1802 and 1819, which aimed to protect children and apprentices, failed because they could not be enforced. The Factory Act of 1833 banned the employment of children under nine, restricted working hours of older children, and provided for the appointment of factory inspectors. Sometimes fiercely opposed by industrialists, it was fought for in Parliament by Christian philanthropists such as Lord SHAFTESBURY. Legislation in Britain (1844 and 1847) extended protection of workers into mines and other industries and reduced the working day to ten hours. A Factory Act (1874) consolidated the ten-hour day and raised the age of children in employment to ten, this being further raised to 12 in 1901 and 14 in 1920. In the 20th century a complicated structure of industrial law developed. Legislation similar to the British was enacted in most European countries, particularly during the 1890s, and also in the USA, where each state developed its own factory laws. These were consolidated by a federal act, the Fair Labor Standards Act of 1938. In the early 20th century conditions of work in much of the Far East remained poor, with child labour often used and excessive hours being demanded, although in British India legislation had begun in 1881 to try to tackle these problems. It was to counter the problem of child labour and the exploitation of factory workers, particularly women, that the INTERNATIONAL LABOUR ORGANIZATION (ILO) was formed by the League of Nations (1919). Despite such initiatives, the exploitation of Third World women and children in such trades as the garment industry remains a matter of serious concern. In Britain workers have been further protected by such legislation as the Employers' Liability (Compulsory Insurance) Act (1969), the Health and Safety at Work Act (1974), and the Employment Act (1989). The so-called 'Social Chapter' of the MAASTRICHT TREATY (1992), harmonizing labour laws throughout the EU, was adopted by all the member states except the UK. The British Conservatives, then in power, and the far-right French National Front were the only mainstream European political parties to oppose this legislation. After the Conservatives were defeated in May 1997, the new Labour government adopted the Social Chapter.

fairs (Latin *feriae*, 'holiday') Seasonal assemblies for the sale of goods, usually with a variety of amusements and entertainment. Fairs were held at religious festivals in China (12th century BC), Greece (including the Olympic Games), and in Rome. The fair of St Denis, near Paris, was probably the first in Western Europe (629). With Europe's economic recovery in the 10th century fairs proliferated in Italy (Pisa, Venice, Genoa), Flanders (Bruges, Ypres), Germany (Cologne, Leipzig), Russia (NOVGOROD), England (Boston, Stourbridge, St Bartholomew's in London). The most important, however, were in Champagne and Brie in France where they were held seasonally at Lagny-sur-Marne (January), Bar-sur-Aube (Lent), St Quirface in Provins (May), Troyes (June and October), and St Ayoul in Provins (September). Merchants from the Middle East and Africa attended these fairs which lasted up to six weeks. Although international trading at fairs generally declined from the 14th century as merchants left long-distance trading to their agents, many continued at such towns as Milan, Frankfurt-on-Main, Brussels, and Paris. Specialist fairs in England were held at Horncastle in Lincolnshire (horses), and at Ipswich in Suffolk (sheep).

Fair Deal The name given by US President TRUMAN to his proposed domestic programme in 1949. By it he hoped to advance beyond the NEW DEAL, to introduce measures on CIVIL RIGHTS, fair employment practices, education, health, social security, support for low-income housing, and a new farm subsidy programme. A coalition of Republicans and conservative southern

Democrats blocked most of his measures in Congress, and although he did secure some advances in housing and social security the bulk of his proposals were lost.

Fairfax, Thomas, 3rd Baron Fairfax of Cameron (1612–71) English Parliamentary general. He was largely responsible for the defeat of the Royalists in the ENGLISH CIVIL WAR. A Puritan, he rose from commander of the Yorkshire cavalry (1642) to commander-in-chief of the NEW MODEL ARMY (1645). He proved to be heroically brave, and popular with his men. His victories included the Battles of MARSTON MOOR (1644) and NASEBY (1645). He disassociated himself from the decision to execute CHARLES I, and resigned his command in 1650, rather than lead the campaign against Royalist resistance into Scotland.

Faisal I (or Feisal) (1885–1933), King of Iraq (1921–33). The son of HUSSEIN IBN ALI, he commanded the northern Arab army in Jordan, Palestine, and Syria in association with T. E. LAWRENCE in the Arab Revolt of 1916–18. In 1920 Faisal was chosen King of Syria by the Syrian National Congress but was expelled by France, the mandatory power. He was then made King of Iraq by Britain, who held the mandate for that territory. As ruler of Iraq (1921–33) he demonstrated considerable political skill in building up the institutions of the new state.

Faisal ibn Abd al-Aziz (1905–75) King of Saudi Arabia (1964–75). Brother of King Saud ibn Abd al-Aziz, he became effective ruler of Saudi Arabia in 1958, dealing with the main consequences for Saudi Arabia of the immense increase of oil revenues. Pro-West, he worked in association with the USA while remaining inflexible in his opposition to Israel's ambitions and unyielding on Arab claims to Jerusalem. Faisal stood against the demands of radical Arab nationalism represented by Egypt under NASSER. He was assassinated by a nephew.

Falange, the (Spanish, 'phalanx') A Spanish political party, the Falange Española. Founded in 1933 by José António Primo de Rivera, the son of General PRIMO DE RIVERA, its members were equally opposed to the reactionary Right and the revolutionary Left. Their manifesto of 1934 proclaimed opposition to republicanism, party politics, capitalism, Marxism, and the class war, and it proposed that Spain should become a syndicalist state on Italian FASCIST lines. During the SPANISH CIVIL WAR Franco saw the potential value of the Falange provided that its aims were made acceptable to traditionalists and monarchists. The death of José António at the hands of the Republicans made it possible for Franco to adopt the movement in April 1937. After World War II it ceased to be identified with fascism and its influence waned. It was formally abolished in 1977.

Falkirk, Battles of Two battles fought at Falkirk, a town 16 km (10 miles) from Stirling in Scotland. The first (22 July 1298) resulted in victory for EDWARD I of England over Sir William WALLACE, leader of the Scottish resistance to English sovereignty. The second (17 January 1746) was a victory for the Jacobite army of Prince Charles Edward Stuart over the government forces in THE FORTY-FIVE rebellion.

Falkland Islands (Spanish, 'Islas Malvinas') A crown colony of the UK, consisting of a group of islands in the South Atlantic.

Physical. The group comprises two main islands and nearly a hundred smaller ones, lying some 480 km (300 miles) off the coast of Argentina. Inland from the jagged coastlines of East and West Falkland the ground rises to heights of about 690 m (2,260 feet), bare of trees and windswept. The moors are the home of many species of bird and hundreds of thousands of sheep, but no cultivation is possible. Winters are long, with much snow, and even summer temperatures seldom rise above 10°C (50°F). South Georgia is an even bleaker island 1,290 km (800 miles) away to the east and further south. The South Sandwich, South Shetland, and South Orkney Islands lie more southward still, only just outside the Antarctic Circle. They are covered with snow and ice all year.

Economy. Wool is the dominant export, though fishing is the largest source of revenue since the declaration of a 241-km (150-mile) fishing zone around the island in 1987. The British government authorized exploration for oil in the 200-mile zone around the islands in 1991 and in 1993 a preliminary report by the British Geological Survey indicated the presence of significant deposits of oil.

History. The Falkland Islands have experienced a complicated diplomatic history since their discovery in the late 16th century, having been claimed at various times by the Spanish, the British, the Argentines, and the French. They were first occupied in 1764 when French settlers began grazing sheep there. Within a year the French were dislodged by the British who claimed the islands on the basis of their discovery in 1592 by Captain John Davis and an expedition a century later under the command of Captain John Strong. When the French were driven out they sold their rights to Spain, and conflict continued over their possession.

In 1806 Spanish rule over Argentina ceased, and in 1820 the Argentinians claimed to succeed Spain in possession of the Falklands. The British objected and reclaimed the islands (1832) as a crown colony. In 1882–83 a British naval squadron occupied the islands for the protection of the seal-fisheries. Since 1833 the Argentinians have exerted their claims and have disputed possession of the Falklands by the British. This rivalry culminated in 1982 with the FALKLANDS (MALVINAS) WAR. The large British naval and military force in the area was reduced following the completion of Mount Pleasant airport in 1985.

CAPITAL:	Stanley
AREA:	12,173 sq km (4,699 sq miles)
POPULATION:	3121 (1991)
CURRENCY:	1 Falkland pound = 100 pence
LANGUAGES:	English

Falklands (Malvinas) War (2 April–14 June 1982) The Argentine–British war in the FALKLAND ISLANDS. Repeated attempts at negotiation for the transfer of the islands from British to Argentine rule having failed, an Argentine warship was sent by General Leopoldo Galtieri's military junta to land a party of 'scrap dealers' on South Georgia on 19 March 1982 with the intention of reclaiming the Falkland Islands. This was followed on 2 April by a full-scale military invasion. Attempts by the UN, the USA, and Peru to secure a peaceful resolution to the conflict failed, and Britain sent a task force of 30 warships with supporting aircraft and auxiliary vessels across 13,000 km (8,000 miles) of sea to recover the islands. Although all but three Latin American nations supported Argentina, the USA, in a difficult position because of close ties to both countries, sided with the British. The ten-week conflict, which claimed the lives of nearly 1,000 British and Argentine servicemen and civilians, ceased with the surrender of the Argentine forces on 14 June. The British victory contributed to the downfall of General Galtieri's government. Argentina officially declared a cessation of hostilities in 1989.

famine Widespread acute starvation in a population associated with a sharp increase in mortality. The victims die not only from starvation but also from diseases that are fatal to the debilitated, and which spread rapidly as a result of massive population movements in search of food. Famine should be distinguished from chronic malnutrition. In India, the last major famine occurred in 1943 (more recent threatened famines having been averted mainly by public intervention), but chronic malnutrition is quite widespread. China, by contrast, has tackled chronic malnutrition more successfully, but fell victim to a famine in 1958–61 in which it is estimated over 20 million people died. Famine is more geographically confined than malnutrition; most famines in recent decades have occurred in sub-Saharan Africa, with a few exceptions, as in Bangladesh in 1974, Cambodia (Kampuchea) in 1979–80 and North Korea in 1996–97. Although a natural disaster such as flood, drought, or crop failure may be the prime initiator of a famine, its impact depends on the organization and prosperity of the society. The most catastrophic recent famines have been exacerbated by war, political rivalries, and the destruction of distribution systems.

Fanti Confederation A loose association of small states along the Gold Coast (Ghana) in West Africa. Having migrated from the north in the 17th century, the Fanti served as middlemen between the slave and gold-producing states of the African interior and European traders along the coast. The coastal states were threatened by the rise of ASANTE power in Kumasi in the 19th century, and they supported the British in the Asante Wars. The Fanti played a prominent role in the affairs of Ghana after independence in 1957.

farmers-general A group of some 40 to 60 financiers in 18th century France, who bought from the crown the right of collecting indirect taxes on wine, tobacco, and salt (a practice known as 'farming' taxes). Employing inspectors to collect the money, they retained the difference between what they paid the crown for this right and what they actually extorted. The salt tax (*gabelle*) was especially harsh. The system was abolished in the French Revolution.

Farnese An Italian family that ruled the duchy of Parma from 1545 to 1731. Originating in the 11th century, its first outstanding member was Alessandro (1468–1549), who became Pope Paul III in 1534 and created the duchy of Parma and Piacenza. His grandson Alessandro (1520–89) was named a cardinal at the age of 14, and remained a powerful figure at the papal court for 50 years; he was a noted patron of the arts.

His nephew Alessandro (1545–92), Duke of Parma from 1586, was the family's most distinguished scion. After serving against the Ottomans at the Battle of LEPANTO (1571), he succeeded Don JOHN OF AUSTRIA as governor-general of the Netherlands and commander-in-

chief of the Spanish forces which were dealing with the DUTCH REVOLTS (1578). By subtle diplomacy he detached the southern provinces from the revolt (1579). Then he conducted a sequence of superbly planned military campaigns further north, including the capture of Antwerp (1585). In 1588 PHILIP II diverted him from his campaigns in the north, ordering him to liaise with the SPANISH ARMADA. In 1590 he was diverted again, this time to intervene in the FRENCH WARS OF RELIGION, where he managed to relieve Paris (1590) and Rouen (1592), but was wounded and died.

Farouk (1920–65) King of Egypt (1936–52). The son of Fuad I, whom the British had installed in 1922, he ruled autocratically, as had his father. His pro-AXIS sympathies during World War II resulted in a clash with the British, who imposed on him (1942) the Wafd leader Mustapha an-Nahas Pasha as a Premier who would support the Allies. Farouk's defeat in the Arab-Israeli conflict (1948), and the general corruption of his reign led to a military coup in 1952, headed by NASSER. He was forced to abdicate in favour of his infant son, Fuad II, in 1952, who was deposed in 1953.

Farrakhan, Louis NATION OF ISLAM.

fasces Bundles of rods bound with thongs that were the sign of regal or magisterial authority both within and outside Rome. After the expulsion of the ETRUSCAN kings, consuls had 12 fasces (a dictator 24), praetors six, lesser magistrates fewer. Originally axes were included in the bundle; but from the early republic the axe was removed in Rome, in deference to the People's ultimate power in capital cases.

fascism A political ideology of the first half of the 20th century, the central belief of which was that the individual should be subjugated to the needs of the state, which in turn should be directed by a strong leader embodying the will of the nation. It arose in opposition to COMMUNISM but adopted communist styles of propaganda, organization, and violence. The term (from the Roman FASCES) was first used by the Fascio di Combattimento in Italy in 1919. MUSSOLINI shaped fascism into a potent political force in Italy and HITLER developed a more racist brand of it in Germany (see NAZISM). Similar movements, which adopted a paramilitary structure, sprang up in Spain (FALANGISTS), Portugal, Austria, the Balkan states, France, and South America. In Britain the National Union of Fascists under Sir Oswald MOSLEY was founded in 1932, and between 1934 and 1936 adopted a strongly ANTI-SEMITIC character. The Public Order Act of 1936, banning private armies and political uniforms in Britain (in this case, the fascists' black shirts) discouraged further activities.

The appeal of fascism lay in its image of order and discipline in contrast to the licentiousness and economic turmoil of the liberal democracies. Once in power (in 1922 in Italy, in 1933 in Germany, and 1939 in Spain) fascists attempted to impose a military discipline on the whole of society at the expense of individual freedom (though, despite the socialist elements in fascist ideology, there was little interference with private ownership). Democratic institutions were replaced by the cult of the single leader, whose pronouncements were unchallengeable. Fascism was thus a form of TOTALITARIANISM, but it attracted mass support in the countries where it came to power and was finally defeated only by military means in the course of World War II. It lingered for some decades after the war in Spain and Portugal.

Some political scientists have detected elements of fascism in subsequent authoritarian regimes, especially military dictatorships in developing countries, but in no instance have these regimes explicitly adopted a fascist ideology. At the same time ideological fascism has remained a latent, if minimal, force in almost every country in the western world. In France the Front National of Jean-Marie Le Pen made considerable gains in the 1986 elections and increased its support to 15% of the electorate in 1991, but did less well in elections in 1993 and 1997. Extreme right-wing parties in Russia and Austria also gained support during the 1990s.

Fashoda incident (18 September 1898) The culmination of a long series of clashes between Britain and France in the 'SCRAMBLE FOR AFRICA'. The French objective, to occupy the sub-Saharan belt from west to east, countered the British aim of linking their possessions from the Cape to Cairo. Thus in 1896 the French dispatched a force under MARCHAND from GABON to occupy the SUDAN, at the same time that KITCHENER was moving up the Nile to recover Khartoum. Both reached Fashoda during the summer of 1898, and as neither side desired conflict, they agreed that both French and British flags should fly over the fort. The matter was referred to London and Paris, and for a while tension between the two countries was extreme. In December the French ordered Marchand to withdraw, and this enabled an agreement to be reached whereby the Nile and Congo watersheds should demarcate the respective spheres of influence by the two countries in Africa.

Fatah, al- (Arabic, 'victory') A militant Palestinian organization. It was founded (1962) in Kuwait to fight for the restoration of PALESTINE to the Arabs. Al-Fatah assumed the leadership of the PALESTINE LIBERATION ORGANIZATION in 1969 and remained the dominant group within the PLO. Its guerrilla units were expelled from Jordan after the civil war in 1970, and it withdrew to southern Lebanon (Fatahland). Subsequently al-Fatah was drawn into the Lebanese imbroglio and became divided; a part was expelled from Lebanon after the Israeli invasion of 1982. Leadership remained in the hands of Yasser ARAFAT, who had led al-Fatah from its foundation. Al-Fatah played a leading role in the achievement of the 1993 peace agreement with Israel. However, divisions within the organization over the progress of PLO–Israeli negotiations became apparent in 1995.

Fatimids The dynasty that reigned in Morocco from 909 until 969, and in Egypt until 1171. They claimed descent from MUHAMMAD's daughter Fatima as proof of their right to be caliphs. The founder, Ubaidallah, claimed to be Mahdi, the divinely guided one, and preached an extreme form of SHIISM. He and his successors steadily conquered north Africa and Sicily and finally Egypt, Syria, and western Arabia in 969, abandoning Kairouan for a new capital of al-Qahira (Cairo). The Fatimids were commercially successful, and had generally good relations with their neighbours, but they suffered decline, partly because of the rise of the SELJUKS and the CRUSADERS, and partly because from the mid-12th century they no longer had rulers of any ability.

Faulkner of Downpatrick, (Arthur) Brian Deane Faulkner, Baron (1921–77) Northern Ireland statesman. A Unionist Member of Parliament at STORMONT (1949–73), he was Minister of Home Affairs (1959–63, 1971–72), and Prime Minister (1971–72). His negotiations with the Westminster government for constitutional changes in NORTHERN IRELAND lost him support in his own party.

Fawcett, Dame Millicent Garrett (1847–1929) British feminist. Sister of Elizabeth Garrett ANDERSON, she was a pioneer of the movement in Britain to secure equality for women in voting, education, and careers. She was strongly supported by her husband, Henry Fawcett, a Liberal politician and academic. In 1897 she became president of the National Union of Women's Suffrage Societies, whose policy was to gain votes for women without the militancy soon to be associated with the SUFFRAGETTES. Though overshadowed by the actions of the latter, the reliance of the 'suffragists' on peaceful methods favourably influenced public opinion.

Fawkes, Guy GUNPOWDER PLOT.

Federal Bureau of Investigation (FBI) The investigative branch of the US Department of Justice. Established by Attorney-General Charles J. Bonaparte (1851–1921) in 1908, it was at first called the Bureau of Investigation. It was reorganized in 1924 when J. Edgar HOOVER was appointed as director, giving it wider powers to investigate violations of federal laws. Hoover successfully led the 1930s drive against gangsters. During World War II the FBI began spying activities against Nazi sympathizers in the USA and Latin America. The later excesses of Hoover, in particular his harassment of political dissidents and radicals such as Martin Luther KING, brought its counter-intelligence activities into disrepute. It was roundly criticized by the Senate in investigations of the WATERGATE SCANDAL in 1975–76.

federalism A form of government in which power is dispersed between one central and several regional legislatures. Federalism contrasts with the unitary system of government, in that sovereignty is shared within a national or possibly supra-national framework. A federal constitution allocates powers to different levels of government, some to the central government, and others to the governments of the territories making up the federation. Powers may be allocated either exclusively to one level, or concurrently to both. Unlike a confederation, where the confederal government usually lacks its own institutions, each level of government in a federal system maintains institutions, imposes its own laws and taxes, and acts directly on the population.

Federalism is often seen as an appropriate constitutional solution for a political system based on an originally limited degree of unity, a diverse or dispersed population, or a large area. An early example of a federal state is that of Switzerland, but it was the USA, whose federal Constitution was devised in 1787, which became a model for many later federations, for example Canada, Australia, the Federal Republic of Germany, and Yugoslavia. For any federal system to succeed, the balance between the powers of each constituent part and those of the central federal government needs to be agreed. In the USA before the AMERICAN CIVIL WAR, the excessive demands for STATES'

RIGHTS ultimately led to the break-up of the Union and to war. The term 'federalist' was early used in the USA to describe those who believed in the need for strong central government. The extent to which the EUROPEAN UNION should be a federal organization remains controversial. Among the disadvantages of federalism are duplication and complexity. The USA, for instance, has 51 complete systems of elections, government, administration, and justice. Relations between levels of government and between the territories in a federation are usually rivalrous and sometimes hostile.

Federalist Party US political party. The first political party to emerge after the CONSTITUTION OF THE USA became operative (1789), it took its name from the *Federalist Papers*, a collection of essays written by MADISON, HAMILTON, and JAY to influence the ratification of the Constitution by New York. The party of George WASHINGTON and John ADAMS, it had support in New England and the north-east generally, both from commercial interests and wealthier landowners. It stood for strong central government and the firm enforcement of domestic laws, was pro-British in foreign affairs, and identified itself with the economic policies of Hamilton. The party's role, which would benefit 'the wise, the good, and the rich', was exemplified in the military campaign in 1794 against the refusal of the WHISKY REBELS to pay excise duty. The emergence of new political issues, disagreements over commercial and foreign policy, and the narrowness of its popular appeal gradually undermined the Party, although it continued to elect members to Congress until it finally disappeared in 1825.

Federation of Rhodesia and Nyasaland CENTRAL AFRICAN FEDERATION.

Feisal I FAISAL I.

feminism A broad-based movement for extending the social, political, and economic rights of women. Its advocates have for the most part demanded equal rights for both sexes, although some have asserted the right of women to separate development. Throughout the ages women had generally been subordinated to men and largely excluded from education, from the ownership of property, from economic independence, and from political representation. A recognizable movement for the elevation of women's status began with the French Revolution. The philosopher Antoine Nicolas Condorcet wrote an essay (1790) on the admission of women to full citizenship, and in Britain Mary Wollstonecraft published the first great document of feminism, the *Vindication of the Rights of Woman* (1792), in which she argued that educational restrictions alone keep women in a state of 'ignorance and slavish dependence'. In the USA the movement grew out of anti-slavery agitation. Abigail Adams, Mercy Otis Warren, and Emma Willard were early campaigners for the rights of women. In 1848 the first feminist convention, led by Elizabeth Cady Stanton and Lucretia Mott, was held at Seneca Falls, New York. In Britain a series of Married Women's Property Acts from 1870 onwards increasingly allowed women to hold and manage property. WOMEN'S SUFFRAGE, first achieved in the US state of Wyoming (1869), became a focus for campaigns in the early 20th century and is now almost universal.

The later 1960s saw the advent of women's liberation (popularly known as Women's Lib), a radical movement that challenged the patriarchal nature of modern society. It demanded the improvement of women's status in society and was concerned with changing stereotypes of both sexes. Women's liberation was especially vocal and active as a movement in the USA; in 1966 the National Organization for Women (NOW) was formed in the USA and has remained active since. Its demands were taken up in other industrialized countries, notably Britain and Australia. Practical demands were focused on the right to equal pay and opportunities. In Britain the Sex Discrimination Acts (1975 and 1986) and the creation of the Equal Opportunities Commission in 1975 gave legal effect to some demands, although many employment practices and financial rewards remain tilted in favour of men.

In developing countries, feminists have been faced with a different order of problem. Women in such countries generally suffer from a greater degree of inequality than in Western countries. Their participation in the paid labour force and their literacy rates tend to be lower, and their fertility rates and maternal mortality rates tend to be higher. Less access to education, low educational attainment, and religious or social traditions which place lower value on women's work than on men's, are responsible for women's limited role in economic, public, and political life. Those who are in paid employment tend to be relegated to low-paid and unskilled occupations, while in general women's workload, including caring for extended families, agricultural work, harnessing fuel and transporting water, is greater than that of men. The revival of ISLAMIC FUNDAMENTALISM, with its enforced social isolation of women, has led to the establishment of segregated systems of banking, commerce, and education in Muslim communities. Nevertheless, in many countries women have tried to improve their status, for example by opposing devisive legal and seclusion codes, and by campaigning against genital mutilation. In Africa, development groups are now supporting women agriculturalists (who produce 70% of the continent's food) by giving women greater access to and control of technology. Women's groups in the developing world tend to be drawn from the better educated, as is, for example, the thriving women's movement in India, which opposes certain social practices such as intimidation over dowry payments. Feminists in many countries have been accused of trying to undermine traditional cultures and religious beliefs. In 1994 the feminist writer Taslima Nasreen fled from Bangladesh following repeated death threats.

Fenians A secret Irish-American revolutionary society founded as the Fenian Brotherhood in the USA by John O'Mahony and as the Irish Republican Brotherhood (IRB) by James Stephens in Ireland (1858). The name Fenian, taken from the Fianna, a legendary band of ancient Irish warriors, was later applied to supporters of Irish republicanism (the modern Irish political party FIANNA FÁIL uses the name). Many early Fenians had been actively involved in the YOUNG IRELAND movement. The society's military wing was known as the IRISH REPUBLICAN ARMY (IRA). Fenian invasions of Canada (1866, 1870, 1871) failed. In England the Fenians attempted to seize Chester Castle; they rescued two of their number in Manchester, and in an unsuccessful rescue of

prisoners in London (1867) killed 12 people. Several
Fenians were executed and hundreds imprisoned. Their
exploits drew attention to Irish discontent and helped
to convince GLADSTONE of the urgent need to find a
solution to Ireland's problems. Several Fenians became
Members of Parliament at Westminster during the HOME
RULE period. In the latter part of the 1860s the Fenian
Brotherhood split into three sections, each in theory
supporting the IRB but in practice sharply divided by
personalities and policies. The organization was
superseded in the USA by Clan-na-Gael, a secret society
headed by John Devoy, and by other open Irish-
American organizations supporting Irish republicanism.

Ferdinand II (1578–1637) Holy Roman Emperor
(1619–37), King of Bohemia (1617–27) and Hungary
(1618–26). He was educated by the Jesuits and developed
into a determined spokesman for the COUNTER-
REFORMATION Catholicism. Before his election to the
imperial throne, he used authoritarian measures against
the Protestants of Inner Austria, with some success, but
in 1619 the largely Protestant Bohemian Diet deposed
him in favour of FREDERICK V (the Winter King). This
crisis was one of the opening moves in the catastrophic
THIRTY YEARS WAR. The first ten years of the conflict did
not go badly for Ferdinand. He reached his high point
when he issued the Edict of Restitution (1629), which
ordered the return of all Roman Catholic property
seized since 1552. Subsequently he was seen as a threat
to German liberty and opposed by both Catholic and
Protestant princes. The interventions of Sweden and
France finally turned the tide of the war against him,
and he was forced to abandon his more extreme
Catholic absolutist ambitions.

Ferdinand V (the Catholic) (1452–1516) King of Castile
and León (1474–1516), King of Aragon as Ferdinand II
(1479–1516), King of Sicily (1468–1516), and King of Naples
(1502–16). He was the son of John II of Aragon. In 1469
he married Princess ISABELLA of Castile, a significant step
towards Spanish unification. He succeeded to the throne
of Aragon in 1479, and in the same year helped Isabella
to win the war of succession in Castile (1474–79). They
began to rule jointly in both kingdoms in 1481, and in
1492 annexed the conquered territory of Granada to
Castile. On Isabella's death in 1504, he was recognized as
Regent of Castile for his daughter JOANNA THE MAD. He
subsequently married Germaine de Foix (1506), and
incorporated Navarre into Castile (1515), thus becoming
personal monarch of all Spain from the Pyrenees to
Gibraltar.

A ruthlessly realistic politician, he was especially
successful in the conduct of foreign policy. He
surrounded France with a network of allies and
acquired Naples. At home he modernized Spain's
governmental institutions, vested in himself the grand
masterships of the wealthy military orders, and won
important ecclesiastical concessions from the papacy,
including the Bull of 1478 authorizing the SPANISH
INQUISITION, a powerful council to combat heresy, to be
controlled by the crown.

Ferdinand VII (1784–1833) King of Spain (1808–33). He
succeeded to the throne after the forced abdication of
his father, Charles IV, and was in turn forced by the
French to abdicate in favour of NAPOLEON's brother,
Joseph Bonaparte, spending the years of the PENINSULAR
WAR in prison in France. Known as 'The Desired One', he

was released in 1814 and restored to the throne. He
abolished the liberal constitution of 1812 and instituted
his own absolutist rule, relying on the support of the
Church and the army. The loss of the colonies in
America (SPANISH-AMERICAN WARS) deprived the
government of a major source of income, and his troops
mutinied. The revolutionaries held him practically a
prisoner until 1823, when French forces came to his aid.
Restored to power, he carried out a bloody revenge on
the insurgents.

Ferry, Jules François Camille (1832–93) French
statesman. Prefect of the Seine (1870–71) during its siege
in the FRANCO-PRUSSIAN WAR, his narrow escape (18 March
1871) from the PARIS COMMUNE left him with a strong
dislike of extremist politics. After serving as French
ambassador in Greece, he was elected to the French
Chamber of Deputies (1876–89) and was in government
1879–85, twice as Prime Minister (1880–81, 1883–85). He
was responsible for much liberal legislation, extending
freedom of association and of the press and legalizing
trade unions. He weakened the grip of the Roman
Catholic Church on education, extended higher
education, created lycées for girls, and made French
elementary education non-clerical (March 1882), free, and
compulsory. His ministries also saw wide French
colonial development in Tunisia (1881), the Congo (1884),
Madagascar (1885), and Indo-China (1885). This latter lost
him support and he fell from office. He narrowly failed
to be elected President of the Republic in 1887.

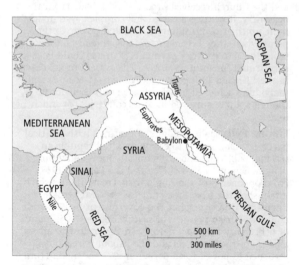

Fertile Crescent *Bounded by mountains in the north and
desert in the south, by the Mediterranean in the west, and
the Persian Gulf in the east, the Fertile Crescent is
interrupted by desert in Mesopotamia, Syria, and Sinai.
Archaeological research suggests that the development of
primitive irrigation, made necessary by the dry summers,
probably preceded the rise of the ancient civilizations of
Babylon, Assyria, and Egypt.*

Fertile Crescent The relatively well-watered area
extending from the head of the Persian Gulf via the
rivers Tigris and Euphrates westward into northern
Syria and then southwards through the LEVANT to the
lower Nile valley. Western scholars have traditionally

regarded it as the cradle of civilization, where empires, such as those of BABYLON, ASSYRIA, and EGYPT created monumental buildings, pyramids, and ziggurats, developed sophisticated craft-skills in pottery, weaving, and metal working, and perfected writing-systems for administrative and ritual purposes. Modern archaeological excavations and scientific techniques such as carbon-dating confirm the existence of settled agricultural communities as far back as 8000 BC. The significance of the region for Western thinking is confirmed by its associations with Judaism, the achievements of HELLENISTIC culture in late antiquity, and the emergence of Christianity. The ARAB CONQUESTS claimed the entire region permanently for Islam and it became therefore the major focus for CRUSADER enterprise before passing under OTTOMAN control.

feudal system A medieval European political and economic system based on the holding of lands on condition of homage or military service and labour. Feudalism probably originated in the Frankish kingdom in the 8th century and spread into northern Italy, Spain, and Germany. It was introduced by the NORMANS into England, Ireland, Scotland, southern Italy, and Sicily. The nobility held lands from the crown and provided troops for the king in times of war. The KNIGHT was the tenant of the noble and a class of unfree peasants (VILLEIN) lived on the land under the jurisdiction of their lord (MANORIAL SYSTEM). Bishops and abbots were invested by secular lords with their livings in return for services and the Church received produce and labour from the peasantry. It became a varied and complex system: lords built up their own military forces and power to the point where they became semi-independent of the king; from the 12th century payments (SCUTAGE) could be substituted for military duties. The system broke down in the 12th and 13th centuries as towns (COMMUNE) and individuals achieved independence from their lords, though SERFDOM survived in some countries for much longer.

Fíanna Fáil (Gaelic, 'soldiers of destiny') Irish political party. Its main aim is to create a united republican Ireland, politically and economically independent of Britain. Eamon DE VALERA founded the Party in 1926 from opponents of the Anglo-Irish Treaty (1921), which established the Irish Free State (see IRELAND, REPUBLIC OF). The Party won control of the government in 1932 and dominated Irish politics for several decades, being out of office only for short periods. In 1973 it lost to an alliance of the Fine Gael and the Labour Party, but returned to power for a period in 1977 and again from 1987 to 1994. Fíanna Fáil began another period of office in 1997.

fief The land held under the FEUDAL SYSTEM by a VASSAL from his lord. Fiefs ranged in size from vast duchies down to the area of land needed to support a single knight, called a knight's 'fee'. Large or small, they provided the agricultural produce which was the source of all wealth. During the early Middle Ages areas which had been forest or barren land came under cultivation and were incorporated into the system.

Field of the Cloth of Gold The site near Calais where HENRY VIII of England met FRANCIS I of France in June 1520, in an attempt to forge a diplomatic alliance. Henry's retinue was made up of more than 5,000 people.

He wrestled, danced, jousted, and tilted with Francis for almost a fortnight, amid scenes of great festivity and pageantry. But the two sovereigns retained their initial mutual suspicions, and within days of leaving Francis, Henry met the French king's arch-rival, Emperor Charles V, at Gravelines.

field systems The visible traces on the landscape of man's present or former agricultural activities. Simple agriculture by digging stick or hoe will leave virtually no trace, and only after prolonged use of the plough, which was available from at least the 4th millennium BC in south-west Asia and Europe, or by deliberate construction will such fields remain visible. Examples are as widely separated as the 'Celtic' fields and lynchets in north-west Europe, where the combined effects of ploughing and gravity on sloping ground transfers soil from the upper to the lower edge of each field, to ancient cultivation plots, levelled and drained, in the forests of Amazonia or Central America. Deliberate terracing leaves a much clearer mark, and is more likely to be maintained in working order since it represents a massive investment of human effort. Andean slopes in South America, vineyards in central and southern Europe, and rice paddies in south-east Asia are major examples still in use. When terraces are abandoned, traces will be largely obliterated over time by different farming practices or natural erosion.

Fifteen, the (1715) A JACOBITE rebellion aimed at removing the Hanoverian GEORGE I from the British throne. Queen ANNE's sudden death in August 1714 had caught the Jacobites by surprise. Their lack of preparedness and their inability to win the English Tories to their cause delayed the rebellion until September 1715. A simultaneous rising in Scotland and England was planned, with Thomas Forster to lead the English northern rebels and the indecisive Earl of Mar to command the Scots. Forster was compelled to surrender his small force at Preston and Mar's inconclusive battle at SHERIFFMUIR virtually ended the rebellion.

Many Englishmen may have sympathized with the Jacobite cause, but few were willing to fight for it. Foreign help had been promised, but LOUIS XIV's death, storms in the English Channel, and the vigour of the English government doomed the rebellion to failure. James Edward Stuart, the Old PRETENDER, arrived in Scotland too late to revive it. By the standards of the day the British government was comparatively lenient towards the rebels: 26 officers suffered the death penalty, and about 700 of the rank and file were sent to the West Indies to serve seven years as indentured servants. Forster escaped from Newgate prison and fled to the Continent, and Mar also died in exile.

Fifth-Monarchy Men An extreme Puritan sect in England in the mid-17th century. They believed that the rule of Jesus Christ and his saints was imminent, and that it would be the fifth monarchy to rule the world, succeeding those of Assyria, Persia, Greece, and Rome. They hoped that, through the BAREBONES PARLIAMENT, the rule of the saints would become a reality, but CROMWELL's establishment of the Protectorate turned them against him. Their agitation became a nuisance, their leaders were arrested, and their abortive rebellions in 1657 and 1661 were suppressed.

Fiji A country comprising a group of islands, in the Melanesian archipelago of the south-west Pacific Ocean.

Physical. Fiji consists of two main islands, Viti Levu and Vanua Levu, and over 800 smaller ones. Being situated some 400 km (248.6 miles) from a plate boundary, they are volcanic. Mountains rise to some 1,300 m (4,265 feet) and have thick rain forest on the wetter slopes. The climate is hot, though not unpleasantly so. The islands lie in a hurricane belt, and there is periodic devastation by tornadoes.

Economy. The economy is agricultural, with sugar the chief crop and export. Other trade is in re-exported petroleum products, coconut oil, fish, and gold. Tourism provides substantial additional revenue. Food-processing is the main industry.

History. The islands first became known to Europeans when Tasman visited them in 1643. Captain Cook landed in 1774. In the 19th century Fuji was notorious for inter-tribal wars and cannibalism, a situation not assisted by an influx of deserting seamen, traders seeking sandalwood, and whalers. The islands became a British crown colony in 1874, the Western Pacific High Commission being set up for the pacification and control of the labour trade. By 1879 Indians began to be imported under the indenture system. By the 1950s Indians outnumbered Fijians and were dominating commercial life, while Fijians owned most of the land. The country became independent in 1970. The election of a government with an Indian majority (1987) brought ethnic tensions to a head, leading to two military coups to restore indigenous Fijian control and to the withdrawal of Fiji from the Commonwealth of Nations. Civilian rule, under a new constitution that guaranteed a Melanesian parliamentary majority, was restored in 1990. There has, since then, been heavy Indian emigration resulting in loss of skills and capital. In 1991 opposition parties attacked the new constitution as racist. There were threats of another military coup, but in 1992 the Fijian Political Party won a majority of seats in the general election and Major General Sitiveni Rabuka, who had led the coups of 1987, became Prime Minister as head of a coalition. The government collapsed in 1994 but was re-elected with Rabuka's party increasing its majority. In 1997 the racial elements in the 1990 constitution were abandoned and Fiji was readmitted to the Commonwealth.

CAPITAL: Suva
AREA: 18,274 sq km (7,056 sq miles)
POPULATION: 802,000 (1996)
CURRENCY: 1 Fiji dollar = 100 cents
RELIGIONS: Christian 52.9%; Hindu 38.1%; Muslim
                   7.8%; Sikh 0.7%
ETHNIC GROUPS: Indian 48.6%; Fijian 46.3%
LANGUAGES: English (official); Fijian; Hindi; local
                   languages
INTERNATIONAL
 ORGANIZATIONS: UN; Commonwealth; Colombo Plan;
                   South Pacific Commission

filibusters A term used originally to describe piratical adventurers or freebooters who pillaged the Spanish colonies in the 17th century. Subsequently it was used of anyone who engaged in unauthorized war against foreign states. From this the term came to be used to describe speakers in the US Congress or any other assembly seeking to delay legislation by making speeches to obstruct business.

Fillmore, Millard (1800–74) Thirteenth President of the USA (1850–53). In 1834 he joined the WHIG PARTY and became its leader in the House of Representatives. He was elected as US vice-president to President Zachary TAYLOR (1848). On Taylor's death in 1850 he became President. While in office, he signed the COMPROMISE OF 1850 and approved of the naval expedition under Matthew PERRY to force trading arrangements with Japan (1853). Denied renomination in 1852 as a result of the split of his party over the issue of slavery, he remained politically active and ran as the presidential nominee of the American (KNOW NOTHING) Party in 1856, but managed to carry only one state (Maryland).

Fine Gael (Gaelic, 'United Ireland') Irish political party. Founded in 1922 as Cumann na nGaedheal, it changed its name in 1933. It originated among supporters of the Anglo-Irish Treaty that created the Irish Free State (see IRELAND, REPUBLIC OF). William COSGRAVE was its first leader (1922–44). Fine Gael was in power as the dominant element in a coalition from 1948 to 1951, with John Costello as its leader. This government in 1949 declared Ireland to be a republic. Since then, Fine Gael has been intermittently in power (1954–57, 1973–77, 1981–82, 1982–87, 1994–97), but has required coalition support to remain so. It has advocated the concept of a united Ireland achieved by peaceful means.

Finland (Suomi) A Baltic country, sometimes considered part of Scandinavia. It is bounded by Norway on the north, Sweden and the Gulf of Bothnia on the west, and Russia on the east.

Physical. A long coastline round the west and south, studded with over 6,000 Åland islands, thrusts into the Baltic Sea. Of the rolling, granitic land area, of which the Fennoscandian Shield forms part, only a tenth is cultivable, some 70% being coniferous forest, 11% tundra, and 9% lakes. Its 60,000 lakes are linked by short rivers, sounds, or canals to form busy waterways. A third of the country lies north of the Arctic Circle and is part of Lapland.

Economy. Finland is an industrialized country with little agriculture. Owing to its extensive forests paper, timber, and wood-pulp are significant exports. Other industries include shipbuilding, and the manufacture of machinery, steel, clothing, and chemicals. The only significant mineral resources are chromium and copper.

History. Occupied between 100 AD and 800 by Finno-Ugrian tribes who drove the original Lapp population into its northernmost regions, Finland was conquered and converted to Christianity by Eric IX of Sweden in the late 1150s, and throughout the Middle Ages found itself at the centre of Swedish-Russian rivalry in the Baltic area. In 1556 GUSTAVUS I (Vasa) made Finland into a separate duchy for his second son John, and following the latter's succession to the Swedish throne as John III in 1568 it was elevated to a grand duchy. Although still dominated by Sweden, Finland was allowed its own Diet and granted a degree of autonomy.

However, the Treaty of TILSIT (1807) between Tsar Alexander I and Napoleon led to the annexation of Finland as a grand duchy of Russia until 1917. Attempts to impose the Russian language and military conscription brought discontent and the RUSSIAN REVOLUTION of 1917 offered opportunities for national assertion. Independence was achieved (1919) under Marshal MANNERHEIM, and a democratic, republican constitution introduced. In 1920 Finland joined the League of Nations, which achieved one of its few successes in resolving the Åland Islands dispute. After the NAZI–SOVIET PACT of 1939, Finland was invaded in the FINNISH-RUSSIAN WAR (1939–40). Finnish resistance excited international admiration but no practical help, and surrender entailed a considerable loss of territory (Karelia and Petsamo). When Germany invaded the Soviet Union in 1941 the Finns sought to regain these territories by fighting on the side of the AXIS POWERS, but capitulated to the Soviet Union in 1944 and were burdened with a huge reparations bill. Since World War II Finland has accepted neutrality in international affairs. In January 1992 the Treaty of Friendship, Co-operation, and Mutual Assistance (1948) with the former Soviet Union was replaced by a new treaty with Russia. Finland's economy suffered from the collapse of eastern European markets, and austerity measures were introduced in April 1992. In 1995 Finland became a member of the EUROPEAN UNION.

CAPITAL:	Helsinki
AREA:	338,145 sq km (130,559 sq miles)
POPULATION:	5.132 million (1996)
CURRENCY:	1 Markka = 100 pennia
RELIGIONS:	Evangelical Lutheran 88.9%; Finnish (Greek) Eastern Orthodox 1.1%
ETHNIC GROUPS:	Finnish 93.6%; Swedish 6.1%; Lapp (Saami) minority
LANGUAGES:	Finnish, Swedish (both official); Lapp (Saami)
INTERNATIONAL ORGANIZATIONS:	UN; EU; OECD; Council of Europe; CSCE

Finnish-Russian War ('Winter War') (1939–40) A war fought between Finland and the Soviet Union. The Finnish government under General MANNERHEIM had rejected Soviet demands for bases and for frontier revisions similar to those accepted by the lesser Baltic states. Soviet armies attacked on three fronts, and at first the Finns' superior skill in manoeuvring on skis on the frozen lakes and across the Gulf of Finland, and in the forests of their country, kept the Soviet forces at bay. After 15 weeks of fierce fighting the Soviets breached the Mannerheim Line and Finland was forced to accept peace on Stalin's terms, ceding its eastern territories and the port of Viipuri (Viborg).

Fire of London A major fire that devastated London in September 1666. The fire began in a baker's shop and, fanned by an east wind, raged for four days, destroying 87 churches, including St Paul's, and more than 13,000 houses mostly build from wood. It was stopped by blowing up buildings in its path. There are eyewitness accounts in the diaries of Samuel PEPYS and John Evelyn. Plans for a modern city with wide streets and squares were abandoned, but Sir Christopher Wren rebuilt St Paul's and a number of other churches and public buildings, and designed the Monument (1677) which commemorates the fire. The fire destroyed the slums where the GREAT PLAGUE still lingered, and gave an enormous boost to the growth of fire insurance.

First World War WORLD WAR I.

Fisher, Andrew (1862–1928) Australian statesman. He was a Member of the Queensland Legislative Assembly (1893–96, 1899–1901) and led the Labor Party (1907–15). He was federal Prime Minister and Treasurer (1908–09,

1910–13, 1914–15). His second government extended social welfare and established the Commonwealth Bank. Wartime stress, and conflict with W. M. HUGHES, led to his resignation, after which he was High Commissioner in London (1916–21).

Fisher, John Arbuthnot, 1st Baron (1841–1920) British sailor and First Sea Lord (1904–10, 1914–15). He successfully persuaded his political masters of the importance of strengthening the British navy before World War I, securing the implementation of the DREADNOUGHT programme. He, together with Winston CHURCHILL, was a prime instigator in 1915 of the GALLIPOLI CAMPAIGN. The failure of this attempt and the resulting strained relations with Churchill led Fisher to resign in May 1915.

five members The five members of the English parliament that CHARLES I attempted to arrest on 4 January 1642. Mounting opposition to the king, culminating in the GRAND REMONSTRANCE (December 1641), had been led by PYM, supported by HAMPDEN, Holles, Hesilrige, and Strode. Charles rashly decided to arrest and impeach them. He entered the House of Commons only to find that the members had fled into the City of London; they returned to the House of Commons a week later. This attempted use of force by the king hardened Parliamentary opposition against him and was a factor leading to the outbreak of the ENGLISH CIVIL WAR. No other monarch has since set foot in the House of Commons; its independence from interference is fundamental to its existence.

Five Nations IROQUOIS.

Five Pillars of Islam The basic duties and religious observances of ISLAM. The first pillar, *īmān* (faith), prescribes regular recitation of the *shahādah*, a summarized confession of belief, itself often referred to as the first pillar, which affirms the unity of God and the sole authority of the Prophet MUHAMMAD: 'There is no god but Allah; and Muhammad is the Messenger of Allah'. The second pillar is daily worship, *salāh* (*salāt*), to which believers are called by the muezzin, performed five times: at dawn, noon, in the afternoon, after sunset, and at night. Three pre-conditions must be observed before worship: a clear conscience, a clean body, and a clean environment. *Wudū*, the observance of ritual cleansing, always precedes worship. A prayer mat or carpet ensures a clean environment, and is placed pointing towards MECCA. Ritual worship is compulsory and follows a fixed pattern of standing, bowing, prostration, and kneeling, and recitation from the KORAN. The third pillar, *sawm*, lays down abstinence from food, drink, and sexual relations during the daylight hours of Ramadan; the rule does not generally apply to children below the age of 12, the infirm, or nursing mothers. *Zakāt* (purification of wealth), an obligation upon those who have enough wealth, demands the donation of 2.5% of yearly income to support the Muslim community, in one of eight prescribed ways. It is administered in some Muslim countries by official collectors. This differs from charity (*sadaqa*), which can be given by any Muslim. The final duty is that all those who are physically and financially able should perform the PILGRIMAGE (*hajj*) to Mecca at least once in a lifetime. The pilgrimage takes place in the twelfth month, *Dhu al-Hajj*, and entails a number of ritual and ceremonial acts, including the adoption of plain white clothing, symbolizing spiritual equality. It culminates, after ten days, in the Festival of Sacrifice, Id ul-Adha. *Jihad* (striving or 'holy war'), is sometimes referred to as a sixth Pillar of Islam, but it has no such official status.

flagellant A religious fanatic who scourged himself in public processions, often to the accompaniment of psalms. Such penitential activities took place in ancient SPARTA and ROME and subsequently throughout the Christian world from about the 4th century. Flagellants appeared periodically in medieval Europe, usually during times of disorder or natural disaster. Major demonstrations came in Perugia in 1260 during political unrest; in 1349 as hysterical reaction to the BLACK DEATH; and in Germany in 1414. Linked, especially in 1349, with anti-Semitism, these demonstrations were critical of the Church establishment, and were condemned by the papacy.

Flanders A historical region in the south-west of the Low Countries, now mainly in BELGIUM. It was taken from Celtic tribes by the FRANKS in the 5th century. In the medieval period it became extremely prosperous, especially through its cloth trade with England, and it allied itself with the English during the HUNDRED YEARS WAR. By 1384 it was a French province, later belonging to BURGUNDY and then coming under HABSBURG control In 1506 it passed to the Spanish crown. After a long period of revolt Philip IV of Spain was obliged to cede the north-western portion to the UNITED PROVINCES, and LOUIS XIV of France acquired the southern part by the treaty of Aix-la-Chapelle in 1668. Following the Napoleonic Wars, during which it was occupied by France, the greater part of Flanders joined the kingdom of the Netherlands (1814). It became part of independent Belgium in 1830 and an autonomous Flemish-speaking region under the federal constitution of 1989.

Fleury, André Hercule de (1653–1743) Cardinal and French statesman. Fleury was tutor to LOUIS XV of France and in 1726 became his chief minister in all but name. His policies were similar to those of WALPOLE: financial retrenchment, encouragement of trade, and peace instead of war. However, Fleury could not prevent France's involvement in the wars of the POLISH and AUSTRIAN SUCCESSION, though he limited the intervention of France in the War of the Polish succession. Fleury also began the negotiations which led to France peacefully annexing Lorraine.

Flodden Field, Battle of (9 September 1513) An important battle that took place between the English and the Scots on the Scottish border; it resulted in a major English victory that gave HENRY VII security in the north for many years. A large army led by JAMES IV was defeated by a somewhat smaller force of about 20,000 English soldiers under the command of Thomas Howard, Earl of Surrey. Long Scottish spears were no match for English bills and longbows, and the Scots lost perhaps as many as 10,000 dead, including James IV himself.

Florence A former city-state in northern Italy. It was founded as a colony for Roman veterans in the 1st century BC, and after the barbarian invasions of the 5th and 6th centuries passed to the CAROLINGIANS in the 8th century. A bishopric, and, by the 11th century, a COMMUNE, it profited from economic boom in the 12th century to become a great banking city, as well as a centre of the cloth trade. In the 13th century it witnessed the rivalry between the papal and imperial factions (GUELPHS and Ghibellines). From 1421 onwards it was ruled by the MEDICI family. There was a brief democratic interlude under SAVONAROLA (1494–1512), and a short republic (1527–30). The Medici ruled as Dukes of TUSCANY until 1737. Florence then passed to the HABSBURGS until 1861, when it became part of independent Italy.

Florida The southernmost state of the US east coast. It was discovered in 1513 by PONCE DE LEÓN and first settled by the Spanish as the city of St Augustine in 1565. Under Spanish control until 1763, Florida embraced much of the Gulf and southern Atlantic coastal regions. It reverted to Spain after British rule during 1763–83, and had troubled relations with the United States until its sale in 1819 under the Adams-Onis treaty.

Foch, Ferdinand (1851–1929) Marshal of France. He fought on the WESTERN FRONT in World War I, co-ordinating the actions of Allied forces in preventing the loss of the Channel ports in 1914, commanded the French troops on the SOMME in 1916, and was appointed Allied commander-in-chief in 1918. He was famous for insisting that constant attack was the sole recipe for victory. Mutual dislike and lack of co-operation between the Allied generals had prevented concerted action until the German offensive in 1918 led to his appointment as Allied commander-in-chief. He achieved final victory in his July counter-offensive and received the German surrender at Compiègne on 11 November.

Fontenoy, Battle of (11 May 1745) A battle in the War of the AUSTRIAN SUCCESSION, fought at Fontenoy, a village in Hainaut in south-west Belgium: it saw a major victory for the French, over Austria and her allies. SAXE, the French commander, had overrun the Austrian Netherlands. The British general, the Duke of CUMBERLAND, was advancing to the relief of Tournai with a British, Austrian, and Dutch force; he found a gap in the French line of fortifications but was driven back.

Food and Agriculture Organization (FAO) An agency of the UNITED NATIONS ORGANIZATION, established in 1945. The FAO is one of the largest and most effective of the UN agencies. It has collected and disseminated facts and statistics, given advice on improvements to food distribution, provided important technical advice for increasing agricultural production, and channelled food aid through its world food programme.

Forbes, George William (1869–1947) New Zealand statesman. A Member of Parliament for the Liberal (later United) Party, Forbes succeeded the Prime Minister, J. G. WARD, in 1930. He attempted to meet the DEPRESSION by balancing the budget and paying 'the dole' only to men who worked on labour-intensive public works schemes. In 1931 Forbes, in coalition with the more dynamic J. G. COATES, won the election on a policy of retrenchment, but in 1935 was swept out of office by Labour with its policy of economic expansion.

Force Acts Popular name for US Acts designed to enforce federal law. Such an Act was passed in 1833 and was designed to counteract NULLIFICATION: it empowered President JACKSON to use the army and navy, if necessary, to enforce the laws of Congress. Four Enforcement Acts of Congress (1870–75) were intended to compel recognition by the South of the CIVIL RIGHTS ACT of 1866, of the FOURTEENTH AMENDMENT and later, the Fifteenth Amendment: Congressional elections were placed under national control, and the acts of armed organizations such as the KU KLUX KLAN were declared tantamount to rebellion.

Ford, Gerald R. (1913–) The 38th President of the USA (1974–77). Ford had replaced Spiro Agnew as Republican Vice-President to NIXON after Agnew's resignation in 1973. When Nixon himself resigned Ford automatically succeeded him as President. He continued with Nixon's attempts to control inflation with some success, although unemployment continued to rise. The VIETNAM WAR was finally ended with an air-lift of some 237,000 troops and refugees out of the country in April 1975. Egypt and Israel were helped by his Secretary of State Henry KISSINGER to settle a territorial dispute. In the election campaign of 1976 he won the Republican nomination, although he was defeated by the Democratic candidate Jimmy CARTER.

Ford, Henry (1863–1947) US industrialist and pioneer in car manufacture, the first to perceive its possibilities as a form of mass transport. Born on a Michigan farm, at 15 he left to work as a machinist's apprentice in Detroit. Later he became chief engineer for the Edison Company. While in Detroit he built his first experimental car (1894). In 1899, with backers, he formed the Detroit Automobile Company, and in 1903 established his own Ford Motor Company. Five years later he built the first Model T ('a motor car for the great multitude'), and by 1913 had developed highly efficient assembly-line techniques that resulted in an eightfold reduction in the production time for a car chassis (see MASS PRODUCTION). At a time when the average wage in manufacturing was $11 a week, he was paying his employees $5 a day and turning out one 'Tin Lizzie' every three minutes. Despite being an advocate of US isolation, in World War I he became a leading producer of aeroplanes, tanks, ambulances, and submarine chasers. Ford ran unsuccessfully for the Senate in 1918 and considered running for President in 1923. His politics were demagogic and right-wing; he opposed trade unions and propagated anti-semitic views.

By the early 1920s Ford had built many overseas plants and one car in two throughout the world was a Ford Model T. In 1927 the Model T was replaced by the Model A, and in 1932 Ford introduced the V-8 engine. In 1936 Ford established the philanthropic Ford Foundation, concerned with the welfare of poorer countries, the arts, and resources management; it is the largest philanthropic trust in the world. During World War II he once more converted his factories to the production of war material. Today Ford is a huge multinational corporation.

Formigny, Battle of (15 April 1450) A battle in the HUNDRED YEARS WAR. English forces were intercepted by French troops on their way to reinforce the garrison at Caen. Despite successes won by their archers, the English were overcome when French reinforcements arrived. This French victory led to the fall of Caen two months later, and the English loss of NORMANDY soon after.

Forrest, Sir John, 1st Baron Forrest of Bunbury (1847–1918) Australian explorer and statesman. He led several major expeditions, including a search for the lost explorer Leichardt (1869), and an expedition from Perth to Adelaide (1870). Forrest was Western Australia's first Premier (a courtesy title not conferred by the Constitution, but by usage) from 1890 until 1901. He was prominent in the AUSTRALIAN FEDERATION MOVEMENT, being a federal politician (Protectionist, Fusion, Liberal, and finally Nationalist) from 1901 until his death. He held various portfolios, serving mostly as Treasurer, and introduced 15 federal budgets.

Forrest, Nathan Bedford (1821–77) US general in the army of the CONFEDERACY. Although he participated with distinction in several of the large engagements in the western theatre of the AMERICAN CIVIL WAR (most notably Shiloh, Murfreesboro, and Chickamauga), he was best known for his brilliant raids behind Union (Northern) lines, tying down large numbers of troops and causing constant confusion and disruption. By the end of the war he was a lieutenant-general, although his reputation had been clouded by his involvement in the alleged massacre of Negro troops at Fort Pillow, Tennessee. After the war he became Grand Wizard of the KU KLUX KLAN but, disapproving of the lawlessness of many of its members, sought to disband the organization in 1869.

Forster, William Edward (1818–86) British statesman and educational reformer. Entering Parliament in 1861, he became Under-Secretary for the Colonies in 1865 and in 1868 vice-president of the Council. As such he, with Lord RIPON, secured the passing of the 1870 Education Act, which laid the foundations of compulsory, government-financed elementary education. In 1880 he was appointed Chief Secretary for Ireland, incurring unpopularity because of the severe measures he used to maintain order. He resigned in 1882 and became an opponent of Gladstone's plans for HOME RULE.

Fort Stanwix A colonial American military stronghold. Named after General John Stanwix, the fort was an important defence point and trading centre located between the Upper Mohawk River and Wood Creek. It fell into disrepair after 1763, but was rebuilt at the beginning of the War of Independence. Fort Stanwix is chiefly remembered as the site of the signing of two treaties with Native Americans in 1768 and 1784, in the second of which the IROQUOIS ceded their territory in Pennsylvania to the US government.

Fort Sumter A military stronghold in Charleston harbour, South Carolina; scene of the first military action in the AMERICAN CIVIL WAR. The Confederates, having seized Federal funds and property in the South, demanded the evacuation of the Federal Fort Sumter. Major Robert Anderson, in command, refused and General Beauregard bombarded it (12–13 April 1861) just as relief for the Federalists approached.

Forty-Five, the (1745) A JACOBITE rebellion in England and Scotland. Its aim was the removal of the Hanoverian GEORGE II from the throne and his replacement by James Edward Stuart, the Old PRETENDER. Jacobite hopes centred on the facts that Britain was heavily engaged in the War of the AUSTRIAN SUCCESSION, and that the Hanoverians had never been popular. The Pretender sent his 25-year-old son Charles Edward (Bonnie Prince Charlie, the Young Pretender) to represent him. Most of Scotland was soon overrun and the Jacobite victory at PRESTONPANS was followed by the invasion of England. But the

English armies of General Wade and the Duke of CUMBERLAND were closing in and, without any significant numbers of English recruits, Charles was advised by his commanders to return to Scotland. The Jacobites turned back at Derby when barely 160 km (100 miles) from London, where panic at their advance had caused a run on the Bank of England. The decision to retreat meant that the rebellion was doomed. The last Jacobite army was routed at the Battle of CULLODEN, which ended any serious Jacobite challenge to the Hanoverian succession.

forum An open public space in a town or city of the Roman empire. From the 6th century BC the Roman forum was a place for civic meetings and religious and military ceremonial. The Curia (Senate House) and COMITIA were situated there, together with markets, libraries, and courts. War trophies were put on display, the most famous being the ram-beaks ('rostra') of Carthaginian galleys taken in the First PUNIC WAR, which decorated the public platform or 'rostra' outside the Senate House. Other forums were built in Rome by early emperors including AUGUSTUS, VESPASIAN, and TRAJAN. The model was followed in virtually every town of the Roman empire.

Fosse Way A Roman road which crossed Britain from Isca (Exeter) to Lindum Colonia (Lincoln) by way of Aquae Sulis (Bath) and Ratae (Leicester). It marked the first and southernmost frontier in Britain after the Roman invasion of 43 AD and was probably laid as a military road along the temporary frontier. Northwards from Lincoln it became ERMINE STREET. The name comes from the 'fossa' or drainage ditch which ran alongside the road.

Foster, William Zebulon (1881–1961) US political leader. He joined the International Workers of the World in 1909, and after organizing the steelworkers' strike in the Chicago area in 1919, became a member of the newly formed US Communist Party. He ran as its presidential candidate in 1924, 1928, and 1932, and in 1945, after the discrediting of Earl Browder, the Party's war-time leader, became its chairman. He died in Moscow.

Fouché, Joseph, duc d'Otranto (c. 1759–1820) French statesman. He was a leading member of the JACOBIN Club in Nantes in 1790. He supported their violent doctrines, demanded the execution of the king, and was used to crush revolts in the west. He helped initiate the atheistical movement which led him into conflict with ROBESPIERRE and to his ejection from the Jacobin Club in 1794. During the next five years his skill and energy enabled him to play a successful part in the coups that overthrew Robespierre and the DIRECTORY. As Minister of Police (1799–1802), and of the Interior under NAPOLEON, he was one of the most powerful men in France until his resignation in 1815.

Founding Fathers The 55 delegates to the Constitutional Convention of 1787 that drafted the CONSTITUTION OF THE USA. They included outstanding public officials, of whom the most respected were George WASHINGTON and Benjamin FRANKLIN, while the leaders were James MADISON and George Mason of Virginia, Governor Morris and James Wilson of Pennsylvania, and Roger Sherman and Elbridge Gerry of Massachusetts. Of the 55 delegates, over half were lawyers, while planters and merchants, together with a few physicians and college professors, made up the rest. Washington was elected president of the Convention and William Jackson secretary. Jackson's notes were meagre, but a report of the debates was given in Madison's journal (and in notes made by other delegates), though, as the Convention was sworn to secrecy, Madison's notes were not published until 1840.

foundling hospital An institution for the care and upbringing of children who had been abandoned by their parents. The earliest known one was established in Milan in the 8th century. A number were founded in various European countries, including the famous Paris foundling hospital, incorporated in 1670. In 1739 Thomas Coram (1668–1751) set up his foundling hospital in London, which was at first reserved for illegitimate children.

Fouquet, Nicolas, vicomte de Melun et de Vaux, marquis de Belle-Isle (1615–80) French statesman in the reign of LOUIS XIV. He was Superintendent of Finances in 1653 and a munificent patron of the arts. On MAZARIN's death in 1661 he hoped to become first minister and invited Louis XIV to a lavish entertainment at his palatial residence at Vaux-le-Vicomte. Colbert persuaded the king that Fouquet's ambitions were a danger to his authority, and Louis XIV, determined not to be controlled by a powerful minister, ordered his arrest. His trial lasted for three years and the eventual sentence was banishment, but Louis had him imprisoned for life.

Four Modernizations Four key aspects of China's post-Mao development. The need to modernize agriculture, industry, national defence, and science and technology was implied in a speech by MAO ZEDONG in 1963, but in the CULTURAL REVOLUTION ideology was considered to be more important than economic development. After DENG XIAOPING came to power, the Four Modernizations began to take priority. Training of scientists, engineers, and managers, and the reform of agriculture by the 'responsibility system' (the transfer of management power from the commune to the individual) are key examples.

Four Noble Truths The basic teaching of the BUDDHA, as set out in his first sermon in the deer park at Varanasi (Benares), when he explained the cause and nature of suffering, and the goal of enlightenment. The Four Noble Truths follow the structure of a medical diagnosis. The first truth recognizes that there is a disease: suffering (*dukkha*), which is the basis of all existence. The second truth determines the cause of the disease: desire (*tanha*). The third truth acknowledges that there is a cure for the disease, and the fourth truth states what that cure is: the following of the Noble Eightfold Path of the Buddha.

Fourteen Points (8 January 1918) A US peace programme, contained in President Woodrow WILSON's address to Congress. They comprised freedom of the seas, equality of trade conditions, reduction of armaments, adjustment of colonial claims, evacuation of Russian territory and of Belgium, the return to France of Alsace-Lorraine, recognition of nationalist aspirations in eastern and central Europe, freedom for subject peoples in the Turkish empire, independence for Poland, and the establishment of a 'general association of nations'. Accepted, with some reluctance, by the Allies, they became in large part the basis for the peace negotiations of the VERSAILLES PEACE SETTLEMENT.

Fourteenth Amendment (1868) The most important of the three AMERICAN CIVIL WAR and Reconstruction amendments to the US Constitution. Drawn up in 1866 by the Joint Committee of Fifteen, the Fourteenth Amendment extended US citizenship to all persons born or naturalized in the USA (and thus, by including ex-slaves, reversed the DRED SCOTT decision). It also prohibited the states from abridging the privileges and immunities of citizens or depriving any person of life, liberty, or property without due process of law, or denying any person the equal protection of the laws. Another clause reduced the representation in Congress of states which denied the vote to Black people. The Fourteenth Amendment has caused more legal controversy than any other part of the constitution. In the late 19th century, it was used as a device to protect big business from state regulation. In the 20th century it has been the main constitutional instrument of the CIVIL RIGHTS movement and, in recent years, of the women's rights movement. (The Fifteenth Amendment, adopted in 1870, provided that the right to vote should not be denied on grounds of race, colour, or previous condition of servitude.)

Fox, Charles James (1749–1806) British statesman. He entered Parliament at the age of 20. At first he supported Lord NORTH, but soon became a bitter critic of North's American policy and favoured American independence. After North's resignation and ROCKINGHAM's death Fox refused to join the SHELBURNE ministry and collaborated with North to bring it down in 1783. The Fox-North coalition lasted only a few months; Fox's India Bill was defeated in the House of Lords, and GEORGE III took the opportunity to dismiss a coalition he detested. Fox spent most of the rest of his career in opposition to the new Prime Minister, the Younger PITT. His friendship with the Prince of Wales, his own blatant dissipations, and his apparently unprincipled efforts to achieve power meant that he never won wide political support, except when his welcome of the French Revolution was briefly in accord with the national mood; but BURKE's attack on the Revolution split the Foxite Whigs and pushed Fox into political isolation. His rivalry with Pitt led him into irresponsible opposition to some of Pitt's earlier reforms, but in 1801 he supported Pitt in his fight for CATHOLIC EMANCIPATION. The two men also shared a dislike of the SLAVE TRADE. When Pitt died in 1806, Fox became a leading member of the new ministry, and through his dying efforts Parliament agreed to an anti-slavery Bill.

Fox, George (1624–91) English founder of the QUAKERS. The son of a Puritan weaver, he left home in 1643 to lead an itinerant life, arguing with religious radicals, then preaching. By 1655 he had attracted thousands of converts. With the help of his wife, Alice Fell (married 1669), he proved to be a tireless organizer. He undertook missionary journeys throughout Britain, and ventured as far as the West Indies and North America (1671–72) and Holland (1677 and 1684). He was repeatedly imprisoned for his beliefs; his *Journal* was published posthumously in 1694.

Foxe, John (1516–87) English clergyman. He is best known as the author of *Acts and Monuments* (Latin edition, Strasburg 1554), a history of the persecution of Christians, and especially of Protestant martyrs from WYCLIF's time to his own. The English edition of 1563, *Acts and Monuments of matters happening in the Church*, complete with sensational woodcut illustrations, was popular with both the government and the clerical establishment. 'Foxe's Book of Martyrs', as it was known, celebrated the struggle and triumph of reformed doctrine in the English nation; it was banned by Archbishop LAUD.

France A country in western Europe, bounded on the north by the English Channel (la Manche), on the west by the Atlantic Ocean, on the south by the Pyrenees and the Mediterranean, and on the east by Belgium, Germany, Luxembourg, Switzerland, and Italy.

Physical. France is Europe's second largest country after Russia. In the north-west the Brittany peninsula with its low granite hills, Normandy with its fertile uplands, the broad Loire valley, and the Seine Basin, all enjoy a temperate climate. The north-east can be colder; but here there is agricultural land on chalk or limestone well drained by rivers. There are also deposits of coal. Southward the ground rises to the Massif Central, a region of high plateaux and rolling country set on volcanic rock. To the west lie the Bordeaux lowlands and the Gironde Estuary, to the south the plains of Languedoc, and to the east the Rhône valley. Extending from south to north along France's eastern border are the Jura Mountains, the Vosges, and the western Alps, falling away on their northern slopes to Alsace-Lorraine.

French overseas departments and dependencies include FRENCH GUIANA, French Polynesia, Guadeloupe, Martinique, Mayotte, New Caledonia, and Réunion.

Economy. France has rich mineral deposits of iron, potash, bauxite, zinc, lead, and gold, but also imports raw materials such as oil for processing. The leading agricultural nation of Western Europe, France is also the fourth most industrialized Western country, with a wide range of manufacturing industry. Services account for some three-fifths of GNP, and principal exports are chemicals, machinery, motor vehicles, iron, steel, and textiles, as well as foodstuffs and wines. Major agricultural crops include wheat, barley, maize, sugar beet, and fruit. Dairy and poultry farming are also substantial. Nuclear power supplies some 70% of electricity, with considerable hydroelectric capacity. The population is concentrated in the north, in the conurbations of Paris and Lyons, and in the south-east.

History. Prehistoric remains, cave paintings, and megalithic monuments attest to a long history of human settlement. The area known as GAUL to the Romans was conquered by the armies of Julius CAESAR, and its native inhabitants thoroughly Romanized by centuries of occupation. After 330 it was invaded by GOTHS, FRANKS, and BURGUNDIANS, and then ruled by Clovis (465–511), a MEROVINGIAN king. It became part of the empire of CHARLEMAGNE and, after repeated assaults from VIKINGS and SARACENS, a CAPETIAN dynasty emerged in 987. Fierce competition with the rival rulers of BRITTANY, BURGUNDY, and, after 1066, with the Norman and Plantagenet kings of England ensued, culminating in the HUNDRED YEARS WAR. France did not emerge as a permanently unified state until the ejection of the

English and the Burgundians at the end of the Middle Ages. Under the VALOIS and BOURBON dynasties France rose to contest European hegemony in the 16th to 18th centuries, notably in the wars of LOUIS XIV. In the 18th century, weak government, expensive wars, and colonial rivalry with England wrecked the monarchy's finances, and mounting popular anger culminated in the FRENCH REVOLUTION (1789).

The First Republic (1792–1804), established after the fall of the Bourbon monarchy, lasted until the First Empire (1804–14) under NAPOLEON I, when France became the dominant political power in Europe. After his fall the monarchy was restored (1814) and, with a brief interval in 1815, lasted until the abdication of Louis Philippe (1848). During this period, having lost influence in India and Canada, France began to create an overseas empire in North Africa. The Second Republic, established in 1848, lasted until 1852, when NAPOLEON III proclaimed the Second Empire (1852–70). It saw further expansion of the French empire, particularly in south-east Asia and in the Pacific. The Third Republic (1870–1940) was established after the capture and exile of Napoleon III and France's defeat in the FRANCO-PRUSSIAN WAR (1870). France took part in the Berlin Conference (1884) on Africa, and by 1914 ruled over Morocco, Tunis, Madagascar, and the huge areas of FRENCH WEST AFRICA and FRENCH EQUATORIAL AFRICA. The Third Republic fell in 1940, following defeat by Nazi Germany. Northern France was occupied by the Germans, unoccupied France to the south was under the VICHY GOVERNMENT, and a FREE FRENCH government was proclaimed in London. The Fourth Republic (1946–58) was replaced by the Fifth Republic (1958–   ), under the strong presidency of Charles DE GAULLE (1959–69). Protracted and costly wars led to the decolonization of Indo-China (1954) and of Algeria (1962), while, from 1956, the rest of the African empire gained increasing independence. After 1945 France regained its position as a major European power and was a founder member of the EUROPEAN ECONOMIC COMMUNITY (1958). As a nuclear power it refused to sign the NUCLEAR TEST-BAN TREATY (1963) and withdrew formally from the military division of NATO in 1966. In 1968 France suffered a wave of social and industrial unrest, including student-led riots in Paris. De Gaulle resigned in 1969, but his conservative and nationalist policies were generally maintained by his successors, Presidents POMPIDOU and Giscard d'Estaing In 1981 François MITTERRAND became the first socialist President for 35 years. A referendum held in 1992 narrowly endorsed the MAASTRICHT TREATY, which created the EUROPEAN UNION. Mitterrand did not contest the presidential elections in 1995 and the conservative Jacques CHIRAC was elected. A socialist government under Lionel Jospin was elected in 1997.

CAPITAL: Paris
AREA: 543,965 sq km (210,026 sq miles)
POPULATION: 58.392 million (1996)
CURRENCY: 1 franc = 100 centimes
RELIGIONS: Roman Catholic 76.4%; other Christian 3.7%; atheist 3.4%; Muslim 3.0%
ETHNIC GROUPS: French 86.8%; Occitan 2.7%; Arab 2.6%; Alsatian 2.3%; Breton 1.0%; Catalan 0.4%
LANGUAGES: French (official); minority languages
INTERNATIONAL
ORGANIZATIONS: UN; NATO; EU; OECD; South Pacific Commission; Council of Europe; CSCE

Franche-Comté A French province bordering the Swiss frontier, of which the chief town is Besançon. It was within the boundary of the Holy Roman Empire and, while the duchy of BURGUNDY was seized by Louis XI in 1477, the Franche-Comté passed eventually to the Spanish HABSBURGS. In the War of DEVOLUTION (1667–68) LOUIS XIV laid claim to it; it was overrun by CONDÉ, but returned to Spain at the Treaty of AIX-LA-CHAPELLE. In 1674 it was reoccupied and since the Treaty of NIJMEGEN (1679) it has been part of France.

Francia, José Gaspar Rodriguez de (1776–1840) Dictator of Paraguay. A leader of the Paraguayan movement for independence from Spain (1811), he dominated the post-independence period by establishing (1814) one of the most absolute dictatorships in 19th-century Latin American history. Dogmatic, anti-clerical, and xenophobic, he placed his country in almost complete isolation from the outside world. At home his autocratic rule earned him the name *El Supremo*. As time went on, he grew more arbitrary and despotic. The extravagances of his later years were considered symptomatic of his insanity, although he held office until his death in 1840.

Francis I (1494–1547) King of France (1515–47). He was in many respects an archetypal Renaissance prince, able, quick-witted, and licentious, and a patron of art and learning, but he developed into a cruel persecutor of Protestants, and devoted the best part of his reign to an inconclusive struggle with the HABSBURGS. He began by recovering the duchy of Milan (1515), but failed in his bid to be elected Holy Roman Emperor (1519). In 1520 he tried to secure the support of HENRY VIII of England against the successful candidate, CHARLES V, at the FIELD OF THE CLOTH OF GOLD, and in 1521 he embarked on the first of four wars against the emperor, which ended with his capture at the Battle of PAVIA (1525). He gained his release from captivity in Spain by renouncing his claims in Italy, but hostilities were resumed and continued intermittently, with the recovery of Milan as a main object, until the Peace of Crespy in 1544. His foreign wars were ruinously expensive, and the prodigality of his court foreshadowed that of LOUIS XIV. The palace of Fontainebleau was rebuilt during his reign, and the artists Leonardo da Vinci, Benvenuto Cellini, and Andrea del Sarto worked at his court.

Francis I (1768–1835) Habsburg monarch, last Holy Roman Emperor (as Francis II, 1792–1805), and first Emperor of Austria (as Francis I, 1804–35). Following defeat at AUSTERLITZ he was forced to abdicate the title of Holy Roman Emperor, losing lands to Russia, Bavaria, and France by the Treaty of Schönbrunn (1809). He had little choice but to allow NAPOLEON to marry his daughter, Marie-Louise, in 1810, but he changed sides with decisive effect in 1813 and played a major part in the eventual downfall of Napoleon. In 1815 at the Congress of VIENNA, he regained much of the territories lost in the war, largely as a result of the diplomatic skill of METTERNICH, responsible for foreign affairs. During the last 20 years of his reign he was identified with the HOLY ALLIANCE and its policy of repression.

Franciscans Friars of the order founded by St FRANCIS OF ASSISI. Their 'rule', which advocated strict poverty, was approved by Pope Innocent III in 1209–10 and confirmed in 1223. They quickly gained popular support through their work with the sick and the poor and others in the secular world. With the spread of the order two factions developed, the 'spirituals', who insisted on a literal interpretation of the rule and the 'moderates', whose views triumphed and allowed the order corporate ownership of property. Reform followed in the 16th century; the Capuchin friars were a reformed group approved by Pope Clement VII in 1528. The Second Order are the nuns known as 'Poor Clares', and the Third Order live and work among the laity.

Francis Ferdinand (1863–1914) Archduke of Austria and heir presumptive to Emperor FRANCIS JOSEPH. He aimed to transform the AUSTRO-HUNGARIAN EMPIRE into a triple monarchy to include a Slavic kingdom. He was opposed by the Hungarians, who refused to make concessions to Slavs, and by extreme Slav nationalists (including Serbs), who saw no future for the emergent nations within the empire. On 28 June 1914, while on an inspection tour at Sarajevo, he and his wife were assassinated by Gavrilo Princip, a Serbian nationalist. The subsequent ultimatum by Austria to Serbia led directly to the outbreak of World War I.

Francis Joseph (or Franz Josef) (1830–1916), Emperor of Austria (1848–1916), King of Hungary (1867–1916). He succeeded to the throne (aged 18) amid the REVOLUTIONS OF 1848. He suppressed all nationalist hopes until forced to meet Hungarian aspirations in the establishment of the AUSTRO-HUNGARIAN EMPIRE (1867). His foreign policy lost Habsburg lands to Italy (1859 and 1866) and led to the loss of Austrian influence over German affairs and to the ascendancy of Prussia. Seeking compensation in the BALKAN STATES, he aroused Slav opposition which ultimately resulted in World War I. His wife Elizabeth was assassinated by the Italian anarchist Lucheni. Opposed to social reform, Francis Joseph maintained administrative centralization and opposed the federalist aspirations of the Slavs.

Francis of Assisi, St (1182–1226) Founder of the FRANCISCAN order of friars. He was born to a wealthy merchant family in northern Italy and initially followed his father's trade. After a period of imprisonment following involvement in a border dispute in 1202 he abandoned this in favour of the religious life. He adopted extreme poverty but remained 'within the world', working and preaching especially to the poor and sick. His example gained for him a large following and Pope INNOCENT III approved the Franciscan order in 1209–10. He was ordained deacon, which position he retained, his humility preventing his acceptance of full priesthood. His teaching reflected a profound love of the natural world and respect for even the lowliest of its creatures. He rejected personal possessions, wearing only the simplest clothing and ruling that his followers should do likewise. He made missionary journeys to southern Europe and visited the sultan al-Kamil in Egypt in an effort to secure peace during the Fifth CRUSADE. A number of miracles and visions were attributed to him, and he was canonized in 1228.

Francis Xavier, St (1506–52) Missionary priest, known as the 'Apostle of the Indies'. Born into a Spanish noble family, he was the first JESUIT missionary in the East. He worked among lepers in GOA, in India, where he baptized thousands of pearl divers, and in the MOLUCCAS and MALACCA. In 1549 he went to Japan where he remained

for two years and made some 2,000 converts. Convinced that the Japanese would readily become Christians if the Chinese were converted, he set out for Guangzhou (Canton) but died on an island near Hong Kong while awaiting an opportunity to enter China. His voluminous correspondence survives.

Franco (Bahamonde), Francisco (1892–1975) Spanish general and head of state. A monarchist, he rose rapidly in the army until 1931, when Alfonso XIII abdicated and was replaced by a republican government. He was temporarily out of favour, but by 1935 was chief of the General Staff. Elections in February 1936 returned a more left-wing government and the army prepared to revolt. At first he hesitated to join in the military conspiracy but in July led troops from Morocco into Spain to attack Madrid and overthrow the republic. After three years of the savage SPANISH CIVIL WAR he was victorious and became dictator of Spain (1939). In 1937 Franco adopted the FALANGE, expanding it into a Spanish fascist party and banning all political opposition. During World War II he remained neutral though sympathizing with Hitler and Mussolini. His government was ostracized by the new United Nations until, with the coming of the COLD WAR, his hostility towards communism restored him to favour. His domestic policy became slightly more liberal, and in 1969 he named Prince Juan Carlos (1938–), grandson of Alfonso XIII, as his successor and heir to the reconstituted Spanish throne. On his death Spain returned to a democratic system of government under a constitutional monarchy.

Franco-Prussian War (1870–71) A conflict between France, under NAPOLEON III, and Prussia. The war was engineered by BISMARCK, who had skilfully isolated the French before provoking them into starting hostilities (the EMS TELEGRAM). Prussian armies advanced into France; the French forces led by MACMAHON were driven out of Alsace whilst a second French army, under BAZAINE was forced to retire to Metz. MacMahon, marching to relieve Metz, was comprehensively defeated by MOLTKE at Sedan. Napoleon was captured and, discredited in the eyes of the French, ceased to be emperor. Bismarck refused to make peace, and in September the siege of Paris began. Hopes of a French counter-attack were dispelled when Bazaine surrendered at Metz and Paris finally gave way in January 1871. An armistice was granted by Bismarck, and a national assembly elected to ratify the peace, but the population of Paris refused to lay down arms and in March 1871 rose in revolt and set up the PARIS COMMUNE. The French government signed the Treaty of FRANKFURT in May and French prisoners-of-war were allowed through Prussian lines to suppress the Commune. For Prussia, the proclamation of the GERMAN SECOND EMPIRE at Versailles in January was the climax of Bismarck's ambitions to unite Germany.

Frank, Anne (1929–45) A Jewish girl who became a CONCENTRATION CAMP victim. She was living with her family in Amsterdam when the Germans invaded in 1940. From July 1942 to April 1944 the family and four other Jews were hidden by a local family in a sealed-off back room, but were eventually betrayed. She was murdered in Belsen. During the years of hiding Anne kept a diary of her experiences which, since its publication in 1947, has attracted a worldwide readership.

Frankfurt, Treaty of (10 May 1871) An agreement that ended the FRANCO-PRUSSIAN WAR. By it France surrendered Strasburg, Alsace and part of Lorraine, together with the great fortresses of Metz to BISMARCK's Germany. An indemnity of five billion gold francs was imposed by Germany on France, and a German army of occupation was to remain until the indemnity had been paid. Bismarck's aim in this treaty was to ensure that France would be entirely cut off from the Rhine.

Frankfurt School An influential group of thinkers based at the Institute for Social Research founded in 1923 at the University of Frankfurt, Germany. During the Nazi ascendancy, many members fled to the USA and the Institute was affiliated to the University of Columbia, New York, between 1934 and 1949. Among its most brilliant scholars were Theodor Adorno (1903–69), Herbert Marcuse (1898–1979), and Jürgen Habermas (1929–   ). The School attempted to integrate disciplines such as philosophy, psychology, and economics and, by building on the work of MARX, to construct new critiques of CAPITALISM. Developing what it called CRITICAL THEORY, it analysed the role of multinational companies, technology, and mass communication. Its members feared the increased control of capitalism over all aspects of life and favoured SOCIALISM.

franklin English freeholder in the 13th and 14th centuries. Franklins paid a rent for their land and did not owe military service to their lord. Their status was above that of the free peasant but below the gentry. After the BLACK DEATH (1349) the status of many franklins improved in the favourable economic climate. The newly rich and socially ambitious franklin was satirized by Chaucer in the Prologue to his *Canterbury Tales*.

Franklin, Benjamin (1706–90) American statesman, journalist, and inventor. He was born in Boston of humble parents and trained as a printer. In 1723 he ran away to Philadelphia. After a visit to London, he became publisher of the *Pennsylvania Gazette* (1730–66) and obtained the lucrative contract for government printing. His *Poor Richard's Almanack* (1732–57), full of advice on success in business, won him intercolonial fame. Influenced by Cotton MATHER, Daniel Defoe, and *The Spectator*, he was a proponent of civic improvements and self-help projects such as the Junto (1727), the Library Company (1731), the Fire Company (1737), the AMERICAN PHILOSOPHICAL SOCIETY (1743), the University of Pennsylvania (1751), and the Philadelphia Hospital (1752). He also pursued scientific inquiries in the spirit of the ENLIGHTENMENT, seeking practical improvements like bifocal spectacles. He invented the Franklin stove in about 1744. From 1746, he took an active interest in the then little understood phenomenon of electricity and gave it a unity and scientific basis. Franklin's famous experiments with a kite (1752) led to the development of the lightning conductor. Appointed Deputy Postmaster-General for the Colonies in 1753, he improved intercolonial communications and developed a federal outlook, shown at the ALBANY CONGRESS in 1754.

Drawn into politics by opposition to the PENN family's privileges and to the pacifism of the ruling Quakers, he was an agent in London for long periods between 1757 and 1775, seeking a new charter and lobbying against revenue-raising measures. He attended the CONTINENTAL CONGRESS before appointment as ambassador to France

(1776–85). Posing as a simple citizen at Louis XVI's court, his popularity helped secure the French alliance (1778) and he was able to arrange favourable terms for America at the Peace of PARIS (1783). In France he continued writing his *Autobiography* which reveals his pragmatic philosophy of personal improvement and natural inquiry. After attending the Constitutional Convention, he died in 1790, the embodiment of the rags-to-riches dream and the public-spirited entrepreneur.

frankpledge (or 'peace-pledge') A system for preserving law and order in English communities from the 10th century to the 14th, when it was superseded by the appointment of Justices of the Peace. Communities were grouped into associations of ten men (a tithing) under a headman (chief pledge or tithingman) and held responsible for the good behaviour of members. Twice a year, in the 'view of frankpledge', sheriffs examined its effectiveness. Frankpledge was not applied to the aristocracy, to certain freeholders, or to vagrants, nor was it found in northern England where the alternative system of Serjeants of the Peace existed.

Franks A group of Germanic tribes who dominated Europe after the collapse of the Western ROMAN EMPIRE. The name was adopted in the 3rd century AD, possibly from their word for a javelin (*franca*). They consisted of Salians from what is now Belgium and Ripuarians from the Lower Rhine. They settled in Gaul by the mid-4th century and ruled it by the following century when the Salians under CLOVIS defeated the Romans at Soissons. Gaul became 'Francia', ruled from the old capital Lutetia Parisiorum (Paris) of the Parisii Gauls. The MEROVINGIAN succession continued until 751. Power then passed from the kings to their palace mayors. In 751 Pepin, son of Charles Martel, became the first CAROLINGIAN ruler of the Franks.

Franz Josef FRANCIS JOSEPH.

Fraser, Peter (1884–1950) New Zealand statesman. He was gaoled during World War I for opposing conscription, and upon his release joined the New Zealand Labour Party. Elected to Parliament in 1918, he became the party's deputy leader in 1933, and Prime Minister (1940–49). One of the architects of the United Nations (1945), he held a life-long commitment to equality in education, and the modern New Zealand education system is perhaps his most enduring monument.

Frederick I (Barbarossa) (*c.* 1123–90) King of Germany and Italy (1152–90), Holy Roman Emperor (1155–90). He was the son of Frederick II, Duke of Swabia. He put down the rebellion of Arnold of Brescia in northern Italy and in 1155 was rewarded by Pope Adrian IV with the imperial crown. From that point onwards, however, he was at odds with the papacy as he tried to strengthen his empire in Italy. He was opposed by the Lombard League (an alliance of north Italian cities) and Pope Alexander III, whom he was eventually obliged to recognize in 1177. He came to terms with the Lombards at the Peace of Constance in 1183. In Germany he had to assert his power over his rival HENRY THE LION. This achieved, he left the empire in the hands of his son, and went on CRUSADE. He won two victories over the Muslims but was drowned crossing a river in Asia Minor.

Frederick I (1657–1713) Elector of Brandenburg from 1688, King of Prussia (1701–13). He lacked the ability of his father, FREDERICK WILLIAM, the Great Elector, and dissipated funds in display and extravagance. In 1700 he supported the Holy Roman Emperor Leopold I in the War of the SPANISH SUCCESSION and with his approval was able to proclaim himself king, taking his title from his territory of East PRUSSIA. In 1713 he acquired Upper Gelders. With his second wife Sophia Charlotte he developed Berlin and established the Academy of Science and the University of Halle.

Frederick II (1194–1250) Holy Roman Emperor (1220–50). The grandson of FREDERICK I (Barbarossa). Frederick II was known as *Stupor Mundi* ('Wonder of the World') because of the breadth of his power and of his administrative, military, and intellectual abilities. He was crowned King of the Germans in 1215 and Holy Roman Emperor in 1220, but his reign was dominated by a long and ultimately unsuccessful struggle for power with the papacy. In 1228 he led a successful crusade to Jerusalem, obtaining, in 1229, Jerusalem, Nazareth, and Bethlehem for Christendom. Twice excommunicated by Pope Gregory IX, and opposed in Italy by the Lombard League, Frederick devolved a great deal of imperial power within Germany on the lay and clerical princes in an effort to maintain their support, and concentrated on building a power base in Sicily, a process completed by the Constitution of Melfi in 1231. He defeated the Lombard League at Cortenuova in 1237 and humiliated Gregory IX prior to the latter's death in 1241, but failed in his efforts to conciliate Innocent IV who appealed to Germany to revolt at the Synod of Lyons in 1245. Frederick's position was crumbling in the face of revolt, papal propaganda, and military defeat when he died in 1250, leaving an impossible situation for his heirs to solve. Many scholars and artists of his court migrated to north Italian cities, becoming precursors of the RENAISSANCE.

Frederick II (the Great) (1712–86) King of Prussia (1740–86). He was the son of FREDERICK WILLIAM I and Sophia Dorothea, daughter of GEORGE I of Great Britain. Able, cultured, a hard-working administrator, and a brilliant soldier, he was an example of an 18th-century enlightened despot. He believed that a ruler should exercise absolute power, but exercise it for the good of his subjects. He established full religious toleration, abolished torture, and freed the serfs on his own estates. He continued the state's tradition of efficient administration, fair though heavy taxation, and above all devotion to the army and its needs.

His foreign policy was unscrupulous. In 1740 he attacked MARIA THERESA and gained Silesia. He fought to keep it in the War of the AUSTRIAN SUCCESSION and the SEVEN YEARS WAR, and greatly increased his prestige by his victories over the French at Rossbach (1757) and the Austrians at Leuthen (1757). He obtained the valuable territory of West PRUSSIA in the first partition of Poland in 1772 and opposed JOSEPH II in the war of the BAVARIAN SUCCESSION. He also built the rococo palace of Sans Souci at Potsdam, played and composed flute music, and corresponded with VOLTAIRE.

Frederick III (1415–93) King of Germany (1440–93), HOLY ROMAN EMPEROR (1452–93). He inherited the HABSBURG domains as Archduke of Austria in 1424. He failed to assert family interest in Hungary, and was troubled by

rival claimants to his own lands, and by Turkish attacks, which became more threatening after the fall of CONSTANTINOPLE in 1453. On good terms with the papacy, he was the last Holy Roman Emperor to be crowned by the pope at Rome. He earned unpopularity by his efforts to suppress John HUSS's followers in Bohemia and Hungary. By arranging the marriage of his son MAXIMILIAN I to Mary, daughter of CHARLES THE BOLD, he greatly extended the dynastic power of the Habsburgs.

Frederick V (the Winter King) (1596–1632) Elector Palatine (1610–20) and King of Bohemia (1619–20). In 1613 he married Elizabeth, daughter of JAMES I of England. He then assumed the leadership of the German Protestant Union, and accepted the Bohemian crown when it was offered, following the deposition of FERDINAND II in November 1619. Thenceforth his fortunes followed the course of the THIRTY YEARS WAR, a struggle in which he took little personal part after his defeat at the Battle of the White Mountain (November 1620). He withdrew to The Hague, and forfeited the Palatinate. GEORGE I of Great Britain (1660–1727) was his grandson.

Frederick Louis (1707–51) British prince, the eldest son of GEORGE II, with whom he quarrelled bitterly. As Prince of Wales his home in London, Leicester House, became the meeting place of the opposition leaders who helped to bring down Sir Robert WALPOLE in 1742. His premature death disappointed the hopes of those politicians who had supported him in the expectation of preferment upon his succession. The throne passed to his eldest son, who reigned as GEORGE III.

Frederick William (the Great Elector) (1620–88) Elector of Brandenburg (1640–88), sometimes called the greatest of the HOHENZOLLERNS. He succeeded to an inheritance impoverished by the THIRTY YEARS WAR but was able, and a good diplomat, and rapidly improved his position and made gains, including East Pomerania, at the Treaty of WESTPHALIA. By 1688 his standing army of 30,000 troops had become the efficient basis of the state, communications were improved, waste lands cultivated, and his territory of East Prussia freed from Polish overlordship. His victory of Fehrbellin (1675) over the Swedes greatly increased his prestige.

Frederick William I (1688–1740) King of Prussia (1713–40). He was the son of FREDERICK I and was known as 'the royal drill-sergeant': he was a strict Calvinist, hardworking, violent tempered, and notorious for his ill-treatment of his son, FREDERICK II. He left a model administration, a large revenue, and an efficient and well-disciplined army. He acquired Stettin in 1720.

Frederick William II (1744–97) King of Prussia (1787–97). He was the nephew of FREDERICK II and a man of little ability, though a patron of the arts. He fought in the early campaigns against the French Revolutionary armies but became more concerned with Poland gaining land, including Warsaw, in the partitions of 1793 and 1795.

Frederick William III (1770–1840) King of Prussia (1797–1840). After his defeat at the Battle of JENA he was forced by the Treaty of TILSIT (1807) to surrender half his dominions by the creation of the kingdom of Westphalia and the grand duchy of Warsaw. In 1811 he joined NAPOLEON in the war against Russia but, following the retreat of Napoleon from Moscow, he signed a military alliance with Russia and Austria. From 1807 onwards he supported the efforts for reform made by STEIN and HARDENBERG, and at the Congress of VIENNA he won back for Prussia Westphalia and much of the Rhineland and of Saxony. He signed the HOLY ALLIANCE, and became progressively more reactionary during the last years of his reign.

Frederick William IV (1795–1861) King of Prussia (1840–61). A patriarchal monarch by temperament, he was the champion of a united Germany, but could not accept the degree of democracy envisaged by the Frankfurt Parliament of 1848 (see REVOLUTIONS OF 1848). He therefore refused (1849) the offer of a constitutional monarchy for the GERMAN CONFEDERATION. For Prussia he promulgated a conservative constitution allowing for a parliament, but with a restricted franchise and limited powers. This remained in force until 1918.

Freedom Riders In the early 1960s, groups of non-violent Black and White protesters against racial discrimination in the US Southern states. They were mostly volunteers from the north who in 1961 began chartering buses and riding through the Southern states to challenge the segregation laws. Many Freedom Riders were arrested or brutally attacked by Southern White racists, but their actions did help to arouse public opinion in support of the CIVIL RIGHTS campaign.

Free French, the A World War II organization of Frenchmen and women in exile. Led by General DE GAULLE, it continued the war against the AXIS POWERS after the surrender and occupation of France in 1940. Its headquarters were in London, where, apart from organizing forces that participated in military campaigns and co-operating with the French RESISTANCE MOVEMENT, it constituted a pressure group that strove to represent French interests. In 1941 its French National Committee was formed and this eventually developed into a provisional government for liberated France. The Free French army in French Equatorial Africa, led by General Leclerc (Philippe, vicomte de Hauteclocque), linked up with the British forces in Tripoli (1943), after completing an epic march of *c.* 2,400 km (1,500 miles) from Lake Chad. A provisional Free French government was established in Algiers, moving to Paris in 1944.

free market An economy in which buying, selling, and other transactions can be conducted on whatever terms the parties choose without intervention by the state. This means, for example, that prices are not fixed, and there is no regulation or subsidization of production or employment. Prices are therefore determined solely by the forces of supply and demand. The ideal of a perfectly free market is central to libertarianism and the NEW RIGHT ideology, on grounds both of freedom of choice and of economic efficiency – see, for instance, FRIEDMAN's *Capitalism and Freedom* (1962). These claims, however, depend on conditions of widespread competition and full information, which are often not fulfilled in reality, and so even governments sympathetic to free-market ideas are obliged to regulate markets to protect consumers and to prevent the emergence of monopolies and cartels. Producer groups, too, may prefer the stability of a regulated market to the hazards of open competition, as the US economist John Kenneth Galbraith argued in *The New Industrial State* (1967). None the less, relatively free markets appear to be indispensable to economic growth, and are being introduced in many countries that are pursuing policies of liberalization in the wake of failures of government planning.

Freemasons An international fraternity of 'Free and Accepted Masons', which declares itself to be based on brotherly love, faith, and charity, and is characterized by elaborate rituals and systems of secret signs, passwords, and handshakes. The rituals are based largely on Old Testament anecdotes and moralities and are illustrated by the tools of a mason, the square and compasses. The original 'free masons' were probably emancipated skilled itinerant stonemasons who (in and after the 14th century) found work wherever important buildings were being erected, all of whom recognized their fellow craftsmen by secret signs. The 'accepted masons' were honorary members (originally supposed to be eminent for architectural or antiquarian learning) who began to be admitted early in the 17th century. The distinction of being an 'accepted mason' became a fashionable aspiration; before the end of the 17th century the purpose of the fraternities seems to have been chiefly social and convivial. In 1717 four of these societies or 'lodges' in London united to form a Grand Lodge, with a new constitution and ritual, and a new objective of mutual help and fellowship among members. The London Grand Lodge became the parent of other lodges in Britain and around the world, and there are now bodies of Freemasons in many countries of the world. The Masonic Order is forbidden to Roman Catholics, as the Church regards certain masonic principles as incompatible with its doctrines.

Free-Silver Movement A movement in the 19th century in the USA for an unlimited silver coinage. Following the GOLD RUSHES of the 1850s and 1860s, large deposits of silver were discovered in the West. Silver miners wished to see unlimited production, but in 1873 Congress refused to include the silver dollar in its list of authorized coins. A protest movement resulted, and in 1878 the silver dollar became legal tender, the US Treasury agreeing to purchase silver to turn into coins. In 1890 the Sherman Silver Purchase Act doubled the agreed issue of silver, but following a stockmarket crisis in 1893 the Act was repealed. Eastern bankers were blamed for a depressed silver market, and the Democratic Party adopted the demand for unlimited free silver in the presidential campaign of 1896. Following the 1900 election, a Republican Congress passed the Gold Standard Act, which made gold the sole standard of currency. Franklin Delano ROOSEVELT passed legislation securing guaranteed US Treasury purchases of silver for use in coins. Supplies of silver decreased during the 1960s and in 1970 the Treasury stopped using silver and sold its surplus stock.

Free Soil Party A minor US political party of the mid-19th century. In 1846 David Wilmot from Pennsylvania proposed to Congress a proviso that slavery would be forbidden in the huge territories then being seized from Mexico in the MEXICAN-AMERICAN WAR. This Wilmot Proviso failed, but its disappointed supporters held a convention in 1848 where they formed a Free Soil Party advocating 'free soil, free labour, and free men'. They gained support from the small farmers as well as from anti-slave groups. The party never won more than 10% of the popular vote in presidential or Congress elections and failed to prevent either the Compromise of 1850 or the KANSAS-NEBRASKA ACT of 1854. It became absorbed after 1854 into the newly formed Republican Party.

free trade A doctrine advocating a free flow of goods between countries to encourage mutual economic development and international harmony by the commercial interdependence of trading nations. A policy of free trade prohibits both tariffs on imports and subsidies on exports designed to protect a country's industry. The doctrine's best early statement was by Adam SMITH in his *Wealth of Nations* (1776). The argument appealed to many British industrialists in the early 19th century, who came to be called the 'MANCHESTER SCHOOL'. It became increasingly government policy with the repeal of the CORN LAWS in 1846, and was fully adopted in 1860. The contrary doctrine, that of protectionism or the imposition of import tariffs to protect home industries, was advocated in the later 19th century in a number of countries, for example the USA, Germany, and Australia. In 1903 Joseph CHAMBERLAIN began a campaign in Britain for TARIFF REFORM, which was a major factor in British politics until 1932, when a conference in Ottawa approved a system of limited tariffs between Britain and the newly created dominions, in the first instance for five years. After World War II the USA tried to reverse the trend to protection. At a conference in Geneva in 1947 a first schedule for freer world trade was drawn up, the GENERAL AGREEMENT ON TARIFFS AND TRADE (GATT). For over a decade after the war Britain also was a strong supporter of moves to restore freer trade. It was a founder member of the EUROPEAN FREE TRADE ASSOCIATION (EFTA) in 1958, but as adverse economic conditions developed in the 1960s Britain sought entry into the EUROPEAN ECONOMIC COMMUNITY (now the EUROPEAN UNION). In Eastern Europe a similar community, COMECON, was established in 1949; after 1987 COMECON, sought co-operation with EU countries. The highly successful growth of the Japanese economy after the war led many countries to seek tariffs against Japan. By the 1990s world economic policies were confused, some policies supporting free trade and others supporting trade protection measures. In 1993, at the conclusion of the Uruguay Round, the members of GATT agreed to further cuts in tariffs and export subsidies and to create the WORLD TRADE ORGANIZATION (WTO). The WTO will enforce GATT rules, especially the agricultural measures agreed in the Uruguay Round, which reduced export subsidies and import duties by 20–36%. The International Trade Centre, founded in 1964 to assist developing countries to increase their export sales, is operated jointly by GATT and the UN Conference on Trade and Development.

Frei (Montalva), Edúardo (1911–82) Chilean statesman. He was President of Chile (1964–70). A founder-member of the Falange Nacional, later Partido Demócrata Cristiano (PDC), he was a severe critic of the US Alliance for Progress programme to aid Latin American countries. The programmes he initiated, including agrarian reform and the 'Chileanization' of the copper industry (whose controlling interest had until then been held by US companies), were ambitious, but his failure to check inflation or to redistribute wealth turned many of his supporters against him. His son, Edúardo Frei Ruiz-Tagle, was elected President of Chile in 1993 (inaugurated in 1994).

Frelimo War (1964–75) A war fought between MOZAMBIQUE nationalist groups united into the Mozambique Liberation Front (Frelimo) and Portuguese troops. In 1963 Frelimo recruits were sent to Algeria and Egypt for political and guerrilla training. Operations, headed by Eduardo Mondlane, began in 1964. The Portuguese failed to contain the conflict, and by 1968 Samora MACHEL claimed one-fifth of the country. A Portuguese resettlement programme (*aldeamentos*), and public and social works failed to satisfy the guerrillas, who were being armed by supplies from China, Czechoslovakia, and the Soviet Union. Brutal Portuguese counter-terrorism made conciliation even more impossible and Portugal conceded independence in 1974. Frelimo became the dominant political force in the new People's Republic of Mozambique.

Frémont, John Charles (1813–90) US explorer, soldier, and political leader. Frémont played an important part in mapping the area between the upper reaches of the Mississippi and Missouri rivers before leading three major expeditions to the West between 1842 and 1846 which earned him the name of the 'Pathfinder'. He was involved controversially in the US conquest of California at the time of the MEXICAN–AMERICAN WAR. In 1856, he was the first presidential candidate of the new Republican Party, but was defeated by BUCHANAN. During the AMERICAN CIVIL WAR, he commanded Union forces in the Department of the West (1861) and in western Virginia (1862) with little success. He briefly challenged Lincoln in the presidential campaign of 1864.

French, John Denton Pinkstone, 1st Earl of Ypres (1852–1925) British field-marshal. Having distinguished himself in the Sudan and the Second BOER WAR (1899), he was appointed commander-in-chief of the BRITISH EXPEDITIONARY FORCE in France (1914). Under instructions from Lord KITCHENER he opposed the German advance through Belgium and Flanders. He and his armies were ill-equipped for the kind of TRENCH WARFARE in which they found themselves involved, and in December 1915 French resigned in favour of Sir Douglas HAIG. At the Irish EASTER RISING in 1916 French dispatched two divisions to suppress the uprising. He served as Lord Lieutenant of Ireland (1918–21) at a time when outrages and reprisals were widespread.

French and Indian wars (1689–1763) Anglo-French conflicts in North America, part of the international rivalry between the two nations. They consisted of KING WILLIAM'S WAR (1689–97), QUEEN ANNE'S WAR (1703–13), KING GEORGE'S WAR (1744–48), and the French and Indian War (1755–63), the American part of the SEVEN YEARS WAR. As a result of an alliance with Prussia, PITT was able to devote more British resources to America. In 1755 the British commander, General BRADDOCK, led forces into Ohio but was defeated at Fort Duquesne. Other forces defeated the French at the Battle of Lake George, but no advantage was taken. The French claimed a number of victories in 1756 and 1757 against the British, already weakened by friction between the new commander, Lord John Loudoun, and the states of Massachusetts and Virginia. In 1759, however, WOLFE defeated the French at the Battle of the PLAINS OF ABRAHAM. Quebec surrendered shortly thereafter, followed by Montreal one year later, all Canada then passing into British hands. By the Treaty of PARIS (1763) Britain gained Canada and Louisiana east of the Mississippi.

French Community (1958–61) An association consisting of France, its overseas territories and departments, and various independent African states formerly part of the FRENCH EMPIRE. Established in 1958, it was a system aimed at associating the former colonies with metropolitan France. Members of the Community were allowed considerable autonomy though they were denied control of their own higher education, currency, defence, or foreign affairs. The West African territory of Guinea immediately voted against the arrangement and became independent. Hostility to the restrictions on autonomy led to a revision of the Constitution in 1960. Nevertheless, some African states left, while continuing to retain close links with France. By 1961 the system had virtually collapsed and some of its institutions were abolished.

French East India Company A commercial organization, founded in 1664 to compete with DUTCH and English EAST INDIA COMPANIES. Until the 1740s it was less successful than its rivals, but led by an ambitious governor, DUPLEIX, the Company then made a bid to challenge English influence in India, notably by alliances with local rulers in south India. Although a number of trading ports, including PONDICHERRY and Chandernagore, remained in French control until 1949, the Company itself collapsed during the French Revolutionary period.

French empire The colonial empire of France. In the 18th century a long rivalry with Britain ended with the loss of QUEBEC and recognition of British supremacy in India. By 1815 only some West Indian Islands, French Guiana, and Senegal and Gabon were left. The 19th century witnessed a rapid growth of the empire. The conquest of Algeria began (1830), while Far Eastern possessions – Cochin China, Cambodia, and New Caledonia – were added. In the SCRAMBLE FOR AFRICA, Tunisia became a protectorate (1881), and by 1912 MOROCCO, MADAGASCAR, and French Somaliland (DJIBOUTI) had been added to FRENCH EQUATORIAL AFRICA and FRENCH WEST AFRICA to make the African empire 20 times the size of France itself. Britain frustrated French aspirations in Egypt and the Sudan, and rivalry at FASHODA (1898) nearly caused war until the ENTENTE CORDIALE brought agreement. After World War I Togoland and the Cameroons, former German colonies, became French MANDATES, as did Syria and Lebanon (1923). Defeat in World War II and short-lived post-war governments prevented urgent reforms, thereby causing the loss of both Far Eastern and African empires. In Indo-China the communist leader, HO CHI MINH, established his Vietnamese republic (1945) which France refused to recognize. Open warfare (1946–54) ended with the French capitulation at DIENBIENPHU and the consequent independence of Cambodia, Laos, and Vietnam. In Algeria almost the entire French army failed to quell an Arab rising (1954). By 1958 DE GAULLE realized that independence was inevitable, it followed in 1962. In 1946 the empire was formed into the French Union, which was replaced in 1958 by the FRENCH COMMUNITY. France still has four Overseas Departments: FRENCH GUIANA, Guadeloupe, Martinique, and Réunion; two Territorial Collectivities: Mayotte and St Pierre et

Miquelon; and four Overseas Territories: French Polynesia, the Wallis and Futuna Islands, NEW CALEDONIA, and the French Southern and Antarctic Territories.

French Equatorial Africa A former French federation in west central Africa. It included the present republics of the Congo, Gabon, Central Africa, and Chad, all originally French colonies. To them was attached (1920) the League of Nations Mandated Territory of Cameroon, now part of Cameroon. The Federation was formed mainly through the efforts of the Franco-Italian empire-builder, Savorgnan de Brazza (1852–1905). Proclaimed in 1908, it was administered centrally from Brazzaville until its constituents became autonomous republics within the French Community in 1958. The member states formed (1959) a loose association called the Union of Central African Republics, before becoming independent nations.

French Foreign Legion A French volunteer armed force consisting chiefly of foreigners. In 1831 LOUIS-PHILIPPE reorganized a light infantry legion in Algeria as the *régiment étranger*, the foreign legion. It fought in numerous 19th-century wars and in both World Wars. Following Algeria's independence in 1962 the legion was transferred to France. No questions are asked about the origin or past of the recruits, whose oath binds them absolutely to the regiment whose unofficial motto is *legio patria nostra* ('the legion is our fatherland').

French Guiana A French possession on the Caribbean coast of South America. The first French settlement was made at Cayenne Island at the beginning of the 17th century. The rivalry with the British, the Dutch, and the Portuguese was intense until 1817, when French possession was finally secured. Immigration schemes were ineffective and the colony was populated by former prisoners from Devil's Island and other off-shore convict settlements. In 1946 it became an overseas department of France and in 1968 the launch site of the European Space Agency was established there. Social unrest, including strikes and sporadic terrorist attacks, increased during the 1970s and 1980s due to high levels of unemployment and a growing independence movement.

French Indo-China Former French colonial empire in south-east Asia. Having gained early influence in the area through assisting Gia-Long in establishing the Vietnamese empire in the early 19th century, the French colonized the area between the late 1850s and 1890s, using the term Indo-China to designate the final union of their colonies and dependencies within Annam, Cambodia, Cochin-China, Laos, and Tonkin. Nationalist movements aiming particularly at the formation of an independent and united Vietnam sprang up between the wars, and French influence in the area was fatally undermined in the early 1940s by the collaboration of the VICHY colonial administration with the Japanese. The VIETMINH resistance movement became active during the war; having consolidated a peasant base, it resisted attempts by the French to reassert their control after 1945. A protracted guerrilla war eventually brought France to defeat at DIENBIENPHU in 1954. In the same year the GENEVA CONFERENCE formally ended French control, transferring power to national governments in Cambodia, Laos, and North and South Vietnam.

French Indo-China War (1946–54) A conflict fought between French colonial forces and VIETMINH forces largely in the Tonkin area of northern Vietnam. The Vietminh began active guerrilla operations during the Japanese occupation of World War II and in September 1945 their leader, HO CHI MINH, proclaimed a Vietnamese Republic in Hanoi. The French opposed independence, and launched a military offensive. Ho Chi Minh was forced to flee Hanoi and begin a guerrilla war in December 1946. By 1950, foreign communist aid had increased Vietminh strength to the point where the French were forced into defensive lines around the Red River delta, but Vietminh attempts to win the war failed in 1951. Guerrilla operations continued until an ill-advised French attempt to seek a decisive engagement led to the encirclement and defeat of their forces at DIENBIENPHU in 1954. The war, and French rule in Indo-China, were formally terminated at the GENEVA CONFERENCE in April–July of that year.

French Revolution (1789) The political upheaval which ended with the overthrow of the Bourbon monarchy in France and marked a watershed in European history. Various groups in French society opposed the *ancien régime* with its privileged Establishment and discredited monarchy. Its leaders were influenced by the American Revolution of the 1770s and had much popular support in the 1780s and 1790s. Social and economic unrest combined with urgent financial problems persuaded Louis XVI to summon the STATES-GENERAL in 1789, an act which helped to set the Revolution in motion. From the States-General emerged the National Assembly and a new Constitution which abolished the *ancien régime*, nationalized the Church's lands, and divided the country into departments to be ruled by elected assemblies. Fear of royal retaliation led to popular unrest, the storming of the BASTILLE, and the capturing of the king by the National Guard. The National Assembly tried to create a monarchical system in which the king would share power with an elected assembly, but after the king's unsuccessful flight to VARENNES and the mobilization of exiled royalists, the Revolutionaries faced increasing military threats from Austria and Prussia which led to war abroad and more radical policies at home. In 1792 the monarchy was abolished, a republic established, and the execution of the king was followed by a Reign of TERROR (September 1793–July 1794). The Revolution failed to produce a stable form of republican government as several different factions (GIRONDINS, JACOBINS, Cordeliers, ROBESPIERRE) fought for power. After several different forms of administration had been tried, the last, the Directory, was overthrown by NAPOLEON in 1799.

French Wars of Religion A series of nine religious and political conflicts in France, which took place intermittently between 1562 and 1598. They revolved around the great noble families fighting for control of the expiring VALOIS dynasty, supported on one side by the Protestant HUGUENOTS and on the other by Catholic extremists. The wars were complicated and prolonged by interventions by Spain, Savoy, and Rome on the Catholic side and by England, the Netherlands, and the German princes on the Protestant side. After the turning-point of the ST BARTHOLOMEW'S DAY MASSACRE (1572), a third party of moderate Catholic 'Politiques' emerged under the Montmorency family. However, its advocacy of mutual religious toleration was undermined in 1576 by the formation of the Catholic extremist HOLY LEAGUE, which opposed HENRY III's tolerant settlement of the fifth war. The Guise-led League grew more militant after the BOURBON Huguenot leader Henry of Navarre became heir to the French throne in 1584. The resulting War of the THREE HENRYS (1585–89), ended with the assassination of Henry III. Henry of Navarre fought on, overcame the League, and drove its Spanish allies out of the country. He adopted Catholicism (1593), and as HENRY IV was able to establish religious toleration in France with the Edict of NANTES (1598). At the Peace of Vervins (1598) he reached a settlement with Spain. Then he applied himself to providing the firm monarchical rule which had been so damagingly lacking since the death of Henry II in 1559.

French West Africa The former federation of French overseas territories in West Africa. In the late 19th century, France sought to extend its colonial interests inland from existing trading settlements on the Atlantic coast. Substantial military force had to be used to overcome local Islamic states, and in 1895 the formation of Afrique Occidentale Française was proclaimed including the present republics of Mauritania, Senegal, Mali, Burkina Faso, Guinea, the Ivory Coast, Niger, and Benin. The neighbouring colony of Togo was captured from Germany in World War I and partitioned as a mandate of the League of Nations between Britain and France. French West Africa supported the VICHY GOVERNMENT from 1940 to 1942, when it transferred its allegiance to the FREE FRENCH cause. In 1958 the constituent areas became autonomous republics within the French community, with the exception of Guinea, which, following a referendum, voted for immediate independence. Full independence was granted throughout the area in 1960.

Freyberg, Bernard Cyril, 1st Baron Freyberg (1889–1963) New Zealand general. A professional soldier, he was appointed commander-in-chief of the New Zealand Expeditionary Forces (November 1939). He commanded the unsuccessful Commonwealth expedition to Greece and Crete (June 1941). He took an active part in the North African and Italian campaigns, where his New Zealand Division greatly distinguished itself, although suffering heavy losses. From 1945 until 1952 he was governor-general of New Zealand.

friar (from the French *frère*, 'brother') A member of a religious order for men. Friars, together with monks, are known as 'regulars' because they follow a written 'rule' for the conduct of their lives, taking vows of poverty, celibacy, and obedience. Unlike monks, who shut themselves off from the secular world, their duty is to work within the world, preaching and healing. They support themselves largely on the gifts they receive from the laity and are therefore sometimes called mendicants. During the 13th century friars achieved immense popularity because of their exemplary lives and the practical help which they offered to the poor and the sick. They helped to counter confusions arising from HERESY and worked to suppress heretical movements.

The four main orders are the AUGUSTINIANS or Austin friars, FRANCISCANS or Grey Friars, DOMINICANS or Black Friars, and CARMELITES or White Friars, the last three being named for the colour of their dress or habit. These orders have survived up to the present day.

Friedman, Milton (1912–   ) US economist. A pioneer of contemporary MONETARISM, Friedman is famous principally for his defence of the self-regulating FREE MARKET economy and his unshakeable hostility to KEYNES' theory of discretionary management by government policy of aggregate demand. Winner of the Nobel Prize for Economics in 1976, Friedman has had enormous influence on economic practice, especially that of conservative governments in the 1970s and 1980s.

Friendly Islands TONGA.

Frisians A Germanic seafaring people. In Roman times they occupied northern Holland and north-west Germany. Apart from records of their revolts against Rome between 12 BC and 69 AD, little is known about them. Some of them served in the Roman army in Britain in the 3rd century. By the 4th century they were under Saxon domination. The FRANKS attempted to convert them to Christianity by force, though this was less successful than the missionary efforts of St Wilfred from England. They were part of the CAROLINGIAN EMPIRE, and in the 16th century became part of the Habsburg empire of CHARLES V. In 1579 they reluctantly joined the Union of UTRECHT against PHILIP II. They continued their independent role in the new state, electing their own Statholder (or President) until 1747.

Froissart, Jean (c. 1337–c. 1410) Flemish poet and court historian. His four *Chroniques* provide a detailed, often eye-witness account of European events from 1325 to 1400. His first book copied the work of an earlier chronicler, Jean le Bel (c. 1290–c. 1370). The others, drawn from extensive travels, especially to the English court, provide an account of events during the HUNDRED YEARS WAR. He travelled in England and France to collect the material for his narrative, which is unparalleled in its depiction of 14th-century life. His style has great vividness, as in his famous depiction of the burghers of Calais and the Battle of Poitiers (1356). Froissart's viewpoint and style were those of the aristocracy. Like his contemporaries, he delighted in feats of chivalry and daring but concerned himself little with the morality of the events described. He took pains to ensure, wherever possible, the truth of his narrative, though the *Chroniques* are not always exact history in the modern sense of that term. The work of Froissart and the other medieval chroniclers Villehardouin and Joinville, whose subject was the Crusades, together with the much more sober narrative of Commines (late 15th century), constitutes the greatest contribution to French prose before the Renaissance. His writings were very popular in western Europe in the 15th century.

Fronde (French, *fronde*, 'boys' game with slings') A name first used by Cardinal de RETZ to describe street fighting in Paris; the word was applied particularly to two revolts against the absolutism of the crown in France during the minority of LOUIS XIV. The First Fronde began in 1648 as a protest by the *Parlement* of Paris, supported by the Paris mob, against war taxation. Disaffected nobles joined in and intrigued with France's enemy, Spain. Peace was restored in March 1649. The Second Fronde began in 1651 with MAZARIN's arrest of the arrogant and overbearing CONDÉ. Throughout France nobles indulged in irresponsible and confused fighting in which certain great ladies, including Condé's sister, Madame de Longueville, and the king's cousin, La Grande Mademoiselle, played a conspiratorial role. Mazarin fled from France, but Condé and the mutinous nobles who supported him soon lost popularity. Mazarin was able to return, giving the command of the army to TURENNE, who had rejoined the royalist party and quickly recovered Paris for the king. The Fronde ended in Paris in October 1652. It was the last attempt of the nobility to resist the king by arms, and resulted in the strengthening of the monarchy. The legacy of the Frondes was Louis XIV's dislike of Paris and the building of the palace of VERSAILLES at a distance from the city.

Front de Libération nationale (FLN) Algerian radical Muslim independence movement. It was formed in 1954 as the political expression of the ALN (Armée de Libération Nationale) when the Algerian war of independence broke out. In spite of differences of opinion between military, political, and religious leaders, the movement hung together, and brought its military leader, BEN BELLA, to power successfully as the first president of Algeria in 1962 following President de Gaulle's successful national referenda on the ÉVIAN AGREEMENT. The principal policies of the party were independence, economic development in a socialist state, non-alignment, and brotherly relations with other Arab states. In 1989 Algeria's constitution was amended so that other political parties were legalized, but the FLN continued to hold all the seats in the National Assembly.

Frontenac, Louis de Buade, comte de (1622–98) Governor of New France (1672–82, 1689–98). He fought with distinction in the THIRTY YEARS WAR. During his first service in Canada, he strengthened the defences of the colony of New France and encouraged exploration, but clashed with Bishop Laval of Quebec and was recalled. Returning to Canada in 1689, he repulsed the New Englanders' attack on Quebec in 1690 and reimposed French authority against the Iroquois in 1696.

Fry, Elizabeth (Gurney) (1780–1845) British philanthropist and prison reformer. The wife of a London Quaker, Joseph Fry, she subsequently became recognized as a preacher in the Society of Friends. After a visit to Newgate prison in 1813, horrified by what she found there, she began to press for more humane treatment for women prisoners. Her unflagging determination resulted in eventual reform. She visited other European countries to advocate improvement in prison conditions and in the treatment of the insane. She also founded hostels for the homeless.

Fuchs, Klaus (1911–88) German-born British physicist and spy. In 1943 he became a member of the team which developed the atomic bomb at Los Alamos. On his return to Britain he worked at the Atomic Energy Research Establishment at Harwell. From 1943 Fuchs passed vital secret information about the atomic bomb and plans for developing a hydrogen bomb to Soviet secret agents. In 1950 he was arrested on the evidence obtained by the USA from confessed communist agents. Fuchs pleaded guilty and was imprisoned. He was released in 1959 and went to the German Democratic Republic, where he became director of the Institute for Nuclear Physics.

Fugger A south German family of bankers and merchants, the creditors of many rulers in the Middle Ages. The family first achieved prominence under Jacob I (1410–69), head of the Augsburg weavers' guild. Ulrich

(1441–1510) supplied cloth, and then lent money to the HABSBURGS. Jacob II (1459–1525), headed the family from 1510 and lent enormous sums to MAXIMILIAN I and CHARLES V, financing Charles's candidacy as HOLY ROMAN EMPEROR in 1519. Resources came from silver and mercury mines in Germany and later from the Spanish empire in South America. The Fuggers were deeply involved in the finances of the PAPACY, and in the sale of INDULGENCES under TETZEL. The family was ennobled and, in 1546 attained a peak of prosperity. Thereafter, Habsburg bankruptcies and the ravages of the THIRTY YEARS WAR damaged their position. They safeguarded their remaining wealth by shrewd management of their extensive estates.

Fugitive Slave Acts US legislation providing for the return of escaped slaves to their masters. After the abolition of slavery in the northern states of the USA, these 'free states' became lax in enforcing the first Fugitive Slave Act of 1793. The second Act, part of the COMPROMISE OF 1850, introduced more stringent regulations, specifically aimed at the UNDERGROUND RAILROAD. Unpopular in the North, it added fuel to the slavery controversy, and 'liberty laws' passed by free states to thwart the Act drove the South further towards rebellion. Fugitive slave legislation was finally repealed in 1864.

Fujimori, Alberto (1938–   ) Peruvian liberal politician; president from 1990. A former agronomist, Fujimori, who is of Japanese descent, was elected on a free-market anti-corruption ticket for the newly formed *Cambio 90* (Change 90) grouping. In 1992 he imposed martial law to combat the threat to democracy from drug cartels and the Maoist Shining Path (*Sendero Luminoso*) guerrilla movement. Having achieved notable success in these aims, Fujimori reinstated constitutional politics and secured re-election in 1995. His personal intervention in a protracted hostage crisis at the Japanese embassy in Lima (December 1996–April 1997) — which ended with the storming of the building, the death of the Tupac Amaru Revolutionary Movement terrorists, and the safe release of almost all the hostages — won him international renown.

Fujiwara A noble Japanese family whose members enjoyed the patronage of the Japanese emperors. In 858 Fujiwara Yoshifusa became the first non-imperial regent for a child emperor. Soon it was customary for every emperor to have a Fujiwara regent. For about three centuries they dominated the court of Kyoto, securing their power by marrying their daughters into the imperial family.

The Fujiwara period (late 9th to late 12th century) saw great artistic and literary development. A court lady, Lady Murasaki, wrote Japan's most famous classic novel *The Tale of Genji* (*c.* 1001–15). But the central administration Prince SHOTOKU had initiated in the 7th century was breaking down into a near feudal society. Tax-free estates proliferated and warrior families came to prominence. The establishment of the KAMAKURA shogunate marked the end of Fujiwara ascendancy, though they acted as important court officials until the Meiji period in the 19th century.

Fulani A people of West Africa. Their origin is disputed, but most probably they were pastoralists forced southwards by the gradual desiccation of the Sahara. They expanded eastwards from Senegal to Cameroon from about the 12th century, and spread their belief in Islam. By intermarriage with pre-existing populations, they produced a number of related groups, the most important being those that initiated the empire of Macina (14th century), which reached its apogee under Seku Hamadu (1810–44); the empire of Futa Jallon (1694); the FULANI EMPIRE OF SOKOTO established by UTHMAN DAN FODIO in the early 19th century; and the chiefdoms of Adamawa and Liptako.

Fulani empire of Sokoto West African Islamic empire. In the late 18th century the Fulani came into contact with the nominally Muslim Hausa states. One of their clerics, UTHMAN DAN FODIO (1754–1817), had built up a community of scholars at Degel in the Hausa state of Gobir, whose new sultan in 1802 enslaved Uthman's followers. A quarrel developed, Uthman was proclaimed 'commander of the faithful', and in the ensuing *jihad* (holy war) all the Hausa states collapsed. By 1810 Uthman had created a vast empire, to be administered by emirs in accordance with Koranic law. High standards of public morality replaced the corruption of the Hausa states and widespread education was achieved. In 1815 he retired, appointing his son Muhammed Bello his successor and suzerain over all the emirates. Bello had built the city of Sokoto, of which he became the sultan, and he considerably extended the empire, establishing control of west Bornu and pushing down into the YORUBA EMPIRE OF OYO. Although losing some of its high ideals, the Fulani empire of Sokoto continued under Bello's successors. In the late 19th century British penetration of the empire increased. Kano and Sokoto were sacked in 1903, when the empire ended, although the emirates survived under the system of indirect rule instituted by the first High Commissioner, Frederick LUGARD.

Fulbright, James William (1905–95) US politician. An early enemy of ISOLATIONISM, he was Chairman of the Senate Foreign Relations Committee from 1959 to 1974. He was an active critic of US foreign policy in the 1960s and 1970s, attacking particularly the US involvement in the VIETNAM WAR, and urging that Congress should have more control over the President's powers to make war. A Rhodes Scholar himself, in 1946 he sponsored the Fulbright Act, which provided funds for the exchange of students and teachers between the USA and other countries.

fundamentalism CHRISTIAN FUNDAMENTALISM; ISLAMIC FUNDAMENTALISM.

Funj A Sudanese kingdom founded, together with the city of Sennar, by Amara Dunkas *c.* 1504–05. Successive rulers expanded it over the Gezira and southern Kordofan, and fought two wars with Ethiopia. In the 17th century the monarchy was kept in power by a great army of slaves, and thereafter declined. When the Egyptians invaded it in 1821, the last king (whose state had been weakened by disunity) offered no resistance.

fur trade Trading in animal furs, which have been used as clothing from the earliest times. MARCO POLO celebrated the rich fur potential of Central Asia, and the Russian penetration of Siberia was pioneered by fur traders. North American settlement was likewise spurred by the profitability of the fur trade, especially beaver pelts popular in hat making. The Pilgrims, New Englanders, New Yorkers, and French Canadians were all active in the trade. Wars were fought for control of rich fur-bearing areas round the Great Lakes. In the 19th century the trade moved west, with 'mountain men' in the Rockies delivering their pelts at rendezvous in the spring to agents of the HUDSON'S BAY or North-West companies or of John Jacob Astor, whose American Fur Company made him the first US millionaire.

fusilier Originally a soldier armed with a 'fusil' (an improved flintlock musket) in the 17th-century French army. The *fusiliers du roi* were an élite force and the first to be armed with bayonets. Later the name was given to various infantry regiments, including machine-gunners.

fyrd The military force of freemen available to the Anglo-Saxon kings. Military service was one of the three duties (the *trinoda necessitas*) required since the 7th century of all freemen – the other two duties being the maintenance of forts and the upkeep of roads and bridges. It was unusual for the fyrd to serve outside the shire in which it was raised. Modified by ALFRED THE GREAT, it continued to be called even under the Norman kings. Henry II reorganized it in his Assize of Arms (1181) and Edward I in the Statute of Winchester (1285). It eventually became the MILITIA.

G

Gabon An equatorial country on Africa's Atlantic coast, bounded inland by Equatorial Guinea, Cameroon, and Congo.

Physical. Along the coast of Gabon are lagoons, mangrove swamps, and large deposits of oil and natural gas. A broad plain covered by thick rain forest rises gradually to a plateau which surrounds a central river valley, and near the head this vegetation gives way to savannah.

Economy. Gabon is the wealthiest mainland African country, with one of the continent's fastest economic growth rates, based on substantial, albeit now falling, revenues from offshore oilfields. Gabon was a member of OPEC from 1975 until 1996. Mineral deposits also include gold and diamonds, manganese, and uranium. The country is also rich in a soft timber, *okoumé*, used for making plywood. Sugar cane, cassava, and plantains are the chief agricultural crops.

History. In 1839 the French made it a naval base to suppress the slave trade. Thus a French colony developed, exploiting the rare woods, gold, diamonds, other minerals, and oil. The country became autonomous within the French Community in 1958 and fully independent in 1960. Almost entirely on the basis of its natural resources it has had one of the fastest economic growth rates in Africa. After early years of political instability, there has been considerable support for the presidency of Omar Bongo (first elected in 1967). In November 1990 his Gabonese Democratic Party won a general election, following a decision to restore multi-party politics. Bongo was re-elected in multiparty presidential elections in 1993 and the Gabonese Democratic Party was re-elected in 1996.

CAPITAL:	Libreville
AREA:	267,667 sq km (103,347 sq miles)
POPULATION:	1.173 million (1996)
CURRENCY:	1 CFA franc = 100 centimes
RELIGIONS:	Roman Catholic 65.2%; Protestant 18.8%; African indigenous Christian 12.1%; traditional religions 2.9%; Muslim 0.8%
ETHNIC GROUPS:	Fang 30.0%; Eshura 20.0%; Mbete 15.0%; Kota 13.0%; Omyene 15.0%
LANGUAGES:	French (official); Fang; Eshura; local languages
INTERNATIONAL ORGANIZATIONS:	UN; OAU; Non-Aligned Movement; Franc Zone

Gadaffi, Moamar al QADDAFI, MUAMAR AL-.

Gadsden Purchase (1853–54) US acquisition of Mexican territory. Following the MEXICAN-AMERICAN WAR and under pressure to construct a transcontinental railway across the south-west of the USA, the administration of President PIERCE sent Senator James Gadsden to negotiate the necessary redefinition of the Mexico–US border. In the resulting transaction, Mexico was paid $10 million for ceding a strip of territory 76,767 sq km (29,640 sq miles) in the Mesilla Valley, south of the Gila River. The area completed the present borders of the mainland USA.

Gage, Thomas (1721–87) British general, appointed British commander in America in 1763, after service in Flanders, at CULLODEN, and in the FRENCH AND INDIAN WAR. His responsibilities shifted from frontier defence to quelling unrest in such towns as New York and Boston. He was appointed governor of Massachusetts in 1774 to enforce the COERCIVE ACTS, but he bungled the Battles of LEXINGTON AND CONCORD, and resigned after BUNKER HILL.

Gaiseric GENSERIC.

Gaitskell, Hugh Todd Naylor (1906–63) British politician. He entered Parliament in 1945, holding several government posts dealing with economic affairs (1945–51), including Chancellor of the Exchequer (1950–51). He became leader of the Labour Party (1955–63). He represented the moderate right-wing of his party and believed in the welfare legislation of 1944–51 and the need for a balance between private and state finance. Gaitskell was particularly vigorous in his opposition to the government over the SUEZ WAR and in resisting the unilateralists within his own party.

Galatia The area in central Asia Minor occupied by the Gauls who crossed the Hellespont from Europe in 278 BC. In 230 they were decisively defeated by Attalus I of Pergamum; Rome later made use of them against Pergamum, and they stayed loyal to Rome during the wars with MITHRIDATES VI. The Roman province of Galatia, established in 25 BC, comprised a much wider area.

Galicia Two separate kingdoms of medieval Europe, so named because they were both originally settled by GAULS. One is a region in north-western Spain that became a kingdom of the GOTHS in the 6th century AD. It became a centre of resistance against the MOORS in the 8th century and in the 13th century passed to Castile. Now an autonomous region of Spain, it retains its own language and culture.

The other Galicia extended west of the Ukraine and east of Hungary, Romania, and Bohemia. In the Middle Ages this second region was an independent kingdom based on Kiev. It extended as far west as Cracow in modern Poland. Under Polish rule from 1349, it passed to Austria in the 18th century.

Gallatin, Abraham Alfonse Albert (1761–1849) US statesman and ethnologist. After serving in Congress, he became Secretary of the Treasury (1801–14), a post he filled with considerable success, carrying out an extensive programme of financial reforms and economies. As one of the US commissioners he helped to negotiate the Treaty of GHENT ending the WAR OF 1812. He undertook ethnological work on the Native Americans and founded the American Ethnological Society.

galleon A sailing warship of the late 16th century. Galleons eventually replaced the less manoeuvrable carracks as the principal type of European trading ship.

About 1550 naval architects began to reduce the top-heaviness of existing larger warships, and, by narrowing the beam to give a GALLEY-like look, they created the galleon. From the designs of Sir John HAWKINS, English galleons were the first to develop the characteristic beaked prow and modestly sized forecastle. These features were later incorporated in the great Spanish and Portuguese galleons which were used for overseas trade. In particular, 'plate fleets' of Spanish and Portuguese galleons brought large quantities of gold and silver from the Americas to Europe during the 16th and early 17th centuries. Spain continued to use galleons until the late 17th century.

galley A warship used principally in the Mediterranean from the 2nd millennium BC. The galley's major weapon was originally a ram on the water-line, used to hole enemy ships or to smash their oars. It was propelled by oars in battle, and carried sails for use in favourable winds. The success of the galley as a warship was due to its great speed and manoeuvrability. This type of galley reached its furthest development in ancient Greece. The best-known type of Greek galley was the TRIREME, with three banks (rows) of oars; a famous trireme battle took place between the Greek and Persian fleets at SALAMIS in 480 BC. The Viking LONGSHIP was a small but durable type of galley. Galleys of various types continued to be important war vessels in the Mediterranean throughout the Roman period and the Middle Ages. In the later period, archers and boarding parties became more important than the ram, and eventually forward-firing guns were used. Byzantium, Genoa, Venice, and other medieval sea powers also built large, elaborate galleys for trading, which by the 13th century were travelling to England and north-west Africa. Galleys continued to be of military importance until the 16th century; LEPANTO (1571) was the last great naval battle involving large numbers of galleys. Galleys continued to be used as convict ships until the 18th century.

Gallicanism In French Roman Catholicism, the tradition of resistance to papal authority; its opposite was Ultramontanism, which granted the papacy complete control over the Church throughout the world. Gallicanism was founded firstly on the assertion of the French monarch's independence from the papacy, secondly on the collaboration of clergy and secular powers to limit papal intervention within France, and thirdly on the superiority of an ecumenical council over the papacy. It figured in disputes dating back to the 13th century, and was authoritatively set out in the *Gallican Articles* (1682), approved by the assembly of the French clergy.

Gallic wars The campaigns (58–51 BC) in which Julius CAESAR established Roman rule over central and northern Europe west of the River Rhine (GAUL). Crossing into Transalpine GAUL, Caesar repelled German tribes in the south and east, Belgae in the north, and Veneti in the west. He even crossed the Rhine to demonstrate Roman control of that crucial natural frontier. With speed and ruthlessness and helped by inter-tribal disunity he subdued the northern and western coasts. He twice (55 and 54 BC) invaded Britain, which was regarded as a Belgic refuge and threat to Rome. In the winter of 53–52 BC, VERCINGETORIX rallied the central Gallic tribes in unusual unity. In a long and bitter war, Caesar defeated him and his successors, and he was executed. Caesar's war dispatches, *De Bello Gallico*, supply most of the information about these events. (See map.)

Gallipoli Campaign (1915–16) An unsuccessful Allied attempt to force a passage through the Dardanelles during WORLD WAR I. Its main aims were to force Turkey out of the war, and to open a safe sea route to Russia. A naval expedition, launched in February and March 1915, failed. A military expedition (relying mainly upon British, Australian, and New Zealand troops), with some naval support, was then attempted. The first landings, on the Gallipoli peninsula and on the Asian mainland opposite, were made in April 1915. Turkish resistance was strong and, although further landings were made, fighting on the peninsula reached a stalemate. The Australian casualties on Gallipoli were 8,587 killed and 19,367 wounded. The Allied troops were withdrawn. Winston CHURCHILL, who was largely responsible for the campaign, was blamed for its failure.

Gambetta, Léon (1838–82) French statesman. After France's defeat at SEDAN and the collapse of the Second Empire he played a principal role in proclaiming the Third Republic and was Minister of War and Minister of the Interior in the provisional government. He opposed the armistice with Prussia, was elected to the National Assembly for Alsace, and left the Assembly when Alsace was ceded to Prussia. He was soon re-elected and in the 1870s led the Republican Party in its campaign to secure the nation for republicans. He died soon after the fall of his brief ministry of 1881–82.

Gambia, The A country on the West African coast.
Physical. The Gambia runs west to east along the lower 320 km (nearly 200 miles) of the River Gambia, entirely surrounded inland by Senegal. The River Gambia is broad and navigable, though its banks are marshy; and its valley is fertile.
Economy. The Gambian economy is heavily dependent on groundnuts, with fish, the re-exporting of imports, mainly to Senegal, and tourism providing additional revenue. Gambia imports about a third of its food requirements.
History. The beginning of the colony was the building of a fort by the British at Banjul in 1816, as a base against the slave trade. Renamed Bathurst, the new town was placed under SIERRA LEONE in 1821. Gambia became a British colony in 1843. The Soninki-Marabout Wars in neighbouring Senegal caused serious disturbances and were ended by Anglo-French intervention in 1889. A British Protectorate over the interior was proclaimed in 1893. Gambia became an independent member of the Commonwealth in 1965, and a republic in 1970, with Sir Dawda Kairaba Jawara as the country's first president. In 1982 The Gambia and Senegal formed a limited confederation, Senegambia, for defence, economic, and foreign policy purposes, but this had lapsed by 1989. In April 1992 Jawara was re-elected President, his fifth term of office. In 1994 Jawara was ousted in a military coup by Lieutenant Yahya Jammeh.

CAPITAL:	Banjul
AREA:	10,689 sq km (4,127 sq miles)
POPULATION:	1.148 million (1996)
CURRENCY:	1 dalasi = 100 butut
RELIGIONS:	Muslim 95.4%; Christian 3.7%; traditional beliefs 0.9%

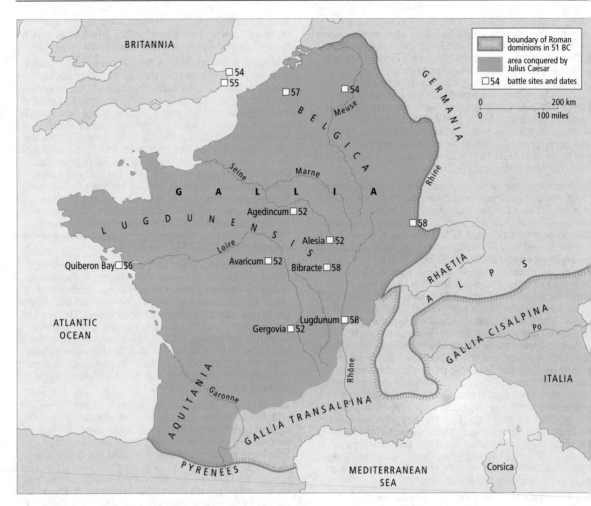

Gallic Wars (58–51 BC) *Julius Caesar was governor of Cisalpine Gaul when he embarked on the Gallic wars in 58 BC. His victory over the Helvetii at Bibracte was the first of a series of conquests in successive campaigning seasons. The Nervii, most powerful of the Belgic tribes, were defeated in 57, and a revolt by the Veneti was put down at Quiberon Bay in 56. These earlier victories were a tribute to superior organization and generalship, but Caesar faced his greatest test in 52, when the Gauls united under Vercingetorix. The rebellion was broken by the siege of Alesia and Gaul was subsequently organized as a Roman province.*

ETHNIC GROUPS: Mandingo 40.4%; Fulani 18.7%; Wolof 14.6%; Dyola 10.3%; Serahuli 6.5%

LANGUAGES: English (official); Mandingo; Fulani; local languages

INTERNATIONAL ORGANIZATIONS: UN; OAU; Commonwealth; ECOWAS; Non-Aligned Movement

Gamelin, Maurice Gustave (1872–1958) French general. As a staff officer in World War I he helped to plan the successful Battle of the MARNE (1914) and served with distinction through the war. In World War II as commander-in-chief of the Allied forces, he was unprepared for the German thrust through the Ardennes which resulted in disaster for his forces. In mid-May 1940 he was replaced by General WEYGAND.

Gandhi, Indira (1917–84) Indian stateswoman. The daughter of Jawaharlal NEHRU, in 1939 she joined the Indian National CONGRESS Party, and spent over a year in

prison for her wartime activities. Her first years in politics were spent as an aide to her father when he was Prime Minister, serving as President of Congress (1959–60). She became Minister for Broadcasting and Information in Lal Bahadur Shastri's cabinet, and in 1966 was chosen to succeed Shastri as Prime Minister. During the following years she was engaged in a protracted struggle with the older leadership of the Congress, but with the aid of the Congress left wing defeated them in 1969–70. After the successful INDO-PAKISTAN WAR of 1971 her popularity stood high, but it waned during the 1970s. When threatened with the loss of her position through a court case for illegal electoral activities, she declared a state of emergency (1975–77) and governed India dictatorially, assisted by favourites such as her younger son, Sanjay. After her defeat in the 1977 elections by Morarji DESAI her career seemed finished, but in 1980 her faction of the Congress Party was re-elected to power and she ruled until her assassination in 1984 by a Sikh extremist. Her elder son, Rajiv Gandhi (1944–91), succeeded her as Prime Minister, remaining in office until his resignation in 1989. He was assassinated while campaigning for re-election. In 1998 Rajiv's Italian-born widow Sonia Gandhi entered politics and was appointed leader of the Congress Party.

Gandhi, Mohandas Karamchand (1869–1948) Indian national and spiritual leader. Born into a family of Hindu Bania (merchant) caste in Porbandar, he was educated in India and Britain, qualifying as a barrister in London. He practised law briefly in India, but moved to South Africa (1893–1914), where he became a successful lawyer. There he developed his technique of *satyagraha* ('truth-force' or non-violent resistance). His campaign for equal rights for Indians in South Africa met with partial success. Returning to India, he formed political connections through campaigns for workers' and peasants' rights (1916–18). Subsequently he led Indian nationalists in a series of confrontations with the BRITISH RAJ, including the agitation against the ROWLATT ACT (1919). From 1920 he dominated the Indian National CONGRESS, supporting the KHILAFAT MOVEMENT and initiating the decision by Congress to promote a non-co-operation movement (1920–22), suffering frequent imprisonment by the British. The SALT MARCH to Dandi (1930) was followed by a campaign of civil disobedience until 1934, individual *satyagraha*, 1940–41, and the 'Quit India' campaign of 1942. As independence for India drew near, he co-operated with the British despite his opposition to the partition of the sub-continent. In political terms Gandhi's main achievement was to turn the small, upper-middle-class Indian National Congress movement into a mass movement by adopting a political style calculated to appeal to ordinary Hindus (using symbols such as the loin cloth and the spinning-wheel) and by creating a network of alliances with political brokers at lower levels. In social and economic terms he stressed simplicity and self-reliance as in village India, the elevation of the status of the Untouchables (*harijans*), and communal harmony. In intellectual terms his emphasis was upon the force of truth and non-violence (*ahimsa*) in the struggle against evil. His acceptance of partition and concern over the treatment of Muslims in India made him enemies among extremist Hindus. One such, Nathuram Godse, assassinated him in Delhi. Widely revered before and after his death, he was known as the Mahatma (Sanskrit, 'Great Soul').

Gang of Four Four radical Chinese leaders of the mid-1970s. Jiang Qing, MAO ZEDONG's fourth wife, Wang Hongwen, Yao Wenyuan, and Zhang Chungqiao all rose to prominence during the CULTURAL REVOLUTION, with a power base in Shanghai. They occupied powerful positions in the Politburo after the Tenth Party Congress of 1973. After the death of Mao in 1976 they are alleged to have planned to seize power, and in 1980 were found guilty of plotting against the state. They have been blamed for the excesses of the Cultural Revolution.

Gao SONGHAY.

Garcia Moreno, Gabriel (1821–75) President of Ecuador (1861–65, 1869–75). An extreme conservative, his goal was to convert Ecuador into the leading theocratic state of Latin America. His 1861 constitution, which accorded wide powers to the president, and his 1863 Concordat with the Vatican almost succeeded in doing so. The Catholic Church enjoyed greater power and privilege during his two administrations than it ever had before. A sound administrator, he put Ecuador on a stable financial basis and introduced material reforms. He was assassinated in 1875.

Garcia y Iñigues, Calixto (1836–98) Cuban nationalist. He led his country's preliminary struggles for independence from Spain. A leader during the Ten Years' War (1868–78), and the Little War (1879–80), his military efforts enjoyed scant success and resulted in his prolonged imprisonment. Cuban troops under his command supported US forces during the SPANISH-AMERICAN WAR, but Garcia, shortly before his death, rejected his erstwhile allies, fearing that Cuba had simply exchanged one master for another.

Gardiner, Stephen (*c.* 1490–1555) Bishop of Winchester (1531–51, 1553–55). A protégé of Thomas WOLSEY, he assisted in the negotiations to secure HENRY VIII's divorce from Catherine of Aragon. He defended the royal supremacy over the Church, most notably in *De Vera Obedientia* (1535), but was opposed to Protestantism. Under EDWARD VI he was imprisoned (1548–53) and deprived of his see. MARY I restored him to Winchester, made him Lord Chancellor, and relied on him until his death.

Garfield, James Abram (1831–81) Twentieth President (1881) of the USA. He served in the AMERICAN CIVIL WAR, retiring as a major-general, and then entered national politics as a Republican Congressman (1863–80). One of the politicians smeared with the CRÉDIT MOBILIER OF AMERICA scandal, he was rescued by James G. BLAINE. During the Republicans' feud between the self-styled 'Half Breeds' (members of that wing of the Republican Party that favoured a conciliatory policy towards the South, and advocated civil service reforms) and 'Stalwarts' (their Republican opponents), he emerged as the compromise candidate to fight, and win, the presidential election of 1880. His assassination within months of taking office by a disappointed office-seeker sealed the fate of the Stalwarts and ensured support for civil service reform in the PENDLETON ACT.

Garibaldi, Giuseppe (1807–82) Italian leader and military commander of the RISORGIMENTO. In 1834 he led an unsuccessful republican plot in Genoa in support of MAZZINI. He fled, and spent the next 12 years in exile in South America, where he became a master of guerrilla warfare and formed his famous 'Redshirts'. He returned to Italy to take part in the REVOLUTIONS OF 1848, and formed a volunteer army to defend the short-lived Roman Republic against French forces intervening for Pope Pius IX. His resistance and his gallant retreat when Rome fell in June 1849 made him a popular hero. He was invited by CAVOUR to help defeat the Austrians in northern Italy. When this was achieved (1859) the 'Thousand' captured Sicily (1860) and then Naples, capital of the kingdom of the Two Sicilies, handing the whole of southern Italy to VICTOR EMANUEL II four months later. In 1862 Garibaldi, in an attempt to secure the Papal States, led his forces unsuccessfully against Rome. In 1867 he was defeated by French and papal forces at Mentana, while attempting once more to capture Rome.

Garvey, Marcus Moziah (1887–1940) Jamaican Black leader. He organized the Universal Negro Improvement and Conservation Association (UNICA) in Jamaica in 1914 to encourage racial pride and Black unity with the slogan 'Africa for the Africans at home and abroad'. In 1916 he went to the USA, promising repatriation of US Black people to a new African republic (to be created out of former German colonies). He established four branches of UNICA in South Africa in 1921, which encouraged the growth of Black movements there in the 1930s. Deeply resented by William DU BOIS, Garvey's followers clashed with more moderate Black people in the 1920s. Although personally honest and sincere, he mismanaged his movement's finances and was convicted (1923) of attempted fraud.

Gascony A former duchy in south-western France. It was named from the Vascones who took it in the 6th century AD and it enjoyed a great degree of independence until 819 when it submitted to King Louis the Pious of France. It came to Henry II of England on his marriage to ELEANOR OF AQUITAINE. Rebel nobles were subdued by Simon de MONTFORT but it was lost to the French in the HUNDRED YEARS WAR. EDWARD III regained it and it was recognized as an English possession by the Treaty of BRÉTIGNY in 1360. The English were finally driven out by the army of Charles VII of France. Royal authority was only fully realized, however, when the House of Armagnac was defeated and Gascony was formally joined to the crown of France by Henry IV.

Gates, Horatio (1728–1806) American general, born in England. He fought under BRADDOCK and AMHERST in the FRENCH AND INDIAN WARS but thereafter supported the American cause in the War of Independence. His victory at SARATOGA (1777) led the Conway Cabal of New England officers to plot for him to replace WASHINGTON. His rout at CAMDEN (1780) ended his military career, though he later served under Washington.

GATT GENERAL AGREEMENT ON TARIFFS AND TRADE.

gaucho A horseman of South America, often Indian or mestizo. Early in the 19th century the gauchos took part in the SPANISH SOUTH-AMERICAN WARS OF INDEPENDENCE, and later were prominent on the Argentine pampas in the development of the cattle industry. By the late 19th century the pastoral economy had given way to more intensive land cultivation in fenced-off estancias (estates), forcing many gauchos to become farmhands or peons.

Gaul The Roman name for the lands of the CELTS in western Europe. The Gauls invaded northern Italy in the 4th and 3rd centuries BC. In 222 BC the territory south of the Alps was declared the Roman province of Cisalpine Gaul. The River RUBICON formed part of the frontier with Italy proper. The area north of the Po was known as Transpadane Gaul, that south of the Po as Cispadane Gaul. Beyond the Alps the southern coast of modern France and its hinterland was known as Transalpine Gaul, or often simply as 'Provincia' (hence modern PROVENCE) after its annexation in 121 BC. Its capital was at Narbo. Julius CAESAR was given command of both the Gallic provinces in 59 BC. He extended Transalpine Gaul to the Atlantic, the English Channel, and the Rhine in the course of his GALLIC WARS. Despite the last stand by VERCINGETORIX, there was generally little unity of resistance. Transpadane Gaul was given Roman citizenship by Caesar in 49 BC and the whole Cisalpine Gaul was incorporated into Italy by AUGUSTUS, thus ceasing to be a province. (Cispadane Gaul had been given Roman citizenship in 90 BC.) Augustus divided Gaul north of the Alps into Narbonensian Gaul under the Senate and Lugdunensian (Lyons) Gaul, Aquitaine, and Belgic Gaul, under his own legates. Lyons was the venue of a provincial assembly of the 'Tres Galliae'. In the later 3rd century usurper emperors created a semi-independent 'Gallic empire' which served as a temporary buffer against Germanic invasions. Increasingly vulnerable as the heartland of the Western empire it was devastated by GOTHS, HUNS, and VANDALS until it was finally ceded to the FRANKS in the 5th century.

Gaunt, John of (1340–99) English nobleman, Duke of Lancaster (1362–99). He was born at Ghent (whence 'Gaunt'), the third surviving son of EDWARD III. Through marriage he accumulated sufficient power to threaten the king, although he proved loyal to his nephew RICHARD II. His father provided him with the vast inheritance of Lancaster by marrying him to the heiress Blanche of Lancaster in 1359; his second marriage, to Constance, elder daughter of King Pedro the Cruel of Castile, gave him a claim to the throne of Castile and León, and his third wife, Katharine Swynford, brought to prominence her family, the BEAUFORTS. He was particularly powerful in 1376–77, as Edward III approached death. By the 1390s Gaunt had outlived many of his rivals, including Thomas of Woodstock. Richard II saw Gaunt as such a threat to the throne that his son Henry of Bolingbroke (HENRY IV) was forbidden from entering into his inheritance.

Gautama Siddhartha BUDDHA.

gavelkind PRIMOGENITURE.

Gaveston, Piers (c. 1284–1312) Favourite of EDWARD II of England. He was from Gascony, but was brought up in the English royal household as the foster-brother of the future EDWARD II, whose infatuation Gaveston shrewdly exploited. Edward gave him the earldom of Cornwall in 1307, and appointed him Regent of England (1307–08). The enraged English barons called for his banishment; Edward twice complied (1308, 1311), but Gaveston returned and in 1312 was killed by the Earl of Warwick.

gay rights activism Political campaigning by homosexual men and women for an end to social and legal discrimination on the grounds of sexual preference. Concerted gay activism originated in the USA, where the 'Stonewall Riots', which took place in New York in 1969, saw the gay community react against sustained police brutality. The work of such pressure groups as the Gay Liberation Front and the gradual liberalization of public opinion have ensured the decriminalization of consenting homosexual acts throughout the Western world. A US Supreme Court ruling of 1996 expressly precluded state and local administrations from denying basic civil-rights protection to homosexuals. In Britain the legal age of male homosexual consent remains higher than that for heterosexual acts, and is the source of continuing debate and controversy. Similarly, discrimination is sometimes still enshrined in civil law, in such diverse matters as inheritance, housing rights, adoption, and insurance cover. CHRISTIAN FUNDAMENTALISTS, with their championing of the heterosexual couple as centre of the family, continue to challenge gay rights. Similarly, many traditionalist societies ranging from the Islamic states of the Arab world to socialist Zimbabwe remain implacably opposed to the acceptance of homosexuality.

General Agreement on Tariffs and Trade (GATT)
An international trade agreement. Established by the UNITED NATIONS in 1948, and with a secretariat in Geneva, Switzerland, it had 125 member countries at the end of 1994. The aim of its members (who together account for some 90% of all world trade) has been to promote international trade by removing obstacles and trade barriers, to lay down maximum tariff rates, and to provide a forum for the discussion of trading policies. GATT promoted the postwar expansion of world trade, but the poorer countries felt that its terms favoured the developed countries, a criticism that led to the founding of the UNITED NATIONS CONFERENCE ON TRADE AND DEVELOPMENT in 1964, and to an agreement in 1965 that developing countries should not be expected to offer reciprocity when negotiating with developed countries. By the 1980s there were demands for modification of the GATT agreements. In 1986 the 'Uruguay Round' of talks (so called because they were held in the Uruguayan capital, Montevideo) undertook to resolve outstanding agricultural issues. The discussions, frequently deadlocked, continued into 1993 seeking a compromise agreement on farm subsidies, prior to talks in Geneva in 1994 for global trade deals. In April 1994 the Final Act of the Uruguay round was formally signed, concluding negotiations for broad cuts in tariffs and export subsidies and for the creation of the WORLD TRADE ORGANIZATION (WTO) as successor to GATT.

General Assembly UNITED NATIONS GENERAL ASSEMBLY.

General Strike (1926)
A national strike in Britain's major industries. It was called in support of the National Union of Mineworkers, whose members were resisting the mine owners attempts to impose longer hours and lower wages because of trading difficulties. The owners had locked out the miners from the pits to try to compel acceptance. The General Council of the Trades Union Congress responded by calling workers out on strike in certain key industries such as the railways, the docks, and electricity and gas supply. This began on 4 May 1926 and ended nine days later. Irresolute trade union leadership, skilful government handling of information to the public, and the use of troops and volunteers to keep vital services running, all led to the collapse of the strike. It was followed in 1927 by a Trade Union Act, restricting trade union privileges.

General strikes have been rare in the USA and Canada; exceptions in the USA include the strikes in Seattle (1919) and San Francisco (1934) and the Winnipeg General Strike in Canada in 1919.

Geneva
A Swiss city situated at the south-western corner of Lake Geneva. It is first mentioned as a settlement of the Celtic Allobroges in the 1st century BC; it later fell to the Romans and became the seat of a bishop. From the mid-12th century to 1401 the bishops effectively ruled the city and region, but from 1401 to 1536 the dukes of Savoy had effective control. In 1535 the citizens rejected the authority of both bishop and duke and accepted the Protestant religion. They turned Geneva into an independent self-governing city-state. In the 16th, 17th, and 18th centuries this 'Protestant Rome' became a haven for religious refugees (who often added considerably to its economic prosperity), and a training-ground for HUGUENOT ministers. It became part of a united federal Switzerland in 1848. In the 20th century Geneva has provided a base for many international organizations, such as the RED CROSS, the LEAGUE OF NATIONS, and the WORLD HEALTH ORGANIZATION.

Geneva Conference (1954)
Conference held in Geneva, Switzerland, to negotiate an end to the FRENCH INDO-CHINESE WAR. Planned by the wartime Allies to settle the future of KOREA and Indo-China, it made rapid progress on the latter after the French defeat at DIENBIENPHU. The resulting armistice provided for the withdrawal of French troops and the partition of Vietnam, with the north under the control of HO CHI MINH's VIETMINH and the south under Saigon. Intended as a prelude to reunification through general elections, the Conference actually resulted in the emergence of two antagonistic regimes which were not to be united until Hanoi's victory in the VIETNAM WAR in 1975.

Geneva Conventions
A series of international agreements on the treatment of victims of war, ratified in whole or partially by the majority of states and certain non-state organizations, such as the PLO (the Palestine Liberation Organization) and SWAPO (the South West Africa People's Organization). The first Geneva Convention was established by the Swiss founder of the RED CROSS, Henri Dunant, in 1864, and concerned the treatment of the wounded in war and the protection of medical personnel. Subsequent Conventions in 1907, 1929, 1949, and 1977 covered the treatment of prisoners of war and the protection of civilians, forbidding such acts as deportation, torture, hostage-taking, collective punishment or reprisals, and the use of chemical and biological weapons. The 1977 Convention dealt with more extensive non-combatant protection, and covered problems arising from internal wars.

Genghis Khan (c. 1162–1227)
Founder of the MONGOL empire. At a time of rapidly shifting alliances among the people of the steppe, he gradually subjected other Mongol tribes. In 1206 a *kuriltai* (assembly) of all the tribes proclaimed him Genghis Khan, Universal Ruler. He proceeded to complete his conquest of the Xi Xia kingdom in Central Asia (1205–09), followed by the JIN in northern China (1211–15), and the Kara Khitai (1211) and Khorezm in Turkistan (1219–21), thus extending his lands up to the Black Sea. Before he died he divided his empire into four KHANATES.

His dynamic leadership and genius for organization largely account for the Mongols' swift rise to power. He was adaptable and had the ability to learn from others. He brought unity to the Mongol peoples and gave them a code of laws supreme over even the khan. An alphabetic script was devised for the Mongol language. He employed a Chinese LIAO prince to establish a system of administration and taxation, which later helped in the Mongol conquest of China. As a commander he created a disciplined military machine. His bowmen could kill at 180 m (200 yards). Used to living on horseback and supplying themselves from plunder, they moved at incredible speed, once covering some 440 km (270 miles) in three days. A master of strategy, he used espionage to outwit his opponents and terror to weaken their wills. Against disunited agrarian and commercial states he acted with overwhelming might and ruthlessness.

Genoa An important port on the coast of north-west Italy. The port and fort established in the 5th century BC were captured by the Romans in the 3rd century BC. After the Roman empire collapsed, Genoa fell to the LOMBARDS in 634, and was repeatedly sacked by the SARACENS, but recovered its fortunes by the 10th century to become an independent republic and a seafaring and trading power. Influence and colonization spread to Sicily, Spain, North Africa, and the CRIMEA. Civil disorder was reduced after a popular coup in 1257 and the office of DOGE was created in 1339. Rivalry with neighbouring powers brought the defeat of Pisa in 1284, and persistent fighting with VENICE, which the Genoese nearly captured in 1380. They also contributed many mercenaries, particularly crossbowmen, to foreign armies. The advance of the OTTOMANS weakened Genoese control of their colonial possessions, and its importance as a major European power diminished.

genocide The systematic destruction of a group or nation on grounds of race or ethnic origin. Following the Nazi's attempted genocide of the Jews and of ethnic groups such as gypsies, the Convention on the Prevention and Punishment of the Crime of Genocide was adopted by the UN in 1948. The Convention establishes that genocide is not to be regarded as a matter of domestic jurisdiction within a state, but rather is to be seen as a matter of fundamental concern to the international community. It also establishes the principle of individual accountability on the part of those carrying out the killings. Since the signing of the Convention, many conflicts in the world have split groups along ethnic or tribal lines (see COMMUNAL CONFLICT), and claims of genocide have been made. Examples include the Nigeria–Biafra conflict in 1969; Uganda in the 1970s; the POL POT regime in Kampuchea (Cambodia) (1976–79); Iraq's treatment of the Kurds (1986–   ); the ethnic cleansing of Bosnian Muslims by Christian Serbs (1992–95); and the attempts by Hutus and Tutsis to annihilate each other in Burundi and Rwanda (1993–   ). The international community has failed in most cases to respond effectively to claims of genocide: firm evidence is hard to obtain; there are problems in determining the appropriate tribunal; perhaps most importantly, states are reluctant to intervene in the domestic affairs of another state on the grounds that this is a violation of national sovereignty.

Genseric (or Gaiseric) (*c.* 390–477 AD) King of the VANDALS from 428. An ARIAN Christian, he was ousted by the GOTHS from his lands in Spain and took his entire nation of 80,000 across to North Africa in 429. He besieged Hippo just after the death of AUGUSTINE OF HIPPO. Carthage fell ten years later and from there he declared an independent kingdom. Three times he defeated the Roman armies. With a fleet he took Sicily and Sardinia. Rome nicknamed the campaign the 'Fourth PUNIC WAR'. In 455 he took Rome and indulged in a fortnight of looting. Fleets sent against the Vandals in 457 and 468 were defeated, and, at his death Genseric was in possession of all of his conquered territories.

Geoffrey of Monmouth (*c.* 1100–55) Bishop of St Asaph in Wales and the author of a chronicle, the

Historia Regum Britanniae ('The History of the Kings of Britain') (*c.* 1136). In this work King ARTHUR was projected as a national hero defending Britain from the Saxon raiders after the departure of the Roman armies. Much of the material was taken from a 9th-century Welsh writer, NENNIUS.

geopolitics An approach to understanding international politics that seeks to explain the political behaviour of states in terms of geographical variables such as size or location. The term is particularly associated with the work of the Swede R. J. Kjellen (1864–1922) and the German Karl Haushofer (1869–1946). Haushofer's perception of geopolitics as involving the struggle between states to occupy the world was taken up by the Nazi Party in Germany to justify its expansionist goals, a connection which helped to bring the subject into disrepute. However, the term is still used to stress the interplay of geographical and political factors in international relations. It is considered particularly helpful in understanding the problems facing strategically sensitive areas of the world.

George I (1660–1727) Elector of Hanover (1692–1714) and King of Great Britain and Ireland (1714–27). His mother Sophia (1630–1714), a granddaughter of JAMES I, and her issue were recognized as heirs to the throne of England by the Act of SETTLEMENT (1701), which excluded the Roman Catholic STUARTS. He succeeded peaceably to the throne on Queen ANNE's death in 1714, and the JACOBITE rebellion a year later helped to unite the country behind him. He had little sympathy for British constitutionalism, the need to accept the limitations of Parliament and ministers, and he disliked England, spending as much time as possible in Hanover. But he developed a good command of English, despite his German accent, and his unswerving support for WALPOLE from 1721 helped to consolidate the supremacy of the Whigs. He ruled without a queen, having divorced his wife, Sophia Dorothea, in 1694.

George II (1683–1760) King of Great Britain and Ireland (1727–60) and Elector of Hanover. He resented his father, GEORGE I, because of his treatment of his mother, Sophia Dorothea. George's own marriage, to Princess CAROLINE OF ANSBACH, was very successful, and through her he learned to accept WALPOLE as his Prime Minister. He had a fiery temper and was intolerant in his dealings with others: he insisted on the execution of Admiral BYNG in 1757, and was always on bad terms with his son, Prince FREDERICK LOUIS. He was the last English king to lead his troops in battle, at Dettingen in 1743 in support of the Empress MARIA THERESA during the War of the AUSTRIAN SUCCESSION. He disliked PITT the Elder and endeavoured to keep him out of office; his final acceptance of Pitt in 1757 paved the way for British success in the SEVEN YEARS WAR.

George II (1890–1947) King of the Hellenes (1922–23, 1935–47). He came to the throne when General Palstiras deposed his father (1922), but the continuing unpopularity of the Greek royal family caused him to leave Greece (1923). In 1935 a plebiscite favouring the monarchy enabled him to return. His position was difficult, for real power lay with the dictatorial General METAXAS. In April 1941 Hitler attacked Greece, driving him into exile again. With strong backing from Britain, the king returned to Greece in 1946, but the Greek communists who had resisted Hitler now waged civil war against the restoration of the monarchy. He died in 1947 and US support for his brother Paul brought the civil war to an end in 1949.

George III (1738–1820) King of Great Britain and Ireland and of dependencies overseas, King of Hanover (1760–1820). He was the first Hanoverian ruler to be born in Britain. The son of FREDERICK LOUIS, he succeeded to the throne on the death of his grandfather GEORGE II, with strong convictions about a monarch's role acquired from BOLINGBROKE and BUTE. He was a devoted family man and a keen patron of the arts, building up the royal art collection with impeccable taste. He disliked the domination of the government by a few powerful Whig families and preferred to remain above politics, which was a major reason for the succession of weak ministries from 1760 to 1770. He was against making major concessions to the demands of the American colonists, and he shared with many Englishmen an abhorrence of the American aim of independence. He suffered from porphyria, a metabolic disease that causes mental disturbances; this manifested itself briefly in 1765, when plans were made for a regency council, and for several months in 1788–89, when his illness was so severe as to raise again the prospect of a regency. Although his political interventions were fewer than have often been alleged, his interference did bring down the Fox-North coalition in December 1783. Increasing reliance on PITT the Younger reduced his political influence, although Pitt always had to take it into account. When the King refused to consider CATHOLIC EMANCIPATION to offset the ACT OF UNION with Ireland, Pitt resigned (1801). In 1811 increasing senility and the onset of deafness and blindness brought about the REGENCY of the profligate Prince of Wales, which lasted until he succeeded as GEORGE IV.

George IV (1762–1830) King of Great Britain and Ireland and of dependencies overseas, King of Hanover (1820–30). As regent (1811–20) and later king, he led a dissolute life and was largely responsible for the decline in power and prestige of the British monarchy in the early 19th century. The eldest son of GEORGE III, he cultivated the friendship of Charles James FOX and other Whigs. In 1785 he secretly and illegally married a Roman Catholic widow, Maria Fitzherbert (1756–1837). Ten years later he reluctantly married Caroline of Brunswick, and separated from her immediately after the birth of their only child, Princess Charlotte. George III became increasingly senile at the end of 1810 and in the following year the prince was appointed regent. He gave his support to the Tories, but soon quarrelled with them too, leaving himself without a large personal following in Parliament. His reign saw the passage of the CATHOLIC EMANCIPATION Act (1829). His attempt to divorce Caroline for adultery in 1820 only increased his unpopularity. He was a leader of taste, fashion, and the arts, and gave his name to the REGENCY period. He was succeeded by his brother WILLIAM IV.

George V (1865–1936) King of Great Britain and Ireland (from 1920, Northern Ireland) and dependencies overseas, Emperor of India (1910–36). The son of EDWARD VII, he insisted that a general election should precede any reform of the House of LORDS (1911). He brought together party leaders at the Buckingham Palace Conference (1914) to discuss Irish HOME RULE. His acceptance of Ramsay MACDONALD as Prime Minister of a minority government in 1924, and of a NATIONAL GOVERNMENT in 1931, contained an element of personal choice. He was succeeded by EDWARD VIII.

George VI (1895–1952) King of Great Britain and Northern Ireland and dependencies overseas (1936–52), Emperor of India until 1947. He succeeded his brother, EDWARD VIII, after the ABDICATION CRISIS. His preference for Lord Halifax rather than Winston CHURCHILL as Prime Minister in 1940 had no effect, but he strongly supported Churchill throughout World War II. Likewise he gave his support to Clement ATTLEE and his government (1945–50) in the policy of granting Indian independence. He and his wife, Elizabeth Bowes-Lyon, will be remembered for sustaining public morale during the German bombing offensive of British cities. He was succeeded by his elder daughter, ELIZABETH II.

Georgia (Asia) A mountainous country in west Asia. It is separated from Russia in the north by the Caucasus Mountains. It has a coast on the Black Sea, shares a border with Turkey to the west, and is bounded by Azerbaijan and Armenia to the east and south.

Physical. About one-third of the land is forest. The climate is subtropical, with cool winters and hot summers, very wet in the west and arid in the east. On the coastal plain and in the central valley fruit trees, palms, and eucalyptus flourish. By contrast, the east is treeless grassland, but rich in minerals.

Economy. Georgia's mineral resources include coal, petroleum, and manganese. Industry is based on the exploitation of these resources; there is also some machinery production and other light industry. Agriculture includes viticulture; tea, tobacco, and citrus are the main crops.

History. Georgia has been a distinctive state since the 4th century BC. In the 3rd century AD it became part of the SASSANIAN EMPIRE but the Persians were expelled *c.* 400. The 12th and 13th centuries saw territorial expansion and cultural achievement cut short by Mongol destruction. Revival was likewise curtailed by the ravages of TAMERLANE (1386–1403) and national decline was confirmed by the decision of Alexander I to split the kingdom between his three sons. After some two and a half centuries of partition, the western half being under OTTOMAN rule, the eastern under Persian, the area was reunited by the Russian conquest of 1821–29.

Throughout the 19th century, Tzarist Russia continued to suppress Georgian nationalism. A strong Social Democrat Party of Mensheviks emerged in Georgia in the early 20th century, which formed a brief republic (1918–21), under British protection. In 1921 Georgia was conquered by the Red Army from Russia, and became part of the Transcaucasian Soviet Federal Socialist Republic with Azerbaijan and Armenia. A large-scale anti-communist uprising was suppressed in 1924 and in 1936 the Georgian Soviet Socialist Republic became a full member of the Soviet Union. Another uprising in the capital Tbilisi in 1956 was suppressed, and in April 1989 there were extensive riots, again brutally suppressed. In April 1991, however, it gained independence under President Zviad Gamsakhurdia. Opposition to Gamsakhurdia's 'dictatorial methods' led to his deposition, following the outbreak of civil conflict in December 1991. In March 1992 Eduard SHEVARDNADZE

(Soviet Foreign Minister 1985–91) returned to his native Georgia to become Chairman of the State Council. In September he was elected President. The civil conflict continued throughout 1992 and 1993 as forces loyal to Gamsakhurdia attempted to gain control. In November, however, with the aid of Russian troops, government forces routed the rebels from Georgia. The country was also beset by other armed conflicts within its borders. In 1989 a rebellion erupted in South Ossetia when the region demanded greater autonomy and secession from Georgia. A ceasefire was eventually agreed in mid-1992 and South Ossetia confirmed its intention to secede. In August 1992 a period of violent armed conflict began, following periodic unrest since 1989, over the region of Abkhazia's demands for independence. By September 1993, after intensive fighting, Georgian forces were defeated and expelled from the region. Following UN-sponsored peace talks, a provisional ceasefire was negotiated in April 1994, when Shevardnadze agreed to cede considerable autonomy to Abkhazia. Meanwhile, in December 1993, Georgia finally agreed to join the COMMONWEALTH OF INDEPENDENT STATES (CIS) and, in February 1994, signed a ten-year treaty of friendship and co-operation with Russia. In March 1995 Shevardnadze signed a military agreement with Russia. He was re-elected in presidential elections later that year. In 1996 an economic co-operation agreement was concluded with the EU.

CAPITAL:	Tblisi
AREA:	69,700 sq km (26,900 sq miles)
POPULATION:	5.361 million (1996)
CURRENCY:	1 lari = 100 tetri
RELIGIONS:	Georgian Eastern Orthodox Church
ETHNIC GROUPS:	Georgian 80.0%; Armenian 8.0%; Russian 6.0%; Azeri 6.0%; Abkhazian and Ossete minorities
LANGUAGES:	Georgian (official); Russian; minority languages
INTERNATIONAL ORGANIZATIONS:	CSCE

Georgia (USA) A state of the USA, on the southern Atlantic coast. It was founded as a British colony in 1732, both as a bulwark against the Spanish in FLORIDA and to provide a new start for English debtors. The trustees under OGLETHORPE established tightly controlled settlements at Savannah (1733) and elsewhere, prohibiting slavery, rum, and land sales, and encouraging silk and wine production. With the relaxation of this regime in the 1750s and immigration from Europe and other colonies, it slowly prospered. Georgia was a strong centre of loyalism during the War of INDEPENDENCE, and did not join the Union until 1782. A member state of the CONFEDERACY during the AMERICAN CIVIL WAR, Georgia suffered heavily, with Atlanta falling to General SHERMAN's army in September 1864. Decline in the state's original source of wealth, cotton growing, in the 20th century has been offset by investment in manufacturing industries. In 1977 the Democratic former state governor of Georgia, Jimmy CARTER, was elected President of the USA.

Germain-en-Laye, St, Treaty of VERSAILLES PEACE SETTLEMENT.

German Confederation (1815–66) An alliance of German sovereign states. At the Congress of VIENNA (1815) the 38 German states formed a loose grouping to protect themselves against French ambitions. Austria and Prussia lay partly within and partly outside the Confederation. The Austrian chancellor METTERNICH was the architect of the Confederation and exercised a dominant influence in it through the Federal Diet at Frankfurt, whose members were instructed delegates of state governments. As the rival power to Austria in Germany, Prussia tried to increase its influence over other states by founding a federal customs union or ZOLLVEREIN. In the REVOLUTIONS OF 1848 a new constituent assembly was elected to Frankfurt, and tried to establish a constitutional German monarchy, but in 1849 the Austrian emperor refused the crown of a united Germany because it would loosen his authority in Hungary, while the Prussian king, FREDERICK WILLIAM IV, refused it because the constitution was too liberal. The pre-1848 Confederation was restored, with BISMARCK as one of Prussia's delegates. In 1866 Bismarck proposed that the German Confederation be reorganized to exclude Austria. When Austria opposed this, Bismarck declared the Confederation dissolved and went to war against Austria. In 1867, after Prussia's victory over Austria in the AUSTRO-PRUSSIAN WAR (1866), the 21 secondary governments above the River Main federated into the North German Confederation (Norddeutscher Bund), with its capital in Berlin and its leadership vested in Prussia. Executive authority rested in a presidency in accordance with the hereditary rights of the rulers of Prussia. The federation's constitution was a model for that of the GERMAN SECOND EMPIRE, which replaced it after the defeat of France in the FRANCO-PRUSSIAN WAR (1871).

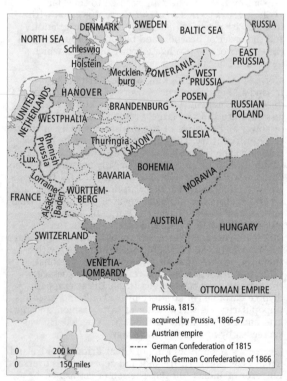

German Confederation *The German Confederation of 1815 spanned 38 states, of which the rival powers of Austria and Prussia were the greatest.*

German Democratic Republic (East Germany) A former eastern European country. It emerged in 1949 from the Soviet Zone of occupation of Germany. Its frontier with Poland on the Oder-Neisse line, agreed at the POTSDAM CONFERENCE, was confirmed by the Treaty of Zgorzelec in 1950. Its capital was East Berlin, but the status of West Berlin, — an enclave of the Federal Republic of GERMANY 150 km (93 miles) inside East German territory, whose existence was guaranteed by the Four-Power Agreement between the victorious allied powers — caused serious problems (see BERLIN AIRLIFT). In the first five years the republic had to pay heavy REPARATIONS to the Soviet Union, and Soviet troops were used to put down disorder in 1953. In 1954, however, the republic proclaimed itself a sovereign state and in the following year became a founder-member of the WARSAW PACT. In 1956 the National People's Army was formed; this organization was instrumental in sealing the GDR's borders in August 1961 (including erecting the BERLIN WALL) to prevent large-scale emigration to West Germany. Walter ULBRICHT (1893–1973) was General Secretary of the ruling Socialist Unity Party (1946–71) and Chairman of the Council of State (1960–71). In 1972 the German Federal Republic, as part of the policy of OSTPOLITIK, established diplomatic relations with the republic. Admission to the UN followed in 1973, after which the republic was universally recognized. Although economic recovery from World War II was slower than in the west, East Germany, under Erich HONECKER (Chairman of the Council of State, 1976–89), succeeded in establishing a stronger industrial base than most of its fellow members of COMECON. However, its highly bureaucratic, centralized system of control steadily atrophied, corruption spread from the top, and its secret police, the Stasi, became ever more ruthless. During 1989 a series of huge demonstrations took place, mostly in Berlin and Leipzig, with a new political grouping, New Forum, demanding democratic reforms. In November 1989 the Berlin Wall was opened and the communist monopoly of power collapsed. The first free elections since 1933 were held in March 1990, with the conservative Christian Democratic Union emerging victorious, and on 3 October 1990 the republic ceased to exist, being absorbed into the Federal Republic of Germany. Criminal proceedings were instituted against those who were deemed to have committed human rights abuses in the GDR regime, but few were punished. The case against Erich Honecker was dropped due to his ill-health. His successor Egon Krenz and several minor officials were found guilty of various crimes, notably for ordering or carrying out the shooting of refugees across the Berlin Wall.

German Second empire (Reich) (1871–1918) A continental and overseas empire ruled by Prussia. (The First Reich was the Holy Roman Empire, which ended in 1806.) It replaced the GERMAN CONFEDERATION and the short-lived North German Confederation (1866–70). It was created by BISMARCK following the FRANCO-PRUSSIAN WAR, by the union of 25 German states under the Hohenzollern King of Prussia, now Emperor William I. An alliance was formed with the AUSTRO-HUNGARIAN EMPIRE in 1879 and German economic investment took place in south-east Europe. In 1884 Bismarck presided over a conference of European colonial powers in Berlin, to allocate territories in Africa. In the same year Karl Peters founded the Society for German Colonization, and

Bismarck was prepared to claim three areas of Africa: German South-West Africa, bordering on Cape Colony; the Cameroons and Togoland, where Britain had long monopolized the trade; and German East Africa, thus threatening British interests in Zanzibar. Northern New Guinea and the Bismarck Archipelago in the Pacific were also claimed. With the accession of William II (1888) colonial activity, especially in the Far East, increased. In 1898 Germany leased the Chinese province of Shandong and purchased the Caroline and Mariana Islands from Spain. In 1899 Samoa was partitioned between Germany and the USA. Potential friction with Britain was averted by a mutual agreement in 1900, following its intervention to crush the BOXER RISING. In that year von BÜLOW became Chancellor (1900–09). The growth of German industry had now made it the greatest industrial power in Europe, and inevitably the search for new markets led to tension with other colonial powers. The expansion of the German navy under von TIRPITZ led to rivalry with the British navy, while competition with France in Africa led to a crisis over MOROCCO (1905). In a second Moroccan Crisis (1911), an international war came close. The assassination at SARAJEVO caught the empire unawares. After some debate it was decided that the 1879 alliance with the AUSTRO-HUNGARIAN EMPIRE must be honoured even if it meant war against Russia and France. During WORLD WAR I most German African territories were conquered and at the VERSAILLES PEACE SETTLEMENT Germany was stripped of its overseas empire, which became mandated territories, administered by the victorious powers on behalf of the LEAGUE OF NATIONS. At the end of the war the emperor abdicated and the WEIMAR REPUBLIC was created.

Germantown, Battle of (4 October 1777) When the British occupied Philadelphia during the American War of INDEPENDENCE the greater part of their army camped at Germantown, north of Philadelphia. After the defeat at BRANDYWINE and the British occupation of Philadelphia, WASHINGTON attempted a surprise counter-attack on the main British camp. Bad weather and bad co-ordination resulted in American defeat, heavy losses, and withdrawal to winter quarters at VALLEY FORGE.

Germany, Federal Republic of A central European country covering an area of almost 357,000 sq km (138,000 sq miles). In the west it extends across the Rhine valley, in the south it includes the central Alps, and in the east it is partially bounded by the River Oder. Germany has borders with Denmark, Poland, the Czech Republic, Austria, Switzerland, France, Luxembourg, Belgium, and the Netherlands.

Physical. The whole of northern Germany, through which run the Weser, the Elbe, and smaller rivers, is set in the North European Plain. The Rhine Basin encompasses some of the most beautiful landscape and best wine-growing regions in Europe. Towards the east, this consists of morainic hills containing fertile loess soil. More than a quarter of the whole of Germany is covered with forest. Among the major ranges of the mid-German highlands are the Teutoburger Wald, the Harz Mountains, the Sauerland, Westerwald, and Taunusgebirge. In the west are the Ruhr coalfields, while in the east there are large lignite deposits. Southward the ground gradually rises to the Black Forest (Schwarzwald), and the Swabian Jura, with dense pine forests and moorland, and potash, salt, and other minerals. In Bavaria, further south, the land becomes rugged. Here are patches of mountain pasture and lakes; to the east is the deep Danube valley.

Economy. Germany has a highly successful industrial economy, which continues to be the dominant economic force in Europe. It also enjoys excellent labour relations, and a high degree of worker participation in management. However, by the end of the 1990s, the huge cost of restructuring the industry of the former GDR, and financial stringencies imposed to meet the requirements of European Monetary Union, began to tell on the German economy. Unemployment rose to an unprecedented postwar level and 'industrial unrest' increased.

Manufacturing industry includes mechanical and electrical engineering, electronics, vehicles, chemicals, and food-processing, with machinery, electronic goods, optical and scientific instruments, transport equipment, and chemical and pharmaceutical products the principal exports. Mineral resources include coal, lignite, salt, and some natural gas. Nuclear power generates around one-quarter of Germany's electricity. The main agricultural crops are potatoes, sugar beet, wheat, and barley. Viticulture is most extensive in the Rhine and Mosel valleys in West Germany and is an important export industry.

History. Germany was originally occupied by Teutonic tribes who were driven back across the Rhine by Julius CAESAR in 58 BC. When the Roman empire collapsed eight Germanic kingdoms were created, but in the 8th century CHARLEMAGNE consolidated these kingdoms under the FRANKS. The region became part of the HOLY ROMAN EMPIRE in 962, and almost 200 years later was invaded by the Mongols. A period of unrest followed until 1438 when the long rule of the HABSBURGS began. The kingdom, now made up of hundreds of states, was torn apart during the THIRTY YEARS WAR; when this ended with the Peace of Westphalia in 1648, the Elector of Brandenburg-Prussia emerged as a force ready to challenge Austrian supremacy. By the end of the NAPOLEONIC WARS, the alliance of 400 separate German states that had existed within the Holy Roman Empire (962–1806) had been reduced to 38. At the Congress of VIENNA these were formed into a loose grouping, the GERMAN CONFEDERATION, under Austrian leadership. The Confederation was dissolved as a result of the AUSTRO-PRUSSIAN WAR (1866), and in 1867 all northern Germany formed a new North German Confederation under Prussian leadership. This was in turn dissolved in 1871, and the new GERMAN SECOND EMPIRE proclaimed. After Germany's defeat in World War I, the WEIMAR REPUBLIC was instituted, to be replaced in 1933 by the THIRD REICH under Adolf HITLER. After the end of World War II the country divided into the Federal Republic of Germany (West Germany) and the GERMAN DEMOCRATIC REPUBLIC (East Germany).

The Federal Republic was created in 1949 from the British, French, and US zones of occupation. It became a sovereign state in 1955, when ambassadors were exchanged with world powers, including the Soviet Union. Konrad ADENAUER, as Chancellor (1949–63), was determined to see eventual reunification of Germany and refused to recognize the legal existence of the German Democratic Republic. A crisis developed over Berlin in 1958, when the Soviet Union demanded the

withdrawal of Western troops and, in 1961, when it authorized the erection of the BERLIN WALL. The Berlin situation began to ease in 1971, during the chancellorship of the social democrat Willy BRANDT (1969–74) with his policy of OSTPOLITIK. This resulted in treaties with the Soviet Union (1970), Poland (1970), Czechoslovakia (1973), and one of mutual recognition and co-operation with the German Democratic Republic (1972), with membership of the UN following in 1973. Economic recovery was assisted after the war by the MARSHALL PLAN. The challenge of rebuilding shattered cities and of absorbing many millions of refugees from eastern Europe was successfully met, as was that of re-creating systems of social welfare and health provision. The Federal Republic joined NATO in 1955, when both army and airforce were reconstituted; large numbers of US and British troops remained stationed there. In 1957 it signed the Treaty of ROME, becoming a founder-member of the EUROPEAN ECONOMIC COMMUNITY in 1958. Although the pace of economic growth slackened, the economy remained one of the strongest in the world, under a stable democratic regime. In 1982 the social democrat coalition of Helmut SCHMIDT collapsed and was replaced by the centre-right coalition under Helmut KOHL.

Following economic and monetary union with the Democratic Republic in June 1990, a Treaty of Unification was signed in August and unification took place in October. Since then, the country has consisted of 16 *Länder* or states, each of which has wide powers over its domestic affairs. Although Chancellor Kohl's Christian Democratic Union won control of four out of the five eastern *Länder*, their economic problems were soon to produce a sense of disillusion, with unemployment rising to 17% and a resurgence of support for the former communists. The cost of restructuring the economy of the former GDR proved far higher than expected, obliging the Bundesbank to maintain very high interest rates. This in turn caused tensions with the ERM (see EUROPEAN MONETARY SYSTEM), and turmoil in the money markets. Germany's liberal policies on asylum resulted in a large influx of migrants, legal and illegal, with accompanying social problems. A resurgence of right-wing extremism in the form of attacks on Jews and foreign citizens led the government to ban four far-right organizations in late 1992: further such groups were proscribed in early 1995. Against a background of recession and political disillusionment in western Germany, further measures were taken in 1993 to fund the restructuring of the eastern German economy. In the presidential elections of May 1994 Roman Herzog was elected to replace Richard von Weizsäcker. In October the federal coalition, led by Helmut Kohl since 1982, was re-elected with a greatly reduced majority. The transfer of the seat of government and administrative departments from Bonn to the capital-designate Berlin is estimated to be complete by the year 2000.

CAPITAL:	Bonn (capital-designate is Berlin)
AREA:	356,954 sq km (137,820 sq miles)
POPULATION:	81.891 million (1996)
CURRENCY:	1 Deutschmark = 100 Pfennige
RELIGIONS:	FRG (1987): Roman Catholic 42.9%; Lutheran 41.6%; Muslim 2.7%; former GDR (1987): Protestant 47.0%; unaffiliated 46.0%; Roman Catholic 7.0%

ETHNIC GROUPS: (nationality) German 93.2%; Turkish
                  2.3%; Yugoslav 0.9%; Italian 0.8%
LANGUAGES: German (official); minority languages
INTERNATIONAL
  ORGANIZATIONS: UN; EU; OECD; NATO; Council of Europe;
                  CSCE

Geronimo (c. 1829–1909) Apache chief. He led his people
in resistance to White settlement in Arizona until 1886.
For 12 years, after 4,000 Apache had been moved to the
inhospitable reservation at San Carlos, Arizona, he
waged war against US troops conducting brutal raids. In
1886 he surrendered on the promise that his braves
could live peacefully in exile in Florida. Instead, they
were imprisoned and moved to Oklahoma.

Gestapo The Nazi secret police or *Geheime Staatspolizei*.
In 1933 Hermann GOERING reorganized the Prussian plain-
clothes political police as the Gestapo. In 1934 control of
the force passed to HIMMLER, who had restructured the
police in the other German states, and headed the SS or
Schutzstaffel. The Gestapo was effectively absorbed into
the SS and in 1939 was merged with the SD or
Sicherheitsdienst (Security Service), the intelligence
branch of the SS, in a Reich Security Central Office
under Reinhard HEYDRICH. The powers of these
organizations were vast: any person suspected of
disloyalty to the regime could be summarily executed.
The SS and the Gestapo controlled the CONCENTRATION
CAMPS and set up similar agencies in every occupied
country.

Gettysburg, Battle of (1–3 July 1863) A battle in the
AMERICAN CIVIL WAR. On 1 July elements of the Army of
Northern Virginia under LEE and the Union Army of the
Potomac under Meade came into contact west of
Gettysburg, Pennsylvania. Although early Confederate
attacks were repulsed, the arrival of reinforcements
forced the Union troops to retreat back through the
town. By the following day, however, fresh Union troops
in strong defensive positions on Cemetery Ridge
repelled Confederate attacks. On the third day, Pickett's
charge against the centre of the Union line was
defeated with heavy losses, and Lee was forced to
abandon his invasion of the North. He lost 20,000 men
from a force of 70,000 and Meade 23,000 from one of
93,000. The retreat from Gettysburg, together with the
simultaneous surrender of VICKSBURG in the west,
marked the turning point of the war, although over a
year and a half of heavy fighting would follow before
Lee was finally forced to surrender.

Ghana A West African country with a south-facing
coast, bounded by the Côte d'Ivoire on the west, Burkina
Faso on the north, and Togo on the east.
  Physical. Ghana's flat and sandy coast is backed by a
rolling plain of scrub and grass, except in the west,
where moderate rains produce thick forest. The forest
extends northward to the Ashanti plateau, which
produces cocoa and tropical hardwoods, as well as
manganese, bauxite, and gold. Further north, up-country
of the valley of the Volta, it is very hot even in winter,
though the harmattan brings relatively cool (and dusty)
conditions from the interior of West Africa.
  Economy. The Ghanaian economy is mainly
agricultural. Exports are cocoa, gold, and timber. Off-
shore oil deposits await development; other mineral
extraction includes gold, manganese, diamonds and

bauxite. There is some light industry and
manufacturing of aluminium. Hydraulic power
accounts for much of the country's electricity
production.
  History. The area now covered by Ghana was composed
of several kingdoms in the middle ages. From the late
15th century, the Portuguese and other Europeans began
trading with the area, which they called the Gold Coast.
It became a centre of the slave trade from the 16th
century onwards. British influence gradually
predominated. In 1850 the British Colonial Office
purchased residual Danish interests in the region and
gave some protection to the FANTI CONFEDERATION. Inland
the area was dominated throughout the 19th century by
the ASANTE confederacy. Britain occupied the capital
Kumasi after wars with the Asante in 1824 and 1874,
when the colony of the Gold Coast was established.
Further wars against the Asante followed in 1896 and
1900. After 1920 economic growth based on mining and
the cocoa industry, combined with high standards of
mission schooling, produced a sophisticated people
demanding home rule. Following World War II, in
which many Ghanaians served, there were serious riots
in Accra (1948) leading to constitutional discussions. In
1957 the Gold Coast and British TOGOLAND to the east
were combined to become the independent Republic of
Ghana, under the leadership of Kwame NKRUMAH, the
first British African colony to be granted independence.
Nkrumah transformed the country into a one-party
state. Economic problems and resentment over political
repression and mismanagement led to his overthrow by
the army in 1966. Since his fall continuing economic and
political problems have unbalanced Ghana. After a
succession of coups, a group of junior officers under
Flight-Lieutenant Jerry RAWLINGS took power in 1979,
executed three former heads of state, and installed a
civilian government. When this failed, Rawlings again
seized power (December 1981), suspending the
constitution and establishing a Provisional National
Defence Council, with himself as Chairman. During the
1980s with IMF support Ghana regained some economic
and political stability, but western aid donors demanded
a move to restore democracy. A Movement for Freedom
and Justice developed, and a new Constitution was
adopted in April 1992, legalizing political parties. In
November 1992 Rawlings was victorious in multiparty
presidential elections, but opposition parties contested
the result. Rawlings was sworn in as President in 1993
and won a second term in December 1996.

CAPITAL: Accra
AREA: 238,533 sq km (92,098 sq miles)
POPULATION: 16.904 million (1996)
CURRENCY: 1 cedi = 100 pesewas
RELIGIONS: Protestant 27.9%; traditional beliefs
21.4%; Roman Catholic 18.7%; African indigenous
churches 16.0%; Muslim 15.7% (of which Ahmadīyah 7.9%)
ETHNIC GROUPS: Akan 52.4%; Mossi 15.8%; Ewe 11.9%; Ga-
Adangme 7.8%
LANGUAGES: English (official); Akan; Mole Dagbani;
local languages
INTERNATIONAL ORGANIZATIONS: Commonwealth; ECOWAS;
Non-Aligned Movement; OAU; UN

Ghana, kingdom of An ancient kingdom in what is
now east Senegal, south-west Mali, northern Guinea, and
southern Mauritania. As early as c. 800 al-Fazari called
Ghana 'the land of gold'. Local tradition claims that

there were 22 princes ruling there before MUHAMMAD, and 22 after, but little is known of this period. The capital was at Koumbi Saleh, with a population of Africans and BERBERS. In 990 the King of Ghana took the Berber kingdom of Audaghost, and so gained control of the gold and salt caravan trade. The capital was in two parts, one of Muslim merchants and scholars, with the royal court 8 km (6 miles) away. It fell to the ALMORAVIDS in 1054, to Sosso in 1203, and finally to SUNDJATA KEITA in 1240. The name was adopted by the former British colony of the Gold Coast when it became independent in 1957.

Ghaznavid TURKISH dynasty whose founder, Sebuktegin, was appointed governor of Khurasan by the Persian Samanids and established his own power in Ghazna, Afghanistan, in 962. His successors extended their realm into Persia and the Punjab, but after the reign of Mahmud (969–1030) it fragmented under SELJUK pressure, although the dynasty clung on in Lahore until 1186, when it was extinguished by the Ghurids, founders of the DELHI sultanate.

Ghent, Pacification of (1576) An alliance forged during the DUTCH REVOLTS. It enshrined the agreement of the Catholic and CALVINIST NETHERLANDS to oppose Spanish rule and to call for the removal of imperial troops. Ruled by Austria from 1714, Ghent was seized by the French in 1792, and was incorporated into the kingdom of Belgium in 1830.

Ghent, Treaty of (1814) A treaty ending the WAR OF 1812 between Britain and the USA. Negotiations to end the war, which was not popular in either country, began in August 1814 in the Belgian city of Ghent. British territorial demands obstructed progress for several months, but general war-weariness eventually brought a settlement. The resulting treaty did not address the issues which had caused the war, but provided for the release of all prisoners, restoration of all conquered territory, and the appointment of a commission to settle the north-eastern boundary dispute. Other questions, including naval forces on the Great Lakes and fishing rights, were left to future settlement.

ghost dance A MILLENNARIAN movement which spread among the Native American PLAINS PEOPLES during the second half of the 19th century. The ghost dance, which involved dancing for days on end to induse a trancelike state, was said to presage the end of the world, when the White settlers would leave and the Native Americans would have their lands restored.

Giap, Vo Nguyen (1912–) Vietnamese general and politician; defence minister (1945–80) and deputy prime minister (1976–80) of (North) Vietnam. Giap's military strategy led to victory first over French colonial forces and then over US troops in the VIETNAM WAR.

Giap joined the Communist Party but fled to China when the party was proscribed in 1939, where he became an aide to HO CHI MINH. He returned to Vietnam in 1945 in command of an exile army (the Vietminh), and drove the Japanese from Hanoi. He then fought the French, who had reclaimed their pre-war colony of Indochina after the Japanese surrender. The French were defeated at Dien Bien Phu in 1954. Giap's use of guerrilla warfare tactics enabled him to defeat the technologically superior US forces that were committed to South Vietnam from 1965 onwards. Giap

masterminded the successful TET OFFENSIVE of 1968 that struck into the heart of Saigon and weakened US morale. The US finally withdrew in 1975 and Giap retired from politics in 1982.

Gibbon, Edward (1737–94) British historian. While on a visit to Rome in 1764 he conceived the plan for what has become the most celebrated historical work in English literature, *The History of the Decline and Fall of the Roman Empire* (1776–88), a six-volume study which traces the connection of the ancient world with the modern, encompassing such subjects as the establishment of the CHRISTIAN CHURCH, the Teutonic tribes, the conquests of ISLAM, and the CRUSADES. The work is distinguished by the author's great erudition and elegant and lucid prose style, and is enlivened by ironic wit.

Gibraltar A fortified town and rocky headland dominating the passage from the Mediterranean Sea to the Atlantic Ocean, 5 km (3 miles) long, near the extreme south of Spain.

Physical. A British dependency, its northern end is a low-lying sandy isthmus, south of which is the famous limestone Rock, containing caves and with a precipitous eastern face. Westward it slopes more gently towards a magnificent bay, which is a natural harbour. The Strait of Gibraltar to the south is the channel, from 15 km (9 miles) to 37 km (23 miles) in width and 56 km (35 miles) long, linking the Atlantic Ocean with the Mediterranean Sea. A surface current flows east and a deeper one west. The Rock of Gibraltar and Almina Point on the facing Moroccan coast are the ancient Pillars of Hercules, marking the limit of the known western world of antiquity.

History. In 711, Gibraltar was captured and fortified by the Moors, who gave it its name, Jabal al-Tariq (Mount of Tariq). It became Spanish in 1462, but in 1704 during the War of the SPANISH SUCCESSION the fortress surrendered to Sir George Rooke, commander of a large Anglo-Dutch fleet, and was retained by Britain at the Treaty of UTRECHT. Spain made repeated attempts to recapture Gibraltar, notably in 1779 when it withstood a long siege by powerful Franco-Spanish forces. Gibraltar was important as a naval base during the two World Wars and remains a British dependency with the support of the inhabitants, some of whom are Italian, Maltese, and Portuguese in origin. In 1969 the border was closed by Spain, which claims possession of Gibraltar, but following an agreement signed in Brussels in 1984, was reopened in 1985. The UK withdrew its ground forces from Gibraltar in 1991. The inhabitants of Gibraltar would like to be independent, but as this is politically unlikely they prefer allegiance to Britain rather than to Spain.

Gilbert, Sir Humphrey (c. 1539–83) English navigator. He had an active and distinguished career as a soldier in France, Ireland, and the Netherlands, but his real interest was in the discovery of a north-west passage to China, and in 1576 he published his *Discourse of a Discovery for a New Passage to Cataia* on the subject. In 1583, with the help of his half-brother Sir Walter RALEIGH, he set off with five ships for NEWFOUNDLAND where he established the first English colony in North America. Fierce storms were met on the return voyage, and the smallest ship of the company, in which Gilbert was sailing, went down off the Azores with all hands.

Gilbert Islands KIRIBATI.

gild GUILD.

Gildas (c. 500–70) British monk and historian. He is best known as the author of a polemical work (c. 550) *De excidio et conquestu Britanniae* ('The Ruin and Conquest of Britain') in which he attacked the British for their wickedness. In spite of its rhetorical tone and historical inaccuracies it is the only substantial written source for the condition of Britain during a crucial period. It recorded the British victory over the Saxons at MOUNT BADON.

'Gilded Age' A term coined by Mark Twain in the title of his novel *The Gilded Age* (1873), which satirizes the gross materialism of the decade following the AMERICAN CIVIL WAR, with its currency inflation and loose business and political morals. Later writers satirized the lawlessness of frontier life, the corruption of presidential elections, and the ruthless business methods of the 'robber barons'.

Gilgamesh A legendary king of the Sumerian city-state of URUK in southern Mesopotamia. The *Epic of Gilgamesh*, one of the best-known works of ancient literature, was written in cuneiform on 12 clay tablets in c. 2000 BC, and discovered among the ruins of Nineveh. Its c. 3,000 lines recount the quest for immortality of the warrior king Gilgamesh, half divine and half human. To curb his power, the god Anu creates a savage, Enkidu, who is brought up in the wilderness. They meet in a trial of strength, which Gilgamesh wins. Enkidu becomes his beloved companion, but is fated to die for having slain the divine bull of Ishtar, goddess of love. Gilgamesh, obsessed with his own mortality, wanders the earth in a quest for the plant that bestows eternal youth. He finds it, only to have it seized from him by a serpent which, by sloughing off its skin, appears to have achieved the renewal of life that has eluded Gilgamesh. The epic contains an account of a great flood that has close parallels with the Biblical story of Noah.

Giolitti, Giovanni (1842–1928) Italian statesman. He dominated Italian politics from 1900 to 1920, being five times Premier. A skilled conciliator and liberal, he introduced universal male suffrage for those over 30 (1912) and did not oppose the growth of trade unionism. He agreed to the conquest of Libya and argued against Italy's entry into World War I (1915). At first he gave some support to the fascists but later attacked the introduction of the corporate state.

Girondins A French political grouping prominent during the FRENCH REVOLUTION, so-called because many of their supporters came from the Gironde region. The Girondins were closely associated with the JACOBINS in the early days of the Revolution. Their radical leaders, BRISSOT, Marguerite Guadet, and Marie-Jeanne ROLAND, quickly gained ascendancy in the Legislative Assembly and, after the king's powers had been abolished, dominated the republican government of the Convention set up in September 1792. They held power at a critical time and were responsible for provoking the wars with France's enemies. The failure of these wars led not only to the king's execution but also to the downfall of the party and the introduction of the Reign of TERROR. The crisis was brought about after the desertion of Charles-François Dumouriez, the

commander-in-chief of the army, to the Austrians in April 1793. The party tried to re-establish itself by appealing to the moderates and arresting HÉBERT. When this failed an immense mob expelled them from the Convention and later more than 20 of their ministers were arrested and guillotined.

gladiator Literally 'swordsman', a slave or prisoner trained to fight other gladiators, wild beasts, or condemned criminals for the entertainment of the people in ancient Rome. Gladiatorial combat originated as a ritual at funerals of dead warriors in Etruria and was introduced to Rome in 264 BC. Here its popularity grew, as politicians used such spectacles as a way of courting public popularity. Gladiators belonged to four categories: the Mirmillo, with a fish on his helmet, and the Sammite, both heavily armed with oblong shield, visored helmet, and short sword; the Retiarius, lightly clad, fighting with net and trident; and the Thracian, with round shield and curved scimitar. Thumbs up or down from the crowd spelt life or death for the loser. Formal combat degenerated into butchery watched by huge crowds. Women and even the physically handicapped sometimes fought. Despite popular antagonism, the emperors CONSTANTINE and THEODOSIUS outlawed the combats.

Gladstone, William Ewart (1809–98) British statesman. He was the outstanding figure in British political life in the Victorian era and four times Prime Minister (1868–74, 1880–85, 1886, 1892–94). He entered Parliament as a Tory in 1832. A firm supporter of FREE TRADE, he had to resign, together with the Prime Minister, Sir Robert PEEL, after the repeal of the CORN LAWS split the Conservative Party in 1846. He later became Liberal Chancellor of the Exchequer (1859–66), introducing an important series of budgets that cut tariffs and restrained government expenditure. Chosen leader of the Liberal Party in 1867, he took office as Prime Minister in 1868. His first administration passed some notable measures, including the disestablishment of the Church of Ireland, a secret ballot at elections, reforms in the legal position of trade unions, in the legal system itself, and in education. He also arranged the settlement of outstanding disputes with the USA through international arbitration. Defeated by Disraeli in 1874, Gladstone became Prime Minister once more in 1880 following his MIDLOTHIAN CAMPAIGN, and secured the passage of the third REFORM ACT in 1884. However, he incurred much unpopularity over the fall of Khartoum and resigned in June 1885. When he took office again in the following year Gladstone introduced a bill to give Ireland HOME RULE. In doing so he split the Liberal Party and his government was defeated. Becoming Prime Minister again in 1892, he made a further attempt with a new Home Rule bill in 1893, but it was rejected by the House of Lords. In 1894 Gladstone resigned for the last time.

glasnost and perestroika The policies of 'openness' and 'restructuring' that led to major changes in Soviet society in the 1980s as well as profoundly influencing the world BALANCE OF POWER and East–West relations. Introduced into Soviet domestic politics by Mikhail GORBACHEV, who became Soviet leader in 1985, the concepts are described in his book *Perestroika* (1987). The twin processes aimed to reduce inefficiency and corruption in the Soviet Union, and to encourage political liberalization. Internally the results of the 'Gorbachev doctrine' were mixed, contributing to growing nationalist demands and economic discontent: by the end of 1991 these forces had brought about the disintegration of the structure of the Soviet Union, the displacement of the Communist party from its formerly dominant position, and the formation of a new COMMONWEALTH OF INDEPENDENT STATES. Externally *glasnost* and *perestroika* contributed to the abandonment of Soviet control over the Eastern bloc, the withdrawal of Soviet troops and support from Afghanistan, as well as a growing rapprochement with the West, which brought the COLD WAR to a close.

glebe Land belonging to a parish church used to support its priest. The size of glebes varied enormously from 1 hectare (2 acres) to a few hundred hectares; priests might afford to engage labourers or be obliged to work the land themselves, and they could sub-lease part or all of the land. Since the glebe was a freeholding, the lord of the manor could not demand labour duties of the priest, although this immunity was not always observed.

Glencoe, Massacre of (13 February 1692) A massacre for political reasons of members of the Macdonald CLAN in Scotland. By failing to swear allegiance to WILLIAM III by 1 January 1692, the rebellious clan Macdonald was technically guilty of treason; their chief's delaying tactics had been compounded by bad weather, and his oath was six days late. The Campbells, hereditary enemies of the Macdonalds, undertook to destroy them, which they attempted after enjoying Macdonald hospitality for 12 days. The clan chief and more than 30 of his followers were murdered, but the rest (about 300) escaped. Although the king probably did not order the atrocity, he did little to punish the perpetrators.

Glendower, Owen (Owain Glyndŵr) (c. 1354–c. 1416) Welsh national leader. Of princely lineage, he fell out with the LANCASTRIAN English rulers of north Wales. In September 1400 he was proclaimed Prince of Wales, and he became leader of a revolt that spread throughout Wales. The castles built by EDWARD I proved to be crucial and it was HENRY IV's control of these, rather than the failure of Glendower's alliances, that ultimately led to the end of the rebellion in 1408. Glendower remains the national hero of Wales.

Glorious Revolution The bloodless English revolution of 1688–89. The term covers the specific events of JAMES II's removal from the throne and his replacement by WILLIAM III and Mary, and in a more general sense refers to the end of Stuart attempts at despotism, and the establishment of a constitutional form of government.

From his accession in 1685, the actions of the Roman Catholic James II aroused both Whig and Tory concern. In defiance of the law he appointed Roman Catholics to important positions in the army, the Church, the universities, and the government. He claimed the right to suspend or dispense with the laws as he pleased, and his two DECLARATIONS OF INDULGENCE suspended penal laws against Roman Catholics and dissenters. He arrested seven bishops and brought them to trial for objecting to the illegality of the second Declaration of Indulgence. The bishops were found not guilty of seditious libel, a verdict which discredited the king. The birth of a son to the king in 1688 appeared to ensure the Roman Catholic

succession and provoked leading politicians of both the main parties to invite the king's Protestant daughter Mary and her husband William of Orange to England. William landed with a Dutch army in Devonshire in November. James's army refused to obey its Catholic officers, his daughters deserted him, and he was allowed to escape abroad. Parliament asked William and Mary to take over the vacant throne. A revival of arbitrary government was made impossible by the BILL OF RIGHTS of 1689, which offered the crown to the new monarchs. James II landed in Ireland with French troops (March 1690), besieged LONDONDERRY, and was defeated at the Battle of the BOYNE (July 1690). He returned to exile in France. The Act of SETTLEMENT of 1701 provided for the Protestant succession.

Gloucester, Humphrey, Duke of (1391–1447) English nobleman, a younger son of HENRY IV. From 1422 he was guardian of his infant nephew HENRY VI, but his claim to be Regent of England was rejected by the House of Lords, and especially Cardinal Henry Beaufort, who distrusted him. He was popular with the House of Commons and the citizens of London, and came to be seen as a threat by Henry VI. In 1441 his wife, Eleanor of Cobham, was imprisoned on a charge of treason and heresy, and his own death six years later was generally accounted murder; within a few years the YORKISTS began fostering the myth of him as the 'Good Duke'.

Goa A district on the west coast of India, a Portuguese colony from 1510 to 1961. Little is known of its early history under Hindu rule until its seizure by Muslims in 1327. The first Portuguese governor, ALBUQUERQUE, captured it in 1510, and expanded the settlement to form an entrepôt for south-east Asian trade. It became the administrative centre of Portugal's Asian empire. When Portuguese power declined elsewhere in Asia, Goa remained as an enclave of European influence. However, it was wrested from the Portuguese by India in 1961 and, together with two other former Portuguese west-coast territories, Daman and the island of Diu, became a Union Territory in 1962. Goa became a State of the Union in May 1987 with three elected Members of Parliament; Daman and Diu remained a Union Territory.

Gobind Singh (1666–1708) The tenth and last of the Sikh GURUS. He became Guru at the age of nine, following the execution of his father, the ninth Guru, Tegh Bahadur, by the Mogul emperor Aurangzeb. Gobind Singh encouraged the militarization of the Sikhs against the Mogul empire. During *Baisakhi* (the new year festival) in 1699, he called upon five Sikhs to give up their lives, but instead of killing the volunteers he rewarded their courage and loyalty by initiating them into the *khalsa*, a newly formed army of soldier-saints. At the time of his death, Gobind Singh declared that there would be no living Guru after him, but that authority would be invested in the *Adi Granth*, the sacred book of the Sikhs.

Gobineau, Joseph Arthur, Comte de (1816–82) French diplomat and scholar, the intellectual founder of racialism. His most famous book, *Essay on the Inequality of Human Races* (1853–55), put forward the thesis that the races are innately unequal and that the White Aryan race is not only the purest but also superior to all others. His writings were to have a sinister influence on the German NAZI theorists, for whom they became a justification for ANTI-SEMITISM.

Goderich, Frederick John Robinson, Viscount and 1st Earl of Ripon (1782–1859) British statesman, Prime Minister (1827–28). He first entered Parliament in 1806 and held a succession of offices, including those of President of the Board of Trade (1818–23), Chancellor of the Exchequer (1823–27), and Secretary for War and the Colonies (1827). As Viscount Goderich he succeeded George Canning as Prime Minister in August 1827, but, ill-suited to the task, resigned the following January. He was created Earl of Ripon in 1833.

Godfrey of Bouillon (Godefroi de Bouillon) (c. 1060–1100) French Crusader and ruler of JERUSALEM. He was a prominent leader of the First CRUSADE and financed a large part of the expeditionary force. Having distinguished himself at the siege of Jerusalem, he was elected Advocate of the Holy Sepulchre – in effect, king – a position which his brother, BALDWIN I, was to assume on his death. His victories against the Muslims confirmed the Crusaders' hold on Palestine and were celebrated in the medieval song cycle, the *Chansons de Geste*.

Godolphin, Sydney, 1st Earl of (1645–1712) English statesman who gave loyal service to CHARLES II, JAMES II, and Queen ANNE. Although he maintained close links with the Jacobites, he served WILLIAM III until he quarrelled with his colleagues in 1696. He was Queen Anne's Lord Treasurer for most of her reign, and in spite of being himself a Tory played an important part in excluding Tories from her government and in securing the Act of UNION with Scotland in 1707. Godolphin's fortunes were linked with MARLBOROUGH'S: he financed the duke's campaigns in the War of the SPANISH SUCCESSION, but when Marlborough lost favour and the Tories regained influence in 1710 his career ended.

Godunov, Boris BORIS GODUNOV.

Godwin (or Godwine) (d. 1053) Earl of Wessex. He was the father of HAROLD II of England. He arranged the accession of both HAROLD I (1040) and EDWARD THE CONFESSOR (1042). When his daughter Edith married Edward (1045) Godwin's dominance in English politics seemed assured. Edward, however, countered his influence by relying on Norman advisers and when Godwin rebelled (1051) he exiled him together with his son Harold. They invaded England in 1052 and Edward was forced to reinstate Godwin and his family.

Godwin, Mary Wollstonecraft WOLLSTONECRAFT (GODWIN), MARY.

Goebbels, (Paul) Joseph (1897–1945) German Nazi propagandist. Rejected by the army because of a club foot, he joined the NAZI Party and founded a new paper for party propaganda, *Der Angriff* ('The Attack'), from now on exploiting his considerable gifts of oratory and manipulation of the masses to further the Nazi cause. His brilliantly staged parades and mass meetings helped HITLER to power. In 1933 he became Hitler's Enlightenment and Propaganda Minister, giving him control over the press, radio, and all aspects of culture until 1945. After Germany's defeat at STALINGRAD he was entrusted with the implementation of 'total war' within Germany. Faced with the advancing Soviet army, he committed suicide in Berlin with Hitler, first killing his wife and six children.

Goering, Hermann Wilhelm (1893–1946) German Nazi leader. As a fighter pilot in World War I he gained the highest award for bravery in the air. He joined the NAZIS in 1922, commanded their BROWNSHIRT paramilitary organization, and fled the country after being wounded in HITLER's unsuccessful MUNICH 'BEER-HALL' PUTSCH. In 1934 he became commander of the German air force, and was responsible for the German rearmament programme. Until 1936 Goering headed the GESTAPO, which he had founded. He was then entrusted by Hitler with the execution of the four-year economic plan and directed the German economy until 1943. In 1937 he became Minister for Foreign Affairs and in 1938 Hitler's first Deputy. Increasingly dependent on narcotics, he was deprived by Hitler of all authority in 1943 and finally dismissed (1945), after unauthorized attempts to make peace with the Western Allies. Sentenced to death at the Nuremberg trials, he committed suicide in his cell by swallowing poison.

Gokhale, Gopal Krishna (1866–1915) Indian nationalist politician. The leader of the moderate faction in the Indian National CONGRESS, he became prominent in the Indian legislative Council established under the MORLEY-MINTO REFORMS in 1910, specializing in finance. He also founded in 1905 the Servants of India Society, an austere organization dedicated to the service of India.

Golan Heights Uplands north-east of the Sea of Galilee (Lake Tiberis), overlooking the Jordan Valley; they are part of south-west Syria but occupied by Israel. The highest peak is Tell-a Shaikha, which stands at over 1,280 m (4,200 feet). The heights provided Syrian artillery with a natural platform from which they could bombard parts of Israel. As a result, the heights were stormed and captured by Israel in the SIX-DAY WAR of 1967. The Golan Heights were again the scene of intense fighting in the YOM KIPPUR WAR of 1973, and were formally annexed by Israel in December 1981. Many KIBBUTZIM have been established in the area (specializing in wine growing), and Israel's insistence on the strategic importance of the Golan Heights in the country's defence has prevented any peace settlement with Syria.

Golconda A ruined city west of Hyderabad city, on India's Deccan plateau. From 1518 to 1687 it was the capital of the Muslim Qutb Shahi sultanate, whose rulers came to power at the expense of the BAHMANI Deccan sultanate. Their control extended from the lower Godavari and Krishna valleys to the eastern coast, but was ended in 1687 by Mogul conquest. Many of the royal tombs and palaces remain in a good state of repair.

Golden Horde The TARTARS of the Mongol KHANATE of the Western Kipchaks (1242–1480). The word 'horde' derives from the Mongol 'ordo', meaning a camp, while 'golden' recalls the magnificence of Batu Khan's headquarters camp. In 1238 Batu, a grandson of GENGHIS KHAN, invaded Russia with a Mongol-Kipchak force. He burned Moscow and in 1240 took Kiev. After a sweep through eastern Europe he established his camp at Sarai on the Lower Volga. Khan of a region extending from Central Asia to the River Dnieper, he claimed sovereignty over all Russia but, apart from demanding tribute in money and military contingents, interfered little with the Russian princes, who in general avoided trouble by co-operating. The destruction of Kiev led to the rise of a more northerly, forest-based Russian civilization, and it was from Moscow that resistance to the Horde started.

Defeat by TAMERLANE in 1391 seriously weakened the Horde. Independent khanates emerged in the Crimea and Kazan. In 1480 the power of the Tartars was broken by IVAN III (the Great).

gold rushes Sudden influxes of people to newly discovered gold fields. The most famous gold rush was to California, where in 1848 gold was found by a Swiss settler, J. A. Sutter. As news spread, adventurers from all over the world made for California. Hard-drinkers and gamblers, the 'forty-niners' created an archetypal saloon society, where more fortunes were made from speculation in land and goods than from gold, as the city of San Francisco boomed. The second great rush was to Australia, where gold was first found near Bathurst in New South Wales in 1851 and later in Victoria at Bendigo and Ballarat, the richest alluvial gold field ever known. A ten-year boom brought diggers back across the Pacific from the declining California field, as well as from Britain, where Cornish tin-mining was declining. The population of Victoria rose from 97,000 to 540,000 in the years 1851–60. Later rushes were to New Zealand (1860), to North Australia, Alaska, Siberia, and South Africa (1880s), and to Klondike in Canada and Kalgoorlie in West Australia (1890s). The most important was probably to Witwatersrand, South Africa, in 1886, where the influx of loose-living miners (*uitlanders* or outlanders) precipitated political tensions which led to the Second BOER WAR.

gold standard A monetary system under which a country's monetary authority maintains convertibility of its currency into gold at a fixed price by standing ready to exchange its currency for gold on demand at the price declared (plus or minus a small margin which reflects the cost of shipping gold). Exchange rates between the currencies of member countries are then necessarily fixed. Each monetary authority has to maintain a certain reserve of gold to honour its obligation; the size of the reserve in relation to the domestic money supply or to changes in it may or may not be established by law. In 1821 Britain became the first country to introduce an official gold standard. It was followed some 50 years later by France, Germany, and the USA, and by 1900 the major countries had adopted the gold standard. Under a 'full' gold standard (or gold specie standard), such as existed before 1914, convertibility applied to all citizens and gold coins circulated as money. Under the 'gold exchange' standard, such as existed in the later 1920s, convertibility applies only among monetary authorities, and there is no circulation of gold coin. The gold standard is not currently in effect anywhere in the world.

Gómez, Juan Vicente (1864–1935) Venezuelan statesman. During his 27-year rule as President (1908–35) he established an absolute dictatorship. The foreign investment that he attracted to Venezuela enabled him to build extensive railways, highways, and other public works. Rich petroleum discoveries (1918) in the Lake Maracaibo basin provided a budgetary surplus which not only enabled Gómez to pay off the foreign debt but

also assured him a favourable reputation abroad. Because of the brutal nature of the dictatorship, this reputation was not shared at home. When he died in office the city of Caracas marched in celebration.

Gomułka, Władysław (1905–82) Polish politician. He was Secretary-General during the crucial period 1943–49 when the Polish United People's Party was being formed. Gomułka's attempted defiance of Stalinism led to his dismissal and imprisonment (1951). He was restored to power (1956) on the intervention of Khrushchev, after Polish and Soviet frontier troops had exchanged fire in the wake of serious rioting in Poznań riots and a workers' trial, in a Soviet attempt at compromise with Poland. He helped to sustain a degree of post-Stalinist liberalism, but resigned in 1970 following popular disturbances against increases in food prices.

Gondomar, Diego Sarmiento de Acuña, Conde de (1567–1626) Spanish diplomat. He achieved notoriety as ambassador to England (1613–18 and 1620–22), when he made himself one of the most influential members of JAMES I's court, much to the chagrin of zealous English Protestants. He was largely responsible for the execution of Sir Walter RALEIGH, and he tried to interest the king in a royal Spanish wife for the Prince of Wales. When his unpopularity in England reached its peak in 1622, he was recalled to Spain.

Good Neighbor Policy The popular name for the Latin American policy of the early administration of President F. D. ROOSEVELT. It was implemented by the withdrawal of US marines from Latin American countries and the abrogation of the Platt Amendment, which had given the US government a quasi-protectorate over Cuba. The Montevideo Conference (1933) declared that 'no state has the right to intervene in the internal or external affairs of another'.

Gorbachev, Mikhail S. (1931–) Russian statesman and Executive President of the Soviet Union (1990–91). A Communist Party member since 1952, he was elected to the General Committee in 1979 and to the Politburo in the following year. On the death of Konstantin Chernenko in March 1985 he became the Soviet leader, exercising control from his position as General Secretary of the Communist Party of the Soviet Union (CPSU). Gorbachev's efforts to carry out *perestroika* (see GLASNOST AND PERESTROIKA), the economic and social reform of Soviet society, led to a gradual process of liberalization and the introduction of high technology to the Soviet Union. Together with his foreign minister, Eduard SHEVARDNADZE, he negotiated (1987) an arms control (INF) treaty with the West to reduce nuclear forces in Europe. On the domestic front he introduced stringent laws against alcohol abuse and encouraged a greater degree of *glasnost* in the face of inefficiency and corruption. He released many political dissidents from restraint, including Andrei Sakharov and, for the first time, the Russian people were told of the enormities of the crimes against humanity perpetrated by Stalin's regime. He initiated a number of constitutional changes, whereby the Congress of People's Deputies was directly elected, the Congress then duly electing him Executive President. He withdrew from Afghanistan, and in August 1990 negotiated with Chancellor KOHL that a united Germany could remain in a reformed NATO. He supported the United Nations policy leading to the GULF

WAR; but he faced increasing resistance from a conservative, bureaucratic hierarchy, while the constituent republics of the Union sought ever-greater independence. Tensions during 1991 culminated in an attempted coup in August, which he survived, but only because of the support given him by his rival Boris YELTSIN. He had by then accepted that the political monopoly of the Communist Party of the Soviet Union had ended, but still believed in his communist ideals, and that the Union could be reformed along evolutionary lines. As the Soviet command-economy disintegrated his power-base collapsed, as did the Union itself. He resigned in December 1991. Gorbachev made an unsuccessful attempt to regain power in the presidential election of 1996, but failed significantly to challenge Yeltsin.

Gordon, Charles George (1833–85) British general and administrator. In 1860 at the request of the Chinese government he entered the Chinese service and turned a small army of 3,500 peasants into a hard-fighting unit to defend Shanghai against TAIPING REBELS. For this he was called 'Chinese Gordon'. In 1873 the governor of Egypt, Khedive Ismail, appointed him Governor of Equatoria (an area of the Upper Nile), where he brought peace and order. In 1880 he resigned, but returned to the SUDAN in 1884 at the British government's request to evacuate Egyptian forces from Khartoum, threatened by an army of the rebellious Muhammad Ahmed, calling himself the MAHDI. In March 1884 the Mahdi besieged Khartoum and, despite Gordon's leadership, the city was captured on 26 January 1885. Gordon and his staff were killed two days before a relief expedition, dispatched belatedly from Britain, reached the garrison. Gordon's death stirred British public indignation and contributed to the collapse of the GLADSTONE government.

Gordon riots Anti-Catholic riots in London in 1780. They were led by Lord George Gordon (1751–93), who objected to parliamentary moves towards CATHOLIC EMANCIPATION. His followers terrorized London for a fortnight. Prisons were broken open, property damaged, and people killed before order was restored. Gordon was acquitted of high treason, but was later convicted of libel and died in Newgate Prison.

Goths Germanic tribes who overran the Western Roman empire in the 5th century. Originally from the Baltic area, by the 3rd century AD they had migrated to the northern Black Sea and the Lower Danube. The eastern group on the Black Sea were known as OSTROGOTHS, the western settlers on the Danube in Dacia were known as VISIGOTHS. In the 4th century the Visigoths settled within the Roman empire under treaty. They expanded their sway over the West, being finally responsible for the fall of the Western empire in 476. Their most famous leader was ALARIC I. The OSTROGOTHS allied themselves to the HUNS and in the 5th century under THEODORIC established their kingdom in Italy. In Spain the Visigothic kingdom survived until it was overrun by the Muslims in 711. Ulfila (c. 311–83) translated the Bible into Gothic and was responsible for the conversion of the Visigoths to ARIANISM. The building style of the 13th century onwards with exaggerated pointed arches and complex embellishment was called 'Gothic' or 'barbarous' by Italian artists of the Renaissance, an unfavourable comparison with Roman and Romanesque simplicity. 'Gothic' script was long used for the printing of German.

Gotland An island in the Baltic Sea, now part of Sweden. Inhabited since the Stone Age, it had extensive commercial contacts during the VIKING period; its capital, Visby, was a town of the HANSEATIC LEAGUE from the 11th to the 14th century. It was of strategic importance in the Baltic; in 1570, by the terms of the Treaty of Stettin, Denmark obtained control of the island, but since the Treaty of Brömsbro (1645) it has been a Swedish possession.

Gottwald, Klement (1896–1953) Czechoslovak politician. He was a founder-member of the Czechoslovak Communist Party in 1921, becoming General Secretary in 1927. After the MUNICH PACT (1938) Gottwald went to the Soviet Union. After World War II he returned to Czechoslovakia. He was Prime Minister in a coalition government in 1946–48 and, after the communist coup in 1948, President (1948–53) in succession to BENEŠ. He dominated the country through purges, forced labour camps, and show trials, culminating in the Slansky trial and the execution (1952) of leading communists. He acquiesced in Stalin's plan of reducing Czechoslovakia's industries to satellite status within COMECON.

Gould, Jay 'ROBBER BARON'.

Gowon, Yakubu (1934–) Nigerian statesman and soldier. He was a colonel in the Nigerian army at the time of the military coup of January 1966. Following a second coup in July he was invited to lead a new government. In a new constitution he divided Nigeria into a federation of 12 states, to replace the federal republic of four regions. The eastern Ibo region rejected the constitution and declared itself the state of Biafra, under General Ojukwu. In the BIAFRA war which followed Gowon did not take field command, and helped to reconcile the defeated Ibo people after the war ended in 1970. He was largely responsible for the creation of the ECONOMIC COMMUNITY OF WEST AFRICAN STATES. By 1975 he was emerging as an international figure, but within Nigeria corruption was rife and he was deposed by the army in July 1975.

Gracchus, Gaius Sempronius (c. 158–121 BC) Roman tribune in 123 and 122 BC; brother of Tiberius Sempronius GRACCHUS. He introduced extensive reforms to alleviate poverty and curb senatorial corruption and abuse of power. Innovations included the introduction of a corn subsidy and the foundation of an overseas colony in the territory of Carthage. He lost popularity when it became clear that he wanted to extend the franchise to Latins and Italians. In 121 a violent incident occurred among his following and the Senate empowered the consul to take strong action. Gaius and his supporters were hounded and killed.

Gracchus, Tiberius Sempronius (168–133 BC) Roman tribune in 133 BC. He introduced a bill to repossess illegal holdings of the 'public land' and redistribute this recovered land among the needy. He bypassed the SENATE and deposed a colleague who attempted to veto him. His disregard of the Senate's authority provoked a violent reaction and when he sought re-election and massed his supporters, the extremists in the Senate, claiming to uphold law and order, charged the crowd and killed many, including Tiberius himself.

Graf Spee PLATE, BATTLE OF THE RIVER.

Grafton, Augustus Henry Fitzroy, 3rd Duke of (1735–1811) British statesman, Prime Minister (1768–70). He was first Lord of the Treasury until PITT the Elder's resignation from office. Although he favoured a conciliatory policy towards the Americans, he was overruled in cabinet. He handled WILKES's return from exile badly, and was subjected to ferocious personal attacks by 'JUNIUS'. He held office again under NORTH in 1771 and under SHELBURNE in 1782, but played little part in politics thereafter.

Gramsci, Antonio (1891–1937) Italian social theorist. As a young man, Gramsci was a revolutionary socialist, active in promoting factory councils as the basis of a socialist society. He helped to found the Italian Communist Party in 1921, but was arrested in 1926 and remained in prison until his death. In *Prison Notebooks* (1947), he expounded a form of MARXISM that played down the determining role of economics in social change. According to Gramsci, human consciousness was by no means a simple reflection of the material world, but played an active and independent role in shaping that world. Thus the key to the struggle between capitalist and working classes was the battle of ideas in which the latter sought to overthrow the hegemony of the former and to become the dominant intellectual force. This meant that Marxists should pay less attention to economics and more to winning control of the cultural institutions through which ideas were disseminated. Gramsci's ideas were later influential among the NEW LEFT.

Granada A province in south-eastern Spain, probably of Roman origin, with the city of Granada as its capital. Granada was conquered by Moorish invaders and survived as a Muslim state long after virtually all the rest of Spain had been seized by the Christians. The Alhambra, an old Moorish citadel and royal palace, gives an indication of the splendour of Moorish civilization in Granada. It finally submitted easily to FERDINAND V and Isabella in 1491. By 1609 the Jews and Moriscos (Muslim converts to Christianity) had been expelled and the INQUISITION was at work in the province. Granada never regained the influence it had enjoyed in Muslim hands.

Granby, John Manners, Marquis of (1721–70) British army officer. He became a hero during the SEVEN YEARS WAR. He was made commander-in-chief of the British army in 1766, but was subjected to bitter political attacks. Unnerved by such savage criticism, and in declining health, he resigned most of his public offices in 1770, and died in debt.

Grand Alliance, War of the NINE YEARS WAR.

Grand Canal, China (Da Yunhe) The world's longest CANAL, extending 1,700 km (1,100 miles). Parts of the 1,000-km (620-mile) southern section were built as early as the 4th century BC, but this whole section was rebuilt between 607 AD and 610, serving to transport grain from the lower Jinsha Jiang (Yangtze) River to the cities of Kaifeng and Luoyang. The northern section of the canal, from Huaian to Beijing, was built between 1280 and 1293, by the engineers Li Yue and Lu Chi. The section crossing the Shandong foothills, completed in 1283, was the earliest example of a 'summit level' canal (one which crosses a watershed). Since its completion, the canal has been periodically enlarged and rebuilt, and some sections are today used by vessels of up to 2,000 tonnes.

Grand Remonstrance (1641) A document drawn up by opposition members of the English LONG PARLIAMENT, indicting the rule of CHARLES I since 1625 and containing drastic proposals for reform of Church and state. Although it passed the House of COMMONS by just 11 votes, with swords being drawn in the chamber over the question of its printing, many saw it as a vote of no confidence in the king. It drove Charles into his disastrous attempt to arrest its prime movers, the so-called FIVE MEMBERS, an act of force that further alienated opposition Members of Parliament.

Grand Siècle The age of LOUIS XIV (1643–1715), the period of France's greatest magnificence, when it replaced Spain as the dominant power in Europe and established its cultural pre-eminence. This pre-eminence was not surprising: France was under strong political control, agriculturally fertile, and its population of some 19 to 20 million was far greater than that of any other European state. The genius of RICHELIEU as chief minister (1624–42) had established the authority of the monarchy and achieved a far greater degree of internal unity for France than was possessed by its rivals. Europe was impressed by the splendours of the court of VERSAILLES. French military predominance was won by the brilliant victories of CONDÉ and TURENNE and the creation of the first modern standing army. The frontiers of France were strengthened by the acquisition of Artois, Alsace, and the FRANCHE-COMTÉ. French fashions in dress were copied everywhere, as were the elegant products of French craftsmanship. The works of the French classical writers Racine, Molière, and La Fontaine were accepted as models, and French became the polite language of Europe, the language spoken by German princes and Russian nobles, the language in which international treaties and learned books were written. The splendour of the *Grand Siècle*, based as it was on heavy taxation of the poorest classes, and a commitment to expensive military campaigns, gave way after the king's death to the more turbulent climate of the 18th century.

Grand Tour A leisurely journey through Europe, often lasting several years, made by young Englishmen in the 18th and 19th centuries. The sons of the aristocracy, often accompanied by a tutor, completed their education by enriching their knowledge of classical art and of European society. The eventual destination was Italy, specifically Naples and Rome, where there were well-established colonies of expatriate painters, architects, and connoisseurs. As well as purchasing antique sculpture these patrons bought contemporary Italian paintings, including portraits of themselves, with which to adorn their houses. The wealth of Greek and Roman statuary and Italian drawings and paintings in the COUNTRY HOUSES and museums of Great Britain are the legacy of the Tour.

Granger Movement A movement begun in 1867 as a social and educational association of mid-western farmers in the USA. It was more properly known as the

National Grange of the Patrons of Husbandry. It believed in the importance of the family farm and opposed what it saw as a drift towards economic monopolies, particularly the abuse of freight rates. It never formed a major political party, but its supporters in a number of states did produce local legislation to fix maximum railway rates. These were validated by the US Supreme Court, which accepted the important new presumption that public regulation of private property was legitimate if the property provided public service. After the mid-1870s the movement declined.

Grant, Ulysses Simpson (1822–85) US general and 18th President of the USA (1869–77). He entered the AMERICAN CIVIL WAR as a colonel of volunteers in support of the Union (Northern states), and success brought him rapid promotion. He was active in most of the early engagements in the western theatre, winning the nickname 'Unconditional Surrender' for his capture of Fort Donelson (12 February 1862). As a major-general, he captured VICKSBURG in 1863 and was again successful at CHATTANOOGA before being promoted to the supreme command of all the Union forces in February 1864. Basing himself in Virginia, he maintained relentless pressure on LEE in a bloody year-long campaign in which Lee was finally forced to abandon Richmond and surrender at APPOMATTOX, bringing the war to an end. Grant served briefly as Secretary of War (1867–68) before being twice elected as Republican President of the USA. His Presidency saw the collapse of the RECONSTRUCTION programme in the South. One of the greatest of all US soldiers, Grant was also one of the least successful US presidents.

Granville, John Carteret, 1st Earl of (1690–1763) British statesman. He was at first Tory in sympathy, but he welcomed the Hanoverian succession and was employed as a diplomat by STANHOPE, who recognized his talent. WALPOLE saw him as a potential rival and sent him to Ireland as Lord Lieutenant (1724). As the opposition to Walpole grew, Carteret became a leading member of it, and on Walpole's fall in 1742 he dominated the new ministry. Yet he relied too exclusively on royal support, and in 1744 he was ousted by Henry PELHAM and the Duke of NEWCASTLE who persuaded George II to dismiss him. He remained in politics, but without power.

Grattan, Henry (1746–1820) Irish statesman, a champion of Irish independence. He was born and educated in Dublin, where he trained as a barrister and entered the Irish Parliament in 1775. A brilliant orator, he led the movement to repeal POYNINGS' LAW, which made all Irish legislation subject to the approval of the British Parliament. After considerable agitation the British government yielded and repealed the Act (1782). He also strongly opposed the ACT OF UNION (1801), which merged the British and Irish parliaments. In 1806 he became member for Dublin in the British House of Commons and devoted the rest of his life to the cause of CATHOLIC EMANCIPATION.

Gravettian culture UPPER PALAEOLITHIC.

Graziani, Rodolfo (1882–1955) Italian general and colonial administrator. He was governor of Italian Somaliland (1935) and, after his success in the Ethiopian War, was made viceroy of Ethiopia. He commanded the Italian forces in Libya that invaded Egypt in September 1940 and reached Sidi Barrani, where he was routed by the British under WAVELL. In Mussolini's rump government of 1943–44 he was defence minister. Arrested in 1945 for collaboration with the Germans after the Italian armistice (1943), he was released in 1950 and became active in the Italian Neo-Fascist Party.

Great Awakening An American revivalist movement, which was a response to the growing formalism and ARMINIANISM of early 18th-century American Christianity. Though revivals began in New Jersey in 1719, Jonathan EDWARDS's preaching, and the resultant conversions in the 1730s gave it widespread recognition and influenced the WESLEYS. George WHITEFIELD's mission (1739–41) won many converts from Pennsylvania to Maine, but his followers Gilbert Tennent and James Davenport precipitated schisms in both Congregational and Presbyterian Churches, which also affected colonial politics. In Virginia, Samuel Davies led revivals (1748–53) among the 'New Side' Presbyterians. Baptists and Methodists also embraced the new movement. By questioning established authority, founding new colleges, and revivifying evangelical zeal, it helped to prepare the revolutionary generation in America.

Greater East Asia Co-Prosperity Sphere The pseudo-political and economic union of Japanese-dominated Asian and Pacific territories during World War II. In the aftermath of Japan's dramatic conquests of 1941–42, some nationalist leaders (for example, Indonesia's SUKARNO and Burma's AUNG SAN) collaborated with the Japanese for tactical reasons. However, the hardships wrought by the Japanese (principally through their requisitioning of supplies and use of forced labour) soon disabused the local populations about Japan's intentions. By the end of the war, the Co-Prosperity Sphere had become an object of hatred and ridicule.

Great Exhibition A major international trade exhibition held in London in 1851 under the sponsorship of Prince Albert. It was housed in the vast Crystal Palace, designed by Joseph Paxton (1801–65), built in London's Hyde Park entirely of glass and iron, except for the flooring and joists. The exhibition, which lasted 23 weeks, attracted 17,000 exhibitors and more than six million visitors. The profits were invested, and are still being used to promote education and science today. The Crystal Palace was dismantled and moved to the London suburb of Sydenham, where it burnt down in 1936. Outwardly, the exhibition presented the UK in an unassailable position as the world's greatest manufacturing nation, although in reality British industry was already in decline and being overtaken by Europe and the USA. One important result of the exhibition was to create a consciously Victorian visual style and, through the newly established School of Design, to encourage industrial design. (See illustration.)

Great Leap Forward (1958–60) In the China of MAO ZEDONG, a drive for industrial and agricultural expansion through 'backyard' industries in the countryside: vastly increased production quotas were to be reached by the people's devotion to patriotic and socialist ideals. Massive increases in the quantity of production were announced, but quality and distribution posed serious problems. In agriculture, COMMUNES became almost universal, but disastrous harvests resulting in famine with an estimated 13 million victims discredited the

Great Exhibition   *An exterior view of the Great Exhibition of 1851, showing the Crystal Palace.*

Leap. As its most important advocate, Mao Zedong, took a back seat until the late 1960s: the CULTURAL REVOLUTION can be seen partly as his attempt to reintroduce radical policies.

Great Northern War NORTHERN WAR.

Great Plague (1664–65) A disastrous epidemic, mainly confined to London and south-east England. Bubonic plague had recurred at intervals since the Middle Ages, but there had been no serious outbreak for 30 years and its violent reappearance was not expected. About a fifth of London's population of almost half a million died. Business in the city came to a standstill. The court and all those able to move into the countryside prudently did so, as the disease was less virulent there. It reached the village of Eyam in Derbyshire, however, in a box of infected clothes, and in order to prevent its spread the villagers agreed to isolate themselves: nearly 300 of the population of 350 died. The ROYAL SOCIETY conducted post-mortems to try to establish the cause of the plague, but without success. At the height of the epidemic plague pits were dug to receive the dead, and hand-carts were taken from house to house, collecting the bodies. The FIRE OF LONDON in the following year destroyed many of the close-packed slums in which the plague flourished, and after 1665 the disease disappeared from London.

great power A state seen as playing a major role in international politics. A great power possesses economic, diplomatic, and military strength and influence, and its interests extend beyond its own borders. The term is usually associated with the emergence of Austria, Russia, Prussia, France, and Great Britain as great powers in Europe after the Congress of Vienna in 1815; they worked together under a loose agreement known as the Concert of Europe. After World War I, the USA grew in importance, while after World War II, the USA and the Soviet Union, through their industrial strength, global

influence, and nuclear capabilities, attained the status of 'superpowers', and world events became dominated by bipolarity. Since the collapse of the Soviet Union in 1991, the only superpower is the USA, though China's growing economic and military strength may assure it superpower status by 2000. The UK and France have declined from their former great power status, although they are still recognized by the UNITED NATIONS, together with the USA, Russia, and China, as permanent members of the UNITED NATIONS SECURITY COUNCIL with power of veto. The number of great powers at any time is considered a key feature of the international system, important in determining the level and nature of war.

Great Schism (1378–1417) A breach in the Roman Catholic Church resulting from the removal of the papacy from Italy to France in 1309. Feuds among the Italian cardinals and their allies among the Italian nobility led to Pope Clement V (1305–14) moving the papal residence from Rome to Avignon in southern France. French interests came to dominate papal policy and the popes, notorious for their luxurious way of life, commanded scant respect. An attempt to return the papacy to Rome was followed by schism as two rival popes were elected by the cardinals, Urban VI by the Roman faction and Clement VI by the French faction. The period of popes and rival ANTIPOPES lasted until the Council of CONSTANCE (1417) elected Pope Martin V of the Roman party and deposed his French rival. The division of the papacy discredited the Church and was criticized by those demanding reform, notably WYCLIF.

Great Trek, the In the 1830s and 1840s, the movement northwards of Boers (Dutch settlers in South Africa) to escape from British administration in the Cape Colony. From 1835 onwards parties of Voortrekkers reached NATAL, where in 1837 Zulu resistance provoked them to kill some 3,000 Zulus at the Battle of BLOOD RIVER in revenge for the death of their leader, Piet Retief. Natal became a British colony in 1843 and migration continued northwards into the Orange River country and the TRANSVAAL.

Great Wall of China A fortification built across northern China as a protection against the nomadic tribes of Mongolia and Manchuria. By the 3rd century BC some Chinese frontier states had built defensive walls. The first Qin emperor SHI HUANGDI ordered that these walls should be joined together and extended, using the forced labour of vast gangs of men and women, many of whom perished. The course of his wall was from the Gulf of Liaodong 2,250 km (1,400 miles) across mountain, steppe, and desert to southern Mongolia. The wall was extended by the HAN to Yumen (Jade Gate) in Gansu province in order to facilitate their expansion into Central Asia. Thereafter much of the wall was rebuilt or reconstructed on different routes, notably by the NORTHERN WEI, the SUI, and lastly by the MING. The wall as seen today is largely of Ming construction. It is approximately 7.5 m (25 feet) high and 3.75 m (12 feet) wide at its top and is constructed of earth, with stone facings on the eastern sections. The wall acted as a demarcation line between the steppe and cultivated land. If adequately manned it could delay raiding parties, but frequently the steppe-dweller was able to ride through its undefended gates. The borders of QING CHINA were far to the north of the wall, which ceased to have any military significance after 1644.

Greece A maritime, mountainous country in south-east Europe, bounded by Albania, Macedonia, and Bulgaria to the north, and by Turkey to the east. The many islands round its long coastline include Corfu, Crete, the Cyclades, and the Sporades. The peninsula is bounded by the Ionian, Mediterranean, and Aegean Seas.

Physical. Thrace in the north-east is mainly low-lying, as are the river deltas of Macedonia. Most of the mainland, however, is a peninsula of mountains, the highest being Olympus. These continue southward beyond the Gulf of Corinth and its isthmus and on to the high Peloponnese peninsula. In winter the northern plateaux are cold and suitable only for sheep grazing. One-third of the country can be cultivated; in areas where the climate is truly Mediterranean, crops include tobacco, tomatoes, and vines.

Economy. Both agriculture and industry are important to the Greek economy, and the manufacturing sector experienced large growth in the 1980s. Important exports include fruit and vegetables, clothing, petroleum products, textiles, and yarns. In addition, shipping and tourism are substantial earners of foreign exchange.

History. Greek history begins *c.* 2000–1700 BC with the arrival in the mainland of Greek-speaking peoples from the north. There followed the MYCENAEAN CIVILIZATION which flourished until overthrown by the DORIANS at the end of the 12th century BC. After an obscure period of history (the Greek 'Dark Ages') the city-state (POLIS) emerged.

In the early 5th century the Greeks repulsed Persian attempts to annex their land. ATHENS and SPARTA were now the major sea and land powers respectively, and after a prolonged struggle it was Sparta who by 404 had crushed Athens and destroyed the Athenian empire in the PELOPONNESIAN WAR. In the 4th century THEBES toppled Sparta, but Greece as a whole was soon forced to bow

before an outside conqueror — PHILIP II of Macedonia. After the death of his son, ALEXANDER THE GREAT, the Greek world was dominated by the Hellenistic kingdoms with the cities of Greece playing comparatively minor parts in the power struggle. Then Rome intervened in the MACEDONIAN WARS, until the year 146 BC saw the defeat of the ACHAEAN LEAGUE, the sacking of Corinth, and the final incorporation of Greece into the Roman empire. Later it was part of the BYZANTINE EMPIRE, but fell under the control of the Ottoman Turks in 1460. It remained under Turkish jurisdiction, apart from a brief period in the late 17th and early 18th centuries when Venice controlled parts of the country, until independence in the early 19th century.

The GREEK WAR OF INDEPENDENCE (1821–33) resulted in the establishment of an independent Greece, with Duke Otto of Bavaria as king. Otto was deposed in 1862 and a Danish prince, William, installed, taking the title George I of the Hellenes (1863–1913). A military coup established a republic (1924–35). GEORGE II was restored in 1935 but fled into exile in 1941. After repulsing an attempted invasion by Italian forces in 1940, Greece was occupied by the Germans in World War II, and the country suffered bitter fighting between rival factions of communists and royalists. The monarchy was restored by the British in 1946, and civil war broke out, lasting until 1949, when the communists were defeated. With the help of aid from the USA, recovery and reconstruction began. Field-Marshal Alexandros Papagos became civilian Prime Minister (1952–55). In 1967 a military coup took place. King Constantine II fled to Rome and government by a military junta (the 'Colonels') lasted for seven years, the monarchy being abolished in 1973. A civilian republic was established in 1974 and in the 1981 general election Andreas Papandreou became the first socialist Prime Minister, remaining in office until 1989. In 1981 Greece had joined the European Community, whose agricultural policies boosted its economy; but as tariff barriers were reduced, a balance-of-payments crisis developed. During 1992 strong opposition emerged to recognizing the proposed republic of Macedonia (see MACEDONIA, FORMER YUGOSLAV REPUBLIC OF), since Greece regards its own northern province as having sole right to the name. This issue and that of the ailing economy led to the fall of the right-wing government of Constantine Mitsotakis in June 1993. Papandreou was subsequently returned to power; his government officially opposed the recognition of Macedonia by other EUROPEAN UNION countries. A dispute over territorial waters in the Aegean threatened war with Turkey in late 1994 and relations between Greece and Turkey further deteriorated in June 1995. In 1996 Costas Simitis became Prime Minister, replacing Papandreou, who had resigned due to ill-health.

CAPITAL:	Athens
AREA:	131,957 sq km (50,949 sq miles)
POPULATION:	10.493 million (1996)
CURRENCY:	1 drachma = 100 lepta
RELIGIONS:	Greek Orthodox 97.6%; Roman Catholic 0.4%; Protestant 0.1%; Muslim 1.5%
ETHNIC GROUPS:	Greek 95.5%; Macedonian 1.5%; Turkish 0.9%; Albanian 0.6%
LANGUAGES:	Greek (official); minority languages

ORGANIZATIONS: UN; EU; NATO; OECD; Council of Europe;
CSCE

Greek city-state POLIS.

Greek-Persian wars Conflicts that dominated the
history of the eastern Mediterranean in the first half of
the 5th century BC. In 499 BC the Greek cities of Ionia in
Asia Minor revolted from the Persian empire. With
some short-lived support from Athens and Eretria, they
captured and burnt the important city of Sardis, but
gradually the Persians regained control, the Greek fleet
being finally crushed at Lade in 494. In 490 a Persian
expeditionary force sailed across the Aegean. The
capture of Eretria – the first goal – was achieved after a
week-long siege and with help from Eretrian traitors.
The Persians then landed in Attica but after a defeat at
MARATHON they were forced to withdraw to Persia.

In 480 a much larger invasion force threatened
Greece, advancing along the northern and western
shores of the Aegean. A small Greek army and a large
Greek fleet were positioned respectively at THERMOPYLAE

and Artemisium, but despite vigorous fighting on land
and sea the Greeks were forced to withdraw to the
Isthmus of Corinth. With central Greece lost, the
Athenians evacuated their city, while the Greek fleet, at
THEMISTOCLES' urging, lured the Persians into battle off
SALAMIS. In these narrow waters the Greek warships had
the advantage and won a decisive victory which caused
the Persian king XERXES to withdraw to Asia. Mardonius,
his second-in-command, remained to continue the
campaign with the army. In 479 Greeks and Persians
met at PLATAEA. The Greeks were eventually successful,
the Spartans and their Tegean allies ensuring victory
when they overcame the élite Immortals (the Persian
royal bodyguards) and killed Mardonius. Meanwhile a
Greek fleet was winning another great victory off
Mycale in Asia Minor. Soon afterwards some of the
Greeks formed the DELIAN LEAGUE to be the instrument
by which they would continue the war against the
Persians.

Greek religion The religion of the ancient Greek
world. It was polytheistic, involving the worship of
several gods and goddesses. The most important deities

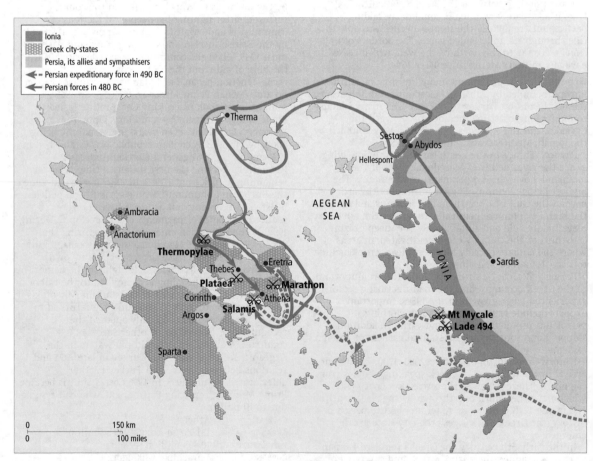

Greek–Persian wars (499–479 BC) *The revolt of the Greek cities in Ionia against the Persian empire was eventually put down, but
it demonstrated to the Greeks that resistance to Persia was not hopeless. Their defeat of Xerxes' punitive expedition at Marathon
further inspired resistance; it also ensured a renewal of the Persian attack (delayed until 480 BC by a revolt in Egypt). The Greek
victory over the Persian fleet at Salamis broke the lines of supply to the Persian land forces and prepared the way for the
destruction of Mardonius' army in 479.*

were the sky-god Zeus (ruler of Olympus), his wife Hera (goddess of marriage), Poseidon (god of sea and earthquakes), the virgin goddess Athene (learning and the arts), Apollo and his sister Artemis (sun and moon, the one patron of music and poetry, the other of chastity and hunting), Hephaestus (fire and metalwork), Aphrodite (love and beauty), Ares (war), Demeter (crops), Hestia (hearth and home), and Hermes, the messenger of the gods. Although all were revered, different cities had different individual gods as their special patrons. Apollo's shrine at DELPHI was recognized throughout the Greek world. Despite the efforts of poets and philosophers the Greek gods never lost their essentially anthropomorphic character, and Greek religion largely lacked that insistence on high standards of personal morality which is associated with Christianity, Judaism, and Islam, and had no developed concept of an 'afterlife'. Its influence was weakened by some of the more mystical aspects of Near-Eastern religion, especially in the period after ALEXANDER THE GREAT's conquest of Asia Minor and Egypt. It was finally superseded, first by Christianity, and then by Islam.

Greek War of Independence (1821–32) The revolt by Greek subjects of the OTTOMAN EMPIRE against Turkish domination. It had its origins in the nationalistic ideas of the Hetairia Philike ('Society of Friends'), who chose Alexander YPSILANTI, a Russian general, and son of the ruler of Wallachia, to lead the revolt. Links were established with Romanian peasants, Serb rebels, and Ali Pasha, the warlord of western Greece. Ypsilanti crossed into Turkish territory in March 1821, but only after his defeat in June did the Greeks rebel. Although atrocities took place on both sides, the revolt gained the popular support of the Christian world and many foreign volunteers (of whom Lord Byron, who went out in 1823, was the most celebrated) joined the Greek forces. By the end of 1821 the Greeks had achieved striking successes on land and sea and in January 1822 an assembly met to declare Greece independent. Four years later, however, MEHEMET ALI of Egypt reconquered the Peloponnese and threatened to restore Turkish control. At the Treaty of London in 1827, Britain and Russia offered to mediate and secure an autonomous Greek state. When the Turks refused, Britain, Russia, and France sent a combined fleet which destroyed the Egyptian fleet at Navarino (1827). The following year the Russian army seized Adrianople and threatened Constantinople. The Turks agreed to make peace (1829), and the Conference of London (1832) confirmed Greek independence. The following year a Bavarian prince, Otto I, was crowned King of GREECE.

Greenback Party A minor political party in the USA, formed in 1874. During the AMERICAN CIVIL WAR the Lincoln government had issued some $400 million of paper money not backed by gold ('greenbacks'), to meet rising Union (Northern) wartime costs. After the war a Greenback Movement urged the retention of this currency. In 1874 the Greenback Party demanded the issue of additional greenbacks to stimulate the economy. However, it could not prevent conservative banking interests from obtaining a Resumption Act (1875) which provided that all greenbacks must be redeemable by the GOLD STANDARD. The Party fought unsuccessfully to have this Act repealed. It won support in Congress (1878) for a general expansion in currency,

backed by gold. After that it disappeared, currency expansionists then turning their attention to silver with a FREE SILVER movement.

Greene, Nathanael (1742–86) American general who led his colony's troops at the Siege of Boston (1775–76) and fought at Long Island, Trenton, BRANDYWINE, GERMANTOWN, and Monmouth. In command in the south (1780–81) he waged a brilliant hit-and-run campaign against CORNWALLIS, eventually recapturing most of the region.

Greenland The world's largest island (2,175,600 sq km/840,000 sq miles), lying more than two-thirds within the Arctic Circle and extending from the Arctic Ocean into the North Atlantic. A part of Denmark, it has internal autonomy.

Physical. Separated from Canada's Ellesmere Island to the north by only 25.6 km (16 miles), Greenland is the most northerly land in the world, its interior covered by thick sheets of ice that conceal 90% of the land area. The coasts are mountainous but are cut by long fiords and surrounded by many smaller islands. Although beset by snow and fogs, the southerly coasts have temperatures above freezing for most of the year, and it is here that cryolite (an aluminium ore) is found. Other resources include uranium, zinc, and lead.

History. Greenland was first sighted in the early 10th century by the Icelander Gunnbjörn Ulf-Krakuson, but it was not until 985–86 that it was settled by ERIC THE RED. Climatic shifts in the North Atlantic rendered the south-western region habitable, and here Eric founded Brattahlid (modern Qagssiarssuk), known as the 'Eastern Settlement'; to the north Gardar, the 'Western Settlement', was established near Julianehaab. Farming was difficult but was supplemented by fishing and the export of furs and walrus ivory. Christianity came with Leif Ericsson *c.* 1000. A chapel was eventually replaced by 12 parish churches, a monastery and nunnery, and a cathedral at Gardar by the 12th century. At its height the population reached *c.* 3,000, but the BLACK DEATH caused it to decrease in the 14th century. The settlements persisted in a poverty-stricken state until their eventual disappearance in the 15th century. However, DENMARK, which had continued to claim the island from 1261 onward, established a colony on Greenland in 1721. Although it remains a sovereign territory of Denmark, Greenland gained self-government in 1979. It joined the EC briefly, but left in 1985.

Green Mountain Boys An association of guerrilla fighters from Vermont, active in the American War of INDEPENDENCE. They were originally organized in 1771 by Ethan ALLEN to defend their settlements against New York claims. Named after Vermont's mountain chain, they came to support the patriot cause, assisting in the capture of TICONDEROGA (1775), the Battle of BENNINGTON, and Burgoyne's surrender at SARATOGA (1777).

Greensboro incident (1960) An incident in the US CIVIL RIGHTS campaign. Four young Black students staged a sit-in at a segregated lunch counter in Greensboro, North Carolina. This led to similar sit-ins in many other Southern towns and sparked off waves of protest against the segregation laws and practices.

Gregorian calendar The modified CALENDAR, also known as the 'New Style', introduced by Pope Gregory

XIII in 1582. It is a modification of the JULIAN CALENDAR and is now in use throughout most of the Christian world. The Gregorian calendar adapted the Julian calendar to bring it into closer conformity with astronomical data and to correct errors which had accumulated because the Julian year of 365.25 days was 11 minutes 10 seconds too long. Ten days were suppressed in 1582 and, to prevent further displacement, Gregory provided that of the centenary years (1600, 1700, etc.) only those exactly divisible by 400 should be counted as leap years. The Gregorian calendar was adopted in Great Britain in 1752, by which time 11 days needed to be suppressed.

Gregory I, St (the Great) (540–604) Pope (590–604). When he became pope Italy was in a state of crisis, devastated by floods, famine, and Lombard invasions, and the position of the Church was threatened by the imperial power at CONSTANTINOPLE; it was owing to Gregory that many of these problems were overcome. He made a separate peace with the Lombards in 592–93, and (acting independently of the imperial authorities) appointed governors to the Italian cities, thus establishing the temporal power of the papacy. One of his greatest achievements was the conversion of England to Christianity, by St AUGUSTINE OF CANTERBURY. Throughout his papacy he effectively opposed the double assault on the Church from paganism and the ARIAN heresy. His interest in music led to developments in the plain chant which bears his name – the Gregorian Chant.

Gregory VII, St (Hildebrand) (c. 1021–85) Pope (1073–85). He argued for the moral reform of the Church and that the Christian West should be united under the overall leadership of the papacy. The latter was opposed by many secular rulers and the prolonged struggles that followed have come to be known as the INVESTITURE contests. His most formidable opponent was the Holy Roman Emperor Henry IV. When in 1077 he submitted to the pope at CANOSSA papal supremacy seemed nearer. However, Henry's submission was merely a tactical one and he later attacked Rome itself, forcing the pope to retreat to Salerno in southern Italy, where he died. He urged celibacy of the clergy and opposed SIMONY.

Gregory of Tours, St (538–94) Frankish churchman and historian in the court of the Frankish king Childebert II. He was educated by his uncle, St Gall, and resisted attacks on the Church during the reign of King Chilperic. Of his many works the best known is his vast *Historia Francorum* ('History of the Franks') a source of early MEROVINGIAN history. He was canonized soon after his death.

Grenada A state comprising the southernmost of the Windward Islands in the Caribbean and several small islands, part of the Grenadines archipelago.

Physical. The island of Grenada is 310 sq km (120 sq miles) in area and contains rugged, forested mountains, rising to Mount Saint Catherine at 838 m (2,749 feet), with crater lakes and springs. The mountains are of volcanic origin and enclose valleys where bananas, spices, and sugar cane are grown.

Economy. Grenada's economy is primarily agricultural, although there is limited manufacturing industry, mostly food-processing, and tourism is a growing source of revenue. The principal exports are nutmeg, bananas, cocoa, and mace. Other crops include coconuts, sugar cane, and citrus. There is a high level of foreign debt.

History. Grenada was discovered by Columbus in 1498. Colonized by the French governor of Martinique in 1650, it passed to the control of the French crown in 1674. The island was conquered by the British during the SEVEN YEARS WAR and ceded to them by the Treaty of Paris (1763). An uprising in 1795 against British rule, supported by many slaves, was put down the following year, and Grenada remained a British colony for almost two centuries. Universal adult suffrage was granted in 1950 when the United Labour Party, led by Matthew Gairy, emerged. The Windward Islands were granted self-government in 1956 and became a member of the West Indies Federation (1958–62) (see WEST INDIAN INDEPENDENCE). Following the break-up of the federation, the various Windward Islands sought separate independence. This was gained by Grenada in 1974, when Gairy became Prime Minister. He was deposed in a bloodless coup (1979) by Maurice Bishop (1944–83), leader of a left-wing group, the New Jewel Movement, who proclaimed the People's Revolutionary Government (PRG) and encouraged closer relations with Cuba and the Soviet Union. He was overthrown and killed in a coup attempt in 1983. Military intervention by the USA prevented a Marxist revolutionary council from taking power. US troops left the island in December 1983, after the re-establishment of democratic government. Under Prime Minister Herbert Blaise (1984–89) political stability was restored, with some economic success which continued through the 1980s. By the end of the decade, however, difficulties with the economy resulted in an INTERNATIONAL MONETARY FUND austerity programme. In June 1995 a general election brought the New National Party (NNP) to power under Prime Minister Keith Mitchell.

CAPITAL:	St George's
AREA:	345 sq km (133 sq miles)
POPULATION:	97,900 (1996)
CURRENCY:	East Caribbean dollar
RELIGIONS:	Roman Catholic 64.4%; Anglican 20.7%; Seventh-day Adventist 3.1%; Methodist 2.1%
ETHNIC GROUPS:	Black 84.0%; mixed 12.0%; East Indian 3.0%; White 1.0%
LANGUAGES:	English (official)
INTERNATIONAL ORGANIZATIONS:	UN; OAS; CARICOM; Commonwealth

Grenville, George (1712–70) British statesman, Prime Minister (1763–65). As premier he was largely responsible for the government's mishandling of the WILKES affair and also for the effort to raise revenue in America that resulted in the STAMP ACT of 1765. George III came to dislike him and some of his fellow politicians objected to his authoritanism, although his budgets were well-received by backbenchers in Parliament. His failures led to his dismissal from office in 1765.

Grenville, Sir Richard (1542–91) English naval commander. He became Member of Parliament for Cornwall (1571), led the unsuccessful expedition to colonize ROANOKE ISLAND planned by his cousin Sir Walter RALEIGH, and supplied three ships to the force assembled against the Spanish Armada. He died after an epic battle off the Azores, during which his ship *Revenge* held out for 15 hours against a powerful Spanish fleet.

Grenville, William Wyndham, Baron (1759–1834) British statesman. He entered the House of Commons in 1782 and served as Secretary of State for Foreign Affairs (1791–1801) under William Pitt the Younger. After Pitt's death he formed the so-called 'Ministry of all the Talents' (February 1806–March 1807). Attempts to end the NAPOLEONIC WARS failed, but a bill for the abolition of the British overseas slave trade succeeded, following a resolution introduced by Charles James FOX. A bill to emancipate Roman Catholics, however, was rejected by George III, and Grenville resigned from politics.

Gresham, Sir Thomas (*c.* 1519–79) English cloth merchant, financier, diplomat, and the founder of the Royal Exchange. His greatest skill lay in negotiating loans for the English government, especially in Antwerp after 1551. He worked with William CECIL, providing him with valuable information from the Continent, and exerting considerable influence over Elizabethan economic policy. He founded Gresham College in 1579 as a venue for public lectures and the ROYAL SOCIETY grew from these meetings at Gresham's house. His principal fame rests on Gresham's Law, wrongly attributed to him in the 19th century, which states that 'bad money drives out good'. According to this law, if there are two coins in circulation with different ratios of face value to intrinsic value (in terms of the precious metal content of the coins), then the coin with the relatively higher intrinsic value will tend to be taken out of circulation for hoarding or melting down.

Grey, Charles, 2nd Earl Grey (1764–1845) British statesman. Entering the House of Commons in 1786, he became an advocate of electoral reform. After he had held office briefly as Foreign Secretary in the coalition government of 1806–07, his liberal views kept him politically isolated for some years. As leader of the Whigs, he was Prime Minister (1830–34) in the government that eventually secured the passage of the first great parliamentary REFORM ACT (1832). In 1833 his government passed important factory legislation and the Act abolishing slavery throughout the British empire. He retired in 1834.

Grey, Edward, Viscount Grey of Fallodon (1862–1933) British politician. He was Foreign Secretary from 1905 to 1916, negotiating the Triple Entente (1907), which brought Britain, France, and Russia together, and in 1914 persuading a reluctant British cabinet to go to war, because Germany had violated Belgian neutrality.

Grey, Sir George (1812–98) British colonial administrator. He served as governor of South Australia (1841–45) and of New Zealand (1845–53, and 1861–68), where he oversaw the introduction of representative government and gained a reputation for suppressing rebellion and promoting the 'amalgamation' of the MAORI people into settler society. After the onset of the TARANAKI WAR, he failed in negotiations with the quasi-nationalist KINGITANGA, and invaded the Waikato in 1863. He ended his governorship in disfavour with the Colonial Office, as the war dragged on.

Grey, Lady Jane (1537–54) The 'Nine Days' Queen' of England in July 1553. As a descendant of HENRY VII's younger daughter Mary, she had some claim to the English throne, and her father-in-law, John DUDLEY, persuaded EDWARD VI to name her as his successor. MARY I ousted her easily, and she was beheaded after her father had incriminated her further by participating in WYATT'S REBELLION.

Griffith, Arthur (1872–1922) Irish statesman. His initial goal was an independent Irish parliament under a dual monarchy of England and Ireland. He helped to found the SINN FEIN Party in 1905. Following the emergence of the militant ULSTER VOLUNTEER Movement in 1912, Sinn Fein became a militant political force and Griffith took part in gun-running for the Irish Volunteers in 1914. He opposed Irish participation in World War I, but did not take part in the EASTER RISING of 1916. Imprisoned by the British (1916–18), he was elected to the Westminster Parliament in 1918, and became instrumental in forming the Dáil Éireann in 1919. When the Irish Republic was declared in 1919 he became Vice-President. He led the Irish delegation that signed the Anglo-Irish Treaty (1921) establishing the Irish Free State (see IRELAND, REPUBLIC OF).

Grotius, Hugo (1583–1645) Dutch jurist and scholar. He distinguished himself in both literary and diplomatic fields. In 1613 he supported his patron OLDENBARNEVELDT in the dispute between the Arminians and the Counter-Remonstrants, for which he was arrested by Maurice of Nassau, tried, and sentenced to life imprisonment. His wife helped him to escape and he took refuge in Paris, entered Sweden's diplomatic service, and was Swedish ambassador to France from 1634 to 1645. His best-known work, *De Jure Belli ac Pacis* ('Concerning the Law of War and Peace', 1625), is generally considered to be the first definitive book on international law.

Group of 7 (G7) An association of the world's seven richest industrial democracies. The G7 was set up in 1975 with the aim of co-ordinating efforts to promote growth and stability in the world economy, and to bring the world's key exchange rates into line. The original five members (France, Japan, the UK, the USA, and West Germany) were joined in 1976 by Canada and Italy, with the EC acquiring observer status in 1977. The G7 has no permanent headquarters, but holds regular meetings between the finance ministers and central-bank governors of member countries. The annual meeting of the G7 heads of state is of growing importance, and now includes discussion of key foreign policy issues. The 1991 summit was marked by the invitation to the then Soviet President Mikhail Gorbachev to attend post-summit discussions on the Soviet economy's transition to a FREE MARKET. Formal admission of Russia to the group seems likely before the year 2000. Attempts to agree on the reduction of agricultural subsidies in order to facilitate the GENERAL AGREEMENT ON TARIFFS AND TRADE talks have been another crucial debate in recent summits.

Guam (USA) Largest and southernmost of the Marianas island chain in the Pacific Ocean which, situated at the junction of the Philippine and Pacific plates, is on a ridge beside the Marianas Trench, the deepest in the world. Guam is volcanic and rises to 400 m (over 1,300 feet). The interior is jungle. Despite its size — 540 sq km (210 sq miles) — it has few natural resources. Discovered by Magellan in 1521, Guam was ruled by Spain (1688–1898), when together with the Philippines it was ceded to the USA after the SPANISH–AMERICAN WAR. Between 1941 and 1944 it was in Japanese hands. It has since been a US naval and air base, and remains one of the most important centres for US strategic intelligence.

Guangzhou (Canton) The capital of Guangdong province, China. It lies on the Zhu Jiang (Pearl River). Under the TANG ARAB and Jewish traders had quarters there and enjoyed extraterritorial rights, not being subject to Chinese laws. From the 16th century it was a trading port for European vessels. After 1757 it was the only port in China open to Europeans, who were restricted to 13 'factories' (trading posts) outside its walls, where they brought tea and silk, and after *c.* 1800 sold increasing quantities of opium.

Guatemala A Central American country, bounded by Mexico on its north and west and by Honduras and El Salvador on its south-east. It has a southern coast on the Pacific Ocean and access to the Caribbean Sea on the east, where it is also bounded by Belize.

Physical. A very high range of volcanic mountains crosses Guatemala from east to west and rivers water the lower slopes, which support crops of coffee. The plateaux have a mild climate, the lowlands a hot one. Earthquakes are frequent, the country lying near a junction of crustal plates.

Economy. Guatemala has a primarily agricultural economy, the largest in Central America, with coffee, cotton, sugar, and bananas accounting for half of exports. Crude oil was discovered in the 1970s, and the revenues from oil production have been used to develop manufacturing industry.

History. In prehistory Guatemala was culturally linked to the YUCATÁN peninsula and witnessed the rise of pre-Maya and MAYA civilizations. (The modern Guatemalan population is largely descended from Maya ancestors.) In the northern and central lowlands arose the great, classic Maya cities such as Tikal, Uaxactún, Altar de Sacrificios, Piedras Negras, Yaxhá, and Seibal; in the southern highlands were the cities of Zacualpa, Kaminaljuyú, Cotzumalhuapa, and others. They had political and economic connections with each other, and with prehistoric cities in southern and central Mexico, such as TEOTIHUACÁN and Monte Albán (in Oaxaca). Spanish CONQUISTADORES arrived in 1523, seeking new American conquests, and the region soon became the Audiencia (a high court with a political role) of Guatemala, under the viceroyalty of NEW SPAIN. For almost 300 years, Guatemala remained under Spanish rule. In 1821 it declared itself independent from Spain and became part of the short-lived Mexican empire of ITURBIDE. When that collapsed (1823), Guatemala helped to found the United Provinces of Central America (1823–38). Strong opposition to federation, led by Rafael Carrera, resulted in its collapse, Guatemala declaring itself an independent republic with Carrera its first President (1839–65). His successors as President became increasingly despotic. A left-wing government under Jacobo Arbenz (1951–54) instituted social reforms, before being forced to resign, following US intervention through the CENTRAL INTELLIGENCE AGENCY. Ten years of disorder were followed by the peaceful election of Julio César Méndez Montenegro as President (1966) on a moderate platform. But military intervention recurred, and during the 1970s and early 1980s there was widespread violation of human rights. In 1985 civilian rule was restored, leading to the election of Vinico

Cerezo as President the following year. In September 1991 Guatemala ended the long dispute over BELIZE, recognizing that country's existence. In 1995 Alvaro Arzu was elected President, retaining power in further elections the following year. A peace treaty was concluded in December 1996 between the government and left-wing URNG guerrillas, bringing to an end Latin America's longest civil war (35 years).

CAPITAL:	Guatemala City
AREA:	108,889 sq km (42,042 sq miles)
POPULATION:	10.928 million (1996)
CURRENCY:	1 Guatemalan quetzal = 100 centavos
RELIGIONS:	Roman Catholic 75.0% (of which Catholic/traditional syncretist 25.0%); Protestant (mostly fundamentalist) 25.0%
ETHNIC GROUPS:	Amerindian 55.0%; Ladino (Hispanic/Amerindian) 42.0%
LANGUAGES:	Spanish (official); Mayan languages
INTERNATIONAL ORGANIZATIONS:	UN; OAS

Guderian, Heinz (1888–1954) German general and tank expert. A proponent of BLITZKRIEG tactics, he used tanks in large formations in the conquest of Poland (1939) and of France (1940). As commander-in-chief of the Panzer (tank) forces, he played a leading role in the German victories of 1940–41, but was dismissed when he disagreed with Hitler's order to stand fast in the 1941–42 Soviet counter-offensive outside Moscow. In 1944 he became chief-of-staff to the German Army High Command, but in March 1945 was again dismissed, this time for advocating peace with the Western Allies.

Guelphs In medieval Germany and Italy, a political faction originating in the German Welf family, who were dukes of Saxony and Bavaria. The Welfs were the traditional opponents of the HOHENSTAUFENS in Germany and Italy (where they were known as Guelphs and the latter were known as the Ghibellines). In the 12th century the Guelph leader was HENRY THE LION and he tended to support the papacy against the aspirations of the Holy Roman Emperors. Guelph support was found mainly in the major Italian towns and cities. Their rivals were the imperial party whose strength came mainly from the great aristocratic families. In local feuds, no matter what the cause, the antagonists came to associate themselves with one or other of the opposing families whose names continued to be used for many years after the original disputes were forgotten.

guerrilla (Spanish, 'little war') A person taking part in irregular fighting by small groups acting independently. The term was coined during the PENINSULAR WAR (1807–14) to describe the Spanish partisans fighting the armies of Napoleon. From Spain the use of the word spread to South America and thence to the USA.

The essence of guerrilla warfare is to avoid full-scale military confrontation while keeping the enemy under pressure with many small-scale skirmishes. The technique is suited to harsh terrain, particularly jungle and mountainous areas, and has been used effectively by materially weak forces against militarily strong opponents, where there are few opportunities for conventional military forces to use superior firepower in well-defined military 'fronts'. It can be used as part of a much larger conventional land war, or as a means of initiating revolutionary war or wars of national iberation, but ultimate military success usually depends on transforming it into conventional warfare. John S. Mosby used guerrilla warfare tactics during the AMERICAN CIVIL WAR of 1861–65 to confuse the Federal army, and in the Arabian desert between 1916 and 1918 T. E. LAWRENCE's highly mobile mounted troops were able to contain superior Turkish forces. MAO ZEDONG, a leading proponent of guerrilla warfare, conducted a large-scale guerrilla campaign during the 1920s and 1930s against the Kuomintang and Japanese in China. It was during WORLD WAR II, however, that guerrillas became most prevalent, when RESISTANCE MOVEMENTS were formed to harass the Japanese and Germans. In post-war years they have become associated with revolutionary movements like those in South America under 'Che' GUEVARA, as well as in Asia, the Middle East, and Africa, with acts of TERRORISM spreading to urban areas.

Guesclin, Bertrand du (*c.* 1320–80) French army commander and Constable of France from 1370. He attracted attention at the Siege of Rennes (1356–57) and was promoted by the regent, CHARLES V, to the office of Constable of France. He fought in campaigns against the English, and, from 1366–69 against Spain where he was defeated and captured at the Battle of Najera in 1367. It was his conduct of the war against the English which helped Charles recover his kingdom.

Guevara (de la Serna), Ernesto 'Che' (1928–67) South American revolutionary and political leader. An Argentine by birth, he joined the pro-communist regime in Guatemala, and when this was overthrown (1954) he fled to Mexico. Here he met Fidel CASTRO and helped him prepare the GUERRILLA force which landed in Cuba in 1956. Shortly after Castro's victory Guevara was given a cabinet position and placed in charge of Cuban economic policy. He played a major role in the transfer of Cuba's traditional economic ties from the USA to the communist bloc. A guerrilla warfare strategist rather than an administrator, he moved to Bolivia (1967) in an attempt to persuade Bolivian peasants and tin-miners to take up arms against the military government. The attempt ended in failure as Guevara was captured and executed shortly thereafter. His remains were discovered in 1997 and returned to Cuba for a state funeral.

Guiana FRENCH GUIANA; GUYANA; SURINAM.

Guicciardini, Francesco (1483–1540) Italian statesman and historian. As Florentine ambassador to Aragon (1512–14), and then in the service of the papacy (1515–34), he showed outstanding administrative ability, and he also became a prolific political writer. In 1536, back in Florence, he began his monumental *Storia d'Italia* ('History of Italy'), which covered the years from 1494 to 1534. Although he died before completing the final revision, it stands as the most objective contemporary history of the country during the period of Italy's wars with France.

guild (or gild) An association of townspeople formed to provide mutual protection of trading practices. Guilds may have developed in Syria and Egypt or in Roman and Byzantine trade associations (*collegia*) but are more likely to have arisen in western Europe in the 7th century. In England they are found in the Anglo-Saxon family associations (frithgilds) which protected members' interests, including those of trade. These early benevolent associations of Europe were usually based in towns, were often religious in character – perhaps dedicated to a saint – and engaged in charity and local administration. Religious guilds, mainly concerned with devotional, charitable, and social activities, remained important in English towns and parishes throughout the Middle Ages. From the early 11th century merchants and traders combined to regulate trade. The merchant guilds they formed controlled markets, weights and measures, and tolls, and negotiated CHARTERS granting their towns borough status. They maintained the charitable work of the earlier religious guilds. However, their monopolistic character forced the small crafts and trades to form their own associations, craft guilds, before the end of the 12th century. Each craft had its own guild which set quality standards and evolved a hierarchy consisting of master, journeymen, and apprentices (serving for up to 12 years). Guilds declined from the 16th century, being unable to adapt to the emergence of new markets.

Che Guevara *Guevara's refusal to commit himself to either capitalism or orthodox communism turned him into an archetypal figure for many radical students, especially during the 1960s and 1970s.*

guillotine The instrument used to inflict capital punishment by decapitation during the FRENCH REVOLUTION. A similar device had been used in Europe since the Middle Ages and had fallen into disuse when Dr Guillotin (1738–1814) suggested its reintroduction. After satisfactory tests on dead bodies it was erected on the Place de Grève in 1792. 'La Guillotine' was used extensively during the TERROR, accounting for 1,376 victims between 10 June and 27 July 1794.

Guinea A West African country with an Atlantic coast, bounded on the north by Senegal and Mali, on the east by Côte d'Ivoire, and on the south by Liberia and Sierra Leone.

Physical. Inland from the marshy coast is a plain with large bauxite deposits. This rises to a sandstone plateau, the Fouta Djallon. Southward is the source of the River Niger; and further south still (the country bends like a hook) are large reserves of iron ore. The climate is hot; the southernmost part is drier than the coast.

Economy. Guinea has a broadly based agricultural economy: the chief crops include cassava, rice, pineapples, coffee, and palm oil. The major exports are bauxite, alumina, gold, and diamonds. Iron-ore mining is being developed.

History. From the 5th to the 8th centuries AD, the far north of modern Guinea formed part of the kingdom of GHANA. This area of the country was incorporated in the Mali Empire in the 16th century. From 1849 onwards, French encroachment upon the region increased, leading to conflict with the empire of SAMORI TOURÉ in eastern Guinea *c.* 1879–91, when Guinea became a French colony. In 1895 Guinea was made part of the huge territory of French West Africa, and remained a French colony until 1958, when a popular vote rejected membership of the FRENCH COMMUNITY, and Ahmed Sékou TOURÉ became first President. His presidency was characterized by severe unrest and repression, and almost complete isolation from the outside world, although before his death in 1984 a degree of liberalization was introduced. This trend has continued under the military regime of President Lansana Conté. The slow pace of democratization, however, together with an IMF-imposed austerity programme, led to a general strike in 1991, after which the government introduced a multiparty system. In 1993, in the country's first multiparty elections, Conté was re-elected. Sidi Touré became the country's first Prime Minister in 1996.

CAPITAL:	Conakry
AREA:	245,857 sq km (94,926 sq miles)
POPULATION:	6.903 million (1996)
CURRENCY:	1 Guinean franc = 100 centimes
RELIGIONS:	Muslim 85.0%; traditional beliefs 5.0%; Christian 1.5%
ETHNIC GROUPS:	Mande 48.0%; Peul 28.0%; Mande-fu 11.0%
LANGUAGES:	French (official); Malinke; Poulor; local languages
INTERNATIONAL ORGANIZATIONS:	UN; OAU; ECOWAS; Non-Aligned Movement

Guinea-Bissau A small tropical country on the coast of West Africa, bounded by Senegal on the north and Guinea on the south. Off-shore is the Bijagós archipelago with a score of inhabitable marshy islands.

Physical. The deeply indented coast of Guinea-Bissau, stretching for some 240 km (150 miles) from north to south, is marshy and contains the mouths of three major rivers. The interior, which extends eastward for some 300 km (185 miles), consists mainly of river valleys filled with rain forest; it rises to above 200 m (650 feet) only in the south.

Economy. Guinea-Bissau has a mainly agricultural economy, whose significant exports are cashews, fish, groundnuts, and palm kernels. Further cash crops are being developed. Bauxite and phosphate reserves are yet to be exploited. Offshore oil deposits have not been developed because of boundary disputes with Guinea and Senegal.

History. Portuguese explorers and traders were active around the coast from the mid-15th century, developing the area into a centre of the slave trade. First incorporated as part of the Portuguese Cape Verde Islands, it became the separate colony of Portuguese Guinea in 1879. Its boundaries were fixed by the 1886 convention with France. In the 1960s a movement for liberation from colonial rule emerged and grew under the leadership of Amilcar CABRAL, and in 1974 Portugal formally recognized its independence. In 1977 an unsuccessful attempt was made to unite with Cape Verde (a newly formed republic of islands to the west). In 1980 a military coup established a revolutionary council with João Vieira as President and a National Assembly elected from the ruling Marxist party, the PAIGC. In 1989 Vieira was re-elected and in 1991 the National Assembly agreed to the introduction of multiparty democracy. The country's first multiparty elections, in 1994, were won by the ruling party and Vieira was re-elected President.

CAPITAL:	Bissau
AREA:	36,125 sq km (13,948 sq miles)
POPULATION:	1.096 million (1996)
CURRENCY:	1 Guinea-Bissau peso = 100 centavos
RELIGIONS:	Traditional beliefs 65.0%; Muslim 30.0%; Christian 5.0%
ETHNIC GROUPS:	Senegambian 60.0%; Peul 20.0%; Manding 13.0%
LANGUAGES:	Portuguese (official); Balante; Fulani; local languages
INTERNATIONAL ORGANIZATIONS:	UN; OAU; Non-Aligned Movement; ECOWAS

Guiscard, Robert (*c.* 1015–85) Norman warrior. He was the son of Tancred de Hauteville, and with his brother Roger established himself in southern Italy. In 1053 they defeated the forces of Pope Leo IX, securing Apulia and Calabria. Pope Nicholas II, enlisting Norman aid against the BYZANTINES, gave him Sicily, though it was not finally conquered till 1090. Excommunicated by Pope Gregory VII for his attack on Benevento, he nevertheless fought for him against the invading HENRY IV of Germany. The brothers sacked Rome in 1084, driving Henry out.

Guise A branch of the ducal house of Lorraine that rose to prominence in 16th-century France. Claude de Lorraine (1496–1550) was created duke in 1528; he had distinguished himself in a number of French military victories, including Marignano (1515). Francis (1519–63), his son and heir, became the most effective commander in the armies of Henry II. He was active throughout the 1550s, capturing Calais from the English (1558) and helping to bring about the Peace of Cateau-Cambrésis in 1559. His brother Charles (1524–74) became Cardinal of Lorraine in 1550, and his sister Mary (1515–60) married James V of Scotland and was the mother of MARY, Queen of Scots.

In 1559, on the accession of Francis II, the Catholic Guise family was the most influential in France. Its dealings with the HUGUENOTS and BOURBONS (1559–62) led directly to the outbreak of the FRENCH WARS OF RELIGION. Francis was assassinated in 1563. His son Henry (1550–88), the third duke, fought in the third and fourth wars, and was one of the instigators of the ST BARTHOLOMEW'S DAY MASSACRE. In 1576 he took the lead in organizing the HOLY LEAGUE, but Henry III had him assassinated in 1588, when he was being put forward as a possible heir to the throne. His brother, Charles (1554–1611), kept the Guise and extremist Catholic causes alive until 1595, when he submitted to HENRY IV. The Guise ducal line died out in 1688.

Guizot, Francois Pierre Guillaume (1787–1874) French historian and statesman. Entering official service in 1815, he lost office in 1822 and led the liberal opposition to CHARLES X's government. Involved in the JULY REVOLUTION of 1830, he returned to official service and, in 1833, introduced a national system of primary education. For the next 18 years he served LOUIS PHILIPPE. A moderate monarchist, he succeeded THIERS as leader of the government in 1840. His passive but immovable resistance to change finally led to his downfall in the REVOLUTION OF 1848.

Gujarat A region of India, consisting of the Kathiawar peninsula on the north-western coast plus a narrow hinterland. INDUS CIVILIZATION sites indicate early urban settlement, followed by absorption into numerous Hindu and Buddhist empires from as early as the MAURYAS (3rd century BC). Its name originated from a Hun tribal dynasty, the Gurjaras (8th–9th century). After earlier contact with Arab traders, its era of Muslim rule began in 1298 with the invasion of the KHALJI Delhi sultan, Ala ud-Din. A strong independent Muslim sultanate, based on the new capital city of Ahmadabad, ruled from 1411 until 1573, when Mogul invasion again reduced Gujarat to provincial subordination. MARATHA expansion in the mid-18th century brought the area under the Marathas, before the region was absorbed into the EAST INDIA COMPANY's Bombay presidency.

Gulf Co-operation Council (Co-operation Council for the Arab States of the Gulf; GCC) An organization of Arab Gulf states, established in 1981 to promote regional co-operation. The GCC has six members: Abu Dhabi, Bahrain, Kuwait, Oman, Qatar, and Saudi Arabia. Its headquarters are in Saudi Arabia. Initially seeking to encourage collaboration in economic, social, and cultural affairs, the GCC later extended its scope to cover common security problems, and in 1984 set up a joint defence force. It supported Iraq in the Iran–Iraq War (1980–88). The organization's failure to offer any decisive response to the Iraqi invasion of Kuwait in 1990 led to suggestions that it be strengthened and expanded. After the GULF WAR ceasefire in February 1991, the GCC countries joined with Egypt and Syria in agreeing to set up an Arab peace force as part of a broader plan to strengthen regional security.

Gulf War (1991) The conflict between Iraq and a US-led multinational coalition that included Britain, France, and may Arab states. On 2 August 1990 Iraqi troops invaded Kuwait, seeking control of its large and valuable oilfields: President Saddam HUSSEIN subsequently declared Kuwait the 19th province of Iraq. The UN Security Council imposed economic sanctions on Iraq, and a US-led coalition of 29 countries was mobilized. Intense diplomatic activity failed, and on 17 January 1991 a massive air attack was launched by the coalition forces stationed in Saudi Arabia. Strategic targets, some placed by Hussein in densely populated areas, were immobilized by electronically guided bombs. By 24 January Allied forces had established air supremacy, 'carpet bombing' Iraqi forces that could not shelter in the deserts of southern Iraq. The land war, named by Hussein as 'the mother of all battles', and by the UN forces under their Commander-in-Chief, General Norman Schwarzkopf, as 'Operation Desert Sabre' lasted from 24 to 28 February, during which time the Iraqi forces were routed by a massive Allied tank advance. The Allied offensive by air was called 'Operation Desert Storm'. On the Allied side the war was fought with sophisticated electronic equipment and weapons systems, notably the F-117 Stealth Fighter, laser-guided bombs, and depleted uranium shells for penetrating armour. Iraq's defence system, which included chemical and biological warheads intended for delivery by Soviet SCUD ballistic missiles, had been rendered ineffective by Allied bombing. By the end of February 1991, Hussein, having set fire to over 700 Kuwaiti oil wells, accepted the UN ceasefire terms. Final casualties of the war numbered some 33,000 Kuwaitis killed or captured, 234 Allied dead, and between 85,000 and 100,000 Iraqi soldiers killed.

gunboat diplomacy Diplomacy supported by the threatened use of force by one country in order to impose its will on another. The term is used specifically with reference to the 19th century when, in furtherance of their own interests, the great maritime nations, notably Britain, employed their naval power to coerce the rulers of small or weak countries. It was used by the British Foreign Secretary, Lord PALMERSTON, during the OPIUM WARS with China. In Egypt in 1882 a British fleet bombarded Alexandria in order to crush a nationalist movement. During the BOXER RISING in China in 1900 the European powers combined their forces in order to protect their interests and punish the rebels. Gunboat diplomacy was also employed by the USA in the Philippines in 1898 and has been used to enforce US policies in Latin America.

gunpowder An explosive consisting typically of a mixture of 75% potassium nitrate, 13% charcoal, and 12% sulphur. The constituents are first ground separately, then mixed, moistened with water, ground together, and dried. Gunpowder was known to the Chinese, and possibly to the Arabs, by the 10th century; its use in European conflicts, where it revolutionized warfare, dated from the 14th century until about 1904. It has now been replaced by other explosives and is rarely used.

Gunpowder Plot A Catholic scheme to murder JAMES I of England and his Parliament at the state opening on 5 November 1605, to be followed by a national Catholic uprising and seizure of power. The plotters, RECUSANTS led by Robert Catesby, saw violent action as the only way to gain toleration for English Catholics. They were subsequently disowned by the majority of their fellow religionists, who had little sympathy for the conspiratorial tradition established by RIDOLFI, THROCKMORTON, and BABINGTON. It has been suggested that Robert CECIL manufactured the plot, in order to discredit the Catholic cause. Cecil learned of the plot through Lord Mounteagle, a Catholic peer. On the eve of the opening, Guy Fawkes (1570–1606) was discovered in the cellar under the House of Lords on guard over barrels of gunpowder. The other plotters were overcome in the Midlands after brief resistance. Fawkes and seven others, including Sir Everard DIGBY were tried before COKE and executed in January 1606. Immediately afterwards, the penal laws against Catholics were stiffened, and an Oath of Allegiance imposed, but to the chagrin of many Puritans and Anglicans, enforcement of the new legislation soon became sporadic. Bonfires, fireworks, and the burning of 'guys' still mark 5 November in Britain.

Guomindang KUOMINTANG.

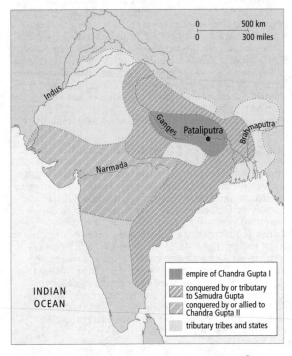

The Guptas: 320–415 *The Guptas exercised their influence over the greater part of India during the 4th century AD. The dynasty was founded in the Ganges valley state around Pataliputra (Patna) by Chandra Gupta I and its influence was roughly doubled by the conquest of his successor Samudra Gupta. In the distant provinces Gupta authority was diffuse and short-lived, but their cultural influence endured.*

Gupta A dynasty ruling from Pataliputra in north-east India from the mid-4th to the mid-6th century AD. The origins and rise of the family are uncertain, but the era is usually dated from the accession of Chandra Gupta I about 320 AD. During the reigns of his son, Samudra Gupta (*c.* 330–80), and grandson, Chandra Gupta II (*c.* 380–415), military conquests achieved direct sway over most of the Indo-Gangetic plain, and suzerainty over much of central and eastern India. Failure to establish tight administrative control over this far-flung empire, and Hun attacks on the northern heartland which began during the next two reigns, caused the collapse of Gupta power by the mid-6th century.

At its height the Gupta empire experienced stable political and economic conditions in which a 'golden' or 'classical' age in religion, philosophy, literature, and architecture was born. Both Hinduism and Buddhism flourished during this period as attested by a Chinese Buddhist monk, Fa Xian, who travelled through northern India in the early 5th century.

guru (Hindi, 'teacher', from Sanskrit, 'heavy') In HINDUISM, a spiritual teacher who assists people in their search for God, leading them from darkness to enlightenment. Hindus are encouraged to seek a guru to help them attain *moksha*, or spiritual liberation. In SIKHISM, the term applies to any of the first ten leaders of the Sikh religion. Sikhism was founded in the 15th century by Guru NANAK, whose authority and personality were transferred to nine further Gurus in succession. They include the third, Amar Das (1479–1574), who introduced the *langar*, or communal kitchen; the fifth, Arjan Dev (1563–1606), who founded the *Harimandir* or Golden Temple at Amritsar, compiled the *Adi Granth*, the Sikh holy book, and was martyred by the Mogul emperor Jahangir; and the tenth, GOBIND SINGH, who founded the *khalsa*, or army of soldier-saints. Before his death, he declared that the religious authority of the Guru was considered to be vested in the *Adi Granth* from that time on. The ten Sikh Gurus are seen as perfect men who have achieved spiritual union with God and have escaped from the cycle of reincarnation.

Gustavus I Vasa (1496–1560) King of Sweden (1523–60) and founder of the Vasa dynasty. He fought against the Danes in 1517–18, but was successful only after 1520, thanks to financial and naval backing from the city of Lübeck. His election as king ended the 126-year-old Union of KALMAR by which Sweden had been subordinated to Denmark. He created a national army of volunteers and built an efficient navy. He also modernized the economy, and in 1527 broke with the Roman Catholic Church for mainly political reasons. In 1544 the Swedish crown was made hereditary in the Vasa family.

Gustavus II Adolphus (1594–1632) King of Sweden (1611–32). He was the grandson of GUSTAVUS I and is generally recognized as Sweden's greatest ruler. His partnership with the Chancellor, OXENSTIERNA, bore fruit in important reforms in the government, the armed forces, the economy, and education. His reign was notable for the absence of friction between crown and aristocracy.

Abroad he inherited three Baltic struggles: the Kalmar War with Denmark (1611–13); the Russian War (1611–17); and the intermittent conflict with Poland. The successes achieved by his mobile, highly motivated, and disciplined forces impressed Cardinal RICHELIEU, who negotiated the Treaty of Altmark (1629) between Sweden and Poland, so that the Swedes could be released for action in the THIRTY YEARS WAR. Leaving the domestic government in the hands of Oxenstierna, Gustavus crossed to Germany in 1630 and proceeded to turn the tide of the war against the imperial forces. He was a devout Lutheran, and his war aims grew more ambitious as his invasion prospered. Originally intending to prevent the Catholic Habsburgs from dominating the Baltic, by 1632 he was pursuing grand imperial designs of his own. He was killed in action at LÜTZEN.

Gutenberg, Johann (*c.* 1398–1468) German pioneer of PRINTING with movable type. From 1430 he experimented in Strasbourg with metal type. By 1448, in partnership with the merchant Johann Furst, he had established a printing operation using movable type in his native Mainz, a metal-working area well supplied with craftsmen able to cast the type and build the presses. In 1455 Gutenberg produced the first printed work in the western hemisphere, a 42-line Bible. Although printing had been pioneered in China in the 11th century, Gutenberg's invention included new features such as metal matrices for moulding the type, and a press akin to a wine press. Gutenberg ultimately lost possession of all his printing equipment after a legal dispute with his partner.

Guyana A country on the north-east coast of South America, extending for 800 km (500 miles) from north to south and for 460 km (285 miles) from east to west.
Physical. Guyana is bordered by the Atlantic Ocean to the north, Surinam to the east, Brazil to the south and south-west, and Venezuela to the west. Much of the country is covered with dense rain forest.
Economy. The economy is based on agriculture and mining. Major exports are bauxite and alumina, sugar (the province of Demerara gave its name to a type of sugar that originated there), and rice. There are rich mineral deposits and huge timber reserves, but these are largely unexploited, and lack of foreign exchange has led to food shortages. There is potential for hydroelectricity which would reduce its dependence on imported oil.
History. The country was first settled by the Dutch in the 17th century. British rule was formally secured in 1831 when three colonies, Essequibo, Demerara, and Berbice (named from the three rivers) were consolidated to form the crown colony of British Guiana. Boundary problems with neighbours dominated the 19th century. During World War II the lease of military and naval bases to the USA proved useful to the Allied war effort. Britain granted independence to the colony in 1966 and Guyana styled itself a Co-operative Republic in 1970. Its Prime Minister, Forbes Burnham, became executive President (1980–86) with supreme authority under an authoritarian constitution. He was succeeded by Desmond Hoyte, who embarked on a policy of restoring good relations with the USA. To boost the economy, his government leased over five million acres of rain forest to foreign companies for exploitation. In the general election of October 1992 a victory by the People's Progressive Party, under the veteran nationalist Cheddi Jagan, ended 28 years of rule by the People's National Congress. Following Jagan's death in 1997 his widow, Janet, became Prime Minister and Samuel Hinds became President.

CAPITAL:	Georgetown
AREA:	215,083 sq km (88,044 sq miles)
POPULATION:	792,000 (1996)
CURRENCY:	1 Guyana dollar = 100 cents
RELIGIONS:	Protestant 30.5%; Hindu 37.1%; Roman Catholic 11.4%; Muslim 8.7%; non-religious 3.7%
ETHNIC GROUPS:	East Indian 51.4%; Black (African Negro and Bush Negro) 30.5%; Mixed 11.0%; Amerindian 5.3%; Chinese 0.2%
LANGUAGES:	English (official); English creole; also Caribbean, Hindi, and Amerindian languages
INTERNATIONAL ORGANIZATIONS:	UN; Commonwealth; CARICOM; Non-Aligned Movement; OAS

Guzmán Blanco, Antonio (1829–99) Venezuelan statesman. Appointed to negotiate loans from London bankers in 1870, he seized power and two years later had himself elected President. He was absolute ruler of Venezuela (1870–89). He fostered railroad construction, public education, and free trade. An efficient administrator, he reformed the civil service and instituted public works. His extravagance gradually alienated the Venezuelan populace and in 1888, while visiting Paris, he was deposed by Juan Paúl.

Gwalior SINDHIA.

Gwyn, Nell (1650–87) English comic actress, and mistress of CHARLES II of England. She sold oranges at Drury Lane Theatre before taking up acting. Charles made her his mistress in 1669, and she bore him two sons. She was always popular with the people, defending herself when a mob attacked her coach in mistake for that of her Roman Catholic rival by proclaiming, 'I'm the Protestant whore'. Charles II's deathbed instruction 'Let not poor Nelly starve' was faithfully carried out by his brother James II, who gave her a pension of £1,500 a year.

Haakon IV (or Haakonsson the Old) (1204–63) King of Norway (*c.* 1220–63). His reign was troubled by internal dissensions and he had Earl Skule executed in 1239. Iceland and Greenland were added to the Norwegian crown but control of the HEBRIDES was lost. This followed his defeat by ALEXANDER III of Scotland in the decisive battle at Largs in 1263.

Haakon VII (1872–1957) King of Norway (1905–57). Formerly Prince Charles of Denmark, he was elected by the Norwegian Storting (parliament) to the throne in 1905. In April 1940 he was driven out by the German invasion. Refusing the suggestion of the government of Vidkun QUISLING to abdicate, he continued the struggle from London. He returned to Norway in 1945. He dispensed with much of the regal pomp attached to the monarchy, and became known as the 'people's king'.

Habsburg (or Hapsburg; also called the House of Austria) The most prominent European royal dynasty from the 15th to the 20th century. Their name derives from Habichtsburg (Hawk's Castle) in Switzerland, built in 1020. The founder of the family power was Rudolf I, who was King of the Romans (1273–91) and conqueror of AUSTRIA and Styria, which lands he bestowed on his two sons in 1282, beginning the family's rule over Austria. Habsburg domination of Europe resulted from the shrewd marriage policy of Maximilian I (1459–1519), whose own marriage gained The Netherlands, Luxembourg, and Burgundy and that of his son, Philip, which brought Castile, Aragon, and the Spanish New World possessions as well as Naples, Sicily, and Sardinia. Habsburgs also ruled Hungary and Bohemia from 1526 to 1918. Thus the zenith of Habsburg power came under Charles I, King of Spain and emperor (as Charles V, 1519–56) in the 16th century. On Charles's death his brother Ferdinand (1503–64) ruled Germany and Austria, while his son, PHILIP II (1527–98), ruled the Spanish inheritance. The Protestant REFORMATION and the Turkish invasion of Eastern Europe forced the two branches to co-operate in preserving European Catholicism throughout the Counter-Reformation and the THIRTY YEARS WAR (1618–48). The long struggle weakened the family despite the addition of Portugal to their territory. In 1700 the Spanish line became extinct and in the subsequent War of the SPANISH SUCCESSION (1703–13) the Spanish inheritance passed to the Bourbons. The Austrian Habsburgs (after 1740 the House of Habsburg-Lorraine) flourished again under MARIA THERESA (1717–80) and her son JOSEPH II (1741–90). The Habsburgs ended the Napoleonic wars with the loss of the Austrian Netherlands, and the title HOLY ROMAN EMPEROR, but continued to rule over Austria. They were increasingly rivals of the kingdom of PRUSSIA, surviving the REVOLUTIONS OF 1848, but being obliged, following the AUSTRO-PRUSSIAN WAR of 1866 to make concessions to Hungarian nationalism with the formation of the AUSTRO-HUNGARIAN EMPIRE. The emperor FRANCIS JOSEPH came increasingly to clash with Russian ambitions in the BALKANS, turning more and more to the GERMAN SECOND EMPIRE, with whom he formed an alliance in 1879. Nationalist aspirations led eventually to the disintegration of his empire during World War I. The last Habsburg monarch, Emperor Charles I of Austria (Charles IV of Hungary), renounced his title in November 1918 and was later deposed.

hacienda A large estate with a dwelling-house, originally given by monarchs in Latin America as a reward for services done. Such estates are known as *estancias* in Argentina and *fazendas* in Brazil. Nineteenth-century land laws made possible the further concentration of land in the hands of a few, and, with population increase, exacerbated tension in rural areas. The first major eruption of violence, calling for the break-up of the haciendas, occurred in Mexico in 1910. Most Latin American countries have experienced similar demands during the 20th century, and they have remained a major political issue.

Hadar A site in the Afar region of Ethiopia where early human fossils dating back to 3.2–2.9 million years ago have been found. The finds were attributed to a new species of AUSTRALOPITHECINE, *Australopithecus afarensis*, but this has been challenged by some scientists who say that they belong to another species, *Australopithecus africanus*, or even that two or more forms are represented at the site. The best-known of the fossils is 'Lucy', a skeleton nearly half complete. She was in her twenties when she died, with a height of only 1.1–1.3 m (3.6–4.3 feet) and a weight of about 27 kg (60 lb). OLDOWAN stone tools from Hadar, dated about 2.5 million years, are the earliest known human artefacts.

hadith (Arabic, 'traditions') The teachings and acts of MUHAMMAD and his followers, constituting the *sunna*, or 'rules of life', the basis of the SHARIA (Islamic law). Although disputed, the *hadith* are highly revered sources of historical, moral, religious, and ritual authority, second only to the authority of the KORAN. Six *hadith* collections, chiefly the one compiled by Bukhari (810–70 AD), are accepted as authoritative by orthodox SUNNIS, whilst five, based upon the authority of the Caliph Ali and the other *imams*, are accepted by SHIITES.

Hadrian (Publius Aelius Hadrianus) (*c.* 76–138 AD) Roman emperor (117–38). He was born in Spain, and became TRAJAN's ward after his parents died. He pursued a successful military career, married Trajan's niece, and was adopted as his heir. Extensive travel characterized his reign after 117. The western empire was covered 121–26 and the eastern parts 128–34. HADRIAN'S WALL was commenced during his visit to Britain 121–22. The BAR COCHBA revolt broke out after his visit to Palestine and his plan for rebuilding a Romanized JERUSALEM. He was a patron of the arts and the ruins of his villa at Tibur (modern Tivoli) remain.

Hadrian's Wall A defensive fortification in northern Britain. It was built 122–26 AD after a visit to Britain by Emperor HADRIAN. It is 117 km (73 miles) long, a stone barricade with a turf section in the west. Large fortress bases, mile-castles, and signal towers marked its length. A road ran along it to the south. Defensive ditches accompanied it on both sides. The wall was damaged several times by the Picts, and was finally abandoned in 383. Long stretches of the wall still stand.

Haganah A Jewish defence force in Palestine. It was established in 1920 first as an independent, armed organization and then under the control of the Histadrut (the Jewish labour organization) to defend Jewish settlements. During the 1936–39 Arab rebellion it was considerably expanded. It gained a general staff and was put under control of the Jewish Agency, acquiring new duties of organizing illegal Jewish immigration and preparing for the fight against Britain, who held the MANDATE over Palestine. In 1941 the Palmah (assault platoons) were formed. In 1948 Haganah provided the nucleus of the Israeli Defence Force, formed to protect the newly created state of Israel.

Haig, Douglas, 1st Earl (1861–1928) British field-marshal. After being chief-of-staff in India (1909) he commanded the 1st Army Corps in Flanders at Ypres and Loos and succeeded Sir John French as commander-in-chief. His strategy of attrition while being prepared to accept huge casualties on the SOMME (1916) and at PASSCHENDAELE (1917) was much criticized. His conduct of the final campaign (1918) ended the war more quickly than FOCH expected. After the war he devoted himself to working tirelessly for ex-servicemen, and instituted the 'Poppy Day' appeal associated with his name.

Haile Selassie (1892–1975) Emperor of Ethiopia (1930–74). Baptized a Coptic Christian under the name of Ras Tafari Makonnen, in 1917 he was named regent and heir apparent by a council of notables. Crowned king in 1928 and emperor in 1930, in 1931 he promulgated a constitution, with limited powers for a Parliament, which proved abortive. From 1935 his personal rule was interrupted by the ABYSSINIAN CAMPAIGNS and Italian colonial occupation. He was forced to seek exile in Britain and regained power in 1941 with British aid. In spite of efforts to modernize Ethiopia, he lost touch with the social problems of his country, and in 1974 he was deposed by a committee of left-wing army officers. He was assassinated the following year. (See also RASTAFARIANISM.)

Hainaut A province in south-western Belgium. Originally inhabited by a tribe called the Nervii, it became part of the Roman empire in 57 BC. It changed hands several times and in the 11th century passed to Flanders and then in 1275 to Count John of Holland. In 1345 it came to the Wittelsbach family and in 1433 went to Duke Philip the Good of Burgundy. LOUIS XIV divided it between France and Austria, but in 1794 the Austrian part was absorbed by France.

Haiti A Caribbean country that occupies the western third of the island of Hispaniola.
Physical. Haiti is mainly mountainous with three main mountain ranges. Much of it is forested but the valleys support agriculture.
Economy. Haiti has a predominantly agricultural economy, with coffee the most important agricultural export; bauxite is also exported.
History. Hispaniola was discovered by Columbus during his first voyage to the New World, and became a Spanish colony in the 16th century. French corsairs settled on the western part of the island in the 17th century and Spain recognized the French claims to the area in 1697 in the Treaty of Ryswick. Known as Saint Domingue in the 18th century, it became a rich source of sugar and coffee for the European market. African slaves replaced a decimated Indian population and by the end of the 18th century the population of Haiti was predominantly Black. French rule was challenged in 1791 by a slave insurrection led by TOUSSAINT L'OUVERTURE.

The country declared its independence (1804) and DESSALINES was proclaimed emperor. After his assassination (1806) a separate kingdom was set up in the north, while the south and west became republican. The country was re-united in 1820 as an independent republic. Haiti and the eastern part of the island (later the DOMINICAN REPUBLIC) were united from 1822 to 1844. In 1859 it became a republic on its own again, whose anarchic history has been exacerbated by hostility between the Mulatto and the Black population. The USA, fearing that its investments were jeopardized and that Germany might seize Haiti, landed its marines (1915) and did not withdraw them until 1934. The country was dominated by President François DUVALIER (1957–71), and by his son and successor, Jean Claude (1971–86). When the latter was exiled to France, a council assumed power. A new constitution and elections followed, but they in turn were followed by a series of military coups and violence. In December 1990 a dissident Roman Catholic priest, Jean-Bertrand Aristide, was elected President. In September 1991 rebel troops seized President Aristide and civil violence flared up against a new military regime. Aristide fled to Venezuela and appealed to the ORGANIZATION DE L'ARMEE SECRETE for help. International aid was suspended and trade sanctions imposed, but negotiations failed. An army-backed government led by Prime Minister Marc Bazin came to power in June 1992. Renewed OAS and US diplomatic efforts at restoring President Aristide to office led to the appointment by Aristide of a new Prime Minister, Robert Malval, in August 1993. An upsurge in army- and police-sponsored violence, however, prevented Aristide's return, while increased sanctions held the economy in a state of crisis. In September 1994 US troops landed on Haiti to oversee the transfer of power to Aristide, following an agreement with military leaders negotiated by former US President Jimmy Carter. Aristide returned in October and, in March 1995, military authority was transferred from the US-led multinational force to the UN Mission in Haiti (UNMIH). In mid-1995 the Lavalas Political Organization, endorsed by Aristide, won legislative elections, but results were contested by opposition parties and the elections were marred by irregularities and violence. Presidential elections in 1995 were won by René Préval, an associate of Aristide.

CAPITAL:	Port-au-Prince
AREA:	27,400 sq km (10,579 sq miles)
POPULATION:	6.732 million (1996)
CURRENCY:	1 gourde = 100 centimes
RELIGIONS:	Roman Catholic 80.3%; (of whom about 90% also practise voodoo); Protestant 15.8% (of which Baptist 9.7%); Pentecostal 3.6%; non-religious 1.2%
ETHNIC GROUPS:	Black 95.0%; Mulatto 4.9%; White 0.1%

LANGUAGES: Haitian (French) creole, French (both official)

INTERNATIONAL ORGANIZATIONS: UN; OAS

Haldane, Richard Burdon, Viscount Haldane of Cloan (1856–1928) British politician. As Secretary for War (1905–12) he showed great organizational skill in his reforms of the British army. Recognizing the growing danger from German militarism, he used his knowledge of the German army to redevelop the military organization in Britain to meet the requirements of modern warfare. A small expeditionary force ready for instant action was formed with a Territorial Army as a reserve, and an Imperial General Staff to organize military planning on an improved basis. Haldane was sent on a mission to Berlin in 1912 to secure a reduction in naval armaments, but failed.

Halder, Franz (1884–1972) German general. As Nazi chief-of-staff from 1938 he was responsible for the planning of the BLITZKRIEG campaigns of World War II. He opposed Hitler's decision to strike against STALINGRAD in 1942, and was dismissed. After the JULY PLOT he was sent to a concentration camp. He was freed in 1945.

Halidon Hill, Battle of (19 July 1333) A battle fought near Berwick-on-Tweed, on the border between England and Scotland, which saw a major victory for Edward BALLIOL over the nationalist Scots. Balliol had been crowned King of Scotland in 1332 but subsequently driven out of the kingdom: his victory at Halidon Hill, which was achieved with the help of English archers supplied to him by EDWARD III, regained him his kingdom – at the price of doing homage for it to the English crown.

Halifax, Edward Frederick Lindley Wood, 1st Earl of (1881–1959) British Conservative politician. From 1925 to 1931 he was governor-general and viceroy of India (as Lord Irwin), and was involved in that country's struggle for independence. Halifax, who favoured DOMINION status for the sub-continent, ordered the imprisonment of GANDHI after the SALT MARCH. As a member of CHAMBERLAIN's government, he visited Germany and met Hitler. An advocate of APPEASEMENT, Halifax accepted the post of Foreign Secretary in 1938 on EDEN's resignation. He accepted, *de facto*, the ANSCHLUSS of Austria and the dismemberment of CZECHOSLOVAKIA after the MUNICH PACT. Halifax refused an invitation to Moscow, thus losing the chance of agreement with the Soviet Union, and leaving the door open for Hitler and Stalin to draw up the NAZI–SOVIET PACT. During World War II he was British ambassador to the USA.

Hallstatt A town in Austria, the site of a famous prehistoric cemetery that has given its name to the culture of the early IRON AGE (c. 750–450 BC). At first cremation was the rule, as were flat or low graves, though later the tumulus or raised BARROW became standard. Then as iron became common, interment was used as well as cremation, and the quality of the geometric-style pottery degenerated. It was superseded by the LA TÈNE culture.

Halsey, William Frederick (1882–1959) US admiral. In 1941, commanding the Pacific Fleet aircraft carriers, he and his fleet were out of harbour when the Japanese attacked PEARL HARBOR. In 1942 he led a spectacular raid against the Marshall and Gilbert Islands and during the campaign of the SOLOMON ISLANDS he took command of the South Pacific area. As commander of the 3rd Fleet at the Battle of LEYTE GULF (1944), he sank a number of Japanese aircraft carriers and in 1945 led the seaborne bombing offensive against Japan.

Hamas An Islamic fundamentalist movement that arose among Palestinians in the Israeli-occupied West Bank and Gaza Strip in the late 1970s, and has since been responsible for terrorist outrages throughout Israel.

The armed wing of Hamas, Al Qassam, was instrumental in organizing the Palestinian uprising against Israel known as the *Intifada* (1987–93). Hamas rejected the 1993 Oslo peace accord between Yasser ARAFAT and Yitzhak RABIN, which gave the PLO control of Jericho and Gaza, and began a campaign of suicide bombings, mostly against civilian targets, such as buses and markets. The Israeli-Palestinian peace process threatens to founder on the question of how vigorously the PLO pursues and eradicates Hamas activity in areas under its jurisdiction.

Hamilcar Barca (d. *c.* 229 BC) Carthaginian general and father of HANNIBAL and HASDRUBAL. He commanded the Carthaginian forces in the later part of the first of the PUNIC WARS and negotiated the peace of 241 BC. When the mercenaries in Carthaginian service rebelled, Hamilcar, along with his rival Hanno, defeated them. In 237 he went to Spain, and brought the southern and eastern areas under Carthaginian control.

Hamilton, Alexander (1755–1804) An artillery company and saw action in campaigns round New York, before becoming Washington's private secretary and aide-de-camp (1777–81). He married into a prominent New York family. He served in the Continental Congress (1782–83) and was a delegate to the Constitutional Convention (1787), where he advocated a strong central government. He wrote more than half of the *Federalist Papers*. As Secretary of the Treasury (1789–95) he devised the US fiscal programme (1790), recommending the treasury to accept old securities at face value in exchange for new bonds, the assumption by the federal government of Revolutionary War debts, the passage of a protective tariff, and the establishment of a Bank of the United States. This 'Hamiltonian System' was supported by the FEDERALISTS and opposed by MADISON and JEFFERSON, helping to precipitate the formation of the Democratic Republican Party. Hamilton resigned from the cabinet (1795) and returned to New York to practise law. In 1800 he thwarted Aaron BURR's ambitions to become President and in 1804 was challenged by Burr to a duel; he was killed by Burr at Weehawken, New Jersey.

Hamilton, James, 3rd Marquis and 1st Duke of (1606–49) Scottish nobleman, a supporter of the CAVALIER cause. CHARLES I appointed him the king's commissioner in Scotland in 1638, but despite negotiating with the COVENANTERS, he was unable to avert the BISHOPS' WARS. Charles kept faith with him on the outbreak of the ENGLISH CIVIL WAR, but his negotiations in Scotland came to nothing in 1643, when he was expelled for refusing to sign the SOLEMN LEAGUE AND Covenant. His attempt to revive the Cavalier cause in 1648 ended in defeat at PRESTON, and his execution.

Hammarskjöld, Dag Hjalmar Agne Carl (1905–61) Swedish diplomat and Secretary-General of the UNITED

NATIONS (1953–61). In 1953 he was elected UN Secretary-General as successor to Trygve LIE. He was re-elected in 1957. Under him, the UN established an emergency force to help maintain order in the Middle East after the SUEZ WAR, and UN observation forces were sent to Laos and Lebanon. He initiated and directed (1960–61) the UN's involvement in the CONGO CRISIS, making controversial use of Article 99 of the UN Charter, which he believed allowed the Secretary-General to exercise initiative independent of the UNITED NATIONS SECURITY COUNCIL or GENERAL ASSEMBLY. While in the Congo he was killed in an aeroplane crash over Zambia.

Hammurabi (d. 1750 BC) Amorite king of BABYLON. He greatly extended the lands he had inherited until they stretched from the Persian Gulf to parts of Assyria. He was much more than a warrior, however, encouraging agriculture, literature, and intellectual pursuits, and drawing up a code of laws which was inscribed on a column found at Susa in 1901.

Hampden, John (1594–1643) English politician, who played a leading part in the opposition to CHARLES I's arbitrary government. In 1627 he was imprisoned for refusing to pay the 'forced loan' imposed by Charles to finance his unpopular foreign campaigns. Ten years later he was prosecuted for refusing to pay SHIP MONEY. As a member of the LONG PARLIAMENT he was prominent in the impeachment of STRAFFORD, and a close ally of John PYM. In 1642 he survived the king's attempt to arrest him (FIVE MEMBERS), and was appointed to the Committee of Safety to organize the parliamentary ENGLISH CIVIL WAR effort. He died of wounds received in action.

Hampton Court Conference (1604) A meeting in which the new king of England, JAMES I, presided over an assembly of bishops and Puritans. The 'Millenary Petition' presented by the Puritans in 1602 had listed Church practices offensive to them and had asked for reform in the ANGLICAN CHURCH. Most of their demands were refused, although it was agreed to produce a new translation of the BIBLE, the Authorized Version of 1611. The conference was held in the Tudor palace on the River Thames near London called Hampton Court. It was given by Cardinal Wolsey in the 1520s to Henry VIII.

Hampton Roads Conference (3 February 1865) An abortive conference to negotiate an end to the AMERICAN CIVIL WAR. At a meeting on a Union (Northern) steamer moored in Hampton Roads, Virginia, Confederate demands, put forward by the Southern President Jefferson DAVIS, that the CONFEDERACY be treated as a sovereign state foundered on the refusal of President LINCOLN to negotiate on any other terms but reunion and abolition of slavery. The conference broke up without result, and the war carried on until the Confederate surrender two months later at APPOMATTOX.

Han (Western Han, 202 BC–8 AD; Eastern Han, 25–220 AD) Chinese dynasty established at the overthrow of the QIN by the rebel peasant Liu Bang. Invoking the glories associated with this dynasty the Chinese still distinguish themselves from other MONGOLOID peoples by calling themselves the Han.

When Wudi ('the Martial Emperor') (141–87 BC) halted XIONGNU onslaughts, Chinese armies penetrated deep into Central Asia. Some marched over 3,200 km (2,000 miles) west of the Western Han capital Chang'an (now Xi'an).

Envoys seeking alliances against the Xiongnu also travelled far west, returning with information about the ROMAN EMPIRE. Camel trains taking out silks, bringing back jade, and 'heavenly' horses, larger than those then known in China, travelled the SILK ROUTE. Much of south China and ANNAM was conquered, though the southern Chinese were not assimilated until later, and Han rule was established over part of KOREA. Gradually the teachings of CONFUCIUS were accepted as the state philosophy.

In 8 AD, the court was oppressed by economic problems and torn by strife. Wang Mang (33 BC–23 AD), chief minister of a boy-emperor he had placed on the throne, seized power and established the Xin (Hsin) dynasty (8–23 AD). He attempted to allay peasant discontent by redistributing landholdings. But the Taoist-inspired 'Red Eyebrows' rebellion in Shandong in 18 AD and renewed Xiongnu invasions brought his downfall.

In 25 AD a Han prince Liu Xiu set up a court in Luoyang. Soon Chinese armies again penetrated central Asia and temporarily subjugated the lands east of the Caspian Sea. The period was noted for its artistic achievement and for advances in technology. The first Buddhist missionaries arrived in China. By the end of the 2nd century the ambitions of empresses and EUNUCHS and the Taoist Yellow Turbans rebellion led to near collapse and the growth of regional armies. The last Han emperor abdicated, and China again became divided during the period of the THREE KINGDOMS.

Hancock, John (1737–93) American Revolutionary leader. A radical Boston merchant who supplemented his inherited fortune by smuggling, he came into open conflict with British customs officers when his sloop *Liberty* was seized (1768). He was a generous backer of the patriot cause, helped to organize the BOSTON Tea Party, and as president of the Second CONTINENTAL CONGRESS was the first to sign the DECLARATION OF INDEPENDENCE. He was first governor of independent Massachusetts.

Hanna, Marcus Alonzo (1837–1904) US businessman and politician. One of the most powerful political organizers of modern times, with the help of unprecedentedly high campaign contributions from big business he achieved William MCKINLEY's defeat of BRYAN in the presidential election of 1896. He supported labour's right to organize and, briefly, opposed US overseas expansion. His major contribution to the Republicans was the introduction of novel sales techniques in elections, paid for by levies on business firms, and the deft use of patronage.

Hannibal (247–183 or 182 BC) Carthaginian general, an outstanding military tactician and leader. He accompanied his father HAMILCAR BARCA to Spain in 237, and helped him establish a province there. He was himself granted supreme command in Spain in 221 and adopted an aggressive policy towards the Romans. His eight-month siege of Saguntum in 219 precipitated the second of the PUNIC WARS, and in 218 he marched over the Alps, into northern Italy, though many of his elephants and troops died during the arduous journey. He inflicted three crushing defeats on the Roman forces, at Trebia (218), Lake Trasimene (217), and CANNAE (216). Despite winning over many of the southern Italian communities, central and northern Italy remained

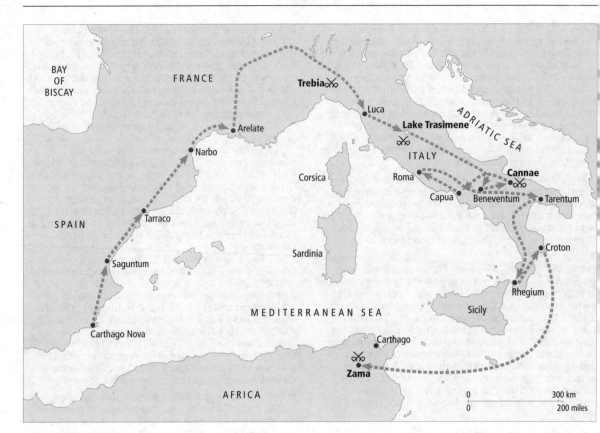

Hannibal   *Hannibal marched north from Carthago Nova (Cartagena) into France in 218 BC and astounded the Romans by crossing the Alps with an army of troops and elephants and descending into Italy. The Alpine crossing, accomplished in a mere 15 days, is regarded as one of the greatest feats of ancient warfare. Despite several devastating victories over the Romans, Hannibal was not strong enough to attack Rome itself and his march on the city in 211 was merely a feint to divert the Romans from their siege of Capua. In 203 he was recalled to Carthago (Carthage). The Second Punic War ended in 201, following Hannibal's defeat at Zama (202).*

largely loyal to Rome. He was unable to break Rome's dogged resistance and gradually the tide of war turned against him, until in 203 he was recalled with his army to Africa. The following year he was defeated at Zama by Publius Cornelius SCIPIO (Africanus). His programme of political reforms in Carthage *c.* 196 provoked his enemies to complain to Rome, and he fled abroad. He spent time at the courts of Antiochus the Great and Prusias of Bithynia, before committing suicide.

Hannibal was one of the great generals of history. His military genius lay in his ability to use cavalry and infantry in combination, and to inspire deep loyalty in a mercenary army.

Hanover A city in northern Germany that gave its name to an electorate (later a kingdom) of Germany. The rulers of Hanover were also the sovereigns of Great Britain and Ireland from GEORGE I to VICTORIA (the House of Hanover). In 1658 SOPHIA, daughter of Elizabeth of Bohemia and granddaughter of James I of England, married Ernest Augustus, Duke of Brunswick-Lüneburg, who subsequently became an Elector of Germany (1692), taking Hanover as his title and capital city. Their son became George I, the first Hanoverian King of Great Britain in 1714. Hanover's territories included the

important towns of Göttingen and Hildersheim and their defence was an important factor in British foreign policy in the 18th century. Hanover became part of the kingdom of Westphalia during the NAPOLEONIC WARS, but in 1815 it was made a kingdom in its own right and was restored to the British crown. Succession in Hanover, unlike Britain, was governed by the Salic Law, which forbids succession through the female line; thus, when Victoria became queen in 1837, her uncle Ernest Augustus became King of Hanover, and on her death in 1901, Saxe-Coburg-Gotha became the British royal house. In 1866 Hanover was annexed by Prussia, whom it had opposed in the AUSTRO-PRUSSIAN WAR. The kingdom was dissolved and it became a province of Prussia within the North German Confederation; it is now part of the German state of Lower Saxony.

Hanseatic League An association of north German cities, formed in 1241 as a trading alliance. Cologne had enjoyed special trading privileges with England and was joined by other traders. An agreement between Hamburg and Lübeck (1241), and a Diet of 1260 marked the origin of the League. The towns of the League dealt mainly in wool, cloth, linen, and silver. In the later Middle Ages the League, with about 100 member towns, functioned as an independent political power with its own army and navy. It began to collapse in the early 17th century and only three major cities (Hamburg, Bremen, and Lübeck) remained in the League thereafter.

Hapsburg HABSBURG.

Harappa A village in south Punjab, Pakistan, an important INDUS CIVILIZATION site. The term 'Harappan culture' is sometimes used to identify common features found at other sites along the Indus valley where urban civilization flourished *c.* 2500 to 1500 BC. Harappa was the first such site to attract the attention of archaeologists. Excavations have revealed a city, built *c.* 2500 BC, which was second only in size and splendour to MOHENJO-DARO. Important constructions were a granary and two cemeteries.

Hara Takashi (or Hara Kei) (1856–1921) Japanese statesman. Leader of the Seiyukai (Friends of Constitutional Government) Party and a strong advocate of government by political party rather than by interest groups, he became the first commoner to hold the post of Prime Minister (1918–22). Attempts to build links with the business community brought him under suspicion of corruption and he failed either to prevent the breakdown of civil order or stop military intervention in the RUSSIAN CIVIL WAR. He planned to end the military administration of Taiwan and Korea but was assassinated by a right-wing fanatic.

Hardenberg, Karl August, Prince (1750–1822) Prussian statesman and reformer. In 1810 he was appointed Chancellor of Prussia and continued the domestic reforms inaugurated by STEIN. These included the improvement of Prussia's military system, the abolition of serfdom and of the privileges of the nobles, the encouragement of municipalities, the reform of education, and civic equality for Jews. In 1813 he persuaded FREDERICK WILLIAM III to join the coalition against Napoleon. He represented Prussia at the Congress of VIENNA where he achieved substantial gains for his country.

Hardie, (James) Keir (1856–1915) British politician. He gained experience of leadership in the National Union of Mineworkers; this cost him his job and he was black-listed by the coal-owners. In 1888 he broke with the Liberal Party and was elected a Member of Parliament for the Scottish Labour Party in 1892, becoming chairman of the INDEPENDENT LABOUR PARTY in 1893. In 1900 he linked it with other socialist organizations to form the Labour Representation Committee. Hardie became leader in the House of Commons of the first Labour group of MPs (1906). An outspoken pacifist and chief adviser (from 1903) to the women's SUFFRAGETTE movement, Hardie gained popular support from his pursuit of improvement in working-class conditions and from his strongly practical Christian beliefs.

Harding, Warren Gamaliel (1865–1923) Twenty-ninth President of the USA (1921–23). He was the tool of the ambitious lawyer Harry Daugherty, who helped him win the office of lieutenant-governor of Ohio (1904–05) and Senator (1915–21), eventually promoting him as the successful compromise Republican candidate for President in 1920. Instructed to straddle the issue on whether or not the USA should join the LEAGUE OF NATIONS, Harding, in his campaign, pledged a 'return to normalcy'. His fondness for his self-seeking friends, the

'Ohio Gang', whom he took into office, resulted in the worst political scandals since the 1870s, notably the TEAPOT DOME scandal. Harding died suddenly before the worst revelations of his administration's incompetence and corruption.

Hardy, Thomas (1752–1832) Scottish radical leader, a champion of parliamentary reform. He moved to London in 1774, where he became a shoemaker. In 1792 he founded the LONDON CORRESPONDING SOCIETY, whose aim was to achieve universal manhood suffrage. The country was at war with Revolutionary France and the government became alarmed at the Society's growing influence. In 1794 Hardy was arrested on a charge of high treason but at the subsequent trial he was acquitted.

Hare Krishna movement (International Society for Krishna Consciousness) A modern Hindu sect brought to the West in the 1960s by A. C. Bhaktivedanta Swami, and based on the teachings of Guru Chaitanya (1486–1534). Members attend temple services or dedicate themselves fully to an austere, monastic life of service and devotion to Krishna. The way of Krishna Consciousness forbids alcohol and demands a vegetarian diet. Followers stress the spiritual benefits of music, ecstatic trance, and chanting, particularly the mantra 'Hare Krishna, Hare Rama', as a way of concentrating the mind in devotion on Krishna's various manifestations.

Harlem A district of New York City, USA: a mostly Black commercial and residential area, it has been a centre of Black culture and politics since the 'Harlem Renaissance' of the 1920s. In 1964 it saw major race riots.

Harley, Robert, 1st Earl of Oxford and Mortimer (1661–1724) British statesman. He entered Parliament as a Whig, and during the early years of Queen ANNE's reign served variously as Speaker of the House of Commons and Secretary of State. He abandoned the Whigs and used the influence of his cousin Abigail Masham, a lady-in-waiting, to undermine MARLBOROUGH's standing with the queen. In 1710 he headed the new Tory government whose greatest achievement was the Peace of UTRECHT (1713). In the subsequent power struggle among the Tories just before Anne's death in 1714 he lost to BOLINGBROKE, and the Whig administration of GEORGE I imprisoned him and began impeachment proceedings against him. He was released two years later, but took no further part in public affairs.

Harmensen, Jakob ARMINIUS, JACOBUS.

Harmsworth, Alfred Charles William, 1st Viscount Northcliffe (1865–1922) British journalist and newspaper proprietor. In 1887 he used his savings to form a general publishing business with his brother, Harold Harmsworth (1868–1940). In 1894 the two brothers acquired the *Evening News* and two years later founded the *Daily Mail*. This opened a new epoch in Fleet Street by presenting news to the public in a concise, interesting style, using advertisements and competitions, and financing schemes of enterprise and exploration. In 1903 the *Daily Mirror* was founded, in 1905 the *Observer* came under Harmsworth's control, and in 1908 he became chief proprietor of *The Times*. He was appointed to head the British War Mission to the USA in May 1917, soon after the USA entered World War I.

Harold I (c. 850–933) First King of all Norway (872–933). A series of battles with minor kings culminated in his decisive victory at Hafrsfjord. He then succeeded in bringing the Orkney and Shetland islands, together with much of northern Scotland, into his kingdom and forced out many Vikings, who went on to conquer Iceland and land in western Europe.

Harold II (c. 1020–66) King of England (1066). He was the second son of Earl GODWIN of Wessex, whom he succeeded in 1053. The Godwin family had great political ambition. Harold's sister Edith was married to EDWARD THE CONFESSOR, and his brother Tostig was Earl of Northumbria (1055–65). Exiled after an abortive attempt to intimidate the king, Harold and his father returned (1052) to dominate political affairs in England. Harold succeeded Edward the Confessor in 1066, despite the Norman claim that Edward had designated Duke William of Normandy as his heir and that Harold had recognized William's right. Tostig, who had been dispossessed of his earldom, raided the south-east coast before joining the invasion by Harald Hardrada of Norway in northern England. Harold defeated them at STAMFORD BRIDGE and then marched 402 km (250 miles) south to meet William's invasion at the Battle of HASTINGS, where he died.

Harrington, James (1611–77) English philosopher and political theorist. He sympathized with republicanism, as his work *The Commonwealth of Oceana* (1656) showed, but he was a friend of CHARLES I and briefly shared his imprisonment with him. Even so CHARLES II had him arrested in 1661 for alleged conspiracy. His ideas are said to have influenced the makers of the US Constitution, especially in his insistence on a written constitution and a two-chamber legislature.

Harrison, Benjamin (1833–1901) Twenty-third President of the USA (1889–93), grandson of President William Henry HARRISON. During his Republican administration US interests helped to stimulate the PAN-AMERICAN MOVEMENT, while Pacific imperialist interests were advanced in Hawaii and Samoa. At home Congress passed the Sherman ANTI-TRUST Act, the MCKINLEY Tariff Act, and the Sherman Silver Purchase Act. Harrison honoured promises to implement the Pendleton Act for reform of the civil service, at the cost of some popularity within the Republican Party, and became personally involved in opening OKLAHOMA INDIAN TERRITORY to settlement in 1889.

Harrison, William Henry (1773–1841) Ninth President of the USA (1841). While governor of the Indiana Territory (1801–12), he defeated the Indian leader TECUMSEH at TIPPECANOE (1811), and as a major-general in the WAR OF 1812, he recaptured Detroit and established US supremacy in the west by defeating a British and Indian force at the Battle of the THAMES (1813). He served in the House of Representatives (1816–19) and the Senate (1825–28), and was elected President in 1840, running with John Tyler on the Whig ticket under the slogan 'Tippecanoe and Tyler too', but died one month after his inauguration.

Harsha (c. 590–647) Buddhist ruler of a large empire in north India (c. 606–47). He dominated the entire Gangetic plain, and also parts of the Punjab and Rajasthan, but was repulsed from the DECCAN. He allowed conquered rulers to keep their titles in return for tribute, and he is considered an enlightened and talented ruler. He organized Buddhist assemblies, established charitable institutions, and patronized learning, particularly poetry. His reign is well documented, notably by his celebrated court poet, Bana, and by a Chinese Buddhist pilgrim, Xuan Cang.

Hartford Convention (1814–15) US political conference, held by FEDERALIST supporters to consider the problems of New England in the WAR OF 1812. Dominated by moderates rather than extremists, the Convention adopted the establishment of an inter-state defence machinery independent of federal government provision, the prohibition of all embargoes lasting more than 60 days, as well as a series of constitutional amendments. The Treaty of GHENT brought an abrupt end to its deliberations, and the adverse publicity which it attracted accelerated the decline of the FEDERALISTS.

Harun al-Rashid (literally, 'Aaron the rightly guided') (c. 763–809) The fifth ABBASID caliph (786–809). Under him Baghdad reached its greatest brilliance, partly thanks to the ability of the Persian VIZIERS of the house of Barmak (until their fall in 803). He was a competent commander and a patron of learning and the arts. His court and capital provided the setting for many of the stories in the *Thousand and One Nights*. His division of the empire among his heirs led to conflict after his death (809–18). According to French chronicles, there was an exchange of embassies between Harun and CHARLEMAGNE.

Hasan, Muhammad Abdille Sayyid (1864–1920) Somali nationalist leader, known to the British as the 'Mad Mullah'. After a visit to Mecca he joined the Salihiya, a militant and puritanical Islamic fraternity. He travelled to the Sudan, Kenya, and Palestine before coming to Berbera on the Gulf of Aden. He believed that Christian colonization was destructive of Islamic faith in Somaliland and in 1899 he proclaimed a *jihad* (holy war) on all colonial powers. Between 1900 and 1904 four major expeditions by the British, Italians, and Ethiopians failed to defeat him. After a truce (1904–20) he resumed war again and was routed and killed by a British attack in 1920.

Hasdrubal (d.207 BC) Carthaginian general and son of HAMILCAR BARCA. He remained in Spain when his brother HANNIBAL invaded Italy in 218. Despite mixed fortunes, by 211 he had established Carthaginian power as far north as the River Ebro. Defeated at Baecula by Publius Cornelius SCIPIO (Africanus) in 208, he extricated most of his troops and marched to Italy in an attempt to join forces with Hannibal but was intercepted by two Roman armies and defeated and killed at Metaurus in 207.

Hasidim (from Hebrew, 'pious') A mystical movement within JUDAISM, which first found expression in 12th-century Germany. Modern Hasidim evolved in 18th-century Poland, where its leader, Ba'al Shem Tov (1700–60), taught a return to faith and piety. The movement was influenced by the KABBALAH, and advocated repeated prayer, song, chanting, and dance as joyous ways of perceiving God in all aspects of daily life. After rapid growth amongst the repressed Jewish communities of eastern Europe, the movement was curtailed by the rise of modernism. Today the largest groups of Hasidim are to be found in the USA and Israel, where their leaders, *zaddikim* ('saints'), are in the forefront of the movement for religious legislation, and are determined defenders of ORTHODOX JUDAISM. Followers are distinguished by their black dress, reminiscent of clothes worn in Poland in the 17th–18th centuries, and curled side-locks, as well as by their acceptance of the Orthodox Jewish prohibition against cutting the beard, which probably originated in a wish to be distinguished from unbelievers.

Hastings, Battle of (14 October 1066) A battle fought at Senlac, inland from Hastings (south-east England) between the English under HAROLD II and an invading army under Duke William of Normandy (WILLIAM I). Harold heard the news of the Norman invasion after his defeat of Harald Hardrada at STAMFORD BRIDGE, near York, and immediately marched southwards with his troops. The English resisted the Norman attack throughout a long day's fighting but the Norman cavalry and crossbowmen were superior to the English soldiers, fighting on foot and armed with axes. Harold was killed, traditionally by an arrow piercing his eye, and William, the victor, marched towards London.

Hastings, Warren (1732–1818) Governor-general of BENGAL (1774–85). He consolidated CLIVE's conquests in north-eastern India, but was afterwards impeached by his enemies. He worked his way up from a clerkship in the EAST INDIA COMPANY's service, gaining experience in both commerce and administration, and a deep and sympathetic insight into Indian culture. Although well equipped for the governorship, he faced insurmountable difficulties when enemies on his council continually vetoed his policies. A quarrel with Philip Francis ended in a duel; both survived and Francis carried home tales of Hastings's alleged malpractices. Among the subsequent impeachment charges were the waging of unjustified wars, extortion from Indian rulers and their families, and the judicial murder of an Indian moneylender who had threatened him. After a seven-year trial he was finally acquitted in 1795, and lived on to see his policies vindicated by the Company's success in India.

Scholarly opinion now holds that Hastings, although not entirely blameless, did not wittingly exceed the limits expected of a colonial administrator of his day. Indeed his constructive plans for improving the administration of Bengal, and his scholarly interest in India, make him in retrospect one of the most admirable of the first generation of British rulers of India.

Hatshepsut (c. 1540–c. 1481 BC) Egyptian ruler, the daughter of Thutmose I. After the death of her half-brother and husband, Thutmose II, the young THUTMOSE III succeeded, but she soon replaced him as the effective ruler and reigned until her death 20 years later. As well as furthering her father's building programme at KARNAK, she had a magnificent temple constructed at Deir al-Bahri.

Hausa The people of north-western Nigeria and southern Niger. The original Hausa states, which include KANO and ZARIA, were for many years the vassals of KANEM-BORNU. Muslim missionaries seem to have come in the 14th century, but during the reign of Muhammad Rumfa of Kano (1463–99) the celebrated divine al-Maghili is said to have introduced the SHARIA (the Muslim code of law), Sufism, and a body of constitutional theory. The Hausa states were conquered by the SONGHAY in 1513 and by the FULANI in the early 19th century.

Their traditional trading activities contributed to the spread of the Hausa language as a lingua franca throughout most of West Africa. Their society is hierarchical, consisting of several hereditary classes. In the wet season, the land is cultivated collectively by members of a patrilineage; millet, sorghum, and maize are grown for subsistence, while cotton, tobacco, and groundnuts are important cash crops. In the dry season, the Hausa take time off to travel or to trade.

Havel, Václav (1936–) Czech statesman and playwright, President of Czechoslovakia (1989–92) and of the Czech Republic (1993–). Born in Prague to a family of 'bourgeois descent', he was excluded from university. Instead he held various jobs before gaining entry into a theatrical academy as a stagehand. He wrote and published a number of plays before 1968, when his work was forbidden and declared subversive. He managed, however, to continue to write and to publish abroad, becoming the outstanding literary-philosophical analyst of the Central European experience under communism. His first play, *The Garden Party* (1963), uses the techniques of the Theatre of the Absurd to satirize post-war Czechoslovak society. *Largo Desolato* (1984) and *Temptation* (1985) continue his preoccupation with the individual at odds with a pervasive bureaucracy, while *Letters to Olga* (1989), based on letters addressed to his wife from prison, reflects on the interior life of the individual under state socialism.

In 1977 Haval formed a Committee for the Defence of the Unjustly Persecuted (VONS) and signed CHARTER 77. He was imprisoned (January–May 1977), held under house arrest (1977–79), and imprisoned again (1979–83) for alleged sedition. Arrested again in January 1989 for 'incitement and obstruction', he was released in May, by now the leading spokesman for political liberalization. He helped to form Civic Forum, which in December achieved the resignation of the government and the downfall of communism in his country. He was elected president by popular vote on 29 December 1989, but almost at once found himself under pressure from Slovakia, which opposed the free-market reforms of his Finance Minister, Václav Klaus. He resigned as President of Czechoslovakia when the country broke into the Slovak and Czech nations in 1993 and was elected President of the new Czech Republic (re-elected in 1998).

Havelock, Sir Henry (1795–1857) British general. He spent almost his entire career in India, where he took part in the first ANGLO-AFGHAN WAR (1839), the SIKH WARS (1843–49), and the INDIAN MUTINY, in which he led the troops which re-took Cawnpore (Kanpus) where the British garrison had been massacred. In September 1857 he relieved LUCKNOW, but had insufficient troops to be able to evacuate the Residency, where he died of cholera in November.

Hawaii (USA) The largest of a score of volcanic islands in the Central Pacific Ocean, which together comprise the US state of the same name.

History. The populated islands, inhabited by Polynesians and ruled by kings, were first named by Captain Cook (1778) after his patron, the Earl of Sandwich. Americans entered the islands from the 1820s and helped evolve a written language and the first constitution (1839). By 1893 a number of the new settlers wanted US annexation and were powerful enough to overthrow the Hawaiian monarchy under Queen Liliuokalani, though not to persuade the USA into annexation until 1898. The increasing interest in the mid-Pacific led the USA to declare Hawaii an organized territory (1900), and to install its chief Pacific naval base in PEARL HARBOR. Hawaii became the 50th state in 1959. In 1996 Hawaiians voted in favour of self-government in a referendum.

Hawke, Bob (Robert James Lee) (1929–) Australian statesman; Labor Prime Minister (1983–91). Hawke was president of the Australian Council of Trade Unions (1970–80) before becoming president (1973–78) and leader (1983–91) of the Labor Party. In 1990 he proposed a radical and controversial privatization programme but nevertheless won a fourth election victory, resigning a year later after losing his party's support.

Hawke, Edward, 1st Baron (1705–81) British admiral. He won fame by his great victory over the French at Finisterre in 1747. During the SEVEN YEARS WAR he blockaded the French Atlantic fleet at Brest, and when it broke out in 1759 he destroyed it at the Battle of QUIBERON BAY, thus effectively cutting France's communications with its Canadian colonies. Hawke then retired from active service.

Hawkins, Sir John (1532–95) English seaman. He made the first English slave-trading voyage from Africa to the West Indies in 1562. His third such voyage (1567–69) ended in disaster, when Spaniards attacked his ships at San Juan de Ulua, Mexico, thus exacerbating Anglo-Spanish tension. He became a Member of Parliament (1572), and succeeded his father-in-law as Treasurer of the Navy (1577). He was largely responsible for creating the fleet which defeated the SPANISH ARMADA (1588), was third in command after Lord Howard of Effingham and his own kinsman, Sir Francis DRAKE, and was knighted at sea during the battle. He died on an expedition to the Spanish West Indies.

Hawkins, Sir Richard (1560–1622) English commander in the Elizabethan navy. The son of Sir John HAWKINS, he served against the SPANISH ARMADA (1588). In 1593 he left England with the intention of surveying eastern Asia, where he hoped to establish an English trading empire. On the way, he plundered Valparaiso in Spanish America, and was held by the Spaniards until a ransom was paid in 1602.

Hawley-Smoot Tariff Act (1930) US legislation directed against imported goods and materials. Drafted before the Wall Street crash of 1929, it was endorsed by President HOOVER in the belief that it would help the hard-pressed farmers if increased tariffs were imposed. The Act aroused deep resentment abroad. Within two years, 25 countries had established retaliatory tariffs, and foreign trade, already declining, slumped even further.

Haya de la Torre, Victor Raúl (1895–1979) Peruvian statesman. He founded and led the Alianza Popular Revolucionaria Americana (APRA), known as the Aprista Party (1924), which became the spearhead of radical dissent in Peru. He advocated social and economic reform, nationalization of land and industry, and an end to US domination of South American economies. After the LEGUÍA regime fell he urged his APRA followers to overthrow the army-backed conservative oligarchy. He stood for President in 1931, but ballots were rigged and Colonel Sánchez Cerro was proclaimed victor. He was imprisoned 1931–33 and, after the latter's assassination, was in hiding in Peru (1935–45), becoming widely known through his writings. In 1945 the Aprista Party took the name Partido del Pueblo (People's Party) and supported José Luis Bustamante as President, but when he was overthrown in 1948 Haya took asylum in the Colombian Embassy in Lima until 1954, when he went into exile in Mexico until 1957. He contested the 1962 Presidential election, but the army intervened and Terry BELAÚNDE was declared the winner. In 1979 Haya de la Torre drafted the new constitution which restored parliamentary democracy, but he died before his party came to power.

Hayek, Friedrich August von (1899–1992) Austrian-born economist and political scientist. A prolific writer, Hayek was a libertarian, famous for his strong defence of *laissez-faire* liberalism and FREE MARKET economics. His tract, *The Road to Serfdom* (1944), condemned social democracy and the WELFARE STATE as harbingers of TOTALITARIANISM. In economic theory he emphasized the importance of market prices as disseminators of information to market participants, both about each others' behaviour and about technological possibilities.

Hayes, Rutherford B(irchard) (1822–93) Nineteenth President of the USA (1877–81). An Ohio Whig who turned Republican, he sat in the House of Representatives (1865–67) and became President by one electoral vote, following the disputed, fraudulent election of 1876. Congress decided to concede the victory to him, rather than to the Democratic candidate Tilden, who had the majority of popular votes, on condition that Hayes ended the process of radical reconstruction (RECONSTRUCTION ACTS) in the South by withdrawing Federal (Northern) troops. Senator Roscoe CONKLING, who had connived at Hayes's election, tried to undermine his authority by obstructing Hayes's attempts to reform the civil service. This led to bitter division in Republican ranks between 'Stalwarts' (professional politicians, led by Conkling) and 'Half Breeds' (reformers led by James G. BLAINE). Although Hayes ousted some of Conkling's supporters, including Chester A. ARTHUR, he was firm in his resolve not to seek a second term in 1880.

Haymarket Square riot (1886) An outbreak of violence in Chicago, USA. A protest at the McCormick Harvester Works culminated in a riot in which 100 people were wounded and several died. Eight anarchists were convicted of incitement to murder, and four were hanged. The international sympathy aroused for the accused led Governor John P. Altgeld to pardon the survivors on the grounds of judicial prejudice and mass hysteria.

Hay Treaties (1901, 1903) US treaties concerning the construction of a Central American canal linking the Atlantic and the Pacific. Negotiated by US Secretary of State John Milton Hay, the Hay–Pauncefote Treaty (1901) nullified the Clayton–Bulwer Treaty of 1850, which had prevented British or US acquisition of territory in Central America. The Hay–Herrán Treaty of 1903 leased the USA a canal zone from Colombia. Agreement broke down and was followed by a revolt in PANAMA (then a department of Colombia), undertaken with US connivance. Independence of Panama (1903) was followed by a new treaty, the Hay–Bunau–Varilla Treaty, which granted the USA a larger zone in perpetuity. President Roosevelt (rather than Secretary Hay) has, however, been held more responsible for this treaty.

health services The provision of organized hospital, medical, and dental services. During the 19th century there was startling progress in medical science, but also an increased awareness of health hazards and the need for improved urban public health. In the late 19th and early 20th centuries the development of public health-service hospitals and clinics became one of the main pillars of the WELFARE STATE, the British National Health Service being introduced in 1946. During the communist regimes of the former Soviet Union and east European republics, state health services alone were officially available, which is still the case in communist Cuba, while in Britain and many western countries health services through privately financed insurance schemes are an alternative to state services. In the USA most health facilities are so funded, apart from MEDICARE and Medicaid. Rising pharmaceutical costs, increased surgical skills, and higher life-expectancy are putting ever greater strains on public health services.

Hearst, William Randolph (1863–1951) US newspaper publisher and journalist. His exaggerated account of Cuba's struggle for independence from Spain was popularly believed to have brought on the SPANISH–AMERICAN WAR (1898). He opposed US entry into World War I and was unremittingly hostile to the League of Nations. From newspapers he branched into magazines and films, amassing a colossal fortune. But his own incursions into politics, for example as candidate for mayor of New York, were consistently unsuccessful.

Heath, Edward (1916–) British Conservative Prime Minister (1970–74). It was during his ministry that Britain became a member of the EUROPEAN ECONOMIC COMMUNITY (January 1973), a move to which Heath was personally deeply committed. Meanwhile, the troubles in NORTHERN IRELAND worsened and direct rule from London was introduced. In domestic and economic affairs the Heath ministry was beset with difficulties. The problems of inflation and balance of payments were serious and were exacerbated by the great increase in oil prices by OPEC in 1973. However, attempts to restrain wage rises led to strikes in the coal, power, and transport industries in the winter of 1973–74. After a national stoppage in the coal industry, Heath called an election to try to strengthen his position, but was defeated. Harold WILSON became Prime Minister. Heath was replaced as party leader by Margaret THATCHER in 1975.

Hébert, Jacques René (1757–94) French journalist and Revolutionary. He became a prominent member of the Cordeliers Club (an extreme Revolutionary club) in 1791. The following year he was a member of the Commune of Paris and was arrested in 1793 after his violent attacks on the GIRONDISTS. Although he was always popular with the mob, he and his followers, the Hébertistes, came into conflict with ROBESPIERRE when he

organized 'The Worship of Reason'. This substitute for the worship of God led to his arrest and execution in March 1794.

Hebrides Two groups of islands (Inner and Outer) off the north-west coast of Scotland. The Inner Hebrides include Skye, Mull, Jura, and Islay (the four largest), and Rhum, Eigg, and the island of Iona among many others. The Outer Hebrides, or Western Isles, which lie in an arc beyond the Little Minch Channel and the Sea of the Hebrides, include Lewis and Harris (the name of a single island), North and South Uist (two islands), Benbecula, and Barra in the south.

History. The largest few dozen islands have been inhabited since *c.* 3800 BC, settled by PICTS and then, from the 3rd century AD, by Scots. Except in the VIKING era, their way of life changed little until the 19th century, when large-scale sheep farming and subsequent clearances of crofters caused depopulation and widespread deprivation.

hedonism An ethical and psychological theory that sees the desire for pleasure as the central factor in human life. As an ethical view, hedonism (from the Greek *hēdonē*, 'pleasure') states that the only things that have value in themselves are states of pleasure or happiness. As a psychological theory, hedonism states that all action is determined and explained by the desire for pleasure or happiness. Hedonism in this second sense seems to conflict with the view that people are, at least sometimes, motivated by moral requirements and that they may prefer to sacrifice their own prospects for the sake of others. Hedonism has been professed in various forms throughout the ages. The Cyrenaics, a minor school of philosophers who flourished in the 4th century BC, saw the satisfaction of immediate, sensual pleasures as the single dominating factor in life. A more subtle and complex theory of hedonism was professed by the EPICUREANS, though their philosophy has often been misunderstood. It came under great pressure from the rise of Christianity, and doctrines of asceticism. MILL defended hedonism in both senses as part of his argument for UTILITARIANISM.

Hegel, George Wilhelm Friedrich (1770–1831) German philosopher of history. Strongly influenced by Romanticism and Idealism Hegel began by modifying KANT's metaphysical system in two fundamental respects: he argued that Kant's division of reality into knowable and unknowable realms was incoherent, and he introduced the dimension of history. The system that resulted (elaborated in *The Phenomenology of Mind*, 1807) viewed the world as the evolution of *Geist*, or Spirit, in a direction of increasing rationality, as *Geist* attained ever higher levels of self-consciousness. This process was for Hegel to be described by means of the 'dialectic', a form of logic quite different from deduction, in which each stage of history is composed of a thesis, contradicted by an antithesis, out of whose conflict there emerges a new and higher thesis, which is contradicted by a new antithesis, and so on. Hegel's world-view, in which history is governed by necessary laws and the world forms an organic whole, proclaimed that 'the rational is the real'.

hegira (Arabic, *hijra*, 'exodus', 'migration', or 'breaking of ties') MUHAMMAD's secret departure from MECCA in 622, accompanied by ABU BAKR, to live among the people of

Yathrib, later MEDINA, thus founding the first Muslim community. Under the second caliph, UMAR, this key event in the history of Islam was chosen as the starting-point for the Muslim calendar.

Hejaz The Red Sea coastal plain of the Arabian peninsula. The region has immense historical and cultural importance as the cradle of ISLAM and the site of the holy cities of MECCA and MEDINA. Under the OTTOMAN EMPIRE the Hejaz was opened up through the improvement of communications: first the construction of the SUEZ CANAL, then the opening of the Pilgrim Railway (1908), which linked Medina with Damascus. Following the 1916 Arab Revolt, which began in the region, and the subsequent fall of the Ottoman Empire, HUSSEIN IBN ALI became King of independent Hejaz. He subsequently abdicated (1924) in favour of his son, Ali, who also abdicated (1925) in the face of a WAHHABI invasion. The Wahhabi leader Ibn Saud, the sultan of Najd, assumed the title of King of Hejaz (1926) before uniting most of the Arabian Peninsula under his control to form the kingdom of Saudi Arabia in 1932.

Helena, St (c. 250–c. 330) Wife of Emperor Constantius Chlorus and mother of the Roman emperor CONSTANTINE, the first Christian emperor. When he became emperor he made her empress dowager. Aged over 60, she was converted to the Christian faith and thereafter was noted for her piety and acts of charity. She died while on PILGRIMAGE to Palestine and was buried in Rome. Legend associates her with the finding of the wooden cross on which JESUS CHRIST was crucified.

Helgoland (or Heligoland) A small island in the North Sea. Originally the home of Frisian seamen, it was Danish from 1714 until seized by the British navy (1807). It was ceded to Britain (1815) and held until exchanged with Germany for ZANZIBAR and Pemba (1890). Germany developed it into a naval base of great strategic importance. Under the terms of the VERSAILLES PEACE SETTLEMENT its naval installations were demolished (1920–22). They were rebuilt by the Nazis and again demolished (1947). It was returned to the Federal Republic of Germany (1952).

Heliopolis ('Sun City') The Greek name for the Egyptian city of Iunu or Onu, now a suburb of Cairo, important as the centre of the worship of Ra, the sun god, whose symbols were the pyramid and the obelisk. The temple there was the largest in Egypt after that of Amun at KARNAK. The temple has not survived, but many obelisks have, most notably two erected by Thutmose III, the so-called Cleopatra's Needles now in London and New York.

Hellenistic civilization The civilization that resulted from the spread of Greek language and culture throughout the Mediterranean between the late 4th century BC and the late 1st century BC. (Hellas, an area of southern Thessaly, was synonymous with Greece from the 7th century BC.) It has come to refer specifically to the civilization that arose in the wake of the conquests of ALEXANDER THE GREAT. The many cities founded by him and his successors were the centres for a fusion of Greek and 'barbarian' ways of life, with ALEXANDRIA in Egypt becoming the literary focus of the Mediterranean world. An important element in the diffusion of the new culture was the development of a common Greek dialect, *Koine*.

Hellespont The strait that joins the Aegean Sea with the Sea of Marmara, and which separates Europe from Asia. It has long been a key strategic point. Ancient Troy stood at its western end. King Xerxes crossed it with his Persian army over a bridge of boats (c. 481 BC); it was also crossed by Alexander the Great in 334 BC. Control of it in 405 BC enabled the Spartans to cut off corn supplies to Athens from the Black Sea area and thus bring the PELOPONNESIAN WAR to a conclusion. In course of time it became known as the Dardanelles.

Hellfire Club (1745–63) A notorious English society that met in the ruins of Medmenham Abbey in Buckinghamshire. It was founded by Sir Francis Dashwood in 1745, and its members reputedly indulged in debauchery and in the mocking of organized religion by the performance of blasphemous 'black masses'. Its membership included many politicians, the most famous of whom were WILKES, BUTE, and Sandwich.

helot An inhabitant of ancient Greece forced into serfdom by conquering invaders. Helots were used as agricultural labourers and in domestic service. The Messenians, subjected by SPARTA, greatly outnumbered the Spartan citizens, and fear of their rebellion caused the city to keep them under ruthlessly tight military control.

Helsinki Conference (1973–75) A series of meetings at Helsinki and later Geneva at which the Conference on Security and Co-operation in Europe (CSCE) was launched (1975). They were attended by leaders of 35 nations representing the entire membership of NATO, the WARSAW PACT, and the non-aligned countries. The conference was proposed by the Soviet Union with the motive of securing agreement to the permanence of the post-1945 frontiers, of furthering economic and technical co-operation, and of reducing East–West tension. The conference produced the Helsinki Final Act containing a list of agreements concerning political freedom, mutual co-operation, and human rights; it can be considered the major achievement of DÉTENTE. All signatories to the agreement, including the leaders of Soviet-bloc countries, agreed to respect 'freedom of thought, conscience, religion, and belief'. Follow-up meetings were held in Belgrade (1977), Madrid (1980), Ottawa (1985), and Paris (1990), when a permanent secretariat for the CSCE was established (based in Prague) and NATO and Warsaw Pact countries signed an unprecedented Treaty on Conventional Armed Forces in Europe, renouncing the use of force, and agreed that NATO and the Warsaw Pact states no longer regard one another as enemies. The 34 heads of state also adopted the Charter of Paris for a New Europe. In 1992 the CSCE decided to create its own armed peacekeeping force; it now has 53 member states.

Helvetii Celts who migrated from southern Germany to regions south and west of the Rhine in the 2nd century BC. In 102 BC they joined the Cimbri and Teutones in invading Italy and were defeated by Emperor MARIUS. Under pressure of Germanic migrations they attempted a mass migration into Roman GAUL in 58 BC. Julius CAESAR drove them back. AUGUSTUS incorporated their territory into Belgic GAUL. Overrun in the 5th century by a succession of Alemanni, FRANKS, Swabians, and Burgundians their name is preserved in the formal name for SWITZERLAND — the Helvetic Confederacy.

Helvétius, Claude Adrien (1715–71) French philosopher. He was a wealthy French financier whose book *De l'Esprit*, published in 1758, was condemned as immoral by both the Church and *parlement*, and was publicly burned. Its theme was that self-interest is the mainspring of all human activity and should be utilized by government for the promotion of public interest. This doctrine gave the Philosophical movement of the 18th-century ENLIGHTENMENT the foundation for a practical programme: the well-being of the human race could be secured by enlightened government without changing human nature. Helvétius was exiled to the country and finally went to England in 1763.

Hengist and Horsa JUTISH brothers, leaders of the first Anglo-Saxon invasion of England. According to BEDE, they were invited by King VORTIGERN to help reinforce British resistance to the raiding Picts and Scots (*c.* 449). The ANGLO-SAXON CHRONICLE claimed that Hengist and Horsa were joint kings of Kent and that when Horsa was killed (455) in battle, Aesc, the son of Hengist (d. *c.* 488), succeeded him.

Henrietta Maria (1609–69) French princess, Queen consort of CHARLES I of England from 1625. At first she was eclipsed in her husband's affection by BUCKINGHAM, but after his death (1628) she became closely identified with the king's politics and tastes. Her Catholicism made her unpopular and heightened public anxieties about the court's religious sympathies. As the Puritan opposition strengthened she began to intervene in politics. The rumour that Parliament was to impeach the queen drove Charles to attempt to arrest five Members of Parliament (FIVE MEMBERS), a contributory cause of the ENGLISH CIVIL WAR. From 1644 she lived mainly in France.

Henry I (the Fowler) (*c.* 876–936) Duke of Saxony (912–36) and King of Germany (919–36). He was elected king by the Franks and Saxons in 919 and was the first king of the Ottonian dynasty. He developed a system of fortified defences against Hungarian invaders whom he defeated in 933 at the Battle of the Riade. Despite challenges from the nobility, he laid a strong foundation for his son OTTO I.

Henry I (1068–1135) King of England (1100–35). He was the fourth and youngest son of WILLIAM I. When his brother WILLIAM II died, Henry seized the treasury at Winchester and was crowned three days later in London, while his elder brother Robert was still on Crusade. Although Robert received the duchy of Normandy in compensation and exacted an annual pension of £2,000 (1101), Henry invaded Normandy in 1106. Robert defeated at Tinchebrai and imprisoned at Cardiff Castle until his death in 1134. Louis VI of France exploited the situation in Normandy but in two campaigns (1111–13, 1116–20) he failed to take the duchy.

A determined ruler, Henry clashed with Archbishop ANSELM over his claim to appoint bishops (lay INVESTITURE). He improved royal administration, particularly in the EXCHEQUER, and extended and clarified the judicial systems. His law code, the *Leges Henrici Primi*, embodied much that had survived from Anglo-Saxon law. Unfortunately the death by drowning (1120) of his only legitimate son William whilst journeying to England

from Normandy led to the accession of Henry's nephew STEPHEN and a period of anarchy and civil war between Stephen and Henry's daughter, MATILDA.

Henry II (1133–89) King of England (1154–89). He succeeded King STEPHEN, who by the Treaty of Winchester (1153) had recognized Henry as his heir. As the son of Geoffrey, Count of Anjou, Henry also inherited Normandy, Maine, Touraine, Brittany, and Anjou (this last title making him the first ANGEVIN king of England). His marriage to ELEANOR OF AQUITAINE (1152), the repudiated wife of Louis VII of France, brought Henry even greater estates in France so that his kingdom stretched from northern England down to the Pyrenees. These territorial gains were reinforced by the homage of Malcolm III of Scotland (1157) and by his recognition as overlord of Ireland (1171).

Henry's immediate task on becoming king was to end the anarchy of Stephen's reign. He dealt firmly with barons who had built castles without permission, and undertook the confirmation of SCUTAGE (1157), an overhaul of military obligations in a review of feudal assessments (1166), and the introduction of a law that his subjects should equip themselves for military service (1181). He initiated a number of important legal reforms in the Assizes of CLARENDON (1166) and of Northampton (1176), and in his reign the land-law was developed to meet the needs of a more complex society. His reign, however, also saw rebellions led by his sons (1171–74) and the murder of the Archbishop of Canterbury, Thomas à BECKET (1170), a crime of which Henry was later absolved by Pope Alexander III (1172).

Henry III (1207–72) King of England (1216–72). He succeeded his father JOHN at the age of nine. During his minority (until 1227) England was managed by William Marshal, the first Earl of Pembroke, Peter des Roches, Bishop of Winchester, and Hubert de Burgh. Henry's personal rule soon proved his general incompetence as king, his preoccupation with aesthetic pursuits, including the rebuilding of Westminster Abbey, and his preference for foreign advisers and favourites. He received an early warning of baronial frustration when a rebellion broke out (1233–34) led by Richard Marshal, the third Earl of Pembroke. In 1258, one of the king's French favourites, Simon de MONTFORT, led the English barons to draft a series of reforms (the Provisions of Oxford). While appearing to accept these, Henry sought to recover his independence. The ensuing civil war (1264–67) led to the temporary control of England by de Montfort following his victory at Lewes (1264). Although Henry recovered control after the Battle of Evesham (1265), where de Montfort was killed, he became increasingly dependent upon his son, the future EDWARD I.

Henry IV (1366–1413) King of England (1399–1413). He was the only legitimate son of John of GAUNT, and would have inherited vast estates on his father's death (in 1399) had RICHARD II not banished him. He retaliated by invading England and forcing Richard to yield both the estates and the crown of England. Henry's position as king was not a strong one. He needed the support of the Church (which caused him to be a persecutor of LOLLARDS), the nobility (who dominated his councils), and the House of Commons (which resented his frequent requests for money). Until 1408 he had to deal with the rebellions of Owen GLENDOWER and the PERCYS, and for the remaining five years of his short life he was in poor health.

Henry IV (1553–1610) King of Navarre (1572–89) and first BOURBON King of France (1589–1610). He was educated as a Calvinist, mainly under the supervision of his mother, Queen Jeanne d'Albret of Navarre. As a leading Protestant nobleman, he was recognized by COLIGNY as the nominal head of the HUGUENOTS. In 1572 he married Marguerite de Valois, daughter of Catherine de MEDICI, and a few days later narrowly escaped with his life during the ST BARTHOLOMEW'S DAY MASSACRE by professing himself a Catholic. He was kept a virtual prisoner at court until 1576, when he escaped, resumed his Protestant beliefs, and played a major part in the subsequent FRENCH WARS OF RELIGION.

He fought the War of the THREE HENRYS (1585–89) in a successful bid to secure his succession to the French throne, professed himself a Catholic again in 1593, and brought peace to France at last in 1598. By the Edict of NANTES he established political rights and some religious freedom for the Huguenots. With the aid of his Huguenot chief minister, SULLY, he reconstructed his war-torn kingdom, while continuing to pursue an anti-Habsburg foreign policy. He is sometimes regarded as the founder of the absolute, centralized regime of later 17th-century France, but the breakdown of royal authority after his assassination by a Catholic fanatic showed that his power had depended on his own personal popularity.

Henry V (1387–1422) King of England (1413–22), eldest son of HENRY IV. He was a skilful military leader, with experience gained in campaigning against Owen GLENDOWER, and took advantage of French weakness by claiming the French crown (1413) and then invading France (1415), where he won the magnificent victory of AGINCOURT. In 1417 he invaded France again, and again fortune favoured him. He was able to conclude the very favourable Treaty of Troyes (1420), by which he was to succeed to the French crown at Charles VI's death and meantime to marry Charles's daughter, Katherine of Valois. However, he died only 15 months later. He was a popular hero, as celebrated in Shakespeare's play *Henry V*, and restored civil order in England in addition to his French campaigns.

Henry VI (1422–71) King of England (1422–61, 1470–71). He inherited the throne from his father HENRY V when only nine months old. During his minority, the court was divided by a power struggle between Humphrey, Duke of GLOUCESTER, and the BEAUFORTS, which led to the Wars of the ROSES. A pious and withdrawn man, he suffered from insanity from 1453. His marriage to MARGARET OF ANJOU brought him a son, Edward, in 1453, who displaced Richard Plantagenet, 3rd Duke of YORK as heir to the throne. Richard claimed it for himself in 1460 and when he was killed at WAKEFIELD, his son Edward seized it in March 1461 and was crowned Edward IV. Henry was later captured, and spent the rest of his life in the Tower of London apart from the brief period when WARWICK restored him to the throne (1470–71), but Edward then defeated Warwick and reimprisoned Henry. When Henry's son, Prince Edward was killed at TEWKESBURY in 1471, Edward IV won back the throne and had Warwick put to death.

Henry VII (1457–1509) King of England (1485–1509), the son of Edmund TUDOR and Margaret BEAUFORT. Through his mother he was an illegitimate descendant of John of GAUNT and so had a tenuous claim to the throne, but rivals' deaths in the Wars of the ROSES strengthened his position as the Lancastrian claimant and enabled him to oust RICHARD III at the Battle of BOSWORTH FIELD. He established the Tudor dynasty on firm foundations. The children of his marriage to Elizabeth of York were married to foreign royalty (his son Arthur to CATHERINE OF ARAGON, and his daughter Margaret to James IV of Scotland), while he built up the crown's financial resources so that he was not dependent on Parliament and was able to leave a considerable fortune to his son, HENRY VIII.

Henry VIII (1491–1547) King of England (1509–47). The second son of HENRY VII and Elizabeth of York, he succeeded to the throne aged 18 and began his reign by executing Dudley and Empson, two of his father's financial officers. From 1513 to 1529 Thomas WOLSEY managed affairs of state and diplomacy while Henry played the part of the Renaissance prince, preferring hunting and dancing to government.

From 1525 he turned against his wife CATHERINE OF ARAGON because of her failure to provide him with male heirs. The pope's refusal to annul his marriage led to England's break with the ROMAN CATHOLIC CHURCH. With the assistance of Thomas CROMWELL and a compliant, anticlerical Parliament (1529–36), legislation was passed to sever the English Church from papal jurisdiction and Henry became Supreme Head of the English Church (1534). He exploited the Dissolution of the MONASTERIES for his own profit and used the revenues from the dissolution to pay for his military campaigns of the 1540s. But he remained conservative in doctrine, believing in Catholicism without the pope and retaining the title 'Defender of the Faith' granted him by the pope in 1521 for his treatise against LUTHER. Meanwhile he married Anne BOLEYN and subsequently Jane SEYMOUR, ANNE OF CLEVES, Catherine HOWARD and Catherine PARR, of whom only Jane Seymour bore him a son, the future EDWARD VI.

Little was achieved by his expensive wars with France and Scotland, but a powerful English navy was created. His attempts to capitalize on the struggles of FRANCIS I of France and CHARLES V of Spain severely undermined the English economy.

Henry, Patrick (1736–99) American patriot, born of Scots-Irish parents in Virginia. He attracted notice as the anti-establishment lawyer in the Parsons' Cause, in which he argued that the use of a royal veto (obtained by clergy wishing to reverse a new law requiring them to be paid in money, at a discounted rate, rather than tobacco) was improper as it was against the public good. As the author of the Virginia Resolves (1765) against the STAMP ACT, he became leader of the frontier radicals, declaiming in 1775: 'Give me liberty or give me death'. He was the first governor of the state and opposed the CONSTITUTION OF THE USA on states' rights grounds, but in the 1790s he supported the FEDERALIST PARTY.

Henry the Lion (1129–95) Duke of Saxony and Bavaria. He was the son of Henry the Proud of the German Welf family. He obtained his duchies with the help of Emperor FREDERICK I (Barbarossa), expanding his territories and influence as far as the Baltic, and encouraging trade. Ambitious and powerful, he lost the emperor's favour and was banished in 1180. He was welcomed in England, as his second wife was the daughter of HENRY II and he became a power in ANGEVIN political life. By 1190 he had regained much of his former territory. His son, Otto IV, continued the challenge to the HOHENSTAUFEN.

Henry the Navigator (1394–1460) Portuguese prince, the third son of John I of Portugal and grandson of John of GAUNT. He did not himself undertake any voyages of EXPLORATION, but was the patron of a succession of Portuguese seamen who made voyages of discovery among the Atlantic islands and down the west coast of Africa as far south as Cape Verde and the Azores, which led, after his death, to the discovery of the Cape of Good Hope and the sea route to India. With the aim of finding a new route to the Indies, as governor of the Algarve he established a school at which navigation, astronomy, and cartography were taught to his captains and pilots, and constructed the first observatory in Portugal.

Heraclius I (575–642) Byzantine emperor (610–41). He came to power having ousted the usurper Phocas, and set about the reorganization of the empire and its army, driving back the Persians in Asia Minor and securing a peace treaty. He then turned his attentions to the north, coming to terms with the invading AVARS, and strengthening the frontier. He then devoted his energies to the study of religion, neglecting the empire and losing Syria and Egypt to the Muslims.

heraldry The study of coats of arms and of their accessories of crests, badges, mottoes, and flags. Its origins are military. Soldiers in armour and helmets could not easily be identified in battle and so the practice evolved of displaying a sign or device on the shield and on the linen surcoat worn over the armour (from which the terms 'coat-of-arms' and 'court armoury' derive). The first heraldic designs may have been worn by the Crusaders, but their use became widespread in Europe in the 12th century. A similar system also emerged in Japan during the 12th century.

By the 13th century heraldry had so developed that it had its own terminology, based on Old French. Its colours are called 'tinctures' of which there are two metals – gold (*or*) and silver (*argent*)—and five colours – blue (*azure*), black (*sable*), green (*vert*), purple (*purpure*), and red (*gules*). In England heralds were formed into the College of Arms (1484). Scotland has its Court of the Lord Lyon (1592).

Herculaneum A small Roman town near Naples, in Italy: lying near the volcano Vesuvius, it was the first to be buried in the eruption of 79 AD, which also claimed POMPEII. Over 20 cm (8 inches) of ash fell on 24 August. This was followed by blast clouds and glowing avalanches of lava early the following day. Many of the population are now thought to have been caught in flight on the beach, buried, like the town, under 20 m (over 60 feet) of volcanic mud 0.5 km (0.25 mile) from the present coastline. It was discovered accidentally by a well-digger in 1709. Systematic archaeological excavation of the site only began in the 19th century.

Herero Wars (1904–08) Campaigns by German colonialists against the Herero people in German South-West Africa. A Herero rebellion resulted in the near-extermination of the population by the Germans, their numbers falling from over 100,000 to 15,000. The survivors were resettled in the inhospitable desert land of contemporary Hereroland in NAMIBIA.

heresy Belief in a doctrine held to be false by the Christian Church. During the Middle Ages it was believed to be necessary to follow the one 'true' religion, which provided the only guarantee of salvation and afterlife. Consequently those who came to believe that orthodox teaching was inadequate or wrong risked being declared heretics. Since the Church sought to maintain the unique validity of its declared doctrine conflict was inevitable.

The early Church condemned Gnostics in the 2nd century and the ARIANS and NESTORIANS in the 4th century. The ICONOCLASTS were condemned at the Council of NICAEA in 787. The condemnation of the CATHARS in southern Europe led to the ALBIGENSIAN crusade. Later dissatisfaction with orthodox teaching led ultimately to PROTESTANTISM. The INQUISITION from its earliest days upheld the Church's doctrine and became responsible for the rooting out of unorthodoxy.

Hereward the Wake (11th century) A semi-legendary Anglo-Saxon outlaw best known for his resistance to the Norman conquerors of England and as the leader of a rebellion against them (1070–71). He supported a Danish raid on the monastery of Peterborough in retaliation for the recent appointment of a Norman abbot. Subsequently he set up camp on the Isle of Ely in eastern England where he was joined by Morcar, the English Earl of Northumbria. Although Morcar later surrendered, Hereward escaped capture; his exploits inspired many legends.

hermit (from the Greek word for 'desert') Someone who for religious reasons takes up a solitary life. The first Christian hermits, from the late 3rd century onwards, were most numerous in and around Egypt; some of them were highly influential and were visited by pilgrims. St Basil the Great (*c.* 330–79) prepared a monastic rule that is still followed in the Eastern Church. The eremitic way of life influenced European monastic orders such as the CARTHUSIANS and CARMELITES.

Herod family A dynasty of Idumaean Jews who ruled in Palestine with the support of Rome. Its founder, Antipater, was appointed governor of Judaea in 47 BC by Julius CAESAR and murdered in 44 BC. Herod the Great was appointed 'King of the Jews' in 40 BC and he ruled Judaea (37–34 BC) with ruthlessness and skill, maintaining an unaccustomed peace. His encouragement of Greek culture was resented by Jewish nationalists and the end of his reign was marked by violent palace feuds. After his death, the kingdom was divided between three of his sons. Archelaus ruled Judaea, Idumaea, and Samaria (4 BC–6 AD); he was deposed and his territory put under a Roman governor. Herod Antipas ruled Galilee and Peraea (4 BC–39 AD); JOHN THE BAPTIST criticized him for marrying his brother's wife *c.* 27 AD. After religious riots, Caligula exiled him. Philip ruled the territory east of Galilee (4 BC–34 AD). By 41 Herod Agrippa I, a grandson of Herod the Great who had been educated at the imperial court in Rome, had, with the help of CLAUDIUS, reunited these territories which he ruled as king (41–44). His son Herod Agrippa II, the last of the dynasty, only ruled in northern Palestine (50–c. 93). He helped the Romans crush the JEWISH REVOLT (66–70).

Herodotus (c. 490–480 to c. 430–420 BC) Greek historian, accorded the title the 'Father of History', since he wrote on a scale that had never been attempted before. He wrote a comprehensive nine-book account of the GREEK–PERSIAN WARS. The scope of his work, which included an account of the earlier history of the Persian empire and a long digression on Egypt, reflects both his inquiring mind and his extensive travels; he visited places as far apart as Athens, Babylon, Egypt, and the Black Sea. Information was elicited from people encountered on his journeys and from his own observations, though he may often have accepted too readily what he heard, failing to subject these accounts to critical scrutiny. Nevertheless, his *History*, full of information about the contemporary Persian and Greek worlds, was an outstanding achievement. His style is simple, clear, and graceful, and his narrative has great charm.

Herrin massacre (22 June 1922) A clash between unionized strikers and non-unionized miners in the USA. It occurred in Herrin, Illinois, where the employers had attempted to break a strike by importing non-union men. Striking miners forced these to stop working, promised them safe-conduct, marched them from the mine, and then opened fire, killing around 25 men. A grand jury returned 214 indictments for murder and related offences, but local feeling prevented convictions.

Hertzog, James Barry Munuik (1866–1942) South African statesman. In the Second BOER WAR he was a brilliant guerrilla leader. In 1910 he joined the first Union of South Africa cabinet. In 1912 he opposed BOTHA and in 1914 he formed the NATIONAL PARTY, aiming to achieve South African independence and oppose support for Britain in World War I. From 1924 to 1929, as Prime Minister, he made Afrikaans an official language, instituted the first Union flag, and was a protectionist. In 1933 he formed a coalition with J. C. SMUTS, and in 1934 they united the Nationalist and South African Parties as the UNITED PARTY. In racial affairs he was a strict segregationist. Although he won the 1938 election, his opposition to joining Britain in World War II brought about his downfall (1939).

Herzen, Alexander Ivanovich (1812–70) Russian author and revolutionary. He was exiled to Viatka in 1835 after being suspected of sympathy with the DECEMBRISTS. He returned to Moscow in 1842, where he became a leader of the 'Westernizers' who believed that Russia must adopt the free institutions and secular thought of western Europe in order to progress. He left Russia in 1847. An exile in London, Geneva, and Paris, he wrote prolifically, supporting both moderate reform and radical revolution in turn and influencing Russian liberals and communists alike.

Herzl, Theodor (1860–1904) Hungarian Jewish writer and founder of modern ZIONISM. As correspondent of a Vienna newspaper he was sent to Paris to cover the DREYFUS trial (1894). The ANTI-SEMITISM he witnessed there confirmed his resolve that the only solution to the Jewish problem was the establishment of a Jewish national state. In the pamphlet *Der Judenstaat* (1896) he set out his aims, and convened the first Zionist Congress

at Basle (1897). His arguments were forcibly underlined by a series of POGROMS against Jews in Russia. He approached rulers, statesmen, and financiers in many countries, hoping for their support for a Jewish national home in PALESTINE, but died before his efforts could be realized.

Hess, (Walther Richard) Rudolf (1894–1987) German Nazi leader. He shared imprisonment with HITLER after the MUNICH 'BEER-HALL' PUTSCH, and was his deputy as party leader and Minister of State. In 1941, secretly and of his own volition, he flew to Scotland to negotiate peace between Britain and Germany. He was imprisoned by the British for the duration of the war and then, for life, by the Allies at the NUREMBERG TRIALS. From 1966 he was the sole inmate of Spandau Prison in Berlin, where he committed suicide.

Hesse A state within the Federal Republic of Germany. In the 19th century the name was used for both the Grand Duchy of Hesse-Darmstadt, and the electorate of Hesse-Kassel. Hesse-Kassel allied with Austria in 1866, whereupon Prussian troops invaded and the electorate was annexed by Prussia, who imposed reforms. In 1815 Hesse-Darmstadt regained territories on the Rhine (Rheinhessen) from France, joined the ZOLLVEREIN (1828), and saw considerable economic growth. After 1848, under the reactionary Chief Minister Baron Dalwigk, Roman Catholicism was encouraged to oppose the ambitions of Protestant Prussia. In 1871 it became one of the states of the new GERMAN SECOND EMPIRE, after which it was simply termed Hesse. Louis IV (1877–92) married a daughter of Queen Victoria; through their daughter, who became the last empress of Russia, the disease of haemophilia was transmitted to the imperial family of Russia. The last grand duke abdicated in 1918. In 1945 most of the Hesse territories and part of old Nassau were merged to form the *Land* of Greater Hesse (Gross-Hessen), later called simply Hessen.

Hexham, Battle of (15 May 1464) A battle of the Wars of the ROSES in which a YORKIST force led by John Neville, Earl of Montagu, captured Henry BEAUFORT, 3rd Duke of Somerset, three miles from the town of Hexham, in Northumberland. Somerset was beheaded on the field of battle and many of his followers were executed soon afterwards, while Neville was rewarded with the estates of the PERCY family and the earldom of Northumberland.

Heydrich, Reinhard (1904–42) German Nazi police official. He joined the SS in 1931, and in 1934 became deputy head of the GESTAPO. He played a leading part in several of the darkest episodes of Nazi history, and from 1941 administered the Czechoslovak territory of Bohemia-Moravia, his inhumanity and his numerous executions earning him the names the 'Hangman of Europe' and 'the beast'. He was assassinated by Czech nationalists in 1942. The Germans retaliated with one of the most extreme reigns of terror in World War II, set to paralyse Czech opposition both in Prague and in the rural areas. Civilians were indiscriminately executed and the entire male population of the villages of Lidice and Ležáky murdered.

Hezekiah (d. 687 BC) King of Judah (715–687 BC). When he came to power, Judah was a vassal state of the ASSYRIAN empire, and with the leaders of neighbouring states he was involved in a number of planned rebellions. The prophet ISAIAH spoke against these, but eventually Hezekiah did rebel and was heavily defeated in 701, when SENNACHERIB invaded, the land was devastated, and only Jerusalem escaped destruction. The Bible describes his work of religious reform, destroying local shrines and various cult objects, and attempting to suppress the worship of local gods. The reform was short-lived, pagan practices being re-introduced after his death by his son and successor Manasseh.

Hidalgo y Costilla, Miguel (1753–1811) Mexican priest and freedom fighter. He inspired (16 September 1810) the Mexican War for Independence from Spain with his *Grito de Dolores* ('Cry of Dolores'), proclaimed from the pulpit of his parish church at Dolores. Within a few months he had amassed an army of almost 80,000, but lacking the military skill necessary to complement his well-developed social ideology, the movement was defeated after much bloodshed at the hands of the royalist army. Captured in 1811, he was tried by the Inquisition and referred to the secular authorities for execution.

Hideyoshi (1536–98) Japanese warrior. He continued ODA NOBUNAGA's work of unifying the country that had been fragmented by the feuds between DAIMYO. Between 1582 and 1591, by a mixture of military strategy and skilful diplomacy he broke their power. Mistrustful of the power of Buddhist monks, for a time he encouraged Catholic missionaries but later savagely persecuted Christians in Nagasaki. He built castles, carried out land surveys, and disarmed peasants. His ambition was to conquer China, and when in 1592 KOREA, a vassal state of China, refused passage to his troops, his army numbering 200,000 captured Seoul and advanced north until MING armies forced him to retreat. The Koreans routed him at sea. A second campaign was abandoned when Hideyoshi died. He appointed TOKUGAWA IEYASU a guardian of his son, Hideyori.

hieroglyphs The signs used for formal inscriptions in ancient EGYPT. They were devised *c.* 3000 BC and were used, mainly for religious and monumental purposes, until the late 3rd century AD. They were representational in design, and were held to have near-magic powers. For practical purposes the structure of the script, as well as its form, was much too clumsy, and even cursive or 'long-hand' versions, the hieratic and demotic scripts, required long professional training to learn. Hieroglyphs have played an important part of archaeological research (ROSETTA STONE), extending written history by 2,000 years beyond classical times. The term has been applied more loosely to other complicated but ornamental scripts used by the MINOAN CIVILIZATION, the HITTITES, and the MAYA.

Highland Clearances The deliberate removal of Scottish 'crofter' peasants by landlords during the 19th century. In the later 18th century, Scottish society in the Highlands suffered severely with the collapse of the system of chiefs and fighting clans. Subsistence farming could not sustain an increasing population and this was aggravated by the policy of many major landowners of clearing their land for sheep farming by expulsion of crofters and the burning of their cottages. The potato famine during the HUNGRY FORTIES aggravated the problem and in the 1880s, after the arrival of the railway, sheep were replaced by deer. In 1882 there were outbreaks of violence, the 'Crofters War', which was investigated by a Royal Commission. In 1885 the crofters voted for the first time in a general election, and an Act of Parliament in 1886 gave them some security of tenure. Yet depopulation steadily continued. Many Scottish Highlanders emigrated throughout the British empire.

highwaymen Robbers who plagued Britain's main roads during the 17th and 18th centuries. There had been thieves and footpads from Anglo-Saxon times, but improved roads, more frequent travelling, and the growth of coaching inns made rich pickings for mounted thieves who sometimes worked in gangs in collusion with innkeepers. They were in reality much less romantic than is generally shown in fiction; the fear of being identified made them only too willing to murder their victims. Some, such as Swift Nick Levison, hanged at York in 1684, Dick Turpin (1705–39), and Jack Sheppard (1702–24), became folk heroes, but in fact highwaymen were always dangerous, and their appearance in central London in broad daylight in the mid-18th century provoked vigorous efforts to stamp them out. By the early 19th century the menace of highwaymen had been largely overcome.

highwaymen *An engraving of a highwayman named Maclaine robbing Lord Eglington on Hounslow Heath on 26th June 1750. Maclaine's accomplice, knowing that Lord Eglington was armed with a blunderbuss, used his coach driver as a human shield, while Maclaine came up from behind and ordered Lord Eglington to throw down his weapon or 'he wou'd blow his brains through his face'. The highwaymen escaped with a portmanteau and 50 guineas but a month later Maclaine was arrested and sent to prison.*

Hill, James Jerome (1838–1916) Canadian-born US railway builder. He opened the Great Northern Railway line to Seattle, Washington, in 1893, building it without government subsidies. He gained control of the Northern Pacific and the Chicago, Burlington, and Quincy lines. His holding company, the Northern Securities Company, was outlawed by the US Supreme Court in 1904, but he remained a potent financial force.

Hill, Sir Rowland (1795–1879) British administrator and inventor. He was the originator of the penny postage-stamp system, subsequently adopted throughout the world. In 1837 he published a pamphlet, *Post Office Reform*, in which he proposed that a uniform, low rate of postage, prepaid by the sender, should be introduced. In it he described his invention of the postage stamp, 'a bit of paper just large enough to bear the stamp, and covered at the back with a glutinous wash'. He adopted the notion from Charles Knight's proposal in 1834 that the postage of newspapers should be collected by means of uniformly stamped wrappers. Despite bureaucratic opposition, his proposals were put into effect in 1840.

Himmler, Heinrich (1900–45) German Nazi police chief. He began life as a poultry farmer in Bavaria; as an early member of the Nazi Party he took part in the MUNICH 'BEER-HALL' PUTSCH (1923). He became chief of the SS in 1929. With the help of HEYDRICH he founded the SD (security service) in 1932. In 1936 he became chief of all the police services, including the GESTAPO, and as head of the Reich administration from 1939 extended his field of repression to occupied countries. From 1943 he was Interior Minister, and commander of the reserve army. From a position of supreme power he was able to terrorize his own party and all German-occupied Europe. Although personally nauseated by the sight of blood, he established and oversaw CONCENTRATION CAMPS in which he directed the systematic genocide of Jews. He ruthlessly put down the conspiracy against Hitler in the JULY PLOT of 1944, but a few months later was himself secretly negotiating German surrender to the Allies, hoping to save himself thereby. Hitler expelled him from the party, and Himmler attempted to escape. he was caught (1945) by British troops and committed suicide by swallowing poison.

Hindenburg, Paul von (1847–1934) German general and statesman. He fought at the Battle of Königgratz (Sadowa) and in the FRANCO-PRUSSIAN WAR (1870–71) and retired in 1911. He was recalled to active service at the outbreak of WORLD WAR I and crushed the Russians at Tannenberg in east Prussia (August 1914). In 1916 he became chief of the general staff. After the failure of Germany's offensive (1918) he advised the need to sue for peace. After the war he came to tolerate the WEIMAR REPUBLIC and in 1925 was elected as President in succession to EBERT. Re-elected (1932), he did not oppose the rise of HITLER, but appointed him as Chancellor (January 1933) on the advice of Franz von PAPEN.

Hinduism The religious beliefs and social customs that originated in India. These are a complex mixture of elements from the Indo-European culture brought by the ARYAN invasions of 1500 BC onwards, and from the indigenous pre-Aryan and Dravidian societies. Because of its evolution over such a long period, Hinduism embraces a vast diversity of religious beliefs and practices, and is neither dogmatic nor evangelical.

Despite the lack of a binding theological creed, several features unify Hindu consciousness. One is respect for the VEDAS, the earliest Hindu sacred texts. Fundamental to many schools of Hindu philosophical thought (in particular Vedanta) is the belief in an eternal and all-pervading principle of ultimate reality, Brahman. Brahman itself is without individual personality, but for most Hindus, religious worship on a practical level is directed towards numerous personal gods and goddesses, the most important being Vishnu, Shiva, and the Great Goddess (Shakti, Durga, or Kali). Each of these is the object of monotheistic devotion, and their individual cults (Vaishnavism, Shaivism, and Shaktism) constitute in practice the three major forms of Hinduism. Most Hindus regard the sacredness of the land of India and the CASTE SYSTEM as central to their religion.

Other common teachings concern the moral law of cause and effect (*karma*), the nature of the soul (*atman*), reincarnation (*samsara*), and, for many Hindu traditions, the possibility of union with Brahman through *moksha*, or spiritual liberation. Running through Hinduism is a constant tension between the importance of one's duty in society (*dharma*) and the ideal of world renunciation, a conflict which is illustrated in the BHAGAVADGITA (Song of the Lord), part of the epic poem the Mahabharata. Hindu worship (*puja*) is based at home, at a local shrine, or within the *mandir* (Hindu temple), and it includes essential daily rituals, popular public celebrations of festivals, familial rites of passage, and non-essential but highly regarded acts such as pilgrimage to one of India's many sites of religious significance, most notably the River Ganges and the town of Varanasi (Benares). Hinduism is followed by approximately 600 million Indians, and, through migration, has spread to East Africa, South Africa, South-east Asia, the Caribbean, Canada, the USA, and Britain.

In the 19th century there were many reform movements that varied in their response to the catalyst of Western influence (see also HINDU REVIVALISM). The foremost reformer of the 20th century was Mohandas GANDHI, champion of the deprived and the untouchables, revered and reviled for his advocacy of non-co-operation, *ahimsa* (non-violence), *satyagraha* (truth-force), and *swaraj* (self-rule). Hinduism, like other religions, today contends with increasing secularization.

Hindu Mahasabha A Hindu communal organization. It was first established in the Punjab before 1914, and became active during the 1920s under the leadership of Pandit Mohan Malaviya (1861–1946) and Lala Rajpat Rai (1865–1928), when it campaigned for social reform and for the reconversion of Hindus from Islam. Its attitude towards Hindu–Muslim relations strained the relations of the Mahasabha with CONGRESS and in 1937 it broke away from Congress. After independence the party declined in importance as the Jana Sangh became the leading exponent of Hindu communal ideas.

Hindu revivalism Hindu responses to the encounter with the West in the 19th and early 20th centuries (see HINDUISM). These are sometimes described as a 'reformation', a 'renaissance', or 'neo-Hinduism'. Hindu revivalism is characterized either by the Hinduization of Western concepts or by an interpretation of indigenous concepts in the light of Western categories. There are many thinkers and ideas associated with this process. Raja Ram Mohun ROY (1772–1833) was the forerunner of new Hinduism; he learned English, located Hindu ideas in the context of Western ones in order to promote Hindu self-understanding, and founded the reform movement the BRAHMO SAMAJ (Society of God). Debendranath Tagore (1817–1905) was his successor as leader of the Society; he explicitly questioned the infallibility of the VEDAS and called for an experimental spirituality based on the aphorisms of the UPANISHADS. Keshab Chandra Sen (1838–84) sought inspirational sources within Hinduism which could demonstrate the universal harmony between experience in different religions, especially CHRISTIANITY and Vedanta Hinduism. The most famous figure was Swami VIVEKANANDA (1863–1902), who claimed that Vedanta was the Hindu exemplification of that oneness to which all religions aspired, and that the idea and practice of tolerance and universality were India's gift to the world; he admired Western self-confidence and scientific success, and formed a model of mutual influence in which the West taught its material skills to India, which reciprocated with its spiritual teachings. Bankim Chandra Chatterji (1838–94) put forward a secular and humanistic reading of the Hindu religious tradition that also supported India's claims to national self-assertion. Dayanand Saraswati (1824–83), founder of the ARYA SAMAJ (Society of Aryans), tried to emphasize the global significance of Vedic teachings by discerning scientific and technological ideas in them.

The term 'Hindu revivalism' is also used to describe an ideology of NATIONALISM based on allegedly Hindu values that is professed by some groups (notably the BJP party) in contemporary Indian politics.

hippodrome A course on which the ancient Greeks and Romans held CHARIOT and horse races. The courses were U-shaped with a barrier down the centre. The competitors would race down one side and then back up the other. Spectators watched from tiered stands. OLYMPIA had an early example, and hippodromes were a typical feature of major Greek cities of classical and Hellenistic times. The one at CONSTANTINOPLE held about 100,000 spectators and was the scene of fierce rivalry among partisan supporters. The Circus Maximus at Rome was modelled on the Greek hippodrome.

Hirohito (1901–89) Emperor of Japan (1926–89). The eldest son of Crown Prince Yoshihito (later the Taisho Emperor), Hirohito was appointed Regent in 1921 and, after surviving an assassination attempt, succeeded to the throne in 1926, initiating the Showa era. Although he did not approve of military expansion, he had little opportunity to exercise his full technical sovereignty, allowing the political triumph of TOJO and the militarists. He continued to follow his counsellors' advice not to weaken the throne by becoming involved in politics until 1945 when, convinced of the need to end World War II, he intervened to force the armed services to accept unconditional surrender. Saved from trial as a war criminal by MACARTHUR, Hirohito renounced his divinity but retained the monarchy, albeit as a symbol without governmental power, in the new constitution of 1947.

Hiroshima Japanese city in southern Honshu. Hitherto largely undamaged by the US bombing campaign, Hiroshima became the target of the first atomic bomb attack on 6 August 1945, which resulted in the virtual obliteration of the city centre and the deaths of about one-third of the population of 300,000. The attack on Hiroshima, together with that on NAGASAKI three days later, led directly to Japan's unconditional surrender and the end of World War II.

Hispaniola The second largest of the Caribbean Islands, divided between two countries (the DOMINICAN REPUBLIC and HAITI), and lying between Cuba and Puerto Rico.

Physical. In the centre, mountains rise to about 3,000 m (9,900 feet), and north-east trade winds bring heavy rain to the windward slopes.

History. Hunter-gatherer Ciboney Indians from South America had settled in the island by 5000 BC. Agriculture reached the island with the arrival (*c.* 1000 BC) of Arawak Indians from north-western South America. From *c.* 200 AD, under the influence of Mexico, a Taino Arawak culture, which included the growing of maize, the construction of ceremonial centres, and the worship of human and animal representation of spirits, developed and spread to other islands. In 1492 COLUMBUS landed on the island and in 1496 the town of Santo Domingo was established, the first European settlement in the Americas. Spaniards developed plantations at the eastern end of the island but lost control of western Hispaniola to France, who established the colony of Santo Domingue (Haiti). Exploitation and European diseases made the Taino Arawak virtually extinct by the 18th century.

Hiss case (1949–50) A US legal case involving allegations that Alger Hiss (1904–96), a State Department official, committed espionage. In 1950 Hiss was found guilty of perjury for having denied on oath the charge that he had passed secret documents to Whittaker Chambers, a self-confessed Communist Party courier. Although Hiss maintained his innocence, and high government officials testified for him, he was sentenced to five years in prison. His controversial trial came to symbolize the fears and suspicions aroused by the COLD WAR; although most Americans believed in his guilt, others alleged that the FEDERAL BUREAU OF INVESTIGATION had tampered with evidence so as to obtain his conviction. He was released in 1954 and spent the rest of his life in attempts to clear his name. Some experts feel that documents released by the Russians since the collapse of communism support the view that Hiss was guilty.

historiography The study and writing of history. The recording and interpretation of past events began with the retelling of legends handed down through oral traditions: the epic tales of HOMER were the poetic expression of oral history, while in the classical age of ancient Greece HERODOTUS and THUCYDIDES wrote narrative histories of their own times. In China SIMA QIAN (*c.* 145–*c.* 85 BC) is known as the 'Father of Chinese History'. The Roman historians, who include TACITUS, LIVY, and SUETONIUS, wrote works which served as models for later medieval and Renaissance historians. In the Arab world al-Tabaric (838–923) wrote the *Annals*, a history of the world from its creation to 915, and Ibn Khaldun (1332–1406) the *Kitab a'ibar* (Book of Examples), a major history of Islam. In medieval Europe history was written by the literate clergy (BEDE) and was mostly confined to chronicles (ANGLO-SAXON CHRONICLE, FROISSART). In the 15th and 16th centuries the Italian historians MACHIAVELLI and GUICCIARDINI wrote political analyses of the state and its rulers. The 18th century ENLIGHTENMENT injected a considerable measure of rationalism and scepticism into historical writing, producing such masterpieces as GIBBON's *The History of the Decline and Fall of the Roman Empire.*

In the early 19th century the German historians Barthold Georg Niebuhr (1776–1831) and Leopold von Ranke (1795–1886) transformed the writing of history. Seeking to explain 'how it actually happened', Ranke set new standards of historical research based on primary evidence subjected to critical evaluation. Still narrowly nationalistic, this 'scientific history' led to systematic collection and cataloguing of sources (for example, *Monumenta Germaniae Historicae,* 1825–1925), and to more rigorous academic teaching. This approach was slower to develop in Britain, where history was dominated by the literary Whig tradition of Thomas Babington MACAULAY. Another form of 'scientific history', the positivist belief in underlying general laws, was pioneered by the French historian Auguste Comte (1798–1857). Karl MARX, in his theory of dialectical materialism, presented one such general law – change through class struggle. Its focus on the economic infrastructure of society challenged narrow political interpretations. This challenge continued in the 20th century. The Annales approach, pioneered in the journal *Annales d'histoire economique et sociale* launched in 1929 by Lucien Febvre (1878–1956) and Marc Bloch (1836–1944) and developed in the work of Fernand Braudel (1902–83), sought 'total history', an understanding of the structures within which people act, and of 'mentalities', drawing on psychology and other social sciences. With the development of computers, quantitative techniques have become important to economic, demographic, and social historians, although few share the supreme confidence in statistical theory of the 'cliometricians', such as Robert W. Fogel (1926–), who claim mathematical objectivity for Clio, the muse of history. British Marxist historians, for example, Christopher Hill (1912–), Eric Hobsbawm (1917–), and E. P. Thompson (1924–93), rejecting rigid dogmas of an all-determining infrastructure, have applied Marxist ideas creatively to intellectual history and to 'history from below'. The study of the role of women, developed as part of mainstream historiography by the women's movement of the 1960s, has broadened to encompass the history of gender. Yet concern with political history remains strong, especially in the empirical approach of A. J. P. Taylor (1906–90) or Sir Geoffrey Elton (1921–94), who emphasize individuals and the importance of the unexpected.

Hitler, Adolf (1889–1945) German dictator. He was born in Austria, the son of Alois Hitler and his wife Klara Poelzl. He volunteered for the Bavarian army at the start of World War I, became a corporal, twice won the Iron Cross medal for bravery, and was gassed. After demobilization he joined a small nationalist group, the German Workers' Party, which later became the National Socialist German Workers (or NAZI) Party, and discovered a talent for demagoguery. In Vienna, he had imbibed the prevailing ANTI-SEMITISM and this, with tirades against the VERSAILLES PEACE SETTLEMENT and against Marxism, fell on fertile ground in a Germany humiliated by defeat. In 1921 he became leader of the Nazis and in 1923 staged an abortive uprising, the MUNICH 'BEER-HALL' PUTSCH. During the months shared in prison with Rudolph HESS he dictated *Mein Kampf,* a

political manifesto in which he spelt out Germany's need to rearm, strive for economic self-sufficiency, suppress trade unionism and communism, and exterminate its Jewish minority. The Great DEPRESSION beginning in 1929 brought him a flood of adherents so that, aided by violence against political enemies, his Nazi Party flourished. After the failure of three successive Chancellors, President HINDENBURG appointed Hitler head of the government (1933). As a result of the REICHSTAG fire, Hitler established his one-party dictatorship, and the following year eliminated his rivals in the 'NIGHT OF THE LONG KNIVES'. On the death of Hindenburg he assumed the title of President and 'Führer of the German Reich'. He began rearmament in contravention of the Versailles Treaty, reoccupied the RHINELAND in 1936, and took the first steps in his intended expansion of his THIRD REICH: the ANSCHLUSS with Austria in 1938 and the piecemeal acquisition of Czechoslovakia, beginning with the SUDETENLAND. He concluded the NAZI–SOVIET PACT of non-aggression with Stalin in order to invade Poland in 1939, but broke this when he attacked the Soviet Union in June 1941. His invasion of Poland had meanwhile precipitated WORLD WAR II. Against the advice of his military experts he pursued 'intuitive' tactics and at first won massive victories; in 1941 he took direct military control of the armed forces. As the tide of war turned against him, he intensified the mass assassination of Jews that culminated in the HOLOCAUST. He escaped the JULY PLOT to kill him (1944), and undertook a vicious purge of all involved. In 1945, as the Soviet army entered Berlin, he went through a marriage ceremony with his mistress, Eva Braun. All evidence suggests that both then committed suicide and had their bodies cremated in an underground bunker.

Hitler Youth A NAZI agency to train and indoctrinate young Germans. In 1931 Baldur von SCHIRACH was appointed Youth Leader of the Nazi Party. In 1936 HITLER outlawed all other youth organizations and announced that all young Germans should join the Jungvolk (Young Folk) at the age of ten, when they would be trained in out-of-school activities, including sports and camping, and receive Nazi indoctrination. At 14 the boys were to enter the Hitler Youth proper, in which they would be subject to semi-military discipline, outdoor activities, and Nazi propaganda, and girls the League of German Maidens, in which they would learn motherhood and domestic duties. At 18 they would join the armed forces or the labour service. By 1936 3.6 million members had been recruited, and by 1938 7.7 million, but efforts to enrol young people were failing, so that in March 1939 a conscription order was issued.

Hittites The ancient people of Asia Minor who flourished from 1700 to 1200 BC. They were Indo-Europeans, probably from north of the Black Sea, and entered Anatolia towards the end of the 3rd millennium BC. They established Hattush as their capital and gradually extended their power through much of Anatolia and into Syria. Mursilis I even penetrated as far as Babylon *c.* 1595 BC, but his death was followed by considerable internal discord. The high-point of Hittite rule was achieved under Suppiluliumas (*c.* 1375–1335). In *c.* 1285 the Hittites met the Egyptians at Kadesh in a famous but indecisive battle. The two great powers then made peace, but *c.* 1200 the Hittite empire collapsed before the invasions of the SEA PEOPLES. Hattush (near modern Boğazköy) has yielded an invaluable collection of Hittite records, written in CUNEIFORM.

Hobbes, Thomas (1588–1679) English philosopher and political theorist. After receiving his degree from Oxford University in 1608, he became a tutor to the Cavendish family, and travelled extensively in Europe with his pupils, meeting such thinkers as Galileo and Descartes. Hobbes's philosophy arose from a project of investigating the nature of matter, of man, and of society. He planned to write a three-part work of philosophy but it was his ideas on the state, published as *Leviathan* in 1651 as part of the debate surrounding the English Civil War (1642–49), that were most controversial. His political thinking was grounded in a materialist metaphysics and a pessimistic view of human beings as driven by innate passions, especially the fear of violent death. In the absence of government, these passions would lead men into interminable conflict with one another for the means of survival; human life would be 'solitary, poor, nasty, brutish and short'. Understanding this, rational men would agree to surrender all their rights to a sovereign (the Leviathan) capable of enforcing peace. The sovereign must have unlimited authority, and must permit no internal divisions of power, since, according to Hobbes, any such limitation or division would be a source of renewed conflict. Hobbes's bleak but remorselessly consistent philosophy won him few friends, but his case for unconditional submission to any government capable of preserving order remains a challenge to more liberal SOCIAL CONTRACT theories. The Royalists regarded Hobbes's views as an inducement to CROMWELL to set himself up as an absolute ruler and the book was condemned by Parliament. However, Hobbes returned from exile in Paris at the end of the English Civil War and accepted the RESTORATION settlement.

Ho Chi Minh (born Nguyen Tat Thanh, also called Nguyen Ai Quoc) (1890–1969) Vietnamese statesman. In 1917 he moved to Paris where he became active in left-wing politics. He travelled to the Soviet Union and in 1924 went to Guangzhou in southern China as a COMINTERN agent. In 1930 he presided over the formation of the Vietnamese Communist Party, re-named the Indo-Chinese Communist Party, and played a key role in its development. After a failed conspiracy in 1940, he took refuge in China and was imprisoned by the nationalist regime of CHIANG KAI-SHEK. In 1943 he returned to the north of Vietnam to found the VIETMINH guerrilla movement to fight the Japanese occupying forces, adopting the name Ho Chi Minh ('he who enlightens'). In 1945 after the Japanese surrender, he proclaimed the Democratic Republic of Vietnam but was forced back into guerrilla war after the return of French colonial forces. The GENEVA CONFERENCE (1954) accepted the Vietminh triumph over the French and left Ho in control of North Vietnam. From 1963 he committed his forces on an ever-increasing scale to the communist struggle in South Vietnam (VIETNAM WAR) and until his death he remained unswervingly committed to the reunification of Vietnam under communism, subordinating social and economic reform to the needs of the military struggle with the USA and the Saigon government.

Hofer, Andreas TYROL.

Hohenstaufen A German royal house, members of which held the throne of the Holy Roman Empire (1138–1254), the rivals of the HOHENZOLLERNS. The emperor Henry IV (1084–1106) gave them the duchy of Swabia and in 1138 Duke Conrad became emperor as Conrad III. The family provided many emperors, including FREDERICK I (Barbarossa) who attempted to build up German power in Italy. The relationship between the papacy and the Hohenstaufen was frequently acrimonious, resulting from their respective claims to land and personal powers. The empire grew to include Germany, northern Italy, and Sicily but proved too large to be managed in the face of papal and Lombard opposition, and the dynasty's last ruling member, Manfred of Sicily, was killed in battle in 1266.

Hohenzollern A former Prussian province (now part of the state of Baden-Württemberg in Germany) that gave its name to a powerful German princely family whose roots can be traced back to the 11th century. From 1415 they ruled the electorate of BRANDENBURG and the following century saw great expansion, Margrave Albert becoming grand master of the TEUTONIC KNIGHTS in 1511. In 1614 the duchy of Cleves was acquired and in 1701 the Elector Frederick III of Brandenburg took the title of Frederick I of PRUSSIA. In 1871 William I of Prussia took the title Emperor William I of the German Empire. His grandson WILLIAM II abdicated in 1918. A member of a second branch, Prince Charles Hohenzollern-Sigmaringen, was elected Prince of ROMANIA in 1866, becoming King Carol in 1881. His brother Leopold was offered the throne of Spain in 1870 and turned it down, an incident that Bismarck used to provoke war with France by altering the EMS TELEGRAM.

Hojo A branch of a powerful family in medieval Japan, the Taira. After MINAMOTO YORITOMO's death they provided regents for puppet SHOGUNS, nominated by themselves. From 1219 the regency was hereditary, and the country prospered under them until *c.* 1300. They refused tribute to KUBLAI KHAN and executed his envoys. His two invasions, though failures, weakened Hojo power. Vassals the Hojo were unable to reward for their victories turned against them. From 1331 there was war between the regent's forces and those attempting to restore imperial rule under Go-Daigo. Their power ended (1333) when ASHIKAGA Takanji, a Hojo vassal, defected to the emperor and another vassal took KAMAKURA. The last regent and his family committed *seppuku* (ritual suicide).

Holkar An Indian MARATHA family of peasant origin that became rulers of one of the most powerful of the Māratha confederacy of states. The family's founder, Malhar Rao Holkar, rose through military service to the Peshwas to establish by 1766 virtually independent control of the Malwa region. The family's control was consolidated in the late 18th century, but succession disputes and quarrels with other Māratha chieftains offset the gains. During the reign of Jaswant Rao Holkar (1797–1811) British expansion destroyed Holkar claims in north India. After defeat in 1804 the Holkars had to accept British protection, remaining a Princely State until 1947.

Holland NETHERLANDS.

Holland, Sir Sidney George (1893–1961) New Zealand statesman. As leader of the National Party from 1940 and Prime Minister (1949–57), he was noted for his staunch support of private enterprise, for his vigorous handling of the 1951 waterfront strike, and for the abolition of the Legislative Council – the Upper House of the New Zealand Parliament. In the tradition of pragmatic conservatism Holland retained and even strengthened much of the welfare state and economic regulatory machinery put in place under Labour.

Holocaust, the (Hebrew, *Shoah*) The ordeal suffered by the Jews in NAZI Europe from 1933 to 1945. Conventionally it is divided into two periods, before and after 1941. In the first period various ANTI-SEMITIC measures were taken in Germany, and later Austria. In Germany, after the Nuremberg Laws (1935) were passed, Jews lost citizenship rights, the right to hold public office, practise professions, inter-marry with Germans, or use public education. Their property and businesses were registered and sometimes sequestrated. Continual acts of violence were perpetrated against them, and official propaganda encouraged 'true' Germans to hate and fear them. As intended, the result was mass emigration, halving the half-million German and Austrian Jewish population. The second phase, which affected Jews throughout Nazi-occupied Europe during World War II, involved forced labour, mass shootings, and CONCENTRATION CAMPS, the latter being the basis of

the Nazi 'final solution' (*Endlösung*) of the so-called Jewish problem through mass extermination in gas chambers. This final solution was decided upon at the Nazi conference held at Wannsee in 1942. At this conference the grotesque plan and schedules were laid down, to be administered by Adolf EICHMANN. During the Holocaust an estimated six million Jews died. Out of a population of three million Polish Jews less than half a million remained in 1945, while Romania, Hungary, and Lithuania also suffered grievously.

Holt, Harold Edward (1908–67) Australian statesman. He represented the United Australia Party and then the Liberal Party, holding a series of portfolios from 1939. After MENZIES retired in 1966, Holt became Prime Minister. His term of office coincided with Australia's increasing and controversial involvement in the VIETNAM WAR.

Holy Land PALESTINE.

Holy Alliance (1815) A loose alliance of European powers pledged to uphold the principles of the Christian religion. It was proclaimed at the Congress of VIENNA (1815) by the emperors of Austria and Russia, and the king of Prussia. All other European leaders were invited to join, except the pope and the Ottoman sultan. The restored French king Louis XVIII did so, as did most

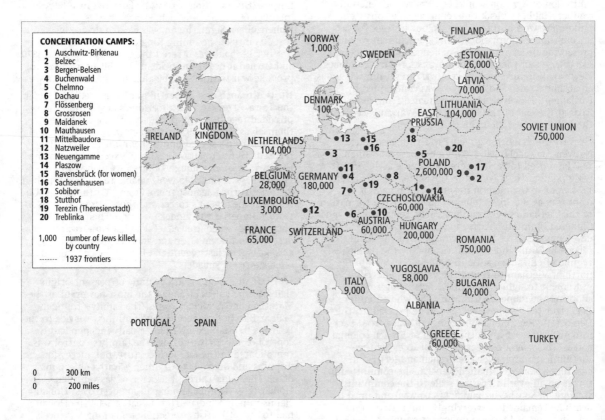

CONCENTRATION CAMPS:

1 Auschwitz-Birkenau
2 Belzec
3 Bergen-Belsen
4 Buchenwald
5 Chelmno
6 Dachau
7 Flössenberg
8 Grossrosen
9 Maidanek
10 Mauthausen
11 Mittelbaudora
12 Natzweiler
13 Neuengamme
14 Plaszow
15 Ravensbrück (for women)
16 Sachsenhausen
17 Sobibor
18 Stutthof
19 Terezin (Theresienstadt)
20 Treblinka

1,000   number of Jews killed, by country
------- 1937 frontiers

0   300 km
0   200 miles

NORWAY 1,000
FINLAND
SWEDEN
ESTONIA 26,000
LATVIA 70,000
DENMARK 100
LITHUANIA 104,000
EAST PRUSSIA
SOVIET UNION 750,000
IRELAND
UNITED KINGDOM
NETHERLANDS 104,000
BELGIUM 28,000
GERMANY 180,000
LUXEMBOURG 3,000
POLAND 2,600,000
CZECHOSLOVAKIA 60,000
AUSTRIA 60,000
HUNGARY 200,000
ROMANIA 750,000
FRANCE 65,000
SWITZERLAND
YUGOSLAVIA 58,000
BULGARIA 40,000
ITALY 9,000
ALBANIA
PORTUGAL
SPAIN
GREECE 60,000
TURKEY

The Holocaust   *The Nazi determination to rid Europe of Jews was rooted in the anti-Semitism of Central and Eastern Europe. From the earliest years of the Third Reich Jews were persecuted and from 1941 onwards a programme of extermination began, with certain camps in Eastern Europe equipped with gas-chambers for systematic slaughter. It is estimated that four million Jews died in these camps. Perhaps a further million died in ghettos by starvation and disease and over a million were shot by mobile killing squads (Einsatzgruppen).*

others; Britain did not. As a diplomatic instrument it was short-lived and never effective and it became associated with repressive and autocratic regimes.

Holy League A name given to several European alliances formed during the 15th, 16th, and 17th centuries. The League of 1511–13 was directed against French ascendancy in Italy. The coalition was organized by Pope Pius II, and included England, Spain, Venice, the Holy Roman Empire, and Switzerland. It succeeded in its initial aims, but then there was squabbling over strategy and the hard-pressed French were able to conclude separate peace treaties with each member. The Holy League of 1526 was formed against emperor CHARLES V by France, the papacy, England, Venice, and Milan. It achieved little in the subsequent war, and FRANCIS I of France made peace with Charles at Cambrai in 1529.

The French Holy League of 1576, also known as the Catholic League, was led by the GUISE faction during the FRENCH WARS OF RELIGION. Henry III ordered its dissolution in 1577, but it was revived in 1584 to play a major part in the War of the THREE HENRYS (1585–89). Its power waned after HENRY IV accepted Catholicism in 1593.

The Holy (or Catholic) League of 1609 was a military alliance of the German Catholic princes, formed at the start of the War of the Jülich Succession (1606–14). During most of the THIRTY YEARS WAR its forces served the imperial cause, with TILLY as its principal commander.

Holyoake, Sir Keith Jacka (1904–83) New Zealand statesman. A farmer active in agricultural organizations in the 1930s and 1940s, he entered Parliament in 1932, becoming leader of the National Party and Prime Minister in 1957 and 1960–72. An able politician in the tradition of pragmatic conservatism, he led New Zealand skilfully in the decades of growing racial tension. He served a term as governor-general of New Zealand after his retirement from politics.

Holy Roman Empire (962–1806) An empire in West central Europe, conceived as a successor to the Christian empire of CHARLEMAGNE and to the earlier rule of Rome. The creation of the medieval popes, it has been called their greatest mistake; for whereas their intention was to appoint a powerful secular deputy to rule Christendom, in fact they generated a rival.

From OTTO I's coronation in 962, the empire was always associated with the German crown, even after it became a HABSBURG (Austrian) title in the 15th century. The empire consisted of duchies, counties, and bishoprics owing formal allegiance to the emperor. In practice there were often clashes between the emperor and the nobility (ELECTOR), especially as the emperor's claims to sovereignty over Italy resulted in frequent absences from Germany. Emperor Henry IV (ruled 1084–1106) had a long struggle with the Church over the right to appoint bishops and senior clergy (INVESTITURE). Emperor Frederick I (ruled 1155–90) made a sustained attempt to bring Italy and the papacy under military subjugation but was finally defeated at the Battle of Legnano in 1176. Open warfare broke out between the GUELPHS (allies of the pope) and the Ghibellines (the imperial party). After the death of Emperor FREDERICK II in 1250 German imperial power, both in Italy and within Germany, waned.

The empire became virtually hereditary, ruled by successive members of the same princely family. The first HABSBURG emperor was Rudolph I (from 1274) and the empire remained in Habsburg hands until its dissolution. King Charles I of Spain was crowned as the Holy Roman Emperor CHARLES V in 1530. His empire included Spain, Germany, the Netherlands, Sardinia, and Sicily, together with newly conquered territory in the Americas (NEW SPAIN). But the REFORMATION and the THIRTY YEARS WAR saw challenges to the power of the Catholic Habsburgs and the emperors suffered a loss of prestige and power during a series of wars against LOUIS XIV. In the 18th century PRUSSIA under FREDERICK II emerged as the leading German power, and, in 1806, the imperial crown was surrendered to Napoleon. The empire was not revived after his downfall.

Holy Roman Empire: *c.* 1100   *By the end of the 11th century the Holy Roman Emperor was the crowned ruler of Germany, Burgundy, and northern Italy, in addition to his imperial role as temporal leader of Christendom, and the empire was close to its height in terms of cohesion and extent. The degree of power he exercised varied, however, at different times. Within Germany there was constant rivalry between the emperor and the rulers of the margraviates, duchies, and kingdoms.*

Home Guard In World War II, a volunteer force raised in Britain to meet the threat of invasion. The Home Guard, known originally as the Local Defence

Volunteers, existed from 1940 to 1944. In 1942 enrolment in the force became compulsory for sections of the civilian population. About a million men served in their spare time, and in its first vital year it possessed considerably more men than firearms. It was never put to the test, but it helped British morale in 1940–41.

Homer The principal figure of ancient Greek literature, traditionally regarded as the author of the *Iliad* and the *Odyssey*, the greatest of the early Greek epic poems. He seems to have lived before 700 BC, probably in Ionia (present-day western Turkey). Tradition suggests that he was blind, and may well have sung at the courts of kings as bards do in the *Odyssey*. The *Iliad*, while recounting the enmity between Achilles and Agamemnon, encapsulates much of the mythology surrounding the ten-year war at Troy. Similarly the *Odyssey*, while recounting Odysseus' return to Ithaca and his revenge on the suitors of his wife, is set against a wider background of the return of the Greek heroes, and gives much detail of other phases of Odysseus' life, at Troy and elsewhere. The poems may not have been the work of one person. They arose from a long oral bardic tradition which told the stories and legends of the heroic age of Greece, roughly the end of the MYCENAEAN period, but they also contain elements which are later than that. As the earliest surviving literary record, they are of great use in helping to reconstruct the early history of Greece, but their evidence is often contentious and has to be treated with circumspection. By about 500 BC, prose histories began to be written, superseding the older medium of verse.

Home Rule, Irish A movement for the re-establishment of an Irish parliament responsible for internal affairs. In 1870 an association was founded by Isaac Butt to campaign for repeal of the ACT OF UNION (1800) between Britain and Ireland. This became a serious possibility when Charles PARNELL persuaded the Liberals under GLADSTONE to introduce Home Rule Bills. The first (1886) was defeated in the House of Commons. It provided for an Irish Parliament at Dublin, with no Irish representation at Westminster; it ignored the problem of Ulster, where a predominantly Protestant, pro-British population had been settled since the early 17th century. Gladstone's second Bill (1893) was also defeated. The third Bill (1912), introduced by Asquith, was passed by Parliament but its operation was postponed when war broke out in Europe in 1914. It left unresolved the question of how much of Ulster was to be excluded from the Act. When World War I ended the political situation in Ireland was greatly changed. The EASTER RISING in 1916 and the sweeping majority for SINN FEIN in the 1918 general election were followed by unrest and guerrilla warfare. Lloyd George was Prime Minister when the fourth Home Rule Bill (1920) was introduced in the Westminster Parliament. The Bill provided for parliaments in Dublin and Belfast linked by a Federal Council of Ireland. The Northern Ireland Parliament was set up in 1920 while fighting continued in Ireland. Following the Anglo-Irish truce the Irish Free State (see IRELAND, REPUBLIC OF) was set up; the new state had a vague DOMINION status at odds with the independence claimed by Dáil Éireann in 1919. The Anglo-Irish agreement was approved by 64 votes to 57 in the Dáil. The majority group wanted peace and partial independence, the minority group, headed by Eamon DE VALERA, desired the immediate independence of all Ireland and the setting up of a republic.

Homestead Act (1862) A US Act to encourage migration west. The Homestead Act gave any citizen who was head of a family and over 21 years of age 65 ha (160 acres) of surveyed public land for a nominal fee. Complete ownership could be attained after five years of continuous residence or by the payment of $1.25 per acre after a six-month period. While some 15,000 such homesteads were created during the AMERICAN CIVIL WAR years, speculation and the development of mechanized large-scale agriculture reduced the effectiveness of the Act in later years.

Homestead strike (1892) A US labour dispute. It was the bitter climax of deteriorating relations between the Carnegie Steel Company at Homestead, outside Pittsburgh, run by Henry Clay Frick, and the Amalgamated Association of Iron and Steel Workers, who had refused to accept a disadvantageous new contract and ordered a strike. When Frick imported 300 PINKERTON detectives to protect the plant and the non-union workers, they were repulsed in an armed battle in which several people were killed. The state governor introduced state militia to restore order, and the strike failed. The union collapsed after the anarchist Alexander Berkman tried to kill Frick, and unionism in the industry was seriously weakened until the 1930s.

Hominids Members of the family Hominidae, including our own species *homo sapiens*, our presumed forebears *homo erectus* and *homo habilis*, and forms believed to be closely related called collectively the AUSTRALOPITHECINES. Many scientists now also include the African great apes – the two chimpanzees and gorilla – in the human family too, rather than grouping them with the more distantly related Asian apes, the orang-utan, gibbon, and siamang. The traditional way of grouping the large apes (chimpanzees, gorilla, and orang-utan) is in their own family, Pongidae. Estimates of the date of divergence of the ape and human lineages vary. The Asian apes probably branched off 8–12 million years ago and the African apes 10–5 million years ago.

Homo erectus ('upright man') The presumed predecessor of our own species, *homo sapiens*, who lived in Africa and Asia and possibly in Europe. This hominid was larger than the AUSTRALOPITHECINES and *homo habilis* and its brain approached the size of a modern human's. However, the facial bones remained relatively massive and the skull was long and low. One of the hallmarks of this species was a teardrop-shaped stone tool flaked on both sides, the ACHEULIAN handaxe, which was more specialized than the OLDOWAN tools of *Homo habilis*. *Homo erectus* was the first member of the human lineage to control and use fire and this, and perhaps clothing, may have contributed to its spreading so widely from its place of origin in tropical East Africa. It had evolved presumably from *Homo habilis*, by 1.6 million years ago. By around 1 million years ago or not long before these hominids are presumed to have begun their travels that took them as far as China (PEKING MAN) and Indonesia (JAVA MAN). The last representatives disappeared 400,000–200,000 years ago.

Homo habilis ('handy man') The name given to a group of human fossil remains found at OLDUVAI GORGE in Tanzania in the early 1960s, and now known from other eastern African sites, especially KOOBI FORA in Kenya and perhaps also from southern Africa. They date from about 2.5 million to 1.6 million years ago. Although similar in size to the contemporary AUSTRALOPITHECINES, their brains were larger, their faces more human-like, and they very likely evolved into *homo erectus*. They were probably the first makers of stone tools – simple pebble and flake artefacts collectively called the OLDOWAN industry.

Homo sapiens ('wise man') Our own species, that evolved from *homo erectus* by 400,000–200,000 years ago. By this stage the brain had enlarged to the modern size, the skull bones had become less heavy, and the back of the head was rounded. The next development is obscure as the *Homo sapiens* lineage apparently split into two main lines, one leading to the NEANDERTHALS (*Homo sapiens neanderthalensis*), the other to fully modern people (*Homo sapiens sapiens*). The latter development took place gradually during the past 125,000 years. Anatomical and genetic evidence support the idea that this happened in Africa, but it is possible that there was at least one parallel development in the Far East. In the Middle East, anatomically modern humans had appeared by around 50,000 years ago; in Europe, they came slightly later, and more abruptly around 35,000 years ago. The earliest modern Europeans are often called CRO-MAGNONS. It is not known what part, if any, the Neanderthals played in these Middle Eastern and European developments. Very likely they were not our direct ancestors but they may have interbred with modern people entering Europe from Africa via the Middle East.

With the evolution of modern people came marked advances in tool technology, rapid increase in population, the grouping of social activities in dwellings, and the first appearance of art; the cultural period called the UPPER PALAEOLITHIC had begun. These Upper Palaeolithic people almost certainly had a spoken language. With population growth came the colonization of new territories, which seems to have begun soon after the origin of fully modern humans. People had reached New Guinea and Australia from Indonesia by at least 40,000 years ago and developed Australoid characteristics in isolation there. The timing of the first settlement of the New World is more controversial. It was probably before 15,000 years ago but there is little firm archaeological evidence so far for an earlier colonization. Genetic, linguistic, and anatomical evidence of modern AMERINDIANS, however, is increasingly suggesting that the first entry into North America occurred between 40,000 and 30,000 years ago.

Honduras A Central American country bounded on the north and west by Guatemala and El Salvador and on the south by Nicaragua.

Physical. Honduras has a long, north-east coast on the Caribbean Sea and a short, south-west coast on the Pacific Ocean. Most of it is mountainous and heavily forested, and the soil is generally poor and acid. The climate varies with altitude but is predominantly tropical.

Economy. Honduras has an agricultural economy with bananas and coffee the principal exports; there are extensive forests (45% of land area) and timber is also exported. Zinc, lead, and silver are mined, and there is limited light industry.

History. The native inhabitants of Honduras are mestizo Indians. One of the lieutenants of Hernan CORTÉS, Francisco de las Casas, founded the first settlement, the port of Trujillo, in 1523. Honduras was attached administratively to the captaincy-general of GUATEMALA throughout the Spanish colonial period.

When independence came in 1821 it briefly became part of the empire of Agustin de ITURBIDE before joining the United Provinces of Central America (1825–38). Separate independent status dates from 1838, when the union broke up. An uninterrupted succession of CAUDILLOS dominated the remainder of the 19th century. Improvement in the political process came slowly in the 20th century. Military dictators continued to be more prominent than civilian presidents, but the election in 1957 of Ramón Villeda Morales gave hope for the future. This optimism proved premature as the Honduran army overthrew him before he could implement the reform programme he had pushed through the congress. Military entrenchment was further solidified as Honduras fought a border war with El Salvador in 1969. In 1982 a new, US-backed constitution aimed to increase democratic activity. As a condition for US support, however, the country provided a base for 'Contra' rebels from NICARAGUA. In 1985 a new President, José Azcona (1985–90) threatened to stop 'Contra' activity, as well as to reduce the power of the military. Honduras, however, remained economically dependent upon the USA, and in 1989 Rafael Callejas was elected President with US support. He faced economic turbulence, left-wing guerrilla activity, and security forces almost totally out of control, with 40 assassinations and over 4,000 known violations of human rights in one year. Despite assistance loans from the IMF and the World Bank, the government's economic structural adjustment plan, launched in 1990, provoked sustained hostility from unions, peasant groups, and private business, causing social unrest and political instability in 1992. In September the long-standing border dispute with El Salvador was resolved by an INTERNATIONAL COURT OF JUSTICE ruling. In the presidential elections of November 1993 Carlos Roberto Reina, who opposed Callejas, was elected. The declared priorities of the new government were the economy and the reduction of the military's role in politics. Honduras remained the focus of international human rights concern.

CAPITAL:	Tegucigalpa
AREA:	112,088 sq km (43,277 sq miles)
POPULATION:	5.666 million (1996)
CURRENCY:	1 Honduran lempira = 100 centavos
RELIGIONS:	Roman Catholic 94.6%; other (mostly Protestant) 5.4%
ETHNIC GROUPS:	Mestizo 89.9%; Amerindian 6.7%; Black (including Black Carib) 2.1%; White 1.3%
LANGUAGES:	Spanish (official); Black Carib (Garifuna); minority languages
INTERNATIONAL ORGANIZATIONS:	UN; OAS

Honecker, Erich (1912–94) German communist politician; head of state of the German Democratic Republic (East Germany) (1976–89). Owing to his activities in the Soviet Union in the communist resistance to Hitler; Honecker was arrested and sentenced to ten years' imprisonment in 1937. At the end of World War II, as a close ally of German communist leader Walter ULBRICHT, he was given charge of the youth wing of the Socialist Unity Party; in 1958 he was appointed secretary of the Central Committee and head of the East German security forces. In this capacity he was responsible for the construction of the BERLIN WALL in 1961. He succeeded Ulbricht as first secretary in 1971 and undertook rapprochement with the Federal Republic (West Germany) from 1972 onwards (see OSTPOLITIK). However, he maintained his country's strict adherence to Soviet political and economic orthodoxy. Having refused to implement reforms in accordance with Mikhail GORBACHEV's liberalization programme, he was forced to resign after massive public pro-democracy demonstrations in 1989. Although initially imprisoned, he subsequently (1991) travelled to Moscow to undergo an operation and while there sought asylum in the Chilean embassy. He was eventually extradited to face criminal charges in Germany but his trial was then suspended on grounds of ill health. Honecker emigrated to Chile in 1993 and died the following year.

Hong Kong A special administrative region of China, formerly (until 1 July 1997) a British crown colony. It comprises a small part (Kowloon and the New Territories) of the Chinese mainland, the island of Hong Kong itself, and nearly 200 outlying islands, of which Lantau is the largest.

Physical. It is situated at the mouth of the Xi Jiang (Pearl River) and has a total area of 1,060 sq km (410 sq miles) supporting a population of about 6.3 million. Hong Kong island rises steeply to a series of peaks, the highest being Victoria Peak. The New Territories have higher mountains and much of the land is too steep for agriculture or settlement.

Economy. Hong Kong's prosperity was initially based on its excellent harbour (it is the world's largest container port) and trading, but manufacturing industry, especially textiles and electronics, financial services, and tourism are important. Since the 1980s there has been an increase in joint industrial ventures with China, especially with the adjacent Shenzen Special Economic Zone. Despite the resumption of Chinese sovereignty in 1997, Beijing is committed to retain the Hong Kong dollar, the Hong Kong stock exchange, and other attributes of the free-enterprise system for at least 50 years.

History. Hong Kong Island was occupied by the British in 1841 during the First OPIUM WAR and was formally ceded by China in the Treaty of NANJING in the following year. The mainland peninsula of Kowloon was added by the Treaty of Beijing in 1860, and in 1898 the colony's hinterland was extended when the New Territories were leased from China for 99 years. Hong Kong grew as a trading centre, attracting both Europeans and Chinese. After two weeks' fighting it surrendered to the Japanese on 25 December 1941. Reoccupied by the British in 1945, there was an influx of refugees and capital, especially from Shanghai, following the communist victory in China. The United Nations embargo on trade with China during the Korean War stimulated the development of industry and financial institutions, and in the 1970s and 1980s Hong Kong became an important international economic and business centre. With the end of the lease on the New Territories approaching, Britain agreed in 1984 to transfer sovereignty of the entire colony to China in 1997. Although China undertook not to alter Hong Kong's existing economic and social structure for 50 years, there remained much unease within Hong Kong, with increasing pressure for the introduction of more democratic government before 1997. The proposals of Chris Patten, appointed governor of Hong Kong in July 1992, for reform of the colony's political system, initiated a dispute with China, who argued that the reforms contravened the 1984 Sino-British Declaration. By June 1994 the reform package had been passed by the Hong Kong Legislative Council (Legco), despite objections from the Chinese government. Owing to pressure from China (and contrary to British assurances), Legco was abolished in 1996 and replaced by an appointed body dominated by pro-Beijing groups: the reform programme was dropped. Hong Kong was duly transferred to Chinese sovereignty in July 1997. The chief executive of the new 'Hong Kong Special Administrative Region' (HKSAR), businessman Tung Chee-Hwa, promised to uphold the territory's established way of life under the slogan 'one country, two systems'.

Hood, Samuel, 1st Viscount (1724–1816) British admiral. He served in the Seven Years War, the American War of Independence, and the French Revolutionary wars. He entered the navy in 1741, was promoted post-captain in 1756, and in 1759 captured a French frigate after a fierce action. In 1780, with the rank of rear-admiral, he went to the West Indies as second-in-command to Lord RODNEY. There he displayed masterly tactical skills and took a prominent part in the defeat of the French fleet near Dominica two years later. During the French Revolutionary wars he commanded the British fleet in the Mediterranean.

Hooker, Richard (c. 1554–1600) English theologian. He enjoyed a reputation as a controversial London preacher, but in 1591 he took a country parish and there wrote *The Laws of Ecclesiastical Polity* (1594–97). In it he attacked the Puritan idea of basing all human conduct upon the scriptures alone, and he gave the Church of England its first systematized Anglican theology and written justification. Hooker's pragmatic emphasis on reason influenced Tudor statesmen as well as churchmen.

Hoover, Herbert (Clark) (1874–1964) Thirty-first President of the USA (1929–33). A successful mining engineer and businessman, Hoover earned a reputation as a humanitarian, organizing the production and distribution of foodstuffs in the USA and Europe during and after World War I. As Secretary of Commerce (1921–28), he persuaded large firms to adopt standardization of production goods and a system of planned economy. Esteemed as a moderate liberal, he received the Republican nomination for President and easily defeated his Democratic rival, Alfred E. Smith, in 1928. However, his presidency was marked by his failure to prevent the Great DEPRESSION, following the STOCK MARKET CRASH of 1929. He ran for re-election in 1932, but was overwhelmingly defeated by Franklin D. ROOSEVELT. Long after his electoral rout he became a respected elder statesman, co-ordinator of the European Food Program (1947), and chairman of two executive reorganization commissions (1947–49, 1953–55). Many of his recommendations were adopted, including the establishment of the Department of Health, Education, and Welfare.

Hoover, J(ohn) Edgar (1895–1972) US administrator. In 1924 he was appointed director of the Bureau of Investigation, now the FEDERAL BUREAU OF INVESTIGATION, with the task of raising its standards after the disrepute of the HARDING years. He achieved this by vigorous selection and training of personnel, and the creation of a scientific crime detection laboratory and the FBI National Academy. In the 1930s his widely publicized entrapment of certain criminals, while not destroying syndicate crime, earned the FBI a reputation of integrity, but in his late years a persistent interest in the sex lives of various public figures clouded his supposed political impartiality, and his antipathy to CIVIL RIGHTS activities earned widespread criticism.

Hopewell cultures A group of related cultures of the eastern USA, dating *c.* 500 BC–500 AD. They are known for their conical burial mounds, most highly developed in Ohio, and often associated with earthworks in various shapes, the most famous being the Great Serpent Mound of Adams County, Ohio, 213 m (700 feet) in length.

Hopkins, Harry (Lloyd) (1890–1946) US administrator and public servant. When Franklin D. ROOSEVELT was governor of New York State he made Hopkins his adviser on social and welfare policies. This continued throughout the years of the NEW DEAL. Hopkins's record in public social service was, perhaps, without equal; he was head of New York's Temporary Emergency Relief Administration (1931), the Federal Emergency Relief Administration (1933), the WORKS PROJECT ADMINISTRATION (1935), and Secretary of Commerce (1938–40). He was Roosevelt's manager when he ran for a third term as President in 1940. Before and after US entry into World War II Hopkins served as Roosevelt's untitled second-in-command. He played a pivotal role in the San Francisco conference of 1945, which launched the charter of the UNITED NATIONS, and in the last 'big three' conference at POTSDAM.

hoplite A citizen-soldier of the cities of ancient Greece. Each man had to provide his own formidable armour (Greek, *hopla*) — 2.7-m (9-feet) spear, short sword, large round shield, breastplate, and greaves (shin-pads). They fought in the close-packed PHALANX formation, and were extremely effective when operating in the plains of Greece. However, over rough terrain they were vulnerable to fast-moving light infantry. The professional hoplites of SPARTA were pre-eminent in classical times until their defeat by the Thebans in 371 BC.

Horn, Filips van Montmorency, Graaf van (or Hoorn) (*c.* 1524–68) Flemish soldier and statesman. He had a long record of distinguished service to both Emperor CHARLES V and PHILIP II of Spain but, as a member of the regency council in the Netherlands (1561–65), he followed a similar opposition course to that of his colleague, Lamoral EGMONT. In 1566 he aligned himself with the Calvinists at Tournai, but then obeyed the regent's command to return to Brussels. Late in that year, he rejected WILLIAM I (the Silent)'s plan for armed resistance to the Spaniards, and withdrew to his home

in Weert. In 1567 ALBA found him out, had him convicted of treason and heresy by the Council of Troubles, and he was beheaded.

Horthy de Nagybánya, Nikolaus (1868–1957) Regent of Hungary. He commanded the Austro-Hungarian fleet in World War I. In 1919 he was asked by the opposition to organize an army to overthrow Béla KUN's communist regime. In January 1920 the Hungarian Parliament voted to restore the monarchy, electing Horthy regent. This post he retained, but thwarted all efforts of Charles IV, the deposed King of Hungary, to support the HABSBURG claim. He ruled virtually as dictator. He agreed to Hungary joining Germany in World War II and declared war on the Soviet Union, but in 1944 he unsuccessfully sought a separate peace with the Allies. He was imprisoned by the Germans (1944) and released by the Allies (1945).

Hospitaller KNIGHT HOSPITALLER.

Hotspur PERCY.

Houphouët-Boigny, Félix (1905–93) African statesman. In 1944 he was a co-founder of the Syndicat Agricole Africain, formed to protect Africans against European agriculturalists. He represented CÔTE D'IVOIRE (formerly the Ivory Coast) in the French Assembly (1945–59), and in 1946 formed the Parti Démocratique de la Côte d'Ivoire. At first allied with the Communist Party, he broke with it in 1950, and co-operated with the French to build up the economy of his country. When Côte d'Ivoire was offered independence in 1958, he campaigned successfully for self-government within the FRENCH COMMUNITY. He became President of Côte d'Ivoire in 1960 in a one-party state, and his international policies have been recognizably moderate. He also maintained close links with France. In May 1990 opposition parties were allowed to function, and he was re-elected in presidential elections later that year. Following his death in 1993 he was succeeded as President by Henri Konan Bedie.

House of Commons (UK) The lower chamber of the British PARLIAMENT. It began as an element of the Parliaments summoned by the king in the later 13th century: both knights of the shire and burgesses of BOROUGHS were summoned to Simon de MONTFORT'S Parliament in 1265. It took over 500 years for the Commons to become supreme in the tripartite division of power between it, the HOUSE OF LORDS, and the monarchy. In the 14th century both Houses gained constitutional rights in relation to the monarchy; many of the struggles between RICHARD II and his opponents were waged through the Commons – notably in the Merciless Parliament of 1388.

In the early 17th century, when differences between the monarchy and Parliament first surfaced, the Commons took the lead in, for instance, the PETITION OF RIGHT (1628), winning CHARLES I's acceptance of the principle of no taxation without parliamentary assent. The LONG PARLIAMENT (1640–60) abolished the House of Lords and set up the COMMONWEALTH, and it was the Commons that was instrumental in inviting CHARLES II to take up the throne, just as it promoted the BILL OF RIGHTS (1689) and Act of SETTLEMENT (1701) that defined the relations between Commons, Lords, and the monarchy.

Although the Commons had gained considerable constitutional powers during the 17th century and had

had some notable Prime Ministers, such as Robert Walpole and William Pitt, it was still, at the beginning of the 19th century, no more than an equal partner with the House of Lords. Extension of the franchise and the influence of such powerful members as Robert Peel, Lord Palmerston, Lord John Russell, and William Gladstone did much to extend its power, so that by the end of the century it was effectively regarded as the voice of the people. Following a series of REFORM ACTS and other legislation (1832, 1867, 1884, 1918, 1928, 1945, 1969) members of the House of Commons are today elected by universal adult suffrage. By the Parliament Act of 1911, the maximum duration of a Parliament became five years.

The life of a Parliament is divided into sessions, usually of one year in length. As a rule, Bills likely to raise political controversy are introduced in the Commons before going to the Lords, and the Commons claim exclusive control in respect of national taxation and expenditure. Since 1911 Members have received payment.

Members of Parliament are elected from 650 single-member constituencies in plurality (first-past-the-post) elections. The presiding officer of the Commons is an elected Speaker, who has power to maintain order and functions in a strictly non-partisan way. The House of Commons is organized along adversarial lines, its proceedings normally controlled by a disciplined party majority. The exercise by the House of Commons of its powers in matters of legislation, finance, scrutiny, and enquiry are thus in practice largely party-dominated, subject to the rights conventionally accorded to the opposition. On the other hand, an increasing role is played by all-party committees, such as standing committees, which consider and amend bills, or select committees, which monitor the workings of government departments, taking evidence, questioning witnesses, and issuing reports. Following a general election, or a change of leadership, the leader of the party commanding an overall majority in the House of Commons is invited by the monarch to become Prime Minister and form a cabinet.

House of Lords (UK) The upper chamber of the British PARLIAMENT. It derived from the medieval kings' Great Council. In the 13th and 14th centuries, as the councils gave way to parliaments, the Lords evolved into a separate body which, together with the HOUSE OF COMMONS, presented bills to the crown for enactment as statutes. The immense individual importance of many peers did not prevent them gradually losing to the Commons the right to levy taxes on the king's behalf, and from the 16th century the Commons were the more powerful political force. The House of Lords was abolished in 1649 and revived in 1660. It was put on what is still its constitutional basis *vis-à-vis* the crown and the House of Commons by the GLORIOUS REVOLUTION 1688–89. Following the 1832 REFORM ACT, its influence gradually declined as that of the House of Commons increased. The Parliament Act of 1911 reduced the Lords' powers to a 'suspensory veto' of two years (further reduced to one year in 1949). By it bills can be delayed, but if passed again by the Commons, become law. The House of Lords has no power to revise or delay money bills. It still performs several useful parliamentary roles. These include the revision of bills from the Commons, the initiation of non-controversial legislation, scrutiny

of the executive, and enquiry by select committee. Debate in the Lords is less raucously partisan and sometimes better informed than in the Commons. The House of Lords is the highest court of appeal in the UK legal system, but only the Law Lords take part when it acts in this capacity.

Members of the House of Lords include the Lords Spiritual (26 archbishops and bishops in order of seniority), the Lords Temporal (approximately 1,000 hereditary and life peers), and the Lords of Appeal in Ordinary (Law Lords), the most senior members of the judiciary. Non-hereditary peers have been created since the Life Peerage Act of 1958; they tend to be more active members of the Lords than many hereditary peers. In 1997 the incoming Labour government pledged to remove the remaining hereditary element in the Lords.

House of Representatives The lower chamber of the two chambers of the US Congress, the other being the SENATE. The powers and composition of the House of Representatives are set out in Article I of the Constitution and it first met in 1789. The House of Representatives comprises 435 members, the number for each state being determined by population, although every state is entitled to at least one Representative. The size of the House increased with the USA's population until 1929 when the number of representatives was fixed. Seats are apportioned every ten years. Members are elected for a two-year term, all terms running concurrently. A Representative (popularly called Congressman) must be at least 25 years of age, a US citizen for at least seven years, and an inhabitant of the state represented. The presiding officer of the House, the Speaker, is elected by members and is third in line for executive power after the President and Vice-President.

The House and the Senate have an equal voice in legislation; however, the right to originate finance bills is given to the House by the Constitution. The House also has the power to begin IMPEACHMENT proceedings, through which the President, a judge, or other official can be removed from office for misbehaviour, if the resolution of the House to impeach is adopted by the Senate.

The House of Representatives is organized along party lines, by majority and minority party leaderships. The majority party in the House does not necessarily coincide with the majority party in the Senate, or the party of the President. A noted feature of both the House of Representatives and the Senate is the system of specialized standing committees and numerous subcommittees, through which most of the legislature's work is accomplished; these committees, which often display striking autonomy in their decisions, conduct most congressional business, dealing with different classes of bills, as well as scrutinizing government departments.

Houston, Samuel (1793–1863) US military leader and statesman. Houston lived for a time with the Cherokee and became a popular hero as a result of his exploits, while serving under Andrew JACKSON, against the Creek in 1814. In 1835–36, as military leader of the Texan insurgents, he defeated and captured SANTA ANNA at the Battle of SAN JACINTO, thus securing Texan independence. He was twice President of the TEXAN REPUBLIC (1836–38, 1841–44), and after Texas joined the United States served the Senate from 1847 to 1859. In 1859 his popularity won him election as governor of his adopted state, but when Texas joined the CONFEDERACY in 1861, Houston was deposed.

Howard, Catherine (c. 1521–42) Queen consort of HENRY VIII of England from 1540. She was the king's fifth wife, her marriage in 1540 the result of the ambitions of her Catholic relatives, the dukes of Norfolk (the Howard faction). After the king's marriage to ANNE OF CLEVES failed, they engineered the downfall of Thomas CROMWELL and promoted the 19-year-old Catherine. Protestant enemies of the Howards subsequently accused her of infidelity and she was beheaded. After her death the Howards continued to promote Catholicism. Thomas Howard, 3rd Duke of Norfolk (1473–1554) was imprisoned by EDWARD VI but was favoured by MARY I. Thomas Howard, 4th Duke of Norfolk (1536–72) was involved in the RIDOLFI PLOT and was executed.

Howard, John (1726–90) British philanthropist and reformer. He first experienced prison conditions when captured by the French in 1756 while on his way to help the survivors of the Lisbon earthquake. Later, as high sheriff of Bedfordshire in 1773, his responsibilities aroused his interest in prison conditions. He published several works on the subject and secured some important prison reforms through Parliament. His name is preserved in the Howard League for Penal Reform.

Howe, Richard, 4th Viscount and Earl (1726–99) British naval officer, who served with distinction in the American War of INDEPENDENCE and the French Revolutionary wars. He entered the navy in 1739, and gave early proof of his abilities during the SEVEN YEARS WAR. He was promoted vice-admiral in 1775 and put in command of the North American station in the following year to enter into peace negotiations with the rebellious American colonists. When these proved fruitless his fleet helped the British army to capture New York and Philadelphia. In 1782 he raised the Siege of Gibraltar after defeating a combined Franco-Spanish force. He brought his career to a triumphant conclusion with his victory over the French fleet off Ushant in 1794 in the Battle of the 'Glorious First of June'.

His brother, **William, 5th Viscount Howe** (1729–1814), joined the army in 1746 and, after winning rapid promotion, took part in the successful assault on QUEBEC in 1759, leading the march to the PLAINS OF ABRAHAM. Although, like his brother, he sympathized with the American colonists, he was made supreme commander of the British forces in North America in 1776 and inflicted a series of defeats on WASHINGTON's army. In 1778 he resigned his position and returned home.

Hoxha, Enver (1908–85) Albanian Communist leader, head of state from 1954 until his death. After a career as a diplomat and teacher, Hoxha founded (1940) the Albanian Communist Party, which undertook partisan activity to resist Italian occupation during World War II. He became prime minister of the liberated country in 1944. In 1949 he broke with Marshal TITO's Yugoslavia, which had supplied aid to his movement, and maintained a Stalinist stance that guaranteed isolation from the Soviet bloc after Stalin's death in 1953. From 1960, Hoxha allied Albania to the People's Republic of China but severed relations with this country in 1978. In 1974 he survived an attempted coup. He died in office in 1985; his legacy was an impoverished and isolated Albania that descended into armed factionalism in the 1990s.

Hoysala An Indian dynasty, first Jain and later Hindu, which ruled the south Deccan from c. 1006 until 1346, with its capital at Dwarasamudra (near Mysore). Beginning as marauding hill chieftains, they finally established sway over a region corresponding to the later MYSORE state. Visnuvardhana (c. 1110–41) expelled the powerful CHOLAS from the Deccan, and during the reign of his grandson, Ballala II (1173–1220), they became a force to be reckoned with in south India. However, their strength finally depended on the acquiescence of Hindu rivals whom they antagonized by rendering assistance to Muslim invaders. On their downfall in the mid-14th century, their territories fell to the VIJAYANAGAR empire. The Hoysalas were patrons of learning and the arts, notably architecture and sculpture.

Hsia XIA.

Hsiung-nu XIONGNU.

Hua Guofeng (or Hua Kuo-feng) (1920–   ) Chinese Communist statesman. He served for 12 years with the 8th Route Army before rising through the provincial bureaucracy to become deputy governor of Hunan province. The leading provincial official to survive the CULTURAL REVOLUTION, Hua won a succession of key posts between 1968 and 1975, becoming acting Premier after the death of ZHOU ENLAI in 1976. He succeeded MAO ZEDONG as chairman of the Central Committee, having defeated a challenge from the GANG OF FOUR. His appointment only disguised the power struggle in which DENG XIAOPING was emerging as the victor. Hua resigned as Premier in 1980 and as chairman in 1981. He was re-elected to the CCP Central Committee in 1987, and again in 1992.

Hudson's Bay Company A company chartered in 1670 to Prince RUPERT and 17 others to govern and trade in the huge area of the Canadian north-west, called Rupert's Land, which drained into Hudson Bay. Although huge profits accrued from the FUR TRADE, the company was, until 1763, threatened by competition and military attack from the French. From 1787 there was occasionally murderous conflict with the North-West Company over control of the fur trade until the two companies amalgamated in 1821.

hue and cry The practice in medieval England whereby a person could call out loudly for help in pursuing a suspected criminal. All who heard the call were obliged by law to join in the chase; failure to do so would incur a heavy fine and any misuse of the hue and cry was also punishable. The system was regularized by Edward I in the Statute of Winchester (1285), which rationalized the policing of communities. The obligation on the public to assist the police in the arrest of a suspect has survived in principle to the present day.

Huerta, Victoriano (1854–1916) Mexican statesman and general. Appointed (1912) as commander of the federal forces, he became President of Mexico (1913–14) by leading a coup against Francisco MADERO. He instituted a ruthless dictatorship in which torture and assassination of his political opponents became commonplace. He was forced to resign under insurgent military pressure, supported not only by his Mexican opponents but also by the government of Woodrow WILSON in the USA. An attempted return to power in 1915 ended unsuccessfully when he was arrested by US agents while attempting to cross the US–Mexican border.

Hughes, Charles Evans (1862–1948) US jurist and statesman. He fought, and lost, the presidential election of 1916 as Republican candidate against Woodrow WILSON. As HARDING's Secretary of State (1921–25), he organized the successful Washington conference on naval limitation (1921–22). His career was crowned by his years as Chief Justice of the US Supreme Court (1930–41), during which he enhanced the efficiency of the federal court system, and gave firm support to the freedoms guaranteed to citizens against state actions under the First Amendment. He was largely instrumental in defending the Supreme Court against a plan of F. D. ROOSEVELT (1937) to 'pack' it by adding judges.

Hughes, William M(orris) (1862–1952) Australian statesman. He became a Labor Member of the House of Representatives in 1901, where he served for over 50 years. He was Prime Minister of the Commonwealth of Australia (1915–23), and represented Labor until it split in 1916. In 1917 he helped to form the Nationalist Party, which he led until 1923, when the Country Party, now in coalition with the Nationalists, refused to serve with him. In 1929, he gave his support to the Labor Party over a matter of industrial relations and the Nationalists expelled him. The United Australia Party, which he led from 1941 until 1943, was transformed by MENZIES into the Liberal Party in 1944 and Hughes became a back-bench member.

Huguenots French Protestants of the 16th and 17th centuries who followed the beliefs of CALVIN. By 1561 there were 2,000 Calvinist churches in France and the Huguenots had become a political faction that seemed to threaten the state. Persecution followed and during the FRENCH WARS OF RELIGION the Huguenots fought eight civil wars against the Catholic establishment and triumphed when, by the Edict of NANTES in 1598, HENRY IV gave them liberty of worship and a 'state within a state'. Their numbers grew, especially among merchants and skilled artisans, until they were again persecuted. The centre of their resistance in 1627 was LA ROCHELLE, which the RICHELIEU government had to besiege for over a year before capturing it. In 1685 the Edict was revoked; many thousands of Huguenots fled to England, the Netherlands, Switzerland, and Brandenburg, some settling as far away as North America and the Cape of Good Hope. All these places were to benefit from their skill in craftmanship and trade, particularly as silk-weavers and silversmiths.

Hukbalahap A Filipino peasant resistance movement with roots in the pre-war *barangay* (village) and tenant organizations in central Luzon. Led by Luis Taruc, the movement developed during World War II into the Anti-Japanese People's Army, a left-wing guerrilla organization that was as much opposed to the Filipino landlord élite and their US backers as to the Japanese. Active against the latter from 1943, the 'Huks' controlled most of central Luzon by the end of the war, but were denied parliamentary representation and went into open rebellion against the Manila government until all but destroyed by government forces between 1950 and 1954.

Hull, Cordell (1871–1955) US statesman. As Secretary of State (1933–44), he achieved a progressive tariff by the Reciprocal Trade Agreements Act of 1934. His GOOD NEIGHBOR POLICY resulted in the US withdrawal of marines from Haiti (1934) and the cancellation of the PLATT amendment. He worked steadily for modification of the isolationist NEUTRALITY ACTS (1935–39). F. D. Roosevelt, however, found him too cautious for his purposes and continually by-passed him in planning wartime policies.

humanism An outlook that places man at the centre of the universe, originating in a philosophical and cultural movement that formed part of the 15th-century European RENAISSANCE. There is no systematic theory of humanism, but any world-view that claims that the only source of value in the world is man, or more loosely that man supplies the true measure of value, may be described as humanist. The relations between humanism and religious thought are complex, but humanism is in some respects opposed to religious belief, by virtue of the humanist's belief in human perfectibility, contradicting the doctrine of original sin. In this way humanism also has connections with individualism, the notion that the goal for man includes the fulfilment of each person by the cultivation of his or her own individual nature, and with a belief in the possibility of social progress.

Historically, humanism was fully articulated for the first time in the 15th-century Renaissance. The original Humanists were Christian scholars who studied and taught the humanities (grammar, rhetoric, history, poetry, and moral philosophy), with particular emphasis on the rediscovered classical Latin texts, and later also Greek and Hebrew texts. They came to reject medieval SCHOLASTICISM, and made classical antiquity the basis of western Europe's educational system and cultural outlook. Among their ranks can be numbered Petrarch, Guicciardini, and MACHIAVELLI. They had no coherent philosophy, but shared an enthusiasm for the dignity of human values in place of religious dogma or abstract reasoning.

The invention of PRINTING enabled the movement's ideas to spread from its birthplace in Italy to most of western Europe. Thomas MORE, ERASMUS, and John Colet all contributed to the humanist tradition. Its spirit of sceptical enquiry prepared the way for both the REFORMATION and some aspects of the COUNTER-REFORMATION.

MARX may be correctly described as a humanist, and in this century humanism has been given expression, in both secular and religious forms, in existentialism.

Humayun (1508–56) The second MOGUL emperor of India (1530–40, 1554–55). His name means 'fortunate', yet after ten years of precarious rule he was driven into exile in Persia, recovering his empire only shortly before his death in an accident. His reign is significant mainly because of the introduction of Persian influences into India when he returned from exile accompanied by Persian scholars and artists. Persian became the court language, and pockets of SHIITE religious influence grew up in India.

Hume, David (1711–76) Scottish philosopher and historian. He published his *Treatise of Human Nature* in 1739. It provoked accusations of atheism, which lost him a hoped-for professorship at Edinburgh University. During the War of the AUSTRIAN SUCCESSION he became secretary to General St Clair and was later sent on diplomatic missions. Between missions he wrote his famous *History of Great Britain*. Service at the British embassy in Paris brought him into contact with ROUSSEAU, whom he befriended, and after further government service he returned to Edinburgh in 1769.

Hume enjoyed a great reputation as a historian in his own day but is now remembered as a philosopher, as probably the most influential writer of the empiricist school. His guiding thought that the sole origin of knowledge is in experience led him to criticize the common views of causation and induction. He argued that as we cannot literally perceive the connection between a cause and its effect, our knowledge of causal phenomena is merely that the appearance of certain objects regularly follows certain others, and that an inductive inference is not truly a process of reasoning, but one of custom or habit. His philosophy limited the role of reason in our knowledge of the world, and emphasized that many human responses are in line with animal habit. These conclusions stirred KANT into producing a philosophical system that re-emphasized the role of reason. His other writings made an important contribution to the development of economic theory, and in their political discussion they influenced the makers of the American Constitution.

Hume, Joseph (1777–1855) British radical politician and advocate of social reform. Associated with the radical reform group led by Francis PLACE, he entered Parliament in 1812, re-entered as a Radical MP in 1818, and soon made a name for himself by his ruthless scrutiny of government expenditure. He played an important part in securing the repeal of the COMBINATION ACTS (1824) and campaigned for the abolition of flogging in the army.

Humphrey of Gloucester GLOUCESTER, Humphrey, Duke of.

hundred An administrative subdivision of an English SHIRE between the 10th century and the Local Government Act (1894), which established District Councils. Hundreds were probably based upon units of 100 hides. (A hide was a measure of land, calculated to be enough to support a family and its dependants, ranging from 25 to 50 ha (60–120 acres) according to locality.) They did not exist in every shire. Their equivalents in the DANELAW were wapentakes, in Kent lathes, in Yorkshire ridings, and in Sussex rapes. The hundred court of freeholders met once a month to deal with military defence, private pleas, tax levies, and to prepare indictments for the royal justices. The hundred bailiff served the sheriff's writs and the constable maintained law and order.

Hundred Days (20 March–28 June 1815) The period between NAPOLEON's return from the island of Elba and the second restoration of LOUIS XVIII. Napoleon landed at Cannes on 1 March while the European powers were meeting at the Congress of VIENNA. He won great popular acclaim as he moved north through Grenoble and Lyons. He arrived in Paris on 20 March, less than 24 hours after Louis had fled. Napoleon's attempt to win over moderate royalist opinion to a more liberal conception of his empire failed. Moreover, he failed to persuade the Allies of his peaceful intentions, and had to prepare to defend France against a hastily reconstituted 'Grand Alliance'. By the end of April he had only raised a total strength of 105,000 troops, the Allies having a force of almost 130,000 men. Nevertheless, Napoleon took the offensive and forced the Prussians to retreat at Ligny. Two days later, on 18 June, Napoleon was defeated at WATERLOO. He returned to Paris and on 22 June abdicated for the second time. Six days later Louis XVIII was restored to power.

Hundred Days Reform (1898) Chinese reform campaign. Inspired by KANG YOUWEI, and supported by Liang Qichao (1873–1921), it attempted to reform the QING state. Kang utilized official disenchantment with the measures of the SELF-STRENGTHENING MOVEMENT and concern at renewed foreign intrusions in the wake of the SINO-JAPANESE WAR of 1894–95 to have extensive reforms, based on Western thinking, adopted by Emperor Guangxu. These included a constitutional monarchy and modernization of the civil service. After a period of 103 days the reform programme was destroyed by a conservative backlash, the empress dowager CIXI launching a palace coup in which the emperor was imprisoned, the reforms rescinded, and the reformers themselves exiled, dismissed, or put to death. Many of these reforms were finally implemented between the RUSSO-JAPANESE WAR of 1904–05 and the Revolution of 1911.

Hundred Flowers Movement (1956–57) A brief period of political and intellectual debate in Communist China. Drawing its name from a slogan from Chinese classical history, 'let a hundred flowers bloom and a hundred schools of thought contend', the campaign was initiated by MAO ZEDONG and others in the wake of Khrushchev's denunciation of Stalin. Mao argued that self-criticism would benefit China's development. After some hesitation, denunciation of the Communist Party and its institutions appeared in the press and there was social unrest. The party reacted by attacking its critics and exiling many to distant areas of the country in the Anti-Rightist Campaign.

Hundred Years War A period of conflict between France and England that stretched over more than a century between the 1330s and 1450s: it was not one continuous conflict but rather a series of attempts by English kings to dominate France. The two key issues were the sovereignty of Gascony (the English king was Duke of Gascony and resented paying homage for it to the kings of France), and EDWARD III's claim, through his mother, to the French throne, following the death of the last CAPETIAN king. Rivalry over the lucrative Flanders wool trade and provocative French support for the Scots against England also contributed.

In 1328 Philip VI of Valois was crowned King of France and his subsequent confiscation of AQUITAINE (1337) provoked Edward's invasion of France (1338). The English won a naval battle at Sluys (1340) and major military victories at CRÉCY (1346), Calais (1347), and POITIERS (1356), where EDWARD THE BLACK PRINCE captured and later ransomed Philip's successor John II. In 1360 the Treaty of Brétigny gave Edward considerable territories in France in return for abandoning his claims to the

Dates	The English	The French
	FIRST PHASE	
1337	Edward III rules French territories of Guyenne and Gascony as Duke of Aquitaine	
		Philip VI tries to extend his rule over the whole of France and confiscates Edward's duchy of Aquitaine
	Edward sends letters of defiance to Philip and claims French throne	
1338	Edward invades France	
1340	Edward assumes title 'King of France'	
	English win major naval battle at Sluys, gaining control of the Channel	
1346	English victorious at Crécy	
1347		*Calais surrenders to Edward III*
1347–56	FREQUENT TRUCES. THE BLACK DEATH SUBDUES MILITARY ACTIVITY	
1350		*Philip VI dies; succession of John II*
1356	Edward the Black Prince victorious at Poitiers; John II captured, but Edward III fails to take advantage	
	SECOND PHASE	
1360	Treaty of Brétigny temporarily ends hostilities: considerable territories transferred to Edward on condition that he gives up his claim to the French throne	
1364		*John II dies; succession of Charles V*
1369	Edward III reassumes title 'King of France' following sporadic fighting and violation of the Treaty of Brétigny	
		Charles V reclaims Edward's French possessions; fighting resumes
1377	Edward III dies; succession of Richard II. England only holds Calais and part of Gascony	
1380		*Charles V dies; succession of Charles VI*
1396	Peace of Paris; Richard II marries Charles VI's daughter – 28-year truce	
1399	Deposition of Richard II; succession of Henry IV	
1410		*Civil War (Burgundians v. Orleanists) weakens France*
	THIRD PHASE	
1413	Henry IV dies; succession of Henry V	
1415	Henry V renews claims to France; captures Harfleur; wins the Battle of Agincourt	
1417	Henry begins systematic occupation of Normandy, helped by an alliance with John the Fearless, duke of Burgundy	
1420	Henry V marries daughter of Charles VI and by Treaty of Troyes becomes heir to French throne	
		Paris occupied by English
1422	Henry V dies	*Charles VI dies*
	Henry VI (aged 10 months) rules France N of the Loire	
		Charles VII rules France S of the Loire
1429		*Joan of Arc leads a French revival and raises siege of Orleans*
		Charles VII crowned King of France at Rheims
1430		*Joan of Arc captured by Burgundians*
	Henry VI maintains control in Paris	
1431	Joan of Arc burned at the stake	
1435		*Charles VII forms alliance with Burgundians by Treaty of Arras*
1436		*Charles recaptures Paris*
1450–53		*Charles reconquers Normandy (1450), Guyenne (1451), and Bordeaux (1453)*
1453	England only holds Calais. Weakened and distracted by the Wars of the Roses, England gives up trying to conquer France.	

Hundred Years War *Phases of the Hundred Years War.*

French throne. The French gradually improved their position and in the later part of the reign of Edward's successor, his grandson, RICHARD II, hostilities ceased almost completely.

The English retention of Calais and Bordeaux, however, prevented permanent peace, and English claims to France were revived by HENRY V (invoking SALIC LAW). He invaded Harfleur and won a crushing victory at AGINCOURT (1415), followed by occupation of Normandy (1419) and much of northern France. The Treaty of Troyes (1420) forced Charles VI of France to disinherit his son, the dauphin, in favour of the English kings. However, following Henry V's early death (1422) the regents of his ineffectual son HENRY VI gradually lost control of conquered territory to French forces under the leadership of JOAN OF ARC. The English were defeated at Orleans (1429) and by 1450 France had conquered Normandy and much of Gascony; Bordeaux, the last English stronghold, was captured in 1453. This effectively ended the war and thereafter the English retained only Calais (until 1558). The English were forced to turn attention to internal affairs, notably the Wars of the ROSES and gave up all claims to France. In France the virtual destruction of the nobility saw the VALOIS monarchy emerge in a strong position.

Hungarian Revolution (1956) A revolt against Communist rule in Hungary (23 October–4 November). It was provoked by the presence in the country of Soviet troops, the repressive nature of the government led by Erno Gerö, and the general atmosphere of de-Stalinization created in February at the TWENTIETH CONGRESS of the CPSU. Initial demonstrations in Budapest led to the arrival of Soviet tanks in the city, which served only to exacerbate discontent, Hungarian soldiers joining the uprising. Soviet forces were then withdrawn. Imre NAGY became Prime Minister, appointed non-communists to his coalition, announced Hungary's withdrawal from the WARSAW PACT, and sought a neutral status for the country. This was unacceptable to the Soviet Union. Powerful forces — mainly Soviet but partly Hungarian attacked Budapest and resistance in the capital was soon overcome. Nagy was replaced by János KÁDÁR, while 190,000 Hungarians fled into exile. The Soviet Union reneged on its pledge of safe conduct, handing Nagy and other prominent figures over to the new Hungarian regime, which executed them in secret.

Hungary A central European country, bounded by Czech Lands on the north, Romania on the east, Croatia and Serbia on the south, and Austria on the west; it is also conterminous with Ukraine in the north-east.

Physical. From north to south through the centre flows the Danube, in a broad plain (the puszta) which extends eastward to the River Tisza across pastureland and areas suited to agriculture. West of the river is the Bakony Forest of mainly deciduous trees, Lake Balaton (the largest and shallowest lake in central Europe), and a fertile plateau with granite hills. The climate, with cold winters and hot summers, is continental.

Economy. The principal crops are wheat, maize, barley, sugar beet, potatoes, and grapes, while mineral resources include bauxite, brown coal, lignite, and copper. Increases in Western joint ventures, new management techniques, and the replacement of outdated machinery are measures which aim to revive

dustrial profitability. Hungary's main exports are
achinery and transport equipment, agricultural
roduce, and computer software. Tourism is an
xpanding source of revenue.

History. The region comprising the Roman provinces
f Pannonia and Dacia was overrun by Germanic tribes
1 the DARK AGES and then conquered by CHARLEMAGNE. By
96 elected MAGYAR ARPAD leaders ruled and Hungary
merged as the centre of a strong Magyar kingdom in
he late Middle Ages. A Mongol invasion devastated the
opulation in 1241 and the Arpad line ended in 1301.
hereafter, the crown was usually passed to a foreigner.
he advance of the OTTOMAN EMPIRE threatened, especially
fter the Battle of Nicopolis in 1396, when Sigismund,
ing of Hungary, was defeated by the Turks. John
unyadi (d. 1456) and his son MATTHIAS CORVINUS brought
evival, but in 1490 the Jagiellons gained the throne,
nd, in 1515, a HABSBURG claim arose. The disastrous
efeat of the Hungarian king, Louis II, at MOHÁCS (1526),
d to the partition of Hungary between the Habsburgs
nd the Ottomans although TRANSYLVANIA retained its
idependence. By 1711 all of Hungary had come under
Iabsburg rule and remained part of the Habsburg
mpire until 1919.

In the 19th century Magyar nationalism was
ntagonized by the repressive policies of METTERNICH,
eading to rebellion under KOSSUTH in 1848. The
ustrians, with Russian help, reasserted control. After
efeat by PRUSSIA the Austrians compromised with the
Iagyars in 1867, setting up the AUSTRO-HUNGARIAN EMPIRE,
r Dual Monarchy, which was first and foremost an
lliance of Magyars and Austrian Germans against the
lav nationalities. Defeat in World War I led to
evolution and independence, first under Károlyi's
emocratic republic, then briefly under Béla KUN's
ommunist regime. Dictatorship followed in 1920 under
ORTHY, and lasted until 1944. Allied to the AXIS POWERS in
Vorld War II, defeat brought Soviet domination and a
ommunist one-party system. This was resented and,
riefly, in 1956, the HUNGARIAN REVOLUTION saw resistance
o the Soviet Union. Hungary experienced some degree
f liberalization during the latter years of János Kádár's
egime (1956–88). Demonstrations in Budapest in 1988
esulted in multiparty politics being restored. Elections
rought to power the Hungarian Democratic Forum
MDF) early in 1990; but after the collapse of COMECON,
rade fell and there was rising unemployment and
opular discontent. Refugees from Romanian
ransylvania and from disintegrating Yugoslavia caused
dditional problems. A programme of ambitious
eforms to revive the economy and introduce a free-
narket system were launched in 1990. These reforms
rogressed steadily with the privatization of many
ompanies in 1991, accompanied by increasing foreign
nvestment. However, continued economic recession and
omestic political problems resulted in heavy defeat for
he MDF in the general election of May 1994. A new
oalition, led by the Hungarian Socialist Party under
yula Horn, took office. Despite a continuing sense of
conomic crisis, which led to the introduction of
overnment austerity measures, modest economic
rowth was recorded in 1995–96. In 1997 Hungary was
ormally invited to join NATO, a suggestion that
eceived enthusiastic backing in a subsequent
eferendum.

APITAL: Budapest

AREA:	93,033 sq km (35,920 sq miles)
POPULATION:	10.201 million (1996)
CURRENCY:	1 forint = 100 filler
RELIGIONS:	Roman Catholic 62.4%; Protestant 23.4%; atheist and non-religious 12.9%; Orthodox 0.5%; Jewish 0.8%
ETHNIC GROUPS:	Magyar 96.6%; German 1.6%; Slovak 1.1%; Romanian and gypsy 0.7%
LANGUAGES:	Hungarian (official); minority languages
INTERNATIONAL ORGANIZATIONS:	UN; CSCE; Council of Europe; North Atlantic Co-operation Council

Hungry Forties A period in the early 1840s when
Britain experienced an economic depression, causing
much misery among the poor. In 1839 there was a
serious slump in trade, leading to a steep increase in
unemployment, accompanied by a bad harvest. The bad
harvests were repeated in the two following years and
the sufferings of the people, in a rapidly increasing
population, were made worse by the fact that the CORN
LAWS seemed to keep the price of bread artificially high.
In 1845 potato blight appeared in England and Scotland,
spreading to Ireland later in the year and ruining a
large part of the crop. The potato blight returned in
1846, bringing the IRISH FAMINE.

Huns Pastoral nomads famed for their horsemanship,
who entered history *c.* 370 AD when they invaded south-
eastern Europe and conquered the OSTROGOTHS. In 376
they drove the VISIGOTHS into Roman territory and early
in the 4th century themselves advanced west, driving
the ALANS, VANDALS, and others west into Gaul, Italy, and
finally Spain. Under ATTILA (434–53) they ravaged the
Balkans and Greece, but a defeat was finally inflicted on
them in 451 at the CATALAUNIAN FIELDS by the Romans and
Visigoths under the command of Aetius. However that
did not prevent them penetrating and plundering Italy
the following year. Two years after the death of Attila
they were decisively defeated near the unidentified
River Nedao, and thereafter ceased to be of historical
significance. The White Huns occupied Bactria and
territory west towards the Caspian Sea. They vigorously
attacked the power of the SASSANIAN EMPIRE, defeating
and killing Peroz in 484, but then moved south to
establish an empire in northern India at the expense of
the GUPTAS.

Hunt, Henry ('Orator Hunt') (1773–1835) British political
reformer. He advocated, among other things, full adult
suffrage and secret ballots. An outstanding public
speaker, in August 1819 he addressed the crowd at the
great meeting at St Peter's Fields (PETERLOO MASSACRE),
Manchester. For this he was subsequently sentenced to
two years' imprisonment. During 1830–33 he was Radical
Member of Parliament for Preston.

hunter-gatherers People who subsist from the
natural environment, without involvement in
agriculture or animal husbandry. They survive by
gathering wild fruit and vegetables, and by hunting.
Theirs is the earliest and simplest form of human
organization, and has been found all over the world:
Australian ABORIGINES, the Arctic Inuit, and the !Kung-San
in southern Africa are all examples of hunter-gatherers.
They have a nomadic way of life, following seasonal
food supplies. They are organized in bands consisting of
close kin, but these bands fluctuate in size as members

move in and out, according to food availability. Marriage is a very loose institution, and lineage is not considered of great importance. Hunter-gatherer society is egalitarian: leadership is usually based on individual ability and is not hereditary. Relations between men and women are also more egalitarian than in many sedentary societies, though there is a basic division of labour, the men hunting game while the women do most of the gathering. Today, many hunter-gatherers are threatened by economic development, which is destroying the natural environment upon which their survival depends. (See also PALAEOLITHIC; STONE AGE; UPPER PALAEOLITHIC.)

Hurons A confederacy of five Iroquoian-speaking tribes of Native Americans with a farming economy who lived in large fortified villages in southern Ontario. They were first encountered by Europeans in the 17th century, when the name 'Huron' was given them by the French. In 1609 they were met by Samuel de CHAMPLAIN, who drew the French into a conflict between the Hurons and the culturally similar IROQUOIS to the south, particularly the SENECA. By the 1620s the Hurons had become important suppliers of furs to the French. From 1635 Jesuits founded several missions among them, two of which were destroyed in Iroquois raids of 1648–49. Those Hurons who were not killed dispersed into other tribes to the west or settled near Quebec. By the mid-19th century the Huron were living in Kansas; they were later resettled in north-east Oklahoma.

Huskisson, William (1770–1830) British statesman. He encouraged the incipient movement towards FREE TRADE in Britain. A supporter of William PITT THE YOUNGER, he held a number of minor posts before being appointed President of the Board of Trade in 1823. He reduced duties on a wide range of articles, removed restrictions on colonial trade, and proposed a relaxation of the CORN LAWS. He was killed by a train at the opening of the Liverpool and Manchester Railway.

Huss, John (c. 1372–1415) Bohemian religious reformer. A preacher in Prague and an enthusiastic supporter of WYCLIF's views, he aroused the hostility of the Church, was excommunicated (1411), tried (1414), and burnt at the stake. By his death he was acclaimed a martyr and his followers (HUSSITES) took up arms against the HOLY ROMAN EMPIRE and inflicted a series of dramatic defeats on the imperial army.

hussar A soldier of a light cavalry regiment. Hussars were originally mounted troops raised in 1485 by MATTHIAS CORVINUS, King of Hungary, to fight the Turks. As good light cavalry was scarce, other countries soon developed their own hussars: FREDERICK the Great proved the superiority of Prussian hussars over those of Austria during the War of the AUSTRIAN SUCCESSION. Britain hired hussars from several German states in the 18th century, sending them to America where they were hated by the patriots.

Hussein, ibn Ali (1856–1931) Arab political leader. A member of the Hashemite family, he was sharif of Mecca and leader of the 1916 Arab revolt against Ottoman rule. In 1916 he assumed the title of King of the Arab Countries, but the Allies only recognized him as King of the HEJAZ. As ruler of the Hejaz (1916–24) he came into conflict in 1919 with Ibn SAUD, the Emir of Najd. He abdicated in favour of his son Ali in October

1924. His son Abdullah became ruler of Trans-Jordan, thus founding the royal line of Jordan, and another son, FAISAL I, became king of Iraq.

Hussein, ibn Talal (1935–) King of Jordan (1953–). Grandson of Abdullah ibn Hussein, he succeeded his father Talal, who was deposed in 1952 as insane. Socially conservative and strongly backed by his army, in the early years of his reign he met continuing opposition from pro-Egyptian factions. Although backed and armed by the USA, he suffered defeat in the SIX DAY WAR of 1967, when he lost the West Bank to Israel. Palestine Liberation Organization (PLO) guerrillas based themselves in JORDAN, but in 1971 fighting developed between these and his army, who expelled the PLO. Generously funded by Saudi Arabia, he reasserted his authority and survived accusations by many of his Arab neighbours that he undermined Palestine resistance. From 1979 his policies became more flexible. He was reconciled with Yasser ARAFAT of the PLO, and was at the centre of a continuing peace initiative in the Middle East. In 1988 he renounced all Jordanian claims to the West Bank. Following the outbreak of the GULF WAR, King Hussein made a controversial speech attacking US policy and called for a ceasefire and US-Iraqi talks. In the same year he repealed almost all of the martial law provisions in place since the 1967 Arab-Israeli War. He improved relations with the USA in 1993, when he met US President Bill Clinton for talks while visiting the country. In 1994 he held talks with Israeli Prime Minister Yitzhak RABIN, signing a formal peace treaty with Israel in October. He subsequently relaxed a 34-year ban on political parties as part of his country's development towards multiparty democracy.

Hussein, Saddam (1937–) President of Iraq (1979–). He joined the Ba'ath Socialist Party in 1957 and was involved in various coups and plots early in the 1960s. In July 1968 he took part in the revolution which brought General Ahmed Bakr to power. In 1969 he became deputy-chairman of the Revolution Command Council (RCC), following the execution of 51 prominent Iraqis on charges of espionage. In 1976 he was granted the rank of general, and in 1979 he succeeded Bakr as Chairman of the RCC and President of Iraq. Soon after launching the IRAN–IRAQ WAR in 1980 he purged the Ba'ath Party of Iraq. He was provided with considerable technical support from the West to fight the war. From 1988 onwards he carried out a systematic campaign of repression against the Kurdish population of Iraq, including the use of chemical weapons and poison gas on civilians. In August 1990 he ordered the occupation of Kuwait, leading to war with a US-led coalition in January-February 1991 (GULF WAR). Following Iraq's military defeat he accepted the UN terms for a ceasefire. However, his policy has since been to defy the UN terms wherever possible, leading to US military action in 1993 and 1996 and a further crisis in 1997–98. In order to win and maintain popular Arab support through the Middle East and Africa, he has moved towards ever-greater deference to Islam, in spite of the secularism of his Ba'ath state.

Hussites Followers of John HUSS, the Bohemian religious reformer who was condemned for heresy and put to death by the Council of CONSTANCE in 1415. Even before his death Huss had a large following in various parts of his native country BOHEMIA and his execution at the stake sparked a nationwide protest in Bohemia, notably in the signing of a solemn protest by 452 nobles on 2 September 1415. Later the Hussite movement split into two main parties: the moderate Utraquists and the Taborites (named after Mount Tabor, their fortified stronghold), who held more extreme theological and social views. The Taborites were eventually defeated by an alliance of Utraquists and Roman Catholic forces at the Battle of Lipany in 1434. Most of the Utraquist demands were granted by the Church at the Compactata of Prague in 1436. Some groups of Hussites survived until today, under various names, but the movement was largely overtaken by the Reformation in the 16th century.

Hyde, Edward CLARENDON.

Hyderabad One of the largest and most important PRINCELY STATES in south-central India. Its rise to dominance was the achievement of the Mogul viceroy, Asaf Jah Nizam ul-Mulk, who in 1724 established virtually independent rule. His successors ruled until 1948 as nizams (governors) of Hyderabad. Absolute power was short-lived, however, for inability to challenge European expansion soon dictated co-operation with the British, whose protection was extended to Hyderabad in 1798 in return for the upkeep of EAST INDIA COMPANY troops. Although internal control was retained, British influence became dominant in the 19th century. On British withdrawal from India in 1947, the nizam acceded to the Indian Union. In 1956 the territories of Hyderabad were divided among the new linguistically based states.

Hyder Ali (1722–82) Sultan of MYSORE, south India (1761–82). Born in relative obscurity, he managed to supplant the Hindu ruler of Mysore. However, he soon had to face the expanding EAST INDIA COMPANY armies, aided by Indian allies. In wars with the Company (1767–69 and 1780–84) he proved himself one of its most formidable obstacles, winning, with some French mercenary assistance, a series of remarkable victories. But heavy defeats in 1781 persuaded him that further struggle was pointless, and he urged his son, TIPU SULTAN, to seek terms with the Company.

Hyksos (rulers of foreign lands) Invaders, probably from Palestine, who ruled Lower Egypt and part of Upper Egypt from *c.* 1674 BC. Their power lasted until *c.* 1550 BC, when they were overthrown by a rebellion started by the Egyptians of Thebes. The introduction of the horse and CHARIOT was attributed to them, but for the most part they seem to have deferred to the native culture and gods. Egyptian remained the official language.

Ibarra, Francisco de (1539–75) Spanish explorer credited with the exploration and colonization of Nueva Vizcaya, the huge area of Mexico that today encompasses most of the states of Durango, Chihuahua, and part of Sonora. With funds provided by his uncle, who had made a fortune in the Zacatecas silver mines, Ibarra, as governor of Nueva Vizcaya, opened up much of the northern frontier of NEW SPAIN in the 1560s before returning to Mexico City.

Iberians Early inhabitants of southern and eastern Spain. In the north of the peninsula they intermingled with the Celts to produce the Celtiberian tribes. From the 9th century BC they came into increasing contact with CARTHAGE, and Iberian and Celtiberian mercenaries were a vital element of the armies with which Carthage fought the Greek cities of Sicily and the Romans.

IBRD WORLD BANK.

Iceland An island country just south of the Arctic Circle in the north-east Atlantic Ocean.

Physical. Only Iceland's coastal areas can be used for settlement and agriculture because the rest is a wasteland of ice, ash, and lava flows. It lies at the edge of the Eurasian plate, on the Mid-Atlantic Ridge, so Iceland has many volcanoes, geysers, and hot springs.

Economy. Hydroelectric power stations provide most of the country's electricity needs and geothermal energy is abundant. Most of the land area is agriculturally unproductive. The fishing industry is of vital importance to the economy.

History. Iceland was conquered by the VIKINGS between 874 and 930. Its capital, Reykjavik, was founded, and the country was governed by some 36 chieftains, who met periodically in the Althing, an official assembly. A lawspeaker was appointed, and, in 1005, a Supreme Court. Authority, once derived from the pagan priests and temples, changed with conversion to Christianity in *c.* 1000 to a partnership of Church and Althing. In 1262 Iceland passed to Norway and, in 1380, with Norway to the Danish crown. Under the rule of Denmark since 1380, a nationalist movement achieved the restoration of the Althing in 1845. Iceland acquired limited autonomy in 1874 and independence in 1918, although it shared its king with Denmark until 1943. It became an independent republic in 1944. An Allied base during WORLD WAR II, it joined the UNITED NATIONS and NATO (1949). It engaged in sometimes violent disputes with Britain over fishing limits, resulting in the COD WAR of 1972–76. In the late 1970s strong opposition to the presence of US bases developed, and Iceland became a nuclear-free zone in 1985. In 1990–91 Iceland attempted to restrict fishing within its territorial waters during negotiations between the EUROPEAN FREE TRADE ASSOCIATION and the EUROPEAN COMMUNITY over a common European Economic Area (EEA), which it boycotted. However, following the election of a new centre-right coalition government in April 1991, Iceland managed to secure a restriction on fishing in its waters and introduced measures of economic liberalization, leading to the privatization of many state-owned industries. It also favoured closer relations with the USA, which maintained NATO naval bases in Iceland. The country's worsening economic situation in 1992, caused by losses in the fishing industry, led the government to introduce emergency measures and to devalue the króna in 1993. Having finally approved the EEA agreement Iceland made moves towards applying for membership of the EUROPEAN UNION, following the example of Sweden and Finland. In April 1995 a new coalition government was formed, led by David Oddsson, following a general election, and in 1996 Olafur Ragnar Grimsson was elected President.

CAPITAL:	Reykjavik
AREA:	103,000 sq km (39,769 sq miles)
POPULATION:	270,000 (1996)
CURRENCY:	1 króna = 100 aurar
RELIGIONS:	Evangelical Lutheran 92.9%; other Lutheran 3.4%; non-religious 1.3%; Roman Catholic 0.9%
ETHNIC GROUPS:	(Place of birth, 1988): Iceland 96.3%; Denmark 0.9%; USA 0.5%; Sweden 0.4%; Germany 0.3%
LANGUAGES:	Icelandic (official)
INTERNATIONAL ORGANIZATIONS:	UN; EFTA; OECD; NATO; Council of Europe; CSCE

Iceni A pre-Roman tribe of eastern England. By the time of the Roman invasion of 43 AD they were part-Romanized and had come under the rule of the dynasty of CUNOBELINUS. Their ruler Prasutagus was a treaty ally of Rome until his death in 60 AD. The treaty was broken by Rome and his widow BOUDICCA led the tribe in a revolt which was brutally suppressed.

Iconoclastic controversy (from the Greek, 'breaking of images') A conflict within the Eastern Christian Church in the 8th and 9th centuries over the veneration of icons (both religious paintings and statues), which the so-called iconoclasts condemned as idolatry. Emperor Leo III banned such veneration in 726 and despite popular antagonism the decision was confirmed by Constantine V in 753. In the seventh ecumenical council of 787 at NICAEA Empress IRENE overturned the decrees but they were again enforced under the emperors Leo V, Michael II, and Theophilus. Veneration of icons was finally restored in 843 and the practice survives today in the Eastern Orthodox Church.

IDA WORLD BANK.

ideology A political belief-system that both explains the world as it currently is and suggests how it should be changed. The term was given currency by MARX, who used it to describe the belief-systems of social classes, and especially that of the capitalist class or bourgeoisie. Bourgeois ideology involved 'false consciousness', in contrast to the 'scientific' outlook that Marx held to represent the true consciousness of the working class.

his ideology/science contrast has since generally been dropped in favour of the view that all political outlooks rest on assumptions that cannot be proved, and are to that degree ideological. Some have sought to reserve the term ideology for especially dogmatic or extreme political positions. Some social and political commentators have identified 'the end of ideology' in Western societies, citing as evidence the demise of MARXISM as an all-embracing vision of society. Others prefer to regard ideology as an all-pervasive mechanism by which people order their perceptions of the social world, whether or not they consciously subscribe to a political doctrine.

Ife A holy city in Oyo Province, south-west Nigeria. For the Yoruba people it is the legendary birthplace of all mankind, allegedly founded by the diviner Ifa. According to Yoruba belief Ife, meaning wide, is the place where creation began, and Ile-Ife ('the house of Ife'), the sacred city, is the Yoruba people's place of origin. It was the capital of a kingdom of the same name, already established by the 11th century, and by the following century its craftsmen had produced the terracotta sculptures and bronze heads for which it is famous. Ife began to lose political influence among the Yoruba during the 16th century as the power of OYO increased.

Iguala, Plan of (1821) A set of constitutional guarantees for an independent Mexico proclaimed in the Mexican town of Iguala by the Creole leader ITURBIDE, with the support of the guerrilla leader, Vincent Guerrero. The plan stated that Mexico would be organized as a constitutional monarchy under Ferdinand VII or another European prince, that Roman Catholicism would be the state religion, and that any person, regardless of race, could hold office. The Viceroy Apodaca was deposed and his successor confirmed the guarantees by the convention of Córdoba, but the Spanish government rejected them. The Plan was discarded when Iturbide proclaimed himself emperor (1822).

Ikeda Hayato (1899–1965) Japanese statesman. He entered the government tax service and rose by 1945 to become head of the National Tax Bureau. Having served as Vice-Minister of Finance in the YOSHIDA SHIGERA cabinet of 1947, he was elected to the House of Representatives in 1949 and became successively Minister of Finance and Minister of International Trade. Serving in a succession of high ministerial posts throughout the 1950s, Ikeda became Prime Minister (1960–64) and devoted himself to sustaining Japanese economic growth through a broadening of international trading connections.

Ikhnaton AKHENATEN.

Ile de France The area at the centre of the Paris basin, where the rivers Marne and Ouse join the River Seine. It is well-populated and fertile, supplying Paris with vegetable and dairy produce. As the original duchy of France it was the cradle of the French monarchy: in 987 Duke Hugh CAPET was chosen as king and his domains were the nucleus of the ever-growing crown lands. It became a province in the 15th century but was partitioned after the French Revolution.

Ilium TROY.

Illyria An area on the eastern coast of the Adriatic, north-west of Greece. In ancient times it was inhabited by a number of related Indo-European tribes from c. 1000 BC. They caused considerable trouble to neighbouring Epirus and Macedonia, though PYRRHUS annexed their southern territory in the 290s BC. Subsequently they reasserted their power southwards, the threat they posed to shipping eventually causing the Romans to declare war and suppress their ambitions (228–227 and 219). They supported the Romans against Macedonia at Cynoscephalae (197) but after supporting King Perseus of Macedonia at Pydna (168) their territory was divided into three. The Roman province of Illyricum was disturbed by rebellion in 6 AD, which TIBERIUS had suppressed by 9 AD. It was later divided into two provinces, known as Dalmatia and Pannonia.

IMF INTERNATIONAL MONETARY FUND.

Imhotep Architect, astrologer, and chief adviser to King Zoser (fl. c. 2700 BC) of Egypt. To him are credited the first temple at Edfu and the first of the PYRAMIDS, the so-called Step Pyramid at Saqqara. In later times he was the patron of craftsmen, and identified as a sage and physician. Imhotep is depicted with cropped or shaven head, seated with a roll of papyrus on his lap. The Greeks identified Imhotep with Asclepius because of his healing powers. Imhotep is important among Egyptian gods as one of the few mortals to achieve a sort of sainthood. He was thought to have been the son of Ptah of Memphis and a mortal woman called Khredu-ankh.

impeachment A judicial procedure by which a public official may be tried by the legislature for treason or other serious crime. In Britain, the impeachment procedure has passed into disuse since the 18th century, but has never been abolished. It was most frequently used in the 17th century against CHARLES I's supporters and ministers including BUCKINGHAM, STRAFFORD and LAUD. It was last used in England against Viscount Melville (1806). In the USA, the House of Representatives institutes the impeachment proceedings and the Senate acts as judge. In 1974 the House of Representatives was preparing articles of impeachment against President Richard NIXON on the grounds of obstruction of justice and misuse of power after he refused to co-operate with inquiries into the illegal electronic surveillance of his political opponents at the Watergate Hotel in Washington, DC. He preempted proceedings by resigning.

imperialism The policy of extending a country's influence over less powerful states. Historically imperialism has existed in all periods: Greece, Rome, Ottoman Turkey, Spain, and Britain have all extended their respective domains over societies at different times, giving way to forms of imperial rule. The INDUSTRIAL REVOLUTION introduced a new form of imperialism, as European countries competed throughout the world both for raw materials and for markets. In the late 19th century imperial ambitions were motivated in part by the need for commercial expansion, the desire for military glory, and diplomatic advantage. Imperialism generally assumed a racial, intellectual, and spiritual superiority on the part of the newcomers. The effects of imperialism, while in some measure beneficial to the indigenous population, often meant the breakdown of traditional forms of life, the disruption of native civilization, and the imposition of new religious beliefs and social values. The dreams of imperialism faded in the 1920s as anti-imperialist movements developed, and from the 1940s colonies gained their independence.

The term 'neo-imperialism' is sometimes used to describe certain (usually economic) policies of the developed world, notably the USA and the former Soviet Union, towards the DEVELOPING COUNTRIES in the post-World War II era. Explanations for the causes of imperialism, be they political, military, economic, or religious, have stimulated a long intellectual debate, notable contributions to which are John Atkinson Hobson's *Imperialism, A Study* (1902) and Vladimir Ilyich Lenin's *Imperialism, the Highest Stage of Capitalism* (1917).

Impressed ware cultures The early NEOLITHIC farmers who spread round virtually the whole coastline of the western Mediterranean from 6000 BC. Their characteristic pottery consists of round-bottomed bowls decorated with impressed designs, particularly using the crinkled edge of the cockle shell (the so-called Cardial ware). Material comes from both caves and open villages. By the 4th millennium the culture had split into many regional variants.

Inca The pre-Columbian Indian people of western South America. They comprised Quechua-speaking tribes round CUZCO (their capital), who formed a state contemporary to, and eventually superseding that of CHIMÚ. 16th-century records indicate that the ruling dynasty was founded *c*. 1200 AD by Manco Capac, but real expansion did not take place until 1438, forming an empire stretching from northern Ecuador, across Peru, to Bolivia and parts of northern Argentina and Chile by 1525 (some 3,500 km, 2,175 miles, north to south). Three important rulers carried out these conquests and the development of the imperial administration: Pachacuti (1438–71), TOPA INCA (1471–93), and Huayna Capac (1493–1525). After Huayna Capac civil wars broke up the empire of his son ATAHUALPA just before Spanish troops led by Francisco PIZARRO landed on the coast in 1532. Atahualpa was captured in 1533 and killed shortly thereafter. In the same year Pizarro captured Cuzco, and by 1537, after the defeat of Manco Capac, most of the empire had been subdued by Spain.

The Sapa Inca, 'Son of the Sun', ruled by divine right and was worshipped as a god in his own lifetime. Under him was a vast administrative bureaucracy, which regulated a complex system of regional capitals (for example, QUITO), agriculture, food collection and redistribution, craft production, and roads and bridges. An efficient army, including a messenger system and strategically placed fortresses (for example, Machu Picchu), kept control; and rebellious populations were transferred wholesale to other parts of the empire. Although writing was unknown, records were kept on *quipus*, sets of cords of different colours and thicknessess tied with a system of coded knots.

Inca technology was of a high standard and included specialized factories and workshops producing ceramics, textiles, and metal artefacts, with fine decoration, incorporating many regional styles. Architecture included accurately fitted stone masonry. Agriculture was based on systems of hillside terracing and included the potato, quinoa, and maize, and the guinea pig (for

food), domestic dog, llama, and alpaca. Religion was centralized, local gods being respected but secondary to the Sun cult as the divine ancestor of the ruling dynasty and Viracocha, the creator god.

Dates	Major Events
c. 1200	Manco Capac, first Lord Inca, establishes ruling dynasty with its capital at Cuzco
c. 1250	Inca culture thrives in Cuzco valley. Incas vie for supremacy with their neighbours, the Chanca, Colla, Lupaca, and others in the southern Andes
c. 1300	Rise of the Chimú empire, rivals to the Incas
c. 1350	Mayta Capa initiates Inca expansion
c. 1380	Chimú empire extends over 960 km (600 miles)
c. 1437	Viracocha, 8th Lord Inca, continues Inca expansion outside Cuzco area. Cuzco besieged by Chanca tribe
1438	Chancas defeated by Inca army led by Yupanqui, son of Viracocha. Proclaimed 9th Lord Inca, he takes the name of Pachacuti
1450	Pachacuti enlarges Inca empire, completing conquest of Titicaca basin
1463	Pachacuti wages war on Lupaca and Colla tribes. Quechua, the Inca language, is established. Pachacuti entrusts control of the army to his son Topa
1466	Chimú empire overrun by Inca troops commanded by Topa
1471	Topa Inca becomes 10th Lord Inca. Era of road-building
1485	Topa Inca conquers Chile as far as the Maule River, the south coast of Peru, and north-west Argentina
1493	Huayna Capac becomes 11th Lord Inca. Quito founded as second capital, a decision that later leads to civil war between Huayna's sons Atahualpa and Huascar
1498	Huayna Capac extends Inca territory beyond Quito into Columbia. Andean highway completed
1519	Atahualpa (last independent Inca) takes part in military campaigns
1525	Death of Huayna Capac. Civil war breaks out between Huascar (crowned 12th Lord Inca) and his brother Atahualpa who dominates the north
1532	Huascar defeated. Francisco Pizarro begins his conquest of the Inca empire for Spain and takes Atahualpa captive
1533	Atahualpa executed by the Spaniards
1535	Inca empire completely subjugated by the Spaniards

Inca   *The history of the Incas.*

incident of 26 February 1936 Attempted military coup in Japan. Young extremists of the Imperial Way faction (*Kodo-ha*) had been active within the Japanese army since the late 1920s, intent on using violent means to overthrow the conservative civilian government and set Japan on a course of military expansion, particularly in China. Their activities culminated in the attempted coup in which several prominent politicians were murdered (the Prime Minister Okada Keisuke only escaping through a case of mistaken identity) and much of central Tokyo seized. The revolt was put down on 29 February and most of its leaders executed, after which leadership of the military expansionist cause passed to the more moderate Control faction (*Tosei-ha*).

income tax A tax levied on the income of an individual. In Britain it was imposed on the incomes of the propertied classes for the first time in December 1798 by William PITT THE YOUNGER, to help finance the war with France. It was temporarily abolished by Parliament against the government's wishes in 1816. It was revived in 1842 by PEEL in exchange for a reduction in customs and excise duties. In the 1850s GLADSTONE planned to abolish it gradually, but was in fact obliged to raise it to finance the Crimean War, and by the 1860s it had become accepted as a permanent necessity on higher incomes.

In the 20th century tax liability tended to reach further down the social scale so that by World War II most full-time employees were taxed. Income taxes were introduced in some European countries during the 19th century and in the British dominions from 1891. In the USA federal income tax was imposed in 1862 to help finance the American Civil War. An attempt by the federal government to reintroduce it in 1894 was declared unconstitutional by the Supreme Court, and a federal tax did not become effective until 1913. By then most individual US states had their own income tax.

Independence, American War of (also known as the American Revolution) (1776–83) The revolution against British rule in America. It was triggered by colonial resentment at the commercial policies of Britain and by the lack of American participation in political decisions that affected their interests. Disturbances such as the BOSTON Tea Party (1773) developed into armed resistance in 1775 (for example at LEXINGTON AND CONCORD and BUNKER HILL), and full-scale war, with the DECLARATION OF INDEPENDENCE in 1776. Britain, fighting 3,000 miles from home, faced problems of supply, divided command, slow communications, a hostile population, and lack of experience in combating guerrilla tactics. America's disadvantages included few trained generals or troops, a weak central authority unable to provide finance, intercolonial rivalries, and lack of sea power. The French Alliance (1778) changed the nature of the war. Though France gave only modest aid to America, Britain was thereafter distracted by European and West and East Indian challenges.

The course of the war can be divided at 1778. The first, northern, phase saw the British capture of New York (1776), their campaign in the Hudson valley to isolate New England culminating in defeat at SARATOGA (1777), and the capture of Philadelphia (1777) after the victory of BRANDYWINE. The second phase switched British attentions to the south, where large numbers of Loyalists could be recruited. Philadelphia was relinquished (1778) and WASHINGTON camped at West Point to threaten the British headquarters at New York. After CLINTON's capture of Charleston (1780), CORNWALLIS vainly chased the Southern Army under GREENE before his own exhausted army surrendered at YORKTOWN, Virginia (October 1781), effectively ending hostilities. Peace was concluded at PARIS (1783).

Despite frequent victories, the British did not destroy Washington's or Greene's armies and could not break the American will. America's success has been depicted as influencing the French Revolution (1789) and subsequent revolutions in Europe and South America.

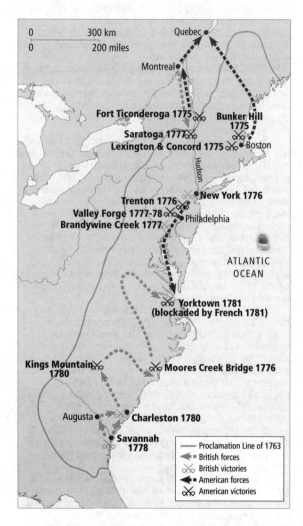

American War of Independence (1776–83) *The British strategy of attempting to break up the union of the colonies was initially successful, when Howe captured New York and forced Washington to retreat to Pennsylvania. However, Burgoyne's surrender at Saratoga raised American morale and persuaded the French to make an alliance with them. Having failed to cut off New England, the British began a southern campaign. Over 5,000 Americans surrendered at Charleston, but Cornwallis was trapped at Yorktown and, denied reinforcements by the French blockade, was forced to admit defeat.*

Independent Labour Party (ILP) British socialist organization. It was founded at Bradford in 1893 under the leadership of Keir HARDIE. Its aim was to achieve equality in society by the application of socialist doctrines. The ILP was one of the constituent groups of the Labour Representation Committee (1900), which in 1906 became the LABOUR PARTY. A split developed between the ILP and the Labour Party between the two World Wars. The sympathy of the ILP for communism, its pacifism, and its theoretical approach to politics were regarded as electoral liabilities by leading Labour politicians; from 1939 its influence declined.

India A South Asian country occupying most of the southward-pointing peninsula of the Indian subcontinent. It is bounded by Pakistan on the north-west, China, Nepal, and Bhutan on the north, and Myanmar (Burma) on the east.

Physical. India is roughly triangular in shape, most of the northern frontier following the Himalayas, the world's highest mountains. The two southern sides are formed by a coastline on the Arabian Sea and another on the Bay of Bengal: they are backed by the ranges of the Western and Eastern Ghats.

Economy. India's economy is largely agrarian, and India has become self-sufficient in food, although agricultural yields are comparatively low and malnutrition is a perennial problem. Manufacturing industry has been developed since independence in 1947, with considerable state investment and control. The state also controls most mining, of which coal and iron ore are the most important products. Electricity is produced by thermal, hydroelectric, and a minority of nuclear power plants. The principal exports are gems, engineering products, garments, and leather goods. The main crops are rice, sugar cane, tea, cotton, and jute, and the chief industrial products are steel, transport equipment and machinery, textiles, and cement.

History. Inhabited from an unknown date by Dravidian peoples, the INDUS civilization sites, dating from c. 2500 BC, indicate one of the world's earliest urban cultures. The Indus civilization was destroyed in about 1500 BC, possibly by the ARYAN invasions. The next 1,000 years saw the evolution of the religious and social systems which remain characteristic of HINDUISM. Regional kingdoms rose and fell under Hindu, and later Buddhist, dynasties, but mastery over the entire subcontinent was rarely achieved. The MAURYAN EMPIRE (c. 325–185 BC), was the first all-India empire, only the southern tip remaining outside its influence. After its disintegration, fighting between local powers was widespread and persistent.

Waves of invasion from from Central Asia from the 11th to the 16th century resulted in Muslim control over the north and the Deccan plateau. Through immigration and conversion, Muslims became India's largest minority. Only in a few areas, notably the RAJPUT states and VIJAYANAGAR, was Hindu political power maintained. Rule by the MOGULS (1526–1857), who claimed most of the subcontinent, marked the height of Indo-Muslim civilization. On their decline European trading powers were poised to take advantage of the power vacuum and the renewal of internecine struggle. The English EAST INDIA COMPANY laid the basis in the 18th century for the subsequent hegemony of the BRITISH RAJ. Following the INDIAN MUTINY control of India passed, via The Act for the Better Government of India (1858) from the English East India Company to the British Crown. The INDIA ACTS of the late 19th and early 20th century granted greater Indian involvement in government. The Indian National CONGRESS was founded in 1885 and conducted major campaigns for self-rule and independence under the leadership of M. K. GANDHI. During 1945–47 Congress negotiated with Britain for independence, which was achieved in 1947 when Britain transferred power to the new states of India and PAKISTAN.

The Republic (or Union) of India opted to remain within the COMMONWEALTH even though it adopted a republican constitution. The PRINCELY STATES within the boundaries of the Indian Union plus KASHMIR all acceded to the Union, though pressure had to be used in some instances, especially Travancore-Cochin and HYDERABAD. Eventually the Princely States were integrated or set up as separate states. The French voluntarily surrendered their few possessions in India, while the Portuguese territories agitating for accession were integrated through military action. The semi-autonomous state of Sikkim was absorbed into India through political pressure but without bloodshed. PAKISTAN's claims over Kashmir, the bulk of which is formally integrated with India, remain a source of dispute. India is a federation of 25 states and 6 Union territories organized primarily on a linguistic basis. Since independence it has had three wars with Pakistan and one with China, and the relationship with SRI LANKA is strained by the Indian Tamils' support for the Sri Lankan Tamils' movement for autonomy. The Sikh demand for autonomy and their terrorist action remain intractable problems in the Punjab. India's first Prime Minister was Jawaharlal NEHRU (1947–64), who initiated a policy of planned economic growth and non-alignment. Indira GANDHI, his daughter, became Prime Minister in 1966. After splitting the CONGRESS Party and experimenting with autocratic rule (1975–77), she suffered electoral defeat. She returned to power (1980) and adopted a firm approach to separatists in 1984 when she suppressed a militant Sikh movement that demanded autonomy for the Punjab. She was assassinated by a Sikh in the same year. Her son Rajiv Gandhi (1944–91), succeeded her as Prime Minister (1984–89). In 1987–89 India undertook large-scale military intervention in Sri Lanka to subdue Tamil rebels. Rajiv failed to win the 1989 election but, after his assassination by Tamil militants the Congress (I) Party under Narasimha Rao regained political control with a minority government. In December 1992 Hindu extremists demolished the ancient Babri mosque at Ayodhya, Uttar Pradesh, which led to severe sectarian clashes in 1993. Following the poor performance of the ruling Congress (I) Party in the 1994 state elections, the authority of Narasimha Rao was further undermined by a leadership crisis and split in the party. International attention was once again focused on the Kashmir dispute when a militant Kashmiri group kidnapped five foreign nationals in the region, one of whom was brutally murdered in August 1995. Following the exposure of widespread government corruption, Rao's Congress Party was heavily defeated in the general election of 1996. There followed a period of political instability in which a series of short-lived coalition governments succeeded one another: in November 1997 I. K. Gujral, India's third Prime Minister in 18 months, resigned. Following the subsequent indecisive elections Atal Behari Vajpayee, leader of the militant Hindu BVP, formed a minority government.

CAPITAL: New Delhi
AREA: 3,166,414 sq km (1,222,559 sq miles)
POPULATION: 952.969 million (1996)
CURRENCY: 1 Indian rupee = 100 paisa
RELIGIONS: Hindu 82.64%; Muslim 11.35%; Christian 2.43%; Sikh 1.97%; Buddhist 0.71%; Jain 0.48%; Parsee 0.01%
ETHNIC GROUPS: (based on language) Hindi 28.1%; Telugu 8.2%; Bengali 8.1%; Marathi 7.6%; Tamil 6.9%; Urdu 5.2%; Gujarati 4.7%; Malayalam 4.0%; Kannada 3.9%; Oriya 3.6%; Bhojpuri 2.6%; Punjabi 2.5%; Assamese 1.6%; Chhattisgarhi 1.2%; Magadhi 1.2%; Maithili 1.1%
LANGUAGES: Hindi, English (both official); Gujarati, Bengali, Marathi, Telugu, Tamil, Urdu, Oriya, Malayalam, Kannada, Punjabi and Bhojpuri are each spoken by over 20 million people
INTERNATIONAL
 ORGANIZATIONS: UN; Commonwealth; Colombo Plan; Non-Aligned Movement

India Acts British parliamentary Acts for the government of India. The Act for the Better Government of India (1858) replaced rule by the English EAST INDIA COMPANY by that of the crown. The viceroy would be assisted by a Council, which from 1861 was to have Indian as well as European members. The India Act (1909) allowed Indians a share in the work of legislative councils (MORLEY-MINTO REFORMS). The Government of India Act (1919) following the MONTAGU-CHELMSFORD PROPOSALS, established a two-chamber legislature at the centre, enlarged provincial legislatures, and gave both an elected majority. Central government remained under the control of the viceroy's Executive Council, but in the provinces a measure of self-government was conceded through the system known as DYARCHY. The Government of India Act (1935) separated Burma from India, and provided for provincial autonomy in British India, a federation of Indian princes, and for a dual system of government at the centre based on the principle of dyarchy. The provisions of this Act were never fully implemented.

Indian Mutiny (1857–58) An uprising against British rule in India. It began as a mutiny of Indian sepoys in the army of the English EAST INDIA COMPANY, commencing at Meerut on 10 May 1857, and spreading rapidly to Delhi and including most regiments of the Bengal army as well as a large section of the civil population in Uttar Pradesh and Madhya Pradesh. The immediate cause was the soldiers' refusal to handle new cartridges that had been removed to be greased with pig and cow fat (an outrage to Muslims and Hindus respectively). The rapid introduction of European civilization coupled with harsh land policies carried out by governor-general Dalhousie and his successor Lord Canning were contributing factors to its rapid spread into the civilian population, to become a full-scale civil rebellion. The mutineers seized Delhi. The rebels restored the former Mogul Emperor Bahadur Shah II to his throne, whereupon the movement spread to LUCKNOW, which was besieged, and to Cawnpore (now Kanpur), where

the massacre of the British garrison is believed to have been instigated by Tantia Topi, a Maratha Brahman who became the military leader of the rebels. The recapture of Delhi by forces from the Punjab on 14 September 1857 broke the back of the mutiny. The fighting was marked by atrocities on both sides. The rebels were ruthlessly crushed in 1858 in a series of campaigns by Sir Hugh Rose in central India. These included the defeat of Lakshmi Bai, the Rani of Jhansi, who was killed in battle. Bahadur Shah was exiled and many civilians executed without trial. Tantia Topi became a fugitive, but was betrayed and executed. Following the restoration of British control, the East India Company's rule was replaced by that of the crown.

Indian National Congress CONGRESS, INDIAN NATIONAL.

Indian reservations Land set aside in the USA for the occupancy and use of NATIVE AMERICANS. The reservations were first created by a policy inaugurated in 1786. President JACKSON first practised removal to reservations on a large scale after Congress passed the Indian Removal Act of 1830. This sent the Creek, Seminole, Chickasaw, Choctaw, and CHEROKEE tribes to an 'Indian territory' in modern Oklahoma. In all some 200 reservations were set up in over 40 states. All but a handful proved economically unviable, so furthering the indigenous peoples' poverty.

Indian subcontinent A geopolitical region comprising India, Pakistan, Bangladesh, Nepal, Bhutan, and Sri Lanka. By 1800, the English EAST INDIA COMPANY had emerged as the paramount power in India. The MARATHA WARS (1803–18) and the annexation of the PUNJAB (1848–49) extended its power to all parts of the sub-continent. A mutiny of the Company's Indian soldiers (INDIAN MUTINY) followed by a rebellion of the civil population in several parts of India in 1857 led to the assumption of power directly by the British government. Administrative consolidation, new systems of land tenure, modern irrigation, and transport and communication systems, initiated in the 1830s, were developed further.

The development of Western-style higher education began in 1817 with the establishment of the Hindu College, Calcutta. The new Western-educated middle classes were attracted by the ideology of nationalism and liberal democracy. Initially enthusiastic about British rule, they became increasingly critical, for example in social reform movements like the BRAHMO SAMAJ and the ARYA SAMAJ. The Indian National CONGRESS, established in 1885, provided an all-India forum for political activity. The government provided for limited association of representative Indians within the legislatures by the Councils Act of 1909, promised 'progressive realization of responsible government' in 1917, and transferred some responsibilities to elected ministers in the provinces by the Government of INDIA ACT in 1919. Agitation organized by Mohandas GANDHI against a bill for suppression of sedition led to the notorious massacre at AMRITSAR. The campaign of SATYAGRAHA and NON-CO-OPERATION launched by Gandhi was aimed at achieving *swaraj* (self-government) and had the support of the KHILAFAT MOVEMENT. The Civil Disobedience Movement (1930–34) demanding independence, and the 'Quit India' Movement, which followed the arrest of Gandhi and other leaders in 1942, consolidated the popular support for the Congress. After World War II, the British opened negotiations for transfer of power. Ever since the 1880s, politicized Muslims were anxious to protect their interests against possible encroachment by a Hindu majority. The MUSLIM LEAGUE, founded in 1905, co-operated with the Congress in 1916 and the Khilafat agitation, but after 1937 emphasized the Muslims' separate aspirations and demanded a separate Muslim homeland, Pakistan, in 1940. Under M. A. JINNAH's leadership the League gained the support of the majority of Muslims. The demand for PAKISTAN was conceded and a separate state created in 1947 comprising the Muslim majority areas in north-western and eastern India. The two states of INDIA and Pakistan fell out over the accession of Kashmir to India and fought three wars, the last leading to the secession of East Pakistan (1971) as BANGLADESH. In foreign policy, Pakistan has been closely associated with the USA, especially after Soviet intervention in Afghanistan, while India, despite its emphasis on non-alignment, had a close relationship with the Soviet Union after the 1971 war and became a nuclear power in 1974. Despite a measure of economic growth, both nations have problems of mass poverty, a high rate of population growth, and several ethnic groups within their borders aspiring towards autonomy.

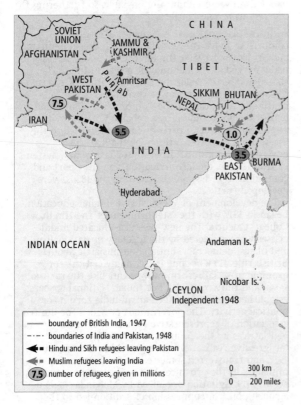

Indian subcontinent (1948) *The Indian subcontinent was steadily subjected to British control in the first half of the 19th century. In 1947 Pakistan (largely Muslim) and the Union of India (largely Hindu) were created as independent nations. The latter is now a federal republic of 25 states and six Union territories, organized on an ethnic basis. In 1971 East Pakistan became independent as Bangladesh.*

Indians, North American NATIVE AMERICANS.

Indian technology Technology derived from the ancient civilizations of the INDIAN SUBCONTINENT. Although far less closely studied, the Harappan civilization, which flourished in the Indus Valley (in modern Pakistan) around 4,000 years ago, ranks with those of Egypt, Mesopotamia, and China. The ancient town of Mohenjo-Daro covered 85 ha (210 acres), and had an advanced town-planning scheme. In historic times Indian science and technology has made important contributions to Western civilization. Wootz steel (a type of crucible steel made in southern India) was prized by the Romans. The great 8-m (26-foot) iron pillar at Delhi (5th century AD) testifies to the skill of early Indian metalworkers. Early Hindu surgeons such as Suśruta performed advanced eye operations and practised lithotomy (surgical removal of a stone from the urinary tract) and plastic surgery. Variolation (a form of immunization) was used for protection against smallpox from at least the 5th century AD. Indian philosophers were skilled in astronomy and mathematics – especially algebra and geometry – and their decimal notation found its way to the West via the Arab world.

Indo-Chinese War (20 October–22 November 1962) A border skirmish between India and China in the Himalayan region, which China claimed had been wrongly given to India by the MCMAHON LINE decision in 1914. Chinese forces began an offensive across the McMahon Line into India. Indian forces retreated and Assam appeared to be at the mercy of China, when the latter announced a ceasefire and withdrew to the Tibetan side of the Line, while retaining parts of Ladakh in Kashmir. Some of the border areas are still disputed.

Indo-Greek dynasties Rulers of parts of north-west India from the 3rd to the 1st century BC. In 326 BC ALEXANDER THE GREAT's army had invaded India and explored the Indus valley. His direct impact was slight, but in the next century Greek commanders, who already held BACTRIA in Central Asia again crossed the Indus, this time to establish power in the Punjab. Their successors were driven out of India after 200 years, but the 'Yavana' (Greek) rulers had an important impact on art and architecture, astrology and medicine. Evidence for Greek activity in India comes mainly from their inscribed coins.

Indonesia A country composed of hundreds of tropical islands in south-east Asia, in the region where the Pacific and the Indian Oceans meet.

Physical. Its east–west length is greater than the width of Australia or the USA, for among its larger islands are included parts of New Guinea (Irian Jaya) and Borneo (Kalimantan) and all of Sumatra, Java, and Sulawesi (formerly called Celebes). Among its smaller islands are Bali, Timor, Flores, and the Moluccas. This vast area lies at the edge of the Eurasian plate. It contains over 70 volcanoes, some periodically active like Krakatoa, and it is subject to severe earthquakes.

Economy. Agriculture is important, principal exports being timber, coffee, rubber, shrimps, pepper, and palm oil, and Indonesia is the most important oil producer of the region. Other mining products include nickel, bauxite, copper, iron, and tin. There is some light industry, and manufacturing is increasing in importance.

History. The Hindu SRIVIJAYA Empire, based on Palembang, flourished between the 7th and 13th centuries AD. Towards the end of the 12th century the MAJAPAHIT kingdom, which was based on JAVA began to dominate the area of present-day Indonesia. During the 16th century the area was occupied by the Portuguese, the British, and the Dutch. The Dutch East India Company had acquired control of most of the islands of Indonesia by the end of the 17th century, with headquarters in present-day Jakarta (then Batavia).

The islands were formed into the Netherlands-Indies in 1914. By the 1920s, indigenous political movements were demanding complete independence. Prominent here was SUKARNO's Indonesian Nationalist Party (*Partai Nasionalis Indonesia*), banned by the Dutch in the 1930s. The Japanese occupation of 1942–45 strengthened nationalist sentiments, and, taking advantage of the Japanese defeat in 1945, Sukarno proclaimed Indonesian independence and set up a republican government. Dutch attempts to reassert control were met with popular opposition (the INDONESIAN REVOLUTION), which resulted in the transfer of power in 1949. By 1957 parliamentary democracy had given way to the semi-dictatorship or 'Guided Democracy' of President Sukarno, a regime based on the original 1945 constitution, with a strong executive and special powers reserved for the army and bureaucracy. Sukarno's popularity began to wane after 1963, with the army and right-wing Muslim landlords becoming increasingly concerned about the influence of communists in government. Rampant inflation and peasant unrest brought the country to the brink of collapse in 1965–66 when the army under General SUHARTO took advantage of a bungled coup by leftist officers to carry out a bloody purge of the Communist Party (PKI) and depose Sukarno (1967). Despite his initial success in rebuilding the economy and restoring credit with its Western capitalist backers, Suharto's regime remained authoritarian and repressive, moving ruthlessly against domestic political opponents. His regime achieved a high growth rate in the economy, but there was growing international concern over the pace of deforestation, as well as over abuse of human rights. In 1976 Indonesia annexed the former Portuguese colony of East TIMOR, causing thousands of civilian deaths. The United Nations (UN) disputed the action and conflict between the independence movement and government forces in East Timor continued in the early 1980s. In 1992 Indonesia and Portugal agreed to resume talks over East Timor under UN auspices and in 1994 Indonesia agreed to allow access to East Timor for human rights and UN organizations. Conflict also erupted in the province of Irian Jaya, part of the island of New Guinea, where a rebellion was staged in support of unification with PAPUA NEW GUINEA. New border arrangements agreed between the two countries put a stop to fighting in 1979, but conflict broke out again in 1984, causing many refugees to flee from Irian Jaya to Papua New Guinea. Accords were signed by Indonesia and Papua New Guinea over security and trade issues in 1992, but further clashes between government troops and separatist rebels occurred in 1993. Although in 1988 legislation had affirmed the dual military and socio-economic role of the Indonesian Armed Forces (ABRI) in the government of Indonesia, there was growing demand for greater democracy in the country in the early 1990s. While Suharto did appear to accept these demands, the activities of new pro-democracy organizations were met with government repression. In 1990–91 a separatist rebellion in the province of Aceh (Sumatra) was crushed by government forces. In 1993 Suharto was re-elected to serve his sixth term as President, while Try Sustrino, an ABRI candidate, was elected Vice-President. The proclaimed aims of the new government were the pursuit of greater democracy and openness. However, in 1994, there was a government crackdown on the press. New rounds of UN-sponsored talks between Portugal and Indonesia over the East Timor dispute took place in 1995. The arrest of pro-democracy campaigners in 1996 led to demonstrations and civil unrest. In 1997, extensive logging and ground clearance by timber companies led to forest fires over an estimated 688,000 ha (1.7 million acres) and the spread of an enveloping smog throughout the region.

CAPITAL:	Jakarta
AREA:	1,919,443 sq km (741,101 sq miles)
POPULATION:	198.189 million (1996)
CURRENCY:	1 Indonesian rupiah = 100 sen
RELIGIONS:	Muslim 86.9%; Christian 9.6% (of which Roman Catholic 3.1%); Hindu 1.9%; Buddhist 1.0%
ETHNIC GROUPS:	Javanese 40.1%; Sundanese 15.3%; Bahasa Indonesian 12.0%; Madurese 4.8%; Chinese minority
LANGUAGES:	Bahasa Indonesian (official); also Javanese, Sundanese, and many others
INTERNATIONAL ORGANIZATIONS:	UN; OPEC; ASEAN; Non-Aligned Movement; Colombo Plan

Indonesian Revolution (1945–49) Nationalist struggle for independence from Dutch rule in INDONESIA. In 1945, SUKARNO proclaimed Indonesia's independence. Attempts by the Dutch to re-establish their colonial administration led to fighting which was temporarily brought to an end by a compromise agreement (1946). This provided for the establishment of a United States of Indonesia tied to the Netherlands under a federal constitution. But the nationalists refused to accept this, forcing the Dutch to launch a new offensive which recaptured most of the estate areas and ended in a ceasefire in 1947. A second Dutch 'police action' a year later increased international pressure and forced the Dutch to convene a conference at The Hague in 1949. As a result, all of the Dutch East Indies, with the exception of western New Guinea, were transferred to the new state of Indonesia in 1949. Western New Guinea (now Irian Jaya) came under Indonesian administration in 1963.

Indo-Pakistan War (September 1965) A border conflict between India and Pakistan following an attempt by Pakistan to assist Muslim opponents of Indian rule in Kashmir. Fighting spread to the Punjab, but a UN cease-fire was accepted and by the Tashkent Declaration of 11 January 1966, a troop withdrawal was agreed. A renewal of frontier fighting occurred in 1971, at a time when BANGLADESH was seeking independence from Pakistan.

indulgence The cancelling by the Christian Church of the temporal punishment still owed for sins after they have been forgiven. The idea was found in various forms in the early Church, but as a widespread doctrine it dated from the 11th century, especially with the granting of indulgences to those who went on CRUSADES. They could be obtained by saying certain prayers or by performing specified good works, such as helping the needy, taking part in a Crusade, or giving money to churches. It was through the connection with money payments that indulgences were most open to abuse, and that they became a focus for criticism by Martin LUTHER and others at the Protestant REFORMATION.

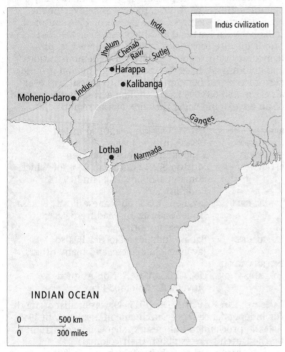

Indus civilization — *Like other early civilizations in Egypt and Mesopotamia, the Indus civilization flourished in a region that despite low rainfall was irrigated by a great river. The civilization covered a very wide area and the discovery of new sites is constantly extending the known range of its cultural influence. The citadels of Mohenjo-daro and Harappa were both built on artificial mounds on riverside sites. Major buildings were substantial and the system of sanitation and drainage with extensive brick culverts, one of the hallmarks of the Indus civilization, implies careful planning under close state control.*

Indus civilization A highly developed urban civilization in the lower valley of the River Indus, in South Asia, which flourished *c.* 2500–1500 BC. Archaeological excavation, which began in the 1920s, is still being carried out and many important questions remain unanswered. City life seems to have ended abruptly *c.* 1500 BC, possible causes being flooding, alteration of the course of the Indus, overpopulation, or an ARYAN invasion.

Among more than 70 sites now excavated, those at MOHENJO-DARO, HARAPPA, Kalibangan, and Lothal seem particularly important for revealing a civilization based on the use of bronze, copper, and stone tools, and also city planning, including granaries, baths, drains, and straight streets. There is evidence of contact with

Mesopotamia, but the script, known by the discovery of seals which were probably used in trade, has not yet been deciphered. The nature of religious worship is also uncertain, although stone and terracotta figures, as well as motifs on the seals, suggest links between the Indus cults and later post-Aryan Hindu religious concepts. The civilization provides evidence of an important stage in India's past, and of one of the world's first highly developed urban communities.

industrial archaeology The systematic study of industrial artefacts. It concerns itself with archaeological remains of all ages – such as the copper mines of Tharsis in Spain and the water-mill at Barbegal, in France, both dating from Roman times – but particularly with commercial enterprises since the INDUSTRIAL REVOLUTION of the 18th and 19th centuries. Although machinery and transport systems are its major areas of interest, it also draws on information from archival material, such as account and order books.

industrialization The process of change from a basic agrarian economy to an industrialized one. It was first experienced by Britain in the INDUSTRIAL REVOLUTION and at much the same time in the New England states of the USA, from which it spread along the eastern seaboard and, after the American Civil War, across the continent. Belgium was the first continental European country to experience industrialization, which then spread to north-east France and, particularly after 1870, to Germany, where its growth was so rapid that by 1900 German industrial production had surpassed that of Britain. During those 30 years all industrialized nations saw rapid development and expansion in such heavy industries as iron and steel, chemicals, engineering, and shipbuilding. Japan was the first non-European power to become industrialized, which it had done by the end of the 19th century. The former Soviet Union saw industrialization on a massive scale under Stalin.

In many less developed countries, industrialization is equated with development, that is modernization, progress, and economic growth, a viewpoint often, though not always, justified by the circumstances of the individual countries. In recent decades there has been rapid industrialization in many developing countries, in particular those known as the NEWLY INDUSTRIALIZING COUNTRIES; economic growth in these countries has generally exceeded that in those benefiting from ample natural resources, excepting certain oil-rich countries. Development plans favouring industrialization via import substitution have been superseded in many countries by policies of export promotion. Industrialization has been welcomed as providing employment for growing populations whom the land could no longer support; but since much industry is located in cities, there have been associated problems of massive URBANIZATION and, often, pollution of the environment. The relationship between industrialization and development continues, therefore, to be debated. In the latter decades of the 20th century, the phenomenon of deindustrialization has been witnessed in industrialized countries. This means that in these countries manufacturing employment accounts for a shrinking proportion of total employment, as a result of the growth both of manufacturing productivity and of tertiary employment.

Industrial Revolution The changes in the organization of manufacturing industry that transformed first Britain and then other countries from rural to urban economies. Improved agricultural techniques that freed workers from the land made it possible to provide food for a large non-agricultural population, leading to people moving to the towns. In Britain this process was under way by about 1750. A combination of economic, political, and social factors, including internal peace, the availability of coal and iron ore, the availability of capital, and the development of STEAM POWER – and later the internal-combustion engine and electricity – led to the construction of factories, which were built for the mass production of manufactured goods. A new organization of work known as the factory system increased the division and specialization of labour. The textile industry was the prime example of industrialization and created a demand for machines, and for tools for their manufacture, which stimulated further mechanization. Improved transport became necessary and was provided by the expansion of the CANAL system and the subsequent development of RAILWAYS and roads. The skills acquired during this period were exported to other countries and this helped to make Britain the richest and most powerful nation in the world by the middle of the 19th century. Simultaneously the process of industrialization radically changed the face of British society, leading to the growth of large industrial cities, particularly in the Midlands, the North, Scotland, and South Wales. As the population shifted from the countryside to the cities a series of social and economic problems arose, the result of such factors as low wages, slum housing, and the use of child labour. Similar changes followed in other European countries, in the USA, and in Japan during the 19th century, while in the 20th century Eastern Europe, China, India, and South-East Asia have undergone a similar industrialization process.

Inkatha Freedom Party A South African Zulu political organization under the leadership of Chief Mangosuthu BUTHELEZI. The party was founded as the Inkatha movement by Buthelezi in 1975 to counter the Xhosa-dominated AFRICAN NATIONAL CONGRESS (ANC). Unlike the ANC, which sought to overthrow the apartheid system through armed struggle, Inkatha was pledged to represent Zulu interests by working within the BANTU HOMELAND system established by the White regime. From the early 1980s onwards, increasingly violent clashes took place between supporters of the two groups, resulting in an estimated death toll of over 5,000 people. The Inkatha movement became a political party in 1990 and changed its name to the Inkatha Freedom Party. In South Africa's first multiracial elections in 1994, Inkatha initially boycotted the poll but eventually participated. It won 43 seats in the new national assembly and Buthelezi was appointed home affairs minister. Inkatha's standing was damaged in the 1990s by revelations that it had been covertly funded and armed by the security forces in the 1980s, in an attempt to increase ethnic tension and destabilize the ANC.

Inkerman, Battle of SEVASTOPOL.

Innocent III (1160–1216) Pope (1198–1216). As pope he was an active and vigorous reformer of the Church. He reasserted control over the PAPAL STATES and was acknowledged as the overlord of SICILY. In Germany he asserted the pope's right to choose between two rival candidates for the imperial crown; he eventually supported FREDERICK II's claims provided that he did homage for Sicily. He intervened in English affairs, excommunicating King JOHN for refusing to recognize Stephen LANGTON as Archbishop of Canterbury and declaring MAGNA CARTA void; he also attempted to curb the independence of PHILIP II of France.

Innocent's overriding concerns were crusades against heresy, and Church reforms. He took steps to improve the quality of the clergy and ordered a crusade against the ALBIGENSIANS in southern France. He supported the disastrous Fourth CRUSADE of 1204, but undeterred by its failure, remained zealous in support of the crusading effort. The Fourth LATERAN COUNCIL, which he summoned in 1215, resulted in 70 decrees for reform and prepared the ground for a new Crusade, though Innocent died of fever the following year. His reign marked the climax of the medieval papacy.

Inönü, Ismet (1884–1973) Turkish soldier and statesman. He served against the Greeks during the Turkish war of independence (1919–22). He was chosen by ATATÜRK as first Prime Minister of the Turkish republic (1923–37) and in 1938 succeeded him as President, remaining in power until the Democrat victory of 1950. Inönü remained leader of the Republican People's Party and served again as Prime Minister (1961–65) in the aftermath of the 1960 military coup.

Inquisition An ecclesiastical court established c. 1232 for the detection and punishment of heretics, at a time when sectarian groups were threatening not only the orthodoxy of the Catholic religion but the stability of contemporary society. The Inquisition came into being when FREDERICK II issued an edict entrusting the hunting-out of heretics to state inquisitors; Pope Gregory IX claimed it as a papal responsiblity and appointed inquisitors mostly drawn from the Franciscan and Dominican orders. He had previously ordered the Dominicans to crush the ALBIGENSIANS (1223). Those accused of heresy who refused to confess were tried before an inquisitor and jury and punishments were harsh, including confiscation of goods, torture, and death. The Index (a list of books condemned by the Church) was issued by the Congregation of the Inquisition in 1557. The SPANISH INQUISITION was a separate organization established in 1479 by the Spanish monarchy with papal approval.

intendant An agent of the French king under the *ancien régime*. The office was developed as an emergency measure to counter disobedience during the 1630s, building on an earlier practice of sending royal officials from the central councils on tours of inspection in the provinces. Under RICHELIEU and LOUIS XIV their authority was extended into every sphere of administration, and they became the principal link between the central government and the provinces. They supervised local courts, oversaw the tax system, and kept the crown informed about the political and economic situation in their *généralités* (administrative units). The office was abolished at the Revolution, but many of the same functions were later performed by the *préfets*.

International Bank for Reconstruction and Development WORLD BANK.

International Brigades International groups of volunteers in the SPANISH CIVIL WAR. They were largely communist, on the side of the republic against FRANCO. Organized by the COMINTERN, their members were largely working people together with a number of intellectuals and writers, such as the English poet W. H. Auden and the writer George Orwell. At no time were there more than 20,000 in the Brigades. They fought mainly in the defence of Madrid (1936) and in the Battle of the River Ebro (1938).

International Court of Justice A judicial court of the United Nations which replaced the Cour Permanente de Justice in 1946 and meets at The Hague in The Netherlands. It is one of the six principal organs of the United Nations, and its main judicial body. It has 15 judges elected for renewable nine-year terms by the General Assembly and the Security Council. It is concerned with disputes between states. By 1966 two international covenants – that on civil and political rights and that on economic, social, and cultural rights – were promulgated. Appeals to the court, based on these covenants, are enforceable only if the state concerned has previously agreed to be bound by its decisions. In 1993 the International Court of Justice found Serbia guilty of promoting acts of genocide in Bosnia-Herzegovina, the first such accusation to be sustained by the court since its inception. This led to the establishment in the same year of an International War Crimes Tribunal for the former Yugoslavia, based in The Hague.

International Development Association WORLD BANK.

International Labour Organization (ILO) An agency founded in 1919 to improve labour and living standards throughout the world. At first affiliated to the League of Nations, in 1946 the ILO became the first specialized agency of the UNITED NATIONS. The ILO sets international guidelines for improving working conditions, trade-union rights, the rights of women and children, minimum wage levels, hours, and health and safety at work. It provides technical assistance to developing countries, promotes employment, and researches and reports on trends in employment and industrial-relations practice and law. The ILO received the Nobel Peace Prize in 1967. The USA withdrew in 1977, claiming that the ILO had become dominated by politics, but rejoined in 1980. By 1993 162 countries were members of the ILO.

International Monetary Fund (IMF) An international economic institution, and specialized agency of the UNITED NATIONS. Proposed at the BRETTON WOODS CONFERENCE in 1944, the IMF was established in 1945 and is based in Washington, DC. In 1991 it had 151 members. Unlike the WORLD BANK, to which it is closely allied, the IMF is not a development agency. Its principal aims are to encourage international monetary co-operation and the expansion of international trade, to stabilize exchange rates, and to eliminate foreign-exchange restrictions. Member states subscribe funds in accordance with their wealth. The Fund has supplemented its resources by borrowing from countries with ample reserves and by creating a new reserve asset, the Special Drawing Right. The Fund offers its members an orderly system for settling financial transactions among themselves. It also makes loans to countries with balance-of-payments difficulties. In recent years most have been developing countries. Such loans are normally conditional on changes in their economic policies designed to improve economic performance. Since these changes often entail cuts in public expenditure, welfare services, and subsidies, and increases in the cost of living, the IMF's conditions have at times been a source of controversy between the IMF and recipient nations. Furthermore, implementation of an IMF-approved programme has typically been necessary for them to secure renewal of their large-scale loans from commercial banks. In 1986 the Fund established a 'structural adjustment facility' to provide assistance to low-income developing countries.

Internationals Associations formed to unite socialist and communist organizations throughout the world. There were four Internationals. The First (1864), at which MARX was a leading figure, met in London but was riven by disputes between Marxists and ANARCHISTS. By 1872 it had become clear that divisions were irreconcilable and it was disbanded (1876). The Second, or Socialist, International (1889) aimed at uniting the numerous new socialist parties that had sprung up in Europe. With headquarters in Brussels, it was better organized and by 1912 it contained representatives from all European countries and also from the USA, Canada, and Japan. It did not survive the outbreak of World War I, when its plan to prevent war by general strike and revolution was swamped by a wave of nationalism in all countries. The Third, usually known as the Communist International or COMINTERN (1919), was founded by LENIN and the BOLSHEVIKS to promote world revolution and a world communist state. It drew up the Twenty-One Points of pure communist doctrine to be accepted by all seeking membership. This resulted in splits between communist parties, which accepted the Points, and socialist parties, which did not. The Comintern increasingly became an instrument of the Soviet Union's foreign policy. In 1943 Stalin disbanded it. The Fourth International (1938), of comparatively little importance, was founded by TROTSKY and his followers in opposition to STALIN. After Trotsky's assassination (1940) it was controlled by two Belgian communists, Pablo and Germain, whose bitter disagreements had by 1953 ended any effective action.

Intifada (Arabic, 'uprising') The Palestinian revolt (1987–93) against Israel, demanding self-determination in the West Bank and the Gaza Strip, the areas illegally annexed by Israel during the SIX-DAY WAR in 1967. The Intifada began as a spontaneous series of demonstrations and acts of civil disobedience by young Palestinians frustrated at security checks and travel restrictions. Later, the uprising became more organized with widespread strikes, boycotts of Israeli goods and shops, and punishment beatings and executions carried out on alleged collaborators. Israel responded by closing Palestinian educational establishments, destroying the houses of supposed ringleaders, and deporting over 400 Shi'ite Muslim activists to South Lebanon. The Oslo Peace Accords of 1993, which transferred control of the occupied territories to the PALESTINE LIBERATION ORGANIZATION, officially ended the Intifada. However, radical groups such as HAMAS and Islamic Jihad, which participated in the revolt and gained much support from young Palestinians, vowed to continue the struggle and were responsible for terrorist attacks in Israel in the mid- to late 1990s.

Intolerable Acts COERCIVE ACTS.

Invergordon mutiny (1931) A mutiny by sailors of the British Atlantic Fleet at the naval port on Cromarty Firth, Scotland. Severe pay cuts imposed by the NATIONAL GOVERNMENT led the ratings to refuse to go on duty. The cuts were slightly revised but foreign holders of sterling were alarmed; an Act suspending the GOLD STANDARD was rushed through Parliament, but the value of the pound fell by more than a quarter. The mutiny ended and the ratings' ringleaders were discharged from the navy.

Investiture The formal act whereby senior clergy receive their offices with their attendant properties and revenues. In the Middle Ages when kings 'invested' bishops with their bishopric, it looked as if bishops were receiving their spiritual powers as well as their property from the semi-sacred figure of the king. In the 11th century radical churchmen questioned this view of royal authority and lay investiture was denounced as a corrupt practice that shackled the Church to the world. Under Pope GREGORY VII (1073–85) the increasingly bitter disputes over the claims of Church and state erupted into the Investiture Conflict, itself part of a wider movement for Church reform that swept Western Europe. Conflict was especially bitter in Germany where Emperor Henry IV, as most exalted lay ruler, had most to lose.

Pope and emperor denounced each other in propaganda campaigns, manoeuvred for diplomatic advantage (CANOSSA), and fought to depose each other. Civil war broke out in Germany until peace was established at the Concordat of Worms (1122) between Pope Calixtus II and Emperor Henry V, whereby the king abandoned investiture of churchmen, and thus claims to spiritual power, but managed to retain much practical control over the appointment of bishops. This was the first great conflict between pope and emperor in the Middle Ages and laid the foundations for papal claims to full authority over the Church.

Iqbal, Muhammad (1876–1938) Indian philosopher, poet, and political leader. He took an active part in politics in the Punjab and was President of the MUSLIM LEAGUE in 1930 when he advanced the idea of a separate Muslim state in north-west India, the beginning of the concept of PAKISTAN.

Iran (formerly Persia) A country of the Middle East in central-west Asia. Bordering on Turkey and Iraq on the west, Turkmenistan on the north, and Afghanistan and Pakistan on the east, it has a northern coast on the Caspian Sea and a southern coast on the Gulf and Arabian Sea.

Physical. Iran consists mostly of arid tableland surrounded by mountains (the Elburz in the north and the Zagros in the south-west) and containing extensive salt deserts: the Great Salt Desert or Dasht-e-Kavir in the north and the Dasht-e-Lut in the south-east. The climate varies from hot to cool according to season and altitude.

Economy. Iran's economy is based on its huge reserves of oil, which accounts for some 95% of exports; however, oil and gas production are restricted due to war damage. Substantial mineral deposits of coal, copper, and iron ore are relatively undeveloped, and ambitious industrial and infrastructural projects embarked on under the Shah have been curtailed. Banks, insurance, and most industries have been nationalized since the revolution. The chief industries are mining, machinery production, and textiles. The neglect of agriculture, which focuses on producing grains and rice, and rearing sheep and cattle, has not yet been successfully reversed, and there is food rationing. Since 1994 there have been a series of financial and economic crises.

History. Early Persian dynasties included the ACHAEMENIDS, whose rule ended with ALEXANDER THE GREAT's defeat of Darius III, and the SASSANIANS who were overthrown by the Arabs. Since the fall of the Sassanian empire in 642, it has been under the rule of Islam. Persians were prominent in the empires of their Arab, Seljuk, and Mongol overlords for nine centuries, until ISMAIL I established a strong Persian state and converted the population to Shiite Islam. After ABBAS I Safavid power declined until the qajars, ruling from Tehran, took power in 1796.

Trade between Muslim countries and European powers had developed throughout the 19th century and both Russia and Britain were anxious to increase their influence over the QAJAR dynasty in Iran. In 1906 Muzaffar al-Din granted a constitution; his successor sought to suppress the *Majlis* (Parliament) which had been granted, but was himself deposed. In 1901 oil concessions were granted to foreign companies to exploit what is estimated as one-tenth of the world's oil reserves. In 1909 the Anglo-Persian Oil Company (later BP) was founded and southern Iran came within Britain's sphere of influence, while Russia dominated northern Iran. Following the RUSSIAN REVOLUTION of 1917 British troops invaded Russia from Iran; at the end of this 'war of intervention' an Iranian officer, Reza Khan, emerged and seized power (1921), backed by the British. In 1925 he deposed the Qajar dynasty and proclaimed himself as REZA SHAH PAHLAVI. In World War II Iran was occupied by British and Soviet forces and was used as a route for sending supplies to the Soviet Union. The Shah abdicated (1941) and was replaced by his son MUHAMMAD REZA SHAH PAHLAVI. It took him 20 years to establish political supremacy, during which time one of his Prime Ministers, MUSSADEGH, nationalized the Anglo-Iranian Oil Company (1951). In 1961 the Shah initiated a land-reform scheme and a programme of modernization, the so-called 'White Revolution' (1963–71). The secularization of the state led ISLAMIC FUNDAMENTALIST leaders such as KHOMEINI into exile (1964), while popular discontent with secular Western, especially US, influence was masked by ever-rising oil revenues, which financed military repression, as well as industrialization. Riots in 1978 were followed by the imposition of martial law. Khomeini co-ordinated a rebellion from his exile in France. The fall and exile of the Shah in 1979 was followed by the return of Khomeini and the establishment of an Islamic Republic that proved strong enough to sustain the IRAN HOSTAGE CRISIS of 1979–81 and to fight the long and costly IRAN–IRAQ WAR (1980–88), which claimed the lives of perhaps a million young Iranians. In February 1989 relations with Western countries were further damaged when Khomeini pronounced a death sentence on the British writer Salman Rushdie for writing *The Satanic Verses*. Following the death of Khomeini in 1989 and a confused power-struggle, Hashemi RAFSANJANI was elected President. A pragmatic and skilful negotiator, he attempted to improve relations with Western states without unduly alienating the Islamic fundamentalists. His government played a key role in achieving the release of Western hostages in the Middle East during 1991, and gave shelter to some 1.5 million Shia and Kurdish refugees from Iraq following the GULF WAR, during which Iran remained neutral. Rafsanjani's programme of social and economic reforms, however, caused discontent and serious rioting occurred in several major cities in 1992. Despite a loss of popular support for his policies, Rafsanjani was re-elected President in 1993. During the early 1990s alleged abuses of human rights in Iran, including attacks against the Kurds, caused international concern. Relations with the USA were further strained by Iran's hostility to US involvement in the region following the Gulf War and to the Israeli–PLO peace accord, signed in September 1993. The question of Iran's military expansion also caused friction. Since the break-up of the Soviet Union in 1991, Iran has strengthened its links with the newly independent states of Central Asia; this has caused some concern in the West over Iran's growing political and religious influence in the region. In 1995 the USA announced complete trade and investment sanctions against Iran in an attempt to halt the country's alleged involvement in international terrorism and its rumoured nuclear weapons programme. The presidential elections of May 1997 resulted in victory for Ayatollah Mohammed Khatemi, who is widely perceived as a moderate reformer.

CAPITAL:	Tehran
AREA:	1,648,196 sq km (636,372 sq miles)
POPULATION:	62.231 million (1996)
CURRENCY:	1 toman = 100 rials
RELIGIONS:	Shia Muslim 91.0%; Sunni Muslim 7.8%; Christian 0.7%; Jewish 0.3%; Baha'i minority
ETHNIC GROUPS:	Persian 45.6%; Azeri 16.8%; Kurdish 9.1%; Gilani 5.3%; Luri 4.3%; Mazandarani 3.6%; Baluch 2.3%; Arab 2.2%; Bakhtiari 1.7%
LANGUAGES:	Farsi (Persian) (official); Azeri Turkish; Kurdish; Arabic and other minority languages
INTERNATIONAL ORGANIZATIONS:	UN; OPEC; Colombo Plan; Non-Aligned Movement

Irangate scandal REAGAN, RONALD.

Iran Hostage Crisis (4 November 1979–20 January 1981) A prolonged crisis between IRAN and the USA. In the aftermath of Iran's Islamic Revolution, followers of the Ayatollah KHOMEINI alleged US complicity in military plots to restore the Shah, MUHAMMAD REZA SHAH PAHLAVI, and seized the US Embassy in Teheran, taking 66 US citizens hostage. All efforts of President CARTER to free the hostages failed, including economic measures and an abortive rescue bid by US helicopters in April 1980. The crisis dragged on until 20 January 1981, when Algeria successfully mediated, and the hostages were

freed. It seriously weakened Carter's bid for presidential re-election in November 1980, and he lost to Ronald REAGAN.

Iran–Iraq War (1980–88) A border dispute between IRAN and IRAQ that developed into a major war. In 1980 President Saddam HUSSEIN of Iraq abrogated the 1975 agreement granting Iran some 518 sq km (200 sq miles) of border area to the north of the Shatt-al-Arab waterway in return for assurances by Iran to cease military assistance to the Kurdish minority in Iraq, which was fighting for independence. Calling for a revision of the border along the Shatt-al-Arab, a return to Iraqi ownership of the three islands in the Strait of Hormuz (seized by Iran in 1971), and for the granting of autonomy to minorities inside Iran, the Iraqi army engaged in a border skirmish in a disputed but relatively unimportant area, and followed this by an armoured assault into Iran's vital oil-producing region. The Iraqi offensive met strong Iranian resistance, and Iran recaptured territory from the Iraqis. In 1985 Iraqi planes destroyed a partially constructed nuclear power plant in Bushehr and bombed civilian targets; this in turn led to Iranian shelling of Basra and Baghdad. The war entered a new phase in 1987 when Iran increased hostilities against commercial shipping in and around the Gulf, resulting in naval escorts being sent to the area by the USA and other nations. Senior officers of the Iranian army began to lose confidence as their troops suffered from shortages of arms and equipment, while Iraq continued to be supplied by the West. Early in 1988 the UN Security Council called for a ceasefire. Iraq agreed, but not Iran. Skilful negotiations by the UN Secretary-General, PEREZ DE CUÉLLAR, however, achieved an armistice in July and a peace settlement in August. Nothing had been gained by either side and an estimated 1.5 million lives were lost.

Iraq A West Asian country bordering on Turkey on the north, Iran on the east, Syria and Jordan on the west, and Saudi Arabia and Kuwait on the south.

Physical. A waterway, Shatt al-Arab, at the delta of the Euphrates, gives Iraq access to the Gulf in the south-east. The Euphrates and its tributary the Tigris traverse the whole country from north-west to south-east, bringing silt to a vast depression which would be widely cultivable were it not for salinity and erosion. This land, once known as Mesopotamia, was the site of early civilizations. To the north are mountains and desert plateaux, to the west all is desert; the climate is one of extremes.

Economy. The economy is based on exports of oil. The main industries are petroleum products and chemicals. Iraq relies on imports of foodstuffs, its main agricultural products being grains, livestock, and dates. The economy has suffered as a result of recent wars, the US-led trade embargo, and the UN ban on exports of oil.

History. As MESOPOTAMIA, the area of present-day Iraq is known as "the cradle of civilization". It became a Muslim state in the 7th century AD following conquest by Arabia. It became a part of the Ottoman Empire in 1534, remaining such until the outbreak of World War I when the Turks were driven out by British forces. Following the British MESOPOTAMIAN CAMPAIGN in World War I, the country was occupied by Britain, which was then granted responsibility under a League of Nations

MANDATE (1920–32). In 1921 Britain offered to recognize amir Ahd Allah Faisal, son of HUSSEIN, sharif of Mecca, as King Faisal I. British influence remained strong until the fall of the monarchy in 1958. Further political rivalries ended with the 1968 coup, which led to rapid economic and social modernization paid for by oil revenues and guided by the general principles of the BA'ATH Socialist Party. A heterogeneous society, of many ethnic and religious groupings, Iraq has long been troubled by periodic struggles for independence for its Kurds. It has often been isolated in Arab affairs by its assertiveness in foreign policy, though the long and bloody IRAN–IRAQ WAR launched against Khomeini's Iran by President Saddam HUSSEIN in 1980 received financial support from formerly critical monarchist Arab states. In 1990 the Iraqi invasion of Kuwait caused and an international crisis, leading to the imposition of UN sanctions and the GULF WAR of January–February 1991. Following Iraq's defeat by a US-led military coalition, uprisings among both Shia and Kurdish peoples were brutally suppressed. The UN-imposed peace terms (a pre-requisite to the lifting of sanctions) included the destruction of chemical and other weapons, acceptance of UN inspectors, and disclosure of Iraq's nuclear capability. Although some progress was made, Iraq refused to accept a UN resolution on the longer-term monitoring of its weapons programme and failed to co-operate with the required inspections. As a result, sanctions remained in place and caused growing hardship. After protracted negotiations, Iraq finally agreed (1996) to a UN proposal that partial oil sales be resumed to fund humanitarian efforts. Renewed attacks by government forces on the Shia communities in southern Iraq in 1992–93 led to the establishment by Western powers of an exclusion zone over the area. Violation of the zone by Iraqi forces resulted in air attacks by Western forces in 1993. The following year President Saddam Hussein assumed the additional title of Prime Minister and formally recognized the sovereignty of Kuwait. Fighting between rival Kurdish groups also broke out in northern Iraq and continued in 1995–96. In 1996 government forces (assisted by members of one of the Kurdish factions) attacked Kurdish towns in the north of the country. In response, the USA bombed strategic targets in southern Iraq. From late 1997 a further crisis arose in Iraq's relations with the international community, as weapons inspectors sent by the UN to dismantle Iraq's weapons of mass destruction were denied access. War between Iraq and the USA over this issue was narrowly averted in 1998.

CAPITAL:	Baghdad
AREA:	435,052 sq km (167,975 sq miles)
POPULATION:	21.442 million (1996)
CURRENCY:	1 Iraqi dinar = 20 dirhams = 1,000 fils
RELIGIONS:	Shia Muslim 53.5%; Sunni Muslim 42.3%; Christian 3.5%
ETHNIC GROUPS:	Arab 77.1%; Kurdish 19.0%; Turkmen 1.4%; Persian 0.8%; Assyrian 0.8%
LANGUAGES:	Arabic (official); Kurdish and minority languages
INTERNATIONAL ORGANIZATIONS:	UN; Arab League; Non-Aligned Movement; OAPEC; OPEC

Ireland An island off the north-west coast of Europe, the furthest west of the British Isles. Situated on the continental shelf, it is surrounded on three sides by the Atlantic Ocean and is separated from Great Britain by the Irish Sea. About 370 km (230 miles) long by 225 km (140 miles) wide, Ireland comprises the Republic of IRELAND and NORTHERN IRELAND, which is a province of the UK.

History. Ireland was inhabited by Goidelic CELTS as early as the 6th century BC, by Bretonnic Celts from the 3rd century, and by PICTS from the 1st century AD. It was never conquered by the Romans, who gave it the name Hibernia, and Irish raiders frequently attacked Britain and Gaul as the Romans withdrew. Its Celtic society, ruled by numerous petty kings and chiefs, lasted into the medieval period. The CELTIC CHURCH which evolved from the 4th century, was based on this feudal model, with bishops subordinate to the heads of land-owning communities. Viking raids and domination by Viking settlers from the late 8th century ended at Clontarf (1014), when the High King BRIAN BORU decisively defeated the Scandinavians. From 1169 Anglo-Norman barons invaded and seized land, until in 1172 HENRY II of England was formally acknowledged as King of Ireland.

For the next 400 years English monarchs made successive attempts to subdue Irish resistance to their rule. Bitterness increased with the imposition of Protestantism by HENRY VIII and the establishment of 'plantations' of English and Scottish settlers in Ulster under ELIZABETH I. In 1599 the queen sent ESSEX to put down a revolt led by the Earl of TYRONE and the Irish were defeated in 1601. Religious oppression and settlements continued and, with the extortionary policies of CHARLES I, led to the Irish Rebellion, which was not finally put down until Oliver CROMWELL led the Parliamentary army to Ireland (1649). He ruthlessly extended Protestant settlement. After the GLORIOUS REVOLUTION (1688) the 'Protestant Ascendancy' was further confirmed. In 1782 Henry GRATTAN's party in the Irish Parliament secured the repeal of POYNINGS' LAW and limited independence, but the rising of the UNITED IRISHMEN (1798) helped bring about the ACT OF UNION (1801), as a result of which Ireland lost its parliament and became subject to direct rule from London. In the 1840s, the failure of the potato crop resulted in the IRISH FAMINE. Continuing social and economic problems produced resentment against British rule and made the campaign for HOME RULE the dominant issue in domestic politics in the second half of the 19th century. The granting of Home Rule was delayed by the outbreak of World War I, and armed resistance to British rule finally broke out in the EASTER RISING of 1916. In 1920 the Government of Ireland Act provided for two Irish parliaments, one (STORMONT) for six of the counties of Ulster in the north and one for the remaining 26 counties of Ireland. The Anglo-Irish Treaty of 1921 suspended part of the 1920 Act: while Northern Ireland remained part of the United Kingdom, the 26 counties gained separate dominion status as the Irish Free State and in 1949 attained full independence as the Republic of Ireland.

Ireland, Northern NORTHERN IRELAND.

Ireland, Republic of A country in western Europe comprising four-fifths of the island of IRELAND, to the west of Great Britain.

Physical. A flat and fertile plain surrounds a central lake, Lough Ree, and the basin of the River Shannon. It is surrounded by coastal areas of great beauty: the

Wicklow Mountains in the south-east reach to nearly 1,000 m (3,040 feet); the Connemara Mountains in the west stand up above great lakes, while those of Kerry in the south-west reach to over 1,000 m (3,415 feet) and point like rugged fingers to the sea. Many islands, among them Aran, lie in the deep bays of the western coast, where there are sandy beaches among the rocks. Warm, damp winds from the Atlantic keep the country largely free of frost, while rainfall is moderate to heavy.

Economy. Ireland has a diversified economy in which agriculture predominates, although industry has become increasingly important; the chief exports are foodstuffs (especially beef), electrical machinery, and chemicals. Other industries include textiles, and tourism is also important. The country generates 15% of its electricity by burning peat, of which there are extensive reserves. Until recently Ireland had a higher rate of emigration than any other member of the EU. However, in the 1990s the economy has boomed, with inflation remaining low: in the period 1994–98 Ireland had the fastest growing economy in the developed world. Irish citizens have had the right to reside, work, and vote in the UK since independence.

History. After years of intermittent fighting, the Anglo-Irish Treaty of December 1921, concluded by Lloyd George with the SINN FEIN leaders, gave separate DOMINION status to Ireland (as the Irish Free State) with the exception of six of the counties of Ulster, which formed the state of NORTHERN IRELAND. Irish republicans led by DE VALERA rejected the agreement and fought a civil war against the Irish Free State forces, but were defeated in 1923. After the FÍANNA FÁIL Party victory in the election of 1932, de Valera began to sever the Irish Free State's remaining connections with Great Britain. In 1937 a new constitution established it as a sovereign state with an elected president; the power of the British Crown was ended and the office of governor-general abolished. The title of Irish Free State was replaced by Republic of Ireland; in Irish, Eire. An agreement in 1938 ended the British occupation of certain naval bases in Ireland. Having remained neutral in World War II, Ireland left the COMMONWEALTH OF NATIONS and was recognized as an independent republic in 1949. De Valera was elected president in 1959. He was succeeded as Taoiseach (Prime Minister) by Sean Lemass (1959–66) and Jack Lynch (1966–73). In 1973 Ireland joined the European Community and a FINE GAEL–Labour coalition led by Liam Cosgrave came to power. Subsequent governments were controlled alternately by the Fíanna Fáil under Charles Haughey (1979–81; 1982; 1987–92) and the Fine Gael–Labour coalition under Dr Garret Fitzgerald (1981–82; 1982–87). In November 1985 Ireland signed the Anglo-Irish Accord (the Hillsborough Agreement) giving the Republic a consultative role in the government of Northern Ireland. The agreement thus ensured a role for the Republic on behalf of the nationalist minority in the north. The election as President, in December 1990, of Mary Robinson, of the Irish Labour Party, represented a move towards greater liberalism within Irish society; but opposition to abortion remained strong. Economically the republic has gained from its membership of the European Community (now the EUROPEAN UNION), which it continues strongly to support. In 1992 Haughey was replaced by Albert Reynolds, who resigned in 1994 following the collapse of his coalition.

The Fine Gael leader, John Bruton, became Prime Minister at the head of a new coalition with Labour and the Democratic Left. In December 1993 Albert Reynolds had joined the UK Prime Minister John Major in issuing the DOWNING STREET DECLARATION, which set out general principles for the holding of future peace talks on NORTHERN IRELAND and represented a significant step towards peace in the province. In August 1994 the IRISH REPUBLICAN ARMY (IRA) announced a complete ceasefire. Despite the presentation by John Major and John Bruton of a joint framework document for all-party talks in early 1995, further progress stalled over the British government's insistence on the IRA decommissioning of weapons before any talks began. The IRA's ceasefire broke down in early 1996 but was restored in July 1997: talks involving both governments and most of the Northern Ireland parties finally began in September. These resulted in the Good Friday agreement of 1998, which proposed the removal from the Republic's constitution of its claim to Northern Ireland. Mary Robinson was succeeded as President in November 1997 by Mary McAleese, a Northern Ireland nationalist.

CAPITAL:	Dublin
AREA:	70,285 sq km (27,137 sq miles)
POPULATION:	3.599 million (1996)
CURRENCY:	1 Irish pound = 100 new pence
RELIGIONS:	Roman Catholic 93.1%; Church of Ireland (Anglican) 2.8%; Presbyterian 0.4%
ETHNIC GROUPS:	Over 94.0% Irish nationality
LANGUAGES:	English, Irish (both official)
INTERNATIONAL ORGANIZATIONS:	EU; OECD; UN; Council of Europe; CSCE

Irene (c. 752–803) Byzantine empress (780–802). After her husband Leo IV died (780) she ruled jointly with her son, Constantine VI, until 790 when he banished her. She soon returned, had him blinded and imprisoned and ruled as emperor (not empress) until again exiled (802) to Lesbos. She strongly opposed the iconoclasts (ICONOCLASTIC CONTROVERSY). For her zeal in this cause she was canonized by the Greek Orthodox Church.

Ireton, Henry (1611–51) English ROUNDHEAD commander and politician. After fighting at Edgehill (1642) and Marston Moor (1644), he was instrumental in pushing through the SELF-DENYING ORDINANCE (1645). In 1646 he married CROMWELL's daughter Bridget, and in 1647 opposed the LEVELLERS' extreme demands at the Putney debates. He figured prominently in the moves that led to PRIDE'S PURGE and the execution of CHARLES I. After serving as Cromwell's second-in-command on his Irish campaign (1649–50), he was made Lord Deputy of Ireland. He died of plague.

Irgun (Hebrew, 'Irgun Zvai Leumi', National Military Organization, byname ETZEL) An underground ZIONIST terrorist group active (1937–48) in Palestine against Arabs and later Britons. Under the leadership of Menachem BEGIN from 1944, it carried out massacres of Arabs during the 1947–48 war, notably at Dir Yassin (9 April 1948), and blew up the King David Hotel in Jerusalem (22 July 1946), with the loss of 91 lives.

Irigoyen, Hipólito (1850–1933) Argentine statesman. A leader of the Radical Party, he was elected to the presidency (1916–22). He actively supported organized labour until a series of strikes in 1918 and 1919 threatened economic paralysis. He then turned against the union movement with the same enthusiasm that he had shown in previously supporting it. Sitting out one term, Irigoyen was elected for a second time in 1928. It was an unstable period in Argentine history when corruption, continued labour unrest, and large budget deficits were all exacerbated by the Great DEPRESSION. The Argentine military stepped in to overthrow Irigoyen in 1930.

Irish Famine (1845–51) Period of famine and unrest in Ireland. In 1845 blight affected the potato in Ireland and the crop failed, thus depriving the Irish of their staple food. Farmers could not pay their rents; often they were evicted and their cottages destroyed. Committees to organize relief works for such unemployed persons, together with soup kitchens, were set up, and, especially in the western counties, large numbers sought refuge in workhouses. Deaths from starvation were aggravated by an epidemic of typhus, from which some 350,000 died in the year 1846–47. The corn harvest in 1847 was good and, although the blight recurred, the worst of the famine was over. It is estimated that one million people died in Ireland of starvation in the five years 1846–51 and another million emigrated to the USA or elsewhere.

Irish Free State IRELAND, REPUBLIC OF.

Irish Republican Army (IRA) Terrorist organization fighting for a unified republican Ireland. Originally created by the FENIAN Brotherhood in the USA, it was revived by SINN FEIN in 1919 as a nationalist armed force. Its first commander in Ireland was Michael COLLINS, who organized guerrilla attacks on British forces during Ireland's War of Independence (1919–21). The IRA was defeated by the Free State army during Ireland's Civil War (1921–23) but remained in being as a secret terrorist organization thereafter. Since its establishment the IRA has been able to rely on support from sympathizers in the Irish-American community. Bomb explosions for which the IRA was held responsible occurred in England in 1939 and hundreds of its members were imprisoned. During World War II hundreds of members were likewise interned without trial in Ireland. In 1956 violence erupted in NORTHERN IRELAND and the IRA performed a series of border raids. Following the outbreak of the current 'troubles' in the late 1960s, the IRA split into Provisional and Official wings (1969). In subsequent decades the Provisional IRA (PIRA) and the Irish National Liberation Army (INLA) staged demonstrations, assassinations, and bombings in both Northern Ireland and Britain. These include the murder of Lord Mountbatten and the British MP Airey Neave in 1979, a bomb attack on the entire British cabinet in Brighton in 1984, a bombing in Enniskillen on Remembrance Day 1987, attacks on British military bases in England and Germany in 1989, the murder of Ian Gow MP in 1990, mortar attacks on Downing Street (1991) and on Heathrow Airport (1994), a bomb in the City of London (1992), and another in Warrington in 1993. In August 1994 the IRA announced a complete cessation of its military operations, following peace initiatives by the British and Irish governments and by Northern Ireland politicians. The issue of decommissioning IRA weapons then became the main stumbling block in progress towards all-party talks on a lasting settlement for Northern Ireland. The ceasefire broke down in early 1996, with the resumption of IRA bombing campaigns in mainland Britain, notably in London Docklands and Manchester. Consequently the IRA's political wing, Sinn Féin, was excluded from talks in mid 1996. However, talks involving Sinn Féin and most of the other parties began in September 1997, after the IRA called a new ceasefire. The Good Friday agreement of 1998 proposed a comprehensive settlement for the province.

Irish Republican Brotherhood (IRB) A secret organization founded in Dublin in 1858 by James Stephens (1824–1901) to secure the creation of an independent Irish republic. It was closely linked with the FENIAN Brotherhood in the USA and its members came to be called Fenians. The primary object of the IRB was to organize an uprising in Ireland; the Fenian Brotherhood worked to support the IRB with men, funds, and a secure base. The British government acted swiftly and IRB leaders including Stephens were arrested. The 1867 Fenian Rising, led by Thomas Kelly, was a failure. The HOME RULE League, the LAND LEAGUE, the Irish Volunteers, and SINN FEIN appeared to supersede the IRB as political forces; but Fenians were active in all these organizations. The Home Rule Bills failed to satisfy them and in World War I the IRB, led by Pádraic Pearse, sought German help for the abortive EASTER RISING. The IRB was subsequently superseded by the IRISH REPUBLICAN ARMY.

Iron Age The period of prehistory distinguished technologically by the use of iron. This was first mastered on a large scale by the HITTITES in Anatolia between 1500 and 1200 BC, and spread to the Aegean, and thence to south-east and central Europe and Italy. The spread was slow across Europe, as it only gradually replaced bronze. In Africa the Iron Age immediately followed the STONE AGE, bronze entering much later. In America, iron was not discovered before being introduced from Europe.

ironclads The first wooden battleships protected by armour-plating. As a result of the loss of French and British wooden battleships during the CRIMEAN WAR, the French government ordered the construction of five armour-plated vessels for service in the Black Sea, the first, the frigate *Gloire*, entering service in 1859. The second ironclad to enter service, built entirely of iron with an internal wooden backing, was the British Battleship *Warrior*, launched in 1860. In 1862, during the AMERICAN CIVIL WAR, the first ironclad battle, MONITOR V. MERRIMACK, took place. The design was quickly adopted by most nations until succeeded by steel-framed, DREADNOUGHT-type battleships at the beginning of the 20th century.

Iron Curtain A popular name for the former barrier frontier between East European countries dependent on the former Soviet Union and Western non-communist countries. Its application to countries within the Soviet sphere of influence originated in a leading article by GOEBBELS in *Das Reich*, February 1945. This was reported in British newspapers, and the phrase was first used in English by Churchill: 'I view with profound misgivings the descent of an iron curtain between us and everything to the eastward.' The Iron Curtain was generally agreed to have gone by 1990, with the disintegration of Soviet influence in eastern Europe and the fall of the Berlin Wall in 1989.

Iron Mask, Man in the 'MAN IN THE IRON MASK', THE.

Ironsides NEW MODEL ARMY.

Iroquois Native Americans of the north-eastern woodlands of the USA and Canada. Unlike the PLAINS PEOPLES, the Iroquois traditionally lived in permanent fortified villages. The men were HUNTER-GATHERERS, while the women grew crops of maize, squash, and beans. Descent was matrilineal, and women had a high status. The Iroquois were not a distinct tribe, but a confederation or league, consisting of five tribes. This was highly organized, with decisions being taken by voting among the tribal members, and then in council by each tribal representative. The Iroquois were also skilled warriors, and expanded the confederation by conquest, until the height of their powers in the mid-17th century.

In the FUR-TRADE rivalry that formed in the 17th century between the Dutch and English at Albany, New York, and the French at Montreal, the Iroquois were tied to Albany. They attempted to control the beaver lands in the north-west by raiding French settlements on the St Lawrence and (in Seneca raids in 1648–49) the HURONS, who lived near Georgian Bay in south-eastern Ontario, virtually destroying them as a nation. In 1784 the Iroquois, who had been allies of the British against the French and later of the rebelling colonies, were rewarded with a large land grant and moved to the Grand River (Ontario), led by Joseph Brant, and the Bay of Quinte (Desoronto, Ontario).

Irredentism (derived from *Italia irredenta*, Italian, 'unredeemed Italy') An Italian patriotic movement of the late 19th and early 20th centuries. Its members aimed at liberating all lands, mainly in the Alps and on the Adriatic, inhabited by Italians and still held by the Austro-Hungarian empire after 1866. Its activities were restrained when the Italian government entered into the TRIPLE ALLIANCE with the Austro-Hungarian empire and Germany in 1882, but the movement headed the campaign for Italy's intervention in World War I in 1915. The Settlement of VERSAILLES satisfied most of its claims.

Irwin, Baron HALIFAX, 1ST EARL OF.

Isabella I (the Catholic) (1451–1504) Queen of Castile (1474–1504). She united her kingdom with that of Aragon by her marriage with its king, Ferdinand II (FERDINAND V of Castile), in 1469, retaining sole authority in Castilian affairs. On the death of Henry IV, her half-brother, in 1474, Isabella's claim to the throne was contested by his heiress Juana la Beltraneja. The skilful generalship of Ferdinand, however, helped Isabella to defeat Juana.

Isabella was noted for her Catholic piety, her encouragement of the SPANISH INQUISITION, and her intolerance towards Jews and Muslims. She patronized Spanish and Flemish artists, and most notably supported the exploration of the Americas by sponsoring COLUMBUS.

Isabella II (1830–1904) Queen of Spain (1833–70), the daughter of FERDINAND VII. Her accession to the throne as a young child was contested by her uncle, Don Carlos, leading to the CARLIST wars that raged until 1839. After two unpopular regencies, her reign was a succession of personal scandals, governmental changes, and conflicts

between political factions. Isabella finally fled to France after an insurrection (1868), and was deposed. The crown, offered by the new constitutional Cortes to five successive candidates, was accepted by the sixth, the Duke of Aosta (1845–90), the second son of Victor Emanuel I of Italy. As Amadeus I he ruled from 1871 to 1873, when he abdicated and the first Spanish republic was declared.

Isabella of France (1292–1358) Queen of England (1308–27). She was the daughter of PHILIP IV of France, and was married in 1308 to EDWARD II. She bore Edward four children, including the future EDWARD III, between 1312 and 1321, but seems to have become alienated from him in 1322, resenting the influence of the DESPENSERS. In 1325 she became the mistress of Roger MORTIMER in Paris, and in September 1326 they invaded England, imprisoning and then ordering the murder of Edward II. They effectively ruled England until Edward III captured them both in October 1330; Isabella was pensioned off with £3,000 a year.

Isabella I *Her resumption of the Spanish Inquisition led to brutal persecution of heretics and non-Christians: some 170,000 Jews were expelled from Spain. However, in her will she called for fair treatment of Native Americans in the New World.*

Isaiah (8th century BC) Hebrew prophet, who preached during the reigns of Jotham, Ahaz, and HEZEKIAH. Isaiah's message was that the safety of Judah was in God's hands and the king should trust him and not rely on foreign allies. He advised Hezekiah to acknowledge Assyrian power and not ally with Egypt; when Judah was invaded by Israelites and Syrians in 735 BC, and by the Assyrians in 710 BC, and again in 703–701 BC, Isaiah promised that faith in God would guarantee the people's deliverance. According to one tradition Isaiah was martyred in the reign of Manasseh by being sawn in two. The biblical Book of Isaiah incorporates many prophecies from a later age, concerning the Babylonian Exile, the victories of Cyrus, and the deliverance of the Jews. The fulfilment of these prophecies increased Isaiah's fame posthumously. In Christianity his prophecies concerning the Messiah are seen as fulfilled in the person of Jesus.

Isandhlwana, Battle of (22 January 1879) A battle fought between Zulu and British forces in South Africa. The ZULU WAR had begun on 11 January when CETSHWAYO ignored the British ultimatum to disband his army of 30,000 Impis gathered in Ulundi. A British force, under Lord Chelmsford, of some 7,000 regulars, with as many African levies, advanced on Ulundi. The British were caught unawares at Isandhlwana, with 1,600 killed in close-combat fighting. That night a force of Zulu warriors went on to attack a mission hospital at Rorke's Drift on the Buffalo River. Eighty defenders under Lieutenant Chard killed some 470 Zulus before being relieved by Chelmsford.

Islam The religion of Muslims, revealed through MUHAMMAD, the Prophet of Allah. The name comes from Arabic, meaning 'submission' to God. The cardinal principle of Islam is *tawhīd* ('making one'), the absolute unity of God, Allah, the universal creator whose omnipotence is supreme. This is expressed in the *shahādah*: 'There is no god but Allah and Muhammad is his Messenger'. Human authority lies with a succession of prophets, of whom the most important are Noah, Abraham (regarded by Muslims as 'the father of Islam'), Moses, and Jesus, with Muhammad as the final 'Seal of the Prophets'. Divine origin and authority are attributed to the KORAN, the 'recitation' of the word and will of God, as revealed by the Angel Gabriel to Muhammad, and the Sunna, Muhammad's words and actions recorded by his companions but not written by him. Religious practice is based upon observance of the FIVE PILLARS OF ISLAM: to accept the basic creed ('I testify that there is no god but Allah and that Muhammad is the prophet of Allah'); to offer prayers five times a day; to pay *zakat*, a charitable levy; to fast during daylight in the month of Ramadan; and, once in a lifetime, to undertake the *hajj*, the pilgrimage to the Kaaba at MECCA. Public worship occurs in a mosque, where prayer is led by an *imam* (spiritual leader). Attendance at the mosque, which is not required of women, is compulsory for men on Fridays and special festivals and meritorious on all days. Moral and religious law is disseminated through the SHARIA, a legal code based on the Koran, and the HADITH, a canon of belief and social regulation. There are four schools of law in Sunni Islam; disputes have traditionally been resolved by *aijma'*, or consensus. Islam does not recognize a clergy that intermediates between the individual and God; however, religious and legal officials exist to give leadership on matters of faith and doctrine, particularly within the Shia branch of Islam. Parallel to the formal practice of Islam is the Sufi or mystical tradition through which an individual may

Islam   *The first page of a general history of the Islamic world by Ibn Khaldun (d. 1406). History writing was an important tradition in the Islamic world; many places, India in particular, had no written histories until after Islamic conquest. Ibn Khaldun's work was well researched and much was based on what he learned during his many diplomatic missions. Many of his sociological theories and general analyses are still respected today.*

experience direct intuitive awareness of God. Sufi fraternities such as dervishes form an important element in Muslim spiritual life and society.

In the 7th and 8th centuries, Muslim armies from Arabia, driven on by the concept of JIHAD (holy war) against unbelievers, spread the religion throughout the Middle East and North Africa and into Spain, creating a vast Islamic empire by the 9th century. By the early 14th century Islam was the official religion of the OTTOMAN EMPIRE, whose sultan was CALIPH (the temporal and spiritual leader of the Muslim world) from 1517: Islam also spread into sub-Saharan Africa, the Balkans, central Asia, the Indian sub-continent, and the East Indies. Today Islam is the official religion of approximately 45 nations with some 800 million believers. New communities of Muslims have become established in all European countries as well as in North and Latin America, and it has been estimated that there are some seven million in Europe and 12 million in the former Soviet republics. The course of African history in the 19th century was affected by Islamic movements among the SANUSI in Libya, the Fulbe and FULANI in West Africa, the MAHDISTS in the Sudan, all influenced by the Persian teacher, Jamal al-Din al-AFGHANI. With the fall in 1922 of the Ottoman empire and the discontinuation of the caliphate in Constantinople, a tide of Muslim nationalism emerged. The early 20th century witnessed two well-organized movements for the revival of fundamental Islamic beliefs and the countering of Western influences: the Society of Muslim Brothers (al-Ikhwan al Muslimun) founded in 1928 by Hasan al-Banna (1906–49) in Egypt, which has since spread throughout the Middle East, and the Islamic Society (jamma'at-i-Islami) founded in 1941 by Syed Abu al-Mawdudi (1903–79) in India. Both of these have influenced other Islamic movements across the world, including that initiated by Ayatollah KHOMEINI in IRAN. All emphasize the social and political reconstruction of Islamic society and of the Islamic state.

The two major sects of Islam are the SUNNI, comprising the main community in most Muslim countries today, and the SHIITE, which is now centred chiefly in Iran. Both adhere to the same body of tenets, but differ in community organization and in theological and legal practices. Central to these is the Shiite belief that only the descendants of the prophet Muhammad may adopt the title and role of *imam*, while the Sunni choose the latter by consensus. The tensions between Sunni and Shiite have been a major cause of social and political unrest in Middle Eastern countries during the 20th century, while the rise of ISLAMIC FUNDAMENTALISM since the late 1970s has created a significant new element in world politics.

Islamic fundamentalism The belief that the revitalization of Islamic society can only come about through a return to the fundamental principles and practices of early Islam. Fundamentalist movements have often been a response to political and economic decline, which is ascribed to spiritual and moral decay. For example, in the 18th and 19th centuries, the disintegration of Muslim political and economic power and the ascendancy of the West were instrumental in the emergence of a number of differing revivalist movements. Despite major differences, these movements shared the belief that religion is integral to both state and society and advocated a return to a life

patterned on the 7th-century political community of the faithful established by Muhammad at Medina, governed by the SHARIA (Islamic law), and supported if need be by JIHAD (holy war). In the 20th century, activist organizations such as the Muslim Brotherhood, which was founded in Egypt in 1928 and has or had independent national organizations in Jordan, Kuwait, Palestine, Sudan, and Syria, and other more radical groups, such as HAMAS and Hezbollah (Party of God) have become prominent. Such groups are characterized by emphasis on the literal interpretation of the Koran and *sharia*. By contrast with ISLAMIC MODERNISM, fundamentalism tends to stress the penal code and restrictions on women contained in the *sharia*, at least in part because such provisions have become symbols of cultural identity and antagonism to WESTERNIZATION. The Muslim Brotherhood advocates presidential rule with an elected consultative council replicating the *shūra* of Muhammad's day. Many fundamentalists regard multiparty politics as divisive of the Muslim community. Some may be Islamic socialists, who are careful to denounce the materialism and atheism of MARXISM, but deplore the inequities of CAPITALISM, especially its reliance on usury, which is forbidden in the Koran. Some Western observers have regarded the recent resurgence in Islamic religious practice and the Iranian Revolution of 1979 as further examples of fundamentalism, but it is not accurate to regard all Muslim religious practice, however strict, as fundamentalist, while scholarly examination of the constitutional structure of the Islamic Republic of Iran reveals radical innovations that are not fundamentalist. There is, however, no doubt that the Iranian revolution has been an inspiring example to many Muslims of all persuasions throughout the world.

Islamic modernism A movement in Islamic thought that seeks to reinterpret Islam to meet the changing circumstances of contemporary life. By contrast with ISLAMIC FUNDAMENTALISM, Islamic modernism is a response to Western imperialism and economic dominance that attempts to reform legal, educational, and social structures. From the 19th century leading Muslim thinkers such as Jamal al-Din al-AFGHANI and his followers in Egypt, Muhammad Abduh (1849–1905) and Rashid Rida (1865–1935), were concerned at the stagnation they perceived in Muslim intellectual, political, and social life. They advocated the reform of the SHARIA by reopening the door of *ijtihād*, or reinterpretation, which orthodox Sunni Muslims have regarded as closed since the 9th century. Western scientific advances should not be rejected as incompatible with Islam, but should be integrated into the structure of a religion that is essentially scientific. Abduh distinguished between an inner unchanging core of Islamic belief and practice, and outer layers of regulations that could be varied in accordance with contemporary social practice. His reinterpretation of the law on these lines was continued by Rida, who drew on a traditional legal principle of public interest to formulate new laws. The Egyptian modernists' concern with the establishment of a modern Muslim state was echoed in India, most influentially by the poet-philosopher, lawyer, and politician Muhammad IQBAL. Influenced by his study of Western philosophers such as HEGEL, Fichte, and Nietzsche, Iqbal developed his own synthesis and interpretation of Islam. His view of the community as a religio-political state based on the supremacy of the *sharia* was influential in the establishment of PAKISTAN in 1947. Islamic modernism has had widespread influence in most Muslim countries, but despite its emphasis on the reform of the *sharia*, no systematic reform has ever been undertaken.

Islamic Salvation Front (French, *Front Islamique du Salut*, FIS) Algerian ISLAMIC FUNDAMENTALIST political party. The FIS was formed by an alliance of five smaller Muslim parties after the introduction of multiparty politics in Algeria in 1989. After violent clashes between the FIS and supporters of the ruling party, the FLN, a state of emergency was declared in 1991. In the first round of parliamentary elections later that year, the FIS scored a clear victory but the second round was suspended and the party was outlawed in 1992. Since then, Algeria has been caught in a spiral of increasing violence; the FIS has officially renounced armed struggle but a group known as the Armed Islamic Group (GIA) has undertaken a series of massacres of civilians. Covert government involvement in the atrocities to discredit the Islamist cause has been suspected and in 1998 EU foreign ministers proposed sending a fact-finding mission to work for a negotiated settlement.

Islam, Nation of NATION OF ISLAM.

Ismail I Safavi (d. 1524) First ruler of the Safavid dynasty in Persia (1501–24). His ancestor Safi ud-Din 1252–1334) was a Sufi holy man and founder of the Safaviyya, the mystic brotherhood after which the dynasty is named. Supported by Turcoman tribesmen, he established his rule over Persia, extending it into KURDISTAN and driving the UZBEKS from Khurasan in the north-east. His expansion was checked in the west by the OTTOMAN sultan Selim I at Chaldiran in 1514. His most enduring achievement was to convert his realm from SUNNI to SHIITE Islam.

Ismaili A branch of SHIITE ISLAM that recognizes seven rather than 12 *imams* (spiritual leaders). They include Mustalians in India and Yemen, and Nizāris in Afghanistan, East Africa, India, Iran, and Syria. Ismail, the eldest son of the sixth *imam*, Jafar al-Sadia (d. 765) was disinherited and most Shiites recognized his brother Musa al-Kazim as *imam*. Ismailis regarded Ismail as the seventh and last *imam* and expected that he would soon return as the Mahdi (expected one) to overthrow existing corrupt governments and establish justice on earth. The FATIMID dynasty (909–1171) promoted their beliefs in Egypt and Syria but attempted no mass conversions among the SUNNI majority. The Ismailis developed the idea that the religious precepts have a secret inner meaning, passed from MUHAMMAD to Ali and from him to later imams, who could thus instruct the ignorant. This encouraged major contributions to Islamic philosophy, though doctrinal differences led the movement to split into various sub-groups, such as the ASSASSINS, Druzes, and Khojas. The family of the Aga Khan claims descent from Ismail.

Isolationism An approach to US foreign policy that advocates non-participation in alliances or in the affairs of other nations. It derives its spirit from George Washington's proclamation of neutrality in 1793, and was further confirmed by the MONROE DOCTRINE (1823). It foiled Woodrow Wilson in his attempt to take the USA into the LEAGUE OF NATIONS (1919 and 1920), and it hindered Franklin D. Roosevelt's support for Britain, France, and China before and during World War II, by ensuring passage of restrictive Neutrality Acts (1935–37). Present-day isolationists favour political and military withdrawal from overseas bases as well as the establishment of a 'fortress America' protected by military systems such as the STRATEGIC DEFENSE INITIATIVE.

Isonzo A river in north-east Italy, the scene of fierce battles between Italian and Austrian forces following Italy's entry into World War I on the Allied side (1915). Some dozen battles, in which Italy had twice as many casualties as Austria, were fought along this front between May 1915 and October 1917, culminating in the Italian disaster at CAPORETTO (1917).

Israel A country of south-west Asia at the eastern end of the Mediterranean Sea. It is bounded on the north by Lebanon, on the east by Syria and Jordan, and on the south by Egypt.

Physical. The coastal plain is very warm in summer and suited particularly to the growth of citrus fruits. The north includes the Sea of Galilee and part of the River Jordan, while the east extends to the Dead Sea with its deposits of potash and reserves of natural gas. Southward is a hot and arid Rift Valley (part of the Great Rift Valley system) running down the eastern side of the rocky Negev Desert. Massive irrigation programmes have brought large areas of former desert under cultivation.

Economy. The Israeli economy has a well-developed manufacturing base, the main products being chemicals and small metal manufactures. However, high military expenditure and reliance on imported fuels and minerals have resulted in a high rate of inflation and dependence on foreign, mostly US, aid. Agriculture, largely carried out by communes (*kibbutzim*) and co-operatives (*moshavim*), has been successfully developed by irrigation, and Israel is self-sufficient in food. Exports include diamonds, chemicals, small metal manufactures, and fruit.

History. The modern state of Israel has developed from the ZIONIST campaign for a Jewish state in PALESTINE and the BALFOUR DECLARATION (1917), in which the Jewish demand for a national home was supported by Britain. Under the British MANDATE (from 1922) in Palestine the Jewish community increased from about 10% of the population in 1918 to about 30% in 1936. In 1937 the Peel Commission recommended the partition of Palestine and the formation of separate Jewish and Arab states. After Britain's referral of the Palestine problem to the United Nations in 1947, a United Nations Special Commission likewise recommended partition and a resolution to that effect passed the General Assembly. The British mandate ended on 14 May 1948 and the independent Jewish state of Israel in Palestine was established. The creation of the state was opposed by the Palestinian Arabs supported by Syria, Lebanon, Jordan, and Egypt, but after a violent conflict Israel survived and considerably enlarged its territory at the expense of the proposed Arab state. A substantial Palestinian refugee problem was created as many Arabs fled from Israel-controlled territory. Further Israeli-

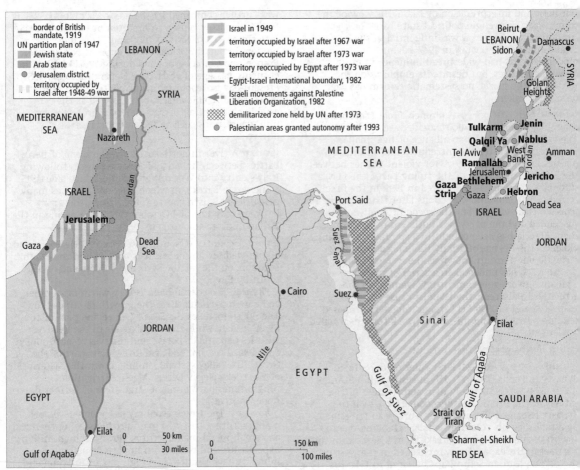

Israel   *When Israel proclaimed itself a state (May 1948) the surrounding Arab states of Egypt, Jordan, Lebanon, and Syria declared war. After fierce fighting Israel agreed to a UN armistice. Israel made substantial gains, including territory beyond Nazareth. Following the Suez War (1956) a UN force was stationed in the Sinai desert and along the Gaza Strip. This was withdrawn in 1967, whereupon Egypt blockaded the Gulf of Aqaba. Israel again went to war against its Arab neighbours, occupying the Gaza Strip, the Sinai desert, West Jordan, and the Golan Heights, all within six days. Jewish settlers quickly moved into these areas, often expelling Arab inhabitants. After a fourth war – the Yom Kippur War – in 1973 Israel, under pressure from both the USA and the Soviet Union, agreed to a phased withdrawal from Sinai, and UN troops were reinstated in the buffer zones.*

In 1993 Israel agreed to grant the Palestinians autonomy in the Gaza Strip and areas of the West Bank.

Arab wars took place in 1956 (SUEZ WAR), 1967 (SIX-DAY WAR), 1973 (YOM KIPPUR WAR), and 1982 (Lebanon War). As a result of these wars Israel extended its occupation to include all the territory of the former British mandate. After 1948 Jewish immigration into Israel took place from over 100 different nations, especially from communist and Arab countries, as well as from Europe, raising the population from about 700,000 in 1948 to nearly 5.5 million by 1996. Despite a high inflation rate, the development of the economy has made Israel the most industrialized country in the region, greatly aided by funding from the USA and European powers. The right-wing leader of the Likud Party, Yitzhak SHAMIR led a government (1986–92) firmly opposed to any concessions over the Palestine problem. Under his successor as Prime Minister, the Labour leader Yitzhak RABIN, progress towards an eventual settlement began.

From 1991 intense diplomatic efforts, led by the USA, resulted in several sessions of Middle East peace talks. Despite escalating violence in the occupied territories in 1992–93, there was an unexpected breakthrough in negotiations between Israel and the PLO, led by Yasser ARAFAT, resulting (1993) in a declaration of principles on Palestinian self-rule in the occupied territories. Although the declaration was welcomed internationally, there was widespread opposition from right-wing Israeli political groups. During 1994–95 Israel granted autonomous status to the Gaza Strip and Jericho, handing over administrative powers to a new Palestinian National Authority. Israel signed a peace treaty with Jordan in 1994. However, the assassination of Prime Minister Rabin by a Jewish extremist in November 1995 cast doubt over the future of the Middle East peace process. Shimon PERES succeeded Rabin. In

1996 HAMAS launched a number of suicide bomb attacks in Israeli cities, while attacks by Hizbollah fighters based in south Lebanon provoked Israel to mount an offensive in the region, with heavy civilian casualties. In the elections of May 1996 Peres, a supporter of the peace process, lost to the hawkish Binyamin NETANYAHU. In September 1996 fighting broke out between West Bank Palestinians and Israeli forces, resulting in over 70 deaths. Terrorist attacks and Israeli reprisals continued throughout 1997, while peace was further threatened by the Likud government's revival of the controversial policy of building Jewish settlements in Arab areas.

CAPITAL:	Jerusalem
AREA:	20,700 sq km (7,992 sq miles)
POPULATION:	5.481 million (1996)
CURRENCY:	1 New (Israeli) sheqel = 100 agorot
RELIGIONS:	Jewish 82.0%; Muslim (mostly Sunni) 13.9%; Christian 2.3%; Druze and other 1.8%
ETHNIC GROUPS:	Jewish 83.0%; Arab 16.8%
LANGUAGES:	Hebrew, Arabic (both official); Yiddish; Russian; Romanian; English
INTERNATIONAL ORGANIZATIONS:	UN

Italian Campaign (July 1943–May 1945) The World War II military campaign in which Allied troops liberated Italy. Following the NORTH AFRICAN CAMPAIGNS, MONTGOMERY and PATTON prepared British and US troops to invade Sicily. The landing was launched (July 1943) from Malta, and by the end of the month both the island's principal cities, Palermo and Catania, were captured: on the mainland MUSSOLINI was deposed and arrested. The German army under KESSELRING was withdrawn from Sicily and British and US forces landed in southern Italy (September 1943). An armistice was signed, ending hostilities between the Anglo-American forces and those of the new government of BADOGLIO. A third surprise Allied landing on the 'heel' of Italy captured the two ports of Taranto and Brindisi, and on 8 October 1943 Italy declared war on Germany. A large and well-organized partisan force now harassed the Germans, but reinforcements successfully reached Kesselring, who took a stand at Monte Cassino (late 1943), site of the ancient monastery of St Benedict. The Allies decided to by-pass this, landing 50,000 men at Anzio (January 1944), south of Rome, while also bombing the monastery, which was finally captured (May 1944) by Polish troops. Rome fell (June 1944), and Florence was captured after bitter fighting (August 1944). The Germans consolidated in the River Po valley and fought a hard battle through the autumn of 1944. In April 1945 the Allied armies launched their final attacks, and on 2 May ALEXANDER OF TUNIS accepted the surrender of the whole German army group serving in northern Italy and southern Austria.

Italy A country consisting of a peninsula in the Mediterranean Sea, bounded on the north by France, Switzerland, Austria, and Slovenia, together with the islands of Sardinia, Sicily, Ischia, and Capri.

Physical. Among the southern foothills of the Alps in the north of the mainland are the Italian Lakes. Below them the River Po runs west–east across the fertile Lombardy Plain to the Adriatic Sea. The Apennines are the backbone of the peninsula itself. To their west are the hills and plains of Tuscany; further south the Tiber flows across the Pontine Marshes to the Tyrrhenian Sea. Further south still the coastal plain is enriched by the debris of Vesuvius and the climate becomes warmer. To the south is Calabria, where the mountains fall steeply to the sea and in summer the land bakes brown.

Economy. With a developed industrial economy, Italy's main exports include electrical machinery (especially office equipment), chemicals, clothing, motor vehicles, textiles, and footwear. The public sector is significant, and industry is concentrated in north and central Italy with the south remaining predominantly agricultural and relatively poor. The tourist industry is significant. There is only a small degree of mechanization of agriculture compared with other European countries.

History. Italy had come under ETRUSCAN, Greek, and Celtic influence before it was united in *c.* 262 BC under Roman rule. In the 5th century it was overrun by the barbarian GOTH and LOMBARD tribes. In 775 CHARLEMAGNE conquered the north and it became part of the Carolingian empire, while the south was disputed between the Byzantine empire and the Arab conquerors of Sicily. By the 12th century city-states had emerged in northern and central Italy and the south united under first Norman and then, in 1176, Spanish control. The 14th century was a time of great commercial activity, followed by the RENAISSANCE period. The country, now divided between five major rival states, came under first Spanish (1559–1700) and then, after the Treaty of UTRECHT in 1713, Austrian domination. In 1796–97 Italy, having been used to maintain the balance of power in Europe, was invaded by NAPOLEON and hopes of independence and unification re-emerged. However, in 1815, the country reverted to a grouping consisting of Lombardy and Venetia, ruled by the HABSBURGS from Vienna; the kingdom of Piedmont Sardinia, which then consisted of most of Savoy, Piedmont, and the island of Sardinia; the Papal States, ruled by the popes in Rome; the duchies of Tuscany, Parma, and Modena, also ruled by the Habsburgs; and the Kingdom of the Two Sicilies, now ruled by restored Bourbons from Naples. France ruled part of Savoy and Corsica, but had lost Genoa to Piedmont. Revolutionary societies, such as the CARBONARI and YOUNG ITALY, were formed. The new forces of the RISORGIMENTO created hopes of independence from Austrian and French rule. Under such leaders as CAVOUR, MAZZINI, and GARIBALDI, unification of Italy was finally achieved, and in 1861 VICTOR EMANUEL II was crowned king of Italy. In an effort to join the SCRAMBLE FOR AFRICA the Italian Premier and Minister of Foreign Affairs, Francesco CRISPI, claimed (1889) the colony of ERITREA, but the abortive bid for ETHIOPIA led to a decisive defeat (1896) at the Battle of ADOWA. During the Turko-Italian War (1911–12), Italy conquered north Tripoli and by 1914 had occupied much of Libya, declaring it an integral part of the country in 1939. In World War I Italy supported the Allies, regaining Trieste and part of the Tyrol. The fascist dictator MUSSOLINI, determined to establish an Italian empire, successfully invaded (1935) Ethiopia, combining it with Eritrea and Italian Somaliland to form Italian East Africa. In World War II Mussolini allied himself with Hitler, but by 1943 the country had lost its North African empire and he was deposed: that same year Italy declared war on Germany. In 1946 the king abdicated in favour of a republic. The immediate post-war period brought remarkable and sustained economic growth but also political instability, characterized by frequent changes of government. The Italian Communist Party successfully adjusted to democracy, but during the 1970s there were RED BRIGADE terrorist kidnappings and outrages. Governments of the republic have mostly been formed by elaborate coalitions, dominated by the Christian Democrats, but during the 1980s and early 1990s Italian politics became increasingly chaotic and incompetent. As a result, President Francesco Cossiga (1985–92) and others called for constitutional reform. Continued attempts to eliminate the MAFIA largely failed. In 1992 President Cossiga resigned and was succeeded by Oscar Luigi Scalfaro. Allegations of corruption against politicians and public figures in 1993–94 further undermined the authority of the political system. In 1994 the country's electoral process was changed from a proportional representation system to a first-past-the-post system, after overwhelming approval by the populace in nationwide referendums. The general election of 1994 brought to power, under the new electoral system, a right-wing coalition government led by *Forza Italia*, a party formed by media magnate, Silvio Berlusconi, who became Prime Minister. However, owing to conflicts of interest between Berlusconi's political and commercial interests, he was forced to resign in 1995 and Lamberto Dini became Prime Minister. A general election held in 1996 was won by a left-wing coalition headed by Romano Prodi. The early 1990s saw Mafia violence escalate, provoking public outrage at the authorities' inability to curb it. The government responded by increasing police and judiciary powers and key arrests were made. By 1994 official reports indicated a significant reduction in Mafia-related crimes. The late 1990s have seen a growing movement for separatism in Italy's more prosperous northern regions.

CAPITAL:	Rome
AREA:	301,277 sq km (116,324 sq miles)
POPULATION:	57.500 million (1996)
CURRENCY:	1 lira = 100 centesimi
RELIGIONS:	Roman Catholic 83.2%; non-religious 13.6%; atheist 2.6%
ETHNIC GROUPS:	Italian 94.1%; Sardinian 2.7%; Rhaetian 1.3%
LANGUAGES:	Italian (official); Sardinian; minority languages
INTERNATIONAL ORGANIZATIONS:	EU; NATO; OECD; UN; Council of Europe; CSCE

Ithaca A small island off the north-west coast of Greece. Mycenaean remains testify to the importance of the island in early times, which was due in part to the fact that it was a staging-post for Corinthian trade with Sicily and southern Italy. By classical times it had declined, never again to regain its significance. At the beginning of the 16th century it was virtually uninhabited and Venetian traders had to encourage resettlement.

Ito Hirobumi (1841–1909) Japanese statesman. As a young SAMURAI of the Choshu clan, he opposed Westernization before becoming aware of the benefits offered by modernization. He became one of the major political figures after the MEIJI RESTORATION (1868), travelling in Europe in search of a model for the MEIJI CONSTITUTION which he subsequently framed, and serving four times as Prime Minister, first in 1885. After the

politics of the 1890s had shown the considerable veto power that political parties were able to exercise, and when YAMAGATA ARITOMO had given the armed services the power to break civilian governments, Ito formed (1901) the Seiyukai (Friends of Constitutional Government) Party. He retired from active politics soon after and exercised a moderating influence on imperial policy as first resident-general (1905–09) of the Korean protectorate. After his resignation he was assassinated by a Korean nationalist.

Iturbide, Agustín de (1783–1824) Mexican independence leader. A Creole officer in the Spanish royalist army, his decision to join the movement for independence from Spain and to proclaim the Plan of IGUALA was significant, as many other royalist officers followed his lead. With the defeat of the Spanish forces (1821) Iturbide managed to have himself proclaimed by his soldiers as Emperor Agustín I, and persuaded (1822) a hostile Congress to ratify the proclamation. On his accession he revoked the Plan of Iguala, refused to carry out his promised social reforms, and instituted a dictatorial government. A revolution led by SANTA ANNA and Guadalupe Victoria overthrew the empire after 11 months. Iturbide left for Europe but when he returned in 1824 he was arrested, tried by the Congress of Tamaulipas, and executed.

Ivan III (the Great) (1440–1505) Grand Prince of MUSCOVY (1462). He was responsible for extending the territories of Muscovite Russia, becoming independent of the TARTARS, and subjecting the principalities of Livonia and Lithuania. Introducing a legal code in 1497, he claimed the title of 'Ruler of all Russia', reorganized and reduced the independence of the nobility, and built up a class of new, loyal, dependent officials. Influenced by contemporary Italy and Byzantium, he claimed leadership of the EASTERN ORTHODOX CHURCH. His authority subsequently declined as alcoholism, conspiracy, and succession problems diminished his effectiveness.

Ivan IV (the Terrible) (1530–84) Grand Prince of Muscovy (1533–84), the first ruler to assume the title of Tsar (Emperor) of Russia (1547). He had a violent and unpredictable nature, but his nickname (Russian, *grozny* is better translated as 'awe-inspiring' rather than 'Terrible'. From 1547 to 1563 he pushed through a series of legal and administrative reforms. He also continued to expand Russian territory although his campaigns against the Mongols and in Siberia were more successful than those in the west. In 1564 he entered on a reign of terror, caused partly by his deteriorating mental condition, and partly by his determination to wrest power from the BOYARS. He used a special body of civil servants, the *oprichniki*, to break the power of the nobility. Shortly before his death, he precipitated further turmoil for Russia by killing in a fit of rage his gifted son and heir, Ivan: although another son, Fyodor, succeeded him, power soon fell into the hands of his favourite, BORIS GODUNOV.

Ivory Coast CÔTE D'IVOIRE.

Izetbegović, Alija (1925–) Bosnian politician, President of Bosnia-Herzegovina from 1992, from 1996 as part of a rotating tripartite presidency. Izetbegović's championing of Islam brought him into conflict with the secular communist state of former Yugoslavia and he was imprisoned several times. In 1990, he formed the anti-communist Party of Democratic Action, which won power in the regional elections in Bosnia-Herzegovina; he was appointed President of a seven-member collective state presidency. When the republic declared its independence in 1992, a bloody civil war ensued, in which Izetbegović took a conciliatory line, attempting to keep the country intact with a constitution guaranteeing equal rights for all ethnic groups and religious toleration. After the secession of the Bosnian Serbs and violent acts of 'ethnic cleansing', he eventually signed the Dayton Peace Accord in 1995, which formalized partition of the republic. He was re-elected President of the joint presidency in 1996.

J

Jackson, Andrew (1767–1845) Seventh President of the USA (1829–37). Trained as a lawyer, he helped draft the constitution of the state of Tennessee. After two years in the Senate (1797–98), he became judge of the Tennessee Supreme Court (1798–1804), but was forced out of politics as the result of a series of duels. On 8 January 1815 he won a victory over the British at the Battle of NEW ORLEANS, and in 1818–19 he invaded Florida during the SEMINOLE WAR, clearing the way for its inclusion in the USA. Entering national politics, Jackson rapidly became a leading figure in the Democratic Party. He narrowly lost the presidential election of 1824, but won easily in 1828 and was re-elected in 1832. During his Presidency, the new two-party system of DEMOCRATS and WHIGS took shape. It featured the SPOILS SYSTEM, party-nominating conventions, and the establishment of the KITCHEN CABINET. Jackson responded robustly to the NULLIFICATION challenge from South Carolina. He vetoed the renewal of the charter of the Bank of the United States, while his 'hard money' policies helped to precipitate a financial panic in 1837. Depending on his reputation as a hard-headed frontiersman, Jackson greatly increased the power and independence of the Presidency, while promoting a new style of popular democratic politics.

Jackson, Robert Houghwout (1892–1954) US lawyer and judge. He was a committed supporter of President Franklin D. Roosevelt's NEW DEAL policy in the 1930s, and defended New Deal laws in hearings before the Supreme Court. As a Justice of the Supreme Court, his decisions reflected his opposition to monopolies and vested interests, and he continually stressed that judges should display independence. He also acted as the chief US counsel at the NUREMBERG TRIALS in 1945–46.

Jackson, Thomas Jonathan ('Stonewall') (1824–63) US general in the army of the Southern CONFEDERACY. He joined the Confederate army at the beginning of the AMERICAN CIVIL WAR and earned his nickname 'Stonewall' at the first Battle of Bull Run (July 1861), when his troops held off assaults by Union (Northern) troops at a crucial phase of the engagement, paving the way for a Southern victory. He emerged as the most trusted lieutenant of General LEE and one of the best fighting leaders on either side. He successfully immobilized a superior enemy force in the Shenandoah Valley campaign and played a major part in Confederate victories at the second Battle of Bull Run (August 1862), Fredericksburg, and Chancellorsville (May 1863). During the latter, he was fatally wounded in an accident involving some of his own men.

Jacobin Club The most famous of the political clubs of the FRENCH REVOLUTION. It had its origins in the Club Breton which was established after the opening of the STATES-GENERAL in 1789, and acquired its new name from its headquarters in an old Jacobin (Dominican) monastery in Paris. Its membership grew steadily and its carefully prepared policies had great influence in the NATIONAL ASSEMBLY. By August 1791 it had numerous affiliated clubs and branches throughout the country. Its high subscription confined its membership to professional men who, at first, were not distinguished by extreme views. By 1792, however, ROBESPIERRE had seized control and the moderates were expelled. The club became the focus of the TERROR the following year, and in June was instrumental in the overthrow of the GIRONDINS. Its success was based on sound organization and the support of the SANS-CULOTTES. It was closed after the fall of Robespierre and several attempts to reopen it were finally suppressed in 1799.

Jacobites Scottish or English supporters of the exiled royal house of STUART. The Jacobites took their name from Jacobus, the Latin name for JAMES II, who had been deprived of his throne in 1688. Their strength lay among the Highland CLANS of Scotland, whose loyalty was personal; the weakness of Jacobitism was that it failed to win over the Tories in England, who might have made it a more powerful and dangerous movement. The Jacobites were politically important between 1688 and 1745. The FIFTEEN and the FORTY-FIVE were their major rebellions, but neither succeeded and after 1745, with the government's suppression of the clans, Jacobitism ceased to have a firm political base.

Jacquerie A rebellion of French peasants in northern France (May–June 1358), named after 'Jacques Bonhomme', the aristocrats' nickname for a French peasant. A leader, Guillaume Karle (or Cale) emerged, and a bourgeois revolt in Paris helped the movement. The BLACK DEATH, the French defeat at POITIERS, the ravages of brigands, feudal burdens, and governmental demands for extra fortification work were all contributary causes. Castles were demolished and looted; but the rebellion was short-lived, collapsing after the execution of Karle and the massacre of a mob at Meaux.

Jagiellon A Polish dynasty that reigned in Lithuania, Poland, Hungary, and Bohemia in the 14th, 15th, and 16th centuries. The family gained prominence under Jagiello, Grand Duke of Lithuania (c. 1345–1434), who became King of Poland, as Ladislas I, in 1386. A descendant, Ladislas III, King of Poland (1434), governed Hungary as Lazlo I (1440) but was killed by the Turks at Varna in 1444. His brother, Casimir IV of Poland, fought the Teutonic Knights and gained the throne of Bohemia for his son, Ladislas II, and in 1490, as Lazlo II, of Hungary. His son was defeated and killed at the Battle of MOHÁCS (1525). The line died out with Sigismund II Augustus, King of Poland (1548–72).

Jahangir (or Jehangir) (1569–1627) Emperor of India (1605–27), whose contribution to MOGUL greatness was artistic rather than military. His name means 'holder of the world', but control over the huge empire he inherited was threatened by court quarrels and by the dominance of his Persian wife, Nur Jahan. The fame of the Mogul empire had reached Europe during the reign of his father, AKBAR, when Jesuit missionaries reached

gra. In Jahangir's time there were visits by English
mbassadors. He was criticized for addiction to
lcohol and opium, but his own artistic interests
ncouraged a new naturalism in the work of his court
ainters.

ainism An Indian religion whose recorded history
oes back to the 6th century BC, but which is certainly
f greater antiquity. It is based on the teaching of 24
rthankaras or jinas ('conquerors'), the last and greatest
eing the founder, Vardhamana Mahavira (c. 599–527 BC),
ho like his near contemporary, the BUDDHA, protested
gainst the dominant HINDU ritualistic cults.
Jainism teaches a strict moral code centred on *ahimsa*
voidance of injury to any living creature) and a path
f spiritual training through austerity, leading to
rvana (absorption into the supreme spirit). Belief in a
eator god is rejected. The two main sects are named
om the dress of their monks, Svetambara ('white-
obed') and Digambara ('sky-clad' or naked). Jainism
ever spread beyond India: it is tolerant towards other
eligions, and is not evangelical. In India its followers
e mainly found in Gujarat and Maharashtra states.
lthough their relative size has been small throughout
story, the influence of the Jains on Indian culture and
ne continuity of their history have been such that they
e regarded as one of India's major religious traditions.
ahatma GANDHI's non-violent movements were
gnificantly influenced by the Jains. Jainism now
umbers some three million adherents.

aipur A former state in Rajasthan, north-west India. It
as a leading RAJPUT state from the 12th century. The
ty of Jaipur, built in 1727 by Raja Saiwai Jai Singh II (c.
99–1743) is renowned for its outstanding pink-
oloured palace. Its rajas held off Mogul interference by
dvantageous bargaining, but in the 18th century fell
ctim to MARATHA, and then British, expansion, finally
knowledging British paramountcy in 1818.

aja of Opobo (d. 1891) Nigerian merchant prince. A
ormer slave, he became head of the Anna Pepple
ading house at Bonny in the Niger Delta, acting as a
iddleman between the coastal markets and the
igerian interior. He established (1869) his own state at
pobo on the Gulf of Guinea. From here he was able to
revent rival supplies from reaching the coast. In 1873
ja was recognized as King of Opobo. In the 1880s Jaja
pposed increasing British influence in the area, and in
87 was deported by Britain to the West Indies.

amaica A Caribbean island country lying south of
uba.
Physical. Jamaica is about 235 km (146 miles) from
est to east and 80 km (50 miles) from north to south at
s widest point, the third largest island in the
aribbean. Along its spine is a range of limestone hills,
hich rises to the Blue Mountains in the east. Streams
ow both north and south, the northern rivers reaching
coast which is very beautiful, with palm-fringed
eaches and long, sandy bays.
Economy. Jamaica is a major producer of bauxite;
auxite and alumina dominate exports. Both agriculture
d industry are important, with sugar, bananas, and
offee the principal agricultural exports, and there is
so a developing manufacturing industry. Tourism is
a important source of foreign exchange.

History. Originally inhabited by Arawak Indians,
Jamaica was discovered by Columbus in 1494 and settled
by the Spanish in 1509. In 1655 it was captured by the
British and prospered as a BUCCANEER base. The
importation of slaves to work on sugar cane PLANTATIONS
made Jamaica the leading sugar producer of the 18th
century. Slavery was abolished in 1833 but this was
followed by economic depression. Many former slaves
rebelled against British colonial rule in 1865 but the
rebellion was ruthlessly suppressed by Governor Eyre. In
1866 Jamaica became a crown colony and representative
government gradually developed from 1884.
In the 1930s there was widespread rioting, as a result
of racial tension and economic depression, and in 1944
self-government, based on universal adult suffrage, was
granted. Economic recovery followed World War II. In
1958 Jamaica became a founding member of the
Federation of the WEST INDIES. When this collapsed, the
Jamaican Labour Party (JLP) under William A.
BUSTAMANTE negotiated independence as a dominion in
the COMMONWEALTH OF NATIONS. Administrations have
alternated between the JLP and PNP (People's National
Party), whose leader Michael Manley introduced many
social reforms in the 1970s. In 1980 the JLP returned to
office under Edward Seaga, whose conservative
economic policies failed to reverse economic decline.
The PNP returned to power in 1989 under Michael
Manley, an enthusiast for the CARIBBEAN COMMUNITY AND
COMMON MARKET. Inheriting both high inflation and rising
unemployment, his policy was to deregulate the
economy. This resulted in protests that the PNP had
betrayed its social democratic principles. Ill-health
obliged Manley to retire in March 1992. He was replaced
as Prime Minister and as leader of the PNP by Percival J.
Patterson, who despite his continuation of economic
austerity policies, boosted the government's popularity.
The general election called in 1993 was preceded by
violent clashes between rival party supporters; a
landslide victory for the PNP was disputed by the JLP,
amid allegations of fraud and thuggery involving police
members. The JLP boycotted the new parliament,
demanding electoral and police reforms, and in 1994 the
two parties agreed to suspend all general and municipal
elections pending electoral reform.

CAPITAL:	Kingston
AREA:	10,991 sq km (4,244 sq miles)
POPULATION:	2.505 million (1996)
CURRENCY:	1 Jamaican dollar = 100 cents
RELIGIONS:	Church of God 18.4%; non-religious or atheist 17.7%; Baptist 10.0%; Anglican 7.1%; Seventh-day Adventist 6.9%; Pentecostal 5.2%; Roman Catholic 5.0%; Rastafarian 5.0%
ETHNIC GROUPS:	Black 76.3%; Afro-European 15.1%; East Indian and Afro-East Indian 3.4%; White 3.2%; Chinese and Lebanese minorities
LANGUAGES:	English (official); English creole; Hindi; Chinese
INTERNATIONAL ORGANIZATIONS:	CARICOM; Commonwealth; Non-Aligned Movement; OAS; UN

James I (1394–1437) King of Scotland (1406–37). The
third son of ROBERT III, he was shipwrecked and held
captive in England from 1406 until his ransom was
arranged in 1423. His rule was firm and effective,
particularly once he had arrested most of his opponents

who had governed Scotland during his absence, but his policy of reducing the powers of the nobility and making more use of the Scottish Parliament ultimately led to a reaction. In February 1437 he was killed by Sir Robert Graham, leader of a conspiracy against him.

James I (1566–1625) King James VI of Scotland from 1567, King of England (1603–25). He succeeded ELIZABETH I of England, since she had never married and the TUDOR dynasty was ended. He was the son of MARY, Queen of Scots and Henry, Lord DARNLEY. As King of Scotland he survived several plots and assassination attempts, while he strengthened the power of the crown over Parliament, Kirk (Church of Scotland), and sectarian religious groups, and fostered good relations with England. As King of England, he lacked the shrewd judgement of his predecessor, his reign being marked by several errors of policy. He angered the Puritans by refusing to hear their demands at the HAMPTON COURT CONFERENCE and by his insistence on the maxim 'no bishop, no king' to counter their demands for the abolition of bishops, which put an end to their hopes of reform. His court was tainted by sexual and financial scandal and although CECIL attempted reform, the king's promotion of BUCKINGHAM from 1618 led him into costly and extravagant schemes that alienated Parliament. Although learned, he was tactless in his handling of Parliament, insisting repeatedly on his prerogatives as king. However the unsettled financial and religious position was his legacy from Elizabeth and it was an achievement that his reign was largely peaceful.

James I *James I of England (James VI of Scotland) with his wife, Queen Anne.*

James II (1430–60) King of Scotland (1437–60), son and successor of JAMES I. During his minority successive earls of Douglas vied for power, and when he began to reign in his own right the Douglases remained a threat to his authority. He improved the courts of justice and regulated the coinage. He was killed by an accidental cannon blast while leading a siege against Roxburgh Castle, held by the English.

James II (1633–1701) King of England and Scotland (1685–88), the second son of CHARLES I. As Duke of York he was Lord High Admiral in the second and third Anglo-Dutch Wars, during which the Dutch settlement of New Amsterdam was captured and renamed New York in his honour (1664). He became a Roman Catholic and married Mary of Modena, also a Roman Catholic, in 1673, resigning as admiral in that year under the TEST ACT; attempts were made to exclude him from the succession during the years 1679–81, but on the death of CHARLES II he ascended the throne without opposition. MONMOUTH'S REBELLION came early in his reign, and the BLOODY ASSIZES that punished it were resented. Within three years of his accession he had provoked the widespread opposition that culminated in the GLORIOUS REVOLUTION, which replaced him on the throne by William and Mary. He died in exile in France.

James III (1452–88) King of Scotland (1460–88), son and successor of JAMES II. He came to the throne aged nine and after his mother died in 1463 his rule was challenged by members of his family and their supporters from the nobility. He did not take control of his kingdom until 1469. In 1479 he imprisoned his brother, Alexander Stuart, Duke of Albany, who later led a rebellion against him. He was defeated and killed in battle by his own nobility, supported by his son (who succeeded him as James IV), at Sauchieburn, close to Bannockburn.

James IV (1473–1513) King of Scotland (1488–1513). An able and popular king, he was successful in restoring order to Scotland, quelling an uprising of discontented nobles, and improving the prosperity of the kingdom. He made peace with England by the Treaty of Ayton (1497–98), and married HENRY VII's daughter Margaret Tudor, which brought the STUART line to the English throne in 1603. He led his country into a disastrous war with Henry VIII of England and was himself killed at FLODDEN FIELD.

James V (1512–42) King of Scotland (1513–42). He succeeded his father James IV at the age of only two months. His mother, her husband, Archibald Angus, Earl of Douglas, and John Stuart, Duke of Albany, struggled for control of the kingdom during his minority. When he came to power he began to ally himself with France against his uncle HENRY VIII of England, and made diplomatic marriages to Madeleine, daughter of FRANCIS I of France (1536), and on her death to Mary of GUISE. His only child was a daughter, who succeeded him as MARY, Queen of Scots.

James, Jesse (Woodson) (1847–82) US outlaw. During the AMERICAN CIVIL WAR he joined the Quantrills Raiders supporting the CONFEDERACY forces. After the war he joined with his brother Frank (1843–1915) and the Younger brothers to form the most notorious band of outlaws in US history, specializing in bank and train

bberies. The reward offered for the James brothers
orrupted one of the gang, Robert Ford, who shot Jesse.
rank lived out his life in obscurity on a Missouri farm.

ameson raid (1895–96) An armed raid on the
ransvaal led by a British colonial administrator Dr
eander Starr Jameson, who planned to overthrow the
overnment of Paul KRUGER. Privately financed by RHODES,
  sought to take advantage of a rebellion of the
TLANDERS against the TRANSVAALERS, and to further
hodes' ambition for a united South Africa. Jameson's
nall band of volunteers was soon halted by the Boers,
nd Jameson himself captured and handed over to the
ritish for punishment. The episode contributed to Boer
islike for Britain. Rhodes was forced to resign as
remier of Cape Colony because of his knowledge of the
onspiracy. Jameson himself was tried in London and
entenced to imprisonment but was soon released. The
efeat of Jameson's raid prompted WILLIAM II of
ermany to congratulate the Boers in the famous
elegram to President KRUGER.

amestown A town in Virginia, USA; the first
ermanent English settlement in North America,
ounded by an expedition despatched by the Virginia
ompany from London in 1607. The site 64 km (40 miles)
p the James River was chosen mainly for strategic
easons, but the surrounding malarial swamp and
yphoid infected river water caused endemic illness.
nly John SMITH's determination saved the new outpost.
amestown was the seat of the colonial assembly from
519; it was burned in BACON'S REBELLION, after which
Villiamsburg became the effective capital.

anata Party Indian political organization. A grouping
f mostly right-wing Hindu political parties, it was
ased upon the Jana Sangh (People's Party, founded 1951).
he so-called Janata Front was a broad coalition formed
o oppose Indira GANDHI in 1975. The Janata Party proper
vas formed in 1977 as a coalition under Morarji Desai; it
von the 1977 election and formed a government that
ndured until the end of 1979. In 1989 an anti-Congress
ational Front, Janata Dal, was formed by V. P. Singh,
vho was briefly Prime Minister (1990); but the party
plit over the issue of the Untouchables (see CASTE
YSTEM), and the Congress (I) Party returned to power.

anissaries (Turkish, *yeni cheri*, 'new troops') An élite
orps of slave soldiers, bound to the service of the
TTOMAN sultans. They were originally raised from
risoners of war, but from the time of BAYEZID I
389–1403) they were largely recruited by means of the
evshirme ('gathering'), a levy of the fittest youths among
he sultan's non-Muslim subjects. Having been
onverted to Islam, most, after intensive training,
erved as foot soldiers, while the ablest passed into civil
dministration. Decimation in the great wars against
ersia and Austria (1578–1606) lowered the traditionally
igh quality of the intake and opened the corps to
1uslims. They exercised a powerful role in political life
ntil their abolition in 1826.

ansen, Cornelius Otto (1585–1638) Dutch bishop, the
ounder of the Catholic school of theology known as
ansenism. After studying at Louvain and Paris, he
ecame the director of a newly founded college at
ouvain (1617). In 1626–27 he publicly opposed the
esuits at Madrid, and in 1636 he was made Bishop of
pres. His ideal was the reform of Christian life

through a return to St AUGUSTINE OF HIPPO, and in 1628 he
began to write his *Augustinus*, published posthumously
in 1640. This work was condemned by the Sorbonne
(1649) and then by Pope Innocent X (1653). Although
Jansen himself insisted upon his Catholic orthodoxy, a
number of his tenets resembled those of CALVIN.
Jansenists suffered persecution in France during most
of the 18th century, but they were tolerated in the
Netherlands, and in 1723 the Dutch Jansenists
nominated a schismatic bishop of Utrecht. The best-
known Jansenist was the French writer Blaise PASCAL.

Japan (in Japanese, Nihon or Nippon) A country
occupying an archipelago off the coast of east Asia. It
stretches about 2,400 km (1,500 miles) from Hokkaido in
the north-east through Honshu, Shikoku, and Kyushu to
the Ryukyu Islands in the south-west. Japan is separated
from China to the south-west by the East China Sea,
from Siberia and Korea to the west by the Sea of Japan,
and from the islands of Sakhalin and the Kuriles to the
north and north-east by the Sea of Okhotsk and the
Nemuro Strait.

Physical. The deeply indented coastlines are
surrounded by many smaller islands, with the Inland
Sea forming an important constituent of the country.
The islands curve along the edge of the Eurasian plate,
one of the Earth's geologically most active zones,
creating almost perpetual earthquake and much
volcanic activity. Mountains cover two-thirds of Japan's
surface and the rivers are generally unsuited for
navigation. During the seasonal periods of heavy rainfall
and typhoons, flooding becomes a major problem.

Economy. The Japanese economy is the second largest
in the world and is still growing rapidly. Economic
growth has been built on a huge level of exports but as
the so-called 'tiger economies' of south-east Asia
continue to grow and Japanese labour costs increase, so
its regional economic preeminence is being challenged.

Japan leads the world in the manufacture of electrical
appliances and electronic equipment, which, along with
motor vehicles, iron, and steel, make up most of the
country's exports. The shipping and chemicals industries
are also important. The Tokyo stock market is one of
the world's foremost financial centres. There are gas
fields around the main island of Honshu, but Japan is
short of mineral and energy resources and is the world's
largest importer of oil. It has a substantial nuclear and
hydroelectric energy capacity. Only one-sixth of Japan's
land can be farmed or is habitable; a quarter of food
needs must be met by imports. Japan has invested
heavily overseas and contributed increasing amounts of
aid, often in the form of Japanese goods and services, to
developing countries. Friction between the USA and
Japan over trade issues – particularly Japan's trade
surplus with the USA eased slightly in the early 1990s as
a series of trade agreements were reached, improving
access to Japan's markets. However, talks to end the
dispute over the valuable sector of cars and components
failed and a trade war was narrowly avoided in 1995.

History. Originally inhabited by native Ainu, the
Japanese themselves are thought to be descendants of
people who migrated from various areas of mainland
Asia. By the 5th century AD the YAMATO clan loosely
controlled much of Japan and began to establish
imperial rule. The developing state was much influenced
by Chinese culture. BUDDHISM was introduced in the 6th
century and, after a brief conflict, coexisted with the

Japanese religion, SHINTO. In the 7th century Prince SHOTOKU was partially successful in establishing an administrative system based on that of SUI China. However, by the 9th century the FUJIWARA family had gained control over the imperial court and its power was undermined.

The growing strength of feudal lords and of Buddhist monasteries resulted in civil war for most of the 12th century, the ultimate victor being MINAMOTO YORITOMO, who in 1192 became the first SHOGUN and established a military administration. From then effective power lay with the shogun rather than the emperor. Yoritomo's KAMAKURA shogunate was replaced in 1333 by the ASHIKAGA shogunate, but its rule was one of prolonged civil strife. In the late 16th century three warriors, ODA NOBUNAGA, HIDEYOSHI, and TOKUGAWA IEYASU broke the power of the feudal lords (DAIMYO), and Ieyasu's TOKUGAWA shogunate provided stable but repressive rule until the restoration of the emperor in 1868.

Europeans had begun to trade with Japan in 1542 and Catholic missionaries, including Matteo RICCI, made numerous converts. The Tokugawa shogunate excluded all foreigners in 1639, except for a few Dutch and Chinese at Nagasaki, and proscribed Christianity. During the 18th and 19th centuries the wealth and power of merchants began to increase and Japan extended its influence over the northern island of Hokkaido.

In the first half of the 19th century Tokugawa power was gradually undermined by economic problems, insurrection, and the arrival of Western trading and naval expeditions, most notably those of the US Commodore PERRY (1853–54). The shogunate's failure to resist foreign penetration served as the catalyst for armed opposition, which in 1868 finally succeeded in replacing the shogunate with a new regime led formally by the emperor Meiji (MEIJI RESTORATION). In the succeeding decades feudalism was dismantled and a centralized state created that was dedicated to the rapid modernization of society and industrialization. Japan's new strength brought victory in the SINO-JAPANESE WAR (1894–95) and the RUSSO-JAPANESE WAR (1904–05), and established it as the dominant power in north-east Asia.

Japan fought on the Allied side in World War I, but thereafter its expansionist tendencies led to a deterioration in its diplomatic position, most notably vis-à-vis the USA. In the inter-war period, expansionist-militarist interests gradually gained power within the country, and, after the occupation of Manchuria (1931) and the creation of MANCHUKUO (1932), full-scale war with China was only a matter of time. The Sino-Japanese War finally broke out in 1937, and, having already allied itself with Germany and Italy in the ANTI-COMINTERN PACT, Japan finally entered World War II with a surprise attack on the US fleet at PEARL HARBOR in December 1941. Having initially overrun the colonial empires of south-east Asia at great speed, Japanese forces were eventually held and gradually driven back (PACIFIC CAMPAIGNS). In September 1945, after the dropping of two atomic bombs, Japan was forced to surrender and accept occupation (see JAPAN, OCCUPATION OF). A new JAPANESE CONSTITUTION was introduced, and full independence was formally returned in 1952.

From the 1960s onwards Japan embarked on another period of rapid industrial development, to become one of the major economic powers in the world. Its relations with China and south-east Asian countries improved, but the large imbalance in its favour in its trade with Western nations (particularly the USA), resulted in economic instability. The LIBERAL DEMOCRATIC PARTY (LDP) held office continually throughout these years, surviving numerous financial scandals. In the early 1990s a further series of scandals threatened the stability of the government, led by Kiichi Miyazawa, while Japan's economy suffered from the global recession. In 1993 the government was defeated in a vote of no confidence and a general election was called in which the LDP split and lost its overall majority. The opposition formed a seven-party coalition and ejected the LDP from office for the first time since its formation in 1955. Three short-lived coalitions governed during the period 1993–95. In January 1995 a large earthquake caused extensive damage to the city of Kobe, killing more than 5,000 and leaving 310,000 homeless. In 1995 the main opposition party, the Social Democratic Party of Japan, disbanded and in early 1996 the LDP's Ryutaro Hashimoto became Prime Minister of a new coalition. To mark the 50th anniversary of the end of the Pacific War, the government agreed to issue an official apology for Japan's actions during the conflict. A large economic stimulation package was also unveiled in an attempt to bring the economy out of its longest recession since 1945. Following the inconclusive general election of October 1996 Hashimoto formed a minority LDP government.

CAPITAL:	Tokyo
AREA:	377,835 sq km (145,883 sq miles)
POPULATION:	125.612 million (1996)
CURRENCY:	Yen
RELIGIONS:	Joint adherents of Shinto and Buddhism 80.0%; Christian 1.2%
ETHNIC GROUPS:	Japanese 99.4%; Korean 0.5%; Chinese and other 0.1%
LANGUAGES:	Japanese (official)
INTERNATIONAL ORGANIZATIONS:	OECD; UN; Colombo Plan

Japan, Occupation of (1945–52) The Allied occupation of Japan after World War II. After Japan's unconditional surrender on 2 September 1945, it came under the control of the Allied forces of occupation led by General Douglas MACARTHUR in his capacity as Supreme Commander of the Allied Powers (SCAP). Although technically backed by an 11-nation Far Eastern Commission and a Four-Power Council (Britain, China, USA, and the Soviet Union), the military occupation was entirely dominated by the USA, with policy remaining in the hands of MacArthur and, after his removal in April 1951, of his successor General Matthew Ridgway. US occupation policy had two main goals, the demilitarization of Japan and the establishment of democratic institutions and ideals. The first objective was achieved through the complete demobilization of the army and navy and the destruction of their installations, backed up by the peace clause of the new JAPANESE CONSTITUTION. The second was much more difficult, and although the new Constitution was in operation before the occupation was formally terminated in 1952, the real impact of US-inspired reforms on Japanese socio-political institutions has been questioned. Although a few ZAIBATSU were dissolved, most survived. At the same time close links with the USA resulted in rapid economic recovery and expansion.

Japanese Constitution (1947) A constitution introduced during the Allied occupation after World War II, with the emphasis placed on the dismantling of militarism and the extension of individual liberties. Drafted under US influence, it was finally adopted on 3 May 1947. The constitution left the emperor as head of state but stripped him of governing power, vesting legislative authority in a bicameral Diet, the lower House of Representatives (originally 466, now 512 seats) being elected for four years and the upper House of Councillors (252 seats) for six (half at a time at three-year intervals). Executive power is vested in the cabinet, which is headed by a Prime Minister and is responsible to the Diet. The constitution specifically renounces war but has been interpreted as allowing self-defence: accordingly, Self Defence Forces have been created, although defence expenditure remains low by Western standards. In 1992 legislation was finally passed allowing Japan's Self Defence Forces to serve overseas in UN peace-keeping operations.

Japan-United States Security Treaty (1951) A defence agreement between Japan and the USA. Negotiated as part of the package of arrangements attending the formal return of Japanese independence after defeat in World War II, the treaty established the USA as the effective arbiter of Japan's defence interests, granting it a large military presence in Japanese territory. Renewal of the treaty in 1960, as a Mutual Security Treaty, with revised terms, produced a major political crisis in Japan: when renewal next became due in 1970, both countries agreed to a process of automatic extension on the condition that revocation could be achieved on one year's notice by either.

Jaurès, Jean (1859–1914) French socialist leader. After entering parliament in 1885, he led a campaign on behalf of DREYFUS and against ANTI-SEMITISM that strengthened socialist support in France. In 1905 he formed the United Socialist Party, which put pressure on the radical governments of the day to implement reforms for the working class. He opposed militarism, but tried to reconcile socialist internationalism and French patriotism. He was assassinated by a French nationalist in 1914.

Java One of the Sunda islands, now the heartland of Indonesia, between the larger island of Sumatra, to the west and the much smaller one of Bali.
   History. In the early centuries AD Hindu principalities emerged on Java. About 700 Buddhism briefly displaced Hinduism in central Java; Borobudur, said to be the largest Buddhist temple in the world, a lasting monument to this period, was constructed by the Sailendra dynasty that ruled an area around Jogjakarta. Hinduism then re-established itself under a succession of kingdoms, the last of which was MAJAPAHIT (1298–1520). During the 16th century Islam started to spread throughout Java. In 1619 the Dutch captured Jakarta on the north coast, renamed it Batavia after the Batavii, the Celtic tribe who lived in the Netherlands in Roman times, and made it the headquarters of the DUTCH EAST INDIA COMPANY. In 1628 and 1629 Sultan Agung (1613–46), the ruler of the kingdom of Mataram, besieged it unsuccessfully and the Dutch consolidated their position. By the mid-18th century the whole island was under direct or indirect Dutch rule. (See INDONESIA.)

Java man Name given to fossilized bones found at Trinil on the River Solo in Java. Originally classified as *Pithecanthropus erectus* ('erect ape-man'), these remains are now included within the species *Homo erectus*. Their date is uncertain but is probably 750,000–500,000 years ago. Subsequent finds of hominids, probably also *Homo erectus*, in Java were made at Sangiran and Modjokerto. Some of these may be rather older (up to 1.3 million years ago) than the Trinil remains.

Java War (1825–30) War fought against the Dutch and their Javanese allies in central Java, led by DIPONEGORO. The uprising proved difficult to suppress until the adoption by the Dutch of a system of rural strong points (*bèntèng*) and the use of mobile columns. Deprived of peasant support, Diponegoro was forced to negotiate with the Dutch and, when he refused to renounce his claim to the title of sultan and the status of Protector of Religion (*Panatagama*) in Java, he was arrested and banished. Thus ended the last and most serious challenge to the extension of Dutch rule in Java.

Jay, John (1745–1829) American statesman and jurist. He was a member of the first and second CONTINENTAL CONGRESSES, became Chief Justice of New York, a member of Congress, Minister to Spain (1780–82), and a member of the delegation that negotiated peace with Britain (1783). A conservative Federalist, he was Secretary of Foreign Affairs (1784–90), before becoming Chief Justice of the USA (1789–95). As special envoy to England he negotiated the Jay Treaty (1794) to settle outstanding differences resulting from the War of Independence. It enforced the terms of the Peace of PARIS (1783) and ordered the British to leave their trading post in the north-west of the country. The British lost control of the lucrative FUR TRADE and ceded a share in the trade with the West Indies to the Americans.

Jefferson, Thomas (1743–1826) Third President of the USA (1801–09). He was a delegate to the House of Burgesses (1769–75) and to the CONTINENTAL CONGRESS (1775–76). He drafted the Declaration of Independence, was active in Virginia during the War of INDEPENDENCE, and was governor of the state (1779–81). A slave owner who favoured gradual emancipation, he never felt able to implement such a policy. After service as US minister to France (1785–89), he was WASHINGTON's first Secretary of State. His opposition to HAMILTON's economic policies led to his resignation in 1794. He later became leader of the Democratic-Republican Party and was Vice-President under John ADAMS before becoming President in 1801. His administration was marked by retrenchment and reduction in the scale of government itself, but also by the TRIPOLITAN WAR, which ended tribute payment to Barbary pirates, the LOUISIANA PURCHASE, the LEWIS and Clark expedition (the first overland expedition to the Pacific Coast of America), and the Embargo Act in defence of the US neutral rights. Jefferson, who believed in the virtues of an agrarian republic and a weak central government, has been a uniquely influential figure in the evolution of the US political tradition.

Jeffreys of Wem, George Jeffreys, 1st Baron (1645–89) English judge and Lord Chief Justice. He presided at the trials of the RYE HOUSE PLOT conspirators, of those implicated in the POPISH PLOT, and of Richard BAXTER, but he is chiefly associated with the BLOODY

ASSIZES (1685) that followed MONMOUTH'S REBELLION. Contemporary reports of his brutality may have been prejudiced, but he certainly browbeat witnesses and his sentencing of the 80-year-old Alice Lisle to be burnt for treason caused widespread revulsion. Following the GLORIOUS REVOLUTION he was imprisoned, but died before proceedings could be taken against him.

Jehangir JAHANGIR.

Jellicoe, John Rushworth, 1st Earl (1859–1935) British admiral. He commanded the Grand Fleet at the inconclusive Battle of JUTLAND (1916) and then became First Sea Lord with an influence on strategic planning. He implemented the CONVOY SYSTEM introduced by LLOYD GEORGE, but was dismissed from office in December 1917. After the war he was appointed governor-general of New Zealand (1920–24).

Jena, Battle of (14 October 1806) A battle between the Prussian army, led by Prince Hohenlohe, and NAPOLEON'S French forces, fought near the German town of that name. The Prussians underestimated the size of the French force and were comprehensively defeated. The defeat by DAVOUT of the Duke of Brunswick's main Prussian army at Auerstädt on the same day left the road to Berlin unprotected. After its double defeat Prussia embarked on a series of military, political, and social reforms in order to be able to challenge the French.

Jenkins's Ear, War of (1739–41) A war between Britain and Spain that broke out as a result of Britain's trade with South America. The Peace of UTRECHT, which gave the British South Sea Company a limited trade monopoly with the Spanish American colonies, caused general friction, but the main trouble-makers were illicit traders who defied both the Company and the Spanish government. In 1737 British merchants were protesting at a tightening-up of Spanish control. The Spanish government and WALPOLE both wanted peace but Walpole's enemies made it an excuse to attack him: a merchant captain named Jenkins was produced to tell a story of torture and the loss of an ear. Popular clamour was such that Walpole consented reluctantly to declare war. Admiral VERNON captured Porto Bello and France sent two squadrons to the West Indies. In 1740 the war merged into that of the AUSTRIAN SUCCESSION.

Jeremiah (born c. 640 BC) Hebrew prophet. He was called to prophesy during the reign of King JOSIAH. As Babylonian power increased, he maintained that resistance was useless and that the fall of Jerusalem was inevitable, views popular neither with the king nor with the people. After the fall of Jerusalem in 586 BC, he remained in the city until taken to Egypt by Jewish dissidents. His messages, always intensely personal, were preserved and edited by his scribe-secretary Baruch.

Jericho An ancient city, now in the Palestinian-administered West Bank of the River Jordan. A well-watered oasis near the Jordan river-crossing at the head of the Dead Sea, it was of strategic importance, located at the junction of the trade routes of antiquity. It was occupied from c. 9000 BC and is one of the oldest continuously inhabited cities in the world. The principal mound, one of the best known of all Near Eastern TELLS, accumulated over 15 m (50 feet) of deposit, even though the later occupation levels, from 2000 to 500 BC, have been swept off the summit by erosion. The most

interesting layers are of the pre-pottery NEOLITHIC period c. 7000 BC, when Jericho was already a walled settlement of some 4 ha (10 acres). Little remains of the late Bronze Age period, the probable date of its destruction by Joshua recorded in the Old Testament of the Bible. Jericho was granted Palestinian self-rule in 1994, as part of the 1993 peace agreement between Israel and the PALESTINE LIBERATION ORGANIZATION.

Jeroboam I (d. c. 901 BC) First king of the northern kingdom of ISRAEL (c. 922–c. 901 BC). After SOLOMON'S death, his successor REHOBOAM failed to gain the support of the northern part of Israel, which seceded under the leadership of Jeroboam. He then extended and strengthened the kingdom, taking advantage of Syrian and Assyrian weakness. He made the kingdom prosperous, but the prophet Amos spoke against his oppression and injustice. He was also criticized for encouraging the sanctuaries at Dan and Bethel to rival the Temple at Jerusalem.

Jerome, St (Eusebius Sophronius Hieronymus) (c. 342–420) Christian writer and translator of the Bible into Latin. During a period spent as a hermit in the Syrian desert he learned Hebrew. From 382 he was Papal Secretary for two years during which he began his Bible translation. When the pope died he settled in Bethlehem where he completed his translation, known as 'The Vulgate' ('popular tongue'), and founded a religious house. He was a vigorous disputer, attacking among others Pelagius (PELAGIANISM) and AUGUSTINE OF HIPPO. He advocated asceticism, notably celibacy.

Jerusalem A holy city to Jews, Christians, and Muslims. It was originally a Jebusite settlement, captured by DAVID c. 1000 BC. Solomon's Temple, the central shrine of Judaism, destroyed by NEBUCHADNEZZAR II in 586 BC, was rebuilt in 516 BC and even more magnificently by HEROD the Great. Jerusalem was razed by the Romans in 70 AD and the Temple destroyed; in 135 they built the city of Aelia Capitolina on its site. St PAUL regarded it as the home of the original Christian congregation, headed until his death in 62 by James, the apostle of JESUS CHRIST. Constantine marked its significance by building the Church of the Holy Sepulchre (c. 335) over the supposed tomb of Christ. Muslim rule from 637 was symbolized by the building of the Dome of the Rock, the city's holiest Muslim Shrine, in 691. The Christian knights of the CRUSADES controlled the city from 1099 to 1187, when it fell to SALADIN. The Ottoman Turks conquered Jerusalem in 1516 and Suleiman the Magnificent built the walls still enclosing the old city in 1538. During World War I the British took over Jerusalem (1917) and held it under the Palestine mandate from 1922 to 1948. When the State of Israel was declared in 1948, Jerusalem was divided between Israel and Jordan. Jerusalem was declared the capital of Israel in 1950, although this is not internationally recognized. During the SIX-DAY WAR in 1967, the Arab sector of Jerusalem was taken over by Israel, which has retained the entire city ever since, the status of occupied East Jerusalem remains a major issue in Israeli-Palestinian negotiations. The city's unique historical importance to three religions has made it a constant focus of religious and ethnic unrest.

Jervis, John, 1st Earl of St Vincent (1735–1823) British admiral. He served with KEPPEL and HOWE during the American War of INDEPENDENCE. At the outbreak of the French Revolutionary War in 1793 he captured Martinique and Guadeloupe in the Caribbean. His greatest victory was his destruction of the Spanish fleet at Cape St Vincent in 1797, where NELSON was one of his captains. He was First Lord of the Admiralty from 1801 to 1804.

Jesuits The Society of Jesus (SJ), a Roman Catholic religious order founded by St Ignatius LOYOLA (1534), and approved by Pope Paul III (1540). Its original aim was to convert Muslims to Christianity but it acted to foster reform within the Roman Catholic Church, especially in the face of the challenge presented by the Protestant REFORMATION.

By the early 17th century Jesuits had contributed incalculably to the success of the COUNTER-REFORMATION, distinguished themselves as educationists, and established missions in India, China (where Matteo RICCI gained the confidence of the Ming emperor, Wanli), Africa, and South America; but before the end of the century they had run into serious opposition within the Roman Catholic Church. The Dominicans, Jansenists, and others accused them of laxity in their ethical code and condemned their incorporation of local customs into their Christian teachings. Their opponents secured their expulsion from France (1764) and Spain (1767), and in 1773 they were suppressed by Pope Clement XIV. Jesuits continued to teach in Germany and Austria and also survived in England. The order was formally restored by Pope Pius VII in 1814.

The Jesuits remain a powerful intellectual body. Governed by a General Congregation, they elect a Superior General with life tenure. A special vow of obedience to the pope is taken. Jesuits have traditionally engaged in international missionary and educational work. Since the Second Vatican Council (1962–65), they have played a leading role in Roman Catholic reforms.

Jesus Christ (c. 6 BC–c. 30 AD) The central figure of CHRISTIANITY, believed by his followers to be the incarnate Son of God. In Christian belief the man Jesus Christ is fully divine, of one essence with God the Father and God the Holy Spirit (the doctrine of the TRINITY). The Gospels of the BIBLE are the main sources of information about Jesus. According to them, Jesus was born at Bethlehem to Mary, by tradition a virgin, in the reign of Augustus Caesar. He was brought up at Nazareth in Galilee and received a traditional Jewish education. He may have been a carpenter, the trade of Mary's husband, Joseph. About 27 AD he was baptized in the River Jordan by JOHN THE BAPTIST and shortly thereafter started his public ministry of preaching and healing (with reported miracles). Through his popular style of preaching, with the use of parables and proverbs, he proclaimed the imminent approach of the Kingdom of God and the ethical and religious qualities demanded of those who were to enjoy it (summarized in the Sermon on the Mount). His interpretation of Jewish law did not reject ceremonial observances but placed them in subordination to the fundamental principles of charity, sincerity, and humility. From among his followers in Galilee he selected 12 DISCIPLES to be his personal companions and to teach his message. His preaching brought him into conflict with the Jewish authorities. In the knowledge of this he travelled to Jerusalem where he was betrayed by Judas Iscariot, one

of his disciples, and condemned to death by the Sanhedrin, the highest Jewish court. Jesus then appeared before the Roman governor, Pontius PILATE, who sentenced him to death by crucifixion. His followers claimed that after three days the tomb in which his body had been placed was empty and that he had been seen alive in a glorified but recognizable form. Belief in his resurrection from the dead spread among his followers, who saw in this proof that he was the Messiah or Christ ('anointed one' in Hebrew and Greek respectively), the fulfilment of the hopes of Israel (as recorded in the Old Testament) and of all men. His followers started to form Christian communities around Jerusalem from which grew the CHRISTIAN CHURCH. The compassion he displayed in life to the poor and lowly is seen as the pattern of Christian conduct, and his sacrifice of his life is the core of the doctrine of atonement, by which God redeems humanity from sin. The drama of his life, suffering, death, and resurrection lies at the heart of Christian ritual and belief.

Jewel, John (1522–71) Bishop of Salisbury, one of the key figures in the early ANGLICAN CHURCH. He came from a Devonshire family, and came into contact with Protestantism at Oxford University. In the reign of MARY I, he fled abroad in 1555, but returned at the accession of ELIZABETH I and was consecrated bishop in 1560. His best-known work was the *Apology for the Church of England* (1562) in which he justified the Anglican Church as a true Church, not a mere compromise between Catholicism and extreme Protestantism.

Jewish people A people descended from the ancient Israelites, whether residing in modern Israel or, as part of the DIASPORA throughout the world. During the EXILE (597–538 BC) following the Babylonian conquest, their religion (JUDAISM) developed from a sacrificial temple cult into an elaborate code for daily living that became the basis for communal identity. The revolt of the MACCABEES in 167 BC showed their determination to preserve that identity, which survived the Roman destruction of the Temple in 70 AD and of JERUSALEM in 135 AD. They were subsequently dispersed throughout the Roman empire.

During the Middle Ages, they suffered much discrimination at the hands of Christian society and often welcomed ARAB conquests that brought greater toleration. In Spain and Cairo they prospered both materially and intellectually. In Christendom, they were free to engage in usury, a sin for Christians, and were herded into ghettos. Though they were tolerated for their usefulness, they suffered periodic persecution. Having been expelled from Spain in 1492, the Sephardim, speaking Ladino, a Spanish dialect, found refuge in north Africa, the Levant, the Ottoman Empire, and Italy. The Ashkenazim, speaking Yiddish, a variant of German, established themselves in north-west and eastern Europe, greatly assisting the economic development of Germany and Romania. Secularization of political life in western Europe enabled them to gain civil liberties from 1789 onwards.

It is estimated that there are today some 15 million Jews worldwide, with about 40% in the USA, 20% in ISRAEL, 12% in the republics of the former Soviet Union, and significant numbers in Argentina, Brazil, Canada, France, South Africa, and the UK. The Falasha, a people of Ethiopia, are also recognized as Jewish. A tiny Jewish community in Mali was discovered in 1996: although they had been forced to stop practising Judaism at the end of the 15th century they have retained Jewish names and symbols. Mainly city-dwellers in their recent history, many Jews live where they do today owing to mass emigration to escape ANTI-SEMITISM. This found its most violent expression in the Nazi HOLOCAUST of World War II, when an estimated 6 million Jews were murdered. More recently, large numbers of Russian Jews have emigrated to Israel, following the relaxation of Soviet emigration laws. However, in most societies Jews are now more assimilated than ever before, although retaining their cultural and religious identity; they retain prominence far beyond their numerical significance in world political, artistic, and economic affairs.

Jewish identity today is based more on a sense of shared history than ethnic or linguistic attributes. A common religious faith is no longer a unifying factor, with growing secularism (particularly in the West) on the one hand, and increased sectarian division on the other. ORTHODOX JEWS, for example, do not recognize many of the other branches of Judaism, some of whom they regard as idol-worshippers, and many deplore the secularism of ZIONISM.

Jewish Revolt A serious nationalist uprising led by the ZEALOTS against Roman rule (66–70 AD). In response VESPASIAN invaded Palestine with 60,000 troops and by 68 the rebels were confined to the Jerusalem area. After Vespasian's deposition in the civil wars of 68–69, his son Titus besieged the city, which fell district by district, the Temple being destroyed. Prisoners were taken to Rome and used as slave labour to build the COLOSSEUM. The last insurgents held out at MASADA until 73. In 132–35 BAR COCHBA led another revolt, which ended with the sack of Bethar and Cochba's death.

Jiang Jiehi CHIANG KAI-SHEK.

Jiangxi Soviet A Chinese communist rural base formed in 1931. Under KUOMINTANG attack in 1927, some communists moved to the countryside, maintaining their strength through guerrilla warfare in remote mountain regions. The group led by MAO ZEDONG, which first established itself on the Hunan–Jiangxi border, merged with a group led by ZHU DE, and the First National Congress of the Chinese Soviet Republic was held in November 1931. Four nationalist 'Encirclement Campaigns' were thwarted by guerrilla tactics between December 1930 and early 1933, but a fifth, beginning in October 1933, forced the evacuation of the Soviet and the commencement of the LONG MARCH a year later. Many communist policies, including land reform, were first tried out in the Jiangxi Soviet which, at its height, had a population of some nine million.

Jiang Zemin (1926–) Chinese Communist politician, President of the People's Republic of China from 1993, Chairman of the Central Military Commission from 1990, and General Secretary of the Chinese Communist Party from 1992. Jiang Zemin studied as an engineer, worked in several factories, including an automobile plant in Moscow, and served as a diplomat before being appointed a member of the Politburo in 1967. An economic reformer, but conservative on questions of internal reform, he was appointed General Secretary of

the Communist Party after his predecessor, the liberal Zhao Ziyang, had lost favour following the massacre of pro-democracy protestors in Tiananmen Square in 1989.

jihad An important concept in Islam, usually translated from the Arabic as 'holy war', but literally meaning 'struggle'. One of the basic duties of a Muslim, prescribed both by the KORAN and by tradition, is to struggle against external threats to the vigour of the Islamic community and also against personal resistance to the rules of divine law within oneself. Jihad is in theory controlled by the strict laws of war in Islam, which prescribe conditions under which war may be declared, usually against an enemy who inhibits the observance of the faith. In practice it has often been used by ambitious Muslim rulers to cloak political aims with religious respectability. Famous jihads include the early ARAB conquests, resistance to the Crusades, and the conquests of the Hausa reformer, UTHMAN DAN FODIO in northern Nigeria in the early 19th century. Those who die fighting in a jihad are accorded a MARTYR's place in heaven. In recent years, the concept of jihad has played a significant role in ISLAMIC FUNDAMENTALISM and revivalism, justifying political violence or TERRORISM.

'Jim Crow' laws The former US discriminatory statutes against Black people. 'Jim Crow', as a synonym for Black people, derives from the minstrel show of that name in about 1828. Applied to legislation, it distinguishes a body of US state laws, enacted between 1881 and 1907, that established racial segregation in respect of public transport, schools, restaurants and hotels, theatres, and penal and charitable institutions. This condition was not effectively challenged until after World War II, by which time racial barriers had been eroded.

Jin (Chin) (1126–1234) A dynasty that governed Manchuria, part of Mongolia, and much of northern China. It was founded by the Juchen, nomad huntsmen, who came from around the Amur and Sungari rivers. They were ancestors of the MANCHUS. When the Northern SONG set out to overthrow the LIAO, to whom they were tributary, they allied with the Juchen, hoping to play off one alien people against another. The latter, however, once having conquered the Liao, sacked the Song capital, Kaifeng, in 1126. The Song retreated south, establishing their new capital at Xingsai (Hangzhou).

The Juchen were in time tamed by their Chinese subjects, who far outnumbered them. Their frontier with Southern Song was stabilized. Jin emperors studied the Chinese classics and wrote poetry in Chinese. Their nomad vigour was sapped by a sedentary life. By 1214 much of their territory, including Beijing, their central capital, was in GENGHIS KHAN's hands. The dynasty survived, ruling from Kaifeng, until a final Mongol onslaught 20 years later.

Jin, Western WESTERN JIN.

jingoism A mood of inflated patriotism. The term originated in 1878, when Russian successes in a war against the OTTOMAN EMPIRE had created at the Treaty of San Stefano a Bulgaria that Britain regarded as a threat to its Eastern interests; a popular music-hall song of the time began with the lines: 'We don't want to fight, but by Jingo if we do; We've got the ships, we've got the men, we've got the money too!' Strong anti-Russian feeling developed in Britain, where DISRAELI called up reserves for army service and war-fever gripped the country.

Jinnah, Muhammad Ali (1876–1948) Founder of Pakistan. He entered Indian politics as a strong supporter of the moderates in CONGRESS and as a proponent of Hindu-Muslim unity. In 1916 he was one of the principal architects of the Congress League Lucknow Pact, in which Congress conceded that Muslims should have adequate legislative representation. After 1919 he became increasingly disillusioned with GANDHI's leadership of Congress and in 1930 he went to London. Returning to India in 1934 he led the MUSLIM LEAGUE in the 1937 elections. Thereafter he devoted his energies to extending the hold of the Muslim League over the Muslims of British India; in 1945–46 the Muslim League won an overwhelming victory in Muslim seats, confirming Jinnah's claim to speak for Indian Muslims. He also led his party to espouse the demand for an independent Muslim state of Pakistan (Lahore 1940). In 1946–47 his determined rejection of attempts to find a compromise led to the partitioning of India and the creation of the state of Pakistan, of which he became the first governor-general (1947–48) and President of its constituent assembly.

Joachim of Fiore (c. 1132–1202) Italian mystic. He was the abbot of the Cistercian monastery of Corazzo in Italy, but left in 1189 to found a new reformed community at San Giovanni, in Fiore, which received papal sanction in 1196. From this developed the small but for a time very influential Florensian order. Joachim's work, *Concordia Novi*, claimed that there are three ages of creation: that of God the Father was past, that of the Son was drawing to a close, and that of the Holy Spirit was imminent.

Joanna the Mad (1479–1555) Nominal Queen of Castile (from 1504) and of Aragon (from 1516). She was the daughter of FERDINAND V and ISABELLA of Spain and the wife of PHILIP IV of Burgundy. After Philip's death in 1506 she became insane. In 1509 she retired to Tordesillas, accompanied by Philip's embalmed corpse. Her sons later became the emperors CHARLES V and FERDINAND I.

Joan of Arc, St (c. 1412–31) French heroine, sometimes called the 'Maid of Orleans'. The daughter of prosperous peasants, from the age of 13 she heard mysterious voices that she identified as the urgings of Saints Michael, Margaret, and Catherine. They insisted she help the French forces who, in 1429, were engaged in defending Orleans against English troops. A local commander was convinced of her claims, as was the dauphin. Given command, she carried out her mission of relieving Orleans and crowning the dauphin, Charles VII, at Reims Cathedral. This was a turning point in the HUNDRED YEARS WAR. The jealousy of rival advisers, and doubts over her military skills, reduced her influence. Wounded and defeated at Paris, she was captured by the Burgundians in 1430, sold to the English, and tried as a witch. She was burnt at Rouen in May 1431, but an ecclesiastical court reversed the guilty verdict in 1455 and she was canonized in 1920.

Jodhpur A city in north-west India, from 1459 to 1947 the capital of the RAJPUT Princely State of the same name. Formerly known as Marwar, the state had existed since the early 13th century, but reached its peak after the construction in 1459 of a new capital, named after its founder, Raja Rao Jodha. Jodhpur occupies a magnificent site, its red sandstone fortress commanding the city from a rocky outcrop. Despite Mogul invasions in the 16th and 17th centuries, its rajas maintained their independence, but fell under MARATHA control in the 18th century. The state became part of Rajasthan in 1947.

Jodl, Alfred (1890–1946) German Nazi general. Throughout World War II he was chief of the Armed Forces' Operations Staff, and was Hitler's closest adviser on strategic questions. He was executed as a war criminal after the NUREMBERG TRIALS. His diaries reveal his complicity in many of Hitler's war crimes, counselling terror BOMBING OFFENSIVES on British cities and signing orders to execute prisoners-of-war.

Joffre, Joseph Jacques Césaire (1852–1931) Marshal of France and French commander-in-chief on the WESTERN FRONT (1914–16). As chief of the general staff (1911) he had devised Plan XVII to meet a German invasion. Its effectiveness was proved in the first Battle of the MARNE (1914), which frustrated German hopes of a swift victory. As commander-in-chief of all French armies (1915), he took responsibility for French unpreparedness at Verdun (1916) and resigned.

John (1167–1216) King of England (1199–1216). He was the youngest son of Henry II, and succeeded his brother Richard I, supplanting Prince Arthur of Brittany. He was nicknamed John 'Lackland' because, unlike his elder brothers, he did not receive lands from his father. With Richard's accession (1189) John received the earldom of Gloucester, but during Richard's absences on Crusade intrigued against him with PHILIP II of France.

John's reign was marked by the effects of spiralling inflation, which forced him to exploit all possible means of raising the royal revenues. The first crisis of the reign was the loss (1206–14) to Philip II of royal and baronial lands in Normandy, Anjou, Maine, and Brittany. The second crisis arose from his refusal to recognize LANGTON as Archbishop of Canterbury, which led to John's excommunication and England being placed under papal interdict (1208–14). The final crisis reflected baronial discontent with John's financial policies and arbitrary style of government. John's opponents presented him with a formal statement of his obligations in the form of MAGNA CARTA (1215). His repudiation of it led to the first BARONS' WAR, which only ended with his death.

John I (the Great) (1357–1433) King of PORTUGAL (1385–1433), the illegitimate son of Pedro I. He led nationalist sympathizers against the CASTILIANS, who supported Queen Eleanor, his rival. Defeating their invasion he went on to ally with England (through his marriage to Philippa, daughter of John of GAUNT) and to encourage African and Western exploration. His reign was the start of Portugal's period of colonial and maritime expansion; his sons, including HENRY THE NAVIGATOR, consolidated his achievements.

John II (the Perfect) (1455–95) King of Portugal (1481–95). He destroyed his rival, the Duke of Braganza in 1483, and crushed a conspiracy led by his brother-in-law in 1484. He sponsored African and American exploration, and negotiated the Treaty of TORDESILLAS, which divided the lands of the New World between Spain and Portugal.

John III (the Pious) (1502–57) King of Portugal (1521–57), grandson of John II. He married CHARLES V's sister and Charles married John's sister to create the HABSBURG claim to the Portuguese throne. He encouraged Portuguese settlement in Brazil, claimed the Moluccas, traded with Siam, and in 1535 conquered the Indian island of Diu. He was a fanatical Catholic noted for his sponsorship of the INQUISITION and the JESUITS, who went as missionaries to Brazil. Agricultural decline and falling population overshadowed the end of his reign.

John IV (the Fortunate) (1605–1656) King of Portugal (1640–56). The founder of the Braganza dynasty, he expelled a Spanish usurper and proclaimed himself king in 1640. He defeated the Spanish at Montijo in 1644, drove the Dutch out of Brazil in 1654, and generally restored Portugal's international position.

John VI (1769–1826) King of Portugal (1816–26). The son of Maria I and Peter III, he took over the control of the government in 1792 from his mother, who had become insane, and assumed the title of regent in 1799. A repressive monarch, he was submissive to Napoleon, who nevertheless forced him into exile in BRAZIL in 1807. In 1816 he was recognized as King of Portugal but continued to live in Brazil until 1822, when he returned to accept the role of a 'constitutional monarch'. In the same year he overcame a rebellion by his son Dom Miguel. In 1825 he recognized his other son, Dom Pedro, as emperor of an independent Brazil.

John XXIII (Angelo Giuseppe Roncalli) (1881–1963), Pope (1958–63). During his pontificate he made energetic efforts to liberalize ROMAN CATHOLIC policy, especially on social questions. Particularly notable were his encyclicals, *Mater et Magistra*, on the need to help the poor, and *Pacem in Terris*, on the need for international peace. He also summoned the Second Ecumenical Vatican Council (1962–65) to revitalize the life of the Church by bringing up to date its teaching, discipline, and organization, with the unity of all Christians as its ultimate goal. He was succeeded by PAUL VI.

John Birch Society US political organization. Named after John Birch, a Baptist missionary and US Army intelligence officer killed by Chinese communists in 1945, it was formed in 1958 in Massachusetts with the aim of exposing the 'communist conspiracy' that was allegedly infiltrating the highest federal offices. Accused by its detractors of using smear tactics associated with MCCARTHYISM, it favoured STATES' RIGHTS and a reduction in federal powers. It gained most support in California and the southern states and bitterly attacked Chief Justice WARREN for his part in forcing the southern states into DESEGREGATION.

'John Bull' A character invented by John Arbuthnot in *The History of John Bull* (1712), who was soon regarded as representative of the typical patriotic Englishman, and even of England itself. He was much used by caricaturists in the late 18th century in various (not always flattering) situations. He later gained a new lease of life from the cartoonists of *Punch* magazine, who made him so universally known that he was often used as a symbol for anything British.

John of Austria, Don (1545–78) Spanish general and admiral. He was an illegitimate son of Emperor CHARLES V, educated in Spain, and recognized as his half-brother by PHILIP II. He was appointed commander-in-chief of the Spanish navy in 1568, and organized the suppression of the Revolt of the Moriscos (1569–70). He commanded the HOLY LEAGUE fleet which defeated the Turks at LEPANTO (1571), and went on to conquer Tunis (1573). His career began to founder after his posting to the Netherlands as governor-general (1576), at a critical point in the DUTCH REVOLTS. His impatience with negotiation led to the resumption of hostilities in 1577–78; and meanwhile he entertained grandiose schemes of marrying MARY, queen of Scots and replacing ELIZABETH I on the English throne. He died of typhus before he could effect these plans.

John of Salisbury (*c*. 1115–80) English philosopher and theologian. He studied under Peter ABELARD and, after a short period at the papal court, was appointed secretary to Archbishop Theobald of Canterbury (*c*. 1148). He continued as secretary to Theobald's successor Thomas à BECKET, went with him into voluntary exile in France (1164–70) during Becket's dispute with HENRY II of England, and was with Becket on the day of his murder (1170). In 1176 he became Bishop of Chartres. He was the author of a number of works, the most important being the *Matalogicon* and the *Policraticus*, which outlines his ideal society.

John of the Cross, St (1542–91) Spanish Christian mystic and poet. He helped St TERESA of Avila to found the Order of the Discalced CARMELITES. A Carmelite monk himself, he was ordained priest in 1567. His collaboration with St Teresa led to friction with the Calced Carmelites, and in 1577 he was imprisoned at Toledo. He escaped, and subsequently attained high office in the Discalced Carmelite order. His rigorously intellectual verse has been called the finest poetic expression of Spanish Christian mysticism. He was canonized in 1726.

John Paul II (Karol Wojtyla) (1920–) Pope (1978–). A Pole, he has travelled more widely on papal missions than any other pope. He survived an assassination attempt in St Peter's Square, Rome, in 1981. On his visit to Britain in 1982 he took part in a service in Canterbury Cathedral, the first pope to enter the building since the Reformation. Since then he has remained cautious about ecumenicism between the Christian Churches. While actively engaged in the revival of Catholicism in eastern Europe both before and after the collapse of communism (1989–91), he has shown less support for left-wing worker-priests in Latin America (see LIBERATION THEOLOGY). His term of office has seen a slowing down of reforms advocated in the wake of the Second Vatican Council (1962–65), notably on the devolution of responsibility to the priesthood and laity. He has maintained the Church's traditional opposition to the ordination of women, to artificial birth control, and to practising homosexuals.

Johnson, Andrew (1808–75) Seventeenth President of the USA (1865–69). As the only southern senator to support the Union in the AMERICAN CIVIL WAR he was appointed military governor of Tennessee. Having been elected as Vice-President to Abraham LINCOLN in 1864, he became President as a result of Lincoln's assassination in April 1865. His reconstruction policy, which failed to protect the interests of former slaves in the ex-Confederate states, brought him into bitter conflict with the Republican majority in Congress: his vetoes of several reconstruction measures were overridden by two-thirds majorities in Congress. His dismissal of his Secretary of War, Edwin Stanton (in defiance of a Tenure of Office Act) led to his impeachment (a US legal procedure for removing officers of state before their term of office expires), and Johnson only survived by a single vote in the Senate (1868). He returned to the Senate in 1875 but died soon after.

Johnson, Lyndon B. (1908–73) The 36th President of the USA (1963–68). A Democrat, Johnson represented Texas in Congress from 1937 to 1961, when he became Vice-President to John F. KENNEDY. When Kennedy was assassinated, he was immediately sworn in as President. Johnson acted decisively to restore confidence and pressed Congress to pass the former President's welfare legislation, especially the CIVIL RIGHTS proposals. He won a sweeping victory in the presidential election of 1964, with Hubert Humphrey as Vice-President. The administration introduced an ambitious programme of social and economic reform. It took his considerable negotiating skills to persuade Congress to support his measures, which included medical aid for the aged (MEDICARE) through a health insurance scheme, housing and urban development, increased spending on education, and federal projects for conservation. In spite of these achievements, urban tension increased. Martin Luther KING and MALCOLM X were assassinated and there were serious race riots in many cities. The USA's increasing involvement in the VIETNAM WAR overshadowed all domestic reforms, and led Johnson on an increasingly unpopular course involving conscription and high casualties. By 1968 this had forced Johnson to announce that he would not seek re-election.

Johnson, Sir William (1715–74) British FUR TRADER and superintendent of Native Americans in northern New York. Johnson travelled from Ireland to the Mohawk valley as an estate manager in 1738. His honesty and geniality won the trust of the IROQUOIS, who gave him huge tracts of land. His intimacy with the Native Americans was a vital element in the FRENCH AND INDIAN WAR, and after his victory at LAKE GEORGE (1755) he was knighted and appointed Superintendent of Indian Affairs (1756). He was influential at the ALBANY CONGRESS and in the promulgation of the PROCLAMATION LINE.

John the Baptist, St (d. 28–30 AD) Jewish preacher and prophet. According to the New Testament he was the son of Elizabeth, a relative of Mary the mother of JESUS CHRIST, and of the temple priest Zechariah. Living an ascetic life in the Judaean desert until he was about 30 (in c. 27 AD), John then started preaching of the imminence of God's Final Judgement; he also preached against social injustices and the religious hypocrisy of the PHARISEES and SADDUCEES, baptizing those who repented, in the River Jordan. Among those who came to him was Jesus, whom he baptized, hailing him as the Messiah. He was imprisoned for denouncing HEROD Antipas' marriage to Herodias, formerly the wife of Herod's half brother. He was beheaded at the request of Herodias' daughter, Salome, in return for dancing at Herod's birthday feast. As the prophet Yahya, John has a prominent place in the Koran, being esteemed for his gentleness and chastity. In Islamic legend, the blood from his decapitated head is said to have boiled. A tomb, alleged to be that of Yahya, is in the Great Mosque of Damascus.

Johore A Malay sultanate founded by Sultan Mahmud, the last sultan of MALACCA before it was captured by the Portuguese in 1511. He tried unsuccessfully to retake Malacca a number of times but was finally defeated in 1526. Thereafter Johore was in frequent conflict with ACHEH, an emerging north Sumatran state. After Johore assisted the Dutch capture of Malacca in 1641, it established its rule over much of the southern Malay peninsular. However, an argument over a royal marriage led to its defeat by the Sumatran state of Jambi in 1673. Its capital moved to Rhio (on the island of Bintang) and a much weakened state only continued with support of BUGIS mercenaries.

joint-stock company A company whose capital ownership is split into small equal parts known as shares (or common stock in the USA). Numerous investors can own different proportions of the company, all protected by limited liability for the company's debts. Thus any company with shares is a joint-stock company, including all public limited companies (PLCs). (See also CHARTERED COMPANY.)

Joinville, Jean de (1224–1317) French historian and courtier. He was a friend and confidant of LOUIS IX, accompanying him on the Seventh CRUSADE (1248–54). He advised against the Eighth Crusade and did not join it. His *Histoire de St Louis* was principally an account of the Seventh Crusade, written with humour and sincerity.

Jones, John Paul (1747–92) US admiral. He was born in Scotland and went to sea aged 12. He was employed in the slave trade and rose to the rank of mate, but his killing of a mutinous sailor led to his settling in America in 1773. He joined the navy of the rebellious American colonies in 1775, and as a captain commanded a privateer in the West Indies (1776–77). He carried the news of SARATOGA (1777) to France, his base for a series of breathtaking exploits round the northern coasts of Britain. He spiked the guns of his old home port, Whitehaven, and captured HMS *Drake*. In a spectacular night battle off Flamborough Head (1779) his shattered *Bonhomme Richard* forced HMS *Serapis* to surrender. His own response to a demand to surrender, 'I have not yet begun to fight', made him a popular hero in the USA and France. After serving as admiral in the Russian navy against the Turks (1788–89), he died in Paris.

Jordan A mainly inland Middle Eastern country, correctly the Hashemite Kingdom of Jordan, a part of historical Palestine. It borders on Syria in the north, Iraq in the east, Saudi Arabia in the south-east, and Israel in the west.

Physical. Jordan's natural resources are meagre, and its only outlet to the sea is the port of Aqaba at the north-east end of the Red Sea. Most of the country is on a desert plateau that has only about 250 mm (10 inches) of rain a year; but in the west is the River Jordan valley where some crops can be grown.

Economy. Jordan's economy is dependent on foreign aid and remittances from Jordanian workers abroad, particularly those working in the Gulf states; the loss of income caused by the 1991 Gulf War was disastrous and was compounded by the fact that Iraq had been the major trading partner. Phosphates, potash, and agricultural produce are the mainstay of the economy. In 1996 the doubling of food prices led to riots.

History. The region was part of the OTTOMAN EMPIRE until 1918, when it came under the government of King FAISAL I in Damascus. In 1920 Transjordan, as it was then called, was made part of the British MANDATE of Palestine. In 1921 Britain recognized Abdullah ibn Hussein as ruler of the territory and gave him British advisers, a subsidy, and assistance in creating a security force. In 1946 the country was given full independence as the Hashemite Kingdom of Jordan, with Abdullah as king. In 1948–49 the state was considerably enlarged when Palestinian territories on the West Bank, including the Old City of Jerusalem, were added. As a result of the SIX-DAY WAR in 1967, these West Bank territories passed under Israeli occupation. The king was assassinated in 1951, his son Talal was deposed in 1952 as mentally unstable, and since 1953 Jordan has been ruled by Talal's son, Talal ibn HUSSEIN (1935–   ). During the late 1960s Palestinian refugees from territory under Israeli occupation established a commando force (*fedayeen*) in Jordan to raid Israel. Hostility from Palestinian refugees to the moderate policies of Hussein led to violence between the guerrillas and Jordanian forces in 1970. The mainly Bedouin regiments loyal to the king broke up the military bases of al-FATAH, and the PALESTINE LIBERATION ORGANIZATION moved its forces (1971) to Lebanon and Syria. During the YOM KIPPUR WAR Jordan sent tanks to aid Syria, but there was no fighting along the Jordan frontier. In 1974 Jordan's relations with other Arab countries improved when it accepted that 'the PLO is the sole and legitimate representative of the Palestinian people'. Jordan relinquished its territorial claim to the West Bank in 1988. It supported Iraq in the IRAN–IRAQ WAR and suffered severely from the effects of the GULF WAR, which included the return of many thousands of expatriates from the Gulf. In June 1991 the 34-year ban on political parties was lifted; among those to form an opposition was the Moslem Brotherhood, which opposed the important role that Jordan was playing in the Middle East peace process. Jordan gradually distanced itself from Iraq as it continued to participate in Middle East peace talks. In 1993 the first multiparty election since 1956 was held in which independent candidates loyal to the king were victorious. Despite the signing of the Israeli–PLO peace accord (1993), Jordan continued its own negotiations with Israel. In 1994 the two countries signed a declaration formally ending the state of conflict between them and agreed a peace treaty. Opposition parties continued to oppose any agreement with Israel, while relations with Saudi Arabia, strained during the Gulf crisis, improved.

CAPITAL:	Amman
AREA:	88,947 sq km (34,342 sq miles)
POPULATION:	4.333 million (1996)
CURRENCY:	1 Jordanian dinar = 1,000 fils
RELIGIONS:	Sunni Muslim 93.0%; Christian 4.9%
ETHNIC GROUPS:	Arab (including Palestinian and Bedouin) 99.2%; Circassian 0.5%; Armenian 0.1%; Turkish 0.1%; Kurdish 0.1%
LANGUAGES:	Arabic (official); minority languages
INTERNATIONAL ORGANIZATIONS:	UN; Arab League; Non-Aligned Movement

Joseph (*c.* 1840–1904) Chief of a group of North American Nez Percé people. He defied the efforts of the US government to move his people from their traditional Oregon lands, and was one of the leaders in a campaign (1877) against overwhelming military odds. He was finally defeated during a retreat to Canada. He spent his later years on a reservation, devoting his life to the welfare of his people.

Joseph II (1741–90) Holy Roman Emperor (1765–90). He was co-regent of Austria with his mother MARIA THERESA from 1765 and sole ruler from 1780 to 1790. Intelligent, dedicated to the principles of the ENLIGHTENMENT, and hoping to improve the lives of his subjects, he was nonetheless autocratic and too hasty. Attempts at major reforms brought many parts of the empire close to revolt. His most lasting achievements were the edicts in 1781 granting toleration to Jews and Protestants. He abolished serfdom and curtailed the privileges of the nobles. In German affairs he was outmanoeuvred by FREDERICK II of Prussia and his alliance with CATHERINE II (the Great) of Russia led to a disastrous war against the Turks.

Josephat, Israel Beer REUTER, PAUL JULIUS, BARON.

Joséphine, Marie Rose Tascher de la Pagerie (1763–1814) Empress of the French (1804–09) and wife of NAPOLEON I. Briefly imprisoned during the Reign of Terror, Joséphine married Napoleon in 1796, two years after her first husband, the Vicomte de Beauharnais, had been executed by the Jacobins. In 1810 Napoleon had the marriage annulled because of her alleged sterility, taking Marie Louise, daughter of FRANCIS I, as his wife.

Josephus, Flavius (Joseph ben Matthias) (born *c.* 37 AD) Jewish historian, priest, and soldier. A visit to Rome in 64 AD left in him a lasting impression of Rome's power and culture. Although hostile to the nationalist extremists, he was given command in Galilee in the Jewish revolt against NERO, but after his capture in 67 went over to the Romans. Settled in Rome, he became a Roman citizen and was given a pension. His most important works were his histories of the revolt and its antecedents (*Bellum Judaicum*, The Jewish War), and of the Jewish people from the Creation to the reign of Nero (*Antiquitates Judaica*, Antiquities of the Jews). His *Vita* (Life) is less an autobiography than an explanation of his conduct during the revolt.

Josiah (649–609 BC) King of JUDAH (640–609 BC) in succession to his father Amon. At the age of 17 he undertook a major reform of worship in and around Jerusalem, suppressing the worship of local gods, closing down outlying shrines, and making the Jerusalem Temple the sole centre of worship. Because of his concern for the Jewish faith, he is described in the Bible as a model king, the last good king of Judah. He died at the Battle of Megiddo, defeated by the Egyptians.

journeyman A qualified artisan working for someone else. Journeymen were workers (paid daily) who had served their apprenticeship and were not yet in a financial position to set up as masters. The late medieval craft GUILDS, by restricting the number of masters without limiting the number of apprentices, created increasing numbers of discontented and sometimes unemployed journeymen: in the 16th century it was found necessary in England for Parliament to pass legislation to compel masters with apprentices to employ journeymen. This legislation was no longer enforced by the 18th century, if it ever had been, and the Industrial Revolution with its factory system and demand for unskilled labour spelled doom for the journeyman. Associations of journeymen were the earliest trade unions (as distinct from guilds) in both Britain and the USA, one of the longest-lived being the Federal Society of Journeymen Cordwainers in Philadelphia.

Juan-Juan AVARS.

Juárez, Benito (1806–72) Mexican statesman. His Plan of Ayutla (1854), calling for a constituent assembly within a federal constitution, paved the way for the War of Reform (1858–61), which exiled SANTA ANNA and established a liberal government under Juárez. He was unable to prevent France's attempt to establish a Mexican empire (1864–67) under MAXIMILIAN but was re-elected President on the emperor's assassination. He reduced the privileges of the army and Church, but his reforms were curtailed by division among the liberals.

Judah (or Judaea) The southern part of ancient Palestine, named after the fourth son of Jacob and his first wife, Leah. After SOLOMON's death the kingdom of Judah resisted repeated invasions before falling to NEBUCHADNEZZAR II of Babylon, who destroyed its capital, JERUSALEM, in 586 BC. When the Jews returned from EXILE in Babylon, the land they occupied was named Judaea. SELEUCID desecration of the Temple in 167 BC prompted the revolt of the MACCABEES. Independence lasted until the Roman conquest of 63 BC. In 135 AD the area was absorbed into Roman Syria.

Judah Ha-Nasi (the Prince) (135–c. 220) Patriarch of Judaea. He is best remembered for organizing the compilation of the *Mishnah*, the first comprehensive statement of Jewish religious law. He won the favour of Roman emperors, forged closer links with the Jews of the DIASPORA, and worked to raise the status of the Hebrew language.

Judaism The religion of the JEWISH PEOPLE. The central belief of Judaism is faith in one God, summarized in the Shema, recited in all public and private devotions, the first verse of which is translated, 'Hear, O Israel: the Lord our God, the Lord is one'. Jews believe that God created both heaven and earth and ordained the Jewish people as the inheritors of a unique relationship with God, through the Covenant he made with Abraham. There is also a MILLENARIAN belief in the prophesied appearance of a Messiah, an 'anointed' figure who will initiate a time when all Jews will be gathered back to the land of Israel, a land promised by God to Abraham and his descendants. Jewish religious practice is based on obedience to the Torah, which governs every aspect of spiritual, religious, and moral life and is summarized in the Ten Commandments. In rabbinic tradition, the total number of biblical commandments (*mitzvot*) is given as 613. Further commentaries and oral traditions are codified within the Mishnah and TALMUD. Public worship occurs in the local synagogue and religious authority is vested in the rabbi, but many distinctive features of religious observance, particularly those surrounding diet and the Sabbath, are centred in the home.

Many of the characteristics of Judaism emerged during the Babylonian EXILE, when the importance of teaching and prayer was emphasized. Jewish communities became widely scattered (the DIASPORA) after the destruction of the Temple at Jerusalem (the central sanctuary of Judaism) in 70 AD by the Romans. Leaders of these communities (rabbis) encouraged a greater loyalty to the Torah and its daily demands; the lives of these groups revolved around the synagogue, their own laws, and their own calendar (as far as the state permitted).

Over the centuries Jews spread to Mediterranean countries (the Sephardim), to Holland, Germany, the Baltic states, and into Central and Eastern Europe (the Ashkenazim), where they lived in ghettos or legally enforced residence areas. By the 18th century pressures were growing within the Jewish community for the granting of equal rights and the abandonment of the ghetto. In Berlin the philosopher Moses Mendelssohn (1729–86) campaigned for Jewish emancipation. From his work there developed the Haskalah, or Jewish Enlightenment, which spread into Eastern Europe in the early 19th century. Jewish religious reform, as well as ANTI-SEMITISM and POGROMS, led to large-scale emigration, especially to the USA. Legal limitations to Jews were abolished in most European countries during the course of the 19th century. Three strands of Judaism emerged: Reform, Orthodox, and Conservative. Followers of Mendelssohn sought to reconcile Judaism with contemporary Europe by means of a Reform Movement, which among other things allowed the language of the country to be used in the synagogue (see REFORM JUDAISM). The movement came to Britain and the USA in the 1840s, gaining many middle-class adherents. In reaction were Orthodox Jews, seeking to reject secular culture and to preserve ancient practices based on the sole authority of the Torah, and supporters of HASIDISM, an influential, mystical movement that stressed the development of a personal spiritual life and attacked any manifestations of modernity. Between these poles emerged Conservative Judaism. Its forerunner was Zacharias Frankel (1801–75), whose 'Positive Historicism' sought to harmonize Jewish tradition with modern knowledge. When ZIONISM emerged in the later 19th century, expressing religious and nationalistic demands, both Reform and Conservative Judaism supported it, although a majority of Orthodox Jews were and have remained suspicious of the concept of a Jewish state. During the 20th century Jews were decimated by the HOLOCAUST, but succeeded in establishing the state of ISRAEL (1948). Most Jews outside Israel have continued their assimiliation into the population of their country while preserving some traditions of the Jewish community.

Judas Maccabaeus MACCABEES.

Jugurtha (c. 156–104 BC) King of NUMIDIA. He contested the throne with his two brothers following the death of his adoptive father Micipsa in 118. A Roman commission divided the kingdom between them, but Jugurtha attacked and killed one brother, Adherbal, in 112. Armed intervention by Rome followed disturbances, but Jugurtha resisted stubbornly until SULLA, the legate of MARIUS, induced Bocchus of Mauretania to hand the Numidian king over. After Marius had celebrated a triumph in Rome, Jugurtha was executed.

Julian (the Apostate) (Flavius Claudius Julianus) (*c.* 331–63) Roman emperor (360–363). He was born at CONSTANTINOPLE, a nephew of CONSTANTINE. After receiving a classical Greek education he gave up Christian belief for NEOPLATONISM, earning himself his posthumous insulting title. He blamed CHRISTIANITY for sapping Rome's traditional strengths. Reversing the Edict of MILAN, he reopened temples and restored paganism as the state cult in place of Christianity, but this move was reversed after his death on campaign against the Persians.

Julian calendar The CALENDAR introduced by Julius Caesar in 46 BC and slightly modified under Augustus, in which the ordinary year has 365 days, and every fourth year is a leap year of 366 days. It has largely been superseded by the GREGORIAN CALENDAR, but it is still used in some of the former Soviet republics. Unlike more primitive calendars the Julian calendar contains months that are whole numbers of days in length.

Julius II (Guiliano della Rovere) (1443–1513), Pope (1503–13). He strove to restore and extend the PAPAL STATES and to establish a strong independent papacy. He crushed Cesare BORGIA and sponsored the League of CAMBRAI and the HOLY LEAGUE against France in 1510. Before the end of 1512 the French were forced to leave Italy and several new territories were added to the papacy's holdings. When Julius died he was mourned as the liberator of Italy from foreign domination.

Politics and war dominated his reign and he devoted little time to Church reform. He did, however, send missionaries to India, Africa, and America, and was a noted artistic patron, commissioning work from Michelangelo, Raphael, and Bramante.

July Plot (20 July 1944) A plot to assassinate Adolf HITLER. Disenchanted by the NAZI REGIME in Germany, an increasing number of senior army officers believed that Hitler had to be assassinated and an alternative government, prepared to negotiate peace terms with the Allies, established. Plans were made in late 1943 and there were a number of unsuccessful attempts before that of July 1944. The plot was carried out by Count Berthold von Stauffenberg, who left a bomb at Hitler's headquarters at Rastenburg. The bomb exploded, killing four people, but not Hitler. Stauffenberg, believing he had succeeded, flew to Berlin, where the plotters aimed to seize the Supreme Command headquarters. Before this was done, however, news came that Hitler had survived. A counter-move resulted in the arrest of some 200 plotters, including Stauffenberg himself, Generals Beck, Olbricht, von Tresckow, and later Friedrich Fromm. They were shot, hanged, or in some cases strangled. Field-Marshal ROMMEL was implicated and obliged to commit suicide. The regime used the occasion to execute several prominent protesters such as Dietrich BONHOEFFER.

July Revolution (1830) A revolt in France. It began when CHARLES X issued his ordinances of 25 July, which suspended the liberty of the press, dissolved the new chamber, reduced the electorate, and allowed him to rule by decree. His opponents erected barricades in Paris and after five days of bitter street fighting Charles was

forced to abdicate. The duc d'Orléans, LOUIS-PHILIPPE, was invited to become 'King of the French', a title which replaced the more traditional 'King of France'. His accession marked the victory of constitutional liberal forces over arbitrary and absolutist rule.

June War SIX-DAY WAR.

'Junius' The pen-name of an unknown British writer of 70 political letters, published in the London *Public Advertiser* between 1769 and 1772. The letters were informed, satirical, and vicious, and directed their attack mainly against the Duke of GRAFTON, particularly on behalf of WILKES. The letter to GEORGE III, a model of studied impertinence, made 'Junius' famous. To this day there is no certainty of the writer's identity – Sir Philip Francis seems the most likely candidate, but many politicians and authors have been credited with the letters.

junta (Spanish, 'council', 'meeting') A group of political or military leaders forming an administrative council or committee, particularly in the aftermath of a coup d'état or revolution when there is no legal government. The term has been widely used in Latin America to describe military regimes such as that of General Galtieri in Argentina during the 1980s. If a single dominant leader or small group emerges from a junta, it can be transformed into a dictatorship.

jury A group of lay persons (usually 12) summoned to a court of law or an inquest in order to decide the facts of a case and give a verdict. The jury system's development was exclusive to England. Initially, jurors were regarded as sworn (Latin, *jurati*) witnesses to the accuracy of a claim. In the Anglo-Saxon 'compurgation' an accused person could be cleared simply on the sworn word of 12 neighbours to his good character. The Assize of Clarendon (1166) instructed jurors to present their evidence and suspects before the king's justices. Trial by jury was adopted in civil cases when the Lateran Council (1215) forbade the trial by ORDEAL, and it became compulsory for certain criminal cases under the Statute of Westminster (1275).

Trial by jury is currently found almost only in the UK and in countries influenced by the English legal system. In the UK, juries are used in criminal trials and in certain types of civil cases, such as libel. In the USA there are two types of jury: the grand jury, which investigates possible criminal wrongdoing, hears the state's evidence, and if satisfied that a trial should take place, hands down a formal accusation or indictment; and the petit or trial jury, which is used in both criminal and civil trials.

The members of a jury are randomly selected, but the defendant has the right to challenge the composition of the jury and to object to jurors on the grounds of prejudice or unsuitability. In the UK jurors may not be challenged with no reason being given. The role of the jury is to decide on questions of fact and to issue a verdict, while the judge directs them on matters of law and sums up the evidence for them. The verdict of the jury is traditionally expected to be unanimous, but where this is impossible, a majority verdict may be sufficient. The use of a jury is intended to ensure that the defendant is given a fair trial by ordinary people, chosen at random, who bring to the proceedings impartiality and common sense. On the other hand, it is sometimes argued, particularly in complex cases involving fraud, for instance, that juries of lay people may be incapable of understanding the issues or the evidence put before them.

Justinian I (482–565) Byzantine emperor (527–65). Throughout much of his reign his troops were engaged in a defensive struggle against Persia in the east and a successful war against the barbarians in the west. Believing that they had lost their initial vigour, he hoped to revive the old Roman empire. His general, BELISARIUS, crushed the Vandals in Africa (533) and the Ostrogoths in Italy (535–53), making Ravenna the centre of government. His greater claim to fame lay in his domestic policy in which he was strongly influenced by his powerful wife, THEODORA. He reformed provincial administration and in his *Corpus Juris Civilis* he codified 4,652 imperial ordinances (*Codex*), summarized the views of the best legal writers (*Digest*), and added a handbook for students (*Institutes*). A passionately orthodox Christian, he fought pagans and heretics. His lasting memorial is the Church of St Sophia in Constantinople.

Justo, Agustín Pedro (1876–1943) Argentine statesman. Justo participated in the conservative military coup that overthrew President Hipólito IRIGOYEN in 1930 and was rewarded with the presidency (1932–38). Faced by the effects of revolution, high unemployment, and the economic decline that was caused by the Great DEPRESSION, his regime was autocratic; for example, he outlawed the Communist Party in 1936. However, he supported PAN-AMERICAN co-operation and closer links with Britain. He was defeated in the 1937 presidential election by Roberto Ortiz, despite having been

instrumental in ending the CHACO WAR. A supporter of the Allies in World War II, he enlisted in the Brazilian army in 1942 and was killed.

Jutes A Germanic tribe who invaded Britain in the 5th century AD, traditionally under the leadership of HENGIST AND HORSA. Their name is preserved in Jutland and Juteborg. According to BEDE (and he is supported by archaeological evidence) they occupied the Isle of Wight, the Hampshire coast, and Kent, the former land of the Belgic Cantii with its capital at Canterbury. Here they permitted AUGUSTINE OF CANTERBURY's mission to re-Christianize Britain. In the 11th century the New Forest in Hampshire was still known as 'Ytene' ('of the Jutes').

Jutland, Battle of (31 May 1916) A naval battle between Britain and Germany, fought in the North Sea off the coast of Jutland. The only major battle fought at sea in World War I, it began between two forces of battle cruisers, the British under BEATTY and the German under von Hipper. Suffering heavy losses, Beatty sailed to join the main British North Sea Fleet under JELLICOE, which then engaged the German High Seas Fleet under SCHEER. Battle began at 6 p.m. at long range (approximately 14 km or 9 miles), but as the Germans headed for home in the night, they collided with the British fleet, several ships sinking in the ensuing chaos. Both sides claimed victory. The British lost 14 ships, including three battle cruisers; the Germans lost 11 ships, including one battleship and one battle cruiser; but the British retained control of the North Sea, the German fleet staying inside the Baltic for the rest of the war.

K

Kaaba The sacred shrine in MECCA, Saudi Arabia, towards which Muslims face daily during prayers, and the focal point for Muslim pilgrimage. It is a cube-shaped building covered with a black cloth, embroidered in gold with Koranic quotations. In a wall of the Kaaba is embedded a sacred black stone. A tradition says that the black stone was given to ABRAHAM by the Angel Gabriel, and it is believed to symbolize God's covenant with the worshipper. The authentic Muslim tradition, according to the Koran, goes that the Kaaba was originally built by Abraham and Ishmael. (See also FIVE PILLARS OF ISLAM.)

Kabbalah (Hebrew, 'tradition') The main tradition of Jewish mysticism. Kabbalistic belief maintains the possibility of a direct 'vision' of divine attributes, based upon astrology and the study of occult interpretations of the Old Testament and other texts, which define the spiritual and symbolic value of numbers and letters. The main Kabbalistic work, the *Zohar* ('Splendour'), a 13th-century mystical interpretation of the Torah, was influential in modern HASIDIC teaching. It taught ten ways of understanding God, whilst maintaining that God himself is beyond comprehension.

Kabila, Laurent-Desire (1939–) Congolese politician and soldier, President of the Democratic Republic of Congo (formerly Zaïre) from 1997. In late 1996 opponents of the increasingly oppressive regime of MOBUTU Sese Seko in Zaïre formed the Alliance of Democratic Forces for the Liberation of Congo (ADFL), led by Kabila. By early 1997, his forces, supported by the neighbouring countries of Angola, Uganda, and Rwanda, had defeated Mobutu's army, and were advancing from the east on the capital, Kinshasa. Mobutu relinquished power and fled, and Kabila appointed himself president, renaming the country. His Tutsi troops have been accused by international aid agencies of undertaking atrocities against Hutu refugees from Rwanda and Burundi.

Kabir (1440–1518) Indian mystic and poet, who preached the unity of all religions. There is uncertainty about his origins, but it is believed that he was adopted by a Muslim weaver after being abandoned by his Brahmin Hindu mother. His borrowings from both Hinduism and Islam resulted in the preaching of a new mystic path, the *Kabir panth*, and the founding, by one of his disciples, of the SIKH religion. His mystical poems, stressing the oneness of God, together with his rejection of caste, have made Kabir one of the most popular religious figures in his country's history.

Kadafy, Moamar al QADDAFI, MUAMMAR AL-.

Kádár, János (1912–89) Hungarian statesman who joined the illegal Communist Party in Budapest in 1931 and was frequently arrested. He helped to organize RESISTANCE MOVEMENTS during World War II, after which he was appointed Deputy Chief of Police (1945) and then Minister of the Interior (1949). Imprisoned (1951–54) during the RAKOSI regime, he joined the short-lived

government of Imre NAGY, who had pledged liberalization. The HUNGARIAN REVOLUTION which followed (October 1956) resulted in the fall and execution of Nagy and harsh Soviet military control. Kádár survived, becoming First Secretary of the Communist Party of Hungary (General Secretary from 1958); he was installed by the Soviet Union to curb revolt through repressive measures and became the effective ruler of Hungary. While remaining loyal to Moscow in foreign affairs, his later policies at home allowed for an increasingly diversified economy and a higher standard of living. He retired in 1988.

Kalmar, Union of (1397) The joining together of the crowns of Denmark, Sweden, and Norway. Margaret I (1353–1412), daughter of the King of Denmark and wife of Haakon VI of Norway (d. 1387) defeated (1389) the King of Sweden and persuaded the Diets of Denmark, Norway, and Sweden to accept Eric of Pomerania, her grandnephew, as king. He was crowned in 1397 at the beginning of the Union of Kalmar, though Margaret herself ruled the three kingdoms until her death. The union was dissolved by GUSTAVUS I of Sweden in 1523.

Kamakura A city south-west of Tokyo, the headquarters of Japan's first SHOGUNATE. There, near his estates and remote from court influence, MINAMOTO YORITOMO set up a military administration, the *bakufu* (tent government). After his death the HOJO family acted as regents of the shoguns. The Kamakura shogunate (1192–1333) saw the emergence of the SAMURAI and the organization of military power. The bronze Daibutsu (Great Buddha) (1252), 15.8 m (52 feet) high, showed the popularity of ZEN BUDDHISM among the warrior class.

Kamenev, Lev Borisovich (1883–1936) Soviet leader who joined the Social Democratic Party (1901) and sided with the BOLSHEVIK faction when the party split in 1903. He was exiled to Siberia for ordering Bolshevik deputies in the Duma to oppose World War I. In 1917 he presided over the Second All-Russian Congress of Soviets. On LENIN's death in 1924 Kamenev, ZINOVIEV, and STALIN formed a triumvirate to exclude Kamenev's brother-in-law, TROTSKY, from power. In 1936 he was accused of complicity in the murder of Kirov in the first public show trial of Stalin's great purge, and was shot.

kamikaze (Japanese, 'Divine Wind') Originally used to refer to the fierce storms that twice saved Japan from MONGOL invasion (in 1274 and 1281), the term was adopted in World War II to describe an aircraft laden with explosives and suicidally crashed by the pilot into an enemy ship. The Japanese naval command resorted to these desperate measures in 1944 in an attempt to halt the Allied advance across the Pacific. At first volunteers were used, but the practice soon became compulsory. Off OKINAWA in 1945, when these tactics came closest to repelling an Allied attack, over 300 kamikaze pilots died in one action.

Kampuchea CAMBODIA.

Kanagawa, Treaty of (also called Perry Convention) (31 March 1854) A treaty between Japan and the USA, establishing trading and diplomatic relations. After three years of negotiation, the US Commodore PERRY came to an agreement with the Tokugawa SHOGUNATE, opening two ports to US vessels, allowing the appointment of a consul, and guaranteeing better treatment for shipwrecked sailors. The Treaty of Kanagawa was followed within two years by similar agreements with Britain, Russia, and the Netherlands, and in 1858 by the more wide-ranging Treaty of EDO with the USA, and marked the beginning of regular political and economic intercourse between Japan and the Western nations.

Kanakas A term used indiscriminately by Europeans to describe Pacific Islanders, mainly from the New Hebrides and the Solomon Islands, who were brought to Australia between 1863 and 1904 as cheap labour. Theoretically, they voluntarily entered contracts for fixed terms. In practice, they were subjected to abuses which included kidnap, slavery, and murder. Their entry to Australia was banned in 1904. Most of those in Australia were deported back to the islands from 1906 onwards, as part of the WHITE AUSTRALIA POLICY.

Kanem-Bornu Two successive major African states that flourished in the Lake Chad region between the 11th and the 19th centuries. Ethnically and linguistically the peoples were mixed. They include Arab, Berber, as well as other African elements, and were mostly Muslims. An Islamic sultanate of Kanem, ruled by the Seyfawa family, existed by the 11th century, which, under Muhammad Dunama (1221–59), came to extend from the regions of Fezzan and Wadai to the River Niger, and included the kingdom of Bornu. Following civil wars this empire collapsed in 1398, but a new state of Bornu was founded with Birni Ngazargamu as its capital, and Kanem as a province. Idris Aloma (ruled 1571–1603) introduced firearms into the army and Bornu reached the peak of its power under his rule. A long period of stability followed until 1808, when the FULANI sacked Birni Ngazargamu. Muhammad al-Kanemi, a leading chief, restored the titular kings, retaining effective power himself. The last Mai, or titular king, was executed in 1846.

Kangxi (K'ang-hsi) (1654–1722) Second QING Emperor of China (1662–1722). He extended the Qing empire by a series of military campaigns, subduing opposition to Manchu rule in southern China (1673–81), incorporating TAIWAN into China for the first time in 1683, and personally leading a campaign into Outer MONGOLIA (1693). He opened certain ports to overseas traders and the Treaty of NERCHINSK (1689), established diplomatic contact with Russia. In 1692 he permitted Catholic missionaries to make converts and he employed JESUITS to teach astronomy and mathematics. He was renowned for his tours of inspection of China and for his sponsorship of scholarship, including a history of the Ming dynasty and an encyclopedia of literature.

Kang Youwei (or K'ang Yu-wei) (1858–1927) Chinese philosopher and political reformer. A scholar, whose utopian work *Da Tong Shu* (*One World Philosophy*, 1900) portrayed Confucius as a reformer, Kang Youwei believed that China's crisis could only be solved through the modernization of institutions along modified

western lines. In 1898, at a time when foreign intervention presented particular dangers, he persuaded the emperor Guangxu to adopt his policies. The resulting HUNDRED DAYS REFORM was brought to a premature end by the empress dowager CIXI's conservative coup, and Kang spent the next fifteen years in exile. He remained a monarchist in spite of the republican trend and spent his last years trying unsuccessfully to engineer an imperial restoration.

Kano A city in northern Nigeria. According to tradition, it was founded in the 10th century, and probably became Muslim in the 14th century. It was one of the seven HAUSA city-states, and was an important trading and commercial centre. In the 16th century the Muslim teacher al-Maghili made it famous, teaching law and mysticism. In the 15th century it was probably subject to the state of KANEM-BORNU, and in the 16th it came under the SONGHAY empire, but it was always ruled by an indigenous vassal.

Kansas–Nebraska Act (1854) An Act of the US Congress concerning slavery. Following the MEXICAN–AMERICAN WAR, the COMPROMISE OF 1850 had allowed SQUATTERS in New Mexico and Utah to decide by referendum whether they would enter the Union as 'free' or 'slave' states. This was contrary to the earlier MISSOURI COMPROMISE. The Act of 1854 declared that in Kansas and Nebraska a decision on slavery would also be allowed, by holding a referendum. Tensions erupted between pro-and anti-slavery groups, which in Kansas led to violence (1855–57). Those who deplored the Act formed a new political organization, the REPUBLICAN PARTY, pledged to oppose slavery in the Territories. Kansas was to be admitted as a free state in 1861, and Nebraska in 1867.

Kant, Immanuel (1724–1804) German philosopher, responsible for the doctrine of transcendental idealism. He spent his whole life in East Prussia: from 1770 he was professor of logic at Königsberg University in spite of some difficulties with the authorities due to the divergence of his teaching from orthodox Lutheranism. Kant's metaphysical system is presented in the *Critique of Pure Reason* (1781), his most important work. Kant sought to transcend the opposition between rationalism and empiricism by showing how knowledge of the external world necessarily involves both experience and the application of metaphysical concepts which do not themselves derive from experience. Kant's proofs of the necessity of presupposing such concepts as substance and causality in all judgements about the external world take the form of transcendental arguments. Kant took it to be a consequence of his arguments that we cannot legitimately claim to have knowledge of (although we can form thoughts about) the world as it really is. The world thus divides for Kant into a realm of objects partly constituted by the human mind (appearances or 'phenomena'), and a realm of unknown independent objects (things-in-themselves or 'noumena'). Speculation about the latter, according to Kant, inevitably ends in contradictions. Kant thought that scepticism could in this way be defeated and idealism that denies the physical world completely, such as that of George BERKELEY, could be avoided. In *Critique of Practical Reason* (1788) and *Critique of Judgment* (1790) Kant elaborated the consequences of his metaphysics for ETHICS and aesthetics, respectively.

Kapp putsch (March 1920) The attempt by Wolfgang Kapp (1858–1922), a right-wing Prussian landowner and politician, to overthrow the WEIMAR REPUBLIC and restore the German monarchy. Aided by elements in the army, including LUDENDORFF, and the unofficial 'free corps' which the new government was trying to disband, Kapp's forces seized Berlin, planning to set up a rival government with himself as Chancellor. The *putsch* was defeated by a general strike of the Berlin workers and the refusal of civil servants to obey his orders.

Kara George, Petrović (1766–1817) Serbian revolutionary leader, founder of the dynasty of Karageorgević. The son of a peasant, in 1804 he became leader of a Serbian revolt against the Turkish army and played a major role in forcing the Turks out of SERBIA. Four years later he was proclaimed leader of Serbia but his ruthless and autocratic rule led to unrest. In 1813 his army was defeated by the Turks and he fled. He returned in 1817 only to be murdered, probably by his rival Milos OBRENOVIĆ. His son, Alexander, ruled Serbia as prince from 1843 to 1858, but was displaced by an Obrenović. Alexander's son, Peter, became King of Serbia in 1903; his grandson became ALEXANDER I of Yugoslavia.

Karnak The religious centre of ancient THEBES, situated on the east bank of the Nile, where the great temple of Amun was constructed. This complex of buildings, which took some 2,000 years to construct, includes the Hypostyle Hall with 134 columns, each *c.* 24 m (79 feet) high. It was begun by Ramesses I and completed by Seti I and RAMESSES II. A road lined with statues of sphinxes linked the site to nearby Luxor.

Károlyi, Mihály, Count (1875–1955) Hungarian statesman. A liberal, he favoured a less pro-German policy for the AUSTRO-HUNGARIAN EMPIRE and supported equal rights for all nations within it. There was no hope of achieving this until the empire collapsed (November 1918), when Hungary proclaimed itself a republic with Károlyi as President. When in March 1920 he learned that Hungary must cede territory to Romania, Czechoslovakia, and Yugoslavia he resigned and was replaced by Béla KUN's Communist regime.

Kasavubu, Joseph (1910–69) Congolese statesman. He became the first President (1960–65) of the Republic of the Congo (now the Democratic Republic of Congo). He was a member of undercover nationalist associations to free the Congo of the Belgians. In 1955 he became President of Abako (Alliance des Bakongo), a cultural association of the Bakongo tribe, and turned it into a powerful political organization. Congo gained independence in 1960 and Kasavubu became Head of State. His Abako party formed a coalition with Patrice LUMUMBA's party, and then ousted him as premier. In 1965 Kasavubu himself was deposed from the Presidency by MOBUTU in a bloodless military coup.

Kashmir A former state on the border of India, now part of Jammu-Kashmir, since 1947 disputed between India and Pakistan. The state, exposed successively to Hindu and Muslim rule, was annexed (1819) to the expanding Sikh kingdom. After the first SIKH WAR the territory was acquired by Gulab Singh, then Hindu raja of the Jammu region. It was a PRINCELY STATE for the rest of the British period. The Maharaja, a Hindu ruling over a predominantly Muslim population, initially hoped the state would remain independent in 1947, but eventually acceded to the Indian Union. War between India and Pakistan (1948–49) over Kashmir ended when a United Nations peace-keeping force imposed a temporary ceasefire line which divided the Indian Union state of Jammu and Kashmir from Pakistan-backed Azad Kashmir. Kashmir remains divided by this line. Conflicts between India and Pakistan over Kashmir flared up again in 1965 and 1971, together with demands for a UN-supervised plebiscite. In 1989 militant supporters of either Kashmiri independence or union with Pakistan intensified their campaign of violent civil unrest and Indian government troops were sent into the state. Direct rule by the President was imposed in 1990 and fighting has continued.

Kassites BABYLON.

Kato Komei (or Kato Takaaki) (1860–1926) Japanese statesman who served as ambassador to Britain (1909) and Foreign Minister (1914–15), but was forced to resign after his presentation of the TWENTY-ONE DEMANDS to China. He reorganized and led the conservative Kenseikai, and as Prime Minister (1924–25) pursued a moderate foreign policy while introducing universal manhood suffrage, cutting expenditure, and reducing the size of the army. He also introduced the stringent Peace Preservation Law to balance the possibly destabilizing effects of manhood suffrage. His cabinet was called the 'Mitsubishi government' because both he and his foreign minister Shidehara Kijuro had marriage ties with the Mitsubishi ZAIBATSU.

Katyn massacre A massacre in Katyn forest in the western Soviet Union. In 1943 the German army claimed to have discovered a mass grave of some 4,500 Polish officers, part of a group of 15,000 Poles who had disappeared from Soviet captivity in 1940 and whose fate remained unknown. Each victim had a bullet in the base of his skull. The Soviet Union denied involvement in the massacre until April 1990, when it was confirmed that the assumption of Western historians that the officers had been killed in the early days of close Nazi–Soviet collaboration, by order of Stalin, was correct. The incident resulted in a breach between the exiled Polish government of General SIKORSKI in London and the Soviet Union and led to the agreement at Teheran (1943) that the post-war Polish-Soviet border should revert to the so-called CURZON line (1920).

Kaunda, Kenneth David (1924–   ) Zambian statesman. At first a schoolmaster, in 1949 he joined the AFRICAN NATIONAL CONGRESS (ANC). In 1959 he became its President and led opposition to the CENTRAL AFRICAN FEDERATION, instituting a campaign of 'positive non-violent action'. For this he was imprisoned by the British, and the movement was banned. He was released in 1960 and was elected President of the newly formed United National Independence Party (UNIP). The UNIP became the leading party when independence was granted to Zambia in 1964 and Kaunda became the first President of the new republic. During his presidency education expanded and the government made efforts to diversify the economy to release Zambia from its dependence on copper. Ethnic differences, the Rhodesian and Angolan conflicts, and the collapse of copper prices engendered unrest and political violence, which led Kaunda to institute a one-party state (1973). Later, with the civil war in ANGOLA, he assumed emergency powers.

Nevertheless, he was re-elected President in 1978, again in 1983, and in 1988. He legalized opposition parties in 1990, but was defeated by the trade-union leader Frederick Chiluba in the multiparty presidential election held in November 1991. In January 1992 he resigned as leader of the UNIP. He was a staunch supporter of the COMMONWEALTH OF NATIONS and took a strong line in demanding sanctions against South Africa for its policy of apartheid. In late 1997 he was arrested and accused of inciting a coup.

Kaunitz, Wenzel Anton, Count von (1711–94) Austrian diplomat and statesman. As Chancellor (1753–92) he controlled foreign policy under Empress MARIA THERESA and Emperor Joseph II. He was convinced that Prussia was Austria's most dangerous enemy and his main diplomatic feat was to reverse (1756–57) long-standing European alliances, but Britain remained opposed to France and Austria stayed allied to Russia. However, when Britain formed an alliance with its former enemy, Prussia, in order to protect Hanover, Kaunitz negotiated an alliance with France, thus isolating Prussia on the Continent. Although the ambitions of FREDERICK II (the Great) were not fully checked, Kaunitz was a leading negotiator of the Treaty of Paris (1763).

Kazakhstan A country in western central Asia, stretching for some 3,200 km (2,000 miles) from the Caspian Sea to Xinjiang. It is bounded by China on the east, Kyrgyzstan and Uzbekistan on the south, the Caspian Sea and Turkmenistan on the west, and Russia on the north.

Physical. In the north a belt of fertile steppe with rich, black earth (chernozem) provides scope for cultivation. Southward, however, it becomes more arid, degenerating into the Kara-Kum desert. On the east Caspian coast, oil and natural gas are found. Further east, towards the Aral Sea, is a clay desert plateau; east and south-east of it, sand desert. To the east of this are the stony Kazakh uplands with huge coal deposits in their northern slopes and copper in their southern ones. Here is the extensive and partly saline Lake Balkhash, which is slowly evaporating.

Economy. Kazakhstan has rich and varied mineral deposits, including tungsten, copper, lead, uranium, diamonds, coal, iron ore, natural gas, and petroleum. Industry is largely based on the exploitation of these reserves. There is also some light and manufacturing industry. Grain production and sheep-rearing dominate agriculture.

History. For centuries, the steppelands of Kazakhstan were the home of nomadic Kazakh herdsmen, ruled by Mongol khans, whose territories were steadily annexed by Tsarist Russia during the 19th century, the KHANATE being abolished in 1848. A nationalist movement developed in the early 20th century and there was a bloody anti-Tsarist revolt in 1916. In 1917 a national government was proclaimed in the capital Alma Ata; but this was suppressed by the Red Army, which occupied the country (1919–20), and large numbers of Russians and Ukrainians moved in. It became the Kazakh Autonomous Soviet Socialist Republic, which in 1936 became a full republic within the Soviet Union. Vast areas (some ten million acres) were developed for agriculture as state farms, while there was also heavy industrialization during the 1930s and 1940s. Large

mineral deposits, including uranium, were discovered and exploited, particularly around Lake Balkhash. After 1941 Stalin's regime forcibly moved German, Greek, and Armenian deportees into the republic. In October 1990 Kazakhstan proclaimed its sovereignty, and in December 1991 its independence was recognized. The Communist Party remained in power, as the Socialist Party, under President Nursultan NAZARBAYEV. In 1994 Kazakhstan's first multiparty elections were won by supporters of Nazarbayev; however, the results were invalidated in 1995 and Nazarbayev announced that he would rule by decree until fresh elections could be held. Kazakhstan is a member of the COMMONWEALTH OF INDEPENDENT STATES. In 1997 the capital transferred to Akmola.

CAPITAL:	Akmola
AREA:	2,717,300 sq km (1,048,887 sq miles)
POPULATION:	16.677 million (1996)
CURRENCY:	tenge
RELIGIONS:	Sunni Muslim; Eastern Orthodox
ETHNIC GROUPS:	Kazakh 40.0%; Russian 38.0%; Ukrainian 5.0%; Tatar, Armenian, Azeri, German, Greek, and Korean minorities
LANGUAGES:	Kazakh (official); Russian; minority languages
INTERNATIONAL ORGANIZATIONS:	UN; CSCE; Commonwealth of Independent States; North Atlantic Co-operation Council

Keating, Paul (1954–) Australian statesman; Labor Prime Minister (1991–96). Keating served as finance minister (1983–91), introducing sweeping economic reforms. As prime minister he supported the ending of Australia's constitutional links with the UK. In 1996 he led Labor to defeat in the general election.

Kefauver, Carey Estes (1903–63) US politician. A state Senator (1949–63), he came to national prominence in the early 1950s when, as chairman of a US Senate committee investigating organized crime, he exposed nationwide gambling and crime syndicates, which had infiltrated legitimate business and gained control of local politics. The evidence of corruption among federal tax officials led to several dismissals and the resignation of the commissioner of Internal Revenue. Kefauver won the Democratic Party's nomination for Vice-President (1956), but President EISENHOWER (Republican) was re-elected.

Keitel, Wilhelm Bodewin Johann Gustav (1882–1946) German field-marshal. As chief-of-staff of the High Command of the German armed forces (1938–45), he handled the armistice negotiations with France in 1940 and ratified the unconditional surrender of Germany in 1945. He was a close adviser of HITLER, and bore some of the responsibility for repressive measures taken by the army in occupied territory. He was hanged after the NUREMBERG TRIALS.

Kellogg-Briand Pact (or Pact of Paris) (1928) A multilateral agreement condemning war. The Pact grew out of a proposal by the French Premier, Aristide BRIAND, to the US government for a treaty outlawing war between the two countries. The US Secretary of State, Frank B. Kellogg, proposed a multilateral treaty of the same character. In August 1928, 15 nations signed an agreement committing themselves to peace; the US ratified it in 1929, followed by a further 46 nations. The failure of the Pact to provide measures of enforcement nullified its contribution to international order.

Kempis, Thomas à (1379–1471) AUGUSTINIAN canon and religious writer. He was the author of the *Imitatio Christi*, an influential work which emphasized the need for asceticism, and reacted against the worldliness of the 15th century Catholic establishment.

Kenilworth, Siege of (June–December 1266) An episode during the BARONS' wars when HENRY III attacked Kenilworth Castle, refuge of the de MONTFORTS and their supporters. The Dictum of Kenilworth (31 October 1266) asserted the king's powers over the barons and offered inducements to peace by allowing them to recover their confiscated lands: the beseiged earls finally surrendered in December.

Kennedy, John Fitzgerald (1917–63) Thirty-fifth President of the USA (1961–63). After service in the US Navy in World War II, he became a Democratic member of the House of Representatives and subsequently a Senator. In 1960 he won the Democratic nomination and defeated Vice-President Nixon in the closest presidential election since 1884. Soon after his inaugural address in which he made the statement, 'ask not what your country can do for you – ask what you can do for your country', Kennedy brought a new spirit of hope and enthusiasm to the office. Although Congress gave support to his foreign aid proposals and space programme, it was reluctant to accept his domestic programme known as the 'New Frontier' proposals for CIVIL RIGHTS and social reform. In foreign affairs, he recovered from the failure of the attempted invasion of Cuba at the BAY OF PIGS and resisted the Soviet premier Khrushchev's threat to sign a separate peace treaty with East Germany in 1961. He also successfully handled the CUBAN MISSILE CRISIS in 1962. Kennedy then helped to secure a NUCLEAR TEST-BAN TREATY in 1963. He became increasingly involved in Vietnam, by despatching more and more 'military advisers' and then US troops into combat-readiness there. Kennedy established (1961) the Alliance for Progress to provide economic assistance to Latin America. In November 1963 he was assassinated while visiting Dallas, Texas. The Warren Commission, appointed by his presidential successor, Lyndon B. Johnson, concluded that he had been killed by Lee Harvey OSWALD. John F. Kennedy was a member of a noted political family. His brother Robert F. Kennedy (1925–68) was Attorney-General (1961–64), and was a candidate for the Democratic presidential nomination in 1968. However, just as his support was growing, he also was assassinated. His brother Edward M. Kennedy (1932–   ) is a Senator and an influential figure in the Democratic Party.

Kenneth I (MacAlpine) (d. *c.* 859) King of Scotland (*c.* 843–58). He united the Scots and Picts to form the kingdom of Scotia (*c.* 843), having succeeded in *c.* 841 as King of Dalriada in the Highlands. In *c.* 848 he moved the relics of St COLUMBA to Scone, where the kings of Scotland were crowned.

Kenneth II (d. 995) King of Scotland (971–95). In return for recognizing the lordship of King EDGAR of England, Kenneth received Lothian two years after his accession in 971. He was murdered by Constantine III who, in

turn, was killed by Kenneth III (d. 1005), whose brief reign of civil wars from 997 ended with the accession of Malcolm II.

Kenya An equatorial country in east Africa, bounded inland by Somalia on the east, Ethiopia and Sudan on the north, Uganda on the west, and Tanzania on the south.

Physical. In the south-east of Kenya is a hot, damp coast on the Indian Ocean, into which run two long rivers, the Tana and the Galana. They rise in the central highlands, a region containing Mount Kenya and cool slopes and plateaux suitable for farming, particularly the cultivation of tea and coffee. The highlands are split by part of the Great Rift Valley, a region of lakes, and to the west fall away to the eastern shore of Lake Victoria. Northward is a rift-valley lake, Turkana (once called Rudolf), and to its east is a vast, hot, dry region with thorny scrub.

Economy. Kenya has an agricultural economy with a developing industrial sector. Main exports are coffee, tea, and petroleum products (from imported crude oil) from the oil refinery at MOMBASA. Tourism is an important sector of the economy, while the textiles, chemical, and vehicle-assembly industries are also significant. There is a developed financial services sector, and a flourishing informal sector. Agriculture is diverse: the highlands produce maize, coffee, tea, and sisal, while lowland crops include coconuts, cashew nuts, and cotton.

History. In areas of the Great Rift Valley, such as Lake Turkana, palaeontologists have discovered some of the earliest fossil HOMINID remains. Arabs settled on the coast during the 7th century. During the 16th and 17th centuries, Portuguese traders operated in the region. The Masai pastoral people came into the area in the 18th century from the north, but during the 19th century they were largely displaced by the agricultural Kikuyu, who steadily advanced from the south. British coastal trade began in the 1840s, and in 1887 the British East African Association (a trading company) secured a lease of coastal strip from the Sultan of Zanzibar. The British East Africa Protectorate was established in 1896, when thousands of Indians were brought in to build railways. The British crown colony of Kenya was created in 1920. By then a great area of the 'White Highlands' had been reserved for white settlement, while 'Native Reserves' were established to separate the two communities. During the 1920s there was considerable immigration from Britain, and a development of African political movements, demanding a greater share in the government of the country. Kikuyu nationalism developed steadily, led by Jomo KENYATTA. From this tension grew the Kenya Africa Union, and the militant MAU MAU movement (1952–57). An election in 1961 led to the two African political parties, the Kenya African National Union (KANU) and the Kenya African Democratic Union (KADU), joining the government. Independence was achieved in 1963, and in the following year Kenya became a republic with Kenyatta as President. Under him, Kenya remained generally stable, but after his death in 1978 opposition to his successor, Daniel arap Moi, mounted, culminating in a bloody attempted coup in 1982. Elections in 1983 saw the return of comparative stability with Moi still President, but of an increasingly corrupt and autocratic regime. In December 1991 Moi reluctantly agreed to end single-party politics, as a result of pressure from the Forum for the Restoration of Democracy (FORD), supported by Western aid-donor nations. Multiparty elections, held in 1992 and in 1998, were won by Moi amid allegations of electoral fraud. Sporadic outbreaks of ethnic and political violence have continued, notably in mid 1997 when opposition protestors demanded sweeping constitutional change.

CAPITAL:	Nairobi
AREA:	582,646 sq km (224,961 sq miles)
POPULATION:	29.137 million (1996)
CURRENCY:	1 Kenya shilling = 100 cents
RELIGIONS:	Protestant 26.5%; Roman Catholic 26.4%; traditional beliefs 18.9%; African Indigenous 17.6%; Muslim 6.0%; Orthodox 2.5%
ETHNIC GROUPS:	Kikuyu 20.9%; Luhya 13.8%; Luo 12.8%; Kamba 11.3%; Kalenjin 10.8%; other African 29.2%; other including Asian 1.2%
LANGUAGES:	Swahili (official); English; local languages
INTERNATIONAL ORGANIZATIONS:	Non-Aligned Movement; OAU; UN; Commonwealth

Kenyatta, Jomo (c. 1892–1978) Kenyan statesman. He visited England in 1928 as Secretary of the Kenya Central Association, campaigning for land reforms and political rights for Africans. He remained in Britain from 1932 to 1946, taking part with Kwame NKRUMAH in the Pan-African Conference at Manchester (1945). He returned to Kenya in 1946, and became President of the Kenya African Union. In 1953 he was convicted and imprisoned for managing the MAU MAU rebellion, a charge he steadfastly denied. He was released in 1961 and shortly afterwards entered Parliament as leader of the Kenya African National Union (KANU), winning a decisive victory for his party at the 1963 elections. He led his country to independence in 1963 and served as its first President from 1964 to his death in 1978. Once in power, he reconciled Asian and European Kenyans by liberal policies and economic common sense, but he was intolerant of dissent and outlawed opposition parties in 1969.

Keppel, Arnold Joost van, 1st Earl of Albemarle (1669–1718) Dutch soldier, who entered the service of WILLIAM III (of Orange) and accompanied him to England in 1688. He served William in various capacities in England, but returned to Holland after William's death and fought with distinction at the Battles of RAMILLIES (1706) and OUDENARDE (1708).

Kerala A region in India which occupies the narrow Malabar coastal plain between the Western Ghats and the Arabian Sea. Its name evokes an ancient kingdom, Keralaputra, to which there are references in ASOKA's inscriptions (3rd century BC). From early times trade developed with distant parts of the world. The dominant rulers up to the 5th century AD were the Cheras, but the region subsequently fragmented into separate kingdoms and was never again united. However, the evolution of the Malayalam language maintained some cultural unity.

The arrival of Vasco DA GAMA at Calicut in 1498 began an era of European dominance of the spice trade. Cochin, which developed as a Portuguese port, was conquered by the Dutch in 1663. By the late 18th century British influence predominated, signalled by the annexation of Malabar District (1792). In 1795 the southern princely state of Travancore accepted British protection.

Kerensky, Alexander Feodorovich (1881–1970) Russian revolutionary. He was a representative of the moderate Labour Party in the Fourth Duma (1912) and joined the Socialist Revolutionary Party during the RUSSIAN REVOLUTION. After the emperor's abdication in March (February, old style calendar), he was made Minister of War in the Provisional Government of Prince Lvov, succeeding him as Premier four months later. Determined to continue the war against Germany, he failed to implement agrarian and economic reforms, and his government was overthrown by the BOLSHEVIKS in the October Revolution. He escaped to Paris, where he continued as an active propagandist against the Soviet regime.

Kesselring, Albrecht (1885–1960) German field-marshal. He commanded the BOMBING OFFENSIVE over Poland, the Netherlands, and France before commencing the Battle of BRITAIN, when he was hampered by interference from GOERING and HITLER. He was posted to the Mediterranean soon after and from 1943 to 1945 commanded all German forces in Italy, and then in 1945 in the West. Condemned to death as a war criminal in 1947, he had his sentence commuted to life imprisonment and was freed in 1952.

Kett's Rebellion (July–August 1549) An orderly English peasant protest against the profiteering and ENCLOSURES of local Norfolk landlords. Led by Robert Kett, a well-to-do tradesman, 16,000 small farmers encamped outside Norwich, and eventually gained control of the city. By their disciplined self-government, the rebels aimed to impress the authorities and shame the local magnates. The rebellion was suppressed by forces under John Dudley (later Duke of NORTHUMBERLAND) who routed the rebels at Dussindale on 27 August. Kett and his brother William were among those executed.

Keynes, John Maynard (1883–1946) British economist, and founder of modern macro-economics. Keynes first achieved national prominence when, in *The Economic Consequences of the Peace* (1919), he criticized the damaging effects on the international economy of the vindictive REPARATIONS policy towards Germany. In his seminal work *The General Theory of Employment, Interest and Money* (1936) Keynes argued that, contrary to the presuppositions of classical and neo-classical economics, a market economy will not invariably maintain or move towards full employment of resources, but may, on the contrary, become stuck in a situation of underemployment. This is because the movement of prices and interest rates may not in themselves provide the necessary incentives for producers to employ idle resources. In particular, Keynes rejected the idea that wage cuts would be a reliable cure for unemployment as resting on an erroneous view of the labour market, which assumed that the price of labour could be altered without significantly affecting demand (or supply) conditions in the rest of the economy at large. In correcting this error, Keynes argued first that cuts in money-wages did not directly bring cuts in real wages but resulted rather in lower prices and thus in an increased purchasing power of the economy's money supply. This in turn would raise aggregate demand and therefore employment only in so far as it led to lower interest rates and thence to higher investment expenditure. Such expenditure would also increase consumption demand through the multiplier effect on household incomes. If the private sector's will to invest could not be adequately stimulated, the government would have to step in with outlays on public works or other (relatively) direct boosts to aggregate demand. Keynes played a major role in the BRETTON WOODS CONFERENCE (1944), which led to the establishment of the INTERNATIONAL MONETARY FUND and the WORLD BANK. His views became so well-respected as to be raised almost to the level of orthodoxy, underpinning the post-war foundation of the British WELFARE STATE, as originally set forth in William BEVERIDGE's report of 1942. However, with the rise of MONETARISM in the 1980s, the validity of 'Keynesian economics' was called into question.

KGB (Russian: Komitet Gosudarstvennoy Bezopasnosti) The Committee of State Security in the Soviet Union, a political police and security agency. Formed in 1953, the KGB was responsible for external espionage, internal counter-intelligence, and internal 'crimes against the state'. The most famous chairman of the KGB was Yuri Andropov (1967–82), who was Soviet leader (1982–84). He made KGB operations more sophisticated, especially against internal dissidents. In 1992 the KGB was dissolved, to be replaced by the Central Intelligence Service of the Russian Republic. This pledged itself to work with Western Intelligence in the prevention of nuclear proliferation and the development of chemical and biological weapons, and to fight terrorism and drug trafficking.

Khalifa, Abdallah (Muhammad al-Ta'a'ishi) (c. 1846–99) The successor of the Sudanese MAHDI. In 1883 the Mahdi made Khalifa commander of the army, and he was largely responsible for the victory over the British at Khartoum in 1885. When the Mahdi died Khalifa eliminated the remaining Egyptian garrisons, and waged war on ETHIOPIA until 1889. After his defeat by KITCHENER at Omdurman he fled to Kordofan, where he died in battle.

Khalji A Muslim dynasty of Turkish origin which seized power in northern India in 1290. Its three kings successively ruled the DELHI sultanate for the next thirty years. Ala ud-Din (1296–1316), the second sultan, was the most successful. His armies held off Mongol threats, subdued large parts of Rajasthan and Gujarat, then carried Islam to Madurai in the extreme south of the subcontinent. Their object was pillage rather than permanent empire, yet Khalji expansion began a new era of Muslim penetration of Hindu southern India. On Ala ud-Din's assassination the dynasty declined, to be replaced in 1320 by the TUGHLUQ dynasty.

Khalsa (Punjabi, 'pure ones') A group within SIKHISM consisting of those who have accepted full initiation into the faith. The Khalsa was instituted by the tenth Sikh GURU, GOBIND SINGH, in 1699, when he formed an army of soldier-saints, prepared to fight for their faith. Nowadays, both men and women can be initiated into the Khalsa by drinking *amrit* ('nectar'; a mixture of sugar and water) in the presence of five Sikhs, and promising to wear the 'five Ks': uncut hair (*kesh*); a comb (*kangha*); a bracelet (*kara*); shorts (*kaccha*); and a sword or

dagger (*kirpan*). To these male members added the turban, giving the Sikhs a distinctive appearance. In addition, smoking, alcohol, and sexual incontinence are forbidden. Members of the Khalsa must accept the teachings of the GURUS, and be prepared to sacrifice all for the faith. Men who are initiated are given the additional name of *Singh* ('lion'), while women adopt the additional name of *Kaur* ('princess').

Khama, Sir Seretse (1921–80) Botswanan statesman, first President of Botswana (1966–80). He inherited the chieftainship of the Ngwato people when he was four. He was educated in South Africa and Britain, where his marriage to an Englishwoman led to the British government demanding he renounce his chieftainship before returning to Botswana. In 1956 he returned to BOTSWANA and established the Bechuanaland Democratic Party. The party won the 1965 elections, and Seretse Khama became his country's leader. Botswana became independent in 1966 with Seretse as its first President. A strong believer in multiracial democracy, he strengthened the economy of Botswana and achieved universal free education.

khanate A region ruled by a khan (a Mongol-Turkic word meaning a supreme tribal leader elevated by the support of his warriors). On GENGHIS KHAN's death in 1227 his empire was divided into four parts, each ruled by one of his descendants. By the mid-13th century the MONGOL empire consisted of four khanates; the khanate of the Western Kipchaks (the GOLDEN HORDE); the khanate of Persia, whose ruler was called the Il-khan; the khanate of Turkistan (the White Horde of the Eastern Kipchaks), and the khanate of the Khakhan in East Asia. The three khans were subject to the Khakhan (the Great Khan), but were generally resentful in their relations with him. After the death of KUBLAI KHAN (1294) the Khakhan's authority was nominal. In 1368 the Mongols were driven out of China and by c. 1500 all four khanates had disappeared. A number of lesser khanates emerged; the khanates of Kazan, Astrakhan, the Crimea, Khiva, Bukhara, Tashkent, Samarkand, and Kokand. These presented a threat to the communities surrounding them for many years. One by one all were absorbed by Russia, the last to fall being Kokand (1876).

Khandesh A medieval Muslim kingdom occupying a narrow strip of territory between the Satpura and Ajanta hills in the Tapti valley of western India. From 1382 to 1599 Khandesh was an independent sultanate, but following conquest by AKBAR it became a province of the Mogul empire. Under subsequent Maratha and British rulers it was absorbed into larger units, and the region, a cotton-growing area, is now part of Maharashtra state.

Khilafat Movement An Indian Muslim movement that aimed to rouse public opinion against the harsh treatment accorded to the OTTOMAN EMPIRE after World War I and specifically against the treatment of the Ottoman sultan and caliph (khalifa). The movement began in 1919 and, under the leadership of the Ali brothers, Muhammad Ali (1878–1931) and Shaukat Ali (1873–1938), assumed a mainly political character. It formed an alliance with the Indian National CONGRESS, adopting the non-co-operation programme in May 1920.

The Khilafat movement had considerable support from Muslims but was extinguished in 1924 after the abolition of the caliphate by ATATÜRK.

Khmer A subject of the Hinduized kingdom of Funan, based in the Mekong valley in the 1st century AD. In the 6th century the Khmers overthrew their rulers, whose title 'Kings of the Mountain' was taken over by the Khmer kings. The Khmers were Buddhists, but their kings, with two exceptions, remained Hindus. Early in the 9th century Jayavarman II expelled Javanese invaders, re-united his country, and instituted the cult of the god-king. He and his successors ruled from the city of ANGKOR or its vicinity. They built cities and temples with forced labour, constructed canals and reservoirs which supported a rice-growing economy, and engaged in savage wars against their neighbours. At the end of the 12th century under Jayavarman VII the Khmers were at the height of their power. Jayavarman VII defeated CHAMPA, extended Khmer territory, and rebuilt Angkor Thom, providing rest-houses and hospitals.

During the 13th century the Khmers were converted from Mahayana Buddhism, which accepted the idea of god-kings, to Hinayana Buddhism, which rejected such concepts. Oppressed by forced labour and decimated by wars, they became unwilling to build temples for god-kings; the complex irrigation systems broke down and the Thais of Siam, former tributaries, attacked Angkor. After repeated defeats the Khmers abandoned Angkor in 1431 and made the village of Phnom Penh, further from the Siamese frontier, the new royal capital of Cambodia. The kingdom lost further lands to its stronger neighbours of Siam and ANNAM in the 18th century.

Khmer Rouge Cambodian communist movement that was formed to resist the right-wing, US-backed regime of Lon Nol after the latter's military coup in 1970. The Khmer Rouge, with Vietnamese assistance, first dominated the countryside and then captured the capital Phnom Penh (1975). Under POL POT it began a bloody purge, liquidating nearly the entire professional élite as well as most of the government officials and Buddhist monks. The majority of the urban population were relocated on worksites in the countryside where large numbers perished. The regime was responsible for an estimated 2 million deaths in CAMBODIA (Kampuchea), and for the destruction of the country's infrastructure. Frontier disputes with Vietnam provoked an invasion in 1978, which led to the overthrow of the Khmer Rouge regime, although its forces continued a guerrilla war against the Vietnamese-backed Heng Samrin regime from bases in Thailand. As the Party of Democratic Kampuchea, with its former leader Pol Pot still influential, it agreed to join the UN-backed Supreme National Council, following the peace agreement of October 1991. However, the Khmer Rouge refused to participate in multiparty elections in 1993 and has continued to wage a guerrilla war against the elected government. Since 1996 the movement has been riven by internal conflicts. In 1997 elements of the Khmer Rouge imprisoned Pol Pot, announcing that he had been tried and given a life sentence; he died the following year.

Khomeini, Ruhollah (c. 1900–89) Iranian religious and political leader. The son and grandson of Shiite religious leaders, he was acclaimed as an *ayatollah* (Persian, from Arabic, 'token of God', i.e. major religious leader) in 1950. During the anti-government demonstrations in 1963 he spoke out against the land reforms and Westernization of IRAN by MUHAMMAD REZA SHAH PAHLAVI, and was briefly imprisoned. After exile in Iraq (1964), he settled near Paris (1978), from where he agitated for the overthrow of the Shah. Khomeini returned to Iran in 1979 and was proclaimed the religious leader of the revolution. Islamic law was once more strictly imposed, and he enforced a return to strict fundamentalist Islamic tradition. The IRAN HOSTAGE CRISIS confirmed his anti-US policy, and the IRAN–IRAQ WAR his militancy; only with deep bitterness did he accept the UN armistice of 1988. He supported Islamic revolution throughout the Middle East.

Khosrau I (d. 579 AD) King of Persia (531–79), whose reign, after a long period of turbulence, marked the highest point of the SASSANIAN EMPIRE. Khosrau I restored royal authority over the army, bureaucracy, and lower nobility, reformed taxation, and restored defences and public works. He invaded Byzantine Syria in 540 and took Antioch. In 565, in alliance with the western Turks, he destroyed the Hephthalite empire on his eastern frontier. He also annexed YEMEN and died during negotiations with Byzantium over his invasion of Mesopotamia.

Khosrau II (d. 628 AD) King of Persia (590–628) who succeeded to the throne after the deposition of his father, Hormidz. After being unseated by a coup, he accepted Byzantine aid to regain his throne in return for most of Armenia. He recovered his territory, with Edessa and Caesarea, in 610. In 611 JERUSALEM was taken and several thousand Christians massacred. In 616 Khosrau II simultaneously invaded Egypt, captured Ankara, and besieged Constantinople. A Byzantine counter-attack drove him back to Ctesiphon, where he was assassinated. He had overtaxed the resources of his empire, which fell to ARAB conquest within a decade of his death.

Khrushchev, Nikita Sergeyevich (1894–1971) Soviet statesman. During World War II he organized resistance in the Ukraine. He was actively involved in agriculture after the war, creating and enlarging state farms to replace collectives. On the death of STALIN he became First Secretary of the Communist Party (1953–64) and Chairman of the Council of Ministers (1958–64). In a historic speech at the TWENTIETH CONGRESS (1956) he denounced Stalin and the 'cult of personality'. At home he attempted to tackle the problem of food supply by arranging for cultivation of the 'virgin lands' of Kazakhstan. He continued the programme of partial decentralization, and introduced widespread changes in regional economic administration. He restored some legality to police procedure and closed many PRISON CAMPS. In foreign affairs he subdued both the Poles under GOMULKA and the HUNGARIAN REVOLUTION. In 1962 he came close to global war in the CUBAN MISSILE CRISIS, but agreed to the withdrawal of Soviet missiles. His ideological feud with MAO ZEDONG threatened a Sino-Soviet war. However, his policy of 'peaceful coexistence' with the West did notably ease the international atmosphere. He was dismissed from office in 1964, largely as a result of the repeated failures in agricultural production.

Khyber Pass A route through the eastern end of the Himalayas, between north-west Pakistan and the Kabul plain of Afghanistan highest point 1,072 m (3,517 feet). For part of its length (53 km (33 miles)) the Pass runs through a gorge cut by stream erosion, and for a distance of 8 km (5 miles) it narrows to a defile little more than 180 m (600 feet) wide. It is the most northerly and most important of the passes between Pakistan and Afghanistan. All invaders of India came through the Kyber Pass: Aryans, Persians, ALEXANDER THE GREAT, MONGOLS, and MOGULS. The British in India fought a number of engagements against Afghan tribes to secure the Pass (1841–42; 1878; 1919).

Kiakhta, Treaty of (1727) A treaty between Russia and China signed at Kiakhta, a town in Russia immediately north of the Mongolian frontier. A border was agreed between Siberia and Mongolia, China losing a large amount of peripheral land to Russia. Trade in Chinese silks, tea, and porcelain and Russian furs was permitted but limited to Kiakhta. The Russians were also allowed to send language students to Beijing and to build a church for them there.

kibbutz (Hebrew, 'gathering', 'collective') An Israeli collective settlement, usually agricultural but sometimes also industrial. Land for kibbutzim was originally held in the name of the Jewish people by the Jewish National Fund, and is now owned or leased at nominal fees by its members, who also manage it. The first kibbutz, Deganya, was founded in 1910, and they now number over 300 in Israel.

Kidd, William (c. 1645–1701) Scottish privateer, based as a shipowner and trader in New York from 1689 to 1699. After service in the Caribbean in KING WILLIAM'S WAR and anti-privateering ventures for New York, he was commissioned by the crown to put down piracy in the Indian Ocean and attack French shipping. Though he obeyed the latter order, he joined up with other pirates in Madagascar and ravaged the Malabar coast of India (1687–89). He was arrested on his return to America and hanged in London in 1701.

Kiel Canal An artificial waterway connecting the North Sea with the Baltic. Conceived by BISMARCK (1873) so as to give German ships quick access to the North Sea, it was built 1887–95. The construction of larger battleships (1907) forced Germany to widen the Canal. It was internationalized in 1919 because of its strategic importance, but Hitler repudiated its international status in 1936, a condition re-imposed after World War II.

Kiev Rus The historical nucleus of Russia. Kiev, now in the Ukraine, was probably founded in the 6th or 7th century, the centre of a feudal state ruled by the Rurik dynasty from the 9th to the 13th century. About 878 Igor advanced along the Dnieper River from Novgorod and made Kiev capital of the Varangarian–Russian principality. As the oldest established city it is known as 'the mother of Russian cities' and also 'the Jerusalem of Russia' as the first centre of the Greek Orthodox Church in Russia.

Killiecrankie, Battle of (27 July 1689) A battle fought in a narrow densely wooded pass near Pitlochry in Scotland when John Graham of Claverhouse, Viscount Dundee, led the first JACOBITE attempt to restore JAMES II to the English and Scottish thrones. He overwhelmed the inexperienced forces of General Mackay, who lost 2,000 dead and 500 taken prisoner, but Dundee was killed at the moment of victory. The Highlanders were subsequently unable to follow up their success.

Kilwa An island off the Tanzanian coast. It was a sultanate founded by Arabs in c. 957, and by 1200 it had a monopoly of the ZIMBABWE gold trade. Its agents reached MALACCA. After 1500 the Portuguese ruined its economy, and in 1587 the Zimba, marauders from the Zambezi valley further reduced the population. Kilwa recovered briefly; in the 17th century ivory was traded there; in the 1770s French slave-traders used it as a base.

Kim Il Sung (1912–94) North Korean politician, Communist Party leader (1946–94) and President (1972–94). As a young man he emigrated to Manchuria where he was active as a communist in the resistance to the Japanese invasion (see SINO-JAPANESE WAR). After the Soviet Union had expelled the Japanese forces from Korea, he returned, and was appointed Prime Minister of the newly-formed Democratic People's Republic of Korea in 1948. Following the KOREAN WAR Kim Il Sung was initially reliant upon aid from the Soviet Union and from communist China, which had supplied military help during the Korean War. However, his adherence to Stalinism led to his isolation from both Moscow and Beijing; he fostered a personality cult, styling himself the Great Leader and making North Korea one of the world's most closed societies. Before transferring power to his son Kim Jong Il (1942–   ) in 1992 he annulled his country's agreement to nuclear non-proliferation and barred international inspectors from nuclear installations, fuelling suspicion that North Korea was developing nuclear weapons.

King, Martin Luther, Jr (1929–68) US pastor and CIVIL RIGHTS leader. As a Baptist pastor in Black churches in Alabama and Georgia, he won national fame by leading (1955–56) a Black boycott of segregated city bus lines in Montgomery, Alabama, which led to the desegregation of that city's buses. He then organized the Southern Christian Leadership Conference, and through this launched a nationwide civil rights campaign. A powerful orator, he urged reform through non-violent means, and was several times arrested and imprisoned. He organized (1963) a peaceful march on the Lincoln Memorial in Washington, in which some 200,000 took part. In 1964 he was awarded the Nobel Peace Prize. His campaign broadened from civil rights for the Black population to a criticism of the Vietnam War and of society's neglect of the poor. He was about to organize a Poor People's March to Washington when he was assassinated in Memphis, Tennessee (4 April 1968).

King, (William Lyon) Mackenzie (1874–1950) Canadian statesman. He entered the Canadian Parliament as a Liberal in 1908 and was appointed Minister of Labour (1909–11) under Sir Wilfrid LAURIER. Chosen (in 1919) as leader of the Liberal Party of Canada, he became Prime Minister in 1921, a post he filled, except for a brief interval in 1926, until 1930. He again served as Prime Minister from 1935 to 1948. He never had a stable majority in Parliament, and combined his support from French-Canadian Liberals with endorsements from the Progressives, the farmers' party of Western Canada. This was reflected in his policies with their assertion of Canadian sovereignty, maintenance of political unity between English- and French-speaking Liberals, and cautious extension of social and economic reform measures. He led the Canadian war effort in World War II, but delayed conscription as long as possible. After the war he promoted the Canadian role in reconstruction, the United Nations, and NATO.

King George's War (1744–48) North American component of the War of the AUSTRIAN SUCCESSION, which saw the capture of LOUISBURG on Cape Breton Island by a combined British Navy–New England force under William Pepperell in 1745. A subsequent campaign against the St Lawrence valley was abandoned. The fortress was returned to France in exchange for Madras in 1748.

King, Martin Luther, Jr *King's 'I have a dream' address to a peaceful civil rights rally in 1963, in which he used biblical imagery to illustrate his vision of a racially just and harmonious society, is one of the most inspirational speeches of the 20th century.*

Kingitanga A MAORI movement in New Zealand intended to unify the Maori under an hereditary kingship and restrain individual chiefs from selling land. In 1858, under the guidance of Wiremu Tamihana (the king-maker), POTATAU, the first king, was recognized by tribes of central North Island. The Kingitanga sought to establish and enforce its own laws, but its more

moderate leaders, including Tamihana, were willing to contemplate a defined authority under the British crown. Governor George GREY was disinclined to recognize a movement which would hinder British authority and settlement. Independent-minded members of the Kingitanga such as Rewi Maniapoto became involved in the TARANAKI war and gave Grey grounds for invading the Waikato in 1863. Even so, for many years, government authority did not run in 'the King Country'. In 1883, the King Country chiefs admitted settlement and King TAWHIAO returned to his traditional land in lower Waikato. In the 20th century, largely under the influence of TE PUEA, the Kingitanga came to terms with government and became a focus for economic and cultural revival.

King Philip's War (1675–76) A Native American rising which resulted from encroachments on Native American lands in New England. It was led by Metacomet (or King Philip), chief of the Wampanoag, whose lands were in southern Massachusetts, but Mohawks of the IROQUOIS confederacy devastated frontier settlements in northern and western interior New England as well. Before Philip was betrayed and killed by CHURCH in 1676 near Kingston, Rhode Island, Native Americans had raided within 32 km (20 miles) of Boston and one out of every ten adult males in Massachusetts had been killed.

King William's War (1689–97) A North American frontier war between the French and the English and their Native American allies, which was a colonial adjunct to the War of the League of AUGSBURG in Europe. The two main theatres were the northern coast and the Upper Hudson–Upper St Lawrence valleys. In 1690 Sir William Phipps's New England expedition sacked Port Royal in Acadia, but an intercolonial campaign against Quebec and Montreal ended in disaster. FRONTENAC organized Abuski raids on English outposts in Maine and successfully intimidated the IROQUOIS. Both sides lacked resources for full-scale war, and assistance from Europe was thwarted. The war was ended by the Treaty of Ryswick (1697) and a truce in Maine (1699).

Kinnock, Neil Gordon (1942–) British Labour politician, leader of the opposition (1983–92). Elected to Parliament in 1970, he was elected Leader of his Party in 1983 and thus led the Opposition to THATCHER's second administration. Following Labour's third successive electoral defeat in 1987 he set in motion a radical reform of the Party, in order to win back public confidence. In doing so he faced opposition from both the Left and Right wings of the Party, but he reconciled them to an agreed programme by 1992. Although the Party made some gains in the general election of that year, it again failed to win a majority, and Kinnock resigned. In 1994 he became a European Commissioner.

Kiribati (pronounced Kiribas) A country comprising a widely scattered archipelago of 33 islands in the Pacific Ocean, lying either side of the Equator and between longitudes 169° W and 147° E.
Physical. Many of the islands are coral atolls not more than 1 km (0.5 miles) across. Kiribati comprises the 16 former Gilbert Islands, eight of the Line Islands, the eight Phoenix Islands, and Ocean Island (Banaba).
Economy. The economy of Kiribati is based on fishing and subsistence farming. The main resource is the

coconut palm, from which copra is produced for export. The phosphate deposits on Ocean Island, once a major source of revenue, are now exhausted.

History. Inhabited by Micronesians when sighted by the Spanish in the 16th century, the largest island group was named the Gilbert Islands in the 1820s by the Russian hydrographer Adam Krusenstern (1770–1846). From 1837 European sperm whale hunters and traders began to inhabit the group, over which Britain declared a protectorate in 1892. In 1916 the group became the crown colony of the Gilbert and Ellice Islands. In 1942 Japanese naval forces occupied the islands, and in 1943 US marines landed and crushed Japanese resistance after fierce fighting. In 1974 the Ellice Islanders voted to secede from the colony, and the Ellice Islands became independent as TUVALU in 1978. The Gilbert Islands became the independent nation of Kiribati in 1979. Falling exports in copra and fish resulted in a trade deficit in 1990 of $24 million, with which the government of Teatao Teannaki (elected May 1991) had to contend. In 1994 Teannaki's government lost a vote of confidence and Teburoro Tito was elected President.

CAPITAL:	Bairiki (on Tarawa Atoll)
AREA:	811 sq km (313 sq miles)
POPULATION:	81,800 (1996)
CURRENCY:	1 Australian dollar = 100 cents
RELIGIONS:	Roman Catholic; Protestant
ETHNIC GROUPS:	I-Kiribati (over 97%)
LANGUAGES:	English (official); I-Kiribati
INTERNATIONAL ORGANIZATIONS:	Commonwealth; South Pacific Forum

Kirk, Norman (1923–74) New Zealand statesman. A long-time Labour Party member, he entered Parliament in 1957 and successfully challenged A. H. Nordmeyer as parliamentary party leader in 1965. After two defeats, Kirk led the party to a landslide victory in 1972. As Prime Minister he embarked on a programme of social reform. After Kirk's death in 1974, his government swiftly lost popularity and was defeated in the 1975 general election.

Kirov, Sergei Mironovich (1886–1934) Russian-born revolutionary leader. A strong supporter of STALIN, he began his revolutionary activities in Caucasia but moved to Leningrad (1928) and became a member of the POLITBURO (1930). In 1934 he was assassinated by a young party member, Leonid Nikolayev, possibly at Stalin's instigation. Stalin used Kirov's murder to launch the show trials and party purges of the late 1930s.

Kishi Nobusuke (1896–1987) Japanese statesman. A member of TOJO's government, he was increasingly opposed to Japan's policies later in World War II. Imprisoned in 1945, he was released without trial. Elected to the Japanese House of Representatives (1953), he emerged as leader of the LIBERAL DEMOCRATIC PARTY, becoming Prime Minister in 1957. In foreign affairs he aimed to ease tensions with neighbouring Asian countries, while encouraging the US–Japanese link. His domestic policy was conservative, especially in education and over law and order. He resigned in 1960, following a riot within the Japanese Diet building, allegedly over his revised JAPAN–UNITED STATES SECURITY TREATY.

Kissinger, Henry Alfred (1923–) US statesman. He acted as government consultant on defence (1955–68) and was appointed by President Nixon as head of the National Security Council (1969–75) and as Secretary of State (1973–77). He was largely responsible for improved relations (*détente*) with the Soviet Union, resulting in the STRATEGIC ARMS LIMITATION TALKS (SALT) of 1969. In addition, he helped to achieve a resolution of the Indo-Pakistan War (1971), rapprochement with communist China (1972), which the USA now recognized for the first time, and above all the resolution of the VIETNAM WAR. This he had at first accepted, supporting the bombing offensive against Cambodia (1969–70), but he changed his views and after prolonged negotiation he reached agreement for the withdrawal of US troops in January 1973. He was awarded the Nobel peace prize jointly with the Vietnamese representative Le Duc Tho, who refused the honour. Later in that year he helped to resolve the Arab–Israeli War and restored US diplomatic relations with Egypt. After the WATERGATE SCANDAL and President Nixon's resignation, he remained in office to advise President FORD. He has since been a consultant and respected commentator on international affairs.

Kita Ikki (d. 1937) Japanese revolutionary and political thinker. A former socialist and member of the nationalist Kokuryukai (Black Dragon Society), Kita played a key role in the upsurge in violent right-wing militarism in the 1930s, inspiring young dissidents with his call for a revolutionary regime, headed by the military, which would nationalize wealth, sweep away existing political forms, and prepare Japan to establish leadership over all of Asia. He was executed in 1937 for alleged involvement in the INCIDENT OF 26 FEBRUARY 1936.

kitchen cabinet Unofficial advisers to a President or Prime Minister. The term was coined during the first years of Andrew JACKSON'S Presidency in the USA (1829–37). In his first years of office Jackson's official cabinet contained many strong but opposed personalities, including his first Vice-President, John CALHOUN, and his Secretary for War, John Eaton. Thus while official cabinet meetings were held as seldom as possible Jackson took most of his advice from VAN BUREN (later his second Vice-President and successor), John Eaton, Amos Kendall, Francis Blair (newspaper editors), and various personal friends appointed as minor government officials. After a cabinet reorganization in 1831 the President relied rather more on members of his official cabinet.

Kitchener of Khartoum and of Broome, Horatio Herbert, 1st Earl (1850–1916) British general. He commanded the Anglo-Egyptian army which conquered the SUDAN (1896–98). His organization of supplies and the effective use made by his troops of the machine-gun, a recent invention, enhanced his reputation and made him a popular hero. In the Second BOER WAR he was chief-of-staff to Lord Roberts, and had to curb the activities of Boer guerrilla fighters in 1900–02. The destruction of Boer farmhouses and placing of non-combatants in CONCENTRATION CAMPS earned him criticism from Liberal politicians and members of the public. Nevertheless, the peace terms of the Treaty of VEREENIGING (1902) owed much to him. He served in India as commander-in-chief and in Egypt (1911–14) before being appointed Secretary of State for War. Unlike many of his colleagues, he realized that the war would be a long one and campaigned successfully to secure volunteers. It was largely due to his determination that Britain survived the disasters of the first two years of the war. Set-backs on the WESTERN FRONT, blunders over the supply of artillery shells, and Kitchener's advice to abandon the DARDANELLES campaign, which ended disastrously, provoked considerable criticism from government colleagues, but he refused to resign. He drowned in 1916 on his way to Russia.

knighthood The special honour bestowed upon a man by dubbing (when he is invested with the right to bear arms) or by admission to one of the orders of chivalry. In England the emergence of knighthood was slow (the Anglo-Saxon word *cniht* means 'servant'). In the late 11th and early 12th centuries, knights were the lowest tier of those who held land in return for military service. During the 12th century their economic and social status improved, as society became more complex, and the market in free land developed. They became involved in local administration, and the new orders of knights which emerged in Europe in the aftermath of the CRUSADES helped to give them a distinct identity. First to appear were the military orders of the KNIGHTS HOSPITALLERS (*c.* 1070), the Knights of the Sepulchre (1113), and the KNIGHTS TEMPLAR (1118). Their potential for military colonization was best realized by the German Order of the TEUTONIC KNIGHTS (1190) which pushed eastwards on the frontiers with Poland and acquired Prussia for itself. The Order of the Livonian Knights gained similar successes along the Baltic. The Order of the Garter (1348) was England's first and most important, followed by the Order of the Bath (1399). France created the Order of the Star (1352), and BURGUNDY the Order of the Golden Fleece (1429).

Knights Hospitallers A military religious order, formally the Knights Hospitallers of St John of Jerusalem, so called after the dedication of their headquarters in Jerusalem to St John the Baptist. From 1310 they were known as the Knights of Rhodes, from 1530 the Knights of Malta. They began in *c.* 1070 with Muslim permission to run a hospital for sick pilgrims in Jerusalem, and were made a formal order when the city fell in 1099 to the First CRUSADE. They adopted a black habit bearing a white eight-pointed (Maltese) cross. Under the first Master their function became primarily military and spread to Western Europe. They followed the AUGUSTINIAN rule and were divided into three classes: knights, chaplains, and serving brothers. When they were driven out by SALADIN they went to Acre, only to be expelled a century later, and then they made Cyprus their headquarters. In 1310 they captured the island of Rhodes and retained it till 1522. Given the island of Malta by Emperor CHARLES V they held it, having fought off the assaults of the Turks, until it finally fell to NAPOLEON I. By this time the order had lost its former influence. Some members moved to Russia where Paul I was made Grand Master. His death in 1801 led to a period of confusion. The English branch of the order was revived in the 1830s and today cares for the sick.

Knights of Labor A US industrial trade union, founded in 1869 at a tailors' meeting in Philadelphia. By 1879 it was organized on a national basis, with membership open to all workers. Its goals were reformist rather than radical, and included the demand for an eight-hour day. Its growth was phenomenal. In 1882 the Knights helped push through Congress the Chinese Exclusion Act, prohibiting the entry into the USA of Chinese labourers. The union was at its height in 1886 under the leadership of Terence V. Powderly, with a membership of almost a million, but declined thereafter, partly due to involvement in unsuccessful strikes and to general antipathy to labour organizations after the HAYMARKET SQUARE RIOT. Factional disputes reduced its membership after the AMERICAN FEDERATION OF LABOR was founded, and by 1900 it was virtually extinct.

Knights Templar A military religious order properly called the Poor Knights of Christ and of the Temple of Solomon, founded in 1118 by Hugh de Payens, a knight of Champagne in France. He and eight companions vowed to protect pilgrims travelling on the public roads of the Holy Land (PALESTINE). At the Council of Troyes (1128) approval was given to their version of the BENEDICTINE rule. They quickly became very influential, attracting many noble members and growing in wealth, acquiring property throughout Christendom. When Jerusalem fell in 1187 they moved to Acre together with the KNIGHTS HOSPITALLERS and great rivalry and hatred developed between the orders. In 1291 when Acre also fell, the Knights Templar retreated to Cyprus. In Cyprus their great wealth enabled them to act as bankers to the nobility of most of Europe and this affluence attracted much hostility, in particular that of PHILIP IV of France. In 1307 they were charged with heresy and immorality. Though some of the charges may have been true, envy of their wealth seems to have been the reason for their persecution. They were condemned, their wealth confiscated, and the order suppressed. The Grand Master and many others were burned at the stake.

Knossos The leading city of the MINOAN civilization, situated a few miles inland from the north coast of the island of Crete. Knossos was excavated by the British archaeologist Sir Arthur Evans (1851–1941) from 1900 onwards. The ancient city was dominated by a palace built originally (*c.* 2000 BC) on the remains of a Neolithic settlement. The palace was destroyed *c.* 1700 BC, probably *c.* 1550 BC, and again shortly afterwards as a result of the massive explosion of the volcano at Thera (modern Santorini). The city seems to have been taken over by Mycenaean invaders *c.* 1450 BC, and the palace was devastated again *c.* 1375 BC. Inhabitation of Knossos continued, but its wealth and power had been destroyed – none of the magnificent decorative frescos on the walls of the palace date from after this disaster. Although Knossos never regained its lost glory, it remained one of the leading cities of CRETE, an often bitter rival of Gortyn. It was captured and destroyed by the Romans in 68–67 BC.

Know-Nothings (or American Party) A US political party, formed in New York in 1849 as a secret oath-bound society calling itself the Star Spangled Banner, opposing immigration, in particular of Irish Catholics. The Party derived its later name from the members' standard response to questions about their activities. In reaction to increasing Irish immigration, the Party called for a 21-year naturalization period and the exclusion of Catholics and foreigners from office, and began to win local and state elections in many parts of the country. In 1854, after the passing of the KANSAS–NEBRASKA ACT, the Party abandoned secrecy and entered the national stage as the American Party. It was joined by seceding WHIGS under ex-President FILLMORE, but was increasingly divided over the slavery issue. It failed badly in the 1856 presidential election and its membership disbanded.

Knox, Henry (1750–1806) American general, who commanded the Continental Artillery during the War of INDEPENDENCE. In 1775 he hauled the guns from Ticonderoga 124 km (200 miles) through the wilderness to Boston, forcing British evacuation. He was George WASHINGTON's right-hand man throughout the War, and after it organized the Veterans' Society of the Cincinnati (1783). A Federalist, he was Secretary of War to the Confederation and under President Washington (1785–94), but his scheme for a national militia was thwarted.

Knox, John (c. 1513–72) Scottish Protestant reformer. He played the key role in the establishment of the Scottish Kirk or Church of Scotland. By 1546 he had fallen under the influence of the Protestant preacher George WISHART. His association with the assassins of Cardinal BEATON led to his capture by the French and nineteen months of forced labour. In 1551 he became chaplain to EDWARD VI of England, but on the accession of MARY I (1553) he fled to Frankfurt, then Geneva, where he ministered to Protestant refugees from Britain and met John CALVIN.

His *First Blast of the Trumpet against the Monstrous Regiment* (meaning 'rule') *of Women* (1558), was intended to undermine the English, Scottish, and French Catholic queens who were suppressing Protestantism. However, it also served to alienate him from the newly crowned Protestant ELIZABETH I of England. She later approved of his return to Scotland in 1559, to lead the Protestant anti-French faction. Appointed minister of St Giles, Edinburgh, he was closely involved in drawing up the *Scots Confession* (1560) and *First Book of Discipline* (1560). He was a fierce opponent of MARY, QUEEN OF SCOTS.

Knox, Philander Chase (1853–1921) US statesman. Born in Pennsylvania, he served in the cabinets of three Presidents (MCKINLEY, T. ROOSEVELT, and TAFT) and also served in the US Senate (1904–09, 1917–21). He initiated the policy referred to as DOLLAR DIPLOMACY by his methods of protecting US financial and big business interests abroad. He was most criticized for having US marines occupy Nicaragua to save New York bankers from loss during the revolution of 1912.

Kohl, Helmut (1930–) German statesman and Chancellor of the Federal Republic of Germany (1982–). Elected to the Bundestag in 1976 as a member of the Christian Democratic Union (CDU), he successfully challenged Helmut Schmidt (1918–) for the chancellorship in 1982, and was re-elected in 1987. In 1989 his government gave asylum to an ever-increasing number of refugees from the German Democratic Republic; the Soviet Union abandoned its control over eastern Europe, and in October 1990 East and West Germany were re-united. In December 1990, in the first all-German parliamentary elections following reunification, Kohl was re-elected. He adopted a positive stance towards the eastern part of his country, offering a currency unification on the basis of 1:1, and agreed to meet the cost of Soviet troops remaining on East German territory. However, the cost of unification and of modernizing eastern Germany proved far higher than he had calculated. High unemployment in the east,

increased taxation, high interest rates, and the presence in Germany of an estimated 1.5 million migrants and asylum seekers led to a loss of public support. In 1992 Kohl's Liberal coalition partner, the foreign secretary Hans-Dietrich Genscher (first appointed 1974), resigned, and Germany experienced a wave of neo-Nazi attacks. Nevertheless, Kohl was re-elected with a reduced majority in 1994, becoming in 1996 the longest-serving German leader since Bismarck. He imposed severe austerity measures on the German economy in the late 1990s so that the country would meet the criteria for entry to the proposed single European currency. The effects of these measures included the highest levels of unemployment in Germany since the 1930s.

Kolchak, Aleksander Vasileyvich (1874–1920) Russian admiral and explorer. After Russia's defeat by Japan (1905), he helped to reform the navy and explored a possible route between European Russia and the Far East. After the RUSSIAN REVOLUTION he became War Minister in an anti-BOLSHEVIK government at Omsk (October 1918), and proclaimed himself supreme ruler of Russia. With DENIKIN he fought the Bolsheviks, clearing them from Siberia, but ultimately failed, owing to defections among his supporters. Betrayed to the Bolsheviks, he was shot.

Konfrontasi A diplomatic and military confrontation between INDONESIA and MALAYSIA (1963–66). It centred around the formation of the Federation of Malaysia (1963) which President SUKARNO saw as a Western-inspired ploy to oppose anti-colonist forces in south-east Asia. Asserting that the Federation was part of a British plot against Indonesia, Sukarno launched a guerrilla war in Malaysia's Bornean territories, Sarawak and Sabah, in April 1963, hoping for support from local Chinese communist elements. His 'confrontation' policy, however, only served to increase support for the new federal arrangements within the Malaysian states (only BRUNEI, with its massive oil reserves, remaining aloof). It led to increased disaffection in the Indonesian army which ultimately contributed to his downfall. With the guerrilla forces defeated by the Malaysians with British, Australian, and New Zealand help, Sukarno's successor General SUHARTO ended Konfrontasi in 1966.

Kongo A kingdom in Central Africa that was established south of the River Congo by 1300 and became one of the most powerful kingdoms in the region. The Kongo people traded over long distances, exploiting iron and salt mines. On Loanda Island they had a monopoly of *nzimbu* shells, which provided a local currency. It was the first African kingdom after Ethiopia to be converted to Christianity, mainly by Portuguese missionaries in the 16th century. The Portuguese also brought the slave trade, which encouraged civil wars, which had severely weakened the Kongo kingdom by the mid-17th century.

Koniev, Ivan Stepanovich (1897–1973) Soviet field-marshal. He joined the RED ARMY and the Communist Party in 1918. Having escaped STALIN's purge of the Red Army, he commanded several army groups in World War II. In 1945 his 1st Ukrainian Army Group advanced through Poland and Silesia and played a major part in the capture of Berlin.

Königgrätz SADOWA.

Konoe Fumimaro (1891–1945) Japanese statesman. He entered politics after World War I and as a member of the upper house emerged as a leading advocate of popularly based parliamentary democracy and an opponent of the military domination of government. As Prime Minister (1937–39, 1940–41), he strove unsuccessfully to control the political situation and prevent war with the USA, but in October 1941 was forced out of office by his War Minister, TOJO HIDEKI. He committed suicide in December 1945 when summoned to answer charges of war crimes.

Koobi Fora A large area in northern Kenya where early HOMINID remains (from over 160 individuals), have been found, including the remarkably complete '1470 skull' found in 1972. The dating of the hominids and tools was once controversial but it now seems clear that most of the finds date to between 2 and 1.4 million years ago. The '1470 skull' is evidence of a large-brained hominid in East Africa at an early date in human evolution. Scientists still question its affinity but most now agree that it is an early representative of *Homo*, possibly *Homo habilis*, and was the maker of the OLDOWAN tools of the same age (about 2 million years old). By 1.6 million years ago, *Homo erectus* appeared with advanced Oldowan tools called the Karari Industry; ACHEULIAN tools came a little later.

Köprülü An influential family of able administrators who through the office of VIZIER dominated OTTOMAN affairs for half a century. Muhammad (1656–61) crushed internal discord and bolstered the war effort against Venice. His son Ahmed (1661–76) ended the conflict successfully, acquiring Crete, and also won Podolia from Poland. Mustafa (1689–91) died in a counter-offensive in the lengthy war (1683–99) against Austria. Hüseyn (1697–1702) ended that conflict by the Peace of Carlowitz (1699), ceding many territories. By their energy the Köprülü had arrested the decay of the empire, but their demise saw it enter its long decline from greatness.

Koran (or Qur'an) The Holy Scripture of ISLAM. Muslims believe the Koran to be the word and will of God, as revealed to his messenger Muhammad (570–632) through the angel Jibril or Gabriel over the period 610–32. Written in classical Arabic, it consists of 114 *sūras* (chapters) of varying length, each *sūra* being composed of a number of *āyas* (normally translated as verses because assonance is involved, although the Koran is a prose work). The first revelation on *Lailat al-Qadr*, the Night of Power, is commemorated during Ramadan (the ninth month of the Islamic calendar, devoted to fasting, almsgiving, and prayer). The early revelations are highly charged and rhetorical, but the style becomes more relaxed later. The contents are diverse, particularly prominent themes being the omnipotence of Allah, the duty to believe in Allah alone, descriptions of the Day of Judgement, heaven, and hell, stories of the Prophets, and, in the latest phase, social legislation. Since the Koran is regarded by Muslims as a literal transcription of God's revelations, for many years translations of the text were not permitted, and although today translations do exist, Muslims are taught to memorize and chant the original Arabic text. Calligraphic renditions of the text are a distinctive aid to worship in Islam.

Korea A former country in north-eastern Asia. Although deeply indebted to Chinese culture, the Korean people and language developed upon quite distinct lines. The earliest Korean state was Choson (Morning Calm), which flourished in about the 3rd century BC in northern Korea. Chinese influence, already strong, increased following conquest and colonization by the Western HAN. Meanwhile the states in southern Korea acted as a cultural bridge between the mainland and Japan. In the 1st century AD the kingdom of Koguryo appeared in the north and by the 4th century Buddhism had reached Korea. Koguryo repulsed Chinese attacks but was overrun when the Silla kingdom, established in the south *c.* 350, allied itself with the TANG (668). The Silla became a tributary state of China and ruled a unified Korea for 200 years. A period of civil war ended with the supremacy of the KORYO kingdom (918–1392). After Mongol incursions the Koryo allied with them, but following the fall of the YUAN dynasty in 1392, Yi Song-gye, supported by the MING, seized power.

Under the Yi dynasty (1392–1910) Korea was greatly influenced by Ming China. A new capital was built at Seoul, and Confucianism largely displaced an increasingly degenerate Buddhism. From the late 15th century the administration was weakened by factional disputes. The Japanese invasion, led by HIDEYOSHI in 1592 took six years to repel and further weakened the state. Shortly thereafter the MANCHUS invaded and in due course Korea became a vassal state of China. The Yi dynasty continued only through the support of the QING. Unwilling to consider change they were more devoted to traditional Confucianism than the Chinese themselves.

In the 19th century, Korea became the object of intense Russian and Japanese rivalry. Opened to Japanese trade in 1876, Korea was granted independence by the Treaty of SHIMONOSEKI in 1895, but became a battle ground during the RUSSO-JAPANESE WAR (1904–05) and was eventually annexed by Japan in 1910. After WORLD WAR II, Korea was divided into US and Soviet zones of occupation along the 38th parallel before the proclamation of the independent Korean People's Democratic Republic (KOREA, NORTH) and Republic of Korea (KOREA, SOUTH) in 1948.

Korea, North (Democratic People's Republic of Korea) North-east Asian country. Consisting of the northern half of the Korean peninsula, mostly above the 38th parallel, North Korea was formed from the zone occupied by the Soviet Union at the end of World War II. It borders to the south with South Korea and to the north with the People's Republic of China.

Physical. North Korea is largely mountainous with narrow valleys, extensive forests, and rivers which freeze in winter.

Economy. North Korea is rich in metal deposits such as iron ore, magnesite, phosphate, sulphur, zinc, and copper, which are major exports. About 90% of cultivated land is owned by co-operatives producing the principal crops of rice, maize, and potatoes. The main trading partners have been the former Soviet Union and China; North Korea received substantial aid from the former. It is believed that over a quarter of GNP is spent on the armed forces, which are thought to be amongst the world's largest.

History. The Democratic People's Republic was proclaimed an independent state on 1 May 1948. Intent on reuniting Korea, North Korea launched a surprise attack on South Korea in June 1950, suffering considerable damage and loss of life in the following three years of the indecisive KOREAN WAR. After the war, the ruling Communist Party of KIM IL SUNG (President and General Secretary since 1948) undertook a programme of reconstruction, using the country's mineral and power resources to finance economic development. From the early 1980s, however, the economy was stagnant and then in decline. This was a factor in the decision in 1985 to hold a series of economic talks with South Korea, after the many years of tension. The result was a marked upturn in trade between the two countries ($25 million in 1990 to $192 million in 1991). Kim Il Sung, the ageing President, was re-elected in 1990; he supported a policy of seeking 'normalization' with South Korea, but not of reunification. Talks between respective premiers began in September 1990 and continued into 1992, when an economic agreement was signed. Tensions flared again in 1994 when North Korea refused to allow international inspectors to examine its nuclear reactors, amid allegations that it was building nuclear weapons. Kim Jong Il succeeded his father as President in 1994. The following year floods left hundreds of thousands homeless, leading to famine and disorder. Indeed, some reports from this highly secretive country suggest that the whole economic and political system may be close to collapse. Friction between the two Koreas rose again in 1996–97, when North Korean forces made incursions into the border zone and South Korea itself. Nevertheless, talks to bring about a lasting settlement began in August 1997; these involved China and the USA as well as both Koreas.

CAPITAL:	Pyongyang
AREA:	122,400 sq km (47,300 sq miles)
POPULATION:	23.904 million (1996)
CURRENCY:	1 won = 100 chon
RELIGIONS:	Atheist or non-religious 67.9%; traditional beliefs 15.6%; Ch'ondogyo 13.9%; Buddhist 1.7%; Christian 0.9%
ETHNIC GROUPS:	Korean 99.8%; Chinese 0.2%
LANGUAGES:	Korean (official); Chinese
INTERNATIONAL ORGANIZATIONS:	UN

Korea, South (Republic of Korea) North-east Asian country. Consisting of the southern half of the Korean peninsula, mostly beneath the 38th parallel, South Korea was formed from the zone occupied by US forces after World War II.

Physical. The terrain of South Korea is made up of low hills and wide valleys. Numerous small islands in the sovereign territory of South Korea lie off its western coast, in the Yellow Sea. The climate is milder than in the north of the peninsula.

Economy. South Korea has a mixed economy with a rapidly expanding and successful export-based industrial sector, and an agricultural sector which provides self-sufficiency in food and high yields in rice production. The principal manufacturing industries are petrochemicals, shipbuilding, textiles, and electronics. The chief exports are transport equipment, electrical machinery, footwear, and textiles. South Korea has few minerals except for large tungsten deposits. South

Korea is regarded as a successful example of a newly industrializing country, and it plays an increasingly important role in worldwide investment.

History. The independent Republic of Korea was proclaimed on 15 August 1948. Badly damaged by the KOREAN WAR (1950–53), the South Korean economy was initially restricted by its lack of industrial and power resources and by a severe post-war refugee problem. Unemployment and inflation damaged the reputation of the government of President RHEE, and its increasing brutality and corruption finally led to its overthrow in 1960. After a second civilian government had failed to improve the situation, the army, led by General Park Chung Hee, seized power in 1961. Park, who assumed the powers of a civilian president (1963–79) organized an extremely successful reconstruction campaign, which saw South Korea emerge as a strong industrial power, but his repressive policies soon engendered serious unrest. Tension with North Korea remained high during this period, until an agreement between the two governments, signed in July 1972, laid foundations for possible future reunification. Park Chung Hee was assassinated by the head of the South Korean Central Intelligence Agency in a coup in 1979. His successor, General Chun Doo Hwan, continued his policies until forced partially to liberalize the political system after student unrest in 1987. A referendum was held and a new constitution proclaimed. President Roh Tae Woo (1932–) was elected, and in 1990 his party, the Democratic Justice Party, amalgamated with others to form the Democratic Liberal Party (DLP), which advocated reunion with the north and normalization of relations with the Soviet Union and, later, Russia. There were student demonstrations in 1991, and feuding within the DLP, which lost its overall majority in the general election of 1992. Relations with North Korea worsened in 1994, with the latter's refusal to submit its nuclear energy programme to inspection by the International Atomic Energy Agency, and again in 1996–97. In 1996 General Chun Doo Hwan was sentenced to death for his role in the 1979 coup and Roh Tae Woo received a long prison sentence (both were subsequently released). In 1997 there was a financial crisis and the economy suffered a dramatic downturn. At the end of that year, Presidential elections resulted in victory for Kim Dae Jung, the first successful opposition candidate since the introduction of democracy.

CAPITAL:	Seoul
AREA:	99,237 sq km (38,316 sq miles)
POPULATION:	45.232 million (1996)
CURRENCY:	1 South Korean won = 100 jeon
RELIGIONS:	Atheist or non-religious 57.4%; Buddhist 19.9%; Protestant 16.1%; Roman Catholic 4.6%; Confucian 1.2%
ETHNIC GROUPS:	Korean 99.9%
LANGUAGES:	Korean (official)
INTERNATIONAL ORGANIZATIONS:	UN; Colombo Plan

Korean War (1950–53) War fought between North Korea and China on one side, and South Korea, the USA, and United Nations forces on the other. From the time of their foundation in 1948, relations between North and South Korea were soured by rival plans for unification, and on 25 June 1950 war finally broke out with a surprise North Korean attack that had pushed US and South Korean forces far south towards Pusan by

September. In the temporary absence of the Soviet representative, the Security Council asked members of the UN to furnish assistance to South Korea. On 15 September US and South Korean forces, under command of General MACARTHUR, launched a counter-offensive at Inchon and by the end of October UN forces had pushed the North Koreans all the way back to the Yalu River, the frontier with the People's Republic of China. Chinese troops then entered the war on the northern side, driving south to recapture the South Korean capital of Seoul by January 1951. After months of fighting, the conflict stabilized in near-deadlock, close to the original boundary line (the 38th parallel). Peace negotiations, undertaken in July 1951 by General M. B. Ridgway (who had succeeded MacArthur in April of that year), proved difficult, and it was not until 27 July 1953 that an armistice was signed at Panmunjom and the battle line was accepted as the boundary between North and South Korea.

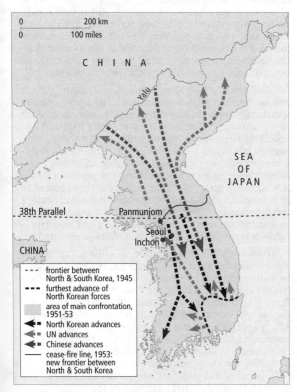

Korean War (1950–53)   *In 1945 Japanese forces surrendered in North Korea to the Soviet Union and in the south to the USA. Two new nations were created, with a frontier along the 38th parallel. US troops withdrew in 1949, whereupon North Korea attempted unification by force. The UN sent reinforcements, mainly US servicemen, to South Korea, and the Chinese aided the North. In 1953 a ceasefire was negotiated by General Ridgway. Of more than 10,000 US soldiers captured, only 3,746 returned after the war.*

Koryo A Korean kingdom that gave its name to the whole country. From 986 its kings ruled a united Korea from their Chinese-style capital, Kaesong. Chinese influence was strong in the administration of the kingdom and Buddhism flourished. A period of disorder in the 12th century was checked after 1196 by military families with powers similar to those of the Japanese SHOGUNATE. Tributary to the SONG, Koryo also had to pay tribute to the LIAO and JIN. After 1231 the Mongols repeatedly invaded and despoiled Koryo, which later depended entirely on YUAN support. After the overthrow of the Yuan, a Koryo general, Yi Song-gye, seized Kaesong and in 1392 established the Yi dynasty.

Kosciuszko, Tadeusz Andrzej Bonawentura (1746–1817) Polish soldier and statesman. He volunteered for service during the American War of INDEPENDENCE after serving for two years in the Polish army. After distinguishing himself at YORKTOWN, Kosciuszko was rewarded with American citizenship and a pension. He returned to Poland and played a leading part in the war of 1792. Kosciuszko then spent three years in Leipzig before returning to lead the Polish forces against the powers attempting further partition of Poland. However, he was defeated and wounded in October 1794. He moved to Paris four years later but refused Napoleon's offers of command. He spent the final years of his life in Switzerland.

Kossovo (or Kosovo Polje, the Field of Blackbirds) The site (in what is now Serbia) of a decisive battle (28 June 1389) when the troops of the SERBS were defeated by an OTTOMAN force. Although the Serbs enjoyed early success and Sultan MURAD I was killed before battle commenced, his son BAYEZID I took command, and won the battle. Victory opened the way for Turkish invasion of central Europe. A second battle, between Hungarians and Turks took place nearby in 1448 at which MURAD II defeated the Hungarians.

Kossuth, Lajos (1802–94) Hungarian public official and revolutionary. He made his name as deputy for an absentee count in the Hungarian Diet of 1832–36. His reports on the proceedings (the debates were not officially published) were widely read and led to his arrest in 1837. Popular agitation persuaded METTERNICH to release him three years later, but he intensified his demands for national independence. He led the extreme liberals in the Hungarian Diet of 1847, and in 1848 became Minister of Finance in the government of a semi-autonomous Hungary. When Austria and Hungary went to war at the end of 1848, he became the virtual dictator of the nation, declaring its independence (1849) with himself as President. Hungarian forces repulsed Austrian military intervention, but when Russian troops intervened in favour of Austria, Kossuth surrendered and fled the country, and his republic collapsed.

Kosygin, Alexei Nikolayevich (1904–81) Soviet politician. He joined the Communist Party in 1927 and became an expert in economics and industry. He was Chairman of the Council of Ministers from 1964 to 1981. During his period in office he shared power with BREZHNEV, who came to overshadow him. Kosygin achieved a notable diplomatic success in bringing the 1965–66 INDO-PAKISTAN WAR to an end.

Krisna Deva Raya VIJAYANAGAR.

Kronstadt Mutiny (1921) Mutiny against the Bolshevik government of Russia. The Kronstadt naval garrison had enthusiastically supported the Bolsheviks in 1917, but in March 1921 the sailors rose against what they regarded as a Communist dictatorship, demanding political freedom and economic liberalism. The rising was brutally suppressed by Lenin, but the incident did cause a partial reassessment of economic planning along more progressive lines, with Lenin's New Economic Policy of 1922.

Kropotkin, Peter, Prince (1842–1922) Russian ANARCHIST. From 1872, after meeting leaders of the First INTERNATIONAL in Switzerland, he became interested in revolutionary ideas. Imprisoned in France (1883–86) for his anarchist views he moved to Britain where he was welcomed as a scholar. In his most famous book, *Mutual Aid* (1902), he refuted the Darwinian theory of human society as essentially competitive, and in *Fields, Factories and Workshops* (1898) he outlined a social organization based upon communes of producers linked with each other through free contract. Returning to Russia (1917) he supported KERENSKY, and remained an outspoken critic of BOLSHEVISM.

Kruger, (Stephanus Johannes) Paul(us) (1825–1904) South African statesman. From 1864 he was Commandant-General of the South African Republic (TRANSVAAL) until it was annexed by the British in 1877. After it regained its independence (1881) he was elected President (1883), and re-elected in 1888, 1893, and 1898. He consistently pursued an expansionist policy, in Bechuanaland (now BOTSWANA), RHODESIA, and ZULULAND, so as to enlarge the Transvaal frontiers. He successfully defeated the JAMESON RAID, receiving a telegram of congratulations from the German emperor, WILLIAM II (1896). Kruger's refusal to allow equal rights to non-Boer immigrants (UITLANDERS) was one of the causes of the Second BOER WAR. When Bloemfontein and Pretoria were occupied in 1900, he retired to Utrecht, where his efforts to rouse European support for the Boers were unsuccessful.

Kubitschek, Juscelino (1902–76) Brazilian statesman. He was governor of the Province of Minas Gerais (1950–56), where he initiated a programme of industrial and agricultural development. He then served as President of Brazil (1956–61). Determined to diversify the economy and reduce unemployment, he embarked on a massive public works programme, including the creation of the new capital city of Brasília. Economic prosperity followed, but at the cost of high inflation. Brazil's national debt rose to $4 billion, while its population soared to over sixty million. He was forced into exile for three years by his successor Castel Branco.

Kublai Khan (1214–94) First YUAN emperor of CHINA (1279–94), a grandson of GENGHIS KHAN. Elected Khakhan (Great Khan) in 1260 on the death of his brother Mangu, he completed the conquest of China. In 1276 Hangzhou fell and in 1279 the Song fleet was defeated off southern China. Contrary to Mongol practice, he did not entirely lay waste the country. In 1267 he made Khanbaligh (Beijing) the Mongol capital. His rule, according to Chinese historians, was harsh, though MARCO POLO, who served him from 1275 to 1292, described it as mild. He followed Chinese precedents of government, though civil service examinations were temporarily abandoned. Many foreigners, particularly Muslims from Central Asia, were appointed to civil and military posts. A curfew and much spying enforced obedience. The Grand Canal, linking north with central China was

reconstructed, post roads were built, and food stored for periods of shortage. Zhangzhou (Zayton), exporting silk and porcelain, was the busiest port in the world. His military adventures in Annam, Champa, Burma (modern Myanmar), and Java had limited success. Campaigns against Japan (1274 and 1281) failed dismally.

Ku Klux Klan A secret society founded in 1866 in the southern USA after the AMERICAN CIVIL WAR to oppose RECONSTRUCTION and to maintain White supremacy. Famous for its white robes and hoods, it spread fear among Black people to prevent them voting. It was often used as a cover for petty persecution and soon alienated public opinion, leading to laws in 1870 and 1871 attempting to suppress it. The Klan reappeared in Georgia in 1915 and during the 1920s spread into the north and mid-west. It was responsible for some 1,500 murders by lynching. At its height it boasted four million members and elected high federal and state officials, but it also aroused intense opposition. A series of scandals and internecine rivalries sent it into rapid decline. Klan activity increased during the 1950s and 1960s, as it violently opposed the CIVIL RIGHTS movement (see also FREEDOM RIDERS). It survives at the local level in the southern states and during the early 1990s there was concern that support for the Klan was increasing.

kulak (Russian, 'fist') Moneylenders, merchants, and anyone considered to be acquisitive. The term became specifically applied to wealthy peasants who, as a result of the agrarian reforms of STOLYPIN (1906), acquired relatively large farms and were financially able to employ labour. As a new element in rural Russia they were intended to create a stable middle class and a conservative political force. During the period of Lenin's NEW ECONOMIC POLICY (1921) they increasingly appeared to be a potential threat to a communist state, and Stalin's COLLECTIVIZATION policy (1928) inevitably aroused their opposition. Between 1929 and 1934 the great majority of farms were collectivized and the kulaks annihilated.

Kulturkampf (German, 'conflict of cultures' or 'beliefs') The conflict between the German government headed by BISMARCK and the Roman Catholic Church (1872–87) for the control of schools and Church appointments. Bismarck, anxious to strengthen the central power of the GERMAN SECOND EMPIRE in which southern Germany, Alsace-Lorraine, and the Polish provinces were predominantly Catholic, issued the May Decrees (1873), restricting the powers of the Catholic Church and providing for the punishment of any opponents. By 1876 1,300 parishes had no priest: opponents had become martyrs. Needing Catholic support in the Reichstag, Bismarck repealed many of the anti-Church laws or let them lapse.

Kun, Béla (1886–1937) Hungarian communist leader. In World War I he was captured on the Russian front and joined the BOLSHEVIKS. He was sent back to Hungary to form a communist party and in March 1919 persuaded the Hungarian communists and Social Democrats to form a coalition government and to set up a communist state under his dictatorship. His Red Army overran Slovakia, but the Soviet assistance that had been promised was not forthcoming. In May 1919 Kun was defeated by a Romanian army of intervention. He fled Hungary and is assumed to have been killed in one of Stalin's purges.

Kuomintang (or Guomindang; National People's Party)
Chinese political party. Originally a revolutionary
league, it was organized in 1912 by Song Jiaoren and SUN
YAT-SEN as a republican party along democratic lines to
replace the Revolutionary Alliance which had emerged
from the overthrow of the QING dynasty. Suppressed in
1913 by YUAN SHIKAI, it was reformed in 1920 by Sun Yat-
Sen and reorganized with COMINTERN assistance in 1923 in
an arrangement that allowed individual communists to
become members. At the party congress in 1924 it
formally adopted the 'Three Principles of the People':
nationalism, democracy, and 'people's livelihood'. In 1926
its rise to power began in earnest with the
commencement of CHIANG KAI-SHEK'S NORTHERN EXPEDITION.
The communists were purged in 1927 and the capture of
Beijing in 1928 brought international recognition for its
Nanjing-based Nationalist Government. It fought the
CHINESE CIVIL WAR with the communists and retreated to
Chongqing after the Japanese invasion of 1937. After
World War II, the civil war recommenced, and by 1949
the Kuomintang's forces had been decisively defeated
and forced to retreat to TAIWAN, where it still continues
to form the government of Taiwan (the Republic of
China), having won the country's first multiparty
elections in 1991. Further elections, in 1995, saw the
Kuomintang narrowly retain its majority, yet with its
lowest vote (46%) since 1945.

Kurdistan A mountainous region of the Middle East.
Many of the mountains are over 2,000 m (6,600 feet)
high, the highest rising to 4,168 m (13,675 feet), and they
form a watershed between the Tigris in the south and
the inland lakes of Van, Urmia, and the Caspian Sea in
the north. The terrain generally is difficult, the climate
hot and dry in summer, and the pasture poor. Oil is the
main natural resource.
    Kurdistan is the homeland of the Kurds, a pastoral
people. It is centred on the Zagros and Taurus
mountains and is at present divided between Iran,
Turkey, Iraq, Syria, and Armenia. The area was
conquered by the Arabs in the 7th century and
converted to Islam and became successively part of the
SELJUK, MONGOL, and OTTOMAN EMPIRES. The Kurdish
Shaddadids ruled Armenia from 951 to 1174 and the
Ayyubids, a dynasty established by SALADIN, ruled Egypt
and Syria from 1169 to 1250. Kurdish nationalism in the
Ottoman empire developed during the late 19th century;
after World War I the Treaty of Sèvres promised an
independent Kurdistan, but this never materialized. In
the years 1944–45 a short-lived Kurdish Republic of
Mahabad was formed in Iran with Soviet help. An
armed struggle for autonomy in Iraq (1958–74) resulted
in a plan for limited autonomy in 1974, but fighting
resumed in 1975 with military assistance from Iran. In
1979 Iran granted its Kurds limited autonomy in the
province of Kordestan. In 1988 the patriotic Union of
Kurdistan (PUK) and the Democratic Party of Kurdistan
(KDP) joined forces in Iraq. Unrest in the Kurdish
population brought retaliation by Saddam HUSSEIN in the
form of chemical warfare which killed thousands of
Kurds. Hussein forcibly removed approximately 1.5
million Kurds from their mountain villages to
townships. The Gulf War of 1991 precipitated a Kurdish
revolt, ruthlessly suppressed until UN intervention.
Over one million Kurdish refugees fled to Turkey, but a
further half million were turned back. In May 1992
elections were held for an Iraqi-Kurdistan National

Assembly but violent disputes between the PUK and
KDP have continued. Iraqi forces launched further
attacks against the Kurds in 1996. In Turkey, there has
been fighting in Kurdish provinces since 1984 between
guerrillas of the separatist Marxist Kurdish Workers'
Party (PKK) and government troops. There was an
upsurge of violence in 1992, with border fighting
between PKK forces and Iraqi Kurds. Turkish
government forces bombed PKK bases in Iraq and Syria.
The Turkish government has been accused of violating
the human rights of people who promote Kurdish
language and culture.

Kursk, Battle of (5–15 July 1943) A fierce tank battle
between the Red Army and German invasion forces
around Kursk in the central European Soviet Union.
Hitler had ordered the elimination of the important
railway junction of Kursk. Under Field-Marshal Walter
Model he concentrated 2,700 tanks and assault guns on
the city, supported by over 1,000 aircraft. They were
confronted by Marshal ZHUKOV's Tank Army, backed by
five infantry armies. Many of the large German tanks
were mined and others became stuck in the mud. The
Russians had more guns, tanks, and aircraft, and when
they counter-attacked, the Germans were forced to
retreat, losing some 70,000 men, 1,500 tanks, and 1,000
aircraft. The battle ensured that the German army
would never regain the initiative on the Eastern Front.

Kush (or Cush) NUBIANS.

Kut, Siege of (December 1915–April 1916) Successful
siege of the town of Kut-al-Amara, now in Iraq, by
Turkish troops in World War I. Kut-al-Amara is on the
River Tigris and was garrisoned by a British imperial
force under General Townshend, who had retreated
there after his defeat by the Turks at Ctesiphon. Badly
organized relief forces failed to break through and the
garrison capitulated on 29 April 1916 after a four-month
siege. Ten thousand prisoners were marched across the
desert, two-thirds dying on the way, while some 23,000
troops of the relieving force were also lost. The defeat
severely weakened Britain's prestige as an imperial
power although Kut-al-Amara was recaptured in
February 1917.

**Kutuzov, Mikhail Ilarionovich, Prince of
Smolensk** (1745–1813) Russian field-marshal. He
distinguished himself in the Russo-Turkish War
(1806–12), bringing Bessarabia into Russia. He
commanded the Russian armies in the wars against
Napoleon and was forced to retreat after the defeat of
BORODINO (7 September 1812). Kutuzov's decision to
disperse in the face of the advancing *grande armée*
undermined Napoleon's plans for a swift victory, and
forced him to retreat from Moscow before the severe
Russian winter.

Kuwait A small country in the north-west corner of
the Gulf, flanked by Iraq and Saudi Arabia.
    Physical. Kuwait is mainly low desert, very hot in
summer but cool in winter, and extremely arid.
    Economy. With an estimated 10% of the world's
petroleum reserves, Kuwait's economy is based on oil
extraction, refining, and petrochemical industries; there
is also an entrepôt trade, and income from overseas
investments is believed to equal that from oil
production before the Iraqi occupation.

History. Kuwait was founded in the early 18th century by members of the Utub section of the Anaiza tribe, and has been ruled since 1756 by the al-Sabah family. In 1899 the ruler, Muvarak, signed a treaty with Britain which established a *de facto* British protectorate over Kuwait, although it remained under nominal Ottoman suzerainty until 1914, when the protectorate was formalized. Kuwait became independent in 1961, when an Iraqi claim was warded off with British military assistance. Oil had been discovered in 1938; after World War II, Kuwait became one of the world's largest oil producers. The country's defensive pact with Britain lapsed in 1971, after which it tried to pursue a policy of neutrality. Its massive wealth was in part channelled into modernization programmes. In 1990 Iraq revived the frontier dispute of 1961, and on 2 August 1990 began its seven-month occupation of Kuwait. In the period before liberation in the GULF WAR, thousands of Kuwaitis were killed, kidnapped, or taken hostage. After the war, reconstruction costs were estimated at up to $100 billion, with serious environmental damage caused by Iraqi sabotage of 732 oil wells. In 1992 the first parliamentary elections in the country's history were held, in which only 13% of the population was eligible to vote; the franchise only extended to male Kuwaiti nationals over the age of 21, whose families had lived in Kuwait since before 1921. Even so, many opposition candidates were elected. Further minor raids by Iraqi troops in 1993 led to the UN moving the border a few metres northwards, into Iraq.

CAPITAL:	Kuwait City
AREA:	17,818 sq km (6,880 sq miles)
POPULATION:	2.070 million (1996)
CURRENCY:	1 Kuwaiti dinar = 1,000 fils
RELIGIONS:	Sunni Muslim 63.0%; Shiite Muslim 27.0%; Christian 8.0%; Hindu 2.0%
ETHNIC GROUPS:	Kuwaiti Arab 40.1%; non-Kuwaiti Arab 37.9%; Asian 21.0%; European 0.7%
LANGUAGES:	Arabic (official); minority languages
INTERNATIONAL ORGANIZATIONS:	UN; Arab League; Gulf Co-operation Council; OPEC; OAPEC

Kyrgyzstan (formerly Kirghizia) A country in central Asia bounded by Kazakhstan on the north and north-west, Uzbekistan on the south-west, and Tajikistan on the south.

Physical. On the south-east the Tian Shan range of mountains, which rise to 7,439 m (24,406 feet), shares a border with China. Kyrgyzstan is a mountainous country with many snowfields, glaciers, and deep lakes. Its lower plains are exposed to hot desert winds. Its middle reaches are forested, while the lower slopes provide pasture for millions of sheep.

Economy. Kyrgyzstan has substantial mineral reserves, including coal, petroleum, and natural gas, but other than coal-mining these have not been fully prospected or exploited. Industry is based on mineral extraction and processing, and there is also some light industry such as food-processing and textile manufacture. Agriculture is based on livestock-raising and crops such as fruit, cereals, cotton, sugar beet, tobacco, and opium poppies.

History. Absorbed into the Russian empire during the 19th century, Kyrgyzstan became an autonomous province of the Soviet Union in 1924 and the Kirghiz Soviet Socialist Republic in 1936. In 1990 Askar Akayev, a supporter of reforms and of independence for Kyrgyzstan, was elected President. He survived an attempted coup in 1991 and resigned from the Communist Party of the Soviet Union. The Kirghiz Communist Party then dissolved itself and the country became independent as Kyrgyzstan. New constitutions were adopted in 1993 and 1994 and the first multiparty elections were held in 1995. Akayev remained President and continued to introduce economic reforms.

CAPITAL:	Bishkek
AREA:	198,500 sq km (76,460 sq miles)
POPULATION:	4.512 million (1996)
CURRENCY:	1 som = 100 tyiyn
RELIGIONS:	Sunni Muslim; Eastern Orthodox
ETHNIC GROUPS:	Kirghiz 52.0%; Russian 22.0%; Uzbek 12.0%; Ukrainian and Tatar minorities
LANGUAGES:	Kirghiz (official); Russian; minority languages
INTERNATIONAL ORGANIZATIONS:	CSCE; UN; Commonwealth of Independent States; North Atlantic Co-operation Council

Labor Party (Australia) The oldest surviving political party in Australia. Founded in the 1880s and 1890s, the title of the Labor groups varied from state to state until 1918, when all adopted the name Australian Labor Party. Labor governments existed briefly in 1904 and 1908–09, and at the federal general election of 1910 Labor obtained clear majorities in both houses, remaining in power until 1912. Under W. H. HUGHES (1915–17) the government established some social reforms, but split in 1916 when a majority voted against conscription. The Labor government was replaced by a Nationalist-Country Alliance, until the general election of 1929 returned it to power under J. H. Scullin (1929–31). Labor split again over policy differences during the Great DEPRESSION. Some Labor followers combined with the Nationalist Party to form the United Australia Party under J. A. Lyons, which, together with the Country Party, dominated federal and state politics until 1937, usually in coalition governments. The Labor Party was again in power 1941–49. A breakaway Labor group emerged in 1955 over the attitude of the Party to communism, a group of federal Labor members forming the new Anti-Communist Labor Party, which later became the Democratic Labor Party. The Party suffered the WHITLAM CRISIS in the 1970s, but returned to power. Bob Hawke's ministry (1983–91) introduced a programme of economic austerity. His successor, Paul Keating, sought to encourage Australia's involvement with its Asian neighbours and was in favour of Australia becoming a republic. Following Labor's defeat in the general election of 1996 Keating was succeeded as leader by Kim Beazley.

Labourers, Statute of (1351) A statute passed after a large part of the English population had died of the BLACK DEATH. It followed an ordinance of 1349 in attempting to prevent labour, now so much scarcer, from becoming expensive. Everyone under the age of 60, except traders, craftsmen, and those with private means, had to work for wages which were set at their various pre-plague levels. It was made an offence for landless men to seek new masters or to be offered higher wages. The statute was vigorously enforced for several years and caused a great deal of resentment; it was specifically referred to in the PEASANTS' REVOLT of 1381.

Labour Party (Britain) A major political party in Britain. Following the third REFORM ACT (1884), a movement developed for direct representation of labour interests in Parliament. In 1889 a Scottish Labour Party was formed, winning three seats in 1892, including one by Keir HARDIE, who next year helped to form the INDEPENDENT LABOUR PARTY, advocating pacifism and SOCIALISM. In 1900 a Labour Representative Committee was formed, which in 1906 succeeded in winning 29 seats and changed its name to the Labour Party, although it remained a loose federation of trade unions and socialist societies. In 1918 the Party adopted a constitution drawn up by Sidney WEBB, a FABIAN. Its main aims were a national minimum wage, democratic control of industry, a revolution in national finance, and surplus wealth for the common good. By 1920 Party membership was over four million. The Party now became a major force in British municipal politics, as well as gaining office with the Liberals in national elections in 1923 and 1929. The Party strongly supported war in 1939 and through leaders such as ATTLEE, BEVIN, and MORRISON played a major role in Winston CHURCHILL's government (1940–45). In 1945 it gained office with an overall majority and continued the programme of WELFARE STATE legislation begun during the war. It was in power (1964–70) when much social legislation was enacted, and 1974–79, when it faced grave financial and economic problems. During the 1970s and early 1980s left-wing activists pressed for a number of procedural changes; for example in the election of Party leader. From the right-wing a group of senior Party members split from the Party in the 1980s to form the SOCIAL DEMOCRATIC party. After its defeat in 1987 it embarked, under its leader Neil KINNOCK (1983–92), on a major policy review which recommended more democratic processes and a less ideological approach to foreign affairs and economic problems. This, however, failed to persuade the electorate, the party again receiving only 34% of the vote in the general election of 1992. Tony BLAIR, who became leader in 1994, has supported private enterprise and promoted reform within the party. In 1994 he oversaw the removal from the Labour Party constitution of the controversial Clause IV, which had committed the Party to the principle of collective ownership of industries. In May 1997, the Party won a landslide victory in the general election, securing a 179-seat majority in the House of Commons.

Labour Party (New Zealand) A major political party in New Zealand. It was formed in 1910 out of the trade union movement but was rivalled by the militant 'RED FEDS'. Re-formed in 1916, the Party supported compulsory industrial arbitration and constitutional change. Its policies favoured nationalization of much industry and state leasehold of land, and these were further modified before it won office in 1935 under Michael SAVAGE. The first Labour government (1935–49) effected radical change, stimulating economic recovery through public works, state support for primary produce marketing, and minimum wages. It introduced SOCIAL SECURITY, including free medical care. In World War II the Labour government declared war on Germany, introduced conscription for military service, and entered strongly into collective security arrangements. The Labour Party held office again (1957–60, 1972–75, 1984–90). Under its Prime Minister David Lange (1984–90) it carried its non-nuclear policy to the point of banning all nuclear-powered or nuclear-armed ships. The party was decisively defeated in the general election of October 1990, at a time of severe economic difficulty.

Laetoli A site in northern Tanzania some 40 km (25 miles) south-west of OLDUVAI GORGE, where a human-like trail of footprints was found. With a date of 3.75–3.6 million years ago, they are the earliest known human footprints and show that upright stance and walking on two legs were developed at this early time in human evolution. A small collection of AUSTRALOPITHECINE hominid remains, mostly jawbones and teeth, is also known from Laetoli. These hominids, along with those from HADAR in Ethiopia, have been attributed to a new species, *Australopithecus afarensis*.

Lafayette, Marie Joseph, marquis de (1757–1834) French soldier and aristocrat who was a youthful enthusiast for the American War of Independence and joined the struggle there in 1777 as a volunteer. He was befriended by WASHINGTON and fought at BRANDYWINE, endured VALLEY FORGE, and fought again at Monmouth (1778). In 1779 he went back to France, where his wealth and court connections won the promise of naval reinforcements. He arrived in America again in 1780 and was given command in Virginia in 1781, playing an important part in the siege of YORKTOWN.

Lafayette returned to France in 1782: an early supporter of the French Revolution in the STATES-GENERAL and the NATIONAL ASSEMBLY, he was put in charge of the national guard of Paris. His troops ensured Louis XVI and Marie-Antoinette were saved from the mob that attacked Versailles. However, his liberal humanist republicanism was swept aside by radical JACOBINISM and he failed to suppress his anti-monarchist opponents. He fled France in 1792 and was imprisoned by the Prussians and Austrians. He retired to private life under Napoleon but was active as a liberal spokesman under the restored monarchy (1815–30). A lifelong advocate of liberty, endowed with great charm, his visit to the USA (1824–25) brought him fame and popularity.

La Fontaine, Sir Louis-Hippolyte (1807–64) French-Canadian statesman. A member of the legislative assembly of Lower Canada (1830–37), he opposed PAPINEAU'S REBELLION and was not in sympathy with MACKENZIE'S REBELLION of 1837. An outspoken advocate of nationalism, he was arrested in 1838, but soon released, and, after the union of UPPER AND LOWER CANADA (1841), assumed political leadership of the French-Canadian reformers. In partnership with Robert BALDWIN he twice formed the government of United Canada (1842–43, 1848–51), on the second occasion serving as Prime Minister in an administration which was notable for its reforms and its achievement of full parliamentary ('responsible') government in Canada. He left politics in 1851.

laissez-faire (French, 'let do') Government abstention from interference with individual action. The expression was originally employed by the French physiocrats in the 18th century. They maintained that society should be governed according to an inherent natural order, and that the soil is the only source of wealth and proper object of taxation. Subsequently taken up by CLASSICAL ECONOMISTS like Adam SMITH, it signifies minimum government intervention in the economic system, and maximum scope for market forces. The policy of non-interference was applied in 19th-century Britain. In time the expression came to be associated with the absence of any general government schemes for the relief of poverty. (See also ECONOMICS, SCHOOLS OF.)

lake dwelling A house built either beside or over shallow water in lakes, river, and swamps. Lake dwellings have been constructed since prehistoric times. Probably not all were raised on piles, as in Thailand, Borneo, and elsewhere today; some may have been on artificial mounds on or near the shore. Even so, the site gave access to water for drinking, washing, refuse disposal, fishing, fowling, transport, and defence, and the wet land was good for some crops. Such sites were used on all continents and round the lagoons of the Pacific islands. In the British Isles they are called crannogs; an example is a 1st-century village excavated near Glastonbury. Other examples were lake-side villages in NEOLITHIC Switzerland and TENOCHTITLÁN.

Lake Erie, Battle of (10 September 1813) A naval engagement in the WAR OF 1812. Control of Lake Erie was of critical importance to both the USA and the UK, and by the late summer of 1813 each had commissioned a locally built and manned squadron of warships. Ten US vessels under Commodore Oliver Hazard Perry met six British vessels under Captain James Barclay off Put-in-Bay. After hard fighting, Perry captured the entire British squadron. His victory opened the way for a renewed US attack on Canada.

Lake George, Battle of (8 September 1755) An engagement in the FRENCH AND INDIAN WAR fought 80 km (50 miles) north of Albany, New York. New England and New York militia and Iroquois commanded by William JOHNSON defeated a French force and halted their advance. This victory offset BRADDOCK's defeat of the summer.

Lally, Thomas Arthur, comte de, baron de Tollendal (1702–66) French general, the son of an Irish Jacobite, Sir Gerard O'Lally. From 1756 Lally was an able commander of the French army in India during the SEVEN YEARS WAR. He had to give up the siege of Madras through lack of supplies, and surrendered Pondicherry after being defeated by the British commander Eyre Coote in January 1760. This put an end to the French empire in India, and on his return to France he was tried for treason and executed after two years imprisonment. VOLTAIRE worked with Lally's son to obtain a posthumous vindication; the condemnation was declared unjust in 1778 and Voltaire, on his death-bed, recorded his pleasure that his efforts to clear Lally's name had succeeded.

Lamaism A form of BUDDHISM practised in TIBET and MONGOLIA. Lama, meaning 'Superior One', is the name given to its higher clergy. Lamaism is a fusion of Bon, the native animist religion of Tibet, with Mahayana Buddhism introduced from north-west India in the 8th century by the scholar Padmasambhava. In times of disorder monks built fortress monasteries and by the 13th century spiritual and temporal power had fused. In the 14th century the Red Sect, whose lamas wore red robes, was discredited, though not entirely displaced, by the new Yellow Sect. Red Sect lamas were not celibate, sons succeeding fathers as abbots of monasteries. The Yellow Sect, by contrast, demanded of its lamas a life of celibacy and poverty. The head of the Yellow Sect, the Dalai ('All-Embracing') Lama, based in Lhasa, became Tibet's priest-ruler. Below him was the Panchen Lama, based in Shigatse. When either of these lamas died a child believed to be his reincarnation succeeded him.

Lambert, John (1619–83) English major-general. He rose to prominence as a ROUNDHEAD officer during the ENGLISH CIVIL WAR. He accompanied CROMWELL as second-in-command on the invasion of Scotland (1650). He entertained high political ambitions and was chiefly responsible for drafting England's first written constitution, the *Instrument of Government* (1653). He supported Cromwell loyally (1653–57), but then resigned all his commissions when his own path to power seemed blocked. In 1662, after the RESTORATION, he was tried for treason, and spent the rest of his life in captivity.

Lancastrians Descendants or supporters of John of GAUNT, Duke of Lancaster. The Lancastrians held the throne of England as HENRY IV, V, and VI (their badge was a red rose). In the Wars of the ROSES, a series of battles for the throne fought with the YORKISTS from 1455 onwards, the Lancastrians suffered a major reverse when Henry VI was displaced by EDWARD IV in 1461. They took refuge in France and, under the leadership of MARGARET OF ANJOU, invaded England, restoring Henry to his kingdom in October 1470. Henry's rule was ended after a few months by the Yorkist victories at BARNET and TEWKESBURY; most of the remaining Lancastrian leaders died in the latter battle. However, the Lancastrian party was ultimately successful, as it supported Henry Tudor, who in 1485, following his victory at BOSWORTH FIELD, became king as HENRY VII.

Land League An agrarian organization in Ireland. It was founded in 1879 by an ex-FENIAN, Michael DAVITT, to secure reforms in the land-holding system. With Charles PARNELL as president, it initiated the BOYCOTTING of anyone replacing a tenant evicted because of non-payment of rent. The campaign for land reform was linked with parliamentary activity by the Irish HOME RULE Members of Parliament. The British government declared the Land League illegal and imprisoned Davitt and Parnell. Branches of the League were formed in Australia, the USA, and elsewhere. Between 1881 and 1903 British governments passed Land Acts to remove the worst features of the landlord system in Ireland.

land reform The changing of systems of land tenure, usually at government initiative. Systems of land tenure vary considerably, and have great importance for the social and political structure of a society. Land may be held corporately by lineages, in small individual plots, or by a tiny number of wealthy landowners. Land reform has varied purposes and takes different forms: it may aim to create a more equal society by abolishing feudalism, winning the support of peasants, and giving them a greater stake in society; it may also aim to increase economic efficiency by creating a pattern of landholding which maximizes investment and productivity; or it may seek to impose a socialist pattern of ownership, where individual land ownership is not in general permitted. Reforms have varied from the redistribution of land, to the imposition of land ceilings (so that no single owner controls more than a certain area), and from the complete abolition of private ownership, to attempts to alter the terms under which tenants work private owners' land, such as the terms of SHARECROPPING agreements. In modern times, the first land redistribution was that in France following the Revolution (1789), which established the pattern of small family farms that continues today. In Britain there have not been any reforms initiated by the government, but

the Enclosures movement (16th to 19th centuries) pushed many peasants off the land into the towns and led to the development of industry and of large-scale farming. In Russia, limited land reform giving the land to the peasants accompanied the emancipation of the serfs in 1861, but the land was taken away again from 1918 with the abolition of private ownership of land and extensive COLLECTIVIZATION. A similar process occurred in much of Eastern Europe but the individual right to own land was reintroduced in the early 1990s. In countries that espouse COMMUNISM, such as China, Cuba, and Vietnam, there has also been extensive collectivization, while in Mozambique and Ethiopia all land title was declared the nation's and the rights of the tillers of the land and their descendants guaranteed. Some land reforms in Asia have been very effective in increasing land ownership among peasants, including those in Taiwan, South Korea, and Malaysia, where a system of co-operative land settlement, resembling the Israeli use of kibbutzim, has been employed. In Latin America, attempts at reform have often been impeded by such factors as the high level of foreign ownership, prevalence of very large PLANTATIONS, and opposition from politically powerful landowners. In the Middle East, a successful reform in Egypt in 1952 has been the model for reforms elsewhere, with varying degrees of success. State compensation to landowners whose land is expropriated often takes the form of state bonds; a noteworthy exception being in Taiwan, where shares in public industry were given in compensation. This illustrates the need for INDUSTRIALIZATION to provide employment in countries where rapid population growth means that the land, however equitably distributed, cannot provide a living for all. The redistribution of land from large estates into small peasant farms has nearly always had the effect of raising productivity and reducing poverty; there has been renewed interest in land reform since World War II. However, powerful vested interests often prevent effective reform. (See also AGRICULTURE.)

Lanfranc (*c.* 1010–89) Scholar, teacher, and Archbishop of Canterbury (1070–89). He was born in Italy, and set up a school at Avranches, Normandy (1039). He studied as a monk at the abbey of Bec, Normandy (1042), becoming its prior (1046) and making it into one of the finest schools in Europe, whose pupils included ANSELM and Theobald, both future archbishops of Canterbury. Lanfranc's association with WILLIAM I began with his negotiation of papal approval for William's marriage while he was Duke of Normandy (1053) and continued after the conquest of England. Lanfranc sought to reform the English church and to unite it under Canterbury, but he also recognized the king's right to intervene in church affairs. He supported WILLIAM II in the rebellion of 1088.

Lange, David Russell (1942–) New Zealand politician; Labour Prime Minister (1984–89). Lange trained as a lawyer and became an MP in 1977. In 1979 he was appointed deputy leader of the opposition, becoming leader in 1983. He led his party to victory in the 1984 elections pledging a commitment to a non-nuclear defence policy. His banning of nuclear-armed and nuclear-powered ships from New Zealand's ports caused anger in the USA. He introduced free-market reforms and reduced national spending.

Langton, Stephen (d. 1228) Archbishop of Canterbury (1207–28). He was one of the main figures in the drafting of MAGNA CARTA (1215). Langton's appointment as archbishop was bitterly opposed by King JOHN, who agreed to it in 1213 only after England had been placed under papal interdict. Langton sought to mediate between John and his barons but was suspended by Pope Innocent III and summoned to Rome to explain his actions. He returned to Canterbury in 1218 and was responsible for a revision of the relations between church and crown.

Languedoc A former province in south-east France. It was colonized by the Romans, and overrun by Visigoths in the 5th century, and later settled by the CAROLINGIANS. It suffered during the ALBIGENSIAN crusade and passed to the French crown in 1271. Traditional local independence, language (*langue d'oc*), and culture survived, and its *parlement*, founded in 1443 was second in importance only to that of Paris. A 16th-century Protestant stronghold, its towns fostered the CAMISARD rebellion.

Lansbury, George (1859–1940) British Labour politician and pacifist. As leader of Poplar Council in east London in 1921, he went to prison rather than reduce relief payments for the unemployed. Refusing to join the NATIONAL GOVERNMENT in 1931, he became leader of the rump of the Labour Party (1931–35). His rejection of sanctions against Italy, following that country's invasion of Ethiopia in 1935, alienated his colleagues, and he resigned.

Lansdowne, Henry Charles Keith Petty-Fitzmaurice, 5th Marquis of (1845–1927) British statesman. As Foreign Secretary in the SALISBURY and then BALFOUR governments (1900–05) Lansdowne negotiated the ANGLO-JAPANESE ALLIANCE (1902) and the *entente cordiale* (1904) with France. From 1906 Lansdowne led the Conservative Opposition in the House of Lords. His use of the veto on legislation from the House of Commons resulted in the Parliament Act (1911), which reduced the power of the LORDS to a two-year suspensory veto. He was the author of the Lansdowne letter of November 1917 in the *Daily Telegraph* advocating a negotiated peace with Germany.

Lansdowne, William Petty Fitzmaurice SHELBURNE.

L'Anse aux Meadows An important archaeological site in northern Newfoundland, the only confirmed VIKING settlement in the Americas. Excavations have uncovered foundations of turf-walled houses unlike any dwellings built by indigenous cultures, but identical to Viking structures in Iceland and Greenland. Norse construction is proved by associated finds, including a spindle-whorl, a stone lamp, a bronze ring-headed pin, iron nails, and a smith's hearth. Radio-carbon datings from the structures range from 700–1080 AD, concentrating in the late 10th century, thus corresponding to the period of Norse VINLAND sagas. Identification with LEIF ERICSSON, however, is purely speculative.

Laos A long, thin, landlocked country in south-east Asia, bordering China and Myanmar (Burma) on the north, Thailand on the west, Cambodia on the south, and Vietnam on the east.

Physical. Laos is mostly high and hilly, with evergreen forest, this terrain also supporting maize. The Mekong River runs through the north of the country, down the western boundary, and through it again in the south; and its wide valley, swept by a summer monsoon, is ideal for rice growing.

Economy. The Lao economy is mainly agricultural, rice being the chief crop and coffee an export crop. The forests are rich in teak wood, a major export to Thailand at the cost of the destruction of much forest land. High-grade tin is mined. The development of hydroelectric power has made exports of electricty to Thailand the largest export. Limited industry includes food-processing and textiles.

History. The Lao, originating in southern China, were forced south by the MONGOLS. In 1354, following a period of Khmer rule, they set up the Buddhist kingdom of Lanxang ('Million Elephants'), which for a time was very powerful. Laos broke up into rival kingdoms in the 18th century and gradually fell under Siamese (Thai) domination before Siam was forced to yield its claim to France in 1893. Occupied by the Japanese during World War II, Laos emerged briefly as an independent constitutional monarchy (1947–53) but civil war broke out as a result of the increasing influence of the communist PATHET LAO as a political force. A coalition government was established under Prince SOUVANNA PHOUMA in 1962 but fighting broke out again soon after, continuing into the 1970s, with Laos also suffering badly as a result of its involvement in the VIETNAM WAR. A ceasefire was signed in 1973 and a year later Souvanna Phouma agreed to share power in a new coalition with the Pathet Lao leader, his half-brother Prince Souphanouvong (1902–95). By 1975 the Pathet Lao were in almost complete control of the country and on 3 December the monarchy was finally abolished and the People's Democratic Republic of Laos established. The country, under Kaysone Phomvihane (Prime Minister 1975–92), maintained close links with Vietnam. In 1989 there began some relaxation of his regime and restructuring of the economy. A new constitution was promulgated in 1991, which envisaged a strong presidency, but made no moves towards multiparty democracy. In 1992 Kaysone was elected President, but died later that year; he was succeeded by Nouhak Phousavanh. The USA restored full diplomatic relations and in May 1992 an IMF loan was negotiated. In 1995 the USA lifted its embargo on aid donations to Laos. The country was admitted to the ASSOCIATION OF SOUTH-EAST ASIAN NATIONS in 1997.

CAPITAL:	Vientiane
AREA:	236,800 sq km (91,400 sq miles)
POPULATION:	5.023 million (1996)
CURRENCY:	1 kip = 100 at
RELIGIONS:	Buddhist 57.8%; tribal religions 33.6%; Christian 1.8%; Muslim 1.0%; atheist 1.0%
ETHNIC GROUPS:	Lao 67.1%; Palaung-wa 11.9%; Tai 7.9%; Miao (Hmong) and Man (Yao) 5.2%; Mon-Khmer 4.6%
LANGUAGES:	Lao (official); minority languages
INTERNATIONAL ORGANIZATIONS:	UN; ASEAN

Laozi (Lao-tzu, 'Master Lao') A probably mythical Chinese philosopher, long honoured in China as the founder of Daoism. He is said to have beaten CONFUCIUS, reputedly his junior, in debate. The *Daodejing* (*Dao Te Ching*), which dates from about the 3rd century BC (about 300 years after Confucius), was attributed to him.

Daoists later claimed he was an immortal who left China for India, where he converted the BUDDHA to Daoism.

Largo, Caballero Francisco (1869–1946) Spanish statesman. As a socialist he was imprisoned for life in 1917 for taking part in a general strike, but released on his election to Parliament in 1918. After the fall of PRIMO DE RIVERA (1930) he joined the government of the Second Republic as Minister for Labour. After this collapsed he was imprisoned again (1934–35) for supporting an abortive rising, but was acquitted and released. He was leader of the Popular Front, which won the elections of February 1936, but did not become Prime Minister until September 1936, two months after the outbreak of the SPANISH CIVIL WAR, when he headed a coalition of socialists, republicans, and communists. He resigned following a communist take-over in Barcelona in May 1937.

La Rochelle A port in south-west France. As part of the county of Poitou it was controlled by the kings of England (1154–1224) until it was captured by the French. It was a HUGUENOT stronghold in the FRENCH WARS OF RELIGION, and was besieged by Catholic forces in 1573. Attacked again by Cardinal RICHELIEU (1627–28), it was the scene for a disastrous English intervention under the Duke of BUCKINGHAM in 1629. Its inhabitants were finally besieged and starvation forced the Huguenots to surrender. La Rochelle went into decline following the Revocation of the Edict of NANTES and its transatlantic trade suffered from the French loss of Canada in 1763.

La Salle, René-Robert Cavalier, sieur de (1643–87) French explorer in North America. He went to Canada in 1666 and in 1682, after exploring the Great Lakes, descended the Mississippi River to its mouth. He took possession of the whole valley, and named it Louisiana in honour of his king, LOUIS XIV. On his return to Paris he was appointed Viceroy of North America and given authority to govern the whole region between Lake Michigan and the Gulf of Mexico. He set out with four ships for the Gulf but could not find the mouth of the Mississippi. The ships separated and he and his men landed on the Texas shore and attempted to find the way overland. Eventually the men became mutinous and murdered him. It was another 12 years before the French established a settlement in Louisiana.

Las Casas, Bartolomé de (1474–1566) Spanish missionary priest, the 'Apostle of the Indies'. He was a Dominican friar who criticized the conquest and exploitation of the Indians of the Spanish colonies. He had himself participated as a settler in HISPANIOLA in 1502 and as a member of the expedition to Cuba in 1511–12. His change of heart came in 1514, and for the next fifty years he travelled between the colonies and Spain advocating humanitarian reform, especially the abolition of Indian slavery, and writing books arguing the equality of Indians as subjects of the king. The most famous work was his *Brief History of the Indies* (1539). In 1542 his campaigning led to the New Laws to protect Indians in Spanish colonies. Their effectiveness, however, was limited by the opposition of the conquistadores.

La Tène An archaeological site near Lake Neuchâtel, Switzerland, which has given its name to the Celtic culture of the late IRON AGE. It began in *c.* 450 BC,

superseding HALLSTATT, when the Celts came into contact with Greek and Etruscan civilization. It lasted, with various developments, until the 1st century BC, when most of the Celts came under the aegis of the Roman empire. A distinct artistic style developed, characterized by such devices as s-shapes, spirals, and circular patterns, which show that La Tène artists were influenced by Greek and Etruscan motifs. The finest examples of La Tène art display a remarkable mixture of abstract and figurative animal and vegetable representations. The society fragmented from about 400 BC but certain items including long iron swords, decorated scabbards, belts, shield bosses, hammers, sickles, and plough shares continued to be found throughout the area. Invaders from the north at first brought new artefacts and artistic devices, but the culture eventually disappeared.

Lateran Council One of the synods or meetings of senior churchmen held at the Lateran Palace in Rome. The First in 1123 was to bring to an end the Investiture contests and to specify which aspects of life should be governed by the church and which by the secular authorities. The Second was called in 1139 to clarify doctrine and to heal the schism which had been caused by the activities of the antipope Anacletus II. In 1179 the Third Council condemned SIMONY and regularized papal elections.

The Fourth Lateran Council (1215) is known as the 'Great Council' and was called by Pope INNOCENT III. It condemned the ALBIGENSIAN heresy and clarified church doctrine on the Trinity, the Incarnation, and transubstantiation. The Fifth Council from 1512 to 1517 condemned heresy and additionally revoked the PRAGMATIC SANCTION of Bourges by which Charles VI of France had claimed authority over the church.

Lateran Treaties (11 February 1929) Agreements between MUSSOLINI's government and Pius XI to regularize relations between the Vatican and the Italian government, strained since 1870 when the Papal States had been incorporated into a united Italy. By a treaty (CONCORDAT) and financial convention the VATICAN CITY was recognized as a fully independent state under papal sovereignty. The concordat recognized Roman Catholicism as the sole religion of the state. The Vatican received in cash and securities a large sum in settlement of claims against the state.

Latimer, Hugh (*c.* 1485–1555) English Bishop of Worcester. He was appointed to his bishopric in 1535 after HENRY VIII had broken with the pope, but resigned over the passage of the Act of Six Articles (1539), which limited the introduction of REFORMATION DOCTRINE. Best known for his vigorous Protestant preaching, he also spoke out against social injustice during EDWARD VI's reign. On MARY I's accession (1553), he refused a chance to escape abroad before being arrested for his 'heretical' views. Along with CRANMER and Nicholas Ridley (1500–55), Bishop of London, he was made to take part in a theological disputation at Oxford in 1554. Condemned for heresy, he, Cranmer, and Ridley were burned at the stake in Oxford (1555), providing the Anglican Church with three of its most celebrated martyrs.

Latin American Integration Association (LAIA; Spanish: *Asociación Latinoamericana de Integración* (ALADI)) An economic alliance of 11 Latin American countries. The permanent members of LAIA are

Argentina, Bolivia, Brazil, Chile, Colombia, Ecuador, Mexico, Paraguay, Peru, Uruguay, and Venezuela. The association was formed by the Treaty of Montevideo (1980) to replace the Latin American Free Trade Area (LAFTA); it began operations in 1981. LAFTA had been established in 1960 to increase trade between member countries and to promote their economic and social development. LAFTA, however, had only limited success, being considered overambitious and inflexible. LAIA was created by the members of LAFTA to continue LAFTA's policies, but without fixed timetables for the introduction of such measures as reductions in trade tariffs and with greater allowance for differences between member nations.

La Trobe, Charles Joseph (1801–75) British colonial administrator. He became superintendent of the newly settled Port Phillip District of New South Wales in Australia in 1839. When it was separated from New South Wales (and re-named VICTORIA) in 1851, he became lieutenant-governor. Almost immediately he was confronted with the GOLD RUSHES, when the population of Victoria rose in six months from 15,000 to 80,000. He introduced, among other measures, the licence system which later became a cause of the EUREKA REBELLION.

Latvia A country lying on the shores of the Baltic Sea and the Gulf of Riga. It borders on Estonia to the north, Russia to the east, and Lithuania to the south.

Physical. Latvia is generally flat, though hilly in the lakelands of the east and well forested with fir, pine, birch, and oak. It has a modified continental climate.

Economy. Mineral resources are limited, although there are unexplored reserves of oil. Latvia produces about half its energy requirements (the Dvina and its tributaries are the source of hydroelectric power) and is dependent for the rest on imports and the unified grid of the former Soviet Union's north-west region. Manufacturing industry concentrates on machinery, metal engineering, and durable consumer goods; light industry is also well developed. Agriculture specializes in dairy and meat production, and grains.

History. Originally inhabited by Lettish peoples, Latvia was overrun by the Russians and Swedes during the 10th and 11th centuries, and settled by German merchants and Christian missionaries from 1158. In the 13th century the HANSEATIC LEAGUE forged commercial links, while the TEUTONIC KNIGHTS and German bishops imposed feudal overlordship. With Estonia it became part of Livonia in 1346, was partitioned under IVAN IV (the Terrible) of Russia, and came under Lutheran influence in the REFORMATION. It then fell to the Poles, and in the 17th century to the Swedes. Their rule lasted until 1721, when parts again reverted to Russia, the remainder succumbing in the partitions of POLAND. From the 1880s Tzarist governments imposed a policy of Russification to counteract growing demands for independence, which was proclaimed in April 1918. After a confused period of war between Latvians, Germans, and Bolshevik Russians, international recognition was gained in 1921 and the Constitution of the Republic agreed in 1922. During the years 1922–40 sea-ports and industry declined with the loss of Russian markets, but agriculture flourished, many of the great estates being broken up. In 1934 a neo-fascist regime was formed by Karlis Ulmanis, who vainly tried to win Hitler's support, but was forced to resign following the Nazi–Soviet Pact

of 1939, then was arrested and deported to Russia. The Red Army occupied it in June 1940, but German troops took Riga on 1 July 1941 and were welcomed. Re-occupied by the Red Army in October 1944, Latvia became a constituent republic of the Soviet Union. Latvian nationalism never died however, and in May 1990 a newly elected Supreme Soviet passed a resolution demanding independence from the Soviet Union, based on the Constitution of 1922. Negotiations began in Moscow, and independence was recognized by the Soviet Union in September 1991. A new citizenship law excluded from political activity everyone except for citizens of pre-war Latvia or their descendants, thus excluding 48.2% of the population, most of whom were Russians. A new government was elected in 1993 under President Guntis Ulmanis. In 1994 the citizenship law was modified slightly but tensions between the Russian and Latvian communities have continued. The last Russian troops were withdrawn from Latvia in August 1994. General elections in 1995 produced no clear winner and a coalition government was formed. In 1996 parliament re-elected Ulmanis President.

CAPITAL:	Riga
AREA:	63,718 sq km (24,595 sq miles)
POPULATION:	2.490 million (1996)
CURRENCY:	1 lats = 100 santimi
RELIGIONS:	Lutheran; Eastern Orthodox, Roman Catholic
ETHNIC GROUPS:	Latvian 52.0%; Russian 35.0%; Belarussian, Polish, and Ukrainian minorities
LANGUAGES:	Latvian (official); Russian; minority languages
INTERNATIONAL ORGANIZATIONS:	UN; CSCE; North Atlantic Co-operation Council

Laud, William (1573–1645) Archbishop of Canterbury. The son of a Reading clothier, he was ordained in 1601. He became president of St John's College, Oxford in 1611, and attached himself to the party of BUCKINGHAM at court. From early in his career he sought to return to some pre-Reformation practices in the Anglican Church rituals. Promotion to the bishopric of St David's (1621) and further preferment followed, despite James I's fears about his 'restless spirit' and the antagonism that his doctrinal attitudes would arouse. He did not adhere to the prevailing Calvinist belief in Predestination and was suspected of wanting to promote Catholicism. As Bishop of London (1628), he became one of Charles I's closest advisers and as archbishop (1633) supported Charles's absolute rule. A considerable opposition party developed as Laud and HENRIETTA MARIA were suspected of plotting together. Resistance came first from Scotland, where his attempt to 'Anglicanize' the Kirk (Church of Scotland) provoked the BISHOPS' WARS (1639–40). Arrested and impeached by the Long Parliament, he was found innocent of treason by the Lords, but then executed by Act of Attainder. His dogmatic policies were instrumental in precipitating the ENGLISH CIVIL WAR.

Laurier, Sir Wilfrid (1841–1919) Canadian statesman. He entered QUEBEC politics as an anti-clerical Liberal, and was elected to the Canadian House of Commons in 1874, where he held a seat until his death. He became Liberal leader in 1887 (the first French-Canadian to lead a national party) and was victorious in the elections of 1896, 1900, and 1904, remaining Prime Minister until 1911.

His policies sought to avoid closer ties with the British empire and to establish greater Canadian autonomy, while advocating a removal of economic barriers with the USA. He could not, however, escape the growing disapproval of Quebec nationalists, led by his former supporter, Henri Bourassa. Nevertheless, he supported Canadian entry into World War I, while opposing, as far as possible, conscription.

Lausanne, Treaty of VERSAILLES PEACE SETTLEMENT.

Laval, Pierre (1883–1945) French politician. He trained as a lawyer before entering politics as a socialist. His views became increasingly right-wing during the 1930s. He was Prime Minister in 1931–32 and 1935–36 but was best known as Foreign Minister (1934, 1935–36), when he was the co-author of the Hoare–Laval pact for the partition of Ethiopia between Italy and Ethiopia. He fell from power soon after, but after France's defeat in 1940 he became chief minister in the VICHY GOVERNMENT. He advocated active support for Hitler, drafting labour for Germany, authorizing a French fascist militia, and instituting a rule of terror. In 1945 he was tried and executed in France.

Law, (Andrew) Bonar (1858–1923) British politician. He became leader of the Conservative Party in 1911, and supported Ulster's resistance to HOME RULE. A tariff reformer, in 1915 he joined ASQUITH's coalition as Colonial Secretary and continued under LLOYD GEORGE, serving as Chancellor of the Exchequer (1916–19) and Lord Privy Seal (1919–21). In 1922 the Conservatives rejected the coalition government of Lloyd George and Law was appointed Prime Minister. He resigned the following May for reasons of ill health.

Law, John (1671–1729) Scottish financier based in France. He was an exiled Scotsman who believed that increased circulation of paper money and proper organization of credit would bring prosperity. The Regent of France, Philippe, duc d'ORLÉANS, facing financial crisis, allowed him to set up a state bank and a trading company, the 'Compagnie du Mississippi', to trade with LOUISIANA, and later gave it a monopoly of overseas trade. In January 1720 Law became Controller-General of Finance, but in December 1720 a wave of speculation brought his system to an end. The episode, which brought fortune to a few and ruin to many, is similar to the SOUTH SEA BUBBLE.

Lawrence, John Laird Mair, 1st Baron (1811–79) British colonial administrator. As civil servant under the East India Company, he joined his brother, Sir Henry Lawrence (1806–57) on the Punjab Board in 1849, and in 1853 became chief commissioner of the Punjab, distinguishing himself by his control of that province during the INDIAN MUTINY. Returning to London, he was appointed viceroy (1864) in succession to Lord Elgin. He encouraged the expansion of public works programmes in India but opposed the expansionist policies that led to the Second ANGLO-AFGHAN WAR.

Lawrence, T(homas) E(dward) (1888–1935) ('Lawrence of Arabia') British soldier, scholar, and author. He worked as an archaeologist in the Near East before World War I, when he joined the Arab Bureau in Cairo. He played a major role in support of the Arab Revolt, notably with Amir Faisal (later FAISAL I). He took part in the capture of Damascus (1918) and subsequently argued for British support of Arab claims in Syria. In 1921 Lawrence joined Churchill's new Middle Eastern Department as adviser and helped to plan the Middle East settlement of that year. He then withdrew from public life and enlisted in the ranks of the Royal Air Force under the name of John Hume Ross. In 1923 he joined the Tank Corps as T. E. Shaw, but returned to the RAF in 1925. His account of the Arab Revolt entitled *The Seven Pillars of Wisdom* (1926) became a classic.

League of Nations An organization for international co-operation. It was established in 1919 by the VERSAILLES PEACE SETTLEMENT. A League covenant embodying the principles of collective security, arbitration of international disputes, reduction of armaments, and open diplomacy was formulated. Germany was admitted in 1926, but the US Congress failed to ratify the Treaty of Versailles, containing the covenant. Although the League, with its headquarters in Geneva, accomplished much of value in post-war economic reconstruction, it failed in its prime purpose through the refusal of member nations to put international interests before national ones. The League was powerless in the face of Italian, German, and Japanese expansionism. In 1946 it was replaced by the UNITED NATIONS.

Lebanon A country in the Middle East at the eastern end of the Mediterranean Sea, bounded by Syria on the north and east and Israel on the south.

Physical. Lebanon is some 200 km (125 miles) from north to south and 50–80 km (30–50 miles) from east to west. On the narrow coastal plain summers are sunny and warm; fruits of all kinds grow well. Inland the ground rises quickly, to two ranges of high mountains, where there is much winter frost and snow. Between them is the fertile Bekaa Valley, well suited to agriculture, while much of the eastern boundary resembles steppe.

Economy. Agriculture, industry, and commerce have been devastated by the civil war; however, food and drink, machinery, and textiles are among the major exports. Fuels have to be imported. Beirut, formerly the Middle East's leading centre of finance, trade, and tourism, faces a period of reconstruction: the stock market was reopened in 1995.

History. Much of present-day Lebanon formed part of PHOENICIA, including the important trading towns of Tyre, Sidon, Byblos, and Arvad, which retained their importance under Roman rule. Mount Lebanon was a refuge for persecuted minorities, such as the Christian Maronites, who settled there from the 7th century AD, and the Muslim Druze, who occupied the southern part of the mountain from the 11th century. After the Arab conquest during the 7th century Arab tribesmen settled in Lebanon. Successive governments in the region usually left the people of the mountain to manage their own affairs and contented themselves with exercising authority on the coastal plain. Part of the Ottoman empire from the 16th century, Lebanon became a French MANDATE after World War I. A Lebanese republic was set up in 1926. The country was occupied (1941–45) by FREE FRENCH forces, supported by Britain.

Independence was achieved in 1945. Growing disputes between Christians and Muslims, exacerbated by the presence of Palestinian refugees, undermined the stability of the republic. Hostility between the differing Christian and Muslim groups led to protracted civil war and to the armed intervention (1976) by Syria. The activities of the PALESTINE LIBERATION ORGANIZATION brought large-scale Israeli military invasion and led to Israeli annexation in 1978 of a part of southern Lebanon. A UN peace-keeping force attempted unsuccessfully to set up a buffer zone. A full military invasion (1982) by Israel led to the evacuation of the Palestinians. A massacre by the Phalangist Christian militia of Muslim civilians in the Chabra and Chatila refugee camps in Israeli-occupied West Beirut brought a redeployment of UN peace-keeping forces. Syria again intervened in 1987, but many problems remained unresolved. Israel established a South Lebanon Army (SLA) and there were twenty Israeli air-raids during 1988. In March 1989 the MARONITE CHRISTIAN GENERAL AOUN launched an all-out war against Syrian troops. In October 1989 the ARAB LEAGUE successfully negotiated an Accord in Taif, Saudi Arabia, whereby the Maronite dominance in government would be reduced. This Taif Accord was reluctantly accepted, and a frail peace established under continued Syrian protection, formalized by a treaty in May 1991. In 1992 the first general elections since 1972 were largely boycotted by Maronite Christian parties, enabling the Muslim parties, Amal and Hezbollah, to gain the most seats. Rafic Hariri became Prime Minister and began to implement a programme of economic reconstruction. Tension in southern Lebanon continued, with attacks by the radical, Iran-backed Hezbollah guerrillas against the Israeli-supported SLA. In 1996 there were further violent clashes in southern Lebanon between Hezbollah and Israeli troops. Thousands of civilians fled following Israeli air attacks.

CAPITAL:	Beirut
AREA:	10,230 sq km (3,950 sq miles)
POPULATION:	3.776 million (1996)
CURRENCY:	1 Lebanese pound = 100 piastres
RELIGIONS:	Shia Muslim 32.0–41.0%; Sunni Muslim 21.0–27.0%; Maronite Christian 16.0–24.5%; Druze 7.0%; Armenian Christian 4.0%; Greek Catholic 3.0–4.0%; Greek Orthodox 5.0–6.5%
ETHNIC GROUPS:	Lebanese Arab 82.6%; Palestinian Arab 9.6%; Armenian 4.9%; Syrian, Kurdish, and other 2.9%
LANGUAGES:	Arabic (official); Armenian; French; Kurdish
INTERNATIONAL ORGANIZATIONS:	UN; Arab League

Lebensraum (German, 'living-space') NAZI political doctrine advocating the acquisition of more territory in order to accommodate the expanding German nation. The term was first introduced as a political concept in the 1870s, but was given patriotic significance by HITLER and GOEBBELS. The corollary to *Lebensraum* was the *Drang nach Osten*. (German, 'drive to the East'), which claimed large areas of eastern Europe for the THIRD REICH as territories where the Nazi master race should subjugate and colonize the Slavic peoples.

Lebrun, Albert (1871–1950) French statesman, 17th and last President (1932–40) of the Third Republic. A moderate conservative, he pursued a respected but unspectacular parliamentary career (1920–32) until his election to the Presidency. He acquiesced in the French armistice (1940) that led to the VICHY GOVERNMENT of Marshal PÉTAIN. He was interned in Austria (1943–44) until the liberation of France, when he acknowledged DE GAULLE as head of the provisional government.

Lechfeld, Battle of (955) A major battle fought near Augsburg, in Germany, when the forces of the Holy Roman Emperor OTTO I defeated the MAGYARS. This put an end to their westward expansion and the long period of harassment which they had inflicted on the German empire.

Lee, Robert Edward (1807–70) US general in the army of the Southern CONFEDERACY. A member of a prominent Virginia military family, Lee served in the MEXICAN–AMERICAN WAR. While on leave from a posting in Texas, he supervised the capture of John BROWN at Harper's Ferry in 1859. Offered the field command of the Union (Northern) army at the outbreak of the AMERICAN CIVIL WAR, he refused, but instead became military adviser to President DAVIS, and then in June 1862 Commander of the (Confederate) Army of Northern Virginia. He ended the threat of General McClellan to Richmond in the Seven Days' battle and then forced the Union Army to retreat from Virginia after the second Battle of Bull Run (August 1862). Although his first invasion of the north was checked at ANTIETAM, he won major victories at Fredericksburg (December 1862) and Chancellorsville (May 1863) and invaded again, only to be defeated at GETTYSBURG. He then held off attacks by General GRANT on Richmond for almost a year in the Wilderness and Petersburg campaigns, before being forced to surrender at APPOMATTOX. A master of both strategy and tactics, Lee was idolized by his men and did more than any other leader to keep the Confederate cause alive during the war.

Lee Kuan Yew (1923–) Singapore statesman, Prime Minister (1959–90). In 1955 he formed the People's Action Party, a democratic socialist organization, which under his leadership dominated politics in Singapore from the late 1950s. He led Singapore as a component state of the newly formed Federation of MALAYSIA in 1963, and then as a fully independent republic. His policies developed along increasingly authoritarian socialist lines. They centred on the establishment of a one-party rule and a free-market economy, tight government planning, and a hard-working population supported by an extensive social welfare system. The result was one of the world's most successful economies. He resigned as Prime Minister in 1990 but remained a senior minister in government.

Left (in politics) Ideas, movements, and parties of a radical or progressive character, usually associated with SOCIALISM. Following the example of the representatives of the Third Estate at the time of the French Revolution (1789), members of legislative assemblies holding liberal, democratic, or egalitarian views have tended to sit on the left of their chambers. What counts as 'Left' varies with time and place: classical LIBERAL views on economics, for instance, would count as 'Right' nowadays, but were 'Left' when first espoused in the late 18th century.

legion ROMAN LEGION.

Leguía, Augusto Bernardino (1863–1932) Peruvian statesman. As leader of the Civilian Party he was Prime Minister of Peru (1903–08) and President (1908–12,

1919–30). During his first term in office he settled frontier disputes with Bolivia and Brazil, introduced administrative reforms, and improved the public health system. He was reinstated as President by the army in 1919, introducing a new constitution in 1920. He chose largely to ignore this, governing by increasingly dictatorial methods. His second term saw rapid industrialization, but was adversely affected by the Great DEPRESSION and fall in commodity prices. Criticized also for the TACNA–ARICA SETTLEMENT, he lost popularity and was forced from office by the military.

Leicester, Robert Dudley, 1st Earl of (c. 1532–88) Courtier and favourite of Elizabeth I. The queen honoured him with offices and lands, and it was rumoured that he hoped to marry her. However, the convenient death of his wife, Amy Robsart, in mysterious circumstances, tarnished his reputation. He was given command of a military force to the Netherlands in 1585, to aid the Dutch in their revolt from the rule of Spanish Catholic monarchs. He was a poor commander and was recalled to organize land troops to fight the Spanish Armada, but died the same year.

Leif Ericsson ERIC THE RED.

Leipzig, Battle of (also called the 'Battle of the Nations', 16–19 October 1813) A decisive battle in the NAPOLEONIC WARS. It was fought just outside the city of Leipzig in Saxony, by an army under Napoleon of some 185,000 French, Saxon, and other allied German troops, against a force of some 350,000 troops from Austria, Prussia, Russia, and Sweden, under the overall command of SCHWARZENBERG. Napoleon took up a defensive position and at first successfully resisted attacks by Schwarzenberg from the south and BLÜCHER from the north. The next day Russian and Swedish troops arrived, while Napoleon's Saxon troops deserted him. The battle raged for nine hours, but at midnight Napoleon ordered a retreat. This began in an orderly fashion until, early in the afternoon of 19 October, a bridge was mistakenly blown up, stranding the French rear-guard of 30,000 crack troops, who were captured. Following the battle French power east of the Rhine collapsed as more and more German princes deserted Napoleon, who abdicated in 1814.

Leisler, Jacob (1640–91) US rebel, who migrated from Germany to New Amsterdam in 1660. Leisler and other merchants resented English control of the colony from 1664. As a militia officer in the GLORIOUS REVOLUTION in New York, he led the humbler residents against both JAMES II and the aristocratic patroons (lords of the manor) and assumed the governorship in 1689. When Governor Slaughter arrived from England in 1691 Leisler resisted and was captured; he was tried for treason and hanged. His execution precipitated factional conflict for a generation.

Lenclos, Anne (or Ninon de Lenclos) (1620–1705) French courtesan. She was well-read, she studied Epicurean philosophy, and delighted in conducting philosophical discussions in her Paris salon, which was frequented by men of letters including the writers Racine, Molière, Duc de La Rochefoucauld, and Marie, Marquise de Sévigné. She was a disciple of Montaigne and a professed free-thinker in religious matters.

Lend-Lease Act An arrangement (1941–45) whereby the USA supplied equipment to Britain and its Allies in World War II. It was formalized by an Act passed by the US Congress allowing President F. D. ROOSEVELT to lend or lease equipment and supplies to any state whose defence was considered vital to the security of the USA. About 60% of the shipments went to Britain as a loan in return for British-owned military bases. About 20% went to the Soviet Union.

Lenin, Vladimir Ilyich (1870–1924) Russian-born revolutionary statesman. Born Vladimir Ilyich Ulyanov, a formative influence on his life may have been the execution (1887) of his elder brother at the age of 19, for implication in a plot against the emperor. Lenin himself was arrested in 1895 for propagating the teachings of Karl MARX among the workers of St Petersburg, and was for a period exiled in Siberia. Living in Switzerland from 1900, he became the leader of the BOLSHEVIK party and took a prominent part in socialist organization and propaganda in the years preceding World War I. He returned to Russia on the outbreak of the RUSSIAN REVOLUTION and quickly established Bolshevik control, emerging as chairman of the Council of People's Commissars and virtual dictator of the new state. He took Russia out of the war against Germany and successfully resisted counter-revolutionary forces in the RUSSIAN CIVIL WAR (1918–21). His initial economic policy (called war communism), which included nationalization of major industries and banks, and control of agriculture, was an emergency policy demanded by the civil war, after which his NEW ECONOMIC POLICY (NEP), permitting private production and trading in agriculture, was substituted. It came too late to avert terrible famine (1922–23). He did not live to see the marked recovery as agricultural and industrial production increased. Lenin's own outlook and character deeply affected the form that the revolution took; he set an example of austerity and impersonality which long remained a standard for the Party. Perhaps the greatest revolutionary of all time, later communist leaders continued to look to his writings for their inspiration. (See COMMUNISM.)

Leningrad, Siege of (September 1941–January 1944) The defence of Leningrad (now St Petersburg) by the Soviet army in World War II. The German army had intended to capture Leningrad in the 1941 campaign but as a result of slow progress in the Baltic area and the reluctance of Germany's Finnish ally to assist, the city held out in a siege that lasted nearly 900 days. As few preparations had been made, and as evacuation of the population was not permitted by the Soviet government, there may have been a million civilian deaths in the siege, caused mainly by starvation, cold, and disease. Over 100,000 bombs were dropped over the city, and between 150,000 and 200,000 shells fired at it. Soviet counter-attacks began early in 1943, but it was nearly a year later before the siege was completely lifted.

Leo I, St (the Great) (c. 390–461) Pope (440–61). He established the authority of the papacy by defending orthodoxy in regions far distant from his authority in Italy, most notably in Spain, Gaul, Africa, and the East. The PELAGIANS and MANICHEANS were particular threats to papal control. At CHALCEDON in 451 he obtained agreement between Eastern and Western churches on defining for Christian believers the relationship of God the Father to the Son. The following year he persuaded the barbarian ATTILA to leave Italy. In 455 he saved Rome from VANDAL destruction.

Leo III (c. 750–816) Pope (795–816), succeeding Hadrian I, who had tried to maintain papal independence by supporting the Byzantine emperor against the power of CHARLEMAGNE. Leo reversed this policy, acknowledging the temporal suzerainty of Charlemagne. Accused of perjury and adultery by Hadrian's relatives, he was waylaid and imprisoned but escaped to Charlemagne at Paderborn. After sending him back safely, Charlemagne went to Rome (800), heard the accusations, and acquitted him. On Christmas Day in St Peter's, apparently unexpectedly, Leo crowned Charlemagne as Emperor of the West, establishing the precedent that only a pope could crown an emperor.

Leo IX, St (1002–54) Pope (1048–54). An able church reformer, he enlisted like-minded churchmen to assist him including Hildebrand (later Pope GREGORY VII). His chief concerns were SIMONY and clerical celibacy; at the Easter synod of 1049 celibacy was enforced on all clergy. Attempting to establish papal control in southern Italy, Leo's forces were defeated by the Normans and he was made prisoner. His interference in south Italy in areas claimed by the BYZANTINE EMPIRE led to the EAST–WEST SCHISM of 1054 when the Patriarch of Constantinople was excommunicated. He died soon after being released from prison and, for his work in restoring the prestige of the papacy, was declared a saint.

León A province in northern Spain, once an independent kingdom. It was captured from the Iberians by the Carthaginian general HANNIBAL in 217 BC and later became the Roman province of Lusitania. It was conquered by the VISIGOTHS in the 5th century and fell to the MOORS in the 8th century. It was freed from Muslim control by the Asturians and united with Asturias and Galicia in the 10th century. Ferdinand I of Castile seized it and it was finally united with Castile in 1230. The armies of the kingdom were important in the reconquest of Spain from the Moors.

Leonidas (d. 480 BC) King of Sparta. He won immortal fame when he commanded a Greek force against the invading Persian army at the pass of THERMOPYLAE. He held the pass long enough to make possible the naval operation at Artemisium (GREEK-PERSIAN WARS). When counter-attacked he remained behind with 300 Spartans and 700 Thespians, and died fighting, allowing his allies to escape.

Leopold I (1640–1705) Holy Roman Emperor (1658–1705). Originally intended to enter the Church, he was ill-equipped to rule, and relied heavily on his ministers and generals. His long reign nevertheless saw a major revival of Habsburg power, particularly after the OTTOMAN attack on Vienna in 1683 was repulsed by an army led by King John SOBIESKI of Poland. The subsequent eastern campaigns brought the reconquest of Hungary, confirmed by the Peace of Carlowitz (1699). Increasing resentment at LOUIS XIV's intervention in German affairs also allowed him to re-establish imperial leadership in Germany, an important contributory factor to the coalitions that inflicted heavy defeats on France between 1689 and 1713. After the removal of the Ottoman threat Vienna became a major European capital.

Leopold I (1790–65) King of the Belgians (1831–65). The son of Francis, Duke of Saxe-Coburg-Saalfeld and uncle of Queen VICTORIA, he declined the throne of Greece (1830) before accepting that of the newly formed Belgium in 1831. In 1832 he married the daughter of LOUIS-PHILIPPE, King of the French. In 1839 he successfully negotiated peace with William I of Holland. He spent the remainder of his life in maintaining the independence of his kingdom and instituting reforms.

Leopold II (1835–1909) King of the Belgians (1865–1909). His reign saw considerable industrial and colonial expansion, due in large part to the wealth gleaned from the CONGO. The Berlin Colonial Conference (1884–85) had recognized Leopold as independent head of the newly created Congo Free State and he proceeded to amass great personal wealth from its rubber and ivory trade. Thanks to the report of an Englishman, Edmund Morel, his maltreatment of the Congo native population became an international scandal (1904) and he was forced to hand over the territory to his parliament in 1908.

Lepanto, Battle of (7 October 1571) A great sea-battle near the northern entrance to the Gulf of Corinth. On one side were the OTTOMANS, who were seeking to drive the Venetians out of the eastern Mediterranean. On the other were the HOLY LEAGUE forces of Venice, Spain, Genoa, and the papacy, under Don JOHN OF AUSTRIA. Despite the Ottomans' superior number of GALLEYS, the League won the battle. Lepanto was the last naval action fought between galleys manned by oarsmen and the first major Turkish defeat by the Christian powers, but it was not followed up, and had little long-term effect on Ottoman power.

Lesotho A small landlocked country entirely surrounded by the Republic of South Africa.

Physical. Lesotho lies in the central and highest part of the Drakensberg Mountains, where summer rains cause severe soil erosion and in winter the temperature can be as low as −16°C (2°F). The Orange River rises here, in a terrain most suitable for grazing sheep and mountain goats, and only in its lower valley and to the west is there much scope for cultivation.

Economy. South Africa dominates the economy of Lesotho, being the principal trading partner. Almost half Lesotho's adult male population work as migrant workers in South Africa, and their remittances are an important source of revenue. The major exports are manufactures, wool and mohair, food, and livestock. Lesotho is a member of the Southern African Customs Union.

History. Lesotho was founded as Basutoland in 1832 by Moshoeshoe I (who built a stronghold on Thaba Bosigo and unified the Sotho (Basuto) people). After fighting both Boers and British, Moshoeshoe put himself under British protection in 1868, and until 1880 Basutoland was administered from Cape Colony. In 1884 it was restored to the direct control of the British government with the Paramount Chief as titular head. When the Union of South Africa was formed in 1910, Basutoland came under the jurisdiction of the British High Commissioner in South Africa. It was re-named Lesotho and became independent in 1966 as a constitutional monarchy, with a National Assembly (1974) to work with hereditary chiefs. The National Assembly was disbanded in 1986 after a South African-backed military coup, by which the King was to rule through a Military Council. In November 1990 King Constantine Moshoeshoe II was deposed and replaced by his son, Letsie III. As chairman of the Military Council, Colonel Elias Ramaena held all effective power. He was ousted in a bloodless coup in 1991 by Major-General Justin Lekhanya, who established a democratic constitution. Multiparty elections were held in 1993 but tensions between the government and opposition parties led to a political crisis. Letsie III suspended the government and the constitution in 1994. After a negotiated settlement the government was restored and Letsie III abdicated in favour of his father, who returned to the throne in 1995. King Moshoeshoe II was killed in a car accident in 1996 and Letsie III again became king.

CAPITAL:	Maseru
AREA:	30,355 sq km (11,720 sq miles)
POPULATION:	1.971 million (1996)
CURRENCY:	1 loti = 100 lisente
RELIGIONS:	Roman Catholic 43.5%; Protestant (mainly Lesotho Evangelical 29.8%; Anglican 11.5%; other Christian 8.0%; tribal 6.2%
ETHNIC GROUPS:	Sotho 99.7%
LANGUAGES:	Sotho, English (both official)
INTERNATIONAL ORGANIZATIONS:	UN; OAU; SADC; Commonwealth

Lesseps, Ferdinand-Marie, vicomte de (1805–94) French civil engineer. In 1849, he sought to further a long-cherished scheme to build a CANAL across the isthmus of Suez. This became feasible when his friend Muhammad Sa'id became Khedive (Viceroy of Egypt) in 1854; work began in 1859 and the canal was completed in 1869. In 1881 Lesseps began work on the PANAMA CANAL, but in 1892–93 the management was charged with breach of trust by the French government.

Leticia dispute (1932–34) A border dispute between Colombia and Peru. The territory of Leticia on the upper Amazon River was ceded to Colombia by a treaty in 1924; it became an object of contention again in 1932 when Peruvian citizens seized the territory and executed Colombian officials. Colombia carried the dispute to the LEAGUE OF NATIONS, which awarded Leticia to Colombia (1934). The active involvement of the USA with the League established a precedent, allowing the interference by an international body in territory protected by the MONROE DOCTRINE. The successful reconciliation in the Leticia dispute was only one example of how the League of Nations was a striking success in Latin America.

Levant The countries bordering the Mediterranean from Egypt to Turkey, Syria, and Lebanon in particular. The coast has been a trading region since Phoenician days and saw the main confrontations between Muslims and Christians at the time of the CRUSADES. The Levant Company was an English CHARTERED COMPANY with a monopoly of trade with the Levant region. It was formed in 1592, on the amalgamation of the Turkey Company and the Venice Company. Cloth was the staple item of trade from England; currants, silk, oils, wines, and cottons came from the Levant. The ANGLO-DUTCH

WARS (1652–74) disrupted the trade, as did later competition from the EAST INDIA COMPANY and the Levant Company ceased trading in 1821.

Levellers English radicals of the mid-17th century. The Levellers were led by John LILBURNE, William Walwyn, and John Wildman, and their early strength lay with the London poor. By 1647 they had won considerable support among the lower ranks of the NEW MODEL ARMY. In that year Leveller 'Agitators' were elected from each regiment to participate in discussions, known as the Putney debates, with CROMWELL and the Army Grandees, in an attempt to resolve disagreements. Their political programme, embodied in documents like the *Agreement of the People*, was less radical than that of the True Levellers or DIGGERS. It demanded the abolition of the monarchy and House of Lords, sovereignty for the people, manhood suffrage, social reform, liberty of conscience, and equality before the law. Exasperated by the conservatism of the Grandees and Parliament, they mutinied in 1647 and 1649. By May 1649 both the civilian and military wings of the movement had been broken.

Lewis, John Llewellyn (1880–1969) US labour leader. He worked as a miner and rose to become President of the United Mine Workers of America (1920–60). He built the union up into one of the strongest in the USA, securing considerable improvements in the wages and conditions of his members. Although he initially supported President F. D. Roosevelt, he led many bitter strikes in the 1930s and during World War II, breaking from the AMERICAN FEDERATION OF LABOR in 1936. Although not a communist, he defied the restrictive TAFT–HARTLEY ACT by refusing to declare on oath that he was not a communist (1947).

Lewis, Sir Samuel (1843–1903) African jurist and statesman. The son of freed slaves, he trained in England as a barrister, practising in Sierra Leone, Gambia, Nigeria, and the Gold Coast. He served twice as Chief Justice of Sierra Leone. He was a Member of its Legislative Council from 1882 to 1902, and elected (1895) the first Mayor of Freetown. He was the first African to receive a knighthood (1896).

Lewis and Clark expedition (1804–06) The most important transcontinental journey in US history. The expedition was commissioned by President JEFFERSON to explore the vast area acquired as a result of the LOUISIANA PURCHASE. Commanded by Meriwether Lewis and William Clark, it left St Louis in 1804 and sailed up the Missouri to winter in North Dakota before crossing Montana to the foothills of the Rockies. Crossing the Continental Divide at Lemhi Pass, Idaho, the expedition then moved north and in November 1805 reached the Pacific via the Clearwater, Snake, and Columbia rivers. In 1806, after crossing the Rockies, the expedition returned.

Lexington and Concord, Battle of (19 April 1775) The first engagement of the American War of INDEPENDENCE. When General GAGE learnt that patriots were collecting military stores at Concord, 32 km (20 miles) north of Boston, he sent a force of about 800 men to confiscate them. Forewarned by Paul Revere and others, the troops were met by 70 militia (the MINUTEMEN) at Lexington. It is not known who fired the first shot, but in the ensuing skirmish eight minutemen were killed. The British marched on to Concord and confiscated some weapons, but retreated to Boston the same day, harried by patriots, who inflicted over 250 casualties on them.

Leyte Gulf, Battle of (October 1944) A naval battle off the Philippines. In the campaign to recover the Philippines, US forces landed on the island of Leyte. Four Japanese naval forces converged to attack US transports, but in a series of scattered engagements 40 Japanese ships were sunk, 46 were damaged, and 405 planes destroyed. The Japanese fleet, having failed to halt the invasion, withdrew from Philippine waters.

Liao (945–1125) A dynasty which ruled much of MANCHURIA and a small part of north-east China. It was founded by the Qidan (Khitan) tribesmen of Tungus stock, whose homeland was around the Liao River in Manchuria. From their name came the Russian *Kitai* and Marco Polo's Cathay. Qidan strength lay in cavalry. In 1004 their frontier with the Northern SONG was stabilized. Gradually they adopted Chinese habits, accepting the teachings of CONFUCIUS, holding civil service examinations, and performing the customary Chinese rites. Overthrown by the Juchen, nomad huntsmen who founded the JIN dynasty, some of them migrated westward to become the Kara Khitai of Central Asia.

Liaqat Ali Khan, Nawabzada (1895–1951) First Prime Minister of Pakistan (1947–51). He began his political career in British India as a Muslim leader in the United Provinces, and from 1933 became JINNAH's right-hand man in the MUSLIM LEAGUE. In 1946 he became Finance Minister in the Interim Government. Between the death of Jinnah in 1948 and his own assassination in 1951 he was the most powerful politician in Pakistan, when he endeavoured to achieve a reconciliation with India via the Delhi Pact (1950).

Liberal Democratic Party (Japan) Japanese political party that has been the dominant party since World War II. Political alignments were slow to coalesce in post-war Japan, but in 1955 rival conservative groups combined to form the Liberal Democratic Party, which succeeded in holding power continuously until 1993. The Party's early leaders included KISHI NOBUSUKE, his brother SATO EISAKU, and TANAKA KAKUEI, who was forced to resign in 1974 as a result of a bribery scandal. Four leaders followed Kakuei in the space of eight years as the party's fortunes waned before some degree of recovery was achieved under the forceful leadership of NAKASONE YASUHIRO, who served as Prime Minister and LDP president from 1982 to 1987. The party developed close links with business and with interest groups such as fisheries and agriculture. A key feature has been its structure of internal factions, less concerned with policy than with patronage, electoral funding, and competition for party leadership. The party has also been involved in numerous financial and sexual scandals. Even so, it continued to appeal to a wide range of the electorate. The future of the party was threatened in 1992 by divisions arising from the uncovering of a further series of financial scandals. The LDP government lost a vote of confidence in 1993, lost the subsequent general election, and was ousted from office for the first time in its history. Two coalition governments collapsed and in 1994 the LDP joined the Social Democratic Party (SDP) of Japan and the Sakigake Party to form a coalition government. The SDP disbanded and the LDP formed a new coalition in 1996.

liberalism A political outlook attaching supreme importance to safeguarding the freedom of the individual within society. Liberal ideas first took shape in the struggle for religious toleration in the 16th and 17th centuries. The liberal view was that religion was a private matter; it was not the business of the state to enforce a particular creed (see RELIGION AND POLITICS). This later developed into a more general doctrine of the limited and constitutional state, whose boundaries were set by the natural rights of the individual (for instance in the political thought of LOCKE). In about 1800 liberalism began to be associated with the doctrines of the FREE MARKET and *laissez-faire*, and of reducing the role of the state in the economic sphere. This tendency was reversed later in the 19th century with the arrival of 'New Liberalism', committed to social reform and welfare legislation. In contemporary debate both schools of thought are represented, some liberals harking back to the CLASSICAL ECONOMIC ideas of the late 18th century (for instance, HAYEK), others embracing the mixed economy and the WELFARE STATE (for instance, Rawls). Despite their economic disagreements, liberals unite in upholding the importance of personal liberty in the face of encroachment by the state, leading to demands for constitutional government, civil rights, and the protection of privacy.

Liberal Judaism A Jewish movement which began in about 1780 in Germany, in response to the need to redefine the meaning and practical observance of the TORAH in a changing society. Liberals saw the Torah's revelations as progressive rather than static, expressing God's teaching rather than God's law. This allowed for evolution in religious law and practice and resulted in dramatic changes in both diet and custom, including the use of the vernacular in services and the relaxation of Shabbat laws. In Europe the movement is also known as Progressive, and is roughly equivalent to US REFORM JUDAISM.

Liberal Party (Australia) A major political party in Australia. The original party emerged in 1910 as an alliance of various groups opposed to the Australian LABOR PARTY, led by FORREST. They were known for a while as the Fusion Party, adopting the title Liberal in 1913. When Labor split in 1916 over the issue of conscription, they joined with elements of Labor to form the Nationalist Party. Shedding the Labor elements in 1922, they joined with the more right-wing Country Party, staying in power until 1929. In 1931 a new United Australia Party was formed, which was in power with the Country Party until 1941. The new Liberal Party was created in 1944 by Robert MENZIES, and a Liberal-Country coalition has alternated with Labor since then, being in office under Malcolm Fraser (1975–83). After five successive Labor governments, the Liberal Party returned to power in 1996 under John Howard.

Liberal Party (Britain) A political party in Britain. The Liberal Party emerged in the mid-19th century as the successor to the Whig Party and was the major alternative party to the CONSERVATIVES until 1918, after which the LABOUR PARTY supplanted it. Lord Palmerston's administration of 1854 is regarded as the first Liberal government. It was identified with FREE TRADE and the need for civil and political liberty. GLADSTONE's Liberal government (1868–74) established a national SCHOOL SYSTEM, voting by secret ballot, and the legalization of trade unions, as well as overseeing reconstruction of the army and reform of the judicial system. Although the Party split in 1886 over Irish HOME RULE and again in 1900 over the Second BOER WAR, it won a sweeping victory in 1906 and proceeded to implement a large programme of social reform, introducing old age pensions, free school meals, national insurance against unemployment and ill-health, and a fairer taxation system; it also passed a Bill to disestablish the Anglican Church in Wales, and the third Home Rule Bill. After the outbreak of war (1914) it formed a coalition with the Conservatives (1915) and was in five coalition governments between 1916 and 1945. Following World War II it became an opposition party of varying fortune, forming a Lib–Lab pact with the Labour government (1977–78). From 1983 to 1987 it formed the Alliance with the SOCIAL DEMOCRATIC Party, with which it merged in 1988 to form the Social and Liberal Democrats (renamed the Liberal Democrats in 1989). The Liberal Democrats gained over 50 seats in the General Election of May 1997; their leader, Paddy Ashdown, was subsequently invited to attend meetings on co-ordinating policy with the new Labour administration.

Liberal Party (Canada) A major political party in Canada. Before the MACKENZIE'S REBELLION of 1837 a group of reformers emerged that gained a voice in the government of the Province of Canada in the mid-1850s. Following the Confederation of Canada in 1867, a Liberal Party took shape as a major political force and remained so, forming a government (1873–78) under Alexander Mackenzie. The Liberal Party has appealed to French Canadians, who have produced three distinguished Liberal Prime Ministers: Wilfrid Laurier (1896–1911), Louis St Laurent (1949–57), and Pierre Elliott Trudeau (1968–79, 1980–84), who succeeded Lester PEARSON (1963–68). In the first half of the century its policies were less sympathetic to the idea of empire and keener on Canadian autonomy than those of the Conservatives. Its longest-serving leader, Mackenzie KING (1921–26, 1926–30, 1935–48), was a powerful influence in bringing about the Statute of WESTMINSTER. With its power base in Quebec, the Party suffered from the *Québecois* secessionist demands, and failed to win federal office after 1984. It endorsed the all-party constitutional proposals of 1992 designed to prevent the break-up of the Canadian federation, although this in fact was rejected in a referendum in 1992. In 1993 the Liberal Party was re-elected and Jean CHRÉTIEN, its leader since 1990, became Prime Minister. The Party was again returned to power, with a much reduced majority, in 1997.

liberation theology (in Christianity) A theological movement developed in the 1960s principally by Latin American ROMAN CATHOLICS. Liberation theology is a response to the widespread poverty and social injustice found in much of Latin America. Drawing on MARXISM and the ideas of dependency theory, which viewed the inequalities of the THIRD WORLD as springing from dependence on the exploitative capitalism of the developed world, liberation theology attempts to address the problems of political and social inequality in addition to the spiritual matters often regarded as the only legitimate concern of the Church as societies became more secular in the 19th century. Liberation theology raises controversial questions about the Church's relationship with non-Christian ideologies, about the connection between religion and politics, and the Christian response to social inequality and poverty, which have led to its rejection by some Roman Catholic authorities.

Liberia A tropical country on the Atlantic coast of West Africa, flanked by Sierra Leone, Guinea, and Côte d'Ivoire.

Physical. The climate is hot and very wet. Rain forest and swamp cover the coastal plain, which is traversed by several rivers flowing down from savannah-covered uplands.

Economy. There are links with Guinea and Sierra Leone through the Mano River Union. Iron ore is Liberia's chief export. Rubber, diamonds, timber, and coffee are the other main exports. Cassava, rice, and sugar cane are important crops. Industry is limited to food-processing. Shipping registration fees contribute substantial revenues; ships are registered in Liberia because of its low taxation and lenient inspection policies. Monrovia is a free port. The civil war and low world commodity prices have contributed to economic decline.

History. Liberia is the oldest independent republic in Africa (1847). It owes its origin to the philanthropic AMERICAN COLONIZATION SOCIETY. US negotiations with local rulers for a settlement for the repatriation of freed slaves began in 1816. The first settlements were made in 1822, and the name Liberia was adopted in 1824. Independence was proclaimed by Joseph Jenkins Roberts, first President, in 1847. The real beginning of prosperity was in the 1920s, when the Firestone Rubber Company provided a permanent and stable market for rubber. W. V. S. TUBMAN was President from 1944 until his death in 1971. With a decline in world rubber prices, the economy suffered in the 1970s and a bloody revolution in 1980 brought in the People's Redemption Council, a military government, under Master-Sergeant Samuel Doe. The latter was named President and Commander-in-Chief, and his ten-year autocratic rule was one of deep corruption, ending in 1990 with civil war. Two rebel groups, one led by Charles Taylor and a second by Prince Yormie Johnson, assailed the capital Monrovia, and some 150,000 refugees fled the country. A peace-keeping force from the ECONOMIC COMMUNITY OF WEST AFRICAN STATES (ECOWAS) intervened, Doe was murdered, and a ceasefire arranged in 1990. Fighting between rival factions continued, while ECOWAS negotiators tried to restore peace. A peace agreement made in 1991 was not upheld, but in 1993 a further agreement was signed, which included provisions for the implementation of multiparty democracy. A transitional legislature was set up in 1994 but the peace process remained fragile and violence continued. A peace accord was formulated in 1995, but factional fighting broke out again in 1996. Ruth Perry was sworn in as head of state in September 1996, with presidential elections in 1997 won by Charles Taylor.

CAPITAL:	Monrovia
AREA:	111,400 sq km (43,000 sq miles)
POPULATION:	2.110 million (1996)
CURRENCY:	1 Liberian dollar = 100 cents

RELIGIONS: Christian 67.7%; Muslim 13.8%;
                  traditional beliefs and other 18.5%
ETHNIC GROUPS: Kpelle 19.4%; Bassa 13.8%; Grebo 9.0%; Gio
                  7.8%; Kru 7.3%; Mano 7.1%
LANGUAGES: English (official); Mande; Kru-Bassa
INTERNATIONAL
ORGANIZATIONS: UN; OAU; ECOWAS

liberty An area or individual enjoying a special
privilege of freedom from royal jurisdictions. Liberties
of all kinds abounded in the Middle Ages: a ruler could
grant privileges to people or places, and these would
then be enforceable for ever, cutting across other laws
and customs. In England the word 'liberty' was usually
taken to mean a territorial area held by some lay or
ecclesiastical magnate; most of these liberties dated
back to Anglo-Saxon times. The greatest liberties were
the palatinate franchises of the bishops of Durham and
the dukes of Lancaster.

Libya A country on the north coast of Africa, bounded
by Tunisia and Algeria on the west, Niger and Chad on
the south, and Sudan and Egypt on the east.
  Physical. The north-west region, Tripolitania, is
cultivable near the coast, which has a Mediterranean
climate; while inland the ground rises to a high desert
of mainly limestone rocks. In Cyrenaica, the north-east
region, some of the coast is high tableland, with light
rain supporting forests. Southward the ground is low
and sandy, though studded with oases. Here there are
reserves of oil in huge quantities. The south of the
country lies within the Sahara; but to the west, in the
Fezzan region, there are a few large oases among the
otherwise bare, stony plains and scrub-covered hills.
  Economy. The economy and exports are dominated by
crude oil. Attempts at diversification and infrastructural
development, such as the ambitious project (Great Man-
Made River) to bring water from the Mediterranean to
the south, have been slowed by declining oil revenues.
Industry is limited mainly to petroleum by-products
and agriculture is limited by the arid nature of most of
the country. In 1989 it joined the Maghreb Union, a
trading agreement of north-west African states.
  History. During most of its history Libya has been
inhabited by Arab and BERBER NOMADS, only the coastlands
and oases being settled. Greek and Roman colonies
existed in ancient times; under the Arabs the cultivated
area lapsed into desert. Administered by the Turks from
the 16th century, Libya was annexed by Italy after a
brief war in 1911–12. The Italians, however, like the
Turks before them, never succeeded in asserting their
full authority over the Sanussi tribesmen of the interior
desert.
  Heavily fought over during World War II, Libya was
placed under a military government by the Allies before
becoming an independent monarchy in 1951 under Emir
Sayyid Idris al-Sanussi, who in 1954 granted the USA
military and air bases. Idris was overthrown by radical
Islamic army officers in 1969, and Libya emerged as a
radical socialist state under the charismatic leadership
of Colonel Muammar QADDAFI. It has used the wealth
generated by exploitation of the country's rich oil
resources to build up its military might and to interfere
in the affairs of neighbouring states. Libya seized the
Aouzou Strip, in Northern Chad, in 1973; the two
countries did not reach a peace agreement until 1994.
Libyan involvement in Arab terrorist operations has
blighted its relations with western states and produced
armed confrontations with US forces in the
Mediterranean. In April 1986, there were US air strikes
against Tripoli and Benghazi. President Qaddafi
condemned the Iraqi occupation of Kuwait in 1990,
taking a neutral stance. However, Libya again clashed
with the USA during 1992 over its refusal to extradite
two Libyans accused of organizing the bombing of a
PanAm aircraft over Lockerbie in 1988 and in April 1992
the UN Security Council imposed sanctions. The
sanctions were tightened in 1993 and began to affect the
economy.

CAPITAL: Tripoli
AREA: 1,757,000 sq km (678,400 sq miles)
POPULATION: 5.445 million (1996)
CURRENCY: 1 Libyan dinar = 1,000 dirhams
RELIGIONS: Sunni Muslim 97.0%
ETHNIC GROUPS: Libyan Arab and Berber 89.0%
LANGUAGES: Arabic (official)
INTERNATIONAL
ORGANIZATIONS: UN; OAU; OAPEC; OPEC; Maghreb Union;
                  Arab League

Lie, Trygve Halvdan (1896–1968) Norwegian politician
and first secretary-general of the UNITED NATIONS
(1946–53). He held several ministerial posts in the
Norwegian Parliament before having to flee (1940) to
Britain, where he acted as Foreign Minister until 1945.
He was elected secretary-general of the United Nations
as a compromise candidate. When forces of the Soviet-
sponsored Republic of North Korea crossed the border
into South Korea (1950), Lie took the initiative in sending
UN forces to restore peace, thus incurring the enmity of
the Soviet Union. He later re-entered Norwegian politics.

Liebknecht, Wilhelm (1826–1900) German political
leader. An early interest in SOCIALISM led to his expulsion
from Berlin in 1846 but, after the outbreak of the
REVOLUTIONS OF 1848, he returned to Germany to help set
up a republic in Baden. Forced to flee, he went to
England, where he spent 13 years in close association
with MARX. He returned to Germany in 1861 and in 1863
founded the League of German Workers' clubs with
August Bebel. A pacifist, he refused to vote for war
credits for the war with France in 1870, was convicted
of treason, and spent two years in prison. In 1874 he
returned to the Reichstag and in 1875, with the
followers of the late Ferdinand Lassalle (1825–64), helped
to form the German Social Democratic Labour Party,
which became the German Social Democratic Party (SPD)
in 1891.

Liechtenstein A country in central Europe, one of the
smallest countries in the world. It lies on the border
between Austria and Switzerland, to the south of Lake
Constance.
  Physical. The western section of Liechtenstein occupies
part of the floodplain of the upper Rhine, while to the
east it extends up the forested and then snow-covered
slopes of the Rätikon Massif, part of the central Alps.
  Economy. The economy is based on manufacturing
industry; tourism and agriculture play a role. The
registration of foreign holding companies provides a
source of tax income and stimulus to financial activity.
There is a customs and monetary union with
Switzerland. In 1992 a referendum approved
Liechtenstein's entry into the European Economic Area.

History. The principality of Liechtenstein was founded in 1719 when the two independent lordships of Schellenberg and Vaduz were united within the Holy Roman Empire. Liechtenstein remained part of the Empire until 1806, when it became part of the Rhine Federation. It joined the German Confederation in 1815 and became independent in 1866. A unicameral parliament was established by the 1921 constitution but the country has remained a monarchy, headed by the Prince. Any 900 persons or three communes may initiate legislation in the Diet (parliament). In 1989 Prince Hans-Adam II (1945–) succeeded his father, Prince Franz Joseph II (1906–89). Liechtenstein became industralized after World War II. Women were given the right to vote on national, but not local, issues in 1984. A constitutional row began to develop in 1996 following the stated intention of the government to remove certain powers from Prince Hans-Adam II, who announced that he would abandon the country unless he retained his full rights. The coalition government that had ruled the country since 1938 broke down following elections in 1997: Mario Frick remained Prime Minister.

CAPITAL:	Vaduz
AREA:	160 sq km (61.6 sq miles)
POPULATION:	31,400 (1996)
CURRENCY:	1 Swiss franc = 100 rappen (or centimes)
RELIGIONS:	Roman Catholic 87.0%; Protestant 9.0%
ETHNIC GROUPS:	Liechtensteiner 63.9%; Swiss 15.7%; Austrian 7.7%; German 3.7%
LANGUAGES:	German (official); Italian; French
INTERNATIONAL ORGANIZATIONS:	CSCE; EFTA; Council of Europe

Light Brigade, Charge of the BALAKLAVA.

Li Hongzhang (or Li Hung-chang) (1823–1901) Chinese statesman. He formed the regional Anhui army to help suppress the TAIPING REBELLION. In 1870 he became governor-general of Zhili (or Chihli) and High Commissioner for the Northern Ocean, becoming responsible for Chinese foreign affairs until 1895. Recognizing the superiority of foreign military technology, he became the leader of the SELF-STRENGTHENING MOVEMENT, establishing arsenals and factories and creating the Beiyang fleet (China's first modern navy). His reforms were piecemeal, however, and his prestige suffered when his forces were defeated in the SINO-JAPANESE WAR.

Lilburne, John (*c.* 1614–57) English political radical, the leader of the LEVELLERS. He was gaoled for smuggling Puritan pamphlets into England in 1638. Released by the Long Parliament, he fought as a ROUNDHEAD in the English Civil War, rising to the position of lieutenant-colonel, but resigned in 1645 in opposition to the SOLEMN LEAGUE AND COVENANT. 'Freeborn John' always spoke and wrote about the rights of the people, rather than those of kings or parliaments. He attacked in turn all constituted authorities, and suffered frequent imprisonment for his opinions. He became a member of the QUAKERS shortly before he died.

Lin Biao (or Lin Piao) (1908–71) Chinese general and statesman. Graduating from the KUOMINTANG'S Whampoa Military Academy in 1926, he joined the Communist Party and rose rapidly through their military command, leading an army in the LONG MARCH of 1934–35 and

operating successfully against the Japanese. He became commander of the North-West People's Liberation Army in 1945 and conquered Manchuria in 1948. He led the Chinese forces in the KOREAN WAR (1950–53), was elevated to the rank of marshal in 1955, became Minister of Defence in 1959, and popularized the concept of the 'people's war'. He politicized the People's Liberation Army and collaborated closely with MAO ZEDONG during the CULTURAL REVOLUTION. In 1969 he was formally designated as Mao's successor, but in September 1971 he apparently attempted a coup and was killed in an aircraft crash in Manchuria when trying to flee the country.

Abraham Lincoln   *A self-educated man born to poor parents in a log cabin, Lincoln came to embody the ideals of American democracy. His place in history now rests above all on his role in ending slavery in the USA.*

Lincoln, Abraham (1809–65) Sixteenth President of the USA (1861–65). Born into a poor Kentucky frontier family, Lincoln moved westwards with his parents, eventually settling in Illinois. He served as a WHIG in the state legislature and was elected to Congress in 1846. His opposition to the MEXICAN–AMERICAN WAR cost him support and he did not stand for re-election in 1848. His opposition to the KANSAS–NEBRASKA ACT led him into the newly formed REPUBLICAN PARTY and he won national fame as a result of his campaign against the Democratic incumbent, S. A. Douglas, in the Illinois senatorial election in 1858. Although Douglas won the contest, Lincoln's performance established him as the national spokesman for a strong federal union in opposition to the further extension of slavery and helped him to win the Republican nomination for the 1860 presidential election. Lincoln's subsequent election on an anti-slavery programme precipitated the secession of a number of Southern states and then the AMERICAN CIVIL WAR. Through his exercise of executive authority and skilful management of those around him, Lincoln steered the Union (Northern) war effort through many storms, and although his *Proclamation for the Emancipation of Slaves* (1862) was the most dramatic statement of his presidency, he consistently made the salvation of the Union his priority. He won re-election in 1864 and refused to consider a compromise peace at the Hampton Roads Conference in 1865. By the time of the surrender of Robert E. LEE at APPOMATTOX, Lincoln was looking ahead to the problems of peaceful reconciliation with the defeated South, and justice for the freed slaves, but he was fatally wounded by the Southern fanatic John Wilkes BOOTH in Ford's Theater, Washington. As the saviour of the Union, the emancipator of the slaves, the embodiment of the log-cabin-to-White House legend, and the eloquent champion of democracy, Lincoln occupies a unique place in US history.

Lin Zexu (or Lin Tse-hsu) (1785–1850) Chinese imperial administrator. In 1838 he was sent to Guangzhou (Canton) as imperial commissioner to stop the illegal opium trade. He ordered foreign traders (mainly British) to surrender their opium and tried to suppress the domestic trade in the drug. Under increasing pressure from the Chinese, including the terminating of all trade, the British representative handed over 21,306 cases of opium, which Lin destroyed. His apparent success won him promotion, but when Britain reacted militarily in the OPIUM WAR, he was disgraced and exiled. He was rehabilitated just before his death.

Li Peng (1928–) Chinese communist politician, Prime Minister of the People's Republic of China from 1988. Li Peng was born at Chengdu in Sechuan; his father, a writer, was executed in 1930 by the KUOMINTANG for being a communist. Li Peng was looked after from 1939 by the wife of the veteran leader ZHOU ENLAI. After working as a hydroelectric engineer, he became minister of water resources and electricity. In 1982 he joined the Central Committee of the Communist Party, was appointed to the Politburo in 1985, and to the post of Prime Minister in 1988. Two years into his premiership, he adopted a hard line towards the pro-democracy student movement, and presided over the Tiananmen Square massacre and subsequent mass arrests and executions.

Lithuania A Baltic country, lying between Latvia to the north, Belarus to the east, and Poland to the south.

Physical. Lithuania has just some 25 km (15 miles) of Baltic Sea coast, and is predominantly flat, though hilly in the east, where there are many lakes. The lowland plain is forested and fertile; it is drained by the Nemen and its tributaries.

Economy. Lithuania is agriculturally self-sufficient, specializing in meat and milk production, but it depends on imports for supplies of energy and raw materials. Lithuania's main industries are machinery, shipbuilding, electronics, chemicals, and oil-refining, together with light industries such as food-processing.

History. Lithuania was a vast grand-duchy during the Middle Ages, stretching at one time from the Baltic to the Black Sea and almost to Moscow. By 1569 it had united with Poland and in 1795 was absorbed into Russia in the Third Partition. After an uprising in 1863 the Lithuanian language was forbidden, but nationalist and strong Social Democrat movements developed from the 1880s. It was occupied by German troops (1915–18) and in March 1918 a German king was elected. He was deposed in November 1918 and a republic proclaimed. Bolshevik troops invaded from Russia and a short Russo-Lithuanian War ended in March 1920 with the Treaty of Moscow. Lithuania gained the German-speaking town of Memel, but it failed to gain Vilna (the present capital Vilnius), which went to Poland. At first a democratic republic, its politics polarized and a neo-Fascist dictatorship under Antanas Smetona was established in 1926. In October 1939 a Soviet-Lithuanian Pact allowed Lithuania to claim Vilna, Memel having been lost to the Germans. In July 1940 the Assembly voted for incorporation into the Soviet Union; but the country was occupied by the Germans (1941–44), when its large Jewish population was almost wiped out. Re-occupied by the Red Army in 1944, it became again a constituent Republic of the Soviet Union. In 1956 there were serious anti-Soviet riots, ruthlessly suppressed. In March 1990 a unilateral declaration of independence was made. The Soviet Union at first responded by an economic blockade, cutting off oil and gas supplies, but in May it agreed to negotiate, and in September 1991 recognized independence. In December citizenship was restricted to those with ten years residence, a knowledge of the language and constitution, and a source of income. During 1992 Lithuania negotiated a treaty of friendship with Poland and was granted IMF membership. A new constitution gave increased executive powers to the President. The Lithuanian Democratic Labour Party (the renamed Communist Party) won elections in 1992 and the former Communist leader Algirdas Brazaukas became President the following year. In 1996 Prime Minister Adolfus Slezevicius was forced out of office for his part in a financial scandal. The subsequent elections resulted in the formation of a centre-right government under Gediminas Vagnorius. In June 1996 parliament ratified a treaty of association with the EU. Valdas Adamkus was elected President in 1997. With the other Baltic states of Estonia and Latvia, Lithuania is a member of the Baltic Council.

CAPITAL:	Vilnius
AREA:	65,207 sq km (25,170 sq miles)
POPULATION:	3.707 million (1996)
CURRENCY:	1 litas = 100 centai
RELIGIONS:	Roman Catholic; Eastern Orthodox; Lutheran
ETHNIC GROUPS:	Lithuanian 80.0%; Russian 9.0%; Polish 7.0%
LANGUAGES:	Lithuanian (official); Russian; minority languages

INTERNATIONAL
ORGANIZATIONS: UN; CSCE; North Atlantic Co-operation
Council

Little Big Horn, Battle of (25 June 1876) General
CUSTER's last stand in South Dakota when he and 266
men of the 7th Cavalry met their deaths at the hands of
larger forces of Sioux. The battle was the final move in
a well-planned strategy by the Sioux leader CRAZY HORSE,
following the invasion of the Sioux Black Hills by White
GOLD RUSH prospectors in violation of a treaty of 1868.

Little Entente (1920–38) Alliance of Czechoslovakia,
Romania, and the new Kingdom of Serbs, Croats, and
Slovenes (later termed Yugoslavia). It was created by the
Czech Foreign Minister Edvard BENEŠ, who in August
1920 concluded treaties (extended in 1922 and 1923) with
both Romania and Yugoslavia. The principal aim of the
Entente was to protect the territorial integrity and
independence of its members by means of a common
foreign policy, which would prevent both the extension
of German influence and the restoration of the
Habsburgs to the throne of Hungary. France supported
the Entente, concluding treaties with each of its
members. In 1929 the Entente pledged itself against
both Bolshevik and Hungarian (Magyar) aggression in
the Danube basin, while also seeking the promotion of
Danube trade. In the 1930s, however, the members
gradually grew apart. Romania under CAROL II (1930–40)
leaned towards Hitler's THIRD REICH, Czechoslovakia
signed a non-aggression treaty with the Soviet Union
(1935), while in February 1934 Romania and Yugoslavia
joined Greece and Turkey to form the so-called Balkan
Entente. In 1937 Yugoslavia and Romania were unwilling
to give Czechoslovakia a pledge of military assistance
against possible aggression from Germany and, when
the SUDETENLAND of Czechoslovakia was annexed
(September 1938), the Entente collapsed.

Little Rock The capital of Arkansas, USA. It achieved
notoriety when (1957) the state governor, Orval Faubus,
called out national guards to prevent Black children
from entering local segregated schools. A federal court
injunction required the guards to be removed, and
President Eisenhower sent federal troops to secure the
entry of the Black children to the schools. After this
incident segregation in US schooling rapidly declined.

Litvinov, Maxim Maximovich (1876–1951) Soviet
revolutionary politician. He joined the BOLSHEVIKS (1903),
and from 1917 to 1918 was Soviet envoy in London. He
headed delegations to the disarmament conference of
the League of Nations (1927–29), signed the
KELLOGG–BRIAND PACT (1928), and negotiated diplomatic
relations with the USA (1933). An advocate of collective
security against Germany, Italy, and Japan, he was
dismissed in 1939 before STALIN signed the NAZI–SOVIET
PACT.

Liu Shaoqi (or Liu Shao-ch'i) (1898–c. 1974) Chinese
statesman. He served as a Communist trade union
organizer in Guangzhou (Canton) and Shanghai before
becoming a member of the Central Committee of the
Chinese Communist Party in 1927 and then its chief
theoretician. On the establishment of the People's
Republic in 1949 he was appointed chief vice-chairman
of the party. In 1959 he became chairman of the
Republic, second only to MAO ZEDONG in official standing,
but during the CULTURAL REVOLUTION he was fiercely

criticized by RED GUARDS as a 'renegade, traitor, and scab'.
In 1968 he was stripped of office; his death was
announced in 1974. In 1980 he was posthumously
rehabilitated.

Liverpool, Robert Banks Jenkinson, 2nd Earl of
(1770–1828) British statesman. He was first elected to
Parliament in 1790. He was appointed Foreign Secretary
in 1801 and helped to negotiate the Peace of Amiens
with France in the following year. He was Home
Secretary during 1804–06 and declined the premiership
on the death of William Pitt. He became Secretary for
War and the Colonies in 1809, reluctantly taking office
as Prime Minister (1812–27) after the assassination of
Spencer PERCEVAL. After the NAPOLEONIC WARS his
government used repressive measures to deal with
popular discontent (PETERLOO MASSACRE), opposing both
parliamentary reform and CATHOLIC EMANCIPATION.
Towards the end of his tenure the more liberal
influences of men like PEEL and HUSKISSON led him to
support the introduction of some important reforms.

livery company One of the London city companies
that replaced the medieval craft GUILDS, so called on
account of the distinctive dress worn by their members.
The liverymen constituted the freemen of the City of
London, indirectly responsible for electing the mayor as
well as the aldermen, while several of their companies,
such as the Goldsmiths and Merchant Taylors, played an
important role in the regulation of their trade and had
monopoly powers within London. Since the 17th century
there have been nearly 100 London livery companies but
few have retained any importance other than as social
and charitable institutions.

Livingstone, David (1813–73) British missionary
doctor and explorer. He was first sent to southern
Africa by the London Missionary Society in 1841,
travelling extensively in the interior, discovering Lake
Ngami (1849) and the Zambezi River (1851). He then
undertook a great journey from Cape Town to west
central Africa (1852–56) on which he first reported the
existence of the Victoria Falls. Welcomed back to Britain
in 1855 as a popular hero, Livingstone returned to Africa
as consul at Quelimane (1858–64). He made further
expeditions into the interior in the Zambezi region on
behalf of the British government before returning once
again to Britain to attempt to expose the Portuguese
slave trade. He returned to Africa for the last time to
lead an expedition into central Africa in search of the
source of the Nile (1866–73). His disappearance became a
Victorian *cause célèbre* and he was eventually found in
poor health by the explorer and journalist H. M. STANLEY
at Ujiji on the eastern shore of Lake Tanganyika, in
Tanzania, in 1871. He died in Africa; his guides carried
his embalmed body over 1,500 km (900 miles) back to
Zanzibar before it was returned to Britain. He was
buried in Westminster Abbey.

Livonia A historic region of Russia, corresponding to
nearly all of modern Latvia and Estonia. The Livs or
Livonians were a Finno-Ugric Baltic tribe, absorbed by
the Letta and Estonians during the Middle Ages. The
Knights of the Sword (the Livonian Order) conquered
and Christianized the region during the 13th century.
They subsequently emerged as the dominant estate
within the Livonian confederation, which also consisted
of ecclesiastical states and free towns. By 1558 rivalries

within the order had combined with peasant discontent and religious disunity to render Livonia vulnerable to foreign intervention.

The Livonian War (1558–83) was a protracted struggle between Russia, Poland, Sweden, and Lithuania for control of the territory, it overlapped with the SEVEN YEARS WAR OF THE NORTH. By the peace treaties of 1582–83, IVAN IV the Terrible of Russia renounced his claims, thus acquiescing in the seizures of Livonian land by Russia's three rivals; but after the Great NORTHERN WAR (1700–21) Russia gained Sweden's considerable holdings in the region and then absorbed the Polish sections as a result of the 18th-century partitions of Poland.

Livy (Titus Livius) (59 BC–17 AD) Roman historian. He came from Padua to Rome where he was tutor to CLAUDIUS. He wrote a history of Rome in 142 books; 35 survive in full, the rest in summary and fragments. He narrated dramatic history following the ANNALS, reconstructing speech and blending fact with tradition and legend. In part his work was a 'eulogy' of the return to Roman ideals and values in the 'new age' of AUGUSTUS.

Lloyd George of Dwyfor, David, 1st Earl (1863–1945) British statesman. He was Liberal Member of Parliament for Caernarvon Boroughs from 1890 to 1945. In 1905 he was appointed President of the Board of Trade and in 1908, when ASQUITH became Prime Minister, Lloyd George succeeded him as Chancellor of the Exchequer. He was responsible for the NATIONAL INSURANCE Act (1911), which protected some of the poorest sections of the community against the hazards of ill health and unemployment. In later life he regarded this as his greatest achievement. His budget of 1909 was challenged by the House of LORDS; as a result the Parliament Act (1911) was brought in, which reduced the Lord's powers, and provided an opportunity for Lloyd George to use his oratorical skills. He became Minister of Munitions in 1915 and his administrative drive ended the shell shortage on the WESTERN FRONT. In 1916 he became Prime Minister, replacing Asquith and forming a coalition government. He galvanized the Admiralty into accepting the CONVOY SYSTEM against U-boat attacks. During the VERSAILLES PEACE SETTLEMENT, fearing the consequences of French vindictive REPARATIONS against Germany, he strove for moderation. At home, the Conservatives, disliking his individualistic style of government, left the coalition and Lloyd George resigned as Prime Minister in 1922. The Liberal Party, split between followers of Asquith and of Lloyd George, was overtaken in the 1920s by the LABOUR PARTY as the alternative to Conservative governments. In the 1930s he opposed the NATIONAL GOVERNMENT over the OTTAWA AGREEMENTS but supported Britain's entry into the war in 1939.

Llywelyn (the Great) (d. 1240) Prince of Gwynedd (north Wales). The most powerful ruler in medieval Wales, his authority over other Welsh leaders was confirmed by the Treaty of Worcester (1218). Although married (1205) to Joan, the illegitimate daughter of King JOHN, Llywelyn took advantage of the political confusion in England to extend his influence over South Wales. He also had close ties with the MARCHER LORDS.

Llywelyn ap Gruffydd (d. 1282) Prince of Wales. He encouraged the further development of feudalism in Wales and was recognized as Prince of Wales by HENRY III

in the Treaty of Montgomery (1267). Forced into two disastrous wars (1277 and 1282) against EDWARD I, Llywelyn was killed near Builth.

Lobengula (c. 1836–94) Ndebele leader. The son of MZILIKAZI, he was the second and last NDEBELE king (1870–93). After his father's death there was civil war until 1870, when Lobengula acceded to the throne. He compromised Ndebele independence by land concessions to the British (1886) and in 1888 signed the concessions which gave mining rights to RHODES's British South Africa Company. Later, Lobengula tried to resist the expanding European settlement and influence in his country. In 1893 he went to war against the British, but was defeated. He died as he was escaping from Bulawayo, his capital.

Locarno, Treaties of (1 December 1925) A series of international agreements intended to ease tension by guaranteeing the common boundaries of Germany, Belgium, and France as specified in the VERSAILLES PEACE SETTLEMENT in 1919. STRESEMANN, as German Foreign Minister, refused to accept Germany's eastern frontier with Poland and Czechoslovakia as unalterable, but agreed that alteration must come peacefully. In the 'spirit of Locarno' Germany was invited to join the LEAGUE OF NATIONS. In 1936, denouncing the principal Locarno treaty, HITLER sent his troops into the demilitarized Rhineland; in 1938 he annexed the SUDETENLAND in Czechoslovakia, and in 1939 invaded Poland.

Locke, John (1632–1704) English philosopher and liberal political theorist, one of the most influential of English political thinkers. A friend of SHAFTESBURY, he fell under suspicion of treason and fled to Holland in 1683, returning after the GLORIOUS REVOLUTION (1688), of which he became the principal theoretical defender. He was employed from time to time by WILLIAM III, but spent his last years in writing and in defending his often controversial views.

As a philosopher he was an empiricist, insisting in *An Essay Concerning Human Understanding* (1690) that knowledge can be based only upon human experience, and that there is no innate or revealed knowledge.

His political views, in his *Treatise on Civil Government* (1690), insist on the superiority of natural over man-made law, reject the Divine Right of Kings, and exalt the theory of private property. He developed arguments against taxation without representation, and believed in a mixed form of constitution with a balance of power: the makers of the CONSTITUTION OF THE USA were much influenced by Locke's ideas. He argued vigorously for toleration of dissenters, although not of atheists or Roman Catholics.

Lodge, Henry Cabot (1850–1924) US politician. A conservative Republican, he led the fight against US membership of the LEAGUE OF NATIONS. A close friend of Theodore ROOSEVELT, he supported the GOLD STANDARD and a high protective tariff, and was a bitter foe of Woodrow WILSON's peace policy.

Lodi A family of Afghan origin whose rule over northern India (1451–1526) marked the last phase of the DELHI sultanate era. Their founder, Bahlul (1451–89), who already had a strong base in the Punjab, took advantage of SAYYID weakness to seize power in Delhi. He and his two successors extended power eastwards through Jaunpur to the borders of Bengal and threatened Malwa to the south.

Sikander (1489–1517) consolidated his father's gains but was also renowned as a patron of poets, musicians, and other scholars. However, attempts by his successor, Ibrahim (1517–26), to secure greater centralization alienated many local governors. In retaliation, Daulat Khan, governor of the Punjab, invited the ruler of Kabul, the Mogul prince, BABUR, to invade India. His defeat of the Lodis in the ensuing battle at PANIPAT (1526), resulted in the destruction of the dynasty and the establishment of the MOGUL empire.

Lollards Followers of John WYCLIF, thought later the name was applied vaguely to anyone seriously critical of the Church. Lollard is probably derived from the Dutch word *lollaerd*, meaning a mumbler (of prayers). Lollardy began in the 1370s as a set of beliefs held by Oxford-trained clerks who were keenly interested in Wyclif's teachings on papal and ecclesiastical authority; in an age unsettled by war and threatened by disease (especially the BLACK DEATH), it also appealed to other educated sectors of society. They attacked clerical celibacy, INDULGENCES, and pilgrimages. RICHARD II, who was himself an opponent of calls for ecclesiastical egalitarianism, nonetheless retained in his household some knights known to favour Lollardy. The nobility abandoned it only when HENRY IV came to the throne and backed Archbishop Arundel in a vigorous persecution of Lollards. Further reaction against the Lollards among the gentry also resulted from the abortive Lollard uprising attempted by Sir John Oldcastle in January 1414. Thereafter, Lollardy's appeal seems to have been limited to craftsmen, artisans, and a few priests in the larger towns.

Lombardy A region of central northern Italy, named after the Lombards, a tribe from the Danube region who arrived there in the 6th century having been driven south by the AVAR tribe. Though at first they were allies of the Byzantines, they later captured Ravenna from them. They were converted to Catholicism and formed a powerful kingdom until CHARLEMAGNE conquered it in the late 8th century. By the mid-12th century the cities of the area (e.g. Milan) had become economically and politically powerful and formed the Lombard League to challenge the ambitions of FREDERICK I (Barbarossa) in the area; he was defeated at the battle of Legnano (1176). Later the region was ruled by Spain, France, and Austria before becoming part of Italy in the 19th century.

London Corresponding Society An organization founded in London in 1792 by Thomas HARDY to agitate for universal manhood suffrage. It was the first real working-class political movement to appear in Britain – its members were mainly artisans of humble origin – and it rapidly established contact with similar societies in other towns, for example the Sheffield Society of Constitutional Information. The aim of the societies was to circulate letters and pamphlets and to initiate orderly debates on reform proposals. PAINE's writings were a stimulus to the popular societies. When there was talk of a national convention the government, then at war with Revolutionary France, became alarmed. The London Corresponding Society was believed to have

been involved in the NORE MUTINY: in 1798 all the Society's committee members were imprisoned without trial and in 1799 the Society itself was suppressed.

Londonderry (or Derry) A city on the River Foyle, in Northern Ireland. It grew up from the monastery founded by St Columba in 546 and was frequently attacked by the Norsemen. In 1613 it was granted to the city of London for colonization, taking the name of Londonderry and becoming staunchly Protestant. It suffered in the Irish rising of 1641, and in 1688–89 its Protestant defenders were besieged for 105 days by the deposed JAMES II of England; the city did not give in and its watchword 'No surrender!' dates from the siege.

London Dockers' strike (1889) A successful strike, one of the major episodes in the history of British trade unionism. The London dockers, objecting to low pay and casual employment, went on strike to secure pay of sixpence an hour instead of fivepence, and a minimum working engagement of four hours. The episode signalled the beginning of 'New Unionism', characterized by the increasingly effective use of strikes.

Long, Huey (Pierce) (1893–1935) US politician. A demagogue, he rose through various political offices in Louisiana to become governor (1928–31) and Senator (1931–35). He used dictatorial methods to modernize Louisiana and had roads, bridges, and privately owned public buildings constructed, fighting the vested interests of the public utility companies. Despite initial support, Long quickly turned against Franklin D. ROOSEVELT, seeing the NEW DEAL as a rival programme to his own 'Share Our Wealth' by the redistribution of income. His charismatic if neo-fascist appeal came close to dividing the Democratic Party, but he was assassinated before he could run for the presidency.

Long March (1934–35) The epic withdrawal of the Chinese Communists from south-eastern to north-western China. By 1934 the JIANGXI SOVIET was close to collapse after repeated attacks by the KUOMINTANG army. In October a force of 100,000 evacuated the area. MAO ZEDONG took over the leadership of the march in January 1935. For nine months it travelled through mountainous terrain cut by several major rivers. In October Mao and 6,000 survivors reached Yan'an, having marched 9,600 km (6,000 miles). Other groups arrived later, in all about 20,000 surviving the journey. The march established Mao as the effective leader of the Chinese Communist Party, a position he consolidated in his ten years in Yan'an.

Long Parliament (1640–60) The English Parliament that was called by CHARLES I after the BISHOPS' WARS had bankrupted him. Led by John PYM, by August 1641 it had made a series of enactments depriving the king of the powers that had aroused so much opposition since his accession. These reforms were intended to rule out absolutism for the future, and were eventually incorporated in the Restoration settlement, and again during the GLORIOUS REVOLUTION. The Parliament was also responsible for the execution of the king's advisers LAUD and STRAFFORD. Without its Cavalier members, the Long Parliament sat on throughout the ENGLISH CIVIL WAR, since it could be dissolved only with its own consent. Serious divisions emerged between the Presbyterian and Independent members, culminating in PRIDE'S PURGE

(1648). The remnant, the Rump Parliament, arranged the trial and execution of Charles I, and the establishment of the COMMONWEALTH (1649). CROMWELL ejected the Rump by force in 1653, but it was recalled after his son's failure as Lord Protector in 1659. In the next year General MONCK secured the reinstatement of those members 'secluded' by Pride. Arrangements for the Convention Parliament were made, and the Long Parliament dissolved itself in March 1660.

Long Parliament of the Restoration CAVALIER PARLIAMENT.

Longshan (Lung Shan) The Dragon Mountain of Shandong province in China, which gave its name to the later NEOLITHIC culture of the lower Huang He (Yellow River) valley, which flourished between 2500 and 1700 BC. Neolithic culture developed from the YANGSHAO culture and was in turn ancestral to the SHANG civilization. Its economy was based primarily on millet, harvested with polished stone reaping knives, and on pigs, cows, and goats. Its distinctive pottery was the first in the Far East to be made on the fast wheel, and was kiln-fired to a uniform black colour.

longship A VIKING ship, strictly referring only to warships. Longships were built usually of fir planks, and differed from the vessels of the Angles, Saxons, and Frisians in having a massive vertical keel of oak instead of a shallow horizontal one; this enabled them to carry a mast and sail. The clinker-built construction of overlapping planks secured by clench nails conferred great strength with flexibility, and the hulls were waterproofed with tar, seams between the planks being caulked with wool and hair. Later examples were over 46 m (150 feet) long and could carry hundreds of warriors, who also rowed. Longships were of extremely seaworthy design, and the addition of sails made very long voyages feasible, while the shallow draught meant that raiders could penetrate far inland by river. The violent expansion of the Norse peoples was dependent on the skilful use of such vessels.

López, Carlos Antonio (1792–1862) Paraguayan statesman, President of Paraguay (1844–62). His domestic policy, although authoritarian, promoted highway and railroad construction, reorganized the country's judicial system and its military, and attempted to strengthen the economy by creating government monopolies. He abandoned the isolationist foreign policy of his predecessor, but in the process involved his country in a series of disputes with the USA, the UK, Argentina, and Brazil.

López, Francisco Solano (1827–70) Paraguayan statesman. Son of Carlos Antonio LÓPEZ, he became President (1862–70) on his father's death. He initiated grandiose building schemes and then led his country into a disastrous war with Brazil, Argentina, and Uruguay. This war (1865–70) was one of the fiercest and bloodiest ever fought in the New World. It halved the population of Paraguay and left the country in a state of economic collapse; López himself was defeated and killed. Considered a cruel and dictatorial CAUDILLO in his lifetime, he afterwards came to be regarded as the champion of the rights of small countries against more powerful neighbours.

López, Narciso (1797–1851) Spanish-American field-marshal and politician. A Venezuelan by birth, he

enrolled in the Spanish imperial army during the revolution against Spain. He was sent as governor to a province of Cuba, where he began to plot a revolt against Spain, hoping that with independence Cuba would become a state within the USA. With the help of pro-slavery Southern volunteers he twice led an unsuccessful military invasion against Cuba. His third expedition (1851) ended in disaster; the expected popular uprising failed to happen and López, together with 50 volunteers, was caught by Spanish forces near Havana, and executed.

Lord Appellant One of five nobles who 'appealed' (accused) certain of the leading friends of RICHARD II of England of treason in November 1387. Thomas of Woodstock, Duke of Gloucester, Richard Fitzalan, Earl of Arundel, Thomas de Beauchamp, Earl of Warwick, Henry BOLINGBROKE, Earl of Derby, and Thomas Mowbray, 3rd Earl of Nottingham were opposed to the king's policy of peace with France. His position had been weakening for some months, and he was forced to summon a parliament to be held in February 1388; at this, the 'Merciless Parliament', the Archbishop of York and others of his friends and their associates were accused of treason or were impeached. Four men, including a former Chief Justice, were executed. Richard II bided his time, gradually restoring his authority until in 1397 he was able to arrest the surviving Lords Appellant and have them accused of treason.

Lord Lieutenant An English magnate, originally commissioned to muster, administer, and command the militia of a specified district in times of emergency. HENRY VIII was the first to appoint Lords Lieutenant and in 1551 during Edward VI's reign there were attempts to establish them on a permanent basis. From 1585 it became usual for every shire to have a lieutenant, and deputy lieutenants, and by the end of the 16th century they assumed additional roles, exercised on behalf of the sovereign, including the appointment of magistrates. They lost their military responsibilities in the army reforms of 1870–71, but still represent the crown in the counties.

The title Lord Lieutenant was also given to the British viceroys of Ireland.

Lord Ordainer A member of a committee chosen in March 1310 by the English lords who were opposed to EDWARD II. They had forced Edward II to agree to the appointment of this committee of 21 lords, with full power to reform both his household and realm; he had infuriated many peers by his infatuation with GAVESTON, and they wished to make the crown's officials answerable to Parliament. The resultant ordinances were drawn up by August 1311, and the Ordainers enforced them until Edward II won the battle of Boroughbridge (1321) and at the Parliament of York in 1322 annulled all the ordinances and reasserted his authority.

Lords, House of HOUSE OF LORDS.

Lorenzo the Magnificent MEDICI, Lorenzo de.

Lorraine A former duchy in north-eastern France. After the death of CHARLEMAGNE, under the terms of the Treaty of VERDUN in 843 the duchy passed to Emperor Lothair I. As Lotharingia it was divided between Charles the Bald (CHARLES II) and his brother, Louis the German, in the Treaty of Mersen of 870. In 911 it passed to the

Frankish kingdom, then back to the German in 923 as the duchy of Lorraine. In the 10th century it was divided into Upper and Lower parts of which only the former retained the name, continuing as a duchy until 1736. Stanislaus Leszczynski, formerly King of Poland, was given title to it in 1737, but it reverted to the French crown on his death in 1766.

Lorraine, House of GUISE.

Louis I (the Pious) (778–840) King of the Franks, German emperor (813–40), a son of CHARLEMAGNE. He administered the empire well but failed to organize his succession, thus jeopardizing the unity of the Frankish kingdom. He had four sons, the youngest by his second wife, and tried originally to settle the empire and its title on the oldest. This plan faltered as father and sons fought for control, causing Louis I to lose the throne briefly in 833.

Louis I (the Great) (1326–82) King of Hungary (1342–82) and of Poland (1370–82). He succeeded his father, Charles I, in Hungary and his uncle, Casimir III, in Poland. He fought two successful wars against Venice (1357–58, 1378–81), and the rulers of Serbia, Walachia, Moldavia, and Bulgaria became his vassals. Under his rule Hungary became a powerful state, though Poland was troubled by revolts. His daughters Mary and Jadwiga succeeded him in Hungary and Poland respectively.

Louis IX, St (1214–70) King of France (1226–70). He succeeded his father, Louis VIII, and worked effectively to stabilize the country and to come to terms with the English who maintained territorial claims in France. Henry III of England was forced to acknowledge French suzerainty in the disputed region of Guienne. He had a profoundly religious nature and built the Sainte-Chapelle in Paris, to house holy relics brought from Constantinople. Prompted by his recovery from a severe illness he raised the Seventh Crusade, which was directed against Egypt, and sailed in 1248. After initial successes he was captured by Sultan Turanshah and only released upon payment of a ransom in 1250. His involvement in the Crusades was recounted by JOINVILLE. He later mounted another Crusade to Tunis where he died. He was canonized by Pope Boniface VIII in 1297, his sanctity conferring immense prestige on the Capetian dynasty.

Louis XI (1423–83) King of France (1461–83). He was exiled for plotting against his father, Charles VII, but succeeded to the throne in 1461. As king he imposed new taxes, dismissed his father's ministers, and attempted to curb the powers of the nobility. They retaliated by forming a coalition against him which waged the 'War of Common Weal'. CHARLES THE BOLD of Burgundy led a group including the Duke of Brittany, the Duke of Bourbon, and Louis XI's brother, Charles of France, supported by some lesser magnates, clergy, and a few towns. The Battle of Montlhéry (July 1465) ended in stalemate, and Louis was able to gain the upper hand after Charles the Bold was defeated by the Swiss in 1477. He pursued a successful policy of territorial acquisition and centralization: by the time of his death only the duchy of Brittany remained largely independent.

Louis XI established firm government but nonetheless bequeathed a troubled legacy at his death. The minority of his son, Charles VIII, saw further outbreaks of discontent amongst the nobility and attempts by the dukes of Brittany to undermine the monarchy.

Louis XIV (1638–1715) King of France (1643–1715). On his father's death in 1643, his mother ANNE OF AUSTRIA became regent and MAZARIN chief minister. Louis survived the FRONDE, was proclaimed of age in 1651, and married the Infanta Maria Theresa of Spain in 1660. He took over the government on Mazarin's death in 1661 and embarked on a long period of personal rule.

Domestic policy was aimed at creating and maintaining a system of absolute rule: the king ruled unhampered by challenges from representative institutions but with the aid of ministers and councils subject to his will. The States-General was not summoned, the *Parlement* largely ignored, the great nobles were generally excluded from political office, and loyal bourgeois office-holders were promoted. Jean-Baptiste COLBERT expanded the merchant marine and the navy, and encouraged manufacturing industries and trade, though he largely failed in his attempts to improve the tax system. In the provinces the *intendants* established much firmer royal control. The French army became larger and more efficient; in his later years Louis was able to put between 300,000 and 400,000 men into the field. The greatest victories came in the earlier years, when the generals TURENNE and CONDÉ were available to take command. Victories were won in the War of DEVOLUTION and the Dutch War, with the French frontiers strengthened by a series of strategic territorial gains, reinforced by the fortifications of VAUBAN. The NINE YEARS WAR and the War of the SPANISH SUCCESSION saw France hard-pressed as Europe united to curb Louis's aggressive policies; after 1700 France suffered a series of crushing defeats. The country was seriously impoverished by the burden of taxation.

Religious orthodoxy was strictly imposed, particularly after the Revocation of the Edict of NANTES (1685) and the forced conversion of the HUGUENOTS, at least 200,000 of whom illegally fled the country. Within the Catholic church Jansenists, Quietists, and other deviants were also persecuted. On the positive side, the achievements of the reign in literature and the arts based on the court at VERSAILLES have given it the name *Le grand siècle*. There was, however, a marked decline in these fields during the later part of the reign, and at his death Louis XIV left a series of political, economic, and religious problems of his great-grandson, LOUIS XV.

Louis XV (1710–74) King of France (1715–74), a great grandson of LOUIS XIV. During his minority Philippe, duc d'Orléans was regent, followed by Cardinal FLEURY. After Fleury's death in 1743 Louis decided to rule without a chief minister, but he proved to be a weak king who reduced the prestige of the French monarchy both at home and abroad.

At the age of 15 Louis married Marie Leszczynska, daughter of the King of POLAND, and France intervened in the War of Polish Succession, gaining the duchy of Lorraine in 1766. In foreign affairs France was involved in almost continuous warfare; in the War of the AUSTRIAN SUCCESSION, in alliance with FREDERICK II of Prussia until hostilities were concluded at AIX-LA-CHAPELLE. The SEVEN YEARS WAR saw France and Austria fighting Prussia and Great Britain but with little success. The Treaty of PARIS (1763) marked the loss of most of France's overseas territories.

In domestic policy Louis XV was influenced by a succession of favourites and mistresses, including Madame de POMPADOUR and Madame DU BARRY, on whom he lavished enormous amounts of money. The extravagance of the court and the high cost of war absorbed all of France's resources and efforts to rationalize the tax system failed. The *Parlement* of Paris secured the suppression of the JESUITS in 1764 but otherwise failed to achieve reforms. The members of the *Parlement* were banished and a compliant *Parlement* appointed in their place in 1771. The reign saw the aristocracy and the wealthy bourgeoisie prosper, though the country was close to bankruptcy. The king's failure to solve his financial affairs left an insolvent government for his successor, LOUIS XVI.

Louis XVI (1754–93) The last King of France (1774–92) before the FRENCH REVOLUTION. Weak and vacillating, unwisely advised by his Austrian wife, MARIE ANTOINETTE, he could neither avert the Revolution by supporting the economic and social reforms proposed by TURGOT and NECKER, nor, lacking all understanding of popular demands, become its popular leader. To meet the situation he summoned the largely aristocratic Assembly of Notables (1787), which achieved nothing, and then (1789) the STATES-GENERAL, which had not been called for 175 years. This marked the start of the Revolution. The royal family was forcibly brought back from VERSAILLES to Paris (October 1789) and their attempt to flee the country was stopped at VARENNES (1791). Thereafter they were virtually prisoners. The monarchy was abolished (September 1792) and Louis was guillotined in January 1793. His wife was executed six months later.

Louis XVIII (1755–1824) King of France (1795–1824). The brother of Louis XVI, he became titular regent after the death of the latter in 1793, and declared himself king on the death in prison of the ten-year-old Louis XVII. Known as the comte de Provence, he had fled to Koblenz, and then to England, where he led the counter-revolutionary movement. His exile ended in 1814 and with the help of TALLEYRAND he returned to the throne of France and issued a constitutional charter. He appointed Marshal Soult (1769–1851) as his Minister of War, the latter going on to a long political career. Many of NAPOLEON's reforms in the law, administration, church, and education were retained, but after the assassination (1820) of his nephew the duc de Berry, he replaced moderate ministers by reactionary ones. Civil liberties were curbed, a trend which continued under his younger brother and successor, CHARLES X.

Louisburg A French fortress on the southern coast of Cape Breton Island, Canada, built in 1720 after the ceding of Acadia (NOVA SCOTIA). As a threat to New England fishermen and shipping and to Nova Scotia, it was captured by Pepperell's combined operation (1745) during KING GEORGE'S WAR. To the disgust of the colonists Louisburg was exchanged for Madras in 1748, but it was again taken by AMHERST and BOSCAWEN in 1758 prior to WOLFE's attack on QUEBEC.

Louisiana A French American colony around the delta and valley of the Mississippi, explored by LA SALLE's expedition from Canada in 1682 and named after Louis XIV. Its capital, New Orleans, was founded in 1718 as part of a chain of French forts and trading posts ringing British settlements in North America. The name Louisiana was extended to cover French claims on the Gulf Coast and in the west. In the FRENCH AND INDIAN WARS it was a serious threat to southern British colonies and West Indian possessions, especially after some 2,000 Acadians, expelled from NOVA SCOTIA, swelled its population in 1755. It was ceded to Spain in 1762, returned to France in 1800 and sold to the USA in 1803.

Louisiana Purchase (1803) US acquisition from France of over two million sq km (828,000 sq miles) of territory stretching north from the mouth of the Mississippi to its source and west to the Rockies. France had ceded Louisiana to Spain in 1762 but regained it by treaty in 1801. Concerned at the possible closure of the Mississippi to commerce and the related threat to US security, President JEFFERSON sent James MONROE to France in 1803 to help negotiate free navigation and the purchase of New Orleans and west Florida. At war again with Britain, Napoleon was anxious not to have extensive overseas territories to defend and sold the whole of Louisiana to the US for $15 million. Although the Constitution gave no authority to purchase new territory or promise it statehood, the Senate confirmed the agreement, increasing US territory by some 140% and transforming the USA into a continental nation.

Louis-Philippe I (1773–1850) King of France (1830–48). The son of the duc d'Orléans he, along with his father, renounced his titles and assumed the surname Égalité. On the restoration of LOUIS XVIII to the French throne he recovered his estates, and was elected King of the French, the 'citizen king', after the JULY REVOLUTION in 1830. During his reign political corruption, judicial malpractices, and limited parliamentary franchise united liberals and extremists in a cry for reform. After 1840, a series of disastrous foreign ventures and alliances with reactionary European monarchies alienated the liberal opinion on which his authority had been based. His rule ended in February 1848 when, after popular riots, he agreed to abdicate, and escaped to England as 'Mr Smith'.

Lovett, William (1800–77) British radical political reformer. He became involved in working-class radical groups, and in 1836, with Francis PLACE, set up the London Workingmen's Association. Lovett outlined a programme of political reform, which in 1838 was presented as the People's Charter. He was secretary of the first CHARTIST convention in 1839, but was imprisoned following violent incidents in Birmingham. He subsequently gave up all political activity.

Low Countries A term sometimes used, especially historically, to describe the three adjacent north-west European countries of the NETHERLANDS, BELGIUM, and LUXEMBOURG. Much of the Netherlands and small parts of Belgium are in fact below sea-level. Southern Belgium and Luxembourg are higher, rising to over 600 m (2,000 feet) in the Ardennes.

Lowell, Francis Cabot (1775–1817) Founder of the US cotton industry. A Boston merchant, in 1814 he established the first US factory to use both spinning and weaving machinery (and the first in the world to manufacture cotton cloth using power machinery enclosed in a single building) at Waltham, Massachusetts. Lowell was singular among early US industrialists for the paternalistic concern he demonstrated for his workforce and for their living and working conditions.

Lower Canada QUEBEC.

Loyola, Ignatius, St (1491–1556) Spanish ecclesiastical reformer, founder and first general of the Society of Jesus (the JESUITS). Born into a noble family, he attached himself to the court of Ferdinand II of Aragon. His military career was ended by a leg-wound received while fighting for Navarre against France (1521). During his convalescence he underwent a spiritual transformation. He spent almost a year in prayer and penance (1522–23) and wrote the first draft of his *Spiritual Exercises*, an ordered scheme of meditations on the life of Jesus Christ and the truths of the Christian faith. After a pilgrimage to Jerusalem in 1523 he attended the University of Paris (1528–35). There he collected a band of like-minded followers, who worked through the *Exercises*. In 1534 he and six others took vows of poverty, chastity, and obedience to the pope, and Pope Paul III recognized their 'Society of Jesus' as an order of the Church in 1540. By the time of his death there were over 1,000 Jesuits in nine European provinces as well as those working in foreign missions.

Luba A Bantu kingdom founded *c.* 1500, lying north of Lake Kisale in modern Democratic Republic of Congo (formerly Zaïre). The founders, the Balopwe clan, came from further north, and imposed their sovereignty over existing chiefdoms. Some of the Luba moved eastwards *c.* 1600, and founded a kingdom among the Lunda; from there a large number of small chiefdoms proliferated stretching from eastern Angola to north-eastern Zambia, and making previously existing chiefdoms their vassals. The largest was the kingdom of Mwata Yamvo; others were the Bemba in north-eastern Zambia, Kazembe in the Luapula valley, and Kasanje in central Angola. They all paid tribute to the central kingdoms, but the organization was decentralized, and the kings served as settlers of disputes between communities. These were occupied not only by agriculture, but also in mining and trade in copper and salt against European goods obtained from the Portuguese. Kazembe was the richest and most important.

Lucknow, Siege of (1857–58) A siege of the British garrison during the INDIAN MUTINY. The abolition by the British of the Kingdom of Oudh, whose capital Lucknow had been, became one of the causes of the Mutiny. On the outbreak of hostilities the British and Indian garrison, together with women and children, were confined to the Residency, and during the ensuing five-month siege they suffered heavy casualties. Lucknow was relieved first on 26 September by troops under Sir Henry HAVELOCK. He in turn was besieged, and only relieved on 16 November by troops under Sir Colin Campbell. The city was not finally restored to British possession until 21 March 1858.

Luddites A 19th-century protest group of British workers, who destroyed machinery that they believed was depriving them of their livelihood. The movement began in Nottinghamshire in 1811, when framework knitters began wrecking the special type of 'wide frames' used to make poor-quality stockings, which were undercutting the wages of skilled craftsmen. The men involved claimed to be acting under the leadership of a certain 'Ned Ludd' or 'King Ludd', although it is doubtful whether such a person ever existed. The outbreaks of violence spread rapidly and by the early part of 1812 were affecting Yorkshire and Lancashire. Large groups of men stormed the cotton and woollen mills in order to attack the power looms. The government responded harshly by making machine-breaking an offence punishable by death. There were further sporadic outbreaks in 1816 but the movement subsequently died out.

Ludendorff, Erich (1865–1937) German general. A brilliant strategist, in World War I he helped to revise the proposals of SCHLIEFFEN for war in the West by extending the German army's southern flank, and largely planned the battle of Tannenberg (1914). With HINDENBURG he exercised a virtual military dictatorship from 1917 and forced the resignation of the Chancellor, BETHMANN-HOLLWEG. He directed the war effort with Hindenburg until the final offensive failed (September 1918). He fled to Sweden, returning to attempt to overthrow the WEIMAR REPUBLIC in the KAPP PUTSCH (1920). He joined HITLER in the abortive MUNICH 'BEER-HALL' PUTSCH (1923) and sat in the Reichstag as a National Socialist (1924–28). He became a propagandist of 'total war' and of the new 'Aryan' racist dogma and wrote pamphlets accusing 'supranational powers' — the Roman Catholic Church, the Jews, and the Freemasons — of a common plot against Germany.

Lugard, Frederick Dealtry, 1st Baron (1858–1945) British colonial administrator. After early service in the army, he joined the British East Africa Company and was posted (1890) to Uganda. He persuaded the British government to assume a protectorate over Uganda in 1894. He was sent to NIGERIA, becoming High Commissioner in 1900, and by 1903 had effectively occupied northern Nigeria. He was governor of HONG KONG (1907–12) and served as governor-general in Nigeria (1912–19), administratively amalgamating the northern and southern protectorates. He developed the doctrine of indirect rule, believing that the colonial administration should exercise its control through traditional native chiefdoms and institutions.

Lumumba, Patrice (Emergy) (1925–61) Congolese nationalist and politician. He founded the influential MNC (Mouvement National Congolais) in 1958 to bring together radical nationalists. He was accused of instigating public violence and was jailed by the Belgians, but was released to participate in the Brussels Conference (January 1960) on the Congo. He became Prime Minister and Minister of Defence when the Congo became independent in June 1960. Sections of the army mutinied, the Belgian troops returned, and Katanga province declared its independence (see CONGO CRISIS). Lumumba appealed to the UNITED NATIONS, which sent a peace-keeping force. President Kasavubu, his rival in power, dismissed him and shortly afterwards he was put under arrest by Colonel MOBUTU. He escaped, but was recaptured and killed.

Lusitania British transatlantic liner, torpedoed (7 May 1915) off the Irish coast without warning by a German submarine, with the loss of 1,195 lives. The sinking, which took 128 US lives, created intense indignation throughout the USA, which until then had accepted Woodrow WILSON's policy of neutrality. Germany refused to accept responsibility for the act, and no reparations settlement was reached. Two years later in 1917, following Germany's resumption of unrestricted submarine warfare, the USA severed diplomatic relations and entered the war on the side of the Allies.

Martin Luther *Luther emerged as a controversialist when he fastened his Ninety-Five Theses, which attacked the sale of Indulgences, to the door of All Saint's Church, Wittenberg on 31st October 1517.*

Luther, Martin (c. 1483–1546) German theologian, the principal initiator of the Protestant REFORMATION in Europe. He attended Erfurt University (1501–05) before joining the Augustinian Friars. Ordained a priest in 1507, he took the chair of biblical theology at Wittenberg University in 1512. In evolving his doctrine of justification by faith alone, he challenged the hierarchy of the Catholic Church over such issues as the roles of the papacy and the priesthood, and the necessity of certain sacraments and observances (see INDULGENCE). At the Diet of WORMS in 1521 he defended his doctrines before CHARLES V, but he was excommunicated by the pope and made an outlaw of the Holy Roman Empire. Yet his challenge to the Catholic Church had been well publicized; his many pamphlets, including *To the Christian Nobility of the German Nation* (1520), had not fallen on deaf ears. By mid-century, a host of German and Scandinavian rulers had severed their links with Rome and set up new 'Lutheran' churches in their territories.

Luther's original intention had not been to split Christendom in this way, but he reluctantly accepted the inevitable when the Catholic establishment proved resistant to his proposals for reform. His fear of anarchy and his conservative political attitudes led him into acrimonious dispute with more radical Protestants such as the ANABAPTISTS. He spent the last 25 years of his life under the protection of Elector Frederick the Wise of Saxony. He married Katherine von Bora (1525) and had six children. His translation of the Bible into German provided the foundation of the literary language of northern Europe.

Luthuli, Albert John (1898–1967) South African political leader. A Zulu by birth, he served as a tribal chief (1936–52) and was a member of the Native Representative Council until its dissolution in 1946. In 1952 he was elected President of the AFRICAN NATIONAL CONGRESS and became universally known as leader of non-violent opposition to APARTHEID. From 1956 he suffered frequent arrests and harassment by the South African government. In 1959 the government banished him to his village and in 1960 outlawed the ANC. In 1961 he was awarded the Nobel Peace Prize.

Lützen, Battle of (16 November 1632) A battle during the THIRTY YEARS WAR between the Protestant forces under GUSTAVUS Adolphus and Bernard, Duke of Saxe-Weimar and imperial Catholic troops commanded by WALLENSTEIN. The Protestant attack was delayed by foggy conditions and the numerically superior imperial forces came close to victory. Gustavus was killed but Bernard eventually secured a victory for the Protestants.

Luxembourg, Grand Duchy of A small country in north-west Europe surrounded by Belgium to the west and north, Germany to the east, and France to the south.

Physical. The climate is temperate continental and there are sizeable forests, but the ground is hilly and rocky with little fertile soil.

Economy. Although steel is a major industry (iron ore being abundant), chemicals and machine manufacture are also significant. Attractive conditions including banking secrecy have made international financial services increasingly important. There is concern that EU fiscal harmonization may jeopardize Luxembourg's status as a leading financial centre.

History. Luxembourg was occupied by the Romans, then by the FRANKS in the 5th century, passing to the counts of Luxembourg in the 11th century. The duchy of Luxembourg was created in 1354. Seized by BURGUNDY in 1443, it passed to the HABSBURGS in 1477 and to SPAIN in 1555. The French occupied it from 1684 until 1697. The first Count of Luxembourg was Conrad, who took the title in 1060. Luxembourg passed again to the Habsburgs after the War of the Spanish Succession (1701–14). In 1815 it was handed over to the Netherlands but joined the Belgians in the revolt of 1830; in 1831 Luxembourg was divided, the Walloon-speaking region becoming part of Belgium. The rest of Luxembourg remained within the Netherlands and became the Grand Duchy of Luxembourg in 1839 with its own government. In 1890 the King of the Netherlands died without a male heir and from then on the two countries were headed by different royal families. Grand Duke Jean (1921–   ) succeeded in 1964 when his mother, Grand Duchess Charlotte (1896–1985), abdicated in his favour. Luxembourg entered into an economic union with Belgium in 1921. The Netherlands joined this union in 1948, forming the Benelux Economic Union, which was the first free-trade area in Europe. Luxembourg was a founder member of the EUROPEAN ECONOMIC COMMUNITY (now the EUROPEAN UNION). The socialist coalition, which has held power since 1984, was re-elected in 1994.

CAPITAL:	Luxembourg
AREA:	2,586 sq km (999 sq miles)
POPULATION:	415,000 (1996)
CURRENCY:	1 Luxembourg franc = 100 centimes (Belgian currency also legal tender)
RELIGIONS:	Roman Catholic 93.0%; Protestant 1.3%
ETHNIC GROUPS:	Luxembourger 73.8%; Portuguese 8.1%; Italian 5.4%; French 3.3%; German 2.3%; Belgian 2.3%
LANGUAGES:	French, German (both official); Letzeburgesch; minority languages
INTERNATIONAL ORGANIZATIONS:	UN; EU; OECD; NATO; Council of Europe; CSCE

Luxemburg, Rosa (1871–1919) Polish revolutionary socialist. A brilliant writer and orator, she defended the cause of revolution against moderates in the German Social Democratic Party. She took part in the RUSSIAN REVOLUTION of 1905 in Poland and argued that the mass strike, not the organized vanguard favoured by LENIN, was the most important instrument of the proletarian revolution. She was active in the second INTERNATIONAL and, with Karl LIEBKNECHT, founded the SPARTAKIST MOVEMENT. A founder of the German Communist Party, she was captured by right-wing irregular troops (*Freikorps*) in Berlin and, together with Liebknecht, was murdered during the Spartakist Revolt of 1919.

Lydia A territory in western Asia Minor. It derived much prosperity from trade as it lay athwart the two main roads which linked the coast to the interior. The first minting of coins is ascribed to it in the 8th century BC. It reached its apogee of independent power under CROESUS, thereafter entering the Persian empire. It later came under the control of the Seleucids and Pergamum, before being incorporated into the Roman province of Asia in 133 BC. Under Diocletian it became a separate province. Then, as previously, Sardis was its principal city.

Lyons, Joseph Aloysius (1879–1939) Australian politician. He was a Labor politician in Tasmania from 1909 until 1929 and was Premier there from 1923 until 1928. He became a federal politician in 1929. When the Labor Party split in 1931, Lyons and others left, joining with the Nationalists to form the United Australia Party. Lyons led the Opposition from 1931 until 1932, when he became Prime Minister (1932–39). He foresaw war and embarked in 1937 on a rigorous programme of armament.

Lysander (d. 395 BC) Spartan admiral and statesman. He did much to bring about the defeat of Athens in the PELOPONNESIAN WAR. He revived Peloponnesian fortunes largely as a result of the friendship which he struck up with CYRUS II (the Great), son of the king of Persia. With his financial support he increased and improved the Peloponnesian fleet, and eventually sealed the Athenian fate with victory at AEGOSPOTAMI (405) and the subsequent blockading of the HELLESPONT. Nevertheless, his high-handedness and lack of restraint made him many enemies at Sparta and elsewhere. He was killed on campaign in Boeotia.

Maastricht Treaty (1992) A treaty, agreed by the leaders of the then 12 member states of the EUROPEAN COMMUNITY, establishing the conditions for the creation of the EUROPEAN UNION following ratification at national level. The treaty – officially known as the 'Treaty on European Union'—envisaged political union, with the concept of 'union citizenship'; eventual monetary union under a European Central Bank; common policies on foreign affairs and security, with the WESTERN EUROPEAN UNION becoming the military arm of the Community; greater co-operation on domestic and environmental matters; some strengthening of the European Parliament; and 'subsidiarity', that is, an effective level of demarcation between the powers and responsibilities of the EU institutions and individual member states. The ratification process was complicated by disagreements over certain clauses of the treaty. Because Britain refused to accept the Social Chapter (proposed in 1989), a section of the treaty that protects the rights of employees, this was eventually omitted from the treaty and signed by the other member countries as a separate protocol. However, on winning power in May 1997, the new Labour administration in Britain immediately revoked this decision and signed the protocol. Britain also secured the right to refuse to adopt the single European currency. Denmark at first rejected the treaty in a referendum, but agreed to ratify it in a second referendum, having negotiated the right to 'opt out' of various provisions regarding monetary union, citizenship, and defence. The Maastricht Treaty finally came into effect on 1 November 1993.

Macao (Aomen) A Portuguese territory on a narrow peninsula on the Zhu Jiang (Pearl River) estuary, near Guangzhou (Canton), China. The territory covers a total area of 16 sq km (6 sq miles), with the city of Macao occupying almost the entire peninsula. Portuguese traders and missionaries established themselves there in 1557 with permission of the local authorities and called their settlement City of the Name of God in China. From its foundation until the late 17th century it had a flourishing trade with Japan. After the SHIMABARA rebellion in 1637 Japanese Christians sheltered there. It became the staging-post and refuge for Europeans trading with or trying to enter China. Sovereignty will revert to China in 1999.

MacArthur, Douglas (1880–1964) US general. The US army chief-of-staff from 1930 to 1935, he was recalled in 1941 by President F. D. Roosevelt to build up a US defence force in the Philippines. In 1941 Japanese troops successfully invaded the islands, and MacArthur transferred to Australia. He commanded the Allied counter-attack (July 1942–January 1943) in the Papuan campaign in New Guinea. From here (1943–44) his troops advanced towards the Philippines, which were recaptured in the spring of 1945. By now he was commander of all US army forces in the Pacific and received the Japanese surrender on board the USS *Missouri* (2 September 1945). As commander of the Allied

occupation forces (JAPAN, OCCUPATION OF), he took an active role in many reforms, as well as in the drafting of the new JAPANESE CONSTITUTION. Appointed UN commander in the KOREAN WAR he led his troops into North Korea (October 1950) but was forced to retreat by an invading Chinese army. In 1951 he resumed the offensive, but tension arose with President TRUMAN, who believed that MacArthur was prepared to risk a full-scale atomic war, and he was dismissed in April 1951.

Macassar (or Makasar; now Ujung Pandang) A city in the south of Sulawesi, an island of eastern Indonesia. After MALACCA fell to the Portuguese in 1511 many Malays transferred their business there. By 1600 Chinese, Indians, Arabs, and Javanese crowded its markets. The conversion of its people to Islam *c.* 1600 added religious zeal to their commercial activities. After 1600 Dutch policies in the MOLUCCAS made Macassar increasingly attractive to smugglers and monopoly breakers. By 1630 its empire extended over much of Sulawesi, eastern Borneo, and many neighbouring islands. In 1667 the Dutch besieged Macassar and achieved its complete submission. Dutch overlordship and monopoly of trade were established.

Macaulay, Thomas Babington, 1st Baron (1800–59) British historian, essayist, and politician. His essay on Milton for the *Edinburgh Review* in 1825 brought him instant fame, and for the next 20 years he wrote many articles on historical and literary topics for the journal. Macaulay embarked on his long parliamentary career in 1830, and became a prominent advocate of reform, religious toleration, and the abolition of slavery. During 1834–38 he worked in India as a member of the Supreme Council, where he played a large part in drafting the penal code which became the foundation of India's criminal law. On his return to England he wrote his partially completed *History of England* (1849–55). This work was notable for its declamatory style, its thorough research, and its biting wit, and was to exert a great influence on liberal perceptions of British history.

Macbeth (*c.* 1005–57) King of Scotland (1040–57). He was the grandson of Malcolm II and cousin to Duncan I, whom he challenged for the Scottish throne, defeating and killing him in battle near Elgin (1040). Previously he had been Mormaer (Earl) of Moray and had married Gruoch, a granddaughter of Kenneth III. Both Macbeth and his wife generously supported the Church and in 1050 he went on pilgrimage to Rome. He was killed in the battle of Lumphanan, Aberdeenshire, by Duncan's son MALCOLM III.

Maccabees A Jewish dynasty founded by Judas Maccabeus (the Hammerer) in the 2nd century BC. In 167 the Syrian king Antiochus IV plundered the Temple in Jerusalem, set up an altar to the Greek god Zeus, and proscribed Jewish religious practices. A Jewish revolt began, led by Mattathias, an elderly priest, and guerrilla tactics were used against the Syrians. When Mattathias died in 166, his second son, Judas, assumed leadership. After a series of successful encounters with Syrian forces he retook the Temple area in 164 and cleansed the Temple in a ceremony that has from that time been commemorated annually as the feast of Hanukkah. Judas died in 160 and his brothers continued the struggle until independence from the Syrians was achieved, the third brother, Simon, becoming high priest, governor, and commander. The conquests and forced conversions of later rulers caused much discontent, and the dynasty ended with the arrival of the Romans in 63 BC.

McCarran Act (1951) A US Act that required the registration of communist organizations and individuals, prohibited the employment of communists in defence work, and denied US entry to anyone who had belonged to a communist or fascist organization. It arose out of the fear in the early 1950s of a communist conspiracy against the USA. In 1965 the Supreme Court ruled that individuals could refuse to admit being communists by claiming the constitutional privilege enshrined in the Fifth Amendment against self-incrimination.

McCarran–Walter Act (1952) A codification of US immigration laws. Passed over the President's veto, it maintained the quota system, whereby immigrant quotas were allocated by nationality, but it tightened up laws governing the admission and deportation of aliens, limited immigration from eastern and south-eastern Europe, removed the ban on the immigration of Asian and Pacific people, provided for selective immigration on the basis of skills, and imposed controls on US citizens abroad.

McCarthy, Joseph Raymond (1908–57) US politician. A Republican Senator from Wisconsin (1947–57), he launched a campaign in the early 1950s alleging that there was a large-scale communist plot to infiltrate the US government at the highest level. Despite the conclusions reached by a Senate investigating committee under Millard Tydings that the charges were a fraud, McCarthy continued to make repeated attacks on the government, the military, and public figures. The term 'McCarthyism' became synonymous with the witch-hunt that gripped the USA from 1950 to 1954. In 1953, as chairman of the Senate Permanent Subcommittee on Investigations, McCarthy conducted a series of televised hearings in which his vicious questioning and unsubstantiated accusations destroyed the reputations of many of his victims. At length his methods were denounced by President EISENHOWER, and the Senate censured him for his conduct. After the 1954 election, with the Democrats again in control of Congress, McCarthy's influence declined.

McClellan, George Brinton (1826–85) US general. Given command of the Department of Ohio at the beginning of the AMERICAN CIVIL WAR, McClellan secured a series of minor victories in West Virginia, and in November 1861 succeeded Winfield SCOTT as general-in-chief of the Union (Northern) armies. While he lost this post in March 1862, he retained command of the Army of the Potomac. His attempt to capture Richmond in the Peninsular campaign proceeded too slowly and was then ruined by counter-attacks from forces of the CONFEDERACY in the Seven Days' battles. He checked LEE at ANTIETAM, but missed the opportunity to destroy his opponent and bring the war to an end, and was subsequently removed from command. McClellan unsuccessfully ran as the Democrat presidential candidate against LINCOLN in 1864.

Macdonald, Flora (1722–90) Scottish Jacobite. She gave invaluable assistance to Prince Charles Edward (the Young PRETENDER) after the collapse of the FORTY-FIVE rebellion. Disguised as her maid-servant, he was able to escape from Scotland to France (June 1746). She was arrested, but released in 1747.

Macdonald, Sir John (Alexander) (1815–91) Canadian statesman. Elected a Tory member of the House of Assembly of United Canada in 1844, he was the leading figure in bringing about Confederation (1867) of the provinces of British North Canada as the Dominion of Canada after the passage of the BRITISH NORTH AMERICA ACT. He became the first Prime Minister (1867–73) of the new Dominion of Canada. During his years in office, which continued from 1878 to 1891, Canada expanded territorially and experienced growth in its economy, its internal communications, and its sense of national purpose.

MacDonald, (James) Ramsay (1866–1937) British statesman and first Labour Prime Minister (1924, 1929–31). In 1906 he was elected a Labour Member of Parliament, and became leader of the Parliamentary Labour Party in 1911. At the outbreak of World War I his belief in negotiation, not war, with Germany made him unpopular, and he resigned. He was leader of the Opposition (1922–23), and then Prime Minister. His ministry of 1924, the first time Labour had formed a government, was too brief for any significant achievement. His second Labour government (1929–31) broke down through cabinet divisions over proposals to reduce unemployment benefits. MacDonald, however, was able to continue as Prime Minister of a NATIONAL GOVERNMENT (1931–35). A section of the Labour Party, led by George LANSBURY, refused to support the government, feeling that MacDonald, though a social reformer, had ceased to have sufficient regard for socialism. MacDonald was closely involved in the international disarmament schemes of the early 1930s. Like many others he did not discern the menace of Nazism. Failing health led to his resignation of the premiership in 1935.

Macedonia A historic region of the Balkan peninsula, now comprising the Former Yugoslav Republic of MACEDONIA (FYROM) and the region of Macedonia in northern Greece.

History. Macedonia was settled by migrating tribes during the Neolithic period. Perdiccas I established a kingdom in the southern plains *c.* 640 BC, but nearly three centuries passed before PHILIP II added mountainous Upper Macedonia to it. Under him the kingdom became the leading power in Greece and under ALEXANDER THE GREAT the leading power in the known world. Macedonia had geographical advantages that helped Philip to dominate Greece – in particular the fertile plains were good for horse breeding and cavalry training.

Macedonia was prominent in the wars that followed Alexander's death. Upper Macedonia came briefly under PYRRHUS's control, but Antigonus II (ruled 276–239 BC) wrested it back and restored the kingdom's strength.

However, it was unable to match the expanding power of Rome, and the MACEDONIAN WARS resulted in its being first partitioned into four republics and then (146 BC) turned into a Roman province. Large numbers of Slavs settled there in the 6th and 7th centuries AD. It was part of the Bulgarian empire until its collapse in 1014, and came under Turkish rule in 1389.

Although Macedonia remained part of the Ottoman Empire for the next five centuries, a nationalist movement IMRO (Internal Macedonian Revolutionary Organization) was founded in 1893, aiming at independence. After a confused period of fighting, the Treaty of Bucharest (August 1913) partitioned it between Serbia and Greece. Macedonia was the scene of fierce fighting during World War I: an Allied force landed at Salonika in October 1915 and, in September 1918 under General Franchet d'Esperey, advanced against Bulgaria. After the war, the Treaty of Neuilly, in the VERSAILLES PEACE SETTLEMENT, confirmed that northern Macedonia would be known as southern Serbia, while southern Macedonia, with Salonika, would remain Greek. Between the wars IMRO terrorists were supported by Bulgaria, from which they operated against both Yugoslavia and Greece. During World War II Macedonia was occupied by Bulgaria, ally of Nazi Germany. The Treaty of Paris (1947) confirmed that of Neuilly and 'southern Serbia' became the Republic of Macedonia, within the Federal Republic of Yugoslavia. Some half a million Macedonians continued to live in Bulgaria, while a sizeable minority of the Republic of Macedonia's population came from Albania. The Republic of Macedonia became independent as the Former Yugoslav Republic of Macedonia (FYROM) in 1993.

Macedonia, Former Yugoslav Republic of

(FYROM) A landlocked country in the Balkan peninsula bordering Serbia in the north, Albania in the west, Greece in the south, and Bulgaria in the east; formerly a constituent republic of YUGOSLAVIA.

Physical. Most of the republic's territory is a plateau, from which rise forested mountain peaks.

Economy. Mineral resources include iron ore, lead, zinc, and nickel. Macedonia is almost agriculturally self-sufficient, the chief crops being cereals, rice, and tobacco. Sheep and cattle are also reared. Industry comprises steel, chemicals, and textile production. An estimated 100,000 Macedonians are migrant workers in Germany and Switzerland.

History. The country comprises part of the historic Balkan region of MACEDONIA, which was divided in 1913 between Greece and Serbia. The Serbian part of Macedonia was known as southern Serbia from 1918 until 1947, when it became the Republic of Macedonia within the Federal Republic of Yugoslavia, with its own regional Parliament. Following elections in 1990 the anti-Communist Democratic Party was the largest in a hung Parliament. In January 1991 it declared the Republic of Macedonia 'sovereign and independent', while not at this stage rejecting membership of a Yugoslav Union of States. The declaration was overwhelmingly supported by a referendum and Parliament adopted a new constitution. The country's independence was recognized by Bulgaria and Turkey, but, although it had rejected 'all territorial claims on other countries', Greece persuaded the EC to delay recognition, on the grounds that Greek Macedonia was the only region entitled to the name Macedonia. In 1993 Greece agreed to recognize

the country on condition that it be known as the Former Yugoslav Republic of Macedonia (FYROM). Negotiations over the name and the use of symbols and emblems considered by Greece to be Greek property continued. FYROM agreed in 1995 to change its national flag. Kiro Gligorov was elected President in 1991 and was re-elected in 1994. He was seriously injured in an assassination attempt in 1995.

CAPITAL:	Skopje
AREA:	25,713 sq km (9,928 sq miles)
POPULATION:	1.968 million (1996)
CURRENCY:	1 deni = 100 paras
RELIGIONS:	Eastern Orthodox
ETHNIC GROUPS:	Macedonian 65.0%; Albanian 21.0%; Turkish, Serb, Romany, and Vlach minorities
LANGUAGES:	Macedonian; Serbo-Croat; minority languages
INTERNATIONAL ORGANIZATIONS:	UN

Macedonian wars Conflicts fought between Rome and Macedonia in the 3rd and 2nd centuries BC. In the first war (211–205) Philip V was opposed by an alliance of Rome, Aetolia, and Pergamum, but with Rome also deeply involved in the second of the PUNIC WARS he was able to force Aetolia to accept terms, and then to agree favourable ones with Rome itself. But war broke out again (200) and this time Philip was defeated decisively at Cynoscephalae (197). Philip's son Perseus came to the throne in 179, and set about winning influence and friends in Greece. This caused Roman suspicion, leading to the outbreak of a third war and another Roman victory, this time at Pydna in 168. Macedonia was divided into four republics. In 149–148 Andriscus, claiming to be a son of Perseus, attempted to set himself up as king but was defeated and Macedonia became a Roman province.

Machel, Samora Moises (1933–86) Mozambique statesman. He trained as a guerrilla in Algeria and became commander-in-chief of the Mozambique Liberation Front, Frelimo (Frente de Libertaçao de Moçambique) in 1966, and one of its leaders in 1969. He led the FRELIMO WAR against the Portuguese (1964–74), and became the first President (1975–86) of the People's Republic of Mozambique. A Marxist, he nationalized multinational companies, and allowed his country to be used as a base for nationalist guerrilla forces operating in RHODESIA and SOUTH AFRICA. Nevertheless, his politics became increasingly pragmatic, accepting Portuguese aid and contact with South Africa. He died in an air crash, which some believe to have been deliberately caused.

Machiavelli, Niccolò (1469–1527) Italian statesman and political theorist, one of the outstanding figures of the RENAISSANCE. By 1498 he had become Secretary and second Chancellor to the republic of Florence, and on his diplomatic missions (1499–1508) he encountered some of the most powerful political figures of the age. After the MEDICI restoration in Florence (1512), he was excluded from public life, and he retired in some frustration to produce works on the art of war and on political philosophy. Machiavelli is most famous as author of *Il Principe* (1513; 'The Prince'), a book of advice to monarchs on the best means to acquire and retain power. In apparent disregard of traditional morality, Machiavelli argued that princes should use cruelty, deception, and other such devices to strengthen themselves in the eyes of their people. 'Machiavellian' has since come to be applied to one who uses deception and opportunism to manipulate others, but this does a considerable injustice to Machiavelli's far subtler view of the relationship between ethics and politics. His fundamental belief was that a strong state was necessary to achieve all other human ends. This conviction also informed his *Discourses on the First Ten Books of Titus Livius* (1513–21), in which the achievements of the Roman republic were analysed in order to understand what successful republican government required. Machiavelli stressed the need for a vigorous political code of morality, in order to preserve the public spirit or *virtu* of the citizens from corruption. He wrote as a political realist, conveying lessons learnt by observing the world as it is.

In 1520 he was appointed chief historiographer of Florence. After the Medici fell again in 1527, his hopes of securing a position in the new republic were dashed, and he died soon afterwards.

MacGregor, Robert ROB ROY.

Mackenzie, Alexander (1822–92) Canadian statesman. After the creation of the Dominion of CANADA in 1867 he became leader of the Liberal opposition in the first House of Commons. One of the dominant figures of Canada's early days of nationhood, Mackenzie defeated the Conservatives under Sir John (Alexander) MACDONALD to become the country's first Liberal Prime Minister (1873–78). During his term in office voting by ballot was introduced, the Canadian Supreme Court formed, and the territorial government of the Northwest Territories successfully organized.

Mackenzie's Rebellion (1837) A popular uprising in Upper Canada (now part of Ontario). Growing pressure for democratic reform in Upper Canada could find no peaceful outlet after the defeat of the Reformers by the Tories in the election of 1836. The radical Reformers, led by the Scottish-born journalist and political agitator William Lyon Mackenzie (1794–1861), attempted an armed uprising on York (now Toronto) that was soon put down. Mackenzie fled to the USA where he set up a provisional government. In 1849 all those exiled as a result of this rebellion and PAPINEAU'S REBELLION in Lower Canada, were pardoned, and in 1850 Mackenzie returned to Canada, settling in Toronto.

McKinley, William (1843–1901) Twenty-fifth President of the USA (1897–1901). He served in the Union army during the AMERICAN CIVIL WAR and entered Congress as a Republican in 1876, giving his name to the tariff of 1890 that steeply raised import duties on foreign goods. With the aid of Marcus HANNA he was elected governor of Ohio (1892–96), and his support for the GOLD STANDARD brought him the Republican nomination against BRYAN in 1896. Elected as President, he supported high tariffs on imported goods and US expansion into the Pacific, fighting the SPANISH–AMERICAN WAR, and accepting the consequent acquisitions of Puerto Rico, Guam, and the Philippines as well as annexing Hawaii. He won re-election in 1900, again against Bryan, on the issue of prosperity, but was assassinated by the anarchist Leon Czolgosz in Buffalo. His vice-president, Theodore ROOSEVELT, succeeded him.

MacMahon, Marie Edme Patrice Maurice, Comte de (1808–93) French statesman. Of Irish descent, he fought successfully in the Crimea and at the battles of MAGENTA and SOLFERINO in 1859. As a general in the FRANCO-PRUSSIAN WAR he was defeated at Worth (1870) and, with NAPOLEON III, capitulated at SEDAN, but he commanded the army that crushed the PARIS COMMUNE in 1871. He had little sympathy with the new (Third) republic but did not support a royalist restoration and agreed to succeed THIERS as President (1873–79). Dislike of the Chamber of Deputies as too republican led him to dissolve it, but the electorate returned an even more republican Chamber (1877). This incident established the principle of ministerial accountability to the Chamber rather than to the President.

McMahon Line The boundary dividing Tibet and India. It was marked out by the British representatives led by Sir Henry McMahon at the Simla Conference (1914) between Britain, Tibet, and China. The Chinese government refused to ratify the agreement, and after the reassertion of control by China over Tibet in 1951 boundary disputes arose between India and China culminating in the INDO-CHINESE WAR OF 1962.

Macmillan, (Maurice) Harold, 1st Earl of Stockton (1894–1987) British Conservative statesman, Prime Minister (1957–63). During the 1930s he was a critic of APPEASEMENT and of his party's economic policy. In 1940 he joined the government of CHURCHILL. In 1951, as Minister for Housing and Local Government, he was responsible for the largest local authority building programme yet seen in Britain. He became Minister of Defence (1954) under Churchill, and Foreign Secretary and Chancellor of the Exchequer (1955) under EDEN, whom he succeeded as Prime Minister (1957–63) when Eden resigned after the SUEZ WAR. During the Macmillan period Britain started to taste the fruits of affluence and the majority of people agreed with the Prime Minister's comment in a speech (1957) given in Bedford, 'Most of our people have never had it so good' – as was confirmed by the Conservatives' success in the 1959 general election. Life-peerages were introduced (1958), and the National Economic Development Council ('Neddy') was set up. Legislation in the form of the Commonwealth Immigration Act (1962) was passed to limit uncontrolled entry into the UK. Overseas, Macmillan enjoyed friendly relations with President KENNEDY, supporting him over the CUBAN MISSILE CRISIS and reaching the Nassau agreement (1962) that the US should furnish nuclear missiles for British submarines. In Africa, Britain accepted the need for independent statehood ('WIND OF CHANGE'). However, the government was frustrated by DE GAULLE's veto on Britain's application to join the EUROPEAN ECONOMIC COMMUNITY (1963). Macmillan's government was weakened by public concern about an alleged Soviet espionage plot (June 1963) involving his Secretary of State for War, John Profumo, but it succeeded (July 1963) in negotiating a NUCLEAR TEST-BAN TREATY between the USA, the Soviet Union, and Britain.

Macquarie, Lachlan (1762–1824) Australian governor. He was appointed governor of the convict settlement of New South Wales in Australia after the RUM REBELLION (1808). He was the last Australian governor with virtually autocratic power. In his view the colony was a settlement for convicts in which free settlers had little place, and where convicts should be given every encouragement. The colony's nature was changing; there was conflict between EMANCIPISTS and EXCLUSIONISTS; many exclusives, notably Jeffrey Hart Bent, the first judge of the Supreme Court of New South Wales, clashed with Macquarie. The BIGGE INQUIRY into the condition of the convict population was held during Macquarie's term of office.

Madagascar A large island country lying 450–900 km (280–560 miles) distant from the south-east African coast, to which it runs parallel.

Physical. A broad plain in the west rises to the Ankaratra Mountains, which slope steeply eastward to the Indian Ocean. The eastern coast is hot, very wet, subject to cyclones, and densely clad with rain forest. The south and west are drier, and the centre mild. Here, on upland plateaux, there is fine grazing. As a result of the island becoming separated from Africa during the period of continental drift, many of its plant and animal species, for example lemurs (prosimians), are unique.

Economy. Economic activity in Madagascar is mainly agricultural: coffee, vanilla, and cloves are major exports. Rice, cassava, and sweet potatoes are the chief food crops; cattle-breeding is extensive. Mining of chrome ore is significant, and there are bauxite deposits. An oil refinery produces petroleum-based products. Industry is limited mostly to food-processing.

History. The Madagascan people are of Indo-Melanesian and Malay descent, mixed with some Bantu, Arabs, Indians, and Chinese. The time of arrival of different groups is controversial. Arab traders were probably visiting by the 10th century. In 1500 a Portuguese sea captain, Diego Dias, chanced on the island, calling it São Lourenço. However, MARCO POLO had already named it Madagascar from hearsay knowledge, and this name endured. In the following centuries Dutch, English, and Portuguese vessels made frequent visits, and the French set up trading centres. Many of these were used as pirate bases. By the beginning of the 17th century a number of small Malagasy kingdoms emerged, and later the Sakalawa, from the west of the island, conquered northern and western Madagascar, but their kingdom disintegrated in the 18th century. The Merina people of the interior were later united under King Andrianampoinimerina (ruled 1787–1810), and became the dominant group on the island by the early 19th century.

In 1860 King Radama II gave concessions to a French trading company. This led in 1890 to a French Protectorate, although resistance lasted until 1895. After 1945 Madagascar became an Overseas Territory of the French Republic, sending Deputies to Paris. It became a republic within the French Community in 1958, and regained its independence (1960) as the Malagasy Republic, changing its name back to Madagascar in 1975. Severe social and economic problems have caused recurrent unrest and frequent changes of government. Admiral Didier Ratsiraka was elected President in 1982 and again in 1989, working closely with a Supreme Revolutionary Council. Although he ended one-party rule in 1990, there were anti-government riots in April 1991. In October 1991 the Revolutionary Council and National Assembly were both dissolved, pending agreement on a new constitution. The new multiparty constitution was adopted in 1992 and Albert Zafy became President following elections in 1993. After elections in 1996 Norbert Ratsirahonana was named Prime Minister. Zafy resigned later that year following attempts by the government to remove him from office. Didier Ratsiraka won the presidential election held in December 1996.

CAPITAL:	Antananarivo
AREA:	587,041 sq km (226,658 sq miles)
POPULATION:	13.671 million (1996)
CURRENCY:	1 Malagasy franc = 100 centimes
RELIGIONS:	Roman Catholic 26.0%; Protestant 22.8%; traditional beliefs 47.0%; Muslim 1.7%
ETHNIC GROUPS:	Malagasy 98.9% (Merina 26.6%; Betsimisaraka 14.9%; Betsileo 11.7%; Tsimihety 7.4%; Sakalava 6.4%; Antandroy 5.3%; Comorian 0.3%; Indian and Pakistani 0.2%; French 0.2%; Chinese 0.1%
LANGUAGES:	Malagasy, French (both official)
INTERNATIONAL ORGANIZATIONS:	UN; OAU

Madeira The largest of a group of five small volcanic islands lying in the Atlantic Ocean some 560 km (350 miles) off the north-west African coast. Madeira is also the name of the island group as a whole, which belongs to Portugal. Only two of the islands are habitable, Madeira itself and Porto Santo.

Madeira was discovered in the 14th century by Portuguese colonists. They chiefly cultivated sugar and vines. Later the Portuguese were joined by Dutch, Spanish, and Italian immigrants, by Jews and Moors expelled from Spain, and yet later by slaves from Africa.

Madero, Francisco Indalécio (1873–1913) Mexican statesman. President of Mexico (1911–13), he assumed leadership of the MEXICAN REVOLUTION of 1910. Thwarted in his attempt to unseat the dictator Porfirio DÍAZ, he fled to the USA, from where he organized an armed movement that was unleashed on 20 November 1910. The Díaz dictatorship fell six months later and in the ensuing elections Madero won the Mexican presidency. He was unable to put into effect any of his political and social reforms because of dissent among his supporters and his own administrative inability. After putting down five insurrections against him, Madero fell victim to the sixth led by General Victoriano HUERTA in 1913. He was murdered a few days after being deposed.

Madison, James (1751–1836) fourth President of the USA (1809–17). He helped draft the Virginia State Constitution, served in the CONTINENTAL CONGRESS (1780–83), and was the author of *Memorial and Remonstrances* (1784) in which he opposed taxation to support religious teachers and secured JEFFERSON's bill for religious freedom. He played an influential role in the Constitutional Convention (1787) and was author of 29 of the *Federalist Papers*; he also proposed the BILL OF RIGHTS (1791). He became leader of the Democratic-Republican Party, and drafted the Virginia Resolves of 1798, condemning the Alien and Sedition Acts. Serving as Secretary of State under Jefferson (1801–09), he was involved in disputes with France and England over the USA's right to neutrality. After his election as president he lost popularity through his poor leadership in the WAR OF 1812 against Britain, referred to in New England as 'Mr Madison's War'. Despite his dislike of a powerful central government and fiscal system, he signed the bill incorporating the Second Bank of the USA and introduced the first protective US tariff.

Mafia An international secret society originating in Sicily. In its modern form the Mafia (Italian 'boldness') can be said to date from the period 1806–15, when, under British pressure, attempts were being made to break up the huge estates of the Sicilian feudal aristocracy. Their disbanded private armies often became brigands. They represented an alternative system of control and justice beyond the purview of the legal authorities. In 1860 the new government of VICTOR EMANUEL II tried to rid Sicily of them, but by now they controlled many police and government officials. In the 1880s many Sicilians emigrated to the USA and the Mafia, as Cosa Nostra (Our Business), became established in New York and Chicago. In the 1920s the fascist government in Italy brought Mafia leaders to trial, but some escaped to the USA, where they were active during the PROHIBITION ERA. After World War II, notably after the opening-up of the former Soviet bloc, Mafia activities spread worldwide, increasingly centred on the drug trade. The Mafia is also involved in organized prostitution, fraud, theft, and kidnapping. In the USA, the Mafia is notable also for its infiltration of legitimate business – for example, in transport, construction, gambling, and fast-food – and its use of these businesses for money-laundering. In Italy periodic, much-publicized trials failed to eradicate its influence, particularly in the South and in Sicily, where assassinations continue to be perpetrated. Mafia members are required to live by a code of silence and to eschew all co-operation with legitimate authorities: any violation of this code is severely punished.

Magadha A centre of ancient regional kingdoms, and intermittently of extensive empires, corresponding to the Patna and Gaya districts of modern Bihar in north-eastern India. Its position on the middle Ganges explains the economic and strategic advantages that drew successive rulers there from the 6th century BC to the 7th century AD. Among them were the MAURYAS (c. 325–185 BC) and GUPTAS (mid-4th–6th century AD). After Muslim invasions in the 12th century Magadha ceased to exist as a separate region.

Magdala A small fortified town in the Ethiopian Highlands, the scene of fighting between British and Ethiopian forces in 1868. After the Foreign Office allegedly failed to answer a letter addressed to Queen VICTORIA by Tewodros II, the latter imprisoned the British consul and his aides at Magdala. After further misunderstandings, a British force of 32,000 landed in 1868 under Sir Robert Napier and marched inland. On 13 April it stormed Magdala almost without loss, and released the captives, only to find that Tewodros had died by his own hand. A short, punitive campaign against Ethiopia followed and John IV succeeded to the throne in 1872.

Magdalenian UPPER PALAEOLITHIC.

Magellan, Ferdinand (c. 1480–1521) Portuguese navigator. On Portuguese service in the East Indies in 1509–12 he explored the Spice Islands (MOLUCCAS), but in 1517 offered his services to Spain to undertake a voyage to the same islands by a westward route. He left Spain with five ships in 1519 and sailed down the coast of

South America and through the long and tortuous strait that now bears his name. When they emerged into a peaceful new ocean to the west, he named it the Pacific. It took more than three months of hardship before they reached the Philippines in 1521. Magellan was killed in a skirmish between the islanders of Cebu, but one of his ships, the *Vittoria*, reached Spain by the Cape of Good Hope, thus becoming the first vessel to circumnavigate the world.

Magenta, Battle of (4 June 1859) A battle fought in Lombardy, between the French and the Sardinians on one side and the Austrians on the other. The Italian patriotic movement known as the RISORGIMENTO had been offered French military support at a meeting (1859) at Plombières between NAPOLEON III and CAVOUR. When war broke out, the French and Sardinian forces defeated the Austrians in a disorganized fight at Magenta, which opened the way to the occupation of Lombardy and Milan. Two weeks later it was followed by the decisive battle of SOLFERINO.

Maginot Line A series of defensive fortifications in France. Begun in 1929, it eventually stretched along France's eastern frontier from Switzerland to Luxembourg. Named after the Minister of War, André Maginot, it was built because French military theorists believed that defence would predominate in any future war and because it reduced the demand for soldiers. Partly because of objections from the Belgians, who were afraid they would be left in an exposed situation, the line was not extended along the Franco-Belgian frontier to the coast; consequently it could be outflanked, as indeed happened in spring 1940. However, the Maginot defences proved impregnable to frontal assault and so fulfilled their original purpose.

Magna Carta The document that the English barons, aided by Stephen LANGTON, forced King JOHN to seal at Runnymede on 15 June 1215. It was a charter of 61 or 63 clauses (the final clause is sometimes subdivided into three) covering a wide range of issues. There were clauses dealing with weights and measures, fish weirs, and foreign merchants. The powers of sheriffs were restricted, and the liberties and privileges of boroughs preserved. The crown agreed not to interfere with the rights of the church, not to levy SCUTAGE or any special tax without the consent of the king's council, and not to demand from the barons more than was due according to feudal practice and convention. Clause 39 guaranteed the right of trial to all freemen, and clause 40 justice to everyone. The charter was safeguarded by clause 61, which set up a group of 25 barons empowered to take up arms against the king if he failed to observe its conditions. John sought and obtained papal condemnation of the charter on 18 June 1215, which led to the first BARONS' WAR four months later. Although the charter was often violated by medieval kings, it came to be seen as an important document defining the English Constitution.

Magyars A race speaking a Finno-Ugric language, whose ancestors came from an area round the River Volga in Russia. Under Prince Arpád, they entered what became HUNGARY in the 9th century. They harassed the German kingdom but were finally defeated and repulsed by Otto I at the Battle of LECHFELD. Pope Sylvester crowned Stephen as the first king of their country in 1000 and he established unity and introduced Christianity. He was canonized after his death.

Mahayana A major grouping within BUDDHISM, distinct from THERAVADA BUDDHISM. It arose during the 1st century AD and spread mainly throughout north-eastern Asia. It is sometimes called Northern Buddhism. Whilst nominally accepting the Theravāda canon, essential Mahayana beliefs are based upon supplementary texts, written in Sanskrit, rather than Pali, particularly the Lotus Sutra. Mahayana belief emphasizes universal enlightenment; its followers belong to all sections of society and need not be monks, hence its name, which means 'Great Vehicle'. Followers seek personal enlightenment for the sake of all, rather than the individual. This distinctive notion is best displayed in the ideal of the Bodhisattva, the being whose essence is enlightenment but who remains on earth to use his or her wisdom and compassion for the benefit of others. There are two main philosophical schools within Mahayana Buddhism: the Mādhyamika school, which emphasizes the illusory and essentially empty nature of all things, as well as the importance of *prajñā* (wisdom); and the Yogāchāra school, which lays stress on meditative concentration.

Mahdi, the The Islamic spiritual and temporal saviour. According to Islamic teaching he will be sent by divine command to prepare human society for the end of earthly time by means of perfect and just government (MILLENARIANISM). Many have claimed to be the Mahdi at different times. Best known was **Muhammad Ahmad bin Abdallah** (1843–85). Of Nubian origin, he claimed descent from Muhammad. Feeling called to purify the world from wantonness and corruption, he gathered many followers and proclaimed himself Mahdi in 1881. In 1882 the Egyptian government sent expeditions against him, but by 1884, with the capture of Khartoum, he made himself master of Sudan. General GORDON was killed in Khartoum on 30 January 1885; the Mahdi himself died, probably of typhus, five months later. Politically his struggle was carried on by the KHALIFA Abdallah until KITCHENER defeated him at Omdurman in 1898.

Mahicans (or Mohicans) A Native American people who inhabited the Hudson River valley. They shared many traits with the IROQUOIS to the west. European contact began when Henry Hudson sailed up the Hudson River in 1609. Beaver and other pelts were exchanged for beads and knives, and regular trade became centred round the Dutch Fort Orange (later Albany). As middlemen for other tribes they jealously kept the MOHAWK IROQUOIS at bay until their control was finally broken in wars of 1662–69. Thereafter epidemics and dispersal by Dutch, then English and American, colonial pressures relegated them to an increasingly lesser role through the 18th century, and, like the DELAWARE, they were eventually officially relocated to midwestern reservations in the 19th century.

Mahmud II (1784–1839) Ottoman Sultan (1808–39). He came to the throne on the deposition of his brother, Mustafa IV, and continued the reforming policies of his cousin, Selim III (1789–1807). He rid himself of the JANISSARIES, the traditional military corps that had become unruly and inefficient, by having them

massacred, and established a new, European-style army. He curbed the power of the religious classes, centralized government, and reduced provincial autonomy. He was attacked by MEHEMET ALI of Egypt, and his army defeated in the battle of Nizip (1839) in Syria.

Mahmud of Ghazna (969–1030) Muslim ruler of the Ghaznavid dynasty of Afghanistan and Khurasan (999–1030). He led 17 raids into northern India in the name of Islam. Sapping Hindu power in the process, he paved the way for Muslim conquest of the subcontinent. He also extended his power into Transoxania, Persia, and Mesopotamia.

Maimonides, Moses (Mosheh ben Maymun) (1135–1204) Jewish physician and philosopher. He was born in Córdoba in southern Spain, but was driven out by the persecution of the conquering ALMOHAD dynasty. He settled in Egypt in 1165, where he wrote two major scholarly works, the *Mishnah Torah*, a massive codification of rabbinical law and ritual, and a *Guide for the Perplexed*, which, attempting to reconcile religious doctrine and reason, caused much controversy among orthodox Jews.

Maine The north-easternmost state of the USA, named after Queen HENRIETTA MARIA's French property. Discovered by Sebastian CABOT (1496) and settled by Sir Ferdinando Gorges and his heirs in the early 17th century, it was infiltrated by settlers from Massachusetts who contended for control. It was purchased by Massachusetts in 1677, and its outposts were devastated by Abnaki Native Americans in alliance with the French (1687–99). Maine prospered after the American War of INDEPENDENCE and became an independent state in 1820.

Maine US battleship destroyed by an explosion in Havana harbour in 1898 with the loss of 260 lives. The US naval inquiry found the cause of sinking to be a submarine mine, while the Spanish inquiry concluded that it was due to an explosion in the forward magazine. The truth was never known, but the episode precipitated the SPANISH–AMERICAN WAR.

Majapahit A Hindu empire based in the fertile valley of the Brantas River in eastern JAVA, which flourished between 1293 and the latter part of the 15th century. It experienced its 'golden age' under its last great ruler Hayam Wuruk (1350–89) whose reign is extolled in an epic poem, *Nagarakertagama* (1365). This poem claimed an empire for Majapahit covering much of peninsular Malaya, Sumatra, Borneo, Sulawesi (Celebes), Bali, and other islands, though its control in the more far-flung areas must have been weak. Its chief minister, Gajah Mada (d. 1364), codified its laws and is said to have bequeathed a more centralized administration. After it was partitioned between Wuruk's sons there was decline. By *c.* 1527 the last remnants of Majapahit's authority had been extinguished and many of its royal family had fled to Bali.

Maji-Maji A rebellion in German East Africa (1905–07) in the south and centre of present-day TANZANIA. The African warriors believed that magic water (*maji*) could make them immune to bullets. German settlers, missionaries, and traders were murdered, and the towns of Liwale and Kilosa sacked. The Germans adopted a scorched-earth policy which ended the rebellion but greatly retarded economic development.

Major, John (1943–) British statesman and Prime Minister (1990–97). Son of a former circus performer, he left school at 16, later joining a bank as an accountant. He was a member of Lambeth Borough Council (1968–71) and became a senior executive of the Standard Charter bank before his election to the House of Commons in 1979. Under the patronage of Margaret THATCHER he held a number of Cabinet posts, including Foreign Secretary and Chancellor of the Exchequer. He succeeded Thatcher as Leader of the Conservatives and Prime Minister in 1990, having taken Britain into the European Monetary System (EMS). Against the predictions of the opinion polls, he comfortably won the general election of April 1992, but his government soon faced grave economic problems. The exchange rate proved impossibly high, and a currency crisis developed in September, when he was obliged to withdraw from the European Exchange Rate Mechanism (see EUROPEAN MONETARY SYSTEM). At the same time he faced criticism for having agreed to the MAASTRICHT TREATY from members of his party who objected to the increasing influence of the European Parliament in British affairs. In 1993 Major signed the DOWNING STREET DECLARATION, a document that set out conditions for negotiations over the future of Northern Ireland. He continued Thatcher's privatization programme, despite increasing criticism of the management of many of the privatized companies. In 1995 he survived a leadership challenge, but by 1997 his parliamentary majority had been reduced to single figures. Following his resounding defeat in the May 1997 general election, he resigned as party leader.

Makarios III (Mihail Christodoulou Mouskos) (1913–77) Greek Cypriot archbishop and statesman. Primate of the Greek Orthodox Church in CYPRUS (1950–77), he reorganized the movement for *enosis* (the union of Cyprus with Greece). He was exiled (1956–59) by the British for allegedly supporting the EOKA terrorist campaign of Colonel Grivas against the British and Turks. Following independence, Makarios was elected President of Cyprus (1960–76). A coup by Greek officers in 1974 forced his brief exile to London, but he was reinstated in 1975 and continued in office until his death.

Makasar MACASSAR.

Malacca (or Melaka) A Malayan port commanding the strait connecting the Indian and Pacific Oceans. It was founded by a refugee Hindu prince from SRIVIJAYA in 1402; he was later converted to ISLAM and took the title Iskandar Shah. Following visits by the Chinese admiral CHENG HE, it became a Chinese vassal, thus securing itself against Thai and Javanese attacks. By 1500 it was an entrepôt where merchants traded in spices from the MOLUCCAS, Chinese silk and porcelain, camphor from Borneo, teak from Burma, Indian cloths, and woollens from Europe. During the 16th century the merchants of Malacca greatly assisted the spread of Islam in south-east Asia. It was captured by ALBUQUERQUE in 1511 and the Portuguese repulsed attacks from ACHEH, JOHORE, and Java. In 1641 it fell to the Dutch, aided by Johore, but with their headquarters in Java, the Dutch regarded it as of little importance.

Malan, Daniel F(rançois) (1874–1959) South African statesman. Rising to prominence in the National Party in Cape Province, he was elected to Parliament in 1918. His political thinking was dominated by desire for secession from Britain and republicanism. He was Prime Minister (1948–54), and initiated the racial separation laws known as APARTHEID.

Malawi A long, narrow, landlocked country running north to south in south-eastern Africa. Its eastern boundary includes much of Lake Malawi; Tanzania is to the north and Zambia to the west, while Mozambique almost encloses its southern half.

Physical. Malawi lies at the southern end of the Great Rift Valley. The Shire River falling from Lake Malawi is flanked by high ground until it enters swampland, with three smaller lakes. A very warm, wet summer permits the growth of rice and sugar.

Economy. The economy is mainly agricultural, exports being dominated by tobacco, sugar, and tea. Groundnuts, cotton, and maize are also grown. The only mineral resource is bauxite. Industrial development is being financed through foreign aid. Electricity is generated mainly from hydroelectric sources.

History. The area has been inhabited since at least 8000 BC, and several kingdoms had risen and fallen before Malawi was first explored by the Portuguese in the 17th century. Slave-traders from ZANZIBAR raided the area frequently in the 1840s, and its desolation was described by LIVINGSTONE in 1859. In 1875 Scottish missionaries settled, and for a while governed parts of the country. Colonial administration was instituted when Sir H. H. Johnston proclaimed the Shire Highlands a British Protectorate in 1889. This became British Central Africa in 1891, then Nyasaland from 1907 until 1964. Unwillingly a member of the CENTRAL AFRICAN FEDERATION (1953–63), it gained independence (1964) as Malawi, with Dr Hastings BANDA as first Prime Minister. When the country became a republic in 1966, he became President and was proclaimed Life President in 1971. Regular elections were held to the National Assembly, but all candidates had to be members of the Malawi Congress Party. At its convention in 1991 the party voted to retain the one-party system; but increasing opposition to this developed early in 1992 and the opposition leader Chakufwa Chilana was arrested. Despite violent riots and the suspension of all non-humanitarian aid from the West, the one-party system continued for the general election of June 1992. Following continued unrest, Banda held a referendum in October 1992, and the adoption of a multiparty political system was approved. A new constitution was adopted in 1993 and elections in 1994 were won by the United Democratic Front (UDF), with Bakili Muluzi becoming President.

CAPITAL:	Lilongwe
AREA:	118,484 sq km (45,747 sq miles)
POPULATION:	9.453 million (1996)
CURRENCY:	1 kwacha = 100 tambala
RELIGIONS:	Protestant 33.7%; Roman Catholic 27.6%; traditional beliefs 19.0%; Muslim 16.2%
ETHNIC GROUPS:	Chewa 46.0%; Lomwe 19.0%; Yao 14.0%; Ngoni 9.0%; Tumbuka 6.0%
LANGUAGES:	English, Chichewa (both official); Lomwe; local languages
INTERNATIONAL ORGANIZATIONS:	UN; Commonwealth; Non-Aligned Movement; OAU; SADC

Malaya (now West Malaysia) A region in south-east Asia, since 1963 part of the Federation of MALAYSIA.

History. Originally inhabited by Negritos, it was later settled by people from YUNNAN. By *c.* 400 AD Indian influence was apparent in Kedah and Perak in north-western Malaya. Later SRIVIJAYA, MAJAPAHIT, and Siam exerted some control. It remained relatively backward until, following MALACCA's foundation in 1402, Islam was introduced. After Malacca fell to the Portuguese in 1511, sultanates were established in JOHORE, Pahang, and Perak. Manangkabau Malays from Sumatra settled in Negeri Sembilan and BUGIS in Selangor. The Dutch, influential after they took Malacca in 1641, came under pressure following the British occupation of Penang in 1786. Following the British acquisition of Singapore in 1819, the Dutch withdrew from Malaya in 1824, and it was ruled until 1867 from British India. In 1874 Perak accepted a British resident whose advice the sultan had to follow in all matters except religion and customs. By 1888 Britain had extended the residency system to all the west-coast states except Johore. These were linked as the Federated Malay States in 1896, and made rapid economic progress after the introduction of rubber and of western tin-mining technology. The immigration of Chinese and Tamil labourers turned Malaya into a multiracial society with the indigenous (*bumiputra*) Malays in danger of becoming a minority within their own land. The prosperity of the Federated States led Kedah, Perlis, Kelantan, and Trengganu to accept British protection (1909) with agreement from Siam, their former suzerain. These Unfederated States were relatively loosely controlled. Johore accepted a British adviser in 1914. After the Japanese invasion and occupation during World War II, the British experimented briefly with a centralized Union of Malaya (1946), and then set up a Federation of Malaya (1948) to include Johore, Kedah, Kelantan, Labuan, Melaka, Negeri Sembilan, Pahang, Pinang, Perak, Perlis, Selangor, and Terengganu. The legacy of inter-communal conflict in 1945, and the strength of the Chinese-dominated Communist Party, which resented Malay dominance within the Federation, helped to spark the armed insurrection of 1948–60 known as the MALAYAN EMERGENCY. Despite this, the Federation achieved sovereign independence in 1957 and was finally expanded into Malaysia in 1963.

Malayan Campaign (December 1941–August 1945) A military campaign in south-east Asia in World War II. After taking over military bases in Vietnam in July 1941 through an agreement with the VICHY administration, and securing a free passage through Thailand, Japanese troops under General YAMASHITA TOMOYUKI invaded northern Malaya in December 1941 while Japanese aircraft bombed Singapore. The British, Indian, and Australian troops retreated southwards, where they were taken prisoner after the Fall of SINGAPORE in February 1942. During the retreat a small guerrilla resistance force was organized to conduct sabotage, operating behind Japanese lines. Known as the Malayan People's Anti-Japanese Army (MPAJA), it consisted largely of Chinese, most of whom were communists. In May 1944 Allied troops, advancing from Imphal, began the gradual reconquest of Burma, and liberated Malaya in 1945.

Malayan Emergency A communist insurgency in Malaya (1948–60). After World War II, minority Chinese resentment of Malay political dominance of the new Federation of Malaya was exploited by the (mainly Chinese) communist guerrillas who had fought against the Japanese. They initiated a series of attacks on planters and other estate owners, which between 1950 and 1953 flared up into a full-scale guerrilla war. Led by Chin Peng and supported by their own supply network (the Min Yuen), the communist guerrillas of the Malayan Races Liberation Army caused severe disruption in the early years of the campaign. However, during the time of TEMPLER's period in charge of British and Commonwealth forces (1952–54), the insurgents were gradually defeated through the use of new jungle tactics, and the disruption of their supply network. The loyalty of the Malay and Indian population to the British, and the skilful use by the British of local leaders in the government committees, facilitated the peaceful transition to independence in 1957. By then the insurrection had been all but beaten, although the emergency was not officially ended until 1960.

Malaysia A country in south-east Asia, having two parts, West and East, separated by the South China Sea.

Physical. East Malaysia comprises SARAWAK and SABAH in the north and north-west of the island of Borneo. West, or Peninsular, Malaysia (the former Federation of MALAYA) occupies the southern end of the Malay Peninsula, extending south from the south-east Asian mainland and bounded on the north by Thailand and on the south by Singapore; it has a south-western coast on the Strait of Malacca. The climate of Malaysia is very warm and affected by the monsoons, which bring about 2,300 mm (90 inches) of rain in a year. The red soil provides for paddy-fields in the lowland areas, where rice is cultivated, and high-yield rubber, oil palm, and cocoa plantations in the west of the peninsula. Inland, the Malayan highlands are forested and provide tropical hardwoods. East Malaysia and off-shore waters are rich in mineral oil.

Economy. Manufacturing industry produces automobiles, electronics, cigarettes, tyres, sawn logs, and cement. Crude oil is an important export. Agriculture, with rice the principal subsistence crop, remains the mainstay of the economy, despite high industrial growth in recent years. Malaysia is the world's largest producer of rubber, palm oil, and tin; timber is also an important export. Other mineral resources include bauxite, iron ore, and copper. The New Economic Policy (NEP), initiated after ethnic riots in 1970, introduced ethnic quotas in an attempt to promote economic growth and eradicate the association of race with occupation. The collapse of the Malaysian stock market and currency in September 1997 precipitated an economic and political crisis.

History. The Federation of MALAYSIA was established in 1963. Although originally included, SINGAPORE was forced to secede in 1965 because of fears that its largely Chinese population would challenge Malay political dominance. BRUNEI refused to join the Federation. The establishment of Malaysia was first suggested (1961) by Tungku Abdul RAHMAN, who became its first Prime Minister (1963–70). The Federation aroused deep suspicion in Indonesia, and provoked President SUKARNO's policy of confrontation (KONFRONTASI), resulting in intermittent guerrilla war in Malaysia's Borneo territories, which was only defeated with Commonwealth military assistance (1963–66). In 1969 inequalities between the politically dominant Malays and economically dominant Chinese resulted in riots in Kuala Lumpur, and parliamentary government was suspended until 1971. As a result, there was a major restructuring of political and social institutions designed to ensure Malay predominance, the New Economic Policy being launched to increase the Malay (*bumiputra*) stake in the economy. The largest single political party remained the United Malays National Organization, which had been created by Tunku Rahman. Since 1971 this has ruled in uneasy alliance with the Malaysian Chinese Association and some other ten parties in a coalition, the National Front. Mahathir bin Mohamed became its leader and Prime Minister in 1981. A leading member of the ASSOCIATION OF SOUTH-EAST ASIAN NATIONS, Malaysia replaced the New Economic Policy in 1991 by a New Development Policy, whose aim was to diversify the economy. At the same time it has incurred international criticism for its exploitation of its rainforests. During 1994 a scandal over Britain's lending Malaysia £234 million to build the Pergau dam in an aid-for-trade agreement caused controversy in Britain and strained relations between the two countries. The ruling coalition was re-elected in 1995. In September 1997 the Malaysian stock market and currency crashed, precipitating an economic and political crisis.

CAPITAL:	Kuala Lumpur
AREA:	330,442 sq km (127,584 sq miles)
POPULATION:	20.359 million (1996)
CURRENCY:	1 ringgit = 100 sen
RELIGIONS:	Muslim 52.9%; Buddhist 17.3%; Chinese popular religions 11.6%; Hindu 7.0%; Christian 6.4%
ETHNIC GROUPS:	Malay, Orang Asli, Iban, Land Dayak, Bajan, and Kadazan 60.0% Chinese 31.0%; Indian, Pakistani, and Bangladeshi 8.0%
LANGUAGES:	Malay (official); English; Chinese; Tamil; minority languages
INTERNATIONAL ORGANIZATIONS:	UN; Commonwealth; Non-Aligned Movement; Colombo Plan; ASEAN

Malcolm III (Canmore) (*c.* 1031–93) King of Scotland (1058–93). Malcolm was brought up at the English court of EDWARD THE CONFESSOR after which MACBETH murdered his father, Duncan I. With English assistance he defeated Macbeth in 1054, and killed him in 1057. Malcolm married (1068) Margaret, the granddaughter of EDMUND II (Ironside). His support of Saxon exiles (including EDGAR THE AETHELING) fleeing from the Normans, led to an invasion (1072) by WILLIAM I and Malcolm's homage to him. Tension continued, and Malcolm was killed at Alnwick while on his fifth invasion of England.

Malcolm X (1925–65) US Black leader. Born Malcolm Little, he renounced his surname (in common with other BLACK MUSLIMS), in favour of 'X', a sign indicating the lost tribal names that had been taken from his ancestors on their capture and transportation as slaves. He rejected the co-operation with White liberals that had marked the CIVIL RIGHTS movement. He became a leading spokesman for the Black Muslims in the 1950s but was suspended by the movement's leader, Elijah Muhammad, for a controversial speech delivered after the assassination of President Kennedy. In 1964, after conversion to orthodox Islam, he preached brotherhood

between Black and White people and formed the Organization of Afro-American Unity. He was assassinated in 1965.

Maldives A country consisting of a chain of coral islands in the Indian Ocean some 650 km (400 miles) south-west of Sri Lanka.

Physical. The islands comprise some 1,800 small atolls and sandbanks built on the summits of old, submerged volcanoes.

Economy. The economy of Maldives is based on fishing, clothing, shipping, and tourism. Ecological change threatens the future of the country, since many of its islands are a mere 1.8 m (6 feet) above sea level.

History. From 1887 to 1952 the islands were a sultanate under British protection. Maldivian demands for constitutional reform began in the 1930s; internal self-government was achieved in 1948 and full independence in 1965. In 1968 the sultanate was abolished, and a republic declared. The Maldives became a full member of the COMMONWEALTH OF NATIONS in 1985. In 1988, with Indian help, President Maumoun Abdul Gayoom (first elected 1978) suppressed an attempted coup. He was re-elected that year, and again in 1993, but faced continuing criticism from young Maldivians who demanded a fully-elected Citizens' Assembly.

CAPITAL:	Male
AREA:	298 sq km (115 sq miles)
POPULATION:	266,000 (1996)
CURRENCY:	1 Maldivian rufiyaa = 100 laaris
RELIGIONS:	Virtually 100% Sunni Muslim
ETHNIC GROUPS:	Majority Sinhalese and Dravidian; Arab, African, and Negrito minorities
LANGUAGES:	Divehi (official)
INTERNATIONAL ORGANIZATIONS:	UN; Commonwealth; Colombo Plan

Maldon, Battle of (August 991) A major battle fought near Maldon in Essex between the East Saxons, under the leadership of Byrhtnoth, and Danish raiders, led by Anlaf. The battle is the subject of a short but moving poem written by an eyewitness, in which the heroism of the defeated East Saxons is celebrated.

Mali A landlocked country in north-west Africa, sharing boundaries with Mauritania, Algeria, Niger, Burkina Faso, Côte d'Ivoire, Guinea, and Senegal.

Physical. The northern part of Mali is in the dry Sahara and its south is in the tropics where there is about 1,200 mm (nearly 50 inches) of rainfall each year. From the south-west, and through its centre flows the Niger, which provides fish. The Niger here has an inland delta that permits the seasonal growing of rice, while other areas contain sufficient pasture for cattle, sheep, and goats.

Economy. Mali is amongst the world's poorest countries. The economy is agricultural, with livestock-rearing predominant in the drought-ridden north, and cotton cultivation in the southern savannah. Cotton, livestock, and gold are the chief exports. Millet, sorghum, and rice are also important subsistence crops. Light industry is based on clothing and food-processing. Hydroelectric power contributes substantially to electricity supplies. There are deposits of gold, marble, limestone, salt, and phosphates.

History. The Mali empire in the upper Niger region of West Africa was established in the 13th century. The founder, SUNDJATA KEITA, conquered the remains of the empire of GHANA c. 1235–40 with his army of Malinke soldiers. Mali soon controlled the rich trade across the Sahara and became a major supplier of gold. The empire reached its peak in the early 14th century under MANSA MUSA, who established an efficient administration. The Muslim traveller Ibn Battuta (1304–78) visited Mali in 1351–52 and gave a detailed account of the court and trade. However, by then the empire was beginning to decline. In 1335 SONGHAY became independent of Mali and by the 15th century had conquered the rest of the empire. After the Moroccan invasion of 1591, the Songhay empire collapsed. Mali was only freed from Moroccan rule at the end of the 18th century, when it was divided among the Tuareg, Macina, and Ségou. France colonized it in the late 19th century. In 1946 it became an Overseas Territory of France. It was proclaimed the Sudanese Republic in 1958, an autonomous state within the FRENCH COMMUNITY. It united with Senegal as the Federation of Mali in 1959, but in 1960 Senegal withdrew and Mali became independent. A military government took over in 1968, under Lieutenant Moussa Traoré, who gradually re-introduced some degree of civilian participation. As General Traoré he was elected President in 1974 and re-elected in 1985. Pro-democracy rioting began in 1990, and in 1991 Traoré was arrested and a National Reconciliation Council took charge under Lieutenant Colonel Amadou Toumani Touré. More than 40 political parties emerged, of which the Alliance for Democracy in Mali won a majority in the general election of 1992, its leader Alpha Oumar Konare being elected President. His policy has been to pacify rebellious Tuareg tribesmen in the north (a peace agreement was reached in 1992) and to seek UN support to rebuild the economy that has suffered severely from drought.

CAPITAL:	Bamako
AREA:	1,240,192 sq km (478,841 sq miles)
POPULATION:	9.204 million (1996)
CURRENCY:	1 CFA franc = 100 centimes
RELIGIONS:	Muslim 90.0%; traditional beliefs 9.0%; Christian 1.0%
ETHNIC GROUPS:	Bambara 31.9%; Fulani 13.9%; Senufo 12.0%; Soninke 8.8%; Tuareg 7.3%; Songhai 7.2%; Malinke 6.6%; Dogon 4.0%; Dyula 2.9%; Bobo 2.4%; Arab 1.2%
LANGUAGES:	French (official); Bambara; Fulani; local languages
INTERNATIONAL ORGANIZATIONS:	UN; OAU; Franc Zone

Malplaquet, Battle of (11 September 1709) A battle fought in north-east France, close to the Belgian frontier, that saw MARLBOROUGH's last victory over the French in the War of the SPANISH SUCCESSION. Marlborough's invasion of France in 1709 was an attempt to make LOUIS XIV agree to the allies' harsh peace terms. Though Malplaquet was a victory, the losses of the combined forces of England and the Holy Roman Empire exceeded those of France and the invasion attempt was abandoned.

Malta A country in the central Mediterranean Sea between Tunisia and Sicily, consisting of the main island, Malta, the smaller Gozo, and the tiny Comino.

Physical. The main island is some 27 km (17 miles) long by 14 km (9 miles) wide and rises to hills in the south-

west. The climate is very warm and rather dry, with fierce winds, and the land is barren in appearance, with few trees and no rivers or streams.

Economy. Malta's major exports incude clothing, machinery, and instruments; ship repair is significant and an offshore financial sector is being developed. Offshore oil exploration is being undertaken, and tourism is an important economic activity intended to replace loss of income from UK defence expenditure after the UK naval base was removed in 1979. Malta is the most densely populated country in Europe, with two-thirds of the population under 40.

History. Malta was settled, possibly as long as 6,000 years ago, during the NEOLITHIC era. In historic times it was a Carthaginian centre, falling to the Romans in 218 BC who named it Melita. The Byzantine empire controlled it until 870 when it was conquered by the Arabs. The NORMANS annexed it to their kingdom of SICILY, but, after having been retaken by Muslim forces, it finally fell to the Spanish kingdoms of Aragon and Castile and thence to Spain itself. Under Emperor Charles V it was given to the KNIGHTS HOSPITALLERS (1530), who defended it against Turkish attacks and fortified and enriched it. They were eventually expelled by Napoleon I of France (1798) and the island was taken by the British in 1800. The Treaty of Amiens (1802) returned Malta to the Knights Hospitallers but the Maltese people protested and requested British sovereignty, provided that Malta remained Roman Catholic and that the Maltese Declaration of Rights was honoured. Britain accepted these terms and the country was formally ceded to Britain by France in 1814. Malta developed as a strategic air and naval base and was awarded the George Cross for its resistance to German attack (1940–42). It gained full independence within the COMMONWEALTH OF NATIONS in 1964 and in 1974 became a republic. Malta applied to join the European Community (now the EUROPEAN UNION) in 1990 and in 1993 the European Commission instructed it to carry out a series of economic reforms before the start of formal accession negotiations. However, the general election of 1996 saw victory for the Labour Party under Alfred Sant, which had campaigned against EU membership.

CAPITAL:	Valletta
AREA:	316 sq km (122 sq miles)
POPULATION:	373,000 (1996)
CURRENCY:	1 Maltese lira = 100 cents = 1,000 mils
RELIGIONS:	Roman Catholic 97.0%; Anglican 1.0%
ETHNIC GROUPS:	Maltese (of Italian, British, and Phoenician origin) 96.0%; British 2.0%
LANGUAGES:	Maltese, English (both official)
INTERNATIONAL ORGANIZATIONS:	UN; Commonwealth; Council of Europe; CSCE

Malthus, Thomas Robert (1766–1834) British political economist and demographer. In 1798 he published his *Essay on the Principle of Population*, in which he put forward the argument that the general standard of living could not be raised above subsistence level, since a nation's population always grows more rapidly than food supplies. Numbers are kept down only by natural disasters such as famine and war. Malthus's theories, which contradicted optimistic opinions about human progress, had considerable influence on 19th-century political thought.

Maluku MOLUCCAS.

Malvinas FALKLAND ISLANDS.

Mamelukes (Arabic, *mamluk*, 'possessed' or slave) Two dynasties who ruled Egypt from 1250 to 1517 and sporadically thereafter. Mamelukes or slave soldiers were a distinctive feature of Islamic armies from the 9th century. Captured in childhood, they were trained in every branch of warfare and had an exacting academic education. Turkish and Mongol slaves were bodyguards of the Ayyubid sultan al-Salih (1240–49). On his death a popular power struggle developed and the Bahri mameluke generals elected one of their number as sultan al-Malik al Muizz. After some confusion, succession became hereditary and in 1291 the last Franks were driven from Egypt.

In the 14th century Bahri sultans recruited Burji slaves as bodyguards, stationing them in Cairo's citadel. These were chiefly Circassian (from the Caucasus). In 1390 they too usurped the sultanate under al-Malik an-Nasir. Under the Burji Mameluke rule extended over Egypt and Syria (including the present Israel, Jordan, Lebanon, and western Arabia). There was an elaborate court, and a highly organized civil service and judiciary. Active encouragement of trade and commerce brought great prosperity throughout their dominions, as is witnessed by the splendid monuments that they built in Cairo and elsewhere. Their external trade reached across Africa as far as Mali and Guinea, and throughout the Indian Ocean as far as Java. In 1517 the OTTOMAN Turks captured Cairo and overthrew the Mamelukes. As Turkish power waned they re-established themselves as rulers. NAPOLEON defeated them in 1798 and they were finally brought down by Muhammad Ali in 1811.

Mameluke sultanate (Slave sultanate) A series of Muslim kings based in Delhi who ruled a north Indian empire from 1206 to 1290. The founder, Qutb ud-Din Aibak (ruled 1206–11) had risen in the service of Muhammad of Ghor, the previous ruler of Delhi. One of Delhi's most famous monuments, the Qutb Minar, a carved red sandstone minaret, was built during his reign. His son-in-law and former slave Iltutmish (1211–36) consolidated his hold on the Punjab, Bengal, and Rajputana, conquered Sind, and expanded south as far as the River Nerbudda. Having survived Mongol threats in the mid-13th century, the sultanate reached its peak under Ghiyas ud-Din Balban (1266–87). Soon afterwards Delhi fell to the KHALJIS (1290).

Manchester School A group of economists, businessmen, and politicians who became influential in Britain in the 1840s. Based in Manchester, the centre of the cotton industry, and led by such men as John BRIGHT and Richard COBDEN, the group followed the *laissez-faire* philosophy of Adam SMITH and David RICARDO. They supported FREE TRADE and political and economic freedom, and opposed any interference by the state in industry and commerce. Their influence faded in the 1860s, when many European countries began to favour state intervention in economic matters.

Manchukuo Japanese puppet state in Manchuria (1932–45). Using the MUKDEN INCIDENT as a pretext, the Japanese seized the city of Mukden in September 1931 and within five months had extended their power over all Manchuria. Manchukuo was established as a puppet state under the notional rule of the last Chinese emperor PUYI, but effective control remained in the hands of the Japanese army. Japanese expansion to the west was halted by the Soviet army in 1939, but the Japanese remained in control of Manchukuo, managing a partial development of its mineral resources, until the Chinese communists (with support from the Soviet Union, who removed large quantities of industrial equipment) took over at the end of World War II.

Manchuria (Pinyin, Dongbei, 'North-east') An area of north-east China at the head of the Yellow Sea, north of Korea. The Hinggan Mountains and forests ring the northern part, while in the south-east, below the valley of the Sunghua River, more forested mountains thrust towards the Liaodong Peninsula, which extends into the Yellow Sea. The highest peak is Paektu on the Korean border at 2,744 m (9,003 feet). In the centre is a rolling plain of great fertility, supporting wheat, soya beans, and other crops. An extension of the Gobi Desert lies in the west. Coal and oil are the main resources, and there are significant metal deposits.

Between 200 BC and 900 AD China exercised little influence over Manchuria's various nomadic peoples except in the extreme south. A succession of dynasties established by different tribes then ruled it – for example the LIAO and the JIN, both of whom extended their empires into China. By the early 17th century the MANCHUS, from whom its name derives, were in control. From 1644, with China under Manchu rule, it was part of the QING empire.

Manchus A nomadic people who conquered China and established the QING dynasty in the 17th century. Previously vassals of the MING, their base was north of the Liaodong Peninsula in MANCHURIA. After 1582 their chief, Nurhachi (1559–1626), made alliances with neighbouring tribes, built a strong castle, and imported Chinese technicians and advisers. Everyone – tribesman, captive, serf, or slave – was registered under a distinctive banner, making possible an efficient system of taxation and military control. In 1616 Nurhachi took the title of emperor and in 1625 made Shenyang, renamed Mukden, his capital. When he died he had built his bannermen into a nation. His son, Abahai, campaigned extensively in Korea, Mongolia, and northern China. Twice he attacked Beijing. He ordered his people to call themselves Manchus, a name of obscure origin, and in 1636 proclaimed the Da Qing (Great Pure) dynasty. Eight years later Nurhachi's grandson became the first Qing emperor of China. While the Manchus adopted many aspects of Chinese life, they remained segregated from them, intermarriage with Chinese was forbidden, and they had separate quarters in all Chinese cities. During the 19th century segregation began to break down and in the 20th century they have merged into the mass of the Chinese people.

mandarin (Portuguese *mandarim*, from the Sanskrit *mantrin*, 'counsellor') A European name for a senior official in imperial China. From the Song dynasty (960 AD), officials were recruited predominantly by examination in the Confucian classics. (Since the HAN dynasty (206 BC) examinations had been used within the civil service.) There were nine grades of mandarin.

mandate A form of international trusteeship devised by the LEAGUE OF NATIONS for the administration of former German and Ottoman colonies after World War I. In 1919 the League assigned a mandate for each territory to one of the Allied nations (principally, Britain and France). Marking an important innovation in international law, the mandated territories were neither COLONIES, nor independent countries, but were to be supervised by the League's Permanent Mandates Commission. The latter, however, had no means of enforcing its will on the mandatory power, which was responsible for the administration, welfare, and development of the native population until considered ready for self-government. Most mandated territories, with the important exceptions of Palestine and Namibia, had achieved independence by World War II. In 1946 the mandate system was replaced by the United Nations' trusteeship system for the remaining mandates.

Mandela, Nelson Rolihlahla (1918–) South African statesman. Under the APARTHEID system, he became a leader of the AFRICAN NATIONAL CONGRESS (ANC) and a member of its militant subsidiary, the Spear of the Nation. He was banned from the country (1953–55) but a year later was among those charged in a mass treason trial. The trial lasted until 1961, when all were acquitted. He continued to campaign for a free, multiracial, and democratic society but was arrested in 1962 and imprisoned for five years. Before this sentence expired, he was charged under the Suppression of Communism Act and after a memorable trial (October 1963–June 1964), in which he conducted his own defence, he was sentenced to life imprisonment. His authority as a leader of Black South Africans did not diminish, though his absence from the political scene enabled a more militant generation of leaders to emerge. Although offered a conditional release by the South African government, Mandela refused to compromise over the issue of apartheid. Following his eventual release in February 1990, he persuaded the ANC to suspend the armed struggle, and took part in negotiations for the dismantling of apartheid. In 1993 a new (transitional) multiracial constitution was adopted (this was replaced by a permanent constitution in 1996). Mandela was elected President in South Africa's first multiracial elections, held in 1994. Although he has attempted to foster national reconciliation, sporadic outbreaks of violence, particularly between ANC and INKATHA FREEDOM PARTY supporters, have continued. In 1996 he visited the UK, where he was entertained by the Queen and fêted in the streets. One of the world's most respected statesmen, he has received numerous honours, including the 1993 Nobel peace prize (jointly with F. W. DE KLERK). In December 1997 he handed over the presidency of the ANC to Thabo MBEKI: although he remains President of South Africa, his role is now mainly a ceremonial one.

His wife Winnie Mandela (1934–) had actively campaigned for her husband's release throughout his years in prison, but a number of scandals led to their separation soon after he was freed. Their marriage was dissolved in 1996. Winnie Mandela's politics became increasingly extremist. In 1994 she was appointed Deputy Minister for Arts, Culture, Science, and Technology but was dismissed in 1995. In appearances before South Africa's Truth and Reconciliation Commission in 1997, Winnie Mandela was accused of personal involvement in the murder of suspected police informers during the apartheid period.

Manfred (1231–66) King of Sicily (1258–66). The illegitimate son of the Holy Roman Emperor FREDERICK II, he ruled in Italy on behalf of Conradin, his half-brother, and with support from the Saracens took the Kingdom of the Two Sicilies (1257). He was excommunicated by Pope Alexander VI but invaded papal territories in Tuscany. He was again excommunicated by Pope Urban IV who gave his crown to Charles I of Anjou, and he was finally defeated and killed at the battle of Benevento.

Manhattan Project The code name for the secret project to develop the atomic bomb in the USA during World War II. When it became apparent in the late 1930s that it was feasible to build such a bomb and that German scientists were working on the technology, the project received high priority. The task of designing and assembling the bomb at Los Alamos, New Mexico, was directed by Robert OPPENHEIMER, who had the collaboration of the University of Chicago, where Enrico Fermi built the first atomic pile. Also involved were Columbia University, New York; the Berkeley Radiation Laboratory, University of California; and scientists from the UK. The fissile material uranium-235 for the HIROSHIMA bomb (known as 'Tallboy') was produced at Oak Ridge, Tennessee, while plutonium-239 for the NAGASAKI bomb (known as 'Fat Max') was made at an atomic plant at Hanford, Washington state. The project resulted in the successful explosion of the first atomic bomb at Alamogordo, New Mexico, on 16 July 1945.

Manichaeism The teaching of Manes (c. 216–76), a Persian influenced by MITHRAISM, CHRISTIANITY, and Gnosticism. He taught a dual principle of Good and Evil in conflict, symbolized as Light against Darkness, God against Satan. He counselled asceticism for an elect group following the teaching of the Jewish prophets, JESUS CHRIST, BUDDHA, and himself. ZOROASTRIANS drove him into exile in India, flayed him alive, and crucified him. His followers were condemned by DIOCLETIAN, though this did not prevent their influence spreading to Rome and Africa by the 4th century. The sect survived in Chinese Turkistan until the 10th century and influenced various heresies in medieval Christianity.

manifest destiny A 19th-century US political doctrine advocating territorial expansion. It was proclaimed by John O'Sullivan as 'Our manifest destiny to overspread the continent allotted by Providence for the free development of our yearly multiplying millions'. A tenet of the Democratic Party, it gained support among Whig, and later Republican, interests, and played a significant part in raising popular support for the annexation of TEXAS (1845) and the MEXICAN–AMERICAN WAR (1846–48). It was later invoked by SEWARD in the purchase of ALASKA (1867), and re-emerged in the 1890s with the annexation of HAWAII and the acquisition of Spanish territories after the SPANISH–AMERICAN WAR.

Manila Bay, Battle of (1 May 1898) Naval engagement during the SPANISH–AMERICAN WAR in the Philippines, in which a US fleet under George DEWEY sank a Spanish fleet at dawn without losing a man. Dewey's objective had been to paralyse the Spanish fleet at the outset of the SPANISH–AMERICAN WAR of 1898 over Cuba, but his overwhelming victory widened the scope of the war by opening the way for US expansion in the Pacific.

'Man in the Iron Mask', the (17th century) One of history's mystery figures, the hero of a legend largely

eated by VOLTAIRE. The unknown prisoner incarcerated
y LOUIS XIV in Pignerol and later in the Bastille is
ought by some to have been Count Ercolo Antonio
Mattioli, an agent of the Duke of Mantua, who had
eceived the king over a secret treaty to purchase the
rategic fortress of Casale. Others suggest that he was a
rother or son of Louis XIV or even FOUQUET. The
risoner, who died in the Bastille in 1703, actually wore
velvet mask.

Mannerheim, Carl Gustav Emil, Baron von
867–1951) Finnish military leader and statesman.
rained as an officer in the Tsarist army, he rose to the
ank of general, and, defeating the Finnish Bolsheviks
918), he expelled the Soviet forces from Finland. He
as appointed chief of the National Defence Council
930–39), and planned the 'Mannerheim Line', a fortified
ne of defence across the Karelian Isthmus to block any
otential aggression by the Soviet Union. When Soviet
orces attacked (1939) he resisted in the FINNISH–RUSSIAN
AR, and in alliance with Germany renewed the war
941–44). In 1944 he signed an armistice with the Soviet
nion. The Finnish Parliament elected Mannerheim as
resident (1944–46). In March 1945 he brought Finland
ato the war against Germany.

Manning, Henry Edward (1808–92) British cardinal.
fter becoming a Church of England priest in 1832, he
as strongly influenced by the Oxford Movement (see
EWMAN, JOHN HENRY) and by the pre-Reformation
atholic Church. Received into the Roman Catholic
hurch in 1851 he became Archbishop of Westminster in
865, and a cardinal in 1875. Theologically conservative,
e supported the proclamation of papal infallibility
870). He was an early supporter of TRADE UNION rights
nd showed his sympathy for the Agricultural
abourers' Union in the 1870s. His mediation helped to
ecure a just settlement in the LONDON DOCKERS' STRIKE
889); and he supported HOME RULE for Ireland.

manor house The home of the lord of an estate in
medieval times. As well as housing the lord – or his
esident BAILIFF — the house was the administrative hub
f the feudal estate (see MANORIAL SYSTEM). Throughout
urope, manor houses varied considerably in size and
esign, depending upon what materials were locally
vailable and how much fortification seemed necessary.
a France, and elsewhere in battle-scarred Europe,
efensive considerations pre-dominated until the 17th
entury. Rectangular, fortified tower-houses within
alled and moated enclosures were familiar sights on
he landscape. In England, the move toward more
uxurious accommodation began earlier. Already by the
4th century, interiors were being divided up into
rivate living apartments and service rooms, rather
han being dominated by the traditional great halls. By
he 17th century the manor house had evolved into the
OUNTRY HOUSE. (See illustration.)

manorial system The social, economic, and
dministrative system (also called seigneurialism) that
merged in 5th century Europe from the chaos and
nstability following the collapse of the Roman empire.
armers sought the protection of powerful lords and in
eturn surrendered certain rights and control over their
nds. Gradually a system of obligations and service
merged, especially relating to manorial agrarian
management, and set down in records called custumals.

The manor consisted of demesne land (private land of
the lord) and tenants' holdings. Tenants were free or
unfree (villeins), rank being determined by personal
status or the status of their land. Not all manors had
this balance of demesne, free land, and unfree land. In
addition, meadow land for grazing livestock was
available to all, and thus known as common land. Access
to woodland for timber and grazing of pigs might be a
further facility. The lord presided over the manorial
court and received money or labour services from his
tenants regularly (week work) or seasonally (boon work).
A tendency in the 12th century for labour services to be
commuted to cash rents was reversed after c. 1200, when
inflation encouraged landlords again to exact services in
kind. Labour shortages following the BLACK DEATH (1348)
when Europe's population fell from 80 million to 55
million, enclosures, tenant unrest, and rebellions such as
the PEASANTS' REVOLT (1381) effectively ended the manorial
system in England by c. 1500.

Mansa Musa (ruled 1307–37) The most celebrated of
the rulers (kankans) of MALI, chiefly because of his
spectacular pilgrimage to MECCA in 1324. He caused a
sensation in Cairo with his 500 slaves and 80–100 camels
carrying gold. In his absence one of his generals
acquired Gao, the capital of the neighbouring SONGHAY
state for him. He returned from Mecca with the
Andalusian poet-architect Es-Saheli, who built the palace
and Great Mosque of TIMBUKTU. He greatly expanded the
commerce and prosperity of Mali, and gave
encouragement to Islamic learning and culture.

Manzikert, Battle of (1071) Battle fought at a site
near Lake Van in Turkey. SELJUK Turks, recent converts
to ISLAM, routed a Byzantine force, capturing its leader,
Emperor Romanos Diogenes IV. Alp Arslan, the Seljuk
leader released him, but the defeat left Anatolia open to
Turkish invaders and the weakening of Byzantine
control that was indirectly to provoke the First CRUSADE.

Maoism The communist doctrines of MAO ZEDONG. Mao
devoted considerable time to the theoretical basis of the
communist state in China, and his ideas reflect the
influence both of traditional Chinese thought and of the
structure of Chinese society. Maoism's principal
difference from Marxist-Leninism is the importance it
attaches to the peasantry as the powerhouse of the
revolution and communist state, rather than to the
urban proletariat, which was at the time not well
developed in China. A central idea is that of permanent
revolution, which led to the radical reform movements
known as the GREAT LEAP FORWARD (1958) and the CULTURAL
REVOLUTION (1966). By contrast with the former Soviet
Union, where large-scale INDUSTRIALIZATION was favoured
and a ruling communist élite emerged, Maoism
emphasized the continuing importance of the peasantry,
small-scale industry, and agricultural COLLECTIVIZATION. In
order to avoid the emergence of a bourgeois élite, city
workers and intellectuals were sent to the countryside
to perform compulsory 'educational' agricultural labour.
Such policies proved economically and socially disastrous
and have been largely reversed in present-day China.
However, Maoist revolutionary theory and strategies for
guerrilla warfare are still influential in some developing
countries.

Maori A branch of the eastern POLYNESIAN race living in
New Zealand. The Maori migrated to New Zealand from

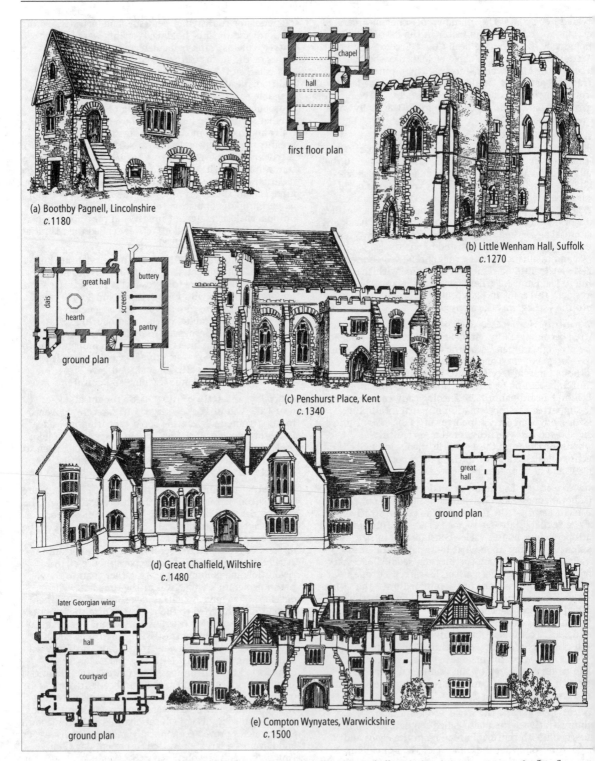

(a) Boothby Pagnell, Lincolnshire
c.1180

(b) Little Wenham Hall, Suffolk
c.1270

first floor plan

chapel

hall

great hall

dais

hearth

screens

buttery

pantry

ground plan

(c) Penshurst Place, Kent
c.1340

(d) Great Chalfield, Wiltshire
c.1480

great hall

ground plan

later Georgian wing

hall

courtyard

ground plan

(e) Compton Wynyates, Warwickshire
c.1500

manor house *Early manor houses were fortified buildings, centred on a great hall, with their living quarters on the first floor. The stone manor at Boothby Pagnell (a) is one of the earliest surviving examples, while Little Wenham Hall (b) is the earliest extant brick manor. Penshurst Place (c) is similar in design, with an additional wing for service rooms. Great Chalfield (d) retained the great hall as an important feature but the house has a more domestic appearance. By early Tudor times the need for defence had disappeared and is no longer apparent in the design of Compton Wynyates (e).*

the central Pacific from about 800 AD in several waves. By the 18th century a settled population of more than 100,000 had developed. Tribal structure was traditionally based on common ancestry, and sub-tribes were the landholding groups. The family was the basis for agricultural production, and also for ritual events. Common language and customs, inter-marriage, and trade linked almost all the tribes, yet there was constant feuding between them. The term 'Maori' (meaning 'normal' or 'ordinary') was adopted when the tribes perceived a common identity in the face of European settlement. They responded to contact positively while attempting to control the intruders and preserve some selectivity. Hence the welcoming of traders but increasing resistance to shore-based settlement. This policy of accommodation also led, in 1840, to the chiefs' signing of the Treaty of WAITANGI. Similarly they created the KINGITANGA to help preserve the land and a measure of independent Maori authority. By the Treaty direct purchase of land from the Maoris was forbidden, but the ANGLO-MAORI WARS were mainly caused by the rapid acquisition of Maori land by the government and pressure by settlers for direct purchase. The wars were followed by participation in elections for the four Maori seats in Parliament and the establishment of village schools teaching in English. The process of putting land through the Maori Land Court, established in 1865, and replacing customary title with a crown-granted title before sale, was accompanied by the transfer of most good land from Maori possession to the settlers. Disease reduced Maori population to a low of 42,000 in 1896. After World War II the Maori migrated systematically to towns in search of wider opportunities. Their numbers increased; but threatened by rising unemployment and loss of identity, they have in recent years again launched protests and demanded recognition of their language, values, and culture in national life, and the preservation of remaining Maori land. Since the mid 1990s the New Zealand government has agreed to pay compensation to several tribal groups whose land had been seized illegally by settlers and to return traditional Maori lands in the government's possession. Many more Maori claims to land are under consideration.

Mao Zedong (or Mao Tse-tung) (1893–1976) Chinese revolutionary and statesman. He served in the revolutionary army during the CHINESE REVOLUTION OF 1911, and became involved first in the MAY FOURTH MOVEMENT (1919) and then in the CHINESE COMMUNIST PARTY in Beijing. Converted to Marxism, Mao moved to Shanghai in 1923 to become a KUOMINTANG political organizer. After the Kuomintang turned on its communist allies in 1927, Mao used his experience of organizing the peasantry and his belief in their potential as a revolutionary force to establish the JIANGXI SOVIET. With ZHU DE he developed the GUERRILLA tactics which were to be the secret of his success in the long civil war with the Kuomintang. In 1931 he became chairman of the Jiangxi Soviet, but following its successful blockade by Chiang Kai-shek's nationalist forces, he eventually led his followers in the LONG MARCH (1934–35) to a new base in north-west China. Having emerged as the *de facto* leader of the Chinese Communist Party, he devoted considerable time to the theoretical writings that were to provide the ideological basis for the future communist state (MAOISM). Mao's

well-organized guerrilla forces, capably led by such men as Zhu De and LIN BIAO, resisted the Japanese and defeated Chiang Kai-shek's nationalist forces. On 1 October 1949 he proclaimed the establishment of the People's Republic of China. Although he served as chairman of the new state from the time of its formation, Mao took little active part in administration until the mid-1950s, when he pioneered a series of reform movements, most notably the GREAT LEAP FORWARD, in an attempt to galvanize economic and political development. The rift with the Soviet Union, which increasingly refused to support the Chinese communist struggle, reached its climax in the early 1960s. In 1959 Mao retired from the post of chairman of the Republic, but re-emerged in 1966 to initiate the CULTURAL REVOLUTION, a dramatic attempt to radicalize the country and prevent the revolution stagnating. Thereafter he gave his tacit support to the radical GANG OF FOUR, but their bid for power was stopped by his nominated successor, HUA GUOFENG, after Mao's death.

maps and charts Diagrammatic representations of all or part of the Earth on a plane surface. The term 'map' is usually confined to land areas, whereas a representation of a sea area is called a 'chart'. The earliest maps of which we have knowledge were made by the Babylonians on clay tablets, dating from around 2300 BC. The ancient Greeks drew maps of the known world and speculated on its form: around the 3rd century BC Greek geographers agreed that the Earth was spherical; at this time the Greek astronomer and and geographer Eratosthenes estimated its circumference to be around 46,000 km (28,750 miles), not far from modern values of around 40,000 km (25,000 miles). Chinese map-making from the 3rd century BC was based on the use of a reference grid of parallel lines running N–S and E–W, and on-the-spot surveys. These maps were remarkably accurate, but Chinese world maps remained poor until the introduction of Western cartography in the 17th century. Probably the greatest figure of early geography was PTOLEMY, whose *Guide to Geography* included a world map that was revived in Europe in the early 15th century. Medieval European geographers believed that the known world of Europe, Asia, and Africa covered only one-quarter of the Earth's surface. In their *mappa mundi* (world maps) they often drew only this portion of the Earth, and the locations of features upon it were not mathematically related to their true positions on the globe. In the Arab world, however, classical astronomy and cartography continued to be studied. Islamic geographers drew world maps, based on new tables of latitude and longitude, in which the habitable world extended well south of the equator, and the Indian Ocean was open towards the Far East. In the 13th and 14th centuries the travels of Europeans across Asia, and the introduction of sea-charts based on magnetic compass directions improved the detail of world maps. In the 15th and 16th centuries the translations of Greek and Arabic geographical works introduced European cartographers to the concept of map projection, while the discoveries of such explorers as Christopher COLUMBUS led to a more accurate view of the globe. The best-known cartographer of the period was Gerardus Mercator, whose method for projection of the globe on to a flat surface enabled navigators to plot bearings as straight lines. In the 18th century a more scientific approach to map-making began to predominate, and many European countries began systematic national topographic surveys. Others followed suit, but some parts of the world remained largely unmapped until World War II, when vast areas were mapped using information from aerial photographs.

Maquis (Corsican Italian, *macchia*, 'thicket') The French RESISTANCE MOVEMENT in World War II. After the fall of France in 1940, it carried on resistance to the Nazi occupation. Supported by the French Communist Party, but not centrally controlled, its membership rose in 1943–44, and constituted a considerable hindrance to the German rear when the Allies landed in France. Its various groups, often operating independently, were co-ordinated into the Forces Françaises de l'Interieur in 1944.

Marat, Jean Paul (1743–93) French Revolutionary leader. He practised as a doctor in London, where in 1773 he published a *Philosophical Essay on Man*; this criticized HELVÉTIUS's view that science was unnecessary for a philosopher. Having returned to Paris to edit the radical journal *L'ami du peuple*, he became a leader of the extremist Cordelier Club and a key figure in the FRENCH REVOLUTION. His attacks on those in power led to his brief exile in 1790 but in 1792 he was elected to the Assembly where he opposed the GIRONDINS. Their defeat in May 1793, a triumph for Marat, led to his murder by Charlotte CORDAY D'ARMONT.

Maratha A Hindu warrior people of western India who in the 17th and 18th centuries led a military revival against Muslim expansion. They rose to prominence under the inspired leadership of SIVAJI, who, after victories against the MOGULS, established a Maratha kingdom in 1674. Their great age was the early 18th century when, after a temporary collapse, they benefited from Mogul decline to sweep over the north and central Deccan. They seemed poised for all-India mastery, but failure in 1761 of their bid to take Delhi (in the battle of PANIPAT) was followed by increasing internal disunity. Authority had passed from Sivaji's line to a Brahmin family based at Pune, who as hereditary *peshwas* (ministers) struggled to hold the dissident chiefs together. Rivalry among these 'confederates', notably the SINDHIA, HOLKAR, Bhonsla, and Gaekwar families, prevented a united stand against expanding British power.

Maratha Wars (1774–82, 1803–05, 1817–18) Wars between the MARATHA peoples of India and troops of the English EAST INDIA COMPANY. By the late 18th century the Maratha Hindus, divided into over 90 clans, had formed an uneasy confederacy that became a significant force in northern and central India. Rivalries between chiefs were exploited by the British. In the Second War Sir Arthur Wellesley (later Duke of WELLINGTON) won the battles of Assaye and Argaon. The Charter of the East India Company was renewed in 1813, when no further British acquisitions were envisaged, but in 1817 Company troops under Lord Hastings invaded Maratha territory to put down PINDARI robber bands supported by Maratha princes, and finally made British power dominant within the subcontinent.

Marathon A plain in north-east ATTICA, scene in 490 BC of a battle in which the Athenians, with their PLATAEAN allies, defeated the invading Persians. The 11,000 Greeks used tactics that prevented encirclement of their flanks and inflicted some 6,400 casualties. They then marched swiftly back to Athens, thereby deterring a sea-borne Persian attack on the city itself. The Athenian herald Phidippides ran to Sparta to summon help, covering 240 km (150 miles) in two days. The modern marathon race of 42.2 km (26 miles 38 yds) commemorates a tradition that a messenger ran that distance to Athens with news of victory – and fell dead on arrival.

Marchand, Jean-Baptiste (1863–1934) French explorer and general. He served in Africa from 1887 until 1895. In 1897, having been instructed to obtain French control of the region between the Niger and the Nile, he made a heroic journey through unexplored territory, reaching FASHODA in 1898. Here he was confronted by an Anglo-Egyptian army led by Lord KITCHENER, who claimed the town for Egypt. Marchand's mission was withdrawn and France yielded its claim to the upper Nile region. Subsequently he served in the BOXER RISING and in World War I.

marcher lord In the Middle Ages, a holder of land (a lordship) lying on the border (or march) between countries. The term applied to Italy (marche), Germany (mark), and in England along its borders with Scotland and Wales. The marcher lords on the Welsh border were particularly powerful. Between 1067 and 1070 three large marcher lordships were created, based on Chester, Shrewsbury, and Hereford. They extended their power into Wales despite Welsh resistance in the 12th century led by Owain Gwynedd and Rhys ap Gruffydd. About 140 lordships and sub-lordships were created, the most powerful being Glamorgan, Pembroke, and Wigmore. The crown sought to deal with them by first setting up the Council of the March in Wales (1472) and then abolishing them in the second Act of Union (1543). Their lands were attached to the six existing and the seven new Welsh shires and to the English border counties.

Marco Polo (*c.* 1254–1324) Venetian traveller. Between 1271 and 1275 he accompanied his father and uncle on a journey east from Acre into central Asia along the SILK ROUTE, eventually reaching China and the court of KUBLAI KHAN. He entered the service of the khan and travelled widely in the MONGOL empire during the next 17 years. In 1292–95 the three Venetians returned home by sea, calling at Sumatra and southern India before reaching Persia and making the last part of their journey to Venice overland. Three years later Marco Polo was captured by the Genoese in a sea battle, and during his imprisonment he dictated an account of his travels. His book was widely read and stimulated European interest in the East and its riches. Doubts have been cast by some modern scholars on the authenticity of Maro Polo's accounts.

Marcos, Ferdinand Edralin (1917–89) Filipino statesman, President (1965–86). He entered Congress in 1949, subsequently becoming Senate leader in 1963. A ruthless and corrupt politician, he initially achieved some success as a reformer and increased links with the USA. However, after his election to a second term he became increasingly involved in campaigns against nationalist and communist guerrilla groups, and in 1972–73 he first declared martial law and then assumed near dictatorial powers. Although martial law was lifted in 1981 and some moves were made towards the restoration of democracy, hostility to Marcos intensified after the murder of the opposition leader Benigno Aquino Jr in 1983. US support for his regime waned as a result of his failure to achieve consensus, and in February 1986 he was forced to leave the country after his attempts to retain power in a disputed election caused a popularly backed military revolt. This gave uncertain support to Corazon Aquino, widow of the slain opposition leader. Marcos's body was returned to the Philippines for burial in 1993. His flamboyant wife Imelda Marcos (c. 1930–) was convicted in the same year of embezzlement and sentenced to at least 18 years imprisonment, but remained free on bail and was elected to the Philippines House of Representatives in 1995.

Marcus Aurelius, (121–80 AD) Roman emperor (161–80) and STOIC philosopher. He was born of Spanish parents, and adopted as HADRIAN's grandson. A student of literature, philosophy, and law, he was plunged into military activity on frontiers in the Balkans, Dacia, Pannonia, and Syria immediately on his accession. His *Meditations*, largely written on campaign, survive with some of his letters. While an admirer of EPICTETUS, he persecuted the Christians.

Margaret, Maid of Norway (c. 1283–90) Queen of Scotland (1286–90). She was the daughter of Erik II, King of Norway, and the granddaughter of ALEXANDER III of Scotland. She became Queen of Scotland at the age of three, although six guardians were appointed to govern the kingdom during her minority. Edward I of England proposed a marriage between Margaret and his son Edward, the first English Prince of Wales. Her death by drowning when crossing the North Sea from Norway to Scotland brought to an end the dynastic House of Canmore, which had ruled since 1057, and led to a dispute (1291–92) over the succession involving 13 claimants. Edward I of England judged in favour of John BALLIOL.

Margaret, St (c. 1046–93) Queen consort of MALCOLM III of Scotland from 1069. She was descended from the House of Wessex, being the daughter of Edward the Atheling and the granddaughter of Edmund Ironside. A pious woman, Margaret encouraged the Scottish Church to adopt the Roman form of Christianity. She refounded Iona and brought the Benedictine monastic order to Scotland. She was canonized in 1250.

Margaret of Anjou (1430–82) Queen of England. Her marriage to HENRY VI in 1445 ensured a truce in the war between England and France. During the Wars of the ROSES Henry's weakness caused the LANCASTRIAN party to centre on his indomitable wife; in February 1461 she won the second battle of ST ALBANS but by her hesitation lost the chance to keep Henry on the throne, and she had to flee to Scotland and thence to France. Except for the few months that Henry regained the throne in 1470–71, she spent most of the rest of her life in her native Anjou.

margrave (German, *Markgraf*, 'count of the mark') A governor appointed to protect vulnerable areas known as marks in the Holy Roman Empire. They were the equivalent of English marches (MARCHER LORD) and were usually frontier territories. Charlemagne introduced

this office, which in the 12th century became hereditary, and the title came to rank equally with a prince of the empire.

Maria Theresa (1717–80) Ruler of the Habsburg dominions (1740–80). As the daughter of Charles VI, she succeeded to the Habsburg lands in Austria, Bohemia, Hungary, the southern Netherlands, and north Italy in 1740 according to the PRAGMATIC SANCTION. Though only 23, she was a woman of great courage and determination, and rallied her peoples to defend her territories in the War of the AUSTRIAN SUCCESSION and the SEVEN YEARS WAR. She lost Silesia but gained Galicia in the First Partition of Poland. Her husband Francis of Lorraine became Holy Roman Emperor in 1745, and on his death in 1765 her son JOSEPH II succeeded and became co-regent with his mother until her death.

She was a benevolent and practical woman and chose able ministers, notably KAUNITZ, Haugwitz, and Chotek. Hungary remained strongly independent but Austria and Bohemia were brought under more centralized control, local government and taxation were reorganized, and important steps were taken in army and educational reform. Her improvements were gradual but proved more enduring than the more radical changes imposed by her son.

Marie Antoinette (1755–93) Queen of France. She was the daughter of MARIA THERESA and FRANCIS I of Austria, and was 14 when her arranged marriage to the Dauphin of France took place. Her brief popularity as LOUIS XVI's queen from 1774 was sacrificed by her frivolous and extravagant behaviour, associated with the *Petit Trianon*, a small country house near Versailles, given by Louis XVI to the queen and used for parties. Throughout the difficult days of the FRENCH REVOLUTION she displayed remarkable courage and dignity. Several attempts were made to free her, but her close relationship with Austria and support for an allied invasion led to her trial and execution.

Maritime strike (1890) A shipping, mining, and shearing strike in Australia. It was a time of economic depression and workers were fighting for trade union recognition (including the 'closed shop'), although other issues were also involved. The unions were defeated, some collapsing completely. This defeat has been seen as being a catalyst in the development of the labour movement and the formation of the Australian LABOR PARTY.

Marius, Gaius (157–86 BC) Roman general and seven times consul. He was a commander in the Numidian campaign and concluded the war by capturing JUGURTHA in 105. From 104 to 101 he fought the Cimbri and Teutones who threatened Italy and defeated them in two major battles. For the African war he had broken with precedent by recruiting men of no property and creating a professional army. In Gaul he introduced rigorous training and established the cohort and the century (CENTURION) as the essential units of the legion. His soldiers were nicknamed 'Marius' mules' because they carried everything on their backs. In 88 he attempted to deprive SULLA of his command against Mithridates. When Sulla marched on Rome to maintain his position, Marius fled. After Sulla's departure for the

East, he captured the city with his partisans and massacred his enemies. He died just after entering on his seventh consulship in 86.

Mark Antony (Marcus Antonius) (83–30 BC) Roman general. He had served with CAESAR at the end of the GALLIC WARS. As tribune in 49 he defended Caesar's interest in the Senate as civil war loomed. He was present at PHARSALUS, and represented Caesar in Italy. His offer of a crown to Caesar was refused. After Caesar's murder he took the political initiative against the assassins, and delivered the funeral speech. Octavian (AUGUSTUS), however, was Caesar's designated heir and hostility arose between the two. During Antony's struggle for ascendancy over the Senate led by CICERO, he was denounced in the 'Phillippic' orations and defeated at Mutina by the forces of the consuls and Octavian. He was then reconciled with Octavian, and together with Lepidus they formed the Second Triumvirate, disposed of enemies including Cicero and defeated the 'Liberators', BRUTUS and Cassius, at PHILIPPI in 42.

Antony received the government of the eastern Mediterranean and began (42) his liaison with CLEOPATRA. Although a powerful ally she cost him much support at Rome. Their marriage, Antony's fifth, was illegal in Roman law. In 34 he declared Caesarion (Cleopatra's son allegedly by Caesar) as Caesar's heir in Octavian's place and divided the east among his family. War followed. After his defeat at ACTIUM he committed suicide in Egypt.

Markiewicz, Constance WOMEN'S SUFFRAGE.

Marlborough, John Churchill, 1st Duke of (1650–1722) English general, one of the most outstanding strategists in English military history. He showed military ability in his early campaigns and political sagacity in his marriage to Sarah Jennings, the favourite of Princess ANNE. JAMES II appointed him second-in-command against MONMOUTH'S REBELLION in 1685, but he failed to support James's Roman Catholic aims and deserted him in 1688 to welcome WILLIAM III (of Orange). When William's wife Mary quarrelled with her sister Anne, Churchill fell from royal favour, but began to recover his influence after Mary's death in 1694.

By 1701 war seemed inevitable over the SPANISH SUCCESSION and the king appointed Churchill commander-in-chief of the English forces. Anne became queen in 1702 and he received a dukedom and became commander-in-chief of the allied armies. His brilliant campaigns in Europe led to a series of spectacular victories at BLENHEIM (1704), RAMILLIES (1706), OUDENARDE (1708), and MALPLAQUET (1709); however, the increasingly heavy casualties brought criticism at home. The Tory revival in 1710 led to his dismissal in the following year. He resumed his old offices on the accession of George I in 1714, but two strokes in 1716 incapacitated him and ended his career.

His wife Sarah (1660–1744) was as loyal and devoted to her husband as she was quarrelsome and vindictive to everyone else, including her own children. Her influence over Queen Anne was undermined by her cousin Abigail Masham, working for HARLEY, and Sarah was dismissed by the queen when the Whigs fell in 1710. After the duke's death Sarah supervised the completion of Blenheim Palace, the country house given by the nation to her husband as a reward for his victories. In 1742 she published an account of her long and stormy public life.

Marne, Battles of the (5–12 September 1914, 15 July–7 August 1918) Two battles along the River Marne in east central France in World War I. The first battle marked the climax and defeat of the German plan to destroy the French forces before Russian mobilization was complete. By September the Germans were within 24 km (15 miles) of Paris and the government moved to Bordeaux. JOFFRE's successful counter-offensive has been hailed as one of the decisive battles in history. The retreating Germans dug themselves in north of the River Aisne, setting the pattern for TRENCH WARFARE on the WESTERN FRONT. The second battle ended LUDENDORFF's final offensive, when, on 18 July, FOCH ordered a counter-attack.

Maronites Members of an Eastern-rite community of the ROMAN CATHOLIC CHURCH, founded by a 4th-century patriarch, Maron: today it has approximately 1.5 million adherents, mainly living in LEBANON, but with important groups in Cyprus, Palestine, and Egypt. The Maronite liturgy is in Syriac and their ecclesiastical head, under the pope, is the patriarch of Antioch (Antakya in present-day Turkey), who resides in Lebanon. Since the 19th century a few Maronites have migrated to the Americas, Australia, and Africa. The massacre (1860) of Maronites by the DRUZE brought French intervention and established French control in Lebanon and Syria. Following the dissolution of the OTTOMAN EMPIRE in 1920 the Maronites in Lebanon became self-ruling under French protection. After the establishment (1945) of an independent Lebanon, they formed the dominant religious and political group, a convention being devised that the President would always by a Maronite, the Prime Minister a Sunni Muslim, and the Speaker of Parliament a Shia Muslim, with the elected chamber of Deputies having Maronites and Muslims in the ratio of 6:5. The Maronites' traditional enemies remained the Druze. Rivalry between Maronite clans resulted in two main political factions developing: the right-wing Phalange, founded in the 1930s by Pierre Gemayel, and the more moderate Chamounists founded by ex-President Camile Chamoun in 1958. Inter-communal feuding gave the Phalange greater control over Christian Lebanon and at the beginning of the Lebanese civil war (1975), the Phalangists attempted unsuccessfully to extend their authority over all Lebanon. The Maronites lost their built-in political majority over the Muslim population of Lebanon in October 1989, by the so-called Taif Accord.

Marprelate tracts Satirical English pamphlets signed by the pseudonymous 'Martin Marprelate', which appeared in 1588–89. They featured scurrilous attacks on Anglican bishops, and were the work of Presbyterians who wished to discredit the episcopacy. ELIZABETH I, angered by them, prompted a search for the secret presses on which they were printed. Star Chamber prosecutions of leading ministers followed. Having appeared at a time when Presbyterian fortunes were already at a low ebb, the tracts probably served to discredit the movement still further with the public.

Marquesas, the A group of 12 volcanic islands in the South Pacific. They are all rugged and mountainous, Hiva Oa reaching 1,250 m (4,100 feet). Their vegetation includes pandanus trees (screw-pines), breadfruit trees, and the orchid from which vanilla is obtained.

From an estimated 50,000 people living on the Marquesas in 1813, foreign diseases had more than halved the population by 1842, when France annexed the islands. By 1926 the population was down to a little more than 2,000 but the development of agriculture, it has recovered to some 6,000. They are now administered as a division within French Polynesia, a French Overseas Territory.

Marshall, George Catlett (1880–1959) US general and statesman. As army chief of staff (1939–45), he was responsible for enlarging the US army when his country entered World War II, and for overall strategic military planning. In late 1945 he led an abortive mission to bring about a settlement between the KUOMINTANG and the communists in China. As Secretary of State (1947–49) he organized aid to Greece and Turkey, and fostered the European Recovery Program, the so-called MARSHALL PLAN, to promote economic recovery. Following the collapse of his economic aid plan for Eastern Europe because of the Soviet Union's hostility to it, he helped to create NATO and supported the firm line taken by the Western Powers over the Soviet blockade of Berlin. He was Secretary of Defense (1950–51).

Marshall, John (1755–1835) US lawyer. Elected to Congress as a Federalist in 1799, he became Chief Justice (1801–35). He raised the power and prestige of the US Supreme Court, and moulded the Constitution through his interpretations, despite the fact that he frequently held opposing views to those of incumbent Presidents. Marshall established the practice whereby the Court reviewed state and federal laws and pronounced final judgment on their constitutionality. In a series of major decisions between 1810 and 1830, the Marshall Supreme Court proved the Constitution on the one hand to be a precise document that established specific powers, and on the other a living instrument to be broadly interpreted both to give the federal government power to act effectively and to limit the powers of the states.

Marshall Islands A country consisting of a cluster of 29 low-lying atolls and five islands in the central Pacific, within the MICRONESIA region of Oceania.

Physical. The archipelago comprises two parallel chains of islands, the Ratak (sunrise) chain to the east and the Ralik (sunset) chain to the west. The islands are coral caps over dome volcanoes and have a tropical climate.

Economy. Farming and fishing are the main economic activities. Coconut oil and copra are exported.

History. The islands were originally inhabited by Micronesians. Although sighted by European sailors in 1529 they were not exploited. The islands were named after a British captain who visited them in 1788. In 1886 the Marshall Islands became a German protectorate. After World War I the islands were administered by Japan, and after World War II they became a UN Trust Territory under US administration. From 1946 the US used BIKINI and other atolls in the group for atomic bomb tests. In 1986 they were given semi-independence in a 'compact of free association' in which the USA maintained control over military activities. The Trusteeship was terminated in 1990 and the country joined the United Nations the following year. Amata Kabua became President in 1980 and was re-elected in 1984, 1988, and 1992: following his death in 1996 his cousin Imata Kabua was elected President. The islands,

which have the highest reported rates of certain cancers in the world, were used by the USA as sites for the testing of nuclear weapons (1946–58). In 1992 the US government made the first payments of compensation for personal injury to islanders. In 1993 the Australian government commissioned the building in the islands of a research station to monitor changes in sea-level; even a comparatively small rise in sea-level (one of the predicted consequences of global warming) could submerge the entire country.

CAPITAL:	Majuro
AREA:	181.48 sq km (7007 sq miles)
POPULATION:	58,500 (1996)
CURRENCY:	1 US dollar = 100 cents
RELIGIONS:	Protestant 90%; Catholic 8.5%; other 1.4%
ETHNIC GROUPS:	Marshallese 96.9%
LANGUAGES:	Marshallese (Kajin-Majol); English
INTERNATIONAL ORGANIZATIONS:	UN

Marshall Plan (European Recovery Program) US economic aid programme to European nations after World War II. Passed by Congress in 1948 as the Foreign Assistance Act, it was named after the Secretary of State, George MARSHALL. It invited the European nations to outline their requirements for economic recovery in order that material and financial aid could be used most effectively. The Soviet Union refused to participate and put pressure on its East European satellites to do likewise. To administer the plan, the Organization for European Economic Co-operation was set up, and between 1948 and 1951 some $13.5 billion was distributed. The Marshall Plan greatly contributed to the economic recovery of Europe, and bolstered international trade. In 1951 its activities were transferred to the Mutual Security Program. All activities ceased in 1956.

Marston Moor, Battle of (2 July 1644) A decisive victory for the ROUNDHEADS and Scots during the ENGLISH CIVIL WAR. The CAVALIER general Prince Rupert had pursued them to Marston Moor, Yorkshire, after his relief of York. They attacked him unexpectedly in the evening, and Cromwell's disciplined cavalry routed the Royalist troops. The Cavaliers lost perhaps 3,000 men through casualties, and 4,500 prisoners. After the encounter few northern fortresses held out for the king.

Martov, L. (born Yuly Osipovich Tsederbaum) (1873–1923) Russian revolutionary and leader of the Menshevik Party in opposition to LENIN'S BOLSHEVIKS. He had at first co-operated with Lenin as joint editor of *Iskra* ('The Spark'), but, at the meeting of the second Russian Social Democratic Party in London (1903), they disagreed over the degree of revolutionary class-consciousness in the labour movement and the extent to which it had to be controlled by a small party. Mensheviks favoured a mass labour party. After 1917 he supported Lenin against the 'White' armies but continued to oppose his more dictatorial policies. He left the Soviet Union in 1920.

martyr Someone who dies for his or her religious, political, or moral beliefs. Originally meaning a legal 'witness', the term came to denote anyone who died for professing the Christian faith after St Stephen, the first Christian martyr, was stoned to death in Jerusalem (*c.*

35). Martyrs ranked before all other saints, were venerated for their courage and faith, and were considered powerful intercessors between man and God. Martyrs' graves became shrines, from the Roman CATACOMBS to that of St Alban outside Verulamium (modern St Albans). After the last Roman persecution in the early 4th century their remains were either transferred to or marked by new churches. Relics were prized, and services were celebrated over a martyr's remains. Later centuries provided countless martyrs, including the Protestant and Catholic martyrs of Tudor England and missionaries sent abroad to the expanding European empires.

In Islam, the *shahīd* ('witness') is a similar concept: those who die in a *jihad* or holy war are considered martyrs, and are guaranteed a place in heaven. Shiite Muslims regard the martyrdom of Husain (in 680 AD), commemorated on the holy day of *ashura*, as the turning-point in their history. Sikhs commemorate the martyrdoms of two of their GURUS, Arjan and Tegh Bahadur. In Judaism, the six million Jews murdered during World War II are remembered as martyrs.

Karl Heinrich Marx *Marx was a student in Prussia (Germany) before moving to Paris, where he met Engels. They both spent some time living in Brussels until Marx returned to Germany and lived in Cologne. He was expelled from Cologne and settled permanently in London, where he is buried.*

Marx, Karl Heinrich (1818–83) German social philosopher, the most important figure in the history of SOCIALISM. Originally a disciple of HEGEL, Marx's involvement with radical groups in Germany and France during the 1840s led him to formulate a far-reaching critique of CAPITALISM, a system that he condemned as the major source of human alienation. Convinced of the centrality of economics to human life, he reversed Hegel's formulation that mind or spirit determines the course of human history, to develop the materialist interpretation of history that came to form the core of MARXISM.

Marx was thwarted in his ambition to follow an academic career at Bonn because of his radicalism. He helped to run (1842) an anti-government newspaper at Cologne, which in turn was suppressed by the censor. Moving to Paris, he met Friedrich ENGELS, and from then on collaborated with him in works of political philosophy. In 1845 he went to Brussels, joined (1847) the Socialist League of the Just, later renamed the Communist League, and in conjunction with Engels wrote for it the *communist manifesto* (1848). The outbreak of the REVOLUTIONS OF 1848 made it possible for him briefly to return to Cologne. Expelled soon after from most European countries, he finally settled in London, where he lived, supported by Engels, for the rest of his life. He envisaged a global political and social revolution as a result of the conflict between the working classes and the capitalists, who used the state to enforce their own dominance. His goal was to unite all workers in order to achieve political power. He was a key figure in inspiring the foundation of the First INTERNATIONAL and was later chosen as its leader. The ideological clash between Marx and BAKUNIN led to its disintegration in 1876. Marx's theories were developed at length in *Das Kapital* (1867; ed. by Engels, 1885–94) and inspired the COMMUNIST movements of the 20th century.

Marxism The system of economic and political ideas first developed by Karl MARX and Friedrich ENGELS and later developed by their followers together with dialectical materialism to form the basis for the theory and practice of COMMUNISM. At the heart of Marxism lies the materialist conception of history, according to which the development of all human societies is ultimately determined by the methods of production that people adopt to meet their needs. A particular technique of production determines first of all a set of property relations to organize production (for instance slavery, feudalism, CAPITALISM), and secondly the politics, religion, philosophy, and so on of a given society. The conflict between the particular social classes that emerged led to the next stage of social evolution. Feudalism had been followed by capitalism, which was destined to make way for SOCIALISM. In this way Marx and Engels sought to establish the centrality of classes and the class struggle. Their attention was focused on capitalist societies, which they viewed as increasingly polarized between an exploiting capitalist class and an impoverished working class. Marx believed that the development of industry would render capitalism obsolete, at which point the working class would be ready to overthrow the system by revolutionary means and establish a socialist society.

Marx and Engels conducted a detailed economic analysis of capitalism but said little about the economics and politics of socialism. After their death,

LENIN and his followers in the Soviet Union and elsewhere used Marxist ideas to underpin communism, the ideology later being dubbed 'Marxist–Leninism'. Other Marxists were critical of communist methods and regarded the Russian revolution (1917) as premature. Since then Marxists have had to grapple with the political and economic failure of the communist societies in Eastern Europe and elsewhere, with the rise of fascism in the 1930s, and the worldwide revival of free-market economics in the 1980s, all of which appear to contradict historical materialism. Hence to embrace Marxism wholesale now requires a considerable leap of faith. However, Marx's injunction that to understand a society we should first investigate its mode of production continues to influence many social scientists and historians who would not remotely regard themselves as Marxists.

Mary I (1516–58) Queen of England and Ireland (1553–58), the only surviving child of HENRY VIII and Catherine of Aragon. During her parents' divorce proceedings, she was separated from her mother (1531), never to be reunited. She was banished from court, declared illegitimate, and barred from the throne before being restored to the succession in 1544.

During the reign of her half-brother EDWARD VI she clung tenaciously to her Catholic faith. Then she outmanoeuvred Lady Jane GREY to win the throne, and appeared to enjoy considerable public support, despite being the first ruling queen since MATILDA. Many people had remained loyal to the old Catholic religious forms, and there was little opposition to her reversal of Edward VI's Protestant legislation, but her projected marriage to the future PHILIP II of Spain (1554) provoked WYATT'S REBELLION. She proceeded with the marriage, which turned out to be unhappy and childless.

After 1554 she relied increasingly on Reginald POLE for guidance in the reversal of Henry VIII's Reformation, except for the Dissolution of the MONASTERIES, and the revival of severe heresy laws. Between 1555 and 1558 nearly 300 Protestants were executed including CRANMER, Ridley, and LATIMER, earning her the name 'Bloody Mary'. She also lost popularity through her foreign policy. In 1557 Philip dragged England into the final phase of the European Habsburg-Valois struggle and England lost Calais, its last outpost on the Continent.

Mary II (1662–94) Queen of England, Scotland, and Ireland (1689–94), the daughter of JAMES II by his first wife Anne Hyde. She married William of Orange in 1677, and in 1688–89 supported her husband against her father during the GLORIOUS REVOLUTION. She always deferred to her husband and refused to become queen in 1689 unless he was made king. Her popularity both in the UNITED PROVINCES and in England enabled WILLIAM III to trust her with the administration of England during his frequent absences abroad. Her lack of children and her quarrel with her sister ANNE, the successor to the throne, saddened her last years.

Mary, Queen of Scots (1542–87) Queen of Scotland (1542–67), the daughter of JAMES V of Scotland and Mary of GUISE. She was betrothed to the future EDWARD VI of England in 1543 but Cardinal BEATON's veto led to war with the English, and the Scottish defeat at PINKIE (1547). Mary was then sent to the French court, where she received a Catholic upbringing under the supervision of her Guise uncles. She married the dauphin Francis (1558), who succeeded to the French throne in 1559 and died in 1560. By 1561 she had returned to Scotland, and had also proclaimed herself the rightful queen of England, as granddaughter of HENRY VIII's sister, Margaret Tudor.

She had to adapt to the anti-monarchical, anti-Catholic, anti-French atmosphere of Reformation Scotland. Her unpopular romantic marriage to DARNLEY (1565), although it produced a son, the future James VI (JAMES I), was disastrous. Darnley murdered Mary's secretary RIZZIO and was then murdered himself. Soon after she married BOTHWELL, despite having been abducted by him. The subsequent rising of the Scottish lords resulted in her military defeat and flight to England. There she threw herself on the mercy of ELIZABETH I, who kept her confined in various strongholds until her death. Wittingly or not, she was involved in a number of Catholic conspiracies against Elizabeth, figuring in the scheming behind the NORTHERN RISING as well as the RIDOLFI and THROCKMORTON PLOTS. Her implication in the BABINGTON PLOT (1586) provided enough damaging evidence for a commission to find her guilty of treason. For years Elizabeth had turned a deaf ear to Protestant pleas to execute this fellow monarch. Even now she delayed signing the death warrant, and then disclaimed responsibility for the execution of Mary at Fotheringhay.

Mary, Queen of Scots *The archetypal Renaissance princess, Mary was educated in several languages and was skilled in hunting and dancing. However, her marriages angered the Scottish nobility and led to her downfall.*

Maryland A state on the central east coast of the USA, at the northern end of Chesapeake Bay. It was founded as a proprietary colony by the Roman Catholic Lord Baltimore in 1632 and named after Queen HENRIETTA MARIA. It became a major tobacco producer. Despite its Toleration Act (1649) it suffered religious uprisings from Puritan settlers in the 1650s and a revolution in 1689, after which it became a royal colony, though in 1715 it reverted to being a proprietary colony. In the American War of INDEPENDENCE, Maryland was responsible for forcing other states to cede their western lands to the national government.

Masada A mountain fortress in the JUDAEAN desert, 395 m (1,300 feet) above the western shores of the Dead Sea. Between 37 and 31 BC HEROD the Great strengthened fortifications possibly dating from the 2nd century BC and added two palaces, a bath-house, and aqueducts. In 66 AD Masada was seized from its Roman garrison by the ZEALOTS, an extremist Jewish sect, who held it until 73 AD when, after a two-year siege, it fell to the 15,000 men of the Tenth Legion. The 1,000 defenders, with the exception of two women and five children, committed suicide rather than surrender.

Masaryk, Jan (1886–1948) Czechoslovak diplomat and statesman. The son of Tomáš MASARYK, he helped in establishing the Czechoslovak republic and thereafter was mainly involved in foreign affairs. As ambassador to Britain (1925–38), he resigned in protest at his country's betrayal by the MUNICH PACT (1938). On the liberation of Czechoslovakia by the Allies (1945) he became Foreign Minister, and was dismayed at the Soviet veto of Czechoslovak acceptance of US aid under the MARSHALL PLAN. At the request of President BENEŠ, he remained in his post after the communist coup of February 1948, but he either committed suicide or was murdered three weeks later.

Masaryk, Tomáš Garrigue (1850–1937) Czechoslovak statesman. As a member of the Austrian Parliament (1891–93 and 1907–14), he achieved fame by defending Slav and Semitic minorities. During World War I he worked with BENEŠ in London for Czech independence and for his country's recognition by the Allies. By their efforts Czech independence was proclaimed in Prague (1918) and he was elected President. He favoured friendly relations with France, Germany, and Austria, and was a strong supporter of the League of Nations. He felt that the rising NAZI menace required a younger President and he resigned (1935) in favour of Beneš.

Mason–Dixon line The line surveyed (1765–68) by Charles Mason and Jeremiah Dixon to determine the disputed southern border of Pennsylvania with Maryland. As the dividing line between a slave and a free colony, its name was later used to designate the westward boundary between slave and free states, 36° 30′ N, laid down in the Missouri Compromise (1820).

Massachusetts A state of the north-eastern USA, founded as a New England colony by the Puritan Massachussetts Bay Company in 1630. Persecution and economic depression in England drove some 20,000 people to emigrate in the 1630s, including leading Puritan ministers and gentry. They were granted a charter authorizing trade and colonization. The first governor, John WINTHROP, chose Boston as capital and seat of the General Court, the legislature, and established a strict congregational regime. Massachusetts fought a delaying battle against royal interference, but its charter was revoked in 1684 and direct government substituted. After 1689 it became a royal colony in which PLYMOUTH COLONY was incorporated. It played a leading role in the American War of INDEPENDENCE. After SHAYS'S REBELLION (1786), in which state troops had to defend a federal arsenal, its élite clamoured for a new federal constitution to strengthen central government. The Massachusetts constitution became a pattern for later US states.

Massey, William Ferguson (1856–1925) New Zealand statesman. He founded the Reform Party which campaigned for freehold tenure and free enterprise. As Prime Minister (1912–25) Massey also made extensive purchases of remaining MAORI land. He was challenged by militant unionists (RED FEDS) and broke the strikes of 1912–13, having enrolled farmers as special constables—'Massey's Cossacks'. He committed New Zealand manpower heavily in World War I, but his hold on domestic politics weakened with increasing urbanization.

mass production A system of industrial production involving the manufacture of a product or part in large quantities at comparatively low unit cost. The theoretical basis for mass production is provided by the concept of division of labour advocated by Adam SMITH in his book *The Wealth of Nations* (1776); this identified efficiency with the breaking down of a process into a large number of specialized operations. Probably James Watt in Britain was the first to apply the principles of mass production, when he designed standard and interchangeable parts for his steam-engine in the 1780s; while in the USA in 1798 Eli Whitney initiated the mass production of muskets by making highly accurate machine tools to turn out the various parts of the firearm. Its opponents during the 19th century, such as John Ruskin and William Morris, criticized the loss of a sense of craftsmanship, which was being replaced by monotonous factory operations. It was in the automobile industry, initially in the US Ford Company in 1913, that the age of mass production was fully inaugurated. AUTOMATION enabled standardized parts to be brought together on a moving assembly line in order to turn out standardized cars at low cost, but with high wages and profits. At the same time, time-and-motion studies were undertaken to analyse and improve efficiency. Mass production methods thereafter were steadily introduced into other areas of manufacturing, for example in World War II in shipbuilding and aircraft manufacture.

Masurian Lakes The scene of heavy fighting in East Prussia in World War I. In August 1914 two Russian armies advanced quickly into the region to relieve pressure on France, but were not fully prepared and the Lakes separated their attack. Prittwitz, the German commander, was indecisive, and only the despatch of LUDENDORFF to the Eastern Front and the resulting battle of Tannenberg saved Germany. In February 1915 Ludendorff continued his offensive. Taking advantage of frozen swamps, he captured four Russian divisions in the region of the Lakes.

Matabeleland ZIMBABWE.

Match Girls' strike (1888) A landmark industrial dispute in Britain. It involved the girls at the factory of Bryant and May in the East End of London, who complained about their low pay and the disfigurement of the jaw, nicknamed 'phossy jaw', caused by the phosphorus used in match-making. Annie BESANT, a journalist and a FABIAN, organized their strike. Demonstrations, partly to show their disfigurement, won public sympathy. Their success in gaining an increase in pay was a small-scale prelude to the growing strength of TRADE UNIONISM.

Mather, Cotton (1663–1728) American Puritan clergyman. The son of Increase MATHER, he became his father's clerical colleague in 1685. Immensely learned, often pedantic, he published nearly 500 works on theology, history, political questions, science, medicine, social policy, and education. Although he did not support the SALEM WITCH TRIALS, his *Memorable Providences relating to Witchcraft and Possessions* (1689) helped to stir emotions. After being passed over as president of Harvard, he helped found Yale University (1701), advocated Puritan involvement in social welfare, and championed smallpox inoculation. He was the first American-born member of the ROYAL SOCIETY.

Mather, Increase (1639–1723) American Puritan clergyman. The son of Richard Mather (1596–1669), who had helped define Congregational orthodoxy in 1648, he became a Boston minister in 1664 and married the daughter of John Cotton. He was a conservative president of Harvard College (1685–1701) but as colonial agent in London (1688–92) he negotiated a liberal royal charter for the state of Massachusetts. On his return he helped end the SALEM WITCH TRIALS. He was a forceful preacher against 'declension' (spiritual decline) as well as a prolific author, and was the foremost minister of his generation.

Matilda (or Maud) (c. 1102–67) The only daughter of HENRY I of England and, after the death (1120) of his heir, William the Aetheling, his only legitimate child. Married (1114) to Henry V, Emperor of Germany, Matilda returned to England after his death (1125) to be recognized by the English barons (1127) as Henry's successor. However, after her unpopular marriage to Geoffrey, Count of Anjou (1128), the barons accepted Henry's nephew STEPHEN as king (1135). Matilda's invasion of England (1139) and the defeat and capture of Stephen at Lincoln (1141) proved but temporary successes. She returned (1148) to Normandy but lived to see her son succeed Stephen as HENRY II.

Matteotti, Giacomo (1885–1924) Italian socialist leader. A member of the Italian Chamber of Deputies, he began in 1921 to organize the United Socialist Party. He openly accused MUSSOLINI and his BLACKSHIRTS of winning the 1924 parliamentary election by force, giving examples of attacks on individuals and the smashing of the printing presses belonging to opposition newspapers. Within a week he was found murdered. How far Mussolini was personally responsible is uncertain, but in January 1925 he took full responsibility for the crime, and proceeded to tighten up the fascist regime.

Matthias I (Corvinus) (1443–90) King of Hungary (1458–90). He was the son of the Hungarian leader and hero John Hunyadi. He was 18 on his father's death and

for the first few months of his reign he was under the control of a regent, his uncle. He had to repulse a military threat from Emperor Frederick III, and fight the Turks, before he was officially crowned in 1464. His reign saw almost continuous warfare; his military successes were based on army and fiscal reforms. In 1468 he accepted an overture from the papacy to lead a crusade to challenge the HUSSITES in Bohemia; meanwhile he continued to wage war against the Turks who remained a constant threat. After the death of King George of Bohemia (1471) Matthias was successful over Bohemia, and the Peace of Olomuc (1478) granted him extensive territories and the (shared) title of King of Bohemia. In 1477 his armies moved into Austria and in 1485 he beseiged and captured Vienna. As well as administrative reforms, he also codified the law, founded the University of Buda, and encouraged the arts and learning. At the time of his death he was lord of an empire that dominated south-central Europe but his successes were short-lived, as the JAGIELLON dynasty came to power.

Mattioli, Ercolo 'MAN IN THE IRON MASK', THE.

Maud MATILDA.

Mau Mau A militant nationalist movement in Kenya. Its origins can be traced back to the Kikuyu Central Association, founded in 1920, and it was initially confined to the area of the White Highlands, which Kikuyu people regarded as having been stolen from them. It imposed fierce oaths on its followers. It was anti-Christian as well as anti-European. From 1952 it became more nationalist in aim and indulged in a campaign of violence, killing some 11,000 Black Africans who were opposed to its brutalities and some 30 Europeans. Jomo KENYATTA was gaoled as an alleged Mau Mau leader in 1953. In a well-organized counter-insurgency campaign the British placed more than 20,000 Kikuyu in detention camps. Widespread political and social reforms followed, leading to Kenyan independence in 1963.

Mauritania A coastal country in north-west Africa, bounded by Morocco and Algeria on the north and by Mali and Senegal on the east and south.

Physical. Most of Mauritania lies in the Sahara. Except in the south-west corner it is arid, and everywhere it is hot. Inland from the Atlantic Ocean a region of smooth sand dunes slowly rises, over large deposits of copper and iron ore, to sandstone ridges and the granite highlands of the north-east of the country. In the east there are a few oases, where date palms grow, and in the south groundnuts and some cereals are cultivated.

Economy. Mauritania's exports are dominated by iron ore and fish. Agriculture, confined mainly to the Senegal River valley in the south, despite attempts to extend irrigation by constructing dams, includes the growing of millet, dates, and rice. Nomadic livestock-rearing has declined with periodic droughts and the expansion of mining. Apart from mining, industrial activity involves a small amount of light manufacturing. There are deposits of copper, gypsum, phosphates, sulphur, gold, and uranium.

History. Dominated from c. 100 AD by nomadic Berber tribes (who still form one-quarter of its population), Mauritania was first sighted by Europeans in the 15th century. French penetration of the interior began in

1858, and in 1903 the country became a French protectorate. In 1920 Mauritania was made a territory of French West Africa. It became an autonomous republic within the FRENCH COMMUNITY in 1958, and fully independent in 1960. Following the Spanish withdrawal from WESTERN SAHARA in 1976 MOROCCO and Mauritania divided between them the southern part of this territory, known as Tiris-el-Gherbia. Bitter war with the Polisario Front (who demanded Western Saharan independence) ensued, but in 1979 Mauritania relinquished all claims and withdrew, leaving Morocco to annex the formerly Mauritanian region. The country's first president, Moktar Ould Daddah, was replaced in 1978 by a military government, the Military Committee for National Salvation (CMSN), which assumed the power to appoint a President and civilian Council of Ministers. In 1991 the electorate voted overwhelmingly in support of a new constitution, establishing an 'Islamic, African, and Arab republic' with multiparty politics and an elected executive president. In January 1992 Colonel Moaouia Ould Sidi Taya was duly elected, having been first appointed President by the CMSN in 1984. In 1989 some 40,000 Black Mauritanians were expelled to Senegal, following ethnic violence in both countries. A border war with Senegal lasted from 1989 until April 1992. Ethnic tensions within Mauritania have continued.

CAPITAL:	Nouakchott
AREA:	1,030,700 sq km (398,000 sq miles)
POPULATION:	2.333 million (1996)
CURRENCY:	1 ouguiya = 5 khoums
RELIGIONS:	Muslim 99.0%; Christian 0.5%
ETHNIC GROUPS:	Moor (mixed Arab-Berber and African-Sudanic) 81.5%; Tukulor 8.0%; Fulani 5.0%
LANGUAGES:	French, Arabic (both official); ethnic languages
INTERNATIONAL ORGANIZATIONS:	UN; OAU; Arab League; Maghreb Union

Mauritius An island country in the southern Indian Ocean, about 800 km (500 miles) east of Madagascar; it is also the name of the chief island (the others are Rodriguez and the Agalega Islands).

Physical. The main island, Mauritius itself, is volcanic in origin and nearly 2,000 sq km (770 sq miles) in area, having steep hills and plains of lava, which have weathered into fertile soil. The slopes are forested, and the plains are green throughout the year with natural vegetation.

Economy. The main exports of Mauritius are textiles and sugar. Tourism is an important source of revenue. Tea, fruit, and vegetables are important agricultural crops. There are no significant minerals.

History. Visited by the Arabs in the 10th century and discovered by the Portuguese in 1511, the island was held by the Dutch (1598–1710), and the French (1710–1810). The British took it in 1810, and under their rule massive Indian immigration took place. Mauritius became an independent state within the COMMONWEALTH OF NATIONS in 1968. Sugar has always been the principal crop, and the fall of world prices in the 1980s resulted in a vigorous programme of agricultural diversification. Politically it has maintained stability as a multicultural state, with the Mauritian Socialist Party, led by Sir Aneerood Jugnauth, in power from 1982 until 1995. In 1992 the Party carried through a constitutional change, whereby Mauritius became a republic but remained within the Commonwealth. Caseem Uteem was elected to the largely ceremonial role of President in 1992. General elections were held in 1995 following the collapse of the government and the opposition alliance, led by Navin Ramgoolam, was elected.

CAPITAL:	Port Louis
AREA:	2.040 sq km (788 sq miles)
POPULATION:	1.141 million (1996)
CURRENCY:	1 Mauritian rupee = 100 cents
RELIGIONS:	Hindu 52.5%; Roman Catholic 25.7%; Muslim 12.9%; Protestant 4.4%; Buddhist 0.4%
ETHNIC GROUPS:	Creole 55.5%; Indian 39.6%; European 3.8%; Chinese 0.6%
LANGUAGES:	English (official); French creole; Bhojpuri; Hindi; other Indian languages
INTERNATIONAL ORGANIZATIONS:	UN; Non-Aligned Movement; Commonwealth; OAU; SADC

Mauryan empire (*c.* 325–185 BC) The first empire in India to extend over most of the subcontinent. The dynasty was founded by Chandragupta Maurya (*c.* 325–297 BC), who overthrew the MAGADHA kingdom in north-eastern India. He established his capital at Pataliputra, then expanded westwards across the River Indus, annexing some trans-Indus provinces deep into Afghanistan from ALEXANDER THE GREAT's Greek successors. His son, Bindusara (*c.* 297–272 BC), moved south, annexing the Deccan as far as Mysore. Although the third emperor, ASOKA (*c.* 265–238) soon renounced militarism, his reign marked the high peak of Mauryan power, for his humane rule permitted the consolidation of his father's huge empire. On his death decline quickly set in, and the dynasty finally ended with the assassination of Birhadratha (185 BC) by the founder of the subsequent Sunga dynasty.

At its height the empire was a centralized bureaucracy organized round the king. It was divided into four provinces, each headed by a prince, and revenue was drawn from the land and from trade. Royal patronage of Buddhism appears to have ceased on Asoka's death. Sources for the extent and character of the empire include the account of Megasthenes, a Greek envoy to Chandragupta's court, and the rock and pillar inscriptions of Asoka's reign. Examples of sculpture that survive indicate that the fine arts flourished during this period.

Maximilian (1832–67) Austrian Archduke and Emperor of Mexico. A brother of the Austrian emperor Francis Joseph, he was persuaded by the French emperor NAPOLEON III and Mexican royalists to accept the crown of the newly founded Mexican empire (1864–67). He soon lost the support of the conservatives by his liberal tendencies, and confirmed the hostility of Benito JUÁREZ's followers by ordering the summary execution of their leaders (1865). Maximilian's only protection was the presence of French troops, and, when these were withdrawn (1866–67), he took personal command of his soldiers. After a siege at Querétaro he was captured, tried by a court martial, and shot.

Maximilian I (1459–1519) King of the Romans (1486–93) HOLY ROMAN EMPEROR (1493–1519). By marrying Mary, daughter and heiress of CHARLES THE BOLD (1477), he added the duchy of Burgundy (which included the Netherlands) to the HABSBURG lands, thus earning the

enmity of France. He defeated the French at the battle
of Guinegate (1479) but the Habsburg–Valois rivalry
continued in the Netherlands and Italy.

In 1490 he drove out the Hungarians, who, under
MATTHIAS CORVINUS, had seized much Austrian territory,
and by the Treaty of Pressburg (1491) he was recognized
as the future king of Bohemia and Hungary. After
repulsing the Turks in 1493, he turned to Italy where
war was waged between French and Habsburg troops
until 1516. He was at a military disadvantage since the
German princes refused to finance his campaigns and,
despite allying with England against France, he was
forced to cede Milan to France and Verona to the
Venetians, and to sign the Treaty of Brussels with
Francis I in 1516. He was also forced to grant the Swiss
independence from the Holy Roman Empire in 1499.

Dynastically he had great success; his son Philip's
marriage to the Infanta Joanna (daughter of FERDINAND V
and Isabella) united the Habsburgs and Spain, and his
grandson's marriage to the daughter of the King of
Bohemia and Hungary secured his inheritance to those
lands. In Germany Maximilian's attempt to impose
centralized rule on the princes and cities was resisted,
since they were determined to remain self-governing.
His achievements were in increasing Habsburg territory
far beyond Germany, notably by linking it to Spain, and
thus to Spain's empire in the Americas.

Maya An indigenous people of Central America, the
dominant cultural and linguistic group in southern
Mexico, Guatemala, and the Yucatán peninsula until the
15th century. Their area of influence is divided by
archaeologists into a southern region – the Guatemalan
Highlands; a central region – the Petén (central
Guatemala), and regions to east and west called the
Southern Lowlands; and a northern region – the
Yucatán peninsula – called the Northern Lowlands. They
built cities throughout these regions: in the period c.
300–800 AD the Southern Lowlands were dominant with
sites like Tikal, Uaxactún, and Palenque; the emphasis
later shifted to the Northern Lowlands, at sites like
Chichén Itzá, Uxmal, and Dzibilchaltún. In the later
period (c. 1200–1450 AD) MAYAPÁN became the most
powerful city until it was overthrown in 1441 AD and
several smaller Maya states were established. In the
highlands Kaminaljuyú and San Antonio Frutal were the
earliest important cities, while Zacuelu, Utatlán, and
Iximché (forming the Quiché Maya state) were later
more important. All the regions had political and trade
connections with the cities of southern and central
Mexico.

Significant features of Maya culture include their use
of hieroglyphic writing, still only partly deciphered;
codices; the Calendar Round, a 52-year ritual cycle
combining a solar and a sacred calendar, and a 'Long
Count' calendar in which absolute dates were calculated
from a zero date (corresponding to our 3113 BC);
ceremonial plazas with steeply stepped pyramids,
temples, and vast multi-roomed palaces decorated with
several different artistic styles through the ages; the
ritual ball game; use of the corbel or false arch; and
their polychrome painted pottery.

Mayapán The most powerful MAYA city of Yucatán in
the late prehistoric period. In c. 1200 AD its ruler, Hunac
Ceel, conquered its principal rival, Chichén Itzá, and
dominated politics and trade until a coalition of other

cities, led by the city of Uxmal, defeated and sacked it in
1441 AD. Its circuit wall, over 9 km (5.6 miles), enclosed
an area, of 4.2 square km. (1.6 square miles) with nearly
4,000 structures inside.

Mayflower PILGRIM FATHERS.

May Fourth Movement Chinese nationalist
movement that began on 4 May 1919 with the student
protest in Beijing at the VERSAILLES PEACE SETTLEMENT
decision that Japan should take over former German
concessions in Shandong. In the New Culture Movement
that emerged intellectuals grappled with Marxism and
liberalism in their search for reforms. Socialist ideas
became popular, and the movement played a major role
in the revival of the KUOMINTANG and the creation of the
CHINESE COMMUNIST PARTY.

Mayhew, Henry (1812–87) British journalist. As a
young man he abandoned the law for journalism and
was associated with two periodicals before he helped to
found *Punch* in 1841. His chief work, *London Labour and
the London Poor* (1851–62), based on a series of interviews,
was a remarkable piece of reporting, combining
sensitive observation with shrewd economic and social
analysis.

Mazarin, Jules (1602–61) French statesman and
cardinal. An Italian by birth, he acted as an envoy for
Pope Urban VIII. From 1631 to 1639 he acted as France's
unofficial representative at Rome, and then joined
RICHELIEU's French service permanently. After the deaths
of Richelieu (1642) and Louis XIII (1643), he became
France's chief minister during the minority of LOUIS XIV,
deriving his authority mainly from his close
relationship with the queen mother, Anne of Austria.
He secured good terms for France at the Treaty of
WESTPHALIA (1648), but his decision to continue the war
against Spain led to the upheavals of the FRONDE
(1648–53). He survived that crisis, then brought the
Spanish War to a successful conclusion at the Treaty of
the Pyrenees (1659). His continuation of Richelieu's
policies enabled him to bequeath to Louis XIV the most
powerful kingdom in Europe.

Mazzini, Giuseppe (1805–72) Italian patriot and
revolutionary. The militant leader of the RISORGIMENTO
movement for a united Italian republic, his membership
of the CARBONARI led to his arrest and exile in 1830 and
to his formation of the YOUNG ITALY Society in Marseilles
the following year. In 1834 he led a fruitless invasion of
the Piedmontese province of Savoy from Switzerland,
was sentenced to death *in absentia*, and spent a period of
exile in London from 1837. During the REVOLUTIONS OF
1848, he was active in Italy. The flight from Rome of PIUS
IX led to his setting up the short-lived Roman republic
in 1849. This failure and abortive risings in Mantua
(1852) and Milan (1853) greatly weakened his influence
and he returned to London. He was considered a
dangerous and irresponsible agitator by CAVOUR and
played an insignificant part in events in northern Italy
of 1859–60.

Mbeki, Thabo (1942–) South African politician;
executive Deputy President since the country's first free
elections in 1994. Mbeki was a student activist in the
AFRICAN NATIONAL CONGRESS in the 1960s and was
imprisoned by the Pretoria regime for his activities. He
worked in the ANC's London information offices,
undertook military training for its armed wing

Umkhonto We Sizwe ('Spear of the Nation') in the Soviet Union, and represented the organization in other African countries in the late 1970s. He was elected ANC national chairman in 1989 and was a leading negotiator in CODESA (Commission for a Democratic South Africa), the body established by F. W. DE KLERK to oversee the transition from apartheid to multiparty democracy. Mbeki is regarded as the natural successor to Nelson MANDELA as President of South Africa, having already taken over many of the executive functions of government. He succeeded Mandela as leader of the ANC in 1997.

Mboya, Tom (1926–69) Kenyan political leader. He served as treasurer of the Kenya Africa Union and was the chief trade-union organizer in Kenya in the late 1950s. In 1960, as leader of the Kenya Independence Movement, he attended a conference in London on the future of Kenya, and was instrumental in securing a constitution which would give Africans political supremacy. In 1960 he became Secretary-General of the newly formed Kenya African National Union. After Kenya gained its independence (1963) he served in various senior ministerial posts. He was assassinated in 1969.

Mecca The capital of the HEJAZ province of Saudi Arabia, the birthplace of the Prophet MUHAMMAD, and the holiest city of Islam. Lying in a narrow valley in an arid region, it nevertheless prospered from trade and from the cult associated with its central shrine, the KAABA. Muhammad's teachings were strongly critical of his native city, and his life was crowned by the incorporation of pilgrimage to the Kaaba into Islam. Although it has retained its sacred character ever since, the city soon lost its commercial significance, its prosperity resting henceforth on the PILGRIMAGE. It was sacked in 930 by the Qarmatians, a radical ISMAILI sect, and fell under OTTOMAN suzerainty in 1517.

Mečiar, Vladimir (1942–   ) Slovak politician; Prime Minister of the Slovak republic (1992–94; 1994–   ). After serving the Communist regime of the former Czechoslovakia in a number of capacities, Mečiar was expelled as a dissident in 1970. He joined the Public Against Violence movement (the Slovak counterpart of the Czech Civic Forum) in 1989 as communism began to collapse in Eastern Europe. In the new Czech and Slovak Federative Republic, Mečiar, a populist nationalist, became premier of the Slovak region. He formed the Movement for a Democratic Slovakia (Slovak HZDS) to campaign for greater Slovak autonomy, which led to his dismissal. However, the following year, the HZDS won a resounding victory in assembly elections, hastening creation of a separate Slovak state in January 1993 with Mečiar as Prime Minister. He resigned following a vote of no confidence in March 1994, but won a general election in October.

Medes An Indo-European people who occupied Media, an area south-west of the Caspian Sea. It seems to have been Phraortus (*c.* 675–653 BC) who established the Median empire. His son Cyaxares (625–585) extended it and, in alliance with Babylon, conquered the Assyrians, capturing NINEVEH in 612. He was succeeded by Astyages, who added various Babylonian territories to his domain before being overthrown by a vassal, CYRUS II (the Great), who established the Persian empire of the ACHAEMENIDS.

Medicare The provision of medical care and assistance to persons aged 65 and over in the USA. It was introduced in 1965 by President JOHNSON as one of a series of reforms for his Great Society, which also included Medicaid for sick people with absolutely no personal resources. Both schemes were to be financed from social security taxes. President CLINTON attempted to reform the health-care system to provide cover for all US citizens but his plans were opposed by private insurance companies and in 1994 Congress voted against his proposed legislation.

Medici, Catherine de (1519–89) Queen consort of HENRY II of France. She was the daughter of Lorenzo de Medici and was married to the duc d'Orléans (later Henry II) in 1533. On the accession of her second son, Charles IX, to the throne of France in 1560, she acted as his regent and then as his adviser until his death in 1574. The outbreak of the FRENCH WARS OF RELIGION saw her abandon an initial policy of conciliation in favour of an alliance with the Catholic GUISE faction against the HUGUENOTS, which led to the ST BARTHOLOMEW'S DAY MASSACRE (1572), in which hundreds of Protestants were killed. After the accession of her third son, Henry III, she still ruled the court and tried once more to reconcile Catholics and Protestants, but was trusted by neither faction.

Medici, Cosimo de (1389–1464) Florentine banker, the first member of the Medici family to rule Florence. In Florence the struggle for power between rival patrician families was intense and Cosimo was expelled from the city in 1433 before triumphing over his rivals in 1434. The basis of his wealth was the Medici bank and he managed it prudently and expanded the family's financial dealings into other areas of commerce. In *c.* 1455 he owned a company for the manufacture of silk, two companies for the manufacture of wool, and a bank (all in Florence), and branch banks in Geneva, Bruges, London, Avignon, Rome, Milan, Pisa, and Venice. He was a keen patron of the arts.

Medici, Lorenzo de (Lorenzo the Magnificent) (1449–92) Italian Renaissance ruler and patron of the arts. Aged 20 he became joint ruler of Florence with his brother Giuliano. In 1478 the brothers were the targets of a plot organized by the rival Pazzi family and the pope: Giuliano was killed but Lorenzo survived. His main concern was the promotion of his family, and he was rewarded by seeing his second son become Pope Leo X. He was a collector of antiquities and was Michelangelo's first patron.

Medina A city in the HEJAZ province of Saudi Arabia, the second holiest city of Islam. Originally an oasis settlement called Yathrib, it welcomed MUHAMMAD after his HEGIRA from Mecca in 622 and became the first Muslim community. It grew rapidly until 661, and became known as Madinat al-Nabi – the city of the Prophet. When the UMAYYADS shifted the capital to Damascus, Medina declined and came under OTTOMAN control from 1517. The tombs of Muhammad and the caliph UMAR are both in Medina.

Medina Sidonia, Alonso Pérez de Guzmán, Duke of (1550–1619) Spanish nobleman. He succeeded to his title in 1555. In 1588 PHILIP II charged him with responsibility for commanding the SPANISH ARMADA against England. He begged to be relieved of the commission, on grounds of ill health and inexperience, but without success. He organized his fleet with great efficiency, and was by no means exclusively to blame for the Armada's eventual failure. He subsequently served Philip III.

megalith Large blocks of stone built into tombs and other monuments in western Europe in the NEOLITHIC to BRONZE AGE, *c.* 4000–1500 BC. They were once thought to have been derived from a single source, but further study and close dating suggest that that is too simple a view, and that many areas were involved.

While many monuments consist of separate stones raised on end as MENHIRS, stone circles (as at STONEHENGE), and avenues (as seen at CARNAC, in France), the same technique was often used in creating walled chambers. Roofs could be of horizontal capstones to make the so-called dolmens, or of oversailing courses of slabs, which are known as corbelled vaults. The largest block recorded is the capstone of the tomb at Browneshill, County Carlow, Ireland, estimated to weigh 100 tonnes. The movement, handling and dressing of such large stones, and, in some cases, their precise orientation, indicate that those responsible had considerable skill in mechanics, mathematics, and the organization of labour.

Mehemet Ali (*c.* 1769–1849) Pasha (or viceroy) of EGYPT (1805–49). An Albanian by birth, he rose from the ranks to command an Ottoman army in an unsuccessful attempt to drive NAPOLEON from Egypt. In 1801 he returned to Egypt in command of Albanian troops and by 1811 he had overthrown the MAMELUKES, who had ruled Egypt almost without interruption since 1250. Technically viceroy of the Ottoman sultan, MAHMUD II, he was effectively an independent ruler and reorganized the administration, agriculture, commerce, industry, education, and the army, employing chiefly French advisers, making Egypt the leading power in the eastern Mediterranean. He occupied the SUDAN (1821–23), and campaigned for the OTTOMAN government in Arabia (1811–18) against the WAHHABIS, and in Greece (1822–28), when his fleet was destroyed by a combination of British, French, and Russian navies at the Battle of Navarino (1827). He took Syria (1831–33) and defeated the Ottoman troops at the battle of Nizip (1839). Threatened by united European opposition, he agreed to accept the suzerainty of the Ottoman sultan in 1841 and in return was granted a request that his family be hereditary pashas of Egypt.

Mehmed II (Muhammad II, the Conqueror) (1430–81) OTTOMAN sultan (1451–81). He was frustrated while ruling briefly (1444–46) during the retirement of his father, MURAD II, but on coming to power backed expansionist factions, and by 1453 had achieved the long-standing Ottoman objective of taking CONSTANTINOPLE and thus uniting the European and Asian parts of the empire. Ceaseless campaigns brought further gains in the Balkans, consolidated control of Asia Minor, and took Otranto in Apulia, but failed to wrest Rhodes from the Knights of St John. He modernized his forces by equipping them with firearms and artillery, and created the institutional framework of the developed Ottoman state.

Meiji Constitution (1884–89) The constitution of the restored imperial Japanese state. Framed by ITO HIROBUMI and modelled on the existing German form, the Meiji Constitution was gradually developed from 1884 with the institution of a European-style peerage (1884), a cabinet system (1885), and a privy council (1888), and formally completed in 1889. It involved a bicameral system with an elected lower house and an upper house of peers, but effective power rested with the executive as representatives of the emperor, in whom ultimate power still resided. Although political leaders always experienced difficulties in controlling the lower house (which by 1925 was elected through universal manhood suffrage), policy in the earlier period was usually dominated by a group of highly influential senior statesmen, including such men as Ito Hirobumi and YAMAGATA ARITOMO, and later fell under military influence. The old constitution was finally replaced by a new JAPANESE CONSTITUTION, prepared under US supervision, on 3 May 1947.

Meiji Restoration The restoration of imperial rule in Japan, often defined as the overthrow of the Tokugawa SHOGUNATE in 1868, but sometimes considered to stretch from that date to the formal institution of the new MEIJI CONSTITUTION in 1889. The Tokugawa shogunate was faced by increasingly severe internal problems in the first half of the 19th century, and its failure to deal effectively with foreign incursions into Japanese territory resulted in the uniting of opposition forces behind a policy of restoring the emperor to full power. Faced by a powerful alliance of regional forces, the last shogun formally surrendered his powers to the Meiji emperor Mutsuhito, who resumed formal imperial rule in January 1868, moving his capital to Tokyo a year later. Thereafter, the feudal DAIMYO and SAMURAI systems were quickly dismantled, a Western-style constitution introduced, and a policy of government-sponsored industrial development implemented, which would transform Japan into a centralized modern state.

Meir, Golda (1898–1978) Israeli stateswoman. Born as Golda Mabovitch in Kiev, Ukraine, she was brought up in the USA before emigrating to Palestine in 1921. She worked for several organizations before becoming (1946–48) head of the Political Department of the Jewish Agency, and involved in negotiations over the foundation of Israel. She served from 1949 to 1956 as Minister of Labour, and from 1956 to 1966 as Foreign Minister. In 1966 she became Secretary General of the Mapai Party and in 1967 oversaw its merger with two dissident parties to form the Israel Labour Party. She was Prime Minister (1969–74) of a coalition government, and faced criticism over the nation's lack of readiness for the YOM KIPPUR WAR. She was succeeded by General Yitzhak RABIN.

Melaka MALACCA.

Melanchthon, Philip (1497–1560) German religious reformer. He became professor of Greek at Wittenberg in 1518, and came under the influence of LUTHER, whose teachings he helped to systematize. After 1521 he assumed an even more prominent role in the Reform movement: his *Loci Communes* (first published in 1521) was the first ordered presentation of Reformation doctrine; he took part in the Diet of Speyer (1529) and the Colloquy of Marburg (1529) and was largely responsible for drawing up the AUGSBURG confession (1530). A conciliatory man influenced by Christian HUMANISM, he was particularly active in reforming

Germany's educational system. In 1537 he signed the Schmalkaldic Articles (a statement on doctrine drawn up by Luther) with the reservation that he would accept the papacy in a modified form.

Melanesians The indigenous peoples of the islands of the central Pacific, lying between the Equator and the Tropic of Capricorn. This region, which includes New Guinea and the Trobriand Islands, contains a diversity of cultures, as well as many distinct languages, which are part of the Austronesian languages group. Melanesians were once assumed to be closely related to the NEGROIDS of Africa, but recent work on blood groups now links them more closely to the neighbouring Australoids and MONGOLOIDS of East Asia. The usual form of settlement is small villages, with the inhabitants practising shifting cultivation as well as rearing pigs and chickens, while hunting and gathering, as well as fishing, add to the basic crop cultivation. The region as a whole has been greatly affected by contact with Europeans; one result has been the growth of MILLENARIAN movements such as cargo cults.

Melbourne, (Henry) William Lamb, 2nd Viscount (1779–1848) British statesman. He was elected to Parliament in 1806 as a Whig, becoming Chief Secretary for Ireland in 1827–28. As Home Secretary (1830–34) he dealt harshly with agrarian riots in southern England in 1830–31 and gave reluctant support to the REFORM ACT OF 1832. Briefly Prime Minister in 1834, he upheld the sentences passed on the TOLPUDDLE MARTYRS. He became Prime Minister again in 1835 and the trusted adviser of Queen VICTORIA during the early years of her reign, remaining in office until 1841.

Mellon, Andrew William (1855–1937) US financier and philanthropist, who served as Secretary of the Treasury (1921–32) under HARDING, COOLIDGE, and HOOVER. Mellon opposed high expenditure by federal government, working to reduce taxes. He presided over the boom of the 1920s, convinced that government was an extension of big business, to be run on business lines. His tax-cuts purposely helped the rich to aid their investments which, he felt, would in time bring employment and other benefits to the less well off. In face of the accelerating Depression he had no policy other than increasing retrenchment. He donated his considerable art collection together with funds, to establish the US National Gallery of Art (1937).

Memphis The capital city of Egypt throughout the Old Kingdom (c. 2700–2200 BC). Tradition attributes its foundation to King Menes who supposedly united Upper and Lower Egypt, on whose boundary near the head of the Nile delta the city stands. It was the centre of worship of the god Ptah. The most impressive remains from the site are two colossal statues of RAMESSES II and an alabaster sphinx.

Menchú, Rigoberta (1959–) Guatemalan human rights campaigner. Menchú was born into a Quiché Maya farming family in the Guatemalan Highlands. Her community was subject to repeated atrocities by the state's security forces because they campaigned for humane working conditions and land rights; in 1979–80 her brother was tortured and mutilated and both her father and mother murdered. In danger of losing her own life, Menchú went into exile in Mexico in 1981 and began to publicize the systematic killing of the Maya

people. She helped found the UN working group on the rights of indigenous peoples in 1982 and was awarded the Nobel peace prize in 1992.

Mencius (Mengzi, Meng-tzu) (c. 372–289 BC) Chinese philosopher. His impact on China was second only to that of CONFUCIUS and he consistently championed Confucius's school. He argued that an individual's innate goodness would be revealed in the right environment. By pithy examples he demonstrated that a ruler who saw to the welfare of the state would attract all people to his sway; 'all under Heaven' would obey him. He argued that rebellion against oppressive rule is justified. Like Confucius he went from court to court but failed to win high office. His teachings later became part of the Chinese classics.

Mendès-France, Pierre (1907–82) French statesman. Elected as a Radical-Socialist deputy in 1932, he became an economics minister in the government of Léon BLUM in 1938. He was imprisoned by the VICHY GOVERNMENT, escaped to London (1941), and joined the exiled Free French government of General DE GAULLE. After the war he was critical of France's policy in Indo-China. He became Premier in May 1954, after the disaster of DIENBIENPHU, promising that France would pull out of Indo-China. He honoured this pledge, rejected the plan for a European Defence Community, prepared TUNISIA for independence, and supported claims for ALGERIAN independence. An austere economic policy led to his downfall in 1955. He served in the government of Guy Mollett (1956), but was unhappy with the constitution of the French Fifth Republic created by de Gaulle in 1958. He resigned from the Radical Party in 1959, after which he never had an effective power-base. He became increasingly opposed to the autocratic use of presidential power by de Gaulle and supported the bid by François MITTERRAND to replace him in 1965. He retired from political life in 1973.

Mendoza, Antonio de (1490–1552) Spanish aristocrat, appointed first viceroy of Mexico by CHARLES V. He served in that important position from 1535 to 1550 and provided the new colony with resolute leadership. During his administration he improved relations between Spaniards and Indians, fostered economic development, especially in mining, and lent his support to important educational initiatives for both the Spanish and Indian populations. In 1551 CHARLES V named him viceroy of Peru but he served in Lima for only a year before his death.

Menelik II (1844–1913) Emperor of Ethiopia (1889–1913). Originally ruler of Shoa (1863–89), with Italian support he seized the throne after Emperor John IV died. He made the Treaty of Ucciali (1889) with Italy, but when he learnt that the Italian wording of the treaty made Ethiopia a protectorate of Italy, he denounced the agreement. Italy's invasion and subsequent defeat at ADOWA greatly strengthened Menelik's position. He modernized Ethiopia, initiated public education, attempted to abolish slavery, and gave France a railway concession from DJIBOUTI, which opened up commerce. His conquests doubled the size of the country, and brought south Ethiopia into his domain.

Mengistu, Haile Mariam (1937–) Ethiopian soldier and politician; President of Ethiopia (1987–91). An army officer, Mengistu first came to prominence in 1974, when the army staged a successful coup against the regime of Emperor HAILE SELASSIE. Appointed acting chairman of the provisional army council, he became head of state in a second coup in 1977. With aid from the Soviet Union and Cuba, he made Ethiopia into a Marxist–Leninist republic, ruthlessly suppressing all opposition. He imposed agricultural collectivization and mass deportations. He pursued the war against the breakaway province of ERITREA, building his forces into the largest army in Africa. In 1984–85 his policies exacerbated one of the worst periods of famine and drought to affect the Horn of Africa, during which many thousands of Ethiopians died. In 1987 Mengistu introduced civilian rule; having banned all but his Workers' Party, he took the Presidency unopposed. After surviving one attempted coup in 1989, his downfall and exile came in May 1991, when a coalition of resistance movements from Eritrea and Tigray, which had made steady advances since the mid-1980s, overran Addis Ababa. In 1995 Mengistu, who had taken refuge in Zimbabwe, was found guilty *in absentia* of genocide in his native country.

menhir A standing stone. The practice of raising MEGALITHS on end spread widely in western Europe in the 3rd to 2nd millennia BC, and occasionally elsewhere. They could stand isolated, or in avenues as at CARNAC, or in circles as in Britain (STONEHENGE, Avebury). In some areas round the central Mediterranean they were given human features by the addition of carved breasts, shoulders, eyes, or weapons. Whether they were raised to commemorate the dead, to serve as places of worship or congregation, as route-markers, or as astronomical observation points remain matters for debate.

Mennonites A Protestant group founded in Friesland in the Netherlands by Menno Simons (1496–1561), a Dutch ex-priest who became an ANABAPTIST in 1536. In accordance with their emphasis on the autonomy of the local Church, Mennonite beliefs are varied, but they unite in upholding adult Baptism and PACIFISM, and rejecting worldly concerns in favour of withdrawal from society. Persecution drove many Mannonites to emigrate from Holland and Switzerland from 1663 onwards. There are now about 500,000 full members, mainly in North America. The Amish Church of the USA, whose members are known for the strict anti-modernism of their way of life, is a conservative branch of the Mennonites.

Menon, (Vengalil Krishnan) Krishna (1896–1974) Indian politician. A prominent spokesman in Britain for the Indian nationalist cause, he subsequently served as India's High Commissioner in London (1947–52) and as India's representative at the United Nations. As Minister of Defence (1957–62) he was heavily criticized for his autocratic decisions and for the defeat in the INDO-CHINESE WAR OF 1962, and he was forced to resign.

Menshevik BOLSHEVIK.

Menzies, Sir Robert Gordon (1894–1978) Australian statesman. From 1934 he served in the Victorian Parliament, representing the Nationalist Party and later the United Australia Party. He held various offices, including that of Deputy Premier. He moved to the federal Parliament in 1934, representing the United Australia Party. A conservative and avowed anti-communist, Menzies was Prime Minister from 1939 until

1941 and leader of the Opposition from 1943 until 1949, during which time he founded the Liberal Party to replace the United Australia Party. He was again Prime Minister from 1949 until his retirement in 1966. He unsuccessfully attempted to ban Australia's Communist Party (1951) and sent Australian troops to assist the USA in the VIETNAM WAR.

mercantilism An approach to economics that aimed to exploit natural resources fully in order to promote exports and limit imports. The term was coined in the 18th century to describe the previous century's commercial practices and beliefs. Mercantilists believed that the possession of gold or 'bullion' was all-important and countries without a source of precious metal must obtain it by commerce; a nation's wealth was seen as chiefly dependent on its balance of trade. Trading was controlled by government-backed companies, tariffs were imposed, and trade wars such as the ANGLO-DUTCH WARS were fought. Mercantilism is particularly associated with COLBERT, who hoped to strengthen France by improving its public finance, though in reality prolonged warfare meant higher taxes which weakened industrial prosperity. Later supporters of free trade (*laissez-faire*) opposed the mercantilist theory that the volume of trade is fixed and that to increase one's share one must lessen that of others. In a celebrated essay of 1752, HUME contradicted the mercantilist view, arguing that a country's bullion reserves were essentially determined by the size of its economy and its consequential need for MONEY as a circulating medium, and would not be permanently influenced either way by government interference with trade.

Merchant Adventurer Originally any English merchant who engaged in export trade. A trading company of Merchant Adventurers was incorporated in 1407 and flourished in the 15th and 16th centuries. It derived from loosely organized groups of merchants in the major English ports who sold cloth to continental Europe, especially the Netherlands. They acquired royal CHARTERS in cities such as Bristol (1467) and London (1505) and in their European settlements. They became dominant in England's foreign trade, ousting their rivals, the German merchants of the HANSEATIC LEAGUE. Until 1564 their principal continental market was in Antwerp, the commercial capital of north-western Europe; from 1611 they made Hamburg their foreign centre, but their main base had long been London. They were the forerunners of the great CHARTERED COMPANIES, and declined in importance in the 18th century.

Merchant Stapler (or member of the Company of the Merchants of the Staple) Any English merchant who traded in wool through the WOOL STAPLE at Calais, the fixed place for its marketing in continental Europe from the 13th to 16th century. The setting up of the Staple (which had between 26 and 38 members) had the effect of keeping down the price paid for wool in England, and thus of encouraging the rise of the English cloth industry and its merchants, such as the Clothworkers and MERCHANT ADVENTURERS. However, the Merchant Staplers were pre-eminent in English overseas trade well into the 16th century as a result of their monopoly in the trading of wool.

Mercia The kingdom of central England formed in the 7th century largely from the settlements made by the

Angles in the 5th century. The original communities in the valley of the Trent had been formed by tribes from the Fenland in the east and from the Humber estuary to the north. This loose tribal confederation was first welded into a kingdom in the 7th century through the military and political skills of its rulers PENDA and his son Wulfhere. The borders of Mercia were extended to meet Wales in the west, Wessex in the south, the eastern coastline, and the northernmost regions. In the 8th century, during the reigns of Ethelbald and OFFA, Mercian supremacy was recognized throughout England south of the Humber and by CHARLEMAGNE and the caliph HARUN AL-RASHID. In the 9th century Mercia collapsed dramatically and was partitioned between the DANELAW and Wessex (877).

Mercier, Honoré (1840–94) French-Canadian statesman. He opposed Confederation (1867) of the British North American provinces and founded (1871) the Parti National to represent the French element in Canada. He served in the Canadian House of Commons from 1872 to 1874. Elected to the legislative assembly of the province of Quebec in 1879, he became leader of the Liberal Party of Quebec in 1883, and in 1886, in the wake of the RIEL REBELLION, defeated the Conservatives to become Premier of Quebec. His immense popularity was eventually undermined by charges of corruption in connection with railroad subsidies, and in 1891 he was dismissed from office and defeated in the subsequent election. The new government acquitted Mercier of the charges.

Mercosur (Portuguese, 'Mercosul') A regional trade organization in South America, also known as the Southern Cone or South American Common Market. Founded in March 1991, with the aim of creating a common market in the area, Mercosur's member states are Argentina, Brazil, Paraguay, and Uruguay. Following protracted negotiations on tariffs, the final presidential accord to create the customs union was signed on 17 December 1994 and Mercosur was inaugurated on 1 January 1995. Chile joined as an associate member in 1996. Mercosur and the European Union signed a co-operation agreement in 1995 and pledged to open negotiations on the eventual creation of a Mercosur–EU free trade zone.

Meredith incident (1962) An episode in the US CIVIL RIGHTS struggle. Officials of the state of Mississippi defied a federal court order requiring the University of Mississippi to allow a Black man, James Meredith, to enrol as a student. The governor made defiant statements, thus encouraging thousands of segregationists to attack the federal marshals assigned to protect Meredith as he entered the university. President KENNEDY sent in national guardsmen and regular army troops to restore peace, enforce the court's orders, and secure the entry of Meredith as the university's first Black student.

Meroë An ancient city on the Nile c. 200 km (125 miles) north of Khartoum. It was the capital of the Kush kingdom from the early 6th century BC until c. 320–25 AD when it seems to have fallen to conquerors from AXUM. Excavation has revealed extensive remains of the ancient city, including palaces, temples, houses, streets, baths, and, not far distant, pyramids. It was an important centre of iron-working as early as c. 500 BC.

Merovingians A dynasty of kings of the FRANKS, named after Merovée (d. 458), the grandfather of CLOVIS. The Merovingians were warriors rather than administrators, few of them showing any interest in government. After the death of Dagobert I in 638, power passed from the kings to the 'mayors of the palace'. The mayor of the palace was originally the head of the royal household and came to represent royal authority in the country, administer the royal domains, and command the army in the king's absence. The most notable mayors of the palace were Pepin (ruled 687–714), CHARLES MARTEL (ruled 714–41), famous for his victories over SARACEN invaders from Spain, and PEPIN, the father of CHARLEMAGNE, who in 751 deposed the last of the Merovingian kings and usurped the throne.

Mesoamerican technology The technology of civilizations existing in the central region of the Americas before the European discovery of the continent in the 16th century. The MAYA civilization of southern Central America developed an urban civilization from about 300 BC, with cities of up to 40,000 people and well-developed systems of irrigation and terraced agriculture. The principal buildings were flat-topped PYRAMIDS on which temples were built; these and other major buildings were usually of stone, covered with plaster and stucco and then painted. Many houses had underground cisterns for drinking water.

In western South America the INCA empire reached its peak between 1476 and 1525. It had few large settlements but well-developed systems of agriculture, irrigation, and road communication. There was no written language, but knotted strings (*quipu*) were used for numerical records.

The AZTECS of Central America (13th–16th centuries) developed extremely large urban communities (up to 250,000 people), and a complex system of agriculture and commerce. The main city, Tenochtitlán (now Mexico City) was built on reclaimed swampland, and the Aztecs built dykes, canals, pipes, and aqueducts to carry water for drinking and for irrigation.

Mesolithic ('Middle Stone Age') The transitional period between the PALAEOLITHIC and NEOLITHIC ages. Its people were the hunting and gathering groups that existed about 10,000 years ago as the climate became warmer at the end of the last Ice Age. The term is most applicable to western Europe, where Mesolithic hunting societies continued to exist contemporaneously with Neolithic farming groups further east.

Mesopotamia (from the Greek, 'between rivers') The land lying between the rivers Euphrates and Tigris in the Middle East. This region is often referred to as the 'cradle of civilization', because of the many ancient civilizations that arose there. By the end of the 4th millennium BC a number of city-states had been established by the SUMERIANS in the south where agriculture (helped by irrigation), trade, and industry developed. The first Mesopotamian empire was forged by Sargon of AKKAD c. 2350 BC and lasted approximately 150 years. The second was centred on the Sumerian city of UR c. 2150–2000. Thereafter the area came under the influence of Amorites from Canaan, a new empire being established by Sumuabum in 1894 BC with its centre in BABYLON. Northern Mesopotamia had by this time been occupied by the ASSYRIANS. Both powers subsided with the appearance of more invaders from the north in the second half of the 2nd millennium BC, but the Assyrians re-emerged to create a great empire (744–609) that extended as far as Egypt. This was shattered by the Chaldean dynasty of Babylon, which also established a regime extending to the Mediterranean until conquered in 539 by CYRUS II (the Great). From then on Mesopotamia came under the aegis of several major empires – the ACHAEMENIDS, the SELEUCIDS, the PARTHIANS, and the SASSANIANS. Arab conquest (635–37), followed by a century of intra-Muslim rivalry with Syria, culminated in the ABBASID dynasty's building of a new capital, Baghdad. The area was devastated by Mongols in 1258 and 1401, and eventually became a loosely ruled part of the OTTOMAN EMPIRE. Mesopotamia is of cardinal importance as one of the first great civilizations of antiquity. Here urban life and a written language first developed, and excavation has revealed the area's artistic legacy.

Mesopotamia Campaign (World War I) A British military campaign against the Ottoman Turks in Mesopotamia (southern Iraq). In 1913 Britain had acquired the Abadan oilfield of Persia (now Iran), and when war broke out in 1914, it was concerned to protect both the oilfields and the route to India. When Turkey joined the war in October 1914, British and Indian troops occupied Basra in Mesopotamia. They began to advance towards Baghdad, but were halted and suffered the disaster of KUT. General Sir Frederick Maude recaptured Kut in February 1917, entering Baghdad on 11 March. One contingent of British troops reached the oilfields of Baku (May 1918), which it occupied until September, when the Turks reoccupied the area. A further contingent moved up the River Euphrates to capture Ramadi (September 1917) and another up the River Tigris as far as Tikrit (July 1918), before advancing on Mosul. Meanwhile from Egypt General Sir Edmund Allenby was driving north into Palestine and Syria, aided by Arab partisans organized and led by T. E. LAWRENCE, a campaign that resulted in the military collapse of Turkey in October 1918. After the armistice of Mudros (30 October), British troops briefly reoccupied Baku (November 1918–August 1919), aiming to deprive the BOLSHEVIKS of its oil and to use it as a base in the RUSSIAN CIVIL WAR. Britain had now occupied all Mesopotamia, and for a brief while considered the possibility of creating a single British dominion, consisting of Palestine, Jordan, Iraq, and Iran, linking Egypt with India and providing a bulwark against Bolshevism.

Mesopotamian technology EGYPTIAN AND MESOPOTAMIAN TECHNOLOGY.

Metaxas, Ioannis (1871–1941) Greek general and statesman. He became chief of staff in the Greek army, but was exiled (1917) when Greece joined the Allies in World War I. He returned (1920), and, after leading a coup, was exiled again (1923–24). A strong monarchist, he held several ministerial posts from 1928 to 1936. With royal approval he dissolved Parliament and became dictator of Greece (1936–41). Under him a united country successfully repelled an Italian invasion in 1940, but in 1941 Hitler's forces intervened and occupied Greece.

Methodist Church A PROTESTANT movement founded by John WESLEY in the 18th century. Stressing the individual believer's personal relationship with God, Wesley organized his followers into 'societies' with emotional class-meetings, regular attendance at which

was a prerequisite of membership. Wesley wished his followers to remain within the ANGLICAN CHURCH, but after his death Methodism's rejection of theological doctrine and traditional ecclesiastical authority led to its development as a distinct Church. In Wales the religious revival inspired by Howel Harris and Daniel Rowlands in the 18th century led to the establishment in 1811 of a dominant CALVINIST form of Methodism. The Church has suffered many secessions, especially of the Methodist New Connexion, the Primitive Methodist Church, and the Bible Christians. In the USA the Methodist Church divided into many groups, largely over attitudes towards slavery. In the 20th century the various Methodist bodies came together again, notably by the merging of the Wesleyan Methodists, the Primitive Methodists, and the United Methodists as the Methodist Church in Britain in 1932, and by the uniting of three Methodist Churches as the Methodist Church in the USA in 1939. This merged with the Evangelical United Brethren Church in 1968 to form the United Methodist Church. The United Methodist Church is the largest single Methodist church; it had almost nine million members in 1989. The World Methodist Council, founded in 1881, provides a link between the 40 million Methodists in the world.

Metternich Winneburg, Clemens Wenzel Nepomuk Lothar, Prince (1773–1859) Austrian statesman. At NAPOLEON's request he became Austrian ambassador in Paris (1806), and took part in all the major negotiations with the emperor. Following Napoleon's victory at Wagram, he returned to Vienna as Chancellor and Foreign Minister. As such he negotiated the marriage of Napoleon to Princess Marie-Louise. Following Napoleon's defeat at the battle of LEIPZIG he signed the Treaty of Paris (April 1814) with LOUIS XVIII and dominated the Congress of VIENNA, which followed. From 1821 to 1848 he was Austrian Court Chancellor and Chancellor of State. His 'system', based upon co-operation between the great powers and the suppression of revolutionary movements, created stability at the cost of liberal reform in Europe. He sought to maintain the AUSTRIAN EMPIRE, the majority of whose subjects were non-German speaking, against the forces of nationalism by the use of police despotism. In the REVOLUTIONS OF 1848 he fled to England, returning in 1851 to live in retirement in his castle on the Rhine.

Mexican-American War (1846–48) A conflict between the USA and Mexico. Hostilities between the two countries began shortly after the USA annexed (1845) the Mexican state of TEXAS and sought to expand the boundaries of the state to include still more territory. In the ensuing war General Stephen Kearny took over the New Mexico territory and Captain John FRÉMONT annexed the California territory almost without a fight. In northern Mexico stiffer opposition was encountered as General Zachary Taylor invaded from across the Rio Grande and defeated General Antonio López de SANTA ANNA in the bloody battle of Buena Vista (22–23 February 1847). The fiercest fighting occurred in central Mexico. General Winfield Scott's order of a mortar bombardment of Vera Cruz resulted in the deaths of hundreds of civilians. The US army then moved inland to Mexico City, where hotly contested engagements were fought at Molino del Rey, and Chapultepec Hill (12–13 September 1847). The US capture of the capital city (1847) occasioned the Mexican surrender. The Treaty of Guadalupe Hidalgo (1848) ended hostilities. By the terms of the treaty the USA confirmed its claim to Texas and gained control of the area that would later become the states of New Mexico, Arizona, and California (where gold had recently been discovered). The USA agreed to pay Mexico US 15 million dollars in return.

Mexican Revolution (1910–40) A period of political and social turmoil in MEXICO. The roots of the revolution can be traced to the demographic, economic, and social changes that occurred during the rule of President Porfirio DÍAZ, known as the Porfiriato (1876–1911). The regime became increasingly centralized and authoritarian, favouring Mexico's traditional and newly emerging élites, but failing to incorporate growing urban middle-class and labour groups into national politics. In 1910 Francisco MADERO, the leader of the Anti-Re-electionist movement, received an enthusiastic response to his call to arms to overthrow the dictator. Although Díaz resigned in May 1911 and Madero was elected President, he failed to satisfy either his radical supporters or his Porfirian enemies, and was assassinated in a counter-revolutionary coup led by General Victoriano HUERTA in 1913. Huerta was defeated by an arms embargo, diplomatic hostility from the USA, and a coalition of revolutionary factions led by Emiliano ZAPATA, Pancho VILLA, Venustiano CARRANZA, and Alvaro Obregon. The victorious revolutionaries split into Constitutionalists (Carranza and Obregon), who sought to reform the 1857 Liberal Constitution, and Conventionists (Zapata and Villa) who wished to implement the radical proposals of the convention of Aguascalientes (1914). The civil war which ensued was protracted and bitter. In February 1917 the reformed Constitution was promulgated. However, the document was largely ignored, and Carranza's procrastination prompted his overthrow and assassination in 1920. Mexico's new revolutionary leaders faced the difficult tasks of economic regeneration and the reconstitution of central political authority, but were hampered by strong opposition from the Catholic Church. Tension culminated in the so-called War of the Cristeros (1928–30), in which thousands of Christian peasants arose in protest against the new 'godless' state, and were finally defeated at the battle of Reforma (1930). When President Avila Camacho (1940–46) was elected, a period of consolidation and reconciliation began, marking the end of the revolution.

Mexico A country lying partly on the North American continent, bordering on the USA in the north, and partly in Central America, bordering on Guatemala and Belize in the south: it has extensive coastlines on the Atlantic and Pacific Oceans.

Physical. Geographically, Mexico divides into several distinct areas. The Isthmus of Tehuantepec, together with the eastern coastal plain and the north-eastward-thrusting Yucatán Peninsula, constitutes the main lowland area. In the far north-west, the splinter-like peninsula of Lower California, with its high sierras, is a southward extension of the Sierra Nevada. So also is the western Sierra Madre on the mainland, while the eastern Sierra Madre is an extension of the Rocky Mountains. The narrow plain facing the Pacific Ocean in the west is largely covered by forests, yielding

mahogany in southern areas, where rain is abundant. In clearings, sisal and sugar can be grown; on the mountain slopes, cotton, coffee, and tobacco. Between the mountains lie high plateaux where, in the more temperate climate, cacti grow. There are several large lakes from which streams run in torrents through deeply cut canyons. Most of the country is subject to humid trade winds from the east between May and August and tropical hurricanes from August to October.

Economy. Crude oil accounts for a majority of Mexico's foreign earnings, and oil revenues have been used to develop an industrial base. However, the economy has suffered from a massive external debt, with high unemployment. There is considerable mineral wealth, particularly oil reserves, silver, and zinc, as well as uranium and copper, not all of which has been fully exploited. Mexico supplies a quarter of the world's requirements in fluorspar. Mexico's main exports are chemicals, non-ferrous ores, motor vehicles, and petroleum products. Agriculture relies on irrigation. The main food crop is maize, and export crops include fruit, vegetables, and coffee. In 1993, Mexico concluded the NORTH AMERICAN FREE TRADE AGREEMENT with the USA and Canada. However, despite this and the establishment of *maquiladoras*—assembly plants set up in Mexico by mainly North American companies – large numbers of illegal emigrants enter the USA annually in search of work. Mexico City is the world's largest urban centre, with severe problems of pollution, infrastructure, and overcrowding.

History. In prehistory Mexico formed the greater part of ancient Mesoamerica, within which arose a succession of related civilizations which shared many cultural traits: socio-political organization based on cities; ceremonial plazas of pyramids, platforms, and temples; similar deities; calendrical systems; long-distance trading; and the ritual ball game. These civilizations included the OLMEC (Gulf Coast), MAYA (Yucatán), TEOTIHUACÁN (Central Valley), MIXTEC (Oaxaca), TOLTEC (North Central), and AZTEC cultures.

The conquest of the Aztec empire by CORTÉS was complete by 1521, and NEW SPAIN became the first Spanish-American viceroyalty, eventually including all of ancient Mesoamerica, northern Mexico, the Caribbean, and most of the south-western USA. A rigid colonial administration, characterized by repression and exploitation of the native population, lasted for the next 300 years. As much as 90% of the indigenous population had died of European-introduced diseases by the early 17th century, and thereafter their numbers only slowly increased.

In the early 19th century, inspired by French revolutionary ideas, an independence movement developed, led by two priests, Miguel HIDALGO Y COSTILLA and José Maria MORELOS Y PAVÓN, both of whom were captured and shot by the Spanish authorities (1810 and 1814). In 1821 Augustín de ITURBIDE briefly created an independent Mexican empire, which included the captaincy-general of GUATEMALA. Following his exile (1823), the first Mexican constitution was proclaimed (1824), based on the US constitution. Two parties, the Federalist and the Centralists, quickly appeared, and in 1833 the liberal federalist Antonio López de SANTA ANNA emerged as President. He was not able to prevent the declaration of independence of TEXAS (1836) nor the MEXICAN–AMERICAN WAR (1846–48), which resulted in the loss of huge territories, added to by the GADSDEN PURCHASE of Arizona in 1853. A period of reform followed, and a new constitution (1857) was promulgated. But economic difficulties and French imperialist dreams resulted in the imposition of the Habsburg prince MAXIMILIAN as emperor (1864–67). When French troops were withdrawn, Maximilian was defeated, captured, and shot. There followed the long dictatorship of Porfirio DÍAZ (1876–1910) and then the prolonged MEXICAN REVOLUTION (1910–40). Under President Miguel Alemán (1946–52), the process of reconciliation begun by his predecessor, Avilo Camacho, continued. Since then a succession of governments dominated by the PRI (Partido Revolucionario Institucional) have sought further to modernize the economy, bolstered by oil revenues. The presidency of Miguel de la Madrid Hurtado (1982–88) was faced by a fall in oil prices and one of the fastest growing birth-rates in the world. His successor, Carlos Salinas de Gortari, continued the austerity programme initiated by Hurtado, but at the same time entered into discussions with Canada and the USA, leading to the North American Free Trade Agreement, which was ratified in 1993. In spite of massive foreign debt, Mexico continued to enjoy the advantages of a strong manufacturing base, self-sufficiency in oil and natural gas, and large capitalist investment in a modernized agricultural system. The PRI candidate, Ernesto Zedillo, was elected President in August 1994 amid allegations by the opposition of electoral fraud. In early 1995 there was an armed uprising in the poverty-stricken state of Chiapas, led by an Indian guerrilla group, the ZAPATISTA NATIONAL LIBERATION ARMY (EZLN), who demanded social and economic reforms. Another guerrilla movement, the Peoples' Revolutionary Army (ERP), emerged in the south in 1996. Following mid-term elections in 1997 the PRI lost control of the Mexican legislature for the first time in nearly 70 years.

CAPITAL:	Mexico City
AREA:	1,958,201 sq km (756,066 sq miles)
POPULATION:	92.711 million (1996)
CURRENCY:	1 peso = 100 centavos
RELIGIONS:	Roman Catholic 92.6%; Protestant (incl. Evangelical) 3.3%; Jewish 0.1%
ETHNIC GROUPS:	Mestizo 55.0%; Amerindian 30.0%; European 15.0%
LANGUAGES:	Spanish (official); Amerindian languages
INTERNATIONAL ORGANIZATIONS:	UN; OAS; NAFTA

MI5 and **MI6** (Military Intelligence) Respectively, the Security Service and the Secret Intelligence Service in Britain. The sphere of MI5, founded in 1909, includes internal security and counterintelligence on British territory while MI6, formed in 1912, covers all areas outside the UK. During World War II, MI6's successful co-operation with RESISTANCE MOVEMENTS overseas contributed considerably to the outcome of the war. Since then, however, it has received adverse public exposure through disclosures that some of its employees, notably intellectuals recruited in Cambridge in the 1930s, such as Philby, Burgess, Maclean, and Blunt, were double agents whose final allegiance lay with the communist bloc. Strong evidence emerged in the 1980s of MI5's extra-constitutional role during the years of the Labour governments (1974–79), which it was seeking to destabilize. A campaign for more liberal legislation,

which would reduce government powers to keep secret matters that should be publicly known, has so far largely failed. Although a Security Service Act of November 1989 placed MI5 and MI6 on a 'statutory basis', the accompanying Official Secrets Act increased government powers against 'unauthorized disclosures' of official information. Stella Rimington, director-general of MI5 from 1992 to 1995, was the first head of MI5 whose identity was officially confirmed. Since the disintegration of the Soviet Union MI5 and MI6 have sought a new role, and in 1995 plans to use them in the fight against organized crime were announced.

Michael VIII Palaeologus (c. 1225–82) Byzantine emperor (1259–82). He usurped the throne of the young emperor of NICAEA, John IV, for whom he had been regent. He then recovered CONSTANTINOPLE and returned the Byzantine capital there, and was crowned Byzantine emperor. He attempted to reconcile the two branches of the church at Constantinople and Rome, though a voluntary union between them agreed at the Council of Lyons (1274) was for immediate political purposes and only lasted until 1289. His great rival was Charles I of Anjou and Naples; after the SICILIAN VESPERS (1282) Angevin power was reduced and Michael's successor, Andronicus, withdrew from the union with Rome, no longer needing the pope as an ally.

Micronesia A division of Oceania in the west Pacific Ocean (South Seas). Micronesia includes KIRIBATI, GUAM, the MARSHALL ISLANDS, NAURU, TUVALU, and the Federated States of MICRONESIA.

Micronesia, Federated States of A country in the west Pacific Ocean, comprising a group of islands divided into four states: Yap, Chuuk (formerly Truk), Pohnpei (formerly Ponape), and Kosrae.

Physical. The Federated States of Micronesia forms part of the Caroline Islands group, one of the archipelagos east of the Philippines. The islands are low coral caps surmounting submerged extinct volcanoes. The climate is tropical, and the area is prone to typhoons.

Economy. Micronesia's principal crops are coconuts (providing the main export, copra), cassava, breadfruit, and sweet potatoes. Industry is confined to garment production.

History. The first settlers on the islands were probably Melanesians who arrived in about 1500 BC. Micronesia was colonized by Spain in the 17th century and was sold to Germany in 1898. The islands were occupied by Japan from 1914 until their capture by US forces in 1944. In 1947 Micronesia became part of the UN Trust Territory of the Pacific Islands, administered by the USA. From 1965 there were increasing demands for autonomy and Micronesia became independent in 1979. The US administration was not formally ended until 1986 and was not ratified by the UN until 1990. A compact of free association was signed with the USA in 1982, giving the USA responsibility for Micronesia's defence. Micronesia's economy is weak and the country depends on financial assistance from the USA. Bailey Olter, first elected in 1991, was re-elected in 1995.

CAPITAL:	Palikir (on Pohnpei)
AREA:	701 sq km (270 sq miles)
POPULATION:	106,000 (1996)
CURRENCY:	1 US dollar = 100 cents
RELIGIONS:	Christianity

ETHNIC GROUPS: Trukese 41.1%; Pohnpeian 25.9%;
Mortlockese 8.3%; Kosraean 7.4%; Yapese
6.0%

LANGUAGES: English (official); Micronesian languages

INTERNATIONAL
ORGANIZATIONS: UN

Middle Ages

The period in Europe from *c.* 700 to *c.*
1500 (though this is not a period for which precise dates
can be given). The decline of the Roman empire in the
West and the period of barbarian invasions in the 5th
and 6th centuries (DARK AGES) was followed by the
emergence of separate kingdoms and the development
of forms of government. The coronation of CHARLEMAGNE
in 800 AD is held to mark the end of anarchy and the
revival of civilization and learning. England, under
ALFRED, similarly saw the encouragement of learning and
the establishment of monastic houses. Territorial
expansion by VIKINGS and NORMANS throughout Europe in
the 9th and 10th centuries, initially violent and
disruptive, led to their assimilation into local
populations. Trade and urban life revived.

The High Middle Ages (12th and 13th centuries) saw a
growth in the power of the papacy which led to clashes
between the pope and secular rulers over their
respective spheres of jurisdiction. The creation of new
monastic orders encouraged scholarship and
architecture. The obsession with PILGRIMAGE to holy
shrines was the impetus behind the CRUSADES, in which
thousands of Christian knights went to Palestine to
fight the Muslims and convert them to Christianity.
Society was organized on a military basis, the FEUDAL
SYSTEM in which land was held in return for military
service. But although war dominated this period, it also
saw the growth of trade (notably the English wool
trade), the foundation of UNIVERSITIES, and the flowering
of scholarship, notably in philosophy and theology
(SCHOLASTICISM). Gothic art and architecture had its finest
expression in the cathedrals built from the 12th
century.

During the 13th and 14th centuries various factors
combined to cause social and economic unrest. The BLACK
DEATH, and the HUNDRED YEARS WAR between France and
England, resulted in a falling population and the
beginnings of ANTICLERICALISM. In the 15th and 16th
centuries the RENAISSANCE in Italy marked a new spirit of
sceptical enquiry and the end of the medieval period.

Midlothian Campaigns

(1879–80) A series of speeches
by William GLADSTONE to mass audiences in Britain,
marking a new phase in party electioneering. Queen
Victoria and DISRAELI, the Conservative Prime Minister,
regarded the tactic as unconstitutional, but it helped
the Liberals to win a large majority in the general
election of 1880. The campaigns recognized the
importance of the new mass electorate created by the
1867 REFORM ACT, and of the growing influence of
newspaper reports of political speeches. Before setting
out by train from London to the Edinburgh
constituency of Midlothian, Gladstone addressed the
crowds, repeating this at stations where the train
stopped. The climax came in speeches at Edinburgh and
other Scottish cities in which he strongly criticized the
government. He gained the Midlothian seat from the
Conservative, Lord Dalkeith.

Mihailovich, Draza

(1893–1946) Serbian army officer
who, after the fall of Yugoslavia in World War II,
organized royalist partisans against German forces. He
structured his forces into bands (četa, prounced cheta),
and these became known as chetniks. Their relations
with the communist partisans of TITO were often
hostile. After Tito gained power, Mihailovich was tried
and shot for collaboration with the Germans and war
crimes.

Mikoyan, Anastas Ivanovich

(1895–1978) Soviet
politician. He joined the Communist Party in 1915,
taking part in the RUSSIAN REVOLUTION and fighting in the
RUSSIAN CIVIL WAR. He held several ministerial posts
(1926–55), mainly in the field of trade. He associated
himself with KHRUSHCHEV's denunciation of STALIN and
became his negotiator in Soviet relations with
discontented East European states. He was President of
the Praesidium of the Supreme Soviet (1964–65).

Milan

A city of northern Italy, the capital of LOMBARDY.
Originally an Etruscan settlement, in 222 BC it became
the roman town of mediolanum and developed into the
prosperous second city of the early roman empire. it
gave its name to the edict of milan issued by
CONSTANTINE in 313 which recognized Christianity and
gave universal religious toleration. Towards the end of
the 4th century its governor AMBROSE became its most
famous bishop. After CHARLEMAGNE defeated the
Lombards the city, which had briefly functioned as
capital of the old Western empire, was ruled by a
patriarch or prince-bishop. In the 16th century it passed
to Spain and in the 18th century to Austria. During the
Napoleonic era it became the capital of French-occupied
Italy. In 1861 it was incorporated into the kingdom of
Italy.

Miletus

One of the leading Ionian cities of Asia Minor.
It established a number of colonies on the Hellespont
and Black Sea coasts in the 7th and 6th centuries BC, and
traded widely. It continued to thrive even after coming
within CROESUS's sphere of influence, and in 499 led the
revolt of the Ionians against Persia. After its final defeat
in 494 it was razed, and never thereafter recovered its
former power. It revolted from the Athenian empire in
412, but then came under Persian control. The city's
economic decline was hastened by the silting up of the
harbour while it was part of the Roman empire.

military technology

WAR, TECHNOLOGY OF.

militia

A military force composed of citizens, enlisted
or conscripted in times of emergency, usually for local
defence. In England, it developed during the Middle
Ages from the Anglo-Saxon FYRD. Its forces were usually
raised by impressment (forcible recruiting), and until
the 16th century it was supervised by the local sheriff.
Then the Lord Lieutenants were given the responsibility
until the later 19th century. Control of the militia was
disputed in 1642 between CHARLES I and Parliament.
Parliament prevailed, but at the Restoration the militia
was again placed under royal command. It declined in
importance as a standing army emerged in the late 17th
century, a tendency that was repeated throughout
Europe. In colonial America, however, the militias were
the only form of defence and the so-called MINUTEMEN
played a significant part in the Revolution. The Militia
Act (1792) required every free, able-bodied, White, male
citizen between the ages of 18 and 45 to be enrolled in
the militia by local and state authorities. The law went
unenforced, and during the next century voluntary

militias developed into the National Guard, local organizations supervised, armed, and paid by the federal government.

Modern militias fulfil a variety of roles. Although generally restricted to infantry or light-armoured roles on land, in certain cases (for example, the US National Guard), they are also deployed in air and coastal defence. Such countries as Israel, Switzerland, and Sweden have based much of their defence planning on the use of militia units, and people's militias were a feature of former communist states such as East Germany and Czechoslovakia. Militia forces can also play an important role in internal conflicts, where they may be raised and controlled by factions; in such cases, the dividing line between militia and GUERRILLA forces can be blurred.

Mill, John Stuart (1806–73) Scottish philosopher and economist. Mill was strictly educated by his father, the historian James Mill, in the UTILITARIAN school of moral and political philosophy. His own contribution was to broaden the basis of that philosophy with insights from continental thought, especially the need for a historical understanding of contemporary institutions. The upshot was a sophisticated statement of LIBERALISM. In *On Liberty* (1859), he argued that a protected sphere of personal freedom was essential to individual self-development, and defended the principle that society might only interfere with an individual's thought or behaviour in order to prevent harm to others. His work *Considerations on Representative Government* (1861) outlined a political system that would combine widespread popular participation with the protection of minorities and a proper role for the intellectual élite. In *Utilitarianism* (1863), Mill expounded the view that BENTHAM's doctrine of the greatest happiness of the greatest number should be achieved through legislation. He was a leading exponent of CLASSICAL ECONOMICS, and wrote widely on economic issues, tempering a liberal belief in *laissez-faire* with enthusiasm for a more equal distribution of social resources. Mill was also an early advocate of equality for women – his *The Subjection of Women* (1869) remains a classic exposition of the case for female emancipation.

millenarianism (or millennialism) Belief in the imminent end of the present world order and the establishment of a new and radically different one. Millenarian movements, which are found all over the world in many different societies, usually occur at times of change and upheaval. The millenarian idea that divine or supernatural intervention will bring about a reversal of worldly expectations resulting in an earthly paradise, tends to appeal to those who are dispossessed both culturally and economically. Millenarianism may often be interpreted as a form of political or social protest; the world is perceived as dominated by enemies who will be overthrown by the forces of good. The awaited new order may be a return to a traditional way of life, as in the GHOST DANCE movement of the Native American PLAINS PEOPLES, or a fusion of both old and new, as in the cargo cults of Melanesia. Much millenarianism has its roots in the Jewish expectation of the coming of the Messiah. It takes its name from the early Christians' anticipation of Christ's Second Coming, to be followed by a millennium, or thousand-year reign of peace and tranquillity. In Christianity, the early expectation of Christ's imminent return to this world was replaced by

St AUGUSTINE OF HIPPO's allegorical model of an other-worldly City of God. Millenarian Christian beliefs thereafter became associated with dissident sects, and are found today in the beliefs of such groups as the Jehovah's Witnesses, Seventh Day Adventists, Christadelphians, and MORMONS. The idea of establishing Christ's kingdom on earth in the New World was found amongst 17th- and 18th-century settlers, and is echoed in an inchoate belief in the USA that the country's role in the world has God's backing. In Islam, SHIITE Muslims and sects such as the DRUZE await the return of the hidden *imam* or MAHDI; in the Islamic Republic of Iran, the spiritual leader, the *Walī Faqīh*, is stated to be the leader in the absence of the *mahdi*. The BAHA'I religion originates from a millenarian proclamation in 1844, the 1,000th anniversary of the hidden *imam*'s disappearance. For many Jews, the establishment of the state of Israel was the fulfilment of millenarian beliefs (see ZIONISM), and the Afro-Caribbean RASTAFARIAN cult envisages the Black people's repatriation to Africa. Millenarian beliefs are less prominent in Buddhism, but in Hinduism, Kalki, the last avatar of Vishnu, is expected to destroy the degeneration of this age and instigate a new cosmic era. The philosopher Bertrand Russell pointed out that even a strictly secular ideology such as MARXISM is patterned on millenarian beliefs in its expectation of an ideal society in the future.

Milner, Alfred, Viscount (1854–1925) British statesman and colonial administrator. As private secretary to G. J. Goschen when Chancellor of the Exchequer, he developed a capacity for finance, which he later applied in Egypt (1889–92) and as Chairman of the Board of Inland Revenue (1892–97). As High Commissioner for SOUTH AFRICA (1897–1905), his policies precipitated the Second BOER WAR, but he made preparations for peace in the settled areas by schemes of reorganization and reform, by which stability was given to the new South Africa. He joined Lloyd George's War Cabinet in 1916 and was Secretary of State for the Colonies (1919–21).

Milošević, Slobodan (1941–) Serbian politician; President of Serbia (1989–) and of the self-declared Yugoslav Federal Republic (Serbia and Montenegro) since 1997. Milošević trained as a lawyer and became director of the Belgrade Bank in 1978. He was elected as First Secretary of the Serbian Communist (later Socialist) Party in 1987 and won the presidential election in the republic two years later. A champion of Serbian hegemony over the constituent republics of the former YUGOSLAVIA, Milošević organized the intervention of the Yugoslav federal army in Slovenia and Croatia in 1991–92 and supported the secession of the Bosnian Serbs that began the war in BOSNIA-HERZEGOVINA in 1992–95. After putting pressure on his allies to resolve the Bosnian war through negotiation, he helped to bring about the Dayton peace accord in November 1995. Internally, his presidency has been marked by repression; he stifled agitation for autonomy by the Albanian majority in the southern province of Kosovo and used riot police to disperse demonstrations against him in Belgrade in 1991–92 and 1996–97.

Minamoto Yoritomo (1147–99) Japanese general, founder of the KAMAKURA Shogunate. His family, like their rivals, the Taira, had risen to prominence when imperial factions called for military support. In 1160 the

Taira, having slain his father, placed him under the surveillance of their HOJO kinsmen. Taira power reached its zenith in 1180 when Taira Kiyomori made his infant grandson, Antoku, emperor. However, by 1185 Yoritomo was master of Japan. The victories that swept him to power were won largely by his younger brother, Yoshitsune, later enshrined in history and legend as a tragic hero. After destroying the Taira's Inland Sea bases he annihilated their fleet on 25 April 1185 at Dan-no-ura at the southern tip of Honshu. Antoku was drowned.

In 1192 another child-emperor appointed Yoritomo as the first SHOGUN, whereupon he set up his military administration in Kamakura, which effectively became the central government of Japan. Yoshitsune and other Minamoto rivals had already been killed on Yoritomo's orders, but his supporters were given estates and were to become the basis of the DAIMYO. On Yoritomo's death Hojo Tokimasa, whose daughter had married Yoritomo, made himself regent. By 1219 Yoritomo's own line was extinct.

Minden, Battle of (1 August 1759) A battle in the SEVEN YEARS WAR. A French army seized the town of Minden, a German city guarding access to Hanover, but was surrounded by a large force of British, Hanoverian, and Hessian troops under Prince Ferdinand of Brunswick. On 1 August the French were severely defeated and Hanover was saved. This was the only pitched battle in which British troops were involved during the Seven Years War.

Mindszenty, József (born József Pehm) (1892–1975) Hungarian prelate. He was imprisoned by the Hungarian puppet government (1944–45) and sentenced to penal servitude for life, commuted to house detention. Freed at the time of the HUNGARIAN REVOLUTION, on the return of Soviet forces he sought refuge in the US Legation in Budapest, staying there until 1971.

Ming (1368–1644) The last dynasty of native-born Chinese rulers. It was founded by Zhu Yuanzhang, who in 1368 drove the Mongol YUAN dynasty from Beijing. Orphaned during a famine, he learned to read as a Buddhist novice and for a time begged for a living. As Emperor Hong Wu (Extremely Martial) he invaded Mongolia, brought YUNNAN for the time being under effective rule, and obliged KOREA to pay tribute. After YONGLE's reign (1403–24) the Ming abandoned expansionist policies. A hundred and fifty years of peace were marred only by the depredations of Chinese and Japanese pirates and brief Mongol incursions. Meanwhile the administrative system established by the Yuan was improved, for example by the appointment of provincial governors and governors-general. Great public works were undertaken. From 1517 Portuguese and other Europeans, traders and missionaries, appeared on the coast. The Portuguese were permitted to settle in MACAO whilst Matteo RICCI and other Jesuits were allowed into Beijing. During this period southern Chinese began settling in south-east Asia, where their presence has remained significant.

The invasion of Korea by the Japanese military ruler HIDEYOSHI in 1592 threatened China. Although the Ming successfully resisted any incursion into China, it destabilized the country. The MANCHUS began to make attacks on Beijing. Banditry became rife in the provinces, and the bureaucracy fell into disorder.

Pressure of population on fertile land brought famine and discontent. A rebellion by a bandit, Li Zicheng, which started in Shaanxi Province, cost a million lives. In 1644 Li occupied Beijing and the last Ming emperor hanged himself. The QING dynasty followed.

Minghuang (or Xuanzong) (684–762) TANG Emperor of China (712–56). He came to the throne when the Tang were at their zenith. An army he dispatched to prevent the Tibetans allying with the Arabs crossed the Pamirs and reached the Hindu Kush. In 745 the emperor took as his consort Yang Guifei, formerly his son's concubine, and began to neglect his imperial duties. In 751 the Arabs defeated the Chinese at the Talas River, resulting in the loss of earlier Tang gains in Central Asia. In 755 An Lushan, a general Yang Guifei favoured, rebelled and took Luoyang. The court fled from Chang'an, Yang was executed, and the emperor abdicated. The revolt, which dragged on until 763, was suppressed only by calling in Uighur troops from Central Asia.

Minoan civilization The civilization of Bronze Age Crete. The first great European civilization, it was named after the legendary King Minos by the British archaeologist Sir Arthur Evans, who first revealed evidence of Minoan culture in 1900.

Minoan civilization developed in Crete from *c.* 3000 BC, its two leading cities being KNOSSOS and Phaestus. The evidence of early Minoan pottery suggests a possible influx of settlers from the east and strong trade contacts with Egypt during the early Minoan period (*c.* 3000–2000 BC), though it is not clear whether the Minoan civilization originated with immigrants or grew from the previous NEOLITHIC culture. Minoan civilization enjoyed its greatest prosperity *c.* 2200–1450 BC, due largely to the Minoans' control of the sea, which for the most part rendered major land defence works unnecessary. The large Minoan palaces were of complex design, each centred on a large courtyard, with many staircases, smaller courtyards and rooms for cult worship. Magnificent frescos adorned the walls. Pottery, metal-working, gem-engraving, and jewellery-making reached high artistic standards. Bull-leaping seems to have been part of religious or magical rites. The palaces at Knossos and Phaestus suffered destruction *c.* 1700 BC— either through war or as a result of an earthquake – but were rebuilt. The exquisite freshness of the earlier painting was succeeded by a more grandiose style, which depicts, among other themes, the religious ceremonial of catching a bull by the horns and leaping over it. The delicate pottery was replaced by great wine jars and vases patterned with dark brown or red varnish on a light ground, with naturalistic floral or marine designs or running spirals. A further destruction occurred *c.* 1500 BC, and soon after that the massive eruption of the volcano on Thera (Santorini) which overwhelmed much of Crete.

MYCENAEAN invaders may have taken over Knossos *c.* 1450 BC. Within a century it had suffered its last major destruction. This final period was a prosperous one for the city, to judge from the grave finds and the continued occupation of the palace. Subsequently, however, the indications are of a civilization under pressure from outside, with communities forsaking the coast for safer sites in the mountains, though Knossos continued to be occupied.

The early Minoan period used a form of pictorial writing that c. 1800 BC was superseded by the still undeciphered Linear A. This in turn was superseded by Linear B, which represented an early form of the Greek language. It was a sophisticated society with the beginning of a palace bureaucracy that used written tablets.

minutemen American Revolutionary militiamen ready at a minute's notice to take up arms in defence of their property or country. Minutemen distinguished themselves in local short-term skirmishes and guerrilla actions such as LEXINGTON AND CONCORD, but proved so unreliable in long campaigns and pitched battles that George WASHINGTON turned to long-term recruits. The Second Amendment to the CONSTITUTION OF THE USA, guaranteeing the right to bear arms, is said to owe its enactment to the 'minuteman philosophy'.

Mirabeau, Honoré Riqueti, Vicomte de (1749–91) French orator and statesman. Until 1789 he led a life of violent excesses, and was often in gaol or exiled. He was the author of numerous political pamphlets, and when the STATES-GENERAL was summoned in 1789 he was elected as a delegate from Aix-en-Provence, for the Third Estate, not as a noble. At the royal session of 23 June LOUIS XVI disregarded the TENNIS COURT OATH and ordered the delegates to deliberate separately from the nobles and clergy. When they were ordered to leave the hall Mirabeau declared: 'We are here by the will of the people and will not leave our seats unless forced by bayonets'. He hoped for the establishment of a constitutional monarchy, allowing some power to the king, in which he hoped to play a major part as chief minister. He was the dominating figure in the events of 1789–91; in 1790 he established secret communications with the court and tried to advise the king but was opposed by the queen.

Miranda, Francisco de (1750–1816) South American revolutionary. He was a Creole born in Caracas, who received a commission in the Spanish army and fought against the British in Florida and the West Indies during the American Revolution. When that conflict ended with the independence of the 13 colonies he dedicated himself to the advancement of the same cause on the South American continent. From 1783 until his death he was the most active promoter of the idea of Spanish American independence. More successful as a political propagandist than as a military leader, he was ultimately captured by Spanish forces and died in a Cádiz prison.

missionary One who propagates a religious faith, especially to those of a different country or culture. Missionary activity has been a major feature of CHRISTANITY since its earliest days. Most Roman Catholic missionary activity is administered by the Rome-based Congregation for the Propagation of the Faith, known as the Propaganda. Foreign missions are run by the various religious orders and lay missionary societies who report to the Propaganda. Protestant missionary activity expanded with the development of trading companies and colonization from the 17th century. In the early 19th century a new missionary spirit was aroused in Great Britain, the USA, and Germany, through the growing evangelical movements within the Protestant Church. In the wake of IMPERIALISM, Roman Catholic and Protestant missionaries went to India, Africa, China, and to the South Seas from Europe. US mission societies took their faith to Native Americans, Black people (both slave and free), and Inuit (Eskimos) in the Arctic. Missionaries provided medical services and education as well as spiritual teaching; among noted missionary doctors and nurses have been David LIVINGSTONE, Albert Schweitzer, and Mother Teresa of Calcutta.

Following World War II, many states restricted proselytizing missionary activity, sometimes, as in China, for ideological reasons, and sometimes, as in the newly independent states of Africa, because it was felt to be a form of cultural imperialism through its association with the process of colonialism. The Second Vatican Council (1962–65) acknowledged such sensibilities in stressing the need to understand different peoples and cultures, whilst continuing to emphasize the importance of mission activity. The social aspects of mission work, such as medicine and education have increasingly become the preserve of governments and international aid agencies, which include among their number non-governmental organizations with a Christian complexion such as Christian Aid. The Christian emphasis on recruiting new converts is not found in other religions; in Islam conversion is deemed desirable, but it is not a religious duty, while in Orthodox Judaism the process of conversion is deliberately arduous.

Mississippi cultures A group of interrelated Native American cultures in the central and lower Mississippi valley from c. 700 to 1700 AD. Three principal new features distinguish them from the preceding HOPEWELL CULTURES. Most famous are the huge politico-religious centres of pyramidal, flat topped, earthen temple mounds, which were part of special religious practices, known as the SOUTHERN CULT. They were surrounded by the wattle-and-daub houses of farmers. Inspiration for these ceremonial centres was ultimately derived from the cultures of Mexico (Mesoamerica), but exactly how is unclear. Famous sites include Cahokia (Illinois), Aztalan (Wisconsin), and Macon (Georgia), with vast mound complexes, the last two fortified. A second feature was the much decreased importance of burial mounds, and a third was the appearance of completely new pottery styles, also showing indirect Mesoamerican influence.

Missouri Compromise (1820–21) A series of measures passed by the US Congress to end controversy over the extension of slavery in the territories beyond existing state boundaries. It was agreed that Maine would enter the Union of the United States as a free state and Missouri as a slave state and that slavery would be prohibited elsewhere in the LOUISIANA PURCHASE north of 36° 30'. This held out to the South the prospect of Florida and Arkansas being admitted as slave states, while securing the greater proportion of unsettled territory to the free North. The Compromise of 1820 temporarily laid the issue of slavery to rest, but the drawing of precise geographical lines between slave and non-slave areas led to fresh divisions.

Mitchel, John YOUNG IRELAND.

Mithras The central figure of a cult popular among Roman soldiers of the later empire. Scholars are divided as to whether there is real continuity between this cult and the reverence for 'Mithra', an Indo-Iranian creator sun-god, shown in much earlier scriptures of HINDUISM and ZOROASTRIANISM. The Roman cult focused on secret rituals in cave sanctuaries devoted to sculptures of Mithras killing a cosmic bull. Initiates underwent severe tests which demonstrated the cult's concern with the soldierly virtues of courage and fortitude. Women were excluded. Mithraism flourished along the empire's frontiers – the rivers Danube, and Rhine, and Britain – but finally succumbed to the challenge of Christianity.

Mithridates VI (Eupator) (120–63 BC) King of PONTUS in Asia Minor, which he led to its period of greatest power. He brought under his control the northern coast of the Black Sea and expanded his domains within Asia Minor. In 88 BC he swept through the Roman province of Asia, and then advanced into Greece, but his armies were crushed at CHAERONEA and he made peace with SULLA in 85. The second and third Mithridatic wars followed before POMPEY inflicted a final defeat on him in 66. He failed to re-establish himself in the Crimea and ordered one of his guards to kill him.

Mitterrand, François (1916–96) French statesman. A leader of the French RESISTANCE MOVEMENT during World War II, he was elected Deputy in the French National Assembly in 1946. He served in all the governments of the French Fourth Republic. Seeking to build a coalition between French parties of the Left – Radical, Socialist, and Communist – he founded (1965) the Federation of the Democratic and Socialist Left, when he stood for President against DE GAULLE, winning seven million votes. After standing unsuccessfully again in 1974, he was finally elected President of France in 1981. Early measures to decentralize government, raise basic wages, increase social benefits, and nationalize key industries were followed by economic crisis and a reversal of some policies. He was re-elected in 1988. A committed supporter of both nuclear power and a nuclear bomb for France, he advocated a strong foreign policy. His commitment to closer political and monetary union within the European Community was narrowly supported in a French referendum in 1992. He retired in 1995, having become France's longest-serving president.

Mixtec A people of the mountainous regions of Oaxaca, Mexico. Several of their historical codices survive, from which their dynastic history can be traced back to 692 AD, including their famous king Eight-Dear-Tiger-Claw. By c. 1000 AD they had formed a loose confederation of city-states and in the 14th century began to infiltrate the valley of Oaxaca where they sometimes fought, and sometimes mixed with, the Zapotec culture there.

Mizuno Tadakuni (1793–1851) Japanese statesman and reformer. As Chief Senior Councillor to the Tokugawa SHOGUNATE, Mizuno responded to the crisis engendered by famine, insurrection, and foreign pressure in the 1830s by instituting a comprehensive programme of social, political, and economic measures known collectively as the Tempo reform. He introduced strict price controls, abolished restrictive merchant guilds, and attempted to bring outlying lands under direct government control through a land requisition scheme. Opposition to the last measure led to Mizuno being driven from office in 1845.

Mobutu Sese Seko (1930–97) African statesman. President of Zaïre (now Democratic Republic of CONGO; 1965–97). He joined the Force Publique (Belgian Congo Army) in 1949 and was appointed commander-in-chief of the new Congolese army following independence in 1960. Following five years of chaos and civil war (CONGO CRISIS), he seized office as President in 1965. While maintaining order by harsh military discipline, he appointed civilians as ministers and struggled to give stability to the economy. As part of the programme of Africanization, he changed the name of the country in 1971 from Congo to Zaïre. In office for over three decades, he at first achieved some degree of political stabilization, while encouraging mineral exploitation and hydro-electric schemes by foreign companies. There were rebel invasions from Angola (1977–78), which he survived. Faced with growing criticism for corruption, in May 1990 he announced political reforms that would end the monopoly of power of his MPR party. A confused political situation developed, with unrest, strikes, and shootings. Mobutu was elected for the last time in 1984; in December 1991 he postponed new presidential elections, amid continued economic and political chaos. A High Council of the Republic was established in 1992 to implement democratic reforms but Mobutu responded by appointing his own rival cabinet. In 1994 a transitional constitution reduced the powers of the President and created a new legislature to implement democratic reforms. In 1996–97 Tutsi-led opposition to Mobutu's rule coalesced around the figure of Laurent KABILA; as Kabila's forces advanced from the east of the country, Mobutu relinquished power under international pressure and went into exile: he died shortly afterwards.

Mochica (Moche) A culture that developed c. 200–700 AD in the Moche and Chicam valleys of PERU. The earliest major civilization on the northern coast, it expanded into adjacent valleys, but was eventually eclipsed by the Huari culture to the south. Its rulers built huge pyramids of adobe bricks, known as Huaca del Sol (Temple of the Sun) and Huaca de la Luna (Temple of the Moon), south of Trujillo, which were painted with polychrome murals. They also constructed extensive irrigation works and fortifications round their ceremonial centres. Craftsmen mass-produced pottery bottles and bowls, including fine-quality water jars, painted with a variety of religious, military, and everyday scenes and its metal-smiths produced cast, alloyed, and gilded artefacts.

Model Parliament The English Parliament summoned by EDWARD I (November 1295) and subsequently idealized as the model for all parliaments because it was supposed to be truly representative of the people. In addition to seven earls, barons (41), archbishops, bishops, abbots (70), heads of religious houses, two knights from each shire, and two representatives from every city or borough, Edward called representatives of the lower clergy (one from each cathedral chapter, two from each diocese). The 'model' was hardly effective. Knights and burgesses did not attend regularly until the mid-14th century. Representatives of religious houses disappeared at the Reformation. The lower clergy preferred their own parliament, Convocation.

Mogadishu A city on the East African coast, now the capital of the Somali Republic. It is first mentioned in history in the 10th century as having the monopoly of the gold trade of ZIMBABWE, which it lost to KILWA in the 12th century, though it remained an important commercial port. It was visited by the Chinese admiral ZHENG HE c. 1432. In the Middle Ages a federation of leading families governed it under a sheikh, with a council of viziers and emirs. This Fakhr al-Din dynasty was succeeded in the 16th century by the Muzaffarids. Its prosperity depended on its relations with the nomads of the hinterland, with whom it was frequently at war.

Moguls (or Mughals) A Muslim dynasty of mixed Mongol and Turkish descent that invaded India in 1526, expanded over most of the subcontinent except the extreme south, and ruled in strength until the early 18th century. The first emperor was BABUR (1483–1530). He was succeeded by a line of remarkable emperors: HUMAYUN, AKBAR, JAHANGIR, SHAH JAHAN, and AURANGZEB. They created a strong administration for the rapidly growing empire, while the official attitude of conciliation towards the majority Hindu population encouraged religious harmony. Culturally, the introduction of the Persian language and Persian artistic styles led to a distinctive Indo-Muslim style in miniature painting and architecture, a legacy remaining today in the tombs and palaces of Delhi, Agra, and several other cities of India and Pakistan.

Internal and external pressure accelerated the weakening of central power during the 18th century. Rival court factions undermined the position of less capable rulers, allowing provincial governors to seize local power. The abandonment of conciliatory religious policies encouraged a resurgence of Hindu power, notably among the MARATHAS. Hostile invasions from central Asia revealed the hollowness of the dynasty's claim to all-India hegemony, so that by 1803, when Delhi fell to the EAST INDIA COMPANY, all real power had already been lost. For another half-century they enjoyed a 'twilight era' as nominal 'kings of Delhi', dependent on British goodwill, but in 1857 the last Mogul king was exiled and the title abolished.

Mohács A town and port on the River Danube, in Hungary. It was the site of two important battles: in 1526 the Hungarian Louis II encountered the invading forces of the Ottoman sultan Suleiman II there, and lost decisively. Louis's death led to civil war and the domination of most of Hungary by the Ottomans. In 1687 a second battle was fought there and an army under Charles of Lorraine routed the Ottomans.

Mohawks A North American Indian people, the easternmost of the Five IROQUOIS nations, living in eastern New York State, west of the MAHICANS. They were the first Iroquois to experience the impact of European trade goods, and as trade rivalry developed between tribes were the prime movers in establishing the Iroquois League. The effectiveness of Iroquois control over trade routes increased as warfare changed with the use of guns, obtained from the English and Dutch from c. 1640. After the destruction of Huronia (1647–49) peace treaties were signed with the French in 1653, 1667, and 1701 at Quebec. Jesuit missionaries converted many in the late 17th and 18th centuries and English missionaries began work among them in 1704. Many moved to new villages near Montreal in the 1670s

and other villages on the St Lawrence in the mid-18th century. In the American War of INDEPENDENCE most sided with the British and as a result any who had remained in New York were driven out in 1777 to join their relatives in Canada, where most remain today. In the 1980s, violent clashes broke out between militant Mohawks and Canadian police over the issue of land rights.

Mohenjo-daro The most important site so far excavated for the understanding of the INDUS CIVILIZATION, which flourished c. 2500–1500 BC. It is situated near the right bank of the River Indus, in SIND province, Pakistan. It is about a mile square, comprising a citadel mound on the west, and a larger lower city, laid out on a grid pattern, to the east. In the citadel is a brick bath, about 2.5 m (8 feet) deep, which was possibly used for ritual bathing. Other civic buildings included a large granary and an oblong hall which may have been a temple.

Mohicans MAHICANS.

Moldova A country in eastern Europe bounded on the north, east, and south by Ukraine, and on the west by Romania. Moldova is also the name of a wider region comprising lands between the Carpathian Mountains in the west and the Dniester River in the east, including the north-east of modern Romania.

Physical. The Prut river waters the western part of Moldova. Although landlocked, the country's proximity to the Black Sea gives it a mild climate. From the north into the centre runs a belt of hills with deep valleys in which vines and fruit trees flourish. Further south are steppes supporting grain, sugar beet, and tobacco.

Economy. Moldova's mineral resources are meagre, but the soil is fertile and agriculture prospers, with viticulture, fruits and vegetables, tobacco, grains, and industrial crops, such as sunflower seeds, of importance. Industry concentrates on food-processing, machinery, and other light industry.

History. Moldova at one time formed part of Bessarabia, control over which was long disputed between Russians and Ottoman Turks, Russian occupation being confirmed in 1812. Although granted autonomy from 1818 to 1828, this was succeeded by a policy of Russification. A nationalist movement developed from 1905 and in November 1917 Bessarabia declared independence, voting in December 1918 for alliance with Romania. In June 1940 the Soviet Union demanded the return of Bessarabia and of northern Bukovina, and the Moldavian Soviet Socialist Republic was created. The northern region of Bukovina and the coastal plain from the Danube to the Dniester went to the Ukraine. Romania briefly re-occupied the area in 1941, but the 1940 situation was restored in 1947. In August 1991 the country declared its independence from the Soviet Union as the Republic of Moldova. The regions of Dnestr and Gagauz, which have sizeable Russian and Ukrainian populations, also declared themselves to be separate republics, but their declarations were annulled by the Moldovan government. Ethnic violence broke out in the Dnestr region and Russian troops were sent in to protect Russian residents. A strong movement for unification with Romania increased inter-ethnic tensions. However, Moldova's first multiparty elections, held in 1994, were won by supporters of Moldovan independence. A new constitution granted autonomous status to the Dnestr and Gagauz regions but, despite the withdrawal of Russian troops from the Dnestr region in 1995 and the election of a pro-Russian Moldovan administration in December 1996, the situation remains tense. Moldova ratified its membership of the COMMONWEALTH OF INDEPENDENT STATES in 1994. In December 1997 the country's first presidential elections with a choice of candidates resulted in victory for Petru Lucinschi, who defeated the incumbent Mircea Snegur.

CAPITAL:	Chişinau
AREA:	33,700 sq km (13,000 sq miles)
POPULATION:	4.372 million (1996)
CURRENCY:	1 leu = 100 bani
RELIGIONS:	Eastern Orthodox
ETHNIC GROUPS:	Moldovan (Romanian) 65.0%; Ukrainian 14.0%; Russian 13.0%; Gagauz, Jewish, and Bulgarian minorities
LANGUAGES:	Romanian (official); Russian; minority languages
INTERNATIONAL ORGANIZATIONS:	UN; CSCE; Commonwealth of Independent States; North Atlantic Co-operation Council

Mollet, Guy (1905–75) French statesman. A long-serving General Secretary of the Socialist Party (1946–69), he served as Prime Minister in 1956–57 and participated in the events leading to the SUEZ WAR. During his ministry the war in ALGERIA also intensified.

Molly Maguires A secret US organization of Irish Americans (c. 1865–75). Its name was based on an anti-landlord organization in Ireland. It dominated the eastern Pennsylvania coalfields, campaigning against anti-union mine-owners and managers. Resorting to murder and intimidation of the police, it was broken after infiltration by a PINKERTON detective.

Molotov, Vyacheslav Mikhailovich (born V. M. Skryabin) (1890–1986) Soviet leader. He joined the Communist Party at 16 and as a student in Kazan was exiled by the Tsarist regime. He played a prominent part in the establishment of the official communist paper *Pravda*, and was its editor during the RUSSIAN REVOLUTION. Working closely with both LENIN and STALIN, he was instrumental in the compulsory nationalization of factories and workshops under the BOLSHEVIKS. For the next 40 years he remained at the heart of the Soviet political élite. He took a leading part in the liquidation of the Mensheviks, and in 1926 put down the ZINOVIEV opposition. In 1939 he was the Soviet signatory in the NAZI–SOVIET PACT and, after Hitler's invasion of Russia (1941), signed the Anglo-Soviet Treaty (1942) against his former allies. At the YALTA and POTSDAM CONFERENCES in 1945 he was Stalin's closest adviser. Surviving Stalin, he was expelled from all his posts by KHRUSHCHEV, who appointed him ambassador to Outer Mongolia. In 1984 he was rehabilitated within the Soviet Communist Party.

Moltke, Helmuth, Graf von (1800–91) Prussian field marshal. As chief of the Prussian General Staff (1857), he was the first European general to appreciate the revolutionary effect of railways on warfare. Men and equipment could be deployed over wider areas, and troops could be maintained in the field throughout the year. His ideas were proved in wars against Denmark (1864), Austria (1866), and France (1870).

Moluccas (or Maluku) A group of volcanic islands in eastern Indonesia. The Moluccas lie on the Equator between Sulawesi and New Guinea. They include the Bandas, Ternate, Tidore, and AMBOINA—the fabled Spice Islands, the source of cloves, nutmeg, and mace. In the 16th century they fell under Portuguese control. Although only newly converted to Islam, the islanders found in religion a focus of opposition to the Portuguese and later to the Dutch. Francis DRAKE visited Ternate in 1579. In 1599 the Dutch made their appearance and by 1666 they had subjugated all the islands. They exercised a tight monopoly, systematically destroying spice trees when over-production threatened. During the French Revolutionary and Napoleonic wars the British twice occupied the Moluccas. Following Indonesian independence in 1949, the south Moluccan islanders fought to secede from the new republic but were defeated by 1956.

Mombasa East African seaport. It was settled by Arabs in the 8th century and became an autonomous city-state and a centre for trade in ivory and slaves. It is mentioned by al-Idrisi, the Moroccan geographer, in the 12th century as a settlement of iron-workers and hunters. Vasco DA GAMA visited it in 1498, and the Portuguese admiral, Francisco d'Almeida, sacked it in 1505. The Turks tried to take it in 1589, and the Portuguese therefore built Fort Jesus, transferring their trading centre there. They lost it, and all the coast, to the sultanate of Oman in 1698. Omani administration of Mombasa was in the hands of the Mazrui family until 1837, when control passed to ZANZIBAR. After Zanzibar had been brought under British rule, in 1890, Mombasa became part of the East African Protectorate (later Kenya), Mombasa became Kenya's principal port.

Monaco A small principality located in the south of France in the hills above the Mediterranean Sea.

Physical. The ancient town and fortress perch on a rocky outcrop that projects into the Mediterranean. On this part of the Riviera, steep white limestone cliffs stand out along the coastline with sheltered intervening bays. The numerous caves and grottoes were long occupied by Palaeolithic peoples.

Economy. Tourism is Monaco's major industry, with gambling the chief attraction; the casino (built in 1861) has been state-run since 1967. Postage stamps also provide an important source of government revenue. Light industry includes electronics and pharmaceuticals. Financial and trading interests are a growing sector. Mineral resources are lacking, and agriculture is very limited.

History. Monaco was held by the Genoese from 1191 until 1297, when it passed to the Grimaldi family. The Grimaldis were allies of France, except for a period of allegiance to Spain (1524–1641), but Monaco was annexed by France in 1793 under the French Revolutionary Regime. The Congress of VIENNA returned the principality to the Grimaldis but placed it under the protection of Sardinia. In 1861 France restored Monaco's independence. Monaco adopted its first constitution in 1911, formalizing its status as a hereditary principality. A more democratic constitution was adopted in 1962, but the monarchy was retained. Prince Rainier III came to the throne in 1949. In 1993 Monaco joined the UNITED NATIONS.

CAPITAL:	Monaco-Ville district is the de facto capital
AREA:	1.95 sq km (0.75 sq miles)
POPULATION:	30,000 (1996)
CURRENCY:	1 French franc = 100 centimes
RELIGIONS:	Roman Catholic 90.0%
ETHNIC GROUPS:	French 46.8%; Monégasque 16.6%; Italian 16.5%
LANGUAGES:	French (official); Italian; Monégasque
INTERNATIONAL ORGANIZATIONS:	UN; CSCE

Monasteries, Dissolution of the (1536–40) The systematic abolition of English monasticism and transfer of monastic property to the Tudor monarchy, part of the English REFORMATION. Thomas CROMWELL, HENRY VIII's vicar-general, pointed the way ahead by commissioning the *Valor Ecclesiasticus* (1535), a great survey of church wealth, and by sending agents to investigate standards within the religious houses. An Act of Parliament (1536) dissolved monasteries with annual revenues of under £200. This provoked an uprising, the PILGRIMAGE OF GRACE. In its aftermath, Cromwell forced certain abbots to surrender larger houses to the king. Another Act (1539) confirmed all surrenders that had been, and were to be, made, and monastic lands passed to the Court of Augmentations of the King's Revenue, a state department. Resistance was minimal. By 1540 all 800 or more English houses were closed. Eleven thousand monks, nuns, and their dependants were ejected from their communities, most with little or no compensation.

The Dissolution had a number of consequences apart from the immediate wholesale destruction of monastic buildings and the despoliation of their libraries and treasures. The nobility and gentry benefited financially from the distribution of former monastic lands, which were used to form the basis of new private estates, and the laity gained a monopoly of ecclesiastical patronage which survived for the next three centuries. The termination of monastic charity and the closure of monastery schools stimulated the introduction of the POOR LAW system and the foundation of grammar schools.

monastery A community of monks living by prayer and labour in secluded, often remote, locations. Such communities, which are meant to further the communal and individual practice of ASCETICISM, are common to most religions. BUDDHA (*c.* 563–*c.* 483 BC) founded a monastic order, the *sangha*, and a code of discipline that was spread by missionaries throughout Asia and is still used. The *sangha*, remains an important element in Theravada Buddhism, with well over 250,000 members despite the hostility of communist governments in China and elsewhere. In return for food and support from ordinary people, monks and, less commonly, nuns offer pastoral advice, education, and religious example. There are also ZEN BUDDHIST monastic orders in which meditation is of prime importance. The 6th century revival in China of Daoism, with its emphasis on individual salvation, prompted the founding of many monasteries on the Buddhist model; however, from the 8th century elements of worship

were taken somewhat indiscriminately from both religions and from CONFUCIANISM. In HINDUISM monasticism takes the form of ashrams, or retreats, where the influence of a guru or holy man and practices such as yoga are important. In the Hindu concept of the four ideal stages of life āshrama, the last two stages, following parenthood, are devoted to contemplation and asceticism. The strictness of JAINIST monastic life, which may include self-mortification to the point of starvation, is perhaps unparalleled in the contemporary world. ISLAM did not fully develop a monastic organization until the Sufis formed the Rifaite and Mawlawite brotherhoods in the 12th century. Although monasticism did not become part of mainstream JUDAISM until the modern era, the Essenes, a messianic sect (2nd century BC) founded a remote community by the Dead Sea.

Christian monasticism evolved from the hermit communities founded in the 3rd century by men fleeing from Roman persecution to the Egyptian and Syrian deserts, where they sought union with God. Although St Antony (*c.* 251–*c.* 356) is usually regarded as the founder of Christian monasticism, it was St Pachomius (*c.* 292–*c.* 346) who founded the first organized community at Tabennisi in Egypt. Monasticism then spread rapidly in Eastern Europe through the Rule of St Basil (*c.* 330–79), the first known Christian monastic rule, and in Western Europe through the Rule of Benedict of Nursia (*c.* 480–*c.* 550). In the EASTERN ORTHODOX CHURCHES monasteries are still based on the Rule of St Basil, with its emphasis on repetitive liturgy. Orthodox monasteries, of which the most famous are at Mount Athos in Greece, are self-governing units which are not part of an order. In ROMAN CATHOLICISM, however, there are numerous orders whose members are often bound by vows of poverty, prayer, and meditation. In addition to their spiritual life, communities have practical functions, such as education and social work. The Benedictine order, whose regime is based on the original Rule of Benedict, emphasizes a balance of prayer, Bible reading, rest, and physical work. From the 10th century the reformed Benedictine Order at CLUNY in France (founded 909) built a series of 'daughter houses' which extended throughout Europe, all under the direct control of the powerful abbot of Cluny. The CISTERCIANS (founded 1098) also built monasteries in Europe and England, though these foundations enjoyed a semi-autonomous position and were only subject to the direct influence of the abbot of Citeaux at an annual council. The Cistercian Order follows the reformed Benedictine Rule; Cistercians of the Strict Observance (Trappist) form the largest contemplative order. Other orders were the Carthusians (1098), the Premonstratensians (1120), and the Gilbertines (1131). The Dominican Order, founded by St Dominic in 1220, and the Franciscan Order, founded by St FRANCIS OF ASSISI in 1209, were originally mendicant orders of friars, living from charity, although now most of their members are based in community houses. The Dominicans are particularly devoted to theological study and preaching.

Monasteries were an integral part of medieval life, as centres of pilgrimage, hostelry, medical care, and learning. Many of the poets and chroniclers of the Middle Ages were monks; monastery libraries housed the classical texts and biblical manuscripts that were the basis of contemporary scholarship. Monastic architecture combined the skills of mason and sculptor: the form of monastic building became more or less standardized in the 11th century, following the Benedictine model.

Monasticism in the ANGLICAN CHURCHES has become more prominent since the 19th-century Anglo-Catholic movement, with the re-foundation of some ancient orders and the establishment of new orders such as the Community of the Resurrection, founded in 1892. The ecumenical Taizé community in France, founded in 1940, is the best-known Protestant order. Although Christian monasticism is declining in Europe, it is expanding in the developing world and plays an important role there in providing educational and other welfare services.

Monck, George, 1st Duke of Albemarle (1608–70) English general, admiral, and statesman. He began his career as a Royalist and was taken prisoner during the ENGLISH CIVIL WAR; however, he was then given a command by Parliament and later completed the suppression of the Royalists in Scotland. In the first ANGLO-DUTCH WAR he fought three naval battles before returning to Scotland in 1654. He was trusted by CROMWELL, but after the Protector's death he acted to secure the restoration of CHARLES II in 1660, and he received many honours. Monck was placed in charge of London during the GREAT PLAGUE (1665) and FIRE OF LONDON (1666).

monetarism A school of economics that emerged mainly in the 1960s and 1970s, with Milton FRIEDMAN as its leading exponent. It is a revival of the CLASSICAL (pre-KEYNESIAN) approach to macro-economics. Monetarist models assume that money, prices, and wages are flexible but that aggregate output and employment will automatically tend towards an optimal equilibrium. Therefore government policy should concentrate on achieving and maintaining the stability of the price level, which monetarists believe depends on proper management of the money supply mainly through monetary rather than fiscal policy. Hence 'monetarism'. Moreover, there is a strong preference for a rigid and rule-based, rather than discretionary, conduct of policy. The right-wing administration of Margaret THATCHER in Britain (1979–90) and the military dictatorship of Augusto PINOCHET in Chile (1974–90) adhered strongly to monetarist policies.

money The general medium of exchange enabling goods and services to be valued in money terms and exchanged for money, rather than traded directly as would occur in a barter economy. In primitive societies goods were exchanged directly in such a barter system, a method that depended upon having suitable goods to exchange and hindered the development of specialization in trade. As trade expanded goods began to be exchanged for portable objects that represented an item of fixed value, for example an ox. Initially these objects included cowrie shells, stones, and precious metals. Coins of fixed values issued by a government first appeared in the 8th century BC both in Lydia, in Asia Minor, and in China. Early Lydian coins were made of electrum, a mixture of gold and silver, but under CROESUS they were made of gold and of guaranteed value. Britain's first coins, of silver and copper, appeared in the 1st century AD. Thereafter until recently most coins have been made of gold and silver, with copper and

bronze used for coins of low value. The style of a head on the obverse and a symbol on the reverse was very widely used from the 4th century BC onwards. Both clipping (cutting small pieces off the coin) and counterfeiting were common practices until the introduction of milled edges in 1724 made this more difficult.

This primary function of money entails three others: money is a unit of account, a store of value, and a unit of deferred payment (a unit of account over time). Historically, commodity money, then token money, and then debt money have developed. Commodity money is money in the form of an ordinary good with intrinsic use value (such as precious metals). Token money (such as banknotes) has an intrinsic value less than its face value. Banknotes were first issued by banks who undertook to pay the sum of money that appeared on the note from their deposits of gold. The BANK OF ENGLAND issued notes from its foundation in 1694 and banknotes are now the principal form of money in . circulation. Debt money is a medium of exchange based on a debt. In particular, a cheque or bank card draws on the debt of a bank to the holder of a bank deposit. Money markets deal in short-term lending and borrowing of money.

Mongkut (1804–68) King Rama IV of Siam (THAILAND) (1851–68). Mongkut remained a Buddhist monk for 27 years following the usurpation of the throne by his elder brother Pra Nang (Rama III) in 1824. After ascending the throne, he made a crucial contribution to the maintenence of Siamese independence at a time when the rest of South-East Asia was falling under European influence. His enlightened policies were continued by his successor, CHULALONGKORN.

Mongol empire An empire founded by GENGHIS KHAN early in the 13th century. The Mongols — loosely related nomadic tribesmen of central Asia who lived in felt huts (yurts) and subsisted on meat, milk, and fermented mares' milk (koumiss) — were united for the first time under his leadership. From Mongolia they swept out to Asia and eastern Europe. Splendid horsemen and archers, they encountered little effective resistance. Khakhans (Great Khans) elected from among Genghis's descendants continued his conquests. Central Russia, Poland, Hungary, Bulgaria, and Romania were overrun, but following the death of the Khakhan Ogodei in 1241 the Mongols withdrew to attend an election in their capital, Karakorum, in Mongolia. However, the GOLDEN HORDE remained in control of Russia. In 1245 an advance towards MESOPOTAMIA began. In 1258 Hulagu, Genghis's grandson, sacked Baghdad, but was defeated by the MAMELUKES at Ain Jalut (1260). The conquest of China, begun under Genghis, was completed 65 years later under KUBLAI KHAN.

The Mongol campaigns were notable for the death and destruction they left behind. But once the empire was established a great peace, the *Pax Mongolica*, descended. Travellers, of whom MARCO POLO was only one, passed to and fro between the CARAVANSERAIS of the empire. There was a steady flow of trade – and ideas and technology – between men of many lands and faiths. For a time NESTORIANS flourished in the steppe areas and parts of northern China. After Kublai shifted the capital to Khanbaligh (now Beijing), it became increasingly difficult to maintain the Khakhan's authority over remote parts of the empire. Quarrels over succession, corrupt and incompetent administration, and revolts accelerated disintegration. After 1300 the KHANATES were fully independent. By 1368 the Mongols were driven out of China and in 1372 a Chinese army burned Karakorum. TAMERLANE and BABUR both claimed descent from Genghis Khan.

Mongolia A country in central Asia, bordered by Siberian Russia on the north and China on the south. It was formerly known as Outer Mongolia (Inner Mongolia is now an autonomous region of China).

Physical. Mainly a high, barren plateau, Mongolia has mountains and saline lakes in the north-west and the Gobi Desert in the south-east. Although rainfall is light, there are areas of steppe on which livestock can be supported, and some grain is grown.

Economy. Mongolia is making the transition from a planned economy to a free-market economy. During the communist era aid from the Soviet Union enabled infrastructural and limited industrial development, but left Mongolia with a large foreign debt, and dependent on trade with Russia, including imports of fuel, equipment, and spare parts. The predominantly nomadic pastoral economy is based on animal-breeding, with meat, livestock, and wool the main exports. However, agriculture, particularly cereal production, is being extended. Mineral resources such as fluorite and copper are exploited. The free-market administration that won power in 1996 abolished all taxes on trade; however, the new market economy and restructuring by the IMF caused widespread unemployment and food shortages.

History. Although Mongolia is named after the MONGOLS, up to the 12th century they only controlled a small area near the sources of the Orkhon River, and other nomadic tribes, such as the Merkit and Naiman, held greater power in the Eastern steppes. In the 13th century, however, the Mongols swept out to create the MONGOL EMPIRE. In the 16th century they were converted to LAMAISM. During the 17th century the MANCHUS won control of Inner and then of Outer Mongolia.

Outer Mongolia remained part of the Chinese empire until the fall of the QING dynasty in 1911, although Russia mounted an increasingly strong challenge for the area in later years. While the neighbouring region of Inner Mongolia remained in Chinese hands, Outer Mongolia seized independence in 1911 and reasserted it after brief Chinese and White Russian occupations in 1919–21. Outer Mongolia became communist in 1924 as the Mongolian People's Republic and remained so, following a policy of alliance with the Soviet Union. In July 1990 it became a multiparty democracy but the Communist Party, now the Mongolian People's Revolutionary Party (MPRP), retained power under Dashiyn Byambasuren. Trade with the former Soviet Union fell and, with price deregulation, an economic crisis developed, with rationing of basic foodstuffs in January 1991. In 1992 the Prime Minister successfully negotiated commercial co-operation with Russia. The country, now called the State of Mongolia, adopted a new democratic constitution, which legalized private ownership. A general election, held in 1992, was again won by the MPRP. Punsalmaagiyn Ochirbat, first elected President in 1990, was re-elected in 1993, in the first direct presidential elections. However, in subsequent elections in 1996, the opposition Democratic Union coalition won a landslide victory and formed the first non-Communist administration for over 70 years. Presidential elections in 1997 resulted in victory for the Communist Natsagin Bagabandi.

CAPITAL:	Ulan Bator
AREA:	1,566,500 sq km (604,800 sq miles)
POPULATION:	2.334 million (1996)
CURRENCY:	1 tugrik = 100 mongo
RELIGIONS:	Buddhism; Shamanism; Islam
ETHNIC GROUPS:	Khalkha 77.5%; Kazakh 5.3%; Dorbed 2.8%; Bayad 2.0%; Buryat Mongol 1.9%; Draiganga Mongol 1.5%
LANGUAGES:	Khalkha Mongolian (official); minority languages and dialects
INTERNATIONAL ORGANIZATIONS:	UN

Mongoloids One of the major human racial groups, distributed widely through Asia from the Caspian Sea eastwards. They are also found on many islands off the Asian mainland and, as Inuits and Aleuts, in northern Canada and in Greenland. The AMERINDIANS, the other indigenous peoples of America, are also sometimes grouped with the Mongoloids. The prehistory of this racial group is unclear. The distinctive physical characteristics of Mongoloids could have developed in isolated populations in the Far East over a long period of time, perhaps many tens of thousands of years, independently of developments in Africa and Asia. In this scheme, which is not widely accepted today, there was a steady evolution from PEKING MAN to Mongoloid *Homo sapiens* in China. Alternatively, Mongoloids developed from a modern human stock that migrated to the Far East from Africa via western Asia and intermixed with indigenous populations. In this latter scheme, Mongoloid characteristics developed relatively recently in human evolution. In historic times, Mongoloids became more widely distributed with the rise of the MONGOL EMPIRE spreading to northern India, Persia, and Central Asia.

Monitor v. Merrimack (March 1862) A naval battle in the AMERICAN CIVIL WAR, the first between IRONCLADS. The troops of the CONFEDERACY had captured the scuttled Union (Northern) frigate *Merrimack* at the beginning of the war and converted her into an ironclad. In the early stages of the battle of Hampton Roads, the *Merrimack* (now renamed *Virginia*) easily defeated a blockading Union squadron. She was then confronted by the *Monitor*, a revolutionary warship designed around a large revolving armoured turret. In the resulting five-hour duel neither vessel was able to inflict major damage on the other, but the Confederate threat to the blockade was countered. Neither vessel played any further part in the war but they had altered the nature of naval combat.

monks MONASTERY.

Monmouth's Rebellion (1685) An insurrection in south-west England against JAMES II, led by the Duke of Monmouth (1649–85), illegitimate son of CHARLES II. Monmouth had failed to gain any political benefit from the crises of his father's reign other than popularity, which was due more to his Protestantism and lenient treatment of rebels than to his rather meagre talents. Following the accession of the Roman Catholic James, the Duke of Argyll led a revolt in Scotland and persuaded Monmouth to launch a rebellion in the south-west. He landed at Lyme Regis in Dorset, and was proclaimed king at Taunton, but could muster only limited support. He failed to take Bristol and, with forces inferior in training, experience, and equipment to the king's army, was routed at SEDGEMOOR. Monmouth was captured a few days later and executed; his followers were harshly punished by the BLOODY ASSIZES.

Monnet, Jean (1888–1979) French economist and administrator. In 1947 he devised and became commissioner-general of a plan bearing his name, whose object was to restore the French economy by means of centralized planning. Monnet was an internationalist and campaigned for European unification, working out the details of the SCHUMAN PLAN and later becoming the first President of the High Authority of the European Coal and Steel Community (1952–55).

Monomatapa MWENE MUTAPA.

Monroe, James (1758–1831) Fifth President of the USA (1817–25). A member of the Virginia legislature (1782–83), the Continental Congress (1783–86), and the Senate (1790–94), Monroe emerged as a firm supporter of STATES' RIGHTS and an opponent of the FEDERALISTS. After serving as minister to France (1794–96) and Governor of Virginia (1799–1802), his political fortunes were transformed by the electoral triumph of the Democratic Republicans under Thomas JEFFERSON. He helped to negotiate the LOUISIANA PURCHASE and served as minister to England, before becoming Secretary of War (1814–15) in the MADISON administration. With Republican power well entrenched, Monroe easily won the presidential election of 1816 and repeated the triumph in 1820. His tenure of office saw the temporary settlement of the slavery issue in the MISSOURI COMPROMISE, the settlement of the Canadian boundary dispute, successful expansion into Florida, and the enunciation of the MONROE DOCTRINE.

Monroe Doctrine US foreign policy declaration warning European powers against further colonization in the New World and against intervention in the governments of the American hemisphere; it also disclaimed any intention of the USA to take part in the political affairs of Europe. The background of the doctrine, spelt out in President James MONROE's annual message to Congress in 1823, was the threat of intervention by the HOLY ALLIANCE to restore Spain's South American colonies, and the aggressive attitude of Russia on the north-west coast of America. The doctrine was infrequently invoked in the 19th century, but after the development of territorial interests in Central America and the Caribbean it became a tenet of US foreign policy. During the early 20th century it developed into a policy whereby the USA regarded itself as responsible for the security of North and South America; this consistently complicated relations with Latin American countries.

Mons Inhabitants of MYANMAR (Burma), akin to the KHMERS of Cambodia. They early established themselves in the Irrawaddy delta, adopted an Indian script that spread throughout Burma, and were converted to Theravada BUDDHISM brought by missionaries from South India and Ceylon. By 825 they had established themselves in Lower Burma and founded the city of Pegu. In the 11th century they were conquered by PAGAN, but after its collapse retained a shadowy rule in the south until overthrown by the TOUNGOO in 1539. They in turn overthrew the Toungoo in 1752 but in 1757 lost their independence to Alaungpaya, the founder of the Konbaung dynasty. Many of the Mons were killed; others fled to Siam.

Montagu-Chelmsford Proposals (1918) Constitutional proposals for British India. They were made in the Report on Indian Constitutional Reforms (1918) by Edwin Montagu (1879–1924), Secretary of State for India, and Frederick John Thesiger, 3rd Baron Chelmsford (1868–1933), governor-general of India (1916–21). They followed the promise of responsible government made in 1917, and envisaged a gradual progress towards devolution of power and Indian self-government. In some ways the Government of India Act (1919) which followed can be seen as a measure to shore up imperial authority by containing opposition; it was regarded by Indian nationalists as inadequate and not a full implementation of the proposals.

Montcalm-Gozon, Louis-Joseph, Marquis de (1712–59) French general. He fought in the Rhineland, Bohemia, and Italy before his appointment as commander in Canada in the FRENCH AND INDIAN WAR (1756). Though initially victorious at Fort Oswego (1756), Fort William Henry (1757), and Ticonderoga (1758), he was surprised by WOLFE's daring attack on Quebec in 1759 and defeated on the PLAINS OF ABRAHAM (1759).

Montenegro The smallest of the constituent republics of the former YUGOSLAVIA. Montenegro borders SERBIA in the north-east, ALBANIA in the south, and BOSNIA-HERZEGOVINA in the north-west. It has a long Adriatic coastline. The south-western part of the republic is a limestone plateau, while the eastern part is mainly forest and fertile highlands. Agriculture consists mainly of sheep- and goat-raising.

History. The only southern Slavic nation to remain outside the Ottoman empire, it engaged in the BALKAN WAR under Nicholas Petrovic Njegos (1910–18) and greatly extended its territory. Having deposed Nicholas in 1918, it became a province of the new kingdom of Serbs, Croats, and Slovenes, which was renamed Yugoslavia in 1929. It was the scene of bitter fighting in World War II, and accepted the federal constitution of Marshal TITO in 1946. A strong spirit of independence survived, yet in the first multiparty elections in December 1990, the Communists held power. When Yugoslavia disintegrated during 1991 Montenegro remained in alliance with Serbia, a decision confirmed by a referendum in 1992. That same year Serbia and Montenegro declared themselves to be an independent country, the Federal Republic of Yugoslavia, but this entity has not so far been recognized by many other countries, owing to Serbian involvement in the civil war in Bosnia-Herzegovina (1992–95). In 1996–97 there was growing friction between Montenegro and the authoritarian government in Belgrade.

Montespan, Francoise Athénais, Marquise de (1641–1707) Mistress of LOUIS XIV (in succession to Mademoiselle de la Vallière) from c. 1667. She had several children by the king and employed as their governess the future Madame de Maintenon. The king was tiring of her by the late 1670s, and her influence was finally destroyed by her implication in the *affaire des poisons*, when she was accused of involvement in black magic.

Montesquieu, Charles de Secondat, Baron de la Brède et de (1689–1755) French political philosopher and man of letters. Trained as a lawyer, in 1721 Montesquieu published the *Lettres persanes*, a fictional account in letter form of the visit of two Persians to Paris. The tale provided him with a vehicle to criticize the abuses of Church and State in contemporary France. His other major claim to fame is his treatise *De l'Esprit des lois* (1748), a comparative study of the origin and nature of the laws governing society, showing his preference for the system of constitutional monarchy established in Britain. In this work Montesquieu carefully described the SEPARATION OF POWERS into executive, judicial, and legislative that influenced the makers of the CONSTITUTION OF THE USA. Both these works reveal Montesquieu's kinship with the early ENLIGHTENMENT in his use of comparative methodology and his application of the spirit of free enquiry to matters of politics and religion. He contributed to the great work of the Enlightenment, Diderot's *encyclopédie*.

Montezuma (more correctly Moctezuma II Xocoyotzin) (*c.* 1480–1520) The ninth AZTEC ruler (1503–21). His priests interpreted the arrival of CORTÉS in 1519 as the return of the legendary god-king, QUETZALCÓATL, from the east. This caused a certain hesitation and indecision on his part, which Cortés exploited by taking him hostage and forcing him to parley with his people. Because he offered to pay tribute to Spain, they deposed him in 1521 and attacked the Spaniards. In the melée that followed he was wounded, dying three days later.

Montfort, Simon de, Earl of Leicester (*c.* 1208–65) The leader of the English barons against HENRY III. Born in Normandy, he came to England (1230) and successfully claimed the earldom of Leicester (1239). His marriage to Eleanor (1240), Henry's sister, and appointment as lieutenant of Gascony (1248–52) appeared to secure his position when Henry subjected him to a five-week trial on uncorroborated charges against his Gascon rule. He was acquitted, but left Gascony to return to England. His support of reforms incorporated in the Provisions of Oxford (1258) led Simon into the BARONS' WAR against the king. Between his victory at Lewes (1264) and death at Evesham he was effectively ruler of England. In that period borough representatives attended Parliament for the first time.

Montgomery of Alamein, Bernard Law Montgomery, 1st Viscount (1887–1976) British field-marshal. He served with distinction in World War I, and in World War II commanded the 8th Army (1942–44) in the NORTH AFRICAN and ITALIAN CAMPAIGNS. He led his troops at El ALAMEIN, one of the most decisive victories of the war, enabling the Allies to begin the advance that removed the Germans from North Africa. From 1944 he commanded the British Commonwealth armies in NORMANDY with considerable success. His attempt at a forward airborne assault on ARNHEM failed, but he played a major role in beating the German counter-offensive in the ARDENNES. He held various senior military posts after the war.

Montrose, James Graham, 5th Earl and 1st Marquis of (1612–50) Head of an ancient Scottish family. He fought for the COVENANTERS, but fearing their control of both church and state later joined CHARLES I in England. In 1644 he was appointed lieutenant-general

of Scotland and commissioned to reconquer the country. His force was small, but in a brilliant campaign he won six battles, entered Glasgow, and summoned a Parliament. Support for the Royalists then faded, however; Montrose was utterly defeated in a surprise attack and escaped abroad. Returning in 1650 to raise an army for CHARLES II, he was betrayed, captured, and hanged by the Presbyterians in Edinburgh.

Moor A term commonly used by European authors from the Middle Ages onwards as a loose synonym for SARACEN. The Spanish and Portuguese used it of the Muslim inhabitants of North Africa and of Spain; and then, by extension, applied it to Muslims as distinct from pagans in Africa, and from Hindus in India. However, the term was particularly applied to the Arab conquerors of Spain, who landed first in 710.

In 711, under TARIQ IBN ZAID, a BERBER army swept the country, and the VISIGOTH kingdom collapsed. The Moors reached the Pyrenees, and crossed into France. Their defeat near Poitiers in 732 marked the limit of their expansion. The new state of al-Andalus (Andalusia) was consolidated by the UMAYYAD amir Abd al-Rahman ibn Mauwiya in 756, and succeeded by a caliphate that lasted from 912 until 1031. Seville was the first capital, but was superseded by Córdoba in 717. Following the collapse of the caliphate, the state dissolved among the Reyes de Taifas, or 'Party Kings' (1031–85), while the Christian kingdoms further north expanded southwards. But in 1090 new North African invaders, the ALMORAVIDS, who were primarily fighting men, made themselves supreme. They gave way in 1145 to another Berber group, the ALMOHADS, whose collapse early in the 13th century gave the Christians their opportunity, and by 1235 only the kingdom of GRANADA remained, covering most of the present Andalusia. Torn by factions, it could not withstand the united monarchy of FERDINAND V (the Catholic) and Isabella who brought an end to Moorish rule in Spain in 1491.

The Moorish period in Spain was the zenith of Islamic culture in learning, law, poetry, art, and architecture. The Great Mosque of Córdoba and the Alhambra of Granada were among their supreme creations.

Moore, Sir John (1761–1809) British soldier. He joined the army in 1776 and served with distinction during the war with France. In 1808 he was appointed commander of the British army in Portugal with orders to drive the French from the Iberian Peninsula. He advanced into northern Spain but was forced to retreat to the coast by overwhelming numbers of French troops. Moore was killed in the successful rearguard action at Corunna which enabled the British army to be safely evacuated.

Moravia An area of the Czech Republic. Occupied during the 4th century by Celtic and Germanic tribes, it was conquered by the Romans, and as the Roman empire declined, came under AVAR, and subsequently MAGYAR domination. It passed to BOHEMIA in 1029. After suppression of the HUSSITE rebellion in neighbouring Bohemia in the 15th century, a moderate form of John Huss's proto-Protestant religion survived in Moravia despite persecution. Gaining from the influence of 16th-century ANABAPTISTS, it evolved as the MORAVIAN CHURCH, whose beliefs survived, often in exile (notably in North America), after the persecutions following the

Bohemian rebellion in the THIRTY YEARS WAR. The HABSBURGS ruled Moravia from 1526 until 1918, when it became a province of the newly created Czechoslovakia.

Moravian Church A small PROTESTANT Church, founded in 1722, that has its origins in the HUSSITE Bohemian Brethren of Central Europe and is closely linked to the LUTHERANS. Worship is kept simple; Moravian hymns are famous, and reflect the Church's emphasis on direct spiritual experience and good conduct rather than elaborate doctrines. Though it has only about 200,000 full members it has been a powerful influence on Protestant thinkers, such as John WESLEY, the founder of METHODISM, and is effective in missionary, educational, and ecumenical activity.

More, Sir Thomas (1478–1535) English statesman and scholar, Lord Chancellor of England (1529–32). He trained as a lawyer and entered Parliament in 1504, becoming Speaker in 1523. By then he had made a European reputation for himself as a leading HUMANIST. His *Utopia* (1516) bitterly attacked contemporary political and social evils. He was appointed Lord Chancellor by HENRY VIII in 1529, becoming known as a stern campaigner against Protestant heresy. His resignation in 1532 was probably hastened by reservations over the king's divorce from Catherine of Aragon and the government's anti-papal stance. In 1534 he refused to acknowledge Henry's supremacy over the English Church. After a trial at which he defended himself, he was executed as a traitor. He was canonized in 1935.

Morelos y Pavón, José María (1765–1815) Mexican mestizo priest and leader of the revolution against Spain. Joining the insurrection in 1810, he led a successful campaign in the south, and assumed command of his country's struggle after the capture and execution (1810) of Miguel HIDALGO Y COSTILLA. From 1812 to 1815 he kept the royalist army on the run with guerrilla warfare. He sponsored the Congress of Chilpancingo (1813), which formally declared Mexican independence and adopted Mexico's first constitution with Morelos as head of government. Before its administrative, social, and fiscal reforms could be adopted, Morelos was captured by Spanish forces and shot.

Moreno, Mariano (1778–1811) Argentine revolutionary. His study of the Enlightenment thinkers led him to challenge Spanish mercantilist policies in the Rio de la Plata region. In his *Memorial of the Landowners*, he argued for free trade in terms similar to those of Adam Smith. Although trade restrictions were eased, Moreno became the secretary of the first revolutionary governing junta in 1810, which deposed the Spanish viceroy. Dispatched to Europe to secure assistance for the independence movement, he died aboard ship.

Morgan, Sir Henry (c. 1635–88) Welsh BUCCANEER, the scourge of Spanish settlements and shipping in the Caribbean between the 1660s and 1680s. Although he had semi-official employment as a privateer, he was little more than a pirate. Among his exploits were the capture and ransom of Porto Bello (1668), the sacking of Maracaibo (1669), and the taking of Chagres and Panama (1670–71). Although knighted and appointed lieutenant-governor of Jamaica in 1674, he continued to encourage piracy and lawlessness. He was disgraced in 1683 but restored just before his death.

Morgan, John Pierpont (1837–1913) US financier and philanthropist. A member of a distinguished family of financiers, he came to New York from Boston in 1857. He established his own company there in 1860, becoming increasingly interested in railways. Morgan believed in the merits of centralization, working to eliminate wasteful competition, but his banking opponents saw him as a monopolist. In 1893 and 1907 his personal weight was sufficient to stabilize critically unbalanced financial markets. He was perhaps the leading private art collector of his day.

Morínigo, Higinio (1897–1985) Paraguayan military dictator. He was an army officer during the CHACO WAR and subsequently became Minister of War. When President José Félix Estigarribia was killed in an air crash (1940), Morínigo became President (1940–48). He suspended the constitution and established a harsh military dictatorship. Housing and public health were improved during his tenure, and, in 1946, political exiles were brought into a more democratic cabinet. When these were ousted on suspicion of treason (1947), civil war broke out and a broadly based opposition, led by the Colorado Party, forced his retirement and exile to Argentina (1948).

Morley-Minto reforms (1909) Constitutional changes in British India, introduced to increase Indian participation in the legislature. They were embodied in the Indian Councils Act (1909) following discussions between John Morley, Secretary of State for India (1905–14), and Lord Minto, viceroy (1905–10). The reforms included the admission of Indians to the Secretary of State's council, to the viceroy's executive council, and to the executive councils of Bombay and Madras, and the introduction of an elected element into legislative councils with provision for separate electorates for Muslims. The reforms were regarded by Indian nationalists as too cautious, and the provision of separate electorates for Muslims was resented by Hindus.

Mormons Members of a Christian MILLENARIAN religious movement, also known as the Church of Jesus Christ of Latter-Day Saints. The Mormon religion was founded in 1830 in New York State by Joseph SMITH and was based on the revelation to him of the Book of Mormon. This was a mixture of religious concepts and mythical history, including the belief that Native Americans were the lost tribe of Israel. Rapidly gathering followers, Smith moved westwards, but local hostility, largely occasioned by the Mormon espousal of polygamy, led to Smith's lynching in Illinois in 1846. Under the leadership of Brigham YOUNG the group made its final westward move to Utah. After many hardships, the Mormons created a self-contained economy centred around Salt Lake City, although continued difficulties with polygamy (renounced in 1890) prevented Utah becoming a state until 1896. Mormons continue to dominate the administration of Utah. Membership of the Mormon Church is now over five million worldwide. Mormon beliefs diverge sharply from orthodox Christianity, which is held to be a corrupt faith. Doctrines include the expectation of the Second Coming of Christ, baptism of adults, and belief in prophecy.

Moro, Aldo (1916–78) Italian statesman. He entered Parliament as a Christian Democrat in 1946. As Minister of Justice (1955–57) he reformed the prison system. He was Foreign Minister in several governments (1965–74), and Prime Minister (1963–68, 1974–76). Moro was kidnapped in 1978 by the RED BRIGADES, who demanded the release of imprisoned terrorists for his return. The government's refusal to accede led to Moro's murder.

Morocco A country in the north-west corner of Africa bounded inland by Algeria and Western Sahara and with coasts on both the Mediterranean Sea and the Atlantic Ocean.

Physical. Much of Morocco consists of the Atlas Mountains, running from the south-west to the north-east. Near the coasts it is warm and wet; in the mountains, arid. South of the mountains begins the Sahara Desert. Rivers from the mountains water the coastal plains and permit a wide variety of crops.

Economy. Morocco's main export is phosphates, of which it has the world's largest reserves; other minerals extracted include anthracite, iron, lead, and manganese. Morocco is dependent on imported fuel for most of its energy needs, and also relies on imports to meet food requirements. Other than phosphate production, industry concentrates on textiles and motor vehicles. Tourism is regarded as an expanding source of revenue. Traditional methods of farming keep exports of crops such as grains, citrus fruit, vegetables, and grapes low. However, vineyards, olive-gardens, and date-palm groves thrive.

History. By the 5th century BC PHOENICIANS had stations on the Moroccan coast. A kingdom of Mauritania was formed in northern Morocco in the 4th century BC and the Romans made this the province of Mauritania Tingitana, based on Tangier. Vandals from Spain occupied the region from 428, but the BERBERS controlled the interior even after the Byzantines had recovered the coast in 533. It did not come under Arab control until Musa ibn Nusayr's conquest in *c.* 705. Under Byzantium the puritanism of the Berber character had been manifested in the DONATIST heresy; under Islam a similarly austere movement, Kharijism, arose. True Arab domination was brief, and Berber dynasties emerged, Idrisids (788–974), FATIMIDS (909–73), ALMORAVIDS (1056–1147), ALMOHADS (1145–1257), Merinids (1248–1548), and finally the SHARIFIAN dynasties from 1524 until the present. Having defeated the Portuguese at ALCAZARQUIVIR (1578), Morocco itself attempted colonial expansion, defeating the SONGHAY empire with the help of firearms in 1591, but ruling it inefficiently.

By the 19th century, Morocco had lapsed into endemic disorder and became the target for French and Spanish imperial ambitions. In the early 20th century, German opposition to French expansionism produced serious international crises in 1905 and 1911, which almost resulted in war. In 1912 it was divided between a French protectorate, a Spanish protectorate, and the international Zone of Tangier. Rif rebels under ABD EL-KRIM fought the Spanish and French occupying powers in the 1920s, and Morocco became an independent monarchy under Muhammad V in 1956 when it absorbed Tangier. Muhammad was succeeded by his son Hassan II in 1961, but opposition sparked the suspension of parliamentary government in 1965, and royal authority has been maintained in the face of abortive military coups in the early 1970s and intermittent republican opposition. In 1980 a new constitution proclaimed the kingdom of Morocco to be a constitutional monarchy. From the mid-1970s Morocco has been involved in an inconclusive desert war in the former Spanish Sahara (see WESTERN SAHARA). A convention was signed in 1976 dividing this mineral-rich area between Morocco and Mauritania; but the latter renounced its claims in 1979 in favour of a nationalist group, the Polisario Front. Morocco annexed the land from which Mauritania had withdrawn, despite violent resistance from the Polisario Front. Major battles were fought in 1979 and 1980, and Moroccan troops built a series of desert walls; but increasing international support was given to the Polisario Front, who in 1976 had proclaimed the Saharan Arab Democratic Republic. A ceasefire was negotiated in 1991, pending a UN-conducted referendum, but little progress has been made in negotiations to secure a permanent peace accord. Morocco was the only Maghreb country to send troops in support of the UN in the GULF WAR. A new constitution, adopted in 1992, increased the powers of the government while retaining the hereditary monarch as head of state. A programme of privatization was launched by the government in 1993. The first general election since 1984 was held in 1993 and the ruling coalition was re-elected.

CAPITAL:	Rabat
AREA:	458,730 sq km (177,117 sq miles)
POPULATION:	26.736 million (1996)
CURRENCY:	1 dirham = 100 francs
RELIGIONS:	Muslim (mostly Sunni) 98.7%; Christian 1.1%
ETHNIC GROUPS:	Arab-Berber 99.5%
LANGUAGES:	Arabic (official); Berber; Spanish; French
INTERNATIONAL ORGANIZATIONS:	UN; Non-Aligned Movement; Arab League; Maghreb Union

Morris, William Richard NUFFIELD, Viscount.

Morrison of Lambeth, Herbert Stanley Morrison, Baron (1888–1965) British politician. As leader of the London County Council (1934–40), he unified the transport system under public ownership and created a 'green belt' around the metropolis. Morrison was Minister of Supply and then Home Secretary in CHURCHILL's coalition government during World War II. He drafted the programme of nationalization and social services in the 1945 Labour manifesto. From 1945 he was deputy prime minister under ATTLEE, but he was defeated by GAITSKELL in the election for leadership of the Labour Party in 1955.

Mortimer, Roger, 8th Baron of Wigmore and 1st Earl of March (1287–1330) A member of a family of MARCHER LORDS of medieval England. While living in exile in France he won Edward II's wife ISABELLA OF FRANCE as his mistress. In September 1326 Roger and Isabella invaded England and forced Edward to abdicate in favour of her son, the young EDWARD III, leaving them as *de facto* rulers of England. Roger's pro-France foreign policy and his financial greed made him unpopular, and in October 1330 Edward III and Henry, Earl of Lancaster, captured him and had him executed.

The family was later restored to favour and Edmund (1352–81), 3rd Earl of March, married Philippa, only child of Lionel, Duke of CLARENCE; in the early 1370s he and EDWARD THE BLACK PRINCE led the so-called constitutional party against the court party of John of GAUNT. His son

Roger (1374–98), the 4th earl, was heir-presumptive of Richard II, but was killed while fighting for Richard in Ireland.

Mortimer's Cross, Battle of (2 February 1461) An important battle in the Wars of the ROSES, which took place at a site near Wigmore in Herefordshire. The YORKIST forces led by Edward, Earl of March, won a major victory over the Earl of Wiltshire's LANCASTRIAN army. It was not negated by the victory of Queen MARGARET OF ANJOU's army at St Albans less than a fortnight later, for Margaret could not win over the Londoners; on 4 March they acclaimed Edward as King EDWARD IV.

Morton, John (c. 1420–1500) English ecclesiastic. He was trained as an academic lawyer; the patronage of Archbishop Bourchier led to his becoming a master in CHANCERY and a member of the king's council. A LANCASTRIAN, he lost all when the YORKISTS seized the crown in 1461 and fled to France; after the battle of TEWKESBURY (1471) he joined the Yorkists and was favoured by EDWARD IV, becoming Bishop of Ely (1479). He then supported Henry Tudor and soon after Henry's accession (as HENRY VII) was made Archbishop of Canterbury (1486) and Chancellor of England (1487), as well as a cardinal (1493). His assistance to Henry in tax gathering has made him known traditionally as the author of 'Morton's Fork'; his two-pronged argument that the rich could afford to pay and the frugal must have savings.

Moses (13th century BC) Hebrew patriarch and prophet, who delivered his people from slavery and founded the religious community called ISRAEL. According to biblical accounts, he was a Hebrew foundling adopted and reared at the Egyptian court. In Midian in north-west Arabia he saw a burning yet unconsumed bush and experienced the voice of God (Yaweh) commanding him to lead his people from Egypt. In the EXODUS that followed, the pursuing Egyptians were engulfed by the Red Sea, which had parted to allow the Israelites to cross. On Mount Sinai (Horeb) Jehovah revealed the Covenant, including the Ten Commandments, between himself and the people of Moses. According to tradition Moses died within sight of CANAAN, the Promised Land, at Moab.

Mosley, Sir Oswald Ernald (1896–1980) British political leader. Mosley was a Member of Parliament successively as Conservative (1918–22), Independent (1922–24), and Labour (1925–31). He formed a progressive socialist movement, the New Party (1931), advocating state intervention. Calling for a dictatorial system of government, he then formed the National Union of Fascists in 1932. ANTI-SEMITIC and FASCIST in character, its blackshirted followers staged violent marches and rallies in the East End of London. Mosley was interned during 1940–43. In 1948 he founded the 'Union Movement', whose theme was European unity.

Mossi West African peoples of the plains and valleys between the upper Black and White Volta rivers. They apparently reached this region in the 10th century. In the 11th century they formed three kingdoms, Yatenga, Wagadugu, and Gurma. In the 12th and following centuries, by skilful organization and the use of cavalry, they ruled a wider area, administered by 393 *nabus* under a *morho-naba*, or emperor, at Wagadugu. In the 16th century they fell to MALI and SONGHAY, but Yatenga and Gurma later managed to recover independence, and continued into the 19th century as sovereign states.

mound-builders Native American peoples in Ohio and Illinois who, from c. 1000 BC, erected richly furnished circular burial mounds, resembling the European BARROWS in shape and function. In the MISSISSIPPI basin some centuries later (c. 700 AD), larger and more complex mounds, presumably for ceremonial gatherings, were raised to support temples. Though most were rectangular, and frequently built in large groups as at Cahokia in Illinois, there are more bizarre ones like the 400 m (1,300 feet) long snake mound in Adams County, Ohio. These may have been influenced from Mexico.

Mountain Men US fur trappers and traders, who explored and developed the Rocky Mountains between the 1820s and 1840s. They caught public attention through their exploits and occupy an important position in the frontier legend. Their living conditions were harsh, and only a handful, such as Kit CARSON, Jedediah SMITH, and Thomas Fitzpatrick, survived long enough to return to a more settled existence after a decline in beaverskin prices in the 1840s.

Mount Badon According to GILDAS, the site of a major battle or siege between the Britons and the invading Saxons c. 500. NENNIUS, 300 years later, claimed that King ARTHUR fought there. The British victory gained for them a brief period of peace, perhaps for half a century. Although the site of the battle is not known, a possible location is the Iron Age hill fort of Badbury Rings near Wimborne, Dorset. Similarly, the date can only be ascribed tentatively to around the year 500.

Mountbatten, Louis Francis Albert Victor Nicholas, 1st Earl Mountbatten of Burma (1900–79) British admiral and administrator. After service in World War I as a midshipman in BEATTY's flagships, he accompanied the Prince of Wales on two empire tours. In 1940–41 he commanded a destroyer flotilla that was badly bombed in the battle of Crete. He became Chief of Combined Operations in 1942 and did much for the subsequent landings in North Africa, Italy, and Normandy. In 1943 he was appointed Supreme Allied Commander, South-East Asia, where he restored the morale and capacity of the hard-hit and neglected Commonwealth forces fighting the Japanese in the BURMA CAMPAIGNS. In 1947 he became the last viceroy of INDIA, charged with the transfer of sovereignty from the British crown. This transfer was promptly effected, although marred by inter-communal massacres. At the invitation of the new Indian government, he stayed on until 1948 as the first governor-general. Resuming his naval career, he rose to Chief of the Defence Staff (1959–65), in which capacity he supervised the merging of the service ministries into a unified Ministry of Defence. Active in retirement, he criticized reliance on nuclear weapons. He was assassinated in 1979 by the IRISH REPUBLICAN ARMY while on a holiday in Ireland.

Mousterian A prehistoric culture associated with NEANDERTHALS and the Middle PALAEOLITHIC in Europe. Tools of this type were named after the Neanderthal cave site of Le Moustier in the Dordogne, France, but have since been found throughout Europe. They date from about 130,000 years ago to about 30,000 years ago, disappearing with the emergence of anatomically modern humans and the start of the UPPER PALAEOLITHIC. They are also found in North Africa and the Near East. Characteristically, Mousterian tools were made from flint. Compared with the earlier ACHEULIAN tools, there was a much greater emphasis on flakes, which allowed a larger range of tools to be produced. Small, neat handaxes and stone and bone projectile points were among other typical Mousterian tools.

Mozambique A country situated on the south-east coast of Africa, and bounded by Tanzania, Malawi, Zambia, Zimbabwe, South Africa, and Swaziland.

Physical. The Zambezi flows across the middle of the country and the Limpopo across the south. The coastal plain is low and broad, with areas of sand between the marshy river valleys. It is wetter inland, where there are regions of fertile soil covered with tropical forest, before the ground rises northward to rocky plateaux with savannah vegetation.

Economy. Mozambique's mineral resources include large reserves of coal, iron ore, tantalite, and unknown reserves of natural gas and precious stones. Many farms have been collectivized; the main crops are cassava, maize, coconuts, and sugar cane. Shrimps and cashew nuts are the main exports. Industry consists primarily of the processing of local raw materials.

History. Mozambique was known to medieval Arab geographers as Musambih. According to the Arab historian al-Masudi it was already exporting gold from mines in the interior of what is now ZIMBABWE in the 10th century. Merchants from MOGADISHU had a monopoly for a time, though it was taken over by KILWA in the 12th century. The Portuguese sacked the port of Sofala in 1505, and built a new town as the seat of a captaincy to control the gold and other trade. Settlers also began to trade in slaves in the 16th century. The present city of Moçambique was begun with a fort in 1508 built by the Portuguese as a refreshment station on the way to GOA. The first inland settlements at Sena and Tete were Arab trading towns, from which they made contact with the MWENE MUTAPA and other hinterland rulers until the 19th century.

The Portuguese gradually suppressed all indigenous resistance movements during the 19th century and Mozambique became an overseas province of Portugal in 1951. In order to rid the country of colonial rule, in 1964 the Marxist–Leninist guerrilla group FRELIMO was formed. By the mid-1970s Portuguese authority had reached the point of collapse, and in 1975 an independent People's Republic was established under the Frelimo leader Samora MACHEL. Support for the guerrilla campaigns in Rhodesia and South Africa led to repeated military incursions by troops of those countries, and the establishment of a stable government within the framework of a one-party Marxist state was further hindered by the weak state of Mozambique's agricultural economy. In 1984 Mozambique and South Africa signed a non-aggression pact, the Nkomati Accord; but South African support of rebel groups, funded by Portuguese ex-colonists, continued with some 10,000 well-armed troops operating in the country. In 1989 Frelimo relaxed its Marxist-Leninist line and President Joaquim Chissano agreed to meet Afonso Dhlakama, leader of the rebel Mozambique National Resistance (RENAMO). A new constitution took effect from November 1990, which was accepted by RENAMO following formal peace talks in 1991. A peace treaty was

agreed in October 1992 and RENAMO became a legitimate political party. Mozambique's first multiparty elections were held in 1994 and Frelimo, under Chissano, was re-elected. In 1995 Mozambique was admitted to the COMMONWEALTH OF NATIONS, thus becoming the first country with no historical links with Britain to join this association. Seventeen years of civil war, together with appalling drought, have left Mozambique one of the poorest countries in the world and famine and social unrest continue to threaten its stability.

CAPITAL:	Maputo
AREA:	802,000 sq km (309,572 sq miles)
POPULATION:	17.878 million (1996)
CURRENCY:	1 metical = 100 centavos
RELIGIONS:	Traditional beliefs 47.8%; Christian (mostly Roman Catholic) 38.9% Muslim 13.0%
ETHNIC GROUPS:	Makua 47.3%; Tsonga 23.3%; Malawi 12.0%; Shona 11.3%; Yao 3.8%; Swahili 0.8%; Makonde 0.6%; Portuguese 0.2%
LANGUAGES:	Portuguese (official); Makua; Tsonga; local languages
INTERNATIONAL ORGANIZATIONS:	UN; OAU; SADC; Commonwealth of Nations

Mubarak, Hosni (1928–) Egyptian statesman; President (1981–). After serving in the Egyptian Air Force, Mubarak was appointed defence minister in 1972 and Vice-President to Anwar SADAT in 1975. He played a significant role in bringing about the CAMP DAVID ACCORD of 1979, which secured peace between Egypt and Israel. After Sadat's assassination by Islamic extremists in 1981, Mubarak assumed the presidency and continued his predecessor's modernizing policies. He was re-elected unopposed in 1987 and 1993. He repaired diplomatic relations with other Arab states, severed since the treaty with Israel, and chaired the Organization of African Unity (1989–90). Egyptian troops formed part of the Western–Arab coalition against Iraq in the Gulf War of 1991. Despite enacting strict measures against fundamentalist groups, Mubarak's government has failed to suppress Islamist terror. He survived an assassination attempt in 1995 and during the 1990s Egypt suffered a series of atrocities against domestic and tourist targets, including the massacre of 62 people (58 foreign tourists) at Luxor in November 1997.

Mugabe, Robert Gabriel (1924–) Zimbabwean statesman. In 1963 he helped to form the Zimbabwe African National Union (ZANU), breaking away from Joshua NKOMO's Zimbabwe African People's Union (ZAPU). Following his imprisonment in 1964 for 'subversive speech', he was elected leader of ZANU. He was freed in 1975, and, with Nkomo, led the guerrillas of the Zimbabwe Patriotic Front against Ian Smith's regime. When the war ended he won a landslide victory in elections held under British supervision in 1980, and became Prime Minister (1980–87). In power his contest with Nkomo sharpened, Nkomo maintaining the supremacy of Parliament, while Mugabe openly declared a Marxist one-party state as his objective. In 1987 he was reconciled with Nkomo after a six-year period of near civil war, and a ZANU-ZAPU Patriotic Front was confirmed by an Accord of Friendship. Mugabe became President of Zimbabwe, securing re-election in 1990 and 1995. A strong supporter of the NON-ALIGNED MOVEMENT and also of the Commonwealth, he took an active role in organizing sanctions against South Africa. In 1991 he abandoned his aim of a single-party Marxist–Leninist state and accepted multiparty politics. By then his country was stricken by both drought and the Aids epidemic but he continued to gain popular support. In contrast to the liberal constitution established by Nelson MANDELA in post-apartheid South Africa, Mugabe's style of leadership has been seen as increasingly autocratic by many critics, who point to his arrest of political opponents on treason charges. In 1998 international pressure forced him to abandon plans to confiscate the land of all the country's remaining White farmers without compensation.

Mughals MOGULS.

Muhammad (c. 570–632) The Prophet of ISLAM. He was born in MECCA of the Hashemite clan of the tribe of Quraish and orphaned in infancy. He won the name 'al-Amin', 'the trustworthy', and married his employer, a wealthy widow, Khadija. Religious contemplation led him to a vision on the 'Night of Power' in 610 and to the revelations that were subsequently compiled as the KORAN. From 613 he preached openly against idolatry and the social evils of his day, proclaiming the oneness of Allah, 'the God', and the inevitability of judgement. The death of Khadija and of his protective uncle Abu Talib in 619 exposed the Prophet and his followers to the hostility of the Meccans and led ultimately to his departure from Mecca (the HEGIRA) of 622 and the establishment of the first community of Muslims at MEDINA. A lengthy period of sometimes violent struggle followed, ending in the capitulation of Mecca to Muhammad and his followers, the purgation of the Kaaba of idols, and the submission to Islam of most of the tribes of the Arabian peninsula. The Prophet's sudden death in 632 led to the establishment of the CALIPHATE and indirectly inaugurated the tide of ARAB CONQUESTS.

As God's messenger, Muhammad is venerated and his example, in word and deed, as recorded in the *Hadith*, is seen as an unchallengeable model of holiness. He is not worshipped in his own right, however, nor does he intermediate between the believer and God. Rather, SUNNITE Muslims believe that Muhammad's life is the culmination of the prophetic era, and that Islam is the fulfilment of the earlier revelations of the prophets of Christianity and Judaism.

Muhammad Reza Shah Pahlavi (1919–1980) Shah of Iran (1941–79). The son of REZA SHAH PAHLAVI he succeeded on the abdication of his father. After the fall of MUSSADEGH in 1953 he gained supreme power and with the aid of greatly increased oil revenues, embarked upon a policy of rapid social reform and economic development, while maintaining a regime of harsh repression towards his opponents. In 1962 he introduced a land reform programme to break landlord power. In 1979 he was deposed by a revolution led by the Islamic clergy, notably Ayatollah KHOMEINI, whose supporters were bitterly opposed to the pro-western regime of the Shah. He died in exile in Egypt.

Mujibar Rahman, Sheikh (1920–75) Bangladeshi statesman. Popularly known as Sheikh Mujib, he came into political prominence as co-founder and general secretary of the AWAMI LEAGUE and as a champion of the Bengalis of East Pakistan, who he feared were being dominated by West Pakistan. He was imprisoned in 1954 under the rule of AYUB KHAN, and again in 1966, but as leader of the Awami League after the death of Suhrawardy, he became the leading politician of East Pakistan. He was released after the fall of Ayub and led his party to victory in the 1970 elections. In the conflict between East and West Pakistan that followed the elections, he was again arrested (1971), but was released in 1972 to head the government of East Pakistan, renamed the People's Republic of BANGLADESH. His leadership was confirmed at the elections of 1973 and in 1975 he became Bangladesh's first President. His attempts at establishing a parliamentary democracy having failed, he assumed dictatorial powers under a new constitution that established one-party Awami League government. In 1975 he and his family were murdered in an army coup.

Mukden incident (18 September 1931) Japanese seizure of the Manchurian city of Mukden (now Shenyang in NE China). A detachment of the Japanese Guandong army, stationed in Manchuria in accordance with treaty rights, used an allegedly Chinese-inspired explosion on the South Manchurian Railway as an excuse to occupy the city of Mukden. Acting without reference to their own government, and in the face of condemnation from the League of Nations, Japanese military authorities then went on to occupy all of Manchuria before the end of 1931, establishing the state of MANCHUKUO. Japan, labelled an aggressor by the League of Nations, withdrew its membership.

Muldoon, Sir Robert (1921–92) New Zealand statesman. Having entered New Zealand politics in 1960 as a member of the National Party, he held various offices before being elected party leader in 1974 and winning a general election in 1975. He was Prime Minister and Minister of Finance (1975–84) at a difficult time for New Zealand, which was faced by grave economic problems. Oil prices had risen steeply in 1973 and its traditional market in Britain for farm and dairy produce had been threatened by the latter's entry into the EUROPEAN ECONOMIC COMMUNITY. He wished to provide economic incentives for industrial growth, but also imposed freezes in prices and wages, leading to conflict with trade unions. He served on the Board of Governors of the World Bank (1979–80). The National Party lost power to Labour in 1984 and he was voted out of the party leadership.

mummy The body of a person or animal embalmed or otherwise treated to ensure its preservation, a practice associated especially with ancient Egypt. Mummification seems to be connected to a belief in life after death, the body being preserved so that the soul could return to it. Artificial methods of preservation were introduced during the Old Kingdom, but the most complex method of embalming was perfected in Dynasty 21 (c. 1100–950 BC). Fine examples of mummification are the bodies of the pharaohs Seti I and Ramesses II. The practice continued into the Roman period, until Christianity gradually made it obsolete. Local conditions also encouraged mummification among the INCAS.

Munich 'beer-hall' putsch (8 November 1923) An abortive rebellion by German NAZIS. In a beer-hall in Munich a meeting of right-wing politicians, who had

gathered to denounce the WEIMAR REPUBLIC and to call for the restitution of the Bavarian monarchy, was interrupted by a group of Nazi Party members led by Adolf HITLER. In a fierce speech Hitler won support for a plan to 'march on Berlin' and there install the right-wing military leader General LUDENDORFF as dictator. With a unit of BROWNSHIRTS (SA), he kidnapped the leader of the Bavarian government and declared a revolution. Next day a march on the centre of Munich by some 3,000 Nazis was met by police gunfire, 16 demonstrators and three policemen being killed in the riot that followed. Many were arrested. Ludendorff was released, but Hitler was sentenced to five years in prison, of which he served only nine months. During this period he dictated the first volume of his autobiography and manifesto *Mein Kampf* (1925) to his fellow prisoner, Rudolf HESS.

Munich Pact (29 September 1938) An agreement between Britain, France, Germany, and Italy concerning the partition of Czechoslovakia. HITLER had long demanded protection for the German-speaking SUDETENLAND and shown readiness to risk war to attain his end. To avert conflict at all costs the British Prime Minister, CHAMBERLAIN, had met Hitler at Berchtesgaden (15 September), and again at Bad Godesberg (23 September), by which time Hitler had extended his demands. He now stipulated the immediate annexation by Germany of the Bohemian Sudetenland and demanded that Germans elsewhere in Czechoslovakia should be given the right to join the THIRD REICH. In a final effort Chamberlain appealed to MUSSOLINI, who organized a conference at Munich where he, Chamberlain, and Hitler were joined by DALADIER, the French Premier. No Czech or Soviet representative was invited. Hitler gained most of what he wanted and on 1 October German troops entered the Sudentenland. As part of the agreement, Poland and Hungary occupied areas of Moravia, Slovakia, and Ruthenia. In March 1939 Bohemia and Moravia were occupied by Nazi troops, and the rest of Slovakia became an independent client state; President BENEŠ had resigned, and he left the country. Germany, which now dominated the entire Danubian area, emerged as the strongest power on the mainland of Europe.

Murad I (c. 1326–89) OTTOMAN sultan (c. 1362–89). He consolidated his empire's hold on Asia Minor by marriage alliances and outright purchase and rapidly extended its Balkan territories, taking Adrianople in 1362, Macedonia after the battle of Cirnomen (1371), and Sofia and Nish in the 1380s. A Serbian counter-offensive was defeated at the first battle of KOSSOVO, in which he was killed.

Murad II (c. 1403–51) Ottoman sultan (1421–51). He overcame early opposition to his claim to the throne and, after significant reverses, routed a Hungarian-led 'crusade' at the battle of Varna and the second battle of Kossovo (1448). He also made the JANISSARIES a basic pillar of the Ottoman state.

Murat, Joachim (1767–1815) Marshal of France, King of Naples (1808–15). He distinguished himself in NAPOLEON's Italian campaigns and was promoted general on the field at Aboukir (1799). Having married Napoleon's sister, Caroline, in 1800, he was made King of Naples (1808) in succession to Joseph Bonaparte, where he undertook

important reforms. He took part in Napoleon's Russian campaign in 1812 but abandoned the emperor during the retreat from Moscow. In order to safeguard his own throne he intrigued unsuccessfully with Austria and England. In 1815, however, Ferdinand IV was restored to Naples as Ferdinand I, King of the Two Sicilies, and Murat escaped to France. He joined Napoleon during the HUNDRED DAYS but was defeated by the Austrians at Tolentino in Italy. In October he was captured, handed over to Ferdinand, and shot.

Muromachi ASHIKAGA.

Muscovy A state, centred on Moscow, which first became a distinct territory in the 13th century. Cut off from the West by the 13th century TARTAR conquest, and by its subscription to the EASTERN ORTHODOX faith, Muscovy evolved into a princedom under Ivan I (1328–41). Major reconquest of former Russian territory ensued under IVAN III (the Great), and under IVAN IV (the Terrible). The state surmounted setbacks in the so-called 'Time of Troubles' (1605–13) and, after 1613, under a new dynasty, the ROMANOVS, became the nucleus of a unified Russia.

Muscovy Company An English CHARTERED COMPANY, incorporated in 1555, with a monopoly of Anglo-Russian trade. It was formed by London merchants, after Richard Chancellor had made contacts with Muscovy in searching for a north-east passage to Asia (1553–54). The trade was largely in cloth and firearms from England, and in naval stores from Muscovy. After the RESTORATION it was reorganized as a regulated company, and its monopoly was ended in 1698.

Museveni, Yoweri Kaguta UGANDA.

musketeer In the 16th and 17th centuries, a foot soldier armed with a musket – a large-calibre smooth-bore firearm that was aimed from the shoulder. Inefficient hand cannons had been used in Europe during the 14th century, and matchlock 'arquebuses' were subsequently used, rather haphazardly, in battle. In the mid-16th century Spanish troops pioneered the use of the more powerful, more accurate *mosquete* (musket). They also evolved complementary battle tactics. Effective as these weapons were, infantrymen still needed forked stands as props for aiming and firing; and since they were slow to load, pikemen had to be included in battalions to protect musketeers from enemy cavalry charges. The 17th-century development of the bayonet eventually removed the need for pikemen. Wheel-lock and flintlock muskets also became practical for military use at this time.

Muskogee CREEK.

Muslim League An Indian political party founded in 1905 to represent the interests of Muslims, many of whom felt threatened by the prospect of a Hindu majority in any future democratic system. The radical nationalist elements in the League forged a pact with the CONGRESS in 1916 on the basis of separate electorates and reserved seats in Muslim minority provinces. A section of the League co-operated with the Congress in the NON-CO-OPERATION MOVEMENT. In the provincial elections (1937), the League captured very few Muslim seats, but it succeeded in convincing the Muslim masses that the elected Congress ministries were oppressing Muslims. In 1940 it put forward the demand for an autonomous Muslim homeland, Pakistan. Its leader, M. A. JINNAH, subsequently demanded that this be a fully independent state during the negotiations to end British rule in India and called for a Direct Action Day in August 1946. Mass rioting followed, whereupon the British and the Congress agreed to partition India. The League was virtually wiped out at the first elections in Pakistan.

Muslims ISLAM.

Mussadegh, Muhammad (1880–1967) Iranian political leader. An Iranian landowner and politician, in 1950 he led the democratic-nationalist opposition to the policies of Muhammad REZA SHAH PAHLAVI in Parliament. A militant nationalist, he forced (1951) the nationalization of the Anglo-Iranian Oil Company, and after rioting in Abadan, was appointed Prime Minister (1951–53). He ruled with left-wing support until he was dismissed by the Shah in 1953.

Mussolini, Benito (1883–1945) Italian dictator. After a turbulent career as a school teacher, he became a leading socialist journalist. During World War I he resigned from the Socialist Party and advocated Italian military support for the AUSTRO-HUNGARIAN EMPIRE. Called up, he became an army corporal and was wounded. After the war he bitterly opposed the VERSAILLES PEACE SETTLEMENT and organized radical right-wing groups, which merged to form the FASCIST Party. Widespread violence by his supporters, the weakness of democratic politicians, and the connivance of the king, who feared a communist revolution, enabled him to take power in 1922 after the so-called 'march on Rome'. Violence, including the murder of his political enemies, and popular esteem as 'Il Duce', enabled him to consolidate his position. His brilliance as an orator and his skill, in conditions of strict censorship, of presenting himself as all-powerful meant that his incompetence was long unnoticed. The VATICAN CITY STATE was set up by the Lateran Treaty (1929). His quest for a new Italian empire led to his annexation (1936) of ETHIOPIA, and Albania (1939). HITLER, one of his early admirers and imitators, became his ally and then a resented senior partner in the AXIS. Having entered WORLD WAR II at the most favourable moment (1940), he nevertheless was unable to avoid a series of military defeats. He was deposed by hitherto acquiescent fascist leaders in 1943, but was rescued by German paratroopers and established a puppet government in the small town of Salo in north Italy. In 1945 he was captured by Italian partisans, who shot him.

Mutesa I (d. 1884) Kabaka (King) of Buganda (now in Uganda) (1857–84). An autocratic monarch, he furthered his country's wealth by opening up trade, often in slaves, with Arab merchants. He strengthened Buganda's army and improved its bureaucracy. He subdued Bunyoro, the leading state in south Uganda. Although a Muslim, he welcomed Christian missionaries. They were followed by the British East Africa Company, causing tensions that were unresolved when he died.

Mutesa II, Sir Edward Frederick (1924–69) last Kabaka of Buganda (1939–63) and President of UGANDA (1963–66). He assumed office after a regency, aged 18. Progressive in spirit, he nevertheless backed the protectorate government in suppressing Buganda nationalist risings in 1945 and 1949. In 1953, fearing the

loss of Buganda's independence, he claimed the right of his kingdom to secede from the Ugandan protectorate. This was denied him by the Ugandan High Court, and he was deported by the British. In 1955 he returned as a constitutional monarch, and in 1963 was elected first President of Uganda. He disagreed with the left-wing policies of the Prime Minister, Dr Milton OBOTE, who deposed him in 1966.

Mutiny Act (1689) English legislation concerning the enforcement of military discipline, primarily over mutineers and deserters. The Declaration of Rights (1689) had declared illegal a standing army without parliamentary consent. To strengthen parliamentary control of the army, the 1689 Mutiny Act was enforced for one year only, theoretically giving Parliament the right of an annual review. In fact there were years (1689–1701) when it was not in force and both army and navy long retained their close connection with the sovereign. Only when the crown ceased to pay for the upkeep of the army did Parliament's annual review become effective.

MVD (Ministry for Internal Affairs) Police organization of the former Soviet Union. Together with the MGB (Ministry of State Security), it replaced the NKVD (People's Commissariat of Internal Affairs) in 1946. The MVD controlled all police forces and administered forced labour in PRISON CAMPS. During the last years of STALIN's rule it became a significant factor in the Soviet economy under the notorious Lavrenti BERIA. The powers of the MGB were extended to supervise and control police agencies throughout the Soviet bloc, and to eliminate all anti-Soviet, anti-communist opposition in the satellite countries. Both agencies were drastically reduced and decentralized between 1953 and 1960, when they were replaced by the KGB.

Mwene Mutapa The title taken by Mutota, founder of the ROZVI EMPIRE in East Africa. It has been translated as 'master pillager' and as 'lord of the conquered mines'. The Portuguese corrupted it to Monomotapa, and used it as a name for the empire. The founder died c. 1470, and was succeeded until 1480 by his son Matope, a great conqueror who took possession of the greater part of eastern Central Africa. On his death his son Changa seized most of the empire from the designated heir, proclaiming himself CHANGAMIRE. The dynasty lasted until the end of the 18th century.

Myall Creek massacre (1838) an incident in which, in retaliation for an alleged 'outrage', White station hands killed 28 Aborigines at Myall Creek in New South Wales, Australia. As a result, 11 White men were tried for murder. They were acquitted, but seven of them were retried, found guilty, and hanged. There was much public protest. Although prosecution of White people for such an incident was unusual, the incident itself was not, and Aborigines continued to be indiscriminately killed as settlers moved into other parts of the continent.

Myanmar (formerly Burma) A country in south-east Asia, with borders on the west with India and Bangladesh, on the north-east with China, on the east with Laos, and on the south-east and south with Thailand.

Physical. Myanmar has a long tropical western coast on the Indian Ocean and is cut off from the rest of Asia by mountains in the north and east. Down the centre of the country run the broad cultivable valley of the Irrawaddy River and several tributary valleys. To the east is the valley of the Salween River. Climatically it is hot and monsoonal.

Economy. Myanmar has a broadly based agricultural economy. Crops include sugar cane, pulses, ground nuts, and maize. Major exports are timber, rice, minerals, and gems. Crude oil is extracted, and production of natural gas is increasing. The small industrial sector includes oil-refining, food-processing, and textiles. Mineral resources include copper, zinc, lead, tin, and silver.

History. There was a Mon Kingdom, Prome, in Burma in the 5th century AD. After the arrival of the Burmans in the 9th century there was much hostility between them and the indigenous peoples. Following a period of Mon ascendancy, the Burmans of PAGAN unified the country for a time (*c.* 849–1287). From the Mons an Indian script and Theravada BUDDHISM spread to Pagan and thence throughout Burma. During the 16th century the country was re-united under the TOUNGOO, but wars against Thai kingdoms and LAOS exhausted it. The last dynasty, the Konbaung, founded by Alaungpaya in 1757, was constantly engaged in wars against Siam, which led to the fall of the Siamese state of Ayuthia in 1767. In 1770 Burma repelled a Chinese invasion. The conquest of ARAKAN brought the Burmese border to the boundary of British India.

Burma was invaded by the British (1824–26; 1852; and 1885). The first two ANGLO-BURMESE WARS led to the cession of territory and the third resulted in the deposition of King Thibaw and the establishment of Upper Burma as a province of British India. In 1931 there was a two-year uprising by the peasantry against European companies, and the Dobama Asi-ayone (Thakin) Party demanded independence. In 1937 Burma became a Crown colony, with a large degree of autonomy, Ba Maw being elected Premier. When Japanese troops moved into Malaya in 1942, the Burma National Army formed under AUNG SAN was at first ready to welcome them. However, this force defected to the Allies during the later campaign of liberation. Full independence was gained in 1948, Burma electing to remain outside the Commonwealth of Nations. Civil war erupted, with challenges to central government by the Karens of the Irrawady Delta and the Chin, Kayah, and Kachin hill tribes. In 1962 U Nu's government succumbed to an army coup, led by NE WIN, who established an authoritarian state based on quasi-socialist and Buddhist principles, and maintained a policy of strict neutrality. When he retired in 1986, U San Yu became chairman of the governing Burma Socialist Program Party, still faced by intransigent ethnic insurgent groups. In September 1988 General Saw Maung seized power, imposing martial law, and changing the country's name to Myanmar. Its social, economic, and political problems only worsened. During 1989, Aung San's daughter Daw AUNG SAN SUU KYI emerged as a leader of the opposition, but was placed under house arrest. Her party, the National League for Democracy (NLD), won a two-thirds majority in elections to a constituent assembly in 1990. However, Saw Maung's State Law and Order Restoration Council (SLORC) refused to allow the assembly to meet and arrested NLD leaders. By now various ethnic separatist guerrilla groups and private armies were roaming the

country, some funded by illegal drug traffic. Fighting in the Muslim majority border state of Rakhine between government forces and Rohingya rebels led to some 200,000 Rohingya Muslims fleeing to Bangladesh in 1992. In April 1992 Saw Maung was replaced by his deputy, General Than Shwe. Some degree of political liberalization followed, but the government's emergency powers remained in force. A national convention to co-ordinate the drafting of a new constitution was inaugurated in 1993, but few meetings were held. Aung San Suu Kyi agreed to hold meetings with SLORC leaders and she was released from house arrest in 1995. Although she was reinstated as leader of the NLD, the official electoral commission vetoed this decision. The NLD boycotted the national convention and was then formally expelled from it by SLORC. By mid-1995 15 guerrilla groups had agreed to ceasefires, but the Karens and the Mong Tai Army continued to fight. During 1996 regular mass pro-democracy demonstrations were held outside the house of Aung San Suu Kyi, while the military junta faced growing international criticism over its suppression of legitimate government. Despite this, Myanmar was admitted to the ASSOCIATION OF SOUTH-EAST ASIAN NATIONS in 1997.

CAPITAL:	Yangôn (formerly Rangoon)
AREA:	676,577 sq km (261,228 sq miles)
POPULATION:	45.976 million (1996)
CURRENCY:	1 kyat = 100 pyas
RELIGIONS:	Buddhist 75.2%; Christian 4.9%; Muslim 16.0%; traditional beliefs 1.1%; Hindu 0.5%
ETHNIC GROUPS:	Burman 69.0%; Shan 8.5%; Karen 6.2%; Rakhine 4.5%; Mon 2.4%; Chin 2.2%; Kachin 1.4%
LANGUAGES:	Burmese (official); minority languages; English
INTERNATIONAL ORGANIZATIONS:	UN; Colombo Plan; ASEAN

Mycenaean civilization The culture that dominated mainland Greece from *c.* 1580 BC to *c.* 1120 BC, when the invading DORIANS destroyed the citadels of Mycenae and Tiryns. Another important Peloponnesian centre was Pylos, and Mycenaean influence spread as far north as southern Thessaly. Mycenaeans seem to have conquered KNOSSOS in Crete in *c.* 1450, and their traders travelled widely in Asia Minor, Cyprus, and Syria. It seems that they also sacked Troy *c.* 1200, though the duration and scale of the expedition were doubtless exaggerated by HOMER in his epic, the *Iliad*. Finds from the early period bear witness to considerable wealth and a high artistic skill. At Mycenae, Tiryns, and Pylos have been excavated palaces, in each of which the central room is the *megaron*, rectangular in shape with one side open and columns supporting a roof; here stood the royal throne and the hearth.

Mysore A former Princely State in south-west India. In early times this region had formed part of successive Hindu kingdoms, including that of the Hoysalas (11th–13th centuries). In the 14th century Muslim expansion from the north led to the emergence of the great Hindu empire of VIJAYANAGAR whose power centred in this region. When Vijayanagar declined the Wadiya family was well placed to set up an independent kingdom. However, strong neighbours prevented consolidation, and in 1761 the Wadiya raja had to surrender power to an enterprising Muslim soldier, HYDER ALI. He and his son, TIPU SULTAN, fought bravely, and with initial success, against EAST INDIA COMPANY forces in four 'Mysore wars' (1767–69; 1780–84; 1797 and 1799), but their capital, Seringapatam, finally fell in 1799. The British annexed almost half of Mysore, but restored the core of the kingdom to the Wadiya rajas.

Mzilikazi (*c*. 1796–1868) NDEBELE leader. The first great ruler of the Ndebele, he united his people into a nation under his leadership. He became a war leader under SHAKA, King of the Zulu, but rebelled in 1822. He led his people away from Zululand to what is now the western Transvaal, and then settled with his subjects in the area of Bulawayo. In 1837 he fled north, subduing the Shona, and ruling the Ndebele until his death.

nabob A servant of the EAST INDIA COMPANY who had amassed fortunes in India, sometimes unscrupulously, which they then used for bettering their economic and social positions in England. The term is corrupted from the Persian title nawab, which originally designated governors administering Indian provinces for the MOGUL emperors and was used as a term of derision, particularly during the 18th century. Rulers of some Muslim Princely States continued to use the title during the British Raj period.

Nadir Shah (1688–1747) Ruler of Persia (1736–47) and scourge of central Asia and India. Of Turkish origin and until 1726 a bandit chieftain, he rose to prominence under the Safavid shahs of Persia, acting as king-maker during an era of disputed succession. In 1736 when the infant shah died he seized the throne and immediately embarked on expeditions against neighbouring states. In 1739 he attacked Delhi, capital of MOGUL India, but retreated after slaughtering the citizens. Campaigns against Russia and Turkey followed but military adventures were by then at the price of Persia's economic stability. His own subjects suffered as much as his enemies from his ruthless methods, and he was assassinated by his own troops.

NAFTA NORTH AMERICAN FREE TRADE AGREEMENT.

Nagasaki Japanese city, capital of the southernmost island of Kyushu. On 9 August 1945, three days after the first atomic bomb attack on HIROSHIMA, Nagasaki became the next target. The hilly terrain protected the population of 230,000 from the full effects of the explosion but 40,000 people were killed instantly and tremendous destruction was caused. On the following day Japan offered to surrender and the ceasefire began on 15 August, the official surrender finally being signed on 2 September.

Nagorno Karabagh ARMENIA; AZERBAIJAN.

Nagy, Imre (1896–1958) Hungarian statesman. He took part in the RUSSIAN REVOLUTION and the RUSSIAN CIVIL WAR. As Hungarian Minister of Agriculture (1945–46) he was responsible for major land reforms and helped in the Communist take-over in Hungary. Prime Minister (1953–55), he became popular because of his policy of liberalization and de-collectivization. Denounced for TITOISM, he was removed from power (1955). Shortly before the outbreak of the HUNGARIAN REVOLUTION he was reappointed. After the collapse of the Revolution, he was seized by Soviet authorities and handed over to János KÁDÁR, who had him tried in secret and executed.

Nakasone Yasuhiro (1917–) Japanese statesman. He was elected to the House of Representatives in 1947. Nakasone succeeded Suzuki as Prime Minister and President of the LIBERAL DEMOCRATIC PARTY in October 1982 and held power until his resignation in 1987, despite the damage done to his party by the involvement of Kakuei Tanaka in the Lockheed corruption scandal. His domestic policies were based on a package of administrative, fiscal, and educational reforms, while internationally he was committed to close ties with the USA and greater involvement in world affairs. He rejoined the party in 1991.

Nakhichevan AZERBAIJAN.

Namibia (formerly South-West Africa) A country in southern Africa with borders on Angola in the north, Botswana in the east, and South Africa in the south.

Physical. In the north-east of Namibia a long sliver of territory, the Caprivi Strip, reaches between Angola and Botswana to Zambia. In the west the Namib Desert stretches down the Atlantic Ocean coast; in the east is the Kalahari. The higher land between is also hot and arid and has no permanent rivers.

Economy. Poor rainfall limits agriculture to livestock-raising, although fishing, millet, maize, and wheat are also important. Exports are dominated by uranium and diamonds. The economy has not recovered from the devastation of the war for independence, and is still highly dependent on South Africa and multinational companies.

History. Namibia was occupied by Khoikhoi (Hottentot), San (Bushman), and Herero peoples when Portuguese navigators explored the coastal areas of the country in the late 15th century. German missionaries went there in the 19th century and in 1884 the German protectorate of South-West Africa was established. In 1915, during World War I, it was captured by South African forces, and in 1920 became a LEAGUE OF NATIONS mandated territory under South Africa. In 1946 the UNITED NATIONS refused to allow it to be incorporated into South Africa and ended the mandate (1964), renaming the territory Namibia. In 1971 the International Court of Justice at The Hague ruled that the continued occupation of Namibia by South Africa was illegal and the UN recognized the Black nationalist group, SWAPO (South West Africa People's Organization), as the legitimate representative of the people of Namibia. A National Assembly for internal government was established by South Africa in 1979 but SWAPO guerrillas continued to operate from Angola, which South African troops invaded. In 1988 South Africa was persuaded by the UN to negotiate with the SWAPO leader Samuel Nujoma. A Geneva protocol was signed in August and SWAPO won elections in November 1989, with Nujoma becoming President. Namibia gained independence as a multiparty democracy in 1990. Walvis Bay, a major port, remained an enclave of South Africa until 1994, when it was returned to Namibia. Nujoma was re-elected President in 1994.

CAPITAL:	Windhoek
AREA:	824,292 sq km (317,818 sq miles)
POPULATION:	1.709 million (1996)
CURRENCY:	1 Namibian dollar = 100 cents
RELIGIONS:	Lutheran 51.2%; Roman Catholic 19.8%; Dutch Reformed 6.1%; Anglican 5.0%

ETHNIC GROUPS:	Ovambo 49.8%; Kavango 9.3%; Herero 7.5%; Damara 7.5%; White 6.4%; Nama 4.8%
LANGUAGES:	Afrikaans; English; German (official); Ambo; Herero; local languages
INTERNATIONAL ORGANIZATIONS:	Commonwealth; UN; OAS; SADC

Nanak (1469–1539) The founder of SIKHISM and the first Sikh GURU. He was born into a Hindu family at Talwandi in the Punjab (now known as Nankana Sahib, in present-day Pakistan). Legends about his life are contained in the four *janam sakhis* ('evidences of his life'). As a child, Nanak learned about ISLAM as well as HINDUISM and he used to compose hymns with a Muslim musician. He was a householder for the first part of his life but at the age of 30 he went travelling in search of spiritual inspiration. He underwent a religious experience in which he had a vision of God. Nanak then proclaimed that he was neither a Hindu nor a Muslim; he gave away all his possessions and became a wandering preacher, hoping to bring Muslims and Hindus together by expounding his message of the oneness of God and the equality of men. He preached a new path to the orthodox Hindu goal of release from the cycle of rebirth and attainment of union with God and practised a form of inward and disciplined meditation on the name of God. He returned to the Punjab after years of travelling and set up a community of disciples, who became known as Sikhs (from Sanskrit, *shishya*, 'pupil'). His teachings in the form of short devotional hymns are contained in the *Adi Granth*.

Nana Sahib (or Brahmin Dhundu Panth) (*c.* 1820–59) Hindu leader. On the outbreak of the INDIAN MUTINY in Cawnpore (now Kanpur) (1857), he reluctantly joined the rebels and accepted the surrender of the British garrison under Sir Hugh Wheeler, promising safe conduct to its people. A reluctant recruit to the Mutiny, he subsequently fled to Nepal and his fate is uncertain, but it is likely that he died in the jungle.

Nanjing, Treaty of (1842) The treaty between Britain and China that ended the First OPIUM WAR. The first UNEQUAL TREATY, it ceded Hong Kong to Britain, broke the Chinese monopoly on trade, and opened the TREATY PORTS of Xiamen (Amoy), Guangzhou (Canton), Fuzhou (Foochow), Ningbo (Ningpo), and Shanghai to foreign trade. Further treaties extended trade and residence privileges to other nations and set up the framework for Western economic expansion in China.

Nansen, Fridtjof (1861–1930) Norwegian explorer, oceanographer, statesman, and humanitarian, who first became famous by crossing Greenland in 1888–89. Four years later, to test his theory of a polar current flowing towards Greenland's east coast, he set course for the North Pole in the *Fram*, a vessel specially constructed with thick-timbered sides. Caught in an ice-floe, it drifted northward for a year and then, as expected, began to drift westwards. At this point Nansen, with one companion, took to sledges and reached latitude 86° N, the nearest to the Pole that man had ever been. The whole journey took three years; and within that time the *Fram* drifted right round the Pole, just as Nansen had foreseen. An active member of the LEAGUE OF NATIONS, Nansen organized relief work among displaced persons, mainly Russian refugees and famine victims.

Nantes, Edict of (1598) A decree promulgated by HENRY IV that terminated the FRENCH WARS OF RELIGION. It was signed at Nantes, a port on the Loire estuary in western France. The Edict defined the religious and civic rights of the HUGUENOTS, giving them freedom of worship and a state subsidy to support their troops and pastors. It virtually created a state within a state and was incompatible with the policies of RICHELIEU and MAZARIN and of LOUIS XIV. The fall of the Huguenot stronghold of La Rochelle to Richelieu's army in 1628 marked the end of these political privileges. After 1665 Louis XIV embarked on a policy of persecuting Protestants and in 1685 he revoked the Edict.

Naoroji, Dadabhai (1825–1917) Indian nationalist leader. He was the first Indian to be elected to the British House of Commons, serving as Liberal Member of Parliament for Central Finsbury (1892–95). His campaign against the drain of wealth from India to Britain, defined in his classic study *Poverty and Un-British Rule in India* (1901), stimulated economic nationalism in the subcontinent. Active in promoting Indian social and political causes, he was a founder of the Indian National CONGRESS, serving as its President (1886, 1893, and 1906).

Napier, Robert Cornelis, 1st Baron of Magdala (1810–90) British field-marshal and civil engineer. He served with distinction in the SIKH WARS and during the INDIAN MUTINY, but made his reputation as the engineer chiefly responsible for the programme of public works in the Punjab from 1849 to 1856. He led an expedition to Ethiopia in which he captured MAGDALA (1868) and compelled the release of British captives. In 1870 he became commander-in-chief in India.

Naples A city on the Bay of Naples in south-east Italy. It was settled by Greeks from Chalcis and Athens, who submitted to Roman conquest in 328 BC. When Roman rule weakened, Naples was invaded by the Goths but under BYZANTINE influence in the 6th century it began to flourish again and survived as an independent duchy until 1139 when it was conquered by the NORMANS. It became part of the Kingdom of the Two Sicilies and passed successively to the Angevins, the Aragonese, and from 1504 to Spain, becoming a key base for Spanish and HABSBURG power in their Italian disputes with the VALOIS kings of France. It passed to the Austrians in the War of the SPANISH SUCCESSION but was conquered for the BOURBONS in 1734. Napoleon gained it in 1799.

Napoleon I (Napoléon Bonaparte) (1769–1821) Emperor of the French (1804–14). Born in Ajaccio, he was a Corsican of Italian descent. He was educated in military schools in France and served in the French Revolutionary army. By the age of 26 he was a general, and placed in supreme command of the campaign against Sardinia and Austria in Italy (1796–97). This provided him with some of the most spectacular victories of his military career and resulted in the creation of the French-controlled Cisalpine Republic in northern Italy. In 1798 he led an army to Egypt, intending to create a French empire overseas and to threaten the British overland route to India. NELSON, by destroying the French fleet at the Battle of the Nile (1798), prevented this plan. Bonaparte returned to France (1799) and joined a conspiracy by SIÈYES which overthrew the Directory and dissolved the First Republic. Elected First Consul for ten years, he became the supreme ruler of France. During the next four years he began his reorganization of the French legal system (see CODE NAPOLÉON), the administration, the Church, and education.

With the Treaties of Lunéville with Austria (1801), and Amiens with Britain (1802), France became paramount in Europe. In 1803 Britain again declared war on France, and Napoleon prepared to invade it. The ruthless execution (1804) of the Duc d'ENGHIEN on suspicion of conspiracy provoked criticism throughout Europe. In the same year Napoleon crowned himself Emperor of the French. He created an imperial court and nobility around himself, while at the same time restricting the liberal provisions of the earlier revolutionary constitution. In 1804–05, a European coalition against Napoleon was formed and he launched his armies against it. He defeated the Austrians at Ulm, occupied Vienna, and won his most brilliant victory over the combined Austrian and Russian forces at AUSTERLITZ (1805). The naval victory by Nelson at the Battle of TRAFALGAR (1805) led Napoleon to seek Britain's defeat by the introduction of the CONTINENTAL SYSTEM, which aimed to stop all trade between Britain and France and its allies on the continent of Europe.

Napoleon I   *This famous oil painting (1821) by Jacques-Louis David shows the young Napoleon leading his troops over the Alps. The rocks beneath him bear the names Bonaparte, Hannibal, and Charlemagne.*

In 1806 the Holy Roman Empire was dissolved and Napoleon consolidated his domination of the continent. The difficulty of enforcing the Continental System, the ill-fated invasion of Russia (1812), and the set-backs of the PENINSULAR WAR (1807–14) all contributed to Napoleon's decline. Following his defeat in the battle of LEIPZIG (18 October 1813) and the proclamation by

TALLEYRAND of the deposition of the emperor, he abdicated in 1814. After a brief exile on Elba he returned, but defeat at the Battle of WATERLOO (1815) ended his rule after only a HUNDRED DAYS. He spent the rest of his life in exile on St Helena. In 1796 he married JOSÉPHINE de Beauharnais, whose failure to give him a son led to their divorce. In 1810 Napoleon married the Austrian princess Marie-Louise. Their only child, Joseph-François-Charles, crowned as the Roi de Rome, died aged 21.

Napoleon III (Charles-Louis Napoléon Bonaparte) (1808–73) Emperor of the French (1852–70). He was the third son of Hortense de Beauharnais stepdaughter of NAPOLEON I and Louis Bonaparte (1778–1846), brother of Napoleon I and King of Holland (1806–10). After the fall of Napoleon I, Napoleon III began a long period of exile in Switzerland, where he was associated with the CARBONARI. On the death of Napoleon I's only son, the Roi de Rome, in 1832, he became Bonapartist pretender to the French throne and twice attempted to overthrow LOUIS-PHILIPPE. After his first attempt in 1836, he was deported to the USA. He went to Switzerland in 1837 to see his dying mother but was forced by the French to leave and so went to Britain in 1838. He came to believe in a political ideology based on the life of Napoleon I and in 1840 embarked upon the disastrous 'Boulogne Conspiracy' to gather supporters. He was arrested and imprisoned in the fortress of Ham. He escaped to London (1846) disguised as a mason by the name of 'Badinguet', which thereafter became his nickname. During the REVOLUTIONS OF 1848, he returned to France, and in December under the new constitution was elected President of the French Republic. In 1852, following a coup against Parliament, he had himself accepted as Emperor of the French. Napoleon III took part in the CRIMEAN WAR and presided over the Congress of PARIS (1856). He at first supported the RISORGIMENTO but concluded a peace treaty with Austria at Villafranca in 1859. His 'Liberal Empire' (1860–70) widened the powers of the legislative assembly and lifted restrictions on civil liberties. His attempts at extending French colonial interests to MEXICO (1861–67) ended in failure. Underestimating BISMARCK, he allowed the latter's belligerent EMS TELEGRAM to provoke him into fighting the FRANCO-PRUSSIAN WAR, the outcome of which brought ruin to the Second Empire. He was captured by the Prussians and deposed, spending the rest of his life in exile in England.

Napoleonic Wars The campaigns carried out between NAPOLEON I and the European powers, including Britain (1796–1815). The first great Italian campaign (1796) under Napoleon I secured a series of decisive victories for the French over the Austrians in northern Italy. In 1798 he led an expedition to Egypt, but the British fleet under Admiral NELSON destroyed the French fleet in Aboukir Bay. In 1799 Napoleon I led an army over the Alps to win the Battle of Marengo (1800) over the Austrians. Britain, apprehensive of Napoleon's threat in the Mediterranean and in continental Europe, was by 1803 once more at war with France. Nelson destroyed the combined Spanish and French fleets at TRAFALGAR (1805), and in the same year Napoleon swung his *grande armée* towards Austria, which, with Russia and Sweden, joined Britain in the Third Coalition. Napoleon's forces encircled the Austrians at Ulm, forcing them to surrender without a battle. Napoleon fought and defeated the emperors of Austria and Russia at the Battle of AUSTERLITZ (1805) and forced Austria to sue for peace. In the following year Prussia joined the Third Coalition but, in a campaign that lasted 23 days, Napoleon broke the Prussian armies at JENA and Auerstädt and accepted the surrender of Prussia. The Russian emperor ALEXANDER I concluded a treaty of friendship and alliance with Napoleon at TILSIT in July 1807. In 1808 a revolt broke out in Spain, which by now was also under French rule. Napoleon sent a large force to quell it but was confronted by the British army under Sir Arthur Wellesley, later Duke of WELLINGTON. Britain won a series of victories in the PENINSULAR WAR, which, though not conclusive, occupied 300,000 French soldiers when they were needed elsewhere. In 1812 Napoleon I defeated the Russians at BORODINO and occupied Moscow, but instead of suing for peace, Alexander I's forces withdrew further into the country. Napoleon I's *grande armée* was forced to retreat from Moscow in the severest winter conditions, which cost the lives of nearly half a million men. After a crushing defeat at LEIPZIG the following year, Napoleon I abdicated and retired to Elba (1814). Next year he returned to France and was finally defeated by Wellington and Blücher at the Battle of WATERLOO (1815).

Narva, Battle of (30 November 1700) The crushing defeat of PETER THE GREAT of Russia by CHARLES XII of Sweden at the beginning of the NORTHERN WAR at the port of Narva, in Estonia. In 1704 Peter the Great recovered the town.

Narváez, Pánfilo de (*c.* 1478–1528) Spanish conquistador. He gained a reputation as a ruthless soldier in the conquest of Cuba in 1511; later, as governor, he watched his men slaughter some 2,500 unarmed Cubans. When he was sent to fetch the rebellious CORTÉS in Mexico in 1520, most of his men deserted, and he lost an eye in the ensuing battle. Leading an expedition to Florida in 1528, he ignored advice from his lieutenant, CABEZA DE VACA, divided his forces, and was lost at sea trying to return to Cuba in makeshift boats.

Nasca NAZCA.

Naseby, Battle of (14 June 1645) A decisive victory for the Parliamentary forces during the ENGLISH CIVIL WAR. The battle took place near Naseby in Northamptonshire, after CHARLES I's storming and sacking of Leicester. Led by Fairfax and Cromwell, the NEW MODEL ARMY outnumbered the CAVALIER force by about one-third. Prince Rupert's cavalry squandered an early advantage, as at EDGEHILL. After a bitter struggle the Roundhead forces proved superior and the Cavaliers suffered extremely heavy losses.

Nash, Richard (1674–1762) English dandy, known in later life as 'Beau' Nash, English dandy. In 1705 Nash moved to Bath when it was a declining health resort, attracted by its gambling. He soon became its most influential resident, organizing such improvements as street lighting and the suppression of duelling, and he was especially famous for defining and insisting upon correct dress. His influence turned Bath into a fashionable SPA TOWN. New anti-gambling laws in the 1740s caused financial difficulties for Nash but in 1758 the city corporation, in gratitude, granted him a pension of £126 a year.

Nash, Sir Walter (1882–1968) New Zealand statesman. A life-long Christian Socialist, he joined the Labour Party, becoming the most important spokesman for its moderate wing. He (and Peter FRASER) turned the Labour Party into a national organization and formulated the policies which led to the election of the first Labour Government in 1935. He played a major role in piloting through Parliament in 1938 the great system of child allowances, and 'free' medicine, which was the most extensive system of social security in the world at that time. He became leader of the Opposition in 1950. Nash led Labour to a narrow victory in the 1957 election, serving as Prime Minister until the party's defeat in 1960. During this period, despite financial stringency, he introduced further important social reforms.

Nasser, Gamal Abdul (1918–70) Egyptian statesman. Together with three other officers in the Egyptian army, he founded the revolutionary Free Officers' Movement with the objective of expelling the British and the Egyptian royal family. In 1952, with 89 Free Officers, he achieved an almost bloodless coup, forcing the abdication of King FAROUK. A republic was declared and a Revolutionary Command Council set up, with Major-General Muhammad Neguib as President. In 1954 he deposed Neguib, and became head of state. In 1956 he promulgated a one-party constitution. With massive Soviet aid he launched a programme of domestic modernization. Failing to receive British and US support for a project to extend the Aswan High Dam, he nationalized the Suez Canal Company (1956), whose shares were mainly owned by British and French investors; his object was to use the canal dues to pay for the Aswan Dam project. Britain, France, and Israel invaded Egypt, but the SUEZ WAR was halted, mainly by US intervention. His attempt to unite the Arab world in a United Arab Republic, a federation with Syria, failed. In 1967 Egypt was disastrously defeated by Israel in the SIX-DAY WAR but Nasser's reputation as a Pan-Arab leader and social reformer emerged untarnished. He died in office.

Natal A former province of the Republic of SOUTH AFRICA. Natal was the smallest of the provinces of South Africa, facing the Indian Ocean. The region comprises a humid subtropical narrow coastal strip with palm trees. A broad inland belt of temperate grassland can support crops of sugar cane, cotton, and tobacco.

History. Natal had been settled, probably since the first millennium, by African farmers. The region was devastated during the Nguni Difagane Wars (1819–38). During this period, European settlers arrived. In 1840 the Boers set up an independent Republic of Natal but Britain annexed it in 1843. Many Boers then migrated to the ORANGE FREE STATE. In 1856 Natal became a self-governing colony. ZULULAND was annexed to it in 1897. Natal was invaded by Afrikaner troops in the Second BOER WAR, but these were checked at Ladysmith in February 1900. Natal joined the Union in 1910. In 1994 the province became part of the new region of Kwazulu-Natal.

Natchez A Native American people of the middle Mississippi River region, especially important because their tribal organization survived long enough for it to be documented, giving a unique insight into the prehistoric MISSISSIPPI CULTURES. Their chiefdoms comprised two or more villages linked under the same authority and were organized into a complex social hierarchy of nobility (comprising 'suns', 'nobles', and 'honoureds') and commoners (called 'stinkards'). Nobility were required to marry commoners, and descent was through the female line. Thus children of stinkard fathers took their mother's rank, while those of commoner mothers were one rank below their fathers.

An attack on Fort Rosalie in 1729 led to a strong French response and many Natchez villages were destroyed. In 1731 450 Natchez captives were sold as slaves and most of the remainder joined the CHICKASAW.

Nation, Carry (Amelia Moore) (1846–1911) US temperance agitator. Born in Kansas, and married to an alcoholic, she became an evangelical Christian and a militant temperance advocate. During the 1890s she became convinced of her mission to destroy the illegal bars in nominally 'dry' states, such as Kansas. A tall powerfully built woman, she was often involved in fights and was arrested 30 times for violent behaviour. Her exploits helped to create a climate for the introduction of PROHIBITION. An advocate of WOMEN'S SUFFRAGE, she received little support from other reform organizations because of her unorthodox conduct.

National Assembly The revolutionary assembly formed by members of the Third Estate on 17 June 1789 when they failed to gain the support of the whole of the French STATES-GENERAL. Three days later the members signed the TENNIS COURT OATH. The Assembly was accepted by LOUIS XVI the following month, having added 'Constituent' to its title. In August it agreed upon the influential declaration of the RIGHTS OF MAN AND THE CITIZEN and two years later its constitution was accepted by the king. Its reorganization of local government into departments, although long lasting, had less immediate success. Renamed the Legislative Assembly (1791) and the National Convention (1792), it was dominated by the GIRONDINS and the JACOBINS before being replaced by the DIRECTORY in 1795.

National governments The British coalition governments of 1931 to 1935. In August 1931 a financial crisis led to a split within the Labour government, nine ministers resigning rather than accepting cuts in unemployment benefits. The Liberal leader Herbert Samuel suggested that the Prime Minister, Ramsay MACDONALD, create a 'government of national salvation', by inviting Conservatives and Liberals to replace them, and the first National government was formed on 24 August. An emergency budget was introduced, increasing taxes and proposing to reduce both benefits and public sector salaries. When naval ratings at Invergordon refused duty in protest, this so-called INVERGORDON MUTINY caused further financial panic and sterling fell by 25%. Britain abandoned the GOLD STANDARD and FREE TRADE, adopting a policy of protection. The Labour Party split, supporters of the government being regarded as traitors to socialism. In October MacDonald won a general election and formed a second National government, but its balance was now strongly towards the Conservative Party. The governments of Stanley BALDWIN (1935–37) and Neville CHAMBERLAIN (1937–40) retained the name National, but they were effectively Conservative governments.

national insurance (or social insurance) A state insurance scheme financed by compulsory contributions from employee and employer. It seeks to provide economic protection against various risks, including sickness and unemployment. Such schemes help to fund social provision within the WELFARE STATE. Pioneered in Germany by BISMARCK, national insurance schemes were introduced in other European countries, including Britain (1911), and in New Zealand before World War I, to provide state assistance in sickness, accident, unemployment, and old age. In Britain, as a result of the BEVERIDGE report (1942), national insurance was extended to all adults in employment. As part of the NEW DEAL in the USA a federal national insurance scheme was introduced by the Social Security Act of 1935. The majority of US citizens, however, rely on private insurance schemes for health, accident, pension, and other provision. In Britain the Conservative governments of the 1980s and 1990s promoted private insurance, especially private pensions, on the grounds that national insurance contributions were failing to provide enough money to meet the claims of an ageing population.

National Federation of Labour RED FEDS.

nationalism The demand by members of a nation for political self-government, which normally entails the founding of an independent state. A nation may be described as a group of people who identify with one another and acknowledge a common loyalty by virtue of descent, language, culture, or religion. National identities have proved remarkably resilient in the modern world and they have been a potent source of political change. Early nationalist movements, such as those in Germany and Italy in the 19th century, were typically concerned to build large and powerful states out of existing small principalities. In the 20th century nationalists have more often sought either to throw off imperial or colonial rule (many developing countries have witnessed nationalist movements aiming at the formation of independent states) or else to break away from an established state. The many minorities or nationalities that sought independence from the Soviet Union in 1991 show nationalism taking this secessionist form. Fierce fighting occurred in Georgia, Armenia, Azerbaijan, and Moldova as different groups sought to establish separate nations for themselves; similarly fighting broke out in the republics of the former Yugoslavia. Liberals and socialists have often been inclined to dismiss nationalism as an irrational phenomenon arising from the most primitive elements in human nature, but few would now deny the mobilizing power of national sentiments and allegiances. (See also COMMUNAL CONFLICT.)

National Party A South African political party. It was originally founded in 1913–15 by General J. B. M. HERTZOG after his secession from Botha's South African Party. In 1924 it became the Nationalist-Labour alliance under Hertzog, who joined SMUTS in the UNITED PARTY in 1934. In the same year D. F. MALAN founded the Purified Nationalist Party, which was reunited in 1939 with Hertzog, emerging as the Afrikaner-dominated party of APARTHEID. It held uninterrupted power from 1948 to 1994. Attempts by President P. W. Botha to meet the twin threats of domestic unrest and international condemnation of apartheid with a programme of mild reforms led to defections by supporters of apartheid to the Conservative Party and extreme right-wing

Afrikaner groups. Under President DE KLERK it opened its ranks to all races in August 1990, winning, at the cost of further defections of right-wingers, some support from moderates among both the coloured and unenfranchised Black population. In South Africa's first multiracial elections in 1994 the National Party won 82 out of 400 seats in the National Assembly and de Klerk was appointed Second Deputy President by Nelson MANDELA. In 1996, following the ratification of a permanent constitution, the National Party withdrew from the government in order to become an opposition party.

National Party of Australia An Australian political party largely representing rural interests. Farmers' representatives were elected to colonial (later state) parliaments from the 1890s onwards. A number of farmers' candidates who had been elected to the Federal Parliament formed the Country Party of Australia in 1916. It has governed federally in coalition with the Nationalist Party (1923–29), the United Australia Party (1934–39, 1940–41), and the LIBERAL PARTY (1949–72, 1975–83). Several of its parliamentary leaders have been Prime Ministers, albeit briefly. They were Earle Page (1939), Arthur William Fadden (1941), and John McEwen (1967–68). It has also governed (under various names), mostly in coalition with other parties, for periods in most states. The party's national name was changed to the National Country Party in 1975 and to the National Party of Australia in 1982.

National People's Party KUOMINTANG.

Nation of Islam Splinter group of the BLACK MUSLIM MOVEMENT, formed in 1985 by the radical African-American preacher Louis Farrakhan (1933–   ), who trained as a teacher and was converted to Islam by MALCOLM X. The Nation of Islam was the original name of the Black Muslims (disbanded in 1985 by the son of their founder Elijah Muhammad) and was adopted by Farrakhan to proclaim his group's adherence to the ideals of the movement, in particular Black separatism. In common with the original organization, the Nation of Islam has gained a reputation for instilling discipline and purpose in its members and working to rid the African-American community of exploitation through crime and drug abuse. In 1995, a 'million-man' march on Washington, DC, was attended by around 400,000 supporters.

Farrakhan has been accused of fomenting racial hatred in his pronouncements. In particular, his alleged ANTI-SEMITISM led to him being banned from entering Britain in 1986 and from Israel in 1997.

Native Americans The original inhabitants of North America, who migrated from Asia from about 30,000 years ago. By the time of European colonization, the indigenous population was probably under 900,000, mostly living along the coasts rather than in the barren interior. They lived in small villages which, except in the south-west, were organized round hunting, with agriculture a secondary activity. The overall social organization was that of the tribe and warfare between tribes was endemic. Conflict with British and French settlers in the north-east forced the Native Americans inland, as did clashes with the Spanish in the south-west. The acquisition of horses from Europeans increased the number of nomadic societies on the Great Plains. The major tribes are usually divided geographically, North-

eastern Woodland (for example, ALGONQUIN, DELAWARE, IROQUOIS), South-east (e.g. CHEROKEE, CHOCTAW, CREEK), Great Plains (e.g. BLACKFOOT, COMANCHE, Dakota), Desert-west (e.g. APACHE, Pueblo, NAVAHO), Far west (e.g. Paiute), Pacific North-west (e.g. Chinook), and Mountain or Plateau (e.g. Nez Percé).

NATO (North Atlantic Treaty Organization) Defence alliance between Western powers. Founded in 1949, it was established primarily to counter the perceived military threat from the Soviet Union and its allies, which in 1955 set up the WARSAW PACT as a counter-measure. According to the Treaty, the members agree that an attack on one of them shall be considered an attack against them all. The Treaty also encourages political, economic, and social co-operation. NATO headquarters are in Brussels, and its highest organ is the North Atlantic Council, which meets at the level of heads of governments, ministers, or permanent representatives. Under the North Atlantic Council is the Military Committee, whose executive agency, composed of representatives of chiefs of staff, is based in Washington, DC. NATO committed the USA to the defence of Europe during the period of poor EAST–WEST RELATIONS (the COLD WAR).

The collapse of communism after 1989 and the dissolution of the Warsaw Pact in 1991 led to a reassessment of the role of NATO in relation to the emerging eastern European democracies. The North Atlantic Co-operation Council (NACC) was established in 1991 as a forum for consultation between NATO and the formerly communist republics, which were invited in 1994 to join a 'partnership for peace'. NATO launched its first-ever aggresive military action in BOSNIA-HERZEGOVINA in February 1994, when it shot down Serb fighter planes that were flying in the UN-established 'no-fly zone' and in April 1994 bombed Serb ground targets. In 1997 the so-called NATO-Russian Founding Act was signed: this gave Russia a formal voice in NATO's affairs in return for acceptance of NATO's expansion into eastern Europe. Shortly afterwards Hungary, Poland, and the Czech Republic were invited to join NATO.

Natufians A group of prehistoric plant-food gatherers and gazelle-hunters in the LEVANT, named after a site discovered in the Wadi el-Natuf. They moved into the region at the end of the last glacial period (between 14,000 and 10,000 years ago), as the northern ice-sheets began to retreat and a period of increased rainfall allowed wild cereals to grow. Their remains have been found both in caves and on campsites underlying the mud brick villages of later farming groups who had progressed from simply collecting food to deliberately sowing and cultivating cereals. Excavations at JERICHO are important illustrations of this transition to settled agriculture.

Nauru A tiny island country just south of the Equator in the south-west Pacific Ocean.

Physical. Nauru is a coral island, with a band of fertile land around the coast rising to a central plateau.

Economy. Nauru's wealth lies in phosphate deposits derived from guano, the excrement of seabirds, which is used as manure. The supply of phosphates is almost exhausted and money has been invested abroad to provide an alternative source of revenue in the future.

History. Nauru was settled by various Polynesian peoples who travelled there from other islands before it

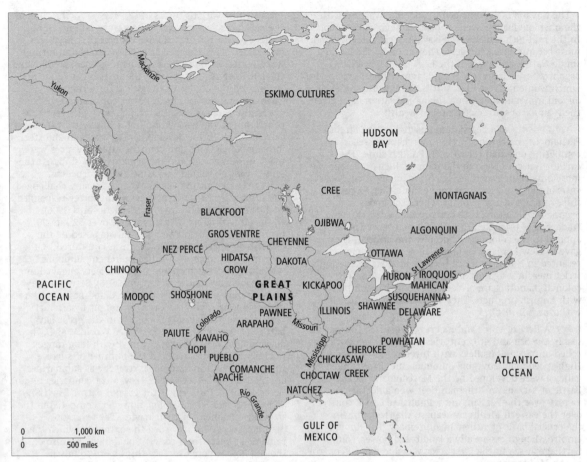

Native Americans (tribal distribution in the late 15th century) *When the first European settlers arrived in North America, the Native American population was scattered widely throughout the whole continent. There were numerous different tribes and an extraordinary diversity of languages and cultures. Some cultural similarities can, however, be found between tribes living in areas of similar geography and climate. For example, in the wooded north-west coastal area, with its hospitable climate and plentiful food supplies, tribes lived a settled life with a well-developed culture; on the central plains the majority of tribes were nomadic, living by hunting buffalo; while in the fertile south-east an agricultural and trading economy was firmly established by the 14th century.*

was discovered by the British in 1798. In 1899 a British company, the Pacific Islands Company, based in Sydney, found that the island comprised the world's richest deposits of phosphate of lime. The company began mining the deposits in 1906. From 1888 to 1914 the island was part of Germany's Marshall Islands protectorate. Thereafter, apart from three years of Japanese occupation during World War II, Nauru was a trust territory of Britain, Australia, and New Zealand, before achieving independence and a limited membership of the Commonwealth in 1968. In 1993 Australia, Britain, and New Zealand agreed to pay compensation for the damage done to the island by the extensive mining of phosphates.

CAPITAL: Yaren (de facto: there is no official
                 capital)
AREA: 21 sq km (8.2 sq miles)
POPULATION: 10,600 (1996)
CURRENCY: 1 Australian dollar = 100 cents

RELIGIONS: Nauruan Protestant Church 43%
ETHNIC GROUPS: Nauruan 61%; other Pacific islanders 21%;
                 Asian 6%; European 2%
LANGUAGES: Nauruan; English
INTERNATIONAL
 ORGANIZATIONS: Commonwealth; South Pacific Forum

Navaho A group of over 50 Native American CLANS, who were originally nomadic HUNTER-GATHERERS and, like the related APACHES, originated in western Canada. They moved southwards to the 'four corners' area of Utah, Colorado, Arizona, and New Mexico between the 11th and 15th centuries, displacing much of the native ANASAZI culture to the south by the end of the 13th century, and raiding the neighbouring Hohokam to the south. Spanish contact began in 1540–42, and from 1609 Spanish missions worked among them. The Navaho adopted horse-breeding and pastoralism from the Spanish, as well as learning Anasazi weaving skills and Spanish silver-working artistry.

The Navaho often engaged in sporadic warfare with the pueblo (village)-dwelling peoples, such as the Hopi. In the mid-19th century, the Navaho were resettled and most became sheep farmers. They are now the largest single Native grouping in the USA. Their kinship organization is based on extended matrilineal groups, in which women have a high status. Recent discoveries of oil and mineral reserves on their reservation have given them an extra source of material wealth.

Navigation Acts Legislation enacted by the English Parliament to prevent foreign merchant vessels competing on equal terms with English ships. The earliest Act goes back to the reign of Richard II, but the most important was that of 1651, requiring that goods entering England must be carried in either English ships or ships of the country where the goods originated. Its aim was to destroy the Dutch carrying trade, and it provoked the ANGLO-DUTCH WARS. The Acts applied to the colonies and despite the impetus they gave to New England shipping, they were widely resented in North America because of their increasingly strict measures against smugglers and against the colonial manufacture of certain goods that competed with English products. They were modified in 1823 and withdrawn in 1849.

navy A fleet of ships and its crew, organized for war at sea. In the 5th and 4th centuries BC Athens and Corinth relied on TRIREMES (galleys with three banks of oars). High-speed manoeuvrable quinqueremes (five-banked galleys) were developed by the Macedonians. At the Battle of SALAMIS an Athenian fleet won a decisive victory over the Persians and established Greek control over the eastern Mediterranean, so the fleet remained the crucial basis of Athenian supremacy. The Roman empire, though essentially a land-based power, fought Carthage at sea in the First PUNIC WAR and gained control of the Mediterranean.

Navies were needed to protect trading vessels against pirates: the BYZANTINE EMPIRE maintained a defensive fleet to retain control over its vital trade arteries. In England, King ALFRED created a fleet in the 9th century in defence against Scandinavian invasions. The CINQUE PORTS supplied the English navy from the 11th to the 16th centuries and it was organized and enlarged under successive Tudor monarchs. The Italian city-states kept squadrons of galleys and adapted carracks (merchant ships) to defend their ports against the OTTOMAN Turks; the Battle of LEPANTO (1571) saw a Christian fleet decisively beat the Ottomans. The 17th century saw naval reorganization in England under PEPYS and the Dutch and French also expanded their fleets as trade and colonial expansion accelerated during the 18th century.

From the early Middle Ages the warship altered from being a converted merchant ship, modified by the addition of 'castles', fortified with land artillery, and manned by knights, into a specially armed vessel. By the 14th century ships were being fitted with guns and by the 16th century special warships were being built with heavy armaments. Success or failure in battle, however, was determined by tactical skill as all sailing ships were at the mercy of the wind.

By 1800 many countries had developed fleets of warships as well as continuing the practice of arming merchant ships in time of war. They were officered by professionals, but relied for their crews on men recruited by various forms of PRESSGANGS. At the time of the NAPOLEONIC WARS, naval vessels were sailing ships, built of wood and armed with cannon that fired broadsides. They engaged at close quarters and ratings were armed with muskets and hand-grenades. Following the Battle of TRAFALGAR (1805), the British navy dominated the oceans of the world for a century. Change came slowly. Steam power replaced sail only gradually, while in 1859 the French navy pioneered the protection of the wooden hull of a ship with iron plates (IRONCLADS). With the development of the iron and steel industry in the late 19th century, rapid advances were made in ship design and the armament of ships. At the same time the submarine, armed with torpedoes, emerged as a fighting vessel. When Germany challenged the supremacy of the British navy, the latter responded with the huge steel DREADNOUGHT battleships (1906), equipped with guns with a range of over 32 km (20 miles). During World War I the threat posed by the German submarine (U-boat) fleet was countered by the CONVOY SYSTEM to protect Allied merchant shipping, while the major British and German fleets engaged in the inconclusive battle of JUTLAND (1916). Between the wars aircraft were rapidly developed and naval warfare in World War II was increasingly fought by aircraft from aircraft carriers, particularly in the great naval battles of the PACIFIC CAMPAIGN. Since World War II, the development of submarines armed with long-range nuclear missiles has reduced the number of surface ships and revolutionized naval strategy as submarines are difficult to detect and destroy. Most countries retain fleets of small, fast vessels for coastal patrol. The USA and the former Soviet Union, however, competed in the size and armament of their navies. The FALKLANDS (MALVINAS) WAR (1982) revealed the extent to which there remained a place for a conventional navy but also showed how exposed surface ships were to missile attack. During the GULF WAR the navies of the Allied forces played an important strategic role. Six aircraft carriers provided launch sites from which air strikes against Iraqi ground targets were made. The small Iraqi coastal defence navy and Iraqi mines were destroyed quickly by Allied naval units. The threat of an Allied invasion of Kuwait from the sea tied down many Iraqi troops in defending Kuwait's coastline. (See illustrations on pp 466–67.)

Naxalite Movement An Indian revolutionary movement named after the village of Naxalbari in the Himalayan foothills in West Bengal, where it first began. The theoretician and founder of the movement, Charu Majumdar, a veteran communist, broke away from the Communist Party of India (Marxist) and established the Communist Party of India (Marxist-Leninist). The CPI (M-L) first organized several armed risings of landless agricultural labourers, especially in eastern India. It developed into an urban guerrilla movement, especially in Calcutta. Its programme of terror was suppressed with considerable violence. The CPI (M-L) eventually split up into several factions, one of which adopted a policy of participating in constitutional politics, but Naxalite atrocities continued into the early 1990s.

Nazarbayev, Nursultan (1940–) Kazakh politician; President of Kazakhstan from 1990. Nazarbayev was Prime Minister of the Kazakh Soviet Socialist Republic from 1984 and leader of its Communist Party from 1989.

Since Kazakhstan's independence, he has adopted economically liberal policies designed to promote the free market but has also taken measures to stifle radical nationalist opposition. He was instrumental in ensuring that the Central Asian republics retained a link to the Russian Federation through the COMMONWEALTH OF INDEPENDENT STATES, and also attracted Western aid. After the first multiparty elections held in Kazakhstan, in 1994, Nazarbayev dissolved parliament for frustrating his economic reforms, and secured the election of more malleable representatives in a ballot held in late 1995. At the same time, he extended his presidential term to the year 2000, endorsed by a referendum that gave him overwhelming support.

Nazca (or Nasca) A culture that developed on the southern Peruvian coast from *c.* 200 BC to 600 AD and was eventually eclipsed by the expansion of the Huari culture of central Peru in the 7th century. Its settlements and population remained modest, due to the dry environment. The Nazca used decorated pottery, which characteristically featured stylized animal and human figures, often painted with several colours. The Nazca Lines are large drawings of animals, abstract designs, and straight lines on the coastal plain, produced by clearing and aligning the surface stones to expose the underlying sand; their purpose is uncertain, but may have been religious.

Nazi A member of the *Nationalsozialistische Deutsche Arbeiterpartei* (NSDAP) or National Socialist German Workers' Party. The Party was founded in 1919 as the German Workers' Party by a Munich locksmith, Anton Drexler, adopted its new name in 1920, and was taken over by HITLER in 1921. The Nazis dominated Germany from 1933 to 1945. Insofar as the party had a coherent programme it consisted of opposition to democracy and a FASCIST belief in a one-party state. It promulgated theories of the purity of the Aryan race and consequent ANTI-SEMITISM, was allied to the old Prussian military tradition and an extreme sense of nationalism, and was inflamed by hatred of the humiliating terms inflicted on Germany in the VERSAILLES PEACE SETTLEMENT. Nazi ideology drew on the racist theories of the Comte de GOBINEAU, on the nationalist fervour of Heinrich von Treitschke, and on the superman theories of Friedrich Nietzsche. It was given dogmatic expression in Hitler's *Mein Kampf* (1925). The success of the National Socialists is explained by the widespread desperation of Germans over the failure of the WEIMAR REPUBLIC governments to solve economic problems during the Great DEPRESSION and by a growing fear of BOLSHEVIK power and influence. Through Hitler's oratory they offered Germany new hope. Only after Hitler had obtained power by constitutional means was the THIRD REICH established. Rival parties were banned, terrorized, or duped, the institutions of state and the German army were won over. Thereafter they were all-powerful agents of Hitler's aim to control the minds of the German people and to launch them on a war of conquest. In the period leading up to WORLD WAR II aspects of Nazi ideology found adherents in countries throughout the Western world. Nazi systems and dogmas were imposed on occupied Europe from 1938 to 1945, and over six million Jews, Russians, Poles, and others were incarcerated and exterminated in CONCENTRATION CAMPS. The German Nazi Party was disbanded in 1945 and its revival officially

forbidden by the Federal Republic of Germany. The defeat of Hitler and worldwide revulsion at his GENOCIDAL policies have ensured the virtual disappearance of Nazism from mainstream politics. However, it retains an influence on certain far Right groups on the fringe of politics. For example, resentment against immigrants at a time of high unemployment in former East Germany precipitated a renewal of neo-Nazi demonstrations in 1992. During the early 1990s there was an increase in racist attacks by neo-Nazis in both Western and Eastern Europe.

Nazi–Soviet Pact (23 August 1939) A military agreement signed in Moscow between Germany and the Soviet Union. It renounced warfare between the two countries and pledged neutrality by either party if the other were attacked by a third party. Each signatory promised not to join any grouping of powers that was 'directly or indirectly aimed at the other party'. The pact also contained secret protocols whereby the dictators agreed to divide POLAND between them and the Soviet Union was given a free hand to deal with the Baltic states.

Ndebele A Bantu-speaking people living in southern ZIMBABWE, in Africa. Traditionally they live in kraals, groups of family homesteads. The women grow maize, the staple crop, and the men herd cattle. Cattle are regarded as a sign of prestige and are used in marriage payments (*lobola*). The Ndebele were NGUNI people from the NATAL area who in 1823 were forced to flee north by SHAKA, King of the Zulus. Their leader was MZILIKAZI and despite raids by the Zulus and by AFRIKANER settlers in the TRANSVAAL, they crossed the Limpopo River, extending their influence over both the Shona and Sotho tribes. Under their leader LOBENGULA they were defeated (1893) by troops of the British South Africa Company. They accepted British control over what was at first called Matabeleland, before it was incorporated into Southern Rhodesia (Zimbabwe). Under colonial rule many Ndebele lost their lands and became industrial or domestic workers. They joined with the more dominant Shona in the independence struggle but ethnic differences are still a source of tension between the two groups.

Neanderthals People who lived in Europe, the Near East, and Central Asia from about 130,000 to 30,000 years ago. No traces of people with characteristic ('classic') Neanderthal features are known from Africa or the Far East. They are named after the Neander valley near Düsseldorf in Germany where part of a skeleton was discovered in 1856. Neanderthals flourished particularly during the last Ice Age and were adapted for living in cold environments. Called *Homo sapiens neanderthalensis* to distinguish them from fully modern people *homo sapiens sapiens*, their features included heavy bones, strong musculature, large brow ridges across a sloping forehead, and larger brains than those of fully modern people. Neanderthals were probably the first people to have burial rites. Flint tools of MOUSTERIAN type are usually found with their remains and characterize the Middle PALAEOLITHIC period.

The part played by Neanderthals in later human evolution is controversial. One widely held view is that none were our direct ancestors. A study of DNA undertaken in 1996 indicated that the Neanderthals were a separate species and neither evolved into modern humans nor interbred with other early humans but

the oar-holes were in
balconies outside the hull,
leaving a long handle inboard

(a) Roman trireme
early 3rd century BC

(b) Viking longship
early 9th century AD

Viking ships were clinker-
built, using individually
shaped, overlapping planks

(c) floating 'castle'
early 14th century

(d) Mediterranean
carrack
late 14th century

(e) *Revenge*
late 16th century

(f) *Sovereign of the Seas*
mid 17th century

navy   *The Roman trireme (a) probably differed little from the earlier Greek trireme but little is known about the appearance of these ships. Well-preserved examples of Viking longships (b) have been found. They were exceptionally well designed and built, ideally suited for long sea journeys. The clumsy floating 'castles' (c) were intended as platforms for conventional troops rather than as naval fighting units. Carracks (d) were primarily merchantmen, adaptable for warfare. Revenge (e) and Sovereign of the Seas (f) were both prototype warship designs. Revenge was a lighter design of galleon. Sovereign was Britain's first 100-gun battleship.*

(a) HMS *Victory*

(b) HMS *Alecto*

(c) *La Gloire*

(d) SMS *Rheinland*

(e) US Essex-class carrier

(f) US nuclear submarine

Sketch (a) is of HMS Victory, Nelson's flagship, launched in 1765. Steam-power was only slowly adopted by the world's navies. Sketch (b) shows a sloop (1845) powered by both sail and paddle. The first ironclad, La Gloire (c) powered by propeller and sail, was protected against exploding shells. Very rapid change from 1880 resulted in vast surface fleets, with Dreadnought-class battleships as in sketch (d), of the early 20th century. Aircraft became the principal means of naval battle in World War II. The submarine (sketch (f)) has nuclear-powered engines and nuclear-armed missiles of strategic capability.

became extinct. An alternative opinion is that some Neanderthal groups evolved into fully modern people or at least some interbreeding between Neanderthals and modern humans took place.

If they were an evolutionary dead end, their extinction 50,000–30,000 years ago remains a mystery (the date varies according to geographical locality). It is possible that they became too specialized and were supplanted by modern people migrating into Europe from elsewhere, probably Africa via the Middle East.

Nebuchadnezzar II (d. 562 BC) A Chaldean who came to the throne of BABYLON in 605 BC, shortly after leading his father's army to victory over the Egyptians at Carchemish. He campaigned vigorously in the west, capturing Jerusalem for a second time in 587 and 'exiling' many of the Judaeans to Babylon. He instituted a major building programme in his capital, including massive city walls and the Hanging Gardens, one of the SEVEN WONDERS OF THE WORLD.

Necker, Jacques (1732–1804) French statesman and financier. He was a Protestant banker from Geneva who was Director-General of Finances in France (1777–81). He analysed the weaknesses of the French taxation system and opposed some of the ideas of the physiocrats, such as free trade in grain. In 1788 he became chief minister. France was bankrupt and a STATES-GENERAL was summoned and reforms introduced. News of Necker's dismissal in July 1789 angered the people and, with other rumours, led to the attack on the BASTILLE. He was reinstated as Controller-General of Finances but finally resigned in September 1790.

Nefertiti (14th century BC) Wife and queen of AKHENATEN, Pharaoh of Egypt. She was a devoted worshipper of the sun god Aten, whose cult was the only one permitted by her husband. She fell from favour and was supplanted by one of her six daughters. She is known to posterity through inscriptions, reliefs, and above all a fine limestone bust which was found at ancient Akhetaton (modern Tell el-Amarna).

Negroids The indigenous peoples of Africa south of the Sahara and their descendants in other parts of the world. Bantu-speaking Negroid pastoralists and crop-growers are traditionally believed to have spread from western to eastern and southern Africa during the past few thousand years but recent evidence suggests that Negroids speaking other languages were in other parts of sub-Saharan Africa much earlier. They may indeed have originated in southern, not western Africa, but this is controversial. Unquestionably, though, they gained knowledge of agricultural techniques and domesticated animals from northern parts of the continent. Negroids are extremely variable in appearance but they can be seen in their most typical form in West Africa; in the east, there has been much intermixing with Hamitic-speaking CAUCASOIDS (for example, Ethiopians and Egyptians); and in the south with the related hunting and gathering San (Bushmen) and the cattle-raising Khoikhoi (Hottentots). The pygmies of Central Africa are a Negroid people but not the MELANESIANS nor the Negritos of southern Asia.

Nehemiah (5th century BC) Jewish leader, the cup-bearer to the Persian king Artaxerxes I. He obtained leave to visit Jerusalem in 444 BC where, despite opposition from local officials and from Samaria, he

supervised the speedy rebuilding of the city walls. In 432 BC he made a second visit to Jerusalem and introduced important moral and religious reforms. His firm action at a time of crisis probably saved the new state of Judaea from collapse and enabled EZRA to undertake his important reforms of Judaism.

Nehru, Jawaharlal (named Pandit, Hindi, 'teacher') (1889–1964) Indian statesman. The son of Motilal NEHRU, he became a leader of the Indian National CONGRESS, where he attached himself to Mohandas GANDHI. He conducted campaigns of civil disobedience, which led to frequent imprisonment by the British. His conviction that the future of India lay in an industrialized society brought him into conflict with Gandhi's ideal of a society centred on self-sufficient villages. On his release from prison (1945) he participated in the negotiations that created the two independent states of India and Pakistan, becoming the first Prime Minister of the independent Republic of India in 1947. As Prime Minister (1947–64) and Minister of Foreign Affairs he had to contend with the first Indo-Pakistan war (1947–49), which ended in the partition of Kashmir, and with the massive influx of Hindu refugees from Pakistan. His government also faced the challenges of integration (sometimes by force) of the PRINCELY STATES and of a communist government (1957–59) in Kerala, as well as the planning and implementation of a series of five-year economic plans to underpin the new state. In 1961 he annexed the Portuguese colony of GOA. In foreign affairs he adopted a policy of non-alignment but sought Western aid when China invaded India in 1962. His daughter, Indira GANDHI, succeeded him.

Nehru, Motilal (1861–1931) Indian political leader. Together with C. R. Das (1870–1925), he organized the Swaraj (Independence) Party in 1922. This set out to participate in the Indian legislative councils but aimed to oppose the British by wrecking the councils from within, as an alternative to Gandhi's NON-CO-OPERATION movement. In 1928 Nehru chaired the All Parties' Committee which produced the Nehru Report, setting out a proposed new Indian constitution with dominion status for India.

Nelson, Horatio, Viscount, (1758–1805) British admiral, whose brilliant seamanship twice broke the naval power of France. The son of a Norfolk rector, he entered the British navy at the age of 12 and became a captain at the age of 20. On the outbreak of war with France in 1793 he was given command of the battleship *Agamemnon* and served under Admiral HOOD in the Mediterranean. He lost the sight of his right eye during a successful attack on Corsica in the following year. In 1797 he played a notable part in the defeat of the French and Spanish fleets at the Battle of CAPE ST VINCENT and was subsequently promoted rear-admiral. Later the same year he lost his right arm while unsuccessfully attempting to capture Santa Cruz de Tenerife in the Canary Islands. In 1798, after pursuing the French fleet in the eastern Mediterranean, he achieved a resounding victory at the Battle of the NILE. While stationed at Naples he began his life-long love affair with Lady Emma Hamilton, the wife of the British ambassador there. In 1801 Nelson was promoted vice-admiral and, ignoring a signal from his commander, Sir Hyde Parker, defeated the Danish fleet at the Battle of COPENHAGEN. Following this engagement he was created a viscount. In

1803, after the renewal of war with France, Nelson was given command of the Mediterranean and for two years blockaded the French fleet at Toulon. When it escaped he gave chase across the Atlantic and back, finally bringing the united French and Spanish fleets to fight at TRAFALGAR in 1805. This decisive victory, in which Nelson was mortally wounded, saved Britain from the threat of invasion by NAPOLEON.

Nennius (*fl. c.* 800) Welsh monk and chronicler, best known for his *Historia Britonum* (History of the Britons) based on earlier chronicles and compilations: it is not clear how much of it Nennius wrote himself. The *Historia* was a source for stories about King ARTHUR and also of HENGIST AND HORSA and was used by GEOFFREY OF MONMOUTH in the 12th century.

Neolithic (New Stone Age) The later part of the STONE AGE, characterized by polished stone axes and simple pottery. The Neolithic discovery of farming brought an end to the slow development of the hunting societies of the PALAEOLITHIC and MESOLITHIC periods and initiated a time of rapid change that soon produced metalworking, cities, states, and empires. The term is thus best applied to the stone-using, farming populations of Asia and Europe, who used polished axes to clear the forests and cooked their grain in pottery vessels. The very first farmers, at sites like JERICHO, had not discovered pottery, and are called pre-pottery Neolithic.

Neoplatonists The followers of PLOTINUS and other thinkers of the school of PLATO in the 3rd century AD: they referred to themselves as simply Platonists. They searched for an intellectually 'respectable' basis for the act of reasonable religious belief. God, described as the 'One' or 'Absolute', was the unifying factor making sense of Plato's two worlds – thought and reality, the mental or 'ideal' and the physical. Mystical experience brought man closer to the 'One'. The experience was known as 'ecstasy' or 'standing outside self'. JULIAN turned to this doctrine from Christianity, AUGUSTINE OF HIPPO from MANICHAEISM.

Plato's work was studied during the RENAISSANCE and such philosophers as Marsilio Ficino (1433–99), who were influenced by both Platonism and ancient Neoplatonism, are also known as Neoplatonists.

Nepal A south Asian country among the peaks and southern slopes of the Himalayas, sandwiched between China (Tibet) and India.

Physical. Nepal contains the highest mountains in the world. The peaks are in the north; below the snow-line rivers run through turfy valleys and fine forests of evergreen, oak, and chestnut before reaching the warm, wet plains of the south.

Economy. Much of the land is not cultivable and deforestation is a major problem. However, the economy is primarily agrarian, industry is limited mainly to agricultural processing.

History. Nepal's first era of centralized control was under the Licchavi dynasty, from about the 4th to the 10th century. Buddhist influences were then dominant, but under the Malla dynasty (10th–18th century) Hinduism became the dominant religion. In 1769 a Gurkha invasion brought to power the present ruling dynasty. From their capital at Kathmandu they wielded absolute power over the indigenous Nepalese tribes. Their incursion into north-west India led to a border

war (1814–16) and to territorial concessions to the British (Treaty of Kathmandu, 1816). Effective rule then passed to a family of hereditary prime ministers, the Ranas, who co-operated closely with the British. Gurkhas were recruited to service in the British and Indian armies. Growing internal dissatisfaction led in 1950 to a coup, which reaffirmed royal powers under the king, Tribhuvan (1951–55). His successor, King Mahendra (1955–72), experimented with a more democratic form of government. This was replaced once more with monarchic rule (1960), which continued under his son, King Birendra Bir Bikram (1972–   ). Following pro-democracy demonstrations and mass arrests from 1989 onwards, the king agreed to legalize political parties, and granted a new constitution in November 1990, establishing a bi-cameral parliament. The first democratic election, in May 1991, was won by the Nepali Congress Party (NCP) led by Girija Prasad Koirala, with the United Communist Party of Nepal (UCPN) forming the official opposition. The government was accused of corruption and economic mismanagement in 1994 and was brought down by a vote of no-confidence. A UCPN-led coalition was formed following elections, but disputes within the government led to its collapse and replacement by a right-wing coalition in 1995, then another Communist-dominated coalition in 1996, with Lokendra Bahadur Chand as Prime Minister.

CAPITAL:	Kathmandu
AREA:	147,181 sq km (56,827 sq miles)
POPULATION:	20.892 million (1996)
CURRENCY:	1 Nepalese rupee = 100 paisa (or pice)
RELIGIONS:	Hindu 89.5%; Buddhist 5.3%; Muslim 2.7%; Jain 0.1%
ETHNIC GROUPS:	Nepalese 58.4%; Bihari 18.7%; Tharu 3.6%; Tamang 3.5%; Newar 3.0%
LANGUAGES:	Nepali (official); Bihari; Tamang
INTERNATIONAL ORGANIZATIONS:	UN; Colombo Plan

Nerchinsk, Treaty of (1689) A treaty between Russia and China signed at Nerchinsk, a town in Russia. It was the first treaty China signed with a western power. Drawn up in Latin by Jesuits from the Chinese emperor KANGXI's court, the treaty fixed the Sino-Russian frontier well to the north of the Amur River. Albazin, a fortress town the Russians had built on the Amur, was dismantled and rebuilt in the Western Hills near Beijing.

Neri, St Philip (1515–95) Italian mystic, known as the 'Apostle of Rome'. He went to Rome in 1533, where he studied, tutored, and undertook charitable works. He established the Confraternity of the Most Holy Trinity (1548) for the care of PILGRIM FATHERS and convalescents. Ordained priest in 1551, he joined the ecclesiastical community at San Girolamo. His popular religious conferences there took place in a large room called the Oratory, built over the church nave. Those who met there, and participated in the devotional, recreational, and charitable activities, were thus called the Congregation of the Oratory or Oratorians (approved in 1575 by Pope Gregory XIII). Philip helped to secure papal absolution from excommunication for HENRY IV of France after his temporary Huguenotism (1595). Philip was canonized in 1622.

Nero, Claudius Caesar Drusus Germanicus (*c.* 37–68 AD) Roman emperor (54–68 AD). He was adopted by

CLAUDIUS, who had married his own niece, Agrippina, Nero's mother. On Claudius' suspicious death in 54 AD Nero succeeded to the throne and poisoned Britannicus, Claudius' son by Messalina. Nero then had his mother murdered, compelled his boyhood tutor and state counsellor SENECA to commit suicide, and had his own wife Octavia executed. Another wife, Poppaea, died as a result of Nero's violence towards her. He was the first emperor to persecute Christians, many of whom were put to death. He saw himself as artist, singer, athlete, actor, and charioteer. Reputedly he set Rome alight in 64 AD, hoping to rebuild it in splendour. The surviving remains of his 'Golden Palace', a massive edifice dominated by a statue of himself as the sun-god, and magnificent coinage show high aesthetic standards. Revolt broke out in Palestine in 66 AD followed by an army rebellion in Gaul and he committed suicide.

Nestorian A member of the Nestorian Church, a sect of the Eastern Orthodox Church. Nestorians followed the teaching of the controversial Syrian Nestorius (d. c. 451), who was appointed Bishop of Constantinople in 428 and exiled to Egypt in 431. He taught that JESUS CHRIST was a conjunction of two distinct persons, one divine and the other human, in whom the human and the divine were indivisible. The implication of this doctrine was that Mary was not the mother of God but simply of Jesus the man. This attack on the popular cult of the Virgin Mary led Nestorius' followers to establish a breakaway church in Edessa. They were expelled in 489 and settled in Persia until they were almost completely wiped out by the 14th-century Mongol invasions. A few Nestorian communities survived, mainly in KURDISTAN. Missionaries had established other groups as far away as Sri Lanka and China. In 1551 some Nestorians joined the Roman Catholic Church and became Chaldeans. A small group joined the Russian Orthodox Church in 1898.

Netanyahu, Binyamin (1949–   ) Israeli politician; Prime Minister from 1996. Netanyahu succeeded Yitzhak SHAMIR as leader of the right-wing Likud Party in 1993, and narrowly won the general election called by Labour caretaker premier Shimon PERES after the assassination of Yitzhak RABIN.

A career diplomat, Netanyahu served in the USA and at the United Nations during the 1980s and became known for his hawkish attitude towards foreign affairs and internal security. After winning power as the first directly elected Prime Minister of Israel, he pledged to maintain the 1993 Oslo Peace Accord with the PALESTINE LIBERATION ORGANIZATION. However, his accusations of PLO collusion in HAMAS terrorist atrocities, and his resumption of building new Jewish settlements on Arab land have, according to many observers, placed the peace process in jeopardy. He renewed military intervention in south Lebanon and was accused of attempting to arrange the assassination of Hamas representatives in Jordan.

Netherlands, the A European country on the North Sea, also called Holland (though this properly refers only to two western provinces). It borders on Germany and Belgium.

Physical. The Netherlands is built up of sediment brought by the Rhine, Meuse, and other rivers. Everywhere, except for the extreme southern corner, is low and flat, much of the land being below sea-level. The coast, partly protected by a chain of sandbanks, has several estuaries and a large lagoon, the IJsselmeer, partly reclaimed from the Zuider Zee. An ongoing programme of maritime land reclamation has increased total land area.

Economy. Trade, banking, and shipping have traditionally been important to the economy, which is now primarily industrial. Many raw materials are imported; petroleum products and chemicals are the principal exports. The manufacturing base includes electrical and other machinery, textiles, and food-processing. Of native minerals, natural gas extraction is substantial and a major source of domestic energy.

History. The area was conquered as far north as the River Rhine by the Romans; the Franks and Saxons moved in during the early 5th century. After the collapse of the Frankish empire in the mid-9th century, there was considerable political fragmentation. Consolidation began under the 14th- and 15th-century dukes of BURGUNDY, and in 1477 the whole of the Low Countries passed to the House of HABSBURG. In 1568 the DUTCH REVOLTS against Spanish Habsburg rule began. The independence of the UNITED PROVINCES OF THE NETHERLANDS was finally acknowledged at the Peace of WESTPHALIA (1648). During the 17th century the Netherlands was a formidable commercial power and it acquired a sizeable DUTCH EMPIRE. It began to decline after the ANGLO-DUTCH WARS and the protracted wars against LOUIS XIV's France. From 1795 to 1814 the Netherlands came increasingly under French control. During those years Britain took over the colonies of Ceylon (now Sri Lanka) and Cape Colony in South Africa, important trading posts of the Dutch East India Company. At the settlement of the Congress of VIENNA the entire Low Countries formed the independent kingdom of the Netherlands (1815). Despite the secession in 1830 of BELGIUM, the Netherlands flourished under the House of Orange, adopting in 1848 a constitution based on the British system. It remained neutral during World War I, suffered economic difficulties during the Great DEPRESSION, and was occupied by the Germans during World War II, when many Jews were deported to CONCENTRATION CAMPS. Until World War II it was the third largest colonial power, controlling the Dutch East Indies, various West Indian islands, and Guiana in South America. The Japanese invaded the East Indian islands in 1942 and installed SUKARNO in a puppet government for all INDONESIA. In 1945 he declared independence and four years of bitter war followed before the Netherlands transferred sovereignty. Guiana received self-government as SURINAM in 1954 and independence in 1975, but Curaçao and other Antilles islands remained linked to the Netherlands. Following the long reign of Queen WILHELMINA (1890–1948) her daughter Juliana became queen. She retired in 1980 and her daughter succeeded her as Queen Beatrix. The Netherlands was a founder member of the European Community, and of NATO. Since 1945 the Netherlands has been ruled by a succession of coalition governments.

CAPITAL:	Amsterdam
AREA:	41.863 sq km (16,163 sq miles)
POPULATION:	15.589 million (1996)
CURRENCY:	1 guilder (florin) = 100 cents
RELIGIONS:	Roman Catholic 36.0%; non-religious 32.6%; Dutch Reformed Church 18.5%; Reformed Churches 8.4%

ETHNIC GROUPS:	Netherlander 96.0%; Turkish 1.0%; Moroccan 1.0%
LANGUAGES:	Dutch (official); minority languages
INTERNATIONAL ORGANIZATIONS:	UN; OECD; NATO; EU; Council of Europe; CSCE

Neuilly, Treaty of VERSAILLES PEACE SETTLEMENT.

Neutrality Acts (1935–39) US laws to prevent the involvement of the country in non-American wars. They grew out of the investigations of the NYE COMMITTEE and included the prohibition of loans or credits to belligerents, as well as a mandatory embargo on direct or indirect shipments of arms or munitions. In a spirit of ISOLATIONISM, the USA declared that it would take no stand on issues of international morality by distinguishing between aggressor and victim nations. During 1940 the Roosevelt administration fought for repeal of the Acts on the ground that they encouraged AXIS aggression and ultimately endangered US security. Gradually they were relaxed, before PEARL HARBOR made them irrelevant.

Neville's Cross, Battle of (17 October 1346) A major victory of the English over the Scots at a site close to the city of Durham, in northern England. EDWARD III's northern barons, the Nevilles and the Percys, and the Archbishop of York, inflicted a severe defeat on the invading army of DAVID II and captured him. It did not gain Edward the kingdom of Scotland but it cost David's people a very expensive ransom for the release of their monarch.

New Amsterdam NEW YORK.

New Australians Immigrants to Australia immediately after World War II. Before 1939 the population of the continent consisted of ABORIGINES and people of predominantly British descent. The war greatly stimulated industrial production and a labour shortage was met by a programme of assisted immigration (£10 from London to Sydney). Of some 575,000 new arrivals between 1947 and 1952, over half were Polish, Austrian, Italian, Maltese, Dutch, Greek, and Yugoslav, and they introduced cultural variety into Australia.

New Brunswick An Atlantic province of Canada, immediately west of the Gulf of Saint Lawrence. First settled in 1604 by the French, it formed part of Acadia (now NOVA SCOTIA) until 1713 when it was ceded to Britain. Its forests, dissected by numerous rivers, were the hunting ground for fur traders and trappers. Small settlements of Scottish farmers in the 1760s were expanded by the arrival of large numbers of loyalists during the American War of INDEPENDENCE.

New Caledonia A group of islands in the South Pacific. The island of New Caledonia was inhabited for at least 3,000 years before being discovered in 1774 by Captain James Cook. The French annexed the island in 1853 and began using it as a penal colony in 1864. With the discovery of nickel in 1863 New Caledonia assumed economic importance for France. The island group was occupied by US troops in 1942–45; in 1946 it was proclaimed a French Overseas Territory, since when there has been a growing movement for independence. A referendum on independence was held in 1987 in

which the electorate voted in favour of remaining French, but many indigenous people boycotted the referendum and another was scheduled for 1998.

Newcastle, Thomas Pelham-Holles, 1st Duke of (1693–1768) English statesman. Born Thomas Pelham, he inherited substantial estates from his uncle John Holles, whose name he added to his own (1711). He became Secretary of State in 1724 and devoted his political career to the management of the House of Commons by using the vast crown patronage at his disposal. He supported in turn WALPOLE and his own brother Henry PELHAM. His own ministry of 1754–56 was a disaster, but his coalition with the Elder PITT, 1757–61, was a triumph and brought success in the SEVEN YEARS WAR. His resignation in 1762 was accepted by George III, who disliked the domination of government by a few powerful Whig families, and he never enjoyed high office again. Thereafter his followers increasingly rallied to the Marquis of ROCKINGHAM.

New Deal The social programme (1933–38) of US President Franklin D. ROOSEVELT in which he attempted to salvage the economy and end the Great DEPRESSION. The term was coined by Judge Samuel Rosenman, was used by Roosevelt in his 1932 speech accepting the presidential nomination, and was made popular by the cartoonist Rollin Kinby. New Deal legislation was proposed by progressive politicians, administrators, and Roosevelt's advisers, the 'brains trust'. It was passed by overwhelming majorities in Congress. The emergency legislation of 1933 ended the bank crisis and restored public confidence; the relief measures of the so-called first New Deal of 1933–35, such as the establishment of the TENNESSEE VALLEY AUTHORITY, stimulated productivity; the WORKS PROJECT ADMINISTRATION reduced unemployment. The failure of central government agencies provoked the so-called second New Deal of 1935–38, devoted to recovery by measures such as the Revenue Act, the Wagner Acts, the Emergency Relief Appropriation Act, and the SOCIAL SECURITY Act. Although the New Deal cannot be claimed to have pulled the USA out of the Depression, it was important for its revitalization of the nation's morale. It extended federal authority in all fields and gave immediate attention to labour problems. It supported labourers, farmers, and small businessmen, and indirectly Black people, who were beneficiaries of legislation designed to equalize opportunity and to establish minimum standards for wages, hours, relief, and security.

New Democratic Party A political party in Canada. It grew out of the Canadian Co-operative Commonwealth Federation (CCF), a political party of industrial workers and small farmers formed in 1932 during the Great DEPRESSION. In 1956 a Canadian Labour Congress of Trade Unions was formed, and in 1961 this amalgamated with the CCF to form the New Democratic Party, a mildly socialist party, committed to a planned economy and extension of social benefits. Leaders of the NDP have been T. C. Douglas (1961–71), David Lewis (1971–75), Ed Broadbent (1975–89), Audrey McLaughlin (1989–95), and Alexa McDonough (1995–).

New Economic Policy A policy introduced into the Soviet Union by LENIN in 1921. It represented a shift from his former 'War Communism' policy, which had been adopted during the RUSSIAN CIVIL WAR to supply the

Red Army and the cities but had alienated the peasants. The NEP permitted private enterprise in agriculture, trade, and industry, encouraged foreign capitalists, and virtually recognized the previously abolished rights of private property. It met with success which Lenin did not live to see, but was ended (1929) by STALIN's policy of five-year plans.

New England A region of the north-eastern USA, comprising the six states of CONNECTICUT, MASSACHUSETTS, RHODE ISLAND, NEW HAMPSHIRE, VERMONT, and MAINE.

History. First named by Captain John SMITH in 1614, the area was granted to the Council for New England in 1620, from whom the PILGRIM FATHERS and the Puritan New England Company (later the Massachusetts Bay Company) obtained permission to settle. Connecticut, Rhode Island, New Hampshire, and Maine were Massachusetts off-shoots. In 1643 the New England Confederation was formed to co-ordinate defence and Indian policy. James II centralized the government of the region into the Dominion of New England (1686–89). Though the region was predominantly agrarian, American merchants and fishermen quickly entered coastal, Caribbean, and transatlantic trades. It was a leading patriot centre in the American War of INDEPENDENCE, and was FEDERALIST in the early national period.

Newfoundland The easternmost province of Canada, comprising the island of Newfoundland in the Gulf of Saint Lawrence and Labrador on the mainland.

History. Claimed for England by John CABOT in 1497, the rich cod banks and deeply indented coastline of the island of Newfoundland quickly attracted European fishermen. Humphrey Gilbert (1583) and Lord Baltimore (1621) attempted colonization, but by 1650 the settlers numbered only 2,000. France contested Britain's claims, and Newfoundland changed hands a number of times. France accepted British sovereignty there in the Peace of UTRECHT (1713) and in 1728 it became a chartered colony. All claims on Newfoundland by France ended with the Treaty of PARIS (1763), although France retained some fishing rights.

New France French possessions in North America discovered, explored, and settled from the 16th to the 18th centuries. Its centres were Quebec (founded in 1608) and Montreal (founded in 1642) on the St Lawrence River. In 1712 New France stretched from the Gulf of St Lawrence to beyond Lake Superior and included NEWFOUNDLAND, Acadia (NOVA SCOTIA), and the Mississippi valley as far south as the Gulf of Mexico. It began to disintegrate when the Peace of UTRECHT was signed in 1713, when France lost Acadia, Newfoundland, and Hudson Bay. As a major competitor for the fur trade and as a threat to the British colonies to the south, New France became embroiled in the FRENCH AND INDIAN WARS. Wolfe's victory on the PLAINS OF ABRAHAM (1759) led to the end of French rule in 1763. New France ceased to exist as a political entity under the terms of the Treaty of PARIS. LOUISIANA, the last French colony on mainland North America, was sold to the USA in 1803.

Under British rule, the territory east of the Ottawa River and north of the St Lawrence River became Lower Canada (1791), Canada East (1841), and the Province of Quebec (1867) in the Dominion of Canada.

New Granada A Spanish colony which embraced much of northern South America. The CONQUISTADORES had occupied the Caribbean coast of present-day Colombia by 1510 but it was not until 1536 that one of them, Gonzalo Jiménez de Quesada, led a two-year campaign into the Andes. By 1538 he had conquered the Chibcha Indians, looted their gold, and founded the city later known as Bogotá. Gold, silver, and precious stones from the mountainous regions of Antioquia and Cauca were exported through Cartagena, which was held to ransom by Sir Francis DRAKE in 1585. In 1564 New Granada became a presidency subject to the viceroyalty of Peru. The distance to Lima created difficulties, however, and in 1717 it became a viceroyalty comprising Colombia, Ecuador, Panama, and Venezuela.

New Hampshire A northern central NEW ENGLAND colony and state of the USA, named by John Mason who received a grant there about 1629 from the Council of New England. New Hampshire was mainly settled from MASSACHUSETTS and CONNECTICUT and became a royal colony in 1679 after long controversies with Mason's family. It was prized by the crown for its ships' timbers and was also attractive to land speculators. Its claims west of the Connecticut River, relinquished in 1782, became VERMONT in 1791.

Ne Win, U (1911–   ) Burmese general and statesman. A member of the extreme nationalist Dobama Asiayone (We-Burmans' Association) from 1936, he served as chief of staff to AUNG SAN's Burma National Army from 1943, defecting with it to the Allied side in 1945. As commander-in-chief after Burmese independence in 1948, he led the campaign against insurgent hill tribes and communist guerrillas and served as Prime Minister (1958–60) in a caretaker government. In 1962 he led a coup against the U Nu administration, abolished the parliamentary system, and proclaimed the Socialist Republic of the Union of Burma, going on to expel 300,000 foreigners in an attempt to regain Burmese control of the economy. Constantly harassed by guerrilla disturbances, he succeeded in maintaining his power as military dictator. Although he stepped down as President in 1981, he remained Chairman of the Executive Committee of the Burma Socialist Programme Party until 1988 and continued to wield considerable influence.

New International Economic Order (NIEO) A set of demands formulated by a group of THIRD WORLD countries at a special session of the UNITED NATIONS GENERAL ASSEMBLY in 1974. The NIEO envisaged a restructuring of the present international economic system to improve the position of the DEVELOPING COUNTRIES (the South) with respect to the advanced industrialized countries (the North). The demands included increased control by developing countries over their own resources, the promotion of INDUSTRIALIZATION, an increase in development assistance, and alleviation of debt problems. While the demand for an NIEO was in part a reflection of frustration at the inability to break out of the cycle of underdevelopment, it also drew inspiration from the experience of OPEC in successfully raising world energy prices. By the 1990s the NIEO had not materialized, having met the joint obstacles of Western resistance, and lack of commitment and support from the developing countries themselves. (See also NORTH–SOUTH RELATIONS, BRANDT REPORT.)

New Jersey A colony and state of the USA situated on the east coast between the Hudson and Delaware estuaries. Originally claimed by the Dutch, it became two English proprietary colonies in 1664 and a united crown colony in 1702. West New Jersey was closely linked with Quaker Pennsylvania and favoured loyalism and union with Britain, while the eastern part was settled by New Englanders and Scottish Presbyterians, supporters of independence. The new state was a battleground in the early stages of the American War of INDEPENDENCE, with actions at Trenton (1776), Princeton (1777), and Monmouth (1778). Its delegates led the smaller states in the Constitutional Convention (1787).

New Learning Educational methods pioneered by 15th and early 16th century European HUMANISTS. Originally New Learning applied new critical techniques to a close scrutiny of the BIBLE and ancient Christian texts in order to reach a deeper understanding of Catholic Christianity. In England humanist thinking also influenced those advocating PROTESTANTISM. This was partly due to the work of great exponents of the New Learning like Sir John Cheke (1514–57), the first professor of Greek at Cambridge University and tutor to EDWARD VI and Nicholas Udall, headmaster of Eton and Westminster schools. Such men helped to establish a new educational ideal: the formal training of gentlemen to become valuable servants of the state. The foundation of their training was rigorous study both of the Bible and of classical literature.

New Left A movement of radical intellectuals in the 1960s, spanning the leading Western societies. The New LEFT was socialist in inspiration but it was critical of orthodox COMMUNISM as practised in Eastern Europe at the time (as well as of existing socialist and communist parties in the West). Its members focused their attention on cultural factors, such as the mass media and the growth of consumer culture, which impeded revolutionary opposition to CAPITALISM. Seminal books were Raymond Williams's *Culture and Society* (1958) and Herbert Marcuse's *One-Dimensional Man* (1964). New Left ideas were influential mainly in such movements as that against the Vietnam War (1964–75) and played a large role in the student uprising in Paris in May 1968, which led to educational and administrative reforms.

newly industrializing country (NIC) A country traditionally placed in the THIRD WORLD or DEVELOPING COUNTRY category which has experienced rapid economic growth since the 1970s. Pacific Rim countries, such as Hong Kong, Singapore, South Korea, and Taiwan are regarded as the leading NICs. Others include Brazil, Malaysia, Mexico, and Thailand. South-east Asian countries among the NICs have become known informally as 'tiger economies', characterized by their achievement of self-sustained, export-led economic growth. Long immune to the debt problems commonly associated with many developing countries (e.g. in Latin America), the NICs of south-east Asia reached a watershed in the late 1990s, when overheating in their economies and loss of confidence by foreign investors brought financial crisis in Malaysia and Thailand, and saw South Korea apply to the INTERNATIONAL MONETARY FUND for a substantial loan.

Newman, John Henry (1801–90) British theologian. He was a leading figure in the Oxford Movement, a group of people who in the 1830s attempted to reform the Church of England by restoring the high-church traditions, and became a prominent convert (1845) to Roman Catholicism. The publication in 1841 of *Tract 90*, which argued that the Thirty-nine Articles of the Church of England could be reconciled with Roman Catholic doctrine, caused a major scandal. In 1846 he went to Rome, where he was ordained priest. A gifted writer, in 1864 he published *Apologia pro Vita Sua*, a justification of his spiritual evolution. He was created cardinal in 1879. His cause for beatification is being examined in Rome.

New Model Army The English ROUNDHEAD force established by Parliamentary ordinance on 15 February 1645. A single army of 22,000 men, it was formed largely from the unco-ordinated Roundhead forces of the first phase of the ENGLISH CIVIL WAR. Its first commander-in-chief was FAIRFAX, with Philip Skippon commanding the infantry and, after the SELF-DENYING ORDINANCE, Oliver CROMWELL in charge of the cavalry. Derided at first by the Cavaliers as the 'New Noddle Army', its men, regularly paid, well disciplined, and properly trained, became known as the Ironsides. Promotion was by merit. Resounding victories, such as those at NASEBY and PRESTON won the war for the Roundheads. The army was inextricably involved in national developments until the Restoration. Religious and political radicalism quickly permeated its ranks, with LEVELLER influence particularly strong between 1647 and 1649. The army was responsible for PRIDE'S PURGE (1648) and formed the basis of government in the following years.

New Orleans, Battle of (8 January 1815) A battle in the WAR OF 1812, fought outside the city of New Orleans. A numerically superior British attempt led by Sir Edward Pakenham to seize New Orleans was brilliantly repelled by US forces commanded by Andrew JACKSON. The battle proved of little military significance, the Treaty of GHENT having formally ended the war two weeks earlier, but Jackson's triumph made him a national hero.

New Plymouth PLYMOUTH COLONY.

Newport Rising (1839) A political insurrection which took place in Newport, Wales, in 1839, following the dissolution of the National Convention of the CHARTISTS. John Frost, a former mayor of Newport, planned to capture the town and release a Chartist leader, Henry Vincent, from gaol. However, the authorities were forewarned and soldiers ambushed the insurgents, killing several of them. Frost and others were arrested and received death sentences, later commuted to transportation.

New Right An intellectual movement of the 1970s and 1980s which sought to reformulate the basis of RIGHT-wing opposition to SOCIAL DEMOCRACY and SOCIALISM. New Right thinkers, whose influence was greatest in the USA and the UK, drew upon the ideas of libertarianism and CONSERVATISM. The libertarian strain could be seen in their defence of the FREE MARKET and their belief that the role of government in the provision of social services had been over-extended and should be reduced. This meant, for example, the privatization of firms and industries owned by the state, the adoption of MONETARIST policies, and a shift away from the WELFARE STATE towards private insurance as a way of coping with ill health and old age. The conservative strain appeared in their curtailment of civil liberties in the name of 'national security' or 'law and order', and in their strong advocacy of the traditional family unit as the exclusive social norm. Some New Right thinkers embraced public choice theory, holding that the actions of governments were to be explained in terms of the self-interest of the politicians and bureaucrats who staffed them. New Right ideas were for the most part not new in themselves, but they marked a radical break with the post-war consensus about the role of the state in society. Their influence was evident in the crusading style adopted by the governments led by Margaret THATCHER and Ronald REAGAN in the 1980s.

New South Wales A state occupying much of the south-eastern quarter of AUSTRALIA, bounded by Queensland on the north, South Australia on the west, and Victoria on the south.

History. Captain James Cook took British possession of the eastern part of Australia (1770), naming it New South Wales. In 1788 Britain established a penal colony, Australia's first White settlement, at Sydney Cove in the Pacific inlet of Port Jackson. Conflicts between governors and officers culminated in the RUM REBELLION (1808). Settlement was confined to an area around Sydney until the crossing of the Blue Mountains in 1813. Increasing numbers of free settlers and EMANCIPISTS led to changes in the colony's nature, as did the BIGGE INQUIRY (1819–21), which recommended liberal land grants to settlers and extensive use of convict labour to open up the country. After the Molesworth Report (1838), convict transportation to New South Wales ended (1840). Partial representative government was granted in 1842, responsible government in 1855. Originally New South Wales comprised all of known Australia. Van Diemen's Land (present-day TASMANIA) was separated from New South Wales in 1825, the Port Phillip District (present-day VICTORIA) in 1851, the Moreton Bay district (present-day QUEENSLAND) in 1859, and land for the Australian Capital Territory (the site of Canberra) was transferred to the Australian Commonwealth in 1911.

New Spain Spain's colonial empire in north and Central America (SPANISH EMPIRE). The formation of the viceroyalty of New Spain began in 1518 with CORTÉS's attack on the AZTEC empire in central Mexico. Following his destruction of Aztec power, Cortés erected a new capital at Mexico City and was named governor and captain-general of New Spain (1522). He and his lieutenants extended Spanish authority south into Salvador, Guatemala, and Honduras, and north into the Mexican hinterland. New Spain grew to encompass California, the American south-west, and Florida, although Spanish settlement in many areas was very limited. In the 18th century Spain's involvement in European wars had affected its colonial possessions. In 1763 it ceded Florida to Britain and received Louisiana from France, regaining Florida in 1783, but being forced to return Louisiana to France in 1800.

New York A state bordering Canada in the north-east of the USA. In 1609 Frenchmen first sailed down Lake Champlain into New York and Englishmen in Dutch service sailed up the Hudson River. The Dutch established Albany as a fur-trading post and in 1625 founded their capital at the mouth of the Hudson on Manhattan Island, which they bought from local Native Americans for trinkets worth $24. They called it New Amsterdam; in 1664 it was captured by the British and renamed New York for the Duke of York (later JAMES II). British colonists joined the Dutch settlers, the IROQUOIS CONFEDERACY prevented French interference, and landowners, merchants, and pirates alike prospered for a century. When the issues leading to the War of INDEPENDENCE arose, New Yorkers were divided. Many were loyalists, and the British, after capturing New York City in 1776, held it throughout the war. Even so, WASHINGTON's triumphal entry into the city (1783) was welcomed tumultuously. His presidential inauguration took place there in 1789 and New York City was briefly (1789–90) the new national capital.

New Zealand A country situated over 1,900 km (1,180 miles) south-east of Australia, comprising the North Island and the South Island together with many smaller islands in the south-west Pacific Ocean.

Physical. The two main islands, separated by the fairly narrow Cook Strait, together stretch north-east to south-west over a distance of some 1,600 km (1,000 miles). The boundary between the Indian (Indo-Australian) plate and the Pacific plate passes just south of North Island and diagonally through South Island. Movements along the boundary are responsible for many of the earthquakes of the region. Mostly the islands lie in the path of westerlies, which bring mild, wet weather across the Tasman Sea; North Cape can be very warm while snow is falling on Stewart Island in the extreme south. Mixed arable and grazing land, with deciduous and evergreen forest, can be found throughout, and both main islands have reserves of coal. The snow-capped Southern Alps, with Mount Cook in the centre, run the length of the South Island. High glaciers and narrow lakes lie among them; their forested south-western slopes fall to the edges of still fiords, as in Fiordland National Park.

Economy. New Zealand has a largely agricultural economy with major exports of meat, wool, and butter. The economy was affected by the loss of preferential treatment by the UK, once the chief trading partner, when the UK joined the EC in 1973. New Zealand imports most manufactured goods and suffers from a balance of payments deficit. In 1984 economic reforms reduced government control of the economy and cut welfare provision. There is some light industry. A treaty for closer economic relations aiming at the gradual introduction of a free market has been signed with Australia.

History. First peopled by the Polynesian MAORI from about 800 AD, European contact began in 1642 with the exploration of the Dutch navigator Abel Tasman. Captain James Cook, in successive explorations from 1769, thoroughly charted the islands and brought them within the British ambit. Commercial colonization began from New South Wales in Australia and from the NEW ZEALAND COMPANY (formerly Association) (1837) of E. G. WAKEFIELD. Humanitarian pressures contributed to the decision formally to annex the islands as the colony of New Zealand in 1840 on the basis that the rule of law was necessary to regulate Maori-settler relations (see Treaty of WAITANGI). In 1846 the British government conferred a limited constitution (rescinded in 1848) on New Zealand, divided into the provinces of New Munster and New Ulster, and in 1852 granted the islands representative government. Responsible self-government came in 1856. Settlement of the South Island prospered, assisted by the GOLD RUSHES of the 1860s. In the North Island, following the rapid acquisition of Maori land by settlers and by the government, the population was drawn into the disastrous ANGLO-MAORI WARS, following which most Maori land was settled. Regulations of 1881 restricted the influx of Asians, who were resented as a threat to the ethnic purity of the New Zealand people. The regulations were confirmed by the Immigration Restriction Act (1920), whose terms were gradually liberalized. The property qualification for voting was abolished and women were enfranchised in 1893. In 1931 New Zealand became an independent dominion, although it did not choose to ratify the Statute of WESTMINSTER formally until 1947. In 1891–1911 (under the Liberal-Labour Party) and 1935–47 (under Labour) New Zealand won a world reputation for state socialism, providing comprehensive welfare and education services. New Zealand actively supported the Allies in both World Wars, enjoying political stability and a high standard of living. After World War II it concentrated its defence policy on the Pacific and Far East, participating in ANZUS (1951–86) and sending a military force to Vietnam. When the LABOUR PARTY returned to power in 1984 it adopted a non-nuclear policy leading to withdrawal from ANZUS. The National Party under Jim BOLGER won the election of 1990 at a time of economic recession. It confirmed Labour's non-nuclear stance, but introduced stringent social welfare cuts, ending free state education and introducing health charges for all. The National Party was re-elected in 1993 but lost its majority in 1996 and Bolger formed a coalition government. In November 1997 Bolger resigned and the right-wing minister Jenny Shipley became New Zealand's first female Prime Minister. Maori activists continued to demand compensation for land seized illegally by European settlers and the government agreed to pay compensation to the Waikato tribe in 1994 and to the Tainui tribal federation in 1995; in 1996 large tracts of South Island were granted to the Ngai Tahu tribe.

CAPITAL: Wellington
AREA: 267,844 sq km (103,415 sq miles)
POPULATION: 3.619 million (1996)
CURRENCY: 1 New Zealand dollar = 100 cents
RELIGIONS: Anglican 24.3%; Presbyterian 18.0%; non-religious 16.4%; Roman Catholic 15.2%; Methodist 4.7%
ETHNIC GROUPS: European origin 82.2%; Maori 9.2%; Pacific Island Polynesian 2.9%
LANGUAGES: English, Maori (both official)
INTERNATIONAL
  ORGANIZATIONS: UN; Commonwealth; OECD; South Pacific Forum; Colombo Plan

New Zealand Company (originally the New Zealand Association) An organization formed in 1837 by E. G. WAKEFIELD to colonize New Zealand. It was denied a charter by the British government, largely because of fears that it would come into conflict with the MAORI. Nevertheless, in May 1834 the company began sending out agents and settlers, buying land from the Maori. The establishment of the crown colony in 1840 led to a review of the company's grandiose land claims. This, and Maori resistance, prevented the settlements developing as planned and in 1843 a rash attempt at Wairau, near

Nelson, to assert authority over the powerful Te Rauparaha resulted in the deaths of 23 settlers. By 1846 the Company had secured recognition from the Colonial Office, a loan, and a settlement of its land claims but it became commercially unviable and was dissolved in 1858.

Ney, Michel, Duc d'Elchingen (1769–1815) Marshal of France. The most famous and popular of NAPOLEON's generals, he served Napoleon in the brilliant campaigns of 1794 and 1795, commanded the army of the Rhine (1799), and conquered the Tyrol. His support was decisive in Napoleon's victory at Friedland (14 June 1807). In the retreat from Moscow (1812) he commanded the defence of the *grande armée* against the Russians and was created Prince of Moscow by Napoleon in 1813. After the Battle of LEIPZIG he urged Napoleon to abdicate (1814). He agreed to take the oath of allegiance to the restored monarchy, but, when sent to check Napoleon's advance (1815) during the 'HUNDRED DAYS', he joined him instead, fighting heroically at WATERLOO, after which he was tried for treason and shot.

Ngo Dinh Diem (1901–63) South Vietnamese statesman, President (1955–63). He was exiled by the French in 1947 after forming the anti-French and anti-communist National Union Front. He returned to South Vietnam in 1954 with joint US and French support and, in the following year, became President of an anti-communist government of South Vietnam. He had commenced military resistance against the VIETCONG by 1960 and had achieved some degree of success with both social and economic reform. However, his harshly repressive regime, in which his brother, Ngo Dinh Nhu, earned particular notoriety as head of political police, aroused strong local resentment and he was killed in a military coup in 1963.

Nguni Several groups of ethnically related people in southern Africa. In the 1820s, the Zulu in the Natal area, under their king SHAKA, developed a superior military force, made up of regiments (or impis), which attacked neighbouring peoples in the Difagane Wars. Refugees from Shaka, copying the military discipline and strategy of their Zulu conquerors, established themselves in the NDEBELE state in Zimbabwe, the Gaza state in Mozambique, the Swazi state in Swaziland, and a group of Nguni states in Tanzania, Zambia, and Malawi. Nguni people came into conflict with European settlers: the British in the Cape Colony moved into the lands of the Xhosa, precipitating the XHOSA (Kaffir) WARS; Boer, and later British, settlers in Natal clashed with the Zulus. Urbanization in the 20th century was accompanied by the policy of APARTHEID. The BANTU HOMELANDS created in South Africa had little connection with original Nguni culture.

Nguyen Van Thieu (1923–) South Vietnamese statesman, President (1967–75). He participated in the post-war struggle against the French but left the VIETMINH because of its communist policies and thereafter became a general in the army of South Vietnam. He participated in the overthrow of NGO DINH DIEM's government in 1963 and together with another military strongman, Nguyen Cao Ky, dominated the politics of his country. Elected President in 1967, and re-elected in 1971, he continued to press hard in the war against the VIETCONG and their North Vietnamese allies despite growing opposition to his dictatorial methods. In the early 1970s the war began to run against him and his US allies drastically reduced their support. In April 1975, with his army in ruins and enemy forces closing on Saigon, he finally resigned his office. He went to live in Taiwan, and later moved to Britain.

Nicaea, Councils of Two councils of the Christian Church, which took place in the city of Nicaea (now Iznik, Turkey). The first Council (325) was summoned by the Roman emperor CONSTANTINE and issued a statement of orthodoxy against ARIANISM, later known as the 'Nicene Creed'. The Second Council (787) was called by the Byzantine empress IRENE to end the ICONOCLASTIC CONTROVERSY.

Nicaean empire (1204–61) A Byzantine principality comprising the territories centred on Nicaea (now Iznik, Turkey). The Nicaean empire was established by Theodore I (1175–1222) following the sack of Constantinople during the Fourth CRUSADE; it adopted the institutions of the Byzantine empire, including emperors and patriarchs. Resisting the pressures of SELJUKS and Crusaders, Theodore I successfully annexed lands from the Komnenoi of Trebizond. His son-in-law John III sustained this miniature empire in exile but the early death of his son, Theodore II (1254–58), enabled MICHAEL VIII to dispossess and subsequently blind and imprison the infant heir, John IV Lascaris, after retaking Constantinople in 1261.

Nicaragua The largest country in Central America, bounded on the north by Honduras and on the south by Costa Rica.

Physical. Nicaragua has a south-western-facing coast on the Pacific Ocean and a longer, eastward-facing one on the Caribbean Sea, the Mosquito Coast. In the west are fertile plains and volcanic mountains. The climate is tropical. In the north are forested hills, and in the south-west two great lakes. The country is subject to earthquakes, being near the junction of crustal plates.

Economy. The civil war in the 1980s devastated the economy, which also suffered from US attempts to enact a trade blockade and suspend foreign aid. The economy is principally agricultural, with coffee, cotton, beef, and bananas the principal exports. There is also some gold-mining. Other mineral resources are silver and copper. Manufacturing industry includes food-processing, petroleum-refining, textiles, and cement.

History. The first inhabitants of Nicaragua were Indians from South America who settled on the coast. From the 10th century AD peoples from Mexico began to immigrate into the region. The first Spanish colonization was undertaken by Francisco Hernándes de Córdoba, who founded the towns of Granada on Lake Nicaragua and León on Lake Managua in 1524. One of the main Indian tribes converted to Christianity, which enabled the Spanish to take control of the area with ease. Administratively part of the viceroyalty of NEW SPAIN and the captaincy-general of Guatemala, Nicaragua grew slowly. It depended upon agriculture, which developed substantially in the 18th century. The country achieved its independence from Spain in 1821. Nicaragua was briefly annexed into the Mexican empire of Agustín de ITURBIDE, and with the collapse of that experiment formed part of the United Province of CENTRAL AMERICA until becoming independent again in 1838. In 1848 the British seized San Juan del Norte, known as the

Mosquito Coast, after a tribe of American Indians, the Miskito. In 1855 a US adventurer, William Walker, seized control of the country and made himself President (1856–57). His ousting helped unite the country, which made peace with Britain and recognized a separate Mosquito kingdom. The 20th century opened with the country under the vigorous control of the dictator José Santos Zelaya, who extended Nicaraguan authority over the Mosquito kingdom. The USA, apprehensive of his financial dealings with Britain, supported the revolution that overthrew him in 1907. The US presence, including two occupations by the marines, dominated the country until 1933. In 1937 Nicaragua fell under the control of Anastasio SOMOZA, who ruled until his assassination in 1956. He was succeeded by his son Luis (1957–63), and then by the latter's brother, General Anastasio Debayle Somoza (1967–72, 1974–79). In 1962 a guerrilla group, the Sandinistas, was formed. It gained increasing support from the landless peasantry and engaged in numerous clashes with the National Guard, ending in civil war (1976–79). Once established as a ruling party, the Sandinistas expropriated large estates for landless peasants. The dispossessed and exiled owners of the estates then organized opposition to the regime, recruiting a 'Contra' rebel army, funded and organized by the CENTRAL INTELLIGENCE AGENCY. Mines and forests were nationalized and relations with the USA deteriorated. In 1981 US aid ended and the regime was accused of receiving aid from Cuba and the Soviet Union. The REAGAN administration sought increasing support from the US Congress to give aid to the exiled Contra forces in Honduras and Miami, but was seriously embarrassed by exposure in 1986–87 of illegal diversion of money to the Contras from US sale of arms to Iran. When President Bush took office in 1989 direct military funding to the Contras ended. Elections were held in 1990 with opposition groups generously funded by the USA. The Sandinistas lost to a coalition group led by Violeta Chamorro. Although she succeeded in winning a $300 million loan from the USA, severe economic recession followed, with the GNP falling by 5.5% and some 1.5 million people unemployed, causing great hardship. President Chamorro only narrowly succeeded in resisting right-wing pressure for *haciendas*, confiscated by the Sandinistas, to be returned to their former owners. In 1992 there were violent clashes between re-armed Contras and Sandinista 're-Compas'. A ceasefire agreement was reached in 1994. In 1996 Chamorro retired and the conservative Arnoldo Aleman was elected President.

CAPITAL:	Managua
AREA:	130,700 sq km (50,464 sq miles)
POPULATION:	4.272 million (1996)
CURRENCY:	1 cordoba = 100 centavos
RELIGIONS:	Roman Catholic 88.3%; other (mostly Baptist, Moravian, and Pentecostal) 11.7%
ETHNIC GROUPS:	Mestizo 77.0%; White 10.0%; Black 9.0%; Amerindian 4.0%
LANGUAGES:	Spanish (official); Amerindian languages
INTERNATIONAL ORGANIZATIONS:	UN; OAS

Nicholas I (1796–1855) Emperor of Russia (1825–55). The third son of Paul I, he succeeded his brother ALEXANDER I, having crushed a revolt by the DECEMBRISTS, who favoured his elder brother Constantine. His rule was authoritarian and allowed for little social reform. Russia was ruled by the army bureaucracy and police, intellectual opposition only expressed itself in study circles and secret societies. These groups polarized into 'Slavophiles', who held that Russian civilization should be preserved through the Orthodox Church and the village community, and 'Westernizers' who wished to see western technology and liberal government introduced. Nicholas embarked on the RUSSO-TURKISH WARS and brutally suppressed the uprising (1830–31) in Poland. Religious minorities, including Jews, were persecuted. In the REVOLUTIONS OF 1848 he helped Austria crush the nationalists in Hungary, and his later attempts to dominate Turkey led to the CRIMEAN WAR (1853–56). He was succeeded by his son ALEXANDER II.

Nicholas II (1868–1918) Last Emperor of Russia (1894–1917). In 1894 he formalized the alliance with France but his Far Eastern ambitions led to disaster in the RUSSO-JAPANESE WAR (1904–05), an important cause of the RUSSIAN REVOLUTION of 1905. He was forced to issue the October Manifesto promising a representative government and basic civil liberties. An elected Duma and an Upper Chamber were set up. Although Russia was prosperous under STOLYPIN (1906–11) and Nicholas II won support for the war against Germany (1914), he unwisely took personal command of the armies, leaving the government to the empress Alexandra and RASPUTIN. Mismanagement of the war and chaos in the government led to his abdication in February 1917 and later his imprisonment. On 16–17 July 1918 the BOLSHEVIKS, fearing the advance of counter-revolutionary forces, murdered him and his family at Ekaterinburg.

Nicopolis, Battle of (23 September 1396) A battle between Crusaders and Ottoman forces. The town of Nicopolis, on the River Danube was besieged by a force of Crusaders under SIGISMUND of Hungary and John, son of Philip the Bold of Burgundy. A combined force of Hungarians and European knights had answered an appeal to relieve CONSTANTINOPLE from Turkish attack. After initial success, they were confronted by the TURKS under Sultan Bajazet I (ruled 1389–1402). The Crusaders were defeated and many of the knights were executed after the battle, although Sigismund escaped.

Niemöller, Martin (1892–1984) German Protestant churchman. A U-boat commander in World War I, he became a priest in 1924. In 1933 he founded the Pastors' Emergency League to help combat rising discrimination against Christians of Jewish background. His opposition to the Nazification of the Church led to his confinement in a CONCENTRATION CAMP (1938–45). A pacifist, he became president of the World Council of Churches (1961–68).

Niger A large, landlocked country in west Africa surrounded by Algeria, Libya, Chad, Nigeria, Benin, Burkina Faso, and Mali.

Physical. The River Niger flows through the country in the extreme south-west, and the northern tip of Lake Chad lies in the extreme south-east. From these points the land rises through dry savannah and thin, thorny scrub to sandy desert and the high plateaux of the Sahara.

Economy. Agriculture is the principal economic activity, concentrating on livestock (the second largest export) and the cultivation of millet, ground-nuts, sorghum, and other arable staples. Drought has continued to be a problem. Uranium accounts for almost three-quarters of exports, with livestock and vegetables also exported. Industry is mainly textiles, cement, and mining.

History. Archaeological evidence shows that the area was inhabited in the PALAEOLITHIC period. The TUAREGS occupied parts of Niger in the 11th century AD and their kingdom of Agadès grew during the 15th century. In the 17th century the Zerma established an empire around the River Niger. The HAUSA, who had been moving into the area since the 14th century, expanded their territory during the 18th century, displacing the Tuaregs. In 1804 the FULANI, ancient competitors for Hausa land, defeated the Hausa in a war and established the kingdom of Sokoto. The French first arrived in 1891 but the country was not fully colonized until 1914. A French colony (part of FRENCH WEST AFRICA) from 1922, it became an autonomous republic within the FRENCH COMMUNITY in 1958 and fully independent in 1960 but there were special agreements with France covering finance, defence, technical assistance, and cultural affairs. From 1974, it was governed by a Supreme Military Council and all political associations were banned. Political activity was re-legalized in 1988. In 1989, under President Ali Saibou, a new constitution was approved by referendum, which set up a new ruling council. Saibou remained opposed to establishing multiparty democracy but strikes and demonstrations throughout 1990 prompted him to agree to implement reforms. Following a National Conference in 1991 a transitional government was formed. A multiparty constitution was approved by a referendum in 1992 and in 1993, following open elections, a coalition government took office and Mahamane Ousmane became President. In 1995 a peace agreement was made with ethnic Tuareg rebels, based in the north of Niger, who had been clashing with government forces since 1991. In January 1996 army officers staged a coup, throwing Ousmane out of office. After pressure from France a presidential election was held. The military leader Ibrahim Mainassara won the election but supporters of Ousmane rioted and instability has continued.

CAPITAL:	Niamey
AREA:	1,267,000 sq km (489,062 sq miles)
POPULATION:	9.465 million (1996)
CURRENCY:	1 CFA franc = 100 centimes
RELIGIONS:	Sunni Muslim 80.0%; traditional beliefs 20.0%
ETHNIC GROUPS:	Hausa 54.1%; Songhai, Zerma, and Dendi 21.7%; Fulani 10.1%; Tuareg 8.4%; Kanuri 4.2%; Teda 0.2%
LANGUAGES:	French (official); Hausa; Songhai; local languages
INTERNATIONAL ORGANIZATIONS:	UN; OAU; Franc Zone

Nigeria A large West African country consisting of a federation of 21 states, with the highest population of any African country.

Physical. Nigeria has a southward-facing coast and is bounded by Benin on the west, Niger and Chad on the north, and Cameroon on the east. The sandy coast is bordered by mangrove swamp, inland of which there is a low plain with tropical rain forest spreading up the valleys of the Niger to the north-west and the Benue to the east. The central Jos Plateau rises to 1,800 m (5,900 feet) with open grassland but north of this the ground falls away to thorn-covered desert.

Economy. Oil accounts for most of Nigeria's exports; other minerals include abundant supplies of natural gas, iron ore, coal, lead, and zinc. Heavy investment in petroleum and other industries such as steel, cement, and vehicles was halted by the drop in world oil prices in the mid-1980s, which led to a massive foreign debt. IMF-backed austerity measures were introduced. These included cuts in subsidies and the development of traditional cash crops and staple crops to reduce dependence on food imports. The austerity measures were achieving some degree of success by the early 1990s but political instability during the mid-1990s has affected the economy badly.

History. The earliest known culture in Nigeria was the NOK CULTURE, which existed from about the 6th century BC to the third century AD. Many different peoples have moved into the region; there are over 250 ethnic groups still living in Nigeria. The kingdom of KANEM-BORNU rose during the 11th century and fell during the 14th century. Islam was introduced to the area during the 13th century. The Portuguese arrived in the 15th century and established a slave trade, supported by the people of the kingdom of BENIN. The British were involved in the slave trade by the 17th century. The HAUSA people broke away from the SONGHAY kingdom and began to mingle with the nomadic FULANI, some of whom settled in Hausa towns. In the early 19th century a Fulani empire emerged. The kingdom of Benin and the YORUBA EMPIRE OF OYO occupied southern Nigeria.

The island of Lagos was a centre for the slave trade when this was banned by the British in 1807. The British had to use military force to stop the slave ships. In 1851 the British attacked and burnt the city of Lagos and ten years later bought it from King Dosunmu, administering it first from Freetown, Sierra Leone, and then from the Gold Coast (Ghana), until in 1886 a separate protectorate (later colony) of Lagos was formed. Explorers worked their way inland but, until the discovery of quinine (1854) to provide protection against malaria, the region remained known as 'the white man's grave'. During the second half of the 19th century trading companies were established, forming the Royal Niger Company in 1886, which was then taken over by the British Colonial Office to become the Niger Coast protectorate in 1893. Following the conquest of the kingdom of Benin, this became the protectorate of Southern Nigeria (1900). The protectorate of Northern Nigeria was proclaimed in 1900. In 1906 the colony of Lagos was absorbed into the southern protectorate and in 1914 the two protectorates were merged to form the largest British colony in Africa, which, under its governor Frederick LUGARD, was administered indirectly by retaining the powers of the chiefs and emirs of its 150 or more tribes. In Northern Nigeria Muslim chiefs of the Fulani tribes maintained a conservative rule over the majority of the country's Hausa population. In the west, the Yoruba dominated; the Ibo tribe was centred in the east.

Under the constitution of 1954 a federation of Nigeria was created, consisting of three regions: Northern, Eastern, and Western, together with the trust territory of Cameroons and the federal territory of Lagos. In 1960 the federation became an independent nation within the COMMONWEALTH OF NATIONS, and in 1963 a republic. In 1967 the regions were replaced by 12 states, further divided in 1976 into 19 states. Oil was discovered off Port Harcourt and a movement for Ibo independence began. In January 1966 a group of Ibo army majors murdered the federal Prime Minister, Sir Alhaji Abubakar Tafawa BALEWA, the Premiers of the Northern and Western regions, and many leading politicians. In July a group of northern officers retaliated and installed General GOWON as Head of State. A massacre of several thousand Ibo living in the North followed. Attempts to work out constitutional provisions failed and in May 1967 the military governor of the Eastern region, Colonel Ojukwe, announced his region's secession and the establishment of the republic of BIAFRA. Civil war between the Hausa and Ibo peoples erupted and Biafra collapsed in 1970. General Gowon was deposed in 1975. In 1979 the military government organized multiparty elections. Corruption and unrest precipitated further military takeovers in 1983 and 1985, when General Ibrahim Babangida became Head of State. Progress towards restoration of full civilian rule was threatened by outbreaks of violence between Shiite Islamic fundamentalists and Christians. Political parties were re-legalized in 1989 but only two parties were allowed to register for elections, both having manifestos devised by the government. Open presidential elections in 1993 were, according to unofficial reports, won by Moshood Abiola but Babangida annulled the elections, prompting serious social unrest. Babangida resigned and handed power over to another military government, promising that an elected civilian government would be installed in 1994. Abiola fled the country and sought international aid; he and his supporters continued to protest that the 1993 elections had been free and fair. The social and political crisis continued and Sanni Abacha took over as head of state in November 1993. He dismantled many existing political institutions and re-instituted the 1979 military constitution but continued to insist that a civilian government would eventually be installed. Abiola returned to Nigeria to campaign for democracy and was arrested in 1994. In 1995 the government announced that civilian rule could not be introduced before 1997, but lifted the ban on political activity. However, in October 1995 nine pro-democracy activists were charged with murder and executed, provoking international outrage. As a result, Nigeria was suspended from the Commonwealth. Social unrest has persisted.

CAPITAL:	Lagos
AREA:	923,768 sq km (356,669 sq miles)
POPULATION:	103.912 million (1996)
CURRENCY:	1 naira = 100 kobo
RELIGIONS:	Muslim 45.0%; Protestant 26.3%; African indigenous and traditional 17.2%; Roman Catholic 12.1%
ETHNIC GROUPS:	Hausa 21.3%; Yoruba 21.3%; Ibo 18.0%; Fulani 11.2%; Ibibio 5.6%; Kanuri 4.2%; Edo 3.4%; Tiv 2.2%; Ijaw 1.8%; Bura 1.7%; Nupe 1.2%
LANGUAGES:	English (official); Hausa; Yoruba; Ibo; local languages
INTERNATIONAL ORGANIZATIONS:	UN; Commonwealth (suspended in 1995); ECOWAS; OAU; OPEC

Nigerian Civil War BIAFRA.

Nightingale, Florence (1820–1910) British hospital reformer. After considerable opposition from her family she received some training as a nurse at Kaiserswerth in Prussia and in Paris in the early 1850s. Her success as superintendent of the Hospital for Invalid Gentlewomen in London led her to be invited in 1854 to take a team of nurses to Scutari in Turkey to look after British soldiers wounded in the CRIMEAN WAR. In the face of much official hostility, she succeeded in improving beyond recognition the state of the British military hospitals, whose insanitary conditions had been largely responsible for the high mortality rate among the wounded. In 1856 she returned home a national heroine, and in 1860 used a gift of money raised by a grateful public to found a training school for nurses at St Thomas's Hospital in London. Throughout the rest of her life, although an invalid, she took an active interest in nursing and hospital matters.

'Night of the Long Knives' (29–30 June 1934) The name coined by HITLER for a weekend of murders throughout Germany. It followed a secret deal between himself and units of his personal bodyguard, the SS. Precise details remain unknown, but the army is believed to have promised to support Hitler as head of state after HINDENBURG's death in return for destroying the older and more radical Nazi private army known as the SA (Sturmabteilung), or BROWNSHIRTS, led by Ernst Röhm. Hitler announced that 77 people had been summarily executed for alleged conspiracy. Subsequent arrests by the SS all over Germany, usually followed by murder, numbered many hundreds, including some non-party figures, and the former Chancellor Schleicher.

nihilism The total rejection of authority as exercised by the church, the state, or the family. More specifically, the doctrine of a Russian extremist revolutionary party active in the late 19th and early 20th centuries. In their struggle against the conservative elements in Russian society, the nihilists justified violence, believing that by forcibly eliminating ignorance and oppression they would secure human freedom. The government of ALEXANDER II repressed the revolutionaries severely and they sought vengeance by assassinating the emperor near his palace on 13 March 1881. After 1917 the small and diffuse cells of nihilists were themselves destroyed by better co-ordinated revolutionaries.

Nijmegen, Treaty of (1678) The Franco-Dutch War (1672–78) was terminated by the treaty signed at Nijmegen, in the Netherlands between France, the United Provinces, Spain, and the Holy Roman Empire; France gained substantially from the terms, which rationalized its frontiers.

Nile, Battle of the (1 August 1798) A naval battle fought at Aboukir Bay on the Mediterranean coast of Egypt, in which a British fleet defeated a French fleet. The French admiral had anchored his fleet of 13 vessels in the bay. He believed his ships to be safe from attack, but NELSON, the British commander, was able partially to encircle the French fleet. Nine French ships were destroyed, including the flagship *L'Orient*. This conclusive victory established Nelson's prestige, destroyed NAPOLEON's plans for Egypt, and encouraged the signing of the second coalition against France.

Nimeiri, Gaafar Muhammad al- (1930–   ) Sudanese statesman. He led campaigns against rebels in the southern Sudan in the 1950s and joined in leftist attempts to overthrow the civilian government.

Following a coup, he became Prime Minister in 1969 and Chairman of the Revolutionary Command Council. President from 1971 to 1985, in 1972 he ended the civil war in the southern Sudan, granting it local autonomy. He switched from socialist economic policies to capitalism, to make the Sudan a major food producer. A devout Muslim, he proposed a new Islamic Constitution in December 1984 that made Islamic law apply to everyone. This was opposed in southern Sudan, where the majority of the population are not Muslim, and a military coup overthrew him in 1985.

Nimitz, Chester William (1885–1966) US admiral. After various surface ship commands and shore appointments, he took over command of the Pacific Fleet in 1941 following the Japanese attack on PEARL HARBOR. From his Hawaii headquarters, he deployed his forces to win the Battle of Midway, and subsequently supervised the moves in the PACIFIC CAMPAIGNS, leading to successful actions off Guadalcanal and in the LEYTE GULF. To a large extent he was responsible for making the Pacific Fleet, weakened by Pearl Harbor, the instrument of Japan's defeat. After the war he was briefly chief of naval operations.

Nineveh An ancient city on the River Tigris. It was selected by SENNACHERIB of Assyria (ruled 704–681 BC) as his capital and he instituted a major building programme there. It was sacked by the MEDES in 612 BC and never thereafter regained its former prestige. Excavations have revealed much of the ancient city, including five of the 15 gateways in the 12 km (7-mile) wall, the royal palaces with magnificent sculptured reliefs, and a remarkable store of cuneiform tablets, which are a valuable source of historical information.

Nine Years War (or War of the Grand Alliance) (1688–97) A conflict that resulted from French aggression in the Rhineland and subsequently became a power struggle between LOUIS XIV of France and WILLIAM III of Britain. In 1688 when French armies invaded Cologne and the Palatinate, the members of the League of AUGSBURG took up arms. Meanwhile William had driven JAMES II from the throne of England and in 1689 a Grand Alliance of England, the United Provinces, Austria, Spain, and Savoy was formed against France. The French withdrew from the Palatinate. James II, supported by French troops, was defeated in Ireland at the Battle of the BOYNE. In 1690 the French navy won a victory off Beachy Head but in 1692 was defeated at La Hogue, although their privateers continued to damage allied commerce. The French campaigns in north Italy and Catalonia were successful but the war in the Spanish Netherlands became a stalemate as one lengthy siege succeeded another. William's one success was the retaking of Namur. The war was a severe defeat for France, despite a good military performance, because its financial resources were not equal to those of Britain and the United Provinces. Peace was finally concluded by the Treaty of RYSWICK.

Nixon, Richard Milhous (1913–94) US lawyer, and 37th President of the USA (1969–74). Elected to the US House of Representatives (1947, 1949), he was prominent in the investigations that led to the indictment of Alger HISS in the MCCARTHY era. He was elected as Vice-President under EISENHOWER and as such (1953–60) earned a reputation for skilful diplomacy. He was narrowly

defeated in the presidential election of 1960 by John F.
KENNEDY and lost (1962) the election for governor of
California. In 1968 he was chosen as Republican
presidential candidate, when he narrowly defeated the
Democrat Hubert Humphrey. In his first term he
achieved many successes, especially in foreign affairs.
His administration initiated a New Economic Policy
(1971) to counteract inflation, which included an
unprecedented attempt to control prices and wages in
peace-time, as well as the reversal of many of the social
policies of President JOHNSON. In an attempt to achieve a
balance of trade, the dollar was twice devalued in 1971
and 1973. The presidency is best remembered for its
achievements in foreign affairs, for which the Secretary
of State Henry KISSINGER was at least partly responsible.
Having inherited the VIETNAM WAR, Nixon began by
extending it, by invading Cambodia (1970) and Laos (1971),
and by saturation bombing. From 1971 onwards,
however, a policy of gradual withdrawal of US troops
began, while negotiations were taking place, ending
with the ceasefire accord of 1973. At the same time
support was being given to the policy of OSTPOLITIK with
a presidential visit to the Soviet Union bringing about
agreements on trade, joint scientific and space
programmes, and nuclear arms limitation. Recognition
was given to the communist regime of the People's
Republic of China as the official government of China
and in February 1972 Nixon paid a state visit to China.
Although Nixon was re-elected President in 1972, his
second term was curtailed by the WATERGATE SCANDAL
(1973–74) and he became the first President to resign
from office (which he did to avoid IMPEACHMENT). He was
granted a pardon by President Ford for any crimes he
may have committed over Watergate. He returned to
politics in 1981 as a Republican elder statesman.

Nizam Shahi Muslim dynasty of Ahmadnagar, based in
the north-western Indian Deccan region, that flourished
from 1490 to 1637. Its founder was Malik Ahmad who
revolted against the BAHMANIS and set up an independent
kingdom centred on a new capital, Ahmadnagar, which
took its founder's name. His main achievement was the
conquest of Daulatabad (1499). He and his successors
then engaged in almost constant warfare. After
abandoning an alliance with the Hindu kingdom of
VIJAYANAGAR, they participated in the final destruction of
that city in 1565. The dynasty presented spirited
resistance to subsequent Mogul encroachment into its
territories but had lost all independent existence by
1637.

Nkomo, Joshua Mqabuko Nyongolo (1917–   )
Zimbabwean politician. He was Secretary-General of the
Rhodesian Railways African Employees Association and
President of the African National Congress (1957–59)
when it was banned in Rhodesia. In 1960 he founded the
National Democratic Party. When this was banned he
instituted the Zimbabwe African People's Union (ZAPU).
He was twice detained (1962–64) and then imprisoned
(1964–74). On release he travelled widely to promote the
nationalist cause. His ZAPU, mainly supported by the
Ndebele in south-western Zimbabwe allied uneasily with
MUGABE's ZANU as the Patriotic Front. He lost the 1980
election to Mugabe and, from 1982 until their
reconciliation in 1987, was his foremost opponent. He
became a senior minister under Mugabe in 1988 and
Vice-President in 1990.

Richard Milhous Nixon   *Although Gerald Ford, Nixon's
successor and former Vice-President, pardoned Nixon for his
role in the Watergate scandal, this itself proved
controversial; officially Nixon had not been found guilty and
so should not have needed a pardon.*

Nkrumah, Kwame (Francis Nwia Kofi) (1909–72)
Ghanaian statesman, Prime Minister of Ghana (1952–60)
and first President (1960–66). After studying in the USA
and Britain, Nkrumah returned to Ghana in 1947 as
General Secretary of the United Gold Coast Convention,
an African nationalist party founded by J. B. Danquah.
In 1949 Nkrumah founded the Convention People's Party
and led a series of strikes and boycotts for self-
government. He became Prime Minister after a short
imprisonment by the British for sedition and led his
country to independence (1957) as GHANA, the first British
African colony to achieve this. His style of government
was autocratic but in his first years in power he was
immensely popular with his policy of Africanization. In
1964 he was declared President for life. Economic
pressures led to political unrest and in 1966, while he
was on a visit to China, a military coup deposed him. He
took refuge in Guinea, where President Sekou TOURÉ
made him 'Co-President'. An outstanding African
nationalist and a firm believer in PAN-AFRICANISM, he died
in exile.

NKVD (initial Russian letters for 'People's Commissariat
for Internal Affairs') The Soviet secret police agency
responsible from 1934 for internal security and the
labour PRISON CAMPS, having absorbed the functions of
the former OGPU. Mainly concerned with political
offenders, it was especially used for STALIN's purges. Its
leaders were Genrikh Yagoda (1934–36), Nikolai Yezhov

936–38), and BERIA until 1946, when it was merged with the MVD (Ministry of Interior). After Beria's fall in 1953 the Soviet secret police was placed under the KGB Committee of State Security).

Nobel, Alfred (1833–96) Swedish industrialist and philanthropist, founder of the Nobel prizes. Born in Stockholm, Sweden, he was brought up and educated in St Petersburg, the capital of imperial Russia. In 1850–52, he travelled widely in Europe and the USA, becoming fluent in five languages and acquiring a good knowledge of chemistry, engineering, and foreign business methods. Nobel became interested in making highly volatile nitro-glycerine safer to handle. In 1867 he patented the invention of dynamite, in which the nitro-glycerine is made less reactive by mixing it with kieselguhr, a siliceous mineral. Nobel's blasting gelatine followed in 1875. The last of his major inventions was ballistite, a smokeless propellant for firearms (1887). On his death, Nobel left the greater part of his vast fortune to support the prestigious international Nobel prizes, first awarded in 1901.

Nok culture The people occupying northern Nigeria from *c.* 500 BC to 200 AD; this culture was important for two reasons. As the earliest known centre of iron-working south of the Sahara, it played a major part in passing on metallurgy and its distinctive terracotta figurines are considered ancestral to the later statuary of IFE.

Nomenklatura A practice of the former Soviet political system, by which the Communist Party exercised control over important appointments. It comprised a list of responsible posts, such as ministerial positions, newspaper editors, factory managers, heads of schools, and other institutions, together with a list of individuals approved by the Party to hold such positions. This created an élite within Soviet society with special rights and privileges, such as access to special shops, hospitals, or schools. It was one of the targets of Mikhail Gorbachev's programme of *glasnost* and *perestroika*.

Non-aligned Movement (NAM) An international organization, linking countries that wanted to remain neutral in EAST–WEST RELATIONS during the COLD WAR. Non-alignment started as an Asian movement, with Prime Minister Nehru of India (1889–1964) as its leading figure. He was soon joined by President Tito of Yugoslavia (1892–1980) and President Nasser of Egypt (1918–70). Inspired by the BANDUNG CONFERENCE of 1955, in which Asian and African states met to discuss world peace and co-operation, the first Non-Aligned Summit was held in Belgrade in 1961, followed by further summits held in different non-aligned capitals, usually at three-year intervals. Gradually the movement was joined by most newly independent nations and the scope of its interests widened. The movement grew in importance during the 1960s and 1970s, becoming the most influential THIRD WORLD grouping, with considerable impact on world politics, particularly in the UN. The Co-ordinating Bureau of Non-Aligned Countries was set up in September 1973 in Algiers with the aim of working towards the establishment of a NEW INTERNATIONAL ECONOMIC ORDER.

By 1993 NAM had 110 members, including the PALESTINE LIBERATION ORGANIZATION. It has pressed for debt alleviation and better terms for trade in tropical raw materials, as well as for basic co-operation between the developing countries. A novel development at the NAM summit in 1989, which followed the revolutions in Eastern Europe, was the guest appearance of former WARSAW PACT member countries. Delegates to its 1991 anniversary meeting chose Indonesia for its chairmanship and concurred that, with the COLD WAR ended, greater attention should be paid to economic development and other economic issues.

Nonconformist (or Dissenter) A Protestant who did not conform to the disciplines or rites of the ANGLICAN CHURCH. A number of groups, including Catholic RECUSANTS, were Nonconformists. The PURITANS wished to purify the Church from within while the PRESBYTERIANS were specific in their demands for the replacement of organization by bishops for a system of elected elders. The separatists under Robert BROWNE left the Anglican Church entirely. All Nonconformists were subject to penalties; the PILGRIM FATHERS emigrated to escape persecution. During the Civil War Nonconformists (especially CONGREGATIONALISTS and BAPTISTS) fought on the Parliamentary side and the Restoration Settlement (1660) enacted harsh measures against all Nonconformist groups. The 1662 Act of Uniformity deprived them of freedom of worship and subsequent persecution led to a further exodus to North America. In 1681 Pennsylvania was founded as a refuge for QUAKERS. The Toleration Act (1689) brought some improvements in England, but until the 19th century Nonconformists were debarred from holding political office.

non-co-operation (in British India) A political campaign by the Indian National CONGRESS organized and led by M. K. GANDHI (1920–22). Its aims were to force further concessions from the British government by organizing the boycotting of the legislative councils, courts and schools, and other symbolic acts. The movement, inspired by Gandhi's SATYAGRAHA campaign, was intended to be non-violent but it degenerated into violence and was called off by Gandhi in February 1922 after the murder of a number of policemen by a mob at Chauri Chaura in the United Provinces. The movement failed to win enough support to paralyse government; its chief effect was to mobilize mass support for Congress and to consolidate Gandhi's position in the leadership of the national movement.

Nootka Sound A harbour on the west coast of Vancouver Island, Canada, lying between it and Nootka Island. The mouth of the sound was visited by Juan Perez in 1774 and by Captain Cook in 1778. In that year a fort was built by John Meares. The seizure of the fort by the Spanish in 1789 led to a controversy with Britain. Agreement was reached in the Nootka Convention of 1790, which opened the West Pacific coast to British settlement.

Nore mutiny (May 1797) A mutiny by sailors of the British navy stationed at the Nore anchorage in the Thames estuary. Encouraged by the earlier naval mutiny at SPITHEAD they demanded improvements in their conditions, the removal of unpopular officers, a greater share in prize money and, under the influence of their ringleader, Richard Parker, certain radical political changes. This time the Admiralty would make no concessions and eventually the mutineers surrendered.

About 19 men, including Parker, were hanged. Alarm at the mutiny probably contributed to the decisive defeat of Grey's parliamentary reform motion of May 1797.

Norman Conquest The period of Norman control of England that opened in 1066 with Duke William of Normandy's victory over the English at the Battle of HASTINGS. As WILLIAM I (1066–87) he established a military superiority over the English, rebellions were crushed (1067–71), and about 5,000 castles were constructed by the time of his death. England's frontiers were protected, first by MARCHER LORDS and then through conquest. Ruthless attention to detail characterized the Norman approach to government. English institutions were either retained and developed (such as the treasury, the king's council, the king's peace, sheriffs, and the shire system) or replaced with Norman versions. Not all changes were popular with the English, who had already lost heavily in terms of status, land holdings, and public office. Taxation was heavier, forest laws were harsh and outside the common law. Norman efficiency produced the unique survey recorded in DOMESDAY BOOK (1086), although it owed a great deal to existing English records. The language of government and of the court was Norman French. England prospered commercially: its towns grew, as did its population. Norman rule probably accelerated, rather than created commercial growth, and similarly reorganization of the English Church, which took place under Archbishop LANFRANC may have occurred anyway. In architecture the Norman style, characterized by rounded arches and heavy pillars, was introduced after the Conquest.

Normandy A former province in north-western France, originally the home of Celtic tribes, and part of the kingdom of CLOVIS. It was in Neustria under MEROVINGIAN rule and suffered from Viking invasions in the 9th century. The Viking ROLLO accepted it in 912 as a FIEF from the French king, who was powerless to prevent its falling to the Vikings, and the present name derives from those invaders. They accepted Christianity and adopted the French language but Norman expansion meant that their power rivalled that of the French kings.

In 1066 Duke William of Normandy conquered England, becoming WILLIAM I. The duchy was recovered for France by Philip Augustus in 1204, but fell once more to England in the Hundred Years War. After the Battle of Formigny in 1450, it was permanently reunited with France.

Normandy Campaign (June–August 1944) Allied counter-offensive in Europe in World War II following the NORMANDY LANDINGS. The US forces under General BRADLEY cut off the Cotentin Peninsula (18 June) and accepted the surrender of Cherbourg. The British army attacked towards Caen, securing it after heavy fighting (9 July), before advancing on Falaise. US troops broke through the German defences to capture the vital communications centre of Saint-Lô, cutting off the German force under ROMMEL. The Germans launched a counter-attack but were caught between the US and British armies in the 'Falaise Gap' and lost 60,000 men in fierce fighting. Field-Marshal Model, transferred from the Eastern Front, was unable to stem Patton's advance, which now swept across France to Paris, while Montgomery moved his British army up the English Channel. Paris was liberated by General Leclerc on 26

August and Brussels on 3 September. By 5 September more than two million troops, four million tonnes of supplies, and 450,000 vehicles had been landed, at the cost of some 224,000 Allied casualties.

Normandy Landings (June 1944) A series of Allied landings on the beaches of Normandy, France, in World War II. Five beaches had been designated for the Allied invasion, codename 'Operation Overlord', for which General EISENHOWER was the supreme commander. All the beaches, given codenames, had been carefully reconnoitred by commandos and at dawn on 6 June 1944 (D-Day) five separate groups landed between St Marcouf and the River Orne: at 'Utah', 'Omaha', 'Gold', 'Juno', and 'Sword'. British and Canadian troops fought across the eastern beaches, US forces the western. Four beaches were taken easily but 'Omaha' encountered fierce German resistance. Allied airforces destroyed most of the bridges over the Seine and the Loire, preventing the Germans from reinforcing their forward units. At the height of the fighting, ROMMEL, who commanded Germany's western defences, was seriously wounded and was recalled. Meanwhile old ships had been towed across the Channel and sunk to provide more sheltered anchorages. On D-Day plus 14 two vast steel-and-concrete artificial harbours (code-name 'Mulberry') were towed across the English Channel. One was sunk by a freak storm but the second was established at Arromanches, on beach 'Gold'. It provided the main harbour for the campaign. Meanwhile a series of 20 oil pipelines (codename 'Pluto') was laid across the Channel to supply the thousands of vehicles now being landed. After months of detailed and meticulous preparation, the greatest amphibious landing in history was complete and the NORMANDY CAMPAIGN launched.

Normans The inhabitants or natives of NORMANDY, France, descendants of a mixed Scandinavian ('Northmen') and Frankish people who were established there by early medieval times. Normandy was secured by ROLLO in 912 from Charles III of France, but was inadequate for settlement since inheritance laws left younger sons without territory; land hunger provided the impetus towards conquest and colonization. Under Duke William the Normans conquered England (1066), and later Wales, Ireland, and parts of Scotland, as well as large areas of the Mediterranean. Their expansion southwards, led by a spirited adventurer Robert GUISCARD, was initially as mercenaries fighting the Muslims but they soon controlled much of Europe. In 1154, the year of ROGER II of Sicily's death and HENRY II's accession to the English throne, Norman power was at its height, witnessed in the highly efficient governments of Sicily and England which were renowned in Europe for their sophisticated legal and administrative systems.

Norseman VIKING.

North, Frederick, Lord (1732–92) British statesman, Prime Minister (1770–82). A statesman of an impeccable WHIG background, he was first given a ministerial post by NEWCASTLE in 1759. He was an able Chancellor of the Exchequer under GRAFTON and he became Prime Minister in 1770, restoring stability after a decade of frequent changes. He kept taxes low and avoided expensive foreign ventures and he tried to cool American passions by withdrawing all but one of the TOWNSHEND ACTS,

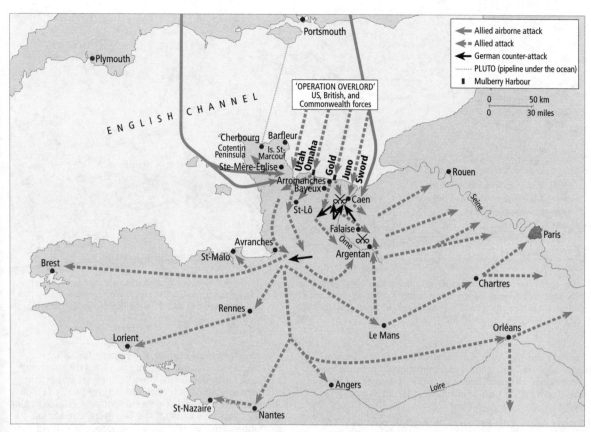

Normandy Campaign   *The Allied plan 'Operation Overlord' succeeded in 1944 largely as a result of meticulous planning. U-boat bases in Brittany were captured in a lightning campaign by US troops, who then swung east. Other US forces, together with British and Commonwealth troops, defeated German defenders at the Battle of Falaise Gap. A swift drive through Normandy led to the capture of Rouen and Paris, and the advance into north-west Europe.*

which imposed import duties on the colonists. He refused to be provoked by incidents such as the Boston Massacre but his divided Cabinet would not allow the BOSTON Tea Party to go unpunished and North was led into a situation that made the American War of INDEPENDENCE inevitable. Defeat in the war brought his resignation in 1782. He had been popular in the House of Commons as a peacetime Prime Minister and in the early years of the American War but increasing frustration with failures in America and opposition propaganda (especially from the ROCKINGHAM Whigs led to suggestions that his ministry was being sustained in power by excessive crown patronage and influence. This led to growing demands for financial reform, which was implemented after his resignation by the Rockingham Whigs. He held office again briefly in the Fox–North coalition of 1783 but failing eyesight from 1786 caused him to withdraw from active politics.

North African Campaigns (June 1940–May 1943) A series of Allied military campaigns in Africa in World War II. When Italy declared war in June 1940, General WAVELL in Cairo with 36,000 Commonwealth troops attacked first, the Italians surrendering Sidi Barrani, Tobruk, and Benghazi between September 1940 and January 1941. In July 1940 the Italians had occupied parts

of the Sudan and British Somaliland but in January 1941 the British counter-attacked and on 6 April 1941 Ethiopia and all of Italian East Africa surrendered, thus opening the way for Allied supplies and reinforcements to reach the Army of the Nile. In March 1941 General ROMMEL attacked and the British withdrew, leaving TOBRUK besieged. Under General AUCHINLECK, an offensive (Operation Crusader) was planned. At first successful, the campaign swung back and forth across the desert, both German and British tank casualties being high. Tobruk fell in June 1942 and the British took up a defensive position at El ALAMEIN in July. From there in October the reinforced 8th Army of 230,000 men and 1,230 tanks now under General MONTGOMERY launched their attack and Rommel fell back to Tunisia. Meanwhile 'Operation Torch' was launched, an amphibious landing of US and British troops (8 November) under General EISENHOWER near Casablanca on the Atlantic and at Oran and Algiers in the Mediterranean. It was hoped that the troops would link up with FREE FRENCH forces in West Africa. The VICHY French troops of General DARLAN at first resisted but after three days they acquiesced. From November 1942 to May 1943 German armies, although reinforced, were being squeezed between the 8th Army advancing from

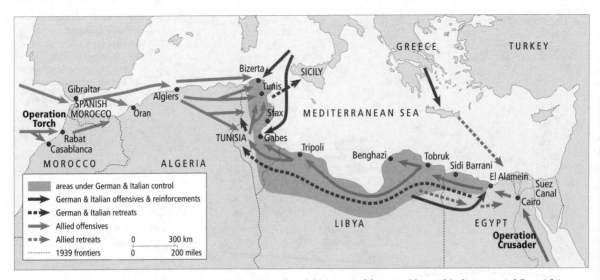

North African Campaign (1941–43)   *In January 1941 British and Commonwealth troops liberated Italian-occupied East Africa. By June 1942 German Panzer troops under General Rommel had reached the Egyptian border, where they were defeated at El Alamein. Rommel was steadily pushed west, while an Allied advance from Casablanca moved east through Algeria. In May 1943 German troops withdrew to Italy.*

the east and the Allied forces advancing from the west. On 7 May Tunis surrendered. Some 250,000 prisoners were taken, although Rommel skilfully succeeded in withdrawing the best troops of his Afrika Korps to Sicily.

North American Free Trade Agreement (NAFTA) An economic pact permitting free trade between the USA, Canada, and Mexico. NAFTA extends a free trade agreement made between the USA and Canada in 1988. The treaty was signed in 1992, ratified in 1993, and took effect in 1994. It provides for the complete removal on all trade tariffs between the member countries, with tariffs on agricultural products to be phased out. Chile applied to join and in 1994 negotiations over its admittance began.

North American Indians NATIVE AMERICANS.

North Atlantic Treaty Organization NATO.

North Carolina A colony and state of the USA on the east coast between Virginia and South Carolina. After Raleigh's ill-fated ROANOKE ISLAND venture, official colonization did not begin until 1663 when CHARLES II granted a charter to colonize the Carolinas to a syndicate of eight proprietors. The northern and southern parts of Carolina developed separately and the colony was divided into North and South Carolina in 1713. It endured recurrent unrest against proprietorial authority, including CULPEPER'S REBELLION, until it became a royal colony in 1729. Scots-Irish and German pioneers settled inland and many supported the REGULATOR movement (1768–71) against the coastal planter oligarchy. After CORNWALLIS's campaign through the back-country (1780–81), the state settled to a planter-dominated regime.

Northern Expedition (1926–28) Military campaign in China waged by nationalist forces under the leadership of CHIANG KAI-SHEK to extend their power from their base

in southern China to much of northern China by defeating local WARLORD armies, initially with military assistance from the Soviet Union. Shanghai and Nanjing were captured in March 1927 and Beijing finally fell on 8 June 1928. A nationalist government was established in Nanjing from 1928 to 1932. The Northern Expedition was notable both for the final emergence of Chiang Kai-shek as the sole leader of the nationalist KUOMINTANG and for his purge of the communists. This resulted in a series of unsuccessful communist risings in August 1927 and the first ten-year phase of the nationalist-communist civil war.

Northern Ireland A province of the UK comprising the six north-eastern historic counties of Ireland, divided into 26 administrative districts.
 Physical. Structurally, Northern Ireland is a south-westward extension of Scotland, separated by the North Channel of the Irish Sea.
 Economy. The traditional linen and shipbuilding industries have declined but remain important, along with engineering and chemical industries. There is some mining. Many people are now employed in the service sector. Agricultural products include barley and potatoes; sheep and cattle are raised.
 History. Northern Ireland was established as a self-governing province of the United Kingdom by the Government of Ireland Act (1920) as a result of pressure from its predominantly Protestant population. Discrimination by the Protestant majority against the largely working-class Catholics (about one-third of the population) over electoral reforms erupted in violence in the 1960s, heralding the decades of 'the Troubles' in Northern Ireland. The civil rights movement (1968) led to outbreaks of violence, and paramilitary groupings such as the IRISH REPUBLICAN ARMY clashed with 'loyalist' militant organizations such as the Ulster Defence Association (UDA) and the Ulster Defence Force (UDF). In 1969 extra British military forces were sent to the

province at the request of the STORMONT government, and have remained there ever since. The British government suspended (1972) the Northern Irish constitution and dissolved the Stormont government, imposing direct rule from London. A more representative Northern Ireland Assembly was elected (1973), but collapsed through extremist Unionist opposition. Leaders such as the Reverend Ian PAISLEY, together with the Ulster Workers Council, which organized a general strike in 1974, paralysed the province, forced the collapse of the non-sectarian Northern Ireland Executive, and foiled attempts at a new governmental framework for power-sharing between both sides. After 1979 closer co-operation between the Republic of Ireland and Britain developed, leading to the Anglo-Irish Accord (the Hillsborough Agreement) signed in 1985, giving the republic a consultative role in the government of Northern Ireland. Sectarian terrorist outrages continued to be committed by extremists of both sides, claiming over 3,000 lives by the early 1990s. In 1991–92 all-party talks (with the exception of SINN FEIN, led by Gerry ADAMS) took place, the first time representatives from the Irish Republic and Ulster Unionists had ever met. Subsequently the DOWNING STREET DECLARATION of 1993 was issued by John MAJOR and Albert Reynolds, the Prime Minister of the Republic of Ireland: this opened the way for negotiations with all parties that were prepared to renounce violence, including Sinn Féin. In 1994 the IRA declared a 'complete cessation' of military activities, which was followed by similar declarations by Loyalist paramilitary groups. However, little progress was made during 1995 as a result of the UK government's refusal to negotiate with Sinn Féin until the ceasefire had been established on a permanent basis by the IRA decommissioning its weapons. In February 1996 the IRA broke the ceasefire by launching bomb attacks on London and Manchester. At a result Sinn Féin was excluded from the talks about the future of Northern Ireland that began in June 1996. In the summers of 1996 and 1997 parades by the Protestant Orange order became a focus for serious rioting. Following a compromise on the issue of decommissioning weapons, the IRA renewed its ceasefire in July 1997. Sinn Féin was consequently admitted to all-party talks in September 1997. The outcome was the Good Friday agreement of 1998, which proposed a comprehensive settlement for the province, to be implemented if supported by the electorates of both Northern Ireland and the Republic in twin referendums. The agreement proposed the creation of three new administrative bodies: an elected Northern Ireland assembly with a power-sharing executive, a North-South ministerial council with cross-border powers, and a 'Council of the Isles' with members drawn from the British and Irish governments, the Northern Irish assembly, and the devolved bodies in Scotland and Wales. It also provided for the decommissioning of all weapons, the phased release of paramilitary prisoners, and reviews of security and policing.

Northern Rising (November–December 1569) An English rebellion, led by the earls of Westmorland and Northumberland. Protesting loyalty to ELIZABETH I, the rebels aimed to remove 'new men' like William CECIL from power, preserve the Catholic religion, and have MARY, Queen of Scots declared heir to the English throne. They ventured south and took Durham before government troops intervened and ended the rising. At the queen's insistence, around 400 rank-and-file rebels were executed. Meanwhile a number of the leaders fled abroad or were allowed to buy themselves pardons.

Northern War (or Great Northern War; 1700–21) A conflict between Russia, Denmark, and Poland on one side, and Sweden opposing them, during which, in spite of the victories of CHARLES XII, Sweden lost its empire and Russia under PETER THE GREAT became a major Baltic power. In 1697, on the accession of the 15-year-old Charles, the Swedish empire included Finland, Estonia, Livonia, and territory in northern Germany. In 1700 Sweden was attacked by a coalition of AUGUSTUS the Strong of Saxony and Poland, Denmark, and Russia, organized by the Livonian exile, Patkul. Charles forced Denmark to make peace, defeated Peter at NARVA, invaded Poland, and placed Stanislaus Leszczynski on the throne. He pursued Augustus into Saxony and in 1706 forced him to recognize Stanislaus as King of Poland. After a diplomatic mission from MARLBOROUGH to persuade him not to invervene in the War of the SPANISH SUCCESSION, Charles turned east and by the summer of 1708 was deep into Russia and won his last victory at Holowczyn. He then turned south but his ally Mazeppa, the hetman (leader) of the Dnieper Cossacks, was defeated by Peter's general Menshikov. The winter was severe and Charles was defeated at POLTAVA. He took refuge in Turkish territory for five years, trying to persuade the sultan to help him while his enemies attacked and his subjects fought desperate rearguard actions. Finally expelled by the Turks, Charles was killed in 1718 and his sister, Ulrica Leonora, began the peace negotiations that Charles had refused to consider. By the Treaties of Stockholm (1719, 1720), the bishoprics of Bremen and Verden were ceded to Hanover and most of Pomerania to Prussia. Finally, after further Russian naval successes, the Treaty of NYSTADT, which ended the war, gave Sweden's Baltic provinces to Russia.

Northern Wei (Toba Wei) (386–535) One of the dynasties that ruled northern China after the empire disintegrated following the collapse of the WESTERN JIN in 311 AD. It was founded by a Mongol group, the Xianbi. Its rulers availed themselves of Chinese administrators and encouraged intermarriage with Chinese. Luoyang, once the Eastern Han capital, became their capital. Land reforms were instituted to build up a stable peasantry and an enduring system of collective responsibility. Its rule ended when tribal frontier garrisons, which were opposed to its policies, revolted.

North Korea KOREA, NORTH.

North–South relations The relationship between the advanced industrialized countries (the North) and the THIRD WORLD, or DEVELOPING COUNTRIES (the South). North–South relations became an issue in international politics following the process of decolonization, which brought a large number of new states into an international system in which they found themselves to be at a serious disadvantage, particularly in economic terms. The developing countries of the South tried through various means to reduce their dependence on the North. They were particularly active in the UN, notably in the UNITED NATIONS CONFERENCE ON TRADE AND DEVELOPMENT (UNCTAD) in 1964, where the framework was established for a set of demands for a new deal on world trade. The position of the South looked stronger by the late 1970s: OPEC (the Organization of Petroleum Exporting Countries) had set an example to all developing countries by successfully raising world energy prices, the demand for a NEW INTERNATIONAL ECONOMIC ORDER had been presented to a UN General Assembly session in 1974, and the issue of North–South relations had been made the subject of an international commission which met from 1977 to 1979 under the chairmanship of Willy Brandt (1913–92). (See BRANDT REPORT.)

Northumberland, John Dudley, Earl of Warwick, Duke of (c. 1502–53) Ruler of England on behalf of Edward VI (1551–53). He began his political career under HENRY VIII and was a member of Edward VI's Privy Council. As Earl of Warwick he sought to undermine SOMERSET's power and was created Duke of Northumberland in 1551 shortly before ordering Somerset's imprisonment and execution. The new government was committed to radical Protestantism and produced a new Prayer Book (1552), supported by a new Act of Uniformity prescribing penalties for not attending Church services. In 1552 CRANMER produced the Forty-Two Articles, a comprehensive statement of Protestant doctrine which formed the basis of the THIRTY-NINE ARTICLES (1571). Though posthumous tradition condemned Northumberland as an evil schemer, his regime promoted stability. He terminated the unsuccessful wars against France and Scotland initiated by Somerset and introduced several important financial reforms. Northumberland brought about his own downfall by trying to ensure the succession of Lady Jane GREY. He was executed and MARY, Henry VIII's daughter, succeeded to the throne.

Northumbria Territory in northern England, the kingdom of the ANGLES formed by the merger of the kingdoms of Bernicia and Deira (604). It extended from Yorkshire to the Firth of Forth. The greatest period of its history was the 7th century when, under a succession of powerful kings (including OSWALD and OSWY) it appeared that Northumbria might create a united England out of the many Anglo-Saxon kingdoms. However, the death of Egfrith at the hands of the Picts in the battle of Nechtansmere (685) revealed the precarious nature of Northumbrian control, which yielded to the kings of MERCIA. In the 7th and 8th centuries Northumbrian learning and monasticism were preeminent, developed by such figures as St Wilfrid, St Cuthbert, and BEDE. It attracted the attention of Danish raiders: the monastery of Lindisfarne was plundered by them in 793 and 875. Northumbria became part of the Danish kingdom of York (876) before being conquered by Wessex in the 10th century and reduced to an earldom in the following century.

North Vietnam VIETNAM.

North-West Europe Campaign (September 1944–May 1945) An Allied military campaign in World War II. Following the NORMANDY CAMPAIGN, MONTGOMERY's forces captured Antwerp (4 September) and crossed the Albert Canal. The US 1st Army captured Namur and Aachen, while the US 3rd Army moved east and reached the Moselle. Montgomery's attempt to seize the lower Rhine by dropping the 1st Airborne Division at ARNHEM ended in failure. In November the Germans consolidated and in December launched a counter-attack in the ARDENNES, the Battle of the Bulge. In January 1945 Montgomery's forces pushed forward to the Rhine. In March a massive bombardment at Wesel preceded a successful crossing of the lower Rhine by Montgomery's troops. The US 7th Army pushed east towards Munich, French forces moved up the upper Rhine to Lake Constance, and the US 3rd Army advanced to Leipzig and across the Austrian border into Czechoslovakia. On 11 April Montgomery reached the River Elbe. Following the capture of Berlin by the Red Army and the suicide of Hitler (30 April), Montgomery received the surrender of the German forces in north-west Europe on Lüneburg Heath on 4 May. Four days later (V-E Day), the war in Europe was declared at an end.

North-West Frontier The mountainous area in Pakistan, inhabited by PATHAN and Baluchi peoples, bordering on Afghanistan. Under British rule from 1849 to 1947, a policy of extending British control into the tribal territories began with the acquisition of Quetta (1876) and of Pishin, Sibi, and Kurram (1879). This led to a number of tribal wars, including those against Hunza and Nagar (1891), Chitral (1895), and Tirah (1897–98). The most troubled area, however, was Waziristan, where resistance was led by the Mulla Powindah until 1913 and by the Fakir of Ipi during the 1930s. To control the frontier the British employed several forces, including the Punjab Irregular Force (founded 1849), various militias, and the Frontier Constabulary. The border with Afghanistan was defined by the Durand Line (1893). The area was constituted a province in 1901 with a number of tribal agencies and after 1947 the Pakistan government withdrew military forces from tribal territory.

Northwest Territory The area in the USA between the Great Lakes and the Ohio and Mississippi rivers, which formed the first national territory of the Indiana, Michigan, Wisconsin, and eastern Minnesota. French explorers and trappers arrived there in the 17th century. It was acquired by Britain in 1763 and transferred to the USA in 1783. The charter grants of individual states had already been transferred to Congress.

The Northwest Ordinance of 1787 was a major achievement of the Confederation. It laid down procedures for government of the territories, survey, division and sale of lands, and the democratically willed acquisition of statehood, on levels of total equality with the original states. Slavery was forbidden in the area, the major difference with the Southwest Ordinance of 1790. The Ohio Company, with large areas of cheap congressional land, was a major colonizer but Native Americans still sympathetic to the British endangered frontier settlement.

Norway A country forming the north-western part of Scandinavia in northern Europe, bordering on Sweden, Finland, and Russia.

Physical. Norway's extensive coast, fringed with innumerable small islands, stretches from the Arctic Ocean to the North Sea. In the north, it is light all 24 hours in high summer – and equally dark in winter. Its climate is warmed by the Gulf Stream, which usually keeps the fiords from freezing. The south is barren moorland plateau cut by forested valleys and the north is mountainous.

Economy. Norway has one of the world's largest reserves of aluminium, though the main resource is North Sea oil and natural gas; north in the Arctic the Svalbard (Spitsbergen) archipelago contains rich deposits of coal. Most electricity is generated by hydroelectric sources. Norway exports machinery, ships, chemicals, and paper. Fur production and conifer forestry are significant. Agriculture is limited since only a small proportion of the land is cultivable. Fishing is a major industry. Norway's defiance of an international ban on whaling has angered environmentalists.

History. Norway was inhabited in prehistoric times by primitive hunting communities. Rivalry between chiefs, and the desire for land provoked excursions by the Norwegian VIKINGS as far as England, Greenland, and Iceland. Political organization strengthened under Harald Fairhair (*c.* 900) and under OLAF I, who brought Christianity. OLAF II furthered the work of Christian conversion, but was killed in a battle with the Danes. Danish rule (1028–35) followed, and thereafter civil war, and, in 1066, an unsuccessful expedition to assert Harald Hardrada's claim to the English throne. The reign of HAAKON IV brought order and, from 1254, Norway traded with the HANSEATIC LEAGUE. In 1397 the Union of KALMAR brought Norway, Sweden, and Denmark together under a single monarch. Danish rule resulted in conversion to LUTHERANISM. The Union was dissolved in 1523, though Norway was ruled by Danish governors until 1814 when it was ceded to Sweden. The country had established its own parliament (Storting) in 1807. A literary revival and a new national consciousness brought demands for complete independence. Responsible government was granted in 1884 and universal male suffrage in 1898. Finally, union with Sweden was unilaterally declared dissolved in June 1905 and Prince Charles of Denmark elected as HAAKON VII. A Liberal Party government introduced women's suffrage and social reform and maintained neutrality during WORLD WAR I. In WORLD WAR II, the Germans invaded, defeating Norwegian and Anglo-French forces at Narvik in 1940 and imposing a puppet government under Vidkun QUISLING. In 1945 the monarchy, and a Labour government, returned. Norway withdrew its application to join the EUROPEAN ECONOMIC COMMUNITY (1972) after a national referendum, while the exploitation of North Sea oil in the 1970s gave a great boost to the economy. Norway had been a founding member of EFTA in 1960, but by 1990 64% of its export revenue was coming from the EC trade, and only 15% from EFTA. Hence Norway was a leading negotiator for the establishment of the European Economic Area in February 1992. Gro Harlem Brundtland (1939–   ), author of the report on sustainable development worldwide, *Our Common Future* (1987), led four minority Labour governments (1981; 1986–89; 1990–93; 1993–96), facing high unemployment and a banking crisis in 1992. Norwegians voted against joining the European Union in a referendum held in 1994. A centrist coalition under Kjell Magne Bondevikwas formed after elections in 1997. King Olav V (1957–91) was succeeded by his son, Harald V.

CAPITAL:	Oslo
AREA:	323,878 sq km (125,050 sq miles)
POPULATION:	4.382 million (1996)
CURRENCY:	1 krone = 100 ore
RELIGIONS:	Church of Norway (Evangelical Lutheran) 88.0%; Penticostalist 1.0%
ETHNIC GROUPS:	Norwegian 98.0%; Danish 0.3%; US 0.3%; British 0.2%; Swedish 0.2%; Pakistani 0.2%
LANGUAGES:	Norwegian (official)
INTERNATIONAL ORGANIZATIONS:	UN; NATO; EFTA; OECD; Council of Europe; CSCE

Nostradamus (Michel de Notredame) (1503–66) French astrologer and physician. He first won fame for his innovative use of medicines and pioneer treatments during outbreaks of the plague at Aix and Lyons (1546–47). His *Centuries* of rhyming prophecies (1555), decidedly apocalyptic in tone, caught the contemporary imagination. An enlarged second edition was dedicated to Henry II of France in 1558. He was appointed physician-in-ordinary to Charles IX on his accession in 1560 and his prophecies continued to excite speculation and controversy. In 1781 they were condemned by the Roman Catholic Congregation of the Index (INQUISITION).

Nova Scotia One of the Atlantic provinces of Canada, claimed by the French in 1603; their settlement at Port Royal became the centre of Acadia. Britain contested their claim, naming the peninsula Nova Scotia in 1621, and launched several invasions (1613, 1654, 1690) before capture in 1710 and cession in 1713. The French retained Cape Breton Island, immediately adjacent, and built LOUISBURG, which was captured in 1745 but returned in 1748. In the FRENCH AND INDIAN WAR, some 6,000 Acadians were forcibly deported to British colonies to the south, some ending up in Louisiana, others eventually returning. The second capture of Louisburg (1757) and the Treaty of Paris (1763) secured Nova Scotia in British hands. Settlement was vigorously encouraged and during the War of Independence large numbers of loyalists emigrated there.

Novgorod A province of north-west European Russia, allegedly the site of the founding of a Russian state under Prince Rurik in 826. Novgorod was forcibly Christianized in 989 and became self-governing in 1019. It survived the invasion of the GOLDEN HORDE but submitted to their suzerainty in 1238. The SWEDES were driven off in 1238 and the TEUTONIC KNIGHTS in 1242 but a struggle with MUSCOVY ensued in which Lithuanian aid was sought and which ended with submission to IVAN III (the Great) in 1478. IVAN IV (the Terrible) inflicted a massacre there in 1570 and it was occupied by the Swedes from 1611 to 1619. It retained political and commercial importance until the building of St Petersburg under PETER THE GREAT.

Nubians A people who live chiefly in Egypt and the Sudan, between the First and Fourth Cataracts of the River Nile. Their recorded history begins with raids by Egyptians *c.* 2613 BC, when their country was called Kush. Then a Nubian dynasty ruling at Napata from *c.* 920 BC conquered all Egypt. The Nubian Shabaka ruled as King of Kush and Egypt with Thebes as his capital but Assyrians forced Taharka, his successor, to withdraw (680–669 BC). After several further struggles, the Nubians drew back to Napata, and *c.* 530 BC their capital moved to MEROË. The dynasty continued until 350 AD, when Aezanas of AXUM destroyed it; its 300 pyramids remain. Nubia was converted to Christianity in *c.* 540 AD. Three Christian kingdoms emerged, but in 652 AD an Egyptian army conquered that at Dongola, granting peace for an annual tribute of slaves and at the end of the 13th century MAMELUKES took the north. The southern kingdom survived until the 16th century, when the FUNJ kingdom of Sennar absorbed it.

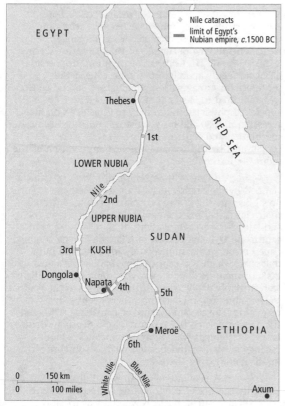

Nubians *The Romans gave the name Nubia to the region of the Nile valley extending roughly from the First Cataract in Egypt to the confluence of the Nile. In the 10th century BC its rulers became pharaohs of Egypt, and Napata, its capital, was briefly the centre of the ancient world.*

nuclear proliferation The spread of nuclear weapons. Vertical proliferation is concerned with the development of more and different types of weapons by the existing nuclear weapons states, often in response to evolutions in nuclear strategy. Such proliferation may be checked by arms control agreements, which set out terms for DISARMAMENT. Horizontal proliferation, on the other hand, refers to the spread of these weapons to currently non-nuclear states. The five declared nuclear weapons states are the USA, Russia, the UK, France, and China. Belarus, Ukraine, and Kazakhstan inherited Soviet nuclear weapons following the collapse of the Soviet Union in 1991. They have all signed the Non-Proliferation Treaty and agreed to give up their nuclear weapons. Belarus suspended its disarmament programme in 1995 but Kazakhstan and Ukraine had transferred all their nuclear weapons to Russia or destroyed them by mid-

1996. It is widely believed that Israel has nuclear weapons and India detonated what it called a peaceful nuclear device in 1974. In 1981, knowing that Iraq was developing a nuclear weapons capability, the Israelis bombed their reactor. Others thought to be capable of producing weapons include Pakistan, Iran, Argentina, Brazil, and South Africa. Fears that North Korea was developing nuclear weapons precipitated a crisis with South Korea during 1994–95. The horizontal proliferation of nuclear weapons is controlled by international constraints, including the 1963 NUCLEAR TEST BAN TREATY; the 1968 Non-Proliferation Treaty (which has not been signed by some countries, such as Israel, India, Pakistan, and South Africa that have the potential for developing nuclear weapons, and was only signed by the declared nuclear powers of China and France in 1992); and the Safeguards Regime of the International Atomic Energy Agency, designed to prevent the transfer of nuclear energy materials into weapons production. However, the weak nature of such constraints was indicated by the confirmation after the 1991 Gulf War of Iraq's attempts to develop nuclear weapons despite its membership of the Non-Proliferation Treaty. Following the demise of the Soviet Union, concern was voiced that Soviet nuclear scientists might contribute to nuclear proliferation by making their expertise available to third-party countries and international diplomacy concentrated on reaching agreement on disarming the nuclear capacity of the Soviet successor states. In 1995 175 signatory states of the Non-Proliferation Treaty agreed to its indefinite extension, although no formal vote was taken.

The 1967 Tlatelolco Treaty prohibits acquisition of nuclear arms by the countries of Latin America and the Caribbean.

Nuclear Test-Ban Treaty (1963) An international agreement not to test nuclear weapons in the atmosphere, in outer space, or under water, signed by the USA, the Soviet Union, and Britain (but not France). The issue of DISARMAMENT had been raised at the Geneva Conference (1955) and discussions on the ban of nuclear testing had begun in Geneva in 1958. In spite of the treaty the spread of nuclear weapons became a major preoccupation of the NATO powers in the 1960s and on 1 July 1968 Britain, the USA, and the Soviet Union signed a Non-Proliferation Treaty, which was endorsed by 59 other states. France and China were already nuclear powers by 1968 and since then Israel, India, and probably Pakistan and South Africa have developed nuclear capacity, whilst both Iran and Iraq, among other countries, have come very close to it. After the break-up of the Soviet Union (1990–91) many of the successor states inherited the capacity, should they decide to develop it. China carried out underground nuclear tests during 1994–95 and declared it would continue testing. France received international condemnation for carrying out a series of six tests in the south Pacific (1995–96) but then announced a permanent end of French tests.

In 1996 a permanent test-ban treaty was signed by the five declared nuclear weapons powers (China, France, Russia, the UK, and the USA).

Nuffield, William Richard Morris, Viscount (1877–1963) British motorcar manufacturer and philanthropist. He set up his own bicycle business at

Cowley, Oxford, when he was 16. In 1902 he designed a motorcycle and, by 1912, he was repairing motorcars. He bought a factory at Cowley, where the Morris Oxford, the first British car planned for middle-class family use, began production in 1913. MASS PRODUCTION kept Morris cars cheap. Business acumen earned him a vast fortune, much of it given away. Nuffield College, Oxford, and the Nuffield Foundation, a trust to encourage educational developments, were established by him.

nullification A US doctrine holding that a state had the right to nullify a federal law within its own territory. The Kentucky Resolutions of 1798–99 asserted the right of each state to judge whether acts of the federal government were constitutional. The nullification theory was fully developed in South Carolina, especially by John CALHOUN, in response to the high protective tariffs of 1828 and 1832. South Carolina's Ordinance of Nullification in 1833 prohibited the collection of tariff duties in the state, and asserted that the use of force by the federal government would justify secession. Although this ordinance was repealed after the passing of new federal legislation in the same year, the sentiments behind nullification remained latent in Southern politics, and were to emerge again in the secession crisis prior to the AMERICAN CIVIL WAR.

Numidia The area to the south and west of Carthage in North Africa, originally inhabited by the Numidae or Nomads. Its inhabitants were renowned in antiquity as horsemen and the cavalry of its king Masinissa played a crucial part in SCIPIO Africanus' defeat of HANNIBAL at Zama in 202 BC. Later JUGURTHA led the Numidians against Rome, a struggle that ended with his capture in 106 BC. Numidia was ruled as a client kingdom of Rome before being incorporated into the province of Africa. It was the centre of the DONATIST movement in the 4th century AD.

nunnery The building that houses a community of religious women. The word 'nun' is reserved for those living under strict vows of poverty, obedience, and chastity. Religious orders for women date from the 4th century and by the 11th century all communities lived lives devoted to prayer, reading, and work (spinning and weaving). From the 16th century sisterhoods were founded for active work, such as teaching and nursing. All communities were abolished in England at the Reformation but some were refounded in the 19th century.

Nupe A kingdom in West Africa, now part of Nigeria. According to tradition, Nupe was founded in the 16th century by Tsoede, who died in 1591 aged 120; he built Gbara and conquered a large amount of territory. Raba, the capital, became highly prosperous. Its wealth was largely dependent on wars to collect prisoners to sell as slaves. In the early 19th century the FULANI asserted overlordship, leading to bitter struggles for independence.

Nuremberg Trials (1945–46) An international tribunal for Nazi war criminals. The trials were complex and controversial, there being few precedents for using international law relating to the conduct of states to judge the activities of individuals. The charges were: conspiracy against peace, crimes against peace, violation of the laws and customs of war, crimes against humanity. As a result of the trials several Nazi organizations, such as the GESTAPO and the SS, were declared to be criminal bodies. Individual judgments against the 24 war-time leaders included death sentences, imprisonment, and not guilty. Ten prisoners were executed, while GOERING and Ley committed suicide. Rudolf HESS was sentenced to life-imprisonment.

Nyasaland MALAWI.

Nye Committee (1934–36) A US Senate committee, chaired by Gerald P. Nye of North Dakota, to investigate the dealings of the munitions industry and bankers and their reputed profits from promoting foreign wars. The findings revealed high profits and a studied hostility to disarmament but no evidence to support the theory that President WILSON had at any time been influenced by the financial 'stake' in his relations with Germany. However, so strong and widespread was the spirit of ISOLATIONISM that the Senate, in an effort to remain aloof from global problems, passed a series of NEUTRALITY ACTS (1935–39).

Nyerere, Julius Kambarage (1922–) Tanzanian statesman, the first Prime Minister of independent Tanganyika (1961) and first President of TANZANIA (1964–86). In 1954 he organized the Tanganyika African National Union (TANU). In 1956 the British administration nominated him as TANU representative in the Legislative Council. In 1957 he resigned, complaining of slow progress, but on Tanganyika's independence (1961) Nyerere became Prime Minister, surrendering his premiership a month later. In 1962 he was elected President of the Tanganyika Republic. In 1964, following a revolution in ZANZIBAR, he effected union between it and Tanganyika as the Republic of Tanzania, bringing it (1967) into the East African Community, a customs union with Uganda and Kenya. In the ARUSHA DECLARATION (1967) he outlined the socialist policies that were to be adopted in Tanzania. He has been a major force in the ORGANIZATION OF AFRICAN UNITY and over the broad range of African politics, especially in relation to Uganda, Zimbabwe, and South Africa. He resigned the presidency in 1985, having been a strong supporter of the Commonwealth. In 1990 he retired as chairman of TANU.

Nystad, Treaty of (1721) The final treaty of the NORTHERN WAR. It was signed at Nystad in south-west Finland. Under this treaty Sweden recognized PETER THE GREAT's title to Estonia, Livonia, Ingria, Kexholm, and part of Finland and so lost its Baltic empire.

OAS ORGANIZATION DE L'ARMÉE SECRÈTE; ORGANIZATION OF AMERICAN STATES.

Oastler, Richard (1789–1861) British social reformer. He began his agitation in 1830 with the support of John Wood, a Bradford manufacturer, who revealed some of the worst abuses of CHILD LABOUR in factories. Oastler, a Tory radical, combined his attack on the factory system with a condemnation of the POOR LAW Amendment Act of 1834. He attained some of his objectives with the Ten Hours Act in 1847, which limited daily working hours.

Oates, Titus POPISH PLOT.

OAU ORGANIZATION OF AFRICAN UNITY.

Obote, Milton (1924–) Ugandan statesman. Politically active throughout the 1950s, Obote served as Prime Minister of Uganda (1962–66), when he overthrew MUTESA II, Kabaka of Buganda, and assumed full power as President. Himself overthrown by Idi AMIN in 1971, Obote returned from exile in Tanzania to resume the presidency in 1980. However, he failed either to restore the economy or to stop corruption and tribal violence, and was once again overthrown in 1985, seeking refuge in Zambia.

Obregón, Alvaro (1880–1928) Mexican general and statesman. President of Mexico (1920–24), he was elected after the most violent decade of the MEXICAN REVOLUTION. He succeeded in bringing about some measure of agrarian, educational, and labour reform, although peonage remained strong. His implementation of the revolutionary programme of 1917 brought him into bitter conflict with the Catholic Church. After turning the presidency over to his successor Plutarco Elías CALLES in 1924, he was elected to a second term in 1928 but was assassinated prior to taking office.

Obrenović Serbian dynasty (1817–1903). It was founded by a former cattle drover, Milos Obrenović I (1780–1860), who became a revolutionary fighting the Turks under KARA GEORGE. After the murder (probably at his instigation) of Kara George, he persuaded the Turks to accept his election in 1817 as Prince of Serbia. His tyrannical rule led to his enforced abdication and the brief reign of Milan Obrenović II. Michael Obrenović III (1823–68) succeeded in 1840 but was forced into exile two years later. Milos was reinstated in 1858 but died in 1860. Michael then resumed his rule, and proved an able and effective leader. He was assassinated in 1868, and his cousin, Milan Obrenović IV (1854–1901), began 30 years of unpopular rule. He declared himself king of Serbia in 1882 but was forced to abdicate in favour of his son Alexander (1876–1903). Alexander's murder in June 1903 ended the dynasty, and the Karageorgević dynasty again came to power.

O'Brien, Smith YOUNG IRELAND.

OCAS ORGANIZATION OF CENTRAL AMERICAN STATES.

O'Connell, Daniel (1775–1847) Irish nationalist leader and social reformer. A lawyer by training, he first came to prominence with his condemnation of the ACT OF UNION (1801). A powerful orator and a skilled organizer, in 1823 he founded the Catholic Association to press for the removal of discrimination against Catholics in tithes, education, the electoral franchise, and the administration of justice. In 1828 he was elected Member of Parliament at the CLARE ELECTION, although as a Catholic he was ineligible for membership of the House of Commons. To avoid the risk of civil disorder the British government passed the Roman Catholic Relief Act (1829), which granted CATHOLIC EMANCIPATION and enabled O'Connell to take his seat. In the 1840s his campaign for the repeal of the Act of Union by constitutional methods was unsuccessful and this lost him the support of many nationalists, including the radicals in the YOUNG IRELAND movement.

O'Connor, Feargus Edward (1794–1855) Irish radical politician and Chartist leader. He was elected Member of Parliament for County Cork in 1832 as a supporter of Daniel O'CONNELL but lost his seat in 1835. In 1837 he founded a radical newspaper the *Northern Star* in England, and it was largely through his tireless energy and his ability as an orator that CHARTISM became a mass movement. After a term of imprisonment for seditious libel, he was elected Member of Parliament for Nottingham in 1847.

Octavian AUGUSTUS.

October Revolution RUSSIAN REVOLUTION (1917).

October War YOM KIPPUR WAR.

Oda Nobunaga (1534–82) Japanese warrior, who overthrew many powerful DAIMYO in an attempt to end the disorder of the ASHIKAGA period. He was assisted by HIDEYOSHI and TOKUGAWA IEYASU — and by the fact that many of his troops were armed with muskets, introduced by the Portuguese after 1542. In 1568 he entered Kyoto and in 1573 he drove out the SHOGUN. He began 'sword hunts' to disarm much of the population and organized land surveys. By the time he was assassinated by one of his followers, firm rule had replaced political chaos in most of central Japan.

Oder–Neisse Line The frontier, formed by these two rivers, established between Poland and Soviet-occupied Germany in 1945: it had once marked the frontier of medieval Poland. As a result of an agreement at the POTSDAM CONFERENCE, nearly one-fifth of Germany's territory in 1938 was reallocated, mainly to Poland. Germans were expelled from these eastern territories, which were resettled by Poles. The frontier, which became the eastern boundary of the German Democratic Republic, was later accepted by the Federal Republic (West Germany) as part of the policy of détente known as OSTPOLITIK, and confirmed in 1990 when reunification took place.

Odoacer (433–93) Gothic chieftain who became the first Germanic ruler of Italy. He and his troops were part of the Roman army and when Romulus Augustus became emperor (476) he led an uprising and deposed him, making Ravenna his capital. This event marked the end of the Western ROMAN EMPIRE. His troops later overran Dalmatia, threatening the power of Zeno, the Eastern emperor, who encouraged THEODORIC, King of the Ostrogoths, to besiege Ravenna. Odoacer surrendered (493) on promise of retaining half of Italy but at a banquet was murdered by Theodoric, who became sole ruler.

OECD (Organization for Economic Co-operation and Development) An organization of industrialized countries, established in 1961, and based in Paris, which seeks to promote co-ordination of economic and social policies among members, to make resources of capital and training available to developing countries, to contribute to the expansion of world trade, and to foster co-operation in fields such as education, energy, and transport. It was created as a replacement for the Organization for European Economic Co-operation, which had been formed in 1948 by those countries receiving aid under the MARSHALL PLAN. In 1998 its members were Australia, Austria, Belgium, Canada, the Czech Republic, Denmark, Finland, France, Germany, Greece, Hungary, Iceland, Republic of Ireland, Italy, Japan, South Korea, Luxembourg, Mexico, the Netherlands, New Zealand, Norway, Poland, Portugal, Spain, Sweden, Switzerland, Turkey, the UK, and the USA. Applications for membership from Slovakia and Russia are under consideration. The OECD prepares an influential annual report on the economy of each member country.

Offa (d. 796) King of MERCIA (757–96). His kingdom was the midland region of Saxon England whose western boundary with Wales is marked by the great dyke he constructed (784–86). His overall supremacy extended to the kingdoms of Kent, Sussex, and Wessex. Offa, anxious to extend his European reputation, re-established direct contact between England and the papacy, and regarded himself as an equal of CHARLEMAGNE. He codified the laws of Mercia, introduced a uniform silver penny that was to remain the basis of English currency until the 13th century, and stimulated its economy, particularly the cloth trade.

Oglethorpe, James Edward (1696–1785) British general, philanthropist, and founder of GEORGIA (USA). He entered Parliament (1722) after serving under Prince EUGÈNE OF SAVOY. Espousing the cause of imprisoned debtors, he led a group of philanthropists who became trustees of the new North American colony of Georgia in 1732. He founded Savannah (1733) and governed the colony on paternalistic lines, encouraging immigration of persecuted Protestants from Europe and of former soldiers. His military preparedness saved the colony from Spanish attack in 1742, after which he returned to Britain, where he fought against the FORTY-FIVE rebellion.

OGPU (Russian acronym for 'United State Political Administration') A Russian security agency established in 1922 as the GPU and renamed after the formation of the UNION OF SOVIET SOCIALIST REPUBLICS (1923). It existed to suppress counter-revolution, to uncover political dissidents, and, after 1928, to enforce COLLECTIVIZATION of farming. It had its own army and a vast network of spies. It was absorbed into the NKVD in 1934.

O'Higgins, Bernardo (1778–1842) South American revolutionary and ruler of Chile. He was the illegitimate son of Ambrosio O'Higgins (c. 1720–1801), governor of Chile, and became the most famous leader of the Chilean movement for independence. His first military effort against royalist forces ended unsuccessfully at the battle of Rancagua (1814). He led the remnants of his army across the Andes and joined the Argentine independence leader José de SAN MARTÍN. The two commanders prepared their combined army for an invasion of Chile and defeated the Spanish troops at Chacabuco in February 1817. With the independence of the new republic secured, O'Higgins was chosen as supreme director of Chile. The reforms that he attempted to introduce during his five-year term met with much opposition and he was forced to resign (1823).

Ojibwa Native Americans who formerly inhabited the territory around Lake Superior in North America. The Ojibwa were hunters and fishers as well as subsistence farmers, and were constantly feuding with the Sioux. They also developed a unique form of picture-writing. During the 17th century they expanded their territory as far as North Dakota, and became one of the largest indigenous peoples of North America. Since the early 19th century they have been living on reservations in North Dakota, Michigan, Minnesota, and Wisconsin.

Okinawa One of the Ryuku islands situated between Taiwan and Japan, captured from the Japanese in World War II by a US assault that lasted from April to June 1945. With its bases commanding the approaches to Japan, it was a key US objective and was defended by the Japanese almost to the last man, with KAMIKAZE air attacks inflicting substantial damage on US ships. After the war it was retained under US administration until 1972, when it was returned to Japan, following a vociferous campaign. The 1990s witnessed growing calls for the closure of US bases on the island.

Oklahoma Indian Territory An early Native American reservation in the western USA. Most of modern Oklahoma came to the USA by the LOUISIANA PURCHASE, which stimulated President JEFFERSON to think that one answer to relations between Whites and indigenous peoples would be to transfer the latter to these newly acquired lands. In 1817 some Cherokees made the journey west to join original inhabitants like the Kiowa, Shawnee, Comanche, and Pawnee. After the Indian Removal Act of 1830 increasing numbers of indigenous peoples were transferred west and in 1867 the general Oklahoma Reservation was established. By the end of the 1880s many Whites had been persuaded that the land was not being used productively, and called for the opening of much of it to White settlement. In 1889 Congress authorized settlement, and in 1890 it organized the White-controlled areas into Oklahoma Territory, which became the 46th state in 1907.

Olaf I (Tryggvessön) (969–1000) King of Norway (995–1000). Exiled when his father was killed, he was brought up in NOVGOROD in Russia. Viking expeditions took him to Iceland, England, and Ireland where he was converted to Christianity. In 995 he was accepted as King of Norway, and established the new religion. He was drowned at sea after a battle with the combined Danish and Swedish fleets.

Olaf II, St (Haraldsson) (c. 995–1028) King of Norway (1015–28). He was converted to Christianity and continued the work of conversion begun by OLAF I but his attempts at reform provoked rebellion and he was killed in a battle with rebel and Danish forces. Canonized as a saint, he is honoured as Norway's national hero.

Oldenbarneveldt, Johan van (1547–1619) Dutch statesman and lawyer who played a key role in the DUTCH REVOLTS. A Calvinist and a keen supporter of WILLIAM I (the Silent), he helped to negotiate the Union of Utrecht (1579). After 1586, as leader of the Estates of Holland, he managed to impose unity on the diverse political, economic, and religious interests of the UNITED PROVINCES. He negotiated a 12-year truce with Spain in 1609, but after this his political differences with Maurice of Nassau became part of a bitter internecine quarrel between two rival schools of Calvinism, and eventually Maurice had Oldenbarneveldt tried and executed on a charge of treason.

Oldowan The oldest tradition of human toolmaking, named after the simple stone tools found at OLDUVAI GORGE but now known from many other early human occupation sites in Africa. The oldest certain stone tools, from the HADAR and Omo regions in Ethiopia and from the eastern Democratic Republic of Congo, were made between 2.5 and 2 million years ago, probably by *Homo habilis*. Usually, the toolmaker started with a large cobble, probably picked out of a stream bed, and flaked it with a hammerstone into the required shape. The detached flakes were also trimmed and put to use. Several distinct types of Oldowan tools were made and were probably used for different tasks. A more advanced tradition, Developed Oldowan, occurred at Olduvai Gorge around 1.5 million years ago, the maker probably being *Homo erectus*.

Olduvai Gorge A ravine in northern Tanzania, East Africa. It lies at the south-east corner of the Serengeti Plain and marks the route of an ancient river that cut deep through the underlying strata to reveal a detailed slice of geological history. The Gorge is a forked cleft 50 km (31 miles) long and up to 100 m (330 feet) deep. It contains an unsurpassed record of human evolution spanning the past two million years. Research carried out since 1935 has produced large quantities of important early human fossils, representing at least three hominid species, together with animal bones and stone tools.

The fossil-rich deposits are numbered I–IV, followed by three later sequences. From Bed I (2–1.7 million years ago) have come AUSTRALOPITHECINES, including the famed *Zinjanthropus* (*Australopithecus boisei*), and also *Homo habilis*, probably the maker of the OLDOWAN tools found in these deposits. *Australopithecus boisei* has also been found throughout Bed II (1.7–1.15 million years ago); in the lower part, the species is associated with *Homo habilis*, in the upper part with *Homo erectus*, the maker of ACHEULIAN handaxes. Acheulian tools and *Homo erectus* continue into Bed III (1.15–0.8 million years ago), and Bed IV (800,000–600,000 years). Later evidence of human activity continues up to 15,000 years ago.

Olmec The ancient indigenous people of the southern gulf coast of Mexico, who were the earliest culture in Mesoamerica (Mexico and northern Central America) to build large ceremonial centres, with huge carved stone heads of imported basalt and serpentine. Three principal sites successively dominated their culture, but overlapped in dates of occupation, between c. 1500 and 400 BC: San Lorenzo, La Venta, and Tres Zapotes. OLMEC ART stressed jaguar figures and a 'baby-face' image, and the style spread widely throughout Central Mexico and as far south as El Salvador and Costa Rica.

Olympia A site in western Greece, location of the most important shrine to the god Zeus (GREEK RELIGION). An oracle of Zeus was there and every four years a festival of competitive games (the Olympiad) was held in his honour. The large complex of religious and secular buildings that grew up survived until the Roman emperor THEODOSIUS decreed the destruction of all pagan sanctuaries. Archaeologists have recovered much, however, most notably many of the sculptures of the temple of Zeus (5th century BC), and also the workshop where the gold and ivory statue of Zeus was created by the Athenian Phidias in the 430s BC.

The first Olympiad is dated 776 BC, though the games are said to have begun before then. The date 776 has become a conventional one marking the 'beginning' of archaic Greece. Originally local, the games soon began to attract Greeks from much further afield. By 472 BC they had expanded from a one-day festival of athletics and wrestling to five days with many events, including horse and chariot racing, wrestling, and a race in full armour. Nevertheless, the most prestigious event continued to be the short foot-race over one length (c. 200 m) of the stadium. Winners received olive wreathes as their prizes, and they brought much glory to their cities, who might reward them with privileges. They might also commission choral poetry in celebration, such as the victory odes of Pindar. The games began and ended with sacrifices and feasting. Theodosius stopped the games in 393 AD.

Olympic Games A world festival of sport inspired by the ancient Greek games held at OLYMPIA until 393 AD. The modern version owes its existence to Baron de Coubertin, a French aristocrat, and was conceived as a championship for amateur sportsmen to be staged every four years. For the first Games in 1896, athletes from 12 nations travelled to Athens to compete in gymnastics, athletics, cycling, fencing, lawn tennis, shooting, swimming, weightlifting, and wrestling. Apart from intervals for the two World Wars (and despite various politically motivated boycotts), the Games have continued ever since, at venues including, in recent years, Mexico City, Munich, Montreal, Moscow, Los Angeles, Seoul, Barcelona, and Atlanta. In 2000 Sydney is host to the 27th Olympic Games in the modern series and in 2004 the Games return to Athens. A separate Winter Olympics began in 1924, at first held in the winter months preceding the summer Games but now held two years after the summer Games. Women's athletic events were introduced to the summer Olympics in 1928. The programme now includes a great diversity of sports, but has become increasingly dominated by nationalism and commercialism. In 1988 professional tennis players were allowed to take part, final evidence that the principle of amateurism had been abandoned.

Oman (formerly Muscat and Oman) A country occupying the eastern corner of Arabia.

Physical. Oman has a coast on the Arabian Sea, and inland it borders on Saudi Arabia and Yemen. Mountains rise steeply from a narrow coastal plain to a plateau which merges into the desert of the 'empty quarter' or Rub al-Khali.

Economy. Crude oil and natural gas are important exports and sources of government revenue, but Oman is not a member of OPEC. The manufacturing base includes oil-refining, copper-smelting, and the manufacture of cement and motor vehicles. The coastal plain is fertile, supporting crops of dates, coconuts, bananas, and sugar cane. Cattle can be bred on the mountains and camels in the oases.

History. Oman was a trading outpost of Mesopotamia, settled by Arabs in the 1st century AD. It was conquered for Islam in the 7th century. Having expelled Portuguese incursions by 1650, the Omanis created a maritime empire with possessions as distant as MOMBASA and ZANZIBAR and trade contacts with south-east Asia. By 1754 Ahmad ibn Said had expelled Turkish invaders and founded the sultanate that still rules Oman. Under SAID IBN SULTAN SAYYID Oman was the most powerful state in Arabia in the early 19th century, controlling Zanzibar and the coastal regions of Iran and Baluchistan (now mainly in Pakistan). Tension frequently erupted between the sultan of Oman and the interior tribes. Oil, now the country's major product, began to be exported in 1967. In 1970 the present ruler, Sultan Qaboos bin Said (1940–), deposed his father Said bin Taimur in a palace coup. An uprising by left-wing guerrillas, the Popular Front for the Liberation of Oman, was defeated in 1975. A member of the ARAB LEAGUE, Oman managed to remain largely unaffected by both the IRAN–IRAQ WAR and the GULF WAR. In the 1990s Sultan Qaboos seemed prepared to consider cautious moves towards allowing the establishment of political parties, and in 1994 the government signalled its intention to allow the election of women.

CAPITAL:	Muscat
AREA:	300,000 sq km (120,000 sq miles)
POPULATION:	2.251 million (1996)
CURRENCY:	1 Omani rial = 1,000 baiza
RELIGIONS:	Muslim 86.0%; Hindu 13.0%
ETHNIC GROUPS:	Omani Arab 77.0%; Indian 15.0%; Pakistani (mostly Baluchi) 3.5%; Bengali 2.5%
LANGUAGES:	Arabic (official); minority languages
INTERNATIONAL ORGANIZATIONS:	UN; Arab League; GCC

Omar UMAR.

Omri (9th century BC) King of Israel (*c.* 876–*c.* 869 BC). After the death of JEROBOAM I (*c.* 901 BC) five kings had ruled ineffectively over the northern kingdom. Omri, an army general, founded his own dynasty in northern Israel. His main achievement was to establish his capital, SAMARIA, where he built a lavish palace and temple as a symbol of political and religious unity for the northern kingdom. Omri expanded the power of northern Israel, aided by Egypt's temporary weakness and Syria's

distraction by the Assyrian revival. Alliances with the Phoenicians were reinforced by his son AHAB's marriage to Jezebel. The Omri dynasty ruled until *c.* 842 BC.

OPEC (Organization of Petroleum Exporting Countries) An international organization seeking to regulate the price of oil. The first moves to establish closer links between oil-producing countries were made by Venezuela, Iran, Iraq, Kuwait, and Saudi Arabia in 1949. In 1960, following a reduction in the oil price by the international oil companies, a conference was held in Baghdad of representatives from these countries, when it was decided to set up a permanent organization. This was formed in Caracas, Venezuela, the next year. Other countries later joined: Qatar (1961), Indonesia (1962), Libya (1962), United Arab Emirates (1967), Algeria (1969), Nigeria (1971), Ecuador (1973), and Gabon (1975). Ecuador left OPEC in 1993 and Gabon withdrew in 1996. OPEC's activities extend through all aspects of oil negotiations, including basic oil price, royalty rates, production quotas, and government profits.

The organization rose to prominence in the mid-1970s after it virtually quadrupled the price of oil over a three-month period at the end of 1973, and imposed an embargo on Western consumers who had supported Israel in the Arab–Israel (Yom Kippur) War. OPEC's successful use of the 'oil weapon' had important repercussions for NORTH–SOUTH RELATIONS, inspiring greater assertiveness among developing countries, and giving weight to their demands for a NEW INTERNATIONAL ECONOMIC ORDER. Some Arab states made large profits from the sale of oil during this period. During the 1980s, however, the influence of OPEC on world oil prices declined slightly as Western industrialized countries, such as Norway and the UK, began to exploit their own oil resources, found alternative forms of fuel, or initiated programmes to cut the use of energy. The Organization of Arab Petroleum Exporting Countries (OAPEC), based in Kuwait, was established in 1968, to co-ordinate the different aspects of the Arab petroleum industry, and safeguard its members' interests.

Opium Wars (1839–42; 1856–60) Two wars between Britain and China. In the early 19th century British traders were illegally importing opium from India to China and trying to increase trade in general. In 1839 the Chinese government confiscated some 20,000 chests of opium from British warehouses in Guangzhou (Canton). In 1840 the British Foreign Secretary, Lord PALMERSTON, sent a force of 16 British warships, which besieged Guangzhou and threatened Nanjing and communications with the capital. It ended with the Treaty of NANJING (1842). In 1856 Chinese officials boarded and searched a British flagged ship, the *Arrow*. The French joined the British in launching a military attack in 1857, at the end of which they demanded that the Chinese agree to the Treaty of Tianjin in 1858. This opened further ports to western trade and provided freedom of travel to European merchants and Christian missionaries inland. When the emperor refused to ratify the agreement, Beijing was occupied, after which, by the Beijing Convention (1860), the Tianjin Agreement was accepted. By 1900 the number of TREATY PORTS had risen to over 50, with all European colonial powers, as well as the USA, being granted trading concessions.

Oppenheimer, (Julius) Robert (1904–67) US physicist. He was appointed in 1942 as Director of the

MANHATTAN PROJECT, based at Los Alamos, New Mexico, which in 1945 made the first atomic bomb. In 1953, at the height of the witch-hunting campaign led by the US Senator Joseph MCCARTHY, Oppenheimer was excluded from sensitive research on the grounds that he had Communist sympathies: subsequently (1963) he was unreservedly rehabilitated.

Oppenheimer, Sir Ernest (1880–1957) South African financier. With the help of Herbert HOOVER, he linked US finance and South African mining enterprise in the Anglo-American Corporation of South Africa in 1917. He extended his interests to diamonds, and established the Diamond Producer's Association (1934).

Opus Dei (Latin, 'work of God') A Roman Catholic organization founded in 1928 by the Spanish priest Josemaria Escrivá (1902–75) de Balaguer. Members, of whom there are 76,000 worldwide, may be either priests or lay people, in which case they are encouraged to retain their social position and pursue their profession. Particularly active in General Franco's Spain (1939–75), the organization has exercised considerable, but controversial, influence on public affairs. It maintains a number of educational establishments, including the Universities of Pamplona and Navarre. There is a separate branch for women, segregation of the sexes being an important principle. Opus Dei emphasizes the austere and conservative aspects of Catholicism; members follow a range of ascetic and spiritual practices, which include daily 'mortification' in the form of brief self-flagellation, and celibacy is encouraged. Active recruitment has resulted in a growing membership worldwide. The movement has attracted considerable criticism for its secrecy and authoritarianism, but Pope John Paul II is a supporter — he beatified de Balaguer in 1992.

oracles Places at which people consulted a particular deity for advice or prophecy. There were many of these in the ancient Greek world, most notably at DELPHI, Didyma on the coast of Asia Minor, Dodona in Epirus, and OLYMPIA. The most famous non-Greek oracle was that of the Egyptian Ammon at Siwah oasis in the Sahara, identified by the Greeks with Zeus and consulted by ALEXANDER THE GREAT in 331 BC. Apollo was the god most favoured as a giver of oracles though many other deities presided over oracular shrines. At the most primitive shrines the god's reply was elicited through the casting of lots and the interpretation of signs. At healing oracles — for instance that of Asclepius at EPIDAURUS — the god's reply came in the form of a dream. At Delphi an entranced priestess conveyed the divine message. Consultations usually concerned religious matters or the seeking of support for political or military actions.

Oracle bones are animal bones that were used in divination by the SHANG kings of ancient China (c. 1600 BC onwards). In many cases the question and/or answer has been written on the bone in pictographic figures.

Orange The ruling house (in full Orange-Châlons) of the principality centred on the small city of Orange, southern France. The city grew up around its Roman monuments, which include a semicircular theatre and a triumphal arch. In the 11th century it became an independent countship, and from the 12th century its rulers were vassals of the Holy Roman Emperor and came to style themselves 'princes'.

After 1530 the related house of Nassau-Châlons succeeded to the title, and in 1544 William of Nassau-Dillenburg became Prince of Orange and subsequently, as WILLIAM I (known as the Silent), STATHOLDER in the Netherlands. His younger son, Maurice of Nassau (1567–1625), assumed the military leadership of the DUTCH REVOLTS in 1584. Until the late 18th century the Orange dynasty continued to play a major part in the politics of the UNITED PROVINCES. The principality itself was conquered by Louis XIV (1672) and incorporated into France by the Treaty of Utrecht (1713); however, the title of Prince of Orange was retained by WILLIAM III (1650–1702), who became King of England in 1689.

Orange Free State A region of the Republic of SOUTH AFRICA, formerly a province. The region is bounded on the north and south by the Vaal and Orange Rivers, whose tributaries drain the plateau on which it stands. Famous for its gold and diamonds, it also has an abundance of coal. In the early 19th century it was inhabited mainly by the Bantu-speaking Sotho people. In 1848 the British annexed the region as the Orange River Sovereignty, with the result that the Boers crossed into TRANSVAAL. In 1852 the British government ordered the province to be relinquished, and by the Bloemfontein Convention (1854) recognized it formally, granting it independence as the Orange Free State. The discovery of diamonds in 1867 caused a rush of mainly British immigrants and helped to cause the First BOER WAR. After the Peace of VEREENIGING the state, as the Orange River Colony, became a crown colony, becoming self-governing in 1907. In 1910 it became a founding province in the Union of South Africa under its earlier title. In the local government reorganization of 1994 the Orange Free State became a region under the new name of Free State.

ordeal A painful technique used in the early Middle Ages to determine the guilt or innocence of suspects by divine intervention, conducted and supervised by the Church. Ordeal by fire required suspects (usually freemen) to carry hot irons, or to walk blindfold and barefoot through red-hot ploughshares or over heated coals. If they emerged unhurt or their wounds healed within three days they were innocent. Immersion of a hand or arm in boiling water was another method. Suspects (often alleged witches) were thrown into cold water and deemed guilty if they floated. Trial by blessed bread was a test for priests, for it was assumed guilty clergy would choke on hallowed food. Ordeals were repudiated by the Church in 1215. They were not particular to Europe; tribes in east Africa and Madagascar practised similar tests.

Oregon Boundary dispute (1843–46) A territorial dispute between the USA and Britain. Since 1818, Britain and the USA had agreed on joint occupation of the Oregon country, an area west of the Rocky Mountains running down into the valley of the Columbia River. However, as settlers moved up the OREGON TRAIL pressure mounted for the territory to become part of the USA. The settlers wanted their northern boundary with the British to be to the north of Vancouver Island on the 54° 40′ parallel, and in 1844 President POLK used the slogan '54 40 or fight' in his victorious campaign. Discussions took place with the British, who at first insisted on the Columbia River as boundary. A compromise agreement between the British Foreign

Secretary Lord ABERDEEN and President Polk was reached in 1846. This was to accept a line well to the south of Polk's original demands, extending the 49th parallel boundary to the Pacific, but excluding Vancouver Island. In 1848, Congress created the Oregon Territory. This was later split up into the state of Oregon (1859), the state of Washington (1889), the state of Idaho (1890), and parts of Montana and Wyoming.

Oregon Trail A wagon trail across the US Rocky Mountains. In the mid 19th century news of the pleasing climate and rich soils in the Pacific north-west began to draw settlers from the east. Each year from 1842 to 1846 some 100 wagons gathered at Independence, on the Missouri River, to make the 3,200-km (2,000-mile) trip to the Pacific. As numbers grew, hostilities arose with the British in Vancouver (the OREGON BOUNDARY DISPUTE, settled in 1846). When gold was found in Montana (1862) John Bozeman (1831–67) charted a branch trail to the goldfield, leaving at Fort Laramie and running up into the Big Horn Mountains. After this gold rush the Bozeman Trail became a CATTLE TRAIL in the 1880s.

Organization de l'Armée secrète (OAS) A French secret terrorist organization based in Algeria, formed in 1961. Its aim was the destruction of the French Fifth Republic in the interest of French colonial control of Algeria. The OAS plotted an unsuccessful assassination attempt on President DE GAULLE in 1962. Its action had little effect on the French government, which by now was determined to grant independence to Algeria. Subsequent riots in Algiers were suppressed, and the OAS itself eliminated (1963) by the capture or exile of its leaders.

Organization for Economic Co-operation and Development OECD.

Organization of African Unity (OAU) An association of African states. It was founded in 1963 to promote unity and solidarity among African states and the elimination of colonialism. All African states have at one time belonged. The leaders of 32 African countries signed its charter at a conference in Addis Ababa in 1963. There is an annual assembly of heads of state and government, a council of ministers, a general secretariat, and a commission for mediation, conciliation, and arbitration. The OAU has attempted to bring about reconciliation in regional conflicts, and supported sanctions against South Africa to bring about the end of apartheid. The 1991 Assembly in Abuja, Nigeria, agreed on the creation of an African Economic Community (AEC). In 1994, South Africa was admitted as the 53rd member of the organization.

Organization of American States (OAS) A regional international organization. Originally founded in 1890 on US initiative for mainly commercial purposes, the OAS adopted its present name and charter in 1948. The major objective of the 35 states which comprise the OAS is to work with the UNITED NATIONS to ensure the peaceful resolution of disputes among its members, to promote justice, to foster economic development, and to defend the sovereignty and territorial integrity of the signatory nations. In general, the OAS has taken an anti-communist stance, and Cuba's membership was suspended in 1962. Canada joined in 1990 and Belize and Guyana in 1991.

Organization of Central American States (OCAS) (1951–60) A regional association comprising Costa Rica, El Salvador, Guatemala, Honduras, and Nicaragua. Founded in 1951, its purpose was to establish the CENTRAL AMERICAN COMMON MARKET. This goal was reached in 1960, but OCAS members co-operated on little else. The San Salvador Charter (1962) expanded the trade and fiscal provisions of the original treaty, envisaging permanent political, economic, and defence councils.

Organization of Petroleum Exporting Countries OPEC.

Orissa An area in eastern India once known as Kalinga. In 261 BC it was conquered by the Buddhist emperor ASOKA, but local dynasties subsequently ruled until its absorption by the CHOLA empire (1023). Its golden age is identified with the Ganga dynasty, founded in 1076 by Anantavarma Codagangadeva. Despite Muslim incursions, Hindu rule was upheld until the 16th century, when an Afghan invasion was followed by absorption into Akbar's MOGUL EMPIRE (1568). MARATHA expansion brought a short return to Hindu rule in the 18th century.

Orkney Islands (UK) An archipelago of over 70 islands off north-east Scotland, separated from the north of Scotland by the Pentland Firth. Only 30 or so are large enough for habitation, the biggest being Pomona (or Mainland), Hoy, and South Ronaldsay, which together shelter the bay of Scapa Flow. The SHETLAND ISLANDS are 80 km (50 miles) to the north-east.

History. Colonized first by the Picts (c. 200 BC), they were already Christian when the first Norse colonists settled in the late 8th century. The Norse earls of Orkney extended their authority over the Shetlands, Caithness, and Sutherland, and their exploits are recorded in the *Orkneyinga Saga* (c. 900–1200). The islands passed to the Scottish crown in 1472 as part of the marriage contract between JAMES III and Margaret of Norway.

Orlando, Vittorio Emanuele (1860–1952) Italian statesman and jurist. He had supported Italy's entry into World War I and after the CAPORETTO disaster (1917) became Premier. At the VERSAILLES PEACE SETTLEMENT he clashed with President WILSON over what Wilson thought were excessive claims by Italy to former Austrian territory. In 1922 he at first supported MUSSOLINI, but after the murder of MATTEOTTI he resigned from Parliament in protest (1925) and fled the country. After the fall of Mussolini (1943) he became a leader of the Conservative Democratic Union.

Orléans, ducs de Several dynasties of French royal princes, two of which (the Valois-Orléans and the Bourbon-Orléans) achieved great historical importance. The title duc de Orléans was borne by younger princes of the French royal family from the 14th century. In 1392 Charles VI of France bestowed the duchy on his brother Louis, the first of the Valois-Orléans. Louis's grandson became Louis XII of France, whose great-grandson became FRANCIS I. The Valois-Orléans ended with the death of HENRY III in 1589. Philippe (1674–1723), the first of the Bourbon-Orléans dynasty, became Regent of France in 1715 during the minority of LOUIS XV. During the 18th and 19th centuries the Orléans branch of the royal family would become a focus for liberal opponents of Bourbon absolutism. Philippe's great-grandson Louis Philippe Joseph ('Philippe Égalité') succeeded to the Orléans title in 1785. He was a supporter of the French Revolution from its beginnings, and in June 1789 he organized the 47 nobles who joined the Third Estate. In 1792 he voted for the death of the king. Nevertheless, his eldest son, LOUIS-PHILIPPE, had him arrested with all the remaining Bourbons, accused of conspiracy, and guillotined (1793). Following the JULY REVOLUTION of 1830, Louis-Philippe was chosen as king, ruling as a constitutional monarch until the REVOLUTION OF 1848.

Ormonde, James Butler, 12th Earl and 1st Duke of (1610–88) Anglo-Irish nobleman and army commander. He fought for CHARLES I against the Irish rebels in 1641–43 and became Lord Lieutenant of Ireland. On Charles's death he proclaimed CHARLES II as King of Ireland, but was defeated by CROMWELL and forced into exile. He served again as Lord Lieutenant throughout most of Charles II's reign. His loyalty to the crown was severely tested by JAMES II's arbitrary actions, some of which he bitterly opposed.

Ormonde, James Butler, 2nd Duke of (1665–1745) Anglo-Irish army commander. A firm Tory, he opposed the Hanoverian succession, and when George I dismissed him from the post of captain-general in 1714 he became a JACOBITE, was threatened with impeachment, and fled to France. Storms prevented him reaching England for the FIFTEEN rebellion; after he had settled in Spain he was given command of an abortive Jacobite expedition in 1719.

Orphic mysteries A religious cult of ancient Greece, prominent in the 6th century BC. It was believed to have been established by the mythological hero Orpheus, who was able to charm all nature with his music. It was based on the belief that there was a mixture of good (divine) and evil in human nature and that the evil should be destroyed by initiation into the Orphic mysteries and by moral purification. Initiates purified themselves and adopted ascetic practices, such as abstaining from meat. It sank to the level of a superstition in the 5th century, though the profound thoughts that underlay it were perceived by PLATO.

Orsini, Felice (1819–58) Italian revolutionary. After being implicated in revolutionary plots, he was condemned in 1844 to life imprisonment. He was later pardoned by Pius IX but took part in Italy in the REVOLUTIONS OF 1848. In 1849 he joined MAZZINI in Rome and then went to Hungary, where he was arrested. After his escape in 1854 he formed a plot to assassinate NAPOLEON III, seen as the principal obstacle to Italian independence. His attempt to blow up the imperial carriage failed (14 January 1858) and he was executed.

Ortega, Daniel NICARAGUA; SANDINISTA NATIONAL LIBERATION FRONT.

Orthodox Church EASTERN ORTHODOX CHURCH.

Orthodox Judaism A major branch within JUDAISM, which teaches that the Torah (the five books of Moses) contains all the divine revelation that Jews require. Religious practice demands the strict observance of 613 rules (*mitzvot*), which govern moral behaviour, dress, religious customs, diet, work, observance of the *Shabbat*, and personal hygiene. When interpretation of the Torah is required, reference is made to the TALMUD, whose religious authority is second only to the Torah. Unlike LIBERAL, REFORM, and CONSERVATIVE JUDAISM, which they do not recognize, Orthodox Jews maintain the separation of sexes in synagogue worship. There is only an Orthodox rabbinate in Israel, with the result that all official religion in that country is Orthodox controlled. While many Orthodox Jews support ZIONISM, they deplore the secular origins of the movement and the fact that Israel is not a fully religious state. For example, the Orthodox recognize a person as Jewish only if he or she has a Jewish mother or undergoes an arduous process of conversion; whereas the Law of Return governing emigration to Israel accepts all those with a Jewish grandmother as potential Israeli citizens.

Osborne judgment (1909) A British court decision concerning the use of trade-union funds for political purposes. It stemmed from an action brought by a Liberal trade unionist, W. V. Osborne, against the practice of using part of trade-union subscriptions to pay salaries to Labour Members of Parliament. The courts found in favour of Osborne. Up to this time Members of Parliament received no Parliamentary salary. This was remedied in 1911. The Trade Union Act (1913) authorized unions to have a political fund but subscriptions to it were optional, members being able to 'contract out'.

Osceola (c. 1800–39) Seminole chief. During the SEMINOLE WAR of 1835–42, Osceola, an extremely capable military leader, held off US attempts to remove his tribe to the west for three years. Frustrated by his successful resistance in the Florida Everglades, General Jessup offered Osceola safe conduct to a peace conference, but treacherously imprisoned him at Fort Moultrie near Charleston, where he died.

Osman UTHMAN.

Osman I (c. 1258–1326) Founder (c. 1300) of the OTTOMAN EMPIRE. He was the leader of the famed 'four hundred tents', who turned his band of Turkish nomads from raiding to permanent conquest. In 1290 he declared his independence from the SELJUK Turks and expanded his territory by capturing minor Christian kingdoms in north-western Turkey.

Ostpolitik (German, 'eastern policy') A policy adopted in the Federal Republic of GERMANY (West Germany) in the early 1970s, according to which that country instituted formal relations with the Eastern bloc. It reversed West Germany's refusal to recognize the legitimacy of the German Democratic Republic (East Germany), as propounded in the Hallstein Doctrine (1955). This asserted that West Germany would sever diplomatic relations with any country (except the Soviet Union) that recognized East German independence. The policy of Ostpolitik was pursued with particular vigour by Willy BRANDT, both as Foreign Minister and as Chancellor of the Federal Republic. A General Relations Treaty (1972) normalized relations between the two Germanys, while treaties between West Germany and both the Soviet Union and Poland gave formal recognition to the ODER-NEISSE LINE (1970–72).

ostracism A method of banishment in ancient ATHENS. At a stated meeting each year, the Athenian assembly voted on whether it wanted an ostracism that year. If the vote was affirmative, an ostracism was held two months later. Every citizen who so wished then wrote a name on a sherd of pottery ('*ostrakon*'), and provided that at least 6,000 valid 'ostraka' were counted, the man with the most against him had to leave Attica for ten years, though he was allowed to enjoy any income from his property there while absent. A vote to ostracize often functioned as a sort of 'general election', constituting a 'vote of confidence' for the policies of the most powerful rival of the man thus named. Such trials of political strength were most notable in the ostracisms of Themistocles (*c*. 471), Cimon (*c*. 462), and Pericles' rival Thucydides (443). Ostracism was not resorted to after 417 or 416.

Ostrogoths Eastern GOTHS originally based on the northern shores of the Black Sea. In the 4th century AD they became vassals of the HUNS, whose migration displaced them westward. Under ATTILA they were defeated by Roman and barbarian allied armies on the CATALAUNIAN FIELDS (451 AD). Forty years later THEODORIC established an Ostrogothic kingdom in Italy. After the murder in 533 of Theodoric's daughter, who was the regent of Italy, JUSTINIAN's general BELISARIUS twice invaded and defeated them, and the Ostrogothic kingdom was crushed by Narses in 552.

Oswald, Lee Harvey (1939–63) Alleged US assassin of President KENNEDY at Dallas, Texas, in 1963. He was arrested leaving the scene, but before he could be tried, he was himself killed by another civilian, Jack Ruby. Many theories have been aired that Oswald had accomplices, but the WARREN Commission concluded that he had acted on his own.

Oswald, St (*c*. 605–42) King of the Northumbrian kingdom of Bernicia (NORTHUMBRIA) (633–42). He gained the kingdom after his victory near Hexham over the Welsh king CADWALADER (633), who had in the previous year invaded Northumbria and killed Oswald's uncle Edwin. Following that invasion Oswald took refuge on Iona, where he became a Christian. On his return he arranged for missionaries from Iona, led by St Aidan, to convert his people (635). Oswald was killed in battle by the pagan king PENDA of Mercia.

Oswy (or Oswiu) (d. 670) King of NORTHUMBRIA (651–70). He succeeded his brother Oswald as ruler of the Northumbrian kingdom of Bernicia in 642 and incorporated the other northern kingdom, Deira, after arranging the assassination of his cousin Oswin (651). Although initially Northumbria was still in the control of PENDA, king of the neighbouring Mercia, Oswy was able to defeat him (655) and establish himself as overlord of England. Oswy's support of St Wilfrid at the Synod of WHITBY (664), called to consider the rival claims of the Roman and Celtic forms of the Christian Church, was critical in gaining the decision in favour of Rome.

Otis, James (1725–83) American lawyer and patriot from Massachusetts. He first achieved fame by his attack on Writs of Assistance (search warrants) in 1761, basing his case on natural rights philosophy. Motivated partly by jealousy against the conservative Thomas Hutchinson, lieutenant governor of Massachusetts (1758–71), he rapidly became the leading orator, pamphleteer, and political spokesman of the patriot cause. After receiving head injuries in a fight with a British customs officer (1769) he became insane, but recovered sufficiently to fight at BUNKER HILL.

Ottawa An Algonquian-speaking group of North American indigenous peoples inhabiting the area around northern Lake Huron, encountered by Samuel de CHAMPLAIN in 1615. Some were dispersed eastwards after 1649 when the IROQUOIS defeated the HURON, whose cultures theirs resembled. Thereafter they relocated their villages round the Great Lakes until the 17th, 18th, and early 19th centuries, when they finally settled on reservations round Lakes Michigan, Huron, and Erie, and in Oklahoma.

Ottawa Agreements (1932) A series of agreements on tariffs and trade between Britain and its DOMINIONS. They were concluded at the Imperial Economic Conference, held at Ottawa, and constituted a system of imperial preference to counter the impact of the Great DEPRESSION. They provided for quotas of meat, wheat, dairy goods, and fruit from the dominions to enter Britain free of duty. In return, tariff benefits would be granted by the dominions to imported British manufactured goods. The economic gains were helpful but not massive. After World War II the benefits were steadily eroded, and, with the prospect of British entry into the EUROPEAN ECONOMIC COMMUNITY, the agreements became increasingly dispensable: although seriously considered during the 1961–63 discussions, they played little part in the entry negotiations of 1971–72 apart from the question of New Zealand dairy products.

Otterburn, Battle of (5 August 1388). A victory for Scottish forces over the English at Otterburn, a village in northern England. The Earl of Douglas captured Henry PERCY the Younger (Hotspur) and jeopardized English control of the north for years to come, in an exploit that was immortalized in the *Ballad of Chevy Chase*.

Otto I (the Great) (912–73) Holy Roman Emperor (936–73). He succeeded his father Henry I, who had established the Saxon (or Ottonian) dynasty on the German throne and so extended royal influence as to make his son's election a virtual formality. Otto I consolidated his position by defeating the independent dukes of south Germany in a three-year war and thereafter keeping most of the great duchies under direct royal control. He went on to restore the empire to its full power, destroying the MAGYAR threat to the eastern frontier at the Battle of LECHFELD in 955, conquering Bohemia, Austria, and northern Italy, and bringing the German church into alliance with the throne despite the opposition of the German nobility. In a series of expeditions into Italy, Otto also established imperial supremacy over the papacy, a process highlighted by his coronation by the pope in 962 and his deposition of papal incumbents who failed to follow his wishes. His reign was also noted for a flowering of culture and learning in the so-called 'Ottonian Renaissance', which was fostered by the imperial court.

Otto III (980–1002) King of Germany and Holy Roman Emperor. He had ambitions of recreating the glory and power of the old Roman empire with himself as leader of world Christianity aided by a subservient pope. His short life was torn between periods of intense religious devotion (he lived for a year in a monastery), and dreams of secular power wielded from Rome, where he lived in oriental seclusion in the palace that he had had built. To control the papacy he installed in turn his cousin Gregory VI (996–99) and his tutor Sylvester II (999–1003) as popes, but this did not prevent rebellions in Italy.

Ottoman empire The Islamic empire established in northern Anatolia by OSMAN I at the end of the 13th century. Inspired by the spirit of JIHAD, it expanded north, west, and south, chiefly at the expense of the BYZANTINE EMPIRE, the capital of which, CONSTANTINOPLE, was taken by MEHMED II in 1453. The army was the basis of the Ottoman expansion, its senior ranks being recruited from the subject Christian families of the Balkans in a five-year levy, the devshirme. Boys were forcibly recruited, converted to the Muslim faith, educated in the palace schools, and entered into the Sipahis (cavalry) and JANISSARIES (infantry) of the army; they also staffed the civil service. At its height, under SULEIMAN I, the empire exercised suzerainty over territories stretching from the Austrian border to Yemen and from Morocco to Persia. The Turkish fleet under the notorious pirate BARBAROSSA, ravaged the coasts of Spain, Italy, and Greece, twice defeating the Italian admiral DORIA, before being beaten at LEPANTO (1571). Internal decline set in as civil service and army appointments became hereditary; moreover, the rule of each new sultan was marked by rivalry and bloodshed as there was no legally accepted line of succession. Although the empire was reinvigorated by the able services of the KÖPRÜLÜ family in the late 17th century, its conservatism condemned it to military backwardness in the face of Europe's industrializing challenge.

During the 18th century cultural links with Europe developed, while territorially Russia made steady advances into the Caucasus. In 1807 the Sultan Mustafa IV led a reactionary movement against western influence, but he was succeeded in 1808 by MAHMUD II (1808–39), who began a long process of reform; this included the destruction in 1827 of the Janissaries and the creation of a new, more westernized army. These changes did not, however, succeed in preventing Greece from becoming independent in 1833. The TANZIMAT reform movement accelerated under Mahmud's two sons Abdulmecid I (1839–61) and Abdulaziz (1861–76). Abdulhamid II (1876–1908) agreed in 1878 to a western-style constitution, the first in any Islamic country. However, the Parliament it created only met once (1878) and was not reconvened until the revolution of 1908. Through the 19th century RUSSO-TURKISH WARS steadily reduced the empire in Europe, and at the Congress of BERLIN in 1878 it abandoned all claims over ROMANIA, SERBIA, MONTENEGRO, BULGARIA and CYPRUS. From 1882 Egypt effectively passed into British control. In the later 19th century a movement for more liberal government produced the YOUNG TURKS revolution in 1908 and the deposition of Abdulhamid II. During World War I Britain and France occupied much of what remained of the empire, encouraging Arab nationalism and creating, after the war, such successor states as JORDAN, SYRIA, LEBANON, and IRAQ, as well as promising (1917) a Jewish national home in PALESTINE. The VERSAILLES PEACE SETTLEMENT attempted to reduce the empire to part of Anatolia, together (reluctantly) with Istanbul. Turkish nationalist feelings rejected the proposals, forcibly expelling Greeks and ARMENIANS and adopting the

present frontiers in 1923. By then the last sultan, Mehmed VI, had been overthrown and the new republic of Turkey proclaimed under Mustafa Kemal ATATÜRK.

Oudenarde, Battle of (1708) Military engagement during the War of the SPANISH SUCCESSION. At the Flemish city of Oudenarde MARLBOROUGH and his Dutch and Austrian allies defeated the French army. It was Marlborough's third great victory and led to the capture of Lille. In 1745, during the War of the AUSTRIAN SUCCESSION, the French took the town and dismantled the fortifications.

Outback The inland grazing lands of Australia, situated beyond the Great Dividing Range of New South Wales. The BIGGE INQUIRY had recommended that EMANCIPISTS and poor settlers should be excluded from taking up land, and in 1829 a vain effort was made to forbid land settlement beyond the '19 counties' of New South Wales, anybody going beyond this boundary being an illegal SQUATTER. However, as the demand for wool grew so did the numbers of such squatters, pressing further west, south-west, and north. In 1836 a £10 per year licence fee gave them rights over any tract of land on which they were already grazing sheep. Vast sheep stations of many thousands of acres developed, and the rich pastoralists became and remain a powerful force in Australian society.

Outremer ('Beyond the Sea') The Frankish name given to the Latin Kingdom of JERUSALEM established in Palestine after the First CRUSADE (1096–99). On Christmas Day 1100 BALDWIN I was crowned as its first king. He ruled over a narrow strip of coastal territory with no clear eastern boundaries, and the kingdom depended for its survival on sufficient settlers coming regularly from Europe. Muslims united against the invaders and Jerusalem fell to them in 1187.

Overbury, Sir Thomas (1581–1613) English courtier, essayist, and poet. He was a close associate of Robert Carr, a favourite of JAMES I of England. Although Overbury opposed the rising influence of the HOWARD faction, Carr, now Earl of Somerset, fell in love with Lady Frances Howard. Despite Overbury's protestations, Carr persuaded James to arrange an annulment of her marriage to the 3rd Earl of Essex. In 1613 Carr and Frances were married, and Overbury was imprisoned in the Tower of London, where he shortly afterwards died, for displeasing the king. In 1615 it was discovered that he had been poisoned. Amid hysterical accusations of adultery and witchcraft, the Carrs were publicly tried and sentenced to death for the crime, but James pardoned them, and kept them in the Tower until 1622. The episode badly damaged the reputation of both king and court, especially in the eyes of PURITANS.

Overland Stage Stage-coach mail-carrying service in the USA, established in 1850 as a government service to run from Independence, Missouri, south-west to Santa Fe and west to Salt Lake City. In 1858 the Southern (Butterfield) Overland Mail was established, running from St Louis to San Francisco. The latter service was expanded into Oregon and Montana before being sold to WELLS FARGO in 1866. By the 1860s thousands of miles of overland route were in use, and, although the expansion of the railways reduced long-distance business, the Overland Mail continued to serve areas not reached by rail for much of the rest of the century.

Owen, Robert (1771–1858) British social reformer, industrialist, and pioneer of the co-operative movement. In 1799 he acquired some textile mills at New Lanark in Scotland and proceeded to create a model community, radically improving the conditions in which his employees worked and lived. He provided amongst other things educational facilities for children, shorter working hours, and better housing. During the period of economic misery after 1815 he proposed the formation of 'villages of co-operation', in which the unemployed would be mutually self-supporting instead of relying on poor relief. He also played an important part in the passing of the 1819 Factory Act. From 1825 to 1829 he lived in the USA, where he attempted, unsuccessfully, to establish co-operative communities run on socialist lines. In 1833 he founded the Grand National Consolidated Trades Union, which collapsed in the following year.

Oxenstierna, Axel Gustaffson, Count (1583–1654) Swedish statesman. He entered the service of the Swedish state in 1602 and joined the Council of State in 1609. GUSTAVUS II (Adolphus) appointed him Chancellor in 1612, and for the next 22 years the two men worked together. An administrative reformer of note, Oxenstierna also made possible the reconciliation of the Swedish aristocracy to the monarchy. He negotiated the Truce of Altmark with Poland (1629), joined Gustavus in Germany in 1631, and after the king's death in 1632 was responsible for directing Swedish policy throughout the THIRTY YEARS WAR. He was also the effective ruler of Sweden from 1636 to 1644, when Queen CHRISTINA reached her majority. His subsequent relations with her were not always harmonious. On his death, his son Erik succeeded him as Chancellor.

Oxford Movement NEWMAN, JOHN HENRY.

Oyo A town in Oyo State in Nigeria, the seat of the Alafin of Oyo, titular head of all the Yoruba people. The original Yoruba capital, Old Oyo, was settled probably in the 10th century, and rose to prominence because of its rich agricultural resources and advantageous trading position. In the 16th century Alafin Oronpoto organized a cavalry force, giving it a military dominance over other Yoruba states. In two wars, 1724–30 and 1738–48, Oyo took the kingdom of DAHOMEY and came into contact with European merchants on the coast, with whom it traded in slaves. By 1817–18 the state had declined as a result of internal dissensions and civil wars, and Old Oyo was destroyed by the FULANI.

P

Pacific, War of the (1879–84) A conflict pitting Peru and Bolivia against Chile over a region in the northern Atacama Desert that was rich in potassium nitrate (saltpetre). British-backed mining companies moved from Chile into the region, whereupon Bolivia and Peru resisted by force. The Chilean navy commanded the Pacific coast and its army was better trained and equipped. Bolivia withdrew, leaving Peru to the Chilean forces, who occupied and sacked Lima in 1881. In the Treaty of Ancón (1883) Chile took most of the disputed territory and left Peru a humiliated nation. Bolivia lost Antofagasta, its Pacific port, and was left landlocked.

Pacific Campaigns (1941–45) The naval and amphibious engagements in the Pacific during World War II. The war spread to the Pacific when Japanese aircraft attacked the US naval base of PEARL HARBOR in 1941. Japan was allied to Thailand and had bases in VICHY-controlled Indo-China. Its landforces quickly occupied Hong Kong, Malaya, Singapore, and Burma. Other Japanese forces captured islands in the Pacific, while convoys sailed to occupy Borneo and the Dutch East Indies following the Japanese naval victory at the Battle of the Java Sea (27 February–1 March 1942). By April the Philippines were occupied, followed by northern New Guinea, and General MACARTHUR withdrew to Australia, where he organized a counter-attack. The Battle of the Coral Sea (5–8 May) between Japanese and US aircraft carriers was strategically a US victory. It prevented Japanese landings on southern New Guinea and ended their threat to Australia. It was followed (3–6 June) by

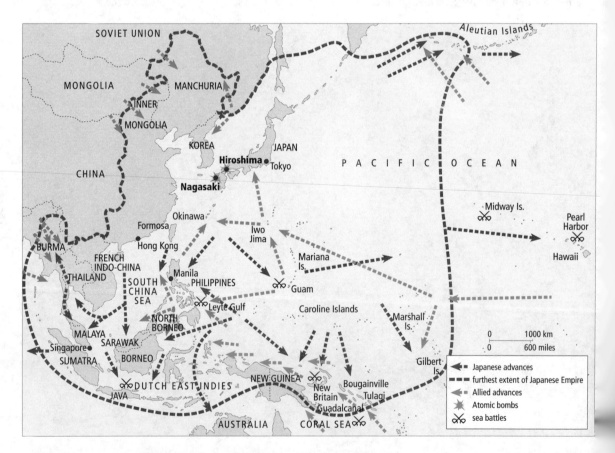

Pacific Campaigns (1941–45) *The rapid Japanese conquest of the countries of south-east Asia and of the Pacific islands was at first supported by anti-colonial nationalist movements. By April 1942 the Philippines were occupied and Australia threatened. The US Pacific Fleet had suffered badly at Pearl Harbor (December 1941), but won a decisive victory at Midway Island (June 1942). From then on a series of naval battles, fought largely by aircraft-carriers, brought US forces steadily nearer to Japan, which was heavily bombed throughout 1945.*

the decisive Battle of Midway Island, which, under Admiral NIMITZ, shifted the balance of naval power to the USA. In August 1942 US marines landed on Guadalcanal and Tulagi in the Solomon Islands, where fighting raged until February 1943. During 1943, the remaining Solomon Islands were recaptured by the USA; Bougainville was reclaimed from the Japanese in November, followed by New Britain early in 1944. In June 1943 MacArthur had launched his campaign to reoccupy New Guinea, and through 1944 US forces gradually moved back towards the Philippines. On 19 June 1944 the Japanese lost some 300 planes in the Battle of the Philippine Sea and in July the USA took the Mariana Islands, from which bombing raids on Tokyo were then organized. In October 1944 the Battle of LEYTE GULF marked the effective end of Japanese naval power, while on the mainland the BURMA CAMPAIGN had reopened land communication with China and begun the process of reoccupation of the short-lived Japanese empire. Manila fell in March 1945, and in April US forces reoccupied OKINAWA against fierce KAMIKAZE air raids, at the cost of very high casualties on both sides. Plans to invade Japan were ended by the decision to drop atomic bombs on HIROSHIMA and NAGASAKI (6 and 9 August), which resulted in Japanese surrender.

Pacific scandal (1873) A Canadian political scandal. British Columbia had entered the dominion of CANADA in 1871 on the understanding that a trans-continental railway line would be built within ten years. In 1872 a contract for such a railway was awarded to a syndicate headed by Sir Hugh Alan, a banker, shipowner, and financial contributor to the Conservative Party. Following a general election in 1872, the defeated Liberals accused the Prime Minister, John MACDONALD, of having given the contract as a reward. Macdonald resigned and the contract was cancelled. The Conservatives were heavily defeated in a new election but the CANADIAN PACIFIC RAILWAY was finally completed in 1885.

pacifism The belief that war is never justifiable, no matter how good the cause or how great the threat to one's country. Pacifism springs either from religious faith, as in the case of QUAKERS, or else from a humanist belief in the sanctity of life; the religious underpinning can be seen in works such as Tolstoy's *Christianity and Pacifism* (1883). In its purest form it prohibits all use of violence, even in self-defence. Pacifists advocate non-violent means of resisting oppression, drawing especially on the experience of Mohandas GANDHI's campaign against the British in India (1920–47). Some pacifists, however, while refusing personally to take part in war, would support the use of force by international bodies such as the UN. In this century many states have respected the beliefs of pacifists by recognizing conscientious objection as a ground for refusing conscription.

Páez, José Antonio (1790–1873) Venezuelan revolutionary and statesman. He was a leader of Venezuela's movement for independence, controlling (1810–19) a band of *Llaneros* (plainsmen) in guerrilla warfare against the Spanish. He led the separatist movement against BOLÍVAR's Colombian republic and became Venezuela's first President. During his first term (1831–35) he governed within the provisions of the Venezuelan constitution, but he became increasingly

oligarchic in his subsequent terms of office (1839–46, 1861–63). He was exiled from 1850 to 1858 but returned in 1861 to become supreme dictator. In 1863 he again went into exile. He encouraged economic development, promotion of foreign immigration, and construction of schools.

Pagan A city on the Irrawaddy River and former state in central Burma (now MYANMAR). It was originally a centre to which the Burmans, a people originating in Yunnan province, south-west China, migrated in the 9th century AD. In the 11th century they brought much of Burma under their rule. With their conquest of the Mon people, Theravada BUDDHISM spread to Pagan and in time throughout Burma. When KUBLAI KHAN, having conquered Yunnan, demanded tribute from Pagan, his envoys were executed. Five Mongol campaigns culminated in the occupation of Pagan (1287–1301), which had already been weakened by Mon and SHAN revolts.

Pahlavi, Muhammad Reza Shah MUHAMMAD REZA SHAH PAHLAVI.

Pai Marire (Maori, 'goodness and peace') A Maori political and religious movement. In 1862 Horopapera Te Ua of south Taranaki began teaching his people to worship the new Pai Marire god whom he saw as the Old Testament Jehovah. His followers danced around *niu* (decorated poles) seeking the gift of prophecy and powers to heal. Renewed war from 1865 saw the movement take a violent turn, becoming known as the Hau-hau. The ritual began to involve the exhibition of heads of White soldiers and missionaries and cannibalism was revived. The movement affected much of the North Island but gradually subsided after 1872.

Paine, Thomas (1737–1809) British writer and political theorist. He lost his post as an excise officer in 1774 after agitating for higher wages in the service. He went to America with a testimonial from Benjamin FRANKLIN and soon became involved in the political controversies that led to American independence. His pamphlet *Common Sense* (1776) influenced the American DECLARATION OF INDEPENDENCE and provided the arguments to justify it. He returned to England in 1787 and in 1791 published the first part of *The Rights of Man*, a reply to BURKE's *Reflections on the Revolution in France*. The radical views expressed in the second part of *The Rights of Man* (1792) stimulated the growth of the LONDON CORRESPONDING SOCIETY but alarmed the British government. Paine was threatened with arrest and fled to France, where he was immediately elected to the Convention. He supported republicanism, but showed courage in opposing LOUIS XVI's execution, on the orders of ROBESPIERRE he was imprisoned for a year, during which he completed *The Age of Reason* (1795), a provocative attack on Christianity. Only his American connection saved him from the guillotine and in 1802 he returned permanently to the USA.

Paisley, Ian (1926–) Northern Irish politician. A staunch Protestant and leader of the Ulster Democratic Unionist Party, he was an MP in the Northern Irish parliament (1970–72) and then in the House of Commons until 1985 when he resigned in protest against the Anglo-Irish agreement. He was re-elected in 1986; he has been an MEP since 1979.

Pakistan A country in the north-west of the Indian subcontinent, bounded by Iran on the west, Afghanistan on the north-west, China on the north-east, and India on the east.

Physical. The Hindu Kush, Karakoram, and Himalaya mountain ranges ring the north of Pakistan. Other ranges sweep down its western side to the Arabian Sea. Below them is the long, broad valley of the Indus. The North-West Frontier Province contains the strategically important KHYBER PASS. To the south is the plateau of the Punjab, or Panjab, meaning 'five rivers', watered by the tributaries of the Indus. To the east is the Thar Desert. Between the Sind Desert, which covers part of the Indus delta, and Baluchistan in the western hills, there are large reserves of natural gas and some oil.

Economy. Pakistan has a mainly agricultural economy, exporting raw and processed cotton, cotton fabrics, and rice. However, Pakistani workers abroad generate more income than exports. Livestock-raising is also substantial. Other products include cement, fertilizer, and chemicals.

History. Prior to 1947, Pakistan formed part of INDIA. Following the British withdrawal from the Indian subcontinent in 1947, Pakistan was created as a separate state, comprising the territory to the north-east and north-west of India in which the population was predominantly Muslim. The 'Partition' of the subcontinent of India led to unprecedented violence between Hindus and Muslims, costing the lives of more than a million people. Seven and a half million Muslim refugees fled to both parts of Pakistan from India and ten million Hindus left Pakistan for India. Muhammad Ali JINNAH, President of the MUSLIM LEAGUE, became the new state's first governor-general. The country's liberal constitution was opposed by the orthodox Muslim sector and in 1951 the Prime Minister, LIAQAT ALI KHAN, was assassinated by an Afghan fanatic. In 1954 a state of emergency was declared and a new constitution adopted (1956). When attempts to adopt a multiparty system failed, Ayub Khan (1907–74) imposed martial law (1958). His decade of power produced economic growth, but also political resentment. The two wings of Pakistan were separated by a thousand miles of Indian territory. Allegations by the Bengalis in East Pakistan against West Pakistan's disproportionate share of the state's assets led to demands by the Awami League, led by MUJIBUR RAHMAN, for regional autonomy. In the ensuing civil war (1971), the Bengali dissidents defeated a Pakistani army, with Indian help, and established the new state of BANGLADESH (1971). In 1970 the first ever general election brought to power Zulfikar Ali BHUTTO (1928–79), leader of the Pakistan People's Party, who introduced constitutional, social, and economic reforms. In 1977 he was deposed and later executed. The regime of General ZIA UL-HAQ (1977–88) committed Pakistan to an Islamic code of laws. With the Soviet invasion of Afghanistan in 1979, over 3 million refugees entered Pakistan. Although martial law was lifted in 1986, with the promise of a return to democracy, Zia's regime ended with his assassination. A general election in December 1988 brought back to power the Pakistan People's Party, led by Zulfikar Ali Bhutto's daughter Benazir Bhutto; her government was short-lived, collapsing in 1990 on charges of corruption. Bhutto's successor Mian Mohammad Nawaz Sharif, leader of the Islamic Democratic Alliance, won an absolute majority

in the Assembly. His government initiated a policy of further 'Islamization', but Sharif himself was criticized for his pro-Western position during the GULF WAR. In 1993, Benazir Bhutto was returned to office to head a coalition government. Her government was dismissed by presidential decree in 1996 following allegations of corruption. The ensuing elections resulted in victory for Sharif's Muslim League. A power struggle between Sharif and President Farooq Ahmed Leghari led to a political crisis and Leghari's resignation in 1997. In the subsequent election Muhammud Rafiq Tarar was elected President.

CAPITAL:	Islāmābād
AREA:	796,095 sq km (307,374 sq miles)
POPULATION:	133.500 million (1996)
CURRENCY:	1 Pakistan rupee = 100 paisa
RELIGIONS:	Muslim 96.7%; Christian 1.6%; Hindu 1.5%
ETHNIC GROUPS:	Punjabi 48.2%; Pashto 13.1%; Sindhi 11.8%; Saraiki 9.8%; Urdu 7.6%
LANGUAGES:	Urdu (official); Punjabi; Sindhi; Pashtu; English
INTERNATIONAL ORGANIZATIONS:	UN; Commonwealth; Colombo Plan

Pala A dynasty of Bihar and Bengal in north-eastern India that ruled from the 8th to the 12th century. Gopala, the founder, was chosen king by the great men of the region. The reign of his successor, Dharmapala (*c.* 770–810) marked the dynasty's apogee, after which power rose and fell intermittently until its final eclipse in the 12th century. The surviving Pala artefacts in both stone and metal are of a particularly fine decorative quality. An important development during their rule was the spread of BUDDHISM to Tibet by missionaries from the University of Nalanda in Bihar, which received Pala patronage.

Palacký, František (1798–1876) Czech nationalist and historian. A leading figure in the Czech cultural and national revival, he presided over the PAN-SLAV Congress in Prague in 1848, advocating Czech autonomy within a federal Austria. After the suppression of the liberal and nationalist uprising of 1848, Palacký retired from active politics until 1861, when he became a deputy to the Austrian Reichstag. After the foundation of the AUSTRO-HUNGARIAN EMPIRE in 1867, he advocated complete Czech independence. His influence on Czech political thought, and on later leaders such as Tomá MASARYK, was immense.

Palaeolithic ('Old Stone Age') The earlier part of the STONE AGE, characterized by flaked stone tools. The term usually includes the entire period during which humans were scavengers, hunters and gatherers, and makers of tools, both before and during the last Ice Age. The term MESOLITHIC describes the hunting groups in Europe in the postglacial period. Among the first tools would have been wooden digging sticks but these have not survived in the archaeological record. However, simple stone tools of OLDOWAN type produced by HOMO HABILIS in eastern Africa up to 2.5 million years ago have been found. More advanced ACHEULIAN handaxes were made by HOMO ERECTUS from 1.5 million years ago. Together, these two traditions in Europe are known as the Lower Palaeolithic. The Middle Palaeolithic began 150,000–125,000 years ago; tools of this time were produced by NEANDERTHAL people and their contemporaries and are more varied than those of the

Lower Palaeolithic. The UPPER PALAEOLITHIC in Europe is associated with the appearance of fully modern populations (HOMO SAPIENS) about 50,000 years ago; they employed more sophisticated stoneworking techniques that produced long, narrow blades struck from a stone core.

Palatinates Two regions in Germany that comprise the Upper Palatinate. FREDERICK I bestowed the title of Count Palatine on his half-brother Conrad, who held lands east and west of the River Rhine (the Lower Palatinate). From 1214 these lands were ruled by the Bavarian Wittelsbach dynasty, whose own lands near Bohemia formed the Upper Palatinate. In 1356 the Counts Palatine were made Electors of the Holy Roman Empire.

The Rhenish (Lower) Palatinate became a centre of the Protestant REFORMATION in the 16th century, but the choice of Elector FREDERICK V as King of Bohemia led to clashes with Catholic Habsburg authority and the outbreak of the THIRTY YEARS WAR. After the Battle of the White Mountain (1621) the Palatinates were partitioned, with Bavaria annexing the Upper Palatinate and the Lower Palatinate passing to Frederick's heirs under the terms of the Treaty of WESTPHALIA. The Lower Palatinate was invaded and brutally devastated by LOUIS XIV in 1688–89. In 1777 the two Palatinates were reunited. However, in the early 19th century, the Upper Palatinate was again absorbed into Bavaria, while the Lower Palatinate was divided between various German states and France. The modern German *Land* of Rhineland Palatinate (Rheinland-Pfalz) occupies a portion of the original Lower Palatinate's territory.

Palau (also known as Belau) A republic comprising over 200 islands in the western Pacific, only eight of which are inhabited.

Physical. The islands are geographically part of the Caroline Islands. The largest island is Babelthaup. Some of the islands are low-lying coral atolls but others are mountainous. The climate is tropical.

Economy. The main economic activities are fishing, farming, and tourism. Palau depends on aid from the USA.

History. Spain acquired the Caroline Islands in 1886 but sold them to Germany in 1899, having been defeated in the SPANISH–AMERICAN WAR. Palau was occupied by Japan during World War I and remained under Japanese control until 1944, when it was captured by Allied forces. The islands were administered by the USA as part of the UN Trust Territory of the Pacific from 1947. The islanders voted against becoming part of the Federated States of MICRONESIA in 1978 and became autonomous in 1981. Palau gained full independence and joined the United Nations in 1994. Under a compact of free association the USA controls the defence of Palau, and has nuclear storage facilities on the islands.

CAPITAL:	Koror
AREA:	488 sq km (188 sq miles)
POPULATION:	17,000 (1996)
CURRENCY:	1 US dollar = 100 cents
RELIGIONS:	Roman Catholic 40.8%; Protestant 24.8%; traditional beliefs 24.8%
ETHNIC GROUPS:	Palauan 83.2%; Filipino 9.8%
LANGUAGES:	Palauan; English; Sonsorolese-Tobian
INTERNATIONAL ORGANIZATIONS:	UN

pale A 14th-century term for a distinct area of jurisdiction, often originally enclosed by a palisade or ditch. Pales existed in medieval times on the edges of English territory, such as around Calais (until its loss in 1558). Later, they were created in Scotland (in Tudor times) and, most importantly, formed a large part of eastern Ireland (from HENRY II's time until the full conquest of Ireland under ELIZABETH I); the actual extent of the Irish pale depended on the strength of the English government in Dublin. CATHERINE II (the Great) in 1792 made a Jewish pale in the lands she had annexed from Poland: Jews had to remain within this area, which ultimately included all of Russian Poland, Lithuania, Belorussia (now Belarus), and much of the Ukraine.

Palestine (or Holy Land) Historically, a region of the eastern Mediterranean comprising parts of JORDAN, EGYPT, and modern ISRAEL. The word 'Palestine' derives from Palaistina or Philistia, the land of the PHILISTINES.

Physical. Palestine stretches from the Mediterranean Sea and the coastal Plain of Sharon in the west to the eastward-lying West Bank country known in biblical times as Judaea and Samaria. The Negev Desert lies to the south, ending in the Gulf of Aqaba. Northward lies the hill country of Galilee, the highest and best-watered part of the region. Inland is the arid valley of the Jordan, which runs below sea-level from the Sea of Galilee south to the Dead Sea. The Jordan Valley is the lowest land surface on earth.

History. By 2000 BC the CANAANITES had settled in the area, though they were subsequently confined to the coastal strip later known as Phoenicia by the Hebrews and Philistines. In time the Hebrews predominated, but after the death of SOLOMON they split into the two kingdoms of ISRAEL and JUDAH. Israel was overthrown by the ASSYRIANS in 722 BC and Judah suffered a similar fate at the hands of NEBUCHADNEZZAR II, who destroyed Jerusalem and transferred many inhabitants to Babylon in 586 BC. When the Chaldean dynasty of Babylon was overthown by CYRUS II (the Great) in 536, the Jews in Babylon were allowed to return to Palestine where, under the leadership of NEHEMIAH and EZRA, Jerusalem was rebuilt and the nation restored. Independence was finally regained when the MACCABEES rebelled against the SELEUCIDS in 168 BC, but in 63 BC Pompey annexed the area for Rome. The HEROD dynasty ruled parts of the area with Roman approval until unrest (the JEWISH REVOLT) caused the Romans to destroy Jerusalem in 70 AD. Further trouble flared in 132 under BAR COCHBA.

Palestine was Christianized under Rome and Byzantium, but it fell to the Arabs in 641 and later successively came under the control of the CRUSADERS, the MAMELUKES, and the OTTOMAN EMPIRE. The Ottoman occupation was the longest, lasting from 1516 to 1918, when Turkish and German forces were defeated by the British at Megiddo (19 September 1918). The name 'Palestine' was revived as an official political title for the land west of the Jordan, which became a British MANDATE in 1923. Following the rebirth of ZIONISM, Jewish immigration, encouraged by the BALFOUR DECLARATION of 1917, increased greatly, and Arab-Jewish tension culminated in a revolt in 1936. The Peel Commission (1937) recommended partition into Jewish and Arab states, but neither group would accept this. After the HOLOCAUST in Europe, pressure for Jewish immigration in 1945 inflamed the situation. Britain ended the mandate in 1948 when the state of ISRAEL was established. In spite of the United Nations plan of 1947 for separate Arab and Jewish states, Palestine ceased to exist as a political entity after the Arab-Israeli War of 1948, being divided between Israel, Egypt (the Gaza Strip), and Jordan (the West Bank of the River Jordan). The West Bank and the Gaza Strip were occupied by Israel in 1967, while over 750,000 Palestinian refugees fled to Lebanon, Jordan, and elsewhere. In December 1987 a spontaneous protest movement or INTIFADA erupted both in Gaza and on the West Bank, suppressed by Israel with considerable violence. An Israeli–Palestinian Peace Accord was signed in 1993, leading to Israel handing over administration of the Gaza Strip and parts of the West Bank to a new Palestinian National Authority in 1994. Israeli troops began to be withdrawn from these areas during 1995 and security transferred to a Palestinian police force. In 1996 Yasser ARAFAT became the first elected President of the Palestinian National Assembly. At this time Israel, under a Labour administration, appeared to accept the creation of a future Palestinian state. However, with the accession to power in June 1996 of a right-wing coalition led by hardline Likud Prime Minister Binyamin NETANYAHU, this prospect seemed much more remote. Although negotiations have continued, progress has stalled over several issues, notably the timing and extent of Israel's withdrawal from the West Bank, the creation of new Jewish settlements there, and the activities of terrorist groups operating from Palestinian-controlled areas.

Palestine Liberation Organization (PLO) A political and military body formed in 1964 to unite various Palestinian Arab groups in opposition to the Israeli presence in the former territory of PALESTINE. From 1967 the organization was dominated by al-FATAH, led by Yasser ARAFAT. The activities of its radical factions caused trouble with its host country, Jordan, and, following a brief internal war in 1970, it moved to Lebanon and Syria. In 1974 the organization was recognized by the Arab nations as the representative of all Palestinians. The Israeli invasion of Lebanon (1982) undermined its military power and organization, and it regrouped in Tunisia. Splinter groups of extremists, such as the 'Popular Front for the Liberation of Palestine' and the 'Black September' terrorists, have been responsible for kidnappings, hijackings, and killings both in and beyond the Middle East. In 1988 Arafat persuaded the movement to renounce violence and its governing council recognized the state of Israel. The PLO was then accepted by an increasing number of states as being a government-in-exile. It took part in the US-sponsored Middle East peace talks in 1992, in spite of East Jerusalem's representatives being rejected by Israel. Following secret negotiations, a peace agreement was concluded in 1993 between the PLO and the Israeli government. As part of this accord, the PLO renounced terrorism, but has been accused of supporting other militant groups, such as HAMAS.

Pallava A south Indian dynasty that maintained a regional kingdom along the Carnatic coast between the 4th and 9th centuries. There is uncertainty about the origins and early history of the Pallava before their emergence to power from a previously subordinate role in the DECCAN. They established their capital at Kanchi and traded in Sri Lanka and parts of south-east Asia. In the late 9th century they lost their territories to their own feudal vassals, the CHOLAS. Their artistic legacy is important. Apart from patronage of music, painting, and literature, some of the greatest south Indian temples were built during their rule, including the 'Shore Temple', carved from solid rock on the coast at Mahabalipuram.

palmers Professional pilgrims in medieval England who made the long and dangerous journey to the Holy Land (Palestine). As evidence of this pilgrimage, palmers displayed a palm leaf. The name was later applied more generally to include those who devoted all their time to pilgrimages and were dependent upon charity for their livelihood.

Palmer Raids (1919–21) The arrests of alleged subversive foreigners, ordered by the US attorney-general Alexander Mitchell Palmer (1872–1936). Fears of a Bolshevik-style revolution resulted in harassment of foreigners believed to be political radicals plotting against the US government. About 3,000 people were rounded up for deportation, all but a few hundred were later released.

Palmerston, Henry John Temple, 3rd Viscount (1784–1865) British statesman. An Irish peer, he entered the House of Commons as a Tory in 1807, serving as Secretary for War from 1809 to 1828. In 1830 he became Foreign Secretary in the new Whig government, holding this position almost continuously until 1841 and then again from 1846 to 1851. During this period he helped BELGIUM to win its independence from the Netherlands, supported the constitutional monarchies of Spain and Portugal against absolutist pretenders, and opposed Russian expansion at the expense of the Ottoman empire in the Near East. However, Palmerston's conduct of foreign policy was to be increasingly characterized by an aggressive nationalism. He initiated the First OPIUM WAR against China in 1840 in defence of British commercial interests and in 1850 intervened against Greece in the DON PACIFICO AFFAIR. In 1855 he succeeded Lord Aberdeen as Prime Minister and brought the Crimean War to a successful conclusion. He kept Britain neutral during the AMERICAN CIVIL WAR, but was unable to save Denmark from defeat by Prussia in 1864. Palmerston's high-handed methods often led him into conflict with his colleagues, but brought him much popular support.

Palmyra An ancient Syrian city that rose to prosperity in the 1st century BC by organizing and protecting caravans crossing the desert between Babylonia and Syria. It was probably incorporated within the Roman empire in 17 AD, but rose to its greatest power in the 3rd century AD under King Odenathus (d. 267) and ZENOBIA, his second wife. She at one point ruled Syria, Egypt, and almost all of Asia Minor, but by 273 AURELIAN had captured her and destroyed Palmyra. Its extensive remains testify to the mixture of Hellenistic and Parthian elements in Palmyran culture.

Pan-Africanism A movement seeking unity within Africa that became a positive force with the London Pan-African Conference of 1900. An international convention in the USA in 1920 was largely inspired by the Jamaican Marcus GARVEY. The invasion of Ethiopia by Italy in 1935 produced a strong reaction within Africa, stimulating anti-colonial nationalism. The Pan-African

Congress in Manchester in 1945 was dominated by Jomo KENYATTA, Kwame NKRUMAH and the 'father of Pan-Africanism', the American W. E. B. DU BOIS. In 1958 a conference of independent African states was held in Accra, followed by two further conferences in Monrovia in 1959 and 1961. In 1963 in Addis Ababa 32 independent African nations founded the ORGANIZATION OF AFRICAN UNITY, by which time Pan-Africanism had moved from being an ideal into practical politics.

Pan-Africanist Congress South African political movement. A militant off-shoot of the AFRICAN NATIONAL CONGRESS (ANC), it was formed in 1959 by Robert Sobukwe. He advocated forceful methods of political pressure and in 1960 sponsored the demonstration at SHARPEVILLE, in which 67 Black Africans were killed and 180 wounded by police. The South African government outlawed both the PAC and the ANC and imprisoned Sobukwe and other leaders. Some PAC members went into exile, continuing their campaign under the Secretary of the Party, Potlako Leballo. Although legalized in 1990 when it was moving away from its commitment to an armed struggle, the PAC at first refused to take part in the Convention for a Democratic South Africa (CODESA) which was set up in December 1991. The PAC participated in the first South African multiracial elections in 1994, winning five seats in the National Assembly, with 1.2% of the vote.

Panama A tropical country occupying the narrow isthmus linking Central and South America, bounded by Costa Rica to the west and Colombia to the east.

Physical. Along the length of the country runs a range of hills, through the centre of which was cut the pass, for the PANAMA CANAL. The Canal gives access to shipping from the Caribbean in the north to the Pacific in the south. The land is fertile, supporting coffee on the higher ground and sugar cane on the coastal plains.

Economy. International finance and shipping are of importance due to Panama's position as a world trade centre. The principal agricultural exports are bananas, shrimps from the coastal waters, and coffee; there are substantial, as yet unexploited, copper reserves, and some light industry, mostly food-processing. There is a petroleum refinery, but its products are of declining importance.

History. Panama was visited in 1501 by the Spaniard Rodrigo de Bastidas. A colony was established in 1510 and the country was explored more thoroughly in 1513 by Vasco Núñez de BALBOA, the first Spaniard to see the Pacific Ocean. The indigenous population was rapidly destroyed by the Spanish and by European diseases. Portobello on the Caribbean coast served as the principal port for the trade of the viceroyalty of Peru. In the 18th century, Panama became part of the viceroyalty of NEW GRANADA. In 1821 the country gained independence from Spain as a province of Gran Colombia. Despite nationalist insurrections against Colombia in the 19th century, the area only became independent as the republic of Panama in 1903 as a protectorate of the USA. The latter had aided Panama's struggle in return for a Panamanian concession to build a canal across the isthmus and a lease of the zone around it to the USA. The volatile, élite-dominated politics which have characterized Panama during much of the 20th century have led to its occupation by US peace-keeping forces in 1908, 1912, 1918, and 1989. From

1968 to 1981, General Omar Torrijos controlled Panama, working to diversify the economy and reduce US sovereignty over the Canal Zone, an object of long-standing national resentment. In 1977 he signed the Panama Canal Treaties, which agree that full control of the canal zone will pass to Panama in 2000, but was killed in 1981. In 1988 General Manuel Noriega seized power. A US military invasion in December 1989 deposed him and installed Guillermo Endara as President; Noriega was convicted of drug trafficking in 1992. Widespread strikes took place against Endara's government, which itself was accused of involvement with drug rings. In 1991 a new constitution abolished the armed forces. A general election in 1994 led to Ernesto Pérez Balladares becoming president.

CAPITAL:	Panama City
AREA:	77,082 sq km (29,762 sq miles)
POPULATION:	2.674 million (1996)
CURRENCY:	1 balboa = 100 centesimos (US $ also in circulation)
RELIGIONS:	Roman Catholic 84.0%; Protestant 4.8%; Muslim 4.5%; Baha'i 1.1%; Hindu 0.3%
ETHNIC GROUPS:	Mestizo 62.0%; Black and mixed 19.0%; White 10.0%; Amerindian 6.0%; Asian 2.0%
LANGUAGES:	Spanish (official); English creole; Amerindian languages
INTERNATIONAL ORGANIZATIONS:	UN; OAS; Non-Aligned Movement

Panama Canal A ship CANAL across the isthmus of Panama, connecting the Atlantic and Pacific oceans. It was begun by a French company under Ferdinand de LESSEPS in 1882, abandoned through bankruptcy, and completed between 1906 and 1914 by the USA at a cost of nearly $400 million. The canal is about 81 km (51 miles) long and can carry ships of up to 80,000 tonnes.

In the Hay-Bunau-Varilla Treaty of 1903, Theodore ROOSEVELT gained for the USA the concession from PANAMA for a 16-km (10-mile) wide Canal Zone under perpetual control of the US government. After World War II Panamanians became more hostile to US sovereignty over the Canal. After years of negotiations, in 1977 the US President, Jimmy CARTER, succeeded in obtaining congressional approval of the Panama Canal Treaties which provide for relinquishing total control of the Canal Zone to Panama by 1 January 2000, while assuring the Canal's perpetual neutrality.

Pan-Americanism The movement towards economic, military, political, and social co-operation among the 21 republics of South, Central, and North America. The first Pan-American conference was held in 1889 in Washington, DC, to encourage inter-American trade as well as the peaceful resolution of conflicts in the region. The seventh conference (Montevideo 1933) was important because the USA, in harmony with Franklin D. ROOSEVELT's 'Good Neighbor' policy, finally adopted the long-espoused Latin American principle of non-intervention, while the conference at Buenos Aires in 1936 adopted a treaty for the peaceful resolution of conflicts between American states. The Conference at CHAPULTEPEC (1945) agreed on a united defence policy for the signatory nations. At the conference held in Bogotá in 1948, the ORGANIZATION OF AMERICAN STATES (OAS) was established, transforming the Pan-American system into a formal regional organization within the framework of the United Nations. The Alliance for Progress conference (1961), attended by representatives of all the American states except Cuba, pledged the members to support one another, by co-ordinating the economies of Latin America and by resisting the spread of communism. Some member states saw the OAS as a cover for extending US influence in Latin America and instead gave greater support to the CENTRAL AMERICAN COMMON MARKET and the Latin American Free Trade Association (see LATIN AMERICAN INTEGRATION ASSOCIATION), both founded in 1960.

Pandya A Tamil dynasty which ruled in the extreme south of India from the 3rd century BC to the 16th century AD. Little is known about their early history during an era of frequent warfare among competing south Indian dynasties. Between the 7th and 14th centuries they expanded into Sri Lanka and Kerala, and northwards into CHOLA and HOYSALA territories. They were at the height of their power during the reign of Jatavarman Sundara (1251–68). They were already weakened by family quarrels when their capital at Madurai was invaded in 1311 by the sultan of Delhi, Ala ud-Din KHALJI. Although they retained local power until the 16th century, they never again aspired to empire. MARCO POLO recorded the prosperity of their realm during its peak years in the late 13th century.

Panipat A town in Haryana state, north India, 70 km (43 miles) north-west of Delhi. It is historically important as the site of three battles which proved decisive for India's future. On each occasion armies moving out to defend the capital of Delhi clashed here with invaders approaching from the north-west. In the first Battle of Panipat (21 April 1526) the MOGUL invader, BABUR, defeated the Afghan sultan of Delhi. The second battle (5 November 1556) marked AKBAR's victory over the Sur Afghans who then held Delhi, and initiated the spread of strong Mogul power in India. In the third battle (14 June 1761) an invading Afghan army ended MARATHA ambitions to fill the power vacuum at Delhi caused by the decline of the Moguls.

Pankhurst, Emmeline (1858–1928) British feminist and leader of the SUFFRAGETTE campaign. She founded the Women's Social and Political Union (WSPU) in 1903 in Manchester. She moved to London in 1906 and at first limited suffragette tactics to attending processions, meetings, and heckling leading politicians. However, as this was achieving little success she turned to more militant methods. Frequently imprisoned for causing disturbances, she responded by going on hunger strike and refusing to sleep, until she was released. She suspended the suffragettes' struggle during World War I, instead recruiting women to work for the war effort. The contribution of women to the war was recognized by the government, who gave women over 30 the vote in 1918. Her daughter, Dame Christabel (1880–1958), trained as a lawyer and was a leading strategist as well as campaigner for the WSPU. Another daughter, Sylvia (1882–1960), an artist, designed publicity materials for the WSPU. However, she believed that the movement was failing working-class women, who she believed saw enfranchisement as less important than economic and social reforms. She left the WSPU in 1913 and as a pacifist campaigned against the war effort.

Pan-Slavism The movement intended to bring about the political unity of all Slavs. It should be distinguished from both Slavophilism, which was purely cultural and acted as a powerful stimulus towards the revival of Slavonic languages and literature, and from Austro-Slavism, which sought to improve the lot of Slavs within the AUSTRO-HUNGARIAN EMPIRE. The aim of Pan-Slavism was to destroy the Austrian and OTTOMAN EMPIRES in order to establish a federation of Slav peoples under the aegis of the Russian emperor. The ideology was developed in Russia, where it took on a militant and nationalistic form and helped provoke the RUSSO-TURKISH WAR (1877–78). Another manifestation was the Balkan League of 1912 by which Russia supported nationalist aspirations of the BALKAN STATES against Austrian ambitions. This led to the crisis that precipitated WORLD WAR I. The Bolshevik government of the newly established Soviet Socialist Republic (1917) renounced Pan-Slavism, but during the COLD WAR period the concept was revived as a justification for dominance by the Soviet Union in Eastern Europe.

Panth, Brahmin Dhundu NANA SAHIB.

papacy The office of the POPE (Bishop of Rome), which derives its name from the Greek *papas* and Latin *papa*, familiar forms of 'father'. In early times many bishops and even priests were called popes, but in the Western Church the word gradually became a title and was restricted to the Bishop of Rome; Pope Gregory VII in 1073 forbade its use for anyone except the Bishop of Rome. The traditional enumeration lists 265 holders of the office, excluding ANTIPOPES, beginning with St PETER and reaching to the present holder John Paul II. The basis of papal authority derives from St Peter's appointment by Jesus Christ as leader of the 12 Apostles, the early tradition that he came to Rome and was martyred there, and the belief that Christ wanted there to be successors to St Peter in the Church. In the early centuries of Christianity the Bishop of Rome exercised authority over the wider Church only in emergencies. Gradually the papacy extended its claims to jurisdiction over the whole Church. These extended papal claims were a major cause of various churches breaking with Rome, notably the EASTERN ORTHODOX CHURCH definitively in 1054, and the Protestant churches at the time of the REFORMATION in the 16th century.

Papal States The lands in central Italy over which the Pope had sovereignty (756–1870). A law of 321 allowed the Church to own land (called the Patrimony of St Peter), but it was the 'Donation of PEPIN' (754), which promised Lombard lands conquered by the Franks to the Pope and guaranteed their protection, which increased the papacy's temporal power. In the early Middle Ages papal control weakened and land was alienated as the papacy 'bought' allies in return for territory. In the 13th century the situation was reversed: the Church's holdings were greatly extended by Pope INNOCENT III and in 1213 Emperor Frederick II confirmed and increased papal possessions. JULIUS II restored and enlarged the temporal power of the papacy: at their greatest extent the Papal States included Romagna (including Ferrara and Ravenna), much of Tuscany, Umbria, and the Patrimony of St Peter. They were taken over by the kingdom of Italy in the 19th century.

Papen, Franz von (1879–1969) German politician. A member of the Catholic Centre Party, he had little popular following and his appointment as Chancellor (1932) came as a surprise. To gain NAZI support he lifted the ban on the BROWNSHIRTS, but HITLER remained an opponent. Attempts to undermine Nazi strength failed and he resigned. He persuaded HINDENBURG to appoint Hitler (January 1933) as his Chancellor, but as Vice-Chancellor he could not restrain him. He became ambassador to Austria (1934), working for its annexation (ANSCHLUSS) in 1938, and to Turkey (1939–44). He was tried as a war criminal (1945) but released.

Papineau's Rebellion (1837–38) A French-Canadian uprising of those seeking democratic reforms and protesting against the proposed union of UPPER AND LOWER CANADA. The Speaker of the Lower Canada Assembly, Louis-Joseph Papineau (1786–1871), led the reformist movement in French Canada (now QUEBEC) and in 1837 he agitated for armed insurrection against the British, but fled to the USA before fighting broke out. Clashes between a few hundred of his supporters and regular troops occurred at Saint Denis in November. The rebellion broke out again in 1838, but was suppressed, and 12 supporters were executed. Papineau received an amnesty in 1844 and returned to Canada in 1845, by which time the establishment of parliamentary 'responsible' government had been achieved by such moderate reformers as Robert BALDWIN.

Papua New Guinea A country consisting of the eastern half of the island of New Guinea north of Australia, together with the Bismarck Archipelago and other adjacent islands in the south-west Pacific Ocean. The western half of the island of New Guinea forms the province of Irian Jaya, part of INDONESIA.

Physical. The mainland is divided by a central range of mountains rising to the highest peak, Mount Wilhelm. A low-lying plain is drained by the Fly River in the south-west, and there are active volcanoes in the east.

Economy. Papua New Guinea exploits extensive copper and substantial gold deposits; these account for half of the country's exports. There are also petroleum reserves. Coffee, timber, cocoa, and palm oil are significant exports, and tropical fruits grow in abundance. Tuna-fishing is also important. Industry is limited mainly to food-processing. Australia contributes about 20% of the annual budget in direct aid.

History. Papua New Guinea may have been inhabited as long as 50,000 years ago and was known to Asian seafarers for centuries before contact with Europe. The Portuguese first sighted the island in 1512 and Jorge de Meneses named the island Ilhas dos Papuas from the Malay word meaning 'frizzy-haired'. The Spaniard Inigo Ortiz de Retes claimed it for Spain in 1545 and called it New Guinea because he was reminded of the Guinea coast of Africa. In 1828 the Dutch annexed the western half of the island, followed, in 1884, by the German and British division of the eastern half. In 1904 the British transferred their territory, now called Papua, to Australia, and at the outbreak of World War I an Australian expeditionary force seized German New Guinea (Kaiser-Wilhelmsland). During World War II Australian troops fought off a determined Japanèse invasion. Formal administrative union of the area as Papua New Guinea was achieved in 1968. Self-government was attained in 1973 and in 1975 Papua New Guinea became an independent nation within the Commonwealth. A defence treaty with Australia was negotiated and democratic political activity, by graduates of the University of Port Moresby (founded 1965), quickly developed. Secessionist demands from some of the offshore islands, especially Bougainville, became a key issue in the 1980s and 1990s, troops being landed on Bougainville in May 1992. Relations between Papua New Guinea and INDONESIA, which had been strained throughout the 1980s over the conflict in Irian Jaya, improved in the early 1990s. In 1994 Sir Julius Chan became Prime Minister. Although a ceasefire was agreed between the government and the Bougainville Revolutionary Army, subsequent peace talks broke down and fighting resumed. A new provincial administration was set up on Bougainville in 1995 to negotiate the future status of the island with the government. In 1997 the government's decision to use foreign mercenaries against the Bougainville rebels sparked an army mutiny, leading to the resignation of Chan as Prime Minister. Following legislative elections in June, a new government was formed under Bill Skate.

CAPITAL:	Port Moresby
AREA:	462,840 sq km (178,704 sq miles)
POPULATION:	4.400 million (1996)
CURRENCY:	1 kina = 100 toea
RELIGIONS:	Protestant 58.4%; Roman Catholic 32.8%; Anglican 5.4%; traditional beliefs 2.5%; Baha'i 0.6%
ETHNIC GROUPS:	Papuan 83.0%; Melanesian 15.0%
LANGUAGES:	English (official); Tok Pisin; about 700 Melanesian and Papuan languages and dialects
INTERNATIONAL ORGANIZATIONS:	UN; Commonwealth; Colombo Plan; South Pacific Forum; Observer status at ASEAN

papyrus A writing material prepared in ancient Egypt from the pithy stem of the aquatic plant *Cyperus papyrus*, from which paper takes its name. Fresh stalks of the grass gathered from the River Nile were teased out with a needle to give strands of damp fibre. These strands were laid out in two crossed layers on a moistened board and compacted in a press, their juice and the added moisture bonding them together to form sheets. After drying, the sheets could be written on using ink. Sheets could be joined by overlapping and meshing the ends together to form continuous scrolls. The extremely dry atmospheric conditions in Egypt have favoured the preservation of papyri. These varied documents – funerary, legal, administrative, and literary – have yielded much detailed information on life in ancient Egypt.

Paraguay A landlocked country in south-central South America, bordered by Bolivia and Brazil on the north and Argentina on the south.

Physical. The navigable Paraguay River, running down the middle of the country, joins the Paraná and provides access to the sea. In the west is the Gran Chaco, a region of black, fertile earth which provides rich pasture and hardwood forests. In the east, the land rises to a low range of forested hills, to the south of which there are swamps and palm-fringed, shallow lakes.

Economy. Paraguay has a primarily agricultural economy, with cotton and soya beans the principal exports, and subsistence crops of cassava and maize. The construction of the Itaipú dam (1985), the world's largest hydroelectric project, benefited the economy, but high inflation and debt remain a problem. Industry is restricted to textiles, food-processing, and cement. Mineral resources are limited.

History. Paraguay was part of Spain's Rio de la Plata territory from the founding of the capital Asunción in 1537. It was only sparsely settled by Spaniards and was dominated by Jesuit mission villages among the Guaraní Indians until their suppression in 1767. The country achieved its independence (1811) when local Paraguayan military leaders led a bloodless revolt against the Spanish governor. The dictator José Gaspar Rodriguez de FRANCIA ruled the new republic from 1813 to 1840, but the rest of the 19th century was dominated by corruption, coups, and chronic bankruptcy. Francisco Solano López led the country to disaster in the PARAGUAYAN WAR (1864–70). Political turmoil continued into the 20th century with the exception of the presidency of the liberal Edvard Schaerer (1912–17), which was marked by foreign investment and economic improvements. In the CHACO WAR (1932–35), Paraguay won from Bolivia the long-contested territory believed to have oil reserves. In 1954 General Alfredo STROESSNER, supported by the USA, seized power. A massive hydroelectric scheme (the Itaipú dam) was begun and some progress made in settling landless peasants, but cattle exports to Europe fell, the economy declined, and the regime became increasingly brutal. Stroessner lost US support and was deposed in 1989. Elections brought General Andrés Rodríguez to office as President. A liberal party, *Asunción Para Todos* (APTO) emerged, but, with military backing, Rodríguez and his Colorado Party retained power. Paraguay's first multiparty elections were held in 1993 and the civilian Juan Carlos Wasmosy was elected President.

CAPITAL:	Asunción
AREA:	406,752 sq km (157,048 sq miles)
POPULATION:	4.964 million (1996)
CURRENCY:	1 guaraní = 100 céntimos
RELIGIONS:	Roman Catholic 96.0%; Protestant 2.0%
ETHNIC GROUPS:	Mestizo 90.0%; Amerindian 3.0%; German 1.7%
LANGUAGES:	Spanish (official); Guaraní
INTERNATIONAL ORGANIZATIONS:	UN; OAS

Paraguayan War (or War of the Triple Alliance) (1864–70) A conflict resulting from rivalries between Paraguay, Uruguay, Brazil, and Argentina. The Paraguayan President Francisco Solano LÓPEZ, alarmed by Brazilian intervention in Uruguay and harbouring desires for Paraguayan territorial expansion and access to the sea, initiated hostilities against Brazil in 1864. Despite traditional rivalry between Brazil and Argentina, the latter joined Brazil and its puppet government in Uruguay in the Triple Alliance pact (May 1865) against Paraguay. Paraguay's well-trained army of 600,000 men did not prove equal to the task, and López's death in March 1870 ended one of the most destructive wars in Latin American history. In addition to losing more than half of its population, Paraguay was also stripped of considerable territory as a result of the war.

pardoners Agents of the Christian Church licensed to sell INDULGENCES. The rapid proliferation of pardoners in the 14th century meant that often they were not licensed. They might carry 'holy' relics to assist sales and they exploited the gullibility of people for their own profit. Pope Boniface IX ordered an enquiry into these abuses (1390) and the abuse of indulgences was one of Martin LUTHER's main quarrels with the Roman Catholic Church. The sale of indulgences was forbidden by the Council of Trent (1563).

Paris, Commune of (15 March–26 May 1871) A revolutionary government in Paris. It consisted of 92 members, who defied the provisional government of THIERS and of the National Assembly. The Commune, which had no connection with communism, was an alliance between middle and working classes. Suspicious of royalist strength and opposing the armistice made with Prussia, the Communards wanted to continue the war and were determined that France should regain the principles of the First Republic. With the victorious German army encamped on the hills outside Paris, government troops were sent to remove all cannons from the city. They were bitterly resisted; Paris, demanding independence, broke into revolt. Thiers decided to suppress the revolt ruthlessly. For six weeks Paris was bombarded by government troops and its centre destroyed. Early in May its defences were breached and a week of bitter street fighting followed. Before surrendering, the Communards murdered their hostages, including the Archbishop of Paris. Over 20,000 people were massacred by the government forces, leaving France deeply divided.

Paris, Congress of (1856) A conference held to negotiate the peace after the CRIMEAN WAR, attended by Britain, Austria, Russia, Turkey, and Sardinia. It marked a defeat for Russia, which conceded part of Bessarabia to Moldavia and Wallachia in the Balkans. The revival of the Straits Convention of 1841 meant that the Black Sea was again closed to all warships and neutralized while navigation of the Danube was to be free. The OTTOMAN EMPIRE was placed under joint guarantee of the West European powers and the sultan agreed to recognize the rights of his Christians. The decline of the Ottoman empire, however, was not halted and Russia, determined to retrieve its Balkan supremacy, was to break the Black Sea clause in 1870.

Paris, Pact of KELLOGG-BRIAND PACT.

Paris, Peace of (1783) The treaty that concluded the American War of INDEPENDENCE. It was mainly engineered by John JAY, Benjamin FRANKLIN, and the Earl of SHELBURNE, and was damaging to Spain, which regained only Florida. The peace recognized American independence, gave it north-eastern fishing rights, and attempted (unsuccessfully) to safeguard creditors, protect loyalists, and settle the frontier between Canada and the USA. These failures led to 30 years' friction, especially in the NORTHWEST TERRITORY, where Britain retained forts in retaliation, and led to the War of 1812.

Paris Peace Settlement VERSAILLES PEACE SETTLEMENT.

Paris, Treaty of (1763) The treaty signed by Britain, France, and Spain which brought the SEVEN YEARS WAR to an end. Britain did not fully exploit the worldwide successes it had enjoyed, as PITT had resigned and the

Earl of Bute was anxious for peace. Under the terms of the treaty Britain gained French Canada and all the territory France had claimed to the east of the Mississippi. France ceded some West Indian islands, including St Vincent and Tobago, but retained the islands of Guadeloupe and Martinique. In India, France retained its trading-stations but not its forts. Britain gained Senegal in West Africa and Florida from Spain; it also recovered Minorca in exchange for Belle Isle. Spain recovered Havana and Manila, and France's claims in Louisiana west of the Mississippi were ceded to Spain in compensation for Florida, which became British until 1783. Britain was supreme at sea and, for the time being, dominated the east coast of North America.

parish The smallest unit of ecclesiastical and administrative organization in England. In the 7th and 8th centuries regional churches ('minsters') were founded, staffed by teams of priests who served large 'parochiae' covering the area of perhaps five to 15 later parishes. These were broken up during the 10th to 12th centuries as landowners founded local churches for themselves and their tenants, though it was only in the 12th century that the territories these served crystallized into a formal parochial system. The *Taxatio Nicholai* (1291), an assessment of clerical incomes, probably understated the number of parishes at 8,085, a more likely figure would be 9,500. The majority of these were rural communities averaging about 300 persons. Probably no more than a few hundred parishes were located in towns: London had about 100, Norwich 50, Lincoln 40, and Cambridge 20. Since the 16th century parishes have performed an administrative role for the state although their boundaries and those of ecclesiastical parishes do not always coincide. In 1555 they were responsible for highways and in 1601 for organizing poor relief.

Park, Mungo (1771–1806) Scottish explorer of the Niger. A surgeon in the mercantile marine, Park undertook a series of explorations in West Africa in 1795–96 on behalf of the Africa Association, sailing up the River Gambia, crossing Senegal and navigating the River Niger before being captured by a local Arab chief. He escaped from captivity four months later and returned to Britain after a year and a half in the interior. His *Travels in the Interior Districts of Africa* (1799), describing his adventures, was an immediate success. Bored with his medical practice in Scotland, Park returned to the Niger in 1805, reaching Bamako and Segou, but was drowned during a fight with Africans at Boussa.

Parkes, Sir Henry (1815–96) Australian politician. He was active in several New South Wales political campaigns, including one against convict transportation, before entering Parliament in 1854, where he remained almost continuously until 1895. He was Premier of New South Wales five times. Parkes, the 'Father of Federation', publicly declared his support for AUSTRALIAN FEDERATION, notably in his now-famous Tenterfield speech in 1889. He died before federation was achieved.

Parlement A sovereign judicial authority in France, the chief being in the capital, PARIS. First established in the 12th century, the Paris *Parlement* functioned as a court of appeal, and as a source of final legal rulings.

There were also provincial *Parlements*, those of Toulouse, Bordeaux, Rouen, Aix, Grenoble, Dijon, and Rennes. Political importance derived from their power to register royal edicts and to remonstrate against them. This power could be overidden by the king, either by order or by *lit de Justice* (a personal intervention). The introduction of hereditary office-holding (the *paulette*), in 1604, considerably enhanced the privileges and power of the *parlementaires*, who challenged the monarchy during the FRONDES. Revolt led to their suppression by LOUIS XIV, but they were restored in 1718 by the regent, Philippe, Duc d'ORLÉANS. They then led opposition to the monarchy, posing as defenders of liberty, but chiefly defending aristocratic privilege and halting royal reforms. Their resistance culminated in the calling of a STATES-GENERAL in 1789. The resulting FRENCH REVOLUTION revealed their selfish motives and they were suppressed in 1792.

Parliament, British The supreme legislature in Great Britain and Northern Ireland, comprising the sovereign, as head of state, and the two chambers, the HOUSE OF COMMONS and the HOUSE OF LORDS. Together, these chambers comprise the Palace of Westminster.

In the 13th century Parliament was simply a formal meeting of the king and certain of his officials and principal lords. It became partly representative, as in Simon de MONTFORT's Parliament (1265), which contained commoners (knights of the shire and burgesses of the boroughs) who were elected in their locality, and Edward I's MODEL PARLIAMENT (1295).

Until the 16th century, both chambers grew in importance *vis-à-vis* the crown, as it came to be accepted that their approval was needed for grants of taxation. HENRY VIII effected the English REFORMATION through the long-lived Reformation Parliament (1529–36). Kings such as CHARLES I tried to manage without summoning a Parliament (1629–40), but by the 17th century the Commons had made themselves indispensable. Charles I had to call Parliament in 1640 in order to raise money, and Parliament, led by John PYM, led the opposition to him. The Parliamentary side won the ENGLISH CIVIL WAR and at the end of the COMMONWEALTH period it was the members of the House of Commons who negotiated the RESTORATION of CHARLES II (1660) and the accession of WILLIAM III and Mary (1688). The legislation enacted in the GLORIOUS REVOLUTION of 1688–89 and the Act of SETTLEMENT (1701) settled the relationship of crown, Lords, and Commons definitively and made clear the ultimate supremacy of the Commons.

Present-day workings of Parliament may be summarized as follows. The Prime Minister and the cabinet (a selected group of ministers from either House) are responsible for formulating the policy of the government. Acts of Parliament in draft form, known as Bills, each of which have to be 'read' (debated) three times in each House, are referred in the House of Commons (and occasionally in the House of Lords) for detailed consideration to parliamentary standing or select committees. The sovereign's powers of government are dependent on the advice of ministers, who in turn are responsible to Parliament. The monarch's prerogatives, exercised through the cabinet or the Privy Council, include the summoning and dissolution of Parliament. The Treaty of Rome, which Britain accepted in 1972 when joining the EUROPEAN COMMUNITY (now the European Union), provided for a gradual development of Community institutions. The Single European Act (1986) laid down that the considerable powers of those institutions take precedence over those of member-states, while the MAASTRICHT Treaty (1992) committed member-states to even closer political, monetary, and economic union. A separate Scottish Parliament and an elected Welsh Assembly will be established in 1999: plans to establish an elected Assembly in Northern Ireland will be put to the province's electorate in a referendum in 1998. The British parliamentary system was adopted by many European countries and by most countries of the COMMONWEALTH OF NATIONS when they gained dominion status or independence.

Parnell, Charles Stewart (1846–91) Irish nationalist. He was the leader of the Irish Members of Parliament agitating for HOME RULE. The son of a Protestant Anglo-Irish landowner, he was elected to Parliament in 1875, where his obstructive tactics, notably the filibuster, drew attention to Irish grievances. He became President of the LAND LEAGUE in 1879, successfully organizing the boycotting of unjust landlords. His advocacy of non-co-operation led to his imprisonment in Kilmainham gaol in 1881. He was released (1882) partly on the understanding that he would curb violence. The PHOENIX PARK MURDERS of two British politicians, following his release, damaged his reputation although a letter allegedly linking him to the murders was shown in court to be a forgery. In 1890 Parnell's involvement in a divorce case ended his career.

Parr, Catherine (1512–48) Sixth and surviving wife of HENRY VIII. She was the daughter of Sir Thomas Parr, controller of the king's household. Herself twice widowed, she became the king's wife in 1543. She skilfully managed him in his decline, helped his daughters MARY and ELIZABETH I to regain their places in the succession, and concerned herself with the education of Elizabeth and the future EDWARD VI. Soon after Henry's death in 1547 she married Thomas, Baron Seymour of Sudeley, but died after bearing his daughter.

Parsi (Parsee) The name given to the Indian followers of the ancient Persian religion of ZOROASTRIANISM. The Parsis emigrated to India from Iran in about the 8th–10th centuries, to avoid persecution by Muslims. Their belief and worship are based on the *avesta*, the scripture attributed to Zoroaster (628–*c.* 551 BC; also known as Zarathustra). Parsis are monotheists, believing in only one God, but they subscribe to the dualist belief that the earth is a battleground for the forces of good (*Ahura Mazda*) and evil (*Angra Mainyu*). Religious practice includes the fire temple, where a sacred flame is kept alight, and the tower of silence, upon which the dead are left exposed. Parsis in India live chiefly in Bombay and surrounding areas. They form a wealthy, well-educated, and influential group, noted for the equal role women play in their society. In Iran, a sect called the Gabars, numbering about 25,000, maintains the traditions of Zoroastrianism. There are also significant Parsi communities outside India, for example in London.

parson A clergyman who held a church living and was supported by its revenues. The term comes from the Latin word *persona* (person), which seems to have been used of clergymen since the 11th century. According to COKE, it derived from the view of a parson as the legal 'person' who holds the property of God in the PARISH. Since the 17th century, however, the term has been used to describe all clergymen, especially those in the Anglican Church.

Parthia An ancient Asian country, originally a SATRAPY of the ACHAEMENID empire, which later passed under the control of the SELEUCIDS. The Parthian empire traditionally began in 247 BC, when Arsaces I led his people in a rebellion against the Seleucids. By the end of the 2nd century BC they ruled from the River Euphrates in the west to Afghanistan in the east and north as far as the River Oxus. In 53 BC they defeated the Romans, led by CRASSUS, at Carrhae. The Parthians never developed beyond being a military aristocracy, though their geographical position allowed them to capitalize on the trade between East and West. Their rule came to an end in 224 AD when Ardashir of Persia defeated Artabanus V in battle, thereby founding the SASSANIAN EMPIRE.

Pascal, Blaise (1623–62) French mathematician, physicist, religious philosopher, and man of letters. As a precociously clever child of 12 he worked out Euclid's *Elements* for himself, and at 16 he wrote a treatise on conic sections so brilliant that the French mathematician René DESCARTES doubted his authorship. He subsequently designed the world's first mechanical calculator and his study of hydrostatics led him to invent the syringe and the hydraulic press. From 1651 to 1654 he suffered from chronically bad health. Part of his work during these years was concerned with laying the foundations for the calculus of probabilities. After a mystical experience in 1654 he withdrew to Port-Royal monastery, the home of French JANSENISM, which taught the corruption of man and his dependence upon divine grace for salvation. Pascal helped the Jansenists in their struggles with the JESUITS by anonymously writing the *Lettres provinciales* (1656–57), which helped significantly to undermine Jesuit prestige and authority. His *Pensées*, published posthumously in 1670, established his influential principle of intuitionism, which taught that God could be experienced through the heart and not through reason. The insights given in the *Pensées* into the grandeur and misery of the human condition are expressed in spare, incisive language.

pasha The highest official title of honour in the OTTOMAN EMPIRE. Used after the proper name, it was personal rather than hereditary, and not given to men of religion and rarely to women. It is derived from the Persian *padshah* and was first used by the SELJUKS. Ottoman usage assigned it to VIZIERS and provincial governors.

Pašić, Nikola (1845–1926) Serbian statesman and a founder of YUGOSLAVIA. Suspicious of Croats on both political and religious grounds, his ideal was a 'Greater Serbia', including much of Croatia and Dalmatia, with Serbs the master race. However, he signed the Corfu Pact (1917) which resulted in a union of Serbs, Croats, and Slovenes into a new kingdom which he represented at the VERSAILLES PEACE SETTLEMENT (1919). He was twice Premier of the new kingdom (1921–24 and 1924–26), which adopted the name Yugoslavia in 1929.

Passchendaele, Battle of (or The Third Battle of Ypres) (31 July–10 November 1917) A battle fought on the WESTERN FRONT in World War I. The name of this Belgian village has become notorious for the worst horrors of TRENCH WARFARE and failure to achieve any strategic gain for over 300,000 British casualties. HAIG, the British commander-in-chief, without French help, remained convinced, despite the SOMME, that frontal assaults in superior numbers must succeed. Torrential rain and preliminary bombardment reduced Flanders to a sea of mud, making advance impossible. Only on the final day did Canadians reach the ruined village of Passchendaele. Even this nominal gain was surrendered in the retreat before LUDENDORFF's final offensive (April 1918).

passive resistance Non-violent opposition to a ruling authority or government. It frequently involves a refusal to co-operate with the authorities or a defiant breach of laws and regulations and has been a major weapon of many nationalist, resistance, and social movements in modern times. One of the most successful campaigns was that waged by GANDHI against British rule in India, when widespread civil disturbances and protests persuaded the British to make major concessions (see also NON-CO-OPERATION). Gandhi's example was an inspiration for the CIVIL RIGHTS movement in the USA from the 1950s, where passive resistance, large-scale demonstrations, and the deliberate breaking of segregation laws brought considerable improvements for the Black population. Similar methods have failed in less liberal regimes, notably in China where demonstrations in Tiananmen Square, Beijing, in 1989 were brutally suppressed.

Patagonia A semi-arid plateau which forms the southernmost part of Argentina, beyond the Negro River. The largest desert in the Americas, it is dissected into several blocks by river valleys that open out on to the Atlantic coastal plain. The northern zone consists primarily of scrubland, but irrigated crops including peaches, grapes, and alfalfa are grown in the valleys.

History. Argentine and Chilean rangers began settling in the territory, occupied by Indians, in the late 19th century; they fell into boundary disputes, resolved by an agreement in 1901. Europeans, notably of BASQUE, Welsh, and Scottish origin, immigrated in the early 20th century. The pastoral economy was challenged in the period after World War II by the discovery of iron ore, manganese, petroleum, uranium, and natural gas deposits that are increasingly being exploited.

Patel, Sardar Vallabhbhai (1875–1950) Indian statesman. Deeply influenced by Mohandas GANDHI, he became the principal organizer of many civil disobedience campaigns, suffering frequent imprisonment by the British. He was elected President of the Indian National CONGRESS in 1931. He played an important role in the negotiations that led to the partition of the subcontinent into India and Pakistan. As Deputy Prime Minister (1947–50) he initiated a purge of communists and with the assistance of V. P. MENON, he integrated the PRINCELY STATES into the Indian Union.

Pathan A Pashto-speaking people of Pakistan and Afghanistan, more especially the tribesmen of the mountainous regions along the NORTH-WEST FRONTIER of Pakistan. After 1849, when control of the region passed from the Sikhs to the British, a series of frontier uprisings took place. In 1893 an international frontier, the Durand Line, was established, with probably about two-thirds of Pathans in British India and one-third in Afghanistan. A Pathan rebellion against this frontier occurred in 1897–98, necessitating an extensive British military occupation, but the frontier was inherited by Pakistan in 1947 when the Pathans of the British North-West Frontier Province voted to join the newly independent Pakistan.

The Pathans consist of 60 tribes and over 5 million people. Each tribe traces its origins to one ancestor and is divided into CLANS and sub-clans. The family is patriarchal, and feuds, which sometimes span generations, can be inherited. Although some Pathans are pastoralists, the majority are farmers, and the rights to land are determined through a complex system of genealogy, while status and rank are also largely inherited. The Pathans are devout Muslims, who have resisted domination by other groups and have a reputation as fierce warriors. An Afghan movement for a Pathan homeland, Pathanistan, was a factor in the civil war in Afghanistan (1979–89).

Pathet Lao Laotian communist movement. In the independence struggle after World War II, Pathet Lao forces co-operated with the VIETMINH against French colonial power. After the Geneva Agreement, it emerged as a major political and military force within Laos, seeking the alignment of their country with communist China and North Vietnam. Between the mid-1950s and mid-1970s the Pathet Lao and its political wing, the Neo Lao Haksat (Patriotic Party of Laos) under the leadership of Prince Souphanouvong, waged a prolonged political and military struggle for power with non-communist government forces, eventually emerging triumphant with the formation of the People's Democratic Republic of Laos in 1975.

Patiño, Simon Iture (1860–1947) Bolivian capitalist. He pioneered the development of Bolivia's tin resources and died one of the world's richest men. Although his modest origins impeded his entry into the Bolivian social élite, by the 1900s Patiño controlled over half of the tin production in Bolivia and exerted considerable influence on his country's government. He is still criticized for not investing in the development of his own country.

patricians The privileged landed aristocrats of early republican Rome. The patricians (meaning 'fathers') gathered after the expulsion of TARQUIN to guide the state. Supported by revered tradition they were hereditary members of the SENATE. They monopolized all magistracies and priesthoods but following the 'struggle of the Orders' with the plebeians they were forced to share power. In 367 BC the consulship was opened to plebeians. Thereafter a 'plebeian nobility' arose, which together with the patricians formed the ruling class. The number of patricians declined and their influence waned in the late republic but the ancient names still carried prestige.

Patrick, St (c. 390–c. 460) Patron saint of Ireland. He was the son of a Romano-British Christian family but was captured by pirates as a boy and spent six years as a slave and herdsman in Ireland. He escaped back to his home in Britain and went to Gaul. He later received a training for the priesthood. He returned to Ireland as a missionary bishop (*c.* 435) and played a leading role in the conversion of the Irish to Christianity. He challenged the influence of the DRUIDS, converted the royal family, and founded the cathedral church at Armagh (444). His *Confession* (450) is the main source for information about his life. The cult of St Patrick gradually spread to Irish monasteries in Europe.

patronage system SPOILS SYSTEM.

Patton, George Smith (1885–1945) US general. In World War II Patton commanded a corps in North Africa and then the 7th Army in Sicily. He lost his command in 1944 after a publicized incident in which he hit a soldier suffering from battle fatigue, but later led the 3rd Army in the NORMANDY CAMPAIGN. His tendency to make rapid military advance, at times with no regard for supporting units or allies, became evident in 1944 in his spectacular sweep through France, across the Rhine, and into Czechoslovakia. As military governor of Bavaria, he was criticized for his leniency to Nazis. He was killed in a road accident while commanding the US 15th Army.

Paul I (1754–1801) Emperor of Russia (1796–1801). He was the disturbed son of the future empress CATHERINE II and Peter III, and was greatly affected by the murder of his father during Catherine's *coup d'état* in 1762. After Catherine's death in 1796 he began a reign of frenzied despotism. He was obsessed by a fear of revolution and joined the coalitions against France. His attempts to violate the order of succession led to a conspiracy, which included his son, Alexander I, and in March 1801 resulted in his murder.

Paul VI (Giovanni Battista Montini, 1897–1978) Pope (1963–78). He continued the work of his predecessor JOHN XXIII by reconvening the Second Vatican Council (1963–65) of the ROMAN CATHOLIC CHURCH. Following the recommendations of the Council, he established important post-conciliar commissions. These investigated the need for reform of the liturgy and curia and ways to promote Christian unity and greater lay participation. A traditionalist by conviction, he was suspicious of any innovation that might undermine the authority of the Church, insisting on the necessity of priestly celibacy and condemning artificial methods of birth control.

Paul, St (1st century AD) Early Christian missionary, originally named Saul. He was born into a Jewish family resident at Tarsus and given a thorough Jewish education. He belonged to the religious party of the PHARISEES and was at first strongly opposed to CHRISTIANITY. He was dramatically converted to it (*c.* 33 AD) after seeing a vision while on a journey by road to Damascus. About ten years after his conversion Paul began to travel as a missionary in Asia Minor and the Aegean. This work expressed his conviction that he was an apostle to the Gentiles (non-Jews). His preaching stressed that Gentiles who became Christians needed only faith in Christ in order to be 'justified' before God, and need not accept Jewish customs. Paul's radical interpretation of the Christian message provoked hostility; a riot against him on a visit to Jerusalem led to his arrest by the Roman authorities. He was eventually taken to Rome, where he is thought to have died a martyr's death (perhaps after a further period of

freedom) in about 64 AD. Several of Paul's letters to early Christian groups have been preserved in the New Testament of the Bible. Through them his influence on Christian life and thought has been greater than that of any other early Christian.

Paulus, Friedrich von (1890–1957) German field-marshal. As deputy chief of staff he planned the German invasion of Russia (Operation Barbarossa) in World War II. In 1942 he failed to capture STALINGRAD, was cut off, and surrendered (February 1943). In captivity, he joined a Soviet-sponsored German organization and publicly advocated the overthrow of the Nazi dictatorship. He lived in East Germany until his death.

Pavia, Battle of (24 February 1525) An engagement in the Habsburg–Valois wars, which involved the papacy and England supporting CHARLES V against FRANCIS I. In October 1524 the French invaded Italy and took Milan, and the Pope changed sides to join them. Then the city of Pavia, in Lombardy, saw a battle between the French and imperial armies. The imperial forces, numbering 23,000 defeated the French army even though it had 5,000 more soldiers, and Francis was taken prisoner. He was released in 1526 and the wars in Italy continued.

Pawnee A Native American people descended from the MISSISSIPPI CULTURES west of the Missouri River in Nebraska. By *c.* 1000 AD they were farmers living in permanent villages and practising seasonal hunting. Some adopted foot nomadism on the Great Plains in the 15th and 16th centuries and in the late 17th and 18th centuries buffalo hunting became increasingly important as horses and, later, firearms were acquired from northern Mexico.

Paxton Boys A group of American rebels in Pennsylvania, who were Scots-Irish frontiersmen from settlements round Paxton. In 1763, threatened by PONTIAC'S REBELLION and agitated by lack of colonial defence and political representation, they first massacred some Christian Native Americans and then marched on Philadelphia, where FRANKLIN managed to pacify them. They were symptomatic of a long-term antagonism between frontier and coastal settlers, having many similarities with BACON'S REBELLION (1676) and the Carolina REGULATORS (1768–71).

Paz Estenssoro, Victor (1907–) Bolivian statesman; President (1952–56, 1960–64, 1985–89). In 1941 he helped to form a left-wing political party, the Movimiento Nacionalista Revolucionario (MNR). In the same year he became Minister of Finance (1941–44), but then went into exile until 1951. In 1952, when the MNR came to power, he became President of Bolivia (1952–56). During this time the tin-mines were nationalized, adult suffrage introduced, and many large estates broken up and transferred to Indian peasants. He was re-elected President (1960–64), when he reached an understanding with international financiers for the re-organization of the tin industry. He was elected for a third time in 1964, but was overthrown by the army and went into exile until 1971. Military government ended in Bolivia in 1982 and in 1985 he was re-elected President in succession to Dr Herman Zuazo. In spite of a drop in world tin prices and consequential economic problems for Bolivia, his government survived until 1989, when he was succeeded by Jaime Paz Zamora.

Pazzi Conspiracy (1478) An unsuccessful plot to overthrow the MEDICI rulers of Florence. Their rivals, the Pazzi family, backed by Pope Sixtus IV, conspired to murder Giuliano and Lorenzo de Medici at High Mass in Florence Cathedral and to seize power. Although Giuliano was murdered as planned, Lorenzo escaped. The mob rallied to the Medici and seized and murdered the main conspirators.

Peabody, George (1795–1869) US philanthropist. He established a prosperous trading business in the eastern USA before settling in London in 1837. He became one of the leading international bankers of his age, amassing a vast fortune, a substantial part of which he devoted to philanthropic ends, including the first educational foundation in the USA, the Peabody Education Fund, set up in 1867 to promote education in the South. He also gave large sums for slum clearance in Britain.

peacekeeping The intervention in a conflict by neutral external forces in order to effect a ceasefire, ensure that a ceasefire is observed, keep the conflicting parties apart, and perhaps prepare the way for mediation. Peacekeeping forces usually have the sanction of a supranational organization, such as the UNITED NATIONS. The members of UN peacekeeping forces are drawn from those member states of the organization who are not nationally identified with the conflict and are subject to strict guidelines (for instance, members may not fire unless fired upon). The peacekeeping mechanism of the UN is now relatively well developed; peacekeeping forces have been sent to such places as the Congo (1960), Cyprus (1964), the GOLAN HEIGHTS (1974), and the former Yugoslavia (1992; see BOSNIA-HERZEGOVINA). The UN also sends unarmed observer missions to countries where there is conflict; for instance, the UN Iran–Iraq Military Observer Group (UNIIMOG), established in 1988, the UN Angola Verification Mission (UNAVEM), established in 1989, or the fact-finding mission sent to Algeria in 1997.

peace-pledge FRANKPLEDGE.

Pearl Harbor A harbour on the island of Oahu in Hawaii. It is the site of a major US naval base where a surprise attack by Japanese carrier-borne aircraft (7 December 1941) delivered without a prior declaration of war, brought the USA into World War II. A total of 188 US aircraft were destroyed and 8 battleships were sunk or damaged. The attack was a strategic failure because the crucial element of the US Pacific fleet, its aircraft carriers, were out of harbour on that day.

Pearson, Lester Bowles (1897–1972) Canadian diplomat and statesman. He served as delegate to the United Nations, where he became President of the General Assembly. Leader of the Canadian LIBERAL PARTY in 1958, he was Prime Minister from 1963 to 1968. His administration saw the implementation of a medical care programme and the adoption of a new Canadian flag (the red maple leaf) signifying the growing Canadian sense of national identity. Pearson's administration, which had no overall majority, was troubled by the problems of Quebec's separatist aspirations and the US struggle in Vietnam.

Peasants' Revolt (1381) A social uprising in England. Widespread unrest caused by repressive legislation such as the Statute of LABOURERS (1351) was brought to a head by the imposition of the POLL TAX of 1380. The revolt drew support from artisans, VILLEINS, and the destitute. Men from Kent and Essex entered London, massacring some merchants and razing the palace of the Duke of Lancaster. The young king Richard II promised cheap land, the abolition of SERFDOM, and free trade. The rebels then occupied the Tower of London and beheaded the Archbishop and the king's Treasurer. The king persuaded the rebels to disperse, promising further reforms. Tyler was murdered by the enraged Mayor of London, and the militant bishop of Norwich crushed the rebels in East Anglia. The government re-established control and reneged on the monarch's promise. The revolt succeeded only as a protest against the taxation of the poor and the further levying of the Poll Tax.

Peasants' War (1524–26) A mass revolt of the German lower classes during the REFORMATION. It began in south-west Germany and spread down the River Rhine and into Austria. Frustrated by economic hardships, the rebels were encouraged by radical PROTESTANT preachers to expect a second coming of Jesus Christ and the establishment of social equality and justice. They raided and pillaged in unco-ordinated bands, driving LUTHER to condemn them in his fierce broadsheet *Against the thieving and murdering hordes of the peasants* (1525). Luther also supported the army of the Swabian League under PHILIP OF HESSE, which helped to crush the main body of insurgents at Frankenhausen. Over 100,000 rebels were eventually slaughtered.

Pedro I (1798–1835) The first Emperor of Brazil (1822–31). The son of John VI of Portugal, he fled from Napoleon to Brazil. Recognizing that Brazilian independence from Portugal was inevitable, Pedro I led the revolt himself (1822) and then governed the new Brazilian monarchy under the executive powers of the constitution of 1824. Republican-inspired uprisings and nationalist resentment over his Portuguese connections undermined Pedro's rule; he abdicated (1831) in favour of his son PEDRO II.

Pedro II (1812–91) Emperor of Brazil (1831–89). The son of PEDRO I, he succeeded under a regency when his father abdicated (1831). The central government was unable to quell the uprisings at Balaiada (1838–41) and elsewhere until the General Assembly declared Pedro to be of age and confirmed (1840) his emperorship. Within 18 months he had established order throughout the country. A popular, moderate leader, he was dedicated to the economic progress of Brazil. After a long rule, with only occasional revolts and foreign conflicts, Pedro eventually alienated his military officers by his refusal to grant them privileges, and the planters by his gradual abolition of slavery (completed in 1888). The army and the Republican Party overthrew him in 1889 and he spent the rest of his life in exile in Europe.

Peel, Sir Robert (1788–1850) British statesman. He entered Parliament as a Tory in 1809, holding office as Secretary for Ireland (1812–18). As Home Secretary (1822–27 and 1828–30) he made sweeping reforms in the penal code, removing about 100 offences from the list of crimes punishable by death, founding the Metropolitan Police, and helping to secure the passage of the act granting CATHOLIC EMANCIPATION. He opposed the Whig government's REFORM ACT of 1832 but in the TAMWORTH MANIFESTO (1834) accepted the principle of moderate reform within the framework of existing institutions that was later to characterize Disraeli's new CONSERVATIVE PARTY. He was briefly Prime Minister in 1834–35, and during his second term of office from 1841 to 1846 he advanced the cause of FREE TRADE by reducing import duties. He introduced the Bank Charter Act of 1844, which monopolized the issue of paper money, and tried to link the issuing of notes to the gold reserve. He is, however, best remembered for his decision in 1846, when faced with the miseries of the IRISH FAMINE, to repeal the CORN LAWS. This action split the Tories, and Peel was forced to resign.

Peisistratus PISISTRATUS.

Peking Man A popular name for the numerous remains of *Homo erectus pekinensis* (originally *Sinanthropus pekinensis*) found at ZHOUKOUDIAN (Choukoutien) in China since 1927 and often used for all *homo erectus* fossils from China. Besides those from Zhoukoudian, important remains are known from Hexian in Anhui province (about 250,000 years old) and from Lantian in Shaanxi province (800,000–600,000 years old), which could be contemporary with JAVA MAN.

Pelagianism The doctrine of the heretical British monk Pelagius (*c.* 350–420). He rejected the pessimistic Christian view which saw mankind as totally depraved and without freedom of will. Instead he insisted that God could be reached, by human effort, through asceticism. His beliefs stemmed partly from a reaction to MANICHAEISM, partly from the necessity for self-survival in the wake of the collapse of the old imperial order. Condemned in 416, he was excommunicated in 418 and disappeared from record. Some of his works survive in fragmentary form. His influence survived particularly in Britain and Gaul which had grown increasingly independent of Rome. The issue later assumed a central importance in the dispute between Protestant and Catholic theologies at the REFORMATION.

Pelham, Henry (1696–1754) English politician and statesman. He was the brother of the Duke of NEWCASTLE with whom he formed a powerful political combination from 1744, with Pelham providing the leadership and Newcastle the patronage and political stability. Pelham reduced the National Debt and in 1748 introduced a period of peace and prosperity by bringing the War of the AUSTRIAN SUCCESSION to an end. His ministry also introduced legislation adopting the Gregorian CALENDAR. His death in office is often regarded as a major factor in producing the political instability of the 1760s.

Peloponnesian War The war waged between Athens and Sparta and their respective allies between 431 and 404 BC. Its history was recorded in detail by THUCYDIDES and XENOPHON. According to Thucydides, the underlying reason for conflict was the growth of Athenian power and the fear this aroused among the Spartans. Corinth was especially vigorous in pressing Sparta to declare war on Athens. Sparta invaded Attica with its allies in 431, but PERICLES had persuaded the Athenians to withdraw behind the 'long walls' that linked Athens to its port of Piraeus, and to avoid a land-battle with Sparta's superior army. Athens relied on its fleet of TRIREMES to raid the Peloponnese and guard its empire and trade-routes. An outbreak of plague in 430 killed

about a third of the population of Athens, including Pericles. Nevertheless, the fleet performed well and a year's truce was made in 423 BC.

The Peace of Nicias was concluded in 421 BC, but Alcibiades orchestrated opposition to Sparta in the Peloponnese, although his hopes of victory were dashed when Sparta won at Mantinea in 418. Alcibiades was also the main advocate of an expedition to Sicily (415–413), aimed at defeating Syracuse, that ended in complete disaster for Athens. War was formally resumed in 413 BC. Athens had lost much of its fleet in Sicily, was desperately short of money, and troubled by political upheaval, with many Athenian allies revolting, and was put under further pressure by the fortification of Decelea in Attica by the Spartans. Nevertheless, and thanks in large part to Alcibiades, Athenian fortunes revived, with naval victories at Cynossema (411), Cyzicus (410), and the recapture of Byzantium (408). There was a further victory at Arginusae in 406. From then on, Persian financial support for Sparta and the strategic and tactical skills of the Spartan LYSANDER tilted the balance. Sparta's victory at AEGOSPOTAMI and its control of the Hellespont starved Athens into surrender in April 404. An oligarchic coup followed immediately, supported by Sparta, which initiated the reign of terror of the 'Thirty Tyrants'. Democracy was restored in 403.

penal settlements, Australian Settlements in 19th-century Australia for convicts who had committed further crimes within the colonies. Newcastle, New South Wales was used as a penal settlement from 1804 to 1824, convicts there worked as coalminers, cedar-cutters, and lime-burners. Port Macquarie (1821–30) and Moreton Bay (1824–39) also were used as penal settlements. Norfolk Island, re-settled in 1825 as a penal settlement, became notorious. It held an average of 1,500 to 2,000 convicts, considered to be of the worst type. Punishment was harsh and a number of mutinies occurred. The last convicts left Norfolk Island in 1856. Port Arthur, in Van Diemen's Land (modern Tasmania), begun in 1830, was finally closed in 1877.

Penda (d. 655) King of MERCIA in the first half of the 7th century. He sought to establish the supremacy of Mercia over the other English kingdoms. He drove the King of Wessex into exile, killed the ruler of East Anglia in battle, and, in alliance with CADWALADER, invaded NORTHUMBRIA. Edwin, its ruler, was defeated and killed in 633 and his successor OSWALD in 642. Although never a Christian, Penda allowed missionaries to preach in his kingdom. He was killed in battle by OSWY, King of Northumbria.

Pendleton Act (1883) An Act to reform the US civil service. Its purpose was to curb the discredited SPOILS SYSTEM and establish the principle of merit in public service. The assassination of GARFIELD by a disappointed office seeker in 1881 stimulated agitation for the reform. The Act, named after its sponsor, Senator George H. Pendleton of Ohio, called on the President to appoint a standing Civil Service Commission of three members (not more than two from any one party), who were required to organize competitive examinations for prospective federal employees in Washington and elsewhere.

Peng Pai (1896–1929) Founder member of the CHINESE COMMUNIST PARTY who pioneered peasant organizations. Peng ran the Haifeng Peasants' Association (1921–24) and set up a Peasants' Bureau which MAO ZEDONG later directed and which successfully organized thousands of peasants in Guangdong province. Peng was executed by the nationalist authorities in 1929.

Peninsular War (1807–14) One of the NAPOLEONIC WARS, fought in Spain and Portugal. War was caused by NAPOLEON's invasion of Portugal (1807) in order to compel it to accept the CONTINENTAL SYSTEM. In 1808 the conflict spread to Spain, whose king was forced to abdicate, Napoleon's brother Joseph Bonaparte being placed on the throne. In June the Spanish revolted and forced the French to surrender at Baylen, whereupon Joseph fled from Madrid. In August Wellesley (later the Duke of WELLINGTON) landed in Portugal, routed a French force at Vimeiro, and expelled the French from Portugal. In November Napoleon personally went to Spain, winning a series of battles, including Burgos, and restoring Joseph to the throne. British hopes of pushing the French out of Spain were destroyed in January 1809, after MOORE's retreat to Corunna. Despite his victory at Talavera, Wellesley withdrew to Lisbon. Here he built a strong defensive line which he centred at Torres Vedras. In 1810 Napoleon sent Massena to reinforce Soult and drive the British into the sea. Massena attempted to lay siege to Torres Vedras, but after four months his army, starved and demoralized, was forced to retreat. Soult, jealous of Massena's command, was slow in coming to his support, but managed to capture Badajoz. Wellington, who had pursued Massena and defeated him

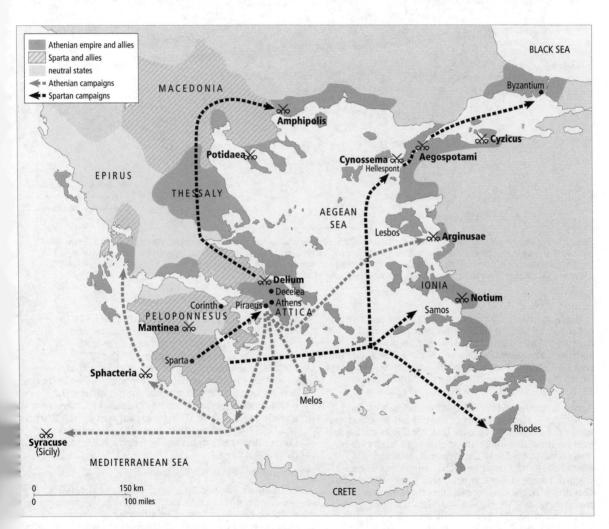

Peloponnesian War (431–404 BC)   *Of the two chief contestants in the Peloponnesian War, Sparta was essentially a land power, while Athens was a naval power. The Athenians were forced to abandon Attica in 431 BC, and it was regularly overrun by the Spartan army thereafter. Sparta was also more successful in gaining Persian aid, which was perhaps the decisive factor ultimately. However, Athens could not be defeated while it retained its maritime supremacy. Despite their disastrous losses at Syracuse, the Athenians inflicted several naval defeats on the Spartans between 411 and 406. Athens' surrender was forced only by the capture of its entire fleet at Aegospotami.*

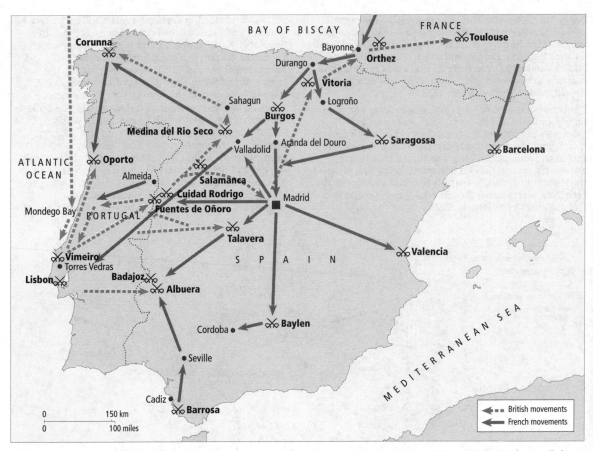

Peninsular War (1807–14) *In 1807, in order to impose the Continental System, Napoleon occupied Portugal. In 1808 he installed his brother Joseph on the Spanish throne. This sparked off a long guerrilla struggle. Napoleon personally intervened in 1809, but after his withdrawal the struggle continued. When French troops were withdrawn to fight in Russia, the British commander, Wellington, entered Madrid. In 1813 he won the decisive Battle of Vitoria.*

at Almeida, withdrew from invading Spain and turned to face Soult. During 1812 Wellington recaptured Badajoz and after defeating Massena's replacement, Marmont, at Salamanca, entered Madrid. The following year he defeated Joseph at the decisive battle of Vitoria. He went on to defeat Soult at Orthez and Toulouse (1814), having driven the French out of Spain.

Penn, William (1644–1718) Quaker founder of PENNSYLVANIA. He was granted the proprietary colony to satisfy debts owed by Charles II in 1681. Persecution and warfare in Britain and Europe ensured a high rate of emigration to his 'Holy Experiment'. Although a tolerationist and friend to Native Americans, Penn's original 'Frame of Government' was paternalistic. Settler discontent forced him to concede representative government by 1701. He was a tireless missionary and propagandist for Quakerism, but spent his later life in England, harassed by financial problems and suffering from apoplexy.

Pennsylvania A colony and state of the USA regarded as a middle Atlantic state, though its only coastline is at its north-west corner on Lake Erie. Founded in 1681 by William PENN, it grew rapidly under Quaker control,

with efficient German farmers, still known as Pennsylvania Dutch (Deutsch), settling the rich farmlands of the coastal plain and Scots-Irish immigrants taming the frontier. By the 1770s Philadelphia was the largest city in the colonies, exporting grain in homebuilt shipping to the Caribbean and Europe. It was the national capital during the Revolutionary period, acting as host to the CONTINENTAL CONGRESS (1774–87). In 1777 it was captured by the British and held for a year. It then hosted the Constitutional Convention (1787) and the new federal government (1790–1800).

penny post HILL, Sir Rowland.

Pentagon Papers An official study of US defence policy commissioned in 1967 to examine US involvement in south-east Asia. Leaked by a former government employee, they revealed miscalculations, deceptions, and unauthorized military offensives. Their publication provoked demands for more open government.

Pentrich Rising (1817) A quasi-political insurrection which took place in Derbyshire, England. Led by Jeremiah Brandreth, a framework knitter, a group of about 200 men from Pentrich and other nearby villages, armed only with primitive weapons, began to march on Nottingham in a protest against the government. Brandreth had been tricked by a government spy into believing that they were taking part in a nationwide insurrection. They were dispersed by a troop of cavalry and Brandreth went into hiding. He was betrayed and later executed, together with two of his associates.

peon (South-American Spanish, 'day-labourer') An unskilled labourer in rural areas of Latin America. Usually the term is associated with agricultural labour or peasants, and it is often linked to the more specific institution of debt peonage, a means of holding agricultural labourers on an HACIENDA. By advancing wages to cover such expenses as religious ceremonies or clothing, landowners encouraged the accumulation of debts by workers who would then be obliged to remain in service until the debt was paid off. The degree to which debt actually signified bondage depended upon market conditions and the availability of labour.

'People's Budget' A controversial British budget in 1909, introduced by LLOYD GEORGE, Chancellor of the Exchequer, to raise revenue for naval defence and social reform, particularly the funding of Old Age Pensions. Increased death duties and the imposition of taxes on land provoked the Conservative-dominated HOUSE OF LORDS to reject this Liberal budget. By constitutional convention the Lords should have automatically approved all financial bills passed by the Commons. Their rejection led to the Parliament Act (1911), a statute that curtailed the power of the House of Lords and asserted the supremacy of the Commons on finance.

People's Party (USA) POPULIST PARTY.

Pepin Three Frankish 'mayors of the palace' under MEROVINGIAN rule who gave rise to the Carolingian dynasty. **Pepin I of Landen** (d. c. 640) was mayor of Austrasia and his son **Pepin II** (d. 714) of both Austrasia and Neustria, the two most important parts of the Merovingian kingdom. **Pepin III** (c. 714–768), the Short, was the grandson of Pepin II and son of CHARLES MARTEL. He ousted the last Merovingian, Childeric III, in 751 and was crowned King of the Franks. A close ally of the papacy, he defended it from Lombard attacks and in 794 made the Donation of Pepin, giving land to the Pope, which was the basis for the PAPAL STATES. He added Aquitaine and Septimania to his kingdom, which passed, on his death in 768, to CHARLEMAGNE and Carloman.

Pepys, Samuel (1633–1703) English naval administrator and diarist. His connection with the navy started in 1660 and in 1673 he became Secretary to the Admiralty Commission and a Member of Parliament. He worked hard for naval reform but his closeness to the Duke of York led to his arrest for alleged complicity in the POPISH PLOT. He was reappointed in 1684 and became president of the Royal Society in the same year; during James II's reign he did his best to rebuild the navy which had again fallen into neglect. Pepys is remembered for his diary, an important document on contemporary life and manners. It includes descriptions of the coronation of Charles II, the FIRE OF LONDON, and the GREAT PLAGUE and is written with engaging sincerity and humanity. Pepys wrote his diary between 1660 and 1669 in a code of his own invention, which was not deciphered until 1825.

Pequot War (1637) A war fought between Native Americans and White settlers in New England. The Pequot had lived peacefully alongside the mainly British settlers from 1620, but tensions increased on both sides. The British took over more and more land while the Pequot would only trade with the Dutch. In 1636 a trader was murdered, the Pequot were blamed, and the authorities destroyed Pequot villages. After several skirmishes, the Pequot camp at Mystic on the Connecticut coast near Rhode Island was surprised and set on fire, killing some 500 of the tribe, which did not recover. Poor colonist co-operation in this war led to the founding of the NEW ENGLAND Confederation (1643).

Perceval, Spencer (1762–1812) British statesman. He entered Parliament in 1796 as a supporter of William PITT in the war against France. He was appointed solicitor-general in 1801 and attorney-general in the following year, holding this post until 1806. In 1807 he became Chancellor of the Exchequer in the Duke of Portland's administration, succeeding him as Prime Minister (1809–12). A moderately competent man and a strong evangelical, Perceval was shot dead in the lobby of the House of Commons by a deranged bankrupt with a grievance against the government.

Percy A family of MARCHER LORDS of medieval England with lands in Northumberland. Henry de Percy (1341–1408), 1st Earl of Northumberland, was the first of the family to be of major importance in the defence of England's northern frontier. The earl's son, Sir Henry Percy ('Hotspur') (1364–1403), was a hero of the Battle of OTTERBURN. When Henry of Bolingbroke landed in the north of England in 1399, the earl and Hotspur helped assure him of the crown; they were well rewarded, but within four years their greed for more offices or money led them into open rebellion. Hotspur and his uncle Thomas, Earl of Worcester, were killed at Shrewsbury in 1403. Five years later Earl Henry invaded England from Scotland, but he too was killed and his estates were forfeited.

  Subsequently restored to their estates, later generations of the family resumed their role as guardians of the northern frontier and rivals of the Nevilles. The male line ended in 1670, but the earldom passed in the female line to Sir Hugh Smithson (1715–86) who took the name of Percy and in 1766 was created Duke of Northumberland.

Peres, Shimon (1923–   ) Israeli politician; Prime Minister (1984–86, 1995–96). Peres emigrated to Palestine from Poland with his parents in 1934. An active Zionist and trade unionist when young, he went on to join the Mapai Party (forerunner of the Israeli Labour Party). Peres specialized in buying weaponry for the defence of the new state of Israel and helped to develop the domestic armaments industry. In the 1960s and 1970s he occupied several ministerial posts and was Prime Minister from 1984 to 1986 in a power-sharing arrangement with the Likud Party under Yitzhak SHAMIR; during this coalition he also acted as Finance Minister and Foreign Minister. Under the new Labour administration of Yitzhak RABIN (1992–95), he was a main instigator of the dialogue with the PALESTINE LIBERATION ORGANIZATION (PLO) and Jordan that led to the Oslo Peace Accord of 1993. For this he was awarded the 1994 Nobel peace prize jointly with Rabin and PLO leader Yasser ARAFAT. Peres briefly held power after the assassination of Rabin by a Jewish extremist in late 1995, but was defeated by Likud under Binyamin NETANYAHU in elections in 1996.

Pérez de Cuéllar, Javier (1920–) Peruvian diplomat and Secretary-General of the United Nations (1982–91). A skilled, careful diplomat, he succeeded Kurt WALDHEIM as Secretary-General in 1982. He became a key figure in the successful peace negotiations in Afghanistan and Namibia, and personally negotiated the end of hostilities in the IRAN–IRAQ WAR. He negotiated the ceasefire for the GULF WAR, and in his last year of office achieved the release of Western hostages, including Terry Waite and John McCarthy, held by the Muslim *Hezbollah* in Lebanon, and a pacification between government and guerrilla opponents in El Salvador in 1991. In presidential elections in Peru in 1995, Pérez de Cuéllar was defeated by the incumbent, Alberto FUJIMORI.

Pergamum An ancient city in what is now Turkey, some 20 km (12 miles) inland from the west coast of Asia Minor. It developed into a major power during the 3rd and 2nd centuries BC under the Attalid dynasty. In particular, Attalus I (ruled 241–197), inflicted a severe defeat on the GALATIANS and for a time wrested most of Asia Minor from the SELEUCIDS. He allied himself to Rome in the first two MACEDONIAN WARS and his pro-Roman policy was followed by his successors. Thus Eumenes II (d. *c.* 160) helped to defeat Antiochus at Magnesia and in accordance with Attalus III's will the kingdom was bequeathed to Rome in 133 BC. It became a province of Asia, and was soon eclipsed by Ephesus as the chief city of the region.

Attalid Pergamum was a brilliant centre of HELLENISTIC CIVILIZATION: its chief glories were its sculpture and its library, where parchment was developed in the 2nd century BC as a more durable material than papyrus for books.

Pericles (*c.* 495–429 BC) Athenian statesman and general. Noted for his oratory, political acumen, and integrity, he dominated Athens throughout the third quarter of the 5th century BC. He supported the democratic leader Ephialtes in his attack on the AREOPAGUS and after his death became champion of the ATHENIAN DEMOCRACY, proposing pay for jurors and other innovations. He was instrumental in strengthening and extending the ATHENIAN EMPIRE and sending out colonists. He personally lead the attack against rebellions at Samos and an expedition into the Black Sea, important as a source of corn. He originated a major building programme, of which the centrepiece was the Parthenon, the temple which dominated the ACROPOLIS. When the spectre of war with the Spartans threatened in the 430s, Pericles determined to resist their demands. After the PELOPONNESIAN WAR broke out, he persuaded the Athenians to abandon the countryside when the Spartans invaded and to rely on their fleet. He was briefly deposed from the generalship when plague shattered Athenian confidence, but was re-elected the following year (429). He died of plague soon afterwards.

Perón, Eva (Duarte de) (1919–52) Argentine political leader. A minor actress, 'Evita', as she was called, became active in politics and organized the mass demonstration of workers (1945) that secured Juan PERÓN's release from prison. After her marriage to him in 1945, she in effect ran the Ministries of Labour and of Health. An opponent of the free press, by 1947 Eva Perón owned or controlled almost every radio station in Argentina, and had closed or banned over 100 newspapers and magazines. She was a gifted orator and a militant champion of women's rights. Her bid for the vice-presidency (1951) was blocked by the army, who opposed her. Her death from cancer at the age of 33 contributed to the decline of Perón's regime.

Eva Perón *As an opponent of freedom of the press, Eva Perón took control of radio stations and newspapers, including the paper* Democrazia, *a copy of which she is reading in this photograph.*

Perón, Juan (Domingo) (1895–1974) Argentine statesman. President of Argentina (1946–55, 1973–74), he was first elected with the support of labour and the military. An army officer who had favoured the fascist governments of Germany and Italy, he fashioned (1946) a revolutionary movement (*peronismo*), calling for a rapid economic build-up leading to self-sufficiency based on the expansion and organization of the urban working class at the expense of agriculture. While trying at first with the support of his wife, Eva PERÓN to implement his programme, Perón became increasingly dictatorial. In 1955 he was deposed by the armed forces. Despite military opposition, Perón was recalled from exile to be re-elected in 1973. He died in office in 1974, and was succeeded (1974–76) by his third wife, María Estela (Isabel) Martínez de Perón (1931–), who in turn was deposed (1975), and replaced by a military triumvirate. Peronism survived the demise of its founder; Carlos Menem, leader of the Peronist party, was elected president of Argentina in 1989, and was re-elected in 1995.

Perry, Matthew Calbraith (1794–1858) US naval officer and pioneer of Western contact with Japan. Perry served under his brother Oliver Perry during the WAR OF 1812. He headed an expedition to Japan entering the fortified port of Uraga in 1853, and Edo (modern Tokyo) Bay in 1854. His display of Western technology, both military and civil, forced the SHOGUNATE to open two Japanese ports to US trade in the Treaty of KANAGAWA. Perry's mission initiated the process which, within half a century, would transform Japan from an isolated feudal country to a highly industrialized world power.

Perry Convention KANAGAWA, TREATY OF.

Persepolis The ceremonial capital of the ACHAEMENID EMPIRE. A festival of tribute was held there each year, it was the burial place of the kings, and its treasury was a repository of enormous wealth. The city was captured, looted, and burnt in 331 BC by ALEXANDER THE GREAT's troops. Excavation of the palaces built by DARIUS I (the Great) and XERXES, and other buildings, while confirming the destruction which took place, has also revealed some magnificent examples of Achaemenid art and architecture, particularly bas-reliefs.

Pershing, John J(oseph) ('Black Jack') (1860–1948) US general. He served in the SPANISH–AMERICAN WAR and later in the Philippines. In 1913 he led the US expedition against Mexico in 1916. In May 1917 he was appointed commander of the American Expeditionary Forces in France and his talent for organization was largely responsible for the moulding of hastily trained US soldiers into well-integrated combat troops. In 1919 he became general of the armies of the USA and from 1921 to 1924 was army chief-of-staff.

Persia IRAN.

Persian wars GREEK–PERSIAN WARS.

Peru A country on the Pacific coast of South America, bounded by Ecuador and Colombia on the north, Brazil and Bolivia on the east, and Chile on the south.

Physical. The north-east of the country is in the upper Amazon basin and comprises equatorial rain forest. In stark contrast, the south-west half is occupied by the Andes mountain ranges. Between the ranges are plateau areas and the high mountain lake, Titicaca, in the extreme south-east. The coastal plain is arid and mostly desert, cooled by the Peru Current and subject to dense mists.

Economy. High inflation and a large foreign debt have caused economic problems for Peru. Exports include copper, zinc, lead, and silver, as well as fishmeal and wool from sheep and llamas. There is a wide range of agriculture, and Peru is almost self-sufficient in food. Peru has a well-established manufacturing sector, which includes petroleum products, although oil production is declining. There is widespread illegal cultivation of coca, which is sent to Colombia for processing into cocaine.

History. Peru was the site of a succession of complex cultures and states from c. 1000 BC: CHAVÍN CULTURE in the central Highlands, MOCHICA on the northern coast, NAZCA on the southern coast, and TIAHUANACO round Lake Titicaca. Between c. 600 AD and 1000 Huari in the central Andes conquered a small 'empire', and the CHIMÚ state rose on the northern coast in about 1000 AD. The INCAS were another such group, based round CUZCO, who began their regional expansion in about 1200 AD and conquered a vast empire stretching from Chile to Ecuador during the 15th century. Spanish invader Francisco PIZARRO's defeat of ATAHUALPA in 1532 was followed by rivalry for control and led eventually to direct rule by the Spanish crown. Inca revolts continued for nearly 50 years. The vice-royalty, with its capital at Lima, attempted to placate the various factions but was not in reasonable control until the mid-16th century. Further Inca insurrections occurred in 1780, led by TUPAC AMARÚ, and again in 1814.

In 1821 José de SAN MARTÍN captured Lima, proclaiming an independent republic and issuing a constitution (1823). In 1824 José de SUCRE won the Battle of Ayacucho, and Spanish troops were withdrawn. Political quarrels in the new republic led to an invitation to Simón BOLÍVAR to accept the powers of a dictator. He tried unsuccessfully to bring Peru into his state of Gran Colombia (which comprised present-day Colombia, Ecuador, and Venezuela). A long period of civil war followed, the situation stabilizing under President Ramón CASTILLA (1844–62), who ended slavery and established an education system. He promoted the extraction of guano (natural nitrates and phosphates produced from sea-bird droppings), which brought immediate prosperity but the guano deposits were soon exhausted. The loss of nitrate revenue and the cost of the War of the PACIFIC (1879–84) led to national bankruptcy in 1889. Civilian politics had emerged in the 1870s with two parties, the Democrats and the Civilians, alternating in office. The latter, led by Augusto LEGUIA, held power (1908–30), introducing progressive legislation and settling the TACNA–ARICA DISPUTE. After World War I a radical group, the Alianza Popular Revolucionaria Americana (APRA), led by HAYA DE LA TORRE, sought to obtain greater participation in politics by the Indians. President Manuel Prado, elected in 1939, aligned Peru with US policies in World War II. Terry Belaúnde gained office in 1963. In 1968 a left-wing military junta seized power, seeking to nationalize US-controlled industries. A more moderate junta succeeded in 1975 and in 1979 elections were again held. In 1980 Belaúnde was re-elected President, when a new constitution was established. In the face of severe economic problems Belaúnde succeeded in re-democratizing the country and in 1985 President Alan Garcia was elected. Confronted by massive rescheduling requirements for Peru's foreign debts, his regime imposed an austerity programme and engaged in a guerrilla war against a strong ultra-left Maoist group, *Sendero Luminoso* (Shining Path). His APRA Party did badly in the 1990 elections, when Alberto FUJIMORI of the Cambio 90 Party, was elected President. Fujimori continued the austerity measures, leading to protests, with strikes and guerrilla attacks across the country. In September 1992, however, his government won a resounding victory against terrorism, by capturing and imprisoning Abimael Guzmán, who had founded and led *Sendero Luminoso* since 1970. A new constitution was introduced in 1993, and Fujimori was re-elected in 1995. In December 1996 Marxist guerrillas took nearly 500 politicians and businessmen hostage at the Japanese embassy in Lima: the four-month siege ended when Peruvian forces stormed the embassy in April 1997.

CAPITAL:	Lima
AREA:	1,285,216 sq km (496,225 sq miles)
POPULATION:	23.947 million (1996)

CURRENCY:	1 new sol = 100 cénts
RELIGIONS:	Roman Catholic 92.4%
ETHNIC GROUPS:	Quechua 47.0%; Mestizo 32.0%; European 12.0%; Aymara 5.0%
LANGUAGES:	Spanish, Quechua (both official); Aymara
INTERNATIONAL ORGANIZATIONS:	UN; OAS; Andean Group

Pétain, Henri-Philippe (1856–1951) French general and head of state. Petain was acclaimed a military hero for halting the German advance at VERDUN (1916) and replaced Nivelle as French commander-in-chief (1917). He later entered politics, becoming Minister of War in 1934. In 1940 he succeeded REYNAUD as Premier and concluded an armistice with Nazi Germany, agreeing that the French forces be disarmed and that three-fifths of France be surrendered to German control. The French National Assembly established its seat at VICHY and conferred on him the power to establish an authoritarian government. He designated LAVAL as his Vice-Premier and Foreign Minister, but later dismissed him for collaborating too closely with Germany. German forces entered unoccupied France and Pétain was forced to reinstate Laval. Thereafter his equivocal dealings with Allies and Germans can only be excused on grounds of failing powers. He was arrested in 1945 and sentenced to death for being a collaborator; the sentence was commuted to life imprisonment by General DE GAULLE.

Peter I (the Great) (1672–1725) Emperor of Russia (1682–1725). He became joint emperor with his mentally disabled half-brother Ivan V (1682–96) at the age of 10: his half-sister Sophia Alekseyevna (1657–1704) was regent while her brothers were minors, from 1682 until Peter seized power in 1689. Russia (Muscovy) was then shut off from Europe by Poland and the Swedish and Turkish empires; Archangel was its only port. From boyhood Peter was fascinated by the sea and ships and with what he learned about Western skills from foreigners visiting Moscow. In 1697–98 he travelled to Germany, Holland, England, and Vienna; his chief preoccupations were learning the techniques of ship-building and recruiting foreign technicians and craftsmen. His attempts to westernize his people were often crude and tactless, but he centralized the government under the senate and brought the church under state control, replacing the patriarch by a Holy Synod. A table of ranks was established, ennobling those who served the state in the higher grades, and requiring service from all. He improved the army and navy and founded St Petersburg as a capital modelled on European examples. He seized but later lost Azov on the Black Sea: in the NORTHERN WAR he defeated CHARLES XII at POLTAVA and by the Treaty of NYSTADT gained the Baltic coastal provinces of Estonia, Livonia, and Ingria. His achievements for his country were marred by his barbaric cruelties, which included even the torturing to death of his own son in 1718.

Peter, St (d. *c.* 64 AD) The leader of the Apostles who followed JESUS CHRIST. He was originally called Simon, but Jesus named him Cephas (Aramaic, 'rock'; Greek *petra*, 'rock') to signify his key role in establishing the early Christian Church. After the death of Jesus, Peter was the undisputed leader of the Church, preaching, defending the new religious movement, and visiting newly established Christian communities. He was the first to accept Gentiles (non-Jews) into the Church but later disagreed with St PAUL over their status. It seems certain that Peter spent the last years of his life in Rome and was probably crucified during NERO's persecution of 64 AD. The PAPACY traces its origins back to Peter and the ROMAN CATHOLIC CHURCH identifies him as the founder and first bishop of the church of Rome, although this cannot be proved.

Peterloo massacre (16 August 1819) A violent confrontation in Manchester, England, between civilians

Peterloo massacre *The killing by cavalry soldiers of 11 peaceful protestors provoked widespread outrage. This cartoon portrays the sabre-wielding cavalry as soldiers at the Battle of Waterloo. One of their speeches reads:*
"Raise up the Trumpet in high-cheerful strain!
Fill the goblets of Rum to the Loyal Yeomen!
How Glorious our Ardour to lay down the Lives
Of defenceless Children, Husbands & Wives."

and government forces. A large but peaceable crowd of some 60,000 people had gathered in St Peter's Fields to hear the radical politician Henry 'Orator' HUNT address them. After he had begun speaking, the local magistrates sent in constables to arrest him. In the mistaken belief that the crowd was preventing the arrest, the magistrates ordered a body of cavalry to go to the assistance of the constables. In the ensuing riot 11 civilians were killed and over 500 injured. The immediate response of LIVERPOOL's government was the passing of the repressive SIX ACTS, but the incident provoked widespread criticism, cartoonists comparing the 'massacre' to that of Waterloo.

Peter's pence The tax paid annually to the Roman Catholic Church to support the papacy. First made compulsory in 787, it was levied in England from the 10th century at the rate of one penny per householder. It was revived by WILLIAM I as a single lump sum of £200 for the whole of England. It was abolished in England in 1534 during the Reformation. The expression is now often used to refer to any voluntary donation of money to the Roman Catholic Church.

Peter the Hermit (1050–1115) French monk, noted for his preaching in support of the First CRUSADE. A charismatic figure, he raised up to 20,000 followers in France and Germany in 1096 but few were trained soldiers. They marched to Constantinople and crossed into northern Turkey where most were massacred or enslaved: this disaster is known as the People's Crusade. Peter lived to participate in the seige of Antioch in 1097 and later became prior of an Augustinian monastery.

Petition of Right A document drawn up in 1628 by opposition members of the English Parliament, led by COKE. It came at the time of CHARLES I's wars against France and Spain, and the lengthy quarrel over TUNNAGE AND POUNDAGE. It stated parliamentary grievances and forbade illegal unparliamentary taxation, the forced billeting of troops, the imposition of martial law, and arbitrary imprisonment. Charles assented to the Petition but it was a limited parliamentary victory and failed to curb Charles's unconstitutional rule during the 11 years of government without Parliament.

Petra An ancient city in Jordan, the capital of the Nabataeans (an Arab tribe) from the 4th century BC to the 2nd century AD. Its prosperity was derived from the caravan trade from southern Arabia, but declined after its annexation by the Romans in 106 AD. The remains of the city, accessible only by a single narrow entrance cut through steep rocks, are extensive and spectacular, particularly the tombs carved in the pink rock of the hills.

petty sessions The HUNDRED courts held by a sheriff in 16th-century England. They were mainly concerned with maintaining order, but were also charged with enforcing terms of service on labourers, prosecuting grain profiteers, and other local economic regulations. They were distinct from the general or quarter sessions, to which they referred more serious criminal cases, and by the 19th century their jurisdiction had been enlarged by innumerable, usually minor, statutory offences.

phalanx A tactical formation of armed infantry, in close ranks. The phalanx was developed in ancient Greece and was usually made up of HOPLITES. Tightly packed phalanxes of pike-armed infantrymen were an important part of the armies of PHILIP II and ALEXANDER THE GREAT as the pikes defended against cavalry attacks. The pike had been extended from a length of 4 to 6.5 m (13 to 21 feet) by the 2nd century BC and this limited the manoeuvrability of the phalanx. It failed to match the more flexible legions of Rome and the Greeks were defeated at Cynoscephalae (196 BC), Magnesia (189), and Pydna (168).

pharaoh The kings of ancient EGYPT. The Egyptians themselves only used the word pharaoh to mean king from 950 BC onwards. It comes from the word for 'palace'. The pharaoh was thought of as a god, the son of Osiris ruling on earth, and acted as an intermediary between gods and men. He wielded immense power as the religious, civil, and military leader of the country. The pharaohs greatly increased Egypt's power and territory. THUTMOSE I conquered much of NUBIA and campaigned as far east as the Euphrates. THUTMOSE III defeated the powerful Mitanni, and strengthened Egyptian rule in Africa. RAMESSES II made peace with the HITTITES and his rule saw great prosperity. The most spectacular legacy of the pharoahs is their magnificent buildings as at KARNAK, THEBES, and HELIOPOLIS.

Pharisee A member of a religious party in ancient Israel which set great store by observance of every detail of the Jewish law. They tended to be rather isolated from other Jews and came into conflict with JESUS CHRIST whose compassion was often at odds with their dry legalism, as is clearly documented in the Gospels of the BIBLE. They continued to have enormous influence on Jews as they were more popular than the conservative, aristocratic SADDUCEES. They were also influential in the development of Judaism after the destruction of the Second Temple of Jerusalem in 70 AD.

Pharsalus, Battle of (48 BC) The battle in which POMPEY was defeated by Julius CAESAR. After Caesar crossed the RUBICON, Pompey retired to Greece to rally his forces. Caesar crushed Pompey's supporters in Spain and then pursued him to northern Greece. Pompey's forces were routed in pitched battle, although he himself escaped.

Philip I (the Handsome) (1478–1506) King of Castile (1504–06). The son of MAXIMILIAN I, Philip I inherited BURGUNDY in 1482 and took over from his father's regency in 1494. His marriage to JOANNA THE MAD of Spain in 1496 brought the HABSBURGS a dynastic link with Spain. When Queen ISABELLA died in 1504, the pair inherited Castile. His wife's increasing madness enabled Philip I to assume considerable power as king consort. He died of fever soon after his arrival at Castile, his claims passing to his son CHARLES V.

Philip II (382–336 BC) King of Macedonia (359–336 BC). Philip II transformed an ineffectual and divided MACEDONIA into a power which dominated the Greek world. His success was based upon exploitation of Macedonia's natural advantages and the highly professional army which he created around a core of pike-armed infantrymen, the PHALANX, and his excellent cavalry. He gradually extended his empire until, after the battle of CHAERONEA, it stretched from the Black Sea to the southern Peloponnese. When an assassin struck him down, he was preparing for the invasion of Persia, a project that his son ALEXANDER III inherited.

Philip II (Augustus) (1165–1223) King of France (1179–1223). One of the CAPETIANS, he succeeded his father Louis VII in 1180 and set about the restoration and expansion of his kingdom. Defeating the Count of Flanders and the Duke of Burgundy, he seized Artois and part of the valley of the Somme. He was obliged initially to accept the homage of King JOHN of England for Normandy, Aquitaine, and Anjou but later recovered Normandy, Anjou, Poitou, and the Auvergne for the French crown. He defeated John and the Holy Roman Emperor jointly at the Battle of Bouvines (August 1214), leaving his country stronger and more united. After these military successes, he devoted his energy to reforming the law and building and fortifying Paris.

Philip II (1527–98) King of Spain, Naples, and Sicily (1556–98) and, as Philip I, of Portugal (1580–98). He was the only legitimate son of Emperor CHARLES V. He was married four times: to Mary of Portugal (1543), to MARY I of England (1554), to Isabella of France (1559), and to Anne of Austria (1570), whose son by him was his successor as Philip III of Spain. He ruled Spain and the SPANISH EMPIRE industriously during its 'golden age', not leaving the Iberian Peninsula at all after 1559. Although he generally subordinated his crusading zeal to more worldly considerations, his strongly Catholic religious policies helped to provoke the DUTCH REVOLTS (1568–1648) and the Revolt of the Moriscos within Spain (1568–70). His intermittent wars against the OTTOMANS, his war with England (1585–1604), and his involvement in the FRENCH WARS OF RELIGION were all largely motivated by interests of state. His personal brand of absolute monarchy left the country economically crippled as a result of his military expenses.

Philip IV (the Fair) (1268–1314) King of France (1285–1314). He inherited the throne from his father and strengthened royal control over the nobility as well as improving the law. Pope Boniface VIII resisted his claim to the right to tax the clergy but was imprisoned by a royal agent and died soon afterwards. The next pope, Clement V, was under the king's control and acquiesced in the removal of the papacy from Rome to Avignon in France, the beginning of 70 years 'captivity'. Coveting the wealth of the KNIGHTS TEMPLAR, he seized much of their property after Pope Clement suppressed their order by royal command in 1313. He also persecuted the Jews and had their property confiscated.

Philip V (1683–1746) King of Spain (1700–46). He was Philip of Anjou, the younger grandson of LOUIS XIV, and succeeded under the terms of the will of the last Habsburg king, Charles II. It was Louis XIV's acceptance of this will that plunged Europe into the War of the SPANISH SUCCESSION. Philip's claim was confirmed at the Peace of UTRECHT. Catalonia was deprived of its liberties when Barcelona surrendered to him in 1714. For the rest of his reign he was dominated by his second wife, Elizabeth FARNESE, whose ambitions for her sons influenced Spanish foreign policy.

Philip VI (1293–1350) King of France (1328–50), the first of the VALOIS kings. His right to the throne was challenged by EDWARD III of England and the HUNDRED YEARS WAR began in 1337. His ill-fated reign also witnessed the BLACK DEATH and war with FLANDERS. Despite the ruinous expense of war and some disastrous

military defeats, the government was strengthened during this period as an organized system of taxation evolved.

Philip of Hesse (1504–67) German prince. He played a leading role in establishing the PROTESTANT religion in Germany and in asserting German princely independence against Emperor CHARLES V. After becoming converted to LUTHER's doctrines (1524), Philip turned Hesse into a Protestant state. He was active at the Diet of Speyer (1529), a subscriber to the AUGSBURG Confession (1530), and became a founder and leader of the Schmalkaldic League, an alliance of Protestant princes and cities (1531). He forfeited the loyalty of some of his followers by marrying bigamously (1540) and after his defeat in the SCHMALKALDIC WAR he was imprisoned by Charles V. He lived to see Lutherans achieve equality with Catholics under the Peace of AUGSBURG (1555).

Philippi, Battle of (42 BC) A battle fought at Philippi, a city in Macedonia in northern Greece, in which CAESAR's assassins under BRUTUS were defeated by the armies of MARK ANTONY and Octavian (AUGUSTUS). Both Cassius and Brutus committed suicide after the defeat.

Philippines A country in south-east Asia comprising over 7,000 islands between the Pacific Ocean and the South China Sea.

Physical. Luzon and Mindanao are the largest islands; in the central Philippines, the islands of Leyte and Samar are linked by a 2,162 m (7,095 feet) long bridge. Lying at a junction of crustal plates, the islands contain volcanoes and are subject to earthquakes. Many of the islands are mountainous and heavily forested with teak, ebony, and sandalwood. Bamboo and coconut palms grow in profusion.

Economy. The economy of the Philippines is predominantly agricultural, but manufacturing industry such as textiles, chemicals, electric machinery, and food-processing is expanding. Mineral resources include coal, nickel ore, copper, chromite, iron, silver, and gold. There is widespread poverty, and land reform is an important issue.

History. The original Negrito inhabitants of the Philippines were largely displaced by waves of Malay peoples migrating from Yunnan province in south-west China after *c.* 2000 BC. By 1000 AD the islands were within the south-east Asian trade network. By the 16th century Islam was advancing from Mindanao and Sulu into the central islands and Luzon. After Spaniards under MAGELLAN visited the islands in 1521, Spanish seamen discovered how to return eastbound across the Pacific to Mexico. In 1543 they named the islands after Prince Philip (later PHILIP II of Spain). In 1564 Miguel de Legazpi, with 380 men, set out from Mexico to establish a settlement, Christianize the Filipinos, open up commerce with East Asia, and secure a share of trade in the MOLUCCAS. A settlement was made in 1565 at Cebu in the western Visayas, but the Spaniards moved their headquarters to Manila in 1571. Manila became the centre for a trade in Chinese silks with Mexico, in return for Mexican silver dollars. From there Spanish influence and control spread out through the Philippine island chain, assisted by missionary activity. Christian outposts founded by Dominicans, Franciscans, and Augustinians grew into towns. Revolts against the harsh treatment of Filipinos by the Spanish were frequent, particularly in the 17th century. During the SEVEN YEARS WAR the British occupied Manila for two years.

In 1896, a nationalist uprising against the Spanish colonial authorities broke out in Manila, led by José RIZAL. After the outbreak of the SPANISH–AMERICAN WAR in 1898, General Emilio AGUINALDO, acting with the support of the USA, declared the country's independence. After Spain's defeat, however, the nationalists found themselves opposed by the USA, and after a brief war (1899–1901), the islands came under US control. Internal self-government was granted in 1935, and, after the Japanese occupation during World War II, the Philippines became an independent republic in 1946 under the Presidency of Manuel Roxas, with the USA continuing to maintain military bases. Successive administrations proved incapable of dealing with severe economic problems and regional unrest. In 1972 President MARCOS declared martial law and assumed dictatorial powers, using as justification civil unrest, in particular the communist guerrilla insurgency conducted by the New People's Army in Luzon and the violent campaigns of the Muslim separatist group, the Moro National Liberation Front, in the southern Philippines. While the Marcos regime achieved some success in dealing with both economic problems and guerrilla activities, the return to democratic government was never satisfactorily achieved and corruption was widespread, epitomized in the amassing of huge personal fortunes by the Marcos family. After the murder of the opposition leader, Benigno Aquino Jr, in 1983, his widow Corazon Aquino and the United Nationalist Democratic Organization became the focus for resistance to the Marcos regime. US support for the Marcos government waned and in 1986, after a disputed election and a popularly backed military revolt, Marcos fled, and Corazon Aquino became President in his place, restoring the country to a fragile democracy. When she came into office it was estimated that 70% of the population of the Philippines remained below the poverty line and the eruption of Mount Pinatubo in 1991 caused immense damage. There were six attempted military coups against President Aquino, who refused to stand for re-election. She was succeeded in 1992 by her ex-Defence Secretary Fidel Ramos, who completed arrangements for the withdrawal of US forces from Subic Bay and other military installations. In 1994 Ramos announced a coalition with the main opposition party, in order to facilitate passage of a common legislative programme, and in 1996 a peace agreement was concluded with Muslim rebels on the island of Mindanao.

CAPITAL:	Manila
AREA:	300,000 sq km (115,800 sq miles)
POPULATION:	71.750 million (1996)
CURRENCY:	1 Philippine peso = 100 centavos
RELIGIONS:	Roman Catholic 84.1%; Aglipayan Philippine Independent Church 6.2%; Muslim 4.3%; Protestant 3.9%
ETHNIC GROUPS:	Tagalog 29.7%; Cebuano 24.2%; Ilocano 10.3%; Hiligaynon Ilongo 9.2%; Bicol 5.6%; Samar-Leyte 4.0%; Pampango 2.8%; Pangasinan 1.8%
LANGUAGES:	English, Pilipino (based on Tagalog) (both official); Cebuano; Ilocano; local languages
INTERNATIONAL ORGANIZATIONS:	UN; Colombo Plan

Philippines Campaign (1944–45) The US campaigns that recaptured the Philippines in World War II. In the Battle of the Philippine Sea, fought in June 1944 by aircraft carriers while US forces were securing required bases in the Marianas, the Japanese naval air service suffered crippling losses. A further Japanese naval defeat was incurred at LEYTE GULF on 25 October, following the landing of US forces on the island five days previously. Troops landed on Luzon in January 1945 and in July General MACARTHUR announced that the whole territory was liberated. However, detached groups of Japanese, in accordance with their instructions to fight to the last man, were still at large after the war ended.

Philip the Bold (1342–1404) Duke of Burgundy (1363–1404). He was the fourth son of John the Good, King of France, and was created Duke of Burgundy in 1363. In 1369 he married Margaret, heiress of the Count of Flanders. In 1380 he helped to quell a revolt by the Flemish burghers against the count, which ended in 1382 with the massacre of 26,000 Flemings. On the death of the count in 1384 Philip inherited Flanders and proceeded to encourage commerce and the arts. During the minority of Charles VI (1380–88) Philip was virtual ruler of France and, when the king became insane (1392), Philip fought for power with Louis d'Orléans, the king's brother, a quarrel carried on after Philip's death by his son, John the Fearless.

Philip the Good (Philip III) (1396–1467), Duke of Burgundy (1419–67). His first act as Duke of Burgundy was to forge an alliance with HENRY V of England, signing the Treaty of Troyes, in which Queen Isabella of France named Henry V as successor to the French throne. Philip was a powerful ally: by the early decades of the 15th century his territories included Namur (acquired 1421), Holland and Zeeland (1428), Brabant (1430), Luxembourg (1435) and the bishoprics of Liège, Cambrai, and Utrecht were under Burgundian control. Some were by inheritance, others had come through marriage, purchase, or conquest and they combined to constitute a formidable 'state'. The Treaty of Arras (1435) released Philip from the duty of doing homage to the French king and rendered him virtually independent of royal control. However, the king of France succeeded in breaking the alliance between France and England and from 1435 France and Burgundy joined forces to wage war on England. The imposition of taxes on the Burgundians provoked a rebellion, led by Ghent, but the rebels (of whom 20,000 were killed) were defeated (1454). Philip's court in Burgundy was the most prosperous and civilized in Europe. He founded an order of CHIVALRY, the Order of the Golden Fleece, and patronized Flemish painters.

Philistines A non-Semitic people, originally a group of the SEA PEOPLES, who settled in southern PALESTINE in the 12th century BC. They established the five cities of Ashdod, Askelon, Ekron, Gath, and Gaza. They gained control of land and sea routes and proved a formidable enemy to the Israelites, inflicting defeats on Samson and SAUL. King DAVID, however, gained decisive revenge and from then on Philistine power declined until they were assimilated with the CANAANITES.

Phoenicians Semitic-speaking people descended from the CANAANITES of the 2nd millennium BC. By 3000 BC they had founded a number of cities on the Levant (eastern Mediterranean) coast, most notably Byblos, Sidon, and Tyre (now in southern Lebanon). By 1000 BC they had invented a system of writing that was the ancestor of the modern alphabet. As they had only a narrow, though fertile, hinterland, they turned to the sea and became the greatest traders of the age, penetrating as far afield as southern Spain and possibly even circumnavigating Africa as early as 600 BC. Phoenician trade and industries included linen, metal, glass, wood, ivory, and precious stones. By 900 BC they were well known in the West, where they established many small trading posts, including the most important, CARTHAGE, which developed into a major city. Conflict with Assyria in the 6th century BC weakened the power of the cities of Phoenicia and they subsequently came under the influence of the BABYLONIANS, the ACHAEMENIDS, ALEXANDER THE GREAT, the SELEUCIDS, and ROME.

Phoenix Park murders (1882) The assassination in Phoenix Park, Dublin, of the British Chief Secretary for Ireland, Lord Frederick Cavendish, and his Under-Secretary, T. H. Burke, by the 'Invincibles', a terrorist splinter group of the FENIANS. In the subsequent climate of revulsion against terrorism, PARNELL was able to gain ascendancy over the Irish National League and strengthen the moderate HOME RULE Party.

Photius (c. 810–c. 893) Patriarch of Constantinople and defender of the independence of the Byzantine Church against the papacy. He was elected in 858 to replace the deposed Patriarch Ignatius, but the papacy refused to recognize him, so he excommunicated the pope. Ignatius was later reinstated and Photius was restored in 886 by Emperor Leo VI. This time Pope John VIII, who urgently needed Byzantine naval assistance against the Moors, recognized him as Patriarch. The dispute, known as the Photian Schism, was also concerned with the presence of Latin missionaries in Bulgaria and doctrinal matters, especially the addition by Rome of a clause meaning 'and from the Son' (filioque) to the Nicene Creed.

Phrygia The territory in north-west Asia Minor occupied by the Phrygians from Europe from about 1200 BC. They clashed with the Assyrians in about 1100 BC and again in the late 8th century BC. They were conquered by the invading Cimmerians from southern Russia in the early 7th century and soon after fell under the sway of Lydia, and subsequently Persia, the Seleucids, and Pergamum. Most of Phrygia was incorporated into the Roman province of Asia in 116 BC, while the eastern sector became part of Roman GALATIA in 25 BC.

Pibul Songgram (1897–1964) Thai statesman. A career soldier, he took part in the bloodless coup which ended absolute rule by the Chakri dynasty in 1932. Emerging as the leader of militarist nationalist forces, he became head of state in 1938 and in January 1942 brought Thailand into World War II on the Japanese side. Overthrown in 1944, he returned to power in 1948 and controlled Thailand dictatorially until 1957, taking an anti-communist line, until overthrown after the corruption of his regime had aroused widespread resentment.

Picts (from Latin *Picti*, 'painted people') The people who lived beyond HADRIAN'S WALL and threatened Britain in the 4th and 5th centuries. A serious invasion took place in 367 AD. Traditionally there were northern and southern Picts. The northern Picts were invaded by SCOTS from Ireland, the southern Picts by the ANGLES. As a result distinct Highland and Lowland cultures developed in Scotland. KENNETH I (MacAlpine) united them into Scotland.

Piedmont A region of Italy centred around Turin, ruled by the dukes of Savoy, who in 1720 became kings of Sardinia. Following the Congress of VIENNA in 1815 Victor Emanuel I returned to Turin from Sardinia. From 1831 under King Charles-Albert, Piedmont became the centre of the movement for Italian unification. Parts of Savoy were forfeited to France in 1860, but in 1861 VICTOR EMANUEL II was proclaimed king of a united Italy.

Pierce, Franklin (1804–69) 14th President of the USA (1853–57). He gained the Democratic presidential nomination in 1852 as a compromise candidate at a time of bitter party divisions. In office, Pierce supported an expansionist foreign policy and was generally under the influence of the southern wing of the Democratic Party. His support for the KANSAS–NEBRASKA ACT lost him the support of northern Democrats and any chance of renomination in 1856.

Pilate, Pontius (*fl.* 1st century AD) The Roman governor of Judaea (26–36 AD) who presided at the trial of JESUS CHRIST. He sentenced Jesus to death by CRUCIFIXION, the standard punishment for non-Romans found guilty of sedition, and his part in the trial is mentioned by TACITUS and in the New Testament of the BIBLE. Depicted in the Gospels as wanting to release Jesus, Pilate, before handing him over to the high priests, attempted to evade responsibility for his death by washing his hands in a symbolic gesture in front of the crowd who demanded his crucifixion. Little is known about Pilate's life although Jewish writers recorded that he was corrupt and insensitive to Jewish customs.

pilgrimage A journey, usually lengthy, to visit a religious shrine or site and undertaken as an act of religious devotion or penance.

Most religions have pilgrimage sites, such as sacred rivers, shrines, or buildings, which have traditional religious significance. Christian pilgrimage was initially made to sites connected with the life of JESUS CHRIST in Palestine (principally Jerusalem, also a sacred site for Jews and Muslims), and Muslim obstruction of this custom helped to provoke the CRUSADES. In the Middle Ages, Christians had a deep reverence for sites connected with particular saints such as Rome (St PETER and St PAUL), Compostela in northern Spain (St James), and Canterbury (associated with Thomas à BECKET after his murder). Most pilgrims travelled in groups, like Chaucer's pilgrims in *The Canterbury Tales*, staying in hostels (known as hospices and usually run by monks) along the main pilgrimage routes. Protestants condemned pilgrimage both theologically and for its commercial debasement.

Pilgrimage to the KAABA at MECCA, well established in pagan Arabia, was incorporated into ISLAM, the detailed rites being based on MUHAMMAD's own practice. Every Muslim tries to undertake the pilgrimage (*hajj* in

Arabic) to Mecca at least once in a lifetime. The *hajj,* undertaken only in the twelfth month of the Muslim calendar, became highly organized, with special caravans and guides. The cities of Karbala and Najaf in Iraq are sacred to Shiite MUSLIMS.

In India, pilgrimage was often linked to HINDU festivals and associated with rivers, such as the Ganges, or sacred cities, like VARANASI (Benares). The Golden Temple at Amritsar in the Punjab is a pilgrimage site for Sikhs. In China and Japan mountains, such as Mount Tai and Mount Fujiyama were early favoured as sites for BUDDHIST pilgrimage. Mendicants and scholars often adopted pilgrimage as a permanent way of life.

Pilgrimage of Grace (1536–37) A series of rebellions in the northern English counties, the most significant of which was led by Robert Aske, a lawyer. He managed, briefly, to weld together the disparate grievances of his socially diverse followers. The main causes of concern were the religious policies of Thomas CROMWELL, notably the Dissolution of the MONASTERIES, although the rebels stressed their loyalty to HENRY VIII, and accepted his promises of pardon before dispersing. Severe retribution followed, as Henry authorized the execution of about 200 of those involved, including Aske.

Pilgrim Fathers The 102 founders of the Plymouth plantation in America who sailed from Plymouth in England in the *Mayflower* in 1620. They were originally called the Old Comers, then the Forefathers, and became known as the Pilgrim Fathers in the 19th century. Some of them had been persecuted as separatists from the Church of England and the nucleus of the group had fled from Scrooby in Nottinghamshire in 1608 to Holland. In 1618 they obtained backing from a syndicate of London merchants and permission to settle in Virginia. On the voyage, having no charter, they subscribed to a covenant for self-government, the Mayflower Compact. They made landfall at Cape Cod, Massachusetts in December and decided to settle there. Only half the party survived the first winter. William BRADFORD wrote a vivid account of their experiences. Fur trading with the Native Americans provided them with a lucrative export, but the plantation grew slowly and was overshadowed by the huge Puritan influx into Massachusetts in the 1630s. In 1643 it joined the NEW ENGLAND Confederation and in 1691 it was incorporated into Massachusetts. The Pilgrim Fathers played a relatively insignificant role in New England history, but as the region's first permanent settlers they are of symbolic importance in the European colonization of North America.

pillory and stocks Devices for punishing wrongdoers, usually located in a prominent place, such as a village green, comprising a wooden frame with holes to secure the head and hands or feet of an offender, who would be exposed to public ridicule. They were used by local communities in the Middle Ages to punish minor offenders convicted in the manor or town court. Even in the time of the STAR CHAMBER (abolished 1641), a court could earn itself a bad name by sentencing someone to stand in the pillory for what might be thought a political offence. The pillory was abolished in 1837.

Pilsudski, Joseph Klemens (1867–1935) Polish general and statesman. His involvement in early revolutionary activity against Tsarist Russia had led to his imprisonment. In World War I he raised three Polish legions to fight Russia, but German refusal to guarantee the ultimate independence of Poland led him to withdraw his support of Germany. After the war, Poland was declared independent with Pilsudski as Chief of State (1918–22) and Chief of the Army Staff (1918–27). He successfully commanded the Poles in the war against the BOLSHEVIKS (1920–21). In 1926, after a military revolt, he assumed the office of Minister of Defence, establishing a virtual dictatorship, and tried to guarantee Poland's independence by signing non-aggression pacts with Germany and the Soviet Union in 1934. He died in office.

Piltdown Man (*Eoanthropus dawsoni*) The supposed fossil remains 'discovered' by Charles Dawson in 1908–13 in gravels in Sussex, England. The association of a modern-looking skull, ape-like jaw, and extinct animal bones appeared to provide exactly the missing link in human evolution that was being keenly sought at the time. It was not until 1953 that the remains were shown by scientific tests to be a forgery, comprising a modern human skull, the jaw of an ape, modern flint tools, and some ancient animal bones that were not from Britain. It has been suggested that a disgruntled museum assistant was responsible for the fraud.

Pinckney, Charles Cotesworth (1746–1825) US statesman. He was appointed minister to France in 1796 and a year later participated in the unsuccessful diplomatic peace mission to avert a naval war with France, known as the XYZ AFFAIR. Pinckney ran with John ADAMS for the FEDERALIST PARTY and was the unsuccessful Federalist candidate for President in 1804 and 1808. His brother Thomas (1750–1828) was also a diplomat and was responsible for negotiating the Treaty of San Lorenzo (popularly known as Pinckney's Treaty) with Spain in 1795, winning US trading rights at New Orleans, free navigation of the Mississippi River, and an agreed southern boundary between the USA and Florida.

Pindaris Groups of mounted marauders in central India, often in the service of the MARATHA princes, who raided MOGUL territory from the 17th century. The Pindaris were not paid but were allowed to forage and plunder freely. After 1807 they extended their depredations to British India, and under Lord Hastings (governor-general 1813–23) a major campaign (MARATHA WARS) was conducted (1817–18) to wipe out the Pindaris. A campaign led by Hastings and involving three British and Indian armies advanced into central India and successfully encircled and defeated some 30,000 Pindaris. Their extirpation confirmed British paramountcy in India.

Pinkerton, Allan (1819–84) Scottish-born US detective. He joined the Chicago police force in 1850 and later that year opened a private detective agency. During the AMERICAN CIVIL WAR, he organized an intelligence network behind the lines of the CONFEDERACY, which was one of the forerunners of the US secret service. The Pinkerton detective agency itself continued to flourish, despite gaining a reputation as a force of strikebreakers (see MOLLY MAGUIRES) in the late 19th century.

Pinkie, Battle of (10 September 1547) Military engagement between the Scots and English, sometimes known as Pinkie Cleuch, which was fought to the east of Edinburgh, Scotland. A large but poorly equipped

Scottish army was defeated by an English expeditionary force under the Duke of SOMERSET, but the expedition failed in its purpose of engineering a marriage between MARY, QUEEN OF SCOTS and EDWARD VI of England and only drove the Scots closer towards alliance with France.

Pinochet, Augusto (1915–) Chilean statesman. Bitterly opposed to the left-wing policies of President ALLENDE, he masterminded a military coup with help from the US Central Intelligence Agency (CIA). Allende was killed (September 1973) in the revolt and Pinochet became President of the Council of Chile (a junta of military officers), which imposed a harsh military rule for three years. During this period, some 130,000 people were arrested and tortured, while thousands were never seen again. Proclaimed President of Chile in 1974, he held plebiscites in 1978 and 1980 to confirm this office. Under a new constitution of 1980 he was proclaimed President again but from 1982 the economy began to collapse and he resigned the presidency in 1990. Despite Chile's adoption of democracy, Pinochet remained commander-in-chief of the army until 1998, when he stepped down and was made a senator for life (thus becoming immune from prosecution for the political murders and other crimes committed during his Presidency).

pipe-roll The financial account presented to the Exchequer by the sheriffs of England. The earliest surviving roll dates from 1130 and there is an almost unbroken series from 1156 to 1832. The rolls were compiled by the clerks of the treasury and included details of rents, leases, and other royal revenues. Their name originated with the practice of enrolling the records on a rod, or 'pipe'.

Piraeus The chief port of Greece, located south-west of Athens. It superseded Phaleron as the harbour of Athens when THEMISTOCLES had it fortified probably in 483–481 BC to protect the large fleet of TRIREMES, which he had just had built. In 461–456 it was joined to Athens by the Long Walls, making a total circuit of 25.7 km (16 miles) and thereafter became the power base and trading centre of the ATHENIAN EMPIRE. It was destroyed in 86 BC when SULLA's troops laid siege to those of MITHRIDATES VI there and was not revived as a port until the 19th century.

pirate A sea robber, operating wherever there is unprotected merchant shipping to attack. Pirates are often described in classical literature and during the Dark Ages the VIKINGS committed piracy throughout European waters. The creation of the Spanish and Portuguese seaborne empires in the 15th and 16th centuries provided irresistible temptations. To Spain heroes like DRAKE or GILBERT were simply pirates, forerunners of 17th-century BUCCANEERS like Blackbeard Teach, MORGAN, and KIDD, who terrorized the Caribbean and India Ocean from their bases in Jamaica, the Bahamas, and Madagascar. As England's international trade grew, its merchantmen became prey to French pirates from Dunkirk, Barbary CORSAIRS in the eastern Mediterranean or African Atlantic Coast, marauding from Algiers, Oran, Tunis, or Salli, and Far-Eastern sea-raiders in the China seas. Piracy generally declined by the middle of the 18th century, though occasional incidents are still reported.

Pisistratus (or Peisistratus) (*c.* 600–527 BC) Tyrant (unconstitutional ruler) of ATHENS from 561 BC. Twice he was forced out of the city, but in 546, with the help of mercenaries, he re-established his tyranny, which he maintained until his death in 527. His rule was generally benevolent. He was conciliatory towards the nobles, yet improved the lot of the poor by encouraging agriculture (thus providing jobs for labourers) and instituting travelling judges. Under him and his sons, Athens thrived in both economic and cultural terms.

Pitt, William (Pitt the Younger) (1759–1806) British Prime Minister (1783–1801, 1804–06), second son of PITT THE ELDER. He became Chancellor of the Exchequer at the age of 23. His refusal to betray Lord SHELBURNE began his long rivalry with FOX, and on the overthrow of the Fox–North coalition in 1783, Pitt became Prime Minister. During the years of peace until 1793 Pitt was nurturing Britain's economic recovery from the American War of INDEPENDENCE, and he showed his brilliance in his handling of finance. From 1793 he symbolized Britain's resistance to the French Revolution and Napoleon, but although he raised three European coalitions and gave subsidies to Britain's allies, he did not fight to restore the French monarchy, only to defend Britain. The French Revolution encouraged rebellion and religious feuding in Ireland, which Pitt believed would only be quelled by political union of Britain and Ireland. When George III refused to consider CATHOLIC EMANCIPATION in exchange for Pitt's ACT OF UNION, he resigned in 1801. Pitt's sympathy with reform evaporated with the war; he suppressed British radicalism as readily as he suppressed Irish revolution. His second term of office was less spectacular, despite NELSON's victory at TRAFALGAR, which ended the threat of French invasion. Although he called himself an independent Whig, his followers, after his early death, were to form the nucleus of the emerging Tory party.

Pitt, William, 1st Earl of Chatham (Pitt the Elder) (1708–78) British Prime Minister (1756–61, 1766–68). Pitt was a brilliant orator and parliamentarian. As a Whig opponent of WALPOLE he earned the mistrust of GEORGE II, but Henry PELHAM and the Duke of NEWCASTLE forced the king to give Pitt a ministerial post in 1746. On Pelham's death he quarrelled with the Duke of Newcastle, but the national emergency of the SEVEN YEARS WAR drew them together in a coalition in 1757. For four years Pitt conducted the war, demonstrating mastery in worldwide strategy and the effective use of sea-power. While public opinion hailed him as a hero, his domineering and aloof nature exasperated his colleagues. By the end of the war Britain was victorious everywhere, but Pitt had already resigned following disagreements with his ministers over war with Spain. In 1764 and 1765 he was twice approached by GEORGE III to form a ministry but declined. His ministry of 1766–68 was severely hampered by his increasing withdrawal from public affairs because of illness. This ill health dogged him in his later years. As an elder statesman he sympathized with the grievances of the Americans, but could not reconcile himself to independence for the colonies, as he showed in his last speech.

Pius II (Aeneas Silvius Piccolomini, 1405–64) Pope (1458–64). Born of an impoverished noble family, Pius II led a dissolute life as a poet but reformed, took holy orders in 1446, and became an outstanding HUMANIST. He became secretary to Felix V, the ANTIPOPE, from 1439, and an ecclesiastical diplomat, to be employed by Emperor FREDERICK III as secretary and poet laureate. As pope he proclaimed a CRUSADE against the OTTOMAN Turks (October 1458) but a congress of Christian rulers summoned to Mantua in 1459 was a failure and despite repeated attempts to launch a Crusade the enterprise came to nothing. He had to face anti-papal movements in France and Germany and frequent quarrels with local rulers prevented him from carrying out his programme of reform. He died, bequeathing the problem of the HUSSITE heresy and Turkish war to his successor.

Pius V, St (Antonio Ghislieri, 1504–72) Pope (1566–72). Pius V was an austere Dominican, Bishop of Nepi and Sutri (1556), cardinal (1557), and Grand Inquisitor from 1558. As pope, he laboured to restore discipline and morality with a sometimes intransigent COUNTER-REFORMATION zeal. His ill-timed Bull calling for the deposition of ELIZABETH I of England (1570) proved ineffectual, but he had more success in helping to organize the HOLY LEAGUE, whose forces defeated the Turks at LEPANTO (1571). He was canonized in 1712.

Pius VII (Luigi Barnaba Chiaramonti, 1740–1823) Pope (1800–23). His predecessor, Pope Pius VI, had seen the Papal States occupied by the French and died a prisoner in France in 1799. Pius VII restored papal fortunes by signing a CONCORDAT with Napoleon I in 1801, which re-established the Roman Catholic faith as the national religion of France. However, his attempts to increase papal influence by refusing to support the CONTINENTAL SYSTEM against Britain led to the annexation of the Papal States in 1808–09. He, too, was imprisoned by Napoleon in France, but returned in triumph after Napoleon's downfall. He renounced his earlier liberalism, condemned revolution and secret societies, and re-established the Society of Jesus (Jesuits) in 1814.

Pius IX (Giovanni Maria Mastai-Ferretti, 1792–1878) Pope (1846–78). Elected as a moderate progressive, he relaxed press censorship, freed political prisoners, set up a council of ministers which included laymen, and opened negotiations for an Italian customs union. After the REVOLUTIONS OF 1848 his Prime Minister was murdered and Pius himself fled in disguise. On the establishment of a Roman republic Pius appealed to the French to come to his aid, and, with their help, he re-entered Rome, which retained a French garrison until 1870. In that year Italian forces occupied Rome, which was then incorporated into the kingdom of Italy. Despite government assurances, Pius saw himself as a prisoner in a secular state, and never set foot outside the Vatican again. In 1854 he defined the doctrine of the Immaculate Conception of the Virgin Mary (the Mother of Jesus Christ) and encouraged the Marian cult. He presided over the First Vatican Council (1869–70), which proclaimed the infallibility of the Pope when speaking *ex cathedra*.

Pius XII (Eugenio Maria Giuseppe Giovanni Pacelli, 1876–1958) Pope (1939–58). As Secretary of State for Pius XI he negotiated a CONCORDAT (1933) with Nazi Germany. HITLER's repeated violations of the Concordat provoked Pius to issue the encyclical, *Mit brennender Sorge* (1937), branding Nazism as fundamentally anti-Christian. As pope he remained politically impartial between the Allied and the AXIS POWERS in World War II. He

supervised a programme for the relief of war victims through the Pontifical Aid Commission and made the VATICAN CITY an asylum for refugees. While unwilling to speak out in public against Nazi atrocities, he gave assistance to numbers of individual Jews. Politically he inveighed against communism, threatening (1949, 1950) its supporters with excommunication, and concluded accords advantageous to the Roman Catholic Church with Portugal (1950) and Spain (1955).

Pizarro, Francisco (c. 1475–1541) Spanish explorer and conquistador. He began his career as an explorer when he joined Vasco Núñez de BALBOA's expedition across Panama, which discovered the Pacific Ocean in 1513. He led his own expeditions in 1524–25 and 1526–27 to explore the Colombian, Ecuadorian, and Peruvian coasts. In 1532 he marched against the INCA empire. At Cajamarca he met the emperor, ATAHUALPA, imprisoned him, demanded a vast ransom, and then had him murdered upon learning of the Inca army marching to his rescue. In the march on CUZCO, the Inca capital, battles were fought at Jauja, Vilcashuamáno, Vilcaconga, and Cuzco itself, which fell in 1533. Another contingent, under his half-brother Hernando Pizarro (c. 1501–78), marched on Pachácamac. Thereafter, he consolidated his position by founding new settlements including Lima, and dividing the spoils of conquest among his supporters. A partner on his earlier expeditions, Diego de Almagro (c. 1475–1538) felt cheated of his share and in 1537 he seized Cuzco and imprisoned Hernando Pizarro, its governor. In 1538 Hernando escaped, defeating Almagro and executing him on the orders of Francisco. Almagro's son took revenge three years later by assassinating Francisco in Lima.

Pizarro, Gonzalo (c. 1506–48) Spanish conquistador and brother of Francisco PIZARRO. He assisted his brother in the conquest of the INCAS and defended CUZCO against the attacks of Manco Capac (1536–37). In 1538 he was appointed governor of Quito. The first viceroy of Peru, Blasco Núñez Vela, proclaimed the New Laws in 1542, drafted by LAS CASAS, to protect Indian rights. Gonzalo became leader of conquistadores opposed to the New Laws and in the ensuing civil war defeated and executed the viceroy in 1546. He was offered a royal pardon by the new viceroy, but rejected it, and was beheaded in 1548 after his army had deserted him.

PKI (after 1924, Partai Kommunis Indonesia) Indonesian Communist Party. Formed in 1920, the PKI was active in trade-union activities, but Dutch repression and the abortive communist uprisings in Banten and West Sumatra in 1926–27 led to its eclipse until 1945. During the 1950s, the PKI became one of the largest communist parties outside China and the Soviet Union, winning 20% of the vote in the 1955 general elections. Rivalry with the army and communist-inspired actions against Muslim landlords in Java provoked the military to move against it after the abortive left-wing coup attempt of 1965. Up to one million PKI members were killed and the party was all but wiped out.

Place, Francis (1771–1854) British radical reformer. In 1799 he opened a tailoring shop in London which became a meeting place for leading radicals. In 1814 he began his campaign for the repeal of the anti-trade-union COMBINATION ACTS, which were eventually abolished in 1824. Place later took a prominent part in the agitation leading to the 1832 REFORM ACT and also helped draft the People's Charter of 1838 (see CHARTISM).

plague A number of epidemic diseases, in particular the infectious bubonic plague caused by bacteria in fleas carried by rodents. The plague which struck Athens in 430 BC, causing the death of the great statesman PERICLES and about a third of the population, cannot now be precisely identified. THUCYDIDES, who caught the plague but recovered from it, described in vivid detail the despair, anguish, and lawlessness it caused.

Plague that had originated in Central Asia devastated the Roman world in the 3rd century, causing hundreds of deaths daily, and again in the time of Justinian (mid-6th century). The plague known as the BLACK DEATH swept through Europe during 1346–50: England may have lost as much as half its population, with severe long-term consequences. In 1665 London was afflicted by the GREAT PLAGUE, which carried off at least 70,000 victims. The following year, the FIRE OF LONDON destroyed in large part the insanitary slums that had made London a fertile breeding-ground for the disease.

Plaid Cymru A political party devoted to the cause of Welsh nationalism. Founded in 1925 as Plaid Genedlaethol Cymru (Welsh Nationalist Party), it seeks to ensure independent recognition for WALES in matters relating to its culture, language, and economy. It became active in the 1960s and 1970s, but its hope that Wales would be able to have a separate representative assembly was rejected by a referendum in Wales in 1979. In 1997, following a vigorous campaign by the new Labour government and Plaid Cymru, a referendum in Wales approved by less than 1% a separate Welsh assembly, without tax-raising powers. Plaid Cymru has not succeeded in wooing the majority of Welsh electors, particularly in the towns, from their support of the major British parties.

Plains Peoples The original inhabitants of the Plains region of North America. Traditionally, there were two main groups, sedentary farmers and nomadic hunters. The introduction of the horse in the early 18th century had a profound effect, with many peoples, such as the Sioux and the CREE, moving into the Plains area. These equestrian nomads became adept buffalo hunters. During the winter months, the tribes split into small groups. In many tribes, like the IROQUOIS, women had a high status. Among men rank was not inherited but had to be achieved through warfare, as well as through generosity towards widows and orphans. The title of chief was largely a matter of prestige, as authority was exercised by the consensus of those of high status, who would act as arbiters in dispute resolution.

Plains of Abraham, Battle of the (13 September 1759) A battle during the FRENCH AND INDIAN WARS that took place on a plateau above the city of QUEBEC, Canada. WOLFE ferried British troops up the St Lawrence past the French fort. Having tricked the sentries into believing them to be French, the British climbed the precipitous Heights of Abraham. In the ensuing battle, the French garrison under MONTCALM was routed and Quebec surrendered. Both commanders died but the British victory ended French rule in Canada.

Plantagenet The English dynasty, descended from the counts of Anjou in France, who were the rulers of England from 1154 to 1485, when the TUDOR line began. The unusual name possibly arose from the sprig of broom plant, *Genista*, which Geoffrey, Count of Anjou (1113–51), wore on the side of his cap. It was Geoffrey's son Henry who became HENRY II (ruled 1154–89) of England and established the Plantagenet dynasty, although it is customary to refer to the first three monarchs Henry II, RICHARD I (ruled 1189–99), and JOHN (ruled 1199–1216), as Angevins (descendants of the House of Anjou). The line was unbroken until 1399 when RICHARD II was deposed and died without an heir. The throne was claimed by Henry Bolingbroke, Earl of Lancaster, Richard's cousin and the son of John of GAUNT (Edward III's third son). In becoming king as HENRY IV he established the LANCASTRIAN branch of the dynasty which was continued by HENRY V (ruled 1413–22) and HENRY VI (ruled 1422–61, 1470–71).

The second branch of the family, the House of YORK, claimed the throne through Anne Mortimer, the great-granddaughter of Lionel (Edward III's second son), who had married the father of Richard, Duke of York. The Yorkist claim succeeded when Edward, Richard's son, became EDWARD IV (1461–70, 1471–83) and was in turn followed by EDWARD V (ruled 1483) and Richard III (ruled 1483–85). In contending for the crown the Houses of Lancaster and York and their supporters resorted to civil war, known romantically as the Wars of the Roses (1455–83), and to murder (of Henry VI, the Duke of Clarence, and Edward V). The Plantagenet line was ousted by HENRY VII.

plantation A farming unit for the production of one of the staple crops in the southern colonies of North America and the British West Indies. Plantation farming may also refer to any tropical crops grown elsewhere, such as rubber, beverage crops, sisal, and oil palm. In North America plantation farming became widespread due to the success of tobacco production after 1614 along with the Virginia Company's emigration inducements of 20 ha (50 acre) 'headright' land grants to each passage-paying settler and grants of private estates ('particular plantations') for investors and company officers. Between 1640 and 1660 Royalists emigrated to the Chesapeake and the Caribbean to grow tobacco and sugar. The Virginia Company's landholders and the Royalists formed the dominant colonial plantation aristocracy. The pattern was copied in South Carolina where rice and indigo were raised. Small profit margins after 1600, credit-worthiness in Britain, access to navigable rivers, and influence with colonial land officers ensured that a tightly knit group of families monopolized staple production. With the increased availability of slaves, after 1650 in the Caribbean and 1700 on the mainland, larger areas could be cultivated and, because tobacco was soil-exhaustive, planters acquired huge areas for future use. Robert 'King' Carter of Nomini Hall, Virginia, owned over 12,000 ha (30,000 acres) in 1732. Successful West Indian sugar planters often returned to England, leaving their estates in the hands of overseers. The larger plantations resembled small towns, with warehouses, smithies, boatyards, coopers' shops, wharves, schools, burial grounds, and slave quarters near the big house of the landowner. Following the abolition of slavery most plantations were divided into small farms but some continue to be worked by low-paid labourers.

Plassey, Battle of (23 June 1757) The village of Plassey in West Bengal, India, was the site of Robert CLIVE's victory over Nawab Siraj ud-Daula, which opened the way for the EAST INDIA COMPANY's acquisition of BENGAL. Clive had prepared Siraj's elimination by buying support from his enemies, notably by promising the nawabship to Mir Jafar, a rival. In the ensuing encounter, in which he was heavily outnumbered, Clive was aided both by good luck and by Mir Jafar's defection from Siraj. After the victory Mir Jafar was made nawab, with Clive as governor.

Plataea A city in southern BOEOTIA. It was helped by Athens in 519 BC to defend itself against Thebes. Hence it alone of the Greek states helped the Athenians against the Persians at the Battle of MARATHON (490), the Spartans arrived too late to take part in the battle. In 479 Plataea was the site of the crucial land-battle of the GREEK–PERSIAN WARS, when Mardonius was defeated. Its citizens were given refuge by Athens in 431 following a Theban attack, and a prolonged siege (429–427) led to the capture and the execution of the garrison who failed to escape.

Plate, Battle of the River (13 December 1939) A naval action between British and German forces in the South Atlantic. It was the first major naval surface engagement of World War II, in which the German battleship *Graf Spee*, which had sunk many cargo ships, was damaged by three British cruisers and forced into the harbour of Montevideo, from which she emerged only to be scuttled by her crew on Hitler's orders.

Plato (*c.* 429–347 BC) Greek philosopher, much influenced by SOCRATES. After the latter's death in 399, he travelled widely before returning to ATHENS in *c.* 387 and founding the ACADEMY. Here he spent the last 40 years of his life, devoting himself to teaching and writing. His *Dialogues* are the first unfragmentary body of Greek philosophical writing to have survived and they had a powerful influence on later philosophers, notably Plotinus (see NEOPLATONISTS). His *Apology* provided a re-creation of the unsuccessful defence which Socrates offered at his trial in 399 BC. The early *Dialogues*, for example *Gorgias* and *Protagoras*, examine the question of the essence of virtue (see ETHICS) and represent a serious questioning of current philosophical thought. These works adopted Socrates' renowned method of argument, whereby a protagonist's definition was demonstrated to be untrue by a series of questions and answers. In the later *Dialogues*, however, the figure of Socrates served more as a mouthpiece for Plato's developing ideas. Thus in the *Republic* he tackled the question of the perfect constitution, arguing that perfect unity would come not through democracy, but through the rule of the enlightened despot. In the *Laws* he rejected the excesses of ATHENIAN DEMOCRACY and argued that extremes of government were to be avoided.

In metaphysics, Plato's Theory of Forms, introduced in the *Phaedo*, postulated the existence of unchanging and eternal objects; each Form Plato regarded as the indivisible essence of a particular thing or concept.

Plato's teachings had a profound influence both on ARISTOTLE and on several Roman authors, notably CICERO, shaping the development of Christian theology and Western philosophy. His works were translated into Latin in the late 15th century and became central to RENAISSANCE scholarship and ideas.

Plato *Plato's philosophy is written in the form of dialogues featuring his mentor Socrates. It is not clear to what extent Plato accurately expressed Socrates' beliefs while using him as a literary device.*

Platt, Thomas Collier (1833–1910) US politician. He was a prominent member of the 'Stalwart' faction supporting the SPOILS SYSTEM. Platt was elected to Congress, serving in the US Senate in 1881, though he resigned shortly afterwards in protest at President GARFIELD's appointment of reform Republicans to federal posts. Again in the Senate (1897–1909), he was largely responsible for the election (1898) of Theodore ROOSEVELT as governor of New York. Threatened by the latter's drive against corrupt political practices, Platt attempted to suppress his initiative by securing him the vice-presidency (1901). Thereafter Platt's power declined.

plebs The common people of ancient Rome, including the poor and landless. In the early republic they were excluded from office and from intermarriage with PATRICIANS. The political history of the early republic reflects largely their increasingly organized claim for greater political participation, which was rewarded by the concession of eligibility for the consulship in 367 BC. During the 'Struggle of the Orders' in the 5th and 4th centuries BC the office of TRIBUNE became a watchdog over the activities of the traditional SENATE. Their vote in COMITIA was a 'plebiscite'.

Plekhanov, Georgi Valentinovich (1857–1918)
Russian revolutionary and Marxist theorist. He became a
leader of the POPULIST MOVEMENT, Land and Liberty, in
1877, but when this turned increasingly to terrorist
methods, he formed an anti-terrorist splinter group to
continue mass agitation. Exiled in Geneva, he became
one of the founders of the League for the Liberation of
Labour, the first Russian Marxist revolutionary
organization (1883), which merged (1898) with the
Russian Social Democratic Workers' Party. In the 1903
split with LENIN he supported the Mensheviks but
always tried to re-unite the party. He returned to Russia
in 1917, but failed to prevent the BOLSHEVIKS from seizing
power.

Pliny (Gaius Plinius Secundus) (23–79 AD) (Pliny the
Elder) Roman lawyer, historian, and naturalist. Of his
many works only the 37 volumes of his *Natural History*
survive, a valuable compendium of ancient scientific
knowledge blended with folklore and anecdote. He died
while leading a rescue (and research) party on the
stricken coastline near POMPEII, during the eruption of
Vesuvius.

Pliny (Gaius Plinius Caecilius Secundus) (61–112 AD) (Pliny
the Younger) Roman senator and consul, nephew of the
Elder Pliny. A close friend of TRAJAN and TACITUS, he
governed Bithynia (in present-day Turkey). His 'Letters',
which are really essays, give a detailed picture of the
lifestyle adopted by wealthy Romans of his class. Other
letters, written after 100, provide the only detailed
accounts of the eruption of Vesuvius in 79, in which his
uncle perished, and the devastation of Campania of
which he was a youthful eyewitness.

PLO PALESTINE LIBERATION ORGANIZATION.

Plotinus (205–c. 269) One of the first NEOPLATONIC
philosophers. He was apparently born in Egypt, though
his name was Roman and his mother tongue was Greek.
From 232 to 242 he studied in Alexandria, then attached
himself to an expedition against Persia in the hope of
learning more about Eastern thought. In 245 he went to
Rome, where he established himself as a teacher,
attracting a wide circle of adherents. At the age of 50 he
began to write the *Enneads*, which record the results of
his deeply felt and closely argued exposition of a
metaphysical, ascetic Platonism. Although he insisted
that everything he taught was to be found in PLATO's
writings, his philosophy was both original and
profoundly influential. The central idea was of the
Three Hypostases: the One, Intellect, and Soul. Although
the *Enneads* were not published until well after his
death (c. 300–305), they established him as the greatest
philosopher since ARISTOTLE and earned him the title of
founder of Neoplatonism.

'Plug' strikes (1842) A succession of strikes
accompanied by rioting in the north of England. The
agitation began as a protest by Staffordshire miners
against cuts in wages, but spread to industries in other
parts of the country. The men involved went from
factory to factory, removing the boiler plugs from
steam engines so that these could not be operated by
anyone else. There were also attempts to use the strike
as a weapon to compel the government to accept the
CHARTIST petition. Hundreds of strikers were arrested
and the ringleaders were transported to Australia.

Plutarch (c. 46–126 AD) Greek writer and philosopher of
wide-ranging interests. His extant works include
rhetorical pieces, philosophical treatises, and, most
memorably, his *Parallel Lives*, paired biographies of
famous Greeks and Romans. He was concerned to
highlight the personal virtues (and sometimes vices) of
his subjects and his work has been an inspiration to
later writers, most notably Shakespeare in his Roman
plays.

Plymouth Brethren A strict PROTESTANT group, so
called because of their early establishment in Plymouth,
England, by John Nelson Darby (1800–82) in 1831. The
Brethren underwent a major division in 1849, becoming
what are known as the 'Exclusive Brethren' and the
'Open Brethren', the latter being the less rigorous. They
advocate adult Baptism and reject clergy.

Plymouth Colony The first permanent NEW ENGLAND
settlement, on the south-eastern Massachusetts coast in
Cape Cod Bay. It was settled by the PILGRIM FATHERS in
1620 and grew slowly under the leadership of William
BRADFORD, profiting from the fur trade with the Native
Americans. Overshadowed after 1630 by MASSACHUSETTS, it
joined the New England Confederation in 1643. KING
PHILIP'S WAR (1675–76) began on its frontier. In 1691 it was
incorporated into Massachusetts.

poaching The unauthorized taking of game or fish
from private property or from a place where hunting,
shooting, or fishing are restricted. Poaching was pursued
by the poor in search of food and by the 18th century
poaching in the English royal forests was a well-
organized and profitable activity. Poachers who were
caught were harshly treated, particularly under the
terms of the Black Act of 1723. The criminal conviction
of poachers was bitterly resented since it was popularly
held that the ENCLOSURE Acts had denied access to
common land.

Pocahontas (c. 1595–1617) Native American 'princess',
the daughter of POWHATAN, Chief of the Native
Americans in the JAMESTOWN region of Virginia. She
befriended the colonists who arrived in 1607 and the
following year John SMITH claimed that she saved him
from torture and death after he had been captured by
her father. She was kidnapped by the British, who were
in conflict with her father. She was apparently treated
kindly and in 1614 she married John Rolfe; having
become a Christian and changed her name to Rebecca.
He took her to England where she was presented at
court, but she died of fever.

pocket borough A British Parliamentary borough
effectively under the control of a single wealthy
individual or family. Before the 1832 REFORM ACT there
was no uniform basis for the parliamentary franchise in
towns and the right to vote tended to be limited to a
small number of people. This made it easier for a local
magnate to ensure the election of any candidate he
chose to put forward. The borough was thus said to be
'in his pocket'. Such pressure on voters was not
effectively ended until the introduction of secret ballots
in 1872.

pogrom (Russian, 'riot' or 'devastation') A mob attack
approved or condoned by authority, frequently against
religious, racial, or national minorities, most often
against Jews. The first pogrom occurred in the Ukraine
following the assassination of ALEXANDER II (1881). After

that, there were many pogroms throughout Russia and Russian Jews began to emigrate to the USA and western Europe, giving their support to HERZL's ZIONIST campaign. After the revolution of 1905, ANTI-SEMITIC persecutions increased in force. Conducted on a large scale in Germany and eastern Europe after HITLER came to power they led ultimately to the HOLOCAUST.

Poincaré, Raymond (1860–1934) French statesman. As President (1913–20) he strove to keep France united during WORLD WAR I and in 1919 supported stringent REPARATIONS against Germany. When Germany defaulted, he ordered French troops to occupy the RUHR (1923) until Germany paid. He could not sustain this policy and resigned in 1924. Reappointed Premier in 1926, he lessened an acute economic crisis by introducing a deflationary policy, balancing the budget, and in 1928 he secured the franc at one-fifth of its former value.

Pocahontas   *The story of Pocahontas has become symbolic of goodwill between peoples and has inspired numerous works of fiction, including an animated Disney film. Many leading families in the Virginia region of the USA claim descent from her, through her son, Thomas Rolfe.*

Point Four Program A US aid project, so called because it developed from the fourth point of a programme set forth in President TRUMAN's 1949 inaugural address, in which he undertook to make 'the benefits of America's scientific and industrial progress available for the improvement and growth of under-

developed areas'. From 1950 Congress annually provided technical assistance for the long-term development of industries, agriculture, health and education in developing countries. The project also encouraged the flow of private investment capital to poorer nations. In 1953 it was merged with other foreign aid programmes.

Poitiers, Battle of (19 September 1356) A battle between the English and French during the HUNDRED YEARS WAR. An English and Gascon force under EDWARD THE BLACK PRINCE was trapped by a superior French army while raiding. The English archers defeated the French and their king, John II, was captured. The JACQUERIE revolt followed soon after.

Poland A country in north Europe with a Baltic Sea coast and bounded by Germany on the west, Russia, Lithuania, Belarus, and Ukraine on the east, and the Czech Republic and Slovakia on the south.

Physical. Poland is on the North European Plain, which is sandy in places, marshy in others and requires careful cultivation, although inland it is well drained by the Odra (Oder), Vistula, and other rivers. There are many small forests of spruce and fir, which increase in size as the land rises through rolling hills and richer land to the Carpathian Mountains in the south-east.

Economy. After the collapse of communism, Poland made the transition to a market economy; however, the economic problems this engendered include high inflation, a large budget deficit, and high foreign debt. In late 1989, an economic reform package, introduced to gain IMF support, reduced wages and removed price subsidies and the Polish stock exchange was opened. The majority of agricultural land is in private hands, wheat, rye, barley, oats, potatoes, and sugar beet being the main crops. Mineral resources include coal (from some of the largest bituminous and lignite coal fields in the world), copper, iron, silver, sulphur, lead and natural gas. Industry is hampered by power shortages and high fuel prices, and financial problems have delayed the nuclear energy programme.

History. Slavic tribes inhabited the area from at least 2000 BC but Poland did not become an independent kingdom until the 9th century. The country was Christianized under Miezko I (962–92). Unity was imposed under Ladislas I (1305–33) and Casimir the Great, who improved the administration and the country's defences, and encouraged trade and industry. JAGIELLON rule (1386–1572) culminated in the brief ascendancy of PROTESTANTISM and the flourishing of the arts and sciences. The 16th century saw Poland at its largest, after Lithuania was incorporated (1447, 1569), stretching from the Baltic to the Black Sea. However, the weakness of a hereditary monarchy took effect and despite the victories of John Casimir (1648–68) and John SOBIESKI (1674–96), internal decline and foreign attack undermined Polish independence and much territory was ceded to Sweden and Russia. Ravaged by the NORTHERN WAR and the War of the POLISH SUCCESSION, it lost its independence in the 18th century. From 1697 the Electors of Saxony took the title of king and Poland was partitioned between Russia, Austria, and Prussia in 1772. Brief resistance under KOSCIUSZKO resulted in two further partitions in 1793 and 1795, mainly to the benefit of CATHERINE II the Great's Russia, and Poland became effectively a protectorate of Russia.

Following the treaties of TILSIT in 1807 Napoleon created the Grand Duchy of Warsaw, under the King of Saxony, introducing the CODE NAPOLÉON, but retaining serfdom and the feudal nobility. The duchy collapsed after the Battle of LEIPZIG and at the Congress of VIENNA, when Poland was represented by Count CZARTORYSKI, parts of the duchy reverted to Prussia and Austria, but the bulk became the kingdom of Poland, which had its own administration but with the Russian emperor Alexander I as king. Revolutions took place in 1830, 1846–49, and 1863. Serfdom was ended in 1864, but policies of repression followed in both Russian and Prussian Poland. This did not, however, prevent the development of political parties demanding democratic government. After World War I in 1918 full independence was granted and Poland became a republic. War against Bolshevik Russia (1920–21) was followed by the dictatorship of Marshal PILSUDSKI. Poland was to have access to the port of Danzig (Gdańsk) via a POLISH CORRIDOR. The status of Danzig and the existence of this corridor provided an excuse for the Nazi invasion in 1939, which precipitated World War II. As a result of the NAZI–SOVIET PACT, Poland lost territory to both countries. After 1945 two million Germans left East Prussia (now divided between Poland and the Russian province of Kaliningrad) for the Federal Republic of Germany, and Poles, mainly from those Polish territories annexed by the Soviet Union, were re-settled in their place. Following the WARSAW RISING a provisional Polish government was established under Red Army protection, which co-operated with STALIN to bring the country within the Soviet bloc. Political opposition was neutralized, and in 1952 a Soviet-style constitution was adopted. In 1956 Polish workers went on strike to protest against food shortages and other restrictions. Under Wladyslaw Gomulka (1956–70) rigid control by the government was maintained, leading to further strikes (1970). The election of a Polish pope, Karol Wojtyla, as John Paul II in 1978, strengthened the influence of the ROMAN CATHOLIC CHURCH in the country. Strikes, organized by the Free Union of the Baltic Coast resulted in the formation of SOLIDARITY at Gdańsk. Martial law was imposed by Prime Minister General Wojciech Jaruzelski (1981–82), military tribunals continuing to operate after it officially ended. By 1987 the government was in crisis and put forward plans for limited decentralization of the economy; the ban on Solidarity was lifted and round-table talks with all groups, including the Roman Catholic Church, began. A new constitution was agreed and multiparty politics was legalized in 1989; in December 1990 Lech WALESA was elected President. Friendship treaties were made with newly united Germany and post-Soviet Russia and with France. In spite of recession, a private sector in the economy grew rapidly. The influence of Solidarity began to wane and in June 1992 Walesa appointed his first non-Solidarity Prime Minister, Waldemar Pawlak, of the Polish Peasant Party. In 1993 the former Communist Party emerged as the largest single party in elections, forming a government under Józef Oleksy. The last Russian troops stationed in Poland left the country in 1994. Walesa was defeated by the former Communist Aleksander Kwasniewski in presidential elections in 1995. Oleksy was forced by charges that he had been a Soviet informer to resign in early 1996 and was replaced as premier by Wlodzimierz Cimoszewicz. Following a referendum in May 1997, the country adopted a new constitution that removed the last traces of the Communist system. Later that year elections resulted in the formation of a Solidarity-led government under Jerzy Buzek.

CAPITAL:	Warsaw
AREA:	312,683 sq km (120,727 sq miles)
POPULATION:	38.731 million (1996)
CURRENCY:	1 zloty = 100 groszy
RELIGIONS:	Roman Catholic 95.0%
ETHNIC GROUPS:	Polish 98.7%; Ukrainian 0.6%; German and other 0.7%
LANGUAGES:	Polish (official); minority languages
INTERNATIONAL ORGANIZATIONS:	UN; CSCE; Council of Europe; North Atlantic Co-operation Council

Pole, Reginald (1500–58) English cardinal and Archbishop of Canterbury. He held a YORKIST claim to the throne of England through his mother, the Countess of Salisbury. This high birth, combined with his devotion to Roman Catholicism, made him very important in the eyes of foreign rulers during the English Protestant Reformation. After 1532 he lived abroad, disenchanted with HENRY VIII's marital and religious policies. He was made a cardinal (1536) and urged France and Spain to invade England in the name of Catholicism. Henry revenged himself on Pole's relatives, executing his brother and his aged mother. In 1554 he returned to England. His task was to assist the new queen, MARY I, in her COUNTER-REFORMATION programme. As Archbishop of Canterbury he began to lay the foundations of a revived Catholicism, although he seems to have disapproved of Mary's persecution of Protestants and his work did not survive after his death.

police A body of civilian officers with particular responsibility for upholding the law and maintaining public order through crime prevention and crime investigation. By the late 18th century large cities in Western Europe, such as Paris and London, had increasing problems of lawlessness and crime. In France, there had developed a centralized system of police spying, which developed into a national police force in the 19th century. From about 1750 in London the Magistrates' Court at Bow Street pioneered a system of unarmed uniformed 'runners' employed to apprehend criminals. These were developed by Sir Robert PEEL in 1829 by the formation of the London Metropolitan Police Force, soon copied in most other major British cities. Police forces have since been adopted by almost all nation-states. The majority of West European countries and all East European countries followed the French pattern of a national police force; this was also adopted by most developing countries. However, in Britain, Denmark, the USA, Canada, and elsewhere a series of local forces has survived, in spite of strong pressures for more centralization.

In some countries, the national police force is supplemented or paralleled by regional or local bodies, or by groups set up for particular purposes, such as riot control, serious crime detection (for example, the US Federal Bureau of Investigation), and such tasks as traffic control. In addition, such national organizations as railway or airport systems frequently develop their own police forces, with powers of arrest and detention within their areas of operation. Military police forces are given the same powers in respect of service personnel. Most police services make a distinction between uniformed and plain-clothes operations; the former patrol the streets and act as a first line of defence against crime, while the latter are detectives who investigate crime and who often have close links with intelligence and counter-intelligence bodies. Since the late 19th century, there has been a notable development of secret or political police forces, charged with the control of social life and the monitoring of dissident or subversive elements.

polis (plural *poleis*) The Ancient Greek city-state. The *polis* may have first emerged in the 8th century BC as a reaction to the rule of the early 'kings'. There were several hundred *poleis* in ancient Greece, many very small. Each consisted of a single walled town surrounded by countryside, which might include villages. At its centre was the CITADEL and the AGORA. In the ATHENIAN DEMOCRACY, which exemplified the *polis* in its highest form, power lay only in the hands of the citizen body, from which, for instance, women, resident foreigners, and slaves were excluded. Freedom, self-reliance, and autonomy were the ideals of the *polis*, but these aspirations were responsible for the innumerable wars between the Greek *poleis*. Even temporary unity in the face of a foreign invader, whether Persian or Macedonian, was very hard to achieve. The rise of the Hellenistic kingdoms at the end of the 4th century BC limited the power of the *polis*.

Polish Corridor The belt of territory separating former East Prussia from Germany and granted to POLAND by the VERSAILLES PEACE SETTLEMENT (1919) to ensure access to the Baltic Sea. Historically, the territory had belonged to Polish Pomerania in the 18th century and was colonized by a German minority. In 1939 Hitler's forces annexed the Polish Corridor, Danzig, Posen, and districts along the Silesian frontier, and placed the rest of Poland under a German governor. As a result of this Britain and France declared war on Germany, the beginning of World War II. After the war the territory reverted to Poland.

Polish Succession, War of the (1733–38) A conflict between Russia and Poland on one side and France. It began after the death of AUGUSTUS II (the Strong): Austria, Russia, and Prussia supported the candidature of his son, while the French supported Stanislaus Leszczynski, the father-in-law of LOUIS XV. Stanislaus was elected but was driven out by Russian troops and Augustus III became king (1733–63). There was fighting in Italy between Austria and Spain, supported by France, and Austria was driven from south Italy. Negotiations began in 1735, though the final treaty was not signed until 1738. Naples and Sicily went to the Spanish Bourbon, Don Carlos; Austria retained Milan and Mantua and acquired Parma; Francis, Duke of Lorraine became Duke of Tuscany, and Lorraine went to Stanislaus (it was to come to France on his death); France accepted the PRAGMATIC SANCTION. The war, which began in Poland, chiefly affected Italy and France.

Politburo The highest policy-making committee of the former Soviet Union and its satellites. The Soviet Politburo was founded, together with the Ogburo

(Organizational Bureau), in 1917 by the BOLSHEVIKS to provide leadership during the RUSSIAN REVOLUTION. Both bureaux were later re-formed to control all aspects of Soviet life.

Polk, James Knox (1795–1849), 11th President of the USA (1845–49). A Jacksonian Democrat, Polk won the presidential election of 1844 on a MANIFEST DESTINY ticket. His term of office resulted in major territorial additions to the USA. Apart from the successful prosecution of the MEXICAN–AMERICAN WAR and the acquisition of California and the south-west, he witnessed the re-establishment of an independent treasury and the settlement of the OREGON BOUNDARY DISPUTE (1846).

poll tax A tax levied on every poll (or head) of the population. Poll taxes were granted by the English House of Commons in 1377, 1379, and 1380. The third of these poll taxes, for one shilling from every man and woman, was acknowledged as a cause of the PEASANTS' REVOLT.

The highly unpopular community charge, a local government tax introduced in Britain (1989–90) by the government of Margaret THATCHER, was also widely dubbed the poll tax.

Pol Pot (1925–98) Cambodian leader. Trained as a Buddhist monk and educated at a French university, he joined the anti-French resistance under HO CHI MINH and rose to a high position within the Cambodian communist movement, supported by the People's Republic of China. After the KHMER ROUGE had overthrown the Lon Nol regime, he succeeded SIHANOUK as Prime Minister in 1976 and presided over the 're-construction' of the country in which as many as two million Cambodians may have been killed. Overthrown in 1979 he retreated with the Khmer Rouge to the borders of Thailand from where he continued to direct guerrilla activity. He was believed still to be exerting considerable influence within the Party of Democratic Kampuchea when it joined the UN-sponsored Supreme National Council for CAMBODIA in 1991. After the Khmer Rouge boycotted UN-monitored multiparty elections in 1993, the group resumed its violent campaign, with Pol Pot apparently still in control. However, in 1997 a rift in the Khmer Rouge led to Pol Pot's being captured and 'tried' by his former colleagues, who sentenced him to life imprisonment.

Poltava, Battle of (1709) PETER THE GREAT's decisive victory over CHARLES XII of Sweden in the NORTHERN WAR. Despite the support of the Cossack hetman (leader) Mazeppa (1644–1709) together with 5,000 of his men, the Russians succeeded in defeating the Swedes at Poltava, near Kiev.

Polybius (*c.* 204–122 BC) Greek historian of the rise of Rome from the Second PUNIC WAR. A man of noble birth and some political importance, he was taken to Rome with other Greek hostages after the Roman intervention in Greece by Aemilius Paullus and joined a circle of intellectuals around his captor. He accompanied his other patron, SCIPIO AEMILIANUS, at the sack of Carthage. His *Universal History* covered the years 220–145. In 40 books he attributed Rome's success to the ROMAN LEGIONS, fair administrators, and a balance of regal, aristocratic, and popular elements in the republican constitution. Only five books survive but his account of the war with Hannibal augments that of LIVY.

Polynesians Inhabitants of the islands of the eastern central Pacific, from Hawaii to Easter Island and New Zealand. They show close affinity in physical features, language, and culture, and probably spread from a focal centre in the area of Samoa and Tonga within the past 3000–2000 years. The principal immigration of MAORIS from the Marquesas into New Zealand is dated to about 1350 AD, though it was not the first. The origins of Polynesians are controversial. Some authorities, on the basis of their fair skin coloration, wavy hair, and stocky build relate them to the CAUCASOIDS; they have also been regarded as close to the MELANESIANS. Probably the widest held view is that they are a distant offshoot of a MONGOLOID population in south-east Asia.

Pombal, Sebastião José de Carvalho e Mello, Marquis of (1699–1782) Portuguese statesman. He was made Minister of Foreign Affairs and War in Portugal on the accession of José I in 1750; the king's indolence gave him control of the country. He regarded the dominance of the church as the chief reason for the retardation of Portugal. He suppressed the Jesuit missions established in South America (part of the PORTUGUESE EMPIRE), and in September 1759 expelled the Jesuits from Portugal. He also brought the INQUISITION under the control of the state. In 1755 when an earthquake devastated Lisbon, Pombal organized relief work and the rebuilding of the city. Although his reduction of ecclesiastical influence was held to be part of the ENLIGHTENMENT, Pombal had little interest in reform.

Pomerania A territory around the River Oder, now in Germany and Poland, with the Baltic to the north. Its name derives from a SLAV tribe that settled there in the 5th century. From 1062 to 1637 it enjoyed much independence, ruled by its dukes, but after the Peace of Westphalia in 1648 it was divided between Sweden and Brandenburg. In 1770 Prussia acquired most of Swedish Pomerania.

Pompadour, Jeanne Antoinette Poisson, Marquise de (1721–64) Mistress of LOUIS XV of France from 1745. She came from the world of wealthy officials and bankers and was a lively witty woman, on friendly terms with the *philosophes* of the ENLIGHTENMENT. The public blamed her for the extravagance of the court and the disasters of the SEVEN YEARS WAR, but her political influence has probably been exaggerated.

Pompeii The largest settlement on the Bay of Naples that was destroyed by the eruption of the volcano Vesuvius in 79 AD. An ancient town of mixed Etruscan, Greek, and Samnite background, it became fashionable and prosperous when it became a colony for veteran Roman soldiers. Dedicated to Venus, its population of 15–20,000 included Greeks, Jews, and Christians. An earthquake damaged many buildings in 62 AD. On 24 August 79 it was engulfed, shortly after Herculaneum, in three days of glowing avalanches of molten lava, and showers consisting of ash, gas, rock, and pumice. A blast cloud from Vesuvius was described by PLINY THE YOUNGER, an onlooker, as 'like an immense pine tree'. PLINY THE ELDER died there as he led a naval party into the burning ash and fumes on a research and rescue mission. Local Jews and early Christians saw the eruption as judgement on immoral behaviour and a sign of the end

of the world. The ruins of Pompeii were discovered in the 16th century, excavation work was begun in 1748 and still continues today.

Pompey (the Great; Gnaeus Pompeius Magnus) (106–48 BC) Roman general and politician. His early military career was meteoric and brilliant. He welcomed SULLA back to Italy with a private army and was dispatched abroad to fight MARIUS. Later the Senate gave him special powers to combat Lepidus, who had raised his own army while proconsul, and Sertorius, who supported the rebellious Lusitani in Spain. On his return from Spain Pompey and CRASSUS, backed by their armies, obtained the consulship for 70 BC, although Pompey was too young and had held none of the statutory offices. Tribunician bills gave him unprecedented powers to clear the Mediterranean of pirates, whom he swept off the sea in only three months. He went on to defeat MITHRIDATES VI and the king of Armenia. By his settlement of Asia and the annexation of Syria, he doubled the revenue of the treasury and vastly increased his personal fortune.

When a hostile Senate refused to ratify his acts and provide land for his army veterans, he was driven into the pact called the First Triumvirate with Crassus and Julius CAESAR, and married Caesar's daughter Julia. His immediate ambitions were satisfied by Caesar as consul in 59, but his relationship with Crassus was strained and he became jealous of Caesar's success in Gaul. Nevertheless he renewed the pact in 56 and obtained a second consulship with Crassus and the governorship of Spain with seven legions to be administered from Rome. In 52 he was made sole consul to deal with gang warfare and anarchy in Rome. Confident of his military superiority, he precipitated the civil war crisis in 49. He finally engaged battle with Caesar at PHARSALUS and was defeated. He escaped to Egypt but was murdered by PTOLEMY's ministers who hoped to gain Caesar's approval.

Pompidou, Georges Jean Raymond (1911–74) French statesman. He served in the RESISTANCE MOVEMENT in World War II and, from 1944, became an aide and adviser to DE GAULLE. While the latter was President, Pompidou held the post of Prime Minister (1962–68) and played an important part in setting up the EVIAN AGREEMENTS. The strikes and riots of 1968 prompted de Gaulle's resignation in 1969 and Pompidou was elected President. In a swift and decisive policy change he devalued the franc, introduced a price freeze, and lifted France's veto on Britain's membership of the EUROPEAN ECONOMIC COMMUNITY.

Ponce de León, Juan (1460–1521) Spanish explorer. He sailed with COLUMBUS on his second voyage in 1493 and as deputy-governor of Hispaniola he founded the first settlement on Puerto Rico in 1508. From there in 1513 he sailed in search of the 'Fountain of Youth', an Indian legend, discovering Florida, which he though to be an island, and probably sighting the coast of Yucatán on his return voyage. He did not realize that he had landed on the mainland of North America and left little description. In 1521 he returned to colonize Florida but was mortally wounded in a battle with Indians.

Pondicherry A French colony (1674–1954) in south-east India, originally established by the FRENCH EAST INDIA

COMPANY. It provoked Dutch and British rivalry and was captured several times in the 18th-century trade struggles. It survived the collapse of the French East India Company to remain the administrative centre for French interests in India throughout the British Raj era.

Pontiac (c. 1720–69) Leader of a Native American tribal confederacy and chief of the Ottawa tribe, for many years allies of the French. After the French defeat in 1759 and British occupation of their forts, he managed to confederate many ALGONQUIN tribes, who were fearful of British expansion and intransigence. Spurred by religious enthusiasm, Ottawa, Ojibwa, Potawatomi, Wyandot, Shawnee, and Delaware tribesmen rose in a concerted frontier attack from the Great Lakes to Virginia in May 1763. Only Detroit and Fort Pitt held out and 200 settlers were killed, many in western Pennsylvania. British punitive expeditions weakened the confederacy, and in 1766 Pontiac made peace. He was murdered in 1769 near St Louis by hired Native American assassins.

Pontus A kingdom in northern Asia Minor whose expansion came to pose a severe threat to Roman power. Pharnaces I, king of Pontus, captured the Black Sea port of Sinope in 183 BC, but was compelled to renounce many other gains. Mithridates IV and V adopted pro-Roman policies, the latter adding GALATIA and PHRYGIA to his territories. MITHRIDATES VI greatly increased the power of the kingdom, but three wars with Rome led to the collapse of his regime, though it was not until 64 AD that eastern Pontus was incorporated into the Roman empire.

Pony Express (1860–61) The horse-borne mail delivery system that operated in the 19th-century US west. It was founded in 1860 by the Missouri freight company of Russell, Majors, and Waddell to prove that there was a viable alternative to the southern route into California for the year-round transportation of overland mail. It operated between St Joseph, Missouri, and Sacramento, California, through Cheyenne, Salt Lake City, and Carson City. It used a relay of fresh ponies and riders and took two weeks to cover the full distance of nearly 3,200 km (2,000 miles). High costs made the operation unprofitable and the coming of the telegraph made it unnecessary, but the Pony Express is still remembered as one of the most picturesque episodes in the opening up of the US frontier.

Poor Laws The legislation that provided the basis for organized relief and welfare payments in England in the 16th century. The Poor Laws gradually reduced the charitable obligations that had been placed upon ecclesiastical institutions, guilds, and other private benefactors in the Middle Ages. With the Dissolution of the MONASTERIES an important source of charity was destroyed. Originally only those physically incapable were deemed worthy of charity and able-bodied beggars were dealt with harshly. However, following local schemes initiated by the town corporations of London, Ipswich, York, Norwich, and Bristol, systematic poor relief evolved. A statute passed in 1576 recognized that men fit and willing to work might be genuinely unable to find employment and were in need of support. Three categories of poor were subsequently recognized: sturdy beggars or vagabonds, regarded as potential trouble-

makers, the infirm, and the deserving unemployed. Justices of the Peace listed the poor in each parish and appointed overseers to raise funds from parishioners sufficient to meet the cost of maintaining the poor and work was organized for able-bodied poor. Vagrants and vagabonds were sent to houses of correction, which became mandatory in all shires from 1601. The government's measures helped to alleviate starvation during years of harvest failure, although there was famine in the northern counties during the 1590s.

By the late 18th century the Poor Law system was becoming increasingly inadequate for coping with problems arising from the greater mobility of the population in search of work. In some rural areas, in addition to direct relief to those without work, there developed the so-called Speenhamland system (named after the district in Berkshire where the system originated in 1795), whereby the wages of low-paid workers were supplemented by a parish allowance. Such a system was clearly unsatisfactory, since it tended both to depress wages and to subsidize landlords and employers. In 1834 a Poor Law Amendment Act tried to end the giving of assistance outside the workhouse; it established the principle that all citizens should have the right to relief from destitution through accommodation. But conditions in the workhouse, often with families separated by sex and age, were to be so severe as to discourage all but the most needy from its care. The workhouses were run by locally elected Boards of Guardians, who raised money through a poor-rate. The system proved inadequate in the growing cities, where the Guardians sometimes resorted to relief without the guarantee of accommodation. The Poor Law was gradually dismantled by social legislation of the 20th century, particularly that of the Liberal governments (1906–14) by important Acts in 1927, 1929 (when Boards of Guardians were abolished), 1930, 1934 (when Unemployment Assistance Boards were created), by SOCIAL SECURITY legislation following the BEVERIDGE report (1942), and by the establishment of the WELFARE STATE.

pope (in Western Christianity) The bishop of Rome (residing at the VATICAN CITY STATE) and the supreme head of the ROMAN CATHOLIC CHURCH. In the EASTERN ORTHODOX CHURCH the patriarch of Alexandria is sometimes called the pope and the title may be used of any priest. Within the Roman Catholic Church, the pope is believed to be the spiritual descendant of St Peter, leader of Jesus' disciples, and his title 'Vicar of Christ' expresses a claim to universal jurisdiction over all Christians. The official doctrine of papal infallibility was promulgated at the First Vatican Council in 1870, to the effect that under certain conditions, when speaking *ex cathedra* (Latin, 'from the throne') on matters of doctrine, faith, or morality, the pope cannot be in error. Since the Second Vatican Council (1962–65), the Roman Catholic Church has emphasized the importance of the bishops working together with the pope on these matters. The pope uses encyclicals (written mandates), circular letters, and, on more important matters, bulls, or apostolic letters, to communicate his views. In recent years, the pope has become an increasingly visible figure, travelling throughout the world on missions to strengthen the Roman Catholic faith and assert the relevance of the Christian message. (See also PAPACY.)

Popish Plot (1678) An alleged conspiracy by Roman Catholics to kill CHARLES II of England and replace him as king by his Roman Catholic brother, James, Duke of York. The plot was invented by Titus Oates (1649–1705), an Anglican priest, who asserted that a massacre of Protestants and the burning of London were imminent. The plot achieved credibility because of SHAFTESBURY's willingness to use Oates as a means to secure James's exclusion from the throne. A nationwide panic ensued during which more than 80 innocent people were condemned before Oates was discredited. He was punished for perjury, but survived to receive a pension from WILLIAM III.

Popular Front A political coalition of left-wing parties in defence of democratic forms of government believed to be threatened by right-wing fascist attacks. Such coalitions were made possible by the strategy adopted by the COMINTERN in 1934, allowing co-operation between Soviet and western communists. In France a socialist and communist alliance gained power after elections in 1936, under the leadership of Léon BLUM, who implemented a programme of radical social reforms. In Spain Popular Front governments were in office from 1936 to 1939 and fought the SPANISH CIVIL WAR against FRANCO and the Nationalists. A Popular Front government ruled in Chile from 1938 to 1947.

population migrations and emigrations Large movements of peoples across and between continents, sometimes under duress. The major 19th-century movement was the great Atlantic migration from Europe to the Americas. This took some 5 million people to Canada, mostly from Britain, some 15 million to South America, mostly from the Mediterranean countries, and some 36 million to the USA (1800–1917), which received succeeding waves from Ireland (about 4.4 million), and the continent of Europe. In the first half of the 19th century the White settlers in turn forced the migration of Native American people to reservations. In total the movement across the Atlantic involved the greatest number of people ever to migrate. The decade 1901–10 saw the greatest influx to the USA, when about 9 million people arrived, many via ELLIS ISLAND. Australian and New Zealand immigration was mostly from Britain until after WORLD WAR II when the NEW AUSTRALIANS, mainly from Asia, began arriving. The empty lands of the Russian empire east of the Urals in the 19th and 20th centuries steadily attracted settlers (some 20 million), of whom some 2 million were political exiles in PRISON CAMPS, used as convict labour. Chinese migration south accelerated in the 19th century, with perhaps as many as 12 million people, often with incentives from the European colonial powers, moving to Vietnam, Thailand, Malaysia, Singapore, and Indonesia. The European colonial powers also moved 'indentured labour' between colonies, where there were labour shortages; for example, Tamils were moved to Ceylon (now Sri Lanka) and other Indians to South Africa and the West Indies.

Most 20th-century migrations have been forced, either by political coercion or famine. STALIN's policy of forcible resettlement of ethnic groupings, such as the Crimean Tartars to Central Asia, left a legacy of national unrest within the Soviet Union. Some 17.5 million refugees resulted from the partition of India and PAKISTAN in 1947; over 10 million Germans were moved from eastern Europe by Soviet authorities after World War II. The war in AFGHANISTAN resulted in over 6 million refugees (although some returned after pacification in 1989), while the civil war and genocide in the central African state of RWANDA in 1994 led to around 2 million people being displaced, seeking refuge in Zaïre (now the Democratic Republic of the Congo), Burundi, and Tanzania. By the early 1990s there were an estimated 19 million refugees who had not found permanent settlement in another country. Modern economic migration includes the process of URBANIZATION that has drawn millions of people from rural hinterlands all over the world into the ever-expanding cities.

population of the world The number of people alive in the world at a given moment in time. Between the collapse of the Roman empire in the 5th century AD and the late 18th century world population appears to have remained fairly stable, with high death rates and occasional plagues. 19th-century Europe saw an unprecedented rise in population, largely because of improved public health and control over infectious DISEASE. In 1803 Thomas MALTHUS propounded the theory that the rapidly growing population would soon increase beyond the capacity of the world to feed it and that controls on population were therefore necessary to prevent catastrophe. Japan instituted the first modern official birth-control policy after World War II, setting an example which other countries followed with China now having the strictest birth-control policy in the world. Since 1950 there has been a population explosion in Asia, Africa, and Latin America, with a total world population rising from 2.5 billion in 1950 to 5.3 billion in 1990. By 2000 AD world population is expected to reach 6 billion, over 80% of which would be living in developing regions, where a large proportion would be in their reproductive years.

The UN forecasts that by the year 2050 world population will reach 9.8 billion. It is predicted that 3 billion of these additional people will live in Africa, Asia, and Latin America, and only 200 million in the developed regions. By that date 84% of the world's population will be living in the developing regions, compared with 67% in 1950. While population predictions are not infallible, particularly for individual countries, global population forecasts have proved reasonably reliable. In the past, population growth was low because in most societies both birth rates and mortality rates were high and roughly balanced each other. With the introduction in many developing countries after World War II of improved health, housing, sanitation, and education, mortality rates fell rapidly, but birth rates and fertility rates remained high, in accordance with traditional values, leading to unprecedented population growth. By the early 1990s, mortality rates were close to their anticipated minimum and birth rates had declined or were starting to decline in most countries. If these trends continue, population growth will eventually return to low rates, with births and deaths stabilized at low rather than at high levels. However, the youthful age structure of the population in the developing world, where a large proportion of young people have yet to reach their reproductive years, means that the absolute number of births, and the total population, will

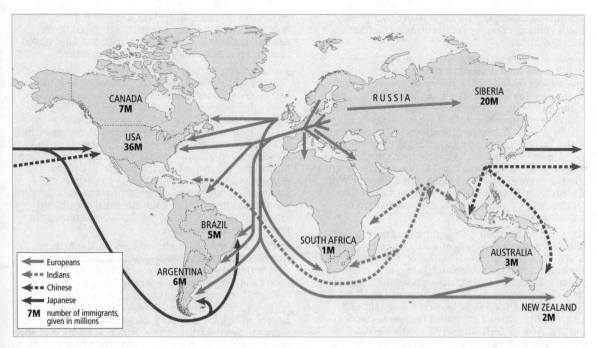

Permanent immigrants 1820–1930.

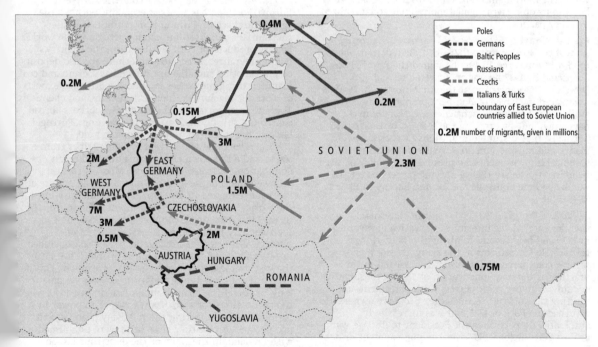

European migrations 1945–52.

population migrations and emigrations   *The last two centuries have seen population shifts on an unprecedented scale. While 19th-century migrants were impelled by the promise of land to be cultivated, grazed, or mined in the Americas, Australia, and Africa, many of their 20th-century counterparts have been victims of wars and persecutions. About 23 million 20th-century migrants were refugees within the subcontinent of India, some 30 million lost their homelands in Europe, about 3 million Jews have entered the newly created state of Israel since 1948, and over 2.5 million Palestinians have become refugees on the borders of Israel. Among migrants in the 1990s are members of former communist countries fleeing ethnic persecution or seeking economic gain.*

continue to rise rapidly for 20 to 30 years, if present trends continue, thereby contributing to increasing overpopulation.

Populist Movement (Russia) A group of agrarian socialists in Russia devoted to radical reform and government by small economic units resembling village communes. The movement was active in the latter half of the 19th century, first under the name of Land and Liberty, when members such as HERZEN, BAKUNIN, Lavrov, PLEKHANOV, and Chernyshevsky advocated the overthrow of the Tzarist regime, being dissatisfied with government reforms; radicals were soon persecuted by the police. In 1879 the most radical wing of the Populist group re-formed under the name of the People's Will Movement and began to adopt terrorist tactics that culminated, two years later, in the assassination of ALEXANDER II.

Populist Party (USA) A US agrarian organization that began in 1889 as a grouping of southern and western interests seeking to remedy the lot of debtor farmers. It drew on the GRANGER MOVEMENT, the Farmers' Alliances, the GREENBACKS, and other protest groups who met in Cincinnati to create the People's Party of the USA. Its members called for a flexible currency system under government control, a graduated income tax, and political reforms including direct election of US Senators. In 1892 its candidate for President, James B. Weaver, won over a million popular and 22 electoral votes. The movement then went into decline, largely because its objectives seemed more likely to be realized by other parties.

Portal, Charles Frederick Algernon, Viscount Portal of Hungerford (1893–1971) British marshal of the Royal Air Force. In 1915 he joined the Royal Flying Corps and by 1937 he was an air vice-marshal and Director of Organization at the Air Ministry. In 1940 he was placed in charge of Bomber Command. The aircraft available had technical deficiencies, especially in navigation, but by carrying the BOMBING OFFENSIVE into Germany, they disrupted munitions factories, power plants, and railway junctions. While introducing technical improvements, he pressed for a policy of 'area bombing' to replace that of specific targets. After the war he became Controller of Atomic Energy in Britain (1945–51).

Portales, Diego (1793–1837) Chilean statesman. Portales entered the interim conservative government in 1830 and held several ministerial offices. He was responsible for reforms in the army, treasury, civil service, commerce, and industry. He assisted in the drafting of the new constitution of 1833, a conservative document, giving great powers to the President and limiting the suffrage to the larger property owners. He returned to office in 1835, but was increasingly autocratic. He persuaded the President to declare war against Peru in June 1837 over the non-payment of debt. This was unpopular in the army, which mutinied and assassinated him.

Porteous Riots A series of disturbances that took place in Edinburgh, Scotland, in 1736. Crowds had rioted during the hanging of a smuggler, and Captain John Porteous of the Edinburgh city guard tried to restore order by opening fire, killing several people. As a result he was condemned to death, but reprieved. An orderly crowd then attacked his prison, dragged him out, and lynched him on the day originally appointed for his execution; for this outrage Edinburgh was fined £2,000 and the Lord Provost was removed from office.

Portsmouth, Treaty of (1905) The treaty that ended the RUSSO-JAPANESE WAR (1904–05). Although the Russians had been decisively defeated on land and at sea in 1904, it was the intervention of the US President Theodore ROOSEVELT that finally brought a successful end to the Russo-Japanese War. The treaty, signed at Portsmouth, New Hampshire, allowed for the mutual evacuation of Manchuria but granted Japan railway rights in southern Manchuria, Russian acknowledgement of Japanese supremacy in Korea, and the ceding to Japan of the Liaodong Peninsula (including Port Arthur, now Lüshun) and the southern half of Sakhalin. Russian eastward expansion was thus halted and Japanese hegemony in north-east Asia confirmed.

Portugal A west European country on the Atlantic west coast of the Iberian peninsula, flanked by Spain on the north and east. The Atlantic archipelago of the AZORES and MADEIRA are also part of Portugal.

Physical. Half of the country lies on the edge of the high and ancient Iberian plateau, in a region of rugged hills, lakes, and deep gorges. Much of the region is covered with forests of pine and cork-oak, and from it flow three great rivers, the Douro, Tagus, and Guadiana.

Economy. One of the poorest countries in Western Europe, Portugal has a mixed economy, with a large agricultural sector. Fishing is important, with a substantial annual sardine catch. Portugal is the world's largest producer of cork. Pyrites form the country's main mineral resource, although there are also deposits of several other metallic ores as well as sodium and coal. Manufacturing industries include the principal exports of clothing, machinery, footwear, textiles, and chemicals. Tourism is important, and Portuguese workers abroad contribute substantially to foreign earnings. Portugal has also benefited from EU development aid.

History. Portugal was settled by Celtic tribes from *c.* 500 BC and was known as Lusitania during Roman domination. Periods of Gothic and Moorish control followed the collapse of the Western Roman empire and Portugal struggled to develop a distinct identity until the papacy recognized the kingship of Alfonso I in 1179. In 1249 the Portuguese completed the reconquest of their country from the MOORS. After a series of unsuccessful wars against Castile, peace was concluded in 1411 and under the ruling house of Avis (1385–1580) the vast overseas PORTUGUESE EMPIRE was acquired. On the expiry of the Avis dynasty, PHILIP II of Spain became king by force. The Spanish union lasted until 1640, when the native House of BRAGANZA was swept to power by a nationalist revolt. During the relatively peaceful and prosperous 18th century close links were established with England. In the wake of the disastrous Lisbon earthquake (1755) the dynamic minister POMBAL exercised the powers of an enlightened despot. During the NAPOLEONIC WARS the Prince Regent John (King John VI from 1816), together with the Braganza royal family, fled to Brazil. Here he met demands for political and economic freedom, Brazil emerging peacefully as an independent empire in 1822. Through most of the rest of the 19th century there was considerable political instability until 1910, when a republic was established. In 1926 there was a military coup, which was followed in 1932 by the establishment of Antonio SALAZAR as Prime Minister, Minister of Finance, and virtual dictator (1932–68), strongly supported by the Roman Catholic Church. Portugal supported the Allies in World War I and in World War II remained theoretically neutral while allowing the Allies naval and air bases. GOA, Diu, and Damao were lost to India in the 1960s, but MACAO in South China was retained. Salazar's autocratic policies were continued by Marcello Caetano until a military coup in 1974. Increasingly bitter guerrilla warfare had developed in Portuguese Africa, especially in ANGOLA and MOZAMBIQUE. These gained independence in 1975, although both experienced civil war, while the state of GUINEA-BISSAU was created in 1974. After two years of political instability at home, a more stable democracy began to emerge following the election of Antonio Eanes as President in 1976. Moderate coalition governments both left and right of centre have alternated, all struggling with severe economic problems. President Mario Soares was elected in 1986, having been Prime Minister since 1983. He was re-elected President in 1991, with Anibal Cavaço Silva of the Social Democrat Party as Prime Minister. Portugal joined the European Community (now the European Union) in 1986. In the general election of 1995, the Socialist Party under António Guterres won power and in 1996 Jorge Sampaio was elected President.

CAPITAL:	Lisbon
AREA:	92,389 sq km (35,672 sq miles)
POPULATION:	9.927 million (1996)
CURRENCY:	1 escudo = 100 centavos
RELIGIONS:	Roman Catholic 95.0%; Protestant 1.0%; Jewish 0.1%
ETHNIC GROUPS:	Portuguese 99.0%; Angolan 0.2%; Cape Verdean 0.2%
LANGUAGES:	Portuguese (official)
INTERNATIONAL ORGANIZATIONS:	UN; OECD; NATO; Council of Europe; EU; CSCE

Portuguese empire The overseas territories accruing to Portugal as a result of the country's leadership of the first phase of European overseas expansion, beginning in the 15th century. Portuguese imperialism was stimulated by a scientific interest in maritime exploration, a desire to profit from the spice trade of the Orient, and a determination to spread the Christian religion in non-Christian lands. By about 1530 the Portuguese empire included the islands of Cape Verde, Madeira, and the Azores, a large part of BRAZIL, fortress settlements in East and West Africa, continuous stretches of the coastlines of Angola and MOZAMBIQUE, Indian Ocean bases like Ormuz, GOA, Calicut, and Colombo, and scattered Far Eastern posts including those in the MOLUCCAS, MACAO, the Celebes, JAVA, and MALACCA.

The empire's wealth derived mainly from coastal entrepôts and its representatives often had to face highly developed Muslim civilizations. Thus, except in Brazil, there was little conquest or colonization along the lines of the contemporary SPANISH EMPIRE. The Portuguese crown was slower than the Spanish to establish a bureaucratic system of administration, but from 1643 the Overseas Council performed a similar role to that of the Spanish Council of the Indies. At the

colonial level, however, the various viceroys, governors, and captains-general retained considerable freedom of action. The empire enriched Lisbon, the court, and an increasingly foreign merchant community, but little of the new wealth was reinvested in the mother country. During the 17th century the DUTCH EMPIRE in Asia was assembled largely at the expense of the Portuguese.

Potatau Te Wherowhero (d. 1860) MAORI leader. Widely respected for his chiefly status, learning, and warrior prowess, Potatau was chosen in 1858 by Waikato and central North Island tribes as their first king in the hope of uniting all the Maori tribes. Potatau supported the KINGITANGA's moves to resist land selling and to secure recognition from the government of *rangatiratanga* (chieftainly authority). Up to his death he tried to avoid involving the Kingitanga directly in the TARANAKI WAR, which broke out in 1860. Potatau's lineal descendants still head the Kingitanga.

Potemkin The battleship whose crew mutinied in the RUSSIAN REVOLUTION of 1905 when in the Black Sea. The crew killed some officers and took control of the ship. As other ships in the squadron were close to mutiny it was thought unwise to open fire on the *Potemkin*. Unhindered, she bombarded Odessa before seeking asylum in Romania. The incident persuaded the emperor to agree to the election of a Duma, but unrest continued until the October Manifesto was issued and a new Russian constitution established.

Potemkin, Gregory (1739–91) Russian soldier and favourite of CATHERINE II. He was a man of great energy and an able administrator who extended Russian rule in the south, carried out a series of army reforms, annexed the Crimea in 1783, and built a Black Sea fleet and a naval base at Sevastopol. In the war with the Turks he was made army commander and died in a year of Russian military victory.

potlatch A ritual based on gift exchange found among North-West Native Americans. Potlatches were ritual feasts in which competitors for positions of status sought to outdo each other by giving more lavish gifts. The arrival of Europeans in the area during the 19th century and the changes this brought to the local economy caused a huge escalation in the scale of potlatches. Large quantities of such European trade goods as blankets were not only given away but were also publicly destroyed to force a rival to equal the gesture.

Potsdam Conference (17 July–2 August 1945) The last of the World War II summit conferences. Held in the former Hohenzollern palace at Potsdam, outside Berlin, the conference was attended by CHURCHILL (replaced by ATTLEE during its course), STALIN, and TRUMAN. It implicitly acknowledged Soviet predominance in eastern Europe by, among other things, accepting Polish and Soviet administration of certain German territories, and by agreeing to the transfer of the ten million or so German people in these territories and other parts of eastern Europe to Germany. It established a Council of Foreign Ministers to handle peace treaties, made plans to introduce representative and elective principles of government in Germany, discussed REPARATIONS, outlawed the Nazi Party, de-monopolized much of German industry, and decentralized its economy. The final agreement, vaguely worded and tentative, was consistently breached in the aftermath of German surrender, as the communist and capitalist countries polarized into their respective blocs. The Potsdam Declaration (26 July 1945) demanded from Japan the choice between unconditional surrender or total destruction.

Potter, Beatrice WEBB, Sidney.

Powhatan Chief of the Native American Algonquin tribes of central coastal Virginia in 1607, when the English settlers arrived to found JAMESTOWN. Earlier contacts with the Algonquin had been made in 1570–71 and 1588 by the Spanish, and in 1584–86 by the English. During the early 17th century Powhatan's position was strengthened by wars of expansion. His daughter POCAHONTAS intervened to save the captured John SMITH and was herself held hostage by the English to force their policy on her father.

Poynings' Law (1494) An act of the Irish Parliament, properly called the Statutes of Drogheda, named after Sir Edward Poynings, Lord Deputy of Ireland (1494–95). By its terms, the Parliament was to meet only with the English king's consent, and its legislative programme had to be approved in advance by the English king. It was intended to bolster English sovereignty and destroy Yorkist influence. It soon became a major grievance to Irish parliamentarians, but it was not until 1782 that Henry GRATTAN managed to have it repealed.

Praemunire, Statute of (1353) English anti-papal legislation. Like the Statute of Provisors (1351), it resulted from a nationalism and anti-papalism that was widespread in later 14th-century England and was designed to protect rights claimed by the English crown against encroachment by the papacy. It was a powerful weapon for the English king; it was used, for instance, to prevent Bishop Henry BEAUFORT from becoming papal legate in England and HENRY VIII several times resorted to it.

praetorian A bodyguard for a Roman general or 'praetor'. In 27 BC AUGUSTUS established nine cohorts of such troops in and near Rome, later putting two prefects in command. Expanded to 12 by CALIGULA and 16 by Vitellius the number of cohorts was fixed at ten by the end of the 1st century. They were an élite, better paid than legionaries, serving shorter engagements and with many privileges. They also became 'king makers' since their support was essential for gaining high political office. At least four prefects became emperor before CONSTANTINE abolished them early in the 4th century.

Pragmatic Sanction An imperial or royal ordinance issued as a fundamental law. The term was employed to denote an arrangement defining the limits of the sovereign power of a prince, especially in matters of the royal succession. The Pragmatic Sanction of Bourges, issued by the French clergy in July 1438, upheld the rights of the French church to administer its temporal property independently of the papacy and disallowed papal nominations to vacant benefices and church livings. In April 1713 the Habsburg emperor Charles VI promulgated a Pragmatic Sanction in an attempt to ensure that all his territories should pass undivided to his children. By 1720 it was clear that his daughter MARIA THERESA would be the heiress and Charles spent his last years in obtaining guarantees of support from his own territories and the major powers of Europe. On his death in 1740 the failure of most of these powers to keep their promises led to the War of the AUSTRIAN SUCCESSION.

Prague, Defenestration of (1618). An act of rebellion by Bohemian Protestant nobles against Catholic HABSBURG rule. The Defenestration of Prague was the ejection of two imperial representatives and a Secretary from a window of the Hradčany Castle in Prague. It precipitated the beginning of the THIRTY YEARS WAR and, following the Habsburg victory at the Battle of White Mountain (1620), near Prague, the city underwent enforced Catholicization and Germanization. In 1635, during the THIRTY YEARS WAR, the Peace of Prague reconciled the German princes to the emperor.

Prasad, Rajendra (1884–1963) Indian nationalist politician. A lawyer by profession, he began working with Mohandas GANDHI in 1917. He was imprisoned by the British (1942–45) for supporting the CONGRESS opposition to the British war effort in World War II. He represented the conservative wing within Congress, of which he was President on four occasions between 1932 and 1947. Prasad became President of India (1950–62) when the republic was proclaimed.

prehistory The period before written records, when the only source of evidence about early societies is archaeology. It thus covers an immense period of time, linking evolutionary biology, archaeology, and history. Prehistory begins with the study of early humans and can be said to have lasted down to recent times in remote parts of the world. It is divided into the STONE AGE (PALAEOLITHIC, MESOLITHIC, and NEOLITHIC), the BRONZE AGE, and the IRON AGE. History, based on written records, begins in about 3000 BC in Egypt and Mesopotamia.

Prempeh I (d. 1931) African leader, Asantehene (Chief) of the ASANTE. He was elected in 1888, but deposed by the British in 1896. In 1924 he was allowed to return to Kumasi and in 1926 was installed as Kumasihene, a simple divisional chief. On his death in 1931 his nephew, Prempeh II, was elected Kumasihene, and then Asantehene in 1935, when the Golden Stool, symbolic of Asante power, was returned by the British and the traditional Asante Confederacy was restored.

Presbyterian A Protestant Christian who subscribes to the anti-episcopal theories of church government and usually to the doctrines of John CALVIN. Presbyterian churches oppose state intervention in religious affairs and advocate the primacy of the Bible as a rule of faith.

At the REFORMATION proponents of the Calvinist system claimed that opposition to church government by bishops was not heretical, but rather a restoration of the original organization of the early Church as described in the Bible. In subsequent centuries Reformed and Presbyterian churches all over the world made various adaptations to the original Calvinist pattern, but they remained essentially similar. Government of Presbyterian churches is by elected representative bodies of ministers and elders. The first Presbyterian Church to be organized on a national basis was in 16th-century France; its members became known as HUGUENOTS and they played a large part in provoking the French Wars of Religion. Reformed congregations contributed to the DUTCH REVOLT and once the

Netherlands secured independence from Catholic Spain the Reformed Church became established there. Elsewhere in Europe, many congregations managed to survive the COUNTER-REFORMATION. In 1628 a Dutch Reformed Church was organized on Manhattan Island. The first American Presbyterian Church was founded in Philadelphia in 1706. The official Church of Scotland, with 1.25 million members, is one of the largest of the Presbyterian churches.

pressgang A detachment of sailors empowered to seize men for service in the British navy. The use of the pressgang had been sanctioned by law since medieval times but the practice was at its height in the 18th century. All able-bodied men were liable for impressment, although in fact the pressgangs confined their attention to the seaport towns where they could find recruits with suitable experience. The navy continued to rely on the pressgangs until the 1830s, when improvements in pay and conditions provided sufficient volunteers. The system was also used to a lesser extent by the army but discontinued after 1815.

Prester John (from Greek *presbyter*, 'priest') A legendary Christian ruler to whom successive generations of Crusaders looked for help against the growing power of Islam. First mentioned in a 12th-century German chronicle, he was variously identified as a Chinese prince, the ruler of ETHIOPIA, and, in a papal appeal of 1177, as 'illustrious and magnificent King of the Indies'.

Preston, Battle of (17–19 August 1648) An encounter in Lancashire that effectively ended the second phase of the ENGLISH CIVIL WAR. On one side were the invading Scottish Engagers under HAMILTON and on the other was Cromwell's NEW MODEL ARMY. The raw Scottish recruits, although greatly superior in numbers, were no match for the English veterans. Cromwell caught up with them at Preston and dispersed them in a series of running battles.

Prestonpans, Battle of (21 September 1745) A military engagement during the FORTY-FIVE Rebellion on the Scottish coast 14.5 km (9 miles) east of Edinburgh. It resulted in a famous JACOBITE victory, when Bonnie Prince Charlie's untrained Scots met Sir John Cope's professional royalist forces and surprisingly routed them in little more than five minutes. The victory attracted many recruits to the Young PRETENDER's standard and paved the way for his invasion of England.

pretender A person who puts themself forward as having a rightful claim to someone else's throne. False claims have been put forward by such pretenders as Lambert SIMNEL and Perkin WARBECK, who claimed the crown of HENRY VII of England, and PUGACHEV during the reign of CATHERINE II the Great of Russia.

In England the Stuart Pretenders were excluded from the throne because of their religion. The Old Pretender, James Edward Stuart (1688–1766), was the son of the exiled JAMES II and in the eyes of loyal JACOBITES became King of England on his father's death in 1701. He was a devout but unimaginative man who failed to win the affection even of his followers. Two Jacobite rebellions, the FIFTEEN and the FORTY-FIVE, were organized by his supporters to accomplish his

restoration, but he arrived in Scotland when the Fifteen was virtually over, and he entrusted the leadership in the Forty-Five Rebellion to his son Charles Edward, the Young Pretender (1720–88). Charles Edward (Bonnie Prince Charlie) had youth and charm, and aroused loyal devotion to his cause, but the Forty-Five was a failure, and Charles's career after his miraculous escape from Scotland was an anti-climax, marred by moral and physical decline.

Pretorius, Andries (Wilhelmus Jacobus) (1798–1853) Boer leader and general. After several frontier campaigns against the Xhosa, he took part in the GREAT TREK and became commandant-general of the Boers after Piet Retief's murder in 1838. He defeated the Zulu at the BLOOD RIVER (1838). In 1847 he organized protests against the British annexation of the land between the Orange and Vaal, but in 1848 he was defeated at Boomplaats by Sir Harry Smith, when the Orange River Sovereignty was established. In 1852 he was instrumental in negotiating the Sand River Convention, which recognized the land beyond the Vaal as the South African Republic (TRANSVAAL).

Pretorius, Martinus Wessel (1819–1901) Boer statesman. He was President of the South African Republic (TRANSVAAL) (1857–71), having followed his father, Andries PRETORIUS, in the GREAT TREK. After fighting the Zulu, he became one of the four Transvaal commandant-generals, and was elected President. He was also elected President of the Orange Free State (1859–63). His claim to diamond fields (1867) on the Vaal River brought him into conflict with British interests. Following the annexation of the Transvaal by Britain in 1877 he was imprisoned. With the outbreak of the First BOER WAR (1880–81) he proclaimed, with Paul KRUGER and Petrus Joubert, a new Boer republic (January 1881). After the victory of Majuba Hill, he was a signatory of the Treaty of Pretoria, which re-established the independent states of Transvaal and Orange Free State.

Pride's Purge (6 December 1648) An English army coup in the aftermath of the ENGLISH CIVIL WAR, in which over 100 Members of Parliament who wished to reach an agreement with CHARLES I were forcibly excluded from the House of Commons by Colonel Thomas Pride, a Puritan army officer. The remaining members continued to sit in the Commons, forming the RUMP PARLIAMENT.

primary elections Elections for the selection of candidates for public office, most significantly for the US Presidency. In the USA in the later 19th century, primaries were pioneered in an attempt to eradicate corruption and patronage in the selection of candidates. Each state selected delegates to send to a national party convention that nominated the party's candidate for President. These delegates were chosen by a closed 'caucus system', that is, senior party members in the state chose the delegates and instructed them how to vote. Beginning with Wisconsin in 1903, however, primary elections steadily replaced the 'caucus primaries'. They are held by the state and the results are legally binding. There are both 'open' and 'closed' presidential primaries. In open primaries any adult voter in a state may take part, regardless of his or her own party preference. In closed primaries, only those who are registered members of the party may vote. The practice of primaries is mainly confined to the USA, but the Australian Labor Party runs a similar 'pre-selection' ballot for the nomination of candidates.

Primo de Rivera, Miguel (1870–1930) Spanish general and statesman, dictator of Spain (1923–30). Believing that widespread disorder was a product of corrupt and inefficient parliamentary government, he led a coup (1923). His authoritarian regime attempted to reunite the nation around the motto 'Country, Religion, Monarchy'. Apart from successfully ending the Moroccan war (1927), he achieved little. His reliance on the landlord class prevented him from introducing urgently needed agricultural reforms. Although he survived three attempts to remove him in 1926, increasing lack of support from the army forced him to resign in 1930.

primogeniture (the condition of being first born) The system whereby the father's estate descends to the oldest son to the exclusion of all other children. It was developed in western Europe and introduced in England in the late 11th century by Norman lawyers as a means of preserving intact the landed wealth of the BARONS as the basis of their military service to the crown. As part of the FEUDAL SYSTEM, primogeniture maintained the political and social status of the aristocracy. Although it was subsequently extended, it never applied to personal or movable property; where previous practice had been for lands to descend to females, then such lands continued to be divided equally amongst the children. Other exceptions to the practice of primogeniture included burghs and the county of Kent, where an alternative system of inheritance existed, known as gavelkind, under which land was divided equally between all sons. Despite the Statute of Wills (1540), which permitted the disinheriting of an oldest son, primogeniture survived in England until 1926 and in Scotland until 1964 and it continues to apply specifically to inheritances of the crown and of most peerages.

Priscus, Lucius Tarquinius TARQUIN.

Primrose League An organization founded by Sir Drummond Wolf and Lord Randolph CHURCHILL in 1883, devoted to the cause of Tory democracy. The League used the emblem of DISRAELI's favourite flower to focus on his concept of Conservatism. This involved defence of traditional features of British life, but also a wish to broaden support for Conservatism by showing its capacity to improve living and working conditions for the masses.

Princely States More than 500 Indian kingdoms and principalities that existed during the BRITISH RAJ period (1858–1947). Although their rulers preserved some autonomy they were bound by treaty to the British. The states, although scattered, made up two-fifths of India's territory. Their princes were Hindu, Muslim, and a few Sikh and Buddhist, some, like those of HYDERABAD and KASHMIR, ruling majorities of other faiths. Most ruled autocratically, but a few, like Mysore, were regarded as progressive. Many princes had been forced to accept indirect British rule during the era of EAST INDIA COMPANY expansion and paramountcy between 1757 and 1857. Mutual rivalries, historical, religious, and social, prevented co-ordinated resistance to British predominance. After 1857, when control of India passed

to the crown, their collaboration was deliberately sought by confirmation of their internal autonomy. After 1877, when Queen Victoria was proclaimed Empress of India, they participated in imperial *durbars*. On British withdrawal in 1947, they came under pressure to join either India or Pakistan. In Kashmir, Hyderabad, and Junagadh crises occurred, but most acceded peacefully, hoping some of their privileges, particularly financial, would be upheld. Many of the smaller states were grouped together into unions, for example the United States of Rajasthan. Legislation in 1970 abolished the special privileges of their ruling families.

printing The process of reproducing copies of text, pictures, or designs on to a material such as paper, board, plastic, or metal, usually by pressing an inked image against the material being printed. Early civilizations in the Far East developed the first known forms of printing. In the 8th century the Chinese produced a million copies of Buddhist texts using wood-blocks and there is evidence of printing from movable wooden (and later metal) type in China and Korea from the 11th century. In the West, monks used wood-blocks in the late 14th century to print pictures of the saints. Johann GUTENBERG in Germany initiated the real development of European printing in the 1450s through his invention of a typesetting mould for casting individual metal letters and William CAXTON set up the first printing press in England in 1476.

This new craft of printing spread rapidly across Europe. By the 1480s, most European countries had printing presses. The development of printing meant that many copies of individual titles could be produced more quickly and cheaply than by scribes copying manuscripts. It enabled ideas to be disseminated more widely, frequently in vernacular languages rather than the Latin of scholars. ERASMUS and LUTHER exploited printing's potential (in 1525 Luther published 183 pamphlets) and universities, lawyers, and doctors benefited from a much wider range of texts.

During the next three centuries, artists, type-founders, artisans, and printers all contributed to advances in the design and quality of printing. New and elegant typefaces were designed, the use of illustration and ornamentation increased, and copper was used for fine engravings. Various non-relief printing processes, such as lithography and gravure, were also developed. Improvements were made to the basic screw press, including a lever action instead of the screw, and metal construction in place of wood. However, output remained relatively low because of the need to redistribute type before setting it again, the slowness of hand presses, and the need to dampen paper before printing on it. The 19th century brought the development of the platen press, in which a plate presses the paper against the type, the flat-bed cylinder press, in which an inked frame carrying the metal type (known as a forme) moves beneath a cylinder carrying the paper, and the rotary press, using curved printing plates that rotate against paper that is either sheet-fed (individual sheets) or reel-fed (continuous sheet).

Later in the century, advances were made in the technologies of typesetting, with the development of linotype and monotype, of stereotyping, and of illustration. The principles of half-tones, offset lithography, colour printing, and photography for platemaking were also laid down during this period, so that by the beginning of the 20th century most of the basic forms of letterpress, lithographic, and intaglio printing had been established. Between the two World Wars print engineering was much improved and photographic methods grew in importance, while modern electronics and computer technology have revolutionized printing methods since 1950.

prison camps, Soviet Punitive institutions for forced labour in the former Soviet Union. The tradition of exiling political protesters and reformers to Siberia was well-established in 19th-century Russia. By a decree of 1919 LENIN maintained such punishment, operating through his police agency, the CHEKA. During STALIN's rule millions were arrested by the MVD, including peasants who resisted COLLECTIVIZATION, Christians, Jews, intellectuals, and political protesters. The prisoners were passed to GULAG (acronym for the Main Administration of Corrective Labour Camps), which was established in 1930 and was responsible for administering the forced labour system. The camps were mostly situated in the east of the Soviet Union and were referred to metaphorically as the 'Gulag archipelago'. Estimates of numbers confined to Gulag camps in the years of Stalin vary, ranging between six and 15 million. After the worst years of the purges in the 1930s thousands continued to be sent to the camps. After the arrest and execution of BERIA (1953) and the de-Stalinization policy of KHRUSHCHEV, there was a decline in the worst excesses of the camps, which were formally replaced in 1955 by Corrective Labour Colonies. Many distinguished Soviet citizens, including the writers Eugenia Ginzberg and Aleksandr Solzhenitsyn, were sent to prison camps; others were 'exiled' to Siberia, placed in 'psychiatric hospitals', or in other ways restrained. The physicist Andrei Sakharov and his wife Yelena Bonner were not allowed to leave Nizhny Novgorod (Gosky). In 1987 in the wake of a new policy of *glasnost* or openness, GORBACHEV ordered the release of some intellectual dissidents. All had allegedly been released by 1992.

Prithviraj III (d. 1193) Hindu (Chauhan Rajput) King of Delhi, who died in a brave attempt to resist the establishment of Muslim power in northern India. Until the Muslim invasions, he was preoccupied with defending his territories in Ajmer and Delhi against rival Hindu kings. Although he was victorious in 1192, in his first encounter with the Turkish invader, Muhammad Ghuri, in 1193 he was defeated and killed thus opening the way for the founding of the DELHI sultanate. Prithviraj III has been immortalized in ballads and folk literature as a figure of romance and heroism.

privateers Licensed sea-raiders in time of war, who had government-issued letters of marque or reprisal allowing them to attack enemy shipping. Privateers were often employed in European wars in the 16th and 17th centuries by the English, French, and Dutch, and they later became common in the Caribbean, North America, and the Indian Ocean during imperial conflicts. The Americans resorted to widespread privateering during the Wars of Independence and 1812; the South followed this example during the Civil War. Privateers were internationally abolished by the Declaration of Paris (1856).

Proclamation Line (1763) A declaration which prohibited American settlement west of the Allegheny Mountains in an attempt by the British government to regularize relations between frontiersmen and Native Americans after the FRENCH AND INDIAN WAR. The royal proclamation also established governments for captured territory and imposed royal control on Native American traders. It antagonized land speculators, pioneers, and war veterans who had been promised land in the west. It was partially amended by subsequent treaties with Native American tribes.

progress, royal A journey around the kingdom, regularly taken by monarchs and their courts in the days of personal rule. When communications were poor and regional control limited, progresses served to assert sovereignty and win loyalty. They also offered opportunities to hunt, to avoid the plagues that thrived in built-up cities, and to share the economic burden of maintaining the court among richer subjects. ELIZABETH I compelled her rich courtiers to entertain her and her retinue at their COUNTRY HOUSES. Emperor CHARLES V, with his widely scattered dominions, was by necessity a 'peripatetic monarch'. Monarchs who refused to make progresses ran the risk of forfeiting their subjects' obedience, as was partly the case with PHILIP II whose reclusive nature failed to inspire his subjects' loyalty.

Progressive Movement (US) (1890–1914) A US movement that sought to provide the basic political, social, and economic reforms necessary for the developing industrial economy. In both the Republican and Democratic parties Progressives were distinguished by a commitment to popular government, free trade, and control of competition-stifling trusts. To secure these ends they advocated direct PRIMARY ELECTIONS for the nomination of candidates, the popular election of Senators (secured in 1913), and ANTI-TRUST legislation. Social reforms were also demanded, for example legislation improving conditions of employment, and PROHIBITION attracted much support. Under Progressive pressure, government extended its activity at municipal, state, and federal levels in the pursuit of equality, efficiency, and social harmony. In different ways, progressive policies were adapted by the Republican Theodore ROOSEVELT and the Democrat Woodrow WILSON.

Progressive Parties (US) (1912, 1924, and 1948) Three US political organizations. In 1912 the first Progressive (the 'Bull Moose') Party, led by the former President Theodore ROOSEVELT, polled more votes in the presidential elections than the Republican candidate, President TAFT. By splitting the Republican vote, it allowed the Democrats to win on an equally progressive platform. In 1924 a revitalized Progressive Party, based on Wisconsin and other farm states, challenged the conservative outlook of both the Republican and Democratic parties. Although securing five million votes, the party carried only Wisconsin. In 1948 Henry A. WALLACE, formerly Democratic Secretary of State for agriculture, campaigned for a more conciliatory policy towards the Soviet Union. His Progressive Party, however, appeared too sympathetic to communism, and failed to challenge either main party.

Prohibition era (US) (1920–33) The period during which alcohol was illegal in the USA. A culmination of the TEMPERANCE MOVEMENT, it began when the Eighteenth Amendment to the Constitution went into effect by the passing of the VOLSTEAD ACT (1919). Despite the securing of some 300,000 court convictions between 1920 and 1930, drinking continued. Speakeasies (illegal bars) and bootlegging (illegal distilling of alcohol) flourished. The success of gangsters like Al CAPONE, who controlled the supply of illegal alcohol, led to corruption of police and city government. In 1931, following the Wickersham Commission's report that the prohibition laws were unenforceable and encouraged public disrespect for law in general, the Eighteenth Amendment was repealed by the Twenty-First Amendment, re-legalizing alcohol. A number of states and counties retained full or partial prohibition, but by 1966 no state-wide prohibition laws existed.

propaganda The attempt to shape or manipulate people's beliefs or actions through the distribution of information, arguments, or symbols. The word derives from the Roman Catholic body established in the 18th century to administer missionary activity, the *Sacra Congregatio de Propaganda Fide*.

Propaganda may be printed, broadcast, or visual, but common to all these forms is the attempt to manage and control communication and thereby to affect people's views of the world. All governments engage more or less in propaganda activities, describing them in many cases as public information programmes, and these can be used to influence opinions and actions both at home and abroad. The extent to which propaganda succeeds depends on the freedom of access to alternative views. One common form of propaganda is the dissemination of information designed to create a favourable image of a government or society, another is the use of 'black propaganda' to create suspicions of either the intentions or the actions of another state. In the 1930s, the German Nazis, led by Hitler's minister of propaganda, Joseph GOEBBELS, conducted a highly skilful propaganda campaign that encompassed not only public information, but also the arts, including literature, the cinema, and the theatre. With a totally cynical disregard for the truth, the German people were indoctrinated by bogus racial theories, urged to seek world domination, and excluded from hearing what the rest of the world thought of them. World War II could be said to have only been possible because German propaganda was so successful. Later, during the COLD WAR (1946–90), Radio Moscow, Radio Free Europe, and the Voice of America were active in promoting the images of their own societies and attacking their opponents. With the growth of international communications systems, propaganda has become an ever more potent political tool, as evidenced, for example, by the attempt by both sides to influence world public opinion through television during the 1991 Gulf War.

Protectorate, English (16 December 1653–25 May 1659) The rule over England established by Oliver CROMWELL. Unable to work with the BAREBONES PARLIAMENT, Cromwell entrusted a council of army officers with the task of drawing up a new constitution. The resulting Instrument of Government made Cromwell Lord Protector, monarch in all but name, who would share power with a single House of Parliament elected by Puritans. Politically it was a failure. Cromwell could not work with his first Protectorate Parliament, so he divided England into 11 military districts ruled by army officers known as major-generals. This was so unpopular that he reverted to parliamentary rule through the second Parliament of the Protectorate in 1656. Although the Protectorate was successful in foreign policy and notable for religious toleration of all faiths other than Roman Catholicism, its stability depended on Cromwell's personal qualities. After his death in 1658 the army removed Richard CROMWELL, his successor, bringing the Protectorate to an end in 1659 in preparation for the RESTORATION of Charles II.

Protestant A member or adherent of any of the Christian Churches that separated from the ROMAN CATHOLIC CHURCH at the REFORMATION. The term was coined after the imperial Diet summoned at Speyer in 1529 and derives from the 'Protestatio' of the reforming members against the decisions of the Catholic majority. These adherents of the Reformation were not merely registering objections: they were professing their commitment to the simple faith of the early Church, which they believed had been obscured by the unnecessary innovations of medieval Roman Catholicism. Since then, the term has been used to identify those who accept the principles of the Reformation, as opposed to Catholic or EASTERN ORTHODOX Christians. Martin LUTHER, Ulrich ZWINGLI, and John CALVIN founded the largest of the original Protestant branches and there were other more radical groups, such as the ANABAPTISTS.

All the early Protestants shared a conviction that the BIBLE was the only source of revealed truth and it was made available to all in vernacular translations. They also believed in the doctrine of justification 'by faith alone' (i.e. rejection of the idea that one could obtain salvation through 'good works'), and in the idea of the universal priesthood of all believers. They minimized the ceremonial aspects of Christianity and placed preaching and hearing the word of God before sacramental faith and practice. Many Protestant sects and churches were formed, largely because the principle of 'private judgement' in the interpretation of the scriptures led to many shades of doctrine and practice. In England, members of both the established ANGLICAN CHURCH and the various NONCONFORMIST churches are usually regarded as Protestants.

Protestant ethic A world-view based on hard work, abstention from luxury, reason, and the steady accumulation of wealth, and associated with northern European Protestantism. The term was coined by the German sociologist Max Weber in *The Protestant Ethic and the Spirit of Capitalism* (1905). Weber held that these qualities had been particularly conducive to the development of CAPITALISM in Europe. Although faith and humility were the mainsprings of Protestantism, financial and professional success came to be identified as outward signs of God's favour; by contrast, Roman Catholicism held that individual grace was not dependent on merit. There has been much debate about Weber's proposition and about whether he stereotyped capitalism and Protestantism. However, a link between the Protestant ethic and the development of capitalism is still widely accepted.

Proudhon, Pierre Joseph (1809–65) French social theorist. In 1840 he published the pamphlet *What is Property?* This began with the famous words '*La propriété, c'est le vol*' (property is theft), and went on to maintain that property was the denial of justice, liberty, and equality, since it enabled some men to exploit the labours of others. For this he was tried by the assize court of Besançon but acquitted. In 1848 he was elected to the National Assembly and took to journalism; he was condemned to three years' imprisonment (1849–52) for attacking the President of the republic. His writings considerably influenced later supporters of ANARCHISM and federalism, but MARX criticized him as a sentimentalist.

Provence A region of south-east France with a Mediterranean coastline. It was named Provincia Gallica Transalpina by the Romans, who annexed it in the 2nd century BC, when it was occupied by Celtic tribes. It also contained Greek and Phoenician settlements and developed a distinct culture, which it managed to retain, even through the chaos of Germanic invasions. As part of the kingdom of Arles it passed to the Holy Roman Empire in the reign of Conrad II but continued to enjoy a large measure of independence, its language, Provençal, remaining substantially different from Middle French. It made a great contribution to the success of the First CRUSADE and its involvement continued throughout the crusading period. The troubadours led a flourishing revival of secular literature and music. Its independence encouraged heresy and CATHARISM took root, resulting in the suppression of the ALBIGENSIANS by the Church. In the 14th and 15th centuries it resisted ANGEVIN claims to sovereignty, but in 1480 René, the last king of Aix, died and it passed, via his nephew, to France.

Provisors, Statute of PRAEMUNIRE, STATUTE OF.

Prussia A former kingdom in north-eastern Europe, originally inhabited by pagan tribes who were conquered by the TEUTONIC KNIGHTS in the mid-13th century. By the 15th century this Christianized region on the south-eastern coast of the Baltic Sea had come under Polish control. The lands east of the River Vistula (Royal Prussia) were ceded to the Polish crown, while the Teutonic Knights recognized Polish suzerainty over the rest in 1466. The HOHENZOLLERN Albrecht of Brandenburg-Ansbach was chosen as High Master in 1511. After the rapid spread of Lutheranism in his territory, he secularized the Teutonic Order and in 1525 became hereditary ruler of ducal Prussia. In 1618 the duchy passed under the control of the Electors of BRANDENBURG. By 1701 Brandenburg-Prussia had evolved into an ascendant Protestant power in Europe and in that year its ruler became known as 'King in Prussia'.

The kingdom's most notable 18th-century ruler was FREDERICK II (the Great) (1712–86). He and his successor Frederick William II (1744–97) added considerably to Prussia's holdings. However, many of these were lost during the NAPOLEONIC WARS, in which FREDERICK WILLIAM III (1770–1840) unsuccessfully tried to maintain neutrality. The territories yielded by Prussia became part of the CONFEDERATION OF THE RHINE, but the Treaty of TILSIT saved the kingdom from extinction. In 1813 it joined the QUADRUPLE ALLIANCE and in 1815 at the Congress of VIENNA gained part of Saxony and important lands on the Rhine. For the rest of his reign Frederick

William III followed METTERNICH's policy of repression. The sponsorship of the customs union or ZOLLVEREIN between almost all German states was important for the economic development of the region. FREDERICK WILLIAM IV (1840–61), was a romantic, whose concessions to the Prussian nobility and Catholic Church alienated the liberal middle classes. When the REVOLUTION OF 1848 began he promised a constitution, and a Prussian assembly met in Berlin, but in April 1849 he refused the crown of a united Germany without Austria. In 1858 he was declared insane and his brother became regent. Prussia vied with Austria for the leadership in the restored GERMAN CONFEDERATION. This struggle was successfully orchestrated by Prussia's chief minister, Otto von BISMARCK. Following the FRANCO-PRUSSIAN WAR (1870), the GERMAN SECOND EMPIRE was founded in 1871, when WILLIAM I was proclaimed emperor. After the defeat of Germany in 1918 a reduced Prussia became a German state in the WEIMAR REPUBLIC. Prussia was eventually abolished in 1947 and was divided between Poland, the Soviet Union, and the GERMAN DEMOCRATIC REPUBLIC.

Prynne, William (1600–69) English Puritan pamphleteer, a fearless campaigner on religious, moral, and political issues. His most famous pamphlet, *Histrio Mastix* (1632), was an attack on stage-plays; he was tried before the Star Chamber for its implied criticism of Queen HENRIETTA MARIA, who was a devotee of plays and masques. He was sentenced to life imprisonment and cropping of the ears (1634). He continued to write anti-episcopal pamphlets and in 1637 the remaining parts of his ears were removed. The LONG PARLIAMENT freed him in 1640. Elected to Parliament himself in 1648, he was expelled at PRIDE'S PURGE, and eventually supported the RESTORATION.

Ptolemies The Macedonian dynasty that ruled Egypt from 323 to 30 BC. Ptolemy I was an officer of ALEXANDER THE GREAT who, after the king's death, was appointed SATRAP of Egypt. He proclaimed himself king in 304 and by the time of his death in 283–282 he had established control over Cyprus, Palestine, and many cities in the Aegean and Asia Minor. The reigns of the Ptolemies who succeeded him were characterized externally by struggles with the SELEUCIDS for control of Syria, Asia Minor, and the Aegean, and internally by dissatisfaction and rebellion among the native Egyptians. Contact with the rising power of Rome came to a head during the reign of CLEOPATRA VII, whose liaison with MARK ANTONY led ultimately to their defeat at Actium, their suicide, and the annexation of Egypt by Octavian (AUGUSTUS).

Ptolemaic Egypt was remarkable for its administrative, financial, and commercial infrastructure, for the most part developed by the first two Ptolemies. The discovery of many PAPYRI has enabled scholars to reconstruct a detailed picture of life in these times. All land except that owned by temples belonged to the state, which rented much of it out to the people. The state provided seed corn, but required that it be repaid in kind at harvest time. It also held monopolies on such goods as oil-producing crops, mining, and salt. Local and central registers of houses, people, and animals facilitated taxation and the close supervision of life that was a pervasive part of the Ptolemaic regime. Ptolemaic Egypt had the most advanced system of banking in antiquity, geared to obtaining the maximum income for the state, with little regard for individual Egyptians, thus attempts to cheat the system and mass unrest were common.

Pueblo ANASAZI.

Puerto Rico An island commonwealth in the Caribbean, between Hispaniola and the Virgin Islands.

History. Originally known as Boriquén, Puerto Rico was inhabited by Arawak Indians when it was discovered by Columbus in 1493. Encouraged by Arawak rumours of deposits of gold, his companion, Juan PONCE DE LEÓN, was granted permission by the Spanish crown to colonize the island. In 1508 he founded the settlement of Caparra and in 1509 he was made governor. Caparra was abandoned and the settlement moved to nearby San Juan in 1521, to take better advantage of the bay for trading. By the end of the 16th century the Arawak were virtually extinct as a result of European-introduced diseases and exploitation. In the 17th and 18th centuries the island remained economically important for its sugar and tobacco plantations, worked by slaves brought from Africa, and strategically as a key to Spain's defence of its trading interests in the Caribbean and Atlantic against France, Britain, and Holland.

Puerto Rico was maintained by Spain as a garrison protecting trade routes until the loss of Mexico in 1821 removed its strategic significance. In 1887 the Autonomist Party was founded to protect home rule under Spanish sovereignty. In 1898, during the SPANISH–AMERICAN WAR, the island came under US military rule and was ceded to the USA at the end of the war. In 1917 an Act of the US Congress (Jones Act) declared Puerto Rican inhabitants to be US citizens. Since the 1940s, with a decline in the sugar industry, there have been successful efforts at industrialization and diversification of the economy. Muñoz Marín (1898–1980) was the first elected governor (1948–64), being re-elected three times. In 1952 the Commonwealth of Puerto Rico was proclaimed and ratified by a plebiscite. The party which has dominated politics since then, the Popular Democratic Party (PPD), has supported the status quo, while urging greater autonomy. Its rival, the New Progressive Party (PNP) would like the island to become the 51st state of the USA. There is also a small Independence Party, but the violent separatist organization, the FALN, has had little support on the island. The UN has regularly urged a plebiscite to decide the island's future. In 1993, Puerto Ricans voted to retain their country's status as a self-governing commonwealth, thereby rejecting both independence and US statehood.

CAPITAL:	San Juan
AREA:	9,104 sq km (3,515 sq miles)
POPULATION:	3.766 million (1996)
CURRENCY:	1 US dollar = 100 cents
RELIGIONS:	Roman Catholic 85.0%; Protestant 5.0%
ETHNIC GROUPS:	Hispanic 75.0%; Black 15.0%; mixed 10.0%
LANGUAGES:	Spanish; English (both official)
INTERNATIONAL ORGANIZATIONS:	CARICOM

Pugachev, Emelian Ivanovich (1726–75) COSSACK and leader of a massive popular uprising in 1773–74 against the rule of CATHERINE II (the Great) of Russia. Deserting the army, he won the support of discontented serfs, cossacks, miners, and such recently conquered peoples as the Bashkirs and Tartars. He captured Kazan and established a court, claiming to be the assassinated Emperor Peter III. He promised the abolition of landlords, bureaucrats, serfdom, taxation, and military service and the restoration of traditional religion. His betrayal and execution were followed by the ruthless suppression of his followers.

Pullman strike (1894) A US labour dispute that began when the Pullman Palace Car Company of Chicago laid off men and cut the wages of others, blaming the economic depression, and refused to discuss grievances with its employees. The cause of the workers was taken up by the powerful American Railway Union, led by Eugene V. DEBS. The strike threatened to paralyse the entire railway network unless Pullman went to arbitration. President CLEVELAND's sympathies were with the company, and the federal circuit court at Chicago issued an injunction declaring the strike illegal. Rioting and bloodshed ensued, and Debs was gaoled in 1895. The injunction remained open to misuse until amended by the Norris–La Guardia Anti-Injunction Act of 1932.

Punic wars The three wars fought in the 3rd and 2nd century BC between Rome and Carthage, so named from 'Poenicus' ('Dark skin' or 'Phoenician'), the term used to describe founders of the North African city. Carthage and Rome were fighting for control of the Mediterranean Sea and Rome was victorious in each war.

The First Punic war (264–241 BC) was fought largely at sea. Rome expanded its navy and took control of Sicily; seizing Corsica and Sardinia a few years later. HAMILCAR BARCA, father of HANNIBAL led the defeated side.

The Second Punic War (218–201 BC) arose from Hannibal's invasion of Italy from Carthaginian bases in Spain. He led a huge force, including squadrons of elephants, into Italy across the Alps, surprising the Romans. Rome suffered disastrous defeats, most notably in the mists by Lake Trasimene and at CANNAE. Italy was overrun by Hannibal but the Italian tribes did not rise against Rome. The strategy of the dictator FABIUS prevented further losses. In a long-drawn out series of campaigns Hannibal's extended lines of supply were threatened by defeats in Sicily and Spain and by the brilliant generalship of SCIPIO. HASDRUBAL, Hannibal's brother, was defeated on the Italian mainland in 207. By 203 Hannibal, who had no effective siege engines, was summoned to withdraw to Africa to defend Carthage itself, now threatened by Scipio. Pursued by Scipio he was defeated at Zama in 202 and the Carthaginians were forced to accept humiliating terms the following year. Spain was acquired as a provincial territory by Rome.

In 149 BC at a peak of its territorial expansion and at the insistence of CATO (the Elder), Rome intervened in an African dispute to side with Numidia against Carthage. In the Third Punic war (149–146 BC) the Younger SCIPIO besieged and destroyed Carthage utterly, sowed the site with symbolic salt and declared Africa a Roman province.

Punjab An area in Asia, formerly a north-western province of British India, now partitioned between India and Pakistan. In 1799 the Sikhs under RANJIT SINGH established a kingdom in the Punjab. After their defeat in the SIKH WARS the region remained under British rule until 1947. As the British withdrawal in 1947 approached, latent tensions between Punjab's Muslim, Hindu, and Sikh communities surfaced. Muslims constituted more than half the province's population and the MUSLIM LEAGUE's winning of Punjabi votes in the 1945–46 election strengthened its demand for a separate Muslim homeland. Growing communal violence pushed Britain and the CONGRESS PARTY into a reluctant acceptance of partition. Violence, during which hundreds of thousands died, increased as Hindus and Sikhs crossed to India and Muslims to Pakistan. Subsequently two wars (1965 and 1971) between India and Pakistan have involved fighting on the Punjabi frontier. Since 1967 Punjabis have been dominant in Pakistan's political life and a new national capital was built at Islamabad in 1966. The Indian state of Punjab was divided on a linguistic basis to provide a predominantly Punjabi-speaking state of Punjab (with a Sikh majority) and a Hindi-speaking state of Maryana, with Chandigarh as a joint capital. Militant SIKHS have continued to campaign for an independent Sikh state (Khalistan) in the Punjab.

Puritans Extreme English Protestants who were dissatisfied with the ANGLICAN CHURCH settlement and sought a further purification of the English Church from ROMAN CATHOLIC elements. Their theology was basically that of John CALVIN. At first they limited themselves to attacking such 'popish' (Roman Catholic) practices as church ornaments, vestments, and organ music, but from 1570 extremists attacked the authority (episcopacy) of bishops and government notably in the Martin MARPRELATE tracts. However, James I resisted their attempts to change Anglican dogma, ritual, and organization, which they had voiced at the HAMPTON COURT CONFERENCE. In the 1620s some Puritans emigrated to North America, but it was the policies of William LAUD and Charles I in the 1630s that resurrected the Puritan opposition of the 1580s. The doctrine of Predestination (that God ordains in advance those who shall receive salvation) became a major source of contention between the Puritans, for whom it was a fundamental article of faith, and the Arminians who rejected it. Religion was a key factor in the outbreak of civil war in 1642. Puritanism was strong among the troops of the NEW MODEL ARMY and in the 1640s and 1650s, with the encouragement of Cromwell, many Puritan objectives were realized. After the Restoration Puritans were mostly absorbed into the Anglican Church or into larger NONCONFORMIST groups and lost their distinctive identity. The term 'Puritan' is now used to refer to many groups and attitudes.

Putnam, Israel (1718–90) American general, who served in the Connecticut militia throughout the FRENCH AND INDIAN WAR and against PONTIAC's rebellion. He was a fervent patriot who joined the continental army at the start of the War of INDEPENDENCE, and fought at BUNKER HILL. He served with Washington's army until 1779 when he became paralysed. He was a mediocre tactician, but his personal bravery, patriotism, and geniality made him a national hero.

Puyi (or P'u-i) (1906–67) The last QING emperor of China (1908–12). Proclaimed Xuantung Emperor at the age of two by the empress dowager CIXI (his great aunt), he reigned until the CHINESE REVOLUTION OF 1911 forced his abdication in 1912. He continued to live in the imperial palace with extensive privileges, serving as a focus for monarchist movements and even experiencing a 12-day restoration in 1917, before being forced to flee by a local WARLORD to the Japanese concession of Tianjin in 1924. After the Japanese seizure of Manchuria, Puyi was placed at the head of the puppet state of MANCHUKUO. Deposed and captured by Soviet forces in 1945, he was later handed over to the communist Chinese, and, after a period of imprisonment, was allowed to live out his life as a private citizen.

Pym, John (1584–1643) English politician. He entered Parliament in 1614, and by the 1620s was making his mark, especially as a manager of the impeachment of BUCKINGHAM (1626), and as a supporter of the PETITION OF RIGHT (1628). In the LONG PARLIAMENT his debating and tactical skills brought him great influence and earned him the nickname 'King Pym'. He was the main architect of the reforming legislation of 1641, including the Acts of ATTAINDER against STRAFFORD and LAUD, and was responsible for having the GRAND REMONSTRANCE printed and published. Pym was one of the FIVE MEMBERS of Parliament whom Charles I ill-advisedly tried to arrest in 1642. Once the ENGLISH CIVIL WAR began, he played a vigorous role on the Committee of Safety (1642) and in the year of his death engineered the SOLEMN LEAGUE AND COVENANT with the Scots.

pyramid A monumental structure especially characteristic of ancient Egypt, often built as a royal tomb and usually made of stone, with a square base and sloping sides meeting centrally at an apex. At first the pharaohs were buried in underground chambers over which were built rectangular *mastabas*, stone structures housing the food and accoutrements the pharaoh would need in the afterlife. The first pyramid was that constructed for King Zoser at Saqqara by IMHOTEP in about 2700 BC, the so-called Step Pyramid which has six enormous steps and is over 60 m (197 feet) high. A pyramid built at Meydum in about 2600 was originally of similar design, but the steps were later filled in with limestone to produce the classical pyramid shape. Most of the best known pyramids date from the Old Kingdom (c. 2700–2200 BC), though some were built during the 11th and 12th dynasties (c. 2050–1750 BC). The pyramids of Khufu, Khafre, and Menkaure at Giza are a spectacular illustration of the skill of Egyptian architects and of the state's ability to organize a large workforce. The Great Pyramid of Giza, constructed of enormous stone blocks of up to 200 tonnes in weight, is estimated to have required a labour force equivalent to about 84,000 people employed for 80 days a year for 20 years.

Stepped pyramids known as ziggurats survive from the 3rd millennium BC in Mesopotamia. Stepped-pyramid structures were also built as bases for temples in pre-Columbian Central America. These were erected by the MAYA, AZTECS, and TOLTECS, for the most part between 250 AD and 1520. The Temple of the Sun in TEOTIHUACÁN in Mexico is perhaps the most impressive.

Pyramids, Battle of the (21 July 1798) The decisive battle fought near the pyramids of Giza that gave NAPOLEON control of Egypt. He took Alexandria by storm on 2 July, and then, with 40,000 men defeated a

MAMELUKE army of 60,000 led by Murad Bey. The victory enabled Napoleon to take Cairo and allowed France to control Egypt until its withdrawal in 1801.

Pyrrhus (319–272 BC) King of EPIRUS in Greece (307–303, 297–272), first as a minor (307–303) and then after his return from exile in 297. After various campaigns against his neighbours, especially MACEDONIA, he aided Tarentum against the growing power of Rome. He was victorious at Heraclea (280) and Asculum (279) and he almost expelled the Carthaginians from Sicily, but because of his limited number of troops he could ill afford the losses that he suffered (hence the expression 'Pyrrhic victory'). After his campaign in Sicily and a third battle with the Romans he returned to Epirus. He was a fine tactician, especially in his use of elephants and was greatly admired by HANNIBAL.

Q

Qaddafi, Muammar al- (1942–) Libyan statesman. Qaddafi served in the Libyan army and overthrew King Idris I in a military coup in 1969. He became Chairman of the Revolutionary Command Council (RCC) and, in 1970, Prime Minister. He then nationalized the majority of foreign petroleum assets, closed British and US military bases, and seized Italian and Jewish properties. He used his nation's vast oil wealth to support the PALESTINE LIBERATION ORGANIZATION and other revolutionary causes and his government became involved in a number of incidents with neighbouring states, most persistently CHAD. In retaliation for alleged acts of terrorism against US nationals, President REAGAN authorized the bombing of the Libyan capital in 1986. In 1979, while remaining actual head of state with the title of chairman, Qaddafi reorganized the Libyan constitution, with 'Basic People's Congresses' theoretically forming an electoral base for the General People's Congress. His ambition for a single North African Arab Federation from Egypt to Morocco remained unrealized, but he did help to form the Maghreb Union, an economic alliance, in 1989. In 1991 he maintained a neutral stance over the crisis leading to the GULF WAR, but was accused of harbouring terrorists responsible for the bombing of a US aeroplane over Lockerbie, Scotland. This led to the imposition on Libya of UN sanctions in 1992. In 1995 Qaddafi again caused controversy by expelling thousands of Palestinian refugees from Libya.

Qajar A Turkic tribe in north-east Iran that produced the Qajar dynasty, which ruled Persia (Iran) from 1794 to 1925. The dynasty was established by Agha Muhammad (1742–97), a eunuch who made Tehran his capital and was crowned Shah in 1796. He was succeeded by his nephew Fath Ali Shah (1797–1834), during whose reign Iran was forced to cede the Trans-Caucasian lands to Russia. The constitutional revolution of 1906 established a parliament. Muhammad Ali (1907–09) was deposed for attacking the constitution and after a lengthy regency, Muhammad Ali's son, Ahmad Shah 1914–25), became the last Qajar ruler, being deposed by an army officer, REZA SHAH PAHLAVI, in 1925.

Qatar A country in the Middle East, bounded by Saudi Arabia inland, with a sea boundary with BAHRAIN to its west.

Physical. Qatar is a hot arid country occupying a peninsula of desert on the southwest of the Persian Gulf.

Economy. The economy and exports of Qatar are dominated by crude oil, which is present in very large quantities both on-shore and off-shore. Industries include oil-refining, gas liquefaction, fertilizers, cement, and steel. The country has one of the highest per capita incomes in the world.

History. Historically linked with Bahrain, Qatar was under Bahraini suzerainty for much of the 19th century. In 1872 it came under Ottoman suzerainty, but the Ottomans renounced their rights in 1913. In 1916 Qatar made an agreement with Britain that created a *de facto* British protectorate. Oil was discovered in 1939 and exploited from 1949. The agreement with Britain was terminated in 1968 and Qatar became fully independent in 1971, under a constitution by which the Emir, Shaikh Khalifa bin Hamad al-Thani would govern as Prime Minister. Qatar provided bases for UN forces in the GULF WAR, after which it strengthened its links with Iran. In 1995 the Emir was overthrown in a bloodless coup by his son, Shaikh Hamad bin Khalifa al-Thani, who embarked on a programme of liberal reforms. This caused tension with Bahrain and Saudi Arabia and led to an attempted coup in 1996.

CAPITAL:	Doha
AREA:	11,337 sq km (4,377 sq miles)
POPULATION:	590,000 (1996)
CURRENCY:	1 Qatar riyal = 100 dirhams
RELIGIONS:	Muslim (mainly Sunni) 92%; Christian 6.0%; Hindu 1.0%; Baha'i 0.2%
ETHNIC GROUPS:	South Asian 34.0%; Qatari Arab 20.0%; other Arab 25.0%; Iranian 16.0%
LANGUAGES:	Arabic (official); South Asian languages; Persian
INTERNATIONAL ORGANIZATIONS:	UN; Arab League; OAPEC

Qianlong (Ch'ien-lung) (1710–99) QING Emperor of China (1735–95). During his rule China reached its greatest territorial extent with campaigns undertaken in Turkistan (XINJIANG), Annam, Burma, and Nepal. In 1757 Qianlong restricted all foreign traders to GUANGZHOU (Canton), where they could trade only from November to March. He rejected in 1793 the requests of a British delegation led by Lord Macartney for an expansion of trade and the establishment of diplomatic relations. Towards the end of his reign his administration was weakened by corruption, financial problems, and provincial uprisings, notably of the WHITE LOTUS SOCIETY in 1796. He was lauded by VOLTAIRE as a philosopher-king, patronizing the arts, writing poetry, and overseeing the compilation of literary collections (in which anything thought critical of the Qing was expunged). Four years before his death he abdicated in favour of his son.

Qin (Ch'in) China's first imperial dynasty (221–206 BC). It was founded by Prince Zheng, ruler of the ZHOU vassal state of Qin. Unlike rival Chinese states, Qin used cavalry rather than chariots in battle and were quick to adopt iron weaponry. The Qin rulers ensured a regular food supply by developing a system for land irrigation. Based in Shaanxi, they began to expand their territories from about 350 BC. Under Zheng, the Qin overthrew the Eastern Zhou and conquered (256–221 BC) all Zhou's former vassal states. Zheng then took the title Huangdi and is best known as SHI HUANGDI (First Emperor). He died in 210 BC and his dynasty was overthrown four years later. From that time, although China was sometimes fragmented, the concept of a united empire prevailed. From Qin is derived the name China.

Qing (Ch'ing) Imperial Chinese dynasty (1644–1912), the last to rule China. Its emperors were MANCHUS. In 1644 a MING general, Wu Sangui, invited Manchu Bannermen, who were massed at Shanhaiguan, the undefended eastern end of the Great Wall of China, to expel the bandit chieftain Li Zicheng from Beijing. The Bannermen occupied the city and proclaimed their child-emperor 'Son of Heaven', establishing the Qing dynasty. They demanded obedience to their emperor and forced Chinese men to braid their long hair into a queue or 'pigtail'. Resistance to the Qing continued for up to 30 years in south China, but was eventually suppressed.

Qing rule differed little from that of the ethnic Chinese dynasties. It emphasized study of the Confucian classics and the Confucian basis of society. The civil service, half Manchu, half Chinese, continued to be recruited through an examination system based on knowledge of the classics. It was during Qing rule that the empire of China reached its widest extent, covering Taiwan, Manchuria, Mongolia, Tibet, and Turkistan. The Qing regarded all other peoples as barbarians and their rulers as subject to the 'Son of Heaven', and were blind to the growing pressure of the West. Under KANGXI (1654–1722) and QIANLONG (1736–96) China was powerful enough to treat the outside world with condescension.

Thereafter, however, the authority of the dynasty was reduced. Faced with major internal revolts, most notably the TAIPING REBELLION (1850–64) and a succession of Muslim uprisings in the far west, the Qing proved unable to contend simultaneously with increasing intrusions from western powers interested in the economic exploitation of China. During the long dominance of the conservative empress dowager CIXI, young, ineffectual emperors failed to inject sufficient force into such modernization schemes as the SELF-STRENGTHENING MOVEMENT and the HUNDRED DAYS REFORM to prevent increasing foreign intervention. Humiliating defeat in the SINO–JAPANESE WAR (1894–95) and the BOXER RISING (1900) weakened Qing power and after the CHINESE REVOLUTION OF 1911, the last Qing emperor PUYI was forced to abdicate in 1912.

Quadruple Alliance An alliance formed in 1813 by Britain, Prussia, Austria, and Russia that committed them to the defeat of Napoleon. The resulting Battle of LEIPZIG (1813) was decisive and the war ended. In November 1815 CASTLEREAGH at the Congress of VIENNA arranged for the Alliance to be maintained to form a permanent league to safeguard 'the general tranquillity of Europe'. However, it became less a means of containing France (the latter joined in 1818 to form the Quintuple Alliance) and more a means of containing revolution. A series of Congresses was held, but Britain became steadily less involved and, after the death of Castlereagh (1822), the alliance had little effective influence.

Quakers (officially 'The Society of Friends') A Christian group that rejects the formal structures of creed and sacraments and usually of clergy and liturgy, emphasizing instead the individual's search for 'inner light'. Founded by the Englishman George FOX in the 17th century, the Quakers became convinced that their 'experimental' discovery of God, sometimes featuring

trembling or quaking experiences during meetings, would lead to the purification of all Christendom. The name 'Quaker' was originally a term of contempt.

By 1660 there were more than 20,000 Quaker converts and Quaker missionaries were at work in Ireland, Scotland, Wales, and the American colonies. They continued to grow in number, despite severe penalization from 1662 to 1689 for refusing to take oaths, attend Anglican services, or pay tithes. After considerable debate, they evolved a form of organization, with regular monthly, quarterly, and annual meetings. This system essentially stands today and any Quaker can attend any meeting.

In 1681 William PENN founded the American Quaker colony of PENNSYLVANIA and Quaker influence in the colony's politics remained paramount until the American War of Independence. Quakers are known for their social reform, pacifism, and support for philanthropic ventures. They played an important role in the abolition of SLAVERY and were instrumental in the foundation of a number of British-based charities, including Oxfam.

Quakers   *This 17th-century print shows an early meeting of the Quaker leadership in England. One of the figures on the platform is William Penn, founder of Pennsylvania.*

Quebec An eastern province of CANADA, extending from south of the Saint Lawrence river north to the Hudson Strait.

History. Quebec city was founded in 1608 by Samuel de CHAMPLAIN on a near-impregnable plateau and served as the capital of NEW FRANCE until it was captured by the British in 1759. When New France was ceded to Britain in 1763, it was renamed the Province of Quebec. The Quebec Act (1774) extended its boundaries at American expense and guaranteed religious tolerance and French Civil Law. This ensured loyalty during the War of Independence and the American campaign to capture Quebec city was repulsed (1775–76). In 1791 the province was divided into two, UPPER AND LOWER CANADA, the latter having a majority of French-speaking Canadians. The WAR OF 1812 confirmed the frontiers with the USA. In 1822 British merchants in Montreal sought a reunion of the two provinces in order to gain an overall English-speaking majority. In 1837 the unsuccessful rebellion led by Louis Joseph Papineau was a protest as much against the increasing dominance of British-Canadians as against any lack of political representation. In the face of French-Canadian opposition, the Act of Union of 1840 joined the two provinces into the new Province of Canada, with a majority of British-Canadians. The BRITISH NORTH AMERICA ACT (1867) once again divided the Province of Canada, creating a separate Province of Quebec within the Confederation of Canada. The Province was expanded by the acquisition of New Quebec in the north in 1912.

The Québecois continue to maintain their separate identity through the use of both written and spoken French, in a country which is predominantly English-speaking. Both languages are now recognized by the government as official. Québecois culture is based on the traditions and folklore of the rural population and includes distinct forms of singing, dancing, and music. Since the early 1960s French-Canadian separatism has been a major factor in Canadian politics. Despite the success in provincial elections of the pro-separatist Parti Québecois secession was rejected in a provincial referendum in 1980. A national referendum in 1992 rejected constitutional changes that included increasing Quebec's autonomy. Nevertheless, the separatist movement continued to gain support and in 1993, with the electoral collapse of the Canadian Progressive Conservative Party, a pro-separatist alliance, the Bloc Québecois became the second-largest grouping in the national Parliament. Complete independence was again rejected, by an extremely narrow margin, in a provincial referendum in 1995.

Quebec Liberation Front A French Canadian separatist movement. Established in the early 1960s, it launched a terrorist and bombing campaign to secure the separation of QUEBEC Province from Canada. The Front de Libération du Québec (FLQ) was greatly encouraged when DE GAULLE used the separatist slogan *Vive le Québec Libre* (Long Live Free Quebec) while visiting Canada in 1967. Its terrorist activities proved unpopular; much more support was given to the constitutional Parti Québecois, which won a majority of the seats in the Quebec legislative assembly in 1976 and remains an important force in the province, playing a significant role in the increasing success of the Bloc Québecois alliance.

Queen Anne's War (1702–13) A war between Britain and France, part of the War of the SPANISH SUCCESSION, that was fought in North America. Frontier warfare in New England with savage French and Indian attacks on outlying settlements broke out again at the start of the 18th century (see FRENCH AND INDIAN WARS). In 1710 the French lost Port Royal in Acadia (known to the British as NOVA SCOTIA), which came under British control. A British attempt to capture Quebec the next year was prevented by storms. In the south, a South Carolinian (British) expedition destroyed the Spanish city of St Augustine, Florida, in 1702 and a retaliatory French attack on Charleston (1706) was repulsed. In the Caribbean, St Christopher (St Kitts) was captured from the French in 1702, but Guadeloupe resisted British attacks in the following year. Thereafter only PRIVATEERS and BUCCANEERS remained active. The main British colonial gains at the Peace of UTRECHT were Nova Scotia, western Newfoundland, and St Christopher.

Queensland A state in north-east AUSTRALIA, bounded by the Northern Territory on the west, South Australia on the south-west, and New South Wales on the south. Queensland's long eastern coast faces the Pacific and is largely sheltered by the Great Barrier Reef, while the Cape York Peninsula points due north to the Torres Strait between the Arafura and Coral Seas. Coal is mined extensively in the centre, and there are plentiful reserves of bauxite, copper, zinc, lead, and other minerals, together with oil and natural gas.

History. In its early years of White settlement, when it formed part of New South Wales, the territory was known as the Moreton Bay district and served as a penal colony from 1824 to 1839. It was separated from New South Wales, re-named Queensland, and granted responsible government in 1859. Gold discoveries in the 1860s and 1870s attracted people to Queensland. The pastoral industry also developed in those years. In 1901 it became a state in the Commonwealth of Australia.

Queen's shilling (or King's shilling) A coin, which, if accepted from a recruiting officer obliged the recipient to serve in the British army. Recruiting sergeants in the 18th century would ply likely young men with drink and if they could persuade them to take the shilling, they were in fact accepting army pay. This ranked as a binding agreement from which escape was very difficult.

Quesnay, François (1694–1774) French physician and economist. He trained as a doctor and became physician to Louis XV; his writings on economics were not published until he was 60. He was the leader of the physiocrats, a group of economists who opposed MERCANTILISM and proclaimed *laissez-faire*. They believed that land was the only source of wealth and that all taxation should be based on land; tax exemptions and all artifical restrictions on the circulation of wealth should cease and in particular there must be a free market in grain. They thought that these changes could best be secured through a strong monarchy. Quesnay was a protégé of Madame de POMPADOUR, his followers met at Versailles.

Quetzalcóatl (literally 'quetzal-bird snake') One of the chief gods of ancient Mesoamerica (Mexico and northern Central America), depicted as a feathered serpent. Quetzalcóatl was also the official title of the AZTEC high priest. Quetzalcóatl was known as a god throughout Mesoamerica and was called Kukulkán by the MAYA. Images and temples to him appear at early sites, such as at TEOTIHUACÁN, but he was especially revered from about 700 to 1520.

Quetzalcóatl was the god of the morning star, wind, life, fertility, wisdom, and practical knowledge, and invented agriculture, the calendar, and various arts and crafts. Human sacrifices were made to him. Quetzalcóatl is also identified with a legendary priest-king who sailed away, promising to return. When Montezuma II, the last Aztec king, heard of the arrival of the CONQUISTADOR Hernán CORTÉS in 1519, he believed it was Quetzalcóatl, and he ordered his men to welcome the Spaniards. This event led to the destruction of Aztec civilization. In addition to his guise as a plumed serpent, Quetzalcóatl was represented as the wind god Ehécatl, shown with a mask and two protruding tubes through which the wind blew.

Quezon, Manuel Luis (1878–1944) Filipino statesman. Quezon followed AGUINALDO in the Philippine wars against Spain and the USA (1896–1901). He served in the Philippines Assembly and became resident commissioner for the Philippines in Washington (1909–16). His successful conduct in this post made him a national hero and he was elevated to the office of President of the Philippine Senate. In 1935 he became first President of the newly constituted Philippine Commonwealth and ruled his country dictatorially until forced into exile by the Japanese invasion in 1942. He headed a government in exile in the USA until his death and was succeeded by his Vice-President, Sergio Osmena.

Quiberon Bay, Battle of (1759) A major British naval victory in the SEVEN YEARS WAR that took place at Quiberon Bay on the west coast of Brittany in northern France. The French were planning to invade Britain. In 1759 Admiral HAWKE was blockading Brest, but in November the French admiral Conflans broke out during a storm. Hawke pursued the French fleet and when most of the ships took shelter in Quiberon Bay he came through the dangerous shoals in a gale. The French lost 11 ships and 25,000 men, and the British only two ships, ending the threat of a French invasion of Britain.

Quisling, Vidkun Abraham Lauritz Jonsson (1887–1945) Norwegian fascist leader. An army officer, he founded the fascist Nasjonal Samling (National Unity) Party and in 1940 helped Hitler to prepare the conquest of Norway. He became head of a new pro-German government and was made Premier in 1942. He remained in power until 1945, when he was arrested and executed. By this time 'Quisling' had become a derogatory term to describe any politician who supported invaders of their country.

Quito The capital of Ecuador, formerly the northern provincial capital of the INCA empire, linked by a long road to CUZCO, the imperial capital. In 1530 it was governed by ATAHUALPA, who used it as a base to seize the rest of the empire, defeating his brother and co-ruler, Huáscar. Under Spanish colonial rule it became a provincial capital, responsible to the viceroy; in 1535 the church and monastery of San Francisco, built on the city's main plaza, became the first Christian foundation in South America.

Qu'ran KORAN.

R

Rabeh, az-Zubayr (d. 1900) Sudanese military leader. Born a slave, he first appeared in the Bahr al-Ghazal region as a lieutenant of the slave-trader Zubayr Pasha. In 1879, when General GORDON defeated Zubayr's son in the course of stamping out the slave trade, Rabeh found himself without a master. Rallying 400 soldiers, he gradually assembled an efficient army. In 1893 he sacked Bagirmi, and then Kukawa, capital of Borno. He gained control of the Chad basin and attacked Sokoto, but was repulsed. He was defeated and killed in 1900 by a French army and his territories were divided between Britain, France, and Germany.

Rabin, Yitzhak (1922–95) Israeli general and statesman. Rabin was chief of staff of the Israeli army (1964–68), commanding the Israeli Defence Forces in the SIX-DAY WAR of June 1967 against Israel's Arab neighbours. As leader of the Labour Party, he was Prime Minister from 1974 until 1977. He regained leadership of the party and the premiership in 1992 and in the following year signed a peace accord with Yasser ARAFAT of the PALESTINE LIBERATION ORGANIZATION. This agreement brought Rabin the Nobel Peace Prize in 1994 (jointly with Arafat and Israeli Foreign Minister Shimon PERES). Arab and Jewish ultra-nationalists remained opposed to the settlement; while attending a peace rally in Tel Aviv in 1995, Rabin was assassinated by a Jewish right-wing extremist.

Race Relations Act (1976) British Act of Parliament that repealed the Acts of 1965 and 1968, strengthened the law on racial discrimination, and extended the 1968 ban on discrimination in housing, employment, insurance, and credit facilities. The Act also established (1977) a permanent Race Relations Commission to eliminate discrimination and to promote equality of opportunity and good relations between different racial groups within Britain. Large numbers of people from Commonwealth countries, especially West Indians, were encouraged to emigrate to Britain in the 1950s, to meet labour shortages. In the early 1960s immigration from India and Pakistan also increased dramatically, rising from an average influx of 7,000 people per annum to 50,000 before the first Immigration Act restricted entry in 1962. In the 1970s the economy went into recession, inflation increased, and unemployment rose. General economic problems, particularly increased unemployment, have tended to produce racial discrimination and prejudice, and the Race Relations Act was intended to ameliorate a deteriorating social situation. In spite of continuing efforts by the Commission, racial tensions flared up in a number of inner-city areas, for example Brixton and Tottenham in London (1981, 1985), Handsworth in Birmingham (1985), Toxteth in Liverpool (1981), and St Paul's in Bristol (1980). The Public Order Act of 1986 contained six offences of inciting racial hatred, while the Criminal Justice Act (1994) included a provision against racial harassment as a form of threatening behaviour.

racism The belief that human characteristics and abilities are determined by race or ethnic group, often expressed as an assertion of superiority by one race or group over another, and prejudice against or even hatred of particular groups. The scientific validity of the concept of race is not widely accepted; the traditional racial groups are no longer considered genetically meaningful, due to interbreeding and population migrations. Often race is confused with 'culture', so that dislike of certain cultural practices is used to condemn a racial group as a whole. Racism is often an underlying issue in the political and economic factors that lead to wars and strife. It is explicit in some political ideologies, such as FASCISM. An extreme example of racism is that of the German NAZIS, whose belief that fair-haired Nordic or Germanic peoples were superior to Jews and other 'non-Aryans' led to the GENOCIDE of millions of Jews, Slavs, and gypsies in Europe during Nazi rule (1933–45). Racism has also been responsible for such political systems as APARTHEID in South Africa, which kept different races apart, ensuring that they used separate facilities and did not meet socially. Even where it is not institutionalized, racism may still have a great influence, affecting the access to education or employment that is given to ethnic groups. Many conflicts, such as the civil wars in BOSNIA-HERZEGOVINA, RWANDA, and BURUNDI in the early 1990s, have involved different ethnic rather than racial groups.

Radek, Karl (1885–c. 1939) International communist leader. He joined the Polish Social Democratic Party and participated in the RUSSIAN REVOLUTION OF 1905 in Warsaw. He crossed Germany with LENIN after the outbreak of the RUSSIAN REVOLUTION (1917) and took part in the BREST-LITOVSK peace negotiations. He helped the communist uprising in Germany (1918–19) and returned in 1923 as an agent of the COMINTERN to organize another communist rising, the failure of which contributed to his declining influence. He was expelled from the party in 1927 for alleged support of TROTSKY but was readmitted after recanting. He assisted BUKHARIN in drafting STALIN's new constitution (1936). Accused of treason at the second show trial (1937), he was sentenced to prison where it is presumed he died.

Radetzky, Josef, Count of Radetz (1766–1858) Austrian field-marshal. He fought in the REVOLUTIONARY WARS and in 1805 was promoted to a command in Italy. After Austria's defeat at WAGRAM, he was appointed to assist SCHWARZENBERG with army reorganization. In 1813 he joined Schwarzenberg in the field and his proposed tactics for the Battle of LEIPZIG were decisive in the defeat of Napoleon. At the beginning of the Italian RISORGIMENTO he was placed in command of the Austrian forces in Lombardy (1831–57). He constructed a quadrilateral of fortresses: Peschiera, Mantua, Verona, and Legnano where in 1849 he successfully withstood the forces of the Risorgimento under Charles Albert of Piedmont. He ruled the Lombardo-Venetian territories of the Austrian HABSBURGS until the age of 91.

Radhakrishnan, Sir Sarvepalli (1888–1975) Indian scholar and statesman. A professor of philosophy at Mysore and Calcutta and professor of eastern religion and ethics at Oxford, he wrote extensively on Hindu religious and philosophical thought. He also served as Indian ambassador to the Soviet Union (1949–52) and as Vice-President (1952–62) and President (1962–67) of India, succeeding Rajendra PRASAD, who was the first President of independent India. As a scholar without political affiliations he occupied a rare and detached position in Indian political life, stressing the need for India to establish a classless and casteless society.

Raeder, Erich (1876–1960) German admiral. Raeder was Admiral Hipper's chief of staff in World War I and from 1928 was commander-in-chief of the German navy, secretly rebuilding it in violation of the VERSAILLES PEACE SETTLEMENT. In the 1930s he elaborated his 'Z-Plan' for building a fleet capable of challenging Britain, but World War II began before this was achieved. He resigned and was replaced by Doenitz in January 1943, after Hitler became outraged by the apparently poor performance of the surface fleet against Allied convoys. His part in unrestricted U-boat warfare led to his imprisonment after the NUREMBERG TRIALS.

Raffles, Sir Thomas Stamford (1781–1826) British colonial administrator. He joined the English East India Company in 1795 and in 1805 was appointed to Pinang. After participating in the capture of Java (1811) he served as its lieutenant-governor (1811–16), instituting wide-ranging and only partially successful administrative and social reforms. As lieutenant-governor of the Sumatran port of Bengkulu (1818–24) he recognized the commercial potential of SINGAPORE. In 1819 he took advantage of a disputed succession to the sultanate of Johore, which contained the territory of Singapore, to found a British settlement without permission from his superiors. Ill-health forced him to return home in 1824, but Singapore went on to become one of the most important trading centres in Asia.

Rafsanjani, Ali Akbar Hashemi (1934–) Iranian cleric and politician; President (1989–97). Rafsanjani studied Islamic law under Ayatollah Ruhollah KHOMEINI. During Khomeini's exile in Paris, Rafsanjani was his deputy within Iran, where he was arrested several times for promoting the cause of ISLAMIC FUNDAMENTALISM. In 1979 he was appointed to the Revolutionary Council and later became speaker, and then leader, of the Iranian parliament, the *majlis*. He led the negotiations with the REAGAN administration to release hostages from the US embassy in Teheran, which resulted in covert arms exports to Iran. After Khomeini's death in 1989, Rafsanjani was made President. He attempted to normalize relations with Western countries and maintained Iranian neutrality during the Gulf War of 1991. He was re-elected in 1993 with a reduced majority and, after growing opposition from more traditionalist clerics, he retired in 1997.

Raglan, FitzRoy James Henry Somerset, 1st Baron (1788–1855) British soldier. He joined the army in 1804, served as aide-de-camp to Arthur Wellesley (Duke of WELLINGTON) during the PENINSULAR WAR, and lost an arm at the Battle of Waterloo. He was appointed to lead the British expeditionary force in the CRIMEAN WAR and

won a victory at Inkerman (5 November 1854) with French assistance, but was criticized for his conduct of the campaign.

Rahman, Tungku (Prince) Abdul (1903–90) Malaysian statesman. He entered the Kedah state civil service in 1931 and in 1952 succeeded Dato Onn bin Jafaar as leader of the UNITED MALAYS NATIONAL ORGANIZATION (UMNO). He played a central role in organizing UMNO's alliance with the moderate Malayan Chinese Association (founded in 1949 by Tan Cheng Lock), which provided the political base for the achievement of independence. After becoming the leader of the Federal Legislative Council in 1955, he became Malaya's first Prime Minister (1957–63) and in 1963 he successfully presided over the formation of the Federation of MALAYSIA, which he led as Prime Minister (1963–70). He remained in office until the political crisis caused by the riots of 1969 between the Malays and the Chinese forced him to stand down.

Raikes, Robert (1735–1811) British printer, newspaper proprietor, and philanthropist. He took up the cause of prison reform early in his career, but his greatest achievement was the Sunday school he established at Gloucester in 1780 to teach reading and the church catechism to children who worked in factories during the rest of the week. This led to a national movement for the establishment of Sunday schools all over Britain.

railways, history of The advent of railways brought together the technology of the steam-engine, developed in the early 18th century, and the horse- or human-powered wagon-ways used in mining since the 16th century. The British engineer Richard Trevithick (1771–1833) built the first steam locomotive to run on such wagon-ways (1804); other early steam-locomotive pioneers, also British, were John Blenkinsop (1783–1831), William Hedley (1779–1843), and George Stephenson. Early locomotives were limited by the weakness of the available railway track: it was not until technical advances were made in track construction that the railway became truly practical.

The Stockton and Darlington Railway (1825) was the first to carry both freight and passengers. In 1830 it was followed by the Liverpool and Manchester Railway, the line that heralded the beginning of the railway era. The selection of the locomotive to be used on the line was made in a series of trials at Rainhill, Lancashire, in 1829: the *Rocket*, designed by George Stephenson, was the outright winner. There followed a period of rapid expansion and development of railways throughout the world. By 1847, 250,000 navvies were employed in railway construction in the UK. In the USA, where railroad companies were the main agents of westward expansion, nearly 34,000 km (21,100 miles) of railway were constructed between 1850 and 1860. By the end of the century railway networks covered Europe, the USA, Canada, and parts of imperial Russia. Railways climbed high into the Alps, the Andes, and the foothills of the Himalayas, spanned wide estuaries, such as the Forth near Edinburgh in Scotland, and tunnelled beneath hills. In Europe cheap and easy travel helped to break down provincial differences, while in Switzerland and the Mediterranean the holiday industry steadily developed. Railways were important for moving troops and supplies for both sides in the American Civil War. In Canada, the need for railways to link new industrial centres across frozen wastes prompted the invention of the rotary snow plough by J. W. Elliot in 1869. The first electric locomotive was demonstrated at an exhibition in Berlin in 1879. Electric traction was commercially applied first on suburban and metropolitan lines, but was quickly adopted for underground railways. One of the earliest users of electric locomotives on mainline routes was Italy, where a line was opened in 1902.

The period before World War I was a time of consolidation, with comfortable, heavy trains running at average speeds of over 95 km/h (60 mph) throughout Europe and North America and freight trains of 1,000–2,000 tonnes carrying goods and raw materials to urban and manufacturing centres. The railways proved strategically important on all fronts in World War I notably for the part they played in transporting German troops to the Western Front in accordance with the SCHLIEFFEN Plan. Many railway companies grouped together as national railway systems or large geographical concerns. Subsequently road and air transport began to challenge railways and improvements to motive power and rolling stock were sought. In the late 1930s the steam locomotive reached its zenith, but electric locomotives were already in widespread use in Europe and Scandinavia, and mainline diesel locomotives were coming into service in the USA.

Following World War II there was a period of reconstruction: new steam locomotives were introduced in the UK and mainland Europe and new diesels were also under test. Steam locomotive production ended in the USA in the 1950s and in Europe in the 1960s, and, as the competition from roads increased, there were major cutbacks in the rail network. In Japan in 1964, the high-speed *shinkansen* or 'bullet' trains began operation, running on specially developed track at speeds of up to 210 km/h (130 mph). Experiments were done to find ground guidance-systems other than conventional track.

In the last quarter of the 20th century, railway construction worldwide has started to grow again, though in developed countries few new lines are being built. In Europe, notably in France and more recently Germany, other high speed trains have been developed following the success of the Japanese *shinkansen* and tilting rolling stock has been introduced on a few lines. There has also been a considerable investment in commuter trains and light railway rapid-transit systems to ease congestion on roads and in response to increasing concern about air pollution from car exhaust. A new development in Jakarta, Indonesia, is the Aeromovel, a light, engineless train powered by compressed air blown through a duct below the track. New underground railways have been built in some of the newer large cities (for example, the Metro in Mexico City), while in China the railway network is growing at a rate of some 1,000 km (600 miles) per year. The Channel Tunnel rail link between England and France began to operate in 1994. Following a model adopted by Sweden in the early 1990s, Britain privatized its rail network in the mid-1990s. In late 1997, an experimental 'Maglev' (magnetic levitation) train in Japan attained a new speed record for locomotives, exceeding the previous record held by the French TGV (*Train à Grande Vitesse*).

Rajagopalachariar, Chakravarti (1878–1972) Indian nationalist politician. He became a close associate of Mohandas GANDHI and was imprisoned on several occasions for NON-CO-OPERATION with the British. Himself a Hindu, he was tolerant of the right of Indian Muslims to demand special minority safeguards and of the creation of the separate state of Pakistan. He served as governor-general of India (1948–50) and chief minister of the Madras government (1852–54). In 1959 he was one of the founders of the conservative Swatantra Party.

Rajput (Sanskrit, 'son of a king') A predominantly landowning class, also called Thakurs, living mainly in central and northern India, who claim descent from the Hindu Ksatriya (warrior) caste. Many leading clans are of royal lineage, but others include cultivators of Sudra (menial) caste. Their clans are divided into four lines: Solar, Lunar, Fire, and Snake.

The Rajput are almost certainly descended from 6th- and 7th-century migrants from Central Asia. They became politically important from the 9th century when their chieftains gained dominance over the desert and hill area now called Rajasthan, between the north Indian plains and the DECCAN. Although they held off Muslim invasions between the 12th and 16th centuries, the MOGULS then penetrated their desert fortresses. However, Emperor AKBAR achieved Rajput acquiesence by allowing them to rule their conquered territories and by drawing them into imperial service. This balance was destroyed, first by less tolerant Mogul rulers, and then by the MARATHA upsurge in the 18th century, which finally ended Rajput independence. When the Marathas fell victim to British arms, their Rajput clients also had to come to terms. However, the leading chiefs, including JODHPUR, JAIPUR, and Udaipur, preserved considerable autonomy as Princely States under British rule.

Rakosi, Matyas (1892–1971) Hungarian politician who played an important role in the Hungarian communist revolution led by Béla KUN in 1919. After four years in Moscow (1920–24), Rakosi returned to Hungary but was arrested and not released until 1940. In 1944 he became First Secretary of the Hungarian Communist Party and during this time established a ruthless Stalinist regime. He was Prime Minister of Hungary from 1952 to 1953. Opposition to his Stalinist policies led to his resignation as Party Secretary and return to the Soviet Union in 1956. The brutality of his secret police contributed to the HUNGARIAN REVOLUTION of 1956.

Raleigh, Sir Walter (c. 1552–1618) English explorer and courtier. Raleigh took part in two privateering expeditions to the West Indies and was then sent to Ireland to suppress a rebellion. On his return to England in 1581 he became a great favourite of ELIZABETH I, who showered honours and rewards on him, including land in Ireland. In 1585–91 he organized several colonizing expeditions to VIRGINIA, all ending in failure. He nevertheless brought back the tobacco plant and the potato, which he introduced as a crop in Ireland. His position as royal favourite was usurped by the Earl of ESSEX in 1592 and he was imprisoned in the Tower of London and later exiled from the court. In 1595 he set out for Guiana in South America where the gold mines of EL DORADO were thought to lie. His account of the voyage, *The Discoverie of Guiana*, is one of the finest narratives of Elizabethan adventure. Raleigh was an accurate topographer and cartographer; as an explorer he also contributed to the study of mathematics as an aid to navigation.

The death of Elizabeth I brought ruin to Raleigh. He was falsely accused of conspiring to dethrone JAMES I and in 1603 was again imprisoned in the Tower, where he remained for 13 years. During this imprisonment he set up a laboratory where he conducted experiments in chemistry, including the condensation of fresh water from salt water. In return for his freedom he promised to discover a gold mine for the king on Guiana, but on condition that there should be no clash with the Spaniards, with whom England was now at peace. When his fleet reached the mouth of the Orinoco River, Raleigh remained at Trinidad, sending five small vessels up the river. They came unexpectedly on a Spanish settlement, fighting broke out, and Raleigh's son was killed. The expedition returned sadly home and Raleigh was arrested and executed at the request of GONDOMAR, the Spanish Ambassador.

Ramanuja (d. 1137) Brahmin (member of the HINDU priestly caste) from southern India, whose teachings inspired the *bhakti* devotional school. He identified Brahman (the supreme soul) with the god Vishnu, whose worship he then encouraged on pilgrimages throughout India. His preaching that the visible world is real and not illusory and that God should be worshipped devotedly, built a bridge between philosophy and popular *bhakti* religion.

Rambouillet, Catherine de Vivonne, Marquise de (1588–1665) French aristocrat who presided over the first of the *salons* which dominated the intellectual life of 17th-century Paris. The Hôtel de Rambouillet was at the height of its influence between 1620 and 1645 and was frequented by such figures as the playwright Corneille, the writer Madame de Sévigné, and the clergyman Bossuet. The Marquise sought to promote philosophical conversation, refinement, and good taste, earning her the description *précieuse*, later mocked in Molière's comedy *Les Précieuses Ridicules*.

Ramesses II (the Great) Pharaoh of Egypt (ruled *c.* 1304–1237 BC). When Ramesses II acceded to the throne Egypt was at war with the HITTITES. In the fifth year of his reign Ramesses II fought the Hittites at Kadesh where he managed to extricate himself from a perilous situation. In the 21st year of his reign the two powers concluded a peace treaty and Ramesses married a Hittite princess. He also undertook campaigns against the Libyans. His reign, which marked a high point in ancient Egyptian history, was one of considerable prosperity and he oversaw a substantial building programme, which included two temples cut out of the cliffs at Abu Simbel, the completion of his father Seti I's hypostyle hall at KARNAK, and temple at Abydos.

Ramesses III Pharaoh of Egypt (ruled *c.* 1188–1156 BC). Ramesses III successfully repelled three major invasions, two by the Libyans and one by the SEA PEOPLES. Peace and prosperity followed, but the last years of his reign were marked by social unrest and an assassination attempt. He was the last Egyptian ruler to hold land in Palestine.

Ramillies, Battle of (23 May 1706) A battle that took place in eastern Belgium between Namur and Louvain, MARLBOROUGH's second great victory during the War of the SPANISH SUCCESSION over the French army under Villeroi. Marlborough duped his opponents into thinking his main attack was coming from the right and smashed through the French line from the left. The

French losses were five times greater than Marlborough's. He went on to overrun much of Flanders and Brabant.

Randolph, Asa Philip (1889–1979) African-American labour leader. He was prominent in many of the struggles for CIVIL RIGHTS. His threat of a march on Washington in 1941 contributed to the end of race restrictions on employment in the defence industries and his activities in 1948 helped to persuade President TRUMAN to end segregation in the armed forces. In 1957, as leader of the Brotherhood of Sleeping-Car Porters, he became a vice-president of the AMERICAN FEDERATION OF LABOR. In 1963 he helped to organize the march on Washington for Jobs and Freedom, one of the largest civil rights demonstrations ever held in the USA.

Ranjit Singh (1780–1839) Ruler of a Sikh kingdom in the Punjab (1799–1839). His state was based on Lahore, which he secured in 1799. In 1801 he took the title 'Maharaja of the Punjab' and in 1802 extended his rule over the Sikh holy city of Amritsar. By agreement with Britain (Amritsar 1809), the eastern boundary of his state remained on the Sutlej River, but with his large army, trained by French officers, he expanded further afield. He extended his rule westwards (1813–21) and also took control of Kashmir. In 1834 he annexed Peshawar. At the end of the SIKH WARS (1849) most of his territory was taken by Britain.

ransom A sum of money paid for the release of a prisoner or for the restitution of property. The demanding and paying of ransoms formed an accepted part of medieval warfare and diplomacy. Knights who were VASSALS of a lord were obliged to pay for the release of their lord if he was captured in war, although in the late Middle Ages family and friends paid as well as a lord's estate. A suitable ransom would be negotiated and raised to secure eventual release. Needless massacre of prisoners, as after AGINCOURT, aroused resentment among would-be captors. Notable ransom victims include John II of France and RICHARD I of England.

Rapallo, Treaties of Two treaties signed at Rapallo, a city in north Italy. The First Treaty of Rapallo (1920) established relations between Italy and the kingdom of Serbs, Croats, and Slovenes (Yugoslavia). Italy obtained the Istrian peninsula while Dalmatia went to Yugoslavia. Fiume (Rijeka) became a free city. The Second Treaty of Rapallo (1922) was more important. It recorded an agreement between Germany and the Soviet Union. The two countries agreed to abandon any financial claims that each might bring against the other following WORLD WAR I. Secretly, in defiance of the VERSAILLES PEACE SETTLEMENT, German soldiers were to be permitted to train in the Soviet Union.

Rashid Ali al-Ghailani (1892–1965) Iraqi statesman. Member of a well-known religious family, he served as Prime Minister on four occasions. In April 1941 he seized power by a military coup that also deposed Abd al-Ilah, regent for the child-king, Faisal II. Believing the new government to be pro-Axis, Britain intervened to expel Rashid Ali in May 1941 and restored the regent.

Rasputin, Grigori Yefimovich (1871–1916) Russian religious fanatic. A Siberian peasant and mystic with healing and hypnotic powers, he earned his nickname, meaning 'debauchee', from his immoral life. He went to St Petersburg in 1903 and met the royal Romanov family. His beneficial treatment of the haemophilic crown prince won him a disastrous hold over the empress. His influence increased when NICHOLAS II left the court to command the army (1915). He and the empress virtually ruled Russia and were responsible in a large measure for the emperor's failure to respond to the rising tide of discontent that eventually resulted in the RUSSIAN REVOLUTION. Rasputin was murdered by a group of nobles led by Prince Yusupov.

Rastafarianism A religious and political movement, originating from a Jamaican cult that worships HAILE SELASSIE (Ras Tafari, 1892–1975), the former Emperor of Ethiopia, as divine. The movement was influenced by the Black activists of the 1930s, particularly Marcus GARVEY (1887–1940), who attempted to 'repossess' Africa for Black people. Rastafarianism combines elements of AFRICAN TRADITIONAL RELIGIONS, Black supremacy, and biblical narrative, particularly exodus and MILLENARIAN liberation themes, along with elements of Afro-Caribbean culture. Its adherents believe the Ethiopians are the lost tribes of Israel, subjected to domination by White people as a punishment for sin, but who will eventually be redeemed by repatriation to Africa to dominate White people. The movement has no clergy or church buildings and ritual practice is largely spontaneous. Rastafarians usually wear their hair in dreadlocks, use the Ethiopian national colours red, black, green, and gold, avoid pork, and occasionally use cannabis as an aid to meditation. Reggae musician Bob Marley (1945–81) popularized Rastafarian ideas.

Ratana, Tahupotiki Wiremu (1870–1939) Maori political and religious leader. In the tradition of Maori prophets such as TE KOOTI and TE WHITI, Ratana emerged as a teacher and healer in 1918. He attacked the traditional fears of *tapu* (power of the spirit world) and sorcery and sought to introduce a heterodox belief in the Christian Trinity. Rejected by the formal Churches, he established his church with its liturgy, temples, and clergy. In 1936 nearly one-fifth of Maori were adherents. Politically he sought advancement of Maori rights through recognition of the Treaty of WAITANGI. Ratana candidates contested the Maori seats in the New Zealand Parliament. In 1931 the Labour Party accepted Ratana candidates as its own. Both the religious and political aspects of this movement survived Ratana's death in 1939. From 1943 the Ratana–Labour candidates, with rare intervals, have held all four Maori seats and influenced legislation on Maori affairs into the 1970s. In 1979 a group of younger Maori politicians, impatient with the Ratana–Labour alliance, formed a new party, Mana Motuhake O Aotearoa, which rapidly gained Maori support.

Rathenau, Walther (1867–1922) German industrialist and statesman. He was responsible for directing Germany's war economy (1916–18) and later became Minister of Reconstruction (1921) and Foreign Minister (1922) in the WEIMAR REPUBLIC. He believed that Germany must fulfil its obligations under the VERSAILLES PEACE SETTLEMENT, including payment of REPARATIONS. Convinced of Germany's ability to gain ascendancy in Europe he negotiated the Second Treaty of RAPALLO (1922) with Russia, establishing military and trade links. He was assassinated by ANTI-SEMITIC nationalists in 1922.

Rawlings, Jerry (John) (1947–) Ghanaian politician; President from 1982. Of mixed Ghanaian and Scottish parentage, Rawlings was born in Accra and educated in military academies. He won a commission in the country's air force in 1969 and was promoted to flight-lieutenant in 1978. In the following year, he was at the head of a group of junior officers that overthrew the government and installed a civilian administration. In 1981, however, Rawlings staged a second coup and declared himself head of state. He has since been re-elected in 1992 and 1996.

Rawlings executed a number of politicians after the 1981 coup for alleged corruption and suspended constitutional rule for a period. In the later 1980s, however, he implemented an IMF/World Bank plan for Ghana's economic recovery and restored multiparty politics. In 1992, after promulgating a new constitution, he resigned and successfully contested the presidential elections as a civilian.

Reagan, Ronald W. (1911–) The 40th President of the USA (1981–89). A Hollywood actor, Reagan became Republican governor of California (1966–74) and won a landslide victory in the 1980 presidential election on a programme of reduced taxation and increased defence expenditure against world communism. He cut federal social and welfare programmes, reduced taxes, and increased defence spending by heavy government borrowing. He campaigned against alleged Soviet involvement in Latin America, especially NICARAGUA and GRENADA. Relations with China steadily improved during the Presidency, with a large increase in trade. There was domestic legislation to strengthen Civil Rights, but increasing disagreements over budget policies. This, together with balance-of-payments deficits, precipitated a serious stock-market collapse in October 1987. Congress steadily obliged the President to reduce proposed defence expenditure in order to give more balanced budgets. Reagan stood for a second term in 1984, overwhelmingly defeating the Democrat, Walter Mondale. Intransigence on the STRATEGIC DEFENSE INITIATIVE blocked advance on nuclear arms control in 1986, at the end of which the Irangate scandal broke. This revealed that in spite of strong anti-terrorist talk, the administration had begun secret negotiations for arms sales to Iran, with profits going illegally to Contra forces in Nicaragua. In the 1986 mid-term elections the Democrats gained control of the Senate. Talks on nuclear arms control began in Geneva in 1985, continued at Reykjavik in 1986, and Washington in 1987, when an Intermediate Nuclear Forces (INF) Treaty was agreed with the Soviet Union, eliminating all ground-based intermediate-range nuclear missiles. The presidency ended with an ever-rising annual Federal budget deficit.

Reason, Age of ENLIGHTENMENT.

Rebecca riots (1839, 1842–43) A series of agrarian riots in south-west Wales. They were a protest against the toll-gates introduced by turnpike trusts. Bands of rioters disguised in women's clothes attacked and broke the gates. Each band was led by a 'Rebecca' after the Old Testament story of Rebecca, 'be thou the mother of millions, and let thy seed possess the gate of those which hate them'. In 1843 a series of massed meetings took place. Troops and a contingent of the Metropolitan Police were sent from London, while a commission to investigate grievances took evidence. In 1844 an Act to 'consolidate and amend the Laws relating to Turnpike Trusts in Wales' ended the protest.

Reconstruction Acts (1867–68) The legislation passed by the US Congress dealing with the reorganization of the South in the aftermath of the AMERICAN CIVIL WAR. The question of the treatment of the defeated CONFEDERACY raised conflicting priorities between reconciliation with White Southerners and justice for the freed slaves. In 1866 an impasse developed between President Andrew JOHNSON and the Republican majorities in Congress. In 1867 Congress passed, over the President's veto, a Reconstruction Act that divided the South into military districts and required the calling of a new constitutional convention in each state, elected by universal manhood suffrage. The new state governments were to provide for Black suffrage and to ratify the FOURTEENTH AMENDMENT as conditions for readmittance to the Union. Further Reconstruction Acts were passed in the following 12 months to counter Southern attempts to delay or circumvent the implementation of the first measure.

recusants The people, usually Roman Catholics, who refused to attend ANGLICAN CHURCH services from the 16th century onward. Fines were imposed on them by Acts of Uniformity (1552 and 1559). Although NONCONFORMISTS could be penalized for recusancy, the term was often used as an abbreviation of 'Catholic Recusants', distinguishing them from 'Church Papists', who were Catholics who attended Anglican services rather than pay the fines. The penal laws against Catholics were extended between 1571 and 1610, but were rarely enforced. They were systematically repealed in a series of Toleration Acts (see CATHOLIC EMANCIPATION).

Red Army The Soviet army formed by TROTSKY as Commissar for War (1918–25) to save the BOLSHEVIK revolution during the RUSSIAN CIVIL WAR. His energy and oratory restored discipline and expertise to the new recruits, most of whom were workers and peasants. For trained officers, Trotsky had to rely on former officers of the Imperial Army. To ensure the reliability of officers and to undertake propaganda among the troops, political commissars were attached to units, often resulting in dual commands. A major offensive against POLAND failed in 1920 when PILSUDSKI successfully organized national resistance. After the Treaty of RAPALLO (1922) close co-operation with Germany led to greater efficiency. Progress was checked by STALIN's purge of army leaders (1937–38) to remove possible opposition, resulting in a lack of leadership in the FINNISH–RUSSIAN WAR. After HITLER's invasion of the Soviet Union (1941) the Red Army became the largest in the world, with five million members by 1945. Precise figures remain unknown, but Red Army casualties in World War II have been estimated as high as seven million men. The name fell into disuse after World War II, the army being called the Soviet Armed Forces, which in turn adopted the titles of the independent republics after the breakup of the Soviet Union in 1991.

Red Brigades A grouping of Italian left-wing terrorists especially active in the period 1977–81. The security forces seemed powerless against them, although some arrests were eventually made. The Red

Brigades were responsible for a number of incidents including the kidnapping and murder of the Italian statesman Aldo MORO in 1978.

Red Cross An International agency concerned with the alleviation of human suffering. Its founder, the Swiss philanthropist Henri Dunant (1828–1910), horrified by the suffering he saw at the Battle of SOLFERINO, proposed the formation of voluntary aid societies for the relief of war victims. In 1863 the International Committee of the Red Cross was established and in the following year 12 governments signed the GENEVA CONVENTION. This drew up the terms for the care of soldiers and was extended to include victims of naval warfare (1906), prisoners of war (1929) and, 20 years later, civilians. Its conventions have now been ratified by almost 150 nations. Its flag is a red cross on a white background. In Muslim countries the cross is replaced by a red crescent.

Red Feds The members of the National Federation of Labour, an association of militant unions formed in 1909 in New Zealand. Never winning the support of a majority of the country's unionists, the Federation briefly became an important force because of the presence of strong unions, such as the miners, in its ranks. In 1912 confrontation between government and Red Feds occurred at the Waihi gold-mine, when a strike resulted in violence and one death before the miners accepted defeat. The United Federation of Labour was formed, which was soon involved in a bitter strike, centred on the Wellington docks and again the government intervened. Thousands of mounted police were recruited and there were violent clashes, but this strike was also broken. The Red Feds and their methods of confrontation were permanently discredited. Since then the New Zealand trade unions have worked amicably through a process of arbitration and a series of Acts were passed to amend the basic Industrial and Conciliation Arbitration Act of 1894.

Red Guards The militant young supporters of MAO ZEDONG during the Chinese CULTURAL REVOLUTION (1966–69). Taking their name from the army units organized by Mao in 1927, the Red Guards, numbering several million, provided the popular, paramilitary vanguard of the Cultural Revolution. They attacked supposed reactionaries, the Communist Party establishment, China's cultural heritage, and all vestiges of Western influence, maintaining the momentum of the movement through mass demonstrations, a constant poster war, and violent attacks on people and property. Fighting between opposing Red Guard groups led to thousands of deaths. After the Cultural Revolution, many were sent into the countryside for forced 're-education'.

Redl, Alfred (1864–1913) Austrian spy. A colonel from a modest background in the Austro-Hungarian army, he was a specialist in counter-intelligence and security. By introducing modern criminological methods his department in Vienna became one of the best equipped intelligence centres in Europe. However, he was a secret homosexual and was being blackmailed for considerable sums of money. He attempted to raise the money by becoming a spy himself, selling military secrets to Russia. When he was eventually detected, he was ordered to commit suicide.

Redmond, John Edward (1856–1918) Irish politician. Redmond was less intransigent than Charles PARNELL, seeking to achieve the same objective of HOME RULE, but by co-operation with British politicians. By 1900 he had united the Irish Nationalist Party under his leadership in the British House of Commons. In return for Redmond's support over the Parliament Act (1911), the Liberal Prime Minister, ASQUITH, introduced the third Home Rule Bill in 1912. However, the outbreak of World War I, in which Redmond supported Britain, postponed implementation of the Bill.

Red River Settlement An early 19th-century agricultural colony in the Red River (now Manitoba) area of central Canada that was granted by the Hudson's Bay Company to Thomas Douglas, 5th Earl of Selkirk (1771–1820). Selkirk endeavoured to settle the dispossessed of Scotland and Northern Ireland there. His first group of settlers succumbed to North West Company pressure to abandon the area soon after their arrival in 1812. The colony was re-established in 1816, but 22 settlers were killed in a massacre at Seven Oaks, led by North West Company men and other attacks followed. Selkirk himself went bankrupt, but the publicity attracted by the affair led to the forced merger (1821) of the North West Company and Hudson's Bay Company and cleared the way for more successful settlement in the area.

Red Shirts A nationalist organization in British India in the NORTH-WEST FRONTIER province. Formed in 1929 by Abdul Ghaffar Khan, a follower of GANDHI, it was correctly entitled Khudai Khidmatgar (Servants of God). It provided the main support for Ghaffar Khan's control of the province until 1946, during which time it was deployed in support of CONGRESS policies. Opposed to partition in 1947 Ghaffar Khan and the Red Shirts campaigned for a separate state of Pakhtunistan. The new government of Pakistan banned the Red Shirts and imprisoned Ghaffar Khan for 30 years.

reeve A local official in Anglo-Saxon and post-Conquest England. The most important were shire reeves (SHERIFFS) who administered royal justice and collected royal revenues within their shire. Manorial reeves organized the peasant labour force on estates and their duties were considerable. They received a money wage, grants of grazing land, and remission of rent and feudal dues. Although often of VILLEIN status those reeves who contrived through annual re-election to make their office hereditary had considerably improved their economic condition by the 14th century, when Chaucer wrote of them in *The Canterbury Tales*.

Reeves, William Pember (1857–1932) New Zealand statesman and journalist. As Minister of Labour in the Liberal government of BALLANCE and SEDDON, Reeves was responsible for a sweeping code of humane labour and factory laws, then for the introduction of compulsory arbitration in industrial disputes. In 1896 Reeves went to Britain as agent-general and then high commissioner (1905–08). He became an associate of the FABIANS and director of the London School of Economics (1908–19).

Reform Acts (UK) A series of legislative measures which extended the franchise in 19th- and 20th-century Britain. In the 1780s William PITT the Younger had proposed to remove some of the worst abuses in the electoral system, but abandoned his attempts in the face of considerable opposition. In the 1820s there was a renewed call for change and the Whigs, who were returned to power in 1830, were pledged to reform. However, the government succeeded in getting its measures through Parliament only after a fierce struggle. The Reform Act of 1832 eliminated many anomalies, such as ROTTEN BOROUGHS, and enfranchised the new industrial towns, which had hitherto been unrepresented. The lowering of the property qualification gave voting rights to the middle classes, but left effective power in the hands of the landed aristocracy. The bulk of the population (all women and five-sixths of men) were still without a vote and agitation continued. The Reform Act of 1867 doubled the size of the electorate and gave many urban working-class men the vote. However, agricultural labourers and domestic servants had to wait a further 17 years to be enfranchised: the Reform Act of 1884 increased the electorate to about five million. The Representation of the People Act (1918) gave the vote to all men over the age of 21 and conceded some of the demands of the SUFFRAGETTES by enfranchising women over 30, but on a property qualification. Universal adult suffrage for everyone over 21 was finally achieved in 1928, when women between the ages of 21 and 30 secured the right to vote and the property qualification was abolished. In 1969 the voting age was lowered to 18.

Reformation The 16th-century movement for reform of the doctrines and practices of the ROMAN CATHOLIC CHURCH, ending in the establishment of Reformed or PROTESTANT Churches. The origins of the movement can be traced back to the 14th century and attacks by LOLLARD and HUSSITE believers on the hierarchical and legalistic structure of the Church. The GREAT SCHISM had also weakened papal authority and there was widespread dissatisfaction with the papacy's worldliness, its financial exactions, and its secular involvement as an Italian territorial power.

The starting point of the Reformation is often given as 1517, when the German theologian Martin LUTHER launched his protest against the corruption of the papacy and the Roman Catholic Church, but he was breaking no new controversial ground. In fact, most of the Reformation movements laid stress not on innovation but on return to a primitive simplicity. Luther's theological reading led him to attack the central Catholic doctrines of transubstantiation, clerical celibacy, and papal supremacy. He also called for radical reform of the religious orders. By 1530 the rulers of Saxony, Hesse, Brandenburg, and Brunswick, as well as the kings of Sweden and Denmark had been won over to the reformed beliefs. They proceeded to break with the Roman church and set about regulating the churches in their territories according to Protestant principles.

In Switzerland, the Reformation was led first by ZWINGLI, who carried through antipapal, antihierarchic, and antimonastic reforms in Zürich. After his death the leadership passed to CALVIN, in whose hands reforming opinion assumed a more explicitly doctrinal and revolutionary tone. Calvinism became the driving force of the movement in western Germany, France, the Netherlands, and Scotland, where in each case it was linked with a political struggle. Calvinism was also the main doctrinal influence within the ANGLICAN CHURCH. In Europe the reforming movement was increasingly checked and balanced by the COUNTER-REFORMATION. The era of religious wars came to an end with the conclusion of the THIRTY YEARS WAR (1618–48).

Reform Judaism A movement in JUDAISM, founded in Germany by Zachariah Frankel (1801–75) in reaction to the perceived laxity of LIBERAL JUDAISM. Frankel questioned the wholly divine inspiration of the Torah, whilst retaining observance of some Jewish laws and traditions. In the UK, Reform Jews might be regarded as being on the 'right' of the Liberal or Progressive movement. In the USA, the term Reform Judaism refers to the whole of the Liberal tradition, brought across by German immigrants in the 19th century. American Reform Jews are roughly equivalent to British Liberal Jews.

refugee A person who, for political, racial, or ideological reasons, or as a result of crises such as FAMINE, war, or disaster, has been forced to flee his or her home country. The 20th century has seen massive and unprecedented numbers of refugees; it was estimated in 1990 that there are 15 million worldwide, with the overwhelming majority in developing countries. The root causes of refugee movements are complex and varied, but the two main contributory factors are armed conflicts or serious internal disturbances, and human rights violations, all of which are exacerbated by NATIONALISM, COMMUNAL CONFLICT, foreign intervention, population growth, and the increasing availability of arms. However, governments are often reluctant to grant political asylum to refugees because they fear damaging relations with the country of origin, encouraging a mass influx, offering protection to ideologically unsound groups, and incurring an economic burden. Despite the explicit terms to the contrary of the 1951 UNITED NATIONS Convention relating to the Status of Refugees, governments close their borders to refugees, treat refugees as illegal immigrants, expel new arrivals, or subject them to incarceration or harassment. Government responses may be motivated by ideological reasons. Thus refugees from the former Eastern bloc from the 1950s to the 1970s were likely to be regarded as defectors possessing valuable intelligence, whereas the response in Europe and North America to growing numbers of refugees from developing countries was to apply increasingly restrictive admissions policies (important exceptions being Chileans and other Latin Americans in the 1970s and the Indo-Chinese in the early 1980s, both of which groups were able to secure popular sympathy). In Pakistan, for example, some 2.8 million Afghan refugees have received massive relief, whereas Iranian refugees receive virtually no government assistance. Even if refugees are successful in obtaining legal status, the problems in rebuilding a satisfactory social and economic life are huge. The office of the UNITED NATIONS HIGH COMMISSIONER FOR REFUGEES and other agencies attempt to mitigate immediate problems, such as lack of food and housing. In the long term, however, the future of many refugees is bleak: they may be unable to return home (repatriation is the wish of most refugees) because the circumstances which they fled remain unchanged, prospects for resettlement in a third country may be slim, and, even where they exist, the facilities to help refugees adapt to a new environment,

such as teaching them a new language or marketable skills may be lacking; many face a future in ill-equipped long-term refugee camps.

Regency, the The period in Britain from 1811 to 1820 when the Prince of Wales, later GEORGE IV, acted as regent for his father, GEORGE III. At first the prince's powers were restricted by an Act of Parliament in case his father should recover, but the king's disability proved to be permanent. Among the major events of the Regency were the WAR OF 1812 involving Britain and the USA, the successful conclusion of the NAPOLEONIC WARS, and the Congress of VIENNA (1814–15). In Britain the post-war period was marked by a slump in the economy, which caused much social unrest. The Tory government used severe measures to quell popular discontent, which culminated in the PETERLOO MASSACRE of 1819.

Regulators (1764–71) American rebels from inland North Carolina who felt aggrieved at the political control of the aristocrats over the coastal region. They turned to violence when legal action failed to increase their representation and reduce their taxation. 'The Regulation', centred in Orange County, attacked magistrates and lawyers until it was overwhelmed by the militia under Governor Tryon at the Battle of the Alamance. Antagonisms between coastal and frontier settlers were not uncommon, as BACON'S, CULPEPER'S, and SHAYS'S REBELLIONS demonstrated.

Regulus, Marcus Atilius (d. c. 251 BC) Roman consul in 256 BC. He defeated the Carthaginian fleet and invaded Africa during the First PUNIC WAR. He took Tunis but was defeated and captured. He was allowed to return to Rome on parole in order to negotiate peace terms involving the exchange of prisoners. He advised the Senate to refuse them, before returning to captivity. A posthumous tradition grew up that he returned to torture and execution.

Rehoboam (10th century BC) The son of SOLOMON by an Ammonite princess and his successor as King of ISRAEL (922–915 BC). On Rehoboam's accession the people of the north, restive from the constraints of Solomon's rule, broke away and set up a new kingdom under JEROBOAM I. Following this break-up of the Hebrew kingdom Rehoboam continued as the first ruler of the southern kingdom of JUDAH. His military efforts to regain control of the north were unsuccessful, partly because of an invasion of Judah by the Egyptian king, Shishak.

Reich HOLY ROMAN EMPIRE.

Reichstag (German, 'imperial parliament') The legislature of the GERMAN SECOND EMPIRE and of the WEIMAR REPUBLIC. Its origins reach back to the DIET of the HOLY ROMAN EMPIRE. The Reichstag was revived by BISMARCK (1867) to form the representative assembly of the constituent states of the North German Confederation and, from 1871, of the German Second empire. Its role was confined to legislation, being forbidden to interfere in federal government affairs and having limited control over public spending. Under the WEIMAR REPUBLIC it enjoyed greater power as the government was made responsible to it. On the night of 27 February 1933 the Reichstag building was burnt. GOERING and GOEBBELS allegedly planned to set fire to the building, subsequently claiming it as a communist plot. The arsonist was a half-crazed Dutch communist, Marinus van der Lubbe. The subsequent trial was an embarrassment as the accused German and Bulgarian communist leaders were acquitted of complicity and only van der Lubbe was executed, but the fire had served its political purpose. On 28 February a decree suspended all civil liberties and installed a state of emergency, which lasted until 1945. Elections to the Reichstag were held on 5 March 1933, but by the Enabling Act of 23 March 1933 the Reichstag effectively voted itself out of existence.

Reid, Sir George Houstoun (1845–1918) Australian statesman. Reid was Premier of New South Wales from 1894 until 1899. His ambivalent attitude towards AUSTRALIAN FEDERATION resulted in his being dubbed 'Yes–No' Reid. He led the Free Traders in the first federal parliament and was Prime Minister, leading a coalition of Free Traders and Protectionists (1904–05). After the defeat of his government, Reid led the Opposition until 1908. He was the first Australian High Commissioner in London (1910–16), after which he was elected to the British House of Commons.

Reith, John Charles Walsham, 1st Baron (1889–1971) First director-general of the British Broadcasting Corporation (1927–38). Reith's strongly Calvinistic temperament moulded the early years of BROADCASTING, with an emphasis on programmes that were educational in the widest sense: classical music, book reviews, news, and drama. His aim was that the BBC should earn respect for its impartiality and sense of responsibility, the more so because of its monopoly of radio broadcasting at that time in Britain. In 1936 he inaugurated British television. In 1940 he was elected National Member of Parliament for Southampton and was appointed Minister of Works by Winston CHURCHILL. During 1943–44 Reith worked at the Admiralty, planning the movement of supplies, war materials, and transport for the invasion of Europe.

relic Part of the mortal remains of, or an object closely associated with, a Christian saint or MARTYR. In the Middle Ages the possession of relics greatly enhanced the prestige of a church or monastery and caused the shrine to become a place of pilgrimage. LOUIS IX of France built the Sainte-Chapelle in Paris to house relics from CONSTANTINOPLE. Abuses led the Fourth LATERAN COUNCIL to forbid their sale and decree that only those authenticated by the papacy might be venerated. Their use was attacked by the later Protestants, which led in 1563 to the Council of Trent confirming the doctrine of the veneration of holy relics simply as aids to devotion.

Religion, Wars of FRENCH WARS OF RELIGION.

religion and politics The relationship between spiritual and secular authority and the effects of religious principles or beliefs on political life has always been fraught with potential conflict. Religion is acknowledged to be a crucial source of legitimacy and political mobilization in all societies, ranging from those that are avowedly secularist, such as communist regimes, to those that are THEOCRACIES, such as Iran, or Tibet before Chinese rule was imposed in 1951, or those where conformity to a state religion plays an important part in national life, as in Saudi Arabia. A complex example is Israel, a state founded on ZIONISM, a secular movement that claims the territory of Israel on historical and religious grounds. Many states have tried to weaken the power of the religious body by creating a state religious body, as in England, Scotland, and most of northern Europe following the 16th-century Reformation, where national churches were legally established in an attempt at control. Likewise, many great Islamic dynasties tried to assimilate the *ulama* (teachers of Islamic law); more recently, the secular government of Turkey attempted to reduce the authority of Islam by creating a State Directorate of Religious Affairs. In the former Soviet Union, religious activity was circumscribed or even banned until 1991 when freedom of belief was reinstated. The authorities had tried to control the remaining religious institutions by bringing them under state supervision. In the USA, by contrast, the separation of church and state is formally enshrined in the First Amendment to the Constitution (1791). This exemplifies the principle of secularism, the view that religion should be separate from public life, which first came to prominence among philosophers of the 18th-century Enlightenment. India has maintained its status as a secular democracy despite recent agitation by rightwing nationalists for a Hindu state.

Secularization and the decline of religious belief and observance were regarded by many as hallmarks of modernization and Western liberal democracy until recent years, but since the Iranian Islamic Revolution (1979) and the spread of ISLAMIC FUNDAMENTALISM, the resurgence of the NEW RIGHT and CHRISTIAN FUNDAMENTALIST values in US political life in the 1980s, and the virtual collapse of most secular communist regimes by the end of that decade, religion has been very widely acknowledged as a powerful element in both individual and public life.

Renaissance The intellectual and artistic flowering that began in Italy in the 14th century, culminated there in the 16th century, and greatly influenced other parts of Europe. Renaissance is French for rebirth and refers to a revival of the values of the classical world, an interest in the Latin classics had begun as early as the 12th century. The concept was used as early as the 15th century and was developed in the 16th century by artist and writer Giorgio Vasari. He held that art had declined in the Middle Ages, had been set on its true path by Giotto, the artist who broke with iconographic tradition and used shading to create depth, and had reached its greatest heights with Michelangelo. The ideal of the 'Renaissance man' (*uomo universale*) arose out of the concept that man was limitless in his capacity for development whether physical, social, or artistic. The idea was brilliantly characterized by Leon Battista Alberti, himself an architect, painter, scientist, poet, and mathematician, and Leonardo da Vinci. Brunelleschi is considered the first Renaissance architect; out of his interest in Roman remains he created buildings that could be compared with the finest ancient examples. In sculpture, the beginnings of the Renaissance are sometimes traced as far back as Nicola Pisano in the late 14th century, because it was known that he was influenced by Roman sarcophagi. However, it was Donatello in the early 15th century who thoroughly assimilated the spirit of ancient sculpture rather than simply borrowed motifs from it. In painting it is harder to define the Renaissance in terms of antique influence because very little classical painting has survived. From classical writings it is known that painters excelled in fidelity to nature and this became a central concern to early Renaissance painters such as Giotto and Masaccio, who brought scientific vigour to the problems of representation, while the invention of perspective assisted in the realistic portrayal of nature. Michelangelo, Raphael, Titian and others broke new ground by introducing the human figure, naturalistically depicted, into their paintings.

In the 15th and 16th centuries the centres of the Renaissance were Florence, Venice, Rome, and the ducal courts of Mantua, Urbino, and Ferrara. Florence in the period around 1425 was the cradle of the Renaissance, but by the early 16th century – the 'High Renaissance'— Venice and Rome were equally important. The MEDICI in Florence and the popes in Rome, particularly Julius II and Leo X, were important patrons. The ideals and imagery of the Italian Renaissance did not generally begin to spread to the rest of Europe until about 1500. The German Albrecht Dürer was the outstanding artist of the 'Northern Renaissance', making it his mission to transplant the new Italian ideas on to German soil.

In literature the Renaissance was led by HUMANIST scholars and poets, notably Petrarch, Dante, and Boccacio in Italy. Poetry and prose began to be written in the vernacular instead of Latin and the invention of PRINTING contributed to the spread of ideas. Among the notable writers of the Renaissance beyond Italy are Erasmus in the Netherlands, Montaigne and Rabelais, and the poets of the Pléiade in France, Lope de Vega and Cervantes in Spain, and Edmund Spenser, Sir Philip Sidney, Shakespeare, and Sir Francis Bacon in Britain. Dramatists introduced classical form and restraint into their works. Based on the architectural works of Vitruvius (*c.* 15 BC), theatre buildings and set design were constructed according to the principles of Roman theatre. A revival of plays by the Roman poet Terence in 15th-century Venice was staged before an audience seated in a horseshoe-shaped auditorium facing a proscenium arch platform and this was to become the model of theatre-building all over the Western world for the next 500 years.

The Renaissance had far-reaching consequences in many other fields. The impulse to explore the world led to the voyages of discovery of DIAZ DE NOVAES, DA GAMA, and MAGELLAN. These in turn led to advances in geography and cartography and the colonization of new lands. The astronomers Copernicus, Kepler, and Galileo (see SCIENTIFIC REVOLUTION) proposed new theories about the movement of the planets and advances were made in biology, chemistry, physics, and medicine. The Flemish anatomist Vesalius wrote *De humani corporis fabricia* (1543), an influential anatomical treatise. The new spirit of enquiry also affected perception of the Church and paved the way for calls for reform.

reparations Compensation payments for damage done in war by a defeated enemy. They were a condition of the armistice for World War I and part of the VERSAILLES PEACE SETTLEMENT. France, who had paid reparations to Germany in 1871, secretly hoped to bankrupt Germany. British civilians had sustained little damage and so LLOYD GEORGE claimed only the cost of war pensions. The US Senate did not ratify the Versailles Treaty and waived all claims on reparations. A sum of £6,500,000,000 was demanded from Germany, a figure which the British economist KEYNES argued was beyond German capacity to pay without ruining the interdependent economies of Europe. Hungary, Austria, and Bulgaria were also to

pay huge sums. Turkey, being more or less bankrupt, agreed to an Allied Finance Commission. To enforce its claims France occupied the RUHR (1923), precipitating an inflationary crisis in Germany. With Britain and the USA unhappy about reparations, various plans were devised to ease the situation. The DAWES PLAN (1924) permitted payment by instalments when possible and the YOUNG PLAN (1929) reduced the amount demanded. In 1932 the Lausanne Pact substituted a bond issue for the reparation debt and German repayments were never resumed. After World War II reparations took the form of Allied occupation of Germany and Japan. Britain, France, and the USA ended reparation collections in 1952. Stalin systematically plundered the East German zone by the removal of assets and industrial equipment. In Japan the USA administered the removal of capital goods and the Soviet Union seized Japanese assets in Manchuria. Since 1953 the Federal Republic of Germany has paid $37 billion (£20.7 billion) as reparations to Israel for damages suffered by Jews under Hitler's regime; in the late 1990s, the Swiss government finally admitted that gold and money deposited by victims of the HOLOCAUST had been held secretly in numbered accounts in the country since World War II and began to pay reparations to the families of those murdered. In the aftermath of the Gulf War (1991), the UN Compensation Commission obliged Iraq, whose invasion of Kuwait had precipitated the conflict, to pay reparations to war victims.

Representatives, US House of HOUSE OF REPRESENTATIVES.

Republican Party A major political party in the USA. The term republican was first used in the USA by JEFFERSON'S Democratic-Republican Party, which was founded in 1796 and was the antecedent of the DEMOCRATIC PARTY. The present Republican Party was formed in 1854, precipitated by the KANSAS–NEBRASKA ACT and by the agitation of the FREE SOIL PARTY; it brought together groups opposed to slavery but supporting a protective trade tariff. The party won its first presidential election with Abraham LINCOLN in 1860 and from then until 1932 lost only four such contests, two each to Grover CLEVELAND and Woodrow WILSON. Its early success was based on the support of the agricultural and industrial workers of the north and west. Its conservative financial policies, tied to tariffs and the fostering of economic growth, remained pre-eminent. The opulence of the 'GILDED AGE', contrasted with increasing poverty among immigrants and the urban proletariat, led to the PROGRESSIVE MOVEMENT and a split in the party when Theodore ROOSEVELT formed his PROGRESSIVE PARTY. After World War I the policy of ISOLATIONISM brought the party back to power, but from 1932 onwards Republicans lost five successive presidential elections, only returning to power through the massive popularity of President EISENHOWER in 1952. Under more recent Republican Presidents NIXON, FORD, REAGAN, and BUSH it became associated with military spending and a forceful assertion of US presence worldwide, especially in Central America. Strongly backed by corporate business, it nevertheless failed to maintain a grip on Congress, which usually had a Democratic majority even when the President was Republican. However, this trend was reversed in 1994, when the Republicans gained control of both the Senate and the House of Representatives for the first time in 40 years.

Repudiation Movement An attempt to set aside land purchase contracts in New Zealand. Ownership of MAORI land had been steadily proceeding through purchases from individual Maori, not tribal communities, ignoring the guarantees of the Treaty of WAITANGI (1840). In 1873 Henare Matua, a Maori chief, appealed to the Hawkes Bay Native Lands Alienation Commission to repudiate land purchase contracts drawn up in the Hawkes Bay area. He received some support from settler-politicians anxious to embarrass the large landed interests. The movement met with little success in overturning contracts, but it did contribute to the growing separatist movement among Maoris, the Kotahitanga.

resistance movements The underground movements that fought against Nazi Germany and Japan during World War II. Their activities involved publishing underground newspapers, helping Jews and prisoners-of-war to escape, conveying intelligence by secret radios, and committing acts of sabotage. In Germany itself resistance to the Nazi regime was active from 1934 onwards, at first expressed by both Protestant and Catholic Churches, but also from 1939 onwards by groups such as the Roman Catholic student group Weisse Rose, and the communist Rote Kapelle, which carried out sabotage and espionage for Russia until betrayed in 1942. Admiral Wilhelm Canaris, head of German Counter-Intelligence (*Abwehr*), was a key resistance figure until betrayed and hanged after the JULY PLOT. In occupied Europe there were often deep divisions between communist and non-communist organizations, notably in France, where the MAQUIS was active, as well as in Belgium, Yugoslavia, and Greece. Communist parties had at first remained passive, but following the German invasion of the Soviet Union (June 1941), they formed or joined underground groups. Dutch, Danish, and Norwegian resistance remained unified and worked closely with London, where in 1940 the British Special Operations Executive (SOE) was set up to co-ordinate all subversive activity, both in Europe and the Far East, and to supply arms and equipment by secret air-dropping. In eastern Europe the long German lines of communication were continually harassed by partisans and the Polish resistance was almost certainly the largest and most elaborate in Europe. Eastern European resistance later turned against the Red Army as it advanced west (1944–45), the Polish WARSAW RISINGS being a tragic example of the tensions between communist and non-communist forces. In the Far East clandestine operations were carried out through British and US intelligence organizations. Much of their effort was devoted to intelligence gathering, psychological warfare, and prisoner-of-war recovery, while the actual sabotaging of selected installations and communication lines was conducted by native-born, nationalist, and often communist-inspired guerrillas. Their leaders, such as HO CHI MINH in Vietnam, went on to form the core of the post-war independence movements against the colonial powers.

Restoration (1660) The re-establishment in England and Scotland of the Stuart monarchy by placing CHARLES II, the exiled son of CHARLES I, on the throne. Oliver CROMWELL had never succeeded in reconciling the royalists to the republican regime and his rule had been based upon the strength of the army rather than popular consent. His death in 1658 undermined the PROTECTORATE and his successor Richard CROMWELL was brushed aside by the army. The careful and deliberate actions of General MONCK in Scotland and England and CLARENDON, in exile with Charles II, brought about the peaceful restoration in May 1660. Before he left Holland Charles's Declaration of BREDA promised forgiveness, reconciliation, and, in effect, a determination to work with Parliament. The Restoration was accompanied by the revival of the Church of England and the growth of Cavalier fortunes (although those who had sold their estates to pay fines could not get them back) and a revival cultural and social life. The Restoration did not restore the absolute authority of the Stuart monarchy, as Charles II was soon to discover.

Retz, Paul de Gondi (1613–79) French statesman and cardinal. The designated successor to his uncle, the Archbishop of Paris, he was extremely ambitious and wished to replace MAZARIN as chief minister of France. He was active in the first years of the FRONDE and was afterwards imprisoned. He escaped and fled to Rome to appeal to the pope, but without success. In exile he was a serious nuisance to LOUIS XIV and it was only in 1662 that he resigned his archbishopric as the price of being allowed to return to France. His memoirs give a spirited, although unreliable, account of the personalities and intrigues of mid-17th-century France.

Reuter, Paul Julius, Baron (original name: Israel Beer Josephat, 1816–99) German-born founder of one of the first news agencies. He established a pigeon-post service between Aachen and Brussels in 1849 to relay commercial information. In 1851 he settled in London, where he opened a telegraph office near the Stock Exchange. Linked by telegraph with correspondents in other countries, he was able to supply the daily newspapers with information about share prices, eye-witness reports of foreign wars such as the Crimean, and other international news. By the 1870s his agency had become a worldwide organization.

Reuther, Walter Philip (1907–70) US labour leader. A foreman in a Detroit automobile plant, he was dismissed in 1932 for union activity. He helped to organize the United Automobile Workers (UAW) and served as its president (1946–70). He pioneered negotiations for guaranteed employment, wage increases tied to productivity, and welfare provisions for his members. An anti-communist, he was president of the Congress of Industrial Organizations (1952–55) and fought strenuously to rid the unions of racketeers. He also helped to organize non-union workers through a short-lived Alliance for Labor Action, formed from the UAW and the TEAMSTERS in 1969.

Revere, Paul (1735–1818) American patriot, a silversmith and engraver of HUGUENOT extraction living in Boston. After service in the FRENCH AND INDIAN WAR he joined the SONS OF LIBERTY and published anti-British cartoons. Immortalized in H. W. Longfellow's account of his midnight ride before LEXINGTON AND CONCORD (1775), he served in New England in the War of Independence and died a wealthy merchant and manufacturer.

revivalism (US) A recurrent Protestant movement of religious evangelization in the USA, initiated by the 'Great Awakening' in the 18th century. A 'Second Awakening' (1797–1805), most spectacular in the West, was started by James McGready who preached at frontier camp meetings for exhortation and prayer. Revivalism in the early 19th century became the accepted method of worship among Congregationalists, Presbyterians, Baptists, and Methodists. The early 20th century saw the rise of professional evangelists, preaching fundamentalism, with large organizations and sophisticated publicity. Revivalists, such as Billy Graham, have continued to attract mass audiences to their meetings, missions, and television shows.

Revolutionary Wars (1792–1802) A series of wars in Europe following the FRENCH REVOLUTION. In 1791 Louis XVI attempted unsuccessfully to escape from France to Germany, to win support from Austria and Prussia. In April 1792 France declared war on Austria, which then ruled Belgium (the Austrian Netherlands). A series of French defeats followed until, on 20 September, an invading Prussian army was defeated at Valmy. In February 1793 war was declared against Britain, Spain, and the United Provinces of the Netherlands. For a year a Reign of Terror operated in France, but, at the same time, under the skill of CARNOT, armies had been steadily raised and trained. At first the aim was to consolidate the frontiers of France along the 'natural frontiers' of the Rhine and the Alps, but from 1795, these armies were to conquer Europe. A number of brilliant young officers emerged, for example Bernadotte (later CHARLES XIV of Sweden), Barthélemy Joubert (killed in battle 1799), and above all NAPOLEON BONAPARTE. All the Netherlands were conquered, Belgium annexed, and the Republic of Batavia created from the United Provinces; French armies advanced across the Rhine and into South Germany. Switzerland was made into the Helvetic Republic (1798). In 1796–97 Napoleon took an army into Italy, defeated the Austrians at Arcola and occupied Venice, creating the Cisalpine and Ligurian Republics. In 1798 he led an expedition to Egypt, but the British fleet under NELSON destroyed his fleet at Aboukir Bay, and Napoleon returned to Paris. Meanwhile Austrian and Russian troops had re-occupied Italy and in 1799 Napoleon again marched across the Alps to win a crushing victory over the Austrians at Marengo. At the same time General Moreau won a second great victory at Hohenlinden. The peace treaties of Lunéville (1801 with Austria) and Amiens (1802 with Britain) were then negotiated, ending the Revolutionary Wars.

Revolutions of 1848 A series of revolutions in western and central Europe. They sprang from a shared background of autocratic government and economic unrest, as well as from the failure of conservative governments to grant representation to the middle classes, and the awakened nationalism of minorities in central and eastern Europe. Revolution erupted first in France, where supporters of universal suffrage and a socialist minority under Louis BLANC caused the overthrow of the July monarchy (see JULY REVOLUTION) and established the Second Republic. In most German states there were popular demonstrations and uprisings and a movement for an elected national parliament to draft a constitution for a united Germany. Rioting in Austria caused the flight of both METTERNICH and the

emperor and the formation of a constituent assembly and the emancipation of the peasantry. A movement for Hungarian independence, headed by KOSSUTH, led to a short-lived republican government from Budapest for all Hungarian lands; Magyar refusal to consider independence for its own minorities resulted in an insurrection by Croat, Serb, and Transylvanian forces and in Hungary's defeat by Austrian and Russian forces. In the Italian states there was a series of abortive revolutions that led to the temporary expulsion of the Austrians and the flight of Pope PIUS IX from Rome, but the united democratic republic dreamt of by Giuseppe MAZZINI did not come about. A PAN-SLAV CONGRESS in Prague inspired Czech nationalist demonstrations to demand autonomy within a federal Austria. By 1849 counter-revolutionary forces had restored order, but the concept of absolute monarchy and the feudal rights of a land-owning aristocracy had been tacitly abandoned.

Reynaud, Paul (1878–1966) French politician. He was Finance Minister (1938–40) and Prime Minister in the emergency of 1940, but, having appointed PÉTAIN and WEYGAND, he was unable to carry on the war when these two proved defeatist. He resigned in mid-June 1940. After the war he was Finance Minister (1948) and Vice-Premier (1953) in the Fourth Republic. He assisted in the formation of the Fifth Republic, but later quarrelled with DE GAULLE.

Reza Shah Pahlavi (Reza Khan) (1878–1944) Shah of Iran (1925–41). An officer of the Persian Cossack Brigade, he achieved power through an army coup (1921) and established a military dictatorship. He was successively Minister of War and Prime Minister before becoming Shah. He followed a policy of rapid modernization, constructing a national army, a modernized administrative system, new legal and educational systems, and economic development, notably through the Trans-Iranian Railway (1927–38). He crushed tribal and other opposition to his policies. In World War II his refusal to expel German nationals led to the invasion and occupation of Iran by Soviet and British forces. He was forced to abdicate in favour of his son, MUHAMMAD REZA SHAH PAHLAVI, and died in exile in South Africa.

Rhee, Syngman (1871–1965) Korean statesman. He was an early supporter of Korean independence from Japan and after a spell of imprisonment (1897–1904) for nationalist activities, he went to the USA and became President of a 'government-in-exile' formed by a small group of his supporters. After World War II he returned to become leader of South KOREA during the US occupation and in 1948 he became the first President of the Republic of Korea, advocating the unification of Korea both before and after the KOREAN WAR (1950–53). Rhee was re-elected in 1952 and 1956, but opposition to his corrupt and autocratic government grew more intense as economic conditions deteriorated and a third re-election in 1960 caused accusations of rigging and serious rioting, which forced Rhee into exile.

Rhineland A former province of Prussia. The success of the French revolutionary armies brought the left bank of the Rhine to France in 1794, but this was ceded by the Congress of VIENNA to Prussia as a bulwark against French expansion. With the formation of the GERMAN SECOND EMPIRE in 1871 the nearby French provinces of ALSACE and Lorraine were annexed, both being rich in iron and coal. In 1918 these were restored to France and the Rhineland 'demilitarized' but allowed to remain within the WEIMAR REPUBLIC. In 1936 HITLER's troops 're-militarized' the area, but met with no effective resistance from France or its allies. The scene of heavy fighting in 1944, it was recaptured by US troops in early 1945 and now forms part of Germany.

Rhode Island A state of the USA, the smallest NEW ENGLAND colony and state, on the southern coast of the region around Narragansett Bay. Originally settled in 1636 by such dissidents from Massachusetts as Roger WILLIAMS and Anne Hutchinson, it was chartered as a colony by Parliament in 1644 and became a Quaker and Baptist refuge. Its internal disunity was pacified under Samuel Cranston's governorship (1698–1727) and its eastern Narragansett country became a prosperous agricultural and horse-breeding area, while Newport and Providence thrived on trade, including slave-trading and rum distilling. It was occupied by British troops and ships during the War of INDEPENDENCE (1776–79), but they withdrew before a French fleet arrived. After the American Revolution, it remained independent in its views. It did not send representatives to the CONTINENTAL CONGRESS and had to be greatly pressured to ratify the CONSTITUTION OF THE USA.

Rhodes (modern Greek, Rodi) An island in the south-east Aegean Sea off the coast of Turkey; now in Greek possession. Rhodes is the southernmost and largest of the 12 Dodecanese islands in the southern Sporades.

History. Rhodes was first settled by the DORIANS, who established the three city-states of Ialysus, Lindus, and Camirus. These sent out colonies, endured tyrannies, and became subject to the Persians, before joining the ATHENIAN EMPIRE in the 5th century BC. In 412–411 they seceded and the subsequent war with Athens brought about a fusion of the three into the federal state of Rhodes. The island was well placed to benefit from trade, and the opening up of the Persian empire by ALEXANDER THE GREAT meant that it became the most prosperous city-state in Greece. It survived a prolonged siege by Demetrius Poliorcetes in 305–304 and managed to sustain remarkably independent policies in the 3rd century. However ambivalent loyalties in the third MACEDONIAN WAR led Rome to declare Delos a free port, which drastically injured Rhodes' trade. Nevertheless it thrived, in a more modest way, under the Romans. Rhodes was part of the Byzantine empire until the capture of CONSTANTINOPLE (1204). It was then held by GENOA and annexed by the emperor of Nicaea (NICAEAN EMPIRE). In 1309 AD the island was occupied by the KNIGHTS HOSPITALLERS of St John of Jerusalem, who were ejected in 1522 by SULEIMAN I, and it became part of the OTTOMAN EMPIRE. Rhodes was captured by Italy in 1912 and ceded to Greece in 1947.

Rhodes, Cecil (John) (1853–1902) British businessman and colonial administrator. He was sent to NATAL in 1870 after a protracted illness. In 1871 diamonds were found at Kimberley and he and his brother were successful in prospecting, which made him financially independent at the age of 19. By the age of 35 he controlled the largest diamond mining and trading companies in South Africa. He fought determinedly for British interests against the AFRIKANER exclusivism of President KRUGER and against German expansion in southern Africa. He was instrumental in acquiring Bechuanaland (BOTSWANA) and

then, through his British South Africa Company, the vast territories of Matabeleland and Mashonaland (ZIMBABWE), which were eventually renamed Rhodesia. He aimed to 'make Africa British from Cape to Cairo' with Afrikaner consent. He became Prime Minister of the Cape (1890–95). Although he was acquitted of responsibility, the abortive JAMESON RAID had his financial support and he resigned, devoting the rest of his life to the development of Rhodesia. In his will he left enough money to provide some 200 annual scholarships for Commonwealth, US, and German students to study at Oxford University.

Rhodesia The former name of a large area of southern Africa. Rhodesia was developed for its mining potential by Cecil RHODES and the British South Africa Company from the last decade of the 19th century. It was administered by the company until Southern Rhodesia became a self-governing British colony in 1923 and Northern Rhodesia a British protectorate in 1924. From 1953 to 1963 the two Rhodesias were united with Nyasaland to form the CENTRAL AFRICAN FEDERATION. After Northern Rhodesia became the independent state of ZAMBIA in 1964, the name Rhodesia was used by the former colony of Southern Rhodesia until the proclamation of the Republic of ZIMBABWE in 1980.

Rhodesia, Northern ZAMBIA.

Rhodesia, Southern ZIMBABWE.

Rhodesia and Nyasaland, Federation of CENTRAL AFRICAN FEDERATION.

Ribbentrop, Joachim von (1893–1946) German Nazi statesman. He joined the Nazi Party in 1932 and became a close associate of Hitler. In 1936–38 he was ambassador in London. As Foreign Minister (1938–45), Ribbentrop conducted negotiations with states destined to become Hitler's victims. The NAZI–SOVIET PACT was regarded as his masterpiece, opening the way for the attack on POLAND and the Baltic States. He was responsible for the Tripartite Pact (1940) between Germany, Italy, and Japan. After the NUREMBERG TRIALS he was executed.

Ricardo, David (1772–1823) British political economist, together with Adam SMITH the founder of British CLASSICAL ECONOMICS and of economics as an independent discipline. His fame rests on his *Principles of Political Economy and Taxation* (1817), in which he made a systematic attempt to establish how wealth was distributed, and put forward his theory that the value of a commodity rests on the amount of labour required for its production – a theory later adopted by Karl MARX. In 1819 Ricardo entered Parliament, where he supported FREE TRADE, a return to the GOLD STANDARD, and the repeal of the CORN LAWS.

Ricci, Matteo (1552–1610) Italian JESUIT missionary. He was received at the court of the MING emperor Wanli in 1601, having arrived in southern China in 1583. He had made himself proficient in Chinese and always dressed in a Chinese scholar's robes. He interested the emperor in clocks brought from Europe, translated numerous books, among them the geometry of Euclid, into Chinese, and made a world map with China, the Middle Kingdom, at its centre. He established beyond doubt that China was Cathay, the land MARCO POLO had described. His tolerance and scholarship impressed influential Chinese, some of whom were converted. The emperor gave land for his tomb in Beijing.

Richard I (the Lionheart) (1157–99) King of England (1189–99). Richard I was the third son of HENRY II and ELEANOR OF AQUITAINE. He was made Duke of Aquitaine at the age of 12 and in 1173 joined his brothers in their rebellion against Henry. Richard spent only six months of his life in England. Soon after his coronation he left with the Third CRUSADE and in PALESTINE in 1191 he captured Acre and defeated SALADIN at Arsuf. The following year, after concluding a three-year truce with Saladin, he set out overland for England. He was imprisoned by Emperor Henry VI of Austria and, according to widespread legend, his whereabouts were discovered by the Minstrel Blondel. In 1194 England paid a ransom of £100,000 for his release. During his absence his brother JOHN had allied himself with PHILIP II of France against him. Within a few weeks of his return he began the military campaigns for the defence of Normandy against Philip that led eventually to his death whilst attacking the castle at Châlus. Richard's military exploits earned him the nickname *Coeur de Lion* (French, 'Lionheart'). However, his absence abroad led to a growth in the power of the barons, a problem inherited by JOHN.

Richard II (1367–1400) King of England (1377–99). He was the only son of EDWARD THE BLACK PRINCE and the grandson of Edward III, whom he succeeded at the age of ten. In 1381 his courage helped prevent disaster in the PEASANTS' REVOLT, but in the next few years he had to face a more direct threat to his power from a group of magnates (LORDS APPELLANT) led by his uncle THOMAS OF WOODSTOCK, Duke of Gloucester. During the session of the Merciless Parliament (1388) they had Richard's chief supporters executed or imprisoned and it was only in 1397 that he was able to strike back at them by punishing the Lords Appellant. His attempt to impose his personal rule upon England alienated support and enabled Henry of BOLINGBROKE to seize the throne with comparative ease in 1399. Richard abdicated and died a few months later in prison. He was a sensitive man but temperamentally unbalanced and incapable of firm rule.

Richard III (1452–85) Duke of Gloucester (1461–85) and King of England (1483–85). He was a younger brother of EDWARD IV and the 11th child of Richard Plantagenet, Duke of YORK. Tudor propaganda, notably the biography by Thomas MORE, portrayed him as a monster from birth, always a traitor to his own family, but as Duke of Gloucester he served Edward faithfully and was an able soldier and a capable administrator in northern England. Upon the accession of his young nephew EDWARD V, he became Protector of England: the council over which he presided included his enemies, the Woodvilles, and he gained in popularity from striking at their power. His usurpation of the throne in June 1483 caused no outright hostility, but in all save the YORKIST north of England there was revulsion when it came to be believed that he had had Edward V and his brother killed in the Tower of London. (When and how they died remains a mystery.) He had long expected a further invasion of England by the LANCASTRIAN Henry Tudor (HENRY VII), but when a battle was fought at BOSWORTH FIELD in August 1485 he was defeated and killed because he had lost the support of his army.

In Shakespeare's play *Richard III* he is portrayed as a villain and a hunchback, but there is no evidence to support the tradition that he was physically deformed.

Richard of York YORK, RICHARD PLANTAGENET, 3RD DUKE OF.

Richelieu, Armand Jean du Plessis, duc de (1585–1642) Cardinal, the chief minister of Louis XIII of France from 1628 to 1642, and architect of royal absolutism in France and of French leadership in Europe. He was consecrated Bishop of Luçon in 1607 and entered the council of the regent, Marie de Medici in about 1616. He was temporarily ousted after Louis XIII's assumption of power, but had gained the king's confidence by 1624 and for the rest of their lives the two men worked together. On the domestic front he destroyed the political power and military capacity of the HUGUENOTS and continued HENRY IV's policies of centralized absolutism. He alienated the Catholic 'Dévot' party, the high nobility, and the judicial hierarchy, but managed to survive a series of plots and conspiracies. His excessive taxation of the lower orders created an endemic state of revolt in many provinces. The money was needed to finance France's active anti-Habsburg foreign policy and during the THIRTY YEARS WAR he subsidized the Protestant Dutch, Danes, and Swedes to fight against the Habsburgs before France declared war on Spain in 1635; he also supported anti-Spanish revolts in Catalonia and Portugal (1640). His successor was MAZARIN, whom he had trained to continue his policies.

Ridolfi Plot (1571) An abortive international Catholic conspiracy, intended to put MARY, QUEEN OF SCOTS on the English throne in place of ELIZABETH I. It took its name from Roberto di Ridolfi (1531–1612), a well-connected Florentine banker who had settled in England. The English Catholics were to rise under Thomas Howard, 4th Duke of Norfolk. Then, with papal finance and Spanish military aid, Elizabeth was to be deposed in favour of Mary, who would marry Howard. Elizabeth's intelligence service uncovered the plot and its leading figures were arrested.

Riebeeck, Jan van (1610–77) Governor of Cape Town (1652–62) and the founder of European settlement in South Africa. He was sent by the Chamber of Amsterdam to found a refreshment station at Cape Town for Netherlands vessels sailing to the East Indies and arrived there on 6 April 1652 with 125 men. As commander he organized a simple government and ruled for ten years. He followed DUTCH EAST INDIA COMPANY policy in regarding the station as an opportunity for profit rather than for colonization. Growing corn and vines and rearing cattle were permitted, but he discouraged trade with Africans. In 1662 he was transferred to MALACCA.

Riel Rebellions (1869, 1885) Two uprisings of the méti or half-Indian population of Manitoba against the Canadian government, led by the French-Indian Louis Riel (1844–85). Expansion westwards led to the uprising in 1869 in which a provisional government under Riel was set up. Riel aroused outrage in the east by executing an Ontario settler, but the arrival of British and Canadian troops coincided with negotiations in Ottawa leading to the area's inclusion within the confederation, with all the local rights demanded by th métis. Riel escaped but increasing resentment of easter domination and economic dislocation produced a second insurrection in 1885. Riel, who returned from the USA to lead it, was supported by several Indian tribes, but alienated most of the White population and was defeated by the Canadian militia. He was then tried and executed for treason.

Rienzo, Cola di (1313–54) Italian popular leader. As spokesman for the Roman populace he attempted to lead a revolution in 1347. Taking the title of tribune, he sought fiscal, political, and judicial reform. Rejected by the papacy and the powerful Orsini and Colonna lords, he was deposed in November 1347 and excommunicated. In 1350 he gained the support of the new pope, Innocent VI, who encouraged him to restore papal authority in Rome. He returned there in triumph in 1354 only to be killed by the mob. He was remembered in the 19th century as a symbol of Italian unity.

Right (or the Right) Political ideas, movements, and parties of a conservative or reactionary character. Following the example of the nobility at the time of the FRENCH REVOLUTION (1789), members of legislative assemblies holding authoritarian, anti-democratic, or anti-socialist views have tended to sit on the right of their chambers. As with 'LEFT', the meaning of 'Right' varies with context, denoting at different times conservative, liberal, or even FASCIST outlooks. Recent trends have been called the NEW RIGHT.

Rights of Man and the Citizen A declaration of the guiding principles of the FRENCH REVOLUTION that was approved by the Constituent National Assembly in August 1789. JEFFERSON, the US minister in Paris, was consulted and the Declaration was influenced by the US example as well as by the ENLIGHTENMENT. It set forth in clear language the principles of equality and individual liberty: 'Men are born and remain free and equal in rights'; 'No body of men, no individual, can exercise authority which does not issue expressly from the will of the nation'. Civil and fiscal equality, freedom from arbitrary arrest, freedom of speech and the press, and the right to own private property were affirmed. Later the Revolution denied many of these rights, but the declaration ensured an initial welcome for the French Revolutionary armies in many European countries and was the charter of European liberals for the next half-century.

Riot Act An Act intended to prevent civil disorder that was passed by the British Parliament in 1715. JACOBITE disturbances following George I's accession alarmed the new Whig government and gave the excuse for new legislation, which applied to any group of more than 12 people. The Act made it a serious crime for anyone to refuse to obey the command of lawful authority to disperse; thus the Act imposed upon the civil magistrates the dangerous duty of attending a riot or a large meeting that might become riotous and reading the Riot Act. Frequent use was made of the Act in the 18th century. Its use declined in the 19th century and it was repealed in 1911.

Ripon, George Frederick Samuel Robinson, 1st Marquess of (1827–1909) British statesman. He entered Parliament as a Liberal in 1853, supporting a scheme to provide working men with opportunities for education. He served as Secretary for War (1863–6), and Secretary for India (1866–68). As President of the Council (1868–73)

he was responsible for the 1870 Education Bill, which his deputy, W. E. FORSTER carried through the House of Commons. In 1873 he became a Roman Catholic and resigned from public office. GLADSTONE appointed him viceroy of India (1880–84) where he introduced a system of local self-government and ended restrictions on the freedom of the vernacular press. His Ilbert Bill (1883) gave qualified Indians jurisdiction over Europeans and established trial by a jury, of which half should be Europeans. On his return to Britain he again held ministerial office in Liberal governments.

Risorgimento   *The vision of a united and liberated Italy inspired the 'Young Italy' movement in 1831 and triumphed in 1861, when Victor Emanuel II was proclaimed King of Italy.*

Risorgimento (Italian, 'resurrection' or 'rebirth') (*c.* 1831–61) A period of political unrest in ITALY, during which the united kingdom of Italy emerged. Much of Italy had experienced liberal reforms and an end to feudal and ecclesiastical privilege during the NAPOLEONIC WARS. The restoration of repressive regimes led to uprisings in Naples and PIEDMONT (1821) and in Bologna (1831), which were then part of the Papal States. Following the French JULY REVOLUTION in 1830, Italian nationalists began to support MAZZINI and the YOUNG ITALY movement. In this they were encouraged by the liberal Charles Albert, who succeeded to the throne of

Sardinia and in 1831 became ruler of Piedmont. In 1847 Count CAVOUR started a newspaper, *Il Risorgimento*, which had a considerable influence on Charles Albert, who in 1848 tried to drive the Austrians out of Lombardy and Venetia. He was defeated at Custozza (1848) and Novara (1849) and abdicated. He was succeeded by his son VICTOR EMANUEL II. During the REVOLUTIONS OF 1848 republicans held power briefly in Rome, Florence, Turin, and Venice and hoped to create a republic of Italy, but were also defeated. Under the guidance of Cavour, Prime Minister of Piedmont from 1852, the French emperor NAPOLEON III was encouraged to ally with Piedmont, in return for promises of Nice and a part of the Alpine region of Savoy and Austria was defeated in the Battles of MAGENTA and SOLFERINO in 1859. Austria evacuated Lombardy and much of central Italy. GARIBALDI liberated Sicily, marched north and almost reached Rome. Plebiscites were held and resulted in a vote to accept Victor Emanuel II as first King of Italy (1861).

Rizal, José (1861–96) Filipino nationalist. While training as a doctor in Spain he wrote two novels attacking Spanish repression in the PHILIPPINES, marking him out as one of the leading spokesmen of the nationalist movement and of the publicity campaign known as the Propaganda Movement. A reformist rather than a revolutionary, Rizal fell foul of the Spanish authorities when he formed a reform society, the *Liga Filipina*, in 1892 and was exiled to Mindanao. Although not involved in the nationalist uprising of 1896, he was executed by the Spanish authorities for supposed complicity in the rebellion.

Rizzio, David (1533–66) Italian-born secretary and adviser to MARY, QUEEN OF SCOTS. He entered service at court in 1561 and by 1564 he had become her Secretary: he possibly arranged her marriage to his friend DARNLEY. By March 1566 'Seigneur' David's arrogant monopoly of power, combined with fears of his being a papal agent, led to his assassination. Darnley, who suspected him of adultery with Mary, was involved in the plot.

Roanoke Island The first English colony in North America, in Albemarle Sound off the north coast of North Carolina. A group of settlers financed by RALEIGH landed there in 1585, but were evacuated, just before relief arrived from England, by DRAKE returning from the Caribbean. A second colonizing group was sent in 1587 under John White, who then had to go back to England to obtain further supplies. His return from England was interrupted by the Spanish Armada, and in 1590 he found the settlement empty. The 'lost colony' has been immortalized by White's paintings of local Native Americans and by Thomas Harriott's *Report* (1588).

'robber baron' A ruthlessly aggressive businessman. The title was first applied in the USA in the 'GILDED AGE' and was conferred on railway operators by aggrieved Kansas farmers in 1880. The earlier generation of 'robber barons' were financiers who made fortunes in the American Civil War and, thereafter, exploited the stock market, railways, and public utilities, a notable example being Jay Gould (1836–92), who made a fortune of $25 million out of railway and bullion speculation. Cornelius VANDERBILT made an even larger fortune out of railways ($100 million), which his son, William Henry,

further extended. Other financial giants who obtained monopolies over industry or markets were J. P. MORGAN, Andrew CARNEGIE, and J. D. ROCKEFELLER.

Robert I (the Bruce) (1274–1329) King of Scotland (1306–29). Robert I had a successful reign, inheriting a contested throne in a country partly occupied by the English, and leaving a securely governed kingdom to his son, DAVID II. He was fortunate in that he was matched by an ineffectual English king, EDWARD II, over whom he won an important victory at BANNOCKBURN in 1314. In 1322 Edward attempted a fresh invasion of Scotland, but Bruce outmanoeuvred him and then invaded England as far south as Yorkshire, nearly capturing Edward himself. In the Treaty of Edinburgh (1328), EDWARD III recognized Bruce's title and Scotland's independence from England, although this was only a temporary lull in Anglo-Scottish hostilities.

Robert II (1316–90) King of Scotland (1371–90). Robert II inherited the throne from his uncle, DAVID II, fairly late in life; as Robert the Steward, he spent most of his active years in virtual opposition to David, leading the Scottish nationalists against the invading armies of EDWARD III while David was in exile in France. Shortly after his accession Robert successfully concluded a treaty with CHARLES V of France that reaffirmed the Franco-Scottish alliance.

Robert III (*c.* 1337–1406) King of Scotland (1390–1406). He was the eldest son of ROBERT II and was christened John but assumed the name Robert on his succession. He had been severely injured by a horse-kick, so power was exercised by a regent – first his brother Robert, Earl of Fife and then his son David, Duke of Rothesay.

Robertson, Sir William Robert (1860–1933) British field-marshal. After service in India and South Africa he became commandant of the Staff College, Camberley, Surrey, in 1910. He was chief of the Imperial General Staff from 1915 until criticisms by LLOYD GEORGE of British strategy led to his resignation in 1918. He subsequently commanded British troops on the Rhine (1919–20).

Robespierre, Maximilien François Marie Isidore de (1758–94) French Revolutionary and 'incorruptible' leader of the JACOBIN CLUB. He trained as an advocate but resigned his post as a judge in 1782 and for a time lived the life of a dandy in Arras. He was a member of the STATES-GENERAL called in 1789 and became an influential voice in the newly formed NATIONAL ASSEMBLY. Two years later he joined the Jacobin Club and began a long and bitter struggle with the powerful GIRONDINS. He was popular with the Paris Commune, despite opposing its violent methods. He argued for the king's execution and the following year he was instrumental in the overthrow of the Girondins and was elected on to the COMMITTEE OF PUBLIC SAFETY. He did not instigate the TERROR or its machinery, but supported moves to rid the Revolution of its enemies. By the end of March 1794 his power seemed secure, HÉBERT and DANTON had been executed and the Terror intensified. On 28 July, however, he was shouted down in the Convention, arrested, and executed the following day.

Robin Hood The legendary English outlaw who stole from the rich to give to the poor. Robin Hood is traditionally represented as the unjustly outlawed Earl of Huntingdon, fighting the corrupt administration of

King JOHN and his local officer the sheriff of Nottingham from Sherwood Forest. The earliest literary evidence of Robin appears in William Langland's poem *Piers Plowman* (written *c.* 1367–86). The fullest account of his exploits, given in the late medieval *Lytell Geste of Robyn Hode* (printed *c.* 1495), locates him in Barnsdale, Yorkshire and a Yorkshire pipe-roll of 1230 mentions an outlaw by that name. Robin's sympathies for the plight of the gentry, not just the peasantry, are best understood in the context of 14th-century disenchantment with royal justice: it has been suggested that the ballads actually describe events of EDWARD III's reign. Post-medieval ballads give Robin Hood companions in Sherwood Forest, among them Maid Marian, Friar Tuck, Little John, Will Scarlett, and Allan-a-Dale.

Robinson, Mary Bourke (1944–) Irish academic and politician, President of the Republic of Ireland (1990–97). Robinson was a law professor, specializing in international law and human rights. In 1969 she won a seat in the Irish upper house, the Senate. She twice ran unsuccessfully for election to the *Dáil*, the lower house, as a Labour Party candidate.

In 1990 Robinson emerged from relative obscurity to win a spectacular victory on the centre-left ticket in the Irish presidential race. She was the first woman to hold the post and campaigned vigorously for women's rights, particularly for reform of the anti-divorce and abortion laws. She was also instrumental in promoting a greater understanding in the Republic of the separate Unionist tradition in NORTHERN IRELAND. In 1997 she became a United Nations High Commissioner for Human Rights. She was succeeded as President by the Northern Irish academic and nationalist representative Mary McAleese.

Rob Roy (Robert MacGregor) (1671–1734) Scottish brigand. He was given a commission by JAMES II in 1688, which he used as an excuse to plunder his neighbours, both by cattle-stealing and blackmail. Ruined by debt, he waged virtual war on the Duke of Montrose whom he blamed for his misfortunes. He was trusted by neither side during the FIFTEEN Rebellion and despite a temporary reconciliation with Montrose in 1722 he was arrested in 1727 and escaped transportation only by the timely arrival of a pardon.

Rockefeller, John D(avison) (1839–1937) US industrialist and philanthropist. He became a partner in a produce business in 1858. His firm entered the oil-refining business in 1862 and became the nucleus of the Standard Oil Company, incorporated in Ohio in 1870. By 1879, due to debatable practices, it controlled 90 to 95% of the nation's oil-refining capacity. The US government sought to limit this monopoly, dissolved eventually in 1911. A pious Baptist, Rockefeller had turned to philanthropy by the 1890s. He gave away $600 million in his lifetime, including $183 million to the Rockefeller Foundation. His son, John D(avison), Jr (1874–1960), bought for the United Nations the site for its headquarters in New York. His son, Nelson Aldrich (1908–79), was attracted by public life and was elected to four consecutive terms as governor of New York (1959–73), also serving as Vice-President (1974–77).

Rockingham, Charles Watson-Wentworth, 2nd Marquis of (1730–82) British statesman and leader of the political faction known as the Rockingham WHIGS.

Most of his supporters were originally followers of the Duke of NEWCASTLE, but from the mid-1760s they transferred their allegiance to Rockingham. He formed a ministry in 1765–66, which repealed the American STAMP ACT and the controversial cider excise. He and his supporters strenuously opposed Lord NORTH and the American War of INDEPENDENCE and argued for financial reforms, which the second Rockingham administration undertook in 1782. On his death in office the Rockingham Whigs split into further factions, of which the most important formed the basis of the new Whig party which was evolving at the end of the 18th century.

Rodney, George Brydges Rodney, 1st Baron (1719–92) British admiral. Rodney gained his early naval expertise with HAWKE at Finisterre in 1747 and at Le Havre in 1759, where he destroyed the French flotilla poised to invade England in the SEVEN YEARS WAR. His greatest victory was at the Battle of Les SAINTES (1782) in the West Indies, where he restored British supremacy at sea in the closing stages of the American War of INDEPENDENCE.

Roger II (Guiscard) (*c.* 1095–1154) King of SICILY (1130–54). The Norman expansion into southern Italy and Sicily was begun by the brothers Robert and Roger GUISCARD, initially in defiance of the pope, but subsequently with his grudging co-operation. The Treaty of Melfi (1059) empowered them to take south Italy from the Greeks and Sicily from the Muslims and by the time of Roger Guiscard's death, Sicily was in Norman hands. His son Roger II effectively ruled Sicily from 1113 but had to assert control over the anarchic Norman barons who threatened his rule, especially when backed by the pope in 1129. From 1130 Roger supported the ANTIPOPE's cause; despite excommunication by Pope Innocent II and internal revolt, he consolidated his power by 1140. He took Malta, Corfu, and many cities on the Greek mainland as well as controlling most of the land in North Africa between Tripoli and Tunis. In 1140 he issued a revised code of laws and in his later years he ruled one of the most sophisticated governments in Western Europe. His court at Palermo enjoyed a high artistic and scholarly reputation.

Rogers, Robert (1731–95) American frontier soldier. He formed the Rogers Rangers, a force of 600 New England frontiersmen who fought with great bravery in the FRENCH AND INDIAN WAR at Lake George (1758) and the capture of Quebec (1759). He served in the relief of Detroit in PONTIAC's Rebellion. His loyalty to the Revolution was questioned and Washington had him arrested as a spy in 1776. Such treatment converted him into a loyalist and in 1780 he went to live in London.

Rokossovsky, Konstantin Konstantinovich (1896–1968) Polish-born Soviet field-marshal. Rokossovsky enlisted in the Tsarist army and joined the RED ARMY in 1919. Arrested during STALIN's purges, he was released from prison camp to become one of the outstanding generals of World War II, taking part in the battles of Moscow, STALINGRAD, KURSK, and others. His Red Army troops stood by (August–September 1944) on the outskirts of Warsaw without helping in the WARSAW RISING against the German occupying forces. After the war he was transferred to the Polish army and became Deputy Premier and Minister of Defence under

President Bierut. Rokossovsky led the army in a bloody suppression (June 1956) of Polish workers in Poznán, who were demonstrating for 'bread and freedom'. On 20 October Polish and Soviet troops exchanged fire; Rokossovsky's troops were recalled to Moscow, and GOMULKA's new nationalist government was able to claim some independence from interference by the Soviet Union.

Roland de la Platière, Marie-Jeanne Philipon

(1754–93) French Revolutionary, whose *salon* became the centre of the GIRONDIN party. Through her political influence her husband, Jean-Marie Roland (1734–93), was appointed Minister of the Interior in 1792. She helped him write a letter, read out in the council, which criticized the actions of LOUIS XVI. He was dismissed in July 1792 but returned to power in August following the overthrow of the monarchy. However, the following year he was forced to resign and, as the power of the Girondins weakened, Madame Roland was arrested. She was executed on 8 November 1793 and two days later her husband, hearing of her death, committed suicide.

Rollo

(c. 860–931) Leader of a band of VIKINGS that invaded north-western France. In 912 as Duke Robert he accepted Normandy as a duchy from the French king Charles III and was baptized, but remained quite independent of French authority. He married a French princess, gave parcels of land in Normandy to his followers, and began the long chapter of NORMAN influence on Europe.

Roman Britain

(43–410 AD) The period when most of Britain was part of the ROMAN EMPIRE. Britain was first visited by the Romans under Julius CAESAR during the GALLIC WARS. It was then the home of Gallic tribes and later a refuge for defeated allies of VERCINGETORIX. CLAUDIUS invaded Britain in 43 AD, attracted by the island's minerals and grain. At first the Belgic tribes were subdued up to the FOSSE WAY. The frontier was then extended into native Celtic territories and established by the building of HADRIAN'S WALL. Native culture absorbed Roman ways: former tribal leaders adopted a Roman lifestyle. Army veterans settled there after discharge, as did traders, scholars, craftsmen, and soldiers from all parts of the Roman empire. Universally acknowledged Christian bishoprics were established. ROMAN VILLAS, ROMAN ROADS, and titles abounded, but little Latin was spoken and the people remained essentially Celtic. In 406 and 409 the Britons rebelled against Roman rule. The Romans withdrew from Britain in 410. The period of Roman decline and the early history of the Saxon kingdoms remains obscure.

Roman Catholic Church

The largest branch of the CHRISTIAN CHURCH in the world, with over 1,000 million members, under the jurisdiction of the POPE (the Bishop of Rome). In the early Church the Bishop of Rome, as the successor of St PETER, exercised a limited measure of authority over all Christians. With the EAST–WEST SCHISM of 1054 however, his authority was restricted to the Western Church. Despite this, the Church and PAPACY reached the zenith of their international power during the MIDDLE AGES. At the REFORMATION of the 16th century this authority was diminished by the secession of the PROTESTANT Churches. It was at this time that the term Roman Catholic Church came to be used, initially by Protestants as a somewhat derogatory term to imply

that the Roman Church was at most one branch of the Christian Church. But the term was also acceptable to many Roman Catholics, inasmuch as it asserted the primacy of the pope over Christians. From the mid-16th century the Catholic Church responded to the challenge of Protestantism with the movement known as the COUNTER-REFORMATION, which brought various reforms and a tightening of Church discipline, the INQUISITION seeking out and destroying those with unapproved attitudes or behaviour. Important developments included the founding (1533) of the JESUIT order, which took a leading role in missionary work, and the convoking of the Council of Trent (1545–63), which determined Catholic teaching, organization, and liturgy for the next 400 years. During the 18th century the Church came under attack from the sceptical spirit of the ENLIGHTENMENT and the anticlerical ideology of the French Revolution. Under Pius VII the papacy signed a CONCORDAT (1801) with NAPOLEON, restoring Catholicism in France, but Pius's refusal to support the CONTINENTAL SYSTEM against Britain led Napoleon to occupy Rome and the VATICAN CITY. In the 19th century the Church and the papacy reacted defensively to the modern world, responding to challenges to their teaching and authority by stressing strict obedience and uniformity of belief. In Prussia, BISMARCK's attempts to subordinate the Church to the state (KULTURKAMPF) failed because of the passive resistance of the clergy and the Catholic population. Following the reunification of Italy (1870) the pope's temporal powers were restricted to the Vatican. At the same time the First Vatican Council (1869–70) under PIUS IX, declared the infallibility of the pope in matters of doctrine. Catholic MISSIONARIES continued to promulgate the faith beyond Europe, into Latin America, Asia and Africa. During World War II Pope PIUS XII, faithful to the LATERAN TREATIES with Italy, retained the strict neutrality of the Church. A second Vatican Council ('Vatican II', 1962–65) was summoned by JOHN XXIII and reconvened by his successor PAUL VI; it set out to modernize the Church's teaching, discipline, and organization. Contacts between the Catholic Church, the EASTERN ORTHODOX and Protestant Churches, and other faiths began to be established. In 1967 the Vatican issued a controversial encyclical that formalized the Church's opposition to artificial contraception. Under JOHN PAUL II (1978–), a Pole, the global mission of the papacy has been emphasized. John Paul's papacy has also been marked by his resistance to any change in the Church's teaching on contraception, abortion, divorce, homosexuality, and the celibacy of the priesthood. In 1984 the Church concluded with the Italian government a revision of the Lateran Treaties, formalizing the separation of the Church and state. By the year 2000 the majority of Roman Catholics will be living in Latin America, where LIBERATION THEOLOGY, the identification of the priesthood with the poor, became a source of controversy within the Church.

The Roman Catholic Church has an elaborately organized centralized hierarchy of bishops and priests, who must be celibate, under the pope, whose authority is based on the doctrine of the Petrine Succession (i.e., that the popes are the spiritual heirs to the power vested in St Peter by Jesus). Owing to the paramount authority accorded to the pope, even rulings that are not technically infallible enjoy great authority. The Roman Catholic Church differs from Protestantism in the importance it attaches to tradition, in addition to the authority of the BIBLE. The importance of the seven sacraments and the celebration of the liturgy have developed as part of the traditions of the Church. The vast majority of worshippers follow the Roman rite, but there are five Eastern-rite groups that accept the authority of the pope. They are the Byzantine, Antiochene, Alexandrian, Chaldean, and Armenian rites, which encompass a number of different churches. Veneration of the Virgin Mary and the saints is a further aspect of Roman Catholic traditionalism. The centralized authority of the Church has led to a high degree of elucidation of doctrine and belief, such as the different categories of sin and the qualities of purgatory, heaven, and hell. Despite this traditionalism, the Church has recognized the need for reform and renewal; the liturgy, once universally held in Latin, is now held in the language spoken by the people. Monasticism remains important, but the importance of lay movements such as the South American 'base communities' is increasingly recognized. The Church participates in the ecumenical movement by sending observers to the WORLD COUNCIL OF CHURCHES. In recent decades the Church has taken a more active role in world events, notably by its sustained opposition to COMMUNISM in Eastern Europe.

Roman civil wars Conflicts that afflicted the last century of the Roman republic (88 BC–*c.* 28 BC) and led to the inevitable institution of the unchallenged authority of one man, the Principate. Political life in Rome was unsettled from the period of SULLA's dictatorship and the Catiline conspiracy (64–63 BC). Rivalry between the republican military leader Julius CAESAR and POMPEY began after the collapse of their alliance. Caesar defeated the Pompeian army in Spain at Ilerda (49 BC) and Pompey himself at Pharsalus (48 BC); he won further victories in Asia and Africa. Cato's suicide in 46 BC signified the collapse of the republican cause. On his return to Rome, Caesar was made dictator and virtually sole ruler. His plans for safeguarding the empire by military expeditions against Dacia and Parthia were cut short by outraged republican traditionalists who murdered him in 44 BC. Further civil wars followed. Initially Octavian (AUGUSTUS), supported by the republican party, struggled against MARK ANTONY. In 43 BC Antony, Octavian, and Lepidus formed a coalition whose forces defeated the republicans led by Brutus and Cassius at PHILIPPI. Antony meanwhile joined forces with Cleopatra and was defeated by Octavian at ACTIUM. The Roman world was united under the sole leadership of Octavian, who annexed Egypt.

In 68 AD civil war broke out in the empire in the struggle for succession after NERO's death. Galba was proclaimed emperor from Spain; he entered Rome in September but was murdered and succeeded by Otho; meanwhile Vitellius was proclaimed emperor in Germany and Otho committed suicide. VESPASIAN then invaded Italy and took the throne, making 68–69 'the year of the four emperors'. This crisis period was followed by the settled rule of VESPASIAN.

Roman empire The period when the Roman state and its overseas provinces were under the rule of an emperor, from the time of AUGUSTUS (27 BC) until 476 AD. The Roman empire was divided in 375 AD by Emperor

Theodosius into the Western and Eastern empires. The term is often used to refer to all Roman territories during both the republic and the empire.

The city of Rome gradually gained power from the time of the Tarquins (6th century BC), subduing the Etruscans, Sabines, Samnites, and Greek settlers, and by the mid-3rd century BC, controlled Italy. It came into conflict with CARTHAGE in the western Mediterranean and with the Hellenistic world in the east. Success in the PUNIC WARS gave Rome its first overseas possessions in Sicily (241), Spain (201), and north Africa (146) and the Macedonian Wars eventually left Rome dominant in Macedonia, Greece, and parts of Asia Minor. Syria and Gaul from the Rhine to the Atlantic were added by the campaigns of POMPEY and Julius CAESAR and Egypt was annexed in 31 BC after the Battle of ACTIUM. AUGUSTUS planned to consolidate the empire within natural boundaries, but in 43 AD CLAUDIUS invaded Britain. TRAJAN, in 106, made Dacia a province in response to raids across the Danube, although it was abandoned in 270. His annexation of Mesopotamia was very brief (114–117).

This vast empire was held together by secure communication and internal peace maintained by the ROMAN LEGIONS. Fleets kept the sea safe for shipping and a network of ROMAN ROADS, built to move troops quickly, facilitated trade, personal travel, and an imperial postal system. The development of a single legal system and the use of a common language (Latin in the west, Greek in the east) helped maintain unity. Roman cities flourished throughout the empire, assisted by efficient water and drainage systems. Roman influence and trade spread even further reaching India, Russia, south-east Asia, and through the SILK ROUTE, China.

The success of the empire also led to its downfall, its sheer size contributing to its collapse, exacerbated by power struggles and the invasion of land-hungry migrating tribes. Rome was sacked by the VISIGOTHS in 410, Carthage was conquered by the VANDALS in 455, and in 476 Romulus Augustulus, the last emperor of the Western empire was deposed. The Eastern empire (BYZANTINE empire) lasted until 1453. GIBBON's *The History of the Decline and Fall of the Roman Empire* (1776–81) is a classic account of the disintegration of imperial Rome. (See map.)

Romania An east European country with its east coast on the Black Sea; it is bounded by Ukraine and the republic of Moldova on the north and east, Hungary and Serbia on the west, and Bulgaria on the south.

Physical. Roughly half of Romania is mountainous. The Carpathians meet the Transylvanian Alps in the centre of the country, where there are large forests. The rest of the country is plain, much of it providing the richest soil in Europe. The Danube forms the southern border as it flows east to its delta on the Black Sea.

Economy. Despite the fall of the repressive communist regime of Nicolae CEAUȘESCU in December 1989, social and economic conditions remain bleak. The policy of promoting exports regardless of domestic needs to pay off foreign debt caused massive hardship. Ceausescu's 'systemization' programme, which forced resettlement in towns, ostensibly to free land for agricultural use, was reversed and collective and state farms have been privatized in the hope of boosting food supplies. Romania is moving towards a market economy and many businesses have been freed from state control; in 1995 a Mass Privatization measure was passed affecting

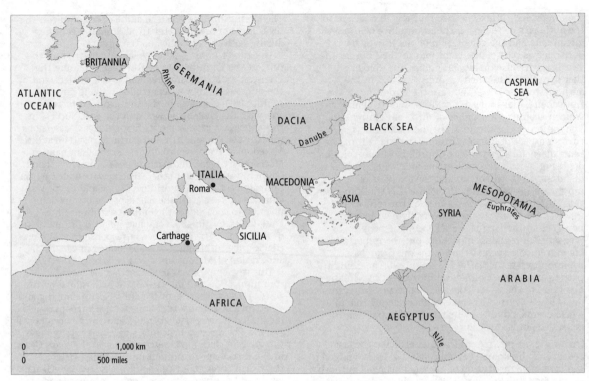

Roman empire *This map shows the expansion of the Roman empire at its greatest extent, in 117 AD. Rome expanded from a small settlement in the 6th century BC to rule most of the known European world by the early 2nd century AD. Having established control over Italy by c. 260 BC, Rome expanded to the east and west. By 133 BC all the territory formerly held by Carthage in the western Mediterranean and north Africa had been absorbed, together with Macedonia and Asia Minor in the east. Expansion continue for a further 150 years, the empire reaching its greatest extent in 117 AD, under Trajan. His successor, Hadrian, attempted to consolidate the empire behind fixed frontiers, drawing back to the Euphrates in the east and building the famous wall in Britain. However, less than 50 years later the decline of the empire had begun.*

over 3,000 businesses. Principal crops are maize, wheat, rye, potatoes, sugar beet, plums, and apples; mineral resources include coal, iron ore, petroleum, and natural gas. Despite heavy subsidies at the expense of agriculture, industry is in great need of modernization. Romania was invited to apply for European Union membership in 1993. Radical economic reform was undertaken by the new conservative administration that took office in 1996.

History. Although the regions known as Moldavia and Walachia were part of the OTTOMAN EMPIRE from the 15th century onwards, Turkish domination was increasingly challenged by both Russia and Austria. In 1812 Russia gained control of north-east Moldavia (present-day Moldova). During the next 40 years Romanian nationalism precipitated many insurrections against the Turks. Following the CRIMEAN WAR, during which the region was occupied by Russia, Walachia and Moldavia proclaimed themselves independent principalities; in 1861 they united to form Romania, electing a local prince, Alexander Cuza, as ruler. On his deposition (1866) Prince Carol Hohenzollen-Sigmaringen was elected. At the Congress of BERLIN independence was recognized and Prince Carol crowned king as CAROL I (1881–1914). His pro-German policy led in 1883 to Romania's joining the Triple Alliance of 1882 (Germany, Austria, and Italy). In

World War I Romania remained neutral until, in 1916, it joined the Allies. At the VERSAILLES PEACE SETTLEMENT the country was rewarded with the doubling of its territories, mainly by the addition of Transylvania from Hungary. Carol I was succeeded by Ferdinand I (1914–27) and then by CAROL II (1930–40), who imposed a fascist regime. He was forced to cede much territory to the AXIS POWERS in 1940. Romanian forces co-operated with the German armies in their offensives (1941–42), but after STALINGRAD the Red Army advanced and Romania lost territory to the Soviet Union and Bulgaria. A communist regime was established in 1948 and for the next 20 years the country became a Soviet satellite. A much greater degree of independence was restored during the presidency of Nicolae Ceauçescu (1967–89), whose rule became increasingly brutal and autocratic. During 1989 a movement towards democracy culminated in a violent revolution and the execution of the President and his wife on Christmas Day. A National Salvation Front (NSF) was formed, led by Ion Iliescu, who was elected President. He and many of his colleagues had been communists and popular demonstrations against the new government were brutally suppressed. Ethnic violence against Hungarians in Transylvania and against the large indigenous gypsy population increased, fomented by far-right nationalist parties. In spite of opposition from groups such as Civic Alliance and the National Convention for the Restoration of Democracy, Iliescu retained power in the 1992 presidential election, having secured a $748 million IMF loan. In elections held in November 1996, the former communists lost power for the first time since the overthrow of Ceauçescu, with the centre-right candidate Emil Constantinescu becoming President.

CAPITAL:	Bucharest
AREA:	237,500 sq km (91,699 sq miles)
POPULATION:	22.670 million (1996)
CURRENCY:	1 leu = 100 bani
RELIGIONS:	Romanian Orthodox 70.0%; Greek Orthodox 10.0%; Muslim 1.0%
ETHNIC GROUPS:	Romanian 86.0%; Hungarian 9.0%; gypsy 4.0%; German and other 1.0%
LANGUAGES:	Romanian (official); Hungarian; Romany
INTERNATIONAL ORGANIZATIONS:	UN; CSCE; North Atlantic Co-operation Council

Roman law The body of law developed in Rome between about 150 BC and 250 AD and codified by the Emperor JUSTINIAN I (482–565) in his *Corpus Juris Civilis* (Body of civil law). Roman law re-emerged in the 11th century as a popular subject of study in the Italian universities; later it evolved into the common core of the civil law (or Romano-Germanic) family of legal systems that were used in the Holy Roman Empire. The ideas of Roman law were dominant in the French CODE NAPOLÉON, adopted in 1804, and in later civil codes adopted in Germany, Switzerland, and Austria. The codification movement appealed to the perceived higher rationality of Roman law as providing a logically consistent set of principles and rules for solving disputes.

Roman legion A division of the army in ancient Rome. Legions evolved from the citizen militia that equipped itself in times of crisis for defence of the state. During the Second PUNIC WAR SCIPIO reorganized the battle array and improved the army's tactics. Under MARIUS, men of no property began to be recruited, a professional army appeared and new training methods were introduced. Ten cohorts, 6,000 soldiers, with standards formed a named and numbered legion with an eagle standard. The cohorts, divided into six centuries (100 men in each century) commanded by a centurion, became the main tactical unit of the army. Cavalry and auxiliaries supported each regiment.

AUGUSTUS established a standing army to man the frontiers of the empire. There appears to have been 28 permanent legions, each having a number and an honorific title. SEVERUS added three legions; CONSTANTINE increased the number but limited them to 1,000 men each to allow flexibility and to avoid mutiny. He also placed them under equestrian prefects instead of the traditional senatorial legates and placed a Christian symbol on their standards. On retirement a veteran in the early days earned a land grant in a 'colony' where he continued to act as a Romanizing and pacifying influence throughout the empire, but from the time of Augustus it was more useful for him to receive money rather than land. Many nevertheless settled in the area where they had served, thus effectively 'colonizing' it.

Romanov The ruling house of Russia from 1613 until the Revolution of 1917. After the Time of Troubles (1604–13), a period of civil war and anarchy, Michael Romanov was elected emperor and ruled until 1645, to be followed by Alexis (1645–76) and Fyodor (1676–82). Under these emperors Russia emerged as the major Slavic power. The next emperors established it as a great power in Europe: PETER THE GREAT (1689–1725) and CATHERINE II (the Great) (1762–96) were the most successful of these rulers.

Roman religion The religion of the Roman republic and empire. In its developed form Roman religion had much in common with GREEK RELIGION, although it originated from Etruscan and other native Italian regional beliefs and practices. The Romans identified their gods with those of Greece: Jupiter = Zeus, Juno = Hera, Neptune = Poseidon, Minerva = Athene, Diana = Artemis, Mars = Ares, Mercury = Hermes, and so on, adopting many Greek myths and legends and applying them to their gods, most of which were originally agricultural and fertility deities. Romans also worshipped spirits of the household (Lares and Penates) at domestic shrines. Religious observances and rites were very closely tied in with politics; from Julius CAESAR onwards, the practice of according divine honours and worship, even temples, to deceased rulers became common (though not all were deified after their deaths) and cults of 'Rome and the Emperor' spread through Italy and the provinces, largely to provide a public and visible focus of loyalty to the regime.

Although CHRISTIANITY became the official religion of the empire from the early 4th century AD, pagan beliefs and practices proved tenacious in many areas, especially away from the cities, and in many places the Christian Church had often to take over Roman festivals and hallowed shrines or sites under a new guise.

Roman republic (Latin *respublica*, 'common business') The Roman state for 400 years after the expulsion of TARQUIN. The rule of a sole monarch yielded to the power of a landed aristocracy, the PATRICIANS, who ruled through two chief magistrates or consuls and an advisory body, the SENATE.

The city of Rome could operate as a 'public concern' as long as the small landed aristocracy managed the state. The simplicity of CINCINNATUS or CATO (the Younger) was an ideal of statesmanship, leaders as ready as their citizen militia to return to their farms after holding power in a crisis. But, with overseas expansion, generals had to be given power to deal with problems abroad, most notably the SCIPIOS, MARIUS, SULLA, POMPEY, Julius CAESAR, MARK ANTONY, and Octavian (AUGUSTUS). They depended on the personal loyalty of their troops. This substantial independence threatened republican tradition with its corporate government and brief periods of high office for individuals in rotation. Eventually the generals simply ignored the law that required generals to lay down their commands on returning to Italian soil. The last of these commanders-in-chief, Octavian, achieved a settlement which appeared to combine republican institutions with personal military power. The ROMAN EMPIRE succeeded the republic.

Roman roads A systematic communications network originating in the Italian peninsula joining Rome to its expanding empire. The APPIAN WAY was the first major stretch, leading into Samnite territory (see SAMNITE WARS). The Via Flaminia, constructed in 220 BC was the great northern highway to Rimini. For travellers landing from Brindisi the Egnatian Way continued overland through Greece and on to Byzantium. By the 1st century AD three roads crossed the Alps and the Domitian Way went from the Rhône valley to Spain. Every province had such roads, which served military and commercial purposes. In Britain major highways fanned out from Londinium (London), some now known by their Anglo-Saxon names: WATLING STREET and ERMINE STREET. Built with several thick layers of stone and concrete, they were drained by side ditches, and maintained by engineers.

Roman Senate The assembly of the landed aristocracy and PATRICIANS which originated in the royal council of the kings of Rome. Entry was widened to include those of plebeian origin by the late 4th century BC. A membership of 600 established by SULLA was standard although it rose to 900 in CAESAR's time. This advisory body consisted of hereditary (patrician) and life (conscript) members, the latter being ex-magistrates. It was summoned by the consuls as chief magistrates and passed decrees which were ratified by the people in assembly. It was expected that all magistrates would submit proposals to the Senate before putting them to the people. This procedure began to be flouted from the time of the GRACCHI onwards. Its power was real but informal, based on prestige and wealth. Even the emperors made at least the token gesture of consulting the 'Fathers'. Until the 3rd century AD all bronze coinage carried the mark 'By Consultative Decree of the Senate'.

Roman villa A Roman house, originally a rural dwelling with its associated farm-buildings, forming the centre of an agricultural holding. Such holdings could vary from small farms chiefly dependent on family labour to large estates worked by slaves or tied-labourers who were effectively SERFS. From the 2nd century BC, villas of increasingly sophisticated design and elegance, usually constructed around a courtyard and often sited to enhance a landscape or command a vista, began to be built as suburban or country or seaside houses for the rich, some of whom owned several in different districts, the attendant estate-land being cultivated by tenants or under the supervision of an estate-manager (*vilicus*). The villa-type of dwelling and estate spread to the provinces and some 60 villas are known in Britain. In post-Roman times the MANOR HOUSE and manor (and their equivalents elsewhere in western Europe) replaced the villa and its dependent estate.

Rome A city on the River Tiber, the capital of Italy and bishopric of the pope. It was at the heart of the ROMAN EMPIRE. It is built on seven low hills and several traditions surround its foundation. According to the most famous legend, the twins, ROMULUS (after whom the city was supposedly named) and Remus, suckled by a wolf, began the first settlement on the Palatine Hill. The date 753 BC became accepted and is well supported by archaeological excavation. ETRUSCAN remains, dating from the time of the TARQUINS (*c.* 650–500 BC) have been discovered. The expansion of provinces under the republic and early empire brought wealth to Rome. AUGUSTUS was said to have turned a city of brick into one of marble and successive emperors added palaces, arches, columns, and temples. NERO burnt much of it, hoping, it was said, to rebuild it and rename it after himself. As the empire declined, Rome was attacked by GOTHS and VANDALS. By then it was politically overshadowed by CONSTANTINOPLE, the capital of the Eastern Roman empire. During the Middle Ages Rome emerged as the seat of the PAPACY and the capital of Western Christianity. It became a centre of the RENAISSANCE and was largely rebuilt in the Baroque style in the 17th century. The city was sacked in 1527 and again in 1798. Rome remained under papal control until the unification of Italy in 1870; it became the capital of the new country in the following year.

Rome, Treaties of (1957) Two international agreements signed in Rome by Belgium, France, Italy, Luxembourg, the Netherlands, and the Federal Republic of Germany. They established the EUROPEAN ECONOMIC COMMUNITY and Euratom (the European Atomic Energy Community). The treaties included provisions for the free movement of labour and capital between member countries, the abolition of customs barriers and cartels, and the fostering of common agricultural and trading policies. New members of the European Community would be required to adhere to the terms of these treaties. The MAASTRICHT TREATY was planned as a development of the Rome Treaties.

Rommel, Erwin (1891–1944) German field-marshal. In 1940 he led a Panzer division in a brilliant assault through the Ardennes to the Channel and in 1941 commanded the Afrika Korps, an élite tank formation which bore the brunt of the battle in Libya, earning for himself the name 'the Desert Fox'. In 1942 he advanced to El ALAMEIN, but British resistance and lack of supplies impeded him and he eventually had to retreat from North Africa. In 1944 he was entrusted with the defence of the Channel coast in northern France against a possible Allied invasion. Wounded in the NORMANDY CAMPAIGN, he was recalled to Germany. The Gestapo believed he was connected with the JULY PLOT against Hitler. No accusations were made publicly against him, but he was forced to commit suicide by taking poison.

Romulus The legendary founder of Rome. He and his twin brother Remus were the children of a Vestal Virgin who had been ravished by Mars; they were abandoned to die, but were suckled by a she-wolf and brought up by a herdsman. In 753 BC Romulus is said to have founded Rome; he killed Remus, who had ridiculed him by jumping over the beginnings of the city wall. After his death, Romulus was regarded as a god and was identified with the god Quirius.

Roosevelt, Franklin D(elano) (1882–1945) 32nd President of the USA (1933–45). In 1921 Roosevelt was stricken with polio and from then on used a wheelchair. A reforming Democrat and governor of New York from 1928, he began his long presidency in 1933, having beaten the Republican incumbent, HOOVER. His NEW DEAL programme tackled with confidence the crisis of the Great DEPRESSION. In the 1936 Presidential election he won a crushing victory against the Republicans. In his second term (1936–40), inherent weaknesses of his New Deal became more obvious and hostility towards him from business and other sections of the community grew. However, he carefully steered his country away from policies favoured by the ISOLATIONISTS. After the fall of France in 1940 he was able to make the USA a powerful supporter of Britain's war effort while remaining, until PEARL HARBOR, a non-belligerent. Such measures as the DESTROYER–BASES DEAL and LEND–LEASE were typical instruments of this policy. He was elected for a third term in the 1940 election and for a fourth term in 1944 but died before the war ended. His wife **Eleanor** (1884–1962) was actively involved in humanitarian projects. As a delegate to the United Nations, she was chairman of the UN Commission on Human Rights and played a major role in the drafting and adoption of the Universal Declaration of Human Rights (1948).

Roosevelt, Theodore (1858–1919) 26th President of the USA (1901–09). Roosevelt served as a Republican member on the New York State Legislature (1881–84), a member of the Civil Service Commission (1889–95), and Assistant Secretary of the Navy (1897–98), before helping to form the ROUGH RIDERS regiment to fight in the SPANISH–AMERICAN WAR (1898). A popular and successful governor of New York (1899–1900), his reform policies threatened to disrupt corrupt political practices there and Republicans under T. C. PLATT attempted to suppress his initiative, nominating him as Vice-President. However, he became President after the assassination of MCKINLEY (1901) and his period of office was notable for the concessions he made to the PROGRESSIVE MOVEMENT. He arbitrated in the coal strike (1902), instituted an anti-monopoly move against the Northern Securities Company (1902), and established the Department of Commerce and Labor (1903). He secured US control of the construction of the PANAMA CANAL. By the Roosevelt corollary (1904) to the MONROE DOCTRINE, he claimed for the USA the right to collect bad debts from Latin America. When TAFT, his successor, failed to maintain Roosevelt's 'Square Deal', he formed a splinter group, the PROGRESSIVE PARTY. Despite his enormous personal popularity he failed to regain the Presidency in 1912 on the Progressive Party ticket. Instead, by dividing the Republicans, he enabled Woodrow WILSON to capture the Presidency for the Democrats.

Root, Elihu (1845–1937) US statesman and diplomat. A Republican, he became Secretary of War (1899–1904) and made drastic reforms in the organization of the army. He formulated the PLATT amendment (1902), which gave the USA greater control over Cuba. He was Secretary of State under Theodore ROOSEVELT and reorganized the consular service. He negotiated the Root–Takahira Agreement (1908) with Japan, upholding the Open Door Policy of US commercial interests in China. From 1909 to 1915 he was US Senator for New York. He opposed US neutrality in 1914 and supported the Allied cause and, with reservations, the League of Nations.

Root-and-Branch Petition (1640) A document drawn up by a London alderman, Isaac Pennington, calling for the abolition of episcopal government (government of the church by bishops), 'with all its dependencies, roots and branches'. The 15,000 signatures showed that there was support for Puritan radicalism in London. A Root-and-Branch Bill was introduced into the LONG PARLIAMENT in May 1641 and was supported by PYM. Eventually it was dropped in favour of more urgent measures, such as the GRAND REMONSTRANCE.

Rosas, Juan Manuel de (1793–1877) Argentine dictator (1835–52). Reacting to the failure of the liberals, who dominated Argentina after independence, Rosas brutally repressed his political enemies and suppressed civil liberties. Often depicted as a CAUDILLO, he was a consummate politician who contributed to the establishment of national unity in Argentina and who stood up to foreign powers like Britain and France when they imposed two blockades (1838–40, 1845–50) as a result of disputes over Paraguay and Uruguay. In February 1852 Rosas was overthrown by another caudillo, Justo José de Urquiza, and fled to England.

Rosebery, Archibald Philip Primrose, 5th Earl of (1847–1929) British statesman. Rosebery served in Gladstone's cabinet as Foreign Secretary (1892–94) and was briefly Prime Minister (1894–95) at the wish of Queen Victoria rather than of the Liberal Party. His support for British imperialism alienated many Liberal supporters, but his concept of regular meetings of colonial Premiers led to the establishment of Imperial Conferences. He was a strong critic of the *entente cordiale* (1904).

Rosenberg case (1953) A US espionage case in which Julius Rosenberg and his wife Ethel were convicted of obtaining information concerning atomic weapons and passing it on to Soviet agents in 1944–45. They became the first US civilians to be sentenced to death for espionage by a US court. The only seriously incriminating evidence had come from a confessed spy and the lack of clemency shown to them was an example of the intense anti-communist feeling that gripped the USA in the 1950s.

Roses, Wars of the (1455–85) A protracted struggle for the throne of England, lasting for 30 years of sporadic fighting. The wars grew out of the bitter rivalry between two aspirants to the throne – Edmund BEAUFORT (1406–55), Duke of Somerset, of the House of Lancaster (whose badge was a red rose) and Richard, 3rd Duke of YORK (whose badge was a white rose). Beaufort the former was a close supporter of HENRY VI and MARGARET OF ANJOU, while Richard of York was their opponent. In 1455 Richard gained power by winning the First Battle of ST ALBANS; a whole series of private enmities and disputes was absorbed into a bitter and openly fought civil war. Richard of York was killed at the Battle of WAKEFIELD (1460) and Henry VI's supporters, the LANCASTRIANS, won a further victory at the Second Battle of St Albans (February 1461). However, their hesitations allowed Richard's son Edward to gain the throne a month later as EDWARD IV, the first YORKIST King of England. In September 1470 a Lancastrian invasion restored Henry VI to the throne (although power was effectively exercised by 'the kingmaker', Richard Neville, Earl of WARWICK), but in April 1471 Edward regained it by the victory of BARNET. Most of the remaining Lancastrian leaders were killed at TEWKESBURY in May 1471, but the struggle ended only in 1485 when Henry Tudor defeated RICHARD III at BOSWORTH FIELD. HENRY VII married Edward IV's eldest daughter, Elizabeth of York, in order to unite the two factions. The wars weakened the power of the nobility and after a bid for the throne from Lambert SIMNEL in 1487, there were no serious challenges to the TUDOR dynasty.

Rosetta stone A slab of black basalt bearing the inscriptions that provided the key to the deciphering of Egyptian HIEROGLYPHS. The stone was found in 1799 by a French soldier during Napoleon's occupation of Egypt and contained three inscriptions, in Greek, in Egyptian demotic, and in Egyptian hieroglyphics. Comparative study of the three texts, which date from 196 BC, was undertaken by Thomas Young and Jean-François Champollion, the latter finally unlocking the secrets of hieroglyphics in 1821–22. The stone is housed in the British Museum in London.

Rosicrucians Members of certain secret societies who venerated the emblems of the Rose and the Cross as symbols of Jesus Christ's resurrection and redemption. Rosicrucians claimed to possess secret wisdom passed down from the ancients, but their origin cannot be dated earlier than the 17th century. The anonymous *Account of the Brotherhood* published in Germany in 1614 may well have launched the movement. It narrated the tale of a mythical German knight of the 15th century, Christian Rosenkreutz, who travelled extensively to learn the wisdom of the East and then founded the secret order. The English physician and philosopher Robert Fludd (1574–1637) subsequently helped to spread Rosicrucian ideas. In later centuries numerous other societies were founded under this name.

Roskilde, Treaty of (1658) A treaty between Sweden and Denmark, named after a port in eastern Denmark. After the defeat of Frederick II of Denmark by Charles X of Sweden, this treaty expelled the Danes once and for all from the Swedish mainland: they surrendered Halland, Scania, Blekinge (provinces), and the island of Bornholm, as well as the Norwegian territories of Trondheim and Bohuslän.

Ross, Sir John (1777–1856) British polar explorer of Scottish extraction. After serving with distinction in the Napoleonic Wars, Ross led an expedition to Baffin Bay in 1818 and another in search of the North-West Passage between 1829 and 1833, during which he surveyed King William Land, Boothia Peninsula, and the Gulf of Boothia (the last two named in honour of the expedition's patron, the distiller and philanthropist Felix Booth).

Rothschild Family A Jewish banking family whose members exerted considerable influence on both economic and political affairs during the 19th and early 20th centuries. Mayer Amschel Rothschild of Frankfurt, who became financial adviser to the Landgrave of Hesse-Kassel, founded the Rothschild banking house in the 18th century. He and his five sons prospered in the years of the REVOLUTIONARY and NAPOLEONIC WARS and moved to London in 1804. They loaned money for the raising of mercenary armies and negotiated means of bypassing Napoleon's CONTINENTAL SYSTEM. After 1815 Rothschild houses were opened as a banking group in all the great cities of Europe. Of Mayer's sons, Anselm (1773–1855) became a member of the Prussian privy council, Salomon (1774–1855) became financial adviser to Metternich in Vienna, and Nathan

(1777–1836) established a branch of the bank in London. His son, Lionel (1808–79), became the first Jew to sit in the British House of Commons (1858) and he lent the British government £4 million in 1875 to buy the SUEZ CANAL shares. His son Nathan (1840–1915) was the first British Jewish Peer and became regarded as the unofficial head of both French and British Jewish communities. It was to his son Lionel Walter (1868–1937), the second Baron and distinguished scientist and scholar, that the BALFOUR DECLARATION was addressed in 1917. The Rothschilds are still prominent in banking in Britain and are notable patrons of the arts and sciences.

rotten borough A British Parliamentary borough that was entitled to elect two Members of Parliament but whose population had virtually disappeared. In 1832 there were more than 50 such boroughs; among the most notorious were Old Sarum with a handful of electors and Dunwich, which had mostly been submerged under the North Sea. Rotten boroughs were abolished by the REFORM ACT of 1832.

Rough Riders The 1st Regiment of US Cavalry Volunteers. They were largely recruited by Colonel Leonard Wood and Lieutenant-Colonel Theodore ROOSEVELT for service in the SPANISH–AMERICAN WAR OF 1898. Comprising rangers, cowboys, Native Americans, and college students, their most notable exploit was the successful charge up San Juan Hill in Cuba, on foot as their horses had been left behind in Florida.

Roundheads The Puritans and Parliamentarians during the ENGLISH CIVIL WAR. It originated as a term of abuse, referring to the Puritans' disapproval of long hair and their own close-cropped heads. Roundhead strength during the Civil War lay mainly in southern and eastern England.

Round Table Conferences The meetings held in London in 1930–32 between Britain and Indian representatives to discuss Indian constitutional developments. The procedure was suggested by the viceroy, Lord Irwin, in 1929. CONGRESS boycotted the first session (November 1930–January 1931), but, following the Gandhi–Irwin Pact (March 1931), GANDHI attended the second session (September–December 1931). With the renewal of the NON-CO-OPERATION campaign, Gandhi was imprisoned and Congress took no part in the final session (November–December 1932). The constitutional discussions formed the basis of the 1935 Government of India Act, with its plan for a federal organization involving the Indian PRINCELY STATES.

Rousseau, Jean-Jacques (1712–78) Swiss-French philosopher and writer, one of the dominant thinkers of his age. The central question of Rousseau's thought was how individuals, with their complex psychological make-up, could be reconciled to the demands of society. In his *Discours sur les sciences et les arts* (1750) he concluded that the natural man or 'noble savage' is preferred to his civilized counterpart, arguing that the development and spread of knowledge and culture, far from improving human behaviour, has corrupted it by promoting inequality, idleness, and luxury. In his *Discours sur l'origine de l'inégalité des hommes* (1755), he argued that human beings were by nature good and had originally lived in a condition of innocent isolation; however, private property and the division of labour had created an artificial social inequality and a false morality. In *Du contrat social* (1762), his most important work, Rousseau applies his trust in human nature to the realm of politics, going beyond the constitutional monarchy admired by MONTESQUIEU to advocate a form of DEMOCRACY. He argued that the people's only means of salvation was to surrender all their natural rights to a sovereign state, in which they themselves would compose the legislature. He envisaged a city-state whose citizens assembled to deliberate on matters of common concern; the 'general will' thus expressed would, Rousseau claimed, necessarily be just. These views had a powerful influence on the radical wing of the FRENCH REVOLUTION.

Rowlatt Act (1919) A piece of repressive legislation enacted in British India, following the report of a committee under Mr Justice Rowlatt. The report had recommended the continuation of special wartime powers for use against revolutionary conspiracy and terrorist activity. The Act aroused opposition among Indian nationalists and this was channelled by Mohandas GANDHI into a nationwide SATYAGRAHA, known as the Rowlatt agitation, which ended with the AMRITSAR MASSACRE.

Rowntree, Joseph (1801–59) British businessman and philanthropist. Rowntree was a Quaker who founded a grocery in York, which later developed into a family cocoa and chocolate manufacturing firm. He was keenly interested in civic affairs and in the development of educational opportunities. His son Joseph (1836–1925), chairman of the firm (1897–1923), was distinguished for his philanthropy and for his care and the welfare of his employees. He created a charitable social service and village trusts, consulting his employees about conditions and providing housing, unemployment insurance, and pensions. An eight-hour day was introduced in 1896, a pension scheme in 1906, and a works doctor was appointed in 1904. 'Social helpers' were recruited to deal with problems faced by women workers and works councils were set up in 1919. His son Seebohm (1871–1954) was chairman of the firm (1923–41) and achieved national prominence for his surveys of poverty in York (1897–98 and 1936) and for his studies of management.

Roy, Ram Mohan (1772–1833) Indian religious and social reformer. He devoted his life to reforming Indian society on the basis of a selective appeal to ancient Hindu tradition. He founded the Atmiya Sabha (Friendly Association) to serve as a platform for his liberal ideas. He evolved a monotheistic form of worship, adapting the ethical and humanitarian aspects of Christianity. He attacked idolatry and popular practices, including the burning of widows (suttee) and polygamy, discrimination against women, and the caste system. He also helped to found the Hindu College in Calcutta (1817) and several secondary schools in which English educational methods were employed. In 1828 he founded the BRAHMO SAMAJ (Society of God), whose influence on Indian intellectual, social, and religious life has been profound.

Royal Academy of Arts The national art academy of Britain, founded in 1768 with the aim of raising the status of the artistic professions and arranging exhibitions of works attaining an appropriate standard of excellence. The Academy succeeded in improving the economic and social status of artists, reflecting the prestige enjoyed by its first President, Sir Joshua Reynolds (1723–92). Until the late 19th century it was the most influential art institution in Britain, but it then came under attack as a bastion of orthodox mediocrity opposed to creative innovation, and the New English Art Club was set up (1886) to challenge its domination. The Academy still enjoys considerable prestige, however; its annual summer exhibition is a popular social event, and it regularly organizes historical exhibitions of the highest quality.

Royal African Company A trading company to which CHARLES II granted a monopoly charter in 1672. It built forts on the west African coast (the 'Gold Coast') and trade was principally in slaves and gold. It lost its monopoly of trade with England by an Act of 1698; in 1750 it was succeeded by the African Company of Merchants. Its castles or forts were trading posts, fortified as much because of quarrels between Europeans as because of attacks from the local Fante chiefdoms, and also against pirates.

Royal Greenwich Observatory (RGO) An observatory founded by King CHARLES II and built by Christopher Wren in 1675 on the foundations of Greenwich Castle in a royal park east of London. Its original purpose was to produce accurate star charts and ephemerides of lunar and planetary motions so that they could be used at sea to enable longitude to be calculated correctly. The first director and Astronomer Royal was John Flamsteed. In 1767 the observatory began publishing the annual *Nautical Almanac*, a compendium of navigational information that is still being produced today. In the same year, John Harrison's marine chronometer solved the problem of longitude, provided that the instrument was accurately set at the start of a voyage. The meridian at Greenwich of the Airy Transit Circle, an instrument for determining times of transit of stars, has become the prime meridian of the world, separating the eastern hemisphere from the western hemisphere. Greenwich has always been associated with the accurate measurement of time. James Pond, Astronomer Royal from 1811 to 1835, introduced the time ball, a visual signal to indicate noon: a 'six-pip' radio signal was introduced in 1924. The transit of the mean sun across the Greenwich Meridian is the basis for Greenwich Mean Time (GMT) on which the international time zone system is based. This became the UK's legal time in 1880. In 1946 Herstmonceux Castle in Sussex was purchased and the observatory moved there over the following years. In the early 1980s the Isaac Newton telescope was relocated to the La Palma Observatory in the Canary Islands and by 1990 the observatory staff had moved to Cambridge (UK) from where the Isaac Newton telescope can be remotely controlled.

Royal Institution A body founded in London in 1799 by the Anglo-American Benjamin Thompson, 'to teach the application of science to the common purposes of life'. In effect, the Royal Institution has devoted itself primarily to scientific research, and to the presentation of science to non-scientific audiences. The change of emphasis resulted from the work of Humphrey Davy (from 1801) and Michael Faraday (from 1813) at the Institution. They were followed in the 19th century by men of equal distinction, including John Tyndall, famous for research on heat; James Dewar, inventor of the vacuum flask; and John Strutt (Lord Rayleigh), discoverer of argon. In the 20th century W. H. Bragg and his son W. L. Bragg, who conducted early research into X-ray crystallography, succeeded one another as directors.

Royal Progress PROGRESS, ROYAL.

Royal Society (of London for Improving Natural Knowledge) One of the world's oldest and most prestigious scientific societies. The first such society in Britain, it was founded in 1660 as a fellowship of some 40 natural philosophers meeting in London and received its first Royal Charter from Charles II in 1662. Its *Philosophical Transactions* (1665–) was the first permanent scientific journal. Among its earliest members were the chemist Robert Boyle, the physicist Robert Hooke, the diarist Samuel Pepys, the architect Sir Christopher Wren, and the physicist Sir Isaac Newton, whose *Principia* was published in 1687 with the active encouragement of the Society. Among its literary members were John Dryden, John Evelyn, and John Aubrey. Political and religious topics were excluded from its discussions and debates and in 1848 the Society became wholly scientific: only those who had made a distinguished contribution to the sciences were eligible for election as Fellows of the Royal Society (FRS).

The Fellowship now numbers around 1,100, including about 100 Foreign Members.

Rozvi empire An empire in East Africa named from a Karanga clan of the Shona, who established the authority of the MWENE MUTAPA in the 15th century. Probably originally spiritual leaders and then military rulers, by 1480 the Rozvi occupied all of present-day Zimbabwe and Mozambique. After about 1500 the central and southern provinces broke away under CHANGAMIRE, while the ports were subject to KILWA. The Rozvi controlled gold-mining in the interior and for a time successfully warded off Portuguese attempts to conquer them, but in 1629 the Mwene Mutapa acknowledged Portuguese suzerainty. The empire was finally broken up by the Ndebele in the 1830s.

Ruanda-Urundi BURUNDI; RWANDA.

Ruapekapeka (Maori, 'the bats' nest') A strongly fortified village (*pa*) in New Zealand defended by the Maori chief Kawiti, an ally of Hone Heke, who, in 1844–45, challenged European sovereignty. The *pa* was attacked by about 1,000 British troops, with artillery, and 500 Maori allies of the British. Kawiti and his people abandoned it, with few casualties, after about 24 hours' fighting.

Rubicon (literally 'reddish coloured') In Roman times a stream in north-east Italy that flowed into the Adriatic and formed part of the border between the province of Cisalpine Gaul and Italy. Roman republican laws demanded that generals who had held commands abroad had to give up their authority when they returned to Italy, a regulation intended to reduce the risk of civil war. Julius CAESAR in 49 BC crossed the Rubicon, entering Italy but refusing to lay down his generalship and thereby committing an irrevocable act of treason.

Ruhr A river in Germany that flows south through North Rhine–Westphalia into the Rhine. In 1802 the Ruhr valley was occupied by Prussia and five years later by Napoleon. Its restoration to Prussia in 1815 marked the beginning of its industrial development, which was helped by the ZOLLVEREIN (customs union), the development of a railway network, and the establishment of the Krupps armament works in Essen. In 1851 new laws, which cut the coal tax, encouraged investment, and within 15 years its coal output was second only to that of Britain. It formed the industrial heart of BISMARCK's united Germany after the creation of the GERMAN SECOND EMPIRE (1871). After World War I France feared that the Ruhr valley might again become an armaments centre. In 1923 the Ruhr was occupied by French and Belgian troops when Germany defaulted on REPARATIONS payments. The loss of resources, production, and confidence resulted in soaring inflation in Germany that year. Two years later the French accepted the DAWES PLAN and withdrew. After 1933 war industries were re-established in the Ruhr as Germany re-armed. After World War II its recovery was monitored by an international control commission. Control passed to the European Coal and Steel Community in 1952 and to the Federal Republic of Germany in 1954.

Rump Parliament The remnant of the English LONG PARLIAMENT that continued to sit after PRIDE'S PURGE (1648). In 1649 it ordered CHARLES I's execution, abolished both monarchy and House of Lords, and established the COMMONWEALTH. Its members were mostly gentlemen, motivated by self-interest, and its policies were generally unpopular. Oliver CROMWELL expelled the Rump in April 1653. Six years later it was recalled to mark the end of the PROTECTORATE; in 1660 the members excluded by Pride were readmitted and the Long Parliament dissolved itself in preparation for the RESTORATION of the monarchy.

Rum Rebellion (1808) A revolt in Australia when colonists and officers of the New South Wales Corps (later known as the Rum Corps because of its involvement in the rum trade) overthrew Governor William BLIGH. The rebellion was fuelled by Bligh's drastic methods of limiting the rum traders' powers and his attempts to end the domination of the officer clique, while an immediate cause was the arrest of the sheep-breeder John MacArthur in his role as liquor merchant and distiller. The officers induced the commander, Major George Johnston, to arrest Bligh as unfit for office. When Governor MACQUARIE took office in 1810, the Corps was recalled, George Johnston was court-martialled in England and cashiered in 1811. Bligh, although exonerated, was removed from office.

Rundstedt, (Karl Rudolf) Gerd von (1875–1953) German field-marshal. Rundstedt was called from retirement in 1939 to command army corps in the Polish and French campaigns of World War II. In 1941 he commanded Army Group South in the invasion of the Soviet Union but was dismissed after he had disobeyed Hitler's orders and withdrawn from Rostov in order to improve his chances of resisting a Soviet counter-offensive. From 1942 to 1945 he commanded the forces occupying France and launched the Battle of the Bulge in the ARDENNES CAMPAIGN in December 1944. Relieved of his command in March 1945, he was captured by US troops in May. He was released in 1949.

Rupert, Prince (1619–82) Son of Frederick V, the Elector Palatine, and Elizabeth, Queen of Bohemia, and the nephew of CHARLES I of England. He grew up in the Low Countries and saw military action during the Thirty Years War. In 1642 he joined the CAVALIERS in England and became commander of the royal army, taking part in all the critical engagements of the first phase of the ENGLISH CIVIL WAR. A daring, skilful cavalryman, he was none the less outwitted at Marston Moor and Naseby. After he surrendered Bristol (1645), Charles I dismissed him. Later he commanded privateers against Commonwealth shipping (1649–52), with diminishing success. Under CHARLES II he was given naval commands in the Second and Third ANGLO-DUTCH WARS.

Russell, John, 1st Earl (1792–1878) British statesman. As Lord John Russell he entered the House of Commons as a Whig in 1813 and first came into prominence with his opposition to the suspension of the Habeas Corpus Act in 1817. A firm advocate of CATHOLIC EMANCIPATION and of the removal of all religious disabilities, he urged the repeal of the Corporation Act and the Test Act (1828) under which no Catholic or Protestant Non-conformist could hold public office. He was largely responsible for drafting the first REFORM ACT. As Home Secretary (1835–39), he brought in the Municipal Reform Bill of 1835 and reduced the number of crimes punishable by death. For two years (1839–41) he was Secretary for War and the Colonies, becoming Prime Minister (1846–52) after the fall of Sir Robert PEEL. Russell's government was overshadowed by the dominant personality of his Foreign Secretary, Lord PALMERSTON, whom he eventually dismissed in 1851. He later served as Foreign Secretary in Palmerston's government from 1859, succeeding him as Prime Minister (1865–66). However, he resigned in the following year when his proposal for a new Reform Bill split his party.

Russia (official name: Russian Federation) A country in northern Asia and eastern Europe. It borders on Norway and Finland in the north, Poland in the north-west, Estonia, Latvia, Lithuania, Belarus, and Ukraine in the west, Georgia, Azerbaijan, Kazakhstan, Mongolia, China, and Korea in the south; its maritime borders meet the Baltic Sea, Black Sea, the inland Caspian Sea, the Arctic, and the Pacific. It is separated from Alaska in the north-east by the Bering Strait.

Physical. The largest country in the world, Russia spans 11 time zones and 160° of longitude – nearly half-way around the Earth. It extends from the Gulf of Finland in the west to the peaks of Kamchatka in the east, from the frozen islands of Novaya Zemlya in the north to the warm Black Sea, the Caucasus Mountains, and the Pamirs and other ranges bordering China and Mongolia in the south. The north–south trending Ural Mountains divide European from Asian Russia. The plateaus and plains of Siberia make up most of the area to the east. To the west of the Urals extends the North European Plain. Great rivers include the Volga flowing south to the Caspian Sea, the Ob, Yenisei, and Lena draining north into the Arctic Ocean, and the Amur entering the Pacific Ocean to the east. East of the Lena is an area of mountains stretching from the Verkhoyanska to the Anadyr Range, which is half the size of Europe. Lake Baikal is Eurasia's largest and the world's deepest, lake. Across the country extend belts of tundra (in the far north), forest, steppe, and fertile areas.

Economy. Since the collapse of the Soviet Union, Russia has embarked on a difficult transition to a free-market economy by freeing prices and introducing measures for privatization and land reform. Chronic food shortages have been worsened by the disintegration of distribution systems and lack of confidence in the monetary system. Potentially of enormous wealth, Russia has rich mineral resources and, in Siberia, the world's largest reserves of petroleum and natual gas. Heavy industry, such as machinery, automobile production, paper and wood industries, and chemicals, dominates the economy, with mining and oil refineries also of importance. There is also light industry, such as textiles and food-processing. Half the agricultural produce of the former Soviet Union was grown in Russia: the principal crops are grain and livestock, as well as commercial crops such as sunflower seeds, sugar beet, and flax. Russia controls the former Soviet Central Bank but it shares responsibility for the Soviet Union's foreign debt with other former Soviet republics. The ownership of certain Soviet assets such as foreign exchange and gold is disputed.

History. In the 9th century the house of Rurik began to dominate the eastern Slavs, establishing the first all-Russian state with its capital at KIEV (now in the Ukraine). This powerful state accepted Christianity in about 985. However, decline had set in long before the Mongols established their control over most of European Russia in the 13th century.

Following the collapse of Mongol rule in the late 14th century, the principality of MUSCOVY emerged as the pre-eminent state. Gradually it absorbed formerly independent principalities, such as NOVGOROD (1478), forming in the process an autocratic, centralized Russian state. IVAN IV (the Terrible) was the first Muscovite ruler to assume the title of Tsar (Emperor) of all Russia in 1547. During his reign the state continued its expansion to the south and into Siberia. After his death a period of confusion followed as BOYAR families challenged the power of Theodore I (ruled 1584–98) and BORIS GODUNOV. During the upheavals of the Time of Troubles (1604–13), there was a period of rivalry over the throne, which ended with the restoration of firm rule by Michael Romanov. The ROMANOV dynasty resumed the process of territorial expansion and in 1649 established peasant SERFDOM. In the early 18th century PETER THE GREAT transformed the old Muscovite state into a partially Westernized empire, stretching from the Baltic to the Pacific.

From this time onward Russia played a major role in European affairs. Under the empresses ELIZABETH I (Petrovna) and CATHERINE II, it came to dominate POLAND and won a series of victories against the OTTOMAN Turks. In 1798–99 the Russians joined Great Britain, Austria, Naples, Portugal, and the Ottoman empire to fight against NAPOLEON. The treaty of TILSIT (1807) enabled it to acquire FINLAND from Sweden, while the early RUSSO-TURKISH WARS led to territorial acquisitions in Bessarabia and the Caucasus. Following Napoleon's defeat, the Treaty of VIENNA (1815) confirmed Russia and Austria as the leading powers on the continent of Europe.

Attempts at liberal reform by the DECEMBRISTS were ruthlessly suppressed and Russia helped Austria to quell Hungarian nationalist aspirations in the REVOLUTIONS OF 1848. Rivalry of interests, especially in south-east Europe, between Russia and the Western powers led to the CRIMEAN WAR. Serfdom was abolished in 1861 and attempts at changes in local government, the judicial system, and education were partially successful, but they fell short of the demands made by the POPULISTS and other radical reform groups. In the late 19th century Russian expansionism, curtailed by the Congress of BERLIN, led to its abandonment of the THREE EMPERORS' LEAGUE and, later, to a Triple Entente with Britain and France (1907). Defeat in the unpopular RUSSO-JAPANESE WAR led to the RUSSIAN REVOLUTION of 1905. A DUMA (Parliament) was established and its Prime Minister, STOLYPIN, attempted a partial agrarian reform. The beginning of the 20th century saw a rapid growth in Russian industry, mainly financed by foreign capital. It was among the urban concentration of industrial workers that the leftist Social Democratic Party won support, although it split after 1903 into BOLSHEVIKS and Mensheviks. Support for BALKAN nationalism led Russia into WORLD WAR I. The hardship which the war brought on the people was increased by the inefficient government of NICHOLAS II. A series of revolts culminating in the RUSSIAN REVOLUTION of 1917 led to the overthrow of the Romanov dynasty and to the RUSSIAN CIVIL WAR and the UNION OF SOVIET SOCIALIST REPUBLICS was established in 1922.

The Russian republic was by far the largest of the Soviet republics, with 70% of the population. In 1978 it received a new constitution as the Russian Soviet Federal Socialist Republic (RSFSR), consisting of six territories, 49 provinces, five autonomous regions, and 16 autonomous republics. The Communist Party of the Soviet Union maintained firm control over the federation until the late 1980s, when pressures developed for greater independence. In 1990 a new constitution created a Russian Congress of People's Republics and a Russian Supreme Soviet, of which Boris YELTSIN was elected Chairman on a ticket of multiparty democracy and economic reform. In June 1991 he was elected President of the Federation by popular vote. Following the disintegration of the Soviet Union and the resignation of President GORBACHEV in December, Russia became an independent sovereign state. It took the leading role in forming a new body, the Commonwealth of Independent States (CIS), which most of the former Soviet republics joined. Problems facing Russia in the early 1990s included tensions between autonomous republics, ethnic conflicts, the re-deployment of military and naval forces and equipment, and of nuclear weapons, and a rapidly collapsing economy. Following endorsement of Yeltsin's economic reforms in a national referendum in 1993, communists staged an unsuccessful coup against his administration. Yeltsin suspended parliament and ruled by presidential decree. In 1994 serious unrest broke out in the Caucasian region of Chechnya, where Muslim Chechens declared an independent republic. Although invading Russian forces devastated the capital, Grozny, resistance continued; all Russian troops were withdrawn by January 1997. Although the republic has *de facto* independence its formal political status remains unresolved. In the mid 1990s, Yeltsin's position was

further weakened by failing health and by the Communist Party's victory in parliamentary elections in 1995. He was, however, re-elected President in 1996. In March 1998 he startled international observers by sacking the entire government and appointing Sergei Kiriyenko, a little-known 35-year-old, as Prime Minister.

CAPITAL:	Moscow
AREA:	17,075,000 sq km (6,590,950 sq miles)
POPULATION:	148.070 million (1996)
CURRENCY:	1 rouble = 100 kopeks
RELIGIONS:	Eastern Orthodox; Jewish; Muslim; and other minorities
ETHNIC GROUPS:	Russian 82%; Tatar 4%; Ukrainian, Mordvin, Lapp, Chuvash, Bashkir, Polish, German, Udmurt, Mari, Yakut, and Ossete minorities
LANGUAGES:	Russian (official); minority languages
INTERNATIONAL ORGANIZATIONS:	UN; CSCE; Commonwealth of Independent States; North Atlantic Co-operation Council

Russian Civil War (or War of Allied Intervention) (1918–21) A conflict fought in Russia between the anti-communist White Army supported by some Western powers and the RED ARMY of the SOVIETS in the aftermath of the RUSSIAN REVOLUTION OF 1917. Counter-revolutionary forces began organized resistance to the BOLSHEVIKS in December 1917 and clashed with an army hastily brought together by TROTSKY. In northern Russia a force made up of French, British, German, and US units landed at Murmansk and occupied Archangel (1918–20). Nationalist revolts in the Baltic states led to the secession of Lithuania, Estonia, Latvia, and Finland, while a Polish army, with French support, successfully advanced the Polish frontier to the Russian Ukraine, gaining an area that was not re-occupied by the Soviet Union until World War II. In Siberia, where US and Japanese forces landed, Admiral KOLCHAK acted as Minister of War in the anti-communist 'All Russian Government' and, with the aid of a Czech legion comprising released prisoners-of-war, gained control over sectors of the Trans-Siberian Railway. He, however, was betrayed by the Czechs and murdered, the leadership passing to General DENIKIN, who sought to establish (1918–20) a 'United Russia' purged of the BOLSHEVIKS. In the Ukraine Denikin mounted a major offensive in 1919, only to be driven back to the Caucasus, where he held out until March 1920. In the Crimea the war continued under General WRANGEL until November 1920. A famine in that year caused further risings by the peasants against the communists, while a mutiny of sailors at KRONSTADT (1921) was suppressed by the Red Army. To win the war, LENIN imposed his ruthless policy of 'war communism'. Lack of co-operation between counter-revolutionary forces contributed to their final collapse and to the establishment of the UNION OF SOVIET SOCIALIST REPUBLICS.

Russian Revolution (1905) A conflict in Russia between the government of NICHOLAS II and industrial workers, peasants, and armed forces. Heavy taxation had brought mounting distress to the poor and Russia's defeat in the RUSSO-JAPANESE WAR aggravated discontent. A peaceful demonstration in St Petersburg was met with gunfire from the imperial troops. Mutiny broke

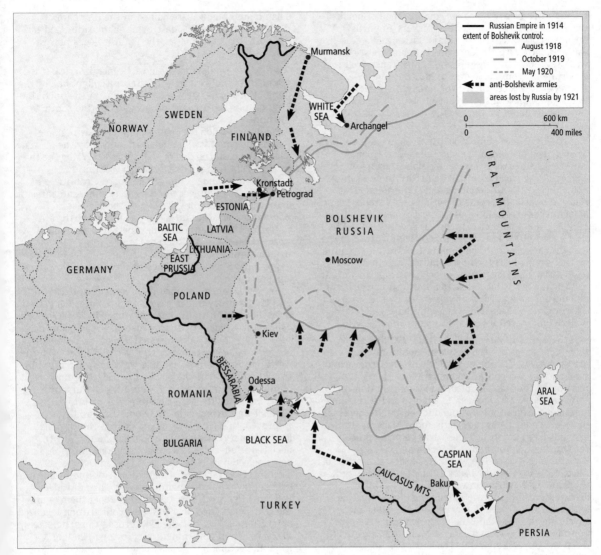

Russian Civil War   *The deployment of troops.*

out on the battleship POTEMKIN and a council of workers' delegates, known as a SOVIET, was formed in St Petersburg. The emperor yielded to certain demands for reform, including the establishment of a legislative DUMA. The SOCIAL DEMOCRATS continued to fight for a total overthrow of the system and were met with harsh reprisals. However, democratic freedoms were curtailed and the government became increasingly reactionary.

Russian Revolution (1917) The overthrow of the government of NICHOLAS II in Russia and its replacement by BOLSHEVIK rule under the leadership of LENIN. It was completed in two stages – a liberal (Menshevik) revolution in March, which overthrew the imperial government, and a socialist (Bolshevik) revolution in November. A long period of repression and unrest, compounded with the reluctance of the Russian people

to continue to fight in World War I, led to a series of violent confrontations, the aim of which was the overthrow of the existing government. The revolutionaries were divided between the liberal intelligentsia, who sought the establishment of a democratic, Western-style republic, and the socialists, who were prepared to use extreme violence to establish a MARXIST proletarian state in Russia. In the March Revolution strikes and riots in Petrograd (St Petersburg), supported by imperial troops, led to the abdication of the emperor and thus to the end after more than 300 years of Romanov rule. A committee of the DUMA (Parliament) appointed the liberal Provisional Government under Prince Lvov, who later handed over to the Socialist revolutionary KERENSKY. He faced rising opposition from the Petrograd Soviet of Workers' and Soldiers' Deputies. The October Revolution was carried through in a nearly bloodless coup by the Bolsheviks under the leadership of Lenin. Workers' Councils (SOVIETS) took control in the major cities, and a ceasefire was arranged with the Germans. A Soviet constitution was proclaimed in July 1918 and Lenin transferred the government from Petrograd to Moscow. The RUSSIAN CIVIL WAR continued for nearly three more years, ending in the supremacy of the Bolsheviks and in the establishment of the UNION OF SOVIET SOCIALIST REPUBLICS.

Russo-Japanese War (1904–05) An important conflict over control of Manchuria and Korea. The Japanese launched a surprise attack on Russian warships at anchor in the naval base at Port Arthur (now Lüshun), Manchuria, without declaring war, after Russia had reneged on its agreement to withdraw its troops from Manchuria. Port Arthur fell to the Japanese, as did Mukden, the capital of Manchuria. The Russian Baltic fleet sailed 28,000 km (18,000 miles) from its base to the East China Sea, only to be sunk in the Tsushima Straits by the Japanese fleet led by Admiral Togo Heihashiro (1846–1934). The victory was important to Japan since it had for the first time defeated a Western power both on land and at sea. The war was ended by the Treaty of PORTSMOUTH. For Russia, it was a humiliating defeat, which contributed to the RUSSIAN REVOLUTION OF 1905.

Russo-Turkish Wars (1806–12, 1828–29, 1853–56, 1877–78) A series of wars between Russia and the OTTOMAN EMPIRE, fought in the Balkans, the Crimea, and the Caucasus for political domination of those territories. The wars enabled the Slavonic nations of ROMANIA, SERBIA, and BULGARIA to emerge and stimulated nationalist aspirations throughout the area to develop. In 1806–12 a vigorous campaign under Marshal KUTUZOV in the Balkans compelled the Turks to make peace, recognizing the autonomy of Serbia and ceding Bessarabia to Russia. The war of 1828–29 was a result of the GREEK WAR OF INDEPENDENCE as Russian ships fought at the Battle of Navarino in which the Turks were defeated, enabling Greece to gain independence. One Russian army invaded Wallachia and Moldavia and, advancing through the Balkans, threatened Constantinople; a second army crossed the Caucasus to reach the Upper Euphrates. The Treaty of Adrianople (1829), which ended the war, gave Wallachia and Moldavia effective independence and granted Russia control over a part of ARMENIA. Russia was opposed in the CRIMEAN WAR of 1853–56 by Britain and France as well as Austria and Turkey, and, at the Treaty of PARIS, ceded territories. In 1876 the Turks quelled an uprising in BULGARIA, causing a European outcry against the 'Bulgarian atrocities'. Russian forces invaded in 1877, allegedly to protect Bulgarian Christians; they again threatened Constantinople. The Treaty of San Stefano (March 1878) (THREE EMPERORS' LEAGUE) which ended the war, provoked criticism from Britain and Germany and was modified by the Congress of BERLIN (June 1878), as it was alleged to have given too much influence to Russia in the Balkans.

Ruyter, Michiel Adrianszoon de (1607–76) Dutch naval commander. He served under Maarten TROMP in the First ANGLO-DUTCH WAR and was the rival of Cornelius Tromp in the Second and Third wars. His most daring coup was in 1667 when, knowing that the English fleet was laid up for lack of money, he sailed up the rivers

Thames and Medway, remained in the Chatham dockyard for two days destroying many ships, and made off with the *Royal Charles*, the English fleet's newest ship.

Rwanda A small country in east central Africa. It is bounded in the west by the Democratic Republic of the Congo (formerly Zaïre) and Lake Kivu, on the north by Uganda, on the east by Tanzania, and on the south by Burundi.

Physical. Rwanda occupies a mountainous region where the equatorial climate is modified by the altitude. Set on the eastern edge of the Great Rift Valley, at the head of Lake Tanganyika, it is also volcanic.

Economy. Rwanda is one of the poorest countries in the world. It is subject to drought, famine, and parasitic and other diseases, but has one of the highest population densities in Africa and a high birth-rate. Coffee and tea are the main exports, and plantains, sweet potatoes, and cassava are staple crops. The principal mineral resource is cassiterite (a tin ore), but exports have been at a standstill since world tin prices collapsed.

History. Rwanda obtained its present boundaries in the late 19th century under pastoral Tutsi kings who ruled over the agriculturalist Bahutu (Hutu). In 1890 Germany claimed it as part of German East Africa. Belgian forces took it in 1916 and administered it under a League of Nations MANDATE. Following civil war (1959) between the Tutsi and Hutu tribes, Rwanda was declared a republic in 1961 and became independent in 1962. The now dominant Hutu forced large numbers of Tutsi into exile, but after the accession to power of President Juvénal Habyarimana in 1973 domestic stability improved. In 1975 Habyarimana's party, the National Revolutionary Movement for Development (MRND) declared itself the sole legal political organization; he was re-elected in 1978, 1983, and 1988. In October 1990 Uganda-based rebels of the Front Patriotique Rwandaise (FPR), many of whose members were Tutsi, invaded. Belgian and French forces helped to repel them, while the OAU negotiated. In 1991 a new constitution legalized opposition parties, but the FPR refused to participate. In 1992 a coalition government was formed pending a general election, but Tutsi–Hutu tension persisted. In 1994, Habyarimana was assassinated. Massacres of Tutsis by the Hutu-dominated army ensued, reigniting the civil war. The FPR emerged victorious, but this provoked millions of Hutus to flee the country for fear of reprisals. Tension mounted during 1995–96 between Rwanda and its neighbour Zaïre (now the Democratic Republic of the Congo), over Tutsi killings of Hutu refugees. Most Hutu exiles returned to Rwanda in 1997, but inter-ethnic violence has continued.

CAPITAL:	Kigali
AREA:	26,338 sq km (10,169 sq miles)
POPULATION:	6.853 million (1996)
CURRENCY:	1 Rwanda franc = 100 centimes
RELIGIONS:	Roman Catholic 65.0%; traditional beliefs 17.0%; Protestant 9.0%; Muslim 9.0%
ETHNIC GROUPS:	Hutu 90.0%; Tutsi 9.0%; Twa 1.0
LANGUAGES:	Rwanda, French (both official); Swahili
INTERNATIONAL ORGANIZATIONS:	UN; OAU

Rye House Plot (1683) A conspiracy of Whig extremists who planned to murder CHARLES II of England and his brother James, Duke of York, after the failure of attempts to exclude James, a Roman Catholic, from the succession. The conspiracy takes its name from the house in Hertfordshire where the assassination was to have taken place. Of those accused of conspiracy, the Earl of Essex committed suicide and Lord Russell and Algernon Sidney were condemned to death on the flimsiest of evidence.

Rymi, Jalal al-Din (also called Maulana or Mevlana) (1207–73) Persian poet, founder of the Mevlevi or 'whirling' dervishes, a Muslim mystical order who are famous for their meditative dance. He was born in Balkh (in modern Afghanistan), but was taken as a child to Turkey, and lived most of his life in Konya, where he is buried. His best-known works are a collection of sonnets and a huge poem called the *Masnavi-yi manavi*, which expresses the philosophy of Islamic mysticism or Sufism through stories.

ryotwari system The system in India of direct settlement of land taxation between the government and cultivators without the intervention of a landlord. In the Madras Presidency the ryotwari system was devised by Governor Thomas Munro in 1820. Elsewhere in India taxation systems operated via the landlord, a system which often worked against the interests of the peasant farmer (the ryot). Tenancy legislation adopting the ryotwari system was later passed to protect the interests of the peasants.

Ryswick, Treaty of (1697) The treaty that ended the NINE YEARS WAR. LOUIS XIV agreed to recognize WILLIAM III as King of England, give up his attempts to control Cologne and the Palatinate, end French occupation of Lorraine, and restore Luxembourg, Mons, Courtrai, and Barcelona to Spain. The Dutch were allowed to garrison a series of fortresses in the Spanish Netherlands as a barrier against France. Strasburg and some towns of Lower Alsace were the only acquisitions made since the Treaty of NIJMEGEN that France retained.

SA BROWNSHIRTS.

Saar River (French, Sarre) A river of France and south-west Germany. In 1792 the Saar valley was occupied by the French, but after the defeat of Napoleon in 1815 most of the area was ceded to Prussia. Its development as a major industrial area really began after the unification of Germany in 1871 and the acquisition of ALSACE-LORRAINE, with its coal and iron deposits. A rapid economic development took place, which was interrupted after World War I, when, as part of the VERSAILLES PEACE SETTLEMENT, the area was placed under the administration of the League of Nations and its mines awarded to France. In 1935 a plebiscite restored it to Germany, but it was again occupied by French troops in 1945. In 1955 a referendum voted for restoration to Germany, and in 1959 the Saarland became the tenth state of the Federal Republic of Germany.

Sabah A state of Malaysia. Controlled in the 19th century by the sultan of Brunei, the area now known as Sabah was leased in 1881 to the British North Borneo Company and in 1888 was taken under British protection as North Borneo. Occupied by the Japanese during World War II, it was united with Labuan as a British crown colony in 1946. In 1963 it became a state within the Federation of MALAYSIA. It was subject to Indonesian attempts at subversion during the KONFRONTASI (1963–66) and to unsuccessful Filipino claims of sovereignty.

Sabines A tribe native to the foothills of the Apennines north-east of Rome. According to tradition they joined the earliest settlement of Rome in the 8th century BC. Legend relates how the Romans abducted the Sabine women during a festival; an army was raised to take revenge but the women appeared on the battlefield with new-born babies and the two sides were reconciled. They became Roman citizens only after conquest.

Sacco–Vanzetti Case The controversial US legal case (1920–27) in which two Italian immigrants, Nicola Sacco and Bertolomeo Vanzetti, were found guilty of murder. Many have alleged that their conviction resulted from prejudice against them as immigrants, ANARCHISTS, and evaders of military service. Following the trial there were anti-US demonstrations in Rome, Lisbon, and Montevideo, and one in Paris, where a bomb killed 20 people. For six years efforts were made to obtain a retrial without success, although the judge was officially criticized for his conduct; the two men were electrocuted in August 1927. The affair helped to mobilize opinion against the prevailing ISOLATIONISM and conservatism of the post-war USA. Later evidence pointed to the crime having been committed by members of a gang led by Joe Morrelli.

Sacheverell, Henry (1674–1724) English divine and preacher. In 1709 he preached two sermons attacking the Whig government's policy of religious toleration,

one of the principles of the GLORIOUS REVOLUTION. The House of Commons condemned the sermons as seditious and Sacheverell was impeached. He attracted a popular following, with crowds shouting 'High Church and Sacheverell' in his support. Although his sentence was a nominal one (a temporary suspension from preaching), the Sacheverell episode was important within a political context; the Tories used the message of 'The Church in danger' to attract support from the conservative Anglican squirearchy against the Whigs, thereby crucially weakening the Whig ministry, which fell in 1710.

Sadat, (Muhammad) Anwar (1918–81) Egyptian statesman. An original member of NASSER's Free Officers association of Egyptian nationalists, he was imprisoned by the British for being a German agent during World War II, and again (1946–49) for terrorist acts. He took part in the coup (1952) that deposed King FAROUK and brought Nasser to power and later succeeded Nasser as President of Egypt (1970–81). By 1972 he had dismissed the Soviet military mission to Egypt and, in 1974, following the YOM KIPPUR WAR, he recovered the Suez Canal Zone from Israel. In an effort to hasten a Middle East settlement he went to Israel in 1977. This marked the first recognition of Israel by an Arab state and brought strong condemnation from most of the Arab world. He entered into talks with the Israeli Prime Minister, Menachem BEGIN, at Camp David, Maryland (1978), under the chairmanship of President Carter, and a peace treaty (the CAMP DAVID ACCORD) between Israel and Egypt was finally signed at Washington in 1979. Mounting disillusionment amongst ISLAMIC FUNDAMENTALISTS within Egypt led to his assassination in 1981.

Sadducee A member of a Jewish sect that was a rival to the PHARISEES in ancient Israel. The Sadducees were drawn mostly from the rich landowners, and were naturally conservative, but by the time of JESUS CHRIST they had declined considerably from their previously dominant position. Nevertheless they still held a number of priesthoods and were a powerful voice in the SANHEDRIN.

Sadowa, Battle of (3 July 1866) A battle fought near the Bohemian town of Sadowa (Königgrätz), between the Prussian army under MOLTKE and Benedek's Austrian army. The Prussians were able to overcome Benedek by their superior mobility and weapons. This battle decided the Seven Weeks War (see AUSTRO-PRUSSIAN WAR) and marked the end of Austrian influence in Germany. Prussian domination in north Germany was confirmed.

Safavid ISMAIL I.

Said ibn Sultan Sayyid (1791–1856) Ruler of Oman and Zanzibar (1806–56). In 1806 he became ruler (Sayyid) of OMAN, with his capital at Muscat on the Persian Gulf. In 1822, assisted by the British, he sent an expedition to Mombasa, whose rulers, the Mazrui family, owed him nominal allegiance, but who were seeking independence. He himself visited Mombasa in 1827 and in the next decade brought many East African ports under his control. In 1837 he ended Mazrui rule in Mombasa and signed commercial agreements with Britain, France, and the USA. He first visited ZANZIBAR in 1828, buying property and introducing clove production. In 1840 he took control of Zanzibar. Said sent trading caravans deep into Africa, seeking ivory and slaves, and Zanzibar became the commercial capital of the East African coast. Although an ally of the British, he was under constant pressure from them to end his trade in slaves, and he signed an agreement to do this in 1845. When he died, he divided the Asian and African parts of his empire between his two sons.

Saigo Takamori (1828–77) Japanese soldier and statesman. A member of a lowly but prestigious SAMURAI family, he played a central role in the overthrow of the SHOGUNATE and the establishment of the MEIJI imperial state. Showered with the highest honours, he initially retired from public life, but in 1871 was persuaded to return to the government as commander of the Imperial Guard. Fearing for the decline of the samurai way of life in the face of the introduction of conscription, Saigo promoted a war of redemption against Korea, to be triggered by his own murder at Korean hands, but retired in 1873 when this plan was vetoed. Subsequently his private school at Kagoshima became a centre for samurai dissatisfaction, and in 1877 he was forced into rebellion by the actions of his followers. Defeated by government forces under YAMAGATA, he had himself killed by one of his own men.

St Albans A town in Hertfordshire, England, the site of two major battles in the Wars of the ROSES which were fought near the town. The first marked the opening of the wars, with Richard, 3rd Duke of YORK, attacking the LANCASTRIAN forces. He won the battle, and with it control of England, on 22 May 1455. The second Battle of St Albans, on 16 February 1461, was a Lancastrian victory, in which MARGARET OF ANJOU's forces outmanoeuvred Richard Neville, Earl of WARWICK, and released HENRY VI from captivity; but her indecision enabled Edward to slip through to London and gain the throne as EDWARD IV.

St Bartholomew's Day Massacre (23–24 August 1572) The mass assassination of HUGUENOT leaders in Paris during the FRENCH WARS OF RELIGION. The Catholic GUISE faction prevailed upon Catherine de Medici to authorize an assassination of about 200 of the principal HUGUENOT leaders. Parisian Catholic mobs used these killings as a pretext for large-scale butchery, until some 3,000 Huguenots lay dead, and thousands more perished in the 12 provincial disturbances that followed. COLIGNY was killed in Paris, while Henry IV of Navarre saved himself by avowing the Catholic faith. Catherine's reputation as a mediator was damaged by the massacre.

Saintes, Les, Battle of (1782) A Caribbean naval battle fought off the coast of Dominica, between a British fleet under RODNEY and a French fleet under de Grasse. Five French ships were captured and one sunk. The engagement was notable because Rodney, taking advantage of the wind, broke the French line in two places, a manoeuvre later perfected by NELSON. This victory somewhat offset the British defeat in the American War of Independence and re-established Britain's maritime supremacy.

St John, Order of KNIGHT HOSPITALLER.

Saint-Just, Louis Antoine Léon Florelle de (1767–94) French Revolutionary leader. He was elected an officer in the National Guard when the FRENCH REVOLUTION began; his great loyalty to ROBESPIERRE led to his appointment to the National Convention in 1792. In his first speech he condemned Louis XVI and he was subsequently instrumental in the overthrow of the GIRONDINS Jacques René Hébert and DANTON. He was the youngest member of the COMMITTEE OF PUBLIC SAFETY, organized the TERROR, and carried out many missions to enforce discipline in the revolutionary armies. He was executed with Robespierre.

Saint Kitts and Nevis (Saint Christopher and Nevis) An island country in the Leeward Islands of the Caribbean.

Physical. Saint Kitts is an oval-shaped volcanic island crossed by rugged mountains and rising to Mount Misery at 1,131 m (3,711 feet). Three kilometres (2 miles) to the south-east, Nevis, which is round and smaller, rises to Nevis Peak at 1,096 m (3,596 feet). Both have an equable, tropical climate. The tiny island Sombrero is included in the group.

Economy. Agriculture has been replaced by tourism as the main source of revenue, and both manufacturing and service industries are developing. The chief crops are sugar cane, coconuts, and fruit, and the leading industries are food-processing, electronics, and clothing. Foodstuffs and machinery are the leading exports.

History. Originally inhabited by Caribs, the islands were visited by Christopher Columbus in 1493, who named the larger island Saint Christopher. English settlers in the early 17th century shortened the name to Saint Kitts; this was the first successful English colony in the Caribbean. The islands, together with Anguilla, were united as a single colony in 1882. In 1958, they joined the West Indies Federation (see WEST INDIAN INDEPENDENCE). Anguilla became a separate British dependency in 1980, while Saint Kitts and Nevis gained independence within the British Commonwealth in 1983. Nevis has its own legislature and retains the right to secede from Saint Kitts at any time should it so choose. In October 1997 the Nevis parliament voted to secede from the federation: the issue will now go to a referendum.

CAPITAL:	Basseterre
AREA:	269.4 sq km (104.0 sq miles)
POPULATION:	39,400 (1996)
CURRENCY:	1 East Caribbean dollar = 100 cents
RELIGIONS:	Anglican 32.6%; Methodist 28.8%; Moravian 8.7%; Roman Catholic 7.2%
ETHNIC GROUPS:	Black 90.5%; mixed 5.0%; East Indian 3.0%; White 1.5%
LANGUAGES:	English (official)
INTERNATIONAL ORGANIZATIONS:	UN; OAS; Commonwealth

St Laurent, Louis Stephen (1882–1973) French–Canadian lawyer and statesman. As Minister of Justice (1941–46) he upheld limited military conscription during World War II in the face of widespread French-Canadian opposition. In 1946 he became Secretary of

State for External Affairs. Having succeeded Mackenzie KING as Prime Minister of Canada (1948–57), he played a significant part in setting up the NATO alliance, and did much to raise the international reputation of Canada. Significant constitutional changes were also made during his administration, with the word 'Dominion' being dropped from Canada's official name and Newfoundland becoming the tenth Province in 1949. After overwhelming victories in 1949 and 1953, he was defeated in the election of 1957. As only the second French-Canadian to become Prime Minister, St Laurent gave notable service in the promotion of good relations between English- and French-speaking Canadians.

Saint Lucia An island country, one of the Windward Islands of the Caribbean.

Physical. Saint Lucia is 43 km (27 miles) in length, roughly oval-shaped, and picturesquely rugged, rising to Morne Gimie at 959 m (3,145 feet). In the south-west is the dormant volcano Qualibou. The fertile volcanic valleys and coastal plains are well watered and the interior has virgin forests and mineral springs. There is a fine harbour.

Economy. Tourism is an important source of revenue, but agriculture is still predominant. Timber, bananas, cocoa, copra, and coconuts are all grown. Manufactured goods include paper products and clothing, both exported, and there is a food-processing industry.

History. The Arawak Indians, the earliest inhabitants of Saint Lucia, were driven out by Carib Indians before Europeans arrived. The British failed in their attempts to colonize the island in 1605 and 1638 and the French settled it, making a treaty with the Caribs in 1660. Saint Lucia changed hands several times before being ceded to Britain in 1814. A representative local government was established in 1924 and Saint Lucia was a member of the Federation of the West Indies from 1958 until 1962. Saint Lucia became an independent member of the British Commonwealth in 1979, after 12 years of internal self-government. The island has been governed since independence by the United Workers' Party. Its economy was severely affected by the fall in prices for bananas (its chief export) in the European market in 1993. Saint Lucia is a member of the CARIBBEAN COMMUNITY AND COMMON MARKET (CARICOM).

CAPITAL:	Castries
AREA:	617.4 sq km (238.4 sq miles)
POPULATION:	144,000 (1996)
CURRENCY:	1 East Caribbean dollar = 100 cents
RELIGIONS:	Roman Catholic 85.6%; Seventh-Day Adventist 4.3%; Anglican 2.7%
ETHNIC GROUPS:	Black 87.0%; mixed 9.1%; East Indian 2.6%; White 1.3%
LANGUAGES:	English (official); English and French creoles
INTERNATIONAL ORGANIZATIONS:	UN; OAS; CARICOM; Commonwealth

Saint-Simon, Claude Henri de Rouvroy, Comte de (1760–1825) French social philosopher and founder of French socialism. He fought in the American War of Independence and was imprisoned in France during the TERROR. Between 1814 and 1825 he published his doctrines on the organization of society, in which he envisaged government not by landowners, lawyers, and priests but by industrialists, scientists, and poets, representing the three faculties of action, thought, and feeling. After his death his theories, summed up in his major work *Nouveau Christianisme* (1825), exerted a far-reaching influence, and a generation of Saint-Simonian technocrats emerged committed to the industrial development of France.

Saint Vincent and the Grenadines An island country in the Windward Islands of the Caribbean, consisting of the main island of Saint Vincent and two islets of the Grenadines.

Physical. The main island, Saint Vincent, is 29 km (18 miles) long. Of volcanic origin, it has forested rugged mountains rising to the active volcano of Mount Soufrière at 1,234 m (4,048 feet). There are picturesque valleys and fertile well-watered tracts. The climate is tropical.

Economy. Luxury tourism is an important source of revenue, with exports headed by agricultural products such as bananas and vegetables. Manufacturing industry includes food-processing and electronics.

History. When Christopher COLUMBUS discovered the islands in 1498 they were inhabited by Carib Indians. Europeans did not colonize the islands until the 18th century when they made treaties with the Caribs. The islands changed hands several times but the British finally gained control in 1796. Most of the Caribs were deported and most of those remaining were killed in volcanic eruptions in 1812 and 1902. The British brought many African slaves to the islands, and after the abolition of slavery in 1834 many Portuguese and Asian labourers were brought in to work on sugar cane plantations. The country was a British colony from 1871 until 1956 when colonial rule was ended. Part of the Federation of the West Indies (1958–62), Saint Vincent and the Grenadines became fully independent in 1979. The country has been governed since 1984 by the right-wing New Democratic Party.

CAPITAL:	Kingstown
AREA:	389.3 sq km (150.3 sq miles)
POPULATION:	113,000 (1996)
CURRENCY:	1 East Caribbean dollar = 100 cents
RELIGIONS:	Anglican 36.0%; Methodist 20.4%; Roman Catholic 19.3%; Seventh-day Adventist 4.1%; Plymouth Brethren 3.9%
ETHNIC GROUPS:	Blacks 74.0%; mixed 19.0%; White 3.0%; Amerindian 2.0%; East Indian 2.0%
LANGUAGES:	English (official); English creole
INTERNATIONAL ORGANIZATIONS:	UN; OAS; CARICOM; Commonwealth

Sakharov, Andrey Dmitriyevich (1921–89) Russian nuclear physicist and human rights activist. Born in Moscow, he worked in the early 1950s as a theoretical physicist to develop the former Soviet Union's first hydrogen bomb, devising, with others, the theoretical basis for controlled thermonuclear fusion. During this time he was made the youngest ever member of the Soviet Academy of Sciences. Disillusioned with his work he publicly protested in 1961 against the testing of a Soviet 100-megaton hydrogen bomb, fearing the effects of widespread radioactive fallout. Thereafter, he and his wife Yelena Bonner (1923–) called for nuclear arms reduction and became active campaigners for human rights. In 1980 he was exiled to the closed city of Gorky (now Nizhnii Novgorod) and not released until 1986 and the era of *glasnost*. After his release he was elected to the Congress of People's Deputies, where he continued to fight for human rights in Russia. He was awarded the Nobel Prize for Peace in 1975.

Saladin (Salah al-Din, literally 'the Welfare of the Faith') (1138–93) The Kurdish founder of the Ayyubid dynasty (1169–93), who reunited Egypt, Syria, and Mesopotamia under one rule. Periodic hostilities with the Crusader kingdom of JERUSALEM led in 1187 to his rout of Christian forces under Guy of Lusignan and the capture of Jerusalem and Acre, thus provoking the Third CRUSADE. The Crusaders eventually recovered Acre in 1191, when RICHARD I also defeated Saladin at Arsuf but, unable to recover Jerusalem, made a truce. Saladin's dynasty fell to the Mongols in 1250, but his fame as a shrewd and chivalrous commander was incorporated into European as well as Muslim legend.

Salamis, Battle of (480 BC). A naval battle fought in the Aegean Sea during the Greek-Persian wars. THEMISTOCLES, the Greek commander, lured the Persian fleet of XERXES, the Persian king, into the narrow waters between the island of Salamis and the mainland. The outnumbered but nimbler and expertly handled Greek triremes took full advantage of the confusion engendered by the confined space to win a victory that offset the earlier reverses at THERMOPYLAE and Artemisium.

Salazar, Antonio de Oliveira (1889–1970) Portuguese statesman. For over 30 years he was Prime Minister and, in effect, dictator of Portugal (1932–68). A successful Finance Minister (1928–32), he was invited to become Premier in 1932. He introduced a new constitution in 1933, creating the New State (*Estado Novo*) along fascist lines and using his authority to achieve social and economic reforms. During the SPANISH CIVIL WAR and WORLD WAR II Salazar was also Minister for Foreign Affairs and maintained a policy of neutrality. His policy of defending Portugal's African colonies (see MOZAMBIQUE, ANGOLA) in the face of mounting nationalism embittered his military leaders, who were forced to wage difficult battles in Africa. He was succeeded by CAETANO.

Salem witch trials (1692) The trial and execution of 19 supposed witches at Salem, Massachusetts. The hunt for witches began when girls in the minister's household believed themselves bewitched. Panic about devil worship and resultant accusations spread through surrounding towns until 50 people were afflicted and 200 had been accused. Increase MATHER and Governor Sir William Phips managed to halt the witch craze in October 1692.

Salic law The legal code of the Salian FRANKS, which originated in 5th century Gaul. It was issued by CLOVIS (465–511) and reissued under the CAROLINGIANS. It contained both criminal and civil clauses and provided for penal fines for offenders. It also laid down that daughters could not inherit land and was later used in France and in some German principalities to prevent daughters succeeding to the throne. The VALOIS kings of France used it against EDWARD III of England, who claimed the French throne through his mother.

Salisbury, Robert Arthur Talbot Gascoigne-Cecil, 3rd Marquess of (1830–1903) British statesman. He became Prime Minister of a 'caretaker' Conservative government in 1885 when the Liberal leader, William GLADSTONE, resigned. Having won an election he

remained as Prime Minister (1886–92) and later returned to head governments at the turn of the century (1895–1900 and 1900–02). In foreign affairs he refused to allow Britain to become embroiled in the alliance-making provoked by Franco-German rivalries but supported the policies that resulted in the second BOER WAR (1899–1902). Domestically his main achievement was administrative, for example in providing a new organizational framework for local government between 1888 and 1899.

Sallust (Caius Sallustius Crispus) (86–34 BC) Roman historian. He was a supporter of Julius CAESAR and later governor of Numidia in north Africa. He was accused of extortion but never brought to trial. In retirement he wrote a history of the Numidian War fought by MARIUS against JUGURTHA and an account of the Catiline conspiracy. Both survive but only fragments exist of his five-book history of Rome.

Sālote Tupou III TONGA.

SALT STRATEGIC ARMS LIMITATION TALKS.

Salt March (12 March–6 April 1930) A march by Indian nationalists led by Mohandas GANDHI. The private manufacture of salt violated the salt tax system imposed by the British, and in a new campaign of civil disobedience Gandhi led his followers from his ashram at Sabarmati to make salt from the sea at Dandi, a distance of 320 km (200 miles). The government remained inactive until the protesters marched on a government salt depot. Gandhi was arrested on 5 May, but his followers continued the movement of civil disobedience.

Salvation Army An international Protestant evangelical and charitable organization, founded in London in 1865 by William BOOTH as the Christian Revival Association. Preaching in the slums of London, Booth used unconventional methods to win people to Christianity, while also insisting on militant teetotalism. In 1878 his mission, which was run on military lines, with a fundamentalist approach to religion, took the name Salvation Army. The Army placed emphasis on welfare work and devoted much time to helping the destitute. It expanded rapidly not only in Britain but also overseas; in the USA Ballington Booth, a son of the founder, set up (1896) a splinter group, the Volunteers of America.

The Salvation Army today is a non-governmental organization operating in 80 countries worldwide with its headquarters in the UK. Officers, who may be men or women, are required to practise obedience and abstinence from alcohol. The organization is well known for helping the poor and homeless and successfully operates a missing persons investigation service.

Samaria An ancient city built to serve as capital of the northern kingdom of Israel after it divided from the southern kingdom of Judah (centred on Jerusalem). In 723 BC it was captured by the Assyrians who deported most of the inhabitants. The descendants of those who remained and those who were imported were subsequently disliked by the Jews for centuries afterwards, more for historical and racial than for religious reasons since they worshipped the same God.

samizdat (Russian, 'self publishing') Unofficial writings circulated in the former Soviet Union and Eastern bloc, expressing the views of dissident groups and individuals in defiance of official censorship and controls. The samizdat movement took shape in the 1950s in the Soviet Union, and was intensified following the death of Stalin and the 'thaw' of the mid-1950s. It experienced rapid growth after the Helsinki Agreement (1975), reporting, for example, on the violation of human rights and on pollution.

Samnite wars A succession of wars fought between ancient Rome and its southern neighbours, the Samnites and the Latins. The first war (343–341 BC) was brief, but the second (326–304) was more protracted: Roman troops experienced the humiliation of having to walk like slaves under a yoke of spears after their defeat at the Caudine Forks. The APPIAN WAY was built in 312 to assist communications between Rome and the war area. Gauls joined against Rome in the third of the wars (298–290), but were defeated. The Samnites were consistently hostile to Rome. They helped HANNIBAL in the Second PUNIC WAR and revolted for the last time in the Social War of 90, after which they became allies of MARIUS. SULLA crushed them and devastated their homelands.

Samoa (formerly Western Samoa) A country consisting of a group of nine islands in the south-west Pacific and forming part of the Samoan Archipelago.

Physical. The country's two major islands, Upolu and Savai'i, are both volcanic and are fringed by coral reefs. The islands have tall, evergreen rain forests and swamps, with 16 species of bird that are unique to the area.

Economy. The economy of Western Samoa is based on agriculture. The main exports are cocoa, copra, and bananas, but tropical fruits and timber are also exported. Tourism is expanding.

History. The Samoan archipelago was first settled in about 1000 BC and was the centre of Polynesian migrations eastwards. Although sighted by the Dutch in 1722, the first European to set foot on the islands was Louis-Antoine de BOUGAINVILLE in 1768. Germany, Britain, and the USA competed for control of the archipelago until 1899 when the western part of Samoa passed to Germany and the eastern islands became American SAMOA. Western Samoa remained a German protectorate until 1914; thereafter it was administered by New Zealand, initially (1920–46) under a League of Nations Mandate and then as a UN Trust Territory. It gained full independence in 1962 as Western Samoa and joined the COMMONWEALTH OF NATIONS in 1970. Susuga Malietoa Tanumafili II became head of state in 1963. He is a constitutional monarch with the power to dissolve the legislative assembly, which is known as the *Fono*. In 1990 universal adult suffrage was introduced and in 1997 the country's official name was changed to Samoa.

CAPITAL:	Apia
AREA:	2831 sq km (1093 sq miles)
POPULATION:	167,000 (1996)
CURRENCY:	1 tala = 100 sene
RELIGIONS:	Congregational 47.2%; Roman Catholic 22.3%; Methodist 15%
ETHNIC GROUPS:	Samoan 88%; Euronesian 10%; European 2%
LANGUAGES:	Samoan; English
INTERNATIONAL ORGANIZATIONS:	UN; Commonwealth; South Pacific Forum

Samoa, American An unincorporated territory of the USA, part of the Samoan Archipelago.

Physical. American Samoa comprises a group of seven islands in the southern Pacific. The islands are volcanic and mountainous.

History. The eastern islands of the Samoan Archipelago were annexed to the USA in 1899, becoming American Samoa. Swain's Island, which lies 336 km (210 miles) north of the Samoan Archipelago, was annexed by the USA in 1925 and is administered as part of American Samoa. A bicameral legislature was established in 1948 as an advisory body and was given limited law-making powers in the new constitutions of 1960 and 1967.

Samori Touré (1830–1900) African military leader. A Muslim, he began to amass a personal following in the mid-1850s, establishing a military base on the Upper Niger. By 1870 his authority was acknowledged throughout the Kanaka region of the River Milo, in what is now eastern Guinea. By 1880 he ruled a vast Dyula empire, from the Upper Volta in the east to the Fouta Djallon in the west, over which he attempted to create a single Islamic administrative system. His imperial ambitions clashed with those of the French and there were sporadic battles between 1882 and 1886. His attempts to impose Islam on all his people resulted in a revolt in 1888. A French invasion in 1891–92 forced him to move eastwards to the interior of the Ivory Coast, where he established himself in Bondoukon (1891–98). French forces, however, captured him and he was exiled to Gabon.

Samuel (11th century BC) Israelite leader and prophet. He was the last judge (leader) of the tribes of ISRAEL before the establishment of hereditary kingship. Ruling during a period of PHILISTINE domination of Israel, he rallied his people in opposition to them. He was instrumental in creating the monarchy by anointing SAUL as the first King of Israel. Samuel provided Saul with prophetic advice until they had a disagreement over his priestly duties; he then secretly anointed DAVID as king in Samuel's place.

samurai (from the Japanese, 'those who serve') Warrior retainers of Japan's DAIMYO (feudal lords). Prominent from the 12th century, they were not a separate class until HIDEYOSHI limited the right to bear arms to them, after which they became a hereditary caste. Their two swords were their badge. Their conduct was regulated by *Bushido* (Warrior's Way), a strict code that emphasized the qualities of loyalty, bravery, and endurance. Their training from childhood was spartan. Their ultimate duty when defeated or dishonoured was *seppuku*, ritual self-disembowelment.

Samurai were active during the KAMAKURA shogunate and with their masters were responsible for the strife of the ASHIKAGA period. They served during Hideyoshi's Korean campaigns and fought for and against the TOKUGAWA at Sekigahara. During the long Tokugawa peace, during which they had little to do except quell peasant revolts, many applied themselves to the pursuit of learning and the development of military skills, and many able samurai became administrators. When their regular incomes were ended by the MEIJI government after 1868 some went into business. Rebellions by discontented former samurai during the 1870s were put down by the newly formed national army.

Sanchi One of the most important Buddhist sites in India, situated in Madhya Pradesh state, central India. During the 19th century a group of well-preserved stupas (shrines) and monasteries dating from the 3rd century BC were rediscovered at this site. The most renowned is the oldest, the Great Stupa, the construction of which was probably begun by the Mauryan Buddhist emperor, ASOKA but was later enlarged. It is enclosed by a stone railing with four richly carved gateways erected in the 1st century AD. The sculpture depicts the previous lives of the BUDDHA, animal life, grotesques, and brackets in the form of female tree-spirits. Later structures include a Gupta temple.

sanctuary A sacred place recognized as a refuge for criminals. Such places existed in both Greek and Roman society and since 399 in the Christian world. In England a fugitive could claim refuge from immediate prosecution in a church or churchyard provided he agreed with the coroner to leave the realm by a specified port within 40 days. Failure to do so would result in prosecution. This right did not apply in cases of treason (1486). Towns having sanctuary privileges were restricted by Henry VIII to Derby, Launceston, Manchester, Northampton, Wells, Westminster, and York. In England criminals lost the right to sanctuary in 1623.

Sandinista Liberation Front (Spanish, *Frente Sandinista de Liberacion Nacional*, or *FSLN*) Nicaraguan guerrilla movement, named after the revolutionary leader César Augusto SANDINO, an early opponent of the dictatorship of the SOMOZA dynasty that ruled the country for 50 years. The Sandinistas were formed by a coalition of left-wing opposition forces in 1961 and began guerrilla activities in 1963. Despite heavy losses and factional in-fighting, their support grew steadily and they won power in 1979, driving Anastasio Somoza into exile. The socialist administration established by their leader Daniel Ortega (President 1984–90) attempted to win recognition both from its traditional allies in the communist bloc and from western states, but found itself embroiled in a bitter civil war against US-sponsored Contra insurgents (see REAGAN). In the elections of 1990, the Sandinistas were defeated by the National Opposition Union under Violeta Chamorro. Ortega stood unsuccessfully in the presidential elections of 1996.

Sandino, César Augusto (1893–1934) Nicaraguan revolutionary general. A guerrilla leader, he tenaciously resisted US intervention in Nicaragua from 1926 to 1933. His anti-imperialist stance attracted wide support in Latin America. After US marines withdrew, Sandino became leader of a co-operative farming scheme. Seen as a liberalizing influence, he was assassinated by Anastasio SOMOZA's National Guard. The SANDINISTA LIBERATION FRONT, which defeated the Somoza dynasty in 1979, considered itself the spiritual heir of Sandino.

San Francisco Conference (1951) A conference held to agree a formal peace treaty between Japan and the nations against which she had fought in World War II. When the treaty came into force in April 1952, the period of occupation (JAPAN, OCCUPATION OF) was formally ended and Japanese sovereignty restored. Japan recognized the independence of Korea and renounced its rights to Taiwan, the Pescadores, the Kuriles, southern Sakhalin, and the Pacific islands mandated to it before the war by the League of Nations. The country was allowed the right of self-defence with the proviso that the USA would maintain its own forces in Japan until the Japanese were able to shoulder their own defensive responsibilities. The Soviet Union did not sign the treaty, but diplomatic relations were restored in 1956, while peace treaties with Asian nations conquered by the Japanese in the war were signed through the 1950s as individual problems with reparations were resolved.

Sanhedrin (Greek, *synedrion*, 'council') The term used by the JEWISH PEOPLE for their supreme court, headed by the high priest, before the fall of JERUSALEM in 70 AD. It was probably founded around the 2nd century BC. Under the Romans its jurisdiction covered Palestinian Jews in civil and religious matters, though capital sentences required Roman confirmation.

San Jacinto, Battle of (21 April 1836) The last important battle of TEXAS's brief struggle to establish an independent republic. Sam HOUSTON, with 800 Texans, defeated a Mexican force of 1,400 at the San Jacinto River and captured the Mexican leader SANTA ANNA. The armistice terms dictated by Houston established *de facto* independence for Texas, and Houston himself was installed as President.

Sankaracharya (*c.* 700–50) Indian religious thinker who expounded and taught the Vedanta system, the most influential of the six recognized systems of Hindu thought. He was born in a Brahmin family in Kerala, south India, but renounced the world to travel all over India as a sannyasi (ascetic), having discussions with philosophers of various schools. His foundation of monasteries throughout India helped to spread his ideas, and he has remained one of the most influential teachers in the Hindu world. Within the Vedanta philosophy his teaching that Brahman (the supreme soul) and Atman (the human soul) are one, and that the visible world is *maya* (illusory), are the chief distinquishing marks of his school.

San Martín, José de (1778–1850) South American revolutionary. Born in Argentina, he trained as a military officer in Spain. On his return to Argentina in 1812, he joined the forces in rebellion against Spain and was sent to take command of the nationalist army in Mendoza. In an outstanding military feat he led his soldiers across the Andes and assured Chilean independence in the Battle of Maipú (April 1818). After landing his troops on the Peruvian coast in 1820, he took Lima unopposed on 28 July 1821. He became Protector of Peru (1821–22). In late July 1822, San Martin met with Simón BOLÍVAR at Guayaquil and decided to withdraw, leaving the liberation of the rest of Peru to Bolívar. In 1824 he sailed for Europe, where he died in 1850.

sansculotte Originally, a member of the volunteer republican 'army' of the early FRENCH REVOLUTION. The term 'sansculotte' ('without knee-breeches'), was chosen by the revolutionaries to describe the labourer's loose-fitting linen garment worn by their supporters. During the Reign of TERROR public functionaries styled themselves *citoyens sansculottes*, with a distinctive costume: *pantalon* (long trousers), *carmagnole* (short-skirted coat), red cap of liberty, and *sabots* (wooden clogs).

Santa Anna, Antonio López de (1794–1876) Mexican military adventurer and statesman. He entered the Spanish colonial army and served as one of the Creole supporters of the Spanish government until 1821, when ITURBIDE made him governor of Vera Cruz. At first a supporter of the Federal Party, he subsequently overthrew (1822) Iturbide and himself became (1833) President of Mexico. His policies led to the uprising at ALAMO, to his defeat and capture in the battle of SAN JACINTO (1836), and to the secession of TEXAS. He was released, and returned to Vera Cruz, where he defended the city against the French (1836–39). In his next presidential tenure during the early 1840s, he discarded the liberal constitution of 1824 and ruled as a dictator. Subsequently, despite defeat in the MEXICAN–AMERICAN WAR and the loss of half of Mexico's territory to the USA, Santa Anna was recalled to the presidency in 1853 by Mexican conservatives. In 1855 the liberal revolution of Ayutla deposed him.

Sanusi Popular name for the *Sanusiyyah*, a Muslim brotherhood that acquired considerable political importance in LIBYA and North Africa. It was founded in Mecca in 1837 as a Sufi religious order by an Algerian, Sidi Muhammad al-Sanusi al-Idrisi, but in about 1843 he retired to the desert in Cyrenaica. The movement spread in Libya under the son and grandson of al-Sanusi; by 1884 there were 100 *zawiyas* or daughter houses, scattered through North Africa and further afield. It became more militant in the 20th century, attacking the British occupation of Egypt in both World Wars and opposing the Italians in Libya. When Libya became independent in 1951, the leader of the order at that time, Idris I, became the country's first king.

São Tomé and Príncipe A country comprising two islands and several islets, lying on the Equator in the Gulf of Guinea, off the coast of West Africa.

Physical. The two main islands are volcanic and both have coastal lowlands rising to central mountainous regions. The island of Príncipe lies about 144 km (90 miles) north of São Tomé. Tropical rainforests cover most of the islands.

Economy. The economy was centrally planned until the mid-1980s, when severe drought and worsening economic conditions, including a drop in world cocoa prices, prompted the government to seek Western aid and reduce state controls. The main export is cocoa, followed by copra. Industry is restricted to food-processing. Since agriculture concentrates on cash crops for exports, most food is imported.

History. The islands were probably uninhabited when they were discovered by the Portuguese in 1471 and were annexed by Portugal in 1522. Independence was gained in 1975, with Portugal's withdrawal from all its African colonies. Multiparty democracy was instituted under a new constitution in 1990. In 1995 President Miguel Trovoada was deposed by Cuban-trained rebel forces but was swiftly restored to power.

CAPITAL:	São Tomé
AREA:	1,001 sq km (386 sq miles)
POPULATION:	134,000 (1996)
CURRENCY:	1 dobra = 100 centimos
RELIGIONS:	Roman Catholic 84.0%; remainder mainly Seventh-day Adventist and indigenous Evangelical Church
ETHNIC GROUPS:	Mixed 43.0%; African 51.0%
LANGUAGES:	Portuguese (official); Portuguese creole
INTERNATIONAL ORGANIZATIONS:	UN; OAU

Saracens Originally nomads belonging to tribes of the Syrian or Arabian deserts but at the time of the CRUSADES the name used by Christians for all Muslims. In a surge of conquest Muslim Arabs swept into the Holy Land (western Palestine), north into the Byzantine territory of Asia Minor, and westward through North Africa during the 7th and 8th centuries. Spain was conquered (MOORS), together with most of the islands in the Mediterranean; they held Sicily from the 9th to the 11th century. Their expansion was halted by the Carolingians in France only with great difficulty. The Crusades against them, though initially effective, did not prove decisive in the long term, and they were not finally expelled from Spain until the 15th century.

Within their conquered territories they had a profound effect on cultural life, particularly in architecture, philosophy, mathematics, and religion. In religion they were often tolerant of local beliefs and customs. The lurid accounts of Saracen bloodshed must be offset by the financial advantages of their presence: Saracen gold, used to pay for European goods, invigorated the Frankish economy.

Saragossa (in Spanish, Zaragoza) A province and its capital city in north-eastern Spain. The city was built on the site of the Roman colony of Caesaraugusta. It was one of the first towns in Spain to receive Christianity, but fell to the Visigoths in the 5th century, and then to the Moors *c.* 714. In 1118 it was seized by the Aragonese, and subsequently prospered as the capital of Aragon. It declined in importance after the unification of Spain, but its citizens' heroic resistance to a long French siege (1808–09) caught the public imagination.

Sarajevo Capital of BOSNIA-HERZEGOVINA. The heir apparent to the Austro-Hungarian throne, Archduke FRANCIS FERDINAND, was assassinated here in 1914, an event that triggered World War I. In the fighting that followed the republic's declaration of independence from YUGOSLAVIA in 1992, Sarajevo was besieged and bombarded by Bosnian Serb forces. The siege was broken in 1995 and a peace accord was signed.

Saratoga campaign (1777) An operation devised by BURGOYNE to isolate New England from the other American colonies during the War of American INDEPENDENCE. He advanced south from Montreal expecting to meet Howe from New York and St Leger from Oswego at Albany and thus secure the line of the Hudson valley. Thanks to bad co-ordination, however, Howe chose this time to embark on his Philadelphia campaign. Burgoyne captured Ticonderoga but his advance was slowed by unsuitable equipment, lack of supplies, and guerrilla attacks. Defeated at BENNINGTON and Freeman's Farm, with no help forthcoming from Howe, he was halted, and forced to surrender to GATES. This British defeat encouraged France to enter the war in 1778 and was a vital tonic to the American cause.

Sarawak A state of MALAYSIA in western BORNEO. Ceded by the sultan of Brunei to Sir James BROOKE in 1841 after the latter had put down a revolt, Sarawak became an independent state under Brooke (the 'White Raja'). Although it became a British protectorate in 1888, it remained under the effective control of the Brooke family until the Japanese occupation of 1942–45. The Brooke family ceded it to Britain in 1946, and it became a crown colony. After a guerrilla war in 1962–63 during the run up to independence, it joined the Federation of Malaysia in 1963. Some fighting occurred there during the KONFRONTASI with Indonesia (1963–66).

Sarekat Islam An Indonesian Islamic political organization. Formed in 1911 as an association of Javanese batik traders to protect themselves against Chinese competition, it had developed, by the time of its first party congress in 1913, into a mass organization dedicated to self-government through constitutional means. Its leader H. Q. S. Cokroaminoto (1882–1934), was viewed by many as a latter-day Messiah, but the organization was weakened from within by the political challenge posed by the emergent PKI in the early 1920s; thereafter it gradually faded away as more radical nationalist parties, most prominently SUKARNO's PNI, were formed.

Sargon I AKKAD.

Sassanian empire An empire that occupied much of south-west Asia from the 3rd to the 7th century. It was founded *c.* 224 by Ardashir (ruled *c.* 224–41), who overthrew Artabanus V, the last PARTHIAN king, in the name of vengeance for the last ACHAEMENID king. The dynasty takes its name from his grandfather Sasan. Territorially the empire stretched from the Syrian desert, where Roman pressure was checked, to north-west India where the Kushan and Hephthalite empires, having restricted valuable trade routes, were eventually destroyed. Politically the empire fluctuated between centralization under strong monarchs like KHOSRAU I (d. 579), who were served by the army and bureaucracy, and local control by great nobles. The religious life of the empire was dominated by ZOROASTRIANISM, established as the state cult in the 3rd century. Christians in Armenia and Transcaucasia survived persecution and, by breaking with the Byzantine Church in 424, threw off the suspicion of alien loyalties. The court at Ctesiphon (in modern Iraq) provided a focus for a brilliant culture, enriched by Graeco-Roman and eastern influences, in which such pastimes as chess and polo were played. The closing years of the dynasty were overshadowed for the masses, however, by lengthy wars, which may explain the empire's rapid disintegration before the ARAB conquest of 636–51.

Satavahana A dynasty that ruled the north-west DECCAN of India, probably from the late 1st century BC until the 4th century AD. Its greatest king, Gautamiputra Satakarni (106–130 AD), consolidated his hold over the north-west Deccan, and extended his sway from coast to coast. Under his successors, Satavahana power gradually declined and had been entirely lost by the early 4th century. The little that is known about the kingdom and its administration depends on inscriptions in the cave temples which are a significant feature of this era, and on numismatic evidence.

Sato Eisaku (1901–75) Japanese statesman. As a supporter of YOSHIDA SHIGERU, he advocated co-operation with the USA in the immediate post-war period. Forced from the cabinet over allegations of corruption in 1954, he returned four years later and between 1964 and 1972 served as Prime Minister. He overcame a period of student violence, oversaw the extension of the revised United States Security Treaty (1970), negotiated with the USA for the return of OKINAWA and the other Ryukyu islands, and normalized relations with South Korea. After leaving office he received a Nobel Peace Prize for his efforts to make Japan a nuclear-free zone.

satrap A provincial governor of the ACHAEMENIDS, as first established by DARIUS I (the Great) who divided his empire up into twenty satrapies. Although the satraps nominally owed allegiance to the king, the considerable power and autonomy vested in them fostered disloyalty and there were frequent uprisings, the most notable being that of 366–358 BC against ARTAXERXES II. Alexander the Great retained the system after his conquest, as did the Parthians, but under the SASSANIAN EMPIRE the term 'satrap' designated a less important figure.

satyagraha (Hindi, 'holding to the truth') A policy of civil disobedience employing PASSIVE RESISTANCE, developed by Mohandas GANDHI in South Africa and widely used in India as a weapon against British rule. Frequently, campaigns of civil disobedience have degenerated into violence, but the method has had some success against liberal governments reluctant to use force. The technique continued to be employed in India and elsewhere after 1947, for example in Goa in 1955, when the satyagrahis were fired on and defeated.

Saud The ruling family of Saudi Arabia. Originally established at Dariyya in Wadi Hanifa, Nejd, in the 15th century, its fortunes grew after 1745 when Muhammad ibn Saud allied himself with the Islamic revivalist Abd al-Wahhab (WAHHABISM), who later became the spiritual guide of the family. The first wave of Saudi expansion ended with defeat by Egypt in 1818, but Saudi fortunes revived under Abd al-Aziz ibn Saud (*c.* 1880–1953), who captured Riyadh (1902), al-Hasa (1913), Asir (1920–26), Hail (1921), and the HEJAZ (1924–25), thus assembling the territories that formed the kingdom of SAUDI ARABIA in 1932. He imposed a settled way of life onto many of the nomadic tribes, but reduced tribal conflicts and crime, especially crimes against pilgrims travelling to Mecca. He granted drilling rights to US oil companies to exploit Saudi oil, much of the revenue from which was spent by the royal family. Abd al-Aziz was succeeded by his sons Saud (1953–64), whose lack of administrative control and extravagant lifestyle almost bankrupted the country, FAISAL IBN ABD AL-AZIZ (1964–75), Khalid (1975–82), and Fahd (1982–   ). Fahd briefly handed power over to Crown Prince Abdullah in late 1995, after suffering a stroke, but resumed control of the country in February 1996.

Saudi Arabia A country in south-west Asia occupying most of the peninsula of Arabia.

Physical. A plateau of deserts rises to mountains in the south and falls away to a low plain in the east. It is dry, hot, and often windy. The ground varies between rock, gravel, and bare sand, and little grows except in the oases and along the Red Sea coast, where slight seasonal rain makes possible the cultivation of dates and a few cereals.

Economy. With a quarter of the world's oil reserves, the Saudi economy and exports are dominated by crude oil, extracted mainly by the state-owned ARAMCO company. Oil-refining, and the manufacture of cement, fertilizers, and steel are the main areas of industry. Agriculture suffers from poor rainfall and moving sands, but investment in irrigation and livestock production has resulted in self-sufficiency in some foodstuffs. The natural resources of the former Neutral Zone with Kuwait are shared.

History. Saudi Arabia was formed from territories assembled by the SAUD family, who were followers of WAHHABISM, and proclaimed as the kingdom of Saudi Arabia in 1932. The early years of the kingdom were difficult, when revenues fell as a result of the declining Muslim pilgrim trade to Mecca and Medina. An oil concession was awarded to the US firm Standard of California in 1933 and oil was exported in 1938. In 1944 the oil company was re-formed as the Arabian American Oil Company (ARAMCO), and Saudi Arabia was recognized as having the world's largest reserves of oil. Since the death of Abd al-Aziz ibn Saud (1953) efforts have been made to modernize the administration by the passing of a series of new codes of conduct to conform both with Islamic tradition and 20th-century developments. The Saudi Arabian Minister for Petroleum and Natural Resources, Sheikh Ahmad Yemani, ably led the OPEC in controlling oil prices in the 1970s. King Fahd succeeded to the throne after the death (1982) of his half-brother, Khalid. There were various Saudi initiatives for peace in the Middle East in the 1980s, and that of 1989 finally resolved the crisis in LEBANON by the Taif Accord. In 1990 a US-led multinational coalition sent troops to protect Saudi oil fields from potential Iraqi invasion. The GULF WAR that followed had destabilizing social effects, with pro-democracy liberals and Islamic fundamentalists voicing criticism of the regime of King Fahd. In 1992 King Fahd announced the creation, by royal decree, of a Consultative Council, comprising 60 members chosen by the King every four years. The council, inaugurated in 1993, is to have an advisory and not a legislative function, the King having expressed his view that democracy is not suited to the Gulf region. There has been international concern over the abuse of human rights and the incidence of public executions in Saudi Arabia.

CAPITAL:	Riyadh (royal); Jiddah (administrative); Mecca (religious)
AREA:	2,240,000 sq km (865,000 sq miles)
POPULATION:	18.426 million (1996)
CURRENCY:	1 Saudi riyal = 100 halalah
RELIGIONS:	Muslim (mostly Sunni) 98.8%; Christian 0.8%
ETHNIC GROUPS:	Saudi Arab (including Bedouin 27.0%) 82.0%; Hemeni Arab 9.6%; other Arab 3.4%
LANGUAGES:	Arabic (official)
INTERNATIONAL ORGANIZATIONS:	UN; Arab League; GCC; OAPEC; OPEC

Saul (11th century BC) The first King of the Israelites (*c.* 1020–*c.* 1000 BC). Following the PHILISTINES' capture of the Ark of the Covenant (the most sacred object of the Israelites) and the destruction of Shiloh and its ruling priesthood, Saul united the tribes of Israel in order to defeat the Ammonites at Jabesh-Gilead, after which he was crowned king. Initially supported by the prophet SAMUEL, he provoked Samuel's anger by usurping some

of his priestly duties. Saul's later years were dominated by DAVID's rise to power. David's military successes and friendship with his son Jonathan provoked Saul's jealousy, and he banished David. This further increased support for David, whom Samuel had secretly anointed king. When Saul and Jonathan were killed fighting the Philistines at Mount Gilboa, David assumed leadership of the tribe of Judah.

Savage, Michael Joseph (1872–1940) New Zealand statesman. Having settled in New Zealand in 1907, he joined the Labour Party on its foundation, entering Parliament in 1919 and becoming deputy-leader in 1923. He took over as leader in 1933 on the death of Harry Holland, and became Prime Minister in 1935 after Labour's landslide victory. Savage, who is best remembered for his insistent advocacy of the Social Security Act, was one of the most popular of the country's political leaders.

Savonarola, Girolamo (1452–98) Italian Dominican friar noted for his vehement denunciations of religious and political corruption. As prior of the convent at San Marco in Florence, he attracted large audiences for his attacks on corruption in church and state in his Lent sermons of 1485–86. His prophecies of doom seemed vindicated when Charles VIII of France invaded in 1494. The feeble policy of the MEDICI led to their expulsion, and Savonarola briefly led a democratic republic of Florence. The Duke of Milan, and the notoriously corrupt Pope Alexander VI opposed him, and, when the French withdrew in 1497, the excommunicated leader was isolated. Refusal to undergo ordeal by fire was followed by his trial, crucifixion, and burning. The Medici were restored to power in 1512.

Savoy A region and former kingdom in north-west Italy. It was ruled by the Savoy dynasty for nine centuries, from 1003. It gained in importance through its strategic control of the Alpine passes, and from the family's ability to hold the political balance between the HOLY ROMAN EMPIRE and the PAPACY, Spain, and France, and subsequently between France and Austria. The power of Savoy in Piedmont increased from the 11th century. A strong military tradition was built up as the dynasty acquired the ducal title of Savoy (1416), and the royal title of King of Sicily (1713). Dominion over Sicily was exchanged in 1720 for control of Sardinia.

Saxe, Maurice, Comte de (Maurice, Count of Saxony) (1696–1750) Marshal of France and one of the best known military theorists of his age. He was an illegitimate son of AUGUSTUS II (the Strong), and was half-German and half-Swedish. In the War of the AUSTRIAN SUCCESSION he won a series of victories, including FONTENOY, and gained control of most of the Austrian Netherlands, which strengthened France's position at the Treaty of AIX-LA-CHAPELLE (1748).

Saxons A group of Germanic tribes, possibly named from their single-edged *seax* ('sword'). Under pressure from the migrating FRANKS they spread from their homelands on the Danish peninsula into Italy and the Frisian lands and engaged in piracy on the North Sea and English Channel between the 3rd and 5th centuries. They appear to have entered Britain, together with ANGLES and JUTES as mercenaries in the late period of the Roman occupation. By the 5th century their settlements had marked the beginning of ANGLO-SAXON England.

Their name survives in Wessex ('West Saxons'), Essex ('East Saxons'), and Sussex ('South Saxons') in England, as well as in Saxony in Germany.

Saxony A former duchy and kingdom in north Germany, now a state (Land) of Germany. The SAXONS expanded their territories in northern Europe during the DARK AGES and conquered many lesser tribes, before they were defeated in battle by CHARLEMAGNE and converted to Christianity. On the collapse of the Carolingian empire the Saxon duchy survived and expanded, reaching its greatest extent under HENRY THE LION; however, the state was dismembered in 1180, with only the part taken by Bernhard of Anhalt retaining the name. In 1423 it came to Landgrave Frederick the Warrior and, as an 'electorate' of the HOLY ROMAN EMPIRE, remained with his descendants.

In 1806 Elector Frederick Augustus III allied with Napoleon; that same year Saxony joined the CONFEDERATION OF THE RHINE and became a kingdom. Despite losing territory to Prussia at the Congress of VIENNA, Saxony remained the fifth largest constituent of the GERMAN CONFEDERATION. Under moderately liberal rulers its constitution of 1831 survived until 1918, while industrialization gained from membership of the ZOLLVEREIN. The kingdom survived the REVOLUTIONS OF 1848 and declared for Austria in the Austro-Prussian war of 1866. This resulted in an indemnity of 10 million thalers to Prussia, and an obligation to join the North German Confederation. Incorporated into the GERMAN SECOND EMPIRE in 1871, it earned the nickname 'Red Saxony' owing to its workers' strong support for the Social Democratic Party. After 1918 it became a state of the WEIMAR REPUBLIC and then of the THIRD REICH. After World War II, Saxony was initially in the Soviet Occupation Zone and, in 1949, became a state of the German Democratic Republic. Saxony became a *Land* (state) of reunified Germany in 1990.

Sayyid dynasty Muslim rulers of the Delhi sultanate in northern India (1414–51). They seized power from the TUGHLUQS, but never equalled their predecessors' imperial pretensions. Rival neighbours soon threatened their claims even in the north, and in 1448 their last sultan abandoned Delhi, to be replaced three years later by the Afghan LODIS. The name 'Sayyid' reflected the family's claim to be direct descendants of the Prophet Muhammad.

scalawag A White supporter of the Republican reconstruction programme in the American South in the early years after the AMERICAN CIVIL WAR. Like the CARPETBAGGERS with whom they associated, the scalawags were a diverse group including some profiteers, but also businessmen, reformers, former Southern Whigs, and poor yeoman farmers who supported the Republican regime.

Scandinavia The northernmost part of Europe, traditionally Denmark, Norway, and Sweden; a broader definition of the area also includes Finland, Iceland, and the North Atlantic islands that have come within Scandinavia's influence during the past thousand years.

Physical. The Scandinavian Peninsula shelters the shallow Gulf of Bothnia and the Baltic Sea. During the Pleistocene Epoch huge and heavy ice-sheets eroded the rocks, leaving innumerable glacial valleys, fiords, and lakes. Jostedalsbreen in western Norway is Europe's largest ice-field outside Iceland: Lake Vänern in southern Sweden is one of Europe's largest lakes. Norway's western mountains rise to the Glittertind Mountains at 2,470 m (8,104 feet), and the fiords cut deeply into them. A ridge of mountains running down the spine of the peninsula has slopes which fall abruptly westwards to the serrated and densely islanded coast of the Norwegian Sea. The peninsula is rich in iron and copper. The north, which contains Lapland, lies within the Arctic Circle, but the western coastal climate is tempered by the North Atlantic Drift. There is frequent snow in winter, when the nights are long and dark and the eastern coasts are ice-bound.

History. In the VIKING Age (c. 800–1050), Scandinavia was an important centre of civilization that sent colonists to Iceland, the North Atlantic islands, and Greenland. Scandinavian rulers also dominated much of England, Ireland, Normandy, Finland, and western Russia. This primarily sea-borne civilization also made contact with the shores of North America. By the early 11th century, the national kingdoms of NORWAY, DENMARK, and SWEDEN were well-established. A period of further overseas conquest was followed by Scandinavian unification when in 1397 the rulers of Denmark set up the Union of KALMAR. The secession of Sweden under GUSTAVUS I (Vasa) in 1523 heralded a long period of disunion, despite common acceptance of reformed religion. Sweden's swift rise to European prominence in the 17th century owed much to the inspirational leadership of GUSTAVUS II (Adolphus) and his Chancellor OXENSTIERNA. It eclipsed Denmark–Norway as a Baltic power, and until the Great Northern War (1700–21) held the balance of power in Europe as a whole. Thereafter it gradually declined in importance. Sweden and Norway were once again united from 1814 until 1905.

Scanian War (1676–78) A struggle between Denmark and Sweden for the latter's southernmost province of Scania. For centuries it was controlled by Denmark but was gained by Charles X of Sweden at the Treaty of ROSKILDE in 1658. Christian V of Denmark invaded Scania and was welcomed by the population. Charles XI of Sweden fought back in a harsh campaign and finally won a pitched battle at Lund (3 December 1676); the victory was acknowledged in the Treaty of Lund (1679), and Scania was ceded to Sweden.

Scapa Flow A stretch of sea in the Orkney Islands, Scotland, used as a British naval base. In May 1919 the terms of the VERSAILLES PEACE SETTLEMENT relating to the surrender of German arms after WORLD WAR I were submitted to the Germans, who protested vigorously. As an act of defiance, orders were given by Admiral von Reuter to scuttle and sink the entire German High Seas Fleet of 71 warships, then interned at Scapa Flow. In October 1939 the defences of Scapa Flow were penetrated when a German U-boat sank HMS *Royal Oak*.

Schacht, Hjalmar (1877–1970) German financier. As Commissioner of Currency (1923) he applied a rigorous monetary policy to stabilize the mark after its collapse in that year. He took part in REPARATIONS negotiations but rejected the YOUNG PLAN (1929). Under HITLER he became Minister of Economics (1934–37), responsible for Nazi programmes on unemployment and rearmament. Rivalry with GOERING caused his resignation. In 1944 he was imprisoned in a concentration camp for his alleged involvement in the JULY PLOT to assassinate Hitler. At the NUREMBERG TRIALS (1946) he was acquitted.

Scharnhorst, Gerhard Johann David von

(1755–1813) Prussian general and military reformer. He served in the Hanoverian army before entering the Prussian army in 1801. Following NAPOLEON's defeats of Prussia (1806–07) Scharnhorst began his reform of the Prussian army, converting it from a mercenary to a conscripted force. He abolished capital punishment and promoted non-aristocrats to the officer corps. He resigned in 1812 when Prussia was forced into an alliance with Napoleon against Russia. France's defeat before Moscow enabled Prussia to join the anti-French coalition (1813), and Scharnhorst returned as chief of staff to BLÜCHER.

Scheer, Reinhard (1863–1928) German admiral. After winning fame as a submarine expert, he commanded the High Seas Fleet during World War I (1916–18). His hopes of dividing and defeating the British Grand Fleet at JUTLAND (1916) failed, but his brilliant manoeuvring saved his own fleet. In October 1918 the German fleet at Kiel mutinied under him, refusing to put out to sea. The mutiny spread rapidly to north-west Germany, and by November Germany had accepted an end to World War I.

Schirach, Baldur von (1907–74) German Nazi youth leader. An enthusiastic Nazi while still a student, from 1933 to 1945 he led the HITLER YOUTH. In 1940 he was appointed governor of Vienna, where he took part in plans to ship Vienna's Jews to CONCENTRATION CAMPS. He was found guilty at the NUREMBERG TRIALS and sentenced to 20 years' imprisonment.

Schleswig–Holstein A state (*Land*) of northern Germany, formerly the subject of a long-running dispute involving Prussia, Austria, and Denmark (the Schleswig–Holstein question). Both Schleswig and Holstein were originally duchies owing allegiance to the Danish crown. At the Congress of VIENNA (1814) Holstein was incorporated into the Austrian-led GERMAN CONFEDERATION. In 1848 Denmark incorporated Schleswig, but the German-speaking population gained support from the German Parliament at Frankfurt and Prussian troops invaded Denmark. Britain, Russia, and France intervened to oblige Prussia to agree to an armistice, and under the London Protocol of 1852 Denmark retained its traditional rights in the duchies. However, Denmark in 1864 again incorporated Schleswig, provoking Prussian and Austrian troops to invade and defeat the Danish army. In 1866, after the AUSTRO-PRUSSIAN WAR, Prussia annexed both duchies. Following World War I there were plebiscites and much of north Schleswig passed to Denmark as the province of South Jutland. Between the wars the existence of a German minority in the province created considerable tension. After World War II over three million refugees from East Germany crowded into Schleswig–Holstein and the area was reorganized to become a West German state.

Schlieffen, Alfred, Graf von (1833–1913) German field-marshal and strategist. He is remembered mainly as the author of the Schlieffen Plan, which formed the basis for the German attack in 1914. According to the plan, Germany could fight on two fronts by descending through Belgium and neutralizing France in a swift

campaign, and then attacking Russia. The plan failed because of French resistance and a lack of manoeuvrability in Germany's armed forces. It was abandoned when Germany's leaders decided to withdraw forces from the WESTERN FRONT to stem Russian advances into East Prussia. In 1940 Hitler successfully employed the principles of the Schlieffen Plan in his BLITZKRIEG or 'lightning war' in the west.

Schmalkaldic War (1546–47) A brief and indecisive phase in the struggle between the Roman Catholic emperor CHARLES V and the Protestant party within the HOLY ROMAN EMPIRE. The defensive League of Schmalkalden was formed in the town of that name by Protestant states in 1531. It was led by PHILIP OF HESSE and John Frederick I of Saxony. The emperor was heavily committed elsewhere and did not come face to face with the League until 1546. Then he crushed the League with the help of Duke Maurice of Saxony, winning a notable victory at the battle of Mühlberg (24 April 1547).

Schmidt, Helmut (1918–) German statesman. A member of the Social Democratic Party, he was elected to the Bundestag (Parliament of the Federal Republic of Germany) in 1953, becoming Minister of Defence (1969–72) and of Finance (1972–74). Elected federal Chancellor in 1974, following the resignation of Willy BRANDT, he served for a second period (1978–82), during which he increasingly lost the support of the left wing of his party and of the Green Party. He sought to continue the Brandt policy of OSTPOLITIK or dialogue with the German Democratic Republic and the Soviet Union.

scholasticism The educational tradition of the medieval 'schools' (universities), which flourished in the 12th and 13th centuries. It was a method of philosophical and theological enquiry that aimed at a better understanding of Christian doctrine by a process of definition and systematic argument. Medieval philosophers often wrote in a very formal style, derived from the dominant pattern of teaching in the universities. First they raised a particular question, then they expounded the views of several previous philosophers or Church authorities on the question and criticized them in turn; finally the author presented and defended his own answer, often drawing attention to minute points of agreement and disagreement with his predecessors.

The writings of Aristotle (translated into Latin by BOETHIUS) and of St AUGUSTINE OF HIPPO played a crucial part in the development of scholastic thought. Scholastics did not always agree on points of theology; AQUINAS and DUNS SCOTUS, for instance, argued from very different standpoints. Scholasticism declined in the later Middle Ages; in the 14th century the writings of WILLIAM OF OCCAM challenged the scholastic position by stressing the opposition between faith and reason.

In the best hands, the scholastic method of presentation conveyed the impression of a powerful, original mind exploiting the resources of an active intellectual tradition. Lesser writers merely adopted the formulas of argument, contributing little but dry and pointless distinctions. The pejorative use of the term derives from this latter group.

school systems Systems for the provision of public primary and secondary education. Until the late 18th century most schooling was controlled by religious

book

organizations and the concept of education for all had only emerged in a few Calvinist countries such as Scotland, the Netherlands, and the New England colonies of America. From this time onward however, state systems began to develop. France (1791) and Prussia (1807) were the first countries to establish secular state primary and secondary schools, with Napoleon imposing the French system on most of Western Europe (in France the system reverted to Church control after 1814). From the early 19th century each state in the USA was obliged by the federal government to provide a secular school system.

In England church schools and SUNDAY SCHOOLS were the main providers of primary education and mass education was pioneered by the monitorial system of Joseph Lancaster. There were not sufficient schools in towns, however, and the Elementary Education Act (1870) required local authorities to provide schools where needed. Secondary education was provided largely by fee-paying grammar schools and 'public' (in fact, private) schools. The Education Act of 1902 established a state system for both primary and secondary education, later supplemented by the Butler Act (1944).

Since the 19th century, many schools throughout the world have been set up according to the systems developed in the industrialized countries of the West. Four systems acted as models: the Prussian, in mid-19th-century Russia and Turkey; the French, in much of western Europe, Egypt, the Middle East, French-speaking Africa, and much of South-east Asia; the US system throughout much of South America, China, and Japan, where a national system of universal education was established in 1871; and the British in India and throughout the COMMONWEALTH. The state system provides the great majority of school places in most countries, but often a parallel system of independent education remains in place. Most schools are co-educational, but traditional single-sex schools survive and are becoming more numerous in Islamic countries. Sometimes control of the system is highly centralized, as in Japan, France, and, formerly, the Soviet Union. In the USA and Australia, responsibility devolves to states. In Switzerland there are said to be as many school systems (26) as there are cantons. The introduction of a National Curriculum in the late 1980s marked a shift towards centralization in Britain.

Some systems, as in the UK and the USA, are comprehensive. That is, children can expect to continue from the beginning of primary education to the end of compulsory schooling without hindrance. Elsewhere secondary school places are limited (as in much of the developing world) or schools are academically selective and entrance is by examination. In some countries, only half day of schooling can be offered. In industrialized countries, children typically learn basic literacy and numeracy in primary school. In secondary school, from about 11, children gradually specialize – often after some three years – in arts or science subjects and vocational studies may begin. Examination success at the end of secondary school, at around 16 to 18 years of age, gains entry to some form of higher education. At every stage, some children drop out from lack of money, pressure to earn, lack of motivation, or simply because there are not enough schools.

Schuman Plan (9 May 1950) A proposal drafted by Jean MONNET and put forward by the French Foreign Minister Robert Schuman. It aimed initially to pool the coal and steel industries of France and the Federal Republic of Germany under a common authority that other European nations might join. The Plan became effective in 1952 with the formation of the European Coal and Steel Community, to which Italy, Belgium, Holland, and Luxembourg as well as France and West Germany belonged. Britain declined to join. Its success ultimately led to the formation of the EUROPEAN ECONOMIC COMMUNITY.

Schuschnigg, Kurt von (1897–1977) Austrian statesman, who became Chancellor following the murder of DOLLFUSS (1934). He considered his main task to be the prevention of German absorption of Austria. Although an Austro-German Agreement (July 1936) guaranteed Austrian independence, Hitler accused him of breaking it. In February 1938 Hitler obliged him to accept Nazis in his cabinet. His attempt to hold a plebiscite on Austrian independence was prevented and he was forced to resign. On 12 March German troops invaded Austria without resistance in the ANSCHLUSS.

Schwarzenberg, Felix, Prince of (1800–52) Austrian statesman. A career diplomat, Schwarzenberg joined the army of Field-Marshal Joseph RADETZKY on the outbreak of the REVOLUTIONS OF 1848. He persuaded the ageing Ferdinand I to abdicate in favour of his nephew, FRANCIS I. Opposed to granting autonomy to Austria's many states, Schwarzenberg drew up a constitution (1849) that transformed the Habsburg empire into a unitary, centralized, and absolutist state with strengthened imperial powers. The Hungarian nationalist uprising was crushed (1849) with Russian aid, and Habsburg supremacy was restored in northern Italy. He secured the revival of a strengthened GERMAN CONFEDERATION, which maintained a precarious balance of power with PRUSSIA.

Schwarzenberg, Karl Philipp, Prince of (1771–1820) Austrian field-marshal. He entered the imperial cavalry in 1787. His courage at the battles of Hohenlinden (1800) and Ulm (1805) saved many Austrian lives, and he was then appointed vice-president of the supreme imperial war cabinet in Vienna, where he was responsible for raising a popular militia to defend Austrian homelands. As general of cavalry he fought at the unsuccessful Battle of WAGRAM (1809), after which Austria made peace with Napoleon in the Treaty of Schönbrunn. Schwarzenberg negotiated (1810) the marriage between Napoleon and Marie-Louise, daughter of the Austrian emperor, who in 1811 agreed to assist Napoleon in his forthcoming campaign against Russia. After Napoleon's failure to capture Moscow (1812) Schwarzenberg skilfully withdrew his troops back to Austria. Next year, when Austria joined Russia, Prussia, and Sweden to fight Napoleon (August 1813), he was appointed commander-in-chief of the Austrian Army and was the senior commander at the battle of LEIPZIG in October. He attended the Congress of VIENNA and then retired.

Scientific Revolution The revolution in human knowledge and understanding of the universe that took place in the 16th and 17th centuries. Although the RENAISSANCE spirit of enquiry led such astronomers as Copernicus (1473–1543), Kepler (1571–1630), and Galileo (1564–1642) to overthrow the medieval notion of the

Earth as the centre of the universe, it was not until the early 17th century that their theories began to gain wide acceptance.

The 17th century was an age of intellectual activity marked by great progress in science. Unbiased enquiry, shrinking from no conclusion merely because it was unorthodox and testing all conclusions by experiment and observation, characterized the work of leading scientists. An early figure was Francis BACON not himself a scientist but a philosopher who saw theology as the study of God's mind and science as the study of God's works by means of experiment. With the emerging division of science into its various branches, progress was made in chemistry by Robert Boyle (1627–91), in medicine by William Harvey (1578–1657), with his discovery of the circulation of the blood, and above all in mathematics and physics by Sir Isaac Newton (1642–1727), whose assurance that everything in heaven or on earth was comprehensible in terms of reason, affected all branches of Western thought and research. Scientific discovery forged ahead in all fields. Electricity was first described by William Gilbert in 1600. Meetings of scientists to exchange information had begun during the English Civil War (1642–49) but their gatherings were given royal patronage by CHARLES II (1662) when the ROYAL SOCIETY was founded. By the 18th century the application of science to industry, with the invention of the steam engine and advances in textile manufacture, marked the beginning of the INDUSTRIAL REVOLUTION.

Scipio, Aemilianus Africanus Numantinus
(185–129 BC) Roman general. Grandson by adoption of Publius Cornelius SCIPIO, he earned the titles 'Africanus' for his destruction of Carthage in the Third PUNIC WAR and 'Numantinus' for his later capture of Numantia in Spain. Rapid promotion gave him command of the war in Africa in 147, during which he blockaded Carthage and levelled the site (146). He died suddenly and suspiciously in 129. He was at the centre of the intellectual group called the 'Scipionic Circle', which included the historian POLYBIUS.

Scipio, Publius Cornelius (236–184 BC) Roman general, later entitled 'Africanus Major' for his part in defeating Carthage on the African mainland in the Second PUNIC WAR. After the Roman defeats at Ticinus and Cannae he rallied the aristocracy and the army. His tactics of aggression led to campaigns in Spain and his landing in Africa in 204 to win the battle of Zama (202). He retired from public life after being accused by CATO (the Elder) of corruption in 184.

Scopes case (July 1925) The US legal case in which John T. Scopes, a biology teacher in Dayton, Tennessee, was charged with violating state law by teaching Darwin's theory of evolution. The state legislature had enacted (1925) that it was unlawful to teach any doctrine denying the literal truth of the account of the creation as presented in the Authorized (King James) Version of the Bible. The judge ruled out any discussion of constitutional legality and since Scopes clearly had taught Darwin's theory of evolution he was convicted and fined $100. On appeal to the Supreme Court the constitutionality of the state's law was upheld, but Scopes was acquitted on the technicality that he had been 'fined excessively'. The law was repealed in 1967.

However, CHRISTIAN FUNDAMENTALISTS in the USA continue to campaign vigorously for a return to creationist teaching.

Scotland A country in the north of Great Britain, a part of the UNITED KINGDOM since 1707.

Physical. Scotland comprises the northern part of the island of Great Britain, together with the Hebrides, Orkneys, Shetlands, and many smaller islands. The mainland, which is approximately 430 km (270 miles) from north to south, is made up of the northern Highlands (the largest part), the central Lowlands, and the Southern Uplands, each running from north-east to south-west. The Highlands include the Grampian Mountains, which rise to Ben Nevis, the highest peak in Great Britain. Scotland is separated from England by the Cheviot Hills and the Solway Firth and bounded on the north and west by the Atlantic Ocean and on the east by the North Sea. It has 3,700 km (2,300 miles) of coastline, because of its deeply indented lochs and firths (estuaries).

Economy. The traditional industries of coalmining and shipbuilding have declined, but manufacturing remains important. Only about one fourth of the land is under cultivation, mainly in the drier eastern valleys. Elsewhere sheep are grazed and cattle are pastured. The herring catch from the North Sea provides exports, as do valuable off-shore oil fields; whisky is also exported. Tourism is an important source of revenue.

History. Scotland was peopled in the early Middle Ages by five different races: PICTS, who by *c.* 500 had retreated to the north-east highlands; Britons, in the south-west; SCOTS, from Ireland, in Argyll and Galloway; ANGLES, in the Lothians; and from *c.* 800, VIKINGS in the far north and west. These peoples spoke different languages, and pursued agricultural and fishing economies when not at war with each other. Scotland was converted to Christianity in the 6th and 7th centuries by such missionaries as St COLUMBA, but the whole country was cut off from the rest of Europe by Norse encirclement.

In 1057 Scotland's first king MALCOLM III (Canmore) and his queen MARGARET established a dynasty that ruled the country for over two centuries. They and their successors, especially DAVID I, did much to civilize the land, introducing burghs and an urban economy, replacing tribal law with FEUDALISM and initiating church reforms (such as diocesan and parish organization).

In the 13th century EDWARD I's attempt to make Scotland subject to him, through the BALLIOL family, led to conflict with England. Intermittent warfare continued for the next 250 years; at times the Scots gained the upper hand, as at BANNOCKBURN under the leadership of ROBERT I (the Bruce), but they were seriously defeated at HALIDON HILL (1333), FLODDEN FIELD (1513), and PINKIE (1547).

In 1560 the Scottish Parliament accepted John KNOX's *Confession of Faith.* The Reformation caused Scotland to turn away from France, its main ally since the early 14th century, and to draw closer to England. James VI o Scotland became JAMES I of England in 1603, and in 1707 an Act of UNION joined the Parliaments of England and Scotland. Union brought great advantage to both countries during Britain's imperial and economic ascendancy, and Scotland experienced a remarkable ENLIGHTENMENT. In the late 18th century Scotland's industrial revolution began in the Lowlands, and the

19th century brought rapid growth in heavy industries. The increasing market for meat and wool led to the HIGHLAND CLEARANCES. In the 20th century Scotland's heavy industries declined, and new industries, such as microelectronics and North Sea oil, slowed but did not halt the country's relative economic decline. The downward trend continued during the 1980s and early 1990s as shipbuilding contracted and the oil-boom ended. This left Scotland facing high unemployment, alleviated in part by EU regional and social funding and UK regional enterprise grants for areas in industrial decline. Partly as a result of economic difficulties, the future of the union with England has been subject to periodic questioning; the SCOTTISH NATIONAL PARTY advocates complete independence from Britain. In 1979 a proposal to introduce devolution (limited home rule), failed to achieve support from the required 40% of the total electorate. Support for devolution rose once more in the 1980s and 1990s and a referendum on the issue in September 1997 saw a comfortable majority in favour of a Scottish parliament with tax-raising powers. Elections to the proposed parliament are scheduled for 1999.

Scots (or Dalriads) Celtic Irish settlers in what is today Scotland. In the early 6th century AD they settled Argyll (Ar Gael) after two centuries of raiding the coasts of Britain and Gaul. They overcame the northern PICTS in the Highlands and introduced the Celtic Gaelic language. The name 'Scotia' (Scotland), formerly a name for Hibernia (Ireland), passed to the land of CALEDONIA and the territories of the Picts.

Scots law The law applicable in Scotland, which remains resistant to the dominant influence of English law within the UK legal system. Scots law came under early Anglo-Saxon–Norman influence in the feudal period (11th to 13th centuries), but Scotland's later political and cultural alliance with France led to the importation during the 14th to 16th centuries of ROMAN LAW doctrines by Scottish law students returning from continental universities. The separate Scottish legal system, court structure, and procedures have been preserved until today, despite the union of the two kingdoms in 1603 and of the two parliaments in 1707. Scots law is more highly systematized, relying, like other civil law systems, more on general principles than on case law and precedent. The chief law officer in Scotland is known as the Lord Advocate and has ultimate responsibility for Crown prosecutions. The superior Scottish civil court is the Court of Session, and the superior criminal court is the High Court of Justiciary. The supreme Scottish civil court is the HOUSE OF LORDS in London.

Scott, Sir Robert Falcon (1868–1912) British polar explorer. Having entered the Royal Navy in 1881, Scott commanded the National Antarctic Expedition of 1900–04, surveying the interior of the continent, charting the Ross Sea, and discovering King Edward VII Land. On a second expedition (1910–12) Scott and four companions (E. A. Wilson, L. E. G. Oates, H. R. Bowers, and Edgar Evans) made a journey to the South Pole by sled, arriving there in January 1912 to discover that the Norwegian explorer Roald AMUNDSEN had beaten them to their goal by a month. On the journey back to base Scott and his companions were hampered by bad weather and illness, the last three finally dying of

starvation and exposure in March. Their bodies and diaries were discovered by a search party eight months later. Scott, a national hero, was posthumously knighted.

Scott, Winfield (1786–1866) US general. He joined the army in 1808 and distinguished himself in the WAR OF 1812. After serving in the BLACK HAWK WAR, acting as presidential emissary during the South Carolina NULLIFICATION CRISIS, and supervising the removal of the CHEROKEE to the south-west, he was appointed general-in-chief of the US Army (1841–61). His successful conduct of the march on Mexico City during the MEXICAN–AMERICAN WAR of 1846–48 made him a national hero. An opponent of secession of the Southern states, Scott was still in post at the outbreak of the AMERICAN CIVIL WAR, but retired some six months later.

Scottish Martyrs A group of political reformers who were persecuted for their beliefs during the period of unrest in Scotland in the 1790s. In 1792 a Society for the Friends of the People was formed to promote parliamentary reform. The government reacted strongly and Thomas Muir, a member of the society, was convicted of treason. In October 1793 a meeting of the Society was broken up by force, three of its delegates being subsequently sentenced to long terms of transportation. A group of radical reformers calling themselves the United Scotsmen continued to meet in secret, but after further trials the movement broke up.

Scottish National Party (SNP) A Scottish political party, formed in 1934 from a merger of the National Party of Scotland and the Scottish Party. The party, which campaigns for the complete independence of Scotland from Britian, gained its first parliamentary seat in 1945 at a by-election in Motherwell. In the October 1974 general election 11 of its candidates won parliamentary seats. In 1979 proposals to set up a Scottish representative assembly failed to elicit the required majority in a referendum and in the 1979 general election all but two of the candidates were defeated. Three were elected in 1987 and in 1992. However, in the 1997 general election the SNP increased its share of the vote and won six of Scotland's 72 parliamentary seats, thereby replacing the Conservatives (who lost all their Scottish representatives) as the main opposition to the Labour Party in Scotland. The SNP joined with Labour and the Liberal Democrats in supporting proposals for an independent Scottish parliament, which were approved in a referendum in September 1997.

Scottsboro case (1931) A US legal case in which nine black youths were falsely accused by two white girls of multiple rape on a train near Scottsboro, Alabama. They were found guilty and sentenced to death or long-term imprisonment. The sensational case highlighted race relations in Alabama and across the USA. The intervention of the Supreme Court and a series of retrials returned a verdict of not proven and all the Scottsboro boys were released in the years 1937–50.

'Scramble for Africa' The rapid European colonization of Africa, which began with the French occupation of Tunis (1881) and ended with the conclusion of the Second BOER WAR (1902). During this period almost the whole of Africa was partitioned between Belgium, Britain, France, Germany, Spain, and Portugal. Later Italy ousted Turkey from TRIPOLITANIA, having already taken possession of ERITREA, while France and Spain partitioned Morocco. The USA maintained an economic foothold in Liberia. Conferences in Berlin (1884) and Brussels (1890) settled the outlines of the new states. In all the events of the period the people most directly concerned, the inhabitants of the new colonies, were seldom consulted. After World War II resistance, until then largely muffled or suppressed, erupted in nationalist movements demanding independence (see AFRICAN DECOLONIZATION; 'WIND OF CHANGE').

Scullin, James Henry (1876–1953) Australian statesman. He was a goldminer, shopkeeper, and organizer for the Australian Workers' Union before becoming a Labor Member of the House of Representatives (1910–13). He was re-elected in 1922, led the Opposition (1928–29), and in 1929 became Prime Minister. In the DEPRESSION he faced deepening divisions within his own party, and deflationary measures brought electoral defeat. From 1932 he led the Opposition until his resignation as leader of the Labor Party in 1935.

scutage (or escutage) (from Latin *scutum*, 'shield') The payment (usually 20 shillings) made by a knight to the English king in lieu of military service. HENRY II raised seven scutages between 1157 and 1187. RICHARD I was tempted (1198) to turn scutage into an annual tax not necessarily connected with military needs. The barons' opposition to John's annual scutages (1201–06) was a factor in their revolt (1214) and was reflected in clause 12 of MAGNA CARTA (1215), which stated that the king was not to levy scutage without consent, except in recognized and reasonable cases.

Scythians A group of Indo-European tribes that briefly occupied part of Asia Minor in the 7th century BC before being driven out by the Medes. They subsequently established a kingdom in southern Russia and traded with the Greek cities of the Black Sea, but in about the 2nd century BC were compelled to move into the Crimea by the related Sarmatian tribe. They were a nomadic people, famed for their horsemanship and their skill as archers. When DARIUS I (the Great) attempted to subdue them in *c.* 512 BC, they successfully adopted a scorched-earth policy and *c.* 325 BC they crushed a large detachment of Macedonian troops before making peace with ALEXANDER THE GREAT. The graves of Scythian kings and nobles have revealed many objects of gold and bronze, which bear witness to outstanding technical and artistic skill.

Sea Peoples The various groups of sea-borne invaders who attacked the countries of the eastern Mediterranean in the later 13th and early 12th centuries BC. They probably included Greeks, Sardinians, and Tyrrhenians, though their activities and identities are indistinctly known. They were instrumental in causing the collapse of the HITTITE empire *c.* 1200 BC, and Egypt was attacked from the sea on several occasions. One group to settle successfully was the PHILISTINES.

SEATO SOUTH-EAST ASIA TREATY ORGANIZATION.

Second Front A term used in World War II to describe the opening of hostilities by US and UK forces on the mainland of Europe. The First Front (a term not used) was that on which the Soviet Union fought the AXIS POWERS in the east. From 1941 the Soviet government pressed for an early opening of the Second Front as a means of relieving heavy German pressure. The hope that it could be opened in 1942 was ended by Churchill's insistence that there was insufficient shipping. The disaster of the DIEPPE RAID (August 1942) confirmed this, although the Soviet and the US governments continued to criticize British hesitancy through 1943. When the NORMANDY LANDINGS eventually opened the Second Front in June 1944 it was clear that the operation was an immense enterprise that could easily have failed had it been undertaken too hastily.

Second Reich GERMAN SECOND EMPIRE.

Security Council UNITED NATIONS SECURITY COUNCIL.

Sedan, Battle of (1 September 1870) A battle fought on the River Meuse, near the Belgian frontier, between French and Prussian forces during the FRANCO-PRUSSIAN WAR. The Prussians, discovering that MACMAHON's army had set out to relieve Metz, diverted two armies marching on Paris and encircled the army of NAPOLEON III at Sedan. The French, under heavy shellfire, surrendered unconditionally. Napoleon III was taken prisoner, together with a large army. In World War II the Germans breached the MAGINOT LINE when they crossed the River Meuse at Sedan (1940).

Seddon, Richard John (1845–1906) New Zealand statesman. Arriving in New Zealand in 1866, he became the miners' advocate and was elected (1881) as parliamentary member for Kumara. He was Minister of Public Works in BALLANCE's first Liberal government and Premier from Ballance's death in 1893. Seddon oversaw the introduction of a range of radical legislation including low-interest credit for farmers, women's suffrage, REEVES's Industrial Conciliation and Arbitration Act old age pensions, free places in secondary schools, and a State Fire Insurance Office.

Sedgemoor, Battle of (6 July 1685) The decisive battle of MONMOUTH'S REBELLION, fought near Westonzoyland in Somerset. Monmouth was blocked in his retreat from Bristol by the army of JAMES II, commanded by Lord Feversham and John Churchill (later Duke of MARLBOROUGH). Monmouth attempted a night attack to give his raw recruits some advantage over the professional royalist army, but his plans miscarried and he suffered a crushing defeat. The battle proved to be the last fought on English soil.

Seeckt, Hans von (1866–1936) German general. He had gained his experience of warfare in eastern Europe and the Balkans in World War I and skilfully rebuilt the German army during the WEIMAR REPUBLIC (1919–33). Although this was limited by the VERSAILLES PEACE SETTLEMENT to 100,000 men, he trained his soldiers as an efficient nucleus for a much larger army. The secret agreement concluded after the Treaty of RAPALLO (1922) permitting German troops to train in the Soviet Union enabled him to circumvent the peace treaty. His work enabled Hitler to expand the army rapidly.

Seku Ahmadu Lobbo (*c.* 1775–1845) West African religious leader. A student of UTHMAN DAN FODIO, Ahmadu participated in Uthman's *jihad* (or holy war) before settling in the province of Macina (in Mali), where he founded an independent Muslim community. Expelled from Macina by the pagan king of Segu, he established new capital at Hamdullahi and in 1818 proclaimed a *jihad*, capturing Macina, and extending his authority around it. He established a strictly theocratic Muslim Fulani state which survived until 1859, when it was absorbed in the Tukulor empire of UMAR IBN SAID TAL.

Selden, John (1584–1654) English lawyer, historian, and antiquary. Although not a Puritan, he used his knowledge of the law on Parliament's behalf in its conflicts with Charles I, and was repeatedly imprisoned. A member of most of the Parliaments after 1621, he was active in the impeachment of BUCKINGHAM (1626), and helped to draw up the PETITION OF RIGHT (1628).

selectors Small farmers in Australia during the second half of the 19th century. By the 1850s, SQUATTERS had acquired much of the best agricultural land. Increasing demands were made, especially by those who had come during the gold rushes of the 1850s, for remaining land to be made available for small farms, at low cost. Selection before survey (hence the name 'selectors') was introduced in all of the colonies between 1858 and 1872. Factors causing the failure of many selectors included the unsuitability of much Australian land for agriculture, lack of capital, and opposition from squatters.

Seleucid The Macedonian dynasty that ruled an Asian empire from 312 BC when Seleucus I, who had served ALEXANDER THE GREAT, gained Media and Susiana to add to Babylon. His subsequent expansion was westwards: he occupied Syria, where he founded Antioch in 300 BC, and by defeating Lysimachus in 281, secured control of Asia Minor. Under his successors Syria and Asia Minor were lost and regained more than once, while in the east Bactria asserted its independence and the Parthian kingdom was established. Antiochus III (ruled 223–187 BC) forced both these kingdoms to acknowledge his lordship. He also recovered Syria and Palestine, but when he conquered Thrace and then invaded Greece, he came into conflict with Rome. He was defeated at THERMOPYLAE and Magnesia, and made peace in 188 on terms which excluded him from Asia Minor. Thereafter Seleucid power declined – Tyre regained its independence in 126 BC, as did other cities and chiefdoms – until in 64 BC Syria became a Roman province.

Self-Denying Ordinance (3 April 1645) An English parliamentary regulation under which all Members of Parliament had to resign their military commands. Oliver CROMWELL was determined to create an efficient national army controlled and paid from Westminster, rather than by the counties. The House of Lords amended the Ordinance, so that it was possible for certain Members of Parliament to be reappointed to the NEW MODEL ARMY, thereby enabling Cromwell to continue his military career as lieutenant-general under commander-in-chief Sir Thomas Fairfax.

Self-help SMILES, SAMUEL.

Self-Strengthening Movement A Chinese military and political reform movement of the second half of the 19th century. Initiated in the early 1860s by Feng Guifen and supported by ZENG GUOFAN, ZUO ZONGTANG, LI HONGZHANG, and Prince Gong, the Self-Strengthening Movement attempted to adapt Western institutions and military innovations to Chinese needs. Prominent among the innovations introduced were the Zongli Yamen (1861), an imperial office established to manage relations with foreign countries, the Jiangnan Arsenal (1865), the Nanjing Arsenal (1867), the Beiyang fleet (1888) (China's first modern navy), and various government-sponsored modern industries. Such reforms, however, were superficial and failed to solve deep-seated institutional problems, as was made clear by China's humiliation in the SINO-JAPANESE WAR of 1894–95.

Selim I (c. 1470–1520) Ottoman sultan (1512–20), known in English as 'the Grim', though 'Relentless' better conveys the meaning of his name in Turkish. Recalled from Crimean exile after an aborted attempt to ensure his own succession, he defeated and killed his brother Ahmed in 1513. In 1514, responding to Safavid-inspired subversion in Asia Minor, he crushed a Persian army at Chaldiran. Turning against the MAMELUKES, he next conquered Syria and Egypt and took the titles of CALIPH and protector of the holy cities of MECCA and Medina.

Seljuks A Turkish dynasty that achieved its greatest power in the late 11th century. Its early members rose to prominence as mercenaries, raising Turkish nomad troops to serve and ultimately to challenge the Ghaznavids. By 1055, under the leadership of Tughrul Beg, they had entered Baghdad and subjected the eastern lands of the Muslim empire to their control, while maintaining the fiction of an ABBASID caliphate and using the existing administrative system and such talented officials as the vizier Nizam al-Mulk. Reaching their apogee under Alp Arslan (1063–72) and Malik Shah (1072–92), they disturbed the existing regional balance of power, crushing the Byzantines at MANZIKERT, and, by interrupting the PILGRIMAGE to Jerusalem, indirectly provoking the First CRUSADE. They were ultimately undermined by the turbulence of their own nomad troops among a settled population and by the rivalries of ambitious subordinates. Their decline in the early 12th century was, however, soon followed by the emergence in Asia Minor of the Seljuk sultanate of Rum, centred on Konya, under Kilij Arslan II (1155–92). Under Kaykobad I (1220–37) this regime achieved great splendour, but it suffered a crushing defeat at MONGOL hands at Kösedagh in 1243 and became a dependency of the Mongol Il-Khans of Persia until its extinction in 1308.

Seminole Wars (1816–18, 1835–42) Two Native American wars in the US south-east. Natives of Florida, the Seminole retaliated against US military forces sent into their area in search of escaped slaves. Andrew JACKSON's subsequent punitive expedition forced the Seminole south into the Everglades. In 1819 Spain ceded east Florida to the USA, and in 1832 the Seminole were forced to sign a treaty involving their removal to the Indian Territory west of the Mississippi (TRAIL OF TEARS). A substantial part of the tribe under OSCEOLA refused to move and held out in the Everglades until Osceola was treacherously captured and most of his followers exterminated. General William T. Worth then ordered (1841) that the Seminoles' crops be burned and their villages destroyed. Starved into surrender, the Seminole signed a peace treaty (1842) and accepted their deportation westwards.

Semites A group of peoples of the Middle East, including the JEWISH PEOPLE and the ARABS. According to the Bible they were descended from Shem, the son of Noah. The original Semites were farmers in Arabia who spread north and west to create some of the major empires of antiquity. The inhabitants of AKKAD who overthrew the Sumerians were Semites, as were the Assyrians, the Aramaeans, the Canaanites, the Phoenicians, and the Hebrews. The earliest known alphabetic writing systems were developed by Semites in about 2000 BC. Modern Semitic languages include Hebrew, Arabic, and Maltese.

Senanayake, Don Stephen (1884–1952) Sinhalese statesman. The chief architect of the independence of SRI LANKA, he entered politics in 1915. He became Vice-President of the State Council in 1936, leader of the constitutional movement and, as head of the United National Party, the country's first Prime Minister (1947–52). He was succeeded as Prime Minister by his son, Dudley Shelton Senanayake (1911–73), who also became leader of the United National Party. Dudley resigned in 1954 in the face of growing pressure from the socialist Sri Lanka Freedom Party of Solomon BANDARANAIKE. However, he led his party again in the elections of 1965 and formed a new government which endured until 1970, pursuing a policy of communal reconciliation.

Senate, Roman ROMAN SENATE.

Senate, US The second, or upper, chamber of the US Congress, representing the 50 states of the union. The powers and composition of the Senate, which first met in 1789, are set out in Article I of the US Constitution. Senators, two from each state, have six-year terms and were chosen by the state legislatures until 1913, when the Seventeenth Amendment provided for their direct election. The terms of one-third of the Senators expire every two years. A Senator must be at least 30 years old, must have been a US citizen for not less than nine years, and must be a resident of the state he or she represents. The Vice-President presides over the Senate, voting only in the case of a tie. The Senate must ratify all treaties, confirm important presidential appointments, and take a part in legislation.

The US Senate is unusual among second chambers in that it is broadly co-equal in power with the HOUSE OF REPRESENTATIVES, the other chamber of the bicameral US legislature. Fewer in number and with the security of a six-year term, senators are more prominent political figures than most Representatives. The Senate, with its committees and subcommittees, constitutes a formidable counterweight to the President. Presidential appointments of high federal officials are subject to the advice and consent of the Senate, which also has the power to ratify foreign treaties and to impeach the President, both by a two-thirds majority (see IMPEACHMENT).

Seneca A Native American people, the westernmost of the five IROQUOIS nations in western New York. They became involved in the FUR TRADE and its wars and French Jesuit missionaries began work among them in 1668. In the AMERICAN REVOLUTION they joined the British, provoking an American expedition to destroy their villages in 1778. New Christian missions began at the end of the 18th century, and simultaneously 'The Code of Handsome Lake', based on Iroquois traditions, was preached by Chief Handsome Lake, both beliefs gaining followers.

Seneca, Lucius Annaeus (Seneca the Younger) (c. 4 BC –65 AD) Roman writer and STOIC philosopher. Seneca was born in Spain; his father, Seneca the Elder,

had been well known in Rome as a teacher of rhetoric. The younger Seneca began his career in law and politics in 31 AD and narrowly avoided being executed by Caligula. He was banished from Rome by Claudius in 42 on suspicion of adultery with the emperor's sister but was recalled in 49 to act as tutor to the 12-year-old Nero. On the young emperor's accession the post evolved into that of political counsellor. At first he and the PRAETORIAN prefect were able to influence Nero. In 59, however, he found himself a reluctant accessory to the murder of Nero's mother Agrippina and composed Nero's explanation for the Senate. He chose retirement in 62. Three years later Nero accused him of treason and he was compelled to commit suicide. His surviving works include nine tragedies on mythological subjects, and a satire on the deification of Claudius, but he is most notable for his prose works: 124 letters; the *Natural Questions*, a treatise on natural science; and a series of essays on philosophical topics, full of point and wit, all marked by an epigrammatic style that uses rhetoric to recommend Stoic principles.

Senegal A West African country with an Atlantic coast.

Physical. Senegal surrounds the Gambia and is bounded inland by Mauritania, Mali, Guinea, and Guinea-Bissau. Its most westerly point (and that of continental Africa) is Cape Verde, to the north of which the coast is straight and sandy and offers a cool dry climate. Inland there is savannah; the south of the country has a marshy coast.

Economy. The predominantly agricultural economy has been weakened by drought and low world prices for agricultural exports. The principal exports are fish, ground-nuts, and phosphates. Other crops include sugar cane, millet, rice, and cotton. Mineral resources include phosphates, and unexploited reserves of iron ore, and gold. Industry includes ship repair and oil-refining in Dakar, and food-processing.

History. Senegal has been part of several ancient empires, including those of GHANA, MALI, and SONGHAY. The Tukulor, one of Senegal's seven main ethnic groups, converted to Islam in the 11th century, but animism remained widespread until the middle of the 19th century. Portuguese navigators explored the coast of Senegal in 1445. Founded by France in the 17th century, the colony of Senegal was disputed by Britain in the Napoleonic Wars. The interior was occupied by the French governor L. L. Faidherbe (1854–61); in 1871 the colony sent its first Deputy to the French Assembly. It became part of French West Africa in 1895, and in 1958 it was made an autonomous republic within the FRENCH COMMUNITY. It became part of the Federation of MALI (1959–60). Under the leadership of Léopold Sédar SENGHOR it became independent in 1960. It briefly federated with The GAMBIA as Senegambia (1982–89). In 1980 Abdou Diouf succeeded SENGHOR as President. Relations between Senegal and MAURITANIA deteriorated sharply in 1989 following the killing of hundreds of Senegalese residents in Mauritania and the expulsion of thousands more. A virtual frontier war lasted through 1990. Faced with rising ethnic tension, President Diouf formed a power-sharing coalition in 1991, which succeeded in restoring a degree of order; diplomatic relations were resumed with Mauritania in 1992. Meanwhile a separatist movement had developed within Casamance in southern Senegal. Diouf was re-elected in early 1993.

Violence by the separatists marred the presidential election, but a ceasefire agreement was concluded later in the year. Despite French and IMF aid, the Senegalese economy was on the verge of bankruptcy; a currency devaluation took place early in 1994. The ceasefire agreement was breached by the Casamance separatists in 1995 but was subsequently restored.

CAPITAL:	Dakar
AREA:	196,722 sq km (75,955 sq miles)
POPULATION:	8.532 million (1996)
CURRENCY:	1 CFA franc = 100 centimes
RELIGIONS:	Sunni Muslim 91.0%; Roman Catholic 5.6%; traditional beliefs 3.2%
ETHNIC GROUPS:	Wolof 38.0%; Fulani-(Peul-)Tukulor 22.0%; Serer 19.0%; Diola 7.0%; Mande 7.0%
LANGUAGES:	French (official); Wolof; other local languages
INTERNATIONAL ORGANIZATIONS:	UN; OAU; Franc Zone

Senghor, Léopold Sédar (1906–) Senegalese statesman and poet, President of SENEGAL (1959–80). In 1946 he was elected to the French National Assembly as a Socialist Deputy and after Senegal became autonomous in 1958 he was elected President. Together with the writers Aimé Césaire and Léon Damas he formulated the concept of *négritude*, which he defined as 'the sum total of cultural values of the Negro-African world'. In 1960 he sought unsuccessfully to achieve federation among the former French West African colonies and in 1975 Senegal joined the West African Economic Community. His collections of lyrical poetry include *Chants d'ombre* (1945), *Nocturnes* (1961), and *Poèmes* (1984).

Sennacherib King of the ASSYRIAN empire (704–681 BC). He was preoccupied with fighting rebels for much of his reign. In 701 he was largely successful in crushing discontent in the west; Tyre and Jerusalem both defied capture, though the latter was compelled to pay a large indemnity. Babylonia was a source of more persistent discontent, and Babylon itself was finally destroyed and looted in 689 after a nine-month siege. Sennacherib carried out a major building scheme at NINEVEH, which included a palace and two city walls.

separation of powers A classic doctrine of liberal government, asserting that the three branches of government – the legislature, the executive, and the judiciary – should be constitutionally separate from each other, both in function and in persons. This doctrine is usually attributed to the French philosopher and political theorist MONTESQUIEU (1689–1755), who argued for such a separation in *The Spirit of the Laws* (1748), although the tripartite division was earlier suggested by ARISTOTLE and LOCKE. In theory, separation of powers produces institutions that are relatively independent from one another and a system of checks and balances, preventing any one branch of government from dominating the others. The doctrine is enshrined in the CONSTITUTION OF THE USA, which provides a formal separation of CONGRESS, President, and Supreme Court. The separation, however, is not total and some collaboration, especially between President and Congress, is necessary if the system is to work at all. In countries with parliamentary government, the executive and legislature are fused and have overlapping functions. In the UK, the executive, formed

from the majority in Parliament, dominates the legislature. The judiciary, however, does stand to one side and is largely independent of legislative and executive processes, although the head of the judiciary, the Lord Chancellor, is a member of the CABINET (executive) as well as the presiding officer of the HOUSE OF LORDS (legislature).

Serbia A republic in south-east Europe, the largest of the republics of the former YUGOSLAVIA.

Physical. Serbia is landlocked, bordering Bosnia-Herzegovina in the west, Montenegro and Albania in the south-west, Macedonia in the south, Bulgaria in the east, Romania in the north-east, Hungary in the north, and Croatia in the north-west. In the south-west are the Šar Mountains and the Kopaonik Mountains, and in the east are the Balkan Mountains, while northern Serbia comprises a low-lying plain crossed by the Sava and Tisa Rivers, which flow into the Danube River.

Economy. Grain and sugar beet are grown in the fertile northern plains, and coal is mined in the more mountainous south. During the 1990s Serbia's economy was badly damaged by the republic's involvement in the Bosnian conflict and consequent international sanctions.

History. Slavic tribes from the Danube region won the area from Greeks and Romanized peoples in the 7th century and established the Slavic state of Rascia. Under threat from Bulgaria in the 10th century, Rascia was obliged to accept the protection of the Byzantine empire, while the rival state of Zeta was supported by Rome. Bogomilism, a dualist heresy, complicated the rivalry between the two major Christian churches, which was finally resolved by acceptance of the EASTERN ORTHODOX faith. The 13th century saw exploitation of mineral resources and much trade, particularly with Venice. Under the rule of STEPHAN DUSHAN (1331–55), the law was codified and the status of the serfs was regularized. Macedonia, Albania, and parts of Greece were annexed, but this expansion came to an abrupt end with disastrous defeats by the OTTOMANS in 1371 and 1389. In 1804 a massed rebellion against the Ottoman Turks by the mainly Eastern Orthodox population under KARA GEORGE was followed by short-lived independence. After a second insurrection, supported by Russian interference, Serbia was granted autonomy (1817) under the suzerainty of the sultan. This was confirmed by the Treaty of ADRIANOPLE (1829) and in 1830 Milos OBRENOVIĆ became hereditary Prince of Serbia, although his autocratic ways led to his abdication in 1839. In 1877 the Serbs allied themselves with the PAN-SLAV movement. In 1878, at the Congress of BERLIN, Serbia gained sovereign nationhood under Prince Milan Obrenović, who had ruled since 1872. In 1882 he was proclaimed king. A period of political unrest followed, including war with Bulgaria (1885–86), culminating in the assassination of Alexander Obrenović in 1903. His successor Peter Karageorgević allowed liberalization and parliamentary government. Austrian fears of Serb expansion into neighbouring BOSNIA-HERZEGOVINA led it to annex the latter in 1908 and attempt to control Serbia. These policies led to the assassination in 1914 of the Austrian archduke FRANCIS FERDINAND by a Serbian nationalist, precipitating World War I.

In 1918 Serbia absorbed Bosnia-Herzegovina and joined with Croatia and Slovenia to form what in 1929 was termed Yugoslavia. Croatia was a reluctant partner, and bitter tensions arose during World War II between

Croats and Serbian partisans. Although the two were re-united into the Yugoslavia of Marshal TITO (a Croat), rivalry continued, reasserting itself in 1990, when the Serbian nationalist Slobodan MILOSEVIC was elected President of Serbia. Full-scale war broke out in 1991 after Croatia and Slovenia declared their independence. Serbia sought to claim Serbian enclaves within Croatia, and to annex the autonomous region of Kosovo against the wishes of its 90% Albanian population. From 1992 a similar policy was pursued in Bosnia, where ethnic Serbs, backed by the Belgrade government, systematically evicted the mostly Muslim communities in the east in the name of a Greater Serbia. UN sanctions were imposed in January 1992, but Serbian policies of aggrandisement continued. In April 1992 Serbia and Montenegro announced the formation of a new Federal Republic of Yugoslavia, although this has so far found little international recognition. During 1995, Serbian expansionism was finally countered, with extensive NATO air-strikes against Bosnian Serb positions and advances by Bosnian government and Croatian forces. A negotiated settlement between Croatia and Serbia saw the return of the region of Eastern Slavonia, including the town of Vukovar, to Croatia. In late 1995 the governments of Serbia, Croatia, and Bosnia-Herzegovina accepted a US-brokered peace settlement (the Dayton Peace Accord). During the winter of 1996–97 the authoritarian rule of Milosevic came under growing pressure and there were mass demonstrations in Belgrade. Nevertheless, Parliament increased his powers by naming him President of the new Yugoslavia (July 1997), a move that provoked tensions with Montenegro. In October-December 1997 presidential and parliamentary elections in Serbia had to be rerun, owing to a boycott by opposition groups and much of the electorate. Constitutional stalemate was finally resolved with the appointment of Milan Milutinovic (a Milosevic supporter) as President and the creation of a government of national unity, including both nationalist hardliners and former dissident leaders. In early 1998 there was renewed violence in Kosovo, as Serb forces attempted to take control of the rebel province.

serf An unfree peasant under the control of the lord whose lands he worked. As VILLEINS or servants of a medieval lord they represented the bottom tier of society. Denied freedom of movement or freedom to marry without permission of their lord, they were obliged to work on their lord's fields, to contribute a proportion of their own produce, to surrender part of their land at death, and to submit to the justice and penalties administered by their lord in the manorial court in the case of wrongdoing. The lord had obligations to his serfs (unlike slaves), most notably to provide military protection and justice (see FEUDAL SYSTEM; MANORIAL SYSTEM).

Serfdom originated in the 8th and 9th centuries in Western Europe and subsequently became hereditary. During the 14th century the system was undermined in the west by the BLACK DEATH and starvation resulting from war, both of which led to acute labour shortages. Commutation of their labour for cash meant that the lord became a rentier and the serf a tenant; in the PEASANTS' REVOLT in England (1381) the main demand was for the abolition of serfdom and the substitution of rent at four pence an acre for services. However, in the eastern regions of Germany and MUSCOVY, the increased power of the nobility and the development of absolutism led to consolidation of serfdom. It was formally abolished in France in 1789, but lingered in Austria and Hungary till 1848, and was abolished in Russia only in 1861.

Settlement, Act of The name of several English Acts, that of 1701 being the most politically significant. It provided for the succession to the throne after the death of Queen ANNE (none of whose children had survived), and was intended to prevent the Roman Catholic Stuarts from regaining the throne. It stipulated that the crown should go to James I's granddaughter, the Electress Sophia of Hanover, or her surviving Protestant heirs. The Act placed further limitations on royal power, and made the judiciary independent of crown and Parliament. On Anne's death in 1714, Sophia's son became Britain's first Hanoverian monarch as King GEORGE I.

Sevastopol A port and naval base on the south-west coast of the Crimean peninsula, now in the Ukraine but formerly in Russia. By the outbreak of the CRIMEAN WAR its strong fortifications had been completed and it was able to sustain an 11-month siege after the battle of BALAKLAVA. It was almost completely destroyed after the Russian withdrawal in September 1855 and its fortifications ordered not to be rebuilt at the Congress of PARIS.

Seven Weeks War AUSTRO-PRUSSIAN WAR.

Seven Wonders of the World The most remarkable man-made sights of the ancient world, the earliest extant list of which dates from the 2nd century BC. The Wonders are usually listed as the PYRAMIDS of Egypt at Giza; the Hanging Gardens of BABYLON (a series of terraced roof-gardens attributed to NEBUCHADNEZZAR II); the statue of Zeus at OLYMPIA (a large statue overlaid with gold and ivory by the Athenian sculptor, Phidias, in approximately 430 BC); the temple of Artemis at Ephesus (built in the mid-6th century BC with assistance from CROESUS, burnt in 356 BC, rebuilt, and finally destroyed by the Goths in 263 AD); the mausoleum of Halicarnassus; the Colossus of RHODES (an enormous (over 30.5 m (100 feet) high) bronze statue of the sun god, Helios, erected (c. 292–280 BC) by the people of Rhodes in their harbour to commemorate their repulse of Demetrius Poliorcetes in 305 BC); the Pharos of Egypt (a huge lighthouse built by Ptolemy II (c. 280 BC) on the island of Pharos outside the harbour of ALEXANDRIA).

Seven Years War (1756–63) A wide-ranging European conflict involving Prussia, Britain, and Hanover on one side and Austria, France, Russia, Sweden, and Spain on the other. It continued the disputes that had been left undecided after the treaty of AIX-LA-CHAPELLE, being concerned partly with colonial rivalry between Britain and France and partly with the struggle for supremacy in Germany between Austria and Prussia. Fighting between Britain and France in North America had continued with the BRADDOCK expedition. Each side was dissatisfied with its former allies and in 1756 FREDERICK II of Prussia concluded the Treaty of Westminster with Britain. This made it possible for MARIA THERESA of Austria and her minister KAUNITZ to obtain an alliance with France (known as the 'diplomatic revolution') by the two treaties of Versailles in 1756 and 1757; she was also allied with ELIZABETH PETROVNA of Russia. At first the advantage was with the French and Austrians, but in July 1757 PITT the Elder came to power in England and conducted the war with skill and vigour. In November Frederick II won his great victory of Rossbach over the French, and in December he defeated the Austrians at Leuthen. Frederick was hard pressed in 1758, but he defeated the Russians at Zorndorf and Ferdinand of Brunswick protected his western flank with an Anglo-Hanoverian army. 1759 was the British year of victories: WOLFE captured Quebec, Ferdinand defeated the French army at MINDEN, and HAWKE destroyed the French fleet at QUIBERON BAY. In India CLIVE had won control of Bengal at Plassey, and in 1760 Montreal was taken. Admiral BOSCAWEN successfully attacked the French West Indies. In 1761 Spain entered the war and Pitt resigned. The death of Elizabeth of Russia eased the pressure on Frederick, as her successor Peter III reversed her policy. All were now ready for peace, which was concluded by the Treaty of PARIS in 1763: overall England and Russia were victorious.

Seven Years War of the North (1563–70) A bitter conflict that resulted from a collision of the expansionist aims of Denmark and Sweden in the Baltic and became entangled with the contemporary war in LIVONIA. Frederick II of Denmark's troops achieved tactical successes on land, but the Swedes compensated with a series of victories at sea. In 1568 the insane Eric XIV of Sweden was deposed by an alliance of the nobility and replaced by John III. The new king swiftly sought peace from the equally exhausted Danes. By the Treaty of Stettin (1570) Denmark's grip on the entrance to the Baltic remained unbroken, but Sweden retained Estonia. The contest for the dominion of the whole Baltic was not resolved until the NORTHERN WAR of 1700–21.

Severus, Lucius Septimius (145–211) Roman emperor (193–211). A professional soldier, he became governor of Pannonia and was proclaimed emperor by his troops in 193. Rivals were eliminated and the PRAETORIANS were disbanded and replaced with his own men. He adopted himself into the ANTONINE dynasty and subjected the Christians to persecution in 203. During a long campaign on the CALEDONIAN border in Britain he died at the military headquarters in Eboracum (York).

Seveso A village near Milan in Italy, the site in 1976 of a major industrial accident at a Swiss-owned chemical plant, resulting in a large cloud of weed-killer being released into the atmosphere. The most toxic substance in the emission was dioxin. As the seriousness of the accident was realized, strong measures were taken to limit the damage and spread of the pollution. The village of Seveso and 30 sq km (12 sq miles) around were evacuated and turned into an exclusion zone, which still exists today. Livestock and crops were destroyed. Pregnant women exposed to the emissions had to consider undergoing abortions because the toxins involved are known to cause foetal defects.

Sèvres, Treaty of (1920) A treaty signed between the Allies and Turkey as part of the VERSAILLES PEACE SETTLEMENT, effectively marking the end of the OTTOMAN EMPIRE. Adrianople and most of the hinterland to Constantinople (now Istanbul) passed to Greece; the Bosporus was internationalized and demilitarized; a

short-lived independent ARMENIA was created; Syria became a French MANDATE; Britain accepted the mandate for Iraq, Palestine, and Transjordan. The treaty was rejected by Mustafa Kemal ATATÜRK, who secured a redefinition of Turkey's borders by the Treaty of Lausanne.

Seward, William Henry (1801–72) US statesman. He served as Whig governor of New York (1839–42) and then as Senator (1849–61). A convinced opponent of slavery, he joined the newly formed REPUBLICAN PARTY in 1855 and served as Secretary of State under LINCOLN during the AMERICAN CIVIL WAR. Wounded in a separate attack at the time of Lincoln's assassination, Seward recovered and stayed in office during the Presidency of Andrew JOHNSON, generally supporting him against the radical Republicans. Seward believed in the need for the USA to expand its influence in the Pacific and was responsible for the US purchase of ALASKA from Russia (1867). He advocated friendly relations with China and pressed for the annexation of Hawaii and other islands to act as coaling stations for a US Pacific fleet.

Seychelles A country comprising an archipelago in the Indian Ocean.

Physical. The Seychelles consists of 92 islands lying 4° S of the Equator and some 1,500 km (930 miles) from the east African coast.

Economy. Tourism is the mainstay of the economy. The main exports are fish and copra.

History. The islands were uninhabited until colonized by the French. They were discovered in 1609 by an expedition of the British East India Company and formally annexed to France in 1756. They were captured from the French by Britain in 1810 during the Napoleonic Wars and were administered from MAURITIUS before becoming a separate British crown colony in 1903. The islands gained universal suffrage in 1970, becoming an independent republic in 1975. In 1977 there was a coup, the Prime Minister, France-Albert René proclaimed himself President. In 1991 he ended his resistance to the legalization of opposition parties. Multiparty elections held in 1993 resulted in a landslide victory for René's Seychelles People's Progressive Front.

CAPITAL:	Victoria
AREA:	453 sq km (175 sq miles)
POPULATION:	76,100 (1996)
CURRENCY:	1 Seychelles rupee = 100 cents
RELIGIONS:	Roman Catholic 90.9%; other Christian (mostly Anglican) 7.5%; Hindu 0.7%
ETHNIC GROUPS:	Seychellois creole (mixture of Asian, African, and European) 89.1%; Indian 4.7%; Malagasy 3.1%; Chinese 1.6%; British 1.5%
LANGUAGES:	Creole, English, French (all official)
INTERNATIONAL ORGANIZATIONS:	UN; Commonwealth; OAU

Seymour, Edward SOMERSET, Edward Seymour, 1st Earl of Hertford, and Duke of.

Seymour, Jane (c. 1509–37) Queen consort of HENRY VIII of England from 1536. She was the king's third wife, supplanting Anne BOLEYN. In 1537 Jane gave birth to a son, the future EDWARD VI, but died 12 days later. Henry had been genuinely fond of her and mourned her death.

Seyss-Inquart, Arthur (1892–1946) Austrian Nazi leader. As Interior Minister in Vienna, he organized the

ANSCHLUSS with Germany in 1938, and was made governor of Austria by Hitler. He later became the Nazi commissioner in the occupied Netherlands, where he was responsible for thousands of executions and deportations to CONCENTRATION CAMPS. He was sentenced to death at the NUREMBERG TRIALS.

Sforza An Italian family that rose to prominence in the 15th and 16th centuries. Muzio Attendolo (1369–1424) was one of the most powerful CONDOTTIERI of the period (his assumed name Sforza means 'force'). His illegitimate son Francesco (1401–66) was also a successful condottiere, whose armies were involved in a three-way war with the Milanese republic and Venice, after which he entered Milan in triumph as duke (1450), and thereafter governed ably.

Ludovico (1451–1508), known as 'Il Moro' (the Moor), usurped the Milanese government in 1480. He helped Charles VIII of France to invade Naples (1494), but he was subsequently driven out of his duchy by Louis XII (1499). In 1512 his son Massimiliano (1493–1530) was restored to Milan with Swiss aid; FRANCIS I of France defeated him at Marignano (1515), and forced him to cede his dominions, granting him a pension of 30,000 ducats. Massimiliano's brother Francesco II (1495–1535) was restored by Emperor CHARLES V in 1522, but his death marked the end of the male ducal line.

Shackleton, Sir Ernest Henry (1874–1922) Irish-born British Antarctic explorer who, having reached latitude 82° S with Robert SCOTT in 1902, tried in 1908 to reach the South Pole. His expedition climbed Mount Erebus, reached the magnetic pole and scaled the Beardmore Glacier; but blizzards forced him back when, at latitude 88° S, he was only 160 km (100 miles) from the Pole. In 1914 he sailed again, planning this time to cross Antarctica from the Weddell to the Ross Sea; but his ship, *Endurance*, was crushed by ice in the Weddell Sea and the party was marooned. By drifting on ice-floes and using the ship's boats, they eventually made Elephant Island in the South Shetlands. Here Shackleton left his main party and sailed for rescue with five men in a small boat to South Georgia, 1,300 km (800 miles) away. In 1921 he began another expedition, but died of a heart attack on board his ship.

Shaftesbury, Anthony Ashley Cooper, 1st Earl of (1621–83) English statesman. He entered Parliament in 1640 as a royalist supporter, but changed sides in 1643, eventually becoming a member of CROMWELL'S council of state. In 1660 he was one of the Commissioners of the Convention Parliament who invited CHARLES II to return, and Charles rewarded him with the Chancellorship of the Exchequer. After CLARENDON's fall he became one of the CABAL, but was dismissed in 1673 because of his support for the TEST ACT and his unwavering opposition to Roman Catholicism. He became leader of the opposition, and used the POPISH PLOT to try to exclude the Roman Catholic James, Duke of York, from the succession (EXCLUSION CRISIS), but his political failure led him to flee into exile in 1682.

Shaftesbury, Anthony Ashley Cooper, 7th Earl of (1801–85) British politician and reformer. A Tory in politics, his first parliamentary campaign was over the abolition of 'suttee' — the Hindu widow's practice of committing suicide on her husband's funeral pyre – in British India. He also persuaded Parliament to pass an Act reforming the treatment of lunatics, and agitated for the abolition of slavery. He was largely responsible for the Ten Hours Factory Act of 1847, which shortened the working day in textile mills to ten hours. He supported charity schools (the 'Ragged Schools') for children in slums, and championed the abolition of boy chimney sweeps. An active reformer in urban housing for the poor, he pleaded for parks and playgrounds, and for the reduction of working hours. He opposed the development of trade-unionism and the REFORM ACTS of 1832 and 1867, fearing that they might provoke class warfare.

Shah Jahan (1592–1666) MOGUL Emperor of India (1628–58) whose outwardly splendid reign ended in imprisonment by his son and successor. He extended Mogul power, notably in the Deccan, and rebuilt the capital at Delhi. His buildings there and in Agra, notably the Taj Mahal, mark the high peak of Indo-Muslim architecture. His severe illness in 1657 caused a succession war between his four sons in which AURANGZEB, the third son, killed his rivals, imprisoned his father in the Agra palace, and seized the throne. On his death Shah Jahan was buried with his favourite wife in the Taj Mahal.

Shaka (or Tshaka, or Chaka) (1787–1828) Zulu chief (1818–28). He was conscripted into DINGISWAYO's army *c.* 1809. Rising rapidly, he became Chief of the Zulu in 1816. He re-organized his army of 40,000 Zulu warriors into regiments (impi), arming them with a stabbing spear, issuing them with distinctive dress, and training them to go barefoot for mobility. Save for veterans, marriage was forbidden, and training was rigorous. In 1818 Shaka profited by Dingiswayo's death to extend his dominions. He subjugated all of what is now Natal. Women's regiments were organized, and the whole nation placed on a war footing against the Boers. In 1828 his half-brother DINGAAN assassinated him.

Shaker (or Shaking Quaker) A member of a religious sect, so-called because of their uncontrolled jerkings in moments of religious ecstasy. They were a revivalist group and held many QUAKER views although they left the Quaker movement in 1747. Ann Lee, who joined in 1758, declared herself the female Christ and, inspired by visions, established a community near Albany in New York colony in 1774. The community prospered and Shakers gained a reputation in New England as skilled craftsmen. The sect reached a peak of about 6,000 members in the 1820s, but a decline set in after 1860. The characteristic Shaker austere wooden furniture and decor has remained popular.

Shamil (*c.* 1798–1871) Leader of Muslim resistance to the Russian occupation of the Caucasus from 1834 to 1859. He became Imam of a branch of the Sufi Naqshbandi order known as Muridism which recommended strict adherence to Islamic law and preached *jihad* (holy war) against Russia. After the Crimean War Russia employed some 200,000 troops in the Caucasus to encircle and subdue Shamil and his followers. He was captured (1859), and imprisoned, but allowed to go on a pilgrimage to Mecca (1870), where he died.

Shamir, Yitzhak (1915–) Israeli politician; Prime Minister (1983–84; 1986–92). Shamir was born in Poland and emigrated to Palestine in 1935. In the struggle leading to the establishment of a Jewish state, he was active in two guerrilla organizations, IRGUN and the STERN GANG. From 1955 to 1965 he worked for the Israeli secret service, Mossad. Shamir then came to political prominence as speaker of the Knesset (1977–80) and thereafter as foreign minister in the Likud Party government of Menachem BEGIN. When Begin resigned in 1983, he became Likud leader and Prime Minister, but lost power in the general election of the following year. Thereafter he served first as deputy premier (1984–86) and then as premier once again in a Labour–Likud coalition, established with Shimon PERES. In 1988 he was able to form a new coalition that was not dependent on Labour support. Despite his reputation as a hard-liner, uncompromising in his opposition to a Palestinian homeland and his support for new Jewish settlements on Arab land, Shamir was pressurized by the US into taking part in a Middle East peace conference in 1991. This lost him the backing of his right-wing coalition partners and his government fell in 1992.

Shang (c. 16th century to c. 11th century BC) China's first verified dynasty. It was authenticated in the 1920s after the discovery of oracle bones ('dragon bones') near ANYANG. Devoted to hunting and war, the Shang kings regulated their activities by consulting diviners. Scratches on the oracle bones, the earliest form of Chinese characters, proved to be their oracular writings. From these records have emerged the traditional names and sequence of the kings of this dynasty, who gradually extended their rule over the Huang He (Yellow River) plain. The Shang developed a complex agricultural society and saw the emergence of skilled artisans, most notably bronze casters.

Shankaracharya SANKARACHARYA.

Shans A people of MYANMAR (Burma). They are akin to people in LAOS and THAILAND, and originated in Yunnan province in south-west China, entering Burma about the 13th century AD. Based in the hills east of the Irrawaddy River, they lived under chieftains thought to have divine powers. There was deep enmity between Burmans and Shans, though the latter, except in very remote areas, adopted Burman culture and Theravada BUDDHISM. A kingdom founded by a Burmanized Shan prince at Ava had considerable power from about 1360 until the unification of Upper Burma under the first TOUNGOO dynasty in the late 15th century.

sharecropping A form of land tenancy in which a landlord allows land to be used in return for a share of the tenant's crops or labour. Sharecropping is found all over the world, especially among peasant societies in developing countries; for example, it is widespread in many parts of Asia, especially in areas where rural population densities are high. It is associated with hierarchical social relations. There is substantial variation in the form of sharecropping agreements. Sometimes the landlord may share production costs (of seeds or labour, for instance) and sometimes not at all. Tenants may face a variety of restrictions, such as in the type of crops produced.

In the USA a sharecropping system developed in the Southern states after the abolition of slavery, involving both black and white tenant farmers who lacked the resources to provide their own equipment or stock. In return for the labour of the farmer and his family, a half share of the crop was provided. Generally, this was diminished in value by the need to obtain credit from the landlord for family needs. As late as 1940, some 750,000 sharecroppers remained, but after World War II their numbers declined as a result of farm mechanization and a reduction in land devoted to cotton cultivation.

Sharia (from Arabic, 'path') The law of Islam. In its widest sense the *sharia* is the way of life ('path') prescribed for Muslims, based on the KORAN and the HADITH. This contains, and is sometimes identified with, *fiḳh* (jurisprudence), the science of the *sharia* worked out by the four orthodox schools in Sunni Islam and by Imam Jafar Sādiq (c. 700–65) and other *imams* in Shiite Islam. Although the *sharia* has no codification as in some Western law systems, the *fiḳh* books may be considered the equivalent of law books. Legal opinions based on *fiḳh* known as *fatwas* are given by scholars known as *muftis*. A religious law, believed to be divinely revealed, the *sharia* may be divided into two major categories: duties to God, which are summarized in the FIVE PILLARS OF ISLAM; and duties to fellow men, including penal, commercial, and family law. In religious terms, all human actions may be classified into the following five categories: obligatory (in this category omission is punished); meritorious; indifferent; reprehensible; and forbidden (a category divided into different types of sin). Each of the schools of law divides actions into somewhat different categories for legal purposes. From the earliest times Islamic rulers have supplemented the *sharia* with secular law based on customary law and edicts issued to meet the political conditions of the day. Beginning in the 19th century, WESTERNIZATION and colonization led to the introduction of Western civil, commercial, and penal codes in many Islamic countries; for example, in the Ottoman empire a commercial code based on the French commercial code was adopted in 1850 and a new system of courts set up to implement it. By the middle years of the 20th century, in the majority of countries with a predominantly or partially Muslim population, the *sharia* was applied only to family law; and in a number of countries the *sharia* courts were abolished and a unified system of courts established. However, Turkey, Albania, and the former Soviet republics with a predominantly Muslim population are the only Muslim countries to have adopted fully secular legal systems and to have abolished the *sharia* entirely. Most other Muslim countries have adopted a mixed system. For example, in Egypt a civil code based on a compromise between Islamic and Western law was drawn up in 1949; this was later adopted by Syria and Libya. In Iran and Saudi Arabia, the *sharia* is the basis of the legal system, with special religio-legal bodies to ensure its correct application in all areas of government. The question of the reintroduction of all or part of the *sharia*, as happened in Iran and Sudan, is an issue for many Muslim countries, causing heated debate between ISLAMIC FUNDAMENTALISTS and ISLAMIC MODERNISTS. Pakistan announced plans to make the *sharia* the supreme law of the land in 1991 whereas in Algeria the authorities closed down the pro-*sharia* Islamic Salvation Front in early 1992.

Sharifian The name given to two MOROCCAN dynasties whose rulers claimed the title of *sharif* (noble) by reason of their descent from al-Hasan, son of MUHAMMAD's daughter Fatima. The *sharifs* of MECCA, and others, claim similar descent.

The Sadian dynasty of *sharifs* originated in Sus in 1509, and speedily conquered all Morocco. Sharif Muhammad traded with Spain and England, a policy followed by his successors. In 1664, after a period of great confusion, a cadet branch of *sharifs* known as Filali supplanted them, and remain the ruling dynasty of Morocco.

Sharpeville massacre (21 March 1960) An incident in the South African township of Sharpeville: the police opened fire on a demonstration against APARTHEID laws, killing 67 Black Africans, and wounding 180. There was widespread international condemnation, and a state of emergency was declared in South Africa. Some 1,700 persons were detained, and the leading Black parties, the AFRICAN NATIONAL CONGRESS and PAN-AFRICANIST CONGRESS were banned. Three weeks later a White farmer attempted to assassinate the Prime Minister, Hendrik VERWOERD, and, as pressure from the Commonwealth against the apartheid policies mounted, South Africa became a republic and withdrew from the Commonwealth (1961).

Shays's Rebellion (August 1786 to February 1787) An armed uprising in the USA led by Captain Daniel Shays (c. 1747–1825), a Massachusetts war veteran. Shays led a group of destitute farmers from western Massachusetts against the creditor merchants and lawyers of the seaboard towns. The Rebellion was caused by the Massachusetts legislature adjourning without hearing the petitions of debt-ridden farmers for financial help. The rebellion prevented the sitting of the courts; the state militia routed Shays's force, but he escaped and was later pardoned. The uprising won concessions, but it also boosted the campaign for an effective constitution and central government for the USA.

Shearers' strikes (1891, 1894) Major strikes in Queensland and New South Wales, Australia. Sheep shearers were fighting for the principles of unionism and the 'closed shop' (an establishment in which only trade-union members are employed), while sheep farmers were fighting for 'freedom of contract' (the right to employ anyone). The strikes were marked by violence and bitterness on both sides. Non-union labour was used. Union leaders, including some from the Barcaldine shearers' camp of 1891, were arrested on charges such as conspiracy, seditious language, and riot. Some were gaoled. The unions were defeated.

Shelburne, William Petty Fitzmaurice Lansdowne, 1st Marquis and 2nd Earl of (1737–1805) British statesman. He joined CHATHAM's ministry in 1766, but failed to build up a political following and was regarded with distrust by many of his colleagues. His ideas were often regarded as impracticable, especially his conciliatory scheme of 1767 for settling the American question. He opposed the American policies of Lord NORTH and in 1782 succeeded Lord ROCKINGHAM as Prime Minister. He was responsible for settling the main outlines of the peace treaty between Britain and America, but before these could be concluded he was brought down by a combination of the supporters of FOX and North in 1783.

Shere Ali (1825–79) Amir (ruler) of Afghanistan (1863–79). He succeeded his father, DOST MUHAMMAD.

During the early part of his reign Afghanistan experienced civil war and his authority was not confirmed until 1868, when he was given British assistance. Shere Ali introduced a number of reforms in Afghanistan including the establishment of a regular, European-style army. In 1878 he admitted a Russian mission to Kabul but refused to accept a British mission, resulting in the Second ANGLO-AFGHAN WAR. Shere Ali fled to northern Afghanistan seeking Russian support, and died.

Sheridan, Philip Henry (1831–88) US general. He emerged as the outstanding cavalry leader on the Union (Northern) side in the AMERICAN CIVIL WAR, distinguishing himself in Tennessee and in the CHATTANOOGA CAMPAIGN (November 1863) before being appointed in April 1864 to command the cavalry of the Army of the Potomac. His campaign in the Shenandoah Valley (September–October 1864) laid waste one of the south's most important supply regions, while his victory at Five Forks on 1 April 1865 effectively forced Robert E. LEE to abandon Petersburg and Richmond. After the war Sheridan commanded the 5th military district in the South, and in 1884 he succeeded SHERMAN as commander-in-chief of the US Army.

sheriff (shire-reeve) The chief representative of the crown in the shires (counties) of England from the early 11th century, taking over many of the duties previously performed by ealdormen. Sheriffs assumed responsibility for the FYRD, royal taxes, royal estates, shire courts, and presided over their own court, the Tourn. That they often abused these powers was shown by an inquest of 1170, when many were dismissed. However, by c. 1550 the office had become purely civil, as a result of the proliferation of specialist royal officials (Coroners from 1170, Justices of the Peace from 1361, and LORDS LIEUTENANT from 1547).

Sheriffmuir, Battle of (13 November 1715) A battle fought in Scotland, the only major battle of the FIFTEEN Rebellion. The JACOBITE army of 10,000 men, commanded by the Earl of Mar, met the much smaller loyalist force of the Duke of Argyll. Although the fighting was inconclusive, Mar was forced on to the defensive, and the chance of Jacobite success disappeared.

Sherman, William Tecumseh (1820–91) US general. He served on the Union (Northern) side in the AMERICAN CIVIL WAR, commanding a brigade at the first Battle of Bull Run and a division at Shiloh, before participating in the VICKSBURG and CHATTANOOGA CAMPAIGNS as General GRANT's most trusted subordinate. He was appointed commander in the western theatre in March 1864 and conducted a successful campaign against Atlanta, which fell to him in September. Determined to carry the war into the heart of the Confederacy, he marched his army through Georgia to the sea and then northward through the Carolinas, taking the surrender of the forces of the CONFEDERACY there (1865). His devastation of the territory through which he marched gravely damaged the Southern war effort and earned him a reputation as a proponent of total war. He became commander-in-chief of the US Army (1869–83).

Sher Shah Suri (c. 1486–1545) Emperor of northern India (1540–45). His short-lived seizure of power from the second Mogul emperor, HUMAYUN, made an important impact on Indian administration. An Afghan of humble origins, he had risen through military service to be well placed to take advantage of temporary Mogul weakness. After defeating Humayun twice (1539 and 1540) he made himself Emperor of Delhi, extending his control to Gwalior and Malwa. Before his death in battle he carried out innovations in the land revenue system and the army that were subsequently built on by the great Mogul administrator, AKBAR.

Shetland Islands A group of islands in the UK, about 160 km (100 miles) off the north coast of Scotland.
Physical. The Shetland Islands form an archipelago of a hundred islands 80 km (50 miles) north-east of the Orkneys, with the isolated Fair Isle between the two groups. Only a score or so are large enough for settlement, by far the biggest being Mainland; of the others only Yell and Uist exceed 16 km (10 miles) in length. Muckle Flugga lighthouse on Uist is the most northerly point in the British Isles. The islands have deep, indented, fiord-like coasts and the winds are continuous and strong.
Economy. Farming and fishing are the main occupations; Shetland sheep are renowned for their fine wool. The discovery of oil in the Brent and Ninian fields of the North Sea, north-east of Shetland, has boosted employment in the region.
History. The islands were settled by the Norse people from the end of the 8th century. The Shetlands were controlled for many centuries by the powerful earls of Orkney, but eventually became part of the kingdom of Scotland in the marriage contract of JAMES III and Margaret of Norway (1472). They subsequently became part of the UNITED KINGDOM.

Shevardnadze, Eduard Amvrosievich (1928–   ) Georgian politician; President of Georgia (1995–   ). During the 1960s he rose steadily through the ranks of the Georgian Communist Party to become minister for internal affairs (1968–72), in which role he campaigned against corruption and instituted economic reforms. He became First Secretary of the Georgian Communist Party in 1972.
Shevardnadze embarked on a national political career when he was appointed to the Central Committee of the Communist Party of the Soviet Union in 1976. In 1985 he became a member of the POLITBURO and Foreign Minister of the Soviet Union; at this time, he became a staunch ally of the reforming Party general secretary, Mikhail GORBACHEV. In tune with Gorbachev's advocacy of GLASNOST AND PERESTROIKA, Shevardnadze's foreign policy was characterized by his promotion of detente and arms control, encouragement of reform in satellite countries, and orderly disengagement of Soviet forces from Afghanistan (1988–89). As the Soviet Union began to break apart in 1990, he resigned his position in protest at growing anti-democratic conspiracies within the Party and the military; after the failure of the attempted coup of 1991, he again briefly took up the post until the formal dissolution of the Soviet Union.
In 1992, Shevardnadze was invited to chair the State Council of his native republic, the newly independent state of Georgia, after its unstable first President, Zviad Gamsakhurdia, had been violently ousted. He was immediately faced with secessionist uprisings in the autonomous regions of Abkhazia and South Ossetia; despite peace agreements, the situation in both areas remains tense. In 1995, shortly before being elected

President by an overwhelming majority, Shevardnadze narrowly escaped assassination in a car-bomb attack. A second attempt on his life was made in 1998.

Shia SHIITE.

Shi Huangdi (Shih Huang-ti) (259–210 BC) First QIN Emperor of China (221–210 BC). He became ruler of the state of Qin in 246 BC and declared himself emperor in 221 BC after overthrowing the ZHOU and their vassal states. He ordered that the frontier walls in northern China should be joined together and extended to make the GREAT WALL OF CHINA and enlarged his empire into southern China. He could not accept the Confucian belief that an emperor should follow traditional rites, and so ordered the burning of all Confucian books, the banning of Confucian teaching, and the killing of scholars. In death as in life he was heavily guarded: close to his burial mound outside Xi'an stood an army of life-size pottery warriors and horses. The dynasty outlasted him by only three years, but he had imposed lasting unity on China by standardizing scripts, weights, and measures.

Shiites (from Arabic, 'sectarians') The minority division within ISLAM, which consists of about one-fifth of all Muslims. Shiites are in the majority in Iran (where Shia Islam is the state religion), southern Iraq, and parts of Yemen, and are also found in Syria, Lebanon, East Africa, northern India, and Pakistan. They originated as the Shiat Ali, the 'party of Ali', who was the cousin and son-in-law of MUHAMMAD. Ali and his descendants are regarded by Shiites as the only true heirs to Muhammad as leader of the faithful. Shiites now differ from SUNNI Muslims in a number of ways but primarily in the importance they attach to the continuing authority of the *imams*, who are the authentic interpreters of the *sunna* (customs), the code of conduct based on the KORAN and *hadith*. The suffering of the House of the Prophet, chiefly of Husain and his martyrdom in Karbala, and the MILLENARIAN expectation of a future *imam* or MAHDI who is currently hidden from the world, permeate much Shiite thinking, providing a set of beliefs in which oppression and injustice figure largely. The tenth day of Muharram marks the martyrdom of Ali and his sons. Shiites also believe in an inner hidden meaning of the Koran. There are hundreds of different Shiite sects: the main ones are the Zaydis, ISMAILIS, and Ithna Ashariya (or Twelvers, who await the return of the hidden twelfth *imam*).

Shimabara A peninsula near NAGASAKI, Japan. In the 17th century it was a Catholic stronghold. Its converts, regarded by the TOKUGAWA as subversive, were persecuted, and in 1637 some 40,000 Christians rebelled against oppression and poverty. Having taken refuge in a castle, they held out for some months against the shogun's army, numbering 100,000, and a Dutch warship sent to his aid. They were virtually annihilated. Japan's few surviving Christians, risking torture and death, continued to practise their rites in secret.

Shimonoseki, Treaty of (17 April 1895) The treaty between China and Japan that ended the SINO-JAPANESE WAR (1894–95). With her navy destroyed and Beijing in danger of capture, China was forced to grant the independence of Korea, pay a large indemnity, grant favourable trade terms, and cede Taiwan, the Pescadores Islands, and the Liaodong peninsula (including the naval base at Port Arthur, now Lüshun). International pressure forced the return of Port Arthur and the abandonment of the claim to the Liaodong peninsula shortly afterwards, but Japanese domination over north China had been established.

Shining Path (Spanish, *Sendero Luminoso*) Peruvian left-wing terrorist group, active from the early 1970s to the early 1990s. The Shining Path gained notoriety for the violence of its campaign against the Peruvian government, which claimed some 28,000 lives. Founded in 1970 by a philosophy professor, Abimael Guzmán, the movement adopted the revolutionary principles of Mao Zedong (see MAOISM); its many recruits came both from universities and from the disadvantaged Amerindian peoples of the Andes. From 1980 it attacked projects established by foreign aid agencies in rural areas, but later moved to the major cities. The emergency powers taken by President Alberto FUJIMORI in 1992, in an attempt to stem political violence, led in the first place to increased guerrilla activity, especially against local politicians, but resulted in the capture and sentencing of Guzmán to life imprisonment in September of that year. Following the arrest of their leader, who called for a cessation of fighting, some 6,000 Shining Path members took advantage of a government amnesty and surrendered. Isolated pockets of resistance remain in more remote areas (where the group has murdered Amazonian Indians opposed to their campaign).

Shinto (Chinese/Japanese, 'the Way of the Spirits') A Japanese religion dating from prehistoric times, based on the worship of ancestors and nature-spirits. Things that inspire awe – twisted trees, contorted rocks, dead warriors – are believed to enshrine *kami* ('spirits'). In early times each clan had its *kami*. With the supremacy of the YAMATO, its sun-goddess, Amaterasu, enshrined at the temple at Ise, became paramount. Shinto is not a highly conceptualized religion; it is tolerant and adaptable, laying emphasis on high standards of behaviour and on daily rituals, rather than on doctrine. It offers no code of conduct or philosophy but stresses ritual purity – which may explain why the Japanese, to the amazement of early Western visitors, bathed frequently. At simple shrines worshippers rinse hands and mouth, bow, and offer food and drink.

The name Shinto was adopted in the 6th century AD to distinguish it from Buddhist and Confucian cults. There is no official Shinto scripture, although the *Kojiki* (Records of Ancient Matters) and *Nihon-gi* (Chronicles of Japan), 8th-century compilations based on oral tradition, contain myths and stories about creation and the gods. During the 5th century AD, the spread of CONFUCIANISM introduced ancestor worship to Shinto and in the 6th century BUDDHIST beliefs became incorporated into the ancient religion.

During the 19th century the rise of the unified Japanese state saw the development of state Shinto: the emperor came to be worshipped as a descendant of the sun goddess Amaterasu. State Shinto was not classed as a religion but as a code of conduct requiring loyalty and obedience to the divine emperor; it informed all public life and encouraged extreme nationalism, until it was rescinded by the emperor (under US pressure) in 1945. It was replaced by the older form, shrine Shinto, the worship of *kami* in shrines or sanctuaries, tended by priests. In the home, the *kami* are housed within a

kamidana, or 'godshelf'. Personal worship involves purification rites and daily prayers to the *kami*. Shinto is regarded as the religion of life, while Buddhism is seen as that of death; marriages are therefore celebrated according to Shinto tradition, while people generally choose Buddhist rites for funerals. Pilgrimages to temples and shrines, particularly those on mountains, are widespread during the new year, spring, and autumn festivals. Festival worship includes the chanting of prayers, the playing of ceremonial music, and the offering of food. A set of different practices, such as simple rites and local festivals, is associated with sect Shinto, new religious movements with a Shinto foundation.

ship money Originally an occasional sum of money paid by English seaports to the crown to meet the cost of supplying a ship to the Royal Navy. CHARLES I revived the tax in 1634, while he was ruling without Parliament. From 1635 he extended it to the inland towns, and raised up to £200,000 a year as a result. In 1637 John HAMPDEN was taken to court for refusing to pay and claimed that Charles needed Parliament's approval to levy such a regular tax. The judges decided by 7 to 5 in Charles's favour, but the narrowness of the victory encouraged widespread refusal to pay tax afterwards. The LONG PARLIAMENT made ship money illegal in 1641.

shire The main unit of local administration in England. Shires evolved as territorial units in Wessex in the 9th century, replacing the Roman system of provinces. They were extended over a wider area of England by ALFRED THE GREAT and his heirs as administrative and political units. The English shire system reveals many different evolutionary processes. Some were based on former kingdoms (Kent, Sussex, Essex); others on tribal subdivisions within a kingdom (Norfolk and Suffolk); others were created during the 10th-century reconquest of the DANELAW or as territories centred on towns (Oxfordshire, Warwickshire, Buckinghamshire, and so on). England north of the River Tees was not absorbed into the shire system until the Norman Conquest when shires were re-styled 'counties'.

Shivaji SIVAJI.

shogunate In Japan, a form of dynastic military government in which power lay in the hands of a *Sei-i dai-shogun* ('barbarian-conquering great general'). During several periods of Japanese history the shoguns exercised civil and military power in the name of the emperors, who became figureheads. In the 8th century generals with the title of shogun had been appointed during the wars against the native Ainu of northern Japan, but their commands were limited in time and purpose. The shogunate as a form of government originated with MINAMOTO YORITOMO's appointment as military overlord without any limit to his authority (1192). After he died the HOJO regents took control of affairs, but in theory they remained subject both to the emperor and the shogun. During the ASHIKAGA period the shoguns were independent of any other authority though their rule was ineffective. Under the TOKUGAWA, who effectively ruled Japan from the beginning of the 17th century, the power of the shogunate was decisive in national politics. From the 1840s, however, their power was progressively undermined by political pressures unleashed by increasing foreign incursions into Japanese territory. Resistance to the shogunate's conservative policies coalesced around advocates of a return to full imperial rule, and between 1866 and 1869 the Tokugawa armies were gradually defeated by an alliance of provincial forces from Choshu, Satsuma, and Tosa acting for the MEIJI emperor, who formally resumed imperial rule in January 1868.

Shotoku Taishi (574–622) Japanese prince. As regent for Empress Suiko, he set out at the age of 20 to convert a clan society into a centralized administration like that of China. He sent embassies to the SUI, brought in Chinese artists and craftsmen, adopted the Chinese calendar, created a constitution, and instituted a bureaucracy based on merit. He promoted both BUDDHISM and CONFUCIANISM. After Shotoku's death, during the Taika ('Great Change') period (645–710), an imperial prince and a FUJIWARA initiated further reforms. Gradually, Chinese practices were adapted to Japanese conditions and a more centralized administration emerged.

Siam THAILAND.

Sicilian Vespers A popular uprising in Sicily that involved the massacre of the island's French occupiers: so-called because it began at the time of vespers (the evening church service) on Easter Tuesday in 1282. It marked the end of the rule of the ANGEVINS in the island and of their dynastic ambitions in Italy. Charles I of Anjou had received the Kingdom of the Two Sicilies from Pope Urban IV in 1266 and to claim it had defeated the Hohenstaufen MANFRED, son of the Holy Roman Emperor Frederick II. His rule was extremely harsh, enforcing heavy taxation, and the French occupation was generally hated. Within a month all the French had been killed or forced to flee. The crown was later given to Pedro III of Aragon, who thwarted Angevin attempts at reoccupation and passed the crown to his son Frederick III of Sicily.

Sicily The largest island in the Mediterranean Sea, south-west of Italy, of which it is now an autonomous region.

Physical. Sicily is separated from the Calabrian mainland by the Strait of Messina, which is only 3 km (less than 2 miles) wide. Much of the island consists of mountain ranges, which culminate in the snowcapped cone of Etna. The main plains are in the south, though even here the interior is hilly, with plateaux where olive bushes, almond trees, and vineyards grow. To the north are the volcanic islands of Ustica, the Liparis, and Stromboli, the most continuously active volcano in Europe. To the south are off-shore deposits of oil.

History. In the 8th century BC Phoenicians founded trading posts in the west of the island, while Greeks colonized the eastern and southern coasts. From the 5th to the 3rd centuries BC conflict between CARTHAGE and the Greeks (led by Syracuse) was a feature of the island's history. In 264 BC the first of the PUNIC WARS between Carthage and Rome began, and by 210 BC the island was totally under Roman control, remaining so until it was occupied by the Vandals and then the Ostrogoths. BELISARIUS took possession of the island for the Byzantine empire in 535 AD, a rule that lasted until the 9th century when the Arabs won control after prolonged and ferocious fighting. Under their benevolent regime Palermo in particular flourished. Two centuries of Arab

rule were ended by NORMAN colonization. From 1139 Sicily was linked to the kingdom of NAPLES under ROGER II. Norman rule was followed by Surabian and ANGEVIN rule, the latter ended by the infamous SICILIAN VESPERS in 1282. There then followed more than five centuries of rule by Aragonese princes and Spanish kings of Naples and Sicily.

In 1799 a French Revolutionary army occupied Naples and King Ferdinand IV of Naples and Sicily sought refuge in Palermo, under British protection. Escorted by Admiral NELSON, he returned to Naples in June and ordered a mass execution of 100 Italian patriots accused of collaborating with the French. In 1806 he had again to seek British protection in Sicily, when Napoleon established first his brother Joseph and then General Joachim MURAT as kings of Naples. The nine years of French rule of the mainland were enlightened, and the power of the aristocracy was broken, but no constitution was granted. In Sicily, under British pressure, Ferdinand issued a constitution in 1812 creating a Parliament along British lines, but was less successful in breaking the power of the feudal lords. In 1815 Ferdinand was restored again in Naples, now as Ferdinand I, King of the Two Sicilies, but his repressive regime was unpopular, as was that of his son Ferdinand II. The kingdom became a centre for nationalist societies seeking Italian unification. A revolt broke out in Naples (1820) and the first of Italy's REVOLUTIONS OF 1848 took place in Palermo. GARIBALDI and his 'Thousand' landed at Marsala in Sicily in 1860 and defeated Ferdinand at a battle near his palace of Caserta. The kingdom voted by plebiscite to join the rest of the kingdom of Italy in October 1861.

Siegfried Line A fortified defensive erected in France from Lens to Rheims in World War I by the Germans, after their failure to capture Verdun. Sometimes known as the Hindenburg Line, it proved useful in 1917, enabling a front to be maintained with depleted forces. In World War II Hitler applied the term to the fortifications along Germany's western frontier. Some of these were briefly used by German troops retreating into Germany in 1944–45.

Sierra Leone A tropical West African country with a south-west-facing Atlantic coast and a fine natural harbour, surrounded inland by Guinea and Liberia.

Physical. Swamps spread up river valleys, through a rain-forested coastal plain to wooded savannah in the interior. In the sand and gravel of these valleys, diamonds are found. The climate is very wet, although in winter the drying harmattan wind blows from the hinterland.

Economy. The leading exports are rutile, diamonds, bauxite, cocoa, and coffee; smuggling of gold and diamonds is widespread. Iron-ore mines are inactive due to lack of financing. In agriculture, the main cash crops are cocoa and coffee, and the main staple crops are cassava, rice, and plantains. Industry is confined to food-processing and other light industry.

History. The Portuguese navigator Pedro de Cintra landed in Sierra Leone in 1462, at about the time the Temne, its chief inhabitants, were reaching the coast. During the 16th and 17th centuries the SLAVE TRADE and opportunities for piracy attracted many Europeans, including Britons, with the result that the coastal population is now racially very mixed. In 1787 the

British Anti-Slavery Society bought the coastal territory from the local ruler as a haven for slaves found destitute in Britain (where escaped slaves had automatically become free since a law of 1772). British philanthropists organized their transport to Cape Sierra Leone, where Freetown was established. In 1791 Alexander Falconbridge formed a transport company, the Sierra Leone Company, which landed the first colonists at Freetown in 1792. This became a crown colony in 1808. After 1815 British warships who captured slave ships brought freed captives there. During the 19th century the hinterland of Sierra Leone was gradually explored and in 1896 it became a British protectorate, which remained separate from the colony of Freetown until 1951. The country gained its independence under Prime Minister Sir Milton Margai (1895–1964) in 1961, but after his death electoral difficulties produced two military coups before some stability was restored by the establishment of a one-party state under Dr Siaka Stevens. Food shortages, corruption, and tribal tensions produced serious violence in the early 1980s, and in 1985 Stevens retired in favour of Major-General Joseph Saidu Momoh. As head of state, he retained a civilian cabinet with the All People's Congress (APC) the sole legal party; its rule was deeply corrupt. In April 1992 an army coup, led by Captain Valentine Strasser, ousted Saidu Momoh and formed a National Provisional Defence Council, committed to the elimination of corruption and the restoration of the economy. Although the ban on political parties imposed in 1992 was lifted in 1995, actions by rebel forces opposed to the government intensified. In 1996 Strasser was ousted by his deputy, Captain Julius Bio, who took over as head of state. In March 1996 democratic elections were won by Ahmad Tejan Kabbah who became President of a civilian government and signed a ceasefire agreement with the rebels. However, Kabbah was forced to flee the country in May 1997, when a military coup led by Major Johnny Paul Koroma toppled the government. An initial attempt by Nigerian forces to crush the coup failed, as did a national strike, but in February 1998 a Nigerian-led coalition of West African forces captured Freetown and President Kabbah was restored.

CAPITAL:	Freetown
AREA:	71,740 sq km (27,699 sq miles)
POPULATION:	4.617 million (1996)
CURRENCY:	1 leone = 100 cents
RELIGIONS:	Traditional beliefs 51.5%; Sunni Muslim 39.4%; Protestant 4.7%; Roman Catholic 2.2%; Anglican 1.2%
ETHNIC GROUPS:	Mende 46.0%; Temne 45.0%
LANGUAGES:	English (official); Krio (English creole); Mende; Temne, other local languages
INTERNATIONAL ORGANIZATIONS:	UN; OAU; ECOWAS; Commonwealth

Sieyès, Emmanuel Joseph (1748–1836) French statesman and abbot, one of the chief theorists of the Revolutionary era. He was vicar-general of the diocese of Chartres when he wrote his famous pamphlet, *What is the Third Estate?* (1788). The following year he became a member of the NATIONAL ASSEMBLY and played a major part in writing the constitution. He voted for the king's execution but refused to serve under the constitution of 1795. Four years later he was appointed to the DIRECTORY but conspired with NAPOLEON to overthrow it and set about producing the 'perfect' constitution. When this was modified by Napoleon he retired from public life and, after the Restoration, left France.

Sigismund (1368–1437) Holy Roman Emperor (1411–37), King of Hungary (1387–1437), Germany (1411–37), Bohemia (1419–37), and Lombardy (1431–37), the last emperor of the House of Luxemburg. In 1396 he was defeated by the Turks at NICOPOLIS but went on to acquire and secure a large number of territories and titles in a long and violent reign that involved warfare with the HUSSITES, Venetians, and rivals for the thrones of Hungary and Germany. An orthodox Catholic, he acted severely against the Hussites, and put pressure on the pope to call a council at CONSTANCE to end the Hussite Schism; Sigismund promised Huss safe-conduct to attend the council, which subsequently ordered his death.

Sihanouk, Norodom (1923–) Cambodian statesman and King of CAMBODIA (1941–55, 1993–). As King, he exploited the complicated political situation immediately after the FRENCH INDO-CHINESE WAR to win full independence for Cambodia in 1953. He abdicated in 1955 to form a political union with himself as Prime Minister and became Head of State in 1960. After attempting to remain neutral in the VIETNAM WAR, he became convinced that communist forces would win and began to lend covert assistance, earning US enmity, which contributed to his overthrow in Lon Nol's military coup in 1970. He supported the KHMER ROUGE from exile in China and returned as nominal head of state following their victory in 1975, but was removed from office in the following year. In exile he sought to overthrow the Vietnamese-backed regime of Heng Semrin, in collaboration with nationalist forces led by Son Sann. In 1982 he allied himself again with the Khmer Rouge, and in 1987 entered discussions that led to a peace agreement and the establishment (1991) of the UN-supported Supreme National Council of Cambodia, with himself as Head of State. After general elections in 1993, a new monarchist constitution restored him as King.

Sikhism (from Sanskrit, *shishya*, 'pupil') A monotheistic religion founded in the Punjab in the late 15th century by Guru NANAK. Sikhism, which derives from both ISLAM and HINDUISM, combines belief in one eternal and omnipotent God with acceptance of the Hindu concepts of karma and reincarnation. It preaches the equality of mankind and rejects the CASTE SYSTEM. The aim of the believer is to root out selfishness and achieve oneness with God through the repetition of his many names. Through union with God, the Sikh achieves *mukti* (the same concept as Hindu *moksha*, liberation from the cycle of birth, death, and rebirth). Nanak was the first of a line of ten GURUS, the fifth and ninth of whom were executed following clashes with the Moguls. The tenth guru, GOBIND SINGH, proclaimed that his successor as perpetual Guru was to be the *Adi Granth*, the Sikhs' holy book. Gobind Singh also established the *khalsa*, a brotherhood of soldier-saints, in 1699. A century later RANJIT SINGH set up a powerful Sikh kingdom in the Punjab, but its shortlived dominance was ended by British annexation in 1849 (see SIKH WARS). Nowadays the *khalsa* consists of both men and women who have undergone full initiation into the faith. The orthodox

Sikh wears 'the five ks': the *kesh* (unshorn hair and beard), the *kungha* (a hair comb), the *kuchcha* (shorts), the *kara* (an iron or steel bangle), and the *kirpan* (a sword or dagger). Sikhism has no priests; any Sikh, of either sex, can conduct a service. Worship may consist of private devotions or public services in the *gurdwara*, or Sikh temple. Apart from the *Harimandir*, or Golden Temple, at AMRITSAR, India, other important places for Sikhs are Patna (the birthplace of Gobind Singh), Anandpur (where the *khalsa* was established), and Nander (where Gobind Singh died). While the majority of Sikhs today live in the Punjab in India, where Sikh separatism has become a militant political movement, many others have emigrated to the UK, the USA, Canada, East Africa, and South Africa. They number about 14 million in all.

Sikh Wars (1845–49) Two conflicts between the Sikhs of Lahore and the English EAST INDIA COMPANY. The First Sikh War (1845–46) took place when Sikh troops crossed the Sutlej River into British India. After the inconclusive battles of Mudki and Firuzshah, the British defeated the Sikhs at Aliwal and Sobraon. By the Treaty of Lahore (1846) Britain obtained the cession of the Jullundar Doab, took Kashmir for Gulab Singh, and established control of the Lahore government through a Resident. Sikh discontent led to the Second Sikh War (1848–49); the bloody Battle of Chillianwallah was followed by the decisive British victory at Gujerat over an army of 60,000 Sikhs. The governor-general, Lord DALHOUSIE, annexed the Punjab in 1849. The battles of the Sikh Wars were the toughest that the British fought in India, the Sikh forces created by RANJIT SINGH being well trained in the European mode of war and determined in battle.

Sikkim A small state in northern India, sandwiched between NEPAL and BHUTAN and lying astride a strategic route between India and Tibet. Much of its north-west frontier is glaciated and dominated by the mighty mountain group of Kanchenjunga. Until 1975 it was a British protectorate, ruled by *chogyals* (kings). In the past Sikkim suffered continual invasions from its Himalayan neighbours, especially Bhutan and Nepal. Its strategic interest to Britain resulted in the Anglo-Sikkimese Treaty (1861), which made it a protectorate of British India. In spite of criticism of his feudal rule, the *chogyal* hoped to retain internal autonomy when Britain left India, but a referendum in 1975 demanded transfer to the Indian Union, which then followed.

Sikorski, Vladislav (1881–1943) Polish general and statesman. He commanded divisions against the BOLSHEVIKS (1919–20) and during 1922–23 headed a non-parliamentary coalition government in Poland. In 1939 he fled to France and organized a Polish army in exile that fought with the Allies in World War II. As head of the exiled Polish government in London he succeeded in maintaining tolerable relations with Moscow until news of the KATYN MASSACRE broke. During his ascendancy Polish prisoners-of-war in the Soviet Union were recruited to form the 'Polish Army in Russia' under General Wladyslaw Anders to fight with the Allies. He was killed in an air crash.

Silesia A region of central Europe, now largely in south-west Poland.

Physical. Lower Silesia is essentially a plain overlying the Silesian Basin. This is oriented north-west to south-east, more or less along the line of the Oder (Odra) River. To the south-east, in Upper Silesia, a corresponding anticlinal structure has brought coalbearing rocks to the surface. These have given rise to an important industrial area.

History. Silesia was a Polish province that passed to BOHEMIA in 1335. From 1526 it was ruled by the Austrian HABSBURGS until captured by PRUSSIA in 1742, Austria retaining only a small area of southern Silesia. After the defeat of the Central Powers in 1918 and a series of plebiscites, Upper Silesia (the coal- and steel-producing area) went to Poland, and most of Austrian Silesia to Czechoslovakia; Germany was left with Lower Silesia. During the years between the wars there was heavy French financial investment in Polish Silesia, but also civil unrest as the interests of Germany, Poland, and Czechoslovakia were disputed. In 1939 Upper Silesia was occupied by the German THIRD REICH; following Germany's defeat in 1945 the POTSDAM CONFERENCE decreed that the whole area should pass to Poland. German nationals were repatriated, mainly to the Federal Republic of Germany.

Silk Route An ancient trade route linking China, Central Asia, and the Levant via the Pamir mountains, the Ferghana valley, Samarkand, and Merv. From the 2nd century BC Chinese silks were exchanged for western bullion, much of the trade being through middlemen. Few merchants and only a small proportion of the goods ever travelled the whole distance. BUDDHISM and NESTORIAN Christianity came to China by this route and, from the 7th century, so did Levantine traders. The Mongol conquests of the 13th century gave the route new life, and MARCO POLO gave it added significance, until in the 15th century it was superseded by east-west trade by sea. (See map.)

Sima Qian (Ssu-ma Ch'ien) (*c.* 145–85 BC) Chinese historian, an official at the court of the HAN emperor Wudi. His *Historical Records* is a history of China from earliest times to the days of Wudi, and is a model for later dynastic histories. As well as recounting ancient myths, he provided much source material, quoting inscriptions from old bronzes and imperial decrees from the archives. One section of the work, *Assorted Traditions*, has lively biographies of generals, poets, scoundrels, and court ladies. Angered by his defence of a general forced to surrender to the XIONGNU, Wudi had him castrated. Although such punishment often led officials to commit suicide he decided to live on to complete his history.

Simnel, Lambert (*c.* 1487–*c.* 1525) English royal PRETENDER. Although he was actually a joiner's son, certain YORKISTS maintained, or genuinely believed, that he was Edward of Warwick, son of the murdered George, Duke of CLARENCE, and on 24 May 1487 he was crowned in Dublin as Edward VI. Next month he was brought to England, but the Yorkists were defeated and HENRY VII, showing mercy, gave him employment in the royal kitchens.

simony In Christianity, the buying and selling of spiritual or church benefits. The practice, which is generally regarded as sinful, is named after Simon Magus who, according to an account in the New Testament, tried to buy spiritual powers from St Peter.

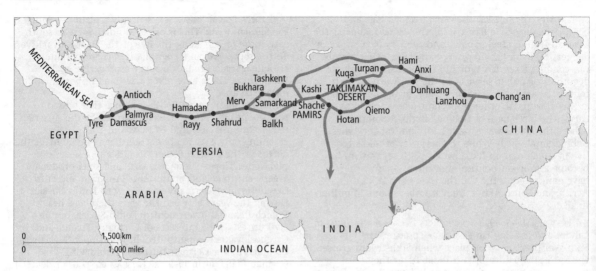

Silk Route *Crossing Asia from eastern China to the Mediterranean, the Silk Route was pioneered by the Chinese in the 2nd century BC. Bactrian camels carried many goods besides silk on the Silk Route, but only a small proportion of the goods, and few merchants, ever travelled its whole length. The route began in the old capital, Chang'an (now Xi'an) and skirted the Taklimakan desert north and south, before climbing into the Pamirs from Kashi (Kashgar) and continuing through Persia to the Mediterranean. From Shache (Yarkand) another route led to India.*

It came to mean the purchase of any office or authority within the ROMAN CATHOLIC CHURCH. The church's policy that its benefices should not be sold for money was often jeopardized because many secular lords claimed that they were theirs to dispose of as they wished. Wealthy families bought offices for their members and used them as a form of patronage. Simony was one of the abuses criticized at the time of the REFORMATION.

Sind A region, now a province of Pakistan, which occupies the predominantly desert region of the lower Indus valley. Several sites, notably MOHENJO-DARO, show that the region was a cradle of early civilization. It was incorporated in the MAURYAN EMPIRE, but for long periods was left to its own devices. In 711 AD Arab invasions initiated an era of Islamicization. AKBAR extended Mogul power to Sind in the 16th century, yet isolation and aridity favoured local independence, which only ended with British expansion in the 19th century.

Sindhia A leading MARATHA family, based at Gwalior in northern India, which dominated the Maratha confederacy in the late 18th century. The founder of the family's fortunes, Ranoji Sindhia (d. 1750), seized control of the Malwa region that he had been appointed to govern. A successor, Mahadaji Sindhia (ruled 1761–94), created a virtually independent kingdom in north India. He became the arbiter of power not only within the Maratha confederacy, but also at the MOGUL court at Delhi, and won victories against the EAST INDIA COMPANY as well as the RAJPUTS. His successors failed to stem British expansion in north India. Daulat Rao Sindhia was defeated in 1803, and in 1818 Gwalior became a Princely State under the Company's protection.

Singapore A south-east Asian island state.
Physical. Singapore comprises an island at the southern end of the Malay Peninsula, only 2° N of the Equator. The climate is hot and damp, and the land is naturally swampy. The country comprises a large low-lying island, about 40 km (25 miles) wide by 22 km (14 miles) from north to south, and many much smaller ones. Its chief physical resource is a magnificent natural harbour.

Economy. The port of Singapore is one of the largest in the world and entrepôt trade has long been important. Manufacturing industry, including shipbuilding, electronics, and refining of imported crude oil, has been developed, and Singapore is a leading financial centre. Tourism is significant, and although agriculture is relatively unimportant, rare orchids and exotic fish are valuable exports. The principal exports are machinery, petroleum products, communications equipment, and clothing. Singapore's capital reserves are among the largest in the world; there is high government spending on social services, with some 20% of the budget used for education.

History. The island of Singapore was formerly known as Tumasik or Temasek. It was inhabited mainly by fishermen and pirates before becoming part of the Sumatran empire of SRIVIJAYA. It then passed to the MAJAPAHIT empire in the 14th century and to the Ayutthaya empire of Siam. In the 15th century it became part of the Malacca empire, and subsequently came under Portuguese and then Dutch control.

The island was acquired for the British EAST INDIA COMPANY by Sir Stamford RAFFLES in 1819 from the sultan of JOHORE, and rapidly developed into an important trading port. In 1867 Singapore was removed from British Indian administration to form part of the new colony of the STRAITS SETTLEMENTS, its commercial development, dependent on Chinese immigrants, migrants, proceeding alongside its growth as a major naval base. In 1942 it fell to Japanese forces under General YAMASHITA TOMOYUKI (SINGAPORE, FALL OF) and remained in Japanese hands until the end of World War II. The island became a separate colony in 1946 and enjoyed internal self-government from 1959 under the leadership of LEE KUAN YEW. It joined the Federation of MALAYSIA in 1963, but Malay fears that its predominantly Chinese population would discriminate in favour of the non-Malays led to its expulsion in 1965. A member of the COMMONWEALTH OF NATIONS, and the ASSOCIATION OF SOUTH-EAST ASIAN NATIONS, it has maintained close ties with Malaysia and Brunei. The People's Action Party has governed since 1965, with Lee Kuan Yew as the world's longest-serving Prime Minister (1965–90). Lee Kuan Yew resigned in 1990, taking the role of Senior Minister. He was succeeded as Prime Minister by Goh Chok Tung. The PAP consolidated its support in the general elections of January 1997.

CAPITAL:	Singapore
AREA:	622 sq km (240 sq miles)
POPULATION:	3.045 million (1996)
CURRENCY:	1 Singapore dollar = 100 cents
RELIGIONS:	Buddhist 28.3%; Christian 18.7%; Muslim 16.0%; Taoist 13.4%; Hindu 4.9%
ETHNIC GROUPS:	Chinese 77.0%; Malay 15.0%; Indian and Sri Lankan 6.0%
LANGUAGES:	Malay, Mandarin, Tamil, English (all official); Chinese
INTERNATIONAL ORGANIZATIONS:	UN; Colombo Plan; Commonwealth; ASEAN

Singapore, fall of (8–15 February 1942) One of the greatest Japanese victories in World War II and the worst defeat in British military history. Although SINGAPORE had strong coastal defences, no fortifications had been built against land attack from the Malay peninsula, apart from providing for the causeway across the 1.6 km (1 mile) Strait of Johore to be blown up. After swiftly overrunning Malaya, Japanese forces under General YAMASHITA TOMOYUKI massed opposite the island at the beginning of February 1942. During the night of 7/8 February armoured landing-craft crossed the Strait of Johore, surprising the garrison of Australian troops opposite. Many Japanese troops followed by swimming across the water. The causeway was blown up and the defenders retreated. The garrison of British, Indian, and Australian troops numbered some 80,000 under General A. E. Percival. However, incessant air-attack by the Japanese destroyed oil tanks and supplies and reduced morale. Having repaired the causeway, further Japanese were sent in and Percival continued to retreat south-east towards the residential area. On 15 February attempts were made to evacuate key personnel by boat, but few survived, and Percival surrendered. The defeat was a significant milestone in the ending of British imperial interests in south-east Asia.

Sinn Féin (Gaelic, 'we ourselves') An Irish political party dedicated to the creation of a united Irish republic. Originally founded by Arthur GRIFFITH in 1902 as a cultural revival movement, it became politically active and supported the EASTER RISING in 1916. Having won a large majority of seats in Ireland in the 1918 general election, Sinn Féin Members of Parliament, instead of going to London, met in Dublin and proclaimed Irish independence in 1919. An independent parliament (Dáil Éireann) was set up, though many of its MPs were in prison or on the run. Guerrilla warfare against British troops and police followed. The setting up of the Irish Free State (December 1921) and the partition of Ireland were bitterly resented by Sinn Féin, and the Party abstained from the Dáil and the Northern Ireland parliament for many years.

Sinn Féin today is the political wing of the Provisional IRISH REPUBLICAN ARMY and has the support of the uncompromising Irish nationalists. In 1994, following a peace initiative by the Irish and British governments, Sinn Féin President Gerry ADAMS announced a complete IRA ceasefire. However, the peace process remained deadlocked throughout 1995, owing to Sinn Féin's refusal to commit the IRA to decommissioning weapons as a precondition to negotiation. In February 1996 the ceasefire was broken by a series of IRA bomb attacks on mainland Britain, and Sinn Féin were excluded from talks on the future of Northern Ireland that began in June. However, when a new IRA ceasefire was announced in July 1997, Sinn Féin representatives were allowed to join multiparty negotiations. In December 1997, Adams became the first Irish Republican leader since Michael COLLINS in the early 1920s to talk directly with a British premier, when he met Prime Minister BLAIR in Downing Street. The negotiations led in 1998 to the Good Friday peace settlement, to be approved in separate referendums by the people of Northern Ireland and the Irish Republic.

Sino-French War (1884–85) A conflict between France and China over VIETNAM. China had assisted Vietnam in partial resistance to French expansion since the 1870s, first with irregular forces of the Black Flag Army and after 1883 with regular forces. In 1884, after both governments had rejected the compromise Li-Fournier agreement, war broke out. The Chinese were unable to resist the French navy, which attacked Taiwan and destroyed Fuzhou (Foochow) dockyard in south-east China, and the QING dynasty's reputation was weakened. In the treaty signed in 1885, France won control of Vietnam.

Sino-Japanese War (1894–95) A war between China and Japan, fought mainly in Korea. After Korea was opened to Japanese trade in 1876, it rapidly became an arena for rivalry between the expanding Japanese state and neighbouring China, of which Korea had been a vassal state since the 17th century. A rebellion in 1894 provided a pretext for both sides to send troops to Korea, but the Chinese were rapidly overwhelmed by superior Japanese troops, organization, and equipment. After the Beiyang fleet, one of the most important projects of China's SELF-STRENGTHENING MOVEMENT, was defeated at the battle of the Yellow Sea and Port Arthur (now Lüshun) was captured, the Chinese found their capital Beijing menaced by advancing Japanese forces. They were forced to sign the Treaty of SHIMONOSEKI, granting Korean independence and making a series of commercial and territorial concessions that opened the way for a Japanese confrontation with Russia, the other expansionist power in north-east Asia.

Sino-Japanese War (1937–45) A conflict on the Chinese mainland between combined nationalist and communist Chinese forces and Japan. China had been the target of Japanese expansionism since the late 19th century, and after the MUKDEN INCIDENT of 1931 full-scale war was only a matter of time. Hostilities broke out, without any formal declaration of war by either side, after a clash near the Marco Polo bridge just west of Beijing in 1937. The Japanese overran northern China, penetrating up the Yangtze and along the railway lines, capturing Shanghai, Nanjing, Guangzhou, and Hankou by the end of 1938. In the 'Rape of Nanjing', over 100,000 civilians were massacred by Japanese troops. The invaders were resisted by both the KUOMINTANG army of the nationalist leader CHIANG KAI-SHEK and the communist 8th Route Army, the former being supplied after 1941 by Britain and the USA. By the time the conflict had been absorbed into World War II, the Sino–Japanese War had reached a state of near stalemate, Japanese military and aerial superiority being insufficient to overcome tenacious Chinese resistance and the problems posed by massive distances and poor communications. The Chinese kept over a million Japanese troops tied down for the entire war, inflicting a heavy defeat upon them at Jiangxi in 1942 and successfully repelling a final series of offensives in 1944 and 1945. The Japanese finally surrendered to Chiang Kai-shek on 9 September 1945, leaving him to contest the control of China with MAO ZEDONG's communist forces.

Sino–Soviet border dispute (March 1969) A brief conflict between China and the Soviet Union over possession of an island in the Ussuri River. The exact position of the border between north-east China and the Soviet Union had long been a subject of dispute. The disagreement turned into a military confrontation because of the ideological dispute between China and the Soviet Union after 1960 and the militant nationalism that was part of the CULTURAL REVOLUTION. In March 1969 two battles were fought for possession of the small island of Zhen Bao (also known as Damansky). The Chinese ultimately retained control of the island, and talks in September 1969 brought the crisis to an end.

Sioux DAKOTA.

Sitting Bull (c. 1834–90) Dakota Sioux chief. He began his career as a warrior against the Crow, and opposed White incursions on to the Great Plains in the 1860s and 1870s. It was his resistance to enforced settlement on a reservation that led to General CUSTER's expedition of 1876 and the Battle of the LITTLE BIG HORN. Despite Custer's defeat, Sitting Bull had to flee to Canada, where he remained until 1881, when he was attracted back by an amnesty. In 1885 he appeared in Buffalo Bill Cody's 'WILD WEST' Show, but he continued to lead the Native Americans in their refusal to sell their lands to the White settlers, and advocated the Ghost Dance religion, preached by WOVOKA. This preached the coming of a Native American messiah who would restore the country to them. In an uprising that followed, Sitting Bull was killed by Native American policemen while 'resisting arrest'.

Sivaji (c. 1630–80) Founder of the MARATHA kingdom in India. He was responsible for a revival of Hindu fortunes in western India at a time of Muslim expansion. He was a member of the Bhonsla family who, at an early age planned the downfall of the Muslim sultanates that surrounded his Deccan home. In confrontations with the sultan of Bijapur and the MOGUL emperor, AURANGZEB, he won unlikely victories, and a reputation for deeds of remarkable daring. When finally defeated by the Mogul army he escaped in disguise to win back and expand his domains. In 1674 he was crowned king and rewarded his subjects' devotion by a fair and firm administration, showing tolerance to all religious communities. His greatest achievements were to withstand Mogul expansion in the west, and to create a nucleus for subsequent Maratha expansion. He is regarded as an Indian hero.

Six Acts (1819) Legislation in Britain aimed at checking what was regarded as dangerous radicalism, in an immediate response to public anger over the PETERLOO MASSACRE. It dealt with procedures for bringing cases to trial, the prohibition of meetings 'for military exercises', the issue of warrants to search for arms, powers to seize seditious or blasphemous literature, the extension of a stamp-duty on newspapers and periodicals, and the regulation and control of all public meetings. The last three were particularly resented and regarded as a threat to freedom. The Acts proved counter-productive by provoking much opposition; three years later the government of Lord LIVERPOOL began to move towards more liberal policies.

Six-Day War (5–10 June 1967) An Arab–Israeli conflict, known to the Arabs as the June War. The immediate causes of the war were the Egyptian request to the UN Emergency Force in Sinai to withdraw from the Israeli frontier, the increase of Egyptian forces in Sinai, and the closure of the Straits of Tiran (the Gulf of Aqaba) to Israeli shipping. An Egyptian, Syrian, and Jordanian military alliance was formed. The war was initiated by General Dayan, Israel's Minister of Defence, with a pre-emptive air strike followed by the occupation of Sinai, Old Jerusalem, the West Bank, and the Golan Heights (9–10 June). The Arab–Israeli conflict erupted again in the YOM KIPPUR WAR of 1973.

Sixtus IV (Francesco della Rovere, 1414–84) Pope (1471–84). Originally a Franciscan monk and teacher, as pope, he was a patron of the arts, and a powerful secular ruler. He organized two military expeditions against the TURKS in 1472–73, and in 1474–76 attempted re-unification between the Russian EASTERN ORTHODOX and the Catholic churches. In 1478 he authorized the setting up of the SPANISH INQUISITION and in 1483 confirmed Tomás de TORQUEMADA as Grand Inquisitor. Thereafter he concentrated on furthering the ambitions of his family (six of the 34 cardinals he created were his nephews), and in strengthening the political and territorial power of the papacy. He was involved in the PAZZI CONSPIRACY, fought against VENICE in 1483, and spent lavishly on military campaigns. He instigated the building of the Sistine Chapel.

Sixtus V (Felice Peretti, 1521–90) Pope (1585–90). A noted Franciscan preacher, with experience of the Venetian Inquisition (1557–60), he was elected to the papacy as a compromise candidate. He attempted to reform the chaotic PAPAL STATES. The resulting increase in revenues enabled him to engage in an extensive building programme that transformed Rome from a medieval into a baroque city, though at the cost of the destruction of several important antique sites. His reform of central church administration, which included limiting the number of cardinals to 70, contributed to the success of the COUNTER-REFORMATION.

Slave Kings MAMELUKE.

slavery The ownership of one person by another, who controls the slave's life and labour. Slaves are viewed by their dominators as property and are bought and sold accordingly. They are usually used for their labour, but sexual rights over them may also be an important element. Slaves are usually not native to the areas where they are held; they are uprooted from their homes and may be deliberately prevented from developing kinship ties. Slavery is closely associated with racial prejudice, the belief that one race is superior to another.

Slavery has a history going back to the earliest civilizations. Thus Linear B tablets of the MYCENAEAN CIVILIZATION refer to persons who were held in some form of captivity. Later, invaders from the north reduced complete populations in Greece to slavery. The HELOTS of Sparta are the best-known example of a slave class: because of their existence, the Spartans had no need for the personal ownership of slaves. By contrast at Athens many families owned one or two slaves for domestic purposes, and private slaves were also employed in factories and in the silver mines. There were also public slaves at Athens. Much of the ancient economy relied on slaves and the sacred island of Delos served as the main slave market of the Aegean. It was very often the practice amongst the peoples of the ancient world to enslave prisoners-of-war, and that was doubtless the major source of slave labour, though traders were often able to purchase slaves. Piracy was another means of supply. The expansion of the Roman empire created an enormous number of slaves, as for instance when EPIRUS was annexed in 146 BC. On three occasions during the 2nd and 1st centuries BC major slave revolts occurred, and were put down only with great difficulty. The coming of Christianity helped to improve the slave's lot, but slavery proved persistent throughout and beyond antiquity.

Slavery was also commonplace in the Arab lands (see SLAVE TRADE, ARAB). In more recent times the most significant episode of slavery was the use of African slave labour in the PLANTATIONS of the Caribbean and the southern states of the USA during the 18th and early 19th centuries (see SLAVE TRADE, AFRICAN). Although the African slave trade was abolished at the end of the 18th century (see SLAVE TRADE, ABOLITION OF), that was not the end of slavery. In Europe, during World War II the Germans made extensive use of slave labour. After the war, the UN defined a slave as anyone who cannot voluntarily withdraw his or her labour; the UN estimates that some 200 million such slaves exist, principally in Asia, Africa, and South America, where bonded labourers (persons who bind themselves and their labour over for a fixed period in order to pay off a debt, earn a fixed sum, or receive other compensation such as transport or housing) and child slavery are widespread.

Slaves, US Proclamation for the Emancipation of (January 1863) The executive order abolishing slavery in the 'rebel' (Confederate) states of the USA. The Proclamation, issued by President LINCOLN as commander-in-chief of the US Armed Forces, was partly a measure designed to win international support for the Union cause. It was of doubtful constitutional validity. Lincoln had issued a preliminary proclamation on 22 September 1862 advising that all slaves would be legally free as from 1 January 1863. This was now confirmed, to be enforced by military authority without compensation. After the war the US Congress passed (1865) the Thirteenth Amendment to the Constitution, abolishing slavery throughout the USA and thus confirming the constitutionality of the President's action.

slave trade, abolition of The ending of SLAVERY. The slave trade reached its peak in the 18th century on the West African coast, where merchants from Europe worked in co-operation with native chieftains and slave raiders who were willing to exchange slaves for Western commodities. Denmark made participation in the Atlantic slave-trade illegal in 1792 and the USA did so in 1794. In Britain a group of humanitarian Christians, including Thomas CLARKSON and William WILBERFORCE (members of the so-called Clapham Sect), argued that if the Atlantic slave-trade were abolished, with its appalling cruelties, plantation owners would treat their slaves more humanely, as being more valuable. They succeeded in getting Parliament to pass a Bill abolishing the British trade in 1807 and at the Treaties of Ghent (1814) and Vienna (1815) Britain agreed to use the Royal Navy to try to suppress the trade, most European countries now supporting the abolition of slavery. However, for the next 40 years illegal smuggling continued, mainly from Africa. Even after slavery was abolished in the British West Indies (1834) trade in slaves between the southern US slave states and such places as Cuba, Costa Rica, Brazil continued. Within the US southern states the breeding, transport, and sale of slaves became highly profitable, there being some four million slaves on the plantations by the time of the Emancipation Proclamation (1863). Slavery in the Caribbean did not cease until it was banned by such countries as Cuba (1886) and Brazil (1888). In the Muslim world the Arab slave trade from Africa operated from Morocco and Zanzibar and stretched throughout the Ottoman empire into Persia and India. In 1873 the Sultan of Zanzibar was finally persuaded by Britain and Germany to close his markets, while the Moroccan trade gradually dwindled with French and Spanish occupation. However, as late as 1935 there was still evidence of trade in slaves in Africa.

slave trade, African The trade whereby Europeans captured people in Africa and transported them as slaves mainly to the Americas, where slave labour enabled colonists to establish PLANTATIONS. Following their 15th-century discoveries, the Portuguese began taking slaves from Senegambia and Guinea-Bissau: they went to Portugal, the Atlantic islands, and later to the Americas; by the 16th century they came also from Angola, and, occasionally, Mozambique. In the 17th century trading forts, stretching from Arguin (now in Mauritania) to Angola, had been established by slavers from Brandenburg, Denmark, Holland, Courland (on the eastern Baltic), England, France, Genoa, and Sweden. These forts could not have operated without active African participation in supplying slaves for shipment to Brazil, and to British, French, Dutch, and Spanish colonies. It is thought that by the mid-19th century 9.5 million Africans had been transported to the New World, in addition to those who died while being captured or in transit. This figure does not include the Arab slave trade nor the flourishing trade in slaves within Africa. Disgust at this treatment of Africans led to demands for emancipation of the slaves and the

abolition of the slave trade in the 19th century. (See also
SLAVERY; SLAVE TRADE, ABOLITION OF; SLAVES, US PROCLAMATION
FOR THE EMANCIPATION OF.)

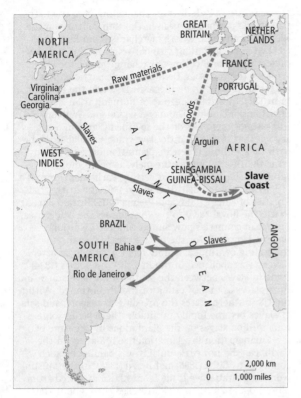

African slave trade   *The African slave trade reached its
height during the 17th and 18th centuries. Several hundred
thousand Africans were transported across the Atlantic each
year, to the plantations of the European colonies in the
Americas. It was a triangular trade. A typical three-leg
voyage set out from Europe to West Africa, carrying cotton
goods, hardware, and, increasingly, guns. These goods were
exchanged for slaves, who were taken to the West Indies and
the southern colonies of North America. The ships returned to
Europe with colonial produce, notably sugar.*

slave trade, Arab A form of commerce in slaves that
existed from earliest times in the Arabian peninsular.
The Prophet MUHAMMAD forbade his followers to enslave
Muslims, but did not free slave converts. His legislation
insisted on humane treatment and gave slaves rights
against oppressive masters. In early Islam slaves were
recruited from prisoners-of-war (including women and
children) and were acquired by raiding and by purchase
in Eastern and Southern Europe, Central Asia, and
Central, East, and West Africa. Under the caliphs the
trade was brisk. Slaves served a variety of purposes:
agricultural, mining, domestic, and clerical, and for
military service. Many slave women employed as
concubines were given the rights of wives. Men and
children often received vocational training after
capture. Through international pressure, the trade was
largely abolished during the 19th century. (See also
SLAVERY.)

Slavs Peoples who occupied eastern Europe in ancient
times and were known to the Romans as Sarmatians and
Scythians. The name is believed to come from *slowo*
('well speaking'). After the collapse of the HUNS in the
5th century the Slavs migrated westwards to the Elbe,
the Baltic, the Danube, the Adriatic, and the Black Sea.
In the 9th century the missionaries Cyril and Methodius
from Constantinople evangelized the Slovenes or
southern Slavs.

Slim, William Joseph, 1st Viscount (1891–1970)
British field-marshal. He commanded an Indian division
in the 1941 conquest of the VICHY French territory of
Syria. In early 1942 he joined the BURMA CAMPAIGN, and in
1943 took command of the 14th Army there. After the
victory at Kohima he pushed down the Irrawaddy River
to recapture Rangoon and most of Burma. After the war
he became Chief of the Imperial General Staff (1948–52)
and governor-general of Australia (1953–60).

Slovakia A central European republic, formerly part of
CZECHOSLOVAKIA.
   Physical. Slovakia covers an area of 49,035 sq km (18,928
sq miles) and is surrounded by Poland to the north,
Ukraine to the east, Hungary to the south, and Austria
and the Czech Republic to the west. The Carpathian
mountains dominate the country reaching a height of
2,655 m (8,711 feet) at the Gerlach Shield in the High
Tatras. Some steppe grasslands are to be found in the
south-eastern lowlands; about one third of the country
is cultivated and two-fifths is covered in forest. The
Danube briefly forms the border between Slovakia and
Hungary as it flows towards Bratislava and finally on to
the Black Sea.
   Economy. Industry is in urgent need of modernization,
and is hampered by the need to import energy, as the
potential for hydroelectric power has not yet been
exploited. Motor vehicles, glass, armaments, footwear,
and textiles are the main exports. IMF resources have
been made available to stabilize the transition from a
communist to a market economy. Slovakia's mineral
resources include iron ore, copper, magnesite, lead, zinc,
and lignite. There are also numerous mineral springs.
The country was invited to apply for EU membership in
1993.
   History. A land belonging to the Hungarian crown
since medieval times, Slovakia experienced an upsurge
in nationalism in the late 18th and early 19th centuries.
A final break with Hungary was made with the collapse
of the Austro-Hungarian empire after World War I;
Slovakia entered into union with the Czech lands.
However, resentment at centralized control from
Prague led to a declaration of autonomy within a
federal Czecho-Slovak state on the eve of the Nazi
annexation of Czechoslovakia in 1938; this was followed
by nominal independence under German protection.
With the end, in 1990, of the communist regime that
had controlled Czechoslovakia since 1948, Slovak
demands for independence grew and the Slovak
Republic (with its capital at Bratislava) came into being
on 1 January 1993 without conflict (the so-called 'Velvet
Divorce', by analogy with the 'Velvet Revolution' that
had ended communism). The nationalist leader Vladimir
MECIAR became Prime Minister. Problems have been
experienced in restructuring the Slovak economy, which
was geared to labour-intensive heavy industry under the
influence of Stalinism in the 1950s. Tensions remain

between the Slovak majority and the ethnic Hungarian minority population. Slovak was made the sole official language of the republic in 1995.

CAPITAL: Bratislava
AREA: 49,035 sq km (18,928 sq miles)
POPULATION: 5.372 million (1996)
CURRENCY: 1 koruna = 100 halierov
RELIGIONS: Roman Catholic 63.8%; non-religious
                    26.7%; Protestant 7.9%; Orthodox 0.6%;
                    other 0.6%
ETHNIC GROUPS: Slovak 86.6%; Czech 1.2%; Hungarian
                    10.9%; other 1.3%
LANGUAGES: Slovak (official); Czech; Hungarian;
                    Romany; other minority languages
INTERNATIONAL
 ORGANIZATIONS: UN; CSCE; Council of Europe

Slovenia A small country in south-east Europe.

Physical. Slovenia is bordered by Austria to the north, Hungary to the east, Italy to the west, and Croatia to the south and east. It has an outlet to the Adriatic Sea. The country is largely mountainous and wooded, with deep and fertile valleys and coal and extensive mineral reserves.

Economy. Industry is well developed, including iron, steel, and textiles. Deposits of coal, lead, zinc, aluminium, and mercury are exploited. Agriculture includes livestock-rearing, viticulture, and crops such as cereals, sugar beet, and potatoes. Tourism is an important source of foreign exchange. Slovenia applied for full membership of the European Union in 1996.

History. The Slovenes, a west Slavonic people, were ruled by the HABSBURGS from the 14th century until 1918. After World War I the majority of the Slovene people were incorporated into the new kingdom of Serbs, Croats, and Slovenes, later renamed YUGOSLAVIA. In 1941 their lands were divided between Italy, Hungary, and the THIRD REICH. In 1945, 1947, and 1954, areas of the Istrian peninsula, including parts of the Free Territory of TRIESTE, were incorporated into the Republic of Slovenia within the Federal Republic of Yugoslavia. The most economically and educationally advanced of the former Yugoslav republics, Slovenia is predominantly Roman Catholic, with a strong Western heritage. During 1989 pressure began to mount for independence, and a coalition of six parties, the Democratic Opposition of Slovenia (DEMOS) emerged. In May 1990 it formed a non-communist government under President Milan Kucan, and in July declared independence, confirmed by a referendum in December. There was intermittent fighting between Slovene partisans and units of the Serb-led Yugoslav army during 1990, before Serbia tacitly accepted the situation. In April 1992 DEMOS split, and the Liberal Democrats under Janez Drnovsek formed a government. Kucan was re-elected President later that year. A new coalition government, led by the Liberal Democrats, was formed in 1993 and retained power in 1997.

CAPITAL: Ljubljana
AREA: 20,251 sq km (7,897 sq miles)
POPULATION: 1.959 million (1996)
CURRENCY: 1 tolar = 100 stotin
RELIGIONS: Roman Catholic 90.0%
ETHNIC GROUPS: Slovene 90.0%
LANGUAGES: Slovenian (official)
INTERNATIONAL
 ORGANIZATIONS: UN; CSCE

Sluys, Battle of (24 June 1340) A naval battle in the HUNDRED YEARS WAR. A force of French, Genoese, and CASTILIAN ships intercepted an English force but was defeated by massed archers. Both French commanders were killed and the victory gave the English control of the English Channel.

Smiles, Samuel (1812–1904) Scottish author and journalist. In 1845 he began delivering lectures to a group of young working-class men in Leeds, who had set up their own evening school for mutual improvement. The lectures were so popular that Smiles had them published as *Self-help* in 1859. The message of the book was that for poor people who wanted to improve themselves the remedy lay in their own hands. If a person worked hard, practised thrift, and tackled problems with determination, he could do almost anything he wanted. The success of *Self-help* was largely due to its celebration of values that most Victorians held dear – notably the promotion of work for its own sake and an optimistic belief in material progress. In the 1908s, Prime Minister Margaret THATCHER referred to Smiles's philosophy in defending her policy of reducing the provisions of the WELFARE STATE.

Smith, Adam (1723–90) Scottish philosopher and economist, the founder of CLASSICAL ECONOMICS. He became professor of moral philosophy at Glasgow University in 1752, and later travelled abroad as tutor to the Duke of Buccleuch. He visited Paris and met a number of the *philosophes*, including QUESNAY, whose ideas confirmed his own hostility to MERCANTILISM. In his revolutionary work, *An Inquiry into the Nature and Causes of the Wealth of Nations* (1776), he focused on the creation of wealth, and noted the importance of manufacturing industry as well as agriculture. He argued that to increase wealth, division of labour and a high proportion of productive to non-productive activity is needed. The larger the market, the greater the scope for specialization and division of labour. Smith ascribed the value of a good to its labour input, but its price to the interaction of supply and demand. Central to his analysis is the role of competition. He argued that, in the presence of competition, individuals pursuing selfish economic ends would be led, 'as if by an invisible hand', to maximize the well-being of society as a whole. From this analysis, he prescribed a minimum of government intervention in the economic system. His ideas had great influence, forming the basis for the development of modern economic theory. (See also *laissez-faire*.)

Smith, Alfred E(manuel) ('Al') (1873–1944) US politician. He rose through his association with TAMMANY HALL and his identification with Irish-American, Roman Catholic, and new immigrant interests in the Democratic Party, to become an able and incorruptible four-term Democratic governor of New York state (1918–20, 1922–28). However, his Catholicism, opposition to PROHIBITION, and Tammany connections prevented him gaining the Democratic nomination for President in 1924, and then from winning the Presidency when he was at last nominated in 1928. Nevertheless, his cultivation of new urban interests helped to develop the Democratic coalition that paved the way for Franklin D. ROOSEVELT's victories of 1932 and 1936, victories that Smith deeply resented.

Smith, Jedediah Strong (1798–1831) US explorer. Born in New York state, he became one of the most famous of the MOUNTAIN MEN who opened up the American north-west. In 1824 he led the third ASHLEY expedition into Wyoming and in subsequent years made the first west–east crossing of the Sierra by a White man. Having opened more territory than any other explorer he was killed by a group of Comanche on the Santa Fe Trail.

Smith, John (1580–1631) Founder of VIRGINIA and promoter of colonization in America. He was born in Lincolnshire and fought against Spain and the Turks (1596–1604). As one of the governing council of Virginia in 1607, his military discipline and firmness with the Native Americans saved JAMESTOWN from collapse. After being burnt in an explosion, he returned to England in 1609. Five years later he explored the New England coast. His optimistic *Description of New England* (1616) was a powerful encouragement to emigration there in the 1620s and 1630s. (See POCAHONTAS.)

Smith, Joseph (1805–44) US founder of the MORMON CHURCH. In 1823 he claimed to have experienced visions and in 1827 a revelation of the existence of mystical religious writings, which he published as the *Book of Mormon* (1829). Smith organized the first Mormon community at Fayette, New York, but persecution as well as disagreements within the community drove him west, first to Ohio, then to Missouri, and finally in 1840 to Nauvoo, Illinois. Opposition increased following Smith's sanctioning of polygamy, and in June 1844, following a general breakdown in order and an ill-considered declaration of martial law, Smith was lynched by a mob in Carthage. Leadership of the Mormons then passed to Brigham YOUNG, who led them to Utah.

smugglers People who move goods illegally from one country to another, to evade payment of customs duties or in defiance of laws prohibiting the importation of merchandise. Smugglers have existed since civilization began: those smuggling cats out of ancient Egypt were subject to the death penalty. The rapid development of organized smuggling came in the late 17th century with higher customs duties and the restrictions of the NAVIGATION ACTS. Smugglers were popular in Britain because they made brandy, tea, silks, and perfumes available at reasonable prices. In colonial America they were regarded as patriotic heroes, who were defying the hated Navigation Acts. The reduction of duties in the late 18th century, the spread of free trade, and the development of the coastguard system, caused a decline in smuggling.

Smuts, Jan Christian (1870–1950) South African statesman, soldier, and scholar. In 1898 he became state attorney in Johannesburg and a member of the KRUGER government. In 1899 he contributed to a propaganda pamphlet, *A Century of Wrong*, explaining the Boer case against Britain, and rose to prominence in the Second BOER WAR as a guerrilla leader of exceptional talent. He was a leading negotiator at the Treaty of VEREENIGING, believing that the future lay in co-operation with Britain. He held a succession of cabinet posts under President BOTHA, but in 1914 rejoined the army and served in South Africa's campaign against German East Africa. In 1917 he joined the Imperial War Cabinet in London, and helped to establish the Royal Air Force. He was an advocate of the LEAGUE OF NATIONS at the Versailles Peace Conference, before returning to South Africa in 1919 to become Prime Minister (1919–24). He led the Opposition until 1933, was subsequently Deputy Prime Minister (1933–39), and once again Prime Minister (1939–48). Among his many achievements was the drafting of the UNITED NATIONS Covenant. His struggle against extreme nationalism found expression in his philosophic study, *Holism and Evolution* (1926).

Snowden, Philip, 1st Viscount (1864–1937) British politician. Permanently crippled in a bicycle accident, he became a socialist and worked for the INDEPENDENT LABOUR PARTY as a journalist. Elected to Parliament for Blackburn in 1906, he became known for his outspoken views, opposing British intervention in World War I, and advocating self-government for India. He served as Chancellor of the Exchequer in 1924 and 1929–31, and again in 1931–32 in the NATIONAL GOVERNMENT. He did not support the GENERAL STRIKE of 1926 and his cautious approach to welfare spending alienated many Labour supporters. His 1931 budget, which reduced unemployment benefits because of the alarming international financial crisis, further antagonized them. The abandonment of FREE TRADE at the OTTAWA conference caused his resignation.

Sobieski, John (1624–96) King John III of Poland (1674–96). He was a member of a great Polish noble family and, after defeating the Turks at Khotin in 1673, was elected king and expelled the Turks from southern Poland, including Lvov. In 1683 he was largely responsible for driving them also from Vienna. He regarded his struggle against the OTTOMAN EMPIRE as a crusade to be pursued at all costs, and can be criticized for not using his great abilities to strengthen the Polish monarchy. He was succeeded by AUGUSTUS II.

socage In Anglo-Saxon and Norman England, a free tenure of land that did not require the tenant to perform military service. He might pay a rent in cash or in kind, and perform some ploughing on his lord's estates. He was liable to pay the three feudal dues — 20 shillings when the lord's son came of age and when the lord's daughter married, and one year's rent to redeem his lord from captivity. In contrast to military tenure, no restrictions attached to the inheritance of the tenure nor to the marriage of the heir.

social contract An agreement among the members of a society to acknowledge the authority of a set of rules or a political regime. The expression was used by the philosophers HOBBES, LOCKE, and ROUSSEAU in their examination of the nature of the state's authority over the individual. Each discussed the condition of man in a state of nature, that is without law and government, and the transition by means of an implied or actual 'contract' to ordered society. Social contract theories became popular in the 16th and 17th centuries as a means of explaining the rightful origin of government and hence the political obligations of subjects. Postulating an original state of nature without political authority, contract theorists such as Hobbes (*Leviathan*, 1651) and Locke (*Two Treatises of Government*, 1689), argued that it would be in each person's interest to agree to the establishment of government. Hobbes considered man without government to be in such a state of fear that he would submit to an absolute authority in order to gain security. Locke, however, believed that man is guided by reason and conscience even in a state of nature and that in accepting government he still retained natural rights. Locke's view influenced the makers of the CONSTITUTION OF THE USA: JEFFERSON held that the preservation of natural rights was an essential part of the social contract. Rousseau disagreed with Locke's description of the state of nature and thought that man, a 'noble savage' in his natural state, acquired a moral and civic sense only when part of a larger democratic community. The terms of the agreement fixed the proper form and scope of government, absolute in Hobbes's case, constitutionally limited in Locke's. For Locke, if the government overstepped the mark, the contract was broken and subjects had the right to rebel. All such theories were later criticized for their unhistorical character.

social credit A theory advanced by the social economist Clifford DOUGLAS, to eliminate the concentration of economic power. It became popular in Canada and New Zealand at the time of the Great DEPRESSION. In Canada a Social Credit Party, led by William Aberhart, won an overwhelming victory in Alberta in 1935 and remained in power until 1971 without, however, implementing many of Douglas's ideas. In 1952 it won an election in British Colombia, but never gained more than a handful of federal seats in Ottawa, and largely disappeared after 1980. A New Zealand Social Credit Party was formed in 1953 and has held from one to three seats in the New Zealand Parliament at various times.

social Darwinism A 19th-century theory of social and cultural evolution. Even before Charles Darwin published the *Origin of Species* (1859), the writer Herbert SPENCER had been inspired by current ideas of evolution to write the *Principles of Psychology* (1855), where he first applied the concept of evolution to the development of society. The theory, based on the belief that natural selection favoured the most competitive or aggressive individual (the 'survival of the fittest'), was often used to support political conservatism. It justified inequality among individuals and races, and discouraged attempts to reform society as an interference with the natural processes of selection of the fittest. In the 20th century it has been used to justify racist ideologies (see EUGENICS) as well as to explain the operations of the 'free economy'.

Social Democrat A member of a left-wing or centre-left party that combines broadly SOCIALIST aims with constitutional methods and an acceptance of at least some aspects of the CAPITALIST system. The name was first adopted by Wilhelm LIEBKNECHT and August Bebel in Germany, when they founded the German Social Democratic Labour Party (1869), based on the tenets of Karl MARX, but advocating evolutionary reform by democratic and constitutional means. In 1875 it was fused with the German Workers' Association, founded (1863) by Ferdinand Lasalle, to form the Social Democratic Party (SDP) of Germany, which was then subjected to anti-socialist legislation by Bismarck. Other parties followed, for example in Denmark (1878), Britain (1883), Norway (1887), Austria (1889), the USA (1897, later becoming the Socialist Party), and Russia (1898), where the Social Democratic Party split in 1903 into BOLSHEVIK

and Menshevik factions. In other countries, for example France, Italy, and Spain, the term 'Socialist Party' was more commonly adopted. The German SDP was the largest party in the Weimar Republic, governing the country until 1933, when it was banned. It was reformed in West Germany after World War II, with a new constitution (1959), ending all Marxist connections. It entered a coalition with the Christian Democrats in 1966, and headed a coalition with the Free Democrats between 1969 and 1982. In East Germany a revived SDP campaigned for office in 1990, following the collapse of the communist regime. In Sweden the SDP, socialist and constitutional in outlook, has been the dominant party since the 1930s, although it was out of office from 1976 to 1982 and from 1991 to 1994. In Britain four prominent members of the Labour Party resigned in 1981 to form a short-lived, Social Democratic Party; most of its members merged with the Liberal Party in 1988 to form the Social and Liberal Democrats (which changed its name to the Liberal Democrats in 1989). After reform by its leaders Neil KINNOCK, John Smith, and Tony BLAIR in the 1980s and 1990s, the British Labour Party may now be more accurately described as a social democratic, rather than a socialist, party.

social insurance NATIONAL INSURANCE.

socialism A political and economic theory that advocates the conscious direction of social life by the State, involving in particular limits on the private ownership of industry. The word first appeared in the early 19th century – in the writings of SAINT-SIMON and Fourier in France and in connection with Robert OWEN's experiments at his New Lanark works in co-operative control of industry. It covers a wide range of positions from COMMUNISM at one extreme to SOCIAL DEMOCRACY at the other, and is therefore difficult to define with precision. It is less easy to say what socialists are for than what they are against, namely untrammelled CAPITALISM, which in socialist eyes enriches the owners of capital at the expense of their employees, provides no security for the poor, and sacrifices the welfare of society to private gain. Most socialists have responded by arguing that the community as a whole should own and control the means of production, distribution, and exchange to ensure a more equitable division of a nation's wealth, either in the form of state ownership of industry, or else in the form of ownership by the workers themselves (see SYNDICALISM). They have also often advocated replacing the market economy by some kind of planned economy. The aim of these measures is to make industry socially responsible, and to bring about a much greater degree of equality in living standards. In addition, socialists have argued for special provision for those in need, in the form, for instance, of a WELFARE STATE. Socialism as a political ideal was revolutionized in the mid-19th century by Karl MARX, who tried to demonstrate scientifically how capitalist profit was derived from the exploitation of the worker, and argued that a socialist society could be achieved only by a mass movement of the workers themselves. Both the methods by which this transformation was to be achieved and the manner in which the new society was to be run remained the subject of considerable disagreement and produced a wide variety of socialist parties, ranging from moderate reformers to ultra left-wing communists dedicated to upheaval by violent revolution. In more recent years, such debates have been overshadowed by the question of whether socialism is a viable alternative to capitalism. Most Western socialists now opt for SOCIAL DEMOCRACY, others for market socialism; in both cases they seek to curb the worst effects of capitalism on society while supporting a free market and ownership of private property. It is only in certain developing countries that traditional socialist aims still attract widespread support among political leaders.

Socialist League A British political organization, set up in 1884 by the designer William Morris, to re-create society on socialist principles. The League published pamphlets, but its main activity took the form of processions and demonstrations, at times resulting in clashes with police and troops. Its membership, consisting partly of moderates seeking working-class progress through parliamentary methods, but partly, also, of revolutionary socialists and ANARCHISTS, was too miscellaneous to endure. By 1890 most moderates had joined the FABIANS, leaving only an extremist and ineffective minority.

social security A system of financial maintenance organized by government to protect individuals against the loss of earnings resulting from sickness, unemployment, old age, and other misfortunes; to meet medical costs; and to give support to families with children. The term covers both social insurance schemes and social assistance schemes. From the late 19th-century onwards such schemes have developed in industrialized countries in response to the emergence of a large class of factory workers dependent on the regular payment of wages, and to the dislocation caused by two World Wars and the economic depression of the 1920s and 1930s.

The first comprehensive scheme in Europe was introduced (1881–89) in BISMARCK's Germany and provided for the payment of insurance benefits by the state in the event of accident, sickness, and old age. Similar schemes were introduced in other European countries and in Australia and New Zealand later in the 19th century: in Britain such provisions were pioneered by LLOYD GEORGE in 1908–11. During World War II the coalition government of Winston Churchill appointed a committee (1941–42) headed by William BEVERIDGE, to review social insurance schemes. Its recommendations, generally known as the Beveridge Report (1942), proposed a comprehensive national insurance scheme that formed the basis of the post-war WELFARE STATE when implemented through the NATIONAL INSURANCE Act, (1946). In the USA (where the term 'social security' originated), the huge increase in unemployment and social distress during the Great DEPRESSION prompted F. D. ROOSEVELT to introduce the NEW DEAL programme and in particular the Social Security Act (based on a payroll tax) in 1935, which provided for old age, widows or widowers, and disability.

By the 1970s almost the entire population of industrialized countries was protected, but rising costs were causing alarm. With social security receipts accounting for a quarter of GDP in some countries, governments have raised insurance contributions and reduced benefits while boosting the importance of occupational and personal insurance. In many countries, including the USA and the UK, social security provision was reduced in scope during the 1980s and 1990s, as costs rose. Increased longevity and long-term structural unemployment mean that governments of many developed countries will continue to face escalating social security costs.

Most developing countries have neither the money nor the administrative infrastructure for social security systems, although some countries, such as Chile and Costa Rica, have insurance schemes and others, such as Thailand, are introducing them.

Society of Friends QUAKERS.

Socinus, Laelius (or Sozzini, Lelio) (1525–62) Italian theologian. After studying law at Bologna, he travelled throughout Europe before settling in Zürich (1548) to study Greek and Hebrew. He corresponded with leading PROTESTANT reformers and conducted his own theological enquiries, but his *Confession of Faith* (1555) showed that he had reached few clear conclusions of his own. His nephew, Faustus Socinus (1539–1604), developed Laelius's views into a well-defined system, which led to the founding of the Socinian sect and contributed to the growth of the UNITARIAN movement.

Socrates (c. 470–399 BC) Athenian philosopher, one of the most remarkable and influential figures of ancient Greece. He was endowed with great courage, both physical and moral. In his early life he seems to have been preoccupied with scientific philosophy, but later he turned to the question of ethical philosophy, or how best to live one's life. He attracted a wide circle of young men, including ALCIBIADES. It was his association with them that may have led to the charges of impiety and corrupting the youth levelled against him in 399 BC. He defended himself at his trial, but was condemned to die by drinking hemlock, which he did, rejecting his friends' offers to help him escape.

Although there is no direct record of Socrates' philosophy the dialogues of his disciple PLATO and the *Memorabilia* of XENOPHON give a vivid picture of his personality, ideas, and methods. Socrates practised philosophy by the method of dialectic, posing questions on such matters as the nature of justice, virtue, or friendship, and subjecting the answers offered to careful analysis and counter-argument. He did not claim to have answers to these questions, but only that he recognized his own ignorance, and that this recognition is a prerequisite of wisdom. Although his investigations are inconclusive, they develop a view of what wisdom would be: a complete and discursive grasp of centrally important concepts. His dialetical method of cross-questioning (the 'Socratic method') was usually ruthless but wryly humorous. He was often critical of the SOPHISTS, whom he accused of attempting to promote immorality by the use of false arguments and rhetoric. Though he professed no fixed set of doctrines, his influence on later thinkers was profound. He believed that virtue was something that could be taught, and applied himself in a systematic philosophical manner to addressing the question of day-to-day conduct and beliefs.

Solemn League and Covenant (1643) The agreement between the English Parliament and Scottish COVENANTERS during the ENGLISH CIVIL WAR. It undertook that the Presbyterian Church of Scotland was to be preserved, and the Anglican Church was to be reformed.

The Scots soon realized that Presbyterianism would not be imposed on England by the specially established Westminster Assembly of Divines. This put considerable strain upon the other aspect of the agreement: Scottish military aid for Parliament in return for £30,000 per month.

Solferino, Battle of (24 June 1859) A battle fought in Lombardy, between the armies of France and Piedmont on one side and Austria on the other. Piedmont, under the leadership of CAVOUR, had persuaded France to give military support to the struggle against Austrian domination in Italy. The French and Piedmont-Sardinians had defeated the Austrians at MAGENTA, and their armies, commanded by NAPOLEON III, captured the elevated position at Solferino and successfully defended it after a fierce counter-attack by the Austrians. The latter, led by FRANCIS JOSEPH, began to retreat. A meeting between the two emperors took place shortly afterwards at VILLAFRANCA, after which hostilities ceased.

Solidarity (Polish, *Solidarnosc*) An independent trade-union and subsequently a political party in Poland. It emerged out of a wave of strikes at Gdańsk in 1980 organized by the Free Union of the Baltic Coast. Demands included the right to a trade union independent of Communist Party control. Under its leader Lech WALESA (1943–) membership rose rapidly, as Poles began to demand political as well as economic concessions. In 1981 the Prime Minister, General Jaruzelski, proclaimed martial law and arrested the Solidarity leaders, outlawing the movement in 1982. In 1989 the government, under pressure from both Left and Right, sponsored round-table talks from which Solidarity emerged as the dominant political organization. In 1990 Walesa was elected President of the republic; but ideological differences soon emerged and the movement broke up into a number of separate political parties, with only one, a minority party, retaining the name. After several years in opposition, Solidarity gained a surprise victory in the general election of 1997 and its leader, Jerzy Buzek, became the head of a coalition government.

Solomon (d. *c.* 922 BC) King of ISRAEL (*c.* 961–*c.* 922 BC). The second son of DAVID and Bathsheba, Solomon succeeded his father and was the last king of a united ISRAEL. His riches and wisdom became legendary and under his rule the nation grew wealthier and alliances were forged with Egypt and Phoenicia. These alliances provoked discontent because they led to the official establishment of foreign religious cults in Jerusalem. Solomon organized the land into administrative districts to facilitate government and introduced a system of forced labour to sustain his extensive building works, including palaces and the Temple at Jerusalem, which became the central sanctuary of the Jewish religion. His fame as sage and poet prompted the queen of Sheba to visit him. The Biblical account, however, also tells of his apostasy and ruthlessness towards his opponents. It was partly because of the high taxes imposed to support court luxury that the northern tribes seceded under JEROBOAM I after his death.

Sulayman (Solomon), a popular figure in Islamic legend, has a prominent place in the Koran, where he is considered an apostle and prophet. It is said he knew the language of the birds and ants and that he had mastery over the jinn, with whose help he built shrines and statues. The Koranic account also says God placed a phantom on his throne to try him but that he repented, which probably refers to Solomon's brief lapse into idolatry.

Solomon Islands An island country in the south-west Pacific.

Physical. The Solomon Islands form a large archipelago comprising a double chain of six large and many smaller islands, lying between 5° and 13° S of the Equator. The largest island, Bougainville, together with a few others in the north-west, is part of PAPUA NEW GUINEA; all the rest constitute a country in which the most important island is Guadalcanal. Lying at the edge of the Pacific plate, the region is subject to earthquakes; and there are volcanoes on the main islands.

Economy. The soil is generally fertile and cocoa and tobacco are grown, although the main resource is copra. Timber and palm oil are exported. Fishing is also important.

History. Occupied for at least 3,000 years, the islands saw the arrival of European missionaries and settlers throughout the 18th and 19th centuries. In 1885 the German New Guinea Company established control of the north Solomons, while Britain declared a protectorate over the southern islands in 1893. During World War II the Solomons witnessed fierce battles between Japanese and Allied forces. The Solomon Islands became an independent member of the COMMONWEALTH OF NATIONS on 7 July 1978. Solomon Mamaloni (Prime Minister since 1989) faced severe criticism during 1991 for allegedly ignoring the constitution and seeking to rule without a mandate. Following an election in 1993, the independent Francis Billy Hilly became Prime Minister. His short-lived administration ended in late 1994, when Mamaloni again won power. Following elections in 1997 Bartholomew Ulufa'alu became Prime Minister. Relations with Papua New Guinea continued to be strained.

CAPITAL:	Honiara
AREA:	28,370 sq km (10,954 sq miles)
POPULATION:	396,000 (1996)
CURRENCY:	1 Solomon Islands dollar = 100 cents
RELIGIONS:	Protestant 75%; Roman Catholic 19%; Baha'i 0.4%; other 2.9%
ETHNIC GROUPS:	Melanesian 94.2%; Polynesian 3.7%; other Pacific islander 1.4%
LANGUAGES:	English (official)
INTERNATIONAL ORGANIZATIONS:	UN; Commonwealth; South Pacific Forum

Solon (*c.* 640–*c.* 560 BC) Athenian statesman and poet. He was the author of a written code of laws that introduced major reforms to ATHENS in the first quarter of the 6th century BC. These included the cancellation of many debts, the restoration to freedom of many who had been made slaves, economic changes intended to stimulate trade and industry, and the division of the citizens into four classes on the basis of wealth, each with particular political responsibilities and prerogatives. This undermined aristocratic power, which was based solely on birth. It seems that Solon may have created a new council (*boule*) to prepare business for the citizen-assembly, thereby undercutting some of the power of the AREOPAGUS. He replaced the DRACONIAN LAW with a less harsh code, which remained the basis of later classical laws.

Solutrian UPPER PALAEOLITHIC.

Somalia A country on the so-called 'Horn of Africa' in the north-east of the continent.

Physical. Somalia has north and south-east coasts on the Gulf of Aden and the Indian Ocean and borders Ethiopia and Kenya inland. Along its north coast, desert plains rise to the red sandstone hills of a northern plateau. There it is hot and arid, the only vegetation being thin thorn-scrub. The south of the country is lower and has one permanent river, the Juba, as a source of irrigation.

Economy. One of Africa's poorest countries and heavily dependent on foreign aid, Somalia has suffered from drought, flooding, famine, civil war, and high foreign debt in recent years. The main exports are livestock and bananas; other crops are sugar cane, maize, and sorghum. Industry is confined mainly to processing agricultural products, although imported petroleum is refined. Mineral resources include lead, gold, zircon, coal, uranium, and kyanite, but most of these are not fully exploited.

History. The kingdom of Punt, mentioned in ancient Egyptian writings, probably occupied the area of Somalia's northern and eastern coastline. Muslim Arabs and Persians established trading routes in the area between the 7th and 10th centuries AD. Somali nomads had lived in the interior area from at least the 10th century AD and Galla peoples lived in the south and west of the country. After the British occupied Aden (now in Yemen) in 1839, European exploration of the region commenced. The area of the 'horn' of Africa was divided between British, French and Italian spheres of influence in the late 19th century. The modern Somali Republic is a result of the unification in 1960 of the former British Somaliland Protectorate and the Italian Trusteeship Territory of Somalia. From then onwards Somalia was involved in border disputes with Kenya and Ethiopia. In 1969 President Shermarke was assassinated in a left-wing coup and the Marxist Somali Revolutionary Socialist Party took power, renaming the country the Somali Democratic Republic under the dictatorship of General Muhammad Siyad Barrah (*c.* 1911–95). There followed 21 years of one-man rule, with a sharply deteriorating economy and an escalating civil war. Fighting broke out in 1988 between government forces and rebel groups, most notably the Somali National Movement (SNM). The country, already hit by drought, now descended into what has been described as the world's 'worst man-made disaster', as refugees fled the insurgents and famine and disease took their toll. Siyad Barrah fled office in January 1991, forming a breakaway grouping, the Somali National Front. The SNM proclaimed a Somaliland Republic in the north, reviving the republic that had briefly succeeded the former British Somaliland protectorate and repudiating the union with ex-Italian Somalia. By mid-1992 some six million people were facing starvation, as rival warlords fought for control of the south of the country and relief agencies, backed by UN troops, sought to alleviate the suffering. After UN peace-keeping forces, led by the USA, had failed to maintain a ceasefire, troops were withdrawn by March 1995. General Muhammad Aidid (1936–96) declared

himself President in 1995, but this was not accepted by the international community. In 1996 he was killed in battle and was succeeded by his son, Hussein Aidid. Factional fighting has continued.

CAPITAL:	Mogadishu
AREA:	637,000 sq km (246,000 sq miles)
POPULATION:	6.802 million (1996)
CURRENCY:	1 Somali shilling = 100 cents
RELIGIONS:	Sunni Muslim 99.8%; Christian 0.1%
ETHNIC GROUPS:	Somali 98.3%; Arab 1.2%; Bantu 0.4%
LANGUAGES:	Somali, Arabic, English (official); Italian; Swahili
INTERNATIONAL ORGANIZATIONS:	UN; OAU; Arab League

Somers, John Somers, Baron (1651–1716) English lawyer and Whig politician. He played a leading part in attacking JAMES II's illegal acts (especially in defending the seven bishops who had objected to the second DECLARATION OF INDULGENCE), and in drafting the BILL OF RIGHTS. In WILLIAM III's reign he presided over the inner cabinet. Although he was the most trusted of William's advisers he was frequently attacked by jealous political rivals, and was dismissed in 1700. He held office only briefly during Queen Anne's reign.

Somerset, Edward Seymour, 1st Earl of Hertford and Duke of (*c.* 1506–52) Protector of England and effective ruler of England on behalf of EDWARD VI (1547–49). On the death of HENRY VIII in 1547 Edward Seymour (brother of Jane SEYMOUR), took the titles of Duke of Somerset and Lord Protector and won an immediate military success against Scotland at the Battle of PINKIE. His attempts to enforce the use of a Protestant English Prayer Book by Act of Uniformity (1549) sparked off the WESTERN RISING. KETT'S REBELLION, coinciding with rising discontent among magnates grouped around his rival, the Earl of Warwick, led to his downfall. He was overthrown in 1549 and executed on the orders of the Duke of NORTHUMBERLAND in 1551.

Somme, Battle of the (July–November 1916) A major battle fought between British and German forces in northern France during World War I. The battle was planned by JOFFRE and HAIG. Before it began the Germans attacked VERDUN, the defence of which nearly destroyed the French army. To relieve pressure on Verdun the brunt of the Somme offensive fell on the British. On 1 July the British advanced from their trenches almost shoulder to shoulder, presenting a perfect target for German machine gunners. The Germans fell back on the Hindenburg Line defences (a barrier of concrete pillboxes armed with machine guns; see SIEGFRIED LINE), while for the loss of some 600,000 men the Allies had gained a few kilometres of mud.

Somoza A family dynasty that dominated NICARAGUA from the 1930s until 1979. Anastasio Garcia Somoza (1896–1956), engineered a successful coup against the liberal regime and took over the presidency in 1936, exercising dictatorial control until his assassination in 1956. Somoza family rule continued under his sons Luis and Anastasio (Tachito) Somoza Debayle (1956–63, 1967–79, respectively). The Somozas used the National Guard to eliminate political opposition while they accumulated vast amounts of Nicaragua's agrarian and industrial resources. Military and economic assistance from the USA helped maintain the Somozas in power until 1979, when economic problems and world outcry against human rights abuses undermined Tachito's control and the SANDINISTA LIBERATION FRONT took power.

Sonderbund (1845–47; German, 'separate league') A league formed by seven Swiss Roman Catholic cantons. Its aim was to safeguard Roman Catholic interests and preserve the federal status of the cantons against the movement by the Radical Party to establish a more centralized government in Switzerland. The Radicals had closed (1841) all monasteries in the Aargau, and a posse had invaded (1844) the canton of Lucerne. The Radical majority in the federal Diet declared the Sonderbund dissolved in 1847, and sent an army against the separatists. The Sonderbund capitulated, and a new federal constitution in 1848 ended the virtual sovereignty of the cantons.

Song (Sung) (Northern Song, 960–1126; Southern Song, 1127–1279) A dynasty that reunited much of China after the period of fragmentation that followed the TANG DYNASTY. It never ruled all China, however – the north-west was a Tibetan kingdom and in the north-east were the LIAO, to whom the Song paid tribute of silk. In 1125–26 JIN horsemen descended on Kaifeng, the Song capital, and took the emperor and 3,000 retainers captive to Manchuria. A Song prince then set up a court in Hangzhou to the south: hoping to regain the north he called the new court Xingzai (Temporary Capital). Thereafter southern China became the heart of the empire. In 1276 KUBLAI KHAN captured Hangzhou. Two little princes escaped, but when the last survivor was drowned near Hong Kong while trying to avoid capture by a MONGOL fleet, all China for the first time came under non-Chinese rule.

The Song's mastery of technology, superior to that of western Europe, included the making of firearms and bombs, shipbuilding, the use of the compass, and clock making. A form of vaccination (variolation) was practised. It was also a time of great sophistication in literature, painting, and ceramics, and Hangzhou became the artistic centre of China.

Songhay (or Songhai, Songhoi) A former West African empire on the Niger River and the name of the people and their language, which is spoken in Mali. Tradition claims that a Berber Christian, al-Yaman, founded Songhay in the 7th century AD on Kukiya Island, below Gao. The rulers became Muslim (c. 1200) and transferred the capital to Gao. In 1325 the MALI empire annexed Songhay, but in 1335 Sonni Ali Kolon, a descendant of al-Yaman made himself king. In about 1464 SONNI ALI made Songhay independent and enlarged it greatly. However, his son, Bakari, was a weakling, and with him the line of al-Yaman failed. In 1493 the new dynasty founded by ASKIA MUHAMMAD I replaced him; he made Songhay the most important empire in western Africa, eclipsing Mali. In 1528 or 1529 Askia Muhammad was deposed by his son. He, and the seven other Askias who followed, were weak, cruel, and debauched, and the empire foundered. In 1591 it fell easy prey to a well disciplined and well armed force of Moroccans who defeated the Songhay army at Tondibi, near Gao. However, they could not control such a large area, and in the 17th century it broke up into a number of smaller states.

Sonni Ali (Ali Ber, Ali the Great) (d. 1492) Ruler of SONGHAY from 1464 or 1465, and the real founder of the Songhay empire. He made Songhay independent and then enlarged its boundaries. In 1469 he took TIMBUKTU, and in 1473 Jenné. Timbuktu chroniclers describe him as cruel, irreligious, and of immoral habits, and report that he persecuted men of religion, despite pretending to be a Muslim. He died by drowning, and was succeeded by his son Bakari, the last of his line.

Sons of Liberty American Revolutionary groups, which sprang up in Massachusetts and New York in 1765 to organize colonial opposition to the STAMP ACT. In both colonies, serious riots, propaganda, and boycotts effectively nullified the measure. The organization spread to other colonies and reactions to English 'tyranny' were synchronized by committees of correspondence. Sons of Liberty were later responsible for the BOSTON TEA PARTY (1773), the radicalization of the CONTINENTAL CONGRESS (1774), and the tarring and feathering of pro-British loyalists.

Sophia (1630–1714) Electress of Hanover (1658–1714). The twelfth child of the Elector Frederick of the Palatinate and Elizabeth, daughter of JAMES I, she married Ernest Augustus of Brunswick-Lüneburg, who became Elector of Hanover. By the Act of SETTLEMENT (1701), as the only surviving Protestant descendant of the STUARTS, she was named as ANNE's successor on the British throne. She died a few weeks before Anne and her son became King GEORGE I, the first Hanoverian king of England and Scotland. She was a cultured woman with a great interest in English affairs.

sophists (Greek *sophistes*, 'wise man') Itinerant professional teachers in Greece, the Greek colonies in Sicily, and southern Italy in the 5th century BC. Sophists offered instruction in a wide range of subjects and skills considered necessary for public life, especially rhetoric, in return for fees. Gorgias of Leontini (c. 483–376 BC) specialized in teaching rhetoric, and his visit to Athens in 427 BC encouraged the development of oratory there. Young Athenian democrats needed rhetoric to persuade the democratic assemblies. By questioning the nature of gods, conventions, and morals, and by their alleged ability to train men 'to make the weaker argument the stronger' through rhetoric, they aroused some opposition. Their readiness to argue either cause in a dispute brought them condemnation from PLATO as self-interested imitators of wisdom lacking any concern for the truth. However, the most renowned sophists, such as Gorgias and Protagoras (c. 485–415 BC) drew relativist or sceptical conclusions from the defensibility of opposed claims, indicating a seriousness of purpose that Plato failed to acknowledge.

During the Roman empire sophists were essentially teachers of rhetoric. The word sophistry, meaning quibbling or fallacious reasoning, reflects both Plato's view and the popular distrust of sophists.

Sousa, Martim Afonso de (1500–64) Portuguese colonist, leader of an exploratory expedition to southern Brazil (1531–33). In 1532 he established the first permanent Portuguese colony in Brazil at São Vicente (near present-day Santos), where he introduced sugar cane. In his efforts to expel French intruders and to find precious metals he explored the coast south from Rio de Janeiro to the Rio de la Plata. In 1534 he was granted the hereditary captaincy of São Vicente but he never returned to Brazil, and later served as governor of India and as a member of the Council of State in Lisbon.

South Africa a country occupying most of the southern part of the African continent.

Physical. In the north the country is bounded by Namibia, Botswana, Zimbabwe, Mozambique, and Swaziland. Southward, the Free State region partly surrounds Lesotho, which forms an enclave. In the east are boundaries with Mozambique, Swaziland, and Lesotho. From Cape Agulhas in the extreme south to the Limpopo River in the extreme north-east is a distance of about 1,600 km (1,000 miles). Two great rivers, the Orange and its tributary the Vaal, traverse the country from the Drakensberg Mountains in the east to the Atlantic in the west. There are rolling grasslands (veld) and deserts. The climate varies widely, from warm dry summers in the south-west to hot wet ones on the eastern coast and to winter frosts on high ground in the north.

Economy. The country has a wealth of minerals, including diamonds, gold, platinum, iron ore, lime, uranium, and coal. There are also reserves of natural gas. Gold and other metal products are the chief exports. Industry is highly developed, and includes metal production, chemicals, engineering, and food-processing. Arms production is also important. Agriculture is vulnerable to droughts and inadequate irrigation; the main crops are cereals, sugar, and fruit, and livestock-raising is also important. International trade and sporting sanctions were imposed in protest against apartheid and not lifted until 1991–92. World recession and low commodity prices have also had adverse effects. There is endemic poverty and high unemployment among Black South Africans who, under the APARTHEID regime, were deprived of access to social services such as health care and education. The Southern African Customs Union links South Africa to Botswana, Lesotho, and Swaziland.

History. South Africa was occupied by the San (Bushmen) and Khoikhoin (Hottentots) about 10,000 years ago. Bantu-speaking peoples had moved into the area and developed mining industries, trading along the east coast of Africa, by the time European exploration began in the 15th century. A Dutch colony was established in 1652; the settlers were at first known as Boers and later as AFRIKANERS. At first the San and Khoikhoin associated and intermarried with the Boers, but later the Khoikhoin were displaced by the Boers and forced to become labourers on their farms. The San withdrew into mountainous areas. Some Boers known as *trekboers*, moved inland and encountered the Xhosa people, who had a settled agricultural society. By the end of the 18th century frontier wars had broken out between the Xhosa and the Boers.

Britain established a colony in 1806 and fought with the Bantu-speaking peoples. In the 1830s large numbers of Boers moved northwards in the GREAT TREK. The Boers refused to form a federation with the British, leading to the BOER WARS. The republics of TRANSVAAL and ORANGE FREE STATE were defeated by the British and were united with the British colonies of Cape and NATAL in 1910 to form the Union of South Africa, a self-governing DOMINION of the British crown. Politically dominated by its small White minority, South Africa supported Britain in the two World Wars, its troops fighting on a number of fronts. After 1948 the right-wing Afrikaner-dominated NATIONAL PARTY (NP) formed a government. It instituted a strict system of apartheid, intensifying discrimination against the disenfranchised non-White majority. This policy entailed brutal repression of dissent (see SHARPEVILLE MASSACRE).

South Africa became a republic (1960) and left the Commonwealth (1961); the AFRICAN NATIONAL CONGRESS (ANC) was banned and its leaders, including Nelson MANDELA, imprisoned. Although its economic strength allowed it to dominate the southern half of the continent, the rise of Black nationalism both at home and in the surrounding countries (including the former mandated territory of NAMIBIA) produced increasing violence and emphasized South Africa's isolation in the diplomatic world. In 1985 the regime of P. W. Botha began to make some attempts to ease tension by interpreting apartheid in a more liberal fashion. This failed, however, to satisfy either the increasingly militant non-White population or the extremist right-wing groups within the small White élite. In 1986 a state of emergency was proclaimed and several thousands imprisoned without trial. The domestic and international sides of the problem remained inseparable, with South African troops fighting against SWAPO guerrillas in Namibia and Angola and support by surrounding states for the forces of the outlawed ANC producing a series of cross-border incidents. In 1988 the US Congress voted to support the 'Front Line' African states in their demand for international sanctions. President Botha retired in 1989 and his successor President DE KLERK began the quest for racial reconciliation. Following the repeal of apartheid legislation in July 1990 sanctions were eased and South Africa re-admitted to international sport. In December 1991 delegations from the government, the National Party, the Democratic Party, the South African Communist Party, ANC, INKATHA FREEDOM PARTY, and from the Indian and Coloured communities, joined to form the Convention for a Democratic South Africa (CODESA). Its deliberations through 1992 were interrupted by a number of violent racial incidents, and it was fiercely attacked by the neo-fascist Afrikaner Resistance Movement. The government was replaced in 1993 by a multiparty Transitional Executive Council. The country's first multiracial elections were held in 1994, with the ANC emerging as clear victors. Nelson Mandela became President, with the ANC's Thabo MBEKI and the NP's de Klerk as Deputy presidents, leading a coalition government of national unity. The same year, South Africa was admitted to the ORGANIZATION OF AFRICAN UNITY and rejoined the Commonwealth. In 1996 a permanent multiracial democratic constitution was adopted and de Klerk and the National Party withdrew from the coalition government in order to form the official opposition. In late 1997, Mandela was succeeded as President of the ANC by Mbeki; although he remained President of South Africa his role became mainly ceremonial.

CAPITAL:	Pretoria (executive); Bloemfontein (judicial); Cape Town (legislative)
AREA:	1,123,226 sq km (433,680 sq miles)
POPULATION:	41.743 million (1996)
CURRENCY:	1 rand = 100 cents
RELIGIONS:	Christian 59.0%; Bantu Churches 17.0%; Hindu 2.0%; Muslim 1.0%; Jewish 1.0%

ETHNIC GROUPS: Zulu 23.8%; White 18.0%; Coloured 10.5%; North Sotho 9.8%; Xhosa 9.7%; South Sotho 7.3%; Tswana 5.7%; Asian 3.3%

LANGUAGES: Afrikaans; English; Zulu; Sotho; Xhosa; Ndebele; Pedi; Swazi; Tsonga; Tswana; Venda (all official)

INTERNATIONAL
ORGANIZATIONS: UN; OAU; Commonwealth; SADC

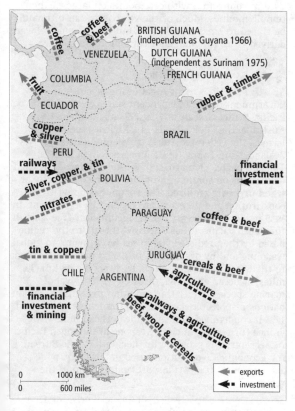

South America: c. 1910   Investment, exports, and imports.

South America The world's fourth largest continent.

Physical. South America lies mainly in the Southern Hemisphere; it is traversed by the Equator in the north and joined to Central America by the narrow Isthmus of Panama. More than two-thirds of it lies within the tropics, while the remainder tapers southward through the temperate mid-latitudes. Structurally it some-what resembles North America, with a plate boundary on its Pacific coast bordered by massive cordilleras, the Andes, and with more ancient highlands towards the Atlantic in the east. It has not one central basin, however, but three: the drainage basins of the Orinoco and Amazon Rivers in the north and that of the River Plate in the south, separated from each other by ancient platforms. The most extensive of these is the Mato Grosso plateau at the centre of the continent. Forming the southern basin is the vast Gran Chaco plain. Rainfall in the equatorial regions is very heavy, especially on the coasts. South of the equatorial forest there are vast expanses of open grazing land, and wide strips of arable land on the east coast. The rain-bearing easterly winds fail to reach

the west coast, however; here the main feature is the arid Atacama Desert. South of the Tropic of Capricorn the forested western slopes of the Andes see rain all year round, while the east is semi-desert and steppe.

Economy. Brazil, Argentina, and Uruguay are the most industrialized South American nations. Agriculture remains undeveloped in many areas, although sugar, cocoa, and coffee are exported and sheep and cattle are reared. The continent is poor in coal but rich in other resources: oil on the coasts and in the basins; iron on the plateaux; nitrates in the desert; and copper, tin, and other metals in the mountains. Melt-water flowing down from the snow-capped Andes provides an enormous source of energy. In many cases, however, remoteness and inaccessibility remain an obstacle to exploitation.

History. The continent was originally settled by AMERINDIANS and a number of sophisticated cultures developed, most notably that of the INCAS. Most of South America was colonized by Spain and Portugal. Spain's claim was based on the discoveries of Christopher COLUMBUS; on his third voyage (1498) he sailed along the Venezuelan coast and landed on Trinidad. In 1500 the Portuguese explorer, Pedro Alvares Cabral, landed near present-day Bahia and took possession of this territory for Portugal. Portuguese BRAZIL and the Spanish viceroyalty of PERU constituted the two principal administrative jurisdictions in South America during the 16th and 17th centuries. In the 18th century, Spain subdivided Peru, adding two new viceroyalties, New Granada (1717) and Rio de la Plata (1776). England, France, and the Netherlands also established small colonies on the north-eastern coast of the continent in the 17th century. Colonial settlement was round the coast and to this day urban centres are concentrated near the coastline and not in the interior.

Between 1816 and 1825 most of Spanish South America achieved independence under the leadership of Simón BOLÍVAR and José de SAN MARTÍN, and subsequently broke into nine separate countries: Venezuela, Colombia, Ecuador, Peru, Bolivia, Chile, Argentina, Uruguay, and Paraguay. Brazil gained independence from Portugal in 1822. British Guiana gained independence from Britain in 1966 as Guyana. Surinam, the Dutch colony, became independent in 1975, but French Guiana continues under French rule. The continent remained politically independent during the 19th century, partly as a result of the MONROE DOCTRINE, which prevented European expansion. At the same time it received some 15 million immigrants from Europe, and was continuously receptive to both cultural and ideological influences from the USA and Europe. There was considerable economic investment, particularly by Britain, in primary production such as minerals and beef, leading to a dependence on such trade. The continent remains predominantly Roman Catholic; in the 19th and early 20th centuries the Church occupied a central political and social position as a conservative force. More recently its stand has been challenged by priests of the LIBERATION THEOLOGY movement, which has sought to involve the Church actively in the politics of poverty and deprivation. Rapid URBANIZATION has overtaken the supply of housing and employment. In an effort to stimulate trade and production, economic groupings such as the CENTRAL AMERICAN COMMON MARKET, the Latin-American Free Trade Association (1960; replaced by the

LATIN-AMERICAN INTEGRATION ASSOCIATION in 1990), and MERCOSUR (the Southern Zone Common Market; 1991) have been established. Extensive development projects and increased oil prices in the 1970s burdened many South American countries with debts which their economies, heavily dependent on the world commodity market, have found almost impossible to service.

South Australia A state in south central Australia.

Physical. South Australia lies between Western Australia and New South Wales. Contiguous also with the Northern Territory, it covers 984,400 sq km (380,000 sq miles) and has a southern shore on the Great Australian Bight. Kangaroo Island lies 40 km (25 miles) off the Yorke Peninsula. In the west is the Great Victoria Desert, from which rise the Musgrave Ranges with Mount Woodroffe at 1,515 m (4,971 feet). South-west is the arid Nullarbor Plain and in the north-east Lake Eyre. In the south-east the Mount Lofty–Flinders ranges presented a major barrier to Westward expansion. The lower reaches of the Murray River provide grass and woodland: here the climate is Mediterranean, permitting a range of crops. Iron ore, gypsum, salt, and low-grade coal are among the minerals found.

History. Sealers began to use Kangaroo Island in the early 1800s. Settlement of the British province of South Australia began in 1836, under the auspices of the Colonial Office and a Colonization Commission. The province went bankrupt, and, after its debts were met by Britain, it became a colony in 1842. In 1851 it became the first British colony to dissolve the connection between church and state. South Australia, which never received convicts, was granted responsible government in 1856. It administered the Northern Territory from 1863 to 1911.

South Carolina A state of the USA on the southern Atlantic coast. CHARLES II granted a charter to colonize the Carolinas to a syndicate of eight proprietors and the first settlement was founded at Charleston in 1670. The northern and southern parts developed separately and the colony was divided into North and South Carolina in 1713. South Carolina's development was influenced by immigrants from the Caribbean and in the 18th century its slave population outnumbered Whites. Its coastlands proved ideal for rice and indigo PLANTATIONS and it was one of the richest and most valued English colonies. Friction between planters and proprietors and the crisis of Native American attacks in the Yamasee War (1715) resulted in its reversion to crown rule in 1729. The colony was divided over independence and while the British occupied Charleston (1780–82) they enjoyed considerable loyalist support.

South-East Asia Treaty Organization (SEATO) A defence alliance established under the South-East Asia Collective Defence Treaty, signed at Manila in 1954, as part of a US policy of CONTAINMENT of communism. The signatories were Australia, Britain, France, New Zealand, Pakistan, the Philippines, Thailand, and the USA. The treaty area covered south-east Asia and part of the south-west Pacific. Pakistan and France withdrew from the organization in 1973 and 1974 respectively. The Organization was dissolved in 1977.

Southern cult A religious cult that held sway throughout the prehistoric MISSISSIPPI and adjacent cultures. It was fully formed by *c.* 1000 AD and appears archaeologically as an interrelated assemblage of ritual objects and design motifs painted or incised on pottery, carved or sculpted on shell, wood, and stone, embossed on thin sheets of native copper, and painted on cloth. These artefacts and motifs are thought to have been used in connection with ceremonies on large earthen temple mounds. Much of the symbolism can ultimately be traced to Mexican religions, but other elements were derived from the indigenous and preceding HOPEWELL CULTURES.

South Korea KOREA, SOUTH.

South Pacific Forum A gathering of heads of government of the independent states of the South Pacific. It met first in 1971. In 1997 its members were Australia, the Cook Islands, Fiji, Kiribati, the Marshall Islands, the Federated States of Micronesia, Nauru, New Zealand, Niue, Papua New Guinea, Solomon Islands, Tonga, Tuvalu, Vanuatu, and (Western) Samoa. Informal discussions on common problems are held annually or when urgently required. The Forum has no written constitution and decisions are reached by agreement. In 1985 it adopted a treaty declaring a nuclear-free zone in the South Pacific. It has discussed threats to the region posed by the predicted rise in sea levels owing to global warming and by overfishing. In 1989 it demanded an end to the use of driftnets, which, by sweeping 48 km (30 miles) of ocean at a time, threaten the survival of marine species. Under this and other pressure, the main nations responsible, Japan and Taiwan, have acceded. In 1995 it condemned, and suspended official links with, France for testing nuclear weapons in the south Pacific. Its secretariat is provided by the South Pacific Bureau for Economic Co-operation based in Suva, Fiji, which also promotes trade, transport, and tourism in the region.

South Sea Bubble A British financial crisis of 1720. Having taken over most of the National Debt (see BANK OF ENGLAND), the South Sea Company, which had been founded in 1711 to trade with South America, needed a rise in the value of its shares. This was achieved not by favourable past trading profits, but by rumours of future ones. Some politicians and even members of the court were bribed with cheap or free South Sea Company shares to promote the company's interests. The shares increased ten-fold in value, and expectations of high dividends rose accordingly. Many bogus companies secured substantial investment by exploiting the speculative fever. When confidence in these bogus companies collapsed, the South Sea Company's shares fell to less than ten per cent of their peak value, and thousands of investors were ruined. Sir Robert WALPOLE began his long period of office by saving the company and restoring financial stability; he managed to limit the political damage to two of George I's ministers who had been implicated in the scandal.

South Vietnam VIETNAM.

South-West Africa NAMIBIA.

South West Africa People's Organization SWAPO.

South Yemen A former country on the south-west Arabian peninsula. It declared its independence in 1967 and, after long negotiations, amalgamated in 1989 with the Yemen Arab Republic to form YEMEN.

Souvanna Phouma, Prince (1901–84) Laotian statesman. A member of the post-war provisional government (1945–46), he opposed French recolonization and was elected Premier in 1951. During his first premiership (1951–54) civil war broke out between the government and the communist-led PATHET LAO movement. He formed a brief coalition (1962–63) with the Pathet Lao (led by his half-brother, Prince Souphanouvong) and after the return of civil war, he continued as Premier. Although he tried to maintain a neutral policy during the Vietnam war, this proved impossible. In 1973 he signed a ceasefire agreement with the Pathet Lao and remained Premier until the People's Democratic Republic of Laos was declared in 1975.

Soviet (Russian, 'council') An elected governing council in the former Soviet Union. Russian Soviets gained their revolutionary connotation in 1905, when the St Petersburg Soviet of Workers' Deputies was formed to co-ordinate strikes and other anti-government activities in factories. Each factory sent its delegates, and for a time other cities were dominated by Soviets. Both BOLSHEVIKS and Mensheviks realized the potential importance of Soviets and duly appointed delegates. In 1917 a Soviet modelled on that of 1905, but now including deserting soldiers, was formed in Petrograd (previously St Petersburg), sufficiently powerful to dictate industrial action and to control the use of armed force. It did not at first try to overthrow KERENSKY's Provisional Government but grew increasingly powerful in its opposition to continuing Russian participation in World War I. Consisting of between 2,000 and 3,000 members, it was controlled by a powerful executive committee. Soviets were established in the provinces and in June 1917 the first All Russia Congress of Soviets met. The Bolsheviks gradually dominated policy, leading to their seizure of power in the RUSSIAN REVOLUTION (1917). During the RUSSIAN CIVIL WAR village Soviets controlling local affairs and agriculture were common. The national Soviet was called the Supreme Soviet, comprising delegates from all the Soviet republics.

Soviet Union UNION OF SOVIET SOCIALIST REPUBLICS.

Soweto A predominantly Black township, south-west of Johannesburg in South Africa. In January 1976 Black schoolchildren demonstrated against legislation proposing to make Afrikaans the compulsory language of instruction, and police broke up the demonstration, using guns and tear gas. This triggered off a wave of violence; by the end of 1976 some 500 Black and Coloured people, many of them children, had been killed by the police. The plans for compulsory teaching in Afrikaans were dropped. Thereafter, until the multiracial elections of 1994 that ended White minority rule, the anniversary of the demonstration was marked by further unrest.

Sozzini, Lelio SOCINUS, LAELIUS.

Spaak, Paul-Henri (1899–1972) Belgian statesman. Having entered Parliament as a socialist in 1932, he served as Prime Minister (1938–39, 1947–49) and later became the first President of the UNITED NATIONS GENERAL ASSEMBLY and of the consultative assembly of the COUNCIL OF EUROPE (1949–51). A firm supporter of a united Europe, he originated proposals for an economic association based on free trade and movement of labour, together with joint social and financial policies, that formed the basis of the EUROPEAN ECONOMIC COMMUNITY.

space exploration Travel beyond the earth's atmosphere for the purpose of gathering information about space and other planets. Space exploration may be said to have begun in 1903, when the Russian physicist Konstantin Tsiolkovsky developed ideas for space rockets fuelled by liquefied gas. By 1926 Robert Goddard in the USA had successfully designed the first liquid fuelled rocket. There followed considerable German research into rockets, culminating in the launch of the V-2 rocket in 1944. In 1957 the Soviet Union surprised the USA by putting the first artificial satellite, SPUTNIK I, in orbit; this was followed by the US Explorer I in 1958. Yuri Gagarin was the first man in space in 1961, followed by John Glenn in 1962. In 1961 President KENNEDY proposed the Apollo programme to achieve a manned lunar landing by 1970, and in 1969 Neil Armstrong and Edwin ('Buzz') Aldrin landed on the moon. The Soviet Union concentrated on unmanned flights, Luna IX achieving a soft landing on the moon in 1966. In the early 1970s space stations were launched by both the USA and the Soviet Union, and in 1975 an Apollo capsule linked up with a Soviet Soyuz capsule. Unmanned flights have been made to Venus and Mars, while the US probe, Voyager 2, launched in 1977, reached Neptune in 1989. In 1981 the USA launched a space shuttle, the first reusable space craft, but its commercial and scientific programme was interrupted for two years by the explosion of the shuttle, *Challenger*, on lift-off in 1986. In 1986 the giant Soviet modular space station, Mir, was launched, with astronauts being ferried to the station by Soyuz spacecraft, followed in 1987 by the placing in space of the powerful Energiya station. In 1987, Soviet cosmonaut Yuri Romanenko set a space endurance record of 326 days in orbit. The Hubble space telescope, which can produce images of other solar systems, was launched from a US shuttle in 1990. Its faulty mirror limited observations until it was repaired by astronauts in the space shuttle *Endeavour* in 1993. An international space station, Freedom, conceived by the USA in 1984, is due to become operational in the late 1990s. Space technology has resulted in numerous applications, and telecommunication satellites have greatly improved global communications. Meteorological satellites provide advance weather information and reconnaissance satellites register the earth's resources and military information.

Spain A country occupying most of the Iberian Peninsula in south-west Europe.

Physical. Spain is bounded by France across the Pyrenees in the north-east and by Portugal on the west of the plateau, the Meseta, on which most of Spain lies. It has a rugged northern coast on the Atlantic Ocean and a gentler one on the Mediterranean Sea, where the Balearic Islands are found. The plateau is very cold in winter, and very warm and arid in summer. Here and there are jagged sierras. In the Cantabrian Mountains to the north, iron ore is mined; and from here the Ebro flows eastward into Catalonia. Across the centre the Tagus runs west-ward to Portugal, while in the south the Guadalquivir flows through the broad valley of

Seville, where oranges are grown. Andalusia and the southern coastal plains are famous for their terraced vineyards, above which rises the Sierra Nevada.

Spain has a semi-federal system of 17 autonomous regions, each with an assembly and government. In the BASQUE and Catalan regions local nationalist parties have formed governments, but there are continuing internal tensions caused by demands for greater autonomy. Spanish territory includes Ceuta, Melilla, Alhucemas, Chafarinas, and Peñón de Vélez in North Africa, which are the subject of territorial disputes with Morocco, and the Canary and Balearic Islands. The sovereignty of GIBRALTAR is disputed with the UK.

Economy. Spain has a broadly based manufacturing sector, which has experienced rapid growth in recent years. Tourism makes a substantial contribution to the economy. Exports include motor vehicles, iron and steel, zinc, petroleum products, and chemicals. Agriculture remains important and concentrates on grains, tomatoes, citrus, and livestock-raising. Mineral resources include iron ore, zinc, and lead. Spain has had a consistently high level of unemployment and a weak system of social security.

History. Spain has been inhabited for at least 20,000 years, and supported at least two early cultures. Celtic peoples began to migrate into Spain during the 9th century BC. After a period of Carthaginian domination, Spain began to come under Roman control from 206 BC. Roman rule was followed, after 415 AD, by that of the VISIGOTHS, who were themselves toppled by Muslim invaders from Morocco (711–18). MOORISH Spain reached its zenith under the UMAYYAD dynasty of al-Andalus (736–1031). During the subsequent political fragmentation, Christian kingdoms became consolidated where Muslim power was weakest, in the north: ARAGON and CASTILE were the most significant of these. By 1248 Christian reconquest had been so successful that only GRANADA remained in Muslim hands. Ferdinand II of Aragon (FERDINAND V) and ISABELLA I of Castile united their kingdoms in 1479, reconquered Granada in 1492, and went on to establish unified Spain as a power of European and world significance. Under their rule the vast SPANISH EMPIRE overseas began to take shape, and under their 16th-century successors, CHARLES V and PHILIP II, Spain enjoyed its 'golden age'. Decline set in during the 17th century and the end of Habsburg rule came in 1700 when Philip V became the first Bourbon monarch. The accession of Philip V led to the War of the SPANISH SUCCESSION (1701–14), in which Spain lost many of its lands in Europe.

In the early 19th century Spain suffered as a result of the NAPOLEONIC WARS and briefly came under French control (1808–14). This defeat encouraged revolution in South America, resulting in the SPANISH-SOUTH AMERICAN WARS OF INDEPENDENCE, which led to the emergence as independent countries of Argentina, Bolivia, Peru, Venezuela, and Mexico. Spain subsequently remained peripheral and undeveloped in a Europe that was fast becoming industrialized. From 1814 onwards the absolutist monarchy was involved in a struggle with the forces of liberalism, and from 1873 to 1875 there was a brief republican interlude. In 1898 the SPANISH–AMERICAN WAR resulted in the loss of Puerto Rico, the Philippines, and Guam, while Cuba, which had been more or less in revolt since 1868, became a US protectorate in 1903. In 1923 General Miguel PRIMO DE RIVERA established a virtual

dictatorship, which was followed by another republican interlude (1931–39), scarred by the savage SPANISH CIVIL WAR (1936–39). Nationalist victory resulted in the dictatorship of General Francisco FRANCO (1939–75). His gradual liberalization of government during the late 1960s was continued by his successor Juan Carlos I, who established a democratic constitutional monarchy. Separatist agitation, often violent, by ETA, an organization seeking independence for the Basque provinces, continued throughout the period. Of its remaining colonies Spain granted independence in 1976 to Spanish Sahara (now WESTERN SAHARA), which was divided between Morocco and Mauritania. King Juan Carlos survived attempted military coups in 1978 and 1981, since when stable, left-of-centre governments have been established under Prime Minister Felipe González (1982–96). Spain joined the EC in 1986. González was defeated in elections in 1996 but the winning right-wing Popular Party gained no overall majority and formed a coalition government, led by José María Aznar.

CAPITAL:	Madrid
AREA:	504,750 sq km (194,885 sq miles)
POPULATION:	39.270 million (1996)
CURRENCY:	1 peseta = 100 céntimos
RELIGIONS:	Roman Catholic 97.0%
ETHNIC GROUPS:	Spanish 73.0%; Catalan 16.0%; Galician 8.0%; Basque 2.0%
LANGUAGES:	Spanish (Castilian) (official); Catalan; Galician; Basque
INTERNATIONAL ORGANIZATIONS:	UN; EU; NATO; OECD; Council of Europe; CSCE

Spanish–American War (1898) A conflict between Spain and the USA. It had its roots in the struggle for independence of CUBA, and in US economic and imperialist ambitions. Sympathetic to Cuban rebels whose second war of independence against Spain had begun in 1895, the USA used the mysterious blowing up of its battleship, the *maine*, in Havana harbour as a pretext for declaring war. The Spanish navy suffered serious defeats in Cuba and the Philippines, and a US expeditionary force (which included the future President Theodore ROOSEVELT and his ROUGH RIDERS) defeated Spanish ground forces in Cuba and in Puerto Rico. Spain surrendered at the end of 1898, Puerto Rico being ceded to the USA and Cuba placed under US protection. The Pacific island of Guam was also ceded while the Philippines were bought by the USA for $20 million. The war signalled the emergence of the USA as an important world power as well as the dominant power in the Caribbean.

Spanish Armada A large naval and military force that PHILIP II of Spain sent to invade England at the end of May 1588. It consisted of 130 ships, carrying about 8,000 sailors and 19,000 infantrymen, under the command of the inexperienced Duke of MEDINA SIDONIA. Having been delayed by a storm off Corunna, the Spanish fleet was first sighted by the English naval commanders on 19 July, then harassed by them with long-range guns, until it anchored off Calais. Unable to liaise with an additional force from the Low Countries led by FARNESE, its formation was wrecked by English fireships during the night and as it tried to escape it suffered a further pounding from the English fleet. A strong wind drove the remaining vessels into the North

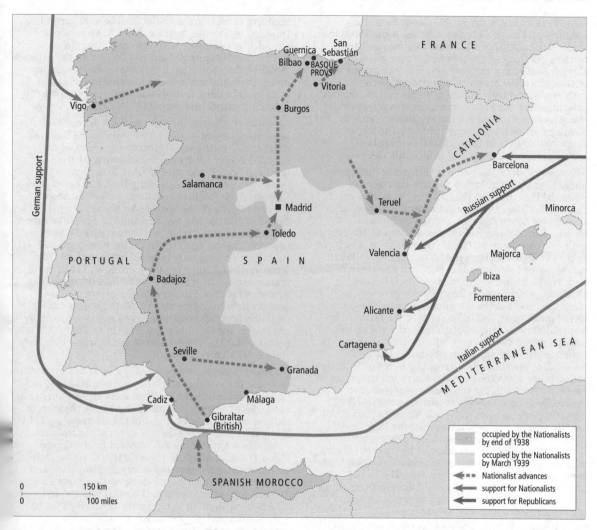

Spanish Civil War (1936–39)   *The early thrust of Nationalist forces under General Franco from Spanish Morocco was westward towards Barcelona, held by the Republicans, and north against the Basques. The latter suffered air-raids including one on the civilian population of Guernica, which inspired the famous painting by Picasso. Internationally, the Civil War was seen as an ideological struggle; its brutalities caused deep bitterness in Spain, which lasted for a generation.*

ea and they were forced to make their way back to pain round the north of Scotland and the west of reland. Barely half the original Armada returned to ort.

panish Civil War (1936–39) A bitter military struggle etween left- and right-wing elements in Spain. After he fall of PRIMO DE RIVERA in 1930 and the eclipse of the panish monarchy in 1931, Spain was split. On the one nd were the privileged and politically powerful roups, such as the monarchists and FALANGE Party, on he other were the Republicans, Catalan and Basque eparatists, socialists, communists, and anarchists. The ections of February 1936 gave power to a left-wing OPULAR FRONT government and strikes, riots, and ilitary plots followed. In July 1936 the generals José njurjo and Francisco FRANCO led an unsuccessful coup gainst the republic from Spanish Morocco and civil

war, marked by atrocities on both sides, began. In 1937 Franco's Nationalists, consisting of Falangists, CARLISTS, and Moroccan troops, overran the Basque region (which, in hope of ultimate independence, supported the Republicans). Nationalists also held the important town of Teruel against Republican attacks, thereby enabling Franco, with German and Italian assistance, to divide the Republican forces by conquering territory between Barcelona and Valencia (1938). The Republicans, weakened by internal intrigues between rival factions and by the withdrawal of Soviet support, attempted a desperate counter-attack. It failed, and Barcelona fell to Franco (January 1939), quickly followed by Madrid. Franco became the head of the Spanish state and the Falange was made the sole legal party. The civil war inspired international support on both sides: the Soviet Union sent advisers and military supplies to the

Republicans, while some 50,000 soldiers from Italy fought with Franco. Germany supplied some 10,000 men to the Nationalists, mostly in the aviation and tank services. Bombing of civilians by German pilots of the 'Condor Legion' and the destruction of the Basque town of Guernica (1937) became the symbol of fascist ruthlessness and inspired one of Picasso's most famous paintings. Left-wing and communist volunteers from many countries fought for the Republican cause as members of the INTERNATIONAL BRIGADES. The war cost about 700,000 lives in battle, 30,000 executed or assassinated, and 15,000 killed in air raids. (See map.)

Spanish empire The overseas territories that came under Spanish control from the late 15th century onwards. They included the Canaries, most of the Caribbean islands, the whole of central America, large stretches of South America, and the Philippines. Christopher COLUMBUS laid the foundations of the empire with his four voyages (1492–1504) in search of a western route to the Orient. Then the CONQUISTADORES followed, colonizing by force in MEXICO, PERU, and elsewhere in the New World. As the wealth of these lands became apparent, private enterprise gradually gave way to direct conciliar rule by the mother power. The Council of the Indies (chartered 1524) stood at the head of the imperial administration until almost the end of the colonial period. Control over all colonial trade was vested in the House of Trade (established in 1503 at Seville). The gold and silver from the New World made 16th-century Spain the richest country in Europe, under Emperor Charles V. The colonies themselves were eventually divided into viceroyalties: NEW SPAIN (1535), PERU (1569), NEW GRANADA (1717), and Rio de la Plata (1776). Despite government regulations like the New Laws (1542) it was difficult to prevent exploitation of the native Indians. English, French, and Dutch depredations of the empire were damaging to Spain throughout this period. Weakened by European wars and internal problems, Spain lost virtually all its overseas territories during the 19th century (see SPANISH-AMERICAN WAR; SPANISH-SOUTH AMERICAN WARS OF INDEPENDENCE).

Spanish Inquisition A council authorized by Pope SIXTUS IV in 1478 and organized under the Catholic monarchs FERDINAND II and ISABELLA I of Spain to combat heresy. Its main targets were converted Jews and Muslims, but it was also used against WITCHCRAFT and against political enemies. The first Grand Inquisitor was TORQUEMADA. Its methods included the use of torture, confiscation, and burning at *autos-da-fé*. It ordered the expulsion of the Jews from Spain in 1492, the attack on the Moriscos (Muslims living in Spain who were baptized Christians but retained Islamic practices) in 1502, and, after the REFORMATION, attacked all forms of Protestantism. In the 16th century there were 14 Spanish branches and its jurisdiction was extended to the colonies of the New World, including Mexico and Peru, and to the Netherlands and Sicily. Its activities were enlarged in the reign of PHILIP II, who favoured it as a COUNTER-REFORMATION weapon. It was suppressed and finally abolished in the 19th century.

Spanish Main Originally, the mainlands of the Americas adjacent to the Caribbean Sea, particularly the coast of South America from the Orinoco River on the east to the Isthmus of Panama on the west, settled by the Spanish in the first half of the 16th century. Later the term came to refer to the Caribbean in general, as travelled by Spanish merchantmen. In literature and legend, it is associated with the early struggles to control Caribbean trade, and especially with the exploits of the English 'sea dogs' John HAWKINS and Sir Francis DRAKE. These and others were involved in early slave trading and raided Spanish shipping, even temporarily capturing islands and ports in the late 16th century.

Spanish Netherlands The southern provinces of the Netherlands ceded to PHILIP II of Spain in the Union of Arras (1579), during the DUTCH REVOLTS. These lands included modern Belgium, Luxembourg, part of northern France, and part of what later became the UNITED PROVINCES. Although Philip II still intended to re-subjugate the rebellious northern provinces, he granted the sovereignty of the Spanish Netherlands to his daughter Isabella and her husband the Archduke Albert (1598). During the Twelve-Year Truce (1609–21) and the unsuccessful war against the United Provinces (1621–48), the region enjoyed only nominal independence from Spain. A great deal of territory was lost to LOUIS XIV of France during the wars of the 17th century, including Artois and part of Flanders. On the expiry of the Spanish Habsburg dynasty in 1700, the region came under French rule until 1706, when it was occupied by the British and Dutch. By the Peace of UTRECHT (1713) it passed under the sovereignty of the Austrian Habsburg Holy Roman Emperors.

Spanish–South American Wars of Independence (1810–25) The emergence, through armed struggle, of Spain's former colonies in South and Central America as independent sovereign states. The roots of the wars of independence are to be found in the attempts made by Spain after 1765 to re-establish imperial control over its American colonies. This was resented by the Creoles (colonial descendants of Spanish settlers), whose local political authority, growing economic prosperity, and increasing sense of national identity were threatened. The precipitant for the armed conflict was the series of international wars in Europe after 1796, which led to Spain's subjugation by France (1807–14). During this period Creoles in Spanish America achieved *de facto* economic independence, and with the abdication of FERDINAND VII (1808), political independence. In 1811 the first declarations of independence were made. Initially the movements were hampered by a counter-revolutionary drive by Spanish royalists. In 1816 Simón BOLÍVAR returned to Venezuela from exile and united with José Antonio PÁEZ and the Ilaneros (plainsmen) of the interior. With the assistance of British mercenaries Bolívar crossed the Andes and won the Battle of Boyacá, and proclaimed the United States of COLOMBIA (1819). The victories of Carabobo (1821) and Pichincha (1822) brought Venezuela and Ecuador into the Colombian Federation. Bolívar then linked up with the independence movement in the south led by SAN MARTÍN, who had crossed the Andes from the United Provinces of La Plata (Argentina) and won the Battles of Chabuco (1817) and Maipo (1818) to liberate Chile. Both movements now closed in on the bastion of the Spanish empire, Peru. The battles of Junin and Ayacucho (1824) were the final victories in the liberation of the continent. Bolivia's Federation of Gran Colombia survived until 1829 when it began to disintegrate. The Creole élites throughout South America were divided over the constitutional

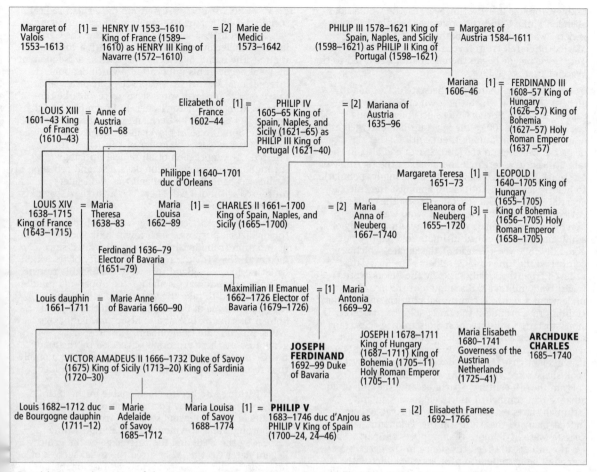

Spanish Succession, War of the (1701–13)   *The lineage of the three claimants — Philip V, King of Spain; Joseph Ferdinand, Duke of Bavaria; and the Archduke Charles.*

foundations of the new nations, every one of which had to grapple with the question of federalism: i.e. how tightly regional autonomy should be subordinate to the central state. These constitutional problems could not hide the fact that the social and economic foundations of the post-independence order showed a remarkable degree of continuity with those of the late Bourbon period.

Spanish Succession, War of the (1701–13) A European conflict arising from the death of the childless Charles II of Spain in 1700. One of his sisters had married LOUIS XIV, the other the Holy Roman Emperor Leopold I: as a result both the French BOURBONS and the Austrian HABSBURGS claimed the right to rule the Spanish empire, which included the southern Netherlands, Milan, Naples, and most of Central and South America. Before Charles II's death WILLIAM III of Britain took a leading part in negotiations to pre-empt the crisis: a partition treaty was signed (1698) between LOUIS XIV and William, agreeing that Spain and its possessions would be shared out between France, Austria, and Joseph Ferdinand, the seven-year old Elector of Bavaria, grandson of Leopold. Charles II meanwhile agreed to leave all of Spain's empire to

Joseph Ferdinand. When he died, Louis and William signed a second partition (1699). However, Charles II left a will bequeathing his whole empire to Louis XIV's second grandson, the future PHILIP V. Louis decided to accept this will rather than his previous agreements, thereby raising European fears of French domination. These fears were exacerbated when he intervened in Spanish affairs, seized the Dutch barrier fortresses, recognized JAMES II's son as King of England, and refused to make it impossible for Philip also to inherit the French throne.

In 1701 William III formed a grand alliance of the English and Dutch with the Austrian emperor and most of the German princes to put the rival Austrian candidate, the Archduke Charles, on the throne; Savoy and Portugal later joined the alliance. William died in 1702 and the war therefore became Queen Anne's War. Fighting took place in the Netherlands, Italy, Germany, and Spain. France's only allies were Bavaria and the people of Castile, who supported Philip V while Catalonia declared for the Archduke Charles. MARLBOROUGH and EUGÈNE OF SAVOY won a series of brilliant victories, including BLENHEIM. France was invaded in 1709 and the allies also prevailed at sea, taking Gibraltar in 1704. However, Castile would not abandon Philip V and the prolonged conflict led to general war weariness on both sides. When Marlborough fell from favour in Britain (1711) the new Tory government began the negotiations that led to the Peace of UTRECHT (1713).

Sparta The usual name for the state of Laconia in ancient Greece, of which the town of Sparta was the capital. Invading Dorian Greeks occupied Laconia (c. 950 BC), and by about 700 BC the Spartans had emerged as the dominant element among them, with a large slave class of HELOTS working on the land. Sparta had also, in the late 8th century, defeated and annexed the territory of Messenia, its western neighbour, reducing its population to helotry and dividing its land amongst the full Spartiate citizens. The Spartan state of the classical period was headed by two 'kings', who were the hereditary commanders of the army. An assembly of all adult male Spartiates had ultimate sovereignty but it generally followed the lead of the Senate, which comprised the kings and 28 'elders'. The Spartiates, relieved from their daily tasks by the helots, were free to cultivate military skills, and from the age of seven underwent a rigorous communal physical and military training that produced the finest soldiers in Greece. The stark austerity, militarism, and discipline of Spartan society were traditionally ascribed to a single great legislator, Lycurgus, variously dated c. 900 and c. 700 BC; it is likeliest that the fully developed Spartan system took shape somewhere between 700 and 600 BC.

From the 6th century, Sparta became the hub of an alliance that comprised most Peloponnesian and Isthmian states except its traditional rival, Argos; indeed, many of these allies in the 'Peloponnesian League' were little more than puppets of Sparta. Sparta led the successful Greek resistance in the GREEK–PERSIAN wars, but later came into protracted conflict with ATHENS in the PELOPONNESIAN WAR. Its final victory in 404 BC left it dominant in Greece and the Aegean. However, after crushing defeats by Thebes at Leuctra (371) and Mantinea (362) and the loss of Messina it declined in importance.

The authoritarian and stratified 'closed society' of Sparta was much admired by some Greeks, most notably by PLATO. But the stifling of individual initiative and hostility to new ideas, the ever-present threat of helot revolts, the instability of its unrepresentative governments, and (from the mid-5th century) a steep decline in the numbers of the exclusive caste of full Spartiates all undermined Sparta's bid for lasting domination of the Greek world.

Spartacus (d. 71 BC) Leader of a slave revolt against Rome. A shepherd, then a Roman military auxiliary, he deserted and on recapture trained as a GLADIATOR in Capua. In 73 BC he led an uprising that occupied the crater of the volcano Vesuvius and went on to defeat two Roman armies. His followers swelled to some 90,000 and devastated southern Italy before CRASSUS and POMPEY defeated him in 71; Pompey also claimed credit for intercepting some of the fugitives. Spartacus was killed and many of his followers were crucified. He has since then been a hero to many revolutionaries, including the early German Marxists who called themselves SPARTAKISTS.

Spartakist Movement A group of German radical socialists. Led by Karl LIEBKNECHT and Rosa LUXEMBURG, it was formed in 1915 in order to overthrow the German imperial government and replace it with a communist regime. The name 'Spartacus' was used as a pseudonym by Liebknecht in his publications, which denounced international warfare as a capitalist conspiracy and called on the modern 'wage slave' to revolt like the famous Roman gladiator leader. In December 1918 the Spartakists became the German Communist Party (KDP) and attempted to seize power in Berlin. The following month Gustav Noske, as leader of the armed forces, ordered the suppression of all radical uprisings throughout Germany. Within days, a second rebellion in Berlin was brutally crushed and the two leaders murdered without trial. There was a further Spartakist rising in the Ruhr in 1920.

spa town A resort containing a mineral spring used for medicinal purposes. Such towns took their designation from Spa, in Belgium, celebrated since medieval times for the restorative quality of its water. In 18th century England spas were fashionable resorts offering cures and amusements; the upper and middle classes flocked to take the waters and attend the Assembly Rooms in Bath (built around the original Roman thermal baths), as also at Epsom, Tunbridge Wells, Buxton, and Cheltenham. The prosperity generated by these visitors is witnessed by the many fine Georgian buildings that grace these towns, notably the crescents in Bath and the Pantiles in Tunbridge Wells.

Sea bathing also became fashionable in the 18th century, encouraged by doctors who recommended the benefits of salt water and sea air. Margate, Ramsgate, Scarborough, and Weymouth were all flourishing resorts by the 1780s and the patronage of the Prince Regent (later George IV) ensured the social success of Brighton in the 1790s. Spas remained fashionable in Europe in the 19th century, particularly the German resort of Baden-Baden.

Speer, Albert (1905–81) German Nazi leader. He became the official architect for the Nazi Party, designing the grandiose stadium at Nuremberg (1934). An efficient organizer, he became (1942) Minister for Armaments and was mainly responsible for the planning of Germany's war economy, marshalling conscripted and slave labour in his *Organization Todt* to build strategic roads and defence lines. He was imprisoned after the war.

Speke, John Hanning (1827–64) British explorer. He reached Lake Victoria (1858) on BURTON's expedition, identifying it as the source of the White Nile. He returned in 1860 with James Grant to confirm the discovery. Working their way up the western shore of Lake Victoria, they came to its northern tip, where Speke found the Ripon Falls. Speke and Grant then followed the Nile down to Khartoum, which they reached in 1863.

Spence, Thomas (1750–1814) British social reformer who advocated the nationalization of land. In 1775 he published a pamphlet, *The Real Rights of Man*, in which he proposed that all land should be placed in the hands of local corporations, who would charge a fair rent for its use and distribute the money earned among the community. He moved to London in 1792 and set up as a printer of radical tracts. He was imprisoned twice, once for publishing PAINE's *Rights of Man*. After his death his followers continued to meet as members of the society of Spencean philanthropists.

Spence, William Guthrie (1846–1926) Australian trade unionist and politician. Spence helped to found several unions, including the Amalgamated Shearers' Union of Australasia (1886) and the Australian Workers' Union (1894). He was President of the former (1886–93), and the latter (1898–1917), then Australia's largest union. He played a prominent role in the Maritime Strike of 1890 and the Queensland SHEARERS' STRIKE OF 1891. He was elected to the Federal House of Representatives for Darling (1901–19).

Spencer, Herbert (1820–1903) British philosopher and sociologist. He received little formal education, and began his career as a railway engineer before turning to writing and the study of philosophy, publishing his first book, *Social Statistics*, in 1851. He welcomed Charles Darwin's *Origin of Species* (1859) and coined the phrase 'survival of the fittest'. He sought to trace the principles of evolution in all branches of knowledge in a projected ten-volume work *A System of Synthetic Philosophy*, of which volume three, *The Principles of Sociology* (1896), was his most influential. He attacked all forms of state interference, which he believed would lead to the loss of individual freedom. His optimistic belief in human progress through evolution won him a large following.

Speransky, Mikhail Mikhailovich, Count (1772–1839) Russian statesman, chief adviser to ALEXANDER I. After the defeat of Russia by Napoleon and the Treaty of TILSIT, he drew up, at the emperor's request, a constitution that proposed popular participation in legislation; this was only partially implemented. He increased the burden of taxation on the nobility and sought to educate the bureaucracy, establishing promotion on the basis of merit. In doing so he incurred the enmity of both the aristocracy and the bureaucrats, and was charged (1812) with treason and secret dealings with the French, and sent into exile. Reinstated four years later, he rejoined the council of state (1821) and spent his final years codifying Russian law.

Spice Islands MOLUCCAS.

Spithead mutiny (April 1797) A mutiny by sailors of the British navy based at Spithead, off the southern coast of England. In April 1797 the fleet refused to put to sea, calling for better pay and conditions, including the provision of edible food, improved medical services, and opportunities for shore leave. The Admiralty, acknowledging the justice of the sailors' grievances and fearing that the mutiny would spread further (by May it had already affected the fleet stationed at the Nore: see NORE MUTINY), agreed to their demands and issued a royal pardon.

spoils system (or patronage system) In US politics, the convention whereby a victorious political party rewards its supporters with public appointments. The term was coined by Senator William Marcy of New York in 1832, in connection with appointments made by President Andrew JACKSON, who replaced 20% of federal office-holders by his political supporters during his two terms. A US President or state governor has considerable patronage at his disposal. After the American Civil War

attempts were made to reduce patronage in the Civil Service, for example by the PENDLETON ACT (1883), which created the Civil Service Commission. The term 'spoils system' is also used to refer to the award of contracts, especially defence contracts, to a state in return for the support of its representatives for presidential policies in Congress, and the granting of public contracts to party contributors on favourable terms.

sports, spectator Sporting events staged before massed spectators. In ancient Greece such events had an important social and even religious function; the original OLYMPIC GAMES, staged at the sanctuary of Zeus at Olympia, may have originated as early as the 14th century BC. Circuses, races, and gladiatorial bouts were of great importance in the Roman world, where large open-air stadiums were built to accommodate big crowds. In later European societies most sporting events were local and rural (one of the most popular being horse-racing) until the mid 19th century. They were often violent, such as boxing, and cruel, such as cock-fighting. One of the few events for massed spectators was the bull-fight in southern France and Spain. In the second half of the 19th century sporting stadiums began to be built in cities, followed by many more in the 20th century. One of the most popular of the new spectator sports was association football or 'soccer'. In its modern form soccer developed at English public schools. Its rules were first codified at Cambridge in 1843 and the Football Association was founded in 1863, with inter-city contests soon following. In 1904 the Fédération Internationale de Football Association (FIFA) was founded in France and thereafter soccer became the world's most popular sport both to watch and play. Its rival in English schools was rugby football, which began at Rugby School in 1823 and spread in varying forms all over the world, and from which are descended American, Canadian, and Australian football. Cricket has been played in England since the 13th century (the Marylebone Cricket Club (MCC), which is the world governing body of the sport, was founded in 1787). The game gained in popularity within the British empire, notably in Australia, where the first Test (international) Match was played in 1877. Tennis, originating from a 12th-century French handball game, was first played in its modern form in Wales in 1873. In 1877 the All England Croquet Club at Wimbledon sponsored the first World Tennis Championship. Athletics contests based on those of ancient Greece were revived by the Olympic Games movement in 1896. The Games gradually extended from track and field events to all sports, attracting ever higher skills and larger crowds; they have also been marred by political tensions, most notoriously the massacre in 1972 of Israeli participants in the Munich Olympics. In Europe violence between supporters of rival club and national football teams has increased in recent years. The rapid growth of satellite television around the world has given many more people, especially in remote regions, the opportunity to watch sports and games.

Spurs, Battle of the Golden COURTRAI, BATTLE OF.

Sputnik A series of Soviet satellites. *Sputnik 1* was the first artificial satellite to orbit the Earth, in October 1957. This event profoundly shocked the USA and sparked the race to put a man on the moon (see SPACE

EXPLORATION). *Sputnik 2* carried the first animal into space, the dog Laika. Subsequent *Sputniks* (11 to 24) were also designated by the name *Cosmos*.

squatter A person who takes unauthorized possession of unoccupied premises or land, usually to live there.

In the USA, from the late 18th century, a squatter was a settler having no normal or legal title to the land he occupied, particularly in a district not yet surveyed.

In New South Wales, Australia, the term was applied from the early 19th century to those, often ex-convicts, who occupied land without authority and stole stock. By the 1830s, its meaning had begun to broaden, often being applied to the many pastoralists settling beyond the official 1829 limits of settlement. They were mostly involved in the wool industry, and in 1836 were granted grazing rights for an annual licence fee. The squatters demanded security of tenure and pre-emptive rights, which they gained in 1847, securing the land most suitable for agricultural and pastoral purposes. Thereafter squatters became a very powerful group, socially, economically, and politically; they often struggled bitterly over land with SELECTORS during the second half of the 19th century. Squatters continued to be known by that name even after they acquired their land freehold. Eventually, the term was applied to all large pastoralists in Australia.

Squatting nowadays generally results from housing shortages, but whereas in rich countries squatters tend surreptitiously to take single buildings, in poorer ones the illegal occupation of land is on so great a scale that the authorities often condone it and sometimes grant squatters legal title. Large-scale land seizures are sometimes carried out rapidly at night after careful planning: this is reflected in some designations for squatter settlements: in Mexico, *barrios paracaidistas* (parachute settlements) and in Turkey, *gecekondu* (built overnight). The land chosen tends to be in public, not private, ownership and to be unwanted by others because, for example, it is on a waste-dump or subject to flooding. Squatters may also squeeze into small patches of land, near motorways for instance. Once the land is occupied, the residents begin to build shelters leading to the creation of shanty towns. When the growth of such settlements initially took off (in Latin America in the 1940s and in sub-Saharan Africa in the 1960s), government reaction was often eviction of residents to distant camps and demolition of the structures. However, when it became apparent that this did not stem migration to cities and destroyed not only housing stock but informal-sector jobs, most governments became more tolerant of squatter settlements. In recent years, rapid URBANIZATION has reduced the supply of accessible public land and increased competition for it.

squire (or esquire) Originally an apprentice KNIGHT in medieval Europe. Usually young men, they served as the personal attendants of fully fledged knights. The title was then one of function rather than birth: it derives from the Latin 'scutarius', referring to the shield-bearing role of the squire. In later medieval England the term came to be applied to all gentlemen entitled to bear arms. By the 17th century, 'squire' had become synonymous with a district's leading landowner, perhaps even the lord of the manor. The considerable local influence, both political and ecclesiastical, of the 'squirearchy' has since diminished.

Sri Lanka (formerly Ceylon) A pear-shaped island country in the Indian Ocean off the south-east coast of India.

Physical. Some 435 km (270 miles) long and 225 km (140 miles) wide in the middle, Sri Lanka has very broad coastal plains which rise at the centre to highlands 2,000 m (6,560 feet) high and more. The climate is monsoonal, with very heavy rainfall; but while the plains are always hot and sticky, the hills are cooler and less humid. At high altitudes the scenery is beautiful, with mixed forests, streams, and waterfalls. On the lower slopes tea is grown; and on the well-rivered plains there are rubber trees, coconut palms, and paddy fields. The flat stretches of coast contain many palm-fringed beaches.

Economy. The economy is largely agrarian, with exports of tea, rubber, precious stones, and coconut products. Manufacturing industry includes textiles, cement, and petroleum-refining. Remittances from emigrant workers are significant, as was tourism until it was disrupted by the civil war.

History. Sri Lanka's early history was shaped by Indian influences and its modern identity by three phases of European colonization. The origins of the dominant Sinhalese racial group go back to Indo-Aryan invaders from north India, whose successors dominated the north central plain from the 5th century BC until about 1200 AD. During the 2nd century BC BUDDHISM spread, following the conversion of the reigning king. An outstanding ruler was Parakramabahu I (1153–86), who exercised strong military and administrative leadership and also reformed the quarrelling Buddhist sects. However, intermittent invasions from south India gradually created an enclave of Tamil Hindu power on the northern Jaffna peninsula and the north-eastern coast. The centre of Sinhalese and Buddhist civilization gradually shifted south-westwards, and political power was divided between a number of kingdoms.

European contacts began in the early 16th century when Portuguese merchants, profiting from the internal disunity, gained trading privileges on the west coast. Dutch traders gradually supplanted Portuguese influence in the 17th century, but were replaced by British forces in 1796. When the embattled interior kingdom of Kandy fell in 1815, the entire island came under the control of the British, who called it Ceylon. By the early 20th century the middle class was pressing for self-government. A new constitution was established in 1931, but racial tensions prevented its full implementation. Although granted an element of self-government, the island remained a crown colony until 1948, when it was granted independence as a dominion within the COMMONWEALTH OF NATIONS. A government was established by the United National Party under Don SENANAYAKE, who was succeeded (1952) by his son, Dudley Senanayake. The Socialist Sri Lanka Freedom Party was in power from 1956 to 1965, with Solomon BANDARANAIKE as its dominant force until his death in 1959. His widow Sirimavo Bandaranaike (1916–), succeeded him as Prime Minister (1960–65, 1970–77, 1994–). A new constitution in 1972 established the island as the Republic of Sri Lanka. Tensions have re-emerged between the majority Sinhalese, traditionally Buddhist, and the minority Tamil, chiefly Hindu, who are of Indian origin and live mainly in northern Sri Lanka. A ceasefire was arranged by the Indian government in 1987 between Tamil guerrilla groups and the Sri Lankan government, but a tense situation remained. During 1989–90 President Ranasinghe Premadasa initiated all-party talks to end civil strife, but these again failed and in 1991 the Defence Minister was assassinated. A state of emergency was declared, but violations of human rights by government forces led to suspension of UK aid. During the years 1990–91 civil strife claimed some 12,000 lives. Although peace talks were again initiated in April 1992, they made little progress. Meanwhile the Sri Lankan economy rapidly declined. Following President Premadasa's assassination in 1993, Chandrika Kumaratunge, the daughter of Solomon and Sirimavo Bandaranaike, was elected Prime Minister in 1994. Later in the same year, Kumaratunge became President and was succeeded as Prime Minister by her mother. Peace negotiations between the Government and Tamil guerrillas were abandoned in 1995, when and renewed fighting erupted. Despite a successful assault by government forces on the Tamil guerrilla stronghold in the Jaffna peninsula in the north of the island, fighting has continued, with a state of emergency being declared throughout the country in 1996

CAPITAL:	Colombo (President and judiciary); Sri Jayewardenepura Kotte (Prime Minister and legislature)
AREA:	65,610 sq km (25,332 sq miles)
POPULATION:	18.318 million (1996)
CURRENCY:	1 Sri Lankan rupee = 100 cents
RELIGIONS:	Buddhist 70.0%; Hindu 15.0%; Christian 8.0%; Muslim 7.0%
ETHNIC GROUPS:	Sinhalese 74.0%; Tamil 18.0%; Moor 7.0%
LANGUAGES:	Sinhalese, Tamil (both official); English
INTERNATIONAL ORGANIZATIONS:	UN; Commonwealth; Non-Aligned Movement; Colombo Plan

Srivijaya A river port near Palembang in southern SUMATRA. It was described by a Chinese Buddhist pilgrim of the 7th century as 'a great fortified city'. Its position some 80 km (50 miles) upstream from the mouth of the Musi River enabled it to trade easily with the mountain peoples of the interior and also protected it from seaborne attack. There were probably two separate states known as Srivijaya, the first flourishing from the 7th to the 9th century, the second from the 10th to the 13th century. The latter grew into a commercial empire extending from Java to Kedah, on the Malay peninsula and had trading contacts with China. Later, raids by Tamils from CHOLA in India weakened its power. In the 14th century it succumbed to MAJAPAHIT. Its port, once the greatest in south-east Asia, declined and became a Chinese pirates' base.

SS (abbr. for *Schutzstaffel*, German, 'protective echelon') The élite corps of the German Nazi Party. Founded (1925) by HITLER as a personal bodyguard, the SS was schooled in absolute loyalty and obedience, and in total ruthlessness towards opponents. From 1929 until the dissolution of the THIRD REICH the SS was headed by Heinrich HIMMLER, who divided it mainly into two groups: the Allgemeine SS (General SS), and the Waffen-SS (Armed SS). Initially subordinated to the SA (BROWNSHIRTS), the SS assisted Hitler in the 'NIGHT OF THE LONG KNIVES' massacre (1934) in which the rival corps

were eliminated. By 1936 Himmler, with the help of Reinhard HEYDRICH, had gained control of the national police force. Subdivisions of the SS included the GESTAPO and the Sicherheitsdienst, in charge of foreign and domestic intelligence work. The Waffen-SS served as an élite combat group alongside but independent of the armed forces. It also administered the CONCENTRATION CAMPS.

Stalin, Josef Vissarionovich (born J. V. Dzhugashvili) (1879–1953) Soviet dictator. The son of a shoemaker, he was born in Georgia, where he attended a training school for priests, from which he was expelled for holding revolutionary views. An early member of the BOLSHEVIK Party, he was twice exiled to Siberia. He escaped after the start of the RUSSIAN REVOLUTION and rose rapidly to become LENIN's right-hand man. After Lenin's death he won a long struggle with TROTSKY for the leadership, and went on to become sole dictator. Features of his rule were: rapid industrialization of the Soviet Union under the five-year plans (which was eventually to turn the Soviet Union into the world's second industrial and military power); the violent COLLECTIVIZATION of agriculture that led to famine and the virtual extermination of many peasants; a purge technique that not only removed, through show trials and executions, those of his party colleagues who did not agree with him but also placed millions of other citizens in PRISON CAMPS. In 1939 Stalin signed the NAZI–SOVIET PACT with HITLER, and, on the latter's invasion (1941) of the Soviet Union, Stalin entered WORLD WAR II on Britain's side, signing the Anglo-Soviet Treaty in 1942. He met with ROOSEVELT and CHURCHILL at the conferences of TEHERAN (1943), YALTA (1945), and POTSDAM (1945). By skilful diplomacy he ensured a new Soviet sphere of influence in eastern Europe, with communist domination in all its neighbouring states. Suspicious of any communist movement outside his control, he broke (1948) with TITO over party policy in former YUGOSLAVIA. Increasingly the victim of his own paranoia, he ordered the arbitrary execution of many of his colleagues. After his death the 20th All-Party Congress (1956) under KHRUSHCHEV attacked the cult of Stalin, accusing him of terror and tyranny. The term 'Stalinism' came to mean a brand of communism that was both national and repressive.

Stalingrad, Battle of (1942–43) A long and bitter battle in World War II, during which the German advance into the Soviet Union was turned back. During 1942 the German 6th Army under General von PAULUS occupied Kursk, Kharkov, the Crimea, and the Maikop oilfields, reaching the key city of Stalingrad (now Volgograd) on the Volga. Soviet resistance continued, with grim and prolonged house-to-house fighting, while sufficient Soviet reserves were being assembled. The Germans were prevented from crossing the Volga and in November Stalin launched a winter offensive of six Soviet armies under Marshalls ZHUKOV, KONIEV, Petrov, and Malinovsky. By January 1943 the Germans were surrounded and von Paulus surrendered, losing some 330,000 troops killed or captured. The Russians then advanced to recapture KURSK, a victory that marked the beginning of the end of German success on the EASTERN FRONT.

Stalwarts In the USA, a faction of conservative Republicans led by Roscoe CONKLING during the

Presidency (1877–81) of Rutherford HAYES. They supported the SPOILS SYSTEM, but opposed both the final ending of Reconstruction in the South (RECONSTREUCTION ACTS), symbolized by the withdrawal of Federal troops in 1877, and any reform of the Civil Service. In 1880 they sought a third term for former President GRANT, but failed. They dubbed their opponents, the anti-Grant wing of the Republican Party, the 'Half-Breeds'. Led in Congress by James BLAINE, the Half-Breeds succeeded in getting their candidate GARFIELD elected in 1880. The nickname 'Stalwart' was dropped after President Garfield was shot (July 1881) by a Stalwart who had been disappointed in his pursuit of office. A direct result of this tragedy was the PENDLETON ACT in 1883, which sought to make entry into the service dependent on merit rather than on reward.

Stamford Bridge, Battle of (25 September 1066) A battle fought at a village on the River Derwent in Yorkshire, north-east England. HAROLD II of England all but annihilated a large invading army under his exiled brother Tostig and the King of Norway, Harald Hardrada, both of whom were killed. Earlier (on 20 September) they had inflicted a heavy defeat on the Saxon forces of Earl Edwin of Mercia and Earl Morcar of Northumbria. Harold's army marched south from Stamford to face the Norman invasion and fight the Battle of HASTINGS.

Stamp Act (1765) A British taxation measure, introduced by GRENVILLE to cover part of the cost of defending the North American colonies. It required that all colonial legal documents, newspapers, and other items should bear a revenue stamp, as in England. Seen by the SONS OF LIBERTY and many other Americans as a first attempt at 'taxation without representation', it was met with widespread resistance. In October 1765, nine colonial delegations met at the Stamp Act Congress in New York and petitioned for repeal. American boycotts of British goods and civil disobedience induced ROCKINGHAM to accede in 1766, though the Declaratory Act reasserted parliamentary power over the colonies. It helped initiate the campaign for American independence.

Stanhope, James, 1st Earl (1673–1721) English soldier and statesman. He served in Spain during the War of the SPANISH SUCCESSION and was appointed commander of the British forces there in 1708. Although he achieved some successes, he was captured in 1710. On his return to Britain he entered politics, and played a major part in securing the succession of GEORGE I. As a leading minister he organized the government's swift response to the FIFTEEN Rebellion. His genius lay in foreign affairs: he ended Britain's isolation, securing a treaty of alliance with its recent enemy France; he put forward a feasible solution to Austro-Spanish rivalry over Italy, and worked for a settlement of the NORTHERN WAR. Accused, probably unjustly, of involvement in ministerial corruption arising from the SOUTH SEA BUBBLE, he died of a stroke while defending himself against his accusers in the House of Lords.

Stanislaus II (formerly Count Stanislaus-Augustus Poniatowski) (1732–98) The last King of Poland (1764–95). He was a lover of CATHERINE II of Russia and her candidate for the Polish throne, which, as the country was under Russian control at that time, he gained. In the first partition of Poland in 1772, Russia, Austria, and Prussia all took slices of Polish territory. From 1773 to 1792 there was a period of national revival encouraged by Stanislaus. However, in 1793 he was forced to agree to the second partition of Poland, which left him with a truncated kingdom and made him almost a vassal of Russia. A rising led by General KOSCIUSZKO was crushed, and the third partition completed the destruction of Poland. In November 1795 Stanislaus was forced to abdicate.

Stanley, Sir Henry Morton (1841–1904) British-born US journalist and explorer. Born John Rowlands, an illegitimate child who was soon orphaned, he was brought up in a Welsh workhouse and ran away to the USA in 1859, travelling as a cabin boy. He was adopted by a New Orleans cotton merchant, Henry Stanley, whose name he took. In the 1860s he served as a soldier on the Confederate side in the AMERICAN CIVIL WAR and as a seaman on US ships before becoming a journalist. He became a widely travelled newspaper correspondent, and in 1871 was sent by the *New York Herald* to Zanzibar to search for David LIVINGSTONE, whom he met on 10 November 1871 on Lake Tanganyika and greeted with the famous words, 'Dr Livingstone, I presume'. Subsequently he traced the course of the CONGO (1875–77) and helped to found, under the auspices of the King of the Belgians, the Congo Free State. He also explored Uganda and opened up central Africa for Europeans. His book *In Darkest Africa* (1890) had an immense sale. He resumed British citizenship in 1892.

Star Chamber An English court of civil and criminal jurisdiction primarily concerned with offences affecting crown interests, noted for its summary and arbitrary procedure. It was long thought to have had its origin in a statute of 1487; in fact, the court of Star Chamber had been developing from the king's council acting in its judicial capacity into a regular court of law since the reign of EDWARD IV. It owed its name to the fact that it commonly sat in a room in the Palace of Westminster that had a ceiling covered with stars. Its judges specialized in cases involving public order, and particularly allegations of riot. Its association with the royal prerogative, and CHARLES I's manipulation of legislative powers in the making of decrees during the period of his personal rule, made it unpopular in the 17th century and caused its abolition by the LONG PARLIAMENT in 1641.

START STRATEGIC ARMS REDUCTION TALKS.

States-General (or Estates-General) Usually a gathering of representatives of the three estates of a realm: the church; the nobility; and the commons (representatives of the corporations of towns). They met to advise a sovereign on matters of policy. The name was applied to the representative body of the UNITED PROVINCES of the Netherlands in their struggle for independence from Spain in the 16th century. As an assembly of the various provinces of the Dutch Republic it wielded considerable power, although delegating authority in emergency to the House of ORANGE. It was replaced in 1795 by a national assembly, but was restored as a legislative body for the kingdom of the Netherlands in 1814.

In France, the States-General began as an occasional advisory body, usually summoned to register specific support for controversial royal policy. Although it was introduced by Philip IV, who held a meeting in 1302 to enlist support during a quarrel with the pope, it was rarely convoked during the following century and the first proper States-General in France was not held until 1484, in the reign of Louis XI. Thereafter it was used by the GUISES during the French Wars of Religion as a political device against the Huguenots and by the nobles in 1614 to attack Marie de Medici – who, however, turned it to her own advantage. The rise of absolutism led to its neglect in the 17th and 18th centuries, but it was urgently summoned in 1789 in an attempt to push through much needed revenue and administrative reforms. The *parlements* and the nobles had resisted these reforms and LOUIS XVI and his minister, NECKER, hoped to break the deadlock. Its summoning and composition were based on the precedent of 1614 and its members were encouraged to draw up *cahiers*, representative lists of grievances. Voting was carried out eventually by head rather than by order (as in 1614), giving radicals a majority. The nobles lost control of the States-General, which then formed itself into a NATIONAL ASSEMBLY, helping to precipitate the FRENCH REVOLUTION.

states' rights A US political doctrine that upholds the rights of individual states against the power of the federal government. The framers of the CONSTITUTION OF THE USA produced a federal system in which the delineation of power between the federal government and the states was open to interpretation, and from the very beginning divergent views on this issue have influenced US politics. In the early years of the USA HAMILTON and the FEDERALIST PARTY saw the Constitution as a sanction for strong central (federal) government, while JEFFERSON and his followers believed that all powers not specifically granted to the federal government should be reserved to the states. The doctrine of states' rights lay behind the NULLIFICATION CRISIS of 1828–33 and provided the constitutional basis of the Southern case in the dispute leading up to the AMERICAN CIVIL WAR. In recent years the doctrine has been central to controversies over CIVIL RIGHTS and welfare expenditure.

state terrorism Repressive measures employed by a government against its own population; or TERRORISM instigated or sponsored by a government against other states or individuals. In the first case, terrorist measures are employed by the state in order to coerce, intimidate, repress, and ultimately eliminate dissidents or ethnic minorities. The most prominent practitioners of state terrorism in the 20th century were the Nazi regime in Germany (1933–45) and the Stalinist regime in the former Soviet Union (1924–53); some contemporary authoritarian states (for example INDONESIA in its illegally annexed province of EAST TIMOR) employ terrorist methods against their own populations, including threats, arbitrary arrest, detention without trial, torture, abduction, and extra-judicial execution.

The second form of state terrorism is often pursued by governments as a means of confronting or subverting other powers, which they do not have the military strength or will to attack directly. For example, the Libyan government of Colonel QADDAFI is alleged to have financed and armed external terrorist groups, such as the Irish Republican Army, while the USA, as emerged in the Iran–Contra scandal of 1986, secretly sold arms to Iran and used the proceeds to fund the Contra rebels in Nicaragua (see REAGAN). In 1997, a German court found Iran guilty of organizing the murder of three Kurdish activists in Berlin; Iran has also been responsible for funding the ISLAMIC FUNDAMENTALIST Hizbollah guerrilla movement, which has attacked Israel from the Lebanon.

statholders Provincial leaders in the Netherlands, as first appointed by the ruling dukes of BURGUNDY in the 15th century. Their duties included presiding over the provincial state assemblies and commanding provincial armies. During the DUTCH REVOLTS (1568–1684), they were elected by the central States-General and subsequently by the provincial state assemblies. In the UNITED PROVINCES the House of Orange-Nassau came to dominate the statholderates. Within the province of Holland there was protracted dispute between the Orange statholders and the states for overall leadership. In 1795 the office of statholder ceased to exist.

Stauffenberg, Claus Graf von JULY PLOT.

steam power The use of steam to power machinery, a major factor in the INDUSTRIAL REVOLUTION. The earliest steam engine, developed by Thomas Newcomen (1663–1729) by 1712, was used to pump water from Cornish tin mines. Major improvements made by James Watt (1736–1819) greatly increased its efficiency and in 1781 he adapted a steam engine to drive factory machinery, thus providing a reliable source of industrial power. Before this many factories depended on water power and were therefore sited in the countryside near swiftly flowing streams, where transport was difficult; moreover, production was always dependent upon the weather. Although steam engines had none of these disadvantages, they were expensive and only large businesses could afford to install them. Factories were henceforth sited near coal mines and large towns grew up to house the factory workers. The use of steam engines in the textile industry and in other manufacturing processes led to a growth in the size of factories while their application in the 19th century to railways and steamships (thanks largely to the innovations of James Watt) led to both faster and cheaper travel and transport of goods. The steam-hammer (1808) enabled much larger pieces of metal to be worked, while such developments as the steam-driven threshing machine greatly accelerated the harvesting cycle and reduced farmers' reliance on wind- and water-mills. The direct use of steam engines began to decline in the early 20th century with the development of petrol and diesel engines and the use of steam-driven turbines to generate electricity, an energy source that can be applied more cleanly and easily in industry.

steamship A ship driven by STEAM POWER. During the late 18th century numerous trials of steam-powered vessels were carried out in France, Britain, and the USA. The steamship *Charlotte Dundas* of 1802 was intended as a canal steamer, but was withdrawn after four days because of fears that its wash would erode the canal banks. The first commercially successful steamers were Robert Fulton's steamer *North River* (*Clermont*) in the USA (1807) and the British engineer Patrick Bell's *Comet* in Scotland (1812). By the mid-1820s paddle-wheel steamers were carrying passengers on rivers and short sea runs in North America and Europe, and navies were beginning to use steam for smaller warships. The marine propeller (or screw) was developed in the late 1830s, and was widely adopted by navies in the 1840s. By that time, steam was replacing sail for carrying passengers and mail on all but the longest oceanic routes. With the introduction of steam colliers in the 1850s, steam also began to take over in cargo-carrying. As steam-engines became more reliable and efficient, the use of steamships continued to grow. As a result of the introduction of the triple-expansion engine at the end of the 1880s, steam tramp ships became the dominant general-purpose cargo carriers, and ships no longer carried sails for assistance and safety. The demonstration of the steam-turbine by Charles Parsons in 1897 led to a change from the reciprocating steam-engine to turbine power. Many of the large ocean liners of the early 20th century used steam-turbines. The marine diesel engine made its appearance in the early 20th century and has steadily increased in importance, although steam-turbines are still used in some large ships. (See also TRANSPORT REVOLUTION.)

Stein, Heinrich Friedrich Karl, Baron vom und zum (1757–1831) Prussian statesman and reformer. After various diplomatic and administrative appointments he became Minister of Commerce in 1804. In 1807 he was dismissed by FREDERICK WILLIAM III for attempting to increase the responsibilities of the ministers of state. However, in the aftermath of the Prussian defeat at JENA, Stein was recalled to begin his enlightened reforms. He persuaded the king to abolish the serf system, to end the restrictions on the sale to non-nobles of land owned by nobles, and to end the monopoly of the sons of the nobility in the Prussian officers corp. He wanted the king to authorize a national insurrection against the French and mobilize patriotic energies by the grant of a 'free constitution', but this alarmed Napoleon, who persuaded the king to dismiss him again (1808). His pleas for a united Germany were ignored at the Congress of VIENNA. Stein subsequently became chief counsellor to ALEXANDER I of Russia (1812–15).

Stephan Dushan (1308–55) King of SERBIA (1331–55). The greatest ruler of medieval Serbia, he deposed his father in 1331 and took the title of Emperor of the Serbs and Greeks in 1345. He also controlled Bulgaria as a result of a marriage alliance. He fought the Byzantine empire, and seized Macedonia, Albania, and much of Greece, and introduced a new code of laws. His achievements were shortlived as his son could not maintain the Serbo-Greek empire against OTTOMAN invasion and regional challenges.

Stephen (c. 1096–1154) King of England (1135–54). He seized the crown after his uncle, HENRY I, had persuaded the English barons (including Stephen) to recognize his daughter MATILDA as his heir. Stephen was supported by his brother, the Bishop of Winchester, and others who disliked Matilda's husband Geoffrey, Count of Anjou.

Stephen's reign was marked by rebellion and intermittent civil war. In 1138 Matilda's half-brother Robert rebelled, and the Scots invaded northern England. Stephen was captured at Lincoln in 1141 and temporarily deposed, but defeats at Winchester (1141) and Faringdon (1145) forced Matilda to withdraw from

England in 1148. However, the year before he died Stephen recognized Matilda's son as his successor, Henry II.

Stephen I, St (975–1036) King of Hungary (997–1038). Crowned by the authority of Pope Sylvester II in 1000, he was chiefly concerned with the thorough Christianization of the country and with the establishment of a durable code of laws. His reign was troubled by persistent warfare, particularly with the Bulgars but later with the German emperor, Conrad II, in which the king was successful. King Stephen's crown remains the outstanding symbol of Hungarian royalty.

Sterkfontein A complex of collapsed limestone caves near Johannesburg, South Africa, one of the most important sites for studies of early human evolution in Africa. In 1936 an AUSTRALOPITHECINE fossil was found there and successive discoveries have made the site the richest source of fossils of the species *Australopithecus africanus*. It has not yet been possible to date the remains exactly but they seem to be from 3 to 2.5 million years old. With the australopithecines are many fossilized animal bones, which suggest that they were preyed upon by leopards and other large cats and by hyenas.

Stern Gang British name for a ZIONIST terrorist group calling itself 'Lohamei Herut Israel Lehi' (Fighters for the Freedom of Israel). It campaigned actively (1940–48) in British-administered Palestine for the creation of a Jewish state. Founded by Abraham Stern (1907–42), the Stern Gang numbered no more than a few hundred. They operated in small groups and concentrated on the assassination of government officials. Their victims included Lord Moyne, the British Minister for the Middle East (1944), and Count BERNADOTTE, the United Nations mediator in Palestine (1948).

Stevens, Thaddeus (1792–1868) US statesman. He served in the Pennsylvania state legislature as a supporter of the ANTI-MASONIC PARTY before his election to Congress as a Whig in 1849. He left the House in 1853 as a result of his strong ABOLITIONIST views and helped to organize the REPUBLICAN PARTY before returning to Congress as one of its representatives (1859–68). His most influential period came after 1865, when he became one of the main champions of the radical reconstruction programme, and one of the chief architects of the FOURTEENTH AMENDMENT and the RECONSTRUCTION ACTS. He chaired the committee that prepared impeachment charges against Andrew JOHNSON.

Stevenson, Adlai E(wing) (1900–65) US statesman. He served in various government posts and in 1948 he was elected governor of Illinois with the largest majority in the state's history. Chosen as the Democratic candidate for the Presidency in the elections of 1952 and 1956, he was badly beaten on both occasions by Dwight D. EISENHOWER. A liberal reformer and internationalist, his Presidential campaigns were marked by brilliant and witty speeches. President KENNEDY appointed him US ambassador to the United Nations (1961–65) with cabinet rank.

Stewart STUART.

Stilwell, Joseph Warren (1883–1946) US general. Popularly known as 'Vinegar Joe' on account of his tactlessness, he served in China between the wars. In

World War II, he commanded US and Chinese forces in south China and Burma, co-operating with the British in the BURMA CAMPAIGN. Technically, his authority was by virtue of his appointment as chief-of-staff in this region by CHIANG KAI-SHEK. Differences of opinion with Chiang led to his recall; he later commanded the US 10th Army at Okinawa.

Stimson, Henry Lewis (1867–1950) US statesman. He was Secretary of War for President TAFT (1911–13) and served in WORLD WAR I. While governor-general of the Philippines (1927–29) he pursued an enlightened policy of conciliation. As Secretary of State (1929–33) in the cabinet of President HOOVER, he promulgated the Stimson Doctrine (or Doctrine of Non-Recognition) in response to the Japanese invasion of Manchuria (1931): a refusal to grant diplomatic recognition to actions that threatened the territorial integrity of China or violated the KELLOGG-BRIAND PACT. He later served as Secretary of War (1940–45) under Franklin D. ROOSEVELT and TRUMAN, in which post he made the recommendation to drop the atomic bomb.

Stock Market Crash (1929) A severe financial crisis in the USA, also known as the 'Great Crash', the 'Wall Street Crash', or the 'Great Panic'. During the first half of 1929 an unprecedented boom took place on the New York Stock Exchange. However, prices began to fall from late September and selling began. In less than a month there was a 40 per cent drop in stock value, and this fall continued over the next three years. Its causes were numerous. Although the post-war US economy seemed to be booming, it was on a narrow base and there were fundamental flaws. The older basic industries, such as mining and textiles, were weak, agriculture was depressed, unemployment at four million was unacceptably high, and international loans were often poorly secured. A new rich class enjoyed a flamboyant life-style, which too many people tried to copy by means of credit and stock-market speculation, within an unsound banking system. Once the business cycle faltered, a panic set in. The effects of the crash were hugely to accelerate a downward spiral: real estate values collapsed, factories closed, and banks began to call in loans, precipitating the worldwide Great DEPRESSION.

stocks PILLORY AND STOCKS.

Stoics Followers of the Stoic doctrine devised by the philosophical school founded by ZENO OF CITIUM in roughly 300 BC. The name derives from the *Stoa poikile* (Painted Colonnade) in ATHENS, where Zeno taught. Zeno's followers propounded various metaphysical systems, united chiefly by their ethical implications. All were variants on the pantheistic theme that the world constitutes a single, organically unified, and benevolent whole, in which the appearance of evil results only from our limited view. Their philosophy had at its core the beliefs that virtue is based on knowledge, reason is the governing principle of nature, and individuals should live in harmony with nature. The vicissitudes of life were viewed with equanimity: pleasure, pain, and even death were irrelevant to true happiness. In time, the idea that only the consummately wise man (the philosopher) could attain virtue was challenged and Stoicism became more engaged with political realities. Later, the Stoic belief in the brotherhood of man helped

the philosophy to make an impact in republican Rome, where it influenced such men as CATO (the Younger), whose suicide brought him a martyr's fame, BRUTUS, and CICERO. Later it underlay much aristocratic opposition to the emperors, but even so its disciples included SENECA, tutor and adviser to NERO, and the emperor MARCUS AURELIUS.

Stolypin, Piort Arkadevich (1862–1911) Russian statesman. The last effective statesman of the Russian empire, he was Premier (1906–11). He was hated for his ruthless punishment of activists in the RUSSIAN REVOLUTION of 1905, for his disregard of the DUMAS, and for his treatment of Jews. His constructive work lay in his agricultural reforms. Believing that a contented peasantry would check revolution, he allowed peasants (KULAKS) to have their land in one holding instead of strips that were periodically re-allocated within the peasant commune. Those taking advantage of this became prosperous, but were not powerful enough to stem the revolutionary tide. He was assassinated in a Kiev theatre.

Stone Ages Those periods of the past when metals were unknown and stone was used as the main material for missiles, as hammers, for making tools for such tasks as cutting and scraping and, later, as spear heads. Hard, fine-grained stone was the material most suitable for flaking. Although the best locally available would have been the material of first choice, stone needed for special purposes was occasionally brought from long distances away, even by early toolmakers of up to two million years ago (as at OLDUVAI GORGE and KOOBI FORA in eastern Africa). Although flint is the material most often associated with flaked stone tools, in Africa, where flint is rare, quartz, chert, and volcanic rocks, such as basalt and obsidian (natural glass), were worked long before early Europeans used flint. In Europe, three Stone Ages are recognized – the Old Stone Age (PALAEOLITHIC), the Middle Stone Age (MESOLITHIC), and the New Stone Age (NEOLITHIC). In other parts of the world, different subdivisions are used. The Stone Ages were followed by the BRONZE and IRON AGES. This division of prehistory into three chronological stages, defined by the main material used for tools (stone, bronze, and iron) – the Three Ages System – was first put to practical use for classifying archaeological material in Denmark in 1819. As it spread to other countries, it became necessary to subdivide the three ages.

Stonehenge A prehistoric MEGALITHIC monument on Salisbury Plain in southern England, built between 3100 and 1800 BC. Archaeological evidence suggests that it was built in three stages: the first, completed in about 2100 BC, consisted of a low circular bank and a ditch of earth surrounding a ring of narrow pits (known as the Aubrey holes). The second, a double ring of standing bluestones (pillars of igneous rock) may have originally formed part of a stone circle elsewhere, and was dismantled before it had been completed. The bluestones, weighing up to four tonnes each, may have been transported from the Preseli Mountains in Wales, 220 km (140 miles) away. The final stage was the present monument, built around 1800 BC. This consists of an inner horseshoe of five trilithons (each consisting of two upright stones of about 40 tonnes and a horizontal lintel), a central altar stone, and an outer ring of 30 uprights (each weighing about 26 tonnes) joined by lintels, all made of a local sandstone known as sarsen.

The function of this monument – whether it was a temple, a secular ceremonial centre, or an astronomical observatory – remains controversial. Certainly it called for a vast outlay of technical effort, and its axis, over the outlying Heel Stone, does indeed align on the summer solstice sunrise. Other examples of megalithic monuments include Avebury Circle in Wiltshire, CARNAC in Brittany, and Callanish on the Hebridean island of Lewis.

Stopes, Marie Charlotte Carmichael (1880–1958) British scientist and writer on parenthood and birth control. She was appointed lecturer in palaeobotany at Manchester University in 1904 and then taught in London. It was, however, her books on sexual and reproductive matters, particularly *Married Love* (1918) and *Wise Parenthood* (1918) that made her famous. With her second husband, H. Verdon-Roe, she founded Britain's first clinic for birth control in London in 1921. Her activities roused opposition but also steadily increasing support among the medical profession and the general public.

Stormont A suburb of Belfast, the former seat of the parliament of NORTHERN IRELAND. Created by the Government of Ireland Act (1920) as a subordinate body to Westminster, the Stormont Parliament was dominated by the ULSTER UNIONIST PARTY until, following the breakdown in law and order in the late 1960s it was suspended in 1972. Direct rule from Westminster was imposed and administered by civil servants of the Northern Ireland Office based in Stormont Castle.

Strafford, Thomas Wentworth, 1st Earl of (1593–1641) English statesman. A Member of Parliament since 1614, he entered the service of CHARLES I in 1628. Although he had previously opposed royal policies, he was a believer in firm government and accepted preferment in order to uphold the king's power. Thenceforth, as Lord President of the Council of the North (1628) and Lord Deputy of Ireland (1633), he was the principal exponent of the policy of 'Thorough', putting the royal will into effect with the utmost authority. His autocratic style made him extremely unpopular, and most of his achievements in the north and Ireland turned out to be temporary. On the outbreak of the BISHOPS' WARS he was recalled by Charles to England. Now at the centre of affairs for the first time, he could not avert the approaching ENGLISH CIVIL WAR. He was created Earl of Strafford in January 1640, but impeached for treason in the same year. Opposition members of the LONG PARLIAMENT claimed that he was about to impose a Catholic dictatorship on England and he was executed under Act of ATTAINDER.

Straits Settlements A former British crown colony comprising territories bordering on the strategic Malacca Strait in South-East Asia. The three English East India colonies of Penang, Malacca, and SINGAPORE were combined as the Straits Settlements in 1826. After 1858 they passed to British Indian control and in 1867 they became a crown colony, to which Labuan was added in 1912. The colony was dismantled in 1946, Singapore becoming a separate colony and Penang, Malacca, and Labuan joining the Malayan Union.

Strategic Arms Limitation Talks (SALT) Discussions between the USA and the Soviet Union, aimed at limiting the production and deployment of nuclear weapons. A first round of meetings (1969–72) produced the SALT I Agreement, which prevented the construction of comprehensive anti-ballistic missile (ABM) systems and placed limits on the construction of strategic (i.e. intercontinental) ballistic missiles (ICBM) for an initial period of five years. A SALT II Treaty, agreed in 1979, sought to set limits on the numbers and testing of new types of intercontinental missiles, but it was not ratified by the US Senate. New STRATEGIC ARMS REDUCTION TALKS (START) began in 1982.

Strategic Arms Reduction Talks (START) Discussions on nuclear arms control between the USA and the Soviet Union (after 1991, between the USA and the four republics of the former Soviet Union that inherited nuclear weapons – Belarus, Ukraine, Russia, and Kazakhstan). START negotiations began in 1982, but were suspended by the Soviet Union at the end of 1983 in protest at US deployment of intermediate nuclear missiles in Western Europe. Resuming in 1985, the talks eventually led to the signing of the treaty known as START I in July 1991, which committed the USA and the Soviet Union to a 30% reduction in their nuclear weapons stockpiles. The four nuclear states that emerged from the break-up of the Soviet Union acceded to START I in November 1993. In the interim, Russia and the USA had signed START II in January 1993, which provided for the dismantling of two-thirds of each country's strategic nuclear warheads.

Strategic Defense Initiative (SDI, 'Star Wars') A research and development programme intended to provide a multi-layer anti-ballistic missile (ABM) space defence system for the USA. It was initiated by President Reagan in 1983 and was based on the use of new weapons, including high-powered laser weapons and particle beams fired from space platforms, to eliminate ballistic missiles, ideally early in flight before they released their warheads. However, the programme was regarded by many as, at best, excessively expensive and, at worst, totally impractical. Allegations that test results had been falsified to obtain continued funding shook public confidence in the project. The BUSH administration reduced the funding and in 1991 it was scaled down and renamed GPALS (Global Protection Against Limited Strikes). This is based on deployment of approximately 1,000 small interceptor missiles in space, an equal number of ground-based anti-missile missiles in the USA, and mobile ground missiles in several other parts of the world. A new type of gun, the rail gun, which uses electromagnetic forces to propel a projectile or shell at extremely high velocities, is being developed as a further layer of defence. Following the end of the COLD WAR, the Russian President Boris Yeltsin proposed a joint global defence system incorporating the Star Wars technology to shield the world from nuclear attack.

Strathclyde and Cumbria A Romano-British kingdom of north-west England and south-west Scotland: formed in the 2nd century AD, it survived until the 11th century, the last kingdom of the Britons to disappear. It survived invasions by Eadbert of Northumbria (750 and 756), plundering by the Danes (870), and the temporary loss of its independence (920) to

Edward the Elder of England. Duncan I acquired Strathclyde in 1018 and united it with three other regions to found the kingdom of Scotland (1034).

Streicher, Julius (1885–1946) German Nazi leader and propagandist. Originally a school-teacher, he expounded his anti-Semitic views in his periodical *Der Stürmer*. He was Party leader (*Gauleiter*) in Franconia (1933–40), and continued to function as a propagandist. He was sentenced to death at the NUREMBERG TRIALS and subsequently hanged.

Stresa Conference (April 1935) A conference between Britain, France, and Italy. Held at Stresa on Lake Maggiore in Italy, it proposed measures to counter HITLER's open rearmament of Germany in defiance of the VERSAILLES PEACE SETTLEMENT. Together these countries formed the 'Stresa Front' against German aggression, but their decisions were never implemented. In June Britain negotiated unilaterally a naval agreement with Germany. In November 1936 MUSSOLINI proclaimed his alliance with Hitler in the Rome-Berlin AXIS.

Stresemann, Gustav (1878–1929) German statesman. As Foreign Minister (1923–29) in the WEIMAR REPUBLIC he ended passive resistance to the French and Belgian occupation of the RUHR. He readily accepted both the DAWES and YOUNG PLANS on REPARATIONS. Personal friendships with BRIAND of France and Austen CHAMBERLAIN of Britain enabled him to play a leading part at LOCARNO (1925) and to negotiate the admission of Germany to the LEAGUE OF NATIONS (1926). In 1928 he signed the KELLOGG–BRIAND PACT. Even so, he was adamant about wanting revision of Germany's eastern frontier, and advocated that Danzig (Gdańsk), the POLISH CORRIDOR, and Upper Silesia should be returned by Poland.

strips Scattered units of unfenced land, the basis of agriculture in much of England between the 10th and 18th centuries. Tenants received a number of strips (also called selions, lands, loons, ridges, and shots) based on their social and economic status: an average holding was 12 ha (30 acres) or one virgate. Each strip was about 0.4 ha (1 acre) in size – usually one furlong (one ploughed furrow) or 210 m (220 yards) in length and 20.1 m (22 yards) in width. Each strip's shape and size was determined by the amount of land ploughed in a day and the nature of the terrain (on sandy soils the strips were wider than on clay soils). Repeated ploughing in one direction produced a 'corrugated' effect ('ridge and furrow') that often survives in pasture-land once under strip cultivation. By the 13th century much of England (except East Anglia and Kent and hill areas mainly in the north and west) had evolved the fully developed common field system, which was based on a three-course CROP ROTATION designed to prevent the soil from becoming exhausted. One field's rotation might be spring grain (in the first year), winter grain (second year), and untilled or fallow (third year). Scattered strips would benefit from this rotation and would also give each tenant a mixture of good and poor soils. ENCLOSURES of consolidated land and the farming improvements of the AGRICULTURAL REVOLUTION destroyed the strip system.

Stroessner, Alfredo (1912–   ) Paraguayan military leader and President (1954–89). The son of a German immigrant, he fought in the CHACO WAR (1932–35) against Bolivia. Having risen from the ranks to become commander-in-chief of the armed forces (1951–54), he

was responsible for the overthrow of President Frederico Chavez in 1954. Basically supportive of the large landowners and international commercial interests, as President he used foreign aid to develop schools, hospitals, highways, and hydro-electric power. His regime remained strongly backed by the army and was essentially totalitarian in that, while allowing for some political dissent, it was guilty of harsh and repressive methods. Stroessner now lives in exile in Brazil.

Stuart (or Stewart) The family name of the Scottish monarchs from 1371 to 1714 and of the English monarchs from 1603 to 1714. The founder of the Stuart house was Walter Fitzalan (d. 1177) who was steward (from which the name Stewart derives) to the King of Scotland. His descendant became the first Stewart king of Scotland as ROBERT II (ruled 1371–90). The marriage of Margaret Tudor, daughter of HENRY VII, to JAMES IV linked the royal houses of Scotland and England, and on the death of ELIZABETH I without heirs in 1603, James VI of Scotland succeeded to the English throne as JAMES I. The Stuarts lost the throne temporarily with the execution of CHARLES I in 1649, regaining it with the Restoration of CHARLES II in 1660. The GLORIOUS REVOLUTION (1688) sent JAMES II into exile and the crown passed to his daughter MARY and her husband William, then to his second daughter ANNE. Her death without heirs in 1714 resulted in the replacement of the Stuart house by the HANOVERIAN family headed by George I. Supporters of the exiled house of Stuart were known as JACOBITES. After the failure of the FIFTEEN and the FORTY-FIVE (1715 and 1745) rebellions, the Stuart cause faded: George III felt able to grant a pension to the last direct Stuart claimant, Henry, Cardinal York, who died in 1807.

Stuart, James Ewell Brown (1833–64) US general in the army of the CONFEDERACY. He resigned from the US Army to join the Confederacy at the outbreak of the AMERICAN CIVIL WAR. In command of a cavalry brigade after the first battle of Bull Run (July 1861), he led raids behind Union (Northern) lines that made him the South's pre-eminent cavalry leader. Stuart served in all the major campaigns of the Army of North Virginia until he was mortally wounded at Yellow Tavern on 11 May 1864.

student revolts Social or political protests by student groups. Students have played an important part in almost every major revolution of the 19th and 20th centuries. In the early 19th century, the German universities produced student movements (*Burschenschaften*) supporting German nationalism and opposing the rule of METTERNICH. In Tsarist Russia students who agitated for liberal reforms were imprisoned, exiled, or executed. In the period between the two World Wars the universities in Germany and Japan had movements supporting mainly right-wing causes and revolutions. After World War II universities in the developing countries often fostered strong nationalist and Marxist movements, while in the 1960s left-wing movements were predominant in many universities and colleges in Europe, the USA, and Japan. The protests at the University of California's Berkeley campus (1964) and the nationwide strike at approximately 200 US campuses (1970) challenged US policy in Vietnam. In Paris French students and workers joined in the movement (1968) to challenge the DE GAULLE regime, while in Japan students acted militantly against the westernization of Japanese society.

Demonstrations by South Korean university students (1987) led to constitutional amendments and the release of political prisoners. Pro-democracy student rallies and hunger strikes in Beijing in 1989 were brutally suppressed by government forces in the Tiananmen Square massacre which left an estimated 2,600 dead and led to the arrest and execution of hundreds more. A series of student demonstrations in Prague in 1989 gained widespread support that led to the downfall of the Czechoslovak communist regime.

sturdy beggars Those classed in the English POOR LAW of 1531 as able-bodied persons who chose not to work. This presumed, wrongly, that there was enough work for everyone who wanted it. Those who took to the roads, seeking jobs or charity, were severely punished. This was because Tudor governments regarded them as threats to public order, especially returned soldiers who organized themselves into bands and robbed travellers. By the end of the century new poor laws made parishes provide work for the genuinely unemployed, while 'incorrigible rogues' were to be whipped, returned to the parishes whence they had come, or even banished overseas for persistent offences.

Stuyvesant, Peter (1592–1672) Dutch colonial governor of the North American colony of New Netherland (1647–64). Though his authoritarian temperament led to friction with the colonists, he gained control of the rival colony of New Sweden in 1655. His own colony had been so infiltrated by English settlers, however, that he was unable to resist the Duke of York's expedition in 1664. New Netherland became the colony of New York.

Sucre, Antonio José de (1795–1830) South American revolutionary. As BOLÍVAR's chief-of-staff, he achieved a victory at the Battle of Ayacucho (9 December 1824) that effectively meant the end of Spanish power in Peru. In 1825, Sucre drove the last Spanish forces from Bolivia and was chosen as that nation's first elected President. He introduced legislation to implement fiscal and educational reforms but resigned the Presidency after an invasion (1828) by Peruvian troops. While working to preserve the union of Gran Colombia (Venezuela, Colombia, and Ecuador), he was assassinated.

Sudan, the A country in north-east Africa. Sudan takes its name from the great belt of open savannah crossing Africa south of the Sahara, from Ethiopia to Cape Verde.

Physical. Sudan has Egypt on its northern boundary, a coast on the Red Sea, and boundaries also with Ethiopia, Eritrea, Kenya, Uganda, the Democratic Republic of Congo (formerly Zaïre), the Central African Republic, Chad, and Libya. The largest country on the African continent, it has equatorial forest in the south and the Nubian Desert in the north; its whole length is traversed from south to north by the River Nile. The mid-south contains the Sudd swamps, which are mainly covered with reeds and papyrus grass. There is a region of savannah, and near the junction of the Blue and White Niles cotton is grown under irrigation on the plains of the Gezira. Further north are areas covered with acacia bushes, the source of gum arabic. In the extreme north years may pass without rain, and the only cultivation is on the river's banks.

Economy. The civil war, drought, and flooding have devastated the economy, which is also crippled by massive foreign debt ($135 billion in 1990), and have led to famine in the south among both Sudanese and the several million refugees from Ethiopia and Chad. The distribution of food aid has been seriously hampered by the war. Agriculture is the principal economic activity, with cotton, gum arabic, and sesame the main exports. Sugar cane, sorghum, and livestock are the other main products. The war has stopped exploitation of oil reserves; other resources include silver, chromite, lead, mica, asbestos, talc, tungsten, diamonds, uranium, copper, zinc, iron ore, and gold. Industry is limited to oil-refining and processing agricultural products such as sugar and cotton.

History. Nubian culture was established in northern Sudan about 30,000 years ago. Most of Nubia gradually came under the control of Egypt from about 4,000 BC. Nubia later formed part of the kingdom of Cush, which lasted from the 11th century BC to the 4th century AD. From about the 6th century AD missionaries established Christianity in the area. From the 13th century Arab nomads began immigrating into Sudan and eventually took control of the Christian areas.

By 1800 northern Sudan consisted of the Muslim empire of the Funji, where an Islamic revival was occurring. The Funji were then conquered by MEHEMET ALI from Egypt (1820–23). In 1874 Khedíve Ismail, viceroy of Egypt, offered the post of governor of the Egyptian Sudan to the Briton Charles GORDON. His anti-slave administration was not popular. In 1881 Muhammad Ahmad declared himself MAHDI and led an Islamic rebellion in the Sudan. Britain occupied Egypt in 1882 and invaded the Sudan where Gordon was killed (1885). The Mahdists resisted Anglo-Egyptian forces until Kitchener defeated them at Omdurman in 1898. Following the FASHODA INCIDENT, an Anglo-Egyptian condominium was created for the whole Sudan (1899) under a British governor. A constitution was granted in 1948 but in 1951 King Farouk of Egypt proclaimed himself King of Sudan. After his fall, Egypt agreed to Sudan's right to independence; self-government was granted in 1953 and full independence in 1956. North–South political and religious tension undermined stability until General NIMEIRI achieved power in 1969 and negotiated an end to the civil war in the south (1972). However, the early 1980s saw the collapse of the economy, widespread starvation, and a renewal of separatist guerrilla activity in the south. Nimeiri was overthrown by the army in April 1985, and a brief civilian coalition government was formed under Sadiq al-Mahdi. But civil war continued; the Sudan People's Liberation Army (SPLA) militarized much of the south, while the Muslim Brotherhood's National Islamic Front (NIF) strengthened its hold in the north. A military coup by General Omar Hassan Ahmad al-Bashir in 1989 was followed by a ban on all political parties. The early 1990 saw an influx of several million refugees from Ethiopia and Chad. The continuing civil war, drought, and flooding led to large-scale destitution and famine. The strongly Islamic Bashir regime has been accused of sponsoring fundamentalist terrorism, particularly in neighbouring Egypt. The first presidential and parliamentary elections since the coup were held in

March 1996, resulting in victory for Bashir and his supporters. In 1997 the SPLA made large gains in the south and east of the country.

CAPITAL:	Khartoum
AREA:	2,503,890 sq km (966,757 sq miles)
POPULATION:	31.065 million (1996)
CURRENCY:	1 Sudanese pound = 100 piastres = 1,000 millimes
RELIGIONS:	Sunni Muslim 73.0%; traditional beliefs 16.7%; Roman Catholic 5.6%; Anglican 2.3%
ETHNIC GROUPS:	Sudanese Arab 49.1%; Dinka 11.5%; Nuba 8.1%; Beja 6.4%; Nuer 4.9%; Azande 2.7%; Bari 2.5%; Fur 2.1%; Shilluk 1.7%; Lotuko 1.5%
LANGUAGES:	Arabic (official); Dinka; Nuba; other local languages
INTERNATIONAL ORGANIZATIONS:	UN; OAU; Arab League

Sudetenland The north-western frontier region of the CZECH REPUBLIC. The region had attracted German settlers for centuries, but their claim to self-determination (1918) was denied and the land awarded to CZECHOSLOVAKIA. The inhabitants had some cause for complaint against the Czech government, but this was whipped up by Konrad Henlein, the region's NAZI leader. His demands for incorporation with Germany gave leverage to Hitler in the negotiations leading to the MUNICH PACT (1938), and he annexed the region into the THIRD REICH, expelling Czech inhabitants. In 1945 Czechoslovakia regained the territory and by the POTSDAM Agreement was authorized to expel most of the German-speaking inhabitants. Bitterness on both sides continued into the late 1990s, when the Czech and German governments signed (1997) a new accord on the region and issued apologies for their past conduct.

Suetonius, Gaius Suetonius Tranquillus (c. 69–140 AD) Roman historian of the early emperors. A lawyer who became the emperor Hadrian's private secretary, he wrote a biography of each of the first twelve Caesars. Part grounded in fact, part drawn from informed anecdote and court gossip, his work has preserved much valuable information. His main flaw as a historian was his failure to judge the accuracy of his raw material. He was one of the earliest non-Christian writers to record the early following of JESUS CHRIST.

Suez Canal A ship CANAL joining the Mediterranean Sea (at Port Said) and the Red Sea (at the Gulf of Suez), built to provide a sea route from Europe to Asia that did not involve having to sail round Africa. The present canal is 171 km (106 miles) long and was built by Ferdinand de LESSEPS between 1859 and 1869. It has no locks, since the two sea-levels are virtually the same and the isthmus reaches a maximum height of only 11 m (36 feet) above sea-level. Twenty thousand labourers carried out the initial excavation until water could be flooded in, after which dredgers were used to deepen and widen the channel. The canal has been further enlarged to accommodate tankers of up to 250,000 tonnes. Opened in 1869, the Canal was purchased by Britain in 1875 and held as a British military base from 1882 to 1955. In 1956 Egypt nationalized the Suez Canal Company, precipitating the SUEZ WAR, which temporarily closed the Canal. The Canal was again closed from 1967 to 1975 after the SIX-DAY WAR and YOM KIPPUR WAR.

Suez War (1956) A military conflict involving British, French, Israeli, and Egyptian forces. It arose from the nationalization of the SUEZ CANAL Company by Egypt in 1956. When attempts to establish an international authority to operate the Canal failed, Britain and France entered into a secret military agreement with Israel. The latter, concerned at the increasing number of raids by *fedayeen* guerrillas, was ready to attack Egypt. On 29 October Israel launched a surprise attack into Sinai, and Britain and France issued an ultimatum demanding that both Israel and Egypt should withdraw from the Canal. This was rejected by President NASSER. British and French planes attacked Egyptian bases and troops were landed at Port Said. Owing to pressure from the USA, the collapse of the value of sterling, and mounting criticism from most other nations, the Anglo-French operations were halted and their forces evacuated. A UN peace-keeping force was sent to the area. The US Secretary of State, J. F. Dulles, formulated the short-lived EISENHOWER DOCTRINE (1957), offering US economic and military aid to Middle East governments whose independence was threatened. Israeli forces were withdrawn in March 1957 following an International agreement to install a UN Emergency Force in Sinai and to open the Straits of Tiran to Israeli shipping.

suffragettes Members of a British militant feminist movement that campaigned for the right of adult British women to vote in general elections (see WOMEN'S SUFFRAGE). The Women's Social and Political Union, which was founded by Emmeline PANKHURST in 1903, gained rapid support, using as its weapons attacks on property, demonstrations, and refusal to pay taxes. There was strong opposition to giving women the vote from the Liberal government of the day, partly from calculations of the electoral consequences of enfranchising women. Frustration over the defeat of Parliamentary bills to extend the vote led the suffragettes to adopt militant methods to press their cause; Parliamentary debates were interrupted, imprisoned suffragettes went on strike, and one suffragette, flinging herself in front of the king's horse in the 1913 Derby horse-race, was killed. These tactics were abandoned when Britain declared war on Germany in 1914 and the WSPU directed its efforts to support the war effort. In 1918, subject to educational and property qualifications, British women over 30 were given the vote (the age restriction was partly to avoid an excess of women in the electorate because of the deaths of men in the war). In 1928 women over 21 gained the vote.

Sufi ISLAM.

Suharto (1921–) Indonesian statesman and general. Having played a prominent role in the INDONESIAN REVOLUTION, he became chief-of-staff of the army in 1965. He crushed a communist coup attempt by the PKI in 1965 and in 1966 President SUKARNO, who had been implicated in the coup, was forced to give him wide powers. Having united student and military opponents of the Sukarno regime, he became acting President in 1967, assuming full powers the following year. He ended the KONFRONTASI with Malaysia and revitalized the Indonesian economy, as well as restoring the country to the Western capitalist fold. Increasingly dictatorial in the 1980s and 1990s, he has faced considerable domestic opposition, most notably from the ISLAMIC FUNDAMENTALIST movement. The sudden collapse of

Indonesia's economy in January 1998 prompted widespread civil disorder, which was met with repressive measures by the government.

Sui (581–618 AD) A dynasty that reunited China after over three centuries of territorial fragmentation. As emperor Yang Qien, the founder of the dynasty, undertook campaigns against TAIWAN, ANNAM, CHAMPA, and SRIVIJAYA. The GREAT WALL OF CHINA was rebuilt to follow a different alignment, and canals, some later to form part of the Grand Canal, were dug. However, defeats in Korea and never-ending demands for labour bred rebellion and second Sui emperor was obliged to flee; betrayed by one of his 3,000 concubines, he was strangled. When an ambitious official Li Yuan, founder of the TANG DYNASTY, seized Chang'an, the last emperor abdicated. Although the dynasty only ruled for a short period, its establishment of a strong central government greatly assisted the development of the Tang dynasty.

Sukarno, Achmad (1901–70) Indonesian statesman and founder of Indonesia's independence. A radical nationalist, he emerged as leader of the PNI (Indonesian Nationalist Party) in 1926 and spent much of the 1930s either in prison or exile. During the Japanese occupation, he consolidated his position as the leading nationalist figure and claimed the title of President of Indonesia in 1945. He then led his country through the INDONESIAN REVOLUTION (1945–49), remaining President after the legal transfer of power from the Netherlands in 1949. A leading spokesman for the non-aligned movement, he hosted the BANDUNG CONFERENCE in 1955, but found that his dictatorial tendencies aroused increasing resistance at home. Economic difficulties, and the KONFRONTASI with Malaysia, further undermined his position in the mid-1960s. Seeking increasing support from the communists, he was implicated in the abortive left-wing officer coup of 1965. Thereafter he effectively lost power to the army. Officially stripped of his power in 1967, he was succeeded as President by General SUHARTO.

Suleiman I (the Magnificent) (1495–1566) OTTOMAN sultan (1520–66). Although he was known to Europeans as 'the Magnificent' from the brilliance of his court, his subjects knew him as *Qanuni* (the Lawgiver) from the many regulations produced by his administration. In three campaigns against Safavid Persia he confirmed Ottoman control of eastern Asia Minor and annexed MESOPOTAMIA. He drove the Portuguese from the Red Sea, taking Aden in 1538, and harried them in the Gulf. He also created CORSAIR states in north Africa, frustrating Christian ambitions to rule there. Having taken Rhodes in 1522, he maintained a naval supremacy in the eastern Mediterranean marred only by a costly failure to take Malta in 1565. His most brilliant victory was at MOHÁCS in 1526, when he crushed the Hungarians and advanced on Vienna, though he could not take the city. Nevertheless he brought the middle Danube under Ottoman rule and made Transylvania a dependency. He died on campaign. Suleiman was a poet and a patron of the arts, and did much to beautify Constantinople.

Sulla, Lucius Cornelius (c. 138–78 BC) Roman soldier and statesman, who assumed the name 'Felix', or 'Fortunate'. Dictator of Rome in 82–79 BC, he served as quaestor (magistrate and paymaster) under MARIUS in

Africa and was instrumental in securing the betrayal of JUGURTHA. He had been accepted by the dominant aristocratic faction in the Senate by 88 BC when he was consul. Deprived of a command at Marius's instigation in 88 BC, he marched on Rome to regain it. After successful campaigning in the East he returned to take Rome a second time in 82 BC. Appointed dictator to reconstitute the state, he restored the Senate's power by imposing strict controls on the tribunes and other magistrates. Shortly before the end of an apparently dissolute life he retired abruptly.

Sully, Maximilien de Béthune, duc de (1560–1641) French statesman. Educated as a Huguenot, he narrowly escaped death during the ST BARTHOLOMEW'S DAY MASSACRE (1572). In 1576 he joined the army of Henry of Navarre; he distinguished himself as a soldier, and contributed significantly to Henry's successful bid for the throne. Under the new king, HENRY IV, he helped to pacify the realm, reorganized the national finances by stringent economies and the reform of abuses, and encouraged agriculture. He was created duc de Sully in 1606, but was forced out of office soon after Henry IV's assassination in 1610.

sultanate A territory subject to sovereign independent Muslim rule. The word 'sultan' is used in the KORAN and the traditions of the Prophet MUHAMMAD to mean 'authority'. MAHMUD OF GHAZNA was the first Muslim ruler to be addressed as sultan by his contemporaries. The term thereafter became a general title for the effective holders of power, such as the SELJUK or MAMELUKE dynasties, though it was also used as a mark of respect under the OTTOMANS for princes and princesses of the imperial house. The term 'sultanate' was also used of a number of virtually independent centres of Muslim power, such as the sultanate of DELHI (1206–1526), the predecessor of the MOGUL empire in India, and the Sulu sultanate, a trading empire in the southern Philippines, which flourished between the 16th and 19th centuries.

Sumatra A very large island in the east of the Indian Ocean, a part of INDONESIA but separated from the Malay Peninsula by the Strait of Malacca and from Java by the Sunda Strait.

Physical. A western coastal plain 1,770 km (1,100 miles) long rises sharply to volcanic mountain ranges that contain, in the north, a great salt lake. From their eastern slopes multitudinous rivers run through otherwise impenetrable jungle to vast areas of swampland, the soil being extremely fertile. Rubber, rice, sugar cane, camphor bushes, tea, and coffee all grow well. There are oilfields, coalfields, deposits of gold and silver and, on smaller islands off the coast, of bauxite and tin.

History. Indian traders introduced Hinduism and Buddhism to the island. In the first centuries AD small states emerged. When SRIVIJAYA's long dominance ended (c. 1300), MAJAPAHIT and BANTAM held sway over southern Sumatra. By 1300 Islam had a footing in the north, thence spreading over Sumatra, through Malaya, and the Indies. In 1613 the sultanate of ACHEH allowed the English to establish a trading station. The Dutch later secured a base at Padang on the west coast and began to incorporate Sumatra into the DUTCH EAST INDIES. There is an armed secessionist movement, the Free Acheh Movement, based in northern Sumatra.

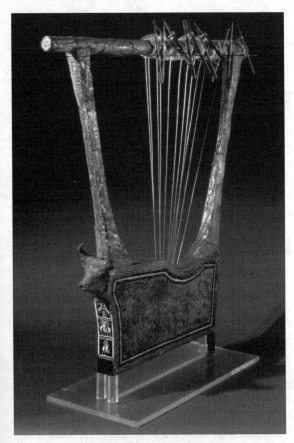

Sumerians   *The Sumerians had a rich and diverse culture and they had a major effect on the cultural development of neighbouring areas. This lyre dates from about 2600 BC and was found at the city of Ur. It has 11 strings that could be tuned by turning the pegs attached to the cross post.*

Sumerians A people living in southern Mesopotamia in the 4th and 3rd millennia BC. By 3000 BC a number of city states had developed in Sumer, such as URUK, Eridu, and UR. The Sumerians are credited with inventing the CUNEIFORM system of writing, which was originally pictographic but gradually became stylized. Many simple inscriptions survive as evidence of this; they also directly attest the increase in administration that accompanied urban growth. Their literature contains references to myths, ritual hymns, and incantations. They developed a legal system, supported by complex political and economic organization. Their technological achievements included wheeled vehicles and potters' wheels, as well as such architectural features as columns, vaults, and domes.

The first great empire of Sumer was established by the people of AKKAD, who conquered the area in about 2350 under the leadership of Sargon. The dynasty founded by him was destroyed in about 2200, and after 2150 the kings of Ur not only re-established Sumerian sovereignty in Sumer but also conquered Akkad. This new empire lasted until roughly 2000 when pressure from the Elamites and Amorites reached its culmination

with the capture and devastation of Ur. The Sumerians at this point disappear from history, but the influence of their culture on the subsequent civilizations of Mesopotamia was far-reaching.

summoner (or apparitor) In medieval England and Scotland a minor official (not a cleric) who summoned people before the ecclesiastical courts. Summoners acquired inquisitorial powers in cases that could incur excommunication, such as non-payment of tithes, heresy (including incidents of Lollardy), usury, slander, and witchcraft. Over 10,000 excommunication writs survive from the 13th century. Summoners were condemned for extortion in the Council of London (1342), by Parliament (1378), and by writers including Chaucer in *The Canterbury Tales.*

Sumner, Charles (1811–74) US statesman. Elected to the Senate in 1851, he served in it for the rest of his life, his powers of oratory making him one of the leading political reformers of his day. He joined the new REPUBLICAN PARTY and emerged as a leading member of the anti-slavery campaign. In 1856 he was assaulted in the Senate Chamber and brutally caned by Congressman P. S. Brooks, whose father, a South Carolina Senator, he had attacked in an anti-slavery speech. He did not resume his seat in the Senate for three years. After 1861 he served as chairman of the Foreign Relations Committee, and pressed hard for emancipation of the slaves. In the years after the AMERICAN CIVIL WAR, he supported the radical RECONSTRUCTION ACTS but constantly attacked the administration of President GRANT for corruption and inefficiency.

Sunday school A school for general and religious instruction of children on Sundays. Probably the first to be so called was established in Gloucester in 1780 by a journalist, Robert Raikes, to teach poor children (who were often at work for the rest of the week) reading and writing and knowledge of the scriptures. Raikes's ideas quickly spread, being greatly assisted by the founding of the London Sunday School Union in 1803. By the early 1800s several hundred thousand children were enrolled in Sunday schools, which were to play an important part in elementary education before William FORSTER's Education Act of 1870. In the USA the Sunday school movement developed rapidly in the 1790s, and the American Sunday School Union, formed in 1817, set out to establish schools all over the country.

Sunderland, Robert Spencer, 2nd Earl of (1641–1702) English statesman. Renowned for his intrigues and double-dealing, he became Secretary of State in 1679 but was dismissed for disloyalty. He won the favour of JAMES II by adopting Roman Catholicism, but meanwhile he was in secret correspondence with WILLIAM III (of Orange), for whom he reverted to Protestantism. Following the GLORIOUS REVOLUTION, William employed him until 1697 and learned from him to govern with a small inner circle of ministers. Nevertheless, Sunderland was despised by both Whigs and Tories, and he resigned to exert his political influence less openly.

Sundjata Keita Founder and ruler of the MALI empire (c. 1235–55) in west Africa. He was sickly as a child, but became a vigorous warrior. In about 1235 he was called on to fight Soumangourou, King of Sosso, and defeated him at Krina. After further victories, he conquered

GHANA and Walata, and then all the neighbouring gold-bearing regions. After *c.* 1240 he devoted himself to administration. He died accidentally, either from an arrow shot at random during a festival or by drowning in the Sankarani River.

Sunni (from Arabic, *sunna*, 'tradition') The belief and practice of mainstream, as opposed to Shia, ISLAM (see SHIITES). Sunni Muslims, constituting over 80% of all believers, follow the *sunna*, a code of practice based on the *hadith* collected in the *Sihah Satta*, six authentic Books of Tradition about the prophet MUHAMMAD. The *Sunna*, variously translated as 'custom', 'code', or 'usage', means whatever Muhammad, by positive example or implicit approval, demonstrated as the ideal behaviour for a Muslim to follow. It therefore complements the KORAN as a source of legal and ethical guidance.

Sunnis recognize the order of succession of the first four CALIPHS, whereas Shias believe authority begins with Ali, the fourth caliph. Sunnis follow one of four schools of law: the Hanafi, prevalent in the Middle East and Pakistan; the Malikite, found in western and northern Africa; the Shafite, found in Egypt, East Africa, Malaysia, and Indonesia; and the Hanbalite in Saudi Arabia.

Sun Yat-sen (or Sun Yixian) (1866–1925) Chinese revolutionary. In 1895 he organized an unsuccessful rising against the QING dynasty and fled the country. Briefly imprisoned (1896) in the Chinese legation in London, his release was negotiated by the British government. In 1905, in Tokyo, he formed a revolutionary society, the Tongmenghui (United League), which became the nucleus of the KUOMINTANG. When the CHINESE REVOLUTION OF 1911 broke out, Sun returned to China and was declared Provisional President (1912) of the republic. He shortly afterwards resigned in favour of YUAN SHIKAI. When Yuan suppressed the Kuomintang (1913), Sun, with WARLORD support, set up a secessionist government in Guangzhou (Canton). In 1923 he agreed to accept Russian help in re-organizing the Kuomintang, thus inaugurating a period of uneasy co-operation with the CHINESE COMMUNIST PARTY. He died in Beijing, trying to negotiate a unified Chinese government. Sun's Three Principles of the People (nationalism, democracy, and 'people's livelihood') form the basic ideology of TAIWAN and he is regarded as the founder of modern China by both nationalists and communists.

Superbus, Lucius Tarquinius TARQUIN.

Supremacy, Acts of (1534 and 1559) Enactments of the English Parliament, confirming respectively the supremacy of HENRY VIII and ELIZABETH I over the ANGLICAN CHURCH. Henry was styled 'Supreme Head' of the Church but Elizabeth, in an attempt to reduce opposition, took the title 'Supreme Governor'. Under the terms of both Acts the 'Oath of Supremacy' was demanded of suspected malcontents to ensure their loyalty.

Supreme Court (Federal) The highest body in the US judicial system. Established by Article III of the CONSTITUTION OF THE USA as a third branch of government, independent of the legislative and executive branches, the Supreme Court has become the main interpreter of the Constitution. Members are appointed by the President, with the advice and consent of the Senate. Between 1789 and 1869, the number of Supreme Court justices varied between five and ten, but since 1869 it

has remained at nine. Early in its history, the Supreme Court established its right to judge whether laws passed by Congress or by the state legislatures conform to the provisions of the Constitution, but it can do so only when specific cases arising under the laws are referred to it. The decisions of the Court have played a central role in the development of the US political system, not only as regards the fluctuating balance of power between the executive and legislative branches, and between the states and the federal government, but also concerning the evolution of social, economic, and legal policies.

Surinam A country on the north-east coast of South America, known until 1948 as Dutch Guiana.

Physical. Surinam is sandwiched between Guyana and French Guiana, with Brazil to the south. The climate is equatorial: hot and very wet. Thick forest covers most of the interior, which rises to highlands in the centre. Rice and sugar cane can be grown on the coast.

Economy. Dutch and US aid, on which the economy depends, was suspended in 1980, following a military coup, but was restored in 1988 after democratic elections. Surinam's exports are dominated by bauxite and its aluminium products but production was disrupted by civil war in the 1980s and early 1990s. Bauxite-smelting and food-processing are the main industries. There are considerable mineral reserves, especially iron ore and gold. Agriculture is restricted to the alluvial coastal area, rice being the main crop.

History. Surinam's name is taken from that of its earliest inhabitants, the Surinen, who had been driven out of the area by other South American Indians by the time Europeans arrived. Surinam was claimed by Spain in 1593 but was colonized by the Dutch from the beginning of the 17th century. The territory alternated between British and Dutch control until the Netherlands received it in a treaty settlement of 1815. In the 17th century African slaves had begun to be imported. By the late 19th century plantation labour was recruited from India and Java. The ethnic diversity of Surinam resulted in increasing racial and political strife after World War II. In 1954 Surinam became an equal partner in the Kingdom of the Netherlands, and full independence was granted in 1975. After several years of party strife the military took over in 1980. In 1986 an extended guerrilla campaign by the Surinamese Liberation Army (SLA) was launched, organized from the jungle in neighbouring French Guyana. Although civilian rule was restored following elections in 1988, the military retained great influence. In 1990 a new military coup was staged, but in 1991 a coalition of opposition parties, the New Front for Democracy and Development, led by Ronald Venetiaan, won elections. A peace agreement with the SLA was made in 1992. Drug trafficking, gun-running, and money laundering all remained problems. In 1996 Venetiaan was succeeded as President by Jules Wijdenbosch.

CAPITAL:	Paramaribo
AREA:	163,820 sq km (63,251 sq miles)
POPULATION:	436,000 (1996)
CURRENCY:	1 Suriname guilder = 100 cents
RELIGIONS:	Hindu 27.0%; Roman Catholic 23.0%; Muslim 20.0%; Protestant (mostly Moravian) 19.0%

ETHNIC GROUPS: East Indian 35.0%; Creole 32.0%;
                  Indonesian 15.0%; African (bush negro)
                  10.0%; Amerindian 3.0%; Chinese 3.0%;
                  European 1.0%
LANGUAGES: Dutch (official); English; Sronan Tongo;
                  Spanish; Hindi; Javanese; Chinese; local
                  Amerindian and pidgin languages
INTERNATIONAL
  ORGANIZATIONS: UN; OAS

Sutton Hoo An important Anglo-Saxon archaeological
site in Suffolk, England, overlooking the estuary of the
River Deben. In 1939 a magnificent ship burial was
uncovered here. It may have been the grave of Raedwald
(d. *c.* 624), King of East Anglia. No body was found, but it
is believed that this may have been destroyed by the
acidity of the soil. The tomb comprises a boat, 24.3 m (80
feet) long and 4.2 m (14 feet) across at its widest beam,
which was propelled by 38 oarsmen. Byzantine spoons
and bowls, Swedish weaponry, Egyptian bowls, East-
Anglian jewellery, and a hoard of 40 gold coins from
Merovingian Gaul make it the greatest single
archaeological find in Western Europe.

**Suvarov, Alexander Vasilevich, Count
Rimniksky, Prince Italysky** (1729–1800) Russian field
marshal. His brilliant campaigns against the Poles (1769)
and the Turks (1773–74) laid the foundations of his
reputation. Further successes against the Turks 14 years
later led CATHERINE II to appoint him a count in 1788. In
1790 he was placed at the head of the army that
subdued the Poles. He was dismissed by the new
emperor PAUL I in 1796, but was recalled to face the
French in Italy three years later. After some early
successes he was forced to retreat and returned to St
Petersburg in disgrace and, worn out and ill, died on 18
May 1800.

Swabia A region of south-west Germany. Taking its
name from the Suevi, a Germanic tribe resident in the
area in Roman times, Swabia emerged as a duchy in the
10th century and was ruled by the HOHENSTAUFEN dynasty
from 1079 to 1268, before being divided among other
rulers. In 1488 the Swabian League was formed by a
group of cities and magnates to counteract the growing
strength of the Swiss Confederation and the Bavarian
Wittelsbach dynasty. It functioned briefly as the
mainstay of imperial power in south-west Germany,
drawing most of the small states of the area into its
ranks, but became divided by religious issues and broke
up in the 1530s.

Swanscombe Man One of the earliest known human
inhabitants of Britain, named after a village in Kent,
England, where three skull bones were discovered in
river gravels in 1935, 1936, and 1955. They belong to an
adult individual, probably a young woman. Around
250,000 years ago, she and her kind camped by the river,
while they hunted deer and other animals. The skull
seems closely related to a similar skull from Steinheim
in Germany; both probably represent a transitional
stage between HOMO ERECTUS and HOMO SAPIENS, while also
appearing to have certain NEANDERTHAL features. A
possible interpretation is that they belong to a
European sidebranch of human evolution.

SWAPO (South West Africa People's Organization) A
nationalist movement in Southern Africa. Nationalist
feeling in South West Africa (now NAMIBIA) began to
grow in the early 1960s as the South African
government attempted to extend its mandate in the
region, which was due to expire in 1966. SWAPO was
formed in 1964–66 out of a combination of existing
nationalist groups. Driven from the country by South
African forces, SWAPO, under the presidency of Sam
Nujoma, began a guerrilla campaign from neighbouring
Angola. Efforts by the United Nations failed to find an
agreeable formula for Namibian independence and the
guerrilla war continued until 1988. SWAPO won
Namibia's first general election in November 1989. In
subsequent elections in 1994, SWAPO secured a two-
thirds majority in the National Assembly.

swastika (from the Sanskrit, *svastika*, 'conducive to
well-being') An emblem in the form of an even-length
cross, with the arms bent at right angles, clockwise or
anti-clockwise. A symbol of prosperity and good
fortune, it was used in ancient Mesopotamia, in early
Christian and Byzantine art, in South and Central
America, and among the Hindus and Buddhists of India.
In 1910 the German poet Guido von List proposed the
swastika (German, *Hakenkreuz* 'hooked cross') as a symbol
for all ANTI-SEMITIC organizations in the mistaken belief
that it was Teutonic in origin. The NAZI Party adopted it
in 1919 and incorporated it (1935) into the national flag
of the THIRD REICH.

Swaziland A small country of southern Africa.
Physical. Swaziland is landlocked by South Africa on
three sides and by Mozambique on the east. In the west
are well-watered hills rich in iron ore and from them
run several rivers to the dry veld in the middle of the
country.
Economy. The economy is heavily dependent on South
Africa; many Swazis find work in South African mines,
and much of Swaziland's electricity is imported from
South Africa. The land is fertile, and sugar, citrus fruit,
pineapples, and cotton are grown for export. Maize and
livestock are important locally, and the forestry
industry produces wood-pulp for export. Tourism is
increasing. Industry concentrates on processing
agricultural products. Coal, diamonds, gold, and asbestos
are mined and exported, but the falling world market
for asbestos has led to unemployment.
History. Swaziland takes its name from the Swazis,
who probably moved into the area during the 16th
century. The name is thought to have been given to the
people in 1836 when Mswati (Mswazi) II became king. A
South African protectorate from 1894, Swaziland came
under British rule in 1902 after the Second BOER WAR,
retaining its monarchy. In 1968 it became a fully
independent kingdom under Sobhuza II (1921–82).
Revisions of the constitution in 1973 in response to
requests from its Parliament, and again in 1978, gave the
monarchy wide powers. All political parties were
banned under the 1978 constitution. As a result, King
Mswati III, who succeeded in 1986, faced increasing
demands (1991–92) for the introduction of democracy.
Parliamentary elections were held on a non-party basis
in 1993, but were widely held to be undemocratic. In
1996 the newly appointed Prime Minister Sibusiso
Barnabas Dlamini announced the creation of a
Constitutional Review Committee that would consider
plans for democratizing the country.
CAPITAL: Mbabane (administrative); Lobamba
                  (royal and executive)

AREA:	17,364 sq km (6,704 sq miles)
POPULATION:	934,000 (1996)
CURRENCY:	1 lilangeni = 100 cents
RELIGIONS:	Protestant 37.3%; African indigenous churches 28.9%; traditional beliefs 20.9%; Roman Catholic 10.8%
ETHNIC GROUPS:	Swazi 84.3%; Zulu 9.9%; Tsonga 2.5%; Indian 0.8%; Pakistani 0.8%; Portuguese 0.2%
LANGUAGES:	English, Swazi (both official); Zulu; local languages
INTERNATIONAL ORGANIZATIONS:	UN; OAU; Commonwealth; SADC

Sweden A country in northern Europe occupying the southern and eastern part of the Scandinavian peninsula.

Physical. Sweden has a long, mountainous boundary with Norway on the north-west and a shorter one with Finland on the north-east. It has island-fringed coasts on the Baltic Sea and the Kattegat, the channel to the North Sea. Sweden's islands include Gotland and Åland in the Baltic. The northern part of the country is within the Arctic Circle. There are glaciers in the northern mountains, which everywhere are heavily forested with conifers. Rivers fall eastwards to the Gulf of Bothnia in rapids and falls, many of which serve hydroelectric power stations, and form at intervals long lakes. High-grade iron ore is found in the mountains, together with many other minerals. A region of hummocky hills and huge lakes lies to the south of the mountain range, and then the land rises again to a rocky, forested plateau. The southern coastal plain is extremely fertile; and the largest island, Gotland, has splendid beaches.

Economy. Sweden has an industrial economy based on the exploitation of abundant natural and mineral resources. Major exports include machinery, motor vehicles, paper, iron, and steel. A leading producer of iron ore, the country also has deposits of copper, lead, and zinc. Commercial forestry is important, though threatened by acid rain, as are the wood-pulp, sawmill, and paper industries. Electricity is generated almost entirely from nuclear and hydroelectric sources, but it is planned that the nuclear programme be discontinued by 2010. Agriculture has declined in importance, although livestock and dairy-farming are still substantial.

History. The country's earliest history is shrouded in legend, but Suiones tribesmen are mentioned by TACITUS and were probably the founders of the first unified Swedish state. Swedish VIKINGS were active in the Baltic area, and also ventured into Russia and the Arab caliphate of Baghdad. Christianity was introduced in the 9th century but the whole population was not converted until much later. In the 13th century parts of Finland and Karelia were occupied, but from 1397 Sweden belonged to the Danish-dominated Union of KALMAR. In 1523 GUSTAVUS I (Vasa) led a successful revolt that ended in independence for Sweden, a national crown for himself and his dynasty, and the introduction of LUTHERANISM as the state religion. During the 16th and 17th centuries Sweden expanded territorially and achieved considerable political status, thanks largely to the efforts of GUSTAVUS II (Adolphus) and Axel OXENSTIERNA. The high point was reached after the Treaty of WESTPHALIA, during the reign of Charles X (1654–60), but the strains of maintaining a scattered empire began

to tell during the reign of CHARLES XII (1682–1718). After the NORTHERN WAR (1700–21) the empire was dismembered, and a form of parliamentary government then prevailed until the coup (1771) of Gustavus III, who remained in power until 1792.

During the NAPOLEONIC WARS Sweden joined the Third Coalition against France (1805), but after France defeated Russia the latter took Finland from Sweden as compensation (1809). In that year the pro-French party in the Swedish estates overthrew the existing monarch, Gustav IV, and elected the aged and childless Charles XIII (1809–18). In 1810 they invited Jean-Baptiste Bernadotte to become crown prince. He subsequently ruled as CHARLES XIV (1818–44), and his descendants have remained monarchs of Sweden ever since. From 1814 to 1905 Norway was united with Sweden. Pursuing a policy of non-alignment, Sweden kept out of both World Wars, and by the 1950s had developed into one of the world's wealthiest and most socially progressive states with an extensive social welfare system. A long Social Democrat hegemony was challenged during the 1970s, but regained by Olof Palme (1982–86), until his assassination. Sweden has played a central role in UN peace-keeping missions. It hosted the conference (1959) that resulted in the creation of the EUROPEAN FREE TRADE ASSOCIATION, but in 1991 applied to join the EUROPEAN COMMUNITY, becoming a member of the European Union in 1995. The Moderate Unity Party under Carl Bildt came to power in 1991, committed to reductions in public expenditure on welfare provision, particularly health and education. The Social Democrat leader Ingvar Carlsson, who had succeeded Palme as Prime Minister in 1986, regained power in 1994 but handed his office to Goran Persson in 1996.

CAPITAL:	Stockholm
AREA:	449,964 sq km (173,732 sq miles)
POPULATION:	8.858 million (1996)
CURRENCY:	1 Swedish krona = 100 ore
RELIGIONS:	Church of Sweden (Evangelican Lutheran) 90.0%
ETHNIC GROUPS:	Swedish 90.0%; Finnish 3.1%; Lapp minority
LANGUAGES:	Swedish (official); minority languages
INTERNATIONAL ORGANIZATIONS:	UN; EU; Council of Europe; CSCE

Sweyn Forkbeard (d. 1014) King of Denmark (*c.* 986–1014). He revolted against his father Harald Bluetooth to establish himself as ruler of Denmark. Thereafter he spent much of his time on VIKING raids, attacking England several times, once in alliance with OLAF I (Tryggvason); he was paid well by its king ETHELRED II (the Unready) to desist. In alliance with Sweden and Norwegian rebels at the Battle of Svolde in 1000 he defeated his former ally, King Olaf, who was drowned. In 1013 he invaded England and captured London, but died suddenly before the conquest could be consolidated. He was the father of CANUTE.

Switzerland A country in central Europe, consisting of a Federation of 23 cantons; three cantons are subdivided making a total of 26 administrative units.

Physical. Switzerland is surrounded by France, Germany, Italy, and the tiny country of Liechtenstein. It is Europe's loftiest country with the Alps stretching across the whole of its southern half. The rivers Rhône and Rhine rise here and form broad valleys. Below the forested mountain slopes, snow-covered all winter, the land is fertile and the summer temperature is warm. Northward the country stands on a hilly plateau that contains the Swiss Lakes and rises again in the north-west to the Jura Mountains, a region important for dairying and forestry, and with vineyards on the southern slopes.

Economy. Switzerland is a prosperous country with the highest GDP per capita in the world. Major exports include machinery, electrical goods, instruments, watches, textiles, and pharmaceuticals. Tourism and international finance and banking are important. Agriculture is mainly livestock- and dairy-farming.

History. Switzerland was occupied by the Celtic HELVETII in the 2nd century BC. Its position astride vital Alpine passes caused the area to be invaded by the Romans, Alemanni, Burgundians, and Franks before it came under the control of the Holy Roman Empire in the 11th century. In 1291 the cantons (Swiss confederacies) of Uri, Schwyz, and Unterwalden declared their independence of their Habsburg overlords, and the alliance for mutual defence was later joined by Lucerne, Zürich, and Bern. During the 15th century this Swiss Confederation continued to expand, and it fought successfully against Burgundy, France, and the Holy Roman Empire, creating a great demand for its soldiers as mercenaries. During the REFORMATION and COUNTER-REFORMATION, its political stability was undermined by civil warfare, but in 1648 the Habsburgs acknowledged its independence in the Treaty of WESTPHALIA.

In 1798 French Revolutionary armies entered the country and established the Helvetic Republic. But at the Congress of VIENNA (1815) Swiss control was restored and the European powers guaranteed the confederation's neutrality. In 1847 a separate Roman Catholic league within the federation, the SONDERBUND, was formed after radicals took power in one of the cantons. After a brief civil war, peace and stability were restored by the new, democratic, federal constitution of 1848. During World War I the country maintained its neutrality despite the contradictory affections of the French and German sections of its population. The Swiss again preserved their armed neutrality during World War II and have since continued to enjoy a high level of economic prosperity. In 1979 the 22 cantons of the confederation were joined by the new Canton of Jura. Women were not allowed to vote on a federal basis until 1971, and suffrage remains restricted in some cantons. Because of its long tradition of neutrality, the International Red Cross and the League of Nations were both based in Switzerland, as are many UN agencies today. In 1992 the Swiss rejected by referendum membership of the European Economic Area, thus freezing the country's application to the EUROPEAN COMMUNITY (now the European Union), which is still being considered. In 1997, following repeated calls for greater openness from the international community, Swiss banks admitted holding the property of Jews murdered in the Holocaust and finally agreed to release these funds as reparations to the families of the victims.

CAPITAL: Berne
AREA: 41,293 sq km (15,943 sq miles)
POPULATION: 7.087 million (1996)
CURRENCY: 1 Swiss franc = 100 centimes
RELIGIONS: Roman Catholic 48.0%; Protestant 44.0%; Jewish 0.3%

ETHNIC GROUPS: German 65.0%; French 18.4%; Italian 9.8%; Spanish 1.6%; Romansch 0.8%; Turkish 0.6%
LANGUAGES: French, German, Italian (all official); minority languages
INTERNATIONAL ORGANIZATIONS: OECD; EFTA; Council of Europe; CSCE

Sykes–Picot Agreement (1916) A secret Anglo-French agreement on the partition of the Ottoman empire after World War I. It was negotiated by Sir Mark Sykes (1879–1919) and François Georges-Picot and provided for French control of coastal Syria, Lebanon, Cilicia, and Mosul, and for British control of Baghdad and Basra and northern Palestine. Palestine was to be under international administration and independent Arab states were to be created in the remaining Arab territories. The agreement reflected the British and French desire to compensate themselves for Russian gains under the secret Constantinople Agreement of 1915 between Russia, Britain, and France (in which the Dardanelles and the Bosporus were to be incorporated into the Tsarist empire in return for British and French spheres of influence in the Middle East). Considerable embarrassment was caused to the Allies when the Bolsheviks revealed the terms of the Agreement in late 1917: its provisions appeared to clash with promises made to the Arabs in the McMahon letters of 1915–16 and to the Zionists in the BALFOUR DECLARATION, as well as the FOURTEEN POINTS of President Wilson.

syndicalism A militant movement among industrial workers, aiming to replace CAPITALISM and the capitalist state with a form of SOCIALISM in which groups of workers would collectively own the means of production. Syndicalists were influenced by the French theorists PROUDHON and Georges Sorel, whose seminal *Refléxions sur la violence* was published in 1908. For radical workers, syndicalism served as an alternative to parliamentary socialist parties. The Syndicalists differed mainly from socialists in that they believed essentially in ANARCHISM, having an abhorrence of the state. Advocating direct action, such as a general strike, to bring about a revolution, syndicalists were active in the late 19th and early 20th centuries, mainly in France, Italy, Spain, Russia, and in the USA. The growing complexity of industrial organization and the attraction of COMMUNISM reduced their influence after 1918.

Syria A country in the Middle East at the eastern end of the Mediterranean Sea.

Physical. Bounded on the north by Turkey, on the east by Iraq, on the south by Jordan, and on the south-west by Israel and Lebanon, Syria has a narrow coastal plain with a Mediterranean climate: citrus fruit and tobacco can be grown. Behind a range of hills the Asi (Orontes) River runs northward, along a rift valley; beyond that the ground rises to a plateau of steppe, where cotton can be grown. This merges into hot, dry desert, relieved only by the upper Euphrates, which runs across the country. In the extreme north-east there is oil.

Economy. Although still largely agricultural, with sheep- and goat-raising the primary agricultural activities, Syria is becoming more industrialized and has benefited in recent years from rising oil exports. Other exports are textiles, clothing, and chemicals. Mineral resources include petroleum, phosphates, salt, and gypsum, and manufacturing industry includes textiles, cement, and chemicals.

History. Syria was settled successively by the Akkadians, Arameans, and Canaanites, and formed a valuable province of successive empires, from the Phoenicians to the Byzantines. After the Arab conquest of the 630s, Damascus became the brilliant capital of the Arab caliphate under the UMAYYADS from 661 to 750. Subsequently, however, Syria became a province ruled by foreign dynasties, such as the FATIMIDS and the MAMELUKES of Egypt. It became a province of the OTTOMAN EMPIRE in 1516, and after the Turkish defeat in World War I Syria was mandated to France. Controlled by VICHY France during the earlier part of World War II, the country was invaded and occupied by British and FREE FRENCH forces, and declared its independence in 1941. Although this was recognized in 1946, political stability proved elusive, with three army-led coups in 1949 and others in 1951 and 1954. An abortive union with Egypt in the UNITED ARAB REPUBLIC provided no solution and was terminated by a further army coup. A leading political grouping, the BA'ATH Socialist Party led one successful and two abortive coups in 1963 but remained split by personal and ideological rivalries. Further coups in 1966 and 1970 saw the eventual emergence of the Ba'athist General Hafiz al-ASSAD as the leader of a new regime, capable of crushing all internal opposition. Despite aspiring to a role of regional dominance, Syria suffered major reverses in the 1967 SIX-DAY WAR and the YOM KIPPUR WAR of 1973 against Israel. It was deeply involved in the civil war in LEBANON (1975–89), and remained generally antagonistic towards Iraq, sending troops to defend Saudi Arabia in the 1991 GULF WAR. In December 1991 a reconciliation took place with the PLO, when Yasser ARAFAT visited Damascus. Relations with other Arab League states improved and Syria took a cautious part in the Middle East peace negotiations of 1992. Unlike its former allies in the Six-Day War (Egypt and Jordan) Syria has not undertaken any major rapprochement towards Israel. However, following the peace agreements between Israel and the PLO and Israel and Jordan (1993; 1994), President Assad has come under increasing pressure to reach an accommodation.

CAPITAL:	Damascus
AREA:	185,180 sq km (71,498 sq miles)
POPULATION:	14.798 million (1996)
CURRENCY:	1 Syrian pound = 100 piastres
RELIGIONS:	Sunni Muslim 72.0%; Alawi (Shia) 11.0%; Druze 3.0%; Christian 9.0%
ETHNIC GROUPS:	Arab 89.0%; Kurdish 6.0%; Armenian and other 4.0%
LANGUAGES:	Arabic (official); minority languages
INTERNATIONAL ORGANIZATIONS:	UN; Arab League; OAPEC

Tabinshweti TOUNGOO.

Tacitus, Publius Cornelius (*c.* 55–*c.* 120 AD) Roman historian and consul. Tacitus followed a political career and served as governor of Asia in 112. He compiled the earliest known account of the German tribes and a biography of his father-in-law, AGRICOLA, governor of Britain. His major works were the *Histories* (dealing with the period from Galba to Domitian, 69–96 AD) and the *Annals*, dealing with the difficult period in Latin history from the death of the emperor Augustus in 14 AD through to the reign of Nero. He is one of the earliest non-Christian writers to record the crucifixion of JESUS CHRIST, which he mentions in connection with the persecution of Christians in 64 AD.

As a historian he has always been admired for his scrupulous accuracy and his epigrammatic style. He saw it as the historian's function to record virtue and to ensure that vice was denounced by posterity, and to this end he created a style as memorable as the events he records: condensed, rapid, and incisive. GIBBON admired Tacitus more than any other ancient historian, and his own biting, concise style comes closest in English to the Latin of his exemplar.

Tacna–Arica Conflict (1883–1929) A territorial dispute between Peru and Chile. The provinces of Tacna and Arica belonged to Peru at the time of its independence from Spain, but after the War of the PACIFIC (1879–84), Chile appropriated Arica and Tacna. In 1929 negotiations between Peru and Chile produced a settlement that returned Tacna to Peru with an indemnity of $6 million and left Arica under Chilean control.

Taff Vale case (1901) A British court action that established the principle that trade unions could be sued for damages. Following a strike by railwaymen employed by the Taff Vale Railway Company, the company sued the Amalgamated Society of Railway Servants for loss of revenue. The House of Lords, on appeal, awarded the company damages and costs. The resentment felt by workers at this contravention of the Trade Union Act of 1871, which had, they thought, established the immunity of union funds, was an important factor in the increased support given to the LABOUR PARTY. The Trade Disputes Act, passed in 1906, effectively reversed the decision by exempting trade unions from this type of action; this remained the situation until the Trade Union Act of 1984, which permitted employers to seek redress if a strike was called without certain preconditions (such as a secret ballot) having been met.

Taft, William Howard (1857–1930) US jurist and 27th President of the USA (1909–13). A Republican, he was appointed (1890) solicitor-general by President Benjamin HARRISON and later served as President Theodore ROOSEVELT's Secretary of War (1904–08). It was Roosevelt who ensured that Taft gained the Republican nomination in 1908. His Presidency is remembered for its DOLLAR DIPLOMACY in the field of foreign affairs, and

tariff laws that were attacked by the PROGRESSIVE MOVEMENT as too sympathetic to big business. Roosevelt and Taft drifted apart and when he ran again in 1912 Taft had to share the Republican vote with Roosevelt running as a Progressive. As a result the Democrat, Woodrow WILSON, was elected. Taft was appointed Chief Justice of the Supreme Court (1921–30), during which time he kept the Court on a conservative course.

Taft–Hartley Act (1947) An act of the US Congress that curbed the power of trade unions. It banned the closed-shop and the secondary boycott, allowed employers to sue unions for breach of contract and for damages inflicted on them by strikes, empowered the President to order a 60-day 'cooling-off period' before strike action, and required union leaders to take oaths stating that they were not communists. Despite protests from the unions, it has remained relatively unchanged.

Tahiti The largest of the Society Islands, in the centre of the South Pacific, administered by France as part of French Polynesia.

Physical. Mountainous, with peaks rising to 2,320 m (7,612 feet), it is a tropical paradise of palms and luxuriant flora, including the climbing orchid from which vanilla is extracted.

History. Tahiti was settled by Polynesians in the 14th century and first visited by Europeans in 1767. At the beginning of the 19th century Protestant missionaries settled on the island, converting the Tahitian chief Pomare II to Christianity in 1815. The French government established a protectorate in 1842 and annexed Tahiti as a colony in 1880. In 1940 the overwhelming majority of Tahitians backed the FREE FRENCH government of General de Gaulle, who made French Polynesia an overseas territory of France in 1946. At that time many Polynesians, led by Pouvanaa a Oopa, demanded independence from France. In 1958 Pouvanaa was sentenced to imprisonment and exile. Since 1977 French Polynesia has had considerable powers of self-government. In 1995 protests against French nuclear testing in the area fuelled the movement for Tahitian independence from France.

taille TALLAGE.

Taiping Rebellion (1850–64) A revolt against the Chinese QING dynasty. Led and inspired by Hong Xiuquan (1813–64), who claimed to be the younger brother of Jesus Christ, the Taiping Rebellion began in Guangxi province. It developed into the most serious challenge to the Qing, bringing most of the central and lower Yangtze region under rebel control, and costing 20 million lives. The rebels captured Nanjing in 1853 and established their capital there before launching an unsuccessful attack on Beijing. Qing resistance depended on such provincial forces as the Hunan Army of ZENG GUOFAN and the Ever-Victorious Army, formed by the American F. T. Ward and later commanded by the British soldier Charles GORDON. The rebellion was crushed with the capture of Nanjing in 1864, Hong Xiuquan having died in the siege, but the Qing regime never really recovered from the long civil war. Taiping ideology was a mixture of Christianity and radical, egalitarian social policies that later revolutionaries, including the Communist Party, drew upon.

Taiwan (Republic of China) A country (not recognized by most other countries and no longer a member of the UN) comprising a large island and several much smaller ones off the south-east coast of China.

Physical. The main island is almost 370 km (230 miles) long from north to south and 130 km (81 miles) wide from west to east. Climatically it is very warm and wet in summer and cooler in winter. High mountains running most of its length, richly forested with camphor, oak, cypress, and cedar, drop steeply eastward to the Pacific Ocean. Westward many rivers flow through plains bearing sugar cane, paddy, and tropical fruits.

Economy. Taiwan is a newly industrializing country with very high growth rates based on exports of manufactured goods, particularly to the USA. Textiles, electronic goods, and information technology are the principal exports. Agriculture, with sugar cane and rice as the main crops, is of little importance, and mineral resources are limited, though silver and gold are mined and there are deposits of coal, oil, sulphur, and iron. Taiwan's economic success has been achieved at the cost of considerable environmental degradation.

History. Portuguese explorers called it Formosa ('Beautiful Island'). Sparsely populated by a non-Chinese people, it was long a Chinese and Japanese pirate base. In the 17th century the Dutch (1624) and the Spaniards (1626) established trading posts, the Dutch driving out the Spaniards in 1642. With the fall of the MING dynasty in 1644, opponents of the QING started to settle on the island and in 1661 'Koxinga' (Zheng Chenggong), a Ming patriot, expelled the Dutch. It was conquered by the Qing in 1683 and for the first time became part of China. Fighting continued between its original inhabitants and the Chinese settlers into the 19th century. Taiwan was occupied by Japan as a result of the Treaty of SHIMONOSEKI in 1895 and remained under Japanese control until the end of World War II. The island was occupied by the Chinese forces of CHIANG KAI-SHEK in September 1945, but Taiwanese resentment at the administration of Chiang's governor Chen Yi produced a revolt that had to be put down by force of arms. When the CHINESE CIVIL WAR began to turn against the KUOMINTANG in 1948, arrangements were made to transfer Chiang's government to Taiwan, a move completed in the following year: by 1950 almost two million refugees from the mainland had also arrived on the island. Supported militarily by the USA, Taiwan maintained its independence from communist China and, until expelled in 1971, sat as the sole representative of China in the United Nations. Chiang Kai-shek remained its President until his death in 1975, and was succeeded by his son, Chiang Ching-kuo. He died in 1988 and was succeeded by President Lee Teng-hui. Since the 1950s Taiwan has undergone dramatic industrialization, becoming one of the world's major industrial nations. In 1986 the creation of new political parties was legalized, but with strict regulations governing their policies. Martial law, in force since 1949, was replaced in 1987 by the slightly less severe National Security law. Pro-democracy demonstrations during the late 1980s and

early 1990s led to further political reforms. The first full multiparty elections since 1949 were held in 1992 and were won by the Kuomintang. The Kuomintang has consistently opposed full independence for Taiwan and sought reunification with the mainland, but only if the mainland regime rejects communism. Negotiations between the two countries have been sporadic and generally unproductive, but in 1991 Taiwan officially ended its state of war with communist China. In 1993 a formal structure for further negotiations on economic and social issues was agreed but relations between the two countries have remained tense. By 1995 Taiwan had been recognized as a separate nation by 29 countries. In 1996 Taiwan's first democratic presidential elections were won by the incumbent, Lee Teng-Hui.

CAPITAL:	Taipei
AREA:	36,000 sq km (13,900 sq miles)
POPULATION:	21.463 million (1996)
CURRENCY:	1 New Taiwan dollar = 100 cents
RELIGIONS:	Buddhist 43.0%; Daoist 21.0%; Christian 7.0%; Muslim 0.5%
ETHNIC GROUPS:	Taiwanese 84.0%; Mainland Chinese 14.0%; Aborigine (Indonesian) 2.0%
LANGUAGES:	Mandarin Chinese (official); Chinese dialects

Taizong (or T'ai-tsung) (596–649) Second TANG Emperor of China (627–49). Taizong was renowned for his military prowess, scholarship, and concern for people. Strong central government was re-established, and he extended Chinese influence in Central Asia, subjugating in 630 the Eastern Turks, who accepted him as their Heavenly Khan. In his capital, Chang'an (now Xi'an), a city of two million people, envoys with tribute from Samarkand, India, and Sumatra mingled with merchants and scholars of many lands and many faiths – Nestorians, Buddhists, Zoroastrians, Manichees, Jews, Muslims, and others. He was a patron of Xuanzang, the Buddhist pilgrim who, in 645, brought back from India Buddhist scriptures, which he translated into Chinese.

Tajikistan A country bounded by Xinjiang (China) on the east and Afghanistan on the south, one of the highest regions of central Asia.

Physical. The Pamir mountains occupy a third of Tajikstan while the Alai range stretches across its centre. Below the snow-line the slopes are generally great stretches of bare red and grey rocks, broken by alpine meadows, there are forests near the tree-line of firs and juniper.

Economy. Tajikstan is the poorest of the former Soviet republics, despite its considerable mineral resources, which include coal, zinc, lead, molybdenum, petroleum, and natural gas; mining and extraction of these are the principal heavy industries. Light industry includes a number of textile mills to process cotton, which is the chief agricultural crop. Silk, fruit, wheat, and natural oils are also produced and cattle are raised. Tajikistan's valleys support vineyards, orchards, and fields of cereal and cotton, while hydroelectricity is available from river power.

History. Tajiks were originally of Iranian stock, but were conquered by Arab people during the 7th and 8th centuries AD. Large numbers of Turkic people moved into the area, which came under the control of the Uzbek khanate of Bukhara from the 15th to the mid-18th century and was then conquered by the Afghans.

By 1868 the whole area had been conquered by the Russians and proclaimed a protectorate. Following the Russian Revolution a Bukharan People's Soviet Republic was proclaimed in 1920. This, however, was conquered by the Red Army and a confused situation lasted until 1929 when the Tajik Soviet Socialist Republic was formed, which in 1936 joined the Soviet Union. During 1990 opposition parties were legalized. In September 1991 independence was proclaimed and Tajikistan joined the COMMONWEALTH OF INDEPENDENT STATES (CIS). Polarization had developed between a nationwide Islamic majority and a Russian minority based in the capital Dushanbe and the industrialized north. There were armed skirmishes, with Russian troops still stationed in the country becoming involved. In 1992 President Rakhmon Nabiyev was removed from office by force. Fighting between government forces and Muslim rebels was halted by a ceasefire in 1994, but sporadic violence continued until 1996. A new constitution was approved in 1994 and Imamoli Rakhmanov, who had been acting head of state since 1992, was elected President. In 1997, the government and the Islamist insurgents concluded a peace treaty that provided for power-sharing.

CAPITAL:	Dushanbe
AREA:	143,100 sq km (55,240 sq miles)
POPULATION:	5.945 million (1996)
CURRENCY:	1 Tajik rouble = 100 tanga
RELIGIONS:	Sunni Muslim; Eastern Orthodox; Ismaili minority
ETHNIC GROUPS:	Tajik 62.0%; Uzbek 23.0%; Russian 7.0%
LANGUAGES:	Tajik (Persian) (official); Russian; minority languages
INTERNATIONAL ORGANIZATIONS:	UN; CSCE; Commonwealth of Independent States; North Atlantic Co-operation Council

Taliban An ISLAMIC FUNDAMENTALIST political and military grouping that seized control of most of Afghanistan, including the capital Kabul, during 1994–96. Taliban means 'seekers' in the Pashto language and the Taliban militia was formed by Islamic theological students in the south of the country in 1994 with the intention of unifying Afghanistan. Rival Mujaheddin factions had been fighting since the withdrawal of Soviet forces in 1989. After initial reverses, the Taliban captured the city of Herat in September 1995 and advanced to take Kabul in August 1996. A strict Islamic code of law was immediately imposed, which debarred women from paid work and education and proscribed television. The Taliban regime is intensely hostile to both Communism and Western interests. Opposition to Taliban rule is concentrated in the north-east of Afghanistan under an alliance of forces known as the United Islamic Front for the Salvation of Afghanistan (UIFSA). Fierce fighting between the Taliban and UIFSA has continued despite attempts by the international community to broker a peace deal.

tallage A tax in medieval Europe that was generally imposed by an estate owner upon his unfree tenantry and its amount and frequency varied. In England it was a royal tax from the 12th century onward, levied on boroughs and royal lands. It was condemned by the barons in MAGNA CARTA in 1215 and became less important with the rise of parliamentary taxation, finally being abolished in 1340.

In France the 'taille' was greatly extended in the 14th century to meet the expenses of the HUNDRED YEARS WAR, although, because it was the monetary equivalent of feudal service, the nobility and clergy were exempted from payment. The main burden of the taille, by now the most important direct tax, lay upon the peasants until it was abolished in the FRENCH REVOLUTION.

Talleyrand-Périgord, Charles Maurice de (1754–1838) French diplomat and statesman. He entered the priesthood in 1778; two years later he became agent-general of the clergy of France and in 1789 was installed as bishop of Autun. He was one of a minority of French clergy who tried to reform the Church to serve the nation. In 1791 he left the Church, began a diplomatic career in London and, six years later, was appointed foreign minister by the DIRECTORY. Involved in the coup that brought NAPOLEON to power, he became the latter's trusted adviser and foreign minister (1799–1807) and took part in most of the peace negotiations during the NAPOLEONIC WARS. He resigned his ministerial office in 1807 and engaged in secret activities with the Allies to have Napoleon deposed. When the Allies entered Paris in 1814, Talleyrand persuaded the Senate to depose him and, as head of the new government, recalled the Bourbon king LOUIS XVIII to the throne. As the king's Foreign Minister, he represented France at the Congress of VIENNA. After his resignation in September 1815 he spent 15 years in semi-retirement. Towards 1830, aware of the growing unpopularity of the government of CHARLES X, he entered into diplomatic relations with LOUIS PHILIPPE. After the 1830 JULY REVOLUTION, as French ambassador to London, he did much to shape the future course of events in Europe. He was a signatory to the Quadruple Alliance (1834) between Britain, France, Spain, and Portugal, aimed at the support of constitutional monarchy in the last two countries against pretenders supported by Austria.

Talmud (Hebrew, 'study') The compilation of scholarly interpretations and commentaries on Jewish oral law codified in the *Mishnah*. The destruction of the Temple in Jerusalem (70 AD) and the growth of the DIASPORA prompted a vigorous effort to preserve traditional teachings. JUDAH HA-NASI compiled the Mishnah (*c.* 200 AD), an organized summary of the oral tradition. This, together with subsequent commentary, the *Gemara*, constitutes the Talmud. There are two major versions: the Palestinian or Jerusalem Talmud (completed *c.* 400 AD) and the Babylonian Talmud (completed *c.* 500 AD). Both are based on the same Mishnah, but the Babylonian Talmud is more extensive and considered more authoritative. The Talmud is primarily a legal compilation, but it also includes non-legal sections known as *Haggadah* (narratives). The standard version of the Talmud prints part of the Mishnah and the relevant Talmud on each page. Summaries of Talmudic teachings were subsequently prepared by scholars like MAIMONIDES in the 12th century and Joseph CARO in the 16th century. The Talmud is the basis of later codifications of Jewish law (*Halakhah*), the most influential of which is Caro's *Shulhan Arukh* (Laid Table) (1565). Study of the Talmud has been central to Jewish intellectual and religious life since its compilation.

Until the 18th century, Jewish communities in Europe had judicial autonomy and were subject to their own rabbinical courts. With the various reform movements thereafter the different branches of Judaism have viewed the Talmud and *Halakhah* differently. ORTHODOX JEWS regard the oral law and the written law of the Pentateuch as equally divine and immutable sources of law, which must be strictly observed. Reform Judaism, however, negates the divinity of the oral law and places emphasis on the authority of the Pentateuch. Conservative Jews take a position between these two, regarding the law as evolutionary. Thus Jewish law on aspects of religious practice, such as diet and keeping the *Shabbat,* applies in differing degrees to Jewish communities throughout the world, with the exception of Israel, where the state acknowledges Jewish law as a source for secular law and recognizes rabbinical courts, which adjudicate exclusively in matters of marriage and divorce concerning Jews, and have concurrent jurisdiction with civil courts in all matters of personal status, if all the parties concerned consent. Questions of constitutional, criminal, and private law are, however, the domain of secular Israeli law, contrary to the declared aim of Orthodox Judaism that Israel become a fully Talmudic state.

Tamerlane   *This representation of Tamerlane's court shows the opulence and splendour for which it was renowned.*

Tamerlane (*Timur Leng,* 'Timur the Lame') (1336–1405) Mongol leader, a descendant of GENGHIS KHAN. He seized Turkistan and from this base conducted brutal and destructive operations against Persia (1380–88, 1392–94), the GOLDEN HORDE (1388–91, 1395), the sultanate of DELHI (1398–99), the MAMELUKE ruler of Egypt and Syria

(1399–1401), and the OTTOMANS, whose ruler BAYEZID I he captured at the Battle of Ankara (1402). He died marching on China.

His genius was military rather than administrative, he simply installed vassal rulers in the areas he had conquered, rather than create a coherent empire; his descendants, the Timurids, ruled only the central Asian heartland. Fighting in the name of Islam, he usually plundered fellow Muslims. He was a keen patron of the arts, and imported foreign craftsmen to beautify his capital, Samarkand.

Tammany Hall Headquarters in New York City of a political organization, the executive committee of the Democratic Party. Founded in 1789 to represent middle-class opposition to the aristocratic Federalists. It was named after Tammanend, a late 17th-century Delaware chief, and based its rites and ceremonies on pseudo-Native American forms. The Society of Tammany acquired, under the control of Aaron BURR, a political importance that endured until the 1950s. The Society became linked with the Democratic Party as both organizations often had the same leader. Tammany gained a reputation as being a source of gifts and benefits, especially to particular religious or ethnic groups and by the mid-19th century, the Society's head, the Grand Sachem, was invariably an Irish Democrat of great influence in New York City politics. Under 'Boss' TWEED, corruption reached a high point between 1867 and 1872. Thereafter, the word Tammany became synonymous with machine politics, graft, corruption, and other abuses in city politics. Its influence was curtailed by President F. D. ROOSEVELT.

Tamworth Manifesto (1834) Election address of Sir Robert PEEL to his constituents at Tamworth, Staffordshire. Peel promised to accept the Whig government's REFORM ACT of 1832. He declared his adherence to a policy of moderate reform, while stressing the need to preserve what was most valuable from Britain's past. This concept of change, where necessary, within existing institutions marked the shift from the old, repressive Toryism to a new, more enlightened Conservatism.

Tanaka Kakuei (1918–93) Japanese statesman. First elected to the House of Representatives in 1947, his career was briefly interrupted by a bribery scandal soon after, but from 1957 he served successively as Minister of Communications, Minister of Finance (in three different cabinets) and Minister of International Trade. In 1972 he became Japan's youngest post-war Prime Minister (1972–74). He was forced to resign as a result of a bribery scandal in December 1974 and in 1976 had to face accusations of responsibility for the Lockheed scandal, relating to the corrupt sale of US military aircraft to Japan. During lengthy legal proceedings against him he remained a powerful force within the ruling LIBERAL DEMOCRATIC PARTY. He was sentenced to four years' imprisonment in 1983, but launched an appeal, which had reached the Supreme Court of Japan by October 1992. He was disabled by a severe stroke in 1985 and by 1987 his intra-party faction had disintegrated.

Tang (618–907) A Chinese dynasty, founded by the SUI official Li Yuan, that first established its power over China with help from nomad troops commanded by his

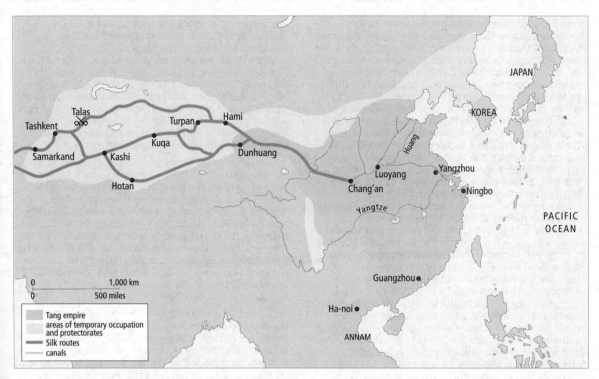

Tang: 618–906   *Under the Tang dynasty, China was initially a highly centralized state. An efficient system of canals augmented river transport and a good road system linked provincial centres with the capital, Chang'an (Xi'an), which was probably the largest and most cosmopolitan city in the world at that time. Standing at the end of the silk route, it attracted merchants from Persia, Arabia, and other parts of Asia. The Tang were especially noted for their sculpture and painting.*

son, who was later to become the second Tang emperor TAIZONG. The unification of China started by the Sui was extended. Chinese armies penetrated central Asia, KOREA, and ANNAM. Until defeated in 751 by the Arabs near the Talas River, West Turkistan, it ruled the largest empire in the world and its vessels voyaged as far as Aden. Printing was invented and gunpowder manufactured for fireworks. The dynasty is famed for its art, literature, and poetry. Neighbouring states, particularly KOREA and JAPAN, sought to make their homelands replicas of China. After MINGHUANG's reign and the abortive rebellion of An Lushan in 755 decay set in. Nomad invasions and revolts brought to power generals who controlled regional armies. When the last emperor abdicated fragmentation under ephemeral 'dynasties' followed.

Tanganyika TANZANIA.

Tan–Zam Railway A railway line in Central Africa. Its construction was formally agreed between ZAMBIA, TANZANIA, and China in August 1970. Its purpose was to free Zambia from dependence on neighbouring countries for railway transport of its vital copper and other exports. China provided an interest-free loan of £169 million, with technical aid. It spanned 1,860 km (1,162 miles), and was completed in October 1975, a year ahead of schedule.

Tanzania A country in East Africa, consisting of the former republic of Tanganyika and the island of ZANZIBAR. Tanzania is bounded by Kenya and Uganda on

the north, Rwanda, Burundi, and the Democratic Republic of the Congo (formerly Zaïre) on the west, and Zambia, Malawi, and Mozambique on the south.

Physical. Tanzania has a coast on the Indian Ocean and several islands; Pemba and Zanzibar islands both have a degree of autonomy. A hot, wet coastal plain rises through thick forest and areas planted with sisal to a warm plateau. To the north is Mount Kilimanjaro, below which the soil is volcanic and coffee can be grown. In the extreme north is Lake Victoria, round which cotton is cultivated, diamonds are found, and animals roam in the Serengeti National Park. Lake Tanganyika lies along the western border, and Lake Malawi in the south, both in the western arm of the Great Rift Valley.

Economy. Tanzania has shifted from socialist principles in economic planning to IMF-backed liberalization policies. Agriculture is the mainstay of the economy, which is dependent on foreign aid, but export cash crops of coffee, cotton, tea, sisal, cashew-nuts, and cloves have all been adversely affected by drought and falling commodity prices; a state of famine was declared in 1997 after poor rains. Cassava and maize are the main staple crops. Mineral resources include diamonds, gold, iron ore, coal, oil, and phosphates; there are unexploited natural gas reserves. Industry is limited, with food-processing, textiles, oil- and metal-refining the principal sectors.

History. In the first millenium BC northern mainland Tanzania was inhabited by Caucasoid peoples, probably from Egypt. Bantu-speaking peoples from western Africa moved into the region and were established there by about 500 AD. Arab slave merchants settled along the coast, clashing occasionally with Portuguese explorers, who first arrived in the late 15th century. German missionaries went to Tanganyika (mainland Tanzania) in the 1840s and were followed by German colonists. By 1907 Germany had taken full control of the country. Tanganyika became a British MANDATE after World War I and a trust territory, administered by Britain, after World War II. It became independent in 1961, followed by Zanzibar in 1963. The two countries united in 1964 to form the United Republic of Tanzania under its first President, Julius NYERERE. In the ARUSHA DECLARATION of 1967 Nyerere stated his policy of equality and independence for Tanzania. In 1975 the TAN–ZAM railway line was completed. Tanzania helped to restore democracy in Uganda in 1986 and gave strong support to political exiles from Zimbabwe, Angola, and Namibia. Nyerere was succeeded by President Ndugu Ali Hassan Mwinyi, who was re-elected in 1990 and whose years in office saw a marked revival of the economy with its very considerable potential. In June 1992 he ended 27 years of one-party rule by the legalization of opposition parties. During 1994 and 1995, some 800,000 refugees from civil war and ethnic violence in the neighbouring countries of RWANDA and BURUNDI fled to Tanzania; some Tanzanian politicians called for their repatriation. Internal tensions also grew in this period, particularly in Zanzibar, where the ruling party encountered growing opposition from Islamic fundamentalists. Multiparty elections, held in November 1995, saw the Party for the Revolution retain power, with Benjamin Mkapa becoming the country's new President.

CAPITAL:	Dar es Salaam
AREA:	945,037 sq km (364,881 sq miles)
POPULATION:	28.838 million (1996)
CURRENCY:	1 Tanzanian shilling = 100 cents
RELIGIONS:	Christian 34.0%; Muslim 33.0%; traditional beliefs and other 33.0%
ETHNIC GROUPS:	Nyamwezi and Sukuma 21.1%; Swahili 8.8%; Hehet and Bena 6.9%; Makonde 5.9%; Haya 5.9%
LANGUAGES:	Swahili, English (both official); Sukuma; local languages
INTERNATIONAL ORGANIZATIONS:	UN; OAU; Commonwealth; Non-Aligned Movement; SADC

Tanzimat reforms (1839–71) A series of reforms in the OTTOMAN EMPIRE. They were promulgated under sultans Abdülmecid I (1839–61) and Abdülaziz (1861–76) in response to western pressure. Under Mustafa Resid Pasha (1800–58) a programme of reform was steadily developed. The army was reorganized, on the Prussian model and the slave trade was abolished. Abuses in the taxation system were to be eliminated and provincial representative assemblies were created. New codes of commercial, land, and criminal law, based on French models, were introduced, with new state courts, separate from the Islamic religious courts. In his last years sultan Abdülaziz lost interest in the Tanzimat and, from 1871, became increasingly autocratic.

Tara The ancient coronation and assembly place of the High Kings of IRELAND, in County Meath. Remains dating back to about 2000 BC have been found there and there

is evidence of a network of halls, enclosures, and fortresses. The pillar stone may have been the inauguration stone of the kings of Tara. In the 4th century there were five tribal kingdoms: Ulster, Meath, Leinster, Munster, and Connaught, which nominally acknowledged the overlordship of the High King (the ruler of Tara). Conn was reputedly the first High King ('Ard Ri'). Niall of the Nine Hostages, possibly the son of a British prince, ruled there in about 400 and his son Leary received St Patrick there in 432. Tara appears to have been abandoned in the 6th century.

Taranaki Wars A major part of the ANGLO-MAORI WARS in New Zealand. In 1859, Governor Browne accepted an offer of land on the Waitara River from Teira (a Maori right-holder), despite the veto of the senior chief, Wiremu Kingi. When the survey was resisted, Browne sent troops to Waitara. Many Maori supported Kingi, believing the purchase to be a breach of the Treaty of WAITANGI. Fighting was inconclusive in 1860–61 and, after a two-year truce, resumed in 1863. Maori resistance on the coast was overcome and much land confiscated. Maori resistance in the interior, increasingly led by the PAI MARIRE, continued through the 1860s.

tariff reform A British fiscal policy designed to end the nation's adherence to FREE TRADE by the use of protective duties on imported goods. Joseph CHAMBERLAIN believed that the use of tariffs would strengthen Britain's revenue and its trading position; it would also strengthen links within the British empire by making possible a policy of imperial preference (the application of lower rates of duty between its member countries). Chamberlain's campaign (1897–1906) failed, it divided the Conservatives and was rejected by the Liberals. Tariff reform was rejected again in 1923 when Stanley BALDWIN and the Conservatives failed to secure an overall majority in an election primarily on that issue. However, the shock caused by the international financial crisis of 1929–31 and the intensification of nationalist political and economic rivalries made Britain's free trade policy even more of an anachronism. The adoption of protectionism by the MacDonald NATIONAL GOVERNMENT from 1931 signalled the ultimate success of the tariff reform policy.

Tariq ibn Zaid (*fl.* 700–12) A freedman of Musa ibn Nusayr, UMAYYAD governor of North Africa. In 711 he was sent to conquer Spain with 7,000 men, landing near the famous rock that has immortalized his name, Jabal al-Tariq (Mount of Tariq), that is, Gibraltar. On 19 July 711 he defeated the Visigoth king Roderick and went on to conquer half of Spain. In 712 Musa crossed to Spain and, out of jealousy at Tariq's success, put him in chains. His subsequent fate is unknown.

Tarquin The fifth and seventh Etruscan kings of Rome, Priscus and Superbus, both subjects of legend and tradition. Lucius Tarquinius Priscus (ruled 616–578 BC) was said to have been the guardian of King Ancus Marcius's sons, but seized the throne on the King's death and was eventually murdered by his sons. Servius Tullius, Priscus's brother-in-law, then became king. Lucius Tarquinius Superbus (ruled 534–510 BC) may have been Servius Tullius's son-in-law, but murdered him and seized the throne. He was a tyrant and executed many senators. A revolt was raised by surviving senators, they expelled Superbus and established the ROMAN REPUBLIC. The stories concerning the Tarquins were largely symbolic, contrasting the decadence of the monarchy with the idealism of the new republic. After this time the word 'king' was used by the Romans as a term of political abuse.

Tartars (or Tatars) A number of Central Asian peoples who, over the centuries, were a threat to civilized peoples in Asia and Europe. More specific names, for example Mongol, Turk, Kipchak, emerge for some of these peoples who were constantly moving, often over great distances, and who spoke a variety of related Turkic and Mongol languages. The name 'Tartars' is applied specifically to tribesmen living south of the Amur who were defeated by the Ming emperor YONGLE in the early 15th century. Papal envoys (c. 1250) to the Mongols consistently called them Tartars, probably by association with Tartarus, the place of punishment in the underworld of Greek mythology. The name was also applied to the GOLDEN HORDE. Some of the Cossacks (originally Kahsaks, 'free men') on the River Dnieper were Tartars. Later any people of Turkish stock in Russia were called Tartars. In the 16th century the khanates of the Volga Tartars came under Russian rule. In the 15th century the Crimean Tartars formed an independent khanate, tributary to the OTTOMAN Turks until annexed by Russia in 1783.

Tasman, Abel Janszoon (c. 1603–59) Dutch navigator and European discoverer of New Zealand. In 1642 Anthony Van Diemen, governor of the Dutch East Indies, gave him command of an expedition to ascertain whether the known part of Australia was linked to a great southern continent. Sailing round western Australia he steered due east and came to land which he named Van Diemen's Land, the island later renamed Tasmania. A month later he sighted high land, the western coast of New Zealand, which he called 'Staten Land'. Exploring northwards he was attacked by Maoris, so he made for the Pacific, there discovering islands in the Tonga and Fiji groups before returning to Java. Two years later, on another voyage, he explored much of the north Australian coast, surveying the Gulf of Carpentaria. By 1653 he had amassed a considerable fortune in the service of the DUTCH EAST INDIA COMPANY and settled down to retirement in Batavia.

Tasmania A state of the Commonwealth of AUSTRALIA. Tasmania is Australia's largest island, lying south of Wilson's Promontory, Victoria, in the south-east of the continent. It has many smaller islands off its own shores.

History. The original inhabitants of Tasmania were a small tribe of Negrito people. The Dutch explorer Abel TASMAN sighted the island in 1642 and named it Van Diemen's Land. British convict settlements were established in 1803 and 1804. The island remained a part of New South Wales until 1825, when it became a separate colony. Sizeable numbers of free settlers began to arrive from the 1820s onwards. The indigenous inhabitants embarked on the Black War (1825) against the settlers, whose efforts to contain them on Flinders Island (1835) failed; the indigenous population became extinct in 1876. Convicts were transported to Van Diemen's Land until 1853, but Port Arthur, the penal settlement, was not closed until 1877. Partial self-government was granted in 1850, extended in 1855 to a cabinet system responsible to an elected Parliament. Its new name, Tasmania, was proclaimed in 1855.

Tata An Indian Parsi commercial and industrial family. It is one of the two (with the BIRLAS) most important merchant families in modern India. The family began in Far East trade, but diversified their operations to create, under Jahangir Ratanji Dadabhai Tata (1904–93), an airline that later became Air India. The Tatas also spent extensively on scientific and other work, founding the Tata Institute of Fundamental Research in Bombay. Their companies continue to be successful.

Tawhiao Son of the Maori king POTATAU and head (1860–94) of the KINGITANGA movement. He led his people in the Second ANGLO-MAORI WAR. Following a truce in 1868 an uneasy peace existed in the 'King Country'. When the government sought to build a railway concessions were made to the Maoris. Tawhiao returned to Lower Waikato in 1883 and continued to press claims for the return of confiscated land and for recognition of Maori *rangatiratanga* (chieftainship).

Taxila A ruined city north-west of Rawalpindi, Pakistan, which was an important centre of trade, learning, and pilgrimage for about a thousand years. In the 5th century BC it was the capital of the Gandhara kingdom. It fell to Alexander the Great in 326 BC and soon afterwards was incorporated in the MAURYAN EMPIRE, becoming a centre of BUDDHISM. The Bactrians, Scythians, Parthians, Kushans, and Sassanians in turn invaded and annexed the city. It had already entered a period of decline when destroyed by Hun invasions in the 5th century and was never rebuilt.

Taylor, Jeremy (1613–67) Church of England divine. He was chaplain to LAUD and CHARLES I and was taken prisoner during the ENGLISH CIVIL WAR. After the RESTORATION he was appointed Bishop of Down and Connor and subsequently of Dromore, in Ireland. His writings, especially *Holy Living* (1650) and *Holy Dying* (1651), had great influence on contemporary religious attitudes. He was one of the earliest Anglican leaders to plead the case for religious toleration.

Taylor, Zachary (1784–1850) Twelfth President of the USA (1849–50). One of the leading US soldiers of the mid-19th century, he fought in the BLACK HAWK and SEMINOLE WARS. His victories in the MEXICAN–AMERICAN WAR, particularly at Buena Vista (23 February 1847), made him a national hero and carried him to the White House as leader of the Whig Party. In the crisis preceding the COMPROMISE OF 1850, he took a firm stand against appeasement of the South. He died after only 16 months in office.

Teamsters, International Brotherhood of A trade union in the USA. Formed in 1903, its members are workers in the transport industry. In the late 1950s its president, David Beck, was indicted for having links with criminals, and his successor, James R. Hoffa, was found guilty of attempting to influence a federal jury while on trial in 1964 for misusing union funds. The revelations of corruption did immense damage to the reputation of unions, but the Teamsters sought to recover by co-operating with more responsible union leaders like Walter REUTHER of the Union of Auto Workers.

Teapot Dome scandal (1922–24) US fraud perpetrated by the 'Ohio gang' surrounding President HARDING. It involved the siphoning of oil, intended for the US navy, from the oil reserves at Teapot Dome, Wyoming, to the Mammoth Oil Company. A second diversion allowed oil from Elk Hills, California, to be siphoned to the Pan-American Petroleum and Transportation Company. Harding died before the full extent of the involvement of the Secretary of the Interior, Albert B. Fall, was exposed by Senator Thomas J. Walsh of Montana in the years 1922–24. Fall was found guilty of accepting a $100,000 bribe and imprisoned (1929–32).

technological revolution A series of technological advances made in the latter half of the 20th century in the manufacturing industries, agriculture, medicine, communications (see COMMUNICATIONS REVOLUTION), energy supply, and warfare. The changes to national economies caused by the INDUSTRIAL REVOLUTION and AUTOMATION were greatly enhanced by the development of high-technology industry since World War II. The productivity, prosperity, and economic growth of nations came to reflect the wealth or otherwise of their electronic, aerospace, chemical, and biotechnological industries. Their national security depended on advanced military technology for weapons and intelligence. Health care increasingly came to depend on sophisticated instruments and treatment as well as on advanced pharmaceuticals. Information was spread around the world through a network of complex telecommunications. Employment in the service and manufacturing sector came to depend on computers and automation. Even the quality of leisure time became, in the technologically advanced nations, based on consumer electronics and on the technological feats of the entertainment industry. Investment in high-technology industry enabled first Japan, the USA, and Europe, and thereafter countries of the Pacific Rim of East Asia (e.g. South Korea, Taiwan), to achieve unprecedented prosperity. By contrast, the economies of the former communist nations, which had invested primarily in obsolescent heavy manufacturing plant and arms manufacture, became non-viable. Today, the world market for the electronics industry alone is worth about $750 billion and is expected to be $2 trillion (million million) by the year 2000. With markets now increasingly competitive, future development in technology is seen in terms of the formation of global consortia, alliances, and collaborations that co-operate and compete at the same time.

Tecumseh (c. 1768–1813) American Shawnee chief in the Ohio Valley. Tecumseh emerged as the most formidable opponent of the White WESTWARD EXPANSION, believing that Native American land was a common inheritance, which could not be ceded piecemeal by individual tribes. Together with his half-brother, the Prophet Tenskwatawa, he formed a confederacy of tribes to negotiate a peaceful settlement with the settlers. This confederacy was defeated at the Battle of TIPPECANOE in 1811 and Tecumseh then sided with the British in the WAR OF 1812, but was killed at the Battle of the THAMES in 1813. This marked the end of Native American resistance in the Ohio Valley. Tenskwatawa retired to Canada with a British pension, but returned in 1826 and accompanied the Shawnee when they were moved, first to Missouri, and then to Kansas, where he died (c. 1837).

Teheran Conference (28 November–1 December 1943) A meeting between CHURCHILL, ROOSEVELT, and STALIN in the Iranian capital. Here Stalin, invited for the first time to an inter-Allied conference, was told of the impending opening of a SECOND FRONT to coincide with a Soviet offensive against Germany. The three leaders discussed the establishment of the UNITED NATIONS after the war and Stalin pressed for a future Soviet sphere of influence in the Baltic States and Eastern Europe, while guaranteeing the independence of Iran.

Te Kooti Rikirangi Te Turuki (c. 1830–93) Maori spiritual leader. A member of the Aitanga-a-Mahaki tribe, he was accused in 1865 of complicity with the PAI MARIRE and its militant offshoot, the Hau-hau, and was deported to the Chatham Islands. In exile he evolved a variation of Pai Marire ritual and belief, the Ringatu. In 1868 his group escaped, seized a government ship, and returned. Challenged by the military, he attacked the settlement at Poverty Bay, killing some Europeans and many more collaborating Maori. The subsequent pursuit and skirmishing lasted until 1872 when Te Kooti found sanctuary in the 'King Country' until pardoned. The Ringatu church survives today.

Tel-el-Kebir, Battle of (12–13 September 1882) A battle between British and Egyptian forces, 83 km (52 miles) east of Cairo. British troops under Sir Garnet Wolseley defeated an Egyptian army led by ARABI PASHA. Cairo fell on the following day, thus confirming the British conquest of Egypt.

tell A mound representing an ancient settlement site. The name is from Arabic and is commonly applied only to examples in the Near and Middle East, but the phenomenon is known in many other areas where long-lived towns were built in mud brick. This decays quite rapidly and is not worth salvaging, so leads to a rapid accumulation of deposit.

Temperance Movements Campaigns to restrict the consumption of alcohol. Early temperance associations appeared first in New England in the USA, where, by 1833, there were some 6,000 local temperance societies. In 1829 the Ulster Temperance Society was formed and the temperance movement then spread to Scotland, Wales, England, Norway, and Sweden. In 1874 the Woman's Christian Temperance Union was founded in Cleveland, Ohio. It quickly spread across the continent, criticizing the masculine 'saloon world', with its hard drinking and prostitution, and coming to the belief that only WOMEN'S SUFFRAGE could end the social degradation of women. In 1883 the Union became a world organization, the first international women's movement its influence spreading beyond the USA to Australia and New Zealand. A PROHIBITION PARTY had been founded in 1869 in the USA, quickly becoming an effective force in US politics, where the Anti-Saloon League was founded in 1893. In 1920 Prohibition was enforced nationally by Congress. In Britain a strong campaigner for temperance in the 1890s was the SALVATION ARMY and temperance legislation was introduced in 1904, 1906, and 1916 in the DEFENCE OF THE REALM ACT, to reduce the number of public houses, exclude people under 18, and impose 'drinking hours'. These acts were confirmed in 1953 and 1961. Many countries have some form of legislation concerned with alcohol consumption and it illegal in most Muslim countries.

Temple, Sir William (1628–99) English diplomat and author. As English ambassador to The Hague, he negotiated the Triple Alliance of 1668 between England, Holland, and Sweden, and brought about the marriage between William of Orange and Princess Mary, daughter of JAMES II, in 1677. His attempt to achieve a compromise solution to the political crisis of 1679 by reviving and strengthening the powers of the Privy Council ended in failure. He refused political honours from William III and devoted the remainder of his life to writing.

Temple, William (1881–1944) British churchman and educationalist. Temple became a priest in 1909 and was Archbishop of Canterbury (1942–44). The achievement of greater equality in the educational system, springing, in part, from his early activities with the Workers' Educational Association, was an important objective for him. He worked with R. A. (later Lord) BUTLER on his Education Bill which became law in 1944. He also sought to secure a greater sense of common purpose between the different religious denominations and his work led to the foundation of the WORLD COUNCIL OF CHURCHES.

Templer, Sir Gerald (1898–1979) British field-marshal. Templer commanded the 6th Armoured Division in World War II and after the war served as vice-chief of the Imperial General Staff before being appointed high commissioner and commander-in-chief in Malaya (1952–54) at the peak of the MALAYAN EMERGENCY. Through a combination of military efficiency, adaptability to local circumstances, and the fostering of good relations with village populations, Templer turned the tide of war decisively against the communist guerrillas.

Tennessee Valley Authority (TVA) An independent federal government agency in the USA. Created by Congress (1933) as part of the NEW DEAL proposals to offset unemployment by a programme of public works, it set out to provide for the development of the whole Tennessee River basin. It took over a project (begun in 1916) for extracting nitrate at Muscle Shoals, Alabama. In addition the TVA was authorized to construct new dams and improve existing ones, to control floods and generate cheap hydro-electric power, to check erosion, and to provide afforestation across seven states.

Tennis Court Oath A dramatic incident which took place at Versailles in the first stage of the FRENCH REVOLUTION. On 17 June 1789 the Third Estate of the STATES-GENERAL under the presidency of Jean Bailly, a representative of Paris, declared themselves the NATIONAL ASSEMBLY, claiming that they were the only Estate properly accredited and that the First and Second Estates must join them. On 20 June they found their official meeting-place closed and moved to the Tennis Court, a large open hall nearby. The Oath bound them not to separate until they had given France a constitution.

Tenochtitlán (literally, 'place of the Tenochca') The island capital of the AZTECS in Lake Texcoco, now modern Mexico City. Traditionally founded in about 1345, it grew to a population of some 300,000 by the early 16th century. It was laid out in a grid of streets and canals round a huge ceremonial precinct of pyramids, temples, and palaces, and surrounded by artificial islands of gardens called *chinampas*. Three wide causeways stretched out across the lake to the mainland.

As the hub of the Aztec empire, its capture by CORTÉS on 13 August 1521 was rapidly followed by complete capitulation.

Tenskwatawa TECUMSEH.

Teotihuacán A site in the Valley of Mexico, north-east of Mexico City, containing well-preserved monumental architecture from about 1st to 7th centuries AD. Teotihuacán was the earliest true city in Mesoamerica (Mexico and northern Central America). Its development began around 100 BC and for some 600 years it dominated Central Mexico economically and perhaps politically. At its height it covered roughly 22.5 sq km (*c.* 8.7 sq miles) with a regular grid of streets, alleys, and apartment-like residential complexes, and a population of about 200,000. It contained the most extensive and sumptuous ceremonial centre of central Mexico in the pre-Toltec period. The focal point of the ceremonial area is the largest and earliest structure, the Sun Pyramid, built up of solid layers over a natural cave. Later ritual platforms are supported on a honeycomb of pillars in-filled with rubble and richly adorned with decorated façades. There are smaller structures, built, like the large pyramids, on platforms, and usually screened by right-angled colonnades, with ornately carved and painted interior spaces. The layout seems to have been determined by a solar ritual, as the face of the central pyramid is aligned with the setting midsummer sun and all the other important buildings are related to it axially. When the Teotihuacán culture collapsed (*c.* 700 AD), features of this architecture seem to have been transferred to sites on the edge of the Valley of Mexico, notably Xochicalco and Cholula.

Te Puea Herangi (or 'Princess' Te Puea) (1883–1952), A niece of the Maori king, TAWHIAO. Thoroughly educated in MAORI language and culture, she took direction of the KINGITANGA movement. She built Turangawaewae, south of Auckland, as a leading *marae* (social, political, cultural, and spiritual centre) and secured recognition of the Kingitanga from the New Zealand government. Her leadership strengthened Maori values and institutions while fostering a controlled accommodation of European influences, including commercial farming and education.

Teresa of Ávila, St (1515–82) Spanish nun and mystic, the originator of the CARMELITE reform. She entered a Carmelite convent at Ávila in 1535, but it was not until 20 years later that she underwent a religious experience. She opened the first reformed convent where the primitive (original) Carmelite rule was observed in 1562 and from 1567 worked with St JOHN of the Cross in nurturing the work of reform. Considerable friction within the order led in 1579 to the granting of independent jurisdiction to Teresa's austere Carmelites, known as Discalced Carmelites. She was canonized in 1622. Her spiritual writings include *The Way of Perfection* and *The Interior Castle*.

Terror, Reign of A period of the FRENCH REVOLUTION that began in March 1793 when the Revolutionary government, known as the Convention, having executed the king, set about attacking opponents and anyone else considered a threat to the regime. A Revolutionary Tribunal was set up to bring 'enemies of the state' to trial and the following month the COMMITTEE OF PUBLIC SAFETY was created. It began slowly but during the ruthless dictatorship that followed the defeat of the GIRONDINS at least 12,000 political prisoners, priests, and aristocrats were executed, including MARIE ANTOINETTE and Madame ROLAND. The Terror was intensified in June 1794 after the execution of HÉBERT and DANTON had left ROBESPIERRE supreme. It ended the following month, after the arrest and execution of Robespierre.

terrorism The practice of using violent and intimidating acts, especially for political ends. STATE TERRORISM implies either the use of terror by state authorities in order to suppress opposition, or state sponsorship of terrorist activities. Terrorism is also used by political groups in order to bring pressure to bear on governments to accede to political demands. Terrorism has been used most commonly by revolutionary groups whose objective is the overthrow of a particular regime and by nationalist groups seeking national self-determination. In 19th-century Russia the ANARCHISTS and NIHILISTS used bombings and assassinations against the Tsarist government, while in the USA organizations such as the KU KLUX KLAN used terrorism and lynchings to intimidate the Black population after the American Civil War. In the 20th century such dictators as Mussolini and Hitler have come to power through the use of terror tactics, while the period after World War II witnessed the growth of nationalist or liberation groups that used terrorism as part of their struggle against an occupying power: for example in CYPRUS, ISRAEL/PALESTINE (IRGUN, the STERN GANG and the PALESTINE LIBERATION ORGANIZATION), IRELAND (the Provisional Irish Republican Army (IRA)), and many countries in Africa, Asia, and the Middle East. A further development was the appearance of terrorist groups struggling against their countries' social and political structure, including the BAADER-MEINHOF gang and the Red Army Faction in Germany, the RED BRIGADES in Italy, Action Directe in France, the BASQUE separatist group ETA in Spain, the TUPAMAROS in Uruguay, and the SHINING PATH in Peru. Some states have been accused of sponsoring international terrorism, including Libya, Syria, Sudan, and the Muslim fundamentalist regime in Iran.

Techniques of terrorism involve bombing and shooting attacks against property and individuals, the assassination of significant persons associated with the established government or security forces, hostage-taking, and hi-jacking of aircraft, trains, ships, and buses. Terrorist acts are rarely indiscriminate (although the immediate effects on victims may be) or random, but they may be intended to appear so in order to create a generalized state of public fear. The major objectives of terrorism are to keep a particular cause in the forefront of public consciousness, to pressure the political authorities to concede the terrorists' demands by inducing public fear, and to induce a government to betray its own commitment to freedom and democracy by imposing illiberal security measures in order to contain such violence. The overthrow of governments or the achievement of national independence have rarely been achieved by terrorist techniques. However, by keeping a cause in the forefront of domestic and international political agendas, terrorism may be seen in retrospect to have played a role if those objectives are ultimately achieved and to have imposed heavy costs on governments, even if they are not.

International collaboration against terrorism has not proved easy since it involves the close co-operation of legal and police authorities from many different states that often have different domestic laws as well as different international and foreign policy interests. The European Convention on the Suppression of Terrorism (1977), the 'Trevi system' of co-operation among EC (now EU) members (1976), which spread to Council of Europe states, the Tokyo summit declaration on terrorism in 1986, and the participation of the former Soviet Union in anti-terrorist collaboration have all helped to establish a climate of international co-operation. However, it is less easy to set up specific mechanisms to counter the terrorist threat. For example, it has often been difficult to get common provisions on airport security and laws on extradition, which are the subject of specific bilateral treaties between states, often produce complex legal problems, the result of which may be that alleged terrorists are not brought to trial.

Tertullian, Quintus Septimius Florens (c. 160–240 AD) A citizen of Carthage, the first Latin-speaking Christian writer, who had had a considerable influence on the development of Christian doctrine. He attacked Gnosticism, contributed to the formulation of a doctrine of the Trinity, urged a rigorous asceticism, and believed that only MARTYRS were assured of salvation.

Test Acts Laws that made the holding of public office in Britain conditional upon subscribing to the established religion. Although Scotland imposed such a law in 1567, the harsh laws against RECUSANTS in England were sufficient in themselves to deter Roman Catholics and dissenters from putting themselves forward for office. In 1661 membership of town corporations and in 1673 all offices under the crown were denied to those who refused to take communion in an Anglican church. In 1678 all Catholics except the Duke of York (the future JAMES II) were excluded from Parliament. In the 18th century religious tests in Scotland were not always enforced, except for university posts, and in England the test could be met by occasional communion, but this was not possible for Roman Catholics. The Test Acts were finally repealed in 1829 and university religious tests were abolished in the 1870s and 1880s.

Tet Offensive (29 January–25 February 1968) An offensive launched in the VIETNAM WAR by Vietcong and regular North Vietnamese army units against US and South Vietnamese forces. In a surprise attack timed to coincide with the first day of the Tet (Vietnamese Lunar New Year) holiday, North Vietnamese forces under General GIAP took the war from the countryside to the cities of South Vietnam. After initial successes, the attackers were repulsed with heavy losses on both sides, but the offensive seriously damaged South Vietnamese morale and shook US confidence in their ability to win the war and brought them to the conference table in Paris in 1969. This led to the Paris Peace Accords of 1973 and the withdrawal of US forces from Indochina.

Tetzel, Johann (1465–1519) A German DOMINICAN friar. An agent for the sale of papal INDULGENCES (to raise money for the rebuilding of St Peter's, Rome) he was responsible for inspiring Martin LUTHER's protest of 1517 which sparked the REFORMATION. He replied to Luther's *Ninety-Five Theses*, but died shortly afterwards, discredited.

Teutonic Knight A member of a military and religious order whose full title was the Order of the

Knights of the Hospital of St Mary of the Teutons in Jerusalem. Founded in 1190 at Acre, it was made up of knights, priests, and lay brothers and was active in Palestine and Syria, although its members retreated to Venice when the CRUSADERS failed to contain the Muslims. The Holy Roman Emperor Frederick II employed the order as missionaries to overcome and convert the pagans beyond the north-eastern border of the empire and in this they were very successful, gaining Prussia in 1229.

In 1234, though in practice independent, they declared that they held the lands they had conquered as a fief from the pope. Joining with the LIVONIAN ORDER, they continued to advance around the Baltic coast, amassing huge territories, but their progress was checked decisively when they were defeated at Tannenberg in 1410 by King Ladislas of Poland. In 1525 the Grand Master, Albert of Brandenburg, became a Lutheran, resigned his office, and the order was declared secular. It remained an order under the control of the Electors of Brandenburg.

Teutons A Germanic tribe, believed to be from Holstein or Jutland, who migrated to southern Gaul and northern Italy with the Cimbri in the late 2nd century BC. In 102 they were defeated by MARIUS at Aquae Sextiae (Aix-en-Provence). They disappeared from history but the name Teuton survived as a synonym for German.

Te Whiti Maori religious leader (*c.* 1820–1907). In 1877, when British government officials began land surveys in South Taranaki without first creating reserves as guaranteed by the Treaty of WAITANGI, Te Whiti organized non-violent resistance. He prophesized success through continued non-violent resistance and 2,000 people flocked to his settlement at Parihaka. In 1881 government forces arrested Te Whiti and dispersed the settlement. After a year in custody Te Whiti rebuilt and modernized Parihaka, where his teachings were promoted for many decades.

Tewkesbury, Battle of (4 May 1471) A battle in the Wars of the ROSES fought between EDWARD IV, fresh from his victory at BARNET and the Lancastrian forces of Margaret of Anjou. Margaret's forces were defeated and her son, Prince Edward, was among those killed.

Texas, Republic of (1836–45) A short-lived independent republic in the south-west of the USA. Texas had only been lightly colonized by the Spanish and in 1821 the Mexican government granted Stephen Austin the right to bring US settlers into the region. Pressure began to build up for independence from Mexican control and a revolt broke out in 1835–36. After defeat at the ALAMO, Texan forces under HOUSTON captured the Mexican general SANTA ANNA at SAN JACINTO. An independent republic of Texas was proclaimed, which was recognized by the USA as the 'Lone-Star' state. The republic lasted for almost a decade before it was admitted to the Union as the 28th state, an event that helped to precipitate the MEXICAN–AMERICAN WAR in the following year (1846).

Texas Rangers A paramilitary US police force. The Texas Rangers were first organized in the 1830s to protect US settlers in Texas against indigenous Mexicans. After the formation of the republic of TEXAS (1836), they were built up by HOUSTON as a mounted border patrol of some 1,600 picked men. They became

renowned for their exploits against marauders and rustlers in the heyday of the great CATTLE TRAILS after the AMERICAN CIVIL WAR.

Thailand (formerly Siam) A country in south-east Asia bounded by Myanmar (Burma), Laos, and Cambodia and, in the south, Malaysia.

Physical. Thailand extends more than half-way down the Malay Peninsula. The north is hilly and covered with dense forest, including teak. In the centre is a great, low-lying plain threaded with rivers that drain into the Gulf of Thailand. The climate is hot and monsoonal.

Economy. A newly industrializing country, Thailand experienced very rapid economic growth in the 1980s and 1990s, based on exports of textiles and machinery and agricultural products such as rice, tapioca, and rubber. Mining and industry are replacing agriculture as the leading economic activities. Rice, once the leading export, dominates agricultural production. Teak production is also important and tourism a significant earner of foreign exchange. Rapid industrial growth concentrated around Bangkok has strained Thailand's infrastructure. In 1997 government mismanagement and imprudent lending by Thai banks precipitated a financial crisis. The crisis provoked plans to repatriate as many as two million foreign labourers (mainly to Myanmar).

History. The Thais, akin to the SHANS and Lao, originated in the Yunnan province of south-west China. Their name means 'free'. MONGOL pressure accelerated their southward movement from Yunnan. They set up kingdoms in Sukhotai and Chiengmai, formerly under KHMER rule, became Theravada BUDDHISTS, and adopted an Indian script. About 1350 Ayuthia became the capital of a new Thai kingdom which, after prolonged fighting, captured ANGKOR in 1431. Ayuthia ruled much of Cambodia and at times Tenasserim and nothern Malaya. Wars with Burma (MYANMAR), whose kings coveted Ayuthia's sacred white elephants, brought no lasting loss of Thai territory.

Among Europeans who became active in Ayuthia the French were dominant. In 1684 Thai envoys presented LOUIS XIV with elephants, rhinoceroses, and a letter engraved on gold. The Burmese finally destroyed Ayuthia in 1767. Under the leadership of General Taskin, the Burmese were expelled from Siam by about 1777. His successor, General Chakri (later Rama I) founded the Chakri dynasty and established Bangkok as his capital. The Chakri dominated much of LAOS and northern Malaya and succeeded in maintaining their country's independence through a policy of conciliation, ceding their vassal state in Laos and Cambodia to France in the late 19th and early 20th centuries. In the reigns of MONGKUT (1851–68) and CHULALONGKORN (1868–1910) Thailand achieved substantial modernization in both the administrative and economic spheres. The middle class produced by the modernization process became intolerant of absolute royal rule and an economic crisis in 1932 produced a bloodless coup that left the Chakri dynasty on the throne but transferred power to a constitutional government. Although technically allied to Japan during World War II, Thailand retained western friendship because of prolonged guerrilla resistance to Japanese forces. Until the early 1970s the country was largely ruled by the army, Marshal PIBUL SONGGRAM maintaining near personal rule from 1946 to 1957. Severe rioting resulted in a partial move to civilian government in 1973 and the introduction of a democratic constitution in 1974, but the threat of communist aggression, particularly on its borders with Cambodia allowed a pronounced military influence. A military coup in 1991 was followed by a new constitution and a general election in 1992. Commander-in-chief General Suchinda Kraprayoon was appointed Prime Minister and he imposed a military crackdown. This resulted in riots, arrests, and the killing of demonstrators, before King Bhumibol (succeeded 1946) was able to restore stability by a political compromise; Suchinda resigned and civilian political parties were re-legalized. Further elections in September 1992 were won by a coalition of pro-democracy parties; the leader of the Democrat Party, Chuan Leekpai, became Prime Minister. Following the collapse of the governing coalition in May 1995, Leekpai called an early general election, which resulted in the formation of a new coalition. Chavalit Yongchaiyudh was elected Prime Minister in 1996. However, the financial crisis of 1997 led to his resignation and a new coalition was formed under Chuan Leekpai.

CAPITAL:	Bangkok
AREA:	513,115 sq km (198,115 sq miles)
POPULATION:	60.003 million (1996)
CURRENCY:	1 baht = 100 satang
RELIGIONS:	Buddhist 95.0%; Muslim 4.0%; Christian 1.0%
ETHNIC GROUPS:	Siamese 54.0%; Lao 28.0%; Chinese 11.0%; Malay 4.0%; Khmer 3.0%
LANGUAGES:	Thai (official); Lao; Chinese; Malay; Mon-Khmer languages
INTERNATIONAL ORGANIZATIONS:	UN; ASEAN; Colombo Plan

Thames, Battle of the (5 October 1813) A military engagement in the WAR OF 1812, fought in present-day south-western Ontario, Canada. Following their abandonment of Detroit, British and Native American forces under General Proctor and TECUMSEH were overtaken and decisively defeated near Chatham on the Thames River by a US force under General HARRISON. The US victory, together with Tecumseh's death in the battle, destroyed the Native American confederacy and the British and Native American alliance and secured the US north-west frontier.

thane (or thegn) A nobleman in Anglo-Saxon England. The status of a thane, as determined by his WERGILD, was usually 1,200 shillings. In return for their services to the crown, thanes received gifts of land, which became hereditary. The king's thanes, members of the royal household, were required to do military service, attend the WITAN, and assist in government.

Thant, U (1909–74) Burmese statesman and third Secretary-General of the United Nations (1961–71). He entered the Burmese diplomatic service in 1948 and served at the United Nations from 1957. In 1961 he succeeded Dag HAMMARSKJÖLD as Secretary-General. He filled the post with great distinction, his achievements including assistance in the resolution of the CUBAN MISSILE CRISIS, the formation of a UN peace-keeping force in CYPRUS, the negotiation of an armistice to end the Arab–Israeli SIX-DAY WAR of 1967, and the admission of communist China to full UN and Security Council membership in 1971.

Thatcher, Margaret Hilda, Baroness (1925–   ) British Conservative Prime Minister (1979–90). Having replaced Edward HEATH as Leader of the Conservative Party in 1975, Thatcher became, after the general election of 1979, the first female Prime Minister in European history. During her first term of office (1979–83) the main thrust of government policy lay in tackling inflation and industrial and public sector inefficiency in Britain. A severe monetary policy was adopted while government control and intervention in industry was reduced. This was the signal for a general reduction in overmanning, and resulted in many bankruptcies and a reduction in manufacturing, made worse by an over-valued pound and high interest rates. A corollary to this policy was the determination to curb public spending, which led to increasing friction between central and local governments, and the curbing of trade-union power. Unemployment rose to levels not seen since the Great Depression, but the FALKLANDS (MALVINAS) WAR produced a mood of national pride that helped to secure a landslide victory for the Conservatives in the 1983 election. During the second term (1983–87) Nigel Lawson as Chancellor of the Exchequer adopted a less rigid economic policy. Inflation was brought under control, helped by lower commodity prices, while a lower pound benefited manufacturing industry. Legislation to limit the power of trade unions was challenged by the National Union of Mineworkers (1984–85); the miner's strike was broken after co-ordinated police action and a number of violent incidents. Lower direct taxation and a wide-ranging programme of public-asset sales, including council housing, helped to extend house ownership and share ownership as well as to reduce public borrowing. In spite of IRISH REPUBLICAN ARMY activity, including an attempt to blow up the cabinet at the 1984 Conservative Party Conference, the Hillsborough Agreement was signed (1985) with the Republic of IRELAND. In 1987 the Conservatives were returned for a third term with a majority of 101, making Margaret Thatcher the first party leader to face three consecutive new parliaments as Prime Minister. Her third administration introduced reforms in education, the legal profession, and the National Health Service. All met strong professional opposition, while the introduction of the Community Charge, or POLL TAX, provoked widespread protest and riots. Her unwillingness to share decision-taking with cabinet colleagues, together with firm rejection of many aspects of European Community policy, led to a challenge to her leadership. She resigned in November 1990 and a three-way struggle for succession was won by John MAJOR. She was made a Baroness in 1992.

Thebes (Egypt) The capital of ancient Egypt in the New Kingdom (c. 1550–1050 BC), on the site of modern Luxor. On the eastern side of the Nile its remains are divided between KARNAK and Luxor. A sphinx-lined road linked Karnak to Luxor, where Amenhotep III built a magnificent temple to Amun. On the western side lie the two royal necropolises – the VALLEY OF THE KINGS and the Valley of the Queens – and various mortuary temples of which the finest may have been that of Amenhotep III (ruled c. 1411–1372 BC). Of the actual temple building only the foundations remain, but also extant are the two 'colossi of Memnon' that represent the pharaoh.

Thebes (Greece) The most important city in BOEOTIA in ancient Greece. From *c.* 519 BC onwards it was a great rival of Athens, which in that year came to the aid of PLATAEA. Thebans fought alongside the Persians in the GREEK–PERSIAN WARS, temporarily lost influence as a consequence, and fought in alliance with the Spartans throughout the PELOPONNESIAN WAR. The peace of 404 did not satisfy Thebes, however, and in the Corinthian War (395–386) it was allied with Athens, Corinth, and Argos against Sparta. From 382 to 378 the Theban citadel was garrisoned by the Spartans, but in 371 Theban troops routed the apparently invincible army of Sparta at Leuctra, thanks to the generalship of Epaminondas (*c.* 418–362 BC). He it was who, together with Pelopidas, guided Thebes to its brief period of supremacy in Greece. However, he died while leading Thebes to a second great victory over Sparta, at Mantinea in 362. Thebans fought alongside the Athenians at CHAERONEA, but to no avail. When Thebes revolted against ALEXANDER THE GREAT, it was destroyed and was never again a power in Greece.

thegn THANE.

Themistocles (*c.* 528–462 BC) Athenian statesman and general. Themistocles survived several attempts at OSTRACISM in the 480s and 470s. He made Athens' naval greatness possible when in 483 he persuaded his fellow citizens to spend the city's wealth on the construction of a fleet of TRIREMES. As one of Athens' generals in 480 BC, he was responsible for inducing the Persians to fight in the confined waters near SALAMIS and it was his skill that ensured the rebuilding of Athens' walls against Spartan wishes in 479–478 BC. He championed anti-Spartan policies and was ostracized in about 471. He fled to Argos and later to Asia Minor, where he was appointed governor of Magnesia-ad-Maeandrum by the Persian king, Artaxerxes I, the son of XERXES.

theocracy A society governed by priests, or one whose government is heavily influenced by religious leaders. Originally it meant a system where divine law was the basis of all humanly enacted law and in which religious and political hierarchies were merged, as in Tibet until Chinese occupation in 1951. There are no theocracies in this strict sense in the modern world, but the term is applied where governments are forced to comply with the edicts of religious authorities, especially over moral issues. The clearest example of a theocracy in this broader sense is IRAN since the fall of the Shah in 1979. See also RELIGION AND POLITICS; SUDAN; TALIBAN.)

Theodora (*c.* 500–548) Byzantine empress. She was probably the most influential woman in the history of the Byzantine empire. Of humble birth, she married JUSTINIAN I, whom she dominated. A woman of courage, she made him stand against rioters anxious to overthrow him. Her influence in affairs of state was decisive and she was merciless in her use of torture and secret police.

Theodoric I (418–51 AD) King of the VISIGOTHS. He was defeated by the Romans at Toulouse in 439 after 15 years warfare. He joined Aetius as an ally against ATTILA but was killed on the CATALAUNIAN FIELDS. His son Theodoric II ruled the Visigothic kingdom of Spain and parts of Gaul until 466.

Theodoric the Great (*c.* 455–526) King of the Ostrogoths (475–526) and ruler of Italy from 493. He invaded Italy and established his capital at Ravenna. At its greatest extent his empire included not only the Italian mainland but Sicily, Dalmatia, and parts of Germany. An ARIAN Christian, his reign brought a degree of authority and stability to the country, though the scholar BOETHIUS was executed on treason charges. His reign saw the beginning of a synthesis of Roman and Germanic cultures. He is a hero of German literature, figuring in the epic *Nibelungenlied*.

Theodosius, Flavius (the Great) (349–95 AD) Roman emperor in the East (379–94) and emperor (394–95). The son of a famous general, Count Theodosius, Gratian appointed him co-emperor in 378. After failing to defeat the GOTHS he formed a treaty with them in 382. He was a champion of strict political and religious orthodoxy. His two sons, Arcadius and Honorius, succeeded him.

Thermopylae A narrow pass on the Malian Gulf that once controlled entry to central Greece from the north-east. In 480 BC it was the scene of a famous defensive action by the Greeks against the invading Persians. The greatly outnumbered Greeks, led by the Spartan king LEONIDAS, resisted a number of frontal assaults, but a traitor, Ephialtes, led the Persians via a mountain track round to attack their rear. Most of the Greeks were sent away, but Leonidas remained with a rearguard. He was killed along with 300 Spartans and 700 men from Thespiae; he has been revered since as a Greek hero. The accompanying Thebans surrendered.

The pass was again outflanked by the Gauls in 279 BC and, in 191 BC, by the Romans under CATO the Elder, who defeated the forces of the SELEUCID empire there.

Thessaly A region of central Greece. It was famous in the ancient Greek world for its horsemen, but was isolated from BOEOTIA and the rest of Greece. The Thessalians conquered the area in the 12th century BC and by the 6th century were a power of some importance. They fought alongside the Persians in the GREEK–PERSIAN WARS, but played little part in the PELOPONNESIAN WAR despite being allied to Athens. Their disunity prevented them from putting up effective resistance to PHILIP II of Macedonia. Rome later allowed the formation of a Thessalian League, which was incorporated into the province of Macedonia in 148 BC. Diocletian created the Roman province of Thessaly *c.* 300 AD and it was later part of the Byzantine empire. After suffering the depredations of successive invaders, it entered Turkish rule in 1393. It finally became part of Greece in 1881.

Thiers, Louis Adolphe (1797–1877) French statesman and historian. In the FRANCO-PRUSSIAN WAR his diplomatic skill helped in the negotiations with BISMARCK that resulted in the Treaty of FRANKFURT. He ordered the ruthless destruction of the Commune of PARIS (1871). He was elected President of the Third Republic in 1871, for, although a monarchist, he believed that national unity demanded a republic. In 1873 he was overthrown by right-wing deputies.

Thing A regular meeting or parliament in Norse communities, comprising nobles, priests, and heads of families, to establish or interpret law and to administer justice. The most famous example is the Icelandic Althing, founded in 930; it survived throughout the long period during which the island was under the Norwegian crown.

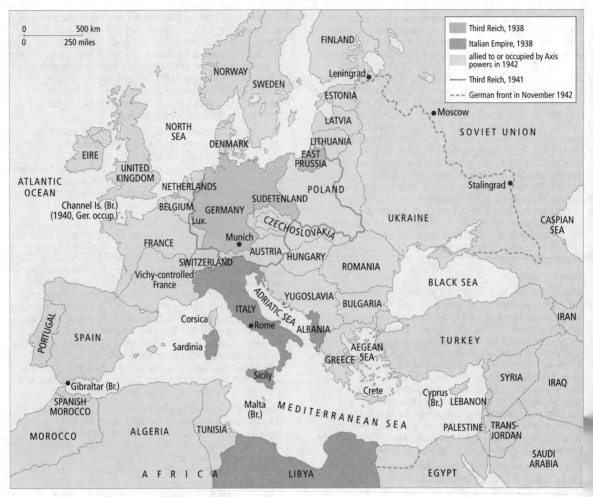

Third Reich *Hitler's control over Europe was at its peak in 1941, but the invasion of the Soviet Union proved disastrous. From December 1942 Nazi Germany was steadily weakened; it lost control of vital oil supplies to the east and was deprived of its industries by Allied saturation bombing.*

Third Reich (1933–45) The period of the NAZI regime in Germany. Adolf HITLER accepted the Chancellorship of Germany in January 1933, after a period of political and economic chaos and assumed the Presidency and sole executive power on the death of HINDENBURG in 1934. He almost immediately engineered the dissolution of the REICHSTAG after a fire, which was blamed on the communists. This led to the Enabling Act, which gave the government dictatorial powers. The Third Reich proved to be one of the most radical reversals of democracy in European history. Germany became a national rather than a federal state, non-Aryans and opponents of Nazism were removed from the administration and the judicial system became subservient to the Nazi regime with secret trials that encompassed a wide definition of treason and meted out summary executions. CONCENTRATION CAMPS were set up to detain political prisoners. All other political parties were liquidated and the National Socialists declared the only party. ANTI-SEMITISM was formalized by the Nuremberg

Laws. Both Protestant and Catholic Churches were attacked. The HITLER YOUTH movement was formed to indoctrinate the young. Most industrial workers were won over by the rapid end to unemployment through rearmament and other public spending. Much of industry was brought under government control, while the small farmer found himself tied more securely to the land. A four-year plan of 1936 set out to attain self-sufficiency in the event of war. Hitler reintroduced compulsory military service in 1935, following the return of the SAAR RIVER Basin by the League of Nations. Having withdrawn from the disarmament conference, Hitler broke the LOCARNO TREATIES by re-occupying the Rhineland; he annexed Austria (ANSCHLUSS) and the SUDETENLAND in Czechoslovakia and sought to break up any system of alliance within Eastern Europe. During the spring and summer of 1939 he made a political and military alliance with MUSSOLINI's Italy and brought the old dispute over the POLISH CORRIDOR to a head, arranging a NAZI–SOVIET PACT with the Soviet Union. On 1

September 1939 he invaded Poland without a declaration of war and Britain and France declared WORLD WAR II. German military occupation of most of continental Europe followed rapidly, until by 1941 Nazi-controlled territory stretched from the Arctic Circle and the English Channel to North Africa and Russia. Britain remained its sole adversary from June 1940 to June 1941, when Hitler invaded the Soviet Union. Total mobilization was introduced early in 1942 and armaments production was increased despite heavy air attacks on industrial and civilian targets. Under Himmler, the SS assumed supreme power. After 1943, the German armies fought a rearguard action and by May 1945 the Third Reich lay in ruins.

Third World The DEVELOPING COUNTRIES of the world. The Third World includes most of Africa (excluding South Africa), Asia (except Japan and parts of South-East Asia), and Latin America. The term is French (*le Tiers monde*) and was originally employed in a UN classification system to distinguish between the developed capitalist countries (First World), the developed communist countries (Second World), and the remaining underdeveloped countries (Third World). The Third World emerged as a distinct entity in international politics following the process known as decolonization, which brought independence to a large group of African and Asian countries in the 1950s and 1960s. Their shared historical experience of IMPERIALISM and common problems, such as poverty and under-development, together with those of Latin America, led them to act as a bloc in international forums, particularly the UN. The Third World advocated NON-ALIGNMENT in East–West relations and formulated a set of demands to reform the existing international economic system known as the NEW INTERNATIONAL ECONOMIC ORDER (NIEO). Like the term developing country or simply the 'South', with which it is used interchangeably, the Third World is in many ways an imprecise and unsatisfactory definition, largely because it encompasses an enormous variety of countries with very different economic, social, and political conditions. It also has a pejorative connotation. However, despite efforts to redefine the term and introduce new categories such as less developed, middle income, and NEWLY INDUSTRIALIZING COUNTRY (NIC), its use is still widespread.

Thirteen Colonies The British colonies in North America that ratified the DECLARATION OF INDEPENDENCE (1776) and thereby became founding states of the USA. They were, with dates of foundation or English colonial status: VIRGINIA (1607), MASSACHUSETTS (1629), MARYLAND (1632), CONNECTICUT (1635), RHODE ISLAND (1636), NORTH CAROLINA (1663), SOUTH CAROLINA (1663), NEW YORK (1664), NEW JERSEY (1664), DELAWARE (1664), NEW HAMPSHIRE (1679), PENNSYLVANIA (1681), and GEORGIA (1732). By 1776 all were ruled by royal governors except Maryland, Pennsylvania, Delaware, Connecticut, and Rhode Island, and all had representative assemblies. Though there were major differences over such issues as slavery or religion and often quarrels between neighbouring colonies, they managed to sustain a fragile unity between 1776 and 1783. This improbable cohesion could be described as the greatest unsought achievement of GEORGE III and his ministers, who, in FRANKLIN's words, 'made thirteen clocks strike as one'.

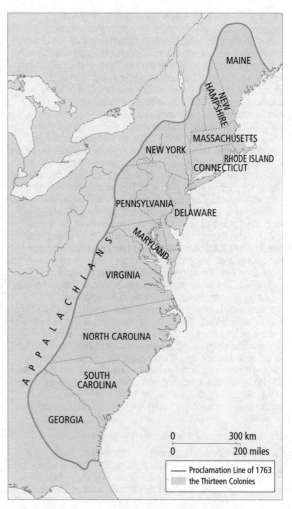

Thirteen Colonies   *The Thirteen British colonies in North America, strung out along the eastern seaboard from Maine to Georgia, had even fewer ties to one another than to the mother country. However, they did share certain underlying interests, one of which was the potential and desire for westward expansion. The Royal Proclamation of 1763, which forbade settlement beyond the Appalachians, was therefore widely resented, particularly since it came at a time when economic recession made the land beyond the frontier especially attractive. The Proclamation was issued as an emergency measure designed to protect Native American lands, but it was widely ignored by the settlers.*

Thirty-Nine Articles The set of doctrinal formulae first issued in 1563 and finally adopted by the ANGLICAN CHURCH in 1571 as a statement of its position. Many of the articles allow a wide variety of interpretation. They had their origin in several previous definitions, required by the shifts and turns of the English Reformation. The Ten Articles (1536) and Six Articles (1539) upheld religious conservatism, but the Forty-Two Articles (1553), prepared by CRANMER and Nicholas Ridley (*c.* 1500–55), were of markedly Protestant character and provided the basis of the Thirty-Nine Articles.

Thirty Years War (1618–48) A series of conflicts, fought mainly in Germany, in which Protestant–Catholic rivalries and German constitutional issues were gradually subsumed in a European struggle. The Thirty Years War began in 1618 with the Protestant Bohemian revolt against the future emperor FERDINAND II, it embraced the last phase of the DUTCH REVOLTS after 1621, and was concentrated in a Franco-Habsburg confrontation in the years after 1635.

By 1623 Ferdinand had emerged victorious in the Bohemian revolt and with Spanish and Bavarian help had conquered the PALATINATE of FREDERICK V. His German ambitions and his Spanish alliance aroused the apprehensions of Europe's Protestant nations and also of France. In 1625 Christian IV of Denmark renewed the war against the Catholic imperialists, as the leader of an anti-Habsburg coalition organized by the Dutch. After suffering a series of defeats at the hands of TILLY and WALLENSTEIN, Denmark withdrew from the struggle at the Treaty of Lübeck (1629) and the emperor reached the summit of his power.

Sweden's entry into the war under GUSTAVUS I (Adolphus) led to imperial reversals. After Gustavus was killed at LÜTZEN (1632), the Swedish Chancellor OXENSTIERNA financed the Heilbronn League of German Protestants (1633), which broke up after a heavy military defeat at Nördlingen in 1634. In 1635 the Treaty of Prague ended the civil war within Germany, but in the same year France, in alliance with Sweden and the United Provinces, went to war with the Habsburgs. Most of the issues were settled after five years of negotiation at the Treaty of WESTPHALIA in 1648, but the Franco-Spanish war continued until the Treaty of the Pyrenees in 1659.

Thistlewood, Arthur CATO STREET CONSPIRACY.

Thomas of Woodstock (1355–97) Earl of Buckingham and Duke of Gloucester, the youngest son of EDWARD III of England. From 1384 he was generally at odds with his nephew RICHARD II and in 1387–88 was one of the five LORDS APPELLANT who attacked Richard's leading counsellors; for some months afterwards Thomas was the most powerful man in England. In 1397 Richard was able to have him arrested, tried for treason, and executed.

Thorez, Maurice (1900–64) French politician. Thorez helped to form the French Communist Party, of which he became General Secretary in 1930. His party supported but never joined the Popular Front Coalition government (1936), which enacted important social and labour reforms. Conscripted in World War II, he deserted and went to Moscow. Sentenced *in absentia*, he was pardoned (1944) and re-elected as a Deputy. He led the Communist Party in the elections of 1945 and 1946 and became Vice-Premier (1946–47). By the late 1950s his authority was reduced by his Stalinist associations and his support of the Soviet invasion of Hungary.

Thrace An area in the Balkans lying between the Black Sea and ancient Macedonia. It was inhabited by various Indo-European tribes. The Thracian tribes had been conquered by the Persians by about 516 BC, on whose side some of them fought in the GREEK–PERSIAN WARS. Later in the 5th century Teres, King of the Odrysae, extended his rule over a number of the tribes, and his son Sitalces allied himself with Athens against

Macedonia. In the following century PHILIP II annexed the area to Macedonia. Following Macedonia's final defeat by Rome in 168 BC, western Thrace was incorporated into the province of Macedonia. The next two centuries saw regular outbreaks of trouble between the Thracians and Rome. It suffered greatly from invasion by Visigoths and Slavs. It is now partitioned between Turkey, Greece, and Bulgaria.

Three Emperors' League (German, *Dreikaiserbund*) An alliance between Prussia, Austria, and Russia. In 1872, following the creation of the new GERMAN SECOND EMPIRE, BISMARCK persuaded the emperors of Austria and Russia to join an unofficial alliance. It was strained by the Treaty of San Stefano (1878) which, in conclusion of the RUSSO-TURKISH WARS, assigned Russia the eastern part of ARMENIA and created a large state of BULGARIA. In June 1881, following the assassination of ALEXANDER II, the league was revived as a more formal alliance. Renewed in 1884, it finally expired three years later, as tension between Russia and Austria-Hungary mounted in the BALKAN STATES.

'Three Fs' The nickname given to the second Irish Land Act (1881) introduced by the GLADSTONE government. The 'Three Fs' were fair rents (to be settled by a tribunal), freedom to sell improvements (involving compensation for improvements tenants had made to a building), and fixity of tenure (so long as rents were paid). The Act failed to win the support of Charles PARNELL and his followers.

Three Henrys, War of the (March 1585–August 1589) The eighth of the FRENCH WARS OF RELIGION. It was precipitated by the efforts of Duke Henry of GUISE to exclude the Huguenot Henry of Navarre from the succession to the French throne. Guise, backed by Spain and the Catholic League (HOLY LEAGUE), forced Henry III to capitulate in the Treaty of Nemours (1585) and to accept the Catholic Cardinal de Bourbon as his heir instead of Henry of Navarre. In the ensuing conflict, Henry III lost control of events and Guise acted as if he were king himself. In late 1588, Henry III had both Guise and the Cardinal de Bourbon murdered. When Henry III was murdered in turn (1589), most of France was in League or Huguenot hands, and Henry of Navarre became king as HENRY IV.

Three Kingdoms (220–280 AD) The period in China immediately following the end of the HAN dynasty. Three kingdoms, the Wei in the north, the Wu in the south-east, and the Shu Han in the west, rose and constantly fought each other for supremacy. The period ended when the Wei general Sima Yen seized power and unified China under the WESTERN JIN dynasty. Many events and legends of this period appear in one of the classics of Chinese literature, *The Romance of the Three Kingdoms*.

Three-Mile Island An island in the Susquehanna River in Pennsylvania, USA, the site of a potential nuclear disaster in March 1979. One of the pumps that circulated water through the steam generators connected to the pressurized-water reactor of the nuclear-power station on the island broke down. Emergency lines then failed to supply extra coolant water and a pressure relief valve stuck open, leading to a loss of water coolant from around the reactor core. The core reached a temperature of over 2,000 °C and underwent partial melt-down. Although many people in the area were evacuated, an official investigation found the levels of radiation in the vicinity (in milk, for example) to be little changed. However, the reactor was damaged beyond repair, and the incident showed that despite elaborate safety precautions, a nuclear accident could still occur. (See also CHERNOBYL.)

Throckmorton Plot (1583) An international Catholic conspiracy, in the manner of the RIDOLFI and BABINGTON plots, to place MARY, QUEEN OF SCOTS on the English throne. Francis Throckmorton (1554–84), a member of a leading English RECUSANT family, helped to contrive the plan. Henry of GUISE would invade England with a French Catholic force, financed by Spain and the PAPACY, then the English Catholics would depose ELIZABETH I in favour of Mary. In late 1583 WALSINGHAM's agents uncovered the plan. Reprisals were moderate, but Throckmorton was tried and executed.

Thucydides (c. 460–c.400 BC) Greek historian. Thucydides wrote an unfinished history of the PELOPONNESIAN WAR (431–404) in eight books, having realized that it was to have a greater importance in the history of Greece than any previous war. The history breaks off in the year 411. In 424 he was a naval commander in the northern Aegean, but failed to save Amphipolis from capture by the Spartan Brasidas, for which he was exiled. He did not return home until the end of the war.

Thucydides referred to his work as a 'possession for all time' and he is recognized as one of the greatest exponents of history writing. He clearly took great care to discover the precise truth of the events about which he wrote. His accounts of the PLAGUE that afflicted Athens, the civil strife at Corcyra (Corfu), the conquest of Melos, and the ill-fated Athenian expedition to Sicily are outstanding examples of his skill. His brilliant but difficult style is well suited to the narration of great events. It has a poetic flavour apparent in the use of slightly old-fashioned forms of words and the use of unnatural word order for emphasis, although his description of actual events is clear and simple.

thug (Hindi, *thag*, 'swindler') A devotee of the Hindu goddess Kali, who was worshipped through ritual murder and sacrifice of travellers. The thuggee centre was in remote central India, where victims were strangled. Eradication of the brotherhoods was difficult because of the secrecy of the cult. It was largely suppressed in the 1830s by the detective skills of William Sleeman, appointed to the task by Lord William BENTINCK. Indians welcomed the intervention and there has been no revival, but the term passed into the English language.

Thutmose I (or Tuthmosis I) Pharaoh of Egypt (c. 1525–1512 BC). He extended his domains deep into Nubia and later penetrated with his army as far as the River Euphrates. He made extensive improvements to the temple of Amun at KARNAK and was the first pharaoh to be buried in the VALLEY OF THE KINGS.

Thutmose III (or Tuthmosis III) Pharaoh of Egypt (c. 1504–1450 BC). During the first 22 years of his reign Thutmose III was overshadowed by his aunt HATSHEPSUT, wife of Thutmose II, who had herself declared regent in 1503. When she died in 1482, he promptly mobilized the army and defeated a coalition of Syrian and Palestinian

enemies near Megiddo, gaining nearly all of Syria for his empire. Further successes followed, culminating in the defeat of the powerful Mitanni beyond the Euphrates. He extended Egyptian rule in Nubia, but generally he concentrated on the administration of his lands. The thriving prosperity of his reign was reflected in much new building at KARNAK.

Tiahuanaco A vast ceremonial site and city near Lake Titicaca in Bolivia, centre of the culture and art style of the same name, which thrived between c. 600 AD and 1000. As a religious centre it fostered the cult of the 'staff god', represented by carvings on a massive, monolithic lava-stone gateway. He has a halo of puma heads and holds two staves tipped with eagles' heads. Similar birds and feline figures were painted on pottery, which has been found as far south as the Atacama Desert in Chile.

Tianjin, Treaty of (1858) OPIUM WARS.

Tiberius, Claudius Nero (42 BC–7 AD) Roman emperor (17–37 AD). Tiberius pursued a brilliant military career in Germany and Pannonia. He was Augustus' stepson, son-in-law, and adoptive son. From 6 BC–2 AD he lived in virtual exile on Rhodes, while Augustus' own grandsons were promoted. After their deaths, Augustus was obliged to acknowledge Tiberius as the only possible successor. Succeeding as emperor in 14 AD he applied stringent economies and had the makings of a good emperor but his reign was marred by an increasing number of treason trials. JESUS CHRIST was crucified during his reign. He became a recluse, paranoid about conspiracy, ordering numerous executions and disliking Rome intensely. Finally he was persuaded by Sejanus, the Prefect of the PRAETORIAN Guard, to leave the city in 26 to live on Capri. His death during a rare excursion to the mainland was rumoured to have been murder.

Tibet (Chinese, Xizang) A mountainous region on the northern frontier of India, an autonomous region of China. Traditionally, Tibetans were primarily agriculturalists, many of whom were tenant farmers, although some nomadic and semi-nomadic groups of yak-herders also existed.

History. Tibet was largely independent from China until the QING dynasty. It was first unified in 607 and by the 8th century a large empire had been established stretching from Lanzhou in China to Kashgar in Central Asia and south to the site of modern Calcutta in India. For a time it was a serious rival to the TANG empire. KUBLAI KHAN conquered eastern Tibet and gave LAMAISM (which controlled every aspect of life) his approval. In the 16th and 17th centuries Mongolia converted to Lamaism and China intrigued over the Dalai Lama's succession. The Qing conducted several Tibetan campaigns and in 1720 established a protectorate, incorporating Tibet into the Chinese empire. The Dalai Lama retained a position of temporal and spiritual authority within Tibet. By the late 19th century Tibet had become virtually independent under the Buddhist leadership of the DALAI LAMA. Fears of Russian influence led to a British invasion in 1904 and the negotiation of an Anglo-Tibetan trade treaty. Tibet became autonomous under British control when the Chinese empire collapsed in 1911 and remained so until Chinese troops returned in 1950, completely occupying the country a year later. After a rebellion in 1959 the present Dalai Lama (1935–) and thousands of his subjects fled. Tibet was administered as a Chinese province until 1965, when it was reconstituted as an autonomous region within the People's Republic. A further revolt was suppressed in 1987 and martial law was imposed by the Chinese authorities in 1989. Serious civil unrest broke out again in 1993 and has continued. The Dalai Lama's calls for negotiations with China over a limited degree of autonomy for Tibet went unheeded by the Beijing regime.

ticket-of-leave In Australia, a certificate that could be granted to a convict during the period of CONVICT TRANSPORTATION. It allowed a convict to be excused from compulsory labour, to choose his or her own employer, and to work for wages. There were some restrictions and the ticket-of-leave could be withdrawn. It usually was granted for good conduct.

Ticonderoga A frontier fortress in New York, USA, commanding the Champlain-Hudson valley between Lake Champlain and Lake George. Built by the French as Fort Carillon in 1755, it held out against British attack in 1758, but the next year fell to AMHERST, who renamed it. In the War of Independence it was surprised by Benedict ARNOLD and Ethan ALLEN in 1775, recaptured by BURGOYNE in 1777, but recovered by the Americans after Saratoga (1777).

Tilak, Bel Gangadhar (1856–1920) Indian scholar and politician. Known as *Lokamanya* (revered by the people), he owned and edited *Kesari* (Lion), a weekly Marathi nationalist paper. He was imprisoned for sedition by the British (1897). Released in 1899, he continued to advocate radical policies within CONGRESS, playing an important role in the radical/moderate split of 1907. In 1914 with Annie BESANT he formed the Indian Home Rule League, but subsequently advocated more moderate, co-operative policies with Muslims in the Lucknow Pact (1916), which recognized separate electorates for Muslim minorities.

Tillett, Benjamin (1860–1943) British trade unionist and politician. His powers as a speaker made him influential in the LONDON DOCKERS' STRIKE (1889), when he succeeded in gaining an assurance for a minimum wage of sixpence an hour and eightpence for overtime. He concentrated on union activities, organizing another dock strike in 1911. A critic of the weakness of the LABOUR PARTY in its early days, he was a Labour Member of Parliament (1917–24, 1929–31).

Tilley, Sir Samuel Leonard (1818–96) New Brunswick and Canadian statesman. He was an important advocate at the Westminster Conference, which drafted the provisions of the BRITISH NORTH AMERICA ACT (1867). He served in John A. MACDONALD's cabinet from 1867 to 1873. On Macdonald's return to office in 1878 he was appointed Minister of Finance. He formulated the protective tariff plan known as the National Policy of Canada.

Tilly, Johannes Tserklaes, Count of (1559–1632) Flemish soldier. Tilly served under FARNESE in the Netherlands and then in the army of Emperor Rudolf II against the OTTOMAN Turks (1594). In 1610 Duke Maximilian of Bavaria appointed him to create an army, which became the spearhead of the Catholic League during the THIRTY YEARS WAR. He was victorious at the Battle of the White Mountain (1620) and went on to

dominate north-western Germany. He crushed the Danes at Lutter (1626) and, on WALLENSTEIN's dismissal, took command of imperial as well as League troops. His brutal destruction of the Protestant city of Magdeburg (1631) blackened his reputation. He was routed by GUSTAVUS II (Adolphus) at Breitenfeld (1631) and killed.

Tilsit, Treaties of (7 and 9 July 1807) Agreements between Russia and France, and Prussia and France. Napoleon I, having won the Battle of Friedland, agreed to meet ALEXANDER I on a raft on the River Niemen near the East Prussian town of Tilsit, now Sovetsk in Russia. Their negotiations, joined by FREDERICK WILLIAM III of Prussia, led to the two treaties. Prussia lost over a third of its possessions, had to pay heavy indemnities to France, and was forced to support a large French army on its soil. The Polish lands annexed by Prussia under the partitions were turned into a French puppet state, the Grand Duchy of Warsaw. Russia recognized the CONFEDERATION OF THE RHINE and was forced to join the CONTINENTAL SYSTEM. Prussia rescinded its treaty in 1813 when it deserted the French, following the latter's invasion of Russia and joined the Russian emperor in a campaign against Napoleon in Germany.

Timbuktu A city in Mali, on the middle River Niger, founded in 1106, according to a 17th-century Arabic source, as a staging post for the then flourishing trans-Saharan trade in gold, ivory, and slaves (which were exchanged for salt, cloth, and pottery from the north). It became one of the main cities of the empire of MALI and was later a cultural centre of the SONGHAY empire, with a university, mosques, and over a hundred schools. Thereafter it declined, being sacked by Moroccan invaders in 1591 and by Tuaregs and others repeatedly afterwards. In the 18th century it was absorbed into the Bambara empire of Segu; it remained famous and several European explorers tried to reach it. Alexander Laing (1793–1826), the first of them to do so, was murdered there.

Timor South-east Asian island. The eastern part of Timor was first colonized by the Portuguese in the 16th century and the western part by the Dutch in the 17th and the island remained divided between the two powers until after World War II (except during the Japanese occupation of 1942–45). Dutch Timor became part of Indonesia in 1949, but Portuguese EAST TIMOR remained an overseas province of Portugal until 1975, when the leftist Fretilin movement proclaimed independence after a brief civil war. Shortly afterwards Indonesian troops invaded. After heavy fighting East Timor was formally integrated into Indonesia in 1976, but this annexation is not recognized by the UN. Sporadic guerrilla resistance has continued, although campaigners for Timorese independence have been violently suppressed.

Timur TAMERLANE.

Tippecanoe, Battle of (7 November 1811) A conflict between US forces and Shawnee people, fought near the Wabash River 240 km (150 miles) north of Vincennes. Governor HARRISON of the Indiana Territory engineered a conflict with the British-supported Native American confederacy of the Shawnee chiefs TECUMSEH and his brother the Prophet Tenskwatawa in order to end Native American resistance to westward US expansion. In the resulting skirmish, Harrison sustained considerable losses but drove away the Native Americans. Tippecanoe was hailed as a major victory, but the British and Native American threat to the north-west frontier was not destroyed until Tecumseh fell in the Battle of the THAMES two years later.

Tipu Sultan (*c.* 1753–99) Sultan of MYSORE (1782–99). He inherited the kingdom recently created by his father, HYDER ALI and was a formidable enemy to both the British and neighbouring Indian states. Failure to secure active French support left him without allies in resisting the British. He was finally besieged in his own capital, Seringapatam, when unfounded rumours that he had secured an alliance with Revolutionary France gave the British the necessary pretext for a final assault. He was killed in the attack.

Tirpitz, Alfred von (1849–1930) German grand-admiral. As Secretary of State for the Navy (1897–1916) his first Navy Bill in 1898 began the expansion of the German navy and led to the naval race with Britain. In 1907 he began a large programme of DREADNOUGHT-class battleship construction. During World War I he made full use of submarines, but following the sinking of the *lusitania* (1915), unrestricted submarine warfare was temporarily abandoned. The policy was resumed in 1917, resulting in US entry into the war.

tithe (Old English, 'tenth') A payment made by parishioners for the maintenance of the church and the support of its clergy. Levied by the early Hebrews and common in Europe after the synods of Tours (567) and Mâcon (585), tithes were enforced by law in England from the 10th century. They were divided into three categories, praedial (one-tenth of the produce of the soil), personal (one-tenth of the profits of labour and industry), and mixed (a combination of the produce of animals and labour). Attempts to abolish them in England were made in 1653 by the BAREBONES PARLIAMENT, but they were not abolished in England until 1936.

Tito (born Josip Broz) (1892–1980) Yugoslav statesman of Croatian origin. He was Prime Minister (1945–53) and President (1953–80) of Yugoslavia. During World War I he served with the Austro-Hungarian infantry and was taken prisoner in Russia. He escaped and fought for the RUSSIAN REVOLUTION. After returning to Yugoslavia he became involved in the Communist Party and was imprisoned for six years. After the German invasion of Yugoslavia (1941), Tito organized partisan guerrilla forces into a National Liberation Front. Tito emerged as the leader of the new federal government. He rejected STALIN's attempt to control the communist-governed states of eastern Europe. As a result Yugoslavia was expelled from the COMINFORM and Tito became a leading exponent of NON-ALIGNMENT in the COLD WAR. Normal relations were resumed with the Soviet Union in 1955, although Tito retained his independence, experimenting with different communist styles of economic organization, including worker-participation in the management of factories. On his death the office of President of Yugoslavia was to rotate between the six republics, but by 1989 this system was in disarray as the country began to disintegrate.

Toba Wei NORTHERN WEI.

Tobruk, Siege of (1941–42) German siege of British and Commonwealth troops in Tobruk in North Africa in World War II. When General WAVELL's army captured

Tobruk in January 1941 some 25,000 Italian troops were taken prisoner. The Afrika Korps of General ROMMEL then arrived (April 1941) and the British withdrew east, leaving a largely Australian garrison to defend Tobruk, which was subjected to an eight-month siege and bombardment. In November 1941, after being reinforced by sea, the garrison broke out, capturing Rezegh and linking up with the 8th Army troops of General AUCHINLECK. But the Germans counter-attacked and in June 1942, after heavy defeats, the British again withdrew leaving a garrison of two divisions, mostly South African and Australian, in Tobruk, which was then subjected to massed attack by German and Italian troops. On 20 June it capitulated, the garrison of 23,000 men surrendering, with vast quantities of stores. It was a major Allied defeat, but Tobruk was recaptured on 13 November 1942 by the troops of General MONTGOMERY.

Tocqueville, Alexis, Comte de (1805–59) French statesman and political analyst. Sent to the USA in 1831 to study its penal system, de Tocqueville carried out a systematic survey of US political and social institutions, publishing the results in *De la démocratie en Amerique* (1835 and 1840). The book immediately found a large readership and became one of the most influential political writings of the 19th century. It remains probably the greatest of all European commentaries on US politics and society.

Togliatti, Palmiro (1893–1964) Italian politician, Secretary of the Italian Communist Party (1926–64). After the fascist take-over Togliatti lived mainly in Moscow (1926–44) and became chief of the COMINTERN in Spain during the SPANISH CIVIL WAR. After World War II he made the Italian Communist Party the largest in Western Europe. Togliatti was undogmatic in his communism: he recognized Roman Catholicism as the state religion of Italy and propounded the doctrine of 'polycentrism', which advocates the existence of several ideologies within a political system. The Russian city of Stavropol on the Volga was renamed Togliatti in his honour in 1964.

Togo A West African country lying between Ghana and Benin.

Physical. Togo has a small southern coastline on the Gulf of Guinea but extends inland as far as Burkina Faso. The tropical coast has sand-bars and lagoons, and inland there is a fertile clay plain. Northward the land rises to low mountains and a rolling sandstone plateau, where it is drier and cooler.

Economy. Drought and falling world commodity prices have affected the economy adversely and loss of income has been exacerbated by a high foreign debt. Agricultural crops for export include cocoa, coffee, and cotton, and staple crops include cassava, maize, and sorghum. Livestock-raising is also of importance. Mining includes phosphates (the principal export), salt, and marble, while industry concentrates on food-processing and cement production. There are also reserves of bauxite and iron ore.

History. Togo's earliest known inhabitants were Gur-speaking Voltaic peoples in the north and Kwa peoples in the south. The Ewé immigrated during the 14th–16th centuries and the Ane (Mina) entered the region in the 17th century. Part of Togo's slave coast was controlled by Denmark during the 18th century and the area formed a buffer zone between the Ashanti and DAHOMEY kingdoms. Annexed by Germany in 1884 as a colony, the area was called Togoland. It was MANDATED between France and Britain after World War I. The western British section joined GHANA on the latter's independence in 1957 and became known as the Volta region. The remainder of the area became a UN mandate under French administration after World War II and achieved independence as Togo in 1960. After two civilian regimes were overthrown in 1963 and 1967, Togo achieved stability under President Gnassingbe Eyadema, who in 1979 was elected executive President, as the sole candidate, and re-elected in 1986. Following violent demonstrations early in 1991, he agreed to legalize political parties. The situation, however, deteriorated, with troops loyal to Eyadema taking the Prime Minister hostage. There was some fighting during 1992 as plans were made for a new constitution and elections. In 1993 Eyadema won the country's first multiparty presidential elections. In the following year, the ruling and opposition parties formed a coalition government. Early in 1994, fighting around the capital, Lomé, left 58 people dead; Togo's relations with Ghana, which was blamed for harbouring insurgents, worsened as a result.

CAPITAL:	Lomé
AREA:	56,785 sq km (21,925 sq miles)
POPULATION:	4.269 million (1996)
CURRENCY:	1 CFA franc = 100 centimes
RELIGIONS:	Traditional beliefs 58.8%; Roman Catholic 21.5%; Muslim 12.0%; Protestant 6.8%
ETHNIC GROUPS:	Ewé-Adja 43.1%; Tem-Kabre 26.7%; Gurma 5.0%; Kebu-Akposo 3.8%; Ana-Ife (Yoruba) 3.2%; non-African 0.3%
LANGUAGES:	French (official); Ewé; Kabre; local languages
INTERNATIONAL ORGANIZATIONS:	UN; OAU; ECOWAS; Franc Zone

Tojo Hideki (1884–1948) Japanese general and statesman. He participated in the war against China in the 1930s, was leader of the militarist party from 1931 onwards, and became War Minister in 1940. He urged closer collaboration with Germany and Italy and persuaded VICHY France to sanction Japanese occupation of strategic bases in Indo-China (July 1941). He succeeded KONOE FUMIMARO as Prime Minister (1941–44) and he gave the order to attack PEARL HARBOR, precipitating the USA into World War II. In 1942 he strengthened his position in Tokyo as War Minister and created a virtual military dictatorship. He resigned in 1944 after the loss of the Marianas to the USA. He was convicted at the TOKYO TRIALS and hanged as a war criminal in 1948.

Tokugawa The last Japanese SHOGUNATE (1603–1867). TOKUGAWA IEYASU, its founder, ensured supremacy by imposing severe restrictions on the DAIMYO (territorial governors). To avoid the effects of European intrusion, Christianity was proscribed in 1641 after the suppression of the Christian SHIMABARA rebellion and all foreigners except a few Dutch and Chinese traders at Nagasaki were excluded. Japanese were forbidden to go overseas. Interest in European science and medicine increased during the rule of TOKUGAWA YOSHIMUNE.

There followed 250 years of almost unbroken peace and economic growth. The economy that had been based largely on barter became a money economy. An influential merchant class emerged whilst some daimyo and their SAMURAI were impoverished; some married into commercial families. The shogunate was faced with growing financial difficulties but under its rule educational standards improved dramatically.

Tokugawa Ieyasu (1542–1616) The founder of the TOKUGAWA shogunate. His base was Edo (now Tokyo). In 1600, at Sekigahara, he defeated DAIMYO loyal to HIDEYOSHI's son Hideyori. Appointed SHOGUN in 1603, he abdicated two years later, but still controlled affairs. In 1615 Hideyori and his retainers, after a hard siege, committed suicide in their moated castle in Osaka. Ieyasu then executed Hideyoshi's grandson, Kunimatsu. Hideyoshi's line was extinct, Ieyasu's power complete.

Tokugawa Yoshimune (1684–1751) Japanese SHOGUN, the eighth TOKUGAWA to hold that office (1716–45). He was extremely capable and, though conservative, was interested in science. In 1720 he allowed European books, hitherto excluded, to be imported by Dutch traders at Nagasaki. Religious books were still banned. He also had a Dutch–Japanese dictionary compiled. The introduction of *rangaku* (Dutch learning) had a profound effect on what had been a closed world. There was particular interest in medicine, cartography, and military science. Yoshimune worked to increase the shogun's authority and improve government finances.

Tokyo Trials The war crimes trials of Japanese leaders after World War II. Between May 1946 and November 1948, 27 Japanese leaders appeared before an international tribunal charged with crimes ranging from murder and atrocities to responsibility for causing the war. Seven, including the former Prime Minister TOJO, were sentenced to death and 16 to life imprisonment (two others receiving shorter terms), but General MACARTHUR refused to allow the trial of the Emperor HIROHITO for fear of undermining the post-war Japanese state.

Toleration Act (1689) The granting by the English Parliament of freedom of worship to dissenting Protestants, that is, those who could not accept the authority or teaching of the ANGLICAN CHURCH. Dissenters were allowed their own ministers, teachers, and places of worship subject to their taking oaths of allegiance and to their acceptance of most of the THIRTY-NINE ARTICLES. The TEST ACTS, which deprived dissenters of public office, remained but from 1727 annual indemnity acts allowed them to hold local offices. Roman Catholics were excluded from the scope of the Act and had to rely on failure to enforce the penal laws.

Tolpuddle Martyrs Six English farmworkers who were charged in 1834 with taking illegal oaths, while establishing a local trade union branch of the Friendly Society of Agricultural Labourers in the Dorset village of Tolpuddle with the aim of obtaining an increase in their wages (then seven shillings a week). The six were found guilty and condemned to seven years' transportation to Australia. The severity of the sentence provoked a storm of protest and mass demonstrations were held in London. After two years, in the face of continuing public hostility, the government was obliged to pardon the men.

Toltecs A northern Mexican tribe who established a military state between the 10th and 12th centuries at Tula, *c.* 80 km (*c.* 50 miles) north of modern Mexico City. They played an important part in the downfall of

TEOTIHUACÁN and were themselves overrun in the mid-12th century by nomadic Chichimec tribes from the north. One of their kings was Topiltzín-QUETZALCÓATL, a religious leader who in their legendary history was driven from Tula by a military faction and sailed east into the Gulf of Mexico, vowing to return one day.

Tone, (Theobald) Wolfe (1763–98) Irish nationalist, who played a leading part in the insurrection of 1798. He was born in Dublin of Protestant parents, studied law, and was called to the Bar in 1789. Inspired by the French Revolution, in 1791 he helped to found the Society of UNITED IRISHMEN, whose initial aim was to establish a democratic Ireland through parliamentary reform. In 1796 Tone sought military support from France to overthrow British rule and accompanied an abortive expedition to Ireland later that year. During the Irish rebellion of 1798 he enlisted further French aid but was captured by the British and committed suicide while under sentence of death.

Tonga (or the Friendly Islands) An island country bordering the Tonga Trench in the South Pacific Ocean.

Physical. Tonga comprises over 150 islands, most of them too small for habitation and even the largest, Tongatapu, measuring only 40 km (25 miles) by 16 km (10 miles). Some are coral and some volcanic, with active craters.

Economy. Oil has been discovered, the only other natural resource being a fertile soil, used for the cultivation of coconuts and bananas.

History. Austronesian-speaking peoples inhabited the islands from at least 1,000 BC. By the 13th century Tongans ruled islands as far-flung as Hawaii. Named the Friendly Islands by Captain James Cook, who visited them in 1773, the country was soon receiving missionaries. King George Tupou I (1845–93) unified the nation and gave it a constitution. In 1900 his son signed a treaty, making the islands a self-governing British protectorate. During World War II Queen Sālote Tupou III (1900–65) placed the island's resources at the disposal of the Allies; in 1968 British control was reduced and in 1970 Tonga became independent within the COMMONWEALTH OF NATIONS. Tonga's first political party was founded in 1994, with an agenda for democratic reform of the constitution.

CAPITAL:	Nuku'alofa
AREA:	749.9 sq km (289.5 sq miles)
POPULATION:	101,000 (1996)
CURRENCY:	1 pa'anga = 100 seniti
RELIGIONS:	Free Wesleyan 43%; Roman Catholic 16%; Mormon 12.1%; Free Church of Tonga 11%; Church of Tonga 7.3%; other 10.6%
ETHNIC GROUPS:	Tongan 95.5%
LANGUAGES:	Tongan, English (both official)
INTERNATIONAL ORGANIZATIONS:	Commonwealth

Tonkin Gulf Resolution (1964) A resolution by the US Congress, giving the President authority to take all necessary measures to repel any attack against the forces of the USA. The resolution was made in response to an alleged attack by North Vietnam patrol boats against the US destroyer *Maddox* in the Gulf of Tonkin. The US involvement in the fighting in the VIETNAM WAR followed. Subsequent investigation revealed that the intelligence information on which it was based was inaccurate and, following the war, the War Powers Act was passed in 1973. This restricts the time a President can commit US troops without Congressional approval to 60 days.

Tonypandy A former mining town in South Wales, which witnessed in 1910 a violent dispute over pay rates for miners. Miners interfered with pit machinery and there was looting and disorder in the town. The local police requested government help and the Home Secretary, Winston CHURCHILL, sent 300 extra police from London and placed military detachments on stand-by. In a subsequent incident in Llanelli a year later troops mobilized by Churchill opened fire on strikers, killing four. Trade union hostility to Churchill was intense.

Tooke, John Horne (1736–1812) British radical politician and philologist. In 1769 Tooke founded the Society of Supporters of the BILL OF RIGHTS, which was largely designed to pay John WILKES's debts and get him into Parliament. In 1771 he founded the Constitutional Society to agitate for British parliamentary reform and self-government for the American colonists. After the Battle of LEXINGTON AND CONCORD, he associated himself with a denunciation of the British forces there as murderers, for which he was imprisoned. He supported the independent Whigs under William PITT the Younger against the rival Whig faction of FOX from 1783 until 1790, but the French Revolution led to public hostility to reformers, and as a leading member of the LONDON CORRESPONDING SOCIETY he was tried for treason but was acquitted in 1794.

tools, history of Tools have been used from a very early stage in human history. The earliest STONE AGE settlements yield abundant evidence of six basic hand tools – the adze, auger, axe, knife, hammer, and chisel – and of products made with these tools. The saw appeared early in the Bronze Age. Primitive forms of drill were also introduced at about this time. These simple tools sufficed to build the ships that sailed the Mediterranean in pre-Christian times, to erect the PYRAMIDS, and to produce the fine examples of craftsmanship recovered from Egyptian tombs. Roman artisans used essentially the same tools, with the important addition of the plane. There were no further major developments until the invention in medieval times of the brace, the tenon saw, and the spoke-shave. The familiar modern hand drill, of all-metal construction with bevel gears, is a 19th-century development. In the 18th and 19th centuries, machine-tools gradually gained in importance over hand tools.

Within each class of tool, there are many differences in design, and even in Stone Age times there were considerable local variations. Indeed, it is possible for archaeologists to deduce the main trade routes of the ancient world from studies of unearthed axe-heads. Most modern hand tools closely resemble those from earlier centuries, but differ in two respects. First, the relatively recent availability of high-grade alloy steels has made possible sharper and longer-lived cutting edges. Second, the introduction of small, reliable electric motors has resulted in the development of a major new set of light power tools.

Topa Inca (d. 1493) Inca emperor (1471–93), son of Pachacuti Inca (ruled 1438–71). While still heir-apparent to the throne he led his father's armies north, to conquer the powerful CHIMÚ state on the north coast of Peru. After his accession to the throne he extended the empire to the south, conquering the northern half of Chile and part of Argentina. He also built the great fortress of Sacsahuaman, overlooking the imperial city of CUZCO. His successor, Huayna Capac (1493–1525) extended the northern boundaries even further, conquering Ecuador and founding QUITO as the second Inca capital.

Tordesillas, Treaty of (7 June 1494) An alliance between Spain and Portugal. It settled disputes about the ownership of lands discovered by COLUMBUS and others. Pope Alexander VI had (1493) approved a line of demarcation stretching between the poles 100 leagues (about 500 km) west of the Cape Verde islands. All to the west was Spanish, to the east Portuguese – an award disregarded by other nations. Portuguese dissatisfaction led to a meeting at Tordesillas in north-west Spain where it was agreed to move the papal line to 370 leagues (about 1,850 km) west of Cape Verde. The pope sanctioned this in 1506. It was modified by the Treaty of Zaragossa (1529) which gave the MOLUCCAS (Spice Islands) to the Portuguese.

Torquemada, Tomás de (1420–98) Spanish Dominican friar. He acted as the notorious first Grand Inquisitor of the SPANISH INQUISITION. As such he was responsible for directing its early activities against Jews and Muslims in Spain and in fashioning its methods, including the use of torture and burnings.

Tory A British political party traditionally opposed to the WHIGS. In the political crisis of 1679 royalist supporters, who opposed the recall of Parliament and supported the Stuart succession, were labelled Tories (Irish Catholic brigands) by their opponents. In the reign of JAMES II many Tories preferred passive obedience to open defiance; they supported the royal prerogative, close links between church and state, and an isolationist foreign policy. The Tories had a brief revival under HARLEY late in Queen Anne's reign, but were defeated in the 1715 general election and reduced to a 'country' party with about 120 Members of Parliament and no effective leaders. The Hanoverian succession dealt a severe blow to the Tories, as George I and George II preferred to trust the Whigs. The political power struggle in the 1760s was between rival Whig factions, despite pejorative accusations of Toryism levelled at BUTE, GRAFTON, and NORTH. William PITT THE YOUNGER, the independent Whig, fought the Foxite Whigs, and it was from the independent Whigs that the new Tory party of the 19th century emerged.

In colonial America loyalists were called Tories, the term being used of anyone loyal to the crown.

totalitarianism A political system in which all individual activities and social relationships are subject to surveillance and control by the state. The idea originated in the 1930s and 1940s, when observers noted points of similarity between NAZISM under Hitler and COMMUNISM under Stalin. These included one-party government headed by a single powerful individual, propagation of an official IDEOLOGY through all media of communication, government control of the economy, and extensive use of terror tactics by the secret police. Together these features pointed to a society in which power was highly centralized and in which no

individual could escape from the attentions of the state. A totalitarian regime is a specifically modern form of authoritarian state, requiring as it does an advanced technology of social control.

Toungoo (1539–1752) A Burman dynasty that brought unified rule after an interregnum following PAGAN's collapse. Its founder, Tabinshweti (1512–50), and his successor, Bayinnaung (*fl. c.* 1570), subdued the SHANS and MONS, conquered Tenasserim, and overran Thai states in SIAM. However, the Thais broke free and in 1600 sacked Pegu, which, except for a brief period, was the Toungoo capital until 1634. From 1635 when Ava, two months' journey by river from the delta, became the capital, there was growing estrangement between the Toungoo and the Mons. Weakened by raids from Manipur, Toungoo fell when the Mons captured Ava.

Touré, (Ahmed) Sékou (1922–84) African statesman, President of GUINEA (1958–84). In 1946, together with other African leaders, including HOUPHOUËT-BOIGNY, he was a founder of the Rassemblement Démocratique Africain. He became Secretary-General of the CGT (Confédération Générale de Travail) for Africa in 1948. In 1955 he was elected Mayor of Conakry and took his seat in the French National Assembly in 1956. In 1957 he became Vice-President in the Guinea cabinet. He was elected President when Guinea became independent in 1958 and broke all links with the FRENCH COMMUNITY. A convinced Marxist, he received aid for Guinea from the Soviet bloc. Following his death in 1984 the armed forces staged a coup.

tourney (or tournament) An armed combat, usually under royal licence, between knights, designed to show their skills and valour. Tournaments were introduced into England from France in the 11th century. Early versions tended to be confused occasions of mock battles between groups of knights, but they were formalized in the 15th century. The elaborate ritual, in which HERALDRY played an important part, included the issuing and accepting of challenges, conditions of engagement, and points scoring (according to the number of broken lances or blows sustained). Fighting could be on horseback with swords (tourney) or on foot. Simple mounted combat (jousting or tilting) with the two knights charging on either side of an anti-collision barrier (the tilt) was the most dramatic, but there were also mock sieges and assaults on defended places. Blunt weapons and padded armour reduced accidents, but deaths did occur, including that of HENRY II of France in 1559.

Toussaint-l'Ouverture, François Dominique (*c.* 1743–1803) Haitian patriot. The self-educated son of slave parents, he organized the successful struggle against French planters in Haiti (1791), and was given the name l'Ouverture (the opening) in 1793 after a series of fast-moving campaigns that secured the emancipation of slaves. He briefly joined the Spanish and British when they invaded the island in 1793, but, with the help of generals DESSALINES and Henri Christophe (1767–1820), secured their withdrawal and established Haiti as a Black-governed French protectorate. He suppressed a mulatto insurrection and in 1800 made himself governor-general of Haiti for life. In 1801 he conquered Santo Domingo, reorganized the government of the island, and instituted civic improvements. In 1802

Napoleon sent a military force under General Leclerc to reassert French control. Toussaint was betrayed, arrested, and transported to France, where he died in prison.

Townsend, Francis Everett (1867–1960) US physician and reformer. He is mainly remembered for his Old Age Revolving Pension scheme, known as the Townsend Plan, that was meant to help the elderly and assist the USA out of the Great DEPRESSION. The plan called for payments of $200 a month to all aged 60 or more. The funds were to be provided by a federal tax on commercial transactions. The popularity of this and other programmes (he secured at least ten million signatures to his petitions) may have persuaded Franklin D. ROOSEVELT to adopt more far-reaching social policies.

Townshend, Charles, 2nd Viscount (1674–1738) English politician and agriculturist. He became Secretary of State in 1714, but quarrelled with George I over foreign policy and was dismissed from the government in 1716. His brother-in-law WALPOLE resigned in sympathy and Townshend was restored as Secretary of State when Walpole came to power in 1721. Walpole at first gave him a free hand in foreign affairs, but Townshend allowed a quarrel with Austria to get out of hand and frequent interference from Walpole led to his resignation in 1730. He retired from politics completely and went back to Norfolk to improve his family estate. He became famous as a pioneer of the AGRICULTURAL REVOLUTION, popularizing four-course rotation of crops (see AGRICULTURE), which enabled farmers to keep many more cattle alive during the winter and to grow more crops without having to keep one field in three fallow every year. He also introduced the widespread cultivation for winter fodder of the turnip, previously only a garden crop, which earned him the nickname 'Turnip' Townshend.

Townshend Acts (1767) A British revenue measure, which was introduced after the failure to raise direct taxes in the American colonies by the STAMP ACT. Faced with a parliamentary revolt against his budget, the Chancellor of the Exchequer, Charles Townshend, grandson of Charles TOWNSHEND, the agricultural reformer, sought revenue through taxes on American imports of paint, paper, glass, and tea. To enforce this trade tax, a new American Board of Customs Commissioners and Vice-Admiralty Courts without juries were established. The revenue was to be used to pay salaries of colonial officials, thus making them independent of the colonial assemblies. American resistance led to the repeal of the duties, except for that on tea, in 1770.

Towton, Battle of (29 March 1461) A desperate encounter near Tadcaster in Yorkshire in a snowstorm between the army of the newly crowned EDWARD IV and the retreating Lancastrian forces of Queen MARGARET of Anjou and HENRY VI. The armies were large (the Lancastrians numbered over 22,000) and the losses on both sides were heavy, but in a late reverse the Lancastrians were routed and some of their ablest leaders killed.

Toynbee Hall A settlement supported by universities, in the east end of London, aimed at improving the lives of the urban deprived. Founded in 1884 by Samuel and Henrietta Barnett, it was named after the young Oxford philosopher Arnold Toynbee. The settlement has attracted reformers, among them William BEVERIDGE and J. M. KEYNES. Its programme of educational and social activities influenced such far-reaching reforms as the National Health Insurance Act (1911) and the Old Age Pension Plan (1908), as well as a changed attitude to young offenders and penal reform, and the establishment of Labour Exchanges (1908). The practical and theoretical reforms initiated there have resulted in similar developments worldwide.

Trades Union Congress (TUC) An organization of British trade unions. It was founded in 1868 with the purpose of holding national conferences on trade union activities. In 1871 it set up a Parliamentary Committee to advance the interests of unions with Members of Parliament. From 1889 onwards, it began to be more politically militant and in 1900 helped to found the Labour Representation Committee, known from 1906 as the LABOUR PARTY, with whom it has had links ever since. The General Council, elected by trade union members, replaced the Parliamentary Committee in 1920. The Congress can urge support from other unions, when a union cannot reach a satisfactory settlement with an employer in an industrial dispute, but it has no powers of direction. After the GENERAL STRIKE relations between the Congress and government (of whatever party) were cautiously conciliatory. It was closely involved in British industrial planning and management during World War II and under successive Labour and Conservative governments until the first THATCHER MINISTRY in 1979. Since then it has tended to be on the defensive, particularly against legislation designed to weaken trade union power in industrial disputes.

trade union An organized association of workers in a particular trade or profession. Unions represent employees in negotiations with employers. In the USA they are referred to as labor unions. In Britain in the late 18th century groups and clubs of working men in skilled trades developed, to regulate admission of apprentices and sometimes to bargain for better working conditions. During the wars with France (1793–1815) COMBINATION ACTS suppressed any such activity, but on their repeal in 1824 limited trade union activity became possible in certain crafts. By 1861 a number of trade unions of skilled workers existed in Britain, forming the TRADES UNION CONGRESS (TUC) in 1868, gaining some legal status in 1871, and the right to picket peacefully in 1875. A parallel development had proceeded in the USA, small local unions appearing in the 1820s. A national organization, the KNIGHTS OF LABOR, flourished (1869–86), having as a main aim the abolition of child labour. It was succeeded by the AMERICAN FEDERATION OF LABOR (AFL) (1886), an organization of skilled workers. With the development of mass-production methods in the industrialized countries large numbers of semi-skilled and unskilled workers were recruited and from the 1880s attempts were made to organize these into unions. These attempts were more successful in Britain and in Europe than in the USA, where cheap immigrant labour was available. Unions emerged in Australia and New Zealand and in other British dominions in the 19th century, first among skilled workers and later among semi-skilled and unskilled. As industrialization proceeded in other countries so trade unions developed, although in South

Africa trade union activity among Black workers was illegal until 1980. In the former Soviet Union and communist Eastern Europe 90% of industrial workers belonged to government-controlled unions, which concerned themselves with training, economic planning and the administration of social insurance. Elsewhere, union membership fluctuates with political and economic vicissitudes, especially in developing countries, where it ranges from under 10 per cent (India) to over 40% (Algeria). The last figure is typical for many industrialized market economies, where membership ranges from 15% (France, Portugal, Spain, USA) to 90% (Finland, Sweden). In Britain, legislation enacted by the right-wing THATCHER MINISTRIES of the 1980s severely diminished the power of the trade unions.

Trade unions are funded by membership subscriptions and are usually run by an elected executive and full-time officials, as well as elected workplace representatives (shop stewards in Britain). Their main economic objectives are to attain good wages, good working conditions, and secure employment for their members. Types of trade union include enterprise or company unions restricted to a single company (common in Japan); craft unions for workers with similar skills in different industries (traditional, and common, for example, in the UK); industrial unions representing all the workers in a specific industry (common in Germany); and general unions, which represent broad groups of workers in different industries and occupations. White-collar (non-manual) and female workers are increasing in total and as a proportion of all trade unionists. Trade unions aim to achieve their workplace industrial relations objectives through collective bargaining, supported when necessary by industrial action. Most unions also have wider political objectives and seek to influence government economic and social policies through national representative organizations, such as the TUC in the UK or the American Federation of Labor and Congress of Industrial Organizations (AFL–CIO) in the USA, and through local trades councils. Trade unions often have links with political parties respectively, for example the Labour Party in the UK. In some European countries, such as France, there are two trade union centres, affiliated to the socialist and communist parties respectively. In the former Soviet Union and other centrally planned economies, trade unions were integrated in government decision-making. A significant development since World War II has been the increasing participation of trade unions in government and tripartite bodies at national or industry level. This is reflected at workplace level, in forms of participation and limited industrial democracy. The two main world organizations of trade unions are the World Federation of Trade Unions (WFTU), with its centre in Paris, and the International Confederation of Free Trade Unions (ICFTU), which has its head office in Brussels.

Trafalgar, Battle of (21 October 1805) A naval engagement between the combined French and Spanish fleets, and the British, fought off Cape Trafalgar near the Spanish port of Cadiz. After failing to lure the British fleet away from Europe to enable NAPOLEON to transport his army to England, Admiral Villeneuve returned to Cadiz and the English Channel fleet, commanded by Cuthbert Collingwood (1748–1810) blockaded the port. On 29 September NELSON arrived in his flagship, *Victory*, to take command. Villeneuve, 20 days later, was ordered by Napoleon to leave Cadiz and threatened by the loss of his command, finally put to sea but hoped to avoid a battle. Nelson, who had kept his main fleet out of sight, divided his fleet of 27 ships and signalled at the beginning of the battle that 'England expects every man to do his duty'. The British lost no ships but took 20 from the French and Spanish. Nelson was mortally wounded by a shot from the French ship *Redoubtable* but British naval supremacy was secured for the remainder of the 19th century.

Trail of Tears The route of enforced westward exile for many Native Americans. As more settlers moved into Georgia and to the states of Alabama, Mississippi, Louisiana, and Florida in the 1830s, it was US policy forcibly to expel the eastern tribes from their lands and move them to Oklahoma territory west of the Mississippi River. The peoples concerned were the CHEROKEE, Creek, Choctaw, Chickasaw, and Seminole, known as the Five Civilized Tribes. Bad weather, neglect, and limited supplies of food caused much suffering and death before the move was completed and the Trail of Tears closed in 1838. In time, even their new homeland became subject to White incursions.

trained band (or trainband) A unit of armed men based in one of the counties of England. The formation of these companies in 1573 was the result of a decision of ELIZABETH I's government that a selection of the most able MILITIA men in each county should be properly trained in the use of pikes and firearms. Freemen in each city were also selected. The bands multiplied in numbers and were extremely active in the early years of the ENGLISH CIVIL WAR. In the 18th century they were replaced by a standing army supported by militia.

Trajan (Marcus Ulpius Nerva Traianus) (*c.* 53–117 AD) Roman emperor (98–117 AD). Trajan was born in Spain and served as a soldier, before becoming consul in 91. Emperor Nerva adopted him as his successor and the PRAETORIANS backed the choice on Nerva's death in 98. He put down the Parthians and the Armenians and fought two DACIAN WARS, which are commemorated on the scenes of reliefs on Trajan's column standing in Rome. Many public works were undertaken including a new section of the APPIAN WAY. He was an excellent administrator and commanded the loyalty of his subjects. He died campaigning against the Parthians.

transport revolution The change in methods of moving goods and people from place to place during th 19th century. At the beginning of the 19th century wind, water, and horse power were relied on for transport. In Britain, as a result of the INDUSTRIAL REVOLUTION, industrialists required improved roads and inland waterways to transport their goods. Turnpike trusts were created, an arbitrary system of road maintenance paid for by fees collected from travellers at tollgates. Civil engineers, such as Thomas Telford and John Macadam, greatly improved the building of roads and bridges and with the abolition of the turnpikes, revenue for road maintenance was derived from taxation. The first steam locomotive to run on rails wa made by Richard Trevithick in 1804 and the first railwa to carry goods and passengers was the Stockton and Darlington railway, opened in 1825. By 1851 there were rail networks in 17 other countries, including France

(1832), Germany (1835), and between St Petersburg and Moscow (1851). High-speed railways are now challenging air travel for short-haul routes (see RAILWAYS, HISTORY OF).

STEAMSHIPS were at first only used in river estuaries and for coastal transport; the first crossing of the Atlantic by a ship using steam alone was in 1838. Steam packet companies were formed by such merchants as Samuel CUNARD to carry passengers and cargo across the Atlantic and from Europe to the colonial empires.

Later in the 19th century bicycles were developed to give convenient personal transport. In 1876 the safety bicycle was invented and in 1889 pneumatic tyres were introduced. In 1884 a German gunsmith, Gottlieb Daimler, invented an engine that burnt petrol and soon afterwards Karl Benz made one of the earliest petrol-driven motor cars. The mass production of motor cars was pioneered by Henry FORD with the construction (1909) of his Model T car. Motor transport created further demands for improved roads and, together with the tramways and underground train system, greatly increased personal mobility and accelerated the growth of suburbia.

Modern air flight was pioneered by two brothers in the USA, Wilbur and Orville Wright, who built and flew the first manned, power-driven flying machine in 1903. Other records followed fast: the Frenchman Louis Blériot flew the English Channel (1909), the Englishmen John Alcock and Arthur Brown flew from Newfoundland to Ireland (1919) and the commercial exploitation of air transport soon followed. After World War II air routes penetrated to all parts of the world, with many nations having their own airlines flying wide-bodied ('jumbo') jet aircraft. The Anglo-French supersonic airliner, Concorde, came into service in 1969.

In 1961 the first manned flight into space took place. The space shuttle was first used in 1982 and is capable of carrying passengers, but space travel remains extremely expensive and is unlikely to become widespread for many decades.

Towards the end of the 20th century increasing concern about the damage done to the environment by exhaust fumes and fears that the reserves of fossil fuels are limited have led to research into alternative fuels and attempts to design small, energy-efficient methods of personal transport.

Trans-Siberian Railway A railway that opened up Siberia and advanced Russian interests in East Asia. It was begun with the aid of French loans in 1891 and was virtually completed in 1904. The suspicion it aroused in Japan was one factor leading to the RUSSO-JAPANESE WAR. From Moscow, it runs east around Lake Baikal to Vladivostok on the Sea of Japan, a distance of 9,311 km (5,786 miles). The express now takes six days to reach Vladivostok.

Transvaal A former province in the north-east of the Republic of SOUTH AFRICA. The area is landlocked, lying south of the Limpopo River and north of the Vaal River. It is high veld country – steppe, with low bush – and very warm with moderate rain and mineral resources include diamonds, gold, uranium, copper, and coal.

History. Inhabited by NDEBELE Africans, the first White settlement was led by Andries Potgieter in 1842. In 1848, after Britain annexed the ORANGE FREE STATE, more Boers crossed the River Vaal under Andries PRETORIUS. The Ndebele leader Mzilikazi (ZIMBABWE) emigrated

northwards and the Boers were granted self-government by the Sand River Convention (1852). In 1877 the Transvaal was annexed by Britain, in an attempt to impose federation, and the First BOER WAR followed. Internal self-government as a republic was regained by the Treaty of Pretoria (1881) under the presidency of KRUGER. After the discovery of gold on the Witwatersrand in 1886, RHODES and others tried unsuccessfully to unite Transvaal with the Cape. The Boers' denial of political rights to and imposition of taxation on foreign workers ('Uitlanders') contributed to the outbreak of the Second Boer War. In 1900 the Transvaal was annexed by Britain and in 1906 self-government was granted. Under Louis BOTHA as Prime Minister, it became a founding province of the Union of South Africa (1910). Under administrative reorganization following South Africa's first multiracial elections in 1994, the Transvaal was divided into four new regions.

Transylvania ('place beyond the forest') A region of Romania, comprising a triangular region of tableland in central and north-west Romania, enclosed by the arc of the Carpathian Mountains, the Bihor Mountains, and the Transylvanian Alps.

History. Transylvania formed the nucleus of Roman DACIA after 106 AD and after the Roman evacuation (*c.* 270), its history is unrecorded until the Hungarian MAGYARS conquered the area in roughly 900. In 1003 it was incorporated into the Hungarian state, but it retained its autonomy, safeguarded by the 'brotherly union' (1437) of its 'three nations' (the noble descendants of Szekler, Saxon, and Magyar colonists). Effective independence was secured in 1566, when Transylvania became an autonomous principality subject to OTTOMAN suzerainty. The 17th century was its 'golden age' as an international power, with a reputation for religious tolerance. In 1699 the Ottomans recognized Austrian Habsburg rule in Transylvania. During the 18th century the Habsburgs deprived the three nations of many of their rights and liberties and the number of Romanians in the region grew until they were more than half of the total population. They were unable to win political recognition as a 'fourth nation', however, and suffered from religious discrimination as Greek Orthodox Christians. The area remained under Austrian domination until it became an integral part of Hungary at the establishment of the AUSTRO-HUNGARIAN EMPIRE (1867). In 1918 the Romanians of Transylvania proclaimed their adhesion to Romania. This was confirmed by the Treaty of TRIANON (1920). Hungary annexed about two-fifths of the land during World War II, but was made to return it again to Romania in 1947. The redistribution of land and the policy of enforced cultural assimilation in turn by Romanians and Hungarians have remained causes of friction between the two countries. There were riots by ethnic Hungarians in Bucharest in 1990 and the Hungarian Democratic Union of Romania (HDUR) was formed. During 1992 this won local elections within Transylvania. Racial tensions continue in the region. Gypsies were lynched by a mob in the town of Tirgu Mures in 1993. Gheorghe Funar, Mayor of the Transylvanian capital, Cluj, and leader of the ultra-nationalist Romanian National Unity Party (RNUP), attempted to foment confrontation with the Hungarian minority throughout 1994 and 1995. In 1996 a treaty was signed in which Hungary renounced any claim to Transylvania and Romania undertook to uphold the rights of ethnic Hungarians.

Travancore KERALA.

treaty ports The Asian ports, especially Chinese and Japanese, that were opened to foreign trade and habitation as a result of a series of UNEQUAL TREATIES in the 19th century. In China, the first five treaty ports were opened as a result of the Treaty of NANJING (1842), 11 more as a result of the Treaty of Tianjin (1858) and the Conventions of Beijing (1860), and approximately 35 more opened before the CHINESE REVOLUTION OF 1911, some on the Yangtze River. Foreigners living in their own concessions in treaty ports had the protection of their home governments and were not required to pay Chinese taxes or to be subject to Chinese laws. This was strongly resented by the nationalist government and all privileges were surrendered by 1943. After the Treaty of Kanagawa (1858), Japan established five treaty ports, but foreign powers were obliged to surrender their privileges in 1899.

Trenchard, Hugh Montague, 1st Viscount (1873–1956) Creator of the British Royal Air Force. In 1913 Trenchard joined the Royal Flying Corps (AIRFORCE), a branch of the army. In August 1915 he became RFC commander in France, where he organized fighter battles against the superior German Fokker monoplane. In addition he began to develop the use of bombers aimed at military targets in Germany and occupied France. In April 1918 he won his fight for the RFC to become independent of the army as the Royal Air Force. As the first Chief of Air Staff he built up the Royal Air Force, continually resisting inter-service rivalry from the army and navy. In 1927 he was created the first Air Marshal. As Commissioner of Police (1932–35), he reorganized the Metropolitan Police, establishing a Police College and Forensic Laboratories at Hendon.

trench warfare A form of fighting conducted from long, narrow ditches in which troops stood and were sheltered from the enemy's fire. At the beginning of World War I the belief that victory came from mass infantry charges dominated military thinking in spite of the introduction of rapid-firing small arms and artillery. After the first Battle of the MARNE thousands of miles of parallel trenches were dug along the Western Front, linked by intricate systems of communication trenches and protected by barbed wire. With such trenches stretching from the North Sea to Switzerland, a stalemate existed and to break it various new weapons were introduced, including hand-grenades, poison gas, trench mortars, and artillery barrages. Consequently casualties hitherto undreamed of followed every mass infantry attack. Not until 1918, with an improved version of the tank (invented in 1915), was it possible to advance across the trenches. World War II by contrast was a war of movement with no comparable trench fighting. Slit trenches, manned by two or three machine gunners, replaced them. In the KOREAN WAR and in VIETNAM fortified bunkers were used. Trench warfare was used by the protagonists in the IRAN-IRAQ WAR of 1980–88.

Trent, Council of (1545–63) An ecumenical council of the Roman Catholic Church, which met in three sessions the city of Trento in northern Italy. It defined the doctrines of the Church in opposition to those of the REFORMATION, reformed discipline, and strengthened the authority of the PAPACY. Its first session (1545–47), produced a ruling against LUTHER's doctrine of justification by faith alone. The brief second session (1551–52) included a rejection of the Lutheran and ZWINGLIAN positions on the Eucharist. By the third session (1562–63), any lingering hopes of reconciliation with the Protestants had disappeared. Various works recommended or initiated by the Council were handed over to the pope for completion, these included the revision of the Vulgate version of the Bible (finally completed in 1592). The Council thus provided the foundation for a revitalized Roman Catholic Church in the COUNTER-REFORMATION.

Trent affair (November–December 1861) An incident between the USA and Britain during the AMERICAN CIVIL WAR. In November 1861 the US warship *San Jacinto* stopped the British mail packet *Trent* at sea and forcibly removed two Confederate (Southern) diplomats and their secretaries. News of the incident produced widespread demands in Britain for war against the Union (the North), but the crisis was averted partly through the intervention of Prince ALBERT and by the decision of US Secretary of State William SEWARD to release the diplomats on the grounds that the captain had erred in not bringing the *Trent* and its 'personal contraband' to port.

Triad Societies Chinese secret societies, originally formed in the late 17th century to overthrow the Manchu QING dynasty and restore its Chinese Ming predecessor. The name was given to various related organizations such as the Three Dot Society, the Three Harmonies Society, and the Society of Heaven and Earth. The societies shared a similar ritual and acted both as fraternal and criminal organizations. They grew in strength during the TAIPING REBELLION and thereafter played an erratic and violent role in China. Some Triad branches assisted SUN YAT-SEN, while others exerted strong political influence in cities like Shanghai.

trial by ordeal ORDEAL.

Trianon, Treaty of VERSAILLES PEACE SETTLEMENT.

tribune (of the people) An official elected by the Roman people for the protection of their interests. In ancient Rome, ten tribunes were elected to protect PLEBS from PATRICIANS and could veto decisions of magistrates and, later, the Senate's decrees. They could also propose legislation of their own. Roman emperors also took the title of tribune, which gave them the constitutional rights of tribunes and a popular image. Military tribunes were senior officers of legions and were also elected.

Trieste An Italian city at the northern end of the Adriatic Sea. As the sole port of the AUSTRIAN EMPIRE it flourished, but became a target of IRREDENTISM and after World War I was annexed (1919) by Italy. During World War II it was occupied by German troops. In a decision disputed by Italy it was awarded to Yugoslavia in 1947. As a compromise, the city and a part of the coastal zone of Istria were made (1947) a 'free territory' of Trieste under the protection of the United Nations. The deadlock between the Italian and Yugoslav claims was resolved after negotiations in London in 1954, when the territory was divided between the two countries, Italy receiving the city of Trieste. The coastal zone is now part of Slovenia and Croatia.

Trinidad and Tobago An island country in the south-east corner of the Caribbean Sea, the larger island, Trinidad, lying only 11 km (7 miles) off the northern coast of South America.

Physical. In the south-west of Trinidad is the great Pitch Lake, a basin of bitumen and across the north of the island is a range of low mountains which contains the Maracas Falls. The densely forested hills of Tobago, to the north-east, are the ridge of an otherwise submerged mountain range.

Economy. The economy is dominated by oil, which, with petroleum products, accounts for the majority of exports. There are also large reserves of natural gas and asphalt. The industrial sector includes an oil refinery, steelworks, and chemicals. With declining oil revenues, tourism, which is comparatively undeveloped, is being encouraged as an alternative source of foreign exchange. Agriculture has been neglected and many staples are imported, although cocoa, sugar, and citrus are grown.

History. The islands were originally inhabited by Arawak and Carib Indians. Trinidad was discovered by Columbus in 1498 during his third voyage. Trinidad was claimed by Spain but left to its indigenous CARIBS until 1532, when settlement was begun. As it lacked precious metals it remained largely ignored until 1595, when Sir Walter RALEIGH landed there for ship repairs and sacked the newly founded town of San José; the Dutch raided it in 1640, and the French in 1677 and 1690. Sugar and tobacco PLANTATIONS were established in the 17th century, worked by imported African slaves. In 1797, during war between England and Spain, a British squadron entered the Gulf of Paria but met little resistance before the island surrendered. In 1802 it was officially ceded to Britain under the Treaty of Amiens. In 1962 the country became an independent member of the British Commonwealth and in 1976 a republic. The first Prime Minister of the new republic was Eric WILLIAMS, founder of the People's National Movement (PNM). Trinidad's first President, Ellis Clarke, was succeeded in 1987 by Noor Mohammed Hassanali. In the same year Tobago achieved full internal self-government. An attempted coup by Black Muslim militants in 1990 failed. The PNM, led by Patrick Manning, won a general election held in December 1991. General elections in 1995 produced no overall winner and Basdeo Panday became Prime Minister, leading a coalition.

CAPITAL:	Port of Spain
AREA:	5,128.4 sq km (1,980.1 sq miles)
POPULATION:	1.262 million (1996)
CURRENCY:	1 Trinidad and Tobago dollar = 100 cents
RELIGIONS:	Roman Catholic 32.2%; Hindu 24.3%; Anglican 14.4%; Muslim 5.9%; Presbyterian 3.7%; Pentecostal 3.4%
ETHNIC GROUPS:	Black 40.8%; East Indian 40.7%; mixed 16.3%; White 0.9%; Chinese 0.5%; Lebanese 0.1%
LANGUAGES:	English (official)
INTERNATIONAL ORGANIZATIONS:	UN; Commonwealth; OAS; CARICOM

Triple Alliance (1882) An alliance between Germany, Austria, and Italy. This was a secret alliance signed in May 1882 at the instigation of BISMARCK. The three powers agreed to support each other if attacked by either France or Russia. It was renewed at five-yearly intervals, but Italy reneged in 1914 by not coming to the support of the Central Powers.

Triple Alliance, War of the PARAGUAYAN WAR.

Tripolitania The western province of Libya, the richest and most populous. The area was settled by Carthaginians and Greeks and was taken by NUMIDIA after the fall of Carthage in 146 BC. It was conquered by the Romans in 46 BC and became an important agricultural area. The Vandals occupied it in 429, but Byzantium recovered it in 533. The Arabs captured it in 643 and a succession of dynasties administered it from without. In the 16th century the Knights of Malta held it briefly, followed by the Ottoman Turks. The Ottoman provincial governors, the Karamanli Beys (1711–35) made it a CORSAIR base, provoking the TRIPOLITAN WAR with the United States (1801–15).

Tripolitan War (1800–15) A conflict between the USA and the Karamanli dynasty of Tripoli, which in 1796 had obtained from the USA the annual payment of $83,000 for the protection of its commerce from piracy. In 1801 the Bey of Tripoli demanded an increase; the USA declined and sent a naval force to blockade the port of Tripoli. In 1803 the Tripolitanians captured the US ship *Philadelphia*. US forces then captured the port of Derna and the Bey agreed to peace, which was concluded in 1805. The Bey received $60,000 as ransom for the *Philadelphia* and renounced all rights to levy tributes on US ships. In 1815, following breaches of the agreement, a US squadron under Captain Stephen Decatur again visited North Africa and compelled the Bey of Algiers to renounce payments for immunity.

trireme The principal warship of antiquity from the 6th to the late 4th century BC. A type of GALLEY, it was lightly built for speed and manoeuvrability and unable to venture very far from land; each trireme carried a crew of some 200 men, the majority being rowers. They were probably seated three to a bench, the bench being angled so that each rower pulled a separate oar. A beak of metal and wood was set at the front of the galley for ramming enemy ships, under the guidance of the steersman. Athens' fleet of triremes played a major part in the Greek victory at SALAMIS and was instrumental in controlling the ATHENIAN EMPIRE.

Tromp, Maarten Harpertszoon (1597–1653) Dutch admiral. A distinguished seaman, he was largely responsible for Dutch naval greatness in the 17th century. In 1639 Tromp completely defeated the Spanish fleet at the Battle of the Downs. In the First ANGLO-DUTCH WAR he defeated BLAKE off Dungeness in December 1652, fought magnificently but unsuccessfully to protect Dutch convoys in the English Channel, and was killed trying to break MONCK's blockade of the Dutch coast. His son Cornelius (1629–91), RUYTER's rival, won victories in the Mediterranean in the Second and Third ANGLO-DUTCH WARS and against Sweden at Gotland.

Trotsky, Leon (born Lev Bronstein) (1879–1940) Russian communist revolutionary and military leader. After the split in the Social Democratic Party (1903) he sided with the Mensheviks and in the RUSSIAN REVOLUTION of 1905 was leader of the St Petersburg SOVIET. In 1917 he joined the BOLSHEVIKS, becoming the principal organizer of the successful October Revolution. With Lenin he now faced two dangers – war with Germany and internal civil war. In the first Soviet government he was Commissar for Foreign Affairs and negotiated the Peace of BREST-LITOVSK (1918) by which, on Lenin's insistence, Russia withdrew from World War I. As Commissar for War (1918–24) his great achievement was the formation of the RED ARMY; his direction of the RUSSIAN CIVIL WAR saved the Bolshevik revolution. On the death of Lenin (1924) he was the obvious successor, but he lacked Lenin's prestige within the party compared to its General Secretary, STALIN. He was an internationalist, dedicated to world revolution, and strongly disagreed with Stalin's more cautious policy of 'Socialism in one country'. Steadily losing influence, he was expelled from the Party in 1927 and exiled. Shortly after founding the Fourth INTERNATIONAL (1937) he was murdered in Mexico. The term Trotskyism is often used indiscriminately to describe all forms of left-wing communism.

troubadour A lyric poet or minstrel in the 11th century in southern France, particularly in Provence. Most troubadours were aristocratic, but members of troubadour bands were also drawn from lower social levels. Their poetry dealt with courtly love, CHIVALRY, religion, and politics, but usually the subject matter was heavily disguised in formal, decorative language. Much of it was heretical and in the 13th century many of the devotees of troubadour poetry were persecuted. William IX, Count of Anjou, is said to have been the first troubadour. Bertrand de Born was received at the court of ELEANOR OF AQUITAINE and through her influence this Provençal poetry reached northern France.

Troy (or Ilium) The city that according to Greek legend as told by HOMER in the *Iliad*, was captured by the Greeks under Agamemnon after a ten-year siege. Historical Troy was discovered by the German archaeologist Heinrich Schliemann at Hissarlik in north-western Asia Minor, a few miles inland from the Aegean sea. The excavations conducted by him from 1870 to 1890 and by others since then, have revealed ten periods of occupation of the city, which was destroyed and rebuilt each time.

The first five settlements at Troy belong to the Early Bronze Age, ending soon after 2000 BC. Troy II in particular was a flourishing community, with impressive fortifications and domestic buildings, but was destroyed by a major fire. Troy VI saw an influx of new settlers who introduced horses, but an earthquake shattered their city in about 1300. It was followed by Troy VIIA, but this phase did not last long before being destroyed by fire. The indications are that this was not an accidental disaster, but accompanied the capture of the city by enemies. The date of destruction, approximately 1250, coinciding with a flourishing Mycenaean civilization in mainland Greece, indicates that it was this event which lies behind the *Iliad*, and that the conquerors of Troy VIIA were Greeks. Troy remained unoccupied for perhaps 400 years before Troy VIII was established. Troy IX lasted into the Roman period.

Trucial States Seven Arab emirates on the Persian Gulf, known as the Trucial States from the early 1820s until 1971, when they were established as the UNITED ARAB EMIRATES. The name was derived from the annual 'truce' obtained by the British in the 1820s, by which the local rulers undertook to abstain from maritime warfare. Other treaties with Britain extended the ban to the arms and slave trades and the Exclusion Agreements of 1892 provided for British control of the external affairs of the states.

Truck Acts Measures passed by the British Parliament in the 19th century regarding the method of payment of wages. Certain employers paid their workmen in goods or in tokens that could be exchanged only at shops owned by the employers – the so-called truck system. The Truck Act of 1831 listed many trades in which payment of wages must be made in coins. It was amended by an Act of 1887, which extended its provisions to cover virtually all manual workers. In 1896 a further Act regulated the amounts that could be deducted from wages for bad workmanship. The Payment of Wages Act of 1960 repealed certain sections of the Truck Acts to permit payment of wages by cheque.

Trudeau, Pierre Elliott (1919–) French-Canadian statesman, Prime Minister of Canada (1968–79, 1980–84). As Minister of Justice and Attorney General (1967) Trudeau opposed any separation of QUEBEC from the rest of Canada. Elected leader of the LIBERAL PARTY and succeeding Lester PEARSON as Prime Minister in 1968, he led his government to victory. In his first period as Prime Minister he sought to secure economic growth by increased government expenditure, but government deficits increased, while inflation and unemployment rose throughout the 1970s. His Bilingual Languages Act (1968) gave French and English equal status throughout Canada and helped to improve relations between English- and French-speaking Canadians. He improved relations with France, but made little real progress in his efforts to make Canada more independent of the USA. By 1979 Canada was experiencing serious economic problems and Trudeau lost the election of that year. The Progressive CONSERVATIVES briefly took office with a minority government. In his second period (1980–84) he continued with his opposition to separatism in Quebec, his policies being supported by a referendum there rejecting sovereignty for the province. He also secured the complete national sovereignty of Canada in 1982, with the British Parliament accepting the 'patriation' of the British North America Act to Canada, thus abolishing formal links with Britain. He retired in 1984 and published his memoirs in 1993.

Trujillo (Molina), Rafael (Léonidas) (1891–1961) Dominican politician, dictator of the Dominican Republic (1930–61). He seized power in 1930 and his regime dominated all aspects of Dominican life, including the economy. He employed authoritarian measures to accomplish material progress and used terrorist methods to repress opposition. In 1937, fearing Haitian infiltration, Dominican troops crossed the border and massacred between 10,000 and 15,000 Haitians. After alienating all of Latin America in an attempt to assassinate the reformer Rómulo BETANCOURT of Venezuela, Trujillo himself was assassinated in 1961.

Truman, Harry S. (1884–1972) 33rd President of the USA (1945–53). From 1935 to 1944 Truman was a Democratic senator and then became Vice-President. On

Franklin D. ROOSEVELT's death in 1945, he automatically succeeded as President. At home, he largely continued Roosevelt's NEW DEAL policies, but was immediately faced with new problems in foreign affairs. He authorized the use of the atom bomb against Japan. His abrupt termination of LEND–LEASE in 1945 was damaging to East–West relations and the TRUMAN DOCTRINE was adopted in response to a perceived threat of Soviet expansion during the COLD WAR period. He defeated Dewey in the 1948 presidential election. His programme, later labelled the 'Fair Deal', called for guaranteed full employment, an increased minimum wage, extended social security benefits, racial equality, price and rent control, and public health insurance. Although Congress allowed little of this to pass into law, he did manage to achieve his 1949 Housing Act, providing for low-cost housing. By his executive authority he was able to end racial segregation in the armed forces and in schools financed by the federal government. He took the USA into its first peacetime military pact, NATO, tried to give technical aid to less-developed nations with his POINT FOUR PROGRAM, and in the KOREAN WAR ensured that western intervention would, formally, be under UNITED NATIONS rather than US auspices. In 1951 he dismissed General MACARTHUR from his Far Eastern command for publicly advocating a war with communist China. He did not run for re-election in 1953, although he remained active in politics long after his retirement.

Truman Doctrine (1947) A principle of US foreign policy aimed at containing communism. It was enunciated by President TRUMAN in a message to Congress at a time when Greece and Turkey were in danger of a communist take-over. Truman pledged that the USA would 'support free peoples who are resisting attempted subjugation by armed minorities or by outside pressures'. Congress voted large sums to provide military and economic aid to countries whose stability was threatened by communism. Seen by communists as an open declaration of the COLD WAR, it confirmed the awakening of the USA to a new global responsibility.

Ts'ao Ts'ao CAO CAO.

Tseng Kuo-fan ZENG GUOFAN.

Tshaka SHAKA.

Tshombe, Moise (Kapenda) (1920–69) African leader in the Belgian Congo (now the Democratic Republic of the Congo, formerly Zaïre). Tshombe founded the Conakat political party, which advocated an independent but loosely federal Congo. He took part in talks that led to Congolese independence in 1960, but then declared the province of Katanga independent of the rest of the country (CONGO CRISIS). He maintained his position as self-styled President of Katanga (1960–63) with the help of white mercenaries and the support of the Belgian mining company, Union Minière. Briefly Prime Minister of the Congo Republic (1964–65), he was accused of the murder of LUMUMBA, and of rigging the elections of 1965, and fled the country when General MOBUTU seized power. In 1967 he was kidnapped and taken to Algeria, where he died in prison.

Tso Tsung-tang ZUO ZONGTANG.

Tubman, Harriet (c. 1821–1913) Black American abolitionist and social reformer. An escaped Maryland slave, Tubman became one of the most effective 'conductors' on the UNDERGROUND RAILROAD. During the AMERICAN CIVIL WAR she served as a nurse and a Union (Northern) spy behind CONFEDERACY lines. After the conflict she worked in the cause of Black education in North Carolina.

Tubman, William Vacanarat Shadrach (1895–1971) Liberian statesman; President of Liberia (1944–71). A member of an Americo-Liberian family, he was elected to the Liberian Senate in 1930 and became President in 1944. He encouraged economic development to remove Liberia's financial dependence on the USA and successfully integrated the inhabitants of the country's interior into an administration which had hitherto extended little beyond the coastline.

TUC TRADES UNION CONGRESS.

Tudjman, Franjo (1922–) Croatian soldier, historian, and politician; President of Croatia (1990–). During World War II, Tudjman was a member of TITO's anti-fascist partisans and after the war became a general in the Yugoslav People's Army. Resigning his commission in 1961, he entered academic life, and was appointed Professor of History at the University of Zagreb in 1963. Tudjman's vociferous advocacy of the Croatian nationalist cause led to his expulsion from the Communist Party in 1967 and his arrest and imprisonment on two occasions (1972, 1981). Tudjman rose to political prominence as founder and leader of the Croatian Democratic Union, which won control of Croatia in 1990 and in the following year declared independence from Yugoslavia. Croatia initially lost territory to the Serb-dominated Yugoslav army in the war that followed, but it was regained in offensives in 1993 and 1995. Tudjman was re-elected in 1992 and 1995. His presidency has been marked by authoritarianism and military support for ethnic Croats during the civil war in the neighbouring state of Bosnia-Herzegovina.

Tudor The English royal house that began as a family of Welsh gentry. Its fortunes started to rise when HENRY V's widow, Katherine of Valois, 'fair Kate', married Owen Tudor (c. 1400–61), her clerk of the wardrobe. He was executed after the YORKISTS' victory of MORTIMER'S CROSS (1461) during the Wars of the Roses but his son Edmund (c. 1430–56), Earl of Richmond, married Margaret BEAUFORT and their son Henry was thus a descendant, though illegitimately, of the House of Lancaster. His claim to the throne became more acceptable after the death of HENRY VI's son Edward in 1471. RICHARD III's loss of the nobility's support paved the way for Henry's invasion of England and taking of the throne as HENRY VII in 1485.

Henry safeguarded his claim to the throne by marrying Elizabeth of York, the Yorkist heiress, she bore him eight children, although four died in infancy. Arthur died soon after marrying Catherine of Aragon and it was his younger brother who succeeded to the throne, as HENRY VIII. Of his children, his only son, EDWARD VI, died in his youth. His elder daughter MARY died in 1558 after a childless marriage to Philip II of Spain and ELIZABETH I never married. With Elizabeth's death (1603) the House of Tudor ended and the throne passed to James VI of Scotland, of the House of STUART.

Tughluq A Muslim dynasty that ruled in India for almost a century (1320–1413). Seizure of power was followed by military campaigns that brought the sultanate of Delhi to its greatest territorial extent, including the extreme south of India. The chief architect of this success was the second sultan, Muhammad ibn Tughluq (1325–51). Some of his controversial actions are deemed to have undermined rather than strengthened the empire. Gifted and well intentioned, he nevertheless gained a reputation for extreme cruelty, which led to rebellions throughout his territories. The invasion of TIMUR in 1398, in which Delhi was devastated, increased the chaos and in 1413 the SAYYIDS seized power from the Tughluqs.

Tuileries A French royal residence in Paris. In June 1792 during the FRENCH REVOLUTION crowds forced their way into the palace and on 10 August it was attacked, the Swiss Guard was massacred, and the royal family took refuge with the Assembly. In 1793 the COMMITTEE OF PUBLIC SAFETY installed themselves there. The palace was burned down in the 19th century.

tumulus BARROW.

Tumulus culture A group of peoples, centred on southern Germany, who occupied most of central and eastern Europe in the Middle BRONZE AGE (1800–1500 BC). The name is taken from the burial rite of individual inhumation, later cremation, beneath a round BARROW or tumulus. The graves were often very richly furnished, serving an élite class. These people had a rich and varied range of bronzework, based on German and Bohemian copper and tin and traded amber from the Baltic. They were succeeded by the URNFIELD CULTURES.

Tunisia A country on the North African coast, between Algeria and Libya, which extends into the Sahara in the south.

Physical. The coastal climate is Mediterranean. In the north-west of the country are hills, mostly covered in scrub though containing forests of cork-oak. Southward it becomes hotter and drier. Salt marshes cover the central belt, where there are also large phosphate deposits. The south is sandy but contains oases.

Economy. Crude oil is the mainstay of Tunisia's economy, but falling production has caused economic problems. Other mineral resource include phosphate, iron ore, zinc, and lead. There is natural gas off-shore. Agriculture, though adversely affected by drought and locust plagues, is well developed, producing cereals, olives, grapes, dates, and citrus. Food-processing, oil, and phosphates are the chief manufacturing industries. Tourism also plays an important part in the economy.

History. Tunisia was the strategic centre of the Mediterranean in the ancient world. PHOENICIANS arrived in the area in about 1000 BC and, traditionally, CARTHAGE, seat of a sea-borne empire, was founded here in 814 BC. BERBER caravans came north to exchange produce for imports. Carthage fell in 146 BC to the Romans who, despite Berber resistance, called the area the province of Africa Proconsularis and made it rich in corn, olives, and vines. VANDALS from Spain took it in 429, but Byzantium (CONSTANTINOPLE) recovered it in 533. The Berbers, nevertheless, held the interior, giving way only when the Arabs built Kairouan as an inland base to control Africa. The Arab caliphate was replaced by an independent local dynasty, the Aghlabids from 800 until 909, when the FATIMIDS took Kairouan. Another local dynasty, the Zirids, replaced them when they moved to Cairo in 969. In revenge, the Fatimids sent thousands of

Arab tribesmen to lay waste the country. In the 12th century the Normans from Sicily held some towns, until the ALMOHADS expelled them. Another local dynasty, the Hafsids (1228–1574) emerged, taking Algiers (1235) and Tlemcen (1242). In 1270 they repulsed the Crusaders under St LOUIS IX. From 1574 until 1881 the Regency of Tunis owed nominal allegiance to the OTTOMANS, but after 1612 a dynasty of Beys (provincial governors) established itself. The Bey of Tunis became increasingly independent and CORSAIRS operated from Tunis, leading to the TRIPOLITAN WAR with the USA. A period of great prosperity ended when the corsairs and the SLAVE TRADE were suppressed (1819). During the 19th century, the Bey's control weakened and, in 1881 France declared Tunisia a protectorate. The rise of nationalist activity led to fighting between the nationalists and the colonial government in the 1950s. Habib BOURGUIBA, the nationalist leader, was imprisoned, but was released (1955) when the country achieved independence. The Bey of Tunis abdicated (1956) and the country became a republic led by Bourguiba and the neo-Destour Party. In the 1970s the government's refusal to allow the formation of other political parties caused serious unrest, while subsequent attempts at liberalization were interrupted by fresh outbreaks of rioting in 1984–85. Bourguiba was deposed (1987) and succeeded by President Zine el-Abidine Ben Ali, who introduced a multiparty system in 1988 and was re-elected in 1994. The Islamic fundamentalist party al-Nahdah, however, was suppressed in 1990, and there were violent incidents throughout 1991. Tunisia took a neutral stance over the GULF WAR, as a result of which both Kuwait and Saudi Arabia withdrew investments and the USA cut aid. From 1982 it provided a refuge for the PLO until a peace agreement was made with Israel (1993).

CAPITAL:	Tunis
AREA:	154,530 sq km (59,664 sq miles)
POPULATION:	9.057 million (1996)
CURRENCY:	1 Tunisian dinar = 1,000 millimes
RELIGIONS:	Sunni Muslim 99.4%; Christian 0.3%; Jewish 0.1%
ETHNIC GROUPS:	Arab 98.2%; Berber 1.2%; French 0.2%; Italian 0.1%
LANGUAGES:	Arabic (official); French
INTERNATIONAL ORGANIZATIONS:	UN; OAU; Arab League; Maghreb Union

tunnage and poundage Duties levied in England on each tun (a large cask) of imported wine and on every pound of most imported or exported merchandise. From the 15th century Parliaments granted the revenues from these duties to English kings for life. By 1625 they ranked as the largest items in the crown's ordinary revenue. CHARLES I's first Parliament granted him the duties for one year only as Members of Parliament, fearing arbitrary customs dues, sought to assert that customs revenue was under parliamentary control. When he continued to collect them, the issue was raised in the PETITION OF RIGHT (1628). They were eventually abolished in 1787.

Tupac Amarú (José Gabriel Condocanqui) (c. 1742–81) Leader of a widespread Indian revolt in the Peruvian highlands (1780–81). As the Indian chief of Tinta, south of Cuzco, Tupac Amarú used his links to the INCA royal dynasty to develop an Indian base of support and his Spanish connections to attract Creole and Mestizo people to his reformist political movement that espoused Inca nationalism, fairer taxes, better courts, and a more open interregional economy. In 1780, reacting to economic abuses, Tupac Amarú plotted the execution of the local Spanish corregidor and then recruited a large indigenous army, led by non-Indian, middle-level, provincial leaders, which occupied much of the highland area, even threatening Cuzco. Although Tupac Amarú was defeated and executed in May 1781, the revolt spread into Upper Peru, becoming more hostile to non-Indians, and finally provoking severe repression that retarded the independence movement in Peru. His name has been used by revolutionary guerrilla groups in modern Peru and by the TUPAMAROS in Uruguay.

Tupamaros Members of the *Movimento de Liberación Nacional* (National Liberation Movement) in Uruguay. An urban guerrilla organization, it was founded in Montevideo in 1963 and led by Raúl Sendic. It sought the violent overthrow of the Uruguayan government and the establishment of a socialist state. Its robberies, bombings, kidnappings and assassinations of officials continued until the early 1970s, when the movement was severely weakened by police and military repression. The Tupamaros derived their name from the 18th-century Inca revolutionary against Spanish rule, TUPAC AMARÚ.

Tupper, Sir Charles (1821–1915) Canadian statesman. Tupper became Conservative Member of the Nova Scotia Assembly in 1855 and Premier in 1863. A Father of the Confederation, he entered the dominion Parliament in 1867 and served under John A. MACDONALD (1870–73 and 1878–84). He became High Commissioner to Britain, holding the post, except for the years 1887–88, until 1896. Returning to Canadian politics, he was Prime Minister for a little over two months. He led the opposition until 1900, when he retired.

Turenne, Henri de la Tour d'Auvergne, vicomte de (1611–75) Marshal of France. A soldier of outstanding ability, he made his reputation on the battlefields of the THIRTY YEARS WAR. During the FRONDE he was briefly persuaded by CONDÉ's sister, Madame de Longueville, to join the antiroyalist faction, but finally supported MAZARIN in establishing order. He captured Dunkirk in 1658 and led the brilliant invasions of Flanders in 1667 and the United Provinces in 1672. In 1674, when LOUIS XIV was threatened from all sides, he showed his supreme ability in deploying troops against superior forces in defending France's eastern frontier. He died on the battlefield.

Turin Shroud A cloth, preserved since 1578 in Turin Cathedral in Italy, which is venerated as the shroud in which JESUS CHRIST was buried. Although its history can be traced with certainty only to 1354, there are various known statements from the earlier period, going back as far as the 5th or 6th century, that Jesus's burial shroud had been preserved. The cloth bears the imprint of a man, about 2 m (6 feet) tall, who had been scourged, and with wounds from nails in his wrists and feet. The arguments for and against its authenticity are complex and technical. Radio-carbon dating in 1988 indicated that it had been woven from 13th- or 14th-century flax and could not therefore be authentic but further tests in 1996 and 1997 cast doubt on these findings.

Turkey A country partly in Asia and partly in Europe.

Physical. The Asian and European parts of Turkey are separated by the Bosporus, the Sea of Marmara, and the channel of the Dardanelles. The smaller, European part is bounded by Bulgaria and Greece. The much larger Asian part comprises the whole of Asia Minor and is known as Anatolia. It has the Black Sea on the north, Georgia, Armenia, and Iran on the east, Iraq and Syria on the south, and coasts on the Mediterranean and Aegean Seas. Here the coastal plains are fertile, as are the valleys leading to them; but the plateau above is less so. In the east rise the Tigris and Euphrates Rivers. The plateau is subject to devastating earthquakes as it lies at a junction of crustal plates.

Economy. Turkey has an expanding industrial sector and prospering agriculture. Although exports, which include textiles, fruit, vegetables, and metals, have risen, high inflation has threatened economic stability as has rapid population growth and rural exodus to the towns. One of the world's four largest chrome producers, Turkey has rich mineral deposits of coal, antimony, copper, iron ore, sulphur, lead, and zinc. Tourism is expanding, and remittances from Turkish workers abroad are an important source of foreign exchange.

History. Modern Turkey evolved from the OTTOMAN EMPIRE, which was finally dissolved at the end of World War I. By the SÈVRES TREATY at the Versailles Peace Conference parts of the east coast of the Aegean around the city of Izmir (Smyrna) were to go to Greece and the Anatolian peninsula was to be partitioned, with a separate state of ARMENIA created on the Black Sea. The settlement triggered off fierce national resistance, led by Mustafa Kemal. A Greek army marched inland from Izmir, but was defeated. The city was captured, Armenia occupied, and the new Treaty of Lausanne negotiated. This recognized the present frontiers, obliging some one and a half million Greeks and some half-million Armenians to leave the country (July 1923). In October 1923 the new Republic of Turkey was proclaimed, with Kemal as first President. His dramatic modernizing reforms won him the title of ATATÜRK, 'Father of the Turks'. The one-party rule of his Republican People's Party continued under his lieutenant Ismel Inonu until 1950, when in the republic's first open elections, the free-enterprise opposition Democratic Party entered a decade of power, ending with an army coup. Civilian rule was resumed in 1961, but there was a further period of military rule (1971–73). Atatürk's neutralist policy had been abandoned in 1952 when Turkey joined NATO. Relations with allies, however, were strained by the invasion of CYPRUS (1974). A US trade embargo resulting from this was lifted in 1978. Tension between left-wing and right-wing factions, hostility to Westernization by the minority Shiites, who seek to enforce Islamic puritanism, and fighting between Turks, Kurds, and Armenians, continued to trouble the country. A military coup, led by General Kenan Evren, overthrew the civilian government of Suleiman Demirel. Under Presidents Evren (1982–87) and Turgut Ozal (1987–93) some political stability developed, with rather more concern for human rights. Martial law was lifted in 1987 and the state of emergency ended in 1988, some political parties having been legalized, including a neo-fascist Nationalist Workers' Party. The Kurdish Workers' Party, claiming to speak for Turkey's 12 million Kurds, continued its armed campaign for an independent KURDISTAN. Turkey contributed to the GULF WAR, and claimed a loss of revenue of some $6,200 million as a result. During 1991–92 it sought to establish a Black Sea Economic Prosperity Zone with former republics and satellites of the Soviet Union. Civilian rule was resumed in 1991, with the re-election of Suleiman Demirel at the head of a coalition. 1993 saw the election of Tansu ÇILLER, Turkey's first female Prime Minister, and Demirel became President. However, the secular nature of the Turkish state became increasingly challenged by the rise of Islamic fundamentalism. In 1995 a military offensive was launched against the Kurds in northern Iraq and unrest within the country led to the collapse of Çiller's government. The pro-Islamic Welfare Party won subsequent elections but the two major centre-right parties formed an anti-Islamic coalition. This collapsed in 1996 and a coalition led by the Welfare Party was formed: this collapsed in June 1997 and a secularist government was formed under Mesut Yilmaz. In 1989 the European Community postponed consideration of Turkey's application for membership (1987), in part as a result of its human rights violations.

CAPITAL:	Ankara
AREA:	779,452 sq km (300,948 sq miles)
POPULATION:	62.650 million (1996)
CURRENCY:	1 Turkish lira = 100 kurush
RELIGIONS:	Muslim (principally Sunni) 99.0%; Eastern Orthodox 0.3%; other Christian and Jewish 0.5%
ETHNIC GROUPS:	Turkish 85.7%; Kurdish 10.6%; Arab 1.6%; Greek, Armenian, and other 2.1%
LANGUAGES:	Turkish (official); Kurdish; Arabic
INTERNATIONAL ORGANIZATIONS:	UN; OECD; NATO; Council of Europe; CSCE

Turkistan A vast and generally arid tract of central Asia that extends eastward from the Caspian Sea to the Gobi Desert and southward from Siberia to Iran, Afghanistan, and Tibet. Western (formerly Russian) Turkistan includes Turkmenistan, Uzbekistan, Tajikistan, Kyrgyzstan and Kazakhstan; Chinese (or Eastern) Turkistan forms part of Xinjiang. It includes both deserts and highlands and the fertile Ferghana valley and among its historic centres are Bukhara, Samarkand, Tashkent, all on the SILK ROUTE.

History. The western part of the region was under Persian rule from the 6th century BC, Muslim control from the 7th century AD, and Russian overlordship from the 18th century. The eastern portion (XINJIANG) was contested between the Chinese empire and various nomadic groups. The Persian trading centres or khanates, for example, Tashkent and Samarkand, along caravan routes were semi-autonomous khanates, which survived until the 19th century when Russia, China, and Afghanistan began to impose centralized government. Tashkent and the other khanates were conquered by Russia in 1867. Following the RUSSIAN CIVIL WAR, four Central Asian Soviet Republics were formed, TURKMENISTAN (1924), UZBEKISTAN (1929), TAJIKISTAN (1929), and KYRGYZSTAN (1936). In 1931 the Turkistan–Siberian railway was completed. Islamic fundamentalism has become an increasingly important factor within the region. Following the collapse of the Soviet Union in 1991, the independent republics of Central Asia have sought to maintain economic and social alliances.

Turkmenistan A country lying east of the Caspian Sea and north of Iran.

Physical. Turkmenistan is in an arid region; it contains the greater part of the Kara Kum desert, which has important mineral resources. Low-lying and hot, the oases produce cotton and mulberry trees for silkworms, while livestock roam the semi-desert areas in search of sparse grass. Oil and natural gas are found in the west, on the Caspian coastal plain.

Economy. Turkmenistan is rich in mineral resources, including coal, sulphur, silver, cotton, lead, high-grade petroleum, and natural gas. Other heavy industry concentrates on chemicals, engineering, and metal-processing; light industry includes carpet-making and food- and textile-processing. Agriculture is largely dependent on irrigation; cotton is the chief crop, and karakul sheep, horses, and camels are raised. Silk is also an important product.

History. The various tribes of Turkmen did not achieve political unity until conquered by the Russians in 1869. Even then fierce resistance lasted until 1881 and there was a rebellion in 1916. In 1918 a Social Revolutionary Transcaspian Republic was proclaimed. It was briefly supported by British troops until April 1919, after which it was conquered by the Red Army. In 1924 the Turkmen Soviet Socialist Republic was formed and incorporated into the Soviet Union in 1925. It declared its sovereignty in August 1990 and its independence in October 1991. Turkmenistan joined the COMMONWEALTH OF INDEPENDENT STATES (CIS) in 1991. A new constitution in March 1992 increased the powers of its executive President Saparmuradi Niyazov and allowed only ethnic Turkmen to work in state enterprises. The extension of President Niyazov's term of office was approved in a referendum in 1994. Legislative elections later that year were won by the former communists, renamed the Turkmen Democratic Party.

CAPITAL:	Ashkhabad
AREA:	488,100 sq km (186,400 sq miles)
POPULATION:	4.574 million (1996)
CURRENCY:	1 manat = 100 tenesi
RELIGIONS:	Sunni Muslim; Eastern Orthodox; Baha'i
ETHNIC GROUPS:	Turkmen 72.0%; Russian 9.0%; Uzbek 9.0%; Kazakh minority
LANGUAGES:	Turkmen (offical); Russian; minority languages
INTERNATIONAL ORGANIZATIONS:	UN; CSCE; Commonwealth of Independent States; North Atlantic Co-operation Council

Turks A central Asian people who were originally nomads from TURKISTAN. During the 6th century AD the Turks controlled an empire stretching from Mongolia to the Caspian Sea. With the conquest of western Turkistan in the 7th century by the ABBASIDS, many were converted to Islam and moved westwards, retaining their distinctive language and culture. In the 11th century, under the SELJUKS they replaced the Arabs as rulers of the Levant and Mesopotamia, then expanded north-west at the expense of Byzantium (CONSTANTINOPLE). The rival house of Osman continued this trend, founding the OTTOMAN empire, which endured for 600 years and embraced most of the Middle East, North Africa, and the Balkans.

Turner, Nat (1800–31) Black American leader of the Virginia slave revolt of 1831. Believing himself a divine instrument to guide his people out of bondage, Turner led about 60 slaves into revolt in Southampton County, Virginia, killing 57 White people before he, his followers, and a number of innocent slaves were killed. Turner's rebellion exacerbated Southern fears of insurrection and led to a tightening of police measures against slaves.

Tuscany A region in north-central Italy, the chief city of which is Florence. Tuscany was ruled by Rome from the 4th century BC, but as the Romans declined it suffered invasion from Goths, Byzantines, and Lombards. The region stabilized under Frankish rule from 774 to 1115, with Lucca as its capital. It was bequeathed to the PAPACY and became a centre for Guelph–Ghibelline rivalry and for struggles between its successful commercial cities. The MEDICI acquired the title of duke after 1569. Medici rule ended in 1737 and Tuscany passed to the Habsburgs. Occupied by French troops in the REVOLUTIONARY WARS, it was ruled by Napoleon's sister Elisa (1809–14). The grand-duke Ferdinand III was restored in 1814 and confirmed many of the reforms introduced by the French. In the REVOLUTIONS OF 1848 Ferdinand's son Leopold II granted a liberal constitution, but revolutionary agitators proclaimed a republic, Leopold fled, and was restored by an Austrian army (1849), after which his regime became more oppressive. He was obliged to flee again in 1859 when Tuscan liberals declared for unification with PIEDMONT. A plebiscite in March 1860 confirmed Tuscany's annexation into the new Kingdom of Italy.

Tutankhamun Pharaoh of Egypt (ruled *c.* 1361–1352 BC). Little is known about his reign and premature death and his importance derives largely from the fact that his tomb alone in the VALLEY OF THE KINGS escaped looting in antiquity. His tomb was hidden by rubble from the construction of a later tomb and was not discovered until 1922 when it was found almost intact by the British archaeologist Howard Carter and his patron, Lord Carnarvon. His mummified body was inside three coffins, the inner one of solid gold; over his face was a magnificent gold funerary mask and the burial chamber and other rooms housed a unique collection of jewellery, weapons, and other items.

Tuthmosis I THUTMOSE I.

Tuthmosis III THUTMOSE III.

Tutu, Desmond Mpilo (1931–   ) South African churchman and peace campaigner. Tutu was ordained a priest in the Anglican Church in 1961. After studying in England in 1962–66, he became a lecturer in theology at the University of Lesotho in 1967 and Bishop of Lesotho in 1976. He also held the post of General Secretary of the South African Council of Churches from 1979–84. Tutu became prominent in the struggle to end the system of APARTHEID, advocating peaceful civil disobedience against state violence; he was awarded the Nobel Peace Prize in 1984. In the same year, he was appointed Bishop of Johannesburg and in 1986 Archbishop of Cape Town. Following the victory of the AFRICAN NATIONAL CONGRESS in South Africa's first multiracial elections in 1994, he was named head of the Truth and Reconciliation Commission, a body set up to investigate human rights abuses during the apartheid era.

Tuvalu A country comprising a scattered archipelago of small islands between Kiribati and Fiji in the South Pacific.

Physical. Funafuti is the chief island in the group of nine coral atolls. The islands experience high temperatures and heavy rainfall and the vegetation consists mainly of coconut palms.

Economy. Tuvalu is almost entirely dependent on foreign aid. The only export is copra, but sales of postage stamps also bring in foreign currency.

History. The first settlers probably came from Samoa and Tonga in the 14th century AD. The islands were sighted by Spanish explorers in the 16th century. They were formerly called the Ellice Islands after a 19th-century British shipowner, Edward Ellice. In the 19th century whalers, traders, missionaries, and 'blackbirders' (KANAKA catchers) for the QUEENSLAND sugar plantations began to take an interest in the atolls, which the British included in the Gilbert and Ellice Islands Protectorate in 1892. In 1974 the Ellice Islanders, who are of Polynesian descent, voted to separate from the Micronesian Gilbertese. They achieved independence in 1978, establishing a constitutional monarchy. The USA claims sovereignty over four of the islands.

CAPITAL:	Fongafale (on Funafuti)
AREA:	23.96 sq km (9.25 sq miles)
POPULATION:	9,600 (1996)
CURRENCY:	1 Tuvalu dollar = 100 cents; Australian currency is also legal tender
RELIGIONS:	Church of Tuvalu 97%
ETHNIC GROUPS:	Tuvaluan 91.2%; other Pacific islander 7.2%
LANGUAGES:	Tuvaluan; English
INTERNATIONAL ORGANIZATIONS:	Commonwealth

Tweed Ring A group of corrupt officials in New York City, USA. It revolved around William Marcy Tweed (1823–78), the New York city political 'boss' and state Senator who had built his power through the influence of TAMMANY HALL. The ring, renowned for corrupt and dishonest dealing and for fraudulent city contracts and extortion, was exposed in the *New York Times* in 1871. Tweed was arrested and convicted but fled to Spain, from which he was extradited. He died in prison in 1878. The operations of the Tweed Ring were estimated to have cost New York City some $100 million.

Twentieth Congress (February 1956) The Congress of the Communist Party of the Soviet Union, noted for KHRUSHCHEV's denunciation of STALIN. After the first and open session of the Congress, Khrushchev, as First Secretary, made three significant doctrinal points, that peaceful co-existence between East and West was possible, that war between them was not inevitable, and that there were 'different roads to socialism' besides the Soviet route. More dramatic was the speech he delivered in the secret session when he denounced the Stalinist cult of personality and STALIN's acts of terror. The speech was carefully constructed to emphasize Stalin's treatment of the Party rather than of the country at large. A fervour of de-Stalinization and demands for liberalization swept through Eastern Europe as well as the Soviet Union. Khrushchev's 'secret' speech was an important contributory factor in prompting the uprisings in POLAND and HUNGARY in 1956 and in the Sino-Soviet quarrel from 1960.

Twenty-One Demands The Japanese attempt to impose domination on China in January 1915. Taking advantage of its favourable international position after entering World War I on the Allied side and capturing the German base of Qingdao on the Chinese mainland, Japan attempted to impose virtual protectorate status on China, which was diplomatically isolated and torn by civil war. Although one group of demands dealing with the appointment of Japanese advisers throughout the Chinese government was not enforced, threat of war left China no choice but to concede the others, including extension of Japanese leases in Manchuria, takeover of former German concessions in Jiaozhou, substantial interests in Chinese mining concerns, and an embargo on future coastal territorial concessions to any other foreign power. The Twenty-One Demands greatly extended Japanese power in China, but provoked serious resentment within China and aroused US fears of Japanese expansionism.

Tyler, John (1790–1862) Tenth President of the USA (1841–45). Tyler entered politics as a Democrat and served in Congress (1817–21), as governor of Virginia (1825–27), and in the Senate (1827–36) before leaving the Party because of the financial policies of Andrew JACKSON and the NULLIFICATION CRISIS. He ran successfully as WHIG candidate for Vice-President in the election of 1840, succeeding HARRISON on the latter's death a month after taking office. His disagreement with the Whig Party leader, Henry CLAY, resulted in the resignation of almost his entire cabinet in 1841. His subsequent alliance with CALHOUN and the Southern Democrats on the issue of STATES' RIGHTS aggravated the geographical polarization of politics between the North and South. At the end of his Presidency, he secured the annexation of TEXAS. In 1861 he chaired the Washington Peace Convention, an unsuccessful attempt to find a compromise to avert the AMERICAN CIVIL WAR.

Tyler, Wat (d. 1381) English rebel, leader of the PEASANTS' REVOLT. He was a former soldier who was accepted as their captain by the Kentish peasants in June 1381. Following him and John BALL, they marched from Canterbury to Blackheath, just outside London, in only two days, 11–13 June. On 15 June RICHARD II met them and ordered Tyler to go home; in an angry exchange of words with the mayor of London, William Walworth, Tyler was pulled from his horse and stabbed to death. Richard proclaimed himself the rebels' leader.

Tyndale, William (1494–1536) English scholar and translator of the Bible. An early Lutheran, he was forced to work abroad by authorities unsympathetic to his Protestantism. His translations of the scriptures into English found a ready illicit English market after 1526. He suffered a heretic's death by strangling at Louvain in the Netherlands. He was immortalized in John FOXE's 'Book of Martyrs', and in the Authorized Version of the Bible (1611), much of which derives from his translations.

Tyre One of the main cities of the PHOENICIANS, famous in early times for its skilled bronze-workers. In the 10th century BC it made treaties with DAVID and SOLOMON of Israel. Conflict with Assyria was a feature of the following centuries, Tilgath-Pileser III capturing the city and exacting tribute in 734–732. In 668 the attacks of the Assyrian king ASHURBANIPAL were beaten off but the city fell to NEBUCHADNEZZAR II in 587. It entered the empire of the ACHAEMENIDS later that century. Alone of the Phoenician cities it resisted ALEXANDER THE GREAT, but fell to him after an epic siege in 332. Despite destruction it revived to become a major commercial centre. The Roman emperor Severus made it the capital of Syrian Phoenicia.

Tyrol An Alpine province of Austria.
History. In 1803 the province was enlarged by the addition of the Italian-speaking province of Trentino, but two years later, after the Treaty of Pressburg, Austria was forced to cede the Tyrol to France's ally, Bavaria. In 1809, when Austria renewed the war on France, Andreas Hofer led a successful revolt against Bavaria and the French. Hofer was made governor of the Tyrol by the Austrians. Austria was defeated at WAGRAM and forced, by the Treaty of Schönbrunn (1809), to cede the Tyrol to Napoleon once more. Hofer's resistance led to his betrayal to the French and his execution, on Napoleon's orders, at Mantua. Tyrol became a centre of IRREDENTIST claims; after World War I the whole of South Tyrol was handed over to Italy and an agreement between Hitler and Mussolini (1938) provided for extensive forced migration of the German-speaking population to Germany. An international meeting in 1946 gave South Tyrol the status of an autonomous region and decided not to change its frontier. Serious tension between Austria and Italy continued. In 1971 a treaty concerning the Trentino–Alto-Adige region was ratified, stipulating that disputes would be referred to the INTERNATIONAL COURT OF JUSTICE at The Hague. During the mid-1990s a movement supporting the formation of an autonomous Tyrol state gained support.

Tyrone, Hugh O'Neill, 2nd Earl of (1540–1616) Ulster chieftain. Tyrone received his earldom from ELIZABETH I of England in 1585. He established himself as the most powerful chief in Ulster and with the support of other Catholic chiefs rebelled against Elizabeth and her religious policies in 1594. After a famous victory at the Yellow Ford (1598), the initiative slipped to the English, under Charles Blount, Lord Mountjoy. Spanish support for the rebels at Kinsale (1601) proved inadequate and in 1603 Tyrone surrendered. In 1607, after another abortive insurrection the earls of Tyrone and Tyrconnel and their households, fled to Flanders in the celebrated 'flight of the earls', and Tyrone died in Rome.

Tz'u-hsi CIXI.

Uganda A landlocked country in East Africa, bounded by Sudan on the north, Kenya on the east, Tanzania and Rwanda on the south, and the Democratic Republic of the Congo (formerly Zaïre) on the west.

Physical. Uganda's tropical climate is alleviated by its height, most of it being over 1,000 m (3,300 feet) above sea-level and over one-sixth of its area is water. Between lakes Victoria (the source of the Nile), Kyoga, and Albert in the southern half of the country are hills with richly fertile slopes and valleys. Round the Ruwenzori Range (the 'Mountains of the Moon') in the south-west and the old volcanic Mount Elgon in the east, coffee is grown. The savannah country in the north supports cotton and grain.

Economy. Coffee accounts for about 95% of the country's exports. Other cash crops are cotton, tea, and maize, and there are livestock-raising, fishing, and subsistence crops of cassava, cereals, plantains, and yams. Mineral resources include copper, mining of which has ceased, apatite, tin, tungsten, and unexploited iron-ore reserves. Industry concentrates on agricultural processing.

History. The area was originally inhabited by Bantu and later by Nilo-Hamitic peoples. By the 18th and 19th centuries the kingdom of Buganda on Lake Victoria became the dominant power in the area under its kabaka (king) MUTESA I. He welcomed the explorers SPEKE and STANLEY, hoping for protection against Arab slave and ivory traders, and allowed Christian missionaries to establish themselves in his kingdom. Following Mutesa's death tensions developed between the Christians and local Muslims and also between British and German interests. In 1890 there was an Anglo-German agreement that the area be administered by the British and the newly formed British East Africa Company placed Buganda and the western states Ankole and Toro under its protection. In 1896 the British government took over the protectorate. After World War II nationalist agitation for independence developed and MUTESA II was deported. In 1962 internal self-government was granted. Uganda was to be a federation of the kingdoms of Ankole, Buganda, Bunyoro, Busoga, and Toro. In September the Prime Minister, Milton OBOTE, renounced this constitution and declared Uganda a republic. Mutesa II was elected first President, but in 1965 he was deposed by Milton OBOTE, who became President himself, only to be deposed in turn by General Idi AMIN (1971). Amin's rule was tyrannical and racist; he ordered the expulsion of Uganda's Asian residents, who were an economically vital group of entrepreneurs. In 1980, after the invasion by Tanzanian forces and Ugandan exiles, Amin fled the country. Obote returned in 1981, but his failure to restore order led to a coup in 1985, the resulting military regime being overthrown by the National Resistance Army of Yoweri Museveni (1944–), who became President in 1986. Under his presidency Uganda tried to recover from the disastrous years under Amin's

regime, which had ruined the economy and cost hundreds of thousands of lives. Most of the armed forces were demobilized in order to secure loans from the World Bank and IMF. However, in the north of Uganda during 1995–96 the terrorist group, the Lord's Resistance Army, became increasingly violent and military strength was increased once more. The ban on political parties, imposed when Museveni took power, was renewed in 1992. In 1994, non-party elections to the Constituent Assembly were won by Museveni's supporters. The country's first direct presidential elections, held in May 1996, resulted in a resounding victory for Museveni.

CAPITAL:	Kampala
AREA:	241,040 sq km (93,070 sq miles)
POPULATION:	20.158 million (1996)
CURRENCY:	1 Uganda shilling = 100 cents
RELIGIONS:	Roman Catholic 49.6%; Protestant 28.7%; traditional beliefs 15.0%; Muslim 6.6%
ETHNIC GROUPS:	Ganda 17.8%; Teso 8.9%; Nkole 8.2%; Soga 8.2%; Gisu 7.2%; Chiga 6.8%; Lango 6.0%; Rwanda 5.8%; Acholi 4.6%
LANGUAGES:	English (official); Swahili; Ganda; local languages
INTERNATIONAL ORGANIZATIONS:	UN; OAU; Non-Aligned Movement; Commonwealth

Uitlanders (Afrikaans, 'outsiders') The non-Boer immigrants into the TRANSVAAL, who came after the discovery of gold (1886). They were denied citizenship, were heavily taxed, and excluded from government.

Ujung Pandang MACASSAR.

Ukraine A country comprising a large region of eastern Europe and stretching from the Carpathian Mountains to the Donetz River. It is bounded on the south by the Black Sea, on the east by Belarus, the east by Poland, Slovakia, Hungary, Romania and Moldova, and on the west by Russia.

Physical. Northern Ukraine is a continuation of the low plains, woods, and marshes of Belarus. To the south is treeless steppe: a vast plain of rich black soil with occasional low hills, deep ravines of streams, and the great Dnieper River flowing down the centre. In the extreme south is the CRIMEA, a peninsula with a milder climate than the steppe.

Economy. After independence Ukraine undertook measures to reduce its economic interdependence with Russia and the other former Soviet republics, including an agreement to import Iranian oil and natural gas to replace Russian supplies. Mineral resources are abundant and varied. Other than mining, heavy industry includes iron and steel production, machinery and transport equipment, aircraft, chemicals, and consumer goods. Grain is the most important agricultural product, followed by potatoes, vegetables, fruit, and grapes; industrial crops are sunflower seeds, sugar beet, and flax. Agriculture has suffered greatly because the nuclear accident at CHERNOBYL in 1986 contaminated large tracts of the rich steppe land, rendering it uncultivable. Despite increasing economic problems, the IMF has approved several loans to Ukraine to aid economic reform. The pace of the economic reforms, such as privatization, has been slowed by government fear of mass unemployment and subsidies to uncompetitive industries still continue.

History. Originally inhabited by Neolithic settlers in the Dnieper and Dniester valleys, Ukraine was overrun by numerous invaders before Varangian adventurers founded a powerful Slav kingdom based on Kiev in the 9th century. Mongol conquest in the 13th century was followed in the 14th century by Lithuanian overlordship until 1569, when Polish rule brought serfdom and religious persecution, which produced an exile community of Cossacks who resisted both Polish and Russian domination. With the partition of Poland in 1795 the region, including the Crimea, under OTTOMAN control from 1478, came under Russian control, a situation that lasted until the break-up of the Soviet Union in 1991. However, Ukrainian nationalism, despite repression, remained strong. In 1918 independence was proclaimed, but by 1922 the area had been conquered by Soviet forces, and became the Ukrainian Soviet Socialist Republic. Stalin imposed COLLECTIVIZATION on the region, which suffered grievously from his purges. It was devastated during the German occupation of 1941–44, although many nationalists welcomed the Germans. Territorial gains from Romania, eastern Poland, and Slovakia completed the union of all Ukrainian lands into one republic by 1945, the Crimea being added in 1954. By 1990 pressure for independence from the Soviet Union was great and the Ukraine Supreme Soviet formally declared independence in August 1991, with overwhelming support in a referendum. Multiparty elections followed and Leonid Kravchuk was elected president. Negotiations took place with Russia over naval and military armed forces, Ukraine declaring itself a nuclear-free zone. The Chernobyl nuclear power-station disaster of 1986 had left thousands of square miles of countryside permanently contaminated; the Ukrainian government has announced its decision to close the plant permanently by 2000. The largely Russian region of the Crimea unilaterally declared itself an autonomous region in 1992, but Ukraine rejected this, creating tension with the Russian minority. Ukraine formally joined the Commonwealth of Independent States (CIS) in 1993. In elections to the Supreme Council, held in 1994, both communists and independent parties fared well. Later in the same year, the former Prime Minister Leonid Kuchma, who advocated economic reform and closer links with Russia, replaced Kravchuk as President. Relations with Russia remained tense, as Ukraine continued to dispute the autonomy of Crimea. A new constitution abolishing Soviet-style institutions and consolidating democracy was adopted in June 1996. In the late 1990s a power struggle between Parliament and President has developed, with serious consequences for political and economic progress.

CAPITAL: Kiev
AREA: 603,700 sq km (171,700 sq miles)
POPULATION: 51.273 million (1996)
CURRENCY: 1 hryvnya = 100 kopiykas

RELIGIONS: Eastern Orthodox; Ukrainian Catholic; Jewish minority
ETHNIC GROUPS: Ukrainian 73.0%; Russian 22.0%; Belarussian, Moldovan, and Polish minorities
LANGUAGES: Ukrainian (official); Russian; minority languages
INTERNATIONAL
ORGANIZATIONS: UN; CSCE: Commonwealth of Independent States; North Atlantic Co-operation Council

Ulbricht, Walter (1893–1973) German statesman. He helped to found the German Communist Party in 1919 and became a communist member of the REICHSTAG (1928–33), fleeing to the Soviet Union to escape Nazi persecution. After World War II he became a member of the communist-dominated Socialist Unity Party in the Soviet zone of Germany, subsequently the GERMAN DEMOCRATIC REPUBLIC. He was Party Secretary (1950–60) and Chairman of the Council of State (1960–71).

Ulster NORTHERN IRELAND; IRELAND, REPUBLIC OF.

Ulster Unionist parties Political parties in NORTHERN IRELAND that support union with Britain. In 1886 Lord Harlington and Joseph CHAMBERLAIN formed the Liberal Unionists, allying with the Conservative Party and pledging to maintain the Union of Ireland with the rest of the United Kingdom. In 1920, when Ireland was divided, the majority party in Northern Ireland was the Unionist wing of the Conservative Party, which called itself the Ulster Unionists, under Sir James Craig, who was Northern Ireland's Prime Minister (1921–40). The party, supported by a Protestant electorate, continued to rule under his successors, until the imposition of direct rule from Westminster in 1972. The policy for handling the increased violence between Nationalists and Unionists after the civil rights campaign of 1968 led to divisions in the party and in 1969 it split into the Official Ulster Unionist Party and the Protestant Unionist Party. The latter, led by the Reverend Ian PAISLEY, was renamed in 1972 the Ulster Democratic Unionist Party, with policies more extreme than those of the Ulster Unionists (led, from 1979 to 1995, by James Molyneaux). Following the Hillsborough Agreement with the Republic of IRELAND (1985) neither Unionist party has had close links with the Conservative Party. In 1995, leadership of the Official Unionists passed to David Trimble. In 1997–98, the Ulster Unionists took part in multiparty negotiations involving representatives of paramilitary organizations, including Sinn Féin: these discussions resulted in the Good Friday agreement of April 1998, which proposed new administrative structures for the province (including cross-border bodies). The Democratic Unionists and a third grouping, the UK Unionists, boycotted the talks and have since campaigned against the agreement.

Ulster Volunteers An Irish paramilitary organization, formed in 1912 to exclude Ulster from the HOME RULE Bil. then about to go through Parliament. Its supporters pledged themselves 'to use all means' to resist this. They were given every encouragement by Sir Edward CARSON and several prominent English Conservatives. The Volunteers were drilled and armed: thousands of rifles were smuggled into Ireland for their use. A clash between these Volunteers and the nationalist Irish Volunteers (formed in Dublin in 1913) became probable but was averted by the start of World War I.

Umar ibn al-Khattab (c. 581–644 AD) Second CALIPH of Islam (634–44). He presided over the first major wave of ARAB CONQUESTS, which were the work of great captains such as Khalid ibn al-Walid. Hostile at first to MUHAMMAD, he became an ardent convert. The bond between them was strengthened by Muhammad's marriage to Umar's daughter Hafsa. His genius was administrative rather than military and his achievements included systematizing the rule of his vast territories, establishing the Islamic calendar, organizing state pensions, and upholding justice.

Umar ibn Said Tal (or al-Hajj Umar or Umar Tal) (c. 1797–1864) Muslim ruler of a state in Mali (1848–64). Born among the Tukolor people, he established the Tukolor empire. He set out on the pilgrimage to Mecca c. 1820, where he was designated caliph for Black Africa. He established himself in the Senegal River area and in 1854 proclaimed a *jihad* (holy war) against all pagans. He created a vast Tukolor empire, but failed to win many converts. He became a harsh ruler. In 1863 he captured Timbuktu but soon lost it to a combined force of Fulani and Tuaregs. He was killed in 1864 but the Tukolor empire survived until 1897, ruled by his son Ahmadu Seku.

Umayyad A Muslim dynasty founded by Mu'awiya and centred on Damascus. The Umayyads wrested control of the Arab empire from Ali, son-in-law of the Prophet MUHAMMAD, in the civil wars following the death of the caliph UTHMAN in 656. They annexed North Africa and Spain, Transoxania and Sind and twice attempted to take Constantinople. Their military achievements were complemented by success in incorporating diverse peoples and territories into a new social and legal order. Their failure to accommodate tribal conflicts and newly arising sectarian jealousies led to their fall at the hands of the ABBASIDS, though one of their number, Abd al-Rahman, escaped to establish an independent Umayyad dynasty in Spain (756–1031).

Umbria A mountainous region in central Italy. The Umbri were an ancient Italic people with a distinctive culture and territory stretching from Ravenna and the Adriatic to the River Tiber. Defeated first by their ETRUSCAN neighbours and then by ROME (c. 290 BC), their land became one of 11 regions of Italy under AUGUSTUS, the first emperor. After the disintegration of the Western Roman empire and the rise of the PAPACY as a political power in Italy after 800 AD, it formed part of the PAPAL STATES.

UNCTAD UNITED NATIONS CONFERENCE ON TRADE AND DEVELOPMENT.

Underground Railroad A secret network in the USA for aiding the escape of slaves from the South in the years before the AMERICAN CIVIL WAR. While the Railroad helped only a small number of slaves a year (perhaps 1,000 per annum after 1850), it served as a valuable symbol for the abolitionist cause and was viewed in the South as a far greater menace than its actual size merited.

unemployment assistance Payments made to involuntarily unemployed persons as part of a system of social insurance. First introduced in Germany by BISMARCK: for health (1883), unemployment (1884), and old age (1889), it was financed in different proportions by employer, employee, and the state. Similar schemes were introduced in Denmark, Sweden, Austria and, in 1911, in Britain, whose first National Insurance Act provided for unemployment assistance for a limited time. In the USA a Social Security Act of 1935 sought to co-ordinate social insurance schemes created by the different US states, while the British scheme was enlarged following the BEVERIDGE Report (1942). By the mid-20th century all industrialized nations had some form of social insurance scheme providing assistance for short-term unemployment. In some countries, such as Britain, short-term unemployment is met by a jobseeker's allowance, while long-term unemployed people receive income support, introduced in 1934 as supplementary benefit and renamed in 1988.

Many developing countries cannot afford any form of state social insurance system. Moreover, statutory unemployment benefit schemes only exist in 40, mainly industrialized, countries, a third of the number in which old-age benefit schemes exist. The difference reflects concern about the effects of unemployment assistance on work incentives and the difficulties of establishing eligibility for benefit, especially in countries where most of the population are self-employed and earn erratically.

Unequal Treaties A number of treaties made between China and various Western powers in the 19th century. The QING dynasty was generally unable to resist foreign pressure for commercial and territorial concessions and in such agreements as the Treaty of NANJING (1842) was forced to agree to Western demands.

UNESCO UNITED NATIONS EDUCATIONAL, SCIENTIFIC AND CULTURAL ORGANIZATION.

UNGA UNITED NATIONS GENERAL ASSEMBLY.

UNHCR UNITED NATIONS HIGH COMMISSIONER FOR REFUGEES.

Unification Church A religious movement founded by Sun Myung Moon (1920–) in South Korea in 1954. Members are popularly known as the 'Moonies'. Its theology, found in the *Divine Principle*, claims that a sinless man (often thought to be Moon himself) could save the world and form the kingdom of God on earth. There are said to be 3 million members. The movement has attracted controversy through its business practices and accusations that it brainwashes new recruits. Moon was imprisoned in the USA for tax evasion in 1984 but released the following year.

Uniformity, Acts of A series of English laws intended to secure the legal and doctrinal basis of the ANGLICAN CHURCH. The first (1549) made the Book of Common Prayer compulsory in church services, with severe penalties on non-compliant clergymen. The second (1552) imposed a revised Prayer Book that was more Protestant in tone and laid down punishments for RECUSANTS. MARY I had both Acts repealed, but the third (1559) introduced a third Book of Common Prayer and weekly fines for non-attendance at church. The fourth (1662) presented a further revised, compulsory Book. Under its terms some 2,000 non-compliant clergymen lost their benefices, creating the Anglican–NONCONFORMIST breach.

Union, Acts of The laws that cemented the political union of Great Britain and Ireland. Following the complete subjugation of Wales by 1284, the Statute of Rhuddlan, never submitted to a formal Parliament, sanctioned the English system of administration there. It was not until 1536 that an Act passed by HENRY VIII incorporated Wales with England and granted Welsh representation in Parliament. The Stuarts united the thrones but not the governments of England and Scotland in 1603. In 1707 an Act of Union between England and Scotland gave the Scots free trade with England, but in return for representation at Westminster they had to give up their own Parliament. The Protestant Irish Parliament enjoyed independence from 1782 to 1800, when legislation (1 August 1800) was introduced to establish the UNITED KINGDOM of Great Britain and Ireland (1 January 1801).

Union of Soviet Socialist Republics (USSR; also called Soviet Union) A former country occupying the northern half of Asia and part of eastern Europe and from 1936 to 1991 comprising 15 constituent republics. The overthrow of NICHOLAS II in the RUSSIAN REVOLUTION of 1917 led, after the RUSSIAN CIVIL WAR, to the triumph of the BOLSHEVIKS under LENIN. At a congress of the first four republics in 1922, the new nation was named the Union of Soviet Socialist Republics. It based its government on the national ownership of land and of the means of production, with legislative power in the hands of the Supreme SOVIET. COLLECTIVIZATION of agriculture was carried out and a series of political purges took place; an estimated 20 million people died during the Stalinist period. The Soviet Union signed a NAZI–SOVIET PACT (1939) and shared with the THIRD REICH in the annexation of POLAND. The Baltic States were annexed (1939) and Finland was invaded in the FINNISH–RUSSIAN WAR. After Germany's invasion of the Soviet Union in 1941 the latter fought on the side of the Allies in World War II. The Soviet Union declared war on Japan (1945) and took part in the TEHERAN, YALTA, and POTSDAM CONFERENCES. It joined the UNITED NATIONS and, during the COLD WAR, formed the WARSAW PACT as a defensive alliance. In foreign affairs, the economic and energy supplies of the Eastern bloc COMECON countries remained closely tied to the Soviet Union. Soviet troops were sent to HUNGARY and POLAND (1956) and to CZECHOSLOVAKIA (1968), to reinforce those countries' governments against liberalization programmes. Ideological differences aggravated relations with CHINA from the late 1950s. In the developing world, the Soviet Union gave aid to pro-Soviet governments and political movements. AFGHANISTAN was invaded (1979) by Soviet troops and a pro-Soviet government under Soviet military protection installed. A pervasive element of Soviet society remained the high degree of police surveillance and state control of private citizens' lives. It was a signatory of the Helsinki Accord (HELSINKI CONFERENCE), but agitation for human rights continued, as political dissidents from prison camps and hospitals began to be released. The appointment of Mikhail GORBACHEV as Secretary-General in 1985 heralded a new style of Soviet leadership committed to liberalization and more open government, international arms control, and an end to bureaucratic corruption. The social relaxation that resulted precipitated demands for independence. A debate on the relation of the Supreme

Soviets of the 15 republics to that of the Union developed during 1989–90, with significant constitutional changes, and multiparty politics were legalized. In August 1991 the Communist Party of the Soviet Union (CPSU) staged a coup against Gorbachev, but was defeated, whereupon it lost its control and the Soviet Union collapsed in December 1991. The Baltic republics and the former SSRs of the Caucasus region and Central Asia became independent. Many of the former Soviet republics have joined the alliance known as the COMMONWEALTH OF INDEPENDENT STATES.

Unitarianism An undogmatic sect based on freedom, reason, tolerance, and a belief in the goodness of human nature. Modern Unitarianism derives from 16th-century PROTESTANT Christian thinkers who rejected the doctrine of the TRINITY and stressed the unity of God. The first Unitarian Church was founded in London by Theophilus Lindsey in 1773, but soon encountered official opposition; holding Unitarian views was technically a legal offence in Britain until 1813 and the movement has never attracted many British adherents. In the USA, however, the influence of Unitarianism has been stronger, especially in New England and above all in Harvard University. Five Presidents of the USA have been Unitarians. In 1961 the Unitarian Universalist Association was founded in the USA by the union of Unitarianism and Universalism, the latter, founded in 1778, having members of diverse religious opinions.

United Arab Emirates (UAE) A federation of seven sheikhdoms (emirates) occupying the southern (Arabian) coast of the Gulf between Qatar and Oman, together with its offshore islands.

Physical. Abu Dhabi in the west is the largest emirate and also the richest in oil and natural gas. Dubai to the east is the second largest emirate and has oil offshore, as has Sharjah. Further east, Ras al-Khaimah and Fujairah are predominantly agricultural, while Ajman and Umm al-Qaiwain are very small. The terrain throughout the emirates is sandy and low-lying.

Economy. The economy of the UAE is based largely on crude oil, which, with natural gas, dominates exports. In addition, Dubai has a substantial entrepôt trade. Industries include petroleum products, cement, and aluminium-smelting. Agriculture suffers from arid conditions and poor irrigation. There is a large immigrant workforce, mainly of Pakistanis, Indians, and Iranians. The collapse of the Bank of Credit and Commerce International (in 1991) cost Abu Dhabi some $10,000 million.

History. The area was traversed by SUMERIAN trade routes in the third millenium BC. It was converted to Islam in about the 6th century, many people eventually becoming Shi'ite. Portuguese traders visited in the 16th century and the British EAST INDIA COMPANY arrived in the 17th century. The various sheikhdoms in the region concluded several treaties with Britain from 1820 onwards. In 1892, they accepted British military protection, becoming known thereafter as the TRUCIAL STATES. The emirates came together as an independent state when they ended their individual special treaty relationships with the British government and signed a Treaty of Friendship with Britain in 1971. The large oil resources of Abu Dhabi were first discovered in 1958. Each of the rulers of the seven constituent emirates has autonomy in his own state. Since 1979 Sheikh Zayed bin Sultan al-Nahayan of Abu Dhabi has been President of the Federation.

CAPITAL: Abu Dhabi
AREA: 77,700 sq km (30,000 sq miles)
POPULATION: 2.5 million (1996)
CURRENCY: 1 UAE dirham = 100 fils
RELIGIONS: Sunni Muslim 80.0%; Shi'ite Muslim 20.0%; Christian minority
ETHNIC GROUPS: UAE Arab 30.7%; other Arab 56.4%; Pakistani and Indian 10.0%; Iranian 1.7%
LANGUAGES: Arabic (official); other immigrant languages
INTERNATIONAL
ORGANIZATIONS: UN; GCC; Arab League; OAPEC

United Arab Republic The union of SYRIA and EGYPT (1958), which was dissolved in 1961 following an army coup in Syria. The United Arab Republic was open to other Arab states to join, but only Yemen entered a loose association (1958), which lasted until 1966. Egypt retained the name United Arab Republic until 1971, when it adopted the name Arab Republic of Egypt.

United Democratic Front (UDF) A South African non-racial political organization. It was formed in 1983 in response to the South African government's proposal to give the Coloured and Indian communities a limited role in government, as part of its campaign to defuse the country's political crisis. The UDF opposed this compromise, demanding full enfranchisement of all ethnic groups. By 1985 it had become a significant opposition group, with an affiliated membership of about 2.5 million. Its activities were banned in the same year.

United Empire Loyalist The title adopted by some 50,000 Americans loyal to the British king George III who emigrated to Canada during the War of INDEPENDENCE. By 1784 about 35,000 had settled in Nova Scotia and some 10,000 in the Upper St Lawrence valley and round Lake Ontario, an area designated Upper Canada (later Ontario) in 1791. They came mainly from New England and New York and among them were several distinguished loyalists, or Tories as they were called, as well as thousands of farmers and artisans. In 1789 the governor-general ordained that all who had arrived by 1783 could put 'UE' for United Empire Loyalist after their and their descendants' names – later arrivals were called 'Late Loyalists'. These 'marks of honour' were treasured throughout the 19th century.

United Federation of Labour RED FEDS.

United Irishmen A society established in Belfast in 1791 by Wolfe TONE and others with the aim of bringing about religious equality and parliamentary reform in Ireland. Inspired by the ideals of the French Revolution, it drew its support from both Catholics and Presbyterians. The British government took steps to remove some grievances, notably with the Catholic Relief Act of 1793. However, after the dismissal of Earl Fitzwilliams, the Lord Lieutenant, who sympathized with the demands for religious equality, the society began to advocate violent revolution in order to overthrow British rule and establish an Irish republic. It sought military assistance from France, but a

French expedition which set forth in 1796 to invade Ireland was scattered by storms. Repression of its members followed. In May 1798 sporadic risings occurred, especially in County Wexford, but two months later another French force was intercepted and Tone captured. Thereafter the society went into decline.

United Kingdom (UK) A country in NW Europe consisting of ENGLAND, WALES, and SCOTLAND, and the province of NORTHERN IRELAND. The Channel Islands and the Isle of Man are British Crown dependencies but are not an integral part of the United Kingdom.

Physical. The United Kingdom consists of Great Britain, a large island off Europe's north-west coast containing England, Scotland, and Wales, and the north east corner of the neighbouring island of Ireland. Scotland comprises mountains with lowland areas in the south and numerous islands. Wales is generally mountainous and includes the isle of Anglesey. England has the Pennine mountains in the north, while the south is mainly lowland. Northern Ireland is bordered by the Republic of Ireland in the south and west and by the Atlantic Ocean and Irish Sea.

Economy. The United Kingdom has a heavily industrialized economy with substantial, though declining, offshore oil production in the North Sea; main exports include machinery, chemicals, electrical equipment, petroleum, and steel. Britain was one of the world's largest steel producers, but its wide range of manufacturing industry has declined in recent decades. There is a growing service sector and high-technology industries are being developed. London is an expanding finance and banking centre. The state sector shrank considerably during the 1980s and 1990s owing to policies of privatization. Coal is mined for domestic consumption and electricity generation. Other mineral resources include iron ore, zinc, tin, and lead. Agricultural productivity has been boosted by mechanization and intensive-farming methods.

History. WALES was incorporated into England in the reign of HENRY VIII. In 1604 JAMES I was proclaimed 'King of Great Britain', but although his accession to the English throne in 1603 had joined the two crowns of ENGLAND and SCOTLAND the countries were not formally united. In the aftermath of the English Civil War, Oliver CROMWELL effected a temporary union between England and Scotland, but it did not survive the RESTORATION. The countries were joined by the Act of UNION (1707), which left unchanged the Scottish judicial system and the Presbyterian church. IRELAND was incorporated into the United Kingdom in 1800 but became independent (except for Northern Ireland) in 1921.

Britain was the first country in Europe to become fully industrialized, developing a predominantly urban, rather than a rural, society by the mid-19th century. A series of parliamentary REFORM ACTS, beginning with the Great Reform Act of 1832, steadily increased the power of the HOUSE OF COMMONS compared to that of the monarch and the HOUSE OF LORDS. Under Queen VICTORIA, colonial expansion of the BRITISH EMPIRE reached its height. However, growing pressure for independence from peoples within the empire meant that during the 20th century British dominions and colonies gradually gained independence; most of them elected to join the COMMONWEALTH OF NATIONS, established in 1931. During WORLD WAR I and WORLD WAR II Britain fought against

Germany and its allies, emerging from both conflicts on the victorious side. A period of austerity, which began to ease in the 1950s, followed World War II. Since 1967 gas and oil from offshore wells have been commercially produced, creating a major impact on the nation's economy. In 1973 Britain became a member of the European Economic Community, subsequently the EUROPEAN UNION. In 1982 Britain fought the FALKLAND (MALVINAS) WAR with Argentina and in 1991 sent troops to support the US-led coalition in the GULF WAR.

The main political parties in Britain are the CONSERVATIVE PARTY, the LABOUR PARTY, and the Liberal Democrats (see LIBERAL PARTY). The Liberals have not been in power since the resignation of LLOYD GEORGE in 1922. During World War II a coalition government under Winston CHURCHILL was formed. The postwar Labour ATTLEE ministries saw the introduction of the National Health Service and the WELFARE STATE, largely following the suggestions of the BEVERIDGE Report. Labour governments have traditionally been supported by TRADE UNIONS and legislated to nationalize service industries. Subsequent Conservative governments, notably those of Margaret THATCHER and John MAJOR, reversed the procedure by privatizing many publicly owned companies; they also passed laws to restrict the power of the trade unions and restricted public spending. In the general election of 1997 the Labour Party was returned to office with a large majority and Tony BLAIR became Prime Minister.

There have been two major referendums in both Wales and Scotland on the issue of devolution. In the first, in 1979, a large majority in Wales voted against devolution while in Scotland a majority of voters backed the proposals, but as they did not win the support of the required 40% of the electorate they failed to pass into law. In 1997 proposals to establish a Scottish Parliament with tax-raising powers were approved by a large majority while a Welsh Assembly with no tax-raising powers was approved by an extremely narrow margin. Since 1969 Northern Ireland has seen recurrent conflict between Catholic supporters of a united Ireland and Protestant supporters of union with Britain. In 1994 the IRISH REPUBLICAN ARMY announced a ceasefire, paving the way for peace negotiations between the various parties. This broke down in 1996, but was renewed in 1997 and multiparty talks began. In April 1998 these talks resulted in a proposed settlement for the province, involving the creation of a devolved Northern Ireland Assembly and various cross-border authorities. The agreement will be put to the electorate on both sides of the Irish border in May 1998.

CAPITAL:	London
AREA:	244,110 sq km (94,251 sq miles)
POPULATION:	58.784 million (1996)
CURRENCY:	1 pound sterling = 100 pence
RELIGIONS:	Church of England 50%; Roman Catholic 13.0%; Church of Scotland 4.0%; Methodist 2.0%; Baptist 1.0%; Muslim 1.0%; Jewish 0.8%; Hindu 0.75%; Sikh 0.5%
ETHNIC GROUPS:	White 94.4%; Asian Indian 1.3%; West Indian 1.0%; Pakistani 0.7%; Chinese 0.2%; African 0.2%; Bangladeshi 0.2%; Arab 0.1%
LANGUAGES:	English (official); Welsh; Scots-Gaelic; other minority languages
INTERNATIONAL ORGANIZATIONS:	UN; EU; Commonwealth; OECD; NATO; Council of Europe; CSCE

United Malays National Organization (UMNO) Malaysian political party. Formed by Dato Onn bin Jaafar, then Prime Minister of Johore, in 1946 in response to British attempts to form the Union of Malaya, UMNO's aim was to fight for national independence and protect the interests of the indigenous population. Since independence in 1957 UMNO has been the dominant party in MALAYSIA, forming the cornerstone of successive electoral alliances, notably the Alliance Party of the 1960s and its successor, the National Front. In 1995, UMNO won its biggest victory since independence. During the southeast Asian financial crisis of 1997–98, its President, Mahathir bin Mohamed blamed foreign speculators for the collapse of the Malaysian economy.

United Nations Conference on Trade and Development (UNCTAD) A permanent agency of the UNITED NATIONS ORGANIZATION, with its headquarters in Geneva. It was established in 1964 to promote international trade and economic growth. The Conference, which meets every four years, called for discrimination in favour of the developing countries, since their industrial products are often subject to quotas and tariffs. UNCTAD has played an important role in devising economic measures to secure advantageous prices for primary commodities and to ensure preferential tariff treatment for developing countries' manufactured goods. In 1968 it proposed that developed countries should give 1% of their gross national product in aid to developing countries, but the gap between rich and poor countries continued to widen (BRANDT REPORT), aggravated by a steady decline in the price of many basic world commodities, which the developing countries produce. Representatives from 150 countries attended its eighth full session in 1992, when it was agreed that increased emphasis in developing countries on domestic policy reforms and efficiency was needed in a changed international climate.

United Nations Convention on the Rights of the Child An international treaty, adopted in 1989. The rights apply to all persons under 18 except in countries where the age of majority is lower. The Convention declares the family to be the natural environment for children and states that in all actions concerning children account should be taken of their best interests. It promulgates the child's right to a name and nationality, to privacy, freedom of association, thought, conscience, and religion. The obligations of others, especially parents and the state, are documented. The state, for example, must provide childcare for those with working parents, education, health care, and protection from child sexual exploitation, child abuse and neglect, drug abuse, and CHILD LABOUR. The treaty indicates the special protection required by vulnerable children, such as the victims of armed conflict, handicapped and REFUGEE children, and the children of minorities. It is binding on states which ratify it, but there is no mechanism for enforcement.

United Nations Educational, Scientific and Cultural Organization (UNESCO) A specialized agency of the UNITED NATIONS ORGANIZATION, founded in 1946 and based in Paris, that promotes international collaboration in education, science, culture, and communication. In education, it supports the spread of literacy, continuing education, and universal primary education; in science, it assists developing countries and encourages international interchange between scientists. It advocates the preservation of monuments and historic sites, and of other aspects of culture, such as oral traditions, music, and dance. By 1989 UNESCO's 'World Heritage List', designed to protect landmarks of 'outstanding universal value', comprised 315 sites in 67 countries. In the field of communication, UNESCO is committed to the free flow of information. In 1980 its supreme governing body approved a New World Information and Communication Order despite opposition from those who believed it threatened press freedom. In 1984 the USA (which had been due to supply about a quarter of UNESCO's budget) and in 1985 the UK and Singapore withdrew, alleging financial mismanagement and political bias against Western countries. The UK rejoined in 1997.

United Nations General Assembly (UNGA) The main deliberative organ of the UNITED NATIONS ORGANIZATION, where representatives of every member country sit and have a vote. The Assembly, based at UN headquarters in New York, can discuss and make recommendations on all questions which fall within the scope of the UN Charter; it is also responsible for the UN budget. It first met in January 1946 and meets for three months annually in regular session, although both special and emergency sessions can also be convened. Such sessions have been held to discuss issues of particular importance, such as the SUEZ WAR in 1956, PALESTINE, disarmament, or the sanctioning of the US-led war against Iraq in 1991. It may also meet when the UNITED NATIONS SECURITY COUNCIL has failed to agree on a course of action in an international dispute, such as occurred in Afghanistan (1980), Namibia (1981), and the Israeli-occupied Arab territories (1982). Decisions on important questions require a two-thirds majority, otherwise a simple majority is sufficient. In the UN's early years, the USA could normally command a majority in the General Assembly, but with the dramatic increase in new members following decolonization, the balance shifted to favour the developing countries, who were often unwilling to endorse the policies of either superpower, preferring to adopt a NON-ALIGNED stance. Since the fall of communism in the Soviet Union and eastern Europe, the General Assembly's numbers have been further swelled by newly independent republics. At the end of 1997 there were 185 member states.

United Nations High Commissioner for Refugees, Office of the (UNHCR) A UN body established in 1951 to replace the International Refugee Organization. Its headquarters are in Geneva and there are five Regional Bureaux. The UNHCR has two primary functions: to extend international protection to REFUGEES under the terms of the 1951 UN Convention relating to the Status of Refugees, and, specifically, to ensure refugees obtain political asylum and are not forcibly returned to a territory where they fear persecution. The UNHCR also seeks to provide refugees with emergency relief, such as food, shelter, and medical assistance, and, in the long term, to assist in their voluntary repatriation or resettlement and integration into a new community.

United Nations Organization (UN) An international organization established in 1945 as successor to the LEAGUE OF NATIONS with the goal of working for peace, security, and co-operation among the nations of the world. Its permanent headquarters are in New York. The term 'United Nations' was first used in a Declaration of the United Nations in January 1942, when representatives of 26 Allied nations pledged their governments to continue fighting together against the Axis powers, but it was only after further conferences held at Dumbarton Oaks, Washington, in 1944, and San Francisco in 1945 that representatives of 50 Allied countries signed the document, known as the Charter, setting up the new organization. The UN grew rapidly as former colonial territories became independent nations and applied for membership. In 1996 the organization had 185 members, most of the countries of the world. Switzerland, which maintains a policy of strict neutrality, is not a member and several south Pacific states have observer status because their populations and economies are too small to support full membership.

In order to carry out its many functions, the UN is served by a wide range of organs and institutions. The six principal organs of the UN are the UNITED NATIONS GENERAL ASSEMBLY (UNGA), the UNITED NATIONS SECURITY COUNCIL, the INTERNATIONAL COURT OF JUSTICE, the Economic and Social Council (which deals with international economic, social, cultural, educational, health and related matters), the Trusteeship Council (which administers those territories held in trust by the UN), and the Secretariat, which is responsible for the general administration of the UN. The Secretariat is headed by the Secretary-General, who is appointed for a five-year renewable term by the General Assembly. There have been eight Secretary-Generals since the UN was founded: Trygve LIE (Norway), 1946–53; Dag HAMMARSKJÖLD (Sweden), 1953–61; U THANT (Myanmar), 1961–71; Kurt WALDHEIM (Austria), 1971–81; Javier PÉREZ DE CUÉLLAR (Peru), 1981–92; Boutros BOUTROS-GHALI (Egypt), 1992–97; and Kofi ANNAN (Ghana) from 1997. The UN is also served by 19 intergovernmental agencies known as the specialized agencies, dealing with economic and social questions. They include the International Atomic Energy Agency (IAEA), the INTERNATIONAL MONETARY FUND (IMF), the UNITED NATIONS EDUCATIONAL, SCIENTIFIC, AND CULTURAL ORGANIZATION (UNESCO), and the WORLD HEALTH ORGANIZATION (WHO). Other organs which are part of the UN system include the UNITED NATIONS CONFERENCE ON TRADE AND DEVELOPMENT (UNCTAD), and the Office of the UNITED NATIONS HIGH COMMISSIONER FOR REFUGEES (UNHCR). (See diagram.)

In 1997 the prominent businessman Ted Turner, founder of the CNN news network and vice-chairman of the Time-Warner conglomerate, announced he would donate $1 billion to the UN, in the form of Time-Warner stock.

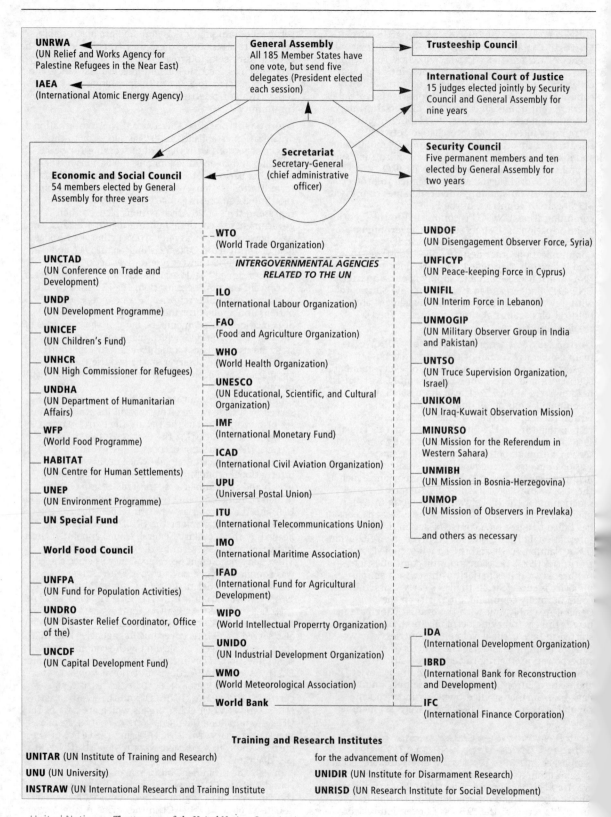

UNRWA
(UN Relief and Works Agency for
Palestine Refugees in the Near East)

IAEA
(International Atomic Energy Agency)

General Assembly
All 185 Member States have
one vote, but send five
delegates (President elected
each session)

Trusteeship Council

International Court of Justice
15 judges elected jointly by Security
Council and General Assembly for
nine years

Secretariat
Secretary-General
(chief administrative
officer)

Security Council
Five permanent members and ten
elected by General Assembly for
two years

Economic and Social Council
54 members elected by General
Assembly for three years

UNCTAD
(UN Conference on Trade and
Development)

UNDP
(UN Development Programme)

UNICEF
(UN Children's Fund)

UNHCR
(UN High Commissioner for Refugees)

UNDHA
(UN Department of Humanitarian
Affairs)

WFP
(World Food Programme)

HABITAT
(UN Centre for Human Settlements)

UNEP
(UN Environment Programme)

UN Special Fund

World Food Council

UNFPA
(UN Fund for Population Activities)

UNDRO
(UN Disaster Relief Coordinator, Office
of the)

UNCDF
(UN Capital Development Fund)

WTO
(World Trade Organization)

*INTERGOVERNMENTAL AGENCIES
RELATED TO THE UN*

ILO
(International Labour Organization)

FAO
(Food and Agriculture Organization)

WHO
(World Health Organization)

UNESCO
(UN Educational, Scientific, and Cultural
Organization)

IMF
(International Monetary Fund)

ICAD
(International Civil Aviation Organization)

UPU
(Universal Postal Union)

ITU
(International Telecommunications Union)

IMO
(International Maritime Association)

IFAD
(International Fund for Agricultural
Development)

WIPO
(World Intellectual Properrty Organization)

UNIDO
(UN Industrial Development Organization)

WMO
(World Meteorological Association)

World Bank

UNDOF
(UN Disengagement Observer Force, Syria)

UNFICYP
(UN Peace-keeping Force in Cyprus)

UNIFIL
(UN Interim Force in Lebanon)

UNMOGIP
(UN Military Observer Group in India
and Pakistan)

UNTSO
(UN Truce Supervision Organization,
Israel)

UNIKOM
(UN Iraq-Kuwait Observation Mission)

MINURSO
(UN Mission for the Referendum in
Western Sahara)

UNMIBH
(UN Mission in Bosnia-Herzegovina)

UNMOP
(UN Mission of Observers in Prevlaka)

and others as necessary

IDA
(International Development Organization)

IBRD
(International Bank for Reconstruction
and Development)

IFC
(International Finance Corporation)

Training and Research Institutes

UNITAR (UN Institute of Training and Research)
UNU (UN University)
INSTRAW (UN International Research and Training Institute

for the advancement of Women)
UNIDIR (UN Institute for Disarmament Research)
UNRISD (UN Research Institute for Social Development)

United Nations   *The structure of the United Nations Organization.*

United Nations Security Council One of the six principal organs of the UNITED NATIONS ORGANIZATION, based at UN headquarters in New York, whose prime responsibility is to maintain world peace and security. The Security Council, which first met in January 1946, consists of five permanent members (the USA, Russia, China, France, and the UK), and ten non-permanent members elected by the UNITED NATIONS GENERAL ASSEMBLY for two-year terms on a rotating basis. With the changes in the economic and political BALANCE OF POWER since the end of the cold war, a change in the permanent membership to admit Germany, Japan, the EU, or other regional powers, is likely to come under discussion. The Security Council can investigate any international dispute and recommend ways of achieving a settlement, including 'enforcement measures', such as sanctions, or the use of force by UN members (as, for example, in Somalia in 1992). It is also responsible for peacekeeping forces such as UNIFIL (United Nations Interim Force in Lebanon), which was established in 1978 to confirm the withdrawal of Israeli forces from southern Lebanon, UNIIMOG (United Nations Iran–Iraq Military Observer Group), established in 1988 to monitor the ceasefire after the Iran–Iraq War, or UNMIBH (United Nations Mission in Bosnia-Herzegovina), established in 1995. Decisions taken by the Security Council require a majority of nine, including all five permanent members. This rule of GREAT POWER unanimity, usually referred to as the right of veto, had been the cause of controversy, as during the cold war, when the activities of the Security Council were frequently paralysed by the failure of the five permanent members to adopt a common position in international crises. The effectiveness of the Council was improved after the collapse of the Soviet bloc in 1991 and it was suggested that its membership needed revision to recognize the new world power-structure. The proposal was advanced in 1994 that permanent Security Council membership be doubled; Germany and Japan made especially strong representations for a permanent seat. The establishment of a UN army, formed from contingents from member nations on permanent standby was proposed in 1992.

United Party (official name: United South African National Party) A South African political party, established in 1934 as a coalition between the followers of HERTZOG's NATIONAL PARTY and SMUTS's South African Party. Although it had AFRIKANER and English backing, it was soon weakened by the defection of MALAN's 'purified' National Party. In 1939 it split when Hertzog attempted to declare South Africa neutral when war broke out. Until the mid-1970s it was the principal opposition party. With the rise of the Progressive Party support for the United Party fell and it was dissolved in 1977.

United Provinces of the Netherlands (or Dutch Republic) The historic state that lasted from 1579 to 1795 and comprised most of the area of the present kingdom of the Netherlands. It was recognized as an independent state by Spain at the conclusion of the DUTCH REVOLTS (1648) and power was subsequently shared between the Holland and Zeeland patricians and the STATHOLDER princes of ORANGE. During its 'golden age' before 1700, the United Provinces developed the vast DUTCH EMPIRE, Dutch merchants traded throughout the world, and the arts flourished. The United Provinces gave refuge to

religious refugees, especially Portuguese and Spanish Jews and French HUGUENOTS, who made a notable contribution to the country's prosperity. A series of wars was fought against England and France in the 18th century. The commercial and military fortunes of the Netherlands declined as those of England and France improved. When in 1794–95 France overran the country during the French Revolutionary wars, there was a Dutch popular movement, inspired by the ideas of the ENLIGHTENMENT, that was ready to overthrow the ruler, William V of Orange, and to set up a Batavian Republic (1795–1806) under French protection in place of the United Provinces.

United States of America (USA) The world's fourth largest country, comprising the central belt of North America together with Alaska, Hawaii, and many small Pacific Ocean islands. Mainland USA is bounded by Canada on the north, and the Great Lakes, and by Mexico on the south.

Physical. The USA contains several topographically very diverse regions. The West Coast is a series of mountain ranges with attendant valleys and plateaux running roughly parallel to the climatically mild Pacific coast. In California, the reverse slopes of the Coast Range descend to the lush Sacramento and San Joaquin valleys, which are fringed inland by the snow-capped peaks of the Sierra Nevada. From here the Great Basin of Nevada and parts of Oregon, Idaho, Utah, and California, an arid and rugged plateau containing its own mountain ranges, extends eastward to the Rocky Mountains. The Rockies are the 'Great Divide', the main watershed of the country. Out of their massive ranges in Montana, Wyoming, Colorado, and New Mexico (the Mountain States), emerge the westward-running Snake and Colorado Rivers, and the eastward-flowing tributaries of the Mississippi. The Great Plains, occupied by the Dakotas, Nebraska, Kansas, Oklahoma, and Texas, have become a great prairie supporting cattle ranching and wheat cultivation. The prairies extend through the Middle West (including Minnesota, Iowa, Missouri, and north-west Arkansas) to the basin of the Mississippi, which intersects the country from north to south. In Louisiana, Mississippi, Tennessee, Alabama, and Georgia, the main crops are cotton, rice, tobacco, and sugar cane and there are oilfields, which extend into the Gulf of Mexico. The peninsula of Florida is renowned for the warmth of its climate and for its citrus fruits. The south-eastern coastal plain is occupied by Virginia, the Carolinas, and eastern Georgia. Mountainous New England, the north-eastern region, experiences harsh winters but contains rich pastures and many areas of great natural beauty.

Economy. The US economy benefits from abundant natural resources and a large internal market. A free-trade treaty was signed with Canada in 1989 and in 1993 the NORTH AMERICAN FREE TRADE AGREEMENT created a free-trade region comprising the USA, Canada, and Mexico. The economy is largely self-sufficient and comparatively unaffected by global economic trends. However, a surge in imports in the 1980s, particularly from Japan, and the uncompetitiveness of exports have caused a trade deficit which, together with the large federal budget deficit, has aroused worldwide concern. Major exports are electrical goods, machinery, chemicals, motor vehicles, cereals, and aircraft. Financial services, entertainment, especially film and television, the computer industry,

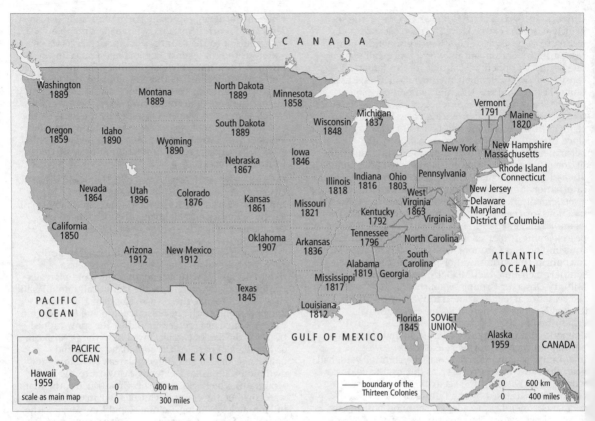

United States of America *An Ordinance of 1787 laid down that when a US territory area reached a population of 60,000 free inhabitants it could petition Congress for admission to the Union as a state. Vermont and Kentucky were early admissions and many western states followed during the 19th century.*

and the arms trade are significant. Regional climatic differences enable agricultural diversity. Fishing, forestry, and livestock are also substantial.

History. The indigenous peoples of North America probably came from Asia across the Bering land bridge over 30,000 years ago. From the territory now occupied by Alaska, they spread out to populate the entire continent (and South America). By 1600 AD, it is estimated that there were around 1.5 million Native Americans in what are now Canada and the USA. European colonization of the eastern seaboard of North America began in the early 17th century, gaining momentum as the rival nations, most notably the British and French, struggled for control of the new territory. The Treaty of PARIS (1763) marked the final triumph of Britain, but by that time the British colonies, stretching from NEW ENGLAND in the north to GEORGIA in the south, had become accustomed to a considerable measure of independence. British attempts to reassert central authority produced first discontent and then open resistance. The First CONTINENTAL CONGRESS met in 1774 to consider action to regain lost rights and the first armed encounters at LEXINGTON AND CONCORD in April 1775 led directly to full-scale revolt and to the formal proclamation of the separation of the THIRTEEN COLONIES from Britain, as the United States of America,

in the DECLARATION OF INDEPENDENCE (4 July 1776). In the War of INDEPENDENCE, which lasted until 1783, the American cause was assisted by France and Spain. The war ended with the Peace of PARIS (1783), which recognized US independence.

A structure of government for the new country was set out in the Constitution of 1787, which established a federal system, dividing power between central government and the constituent states, with an executive President, a legislature made up of two houses, the SENATE and the House of REPRESENTATIVES, and an independent judiciary headed by the SUPREME COURT (see also CONGRESS OF THE USA). Territorial expansion followed with the LOUISIANA PURCHASE of 1803, the acquisition of Florida in 1810–19, and of TEXAS, California and the south-west following the MEXICAN–AMERICAN WAR of 1846–48. The western lands of the Louisiana Purchase and those seized from Mexico were at first territories of the USA, administered by officers of the federal government. When the population reached some 60,000, an area of territory negotiated to be admitted to the Union as a new state. The mid-19th century was dominated by a political crisis over slavery and STATES' RIGHTS, leading to the secession of the Southern states and their reconquest in the AMERICAN CIVIL WAR of 1861–65. The final decades of the century saw the

WESTWARD EXPANSION of European settlement, the purchase of Alaska (1867), and the acquisition of Spanish overseas territories after the SPANISH–AMERICAN WAR of 1898. In the 20th century the USA has participated in the two World Wars and has gradually emerged from ISOLATIONISM to become a world power, a process accelerated by the COLD WAR division. It fought the KOREAN WAR and VIETNAM WAR, and has intervened to prevent left-wing regimes gaining control in South American and Caribbean countries. After the disintegration of the Soviet Union in 1991 US foreign policy has concentrated on the resolution of major regional disputes and on providing military support for UN peacekeeping operations around the world.

CAPITAL: Washington, DC
AREA: 9,529,063 sq km (3,679,192 sq miles)
POPULATION: 265.455 million (1996)
CURRENCY: 1 dollar = 100 cents
RELIGIONS: Protestant 49.1%; Roman Catholic 29.6%; other Christian 8.4%; Jewish 2.7%; Muslim 1.9%; Hindu 0.2%; non-religious and atheist 6.8%
ETHNIC GROUPS: European origin (White, of whom Hispanic 6.4%) 83.2%; Black 12.4%; Asian and Pacific Islander 1.5%; Amerindian 0.6%
LANGUAGES: English (official); Spanish; numerous minority or immigrant languages
INTERNATIONAL
ORGANIZATIONS: UN; OAS; NATO; OECD; Colombo Plan; Anzus; CSCE; NAFTA

Universal Declaration of Human Rights An international declaration, adopted in 1948 by the General Assembly of the UN (with Saudi Arabia, South Africa, and the six Soviet members, Belarussian SSR, Ukrainian SSR, Russia, Poland, Czechoslovakia, and Yugoslavia, abstaining). It declares that all human beings are born free and equal in dignity and rights and are entitled to the rights and freedoms set out in the Declaration without discrimination on the grounds of race, colour, sex, language, political opinion, or religion. The rights enumerated include CIVIL RIGHTS, such as freedom of expression, conscience, movement, peaceful assembly, and association, and economic and social rights such as those to work, to an adequate standard of living, to education, and to participation in cultural life. The exercise of an individual's rights and freedoms is limited only by respect for the rights and freedoms of others. The Declaration is not legally binding but it has underpinned the activities of the UN, affected both national and international law, and widely influenced debates on human rights. In 1966 the General Assembly adopted two Covenants, the International Covenant on Civil and Political Rights and the International Covenant on Economic, Social, and Cultural Rights, which embody the rights in the Declaration and have legal force.

University A centre of higher education with responsibilities for teaching and research. Universities evolved in Europe from *Studia generalia*, schools open to scholars from all countries, established to educate priests and monks beyond standards attainable in cathedral or monastic schools. Originally societies or guilds of foreigners who banded together for protection in a strange land, by the 13th century 'universities of scholars' had developed into corporate bodies with well-

defined administrative structures. At Bologna and Paris foreign students were granted special privileges, such as right of trial for misdemeanours in an ecclesiastical court and the right to strike in protest against unsatisfactory conditions.

Among the earliest European universities were Bologna (1088), Paris (*c.* 1150), Prague (1348), Vienna (1365), and Heidelberg (1386). In Britain Oxford (*c.* 1150) and Cambridge (1209), where college organization developed early, were followed by St Andrews (1411) and Glasgow (1451) in Scotland, and in Ireland by Trinity College, Dublin (1591). The basis of medieval university learning was formed by the seven liberal arts, a curriculum that was organized into a higher division (the *quadrivium*, consisting of arithmetic, astronomy, music, and geometry) and a lower division (the *trivium*, consisting of grammar, rhetoric, and logic). American universities evolved from colleges founded in the 17th and 18th centuries, Harvard (1636) being the earliest. For a long time the seven liberal arts, and later jurisprudence, were the principal subjects of study. However, in Salerno, influenced by Arab culture, there was a renowned medical school that had been established by the 11th century. During the 17th century the SCIENTIFIC REVOLUTION forced the gradual widening of the curriculum.

By 1800 the great European medieval universities such as Bologna, Paris, and Oxford had been augmented considerably, particularly in Italy and Germany, where individual cities or princes wanted the prestige of a foundation that they had sponsored. In both Europe and the USA traditional courses in grammar, logic, and rhetoric, Greek, Latin, and mathematics still dominated, and graduates went into either the Church or government service. It is estimated that some 160 universities existed in 1800. Higher education expanded at a remarkable rate during the 19th and 20th centuries and by the mid-1990s over 5,000 universities existed, including some 400 in the USA, together with several thousand colleges and institutes of higher education. In the early years of the 19th century many German universities pioneered new curricula with a greater emphasis on science, which became the model for the numerous 19th-century foundations, particularly in the USA. In the late 20th century there was accelerated university expansion, in part created by the granting of university status to academies of science in the former communist bloc and by the upgrading of polytechnics and technical colleges to university status in Britain. The Open University system, using radio and television for advanced distance-learning, was launched in Britain in 1969 and has since then been successfully introduced in other countries.

Unrepresented Nations' and Peoples' Organization (UNPO) An international organization, modelled on the UNITED NATIONS ORGANIZATION, that was established in 1991 to represent ethnic or minority groups aspiring to nationhood. Representatives from TIBET, which has been occupied by Chinese troops since 1951 and made into a province of China, were prominent in the founding of the association. Other members include Australian ABORIGINES, the Lakota Sioux people of North America, the people of EAST TIMOR, and many peoples of the former Soviet Union (including the breakaway Caucasian republics of Chechnya and Ingushetia, seeking independence from Russia, and

Abkhazia, hoping to secede from Georgia). The organization's 1997 assembly, held in Estonia, was attended by 38 delegations, representing 100 million dispossessed people.

Upanishads (Sanskrit, 'sitting near', i.e. at the feet of a master) A collection of more than one hundred HINDU sacred texts composed in Sanskrit at an uncertain date (probably after about 400 BC). They contain a distillation of the teaching of the VEDAS and the Brahamanas (commentaries on the Vedas) and are therefore known as the Vedanta ('the end of the Vedas'), but are more philosophical and mystical in character. Scholars identify in the Upanishadic era the first emergence of a concept within HINDUISM of a single supreme God (Brahman) who is knowable by the human self (atman). Hence the *bhagavadgita*, although part of the later Mahabharata epic, is often classed with the Upanishads as providing the highest and most essential Hindu teaching.

Upper and Lower Canada Two British North American colonies or provinces (1791–1841). Following the American War of INDEPENDENCE (1775–83) many loyalists to the British crown came north into the British colony of QUEBEC. Pressure developed among the settlers in the west for separate status, which was granted by the Constitutional Act of 1791. Quebec was divided along the Ottawa River: the eastern area, with its predominantly French population was known as Lower Canada (now Quebec); the western part was called Upper Canada (now Ontario) and adopted English common law and freehold land tenure. Government in both provinces remained in the hands of a governor appointed by the British crown, advised by an appointed executive council and a legislature consisting of an appointed upper house and a lower assembly of elected representatives, who in fact wielded little power. In both provinces movements for reform developed in the 1830s and, on the accession of Queen Victoria in 1837, two abortive rebellions took place led by Louis Joseph PAPINEAU in Lower Canada and William Lyon MACKENZIE in Upper Canada. In the wake of the DURHAM REPORT (1838), an Act of Union was passed (1840) by the British Parliament and the two provinces united to form United Canada, with a legislature in which Canada West and Canada East enjoyed equal representation. The objective of reformers for cabinet government directly responsible to the legislature was achieved in 1848, under Lord ELGIN.

Upper Palaeolithic The final division of the PALAEOLITHIC or Old STONE AGE, associated with the appearance of *homo sapiens sapiens* about 50,000 years ago. It occupies the second half of the last glaciation, ending 10,000 years ago. During the Upper Palaeolithic the early human population increased and formed larger communities, displaying a faster rate of cultural change than in the Middle Palaeolithic. Distinctive regional groups appeared for the first time. The most developed cultures were on the steppe and tundra belts south of the ice-sheets, where there were plentiful herds of horses, reindeer, and mammoths. Several cultures, distinguished by their styles of toolmaking, can be distinguished in Europe: the earliest is Aurignacian, characterized by the first blade tools and a plentiful use of bone for missile heads. This was followed by the Gravettian, stretching from France to the Ukraine, featuring small pointed stone blades with one blunt edge, small female figurines are also associated with Gravettian culture. More localized traditions, such as the Solutrian and Magdalenian, were responsible for the cave art of south-western France and northern Spain. These cultures disappeared with the onset of warmer conditions at the end of the last Ice Age and the spread of forests, which displaced the large herds of game animals.

Ur (modern Muqayyar) A city of the SUMERIANS. It was occupied from the 5th millennium BC, and was at one point damaged by a severe flood. By 3000 BC it was one of a number of sizeable Sumerian cities. It was subject to the rule of AKKAD, but emerged in about 2150 BC as the capital of a new Sumerian empire, under the third dynasty established by Ur-Nammu. The city was captured by the Elamites in about 2000 BC, but continued to thrive under the Chaldean kings of Babylon. It was finally abandoned in the 4th century BC. Remains of the ancient city include a ziggurat (pyramidal tower), a palace and temple built by Nabonidus of Babylon, and private dwellings. CUNEIFORM inscriptions found there shed light on the economy and administration of the city.

Urban II (Odo of Lagery, c. 1042–99) Pope (1088–99). Urban II was a Cluniac monk who was made Bishop of Ostia near Rome in 1078 and then a cardinal by Pope Gregory VII. At the Council of Clermont in 1095 he preached for the sending of the First CRUSADE to recover PALESTINE, which had fallen to the Muslims, hoping to unite the Christian West, then torn by strife between rival rulers. He continued Gregory's work of church reform and his councils condemned SIMONY, lay INVESTITURE, and clerical marriage.

Urban VIII (Maffeo Barberini, 1568–1644) Pope (1623–44). Urban VIII became a cardinal in 1606 and Bishop of Spoleto in 1608. As pope, he canonized Philip NERI and Ignatius LOYOLA, condemned the astronomer Galileo and JANSENISM (a school of Catholic theology), and approved a number of new religious orders. He was a noted poet, scholar, and patron of the arts, but was given to nepotism, appointing his relatives to high office. In diplomacy, his fears of Habsburg domination in Italy led him to favour France during the THIRTY YEARS WAR. He also extensively fortified the PAPAL STATES and fought the War of Castro (1642–44) against the north Italian Farnese Duke of Parma. The result was a humiliating defeat which crippled the papal finances and made him bitterly unpopular with the Roman people, who had already suffered from his lavish expenditure on the beautification of the city.

urbanization The increase in the proportion of a population living in urban areas and the process by which an area loses its rural character and way of life. Urbanization is a consequence mainly of rural-urban migration. This process began in Europe in the 19th century. Although large cities existed before 1800, the vast majority of the world's population lived in small, often self-sufficient village communities. INDUSTRIALIZATION and population growth in Europe in the 19th century resulted in radical change: sometimes the excess peasant population moved to towns to seek paid work, often having to live in unhygienic slums an dying of infectious diseases; where there was no industrial growth, POPULATION MIGRATION to the New World occurred.

Urbanization in the 20th century has proceeded at an unprecedented rate. In 1900 the UK became the first country to be predominantly urban. In 1920 only about 14% of the world's population lived in urban areas but by 1950 the proportion had reached 25% and by 1990, 43%. The TRANSPORT REVOLUTION has ensured that many villages near large cities in Western Europe or the USA have become little more than dormitories for urban workers, who commute daily to the city. If present trends continue, nearly half the world's population will live in towns and cities at the turn of the century and the figure could reach 60% by 2025. Industrialized countries are the most urbanized: in the early 1990s about 75% of their people lived in urban areas, compared with 30% in developing countries. However, patterns of population growth mean that urban settlements in developing countries are growing three times faster than in industrialized countries and that by the year 2000 urban residents will outnumber rural residents in most developing countries. The natural increase of the existing population is the main component of population growth in some of the fastest-growing cities. Elsewhere, for example in Seoul in South Korea and Lagos in Nigeria, migration in search of work accounts for most of urban growth. In industrialized countries, urban growth has become more gradual; the populations of many big old cities have started to shrink, as disadvantages of city life, such as overcrowding, pollution, and crime, have become more pronounced, and as manufacturing industry has relocated in search of lower costs either in the same country or in developing countries. Attempts to reverse the trend to urbanization, for instance by migration controls, have largely failed. However, urban renewal has helped to halt the decline of some inner-city areas. For governments to ensure housing, water, sanitation, and work for the equivalent of 30,000 extra urban dwellers each day in industrialized countries and 140,000 in developing countries is a task of enormous magnitude.

Urnfield cultures A group of BRONZE AGE cultures of central Europe and associated with peoples who were later identified as CELTS. They first became recognizable as a distinct group in east central Europe in about the 15th century BC, with their origins in Hungary and Romania. Thereafter these cultures spread widely, replacing the TUMULUS CULTURE. Their characteristic feature was the use of cemeteries of flat graves containing the ashes of the cremated dead in urns. They spread into northern Italy and as far as Sicily. In the 11th century BC they crossed into France, and in the 8th century on into Spain. They were followed by the HALLSTATT Iron Age.

Uruguay A country in south-east-central South America with a coast on the Atlantic bounded by Argentina on the west and Brazil on the north-east.

Physical. Uruguay has a coast on the estuary of the River Plate, and the Uruguay River flowing down its western boundary is navigable for some 320 km (200 miles). The country is mainly warm, grassy plain (pampas) supporting cattle and sheep. In the centre and north-east the plain is broken by occasional rocky ridges.

Economy. Uruguay has a predominantly agricultural economy dominated by livestock-rearing. Textiles, wool, and meat are the major exports. Mineral deposits are insignificant (there are some deposits of iron), but hydroelectricity is exported to Brazil, and accounts for some 90% of domestic consumption. Food-processing and textiles are the principal industries.

History. Uruguay was inhabited by various indigenous peoples, such as the Chaná and Charnía, prior to the arrival of Spanish and Portuguese colonists in the 16th century. During the colonial period it was known as the Banda Oriental and became a part of the Spanish vice-royalty of Rio de la Plata. In 1814 the leaders of the Banda Oriental, notably ARTIGAS, broke with the military junta in ARGENTINA and led a struggle for Uruguayan independence until occupied by Brazil in 1820. In 1825 an independent republic of Uruguay was declared, which was recognized by the treaty between Argentina and Brazil, signed at Rio de Janeiro in 1828. Under a republican constitution, the liberals (*Colorados*, redshirts) and the clerical conservatives (*Blancos*, whites) struggled violently throughout the 19th century for political control. In 1872 the *Colorados* began a period of 86 years in office. During the first three decades of the 20th century, José BATLLE Y ORDÓÑEZ, while in and out of the presidency, helped mould Uruguay into South America's first WELFARE STATE. Numerous measures for promoting governmental social services and a state-dominated economy were enacted. In 1958 the elections were won by the *Blancos*. Economic and political unrest plagued the nation throughout the 1960s and saw the emergence of the Marxist terrorist group, the TUPAMAROS. The military took over in the 1970s, but civilian rule was restored in 1985, when Julio Sanguinetti became President. After a long campaign he won a referendum in 1989 in support of an Amnesty Law for political prisoners from the military regime of 1973–85. In 1990 Luis Alberto Lacalle Herrera of the *Blanco* Party succeeded him, forming a coalition government with the *Colorados*. Sanguinetti was re-elected in 1995. Uruguay has emerged as one of the most prosperous and literate nations in the continent, in spite of falling world commodity prices and high inflation.

CAPITAL:	Montevideo
AREA:	176,215 sq km (68,037 sq miles)
POPULATION:	3.140 million (1996)
CURRENCY:	1 Uruguayan new peso = 100 centésimos
RELIGIONS:	Roman Catholic 60.0%; Jewish 2.0%; Protestant 2.0%
ETHNIC GROUPS:	European (Spanish/Italian) 90.0%; Mestizo 3.0%; Jewish 2.0%; mixed 2.0%
LANGUAGES:	Spanish (official)
INTERNATIONAL ORGANIZATIONS:	UN; OAS

Uruk One of the leading cities of the SUMERIANS. A community occupied the site as early as 5000 BC and in the 3rd millennium BC the city was surrounded by a 9.5 km (6 mile) wall, which was attributed in later tradition to the hero GILGAMESH. Excavation has revealed much, not least ziggurats (pyramidal towers), dedicated to the two main gods, Anu and Inanna. It continued to be inhabited into Parthian times.

Ussher, James (1581–1656) Irish theologian, Archbishop of Armagh from 1625. In 1640 he escaped to England on the outbreak of the Irish Rebellion and settled there. A Calvinist but also a royalist, he was well treated by Oliver CROMWELL. Among his writings on a wide variety of subjects was an influential chronology of scripture (1650–54), which set the date of the creation as 23 October 4004 BC.

USSR UNION OF SOVIET SOCIALIST REPUBLICS.

Uthman (Osman) (c. 574–656) Third CALIPH of Islam (644–56). He restored representatives of the old Meccan aristocracy to positions of influence, creating considerable discontent. His personal weakness led to rivalry to his authority from Aisha, the youngest wife of MUHAMMAD, from Ali, his cousin and son-in-law, and others. He was murdered by mutinous troops from Egypt. His lasting memorial was the authorized version of the KORAN, compiled at his order.

Uthman dan Fodio (or Usuman dan Fodio) (1754–1817) West African religious and political leader. A Muslim Fulani, he began teaching in about 1775 among the Hausa and established the Emirates of Northern Nigeria (1804–08) after waging a *jihad* (holy war). He conceived the latter as a primary duty, not only against infidels, but against any departure, public or private, from the original and austere ideals of Islam. Under his rule as caliph, and that of his son, Muhammad Bello (d. 1837), Muslim culture flourished in the FULANI EMPIRE.

utilitarianism An ethical doctrine expounded by Jeremy Bentham and refined by John Stuart MILL. In his *Introduction to the Principles of Morals and Legislation* (1789), Bentham identified the goal of morality as 'the greatest happiness of the greatest number', and, in consequentialist fashion, claimed that an action is right in so far as it tends to promote that goal. Bentham devoted much of his time to attacking the abuses in the legal system, but both he and his followers were to have a profound influence on all aspects of political and social reform in Britain during the 19th century. Acting as a pressure group on both Conservative and Liberal governments, they often gave a lead to public opinion. Mill's essay, *Utilitarianism* (1863), gave perhaps the clearest expression to the doctrine.

As a philosophical proposition, utilitarianism is hampered by the fundamental difficulty of comparing quantitatively the happiness of one person with that of another. Nevertheless, it has proved a remarkably persistent doctrine and continues to attract adherents. Part of its appeal lies in its apparent clarity and simplicity: the concept of happiness seems much less obscure than such rival moral concepts as that of a natural right and the rule 'Maximize happiness', seems to offer a decisive and factual procedure for deciding what to do. Utilitarianism is particularly attractive as a method for public decision-making. However, it is difficult to explain in utilitarian terms why we value things other than happiness, such as equality and justice.

Utopianism A form of speculative thinking in which ideal societies are depicted in order to highlight the defects of those we inhabit. The original *Utopia*, published in 1516 by Sir Thomas MORE, depicted a society whose members lived communally and abstemiously, sharing property, and working under the direction of spiritual leaders. Some of More's ideas have reappeared in later Utopian writings: for instance, the idea of a harmonious society in which everyone works together according to a rational plan. Many 19th-century Utopias were SOCIALIST in inspiration, but the genre is not tied to any particular political creed. It is not always easy to say, moreover, whether the aim of Utopian writing is to describe an ideal society, which the author would like to see brought into existence, or simply to satirize present society by imagining a very different set of arrangements. In the 20th century, so-called 'dystopias' extrapolate present trends to present a nightmarish vision of the future (Aldous Huxley's *Brave New World* (1932) and George Orwell's *1984* (1949) are literary examples) in the hope that such developments can be forestalled.

Utrecht, Peace of (1713) The treaty which ended the War of the SPANISH SUCCESSION. After negotiations between the English and French, a Congress met at Utrecht without Austria and signed the treaties. The Austrian emperor Charles VI found he could not carry on without allies and accepted the terms at Rastadt and Baden in 1714. PHILIP V remained King of Spain but renounced his claim to the French throne and lost Spain's European empire. The southern Netherlands, Milan, Naples, and Sardinia went to Austria. Britain kept Gibraltar and Minorca and obtained the right to supply the Spanish American colonies with Negro slaves, the ASIENTO. From France it gained Newfoundland, Hudson Bay, St Kitts, and recognition of the Hanoverian succession. France returned recent conquests, but kept everything acquired up to the Peace of NIJMEGEN in 1679 and also the city of Strasbourg. The Duke of Savoy gained Sicily and improved frontiers in northern Italy. The Dutch secured Austrian recognition for their right to garrison 'barrier' fortresses in the southern Netherlands. French domination had been checked but France was still a great power. Britain made significant naval, commercial, and colonial gains and thereafter assumed a much greater role in world affairs.

Uzbekistan A country in central Asia situated south of Kazakhstan; to the south and east are Turkmenistan, Afghanistan, Tajikistan, and Kyrgyzstan.

Physical. Uzbekistan stretches south-east from the deserts of the Aral Sea to the Alai Mountains on the border with Afghanistan. At the foot of these lie the fertile Fergana valley and several large oases. The Amu Darya (Oxus) flows north-west to the Aral Sea, providing a second fertile belt, between the Kara Kum sand desert and the Kyzyl Kum desert of stony clay.

Economy. Uzbekistan's principal mineral reserves are natural gas, petroleum, coal, and metal ores (including those of copper and lead), all of which are extracted. Heavy industry focuses on machinery production, particularly for the cultivation and processing of cotton. Other agricultural products are silks, fruit, grapes, and livestock, particularly karakul sheep. The increased mechanization of cotton cultivation has cut employment dramatically and the use of defoliants and pesticides has caused health problems and environmental degradation. In recent decades, aluminium factories have produced uncontrolled wastes that are now affecting fruit-growing areas and livestock.

History. Uzbekistan was the centre of the empire of GENGHIS KHAN and its two ancient cities of Samarkand and Tashkent flourished with the silk caravan trade. Divided into three khanates, Bukhara, Khiva, and Kokand, it was repeatedly attacked by Russia from 1717 until its annexation in 1876. Its Sunni Muslim Uzbeks were excluded from office by the Russians and in 1918 staged a rebellion. This was suppressed by the Red Army and a Soviet Socialist Republic was formed in 1929, which joined the Soviet Union in 1936. After 1989 the republic pressed for independence. The former Communist Party of Uzbekistan, renamed the People's Democratic Party, retained power in the country's parliament following elections in 1990. Uzbekistan declared independence from the Soviet Union in August 1991. However, the commitment of the PDP to democratic reform has been questioned; three major opposition parties are officially proscribed. The banned Islamic Renaissance Party claimed that President Islam Karimov was trying to unseat the Mufti of Tashkent, leader of Islam throughout central Asia. Uzbekistan joined the COMMONWEALTH OF INDEPENDENT STATES in 1991. However, dissatisfaction at the Russian dominance of this body led Uzbekistan to form an alternative economic union with Kazakhstan and Kyrgyzstan in 1994. Karimov has called for the five former Soviet republics of Central Asia to unite in a single Turkic republic of 'Turkestan'.

CAPITAL:	Tashkent
AREA:	447,400 sq km (172,741 sq miles)
POPULATION:	23.206 million (1996)
CURRENCY:	sum
RELIGIONS:	Sunni Muslim; Eastern Orthodox; Jewish and minority faiths
ETHNIC GROUPS:	Uzbek 71.0%; Russian 8.0%; Tatar, Tajik, Ukrainian, and Armenian minorities
LANGUAGES:	Uzbek (official); Russian; minority languages
INTERNATIONAL ORGANIZATIONS:	UN; Commonwealth of Independent States; CSCE; North Atlantic Co-operation Council

Uzbeks A Turkish-speaking people, Mongol by descent and SUNNI Muslim by religion. They moved through Kazakhstan to Turkestan and Transoxania between the 14th and 16th centuries to trouble the SHIITE Safavid rulers of Persia. Initially ruled by the Shaybanids and then the Janids, they later split into dynasties based on Bukhara, Khiva, and Kokand.

vagabonds STURDY BEGGARS; POOR LAWS.

Valley Forge (1777–78) An American Revolutionary winter camp 32 km (20 miles) north-west of Philadelphia that was occupied by WASHINGTON's army after it had been defeated at BRANDYWINE and GERMANTOWN and the British had occupied Philadelphia. A bitter winter and lack of supplies came close to destroying the Continental Army of 11,000 men. The Valley Forge winter was the low point in the American Revolutionary struggle; it hardened the survivors and became a symbol of endurance.

Valley of the Kings A narrow gorge in Egypt, in western THEBES containing the tombs of at least 60 pharaohs of the 18th to 20th dynasties (c. 1550–1050 BC), beginning with THUTMOSE I. Although supposedly secret, it was a rich hunting-ground for robbers in antiquity and of those tombs discovered only that of TUTANKHAMUN had not been plundered.

Valmy, Battle of (1792) The first important engagement of the French Revolutionary wars. Near a small village on the road between Verdun and Paris the French commander-in-chief, Charles-François Dumouriez, with the belated assistance of Marshal François Christophe Kellermann, defeated the Duke of Brunswick's German troops. The French, whose morale was low after a series of defeats, were at first obliged to withdraw, but rallied the next day and forced Brunswick to retreat.

Valois A royal family of France, a branch of the CAPETIANS. When Charles IV died in 1328, an assembly of nobles decided that his daughter could not inherit the throne (see SALIC LAW). Philip of Valois, grandson of Philip III, became PHILIP VI. The direct Valois line ended with the death of Charles VIII, but the dynasty continued under LOUIS XII (Valois-Orléans) and FRANCIS I (Valois-Angoulême). The dynasty was crippled by succession problems and a series of regencies after 1559. The rule of Catherine de MEDICI and her three sons coincided with the FRENCH WARS OF RELIGION. The monarchy was challenged by the HUGUENOTS, the dukes of GUISE, and the Spanish. When Henry III died in 1589, the throne passed to the BOURBONS headed by Henry of Navarre (later HENRY IV).

Van Buren, Martin (1782–1862) Eighth President of the USA (1837–41). He became leader in 1820 of the DEMOCRATIC PARTY in New York. He served in the Senate (1821–28) and then as governor of New York, resigning his post in 1829 to become Secretary of State, only to leave in 1831. Van Buren ran successfully as JACKSON's Vice-President in the election of 1832, and was himself elected President in 1836. However, he lost support when the Democrats split over financial policies in 1837 and he accomplished little in the legislative field. He lost the election of 1840 to HARRISON, failed to secure the nomination in 1844, and ran unsuccessfully as nominee of the breakaway FREE SOIL PARTY in 1848.

Vandals A Germanic tribe that migrated from the Baltic coast in the 1st century BC. After taking Pannonia in the 4th century they were driven further west by the HUNS. With the Suebi and Alemanni they crossed the Rhine into Gaul and Spain where the name Andalusia ('Vandalitia') commemorates them. They were then ousted by the Goths. Taking ship to North Africa under GENSERIC they set up an independent kingdom after the capture of Carthage. In 455 they returned to Italy and sacked Rome. BELISARIUS finally subjugated them in 534.

Vandenberg, Arthur Hendrick (1884–1951) US politician. He entered the US Senate in 1928 as a Republican. He supported much of Franklin D. ROOSEVELT's domestic legislation, but he was an avowed ISOLATIONIST. In 1945, however, he responded to changing world conditions by working for a bipartisan foreign policy and supporting US membership of the UNITED NATIONS. Thereafter he was instrumental in securing the Senate's approval of the MARSHALL PLAN and NATO.

Vanderbilt, Cornelius (1794–1877) US railroad magnate. Starting by ferrying passengers and freight around New York City, he later gaining a virtual monopoly over the ferry lines along the coast. When the GOLD RUSH created a demand, he connected New York and California by running his own shipping line to San Francisco via Nicaragua, constructing his own roads for the overland part of the journey. Turning to railways with the AMERICAN CIVIL WAR, he quickly came to dominate the network in and out of New York and as far west as Chicago. Amassing a vast fortune, he made an endowment of $1 million to found Vanderbilt University.

Van Diemen's Land TASMANIA.

Vane, Sir Henry (the Younger) (1613–62) Leading Parliamentarian, son of Sir Henry Vane (the Elder). He served briefly as governor of Massachusetts (1636–37) then played a leading role in the English LONG PARLIAMENT until 1660. A promoter of the SOLEMN LEAGUE AND COVENANT and the SELF-DENYING ORDINANCE, from 1643 to 1653 he was the civil leader of the Parliamentary cause, while CROMWELL directed the army. He opposed the trial and execution of CHARLES I and in 1653 disagreed with Cromwell over the expulsion of the Rump Parliament. After a period out of politics, he helped to bring about the recall of the Rump (1659). At the RESTORATION he was arrested and executed for treason.

Vanuatu (formerly New Hebrides) A country comprising a double chain of over 80 south-west Pacific Ocean islands.

Physical. Only 13 of Vanuatu's islands are suitable for settlement, the largest being Espiritu Santo, Efate, Malakula, Maewo, Pentecost, Ambrym, Erromango, and Tanna. Of volcanic origin, they are hilly and forested.

Economy. Coconuts are the most important cash crop on Vanuatu; copra is the country's major export. The soil on the slopes of the extinct volcanoes that form the island group is suitable for growing coffee, while livestock are grazed on the warm, wet plains.

History. Inhabited for over 3,000 years, the islands were sighted in 1606 by the Portuguese, rediscovered by the French in 1768, and charted by Captain James Cook (1774), who named them the New Hebrides. In 1887 an Anglo-French naval commission took control of the islands. During the 19th century, thousands of the indigenous people of Vanuatu – KANAKAS – were taken to work on sugar plantations in QUEENSLAND, Australia. The population was decimated and took many years to recover. In World War II Vanuatu served as a major Allied base. The islands became an independent republic and member of the Commonwealth of Nations in 1980.

CAPITAL:	Vila
AREA:	12,190 sq km (4,707 sq miles)
POPULATION:	172,000 (1996)
ETHNIC GROUPS:	mainly Ni-Vanuatu, with European and other minorities
LANGUAGES:	Bislama; French; English
INTERNATIONAL ORGANIZATIONS:	UN; Commonwealth

Varanasi (Benares) A city in north India, which has long been renowned as a centre of PILGRIMAGE for HINDUS from all over India. There they seek ritual purification in the sacred River Ganges and cremate their dead on the ghats (flights of steps) that line the river and on other cremation grounds along the river. The city contains hundreds of temples, most of which have been built since the 17th century, Muslim invaders having destroyed many earlier shrines. Its importance has always been religious and cultural rather than political.

Varennes, Flight to (20 June 1791) The unsuccessful attempt by LOUIS XVI to escape from France and join the exiled royalists. He had been prevented from leaving Paris in April 1791 and elaborate plans for an escape were made. On the night of 20 June the royal party, disguised and with forged passports, left Paris. They were recognized by a postmaster, pursued, and stopped at Varennes. The fugitives were returned and became virtual prisoners in the Tuileries.

Vargas, Getúlio (1883–1954) Brazilian statesman. He governed BRAZIL first as head of a provisional government (1930–34), then as constitutional President elected by Congress (1934–37), then as dictator (1937–45), and finally as constitutional President elected by universal suffrage (1950–54). The fraudulence of the 1930 elections, political corruption, and the growing impact of the Great DEPRESSION on Brazil's vulnerable agricultural economy combined to bring an end to the first or Old Republic (1889–1930), and Vargas assumed power. In 1937 he announced a state of emergency, a ban on all political organizations, the dissolution of Congress, and the promulgation of a new Constitution that would create a nationalist corporate unified 'New State' (Estado Novo), backed by the military. His economic strategy concentrated on the diversification of agricultural production, improvements in transport and communication, the promotion of technical education, the implementation of a new labour code, the national ownership of mineral resources and key industries, and the promotion of industrial expansion. World War II offered a favourable climate for economic growth, and growing commercial and diplomatic co-operation with

the USA led to Brazilian participation in the war (1942). The defeat of the Axis powers brought renewed pressure on Vargas to relax the authoritarianism of the Estado Novo. His reluctance to do this prompted a military coup in 1945, but Vargas' national popularity and his courting of the left resulted in his return to power by popular vote in 1950. Thwarted by a growing economic crisis after 1952 and accused of political corruption, Vargas committed suicide in 1954.

vassal A holder of land by contract from a lord. This tenurial arrangement was one of the essential components of FEUDALISM. The land received was known as a FIEF and the contract was confirmed when the recipient knelt and placed his hands between those of his lord. Counts and dukes received their lands from kings in this way, in some cases acquiring more territory and consequently greater power than their nominal masters. Norman kings of England did homage to kings of France for the duchy of NORMANDY. The contract could legally be broken only by a formal act of defiance.

Vatican City State An independent papal state in Rome, the seat of the Roman Catholic Church. Following the RISORGIMENTO, the Papal States (the modern Italian provinces of Lazio, Umbria, Le Marche, and parts of Emilia-Romagna) became incorporated into a unified Italy in 1870 while, by the Law of Guarantees (1871), the Vatican was granted extraterritoriality. The temporal power of the pope was suspended until the Lateran Treaty of 1929, signed between Pope Pius XI and MUSSOLINI, which recognized the full and independent sovereignty of the Holy See in the City of the Vatican. It covers an area of 44 hectares (109 acres) and has its own police force, diplomatic service, postal service, railway station, coinage, and radio station. It has about 1,000 inhabitants.

The **Vatican Bank** is the official bank of the Vatican City and manages and invests money belonging to the Roman Catholic Church. It was at the centre of a financial scandal in the 1980s that involved allegations of state corruption, but no Vatican Bank officials were brought to trial.

Vauban, Sébastien Le Prestre de (1633–1707) French military engineer. Commissioned in the French Army as an engineer (1655), he compiled for the Minister of War an enormously influential treatise on siege warfare in 1669 (published in Leiden, 1740). Over the period 1672–78 he carried out nearly 20 successful sieges in the Low Countries (e.g. Maastricht, Mons, and Namur), using a succession of parallel trenches to give advancing troops constant protection. He constructed many distinctive fortresses, based on geometrical principles of design to eliminate dead ground. He also developed the technique of indirect ricochet fire and the use of the bayonet (first used at Bayonne, 1650). In spite of the royal favour he long enjoyed, he died in disgrace after writing a pamphlet on taxation, *Projet d'une dîme royale* (1707), that met with LOUIS XIV's disapproval.

Vaudois WALDENSES.

Vedas (Sanskrit, 'wisdom') The most authoritative of the HINDU sacred texts, regarded as *shruti*, the product of divine revelation. They are the earliest Sanskrit scriptures of the Indo-Aryans, having been composed at an uncertain date (*c.* 1500–1200 BC) during and following the ARYAN invasions of India. The basic four collections of *Vedas* consist of the *Rigveda* ('The Veda of Verses'), hymns of praise to the nature gods, particularly Agni, the fire god, and Indra, the warrior god; the *Yajurveda* ('The Veda of Sacrificial Texts'), a collection of sacrificial rites; the *Samaveda* ('The Veda of Chants'), containing the melodies and chants required for special sacrifices; and the *Atharvaveda* ('The Veda of the Fire-Priest'); (included later in the canon), which consists of occult formulas and spells. Later on, commentaries were added, stemming from different schools. The *Brahmanas* are detailed explanations of the sacrifices, for the use of priests. The *aranyakas* are works suitable for the hermit, while the *upanishads* are mystical and philosophical works. They are also known as Vedanta, or 'end of the *Vedas*', and form the basis of the philosophical school of the same name.

Vendée A large area of western France, formed in 1790, which was the centre of a series of counter-revolutionary insurrections from 1793 to 1796. The ideas of the Revolution were slow in penetrating this area and the introduction of conscription acts was a signal for widespread rioting. In March republicans were massacred in the towns and the exiled royalists placed themselves at the head of a Catholic and royal army. This Vendéan army, using its superior knowledge of the area and partly equipped with English arms, scored several victories, though republican armies finally crushed the revolts.

Vendôme, Louis Joseph, duc de (1654–1712) Soldier and Marshal of France. In 1702 at the beginning of the War of the SPANISH SUCCESSION he was made commander in Italy. He defeated Prince EUGÈNE OF SAVOY at Cassano, but in 1708 was defeated by MARLBOROUGH at OUDENARDE. In 1710 he was sent to Spain, where his victories helped to keep PHILIP V on the throne.

Veneti An Italic tribe with their own distinctive language who inhabited north-east Italy from the 1st millennium BC. Always in need of protection against major invasions of Italy by the Gauls and by Hannibal, they remained loyal to the Roman empire. Under the later Roman empire their territory became the province of Venetia. Their geographical position put their cities (for example, Aquileia and Padua) in the path of GOTH and HUN invasions of Italy. A gradual migration took place towards the barely inhabited islands, marshes, and sandbanks of the coastal estuaries. The area grew in prosperity largely through trade. In the 9th century, the Republic of St Mark, better known as VENICE was established.

Venezuela A country on the north coast of South America, with a coastline on the Caribbean Sea. It is bounded by Colombia on the west, Brazil on the south, and Guyana on the east.

Physical. The island-fringed coast of Venezuela is tropical, with lagoons. Much oil is found here, notably around the shallow Lake Maracaibo. At the eastern end of the coast is the swampy delta of the Orinoco River. Inland are the llanos and the maritime Andes. The Guyana Highlands lie in the south of the country and contain the Angel Falls, the highest in the world.

Economy. The Venezuelan economy is dominated by state-owned oil production and associated industries, but production has fallen due to a policy of

conservation. Also, attempts have been made to diversify the economy. There are substantial mineral deposits, including bauxite and iron ore, refined by the government-owned steel industry. Although agriculture is potentially rich, Venezuela imports about 60% of its food. The economy has suffered from its over-dependence on oil, high rates of inflation, and foreign debt.

History. Venezuela was visited in 1499 by the explorer Amerigo Vespucci, who gave it its name ('Little Venice') after sighting native houses built on stilts on lake Maracaibo. It was subsequently colonized by the Spanish. By the mid-18th century wealthy Creoles (Spaniards born in the colony) were protesting against trade restrictions imposed by Madrid. It was in its capital Caracas that the Colombian Independence Movement began (1806), resulting in the creation by Simón BOLÍVAR of Gran Colombia. When this collapsed in 1829, Venezuela proclaimed itself a republic under its first President, General José Antonio PÁEZ (1830–43), who, while preserving the great estates, provided a strong administration, allowed a free press, and kept the army under control. The period that followed (1843–70) was politically chaotic and violent. Under President Guzmán BLANCO (1870–88) moves were made towards democracy, with the first election in 1881, and there was growth in economic activity. Despotic government returned under the CAUDILLOS Cipriano Castro (1899–1908) and Juan Vicente GÓMEZ (1909–35). Oil was discovered before World War I and by 1920 Venezuela was the world's leading exporter of oil. Military juntas continued to dominate until Rómulo Betancourt completed a full term as a civilian President (1959–64), to be peacefully succeeded by Dr Raul Leoni (1964–69). Since then, democratic politics have continued to operate, with two parties, Accion Democratica and Christian Democrat, alternating in power, even though extremists of left and right have harassed them with terrorism. A post-war oil boom brought considerable prosperity, but rising population and inflation caused many problems for President Dr Jaime Lusinchi (1983–88). Falling oil prices and increased drug trafficking were additional problems for his successor Carlos Andrés Pérez, who faced serious riots in 1989 for his austerity measures, and two unsuccessful military coup attempts in 1992. In 1993 Pérez was removed from office and charged with corruption (he was found guilty and imprisoned in 1996). Elections in December 1993 saw Rafael Caldera Rodríguez accede to the presidency.

CAPITAL:	Caracas
AREA:	912,050 sq km (352,144 sq miles)
POPULATION:	22.311 million (1996)
CURRENCY:	1 bolivar = 100 centimos
RELIGIONS:	Roman Catholic 92.0%
ETHNIC GROUPS:	Mestizo 69.0%; White 20.0%; Black 9.0%; Amerindian 2.0%
LANGUAGES:	Spanish (official); Amerindian languages
INTERNATIONAL ORGANIZATIONS:	UN; OAS; OPEC; Andean Group

Venice A city built on the islands of a lagoon on the Adriatic coast of north-east Italy. The islands were first inhabited by the VENETI as a refuge from barbarian invasion in the 5th century and by the end of the 6th century were permanently inhabited. They were extended and sea defences were built. From 726 rulers, or DOGES, were elected and Venice became a republic independent of the Byzantine empire in the 9th century. Venice became a maritime power, defeating pirates and growing rich on the profits from trade with the East. Venice was prominent in the CRUSADES: it benefited from the sack of CONSTANTINOPLE (1204). On the mainland of Italy it ruled the large adjoining province known as Venetia and also many Greek islands.

The republic at the height of its powers dominated the Mediterranean, gaining Cyprus in the 15th century and ruling the towns of Bergamo, Brescia, Padua, Verona, and Vicenza: 'the Veneto'. Government was in the hands of a few great families. Although successful at the naval Battle of LEPANTO against the Turks in 1571, it lost Cyprus and its power declined thereafter. Succumbing easily to the French invasion of 1797, it was given to Austria, but in the 19th century joined the kingdom of Italy. In the 20th century, large-scale projects have been undertaken to protect the city from subsidence and the damaging effects of pollution.

Venizélos, Eleuthérios (1864–1936) Greek statesman. Active in the anti-Turkish movement of 1895–1905, he became Premier (1910), modernizing Greek political institutions and joining the Balkan League against Turkey. In 1914 his wish to join the Allies was thwarted by the pro-German King Constantine, who later abdicated, thus enabling Greek troops to fight Germany. At the VERSAILLES PEACE SETTLEMENT he negotiated promises of considerable territorial gains – the Dodecanese, western Thrace, Adrianople, and Smyrna in Asia Minor. In the event, following the challenge of ATATÜRK's army only western Thrace was gained, and he resigned. Greece alternated between monarchy and republic and his periods as Premier alternated with periods in exile.

Vercingetorix (d. 46 BC) King of the tribe of the Averni in Gaul. Towards the end of the GALLIC WARS in 52 BC he revolted against Roman occupation and was acclaimed King of the united Gauls. He was defeated and captured and was finally paraded through Rome as a trophy in CAESAR's triumph (46 BC) and then executed.

Verdun, Treaty of (843) The peace made between the Frankish kings Lothar, Louis, and Charles, the grandsons of CHARLEMAGNE, who had been fighting a civil war. When their father, Louis the Pious, died in 840 he bequeathed them the united CAROLINGIAN EMPIRE, but the brothers could not agree on how to divide the inheritance and they fought until 842. Long negotiations then culminated in the meeting in Verdun where the empire was divided into three kingdoms. Charles and Louis received West and East Francia (roughly, present-day France and Germany), while Lothar held the middle kingdom, a long strip of territory stretching from the North Sea over the Alps to Rome and bordered in the west by the rivers Scheldt, Meuse, and Saône and in the east by the Rhine. The treaty was not governed by geographical factors but was an attempt to satisfy the claims of each brother for a share in the Carolingian family estates, many of which were in the fertile lands of the middle kingdom, Lotharingia. Lotharingia soon lost its own identity and became a battleground for the embryonic kingdoms of France and Germany.

Vereeniging, Treaty of (31 May 1902) The peace treaty that ended the Second BOER WAR. It provided for the acceptance by Boers of British sovereignty, the use of Afrikaans in schools and law courts, a civil administration leading to self-government, a repatriation commission, and compensation of £3 million for the destruction inflicted during the war on Boer farms.

Vermont A state in the USA, in western NEW ENGLAND. Settlement began in the mid-18th century, but as the region was claimed by both New York and New Hampshire, the pioneers formed the GREEN MOUNTAIN BOYS under Ethan ALLEN in 1771 to protect their property rights. After the British defeat at BENNINGTON (1777), the next 14 years were spent in securing US statehood, through negotiations, threats of joining the British empire, or declaring an independent republic. In 1791 it became the 14th state and attracted small farmers from southern New England.

Vernon, Edward (1684–1757) English admiral. In 1739 he was sent to fight against the Spanish in the Caribbean. He captured Porto Bello (now in Panama) in the opening phase of the War of JENKINS'S EAR in 1739, but failed disastrously at Cartagena (now in Colombia) in 1741. His boat-cloak of grogram (a mixture of silk, mohair, and wool) gave him the nickname 'Old Grog'. 'Grog' became the name of the naval rum ration when diluted with three parts of water, as Vernon was in the habit of issuing to his own sailors. He was removed from the active list in 1746 because he was thought to be the author of anonymous pamphlets attacking the Admiralty.

Verrazzano, Giovanni da (c. 1485–c. 1528) Italian (Florentine) navigator in the service of France. He led three expeditions in search of a westward passage into the Pacific and thus to the East. In 1524 he explored the North American coast from North Carolina to New York Bay and continued north to Newfoundland before returning to Dieppe. In 1527 he took a second expedition across the Atlantic and reached Brazil. He set out once more in 1528 but was met in the Antilles by cannibal CARIBS who killed and ate him.

Versailles A city in northern France, the site of a great palace, 16 km (10 miles) from Paris, built by LOUIS XIV of France. In 1682 it became the seat of government; here Louis moved through the day according to a strict pattern of ceremonial and attendance at court was essential to any nobleman who wished to retain the royal favour. Further reconstruction and redecoration was executed under LOUIS XV and LOUIS XVI and MARIE ANTOINETTE. The king was forced to leave the palace in October 1789 during the FRENCH REVOLUTION. It was stripped of much of its contents and today the palace is a museum.

Versailles Peace Settlement (or Paris Peace Settlement) (1919–23) A collection of peace treaties between the Central Powers and the Allied Powers ending World War I. The main treaty was that of Versailles (June 1919) between the Allied Powers (except for the USA, which refused to ratify the treaty) and Germany, whose representatives were required to sign it without negotiation. Germany had concluded an armistice in 1918 based on the FOURTEEN POINTS of President WILSON. By a new 'war-guilt' clause in the treaty Germany was required to accept responsibility for provoking the war. Various German-speaking territories were to be surrendered, including ALSACE-LORRAINE to France. In the east, POLAND was resurrected, and given parts of Upper Silesia and the POLISH CORRIDOR to the Baltic Sea, while Gdańsk (Danzig) was declared a free city. Parts of East Silesia went to Czechoslovakia; the Ardennes towns of Moresnet, Eupen, and Malmédy to Belgium; and the SAAR RIVER valley was placed under international control for 15 years, as was the Rhineland, which, together with Heligoland, was to be demilitarized. Overseas colonies in Africa and the Far East were to be MANDATED to Britain, France, Belgium, South Africa, Japan, and Australia. Germany was henceforth to keep an army of not more than 100,000 men and to have no submarines or military aircraft. REPARATIONS were fixed in 1921 at £6,500 million, a sum that was to prove impossible to pay. Many aspects of the treaty were criticized as excessive and its unpopularity in Germany created a political and economic climate that enabled HITLER to come to power. The treaty established the LEAGUE OF NATIONS and the INTERNATIONAL LABOUR ORGANISATION.

A second treaty, that of St Germain-en-Laye (September 1919), was between the Allied powers and the new republic of AUSTRIA. The HABSBURGS had been deposed and the imperial armed forces disbanded. Austria recognized the independence of Czechoslovakia, Yugoslavia, Poland, and Hungary. Eastern Galicia, the Trentino, South Tyrol, Trieste, and Istria were ceded by Austria. There was to be no union (Anschluss) with Germany. Austria, like Germany, was to pay reparations for 30 years. A third treaty, that of Trianon (June 1920), was with the new republic of HUNGARY, whereby some three-quarters of its old territories (i.e., all non-Magyar lands) were lost to Czechoslovakia, Romania, and Yugoslavia, and the principle of reparations again accepted. A fourth treaty, that of Neuilly (November 1919), was with BULGARIA, whereby some territory was lost to Yugoslavia and Greece, but some also gained from Turkey; a figure of £100 million reparations was agreed, but never paid. These four treaties were ratified in Paris during 1920. A fifth treaty, that of SÈVRES (August 1920), between the Allies and the old OTTOMAN EMPIRE was never implemented as it was followed by the final disintegration of the empire and the creation by Mustafa Kemal ATATÜRK of the new republic of Turkey. The treaty was replaced by the Treaty of Lausanne (July 1923), whereby Palestine, Transjordan, and Iraq were to be mandated to Britain, and Syria to France. Italy was accepted as possessing the Dodecanese Islands, while Turkey regained Smyrna from Greece. The Dardanelles Straits were to be demilitarized and Turkey would pay no reparations.

Verwoerd, Hendrik Frensch (1901–66) South African statesman. As Minister of Native Affairs (1950–58) he was responsible for establishing the policy of APARTHEID. He became Nationalist Party leader and Prime Minister (1958–66). During his government, in the aftermath of the SHARPEVILLE MASSACRE, South Africa became a republic and left the Commonwealth. Harsh measures were taken to silence Black opposition, including the banning of the AFRICAN NATIONAL CONGRESS. He was assassinated in Parliament.

Vesey, Telemaque 'Denmark' (c. 1767–1822) Leader of a planned American slave revolt. A slave who had educated himself and purchased his freedom having won a street lottery, Vesey in 1822 inspired a group of slaves with the idea of seizing the arsenals of Charleston, South Carolina, as a prelude to a mass escape to the West Indies. However, the plan was betrayed by a house servant and Vesey and about 130 of his followers were arrested, 32 were exiled and 35, including Vesey, were hanged. The authorities responded by tightening the restrictive 'black codes' as a means of controlling the slave population.

Vespasian (Titus Flavius Sabinus Vespasianus) (9–79 AD) Roman emperor (69–79 AD), the first of the Flavian emperors. Consul in 51, he became a governor in North Africa in 63. On the outbreak of the JEWISH REVOLT in 66 NERO sent him to quell Palestine, but on Nero's death he suspended operations, leaving his son Titus in command. He refused to accept Vitellius in the imperial civil war and was proclaimed emperor by his legions in 69. He restored discipline in the army after the civil war, pacified the frontiers, and restored the exhausted economy, largely by taxation. He kept the administration under tight control so that, after a peaceful rule, he died leaving Rome solvent.

Vespucci, Amerigo (1451–1512) Italian merchant, navigator, and explorer. While in the service of the king of Portugal, Vespucci made several voyages to the New World and claimed, on dubious authority, to have been the first to sight the mainland of South America (1497). There is no doubt, however, that he was an experienced navigator and he evolved a system for computing nearly exact longitude. The name America is said to have been derived from his own first name, but there are other suggestions of its origin.

Vestal virgin An attendant of VESTA, goddess of fire, hearth, and home. There were six Vestal virgins, chosen by lot from a short list of aristocratic girls. Under vows of chastity they served for 30 years, dressed as brides, cleaning Vesta's shrine and tending its fire. Unchaste Vestals were buried alive. They lived in the House of the Vestals in the FORUM at Rome and wills were deposited with them for safe-keeping.

Vichy government (1940–45) The French government established after the Franco-German armistice in World War II. The Germans having occupied Paris, the government was set up under Marshal PÉTAIN in the spa town of Vichy by the French National Assembly (1940) to administer unoccupied France and the colonies. Having dissolved the Third Republic, it issued a new constitution establishing an autocratic state. The Vichy government was never recognized by the Allies. In 1941 it granted Japan right of access and air bases in Indo-China, from which it was to launch its Malaya and Burma campaigns. It was dominated first by LAVAL, as Pétain's deputy (1940), then by DARLAN (1941–42) in collaboration with Hitler, and once more (1942–44) by Laval as Pétain's successor after German forces moved in to the unoccupied portions of France. After the Allied liberation of France (1944), the Vichy government established itself under Pétain at Sigmaringen in Germany, where it collapsed when Germany surrendered in 1945.

Vicksburg Campaign (November 1862–July 1863) A military campaign in the AMERICAN CIVIL WAR. By the autumn of 1862 the stronghold of the CONFEDERACY forces at Vicksburg in western Mississippi was the last remaining obstacle to Union (Northern) control of the Mississippi River. In late 1862 advances by Generals GRANT and SHERMAN failed to capture the city. In May 1863 Grant started a siege of the city. After six weeks of resistance, Vicksburg surrendered on 4 July. With its capture, the Confederacy was effectively split in half. The Union success at Vicksburg and GETTYSBURG in July 1863 marked a major turning-point in the Civil War.

Victor Emanuel II (1820–78) King of Sardinia (Piedmont) (1849–61) and first King of Italy (1860–78). He succeeded to the throne of Sardinia after the abdication of his father, Charles Albert. He fought in the REVOLUTIONS OF 1848 against Austrian rule and, on his accession to the throne, appointed CAVOUR as Premier (1852). The central figure of the RISORGIMENTO, he sought the support of Britain and France in his bid for the reunification of Italy by entering the CRIMEAN WAR as their ally. Proclaimed King of Italy in 1861, he supported Prussia in the AUSTRO-PRUSSIAN WAR (1866). His troops seized the Papal States (1870), and Rome was made the capital of Italy in 1871.

Victor Emanuel III (1869–1947) King of Italy (1900–46). Succeeding Humbert I, he retained good relations with France and Britain although a member of the TRIPLE ALLIANCE, and maintained neutrality in World War I, until joining the Allies in 1915. With the breakdown of parliamentary government after World War I, he refused to suppress a fascist uprising and asked MUSSOLINI to form a government (1922), fearing the alternative to be civil war and communism. He was created Emperor of Ethiopia (1936) and King of Albania (1939). He dismissed Mussolini (1943), replacing him with BADOGLIO, and concluded an armistice with the Allies soon after. He declared war on Germany in October 1943. In 1946 he abdicated, dying in exile in Egypt a year later.

Victoria (1819–1901) Queen of Great Britain and Ireland and of dependencies overseas (1837–1901) and (from 1876) Empress of India. The last of the House of Hanover, she was the only child of George III's fourth son, Edward, Duke of Kent. She came to the throne in 1837 on the death of her uncle, WILLIAM IV. She was guided in the performance of her duties as a monarch by the Prime Minister, Lord MELBOURNE. Her marriage to Prince ALBERT of Saxe-Coburg-Gotha in 1840 was to prove a happy one; his early death in 1861 was a blow from which she never fully recovered and her withdrawal from public life during the early years of her widowhood did not enhance her popularity. Benjamin DISRAELI persuaded her to take her place once more in the life of the nation, but it was largely at her own instigation that she was declared Empress of India by the Royal Titles Act of 1876. By the 1880s she had won the respect and admiration of her subjects at large. The Golden and Diamond Jubilees were great imperial occasions. Her death in 1901 marked the end of an era to which she had given her name, the Victorian Age, during which Britain had become the world's leading industrial power at the centre of the BRITISH EMPIRE.

Victoria A state of south-east Australia, bounded by South Australia on the west and, along the Murray River, by New South Wales on the north. Victoria has south and east coasts and is separated by Bass Strait from Tasmania.

History. In the early years of White settlement, Victoria formed part of New South Wales. Convict settlements there were short-lived (1803–04, 1826–28). There were no permanent settlements until 1834 and 1835, after when SQUATTERS moved in. The area was separated from New South Wales and named Victoria in 1851. GOLD RUSHES, notably to Ballarat and Bendigo, began that year. The EUREKA REBELLION occurred in 1854. Restrictions on Chinese immigration, imposed in 1855, marked the beginning of the WHITE AUSTRALIA POLICY. Between 1860 and 1890 attempts were made to 'unlock the lands' for SELECTORS. Victoria became a state of the newly created Commonwealth of AUSTRALIA in 1901. Many NEW AUSTRALIAN immigrants arrived in Victoria immediately after World War II.

Vienna, Congress of (1814–15) An international peace conference that settled the affairs of Europe after the defeat of NAPOLEON. It continued to meet through the HUNDRED DAYS of Napoleon's return to France (March–June 1815). The dominant powers were Austria, represented by METTERNICH, Britain, represented by CASTLEREAGH, Prussia, represented by FREDERICK WILLIAM III, and Russia, represented by ALEXANDER I. TALLEYRAND represented Louis XVIII of France. The Congress agreed to the absorption by the new kingdom of the Netherlands of what had been the Austrian Netherlands (now Belgium), but otherwise the Habsburgs regained control of all their domains, including Lombardy, Venetia, Tuscany, Parma, and TYROL. Prussia gained parts of Saxony as well as regaining much of Westphalia and the Rhineland. Denmark, which had allied itself with France, lost Norway to Sweden. In Italy the pope was restored to the VATICAN and the Papal States, and the Bourbons were re-established in the Kingdom of the Two Sicilies. The GERMAN CONFEDERATION was established and Napoleon's Grand Duchy of Warsaw was to be replaced by a restored Kingdom of Poland, but as part of the Russian empire with the Russian emperor also king of Poland. The Congress restored political stability to Europe, but often at the cost of nationalist and liberal aspirations.

Vietcong Communist guerrilla organization operating in South Vietnam (1960–75). Opposition to the Saigon-based regime of NGO DINH DIEM had already produced widespread guerrilla activity in South Vietnam when communist interests founded the National Front for the Liberation of South Vietnam (known to its opponents as the Vietcong) in 1960. As US military support for the Saigon government broadened into the full-scale VIETNAM WAR so Vietcong forces were supplied with arms and supported by North Vietnamese forces brought to the south via the Ho Chi Minh Trail, which passed through neighbouring Laos and Cambodia. They maintained intensive guerrilla operations and occasionally fought large set-piece battles. They finally undermined both US support for the war and the morale of the South Vietnamese army and opened the way for communist triumph and the reunification of Vietnam in 1975.

Vietminh Vietnamese communist guerrilla movement. Founded in 1941 in south China by HO CHI MINH and other exiled Vietnamese members of the Indo-Chinese Communist Party with the aim of expelling both the French and the Japanese from Vietnam, the Vietminh began operations, with assistance from the USA, against the Japanese in 1943–45 under the military leadership of Vo Nguyen GIAP. After the end of World War II, it resisted the returning French, building up its strength and organization through incessant guerrilla operations and finally winning a decisive set-piece engagement at DIENBIENPHU in 1954. This forced the French to end the war and grant independence to Vietnam, partitioned into two states, North and South.

Vietnam A country in south-east Asia, shaped like an 'S', bordering on China on the north and Laos and Cambodia on the west, and having long east and south coasts on the South China Sea.

Physical. In the north of Vietnam the Red and Black Rivers flow from forested mountains across very warm, wet lowlands spread with paddy-fields. The south is even wetter, with rice being cultivated all down the coastal strip and in the Mekong delta. Rubber and other crops are grown in areas where the ground rises to the central highlands.

Economy. Despite policies of economic liberalization and a decision in 1986 to switch to a free-market economy, the Vietnamese government maintains its adherence to communism. Primarily agricultural, the Vietnamese economy has been badly damaged by war, poor climatic conditions, and a US embargo and veto on Western aid. Once-substantial Soviet aid has ceased and many of the Vietnamese migrant workers in the former Eastern bloc have returned home. The chief agricultural crops are rice, sugar cane, tea, coffee, rubber, and fruits, but Vietnam depends on imports to meet its food requirements. There are large reserves of coal, iron ore, manganese, and other minerals, including off-shore oil fields.

History. The kingdom of Nam Viet emerged in about 200 BC but was taken over by China. From the 1st to the 6th century the kingdom of Funan flourished around the Mekong delta. The Chinese were expelled in the 10th century and MONGOL raids were repelled, but the area was occupied by China again from 1407 until 1428. Over the following centuries a Vietnamese nation emerged, comprising the regions of ANNAM, COCHIN CHINA, and Tonkin. The country was divided in 1757 but in 1802 the two states of ANNAM and Tonkin were reunited by the Annamese general Nguyen Anh, who became emperor Gia-Long. Gia-Long was given French assistance and French influence increased in the 19th century. By 1883 Vietnam was part of FRENCH INDO-CHINA, although a weak monarchy was allowed to remain. In World War II the Japanese occupied it but allowed VICHY France to administer it until March 1945. In September 1945 HO CHI MINH declared its independence, but this was followed by French reoccupation and the FRENCH INDO-CHINA WAR. The GENEVA CONFERENCE (1954), convened to seek a solution to the Indochina conflict, partitioned Vietnam along the 17th parallel, leaving a communist Democratic Republic with its capital at Hanoi in the north, and, after the deposition of the former emperor BAO DAI in 1955, a non-communist republic with its capital at Saigon in the south. Ho Chi Minh, the North Vietnamese leader, remained committed to a united communist country and by the time the South Vietnamese president NGO DINH DIEM was overthrown by the military in 1963, communist insurgents of the VIETCONG were already active in the south. Communist attempts to take advantage of the political confusion in the south were accelerated by the infusion of massive US military

assistance and in the late 1960s and early 1970s the VIETNAM WAR raged throughout the area, with the heavy use of US airpower failing to crush growing communist strength. Domestic pressures helped accelerate a US withdrawal and, after abortive peace negotiations, the North Vietnamese and their Vietcong allies finally took Saigon in April 1975; a united Socialist Republic of Vietnam was proclaimed in the following year. Despite the severe damage done to the economy, Vietnam adopted an aggressively pro-Soviet foreign policy, dominating Laos, invading Cambodia to overthrow the KHMER ROUGE regime (1975–79), and suffering heavily in a brief border war with China (1979). In 1989 Vietnamese troops withdrew from Cambodia. Attempts to reorder society in the south of the country produced a flood of refugees, damaging Vietnam's international standing and increasing its dependence on the Soviet Union. Many of these refugees were from the Chinese minority; known as the 'Boat People,' they fled Vietnam in small boats on the South China Sea. With the disintegration of the Soviet Union in 1991, Vietnam was prompted to normalize relations with China and the USA. A new constitution was adopted in 1992, incorporating major economic and political reforms. However, the Communist Party of Vietnam retained its dominant position as the sole political party. Relations with the USA continued to improve during the 1990s with joint investigations taking place into the whereabouts of US servicemen missing in action during the Vietnam War and full diplomatic links were restored in 1995. Economic links were forged with the USA and other countries (e.g. Japan and Britain), notably to exploit oil and natural gas fields in the country's territorial waters. Vietnam became a full member of the Association of South-East Asian Nations (ASEAN) in 1995. Following elections in 1997 Tran Duc Luong became President and Phan Van Khai became Prime Minister.

CAPITAL:	Hanoi
AREA:	331,688 sq km (128,065 sq miles)
POPULATION:	76.151 million (1996)
CURRENCY:	1 dong = 10 hao = 100 xu
RELIGIONS:	Buddhist 55.3%; Roman Catholic 7.0%; Muslim 1.0%
ETHNIC GROUPS:	Vietnamese (Kinh) 88.0%; Chinese (Hoa) 2.0%; Tai 2.0%; Khmer 1.0%; Muong 1.0%; Thai 1.0%; Nung 1.0%
LANGUAGES:	Vietnamese (official); minority languages
INTERNATIONAL ORGANIZATIONS:	UN, ASEAN

Vietnam War (1964–75) The period of the civil war in Vietnam after the commencement of large-scale US military involvement in 1964. Guerrilla activity in South Vietnam had become widespread by 1961, in which year President NGO DINH DIEM proclaimed a state of emergency. Continued communist activity against a country perceived in the USA as a bastion against the spread of communism in south-east Asia led to increasing US concern and after an alleged North Vietnamese attack on US warships in the Gulf of Tonki in 1964, President Johnson was given congressional approval (TONKIN GULF RESOLUTION) to take military action By the summer of 1965 a US army of 125,000 men was serving in the country and by 1967 the figure had risen to 400,000, while US aircraft carried out an intensive bombing campaign against North Vietnam. Contingent from South Korea, Australia, New Zealand, and Thailan fought with the US troops. Although communist forces were held temporarily in check, the war provoked widespread opposition within the USA and after the TET OFFENSIVE of February 1968 had shaken official belief in the possibility of victory, the bombing campaign was halted and attempts to find a formula for peace talks started. US policy now began to emphasize the 'Vietnamization' of the war and as increasing efforts were made to arm and train the South Vietnamese army, so US troops were gradually withdrawn. Nevertheless, US forces were still caught up in heavy

fighting in the early 1970s and the bombing campaign was briefly resumed on several occasions. US troops were finally withdrawn after the Paris Peace Accords of January 1973, but no lasting settlement between North and South proved possible and in early 1975 North Vietnamese forces finally triumphed, capturing Saigon (the capital of South Vietnam; renamed Ho Chi Minh City in 1976) on 30 April 1975. The war did enormous damage to the socio-economic fabric of the Indochinese states, devastating Vietnam and destabilizing neighbouring Cambodia (Kampuchea) and Laos.

vigilante A member of a self-appointed body for the maintenance of law and order in the US West. With the slow development of official policing, vigilance committees, organized and manned by local citizens, frequently took the law into their own hands, meting out rough justice and sometimes resorting to lynch law. They disappeared in the USA with the growth of official institutions in the last decades of the 19th century.

Vijayanagar (Sanskrit, 'City of Victory') A ruined city site on the River Tungabhadra in south India that was, from the 14th to the 17th century, the centre of a powerful Hindu empire. It was founded in 1336, its name reflecting the rise of a new southern dynasty filling the vacuum left by CHOLA collapse. Three dynasties ruled successively, the Sangama (1336–c. 1485), the Saluva (c. 1485–1505), and the Tuluva (c. 1505–65). The empire reached its peak under Krisna Deva Raya (1509–29), but soon afterwards concerted Muslim pressure from the Deccan kingdoms of Bijapur, Ahmadnagar, and Golconda resulted in the massive defeat at the battle of Talikota (1565) in which Vijayanagar was destroyed. Despite some recovery under the upstart Aravidu dynasty, the empire, one of the greatest in India's history, had collapsed by the early 17th century. It had prevented Muslim penetration into south India and had revitalized Hindu religious and literary traditions.

Vikings Scandinavian traders and pirates of the 8th to 12th centuries. In the 8th century the Vikings began one of the most remarkable periods of expansion in history. Setting sail from Denmark and Norway, they voyaged westward in longships through the Shetlands, Iceland, and Greenland, as far as VINLAND (modern Newfoundland). They attacked Britain and Ireland, ravaged the coast of continental Europe as far as Gibraltar, and entered the Mediterranean, where they fought Arabs as well as Europeans. From the Baltic they sailed down the rivers of western Russia to a point from which they threatened Constantinople. In Europe they were able to strike far inland, sailing up the Rhine, Loire, and other rivers. Local rulers often preferred to buy them off, rather than resist.

The Vikings were also traders and farmers in the areas they settled, including Normandy, the north of England, and the area around Dublin in Ireland. They were skilled wood- and metalworkers and manufactured superb jewellery. They had a powerful oral poetic tradition, manifest in their sagas. They were an extremely adaptable people, able to absorb the cultures which they encountered while retaining their own vital qualities. This adaptability was perhaps forced upon them because they were greatly outnumbered by the native populations; it was easier to modify existing forms than to impose their own. They adopted

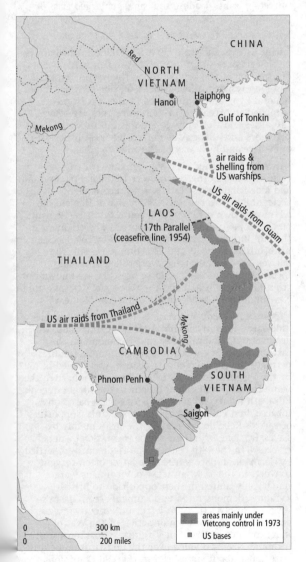

Vietnam War *By 1963 the communist leader of North Vietnam, Ho Chi Minh, had established a network of Vietcong (communist) insurgents in South Vietnam. In the USA strategists argued that all south-east Asia was at risk unless South Vietnam was buttressed against communism and by 1967 some half million US troops were fighting there, with Thailand providing air-bases for US raids against Vietcong strongholds. Two years after the US withdrawal (1973) Saigon was captured and renamed Ho Chi Minh City.*

languages and quickly modified fighting styles to suit land-based operations. The NORMANS were descendants of the Viking ROLLO's settlement in Normandy, they became a powerful element in Europe, the CRUSADES, and throughout the Mediterranean.

Viking ship The type of vessel used by the VIKINGS for trade and warfare (c. 850–1200 AD). Viking warships were long, open, oared vessels, clinker-built and rowed by 40 to 80 men. They had a short mast carrying a single square sail that could be braced to allow some measure of travel into the wind. The larger vessels had a part-deck fore and aft. Viking trading ships ('knorrs') were broader in beam and relied on sails much more than on oar power. The Vikings sailed in such vessels as far as VINLAND (Newfoundland) to the west, northern Africa to the south, and the Black Sea to the east.

Villa, Francisco ('Pancho', born Doroteo Arango) (1877–1923) Mexican revolutionary leader. He pursued an early career as a bandit and a merchant before taking up the cause of Francisco MADERO in the MEXICAN REVOLUTION of 1910. Along with Pascual Orozco, Villa provided the military leadership that was responsible for Madero's defeat of Porfirio DÍAZ. After Madero's assassination in 1913, Villa first joined and then broke with the constitutionalist opposition to the usurper Victoriano Huerta. During 1914–15 Villa held sway in Chihuahua with his cavalry, *los dorados*, expropriating the holdings of large landowners and using their revenues to equip the revolutionary army in Mexico. By late 1915 he had been defeated by CARRANZA and other revolutionary factions. With ZAPATA, he moved north, and for reasons still controversial, ordered an attack (1916) on the US town of Columbus, New Mexico, killing 17 Americans and provoking retaliation from a punitive expedition under General PERSHING. He escaped and lived in retirement until he was assassinated.

Villafranca di Verona, Treaty of (1859) An agreement between France and Austria. After the battles of MAGENTA and SOLFERINO, NAPOLEON III and FRANCIS JOSEPH met at Villafranca, where the Austrians agreed to an armistice. Austria handed Lombardy over to France, who later passed it to Sardinia (Piedmont) but retained Venetia. The rulers of the central Italian duchies were restored. Piedmont acquiesced and CAVOUR resigned.

Villanovans One of the peoples occupying Italy during the IRON AGE. Their territory included Tuscany and Latium as far as Rome and reached out into Campania. They were great bronzesmiths and were the first in their area to work iron. Evidence for them comes largely from rich cremation cemeteries of the 10th to 8th century BC, when they become recognizable historically as the ETRUSCANS, whose cities occupy former Villanovan sites.

Villehardouin, Geoffroi de (c. 1150–1217) French historian and Marshal of Champagne. He took part in the disastrous Fourth CRUSADE and became Marshal of the Eastern empire. His work *Conquête de Constantinople* described and justified the Fourth Crusade and is one of the earliest examples of French prose.

villein (Latin *villanus*, 'villager') A medieval peasant entirely subject to a lord or attached to a manor, similar to a SERF. Both groups were part of the MANORIAL SYSTEM, which dominated Europe between the 4th and 13th centuries. Villeins provided labour services to the lord (in return for tilling their own strips of land). In England these services could vary from region to region. There were few villeins in Kent or East Anglia; labour services in the Midlands were not usually heavy. Ecclesiastical estates, however, tended to make severe demands of their villeins. By the 13th century villeins in England had become unfree tenants. In Europe they had fewer duties and remained essentially free peasants, creating a significant difference in rank to the serfs. By the 15th century, even in England, social and economic changes had blurred the distinctions between free and unfree peasants, leading to a single enlarged class of peasants.

Villiers BUCKINGHAM, GEORGE VILLIERS, 1ST DUKE OF.

Vimy Ridge, Battle of (9 April 1917) An Allied attack on a German position in World War I, near Arras in France. One of the key points on the WESTERN FRONT, it had long resisted Allied attacks. Canadian troops under General Byng and commanded by General Horne launched an offensive. In 15 minutes, despite heavy casualties, most of Vimy Ridge was captured and 4,000 prisoners taken. The Allied offensive was unsuccessful elsewhere and by 5 May had ground to a halt.

Vinland (Vine Land) The Viking name for part of eastern Canada; other parts were Helluland (Stone Land) and Markland (Forest Land). Sagas record their accidental discovery c. 985–986 by Bjarni Herjolfsson, who was blown off course en route to the settlements on GREENLAND, and record the short-lived settlement in the late 10th and early 11th centuries by Leif Ericsson, his brother Thorvald, and Thorfinn Karlsefni. The natives, the Beothuk tribe, were called *Skraellings*. Incontestable traces of a Norse presence are known only from Ellesmere Island and the L'ANSE AUX MEADOWS site in Newfoundland, Canada, and a coin from Maine, USA.

Virginia A colony and state of the USA that consists of 'tidewater' land in the mid-Atlantic coastal plain, which drains into Chesapeake Bay, and Piedmont, on the eastern slopes of the Allegheny Mountains. The first permanent British colony, JAMESTOWN was settled in 1607 by the Virginia Company of London, who inherited the name from RALEIGH's compliment to the 'virgin queen' Elizabeth I. Survival and prosperity were based on tobacco, first cultivated by White servants (supporters of BACON's Rebellion) but after the 1690s mainly by slaves. By then a rural gentry of PLANTATION owners had emerged. In the 18th century the Piedmont was settled by Germans and Scots-Irish, the latter often fervent converts in the GREAT AWAKENING. Virginians were remarkably united in their opposition to British 'tyranny', demonstrated in documents from HENRY's Virginia Resolves (1765) to Jefferson's DECLARATION OF INDEPENDENCE. The last major action of the War of Independence occurred in Virginia, at YORKTOWN (1781). Although deeply divided over the Constitution because of jealousy about states' rights, the 'Old Dominion' provided four out of the first five presidents and became a heartland of the Democratic-Republican party.

Virginia Campaigns (July 1861–65) A series of engagements and campaigns in the AMERICAN CIVIL WAR. The first engagement of the Civil War was fought on 21 July 1861 at the first Battle of Bull Run. In a confused mêlée the CONFEDERACY was saved from defeat by the brigade of 'Stonewall' JACKSON. In the Peninsula

Campaign of April–June 1862 Union (Northern) forces under General McClellan attempted to advance up the peninsula between the James and York rivers to capture Richmond, but in the Seven Days Battle (26 June–2 July) he was forced to withdraw by the Southern commander, General Robert E. LEE. At the same time in the Shenandoah Valley a brilliant campaign by 'Stonewall' Jackson pinned down Union forces. The second Battle of Bull Run followed (29–31 August), when Lee forced the Union army to retreat to Washington. The way was open for an invasion of the North, but it ended in defeat at the Battle of ANTIETAM (17 September). Following the Confederate army's escape back to Virginia, the new Union commander, General Ambrose Burnside, launched an assault on Lee's positions above Fredericksburg (13 December 1862). Burnside withdrew, the reverse severely shaking the Union war effort. In the spring of 1863 a reinforced Union army under General Joseph Hooker, resumed the offensive in the Battle of Chancellorsville (2–4 May 1863). Lee withstood the assault, but suffered heavy casualties, including the death of Jackson. Lee now invaded Pennsylvania, but suffered the major defeat of GETTYSBURG, after which he was on the defensive for the rest of the war. A series of engagements was fought in May and June 1864 in the 'wilderness' region of Virginia, when General GRANT was defeated three times before retreating across the River James, to renew his attacks in the Petersburg Campaign. This last campaign was launched in June 1864 and continued into 1865. Three assaults on Richmond by Grant were repelled by Lee, after which Union forces besieged the Confederate capital through the winter. Lee was thus prevented from sending reinforcements south to repel SHERMAN's advance through Georgia and on 1 April he was defeated at Five Forks and forced to abandon both Richmond and Petersburg. All but surrounded, he surrendered at APPOMATTOX on 9 April, bringing the campaign, and the war, to an end.

Virgin Islands A group of about 100 islands in the Caribbean Sea between Puerto Rico and the Lesser Antilles, divided between British and US administration.
History. Although they were visited by Columbus in 1493, effective settlement of the Virgin Islands, primarily by British and Danish planters, did not occur until the 17th century. Descendants of African slaves imported for the sugar plantation economy account for the majority of the population of the islands today. In 1917 Denmark sold its possessions to the USA, which was interested in their strategic value; the Virgin Islands of the United States comprises over 50 islands, the largest of which is Saint Croix. The British Virgin Islands are a smaller group at the northern end of the Leeward Islands, with Tortola the largest island. From 1872 to 1956 this group was part of the British colony of Leeward Islands, but since 1956 has been administered separately by British governors or administrators who have gradually extended self-government.

Virginius incident (1873) The capture of an arms-running ship fraudulently flying the US flag during the Cuban rebellion against Spain (1868–78). Seized off the coast of Jamaica by a Spanish gunboat, the *Virginius* was taken to Santiago de Cuba. Subsequently her commander, Captain Fry, a US citizen, and 52 others, including British and American citizens, were executed by the Spanish as FILIBUSTERS (persons engaged in

unauthorized warfare against a foreign state). Despite the angry reaction of the USA the dispute was resolved by compromise and Spain paid the families of the executed Americans compensation totalling $80,000. The families of the British victims were also paid compensation.

Visconti, Gian Galeazzo (1351–1402) Italian statesman and patron of the arts. Succeeding his father Galeazzo II in 1378, Gian Galeazzo ruled Milan jointly with his uncle Bernabò until 1385 when he had the latter put to death and assumed sole control as duke. His expansionist policies united independent cities such as Pisa and Siena under Milanese rule and made the Visconti dynasty master of northern Italy. He arranged marriage alliances with most of the western European powers. After his death in 1402, the unity of his dominions was temporarily disrupted before being restored by his son Filippo Maria, who ruled as duke from 1412–47. On his death Milan passed to the SFORZAS.

Visigoths (or western Goths) A people originating in the Baltic area. Migrations in search of farmland took them to the Danube delta and the western Black Sea by the 3rd century AD. They raided Greece and threatened the eastern Mediterranean but were temporarily repulsed by Claudius II 'Gothicus'. AURELIAN conceded Dacia and the Danube to them. Competition over land with the migrating HUNS drove them south in 376 and they defeated the Roman emperor Valens at Adrianople. A treaty of alliance followed but on the death of THEODOSIUS I they ravaged the empire and Rome itself under the leadership of ALARIC I. They occupied parts of Gaul and Spain (Languedoc and Catalonia), assisting Rome against other barbarians, notably against the Huns at the CATALAUNIAN FIELDS in 451. Frankish and Muslim invaders defeated and absorbed the Visigoths in the following two centuries.

Vitoria, Battle of (21 June 1813) A battle fought between the French and the British near the BASQUE city of Vitoria, during the PENINSULAR WAR. WELLINGTON decisively defeated the French under Joseph Bonaparte and Jourdan. News of this victory inspired Austria, Russia, and Prussia to renew their plans to attack France and they declared war on NAPOLEON on 13 August.

Vittorio Veneto, Battle of (October 1918) The scene of a decisive victory in World War I by the Italians over the Austrians. A town in north-east Italy, it is named after VICTOR EMANUEL II, in whose reign Venetia was regained from Austria after the Six Weeks War (1866). Italian forces under General Diaz avenged the CAPORETTO disaster (1917) by routing the Austro-Hungarian army, which resulted in an Austrian request for an armistice.

Vivekananda, Swami (born Narendranath Datta) (1863–1902) Hindu monk who preached the Hindu philosophy of Vedanta in Europe and the USA and established the Ramakrishna Mission, named after his guru (spiritual teacher) Ramakrishna Paramahamsa (1836–86), a mystic who preached that all religions contained the same fundamental truth. A mystic, he renounced the world and, as a wandering *sadhu* (religious man), discovered the poverty of the Indian masses. He went to the USA to raise funds to establish an institution for educating the poor. After his speech at the Chicago Parliament of Religions (1893), he became a celebrity in the West. His patriotic speeches and writings inspired youthful Indian nationalists, especially the early revolutionaries.

vizier (Arabic, *wazir*) A leading court official of a traditional Islamic regime. Viziers were frequently the power behind nominal rulers. At times the office became hereditary, under the early ABBASIDS falling into the hands of the Barmakids and under the OTTOMANS in the late 17th century held by the KÖPRÜLÜ family.

Vladimir I, St (956–1015) Grand Duke of Kiev (978–1015). He was converted to Christianity and married the sister of the Byzantine emperor. By inviting missionaries from Greece into his territories he initiated the Russian branch of the EASTERN ORTHODOX CHURCH, which was rapidly established. He was canonized and became the patron saint of Russia.

Vogel, Sir Julius (1835–99) New Zealand statesman. He came to Otago with the gold rushes and soon dominated provincial politics. He entered national politics in 1863 and, as Colonial Treasurer from 1869 and Premier (1872–74), was responsible for a bold and successful policy of borrowing to promote immigration, road and railway building, and land development. He was responsible for the establishment of the Government Life Insurance Office and the Public Trust, thus launching a tradition of state involvement for which New Zealand is noted. He served as Treasurer again (1884–87).

Volstead Act (1919) US federal PROHIBITION Act, enforcing the Eighteenth Amendment, banning the manufacture, distribution, and sale of alcohol. The Act was devised by the Anti-Saloon League counsel Wayne Wheeler but named after Congressman Andrew Volstead of Minnesota. It proscribed beer and wine as well as distilled spirits, to the surprise of those

moderate prohibitionists who wanted the prohibition of spirits only. It became void by the passage of the Twenty-first Amendment in 1933.

Voltaire (François-Marie Arouet) (1694–1778) French satirist and critic. The Jesuit-educated son of a lawyer, Voltaire was a prolific author. His attacks on political and religious intolerance brought repeated condemnation of his works, causing him to live at different periods in Britain, Prussia, and Switzerland. An early work, the *Lettres philosophiques sur les Anglais* (1734), shows his admiration, shared by MONTESQUIEU, for the British political system, which, in allowing freedom of conscience, made it possible for the arts and sciences to flourish. Voltaire's drama is generally conventional while his poetry is witty and cultivated, and although his plays and poems were very successful in his own day they are now largely forgotten. The satirical poem *Le Mondain* (1736) is interesting as a defence of the luxury of contemporary society and contrasts with the ideal simplicity advocated by the French theologian François Fénelon and ROUSSEAU. Voltaire wrote several historical volumes, including the *Essai sur les moeurs* (1769), which recounts the history of civilization without recourse to divine intervention in human affairs. Voltaire's ideas receive their best literary expression in his philosophical tales, which demonstrate the characteristic clarity and concision of his style. He was a major figure in the French ENLIGHTENMENT.

Voortrekkers GREAT TREK.

Vortigern (Overlord) A legendary 5th-century Romano-British king said by BEDE to have invited HENGIST AND HORSA to Britain as mercenaries in an attempt to withstand the raids by the PICTS and the SCOTS. The plan rebounded on Vortigern when Hengist and Horsa turned against him (455) and seized lands in Kent. He was blamed by the historian GILDAS for his misjudgement and also for the loss of Britain.

Wade, Benjamin Franklin (1800–78) US statesman. Wade served in the Senate from 1851 to 1869, first as a Whig, and then as a Republican, generally on the radical wing of the Party. He sponsored the Wade–Davis Bill (1864), an abortive and punitive blueprint for the RECONSTRUCTION of the South, which was vetoed by President LINCOLN. Wade played an active role in the attempted impeachment of Andrew JOHNSON and as acting president of the Senate would have assumed the Presidency had the move succeeded; its failure and Wade's own defeat in the next election marked the end of his political career.

Wafd (Wafd al-Misri, Arabic, 'Egyptian Delegation') Egyptian nationalist party. Under the leadership of Zaghlul Pasha it demanded freedom from British rule. When Egypt won nominal independence in 1922, the Wafd demanded full autonomy and control of the SUDAN and the SUEZ CANAL. After 1924 there were frequent Wafdist governments, opposing the monarchy. In 1930 the constitution was suspended and Egypt became a royal dictatorship until the Wafdists succeeded in restoring the constitution in 1935. In 1950 the Wafd formed a one-party cabinet and the struggle between King FAROUK and his government intensified. The monarchy fell in 1952 and the new Revolutionary Command Council under Colonel Gamal NASSER dissolved all political parties.

Wagner–Connery Act (officially: National Labor Relations Act) (1935) US labour Act. The Act was introduced by Senator Robert Wagner of New York and was intended to outlaw employer-dominated trade unions and to provide for enforcement of the right of free collective bargaining. It established a National Labor Relations Board, with powers to supervise and conduct elections in which workers would select the union to represent them. The Board survived various attempts to secure a Supreme Court ruling of its unconstitutionality and it served to increase trade-union membership.

Wagram, Battle of (5–6 July 1809) A battle in the NAPOLEONIC WARS fought between the combined French and Italian forces, led by NAPOLEON, and the Austrians under the Archduke Charles, at the village of Wagram, near Vienna. Napoleon, determined to offset earlier setbacks, ordered a massive attack on the well-chosen Austrian position. The first day's fighting was inconclusive and the following day Napoleon renewed his assault and the Austrian army finally began to retreat. The French, who had been close to defeat, claimed the victory, but their losses outnumbered those of the Austrians. It was followed by the Treaty of Schönbrunn, in which Austria lost territory and agreed to join the CONTINENTAL SYSTEM against Britain. Napoleon married the Austrian Princess Marie-Louise in 1810.

Wahhabism The doctrine of an Islamic reform movement. Founded by Muhammad ibn 'Abd al-Wahhab 1703–92) in Nejd, Saudi Arabia, it is based on the SUNNI teachings of Ibn Hanbal (780–855), involving puritanism, monotheism and rejection of popular cults, such as the Sufi veneration of saints and tombs, on the grounds that these constitute idolatry. Under the SAUD family, the Wahhabis raided into the Hejaz, Iraq, and Syria, capturing Mecca in 1806. They were crushed by Ottoman forces in a series of campaigns (1812–18), but the SAUD family gradually consolidated its power within the peninsula. The cult was revived by Abd al-Aziz ibn Saud in his bid for power after World War I, but later crushed, as too fanatical, with British help in 1929 at the Battle of Sibilla. Sunni Wahhabism revived after World War II, with the growth of Islamic fundamentalism, and Wahhabi Mujahidin were fierce participants in the Afghan civil war of 1979–89.

Waitangi, Treaty of (6 February 1840) A treaty between MAORI chiefs and the British government signed at Waitangi, New Zealand. Some 500 local Maori chiefs of the North Island were present and 46 Head Chiefs signed the document drawn up by the governor, recognizing Queen Victoria's sovereignty over New Zealand in return for recognition of the Maori's *rangatiratanga* (chieftainship) and land rights, and their rights as British subjects. The treaty cleared the way for a declaration of sovereignty on 21 May 1840. Subsequent encroachment on their lands led to the ANGLO–MAORI WARS of 1860–72, in which Maori independence was overcome. Since its recognition by New Zealand statutes the treaty has since 1975 assumed new importance as a basis of relations between Maori and non-Maori New Zealanders. The Waitangi Tribunal was reconvened in 1975 to consider Maori land claims and in 1985 was given authority to settle claims dating from 1840. In 1994 and 1995 the government agreed to pay compensation to certain Maori tribes whose land was seized illegally by settlers.

Wakefield, Battle of (30 December 1460) A battle in the Wars of the ROSES fought in Yorkshire. The LANCASTRIANS defeated and killed the YORKIST claimant to the throne, Richard, 3rd Duke of York.

Wakefield, Edward Gibbon (1796–1862) British colonial reformer and writer. In 1829 he published his *Letter from Sydney* using information he had obtained while serving a sentence in Newgate gaol in London. Concerned that Australian settlements were failing because land could be acquired so easily, he proposed a 'sufficient price' for land, which would finance the regulated emigration of labourers and oblige them to work to buy their own land. This would give a balanced colonial society and provide some relief to unemployment in Britain. His ideas were taken up and implemented from 1831, with some 70,000 migrants travelling to Australia in the next ten years. In 1837 Wakefield founded the NEW ZEALAND Association (later COMPANY). He was largely responsible for the succession of systematic settlements in New Zealand. He wrestled for years for self-government for the colonists, emigrating to New Zealand in 1853 and involving himself in colonial politics until ill-health intervened.

Waldenses (or Vaudois) A Christian religious sect established by Peter Valdes (d. 1217) in the 12th century. Assuming a life of poverty and religious devotion, Valdes founded the 'Poor Men of Lyons' in France. They lived simply and taught from vernacular scriptures. They were persecuted as heretics but survived in southern France and in Piedmont in north-eastern Italy. In 1532 they formed an alliance with the Swiss reformed church but were almost destroyed in France and in 1655 the Piedmontese Waldenses, despite support from Protestant groups, were massacred.

Waldheim, Kurt (1918–) Austrian politician and diplomat; President of Austria (1986–92) and Secretary-General of the UNITED NATIONS ORGANIZATION (1972–81). Waldheim occupied ambassadorial posts at the UN (1956–58; 1970–71) and in Canada (1958–60). He served as Foreign Minister in the conservative People's Party government of Josef Klaus, but lost presidential elections in 1971. In the following year, he was appointed as the fourth UN Secretary-General, securing two terms of office until 1981. In 1986 Waldheim was successful in his bid for the Austrian Presidency; however, his term of office was embroiled in controversy after revelations that he had concealed his allegiance to the Nazi Party and his involvement in war crimes while serving as a German Army officer in World War II.

Wales (Welsh, Cymru) The western part of Great Britain and a principality of the UNITED KINGDOM.

Physical. Along the border with England, the Marches, is a stretch of pastureland much broken by hills, woods, and twisting rivers. It rises to the Cambrian Mountains, which stretch down the centre of the country. In the south-east are the Brecon Beacons and in the south-west the Pembroke Peninsula with its rocky coasts. Snowdonia is in the north-west.

Economy. Coal-mining and steel production were the main economic activities in Wales until the 1980s, when depletion of the coal seams led to closure of most of the mines. Coal mined in South Wales was of extremely high quality and the region was the world's chief exporter of coal in the 19th century. Heavy industry developed close to the mines. In the 1930s unemployment rose dramatically and the government encouraged industrial diversification. In the 1990s low wages attracted foreign companies (including Far Eastern ones) to open plants in South Wales. There are oil-refining and petrochemical industries, concentrated in South Wales around the deep-water port of Milford Haven. Forestry and farming, especially the rearing of sheep and cattle, have remained important. Tourism is an increasingly significant source of revenue and employment.

History. The population of Wales, which is Celtic in origin, resisted the Romans (who penetrated as far as Anglesey in a campaign against the DRUIDS), and after the departure of the Romans was increased in size by British refugees from the SAXON invaders (c. 400). By the 7th century Wales was isolated from the other Celtic lands of Cornwall and Scotland. Christianity was gradually spread throughout Wales by such missionaries as St Illtud and St DAVID, but politically the land remained disunited, having many different tribes,

kingdoms, and jurisdictions; Gwynedd, Deheubarth, Powys, and Dyfed emerged as the largest kingdoms, one notable ruler being Hwyel Dda (the Good), traditionally associated with an important code of laws.

From the 11th century the Normans colonized and feudalized much of Wales and Romanized the Church, but the native Welsh retained their own laws and tribal organization. There were several uprisings but as each revolt was crushed the English kings tightened their grip. Although LLYWELYN the Great (ruled 1194–1240) recovered a measure of independence, EDWARD I's invasion in 1277 ended hopes of a Welsh state: Llywelyn II was killed in 1282 and in 1301 Edward of Caernavon (EDWARD II) was made Prince of Wales. Thereafter Wales was divided between the Principality, royal lands, and virtually independent MARCHER LORDSHIPS. The unsuccessful revolt of Owen GLENDOWER in the early 15th century revived Welsh aspirations, but HENRY VIII, the son of the Welsh HENRY VII, united Wales with England in 1536, bringing it within the English legal and parliamentary systems. Welsh culture was eroded as the gentry and church became Anglicized, although most of the population spoke only Welsh, given a standard form in the Bible of 1588, until the 19th century. The strong hold of NONCONFORMISM, especially of the Baptists and Methodists, made the formal position of the Anglican Church there the dominant question of Welsh politics in the later 19th century, leading to the DISESTABLISHMENT of the Church from 1920. The social unrest of rural Wales, voiced in the REBECCA RIOTS, resulted in significant emigration. The INDUSTRIAL REVOLUTION brought prosperity to South Wales but during the Great DEPRESSION in the 1930s many people lost their jobs. Unemployment was exacerbated by the closure of most of the coalfields by the 1980s and remains a problem despite the introduction of a more diversified industry. Political, cultural, and linguistic nationalism survive, and have manifested themselves in the PLAID CYMRU Party, the National Eisteddfod, and Welsh-language campaigns. A Welsh referendum in 1979 overwhelmingly rejecting partial devolution from the United Kingdom was followed, in 1997, by a referendum that narrowly approved the establishment of a separate Welsh Assembly.

Walesa, Lech (1943–) Polish statesman and President (1990–95). A shipyard worker from Gdańsk, he founded the independent trade union movement SOLIDARITY after a wave of strikes in 1980. Further political agitation led to a total industrial stoppage along the Baltic seaboard and the government under General Jaruselski was forced to concede the right to organize themselves independently. In 1981 Solidarity was outlawed and Walesa imprisoned. Released in 1982, he forged close links with the Roman Catholic Church and Pope John Paul II. In 1989 Solidarity was legalized and in 1990 he was re-elected its chairman. Increasingly on the right wing of the movement and with the full power of the Church behind him, he defeated Tadeusz MAZOWIECKI in the presidential election of November 1990. Throughout Walesa's term of office, his governments grappled with the economic challenge of moving towards a free-market economy, and there were a series of political crises and strikes as Walesa himself drifted further away from his Solidarity colleagues. In December 1995, Walesa was defeated in presidential elections by the former communist Aleksander Kwasniewski.

Wallace, George Corley (1919–   ) US politician and state governor. He became an Alabama state congressman (1947–53) and a District Judge (1953–58). When first elected governor of Alabama (1963–66) he resisted the DESEGREGATION of state schools and universities. He stood in the Presidential campaign of 1968 as leader of the newly established DIXIECRAT American Independent Party. His main support was in the South and he polled over ten million votes. In 1972 he sought the Democratic Party's presidential nomination, but his campaign ended when an assassination attempt left him paralysed. He stood again unsuccessfully in 1976, by which time he was becoming reconciled to the issue of CIVIL RIGHTS. For the 1982 election as governor he publicly recanted his opposition to desegregation, polled a substantial number of Black votes, and was re-elected, remaining in office until 1987.

Wallace, Henry Agard (1888–1965) US agricultural reformer and statesman. He developed successful varieties of corn grown throughout the USA and in 1932 he helped swing the state of Iowa to the Democratic Party. In 1933 he became Franklin D. ROOSEVELT'S Secretary of Agriculture, in 1940 his Vice-President, and in 1944 Secretary of Commerce in Roosevelt's last administration, continuing under TRUMAN. A visionary liberal, Wallace soon fell out with Truman's COLD WAR policy, and resigned in 1946. Wallace then moved considerably to the left, exposing himself to charges of 'fellow travelling' with the communists. In 1948 he formed his own 'Progressive Party' and ran against Truman for the Presidency. He won only 1.2 million votes and carried no state. He then retired to continue his agricultural research.

Wallace, Sir William (c. 1270–1305) Scottish soldier who became a national hero for his resistance to English rule. In May 1297 Wallace attacked the English garrison at Lanark and then defeated an English army at Stirling Bridge (1297), after which he was knighted. Wallace proceeded to recapture Berwick and raid northern England. He was then elected governor of Scotland. In 1298 EDWARD I invaded Scotland with 88,000 men and defeated Wallace at the Battle of FALKIRK. He fled to France, but was later captured, tried in London, and beheaded.

Wallenstein, Albrecht Wenzel Eusebius von (1583–1634) Duke of Friedland (1625), Duke of Mecklenburg (1629), Czech magnate and military entrepreneur. At the outbreak of the THIRTY YEARS WAR he remained loyal to Emperor Ferdinand II and in 1621 was made governor of Bohemia, a position from which he profited enormously. He served as commander-in-chief of the emperor's Catholic forces (1625–30), but after driving the Danes from north Germany, he tried to establish his own empire on the Baltic, and the German princes prevailed upon the emperor to dismiss him. He was subsequently recalled as imperial general (1632–34) to deal with the ascendant Swedes and Saxons. Having become embittered by his earlier dismissal, he was determined to build up his personal power and his secret negotiations with the enemy were discovered. Ferdinand again removed him from command and shortly afterwards connived at his assassination.

Walpole, Sir Robert, 1st Earl of Orford (1676–1745) English statesman. He entered Parliament in 1701 and briefly held the offices of Secretary of War and Treasurer of the Navy until he was dismissed with his WHIG colleagues in 1710. The TORIES impeached him for corruption in 1711 and expelled him from Parliament, making him a martyr for the Whig cause. On the accession of George I in 1714 he became Paymaster of the Forces and Chancellor of the Exchequer in 1715, but resigned in sympathy with his brother-in-law TOWNSHEND in 1717. The SOUTH SEA BUBBLE crisis brought Walpole to power in 1721 and he remained in office as leading minister until 1742.

During his long period of power he strove for peace abroad and also did his best to avoid political controversy at home, especially on such contentious issues as religion; he strengthened the economy and by his mastery of the House of Commons and use of patronage he maintained political stability. He regularly presided over CABINET meetings and was thus generally regarded as the first effective Prime Minister; he insisted on cabinet loyalty and moved a long way towards the idea of the collective responsibility of the cabinet. In 1733 his unpopular attempts to impose excise duties on wine and tobacco were defeated in Parliament, but he placed a heavy duty on molasses imported into America, which became a major American grievance. He then faced an increasingly powerful opposition from within his own party in Parliament and lost an important patron when Queen Caroline died in 1737. After reluctantly going to war with Spain in 1739 and seeing Britain increasingly involved in the War of the AUSTRIAN SUCCESSION, he accepted a peerage and resigned in 1742.

Walsingham, Sir Francis (c. 1530–90) English statesman and diplomat. He entered the service of ELIZABETH I in 1568, becoming her joint Secretary of State in 1573. A zealous Protestant, he constantly advocated aggression toward Catholics at home and abroad. Elizabeth generally preferred the more moderate counsels of CECIL, yet she valued Walsingham highly – not least because of his efficient network of diplomats and spies, which spanned Europe. It ensnared such enemies of the state as THROCKMORTON, BABINGTON, and MARY, Queen of Scots and brought him detailed information on the preparation of the SPANISH ARMADA (1588).

Walter, Hubert (d. 1205) English cleric and statesman. After studying law at the University of Bologna he served first under HENRY II and then went with RICHARD I on the Third CRUSADE. On his return in 1193 he was made Archbishop of Canterbury and Justiciar, or Regent, of England. He was appointed papal legate in 1195. Walter's legal and administrative skills were recognized by both Richard I (whose £100,000 ransom he organized) and JOHN (whose accession he secured) who made him Chancellor. During Richard's frequent absences abroad he was virtually the ruler of England. Extensive financial and judicial reforms were made, including improvements to the enforcement of law and order (1195). He was Lord Chancellor from 1199.

Wandewash, Battle of (22 January 1760) One of the last great battles between the English and French East India Companies in south India, fought at the coastal fortress of Wandewash, in South India. Although the French commander, the comte de LALLY, had the advantage of numbers, he was hampered by dissensions among his forces. His attack was repulsed by the able British commander, Eyre Coote. The fall of Pondicherry followed.

Wang Anshi (1021–86) Chinese statesman, chief councillor to the SONG (1069–76). He introduced major financial and administrative reforms and reorganized local policing and the militia, known collectively as the 'New Policies'. The prices of commodities were stabilized and farmers benefited from reduced land tax, low-interest state loans, and a reduction in the levy that replaced forced labour. There was much opposition to his reforms, particularly from officials and landowners, and he was dismissed in 1076. Many of his reforms were reversed shortly thereafter.

war, technology of The technology developed for use in war and warfare. Military technology and military engineering have been important factors in warfare since prehistoric times. The archaeological evidence from excavated skeletons indicates that the first weapons were those used in hunting, such as clubs, axes, knives, and spears. The earliest weapons were made of stone or wood; the arrival of bronze in the 4th millennium BC and of iron around 2,000 years later, made weapons more deadly. The introduction in about 2500 BC of the horse-drawn chariot had a major impact on military strategy. Cavalry appeared soon afterwards; their mobility was improved by the invention of the stirrup.

Rock paintings show the bow and arrow to be at least 30,000 years old; it is technologically significant as the first device in which energy is stored slowly and released quickly. From the 13th century BC the power of the bow was increased by using composite materials, but the major advance was the introduction of mechanical devices to draw the bow, as in the crossbow. Siege weapons were developed from the basic bow, such as the catapult and the onager, a huge sling deriving its power from torsion.

Improved weaponry led to the development of body armour and shields, the culmination of this being the armour of medieval European knights. At a very early date recourse was made to temporary or permanent fortifications strong enough to resist the most powerful weapons of the day. These in turn engendered a range of weapons for siege warfare, such as assault towers and battering-rams.

Incendiary devices were used in war from an early date. The best known was the Greek fire of the 7th century AD, similar in effect to 20th century napalm. It was from such incendiary mixtures that the Chinese derived GUNPOWDER, first used for bombs in the 13th century but developed soon afterwards as a propellant. It was first used in the West early in the 14th century, originally for heavy cannon and subsequently in hand-held firearms. Gunpowder revolutionized war in western Europe. It reigned supreme for some 500 years, until displaced in the late 19th century by other explosives. The 20th century saw the introduction of both the submarine and the aeroplane. The aircraft carrier united naval and air forces. The escape from the surface of the Earth was accentuated by the development of ballistic missiles ascending high into the stratosphere and military satellites in orbit. Two other major military developments in the 20th century were the tank and the self-propelled gun. However, the single most important military development of the 20th century was that of nuclear weapons. Although only two bombs have ever been exploded in war, their effect on military strategy has been enormous.

Warbeck, Perkin (1474–99) PRETENDER to the throne of England. He was in the service of a merchant who was friendly with EDWARD IV of England and posed from 1491 to 1497 as Richard, Duke of York, the younger of Edward's murdered sons. He was well received in Ireland, France, and Flanders by those hostile to HENRY VII, but soon after he had landed in Cornwall in September 1497 he was captured. His large following dispersed, as he made a full confession and was imprisoned and later executed.

technology of war *This picture shows Mongol armies using technology devised and operated by Chinese and Islamic engineers to attack a fortified city.*

war crimes Certain activities in war that violate the rules governing the established rules of warfare, as set out in the Hague and GENEVA CONVENTIONS. In most societies, activities such as the killing of prisoners, their torture or enslavement, hostage-taking and the deportation and killing of civilians, are deemed to be war crimes. Present-day attitudes to war crimes have been influenced by the trials at NUREMBERG and TOKYO in 1945–46 of German and Japanese wartime leaders. In the course of these proceedings, it was made clear that an individual was to be held responsible for his or her actions even if carrying out the orders of a higher authority. During the VIETNAM WAR (1964–75), US soldiers were indicted on charges of killing civilians; Iraq's hostage-taking and maltreatment of prisoners during its occupation of Kuwait (1990–91) also led to calls for those responsible to be tried for war crimes. A war crimes tribunal of the INTERNATIONAL COURT OF JUSTICE, the principal judicial organ of the UNITED NATIONS, was convened in 1993 to try people accused of war crimes committed during the conflict in BOSNIA-HERZEGOVINA.

Ward, Sir Joseph George (1856–1930) New Zealand statesman. A minister of the first and successive Liberal cabinets, he was noted for successful loan raising and for provision of low-interest credit to farmers. As Prime Minister (1906–12) and in coalition with MASSEY (1915–19) he supported waning concepts of empire unity in defence and foreign affairs. He won office as Prime Minister again in 1928 as head of the United Party, partly on his reputation as a 'financial wizard', but failed to solve the crises brought on by the Great DEPRESSION.

Wardrobe A department in the household of the English kings, who found the EXCHEQUER's methods of collecting revenues too cumbersome to meet their financial needs, particularly when travelling. King John had used another household department, the Chamber, but under Henry III the Wardrobe was developed and Edward I treated it virtually as his war treasury to supply military expenditure. By the 15th century, however, the Chamber had become the main financial department.

warlords Chinese regional military rulers of the first half of the 20th century. Following the death of YUAN SHIKAI in 1916, China was divided among many local rulers who derived their power from control of personal armies. In origin, the warlords were mostly former soldiers of the imperial and republican armies, bandits, or local officials. They depended on revenue from towns and agricultural areas in their own spheres of influence to feed the well-equipped troops with which they sought to establish their primacy over local rivals. The most successful warlords generally controlled easily defended areas and the largest of the many wars between rival cliques witnessed the mobilization of hundreds of thousands of soldiers. CHIANG KAI-SHEK's Nanjing government (1928–37) re-established central authority over most warlord areas, but military rulers persisted in the far west of China into the 1940s.

War of 1812 (1812–15) A war between Britain and the USA. US frustration at the trade restrictions imposed by Britain in retaliation for Napoleon's CONTINENTAL SYSTEM, together with a desire to remove British and Canadian obstacles to US westward expansion, led the US Congress to declare war on Britain (June 1812). The USA–British North American (Canadian) border was the main theatre of war. In July, the US General, William Hull, advanced into Upper Canada, but in early August withdrew to Detroit, which was soon after captured by Canadian and British forces under Major-General Isaac Brock. In October 1812 a second invading US force crossed the Niagara River and stormed Queenston Heights, but it too was driven back by a British force, under Brock, who was killed. In October 1813 another US army under General William Harrison won the Battle of the THAMES, in southwestern Ontario, at which the Native American leader TECUMSEH was killed. In November US troops were defeated by a much smaller British force at Crysler's Farm on the St Lawrence. In July 1814, at the Battle of Lundy's Lane, a US force under General Jacob Brown briefly fought at night a British force under General Drummond and then withdrew, after which no more attempts were made to invade Canada. On Lake Erie in September 1813 a US force captured a British squadron of six ships, while the following year (September 1814), in a similar victory on Lake Champlain, a British squadron of 16 ships was forced to surrender. At sea US warships won a series of single-ship engagements, but they were unable to disrupt the British naval blockade, which by 1814 was doing considerable harm to the US economy. In June 1814 a British expeditionary force landed in Chesapeake Bay, Virginia, marching north and burning the new city of Washington. War-weariness now brought the two sides to the conference table and in December 1814 the Treaty of GHENT was signed, restoring all conquered territories to their original owners.

Warren, Earl (1891–1974) US judge and public official. He had been attorney-general and governor of California when in 1948 he became Republican Vice-Presidential candidate. Eisenhower appointed him Chief Justice of the US Supreme Court (1953–69). In 1954 he wrote the Supreme Court ruling that racial segregation in public schools was unconstitutional. In 1964 he was appointed chairman of the Commission to investigate the assassination of President KENNEDY. By establishing the sole responsibility of Lee Harvey OSWALD, the Commission went far to allay the nation's fears of either communist or extreme right-wing conspiracies.

Warsaw Pact (officially: Warsaw Treaty of Friendship, Co-operation and Mutual Assistance) A military alliance of Soviet-bloc powers, signed in 1955 by Albania, Bulgaria, Czechoslovakia, the German Democratic Republic, Hungary, Poland, Romania, and the Soviet Union after the Paris agreement between the Western powers admitting the Federal Republic of Germany to NATO. Yugoslavia refused to join and Albania formally withdrew in 1968. The pact provided for a unified military command, the maintenance of Soviet Army units on member states, and mutual assistance, the latter provision being used by the Soviet Union to launch a multinational invasion of CZECHOSLOVAKIA against the DUBČEK regime in 1968. Following the collapse of the Communist regimes in Eastern Europe in 1989, a summit in Moscow in June 1990 agreed that it be dissolved. In November 1990 the 16 members of NATO and 6 members of the Pact signed a Treaty of Conventional Armed Forces in Europe; as a military alliance the Pact was formally ended in Prague on 1 July

1991. By then Warsaw Pact troops and equipment had been withdrawn from Czechoslovakia and Hungary, while withdrawal from Poland and Germany was completed in 1994.

Warsaw Rising (August–October 1944) Polish insurrection in Warsaw in World War II, in which Poles tried to expel the German Army before Soviet forces occupied the city. As the Red Army advanced, Soviet contacts in Warsaw encouraged the underground Home Army, supported by the exiled Polish government in London, to stage an uprising. Polish RESISTANCE MOVEMENT troops led by General Tadeusz Komorowski gained control of the city against a weak German garrison. Heavy German air-raids lasting 63 days preceded a strong German counter-attack. The Soviet Army under the Polish-born General ROKOSSOVSKY reached a suburb of the city but failed to help the insurgents or to allow the western Allies to use Soviet air bases to airlift supplies to the hard-pressed Poles. Supplies ran out and on 2 October the Poles surrendered. The Germans then systematically deported Warsaw's population and destroyed the city itself. The main body of Poles that supported the Polish government in exile was thus destroyed and an organized alternative to Soviet political domination of the country was eliminated. As the Red Army resumed its advance into Poland the Soviet-sponsored Polish Committee of National Liberation was able to impose on Poland a Communist Provisional Government on 1 January 1945 without resistance.

Warwick, Richard Neville, Earl of (1428–71) English nobleman who earned the title of 'kingmaker' of England, as a result of the influence he exerted during the Wars of the ROSES. He inherited the earldom of Salisbury from his father Richard (d. 1460) and gained that of Warwick by his marriage to Anne Beauchamp. He had the support of the rest of the Neville family, which was central to the YORKIST party. He was an ally of Richard Plantagenet, Duke of YORK, and was largely responsible for putting his son, EDWARD IV, on the throne in 1461. His wealth and power made him easily the most formidable subject of the king until Edward's marriage to the LANCASTRIAN Elizabeth Woodville, after which he and his family gradually lost influence and had to see Edward move towards alliance with BURGUNDY. After Edward declared him a traitor, he fled to France, but invaded England in September 1470 and put HENRY VI back on the throne. He was himself defeated and killed in the Battle of BARNET on 14 April 1471.

Washakie (c. 1804–1900) Native American (Shoshone) chief. He became the leader of the eastern band of his tribe in the 1840s. He chose to ally with White settlers in the Native American wars of the 1870s and was accorded a commission in the US army and a tomb in Fort Washakie.

Washington, Booker T(aliaferro) (1856–1915) US educator. The son of a Black slave and a White father, he was the undeclared leader of those Black people who favoured 'gradualism' as the route to integration and CIVIL RIGHTS. He created economic opportunities for Black people from his base at Tuskegee Industrial Institute, Alabama, by training them as farmers, mechanics, and domestics. In a widely publicized speech of 1895, known as the Atlanta Compromise, he abandoned the effort to achieve civil and political equality for Black people as a priority, advocating that they concentrate on material progress. He was criticized for his emphasis on vocational skills to the detriment of academic development and civil rights by militant intellectuals, such as W. E. B. DU BOIS. His insistence on industrial education encouraged White businessmen to subsidize Black institutions, to provide him with funds for the National Negro Business League of 1900, and to finance court cases against segregation.

Washington, George (1732–99) First President of the USA (1789–97). Washington came from a well-established Virginian planter family. As a young man he saw active service in the last of the FRENCH AND INDIAN WARS, leaving the army in 1758 with the rank of colonel. Politically he was a supporter of resistance to British measures and at the second CONTINENTAL CONGRESS he was elected commander-in-chief. Taking command at Cambridge, Massachusetts, he imposed some order on the 16,000 volunteers and in March 1776 drove the British from Boston. In September, after an inept defence of New York, he brilliantly extricated his army; for the next five years, he played a waiting game against the British in New York and Philadelphia, with occasional raids and skirmishes, such as at Trenton (1776), Princeton, Brandywine, and Germantown (1777), and, after the VALLEY FORGE winter, at Monmouth (1778). French troops arrived as allies in 1780 and he was able to engage in the YORKTOWN campaign, which effectively ended the war.

Washington's main achievement had been to hold his ill-supplied army together while deferring to a divided Congress. Anxious about post-war political anarchy, he encouraged the calling of the Constitutional Convention in 1787 and supported the resultant CONSTITUTION OF THE USA. He was elected unanimously to the presidency and again for a second term in 1792. Although he tried to keep his office above politics, he became identified with FEDERALIST policies; his suppression of the WHISKY REBELLION, his refusal to support Revolutionary France, and his approval of JAY's treaty provoked attacks from Jeffersonian Republicans. His farewell address deplored factionalism and called for US neutrality in foreign affairs. The father of his nation, his powers of leadership, his stoicism, and his integrity together earned him the admiration and respect of his countrymen.

Washington Conference The conference held in the USA between November 1921 and February 1922 to discuss political stability in the Far East and naval disarmament. Summoned on US initiative, the conference was attended by Belgium, Britain, China, France, Holland, Italy, Japan, Portugal, and the USA and resulted in a series of treaties including a Nine-Power Treaty guaranteeing China's independence and territorial integrity, a Japanese undertaking to return the region around Qingdao to Chinese possession, and an Anglo-French-Japanese-US agreement to guarantee each other's existing Pacific territories. Naval discussions resulted in a ten-year moratorium on capital-ship construction. The Washington Conference successfully placed restraints on both the naval arms race and Japanese expansionism, but by the 1930s both problems broke out afresh.

watch and ward The system developed in 13th century England to preserve the peace in local communities. Guards were appointed and the duties of the constables at night (watch) and in daytime (ward) were defined. Town gates remained closed from dusk to dawn, strangers had to produce sureties to prove their identity and business, up to 16 men maintained the watch in cities, 12 in boroughs, and four in smaller communities. Modifications to the system were made regularly throughout the 13th century and were eventually incorporated in the Statute of Winchester of 1285, a collection of regulations aimed at keeping the peace.

Watergate scandal A major US political scandal. In 1972 five men were arrested for breaking into the headquarters of the Democratic Party's National Committee in the Watergate building, Washington, DC, in order to wire-tap its meetings. It was soon discovered that their actions formed part of a campaign to help President NIXON win re-election in 1972. At first the White House denied all knowledge of the incident, but after intensive investigations, initially led by journalists on the *Washington Post*, it became apparent that several of the President's staff had been involved in illegal activities and an attempt to cover up the whole operation. Several White House officials and aides were prosecuted and convicted on criminal charges. Attention then focused on President Nixon and, as extracts from tapes of White House conversations were released, it became clear that he too had been involved. In August 1974 Nixon resigned to avoid impeachment, but he was pardoned for any federal offences he might have committed by the new President, Gerald R. FORD.

Waterloo, Battle of (18 June 1815) A decisive battle between French and British and Prussian forces near the Belgian village of Waterloo. It was fought during the HUNDRED DAYS of NAPOLEON between his hastily recruited army of 72,000 men and WELLINGTON's Allied army of 68,000 men (with British, Dutch, Belgian, and German units) before the Prussians (45,000 men) arrived. There had been a violent storm in the night and Napoleon postponed his attack until midday to allow the ground to dry. By 2 p.m. a first contingent of Prussians arrived and attacked Napoleon on the right. At 6 p.m. Marshal NEY ordered a co-ordinated attack and captured La Haye Sainte, a farmhouse in the centre of the Allied line. The French artillery then began attacking the Allies from the centre. At 7 p.m. Napoleon launched his famous Garde Impériale in a bid to break Wellington's now weakened infantry. At this point, however, BLÜCHER appeared with the main Prussian forces, taking Napoleon in the flank, and Wellington ordered a general advance. The French were routed, with the exception of the Garde, who resisted to the end. In Wellington's words, the outcome of the battle was 'the nearest run thing you ever saw in your life'. On 22 June, Napoleon signed his second and final abdication.

Watling Street A north-westerly Roman road in Britain that ran from Dubris (Dover), via Londinium (London) and Verulamium (St Albans), to Deva (Chester). Much of it was built from about 60 to 70 AD for the advance north of the FOSSE WAY. Its name derives from the Anglo-Saxon name for Verulamium ('Waeclingacaester') and for a paved road ('street').

Wavell, Archibald Percival, 1st Earl (1883–1950) British field-marshal and viceroy of India. In World War I he served in France (where he lost an eye) and in 1937–39 he commanded the British forces in Palestine. In 1939 he became commander-in-chief in the Middle East and won the victory of Sidi Barrani (1940) over the Italians. In 1941, forced to divert some of his forces to Greece and facing new German formations, he had to retreat in North Africa and was dismissed by Churchill. He then served in India, first as commander-in-chief from 1941, then as viceroy (1943–47), where he made it his main task to prepare India for independence.

Wayne, Anthony (1745–96) American Revolutionary general, who led a Pennsylvanian regiment in the abortive invasion of Canada (1776). He displayed conspicuous initiative in such actions as Brandywine, Germantown, and Monmouth. In 1779 his brilliantly planned and executed night attack on Stony Point, a British-held fort on the Hudson, won him the nickname of 'Mad Anthony'. In 1794 he commanded the western army, which defeated the Native Americans at the Battle of Fallen Timbers and opened up the NORTHWEST TERRITORY to settlement.

Webb, Sidney James, Baron Passfield (1859–1947) British social reformer and historian. Initially a civil servant he and his wife Beatrice Webb (1858–1943) (née Potter), became leading members of the FABIAN Society. As members of the Royal Commission on the Poor Law (1905–09) they were the moving spirit behind its minority report that poverty should be dealt with by setting up government organizations to concentrate on specific causes of poverty. This later became the basic approach by British governments to the problem. Two British institutions, the London School of Economics and Political Science (1895) and the journal, the *New Statesman*, owe their foundation to Sidney Webb. His writings, many of them joint studies with his wife, on trade unionism and local government, exerted considerable influence on political theory and social reform. He helped to found the Labour Party, served as a Labour Member of Parliament (1922–29), and was Dominion and Colonial Secretary in the Labour government (1929–31).

Webster, Daniel (1782–1852) US orator, lawyer, and statesman. A native of New Hampshire, he served as a Congressman (1813–17) and Senator (1827–41, 1845–50), and secured his reputation by winning a series of important cases before the Supreme Court. His Second Reply to Senator Hayne of South Carolina in 1830 was a staunch defence of the Union. Through the 1830s and 1840s Webster was one of the leaders of the Whig Party. He failed to fulfil his presidential ambitions in successive elections from 1836 to 1852, but served as Secretary of State (1841–43) under Harrison and Tyler, during which time he was responsible for the WEBSTER–ASHBURTON TREATY, and again as Secretary of State under Fillmore (1850–52).

Webster–Ashburton Treaty (1842) An agreement between Britain and the USA settling the present Maine–New Brunswick border. Negotiated by the US Secretary of State Daniel WEBSTER and the British minister Lord Ashburton, the treaty settled the disputed boundaries in the north-east, awarding the USA more than 18,000 sq km (7,000 sq miles) of the 31,000 sq km (12,000 sq miles) disputed area and opening the St John River to free navigation. The treaty also fixed the

Canadian–US boundary in the Great Lakes region and served as a precedent for the successful settlement of other 19th-century border disputes between Britain and the USA.

Weimar Republic (1919–33) The republic formed in Germany after the end of World War I. On 9 November 1918 a republic was proclaimed in Berlin under the moderate socialist Friedrich Ebert. An elected National Assembly met in January 1919 in the city of Weimar and agreed on a constitution. Ebert was elected first President (1919–25) and was succeeded by HINDENBURG (1925–34). The new republic had almost at once to face the VERSAILLES PEACE SETTLEMENT, involving the loss of continental territory and of all overseas colonies and the likelihood of a vast reparations debt. The terms of the settlement were so unpopular that they provoked a brief right-wing revolt, the KAPP PUTSCH. Unable to meet reparation costs, the mark collapsed, whereupon France and Belgium occupied the Ruhr in 1923, while in BAVARIA right-wing extremists (including HITLER and LUDENDORFF) unsuccessfully tried to restore the monarchy. Gustav STRESEMANN succeeded in restoring confidence and in persuading the USA to act as mediator. The DAWES PLAN adjusted reparation payments and France withdrew from the Ruhr. It was followed in 1929 by the YOUNG PLAN. Discontented financial and industrial groups in the German National Party allied with Hitler's NAZI Party to form a powerful opposition. As unemployment increased, support grew for this alliance, which was perceived as the only alternative to communism. In the presidential elections of 1932 Hitler gained some 13 million votes, exploiting anti-communist fears and anti-Semitic prejudice, although Hindenburg was re-elected. In 1933 he was persuaded to accept Hitler as Chancellor. Shortly after the REICHSTAG fire, Hitler declared a state of emergency (28 February 1933) and on Hindenburg's death in 1934, made himself President and proclaimed the THIRD REICH.

Weizmann, Chaim (Azriel) (1874–1952) Zionist leader and scientist. Born in Russia, he became a British subject in 1910. During World War I his scientific work brought him to the notice of LLOYD GEORGE. Weizmann exploited his contacts to help to obtain the BALFOUR DECLARATION in 1917. At the Versailles Peace Conference Weizmann was the chief spokesman for ZIONISM and thereafter, as President of the World Zionist Organization, he was the principal negotiator with the British and other governments. He played a major role in shaping the PALESTINE mandate and in frustrating the British attempt to restrict Jewish immigration and land purchase in the 1930s. When the state of Israel came into being (1948), Weizmann became its first President (1948–52).

Welensky, Sir Roy (Roland) (1907–91) Rhodesian statesman. He entered politics in 1938 and founded the Federal Party in 1953, dedicated to 'racial partnership'. He was an advocate of the CENTRAL AFRICAN FEDERATION, which was created largely as a result of his negotiations. He was Prime Minister of the Federation from 1956 to 1963. When the Federation was dissolved (1963) Welensky lost the support of the White Rhodesians, who gave their allegiance to the Rhodesian Front of Ian Smith.

welfare state A country with a comprehensive system of social welfare funded both by taxation and schemes

of NATIONAL INSURANCE. The term is believed to have been coined by Archbishop TEMPLE in 1941. The emergence of the strong secular state in 19th-century Europe was characterized by the development of state involvement in an increasing number of areas of social activity, for example education, public health, and housing. Public education systems were first introduced in France and Prussia early in the 19th century, while the need for housing and public health measures accelerated as URBANIZATION increased in Europe. A scheme of social insurance against unemployment, sickness, and old age was pioneered in Germany under BISMARCK, and other European states soon followed. In Britain a similar scheme, together with other social welfare measures, was introduced under the Liberal governments (1906–14). Between the wars significant developments towards the establishment of a welfare state took place in New Zealand under the New Zealand LABOUR PARTY, while F. D. Roosevelt's NEW DEAL in the USA created a series of federal social welfare agencies. In 1942 a report by William BEVERIDGE proposed that the British system of national social insurance be comprehensive. His proposals were implemented after World War II by the ATTLEE ministries, which added other reforms, such as the creation of the National Health Service. In the Soviet Union and East European states welfare provision became an official part of the fabric of society. In the USA and elsewhere in the Western World social welfare is regarded by many people as being at odds with the FREE MARKET economy and so remains highly selective. Sweden is usually taken as the purest example of a welfare state because of its interventionist labour market policy and integrated health care system, but Belgium and The Netherlands have more generous SOCIAL SECURITY systems. In Britain, the heavy public expenditure required to distribute social benefits irrespective of means was increasingly challenged from the mid-1970s and a fundamental revision of the NHS and the social security system took place in the 1980s and early 1990s under the Conservative administrations of Margaret THATCHER and John MAJOR. The results of their policies can be seen in cuts in benefits, deregulation, and contracting-out of services. The Labour government elected in 1997 promised even more sweeping reforms.

Wellington, Arthur Wellesley, 1st Duke of (1769–1852) British soldier and statesman. Wellington joined the army in 1787. He saw action in Flanders in 1794–95 before being posted to India in 1796, where he was to distinguish himself both as a soldier and as an administrator, winning a notable victory over the MARATHAS at Assaye in 1803. On his return home he was knighted. In 1808 he was sent to Portugal to lead an army against the French. Throughout the PENINSULAR WAR he adopted defensive tactics, which aroused much criticism in Britain, but eventually brought about the expulsion of the French from Spain after the victories of Salamanca (1812) and Vitoria (1813). Created Duke of Wellington (1814) in acknowledgement of his services, he attended the Congress of VIENNA and subsequently commanded the forces which defeated Napoleon at the Battle of WATERLOO in June 1815. In 1818 he embarked upon a political career, entering Lord LIVERPOOL's government as Master-General of Ordnance and he represented Britain at the Congress of Verona in 1823. As Prime Minister (1828–30) he reluctantly agreed to

CATHOLIC EMANCIPATION, but his refusal to contemplate parliamentary reform of any kind made him extremely unpopular and he resigned. He served briefly as acting Prime Minister in 1834 and then as Foreign Secretary (1834–35) under Sir Robert PEEL. In 1841 he again joined Peel's government, this time as a minister without portfolio. Wellington retired from public life in 1846 but in 1848 as commander-in-chief of the army he organized a military force to protect London against possible CHARTIST violence.

Wells, Fargo and Company US transport organization, founded by Henry Wells, William C. Fargo, and associates in 1852 to operate between New York and California. Wells and Fargo established a monopoly west of the Mississippi within a decade, succeeding the PONY EXPRESS as the agency for transporting bullion to eastern markets and for 20 years dominated the postal service in the West. In 1918 it merged with a number of other concerns to become the American Railway Express Company.

Welsh Nationalist Party PLAID CYMRU.

Wenceslas, St (c. 907–29) Duke of BOHEMIA, who became the second Christian duke on the death of his father, Uratislas, although part of the dukedom passed to Boleslav, his younger non-Christian brother. He was named king by the Holy Roman Emperor, Henry I, over an area which corresponds approximately to the present Czechoslovakia, but soon afterwards was murdered by his brother in the church of St George in Prague. This event precipitated war and the intervention of the emperor and resulted in the permanent Christianization of the country under Boleslav and his son, Boleslav II.

Wenceslas IV (1361–1419) King of BOHEMIA (1376–1419), King of Germany (1378–1400), and Holy Roman Emperor (1378–1400). A weak king, he was overcome by the ambitions of the imperial princes, the town leagues, and by his brother SIGISMUND. A Bohemian revolt, starting in 1394, deposed him in favour of Sigismund in 1402. He lost the German throne in 1400 in favour of Rupert

Wittelsbach, although he regained it in 1404. Much of his reign was disturbed by the HUSSITE movement; Wenceslas supported Huss and tried to prevent his execution, which was ordered by Sigismund.

Wentworth, Thomas STRAFFORD.

wergild (or 'man-price') The compensation that had to be paid by a murderer to the kinsmen of the victim in Anglo-Saxon England. The amount of an individual's wergild was fixed in law and varied according to his rank in society. An ordinary freeman (ceorl) was valued at 200 shillings, a nobleman (earl) at 1,200 shillings, and the king at 7,200 shillings. Although the unfree had no wergild, compensation for their murder was paid to their owners.

Wesley, John (1703–91) British Anglican priest, the founder of Methodism. He was the leader of an earnest, devout, and scholarly group in Oxford whose members (including his brother Charles) became known as METHODISTS. Their methodical prayer and Bible readings were a reaction against the worldliness of student life rather than a revolt against the Church. He went to the American colony of Georgia to act as priest to the settlers and although his tactlessness led to his early return to England, his fellowship meetings, the hymn-singing, and the contact with the MORAVIANS (an ANABAPTIST sect) brought him invaluable experience. He had a profound spiritual conversion in 1738 and began widespread preaching, taking to the open air as early as 1739. At Bristol in the same year he established a chapel and a school for the religious societies. As the ANGLICAN CHURCH either showed indifference to his work or actively opposed him, he began to found Methodist societies wherever he preached and he chose lay preachers as full-time helpers. In 1744 he drew up his strict rule-book for the regulation of Methodist societies. The American War of Independence had cut his contact with the colonies and in 1784 it became necessary for him to ordain 27 preachers for America, the Anglican Church having refused to do so.

John Wesley   *During his preaching tours Wesley often faced hostile demonstrations. This painting shows him being taunted by a drunken mob in Wednesbury, England.*

During his 50-year ministry he travelled 250,000 miles, mostly on horseback, and delivered 50,000 sermons. He preached in industrial areas where the parish system had broken down. The religious revival for which he was responsible, the GREAT AWAKENING, not only created Methodism but challenged the Anglican Church into reviewing its own evangelism.

His brother Charles Wesley (1707–88), was the co-founder of Methodism. He accompanied John to America and on his return carried out exhausting preaching tours, but his genius lay in hymn-writing.

Wessex The kingdom of the West Saxons, whose royal dynasty achieved the unification of England by the early 10th century. According to the *anglo-saxon chronicle*, Wessex was founded in 495 by two chieftains, Cerdic and Cynric, who landed near Southampton Water before advancing inland over Hampshire and the basin of the upper Thames. The capital of Wessex was established at Winchester. Under Ceawlin (560–91) whose overlordship was recognized by other Saxon leaders, the policy of expansion continued. A victory over the Romano-British at Dyrham (577) extended West Saxon control over the towns of Gloucester, Bath, and Cirencester. However, in the 7th century the growth of Wessex was challenged by the rise of its northern neighbour MERCIA, particularly under its kings Penda (ruled *c.* 626–55) and Offa (ruled 757–96). Wessex continued to expand along the south coast under Ine (688–726) and by the reign of Egbert had established its authority in southern England. Aethelred I (865–871) and ALFRED (871–99) resisted Danish invasions (871–86). Alfred became overlord of all England not held by the Danes. His grandson, Athelstan, ousted the Danes from their remaining English territory and became the first ruler of all England (926). Despite a temporary Danish recovery (939–954) the authority of Wessex was not seriously challenged and by the reign of Edgar the Peaceable (959–75) Northumbria, Mercia, and Wessex were united.

Western Australia A state of AUSTRALIA. The state stretches from its boundary with Northern Territory and South Australia to Shark Bay on its Indian Ocean coast. The centre comprises three immense deserts: the Great Sandy, Gibson, and Great Victoria, and Nullarbor Plain in the south. The plateaux of eroded mountains in the west, such as the Hamersley Range, have seasonal rivers, and there are many seasonal lakes on the interior tableland in the south-west. There are large deposits of a wide range of minerals, notably gold, iron, and coal.

History. In 1826 Governor Darling, acting on British instructions, sent soldiers and convicts to King George Sound in Western Australia to found a settlement. However, this mission proved abortive. In 1829, Britain founded the new free colony of Western Australia. The colony's progress was slow, inadequate labour being a major problem. The colonists eventually requested that convict labour be reintroduced to the area. In consequence, approximately 10,000 convicts (all male) were transported to Western Australia between 1850 and 1868. Western Australia became a state of the Australian Commonwealth in 1901. Western Australians voted in favour of secession at a referendum held in 1933, but Britain rejected the petition the following year. The state experienced a significant mining boom in the 1960s.

Western European Union (WEU) A West European defence organization founded in 1955 by Belgium, France, the UK, Luxembourg, the Netherlands, West Germany, and Italy. The WEU came into being as a successor to the Brussels Treaty organization, after France had refused to ratify the treaty providing for a European Defence Community; its primary function was to supervise the rearmament and accession to NATO of West Germany. The Union formally ended the occupation of West Germany and Italy by the Allies. The social and cultural activities initially envisaged by its founders were transferred to the COUNCIL OF EUROPE in 1960, leaving the Union with the task of improving defence co-operation among the countries of Western Europe. Reactivated in 1984, it was involved from 1987 in arms control and was joined by Spain and Portugal in 1989 and by the former East Germany after German reunification in 1990. The WEU helped to co-ordinate Europe's contribution to the anti-Iraq coalition in the Gulf War in 1991. In 1993 the Eurocorps rapid reaction unit was founded, comprising land-based forces from France, Germany, and Belgium. In 1994, several former Soviet satellite states of Eastern Europe (e.g. Bulgaria, Poland, Romania) were granted associate member status. The Treaty of MAASTRICHT (1992) envisaged it as the defence component of the European Union.

Western Front The line of fighting in WORLD WAR I that stretched from the Vosges mountains through Amiens in France to Ostend in Belgium. Fighting in World War I began in August 1914 when German forces, adopting the SCHLIEFFEN PLAN, were checked in the first Battle of the MARNE. The subsequent German attempt to reach the Channel ports was defeated in the first Battle of Ypres (12 October–11 November). Thereafter both sides settled down to TRENCH WARFARE, the distinctive feature of fighting on this front. The year 1915 saw inconclusive battles with heavy casualties: Neuve Chapelle (March), the second Battle of Ypres (April/May), when poison gas was used for the first time, and Loos (September). In 1916 Germany's heavy attack on Verdun nearly destroyed the French army but failed to secure a breakthrough. To relieve pressure on the French, the British bore the brunt of the SOMME offensive (July), gaining little ground and suffering appalling casualties. Early in 1917 the Germans withdrew to a new set of prepared trenches, the SIEGFRIED LINE (or Hindenburg Line), and in 1917 the Canadians captured VIMY RIDGE. In November the British launched yet another major offensive, the Battle of PASSCHENDAELE (or third Battle of Ypres), and lost 300,000. The entry of the USA into the war (1917) meant that the Allies could draw on its considerable resources. US troops commanded by General Pershing landed in France in June 1917. In March 1918 LUDENDORFF's final offensive began, with his troops again reaching the Marne before being stemmed by US forces at Château-Thierry. FOCH, now Allied commander-in-chief, began the counter-offensive with the third Battle of the Marne (July). British troops broke the Siegfried Line near St Quentin, while the Americans attacked through the Argonne region. By October Germany's resources were exhausted and on 11 November Germany signed the armistice that marked the end of World War I.

westernization The process by which a country or society adopts the customs and institutions that are said

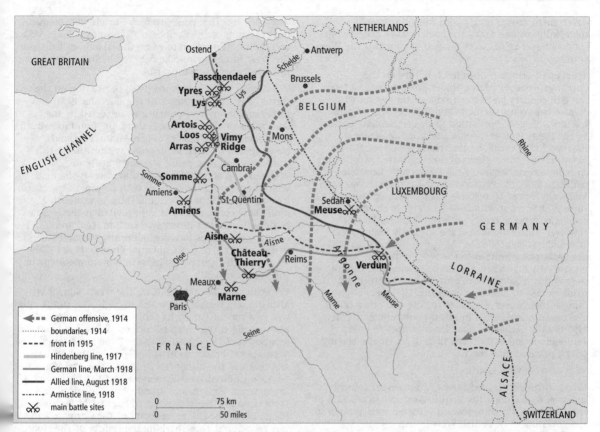

Western Front (World War I) *The Schlieffen Plan, by which the German army planned to encircle and capture Paris early in the war, was checked by the Allies in the first Battle of the Marne. An almost stationary situation of trench warfare then ensued. Stalemate continued into 1918, when a massive German offensive was again checked on the Marne. By now US troops and equipment were reinforcing the Allies, who finally advanced into Belgium in September, an armistice following on 11 November. Each year hundreds of thousands of men died for mere acres of mud, as the Western Front moved backwards and forwards.*

to characterize the Western world. For some governments and élites in DEVELOPING COUNTRIES, westernization has been seen as synonymous with modernization and development and therefore as a desirable goal. Another more recent tendency, however, is to regard westernization as a pernicious process equated with the negative aspects of CAPITALISM, which undermines local customs and values and which should therefore be strongly opposed. The Iranian Revolution of 1979 was, at least in part, a reaction to the westernizing policies of MUHAMMAD REZA SHAH PAHLAVI (1919–80), which neglected the traditional, particularly religious, values in Iranian society, and the anti-Western theme has, to a greater or lesser degree, been taken up by ISLAMIC FUNDAMENTALIST movements throughout the Muslim world.

Western Jin (Western Chin) (265–316) A dynasty that briefly unified China after the period of the THREE KINGDOMS. It was established by Sima Yan, a general of the Wei kingdom. He attempted to curb the power of the dominant families but after his death in 290, Sima princes feuded with each other and the central government collapsed. In the resulting chaos, a XIONGNU invasion occurred and Luoyang (311) and Chang'an (316)

were sacked. One Sima prince in the south-eastern kingdom of Wu established the Eastern Jin dynasty (317–420), but it too lacked strong central government. During this period, the colonization of southern China by HAN Chinese greatly increased.

Western Neolithic The period after 4000 BC during which the indigenous hunting and gathering peoples living along the western coasts of Europe merged with incoming farmers from central Europe (related to the BANDKERAMIK culture) to form new groups of farmers with a basically similar material culture. Their simple round-based pottery has sometimes given them the name 'bowl cultures', but they are better known for the construction of monumental tombs out of large boulders or MEGALITHS.

Western Rising (July–August 1549) An English rebellion in Cornwall and Devon, at the same time as KETT'S REBELLION in Norfolk. The West Country rebels' main grievance was the imposition, by Act of UNIFORMITY, of the first Book of Common Prayer in English. Demanding that no such religious changes should be made until EDWARD VI came of age, they laid siege to Exeter on 2 July. It was not until mid-August that government troops under Lord Russell scattered them, killing some 4,000. The leaders were executed in London; lesser rebels were hanged throughout the West Country.

Western Sahara A disputed territory on the northwest coast of Africa. Under Spanish control from the 19th century (as Spanish Sahara), the region was divided between MAURITANIA and MOROCCO when Spain withdrew in 1975. Opposition to this settlement was led by the *Frente Popular para la Liberación de Saguia el Hamra y Rio de Oro* (Polisario Front), which sought independence, with Algerian backing. After proclaiming an independent Saharan Arab Democratic Republic (SADR) in 1976, the Polisario Front has been at war with Moroccan forces; Mauritania has maintained neutrality since 1979, when it withdrew its claim to the area and concluded a peace treaty with the Polisario Front. However, Morocco invaded the formerly Mauritanian area and has laid claim to the entire territory. In 1982 the SADR was admitted to the ORGANIZATION OF AFRICAN UNITY (OAU). Efforts by the UN to resolve the dispute over Western Sahara have centred on an agreement made in 1988 to hold a referendum. However, disagreements over eligibility to vote and other terms and conditions resulted in several postponements. In 1996 the UN decided to abandon attempts to hold a referendum and withdrew a fifth of its troops, leaving only a peacekeeping force.

Western Samoa SAMOA.

West Indian independence A movement towards independence among the British West Indian colonies in the Caribbean. Pressure towards greater participation in the government of British West Indian colonies developed in the 19th century. A Black uprising in JAMAICA had been ruthlessly suppressed in 1865, but following a Jamaican deputation to London in 1884, elected legislatures, on a limited franchise to advise governors, were steadily introduced throughout the islands. After World War I there were further moves towards more representative government, for example, in TRINIDAD in 1923. By 1940 the British government, aware of the strategic importance of the area, established a Commission for Development and Welfare in the West Indies, substantial financial aid was given and the principle of self-government was accepted. This policy did not, however, prevent large-scale unrest after World War II. Britain believed that individual islands could never be viable as independent states, hence the concept of federation and the attempt to form the West Indies Federation (1958–62). When this failed, Jamaica and Trinidad and Tobago were granted full independence in 1962 and BARBADOS in 1966. New attempts to create a Federation of the East Caribbean also failed (1967), when many smaller islands temporarily became 'associated states of the United Kingdom'. Since then six new member states of the COMMONWEALTH OF NATIONS have emerged: GRENADA 1974; DOMINICA 1978; SAINT VINCENT AND THE GRENADINES 1979; SAINT LUCIA 1979; ANTIGUA AND BARBUDA 1981; and SAINT KITTS AND NEVIS 1983. The island of Anguilla was first associated with Saint Kitts and Nevis, but unilaterally seceded from the association in 1967. The UK intervened and Anguilla was obliged to resume the status of an independent territory of the UK in 1969; it became a separate British dependency in 1980.

West Indies The name given by Christopher COLUMBUS to the islands of the Caribbean. Columbus, who in 1492 was the first European to reach the islands, called them the West Indies because he believed he had arrived near India by travelling westward.

Westminster, Statute of (1931) Legislation on the status of British DOMINIONS. At the 1926 and 1930 Imperial Conferences pressure was exerted by the dominions of Canada, New Zealand, the Commonwealth of Australia, the Union of South Africa, Eire, and Newfoundland for full autonomy within the British COMMONWEALTH. The result was the Statute of Westminster, accepted by each dominion Parliament, which recognized the right of each dominion to control its own domestic and foreign affairs, to establish a diplomatic corps, and to be represented at the League of Nations. It still left unresolved certain legal and constitutional questions, including the status of the British crown. The Consequential Provisions Act (1949) allowed such republics as India to remain members of the Commonwealth.

Westphalia, Treaty of (1648) The treaty signed at Münster and Osnabrück, which brought the THIRTY YEARS WAR to a conclusion. By its terms, the Habsburgs acknowledged the independence of Switzerland and the separation of the UNITED PROVINCES from the SPANISH NETHERLANDS, France secured undefined rights in Alsace and retained the bishoprics of Metz, Toul, and Verdun, Sweden acquired West Pomerania and the bishoprics of Bremen and Verden, and Brandenburg acquired East Pomerania and the succession to the archbishopric of Magdeburg. The full sovereignty of the German states was recognized, thus marking the failure of the Holy Roman Emperor to turn Germany into a centralized Catholic monarchy.

westward expansion, American The growth of the USA from the original White settlements on the east coast to span the entire continent. Between the WAR OF 1812 and the AMERICAN CIVIL WAR, the Mississippi Valley and the Great Lakes region were settled and westward expansion came to the fore as one of the dominant themes of the 19th century. The successful MEXICAN–AMERICAN WAR (1846–48) and the GOLD RUSH in California (1848) played a major role in the opening up of the 'WILD WEST' and the Pacific coast, while in the aftermath of the American Civil War the new Union Pacific Railroad, the spread of the railway network, the pacification of the Native American population, and ever-increasing immigration from Europe began to fill in the area of the Great Plains. By the 1890s the frontier as such had disappeared, although the movement of population within the continent remained generally westwards through the 20th century.

Weygand, Maxime (1867–1965) French general. Weygand was FOCH's chief of staff in World War I and i 1920 was sent by the French government to aid the Poles in their ultimately successful defence against the advancing Soviet RED ARMY. In the military crisis of May 1940 Weygand was recalled to assume command of the French armies attempting to stem the German BLITZKRIEG attack. Advising capitulation, he later commanded the VICHY forces in North Africa, was dismissed at the request of the Germans, arrested by th

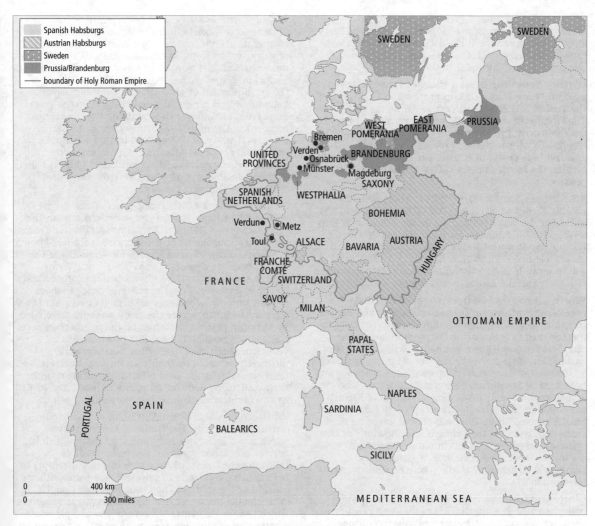

Treaty of Westphalia: Europe in 1648   *The Treaty of Westphalia ended the Thirty Years War and laid down the political framework of Europe until well into the 18th century. It marked the beginning of French ascendancy and the defeat of the imperial ambitions of the Habsburgs. Germany, economically devastated by the long war, was split into more than 300 sovereign states, and the Holy Roman Empire existed in little more than name. France now emerged as the dominant power in Europe and although French territorial acquisitions were small, they were strategically important. Sweden, whose intervention against the Habsburgs had played a decisive role in the war, gained territories in central Europe to add to its growing empire.*

Gestapo, and then freed by the Allies. He was tried and acquitted under the DE GAULLE regime on a charge of collaboration with the Germans.

Whig A British political party traditionally opposed to the TORIES. The Whigs owed their name, like the Tories, to the EXCLUSION CRISIS of CHARLES II's reign. Those who petitioned for the recall of Parliament in 1679 were named Whigs (Scottish Covenanting brigands) by their Tory opponents. The Whigs suffered defeat in Charles's reign, but joined with the Tories in inviting WILLIAM OF ORANGE to England and they alternated with the Tories in power until 1714. Their principles were to maintain the power and privileges of Parliament, to show sympathy with religious dissent, keeping links between church and state to a minimum, and to play an active role in Europe.

From the accession of GEORGE I the Hanoverian kings placed their trust in the Whigs and there followed the long period of Whig supremacy. From the mid-1720s there were Whigs in opposition to WALPOLE and the development of factions within the party became increasingly acute by the mid-century, bringing political instability in the 1760s. The ROCKINGHAM faction, which formed the core of FOX's followers, became the basis of the new Whig party in the late 18th century. The changed political and social conditions of the 19th century caused the break-up of the Whig party. Many of its members, however, formed the core of the British LIBERAL PARTY.

Whig Party A US political party of the second quarter of the 19th century. The Whig Party was formed in the mid-1830s by those who opposed what was perceived as the executive tyranny of President Andrew JACKSON. Dominated by Henry CLAY and Daniel WEBSTER, the Party elected HARRISON to the White House in 1840 and TAYLOR in 1848, but disunity on free-soil and slavery issues weakened it severely and it broke up.

Whisky Rebellion (1794) A rising of farmers in western Pennsylvania, USA, in protest at Secretary of the Treasury Alexander HAMILTON's excise tax of 1791. The frontiersmen who made whisky considered the tax discriminatory. President WASHINGTON called out 15,000 troops to quell the rioting, proving the federal government's power to enforce the country's laws and earning the frontiersmen's hatred of the FEDERALISTS' policies.

Whitbread, Samuel (1758–1815) British politician. A notable champion of reform and of the liberties of the individual, he began his parliamentary career in 1790 as a Whig. He allied himself with Charles James FOX and became the dominant figure in the opposition to the government of William PITT the Younger. Whitbread was to prove himself a fervent advocate of the abolition of slavery and the extension of religious and civil rights.

Whitby, Synod of (664) A church council that resolved the differences between the Celtic and Roman forms of Christian worship in England, particularly the method used for calculating the date of Easter. The CELTIC CHURCH had its own method of fixing the date of Easter; this was a matter of dispute after the arrival of St AUGUSTINE OF CANTERBURY's mission. The Celtic case was presented by St Colman, Bishop of Lindisfarne. The Roman case was put forward by St Wilfrid of Ripon, whose arguments were finally accepted by King OSWY of Northumbria. This decision was crucial, severing the connection with the Irish church and allowing for the organization of the English church under Roman discipline. Theodore, Archbishop of Canterbury, summoned an assembly of the whole English church at Hertford in 672.

White Australia policy A restrictive immigration policy pursued in Australia. In the mid-19th century there was a shortage of labour and SQUATTERS brought in Chinese and KANAKAS (Pacific Islanders) as labour. By the 1880s developing trade unions were calling for a policy to protect the 'White working man'. By 1890 all states had legislation to preserve the purity of White Australia, Alfred DEAKIN being one of its strongest advocates. The new Commonwealth government legislated to exclude non-Europeans (Immigration Restriction Act, 1901). The main device used was to be a dictation test in any European language (any 'prescribed' language from 1905), the language being chosen to ensure failure. This policy of exclusion continued until the 1950s. The Labor administration of Gough Whitlam (see WHITLAM CRISIS) repudiated the policy in the early 1970s. Since then, immigration to Australia from south-east Asia has grown considerably.

Whitefield, George (1714–70) British evangelist. He was one of the early METHODISTS, whom he joined at Oxford in 1732. He followed the WESLEYS to Georgia in 1738 and on his return began open-air preaching, encouraging the Wesleys to follow his example. His Calvinist views caused a temporary breach with John Wesley but the two men were reconciled. He spent a lifetime of preaching in Britain and America.

White Lotus Society (or Incense Smelling Society) A Chinese secret society. It had religious affiliations, tracing its origins to a Buddhist monk of the 4th century AD. The lotus, springing unsullied from the mud, is a Buddhist symbol. In times of trouble, its leaders preached of the coming of the Buddha and of the establishment of a new dynasty. Its supporters, bound by blood ceremonies and claiming magic powers, came from an impoverished peasantry. Major risings occurred in the mid-14th century during the decline of the YUAN dynasty, and from 1796 to 1804, when they successfully opposed Manchu troops in southern Shaanxi province. This setback weakened Chinese belief in the invincibility of the Manchu troops and the authority of the QING dynasty.

White Russians Russian supporters of the Tsarist regime who fought against the Soviet RED ARMY in the RUSSIAN CIVIL WAR (1918–21). The name was derived from the royalist opponents of the French Revolution, known as Whites, because they adopted the white flag of the French Bourbon dynasty. The White Russian Army, though smaller than the Red, was better equipped and had an abundance of Tsarist officers, some of whom offered to serve as ordinary soldiers. Its two main bases were in the south, where the army was successively led by Kornilov, DENIKIN, and WRANGEL, and in Siberia, where KOLCHAK was nominally head of a provisional government at Omsk. The White Russians were ultimately defeated by their own internal quarrels, by their refusal to grant land reforms in the areas under their control, by Red control of the railways, and by Red Army commander Leon TROTSKY's organizing genius.

Whitlam crisis (1975) An Australian political and constitutional crisis. The House of Representatives, which had a Labor majority, and the Senate, which had a narrow non-Labor majority, reached a deadlock following the Loans Affair, which involved attempts by several Labor ministers to raise overseas loans without consulting the cabinet. The Prime Minister, Gough Whitlam, did not agree to a dissolution of Parliament, which the Senate demanded before it would pass the Appropriation Bills. The governor-general, Sir John Kerr, withdrew Whitlam's commission as Prime Minister, and commissioned Malcolm Fraser, the Leader of the Opposition, instead. Fraser advised Kerr to dissolve both houses and the Appropriation Acts were passed. Fraser's Liberal–National Country Party coalition secured majorities in both houses at the subsequent election.

WHO WORLD HEALTH ORGANIZATION.

Wilberforce, William (1759–1833) British philanthropist who played a leading part in the anti-slavery movement. Entering the House of Commons in 1780, Wilberforce became a staunch supporter of William PITT the Younger. An effective parliamentary speaker, he lost no opportunity to denounce the horrors of the slave trade, which was eventually abolished in 1807. He also supported the campaign to outlaw slavery completely within the British empire, which culminated in the passing of the Emancipation Act of 1833, a month after his death.

Wilderness Road A frontier trail in North America opened by Daniel BOONE in 1775 across the Allegheny Mountains. It ran for nearly 482 km (300 miles) from western Virginia through the Cumberland Gap to the upper Kentucky River at Boonesborough. It was commissioned by the Transylvania Company, an association of land speculators, to encourage settlement in Kentucky, Tennessee, and the Ohio valley. For 50 years it was a major route into the eastern Mississippi valley.

'Wild West' The frontier society in 19th-century USA. The mythology of the Wild West developed early in its history, based on tales about the macho, saloon-bar world of the GOLD RUSHES and the COWBOY cattle-drives to the largely unsettled western territories. Bandits such as Billy the Kid and Jesse James were romanticized, as were General CUSTER and his 'last stand'. An early perpetrator of the myths was Edward Z. C. Judson, who, under the pseudonym Ned Buntline, wrote penny (dime) novels romanticizing the exploits of his friend W. F. Cody as 'Buffalo Bill'. The latter in turn organized 'Wild West Shows' from 1883 onwards, which included the appearance of the Native American Chief SITTING BULL and which travelled as far afield as Europe. There is no evidence that the West was much less law-abiding than the rest of the USA. Nonetheless, the 'Wild West' was no purposeless myth; it suggested an arena in which individuals struggled to make order out of chaos and to progress through individual effort and moral worth. There had been a succession of 'Wests' as settlers moved across the North American continent; the 'Wild West' was the last frontier region. It disappeared after 1890, with the end of Native American hostilities, the decline of the long-distance cattle drives, the building of the railways, and the steady growth of population.

Wilhelmina (1880–1962) Queen of the Netherlands (1890–1948). The daughter of William III, she probably played a significant role in maintaining the neutrality of the Netherlands during World War I. When her country was invaded by Germany (1940), she and her ministers maintained a government-in-exile in London. Through frequent radio talks she became a symbol of resistance for the Dutch people. She returned in 1945, but abdicated (1948) in favour of her daughter Juliana.

Wilkes, John (1727–97) British journalist and politician. Wilkes was hailed in both Britain and America as a champion of liberty. In 1763 in issue 45 of his paper the *North Briton* he attacked George III's ministers and by implication the king himself, but when arrested for seditious libel he claimed the privileges of a Member of Parliament to contest the legality of his arrest, which had been made under a general warrant, not specifying him by name. The government then managed to expel him from Parliament on grounds of obscenity, particularly for the publication of his *Essay on Woman*, an obscene spoof on Alexander Pope's *Essay on Man*, and Wilkes fled to France in 1764. He returned in 1768 to fight the general election and to serve a 22 month sentence for his earlier offences. Controversy raged when Parliament refused to let him take his seat, even though he was elected Member of Parliament for Middlesex on four consecutive occasions. He was at last allowed back into Parliament in 1774 and sat for Middlesex until 1790. He supported the parliamentary reform movement and declared an interest in and sympathy for the American cause. All this time he enjoyed the support of the populace and a mob could always be called out to rally to his cause. In 1780, after some hesitation, he supported the action being taken to suppress the GORDON RIOTS and he was considered to have become respectable when he opposed the French Revolution.

Wilkins, Roy (1901–81) US social reformer and civil rights leader. The grandson of a slave, he worked for Black newspapers before he joined the National Association for the Advancement of Colored People (NAACP) in 1931. He was an active leader of the CIVIL RIGHTS movement to improve the status of the Black population. He held high executive office in the NAACP from 1955 to 1977, but came under increasing criticism from Black militants towards the end of his life, for his commitment to non-violence.

Wilkinson, James (1757–1825) US general and adventurer. He distinguished himself in the early days of the War of Independence. Moving to Kentucky, he became a principal figure in the confused politics of the developing south-west. He re-entered the army in 1791 and went on to serve as governor of the Louisiana Territory (1805–06). While there he became involved with Aaron BURR's conspiracy, but betrayed the latter and acted as prosecution witness in the subsequent treason trial. The failure of his campaign to capture Montreal in the early stages of the WAR OF 1812 led to his removal from command and eventual retirement.

Willard, Emma (Hart) (1787–1870) US pioneer of women's education. She opened a seminary at Middlebury, Vermont, in 1814 to teach subjects not then available to women (see FEMINISM). Her appeal to the New York legislature, *Plan for Improving Female Education* (1819), led her to be invited by Governor Clinton to settle in that state, and in 1821 she opened the Troy Female Seminary, offering a college education that became a model for similar establishments in Europe and the USA.

William I (the Conqueror) (or William the Bastard) (1028–87) The first Norman King of England (1066–87). The illegitimate son of Robert I, Duke of Normandy, he succeeded to the dukedom as a child in 1035. His early life was fraught with danger – three of his closest advisers were murdered and an attempt was made on his own life. Twice he faced major rebellions. In 1047 he was saved only by the intervention of the French king, Henry I, who helped him in battle. In 1053–54 Henry failed to seize Normandy for himself. William's claim to the English throne was based on the promise allegedly given to him in 1051 by EDWARD THE CONFESSOR. With papal backing he landed in England and defeated HAROLD II at the Battle of HASTINGS (1066). While the English leaders considered their next move William laid waste parts of Sussex, Surrey, and Hertfordshire. He was crowned on Christmas Day at Westminster Abbey.

The period 1067–71 was characterized by a number of rebellions against his rule in Northumbria, Wessex, Mercia, and the Isle of Ely. His suppression of them was ruthlessly effective. Much of his later life he spent in Normandy fighting against the French king Philip I but before his death he initiated the DOMESDAY BOOK (1086). He died after being wounded on the battlefield, fighting Philip I of France.

William I (the Lion) (1143–1214) King of Scotland (1165–1214), succeeding his brother Malcolm IV. He helped to establish the independence of the Church of Scotland (1188), formulated the first major alliance between his country and France (1168), and stimulated Scotland's urban development. Initially loyal to HENRY II of England, William's determination to recover the earldom of Northumberland led to his support of Henry's three sons in a disastrous civil war, which resulted in William's capture at Alnwick (1175), the acknowledgement of Henry as his feudal superior by the Treaty of Falaise, and, in 1189, the payment of 10,000 marks to RICHARD I to recover his independence.

William I (the Silent) (1533–84) Prince of ORANGE and Count of Nassau-Dillenburg. William I is regarded as the founding father of the UNITED PROVINCES OF THE NETHERLANDS. He was trusted by Emperor CHARLES V and initially by PHILIP II of Spain, who made him STATHOLDER of Holland, Zeeland, and Utrecht (1559) and then of Franche-Comté (1561). Nevertheless he emerged in the 1560s as the leader of the aristocratic opposition to Philip's centralizing absolutism. On ALBA's arrival in the Netherlands (1567) he became the key figure in the first phase of the DUTCH REVOLTS. He was never a great general in the field, but his strengths lay in negotiating financial and military aid from abroad and in providing leadership in a country often torn by rivalries. He was recognized as statholder by the Estates of Holland (1572) and joined the Calvinist church (1573). His dream of a united Netherlands under a national government seemed close to realization with the signature of the Pacification of GHENT (1576); he was powerless to prevent the permanent north–south division of 1579. In 1580 he was outlawed by Philip II and four years later he was assassinated by a Catholic fanatic.

William I (1797–1888) King of Prussia (1861–88) and German Emperor (1871–88). He devoted himself to the welfare of the Prussian army, assuming personal command in suppressing the REVOLUTION OF 1848 in Baden. When he succeeded to the Prussian throne in 1861 he proclaimed a new 'era of liberalism', but this did not last for long. In 1862 he invited Otto von BISMARCK to become his Minister-President and from then on relied increasingly on Bismarck's policies, giving his approval to the growing influence of Prussia. During the FRANCO-PRUSSIAN WAR he took command of troops, receiving the surrender of Napoleon III at SEDAN (September 1870). In January 1871 he was invited by the princes of Germany, at Bismarck's instigation, to become their emperor, thus creating the GERMAN SECOND EMPIRE. Two unsuccessful assassination attempts strengthened his popularity, but also offered a pretext to clamp down on socialists.

William II (or William Rufus, 'red-faced') (c. 1056–1100) King of England (1087–1100). William II was the second son of WILLIAM I (the Conqueror) and Matilda. His succession was challenged by some Norman barons led by his uncle, Bishop Odo of Bayeux, who preferred his elder brother Robert, Duke of Normandy. This rebellion (1088) was crushed as was a second revolt in 1095. Robert's departure on the First CRUSADE (1096) gave William the opportunity to secure Normandy for himself. His successes there against the French king and in neighbouring Maine did much to secure the boundaries of Normandy. William's resistance to ANSELM's appointment as Archbishop of Canterbury contributed to his unpopular image with the chroniclers. His death from an arrow when hunting in the New Forest may have been arranged by his younger brother, who succeeded him as HENRY I.

William II (1859–1941) King of Prussia and Emperor of Germany (1888–1918). A grandson of Queen Victoria and of William I of Prussia, in 1890 he forced BISMARCK's resignation and embarked on a personal 'new course' policy that was regarded abroad as warmongering. He supported TIRPITZ in building a navy to rival that of Britain. His congratulatory telegram to the Boer leader, KRUGER, on the failure of the JAMESON RAID (1896) offended public opinion in Britain. He made friendly overtures to Turkey and dangerously provoked France in the MOROCCO crises of 1905 and 1911. His support of the AUSTRO-HUNGARIAN EMPIRE against SERBIA (1914) led to World War I, although his personal responsibility for the war is less than was once thought. He played little direct part in the war and in 1918 was forced to abdicate.

William III (of Orange) (1650–1702) King of England, Ireland, and Scotland (1689–1702). William III was STATHOLDER of Holland and took over effective rule of the UNITED PROVINCES (1672–1702) after the crisis of the French invasion in 1672. In 1677 he married his cousin, MARY of England, and was invited in 1688 by seven leading English politicians to save England from his Roman Catholic father-in-law, JAMES II. In what became known as the GLORIOUS REVOLUTION, he landed at Torbay, met with virtually no resistance, and in 1689 jointly with Mary accepted from Parliament the crown of England. He defeated James II's efforts to establish a base in Ireland by the victory of the BOYNE and suppressed the highlanders of Scotland. He commanded the Dutch army in the Netherlands and although he scored only one victory, at Namur in 1695, he was able to win a favourable peace at RYSWICK two years later. He was never popular in England and relied heavily on Dutch favourites, such as KEPPEL. Although he preferred the WHIGS to the TORIES, he tried to avoid one-party government. His reputation was affected by his failure to honour the Treaty of Limerick (a treaty (1691) in which William guaranteed political and religious freedom to Irish Catholics and the massacre of GLENCOE (1692).

William IV (1765–1837) King of Great Britain and Ireland and dependencies overseas, King of Hanover (1830–37). The third son of George III, his reign marked decline in the political influence of the crown. He joined the navy as an able seaman in 1779, subsequently becoming a close friend of Horatio NELSON. In 1790 he set up house with an actress, Dorothea Jordan, who bore him ten children. In order to secure the succession to the throne, in 1818 he married Adelaide of Saxe-Meiningen and had two daughters, who both died in infancy. Becoming king on the death of his brother, GEORGE IV, in 1830, he overcame his natural conservatism sufficiently to help ensure the passage of the REFORM ACT of 1832.

William of Malmesbury (c. 1095–c. 1143) Historian of 12th-century England. A librarian at the Benedictine abbey of St Aldhelm in Malmesbury, Wiltshire, he was the author of a history of the English church to 1125 (*Gesta Pontificum Anglorum*). He is best known for his other historical work the *Gesta Regum Anglorum* (Acts the English Kings), dealing with the period from BEDE 1120, and the *Historia Novella* (Modern History), which continues the account to 1142. His work is notable for its attempt to understand and interpret events rather than record them in an uncritical fashion.

William of Occam (or Ockham) (*c.* 1290–*c.* 1347) English theologian and scholastic philosopher. He was a Franciscan friar who developed an anti-papal theory of the state, denying the pope secular authority and was EXCOMMUNICATED in 1328, living thereafter in Munich under Emperor Louis IV's protection. His form of nominalist philosophy saw God as beyond human powers of reasoning and things as provable only by experience or by (unprovable) scriptural authority. Hence his famous maxim, 'Occam's razor', that the fewest possible assumptions should be made in explaining a thing.

William of Wykeham (1324–1404) English administrator and Bishop of Winchester (1367–1404). He is thought to have been a SERF's son; in the 1350s, as a royal clerk, he gained EDWARD III's favour and in the next decade he became the king's right-hand man. As Bishop of Winchester and Chancellor of England from 1367, he aroused parliamentary opposition, which forced him out of the chancellorship in 1371; RICHARD II brought him back as Chancellor (1389–91). He was responsible for two educational foundations, New College, Oxford (1379) and Winchester College (1382).

Williams, Eric (Eustace) (1911–81) West Indian statesman. In 1955 Williams founded the People's National Movement (PNM), which remained unsuccessful during the West Indies Federation (1958–62), but won a landslide victory in the national elections of 1961. In 1962 he led his country to independence, becoming the first Prime Minister (1961–81) of the colony and then of the republic of TRINIDAD AND TOBAGO. An 'empirical' socialist, Williams attracted foreign capital through tax incentives and, by skilful use of foreign aid, made Trinidad and Tobago the wealthiest Commonwealth nation in the Caribbean. He faced increasing militant opposition to his government before his death in 1981.

Williams, Roger (*c.* 1603–83) English founder of the North American colony of RHODE ISLAND. He emigrated to Massachusetts in 1631 and, as a minister at Salem, he soon quarrelled with John Cotton and Governor John WINTHROP. In 1635 he was banished. He founded Providence, Rhode Island, where he developed friendly relations with local Native Americans and established the Baptist Church. He obtained a parliamentary charter for Rhode Island in 1644. Although free of religious persecution, the colony was beset by feuding for most of Williams's life.

Wilson, (James) Harold, Baron Wilson of Rievaulx (1916–95) British Labour Prime Minister (1964–70, 1974–76). Wilson's policies were noted for their non-doctrinal content and were considered pragmatic by his supporters, but unprincipled by his detractors. Throughout their periods in office the Wilson cabinets were plagued by economic problems: in the first period these mainly took the forms of balance-of-payments deficits and sterling crises, the latter leading to a devaluation of the pound in 1967. Experiments to create prices and incomes policy collapsed and the White Paper *In Place of Strife* (1969), which sought to curb trade unions, to end unofficial strikes, and to establish a permanent Industrial Relations Commission, was withdrawn. In February 1968 the government passed an immigration Act to prevent mass entry into Britain of Asians from Kenya and Uganda who held British passports and to restrict entry by all Commonwealth citizens. A RACE RELATIONS ACT was introduced two months later. Important regional development and social reforms, particularly in education, were achieved in the 1960s: the introduction of comprehensive education, the expansion of higher education, changes in the law on sexual relations, divorce, and abortion, the end of the death penalty, and the reduction of the age of adulthood to 18. In 1968 the decision was made to withdraw forces from east of Suez. Overseas, the government failed to solve the problem of Rhodesian UDI in 1965 (ZIMBABWE). During the period 1974–76 the major problem was inflation, which the government unsuccessfully tried to cure by abating wage demands by a 'social contract' with the trade unions. In 1975 the Wilson administration reluctantly confirmed British membership of the EUROPEAN ECONOMIC COMMUNITY after a referendum. A perceived defect in all Wilson's governments was the array of private advisers and the highly personalized style of running public affairs.

Wilson, Jack WOVOKA.

Wilson, (Thomas) Woodrow (1856–1924) 28th President of the USA (1913–21). Wilson entered an academic career in 1883 and was appointed president of Princeton University in 1902. He was responsible for major changes in the educational and social organization of Princeton. In 1910 he resigned to run as governor of New Jersey and was elected. Wilson became a successful reform governor and earned a reputation that helped give him the Democratic nomination for the Presidency in 1912. Once in office, Wilson determined to effect a programme known as the 'New Freedom', designed to stimulate competition, promote equal opportunity, and check corruption. Faced with the outbreak of World War I in 1914, he at first concentrated on preserving US neutrality. Gradually, however, he came to a view that the USA should enter the war on the side of the Allies. German policy of unrestricted submarine warfare from January 1917 led to the declaration of war in April. From then on he worked to realize his vision, proposed in the FOURTEEN POINTS, of a peaceful post-war world. Wilson's Presbyterian background and respect for legal traditions made him favour an international peacekeeping forum, but he fell foul of American ISOLATIONISM, which saw the proposed LEAGUE OF NATIONS as a tool of British and French diplomacy. The isolationists in the Senate defeated Wilson on the issue of US participation in the League, while his exertions in negotiating the VERSAILLES PEACE SETTLEMENT and trying to win its acceptance by the Senate brought on a severe stroke. He never fully recovered, and for the last year of his presidency his wife, Edith Wilson, a lady of powerful personality, largely directed such business as could not be avoided or postponed.

'Wind of Change' A phrase in a speech by the British Prime Minister, Harold MACMILLAN. He used it in his address to both Houses of the South African Parliament on 3 February 1960, to draw attention to the growth of national consciousness that was sweeping like a 'wind of change' across the African continent and warned that SOUTH AFRICA should take account of it.

window tax An English tax on any window or window-like opening, which was in force from 1695 to

1851. It was originally imposed to pay for the losses of the great recoinage of 1695 and was increased six times in the 18th century, particularly by PITT THE YOUNGER. The tax was eventually applied to all windows in excess of six in a building and windows bricked up to avoid the tax can still be seen in older houses throughout Britain.

Windsor, House of The official designation of the British royal family since 1917. Anti-German feeling during World War I was sufficiently strong for George V to feel that it would be an appropriate gesture to remove all references to the German titles of Saxe-Coburg, derived originally from the marriage of Queen Victoria to Prince Albert of Saxe-Coburg-Gotha. 'Windsor' was adopted because Windsor Castle, Berkshire, has long been a main home of British monarchs.

Wingate, Orde Charles (1903–44) British major-general. A brilliant exponent of guerrilla warfare, in the 1930s he helped to establish and train Jewish irregular forces operating against Arabs in Palestine and in 1941 he organized Sudanese and Abyssinian irregulars to fight the Italian occupiers and restore Emperor HAILE SELASSIE to the throne of Ethiopia. He created and led the *chindits*, a Burmese guerrilla group that operated behind Japanese lines. He died in an air crash in 1944 at the outset of his second, and greatly enlarged, *chindit* operation.

Winstanley, Gerrard (*c.* 1609–after 1660) English radical Puritan. He was the leader of the DIGGERS, who cultivated common land in Surrey in 1649–50, when food prices had risen sharply, and were then forced off their land by the authorities. Winstanley later became prominent as a pamphleteer with communistic ideas. In dedicating his most famous pamphlet, *The Law of Freedom in a Platform*, to CROMWELL in 1652, he showed surprising naïvety in thinking that Cromwell would approve the thesis that the ENGLISH CIVIL WAR had been fought against all who were enemies of the poor, including landlords and priests.

Winthrop, John (1588–1649) First governor of the North American colony of MASSACHUSETTS. Born in Suffolk, he became a member of the Puritan Massachusetts Bay Company and left England in 1630 to establish the new colony, based in Boston. Under him a representative government of church members was established, the law was codified, Congregationalism defined, and ARMINIANISM bitterly attacked. He left a vivid account of the period from his departure from England until his death in his *Journal*, sometimes called *The History of New England*.

Winthrop, John (1606–76) Son of John WINTHROP and governor of CONNECTICUT from 1657 until his death. He emigrated from England to Massachusetts in 1631. In 1635 he established the colony of Saybrook, Connecticut, and became the leader of Connecticut colonies. He encouraged industrialization, erected an ironworks at Saugus, Massachusetts (1644), established an efficient administration, and in 1662 obtained the charter for the unified colony of Connecticut and New Haven. A notable physician and scientist, he became in 1663 the first Fellow of the ROYAL SOCIETY to be resident in America.

Wishart, George (*c.* 1513–46) Scottish Protestant preacher and martyr. Wishart fled to England in 1538, then spent some time in Europe before returning to

Scotland. There he opposed the anti-English policies of Cardinal BEATON and was possibly involved in plots to assassinate him. In 1546 John KNOX became his disciple. Wishart was charged with heresy and burned to death.

witan (from Old English *witenagemot*, 'moot', or meeting, of the king's councillors) The council summoned by the Anglo-Saxon kings. The meetings of the witan in the 10th and 11th centuries were a formalization of the primitive councils that existed in the early Saxon kingdoms of the 7th century. These formal gatherings of ALDERMEN, THANES, and bishops discussed royal grants of land, church benefices, charters, aspects of taxation, defence and foreign policy, customary law, and the prosecution of traitors. The succession of a king had usually to be acknowledged by the witan.

witchcraft The malevolent exercise of preternatural powers, especially by women, attributed to a connection with the devil or evil spirits. The witch's male counterpart is named a wizard, sorcerer, or warlock. There are accounts of witchcraft in ancient Greek and Roman texts, for example Medea, who uses sorcery to help Jason win the Golden Fleece. In the Old Testament King Saul consults the Witch of Endor. In the early Middle Ages popular superstition began to associate witchcraft with demonic possession and the rejection of God. By the late 12th century the INQUISITION dealt with cases of witchcraft involving heresy, and secular courts, especially in Germany, punished these supposed crimes with cruelty and burning. Mass persecutions began to take place in the 15th century, and the publication of *Malleus Maleficarum* (Hammer of Witches) in 1487, describing witches' sabbaths, night-flying, intercourse with the devil, transformation into animals, and malicious spells cast on men and cattle, greatly increased superstition and persecution. Witches were popularly depicted with a black cat (the 'familiar') and a broomstick. The 16th-century Reformers further contributed to the persecution of witches, as did the unrest stirred up by the religious wars. The last trials for witchcraft in England were in 1712 and on the Continent (in Prussia) in 1793. In America the belief in witchcraft was rife but the SALEM WITCH TRIALS (1692) caused a general revulsion. Greater scientific knowledge in the 17th century led the educated to reject belief in witchcraft, but popular belief has survived much longer. In the 20th century, in Europe and the USA, a new kind of witchcraft has manifested itself, which claims to be a revival of pre-Christian pagan religion. It is practised by a small number of adherents in covens (groups) or assemblies and has at times been associated with allegations of animal sacrifice and child sexual abuse.

Witt, Jan de (1625–72) Dutch statesman, an opponent of William II of Orange. He was the effective leader of the United Provinces during the minority of WILLIAM III, dominating the other provinces by his political skill and his knowledge of foreign affairs. The republican party sought to limit the powers of the Orange family and in 1654 members were excluded from state offices. In 1668 he signed the defensive Triple Alliance with England and Sweden to thwart LOUIS XIV's designs on The Netherlands. When Louis invaded in 1672 de Witt was caught unprepared and William proved himself an able commander of the Dutch forces. De Witt's power was undermined and he and his brother Cornelius, a naval officer, were attacked and killed by a mob in 1672.

Witte, Sergei Yulyevich, Count (1849–1915) Russian statesman. As Finance Minister (1892–1903) and Premier (1905–06), he believed that if Russia was to become the equal of western industrial nations both government investment and foreign capital were essential. New railways linked the Donetz coalmines with St Petersburg and Moscow and the Trans-Siberian railway was built. He encouraged the start of steel production and sufficient petroleum was produced to satisfy Russia's need and for export. Thus on the eve of political revolution Russia underwent a remarkable industrial revolution. Although Witte's ideal was economic modernization combined with authoritarian rule, during the RUSSIAN REVOLUTION OF 1905 he urged NICHOLAS II to issue the October Manifesto granting Russia a constitution and to summon the DUMA. Nicholas disliked him and dismissed him.

Wittelsbach A German family which formed a ruling dynasty in Bavaria between 1180 and 1918. By a marriage of 1214, the Rhenish Palatinate was added to the family holdings. Duke Louis II (c. 1283–1347) was elected Holy Roman Emperor, and divided the Wittelsbach succession between a younger branch (which received Bavaria) and a senior one (which inherited the Rhenish and Upper Palatinate and was given an electoral title in 1356). During the REFORMATION, the Bavarian branch remained staunchly Catholic. The Palatinate branch espoused the new Protestant faith and during the THIRTY YEARS WAR forfeited both its electoral vote and the Upper Palatinate to Bavaria. By the Treaty of WESTPHALIA (1648) a new electoral vote was created for the Rhenish Palatinate. The Elector Charles Albert of Bavaria (1697–1745) became Holy Roman Emperor (1742–45).

Wolfe, James (1727–59) British general. He was appointed second-in-command to AMHERST in 1758 at the age of 31, after 17 years' outstanding military service in Europe and Scotland. He led the landing on Cape Breton Island in 1758, which forced the surrender of LOUISBURG. In the next year his daring surprise attack on Quebec and his defeat of Montcalm on the PLAINS OF ABRAHAM won Canada for Britain. His training of his troops in disciplined fire-power brought them victory; his determination to lead from the front resulted in his death on the Plains of Abraham.

Wollstonecraft (Godwin), Mary (1759–97) British writer and pioneer of women's rights. The daughter of a violent alcoholic father, Wollstonecraft became a schoolteacher and governess. She wrote *Thoughts on the Education of Daughters* (1787), which established her as a moral and political philosopher. She visited Paris in 1792 to witness the aftermath of the French Revolution, inspiring her to write *Historical and Moral View of the French Revolution* (1794). She wrote several other works but is best known for *Vindication of the Rights of Women* (1792), which argues for equality of education and professional opportunity for women and is regarded as one of the early classics of FEMINISM.

In 1797 she married William Godwin, but died following the birth of their daughter, the future Mary Shelley, author of *Frankenstein* (1818) and wife of the poet Percy Bysshe Shelley.

Wolseley, Garnet Joseph, 1st Viscount (1833–1913) British field-marshal. He served in Burma, the Crimea, the Indian Mutiny, China, and Canada. He furthered the army reforms of Edward CARDWELL at the War Office (1871–72) and in 1873 commanded the ASANTE expedition. His most famous achievement was his brilliant defeat of ARABI PASHA in 1882. In 1884 he was too late to relieve GORDON in Khartoum. An advocate of army reform, he successfully worked for the abolition of the purchase of commissions, shorter periods of enlistment, and the creation of an army reserve.

Wolsey, Thomas (c. 1474–1530) English-prelate and statesman. He rose from humble origins to the favour of HENRY VII and was made royal almoner by HENRY VIII (1509). As privy councillor (1511), then Lord Chancellor (1574), he virtually ruled on Henry's behalf, while as cardinal (1515) and papal legate (1518) he was effectively head of the English church. He acquired a string of rich benefices, culminating in the archbishopric of York (1514), which supported the grandeur of his lifestyle in palaces such as Hampton Court.

Wolsey's ambitions in international affairs were marked by the Treaty of London (1518), which established a temporary peace between France and Spain. Although he generally favoured a peaceful foreign policy Henry committed England to a policy of European warfare, which contributed to Wolsey's unpopularity. His despotism and personal ambition fed the growing anti-clericalism of the times. He supported Henry's wish to divorce Catherine of Aragon, but tried to persuade him to remarry into the French royal house. His failure to secure the divorce finally discredited him with the king. He was arrested on a trumped-up charge of treason, but died before he could be brought to trial.

women's liberation FEMINISM.

women's movement FEMINISM.

women's suffrage The right of women to take part in political life and to vote in an election. Women's suffrage was advocated by Mary WOLLSTONECRAFT in *A Vindication of the Rights of Women* (1792) and throughout the 19th century, in Britain and the USA, calls were made for voting rights for women. These were first attained at a national level in New Zealand (1893). The state of Wyoming, USA, introduced women's suffrage in 1869; in 1893 the National American Woman Suffrage Association (NAWSA) combined two earlier organizations, formed in 1869, and organized state-by-state activity, and in 1920 all women over 21 were given the vote in the USA. The first European nation to grant female suffrage was Finland in 1906, with Norway following in 1913, and Germany in 1919. In Britain, as a result of agitation by the Women's Social and Political Union, led by Emmeline PANKHURST and her daughter Christabel (see also SUFFRAGETTES), the vote was granted in 1918 to those over 30 and in 1928 to women over 21. In 1918 the Irish politician Countess Constance Markiewicz (1868–1927) became the first woman to be elected to the British House of Commons but as a member of SINN FEIN, she refused to take the oath of Allegiance and thus could not take her seat. She later became a member of DE VALERA's Daíl Éireann. In the years following World War I, women were granted the vote in many countries, including Germany, Poland, Austria, and Sweden (1919), and the USA (1920). The

Roman Catholic Church was reluctant to support women's suffrage and in many Catholic countries it was not gained until after World War II; in France it was granted in 1944, in Belgium in 1948, while in Switzerland not until 1971. In Russia women gained the right to vote with the Revolution (1917) and women's suffrage was extended to the Soviet Union from 1922. In developing countries, women's suffrage was usually obtained with independence, and in most Muslim countries women now have the vote. Women still do not have the vote in certain absolute monarchies such as Saudi Arabia and Kuwait (where male suffrage is also restricted). The 20th century has seen the emergence of such outstanding women politicians as Sirimavo BANDARANAIKE (1916–), Golda MEIR (1898–1978), Indira GANDHI (1917–84), Benazir BHUTTO (1953–), and Margaret THATCHER (1925–), although the proportion of women taking an active part in politics remains low.

wool staple One of the towns in England, Wales, Ireland, or in Continental Europe, through which wool merchants traded. They were set up by EDWARD III of England as a means of controlling the principal English export, wool, so that he could be guaranteed the tax due on it at the customs point. By the Ordinance of the Staple (1353) 15 British staple towns were established, but in 1363 Calais was made the wool staple through which all wool exports had to pass; a very profitable monopoly in the wool trade was given to the MERCHANT STAPLERS. A continental staple existed until the ban on exports of wool in 1617.

workhouse A public institution where people unable to support themselves were housed and (if able-bodied) made to work. The 1601 POOR LAW Act made parishes responsible for their own workhouses, but often they were hard to distinguish from the houses of correction, set up to discipline vagrants. The 1723 Workhouse Act denied relief to able-bodied paupers who refused to enter workhouses.

Works Project Administration (or Works Progress Administration) (WPA) A US federal relief measure for the unemployed. An agency of the NEW DEAL, it was established by the Emergency Relief Appropriation Act of 1935. The initiators were Harold Lekes and Harry HOPKINS; they wanted the (estimated) 3.5 million unemployed but able-bodied to be given work and not a dole. Thus, through their wages, they would have money to spend and thereby help business to revive. The WPA employed about two million at one time and by 1941 eight million (20% of the labour force) were engaged in public works. It built roads, bridges, playgrounds, airport landing fields, school buildings and hospitals, and ran a campaign against adult illiteracy. It was also, as even its friends had to admit, a useful source of employment for Democratic Party workers.

World Bank An international economic organization and specialized agency of the UNITED NATIONS ORGANIZATION, based in Washington, DC. Proposed at the BRETTON WOODS CONFERENCE in 1944, it comprises two legally and financially distinct organizations which are, however, administered by the same staff: the International Bank for Reconstruction and Development (IBRD), established in 1945, and the International Development Association (IDA), established in 1960. The World Bank receives its funds from member countries (the USA being the largest contributor) and from borrowing on world money markets. It had 178 members in 1995. Its purpose is to provide funds and technical assistance to help the economies of developing countries and it works closely with the INTERNATIONAL MONETARY FUND. The IBRD lends to countries at a slightly advanced stage of economic growth at just below commercial interest rates. Some of the projects supported by the IBRD, particularly those which have entailed large-scale industrial developments and construction projects, such as dams and roads, have been criticized for overburdening states with debt and harming indigenous development and the environment. In the light of the problems of the North/South divide highlighted in the BRANDT REPORT, the Bank established a Special Fund (1977) to help least developed countries with debt-service relief. Accordingly, it has shifted its emphasis in recent years to investments in projects which involve simpler 'intermediate technology' and has concentrated on supporting rural development, agriculture, small-scale enterprises, education, family planning, health, public hygiene, and nutrition in an attempt directly to improve the well-being of the vast numbers of poor people in developing countries. The World Bank also helps to plan strategies for industrialization. The IDA, which is open to all member states of the World Bank, gives assistance to the poorest countries on more favourable terms than IBRD. IDA credits, which are made only to governments, can be repaid over 40 to 50 years with a grace period of ten years and without interest.

World Council of Churches (WCC) An inter-denominational organization of Christian Churches, created in 1948. Apart from the ROMAN CATHOLIC CHURCH and the UNITARIANS, the Council includes all the major and many minor denominations and nearly all the Eastern Orthodox Churches. Since 1961 the Roman Catholic Church has sent accredited observers to its meetings. The World Council of Churches is the most important of a number of ecumenical movements advocating greater unity amongst the Christian Churches. Most of the work of the Council is advisory, but it also has a number of administrative units; the largest of these is the division of Inter-Church Aid, Refugee, and World Service.

world fairs Displays that emphasize the industrial, scientific, and technological achievements of the participating nations. They seek to promote trade and publicize cultural progress. Early examples were the GREAT EXHIBITION at the Crystal Palace in London in 1851 and the Paris Exhibition of 1861. The first New York Fair was held in 1853–54 and the Philadelphia Centennial Exhibition in 1876. Fairs of particular note in the 20th century include those in New York in 1939–40 and 1964–65, the Brussels World Fair in 1958, the Seattle Century 21 Exposition of 1962, Expo 67 held in Montreal and Expo 92 in Seville.

World Health Organization (WHO) A UNITED NATIONS specialized agency established in 1948 with the broad aim of attaining the highest level of health for all people, and supported by 190 countries. Its head office is in Geneva, Switzerland. WHO does not conduct its own research but promotes biomedical and health research in some 500 collaborating centres worldwide, arranging international medical conferences and the exchange and training of research workers. WHO compiles the *International Pharmacopæia*, monitors epidemics, evaluates new drugs, and advises on biological standards. It publishes quarterly an international journal of health development (*World Health Forum*) in Arabic, Chinese, English, French, Russian, and Spanish. A notable success of WHO has been the eradication of smallpox throughout the world.

WHO advocates a number of public health measures to provide safe drinking water and adequate sanitation, the immunization of all children against major communicable diseases, and the reduction of malnutrition. In addition, it has intensified efforts to prevent and combat endemic diseases, such as malaria and tuberculosis, and to give access to essential drugs and to family planning services.

world population POPULATION OF THE WORLD.

World Trade Organization (WTO) An international economic body, inaugurated on 1 January 1995 as the successor to the GENERAL AGREEMENT ON TARIFFS AND TRADE (GATT). By April 1997 the WTO consisted of all 125 members of GATT and six new member states; another 28 states have applied to join. The WTO has a wider role than GATT, covering commercial activities beyond the remit of the latter body, such as telecommunications, information technology, intellectual property rights, and trade in services.

World War I (1914–18) The war between the Allied Powers (Britain, France, Russia, Japan, and Serbia, who were joined in the course of the war by Italy (1915), Portugal and Romania (1916), the USA and Greece (1917)) against the Central Powers (Germany, the Austro-Hungarian empire, OTTOMAN Turkey, and (from 1915) Bulgaria). The war's two principal causes were fear of

World War I   *In 1914 the empires of the Central Powers – German, Austro-Hungarian, and Ottoman – extended through Central Europe into the Middle East. The Versailles Settlement (1919–23) sought to draw frontiers of the successor states along ethnic lines, and these largely survived, although Czechoslovakia's frontiers were to be challenged by Hitler. Following the Treaty of Brest-Litovsk and the Russian Civil War, the Baltic states of Latvia, Estonia, and Lithuania, together with a reconstituted Poland, became independent.*

Germany's colonial ambitions and European tensions arising from shifting diplomatic divisions and nationalist agitation, especially in the BALKAN STATES. It was fought in six main theatres of war. On the WESTERN FRONT fighting was characterized by TRENCH WARFARE, both sides believing that superiority in numbers would ultimately prevail despite the greater power of mechanized defence. Aerial warfare developed from reconnaissance into bombing and the use of fighter aircraft in air-to-air combat. On the Eastern Front the initial Russian advance was defeated at Tannenberg (1914). With Turkey also attacking Russia, the DARDANELLES expedition (1915) was planned in order to provide relief, but it failed. Temporary Russian success against Austria-Hungary was followed (1917) by military disaster and the RUSSIAN REVOLUTION. The MESOPOTAMIAN CAMPAIGN was prompted by Britain's desire to protect oil installations and to conquer outlying parts of the Ottoman empire. A British advance in 1917 against the Turks in Palestine, aided by an Arab revolt, succeeded. In north-east Italy a long and disastrous campaign after Italy had joined the Allies was waged against Austria-Hungary, with success only coming late in 1918. Campaigns against Germany's colonial possessions in Africa and the Pacific were less demanding. At sea there was only one major encounter, the inconclusive Battle of JUTLAND (1916). A conservative estimate of casualties of the war gives 10 million killed and 20 million wounded. An armistice was signed and peace terms agreed in the VERSAILLES PEACE SETTLEMENT.

World War II (1939–45) A war fought between the AXIS POWERS and the Allies, including Britain, the Soviet Union, and the USA. Having secretly rearmed Germany, HITLER occupied (1936) the Rhineland, in contravention of the VERSAILLES PEACE SETTLEMENT. In the same year the Italian FASCIST dictator, Benito MUSSOLINI, joined Hitler in a Berlin–Rome axis, and in 1937 Italy pledged support for the ANTI-COMINTERN PACT between Germany and Japan. In the 1938 ANSCHLUSS, Germany annexed Austria into the THIRD REICH, and invaded Czechoslovak SUDETENLAND. Hitler, having secured the MUNICH PACT with CHAMBERLAIN in 1938, signed the NAZI–SOVIET PACT with STALIN in August 1939. Germany then felt free to invade the POLISH CORRIDOR and divide Poland between itself and the Soviet Union. Britain, which until 1939 had followed a policy of APPEASEMENT, declared war (3 September) on Germany, and in 1940 Winston CHURCHILL became head of a coalition government. The Soviet Union occupied the Baltic States and attacked FINLAND. Denmark, parts of Norway, Belgium, the Netherlands, and three-fifths of France fell to Germany in rapid succession, while the rest of France was established as a neutral state with its government at VICHY. A massive BOMBING OFFENSIVE was launched against Britain, but the planned invasion of the country was postponed indefinitely after Germany failed to gain air superiority in the Battle of BRITAIN. Pro-Nazi governments in Hungary, Romania, Bulgaria and Slovakia joined the Axis Powers, and Greece and Yugoslavia were overrun in March–April 1941. Hitler, breaking his pact with Stalin, invaded the Soviet Union, where his forces reached the outskirts of Moscow. Without declaring war, Japan attacked the US fleet at PEARL HARBOR in December 1941, provoking the USA to enter into the war on the side of Britain. In 1942 the first Allied counter-offensive began against ROMMEL in North Africa (NORTH AFRICAN CAMPAIGNS) and in 1943 Allied

troops began an invasion of the Italian mainland, resulting in the overthrow of Mussolini's government a month later. On the EASTERN FRONT the decisive battles around KURSK and STALINGRAD broke the German hold. The Allied invasion of western Europe was launched with the NORMANDY landings in June 1944 and Germany surrendered, after Hitler's suicide in Berlin, in May 1945. The PACIFIC CAMPAIGNS eliminated the Japanese navy and the heavy strategic bombing of Japan by the USA, culminating in the atomic bombing of Hiroshima and Nagasaki on 6 and 9 August 1945, induced Japan's surrender a month later.

The dead in World War II have been estimated at 15 million military personnel of which up to 2 million were Soviet prisoners-of-war. An estimated 35 million civilians died, with between 4 and 5 million Jews perishing in CONCENTRATION CAMPS, and an estimated 2 million more in mass murders in Eastern Europe. Refugees from the Soviet Union and Eastern Europe numbered many millions. The long-term results of the war in Europe were the division of Germany and the restoration to the Soviet Union of lands lost in 1919–21, together with the creation of communist buffer-states along the Soviet frontier. Britain had accumulated a $20 billion debt, while in the Far East nationalist resistance forces were to ensure the decolonization of south-east Asian countries. The USA and the Soviet Union emerged from the war as the two largest global powers. Their war-time alliance collapsed within three years and each embarked on a programme of rearmament with nuclear capability, as the COLD WAR developed.

Worms, Diet of (1521) A meeting between LUTHER and CHARLES V that took place in the city of Worms, on the River Rhine, in Germany. Luther committed himself to the cause of Protestant reform and on the last day of the Diet his teaching was formally condemned in the Edict of Worms

Wounded Knee, Battle of (1890) The last major battle between the US army and the Sioux people of the Great Plains. The site is a creek on Pine Ridge reservation, South Dakota, where, after the killing of SITTING BULL, the 7th US Cavalry surrounded a band of Sioux. These were followers of the Native American Ghost Dance religion, evolved around 1888 among the Paiute by WOVOKA, who preached the coming of an Native American messiah who would restore the country to the Native Americans and reunite the living with the dead. In 1890 a Ghost Dance uprising in South Dakota culminated at Wounded Knee, when US troops massacred some 200 Teton Sioux.

In 1973 the massacre was recalled when members of the American Indian Movement occupied the site. They were surrounded by a force of federal marshals; two Native Americans were killed, and one marshal seriously wounded. They agreed to evacuate the area in exchange for negotiation on Native American grievances.

Wovoka (or Jack Wilson) (c. 1865–1932) A Native American (Paiute) prophet, who instigated the *Ghost Dance*, a MILLENARIAN movement in the late 19th century that promised beleaguered Native Americans redemption and freedom from oppression. In 1888 Wovoka experienced a vision in which he claimed the 'Great Spirit' had assured him that the White invaders, who had overrun traditional lands and slaughtered the bison on which the Plains peoples depended, would be put to flight if the Native Americans united in performing the Ghost Dance. This ritual entailed inducing a trance-like state by chanting and dancing for days at a time and soon attracted thousands of desperate devotees. Wovoka's messianic movement failed to help the native North Americans. In 1890 the charismatic Hunkpapa (Dakota) Sioux leader SITTING BULL, who supported the dance, was killed while resisting arrest and shortly afterwards a group of dancers, believing that their ritual garb made them immune to bullets, were massacred by US troops at the Battle of WOUNDED KNEE.

Wrangel, Piotr Nikolayevich (1878–1928) Russian general who became prominent as the leader of the counter-revolutionary armies in the RUSSIAN CIVIL WAR (1918–21). Serving under KOLCHAK and then under DENIKIN, Wrangel became commander-in-chief of all WHITE RUSSIAN armies after Denikin's withdrawal (March 1920) to the Caucasus. In the Crimea Wrangel maintained a base as head of a provisional government. In November 1920 the RED ARMY broke through his defences and he fled to Turkey. His defeat ended White Russian resistance.

writing A system of inscribed signs replacing or recording spoken language. Various writing systems worldwide have developed independently. Writing is closely associated with the appearance of civilization, since in simple societies speech and memory were sufficient and there was no need for writing. It was essential, however, for the administration on which civilized states depend. The *quipus* of the INCAS, which were bundles of variously knotted strings, were a simple form of recording information that served the purposes of accounting but lacked the flexibility of other writing systems, whether carved, painted, scratched, impressed, handwritten, or printed.

People had probably attempted writing by 6000 BC and it developed independently in such places as Egypt, Mesopotamia, China, and South America. The earliest forms of writing used simple pictorial signs to represent objects. The SUMERIANS had developed a pictographical system of writing by about 3400 BC (see CUNEIFORM). The Sumerians and Egyptians also used symbols to represent spoken sounds, such as syllables and words.

The first complete alphabet, comprising symbols representing all the vowels and consonants of a language, was devised by the ancient Greeks. They based their alphabet on earlier sound-based partial alphabets, such as that used by the PHOENICIANS.

Chinese writing uses a system of symbols to represent words or concepts rather than sounds and is not directly linked to pronunciation.

The history of writing has been influenced by technological developments, such as the invention of paper and PRINTING, and by increased literacy due to the expansion of formal education.

Wuchang Uprising (10 October 1911) A revolt in the city of Wuchang that started the CHINESE REVOLUTION OF 1911. An accidental explosion forced republican revolutionaries to begin a planned uprising earlier than intended, but on the next day army units that had been won over to the rebel cause seized the city. The Qing government failed to respond swiftly to the uprising and further provincial uprisings followed, leading to the formation of a Provisional Republican Government on 1 January 1912.

Wyatt's Rebellion (February 1554) A protest in England against MARY I's projected marriage to the future PHILIP II of Spain. Its leader was a Kentish landowner, Sir Thomas Wyatt (1521–54). Wyatt was so convinced that the marriage would turn England into 'a cockleboat towed by a Spanish galleon', that he led 3,000 Kentishmen in a march on London. The rebellion's ultimate aims are uncertain, as is the involvement of Mary's half-sister, Princess Elizabeth, but it led to the execution of Lady Jane GREY. Wyatt found most Londoners' loyalty to Mary was stronger than their antipathy to Spain. He surrendered and was executed, along with 100 others.

Wyclif, John (or Wycliffe) (*c.* 1330–1384) English church reformer. For centuries he was thought to have been the sole translator of the Bible (from Latin into English) in the 14th century. He is now regarded as one of several men who shared in the joint enterprise of producing the 'Wyclif' or LOLLARD Bible. An Oxford academic and ecclesiastic, he wrote various logical and philosophical works, but achieved fame through his theological writings. These writings were condemned as heretical (1382) but gained him the interest and support of the royal family and the king's council in the later years of EDWARD III and the minority of RICHARD II. He died without having been imprisoned and the Lollards kept alive many of his beliefs.

Xenocrates (396–314 BC) Greek philosopher. Xenocrates was a student under PLATO and subsequently became head of the ACADEMY (339–314 BC). He was chosen to be an ambassador on Athens' behalf to the Macedonian king Antipater in 322 BC. As a philosopher he was an imitative follower of Plato, with a strong interest in the nature of the gods and in establishing a practical morality.

Xenophon (c. 428–c. 354 BC) Greek historian, essayist, and military commander from Athens. He left Athens in 401 to join the army of CYRUS II (the Great), who was attempting to win the Persian throne. He was exiled from Athens c. 399 and in 396–394 he fought under the Spartan king Agesilaus. Soon afterwards the Spartans allocated him an estate near Olympia, from where he later moved to Corinth, and finally in 366–365 back to Athens, where he spent the rest of his life. His writings reflect the viewpoint of a conventional and practically minded gentleman who supported aristocratic ideals and virtues. His historical works include the *Anabasis*, an eye-witness account of the expedition of the Persian prince Cyrus II against Artaxerxes (401–399 BC), in which he led the 10,000 Greek mercenaries in their retreat to the Black Sea after they had been left in a dangerous situation between the Tigris and Euphrates. Apart from the *Anabasis*, a number of his other works have survived, most notably the *Hellenica*, a work on the history of Greece and the Peloponnesian War, which covers the period from where THUCYDIDES left off (411) to 362 BC. The *Apology, Memorabilia*, and *Symposium* recall the life and teachings of his friend SOCRATES; the *Cyropaedia* is a historical romance on the education of Cyrus II, seen as the ideal prince. He also wrote treatises on politics, war, hunting, and horsemanship.

Xerxes I (the Great) (c. 519–465 BC) Ruler of the Achaemenid Persian empire from 486 to 465 BC. He personally led the great expedition against Greece, but after watching his fleet being defeated at SALAMIS in 480 BC, he withdrew, leaving behind Mardonius under whose command the army was defeated at PLATAEA in 479. The subsequent activities of the DELIAN LEAGUE deprived him of many Greek cities in Asia Minor. The latter part of his reign was marked by intrigues, one of which led to his murder.

Xhosa Wars (1779–1879) The wars between the Xhosa people and Dutch and British colonists along the east coast of Cape Colony, between the Great Fish and Great Kei rivers. From 1811 the policy of clearing the land of Xhosa people to make way for Europeans began and, following a year of fighting (1818–19), some 4000 British colonists were installed along the great Fish river. As they pushed the frontier east, however, the colonists met greater resistance, cattle raids resulting in retaliation. The war of 1834–35 yielded 60,000 head of cattle to the colonists and was followed by the longer struggle of 1846–53. The war of 1877–79, which yielded 15,000 cattle and 20,000 sheep, was vainly fought by

tribesmen returning from the diamond fields in a last bid to regain their land. Afterwards all Xhosa territory was incorporated as European farmland within Cape Colony (see CAPE PROVINCE).

Xia (or Hsia) (c. 21st century–c. 16th century BC) The first dynasty to rule in China, according to tradition. It was reputedly founded by Yu the Great, a model ruler, who is said to have attempted to control flooding by irrigation schemes. As yet no evidence authenticates the Xia, but it is possible such evidence will be found, as the existence of China's second dynasty, the SHANG, was not verified until the 1920s.

Xi'an incident (December 1936) The kidnapping of the Chinese leader CHIANG KAI-SHEK while visiting disaffected Manchurian troops at Xi'an. Chiang was captured by conspirators headed by Zhang Xueliang, who attempted to force him to give up his campaign against the communists and lead a national war against the Japanese, who had occupied Manchuria in 1931. After Chiang had refused to accede to their demands, the communists, headed by ZHOU ENLAI, also became involved in the negotiations and eventually Chiang was released, having promised to take a more active role against the Japanese and to allow local autonomy to the communists. Zhang Xueliang was imprisoned by Chiang, but the incident led to limited co-operation between the communists and the KUOMINTANG against the Japanese.

Xinjiang (Sinkiang) A vast region in the west of China, bounded by Kazakhstan on the west, Kashmir and Tibet on the south, and Mongolia on the north-east.

History. The region was inhabited by various Turkic-speaking peoples of which the Uighur became the most numerous. The SILK ROUTE connecting east and west Asia ran through its oasis towns. From HAN times the more powerful Chinese dynasties exercised control there. Part of the KHANATE of Turkistan, it was brought under QING military administration in the mid-18th century. However, Xinjiang was a rebellious area, partly because of an Islamic revival among the Uighur tribesmen and partly because of the corruption of local Qing officials. Local Islamic leaders launched unsuccessful *jihads* (holy wars) against the Qing in 1815, 1820–28, and 1857. In 1865 Yakub Beg invaded Xinjiang from Kokand, receiving British support to stem growing Russian influence in the area. Chinese forces defeated Yakub Beg in 1877, reclaiming nearly all of Xinjiang, which became established as a province in 1884. Russian influence in the area remained strong and only after 1950 did it become more closely integrated into China with the settlement of many Chinese in the province. There were border clashes with the Soviet Union in 1969. In 1996–97 a growing Muslim separatist movement was severely repressed.

Xiongnu Nomad horsemen who began harrying northern Chinese states from about 300 BC. Their homelands were in southern Siberia and Mongolia. It was to fend off their incursions that some Chinese states built walls, later joined together to form the GREAT WALL OF CHINA. The most serious attacks came during the rule of the early HAN, after the Xiongnu had formed a league under their Shan Yu (Heavenly Ruler). The Han at first attempted to buy off these great chieftains by conferring titles on them and giving them Chinese princesses as wives. Later, the policy of the Han emperor Wudi of isolating them by making alliances with other Asian peoples was in general successful. In the 1st century BC one group moved westward. The others, nominal vassals of China, were often employed by the later Han as frontier troops and to some extent they adopted Chinese ways. In the confusion following the Han's collapse, claiming descent from Chinese princesses, they set up ephemeral dynasties in northern China. Thereafter Chinese records make no reference to them. The Eastern Turks, who submitted to the Tang emperor TAIZONG, are thought to be their descendants.

Xuanzong MINGHUANG.

XYZ ffair An episode (1797–98) in US–French diplomatic relations. A three-man mission was sent to France to resolve a dispute caused by the USA's unwillingness to aid France in the French Revolutionary wars in spite of treaty obligations made in 1778. The French foreign minister TALLEYRAND refused to see the delegation and indirect suggestions of loans and bribes to France came through Mme de Villette, a friend of Talleyrand. Negotiations were carried on through her with X (Jean Conrad Hottinguer), Y (a Mr Bellamy, an American banker in Hamburg), and Z (Lucien Hauteval). A proposal that the Americans should pay Talleyrand $250,000 caused outrage in the USA. President ADAMS, however, ignored calls for war and reached agreement with the French at the Convention of Mortefontaine (30 September 1800).

Y

Map legend:
- American zone
- British zone
- French zone
- Soviet zone
- annexed by Soviet Union
- countries dependent on Soviet Union from 1948
- ⋯⋯ boundaries in 1937
- —— 'Iron Curtain'

Yalta and Potsdam Conferences *Two conferences in 1945, at Yalta and Potsdam, largely determined the pattern of post-war power blocs. At Yalta (February), Stalin, Roosevelt, and Churchill confirmed that Austria and Germany were to be divided into four zones of occupation, as was the Saarland. The Soviet Union agreed to enter the war against Japan, in return for territories lost during the Russo–Japanese War of 1905. The Potsdam Conference (July–August) confirmed that the Soviet Union was to keep the Polish territory that it had conquered in 1939 and Poland was to receive part of eastern Germany in compensation. Stalin's deft manipulation of agreements reached at the conferences was later to leave the Soviet Union in control of a broad area of 'buffer zones' stretching from the Baltic to the Adriatic and to its emergence as a major World Power.*

Yalta Conference (4–11 February 1945) A meeting between the Allied leaders STALIN, CHURCHILL, and ROOSEVELT at Yalta in the Soviet Union. They discussed the final stages of World War II, as well as the subsequent division of Germany. Stalin obtained agreement that the Ukraine and Outer Mongolia should be admitted as full members to the UNITED NATIONS, whose founding conference was to be convened in San Francisco two months later. Stalin also gave a secret undertaking to enter the war against Japan after the unconditional surrender of Germany and was promised the Kurile Islands and an occupation zone in Korea. The meeting between the Allied heads of state was followed five months later by the POTSDAM CONFERENCE.

Yamagata Aritomo (1838–1922) Japanese soldier and statesman. A member of a samurai family, he was an early opponent of the westernization of Japan, but, having experienced western military supremacy, he became a strong advocate of the modernization of the recently created MEIJI state. Serving in a succession of senior posts, he was the prime architect of the modern Japanese army, shaping a mass conscript army organized on the principle of unswerving loyalty to the emperor. He served as the first Prime Minister (1889–91) after the introduction of the parliamentary system and held the post again (1898–1900). Serving also as chief of the general staff during the RUSSO-JAPANESE WAR he exercised great influence and power, largely behind the scenes, in the years leading up to World War I.

Yamashita Tomoyuki ('The Tiger of Malaya') (1888–1946) Japanese general. In World War II he led his forces in a lightning series of successes, capturing Malaya (1941–42), SINGAPORE (1942), and Burma. In 1944 he assumed control of the PHILIPPINES CAMPAIGN. He surrendered to the Allies under MACARTHUR in 1945, was tried before a military commission for atrocities committed by his soldiers, and hanged.

Yamato The clan from which all the emperors of Japan are descended. Claiming the sun-goddess as ancestress, they had their chief shrine at Ise. Gradually they established control over rival clans and by the 5th century AD much of Japan was subject to them. They were influenced by Chinese culture, initially learning of China through southern Korea. BUDDHISM and the study of Chinese language and literature were introduced in the 7th century and Prince SHOTUKU produced administrative systems based on SUI China. The Yamato chief assumed the title emperor and built capitals based on TANG Chinese designs, first at Nara then at Kyoto. By the 9th century the FUJIWARA family controlled the imperial court, but during the period of the SHOGUNS the imperial family had little power.

Yangshao A site in northern Henan province, China, that has provided archaeological evidence of the Chinese NEOLITHIC period. There were square and round houses of timber post construction with thatched roofs, in villages up to 5 ha (12 acres) in size. The red burnished pottery, often painted in black, was handmade but finished on a slow wheel. Polished stone axes and knives were in general use. The staple crop was millet, grown on terraces, and pigs and dogs were the commonest domestic animals. This culture was distributed over much of the middle Huang He (Yellow River) valley during the 4th and early 3rd millennia BC.

Yeltsin, Boris (1931–) Russian statesman and President of the Russian Federation (1991–). In 1985

Yeltsin was appointed head of the Moscow City Party Committee. He alienated party conservatives by his attempts to eradicate corruption and was dismissed in 1987. He was elected to the Russian Federal Supreme Soviet and in March 1990 became its chairman. From this he went on in June 1991 to become the first President of the Russian SSR elected by popular vote, promising sweeping reforms. In August 1991 he successfully resisted a coup by communist hardliners and was able to assume effective leadership of his country. GORBACHEV's resignation and the disintegration of the Soviet Union followed in December. As President of independent Russia, Yeltsin had to grapple with economic collapse and internal tensions between the republics of the Federation. Yegor Gaidar (1952–   ), an economic reformer, was his acting Deputy Prime Minister from 1992 until 1994. In 1992 Yeltsin set up a Presidential Security Council, with himself as chairman and the conservative Yuri Skokov as secretary, with powers to override all government ministry decrees. By late 1992 the Russian state budget deficit had soared, partly because Yeltsin's reformist government had bowed to conservative pressures to extend vast credits to unprofitable state enterprises. The President resorted increasingly to government by decree, which seemed to carry little authority. Troops loyal to Yeltsin's government suppressed an attempted coup by communists in 1993, while a referendum held later the same year endorsed Yeltsin's economic and social reforms. Yeltsin's handling of regional crises (notably the revolt in the Caucasian republic of Chechnya in 1994–95) attracted widespread criticism, with his presidency being regarded as a hostage to the Russian military. Yeltsin suffered heart attacks in 1995, leading to speculation about his position. His authority was further undermined by the Communist Party's victory in parliamentary elections in 1995. In 1996 Yeltsin was re-elected as President; later that year he underwent a coronary bypass operation fuelling fears about his failing health. His reputation for erratic behaviour was reinforced by his action in sacking the whole government and appointing an inexperienced Prime Minister in March 1998.

Yemen, Republic of A country in the south of the peninsula of Arabia, bordering on Saudi Arabia and Oman on the north.

Physical. Behind the western, Red Sea, coast are high mountains, where cotton and coffee are grown. The lower-lying eastern part has an arid coast on the Gulf of Aden.

Economy. In the north, agriculture, mainly sheep- and goat-raising, and growing cotton, coffee, the narcotic qat, and other food crops, was the mainstay of the economy until oil production began in 1986. However, further oil exploration is jeopardized by a border dispute with Saudi Arabia. In the south, which was formerly a one-party communist republic with a centrally planned economy heavily dependent on Soviet aid, agriculture is the principal economic activity. Yemen is heavily dependent on the remittances of migrant workers and the economy was severely affected by Saudi Arabia's repatriation of a large number of Yemeni workers following Yemen's neutral stance in the 1991 Gulf War.

History. From about 950 to 115 BC Yemen was a flourishing region called Saba – the site of the kingdom of the biblical queen of Sheba. Because of its summer rains it was known to Rome as Arabia Felix ('Happy Arabia'), but it went into decline as its irrigation system collapsed around the 6th century AD. It was converted to ISLAM in the 7th century and came under the rule of the Muslim CALIPHATE. Much of it was under the rule of the Ottomans (1517–1918), although the British established the colony of ADEN in 1839. In 1918, with British support, the territory (excluding Aden) was proclaimed a kingdom under Imam Yahya, but its borders with both Aden and Saudi Arabia were disputed. Yahya was assassinated in 1948, and his son Ahmad ruled until 1962. On his death the army under General Abdullah al-Sallal proclaimed the Yemen Arab Republic (North Yemen), backed by both Egypt and Syria. Saudi Arabia supported those tribes who gave their loyalty to Ahmad's son Imam Muhammad al-Badr. Civil war lasted until 1967, when Nasser withdrew Egyptian troops after Egypt's defeat by Israel in the SIX-DAY WAR. Sallal resigned and a more moderate government was formed. The People's Republic of Yemen (South Yemen) was formed from Aden and neighbouring emirates when British rule ended in 1967. In April 1970 civil war in North Yemen subsided, but in 1979 a month-long war broke out with the neighbouring South Yemen. Intermittent talks to unify North Yemen and South Yemen followed, with a draft constitution agreed in December 1989. The unified state was proclaimed in May 1990, its political capital being Sana'a and commercial capital Aden. A five-member Council was headed by President Ali Abdullah Saleh. The new republic was welcomed to the UN and found itself a member of the Security Council at the time of the Gulf Crisis, when its decision to oppose the US-dominated intervention, leading to the GULF WAR, had strong popular support. However, it resulted in economic reprisals by many of the Gulf States, by Europe, and by the USA. Saudi Arabia expelled some 800,000 Yemeni migrant workers and gave 'substantial financial support' to anti-government Islamic fundamentalists, who had a strong following among the conservative tribes of the interior. Political tensions, focusing on the distribution of oil revenues, culminated in the southern Yemeni leaders declaring secession, which prompted a three-month civil war in 1994. The war ended when forces from northern Yemen captured Aden. A peace settlement was made and the constitution was amended, the ruling Council being replaced by a directly elected President.

CAPITAL:	Sana'a (political); Aden (economic)
AREA:	472,099 sq km (182,336 sq miles)
POPULATION:	16.600 million (1996)
CURRENCY:	1 Yemeni riyal = 100 fils
RELIGIONS:	Sunni Muslim 53.0%; Shi'ite Muslim (mainly in north) 46.9%
ETHNIC GROUPS:	Arab 97.0%; Indian and Pakistani 1.5%; Somali 1.5%
LANGUAGES:	Arabic (official)
INTERNATIONAL ORGANIZATIONS:	UN; Arab League

yeoman A person qualified by possessing free land of an annual value of 40 shillings to serve on juries, vote for knights of the shire, and exercise other rights. In the 13th and 14th centuries yeomen in England were freehold peasants, but by 1400, as many peasants became richer, the term was coming to be applied to all prosperous peasants, whether freeholders or not, as well as to franklins (freehold farmers). In the 15th century some yeoman farmers, leasehold as well as freehold, entered the ranks of the gentry.

Yom Kippur War (or October War) (1973) The Arab–Israeli war that began on 6 October, the Feast of Yom Kippur, Israel's most important holy day. The Israeli name for the war is the Yom Kippur War, while Arabs refer to it as the October War. The war started when Egyptian forces crossed the Suez Canal and breached the Israeli Bar Lev Line. Syrian troops threw back Israeli forces on the Golan Heights, occupied by the latter since the SIX-DAY WAR. The war lasted three weeks, in which time Israel pushed Syrian forces back into Syria and crossed the Canal, encircling an Egyptian army. In the aftermath, disengagement agreements were signed by Israel with Syria in 1974 and with Egypt in 1974 and 1975. The Israeli withdrawal from Sinai was completed in 1982 after the 1978 Israeli–Egyptian peace treaty.

Yongle (Yung-lo) (1359–1424) MING Emperor of China (1403–24). Yongle was a usurper who seized the throne when the second Ming emperor, his young nephew, disappeared in a mysterious palace fire. A man of great enterprise, he obliged Japan to pay tribute and extended the empire by campaigns in the steppes and in ANNAM. He and his successor sent ZHENG HE on prestigious voyages as far as the east coast of Africa. In 1421 he transferred the main capital from Nanjing to Beijing, his power base, and assured its food supplies by restoring the Grand Canal, linking it to the Huang He and Yangtze rivers. He built the great halls and palaces of the Forbidden City in Beijing and arranged for the preparation of definitive editions of the Confucian classics.

York, Richard Plantagenet, 3rd Duke of (1411–60) The son of Richard, Earl of Cambridge, and Anne Mortimer, who until 1453 was heir to the throne of England. He led the opposition to HENRY VI, especially after the death of Humphrey, Duke of GLOUCESTER in 1447 and in 1455 he captured Henry at the first Battle of ST ALBANS and became Protector of the kingdom. In October 1460 he claimed the English throne, but two months later he was defeated and killed by LANCASTRIAN forces in the Battle of WAKEFIELD. The YORKIST party survived him and triumphed at the second Battle of ST ALBANS.

Yorkists Descendants or adherents of Richard, 3rd Duke of YORK (their badge was a white rose). Despite Richard's death at the Battle of WAKEFIELD (1460), his party was soon afterwards successful against the LANCASTRIANS and his son Edward became king as EDWARD IV. The House of York continued on the throne with EDWARD V and then with Edward IV's younger brother, RICHARD II, until HENRY VII began the TUDOR dynasty after his victory at BOSWORTH FIELD in 1485. Henry prudently married the Yorkist heiress, Edward IV's eldest daughter, Elizabeth of York.

Yorktown An American Revolutionary battlefield on the peninsula between the York and James rivers, in Virginia, USA. In August 1781 the British General CORNWALLIS, his southern army exhausted after the vain pursuit of Nathanael GREENE, seized and fortified the area for winter quarters. Thanks to the promise of French naval support from the Caribbean, WASHINGTON was persuaded by the French to march from the Hudson and concentrate all his forces on a siege. With relief by sea cut off by 36 French warships, Cornwallis was forced to surrender on 19 October and American independence was assured.

Yoruba empire of Oyo A loose confederation of Yoruba kingdoms in West Africa. By the early 19th century the Yoruba empire of Oyo was beginning to disintegrate, a process accelerated by the decline of the slave trade and the rise of the FULANI EMPIRE in the north. The Fulani destroyed the old city of Oyo, creating the Muslim emirate of Ilorin. Alafin Atiba, the new ruler of the Oyo empire (1836–59), built a capital, Ago Oja, and allied his empire with Ibadan, but on his death civil war developed. At the same time the influence of the spiritual leader of the Yoruba people, the Oni of Ife, began to decline with the arrival of Christian missionaries. In 1888 a treaty was made with the then Alafin of Oyo, whereby all the Yoruba kingdoms were brought under British protection. In 1900 the empire was incorporated into the protectorate of Southern Nigeria.

Yoshida Shigeru (1878–1967) Japanese statesman. A liberal-conservative politician whose appointment as Foreign Minister had been blocked in 1936 by militarist interests, he was imprisoned for advocating surrender in the closing stages of World War II. He emerged after the war as the leader of the Liberal party. As Prime Minister (1946–47, 1949–54), Yoshida was a major architect of Japan's political rehabilitation and socio-economic recovery, working closely with MACARTHUR and espousing pro-Western policies.

Young, Brigham (1801–77) US MORMON leader. After Joseph SMITH's death in Illinois in 1844, Young became the dominant figure of Mormonism, leading the migration west to Salt Lake City, ruling over the new community with autocratic firmness, and turning a desert waste into a flourishing and expanding city.

Young England A British political movement of young Tory aristocrats in the early 1840s. It aimed at ending the political dominance of the middle classes by an alliance between the aristocracy and the working classes, which would carry out all necessary social reforms. The rather vague, romantic ideas of its members were given some substance by Benjamin DISRAELI, who defined its principles in his novel *Coningsby* (1844). The movement broke up in 1845 over the issue of FREE TRADE and the disputed grant to Maynooth College, the principal institution in Ireland for training Roman Catholic clergy.

Young Ireland An Irish nationalist movement of the 1840s. Led by young Protestants, including Smith O'Brien (1803–64) and John Mitchel (1815–75), who, inspired by Mazzini's YOUNG ITALY, set up their own newspaper, the *Nation*. It called for a revival of Ireland's cultural heritage. At first the members of Young Ireland were associated with Daniel O'CONNELL in his campaign to repeal the ACT OF UNION, but later they turned to more radical solutions. In 1848 they attempted a rebellion, which was easily suppressed, and O'Brien and Mitchel were sentenced to transportation.

Young Italy An Italian patriotic society. Formed in 1831 by Giuseppe MAZZINI and 40 other Italian exiles in Marseilles, it set out to replace earlier secret societies such as the CARBONARI as a prime force in the RISORGIMENTO. Its significance lay in the kindling of national consciousness and thus contributed towards Italian unification.

Young Plan The programme for the settlement of German REPARATIONS payments after World War I. The plan was embodied in the recommendations of a committee that met in Paris (February 1929) under the chairmanship of a US financier, Owen D. Young, to revise the DAWES PLAN (1924). The total sum due from Germany was reduced by 75% to 121 billion Reichsmark, to be paid in 59 annual instalments. Foreign controls on Germany's economy were lifted. The first instalment was paid in 1930, but further payments lapsed until HITLER repudiated all reparations debts in 1933.

Young Turks The European name for a number of late 19th- and early 20th-century reformers in the OTTOMAN EMPIRE who carried out the Revolution of 1908. The most prominent party was the Committee of Union and Progress, which seized power in 1913 and under the triumvirate of ENVER PASHA, Talat, and Jamal Pasha ruled the Ottoman empire until 1918, supporting the Central Powers in World War I.

Ypres PASSCHENDAELE; WESTERN FRONT.

Ypsilanti, Alexander (1792–1828) Greek nationalist leader. Ypsilanti served as a general in the Russian army and was elected leader of the *Philike Hetairia*, a secret organization that sought Greek independence from the OTTOMAN EMPIRE. In 1821 he raised a revolt in Moldavia, proclaiming the independence of Greece, but he lacked the support of Russia or Romania and was defeated by the Turks and imprisoned in Austria. Together with the successful Greek rebellion in the Peloponnese, his uprising marked the beginning of the GREEK WAR OF INDEPENDENCE.

Yuan (1279–1368) The MONGOL dynasty that ruled China following KUBLAI KHAN's defeat of the SONG dynasty. Kublai Khan established a strong central government that in many ways reflected Chinese rather than Mongol practice. His reign and that of his grandson Temur (1294–1307) saw the growth of internal and foreign trade and the re-establishment of direct links with the West along the SILK ROUTE (for a while MARCO POLO worked for the Yuan dynasty). Many religions were tolerated and vernacular literature, particularly drama and novels, flourished. However, after the death of Temur, the empire suffered from neglect, disorder, and rebellion. From 1348 there was continuous conflict, with rebel Chinese armies fighting each other as well as the Mongols. In 1368 the last Yuan emperor fled to Mongolia when the rebel leader Zhu Yuanzhang captured Khanbaligh (now Beijing) and founded the MING dynasty.

Yuan Shikai (or Yuan Shih-k'ai) (1859–1916) Chinese soldier and statesman, who established his military reputation in Korea and returned to China to undertake a programme of army reform. Yuan Shikai supported the empress dowager CIXI in her suppression of the HUNDRED DAYS REFORM. Dismissed from office after her death (1908), he retired to his old power base in northern China. He was recalled by the court when the CHINESE REVOLUTION OF 1911 began, but he temporarily sided with the republicans and advised the emperor to abdicate. In 1912 he became President of the republic. Initially successful in restoring central control, his

suppression of SUN YAT-SEN's KUOMINTANG, dissolution of Parliament, and his submission to Japan's TWENTY-ONE DEMANDS provoked a second revolution in the Yangtze region. He had himself proclaimed emperor in 1916, but died shortly afterwards, leaving China divided between rival WARLORDS.

Yucatán The peninsula of eastern Mexico and the state occupying the northern part of the Yucatán peninsula. The peninsula projects north-eastward from Central America for some 640 km (400 miles) between the Gulf of Mexico and the Caribbean Sea.

History. In prehistory it was the northern area of MAYA civilization, including several long-occupied, powerful cities, some dating from as early as *c.* 750 BC. From *c.* 800 AD many Maya migrated from the Southern Lowlands (Guatemala) into the Northern Lowlands of the peninsula and founded new states at Chichén Itzá, Izamal, MAYAPÁN, and Uxmal, linked by political alliances and trade. At first Chichén Itzá dominated, then Mayapán, and 17 small principalities were formed in the late 15th century. Fernández de Córdoba explored the coast in 1516–17 sighting several cities, but resistance to conquest was strong and they were not fully subdued until the 1540s.

Yugoslavia A country in south-east Europe that is not recognized in its present form by the United Nations. Yugoslavia was created at the end of World War I as the Kingdom of the Serbs, Croats, and Slovenes, from the former Slavic provinces of the AUSTRO-HUNGARIAN EMPIRE (Slovenia, Croatia, Bosnia-Herzegovina), together with Serbia and Montenegro, and with Macedonian lands ceded from Bulgaria. The monarch of Serbia, Peter I, ruled the new kingdom and was succeeded by his son ALEXANDER I. At first the Serbian Premier Nikola PASIC (1921–26) held the rival nations together, but after his death political turmoil caused the new king to establish a royal dictatorship, renaming the country Yugoslavia in January 1929. Moves towards democracy ended with his assassination (1934). During World War II Yugoslavia was overrun by German forces (1941), aided by Bulgarian, Hungarian, and Italian armies. The king fled to London and dismemberment of the country followed, with thousands of Serbs being massacred and the puppet state of CROATIA established under the fascist Ante Pavelić. A guerrilla war began, waged by two groups, supporters of the Chetnik MIHAILOVIC and TITO's Communist partisans. In 1945 Tito, supported by the Soviet Union, proclaimed the Socialist Federal Republic of Yugoslavia, consisting of the republics of BOSNIA-HERZEGOVINA, CROATIA, MACEDONIA, MONTENEGRO, SERBIA, and SLOVENIA, and two autonomous Serbian provinces, Kosovo and Vojvodina. Expelled by Stalin from the Soviet bloc in 1948, Yugoslavia became a leader of the NON-ALIGNED nations and the champion of 'positive neutrality'. Improved relations with the West followed and, after Stalin's death, diplomatic and economic ties with the Soviet Union were renewed (1955).

Tito died in 1980 and was replaced by an eight-man Collective State Presidency, with the office of President rotating annually. In 1989, multiparty systems were introduced in Croatia and Slovenia, and demands for independence soon followed. In 1990 a rebellion by Croatia's 12% Serb population was supported by Serbia, while in the same year Serbia, under its President, Slobodan MILOSEVIC, brutally suppressed the 90%

Albanian majority in the province of Kosovo. Croatia and Slovenia declared independence in 1991, provoking a full-scale military conflict with the Serb-led Yugoslav army. Atrocities were committed by both Croatian and Serb forces, creating large-scale refugee problems. The Belgrade leadership having failed to crush nationalism in Croatia and Slovenia, both states were recognized as independent in January 1991. Bosnia-Herzegovina was also recognized as independent but erupted into fierce civil war between ethnic Serbs (aided by the Belgrade government), Muslims, and Croats. By the end of 1992, after brutal and extensive 'ethnic cleansing', more than two-thirds of Bosnia-Herzegovina was under Serb control. Sanctions were imposed on Serbia by the international community and a UN force was sent to Bosnia to attempt to keep humanitarian relief lines open. After a long period of political indecision in the West, NATO forces finally launched air raids on Serb positions around Sarajevo in 1995. At the end of the year the presidents of Serbia, Croatia, and Bosnia-Herzegovina accepted a US-brokered peace plan for the region and a ceasefire came into force. In Serbia, sanctions and general economic collapse left 40% of the population unemployed and the country suffering from hyper-inflation. The new Federal Republic of Yugoslavia, proclaimed by the Belgrade government in 1992 and comprising Serbia and Montenegro, has so far received little international recognition. The independence of Macedonia was generally recognized in 1993. In 1996 relations between Serbia-Montenegro and Macedonia were normalized; this may lead to international recognition of the new Yugoslav republic by the EU and other countries. The period 1996–97 saw mounting dissatisfaction with the authoritarian rule of Milosevic, who became President in 1997, as well as increasing tension between Serbia and Montenegro. In early 1998 Serbian forces began a new and brutal crackdown on Albanian separatists in Kosovo.

Yunnan A province in south-west China. It was the area from which, over several millennia, Malay and Thai peoples moved into south-east Asia. In the 8th century Thai people set up a kingdom, Nanchao, there. They defied Chinese armies but were overcome by KUBLAI KHAN, accelerating Thai expansion to the south. At this time a Mongol general introduced Islam to Yunnan. Inhabited by a variety of racial groups, it was only integrated into China by the QING dynasty in the 17th century, becoming the site of a major copper industry.

Z

Zagwe (or Zague) An ETHIOPIAN dynasty founded in 1137 that derives its name from its founder. Zagwe and his successors are reckoned as usurpers because they were of Agau origin from Lasta, and not descended from the Solomonic kings of Ethiopia. There are few records of their emergence, but they claimed to have been descendants of the last king of AXUM. The first five Zagwe kings are said to have been Jewish, the later kings Christian. They fought rebels in the south of the country and were powerful enough to stop Egypt attempting to convert the country to Islam. They organized the building of many rock churches and founded the holy city of Lalibela. At the end of the 13th century the Zagwe were overthrown by a faction claiming to be the true heirs of the Axumite kings.

Zaharoff, Sir Basil (born Zacharias Basileios) (1850–1936) International financier and munitions manufacturer. Originating from Anatolia, Turkey, he was known as the 'mystery man of Europe' and was accused of fomenting warfare and of secret political intrigue. He built up profitable connections with British, German, and Swedish armament firms and amassed vast wealth. His sympathies in World War I lay with the Allies, who rewarded him with civil decorations for supplying them with intelligence information.

zaibatsu (literally 'financial clique') Japanese business conglomerates. The zaibatsu were large business concerns, with ownership concentrated in the hands of a single family, that grew up in the industrialization of late 19th-century Japan. They had their origins in the activities of the *seisho* (political merchants), who made their fortunes by exploiting business links with the newly restored MEIJI government. After the government ceased to play a direct role in economic activity, zaibatsu expanded to fill the gap through the ownership of interrelated mining, transport, industrial, commercial, and financial concerns, dominating the business sector in a fashion which had no near equivalent elsewhere in the industrialized world. The five major zaibatsu (Mitsubishi, Mitsui, Okura, Sumitomo, Yasuda) controlled much of Japanese industry and trade up to World War II. In 1948 a decree limited the influence of the traditional zaibatsu families and prevented members of these families from continuing to hold official positions in zaibatsu companies. The influence of the zaibatsu therefore declined; however, they continued in a modified form to provide the characteristic pattern for large Japanese industrial organizations into the 1980s. They are now more usually known in Japan as keiretsu.

Zaïre CONGO, DEMOCRATIC REPUBLIC OF THE.

Zambia A landlocked country lying on a plateau in central Africa, surrounded by Angola, the Democratic Republic of the Congo (formerly Zaïre), Tanzania, Malawi, Mozambique, Zimbabwe, and Namibia (the Caprivi Strip).

Physical. The Zambezi and its tributaries the Kafue and Luangwa run through Zambia, while in the north the Chambeshi drains into swampy areas round Lake Bangweulu. These river valleys are very warm and wet; but the rolling plateaux surrounding them are high, drier, and less hot. In the south-west there are forests of teak.

Economy. With the fourth largest copper reserves in the world, Zambia has rich mineral resources, including coal, lead, zinc, manganese, cobalt, and gemstones; copper accounts for 91% of exports, followed by cobalt and zinc. However, economic development has been restricted by fluctuating world commodity prices, lack of investment in infrastructure, especially in the mining sector, a large foreign debt, and drought. Industry includes vehicle assembly, petroleum refining, cement, and chemicals. Neglect of agriculture has led to a decline in the importance of tobacco, sugar cane, and other cash crops and dependence on food imports; staple crops include maize, cassava and millet, and cattle-rearing is also important.

History. Zambia was settled by NGUNI people in flight from Zululand in 1835, but was also subject throughout much of the 19th century to Arab slave-traders. Agents from Cecil RHODES entered the country (known at this time as Barotseland) in 1890. Rhodes's British South Africa Company had been granted responsibility for it in its charter of 1889 and it began to open up the rich deposits of Broken Hill from 1902. The country was named Northern Rhodesia in 1911. It became a British protectorate in 1924 and between 1953 and 1963 was federated with Southern Rhodesia and Nyasaland, before becoming the independent republic of Zambia under President Kenneth KAUNDA in 1964. Dependent on its large copper-mining industry, Zambia has experienced persistent economic difficulties due to its lack of a coastline and port facilities and to low copper prices. It suffered from economic sanctions against Rhodesia (1965–80), but was assisted by the construction of the TAN-ZAM railway. It gave refuge to political exiles from its neighbours Rhodesia (Zimbabwe), Angola, Namibia, and Mozambique, as well as from the AFRICAN NATIONAL CONGRESS. In September 1990 Kaunda yielded to pressure to hold a referendum on the introduction of a multiparty system and in November 1991 Frederick Chiluba, an ex-trade union leader, was elected President. He inherited both severe economic problems and an inefficient and corrupt civil service, but was helped by promises that Zambia's international debt-loan would be eased. Chiluba's programme of economic reform was hampered by the drought that swept southern Africa in 1992–93. Alleged high-level corruption in government led to the dismissal of a number of ministers. In 1996 Chiluba was re-elected, despite an attempted boycott of the elections by the opposition: he survived an attempted coup in 1997. Subsequently, Kaunda was arrested and imprisoned, accused of supporting the failed coup. He was released shortly afterwards, but placed under house arrest.

CAPITAL:	Lusaka
AREA:	752,614 sq km (290,586 sq miles)
POPULATION:	9.715 million (1996)
CURRENCY:	1 Zambian kwacha = 100 ngwee
RELIGIONS:	Protestant 34.2%; Roman Catholic 26.2%; African Christian 8.3%; traditional beliefs 27.0%; Muslim 0.3%
ETHNIC GROUPS:	Bemba 36.2%; Nyanja 15%; Tonga 19%; Mambwe 8.0%; Barotze 7.0%
LANGUAGES:	English (official); Bemba; Tonga; local languages
INTERNATIONAL ORGANIZATIONS:	UN; Commonwealth; SADC; OAU

zamindar A tax collector or landlord in India under the Mogul empire. The landlord system formed the basis of a system of land-settlement developed in India under British rule. It fell into two distinct groups. In Lower Bengal, the government of Lord Cornwallis fixed the land revenue payable by the zamindars in perpetuity in 1793 in the hope of stabilizing the revenue, providing an incentive for improvement, and creating a class of loyal landlords. The effect was to create a privileged group of large and wealthy landlords. In the North Western Provinces, the government made a settlement during the 1830s, with much smaller landlords for 30-year periods, in the hope of creating a class of small yeoman farmers and retaining a larger revenue for government.

Zanzibar One of two islands (the other being Pemba) belonging to TANZANIA, lying on a coral reef some 32 km (20 miles) off the East African coast. With a climate which is monsoonal, wet, and very warm, the island is renowned for the variety of its lush flora and for its spices, especially cloves.

History. Little of Zanzibar is known in early times but in about 1100 it was importing pottery from the Persian Gulf and became a base for Arab traders. In 1506, when the Portuguese demanded tribute, it was poor and thinly populated. The Portuguese established a trading post and a Catholic mission, but were displaced by the sultanate of OMAN who took it in 1698. It began to prosper in about 1770 as an entrepôt for Arab and French slave traders. Following its development by SAID IBN SULTAN SAYYID, his son Majid became ruler of Zanzibar, but was guided by the British consul Sir John Kirk (1866–87). German trading interests were developing in these years, but Britain and Germany divided Zanzibar's mainland territories between them and, by the Treaty of Zanzibar (1890), Germany conceded British autonomy in exchange for control of the North Sea island of Heligoland. Zanzibar became a British protectorate. In December 1963 it became an independent member of the Commonwealth, but in January 1964 the last sultan was deposed and a republic proclaimed. In April that year it united with Tanganyika to form the United Republic of Tanzania. Zanzibar retained its own administration and a certain degree of autonomy. After the assassination of Sheikh Karume in 1972, Aboud Jumbe and the ruling Afro-Shirazi Party ruthlessly put down all forms of political opposition until growing resentment forced Jumbe's

resignation in 1984. He was succeeded by Ali Hassan Mwinyi who became President of Tanzania in 1985. A new constitution was adopted and Idris Abdul Wakil was appointed President, succeeded in 1990 by Salmin Amour. A banned Islamic fundamentalist movement, Bismillahi, has steadily gained support on the island. The Tanzanian government, fearing a threat to national unity, revoked the island's membership of the Organization of the Islamic Conference (OIC) in 1993. In presidential elections, held in October 1995, Amour narrowly defeated a challenge from the Civic United Front, which advocated greater autonomy for Zanzibar within Tanzania.

Zapata, Emiliano (1879–1919) Leader in the MEXICAN REVOLUTION. A mestizo peasant, Zapata forcefully occupied the land that had been appropriated by the HACIENDAS and distributed it among the peasants. He joined MADERO's revolution, which overthrew the DÍAZ regime. Madero was elected President and Zapata sought to have land returned to the *ejidos* (the former Indian communal system of ownership). When he saw that Madero was not prepared to embark upon major programmes of agrarian reform, he declared against him. For eight years he led his peasant guerrilla armies against the haciendas and successive heads of state before falling victim to an assassination plot at Chinameca. His creed, *zapatismo*, became one with *agrarismo*, calling for the return of the land to the Indians, and with *indianismo*, the cultural, nationalist movement of the Mexican Indian people.

Zapatista National Liberation Front A Mexican guerrilla movement that arose in 1994 in the poor southeastern province of Chiapas. The *Zapatistas*, named after the revolutionary leader Emiliano ZAPATA, embarked on an armed struggle to fight discrimination against Maya Indian people in the allocation of land and jobs. Their grievances were fuelled by the NORTH AMERICAN FREE TRADE AGREEMENT concluded between Mexico, the USA, and Canada in 1993, which they claimed would benefit only the rich. Despite a number of ceasefires and peace accords offering increased Maya Indian regional autonomy and representation in the national parliament, violence continued in the south of the country throughout 1995–97.

Zarathustra (or Zoroaster) (7th–6th century BC) Persian religious reformer, the founder of the ZOROASTRIAN religion. Born in an aristocratic family and probably a priest, he is said to have received a vision from *Ahura Mazda* (the Wise Lord), one of many gods then worshipped, urging belief in one god. After King Vishtaspa's conversion (*c.* 588 BC) the religion spread.

It is difficult to distinguish between Zarathustra's actual teachings and later legends, as the details of his life cannot be reconstructed with accuracy. Claims that he significantly influenced Greek, Judaic, and Christian thought are probably exaggerated. He certainly brought Ahura Mazda, the creator, to the centre of worship as the principle of 'good', but retained the ancient fire cult while abolishing orgiastic sacrificial practices. The *Gathas* (hymns) contain his teachings, but they too are unauthenticated.

Zaria (or Zazzau) One of the original HAUSA states of West Africa. Tradition claims that it had 60 rulers before the FULANI conquest of the early 19th century and that it controlled a large territory. It was converted to Islam in the 14th and 15th centuries. Its city walls were nearly 16 km (10 miles) round, containing the Great Mosque, a palace, and private estates and houses. The emirate was chosen in turn from three families and had several vassals.

Zealots The party of revolt among the Jews of Roman Palestine, named after their zeal and fanaticism. They were also known as Canaans after the early inhabitants of Palestine and have been identified with the 'Daggermen' ('Sicarii') of the JEWISH REVOLT of 66–70 AD and the defenders of MASADA. Simon, one of the DISCIPLES of JESUS CHRIST was also known as 'the Zealot', meaning either that he was a member of the party, or equally likely, that he was of a 'zealous' disposition.

Zeebrugge raid (23 April 1918) A raid on a German U-boat base in Belgium during World War I. During the night of 22–23 April 1918 a force led by Admiral Keyes attacked the base sinking three blockships in the channel and almost closing it. More effective but less dramatic was the line of deep mines that he laid across the Straits of Dover.

Zen (Chinese, *ch'an*, from Sanskrit, *dhyāna*, 'meditation') A BUDDHIST sect of major importance in Japan. Strongly influenced by Daoism, it originated in China in the 7th century and spread to Japan during the KAMAKURA period (12th century). In sharp contrast to such popular sects as Pure Land Buddhism, it seeks salvation through enlightenment – revelation of the Buddha-nature which, it says, is innate to all people. Enlightenment is not achieved through scriptural texts or ritual worship, but through *satori*, a sudden enlightenment experience, which is usually achieved under the guidance of a teacher. Meditation under a master, intellectual exercises, and physical endurance are stressed. Different branches of Zen teach different methods of achieving enlightenment, such as meditation on paradoxical statements, or *kōans*, and seating posture (*zazen*). With its strict discipline it appealed to the SAMURAI. It flowered under the ASHIKAGA, when its masters, emphasizing harmony with nature, had much influence on aesthetics. It was associated with such refinements as the tea ceremony, which emerged under the Ashikaga. Some masters were active in affairs of state and had extensive contacts, often through trading missions, with China.

Zeng Guofan (or Tseng Kuo-fan) (1811–72) Chinese soldier and statesman. An imperial official and scholar, critical of the emperor's behaviour and the government's financial policies, in 1852 he reluctantly agreed to organize imperial resistance to the TAIPING REBELLION, raising the Hunan Army, and played a key role in wearing down resistance. With the crucial help of purchased modern European weapons, foreign military containment of the rebels along the eastern coast, and the capture of Nanjing in 1864, he finally broke their power. He became governor-general of Liang-Jiang, which gave him considerable powers in east-central China. In the 1860s and 1870s he supported the SELF-STRENGTHENING MOVEMENT and developed the Jiangnan arsenal for the manufacture of modern arms and the study of Western technical literature and Western languages.

Zenobia (*fl. c.* 270 AD) Queen of Palmyra (267–273). Zenobia became queen of Palmyra when her husband, King Odenathus, and his heir, her stepson, were murdered. Unlike her husband, Zenobia did not want Palmyra to be an autonomous state within the Roman empire but fully independent. She conquered Egypt and much of Asia Minor, provoking the emperor AURELIAN to send forces to stop her. In 271 Zenobia's armies were defeated at Antioch and Emesa and Palmyra was besieged. The city fell and was largely destroyed in 273. Zenobia was captured and taken to Rome where she married a senator.

Zeno of Citium (*c.* 336–*c.* 264 BC) Greek philosopher, the founder of the STOICS. He attended the ACADEMY in ATHENS, devoting himself first to the Cynic philosophy and then to the Socratic method of enquiry. The school of thought that he originated included a theory of knowledge, ethics, and physics, and a new system of logic. He taught that virtue, the one true good, is the only important thing, the virtue of a wise man cannot be destroyed, and that the vicissitudes of life are irrelevant to a man's happiness.

Zeno of Elea (born *c.* 490 BC) Greek philosopher. He was a pupil of Parmenides and a keen advocate of his theory of monism (the theory that there is only a single ultimate principle or kind of being). He wrote a famous work that drew pairs of contradictory conclusions from the presuppositions of his rivals. This led ARISTOTLE to credit him with the invention of dialectic. His most renowned paradox is that of Achilles, renowned for his speed, and the tortoise, by which it is shown that if Achilles gives the tortoise a start in a race, Achilles can never overtake it, since by the time he arrives where the tortoise was it has already moved on.

Zheng He (Cheng Ho) (d. *c.* 1433) Chinese admiral and explorer, a Muslim court EUNUCH from Yunnan province. He commanded seven remarkable voyages (1405–33) undertaken by order of the Ming emperor YONGLE and his successor. His first voyage in 1405–07, consisting of 62 ships, called in at MALACCA and reached India. Subsequent voyages went to the Persian Gulf and his last voyage in 1431–33 reached the coast of East Africa. His voyages were made possible by the use of the compass and by Chinese advances in navigation and shipbuilding. The purpose of the voyages is unclear, however, as they were used neither to develop trade nor political influence with the countries visited, although Zheng He did return with tribute in the form of gifts to the emperor, including giraffes, ostriches, and zebras from MOGADISHU in East Africa.

Zhou (Chou) (*c.* 11th century BC–256 BC) The second historically authenticated dynasty in China. It was founded by Wu the Martial, who justified his overthrow of the SHANG by claiming that its oppressive rule had led Heaven to transfer its mandate to a new 'Son of Heaven', the title of the emperor of China. The same claim was made by all subsequent founders of dynasties. Western Zhou ruled over feudal vassal states in the Wei valley and far beyond from their capital at Hao near Xi'an until 771 BC. Eastern or Later Zhou, based in Luoyang, never exercised real power. While the emperor performed the ritual sacrifices, his vassals strove for mastery of the kingdom. In 403 BC the era of the

Warring States began. In 256 BC the last Zhou sovereign was overwhelmed by the armies of his most powerful vassal, Prince Zheng of the state of QIN.

Out of the turmoil of the Eastern Zhou came much that became identified with Chinese civilization. There was a flowering of philosophical thought whose prime exponents were CONFUCIUS and MENCIUS. Agriculture developed through the building of irrigation systems and trade grew, encouraged by demand for silk, the use of coins, and transport by canals. The use of bronze spread to southern China and iron was introduced, first for weapons and then for ploughs.

Zhou Enlai (or Chou En-lai) (1898–1976) Chinese revolutionary and statesman, Premier (1949–76). Politically active as a student, he studied in France (1920–24) and became a communist. On his return he became deputy political director of the KUOMINTANG Whampoa Military Academy. He organized an uprising in Shanghai in 1927, which was violently suppressed by CHIANG KAI-SHEK. Escaping to Jiangxi, he took part in the LONG MARCH and became MAO ZEDONG's chief adviser on urban revolutionary activity and his leading diplomatic envoy, representing the communists in the XI'AN INCIDENT and in US attempts to mediate in the civil war in 1946. He became Premier on the establishment of the People's Republic and served as Foreign Minister until 1958. He played a major role in the GENEVA CONFERENCE (1954) and the BANDUNG CONFERENCE (1955) and was the main architect of Sino–US détente in the early 1970s. During the CULTURAL REVOLUTION he actively restrained extremists and helped restore order. He was one of the earliest proponents of the FOUR MODERNIZATIONS policy, which later became associated with DENG XIAOPING.

Zhoukoudian (Choukoutien) A cave complex southwest of Beijing, China, made famous by fossils of PEKING MAN. The fossils are now believed to represent a Chinese variant of *homo erectus* (*Homo erectus pekinensis*), but were once classified in a separate genus, *Sinanthropus*. More than 40 male and female *Homo erectus* individuals are now known from the caves. There are also many tens of thousands of simple flaked stone tools as well as fossilized bones of more than 100 animal species and so-called ash layers that were once interpreted as cooking hearths. The caves were occupied by Peking Man from about 500,000 to 250,000 years ago.

Zhuangzi (Chuang-tzu) A classic text of Daoism, much of which was written by Zhuangzi (*c.* 369–286 BC), a Chinese philosopher from the state of Meng on the border of present-day Shandong. Although Zhuangzi's philosophy differs from that found in the DAODEJING, an earlier Daoist work ascribed to LAOZI, his concept of *Dao* was a further naturalization of Laozi's concept. To him all things change at all moments and although they are different and conflicting, *Dao* transforms and unites them into a harmonious whole. The ideal person does not interfere with the Way of Nature but is at one with it. Thus the mystical and metaphysical features of Daoist thought are ultimately vehicles for addressing human problems. In life the individual must return to the simplicity and purity of the *Dao* in order to achieve true freedom. The *Zhuangzi* also asserts that all ideas and conventions used to judge truth are relative and that individual freedom comes from the identification with the *Dao*. The text is paradoxical and cryptic, a work of religion and literature. A famous passage,

which illustrates its style, is an account of the author dreaming he was a butterfly and, on waking, wondering whether it might have been a butterfly dreaming of being him. The text greatly influenced ZEN Buddhism.

Zhu De (or Chu Teh) (1886–1976) Chinese revolutionary and soldier. He served as an officer in the imperial army and in the republican force that succeeded it. He became a communist in 1925, presenting his inherited wealth to the party. With MAO ZEDONG he organized and trained early units of the People's Liberation Army (1931) in Jiangxi and served as its commander-in-chief until 1954. He was a leader of the LONG MARCH of 1934–35 and commanded the 8th Route Army against the Japanese between 1939 and 1945 before overseeing the communist victory in the CHINESE CIVIL WAR. He became marshal in 1955 and remained influential until purged during the CULTURAL REVOLUTION. He was restored to favour in 1967 and lived out his life in honoured retirement.

Zhukov, Georgi Konstantinovich (1896–1974) Soviet marshal. Zhukov was a peasant who joined the BOLSHEVIKS and fought in the RUSSIAN REVOLUTION (1917), as well as in the RUSSIAN CIVIL WAR (1918–21). In 1939 he led the successful defence against Japanese incursions in the Far East. He was responsible for much of the planning of the Soviet Union's World War II campaigns. He defeated the Germans at STALINGRAD (1943) and lifted the siege of LENINGRAD. He led the final assault on Germany (1945), captured Berlin, and became commander of the Soviet zone in occupied Germany. He was demoted by Stalin, but after the latter's death rose to become Defence Minister (1955). He supported KHRUSHCHEV against his political enemies in 1957 but was dismissed the same year, only to be reinstated after Khrushchev was deposed (1964).

Zia ul-Haq, General Mohammed (1924–88) Pakistani army officer and statesman. In 1977 he led a military coup deposing Zulfilkar Ali BHUTTO, who was later tried and hanged. In 1978 he was proclaimed President of Pakistan, outlawing all political parties and enforcing press censorship. A zealous Muslim, he introduced some aspects of the Islamic code of laws and an Islamic welfare system. After the Soviet invasion of AFGHANISTAN in December 1979 an estimated five million refugees flooded Pakistan and Zia received increasing amounts of economic and military aid, especially from the USA. He was under some pressure to allow wider participation in government and in 1982 he formed a Federal Advisory Council of 350 nominated members. At the time of his death, caused by a bomb in a military aircraft in which he was travelling, he was in serious dispute with his provincial governments. However, it is not clear who was responsible for his assassination.

Zimbabwe A landlocked country in southern Africa. It is surrounded by Zambia, Mozambique, South Africa, and Botswana.

Physical. On the north-west boundary of Zimbabwe with Zambia are the Victoria Falls and Lake Kariba on the Zambezi River and on the boundary with South Africa is the Limpopo River. The country stands mainly on a plateau drained by tributaries of these and other rivers. The height of the plateau modifies the heat; cattle thrive and crops can be grown.

Economy. The main exports are tobacco, gold, metal alloys, and cotton. Mineral resources include gold, nickel copper, tin, chrome, gems, and coal. Beef production is also important. Agriculture has substantially recovered from the devastation of the liberation war, despite recurrent drought. The main industries are food-processing, metal-refining, chemicals, and textiles.

History. Zimbabwe is named after the ancient palace city of Great Zimbabwe, a 24 ha (64-acre) site, that dates from the 11th to the 15th centuries. Gold and copper were exported from more than a thousand mines by the 10th century AD, the trade passing through Sofala, in Mozambique, to Arab hands. In the early 15th century the region's riches enabled the rise of the Shona (Karanga) empire, with the stone-built city as its capital. The sovereign had an elaborate court and constitution and trade links with both sides of Africa; after Portuguese incursions in the 16th century, Zimbabwe's fortunes steadily declined. In 1629 in an attempt to expel the Portuguese resulted in the installation of a puppet ruler. After 1693 the territory was absorbed by the ROZVI EMPIRE. In the early 19th century, the Ndebele, under their leader MZILIKAZI (c. 1795–1868), invaded the country from the south. He created a kingdom of Matabeleland, which for the next 50 years was to be in a state of permanent tension with the Shona to the north, in what came to be called Mashonaland, but he obtained a peace treaty with the new TRANSVAAL REPUBLIC. He was succeeded by his son LOBENGULA. In 1889 the British South Africa Company of Cecil RHODES was founded and in 1890 his Pioneer Column marched into Mashonaland. Following the JAMESON RAID and the Matabele War of 1893, Mashonaland and Matabeleland were united. Rebellion erupted in 1896–97, but it was ruthlessly suppressed. Rapid economic development followed, the country becoming the crown colony of Southern Rhodesia in 1911 and a self-governing colony in 1923.

After the victory of the right-wing Rhodesian Front in 1962, the colony sought independence but refused British demands for Black political participation in government and, under Prime Minister Ian Smith, issued the Unilateral Declaration of Independence (UDI) in 1965, renouncing colonial status and declaring Rhodesian independence. Subsequent British-sponsored attempts at negotiating a political compromise failed and nationalist forces waged an increasingly successful guerrilla campaign. Military pressure finally forced Smith to concede the principle of Black majority rule, but the regime of the moderate Bishop Muzorewa could not come to an accommodation with the guerrilla leaders of the Patriotic Front, Robert MUGABE and Joshua NKOMO. Following the Lancaster House Conference (1979) Robert Mugabe was elected Prime Minister and Rhodesia became the republic of Zimbabwe in 1980.

The decade of the 1980s saw a revival of tension between Shona and Ndebele, personified by Mugabe and Nkomo. The new constitution of 1987 not only eased this, by merging the two parties of which Mugabe and Nkomo were leaders, but also ended racial representation and created the office of executive President. With internal domestic tensions eased, Zimbabwe played a leading role in the politics of southern Africa, while its five-year plan (1986–90) did much to expand the economy. The state of emergency of 1965 was finally ended in July 1990. Since then the country has suffered grievously from an unprecedentedly severe drought in 1991–93. In April 1995, the Zimbabwe African National Union-Patriotic

Front (ZANU-PF), which had ruled the country since the inception of Black majority rule, won its fourth successive election victory with an increased majority. The leader of the only opposition party to win seats, the Rev. Ndabaningi Sithole of ZANU-Ndonga, was arrested on charges of conspiracy to assassinate President Mugabe later the same year. In March 1996 Mugabe was re-elected as President; turnout at the polls was lower than 40% of the electorate. In 1998 international pressure forced Mugabe to abandon a plan to dispossess White farmers of their land and distribute it among Blacks. From late 1997 Mugabe's government faced a series of strikes (including a general strike) in protest at food taxes, government corruption, and the lack of political reform.

CAPITAL:	Harare
AREA:	390,759 sq km (150,873 sq miles)
POPULATION:	11.515 million (1996)
CURRENCY:	1 Zimbabwe dollar = 100 cents
RELIGIONS:	Protestant 17.5%; African indigenous 13.6%; Roman Catholic 11.7%; traditional beliefs 40.0%
ETHNIC GROUPS:	Shona 70.8%; Ndebele Nguni 15.8%; Nyanja 5.0%; European 2.0%; Asian 0.1%
LANGUAGES:	English (official); Shona; Ndebele
INTERNATIONAL ORGANIZATIONS:	UN; Commonwealth; OAU; SADC; Non-Aligned Movement

Zimmermann note (19 January 1917) A German secret telegram, containing a coded message from the German Foreign Secretary, Alfred Zimmermann, to the German minister in Mexico City. This instructed the minister to propose an alliance with Mexico, offering Mexico the territories lost in 1848 to the USA. The British intercepted the message and gave a copy to the US ambassador. The US State Department released the text on 1 March 1917, even as US–German relationships were deteriorating fast over submarine warfare. With the possibility of a German-supported attack by Mexico, the ISOLATIONISTS lost ground and on 6 April 1917 Congress entered WORLD WAR I against Germany.

'Zinjanthropus' An East African AUSTRALOPITHECINE fossil from OLDUVAI GORGE, Tanzania from about 1.8 million years ago, now usually called *Australopithecus boisei*. An almost complete skull of this species has been popularly known as 'Nutcracker Man', because of the very rugged build of its teeth and jaw-bone.

Zinoviev, Grigori Yevseyevich (1883–1936) Soviet communist leader. Despite originally opposing the RUSSIAN REVOLUTION, he became chairman of the COMINTERN (1919–26). In 1924 a letter, apparently signed by him, was sent by the COMINTERN to the British Communist Party, urging revolutionary activity within the army and in Ireland. Published in British Conservative newspapers four days before the general election, it may have swung the middle-class vote away from the Labour Party, who claimed that it was a forgery. On LENIN's death Zinoviev, with STALIN and KAMENEV, formed a triumvirate, but he lost power and was executed after Stalin's first show trial.

Zionism A movement advocating the return of Jews to PALESTINE founded in 1897 under the leadership of Theodore HERZL. Originally a secular movement, Zionism has its foundation in the MILLENARIAN belief that the

Jews, the chosen people of God, will be reunited from DIASPORA (dispersion or exile) in their rightful homeland. After the Russian POGROMS of 1881, Leo Pinsker wrote a pamphlet, *Auto-Emanzipation*, appealing for the establishment of a Jewish colony in Palestine. Zionism assumed a political character, notably through Herzl's *Der Judenstaat* (1896). The issue of the BALFOUR DECLARATION in 1917 and the grant of a MANDATE for Palestine to Britain gave impetus to the movement. During the mandate period (1920–48), under Chaim WEIZMANN the World Zionist Organization played a major part in the development of the Jewish community in Palestine by facilitating immigration, by investment (especially in land), and through the Jewish Agency. The movement was further strengthened by the persecution and massacre of the Jewish people in World War II (the HOLOCAUST). Zionist activities in the USA were influential in winning the support of Congress and the Presidency in 1946–48 for the creation of the state of Israel.

Zionism remains an important issue in Israeli domestic politics and in the politics of the Middle East, since the question of the existence of the state of Israel and its claim to all the biblical territory of Israel has not been satisfactorily reconciled with the rights of the PALESTINIANS. The continuing right of all Jews worldwide, whatever their nationality, to emigrate to Israel and to take Israeli citizenship, is a fundamental principle of Zionism, and the World Zionist Congress, an independent body, exists to support Jewish emigration to Israel.

Zog (born Ahmed Bey Zogu) (1895–1961) King of Albania. An Albanian politician who supported Austria in World War I, he later served as Premier (1922–24), President (1925–28), and King (1928–39) after the Albanian throne had been refused by the English cricketer, C. B. Fry. The new constitution placed power in his hands and he became the champion of the modernization of the country, instituting language reforms, educational development, and religious independence. He relied on Italy for financial help and the Treaty of Tirana (1926) provided him with Italian loans in return for Albanian concessions. By 1939 MUSSOLINI controlled Albania's finances and its army and an Italian invasion ended Albania's independence, forcing him into exile.

Zollverein (German, 'customs union') A customs union that abolished trade and economic barriers between the German states in the 19th century. PRUSSIA abolished internal customs dues in 1818 and signed a free trade pact with Hesse-Darmstadt in 1828. At the same time Bavaria, Württemberg, and later the Palatinate agreed to free trade, and a similar agreement was reached by the central German states. The Prussian Zollverein was founded in 1834 by merging the North German Zollverein with the smaller customs unions, thus increasing Prussian influence. After the AUSTRO-PRUSSIAN WAR (1866) the newly formed North German Confederation entered the Zollverein and by 1888 the union, which excluded Austria, had largely achieved the economic unification of Germany.

Zoroastrians Followers of the religious doctrines originally disseminated in Persia by ZARATHUSTRA in the 6th century BC. Zoroastrianism was the state religion in Persia under the SASSANIAN EMPIRE (3rd–7th century AD),

but Islamic invasion resulted in the persecution and emigration of believers. Isolated groups have survived there, but the focus of emigration was the west coast of India (Gujarat) where Hindus tolerated the new cult whose followers readily adapted themselves to the environment. There they became known as PARSIS (from the Persian *parsi*, 'Persian'). Characteristic religious practices include preservation of the sacred fire, and disposal of the dead by exposure on 'towers of silence'.

Zulu A people of southern Africa, mostly living in South Africa, related to the NGUNI. The Zulus formed a powerful military empire (ZULULAND) in the 19th century, before their defeat by Europeans. Traditional Zulu society is based on the clan system, the clan consisting of several patrilineal households, under the leadership of a chief. Formerly, under the APARTHEID regime, some Zulu lived in the traditional way in the former BANTU HOMELAND of KwaZulu. In recent years the mainly Zulu INKATHA FREEDOM PARTY has clashed violently with other Black groups in South Africa, particularly the AFRICAN NATIONAL CONGRESS.

Zulu Inkatha Movement INKATHA FREEDOM PARTY.

Zululand The area of South Africa that was formerly a Zulu state. Zulu and related NGUNI people are thought to have occupied the region from about the 15th century. Under their chief SHAKA in the early 19th century they reduced rival tribes to vassalage and occupied their territories before confronting Boer settlers migrating north. In 1879 Britain initiated the ZULU WAR, annexing the whole area in 1887. It became a crown colony until 1897, when it was incorporated into Natal. There were rebellions in 1888 and 1906, two-thirds of Zululand being confiscated, the inhabitants being confined to native reserves. These were developed by the Bantu Self-government Act of 1959 into the BANTU HOMELAND of KwaZulu, which was replaced in 1994 by the region of Kwazulu-Natal.

Zulu War (1879) A war fought between Britain and ZULULAND. Until he occupied the TRANSVAAL in 1877, the policy of the Natal Secretary for Native Affairs, Theophilus Shepstone, had been to protect the Zulu empire of CETSHWAYO against Afrikaner aggression. After the annexation, he reversed this policy to placate the Afrikaner population and a scheme was prepared to seize Zululand. Frontier incidents provided opportunities and the British High Commissioner ordered the disbandment of the Zulu army within 30 days. Cetshwayo did not comply and war broke out on 11 January 1879. On 22 January the British suffered disaster at ISANDHLWANA, but reinforcements were sent and the Zulu capital, Ulundi, was burnt. Cetshwayo was captured (28 August) and the war ceased on 1 September.

Zuo Zongtang (or Tso Tsung-t'ang) (1812–85) Chinese soldier and statesman. He rose to military prominence, assisting ZENG GUOFAN in suppressing the TAIPING REBELLION and was appointed governor-general of Zhejiang province (1862). He supported the SELF-STRENGTHENING MOVEMENT, in 1877 recapturing XINJIANG from Yakub Beg, and making possible its incorporation as a Chinese province.

Zwingli, Ulrich (1484–1531) Swiss PROTESTANT reformer. Zwingli studied at Vienna and Basle before becoming pastor at Glarus in Switzerland (1506). He taught himself Greek and was considerably influenced by the humanist precepts of ERASMUS. He also served as chaplain to Swiss mercenaries involved in the Italian wars. As pastor at Einsiedeln (1516–18), he began to reach Lutheran conclusions, possibly independently of LUTHER himself. After becoming Common Preacher at the Great Minster in Zürich (1518), he played a significant part in converting the city's inhabitants to the reformed religion. At a public disputation with a papal representatives in 1523 Zwingli presented his doctrines in 67 theses; these were adopted by the general council of Zürich as official doctrine. The Protestant Reformation thereafter proceeded to make great headway in Switzerland.

The last period of his life was marked by dispute and conflict. He was unable to reach agreement with Luther at Marburg (1529) about the nature of the Eucharist. The division on this matter was so deep that any union of the Protestant branches was impossible. He was killed at the Battle of Kappel, in which Zürich was defending itself against the Catholic cantons (provinces) of Switzerland. John CALVIN then became the principal champion of the Reformation in Switzerland.

CHRONOLOGY OF WORLD EVENTS

All dates BP *(before present)*

c. 4,000,000	Early hominids (*Australopithecus*) evolving in East and southern Africa.

LOWER PALAEOLITHIC

c. 2,000,000	*Homo habilis* evolving in Africa; shapes and uses stones as tools; omnivore, killing small game; also a scavenger.
c. 1,500,000	*Homo erectus* (formerly *Pithecanthropus*) appears in Africa; uses fabricated stone tools; omnivore, killing small animals, scavenging remains of larger ones; camps by lakes and in river valleys. Acheulian hand-axes and cleavers in East and southern Africa.
c. 1,000,000	*Homo erectus* in East and SE Asia; *Australopithecus* dies out.
c. 700,000	*Homo erectus* in Europe.
c. 400,000	Archaic *Homo sapiens* (the earliest form of modern human) appears in Europe.

MIDDLE PALAEOLITHIC

c. 120,000	Neanderthal man emerging in Europe; cave-dweller, using flint scrapers for preparing furs; burial of dead.

UPPER PALAEOLITHIC

c. 35,000	Cro-Magnon man, the first anatomically modern human (*Homo sapiens sapiens*) spreading from Africa through Asia, China, Australia, America (?*c.* 25,000). Variety of tools (knives, axes, harpoons, needles, etc.) and materials (wood, bone, stone, reed, leather, fur, etc.).
c. 27,000	First painting on stone tablets in southern Africa (Namibia).
c. 20,000	Finger-drawings on clay walls, e.g. Koonalda Cave, Australia. Paintings on rock surfaces in Australia.
c. 17,000	First cave-painting and carving SW France (Lascaux). Female figurines across Europe and Russia.
c. 15,000	Tools with blades of stone made in Europe, western Asia, East and southern Africa. High level of art. Personal adornment (beads, pendants).

MESOLITHIC

c. 12,000	Siberia first peopled as ice age ends. Earliest potters in Japan. Microlithic tools widely made throughout the world. Bows, spears, knives in use.

NEOLITHIC

c. 10,000	Climatic changes stimulate new economies and techniques. Beginning of farming in several parts of world.

NEAR EAST, MEDITERRANEAN, AND EUROPE	REST OF THE WORLD

All dates BC

	NEAR EAST, MEDITERRANEAN, AND EUROPE	REST OF THE WORLD
9000	Sedentary societies emerging; Natufian culture in Syria and Palestine; collection of wild cereals, first domestication of dog, pig, and goat.	
8300	Post-glacial warming and spread of forests.	
8000	Pre-pottery neolithic societies in Syria and Palestine, with cultivated cereals and mud-brick villages (Jericho). Rapid retreat of ice in northern Europe and spread of light forest; mesolithic societies, e.g. Maglemosian culture; hunting elk and wild cattle; first evidence of dugout canoe.	Cattle-keeping groups, making pottery, spread into Sahara, which was wetter than it is today.
7000	Domestication of sheep and cattle in Near East; animals used mainly for meat, not milk or wool. Linen textiles. First use of copper for small ornaments, made by hammering and heating pure copper. Obsidian imported to mainland Greece from island of Melos.	Cultivation of root crops in New Guinea and South America.
6000	First pottery in Near East; use of smelting (lead). Major site of Çatal Hüyük in central Turkey. Domestication of cattle. Farming spreads to SE Europe; first neolithic cultures there. Oak forests spread to northern Europe; deer and pig hunted. Cattle first used for traction in Near East (plough, sledge). First evidence of irrigation, in Iraq.	Tropical millet first cultivated in the southern Sahara; temperate millet in China. Wheat and barley introduced to Pakistan.
5000	Copper-smelting in Turkey and Iran. Woollen textiles; use of animals for milk; domestication of horse and donkey. Tree crops (olive, fig, vine) cultivated in the eastern Mediterranean. Growth of population in lowland Mesopotamia; date-palm cultivated. Farming spreads into central Europe. Ertebølle culture in Baltic.	Beginning of maize cultivation in Mexico; rice cultivation in China and India.
4000	Copper-casting and alloying in Near East; development of simple copper metallurgy in SE Europe. Gold-working in Near East and Europe. First urban civilization develops in Sumer, with extensive irrigation. Trading colonies established in Syria; temple-building, craft workshops with extensive importation of raw materials, such as metals and precious stones. First wheeled vehicles and sailing-boats on Euphrates and Nile; use of writing (cuneiform script); spread of advanced farming (plough, tree-crops, wool) and technology (wheel, alloy metallurgy) to SE Europe.	Llama domesticated in highland Peru as pack animal; cotton cultivated in lowland Peru. Pottery comes into use in South America. Jade traded in China.

Farming spreads to western and northern Europe; construction of monumental tombs in Portugal, Brittany, British Isles, Scandinavia. Use of horse leads to expansion of first pastoralist communities on steppes north of Black Sea; burial mounds covering pit-graves. Plough and cart widely adopted in Europe.

3100   Unification of Upper and Lower Egypt; trading expeditions up into the countries of the eastern Mediterranean, where urban societies now exist. Troy an important trading centre in north Aegean; Cycladic culture in the Greek islands. Copper-working in Iberia (at Los Millares).

3000   Egyptian hieroglyphic script develops; pyramid building begins. Royal tombs in Mesopotamia (e.g. Ur) demonstrate high level of craftsmanship in secular city-states. Spread of burial mounds in northern Europe replaces megalithic tradition, though ceremonial monuments (Avebury, first phase of Stonehenge) continue in British Isles. Stone-built temples in Malta.

         Introduction of dog to Australia. Copper and bronze metallurgy in China and SE Asia; silk production.

2500   Extensive Egyptian maritime trade with Phoenician city of Byblos (Lebanon); Ebla a major centre in Syria, in contact with both Byblos and Mesopotamia. Exploration of eastern Mediterranean maritime routes along southern coast of Turkey to Crete, using boats with sails. Beaker cultures bring innovations (copper-working, horse, drinking-cups, woollen textiles) to Atlantic coast.

         Permanent villages with temple mounds and ceremonial centres in Peru. First towns in China (Longshan culture) with trade and specialized production.

2300   Empire of Akkad unites Mesopotamian city-states. Trade with Indus valley civilization in Pakistan. Akkadian becomes diplomatic language of the Near East.

         Spread of pottery-making and maize cultivation in Middle and South America.

2134   Collapse of Old Kingdom in Egypt, and of empire of Akkad.

2040   Middle Kingdom established in Egypt; beginnings of middle Minoan (palatial) period in Crete. Revival of northern Mesopotamian centres (Assur and Mari); Assyrian merchant colonies established in Anatolia. Development of Hittite culture. Babylonian empire expands.

1700   Egypt dominated by Asiatic rulers (Hyksos). Cretan palaces reconstructed after damage caused by earthquake or warfare; expanded trade-links with mainland Greece; growth of Mycenaean civilization. Hittite empire expands; Assyria dominated by Mitanni. Use of bronze now standard in Europe. Appearance of chariot.

         Emergence of Shang civilization in China.

1500   Kassite dynasty in Babylonia; New Kingdom in Egypt following expulsion of the Hyksos; expansion of Egyptian empire in the Middle East. Rulers buried in Valley of the Kings. Akhenaten introduces monotheistic cult c. 1360 and founds new capital. Canaanite cities flourish in the Middle East; use of alphabet evolving.

         Metal-working (copper, gold) in Peru. Expansion of Lapita culture into western Polynesia.

1200   General recession and political collapse in many parts of eastern Mediterranean; end of Mycenaean and Hittite palace centres, decline of Egyptian power; invasion of Sea Peoples. Spread of iron metallurgy. Expansion of nomadic Aramaean tribes in Middle East. Temporary expansion of Assyria, and capture of Babylon. Expansion of agriculture and bronze-working in temperate Europe, associated with expansion of urnfield cultures

         Olmec civilization, with temple mounds and massive stone sculptures, in Mexico.

EUROPE AND THE MEDITERRANEAN	REST OF THE WORLD	CULTURE AND TECHNOLOGY
1000 Development of spice route to Arabia; growth of coastal trade in eastern Mediterranean under Phoenicians; colonization of Cyprus and exploration of central and western Mediterranean. David king of Israel (c. 1000–c. 962); makes Jerusalem his capital. Solomon king of Israel (c. 970–930); extends his kingdom to Egypt and Euphrates.	Zhou dynasty in China. Adena culture with rich burials under large mounds in Ohio and Mississippi valleys. Chavín civilization in Andes. Early cities in Ganges valley.	Hebrew and Greek alphabets developing from Phoenician. Worship of Dionysus enters Greece from Thrace. 957 The Temple built in Jerusalem.
930 Israel divides into kingdom of Israel in the north (c. 930–721) and kingdom of Judah in the south. Phoenician contacts with Crete and Euboea.		Early Hebrew texts (Psalms, Ecclesiastes). Early version of great Hindu epic the Mahabharata.
900 Celts move west to Austria and Germany.	Farming villages on Amazon floodplain.	Geometric-style pottery in Greece.
858 Assyrian empire reaches Mediterranean.		
814 Legendary date at which Phoenicians found Carthage.		
753 Legendary date for foundation of Rome.		First Olympic Games held (776)

EUROPE AND THE MEDITERRANEAN	REST OF THE WORLD	CULTURE AND TECHNOLOGY
750 Greek colonies in southern Italy (Magna Graecia, Cumae) and Sicily. Greek city-state culture through Aegean; Lydia pioneers coinage. Greek colonies spread through Mediterranean.		
721 Assyrians under Sargon II (721–705) conquer Israel; under Sennacherib (705–681) empire expands. Nineveh becomes Assyrian capital.		
712 Cushite king Shabaka conquers Egypt.		
700 Hallstatt culture (Celtic iron-age warriors) in Austria moves west and down Rhône to Spain. Carthage expands through western Mediterranean, occupying Sardinia and Ibiza.	Zhou dynasty in China establishes legal system.	The *Iliad* and *Odyssey* emerge from oral tradition.
660 First Celtic hill-forts.	660 Traditional date for Jimmu, first Japanese emperor.	Dionysiac festivals in Greece leading to drama.
640 Assyrians under Ashurbanipal conquer Elamites.		Library established in Nineveh under Ashurbanipal (c. 668–627).
625 Babylon under Chaldean dynasty (625–539).		
612 Assyria defeated by Medes and Babylonians; sack of Nineveh.		Zoroaster in Persia.
c. 600 Ionian Greeks found Massilia (Marseilles).	Magadha kingdom on Ganges in India.	Doric order appears in Greek architecture. Trireme (Greek warship) created. Hanging Gardens of Babylon built.
594 Solon begins reforms of Athenian law.	New Nubian kingdom of Cush established at Meroe on upper Nile.	Greek lyric poetry (Sappho, Alcaeus). Jeremiah writing.
586 Chaldean Nebuchadnezzar conquers Jerusalem. Israelites taken into Babylonian Captivity. Greeks colonize Spain; import Cornish tin.	The king of Persia (Vishtaspa) converted to Zoroastrianism.	Thales of Miletus developing physical science and geometry.
561 Pisistratus controls Athens 561–c. 527.	550 Cyrus the Great defeats Medes; establishes Persian empire from Susa; captures Babylonia (539).	Aesop: fables.
546 Persian empire extends to Aegean. Ionian Greek cities captured.		Daoism founded in China, traditionally by Laozi (6th–5th century). Pythagoras teaching in southern Italy.
539 Israelites return from Babylonian Captivity and rebuild Temple in Jerusalem.		Ionic order appears in Greek architecture.
509 Roman Republic proclaimed.	Persian empire reaches India.	Siddhartha Gautama (Buddha) teaching.
508 Cleisthenes establishes democratic constitution in Athens.	Chinese bronze coinage.	Athenian pottery at its zenith. Iron-working in China.
500 Etruscans at the height of their power.		Emergence of Greek drama; theatres built.
499 Revolt of Ionian Greek cities against the Persians.	First inscriptions of Monte Albán, Mexico.	Greek philosophical thought emerging (Heraclitus).
490 Persian emperor Darius invades Greece; his army defeated at Marathon.		Confucius teaching in China.
480 Xerxes I, son of Darius, invades Greece with army and navy. Allied with Thebes, he wins land battle at Thermopylae, devastates Attica, but is defeated by Greeks in sea battle at Salamis. Xerxes retreats.		
472 Athens controls Aegean through Delian League.		458 Aeschylus: *Oresteia*.
450 Rome extending power in Latium and against Etruscans. Twelve Tables (set of laws) drawn up.	Persian empire in decline.	

EUROPE AND THE MEDITERRANEAN	REST OF THE WORLD	CULTURE AND TECHNOLOGY
443 Pericles dominates Athenian democracy until 429. Athens rebuilt. Parthenon built. Celtic La Tène culture flourishes in Switzerland.	The Carthaginian explorer Hanno sails to Senegal. Coinage reaches India. Extensive trade links between Mediterranean and Asia.	Sophocles: *Antigone*. Herodotus: *History*. Phidias leading Greek sculptor. Solar calendar in China.
431 Peloponnesian War begins; Athens against Sparta and her allies (431–404, with brief interlude 421–415).		Democritus: atomic theory. Euripides: *Medea*.
415 Alcibiades leads Athenian expedition to Sicily. Disastrous siege of Syracuse; many Athenians put to death.	Nok culture in West Africa (northern Nigeria), lasting until *c.* 200 AD. Iron metallurgy; clay figurines.	Aristophanes: comedies.
405 Spartan naval victory at Aegospotami on the Hellespont; Athens sues for peace (404).		Thucydides: *History of the Peloponnesian War*.
390 Celts sack Rome.	In China Zhou dynasty in decline.	399 Socrates condemned to death in Athens. 387 Plato founds Academy in Athens.
371 Thebes defeats Sparta at Battle of Leuctra and briefly dominates Greece. Rome dominates Latium, building roads and aqueducts.		Hippocrates developing medicine.
338 Macedonia defeats Thebes at Battle of Charonea; controls all Greece under Philip II (359–336).		Iron metallurgy in central Africa.
336 Alexander the Great king of Macedonia (336–323).		
334 Alexander crosses Hellespont, defeats Persians at Battle of Granicus, liberates Ionian cities; captures Tyre and Egypt; marches east.	Alexander master of Persian empire; invades India.	335 Aristotle founds Lyceum at Athens.
323 Death of Alexander at Babylon. Empire disintegrates. Hellenistic kingdom of Attalids established at Pergamum.	Mauryan dynasty established in India.	Epicurean and atomistic theory fashionable. Hellenistic art spreads throughout Asia. Menander: comedies.
311 Seleucid power established in Babylon.		
304 Ptolemy founds dynasty in Egypt.		
280 Pyrrhus of Epirus campaigns in Italy; defeats Romans in several battles but is unable to exploit victory and suffers heavy losses. Rome continues to advance into southern Italy.	Early Maya culture developing in Guatemala.	292–280 Colossus of Rhodes built. 284 Library founded (100,000 volumes) at Alexandria. Euclid teaching there. Catapult and quinquereme warship invented at Syracuse. Elephants first used in battle. Theocritus writes idylls idealizing bucolic life.
264 First Punic War (264–241), Rome against Carthage. Rome expands navy and wins control of Sicily (but not Syracuse), Sardinia, and Corsica.	269 Asoka (*c.* 269–*c.* 232), Mauryan emperor of India. Enthusiastic convert to Buddhism. 256 Zhou dynasty ends in China.	Zoroastrianism spreading in Persia. Greek and Oriental cultures fusing in Hellenistic period.
237 Hamilcar of Carthage conquers SE Iberia.	Extensive trade between China and Hellenistic world.	Latin literature beginning to emerge.
218 Second Punic War (218–201). Hannibal crosses Alps from Spain and defeats Romans but fails to take Rome itself.	221 Qin dynasty established in China. Zhou provinces conquered and country united politically.	214 Archimedes' inventions used to resist Romans in siege of Syracuse.
214 Romans fight first Macedonian War (214–205).	*c.* 210 Construction of Great Wall of China begun.	
202 Scipio Africanus defeats Carthage at Zama and second Punic War ends (201).	206 Han dynasty established in China.	Horse collar and harness in China.
200 Second Macedonian War (200–196). Rome defeats Philip V (197).		
192 Seleucid Antiochus III occupies Athens and Greece.	*c.* 184 Mauryan empire ends in India.	Plautus (later Terence) writing comedies in Rome.
171 Third Macedonian War (171–168).		
167 Revolt of Maccabees in Judaea against	Parthian empire (*c.* 250–*c.* 230 AD) at its	

EUROPE AND THE MEDITERRANEAN	REST OF THE WORLD	CULTURE AND TECHNOLOGY
Seleucids; Judas Maccabaeus establishes Jewish dynasty in Jerusalem (165).	height, from Caspian Sea and Euphrates to the Indus.	
149 Third Punic War begins (149–146).		
146 Carthage destroyed. Rome dominates western Mediterranean. Macedonia becomes Roman province.		Buddhism spreading throughout SE Asia.
133 Rome master of Iberia, occupies Balearic Islands (123). The Gracchus brothers attempt social and legal reforms in Rome 133–121.	127–101 Han armies from China conquer central Asia. Drift west of Asiatic tribes.	Polybius: *Histories* (40 volumes of Roman history, 220–146).
112 Outbreak of war between Rome and Jugurtha, king of Numidia.	Roman envoys to Han China.	Parchment invented in Pergamum to replace papyrus.
107 Gaius Marius elected to the first of his seven consulships at Rome.		
105 Jugurtha captured by the Romans.	Teotihuacán and Monte Albán developing in Mexico.	
c. 100 Celtic Belgae first settle in SE Britain.		Water-mill first described in Greek writings; came from China.
91 Confederacy of Italian tribes on Adriatic and in Apennines rebels against Rome; civil war.		
90 Roman citizenship extended to the Latin and some Italian cities.		
88 Mithridates VI, king of Pontus, invades Greece; defeated by the Roman general Sulla (85).		Buddhism spreading in China.
73 Spartacus leads revolt of slaves against Rome; suppressed by Crassus (71).		
66 Mithridates finally defeated by Pompey.	Civilization in Peru emerging (pyramids, palaces, etc.).	Cicero pleading and writing in Rome.
63 Catiline's conspiracy at Rome.	Romans under Pompey conquer Syria and Palestine; end of Seleucid empire.	
60 First Triumvirate in Rome; Crassus, Pompey, and Julius Caesar co-ordinate their political activities.		
58 Caesar fights Gallic Wars (58–51).		
55 Caesar invades Britain (55, 54).		
53 Crassus killed in battle against Parthians.		
51 Transalpine Gauls defeated by Caesar.		
49 Caesar crosses Rubicon and begins civil war.		
48 Caesar defeats Pompey in Battle of Pharsalus. Pompey murdered in Egypt.		
45 Caesar dictator of Rome.		46 Caesar introduces Julian calendar.
44 Caesar assassinated.		42 Virgil begins to write *Eclogues*.
43 Second Triumvirate (Octavian, Antony, Lepidus).		
31 Battle of Actium. Antony and Cleopatra commit suicide (30). Octavian sole ruler of Rome.		
27 BC Octavian accepts title of Augustus. Date traditionally marks beginning of Roman Empire (to 476 AD).		Pantheon built in Rome. 19 Virgil dies, leaving *Aeneid* unfinished. 17 Herod the Great rebuilds Temple at Jerusalem. Vitruvius: treatise on architecture.
c. 6 BC Jesus of Nazareth born.		Strabo: *Geographica*.

EUROPE AND THE MEDITERRANEAN	REST OF THE WORLD	CULTURE AND TECHNOLOGY
All dates AD		
9 Germans annihilate three Roman legions. Rome withdraws to Rhine.		
14 Death of Augustus. Tiberius emperor (14–37).		Ovid: *Metamorphoses.* *c.* 30 Crucifixion of Jesus.
37 Caligula emperor; assassinated 41.		
41 Claudius emperor (41–54).		
43 Britain occupied under Claudius.		
54 Nero emperor (54–68).		
61 Boudicca's revolt in Britain crushed by Suetonius Paulinus.	Kingdom of Aksum (Ethiopia) flourishes.	
64 Great fire of Rome: Christians blamed and martyred in Rome (64–67), including St Paul and St Peter.	Dead Sea Scrolls hidden at Qumran near the Dead Sea. 66 Revolt of Jews in Judaea.	Hero invents various machines in Alexandria.
69 Vespasian emperor (69–79); first of Flavian emperors; restores imperial economy.	70 Destruction of the Temple at Jerusalem under Titus, son of Vespasian. Jewish Diaspora.	First Gospel (St Matthew).
79 Eruption of Vesuvius. Pompeii and Herculaneum buried.		*c.* 75 Colosseum in Rome begun. Paper, magnetic compass, and fireworks invented in China. 90 Plutarch: *Parallel Lives.*
98 Trajan emperor (98–117); extends empire, defeating Dacians, Armenians, and Parthians. Empire at its fullest extent.	Christianity spreading.	Reform of Buddhism in India. Iron-working in Zambia.
100 Europe, North Africa, and Middle East under Roman control.		Juvenal: *Satires.* Canon of Hebrew Bible (Old Testament) fixed for Judaism.
117 Hadrian emperor (117–138).		Tacitus: *Annals.*
122 Hadrian's Wall built in Britain against northern tribes.		Suetonius: *Lives of the Caesars.*
132 Bar-Cochba leads revolt of Jews against the Romans.	Teotihuacán civilization in Mexico flourishing.	
138 Antoninus Pius emperor (138–161). Founds Antonine dynasty; streamlines imperial government.		
c. 140 Antonine Wall built in Britain.		
161 Marcus Aurelius emperor (161–180); a Stoic philosopher, he campaigns on eastern and northern frontiers of empire.	Parthian empire weakening.	Astronomy developing in school of Alexandria. Marcus Aurelius: *Meditations.*
180 Commodus emperor (180–192); murdered for his wild extravagance and cruelty.	184 Revolt in China as Han dynasty declines.	Galen practising medicine in Rome.
193 Septimius Severus emperor (193–211); resumes persecution of Christians; long campaign in Britain against Picts.		Tertullian: Christian apologetics.
211 Caracalla emperor (211–217); his reign one of cruelty and extortion.		
212 Roman citizenship extended to all freemen of the Roman Empire.		
218 Heliogabalus emperor (218–222); wild and decadent. Murdered in Rome.	220 Han dynasty ends in China.	Neoplatonism in Alexandria.
222 Alexander Severus emperor (222–235); rule remembered as just; re-established authority of Rome.	224 Persians defeat Parthians, whose empire collapses. The Persian Sassanid empire established.	Indian art (sculpture and painting) flourishes. Chinese literature developing.
235 Political tensions in Rome as empire begins to decline.		Gnostic Manichaeism spreads from Persia.

EUROPE AND THE MEDITERRANEAN	REST OF THE WORLD	CULTURE AND TECHNOLOGY
249 Decius emperor (249–251); intense persecution of Christians; Danube and the Balkans overrun by Goths.	*c.* 250 Syrian kingdom of Palmyra rises in power.	Roman architecture covers Europe and Mediterranean.
253 Valerian (253–260) and Gallienus emperors (253–268); Franks invade empire and Sassanids take Syria.	260 Sassanid emperor captures and imprisons Valerian. 265 Foundation of Western Jin dynasty in China (265–317). Bantu-speaking peoples move into southern Africa.	Christian theology emerging in Asia Minor and Egypt.
270 Emperor Aurelian (270–275) abandons Dacia to Goths but regains Rhine and Danube.	272 Kingdom of Palmyra conquered by Aurelian.	
284 Diocletian emperor (284–305); re-establishes frontiers and reorganizes government; divides empire with Maximian (286).	Classic Maya civilization emerging (Tikal, Palenque).	Monastic ideal (hermits) becoming popular (St Anthony).
293 Diocletian establishes tetrarchy; he rules with Galerius in east, Maximian and Constantius in the west.	292 First Mayan stela from Tikal.	Arius of Alexandria founds Arianism, denying divinity of Christ.
303 Diocletian persecutes Christians.		
306 Constantine proclaimed emperor in York (306–337); engages in long and complex civil war.		
313 Edict of Milan allows freedom of worship to Christians in Roman Empire.	317 Foundation of Eastern Jin dynasty in China (317–420).	Pappus last great mathematician of Alexandria.
324 Byzantium rebuilt by Constantine; becomes capital of empire (330); named Constantinople.	320 Foundation of Gupta empire (to *c.* 550) in India (golden age of religion, philosophy, literature, and architecture).	325 Council of Nicaea denounces Arianism and agrees Nicene Creed. Chinese mathematics reducing fractions and solving linear equations.
353 Constantius II emperor (353–360). Saxons invading coasts of Britain.		Chinese bucolic literature flourishing.
360 Julian (the Apostate) emperor (360–363); restores paganism briefly.		
374 St Ambrose elected bishop of Milan; influences emperor and dominates Western Church.		371–397 St Martin bishop of Tours.
378 Visigoths defeat Roman army.		
379 Theodosius I (the Great) emperor (379–395); pious Christian; defeats usurpers and makes treaty with Visigoths (382).	Huns from Asia concentrate on River Volga; moving west.	
391 All pagan worship banned in Roman Empire by Theodosius.		
395 Roman Empire divided into East and West on death of Theodosius; Honorius (395–423) rules from Milan, Arcadius (395–408) from Constantinople.		
396 Roman victories in Britain against Picts, Scots, and Saxons (396–398).		*c.* 400 Text of Palestinian Talmud finalized.
402 Western capital of RomanEmpire moves from Milan to Ravenna.		*c.* 405 St Jerome completes Vulgate (Latin Bible).
408 Visigoths invade Italy.		
410 Visigoths, led by Alaric, sack Rome. Romans evacuate Britain. Franks occupy northern Gaul and Celts move into Breton peninsula.	420 End of Eastern Jin dynasty in China.	Christian theology continues to be defined; Athanasian Creed agreed.
476 Romulus Augustulus, last Western emperor (475–476), is deposed; date traditionally marks the end of the Roman Empire. Saxon settlement in Sussex.		Shinto religion in Japan.

EUROPE AND THE MEDITERRANEAN	REST OF THE WORLD	CULTURE AND TECHNOLOGY
481 Clovis king of Salian Franks (481–511).		Buddhism dominant in China.
488 Theodoric and Ostrogoths invade Italy.		
496 Clovis baptized; establishes Merovingian Frankish kingdom. Wessex occupied by Saxons.	Ecuadorean pottery dated *c.* 500 found in Galapagos Islands, evidence of possible Pacific trade.	
516 British victory (King Arthur) over Saxons at Badon Hill. Visigoths established in Spain; Vandals in Africa (429–534).		
527 Justinian Byzantine emperor (527–565); attempts to recover western part of Roman Empire; drives Ostrogoths from Italy (552).	*c.* 550 End of Gupta empire in India following attacks by Huns.	*c.* 550 St David founds monasteries.
560 Ethelbert (d. 616) king of Kent.		Buddhism in Japan along with Shinto.
c. 563 St Columba founds monastery at Iona.		
568 Lombards invade northern Italy. Anglo-Saxon kingdoms in Britain emerging.	*c.* 570 Birth of Muhammad.	Byzantine architecture spreads throughout Eastern Empire and southern Italy.
577 West Saxons take Bath and Gloucester.	Chinese Sui dynasty 581–618; reunites country and rebuilds Great Wall.	
590 Election of Gregory the Great as pope (590–604).	607 Unification of Tibet, which becomes centre of Buddhism. 618 Tang dynasty established in China (618–907).	Gregorian chant and Roman ritual imposed by Gregory the Great.
627 Angle and Saxon kingdoms in Britain (Mercia, Wessex, and Northumbria) struggle for power.	622 Hegira of Muhammad and friends; Mecca to Medina. In Mexico Mayan civilization at height; temples and palaces in stone (complex astronomical and mathematical knowledge).	Christian missionaries to Germany and England (St Augustine, 597). Sutton Hoo burial. *c.* 625 Isadore of Seville: *Etymologies.* Parchment displacing papyrus.
629 Dagobert, king of Franks (629–639), reunites all Franks.	632 Death of Muhammad. 634 Rapid spread of Islam in Arabia, Syria, Iran, North Africa under Caliph Uma (634–644).	*c.* 632 The 114 chapters or suras of the Koran collected. *c.* 641 The great library of Alexandria destroyed by Arabs.
664 Synod of Whitby.	637–651 Collapse of Sassanid empire. 660 Damascus capital of Umayyad empire of Islam.	644 Windmills in Persia.
678 Constantinople resists Arabs.		
679 Mercia becomes major British power.	Teotihuacán civilization of Mexico declining.	680 Divisions within Islam produce Sunnis and Shiites.
685 Battle of Nechtansmere; Picts defeat Northumbrians. Wessex expanding; Kent, Surrey, and Sussex taken by Saxons.	Zapotec civilization, Monte Albán, flourishing; influenced by Teotihuacán. Afghanistan conquered by Arabs who cross Khyber Pass and conquer the Punjab.	Dome of the Rock in Jerusalem (692) and Umayyad Mosque in Damascus (705–715) built.
711 Muslim Arabs enter Spain, conquer Seville (712).	Tang emperor Xuan Zong (712–756) suffers revolts and drastic incursions by Arabs.	
718 Bulgars pressing south towards Constantinople.		726 Icons banned in Byzantine Church.
732 Battle of Poitiers; decisive victory of Charles Martel, Frankish king, over Constantinople.	Kingdom of Ghana established; to last until 1240.	Block printing in China for Buddhist texts. Bede: *The Ecclesiastical History of the English People.*
751 Pepin III (the Short), son of Charles Martel, ousts last Merovingian, Childeric III, and founds Carolingian dynasty.	Establishment of Abbasid caliphate in Baghdad, 750–1258.	*Beowulf*: Anglo-Saxon poem. Golden age of Chinese poetry (Li Po, 701–761) and art.
754 Pepin the Short crowned by Pope Stephen II; recognizes Papal States (756).		Cordoba centre of Muslim culture in Spain. Irish Book of Kells.
757 Offa king of Mercia (757–796).		
768 Charlemagne king of Franks (768–814); campaigns against Avars and Saxons in east.		Offa's Dyke built. Dravidian temples in India.
774 Charlemagne annexes Lombardy, but is checked in Spain (death of Roland at	Caliph Harun al-Rashid establishes close links with Constantinople and with Charlemagne.	Cotton grown in Spain.

EUROPE AND THE MEDITERRANEAN	REST OF THE WORLD	CULTURE AND TECHNOLOGY
Roncesvalles in 778).	Patronage of learning and the arts (e.g. tales of the *Arabian Nights*). Kyoto capital of Japan.	
794 Viking raids on England and Ireland; Jarrow and Iona (795) sacked.		
800 Charlemagne crowned in Rome by Pope Leo III.		Alcuin at court of Charlemagne; Carolingian Renaissance. 805 Aachen cathedral inspired by Byzantine models.
812 Charlemagne recognized emperor of the West by Byzantine emperor Michael I.		
813 Byzantine army defeats Bulgars. Constantinople besieged by Bulgars and Arab army.		
825 Wessex annexes Essex.		
827 Byzantine loss of Sicily and Crete to Arab Saracens.		833 Observatory in Baghdad; Arabs develop astronomy, mathematics (algebra from India), optics, medicine.
843 Carolingian empire divided; East Franks, West Franks, and Lotharingia (Lorraine). Vikings trading to Volga and Baghdad.		843 Restoration of cult of images in Byzantine Church. Icon art to influence West through Venice. 845 Buddhism outlawed in China. *c.* 850 Windmills in Europe.
c. 859 Novgorod founded as trading centre; Viking and Byzantine merchants. Bulgars accept Christianity.		
866 Danes land on east coast of Britain; Northumbria conquered; Danelaw established.		
867 Danes conquer York.		
870 St Edmund the Martyr murdered by Danes.		Romanesque architecture developing in West.
871 Alfred the Great king of Wessex (871–899).		
c. 880 Kingdom of Kiev established in Russia.		
885 Paris besieged by Vikings.		
896 Magyars settle in Hungary.	Classic Mayan civilization in Mexico ending. *c.* 900 Teotihuacán civilization ends; rise of Toltecs in Mexico based on Tula.	Benedictine Order spreads through Europe.
912 Rollo the Norseman established as first Duke of Normandy.	907 Tang dynasty in China ends; China fragments. 909 Shiite dynasty, the Fatimids, conquers North Africa.	910 Monastery of Cluny established.
925 Athelstan first king of all England (925–939).	Arabs trading along East African coast.	Stone replacing wood as building material in western Europe.
936 Otto I king of Germans (936–973).		Expansion of European agriculture. Buddhism flourishes in Korea.
937 Athelstan defeats Vikings and Scots.		
939 Edmund I king of England (939–946).		
945 Norsemen in Constantinople and Kiev.	947 Liao dynasty from Manchuria (947–1125) extends control over northern China.	943 Dunstan abbot of Glastonbury; under his leadership monasticism re-established in England.
955 Otto I defeats Magyars.		
959 Edgar king of England (959–975).		
960 Dunstan archbishop of Canterbury.	Sung dynasty in China (960–1279); gradually reunites country; high levels of art and literature.	
962 Otto I crowned Holy Roman Emperor in Rome by Pope John XII. Seeks to establish power in Italy.		
971 Bulgaria and Phoenicia conquered by Byzantine armies.	969 Fatimids conquer western Arabia, Syria, and Egypt; Cairo capital.	
975 Edward the Martyr king of England (975–978); murdered by half-brother Ethelred.		

EUROPE AND THE MEDITERRANEAN	REST OF THE WORLD	CULTURE AND TECHNOLOGY
978	Ethelred II (the Unready) king of England (978–1016).		
987	Hugh Capet king of France (987–996).	986 Viking settlements in Greenland. New Mayan empire emerging under Toltec influence.	988 Baptism of Vladimir, prince of Kiev (956–1015).
991	English treaty with Normans.		
996	Otto III crowned Holy Roman Emperor (996–1002); establishes capital in Rome (999); with Pope Sylvester II aims to create universal Christian empire.		Avicenna has lasting influence on West: philosophy and medicine.
1001	Christian kingdom of Hungary established.		c. 1000 Arabic description of magnifying properties of glass lens.
1003	Sweyn Forkbeard, king of Denmark, attacks Britain.		
1013	Sweyn invades England and takes London.		
1014	Death of Sweyn. His son Canute elected king of Danes in England.		
1016	Death of Ethelred and then of his son Edmund Ironside; Canute accepted as king of England (1017–35). Byzantine Empire at height of power and influence under Basil II (976–1025).	Ghaznavid empire extends into Persia and Punjab from Afghanistan.	
1035	Harold I king of England (1035–40).		
1040	Hardecanute king of England and Denmark (1040–42).		
1042	Edward the Confessor king of England (1042–66).		c. 1045 Printing by movable type in China.
1050	Bohemia, Poland, and Hungary become fiefs of Holy Roman Empire.	Toltecs flourish in Mexico; conspicuous Maya influence.	Salerno medical school emerging; Arabic expertise. Cult of Quetzalcóatl in Toltec Mexico.
1054	Great Schism within Christian Church; Orthodox Eastern Churches split from Catholic Rome.		
1066	Harold II (1066) king of England. Normans conquer England; William I king (1066–87).	1064 Seljuk Turks menace Byzantine Empire.	1063 St Mark's Cathedral, Venice, rebuilt. Pisa Cathedral built.
1069	North of England ravaged by William I's troops.	1068 Almoravid Berber dynasty in North Africa; Islamic fanaticism; Marrakesh built.	
1071	Normans established in southern Italy.	Seljuk Turks rout Byzantine army at Battle of Manzikert and threaten Asia Minor.	Bayeux Tapestry.
1081	Normans invade Balkans; Venice aids Constaninople against Normans; Venetian trade expands.	1080 Turks control Asia Minor and interrupt Christian pilgrim routes to Jerusalem.	
1084	Foundation of Carthusian order of monks.		
1086	Domesday Book in England.		
1087	William II king of England (1087–1100).		Omar Khayyám: algebra, astronomy, poetry (The Rubáiyát of Omar Khayyám). 1090 Water-powered mechanical clock in China.
1095	Pope Urban II urges crusade to rescue holy places from Turks.	First Crusade (1096–99).	1094 St Anselm: Cur Deus Homo?
1098	Cistercian order of monks founded.	1099 Jerusalem captured by Crusaders.	Feudal system well established throughout Europe. Urban society developing in Flanders, Germany, and Italy. Chanson de Roland.
1100	Henry I king of England (1100–35).	Christian states in Palestine.	
1108	Louis the Fat king of France (1108–37); Capetian power expanding.		
1120	Henry I's son William drowned.	1115 Jin dynasty in Manchuria (1115–1234). 1118 Knights Templars founded in Jerusalem.	1115 St Bernard abbot of Clairvaux; stresses spiritualism of monasticism. Rediscovery of

EUROPE AND THE MEDITERRANEAN	REST OF THE WORLD	CULTURE AND TECHNOLOGY
	1121 Almohad dynasty founded in North Africa.	Aristotle. Abelard teaching in Paris.
	1126 Sung capital Kaifeng in China sacked by Jin horsemen.	
1137 Catalonia linked by marriage with Aragon.		
1138 Beginning of long medieval struggle; Guelphs (for pope) against Ghibellines (for Holy Roman Emperor).		Gothic architecture beginning.
1139 Civil war in England: Stephen against Matilda.		c. 1139 Geoffrey of Monmouth: *Historia Regum Britanniae.*
1147 The Almohads rule in southern Spain.	Second Crusade (1147–49).	
1152 Henry of Anjou marries Eleanor of Aquitaine. Frederick I ('Barbarossa') crowned Holy Roman Emperor (1152–90); seeks to extend power in Italy.	c. 1150 Khmer temple Angkor Wat built in Cambodia.	c. 1150 Toledo school of translators transmits Arab learning to West.
1154 Henry II king of England (1154–89). Adrian IV pope (1154–59); only Englishman to have been pope.	Toltec capital Tula overrun by Chichimecs from northern Mexico. Toltec power declines.	1158 Bologna University granted charter by Frederick I.
1165 William I ('the Lion') king of Scotland (1165–1214).		
1166 Jury system established in England.	Aztecs moving into Mexico; destroy Toltec empire.	Catharist Manichaean heresy spreading. c. 1167 Oxford University founded.
1170 Murder of St Thomas à Becket.	1169 Saladin conquers Egypt. Drives Christians from Acre and Jerusalem.	c. 1170 Paris University founded. Troubadour songs in France. Early polyphonic music.
1180 Philip II ('Augustus') king of France (1180–1223); greatly expands kingdom.		1171 Averroës teaching in Cordoba.
1182 Massacre of Latin merchants in Constantinople.		
1189 Richard I king of England (1189–99).	Third Crusade (1189–92); Acre retaken (1191). Saladin grants pilgrims access to holy places.	1193 Zen Buddhism in Japan.
1198 Innocent III pope (1198–1216); papacy has maximum authority during these years.		1194 Chartres Cathedral rebuilding begun in Gothic style.
1199 John king of England (1199–1216).	1200 Incas developing civilization based on Cuzco. Chimu civilization in Peru (1200–1465); large urban centres; elaborate irrigation.	
1204 Philip Augustus victorious in Normandy.	Fourth Crusade (1202–04); Constantinople sacked.	1202 Arabic mathematics in Pisa.
1212 Children's Crusade; thousands enslaved.	1206 Genghis Khan proclaims Mongol empire.	1209 Cambridge University established. Franciscan (1209) and Dominican (1215–16) orders founded.
1214 Philip Augustus defeats King John and German emperor Otto IV; gains Normandy, Anjou, and Poitou for France.		
1215 John accepts Magna Carta from barons. Fourth Lateran Council condemns Albigensian heresy; transubstantiation doctrine.	Beijing sacked and Jin empire overrun by Mongols.	Islam spreading into SE Asia and Africa.
1216 Henry III king of England aged nine (1216–72); Earl of Pembroke regent until 1227.		
1220 Frederick II Holy Roman Emperor (1220–50); inherits southern Italy and Sicily, which he makes power base.		
1223 Louis VIII of France (1223–26) conquers Languedoc in crusade against Cathars (1224–26). Mongols invade Russia.		1224 Frederick II founds Naples University; Jews, Christians, and Arabs.
1226 Louis XI king of France (1226–70).	1229 Frederick II negotiates access for pilgrims to Jerusalem, Bethlehem, and Nazareth.	
1236 Cordoba falls to Castile.	c. 1235 Mali empire established in West Africa.	*Roman de la rose.*

EUROPE AND THE MEDITERRANEAN	REST OF THE WORLD	CULTURE AND TECHNOLOGY
1241 Formation of Hanseatic League.	Mongol Golden Horde emerges. 1244 Christians are driven from Jerusalem. Mamelukes establish dynasty in Egypt.	
1250 Italian cities gain power on collapse of Frederick II's empire.		1248 Alhambra begun. Cologne Cathedral begun.
1258 Catalans expel Moors from Balearics.	Mongols take Baghdad.	Thomas Aquinas: *Summa Contra Gentiles.*
1261 Byzantines regain Constantinople.	1259 Kublai Khan elected khan. Establishes capital in Beijing and founds Yuan dynasty.	*c.* 1260 Nicola Pisano: pulpit in Pisa Baptistery; renaissance of classical style.
1264 Battle of Lewes: Simon de Montfort effective ruler of England until 1265.		
1270 Louis IX dies on crusade outside Tunis. Philip III succeeds (1270–85).	Marco Polo travelling 1271–95.	Gothic architecture throughout Europe.
1272 Edward I of England (1272–1307) begins conquest of Wales.		Mechanical clock developed.
1282 Sicilian Vespers; revolt against Angevins (ruled since 1266). Sicily goes to Aragon. Welsh resistance collapses.		Duccio painting in Siena.
1284 English rule of Wales confirmed.		Giotto active in Florence; significant in development of modern painting.
1285 Philip IV king of France (1285–1314).	Inca empire expanding in Peru.	
1290 Jews expelled from England. Scottish throne vacant.		
1297 William Wallace defeats English army at Stirling.	New Mayan empire flourishing in Yucatán (Chichén Itzá).	Roger Bacon teaching philosophy, science, technology; eventually imprisoned for heresy.
1305 Edward I executes William Wallace. Clement V pope (1305–14); papacy moves to Avignon (1309).		Spectacles invented.
1306 Jews expelled from France.		Duns Scotus and nominalists oppose Aquinas's theology.
1307 Knights Templars suppressed in France. Edward II king of England (1307–27). Italian cities flourish as German empire abandons control.	Kingdom of Benin emerging in southern Nigeria.	Dante: *The Divine Comedy* begun *c.* 1309.
1314 Robert the Bruce defeats English at Bannockburn.		
1327 Edward II imprisoned and murdered. Edward III king of England (1327–77); his mother Isabella and her lover Mortimer rule till 1330.	Aztecs adopt cult of Quetzalcóatl from Toltecs.	Spinning-wheel from India in Europe.
1328 Scottish independence recognized. Capetian line of kings ends. Philip VI first Valois king of France (1328–50).	Disease (plague) and famine weaken Yuan dynasty in China.	
1337 Edward III claims French throne and Hundred Years War begins.		
1340 English gain control of Channel.		Paper-mill in Italy. Bruges centre of wool trade; Flemish art emerging.
1346 Battle of Crécy; English victory; cannon used; Calais occupied.	1347 Black Death reaches Europe from China.	*c.* 1344 Order of Garter in England.
1348 Black Death arrives in England; one-third of population dies.	Aztec empire thriving.	Boccaccio: *Decameron.*
1353 Ottoman Turks enter Europe.		Petrarch: *Canzoniere.*
1356 Edward the Black Prince wins Poitiers; French king John II captured.		
1360 England makes peace with France, keeps western France.		
1369 Hundred Years War resumed.	Mongol Tamerlane conquers Persia, Syria, and Egypt (1364–1405). Ming dynasty in China founded (1368–1644); great period for pottery and bronze.	William Langland: *Piers Plowman.* Jean Froissart: *Chronicles.* Siena artists flourish.
1371 Robert II king of Scotland (1371–90); first Stuart.		

EUROPE AND THE MEDITERRANEAN	REST OF THE WORLD	CULTURE AND TECHNOLOGY
1377 Richard II king of England (1377–99). Papacy returns to Rome from Avignon.		
1378 Great Schism in Church; two popes.		Flamboyant architecture in Europe: Beauvais Cathedral in France.
1380 Charles VI king of France (1380–1422).		
1381 Peasants' Revolt in England; Wat Tyler defeated; poll tax withdrawn.		1382 Lollards (John Wyclif) condemned.
1386 Poland and Lithuania unite.		1387 Chaucer: *Canterbury Tales.*
1396 Truce in Hundred Years War.		Ghiberti in Florence: baptistery doors.
1397 Union of Kalmar; crowns of Denmark, Norway, and Sweden unite (1397–1523).		
1399 Richard II deposed; Bolingbroke becomes Henry IV (1399–1413).	*c.* 1400 Foundation of Malacca sultanate.	
1402 Owen Glendower defeats English.	Tamerlane defeats Ottomans at Ankara.	
1403 Prince Henry (later Henry V) defeats Sir Henry Percy ('Hotspur') and Glendower rebellions (1408).		
1413 Henry V king of England (1413–22).	Portuguese voyages of exploration begin under Henry the Navigator.	1410 St Andrews University founded.
1415 Henry V wins Battle of Agincourt; occupies Normandy. John Huss burnt at the stake; Hussites seek revenge for martyr Huss. Great Schism ends (1417).		Painting in oil begins.
1422 Henry VI king of England (1422–61, 1470–71). Charles VII king of France (1422–61).		Thomas à Kempis: *On the Imitation of Christ.* Masaccio: frescoes. 1420 Dome of Florence Cathedral begun by Brunelleschi.
1429 Joan of Arc relieves Orleans.		
1431 Joan of Arc burnt at stake in Rouen.	Thais of Siam take Angkor. Phnom Penh new Khmer city.	
1434 Cosimo de' Medici rules in Florence; patron of learning. Burgundy emerging under strong dukes.	Inca ascendancy in Peru; high level of astronomical and surgical knowledge; cotton and potatoes grown.	Donatello: *David.* Van Eyck: *The Arnolfini Marriage.*
1452 Frederick III (1452–93) first Habsburg Holy Roman Emperor.		1452–66 Piero della Francesca: Arezzo frescoes.
1453 Constantinople falls to Ottoman Turks. Hundred Years War ends. English Wars of Roses begin.		Alberti: façade of Santa Maria Novella; Florence centre of artistic activity. *c.* 1455 Gutenberg Bible. *c.* 1454–57 Uccello: *The Rout of San Romano.*
1461 Edward of York seizes English throne; Edward IV (1461–83). Louis XI king of France (1461–83).		
1469 Ferdinand and Isabella I marry; unite Aragon and Castile (1479).		
1470 Henry VI of England restored; Edward IV exiled.		
1471 Lancastrians defeated at Tewkesbury; Henry VI killed; Edward IV accepted.		
1478 Spanish Inquisition established.	1476 Incas conquer Chimu.	Caxton printing at Westminster. Topkapi Palace built in Constantinople. Botticelli: *Primavera.*
1480 Ivan III overthrows Mongol Golden Horde.		
1483 Edward V; Richard III king of England (1483–85).		
1485 Henry Tudor victorious at Bosworth Field; Henry VII (1485–1509).		Leonardo da Vinci: anatomy, mechanics, painting, etc.
1492 Reconquest of Spain from Moors complete.	Columbus reaches the New World. 1497 John Cabot reaches mainland North America from Bristol.	
1498 Louis XII king of France (1498–1515).	1498 Vasco da Gama rounds Cape of Good	Nanak founds Sikh religion.

EUROPE AND THE MEDITERRANEAN	REST OF THE WORLD	CULTURE AND TECHNOLOGY
	Hope and reaches Calicut; beginning of Portuguese empire.	1501–04 Michelangelo: *David*.
1503 Julius II pope (1503–13).		*c.* 1503–06 Leonardo da Vinci: *Mona Lisa*. 1505–07 Dürer in Italy.
1509 Henry VIII king of England (1509–47).		1506 Bramante designs St Peter's, Rome. 1508–12 Michelangelo: Sistine chapel ceiling. 1509 Watch invented in Nuremberg.
1513 Scots defeated at Flodden; death of James IV.	1511 Portuguese conquer Malacca (Melaka).	
1515 Francis I king of France (1515–47).		1516 Grünewald: Isenheim Altar. King's College Chapel, Cambridge, completed.
1517 Start of Reformation in Germany.	Ottoman Turks conquer Egypt.	
1519 Charles V elected Holy Roman Emperor.	Cortés conquers Aztecs. Magellan crosses Pacific.	
1521 Diet of Worms condemns Luther's teaching.	Suleiman the Magnificent sultan of the Ottoman Empire.	
1525 Reformation moves to Switzerland.	*c.* 1525 Babur invades India and founds Mogul dynasty.	Titian: *Bacchus and Ariadne*.
1526 Battle of Mohács. Ottoman Turks occupy Hungary.		
1527 Charles V's troops sack Rome.		Paracelsus in Basle (new concept of disease).
1529 Ottomans besiege Vienna. Fall of English chancellor Wolsey.	Franciscan mission to Mexico. European spice trade with Asia; trade in sugar/slaves with America.	Early Italian madrigal.
1530 Augsburg Confession states Lutheran position.		
1533 Henry VIII marries Anne Boleyn.	1531–33 Pizarro conquers Inca empire.	
1534 English Act of Supremacy; break with papacy. Anabaptists revolt in Münster, Germany.	Persia conquered by Ottoman Turks.	Luther's translation of the Bible. Rabelais: *Gargantua*. Jesuits founded.
1535 John Calvin in Geneva.		
1536 Dissolution of English and Welsh monasteries.		Calvin: *Institutes of the Christian Religion*.
1538 Pope Paul III excommunicates Henry VIII.		
1540 Henry VIII tries to impose political and religious settlement on Ireland.	1542 St Francis Xavier in India, Sri Lanka, Japan (1549).	1543 Copernicus: *De Revolutionibus Orbium Coelestium*. Vesalius: *De Humani Corporis Fabrica*.
1545 Council of Trent begins (1545–63).		
1547 Edward VI king of England (1547–53). Ivan the Terrible tsar of Russia (1547–84).	Portuguese settling coast of Brazil.	1548 Ignatius Loyola: *Spiritual Exercises*.
1553 Mary Tudor queen of England (1553–58); persecution of Protestants.		1550 Vasari: *Lives of the Most Excellent Painters, Sculptors, and Architects*.
1556 Charles V retires; Philip II king of Spain (1556–98).	Akbar Mogul emperor of India (1556–1605). Expands empire and unites its peoples.	
1558 France recaptures Calais from English. Elizabeth I queen of England (1558–1603).	1557 Portuguese found Macao.	
1559 John Knox active in Scotland.		Tobacco enters Europe.
1562 Start of French Wars of Religion.		
1567 Dutch revolt against Spanish begins. Mary Queen of Scots flees to England.		1566 Palladio starts to build church of San Giorgio Maggiore in Venice.
1571 Battle of Lepanto; Turkish domination of eastern Mediterranean ends. Religious settlement in England; Thirty-nine Articles.		1569 Mercator invents map projection.
1572 Massacre of St Bartholomew (French Huguenots).		

EUROPE AND THE MEDITERRANEAN	REST OF THE WORLD	CULTURE AND TECHNOLOGY
1577 Drake's voyage round the world begins.	Spanish expanding in Mexico and Colombia.	El Greco to Toledo. Tycho Brahe: *De Nova Stella*.
1579 Protestant Dutch unite, form United Provinces. Irish rebels massacred; plantation of English settlers.		
1580 Spain occupies Portugal.	1582 Warrior Hideyoshi unites Japan and campaigns in Korea (1592, 1598).	1580–95 Montaigne: *Essays*.
1585 England and Spain at war.	1584 Walter Raleigh attempts to found colony of Virginia.	
1587 Mary Queen of Scots executed.		
1588 Spanish Armada defeated.		
1589 Henry IV king of France (1589–1610)		Early ballet in France. *c.* 1590 Marlowe: *Doctor Faustus*. 1590, 1596 Spenser: *Faerie Queene*. 1593 Microscope; thermometer; water-closet. 1594 Death of Palestrina and Lassus.
1593 Henry IV accepts Catholicism in France.		
1598 Edict of Nantes ends Wars of Religion in France. Boris Godunov Russian tsar (1598–1605). 1601 Irish revolt suppressed.	1600 East India Company formed.	Shakespeare: *Romeo and Juliet*. Globe theatre built (1599). Giordano Bruno burnt at stake for heretical theory of universe.
1603 James VI of Scotland (1567–1625) becomes James I of England (1603–25).		Shakespeare: *Hamlet*.
1604 Anglo-Spanish peace treaty.		
1605 Gunpowder Plot in English Parliament.	1607 Virginia settled by British. 1608 Quebec settled by Champlain for France.	1606 Ben Jonson: *Volpone*. 1605–15 Cervantes: *Don Quixote*. 1607 Monteverdi: *Orfeo*. 1609 Shakespeare: sonnets. Galileo: telescope. Kepler: laws of planetary motion.
1610 Ulster planted with English and Scottish settlers. Louis XIII king of France (1610–43).		1610 Caravaggio dies. 1611 Authorized Version of the Bible. Shakespeare: *The Tempest*.
1613 Russian Romanov dynasty established.		1614 John Napier: work on logarithms.
1618 Thirty Years War begins in Europe.	1616 Japan ejects Christian missionaries. Tobacco plantations in Virginia expanding.	1619–21 Inigo Jones designs Banqueting Hall at Whitehall. Francis Bacon: *Novum Organum*.
1621 Philip IV king of Spain (1621–65).	1620 Pilgrim Fathers arrive at Cape Cod on the *Mayflower*.	
1624 Richelieu in power in France. Britain and Spain renew war (1624–30).		Frans Hals: *The Laughing Cavalier*.
1625 Charles I king of England (1625–49).	1626 Dutch purchase Manhattan (New Amsterdam).	
1627 Britain and France at war (1627–29). Richelieu defeats Huguenots.		
1629 Charles I governs without Parliament.		1628 William Harvey: *De Motu Cordis*.
1630 Gustavus Adolphus of Sweden joins Thirty Years War.	1630–42 Large-scale British emigration to Massachusetts.	1632 Van Dyck to England.
1633 William Laud elected Archbishop of Canterbury; opposes Puritans in Britain.		Galileo before Inquisition; recants.
1635 France joins Thirty Years War.		
1637 Charles I faces crisis in Scotland over new liturgy.	Japan closed to Europeans.	Corneille: *Le Cid*. Descartes active in Holland.
1640 Long Parliament begins. Braganza dynasty rules in Portugal.		
1642 English Civil War begins (1642–49). Death of Richelieu.	1642–43 Tasman explores Antipodes.	Rembrandt: *Night Watch*. Pascal's calculating machine.
1643 Louis XIV king of France (1643–1715). Mazarin in power.		Torricelli invents barometer.
1644 Charles I defeated at Marston Moor.	Qing dynasty established in China.	
1645 New Model Army formed. Charles I defeated at Naseby. Main phase of war ends (1646).		

EUROPE AND THE MEDITERRANEAN	REST OF THE WORLD	CULTURE AND TECHNOLOGY
1647 Leveller influence in New Model Army.		
1648 Charles I's attempt to regain power with Scottish help defeated. Treaty of Westphalia ends Thirty Years War. Independence of Dutch from Spain recognized.	Atlantic slave trade expanding.	
1649 Charles I tried and executed. Cromwell defeats Irish at Wexford, massacres garrison at Drogheda.		c. 1649 Taj Mahal completed. 1650 Guericke invents air pump.
1651 Cromwell defeats Scots at Worcester.		1651 Hobbes: *Leviathan.*
1652 English and Dutch at war (1652–57).	Dutch found Cape Colony.	
1653 Oliver Cromwell 'Protector' (1653–58).		c. 1655 Poussin: *Et in Arcadia Ego.* 1656 Bernini completes piazza of St Peter's, Rome. Huygens invents pendulum clock. Velázquez: *Las Meninas.*
1660 Restoration of Charles II as king (1660–85).	Aurangzeb Mogul emperor (1658–1707); expansion followed by decline after his death.	1660 Vermeer at work. 1662 Royal Society founded in London. Robert Boyle: Boyle's Law.
1664 English and Dutch at war (1664–67).		1664 Molière: *Tartuffe.*
1665 Great Plague of London. Colbert chief minister in France (1665–83).		
1666 Fire of London.	Hindu Maratha kingdom rises in western India; challenges Moguls.	1666–67 Newton invents differential calculus. Spirit-level invented. 1667 Milton: *Paradise Lost.*
1670 French troops occupy Lorraine.	Rise of Asante (Ashanti) in West Africa.	1670 Versailles palace built. 1670–1720 Wren rebuilds London churches and St Paul's.
1672 English and Dutch at war again (1672–74).	1675 In India Sikhism becomes military theocracy to resist Mogul power.	1676 Van Leeuwenhoek identifies microbes with aid of microscope. 1677 Racine: *Phèdre.*
1678 Franche-Compté annexed to France.		1678–84 Bunyan: *The Pilgrim's Progress.*
1682 Peter the Great tsar of Russia (1682–1725).	Pennsylvania founded.	1681 Pressure-cooker invented.
1683 Turks besiege Vienna.		
1685 Edict of Nantes revoked. James II king of England, Scotland, and Ireland (1685–88).		
1688 English 'Glorious Revolution'; William (1689–1702) and Mary (1689–94) reign. Spain recognizes Portugal's independence.		1687 Newton: *Principia Mathematica.*
1689 England at war with France.		Purcell: *Dido and Aeneas.*
1690 Battle of Boyne; forces of James II defeated.	1692 Witch trials in Salem, Massachusetts.	Locke: *An Essay concerning Human Understanding.* 1693 François Couperin to Versailles as court organist. 1698 Savery: steam engine.
1700 Charles II (Habsburg) of Spain dies childless. Philip V (Bourbon) king of Spain (1700–46). Great Northern War (1700–21); Russia and allies oppose Sweden.		Congreve: *The Way of the World.* Stradivarius: violins.
1701 War of the Spanish Succession (1701–14); Britain, Holland, and Holy Roman Empire against France.		
1702 Anne queen of England, Scotland, and Ireland (1702–14).		
1704 Marlborough wins Battle of Blenheim. British take Gibraltar.		Newton: *Opticks.* 1705 Halley predicts return of his comet.
1706 Battle of Ramillies: Marlborough routs French.		

EUROPE AND THE MEDITERRANEAN	REST OF THE WORLD	CULTURE AND TECHNOLOGY
1707 Act of Union between England and Scotland.		
1708 Battle of Oudenarde: Marlborough's third victory.		
1709 Battle of Poltava in Great Northern War ends Swedish hegemony in the Baltic. Last of Marlborough's victories, at Malplaquet.		First piano in Italy. Newcomen: piston-operated steam engine.
1713 Peace of Utrecht ends War of the Spanish Succession. Frederick William I king of Prussia (1713–40).	Newfoundland, Nova Scotia, St Kitts, and Hudson Bay awarded to Britain.	1712 Handel to London.
1714 George I king of Great Britain and Ireland (1714–27).		Fahrenheit devises thermometer scale.
1715 Louis XV king of France (1715–74). Jacobite rebellion suppressed in Scotland and England.	1717 Shenandoah Valley settled. American Indians evicted.	1716 Couperin: treatise on harpsichord-playing. 1717 Watteau: *L'Embarquement pour l'île de Cythère.*
1720 South Sea Bubble; major financial collapse in London.	Chinese invade Tibet.	1719 Defoe: *Robinson Crusoe.*
1721 Robert Walpole first Prime Minister in Britain (1721–42).	French and English rivals in India.	1724 Bourse opens in Paris. 1726 Swift: *Gulliver's Travels.* Voltaire goes to England.
1727 George II king of Great Britain and Ireland (1727–60).	1728 Danish explorer Bering discovers Straits. 1729 North and South Carolina become Crown Colonies.	1728 Gay: *Beggar's Opera.* Pope: *Dunciad.* 1729 J. S. Bach: *The Passion according to St Matthew.*
1739 War of Jenkins's Ear between England and Spain.		1734 Voltaire: *Lettres philosophiques.* 1735 Linnaeus: *Systema Naturae.* Richardson: *Pamela.*
1740 Frederick II king of Prussia (1740–86); claims Silesia, causing War of the Austrian Succession (1740–48). Archduchess Maria Theresa, queen of Hungary and Bohemia (1740–80).	1741 Bering discovers Alaska.	1742 Celsius devises centigrade scale. Handel: *Messiah.*
1745 Jacobite Rebellion under 'Bonnie Prince Charlie'.		
1746 Battle of Culloden in Scotland: defeat of Jacobites; rebellion ruthlessly suppressed.	English, French, Dutch trading extensively in Asia.	1748 Pompeii excavated. 1749 Bow Street Runners formed in London. Fielding: *Tom Jones.* 1750 Death of J. S. Bach. Symphonic form emerging in music. Ideas of the Enlightenment influential in Europe. 1751 Diderot publishes first volume of *Encyclopédie.* Franklin devises lightning conductor. Jewish naturalization in Britain. Buffon: *Histoire naturelle* (36 vols., 1749–88).
1752 England and Wales adopt Gregorian calendar.		
1755 Lisbon earthquake.		Samuel Johnson: *Dictionary of the English Language.* Neoclassical art fashionable.
1756 Outbreak of Seven Years War (1756–63). Pitt the Elder Prime Minister (1756–61).		
1757 Frederick II wins victories for Prussia.	Robert Clive commands East India Company army. Battle of Plassey: Clive defeats Nawab of Bengal and controls state.	Sextant designed in England. French physiocrats active (early economists). 1758 Voltaire: *Candide.*
1758 Frederick II defeats Russians.		
1759 French defeated by Prussians at Minden and by British at Quiberon Bay.	Wolfe captures city of Quebec; British then take Montreal and whole colony of Quebec.	1759–67 Sterne: *Tristram Shandy.*
1760 George III king of Great Britain and Ireland (1760–1820).		1761 Haydn to court of Prince Esterházy in Hungary.
1762 Catherine the Great empress of Russia (1762–96).	African slave trade begins to attract criticism.	Jean-Jacques Rousseau: *Émile* and *Social Contract.* Gluck: *Orfeo ed Euridice.*
1763 Seven Years War ends.	American colonists move west into Ohio basin.	Compulsory education in Prussia.
1765 American Stamp Act to finance		

EUROPE AND THE MEDITERRANEAN	REST OF THE WORLD	CULTURE AND TECHNOLOGY
defence of colonies. Joseph II Habsburg emperor, supported by his mother Maria Theresa.		
1766 Stamp Act repealed. Pitt the Elder Prime Minister (1766–68).	1766–69 Bougainville's voyage round world, exploring many Pacific islands. Increasing opposition in British American colonies to control from London through royal governors. West African kingdom of Benin declining in power. 1768–71 Cook's voyage in *Endeavour*; charts New Zealand and eastern Australia.	Cavendish isolates hydrogen. Robert and James Adam influential architects.
1769 Russia advancing against Turks and Tartars. Birth of Napoleon.		Improved steam engine using condenser patented by James Watt.
1770 Lord North Prime Minister in Britain (1770–82).	Policies of North government cause growing resentment in Virginia and Massachusetts.	Spinning-jenny patented by Hargreaves. Gainsborough: *Blue Boy*.
1772 First partition of Poland between Russia, Prussia, and Austria.		Horace Walpole rebuilds Strawberry Hill; helps to inspire Gothic revival.
1774 Financial and administrative chaos in France at the end of Louis XV's reign. Louis XVI king (1774–93).	Warren Hastings Governor-General in India; consolidates Clive's conquests.	Goethe: *The Sorrows of Young Werther*. Priestley discovers oxygen.
1776 French support American colonies.	1775 War of American Independence begins (1775–83); Battle of Bunker Hill. 1776 Declaration of Independence signed 4 July by 13 rebel colonies.	1775 Beaumarchais: *The Barber of Seville*. Jenner discovers the principle of vaccination. 1776–88 Gibbon: *The History of the Decline and Fall of the Roman Empire*. 1776 Adam Smith: *Inquiry into the Nature and Causes of the Wealth of Nations*.
1777 Rapid growth of British textile industry. Necker French finance minister (1777–81).	British take New York and Philadelphia but are defeated at Saratoga.	Sheridan: *The School for Scandal*. Lavoisier: work on combustion. *Sturm und Drang* literary movement.
1778 France joins American war.		La Scala in Milan built.
1779 Spain joins American war. Riots against machines in England.		
1780 Gordon Riots in London.	1781 British take Charleston but surrender at Yorktown.	1781 Kant: *Critique of Pure Reason*. Planet Uranus discovered by Herschel.
1782 Political crisis in Britain. Fall of Lord North.		Laclos: *Les Liaisons dangereuses*. Watt: improvements to the steam engine.
1783 Pitt the Younger Prime Minister (1783–1801). Peace of Paris ends War of American Independence; Britain accepts independence of US colonies but retains West Indies and Canada.	1785 Warren Hastings returns to Britain; faces seven-year trial for corruption in India.	First manned flight in a hot-air balloon (France). Cavendish determines composition of water. David: *The Oath of the Horatii*. 1786 Mozart: *The Marriage of Figaro*.
1788 George III's first period of mental illness. France bankrupt; Necker restored.	1787 US constitution written. First British convicts sent to Botany Bay; settle in Sydney Bay and create New South Wales. 1788 US constitution agreed.	1787 Schiller: *Don Carlos*. Charles's Law formulated. Improved horse-drawn threshing machine patented.
1789 French Revolution: States General summoned; Bastille stormed (14 July); National Assembly formed; French aristocrats flee to England and Germany.	George Washington first US President (1789–97). Alexander Hamilton secretary of US Treasury.	Blake: *Songs of Innocence*. Lavoisier establishes modern chemistry.
1790 France: Church lands nationalized; country organized into departments.		Burke: *Reflections on the Revolution in France*. Ambulances in France.
1791 Louis XVI and Marie Antoinette under restraint in Paris. Attempted escape foiled; arrested at Varennes.	US Congress meets in Philadelphia. Slave revolt in Haiti under Toussaint L'Ouverture.	Mozart dies in poverty. Thomas Paine: *The Rights of Man*. Methodists separate from Church of England.
1792 Russian empire extends beyond Black Sea. French Republic proclaimed (September).		Mary Wollstonecraft: *A Vindication of the Rights of Woman*.
1793 Louis XVI executed (January). The Terror begins. Britain declares war on France. Second partition of Poland. Committee of Public Safety under Robespierre.	George Washington's second term as US President.	

EUROPE AND THE MEDITERRANEAN	REST OF THE WORLD	CULTURE AND TECHNOLOGY
1794 Robespierre executed (July).		Eli Whitney patents cotton-gin in USA.
1795 Third partition of Poland. Rural depression and high inflation in Britain. France under Directory.		Hydraulic press in England.
1796 French campaign in Italy; Napoleon victor.		Jenner succeeds with smallpox vaccine.
1797 Talleyrand French foreign minister.	John Adams US President (1797–1801).	
1798 Napoleon to Egypt. Irish rebellion suppressed.	French invade Egypt. Nelson destroys French fleet at Aboukir Bay.	Malthus: *Essay on Population.* Lithography invented. Wordsworth: *Lyrical Ballads.* Coal-gas lighting patented in England.
1799 Napoleon returns to Paris and seizes power as First Consul. European coalition against France. Income tax introduced in Britain.		Gas fire patented (France).
1800 Napoleon defeats Austrians at Marengo. France dominates Italy except for Sicily and Sardinia.		Volta makes first battery. Fichte: *The Destiny of Man.*
1801 Irish Act of Union. First census in Britain. Alexander I tsar of Russia (1801–25).	Thomas Jefferson US President (1801–09)	Chateaubriand: *Atala.* Gauss: theory of numbers. 1802 *Charlotte Dundas* first steamship.
1803 Britain declares war on France and forms new coalition. Rebellion in Ireland suppressed.	Jefferson purchases Louisiana from Napoleon.	Dalton: atomic theory.
1804 Pitt the Younger again Prime Minister (1804–06). Pope crowns Napoleon emperor.	Haiti independent. 1804–06 Lewis and Clark expedition across USA.	Beethoven: *Eroica* symphony. Trevithick: first steam rail locomotive (Wales).
1805 Nelson wins Battle of Trafalgar. French defeat Austrians and Russians at Austerlitz.		
1806 Death of Pitt the Younger. Holy Roman Empire ends. Prussians defeated at Jena.	Britain seizes Cape Province.	Beaufort scale of wind velocity. Fulton: paddle-steamer.
1808 Spanish rising against French occupation; Peninsular War begins (1808–14).	South American independence movement from Spain begins in Venezuela under Bolívar.	Ingres: *Bather.* Gay-Lussac: law of gas expansion. 1808–32 Goethe: *Faust.*
1809 British victory at Corunna. France occupies Papal States.	James Madison US President (1809–17). Macquarie governor of New South Wales (1809–21).	
1810 Wellington in command of British in Peninsular War.		1810–14 Goya: *The Disasters of War.*
1811 George III mentally ill; Prince Regent installed (1811–20). Economic depression in Britain; Luddite riots against machines.	Muhammad Ali overthrows Mamelukes in Egypt. Paraguay independent.	Krupp factory at Essen. Avogadro's law.
1812 Napoleon marches on Russia; forced to retreat from Moscow. British Prime Minister Spencer Perceval assassinated. Succeeded by Lord Liverpool (1812–27).	War of 1812, US against Britain (1812–14).	Brothers Grimm: first volume of fairy tales. 1812–18 Byron: *Childe Harold's Pilgrimage.* 1812–16 Hegel: *Science of Logic.* 1813 Jane Austen: *Pride and Prejudice.* Beethoven: *Fidelio.*
1814 Napoleon abdicates; sent to Elba. Louis XVIII (1814–24) and Ferdinand VII (1808, 1814–33) restored as kings of France and Spain. Congress of Vienna convened.		
1815 Napoleon returns; raises army; defeated at Waterloo; banished to St Helena.	US westward expansion begins. 1816 Argentina declares independence. Shaka forms Zulu kingdom. 1817 James Monroe US President (1817–25).	Davy lamp invented. 1816 Rossini: *The Barber of Seville.* Stethoscope invented (France). 1817–21 Weber: *Der Freischütz.* 1818 Keats: poems. Mary Shelley: *Frankenstein.*
1819 Peterloo massacre in Manchester.	1819 Raffles founds Singapore. USA purchases Florida.	1819 Schubert: 'Trout' quintet. Géricault: *The Raft of the Medusa.* Scott: *Ivanhoe.*
1820 Abortive risings in Portugal, Sicily, Germany, and Spain. George IV king of Great Britain and Ireland (1820–30).	US settlers beyond the Mississippi.	Macadamized roads stimulate coach travel. 1820 Shelley: *Prometheus Unbound.* Street lighting in Pall Mall, London.

EUROPE AND THE MEDITERRANEAN	REST OF THE WORLD	CULTURE AND TECHNOLOGY
1821 Famine in Ireland. Greek war of independence from Turkey starts (1821–30).	Mexico independent.	Constable: *The Hay Wain*.
1822 Castlereagh dies; Canning foreign secretary.	Liberia founded for US freed slaves. Brazil independent. 1823 Monroe Doctrine extends US protection to Spanish-American republics. Costa Rica, Ecuador independent.	Champollion deciphers Egyptian hieroglyphics (Rosetta Stone). Rapid industrialization of NW England and Lowland Scotland (textiles).
1824 British Combination Acts repealed to allow trade unions. Charles X king of France (1824–30).	Peru independent.	Beethoven: Ninth Symphony. National Gallery founded.
1825 Nicholas I tsar of Russia (1825–55). Decembrist revolt suppressed.		Stockton and Darlington railway opened. Saint-Simon: *Nouveau Christianisme*.
1826 Muhammad Ali reconquers Peloponnese in Greek war.	Britain establishes Straits Settlements: Penang, Malacca, and Singapore.	James Fenimore Cooper: *The Last of the Mohicans*.
1827 Britain, Russia, and France send navies and destroy Turkish fleet at Navarino. Canning British Prime Minister; dies and succeeded by Wellington (1828–30).	France intervenes in Algeria.	Beethoven dies in Vienna.
1828 Daniel O'Connell (Catholic) elected to Parliament.		Webster: *American Dictionary of the English Language*.
1829 Full Catholic emancipation granted in Britain. Metropolitan Police formed.	Andrew Jackson US President (1829–37). Western Australia founded.	Braille invented (France). Sewing machine (France). Stephenson: *Rocket*.
1830 First cholera epidemics in Europe. Charles X deposed; Louis Philippe king of France (1830–48). William IV king of Great Britain and Ireland (1830–37). Lord Grey Prime Minister (1830–84). Belgium fights for independence.	Muhammad Ali encourages revival of Arabic culture. France takes Algeria. Colombia, Venezuela independent.	Stendhal: *Le Rouge et le noir*. Berlioz: *Symphonie fantastique*. Joseph Smith founds Mormon Church.
1831 Major cholera epidemic in Britain. Mazzini founds Young Italy movement. Greece gains independence.		Pushkin: *Boris Godunov*. Darwin begins voyage on *Beagle* (1831–36). Bellini: *Norma*.
1832 First Reform Act in Britain.	Forcible settlement of American Indians in Oklahoma.	Industrialization in Belgium and NW France; railways.
1833 British Factory Act: child labour regulated.	Abolition of slavery in British Empire.	Oxford Movement to restore Anglicanism.
1834 British Poor Law Amendment Act. Peel's Tamworth Manifesto. Tolpuddle martyrs transported to Australia.	1835–37 Great Trek by Afrikaners in Africa. 1836 South Australia becomes British colony. Texas independent from Mexico.	1835 Donizetti: *Lucia di Lammermoor*. Revived Gothic architecture widespread. Fox Talbot: first photographic negative. Chopin: *Preludes*. Morse code.
1837 Victoria queen of Great Britain and Ireland (1837–1901).		Railway boom in Britain. Electric telegraph. Dickens: *Oliver Twist*.
1838 *The People's Charter* drawn up in London by Chartists. Anti-Corn-Law League founded in Manchester.		Turner: *The Fighting Téméraire*. Isambard Kingdom Brunel: *Great Western*.
1839 Treaty granting Belgian independence.	First Opium War in China (1839–42).	Daguerreotype photograph. Faraday: theory of electromagnetism.
1840 Penny post in Britain.	Canadian Provinces Act of Union. Treaty of Waitangi between Maoris and settlers in New Zealand.	Edgar Allan Poe: *Tales of the Grotesque and Arabesque*. First bicycle in Scotland. Proudhon: *What is Property?* Schumann: songs.
1841 Robert Peel British Prime Minister (1841–46).	Britain takes Hong Kong. France occupies Tahiti, Guinea, and Gabon.	1842 Verdi's *Nabucco* encourages Italian nationalism. Gogol: *Dead Souls*. Balzac: *La Comédie humaine* (1842–48).
1843 Free Church of Scotland formed in protest against established Church of Scotland.	Britain annexes Sind.	Joule: theory of thermodynamics.
1844 Co-operative Society formed in Rochdale.		Dumas: *The Count of Monte Cristo*. Kierkegaard: *The Concept of Dread*.
1845 Potato famine in Ireland.	USA annexes Texas. Sikh Wars (1845 and 1848–49).	Engels: *The Condition of the Working Classes in England in 1844*. Disraeli: *Sybil*. Galvanized corrugated iron patented (England).
1846 Corn Laws repealed; Peel resigns; Lord Russell Prime Minister (1846–52).	Mexican–US War (1846–48).	Planet Neptune discovered.
1847 Risorgimento in Italy. Factory Act in		Charlotte Brontë: *Jane Eyre*. Emily Brontë:

EUROPE AND THE MEDITERRANEAN	REST OF THE WORLD	CULTURE AND TECHNOLOGY
Britain: ten-hour day.		*Wuthering Heights.*
1848 Last Chartist petition. Revolutions in Europe. Second Republic in France (1848–52). Cholera in Europe.	Gold discovered in California. Irish emigrants to USA. Abolition of slavery in French West Indies.	Marx/Engels: *Communist Manifesto.* Pre-Raphaelite Brotherhood formed.
1849 Revolutions suppressed around Europe.	California gold rush. Britain annexes Punjab and subdues Sikhs. 1850–64 Taiping Rebellion in China. Livingstone crosses Africa.	Safety pin patented. 1850 Courbet: *Burial at Ornans.* Tennyson: *In Memoriam.* Nathaniel Hawthorne: *The Scarlet Letter.* Kelvin: second law of thermodynamics.
1851 Coup by Louis-Napoleon in France.	Gold in Australia; settlers moving into Victoria.	Great Exhibition in Crystal Palace.
1852 Aberdeen British Prime Minister (1852–55). Napoleon III founds French Second Empire (1852–70). Cavour premier of Piedmont (1852–59; 1860–61).		Harriet Beecher Stowe: *Uncle Tom's Cabin.*
1853 Crimean War begins (1853–56); Russia against Turkey.	First railways and telegraph in India. Gadsden Purchase in USA.	Hypodermic syringe (France). Verdi: *La Traviata.*
1854 Crimean War develops; France and Britain join Turkey; siege of Sebastopol; Florence Nightingale works in the hospital at Scutari.	US Republican Party founded.	William Holman Hunt: *The Light of the World.* Catholic dogma of Immaculate Conception.
1855 Palmerston British Prime Minister (1855–58).	Railways in South America: Chile (1851), Brazil (1854), Argentina (1857).	Telegraph news stories of Crimean War. Walt Whitman: *Leaves of Grass.* Mendel outlines laws of heredity.
1856 Crimean War ends.	Britain annexes Oudh. Second Opium War (1856–60).	Synthetic dyes invented (England).
1857 Italian nationalism growing.	1857–58 Indian Mutiny.	Baudelaire: *Les Fleurs du mal.* Flaubert: *Madame Bovary.* Trollope: *Barchester Towers.*
1858 Lionel Rothschild first Jewish MP.	Fenians founded in USA. Government of India transferred from East India Company to British Crown.	Lourdes miracles reported.
1859 French support Italians in struggle for independence from Austria.	John Brown at Harpers Ferry.	J. S. Mill: *On Liberty.* Darwin: *On the Origin of Species.* Wagner: *Tristan und Isolde.* Oil pumped in Pennsylvania.
1860 Garibaldi victorious in southern Italy.	1860–72 War in New Zealand; Maoris against settlers. South Carolina secedes from US Union.	Bessemer: mass production of steel. Huxley defends theory of evolution. George Eliot: *The Mill on the Floss.* Dickens: *Great Expectations.*
1861 Victor Emmanuel II king of Italy (1861–78). Death of Prince Albert. Russia abolishes serfdom.	Lincoln US President (1861–65). American Civil War (1861–65). First Battle at Bull Run.	Siemens developing open-hearth steel production.
1862 Bismarck Minister-President of Prussia.	French Indo-China established. 1863 Battle of Gettysburg; Union victory. Emancipation of US slaves. French protectorate of Cambodia.	Victor Hugo: *Les Misérables.* 1863 Manet: *Déjeuner sur l'herbe.* 1863–69 Tolstoy: *War and Peace.* c. 1863 Rossetti: *Beata Beatrix.* Maxwell: theory of electromagnetism.
1864 First International formed in London (Karl Marx organizes). Red Cross founded.	French install Maximilian emperor of Mexico. Sherman marches through Georgia.	Jules Verne: *Journey to the Centre of the Earth.*
1865 Lord Russell British Prime Minister again (1865–66).	1865–70 Brazil, Argentina, and Uruguay at war with Paraguay; ends in disaster for Paraguay. Confederate commander Lee surrenders; American Civil War ends. Lincoln assassinated; Andrew Johnson US President (1865–69).	Lewis Carroll: *Alice's Adventures in Wonderland.* Pasteur publishes theory of germs causing disease. Whymper ascends the Matterhorn.
1866 Lord Derby British Prime Minister (1866–68).	Livingstone begins third journey in Africa. US Reconstruction under way.	Dostoevsky: *Crime and Punishment.*
1867 Austro-Hungarian empire formed. Fenian rising in Ireland. Second British Reform Act.	US purchases Alaska from Russia. Canada becomes a British dominion. Restoration of imperial power in Japan; end of shogunates.	Karl Marx: first volume of *Das Kapital.* Ibsen: *Peer Gynt.* Japanese art arrives in West.
1868 Gladstone British Prime Minister (1868–74). British TUC formed.		Helium discovered. 1869 Suez Canal opens. Liquefaction of gases (Andrews).
1870 Irish Land Act. Franco-Prussian War (1870–71); Napoleon III defeated at Sedan; dethroned and exiled.	Rockefeller establishes Standard Oil Company in USA.	Doctrine of papal infallibility. British elementary education.
1871 French Third Republic suppresses Paris Commune and loses Alsace-Lorraine to German Empire. Wilhelm I first German emperor (1871–88). British trade unions gain	Stanley finds Livingstone. Ku Klux Klan suppressed in USA. Feudalism suppressed in Japan; modernization begins.	1871–72 George Eliot: *Middlemarch.*

EUROPE AND THE MEDITERRANEAN	REST OF THE WORLD	CULTURE AND TECHNOLOGY
legality. Rome made capital of Italy.		
1872 Voting by secret ballot in Britain. Bismarck opposes Catholic church in *Kulturkampf*.		Air brakes patented (Westinghouse). 1873 Rimbaud: *Une Saison en enfer*. 1873–77 Tolstoy: *Anna Karenina*. 1874 First Impressionist exhibition: Monet, Sisley, Renoir, Pissarro, Degas, Cézanne. Remington typewriter.
1874 Disraeli British Prime Minister (1874–80).	Stanley charts Lake Victoria and traces the course of the Congo (1874–77).	
1875 Britain buys control of Suez Canal.		Bizet: *Carmen*.
1876 Queen Victoria Empress of India.	Battle of Little Bighorn.	Plimsoll line for ships. Bell patents telephone. Brahms: First Symphony. Wagner's *Ring* cycle.
1877 Russo-Turkish War (1877–78).	US Reconstruction collapses; southern states impose racist legislation. Britain annexes Transvaal.	Phonograph (Edison). Tchaikovsky: *Swan Lake*.
1878 Salvation Army created in Britain. Serbian independence. Britain gains Cyprus. Romania independent.		Gilbert and Sullivan: *HMS Pinafore*.
1879 Land League formed in Ireland.		Mary Baker Eddy founds the Church of Christ, Scientist.
1880 Gladstone British Prime Minister (1880–85).	First Boer War (1880–81).	Swan perfects carbon-filament lamp. Burne-Jones: *The Golden Stairs*. Development of seismograph. Rodin: *The Gate of Hell*.
1881 Second Irish Land Act. Assassination of Tsar Alexander II. Jewish pogroms in eastern Europe. Alexander III tsar (1881–94).	Mahdi leads revolt against Egyptian rulers of Sudan.	Ibsen: *Ghosts*. First public electricity supply (Godalming, Surrey).
1882 Triple Alliance: Germany, Austria-Hungary, Italy.	British occupy Egypt.	Manet: *A Bar at the Folies-Bergère*.
1883 Social insurance introduced in Germany.	Jewish immigration to Palestine.	Robert Louis Stevenson: *Treasure Island*. 1883–85 Nietzsche: *Thus Spake Zarathustra*.
1884 Third British Reform Act.	Germany acquires South West Africa.	First part of *Oxford English Dictionary*. Rayon artificial fibres (France).
1885 Lord Salisbury British Prime Minister (1885–86).	Mahdi takes Khartoum; death of General Gordon. Canadian Pacific Railway complete. Indian National Congress formed.	Motor car (Benz). Motorcycle (Daimler). Pasteur: anti-rabies vaccine. Zola: *Germinal*.
1886 Gladstone British Prime Minister but resigns over Irish Home Rule. Liberal Unionists formed in protest against Home Rule. Lord Salisbury Prime Minister (1886–92).	Slavery ends in Cuba. Tunisia under French protectorate. All Burma occupied by British.	Hardy: *The Mayor of Casterbridge*.
1887 Queen Victoria's Golden Jubilee celebrated. Industrial unrest in Britain: 'Bloody Sunday' (Trafalgar Square riots).	Gold discovered in Kalgoorlie, Western Australia.	Conan Doyle: *A Study in Scarlet* (first Sherlock Holmes stories). Radio waves demonstrated (Hertz).
1888 Wilhelm II emperor of Germany (1888–1918).	Slavery ends in Brazil.	Pneumatic tyre (Dunlop). Strindberg: *Miss Julie*.
1889 Second International formed in Paris.		Van Gogh: *A Starry Night*. Eiffel Tower, Paris.
1890 Parnell resigns from Parliament. Chancellor Bismarck forced to resign.	Battle of Wounded Knee.	Death of Van Gogh. Mascagni: *Cavalleria Rusticana*. Dewar: vacuum flask.
1891 Trans-Siberian Railway begun.	Young Turk movement founded.	Gaugin to Tahiti.
1892 Tsar Alexander III forms alliance with France. Gladstone's fourth ministry (1892–94).		1892–95 Dvořák: Ninth Symphony ('From the New World'). Diesel engine patented.
1893 Independent Labour Party formed in Britain.		Tchaikovsky: Sixth Symphony. Edvard Munch: *The Scream*.
1894 Nicholas II tsar (1894–1917). Lord Rosebery British Prime Minister (1894–95). Death duties in Britain. Dreyfus imprisoned in France.	First Sino-Japanese War (1894–95).	Kipling: *The Jungle Book*. Toulouse-Lautrec: *Moulin Rouge* lithographs.
1895 Lord Salisbury British Prime Minister (1895–1902); strongly imperialist government.	Japan takes Taiwan (Formosa). Jameson Raid in South Africa (1895–96).	Lumière brothers: cinema. X-rays discovered (Röntgen). Oscar Wilde: *The Importance of Being Earnest*. Safety razor.
1896 First modern Olympic Games in Athens.	Laurier elected Canada's first French-Canadian and Roman Catholic Prime Minister.	Hardy: *Jude the Obscure*. Radioactivity of uranium (Becquerel).
1897 Queen Victoria's Diamond Jubilee celebrated.	Klondike gold rush (1897–99).	Thomson: the electron. Bram Stoker: *Dracula*. Henri Rousseau: *Sleeping Gypsy*.

EUROPE AND THE MEDITERRANEAN	REST OF THE WORLD	CULTURE AND TECHNOLOGY
Zionist movement founded.		Aspirin marketed.
1898 German naval expansion rapid.	Spanish–American War. British reconquer Sudan.	Zola: *J'accuse*. H. G. Wells: *The War of the Worlds*. Curies: radium.
1899 British fights Second Boer War (1899–1902).	Siege of Mafeking. Boxer Rising in China.	Freud: *The Interpretation of Dreams*. Monet: first in *Water-lilies* sequence. Scott Joplin: 'Maple Leaf Rag'.
1900 Boer War concentration camps arouse European criticism.	Mafeking relieved.	First Zeppelin. Planck: quantum theory. Conrad: *Lord Jim*. Puccini: *Tosca*. First agricultural tractor.
1901 Death of Queen Victoria. Edward VII king of Great Britain and Ireland (1901–10).	Commonwealth of Australia formed. US President McKinley assassinated. Theodore Roosevelt President (1901–09).	1901–04 Picasso: Blue Period. Gorky: *The Lower Depths*.
1902 Balfour British Prime Minister (1902–05).	Treaty of Vereeniging ends Boer War.	Gide: *The Immoralist*. John Masefield: *Salt-Water Ballads*.
1903 Bolsheviks form majority of Social Democratic party in Russia. Pogroms in Russia. Suffragette movement in Britain; Pankhursts.	Mass European emigration to USA. Panama independent; Canal Zone to USA.	Electrocardiograph. Wright brothers: powered flight.
1904 Franco-British *entente cordiale*.	Russo-Japanese War (1904–05).	J. M. Barrie: *Peter Pan*. Chekhov: *The Cherry Orchard*. Photoelectric cell.
1905 First Russian Revolution. Liberal government in Britain; Campbell-Bannerman Prime Minister (1905–08).	Japanese destroy Russian fleet at Tsushima.	Richard Strauss: *Salome*. Einstein: special theory of relativity. Early brain surgery (Cushing in USA).
1906 Labour Party formed in Britain. Russian Duma. Clemenceau French Prime Minister (1906–09).	Muslim League founded in India. Earthquake in San Francisco.	Vitamins discovered (Hopkins).
1907 Triple Entente (Great Britain, France, and Russia).	New Zealand gains dominion status.	George Bernard Shaw: *Major Barbara*. J. M. Synge: *The Playboy of the Western World*. Electric washing machine.
1908 Bulgaria independent. Bosnia-Herzegovina occupied by Austria-Hungary. Old-age pensions introduced in Britain. Asquith British Prime Minister (1908–16).	Young Turk revolution in Turkey.	Klimt: *The Kiss*. Cubist movement. E. M. Forster: *A Room with a View*. Mahler: *Das Lied von der Erde*. Geiger counter invented. Borstal system in Britain.
1909 Lloyd George budget rejected by Lords: constitutional crisis.	Oil-drilling in Persia by British.	Model T car (Ford). Matisse: *The Dance*. Ballets Russes formed (Diaghilev). Schoenberg: *Three Piano Pieces*.
1910 George V king of Great Britain and Ireland (1910–36).	Union of South Africa. Japan annexes Korea.	1910–13 A. N. Whitehead and Bertrand Russell: *Principia Mathematica*. Post-impressionist exhibition, London.
1911 Industrial unrest in Britain.	Amundsen to South Pole. Chinese revolution; Sun Yat-sen establishes republic (1912).	Rutherford: nuclear and model of atom.
1912 Balkan Wars (1912–13).	ANC formed in South Africa. *Titanic* sinks. French protectorate in Morocco.	Jung: *The Psychology of the Unconscious*. First parachute descent from an aircraft. Stainless steel.
1913 Ottoman Turks lose European lands except Constantinople. Crisis in Ireland. British suffragettes.	Woodrow Wilson US President (1913–21).	D. H. Lawrence: *Sons and Lovers*. Stravinsky: *The Rite of Spring*. Alain-Fournier: *Le Grand Meaulnes*. 1913–27 Proust: *À la recherche du temps perdu*.
1914 Assassination at Sarajevo of Archduke Franz Ferdinand. Outbreak of World War I (1914–18). Trench warfare on the Western Front.	Panama Canal opens. Egypt British protectorate.	1914–21 Berg: *Wozzeck*. Joyce: *Dubliners*. Vaughan Williams: *A London Symphony*.
1915 Heavy fighting at Gallipoli. Asquith forms coalition in Britain. Zeppelin raids.	*Lusitania* sunk by German submarine.	Einstein: general theory of relativity. W. G. Griffith: *The Birth of a Nation*.
1916 Battles of Verdun, Somme, and Jutland. Irish Easter Rising, Dublin. Lloyd George British Prime Minister (1916–22).		Dada movement. Parry: musical setting of 'Jerusalem'.
1917 Russian Revolution: Tsar Nicholas II abdicates. Battle of Passchendaele.	USA enters World War I. Balfour Declaration on Palestine.	1917–70 Pound: *Cantos*. Kafka: *Metamorphosis*. First jazz recordings.
1918 Second Battle of the Marne; tanks help final Allied advance. Armistice (November). Women's suffrage in UK.	British take Palestine and Syria; Battle of Megiddo. Ottomans make peace.	Gerard Manley Hopkins: *Poems*. 1918–22 Spengler: *The Decline of the West*.
1919 Spartacist revolt in Germany. Sinn Féin sets up independent parliament in Ireland. Third International formed, in Moscow. Treaty of	Arab rebellion in Egypt against British. Massacre at Amritsar in India.	Elgar: Cello Concerto. Alcock and Brown fly Atlantic.

EUROPE AND THE MEDITERRANEAN	REST OF THE WORLD	CULTURE AND TECHNOLOGY
Versailles. League of Nations established. Weimar Republic formed.		
1920 Separate parliaments established in northern and southern Ireland.	Prohibition of alcohol comes into effect in USA. Gandhi dominates Indian Congress. US Senate rejects Treaty of Versailles. Palestine mandated to Britain.	Edith Wharton: *The Age of Innocence*. Duchamp: *Mona Lisa*.
1921 Southern Ireland becomes Irish Free State; civil war (1921–23).	Chinese Communist Party founded by Mao Zedong and others. King Faisal I in Iraq (1921–33).	Pirandello: *Six Characters in Search of an Author*. 1921–23 William Walton: *Façade*.
1922 Soviet Union formed. Italian Fascists march on Rome; Mussolini forms government. Andrew Bonar Law British Prime Minister (1922–23).	Egypt independent.	Joyce: *Ulysses*. T. S. Eliot: *The Waste Land*. Max Weber: *Economy and Society*.
1923 Rampant inflation in Germany. French occupy Ruhr. Putsch organized by Hitler fails. Baldwin British Prime Minister.	Ottoman Empire ends.	Le Corbusier: *Towards a New Architecture*.
1924 MacDonald first Labour Prime Minister in Britain. Death of Lenin. Baldwin Prime Minister again (1924–29).	Northern Rhodesia British protectorate. US economy booming.	Honegger: *Pacific 231*. André Breton: surrealist manifesto.
1925 Locarno Pact.	Reza Pahlavi is shah in Iran (1925–41). Chiang Kai-shek launches campaign to unify China. Emperor Hirohito in Japan (1926–89).	Hitler: *Mein Kampf*. Eisenstein: *The Battleship Potemkin*. Discovery of ionosphere.
1926 British general strike. Gramsci imprisoned in Italy.		First television. Stanley Spencer: *Resurrection: Cookham*. Buster Keaton: *The General*.
1927 Stalin comes to power; Trotsky expelled from Communist Party.	Lindbergh flies Atlantic.	BBC founded. Al Jolson: *The Jazz Singer*. Walt Disney: Mickey Mouse.
1928 Stalin launches Soviet collectivization. Nazis and Communists compete in Germany. Women over 21 enfranchised in UK.	Kellogg Pact for peace.	W. B. Yeats: *The Tower*. Ravel: *Boléro*. Penicillin discovered.
1929 Depression begins. Trotsky exiled. Yugoslavia formed. Labour government in Britain under MacDonald (1929–31). Lateran Treaty in Italy.	Wall Street Crash. St Valentine's Day Massacre.	Hemingway: *A Farewell to Arms*. Robert Graves: *Good-bye to All That*.
1930 Airship disaster (*R101*) in France.	Revolution in Brazil; Vargas President. Haile Selassie emperor in Ethiopia (1930–74).	Turbojet engine patented by Whittle. Planet Pluto discovered. 1930–31 Empire State Building, New York. First Football World Cup.
1931 Depression worsens. King Alfonso XIII of Spain flees; republic formed. British national government under MacDonald (1931–35).	New Zealand independent. Japan occupies Manchuria.	Virginia Woolf: *The Waves*. Boris Karloff: *Frankenstein*. Salvador Dali: *The Persistence of Memory*.
1932 Oswald Mosley's British Union of Fascists formed. Dictator Salazar in Portugal.	14 million unemployed in USA. Kingdoms of Saudi Arabia and Iraq independent.	Cockcroft and Walton split the atom. James Chadwick: discovery of the neutron. First autobahn, Cologne–Bonn, opened.
1933 Nazi Party wins German elections. Hitler appointed Chancellor. Third Reich formed.	Franklin D. Roosevelt US President (1933–45); New Deal.	Lorca: *Blood Wedding*. Dorothy L. Sayers: *Murder Must Advertise*.
1934 Night of the long knives in Germany. Stalin purges begin.	1934–35 Long March in China.	Henry Miller: *Tropic of Cancer*. Agatha Christie: *Murder on the Orient Express*.
1935 German Jews lose citizenship. Baldwin British Prime Minister (1935–37).	Italy invades Ethiopia.	Marx Brothers: *A Night at the Opera*. Paul Nash: *Equivalents for the Megaliths*.
1936 Edward VIII abdicates; George VI king of United Kingdom (1936–52). Léon Blum Popular Front government in France. Spanish Civil War (1936–39). Rhineland reoccupied by Germany.	King Farouk in Egypt (1936–52). Haile Selassie in exile (1936–41).	A. J. Ayer: *Language, Truth, and Logic*. Keynes: *The General Theory of Employment, Interest, and Money*. Prokofiev: *Peter and the Wolf*. BBC begins television broadcasts.
1937 Chamberlain British Prime Minister (1937–40).	Sino-Japanese War (1937–45).	Picasso: *Guernica*. George Orwell: *The Road to Wigan Pier*. Walt Disney: *Snow White and the Seven Dwarfs*.
1938 Austrian *Anschluss* with Germany. Munich Agreement. Czechoslovakia cedes Sudetenland.		Nuclear fission discovered. Graham Greene: *Brighton Rock*. Fluorescent lighting in USA. Nylon patented in USA.
1939 Molotov-Ribbentrop pact between Germany and Soviet Union. Poland	King Faisal II in Iraq (1939–58).	Pauling: *The Nature of the Chemical Bond*. Judy Garland: *The Wizard of Oz*. John Steinbeck: *The*

EUROPE AND THE MEDITERRANEAN	REST OF THE WORLD	CULTURE AND TECHNOLOGY
invaded. Franco leader of Spain. Britain and France declare war on Germany; World War II (1939–45).		*Grapes of Wrath.*
1940 Occupation by Germany of France, Belgium, the Netherlands, Norway, Denmark. British retreat from Dunkirk. Vichy government in France. Churchill British Prime Minister (1940–45). Battle of Britain.	Trotsky assassinated in Mexico.	Charlie Chaplin: *The Great Dictator.*
1941 Germany occupies Balkans and invades Soviet Union.	Lend-Lease by USA. Atlantic Charter. Pearl Harbor bombed by Japan. USA enters war. Malaya, Singapore, and Burma taken by Japan.	Orson Welles: *Citizen Kane.*
1942 Beveridge Report. Battle of Stalingrad begins.	Midway and El Alamein key Allied victories.	Fermi: nuclear chain reaction. Camus: *The Outsider.* Bogart/Bergman: *Casablanca.*
1943 Allied bombing of Germany (1943–45). Allies invade Italy; Mussolini deposed. Germans surrender at Stalingrad.	Lebanon independent.	Sartre: *Being and Nothingness.* T. S. Eliot: *Four Quartets.*
1944 D-Day invasion; Paris liberated. Civil war in Greece (1944–49).	1944–45 Burma recaptured.	Holmes: *Principles of Physical Geology.* 1944–46 Eisenstein: *Ivan the Terrible.* Olivier: *Henry V.*
1945 Yalta Conference. War ends in Europe (May). United Nations formed. Labour wins British election; Attlee Prime Minister (1945–51). Potsdam Conference.	Death of Roosevelt; Truman US President (1945–53). USA drops atom bombs on Hiroshima and Nagasaki. War ends (September).	Benjamin Britten: *Peter Grimes.*
1946 Cold war begins. Italian Republic formed.	Perón President in Argentina. Jordan independent. Civil war in China (1946–49).	Cocteau: *La Belle et la bête.*
1947 Attlee government nationalizes fuel, power, transport in Britain. Puppet Communist states in eastern Europe.	India independent; Pakistan becomes separate state.	Tennessee Williams: *A Streetcar Named Desire.* Jackson Pollock: action painting.
1948 Berlin airlift. British welfare state. Marshall Plan of aid for western Europe approved by US Congress.	State of Israel established. Ceylon in Commonwealth. 1948–60 Malayan Emergency. Apartheid legislation in South Africa. Gandhi assassinated.	Brecht: *The Caucasian Chalk Circle.* De Sica: *Bicycle Thieves.* 1948–51 Stravinsky: *The Rake's Progress.* Transistor developed in the USA.
1949 Comecon and NATO formed. Republic of Ireland established. Communist regime in Hungary.	Indonesia independent. People's Republic of China declared.	George Orwell: *1984.* Simone de Beauvoir: *The Second Sex.* Genet: *Journal du voleur.*
1950 Labour Party wins election in Britain; retains power.	1950–53 Korean War.	Ionesco: *The Bald Prima Donna.* Kurosawa: *Rashomon.* Stereophonic sound developed. First successful kidney transplant.
1951 Conservatives win election in Britain; Churchill Prime Minister (1951–55).	China extends rule over Tibet. Anzus pact in Pacific.	Ray Bradbury: *Fahrenheit 451.* J. D. Salinger: *The Catcher in the Rye.*
1952 European Coal and Steel Community formed. Elizabeth II queen of United Kingdom (1952–). Conservative government in UK denationalizes iron and steel and road transport (1953).	USA tests hydrogen bomb.	Hemingway: *The Old Man and the Sea.* Beckett: *Waiting for Godot.*
1953 Death of Stalin.	Egyptian Republic formed. 1953–57 Mau Mau in Kenya. McCarthy era in USA. Eisenhower US President (1953–61). Korean War ends. Vietnam independent, partitioned. Algerian War of Independence (1954–62). Nasser in power in Egypt.	Crick and Watson: double helix structure of DNA. Mount Everest climbed for first time (Hillary, Tenzing Norgay). Matisse: *The Snail.*
1954 First commercial TV station in Britain.		1954 William Golding: *Lord of the Flies.* 1954–55 J. R. R. Tolkien: *The Lord of the Rings.* Bill Haley: 'Rock Around the Clock'. Fortran in USA. Roger Bannister runs first four-minute mile.
1955 West Germany joins NATO. Warsaw Pact formed. Anthony Eden British Prime Minister (1955–57).		1955 Marcuse: *Eros and Civilization.* James Dean: *Rebel Without a Cause.* Hovercraft patented.
1956 Khrushchev denounces Stalin. Suez crisis. Polish and Hungarian revolts.	Hundred Flowers in China (1956–57). Morocco independent. Guerrilla conflict in Vietnam.	1956 John Osborne: *Look Back in Anger.* Elvis Presley: 'Heartbreak Hotel'. First commercial nuclear power stations (Britain 1956, USA 1957).
1957 Macmillan British Prime Minister (1957–63). Treaty of Rome; EEC formed. Soviet Sputnik flight.	Ghana independent.	1957 Robbe-Grillet: *Jealousy.* Jack Kerouac: *On the Road.*
1958 Fifth Republic in France. Life peerages introduced in Britain.	Great Leap Forward in China. NASA set up.	Silicon chip invented in USA. Harold Pinter: *The Birthday Party.* Lévi-Strauss: *Structural Anthropology.* Achebe: *Things Fall Apart.*
1959 De Gaulle French President (1959–69). Conservatives win British election. North Sea natural gas discovered.	Cuban revolution (Castro).	Günter Grass: *The Tin Drum.* Marilyn Monroe: *Some Like it Hot.*

EUROPE AND THE MEDITERRANEAN	REST OF THE WORLD	CULTURE AND TECHNOLOGY
1960 EFTA formed. Cyprus independent.	End of Malayan Emergency. Sharpeville massacre in South Africa. Belgian Congo (Democratic Republic of the Congo) independent. OPEC formed. Nigeria independent.	Hitchcock: *Psycho*. Fellini: *La Dolce vita*. Godard: *Breathless*. Lasers built (USA). Oral contraceptives marketed.
1961 Berlin Wall erected.	John F. Kennedy US President (1961–63). Bay of Pigs invasion of Cuba by USA. South Africa becomes a republic, leaves Commonwealth because of apartheid.	Joseph Heller: *Catch-22*. Manned space flight (Yuri Gagarin).
1962 Vatican Council (1962–65).	Cuban Missile Crisis. Jamaica, Trinidad and Tobago, and Uganda independent.	The Beatles: 'Love Me Do'. Andy Warhol: Marilyn Monroe prints.
1963 De Gaulle vetoes Britain's bid to enter EEC. Alec Douglas-Home British Prime Minister (1963–64).	Test-Ban Treaty signed. Kenya independent. President Kennedy assassinated. Lyndon Johnson US President (1963–69). OAU formed.	Betty Friedan: *The Feminine Mystique*. Sylvia Plath: *The Bell Jar*.
1964 Labour Party wins British election; Harold Wilson Prime Minister (1964–70). Khrushchev ousted by Brezhnev (1964–82).	US enters Vietnam War. Nelson Mandela sentenced to life imprisonment in South Africa. PLO formed.	Saul Bellow: *Herzog*. Word processor.
1965 De Gaulle re-elected French President.	UDI in Rhodesia. India and Pakistan clash over Kashmir. Military takeover in Indonesia.	Joe Orton: *Loot*. The Rolling Stones: 'Satisfaction'. Bob Dylan: *Highway 61 Revisited*.
1966 Labour Party gains bigger majority in Britain.	Cultural Revolution in China (1966–68). Indira Gandhi Indian Prime Minister (1966–77).	England win World Cup. Tom Stoppard: *Rosencrantz and Guildenstern are Dead*.
1967 De Gaulle vetoes Britain's second bid to enter EEC. Abortion legalized in Britain.	Biafran war (1967–70). Six Day War between Israel and Arabs.	The Beatles: *Sergeant Pepper's Lonely Hearts Club Band*. First heart transplant (Barnard). First pulsar discovered.
1968 Soviet forces invade Czechoslovakia. Student protest in Paris and throughout Europe. Violent protest erupts in Northern Ireland.	Tet Offensive in Vietnam. Martin Luther King assassinated.	Kubrick: *2001: A Space Odyssey*. Plate tectonics.
1969 British army to Northern Ireland. De Gaulle resigns; Pompidou French President (1969–74). Brandt West German Chancellor (1969–74).	Richard Nixon US President (1969–74). Sino-Soviet frontier war. Gaddafi in power in Libya.	First man on moon (Neil Armstrong). First Concorde flight. Woodstock pop festival.
1970 Conservatives win British election; Edward Heath Prime Minister (1970–74).	Allende President in Chile (1970–73). Biafran war ends.	Germaine Greer: *The Female Eunuch*. Beatles split up.
1971 Internment without trial in Northern Ireland. Decimal currency introduced in UK.	Amin seizes power in Uganda. Bangladesh becomes a state.	Visconti: *Death in Venice*. Open University in UK.
1972 Bloody Sunday in Northern Ireland; direct rule from Westminster imposed. Many Ugandan Asian refugees flee to UK.	Nixon visits China.	Bertolucci: *Last Tango in Paris*. World Trade Center completed. Video cassette recorder marketed.
1973 Denmark, Ireland, and UK enter EEC. Widespread industrial unrest in UK.	Allende killed in Chilean coup. US withdraws from Vietnam War. OPEC raises oil prices. Yom Kippur War.	US Skylab missions. Schumacher: *Small is Beautiful*.
1974 Harold Wilson British Prime Minister (1974–76). IRA bombings of mainland Britain. Dictatorship ended in Portugal. Northern Ireland Assembly fails.	Watergate scandal; Nixon resigns. Gerald Ford US President (1974–77). Cyprus invaded by Turkey. Haile Selassie deposed in Ethiopia.	Philip Larkin: *High Windows*.
1975 Franco dies; Juan Carlos becomes king of Spain.	Angola and Mozambique independent. End of Vietnam War. Khmer Rouge in Cambodia. Civil War in Lebanon.	Apollo and Soyuz dock in space.
1976 James Callaghan British Prime Minister (1976–79).	Death of Mao Zedong; Gang of Four. Soweto massacre.	Richard Dawkins: *The Selfish Gene*.
1977 Democratic elections in Spain. Terrorist activities in Germany and Italy.	Deng Xiaoping gains power in China. Steve Biko dies in police custody in South Africa. Jimmy Carter US President (1977–81).	Pompidou Centre opened. Woody Allen: *Annie Hall*.
1978 Pope John Paul II elected.	Camp David agreement. Boat people leaving Vietnam.	Irish Murdoch: *The Sea, The Sea*. First test-tube baby born.
1979 European Parliament direct elections. Strikes in Britain. Conservatives win British election; Margaret Thatcher Prime Minister (1979–90).	Shah of Iran deposed by Khomeini's Islamic revolution. Soviet Union invades Afghanistan. Pol Pot deposed in Cambodia. SALT II signed. Sandinistas take power in Nicaragua.	Coppola: *Apocalypse Now*. Smallpox eradicated.
1980 Solidarity in Poland.	Zimbabwe independent. Iran–Iraq War (1980–88). US funds Contras in Nicaragua.	Anthony Burgess: *Earthly Powers*. Anglican Alternative Service Book.

EUROPE AND THE MEDITERRANEAN	REST OF THE WORLD	CULTURE AND TECHNOLOGY
	Indira Gandhi Indian Prime Minister (1980–84).	
1981 Privatization begins in Britain. Mitterrand French President.	Ronald Reagan US President (1981–89). President Sadat assassinated in Egypt.	US space shuttle. John Updike: *Rabbit is Rich*.
1982 British victory over Argentina in Falklands War.	Israel invades Lebanon. Famine in Ethiopia.	Alice Walker: *The Color Purple*. Richard Attenborough: *Gandhi*. Steven Spielberg: *ET*. Compact discs introduced. AIDS identified.
1983 Thatcher re-elected Prime Minister.	US troops invade Grenada.	1983 Wajda: *Danton*.
1984 Miners' strike in UK (1984–85). IRA bomb attack during Conservative Party conference in Brighton.	Hong Kong agreement between UK and China. Assassination of Indira Gandhi.	Milan Kundera: *The Unbearable Lightness of Being*.
1985 Gorbachev General Secretary of Soviet Communist Party (1985–91); begins policy of liberalization. Anglo-Irish Agreement.	Greenpeace ship *Rainbow Warrior* sunk by French.	Primo Levi: *The Periodic Table*.
1986 Spain and Portugal join EC. 'Big bang' in UK Stock Exchange.	US bombs Libya.	Chernobyl disaster. Wole Soyinka awarded Nobel Prize for literature.
1987 Single European Act. UK stock-market crisis (Black Monday). Third Thatcher government.	Palestinian intifada.	Genetic fingerprinting in forensic science.
1988 Liberal Democrats formed in Britain. Mitterrand re-elected in France. Lockerbie disaster.	Iran–Iraq War ends. PLO recognizes Israel. Soviet Union begins withdrawal from Afghanistan.	Salman Rushdie: *The Satanic Verses*. Stephen Hawking: *A Brief History of Time*.
1989 Berlin Wall broken. Communist regimes deposed in Hungary, Poland, East Germany, Czechoslovakia, Bulgaria, Romania.	George Bush US President (1989–93). Tiananmen Square massacre. De Klerk South African President (1989–94).	France celebrates 200th anniversary of the Revolution.
1990 East and West Germany reunited. John Major becomes British Prime Minister. Britain joins ERM.	Iraq invades and annexes Kuwait. Nelson Mandela released; ANC talks with South African President de Klerk. Cold war formally ended. Namibia independent.	Hubble Space Telescope launched into orbit. A. S. Byatt: *Possession*.
1991 Soviet Union breaks up; attempted coup fails. Boris Yeltsin President of the Russian Federation. Croatia and Slovenia break away from Yugoslavia; civil war. Warsaw Pact dissolved. Maastricht Treaty agreed.	Gulf War. START agreement signed. Rajiv Gandhi assassinated.	
1992 Conservatives win fourth term in UK. UK withdraws from ERM. Bosnia-Herzegovina declares independence; Sarajevo besieged by Serbs.	UN intervenes in Somalia. Rioting in Los Angeles.	Toni Morrison: *Jazz*.
1993 Single market in Europe; EC becomes EU. Czechoslovakia splits into the Czech Republic and Slovakia.	Israeli and PLO leaders sign peace accord. Bill Clinton US President. Eritrea independent.	Steven Spielberg: *Jurassic Park*.
1994 Channel Tunnel opens to rail traffic. IRA announces ceasefire. Austria, Finland, and Sweden vote to join EU; Norway rejects membership. Russian forces invade Chechnya.	First multiracial democratic elections in South Africa; ANC wins, Mandela becomes President. Ethnic massacres in Rwanda and Burundi. GATT agreement signed.	Steven Spielberg: *Schindler's List*, wins Oscars.
1995 Chirac wins French presidential election. Bosnia-Herzegovina peace accord. Clinton visits Northern Ireland on peace mission.	World Trade Organization established. Yitzhak Rabin assassinated. Ken Saro-Wiwa, writer and political campaigner, hanged in Nigeria; Nigeria suspended from Commonwealth.	Estimated 30–40 million Internet users worldwide. UN-sponsored Intergovernmental Panel on Climate Change confirms global warming is occurring.
1996 Dunblane primary school massacre prompts banning of most handguns in UK. British beef banned worldwide.	USA bombs Iraq for attacking Kurds. Taliban forces occupy Kabul.	European Space Agency's Ariane-5 destroyed on its maiden flight. Anthony Minghella: *The English Patient*
1997 Labour Party election victory ends 18 years of Conservative rule in the UK. Diana, Princess of Wales killed in car crash. Scottish Parliament and Welsh Assembly approved in referendums.	Economic crises in Far East. Hong Kong returned to China. Deng Xiaoping dies. Laurent Kabila overthrows Mobutu Sese Seko in Zaïre. NATO agrees treaty with Russia.	Priceless church art destroyed by earthquakes in Italy. Wole Soyinka charged with treason (Nigeria). A sheep is cloned.
1998 Clashes between Albanian separatists and Serb forces in Kosovo. Northern Ireland peace terms agreed.	Yeltsin dismisses entire Russian government. Pol Pot dies.	James Cameron's *Titanic* wins 11 Oscars. Ted Hughes: *Birthday Letters*.